RECORDS OF NORTH AMERICAN BIG GAME

12TH EDITION

Records of North American Big Game, 12th Edition

Edited by Eldon L. "Buck" Buckner and Jack Reneau

Copyright © 2005 by Boone and Crockett Club

Library of Congress Catalog Card Number: 2005924446
ISBN: 0-940864-51-7
Published August 2005

Published in the United States of America
by the
Boone and Crockett Club
250 Station Drive
Missoula, Montana 59801
Phone (406) 542-1888
Fax (406) 542-0784
Toll-Free (888) 840-4868 — merchandise orders only
www.booneandcrockettclub.com

RECORDS OF NORTH AMERICAN BIG GAME

12TH EDITION

A Book of the Boone and Crockett Club Containing Tabulations of Outstanding North American Big-Game Trophies, Compiled from Data in the Club's Big-Game Records Archives.

Edited by
Jack Reneau
Eldon L. "Buck" Buckner

2005

BOONE AND CROCKETT CLUB

Missoula, Montana

DEDICATION

C. Randall Byers, 1945-2002

GEORGE A. BETTAS
EXECUTIVE DIRECTOR
Boone and Crockett Club

JACK RENEAU
DIRECTOR OF
BIG GAME RECORDS
Boone and Crockett Club

This 12th Edition of the Boone and Crockett Club's All-Time records book is dedicated to C. Randall Byers.

The arrow was broken in sorrow when our friend Randy Byers took the last trail on August 17, 2002. The sport of fair chase hunting lost a forceful champion when Randy died at the Theodore Roosevelt Memorial Ranch at the age of 56. At the time of his death Randy was among some of his closest friends — members of the Boone and Crockett Club — who made a valiant effort to save his life after he suffered a massive heart attack. Randy's untimely death came at a time when he was at the zenith of his academic career at the University of Idaho, as well as his "public service careers" as the President of the Pope and Young Club and Chair of the Boone and Crockett Club's Records of North American Big Game Committee. Randy Byers truly loved life, his family, his career, his students, and his work with the Boone and Crockett and Pope and Young Clubs. His life was characterized by his extraordinary dedication to helping others, a great sense of humor, a love of nature, a strong devotion to his profession, and a tenderness for people.

He was an inspirational professor who made learning interesting and fun for his students. His self-deprecating humor taught his students to take a step back at times and take a good laugh at themselves because "it builds strong character." He was a master teacher who mentored new and veteran faculty members alike. He was a university department Chair who took great pride in making new faculty feel welcome and taught them the rules of the game with such a "light hand" that they never felt inadequate.

He was a dedicated father who over more than 20 years of teaching his two boys the real joys of hunting never once failed to encourage his boys to take the lead.

RANDY AND HIS DOG HUNTING FOR CHUKAR IN IDAHO.

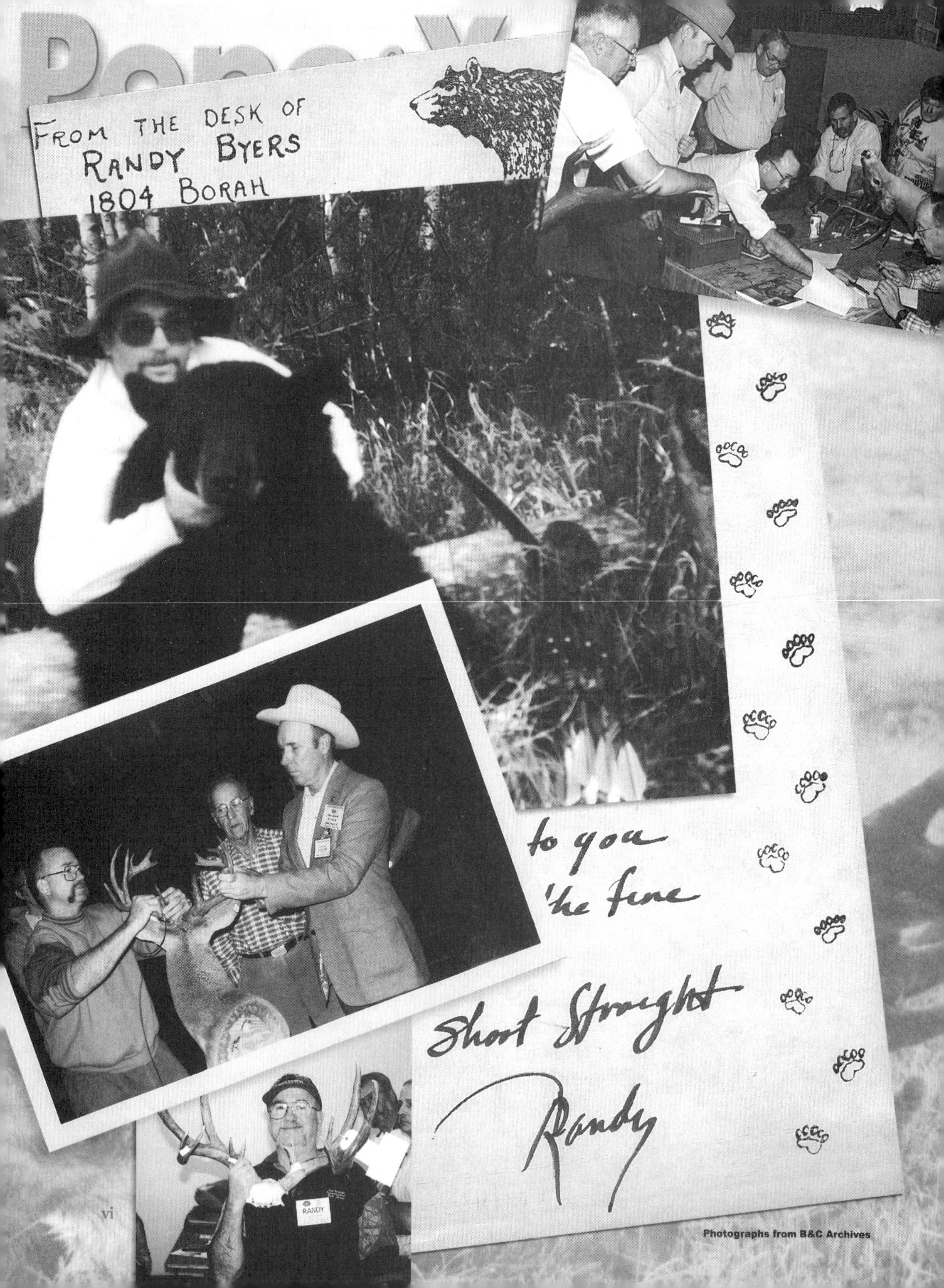

From the desk of
RANDY BYERS
1804 Borah

to you
'he fine

Shoot Straight

Randy

vi

He always wanted them to have the shot or land the fish. He was with them when they shot their first black bear, their first deer, their first elk, and their first cougar. They trudged through snow together, watched the desert sun, fished Idaho's rivers, loved and appreciated the outdoors.

Randy's dedication to Boone and Crockett Club's and Pope and Young Club's North American big game records systems remains unmatched in modern times by anyone other than Randy's mentor, Dr. Phil Wright. In his letter of support for Randy's Regular membership in the Boone and Crockett Club, Phil noted, "I know Dr. Byers well, first from working with him as a measurer with the Pope and Young Club, then as one of his committee members when he became chairman of that Club's Records Committee. He was a participant in June 1985 at the ad hoc committee I convened at the Theodore Roosevelt Memorial Ranch to review the scoring problems of our Club.

He later served as a Judge at the 19th Awards Program in Las Vegas, in 1986. I have corresponded with him at length about scoring problems of interest to both of our organizations. He is one of the truly dedicated Official Measurers who have devoted hundreds of hours of effort into standardizing the measurement techniques now in use by both Clubs. His mature judgment about scoring matters is based upon a profound knowledge of the subject."

This past spring Randy was elected to bowhunting's highest position as President of the Pope and Young Club. Randy became an Associate Member of the Pope and Young Club in 1971, Regular Member in 1977, and an Official Measurer and Senior Member in 1981. He was appointed as Pope and Young Club's Records Chairman in 1983. Randy was appointed as a Boone and Crockett Club Official Measurer in 1981. He became a Regular Member of the Boone and Crockett Club in April 1988.

SHOOT STRAIGHT
FROM TOP TO BOTTOM:
RANDY DISCUSSING
THE FINER POINTS OF
MEASURING AT THE 20TH
AWARDS PROGRAM JUDGES
PANEL IN ALBUQUERQUE,
NEW MEXICO. RANDY
PICTURED WITH HIS
SIGNATURE FLOPPY HAT
AND A SPRING BEAR
TAKEN IN MAY 1987 IN
SASKATCHEWAN. THREE
PILLARS OF THE CLUB'S
RECORDS PROGRAM –
RANDY AND CURRENT CHAIR,
BUCK BUCKNER DISCUSS A
COUES' WHITETAIL TROPHY
WHILE THE LEGENDARY
PHIL WRIGHT WATCHES ON.
RANDY SHOWING JUST HOW
MUCH HE ENJOYED BIG
GAME RECORDS KEEPING
AT THE 24TH AWARDS
PROGRAM.

Walter White recruited Randy for membership in the Boone and Crockett Club because of his leadership with the Pope and Young Club's records program and his expertise in the Boone and Crockett Club's records system.

Although his hunting method of choice was the bow and arrow, Randy had taken the prerequisite big-game animals with a rifle prior to being proposed for the Club. In this regard, Randy followed the same path to Boone and Crockett Regular membership, as did Fred Bear and Glenn St. Charles. In fact, Glenn St. Charles wrote one of Randy's seconding letters.

Throughout his tenure on the Club's Records of North American Big Game Committee, Randy was a strong voice for fair chase hunting and standardized measuring practices. He served as a judge on every Judges' Panel since 1986. He was chairman of the 20th Awards Program Judges' Panel in 1989. He was the obvious choice to chair the Records of North

American Big Game Committee when Walter White decided to step down from the position in 1995. During the seven years he chaired the Records of North American Big Game Committee, Randy's leadership moved the Club and its Awards Program through significant growth and major challenges.

His leadership was instrumental in guiding delicate changes in the Awards Program through the Club's decision-making system. He did this with the same "light hand" that he used in his university teaching and administration career. Randy's thoughtful leadership was fundamental to the success of these major changes in the Awards Program.

Boone and Crockett Club President, Earl Morgenroth, has often made the analogy that the Records of North American Big Game Committee of the Boone and Crockett Club is to the Club as the Fighting Irish football team is to the University of Notre Dame. He noted, "The Club has 21 committees, but the signature committee that brings national recognition to the Boone and Crockett Club is the Records of North American Big Game Committee. Randy Byers was the Knute Rockne of North American Big Game Records Keeping. He died as he had lived and I'm certain the way he would have wanted to: measuring a big game head."

Randy's great-grandparents on both sides of the family were original Idaho settlers and Randy was a fourth-generation Idahoan. The Collister area of Boise was named after one of Randy's great-grandfathers, Dr. Collister, Boise's first doctor. Randy grew up in Meridian, Idaho, on his family's farm and attended elementary school in a one-room schoolhouse. After graduating from Meridian High School in 1964, he attended the University of Idaho and was a member of Delta Tau Delta fraternity. Randy graduated in 1968 from the University of Idaho College of Business and was named as an outstanding graduating senior. Randy went on to receive his master's degree from the University of Wyoming and a Ph.D. from the University of Minnesota. Professor Byers joined the University of Idaho business faculty in 1973 and served as department chairman for 18 years.

Randy was honored with numerous teaching and advising awards and recently returned to the classroom full-time, where he continued his love for teaching, which spanned almost 30 years at the University of Idaho College of Business and Economics. Because he was well-known and admired by so many of his students and advisees, the first floor level in the new J.A. Albertson's College of Business on the University of Idaho campus was named in his honor prior to his death.

He learned to hunt from his father and grandfather and passed on the hunting passion to his sons. He was a bowhunter by choice. As a child he dreamed of big game hunting in Africa. He achieved his dream with five great hunts in the last six years. Randy found hunting challenging, mentally and physically, and was quoted as saying, "It is just part of who I am." A granite brick was placed upon the Boone and Crockett Club's Millennium Circle in Randy's memory through the generosity of Boone and Crockett Club Members.

ABOUT THE AUTHORS: *George A. Bettas, Ed.D., Stevensville, Montana, is the Boone and Crockett Club's Executive Director. He became a Regular Member of the Boone and Crockett Club in 1989 and has served as the Club's Vice-President of Administration, Vice-President of Communications, Chairman of the Associates Committee, and Editor of* Fair Chase *magazine. He has been an Official Measurer and member of the Records Committee since 1990. George is a founder and past president of the Mule Deer Foundation and retired Vice-Provost of Student Life and Dean of Students at Washington State University, Pullman, Washington. George has three Alaska brown bears in the records book and one typical mule deer. He is pictured at left with one of his trophy Alaska brown bears, which scores 28-7/16 points.*

Jack Reneau is a certified wildlife biologist who has been Director of Big Game Records for the Boone and Crockett Club since 1983 and a Professional Member since 1986. He was responsible for the day-to-day paperwork of the Boone and Crockett Club's records-keeping activities from 1976 to 1979 as an information specialist for the Hunter Services Division of the National Rifle Association (NRA) when NRA and Boone and Crockett Club cosponsored the B&C Awards Program.

Jack earned a M.S. in Wildlife Management from Eastern Kentucky University and a B.S. in Wildlife Management from Colorado State University. Jack, far right in the photo above, recently harvested a records-book Coues' whitetail deer while on a hunting trip in Mexico. The buck scores 103-3/8 points.

WILDLIFE
FOR THE 21ST CENTURY: II

RECOMMENDATIONS TO PRESIDENT GEORGE W. BUSH

AMERICAN WILDLIFE CONSERVATION PARTNERS

FOREWORD

ROBERT MODEL
PRESIDENT
Boone and Crockett Club

This 12th edition of *Records of North American Big Game* is published at an important time, not only as a continuation of an important aspect of the Club's history, but also as we settle into the 21st century and work hard to maintain our hunting heritage. I am most honored to have the opportunity to participate in this small way with this 12th edition of the records book. It has been my privilege to be the President of the Boone and Crockett Club during the past three years.

In the early 1990s the Club recognized that we were facing important decisions to meet the challenges of the 21st century. As is our history, the Club, under the leadership of Dan Pedrotti, spent a great deal of energy and time developing a strategic plan identifying the core objectives and principles for the Club. This took shape as a triangle. The cornerstones of our triangle of objectives are the records book, our commitment to hunting ethics, and our conservation programs.

Conservation Programs

As Pedrotti spearheaded this important work with the assistance of Steve Mealey and Dan Dessecker, we branched out in our conservation efforts to include policy. That policy initiative was an outgrowth of the Club's leadership in helping create the American Wildlife Conservation Partners. This began as Pedrotti's dream that became a reality with the commitment by 40 hunter-conservation groups to find common ground in order to speak with a single voice on issues that affect our whole community. This unprecedented cooperation produced *Wildlife for the 21st Century*. This is the first set of recommendations that were published and presented to President George W. Bush and his Administration. With a lot of hard work from our group, the Administration formulated their conservation initiatives based in large part on these recommendations and concerns. The 11 recommendations were:

SECRETARY GALE NORTON OF THE DEPARTMENT OF INTERIOR HOSTED A RECEPTION, AS WELL AS A MINI CONFERENCE ON CONSERVATION IN MAY 2005. THE MAIN PURPOSE OF THE GATHERING WITH REPRESENTATIVES OF NEARLY ALL OF THE 40 AMERICAN WILDLIFE CONSERVATION PARTNERS (AWCP), WAS FOR THE AWCP TO PRESENT THE SECRETARY WITH **WILDLIFE FOR THE 21ST CENTURY: VOLUME II – RECOMMENDATIONS TO PRESIDENT GEORGE W. BUSH.**

- Maintain and Restore Forest and Rangeland Habitats in the West Through Proactive Public Land Management
- Maintain and Restore Forest Habitats in the East Through Proactive National Forest Management
- Reinforce State Authority and Responsibility for Wildlife Management-Funding Issues
- Emphasize Cooperative National Forest Decision Making
- Ensure Effective Federal Natural Resource Leadership
- Support Wildlife Conservation Provisions in the 2002 Farm Bill
- Reaffirm State Authority and Responsibility for Wildlife Management – Legal Issues
- Establish Federal Budget Priorities that will Restore Wildlife Funding to the 1980 Level
- Increase Funding to Provide for Hunter Retention, Recruitment, and Education
- Remove Disincentives and Create Incentives for Private Land Wildlife Conservation
- Initiate an Assessment of Federal Land Laws to Identify Legal and Regulatory Problems Contributing to Federal Land Management "Gridlock"

SECRETARY OF THE INTERIOR, GALE NORTON, PICTURED HERE WITH ATTENDEES REPRESENTING NUMEROUS AWCP GROUPS, PLEDGED TO CONTINUE AND STRENGTHEN THEIR CONSERVATION PARTNERSHIP AGENDA, WITH W21: VOLUME II AS THE PRIMARY FOCUS.

The partnership is in its sixth year, and we have grown stronger and more committed with each year. With President Bush's second term, we have been given the opportunity to update our recommendations based upon some of the successes during the first term, and consistent with other issues that have surfaced since W-21 was first published.

Our new recommendations were presented to the Administration in mid-May 2005. The updated recommendations are:

- Ensure Effective Natural Resource Leadership
- Utilize Comparative Ecological Risk Assessments in Land Management Decisions
- Fully Incorporate the Conservation of Wildlife and Other Natural Resources Into Energy Development
- Support Wildlife Conservation Provisions in the 2007 Farm Bill

PRESIDENT BUSH ADDRESSED THE AWCP, INCLUDING THE CLUB'S PRESIDENT (FAR RIGHT), ON DECEMBER 12, 2003.

- Reaffirm State Authority and Responsibility and Secure Assured State Funding for Wildlife Management
- Create Incentives and Remove Disincentives for Wildlife Conservation on Private Land
- Promote Hunting and Recreational Shooting on Federal Lands
- Maintain and Restore Forest and Rangeland Habitats Through Proactive Public Land Management
- Establish Federal Budget Priorities That Will Restore Wildlife Funding to the 1980 Level
- Coordinate Efforts to Address the Threats from Invasive Species
- Emphasize Cooperative National Forest Decision Making
- Establish a Nationwide Strategy to Sustain Wildlife Health

I recognize that some might ask the question "why is the Boone and Crockett Club involving itself in policy issues?" In the fast moving world that we live in, decisions are being made in Washington that affect sportsmen and sportswomen, and our entire hunting heritage. If we do not have a seat at the table during these discussions, we will be left out of the process and our concerns may be passed by. Therefore, I am proud to have played a small part with fellow members in recognizing how important Dan Pedrotti's vision was, and that it is now being realized. During the past three years, our community was invited to the White House on three separate occasions.

President Bush wanted to thank us for our suggestions, and he also expressed genuine concern and interest for our public and private lands and the importance of good land stewardship.

Another important initiative in our conservation programs is the Professorship we created at the University of Montana. Under the leadership of Hal Salwasser and Jack Ward Thomas, this position has become the model for educating future conservation leaders in wildlife and natural resource policy, an area heretofore overlooked. We have just established another chair at Texas A&M University that will broaden our outreach. We are also working to complete a joint chair with Boise Cascade and Robert Mealey at Oregon State University. We are developing a model for K-12 education and are working with our partners in AWCP to develop and coordinate our individual efforts. The Club is taking the leadership in developing a paradigm we hope will be adopted by our sister organizations. Our plan is to take the best of what we do with education, combine it with the best that the other organizations do regarding education, and create a Conservation Leadership Institute that will provide the best natural resource and wildlife conservation education program for students who will become our future resource managers.

Under the leadership of Winnie Kessler, our grants-in-aids program is well managed. We are identifying the best students to support in their research. Winnie has been very effective in partnering with other organizations to procure added funding sources to support the best research projects.

The Theodore Roosevelt Memorial Ranch is also part of our education outreach. It provides a unique venue for retreats, research, and K-12 education programs. The cattle ranching operation lends itself to practical demonstration, and we are now in full operation. I believe we have achieved the clear vision that Jack Parker, Bill Spencer, Wes Dixon, Tim Hixon, Lowell Baier, Bill Searle, and others had when they bought the ranch to function as a practical example of the Clubs' commitment to integrating ranching while protecting wildlife and natural resource values.

Hunter ethics

Hunter ethics is metamorphosing in the 21st century. The Club has always been the unquestioned leader in defining hunter ethics. In order to understand the historical context under which we developed a code of ethics for hunters, it is important to remember that the success the Club had through the 20th century was an outgrowth of the market hunters, and in reality, their blatant disregard for proper wildlife management. Those early market hunters were killers not hunters. If our big game heritage was to survive, our early members knew we had to put in place rules and regulations, and define fair chase. Fair chase is all about hunter ethics, and the Club has continued to struggle with these challenges. We are faced in the 21st century with different ethical challenges that are an outgrowth of the success we had with stopping market hunting, making hunters responsible, and instilling a code of behavior that insured that hunting was viewed, not as indiscriminate killing, but as a part of man's natural hunter/gatherer instinct.

I point this out here because I believe in ensuing records books we will track the success or failure of what will come in the future. Actually, the future is now. I hope and pray that our leadership in this new century will be as successful as our leadership in the last century.

Records books

From time to time, providence and good luck lead to the right individual surfacing to carry on the important work of our early leaders in our *Records of North American Big Game*. Eldon "Buck" Buckner is such an individual. He comes to us out of the mold of Prentiss Gray, Sam Webb, Jack Parker, Walter White, Grancel Fitz, and Phil Wright. Buck's leadership is so crucial at this time because he clearly understands that the other parts to the triangle (conservation policy and hunter ethics) support our records program.

This ensures that our honored records book is integrated as a part of the whole and not a stand-alone entity. It is important that we focus on this and continue to re-member as we move through this century that the Club's focus is on the whole and not just the individual parts.

I want to thank all the contributors to this 12th edition of *Records of North American Big Game*. I believe this book is a cornerstone publication carrying on our legacy and illustrating our long and cherished hunter-conservation values and visions.

ABOUT THE AUTHOR: *Robert Model, age 62, was born in Greenwich, Connecticut. He is owner and President of Mooncrest Ranch in Cody, Wyoming. Model attended The Browning School and Elon College. He is currently Vice President of Stillrock Management and Vice President of Elmrock Capital, both based in New York. He is a past director of the National Forest Foundation; current Chairman of the American Wildlife Conservation Partners; and board member for the Theodore Roosevelt Conservation Partners. He has previously served as a Direc-tor on the boards of CapMAC, Overhills, Inc., and Piggly Wiggly.*

24th BIG GAME AWARDS
1998-2000 ▲ SPRINGFIELD, MISSOURI

AWARDS JUDGES PANELS

25th BIG GAME AWARDS
2001-2003 ▲ KANSAS CITY, KANSAS

INTRODUCTION

ELDON L. "BUCK"
BUCKNER
CHAIR
Records of North American
Big Game Committee

Boone and Crockett Club published its first record book reflecting the current scoring system in 1952. I first discovered it in the shop of Tucson taxidermist John Doyle about 1956. The late John Doyle was a B&C Official Measurer, veteran Coues' deer hunter, and Irish philosopher. I was simply a teenager enamored with hunting and guns who devoured everything in print that he encountered on these subjects. It was John who measured my first record-class Coues' deer, shared the next (1958) edition of the B&C records book with me, and later mentored me to become an Official Measurer in 1968.

Over the years, the size of *Records of North American Big Game* editions has increased greatly compared to the modest volumes of the Fifties, although the general format has remained similar. In both older and newer books you'll find chapters about Boone and Crockett Club, big game hunting and an extensive records section. This edition is no exception.

Chapters of historical interest in this book include one on the Club's greatest bestowed honor, the Sagamore Hill Award, and another on the National Collection of Heads and Horns now displayed at the Buffalo Bill Historical Center at Cody, Wyoming.

The Boone and Crockett Club was originally founded as a big game conservation organization. This primary focus has not changed. A significant portion of this book reports on the Club's current conservation efforts.

Dr. Jack Ward Thomas, the Club's Professor of Wildlife Conservation, a wildlife research biologist, and former Chief of the U.S. Forest Service, reports on the Club's professorships sponsored at key universities and their purpose. Another conservation education project, Conservation Across Boundaries, is explained by B&C Professional Member Lisa Flowers.

Dr. Winifred Kessler, another B&C Professional Member in charge of the research grants program, de-

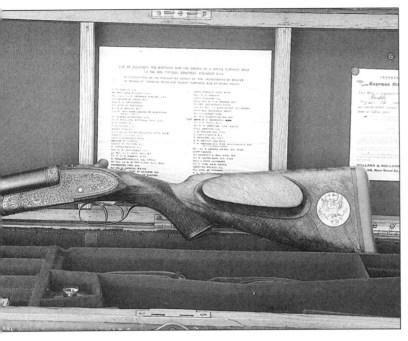

scribes current projects the Club is assisting financially. Jim Heffelfinger, a deer expert with the Arizona Game and Fish Department and author of a soon to be published book on deer of the Southwest, has contributed an informative piece on DNA research as it relates to big game records keeping.

In keeping with the Club's tradition of leadership in the conservation area, Steve Mealey tells of the historic and effective formation of the American Wildlife Conservation Partners while Gary Wolfe relates the formation of the Chronic Wasting Disease Alliance.

Boone and Crockett Club's initiation of the Hunt Fair Chase campaign and its message of a basic Club tenet is covered by Keith Balfourd.

A fascinating article on antlers and factors affecting their growth and development by Dr. Robert Brown of Texas A&M University will be of interest to any deer hunter.

The current trend to dictate wildlife management via the ballot box with misguided initiatives instead of biological facts and proven techniques is reported in Vern Bleich's excellent treatise on the effects of anti-hunting efforts.

One of my favorite chapters in the 1958 records book included photos of selected rifles for hunting North American big game. The special color section of this book features custom and otherwise special rifles that have connections to both current and former Club members and other noted hunters, from Theodore Roosevelt to Jack O'Connor.

A special feature of this 12th Edition is a collection of "most memorable hunt" stories from some of today's well-known outdoor writers. One of my favorites is Gordon Whittington's tale of going back in time to take a deer at the same location and with the same old rifle as he did the first time decades ago. Others I personally connected with were Diana Rupp's elk hunting story, Todd Smith's sheep hunting account, Bob Robb's deer hunt, and Craig Boddington's desert sheep story.

BARREN GROUND CARIBOU
477 points ■ Daniel L. Dobbs

ROCKY MOUNTAIN GOAT
56-6/8 points
G. Wober & L. Michalchuk

TULE ELK
365 points ■ Bryce Evans

NON-TYPICAL COLUMBIA BLACKTAIL
208-1/8 points
Frank S. Foldi

MOUNTAIN CARIBOU
453 points ■ C. Candler Hunt

ROOSEVELT'S ELK
404-6/8 points
Jason S. Ballard

NON-TYPICAL SITKA BLACKTAIL
134 points
William B. Steele, Jr.

12 NEW WORLD'S RECORDS

BIGHORN SHEEP
208-3/8 points
Guinn D. Crousen

MUSKOX
129 points
Craig D. Scott

PRONGHORN
95 points ■ David Meyer

NON-TYPICAL COUES' WHITETAIL
196-2/8 points ■ Native American

PRONGHORN
95 points ■ Dylan M. Woods

The primary reason for a big game records book is for the records themselves. This latest edition stands as a tribute to the success of modern wildlife management and continued conservation of habitat, despite increasing and continuous adverse factors. It includes over 5,000 new entries. The category with the most entries is the whitetail deer, as would be expected. It is somewhat startling to compare whitetail entries in this edition with those in the 1952 book. Back then, 84 typical whitetails were listed that met the then minimum score of 140. This book includes 4,060 that make the current minimum of 170!

This book includes records for the first time of three new categories: non-typical Columbia blacktail deer, non-typical Sitka blacktail deer, and tule elk.

In addition to the three new World's Records in the new categories mentioned, new World's Records have been replaced in eight other categories since publication of the 1999 book. Led by Guinn Crousen's year 2000 bighorn ram that edged out the Weiler ram taken in 1911, other categories with new leaders, or a tie are: non-typical Coues' deer, barren ground caribou, mountain caribou, Roosevelt's elk, Rocky Mountain goat, muskox, and pronghorn. In the pronghorn category two trophies tied for World's Record status.

It will be interesting to see if North America's wildlands and evolving management will produce similar records in the next six years!

ABOUT THE AUTHOR: *Eldon "Buck" Buckner of Baker City, Oregon, is a Regular Member and Vice President of the Boone and Crockett Club. An Official Measurer since 1968, Buck has served as a Judge, Consultant, or Judges Panel Chairman since 1989 and has chaired the Records of North American Big Game Committee since 2002. Buck was formerly a U.S. Forest Service Range Conservationist in the Southwest, now ranches in Oregon and has hunted extensively in North America, Africa, and Europe.*

TABLE OF CONTENTS

Records of North American Big Game
12th Edition

THE FIRST-EVER SPECIAL JUDGES PANEL CONVENED IN MISSOULA, MONTANA, ON AUGUST 15, 2001, FOR THE SOLE PURPOSE OF CERTIFYING TWO NEW WORLD'S RECORDS — GUINN CROUSEN'S BIGHORN SHEEP AND VICENTE SANCHEZ-VALDEPENAS' MUSK OX. THE MUSK OX WAS LATER USURPED BY CRAIG SCOTT'S BULL AS THE REIGNING WORLD'S RECORD. MEMBERS OF THE FIRST SPECIAL JUDGES' PANEL INCLUDE (CLOCKWISE FROM TOP LEFT) FRED KING, JACK RENEAU, ROBERT HANSON, STAN RAUCH, AND RANDY BYERS.

TABLE OF CONTENTS

Continued

RECORDS OF NORTH AMERICAN BIG GAME

12TH EDITION

CHAPTER ONE

B&C and Our Role in Conservation Today

LISA FLOWERS
SELMA GLASSCOCK
HAROLD J. SALWASSER
PROFESSIONAL MEMBERS
Boone and Crockett Club

CONSERVATION ACROSS BOUNDARIES®

An educational strategy for the future

Commercial and unregulated hunting, deforestation, and other habitat alterations contributed to precipitous declines in wildlife populations and habitats in the United States prior to establishment of the Boone and Crockett Club in 1887. Legislation promoted by the Boone and Crockett Club in the late 1800s and early 1900s served to outlaw commercial hunting, support state hunting regulations, and establish highly effective and sustainable forest, park, and wildlife refuge management systems. Later, political advocacy by Club members led to establishment of wildlife research units and teaching programs at land-grant universities across the nation. These programs served to train and educate many of today's professional wildlife managers and scientists. Yet, today, just over 100 years after the establishment of the Boone and Crockett Club, we still are concerned over decline of selected wildlife species in North America.

Why do species and their habitats continue to decline? The answer lies in the changing demographics of the human population. The U.S. population had reached nearly 60 million people when the Boone and Crockett Club was founded, but by the turn of the 21st century our nation's population had more than quadrupled to nearly 295 million people. Worldwide population growth has been exponential, with the global population reaching nearly 6.5 billion in 2005. Secondly, our lifestyles have changed. Once a rural, agrarian-oriented society with strong connections to the land, we are now a technology-dependent, urban society not only physically and psychologically disconnected from the land, but living in cities that continually erode the edges of remaining habitats on working farms, ranches, and forests. Consequently, we must refurbish our conservation toolbox with pioneering strategies to ensure the future of our wildlife heritage.

THE BOONE AND CROCKETT CLUB AND THE WELDER WILDLIFE FOUNDATION SPONSOR THE CONSERVATION ACROSS BOUNDARIES© PROGRAM — A HANDS-ON FIELD COURSE DESIGNED FOR CLASSROOM SCIENCE TEACHERS WHO ARE INTERESTED IN INTEGRATING NATURAL RESOURCE CONSERVATION INTO THEIR CURRICULA. PARTICIPANTS PICTURED HERE ARE TOURING THE CLUB'S THEODORE ROOSEVELT MEMORIAL RANCH IN DUPUYER, MONTANA.

Conservation Across Boundaries® (CAB) is one such tool. CAB was created in 2001, through the joint efforts of the Boone and Crockett Club and the Welder Wildlife Foundation. It has proven to be one of the most innovative teacher in-service training programs to date. CAB is national in scale and was created to combat some of our greatest contemporary challenges. These challenges fall into two principle areas of concern. First, we need to elevate the weak public understanding and concern for wildlife and natural resource conservation, and to promote the vital need to manage and use our natural resources in ethical and domestically sustainable ways. Second, we must combat the abundance of misinformation being spread by groups to sway national policy away from progressive conservation as originally crafted and envisioned by such visionary Club leaders as President Theodore Roosevelt, Gifford Pinchot, George Bird Grinnell, and Aldo Leopold.

The Club understands that teachers are our link to young people and future generations. Fortunately, many teachers have a profound appreciation of wildlife and natural resources. However, due to their urban backgrounds and exposure to environmental perspectives, which often lack a conservation or sustainability context during their formative years, many have limited educational backgrounds regarding wildlife and lack the support and confidence to take students into the field and teach them about wildlife, natural resources, and conservation. They lack training in the disciplines of wildlife ecology and management, and the experience to design the field-based projects necessary to stimulate their students' interest in the natural world. Finally, teachers need to appreciate the vital role of people in stewardship and sustainable use of such resources as a key to society's successful future. Despite these deficiencies, teachers are inspired to learn.

Conservation education programs that share the values and approaches of Conservation Across Boundaries® provide opportunities for educators to learn about, experience, and to discuss conservation-related issues openly with natural resource professionals. Only then will educators be able to assist younger generations in their development of a conservation ethic. Attitudes, behaviors, values, and perceptions concerning the importance of land stewardship, habitat enhancement, best management practices, and ethical uses can be developed given time and education. Teachers serving as mentors can play an important role in the development of an appreciation and respect for healthy lands, plant, and wildlife diversity, and sustainable human interactions with natural systems.

Conservation Across Boundaries® takes the concept of the teacher as a conservation "trailblazer" to a new level. Teachers learn to use a systems approach to integrate scientific knowledge, problem solving, and critical thinking regarding issues of conservation and sustainable use of wildlife and natural resources. Specifically, the course trains teachers to design authentic, inquiry-based field investigations for their students, and within these investigations students learn to integrate their findings with biological and ecological knowledge and natural resource conservation issues

with regional historical and cultural knowledge. Our approach promotes a systems view of the underlying causes and solutions to challenges and opportunities regarding wildlife and natural resources.

Course design includes invited professionals from the fields of natural science and resource management (biology, ecology, forestry, range) who discuss current conservation issues with the Conservation Across Boundaries® teachers. Science and conservation lessons and activities are incorporated into field experiences, such as establishing transects to measure plant and animal diversity, and collecting, identifying, and preserving plant specimens. Teachers also learn to utilize computer modeling, geographic information systems, and mapping technology and how to integrate these into their curricula. We incorporate computer programs that will enable their students to develop multimedia presentations that can be shared with other students and adults. To further emphasize our

THROUGH CONSERVATION ACROSS BOUNDARIES® THE BOONE AND CROCKETT CLUB, IN PARTNERSHIP WITH WELDER WILDLIFE FOUNDATION, HAS BLAZED A NEW TRAIL TOWARDS A FUTURE WHERE MORE STUDENTS AND TEACHERS LEARN TO APPRECIATE AND UNDERSTAND THE NEED FOR CONSERVATION OF OUR WILDLIFE RESOURCES; WHERE ALL MEMBERS OF SOCIETY FEEL COMPELLED TO DEVELOP A PERSONAL CONSERVATION ETHIC; AND, ULTIMATELY, A FUTURE WHERE A COMMON LANGUAGE FOR NATURAL RESOURCE CONSERVATION IS THE NORM AND IS SPOKEN READILY BY OUR FUTURE CULTURAL LEADERS.

systems approach to learning, teachers are exposed to how historical, cultural, and socioeconomic aspects of human settlement and land use activities have shaped, and continue to shape, conservation issues regarding wildlife and natural resources in different ecological regions. In addition to using the outdoors as a scientific "classroom" in two diverse ecosystems, participants learn about the history and economy of Texas and Montana; hunting practices and hunting ethics; the role that agriculture plays in providing wildlife habitat on private lands; and current challenges facing farmers, ranchers, and hunters. Teachers receive 3 hours of graduate-level credit for completing the 2-week program and coursework.

CAB is unique in that it assembles teachers from throughout North America to facilitate the interchange of regional and cultural knowledge pertaining to the use and management of natural resources in their home territories. When established in 2001, the course was restricted to teachers from Texas and Montana. Subsequent courses in 2002, 2003, and 2004 included teachers from 9 additional states, as well as Mexico and South Africa. To date, 68 educators have completed the Conservation Across Boundaries® course.

To cultivate the seeds of their newly gained knowledge about natural resource conservation, teachers are assembled into peer groups to develop cooperative projects that are administered by the teachers in their home classrooms. These projects are designed to guide students in investigation and information sharing with each other and, if at all possible, with "partner classrooms." Ideally, their students will begin to work collectively to research and develop solutions to conservation challenges within their local area or region. Ultimately, these programs will guide them in the development of a personal conservation ethic and help to build a growing culture of conservation. To date, our impact is limited. We must expand the CAB ethic and approach nationwide – a goal for future years.

Individual attitudes and behaviors, which are strongly influenced by human values, are important in establishing cross-boundary relationships as they relate to wildlife conservation and stewardship of natural resources. Cooperation in cross-boundary conservation efforts, whether across ownership, state or international boundaries, are enhanced when people share similar values regarding the natural resources that provide them with food, clothing, shelter, environmental services, and other necessities of life. Conservation Across Boundaries® is one of the Boone and Crockett Club's major strategies for creating a new climate of conservation in the 21st century, what we call the new American Conservation Ethic for the 21st Century.

The Club's vision is a future where educators routinely integrate the principles of sustainability – shared and ethical stewardship and use of domestic natural resources in ways that promote environmental, economic, and community values -- through wildlife and natural resource conservation, ecology, and management with authentic field-based studies within a systems context. To achieve this vision, we must ensure that teachers actively seek and be provided with the highest quality educational opportunities that articulate this new ethic. The Conservation Across Boundaries® model provides the tools for teachers to develop their own models of scientific inquiry and instructional strategies to guide their students' thinking and understanding of the origin and importance of natural resources in their daily lives.

CAB CURRICULUM CONTENT TOPICS

- Ecological and Cultural History
- Geology and Soils
- Weather and Climate
- Fish Ecology
- Coastal Ecology
- Riparian and Wetland Habitats and Ecology
- Plant Identification and Ecology
- Wildlife Indentification and Management
- Wildlife and Water Quality Monitoring
- Habitat Assessment and Evaluation
- Conservation Ethics
- Conservation of Threatened and Endangered Species
- International Wildlife Conservation Issues
- Conservation and Identification of Birds
- Conservation of Wildlife Habitat
- Public and Private Land Management
- Wilderness
- Systems Ecology and Modeling
- PowerPoint Presentations
- Global Positioning Systems
- ARC View and Topo USA Mapping Software

Through Conservation Across Boundaries® the Boone and Crockett Club in partnership with Welder Wildlife Foundation have blazed a new trail towards a future where more students and teachers learn to appreciate and understand the need for conservation of our wildlife resources; where all members of society feel compelled to develop a personal conservation ethic; and, ultimately, a future where a common language for natural resource conservation is the norm and is spoken readily by our future cultural leaders.

WINIFRED B. KESSLER, PH.D.
PROFESSIONAL MEMBER
Boone and Crockett Club

BOONE AND CROCKETT CLUB CONSERVATION GRANTS PROGRAM

The Boone and Crockett Club's tradition of funding wildlife research dates back to 1948, coincident with the formation of the Conservation Committee. The Club's Grants-in-Aid have seeded the careers of over a hundred graduate students, including many who now occupy leadership positions in the wildlife profession. These investments have yielded a wealth of information on biological, management, and policy aspects of North American wildlife. The program remains unique in maintaining a focus on big game species, and in soliciting proposals directly from graduate students.

The Grants-in-Aid Program underwent several milestones in the last 10 years. Prominent among these was the development of a strategic plan that establishes three goals for the program:

- Support the Club's mission to promote the guardianship and provident management of big game and associated wildlife in North America by funding research required by managers and policy-makers.
- Complement the Club's other research programs, the Theodore Roosevelt Memorial Ranch, and the Boone and Crockett Professorships, by supporting graduate student research at diverse locations across North America.
- Assist and encourage promising graduate students who have chosen careers in the wildlife profession.

The strategic plan sets forth a yearly timetable for the solicitation of proposals from all schools in the U.S. and Canada that have graduate programs in wildlife, and establishes a formal process and criteria for the evaluation of proposals.

A second milestone was the creation of an endowment account and the naming of the William I. Spencer Conservation Grants Program to honor the memory of this Boone and Crockett Club leader. Once the endowment is complete, it will provide the program with a stable, long-term revenue source to fund the grants program. Meanwhile, the Club makes available about $25,000 each year to fund a modest program. This would not seem to "buy" much research, given that the cost of Ph.D.-level studies today often run in the hundreds of thousands of dollars. This trend toward larger budgets reflects the greater scales and complexity of information required for management, as well as the cost of modern technologies such as DNA analysis and GPS collars. But a parallel trend is that few studies today are supported by a single funding source. Typically, graduate students use their Boone and Crockett Club support as "seed money" to attract additional, larger grants from a variety of public and private funding sources. Through this leveraging process, the Club serves a vital role in the launching of significant research projects even though its actual monetary contribution is modest.

A third milestone was the initiation of themes that focus each year's grant competition on problems of greatest interest to the Boone and Crockett Club. The 2002 and 2003 theme, *Sustainable Use of Wildlife on Private Lands* and the *Private/Public Land*

Interface, produced one Masters and five Ph.D. projects addressing predator compensation programs, large carnivore conservation, metapopulation dynamics of elk, water influences on desert bighorn sheep, and black bear ecology and restoration. The theme in 2004 and 2005, *Mule Deer Conservation*, initiated several studies that seek causes of the range-wide decline of this highly valued species, or that contribute to the conservation or restoration of mule deer and their habitats.

Other recent changes have improved the effectiveness and efficiency of the program. For several years now, grant recipients have been invited to submit an article about their research for publication in the Club's premier magazine, *Fair Chase*. These articles inform Boone and Crockett Club Members and Associates about the purposes and results of the research, and relate the students' personal experiences in carrying out the work. Awareness of the program is also enhanced by an annual *Fair Chase* article that profiles the students and projects selected for funding in that year.

And today, because of improvements to the Boone and Crockett Club's website, prospective applicants can download Conservation Grants information and forms and submit their applications electronically. Before long, we may be able to eliminate paper copies altogether from the solicitation, application, and evaluation cycle.

Every year, the Conservation Grants Program receives more worthy proposals than it can fund. That is the reason for the recent launching of "Partners for Investment," which invites other groups and individuals to consider the Conservation Grants Program as a convenient and effective way to invest in wildlife research and future professionals. The Conservation Grants Program has an effective system in place to solicit proposals on specified topics or themes, evaluate submissions for quality and merit, and administer the delivery of funds and the receipt of products. By partnering with the Boone and Crockett Club, others who wish to support wildlife research can target their investments for maximum effect, while avoiding the work and expense of soliciting, evaluating, and administering grants.

Funding partnerships can take different forms, depending on the partner's objectives, preferences, and funding capability. We invite interested parties to examine the options outlined on the Club's website,

JAMES W. CAIN, A 2002 GRANTS-IN-AID STUDENT, WAS AWARDED AN ADDITIONAL GRANT TOWARD HIS STUDY ON THE INFLUENCE OF ARTIFICIAL WATER SOURCES ON DESERT BIGHORN SHEEP. JAMES IS ENROLLED IN THE PH.D. PROGRAM AT THE UNIVERSITY OF ARIZONA, WORKING UNDER THE SUPERVISION OF B&C PROFESSIONAL MEMBER, DR. PAUL KRAUSMAN. A COMPLETE LIST OF GRANT RECIPIENTS AND THEIR PROJECTS CAN BE FOUND ON THE CLUB'S WEBSITE.

www.booneandcrockettclub.com. (Click on "Education," then "Conservation Grants," followed by "Partners for Investment.") Better yet, approach us with new ideas on how, together, we can enhance investment in big game research and future wildlife professionals.

In the short term, these investments yield knowledge and tools that promote the guardianship and provident management of our precious wildlife resources. Longer term, they will have a significant role in shaping the next generation of wildlife professionals and conservation leaders.

JACK WARD THOMAS
BOONE AND CROCKETT
PROFESSOR OF WILDLIFE
CONSERVATION
University of Montana

B&C Professorships
A Bridge to the Future

In the early 1990s, the Boone and Crockett Club moved to reenter the arena of wildlife conservation in a significant fashion. Among those bold moves was a two-pronged effort in Montana. The first was the acquisition of a working cattle ranch adjacent to the Lewis and Clark National Forest on the Rocky Mountain Front near Dupuyer. The purpose of this ranch was three fold: preservation from development of this spectacular property that provided prime wildlife habitat; demonstration that accommodating significant wildlife populations was compatible with ranching operations; provision of a "laboratory" for wildlife related research; and service as a center for field oriented education for kindergarten through grade 12 students. Also included in the package was the establishment of an endowed professorship in the College of Forestry and Conservation at the University of Montana in Missoula through a $3 million endowment from the Club to be matched by $3 million from the University. The holder of this chair was to be known as the Boone and Crockett Professor of Wildlife Conservation.

The Chair was intended to be, and has been, occupied by senior, already well-established wildlife professionals with demonstrated skills as a research scientist with a knack for and experience in dealing at the interface of research and land/wildlife management. Communication skills, both written and spoken, were deemed important as the occupant was expected to occupy what the Club's founder, Theodore Roosevelt, called the "bully pulpit" for wildlife conservation. Those professionals who have held the Boone and Crockett Chair have been in high demand as speakers in various forums giving 20-30 presentations per year ranging from testimony before Congress to technical presentations to learned societies to talks to service clubs. Publications including such outlets as popular magazines, technical journals, book chapters, books, editorials, and others have averaged 20 or so per year. Indeed, the Chair provides a bully pulpit.

However, the Club was interested in having the Professor deal, at least to a large extent, with training of students with focus of associated research programs with pragmatic aspects of land and wildlife management. This focus would include: aspects of policy; political science; and economics. Graduates are trained and focused to enter into the arena of the "real world" of wildlife and land management — both in on-the-ground and political/policy positions — in the private, federal, and state sectors.

Students from varied backgrounds (e.g., forestry, range, wildlife, political science, law, biology, economics, social sciences, and business) have been recruited into the program over the years. The ideal graduate of the program was to be intentionally "cross-trained" in several disciplines as opposed to being intensely focused in a single discipline. The resources available to the Professor allowed recruiting carefully selected students who were fully supported for one to two years, and thereby able to carry full course loads – and to make up deficits in forestry/wildlife training – while a suitable research project was developed.

The entire purpose of such relatively "unusual" and prolonged training was to produce graduates who possessed a broad array of skill sets and who were dedicated to becoming leaders in the management arena found at the intersection of biology, politics, philosophy, policy, economics, and business.

Too many graduates of more standard wildlife, forestry, fisheries, and range programs find themselves unable to function effectively in the "real world" as they simply are overwhelmed by lack of understanding of how the world of management actually works. Those who are successful — and remain reasonably sane — learn, on the job, how the social system works and how to make their knowledge and skills valuable and influential within that system. The object of the Boone and Crockett Professorship is to encourage and develop young professionals who emerge from the womb of the university familiar with how the system works and how to bring their skills and values to bear within that system — starting with day number one. Particular emphasis is given to the role of private lands in the conservation of wildlife and sustenance of hunting traditions in North America.

Given the senior status, reputations, and "connections" of the Boone and Crockett Professors, their students have the advantage of facilitated entrée into the natural resources conservation community. This has proven useful in attaining fund-

THE BOONE AND CROCKETT WILDLIFE CONSERVATION PROGRAM ALSO SUPPORTS GRADUATE STUDENTS IN WILDLIFE CONSERVATION AND RELATED FIELDS THROUGH ITS FELLOW PROGRAM. THE CURRENT BOONE AND CROCKETT FELLOWS ARE SHOWN ABOVE WITH PROFESSOR JACK WARD THOMAS AND HIS WIFE AND PROFESSIONAL MEMBER KATHY THOMAS AT THE 2004 ANNUAL MEETING OF THE CLUB.

CURRENT BOONE AND CROCKETT FELLOWS

MARK STEINBACH - Evaluating the Consequences of a Public Land Grazing Permit Buyout Program, Permit Reductions, and Increased Fees on Land Ownership and Open Space in Western States

A.J. KROLL - An empirical assessment of habitat-based species viability procedures using the Dusky Flycatcher (*Empidonax oberholseri*) as a model species

STEPHANIE LYNN GRIPNE - Bartering for Conservation: Are Grassbanks an Effective Tool for Achieving Conservation, Promoting Stewardship, and Building Trust?

BRENDAN MOYNAHAN - Understanding Relationships Between Sage Grouse (*Centrocercus urophasianus*) Habitat and Population Dynamics in Eastern Montana

FORMER BOONE AND CROCKETT FELLOWS

KAUSH ARHA
DAYNA BAUMEISTER
THOMAS BAUMEISTER
JOHN CITTA
KRIS HURLBURT
JASON MOECKEL
ZACH PARSONS
JENNIFER MORGAN RINEHART
GREGORY T.M. SCHILDWACHTER
MATT TUNNO
LAURA VAN RIPER

ing for research proposals, assistance in research activities, and in obtaining suitable employment after graduation.

It was the hope of the founders of the Boone and Crockett Professorship program that these carefully selected and very special young professionals with carefully honed talents and values – attained through their training and exposure to the values and dedication of Club members – would quickly attain positions of influence and leadership in the conservation arena. Upon graduation, each of the doctoral graduates of the program have become professional members of the Club in the hope that continued association will keep the Club's values fresh in their minds and that their ever increasing knowledge, experience, achievements, and insights will, likewise, influence the Club over the years.

Graduates of the program have already begun to have significant impacts in the conservation arena and occupy a wide variety of positions in both private and government sectors – both state and federal. Those "in the pipeline" will, with little doubt do just as well.

Based upon the successful model at the University of Montana, the Boone and Crockett Club's members have endowed two additional Boone and Crockett Chairs at two other leading Universities in the conservation arena — Oregon State University and Texas A&M University. Future graduates of the programs will be at the forefront of the conservation efforts in the new century. The dream that the late Boone and Crockett Club President William "Bill" Spencer, and like-minded Club members dared to make reality in the early 1990s has grown and prospered. The dream of bountiful wildlife in North America that Theodore Roosevelt and the other founders of the Boone and Crockett Club had in 1887 came true. The Boone and Crockett Professorship programs are a significant and growing part of the Club's effort to make sure the dream remains alive and fruitful in this new century. So far, so good.

GARY J. WOLFE
PROFESSIONAL MEMBER
Boone and Crockett Club

Chronic Wasting Disease Alliance
CWD Background

This mysterious disease was first observed in captive mule deer at a Fort Collins, Colorado, research facility in the late 1960s. Biologists did not know what it was, and coined the term Chronic Wasting Disease (CWD) because of the way it affected its victims… They literally wasted away and died. In 1977, Dr. Elizabeth Williams, a veterinarian and graduate student at Colorado State University, determined that this strange new disease was a member of a class of neurological diseases known as Transmissible Spongiform Encephalopathy (TSE). TSEs include scrapie in domestic sheep, bovine spongiform encephalopathy (BSE or Mad Cow Disease) in cattle, and Creutzfeldt-Jakob Disease (CJD) in humans.

CWD was first identified in free-ranging wildlife in 1981 when a wild Colorado elk was diagnosed. This was followed by the confirmation of CWD in wild mule deer in 1985 and wild whitetail deer in 1990.

For many years it was thought that the disease was limited to a small endemic area in north central Colorado and southeastern Wyoming. But in 1996, CWD turned up in cap-

(3)

(40)

(1)

(2)

(1)   (8)   (7)

(1)   (2)

(4)

(12)   (1)

(1)

◯ CWD Infected Wild Cervid Populations

☐ States Where CWD Has Been Found in
Captive Cervid Populations

(#) Indicates total number of captive
herds infected. Many have been eliminated.

Map Up-to-date through
June 1, 2005

Photograph by Neal and Mary Jane Mishler

tive elk on several Saskatchewan game farms, and over the next few years was documented on game farms in nine states and two Canadian provinces. In 2001, the USDA declared an animal health emergency in response to the growing number of CWD outbreaks in game farm elk, and many states adopted a moratorium on the importation of captive cervids. In 2000, CWD was found in wild mule deer in both Saskatchewan and Nebraska, and by 2003 the disease had been confirmed in wild cervids in eight states and Saskatchewan.

The Need

Coinciding with the emergence of CWD in North America was the appearance of BSE in Europe in the mid-1980s. And since the 1996 announcement of an apparent relationship between BSE in cattle and variant CJD in humans, there has been a growing media, public, and animal and human health agency interest in TSEs. Could CWD, like Mad Cow Disease, pose a risk to human health? That question was being asked more and more by the media, sportsmen, and public health agencies.

The Boone and Crockett Club has long been a leader in wildlife conservation and hunting issues. As questions, concerns, and fears about CWD and its impact on wildlife populations and hunting grew; it became clear that strong leadership was needed to ensure that sportsmen had access to timely and accurate information about the disease, as well as a voice in the political debate. In late 2001, under the initiative of Boone and Crockett Club President Earl Morgenroth, three B&C members provided the seed money to allow the Club to develop a CWD initiative. As a wildlife biologist and Professional Member of the Club, I was contracted to develop and coordinate the Club's CWD plan. The Rocky Mountain Elk Foundation (RMEF) and the Mule Deer Foundation (MDF) immediately joined forces with the Club to help fund this important project. This partnership became known as the CWD Alliance, and the partners agreed to pool resources, share information and cooperate on projects and activities to positively impact the CWD issue. The Club's Executive Director, Dr. George A. Bettas, chaired the Alliance's steering committee and B&C Professor of Wildlife Conservation, Dr. Jack Ward Thomas, served as a special advisor to the Alliance.

The first order of the day was to open communications with the wildlife biologists and veterinarians actively working on the problem. Fortuitously, I was acquainted with several of the leading CWD experts and was invited to attend an upcoming Multi-State CWD Working Group meeting held in Cheyenne, Wyoming, in December 2001. The new CWD Alliance was enthusiastically welcomed by the interagency group, which unanimously agreed that the Alliance should focus on communication issues. Due to inaccurate reporting and media sensationalism, it was clear that timely public information and education were vital to the resolution of the CWD dilemma. Thus, the mission of the CWD Alliance was crafted:

> "To promote responsible and accurate communications regarding CWD, and to support strategies that effectively control CWD to minimize its impact on wild, free-ranging deer and elk populations."

CWD Website

Development of a CWD website became a top priority for the Alliance. Discussions were held with wildlife biologists, veterinarians, scientists, and agency administrators to ensure that the Alliance would be promoting scientifically credible information. The new CWD website, www.cwd-info.org, was launched in July 2002 and soon became widely-recognized as the "GO TO" resource for responsible and accurate CWD information, recording more than 82,000 visits during its first six months of operation. It quickly gained credibility with wildlife professionals.

By the end of 2004, the CWD Alliance website was referenced from almost every state and had recorded more than 375,000 visits.

CWD Symposia

The first National CWD Symposium was held August 6-7, 2002, in Denver, Colorado. It was hosted by the Colorado Division of Wildlife, and co-sponsored by several other agencies and organizations, including the CWD Alliance. To everyone's surprise, 453 wildlife biologists, pathologists, veterinarians, university scientists, natural resource administrators, and the press, convened to discuss and learn about CWD. What until recently had been an obscure wildlife disease, was now center stage in North American deer and elk management.

Over the next three years, the CWD Alliance participated in numerous CWD conferences and seminars at such varied venues as the SHOT Show, Outdoor Writers Association of America, Governor's Symposium on North America's Hunting Heritage, Alberta CWD Symposium, and Montana Outfitters and Guides Association. It also was a key co-sponsor of the second National CWD Symposium held July 12-14, 2005, in Madison, Wisconsin.

Congressional Testimony

In May 2002, the Alliance was organized, the House Resources Subcommittee on Forests and Forest Health held a congressional oversight hearing on CWD. The CWD Alliance was the only sportsmen-conservation group invited to testify. Its testimony focused on the need for congressional funding to assist state wildlife agencies in combating CWD, and congressional recognition that state wildlife agencies have the primary responsibility for managing wild cervid populations.

In early 2003, the Alliance took the lead drafting a letter to the House and Senate appropriations committees requesting full funding in fiscal 2004 for the "National Plan to Assist States, Federal Agencies and Tribes in Managing CWD in Captive and Free Ranging Cervids" (National CWD Plan). The letter was ultimately signed by more than 20 wildlife conservation organizations.

The Alliance was invited to address the Congressional Sportsmen's Caucus CWD Task Force Hearing held September 23, 2003, in Washington, D.C., where a presentation was given on the CWD Alliance's activities, and suggestions were made as to how Congress could assist in the effort to control CWD.

In April 2004, the Senate Environment and Public Works Subcommittee on Fisheries, Wildlife, and Water convened a hearing on CWD. Again, the CWD Alliance was the only sportsmen-conservation group invited to provide testimony.

CWD Working Groups and Committees

An important goal of the Alliance is to represent the perspectives of its partner organizations and their members to the various agency task forces and committees charged with addressing CWD management issues. The Alliance has been represented on several key working groups and committees:

- Multi-State CWD Working Group (2002 – 2004)
- National CWD Symposium Planning Committee (2002)
- International Association of Fish and Wildlife Agencies' (IAFWA) Fish and Wildlife Health Committee (2002 – 2004)
- IAFWA CWD Task Force (2003 – 2004)
- National Wildlife Health Center's CWD Data Standards Forum (2003)
- National Wildlife Health Center's CWD Risk Assessment Workshop (2004)

This involvement helps to provide the agencies and wildlife managers with valuable input from the sportsmen's perspective.

Partners and Funding

The Boone and Crockett Club, Mule Deer Foundation, and Rocky Mountain Elk Foundation launched the CWD Alliance in December 2001. The founding organizations were deeply concerned about the impact CWD was having, and may continue to have, on North America's wild deer and elk populations. They were also concerned about the impact this disease may have upon millions of hunters' desire and opportunity to hunt deer and elk each fall, and upon their confidence to continue to put healthful wild venison on their families' tables. By the end of 2004, the Alliance had grown to a total of 18 partners and sponsors (* indicates Sponsors):

- American Wildlife Conservation Fund
- Boone and Crockett Club
- Bowhunting Preservation Alliance
- Camp Fire Conservation Fund
- Dallas Safari Club
- Izaak Walton League of America
- Mule Deer Foundation
- National Fish and Wildlife Foundation
- National Shooting Sports Foundation
- Pope and Young Club
- Quality Deer Management Association

- Rocky Mountain Elk Foundation
- USGS - National Biological Information Infrastructure
- Whitetails Unlimited
- Wildlife Management Institute
- Bio-Rad Laboratories*
- IDEXX Laboratories*
- Cabela's*

During the Alliance's first three years, these dedicated conservation partners contributed approximately $200,000 to support the Alliance's core mission of promoting responsible and accurate communications regarding CWD, and encouraging strategies that effectively control CWD to minimize its impact on wild, free-ranging deer and elk populations.

"The CWD Alliance has brought a much needed resource to the battle against CWD. The provision of current, factual information to the media and general public was the missing ingredient in the effort to keep everyone informed. The CWD Alliance provided this information."

Bruce Morrison, Chair
National CWD Plan Implementation Team

At the time of this writing, there is no evidence that CWD is transmissible to humans. Visit the CWD Alliance website (www.cwd-info.org) for the most current information about CWD and specific recommendations for hunters.

STEPHEN P. MEALEY
PROFESSIONAL MEMBER
Boone and Crockett Club

AMERICAN WILDLIFE CONSERVATION PARTNERS
The First Five Years

The American Wildlife Conservation Partners (AWCP), a loose federation of 40 hunter-conservation organizations seeking a common national agenda for wildlife, and effectiveness through cooperation, has had a "good run" since its origin in August 2000 at Boone and Crockett Club headquarters in Missoula, Montana. Successes include unprecedented unity among the partners, access to President George W. Bush, his staff and key Cabinet members, and effectiveness in achieving important policy priorities. The AWCP and its momentum reflect the Boone and Crockett Club's continuing commitment to national and international conservation leadership.

Background

The Boone and Crockett Club is a great American legacy, a legacy that includes being the first private sportsmen's organization to deal effectively with conservation issues of a national scope; playing a key role in the creation and management of the first National Parks, Federal Forest Reserves (later National Forests), and National Wildlife Refuges; and advancing the conservation, scientific management, and ethical hunting of big game. The conservation idea of wise and managed use of forests and wildlife advocated by the Club and especially by its founder Theodore Roosevelt and members George Bird Grinnell and Gifford Pinchot (first Forest Service Chief), has become the rule for most state and federal resource management agencies. These landmark accomplishments, mostly in the latter part of the 19th Century and early 20th Century, were made in the Club's characteristic quiet manner: building strong coalitions of interest groups with shared priorities and facilitating their achievement of goals to meet the challenges of the times. The Club applied this same "quiet" approach in bringing the AWCP together to respond to the wildlife challenges of the 21st Century.

By 2000, it was clear to Club leaders that America's hunting traditions were being pulled in multiple directions by many factors. These included demographic changes, urbanization, broad concepts like ecosystem management and biological diversity, mass turnover in professional staffs of state and federal wildlife agencies, the shrinking segment of Americans that hunt and fish, and a growing segment of Americans that see preservation or non-use (non-hunting) of resources as the best way to sustainability. In spite of great successes in restoration of wildlife over the past 100 years, the changing structure of our society made it clear to the Club the necessity of wildlife managers and hunter/conservationist organizations working together more effectively than ever before to build on past successes. Further, the decade of 1995-2005 was recognized as critical for wildlife as the die was being cast for its future. Against this backdrop of challenge, hunter/conservationists were arrayed in literally hundreds of organizations potentially diluting their effectiveness. The early successes of Boone and Crockett Club members and citizen-sportsmen of the turn-of-the-century offered a clear example of the value of unity in tackling major conservation challenges. With all this in mind, representatives of 35 wildlife organizations with nearly 4.5 million total members gathered in the heat and smoke of a major fire season in August 2000 at the first AWCP summit as guests of the Boone and Crockett Club at its Missoula headquarters. These dedicated hunter-conservationists met for one purpose: to identify how best to work collectively to help chart the course for the future of wildlife conservation in the 21st Century in the United States.

A Magic Moment: The First Summit
During 2 days of meetings at the AWCP summit, 80 partner sportsmen and sportswomen

agreed to work together to build unity among their organizations and to increase their collective effectiveness; to develop a vision for wildlife; to develop and address a list of key wildlife conservation issues, and to advance the list as a wildlife conservation agenda for the new President and for Congress. The agenda was published in a booklet titled *Wildlife For The 21st Century* (W21) and was sent to the President on March 16, 2001. W21 presented a "short list of issues, which, if not properly resolved soon, could put American wildlife and American wildlife management at risk". It also contained 11 recommendations to the President. The "short list" of issues included:

1. Habitats of federal forests and rangelands are deteriorating; especially those at risk of uncharacteristic wildfire.

2. The authority of state natural resource agencies to manage fish and wildlife populations within their borders is eroding.

3. Actual and projected declines in hunter participation indicate that America's hunting heritage is at risk, and along with it, the tradition of American game management.

4. Public conflict and polarization over wildlife issues is increasing.

5. Incentives for wildlife conservation on private lands are inadequate.

6. The stewardship of federal lands is hampered by the web of laws and regulations guiding the management of these lands.

The Partners also agreed that policy positions would be taken by member organizations and not in the name of AWCP; it was also agreed however, that AWCP partners could and should initiate "sign on" letters advocating policy positions which would be circulated among all members affording each the opportunity to

AWCP published a booklet titled *Wildlife For The 21st Century* that was sent to the President on March 16, 2001. It presented a "short list of issues, which, if not properly resolved soon, could put American wildlife and American wildlife management at risk". It also contained 11 recommendations to the President.

sign and become part of the advocacy. Finally it was agreed to hold an AWCP summit each year in a different part of the country to reinforce unity and chart progress on current and emerging issues.

Fast Forward to 2003

The Partners continued to host Annual Summits and had their first meeting with Secretary Gale Norton and her staff in 2001. However, the year 2003 was particularly active for the AWCP and for Boone and Crockett Club participation. The Club "signed-on" to more than 15 letters during the year, directed to either Congress or the Administration. Each of these letters represented a unique policy position for the signing partners in the AWCP including the Club, on matters of high conservation significance. Club supported letters included those advancing forest health legislation, Clean Water Act authority restoration, Farm Bill appropriations, Conservation Reserve Program "Conserving Use", reprogramming US Forest Service funds for wildfire control, a Memorandum of Understanding between AWCP and federal natural resources agencies, funding for the 2004 Chronic Wasting Disease program, and support for Governor Mike Leavitt as EPA Administrator. Letters also included those opposing curtailment of "bear baiting" on federal land and reprogramming BLM wildlife funding to support the wild horse and burro Program. The Club also initiated and supported letters advocating changes to the US Forest Service planning regulations and to the US Fish and Wildlife Service and National Marine Fisheries Service proposed joint counterpart regulations for consultation under the Endangered Species Act.

SECRETARY OF THE INTERIOR, GALE NORTON, PICTURED HERE WITH ATTENDEES REPRESENTING NUMEROUS AWCP GROUPS, PLEDGED TO CONTINUE AND STRENGTHEN THEIR CONSERVATION PARTNERSHIP AGENDA, WITH W21: VOLUME II AS THE PRIMARY FOCUS.

Perhaps of greatest significance was the AWCP partners' and Club's support for H.R. 1904, the Healthy Forest Restoration Act (HFRA), which passed both the House and the Senate with "sign-on" letter support. HFRA passed through the House/Senate

Conference successfully and through both chambers again as the final conference version November 21, 2003. During this process, several additional letters of support were sent at strategically important times to keep the effort going. Wildlife community support from AWCP was critical to passing the legislation, a primary goal of the President, of W21, and of the Club.

Probably because of this critically important support for the Administration and its pursuit of HFRA as federal law, President Bush invited AWCP organizations to the White House in December 2003 to thank them and to announce his "No Net Loss of Wetlands" initiative that had been advocated by AWCP members. This meeting was a springboard to several subsequent meetings between AWCP members and different Cabinet members on W21 agenda items. It also led to another meeting hosted by the President in April 2004 at his Crawford, Texas, ranch for some AWCP members including AWCP Chairman and Boone and Crockett Club President Bob Model. Here the President reinforced his commitment to wildlife and wildlife habitat and to hunters and hunting.

AWCP/US Department of Interior (USDI) Miniconference
In January 2005, AWCP leaders and Interior Secretary Norton began discussions leading to a decision to hold a joint AWCP/USDI conference May 17-18, 2005, to review and celebrate W21 successes including most notably the President's Healthy Forest Initiative, which led to the HFRA, and wildlife conservation provisions in the 2002 Farm Bill. The conference was also designed as a forum for the AWCP to "roll out" and to discuss with USDI shared opportunities to implement W21, Volume II, developed by AWCP as an updated wildlife conservation agenda to coincide with President Bush's second term. Recommendations include:
1. Ensure Effective Natural Resource Leadership.
2. Utilize Comparative Ecological Risk Assessments in Land Management Decisions.
3. Fully Incorporate the Conservation of Wildlife and Other Natural Resources Into Energy Development.
4. Support Wildlife Conservation Provisions in the 2007 Farm Bill.
5. Reaffirm State Authority and Responsibility and Secure Assured State Funding for Wildlife Management.
6. Create Incentives and Remove Disincentives for Wildlife Conservation on Private Land.
7. Promote Hunting and Recreational Shooting on Federal Lands.
8. Maintain and Restore Forest and Rangeland Habitats Through Proactive Public Land Management.
9. Establish Federal Budget Priorities That Will Restore Wildlife Funding to the 1980 Level.
10. Coordinate Efforts to Address the Threats From Invasive Species.
11. Emphasize Cooperative National Forest Decision-Making.
12. Establish a Nationwide Strategy to Sustain Wildlife Health.

Conclusion

The success of the AWCP partnership over five years has turned largely on its strategy to defer policy positions to partner members via "sign on" letters and to its leadership. The decisions to rotate AWCP chairmanship among partner members on an annual basis and to encourage every partner to choose issues and policy choices that best fit their goals have been keys to success. Today, as evidenced by repeated meetings with top Administration officials, personal visits with the President, and the fact that the AWCP continues as a primary player in the most important challenges facing wildlife and wildlife habitat in the new millennium, the AWCP has proven its thesis of strength through unity and commitment. This is a tribute to the founding partners and to the Boone and Crockett Club leaders who believed in the "magic" of its possibility.

KEITH BALFOURD
PROFESSIONAL MEMBER
Boone and Crockett Club

HUNT FAIR CHASE PROGRAM

Hunting ethics go well beyond whether an act is legal or illegal. This is why it is impossible to legislate or create laws that cover ethics when it comes to hunting. All we can do is lead by good example.

Like many, my father introduced me to hunting. Long before I could carry a weapon in the field he began teaching me his way of hunting, with his set of rules. His teachings didn't have a name. They weren't called anything special. It was almost as if what he was trying to instill in me was above having a name. It was just how it was. "If you want to be a hunter, this is how you hunt."

Past basic firearm safety, my father's rules were simple, easy to follow, and made me feel good when I did it right.

- We always ask permission to hunt someone else's property.
- The landowner is always right, and we offer them part of our take.
- We don't shoot hens.
- Search and search some more for a downed bird until you find them.
- We only shoot game – no signs, fence posts, or songbirds.
- We clean and eat what we take and never take more than our limit.
- If others are here first, we give them the field.
- We only shoot birds in flight – never on the ground or on the water.

Also, like many, my first hunting experiences were for upland birds and small game. I wasn't old enough or skilled enough to carry a rifle for deer. As I grew older, a right of passage of sorts was being invited into deer camp with my father's friends and my uncles. I soon found out they had unwritten rules too — rules without a name. Later in my hunting career I came to learn that these rules did have a name. They were called "fair chase."

THE 2005 AD CAMPAIGN FOR THE HUNT FAIR CHASE PROGRAM DROVE EVEN MORE OUTDOORSMEN TO THE PROGRAM'S WEB SITE – WWW. HUNTFAIRCHASE.COM.

The concept of fair chase was first conceived and promoted as a sportsman's code of ethical conduct by the founding fathers of the Boone and Crockett Club, including Theodore Roosevelt. In the late 1800s the rules for the taking of wild game were loose to say the least – non-existent would be more accurate. In fact there were no rules or written laws. Ethics were left up to the individual, but this system was not working. The general thinking of the time was that an over abundance meant and inexhaustible supply, so why worry about how we hunt or how much we take? Consequently, game populations were in dire straits by the turn of the last century.

There were other factors that influenced the hunting culture of that era, which contributed to this decline. In a land of abundance, free-spirited pioneers and outdoorsmen were naturally resistant to change, laws, and limits. Early European law mandated that all wildlife belonged to the crown; therefore, American pioneers shunned anything that resembled old-world restrictions.

As indicated in Roosevelt's and the Club's Master Plan, a set of guidelines had to be established. An ethical code of conduct for all sportsmen was required. If wildlife was to survive, and for "conservation" (use) to prevail over "preservation" (non-use) sportsman must lead the charge. With the leadership of Roosevelt, the Boone and Crockett Club's "Fair Chase" tenants encouraged laws in the states and provinces to maintain sport hunting at a high level of sportsmanship and ethical action. This "Fair Chase" code directly engaged the hunter conscience to enjoy hunting in an ethical fashion. Born from these efforts was the concept of public stewardship and the realization that wildlife did indeed belong to the people.

Throughout its existence, the Boone and Crockett Club never skirted thorny issues, even when the situation arose. Changing the culture and thinking of the American sportsmen, was perhaps, one of the most difficult yet significant accomplishments of the Club. The Club's Fair Chase statement provided the foundation for hunter ethics, as we know them today. The public image of hunters was raised to that of a sportsman – one who can kill, yet protect and nurture what is taken.

Over a century has passed since sportsmen first accepted and practiced this Fair Chase code. As with any self-imposed, self-policed action time has a way of eroding away intent and practice. To address this slippage and to set a new course for a positive public image of hunters and hunting the Boone and Crockett Club launched a program titled Hunt Fair Chase in 2004. This program brought together hunting industry manufacturers, conservation organizations, and the outdoor media to deliver to all hunters a unified message about the origins of hunting ethics and the important role hunting ethics play in projecting a positive public image. Today, Hunt Fair Chase also reaffirmed a hunter's role as a conservationist by turning back the clock to the time when hunters first embraced the concept of fair chase and helped launch the conservation movement.

Today, more than ever, the traditions of hunting are under attack. Through negative propaganda aimed at the non-hunting public to portray hunting in a negative light, those who would like to see hunting go away altogether have gained ground in misrepresenting hunting and confusing those who do not hunt to the point of turning many against hunting.

Since more than 100 years had passed since the Boone and Crockett Club first promoted the importance of ethical hunting and sportsmanship as a way to save wildlife from pending disaster it only seemed natural that the Club accepted this leadership role once again. Through the Fair Chase tenants set first forth by Roosevelt and the Boone and Crockett Club, sport hunters continue to foster the North American Model of Conservation and public stewardship of wildlife. In one year, Hunt Fair Chase reached over 5 million hunters through print and Internet advertising, educating and reaffirming their role as conservationists. The campaign was a huge success in bringing hunting ethics back to the forefront and rallying hunters to think about their actions in the field and what they teach young hunters. As individuals making ethical choices these hunters will continue to positively affect the image of hunters as perceived by the public.

Since the message of ethical hunting has no sunset, the web site created by this Program (HuntFairChase.com) remains as a portal of information and resources about the origins and importance of hunting ethics to the North American Model for Conservation.

The success achieved by this Program provides a foundation for our continued effort in perpetuating the highest ethical standards among all hunters. The extension of the Hunt Fair Chase program will focus on informing those unexposed to hunting, affording them a clearer understanding of the cultural context in which hunting occurs. The delicate ecosystems in North America benefit from hunters and hunting in numerous ways, including untold conservation dollars that are spent by the hunting community. This support will ultimately lead to healthy wildlife populations and science-backed conservation systems that work. It is imperative that we, as hunters, hunt ethically, and that we do our part in changing negative hunting perceptions.

ABOUT THE AUTHOR: *Keith Balfourd grew up hunting and fishing the farm country of eastern Ohio. He settled in the Northwest after graduation from Oregon State University with a degree in marketing and forestry. His passion for hunting and fly fishing have guided him to a career in the outdoors as an outdoor writer, and in marketing and advertising. In 1995 he started an advertising agency based in Seattle, Washington servicing companies in the hunting and fly-fishing industries. Keith is currently the Director of Marketing and an Official Measurer for the Boone and Crockett Club. He lives in Florence, Montana, with his wife, DeEtte, and their two daughters, Jordyn and Jacklyn.*

CHAPTER TWO

National Collection of Heads and Horns

ROBERT H. HANSON
REGULAR MEMBER
Boone and Crockett Club

The Boone and Crockett Club's National Collection of Heads and Horns has had a storied history since its humble beginnings at the New York Zoological Society's Bronx Zoo in 1906. It continues to be maintained and displayed today under the roof of the Buffalo Bill Historical Center, in Cody, Wyoming, where the Collection is housed in an "Adirondack Cabin" in the Cody Firearms Museum – one of the five constituent museums of the Historical Center.

Conceived as a "zoological "collection, the original premise of the National Collection was to display the various North American big game species, many of which, at that time, were in danger of vanishing from the plains and forests of the world. It was hoped that the Collection would allow future generations to see these species, which, it was feared, were endangered and potentially subject to extinction.

Many eloquent words have been written about the National Collection, and I will not attempt to provide yet another detailed history, but a brief report on the highlights (and in some cases, "lowlights") of the Collection.

It is well known that the National Collection of Heads and Horns was designated as such in December 1906 by William T. Hornaday, following the organization of the New York Zoological Society's Bronx Zoo. The original Collection was augmented in 1907 by the donation of Dr. Hornaday's personal collection. Additional donations came from others, and in a 1910 report of the New York Zoological Society, it was reported that the Collection then housed 12 World's Record heads and 5 number two heads. It should be noted that the present-day Boone and Crockett Club measuring system had not yet been devised, and the according of World's Record status to trophy specimens was done on a basis totally different from the system that is now employed.

By 1922 the entire Collection, which, in addition to North American trophies, displayed species from around the world, was open for public display at the New York Zoological

TODAY THE COLLECTION INCLUDES FIVE OF THE CURRENT WORLD'S RECORDS. CLOCKWISE FROM THE TOP LEFT: WOODLAND CARIBOU 419-5/8 POINTS, ROCKY MOUNTAIN GOAT (TIE) 56-6/8 POINTS, DESERT SHEEP 205-1/8, STONE'S SHEEP 196-6/8 POINTS, AND QUEBEC-LABARDOR CARIBOU 474-6/8 POINTS.

Society, in a building newly-constructed for that purpose. Unfortunately, in the decades that followed, public interest in the display, which had grown to some 2,371 specimens, had waned, and the building that housed the Collection was largely used for storage and office space. A burglary in 1974 resulted in the loss of 13 top specimens. One of the stolen trophies, a non-typical mule deer, taken by Andrew Daum in 1886, was recovered in 2004, and has rejoined the National Collection in Cody.

It was in 1977 that Lowell E. Baier, now a Vice President and veteran member of the Boone and Crockett Club, visited the New York Zoological Society and was shocked to see the deplorable condition to which the Collection had fallen. Notwithstanding an agreement that the Zoological Society had to transfer the Collection to the American Museum of Natural History, the Boone and Crockett Club was able to intercede, and the title to the National Collection officially passed to the Club on January 23, 1978. At that time, there remained only 34 North American big game trophies in the Collection. The Asian, African, and European specimens in the Collection went to Safari Club International.

Until 1981 the National Collection was on public display at the National Rifle Association's headquarters, in Washington, D.C. In that year, William Talley, a Trustee of the Buffalo Bill Historical Center, Cody, Wyoming, felt that the Collection belonged at the Center, and, indeed, it was subsequently moved to the Buffalo Bill Gallery, where I had the privilege of first seeing this display in 1985.

The Adirondack hunter's cabin, which now houses the National Collection, was conceived in 1989, and at the Boone and Crockett Club's annual black-tie dinner that year, members pledged $250,000 toward its construction. Through the generosity of many other contributors, the cabin was built on the outskirts of Cody, and subsequently transferred and assembled at the new Cody Firearms Museum, inside the Buffalo Bill Historical Center. It was officially dedicated in 1991, and when it opened for public display, there were nine

World's Record trophies in the Collection, as well as a number of additional high quality specimens. Among that number were 10 remnants of the original National Collection.

Throughout the decade of the 1990s there ensued a conscientious effort to upgrade the trophies displayed in Cody, and, indeed, the Collection benefited from the donation or loan of many outstanding trophies. In addition, it was felt that the Collection should have the larger goal of being the embodiment of the success of 20th Century conservation and big game management practices. These practices, to a large degree, had not only stopped the declines in big game populations, but had substantially restored their numbers, both in quantity and quality. With respect to quality, it should be noted that the Boone and Crockett Club, as part of its triennial Awards Programs, consistently recognized new World's Records during the last three decades of the 20th Century – a testament to the efficacy of big game management and conservation in North America.

As part of "telling this story," it was decided that the collateral materials that appear in the Adirondack Cabin should be improved and upgraded, and that the signage accompanying a trophy should not just recite the name of the hunter, the official score, and the location of its harvest, but should include far more information. Accordingly, utilizing the considerable talents of Julie T. Houk, the Club's Director of Publications, a new design "template" is now placed with each trophy in the Collection. Multi-colored 13" by 13" signs incorporate a map of the North American continent, on which is overlaid the geographical distribution of the given species, as well as a photograph of that species in its natural habitat. In addition, information is also given with respect to the live weight of the animal, as well as the number of pounds of meat that such live weight generates for human consumption. Recognition of the donor or lender of the trophy is also prominently displayed on the signage.

Additional signage has been dedicated to an explanation of the trophy scoring system utilized by the Boone and Crockett Club, which places particular emphasis on both massiveness and symmetry. Illustrative score charts are provided to assist the visitor in understanding how final scores are derived.

Since 1991, the Boone and Crockett Club has officially recognized a number of additional categories, and the Collection has been quick to reach out for outstanding trophies that are representative of those categories. In addition, it is felt that many North American species are best displayed as full mounts, and at the present time all four species of North American bears are life-sized mounts – highlighted by the impressive polar bear that guards the outside of the cabin. Inside the cabin are additional life-sized bear mounts, as well as full mounts of cougar and muskox.

Of interest is the fact that the National Collection now includes only five World's Record trophies. This is a consequence of the fact, already noted, that new World's Record heads are being consistently taken, even as these words are written in the early years of the 21st Century. The Collection, of course, will continue to endeavor to secure such World's Records, either by loan or donation. A visitor to the Adirondack cabin will not be disappointed by the quality of the trophies on display, as virtually all such trophies appear

70. BOONE & CROCKETT CLUB HOUSE.

BACKGROUND: INTERIOR OF THE BOONE AND CROCKETT CLUB CABIN AT THE 1893 WORLD'S COLUMBIAN EXPOSITION HELD IN CHICAGO. INSET IMAGES FROM THE TOP: EXTERIOR OF THE BOONE AND CROCKETT CLUB CABIN; A NEW BUILDING WAS CONSTRUCTED TO HOUSE THE NATIONAL COLLECTION AT THE NEW YORK ZOOLIGICAL SOCIETY IN 1922; DURING THE COLLECTIONS MOST POPULAR ERA, THE COLLECTION INCLUDED OVER 2,300 SPECIMENS.

Photographs from B&C Archives

in the Club's ***Records of North American Big Game***, many of them highly-ranked. In addition, it is believed that the National Collection in Cody is the only collection in North America that displays specimens of both Atlantic and Pacific walrus.

The famous "Chadwick Ram," which many regard as the most impressive big game trophy ever taken in North America, is actually displayed outside the cabin in the "Boone and Crockett Gallery." It stood by itself for a number of years, until the aforementioned Lowell E. Baier loaned a number of artifacts associated with Lee Sherman Chadwick. Through his extraordinary generosity, the display now includes a number of items associated with Chadwick's hunting career, including the .404 Mauser Model 1898 that he used to harvest the outstanding ram and the original version of his daily diary. Also displayed are the vintage Kodak "Postcard" Camera and Bell & Howell "Filmo" 16mm movie camera that accompanied Mr. Chadwick on his hunting expeditions and captured his famous Stone's sheep during his 1936 trip to northern British Columbia. Another section includes a number of Chadwick's inventions and patents, developed during his distinguished career as an automotive engineer.

The 1993 tenth edition of ***Records of North American Big Game*** listed the trophies that were on display when the Adirondack Cabin was dedicated in 1991, and here follows a similar listing of those trophies now in the Collection in early 2005:

- **Black Bear, 22-13/16 points**, taken by Loren C. Nodolf in Ventura County, California, 1990. (Mount on loan to the National Collection).
- **Grizzly Bear, not scored,** taken by Arthur Carlsberg, near Kotzebue, Alaska, 1973. (Mount on loan to the National Collection)
- **Alaska Brown Bear, not scored,** taken by Richard P. Carlsberg on the Alaska Peninsula, 1968. (Mount owned by the National Collection).
- **Polar Bear, 27-9/16 points,** taken by Pat Auld, off Point Hope, Alaska, 1964. (Mount owned by the National Collection).
- **Cougar, 16-3/16 points,** taken by Gene R. Alford in Idaho County, Idaho, 1988. (Skull only owned by the National Collection).
- **Cougar, 16-1/16 points,** taken by Scott M. Moore in Park County, Wyoming, 1993. (Mount on loan to the National Collection).
- **Atlantic Walrus, 95-6/8 points,** taken by Porter Hicks at Foxe Basin, Nunavut, 2001. (Owned by the National Collection).
- **Pacific Walrus, not scored,** taken by Arthur Carlsberg, near St. Lawrence Island, Alaska, 1978. (On loan to the National Collection).
- **American Elk – Typical Antlers, 417-3/8 points,** taken by Merwin D. Martin in Park County, Wyoming, 1991. (On loan to the National Collection).
- **American Elk – Non-Typical Antlers, not scored,** picked up in Teton County, Wyoming, 1961. (Owned by the National Collection).
- **Roosevelt's Elk, 372-1/8 points,** taken by Robert H. Gaynor in Del Norte County, California, 2000. (On loan to the National Collection).

- **Tule Elk, 351 points,** former World's Record, taken by Quentin Hughes in Solano County, California, 1990. (Owned by the National Collection).
- **Mule Deer – Typical Antlers, 216-2/8 points,** picked up in Coconino County, Arizona, 1994. (Owned by the National Collection)
- **Mule Deer – Non-Typical Antlers, 304-5/8 points,** former World's Record, taken by Andrew Daum, in Elk Creek, Colorado, 1886. (Owned by the National Collection).
- **Columbia Blacktail Deer – Typical Antlers, 154-1/8 points,** taken by Mitchell A. Thorson in Glenn County, California, 1969. (Owned by the National Collection).
- **Sitka Blacktail Deer – Typical Antlers, 121-6/8 points,** taken by James F. Baichtal on Dall Island, Alaska, 1998. (Owned by the National Collection).
- **Sitka Blacktail Deer – Non-Typical Antlers, 126-7/8 points,** taken by Dan L. Hayes on Prince of Wales Island, Alaska, 1984. (Owned by the National Collection)
- **Whitetail Deer – Typical Antlers, 192-2/8 points,** taken by Roger D. Syrstad, in Pope County, Minnesota, 1989. (Owned by the National Collection)
- **Whitetail Deer – Non-Typical Antlers, 212-5/8 points,** picked up in Greenwood County, Kansas, 1998. (Owned by the National Collection).
- **Coues' Whitetail Deer – Typical Antlers, 90-6/8 points,** taken by Basil Bradbury in Arizona, date unknown. (Owned by the National Collection).
- **Coues' Whitetail Deer – Non-Typical Antlers, 158-4/8 points,** former World's Record, picked up in Santa Cruz County, Arizona, 1988. (Owned by the National Collection).
- **Canada Moose, 238-5/8 points,** former World's Record, taken by Silas H. Witherbee, at Bear Lake, Quebec, 1914. (Owned by the National Collection).
- **Alaska-Yukon Moose, 240-7/8 points,** former World's Record, taken by A.S. Reed on the Kenai Peninsula, 1900. (Owned by the National Collection).
- **Shiras Moose, 183-4/8 points,** taken by Norb Voerding in Sublette County, Wyoming, 1940. (On loan to the National Collection).
- **Mountain Caribou, 446-2/8 points,** taken by Irvin Hardcastle in Atlin, British Columbia, 1955. (On loan to the National Collection).
- **Woodland Caribou, 419-5/8 points,** World's Record, taken by H. Casmir de Rham in Newfoundland, prior to 1910. (Owned by the National Collection).
- **Barren Ground Caribou, 465-1/8 points,** former World's Record, taken by Roger Hedgecock at Mosquito Creek, Alaska, 1987. (On loan to the National Collection).
- **Central Canada Barren Ground Caribou, 400-6/8 points,** taken by Dale L. Zeigler at Rendez-vous Lake, Northwest Territories, 1986. (On loan to the National Collection).
- **Quebec-Labrador Caribou, 474-6/8 points,** World's Record, taken by Zack Elbow in Nain, Labrador, 1931. (Owned by the National Collection).
- **Pronghorn, 93 points,** former World's Record, taken by Edwin L. Wetzler in Yavapai County, Arizona, 1975. (On loan to the National Collection).
- **Bison, 124-6/8 points,** taken by Lord Rendlesham in Wyoming, 1892. (Owned by the National Collection).

- **Rocky Mountain Goat, 56-6/8 points,** World's Record (tie), taken by E.C. Haase, in the Babine Mountains, British Columbia, 1949. (Owned by the National Collection).
- **Musk Ox, 113-2/8 points,** former World's Record, taken by an unknown hunter on the Barren Grounds, Nunavut, prior to 1910. (Owned by the National Collection).
- **Musk Ox, 111-6/8 points,** taken by Robert H. Hanson on the Perry River, Nunavut, 1987. (On loan to the National Collection).
- **Bighorn Sheep, 195 points,** taken by Gold White at Sun River, Montana, 1911. (Owned by the National Collection)
- **Desert Sheep, 205-1/8 points,** World's Record, taken by a Native American in Baja California, Mexico, 1940. (On loan to the National Collection).
- **Stone's Sheep, 196-6/8 points,** World's Record, taken by L.S. Chadwick at Muskwa River, British Columbia, 1936. (Owned by the National Collection).

In 1893 the World's Columbian Exposition was held in Chicago and featured many outstanding exhibits. It was also the first opportunity to display the relatively new technology of electricity, earning the Exposition the title of "The White City," a testament to the brilliant lights that illuminated the buildings. A small island featured a replica of a hunter's cabin erected by the Boone and Crockett Club, then an organization only six years old. It was the message of the Club that the frontier was vanishing as civilization moved westward. The candles that were lit in the cabin appeared in stark contrast to the searchlights that filled the skies over the Exposition. How ironic it is that the Club, almost 100 years later, built a similar cabin in Cody, Wyoming, to celebrate the success of modern-day wildlife conservation and game management. George B. Ward, author of ***Heads and Horns: The Sport Hunter and Conservationist in the West***, eloquently summed up the enduring message that has remained constant over the years, as follows.

> *"The 'battle of the searchlight and the candles' continues. It is a dilemma that confronts us today as we attempt to balance our economic growth against our irreplaceable natural heritage. Like the Hunter's Cabin in the middle of the World's Columbian Exposition, the Boone and Crockett Club's collection of heads and horns stands as a visual reminder of that wilderness heritage and the generations of sportsmen who have done so much to preserve it."*

AUTHOR'S NOTE: I am indebted to several individuals whose prior writings on the National Collection of Heads and Horns preceded mine – especially James J. McBride, whose *National Collection of Heads and Horns* chapter appeared in the 1993, tenth edition of ***Records of North American Big Game***. As noted previously, ***Heads and Horns: The Sport Hunter and Conservationist in the West***, authored by George B. Ward, is an important historical accounting of the National Collection. It appears in a 1993 publication of the Buffalo Bill Historical Center, titled ***Boone and Crockett: National Collection of Heads and Horns***.

ABOUT THE AUTHOR: *Robert H. Hanson of Wapiti, Wyoming, is a Regular Member of the Boone and Crockett Club, the Club's Secretary, and a member of the Records of North American Big Game Committee. He is an Official Measurer for the Club and was a member of the 24th and 25th Awards Program Judges Panels. He has hunted extensively throughout North America and Africa and has taken most of the North American big game species, including the Alaska-Yukon moose, scoring 223-4/8 points with which he is pictured above. He is the Club's National Collection of Heads and Horns "Liaison," and is actively involved in the maintenance and enhancement of the Collection.*

New world record Brownie killed
Cold Bay - May 1948
Skull - 19 3/16 in. long (dry)
11 1/2 " wide "
Hide 12 ft. 4 in wide
10 " 4 " long

(See official North American
Big Game Records)

CHAPTER THREE

Sagamore Hill Award

ELDON L. "BUCK" BUCKNER
REGULAR MEMBER
Boone and Crockett Club

The Sagamore Hill Award is the highest award given by the Boone and Crockett Club. Its origin goes back to a Vermont grouse hunt in 1947. During a rest break to admire the colorful autumn leaves, Dr. Richard Derby reminisced to his hunting partner, Archibald B. Roosevelt, how much the latter's father, Theodore Roosevelt, enjoyed the colorful falls of New England and New York. Two other Boone and Crockett Club members, Richard Borden and Fairman Dick, were also present. The idea of some sort of memorial within the Club, to Theodore Roosevelt, its founder and first President soon surfaced.

As Archibald relates in his chapter titled "The Sagamore Hill Medal", first published in the 1964 Edition of **Records of North American Big Game** and reprinted in the 1971 Edition, it was Karl Frederick, Club President, who suggested the memorial be a medal called the Sagamore Hill Medal. He further suggested that it be awarded for the outstanding trophy in the Big Game Competitions, thus honoring both hunting and conservation as Theodore Roosevelt intended the Club to do.

The medal, first awarded in 1949, was and still is given by the Roosevelt family in memory of Theodore Roosevelt, Theodore Roosevelt, Jr., and Kermit Roosevelt. The first recipient was the late Robert C. Reeve, a pioneering Alaskan aviator who founded Reeve Aleutian Airways and later became a Regular Member of the Club. His award winning trophy was a huge Alaska brown bear, killed and entered in the 1948 Annual Competition. The Sagamore Hill Medal was also intended as a special award for Club Members who demonstrated outstanding devotion to Club ideals and objectives. The first such recipient was DeForest Grant in 1952 "for long and distinguished service to conservation."

As interest in trophy hunting continues to grow and questions frequently arise regarding the Sagamore Hill Award, it is timely to address the two versions of Boone and Crockett Club's highest honor.

ROBERT C. REEVE, PICTURED HERE WITH HIS ALASKA BROWN BEAR SCORING 29-13/16 POINTS, RECEIVED THE VERY FIRST SAGAMORE HILL AWARD IN 1948 FOR THIS EXCEPTIONAL TROPHY. THE MEDALLIONS GIVEN OUT TO THE RECIPIENTS OF THE SAGAMORE HILL AWARD WERE DESIGNED BY SCULPTOR GIFFORD PROCTOR, NEPHEW OF SCULPTOR AND CLUB MEMBER A. PHIMISTER PROCTOR.

RECORD DALL SHEEP BAGGED

Dall sheep, unofficially measured at larger than the world's rec by Harry Swank Jr., local sportsman and operator of Van's The sheep's unofficial preliminary measurements totaled 1925 e and Crockett Club hunting standards. That is more than seve an Anchorag tax consultant Frank Cook's present world heep was xen in the Wrangell Mountains. Swank hunte es of the S. Army Engine District, Alaska, and Jack E. Flyi rvice, Gulkana.

BOONE AND CROCKETT CLUB MEMBER, FRANK COOK (TOP LEFT), WAS AWARDED THE SAGAMORE HILL MEDAL FOR HIS OUTSTANDING DALL'S SHEEP TAKEN IN THE CHUGACH MOUNTAINS. THE RAM, SCORING 185-6/8 POINTS, WAS DECLARED A WORLD'S RECORD AT THE TIME. COOK'S RAM STOOD AT THE TOP SPOT UNTIL HIS CLOSE FRIEND AND FELLOW HUNTER, HARRY SWANK, JR., SHOT THE CURRENT WORLD'S RECORD IN 1961 (LEFT AND ABOVE). SWANK ALSO RECEIVED A SAGAMORE HILL AWARD FOR HIS RAM. BOTH MEN'S HUNTS DEMONSTRATED THE FINEST STANDARDS OF FAIR CHASE. A MORE DETAILED ACCOUNT OF SWANK'S HUNT IS ON PAGE 876 OF THIS BOOK.

As noted earlier, the Sagamore Hill Medal for big game trophies was first awarded in 1949 to the outstanding trophy entered in the 2nd Big Game Competition for the year 1948. The 1948 and 1949 competition awards were made before the current Boone and Crockett scoring system was adopted. They were awarded based on the selection by a Judges Panel.

During 1949 a special committee of six men was appointed to devise a scoring system for North American big game. The committee, chaired by Samuel B. Webb of Vermont, included Dr. Harold E. Anthony, Milford J. Baker, Frederick K. Barbour, Dr. James L. Clark, and Grancel Fitz. Although there was rivalry between the latter two committee members who had already devised their own systems, the committee successfully accomplished its goal. The new copyrighted system was put into use in 1950 and received widespread acceptance with publication of the 1952 records book, ***Records of North American Big Game***.

The year 1951 marked the end of the Annual Big Game Competitions, with George Lesser receiving the Sagamore Hill Award for his woodland caribou trophy. Trophy entries received during 1952 and 1953 were the first in a new Biennial Big Game Competition, with awards presented in 1954. Edison Pillmore's Colorado mule deer scoring 203-3/8 points was awarded the Sagamore Hill Award. As in the past, the Competitions were held at the American Museum of Natural History in New York City, where they continued through the 10th Competition in 1962. No trophy was deemed worthy of the Sagamore Hill Award for the 1954-1955 Competition, but Frank Cook's new World's Record Dall's sheep, taken in 1956, received it at the next awards banquet, in 1958.

The 11th Competition for 1962-1963 was held at the Carnegie Museum in Pittsburgh, Pennsylvania, where the Boone and Crockett Club headquarters had been relocated. Norman Blank's Stone's sheep, scoring 190 points received the Sagamore Hill Award. The Carnegie Museum remained the site for the next three Competitions. The last one, the 14th Competition, marked still another change. It was the first to cover a three-year period, 1968 through 1970. It was also the last to be called a "Competition." All future entry periods would be labeled "Awards Programs."

Since the Sagamore Hill Award was first introduced, interest in trophy hunting has increased exponentially. With the increased interest and the development of sport hunting as a major economic factor in many parts of the country have also come changes in modes of transportation and technological advances that were unimaginable just 20 years ago. As "fair chase" and ethical hunting practices are among the oldest tenets of the Boone and Crockett Club, the current entry affidavit that is required of trophy entries has evolved with time. So too has the criterion for awarding the Sagamore Hill Award.

Although there have been many new World's Record trophies honored during the past 15 years, the Sagamore Hill Award has only been presented three times during that period. To be eligible for nomination the trophy must either be a new World's Record or one that is close to it. In addition, the hunt that produced the trophy should be exemplary of those characteristics most highly valued by Roosevelt: fair chase, self reliance, perseverance, intentional selective hunting, and mastery of challenges being some of those. After reviewing the hunt accounts of possible candidates, the Judges Panel may choose to nominate a particular trophy for the Sagamore Hill Award. The nomination is reviewed by the Big Game Records Committee Chair who may choose to make further investigations before recommending the award to the Club. All Sagamore Hill Trophy Awards made to date are listed below.

Year Awarded	Name	Category	Score
1949	Robert C. Reeve	Alaska brown bear	29-13/16
1950	E.C. Haase	Rocky Mountain goat	56-6/8
1951	R.C. Bentzen	typical American elk	441-6/8
1952	George H. Lesser	woodland caribou	405-4/8
1954	Edison A. Pillmore	typical mule deer	203-7/8
1958	Frank Cook	Dall's sheep	185-6/8
1960	Fred C. Mercer	typical American elk	419-4/8
1962	Harry L. Swank, Jr.	Dall's sheep	189-6/8
1964	Norman Blank	Stone's sheep	190
1966	Melvin J. Johnson	typical whitetail deer	204-4/8
1974	Doug Burris, Jr.	typical mule deer	226-4/8
1977	Garry Beaubien	mountain caribou	452
1986	Michael J. O'Haco, Jr.	pronghorn	93-4/8
1989	Gene C. Alford	cougar	16-3/16
1992	Charles E. Erickson, Jr.	non-typical Coues' whitetail deer	155
2001	Gernot Wober	Rocky Mountain goat	56-6/8

Special Sagamore Hill Awards, mentioned earlier, may be recommended by the Sagamore Hill Committee, made up of past Club Presidents, with advice and approval of the Boone and Crockett Club's Board of Directors. Only seven such awards have been made, starting with the first to DeForest Grant in 1952. These presentations are usually well-planned special events made to unsuspecting recipients. Although the actual citations accompanying presentation of the medal may be more detailed, the official club summary for each of the seven distinguished recipients is given below.

SPECIAL SAGAMORE HILL RECIPIENTS

1952 - DeForest Grant "For long and distinguished service to conservation."

1968 - Richard King Mellon "For devoted and dedicated service to the conservation of our North American wildlife heritage."

1977 - Robert Munro Ferguson "For unswerving loyalty to his heritage, his principles, and his friends."

1987 - C.R. "Pink" Gutermuth "For life-long conservation service to the nation and for achievement of the Boone and Crockett Club's goals."

1992 - William I. Spencer "For tenacious focus on the vision of the Club's founders and absolute insistence on the perpetuation of their original mission."

1996 - Philip L. Wright "For lifelong commitment to conservation; For dedication to the principles of fair chase and scientific integrity with the records program."

1997 - George C. Hixon "For steadfast devotion to the preservation of the Club's rich traditions and its historical legacy of wildlife conservation."

The Sagamore Hill Award remains one of the most prized honors that can be bestowed – whether it be to a hunter for an outstanding trophy or a Club Member for extreme dedication to furtherance of the organization's conservation objectives. It is intended to remain such in the future.

THE SAGAMORE HILL AWARD WAS NAMED AFTER THE HOME THAT THEODORE ROOSEVELT BUILT FOR HIS FAMILY IN OYSTER BAY, NEW YORK, IN 1885. SAGAMORE HILL IS CURRENTLY REGISTERED AS A NATIONAL HISTORIC SITE AND IS OPEN AS A VISITORS' CENTER AND MUSEUM WHICH IS OVERSEEN BY THE NATIONAL PARK SERVICE. ABOVE IS A VIEW OF THE TROPHY ROOM THAT ROOSEVELT ADDED TO THE HOME IN 1905. INSET: DEFOREST GRANT RECEIVED THE VERY FIRST SPECIAL SAGAMORE HILL AWARD FOR HIS "LONG AND DISTINGUISHED SERVICE TO CONSERVATION."

Photographs from B&C Archives

41

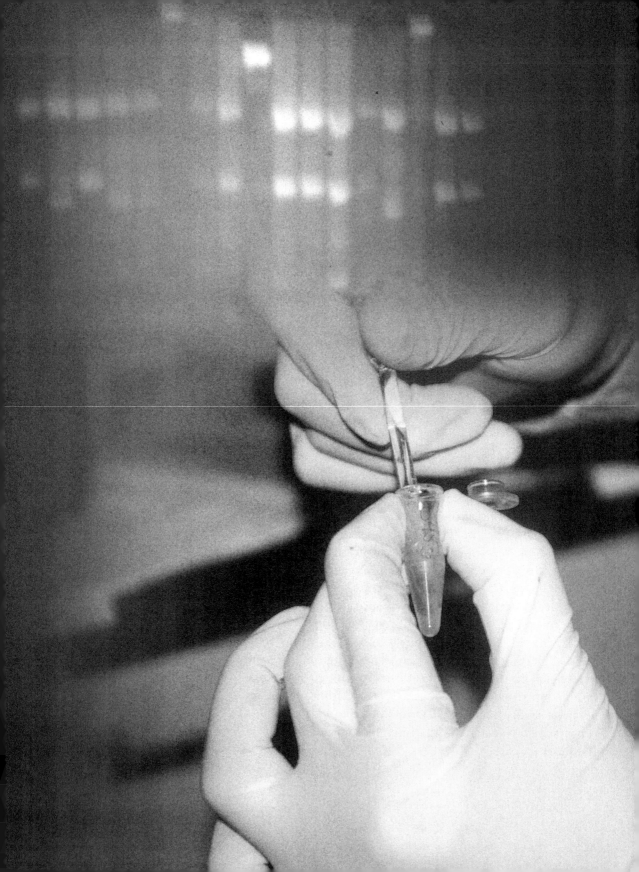

CHAPTER FOUR

Practical Use of Genetics for Wildlife Conservation and Trophy Records Keeping

JIM HEFFELFINGER
WILDLIFE BIOLOGIST
Arizona Game and Fish Department

Humans have always had the propensity to classify everything into neat categories. We all categorize ourselves at one time or another by the groups in which we claim membership. Under different settings we may arrange ourselves into groupings based on heritage, religion, state of origin, social status, political ideology, occupation, hobbies, and more. These cultural categories shape the way we see the world around us and the people in it. For some reason we think of "Texans" as being very different from those living in Kansas just 45 miles away. The world is much neater and easier to understand if we can put everything in a bin with its own tidy name.

This predisposition for categorizing and naming reached a fever pitch during the early days of exploration and study of the natural world. There are many examples of naturalists categorizing to excess in an attempt to describe the natural variation in animals they encountered. The most famous case of this was the designation of 86 different types of grizzly and brown bear (*Ursus spp.*) in North America by C. H. Merriam.

Throughout the geographic range of any species we see a lot of variation in body size, coat color, antler/horn shape, behavior, and other attributes. For instance, animals in the southern latitudes are generally smaller in body size than their relatives in the north. Also, those inhabiting deserts appear lighter in color than those in heavily forested regions. The large degree of physical variation observed in animals led early naturalists to collect specimens from a few geographically distant areas and designate them as different species or subspecies because they differed slightly from one another.

Subspecies: The name game

From these sparse collections of samples, the geographic range of subspecies was drawn somewhat arbitrarily. The purported differences between subspecies were often based on subjective

GENETIC ANALYSIS CAN RELEASE INFORMATION PREVIOUSLY LOCKED INSIDE THE DNA MOLECULE. INCREASINGLY AUTOMATED LABORATORY PROCEDURES MAKE THE ANALYSIS OF DNA AN AFFORDABLE AND POWERFUL TOOL TO ANSWER THE PREVIOUSLY UNANSWERABLE. THERE ARE A LOT OF DIFFERENT WAYS TO ANALYZE DNA DEPENDING ON THE QUESTIONS BEING ANSWERED.

opinions regarding characteristics or measurements of only one or a few specimens. The original lists of subspecies have been altered very little by subsequent biologists and so they still form the foundation for how we view the variation of many species today.

These sometimes-arbitrary subspecies names have been repeated over and over in books, scientific papers, and magazines to the point that everyone assumes there is a solid scientific basis for these categories. One of the most frivolous subspecies assignments was the designation of a new eastern desert mule deer (*Odocoileus hemionus canus*) different from the western desert mule deer (*O. h. eremicus*) based on the antler shape of a single buck skull lying uncatalogued in a museum. The naturalist simply gave the new subspecies a name and drew a distribution for it on the map.

Subspecies' boundaries, when taken literally (as they usually are), frequently create a nonsensical pattern of geographic differences. For example, the map of pronghorn (*Antilocapra americana*) subspecies indicates that pronghorn in central Arizona are the same as those in Alberta, Canada (*A. a. americana*), but different from those in southern Arizona (*A. a. sonoriensis*). Such gross disparities, which challenge common sense, are not supported by any existing evidence.

In light of the uncertainty and confusion that current subspecies designations have produced, some have argued that it is time to discard subspecies names altogether. This would be throwing the baby out with the bathwater. It is meaningful to recognize some geographic differences for improved management, particularly if they provide a useful designation of a population that is physically or ecologically different. Rather than ignore local adaptations or disregard geographic differences, we should describe them accurately based on physical, ecologic, and genetic relationships that show true relatedness and differentiation. Subspecies solidly based in science will be useful units of conservation in the future.

Turning DNA into data

Genetic analysis can release information previously locked inside the DNA molecule. Increasingly automated laboratory procedures make the analysis of DNA an affordable and powerful tool to answer the previously unanswerable. There are a lot of different ways to analyze DNA depending on the questions being answered.

Sometimes "genetic analysis" is thought of as a black box that you put samples in and out pops a tree diagram showing who is more closely related to whom. It is not quite that simple; you actually have to select the right test to get at the question you want answered. Various genetic analyses can differentiate animals at a variety of levels. For example, some analyses can differentiate members of the deer family from those of the cattle or giraffe family. This is useful in studying the evolutionary relationships between these groups of animals. On the other end of the spectrum, there are analyses that can differentiate between individuals in a population.

Genetic analysis starts with the extraction of the DNA out of the tissue or blood samples of interest. There are two kinds of DNA that can be analyzed: mitochondrial DNA (mtDNA) and nuclear DNA (nDNA). Each is useful for different questions; analyzing both together is even more powerful. The most common methods currently in use are the sequencing of a portion of the mtDNA and the use of repeated segments of nDNA called "microsatellites." Using these methods, or a myriad of others, geneticists can collect raw data on the variability of a population or the make-up of an individual. These raw data can then be analyzed with any number of different statistical analyses to yield answers to practical questions.

Some of the most exciting uses of genetic data are testing validity of subspecies, records-keeping accuracy, defining units of conservation, identification of inbreeding and population fragmentation, and forensic law enforcement.

Building a defensible basis for trophy records-keeping categories

Records-keeping categories must be based on real and consistently diagnosed differences. It is particularly important that we evaluate the true geographic distribution of different "types" of animals that are recognized in trophy records keeping. Just one example of this is the blacktail deer/mule deer interface in the Pacific Northwest. Clear delineation of the boundary between blacktails and mule deer is an issue that must be addressed to maintain the integrity of the records books. For example, deer harvested in the central portions of the northwestern states and provinces may be hybrid intergrades. This results in a situation where larger hybrids harvested in an area officially recognized as "blacktail" range have an unfair advantage over pure blacktail deer entered. Drawing lines based on "records-keeping purposes" rather than solid biological information may result in spurious records.

Fortunately, in the case of blacktail vs. mule deer, we already have a foundation of previous genetic research that indicates that blacktails and mule deer differ substantially in their mtDNA. This means we can immediately apply genetic tools to map the current distribution of each type of deer. Nuclear DNA can also be used for something called an assignment test, whereby a sample from an "unknown" deer can be assigned to either "blacktail" or "mule deer" with some level of probability. This will result in information that is directly applicable to records keeping and conservation of this species.

The mule deer vs. blacktail boundary is not the only mule deer boundary that needs to be better defined. For instance, the Inyo, Burro, and desert mule deer, as well as numerous island populations of mule deer in Mexico, are sometimes recognized as being different. It is important to know how many different defensible and well-documented forms of mule and blacktail deer exist. Once this species is evaluated objectively, we may find that some types can be promoted as a destination for hunters similar to the sheep hunter's "Grand Slam." The designation of different mule deer types will benefit the economy of those local areas. Mexico is home to most of the types of mule deer with the highest probability of showing differences. If some of these mule deer types are truly different, this will result in a tremendous opportunity for ranchers to diversify their income from the land. With income generated from hunting, these animals become an asset to be managed for and hunting in that area will be strongly promoted, opening new opportunities for mule deer hunting enthusiasts and conservation efforts.

A similar situation exists with the integrity of whitetail deer (*Odocoileus virginianus*) categories. The Boone and Crockett Club recognizes Coues' whitetail (*O. v. couesi*) in the Southwest as different from other whitetail deer. This deer is different in many physical and ecological aspects. Most experienced Coues' whitetail enthusiasts can recognize this desert variety from its eastern cousin. The accuracy of records in this category relies on being able to distinguish between a medium-sized Arkansas whitetail claimed to have been shot in Arizona, from the real deal. There are physical characters, that can help, but there are those occasional deer that make everyone scratch their heads. A test is needed to weed out the cheaters and those with faulty stories from Grandpa, but not disqualify a genuine new number one. Genetic analysis has this potential, but the difficulty lies south of the border. The Coues' deer gradually blends into the Carmen Mountain whitetail (*O. v. carminus*) and then the Texas whitetail (*O. v. texanus*) as you travel south and east through Mexico. Additionally, it gradually morphs into the Miquihuana whitetail (*O. v. miquihuanensis*) as you go south into the Sierra Madres. Finding a clean separation between records-keeping categories depends on reduced genetic exchange between those categories. The disjunct nature of whitetail habitat in northern Mexico may provide this separation, but only a thorough analysis of a robust collection of Mexican whitetail deer will provide a universally diagnostic test for the Coues' whitetail.

Hybridization between two different species is another burr under the saddle of records-keepers. Although many large mammals have been known to hybridize with other wild and domestic forms, it is the deer family that creates the largest problem for records integrity. Where do you place a huge buck that is half whitetail and half mule deer? The answer is, of course, on the wall because it cannot be recorded with either species. Hybridization is really a problem in the Southwest because the Coues' whitetail is so much smaller. A cross between the larger desert mule deer and the Coues' deer creates a "book" Coues' buck nearly every time. Even without the size difference in the parental species, a phenomenon called "hybrid vigor" causes a first generation hybrid to be larger than either of the parents. The female offspring of a whitetail x mule deer mating are fertile (males are not) and so hybridization can effect subsequent generations. Fortunately, these cases of hybridization are rare, but when they occur it has the potential to pollute the records books.

Currently there is a test available to analyze certain proteins that differ between whitetail and mule deer. When these proteins are analyzed, mule deer produce a band on the gel in a certain location and whitetail show a band in a different location. First generation hybrids show bands in both locations. The problem with this test is that it requires fresh or frozen tissue. Suspected hybrids often come in the form of a cleaned skull plate or a mounted head that is decades old. This is where more recent genetic tools will be useful. Microsatellites (nDNA) offer the most promise for a test to definitively diagnose hybrids. This method can be used with only a few shavings of antler or even a few complete hairs. The technology

THE IMPORTANCE OF BEING ABLE TO PLACE TYPES OF ANIMALS ACCURATELY INTO CATEGORIES GOES FAR BEYOND THE RECORD BOOKS. SOME OF THESE USES OF GENETIC DATA ARE IMPORTANT TO THE CONSERVATION OF THE SPECIES.

is available, it would just require the funding and a large number of samples to identify a suite of microsatellites that show differences between the species and thus can be used to "test" a suspected hybrid. Ongoing research in Arizona has made progress towards finding genetic markers that can be used in this manner.

The records-keeping categories of elk (*Cervus elaphus*) in North America have been greatly clarified by genetic analysis. In 1998, Rene Polziehn and coworkers analyzed elk sampled from all living subspecies and found little difference between Manitoban (*C. e. manitobensis*) and Rocky Mountain (*C. e. nelsoni*) subspecies, but tule (*C. e. nannodes*) and Roosevelt's elk (*C. e. roosevelti*) appeared to be solid categories. Accordingly, the Boone and Crockett Club established the Tule elk as a separate category that year, establishing three classifications of elk for records keeping (American [Rocky Mountain and Manitoban], tule, and Roosevelt's). Researchers used genetic analysis to search for the existence of DNA from the extinct Merriam's subspecies in current Arizona elk. They found no evidence that Merriam's elk survived long enough to interbreed with the elk brought to Arizona from Yellowstone National Park in 1913. From a genetic perspective, Arizona elk look no different than those still in Yellowstone today. This analysis did, however, indicate there might be surprising differences between the native Merriam's elk and the other recognized subspecies. Further work is ongoing, but will be hampered by the fact that there are only three known specimens of Merriam's elk in existence.

There are two species, but four categories of mountain sheep in North America. Both thinhorn species (Dall's and Stone's; *Ovis dalli*) intergrade with one another in southern Yukon and northern British Columbia. The two bighorn subspecies (Rocky Mountain and desert; *Ovis canadensis*) probably do not interbreed at the current time. Several studies have defined genetic markers that can be used to differentiate Rocky Mountain from desert bighorn sheep. Clinton Epps and his coworkers used both mtDNA and nDNA to evaluate a few naturally established desert sheep populations in southern California. Using a high-resolution analysis, they were able to determine from which nearby sheep populations the new populations originated. Arizona Game and Fish Department recently teamed up with

CLEAR DELINEATION OF THE BOUNDARY BETWEEN BLACKTAILS AND MULE DEER IS AN ISSUE THAT MUST BE ADDRESSED TO MAINTAIN THE INTEGRITY OF THE RECORDS BOOKS. FOR EXAMPLE, DEER HARVESTED IN THE CENTRAL PORTIONS OF THE NORTHWESTERN STATES MAY BE HYBRID INTERGRADES. THIS RESULTS IN A SITUATION WHERE LARGER HYBRIDS HARVESTED IN AN AREA OFFICIALLY RECOGNIZED AS "BLACKTAIL" RANGE HAVE AN UNFAIR ADVANTAGE OVER PURE BLACKTAIL DEER ENTERED.

Purdue University to use these same genetic tests for a population that became naturally established between the ranges of Rocky Mountain and desert bighorn. Tests revealed that those animals tested were Rocky Mountain sheep. This same analysis could be used to test an animal being submitted for the record books.

Many genetic analyses have not supported decades-old subspecies designations, which should come as no surprise given the origin of those classifications. However, a recent (2003) analysis of moose subspecies by Kris Hundertmark and others found support for the four subspecies described by Peterson in 1955. This analysis also provides support for the categories used by the Boone and Crockett Club except their analysis showed some limits to gene flow between populations of the Canada moose east and west of the Great Lakes.

Other benefits of genetic research

The importance of being able to place types of animals accurately into categories goes far beyond the records books. Some of these uses of genetic data are important to the conservation of the species. Once genetic analyses are conducted, the data obtained can also be used to test different hypotheses or attempt to answer many different questions. For example, if subspecies or some newly recognized portions of a species range have been genetically isolated, it may be prudent to manage that subspecies differently.

When moving animals around in translocation and reestablishment efforts, managers should strive to keep from mixing populations with drastically different gene pools. For example, genetic analysis of North American pronghorn consistently shows that there is a northern group and a southern group. When restoring pronghorn to formerly occupied range, animals should be chosen that represent the historic genetic, ecologic, and physical attributes of the restored areas as much as possible.

Another under-utilized potential for genetic analysis is the identification of populations suffering from fragmentation and inbreeding depression. We can look at the relatedness of animals within populations and compare that to the variation between populations. This may elucidate areas where fragmentation of the habitat by human or natural factors has resulted in a loss of genetic diversity. Identifying such areas or populations allows managers to use translocation as a potential tool for releasing a population from the depressive effects that losses of genetic diversity and/or inbreeding can have on survival and reproduction. The greatest potential for this is in populations of species such as pronghorn and bighorn that exist in isolated pockets of suitable habitat.

Genetic data can also help us protect lawful hunting by acquiring the knowledge needed to guard against unjust legal actions based on nonsensical subspecies designations. When variations of a species are given the status of a scientific name (like subspecies), the legal repercussions can overshadow questions of subspecies validity. This has happened when poorly defined subspecies were listed as "Endangered Species." Millions of dollars may be spent on populations that do not differ in any consistent way from populations in other parts of that animal's geographic range. Several currently described subspecies are at risk of being used by anti-hunting groups to further infringe on our ability to legally hunt. A court injunction could be granted by a sympathetic judge to stop the hunting of some populations until we "prove" hunting is not detrimental to its persistence. The fact that these animals are thriving under the most successful system of wildlife conservation in the world is not always an adequate defense today.

For years now, wildlife forensic labs have been using genetics to make cases and help officers enforce wildlife laws. One of the most useful law enforcement applications is the ability to match blood or tissue from one source to another. For example, a gut pile located in an area closed to hunting can be matched to a set of antlers or tenderloins in someone's possession. Alternatively, the same test can prove it was not the same animal, thereby absolving the hunter of any wrongdoing. In some cases, genetic testing can estimate the probability an animal was harvested in a particular area. If an analysis is conducted using many samples from several populations, geneticists can infer from which population an animal in question came. In cases where harvest limits or regulations differ by gender, genetic markers can be used to determine the gender of a harvested animal using tissue, a blood smear on a tailgate, or material under a hunter's fingernails.

We need to take advantage of the wonderful and practical things that genetics can do for records keeping and wildlife conservation. There is growing recognition that the animals we admire contain information at the molecular level that can answer our questions and aid in their own conservation.

Using DNA analysis techniques, my study focuses on defining practical units of conservation and records keeping through analysis of genetic differentiation in mule and blacktail deer by evaluating genetic differentiation throughout the range of mule and blacktail deer. The objectives are: 1) Provide a solid, defensible basis for trophy records-keeping categories based on a high-resolution genetic analysis. 2) Revise subspecific taxonomy for mule and blacktail deer in North America and restructure into units of conservation based on evolutionary history, current genetic differences, and restriction to gene flow. 3) Assess populations for evidence of negative genetic effects of isolation and range fragmentation (e.g., inbreeding, genetic drift). 4) Protect lawful hunting of mule deer throughout their range by acquiring the knowledge needed to guard against unjust legal actions based on nebulous subspecies designations. 5) Use findings about genetic variation to determine the probability that a mule or black-tailed deer of interest was harvested from a particular location. 6) Provide a model of how intraspecific differences should be evaluated for animals with a large geographic range. The study draws from a collection of over 2,200 tissue samples taken from deer harvested during normal hunting seasons.

ABOUT THE AUTHOR: *Jim Heffelfinger is a Wildlife Biologist with the Arizona Game and Fish Department. He has been involved with genetic analyses of pronghorn, elk, bighorn, javelina, and deer. His collaborative study on North American mule and black-tailed deer genetics with Drs. Emily Latch and O. E. Rhodes, Jr. was initiated with support from the William I. Spencer Conservation Grants Program.*

CHAPTER FIVE

Deer Antlers: Bones of Contention?

ROBERT D. BROWN
PROFESSIONAL MEMBER
Boone and Crockett Club

PROFESSOR AND HEAD
Department of Wildlife and
Fisheries Sciences
Texas A&M University

First, let's get something straight. There is no such thing as a deer with a good set of horns! Cows, sheep, and antelope have horns; deer, elk, caribou, and moose have antlers. Horns are made of a protein called keratin, the same stuff that fingernails, hair, and animal's hooves are made of; antler is real bone. Both males and females of the species have horns; except for reindeer and caribou, only male cervids have antlers. Horns grow from the base, whereas antlers grow from the tip. And, horns are usually permanent structures, whereas antlers are deciduous — they drop off and are replaced each year.

Why cervids have antlers and how they grow are subjects that have intrigued mankind literally for centuries. The ancient Greek, Aristotle wrote about the phenomenon of antler growth over 2,000 years ago. The fascination with antlers and research about their growth has continued to this day. Naturally, much of the interest has had to do with trying to produce the "muy grande" animal as a hunting trophy, but for the past couple of decades, antler growth has also been studied as a biomedical model for human diseases such as osteoporosis and bone cancer.

Much of the confusion about antlers and some of the frustrations of researchers have to do with the anomalies of antler growth. That is, no matter what physiological function is studied with regards to antler growth, it is not universal across all cervids. For instance, two species of deer, the Chinese water buck and the Asian musk deer, have no antlers at all — they have tusks instead. Others, like the Asian tufted deer and the muntjak, or barking deer, have both small antlers and tusks. The pronghorn has a horn over a bony core. The horn is shed, but the bone is not. Giraffes have knobs that are covered with a skin and hair that look a lot like velvet antlers, but they are permanent structures. Caribou and reindeer females have antlers, and they shed them two to three weeks after giving birth to their young.

These anomalies lead to some obvious questions. Why do deer have antlers in the first place? Why are the antlers of

ONCE THE ANTLERS START GROWING IN THE SPRING OR SUMMER, THEY GROW RAPIDLY — AS MUCH AS AN INCH A DAY IN ELK AND MOOSE. AT THIS POINT THE ANTLER IS "IN VELVET" AND COVERED WITH A SKIN THAT IS HIGHLY VASCULARIZED. THE ANTLER ITSELF IS NOT YET BONE. IT IS MADE OF CARTILAGE, LIKE YOUR NOSE OR EARS. IT HAS ENOUGH MINERAL TO MAINTAIN ITS SHAPE, AND A GOOD BLOOD SUPPLY BOTH THROUGH THE PEDICLE ON THE SKULL AND FROM THE VELVET SKIN.

different species of deer, elk, and moose shaped differently? Why don't all female deer have antlers? What makes antlers grow? What causes the timing of the antler cycle? And, why are antlers shed each year instead of being permanent structures? Biologists like to assume there is a reason for everything. We assume there is a reason for antlers, and that they have evolved differently in the various cervid species and subspecies for a reason. Finding the answers to those reasons is not so easy, however.

Since antlers are found mainly in males, we call them "secondary sex characteristics" like the colorful plumage in birds. Deer tend to be herd animals, with one male servicing a group of females. The antlers seem to be show items to attract females, and they allow the male to fight off other males to protect his harem. Fighting among males is generally never in any buck or stag's best interest, so there is a lot of posturing, display behaviors, and non-lethal sparring that occurs rather than all-out fighting. Sometimes just the display of a large rack is enough to scare off a potential challenger. Males seem to know the shape of their own racks, and since they don't own mirrors, we believe they learn about the shape of their racks during the rut, when they rub off the velvet against trees.

It is amazing to see a buck or elk run through the forest without getting caught up in branches and vines. Some deer, like Sitka blacktail deer, have dangerous antlers shaped like bayonets, but most deer, elk and moose have antlers that are curved and less dangerous to others. Sparring males often carefully lock their antlers, as though they want a good grip that won't slip and stab their opponent. All-out fights between males of about equal size do happen, however, and broken antlers and even fatalities are not all that uncommon. Occasionally sparing cervids lock antlers and both die.

Depending on the species and the part of the world, deer usually begin growing their first set of antlers during the spring of their first year. Some fawns will start growing little "nubs" during their first fall, and they are called "button bucks."

These may not even rub out, or again they may. We know that the male hormone, testosterone, is necessary for the first set of antlers. It was actually Aristotle who experimented with Red deer and found that if he castrated a fawn, it would never grow antlers.

The first set of antlers on a yearling is usually smaller than racks grown in subsequent years. A lot of folklore and conflicting scientific research has gone into what we call the "spike phenomena."

Spikes are antlers without forks, and when found in yearling deer, the deer are usually thought to be inferior animals. Many deer managers have a policy of "culling" all spikes. The thought is that these animals will always be inferior and will never have quality antlers, even as 4- or 5-year-olds. There is also the belief that antlers are an inherited characteristic, and that if spikes are allowed to breed, they will produce more inferior bucks.

A lot of research has been done on this, some at the Kerr Wildlife Management Area of Texas Parks and Wildlife Depart-

THE NATIONAL COLLECTION OF HEADS AND HORNS, WHILE ON DISPLAY AT THE NEW YORK ZOOLOGICAL SOCIETY DECADES AGO, INCLUDED THE INTERLOCKING ANTLER DISPLAY PICTURED HERE. THE CLUB STILL HAS THESE SPECIMENS — KNOWN AS THE "COMBAT COLLECTION" — AT ITS HEADQUARTERS IN MISSOULA, MONTANA.

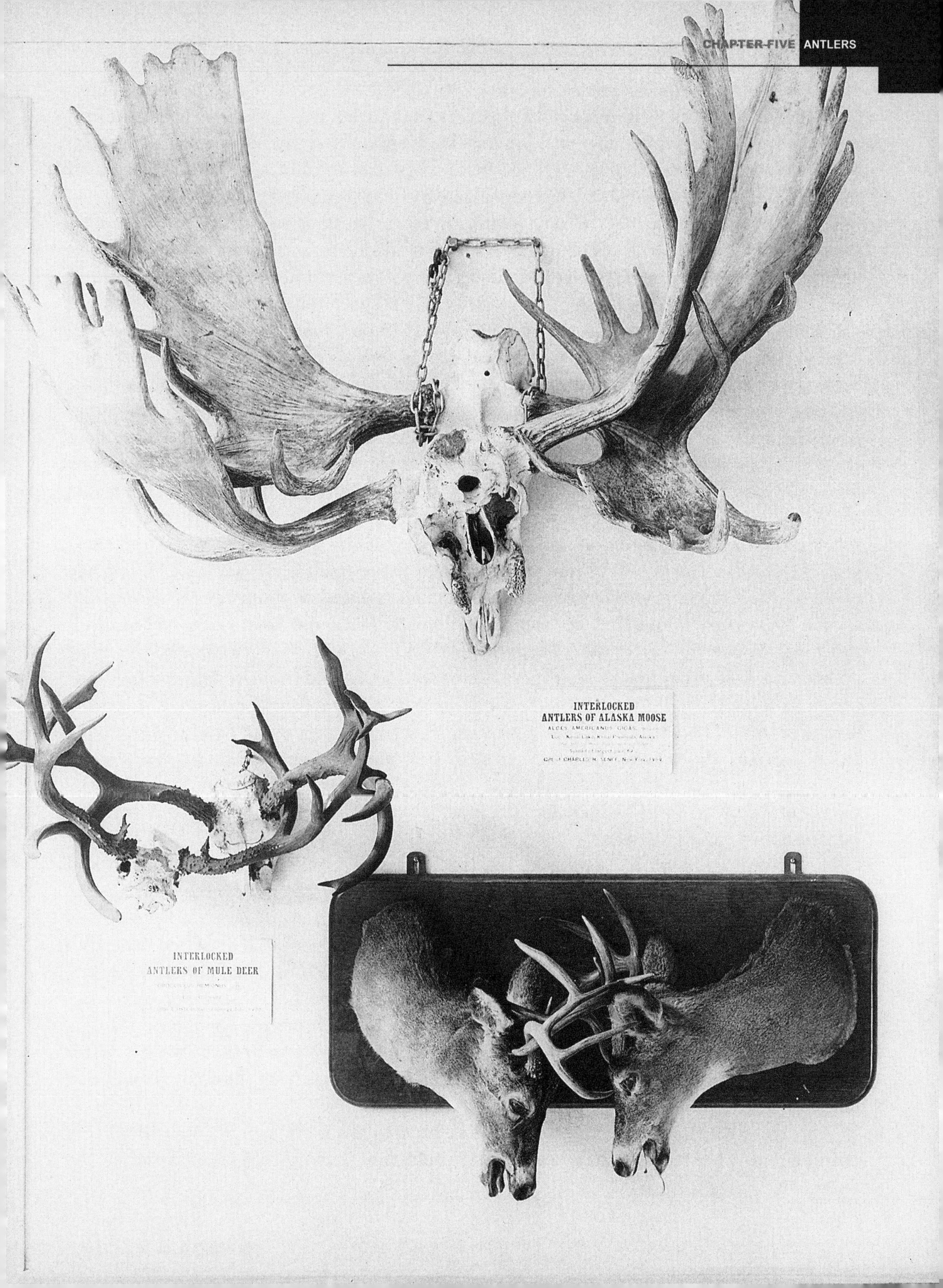

INTERLOCKED
ANTLERS OF ALASKA MOOSE
ALCES AMERICANUS GIGAS

INTERLOCKED
ANTLERS OF MULE DEER

ment, and some at Mississippi State University (MSU). Unfortunately, the results have been conflicting. The Kerr Area work suggests that antler size and shape is determined genetically, and that spike deer will produce more spikes over their lifetimes. The MSU work suggests that some spikes will become quality deer as adults, though maybe never trophies, and that these deer may produce quality offspring.

Why the confusion? First, wildlife genetic work is very difficult. Genetic studies on beef cattle and other domestic species are done with literally thousands of animals. Most deer genetic work is done on a few dozen animals. In addition, deer in pens, where they can be studied, sometimes break their velvet antlers or have other problems that preclude long-term studies. Most importantly, we believe there is an "antler gene," and that it is carried by the doe as well as the buck. Hormone studies have shown that if you remove the ovaries of a doe and give her a shot of testosterone, the doe will grow antlers. We think about half of the genetics for antler growth comes from the doe, and since does do not normally have antlers, we can't select those does that have the best antler genes. Thus, depending on which does he breeds, a trophy buck may produce spike offspring, and a spike buck may produce quality offspring.

Once the antlers start growing in the spring or summer, they grow rapidly — as much as an inch a day in elk and moose. At this point the antler is "in velvet" and covered with a skin that is highly vascularized. The antler itself is not yet bone. It is made of cartilage, like your nose or ears. It has enough mineral to maintain its shape, and a good blood supply both through the pedicle on the skull and from the velvet skin. If you touch or rub the velvet antlers of a tame deer, they will be warm, due to the blood supply. It will also be obvious that there is a nerve supply, and that the deer can feel your touch. Interestingly, if a deer is castrated while it is in velvet, it will remain in velvet the rest of its life. The antlers will keep growing every year, producing what the Germans call a "peruke." Also, if the antler is injured during this time, the resulting antlers, when rubbed out, may be odd-shaped. Most interestingly, if the injury is really severe, the nerves of the pedicle will "remember" the injury, and subsequent sets of antlers will also be misshaped, year after year.

Around mid- to late-summer, the antler begins to mineralize, as calcium and phosphorus are deposited. Unlike most other bones, the antler has no marrow, but becomes solid all the way through. These minerals are deposited so fast that the deer has to raid its own skeleton. The skull, ribs, sternum and long bones will decrease in density as much as 10% during antler mineralization. This seems to be a unique ability of the deer to mobilize minerals from one part of the body and move them to another. Although they don't seem to be able to take minerals out of the antlers and put them back into the skeleton, should a deer break its leg, the leg usually heals in two to three weeks. After antler hardening, the skeletal mineral is replaced by minerals from the diet over a period of months.

The ultimate size of the antlers is related to the body size of the animal to a power of 1.6. That means that if you have one buck that is twice the size of the other, the first buck's antlers will be more than twice the size of the smaller buck's antlers. As the testosterone levels in the buck or stag begin to rise, the antlers start to dry up and itch, and the animal "rubs out" its velvet against trees. During this time you can sometimes see the rubs on trees, or see deer with strips of velvet hanging from their antlers. If you look very closely, you can still see tiny pores in the antlers where the velvet's blood vessels were.

Once the antlers are rubbed out and hardened, the buck or stag enters the rut and prepares to breed. We actually don't know if the larger bucks do the breeding. Nearly all bucks reduce their feed intake during the rut and subsequent winter. They do this even in pens with adequate pelleted feed. A loss in body weight of 15 to 20 percent is not uncommon. They are totally focused on finding does to breed and scaring or fighting off other male challengers. It seems that the really big guys wear out the quickest. Remember that there may be one male for 10 to 20 females, and he has to breed them, be constantly vigilant, and constantly fighting off challengers. All of this while not eating much at all and perhaps during severe winter weather. Studies in South Texas have suggested that these big bucks won't live more than about 5-1/2 years and will die of natural mortality if not harvested by hunters. Studies in pens show breeding bucks can live much longer, but pen studies are not always reflective of what happens in the wild.

Once the rut is over, the males become more docile. Although the buck's blood testosterone levels rose gradually over the summer and fall, when the rut is over, they fall precipitously, often to the level of a doe in a day or two. With the fall in male hormones, we see the fastest degeneration of bone in the animal kingdom — that between the antler and the pedicle. You can literally pick a deer up by its hard antlers one day, and the antlers will fall off the next day. Usually, the two antlers will fall off within a day of each other. There will be a little blood on the pedicle, but deer blood clots quickly. The cast antlers then become a source of minerals for forest or range rodents.

The starting and stopping of the antler cycle depends on the animal's location. Cervids farther from the equator have the most distinct antler and reproductive cycles. Their young are often all born within a two-week period. As you get nearer the equator, however, antler and reproductive cycles spread out, and young may be born over a period of four to six months. On the equator, deer are in and out of antlers, and the young are born year round. Each individual deer has a distinct antler cycle, however, and it repeats it at the same time every year, depending on the time of year it was born.

We know conclusively that antler and reproductive cycles are controlled by light cycles. Experiments with deer under controlled lighting have shown that you can get deer to grow their antlers only every other year by stretching out the annual light cycle over two years. Likewise, you can get up to three sets of antlers a year from one buck by condensing its light cycle to four months. If deer are kept under constant 12 hours of light and 12 hours of darkness daily, they will grow no antlers at all. Temperature changes seem to have little effect, and feed intake effects are conflicting. If you reduce the feed of a penned whitetail by 50 percent, for instance, it will drop its antlers within about two weeks. If you cut

back on the groceries of a European red deer, it will keep its antlers longer. Naturally, if you feed a deer a nutritious diet of all it will eat, it will grow its body size to its genetic maximum, and its antlers will also reach their genetic potential. Ecologically, however, you can do the same thing by adjusting the size of the herd to the carrying capacity of the habitat.

How do light cycles actually control the antler cycle? The study of hormones is called endocrinology, and the endocrinology of deer is very complex. We know that deers' eyes, when exposed to light, send a message to a pea-sized gland at the base of the brain called the pineal gland. The pineal gland produces a hormone called melatonin, and it produces more during periods of darkness. Melatonin seems to control a number of other hormones, especially two of those of the pituitary gland called luteinizing hormone (LH) and follicle stimulating hormone (FSH). These two hormones control things like testosterone production in males and estrogen production and ovulation in does. During winter, with short days and long nights, the increased melatonin produced puts a damper on the pituitary production and release of LH and FSH, and without those, testosterone is barely produced at all. As the days lengthen, less melatonin is produced, LH and FSH get into circulation, and these stimulate testosterone production and release.

But it is not that simple, that is, if you think the explanation so far is simple. Again, we have anomalies, like the Roe deer of Europe, whose bucks rut in the summer and grow antlers in the winter, but whose does make up for it by delayed implantation of the fertilized egg.

Many other hormones, such as prolactin, growth hormone, thyroid hormone, parathyroid hormone, calcitonin, insulin-like growth factors, vitamin D, and hormone receptors seem to be involved in antler growth. It may be that the male hormone, testosterone, is actually converted to estrogen at the receptor in the antler before it has its effect. The "steroid" hormones, like testosterone, estrogen, and cortisol, look very much alike. Deer, when stressed, produce cortisol from their adrenal glands, and that can have an effect similar to that of testosterone. I once had an adult castrate buck in a pen that took ill. It was listless and lost weight, so we separated it in another pen, put it on antibiotics, and gave it extra feed and greens. It recovered, but rubbed out its antlers - no doubt due to the cortisol it was producing, since it had no testis.

In another case, a tule elk in a California zoo looked as if it produced no antlers one year. The veterinarians tranquilized it, and took teste biopsies to show it was normal (at least before the biopsy). It turns out the elk had very small rubbed out nubs about 1-1/2 inch high. The elk had been moved into a new pen with a number of other bulls and cows just at the day it was beginning to grow antlers. Apparently the stress of the move and the new neighbors caused the elk to produce cortisol, and that androgen caused the nub antlers in the velvet to rub out without further growth.

These types of events have been duplicated by experiments, where castrated deer with velvet antlers were given shots of testosterone, estrogen, or cortisol, and all three hormones caused the castrates to rub out. Likewise, a shot of any of these three steroids to a normal buck in velvet will cause him to rub out.

Thus far we've covered the impact of nutrition, light cycles, genetics, and hormones on deer antler growth. For the hunter and wildlife enthusiast, there is no "magic bullet" that will or should produce animals with superior antlers. Stories of some new feed ingredient, additive, or even food plot seed mix that will grow trophy antlers, or of breeding bucks with "powerful genes" that are guaranteed to produce superior offspring are just that — stories. The modern aspects of animal husbandry that are being used to "grow" big deer, including importation of breeding bucks, use of artificial insemination, year-round feeding, and cloning, are both ecologically unwise and unethical for a variety of reasons.

Antlers are one of nature's wonders, and we should admire them as nature intended them to be. Habitat management, buck-doe ratio management, and keeping the cervid population under the carrying-capacity of the land will produce high quality animals that are truly "wild" animals, rather than manufactured "freaks."

I can't leave you without introducing you to the grandest of all cervids — the so called giant Irish elk, *Megaloceros giganteus*. This animal had antlers spanning nine feet and weighing up to 100 pounds, yet its body was no larger than that of a modern moose. Hun-

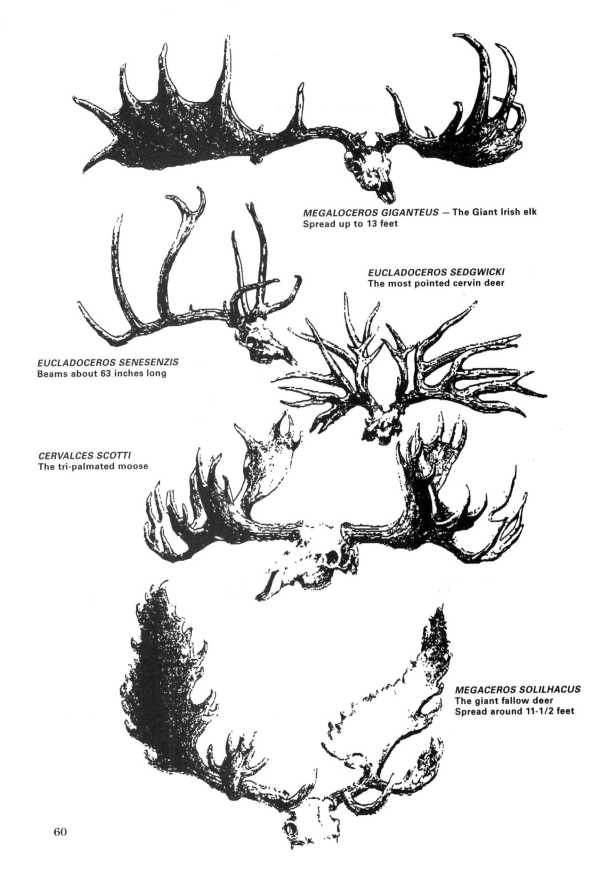

MEGALOCEROS GIGANTEUS — The Giant Irish elk
Spread up to 13 feet

EUCLADOCEROS SEDGWICKI
The most pointed cervin deer

EUCLADOCEROS SENESENZIS
Beams about 63 inches long

CERVALCES SCOTTI
The tri-palmated moose

MEGACEROS SOLILHACUS
The giant fallow deer
Spread around 11-1/2 feet

ANTLER FORMATIONS FROM NOW EXTINCT CERVIDS FROM THE PLIOCENE/ PLEISTOCENE EPOCH. Illustration from *Horns, Pronghorns and Antlers*.

dreds of skeletons of this animal have been found in Irish bogs, but actually the animal has been found from Europe to Japan. Unfortunately, this guy became extinct between 2,500 and 10,000 years ago. Some think its antlers evolved to be so big that it couldn't keep its head up and that its antlers became a heavy burden. Others believe that climatic changes led to a decline in its diet, especially those plants high in the calcium it needed, and it just starved out. Whatever the reason, although we have no Boone and Crockett score set up for this monster, suffice it to say that every one of them would have "made the book."

REFERENCES

Brown, Robert D. (editor). 1983. Antler Development in Cervidae. Caesar Kleberg Wildlife Research Institute, Kingsville, Texas. 480pp.

Brown, Robert D. (editor). 1993. The Biology of Deer. Springer-Verlag, New York. 596pp.

Bubenik, George, and Anthony Bubenik. (editors). 1990. Horns, Pronghorns, and Antlers. Springer-Verlag, New York. 562pp.

Cearley, Kenneth A. and Dale Rollins. (editors). 1998. The Role of Genetics in White-tailed Deer Management. Texas Cooperative Extension, College Station. 129pp.

Gerlach, Duane, Sally Atwater, and Judith Schnell. (editors). 1994. Deer. Stackpole Books. Mechanicsburg, Pennsylvania. 384pp.

Goss, Richard J. 1983. Deer Antlers: Regeneration, Function, and Evolution. Academic Press, New York. 316pp.

ABOUT THE AUTHOR: *Dr. Robert Brown received his B.S. in animal nutrition from Colorado State University and his Ph.D. in animal nutrition with a minor in physiology from Pennsylvania State University. He then joined the faculty of Texas A&I University in Kingsville as an assistant professor of animal nutrition. He was promoted to associate professor in 1979. From 1981 to 1987 he served as a research scientist with the Caesar Kleberg Wildlife Research Institute at Texas A&I University. In 1987, he assumed the position as head of the Department of Wildlife and Fisheries at Mississippi State University. Dr. Brown was appointed professor and head of the Department of Wildlife and Fisheries Sciences at Texas A&M University in 1993, and Director of the Institute for Renewable Natural Resources in 1995. Dr. Brown's research expertise is directed toward comparative wildlife nutrition and physiology. He has edited three books and is the author or co-author for over 100 scientific and popular publications. Dr. Brown has been active in a number of professional associations and is currently president-elect of The Wildlife Society.*

CHAPTER SIX

Management of Mountain Lions in California

VERNON C. BLEICH
PROFESSIONAL MEMBER
Boone and Crockett Club

SENIOR ENVIRONMENTAL
SCIENTIST
California Department of
Fish and Game

BECKY M. PIERCE
ASSOCIATE WILDLIFE
BIOLOGIST
California Department of
Fish and Game

IT IS DOUBTFUL THAT THE ABILITY TO MANAGE MOUNTAIN LIONS IN CALIFORNIA AT A LEVEL THAT WOULD AFFECT POPULATIONS OF OTHER UNGULATE PREY WILL BE RESTORED TO WILDLIFE BIOLOGISTS, WHO ARE THE INDIVIDUALS BEST TRAINED TO MAKE THOSE DECISIONS. THAT ABILITY WAS LOST THROUGH THE VOTING INITIATIVE PROCESS, AND CAN ONLY BE RESTORED THROUGH THE INITIATIVE PROCESS, OR BY A FOUR-FIFTHS VOTE OF THE LEGISLATURE; NEITHER IS LIKELY TO OCCUR IN CALIFORNIA.

Few animals stir as much emotion as cougars, catamounts, or pumas; these are large felines that most commonly are referred to as mountain lions. In California, the birth place of many politically correct trends, mountain lions are of special interest and have a long and varied management history. That history includes the entire spectrum of management strategies, ranging from year-round open-seasons with no limit on take, to that of persecuted predator, nonprotected predator, carefully regulated game animal, and, eventually, to California's only "special protected mammal."

The diverse management history of mountain lions in the Golden State is rivaled only by the variety of landscapes that occur there. During the early part of California's history, mountain lions were fair game, with no legal status. From 1907 to 1963, records indicated that more than 12,000 bounties were paid. Following cessation of the bounty period in 1963, mountain lions were managed as nonprotected, nongame animals, and no records of take were maintained: anyone with a hunting license could pursue these large carnivores in unlimited numbers, and on a year-round basis.

Mountain lions first received protection under modern wildlife management regulations in 1969, when they were classified as game animals by the California Fish and Game Commission; that status was retained until 1972, when a moratorium on take was enacted. During 1969-1972, 4,953 tags were issued, and 118 specimens were harvested. After the moratorium was in place, the California Department of Fish and Game established a system whereby incidents of livestock or pets and mountain lions have been kept with painstaking consistency. As a result, depredation permits are issued to affected property owners and allow them to "take" the offending mountain lion.

Following extensive investigations, mountain lions were again classified as a game mammal in 1986, but recommendations for limited harvests were challenged in court.

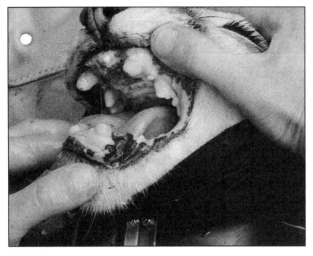

As a result, no hunting season ever occurred and, in 1990, the voters of California passed a ballot initiative, Proposition 117, which afforded mountain lions the status of specially protected mammal. A subsequent ballot measure, Proposition 197, which would have modified the specially protected status, was defeated in 1996 and reaffirmed total protection as the management strategy for mountain lions in California.

There has been much speculation about whether cessation of sport hunting of lions has had a negative effect on large mammal populations in California. Further, some have argued that cessation of sport hunting has resulted in mountain lions becoming emboldened around humans, thereby creating situations in which citizens are exposed to greater danger of being attacked than had been the norm when lions were hunted. Regardless of whether sport harvest of mountain lions has resulted in lower numbers or reduced populations of large game mammals, or if it has increased risks to humans because those carnivores no longer equate the presence of humans with danger, the management of lions in California remains a contentious issue. Certainly, far fewer management options currently exist than in other states that support healthy populations of those carnivores. The initiative process has altered the ability of professional wildlife biologists to use traditional techniques to manage lion populations, or to provide recreational opportunities to those seeking to harvest a trophy animal. Current law even prohibits the use of hounds to pursue lions for the purposes of photography, an interest held by many citizens that have little chance of photographing one of those elusive carnivores in the absence of assistance from professional houndsmen.

To better describe interactions between mountain lions and their prey, we define several basic terms. Among these are nutritional carrying capacity, density-dependent processes, density-independent processes, compensatory mortality, and additive mortality. Nutritional carrying capacity (K) refers to the number of animals of a particular species that a given environment will support, based on the nutrient requirements of the population involved. Density-dependent processes are those that are a function of the current population density relative to K that influence the demographic characteristics of a population; there is a feedback between population density and the recruitment rate (young added to the population per adult female) of the population. Density-independent factors also influence demography, but there is no feedback between those factors and the response of a population to those factors; examples of density-independent factors include severe weather and accidents. Compensatory mortality refers to causes of death that are compensated for by increased survival or reproductive output by animals remaining in a population following the removal of some individuals, and one source of mortality compensates for another. For instance, young deer in poor condition and that were killed by a predator likely would have died anyway from malnutrition during winter. Additive mortality refers to deaths that are not compensated for by enhanced survivorship or reproductive output among animals remaining in a population, and that occur in addition to other causes of death. In this example, winter deaths from malnutrition would be added to losses from predation. All of these terms are applicable both to predators and prey.

Prey species of mountain lions (in particular large ungulates) respond to the removal of individuals in a density-dependent manner. That is, when prey populations are limited by the food supply, reproduction and recruitment are low, and body condition generally is poor. Individuals in such populations die of numerous causes, including predation. Losses to predators under such circumstances are often compensatory mortality, because those losses are compensated for by enhanced survival (or, perhaps, reproductive success) among surviving prey. When a population of animals is in poor body condition, mountain lion control likely has little effect on the number of animals in the population: forage is limiting the number of animals in the population, and lion removal does nothing to enhance the availability of resources to individual prey. In such scenarios, control of mountain lions cannot be expected to result in an increase in the prey population.

When members of an ungulate population are well below K and not affected by nutritional constraints, individual prey are likely to be in excellent body condition, and reproduction and recruitment are expected to be high. In such populations, any animal removed by predation likely would not have died of nutrition-related factors, and the resulting decrease in competition provides little benefit in reproduction for remaining individuals. Therefore, deaths resulting from predation likely are additive, because they occurred in addition to losses from other causes.

Populations of mountain lions were thought to be self-regulating for many years. Sophisticated new techniques, coupled with research questions firmly entrenched in an evolutionary context have, however, produced results that are contrary to previous hypotheses. We were the first to demonstrate that mountain lion populations were regulated by their food supply (that is, population levels were determined by the nutritional carrying capacity of their environment), and not primarily by "social mechanisms." The confusion was a result of the relatively long time lags between growth trends in prey populations and resulting responses in the predator population. Because populations of large carnivores like mountain lions recruit only a small number of individuals each year, effects on recruitment may not be apparent for extended periods of time. Recent work by others has been consistent with our conclusions; together, these results have important implications for the management of mountain lions.

The number of mountain lions inhabiting a particular geographic area is largely determined by the availability of primary prey, which frequently is mule deer. Thus, a population of lions would be expected to increase until food availability became a factor that limited the ability of individual animals to successfully reproduce and recruit young into the population; the rate of growth of the population of lions would vary with its density relative to prey populations, and would exhibit density dependence. If food availability did limit a population of mountain lions, the removal of individual lions (whatever the cause) would represent compensatory mortality because these animals would have died of other causes anyway. To drive such populations downward (that is, to limit the population of lions below what the prey base would support, or K), adult mortality must exceed the ability of the population to recruit young. Intensive harvest, either through the use of bounties, professional hunters, or by sport hunting, is a means by which such a population of lions might be held below the level dictated by the prey base. In most areas, and, especially with a stable prey base, however, removals are not adequate to offset the ability of the population to replace individuals lost to guns or traps.

Under other circumstances, as in an area where a population of mountain lions is responding positively to increasing prey, the removal of individual lions would represent additive mortality, because those deaths are in addition to those that might be expected to occur in the absence of removals by humans. In such scenarios, increases in the population of mountain lions might be slowed relative to what would be expected in the absence of removals, and may speed the rate of increase of prey. Management that results in additive mortality for the predator has potentially important implications for the recovery (or increase) of prey populations that are at low densities, either as a result of predation or for other reasons.

Forage availability, prey, and predators interact in a number of ways, all of which result in feedback mechanisms that have important implications for the management of mountain lions in the absence of political or legislative intervention. Further, the abundance of secondary prey further complicates the responses of mountain lions and other predators to direct management actions, or to actions affecting their primary prey. For example, investigators in New Mexico have reported that beef calves on rangelands appear to have "subsidized" mountain lions where deer are not abundant, and their availability may be a factor exacerbating rates of lion predation on mountain sheep in the absence of intensive lion control.

If a management goal is to maintain populations of ungulates at high levels (e.g., to support a high sport harvest), removal of mountain lions will help do so only when prey populations exhibit characteristics that include good body condition and high reproductive rates and recruitment, among other traits. Thus, in populations of prey that have

GPS RADIO COLLARS ARE ALLOWING FOR MUCH GREATER ACCURACY IN THE MONITORING OF MOUNTAIN LIONS.

declined substantially as a result of a catastrophic event and are not nutritionally constrained, predation can be a factor that limits the growth rate of that population and control of mountain lions could lead to an increased rate of growth in the prey population.

When prey populations decline in the absence of a secondary species of prey (that would help maintain the population of lions at a high level if it were present), however, lion numbers will eventually decline, lagging behind their prey even in the absence of harvest. As a result, additive mortality among prey will decrease, and the prey population will again grow until it reaches a level commensurate with the nutritional carrying capacity of its environment. At that point, lion predation will again become a source of compensatory mortality for the prey population.

Historical levels of removal may have severely affected some mountain lion populations, particularly during periods when bounties were paid. Indeed, there is strong evidence that intensive lion control during the early 1900s was a factor important in the population dynamics of mountain sheep in California's San Gabriel Mountains. There is also evidence that cessation of bounty hunting, when combined with habitat changes resulting from fire suppression, resulted in extreme dynamics of mule deer (the primary prey) and ultimately contributed to the decline of mountain sheep in that range. What is clear is that lion removal was intensive, and it was implemented by individuals that were rewarded financially for their efforts. Whether regulated sport hunting can occur at rates sufficient to effect ungulate population dynamics is unclear; in the absence of high rates of harvest of their primary predators, however, few benefits to ungulate populations are likely to accrue.

The initiative process has "tied the hands" of professional wildlife managers in California by eliminating a number of management options that were formerly available. Further, initiatives in other states have eliminated the use of hounds as a method of pursuing mountain lions. Although lions have been afforded special protection in California, recent legislation has provided the Department of Fish and Game the authority to remove lions that threaten the persistence of any population of mountain sheep. That legislation was passed by a near unanimous vote in the State Legislature, and has returned to the Department some of the authority that had been usurped by the initiative process. As a result, management programs to protect small populations of mountain sheep have been implemented on a localized basis, with good success, and without public outcry. It is doubtful, however, if the ability to manage mountain lions at a level that would affect populations of other ungulate prey will be restored to wildlife biologists, who are the individuals best trained to make those decisions. That ability was lost through the initiative process, and can only be restored through the initiative process, or by a four-fifths vote of the legislature; neither is likely to occur in California.

ABOUT THE AUTHORS: *Vernon C. Bleich (left) received B.S. and M. A. degrees from California State University Long Beach, and a Ph.D. from the University of Alaska Fairbanks (UAF). He holds academic appointments at UAF and at Idaho State University (ISU). Vern has been employed by the California Department of Fish and Game (CDFG) for over 30 years; he is Senior Environmental Scientist and Project Leader for the Sierra Nevada Bighorn Sheep Recovery Program. He and co-author Dr. Becky Pierce began investigating* *ecological relationships between mule deer and mountain lions in 1991, and the resulting Round Valley Project has become well-known as an outstanding, long-term research effort.*

Vern has received numerous awards during his career, including Wildlife Officer of the Year (Shikar Safari International), Professional of the Year (Western Section of the Wildlife Society), Trail Blazer Award (California Chapter of the Foundation for North American Wild Sheep), and the Desert Ram Award (Desert Bighorn Council). In 2002, he was recognized as the Outstanding Alumnus by the College of Science, Engineering, and Mathematics at UAF, and he received the Alumni Achievement Award for Professional Excellence from the UAF Alumni Association that same year. Vern has been a Professional Member of the Boone and Crockett Club since 1998. He lives with his family on the eastern slope of the Sierra Nevada Mountains, one of the most spectacular mountain ranges in North America.

Becky M. Pierce (right) is an Associate Wildlife Biologist with CDFG. She and co-author Dr. Vern Bleich have been studying mountain lions in the eastern Sierra Nevada Mountains since 1991; currently, she is the Predator Ecologist for the CDFG Sierra Nevada Bighorn Sheep Recovery Program. Becky's research has addressed predator-prey interactions between mountain lions and mule deer, and the population biology and behavior of mountain lions. Recently, her focus has been the interactions between mountain lions and endangered Sierra Nevada bighorn sheep. In 2004, Becky received the CDFG Director's Achievement Award for her contributions toward recovery of Sierra Nevada bighorn sheep.

Becky is an affiliate assistant professor in the Department of Biology and Wildlife, and a research associate in the Institute of Arctic Biology at UAF; additionally, she holds an appointment as affiliate faculty at ISU. She serves as an associate editor for Western North American Naturalist, and publishes regularly in the peer-reviewed literature. In her spare time, Becky enjoys the outdoors, is vice president of the Inyo County Search and Rescue (SAR) Team, and is currently training a K-9 for SAR.

CHAPTER SEVEN

A Collection of Hunting Memories

COMPILED BY
KEITH BALFOURD
PROFESSIONAL MEMBER
Boone and Crockett Club

In a very real sense, **Records of North American Big Game** *is a celebration of big game hunting and the success of our conservation and game management systems. It is also a history text, locking in time the events, trophies, issues, and personalities of big game hunting in North America.*

Outdoor magazines have always been an important part of the hunting landscape. They inform, engage, and bring hunters together. The editors of this 12th Edition felt that a history book of this nature would not be complete if it didn't include views and perspectives from some of the most respected and published outdoor writers of this time. This chapter includes contributions from just a few of today's most recognized outdoor personalities, capturing their thoughts and recollections on what hunting has meant in their lives.

CRAIG BODDINGTON
PROFESSIONAL MEMBER
Boone and Crockett Club

A DESERT BIGHORN

Through the spotting scope, from miles away, we had watched the two rams bed on a brushy shelf just below the crest of a ridge. The ideal situation would have been to circle the ridge and come up above and behind them, but the wind was exactly wrong. It was perfect for a frontal assault, but the ridge was very steep; the obvious problem would be seeing the rams.

The last intervening ridge offered possibilities. We got there easily, gaining the top in total concealment with the breeze in our faces. The rams were invisible, but we were pretty sure where they were bedded, in a grove of palo verde on top of a black rock face. Sooner or later they'd get up. Our problem now was that last bit of high ground was nearly 600 yards from the rams, so they might as well be on the moon. My friend, guide, and outfitter Kirk Kelso and I conferred. The only option we could come up with was to circle to our left and come through a saddle below the rams. It was risky and, looking uphill from below that face, most unlikely we could actually see them. But if we didn't spook them we might find a good spot to set up within range and wait for them to move.

Moving as slowly and quietly as we could, we relocated three

CRAIG BODDINGTON WITH A FINE DESERT BIGHORN TAKEN IN SONORA'S SIERRA DEL SERI REGION IN FEBRUARY 2003.

Photograph courtesy of Craig Boddington

times before settling on a little rockpile that jutted up from the valley floor. The top of the face was 330 yards above us, and I doubt we'd been there a minute before Kirk, behind me with his tripoded 20x60 Zeiss, found the ram. A few inches lower and with less magnification in my riflescope, it took me a bit longer. Finally I realized that the odd circular shine, almost a halo behind a pale green screen, was the horn of a bedded ram.

It was at this point that the excitement finally hit me. I hadn't realized it, but up until this moment I had merely been going through the motions. My pack was grounded on a rock shelf and I was lying behind it, rifle steadied at a steep uphill angle. I started shaking uncontrollably.

Thirty years. I had waited 30 years for this moment. My first ram, a Stone's sheep, had come easily in 1973. My first Dall's sheep came a few years later, but by then I'd already started applying for desert sheep permits. In 1978 my old friend, the great Nevada outfitter Jerry Hughes, had told me that, despite the odds, he'd never had a hunter apply more than seven years without drawing a tag. Seven years passed, and Jerry Hughes has now been gone twenty years. I'd applied in Nevada, Arizona, and everywhere else, and I'd never drawn. I couldn't complain too much; I'd drawn Rocky Mountain bighorn tags in both Montana and Wyoming, in '94 and '98. This, of course, made me want a desert sheep even more. From 1994 on, it was a matter of finishing the quest.

I laid plans for this hunt before I went overseas in the wake of 9/11. It seemed reasonable enough at the time, something to look forward to. But in camp in Sonora, scant days after I'd returned home, it seemed the most foolish thing I'd ever done. A whole year of combat pay; surely there were better things I could have done with the windfall! Truthfully, I'd made a half-hearted attempt to get out of the hunt. But it was too late; Kirk had secured the permit, and the loss would be too great.

So I was there, enjoying the mesquite fire at night and the pleasant February days in the Sierra del Seri, but I wasn't sure I wanted to be there. That is, not until the moment that I saw that ram's horn glinting through the palo verde. Now, finally, I understood why I was there. The remaining issue was whether I could control myself enough to do what I had to do.

I took a few deep breaths and partially controlled the shaking, hoping Kelso hadn't noticed. The ram was bedded tight, and it was early. This could be a long wait. It was a very long wait, although as we measure time I doubt it lasted an hour. During those endless minutes I stayed on the riflescope until my neck caught fire, then stretched and went back to the scope. I tried to concentrate on the shot, reminding myself that it was just like any tough shot, nothing special. The years of unsuccessful applications didn't matter, nor did the sweat of nearly a year in the Persian Gulf. All that mattered was the lip of that black rock face, the palo verde beyond, and the partially seen ram it obscured. It didn't matter that my uncle, Art Popham, had taken a ram not far from here with Charlie Ren and Jack O'Connor back in 1935, long before I was born; nor that O'Connor had taken many of his desert sheep within a few miles from where I now lay. Thinking was dangerous, but the mind can't be stopped.

The ram was bedded quartering away with his head to the left. Now and then he shifted, giving us a partial view of heavy bases and a right horn that seemed to match the left. Through the spotting scope at great distance, he had looked good. Now he looked better, but we still weren't sure of him. By the time he stood, the cramps stretched from my neck to the small of my back.

He was broadside, and his head was clear for a moment. Kirk said what I expected him to say: "Craig, I think we'd better take this ram."

It wasn't that simple, not yet. The angle would never get better, but the body was screened by palo verde. I could have tried it, but it might get better. It got worse. He took a couple of steps and was almost swallowed by brush. Then he turned and stepped to the edge of the face, completely clear, quartering toward me. Thirty years of waiting. Now was the time, if I could do it.

For the first time in many minutes the shakes were gone. So was the ache in my back. Three hundred and thirty yards, but strongly uphill. A quartering left crosswind, maybe ten or twelve miles per hour. I held just above the centerline of the body and put the vertical wire a little bit right on the body, into the wind. The shot was gone before I realized.

Down out of recoil, I did not see the second, lesser ram run straight up and over the ridge. I thought I saw my ram run to the right, off the face and into thick mesquite, but the movement stopped so quickly I wasn't sure.

Kirk, seeing the second ram, had instantly and urgently hissed, "Don't shoot again." Then he said, "He's down."

A lifetime earlier he had been too polite to comment as my whole body shook. Now he was too polite to comment as I lay over the rifle, shoulders shaking. In time he asked, "Are you all right?"

I was not all right, not at all. Or perhaps I was more all right than I'd ever been in my hunting life.

ABOUT THE AUTHOR: *Craig Boddington of Paso Robles, California, is the Executive Field Editor for PRIMEDIA Outdoor Group, including* Guns & Ammo *and* Petersen's HUNTING *magazines, and also appears on The Outdoor Channel as co-host for the exciting new series,* Guns & Ammo TV. *He is the author of 16 books including* **Safari Rifles, American Hunting Rifles, Search for the Spiral Horn,** *and* **Where Lions Roar.**

Boddington has been a Professional Member of the Boone and Crockett Club since 1981 and has served 30 years as a Marine Corps Infantry Officer.

JIM DOUGHERTY
PROFESSIONAL MEMBER
Boone and Crockett Club

THE BUCK IN THE CANYON

I'm thinking back on over 50 years of reasonable bowhunting success, one long ago encounter when I was not much more than a kid has never been retired to a dusty corner in my mind, but remains a bright reminder that dedication can pay off. That recollection has to do with a mule deer buck I met one summer evening while glassing a gnarly, deep, thickly brushed canyon in southern California. At the time, the foothills below the east/west line of the Angeles National Forest boundary and the little mountain ranges surrounded by small cities like Glendale, Burbank and La Canada were wild, mostly uncluttered places that have long since surrendered to the incessant human requirement for pavement and housing. It is not that those small mountains we referred to, as "The Hills" were uninhabited, for certainly they were, though less than today, which left hundreds of acres available to us who loved bowhunting. The special Los Angeles County archery season ran from mid-July to the end of the year with two deer of either sex as the legal limit.

On the evening mentioned, an out-of-place white spot near the canyons' bottom caught my attention. A quick focus of my binoculars revealed the whitish muzzle of an exceptionally large buck studying me in return. It seemed that upon realizing he had been spotted his expression changed and he simply took a step backwards and out of my view. But that one quick look was enough to tell me he was easily the biggest deer I had ever seen in "The Hills." It was his body size, not a spectacular rack, that thrilled me though his dark, deeply-forked antlers were well above the norm for deer in that dense, dry habitat. Here mature bucks field-dressed weight would average just 100 pounds, or so it was with the dozens my friends and I had taken in the past. This old boy seemed twice that size with headgear much larger than I'd ever taken. Then and there I made a commitment to hunt only him until I won or the season came to a close. It was the very first time I made such a singular vow; after all, bow shooting any deer in that rough and tumble country was a steep enough challenge in itself. I told my wife about him when I returned after dark but selfishly never mentioned him or his location to anyone else. I figured if he lived there and remained undisturbed our paths would eventually cross. And so, I set out on what was my first true trophy hunting venture; for a long time it did not go well.

The buck's assumed home canyon was not much more than a 20 minute drive from my home. With summer's long evening hours I had plenty of time to search for him after work when the hot days of August and September began to cool with the downward slant of the sun and its cooling long shadows. I saw lots of deer in those purple-pink evenings, mostly does, though once a buck much better than I'd ever taken gave me a slam-dunk chance that reluctantly, with clench jawed determination I let walk, then wondered, "Just what-in-hell were you thinking?" Three days later, I was proud of the decision for just before dark I saw my buck again just down a steep side hill. He was within easy range, but feeding in brush where no arrow could slip through. I watched him with fingers tense on the string as daylight faded and he melted from sight in the gloom: one of those "almost" sort of things a bowhunter must learn to endure.

In October, damp, offshore breezes bring on what passes for fall weather in southern California and those misty cool mornings bring on the rut. Two times I saw the buck dogging a doe and another morning, seriously sparring with the same buck I'd passed up. With the cooler weather and increasing activity I hunted more often though evenings grew shorter. Several times I found the buck within 40 yards yet the ever-present brush denied me a good shot.

By now I knew the canyon nearly as well as the buck — what trails I could quietly negotiate, small clearings where I could hide nearby in wait. All of my free time was spent scouring the canyon. My patient, young wife, though supportive, labeled my mission "obsessive!"

Then, one cool, breezy evening he was standing right before me as I eased around a brushy corner in a trail. I saw the arrow strike him cleanly without clearly realizing I had shot. My trembling legs failed to support me as I followed the sounds of his crashing departure

from my knees. It seemed forever before I could breath, stand, and take up the clear crimson trail.

You won't find my buck recorded in any book of record listings — only an entry in a tattered old notebook dated October 5, 1957, mentioning that I got him after 30 some tries. While there have been many other successes in the near half-century that's followed — some on fine animals of significant size — my private battle with the buck in the canyon, the pure enjoyment and dedication to the challenge, shaped my hunting perspective.

ABOUT THE AUTHOR: *Jim Dougherty has bowhunted 37 states, Canada, Mexico, and Africa with what he terms "reasonable success." A past president and director of the Pope & Young Club he currently serves on its Records Committee. He has been inducted to the National Bowhunters Hall of Fame and The Archery Hall of Fame. Dougherty lives in Tulsa, Oklahoma, with his wife Sue of 48 years and considers raising five sons, all experienced bowhunters, his greatest accomplishment.*

JACK RENEAU
PROFESSIONAL MEMBER
Boone and Crockett Club

MENTORS

There is an individual in most hunters' lives that they can look back on and say, "I am a hunter because that person introduced me to hunting." This brief story is mostly about one such person, and a little about my first deer.

I grew up in rural, western Pennsylvania back in the 1950s when deer were nearly as scarce as hen's teeth. If someone spotted deer tracks, it was a major topic of discussion at dinner that evening. Actual deer sightings were so rare that our family once piled into my grandfather's 1956 Ford sedan to go look at a road-killed deer we had heard about. It was a magnificent animal, with four large points per side.

I don't remember when I first became interested in wildlife and hunting. I do remember, however, that my first lessons about wildlife and the out-of-doors were given to me by my mother's brother, Paul Tomon. The first such lesson took place back in the mid-1950s when I was seven or eight years old.

Uncle Paul was president of the Chewton Rod and Gun Club in the small town where we lived. He was the first hunter/conservationist I met but didn't realize it at the time. Why he latched on to me, he never said, and I never thought to ask. One Saturday he asked if I wanted to join him at the gun club to help with planting a variety of berries and shrubs to improve wildlife habitat. The events of that day come to mind as if they happened only yesterday.

Shortly after we arrived at the gun club, Uncle Paul identified some deer tracks and told me how I could tell the direction it was going. A little later he drew my attention to some rabbit tracks and explained how rabbits run, and which way it was going. Uncle Paul also taught me how to climb a hill that day. "Don't walk straight up the hill," he said "contour the hill by digging in with the sides of your boots." It worked!

All this was new and exciting to me, and I wanted to learn more. For some reason Uncle Paul became my hunting mentor. Perhaps it was because he didn't have any children of his own at the time, or the fact that my father was in the army. I always wanted to hunt deer with him, but it wasn't until I returned from Vietnam in August 1968 that I had my first opportunity. I was 21 years old at the time.

Uncle Paul invited me that fall to hunt deer with him and his older brother, Henry, at his cabin during the first week in December near Pigeon, Pennsylvania. I enthusiastically accepted and asked my boss if I could take time off, even though I hadn't built up enough vacation. He approved it.

In preparation, I purchased a lever-action, Model 99, .300 Savage topped with a 4X Hawk, J. Unertl scope. It turned out to be the exact medicine needed for my first deer hunt. When we arrived in hunting camp in December, I discovered that Uncle Henry coincidentally had the same exact rifle and scope. I knew then and there that if my uncle had one, I surely made the right choice.

On Saturday, opening day, Uncle Paul directed me to a stump along a well-used deer trail just before daylight. At legal shooting time the sounds of gunfire echoed throughout the valleys and woods in all directions. I figured with that much shooting going on that I surely would be tagging my buck in short order. That didn't happen, and none of us saw a deer that day. I couldn't believe it. To this day I still wonder what so many people were shooting at.

The next day was Sunday, and we sat around camp cutting firewood, checking out the zero on our scopes, and doing odd jobs, as there is no Sunday hunting in Pennsylvania. Monday and Tuesday were repeats of Saturday, except there was less shooting. I debated whether or not most of the deer had been killed or if they were now better educated.

We only had a half day to hunt on Wednesday as we were leaving about noon. When the alarm went off that morning, Uncle Paul peered out the cabin's window and announced, "I'm not going out; it looks like there are several inches of new snow on the ground, and it's still snowing."

Henry wasn't feeling well that morning and said that he too was going to sleep in. While they both dozed back off to sleep, I slipped into my hunting gear, grabbed my rifle, and slid out the door as quietly as possible. The snow wasn't going to dampen my enthusiasm.

At the end of the dirt road I intersected the railroad tracks that took me into the forest. The snow was still falling, and the forest was a winter wonderland. I followed the tracks for a few hundred yards before dropping down into the woods to the north of the tracks. There were fresh deer tracks going in all directions.

I still-hunted my way parallel to the tracks for about 20 minutes when I suddenly detected movement ahead to my left. I quickly made out a running deer that was going to pass directly in front of me. When it paused about 75 yards away to check its backtrail I saw its antlers. In what seemed like slow motion, which I still replay in my mind's eye, I placed the crosshairs on the buck's vitals and fired. Before I knew it, I was punching my tag, and the fellow who spooked the buck to me was instructing me on how to field dress my first deer. I couldn't wait to show it to my uncles.

The snow made the drag easy, and I was back at Paul's cabin within an hour and a half of the time I left. It was still overcast, but the snow was turning to sleet and rain. Paul and Henry were still sleeping when I quietly slipped back into the cabin. From under his blankets somewhere Uncle Paul groggily asked, "Did you see anything?"

"Yes, I got one," I answered,

Paul and Henry catapulted out of bed and glanced out the window. Seeing my buck lying next to the cabin, Uncle Paul exclaimed, "He got one! Where's the camera? Let's get pictures!" They were at least as excited for me as I was. Maybe they were even more excited, because I know how excited I was when each of my three sons got their first deer.

After the usual pictures and story telling, we carefully examined the antlers. The rack wasn't large, but there were four well-developed points on the right antler and three on the left. There was one other projection on the left antler near the beam tip, but its status as a point was "debatable." As he took his ring off, Uncle Paul said, "They say it's a point if you can hang a ring on it."

No matter how hard we tried we couldn't get the ring to hang from it. After much discussion, we ultimately concluded the projection did not qualify as a point and that I had taken a 4x3.

We headed home around noon after a brief stop at the check station. At first I figured the checkers were surely wrong when they told us my buck was only one and a half years old. I just knew a 4x3 buck had to be at least nine or ten years old. My uncles eventually convinced me that the checkers knew their stuff. I still wonder to this day how big my buck's rack would have gotten if it had reached its full potential at 4-1/2 to 5-1/2 years old.

Of all the hunting memories I have, this is the one I cherish the most. Not only did I get my first deer, but it is the only time I hunted big game with Uncle Paul, my mentor, and Uncle Henry to whom I was somewhat of a surrogate son. Uncle Henry didn't have any sons of his own so I accompanied him every year to the father-son breakfasts and picnics at his church and wherever else he needed a stand-in son.

Both men have since passed away, and my biggest regret is that I never had another chance to hunt with either of them. Uncle Henry passed away a couple months after the hunt from a series of heart attacks. The first one apparentlly occurred the day before I got my deer, which is why he was sickly the morning I took my deer. He never told Paul or me.

Different mentors come and go at different stages in our lives. It's hard to recognize them at the time, but they leave a permanent imprint on us that we may not even recognize for years.

BOB ROBB

PROFESSIONAL MEMBER

Boone and Crockett Club

THE GORGE

Sometimes, not taking the shot makes the best memories.

When I was a tow-headed young boy growing up behind the firehouse in what was then a rural southern California farm town, once a month my dad – the station captain – would haul me unto the firehouse lounge, prop me up into a chair, and proceed to clipper my hair to the scalp. If I didn't wiggle and fuss too much, my reward was a shiny dime I could toss into an old cigar box in the fridge in exchange for an icy Coca-Cola in a bottle. I was allowed to sit on the couch and read old dog-eared copies of Outdoor Life and Field & Stream as long as the Coke lasted. I learned to nurse a drink long before I ever set foot in my first tavern.

Dad loved to deer hunt and though I never hunted deer with him, just watching him butcher bucks in the garage and sight in his old custom pre-64 Model 70 in .270, along with those magazines, got the fire going in me. Dad had purchased the rifle back in 1946 for $250 — a lot of money for a working man of modest means just back from the war. In high school I inherited that rifle, and together we made forays into the rugged, brush-choked mountains of Ventura County in search of what the old timers called "Pacific bucks" — scrawny mule deer that never got to be more than big forked horns, but were craftier than an owl and harder to kill than a cat with nine lives.

I soon graduated from successful deer hunter to teenage trophy buck hunter. So it was that one hot August afternoon found me way off into the bottom of a deep, brush-choked gorge, where I never saw another hunter, but there was a small seep that drew deer. And after three seasons of searching for the buck that had left tracks almost as big as my hands, I finally spotted him.

When he slowly slipped out of the brush late that afternoon, my heart started pounding harder than it did after my first kiss. At first, all I could see was his backline behind the thick brush. And then his head came up, ears flicking at the bothersome flies, and I saw his antlers for the first time. They were large, and as he turned his head from side to side my heart almost exploded. His antlers were wider than his ears and at least twice as tall, the bases heavy and gnarled, and I could see three points on one side, four on the other. He was larger than any buck I had ever seen, alive or dead.

He stared for a full minute or more – a lifetime – then he flicked his ears, first the left and then the right, and as the nagging black flies became more numerous he shook his entire coat. With that the tension was gone from his eyes, and he moved closer to the seep.

Soon he was but 75 yards off. I waited tensely for the proper moment, and when it came I slowly raised the rifle to my shoulder. The heat and tension and sweat had turned my hands into a sweaty mess; gripping the rifle was about as easy as holding tightly onto those greased pigs we chased as kids at the county fair. As the crosshairs found their way just behind his shoulder I slid my index finger over the trigger and drew a short breath.

"Bang," I whispered.

Then, lowering the rifle, I slowly started to rise. With my first motions the buck started and took a couple of short, quick jab steps. He snapped his head in my direction, saw that I was a danger, and was off like a shot, clattering rocks and snapping twigs as he disappeared through the grove of young oaks. A moment later he reappeared on the ridgeline, a ghost-like silhouette of tan and brown against the darkening afternoon sky.

I stared at the spot where he last stood for some time, hands shaking and sweat dripping off my nose and chin. My knees weren't working so good, so I sat down against an old scrub oak, closed my eyes, and replayed the scene over in my mind. The buck had been mine. I had suffered the heat and dust and bugs and grueling hike for just such an opportunity, yet when the time came I had elected not to squeeze the trigger. Why?

As I replayed the scene over and over again, savoring every detail, I knew.

It has been more than 30 seasons since my encounter with the big buck down in the gorge. Though I made other trips there after that day, I never saw him again. And though I took a couple of other good bucks in the gorge, the day I remember most is the one on which I chose not to pull the trigger.

There are times when I regret that I do not have that great buck mounted in a place of great honor above my fireplace, but those days are rare. More often I think about my hike out of the canyon that evening, and what my late father taught me about ethics.

Even after dark, the walk had been long and hot. Finally I crested the rim and sat on a stump near the old fire road and reached for my canteen, greedily swallowing its remaining contents. The full moon had risen over the hills, illuminating the sky like a downtown streetlight.

I thought of an ancient arrowhead, chipped and polished from a chunk of obsidian that I had found on my very first trek into the gorge years before. That day, as I slipped and slid down the hillside I thought that here, perhaps, was a spot no man had ever set foot on before. The thought thrilled me, and finding that arrowhead was both exciting and, at the same time, disappointing.

In their ceremonial rituals the ancient Indians of Ventura County had danced to "the great bucks of the mountains," believing that such old, great bucks possessed powerful medicine, and that his well-being was vital to the health of the herd. They would vigorously hunt other deer, but to kill this great buck was to place a curse on a most important food source.

I wondered about the ancient hunter who had made his way down into the gorge a hundred years or more before me. Had he, too, seen a great buck? Did he stalk within range with his primitive bow and arrow, just to see if he could, and then hesitate at the moment of truth? And on his way back out of the hot, steamy gorge, did he feel the mixed emotions of pride and disappointment that not taking such a shot brings?

Perhaps. But as I drove back down the mountain that night, I felt that this had indeed been one of the most successful hunts of my life. As dad had taught me, ethics is about doing the right thing when nobody is looking. I knew that this day I had done the right thing, that it would bring me great luck in the future.

And besides, I could always find my meat deer later, on kinder ground.

ABOUT THE AUTHOR: *A full-time outdoor writer since 1978, Bob Robb's stories and photographs have graced the pages of most of the country's major hunting magazines for over 25 years. A former editor of* Western Outdoor News, Petersen's Bowhunting, *and* Bowmasters, *a former senior staff editor for* Petersen's Hunting, *and current editor of* Whitetail Journal, *Bob currently writes regular columns for several major hunting national publications and serves as a pro staff member and consultant to a handful of select industry manufacturers. He's also authored nine books on hunting. Bob's adventures have taken him to six continents and most of the states, including Alaska, where he lived for 14 years and is a licensed assistant hunting guide. Currently he resides in Tucson, Arizona.*

DIANA RUPP
SPORTS AFIELD
Editor-in-Chief

AN ELK-HUNTING EPIPHANY

It had been years since I'd spent an entire day on horseback, and my knees were telling me about it by the time the snug collection of white wall tents came into view. The 14-mile ride from the trailhead north of Missoula to our elk camp in the Scapegoat Wilderness had been an experience all by itself, though—a trip through a stunning landscape of yellow aspens, roiling trout streams, and jagged peaks rising in the distance. When I slid out of the saddle and tied my horse to a tree near the three-walled tent that formed a stable of sorts, the sun was already on the other side of the western ridge.

As the packtrain thundered into camp and we all pitched in to relieve the mules of their canvas-wrapped loads, I felt again the rising excitement that had been building since that morning, when our outfitter, astride his big black horse, had surveyed our group of eager but uncertain hunters perched atop unfamiliar mounts. He'd grinned at us and spurred his horse up the trail with the shout, "Let's go elk hunting!"

Now we had arrived. From this base, in the ensuing days, I would ride up the mountain every morning with a guide and one other hunter, sometimes spending three or four hours in the saddle. The four-legged transportation would take us most of the way, and then we would dismount and spend the rest of the day hiking up eight-thousand-foot peaks, bugling off canyon rims, and skidding down timbered slopes in pursuit of elk.

I'd been fortunate in my hunting life—more so than I'd ever dreamed. I'd killed pronghorn on Wyoming cattle ranches, stalked and shot bears in Canadian clear-cuts, slogged through Newfoundland bogs in search of caribou, and hunted whitetails in second-growth timber. Still, I was in search of something more. I felt sometimes that I was getting away from the heart of what had first drawn me to hunting—the intimate experience with wild country. I wanted to go where the nights were still black-dark, where no engines would shatter the intense quiet, where only two- and four-legged critters would carry the load, and where I might not even

hold the top spot on the food chain. The search for a hunt that would take me to real, honest-to-God wild country brought me, at last, to Montana, to experience what is arguably the finest, most traditional and classic hunting experience left in North America—a wilderness pack trip.

The setting, the lack of vehicles and other hunters, the backcountry camp, and the constant awareness in the back of the mind of the presence of grizzlies brought the experience of hunting back to its essence. There were no property lines to consider, no boundaries except our own physical limitations, no excess of gear and gadgets. It didn't take long for the wilderness to cleanse my mind of complications and reduce life to a refreshingly simple routine: sleep, eat, hunt.

The five all-too-short days between the ride in and the ride out live in my mind as a jumble of experiences and impressions rather than as an orderly time line of events. That's what wilderness does—it places you on a schedule that has nothing to do with a watch. There were the morning rides up the mountain with nobody talking, just the quiet thud of horse hoofs on the damp trail; the lunch breaks on the mountaintop when we savored the incredible vistas below; and the sheer twelve-volt excitement of closing in on a bugling elk, only to have it spot us and bolt. There were other experiences I wouldn't trade for anything: riding back to camp in pitch darkness with the surreal sense of having been stricken blind; clawing my way up a near-vertical slope just to peek over the other side; ravenously inhaling the evening meal through a haze of physical exhaustion; stopping suddenly in the middle of a freezing midnight dash from tent to outhouse to stare in wonder at stars that seemed just an arm's length away.

The jumble of events coalesced into a single moment: When my elk materialized in the dark timber behind a muddy elk wallow, wearing a 6x6 rack that matched the majesty of its surroundings, I raised my rifle. The impact of the bullet forever sealed my connection to this particular elk and to the wild country where it lived. Minutes later, surrounded by the tremendous silence of an ancient spruce forest, I placed my hands on the still-warm flank and held the magnificent rack.

That's when I realized that while all hunts are treasured experiences, the pursuit of game on foot, in true wilderness, enriches the soul and embodies the joy of the hunt in a way that nothing else can.

ABOUT THE AUTHOR: *Diana Rupp was born and raised in Potter County, Pennsylvania, where the opening day of deer season is the most important day of the year. Her parents, both hunters, introduced her to the outdoors at an early age. After earning a B.A. in journalism from Susquehanna University in Selinsgrove, Pennsylvania, Diana joined* Sports Afield *magazine, serving as an associate editor and then contributing editor. She later moved on to editorial jobs at other outdoor magazines, with stints as editorial director of* Pennsylvania Sportsman, New

York Sportsman, *and* Michigan Hunting & Fishing, *and as editor of* Wing & Shot. *In 2002 Diana returned to* Sports Afield *as editor-in-chief, spearheading its re-launch as an upscale big-game hunting magazine. Diana has hunted big game throughout the United States and Canada as well as in Africa and Europe. She lives in Torrance, California, with her husband and favorite hunting partner, Scott, who is the editor of* Petersen's Hunting *magazine.*

J. SCOTT RUPP
EDITOR-IN-CHIEF
Petersen's HUNTING

ALASKA CARIBOU

Low clouds clutched the rocky, spiny ridgetop, and we pushed on through pelting rain and gusty winds, stopping whenever visibility dropped to less than 50 yards. Wes Lang and I had been hunting hard for four days and were running out of time, but there was no sense in blundering into the fog and bumping the caribou we were looking for.

The fact that we hadn't filled a tag wasn't due to a lack of animals; the Lime Hills region of Alaska was full of them, but we were being picky. After the first few days, however, we noticed we were seeing fewer and fewer animals in the broad valley near our spike camp. At the same time we began spotting more herds high on the ridge behind camp, and in a bid to change our luck, we decided to go up for a look.

It took most of the morning to reach the main spine of the ridge. We took shelter in a cluster of boulders to rest and wait out one particularly dense cloud bank, and, as we chatted, a grizzly bear materialized out of the mist just 50 yards away--following the path we'd taken. Wes and I worked the bolts on our rifles, chambering rounds just in case, but the grizzly paused just briefly, glanced at us (with disdain, it seemed) and continued over the top and down the other side.

We laughed nervously, gathered our gear, and moved out. We were just shy of the peak when the clouds suddenly detached themselves from the mountain, revealing bright sun, brilliant blue sky and caribou--hundreds of them gathered in tightly bunched herds in a valley to the northwest.

We took a knee, raised our binoculars and began to look them over, but as had been the case for most of the trip, none of the bulls were what we sought. Then Wes swung his glasses to check back down the ridge and spotted a bachelor herd of about 10 bulls that we'd walked by in the fog.

We made a quick stalk and soon found ourselves belly-down in a field of sharp black rocks, the bulls 250 yards directly below us. Wes gave me first shot, and I put the crosshairs on a good bull and squeezed the trigger, the .30-06 dropping him on the spot. Wes's .270 cracked an instant later, and minutes later we were standing over two fine caribou.

As a kid I'd dreamed of hunting Alaska, but it remained just a dream as I chased whitetails and turkeys up and down the Eastern Seaboard. I'd been working as a magazine editor for a number of years — at NRA's *American Rifleman*, then *Pennsylvania Game News*, then *Pennsylvania Sportsman* — when unexpectedly I was offered the job as editor in chief of *Petersen's HUNTING*. And with that offer, almost simultaneously, came the chance to go to Alaska for caribou.

How could I say no? There was the small detail of packing up and moving from Harrisburg, Pennsylvania, to Los Angeles, California, shortly after my return, not to mention the anxiety of taking the helm of a national magazine. That should have caused me some sleepless nights, but instead I focused on going to Alaska; worrying about the rest could wait until I got back.

Our small plane touched down on a dirt airstrip in the Alaskan bush in mid-August, and by afternoon we were trekking the several miles to our spike camp. We had no guide, although Wes had hunted the area before. Over the next few days, we fought our way through thick stands of alders, sampled the tart sweetness of tundra blueberries, watched a big blond grizzly scatter herds of caribou like a bully on a playground, and listened to the guttural croaks of ptarmigan echoing through the ravines.

We hunted hard every day, slept hard every night, and while our campmates filled their tags, Wes and I held out. And now, high above camp, our reward was at hand--and so was the work. I'd never skinned and butchered an animal in the field before, but before too long we got the quarters and boned meat stuffed into game bags, slung them over our shoulders and lurched dangerously over the wet, sharp rocks to stash them some distance from the carcasses. We'd been hunting without our frame packs, so we trudged back to camp--arriving spent, tired and with not enough time to go back for a load.

We'd killed the bulls a full three miles from camp, all of it uphill. We set out fairly early the next morning, and with campmate Jim Morey along for extra muscle, we reached our cache just as another weather system moved in--drenching us with cold, wind-driven rain that stung our faces. We finished a few last-minute butchering details and lashed the loads to our pack frames. And what loads they were. When Jim's back gave out halfway back to camp, Wes and I divvied up his share and wound up with about 100 pounds each on our backs.

At first I thought that since we were going downhill it wouldn't be so bad. I was wrong. My legs shook with strain on the steeper slopes, and the alder thickets--tough to get through under any condition--seemed like a circle of Hell that even Dante hadn't envisioned. At one point I slipped on a wet rock and tumbled down a ravine, completing two full somersaults before somehow landing on my feet--to the laughter and applause of my partners.

It was nearly 11 o'clock that night when we first caught sight of camp, the white canvas tents barely visible in the deep twilight. I was completely exhausted, and even though the tents were only a couple hundred yards away, I briefly considered dropping the pack and coming back for it later. But I found a last little bit of strength and, drawn by the faint glow of the lanterns and the promise of food, I crossed the distance and shucked my pack for the first time since we'd started down. I staggered into the tent, wolfed down some food ,and slept like the dead.

The next day, Wes and I headed out early for the last of the meat, the capes, and the antlers. The loads were lighter, the weather nicer, and by late afternoon we were back at camp.

The outfitter sent an ATV and trailer to transport the meat and our gear back to base camp, and after it departed we followed on foot--headed for camp and a hot shower.

In the ensuing years I've been on a lot of hunts in a lot of places, and it's been my good fortune to have killed some great trophies, but I'll always treasure my first Alaskan hunt above them all. In many ways it was a test of me as a hunter and as a professional in the outdoor writing field. I'd like to think I passed.

ABOUT THE AUTHOR: *J. Scott Rupp grew up hunting deer, turkeys, and small game in his native Pennsylvania. He served as a shooter/instructor with the U.S. Army Marksmanship Unit in the early 1980s and was an All-American smallbore rifle shooter at Eastern Kentucky University. After earning a bachelor's degree in journalism from EKU in 1986, he began his magazine career as associate editor for* American Rifleman *and, later,* Pennsylvania Game News. *He was editorial director of* Pennsylvania Sportsman, New York Sportsman *and* Michigan Hunting & Fishing *magazines before taking over the helm at* Petersen's HUNTING *in 1999. He has hunted a variety of big game across the Lower 48, Alaska, Canada, Mexico, and Africa. He lives in Torrance, California, with his wife, Diana.*

TODD W. SMITH
OUTDOOR LIFE
Editor-in-Chief

WELCOME TO SHEEP COUNTRY

On the wall of my office hangs an old Dall's sheep ram. He's not very heavy and he's not very long. In fact, almost nothing about him physically can compare to the grandeur of the trophies that are celebrated in these pages, except, perhaps, his snow-white cape.

Yet to me he is no less deserving of honor. Not for his size or even the guile by which he lived to maturity, but for the sheer adventure that hunting him provided—an experience that surpassed everything I had hoped my first trip to Alaska would be.

Twenty years ago I went on my first sheep hunt. I was 31 years old, single and probably in the best physical condition of my life. My outfitter had put the fear of God into me.

"Jog everyday with your pack on," he began matter-of-factly. "Then gradually increase the weight in your pack until you can't lift it onto your back without help. When you can do that, begin preparing yourself mentally for what will be the toughest hunt of your life." He paused for a moment to let that thought sink in then locked onto my eyes. "The Alaskan wilderness is the most beautiful place on earth," he said quietly, "but it will eat you alive if you're not ready."

So I went into training. I started running several miles each morning in the soft sand along the beach where I lived, and I added more and more weight to my pack. I ran up and down the bleachers at the local high school until my lungs burned and lifted weights until I couldn't lift another ounce. Six months later, I thought I was ready.

When the Super Cub dropped me on the gravel bar near our base camp in the Alaska Range and I saw the ice-sheathed mountains rising up thousands of feet above the valley floor, I still thought I was ready. My guide, Pearce Nelson, caught me staring at the sheer cliffs and craggy faces.

"Welcome to sheep country," he said with a smile.

On the 8-mile trek into our spike camp the next day we slogged across jagged talus slopes and skirted the glacier that scraped down one side of Mt. Deborah. The bright sun clouded over, the temperature dropped and a freezing rain that later turned to snow began to fall. Gathered around a sputtering camp stove waiting for our freeze-dried dinner pouches to warm, I watched dumbfounded as Pearce ate handful after handful of uncooked Minute Rice.

"How can you eat that stuff?" I asked.

"I'm cold," he said, swallowing. "My body's screaming for carbs."

Five days later, I was fighting him for the Minute Rice box.

"Alaska will eat you alive if you're not ready," a little voice reminded me. And it will.

Our hunt lasted 16 days. I lost a pound a day while wolfing down more than I have ever eaten before or since. We hunted from dawn until dark; through snowstorms and rain; up steep snow chutes and down; across glaciers and ancient snowfields. By the end of the second week we were so tired that we sometimes simply curled up at the top of some rocky peak and slept on the bare ground, happy just to close our eyes and escape the cold that crept ever more deeply into us. Even in my 4-pound down bag I shook uncontrollably before being overtaken by fitful sleep. My socks froze, my knees burned, my boots were torn to shreds, and my head ached with the dull throb of exhaustion.

But on the 14th day, when I finally knelt beside the fallen body of the ram I had worked so hard to find, I was suddenly overwhelmed by a feeling of peace and joy and triumph—not just over an animal that is perhaps more worthy than anything I have ever hunted, but in triumph over myself. And in that moment I experienced a feeling of freedom and a connection with all the wild whiteness around me that no other earthly experience could provide. That's why I hunt. Every morning when I walk into my office and see my beautiful ram on the wall, I remember that day and that feeling. That, for me, is what hunting is all about.

ABOUT THE AUTHOR: *From Alaska to the Alps to Africa, Todd Smith spent years playing the world's game fields and streams, writing hundreds of stories for various magazines and books before joining* Outdoor Life *as Editor-in-Chief in 1996. Prior to that, he spent 14 years with Petersen Publishing Company, where he served as editor of* Petersen's HUNTING Magazine *and as editorial director for the Outdoor Group. Smith is a graduate of UCLA and the 1998 recipient of the Times Mirror "Editor of the Year" award.*

GREG TINSLEY
FAIR CHASE
Editor-in-Chief

HILL COUNTRY PRAYER BREAKFAST

The place where I grew up is one of the ugliest landscapes in the world. It is almost completely devoid of natural surface water or rain and, often enough, the mostly constant west-to-northwest wind blows up biblical dirt storms, gritty brown-outs dense enough to make the street lights flicker on at noon on an otherwise cloudless day. It's a flat, blank canvas of wispy mesquites where the most interesting days include the sight of an anvil-headed thundercloud, a world-class giant to 30,000 feet, snailing across the great horizon.

The bison, the pronghorns, and all but a remnant population of white-tailed prairie dogs, which the town kept inside the city limits on a rodent reservation called Prairie Pete Park, were shot out 120 years before I arrived.

But just east of there Texas gradually rises to form the Edwards Plateau, which, in difference to my birthplace in Far West Texas, remains one of the great game countries of the world. Whitetail deer, Rio Grande turkeys and even the relocated African kudu thrive in its rocky limestone draws. Understated song birds bathe in the cool overflows that spring from the now threatened Edwards Aquifer before flitting to the nearby branches of sculpted live oaks. Parts of Africa are better thanks to a tremendous array of native wildlife, plus Africa exudes that feeling of "newness" that even Ernest Hemingway battled to describe. And for fractions of the year the northwest and Alaska and the Rockies surely out radiate central Texas with the blinding beauty of ether worlds.

Certainly, I have not traveled much in comparison to those with means or wanderlust. But based on what I've seen, and what I'm likely to see, a more enjoyable and relaxing hunting country does not exist; the mesas of New Mexico and Arizona, the lovely hills of Central California, the remote handsomeness of northern Mexico, all not withstanding.

My first hunting trip to the Texas Hill Country was as the guest of Ernest Broughton. Mister B had purchased his spread near London for $50 per acre before I was born. Altogether it is about a half section of short- and long-stem grasses, cactus, oak mottes, and limestone land that encompassed most of the lower pools of Turkey Creek, an old Comanche campsite and a very distinguished, though modest, stretch of the Llano River. Honoring the truest sense of the term, it was a gentleman's ranch owned by a man who could have been the template for Larry McMurtry's Captain Call. You see Mister B was the real deal. After retiring as a border cowboy, he took a turn as the sheriff of Odessa, Texas, where he nicely kept the peace for that rough boomtown until retiring to a life of brush clearing, pecan picking and painting houses and fences.

The only time I saw Mr. B off duty, without his cowboy hat and not wearing a pressed pearl-button shirt, was the morning of my first deer hunt. It was probably also the first time that I'd ever "breathed smoke," or noticed my breath, inside a walled structure. "Are you awake, Marshal? We've experienced a very short night — shortest night on record and blue cold. Wake up now and hurry on to the kitchen, it may be the only warmth that remains this side of the frozen Red River," he urged.

By God it was fresh and at that very instant I felt like I was old enough to say "By God" aloud for grown people to hear if I wanted too, particularly at such a cold.

In contrast, the tiny kitchen was an Inferno. And it was a little crazy in there, too, with the smell of burned toast and bacon and the sounds of eggs rupturing in 300-degree grease. But it was the sight of Mr. B's bare arms and hatless head, all exposed and whiter than West Texas cloud tops in bright sun that may have been the greatest stunner. "Marshal, I've put a nice, thick char on everything but the eggs and they're hard as a saddle," he lamented, words which broke my fixation on the incredible color transition between his brown hands and face and his exposed arms and forehead long enough to pull out a chair and sit. "Will you take coffee?" he asked, glancing away from the egg blast.

Yet un-warmed and still in some sort of 4:00 a.m. suspension, admittedly concerned about the prospect of a flash fire, I shook him off with a half-hearted smile and a "No'sir. Thank you."

"Well, it's the only thing fit to swallow, so you'll have to try some. If you put enough cream and sugar in it you'll be pleasantly hooked for life," he prophesied. I'd never known Mr. B to talk so much. Catching his breath, he addressed my dad, who was making his way into the room: "Bob, you're just in time to pick through the ruins of what could have been. Convicts eat better than this."

Burned or not, it was the most memorable and remarkable meal I've ever enjoyed.

Afterwards, I stood waiting for Dad at the front door of the ranch house, staring at the pair of bomber 10 pointers Mr. B had killed the first year he owned the ranch, the year he'd given up hunting for piling and burning brush and whitewashing all of the inanimate objects under his domain. They were great bucks, 130- to 140-inch deer and the mounted displays were probably the only extravagances of his otherwise frugal, old-school lifetime.

Terribly underdressed, Dad and I went off into the scrub with full bellies, ascending homemade wooden stands attached to the low forks of live oaks. It was raw cold until maybe midmorning when the sun scorched through, mottling the country with fantastic shafts of light. Eventually a line of big whitetail does appeared in one of those bright spots, and I put each of them carefully into the glass atop the .30-30, holding the crosshairs on each of their glowing bodies, contemplating my options. By God they were neat, shiny and perfect in that light, maybe too perfect to shoot, I thought, just seconds before they abruptly melted away. I wished their return for several hours but all that's left of the experience some 35 years later is Technicolor memory.

Mr. Broughton and his wife, Margaret, have been gone for years, gone before and after the deaths of their great friends, my grandfather and grandmother. I want to believe that the ranch is still owned by "Little Ernie" Broughton out of San Antonio, the grandson. And I would hope that Little Ernie's kids and, perhaps, grand kids, and their friends, have risen before sunrise to the sounds of first-hunt breakfasts, and that they appreciate those basic things and the Hill Country and the compassion and the simple generosity of their mothers and fathers.

ABOUT THE AUTHOR: *Greg Tinsley has been in the publishing business for over 20 years, first as the editor of a family-owned hunting and fishing newspaper,* Texas Outdoor Times, *and then for 13 years as a staff editor/ writer for Petersen's Publishing Company in Los Angeles. Tinsley became the editor of* Bowhunting *magazine holding that spot for six years until moving onto the editorship of* HUNTING *magazine. Tinsley received a degree in agriculture/journalism from Texas State University and is currently the vice president of Axis Media and, in his spare time, serves as the editor-in-chief of the Boone and Crockett Club's quarterly magazine,* Fair Chase.

RANDY ULMER
OUTDOOR WRITER

DESERT SOJOURN

Driving east from Las Vegas you'll pass through a small range of black mountains. Once past these, say good-bye. You have left civilization behind. The next gas station is 50 miles away.

The world seems alien, desolate, sterile, but this is an illusion. Bighorn sheep live here, or so I've been told. Looking at the country for the first time, I have my doubts.

I nose the old Dodge down into a large sandy wash, park, and make camp far enough down the bank to be protected from the wind, but not so far as to be threatened by flash floods. At dawn, I climb a little hill behind camp, raise my binoculars and spot a sheep, a young ram. He's not what I'm looking for, but he's a ram nonetheless. I see no other sheep that day. I return to camp deflated.

The evening before opening day I'm joined by my brother Rusty, and my friend Rich Egly, an ex-military man who resembles Dick Butkus. Before the first hint of sunrise, we climb off the valley floor onto the hulking, multicolored rock mass of Pinto Ridge. While Rich and I glass the local neighborhood, Rusty has his 'Big Eyes' focused on Razorback Ridge — in another zip code. "I've got sheep," he says.

We pull out the spotting scope and see a band of a dozen sheep, including three rams, located about a day's walk to the south. A closer look is warranted, so we descend to the flats and plan a route around the far end of Pinto Ridge. The country looks flat, but turns out to be a web of erosion.

We traverse the length of Pinto Valley, aiming for a saddle we hope will give us a clear view of the sheep. Hours later, we scramble to the top and I look over. Some 150 yards away, a pair of large horns crest a small ridge. We freeze in awkward positions until the ram's head disappears again briefly. Razor sharp rocks cut into our bones and muscles as we hit the ground. The horns reappear.

"What now?" Rich whispers.

"Wait," Rusty says.

So we huddle motionless, winter sun harsh, wind cold. Long minutes later Rusty slowly raises his binoculars. "He's definitely a shooter," Rusty whispers. "He'll go 160. Go shoot him."

I slide back, pull off my boots, and sneak through the loose rock. As I reach the crest of a finger canyon, the ram senses something amiss and trots out for a look around. I load an arrow, hook the release and will myself to pull but can't, or, more accurately, won't. At 40 yards, he stops. His sense of self-preservation overcomes his curiosity and the ram trots over the hill. Placing the arrow back into the quiver, I walk back.

"Too small?" Rusty asks incredulously.

"Too early," I reply sheepishly.

"An old sheep hunter once told me..." Rusty begins. I cringe. I hate Rusty's old sheep hunter (or old elk hunter or old deer hunter) stories. They all have a moral aimed at one of my mistakes. "Never pass up a sheep that you'd take on the last day," he finishes. Little did I know that 20 days later I would be willing to trade my truck for that one chance, refused.

Several days later, I exchange Rich and Rusty for my long-time hunting buddy Jim Rufh. Early the next morning we climb through a city of huge rectangular boulders scattered down the mountainside. We sight no shooters that day or the next or the next, and after eight days all my buddies with real jobs have gone back to work. I am alone. Not bad really, I tell myself. Time for meditation. Communion with nature — feeding the soul. I'm lying. Being alone may be good for the soul, but it's lousy for sheep hunting with a bow. There is no one to help spot sheep, or to give hand signals, or to let you know where the ram is two hours after you start your stalk; no one to relieve your loneliness.

The next morning I swing the heavily laden backpack onto my shoulders and settle under the old familiar weight. I feel the same emotions every time I head into the wilderness alone — anticipation, adventure, determination, a touch of loneliness, and a hint of dread. I strike out into country least likely to have seen a boot track this year.

On the third day out, I'm as far away from a road as is possible to get in this country. I scan a ragged, behemoth of a mountain rising solitary from the plain. I spot a ram near the top. His horns seem as big around as my legs. He's feeding along the base of a towering orange cliff. In order to get above him and down-wind, I'll have to do some serious hiking.

I drop my pack and feel like I might float away, instantly 70 pounds lighter. I circle the mountain, crawl laboriously up the crumbling, rotten rock to the cornice. Slowly, head canted, so as to expose just one eye, I peak over — no sheep. Inching, head up, I glass my surroundings, no sheep. I move my shoulders up a little further. Still no sheep. Then he is standing, where nothing stood before. He disappears like a mirage in the desert.

My story develops a recurring theme: hunter spots sheep; hunter goes around the mountain; sheep is no longer there when hunter peeks over the crest.

I go into town for supplies and call my wife Tammy. God love her, she's always supportive. "You'll get one honey, just don't give up," she says. Oh, if I only had her confidence.

I call Jim. "Have you got anything?" he asks.

"Sore feet," I whine. "Sheep are always gone by the time I move around the mountain. The drought has made food scarce. They're so busy getting groceries they can't stay still. Terrain's so cut up, I could be 40 yards from them and not know they're there."

"Sounds like you could use another set of eyes," he says, reading my plea for help between the lines. "Let me see what I can do. Call me back in five minutes."

"Pick me up at the Vegas airport tomorrow night," he says five minutes later.

Soon it's the last day of Jim's stay and my season is nearly over. This hunt has become a race against the clock. I arrived here 25 days ago and I'm getting tired. And though tired, I'm having trouble sleeping. My head is full of self-doubt, and I miss my family. I feel a deep sense of urgency — desert sheep tags rarely come around twice in a lifetime. I tell myself it is noble to have put my heart and soul into the effort and failed, although that makes the failure no less painful.

My buddies insist I pick up a rifle and, "Just shoot one." And though admission may reveal weakness, the thought has drifted through my mind. But each time, resolve overcomes common sense and the rifle notion. A sacrilege to this wannabe purist, is shunned.

Jim and I hike to a vantage point before dawn, where, at a distance, we can see the mountain island that held the big ram. We see no sheep. We crawl through a cut in the bluffs leading to a saddle between ranges. With only our heads exposed, we scan new territory a mile away. Jim spots a ewe and a good-sized ram on top of a mountain.

My typical stalk has been to circle the mountain, climb the far side and come down on the sheep. My typical stalk has not been working.

"Jim," I say. "It's going to take me a day just to walk around that mountain, so I'm going to attempt a frontal assault."

He looks at me in disbelief.

I try to explain, "I'll move when they're feeding away. When I can't see them any longer, I'll look back for signals."

I wait until both sheep are feeding, then dog-trot down the wash 100 yards, stop, and glass. I repeat this process for a thousand yards. Once at the base of the mountain and out of sight of the sheep, I rely entirely on Jim's signals. He guides me up a narrow rock chute, laterally under a cliff face, then along the base of a small overhang. His signals indicate I'm very close. I ease one eye up, thinking to myself, "Move like the hands of a clock."

My muscles tense spasmodically as I see the ram, his underbelly bracketed by his hind legs, straight above me at 15 yards. I slowly lower my head. Hands trembling, I prepare the shot. I release the arrow. The ram is down faster than the telling of it. I give Jim the hands above the head sign for victory. I slide and hop down to the ram.

I sit beside him, admiring his old gray muzzle and face. I hold his horns in my hands, ten dark rings mark his years. As I wait for Jim, I look out at the mountains beyond, range after range, purple into infinity. Bittersweet this success — elation laced with regret.

That night in my sleeping bag, I bask in the afterglow of eleventh-hour success — a game pulled out at the buzzer. It seems I've been away from home for years. I experience a gnawing discomfort. Other than to be with my family I have no desire to go back. Civilization I do not want. I feel no need to be anything other than a sheep hunter, no desire to go back to talk radio, telephones, freeway — and worry. Life has become simple: wake, hunt, eat, sleep, wake.

I fall asleep and dream of dark canyon walls and the petroglyphs I discovered there, timeless reminders of the continuity of mans existence — ancient, crude figures of sheep and man and bow.

ABOUT THE AUTHOR: *Dr. Randy Ulmer grew up in Arizona with hunting as his passion. He attended Oregon State University where he graduated summa cum laude in 1980. He received his Doctorate from Washington State University, cum laude in 1983.*

Randy is probably best known for his competitive archery achievements. He has won world and national titles in many different venues. These include 2 Archery Shooting Association World Titles, 2 North American Bowhunters World Titles, 2 International Bowhunters Organization World

Titles and 1 Federation of International Target Archers World Title as well as numerous indoor titles.

Randy has been bowhunting for nearly 30 years. He was inducted into the Bowhunters Hall of Fame in 1999. Randy is also an outdoor writer. He pens a monthly column for both Petersen's Bowhunting *and* Bowhunter Magazines. *Randy currently lives in Arizona with his wife Tammy and sons Jacob and Levi.*

WAYNE VAN ZWOLL
PROFESSIONAL MEMBER
Boone and Crockett Club

AN ELK THROUGH THE 'POLES

The mountain was big and misshapen, a sprawling giant with serpentine arms and a snowy cap. Its trees were still clogged with snow from an early blizzard. When I started climbing in late afternoon, three days after the opener, horse trails snaking up the bottoms had been churned to boot-sucking mud. In gusting snow I hiked off that artery to a low ridge, then took an elk trail through aspens toward an open spine.

To find elk, you must know when to climb and when to still-hunt, because most of elk country is empty. Slow hunters must be lucky to find elk. Hunters who move too fast are more apt to find elk, but also likely to spook them first. On the spine, I slowed and got lucky. The elk appeared as tawny smudges in second-growth Douglas-firs. I knelt and glassed. Cows. As I waited for an antler to sift from the timber, my scent pooled and an elk fed too close. Sudden silence. Then she broke, clattering over deadfall. The others followed. Soft earth rumbled to their hoofbeats. Then, again, silence.

I climbed the spine to a wooded ridge. Crosswind, I eased into a bowl of conifers black with dusk.

Listen. Elk make noise. I'd killed an elk here a year ago, just stopping to listen. The cow had put a hoof on a brittle stick just as I was about to move. Minutes later her nose appeared

in an alley through the lodgepoles. Her shoulder followed. I wanted this cow, so I triggered the Savage, a 7mm-08. The animal had forfeited her chance. At the blast, she dashed down the canyon gut, over deadfall, and through wickets of naked pines. Short seconds into the sprint, she stumbled over a dam of jackstraw trunks, and was gone.

Now I stopped again. But the prospects here were poor. The thermals would spread my scent, no matter where in this bowl I went.

Snap.

Elk ghosted through an opening across the drainage. I eased the 6.5x55 to my shoulder. A sleek cow elk slid along my horizontal wire to the occasional clack of limbs. A tall, but short-pointed rack bobbed into view behind a windfall. But the bull's shoulder was hidden by the log, and in an instant he was gone. I tried to move in. But this timber had lost much of its sound-deadening snow, forcing me to throttle down. Again, a cow fed close. Thermals brought me to her in seconds, and when she wheeled, the herd galloped off too.

Sleep came easily that night, in a cabin far below.

An hour before dawn, I returned to the ridge. Heavy skies soon dumped snow. It came so hard that in a thicket I lost my way and had to back-track to find my route. Climbing again, I saw only old tracks. At noon, with nary an elk sighting, I descended to work second-growth Doug-fir.

The north face had lots of trash, and a pitch that made even elk trails a challenge. Predictably, they stayed below the crest; but the most heavily trafficked lay well above the creek bed. They led me into difficult places, made treacherous by nearly a foot of snow. Two hours later I struggled back to the ridgeline, pulling myself up through the brush. My hands were wet through the gloves, my feet damp through boots long ago soaked. I found an old, forlorn Doug-fir and leaned against its thick bark. I wolfed a bagel, sipped icy water, and shivered.

Where had the elk gone? Scrambling about on norths isn't always smart, but pockets hard to reach usually hold elk, especially when hunters are afoot. Sometimes it pays to think of such places in reverse – the best may simply be those that are hard to come from. In mid-afternoon, I looked into such a place.

The bench jutted from one of the mountain's tentacles. Canyons gaped on both sides, with other tentacles curling around them. There were no openings. Elk came here to disappear, not to eat or loaf. The odds of getting a clear shot here were indeed slim, but to shoot game you must first go where it is.

There were two bulls, bedded together. I heard the first go: a swish of branches and the clunk of a hoof behind impossibly thick second-growth. He went right and was lost. But as I tore at my glove with my teeth, a flash of antler appeared to the left. I dashed 20 steps, hurdled a deadfall, then fought my way to the lip. The bull could go down the gut, out of sight.... But he didn't. Flickers of black, a wink of yellow, and then he was in the gap. It wasn't a big gap, or one with anything to recommend it other than it happened to be in front of my rifle when instinct told me to stop moving. I leaned the Howa into a lodgepole, pressed the trigger and cycled the bolt on recoil as my 140-grain softpoint bit. The bull collapsed, then thrashed its way out of the gap and vanished down-canyon.

With no window to the elk's route, patience failed me. I leaped forward, skidding and scrambling through the snowy jungle. I finally spied the bull through a slit in the trees. At my shot, the head dropped. A convulsive kick sent the animal into the bottom of the cut, where the antlers caught under a great fallen tree. I moved, quietly now, down to the bull. Stopping a few yards short, I watched the life drain from his eye. The mountain had lost something I could not replace.

"You can take a horse and packer," said my friend Tim that night. I told him I had skinned and caped the bull that evening and carried the head and cape out. Another day's backpacking would clean up the meat. He shook his head. "A horse will make the day easier."

92

But easy isn't always best. Still-hunting a bull out of his mountain bed is a rare treat. A hunt like that merits a proper finish. Early next morning, I started up the trail with my Kelty. Two loads of boned meat later, in mid-afternoon, I swung the pack off for the last time.

I was very tired. It had been a very good hunt.

ABOUT THE AUTHOR: *Wayne van Zwoll has published hunting and shooting stories since 1975. Now, a dozen books and more than 1,000 magazine articles later, he is also working on television projects for Primedia. A Professional Member of the Boone and Crockett Club, Wayne has hunted world-wide and explored the history and motives of hunting in his Ph.D. dissertation. He has served as an editor for several publications, from* Shooter's Bible *to* Kansas Wildlife. *Teaching is a passion too: English and Forestry at Utah State University, and marksmanship through various shooting programs and his own women's outdoors program,* High Country Adventures. *Wayne has introduced many people to hunting and speaks often for organizations like Safari Club International and the Rocky Mountain Elk Foundation, where he served early on as Northwest field director. Wayne makes his home in north-central Washington State.*

LARRY WEISHUHN
PROFESSIONAL MEMBER
Boone and Crockett Club

BECOMING A HUNTER

Do you remember your first hunting experience?

Quite frankly I do not! And that is with good reason, I started hunting with my father, Lester, and my maternal grandfather, A.J. Aschenbeck, while I was still in diapers, long before I learned to walk or talk. Pre-school days were spent hunting squirrels with my granddad and listening to my dad's coonhounds at night. Between, I roamed the woods behind our country home in search of deer and raccoon tracks.

We hunted whitetails during the season, but due to screw-worms and frequent droughts their numbers were extremely low. If someone from within our Zimmerscheidt Community killed a whitetail buck, there was celebration in our corner of Texas.

As a growing youngster I read everything I could about guns, wildlife, and hunting. While I knew or cared very little about algebraic theorems, conjugating verbs, and the like, I could quote ballistics of most all the popular rounds of the time. I could quote word for word from the writings of Elmer Keith, Jack O'Connor, and Russell Annabel, yet trying to remember two verses of Shakespeare seemed impossible.

Growing in age and stature, work around our livestock farm was tough and the hours hard and long. What spare time I had, if there was any, was spent fishing during the spring and summer and hunting throughout the fall and winter. With each approaching fall my dream remained the same, to take my first whitetail deer. Not only did I want to be a deer hunter, I wanted to be a successful deer hunter!

Along about my fourteenth year the whitetail population in our corner of Texas started making a comeback. That August, with the help of my dad, I hammered a couple of old 2x4s in a leaning oak tree that overlooked a couple of deer trails. I proudly proclaimed it my deer stand.

Come fall I wanted to hunt with a real deer rifle, a Model 94 like my dad and uncles used. But, it was not to be. Dad suggested I hunt with my grandad's single-barrel 12-gauge shotgun. Grandad had passed away when I was nine.

It took many lifetimes, but finally opening day was just one more night's sleep away... Like I was really going to sleep...

I arrived at my deer stand, crawled the 30-plus feet up the leaning oak and sat on the 2x4. Then I waited for another two hours for it to get light enough to see my hand in front of my face. Finally black turned to ashen gray, allowing me to distinguish bushes. Way off in the distance I heard a shot, and hunting season was officially open!

The first 30 minutes of light all I saw were a couple of squirrels. Then off to my left I heard something scurrying through fallen oak leaves. I gripped the old single barrel loaded with "double aught" buck. Slowly I turned to determine the cause of the noise. Movement behind the underbrush, then an emerging form! Heart beating off the chart, I spotted the largest whitetail in the world. No doubt about it, Boone and Crockett would have to rewrite their records book when I shot this one! Thankfully, the new World's Record whitetail was headed my way. If all went well, he would just about pass under my tree, if his antlers weren't too big to do so...

Up came Grandpa Aschenbeck's old single-barrel coming to rest solidly against my shoulder. I tracked the monstrous buck over the top of the barrel and tried to keep the front bead within reasonable distance of the notch in the receiver. Couple more steps and the buck would be in the clear for me to shoot. Oh yeah, cock the hammer. Hammer cocked. Sight down the barrel. Barrel pointed at the awesome buck's shoulder. Don't close both eyes. Pull, don't jerk.

"Blam!" I recoiled from the shot and watched in absolute terror as the world's biggest whitetail limped away. Just then I remembered, I had a second double-aught buckshot shell in my pocket. I broke open the gun to replace the empty hull with a fresh round.

In doing so, I pulled a bit too hard on the forearm, which in turn disengaged the barrel, which in turn, to my horror, allowed the barrel to fall 30 feet to the ground below where it landed with a solid "thud!"

For a moment I seriously considered diving out of the tree to retrieve the barrel. Thankfully buck fever subsided just long enough to nix that decision. I sort of slid down the tree to the ground below.

By the time I picked up the barrel, blew the mud out of it, "rebuilt" my gun and put a fresh round in the barrel, the buck had disappeared into the underbrush.

Slowly I walked to where the new World's Record whitetail disappeared into the thicket, gun at ready. I was scanning ahead when I tripped over something. Looking down, I saw my buck, the biggest whitetail in the world! I said a prayer of thanks, then let out a whoop to proclaim to my dad and mom and the rest of the world, that not only was I now a deer hunter, I was a successful deer hunter.

I knelt at the buck's side and ran my fingers over his antlers again and again. He had a four-inch spike on his right side and a three-inch spike on his left side.

Over the years as a hunter/biologist/writer/television personality, I've gotten to hunt throughout the world. But none of the great animals I have hunted compare in importance of that deer. Those few moments of taking my first deer led to a lifetime in the outdoors and created for me not only a vocation, but also an avocation! The age-worn mount of that little spike buck still hangs on my wall. Every time I look at it, I remember the day I became a hunter.

ABOUT THE AUTHOR: *From his many years spent managing, researching, hunting, and promoting whitetail deer, Larry has become one of the most highly respected and sought after wildlife biologist, outdoor writers, and outdoor television personalities. His expertise in whitetail deer is unequaled. To date, he has been responsible for quality deer management programs on well over 15 million acres.*

His features and columns have appeared in nearly every popular outdoor publication, and he has authored or provided chapters to numerous books on the subject of whitetail deer hunting and management.

GORDON WHITTINGTON
NORTH AMERICAN
WHITETAIL
Editor-in-Chief

COMING FULL CIRCLE

To become a hunter is to become a dreamer, too. No matter at what age we start hunting, we soon begin to fantasize about ever more exotic adventures, to faraway lands inhabited by species straight from magazine pages and television screens. We project ourselves into those scenes and believe that if only we could get there, the high-scoring animals we'd bag would be the most special trophies of our lives.

I feel the magnetic pull of a compass as much as the next guy, and I've given in to it many times. That said, as I bear down hard on age 50, I've concluded that the pursuit of small, simple goals close to home can be as satisfying as hunting a record-book giant a continent away. Indeed, even a globetrotting sportsman's greatest trophy can be what others might see as a wholly unimpressive specimen, taken within plain sight of home.

Growing up in a family of whitetail hunters on a ranch in the Texas Hill Country, I had little choice but to become one myself. There was no minimum legal hunting age, so in 1961, when I was only five, my paternal grandfather began taking me hunting. Although I didn't get a deer that year, I saw and felt enough to know I wanted to be in the woods the next opening morning.

But when it arrived, I wasn't there. I had to accompany Grandma and Grandpa on a shopping trip to San Antonio, an hour away. I was amazed that anyone would even think of shopping on opening day, but my grandparents promised that we'd be home in time for an afternoon hunt in the oat field across the creek from our houses.

Upon our return to the ranch, Grandpa and I set out on my adventure. We crossed the trickling creek, walked another 200 yards and settled into our blind, a shallow depression with

cedar logs stacked around it. The hole was all that remained of what had once been a huge colony of harvester ants, whose burrowing had caused the ground to subside. Grandpa had turned the low spot into a pit blind for hunting deer that came off a nearby ridge to feed every afternoon.

As the hill's shadow flowed over us just before dusk, a doe began walking toward our blind. Sitting on Grandpa's knee and clutching the Winchester Model 92 carbine on loan from my mother's father, I waited for the doe to feed into range. Finally, when she was perhaps 30 yards out, I poked the quivering barrel of the .32-20 through the logs, drew a fine bead where Grandpa had taught me to aim and squeezed the trigger.

The 100-grain bullet lurched out of the barrel at only 1,210 feet per second. But it flew straight into the doe's heart . . . and whitetail hunting flew straight into mine.

Eager to prove myself big enough to handle a "real" gun, I soon began to shoot my way through the family's entire arsenal of scoped deer rifles: a Marlin 336 in .30-30; Remington Model 742s in 6mm Rem. and 30-06; and the first deer gun I could call my own out of the box, a Remington Model 700 in .25-06 Rem. Years later I'd move on to a Model 700 in 7mm Rem. Mag., then a Thompson/Center Encore in the same cartridge.

By the fall of 1995, I'd been editor of *North American Whitetail* magazine for more than a decade, and I'd been on my share of far-flung expeditions for trophy deer. Perhaps that's why I suddenly decided it was time for a different kind of quest. As I thought about what I wanted to do that season, my mind drifted back to 1962, to the first deer I'd ever shot. Although I knew the .32-20 was at best marginal for whitetails, I figured that if I could shoot a small doe with it when I was only six, surely I could do it again. I wanted to take another one with that carbine, to bring my career full circle . . . then retire the old lever action once and for all.

It seemed simple enough. Just before Christmas I'd be flying from my home near Atlanta, Georgia, to South Texas, to hunt the Diamond H Ranch. But while I was there, the only deer that came within easy range of the carbine was a mature 9-pointer that paraded past me at 20 yards several times. Uncomfortable with the idea of shooting a big-bodied deer with such an iffy cartridge, I never even raised the gun.

The next day, Christmas Eve, I drove north about three hours to my family's ranch for a quick holiday celebration before heading back to Georgia. My "easy" doe quest would have to be put on hold for another year.

Well, maybe not. At 8 a.m. on Christmas morning, while sitting in the living room of the old rock house in which I'd grown up, I looked out the window and saw a deer. It was a doe, perhaps 200 yards away across the creek, and she was walking toward the Bermuda-grass cattle pasture that had been the oat field of my youth. I threw on my camouflage, pulled the .32-20 from its case and scrambled out the door.

Minutes later, as I hid behind a pecan tree just a few yards from the cattle pasture, I saw the doe. She was 125 yards off, heading away at a slow walk . . . but then, magically, she turned and started back my way. A minute or so later she was within 30 yards. I nervously cocked the carbine's hammer, eased it around the tree, put the sights low on the deer's chest and fired.

There was no roar — a .32-20 sounds about as much like a .22 as it does a high-powered rifle — but again the little gun did its job. The young doe whirled, ran for a few seconds and fell dead, literally within rock-throwing distance of where I'd shot my first one back in 1962. This deer, like my first, had been shot through the heart.

As I looked across the creek toward home, my mind was flooded with thoughts of my now-late grandfathers and the tiny rifle that still linked me to them. Suddenly, I knew why I'd been so unlucky in my earlier efforts to shoot a doe: I was meant to return to this, the exact site of my first kill, to take a deer that for all I know could have been a descendant of the one I'd shot with the same gun 33 years earlier.

I've now pursued whitetails for over four decades, and in that span I've had the good fortune to take dozens of bucks that hang beautifully on the wall. Strange, then, that when asked to reflect on some of my most memorable deer, among the first to come to mind are two that had nary an antler between them.

I think we should all be so lucky.

ABOUT THE AUTHOR: *Gordon Whittington was editor of* North American Whitetail *magazine for 18 years before becoming editor-in-chief of the magazine, as well as* North American Whitetail Television. *In the course of his 45-year hunting career he has pursued whitetails in more than 20 U.S. states, Canadian provinces and Mexico; he even has hunted them in New Zealand. When the author dropped this doe with his hand-me-down Model 92 Winchester carbine on Christmas morning 1995, it brought him full circle to his first-ever whitetail.*

Gordon authored the book **World Record Whitetails** *and co-authored* **The Art & Science of Patterning Whitetails** *with Dr. James C. Kroll. He also has edited a number of books, including* **Legendary Whitetails, Legendary Whitetails II, Dick Idol's Hunting the 4 Periods of the Rut, Bobby Worthington's Bowhunting Trophy Whitetails, Steve Bartylla's Advanced Stand-Hunting Strategies** *and the Illinois Conservation Foundation's* **Illinois Whitetails.**

A frequent seminar speaker and staff instructor for North American Whitetail University, Gordon lives with his wife, Catherine, in Marietta, Georgia.

BILL WINKE
OUTDOOR WRITER

THE RUSH

As a beginner, I felt wonder in every aspect of the hunt. The process was more important than the results, and taking a trophy animal was a far-off dream.

In this age of growing deer populations and quality deer management, it's hard to escape the mindset that antler score is somehow a mark of success. Peer pressure would seem to demand it.

Granted, shooting a big buck is a lot of fun and creates plenty of excitement. But if you allow yourself to think that the only measure of a successful hunt is the buck's antler score, you start to focus on the results instead of the process, and you lose the simple joy and youthful wonder that makes hunting such a great adventure.

In the past couple of years, I've run into several hunters that whip their tape measure out as soon as a buck hits the ground. If the animal doesn't make a certain minimum they're disappointed with their hunt. If he does make the standard, they're over-joyed. It is the same deer and the events of the hunt are the same; the thing different is what the tape tells them. That's not right. I even had one guy get mad at me because I wouldn't let him score a buck I had just shot a few hours after I shot it. Usually I'll put a tape to my bucks well after the fact — sometimes years later — after I've had plenty of time to burn-in the memories and relive the hunt. I'm not against scoring, I'm for putting the priority where it belongs. I love mature animals with big antlers, but I love the process of hunting even more.

The following story is about a buck I shot in 1995. I had two encounters with him over the span of three days. You might be surprised at what I learned, and maybe it will affect the way you define "success" in your own deer hunting.

November 4 dawned clear, cold and still with a thick coating of frost. It was the perfect morning for bucks to be moving. By 9:15 I had seen several, most of them were in the distance crossing the isolated five-acre corn bottom I watched. I even grunted at a couple of the bigger ones but they had places to go and were too intent on getting there to come toward me.

I had some business to attend to at 10 o'clock, so I was thinking about climbing down when I saw a buck standing along the edge of the woods about 150 yards away. I wasn't sure he was the kind of mature buck I was waiting for until he lifted his head and turned to the side. My eyes probably made an audible POP! I'm sure they instantly doubled in size. Through the binoculars, I could see a wall of long tines. A shot of adrenaline pumped into my blood stream, jolting me.

Up until the buck lifted his head, I had been detached, having already seen several smallish bucks earlier that morning in the same spot where this one now stood. Forget detachment, now I was clawing at my chest pocket for the grunt call.

My heart was racing as I watched to see which direction he would go. If he came my way, I'd be quiet. If he went the other, I would call. His first step was away from me. Uuurrrp.

Nothing. It would need to be louder. URRRRPP! He stopped and looked my way. Another softer grunt brought him along the edge of the woods at a steady walk. It was still cool enough out that I could see steam rising from the buck's nostrils as he walked my way with his head held high. Now the adrenaline was really flowing! As the giant slowly closed the ground between us, I started squirming unconsciously in my stand. The tension was driving me squirrelly. I clipped the release on the string and slid around on the seat until I was positioned for the shot that I knew was only moments away. The tension was building with every step he took. BOOM! BOOM! BOOM! My heart sounded like a base drum. I could hardly bear the excitement.

Still 75 yards away, the buck began to circle out into the foxtail grass that grew on the unplanted end of the cornfield where my stand was located. I didn't worry because he would still be forced within bow range by a thin line of brush on the other side of the field, only 30 yards away. The wind was perfect. Everything looked great until the buck hit the path I had taken to get to my stand. Believing the center of the field to be the least likely place for a buck to approach, I had circled right through the foxtail before entering my stand.

He locked up for only 10 seconds before blowing loudly. I nearly jumped out of my skin it was so loud. He bolted 50 yards in the opposite direction and blew again. Steam whistled from his nostrils. My world had crumbled by the time he was out of sight, but the whole encounter also wonderfully thrilled me. What a privilege just to be there and experience such drama.

I decided to stay out of the area for a little while to let things cool down. Two days later I came back and put up a stand about 300 yards down the narrow finger of cover from where I'd seen the big buck. I didn't really expect to see him again, but there was always hope. Besides, if one big buck was using the area maybe there were two.

The morning of November 7 found me 20 feet off the ground watching the same cornfield from my new stand. I'd brought a lunch and warm clothes, planning to stay all day long. This day dawned cool, crisp and frosty too — almost an exact repeat of the conditions when I last saw the big buck. In other words, it was again perfect. I hadn't been in the stand more than 10 minutes when I heard a buck grunt, and saw a form racing along the far side of the finger.

Directly opposite me, probably only 30 yards away, the buck stopped and peered intently into the cover. I couldn't make out antlers yet, and didn't want to risk pulling the binoculars up either. Something about the width of his intensely white throat patch and his outline suggested that he was a mature buck. After a few moments he put his head down and crashed into the cover, busting back in the direction he'd come from.

I figured he was cutting off a doe that was trying to get to a large block of connected timber beyond my stand. Twenty minutes later, just after the beginning of legal shooting time, a doe stepped out of thick cover about 30 yards away and came straight down the middle of the finger. I didn't move as first one, and then a second buck showed up a few yards behind her. The first buck was a nice eight-pointer, but the second was much bigger. I didn't try to size him up — he was a shooter. Everything happened so fast that I barely had time to get nervous.

Worried to the point of anger by his subordinate, the big buck charged forward. Both he and the doe bounded out into the picked cornfield on my side of the finger as the big buck stopped right under my stand. I'm sure he could smell my scent on the ground at the base of the tree but the fact that he was now on my right-hand side — with me still sitting — was a much more pressing emergency.

It seemed as if deer were crashing everywhere as I jumped to my feet. The buck was walking, but still in range. I was so focused on getting the shot that I never even looked at his antlers. I grunted loudly with my mouth to stop him for a shot, but just as I did, he took one more step and then froze right behind the branches of a fallen tree. I looked for an opening but found none. Within seconds the buck was moving again as I pulled my just visible sight pins ahead of him.

Quickly guessing him at 30 yards, I pulled the correct pin onto his shoulder (to account for the walking pace) and punched the trigger. THUP. It was a good hit! The buck kicked up his hind legs before busting into the cover in a headlong dash. Everything looked positive, but it was a beautiful morning and to play it safe I decided to wait in my stand for a few hours and soak up the scene before tracking him.

After following the buck's running tracks and blood that was almost washed away by thawing frost, I came to the other side of the cover. Glancing farther out into the field in the hope of finding blood, I was shocked to find that I was practically standing on the buck! Fifteen yards away I could see a heavy antler sticking above the short grass that grew under the overhanging limbs. There were six long points on it! After running over to the dead deer I was amazed and thrilled to find that it was the same giant buck that had come part way to my grunt call three days earlier!

As I write these words, it is almost nine years later. Which one of those two encounters with the buck do you think I still remember best? Surprisingly, it was the first one - the day he got away. The adrenaline rush was almost more than I could take and my heartbeat still picks up every time I think of his slow, excruciating approach.

That one day forever changed the way I look at deer hunting success. It reaffirmed that success is not about how many you shoot or how big they are, it's about the thrill of the hunt and the adrenaline rush that comes with close encounters, successful or not. I love to shoot deer but it is such memories that keep me on stand for long hours each fall. A trophy for the wall is just icing on the cake.

ABOUT THE AUTHOR: *Bill Winke has been writing full-time for hunting magazines for 13 years. He specializes in product reviews and articles about hunting strategy, primarily*

whitetail deer. Bill has hunted deer in 16 different states and 3 Canadian provinces. He has also played a leading hand in the management of thousands of acres of land for improved deer hunting. These experiences have given Bill broad exposure to — and great appreciation for — the wonderful challenges that whitetails present.

Bill earned a degree in mechanical engineering from the University of Iowa in 1986 and now lives on a farm in southern Iowa with his wife Pam, their six-year old daughter named Jordan and their five-year old son named Andrew.

JIM ZUMBO
PROFESSIONAL MEMBER
Boone and Crockett Club

HOW IT ALL BEGAN

Some of us believe destiny is totally responsible for our life's path. Others believe we manipulate our lives by making certain decisions, either right or wrong, or by simply being at the right place at the right time, or by meeting people who have had a negative or positive influence. We often examine our lifestyle, and try to determine just how we got where we are.

As one who makes a living by hunting, including writing books, magazine articles, giving seminars, and hosting a TV show, people often ask me how I arrived at my so-called enviable position. I respond by saying that destiny nudged me along, but it wouldn't have happened without mentors. For me, there have been dozens along my path of life, but one stands out as being the most influential.

Ken Taylor is two years older than I, and I met him when I was barely a teenager. Ken was the consummate woodsmen, who always shot more rabbits and squirrels than anyone else, and caught more muskrats and coons in his traps than me and my buddies put together. Because our moms were good friends, Ken took me under his wing and taught me woods skills that helped me understand the quarry. My hunting and trapping improved, but because we were two grades apart in school, we never really became good buddies. He went on to college to study forestry, and I struggled through high school, trying to mix studies with hunting and fishing. I couldn't get enough of the outdoors, and managed to graduate about 100th in a class of 300. There were simply too many critters to hunt; too many fish to catch, and I'd be lying if I didn't place some of the blame on girls and hotrods. But all through school, I wanted a career in the outdoors, preferably being a game warden. I didn't know how to get there, and decided to enter the military as soon as I graduated from high school and worry about a career later. In those days there were no wars going on, Korea being over, and Viet Nam not yet begun.

I was about to go to the enlistment office when a letter from Ken arrived, in fact, I was headed out my door when I found it in the mailbox. He knew about my outdoor interest, and strongly suggested I investigate enrolling at Paul Smith's College in New York's northern Adirondacks. This two year school offered three options of study: liberal arts, hotel management, and forestry. Ken had just graduated, and was off to a western university to earn his Bachelor's, since Paul Smith's offered only an Associate degree. It didn't take long to make a decision. I applied to the college, was accepted, and soon started my studies. Paul Smith's offered two forestry courses: pre-professional, which prepared you for a four year degree elsewhere, or terminal, which trained you to be a woods boss, such as a foreman on a logging crew, sawmill, or other forestry endeavor. I chose the latter. My courses were basic, and I loved them. I studied Dynamiting 101, learning how to blast stumps out of the ground, blow up beaver dams, and build wood roads. Then there was Logging, where we actually cut down trees using crosscut saws (big trees, I might add), and Sawmilling, where we sawed the logs into boards at the college mill, and Sugarbush, where we collected sap from huge maples, and transported the buckets on a horse-drawn sleigh over an honest three feet of snow to the sugar house. Everything we did was hands-on. Three essential items were required before

101

we showed up for field classes, a hardhat, a damned sharp double-bitted axe (the professors checked the axes every day), and snowshoes.

My writing career began when I wrote an article for the college newspaper about a savvy old whitetail buck that many of us hunted. Old Joe was a legend, seen by many hunters, but always elusive in the dense swamps. I cannot tell you how proud I was to see my byline and article in the little paper. I wrote a couple more articles, and soon graduated, not knowing the next step of my career. It took the form of a phone call from Ken Taylor, who had just received his Bachelor's of Science at Utah State University. (I hadn't seen Ken at Paul Smith's, since he had graduated and left when I arrived. I might add that a long distance phone call in those days was a big deal, very rare and very expensive.)

"You need to come out here and get your Bachelor's," Ken said, calling from Utah. "It's vital to your career. If you want to be a game warden or forester, you need a Bachelor's."

"But I took the terminal forestry course," I told Ken. "I'll have to start all over."

"It's worth it," he said. "Get out here."

My brain went into overtime. Ken was right, and I felt cheated about my stay at Paul Smith's. There were 400 men and three women in the college, and there was no social life, no mingling with other students. My classmates and I lived in a dorm off campus which was accessed by a three mile terrible dirt road cut through the forest, and we amused ourselves by hunting, fishing, having tobacco-spitting and axe-throwing contests, and everything else a bunch of young forestry students might do. For a date with a woman, several of us piled into a car after classes on Friday night and drove on icy roads to a state-teacher's college in Plattsburg, about 50 miles away. We'd knock on the door of a women's dorm, and ask the house-mother if any gals were still around. Of course, they were the rejects, but we'd take them to a movie and have them back by a 10pm curfew.

I applied to Utah State, was accepted, and boarded a bus in late August for a long cross-country trip, leaving my mother and father in tears at the bus terminal. Ken had graduated, taken a job with the U.S. Forest Service, and I never saw him. I joined a fraternity immediately, discovered an entirely new campus life, and was asked by one of my fraternity brothers to write a mule deer forecast for the student newspaper. I did, it was well-received, and I became outdoor editor, writing a column each week. Because of my terminal course at Paul Smith's, I was able to transfer only a few credits, and needed three more years to graduate.

At one of our frequent Paul Bunyan parties, which were all-male functions, and where much beer was consumed, a college professor teased me and said he'd wager a case of Lucky Lager beer that I couldn't sell a story to a "real" publication. We shook hands, I queried Outdoor Life on a fishing article about a little fish that lives only in Bear Lake on the Utah-Idaho border and is caught by hand-held nets during the frigid month of January, and waited for a response. Dumb me. I sent the query to the circulation office in Boulder, Colorado instead of the New York editorial office. But somehow it made it to editor Bill Rae several months later, who was instrumental in starting up many new writers in those days. He went for the idea, another professor helped me take pictures, and the magazine bought the article. From there, it was a long, long uphill climb, and the rest is history.

A few years ago I saw Ken Taylor at a sportsmen's show in Oregon. I hadn't seen him in more than 30 years. He had retired from the Forest Service, and we chatted for a long time. While he stood there, I suddenly had a powerful sense of kinship. Had it not been for Ken's insistence that I follow him in two schools, I would never have found my career. Since then we meet at the show every year and share memories. For me, Ken was part of my destiny. I shall be forever thankful.

ABOUT THE AUTHOR: *Jim Zumbo has two degrees in forestry and wildlife, and has been writing for more than 40 years. He joined* Outdoor Life *in 1978 full-time, and is now Hunting Editor. He's written more than 2,000 articles, 23 books, and conducts hunting seminars around the country. He also hosts a new hunting TV show on the Outdoor Channel. He lives outside Cody, Wyoming, and is a professional member of the Boone and Crockett Club.*

CHAPTER EIGHT

Special Firearms

The special color section features custom and otherwise special firearms that have connections to both current and former Boone and Crockett Club members and other noted hunters, from Theodore Roosevelt to Jack O'Connor.

COMPILED BY:
KEITH BALFOURD
PROFESSIONAL MEMBER
Boone and Crockett Club

ELDON L. "BUCK" BUCKNER
REGULAR MEMBER
Boone and Crockett Club

BELOW THEODORE ROOSEVELT'S WINCHESTER MODEL 1876, SERIAL NUMBER 38647, IS ONE OF HIS FIRST AND MOST FAMOUS WINCHESTERS. THE RIFLE, A .45-75, HAS A GOLD INLAY OF A GRIZZLY BEAR ON THE RIGHT SIDE OF THE BUTT STOCK AND WAS INTRICATELY ENGRAVED BY JOHN ULRICH. Courtesy of the Sagamore Hill National Historic Site.

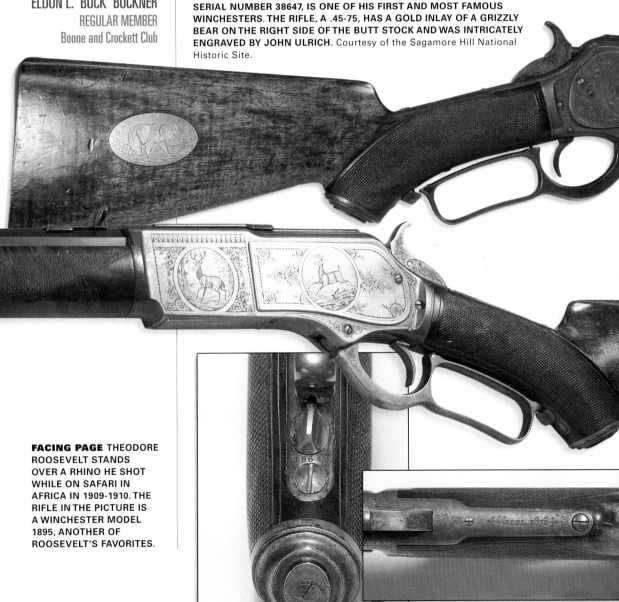

FACING PAGE THEODORE ROOSEVELT STANDS OVER A RHINO HE SHOT WHILE ON SAFARI IN AFRICA IN 1909-1910. THE RIFLE IN THE PICTURE IS A WINCHESTER MODEL 1895, ANOTHER OF ROOSEVELT'S FAVORITES.

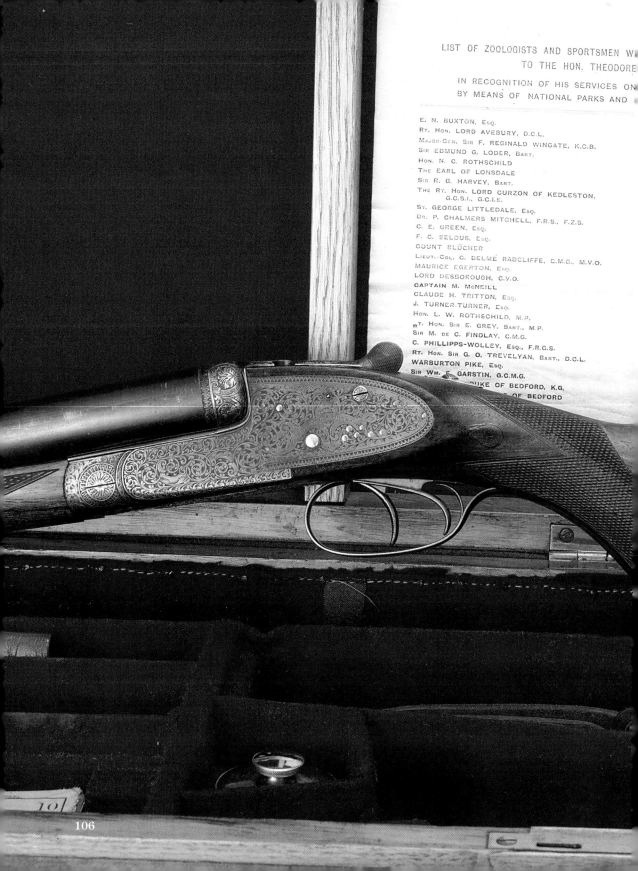

LIST OF ZOOLOGISTS AND SPORTSMEN W...
TO THE HON. THEODORE...

IN RECOGNITION OF HIS SERVICES ON...
BY MEANS OF NATIONAL PARKS AND...

E. N. BUXTON, Esq.
Rt. Hon. LORD AVEBURY, D.C.L.
Major-Gen. Sir F. REGINALD WINGATE, K.C.B.
Sir EDMUND G. LODER, Bart.
Hon. N. C. ROTHSCHILD
The EARL OF LONSDALE
Sir R. G. HARVEY, Bart.
The Rt. Hon. LORD CURZON OF KEDLESTON,
    G.C.S.I., G.C.I.E.
St. GEORGE LITTLEDALE, Esq.
Dr. P. CHALMERS MITCHELL, F.R.S., F.Z.S.
C. E. GREEN, Esq.
F. C. SELOUS, Esq.
COUNT BLÜCHER
Lieut.-Col. C. DELMÉ RADCLIFFE, C.M.G., M.V.O.
MAURICE EGERTON, Esq.
LORD DESBOROUGH, C.V.O.
CAPTAIN M. McNEILL
CLAUDE H. TRITTON, Esq.
J. TURNER-TURNER, Esq.
Hon. L. W. ROTHSCHILD, M.P.
Rt. Hon. Sir E. GREY, Bart., M.P.
Sir M. de C. FINDLAY, C.M.G.
C. PHILLIPPS-WOLLEY, Esq., F.R.G.S.
Rt. Hon. Sir G. O. TREVELYAN, Bart., D.C.L.
WARBURTON PIKE, Esq.
Sir WM. E. GARSTIN, G.C.M.G.
... DUKE OF BEDFORD, K.G.
... OF BEDFORD

ORS OF A DOUBLE ELEPHANT RIFLE
PRESIDENT U.S.A.

THE PRESERVATION OF SPECIES
RVES, AND BY OTHER MEANS.

RD BRASSEY, G.C.B., M.V.O.
N. T. A. BRASSEY
YS WILLIAMS, Esq.
JOR-Gen. A. A. A. KINLOCH, C.B.
Wm. LEE-WARNER, K.C.S.I.
E Rt. Rev. The LORD BISHOP OF LONDON
JOR-Gen. DALRYMPLE WHITE
ONEL CLAUDE CANE
Hon. SYDNEY BUXTON, M.P.
ON C. E. RADCLYFFE,
A. E. PEASE, Bart.
H. H. JOHNSTON, K.C.B., C.C.M.G.
EL CHAPMAN, Esq.
G. MILLAIS, Esq., F.Z.S.
LORT-PHILLIPS, Esq.
KEARTON, Esq., F.Z.S.
H. GURNEY, Esq., F.Z.S.
N. JACKSON, C.B., C.M.G., Lieut-Governor East
African Protectorate
, Sir F. LUGARD, K.C.M.G., C.B., D.S.O.
Y LUGARD
CLEMENT L. HILL, K.C.B., M.P.
H. SETON-KARR, M.P., C.M.G.
AIN BOYD ALEXANDER
J. KIRK, K.C.B., G.C.M.G.
RETON FREWEN, Esq.
EARL OF WARWICK
SLATER

IMPOR

.500/.450 Express

This Rifle is regulate
Cordite
.500/.450 3/4"
our special nickel cover
nose or hollow point.

H. & H. will not guaran
unless their own Amm

NOT

The first shot fired out of a clean a

To avoid this fire a shot out of
st-game; or, if this is not convenient,
barrel out quite dry and free from oil h

To ensure easy extraction of the
slightly grease the chamber of the barre

Ammunition for this Rifle
from Messrs. WALTER LOC
and Lahore.

HOLLAND & HOLLA
98, New Bond

ABOVE THEODORE ROOSEVELT'S HOLLAND & HOLLAND ROYAL GRADE DOUBLE BARREL RIFLE IN .500/.450 CALIBER. THE FINEST RIFLE EVER OWNED BY ROOSEVELT, AND USED BY TR AND SON KERMIT ON THEIR HISTORIC AFRICAN SAFARI OF 1909-1910. PHOTOGRAPHED BY G. ALLAN BROWN FOR R.L. WILSON, AND TO APPEAR IN THE FORTHCOMING BOOK, *THEODORE ROOSEVELT HUNTER-CONSERVATIONIST* (2006). Courtesy of R.L. Wilson.

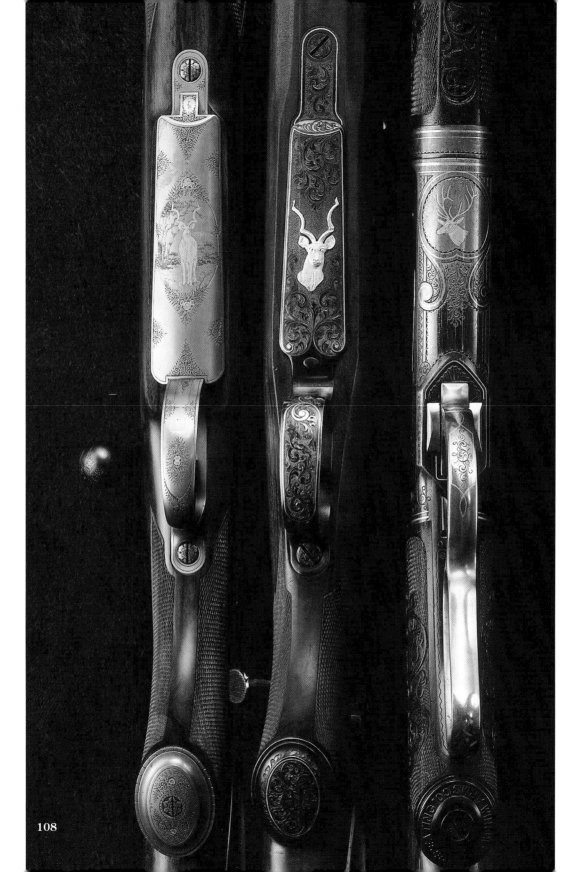

ABOVE & RIGHT ONE OF THE FINEST RUGER RIFLES EVER BUILT, SECOND IN THE LIMITED EDITION "NORTH AMERICAN BIG GAME" SERIES IS THE NO.1 SINGLE SHOT RIFLE: SERIAL NO. 132-65199. GOLD INLAID AND ENGRAVED BY FRANZ MARKTL. THE CONCEPT OF THIS SERIES WAS SUGGESTED TO THE LATE BOONE AND CROCKETT CLUB HONORARY LIFE MEMBER, BILL RUGER, BY THE LATE DAVE WOLFE, PUBLISHER OF *RIFLE* MAGAZINE. Courtesy of R.L. Wilson.

FACING PAGE FROM LEFT TO RIGHT, CUSTOM MODEL 70 WINCHESTER WITH ENGLISH STYLE ENGRAVING. ◼ FN ACTION .35 WHELEN MADE BY AN ALASKAN GUIDE FOR B&C PROFESSIONAL MEMBER, R.L. WILSON, AND USED ON SEVERAL AFRICAN HUNTS; ENGRAVING AND GOLD INLAID BY A.A. WHITE (c. 1982). ◼ THE WINCHESTER, A MODEL 1886 (SERIAL NO. 129666) GOLD INLAID AND ENGRAVED IN FACTORY STYLE NO. 2, WITH STOCKS IN STYLE B; SIGNED BY JOHN ULRICH. Courtesy of R.L. Wilson.

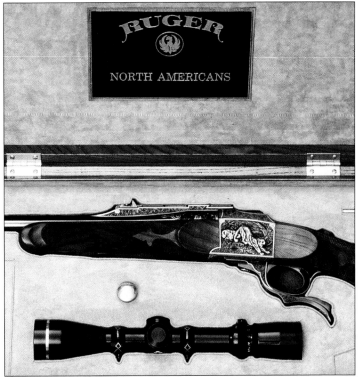

109

CENTER BOONE AND CROCKETT CLUB REGULAR MEMBER AND PAST PRESIDENT PAUL D. WEBSTER HAD THIS CUSTOM MADE-TO-ORDER BROWN PRECISION 7MM MAGNUM WITH MUZZLE BRAKE IN 1976. THIS RIFLE FEATURES A LEUPOLD 4-12 POWER SCOPE WITH A KEVLAR STOCK, THE ORIGINAL SLING AND CARTRIDGE CASE, A MODEL 70 WINCHESTER ACTION AND A DOUGLAS BARREL. WEBSTER HAS HUNTED WITH HIS "THUNDER STICK" ON THE FOLLOWING HUNTS: 1976 Mexico ■ 1977 Mexico, Iran ■ 1978 India, Iran ■ 1979 Nepal, Yukon ■ 1980 Spain ■ 1981 Spain ■ 1982 South Africa ■ 1983 Germany, Yugoslavia ■ 1984 Northwest Territories ■ 1985 Spain, Mongolia, Colorado ■ 1986 Yugoslavia, Pakistan, Azerbaijan, Germany, Spain ■ 1987 Austria, Azerbaijan ■ 1988 China, Pakistan, Bhutan ■ 1989 Pakistan, Russia Georgia ■ 1991 Kyrgizistan ■ 1992 Uzbekistan, China, Turkey ■ 1993 Switzerland, Siberia, Sweden ■ 1994 Kazahkistan, Siberia, Spain ■ 1995 Turkmenistan, Turkey ■ 1997 Siberia, Turkey, Spain ■ 1998 China, Pakistan, Mexico, British Columbia ■ 1999 Austria, Bulgaria, Scotland ■ 2000 China, Mongolia ■ 2001 Austria, Montana, British Columbia ■ 2002 Austria, Mexico, 2003 ■ Austria, Alaska ■ 2004 Mexico, Austria. Courtesy of Paul D. Webster. Photography by Kemmetmueller Photography, Inc.

BELOW IN 1964, PAUL D. WEBSTER SHOT THIS REMINGTON MODEL 32 (4 BARREL SET) AT THE NATIONAL SKEET SHOOTING ASSOCIATION'S WORLD CHAMPIONSHIPS HELD IN RENO, NEVADA. WEBSTER WON THE 20-GAUGE 2-MAN TEAM CHAMPIONSHIP IN CLASS AA. HE CONTINUED TO SHOOT THIS GUN FOR THREE MORE YEARS COMPETITIVELY FOR BOTH TRAP AND SKEET AND PLACED FIRST IN THE CLASS A MINNESOTA TRAP ASSOCIATION'S 16-YARD STATE CHAMPIONSHIP EVENT IN 1966 WITH A SET OF BORROWED BARRELS MOUNTED ON THE SAME MODEL 32 STOCK AND FOREARM HE USED FOR SKEET SHOOTING. Courtesy of Paul D. Webster. Photograh by Bryant Photographics.

BELOW CUSTOM PRE-64 MODEL 70, .270 WINCHESTER BUILT IN 1953 BY AL BIESEN. THIS RIFLE, WITH BARREL SHORTENED TO 22 INCHES AND SEVERAL OTHER CUSTOM FEATURES, BECAME THE FIRST OF JACK O'CONNOR'S FAMOUS PAIR OF FAVORITE .270s. IT FEATURES A CLASSIC FRENCH WALNUT STOCK WITH HIS FAVORITE FLEUR-DE-LIS CHECKERING PATTERN, AND A STITH-KOLLMORGEN 4X SCOPE ON TILDEN MOUNTS. O'CONNOR USED THIS RIFLE ON YUKON SHEEP HUNTS, WYOMING ELK HUNTS, AND ON SAFARI IN CHAD IN 1958 WITH ELGIN GATES. THE RIFLE IS NOW OWNED BY HIS FRIEND HENRY KAUFMAN. O'CONNOR AUTHORED A CHAPTER ON COUES' WHITETAIL DEER IN THE CLUB'S 1939 RECORDS BOOK AND SERVED AS A JUDGE FOR THE CLUB'S BIG GAME COMPETITIONS IN THE EARLY 1960s. Courtesy of Eldon L. "Buck" Buckner. Photography by Mike McElhatton.

ABOVE & RIGHT THIS FN MAUSER ACTION .30-06 WAS BUILT FOR JACK O'CONNOR IN 1947. THE METAL WORK WAS DONE BY BILL SUKALLE, A PHOENIX BARREL MAKER. IT WAS THE SECOND RIFLE CUSTOM STOCKED BY AL BIESEN FOR O'CONNOR. IT IS SIGHTED WITH A LYMAN ALASKAN 2-1/2X SCOPE ON G&H SIDEMOUNTS AS WELL AS A LYMAN 48 RECEIVER SIGHT. THE MAGAZINE FLOORPLATE IS ENGRAVED WITH A GRIZZLY AND OAK LEAF DESIGN. JACK USED THIS RIFLE TO BAG HIS BEST RAM – A DALL'S SCORING 177-1/8 SHOT IN 1950 ON PILOT MOUNTAIN IN YUKON TERRITORY. IN 1959 HE SHOT A 60" KUDU WITH IT IN TANGANYIKA. RIFLE NOW OWNED BY HENRY KAUFMAN OF LEWISTON, IDAHO, WHO USED IT ON A KENYA SAFARI IN 1977, ONE OF THE LAST SAFARIS IN KENYA. Courtesy of Eldon L. "Buck" Buckner. Photography by Mike McElhatton.

ABOVE BOONE AND CROCKETT CLUB REGULAR MEMBER, RICHARD T. HALE'S WINCHESTER MODEL 70. ORIGIINALLY MANUFACTURED IN 1936 AND REBUILT BY GRIFFIN AND HOWE 1979-1980. CALIBER IS A 7MM AND HAS BEEN USED ON MORE THAN 20 HUNTS IN THE LOWER 48 STATES, 16 TRIPS TO CANADA AND ALASKA AND HAS ALSO BEEN USED IN AFRICA AND ASIA. THE RIFLE FEATURES A DOUBLE-LEVER, TOP MOUNT WITH EXTRA SCOPE. THIS RIFLE HOLDS ITS POINT OF IMPACT TO A REMARKABLE DEGREE. Courtesy of Richard T. Hale.

RIGHT BOONE AND CROCKETT CLUB HONORARY LIFE MEMBER ARTHUR C. POPHAM, JR. ACQUIRED THIS CUSTOM SPRINGFIELD .30-06, USED, AT AGE 16 IN 1930. IT WAS CUSTOM BUILT BY JOHN WRIGHT, AN ENGLISH GUN MAKER WHO WORKED FOR HOFFMAN ARMS CO., AS WELL AS GRIFFIN & HOWE. POPHAM USED THIS RIFLE WHILE A STUDENT AT THE UNIVERSITY OF ARIZONA WHERE HE HUNTED WITH HIS JOURNALISM PROFESSOR JACK O'CONNOR. HE SHOT BOTH A DESERT BIGHORN IN SONORA, MEXICO, AND A 6-POINT BULL ELK ON ARIZONA'S MOGOLLON RIM IN 1935 WITH THIS RIFLE WHILE HUNTING WITH O'CONNOR. THE RIFLE IS EQUIPPED WITH A NOSKE SCOPE WITH LONG EYE RELIEF AND THE FIRST PRACTICAL INTERNAL ADJUSTMENTS. VICE PRESIDENT OF THE CLUB'S BIG GAME RECORDS PROGRAM, ELDON L. "BUCK" BUCKNER USED THIS RIFLE ON A KANSAS WHITETAIL HUNT IN DECEMBER 2004. Photographs courtesy of Eldon L. "Buck" Buckner.

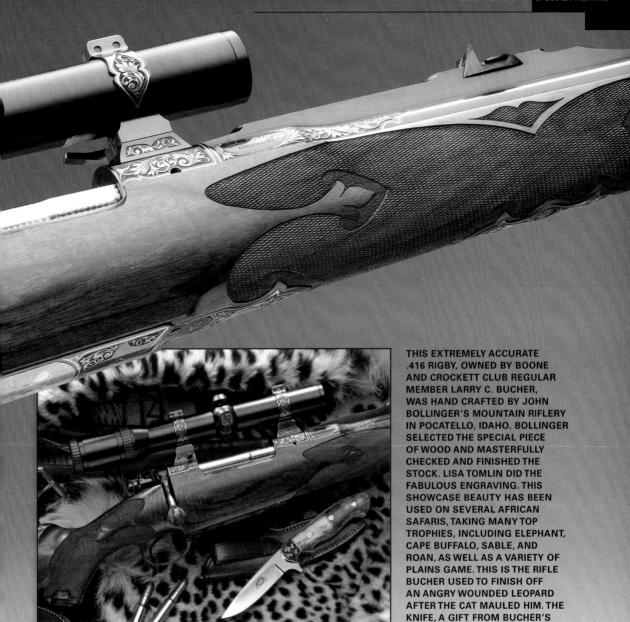

THIS EXTREMELY ACCURATE .416 RIGBY, OWNED BY BOONE AND CROCKETT CLUB REGULAR MEMBER LARRY C. BUCHER, WAS HAND CRAFTED BY JOHN BOLLINGER'S MOUNTAIN RIFLERY IN POCATELLO, IDAHO. BOLLINGER SELECTED THE SPECIAL PIECE OF WOOD AND MASTERFULLY CHECKED AND FINISHED THE STOCK. LISA TOMLIN DID THE FABULOUS ENGRAVING. THIS SHOWCASE BEAUTY HAS BEEN USED ON SEVERAL AFRICAN SAFARIS, TAKING MANY TOP TROPHIES, INCLUDING ELEPHANT, CAPE BUFFALO, SABLE, AND ROAN, AS WELL AS A VARIETY OF PLAINS GAME. THIS IS THE RIFLE BUCHER USED TO FINISH OFF AN ANGRY WOUNDED LEOPARD AFTER THE CAT MAULED HIM. THE KNIFE, A GIFT FROM BUCHER'S SON RICHARD, AND SO INSCRIBED ALONG THE TANG, WAS MADE BY DAVE KAUFFMAN. THE HANDLE IS OF MASTODON TUSK. Courtesy of Larry C. Bucher. Photography by Turk's Head — Mustafa Bilal.

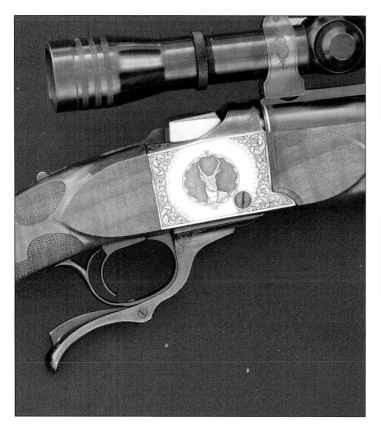

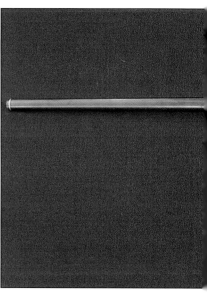

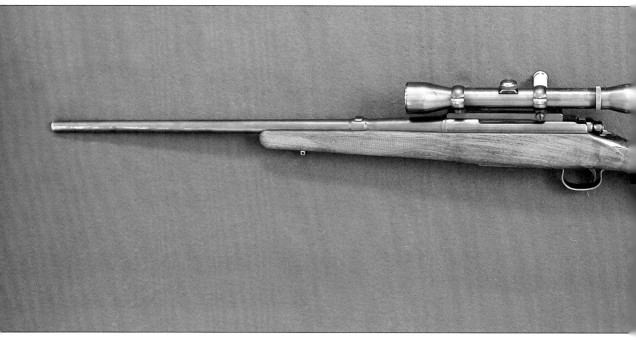

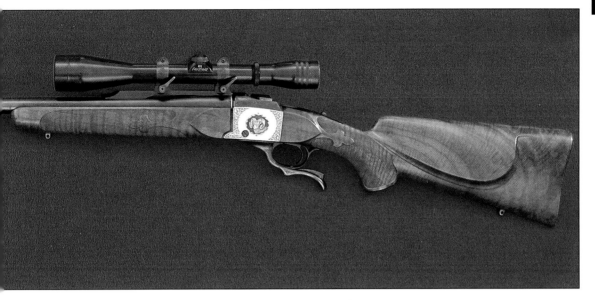

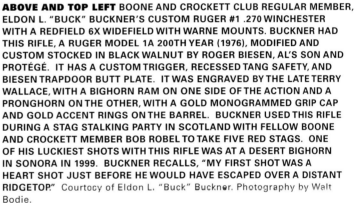

ABOVE AND TOP LEFT BOONE AND CROCKETT CLUB REGULAR MEMBER, ELDON L. "BUCK" BUCKNER'S CUSTOM RUGER #1 .270 WINCHESTER WITH A REDFIELD 6X WIDEFIELD WITH WARNE MOUNTS. BUCKNER HAD THIS RIFLE, A RUGER MODEL 1A 200TH YEAR (1976), MODIFIED AND CUSTOM STOCKED IN BLACK WALNUT BY ROGER BIESEN, AL'S SON AND PROTÉGÉ. IT HAS A CUSTOM TRIGGER, RECESSED TANG SAFETY, AND BIESEN TRAPDOOR BUTT PLATE. IT WAS ENGRAVED BY THE LATE TERRY WALLACE, WITH A BIGHORN RAM ON ONE SIDE OF THE ACTION AND A PRONGHORN ON THE OTHER, WITH A GOLD MONOGRAMMED GRIP CAP AND GOLD ACCENT RINGS ON THE BARREL. BUCKNER USED THIS RIFLE DURING A STAG STALKING PARTY IN SCOTLAND WITH FELLOW BOONE AND CROCKETT MEMBER BOB ROBEL TO TAKE FIVE RED STAGS. ONE OF HIS LUCKIEST SHOTS WITH THIS RIFLE WAS AT A DESERT BIGHORN IN SONORA IN 1999. BUCKNER RECALLS, "MY FIRST SHOT WAS A HEART SHOT JUST BEFORE HE WOULD HAVE ESCAPED OVER A DISTANT RIDGETOP." Courtesy of Eldon L. "Buck" Buckner. Photography by Walt Bodie.

LEFT BUCKNER'S REMINGTON MODEL 721, .270 WITH WEAVER K4 SCOPE ON REDFIELD MOUNTS. BUCKNER RECEIVED THIS, HIS FIRST CENTERFIRE RIFLE, FOR HIS 14TH BIRTHDAY IN 1956. WITH IT, HE SHOT HIS FIRST JAVELINA, FIRST MULE DEER, COUES' DEER, PRONGHORN, CARIBOU, AND DALL'S SHEEP. IN 1970, HE HAD THE BARREL SHORTENED TO 22 INCHES AND CUSTOM STOCKED BY THE LATE HAROLD QUILLEN OF PAYSON, ARIZONA, BEFORE TAKING IT TO ALASKA ON HIS FIRST SHEEP HUNT. IT HAS BEEN CARRIED MANY MILES IN A SADDLE SCABBARD. IN 1962, HE SHOT HIS FIRST B&C RECORDS-BOOK ANIMAL, AN ARIZONA COUES' DEER, WITH THIS RIFLE. Courtesy of Eldon L. "Buck" Buckner. Photography by Walt Bodie.

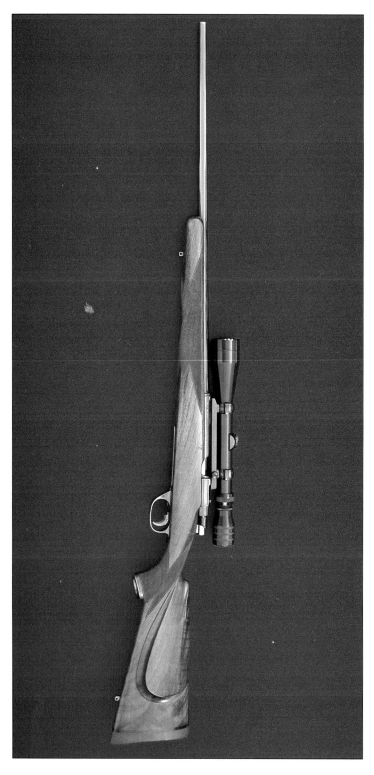

LEFT BOONE AND CROCKETT CLUB REGULAR MEMBER, ELDON L. "BUCK" BUCKNER'S CUSTOM MAUSER 6MM WITH REDFIELD 3X9 SCOPE ON REDFIELD MOUNTS. THIS WAS HIS FIRST FULLY CUSTOM RIFLE, BUILT TO HIS SPECIFICATIONS IN 1973. BASED ON A K98 MAUSER ACTION, WHICH WAS LIGHTENED AND HIGHLY MODIFIED, EQUIPPED WITH A CANJAR TRIGGER, AND BARRELED WITH A 23-INCH AIR-GAUGED DOUGLAS BBL BY ED HAVEN OF FLAGSTAFF, ARIZONA. THE RIFLE WAS CUSTOM STOCKED IN FRENCH WALNUT BY HAROLD QUILLEN WITH 24 LINE/INCH CHECKERING. HARRY LAWSON DID THE METAL BLUEING. BUCKNER INTENDED THIS RIFLE FOR LIGHTER BIG GAME AND VARMINTS, AND HAS TAKEN COUES' DEER, MULE DEER AND TWO RECORDS-BOOK PRONGHORNS WITH IT, AS WELL AS NUMEROUS ROCK CHUCKS. IT IS VERY ACCURATE. Courtesy of Eldon L. "Buck" Buckner. Photography by Walt Bodie.

BELOW JACK SLACK BEGAN HIS EMPLOYMENT AT LEUPOLD & STEVENS, INC. IN 1952 AND RETIRED AS SENIOR VP OF MARKETING IN 1989. JACK'S KEEN INTEREST IN FIREARMS AND HIS LOVE OF HUNTING AND SHOOTING PROVED TO BE A NATURAL FIT FOR THE COMPANY'S EARLY EFFORTS TO ESTABLISH LEUPOLD'S ENTRY INTO THE SCOPE MARKET IN THE EARLY 1950S. JACK'S PRACTICAL KNOWLEDGE OF HOW HUNTING OPTICS PERFORM IN THE FIELD MADE HIM A SIGNIFICANT CONTRIBUTOR TO THE ON-GOING ADVANCEMENT OF LEUPOLD SCOPES. THIS RUGER #1 WAS ONE OF JACK'S FAVORITE RIFLE ACTIONS FOR LONG RANGE VARMINT SHOOTING. HE USED THIS RIFLE ON COUNTLESS TRIPS AFIELD TO SHOOT PRAIRIE DOGS, GROUND SQUIRRELS, AND COYOTES.

LEUPOLD WILL BE CELEBRATING ITS 100TH ANNIVERSARY IN 2007 AND IS PROUD TO BE THE SPONSOR OF THIS EDITION OF *RECORDS OF NORTH AMERICAN BIG GAME*.

THE RIFLE IS A RUGER #1 IN .223 CALIBER STOCKED WITH A BEAUTIFUL PIECE OF ENGLISH WALNUT BY EARL MILLIRON. THE ENGRAVING IS BY FRANZ MARKTL. THE RIFLE HAS GROUPED INTO 1/4" ON A COUPLE OF OCCASIONS.
Courtesy of Mike Slack. Photography by Bryant Photographics.

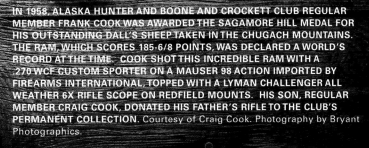

IN 1958, ALASKA HUNTER AND BOONE AND CROCKETT CLUB REGULAR MEMBER FRANK COOK WAS AWARDED THE SAGAMORE HILL MEDAL FOR HIS OUTSTANDING DALL'S SHEEP TAKEN IN THE CHUGACH MOUNTAINS. THE RAM, WHICH SCORES 185-6/8 POINTS, WAS DECLARED A WORLD'S RECORD AT THE TIME. COOK SHOT THIS INCREDIBLE RAM WITH A .270 WCF CUSTOM SPORTER ON A MAUSER 98 ACTION IMPORTED BY FIREARMS INTERNATIONAL, TOPPED WITH A LYMAN CHALLENGER ALL WEATHER 6X RIFLE SCOPE ON REDFIELD MOUNTS. HIS SON, REGULAR MEMBER CRAIG COOK, DONATED HIS FATHER'S RIFLE TO THE CLUB'S PERMANENT COLLECTION. Courtesy of Craig Cook. Photography by Bryant Photographics.

THE SAGAMORE HILL MEDAL IS GIVEN BY THE ROOSEVELT FAMILY IN MEMORY OF THEODORE ROOSEVELT (FOUNDER AND FIRST PRESIDENT OF THE BOONE AND CROCKETT CLUB), THEODORE ROOSEVELT, JR., AND KERMIT ROOSEVELT. IT WAS CREATED IN 1948. IT MAY BE AWARDED BY THE BIG GAME FINAL AWARDS JUDGES PANEL, IF, IN THEIR OPINION, THERE IS AN OUTSTANDING TROPHY WORTHY OF GREAT DISTINCTION. ONLY ONE MAY BE GIVEN IN ANY BIG GAME AWARDS PROGRAM. THE SAGAMORE HILL MEDAL IS THE HIGHEST AWARD GIVEN BY THE BOONE AND CROCKETT CLUB.

ABOVE BOONE AND CROCKETT CLUB REGULAR MEMBER, HERMAN A. BENNETT'S WINCHESTER H&H MODEL 70, .458 MAGNUM, SERIAL NO. 550863. THIS FIREARM WAS MANUFACTURED IN 1961. BENNETT LIKES TO USE THIS RIFLE IN HEAVY TIMBER FOR VERY BIG GAME. BENNETT IS PICTURED HERE (STANDING ON THE RIGHT) WITH THE LATE BASIL C. BRADBURY WHILE ON SAFARI IN ETHIOPIA. BENNETT PUT THIS CHARGING ELEPHANT DOWN WHEN IT WAS ONLY 6 STEPS AWAY FROM HIM. Courtesy of Herman A. Bennett.

BELOW BENNETT'S .264 MAGNUM, HARRY LAWSON RIFLE HAS A STOCK MADE OF BASTOGNE WALNUT AND A REMINGTON 700 LONG ACTION. BENNETT USED THIS RIFLE WHILE ON SAFARI WITH DOUG BENNETT IN BOTSWANA AND RHODESIA, WHICH IS NOW ZIMBABWE. BENNETT IS THE FIRST TO ADMIT A .264 ISN'T THE BEST CALIBER TO TAKE ON SAFARI, BUT HIS PROFESSIONAL HUNTER, DOUG WRIGHT, NOTED, "AVOID BEING SHOT BY HERMAN'S WINCHESTER .264 — APART FROM DANGEROUS GAME, THAT'S ELEPHANT, BUFFALO, AND LION — THIS GUN HAS KILLED ALL THE MAJOR ANTELOPES IN THE COUNTRY AND ALL THE LESSER ANTELOPES. IT'S ONE OF THE GREATEST LITTLE GUNS THAT WAS EVER BROUGHT OUT AND A BIT LIGHT FOR OTHER PEOPLE, BUT I THINK WE HAVE DONE WELL WITH IT ON THIS SAFARI." Courtesy of Herman A. Bennett.

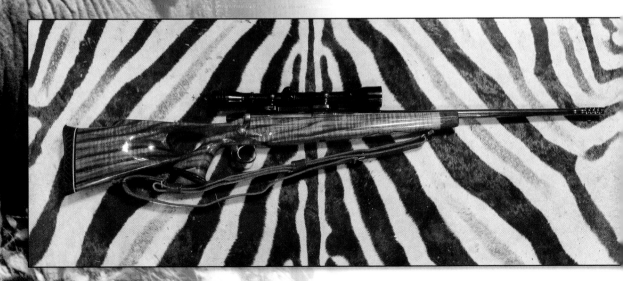

BELOW BOONE AND CROCKETT CLUB REGULAR MEMBER, HERMAN A. BENNETT'S WINCHESTER MODEL 70, .375 H&H MAGNUM, SERIAL NO. 481128, AS MANUFACTURED IN 1941. IT FEATURES A 3X9 LEUPOLD SCOPE. BENNETT SAYS IF HE ONLY HAD ONE RIFLE TO TAKE TO AFRICA, THIS WOULD BE IT. BENNETT IS PICTURED HERE WITH A LION HE TOOK WHILE ON SAFARI IN RHODESIA. Courtesy of Herman A. Bennett.

ABOVE AND RIGHT DELUXE
WINCHESTER MODEL 1866
SPORTING RIFLE, SERIAL NO.
112272, SIGNED BY J.U. FOR
JOHN ULRICH, AND BELIEVED
MADE AS A FACTORY SHOWPIECE.
RIFLE FEATURES SIX RELIEF
SCULPTURED PANEL SCENES,
WITH DIANA, AMERICAN HUNTER,
BIG GAME, GAME BIRD, AND BIRD
DOG MOTIFS. OWNED BY BOONE
AND CROCKETT CLUB REGULAR
MEMBER, ROBERT M. LEE.
Courtesy of R.L. Wilson.

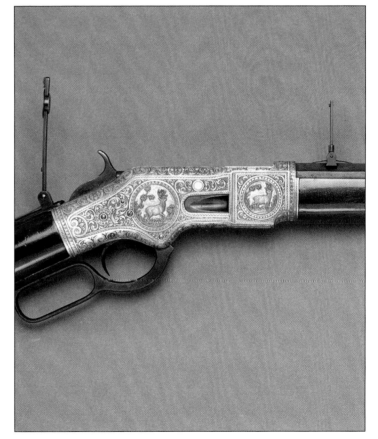

127

ABOVE WINCHESTER MODEL 70, STANDARD GRADE, IN .270 CALIBER — Story by Robert M. Lee

In the '50s, I purchased an "almost new" Winchester Model 70, Standard Grade, in .30-06 caliber. Jack O'Connor's writings had a great influence on me, and Jack was to become a very good friend. I decided that I needed a .270!

I heard about Monty Kennedy's skill as a stockmaker. I wrote to him about getting the rifle re-barreled to .270 and restocked, and he recommended Sam May of Apex Rifle Company. Sam re-barreled the rifle with a light tapered 24" barrel. Monty stocked the rifle with a fine piece of French walnut.

The rifle became a part of my battery on my first safari, which started out as a 30-day safari and wound up taking six months!

After two more safaris in East Africa, I decided to start my own safari company, Lee Expeditions, Ltd. Jack and Eleanor O'Connor were among my first guests in Angola, and Jack's story in *Outdoor Life*, titled "Big Lion of Mucusso," booked me up for two years!

But getting back to the rifle, I used this rifle more than any other light rifle for many years. It accounted for nine lions. The only lion that I had to shoot twice was shot with my .458!

The rifle accounted for virtually all of my plains game, and I collected a number of leopards with it in Africa, India, and Nepal.

In America, I used it on deer, pronghorn, and woodland caribou. Courtesy of the Robert M. Lee Trust.

RIGHT PURDEY CALIBER .500/.465 DOUBLE RIFLE ENGRAVED IN NEW YORK BY JOSEF FUGGER — Story by Robert M. Lee

In 1955, on return from my first safari in East Africa, I stopped in to see Harry Lawrence, who, at the time, was Managing Director at Purdey's. Harry was the Dean of English gunmakers, and was certainly the only Managing Director in the London gun trade who could, in fact, make a "best London gun" lock, stock, and barrel! Having shown Harry a sample of Joe Fugger's work, he agreed to undertake the making of a special .500/.465 double-barrel rifle, to be engraved in New York by Joe Fugger. This was to be the first time in Purdey's history that a gun or rifle was sent overseas for engraving.

Josef Fugger worked for Griffin & Howe, and could not spend all of his time on this project. Seymour Griffin was proud to have an in-house engraver who was one of the best of our time, and allowed Joe to work on my rifle as much as possible. It took about 18 months to finish the engraving.

African game scenes were selected for the theme of this rifle, and I decided that since the rifle was intended for hard use, gold inlays should be minimized. In fact, the only gold inlay is a cobra on the opening lever.

The rifle was finally returned to Purdey and was ready to be picked up prior to my 1959 safari. When I arrived at Purdey's, Harry Lawrence had the new rifle on the big table in the famous "Long Room." He was beaming as he handed it to me. What a magnificent rifle!

On asking Harry what he thought of it . . . he smiled and said, "Bob, this is the most magnificent rifle of our time."

I neglected to mention that the stock was designed by the late Monty Kennedy, who had completed a number of Mauser stocks for me in the past. Monty was, in my opinion, one of the half-dozen best stock makers in America, if not in the world. His book, *Checkering & Carving of Gun Stocks*, is a classic, and no one could checker better than Monty.

Eventually, I took several elephants with this rifle including the one in the photo shown here, which was taken near the Athi River, Kenya, in January 1960. The tusks weigh 95 and 93 pounds. I also used it on rhinos and buffalo. In India, the rifle accounted for my one and only tiger and two gaur. This is still one of my all-time favorites, although I would not want to push my luck and in today's unsettled times, I'd rather not travel with one of my treasures. Courtesy of the Robert M. Lee Trust.

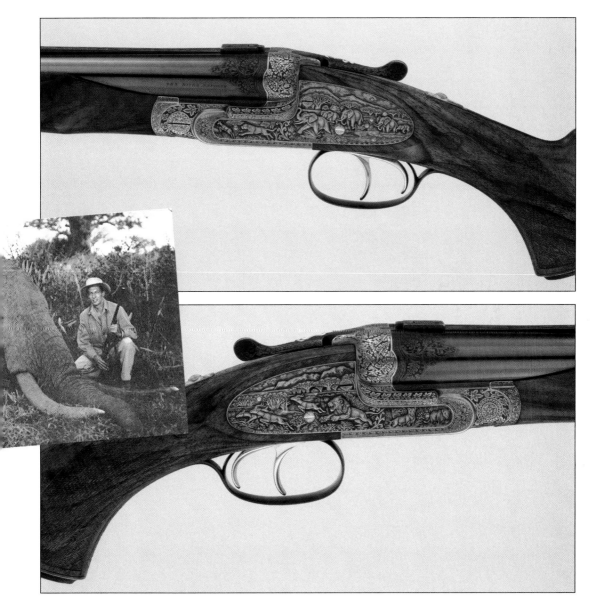

LEFT A MAUSER CUSTOM .243 ON MAUSER SHORT ACTION. THE RIFLE FEATURES A JEWELLED BOLT AND FOLLOWER, A LYMAN ALASKAN ALL-WEATHER SCOPE MOUNTED ON AN O'NEIL/HOPKINS SCOPE MOUNT AND A MONTE KENNEDY STOCK. BOONE AND CROCKETT CLUB REGULAR MEMBER AND PAST PRESIDENT JACK PARKER DONATED THIS RIFLE TO THE CLUB. IT WAS GIVEN TO HIM BY DON HOPKINS AND USED EXTENSIVELY FOR COYOTES ON PARKER'S RANCH, NOT TO MENTION SOME VERY NICE MULE DEER. Courtesy of the Boone and Crockett Club. Photography by Bryant Photographics.

BELOW PARKER RECEIVED THIS RUGER NO. 1 PRESENTATION GRADE .270 FROM MEMBER BILL RUGER. THE RIFLE HAS A GOLD INLAY ON THE RECEIVER, LEVER, AND MUZZLE AND FEATURES A REDFIELD WIDEFIELD 4X SCOPE. RUGER HAD PARKER'S RANCH BRAND AND A PRONGHORN HORN ENGRAVED ON THE SIDES. PARKER ALSO DONATED THIS RIFLE TO THE CLUB. Courtesy of the Boone and Crockett Club. Photography by Bryant Photographics.

LEFT THIS HIGHLY ENGRAVED
MODEL 1892 WINCHESTER .44
REMINGTON MAGNUM ORIGINALLY
BELONGED TO A FRIEND OF C.R.
SMITH WHO DIED IN AN AIRPLANE
ACCIDENT. THIS RIFLE HAS BEEN
PART OF BOONE AND CROCKETT
CLUB HONORARY LIFE MEMBER
JACK PARKER'S COLLECTION FOR
YEARS. THIS RIFLE WAS DONATED
TO THE BOONE AND CROCKETT
CLUB IN 2003 BY PARKER. IT WAS
PURCHASED BY CLUB PRESIDENT,
ROBERT MODEL IN THE CLUB'S
FUND-RAISING AUCTION AT
THE 2004 ANNUAL MEETING IN
NEW ORLEANS, LOUISIANA,
IN DECEMBER 2004. MODEL
DONATED IT BACK TO THE
CLUB AND ASKED THAT IT BE
INCLUDED IN THE CLUB'S
PERMANENT COLLECTION
OF GUNS, IN HONOR OF
JACK S. PARKER. Courtesy
of the Boone and Crockett
Club. Photography by
Bryant Photographics.

ABOVE JACK PARKER'S GRIFFIN & HOWE CUSTOM .270 WEATHERBY MAGNUM WITH A 22-INCH BARREL, FN MAUSER ACTION WITH CHECKERED TRIGGER AND BOLT KNOB, JEWELED BOLT AND FOLLOWER, FIGURED WALNUT STOCK WITH BEADED CHEEKPIECE AND EBONY FOREND TIP, PLUS A BAUSCH AND LOMB BALFOR 4X SCOPE ON LEUPOLD MOUNTS. PARKER USED THIS RIFLE ON NUMEROUS HUNTS IN NORTH AMERICA AND THROUGHOUT THE WORLD. Courtesy of the Boone and Crockett Club. Rifle photography by Bryant Photographics.

ABOVE AND LEFT MEMBER WILLIAM B. RUGER CREATED A SPECIAL SERIES OF BOONE AND CROCKETT MEMBER RIFLES IN RECOGNITION OF THE CLUB'S CENTENNIAL CELEBRATION IN 1988. THESE RIFLES WERE MADE ON THE RUGER MODEL 77 MAGNUM ACTION AND WERE CHAMBERED IN .375 H&H MAGNUM OR .416 RIGBY CALIBER. THEY WERE INDIVIDUALLY NUMBERED AND WERE SOLD ONLY TO BOONE AND CROCKETT CLUB MEMBERS. LESS THAN 100 OF THESE RIFLES WERE MADE. IN ADDITION TO THIS SERIES OF RIFLES, A VERY UNIQUE BOONE AND CROCKETT CLUB MEMBER RIFLE FROM THIS SERIES IN CALIBER .416 RIGBY WAS MADE AND WAS AUCTIONED DURING THE CLUB'S CENTENNIAL CELEBRATION. THIS RIFLE WAS ENGRAVED AND WAS NUMBERED 1 OF 1. CLUB MEMBER GEORGE C. (TIM) HIXON PURCHASED THIS RIFLE. HE DONATED THIS RIFLE TO THE CLUB'S PERMANENT COLLECTION IN 2005.

Courtesy of the Boone and Crockett Club. Photography by Bryant Photographics.

BELOW BOONE AND CROCKETT CLUB EMERITUS MEMBER, ROBERT D. MARCOTTE, DONATED THIS BRITISH-MADE FARQUARSON-ACTION SINGLE-SHOT .450/.400 CALIBER RIFLE TO THE CLUB. THIS IS AN EXTREMELY STRONG ACTION AND WAS POPULAR AROUND THE TURN OF THE 20TH CENTURY. THIS RIFLE WAS MADE BY THE WESTLEY RICHARDS COMPANY IN 1896. THE STOCK AND ENGRAVING ARE NEW, BUT THE ACTION AND BARREL ARE ORIGINAL. Courtesy of the Boone and Crockett Club. Photography by Bryant Photographics.

Recorded Trophies

JACK RENEAU
DIRECTOR OF
BIG GAME RECORDS
Boone and Crockett Club

The trophy data listed on the following pages have been taken from score charts in the Records Archives of the Boone and Crockett Club. Trophies listed are those that continue to meet minimum scores and other stated requirements of trophy entry for the program. This edition includes entries from the 11th edition of the All-time records book, *Records of North American Big Game*, as well as entries from the 24th (1998-2000) and 25th (2001-2003) Awards Entry Periods that meet or exceed the All-time minimum entry score for each category.

The final scores and rank shown are official except for those trophies shown at the end of the list for their category with an asterisk. The asterisk is assigned to trophies in this edition that were subject to verification by either the 24th or 25th Awards Program Judges Panels, but were not sent in for verification. The asterisk can be removed, except in the case of potential World's Records, by submitting two additional, independent scorings by Official Measurers of the Boone and Crockett Club. The Club's Records Committee would then review the three scorings available (original plus two additional), and determine which, if any, will be accepted in lieu of the Awards Program Judges' Panel measurement. When the score has been accepted as final by the Records Committee, the asterisk will be removed and that trophy will take its rightful place in the listings of all future editions of the Club's records books.

An asterisked trophy is listed in one Awards Program records book and one All-time records book. If its score is not verified by publication of the next edition of the All-time records book, it is no longer listed. For example, all trophies listed with an asterisk in the last (11th) edition of the All-time records book (1999) with an asterisk have been dropped from this edition if their score was not verified by additional measurements. The scores of a number of trophies asterisked in the 11th edition were verified so they took their rightful place in the listings. The trophies that were dropped are still eligible for listing in future editions of the Club's records books if their final score is verified as outlined above.

Potential Worlds' Records, which are those trophies with entry scores that exceed the World's Record at the time they are entered, must be verified by either an Awards Program Judges Panel at the end of an Awards Program, or by a Special Judges Panel convened between Final Awards Program Judges Panels with the sole purpose of verifying their score and certifying their World's Record status.

Actually, there are fewer new asterisked trophies in this edition of the All-time records book than in past editions because the scores of a number of entries in the 24th Awards Program have been verified, and the 25th Awards Program was the most successful ever in terms of the number and quality of trophies received and verified by the Judges Panel. The Club announced nine new World's Records in eight categories (two-way tie in pronghorn) from among the 117 trophies received and displayed at Cabela's in Kansas City, Kansas. Prior to the 25th Awards Program, the greatest number of trophies displayed at a single Awards Program was 105 at the 22nd Awards Program held at the Dallas Museum of Natural History, Dallas, Texas, in 1995. We received 30 more trophies in Kansas City in 2004 than were submitted to the 24th Awards Program just three years ago.

There is one significant change in the tabular data worth noting that has taken place since the 11th edition of All-time records book was published in 1999. That is the addition of two new categories for non-typical Columbia blacktail deer and non-typical Sitka blacktail deer, with respective minimum scores of 155 points and 118 points.

This is the second edition to use standard postal code abbreviations for states and provinces. A complete listing of postal codes used in this edition is shown in the table to the left.

The scientific and vernacular names, and the sequence of presentation, follow that suggested in the ***Revised Checklist of North American Mammals North of Mexico***, 1979 (J. Knox, et al., Texas Tech University, Dec. 14, 1979.) Note that "PR" preceding date of kill indicates "prior to" the date shown for kill.

GEOGRAPHIC BOUNDARIES

Geographic boundaries are of considerable importance in records keeping. The Club's Awards Programs are set up only for native North American big-game animals. For such purposes, the southern boundary is defined as the south boundary of Mexico. The northern limit for trophies that may inhabit the offshore waters, such as polar bear and walrus, is the limit of the continent and associated waters held by the

United States, Canada or Greenland. Continental limited and associated waters define the east and west boundaries for all categories.

In addition to the broad geographic boundaries described above, carefully described geographic boundaries are necessary in certain categories that closely resemble each other, due to the fact they are set up to recognize subspecies. Categories for which such boundaries are spelled out include: grizzly and brown bear; American, Roosevelt's, and tule elk; mule, Columbia, and Sitka blacktail deer; whitetail and Coues' deer; Canada, Alaska-Yukon, and Wyoming moose; barren ground, Central Canada barren ground, mountain, woodland, and Quebec-Labrador caribou; bighorn, desert, Dall's, and Stone's sheep; and Atlantic and Pacific walrus. For these cases, specific boundary descriptions are spelled out for the smaller category to prevent specimens of the larger being erroneously entered in the smaller category and thus receiving undue recognition.

In addition, special considerations are also spelled out for certain other animals. For example, bison exist today as wild, free-ranging herds in their original setting only in certain areas of Alaska and Canada. Bison from the lower 48 states are, in many cases, semi-domesticated and regulated as domestic livestock. Thus, hunter-taken trophies from the lower 48 states are acceptable for listing in the records book(s) only if they were taken in a state that recognizes bison as wild and free-ranging, and which requires a hunting license and/or big-game tag for such hunting. If bison from the lower 48 states are invited and sent to an Awards Program Judges' Panel, the trophy can only receive a certificate of merit. Bison from most herds in Canada and Alaska are eligible to receive awards medals.

Detailed descriptions of the applicable geographic boundaries are given in the trophy data section for the affected categories. Additional detailed boundary information can be found in *Measuring and Scoring North American Big Game Trophies*, 2nd Edition. Hunters are encouraged to read and understand such boundaries while planning hunting trips in order to avoid possible disappointment.

SAGAMORE HILL AWARD

The Sagamore Hill Medal is given by the Roosevelt family in memory of Theodore Roosevelt (Founder and first President of the Boone and Crockett Club), Theodore Roosevelt, Jr., and Kermit Roosevelt. It was created in 1948. It may be awarded by the Big Game Final Awards Judges' Panel, if in their opinion there is an outstanding trophy worthy of great distinction. Only one may be given in any Big Game Awards program. A special award may also be presented by the Executive Committee of the Boone and Crockett Club for distinguished devotion to the objectives of the Club. The Sagamore Hill Medal is the highest award given by the Boone and Crockett Club. This edition of the All-time records book highlights those trophies that have received this distinguished award by listing the trophy in bold type and including an image of the Sagamore Hill Medal next to the trophy photo, where available, and listing.

BLACK BEAR
WORLD'S RECORD

RANK
World's Record

SCORE
23 $^{10}/_{16}$

LOCATION
Sanpete Co., UT

HUNTER
Picked Up

OWNERS
A.R. Lund and
M. Daniels

DATE KILLED
1975

On July 1, 1975, the World's Record skull for a black bear (*Ursus americanus*) was found along the edge of the Manti-La Sal National Forest, about seven miles east of Ephraim, Utah. Out west, black bears are occasionally seen in sub-alpine meadows, but they generally prefer the shelter of trees, where they quietly move in and out along the edges of the forest. Such was the setting where Merrill Daniels and Alma Lund contemplated their discovery. Daniels and Lund were unable to determine the cause of death but did recognize the immensity of the old carcass that was slowly decaying in the summer heat. In the past, when many trophy-sized black bears were scored by measuring hides, this could have been a tough call. Using Boone and Crockett's system for measuring the bear's immense skull, the duo received an entry score of 23-10/16. However, because the score exceeded the previous record by more than an inch, their incredible find was greeted with skepticism. With the concurrence of the trophy owners, the skull was shipped to the Club's office in Washington D.C., where it was examined by experts at the Smithsonian Institution.

After undergoing careful comparisons with type specimens, as well as other identification criteria, the final assessment was that this was indeed a bona fide black bear skull. In 1980, the trophy was awarded a Certificate of Merit in recognition of outstanding trophy characteristics at the 17th North American Big Game Awards Program. Pick-ups are included, in order to enhance the scientific value of the records and complete the standard which sportsmen can judge their best trophies. San Pete County, Utah, was also the location of the previous state record trophy taken by Rex W. Peterson accompanied by Richard Hardy in 1970, which scored 22-6/16. Bears taken in Arizona and Colorado during the 1960s have also received impressive scores. ∎

250 Station Drive
Missoula, MT 59801
(406) 542-1888

BOONE AND CROCKETT CLUB®

OFFICIAL SCORING SYSTEM FOR NORTH AMERICAN BIG GAME TROPHIES

BEAR

KIND OF BEAR (check one)
- ■ black bear
- ☐ grizzly
- ☐ Alaska brown bear
- ☐ polar

| | MINIMUM SCORES | |
	AWARDS	ALL-TIME
black bear	20	21
grizzly bear	23	24
Alaska brown bear	26	28
polar bear	27	27

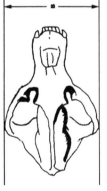

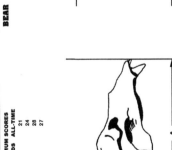

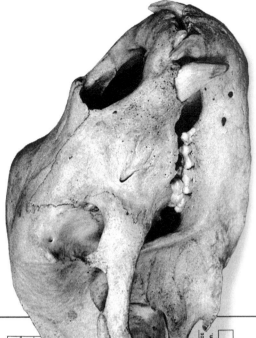

SEE OTHER SIDE FOR INSTRUCTIONS	MEASUREMENTS
A. Greatest Length Without Lower Jaw	14 12/16
B. Greatest Width	8 14/16
FINAL SCORE	23 10/16

Exact Locality Where Killed: Sanpete Co. UT

Date Killed: July 1, 1975   Hunter: Picked Up

Owner: Alma R. Lund and Merrill Daniels   Telephone #:

Owner's Address:

Guide's Name and Address:

Remarks: (Mention Any Abnormalities or Unique Qualities)

I, **Glenn C. Sanderson** , certify that I have measured this trophy on **MM/DD/YYYY**
PRINT NAME

at **Missouri Department of Conservation**   **Jefferson City**   **MO**
STREET ADDRESS   CITY   STATE/PROVINCE

and that these measurements and data are, to the best of my knowledge and belief, made in accordance with the instructions given.

Witness: _____ **F. Cook** _____   Signature: _____ **Glenn C. Sanderson** _____   I.D. Number ☐☐☐☐
B&C OFFICIAL MEASURER

BLACK BEAR
WORLD'S RECORD SCORE CHART

BLACK BEAR

Ursus americanus americanus and related subspecies

Score	Greatest Length of Skull Without Lower Jaw	Greatest Width of Skull	Locality	Hunter	Owner	Date Killed	Rank
23 10/16	14 12/16	8 14/16	Sanpete Co., UT	Picked Up	A.R. Lund & M. Daniels	1975	1
23 7/16	14 8/16	8 15/16	Lycoming Co., PA	PA Game Commission	PA Game Comm.	1987	2
23 3/16	13 15/16	9 4/16	Mendocino Co., CA	Robert J. Shuttleworth, Jr.	Robert J. Shuttleworth, Jr.	1993	3
22 15/16	13 14/16	9 1/16	Kuiu Island, AK	Craig D. Martin	Craig D. Martin	1996	4
22 14/16	14 5/16	8 9/16	McCreary, MB	John J. Bathke	John J. Bathke	1998	5
22 13/16	14 1/16	8 13/16	Ventura Co., CA	Loren C. Nodolf	Loaned to B&C Natl. Coll.	1990	6
22 13/16	14	8 13/16	Luzerne Co., PA	Joseph E. Mindick	Joseph E. Mindick	1998	6
22 11/16	14 5/16	8 6/16	Bradford Co., PA	Chad M. Reed	Chad M. Reed	1991	8
22 11/16	13 13/16	8 14/16	Bronson Lake, SK	Stanley Benson	Stanley Benson	1997	8
22 10/16	13 14/16	8 12/16	Lincoln Co., WI	Daniel J. Kufahl	Daniel J. Kufahl	2002	10
22 9/16	14 6/16	8 3/16	Greenlee Co., AZ	William H. Slater	William H. Slater	1987	11
22 9/16	14 7/16	8 2/16	Jefferson Co., PA	Frank A. Rottman	B&C National Collection	1991	11
22 9/16	13 12/16	8 13/16	Carbon Co., PA	Joseph M. Legotti	Joseph M. Legotti	1991	11
22 9/16	13 14/16	8 11/16	Prince of Wales Island, AK	Mark T. Young	Mark T. Young	1993	11
22 8/16	14 6/16	8 2/16	Porcupine Plain, SK	Calvin Parsons	Calvin Parsons	1977	15
22 8/16	14 1/16	8 7/16	Gila Co., AZ	Fred Peters	Fred Peters	1985	15
22 8/16	13 13/16	8 11/16	Rockingham Co., VA	Roger O. Wyant	Roger O. Wyant	1994	15
22 8/16	14	8 8/16	Monroe Co., PA	Thomas Q. Vasey	Thomas Q. Vasey	1995	15
22 8/16	13 11/16	8 13/16	Schuylkill Co., PA	Elwood W. Maurer	Elwood W. Maurer	1997	15
22 7/16	13 11/16	8 12/16	Sevier Co., UT	Picked Up	UT Div. of Wildl. Resc.	1982	20
22 7/16	13 14/16	8 9/16	Owl River, AB	Dan B. Pence	Dan B. Pence	1999	20
22 6/16	13 11/16	8 11/16	Sanpete Co., UT	R.W. Peterson & R.S. Hardy	Rex W. Peterson	1970	22
22 6/16	14 3/16	8 3/16	Gila Co., AZ	Roy A. Stewart	Roy A. Stewart	1978	22
22 6/16	13 11/16	8 11/16	Lycoming Co., PA	John C. Whyne	John C. Whyne	1983	22
22 6/16	13 12/16	8 10/16	Gronlid, SK	Floyd Forster	Floyd Forster	1992	22
22 6/16	13 12/16	8 10/16	Bedford Co., PA	James E. Deneen	James E. Deneen	1995	22
22 5/16	14 3/16	8 2/16	Hubbard Co., MN	Brian A. Gross	Brian A. Gross	2000	27
22 4/16	13 9/16	8 11/16	Apache Co., AZ	R.R. Barney & H.E. Booher	Richard R. Barney	1968	28
22 4/16	14 1/16	8 3/16	Ft. Apache Res., AZ	Jimmie C. James	Jimmie C. James	1971	28
22 4/16	13 15/16	8 5/16	Nestor Falls, ON	Vicki M. Blender	Vicki M. Blender	1995	28
22 4/16	13 11/16	8 9/16	Greenlee Co., AZ	Brian Reece	Brian Reece	1996	28
22 4/16	13 11/16	8 9/16	Rusk Co., WI	Ben R. Brandstatter	Ben R. Brandstatter	2000	28
22 4/16	14 1/16	8 3/16	Woodridge, MB	Peter U. Funk	Peter U. Funk	2000	28
22 3/16	13 13/16	8 6/16	Frog Lake, AB	Darren Daniel	Darren Daniel	1983	34
22 3/16	14 1/16	8 12/16	Aitkin Co., MN	Picked Up	Greg & Gary Kullhem	1992	34
22 3/16	13 7/16	8 9/16	Barron Co., WI	Mike T. Losey	Mike T. Losey	1995	34
22 3/16	13 12/16	8 7/16	Kanabec Co., MN	Corey A. Gilbertson	Corey A. Gilbertson	1996	34
22 3/16	13 12/16	8 7/16	Menominee Co., MI	James W. Henney	James W. Henney	2000	34

Score			Locality	Owner	Hunter	Date Killed	Rank
22 3/16	13 12/16	8 7/16	Burnett Co., WI	Dustin Luke	Dustin Luke	2003	34
22 2/16	13 13/16	8 5/16	Graham Co., AZ	Peter C. Knagge	Peter C. Knagge	1982	40
22 2/16	13 11/16	8 4/16	Sanpete Co., UT	Larry W. Cox	Larry W. Cox	1987	40
22 2/16	13 14/16	8 6/16	Queen Charlotte Islands, BC	Craig N. Beachy	Craig N. Beachy	1988	40
22 2/16	13 12/16	8 12/16	Kern Co., CA	Danny R. Thomas	Danny R. Thomas	1988	40
22 2/16	13 6/16	8	Mendocino Co., CA	Jay Bromley	Jay Bromley	1991	40
22 2/16	13 8/16	8 10/16	Clark Co., WI	Daniel L. Kizewski	Daniel L. Kizewski	1993	40
22 2/16	13 13/16	8 5/16	Mendocino Co., CA	Chris Brennan	Chris Brennan	1995	40
22 2/16	13 15/16	8 3/16	Ashland Co., WI	Kris J. Freimuth	Kris J. Freimuth	1998	40
22 2/16	13 15/16	8 5/16	Delta Co., CO	James B. George	James B. George	1998	40
22 2/16	13 15/16	8 3/16	Rusk Co., WI	Dean R. Ecker	Dean R. Ecker	2001	40
22 2/16	14 1/16	8 1/16	St. Croix Co., WI	Gary L. Kurtz	Gary L. Kurtz	2002	40
22 1/16	13 11/16	8 6/16	Uintah Co., UT	Hal Mecham	Hal Mecham	1975	51
22 1/16	13 13/16	8 4/16	Arran, SK	Harry Kushniryk	Harry Kushniryk	1981	51
22 1/16	13 15/16	8 2/16	Fox Creek, AB	Richard Raiwet	Richard Raiwet	1992	51
22 1/16	13 12/16	8 5/16	Snake Lake, MB	Edward J. Blair	Edward J. Blair	2000	51
22	13 6/16	8 10/16	Hahns Peak, CO	W.L. Cave	W.L. Cave	1964	55
22	13 8/16	8 8/16	Graham Co., AZ	Thomas E. Klepfer	Thomas E. Klepfer	1972	55
22	13 12/16	8 4/16	Garfield Co., CO	Joseph R. Maynard	Joseph R. Maynard	1977	55
22	13 10/16	8 6/16	Hamilton Co., NY	Samuel A. Johnson	Samuel A. Johnson	1986	55
22	13 13/16	8 3/16	Maknak, MB	Cory A. Pardon	Cory A. Pardon	1986	55
22	13 7/16	8 9/16	Roscommon Co., MI	Matthew A. Gettler	Matthew A. Gettler	1987	55
22	13 11/16	8 5/16	Carbon Co., UT	Michael J. Hreinson	Michael J. Hreinson	1987	55
22	13 7/16	8 9/16	Prince of Wales Island, AK	John W. Simons	John W. Simons	1987	55
22	13 12/16	8 4/16	Prince of Wales Island, AK	George P. Mann	George P. Mann	1991	55
22	13 14/16	8 2/16	Prince of Wales Island, AK	Stanley L. Parkerson	Stanley L. Parkerson	1991	55
22	13 10/16	8 6/16	Gila Co., AZ	Steven J. Stayner	Steven J. Stayner	1991	55
22	13 10/16	8 6/16	Los Angeles Co., CA	Joe L. Clay	Joe L. Clay	1992	55
22	13 8/16	8 8/16	Lycoming Co., PA	Clarence G. Eppley	Clarence G. Eppley	1992	55
22	13 9/16	8 7/16	Menominee Co., MI	Michael L. Hesyck	Michael L. Hesyck	1992	55
22	14 2/16	7 14/16	Tioga Co., PA	Ronald E. Andrus	Ronald E. Andrus	1994	55
22	13 6/16	8 10/16	Aitkin Co., MN	Joel J. Stang	Joel J. Stang	1995	55
22	13 11/16	8	Pine Co., MN	Darrin G. Stream	Darrin G. Stream	1995	55
22	14	8	Essex Co., NY	Anthony J. Ploufe	Anthony J. Ploufe	1996	55
22	14 2/16	7 14/16	Hertford Co., NC	Joseph C. Lowe	Joseph C. Lowe	1997	55
22	13 11/16	8 5/16	Lycoming Co., PA	John T. Zerbe	John T. Zerbe	1997	55
22	13 4/16	8 12/16	Burntwood River, MB	Ken R. Malehorn	Ken R. Malehorn	1998	55
22	13 12/16	8 4/16	Kuiu Island, AK	Ricky Smith	Ricky Smith	1999	55
22	14 4/16	7 12/16	Mille Lacs Co., MN	Roy C. Basham	Roy C. Basham	2000	55
22	13 15/16	8 1/16	Suffolk Co., VA	Michael P. Haberman	Michael P. Haberman	2000	55
22	13 6/16	8 10/16	Lycoming Co., PA	Donald W. Howard	Donald W. Howard	2002	55
22	13 10/16	8 6/16	Polk Co., WI	Steve D. Flook	Steve D. Flook	2002	55
22	13 11/16	8 5/16	Polk Co., WI	Dale Ostenson	Dale Ostenson	2002	55
22	13 3/16	8 12/16	Sturgis, SK	Rupert M. Satterthwaite	Rupert M. Satterthwaite	2003	55
21 15/16	13 3/16	8 12/16	Land O'Lakes, WI	Ed Strobel	Ed Strobel	1953	84
21 15/16	13 13/16	8 2/16	Swan River, MB	Jim E. Russell	Jim E. Russell	1973	84

BLACK BEAR

Ursus americanus americanus and related subspecies

Score	Greatest Length of Skull Without Lower Jaw	Greatest Width of Skull	Locality	Hunter	Owner	Date Killed	Rank
21 15/16	13 5/16	8 10/16	Lincoln Co., WY	C. William Redshaw	C. William Redshaw	1976	84
21 15/16	13 12/16	8 3/16	Clearfield Co., PA	Dwayne B. DeLattre	Dwayne B. DeLattre	1987	84
21 15/16	13 9/16	8 6/16	Russell, MB	Gerry Mushumanski	Gerry Mushumanski	1987	84
21 15/16	13 12/16	8 3/16	Gila Co., AZ	Thomas Alvin	Thomas Alvin	1990	84
21 15/16	14 6/16	7 9/16	Birdtail Creek, MB	Barry Minshull	Barry Minshull	1990	84
21 15/16	13 12/16	8 3/16	Cambria Co., PA	Frank J. Mehalko, Sr.	Frank J. Mehalko, Sr.	1992	84
21 15/16	13 9/16	8 6/16	Riverton, MB	Samuel J. Amodeo	Samuel J. Amodeo	1995	84
21 15/16	13 13/16	8 2/16	Queen Charlotte Islands, BC	Philip Giesbrecht	Philip Giesbrecht	1995	84
21 15/16	13 10/16	8 5/16	Graham Co., AZ	Mark D. Morris	Mark D. Morris	1995	84
21 15/16	13 14/16	8 1/16	Shawano Co., WI	Rick A. Much	Rick A. Much	1997	84
21 15/16	13 14/16	8 1/16	Schuylkill Co., PA	Glen J. Hendricks	Glen J. Hendricks	1998	84
21 15/16	14	7 15/16	Santa Barbara Co., CA	Eliseo Pizano	Eliseo Pizano	1998	84
21 15/16	13 14/16	8 1/16	Bronson Lake, SK	Daniel Valette	Daniel Valette	2000	84
21 15/16	13 11/16	8 3/16	Smithers, BC	Native American	Jack Adams	1975	99
21 14/16	13 10/16	8 4/16	Lincoln Co., WI	Robert P. Faufau	Robert P. Faufau	1981	99
21 14/16	13 7/16	8 7/16	Grant Co., NM	Mark J. Miller	Mark J. Miller	1983	99
21 14/16	13 12/16	8 2/16	Hirsch Creek, BC	Cecil W. Brown	Cecil W. Brown	1984	99
21 14/16	13 9/16	8 5/16	Luzerne Co., PA	Adrian C. Robbins	Adrian C. Robbins	1989	99
21 14/16	13 12/16	8 2/16	Tyrrell Co., NC	Albert J. Blase	Albert J. Blase	1996	99
21 14/16	13 15/16	7 15/16	Polk Co., MN	Picked Up	MN Dept. of Natl. Resc.	1996	99
21 14/16	13 9/16	8 5/16	Chimdemash Creek, BC	Randy Kucharyshen	Randy Kucharyshen	1997	99
21 14/16	13 14/16	8	Weldon, SK	Ron S. Bodnarchuk	Ron S. Bodnarchuk	1998	99
21 14/16	13 10/16	8 4/16	Lackawanna Co., PA	Jeff J. Kozar	Jeff J. Kozar	1998	99
21 14/16	13 10/16	8 4/16	Lake of the Woods, ON	Greg D. Daniels	Greg D. Daniels	1999	99
21 14/16	13 10/16	8 4/16	Benton Co., MN	Randy J. Hamers	Randy J. Hamers	1999	99
21 14/16	14	7 14/16	Hyde Co., NC	Gurnwood L. Radcliff, Jr.	Gurnwood L. Radcliff, Jr.	1999	99
21 14/16	13 9/16	8 5/16	Crow Wing Co., MN	Ricky J. Carlson	Ricky J. Carlson	2000	99
21 14/16	13 12/16	8 2/16	Mille Lacs Co., MN	Charles D. Huber	Charles D. Huber	2000	99
21 14/16	14 1/16	7 13/16	Point Lookout, AK	Mark L. Wilson	Mark L. Wilson	2000	99
21 14/16	13 8/16	8 6/16	Monroe Co., PA	Scott H. Mosier	Scott H. Mosier	2001	99
21 14/16	13 11/16	8 3/16	Echols Co., GA	Everett D. Sirk	Everett D. Sirk	2002	99
21 14/16	13 8/16	8 6/16	Carswell Lake, SK	Richard P. Smith	Richard P. Smith	2002	99
21 13/16	13 9/16	8 4/16	Ft. Apache Res., AZ	G. Boyd, P. Ellsworth & G. Brewer	Greg Boyd	1964	118
21 13/16	13 7/16	8 6/16	Tatlanika River, AK	Barry W. Campbell	Barry W. Campbell	1966	118
21 13/16	13 8/16	8 5/16	Ft. Apache Res., AZ	Gary W. Sholl	Gary W. Sholl	1969	118
21 13/16	13 9/16	8 4/16	Graham Co., AZ	Bruce Liddy	Bruce Liddy	1976	118
21 13/16	13 6/16	8 7/16	Carbon Co., PA	Robert F. Kulp	Robert F. Kulp	1983	118
21 13/16	13 7/16	8 6/16	Big River, SK	William Dear	William Dear	1985	118

Score			Locality	Hunter	Owner	Date	Rank
21 13/16	14 6/16	7 7/16	St. Johns Co., FL	Picked Up	FL Game & Fresh Water Fish Comm.	1985	118
21 13/16	13 12/16	8 1/16	Aitkin Co., MN	Picked Up	MN Dept. of Natl. Resc.	1988	118
21 13/16	13 4/16	8 9/16	Menominee Co., MI	Andrew M. Bray	Ray Bray	1989	118
21 13/16	13 3/16	8 10/16	Price Co., WI	John W. Marshall	John W. Marshall	1993	118
21 13/16	14	7 13/16	Douglas Co., WI	Annette C. Lehman	Annette C. Lehman	1995	118
21 13/16	13 12/16	8 1/16	White Co., GA	John M. Wood	John M. Wood	1995	118
21 13/16	13 5/16	8 8/16	Prince of Wales Island, AK	Dyrk T. Eddie	Dyrk T. Eddie	1996	118
21 13/16	13 3/16	8 10/16	Sullivan Co., NY	Thomas V. Schields	Thomas V. Schields	1998	118
21 13/16	13 10/16	8 3/16	Kupreanof Island, AK	Peter D. Rowe	Peter D. Rowe	1999	118
21 13/16	13 10/16	8 3/16	Nut Mt., SK	Earl Smith	Earl Smith	1999	118
21 13/16	13 8/16	8 5/16	Rusk Co., WI	Robert A. Brunkow	Robert A. Brunkow	2000	118
21 13/16	13 11/16	8 2/16	Bedford Co., PA	John W. Colliflower, Sr.	John W. Colliflower, Sr.	2000	118
21 13/16	14	7 13/16	Aitkin Co., MN	Thomas A. Kubiak	Thomas A. Kubiak	2000	118
21 13/16	13 11/16	8 2/16	Apache Co., AZ	R. Terrell McCombs	R. Terrell McCombs	2000	118
21 13/16	13 12/16	8 1/16	Ventura Co., CA	Loren C. Nodolf	Picked Up	2000	118
21 13/16	13 3/16	8 10/16	Pouce Coupe, BC	Dan R. Therrien	Dan R. Therrien	2000	118
21 13/16	13 13/16	8	Lycoming Co., PA	Scott L. Cummings	Scott L. Cummings	2001	118
21 13/16	13 9/16	8 4/16	Rusk Co., WI	Daryl Risler	Daryl Risler	2001	118
21 13/16	13 1/16	8 12/16	Luzerne Co., PA	Earl J. Cichy, Jr.	Earl J. Cichy, Jr.	2002	118
21 13/16	13 9/16	8 4/16	Searchmont, ON	Gregory E. Meredith	Gregory E. Meredith	2002	118
21 13/16	14	7 13/16	Navajo Co., AZ	Nick C. Williams	Nick C. Williams	2003	118
21 12/16	13 3/16	8 9/16	Delta Co., CO	Quincy Hines	Quincy Hines	1967	145
21 12/16	13 10/16	8 2/16	Bayfield Co., WI	Byron Bird, Jr.	Byron Bird, Jr.	1976	145
21 12/16	13 14/16	7 14/16	California Creek, AK	Boyd J. Blair	Boyd J. Blair	1976	145
21 12/16	13 8/16	8 4/16	Gila Co., AZ	Mike Lisk	Mike Lisk	1984	145
21 12/16	13 10/16	8 2/16	Garfield Co., UT	Clint Mecham	Clint Mecham	1985	145
21 12/16	13 11/16	8 1/16	Greenwater Lake, SK	John Woulfe	John Woulfe	1987	145
21 12/16	13 4/16	8 8/16	Huerfano Co., CO	Harvey R. Newcomb	Harvey R. Newcomb	1988	145
21 12/16	13 5/16	8 7/16	Lily Lake, BC	James C. Zevely	James C. Zevely	1990	145
21 12/16	14	7 12/16	Chowan Co., NC	George D. Copeland, Sr.	George D. Copeland, Sr.	1991	145
21 12/16	13 8/16	8 4/16	Makinak, MB	Wendell Hanson	Wendell Hanson	1991	145
21 12/16	13 10/16	8 2/16	Alonsa, MB	Cory Mozdzen	Cory Mozdzen	1991	145
21 12/16	13 8/16	8 4/16	Prince of Wales Island, AK	Kleigh C. Hirschi	Kleigh C. Hirschi	1992	145
21 12/16	13 8/16	8 4/16	Ventura Co., CA	Joey La Salle	Joey La Salle	1992	145
21 12/16	13 9/16	8 3/16	Gila Co., AZ	John W. Oberg	John W. Oberg	1992	145
21 12/16	13 12/16	8	Pine Co., MN	Fred Olander	Fred Olander	1992	145
21 12/16	13 2/16	8 10/16	Trinity Co., CA	Blue Millsap	Blue Millsap	1994	145
21 12/16	13	8 12/16	Graham Co., AZ	Lee A. Malaby	Lee A. Malaby	1995	145
21 12/16	13 11/16	8 1/16	Maricopa Co., AZ	Trent P. Thornton	Trent P. Thornton	1995	145
21 12/16	14 1/16	7 11/16	Tyrrell Co., NC	Jim Williams	Jim Williams	1997	145
21 12/16	13	8 12/16	Greene Co., NY	Edward B. Rivenburg, Jr.	Edward B. Rivenburg, Jr.	1998	145
21 12/16	13 10/16	8 2/16	Fishing Lake, AB	LeRoy C. Haug	LeRoy C. Haug	1998	145
21 12/16	13 8/16	8 4/16	Pike Co., PA	Jeffrey N. Lee	Jeffrey N. Lee	1998	145
21 12/16	13 4/16	8 8/16	Ventura Co., CA	Loren C. Nodolf	Loren C. Nodolf	2000	145
21 12/16	14 1/16	7 11/16	Hyde Co., NC	Jeffrey D. Gibbs	Jeffrey D. Gibbs	2000	145
21 12/16	13 8/16	8 4/16	Langlade Co., WI	Cary W. Krueger	Cary W. Krueger	2001	145
21 12/16	13 8/16	8 4/16	Peace River, AB	Ronny F. Register	Ronny F. Register	2001	145

Score	Greatest Length of Skull Without Lower Jaw	Greatest Width of Skull	Locality	Hunter	Owner	Date Killed	Rank
21 12/16	13 7/16	8 5/16	Sublette Co., WY	Dan W. McCann	Dan W. McCann	2002	145
21 11/16	13 5/16	8 6/16	Mendocino Co., CA	E.J. Vamm	Univ. of CA Museum	1928	172
21 11/16	13 6/16	8 5/16	Gila Co., AZ	Clay Warden	Milo Warden	1975	172
21 11/16	13 5/16	8 6/16	Menominee Co., MI	Ray Bray	Andy Bray	1984	172
21 11/16	13 5/16	8 6/16	Kern Co., CA	George H. Hershberger	George H. Hershberger	1985	172
21 11/16	13 7/16	8 4/16	Karta Bay, AK	Donald J. McNeil	Douglas A. McNeil	1985	172
21 11/16	13 15/16	7 12/16	Hyde Co., NC	Gurnwood L. Radcliff, Jr.	Gurnwood L. Radcliff, Jr.	1986	172
21 11/16	13 6/16	8 5/16	Cass Co., MN	Anne M. Zahalka	Anne M. Zahalka	1986	172
21 11/16	13 11/16	8	Prairie River, SK	Gregory Stabrylla	Gregory Stabrylla	1987	172
21 11/16	13 7/16	8 4/16	Queen Charlotte Islands, BC	Kurt M. Saffarek	Kurt M. Saffarek	1988	172
21 11/16	13 6/16	8 5/16	Prince of Wales Island, AK	Richard J. Asplund	Richard J. Asplund	1990	172
21 11/16	13 15/16	7 12/16	Porcupine Hills, SK	Richard K. McLean	Richard K. McLean	1990	172
21 11/16	13 5/16	8 6/16	Ventura Co., CA	Marsha Vaughan	Marsha Vaughan	1990	172
21 11/16	13 9/16	8 2/16	Tyrrell Co., NC	Hank D. Rose, Jr.	NC Wildl. Resc. Comm.	1993	172
21 11/16	13 13/16	7 14/16	Rusk Co., WI	Gregory J. Baneck	Gregory J. Baneck	1995	172
21 11/16	13 6/16	8 5/16	Washburn Co., WI	Keith W. Dahlstrom	Keith W. Dahlstrom	1996	172
21 11/16	13 4/16	8 7/16	Olha, MB	Gary G. Lex	Gary G. Lex	1996	172
21 11/16	13 5/16	8 6/16	Luzerne Co., PA	Gerard E. Dessoye	Gerard E. Dessoye	1997	172
21 11/16	13 8/16	8 3/16	Prince of Wales Island, AK	Kurt G. Kruger	Kurt G. Kruger	1997	172
21 11/16	13 13/16	7 14/16	Hyde Co., NC	Gary D. McMahan	Gary D. McMahan	1998	172
21 11/16	13 9/16	8 2/16	Riding Mt., MB	Mike Minshull	Mike Minshull	1998	172
21 11/16	13 8/16	8 3/16	Huntingdon Co., PA	Marty W. Snyder	Marty W. Snyder	1998	172
21 11/16	13 6/16	8 5/16	Bronson Forest, SK	Rhodney N. Honeycutt	Rhodney N. Honeycutt	1999	172
21 11/16	13 9/16	8 2/16	Paradise Hill, SK	Kolby Morrison	Kolby Morrison	1999	172
21 11/16	13 10/16	8 1/16	Carbon Co., UT	Matthew Christy	Matthew Christy	2000	172
21 11/16	13 10/16	8 1/16	Prince of Wales Island, AK	Kelly J. King	Kelly J. King	2001	172
21 11/16	13 14/16	7 13/16	Apache Co., AZ	Ty Ryland	Ty Ryland	2001	172
21 10/16	13	8 10/16	Mendocino Co., CA	Andy Bowman	Univ. of CA Museum	1930	198
21 10/16	13	8 10/16	Custer Co., ID	Robert L. Caskey	Robert L. Caskey	1967	198
21 10/16	13 5/16	8 5/16	Lake Co., OR	Martin V. Pernoll	Martin V. Pernoll	1967	198
21 10/16	13 12/16	7 14/16	Piscataquis Co., ME	J.D. Flowers	J.D. Flowers	1980	198
21 10/16	13 4/16	8 6/16	Grande Cache, AB	Laurier Adam	Laurier Adam	1984	198
21 10/16	13 8/16	8 2/16	Gila Co., AZ	Harold W. Mosser	Harold W. Mosser	1985	198
21 10/16	13 9/16	8 1/16	Prairie River, SK	Tim P. Matzinger	Tim P. Matzinger	1989	198
21 10/16	13 2/16	8 8/16	Gila Co., AZ	Fred Peters	Fred Peters	1989	198
21 10/16	13 10/16	8	Alcona Co., MI	Randy L. Schultz	Randy L. Schultz	1989	198
21 10/16	13 7/16	8 3/16	Graham Co., AZ	S. Kim Bonnett	S. Kim Bonnett	1990	198
21 10/16	13 6/16	8 4/16	Bucareli Bay, AK	Dwight B. Leister, Jr.	Dwight B. Leister, Jr.	1990	198

			Locality	Hunter	Owner	Year	Rank
21 10/16	13 3/16	8 7/16	Sullivan Co., NY	Daniel O'Keefe	Daniel O'Keefe	1991	198
21 10/16	13 2/16	8 8/16	Ventura Co., CA	Chris Ames	Chris Ames	1992	198
21 10/16	13 7/16	8 3/16	Sawyer Co., WI	Brad A. Beise	Brad A. Beise	1992	198
21 10/16	13 8/16	8 2/16	Grant Co., WV	Carnie Carr, Jr.	Carnie Carr, Jr.	1993	198
21 10/16	13 10/16	8	Peace River, AB	Richard A. Walker	Richard A. Walker	1993	198
21 10/16	13 4/16	8 6/16	Glenn Co., CA	John H. Knight	John H. Knight	1994	198
21 10/16	13 6/16	8 4/16	Graham Co., AZ	Jeffrey D. Warren	Jeffrey D. Warren	1994	198
21 10/16	13 13/16	7 13/16	Prince of Wales Island, AK	Gerald Baty	Gerald Baty	1996	198
21 10/16	13 10/16	8 1/16	Marathon Co., WI	David S. Williamson	David S. Williamson	1996	198
21 10/16	13 9/16	8 7/16	Qu'Appelle River, SK	Lyle Gorecki	Lyle Gorecki	1997	198
21 10/16	13 3/16	8 7/16	Pike Co., PA	Reynold L. Morey	Reynold L. Morey	1998	198
21 10/16	13 8/16	8 2/16	Prince of Wales Island, AK	Ian K. Chase-Dunn	Ian K. Chase-Dunn	1999	198
21 10/16	13 1/16	8 9/16	Chelan Co., WA	Robin L. Radach	Robin L. Radach	1999	198
21 10/16	13 6/16	8 4/16	Wayne Co., PA	Joseph Simyan, Jr.	Joseph Simyan, Jr.	1999	198
21 10/16	13 6/16	8 1/16	Bradford Co., PA	Stephen E. Watkins	Stephen E. Watkins	2000	198
21 10/16	13 6/16	8 6/16	Sawyer Co., WI	LeRoy McGary	LeRoy McGary	2000	198
21 10/16	13 9/16	8 1/16	Peace River, AB	Randy L. Stadler	Randy L. Stadler	2002	198
21 10/16	13 9/16	8 1/16	Kelwood, MB	John N. Pardun, Sr.	John N. Pardun, Sr.	2002	198
21 10/16	13 9/16	8 5/16	Garfield Co., CO	Robert C. Maurer	Robert C. Maurer	2003	198
21 9/16	13 4/16	8 6/16	Collbran, CO	O.K. Clifton	O.K. Clifton	1955	227
21 9/16	13 3/16	8 3/16	Williams Fork Rive:, CO	Clyde Stehle	C. Stehle & J. Grove	1957	227
21 9/16	13 6/16	8 5/16	Vilas Co., WI	Neal Long Taxidermy	WI Dept. of Natl. Resc.	1958	227
21 9/16	13 4/16	8 4/16	Mesa Co., CO	Hartle V. Morris	Hartle V. Morris	1959	227
21 9/16	13 5/16	8 2/16	Clinton Co., PA	Donald Sorgen	Donald Sorgen	1962	227
21 9/16	13 7/16	8 7/16	Vilas Co., WI	John J. Volkmann	John J. Volkmann	1968	227
21 9/16	13 2/16	8 5/16	Ouray Co., CO	Thomas C. Middleton	Thomas C. Middleton	1973	227
21 9/16	13 4/16	8 3/16	Zeballos, BC	Gary M. Biggar	Gary M. Biggar	1978	227
21 9/16	13 6/16	7 14/16	Catron Co., NM	Sam Ray	Sam Ray	1983	227
21 9/16	13 11/16	8	Tyrrell Co., NC	Larry D. Bailey	Larry D. Bailey	1983	227
21 9/16	13 9/16	8 6/16	Tioga Co., PA	Thomas B. Gamble	Thomas B. Gamble	1987	227
21 9/16	13 3/16	7 12/16	Pelican Lake, MB	Rick D. Oliphant	Rick D. Oliphant	1987	227
21 9/16	13 13/16	8 7/16	Collier Co., FL	Picked Up	FL Game & Fresh Water Fish Comm.	1988	227
21 9/16	13 7/16	8 6/16	Thorne River, AK	Ernest W. McLean	Ernest W. McLean	1989	227
21 9/16	13 7/16	8 2/16	Deena Creek, BC	William H. Hintze	William H. Hintze	1992	227
21 9/16	13 3/16	8 5/16	Burnt Bay, NL	Ewen K. Whiteway	Ewen K. Whiteway	1992	227
21 9/16	13 7/16	8 4/16	Ouray Co., CO	Lee Gabardi	Lee Gabardi	1993	227
21 9/16	13 4/16	8 1/16	Sawyer Co., WI	Kevin R. Samuel	Kevin R. Samuel	1993	227
21 9/16	13 8/16	8 8/16	Dunn Co., WI	Richard E. Anderson	Richard E. Anderson	1995	227
21 9/16	13 1/16	8 9/16	Rusk Co., WI	Dennis F. Grimme	Dennis F. Grimme	1995	227
21 9/16	13 1/16	8 8/16	Simonette River, AB	Kirk G. Garner	Kirk G. Garner	1997	227
21 9/16	13	8 8/16	Carbon Co., PA	Elwood P. Yaich	Elwood P. Yaich	1997	227
21 9/16	13 1/16	8 8/16	Prince of Wales Island, AK	David K. Mueller	David K. Mueller	1998	227
21 9/16	13 7/16	8 2/16	Chitek Lake, SK	Steve Grassmid	Steve Grassmid	2000	227
21 9/16	13 12/16	7 13/16	Oconto Co., WI	Todd E. Lackey	Todd E. Lackey	2000	227
21 9/16	13 5/16	8 4/16	Price Co., WI	Troy M. Collins	Troy M. Collins	2001	227
21 9/16	13 7/16	8 2/16	Mantagao Lake, MB	Bruce V. Huewan	Bruce V. Huewan	2001	227
21 9/16			Delta Co., CO	Bryan Livengood	Bryan Livengood	2001	227

147

BLACK BEAR

Ursus americanus americanus and related subspecies

Score	Greatest Length of Skull Without Lower Jaw	Greatest Width of Skull	Locality	Hunter	Owner	Date Killed	Rank
21 9/16	13 4/16	8 5/16	Shawano Co., WI	Dale Van Gheem	Dale Van Gheem	2001	227
21 9/16	13 5/16	8 4/16	Comox Lake, BC	Chantelle R. Bartsch	Chantelle R. Bartsch	2002	227
21 9/16	13 5/16	8 4/16	Prince of Wales Island, AK	Ian K. Chase-Dunn	Ian K. Chase-Dunn	2002	227
21 9/16	13 3/16	8 6/16	Navajo Co., AZ	Lon Hoffman	Lon Hoffman	2002	227
21 9/16	13 5/16	8 4/16	Saddle Hills, AB	David W. Watson	David W. Watson	2003	227
21 8/16	13 1/16	8 7/16	Gallatin River, WY	J.P.V. Evans	U.S. Natl. Museum	1914	261
21 8/16	13 9/16	7 15/16	Bayfield Co., WI	Earl B. Johnson	Earl B. Johnson	1953	261
21 8/16	13 8/16	8	Lincoln Co., WY	Picked Up	Matt Failoni, Jr.	1965	261
21 8/16	13 5/16	8 3/16	Forest Co., WI	Richard Ruthven	WI Buck & Bear Club	1968	261
21 8/16	13 5/16	8 3/16	Chiricahua Butte, AZ	W.O. Morrison	W.O. Morrison	1969	261
21 8/16	13 6/16	8 2/16	Lincoln Co., WY	Charles R. Nixon	Charles R. Nixon	1973	261
21 8/16	13 7/16	8 1/16	Augusta Co., VA	Joseph R. Lam	Joseph R. Lam	1977	261
21 8/16	13 4/16	8 4/16	Ventura Co., CA	James B. Wade	James B. Wade	1977	261
21 8/16	13 1/16	8 7/16	Apache Co., AZ	Joseph H. Lyman	Fred Peters	1978	261
21 8/16	13 7/16	8 1/16	Rossburn, MB	Unknown	Randall J. Bean	1980	261
21 8/16	13 3/16	8 5/16	Garfield Co., CO	Robert W. Jackson	Robert W. Jackson	1980	261
21 8/16	12 14/16	8 10/16	Harrison Hot Springs, BC	Domenico Abbinante	Domenico Abbinante	1982	261
21 8/16	13 5/16	8 3/16	Bonneville Co., ID	George R. Adams	George R. Adams	1982	261
21 8/16	13 6/16	8 2/16	Gila Co., AZ	Rick Corven	R. Corven & R. Gifford	1983	261
21 8/16	13	8 8/16	Pike Co., PA	Paul D. Longenbach	Paul D. Longenbach	1983	261
21 8/16	13 11/16	7 13/16	Douglas Co., WI	Picked Up	WI Dept. of Natl. Resc.	1984	261
21 8/16	13 6/16	8 2/16	Marshall Co., MN	James E. Kelley	J. & B. Zimpel	1984	261
21 8/16	12 15/16	8 9/16	Mesa Co., CO	Rem B. Bennett, Jr.	Rem B. Bennett, Jr.	1986	261
21 8/16	13 6/16	8 2/16	Navajo Co., AZ	Fred Peters	Fred Peters	1987	261
21 8/16	13 10/16	7 14/16	Sarkar Creek, AK	Robert F. Ellebruch	Robert F. Ellebruch	1988	261
21 8/16	13 5/16	8 3/16	Lake Co., FL	Picked Up	FL Game & Fresh Water Fish Comm.	1989	261
21 8/16	13 4/16	8 4/16	Gila Co., AZ	Don Hoey	Don Hoey	1989	261
21 8/16	13 3/16	8 5/16	Stove Lake, SK	David Prince	David Prince	1990	261
21 8/16	13 2/16	8 6/16	Clinton Co., NY	Todd F. Rabideau	Todd F. Rabideau	1990	261
21 8/16	13 4/16	8 4/16	Prince of Wales Island, AK	James W. Cook	James W. Cook	1992	261
21 8/16	13 5/16	8 3/16	McKean Co., PA	Donald L. Magno	Donald L. Magno	1992	261
21 8/16	13 6/16	8 2/16	Westmoreland Co., PA	Wayne E. Toth	Wayne E. Toth	1993	261
21 8/16	13 11/16	7 13/16	Bradford Co., PA	Robert C. Beebe	Robert C. Beebe	1994	261
21 8/16	13 5/16	8 3/16	Bladen Co., NC	Michael Burgess	Michael Burgess	1994	261
21 8/16	13 7/16	8 1/16	Piney, MB	Paul E. Asmundson	Paul E. Asmundson	1995	261
21 8/16	13 7/16	8 1/16	Florence Co., WI	Richard T. Slattery	Richard T. Slattery	1995	261
21 8/16	13 6/16	8 2/16	Sullivan Co., PA	John C. Koller	John C. Koller	1996	261
21 8/16	13 1/16	8 7/16	Grant Co., NM	Mark J. Miller	Mark J. Miller	1996	261

Score	Length	Width	Locality	Hunter	Owner	Date	Rank
21 8/16	13	8 8/16	Sandoval Co., NM	Thomas D. Stromei	Thomas D. Stromei	1996	261
21 8/16	13 11/16	7 13/16	Rennell Sound, BC	Philip Giesbrecht	Philip Giesbrecht	1997	261
21 8/16	13 5/16	8 3/16	Two Hills Lake, AB	Lionel L. Rogers	Lionel L. Rogers	1997	261
21 8/16	13 3/16	8 5/16	Prince of Wales Island, AK	Eric H. Wietfeld	Eric H. Wietfeld	1997	261
21 8/16	13 7/16	8 1/16	Sullivan Co., NY	Frederick A. DeBoer	Frederick A. DeBoer	1998	261
21 8/16	13 4/16	8 4/16	Jefferson Co., PA	Lanny L. Kunselman	Lanny L. Kunselman	1998	261
21 8/16	14 1/16	7 7/16	Washington Co., NC	Don W. Noah	Don W. Noah	1998	261
21 8/16	13 4/16	8 4/16	Burnett Co., WI	Daniel R. Sylte	Daniel R. Sylte	1998	261
21 8/16	13 10/16	7 14/16	Beaufort Co., NC	Danny L. Bowling	Danny L. Bowling	2000	261
21 8/16	13 10/16	7 14/16	Sawyer Co., WI	James M. Slepika, Sr.	James M. Slepika, Sr.	2000	261
21 8/16	13 8/16	8	Duck Mt., MB	Jeffrey A. Lute	Jeffrey A. Lute	2001	261
21 8/16	13 12/16	7 12/16	Lycoming Co., PA	Anthony F. Campana	Anthony F. Campana	2002	261
21 8/16	13 8/16	8	Clam Cove, AK	Thomas J. Stevens	Thomas J. Stevens	2003	261
21 7/16	13 2/16	8 5/16	Mariposa Co., CA	Bert Palmberg	Bert Palmberg	1957	307
21 7/16	13 2/16	8 5/16	Wales Is., AK	L.R. Hall	Picked Up	1962	307
21 7/16	13 3/16	8 4/16	Megal Mt., NL	Ben Hillicoss	Ben Hillicoss	1963	307
21 7/16	13 7/16	8	Albemarle Co., VA	Grover F. Sites	Grover F. Sites	1964	307
21 7/16	13 3/16	8 4/16	Pierce Co., WA	Tracy Johnson	T. Johnson & B. Paque	1968	307
21 7/16	13 6/16	8 1/16	McKean Co., PA	PA Game Comm.	Picked Up	1969	307
21 7/16	13 4/16	8 3/16	Douglas Co., WI	Kenneth J. Burton	Kenneth J. Burton	1972	307
21 7/16	13	8 7/16	Nordegg, AB	Leo F. Hermary	Leo F. Hermary	1977	307
21 7/16	13 4/16	8 3/16	Pierceland, SK	Bryce Burgess	Bryce Burgess	1980	307
21 7/16	13 12/16	7 11/16	Sevier Co., UT	Milton L. Robb	Milton L. Robb	1980	307
21 7/16	13 4/16	8 4/16	Iron Co., WI	Gary G. Johnson	Gary G. Johnson	1982	307
21 7/16	13 10/16	7 13/16	Flat Lake, AB	Dale Loosemore	Dale Loosemore	1983	307
21 7/16	13 8/16	7 15/16	Simonette River, AB	Richard Mellon	Richard Mellon	1983	307
21 7/16	13 4/16	8 3/16	Gila Co., AZ	D. Highly Falkner	D. Highly Falkner	1984	307
21 7/16	13 3/16	8 4/16	Cholmondeley Sound, AK	Philip A. Indovina	Philip A. Indovina	1984	307
21 7/16	13 11/16	7 12/16	Peesane, SK	Peter Janzen	Peter Janzen	1984	307
21 7/16	13 3/16	8 4/16	Fox Creek, AB	William Hellebrand	William Hellebrand	1985	307
21 7/16	13 4/16	8 3/16	Tokeen, AK	Terry D. Denmon	Terry D. Denmon	1986	307
21 7/16	13 2/16	8 1/16	Somerset Co., PA	Ralph T. Meyers	Ralph T. Meyers	1987	307
21 7/16	13 6/16	7 14/16	Loon Lake, SK	Wyatt Barnes	Wyatt Barnes	1988	307
21 7/16	13 9/16	8	Smoky River, AB	Gary G. Dumdei	Gary G. Dumdei	1989	307
21 7/16	13 7/16	8 1/16	Kupreanof Island, AK	David K. Mueller	David K. Mueller	1989	307
21 7/16	13 6/16	8 5/16	Carrot River, SK	Hanz F. Meyer	Hanz F. Meyer	1991	307
21 7/16	13 2/16	8 1/16	Douglas Co., WI	Richard J. Rohlfs	Richard J. Rohlfs	1991	307
21 7/16	13 11/16	7 12/16	Gordondale, AB	Zigmund J. Kertenis, Jr.	Zigmund J. Kertenis, Jr.	1993	307
21 7/16	13 6/16	8 1/16	Clearfield Co., PA	James A. Mihalko	James A. Mihalko	1993	307
21 7/16	13 4/16	8 3/16	Roseau Co., MN	Kevin D. Johnson	Kevin D. Johnson	1994	307
21 7/16	13 2/16	8 5/16	McAuley, MB	Jamie B. Poole	Jamie B. Poole	1994	307
21 7/16	13 2/16	8 1/16	Price Co., WI	Donald L. Cramer	Peter E. Dickmann	1996	307
21 7/16	13 1/16	8 6/16	Montmorency Co., MI	R. Dennis Desgrange	R. Dennis Desgrange	1996	307
21 7/16	13 1/16	7 15/16	Ventura Co., CA	Mark Karluk	Mark Karluk	1996	307
21 7/16	13 8/16	8 7/16	Clinch Co., GA	Danny Hinson	Danny Hinson	1997	307
21 7/16	13	8	Menominee Co., MI	Jacqueline M. Piatt	Jacqueline M. Piatt	1997	307
21 7/16	13 10/16	7 13/16	Poplarfield, MB	Stephen R. Mills	Stephen R. Mills	1999	307

BLACK BEAR

Ursus americanus americanus and related subspecies

Score	Greatest Length of Skull Without Lower Jaw	Greatest Width of Skull	Locality	Hunter	Owner	Date Killed	Rank
21 7/16	13 6/16	8 1/16	Burnett Co., WI	Craig M. Wyszynski	Craig M. Wyszynski	1999	307
21 7/16	13 1/16	8 6/16	Mendocino Co., CA	Ronald L. Koch	Ronald L. Koch	2000	307
21 7/16	13 6/16	8 1/16	Bayfield Co., WI	Jane M. Paulson	Jane M. Paulson	2000	307
21 7/16	13 6/16	8 1/16	Becker Co., MN	Michael J. Honek	Michael J. Honek	2001	307
21 7/16	13 4/16	8 3/16	Burnett Co., WI	Picked Up	Bill Klugow	2001	307
21 7/16	13 8/16	7 15/16	Sawyer Co., WI	Daniel A. Solie	Daniel A. Solie	2001	307
21 7/16	13 12/16	7 11/16	Rusk Co., WI	Audrey M. Vandeberg	Audrey M. Vandeberg	2002	307
21 7/16	13 3/16	8 4/16	Sheffield Lake, NL	Jerry L. Beck	Jerry L. Beck	2003	307
21 6/16	13 1/16	8 5/16	Prince of Wales Island, AK	Picked Up	Robert Kase	PR 1954	349
21 6/16	13 13/16	7 9/16	Sandpoint, ID	Ronald L. Book	Ronald L. Book	1969	349
21 6/16	12 12/16	8 10/16	Franklin Co., NY	James Donner	James Donner	1970	349
21 6/16	13 5/16	8 1/16	Reserve, NM	C.J. McElroy	C.J. McElroy	1970	349
21 6/16	13 11/16	7 11/16	Pike Co., PA	Robert Loux	Robert Loux	1971	349
21 6/16	13 2/16	8 4/16	Prince of Wales Island, AK	John Stubbs	John Stubbs	1973	349
21 6/16	13 6/16	8	Bayfield Co., WI	Larry L. Frye	Larry L. Frye	1975	349
21 6/16	13 10/16	7 12/16	Carbon Co., UT	R. Peterson & R.S. Hardy	Rex W. Peterson	1975	349
21 6/16	13	8 6/16	Humboldt Co., CA	Dean Earley	Dean Earley	1977	349
21 6/16	12 13/16	8 9/16	Pitkin Co., CO	Chris Green	Chris Green	1980	349
21 6/16	13 2/16	8 4/16	Thorne Bay, AK	Tod L. Reichert	Tod L. Reichert	1985	349
21 6/16	13 3/16	8 3/16	Klawock, AK	Tom R. Engel	Tom R. Engel	1987	349
21 6/16	13 6/16	8	Grant Co., WV	Carnie Carr, Sr.	Carnie Carr, Sr.	1988	349
21 6/16	13 7/16	7 15/16	Graham Co., AZ	Timm J. Haas	Timm J. Haas	1988	349
21 6/16	13 8/16	7 14/16	Cattaraugus Co., NY	John M. Abrams, Sr.	John M. Abrams, Sr.	1989	349
21 6/16	13 5/16	8 1/16	Potter Co., PA	Earl E. Carolus	Earl E. Carolus	1989	349
21 6/16	12 13/16	8 9/16	Craven Co., NC	Todd A. Brewer	Todd A. Brewer	1991	349
21 6/16	13 2/16	8 4/16	York Co., NB	Kenneth J. Fluck	Kenneth J. Fluck	1991	349
21 6/16	13 1/16	8 5/16	Mendocino Co., CA	R. Larry Hyder	R. Larry Hyder	1991	349
21 6/16	13 4/16	8 2/16	Plumas Co., CA	Monty D. McCormick	Monty D. McCormick	1992	349
21 6/16	13 4/16	8 2/16	Taylor Co., WI	Kenneth R. Cisewski	Kenneth R. Cisewski	1993	349
21 6/16	13 5/16	8 1/16	Gila Co., AZ	Becky Jo Smith	Becky Jo Smith	1993	349
21 6/16	12 14/16	8 8/16	Mendocino Co., CA	Lawrence E. Taylor	Lawrence E. Taylor	1993	349
21 6/16	13 5/16	8 1/16	Menominee Co., MI	Linda K. Nowack	Linda K. Nowack	1995	349
21 6/16	13 4/16	8 2/16	Price Co., WI	Patrick H. Sheldon	Patrick H. Sheldon	1995	349
21 6/16	13 10/16	7 12/16	Mahnomen Co., MN	Michael J. Ahles	Michael J. Ahles	1996	349
21 6/16	13 7/16	7 15/16	Oakburn, MB	Marv Biadasz	Marv Biadasz	1996	349
21 6/16	13 4/16	8 2/16	Clark Co., WI	Larry L. Osegard	Larry L. Osegard	1996	349
21 6/16	13 4/16	8 2/16	Clearfield Co., PA	Barry R. Henry	Barry R. Henry	1997	349
21 6/16	13 6/16	8	Otter Lake, MB	Timothy J. Laha	Timothy J. Laha	1997	349

Score	Length	Width	Locality	Hunter	Owner	Date	Rank
21 6/16	13 3/16	8 3/16	McBride Lake, SK	Dennis H. Hextall	Dennis H. Hextall	1999	349
21 6/16	13 4/16	8 2/16	Pamlico Co., NC	Randall K. Russell	Randall K. Russell	1999	349
21 6/16	13 4/16	8 2/16	Tehama Co., CA	Picked Up	Matthew A. Reno	2000	349
21 6/16	13 4/16	8 2/16	Tyrrell Co., NC	Terry L. Sherman	Terry L. Sherman	2000	349
21 6/16	13 3/16	8 3/16	Prince of Wales Island, AK	Picked Up	James F. Baichtal	2001	349
21 6/16	13 6/16	8	Ventura Co., CA	Kevin J. Edwards	Kevin J. Edwards	2001	349
21 6/16	13 10/16	7 12/16	Hyde Co., NC	James P. Pridgen	James P. Pridgen	2001	349
21 6/16	13 6/16	8	Catron Co., NM	Ernest R. Gutierrez	Ernest R. Gutierrez	2002	349
21 6/16	13 10/16	7 12/16	Lac du Bonnet, MB	Jason M. Singbeil	Jason M. Singbeil	2002	349
21 6/16	13 2/16	8 4/16	Ashland Co., WI	James D. Truttschel	James D.Truttschel	2002	349
21 6/16	13 2/16	8 4/16	Mesa Co., CO	M. Scott Ghan	M. Scott Ghan	2003	349
21 5/16	13 1/16	8 4/16	Colorado	E.T. Seton	U.S. Natl. Museum	1897	390
21 5/16	12 15/16	8 6/16	Yarmouth Co., NS	John L. Bastey	John L. Bastey	1945	390
21 5/16	13 4/16	8 1/16	Centre Co., PA	Picked Up	Wayne B. Harpster	1946	390
21 5/16	13 3/16	8 2/16	Rockbridge Co., VA	Richard L. Merchant	Richard L. Merchant	1953	390
21 5/16	13	8 5/16	Buffalo Park, CO	John L. Howard	John L. Howard	1958	390
21 5/16	13 5/16	8	Coburn Lake, CA	Lauren A. Johnson	Lauren A. Johnson	1960	390
21 5/16	13 2/16	8 3/16	Olympic Pen., WA	Bert Klineburger	Bert Klineburger	1963	390
21 5/16	12 15/16	8 6/16	Cynthia, AB	R. LeVoir	R. LeVoir	1968	390
21 5/16	13 5/16	8	Mendocino Co., CA	Gene H. Whitney	Gene H. Whitney	1971	390
21 5/16	13 5/16	8	Vilas Co., WI	Michael G. Duwe	Michael G. Duwe	1972	390
21 5/16	13 4/16	8 1/16	Lincoln Co., WY	Gregg G. Fisher	Gregg G. Fisher	1975	390
21 5/16	13 7/16	7 14/16	Gila Co., AZ	Larry S. Behrends	Larry S. Behrends	1976	390
21 5/16	13 11/16	7 10/16	Langlade Co., WI	Michael Steliga	Michael Steliga	1981	390
21 5/16	13 5/16	8	Santa Barbara Co., CA	Picked Up	John L. Mussell	1982	390
21 5/16	13 8/16	7 13/16	Rockingham Co., VA	Roger O. Wyant	Roger O. Wyant	1984	390
21 5/16	13	8 5/16	Mendocino Co., CA	John Jacobs	John Jacobs	1985	390
21 5/16	13 2/16	8 3/16	Navajo Co., AZ	D. Howard Mullins	D. Howard Mullins	1986	390
21 5/16	13 4/16	8 1/16	Gila Co., AZ	Neil L. Sullivan	Neil L. Sullivan	1986	390
21 5/16	13 8/16	7 13/16	Pine Co., MN	Harland Johnson	Harland Johnson	PR 1987	390
21 5/16	13 3/16	8 2/16	Prince of Wales Island, AK	Mark S. Rodin	Mark S. Rodin	1987	390
21 5/16	13	8 5/16	Rio Blanco Co., CO	Jason Steiner	Jason Steiner	1987	390
21 5/16	13 2/16	8 3/16	Potter Co., PA	Gary R. Sellers	Gary R. Sellers	1989	390
21 5/16	13 8/16	7 13/16	Hudson Bay, SK	Jim Strini	Jim Strini	1989	390
21 5/16	13 3/16	8 2/16	Rusk Co., WI	James J. Heberlein	James J. Heberlein	1990	390
21 5/16	13 6/16	7 15/16	Swan River, MB	Linda A. Nuss	Linda A. Nuss	1990	390
21 5/16	12 14/16	8 7/16	Sawyer Co., WI	Mark R. Heath	Mark R. Heath	1991	390
21 5/16	13 6/16	7 15/16	Swan River, MB	Richard C. Weber	Richard C. Weber	1991	390
21 5/16	13 13/16	7 8/16	Sawyer Co., WI	Stephan E. Bouton	Stephan E. Bouton	1992	390
21 5/16	13 2/16	8 3/16	Forest Co., PA	Raymond A. Egan III	Raymond A. Egan III	1992	390
21 5/16	13 4/16	8 1/16	Meadow Lake, SK	Jack B. Kambeitz	Jack B. Kambeitz	1992	390
21 5/16	13 2/16	8 3/16	Kuiu Island, AK	David K. Mueller	David K. Mueller	1992	390
21 5/16	12 12/16	8 9/16	Williams Creek, BC	Wayne P. Topolewski	Wayne P. Topolewski	1992	390
21 5/16	13 4/16	8 1/16	Round Lake, SK	Floyd Forster	Floyd Forster	1994	390
21 5/16	13 7/16	7 14/16	Rossburn, MB	Curtis L. Hahn	Curtis L. Hahn	1994	390
21 5/16	12 15/16	8 6/16	Garfield Co., CO	Ted R. Bina	Ted R. Bina	1995	390
21 5/16	13 9/16	7 12/16	Deep Lake, MB	Kenneth B. Cherepak	Kenneth B. Cherepak	1995	390

BLACK BEAR

Ursus americanus americanus and related subspecies

Score	Greatest Length of Skull Without Lower Jaw	Greatest Width of Skull	Locality	Hunter	Owner	Date Killed	Rank
21 5/16	13 6/16	7 15/16	Horseshoe Lake, AB	Darren Daniel	Darren Daniel	1995	390
21 5/16	13 5/16	8	Shawano Co., WI	Scott A. Johnson	Scott A. Johnson	1995	390
21 5/16	13	8 5/16	San Bernardino Co., CA	Rahul T. Mathur	Rahul T. Mathur	1995	390
21 5/16	13 5/16	8	Lincoln Co., WI	Richard H. Rollmann	Richard H. Rollmann	1995	390
21 5/16	13 11/16	7 10/16	Hyde Co., NC	David M. Blalock	David M. Blalock	1996	390
21 5/16	13 2/16	8 3/16	Falher, AB	Stephen L. Collins	Stephen L. Collins	1996	390
21 5/16	13	8 5/16	Delaware Co., NY	William S. Hoover	William S. Hoover	1996	390
21 5/16	13 3/16	8 2/16	Prince of Wales Island, AK	David K. Mueller	David K. Mueller	1996	390
21 5/16	13 1/16	8 4/16	Carswell Lake, SK	David A. Whitcomb	David A. Whitcomb	1996	390
21 5/16	13 1/16	8 4/16	Beltrami Co., MN	Deloris M. Ekstrom	Deloris M. Ekstrom	1997	390
21 5/16	13 4/16	8 1/16	Washington Co., NC	Michael T. McCorquodale	Michael T. McCorquodale	1997	390
21 5/16	13 15/16	7 6/16	Stenen, SK	J. Stephen Williams	J. Stephen Williams	1997	390
21 5/16	13 4/16	8 1/16	Gunnison Co., CO	Brian Curtis	Brian Curtis	1998	390
21 5/16	13 5/16	8 1/16	Aitkin Co., MN	Wayne E. Haeg	Wayne E. Haeg	1998	390
21 5/16	13 6/16	7 15/16	Wolf Lake, AB	W.E. Haeg & M.K. Kiekow	Thomas G. Lester	1998	390
21 5/16	13 2/16	8 3/16	El Capitan Peak, AK	Thomas G. Lester	Steven R. Martin	1998	390
21 5/16	13 1/16	8 4/16	Red Deer River, SK	Steven R. Martin	William A. Pace	1998	390
21 5/16	13 5/16	8 4/16	Gila Co., AZ	William A. Pace	Richard S. Rosenberg	1998	390
21 5/16	13 3/16	8	Hyde Co., NC	Richard S. Rosenberg	Thomas C. Rowland III	1998	390
21 5/16	12 15/16	8 6/16	Mono Co., CA	Thomas C. Rowland III	Gregory W. Brackett	1999	390
21 5/16	13 7/16	8	Portage Co., WI	Gregory W. Brackett	Craig E. Solinsky	1999	390
21 5/16	13 5/16	7 14/16	Nechako River, BC	Craig E. Solinsky	Dean McNolty	1999	390
21 5/16	13 8/16	8	Rossburn, MB	Dean McNolty	William E. Clink	2000	390
21 5/16	13 13/16	7 13/16	Cass Co., MN	William E. Clink	Mike Mellema	2001	390
21 5/16	13 13/16	7 8/16	Shawano Co., WI	Mike Mellema	Diane M Henry	2001	390
21 5/16	13 11/16	7 13/16	Washburn Co., WI	Diane M Henry	Armand D. Van Vleet	2002	390
21 5/16	13 13/16	7 11/16	Rossman Lake, MB	Armand D. Van Vleet	John R. Evans	2002	390
21 5/16	13 11/16	7 10/16	Buckingham Co., VA	John R. Evans	Michael D. Nixon	2003	390
21 4/16	13 3/16	8 1/16	Cochise Co., AZ	Michael D. Nixon	Univ. of CA Museum	2003	454
21 4/16	13 6/16	7 14/16	Los Angeles Co., CA	Unknown	Anselmo Lewis	1928	454
21 4/16	13 6/16	7 14/16	Shoshone River, WY	Picked Up	Loren L. Lutz	1952	454
21 4/16	13 8/16	7 12/16	Michigan	Loren L. Lutz	Albert Erickson	1956	454
21 4/16	13 2/16	8 2/16	Arizona	Albert Erickson	Paul B. Reynolds	1957	454
21 4/16	12 11/16	7 11/16	Olympic Pen., WA	Paul B. Reynolds	Bert Klineburger	1965	454
21 4/16	12 12/16	8 8/16	Curry Co., OR	Bert Klineburger	Joe W. Latimer	1967	454
21 4/16	12 11/16	8 9/16	Sawyer Co., WI	Joe W. Latimer	Ted Roberts	1968	454
21 4/16	13 1/16	8 3/16	Hudson Bay, SK	Ted Roberts	Neil Southam	1968	454
21 4/16	13 1/16	8 3/16	Williams Co., AZ	Neil Southam	James E. Coy	1969	454
21 4/16	13 1/16	8 3/16			James E. Coy	1970	454

152

Score			Locality	Hunter	Owner	Date Killed	Rank
21 4/16	13 6/16	7 14/16	Snowmass, CO	Ronald D. Vincent	Ronald D. Vincent	1974	454
21 4/16	13	8 4/16	Marquette Co., MI	David L. Pietro	David L. Pietro	1975	454
21 4/16	13 7/16	7 13/16	Tehama Co., CA	Jim Cox	Jim Cox	1980	454
21 4/16	13 7/16	7 13/16	Pinal Co., AZ	Bruce R. Gifford	Bruce R. Gifford	1980	454
21 4/16	13 2/16	8 2/16	Khyex River, BC	Edward Dickens	Edward Dickens	1982	454
21 4/16	13 2/16	8 2/16	Sawyer Co., WI	Harvey W. Klein	Harvey W. Klein	1982	454
21 4/16	13 4/16	8	Vanderhoof, BC	William Stanley	William Stanley	1985	454
21 4/16	13	8 4/16	Mille Lacs Co., MN	Timothy J. Dusbabek	Timothy J. Dusbabek	1987	454
21 4/16	13 7/16	7 13/16	Greenlee Co., AZ	Bart Bledsoe	Bart Bledsoe	1988	454
21 4/16	13 1/16	8 3/16	Navajo Co., AZ	Fred Peters	Fred Peters	1988	454
21 4/16	13 5/16	7 15/16	Catron Co., NM	Gary L. Raney	Gary L. Raney	1988	454
21 4/16	13 2/16	8 2/16	Peace River, BC	Ivan Brausse	Ivan Brausse	1989	454
21 4/16	13 2/16	8 2/16	Pasquia Hills, SK	Patrick G. Povah	Patrick G. Povah	1989	454
21 4/16	13	8 4/16	Aroostook Co., ME	John S. Drost	John S. Drost	1990	454
21 4/16	13 9/16	7 11/16	Shasta Co., CA	Richard L. Moore	Richard L. Moore	1990	454
21 4/16	13 3/16	8 1/16	Crow Wing Co., MN	Robert H. Hartigan	Robert H. Hartigan	1991	454
21 4/16	12 15/16	8 5/16	Alpena Co., MI	Fred C. Webber	Fred C. Webber	1992	454
21 4/16	13	8 4/16	Cass Co., MN	Bradley T. Anderson	Bradley T. Anderson	1993	454
21 4/16	13 4/16	8	Greenlee Co., AZ	Brody J. Bonnett	Brody J. Bonnett	1993	454
21 4/16	13 4/16	8 2/16	Prince of Wales Island, AK	George P. Mann	George P. Mann	1993	454
21 4/16	13 2/16	8	Menominee Co., MI	Todd D. Powers	Todd D. Powers	1993	454
21 4/16	13 5/16	8 2/16	Mendocino Co., CA	Steven W. Shelton	Steven W. Shelton	1993	454
21 4/16	13 2/16	7 15/16	Greenlee Co., AZ	Steven J. Stayner	Picked Up	1993	454
21 4/16	13 6/16	8 2/16	Gila Co., AZ	Fred Peters	Fred Peters	1994	454
21 4/16	13 6/16	7 14/16	Prince of Wales Island, AK	Carl F. Sellers	Carl F. Sellers	1994	454
21 4/16	13 7/16	7 14/16	Lake Mantagao, MB	Joseph D. Belas	Joseph D. Belas	1995	454
21 4/16	13 8/16	8	Wadena Co., MN	Bonita G. Newhouse	Bonita G. Newhouse	1995	454
21 4/16	12 14/16	7 13/16	Porcupine Plain, SK	Royce P. Reavley	Royce P. Reavley	1995	454
21 4/16	13 4/16	7 12/16	Chippewa Co., WI	Lavern M. Vetterkind	Lavern M. Vetterkind	1995	454
21 4/16	13 8/16	8 6/16	Graham Co., AZ	Tommie Harendt	Tommie Harendt	1996	454
21 4/16	13 1/16	8	Greenlee Co., AZ	Bill Hudzietz	Bill Hudzietz	1996	454
21 4/16	13	7 12/16	Beltrami Co., MN	Larry D. Johnson	Picked Up	1996	454
21 4/16	13 12/16	8 3/16	Gila Co., AZ	Leonardo E. Murdock	Leonardo E. Murdock	1996	454
21 4/16	13 10/16	8 4/16	Roanoke Co., VA	Chester A. Scott	Chester A. Scott	1996	454
21 4/16	13	7 8/16	Mille Lacs Co., MN	James Schug	James Schug	1998	454
21 4/16	13 4/16	7 10/16	Hyde Co., NC	Daniel A. Hoffler	Daniel A. Hoffler	1999	454
21 4/16	13 4/16	8 4/16	Mink Creek, MB	Leonard R. Bull	Leonard R. Bull	2000	454
21 4/16	13 5/16	7 14/16	Prince of Wales Island, AK	Brian Crawford	Brian Crawford	2000	454
21 4/16	13 6/16	8	Sanpete Co., UT	Justin Rasmussen	Justin Rasmussen	2000	454
21 4/16	13 6/16	7 15/16	Chippewa Co., WI	Rick A. Sokup	Rick A. Sokup	2000	454
21 4/16	13 3/16	7 14/16	Oscoda Co., MI	Gus Harris	Gus Harris	2001	454
21 4/16	13 3/16	7 14/16	Richards Lake, SK	M.R. James	M.R. James	2001	454
21 4/16	13 4/16	8 2/16	Shasta Co., CA	Sal E. Santoro	Sal E. Santoro	2002	454
21 4/16	13 4/16	8 1/16	Prince of Wales Island, AK	William A. Fedorko	William A. Fedorko	2002	454
21 4/16	13 4/16	8	Price Co., WI	Tim Gehrke	Tim Gehrke	2002	454
21 4/16	13 4/16	8	Kelvington, SK	Mike J. Ryan	Mike J. Ryan	2002	454
21 4/16	13 10/16	7 10/16	King Co., WA	Tyler Seubert	Tyler Seubert	2003	454

BLACK BEAR

Ursus americanus and related subspecies

Score	Greatest Length of Skull Without Lower Jaw	Greatest Width of Skull	Locality	Hunter	Owner	Date Killed	Rank
21 3/16	13 6/16	7 13/16	Queen Charlotte Islands, BC	C. de Blois Green	Univ. of CA Museum	1911	511
21 3/16	13 2/16	8 1/16	Bayfield Co., WI	G. Michaels	Gerald M. Weber	1966	511
21 3/16	13 8/16	7 11/16	Alberta	James C. Wynne	James C. Wynne	1966	511
21 3/16	12 15/16	8 4/16	Alberta	F.A. Stromstedt	Univ. of Calgary	1967	511
21 3/16	13	8 3/16	Thurston Co., WA	Hugh M. Oliver	Hugh M. Oliver	1969	511
21 3/16	13 1/16	8 2/16	Graham Co., AZ	O. Dale Porter	O. Dale Porter	1970	511
21 3/16	12 15/16	8 4/16	Eagle Co., CO	Charles T. Coffman	Charles T. Coffman	1971	511
21 3/16	13 4/16	7 15/16	Ashland Co., WI	Herman Straubel	Herman Straubel	1972	511
21 3/16	12 13/16	8 6/16	Madison Co., MT	Gerald D. Morgan	Gerald D. Morgan	1974	511
21 3/16	13 1/16	8 2/16	Stonecliffe, ON	Robert M. Weir	Robert M. Weir	1974	511
21 3/16	13 1/16	8 2/16	Oneida Co., WI	Fred C. Hageny	Fred C. Hageny	1975	511
21 3/16	13 4/16	7 15/16	Gila Co., AZ	Kae L. Brockermeyer	Kae L. Brockermeyer	1977	511
21 3/16	12 15/16	8 4/16	Carbon Co., WY	Hugh D. Beavers, Jr.	Hugh D. Beavers, Jr.	1981	511
21 3/16	12 14/16	8 5/16	Routt Co., CO	Picked Up	Steven R. Beckwith	1981	511
21 3/16	13 3/16	8	Clinton Co., PA	Orwin W. Srock	Orwin W. Srock	1981	511
21 3/16	12 15/16	8 4/16	Slave Lake, AB	Dwight E. Diehl	Dwight E. Diehl	1982	511
21 3/16	12 11/16	8 8/16	Yolo Co., CA	Walter D. Foster	Walter D. Foster	1983	511
21 3/16	13 1/16	8 2/16	Neck Lake, AK	F.A. Lonsway, Jr.	F.A. Lonsway, Jr.	1983	511
21 3/16	13 5/16	7 14/16	McBride Lake, SK	Maurice Maurer	Maurice Maurer	1984	511
21 3/16	12 10/16	8 9/16	Chuwhels Mt., BC	Ronald J. Couture	Ronald J. Couture	1986	511
21 3/16	13 1/16	8 2/16	Valleyview, AB	Alfred Heschl	Alfred Heschl	1986	511
21 3/16	13 7/16	7 12/16	Minitonas, MB	Scott Ward	Scott Ward	1986	511
21 3/16	13 6/16	7 13/16	Washington Co., ME	John S. Barmby	John S. Barmby	1987	511
21 3/16	13 2/16	8 1/16	Lincoln Co., WI	Daniel L. Lemke	Daniel L. Lemke	1987	511
21 3/16	13 2/16	8 1/16	Whiteshell Lake, MB	Paul D. Pauls	Paul D. Pauls	1987	511
21 3/16	13 3/16	8	Mesa Co., CO	Marilyn J. Scott	Marilyn J. Scott	1987	511
21 3/16	13	8 3/16	Eaglehead Lake, ON	Ty Sweeney	Ty Sweeney	1987	511
21 3/16	12 14/16	8 5/16	Coconino Co., AZ	Russell M. Watkins	Russell M. Watkins	1987	511
21 3/16	13 4/16	7 15/16	Aitkin Co., MN	Picked Up	S. & P. Gelhar	1988	511
21 3/16	13 8/16	7 11/16	Jim Lake, SK	James A. Lynn	James A. Lynn	1988	511
21 3/16	13	8 3/16	Red Deer River, SK	Gordon Paproski	Gordon Paproski	1988	511
21 3/16	13 2/16	8 1/16	Kuiu Island, AK	Michael D. Speigle	Michael D. Speigle	1989	511
21 3/16	13 8/16	7 11/16	Westmoreland Co., PA	Clyde A. Tantlinger	Clyde A. Tantlinger	1989	511
21 3/16	13 3/16	8	Prince of Wales Island, AK	George P. Mann	George P. Mann	1990	511
21 3/16	13 1/16	8 2/16	Catron Co., NM	John M. Burton, Jr.	John M. Burton, Jr.	1991	511
21 3/16	13 6/16	7 13/16	Ft. McMurray, AB	Karl F. Falch	Karl F. Falch	1991	511
21 3/16	13 7/16	7 12/16	Canora, SK	Rodney S. Petrychyn	Rodney S. Petrychyn	1991	511
21 3/16	13 3/16	8	Prince of Wales Island, AK	L. Scott Robinson	L. Scott Robinson	1991	511
21 3/16	13 6/16	7 13/16	Fort a la Corne, SK	Larry Zens	Larry Zens	1992	511

Score	Length of Skull	Width of Skull	Locality	By Whom Killed	Owner	Date Killed	Rank
21 3/16	13 3/16	8	Oldman Lake, SK	Robert L. Fitzsimonds	Robert L. Fitzsimonds	1994	511
21 3/16	13 4/16	7 15/16	Socorro Co., NM	William F. Gorman	William F. Gorman	1994	511
21 3/16	13 6/16	7 13/16	Gila Co., AZ	Gary D. Gorsuch	Gary D. Gorsuch	1994	511
21 3/16	13 8/16	7 11/16	Georgetown Co., SC	Picked Up	SC Dept. of Natl. Resc.	1994	511
21 3/16	13 3/16	8	Greenwater Lake, ON	Kevin J. Wagner	Kevin J. Wagner	1994	511
21 3/16	13 7/16	7 12/16	Apache Co., AZ	Benny White	Benny White	1994	511
21 3/16	13 2/16	8 1/16	Lincoln Co., WI	Jesse J. Hoffman	Jesse J. Hoffman	1996	511
21 3/16	13 5/16	7 14/16	Rappahannock Co., VA	Michael A. Presgraves	Michael A. Presgraves	1997	511
21 3/16	13 3/16	8	Beaver River, SK	Jason Toews	Jason Toews	1997	511
21 3/16	13 5/16	7 14/16	Kupreanof Island, AK	Richard L. Tshudy	Richard L. Tshudy	1997	511
21 3/16	13 5/16	7 14/16	Presque Isle Co., MI	Brian M. Zdanowski	Brian M. Zdanowski	1999	511
21 3/16	12 15/16	8 4/16	Bayfield Co., WY	Michael R. Cunningham	Michael R. Cunningham	1999	511
21 3/16	13 6/16	7 13/16	Pine Falls, MB	Fred Souders	Fred Souders	1999	511
21 3/16	13 3/16	8	Pike Co., PA	Mathew J. Wierzbowski	Mathew J. Wierzbowski	2000	511
21 3/16	12 13/16	8 6/16	Morrison Co., MN	Linda Brummer	Linda Brummer	2000	511
21 3/16	13 8/16	7 11/16	Desbergeres Lake, QC	Chris S. Carson	Chris S. Carson	2000	511
21 3/16	13 1/16	8 2/16	Big River, SK	Warren K. Dugan	Warren K. Dugan	2001	511
21 3/16	12 13/16	8 6/16	Gila Co., AZ	Fred Peters	Fred Peters	2001	511
21 3/16	13	8 3/16	Besnard Lake, SK	Tony Milliken, Sr.	Tony Milliken, Sr.	2002	511
21 3/16	13 2/16	8 1/16	Koochiching Co., MN	Kirby D. Sorensen	Kirby D. Sorensen	2002	511
21 3/16	13 1/16	8 2/16	Bronson Lake, SK	Stanley C. Benson	Stanley C. Benson	2002	511
21 3/16	13 5/16	7 14/16	Oconto Co., WI	Christopher J. Burg	Christopher J. Burg	2002	511
21 3/16	13	8 3/16	Marshall Co., MN	Michael R. Powell	Michael R. Powell	2003	511
21 3/16	13 6/16	7 13/16	Prince of Wales Island, AK	William T. Stevens	William T. Stevens	2003	511
21 2/16	12 14/16	8 4/16	Beatty Brook, NB	Jay S. Conrad	Jay S. Conrad		576
21 2/16	13 1/16	8 1/16	Gila Co., AZ	Scott Keetch	Scott Keetch		576
21 2/16	13 3/16	7 15/16	Kuiu Island, AK	L.W. Potter	L.W. Potter	1951	576
21 2/16	13	8 2/16	Lincoln Co., WY	R. Langford & W.R. Ryan	Ralph Langford	1955	576
21 2/16	13 6/16	7 12/16	Essex Co., NY	William R. Waddell	NY Dept. of Env. Cons.	1955	576
21 2/16	12 12/16	8 6/16	Los Angeles Co., CA	Leo J. Reihsen	Leo J. Reihsen	1961	576
21 2/16	13 3/16	7 15/16	Mammoth Mt., CA	Clarke Merrill	Clarke Merrill	1963	576
21 2/16	13 2/16	8	Chinitna Bay, AK	Basil C. Bradbury	Basil C. Bradbury	1964	576
21 2/16	13 12/16	7 6/16	Chelan Co., WA	Virgil R. Bedient	Virgil R. Bedient	1965	576
21 2/16	12 15/16	8 3/16	Collbran, CO	R.R. Lyons & H.V. Morris	Raymond R. Lyons	1965	576
21 2/16	12 12/16	8 6/16	Shasta Co., CA	Ivan L. Marx	Ivan L. Marx	1965	576
21 2/16	13 5/16	7 13/16	Mesa Co., CO	Waldemar R. Kuenzel, Jr.	Waldemar R. Kuenzel, Jr.	1966	576
21 2/16	13	8 2/16	Trinity Co., CA	Picked Up	Robert E. Frost	1967	576
21 2/16	13	8 2/16	Raven Lake, BC	Robert G. Wardian	Robert G. Wardian	1967	576
21 2/16	12 14/16	8 4/16	Montrose Co., CO	Earl L. Markley	Earl L. Markley	1970	576
21 2/16	12 10/16	8 8/16	Clam Lake, WI	Picked Up	M. Reynolds & J. Olson	PR 1971	576
21 2/16	13 7/16	7 11/16	Sublette Co., WY	A. Jack Welch	A. Jack Welch	1971	576
21 2/16	14 1/16	7 1/16	Lake Co., CA	David C. Sharp	David C. Sharp	1972	576
21 2/16	13 3/16	7 15/16	Gila Co., AZ	Daniel J. Urban	Daniel J. Urban	1972	576
21 2/16	13 6/16	7 12/16	Gunnison Co., CO	Dick Cooper	Dick Cooper	1977	576
21 2/16	13 4/16	7 14/16	Gila Co., AZ	Robert E. Barnes	Robert E. Barnes	1978	576
21 2/16	13 1/16	8 1/16	Ethelbert, MB	Paul A. Bormes	Paul A. Bormes	1979	576
21 2/16	13 1/16	8 1/16	Lodgepole, AB	Jim H. Van Manen	Jim H. Van Manen	1979	576

Ursus americanus and related subspecies

Score	Greatest Length of Skull Without Lower Jaw	Greatest Width of Skull	Locality	Hunter	Owner	Date Killed	Rank
21 2/16	13 8/16	7 10/16	Graham Island, BC	Roger Britton	Roger Britton	1982	576
21 2/16	13 2/16	8	Fox Creek, AB	Brent E. Eeles	Brent E. Eeles	1982	576
21 2/16	13 2/16	8	Preeceville, SK	David S. Hodgin	David S. Hodgin	1982	576
21 2/16	13	8 2/16	Goose River, AB	T. Barker & R. Mompere	Thomas Barker	1983	576
21 2/16	12 12/16	8 6/16	Marquette Co., MI	Gerald J. Isetts, Sr.	Gerald J. Isetts, Sr.	1984	576
21 2/16	13 3/16	7 15/16	Hudson Bay, SK	Neil Southam	Neil Southam	1984	576
21 2/16	13	8 2/16	Terra Nova River, NL	James A. Young	James A. Young	1984	576
21 2/16	13 2/16	8	Montmorency Co., MI	Kenneth R. Reed	Kenneth R. Reed	1986	576
21 2/16	12 12/16	8 6/16	Hamilton Co., NY	Kerry Rogers	Kerry Rogers	1986	576
21 2/16	12 15/16	8 3/16	Gallatin Co., MT	Steven M. Steele	Steven M. Steele	1986	576
21 2/16	13	8 2/16	Caribou Co., ID	Ronald J. Thompson	Ronald J. Thompson	1987	576
21 2/16	13 3/16	7 15/16	Beltrami Co., MN	Douglas P. Budensiek	Douglas P. Budensiek	1987	576
21 2/16	13 9/16	7 9/16	Gila Co., AZ	Jesse L. Enterkin, Jr.	Jesse L. Enterkin, Jr.	1987	576
21 2/16	13 8/16	7 10/16	Marco, MB	Erwin Weidenfeld	Erwin Weidenfeld	1988	576
21 2/16	12 13/16	8 5/16	Pencil Lake, ON	Michael F. Gerber	Michael F. Gerber	1988	576
21 2/16	13 3/16	7 15/16	Cass Co., MN	Toni M. Gross	Toni M. Gross	1988	576
21 2/16	13 8/16	7 10/16	Burnett Co., WI	Bill Klugow	Bill Klugow	1988	576
21 2/16	13 2/16	8	Kuiu Island, AK	Robert M. Teskey	Robert M. Teskey	1988	576
21 2/16	13 4/16	7 14/16	Turtle Lake, SK	Tony L. Johnson	Tony L. Johnson	1989	576
21 2/16	13 2/16	8	Cold Lake, AB	Dean Herron	Dean Herron	1990	576
21 2/16	13 3/16	7 15/16	Bjorkdale, SK	Clayton R. Shiels	Clayton R. Shiels	1990	576
21 2/16	12 14/16	8 4/16	Humboldt Co., CA	Conrad H. Will	Conrad H. Will	1990	576
21 2/16	13 4/16	7 14/16	Chinaman Lake, BC	Fred Becker	Fred Becker	1991	576
21 2/16	13 4/16	7 14/16	Craven Co., NC	Eddie C. Bridges	Eddie C. Bridges	1991	576
21 2/16	13 1/16	8 1/16	Moresby Island, BC	Roger W. Robinson	Roger W. Robinson	1991	576
21 2/16	12 12/16	8 6/16	Mitkof Island, AK	Robert W. Anderson	Robert W. Anderson	1993	576
21 2/16	13	8 2/16	Rogersville, NB	Larry Dominguez	Larry Dominguez	1993	576
21 2/16	13 1/16	8 1/16	King Co., WA	Timothy C. Fish	Timothy C. Fish	1993	576
21 2/16	13 7/16	7 11/16	Price Co., WI	Picked Up	William D. Janak	1993	576
21 2/16	13 11/16	7 7/16	Clinton Co., PA	Richard T. Kordes	Richard T. Kordes	1993	576
21 2/16	13 5/16	7 13/16	San Bernardino Co., CA	Rodney K. McGee	Rodney K. McGee	1993	576
21 2/16	13 3/16	8	Clearfield Co., PA	Donald C. Miller III	Donald C. Miller III	1993	576
21 2/16	13 3/16	7 11/16	Tyrrell Co., NC	Ed Wilkerson	NC State Mus. Natl. Sci.	1993	576
21 2/16	13 7/16	7 11/16	Kuiu Island, AK	Thomas E. Phillippe, Sr.	Thomas E. Phillippe, Sr.	1993	576
21 2/16	13 8/16	7 10/16	Craven Co., NC	Eddie C. Bridges	Eddie C. Bridges	1994	576
21 2/16	13 3/16	7 15/16	Fort a la Corne, SK	Gerald Gilmore	Gerald Gilmore	1994	576
21 2/16	12 13/16	8 5/16	Pine Co., MN	Picked Up	MN Dept. of Natl. Resc.	1994	576
21 2/16	13	8 2/16	Catron Co., NM	Joe W. Murdock	Joe W. Murdock	1994	576

Score	Length	Width	Locality	Hunter	Owner	Date Killed	Rank
21 2/16	13 6/16	7 12/16	Hyde Co., NC	Stephen R. Bathon	Stephen R. Bathon	1995	576
21 2/16	13 5/16	7 13/16	Rockingham Co., VA	Charles G. Carter	Charles G. Carter	1995	576
21 2/16	13 4/16	7 14/16	Oconto Co., WI	Patrick J. Gauthier	Patrick J. Gauthier	1995	576
21 2/16	13 9/16	7 9/16	Clarion Co., PA	Todd W. Miller	Todd W. Miller	1995	576
21 2/16	13 8/16	7 10/16	Onslow Co., NC	John R. Sewell	John R. Sewell	1995	576
21 2/16	13 3/16	7 15/16	Rusk Co., WI	Rainer J. Bidinger	Rainer J. Bidinger	1996	576
21 2/16	13	8 2/16	Hodgson, MB	Linda Cherepak	Linda Cherepak	1996	576
21 2/16	13 7/16	7 11/16	Perry Co., AR	Dillard R. Graves	Dillard R. Graves	1996	576
21 2/16	13 6/16	7 12/16	Mesa Co., CO	Stephen J. Gray	Stephen J. Gray	1996	576
21 2/16	13 3/16	7 15/16	Preeceville, SK	David O. Guthrel	David O. Guthrel	1996	576
21 2/16	13 10/16	7 8/16	Coos Co., NH	Gary J. Russell	Gary J. Russell	1996	576
21 2/16	13 8/16	7 10/16	Jones Co., NC	Forrest P. Boone	Forrest P. Boone	1997	576
21 2/16	13 9/16	7 9/16	Hyde Co., NC	Steve Hyde	Steve Hyde	1997	576
21 2/16	13	8 2/16	Wadena Co., MN	Wade A. Kern	Wade A. Kern	1997	576
21 2/16	13 3/16	7 15/16	Pike Co., PA	William S. Sinclair	William S. Sinclair	1997	576
21 2/16	13	8 2/16	Nez Perce Co., ID	Brice J. Barnes	Brice J. Barnes	1998	576
21 2/16	13 6/16	7 12/16	Hyde Co., NC	Michael B. Davis	Michael B. Davis	1998	576
21 2/16	13	8 2/16	Aroostook Co., ME	Linda L. Harlow	Linda L. Harlow	1998	576
21 2/16	13 1/16	8 1/16	Carrot River, SK	Dan S. Meske	Dan S. Meske	1998	576
21 2/16	13 4/16	7 14/16	Lintlaw, SK	Donald Schemenauer	Donald Schemenauer	1998	576
21 2/16	13 2/16	8	High Prairie, AB	Chris P. Thomas	Chris P. Thomas	1998	576
21 2/16	12 12/16	8 6/16	Las Animas Co., CO	Roger L. Bell	Roger L. Bell	1999	576
21 2/16	13 2/16	8	Lac La Biche, AB	Ralph R. Brausen	Ralph R. Brausen	1999	576
21 2/16	13 2/16	8	Washburn Co., WI	Jesse M. Hill	Jesse M. Hill	1999	576
21 2/16	13 4/16	7 14/16	Wexford Co., MI	Michael D. Horton	Michael D. Horton	1999	576
21 2/16	13 5/16	7 13/16	Duck Mt., MB	R. Steve Martin	R. Steve Martin	1999	576
21 2/16	13 3/16	7 15/16	Washburn Co., WI	Paul C. Arnold	Paul C. Arnold	2000	576
21 2/16	13 2/16	8	Smoky River, AB	James S. Eason	James S. Eason	2000	576
21 2/16	13 5/16	7 13/16	Kittitas Co., WA	John J. Heinz	John J. Heinz	2000	576
21 2/16	13 4/16	7 14/16	Burnett Co., WI	Don S. Karastes	Don S. Karastes	2000	576
21 2/16	13	8 2/16	Okanogan Co., WA	Jeffery G. Randall	Jeffery G. Randall	2000	576
21 2/16	13 2/16	8	Washburn Co., WI	Peter Schomin	Peter Schomin	2000	576
21 2/16	13 3/16	7 15/16	Menominee Co., MI	Chris M. Christophersen	Chris M. Christophersen	2001	576
21 2/16	13 4/16	7 14/16	Craven Co., NC	Thomas J. Denesha	Thomas J. Denesha	2001	576
21 2/16	13 4/16	7 14/16	Gila Co., AZ	Fred Peters	Fred Peters	2001	576
21 2/16	13 3/16	7 15/16	Langlade Co., WI	Harvey R. Roth	Harvey R. Roth	2001	576
21 2/16	13 3/16	7 15/16	Price Co., WI	James F. Voborsky	James F. Voborsky	2001	576
21 2/16	13 6/16	7 12/16	Fish Lake, MB	David R. Bryce	David R. Bryce	2002	576
21 2/16	13 2/16	8	Sullivan Co., NY	Charles W. Hahl	Charles W. Hahl	2002	576
21 2/16	12 15/16	8 3/16	Athabasca River, AB	Walter Krom	Walter Krom	2002	576
21 2/16	13 3/16	7 15/16	Gila Co., AZ	Robert L. Long, Jr.	Robert L. Long, Jr.	2003	576
21 2/16	13 3/16	7 15/16	Chitek Lake, SK	John H. Vance	John H. Vance	2003	576
21 1/16	13 3/16	7 14/16	Indian Lake, LA	B.V. Lilly	U.S. Natl. Museum	1904	677
21 1/16	13 7/16	7 10/16	Coahuila, MX	B.V. Lilly	U.S. Natl. Museum	1906	677
21 1/16	13 2/16	7 15/16	Santa Barbara Co., CA	Charles Tant	Univ. of CA Museum	1940	677
21 1/16	12 12/16	8 5/16	Columbia Co., WA	Glenn Ford	Fred Van Arsdol	1954	677
21 1/16	13 2/16	7 15/16	Mt. Gentry, AZ	Cliff Edwards	Cliff Edwards	1960	677
21 1/16	12 12/16	8 5/16	Paonia, CO	William O. Good	William O. Good	1960	677

BLACK BEAR

Ursus americanus americanus and related subspecies

Score	Greatest Length of Skull Without Lower Jaw	Greatest Width of Skull	Locality	Hunter	Owner	Date Killed	Rank
21 1/16	12 8/16	8 9/16	Steamboat Springs, CO	Norman W. Garwood	Norman W. Garwood	1964	677
21 1/16	13 3/16	7 14/16	Peace River, AB	Don W. Caldwell	Don W. Caldwell	1965	677
21 1/16	13	8 1/16	Piscataquis Co., ME	J.D. Flowers	J.D. Flowers	1966	677
21 1/16	13 2/16	7 15/16	Gila Co., AZ	George L. Massingill	George L. Massingill	1971	677
21 1/16	13	8 1/16	Price Co., WI	J. Hanson & J. Valiga	Joseph Valiga	1971	677
21 1/16	13 3/16	7 14/16	Iron Co., WI	Gerald Brauer	Gerald Brauer	1972	677
21 1/16	12 13/16	8 4/16	San Carlos Indian Res., AZ	Michael D. Gunnett	Michael D. Gunnett	1973	677
21 1/16	13 6/16	7 11/16	Hubbard Co., MN	Dean J. Como	Dean J. Como	1974	677
21 1/16	13 3/16	7 14/16	Graham Island, BC	Roger Britton	Roger Britton	1978	677
21 1/16	12 15/16	8 2/16	Logan Lake, BC	Norman W. Dougan	Norman W. Dougan	1978	677
21 1/16	12 15/16	8 2/16	Greenlee Co., AZ	Michael W. Goodyear	Michael W. Goodyear	1979	677
21 1/16	13 10/16	7 7/16	Graham Island, BC	Roger Britton	Roger Britton	1980	677
21 1/16	13 1/16	8	Spirit River, AB	John Dobish	John Dobish	1982	677
21 1/16	12 15/16	8 2/16	Teller Co., CO	Samuel T. Harrelson, Jr.	Samuel T. Harrelson, Jr.	1982	677
21 1/16	12 13/16	8 4/16	Apache Co., AZ	William J. Morris	William J. Morris	1985	677
21 1/16	12 14/16	8 3/16	Cook Co., MN	K. Johnson, G. Bjerkness, & S. Borud	Kevin R. Johnson	1986	677
21 1/16	12 15/16	8 2/16	Menominee Co., MI	Manfred L. Pfitzer	Manfred L. Pfitzer	1986	677
21 1/16	13 5/16	7 12/16	Valley River, MB	Craig Kozak	Craig Kozak	1987	677
21 1/16	13 4/16	7 13/16	Gila Co., AZ	Daniel G. Robinett	Daniel G. Robinett	1987	677
21 1/16	13 1/16	8	Charlevoix Co., MI	Gerald L. Fuller	Gerald L. Fuller	1988	677
21 1/16	12 13/16	8 4/16	Klakas Inlet, AK	Stephen P. Harvey	Stephen P. Harvey	1988	677
21 1/16	13 5/16	7 12/16	Flatbush, AB	Tom McFadzen	Tom McFadzen	PR 1988	677
21 1/16	12 15/16	8 2/16	Eagle Lake, SK	Randall N. Olejnik	Randall N. Olejnik	1988	677
21 1/16	12 14/16	8 3/16	St. Louis Co., MN	Jonathan E. Polecheck	Jonathan E. Polecheck	1989	677
21 1/16	12 12/16	8 5/16	Orange Co., NY	George E. Decker	George E. Decker	1992	677
21 1/16	13	8 1/16	Prince of Wales Island, AK	Hanson E. Fitte	Hanson E. Fitte	1993	677
21 1/16	13 3/16	7 14/16	Pierce Co., WI	Steven J. Hlavacek	Steven J. Hlavacek	1993	677
21 1/16	13 2/16	7 15/16	Trinity Co., CA	Dorrel K. Byrd	Dorrel K. Byrd	1994	677
21 1/16	12 13/16	8 4/16	Trinity Co., CA	Curt M. Connor	Curt M. Connor	1995	677
21 1/16	13 6/16	7 11/16	Otter Lake, MB	William A. Guelzow, Jr.	William A. Guelzow, Jr.	1995	677
21 1/16	12 10/16	8 7/16	Smoky Lake, AB	Lawrence L. Piquette	Lawrence L. Piquette	1995	677
21 1/16	13 2/16	7 15/16	Bayfield Co., WI	Thomas C. Albrecht	Thomas C. Albrecht	1996	677
21 1/16	13 1/16	8	Prince of Wales Island, AK	Shawn P. Price	Shawn P. Price	1996	677
21 1/16	13 7/16	7 10/16	Ventura Co., CA	Thomas J. Weir	Thomas J. Weir	1996	677
21 1/16	13 3/16	7 14/16	Round Lake, SK	Floyd Forster	Floyd Forster	1997	677
21 1/16	13	8 1/16	Swan River, MB	Richard Barrett	Richard Barrett	1998	677
21 1/16	13 3/16	7 14/16	St. Louis Co., MN	Joseph A. Benedict	Joseph A. Benedict	1998	677
21 1/16	13 8/16	7 9/16	Ventura Co., CA	Kevin D. Colvard	Kevin D. Colvard	1998	677

Score	Length of Skull	Width of Skull	Locality	Owner	By Whom Killed	Date Killed	Rank
21 1/16	13	8 1/16	Tyrrell Co., NC	Marion K. DuPree	Marion K. DuPree	1998	677
21 1/16	12 15/16	8 2/16	Iosco Co., MI	Nicholas E. Uithol	Nicholas E. Uithol	1998	677
21 1/16	12 13/16	8 4/16	Greenlee Co., AZ	Derek W. Doran	Derek W. Doran	1999	677
21 1/16	13 3/16	7 14/16	Grey River, NL	Christopher L. Fischer	Christopher L. Fischer	1999	677
21 1/16	12 15/16	8 2/16	Poplarfield, MB	Stephen R. Mills	Stephen R. Mills	1999	677
21 1/16	13 4/16	7 13/16	Marinette Co., WI	Neal A. Ruechel	Neal A. Ruechel	1999	677
21 1/16	13 7/16	7 10/16	Douglas Co., WI	Larry J. Selzler	Larry J. Selzler	1999	677
21 1/16	12 15/16	8 2/16	Edith Lake, BC	Brittany K. Thomas	Brittany K. Thomas	1999	677
21 1/16	13 3/16	7 14/16	Pacific Co., WA	Greg J. Bryant	Greg J. Bryant	2000	677
21 1/16	13	8 1/16	Prince of Wales Island, AK	Marvin G. DeVore, Sr.	Marvin G. DeVore, Sr.	2000	677
21 1/16	12 12/16	8 5/16	Prince of Wales Island, AK	Dennis Dix, Jr.	Dennis Dix, Jr.	2000	677
21 1/16	13 8/16	7 9/16	Rennell Sound, BC	Philip Giesbrecht	Philip Giesbrecht	2000	677
21 1/16	12 15/16	8 2/16	Little Fishing Lake, SK	Gilbert Groseth	Gilbert Groseth	2000	677
21 1/16	13 7/16	7 10/16	Saddle Hills, AB	Terry D. Hagman	Terry D. Hagman	2000	677
21 1/16	13 6/16	7 11/16	Pine Co., MN	William N. Hegge, Jr.	William N. Hegge, Jr.	2000	677
21 1/16	13 1/16	8	Cass Co., MN	Robert L. Stephan	Robert L. Stephan	2000	677
21 1/16	13	8 1/16	Sawyer Co., WI	William J. Vander Zouwen	William J. Vander Zouwen	2000	677
21 1/16	13 8/16	7 9/16	Pike Co., PA	Timothy M. Biehl	Timothy M. Biehl	2001	677
21 1/16	13 4/16	7 13/16	Itasca Co., MN	John M. Warneke	John M. Warneke	2001	677
21 1/16	13 4/16	7 13/16	Trinity Co., CA	Eric A. Chatham	Eric A. Chatham	2002	677
21 1/16	13 1/16	8	Prince of Wales Island, AK	Kristy J. King	Kristy J. King	2002	677
21 1/16	12 13/16	8 4/16	Menominee Co., MI	Owen R. Koppelberger	Owen R. Koppelberger	2002	677
21 1/16	13 1/16	8	Whitemud Hills, AB	Alfred C. Faber, Jr.	Alfred C. Faber, Jr.	2003	677
21 1/16	12 13/16	8 4/16	Lincoln Co., WI	Timothy J. Grzesiak	Timothy J. Grzesiak	2003	677
21	13	8 1/16	Queen Charlotte Islands, BC	Douglas McIntyre	Unknown	PR 1959	745
21	12 8/16	8 8/16	Vancouver, BC	Elmer E. Kurrus, Jr.	Elmer E. Kurrus, Jr.	1964	745
21	13	8	Hamilton Co., NY	NY Dept. of Env. Cons.	James McIntyre	1965	745
21	12 12/16	8 4/16	Collbran, CO	Cecil E. Alumbaugh, Jr.	Cecil E. Alumbaugh, Jr.	1967	745
21	12 11/16	8 5/16	Oconto Co., WI	Calvin E. Schindel	Calvin E. Schindel	1968	745
21	13 2/16	7 14/16	Overflowing River, MB	Victor Kostiniuk	Victor Kostiniuk	1971	745
21	12 15/16	8 1/16	Garfield Co., CO	J.D. Liles	J.D. Liles	1974	745
21	13 2/16	8 2/16	St. Louis Co., MN	Robert J. Manteuffel	Robert J. Manteuffel	1977	745
21	13	8	Routt Co., CO	Jerome W. Keyes, Jr.	Jerome W. Keyes, Jr.	1980	745
21	13 4/16	7 12/16	Wasatch Co., UT	UT Div. of Wildl. Resc.	Picked Up	1980	745
21	13 4/16	7 12/16	Hamilton Co., NY	Marshall E. Conklin	Marshall E. Conklin	1981	745
21	12 7/16	8 9/16	Fremont Co., WY	Timothy B. Hill	Timothy B. Hill	1981	745
21	12 12/16	8 4/16	Bradford Co., PA	Ray B. Moyer	Ray B. Moyer	1981	745
21	13 2/16	7 14/16	Coconino Co., AZ	Michael P. Whelan	Michael P. Whelan	1981	745
21	13	8	Fort Assiniboine, AB	George Plashka	George Plashka	1982	745
21	13 3/16	7 13/16	Langlade Co., WI	Michael Steliga	Michael Steliga	1982	745
21	12 14/16	7 14/16	Macon Co., NC	C. Rick Jones	C. Rick Jones	1983	745
21	13 2/16	7 14/16	Ostenfeld, MB	Erik Thienpondt	Erik Thienpondt	1983	745
21	13	8	Santa Barbara Co. CA	Marshall Munger	Picked Up	1984	745
21	13 1/16	7 15/16	Cholmondeley Sound, AK	Gerry D. Downey	Gerry D. Downey	1985	745
21	13	8	Garfield Co., CO	Gordon L. Haxton	Gordon L. Haxton	1985	745
21	12 10/16	8 6/16	Echouani Lake, QC	Collins F. Kellogg	Collins F. Kellogg	1985	745
21	13 3/16	7 13/16	Wild Goose, ON	William G. Tellijohn	William G. Tellijohn	1985	745

Score	Greatest Length of Skull Without Lower Jaw	Greatest Width of Skull	Locality	Hunter	Owner	Date Killed	Rank
21	13 3/16	7 13/16	Graham Co., AZ	Mark J. Bensley	Mark J. Bensley	1986	745
21	13 6/16	7 10/16	Ogemaw Co., MI	William D. Massey	William D. Massey	1987	745
21	13 1/16	7 15/16	Carrot River, SK	Demetry Procyk	Demetry Procyk	1987	745
21	13 6/16	7 10/16	Muriel Lake, AB	Edward R. Rempel	Edward R. Rempel	1988	745
21	13 2/16	7 14/16	Gates Co., NC	John W. Whitehurst, Jr.	John W. Whitehurst, Jr.	1988	745
21	13	8	Carbon Co., UT	Lonnie K. Bell	Lonnie K. Bell	1989	745
21	12 13/16	8 3/16	Iron Co., WI	Todd J. Brauer	Todd J. Brauer	1989	745
21	13 2/16	7 14/16	Peace River, AB	Danny de Melo	Danny de Melo	1989	745
21	12 15/16	8 1/16	Brokenhead River, MB	Michael E. Vandenbosch	Michael E. Vandenbosch	1989	745
21	13	8	LeDomaine, QC	Anthony Beceiro	Anthony Beceiro	1990	745
21	13	8	Beaufort Co., NC	Marlow Van Jones	Marlow Van Jones	1990	745
21	12 12/16	8 4/16	Peace River, AB	Kent S. Anderson	Kent S. Anderson	1991	745
21	13 4/16	7 12/16	Onanole, MB	Robert J. Grosfield	Robert J. Grosfield	1992	745
21	12 13/16	8 3/16	Prince of Wales Island, AK	Matthew Heller	Matthew Heller	1992	745
21	13 2/16	7 14/16	Peace River, AB	G. Byron Horn	G. Byron Horn	1992	745
21	12 14/16	8 2/16	Price Co., WI	Paul A. Quinn	Paul A. Quinn	1992	745
21	13 8/16	7 8/16	Indiana Co., PA	William G. Shank	William G. Shank	1992	745
21	13 4/16	7 12/16	Clark Co., WI	Don A. Ziemann	Don A. Ziemann	1992	745
21	13 4/16	7 12/16	Otero Co., NM	Woodie B. Howell	Woodie B. Howell	1993	745
21	13 1/16	7 15/16	Pine Co., MN	Donald J. Lorentz	Donald J. Lorentz	1993	745
21	13 6/16	7 10/16	Hyde Co., NC	Chuck Blalock	Chuck Blalock	1994	745
21	12 15/16	8 1/16	Painted Rock Island, ON	Harry D. Brickley	Harry D. Brickley	1994	745
21	13 4/16	7 12/16	Aroostook Co., ME	George W. Cameron	George W. Cameron	1994	745
21	13 2/16	7 14/16	Lincoln Co., MT	Ian K. Chase-Dunn	Ian K. Chase-Dunn	1994	745
21	12 14/16	8 2/16	Bay Tree, AB	Sedgwick B. Loyd II	Sedgwick B. Loyd II	1994	745
21	13	7 10/16	Hyde Co., NC	Benjamin Simmons III	Benjamin Simmons III	1994	745
21	13 6/16	7 10/16	Hyde Co., NC	Charlie E. Vandiford	Charlie E. Vandiford	1994	745
21	13 7/16	7 9/16	Tyrrell Co., NC	Edward R. Wilkerson	Edward R. Wilkerson	1994	745
21	12 14/16	8 2/16	Tuolumne Co., CA	Stacy J. Willoughby	Stacy J. Willoughby	1994	745
21	12 10/16	8 6/16	Ulster Co., NY	Thomas Nolan	Thomas Nolan	1995	745
21	12 14/16	8 2/16	Washburn Co., WI	Sonjonae L. Setser	Sonjonae L. Setser	1995	745
21	13 3/16	7 13/16	Barron Co., WI	Jeffrey P. Tomesh	Jeffrey P. Tomesh	1995	745
21	13	8	Whale Passage, AK	E. Lance Whary	E. Lance Whary	1995	745
21	13 1/16	7 15/16	Bradford Co., PA	J. Martin Alles	J. Martin Alles	1996	745
21	13	8	Stevens Co., WA	Tom Balis	Tom Balis	1996	745
21	13 3/16	7 13/16	Humboldt Co., CA	Jerry R. Cardoza	Jerry R. Cardoza	1996	745
21	13 7/16	7 9/16	Sawyer Co., WI	Chris L. Duerst	Chris L. Duerst	1996	745
21	13	8	Makinak, MB	Robert C. Missler	Robert C. Missler	1996	745

21	12 11/16	8 5/16	Delaware Co., NY	James D. Muench	James D. Muench	1996	745
21	12 14/16	8 2/16	Marathon Co., WI	Orville J. Sazama	Orville J. Sazama	1996	745
21	13 2/16	7 14/16	Tioga Co., PA	Melvin D. Noll	Melvin D. Noll	1997	745
21	12 14/16	8 2/16	Smeaton, SK	Paul C. Sills	Paul C. Sills	1997	745
21	13 1/16	7 15/16	Tehama Co., CA	Kenneth A. Wilson, Sr.	Kenneth A. Wilson, Sr.	1997	745
21	12 12/16	8 4/16	Mendocino Co., CA	Ralph Allino	Ralph Allino	1998	745
21	13 3/16	7 13/16	Wadena Co., MN	Darrell A. Anderson	Darrell A. Anderson	1998	745
21	12 13/16	8 3/16	Montezuma Co., CO	Joe W. Brunner	Joe W. Brunner	1998	745
21	13	8	Mendocino Co., CA	Peter M. Hoyle	Peter M. Hoyle	1998	745
21	13 13/16	7 3/16	Sidney Lake, SK	Donald Wright	Donald Wright	1998	745
21	13 3/16	7 13/16	Fergus Co., MT	Ross C. Roe, Jr.	Ross C. Roe, Jr.	1999	745
21	13 3/16	7 13/16	Beaver River, SK	Jason Toews	Jason Toews	1999	745
21	13 4/16	7 12/16	Beaver River, SK	Paul J. Allgyer	Paul J. Allgyer	2000	745
21	12 14/16	8 2/16	Peace River, AB	Mikael Andersson	Mikael Andersson	2000	745
21	13 6/16	7 10/16	Carteret Co., NC	David T. Beveridge	David T. Beveridge	2000	745
21	12 15/16	8 1/16	Porcupine Plain, SK	Kirby Fruin	Kirby Fruin	2000	745
21	12 7/16	8 9/16	Beavervale Creek, BC	Brett J. McAllister	Brett J. McAllister	2000	745
21	13 3/16	7 13/16	Iron Co., WI	Donald B. Morris	Donald B. Morris	2000	745
21	12 11/16	8 5/16	Onion Lake, SK	Lannon Nault	Lannon Nault	2000	745
21	13 2/16	7 14/16	Duck Mt., MB	Wayne R. Schatzman	Wayne R. Schatzman	2000	745
21	12 14/16	8 2/16	Mendocino Co., CA	Henry W. Anderson	Henry W. Anderson	2001	745
21	12 15/16	8 1/16	Thorne Bay, AK	Ian K. Chase-Dunn	Ian K. Chase-Dunn	2001	745
21	13 4/16	7 12/16	Frobisher Lake, SK	Robert L. Holder	Robert L. Holder	2001	745
21	13	8	Mount Martley, BC	Steven A. Krossa	Steven A. Krossa	2001	745
21	13 5/16	7 11/16	Polk Co., WI	Michael D. Mader	Michael D. Mader	2001	745
21	12 15/16	8 1/16	Seech Lake, MB	Duane Seiler II	Duane Seiler II	2001	745
21	13 2/16	7 14/16	Chitek Lake, SK	Todd E. Stahley	Todd E. Stahley	2001	745
21	13 5/16	7 11/16	Beaufort Co., NC	Kenneth Bateman, Jr.	Kenneth W. Bateman, Jr.	2002	745
21	13 2/16	7 14/16	Pine Co., MN	Daniel J. Fischer	Daniel J. Fischer	2002	745
21	12 13/16	8 3/16	Yavapai Co., AZ	Todd A. Hyslip	Todd A. Hyslip	2002	745
21	13 4/16	7 12/16	Sundown, MB	Mel A. Ortmann	Mel A. Ortmann	2002	745
21	13	8	Price Co., WI	Thomas P. Stenborg	Thomas P. Stenborg	2002	745
21	13 2/16	7 14/16	Prince of Wales Island, AK	Rudolph O. Wilson, Jr.	Rudolph O. Wilson, Jr.	2002	745
21	13 2/16	7 14/16	Sawyer Co., WI	Robin R. Zillmer	Robin R. Zillmer	2002	745
21	12 13/16	8 3/16	Valleyview, AB	Paul J. Kruger	Paul J. Kruger	2003	745
23*	14 8/16	8 8/16	Montmorency Co., MI	Sharon L. Agren	Sharon L. Agren	1997	745
22 12/16*	14 4/16	8 8/16	Queen Charlotte Islands, BC	Raymond J. Fournier	Raymond J. Fournier	1992	745
22 12/16*	14 5/16	8 7/16	Washburn Co., WI	George Spaulding	George Spaulding	2002	745
22 9/16*	13 9/16	9	Huntington Co., PA	Raymond K. Pruss	Raymond K. Pruss	2001	745

* Final score is subject to revision by additional verifying measurements.

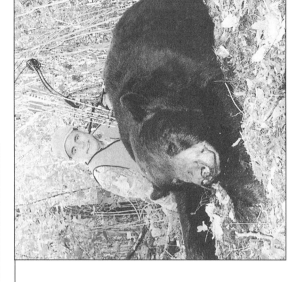

CATEGORY
BLACK BEAR

SCORE
21-4/16

HUNTER
M.R. JAMES

LOCATION
RICHARDS LAKE,
SASKATCHEWAN

DATE OF KILL
JUNE 2001

CATEGORY
BLACK BEAR

SCORE
21

HUNTER
WAYNE R. SCHATZMAN

LOCATION
DUCK MOUNTAIN,
MANITOBA

DATE OF KILL
SEPTEMBER 2000

CATEGORY
BLACK BEAR

SCORE
21-2/16

HUNTER
KERRY ROGERS

LOCATION
HAMILTON COUNTY, NEW YORK

DATE OF KILL
SEPTEMBER 1986

CATEGORY
BLACK BEAR

SCORE
21-1/16

HUNTER
BRITTANY K. THOMAS

LOCATION
EDITH LAKE,
BRITISH COLUMBIA

DATE OF KILL
JUNE 1999

CATEGORY
BLACK BEAR

SCORE
21-1/16

HUNTER
RICHARD BARRETT

LOCATION
SWAN RIVER, MANITOBA

DATE OF KILL
JUNE 1998

CATEGORY
BLACK BEAR

SCORE
21-5/16

HUNTER
THOMAS G. LESTER

LOCATION
WOLF LAKE,
ALBERTA

DATE OF KILL
MAY 1998

CATEGORY
BLACK BEAR

SCORE
21-9/16

HUNTER
DAVID W. WATSON (LEFT)

LOCATION
SADDLE HILLS, ALBERTA

DATE OF KILL
MAY 2003

SCORE
21-1/16

HUNTER
STEPHEN R. MILLS (BELOW)

LOCATION
POPLARFIELD, MANITOBA

DATE OF KILL
MAY 1999

CATEGORY
BLACK BEAR

SCORE
21-10/16

HUNTER
JOHN N. PARDUN, SR.

LOCATION
KELWOOD, MANITOBA

DATE OF KILL
MAY 2003

164

ALASKA BROWN BEAR AND GRIZZLY BEAR BOUNDARIES

The big brown bears are found on Kodiak and Afognak Islands, the Alaska Peninsula, and eastward and southeastward along the coast of Alaska. The smaller interior grizzly is found in the remaining parts of the continent. The boundary between the two was first defined as an imaginary line extending 75 miles inland from the coast of Alaska. Later this boundary was more precisely defined with the current definition as follows (Alaska brown bear is shaded area of map):

A line of separation between the larger coastal brown bear and the smaller interior grizzly has been developed such that west and south of this line (to and including Unimak Island) bear trophies are recorded as Alaska brown bear. North and east of this line, bear trophies are recorded as grizzly bear. The boundary line description is as follows: Starting at Pearse Canal and following the Canadian-Alaskan boundary northwesterly to Mt. St. Elias on the 141 degree meridian; thence north along the Canadian-Alaskan boundary to Mt. Natazhat; thence west northwest along the divide of the Wrangell Range to Mt. Jarvis at the western end of the Wrangell Range; thence north along the divide of the Mentasta Range to Mentasta Pass; thence in a general westerly direction along the divide of the Alaska Range to Houston Pass; thence westerly following the 62nd parallel of latitude to the Bering Sea. ■

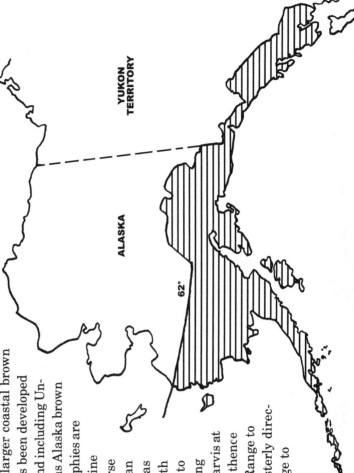

YUKON TERRITORY

ALASKA

62°

GRIZZLY BEAR
WORLD'S RECORD

There is a three-way tie for the World's Record grizzly bear (*Ursus arctos horribilis*) beginning in 1970 with a find in Bella Coola Valley, British Columbia, by James G. Shelton. The final judging on Shelton's pick-up would confirm a score of 27-2/16, which was recorded in the 1981 edition. This trophy would be tied a year later by an equally huge grizzly taken in the same province along the Dean River by Roger J. Pentecost. Pentecost shared his story that colorfully describes the momentous hunting event that he shared with his son.

"Suddenly, off to our left about 70 feet away and partly obscured by a cedar, something started to move slowly up out of the ground. It was a massive head in profile, followed by an enormous shoulder hump. We froze. Here was what we had come all this way for – a good bear. But really, I never wanted it quite so close. As I readied my Husqvarna, I heard Jason close his gun.

"For what seemed to be a long time, I had an excellent side shot. I squeezed the shot off. But, the bear, instead of falling over dead, rose up out of the hollow in the ground and turned toward us. Here it was, coming right at us. I aimed at his shoulder, still hardly believing he wasn't down. This next shot hit his side. This turned him, and he plunged off sideways into a thicket of alders, windfalls, and devils club. As he was going in, I placed a third shot.

"All hell seemed to break loose in that small wooded area. It was too thick to see what was happening, but boy, could we hear the bear snorting, growling, grunting and gasp-

ing draughts of breath. It was a simply enormous and rather frightening sound. I looked back at Jason and Wayne. They looked as apprehensive as I felt. I knew a grizzly could explode out of that cover like an 'express train', with none of the brush slowing him down at all, and leap 15 feet in a bound."

Entered in the 19th Awards, Pentecost's trophy would stand alone for nearly a decade as the largest hunter-taken grizzly. However, it was matched again in 1991 by Theodore Kurdziel, Jr., during a hunt on the frozen landscape along the Inglutalik River near Koyuk, Alaska. Kurdziel gave an equally fine account describing the pinnacle of his hunting story.

"Suddenly the bear appeared about 40 yards ahead, running for me at full speed. Steve could not see him from his position. The bear, his hackles raised, looked as mad as a guard dog protecting his turf. I shouldered my rifle and found the grizzly in my scope. The only shot I had was at the bear's head, so I held off until the bear was about 20 yards away. At that point, he stumbled momentarily and exposed his chest, and I fired instinctively. The bear spun around like a top and ran uphill, more or less angling toward Steve. I shot again, hitting the bear in the neck.

When we walked up to that mountain of a bear, we were awestruck by his size. I did not care at that point whether he was a Boone and Crockett bear or not. All I knew was that I had experienced a close-range encounter with one of the most imposing, gorgeous creatures on earth, and I had survived." ∎

GRIZZLY BEAR
WORLD'S RECORD SCORE CHART

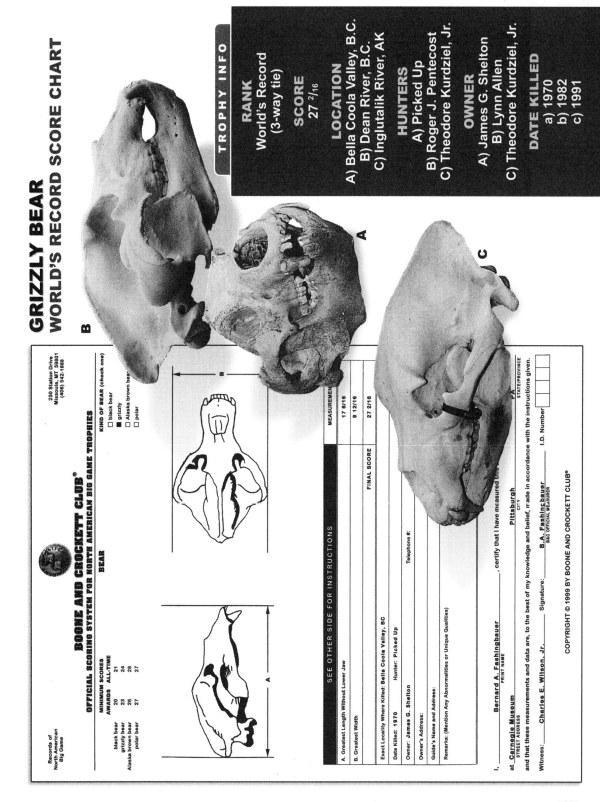

Records of
North American
Big Game

250 Station Drive
Missoula, MT 59801
(406) 542-1888

BOONE AND CROCKETT CLUB®

OFFICIAL SCORING SYSTEM FOR NORTH AMERICAN BIG GAME TROPHIES

BEAR

	MINIMUM SCORES	
	AWARDS	ALL-TIME
black bear	20	21
grizzly bear	23	24
Alaska brown bear	26	28
polar bear	27	27

KIND OF BEAR (check one)
☐ black bear
☑ grizzly
☐ Alaska brown bear
☐ polar bear

B

A

SEE OTHER SIDE FOR INSTRUCTIONS

	MEASUREMENTS
A. Greatest Length Without Lower Jaw	17 6/16
B. Greatest Width	9 12/16
FINAL SCORE	27 2/16

Exact Locality Where Killed: **Bella Coola Valley, BC**

Date Killed: **1970**   Hunter: **Picked Up**

Owner: **James G. Shelton**   Telephone #:

Owner's Address:

Guide's Name and Address:

Remarks: (Mention Any Abnormalities or Unique Qualities)

I, _____ **Bernard A. Fashingbauer** _____ , certify that I have measured this
PRINT NAME

at **Carnegie Museum**   **Pittsburgh**   **PA**
STREET ADDRESS   CITY   STATE/PROVINCE

and that these measurements and data are, to the best of my knowledge and belief, made in accordance with the instructions given.

Witness: **Charles E. Wilson, Jr.**   Signature: **B.A. Fashingbauer**   I.D. Number [ ][ ][ ]
B&C OFFICIAL MEASURER

GRIZZLY BEAR
Ursus arctos horribilis

MINIMUM SCORE 24

Score	Greatest Length of Skull Without Lower Jaw	Greatest Width of Skull	Locality	Hunter	Owner	Date Killed	Rank
27 2/16	17 6/16	9 12/16	Bella Coola Valley, BC	Picked Up	James G. Shelton	1970	1
27 2/16	16 14/16	10 4/16	Dean River, BC	Roger J. Pentecost	Lynn Allen	1982	1
27 2/16	17 3/16	9 15/16	Inglutalik River, AK	Theodore Kurdziel, Jr.	Theodore Kurdziel, Jr.	1991	1
26 14/16	16 14/16	10	Teklanika River, AK	D. Alan McCaleb	D. Alan McCaleb	1989	4
26 14/16	16 6/16	10 8/16	Anahim Lake, BC	Denis E. Schiller	D.E. Schiller & K. Karran	1990	4
26 14/16	16 11/16	10 3/16	Kala Creek, AK	Eugene C. Williams	Eugene C. Williams	2001	4
26 13/16	16 11/16	10 2/16	Wakeman River, BC	Harry Leggett, Jr.	B&C National Collection	1980	7
26 13/16	16 9/16	10 4/16	Devil Mt., AK	Russell J. Lewis	Russell J. Lewis	1993	7
26 12/16	16 6/16	10 6/16	Kuskokwim River, AK	Richard E. Jobe	Richard E. Jobe	2001	9
26 11/16	16 11/16	10	Shaktoolik River, AK	Hans Hartwig	B&C National Collection	1993	10
26 10/16	16 10/16	10	Rivers Inlet, BC	F. Nygaard	Univ. of BC	1954	11
26 10/16	17	9 10/16	Lonesome Lake, BC	J. Turner	Douglas Kenefick	1965	11
26 10/16	16 14/16	9 12/16	Kaltag, AK	Roger D. Hooten	Roger D. Hooten	1999	11
26 10/16	16 9/16	10 1/16	Windy Creek, AK	Kyle R. Moffat	Kyle R. Moffat	2001	11
26 9/16	16 4/16	10 5/16	Ungalik River, AK	Stanley F. Smith	S.F. Smith & G. Fait	1983	15
26 9/16	16 6/16	10 3/16	Anvik River, AK	Thomas M. Sharko	Thomas M. Sharko	1999	15
26 8/16	16 10/16	9 14/16	Yanert Glacier, AK	Xavier T. Riedmiller	Xavier T. Riedmiller	1970	17
26 7/16	16 11/16	9 12/16	Casadepaga River, AK	Carl O. Merchant	Carl O. Merchant	1996	18
26 7/16	16 7/16	10	Lone Mt., AK	Jon D. Seifert	Jon D. Seifert	2000	18
26 6/16	16 6/16	10	Bella Coola, BC	Walter C. Shutts	Walter C. Shutts	1957	20
26 6/16	16 12/16	9 10/16	Farewell Lake, AK	John C. Schwietert	John C. Schwietert	1968	20
26 6/16	16 8/16	9 14/16	Seaskinnish Creek, BC	Paddy H.S. Wong	Fred Y.C. Wong	1982	20
26 6/16	16 5/16	10 1/16	Cluculz Creek, BC	Thomas C. Roberson	Thomas C. Roberson	1983	20
26 6/16	16 10/16	9 12/16	Tonzona River, AK	Fred M. Corriea	Fred M. Corriea	1997	20
26 6/16	16 4/16	10 2/16	Little Tahltan River, BC	Duane A. Enders	Duane A. Enders	1997	20
26 6/16	15 14/16	10 8/16	Nulato Hills, AK	Larry A. Meyer	Larry A. Meyer	2002	20
26 5/16	16 3/16	10 3/16	Kuskokwim River, AK	William G. Farley	William G. Farley	2003	20
26 5/16	16 10/16	9 11/16	Slave Lake, AB	B. Twin & D. Auger	R.W.H. Eben-Ebenau	1953	28
26 5/16	16 5/16	10	Knights Inlet, BC	Thomas N. Bernard	Thomas N. Bernard	1967	28
26 5/16	16 15/16	9 6/16	Swan Hills, AB	Wilfred Hartfelder	Wilfred Hartfelder	1974	28
26 5/16	16 1/16	10 4/16	Devereux Creek, BC	Raymond Ferrieri	Raymond Ferrieri	1994	28
26 5/16	16 2/16	10 3/16	Koyuk River, AK	Remo Pizzagalli	Remo Pizzagalli	1996	28
26 5/16	16 3/16	10 2/16	Vreeland Creek, AK	Leo P. Caito, Jr.	Leo P. Caito, Jr.	2000	28
26 4/16	16 10/16	9 10/16	Elliott Hwy., AK	Unknown	AK Dept. of Fish & Game	1967	34
26 4/16	16 12/16	9 8/16	Tatshenshini River, BC	William G. Underhill	William G. Underhill	1970	34
26 4/16	16 5/16	9 15/16	Ferry, AK	Jamie C. Smyth	Jamie C. Smyth	1973	34
26 4/16	16 1/16	10 3/16	Nulato Hills, AK	Randy A. Tarnowski	Randy A. Tarnowski	1978	34
26 4/16	17	9 4/16	Kakwa River, AB	Klaus Wernsdorf	Klaus Wernsdorf	1979	34

Score	Length	Width	Locality	Hunter	Owner	Date Killed	Rank
26 4/16	16 4/16	10	Nenana River, AK	Stan W. Hughes	Stan W. Hughes	1995	34
26 3/16	17	9 3/16	Tatla Lake, BC	Robert L. Tuma	Robert L. Tuma	1971	40
26 3/16	16 1/16	10 2/16	Buckland River, AK	Bill McDavid	Bill McDavid	1977	40
26 3/16	16	10 3/16	Tok River, AK	Garlen Keen	B&C National Collection	1983	40
26 3/16	16 12/16	9 7/16	Bear Lake, BC	DeVern Gardner	DeVern Gardner	1984	40
26 3/16	16 1/16	10 2/16	Marys Igloo, AK	Mark W. Kelso	Mark W. Kelso	1998	40
26 3/16	16 2/16	10 1/16	Otter Creek, AK	Daniel S. Bolek	Daniel S. Bolek	2001	40
26 2/16	16 10/16	9 9/16	Nechako River, BC	R.J. Nielson	R.J. Nielsen	1971	46
26 2/16	16	10 2/16	Kantishna River, AK	Theodore B. Kelly, Jr.	Theodore B. Kelly, Jr.	1972	46
26 2/16	16 5/16	10 5/16	Kwatna Bay, AK	J.G. Bartlett	J.G. Bartlett	1976	46
26 2/16	16 2/16	9 13/16	Chiroskey River, AK	Harold L. Ahlberg	Harold L. Ahlberg	1992	46
26 2/16	16 2/16	10 5/16	Seal Oil Creek, AK	Ronald O. North	Ronald O. North	1997	46
26 2/16	16 5/16	10 6/16	Post River, AK	Jack J. Tuso	Jack J. Tuso	1997	46
26 2/16	16 9/16	9 13/16	Simonette River, AB	Picked Up	Mikal Christensen	1998	46
26 1/16	16 1/16	9 9/16	Smiths Inlet, BC	Donald M. Swarthout	Donald M. Swarthout	1963	53
26 1/16	16 4/16	10	Camelback Mt., AK	Thomas E. Smith	Thomas E. Smith	1985	53
26 1/16	16	9 13/16	Bendelben Mts., AK	Ronald E. Taig	Ronald E. Taig	1992	53
26 1/16	16 3/16	10 1/16	Klinaklini River, BC	Morris Trace	Morris Trace	1995	53
26 1/16	16 5/16	9 14/16	Inglutalik River, AK	John J. McPartlin	John J. McPartlin	1996	53
26 1/16	15 11/16	9 12/16	Nunavulnuk River, AK	Kenneth S. Orrison	Kenneth S. Orrison	2000	53
26 1/16	16 5/16	10 6/16	Kokrine Hills, AK	Vernon Spencer	Vernon Spencer	2000	53
26 1/16	15 12/16	9 12/16	Kigluaik Mts., AK	Joseph P. Small	Scott C. Babcock	2001	53
26	16	10 5/16	Lake Minchumina, AK	Val J. Blackburn	Val J. Blackburn	1956	61
26	17	10	Bella Coola, BC	J. Harstad	John Lesowski	1959	61
26	16 1/16	9 15/16	Tweedsmuir Park, BC	Michael R. Caspersen	Michael R. Caspersen	1969	61
26	16 8/16	9 8/16	Kobuk River, AK	Charlie Horner	Charlie Horner	1971	61
26	15 12/16	9 14/16	Meziadin Lake, BC	Peter Martinson	Peter Martinson	1987	61
25 15/16	16 3/16	10 3/16	Rapids Roadhouse, AK	H. Herring	H. Herring	1964	66
25 15/16	16 3/16	9 12/16	Bella Coola, BC	Bernard J. Meinerz	Bernard J. Meinerz	1968	66
25 15/16	16	9 12/16	Klinaklini River, BC	Jerry Stubblefield	Jerry Stubblefield	1970	66
25 15/16	15 10/16	9 15/16	Iskut River, BC	Fritz A. Nachant	Fritz A. Nachant	1980	66
25 15/16	16	10 5/16	Tubukutulik River, AK	William A. Brooks, Sr.	William A. Brooks, Sr.	1986	66
25 15/16	15 15/16	10	Tatlawiksuk River, AK	William H. Green	Mrs. William H. Green	1988	66
25 15/16	15 13/16	10 2/16	Morice River, BC	Josef Martinek	Josef Martinek	1991	66
25 15/16	16 7/16	9 8/16	Poplar Lake, BC	Dick Van Barneveld	Dick Van Barneveld	1996	66
25 14/16	16	9 14/16	Telkwa River, BC	Matt Helstrom	Lowell A. Davison	1957	74
25 14/16	16 9/16	9 5/16	Owikeno Lake, BC	Alexander M. Peterson	Alexander M. Peterson	1959	74
25 14/16	15 14/16	9 14/16	Christmas Mt., AK	Mark E. Gilson	Mark E. Gilson	1980	74
25 14/16	16	9 12/16	Muskeg River, AB	Dale B. Kolberg	Dale B. Kolberg	1981	74
25 14/16	16 2/16	9 9/16	Gardner Canal, BC	Steven B. Garland	Steven B. Garland	1984	74
25 13/16	16 5/16	9 14/16	Wood River, AK	Horace Black	Horace Black	1963	79
25 13/16	15 15/16	9 4/16	Bella Coola, BC	Roger L. Adams	Roger L. Adams	1965	79
25 13/16	16 9/16	9 6/16	Spatsizi River, BC	Howard W. Gambrell	Howard W. Gambrell	1985	79
25 13/16	16 7/16	10	Knight Inlet, BC	Kenneth R. Hamer	Kenneth R. Hamer	1998	79
25 12/16	15 13/16	9 15/16	Alaska Range, AK	Elmer R. Schlachter	Elmer R. Schlachter	1971	83
25 12/16	15 13/16	9 10/16	Kwatna River, BC	Robert C. Riggs	Robert C. Riggs	1981	83
25 12/16	16 2/16	9 12/16	Hanna Ridge, BC	Dale T. Dean	Dale T. Dean	1984	83

GRIZZLY BEAR
Ursus arctos horribilis

Score	Greatest Length of Skull Without Lower Jaw	Greatest Width of Skull	Locality	Hunter	Owner	Date Killed	Rank
25 12/16	16	9 12/16	Bond Sound, BC	William Kemp, Jr.	William Kemp, Jr.	1985	83
25 12/16	16 2/16	9 10/16	Klinaklini River, BC	Leonard E. Ellis	Leonard E. Ellis	1991	83
25 12/16	16 6/16	9 6/16	Smithers, BC	Troy N. Ginn	Troy N. Ginn	1995	83
25 12/16	16 7/16	9 5/16	Taku River, BC	David J. Leslie	David J. Leslie	1998	83
25 11/16	16 3/16	9 8/16	Owikeno Lake, BC	W.W. Meeker	W.W. Meeker	1959	90
25 11/16	15 11/16	10	Tatshenshini River, BC	Robert E. Miller	Robert E. Miller	1974	90
25 11/16	16 7/16	9 4/16	Kimsquit River, BC	Norman E. Kinsey	Norman E. Kinsey	1977	90
25 11/16	15 11/16	10	Meziadin Lake, BC	J.D. Jensen & R.S. Curtis	Jae D. Jensen	1979	90
25 11/16	16 4/16	9 7/16	Knight Inlet, BC	Charles E. Gromatzky	Charles E. Gromatzky	1988	90
25 11/16	16 2/16	9 9/16	Babine River, BC	Robert V. Ellis	Robert V. Ellis	1991	90
25 11/16	15 12/16	9 15/16	Paragon River, AK	Gregory D. Yon	Gregory D. Yon	1992	90
25 10/16	16 1/16	9 9/16	Bralorne, BC	Bert Klineburger	Bert Klineburger	1956	97
25 10/16	16 3/16	9 7/16	Dease River, BC	Herb Klein	Dallas Mus. of Natl. Hist.	1960	97
25 10/16	16 2/16	9 10/16	Eagle Creek, WY	Picked Up	L.L. Lutz & H. Sanford	1961	97
25 10/16	16	9 8/16	Brooks Range, AK	John H. Epp	John H. Epp	1965	97
25 10/16	15 6/16	10 4/16	Nabesna River, AK	Jack A. Shane, Sr.	Jack A. Shane, Sr.	1966	97
25 10/16	16 2/16	9 8/16	Kuskokwim River, AK	George Panagos, Jr.	George Panagos, Jr.	1968	97
25 10/16	15 15/16	9 11/16	Tok River, AK	Robert S. Thompson	Robert S. Thompson	1974	97
25 10/16	16	9 10/16	Machmell River, BC	Herbert J. Wenk	Herbert J. Wenk	1975	97
25 10/16	15 14/16	9 12/16	Sheslay River, BC	John Welsh	John Welsh	1983	97
25 10/16	15 14/16	9 12/16	Kuskokwim River, AK	Thomas J. Stolsky	Thomas J. Stolsky	1992	97
25 10/16	16 4/16	9 6/16	Bonnifield Creek, AK	Picked Up	Jerry D. Lees	2000	97
25 9/16	16	9 9/16	Missouri Breaks, MT	E.S. Cameron	U.S. Natl. Museum	1890	108
25 9/16	16 4/16	9 5/16	Klinaklini River, BC	Grancel Fitz	Mrs. Grancel Fitz	1953	108
25 9/16	16	9 9/16	Kitseguecla Mts., BC	Jack Adams	Jack Adams	1975	108
25 9/16	16 3/16	9 6/16	Carpenter Lake, BC	Jim Sprangers	Jim Sprangers	1982	108
25 9/16	16 1/16	9 8/16	Klinaklini River, BC	Homer Harvey	Homer Harvey	1987	108
25 9/16	15 11/16	9 14/16	Tok River, AK	Phillip A. Wolfe	Phillip A. Wolfe	1993	108
25 9/16	15 10/16	9 15/16	Bitter Creek, BC	Dennis R. Beebe	Dennis R. Beebe	1998	108
25 9/16	15 15/16	9 10/16	Anvik River, AK	Gene A. Ott	Gene A. Ott	1999	108
25 8/16	16 2/16	9 6/16	Owikeno Lake, BC	J.C. Russell	J.C. Russell	1957	116
25 8/16	16	9 8/16	Maxan Lake, BC	Alfred E. Matthew	Alfred E. Matthew	1967	116
25 8/16	15 15/16	9 9/16	Wakeman Sound, BC	Dennis King	Dennis King	1969	116
25 8/16	16	9 9/16	Cassiar Mts., BC	Arlow Lothe	Arlow Lothe	1969	116
25 8/16	15 12/16	9 12/16	McKinley River, AK	John R. Cardis	John R. Cardis	1970	116
25 8/16	16	9 8/16	Big River, AK	George Engel	George Engel	1976	116
25 8/16	16 3/16	9 5/16	Prince Rupert, BC	Murray B. Wilson	Murray B. Wilson	1979	116
25 8/16	16 8/16	9	King Salmon Creek, BC	John K. Fritze	John K. Fritze	1980	116

Score	Length	Width	Locality	Hunter	Owner	Date Killed	Rank
25 8/16	15 12/16	9 12/16	Kuskokwim River, AK	Bernard V. Davis	Bernard V. Davis	1983	116
25 8/16	16 2/16	9 6/16	Iskut River, BC	Robin Buchanan	Robin Buchanan	1987	116
25 8/16	15 15/16	9 9/16	Ospika River, BC	Frank H. Gunther	Frank H. Gunther	1987	116
25 8/16	15 12/16	9 12/16	Sand Creek, AK	Picked Up	B. & T. Jorgensen	1994	116
25 8/16	16 8/16	9	Roscoe Creek, BC	Robert Strebel	Robert Strebel	1997	116
25 8/16	15 12/16	9 12/16	Grayling, AK	David G. Imm	David G. Imm	1998	116
25 8/16	15 11/16	9 13/16	Squirrel River, AK	Robert H. McKay	Robert H. McKay	2000	116
25 8/16	15 10/16	9 14/16	Andreafsky Hills, AK	Kenneth L. Wallach	Kenneth L. Wallach	2000	116
25 7/16	15 12/16	9 11/16	Upper Boulder River, MT	Ted Johnston	E.C. Cates	1934	132
25 7/16	16	9 7/16	Tweedsmuir Park, BC	Lloyd B. Walker	Lloyd B. Walker	1950	132
25 7/16	15 13/16	9 10/16	Clearwater River, AB	Jack N. Allen	Jack N. Allen	1957	132
25 7/16	15 4/16	10 3/16	Zohini Creek, BC	Paul R. Beebe	Paul R. Beebe	1967	132
25 7/16	16 10/16	8 13/16	Nordegg, AB	Charles W. Matter	Charles W. Matter	1974	132
25 7/16	15 14/16	9 9/16	Kitlope River, BC	Darryl W. Hodson	Darryl W. Hodson	1975	132
25 7/16	15 4/16	10 3/16	Lakelse River, BC	William J. Harvey, Jr.	William J. Harvey, Jr.	1979	132
25 7/16	16 2/16	9 5/16	Andreafsky River, AK	John C. Bruno	John C. Bruno	1981	132
25 7/16	15 9/16	9 9/16	Toad River, BC	Paul E. Robey	Paul E. Robey	1981	132
25 7/16	15 13/16	9 10/16	Wedeene River, BC	Stuart Haslett	Stuart Haslett	1983	132
25 7/16	15 9/16	9 14/16	Skeena Mts., BC	Thomas J. Grogan	Thomas J. Grogan	1989	132
25 7/16	15 13/16	9 10/16	Bob Quinn Lake, BC	Patrick Kennedy	Patrick Kennedy	1998	132
25 7/16	16 9/16	8 14/16	Chiroskey River, AK	Jonathan G. Schiller	Jonathan G. Schiller	2000	132
25 7/16	15 9/16	9 14/16	Elk River, BC	Harry E. Seratt	Harry E. Seratt	2002	132
25 6/16	16 6/16	9	Slave Lake, AB	R.W.H. Eben-Ebenau	R.W.H. Eben-Ebenau	1944	146
25 6/16	16 1/16	9 5/16	Kleena Kleene, BC	A.W. Travis	A.W. Travis	1961	146
25 6/16	15 9/16	9 9/16	Northway, AK	James A. Johnson	James A. Johnson	1964	146
25 6/16	15 10/16	9 12/16	Edson, AB	Jack Armstrong	Jack Armstrong	1967	146
25 6/16	16	9 6/16	Mussel Inlet, BC	Victor W. Budd	Victor W. Budd	1967	146
25 6/16	15 3/16	10 3/16	Brooks Range, AK	Rusty Pickus	Rusty Pickus	1979	146
25 6/16		10 2/16	Kuskokwim River, AK	Michael T. Carlucci	Michael T. Carlucci	1981	146
25 6/16	15 12/16	9 10/16	Bond Sound, BC	James H. Garner	James H. Garner	1982	146
25 6/16	15 13/16	9 9/16	Liard River, BC	Norman F. Schenk	Norman F. Schenk	1986	146
25 6/16	16 2/16	9 4/16	Bella Coola, BC	G. Thierbach & F. Rad	George Thierbach	1987	146
25 6/16	16 6/16	9	Jennings River, BC	Jeffrey S. Shoaf	Jeffrey S. Shoaf	1993	146
25 6/16	15 12/16	9 10/16	Suskwa River, BC	Debra Nelson	Debra Nelson	1994	146
25 5/16	16 4/16	9 2/16	Casadepaga River, AK	Fred D. Chadwick	Fred D. Chadwick	1995	161
25 5/16	15 3/16	10 3/16	American River, AK	Casey D. Simon	Casey D. Simon	2000	161
25 5/16	15 12/16	9 10/16	Anvik River, AK	Tracy Samuelson	Tracy Samuelson	2001	161
25 5/16	15 13/16	9 8/16	Anahim Lake, BC	Ace Demers	Ace Demers	1951	161
25 5/16	15 14/16	9 7/16	Kwatna River, BC	Walter W. Butcher	Walter W. Butcher	1954	161
25 5/16	15 7/16	10 4/16	Granite Lake, YT	Jim Papst	Jim Papst	1969	161
25 5/16	15 8/16	9 9/16	Kobuk River, AK	Hugh H. Chatham, Jr.	Hugh H. Chatham, Jr.	1971	161
25 5/16	15 12/16	9 13/16	Eutsuk Lake, BC	W.R. Macfarlane	W.R. Macfarlane	1974	161
25 5/16	16 1/16	9 9/16	Brooks Range, AK	Warren K. Parker	Warren K. Parker	1979	161
25 5/16	15 7/16	9 4/16	Scoop Lake, BC	Darrell A. Farr	Dwight E. Farr, Jr.	1981	161
25 5/16	16 4/16	9 1/16	Skowquitz River, BC	Robert G. McEntee	Robert G. McEntee	1981	161
25 5/16		9 14/16	Tonzona River, AK	George G. Houser	George G. Houser	1985	161
25 5/16		9 1/16	Pilgrim Springs, AK	Troy L. Nance	Troy L. Nance	1993	161

GRIZZLY BEAR
Ursus arctos horribilis

Score	Greatest Length of Skull Without Lower Jaw	Greatest Width of Skull	Locality	Hunter	Owner	Date Killed	Rank
25 5/16	15 6/16	9 15/16	Kwiniuk River, AK	Bruce M. Stoner	Bruce M. Stoner	1994	161
25 5/16	15 10/16	9 11/16	Deadlock Mt., AK	Richard R. Lindsay	Richard R. Lindsay	1995	161
25 5/16	15 12/16	9 9/16	Solo Lake, AK	Robert P. Robb	Robert P. Robb	1995	161
25 5/16	15 10/16	9 11/16	Alaska Range, AK	Andrew J. Klejka	Andrew J. Klejka	1998	161
25 4/16	16	9 4/16	Anahim Lake, BC	C.D. Carrington	Univ. of CA Museum	1957	175
25 4/16	16 3/16	9 1/16	Cascade Inlet, BC	Walter A. Frame	Walter A. Frame	1964	175
25 4/16	15 9/16	9 11/16	Salmon River, BC	Al Rand	Al Rand	1964	175
25 4/16	15 8/16	9 12/16	Yanert River, AK	Herbert A. Biss	Herbert A. Biss	1965	175
25 4/16	15 5/16	9 15/16	Anahim Lake, BC	Bernard Nofziger	Bernard Nofziger	1970	175
25 4/16	15 13/16	9 7/16	Kynoch Inlet, BC	P.J. Kennedy	W.G. Hawes	1971	175
25 4/16	15 15/16	9 5/16	Berland River, AB	Donald Brockman	Donald Brockman	1978	175
25 4/16	15 12/16	9 8/16	Alaska Range, AK	David L. Kulzer	David L. Kulzer	1979	175
25 4/16	15 10/16	9 10/16	Gisasa River, AK	Billy R. Deligans, Jr.	Billy R. Deligans, Jr.	1985	175
25 4/16	16 2/16	9 2/16	Dazell Creek, AK	Armand J. Giannini	Armand J. Giannini	1988	175
25 4/16	16 4/16	9	Trapper Lake, BC	John Kloosterman	John Kloosterman	1991	175
25 4/16	15 14/16	9 6/16	Noatak River, AK	A. Dean Chelton	A. Dean Chelton	1999	175
25 3/16	15 7/16	9 12/16	Bella Coola, BC	Umberto Benedet	Umberto Benedet	1957	187
25 3/16	16 4/16	8 15/16	Wrangell Mts., AK	Peter W. Bading	Peter W. Bading	1963	187
25 3/16	15 9/16	9 10/16	Teller, AK	Harry J. Armitage	Harry J. Armitage	1965	187
25 3/16	15 1/16	10 2/16	Motase Lake, BC	Joel Franzoia	Joel Franzoia	1970	187
25 3/16	15 9/16	9 10/16	Anahim Lake, BC	Lloyd E. Nygaard	Lloyd E. Nygaard	1973	187
25 3/16	15 9/16	9 10/16	McClinchy River, BC	Picked Up	Bernie Gano	PR 1974	187
25 3/16	16 2/16	9 1/16	Bella Coola, BC	Richard K. Miller	Richard K. Miller	1975	187
25 3/16	15 8/16	9 11/16	Thutade Lake, BC	James H. Glover	James H. Glover	1977	187
25 3/16	15 5/16	9 13/16	American River, AK	John M. Griffith, Jr.	John M. Griffith, Jr.	1977	187
25 3/16	15 5/16	9 14/16	Andreafsky River, AK	James P. Barkman	James P. Barkman	1980	187
25 3/16	15 9/16	9 10/16	Ogilvie Mts., YT	Stanton E. Wilson	Stanton E. Wilson	1981	187
25 3/16	15 9/16	9 10/16	Kingcome River, BC	Graydon A. Peat	Graydon A. Peat	1983	187
25 3/16	16	9 3/16	Nunakogok River, AK	Randy Jackson	Randy Jackson	1984	187
25 3/16	15 14/16	9 5/16	Boston Creek, AK	Sigurd E. Murphy	Sigurd E. Murphy	1987	187
25 3/16	15 8/16	9 11/16	Salcha River, AK	Danny E. Walker	Danny E. Walker	1987	187
25 3/16	16 1/16	9 2/16	Bella Coola River, BC	Craig A. Crichton	Craig A. Crichton	1996	187
25 2/16	15 10/16	9 8/16	Fremont Co., WY	Unknown	Warren V. Spriggs, Sr.	1947	203
25 2/16	15 14/16	9 4/16	Yellowstone River, WY	Bill Nymeyer	Jack H. White	1960	203
25 2/16	16 2/16	9	Lignite, AK	Leonard Spencer	Leonard Spencer	1963	203
25 2/16	16 2/16	9 5/16	Mentasta Mts., AK	Basil C. Bradbury	Basil C. Bradbury	1965	203
25 2/16	15 13/16	9 5/16	Kotzebue, AK	F.W. Hatterscheidt	F.W. Hatterscheidt	1968	203
25 2/16	16	9 2/16	Bella Coola, BC	Howard Morrisey	Howard Morrisey	1971	203

Score	Length	Width	Locality	Hunter	Owner	Date Killed	Rank
25 2/16	15 6/16	9 12/16	McGrath, AK	Curtis C. Classen	Curtis C. Classen	1974	203
25 2/16	15 8/16	9 10/16	Butedale, BC	Walter R. Peters	Walter R. Peters	1974	203
25 2/16	15 12/16	9 6/16	Parsnip River, BC	Graham Markland	Graham Markland	1977	203
25 2/16	16	9 2/16	Cluculz Creek, BC	Ed Roberson	Ed Roberson	1978	203
25 2/16	15 6/16	9 12/16	Beaver Creek, AK	Picked Up	Abram Walter	1979	203
25 2/16	15 10/16	9 8/16	Blue Ridge, AB	Thomas E. Deacon	Thomas E. Deacon	1983	203
25 2/16	15 2/16	10	Kemano River, BC	Victor L. Sensenig	Victor L. Sensenig	1983	203
25 2/16	15 12/16	9 6/16	Toklat River, AK	Marvin Carkhuff	Marvin Carkhuff	1987	203
25 2/16	15 6/16	9 12/16	Dease Lake, BC	John Flynn	John Flynn	1988	203
25 2/16	15 2/16	10	Noomst Creek, BC	Marc A. Laynes	Marc A. Laynes	1988	203
25 2/16	15 6/16	9 12/16	Banner Creek, AK	Randall K. Russell	Randall K. Russell	1999	203
25 2/16	15 8/16	9 10/16	Mess Creek, BC	Marty Halpern	Marty Halpern	2000	203
25 2/16	15 4/16	9 14/16	Level Mt., BC	George W. Jacobson	George W. Jacobson	2000	203
25 1/16	15 11/16	9 6/16	Teton Co., WY	C.C. Craven	Jackson Hole Museum	1938	222
25 1/16	15 13/16	9 4/16	Knight Inlet, BC	Frederic N. Dodge	Frederic N. Dodge	1954	222
25 1/16	15 14/16	9 3/16	Bella Coola, BC	L. Rowe Davidson	L. Rowe Davidson	1958	222
25 1/16	15 11/16	9 6/16	Caribou Flats, BC	Edward Escott	Edward Escott	1962	222
25 1/16	16 3/16	8 14/16	Yanert River, AK	E.G. Brust, Jr.	E.G. Brust, Jr.	1964	222
25 1/16	15 8/16	9 9/16	Selby River, AK	Kenneth T. Alt	Kenneth T. Alt	1965	222
25 1/16	15 12/16	9 5/16	Bob Quinn Lake, BC	Dave Miscavish	Dave Miscavish	1971	222
25 1/16	15 10/16	9 7/16	Pikmiktalik River, AK	Donald B. Huffines	Donald B. Huffines	1984	222
25 1/16	15 12/16	9 5/16	Euchiniko Lakes, BC	Native American	Mark J. Simonson	1986	222
25 1/16	15 15/16	9 2/16	Morice River, BC	Doug W. Six	Doug W. Six	1991	222
25 1/16	15 14/16	9 3/16	Alsek River, BC	Roy S. Bowers	Roy S. Bowers	1994	222
25 1/16	16	9 1/16	Tatshenshini River, BC	James C. Ranck	James C. Ranck	1998	222
25 1/16	16	9 1/16	Nulato River, AK	Heath Sisk	Heath Sisk	2000	222
25 1/16	15 9/16	9 8/16	Kauk River, AK	Jack B. Robins	Jack B. Robins	2002	222
25	16 3/16	8 13/16	Lewistown, MT	Mildred Connor	U.S. Natl. Museum	1888	236
25	15 9/16	9 7/16	Atnarko River, BC	David Maytag	H.J. Borden	1959	236
25	15 11/16	9 5/16	Nabesna River, AK	Marven A. Henriksen	Marven A. Henriksen	1964	236
25	15	10	Yellowstone Natl. Park, WY	Picked Up	John C. Kirk	PR 1965	236
25	15 4/16	9 12/16	Kotzebue, AK	Glen E. Park	Glen E. Park	1965	236
25	15 3/16	9 13/16	Hart Ranges, BC	T.T. Stroup	T.T. Stroup	1966	236
25	15 4/16	9 12/16	Mt. Hayes, AK	Benjamin H. Robson	Benjamin H. Robson	1968	236
25	15 8/16	9 8/16	Noomst Creek, BC	James G. Shelton	James G. Shelton	1970	236
25	15 10/16	9 6/16	Stikine River, BC	Donald R. McClure, Sr.	Donald R. McClure, Sr.	1971	236
25	15 13/16	9 3/16	Tacu River, BC	W.N. Olson	W.N. Olson	1971	236
25	15 15/16	9 1/16	Hinton, AB	Oliver Hannula	Oliver Hannula	1972	236
25	15 8/16	9 8/16	Whitecourt, AB	Sid Wheeler	Sid Wheeler	1974	236
25	14 14/16	10 2/16	Richland Co., MT	Picked Up	Jack Stewart	1976	236
25	16 1/16	8 15/16	Fortymile River, AK	James B. DeMoss	James B. DeMoss	1980	236
25	15 13/16	9 3/16	Owikeno Lake, EC	Robert K. Fisher	Robert K. Fisher	1981	236
25	15 6/16	9 10/16	Bella Coola River, BC	James G. Shelton	James G. Shelton	1983	236
25	16 9/16	8 7/16	Koyuk River, AK	John Macaluso	John Macaluso	1985	236
25	15 9/16	9 7/16	Chinchaga River, AB	Bernd Licht	Bernd Licht	1989	236
25	15 14/16	9 2/16	Dunedin River, BC	E.M. Takahashi	E.M. Takahashi	1992	236
25			Noatak River, AK	Kenneth C. Thomas	Kenneth C. Thomas	1992	236

GRIZZLY BEAR
Ursus arctos horribilis

Score	Greatest Length of Skull Without Lower Jaw	Greatest Width of Skull	Locality	Hunter	Owner	Date Killed	Rank
25	15 10/16	9 6/16	Ungalik River, AK	Donald R. Card	Donald R. Card	1996	236
25	15 11/16	9 5/16	Klinaklini River, BC	George P. Mann	George P. Mann	1999	236
25	15 13/16	9 3/16	Ungalik River, AK	Aaron I. James	Aaron I. James	2002	236
25	15 8/16	9 8/16	Golsovia River, AK	Dennis G. Rulewicz	Dennis G. Rulewicz	2002	236
24 15/16	15 6/16	9 9/16	Taseko Lakes, BC	A. Cecil Henry	A. Cecil Henry	1956	260
24 15/16	15 4/16	9 11/16	Ootsa Lake, BC	J. Block & D. Vantine	John Block	1965	260
24 15/16	15 7/16	9 8/16	Dudidontu River, BC	Bob Loewenstein	Bob Loewenstein	1965	260
24 15/16	15 14/16	9 1/16	Teller, AK	Jack D. Putnam	Jack D. Putnam	1965	260
24 15/16	15 10/16	9 5/16	Lakelse River, BC	Victor Lepp	Victor Lepp	1968	260
24 15/16	15 12/16	9 3/16	Wrangell Mts., AK	James E. Saxton	James E. Saxton	1977	260
24 15/16	15 13/16	9 2/16	Nusatsum River, BC	Picked Up	Randy Svisdahl	1980	260
24 15/16	15 6/16	9 9/16	Tonzona River, AK	Wayne J. Pensenstadler	Wayne J. Pensenstadler	1982	260
24 15/16	15 5/16	9 10/16	Tetsa River, BC	John J. Belous	John J. Belous	1985	260
24 15/16	15 7/16	9 8/16	Maroon Creek, BC	Roger M. Britton	Roger M. Britton	1988	260
24 15/16	15 15/16	9	Pilgrim River, AK	Daniel R. Fiehrer	Daniel R. Fiehrer	1999	260
24 15/16	15 10/16	9 5/16	Mt. Lathrop, AK	Tor Wittussen	Tor Wittussen	2000	260
24 14/16	16 2/16	8 12/16	Atnarko, BC	F.N. Bard	Chicago Nat. Hist. Mus.	1938	272
24 14/16	15 12/16	9 2/16	Chilcotin, BC	R.J. Pop & J. Beban	R.J. Pop	1954	272
24 14/16	15 7/16	9 7/16	Chisana, AK	Larry Folger	Larry Folger	1957	272
24 14/16	15 9/16	9 5/16	Atnarko River, BC	Carl Molander	Carl Molander	1957	272
24 14/16	15 11/16	9 3/16	Meziadin Lake, BC	Larry T. Spangler	Larry T. Spangler	1962	272
24 14/16	15 4/16	9 10/16	Brooks Range, AK	E. Wayne Gilley	E. Wayne Gilley	1963	272
24 14/16	15 13/16	9 1/16	Alaska Range, AK	Jack Williamson	Jack Williamson	1963	272
24 14/16	15 2/16	9 12/16	Shishmaref, AK	James K. Harrower	James K. Harrower	1964	272
24 14/16	16 3/16	8 11/16	Taku River, BC	Robert J. Lacy	Robert J. Lacy	1964	272
24 14/16	16 3/16	8 11/16	Knights Inlet, BC	Levon Bender	Levon Bender	1965	272
24 14/16	15 7/16	9 7/16	Brooks Range, AK	W.F. Krebill	W.F. Krebill	1966	272
24 14/16	15 6/16	9 8/16	Cassiar Mts., BC	H. Kenneth Seiferd	H. Kenneth Seiferd	1966	272
24 14/16	15 7/16	9 7/16	McGregor Mts., BC	Edward Johnson	Edward Johnson	1967	272
24 14/16	15 9/16	9 5/16	McGregor River, BC	C.C. Carpenter	C.C. Carpenter	1968	272
24 14/16	15 12/16	9 2/16	Telkwa River, BC	Richard Pohlschneider	Richard Pohlschneider	1969	272
24 14/16	15 6/16	9 8/16	Seaskinnish Creek, BC	Thomas D.J. Fulkco	Thomas D.J. Fulkco	1977	272
24 14/16	15 3/16	9 11/16	Klutina River, AK	Robert M. Decker	Robert M. Decker	1979	272
24 14/16	15 8/16	9 6/16	Tatla Lake, BC	Donald L. Gardner	Donald L. Gardner	1980	272
24 14/16	15 10/16	9 4/16	Andreafsky River, AK	James W. Latreille	James W. Latreille	1980	272
24 14/16	15 15/16	8 15/16	Barney Creek, BC	Roy Pattison	Roy Pattison	1984	272
24 14/16	15 4/16	9 10/16	Squirrel River, AK	William M. Eubank	William M. Eubank	1988	272
24 14/16	15 8/16	9 6/16	Grayling Fork, YT	Michael L. Rogers	Michael L. Rogers	1991	272

Score	Length	Width	Locality	Hunter	Owner	Date	Rank
24 14/16	15 12/16	9 2/16	Meziadin Lake, BC	C. Don Wall	C. Don Wall	1991	272
24 14/16	15 5/16	9 9/16	Nazcha Creek, BC	Ken Moffett	Ken Moffett	1992	272
24 14/16	15 3/16	9 11/16	Knight Inlet, BC	Robert E. Sheets	Robert E. Sheets	1992	272
24 14/16	15 10/16	9 4/16	Nation River, YT	Daniel J. Jones	Daniel J. Jones	1993	272
24 14/16	15 8/16	9 6/16	Peace River, BC	Lee Johnson	Lee Johnson	1995	272
24 14/16	15 8/16	9 6/16	Buckland River, AK	Norbert D. Bremer	Norbert D. Bremer	1999	272
24 14/16	15 8/16	9 6/16	Dean Creek, AK	Mark D. Etchart	Mark D. Etchart	2003	272
24 14/16	15 10/16	9 4/16	Salmon Creek, AK	Bradford G. McDavid	Bradford G. McDavid	2003	272
24 13/16	15 7/16	9 6/16	Chisana River, AK	Larry Folger	Larry Folger	1957	302
24 13/16	15 9/16	9 4/16	Livengood, AK	Ada Holst	Ada Holst	1961	302
24 13/16	15 3/16	9 10/16	Tatla Lake, BC	R.D. Brooks	R.D. Brooks	1962	302
24 13/16	15 12/16	9 1/16	Warden Creek, AB	Harvey R. Cook	Harvey R. Cook	1964	302
24 13/16	15 12/16	9 1/16	Chetwynd, BC	William E. Dugger	William E. Dugger	1964	302
24 13/16	15 5/16	9 8/16	Tonzona River, AK	Francis Kernan	Francis Kernan	1964	302
24 13/16	15 4/16	9 9/16	Clarence Lake, AK	E.A. Munroe	E.A. Munroe	1964	302
24 13/16	15 9/16	9 4/16	Slim Lake, BC	Freda Stalder	Freda Stalder	1968	302
24 13/16	15 4/16	9 9/16	Noatak River, AK	John E. Batson	John E. Batson	1970	302
24 13/16	15 11/16	9 2/16	Telkwa Range, BC	Jack Adams	Jack Adams	1978	302
24 13/16	15 15/16	8 14/16	Kilbella River, BC	Larry Sawchuk	Larry Sawchuk	1984	302
24 13/16	15 14/16	8 15/16	Burnt Trail Creek, BC	Tom W. Housh	Tom W. Housh	1985	302
24 13/16	15 8/16	9 5/16	Noatak River, AK	Dave R. Cerenzia	Dave R. Cerenzia	1987	302
24 13/16	15 10/16	9 3/16	Bear River, AK	Richard M. Cowles	Richard M. Cowles	1987	302
24 13/16	15 13/16	9	Trident Glacier, AK	Glenn J. Rasmussen	Glenn J. Rasmussen	1992	302
24 13/16	15	9 13/16	Bella Coola River, BC	Byron K. McGaffey	Byron K. McGaffey	1993	302
24 13/16	15 7/16	9 6/16	Pitmegea River, AK	Scott R. Ravenscroft	Scott R. Ravenscroft	1993	302
24 13/16	15 10/16	9 3/16	Noatak River, AK	Morris A. Link	Morris A. Link	2000	302
24 13/16	15 7/16	9 6/16	Swan Hills, AB	Allan P. Keats	Allan P. Keats	2001	302
24 13/16	15 8/16	9 5/16	Soule Lake, AK	Jeffery Belongia	Jeffery Belongia	2002	302
24 12/16	15 6/16	9 6/16	Spanish Lake, BC	Bill Niemi	Bill Niemi	1953	322
24 12/16	15	9 12/16	Sheep Creek, AB	Robert V. Broadbent	Robert V. Broadbent	1963	322
24 12/16	15 10/16	9 2/16	Brooks Range, AK	Lewis A. Meyers	Lewis A. Meyers	1964	322
24 12/16	15 8/16	9 4/16	Terminus Mt., BC	Herb Klein	Dallas Mus. of Natl. Hist.	1965	322
24 12/16	15 15/16	8 13/16	Kitimat, BC	Hans Lackner	Hans Lackner	1969	322
24 12/16	15 4/16	9 8/16	Burrage Creek, BC	Jack Worthy	Jack Worthy	1970	322
24 12/16	15 10/16	9 2/16	Toklat River, AK	George P. Mann	George P. Mann	1971	322
24 12/16	15 8/16	9 4/16	Bella Coola, BC	Joe M. Colvin	Joe M. Colvin	1973	322
24 12/16	15 7/16	9 5/16	Alaska Range, AK	Earl K. Edstrom	Earl K. Edstrom	1976	322
24 12/16	15 8/16	9 4/16	Wigwam River, BC	Ray S. Koontz	Ray S. Koontz	1977	322
24 12/16	15 12/16	9	Turnagain River, BC	Arthur E. Crawford	Arthur E. Crawford	1980	322
24 12/16	15 6/16	9 6/16	Norton Sound, AK	Lewis E. Henyon	Lewis E. Henyon	1984	322
24 12/16	15 13/16	8 15/16	Tsayta Lake, BC	Vincent A. Pisani	Vincent A. Pisani	1986	322
24 12/16	16 2/16	8 10/16	Teklanika River, AK	Kenneth E. Abel	Kenneth E. Abel	1990	322
24 12/16	15 7/16	9 5/16	Valemount, BC	Mark G. Holt	Mark G. Holt	1992	322
24 12/16	15 4/16	9 8/16	Pilgrim River, AK	Brent E. Chadwick	Brent E. Chadwick	1995	322
24 12/16	15 10/16	9 2/16	Minaker River, BC	Fred A. Parent	Fred A. Parent	1995	322
24 12/16	15 8/16	9 4/16	Telegraph Creek, BC	Keith C. Caldwell	Keith C. Caldwell	1996	322
24 12/16	15 7/16	9 5/16	White River, YT	Roger D. Evans	Roger D. Evans	1996	322

GRIZZLY BEAR
Ursus arctos horribilis

Score	Greatest Length of Skull Without Lower Jaw	Greatest Width of Skull	Locality	Hunter	Owner	Date Killed	Rank
24 12/16	15 8/16	9 4/16	Fraser River, BC	Randy W. Kolida	Randy W. Kolida	1996	322
24 12/16	16	8 12/16	Stupendous Mt., BC	Malcolm R. Bachand	Malcolm R. Bachand	1999	322
24 12/16	15 15/16	8 13/16	Noatak River, AK	Christian Johnson	Christian Johnson	1999	322
24 12/16	15 14/16	8 14/16	Beaver Inlet, BC	Peter G. Klaui	Peter G. Klaui	2000	322
24 11/16	15 2/16	9 9/16	Stevens Lake, BC	R.L. Hambrick	R.L. Hambrick	1965	345
24 11/16	15 4/16	9 7/16	Tok River, AK	Lewis B. Wyman	Lewis B. Wyman	1965	345
24 11/16	15 4/16	9 4/16	Alaska Range, AK	Tony Caputo	Tony Caputo	1967	345
24 11/16	15 14/16	8 13/16	Lesser Slave Lake, AB	Picked Up	James Erickson	1967	345
24 11/16	15	9 11/16	MacMillan Plateau, YT	Paul Yeager	Paul Yeager	1967	345
24 11/16	15 8/16	9 3/16	Butte Inlet, BC	Thomas M. Utigard	Thomas M. Utigard	1970	345
24 11/16	15 6/16	9 5/16	Kuzitrin River, AK	H. Doak Neal	H. Doak Neal	1976	345
24 11/16	15	9 11/16	Toklat River, AK	Timothy A. Sanderson	Timothy A. Sanderson	1976	345
24 11/16	15 3/16	9 8/16	Toad River, BC	Bruce H. Morrill	Bruce H. Morrill	1980	345
24 11/16	15 9/16	9 2/16	Kwatna Bay, BC	Norman C. Roettger	Norman C. Roettger	1982	345
24 11/16	15 9/16	9 2/16	American Creek, AK	Marvin H. Hanebuth	Marvin H. Hanebuth	1986	345
24 11/16	15 6/16	9 5/16	Cadomin, AB	Pemble Davis	Pemble Davis	1987	345
24 11/16	15 13/16	8 14/16	Moses Inlet, BC	Robert E. Johnson	Robert E. Johnson	1989	345
24 11/16	15 9/16	9 2/16	Muskwa River, BC	Benjamin F. Kirkham	Benjamin F. Kirkham	1990	345
24 11/16	15 9/16	9 2/16	Kirbyville Creek, BC	Gary L. Drager	Gary L. Drager	1992	345
24 11/16	15 5/16	9 6/16	Sheep Mt., AK	Norman W. Schmidt	Norman W. Schmidt	1994	345
24 11/16	15 3/16	9 8/16	Koyuk River, AK	Peter J. Pizzagalli	Peter J. Pizzagalli	1996	345
24 11/16	15 6/16	9 5/16	Cheeneetnuk River, AK	Chuck R. Schlindwein	Chuck R. Schlindwein	1999	345
24 11/16	15 6/16	9 6/16	Virginia Creek, AK	Mike L. Wade	Mike L. Wade	2001	345
24 10/16	15 8/16	9 2/16	Camp Island Lake, BC	Harold L. Jones	Harold L. Jones	1965	364
24 10/16	15 8/16	9 6/16	Point Hope, AK	Richard K. Siller	Richard K. Siller	1965	364
24 10/16	15 4/16	9 6/16	Brooks Range, AK	T.W. Bohannan	T.W. Bohannan	1968	364
24 10/16	15 5/16	9 5/16	Seymour Inlet, BC	Tim Fischer	Tim Fischer	1969	364
24 10/16	15 11/16	8 15/16	Wiseman, AK	David L. Howard	David L. Howard	1970	364
24 10/16	15 4/16	9 6/16	Toklat River, AK	Gary Miller	Gary Miller	1972	364
24 10/16	15 2/16	9 8/16	Mosley Creek, BC	Charles Harvey	Charles Harvey	1976	364
24 10/16	15 4/16	9 6/16	Alaska Range, AK	Victor Geibel	Victor Geibel	1978	364
24 10/16	15 6/16	9 4/16	Toklat River, AK	Howard W. Neice	Howard W. Neice	1981	364
24 10/16	15 3/16	9 7/16	Pilgrim River, AK	Karen J. Chadwick	Karen J. Chadwick	1982	364
24 10/16	14 12/16	9 14/16	John River, AK	Rick J. Schikora	Rick J. Schikora	1982	364
24 10/16	15 14/16	8 12/16	Swan Hills, AB	Henry H. Foisy	Henry H. Foisy	1988	364
24 10/16	14 12/16	8 14/16	Mt. Miller, YT	Doug White	Doug White	1990	364
24 10/16	15 12/16	8 14/16	Gold Bridge, BC	J. Gregory Boyd	J. Gregory Boyd	1993	364
24 10/16	14 15/16	9 11/16	Horse Range Creek, BC	Guyle G. Cox	Guyle G. Cox	1993	364

Score	Length	Width	Locality	Owner	Hunter	Date Killed	Rank
24 10/16	15 8/16	9 2/16	Morice River, BC	Tom Wiggins	Tom Wiggins	1993	364
24 10/16	15 2/16	9 8/16	Bond Sound, BC	Marvin S. Maki	Marvin S. Maki	1997	364
24 10/16	15 14/16	8 12/16	Babine Lake, BC	Stephen J. McGrath	Stephen J. McGrath	1999	364
24 9/16	15 5/16	9 4/16	Whiteswan Lake, BC	A.C. Gilbert	A.C. Gilbert	1937	382
24 9/16	15 8/16	9 1/16	Tatla Lake, BC	D. McDermott	D. McDermott	1954	382
24 9/16	15 13/16	8 12/16	Bella Coola, BC	William P. Mastrangel	William P. Mastrangel	1956	382
24 9/16	15 4/16	9 5/16	Atnarko River, BC	Martin Anderson	Martin Anderson	1957	382
24 9/16	15 3/16	9 6/16	Owikeno Lake, BC	Norman W. Garwood	Norman W. Garwood	1960	382
24 9/16	15 7/16	9 2/16	Hulahula River, AK	Richard Sjoden	Richard Sjoden	1963	382
24 9/16	15 4/16	9 5/16	Ray Mts., AK	Mario Grassi	Mario Grassi	1965	382
24 9/16	16 1/16	8 8/16	Anahim Lake, BC	M.V. Nearing	M.V. Nearing	1966	382
24 9/16	15 6/16	9 3/16	Meziadin Lake, BC	Teuvo Pahti	Teuvo Pahti	1968	382
24 9/16	15 5/16	9 4/16	Tok River, AK	John W. Waller	John W. Waller	1968	382
24 9/16	15 1/16	9 1/16	Cape Lisburne, AK	Gerrit N. Vandenberg	Gerrit N. Vandenberg	1969	382
24 9/16	15 9/16	9	Kispiox River, BC	W.J. Love	W.J. Love	1971	382
24 9/16	16	8 9/16	Graham River, BC	Edward F. Lundberg	Edward F. Lundberg	1976	382
24 9/16	14 15/16	9 10/16	Yanert River, AK	Robert J. Barham	Robert J. Barham	1977	382
24 9/16	15	9 9/16	Quesnel Lake, BC	Thomas E. Phillippe, Sr.	Thomas E. Phillippe, Sr.	1978	382
24 9/16	15 13/16	8 12/16	Chuckwalla River, BC	George B. Morris	George B. Morris	1979	382
24 9/16	15 7/16	9 8/16	Motase Peak, BC	Roger L. Pock	Roger L. Pock	1984	382
24 9/16	15 1/16	9 1/16	Brooks Range, AK	Tim D. Hiner	Tim D. Hiner	1992	382
24 9/16	14 13/16	9 12/16	Kukpowruk River, AK	Alan J. Amundson	Alan J. Amundson	1993	382
24 9/16	15 8/16	9 1/16	Mosquito Fork, AK	Richard C. Swisher	Richard C. Swisher	1996	382
24 9/16	15 11/16	8 14/16	Eleven Mile Creek, BC	Clint Cartier	Clint Cartier	1999	382
24 9/16	15 1/16	8 13/16	Ungalik River, AK	William F. Kneer	William F. Kneer, Jr.	1999	382
24 9/16	14 13/16	9 12/16	Ungalik River, AK	Steven A. Persson	Steven A. Persson	1999	382
24 9/16	15 10/16	8 15/16	Taku River, BC	Kent Deligans	Kent Deligans	2003	382
24 8/16	15 2/16	9 6/16	Cassiar Mts., BC	Elgin T. Gates	Elgin T. Gates	1953	406
24 8/16	14 11/16	9 13/16	Mt. McKinley, AK	Howard W. Pollock	Howard W. Pollock	1953	406
24 8/16	15	9 8/16	Bella Coola, BC	H.J. Borden	James A. Perry	1959	406
24 8/16	15 4/16	9 4/16	Big Delta, AK	Harold E. Hogan	Harold E. Hogan	1961	406
24 8/16	15 15/16	9 9/16	Tatla Lake, BC	Harold A. Cowman	Harold A. Cowman	1964	406
24 8/16	15 13/16	8 11/16	Kleena Kleene River, BC	Martin J. Durkan	Martin J. Durkan	1966	406
24 8/16	15 1/16	9 7/16	Brooks Range, AK	Jerry N. Martin	Jerry N. Martin	1968	406
24 8/16	15 2/16	9 6/16	Kotzebue, AK	C.J. McElroy	C.J. McElroy	1968	406
24 8/16	15 1/16	9 7/16	Brooks Range, AK	Rick Reakoff	Rick Reakoff	1969	406
24 8/16	15 2/16	9 6/16	Tweedsmuir Park, BC	T. & C. Ritter	T. & C. Ritter	1970	406
24 8/16	14 11/16	9 13/16	Lakelse River, BC	Kolbjorn Eide	Kolbjorn Eide	1971	406
24 8/16	14 14/16	9 10/16	Miner Lake, BC	Dwight E. Farr, Jr.	Dwight E. Farr, Jr.	1971	406
24 8/16	15 6/16	9 2/16	Coast Range, BC	Laverne D. Hirzel	L.D. Hirzel & J. Petersen	1973	406
24 8/16	14 12/16	9 12/16	Stikine River, BC	Fred P. Grob	Fred P. Grob	1974	406
24 8/16	15 5/16	9 3/16	Colville River, AK	Richard A. McClellan	Richard A. McClellan	1974	406
24 8/16	15 5/16	9 11/16	Tonzona River, BC	Jill L. Nunley	Jill L. Nunley	1976	406
24 8/16	14 13/16	9 6/16	Ogilvie Mts., YT	Vearl Fowler	Vearl Fowler	1977	406
24 8/16	15 2/16	9 4/16	Brooks Range, AK	Calvin Danzig	Calvin Danzig	1978	406
24 8/16	15 4/16	9 1/16	Fraser River, BC	Paul F. Bays, Sr.	Paul F. Bays, Sr.	1978	406
24 8/16	15 7/16	9 1/16	Kugrururok River AK	Bruce A. Moe	Bruce A. Moe	1978	406

Score	Greatest Length of Skull Without Lower Jaw	Greatest Width of Skull	Locality	Hunter	Owner	Date Killed	Rank
24 8/16	15 9/16	8 15/16	Table River, BC	George W. Morris	George W. Morris	1978	406
24 8/16	15	9 8/16	Terminus Mt., BC	William E. Greehey	William E. Greehey	1982	406
24 8/16	15 1/16	9 7/16	Koyuk, AK	K. James Malady III	K. James Malady III	1985	406
24 8/16	15 9/16	8 15/16	Brazeau Mts., AB	Richard F. Edmonds, Jr.	Richard F. Edmonds, Jr.	1986	406
24 8/16	15 9/16	8 15/16	Kuskokwim River, AK	Jerome D. Melbinger	Jerome D. Melbinger	1986	406
24 8/16	14 14/16	9 10/16	Greyling Creek, YT	Lee A. Hickey, Sr.	Lee A. Hickey, Sr.	1987	406
24 8/16	15	9 8/16	Buckland River, AK	Curtis R. Cebulski	Douglas E. Christiansen	1988	406
24 8/16	15 6/16	9 2/16	Norton Sound, AK	Jerry W. Peterman	Jerry W. Peterman	1988	406
24 8/16	15 2/16	9 6/16	Bowser Lake, BC	Raymond J. Kotera	Raymond J. Kotera	1990	406
24 8/16	14 8/16	10	Eli River, AK	Gary A. Habe	Gary A. Habe	1992	406
24 8/16	15 7/16	9 1/16	Tatla Lake, BC	Morris Monita	Morris Monita	1993	406
24 8/16	15 8/16	9	Yukon River, YT	Roger D. Hanover	Roger D. Hanover	1994	406
24 8/16	15 1/16	9 7/16	Tezzeron Creek, BC	Ken Graham	Ken Graham	1996	406
24 8/16	15 5/16	9 3/16	Cariboo River, BC	Peter P.K. Grundmann	Peter P.K. Grundmann	1996	406
24 8/16	15 4/16	9 4/16	Ducette Peak, BC	Rainer Maas	Rainer Maas	1997	406
24 8/16	14 13/16	9 11/16	Kobuk River, AK	Timothy S. Moermond	Timothy S. Moermond	2001	406
24 8/16	15 5/16	9 3/16	Koyuk River, AK	Holly E. Oliver II	Holly E. Oliver II	2001	406
24 7/16	15	9 7/16	Cold Fish Lake, BC	William E. Goudey	William E. Goudey	1956	443
24 7/16	15 8/16	8 15/16	Dease River, BC	John Caputo, Sr.	John Caputo, Sr.	1958	443
24 7/16	15 6/16	9 1/16	Brooks Range, AK	Bobbie J. Cavnar	Bobbie J. Cavnar	1966	443
24 7/16	15 5/16	9 2/16	McClaren Glacier, AK	Gordon S. Pleiss	Gordon S. Pleiss	1967	443
24 7/16	15 7/16	9	Brooks Range, AK	Don Elder	Don Elder	1968	443
24 7/16	15 4/16	9 3/16	Ocena Falls, BC	Richard D. Dimick	Richard D. Dimick	1969	443
24 7/16	15 2/16	9 5/16	Colville River, AK	Alfonso I. Casso	Alfonso I. Casso	1970	443
24 7/16	15 6/16	9 1/16	Grande Cache, AB	Laurier Adam	Laurier Adam	1976	443
24 7/16	15 8/16	8 15/16	Kelly Creek, AK	Rick H. Jackson	Rick H. Jackson	1980	443
24 7/16	15 5/16	9 2/16	Wood River, AK	Kerry Q. Gronewold	Kerry Q. Gronewold	1984	443
24 7/16	14 15/16	9 8/16	Wulik River, AK	Peter W. Dress	Bill Dress	1986	443
24 7/16	15 6/16	9 1/16	Dore River, BC	Brian C. Jeck	Brian C. Jeck	1987	443
24 7/16	14 15/16	9 8/16	Nation River, AK	Robert W. Stenehjem	Robert W. Stenehjem	1987	443
24 7/16	14 15/16	9 8/16	Big River, AK	William J. Schilling	William J. Schilling	1992	443
24 7/16	15 8/16	8 15/16	Raley Creek, BC	Randy Kucharyshen	Randy Kucharyshen	1994	443
24 7/16	15 1/16	9 6/16	Black Lake, YT	Thomas P. Bruner	Thomas P. Bruner	1995	443
24 7/16	15 2/16	9 5/16	Kelly River, AK	Robert H. Mace	Robert H. Mace	1998	443
24 6/16	15	9 6/16	Alaska Hwy. Mile 175, BC	Selmer Torrison	Selmer Torrison	1958	460
24 6/16	15 6/16	9	Willow River, BC	Eric Hanet	Eric Hanet	1962	460
24 6/16	15 2/16	9 4/16	Alaska Range, AK	Hank Kramer	Hank Kramer	1964	460
24 6/16	14 10/16	9 12/16	Yanert River, AK	P.W. LaHaye	P.W. LaHaye	1965	460

Score	Length	Width	Locality	Hunter	Owner	Date Killed	Rank
24 6/16	15 5/16	9 1/16	Alaska Range, AK	Alberto Pipia	Alberto Pipia	1966	460
24 6/16	15 6/16	9	Atlin, BC	Jack E. Carpenter	Jack E. Carpenter	1967	460
24 6/16	15 15/16	9 7/16	Brooks Range, AK	Paul H. Magee	Paul H. Magee	1967	460
24 6/16	14 12/16	9 10/16	Prince George, BC	Wayne H. Laursen	Wayne H. Laursen	1969	460
24 6/16	15	9 6/16	Colville River, AK	E.H. Borchers, Jr.	E.H. Borchers, Jr.	1970	460
24 6/16	15 8/16	8 14/16	Wrangell Mts., AK	Victor W. Bullard	Victor W. Bullard	1971	460
24 6/16	14 14/16	9 8/16	Ogilvie Mts., YT	Philip R. Murphy	Philip R. Murphy	1972	460
24 6/16	15 4/16	9 2/16	Cassiar Mts., BC	Monte Hofstrand	Monte Hofstrand	1975	460
24 6/16	14 11/16	9 11/16	Kelly River, AK	J.B. Goodman & E. Remsing	J.B. Goodman & E. Remsing	1976	460
24 6/16	15	9	Alaska Range, AK	Steve Casey	Steve Casey	1977	460
24 6/16	15 2/16	9 2/16	Murray River, BC	Carl Kortmeyer	Carl Kortmeyer	1980	460
24 6/16	15 4/16	9 4/16	Nalbeelah Creek, BC	Wayne Moon	Wayne Moon	1983	460
24 6/16	15 10/16	8 12/16	Clyak River, BC	Marvin Opp	Marvin Opp	1983	460
24 6/16	15 2/16	9 4/16	Tagagawik River, AK	Roland L. Quimby	Roland L. Quimby	1984	460
24 6/16	15 5/16	9 5/16	Knight Inlet, BC	Norman W. Dougan	Norman W. Dougan	1984	460
24 6/16	15 10/16	8 12/16	Macoun Creek, BC	Martin McIlroy	Martin McIlroy	1984	460
24 6/16	15 2/16	9 4/16	Phillips Creek, BC	Paul L. VanMeter	Paul L. VanMeter	1991	460
24 6/16	15 10/16	8 12/16	Wakeman River, BC	Peter Morrison	Peter Morrison	1992	460
24 6/16	15 5/16	9 1/16	Swift River, BC	Scott Fontaine	Scott Fontaine	1993	460
24 6/16	15	9 6/16	Tetlin River, AK	Zach Pallister	Zach Pallister	1994	460
24 6/16	14 10/16	9 12/16	Shaktoolik River, AK	Charles M. Walraven	Charles M. Walraven	1995	460
24 6/16	15 6/16	9	Nenana River, AK	James E. Boyd	James E. Boyd	1997	460
24 6/16	15 6/16	9	Kelly River, AK	David T. Klein	David T. Klein	1999	460
24 6/16	15 6/16	9	Stikine River, BC	Frank D. Amoretto	Frank D. Amoretto	2000	460
24 6/16	15 8/16	8 14/16	Koyuk River, AK	Terry J. Fricks	Terry J. Fricks	2000	460
24 6/16	15 4/16	9 4/16	Anvik River, AK	Douglas G. Sansone	Douglas G. Sansone	2000	460
24 6/16	15 7/16	8 15/16	Otter Creek, AK	George A. Schiller	George A. Schiller	2000	460
24 5/16	15 6/16	8 12/16	Kitimat, BC	Ewald Kirschner	Ewald Kirschner	1958	491
24 5/16	15 6/16	8 15/16	Bear Berry, AB	Phil Temple	Phil Temple	1958	491
24 5/16	14 6/16	9 15/16	Blackstone River, AB	Wilhelm Eichenauer	Wilhelm Eichenauer	1963	491
24 5/16	15 2/16	9 3/16	Teller, AK	Bill Glunt	Bill Glunt	1965	491
24 5/16	15 7/16	8 14/16	Cassiar Mts., BC	Henry E. High	Henry E. High	1965	491
24 5/16	15 4/16	9 1/16	Nabesna River, AK	C.W. Houle	C.W. Houle	1965	491
24 5/16	14 15/16	9 11/16	Tetachuck Lake, BC	Torben Dahl	Torben Dahl	1966	491
24 5/16	14 10/16	8 5/16	Brooks Range, AK	Robert L. Cohen	Robert L. Cohen	1967	491
24 5/16	16	8 5/16	Edson, AB	Otto Braaz	Otto Braaz	1969	491
24 5/16	14 14/16	9 7/16	Toba Inlet, BC	Jack C. Glover	Jack C. Glover	1970	491
24 5/16	15 7/16	8 14/16	Chatsquot Creek, BC	Roger J. Ahern	Roger J. Ahern	1978	491
24 5/16	14 15/16	8 14/16	Graham River, BC	William J. Fogarty, Jr.	William J. Fogarty, Jr.	1978	491
24 5/16	15 6/16	9 6/16	Selwyn Creek, YT	Rod G. Hardie	Rod G. Hardie	1979	491
24 5/16	14 15/16	8 15/16	Cranberry River, BC	Albert Wong	Fred Y.C. Wong	1982	491
24 5/16	15 6/16	9 6/16	Baird Mts., AK	Howard L. Olson	Howard L. Olson	1985	491
24 5/16	15 4/16	9 1/16	Stikine River, BC	Frederick L. Wood III	Frederick L. Wood III	1986	491
24 5/16	15	9 5/16	Mt. Fairplay, AK	David G. Kelleyhouse	David G. Kelleyhouse	1987	491
24 5/16	15 3/16	9 2/16	Poktonik Mts., AK	John W. Bania	John W. Bania	1989	491
24 5/16	15 6/16	8 15/16	Squirrel River, AK	Walter J. Miller	Walter J. Miller	1990	491
24 5/16	15 1/16	9 4/16	Horton River, NT	Victor E. Moss	Victor E. Moss	1990	491

GRIZZLY BEAR
Ursus arctos horribilis

Score	Greatest Length of Skull Without Lower Jaw	Greatest Width of Skull	Locality	Hunter	Owner	Date Killed	Rank
24 5/16	14 11/16	9 10/16	Ungalik River, AK	Barry Kutun	Barry Kutun	1993	491
24 5/16	14 15/16	9 4/16	Yanert Fork, AK	Randy F. Stout	Randy F. Stout	1994	491
24 5/16	15 1/16	9 4/16	Chalco Creek, BC	Clifton Keel, Jr.	Clifton Keel, Jr.	1997	491
24 5/16	14 9/16	9 12/16	Green Creek, YT	Richard P. Musselman	Richard P. Musselman	1997	491
24 5/16	15 3/16	9 2/16	Quesnel Lake, BC	Michael D. Bright	Michael D. Bright	1999	491
24 5/16	15	9 5/16	Flambeau River, AK	Anthony S. Gorn	Anthony S. Gorn	1999	491
24 5/16	15 6/16	8 15/16	Nass River, BC	Steve Pereira	Steve Pereira	1999	491
24 5/16	15 4/16	9 1/16	Two Pete Mt., YT	Luke R. Viravec	Luke R. Viravec	2001	491
24 5/16	15 7/16	8 14/16	Big River, AK	L.N. Wisner	L.N. Wisner	2003	491
24 4/16	15 8/16	8 12/16	Dease Lake, BC	G.C.F. Dalziel	G.C.F. Dalziel	1956	520
24 4/16	14 13/16	9 7/16	Selkirk Mt., BC	Eli Paulson	Eli Paulson	1957	520
24 4/16	15 10/16	8 10/16	South Hay River, AB	Bert Shearer	Bert Shearer	1957	520
24 4/16	14 6/16	9 14/16	Kotzebue, AK	Don D. Giles	Don D. Giles	1965	520
24 4/16	15 4/16	9	Kuskokwim River, AK	Edward W. Williams	Edward W. Williams	1967	520
24 4/16	14 14/16	9 6/16	Brooks Range, AK	Stanley Blazovich	Stanley Blazovich	1970	520
24 4/16	15 10/16	8 10/16	Bella Coola, BC	Howard Creason	Howard Creason	1971	520
24 4/16	15 7/16	8 13/16	Sheep Creek, AB	Rolly Balzer	Rolly Balzer	1972	520
24 4/16	14 10/16	9 10/16	Nilkitkwa River, BC	Roger Britton	Roger Britton	1976	520
24 4/16	15 4/16	9 1/16	Trout Lake, BC	Paul L. Reese	Paul L. Reese	1982	520
24 4/16	14 12/16	9 8/16	Luwa Mt., BC	Joel B. Benner	Joel B. Benner	1985	520
24 4/16	15 1/16	9 3/16	Knight Inlet, BC	Steven C. Gromatzky	Steven C. Gromatzky	1988	520
24 4/16	15	9 4/16	Gathto Creek, BC	James I. Scott	James I. Scott	1988	520
24 4/16	15 8/16	8 12/16	Thutade Lake, BC	George R. Kennedy, Jr.	George R. Kennedy, Jr.	1992	520
24 4/16	15	9 4/16	Chisana River, AK	Shelby R. Smithey	Shelby R. Smithey	1994	520
24 4/16	15 8/16	8 12/16	Scoop Lake, BC	Mark S. Coles	Mark S. Coles	1996	520
24 4/16	14 10/16	9 10/16	Unalakleet, AK	Stanley R. Godfrey	Stanley R. Godfrey	1997	520
24 3/16	15 2/16	9 1/16	Nabesna, AK	Ernest B. Schur	Ernest B. Schur	1958	537
24 3/16	14 14/16	9 5/16	Moose Creek, BC	R. Angell	R. Angell	1964	537
24 3/16	15 8/16	8 11/16	Gardiner, MT	Marguerite McDonald	Marguerite McDonald	1964	537
24 3/16	15 2/16	9 1/16	Toba Inlet, BC	Kenneth L. Wagner, Jr.	Kenneth L. Wagner, Jr.	1968	537
24 3/16	14 14/16	9 4/16	Likely, BC	Louis Tremblay	Louis Tremblay	1970	537
24 3/16	15 1/16	9 2/16	Alaska Range, AK	Gilbert L. Shelton	Gilbert L. Shelton	1975	537
24 3/16	15 2/16	9 1/16	Parsnip River, BC	Richard O.A. Gunther	Richard O.A. Gunther	1976	537
24 3/16	14 5/16	9 14/16	Tetlin Indian Res., AK	Robert B. Rhyne	Robert B. Rhyne	1976	537
24 3/16	14 13/16	9 6/16	Kuskokwim River, AK	Roger J. Ahern	Roger J. Ahern	1977	537
24 3/16	15 6/16	8 13/16	Big River, AK	Dale G. Moffat	Dale G. Moffat	1977	537
24 3/16	15 8/16	8 11/16	Nusatsum River, BC	Randy Svisdahl	Randy Svisdahl	1983	537
24 3/16	15	9 3/16	White Creek, AK	J.H. Harvey & V. Landt	John H. Harvey, Jr.	1985	537

Score	Length	Width	Locality	Hunter	Owner	Date Killed	Rank
24 3/16	14 15/16	9 4/16	Squirrel River, AK	Robert L. Eubank	Robert L. Eubank	1986	537
24 3/16	14 15/16	9 4/16	Monashee Mts., BC	Georg Frisch	Georg Frisch	1986	537
24 3/16	14 14/16	9 5/16	Sinclair Mills, BC	Steven L. Gingras	Steven L. Gingras	1986	537
24 3/16	15 6/16	8 13/16	Christmas Creek, AK	Charles L. Fuller	Charles L. Fuller	1988	537
24 3/16	14 14/16	9 5/16	Henry Creek, AK	Ray S. Smith	Ray S. Smith	1990	537
24 3/16	15 2/16	9 1/16	Nuka River, AK	Gene Hynes	Gene Hynes	1991	537
24 3/16	15 5/16	8 14/16	Ghost Lake, BC	Thomas J. Pagel	Thomas J. Pagel	1991	537
24 3/16	15 9/16	8 10/16	Owikeno Lake, BC	Robert Smink	Robert Smink	1993	537
24 3/16	15 2/16	9 1/16	Colville River, AK	Thomas D. Suedmeier	Thomas D. Suedmeier	1993	537
24 3/16	15 4/16	8 15/16	Sulphur Creek, BC	Bud Dow	Bud Dow	1996	537
24 2/16	15 1/16	9 1/16	John Hansen Lake, AK	Beverly A. Wiesner	Beverly A. Wiesner	1997	537
24 2/16	15 8/16	8 10/16	Caribou Co, ID	Picked Up	Bill E. Lovely	PR 1900	560
24 2/16	15 3/16	8 15/16	Chisana River, AK	Larry Folger	Larry Folger	1961	560
24 2/16	14 15/16	9 3/16	McDonnell Lake, BC	W.C. Gardiner	W.C. Gardiner	1966	560
24 2/16	15 2/16	9	Dawson City, YT	Donald R. Hull	Ray C. Dillman	1971	560
24 2/16	15 9/16	8 9/16	Bella Coola, BC	Hugh M. Klein	Hugh M. Klein	1972	560
24 2/16	15	9 2/16	Sikanni Chief River, BC	Dale E. Mirr	Dale E. Mirr	1973	560
24 2/16	15 4/16	8 14/16	Quintette Mt., BC	Dennis J. Brady	Dennis J. Brady	1977	560
24 2/16	15 1/16	9 1/16	Chatanika River, AK	Robert L. Nelson	Robert L. Nelson	1981	560
24 2/16	15 9/16	8 9/16	Koeye River, BC	William H. Dunstan IV	William H. Dunstan IV	1983	560
24 2/16	15 10/16	8 8/16	Kuskokwim River, AK	Anthony J. Bianchi	Anthony J. Bianchi	1984	560
24 2/16	15 10/16	8 8/16	Deep Valley Creek, AB	Gerald Desjardins	Gerald Desjardins	1984	560
24 2/16	15	9 2/16	Casadepaga River, AK	Richard L. Hoffman	Richard L. Hoffman	1987	560
24 2/16	14 12/16	9 6/16	Mason River, NT	Gary G. Dumdei	Gary G. Dumdei	1992	560
24 2/16	14 14/16	9 4/16	Noatak River, AK	David M. Smith	David M. Smith	1994	560
24 2/16	14 14/16	9 4/16	Anvik River, AK	Chilton E. Miles, Jr.	Chilton E. Miles, Jr.	1996	560
24 2/16	15 3/16	8 15/16	Chalco Creek, BC	Mark A. Nucci	Mark A. Nucci	1999	560
24 2/16	15 6/16	8 12/16	Wood River, AK	Evan L. Wheeler	Evan L. Wheeler	1999	560
24 2/16	15 7/16	8 11/16	Little Salcha River, AK	Randy A. Cravener	Randy A. Cravener	2000	560
24 2/16	14 12/16	9 6/16	Squirrel River, AK	Tim D. Hiner	Tim D. Hiner	2001	560
24 2/16	14 15/16	9 3/16	Nabesna River, AK	Joseph Rendeiro	Joseph Rendeiro	2001	560
24 2/16	15 2/16	9	Kantishna River, AK	Thomas C. Brown	Thomas C. Brown	2002	560
24 1/16	15 10/16	8 7/16	Owikeno Lake, BC	R.C. Bentzen	R.C. Bentzen	1960	581
24 1/16	15 3/16	8 14/16	Flathead Co., MT	T.H. Soldowski	T.H. Soldowski	1963	581
24 1/16	14 12/16	9 5/16	Brooks Range, AK	Ted Schlaepfer	Ted Schlaepfer	1964	581
24 1/16	14 14/16	9 3/16	Nabesna River, AK	Frank C. Hibben	Frank C. Hibben	1967	581
24 1/16	14 15/16	9 2/16	Quesnel, BC	Larry Chaves	Larry Chaves	1968	581
24 1/16	14 9/16	9 8/16	Toklat River, AK	Ronald Lauretti	Ronald Lauretti	1971	581
24 1/16	14 7/16	9 10/16	California Creek, AK	Boyd J. Blair	Boyd J. Blair	1975	581
24 1/16	15 2/16	8 15/16	Gataga River, BC	James E. Carson	James E. Carson	1977	581
24 1/16	14 15/16	9 2/16	Tatlatui Lake, BC	Paul S. Burke, Jr.	Paul S. Burke, Jr.	1978	581
24 1/16	15 2/16	8 15/16	Sukunka River, BC	Albert R. Heikel, Jr.	Albert R. Heikel, Jr.	1979	581
24 1/16	14 14/16	9 3/16	King Salmon River, BC	Phil Forte	Phil Forte	1981	581
24 1/16	15	9 1/16	Noatak River, AK	Stephen P. Connell	Stephen P. Connell	1984	581
24 1/16	15 1/16	9	Pine River, BC	Brian R. Goates	Brian R. Goates	1985	581
24 1/16	15 5/16	8 12/16	Little Red Rock Creek, AB	Patrick Casey	P. Casey & B. Winters	1987	581
24 1/16	15 1/16	9	Hunter Creek, AK	Leonard L. Taig	Leonard L. Taig	1992	581

GRIZZLY BEAR
Ursus arctos horribilis

Score	Greatest Length of Skull Without Lower Jaw	Greatest Width of Skull	Locality	Hunter	Owner	Date Killed	Rank
24 1/16	15 3/16	8 14/16	Blackman Creek, BC	James A. Springer	James A. Springer	1994	581
24 1/16	15 6/16	8 11/16	Majuba Lake, BC	Scott E. Edwards	Scott E. Edwards	1997	581
24 1/16	14 12/16	9 5/16	Nass River, BC	Marvin Kwiatkowski	Marvin Kwiatkowski	2001	581
24 1/16	15 3/16	8 14/16	Anvik River, AK	Jorge M. Rodriguez	Jorge M. Rodriguez	2001	581
24 1/16	14 15/16	9 2/16	Canyon Creek, AK	Lance M. Cannon	Scott C. Babcock	2002	581
24	15 5/16	8 11/16	Bella Coola, BC	Wynn Beebe	Wynn Beebe	1960	601
24	15 4/16	8 12/16	Wood River, AK	Gordon Studer	Gordon Studer	1963	601
24	15 2/16	8 14/16	Cantwell, AK	Donald R. Johnson	Donald R. Johnson	1964	601
24	14 11/16	9 5/16	Little Tok River, AK	Herbert F. Fassler	Herbert F. Fassler	1966	601
24	15	9	Fernie, BC	James Sloan	James Sloan	1967	601
24	14 14/16	9 2/16	Fairbanks, AK	Rudolf von Strasser	Rudolf von Strasser	1968	601
24	15 12/16	8 4/16	Bella Coola, BC	Alton A. Myhrvold	Alton A. Myhrvold	1969	601
24	14 9/16	9 7/16	Alaska Range, AK	R.A. Schriewer	R.A. Schriewer	1969	601
24	14 14/16	9 5/16	Canyon Lake, BC	Luther E. Lilly	Luther E. Lilly	1970	601
24	14 9/16	9 7/16	Ayiyak River, AK	Tom Toscano	Tom Toscano	1971	601
24	14 12/16	9 4/16	Kuskokwim Mts., AK	James V. Travis	James V. Travis	1974	601
24	15 4/16	8 12/16	Ram River, AB	Howard Bugg	Howard Bugg	1976	601
24	14 12/16	9 4/16	Andreafsky River, AK	Bruce K. Kent	Bruce K. Kent	1980	601
24	15 5/16	8 11/16	Kitsumkalum River, BC	Bill Gourlie	Bill Gourlie	1984	601
24	14 11/16	9 5/16	Kelly River, AK	Thomas W. Becker	Thomas W. Becker	1986	601
24	14 12/16	9 4/16	Stikine River, BC	Lynn F. Greenlee	Lynn F. Greenlee	1987	601
24	15 1/16	8 15/16	Draney Inlet, BC	Tim Dernbach	Tim Dernbach	1988	601
24	14 14/16	9 2/16	Nome River, AK	Samuel J. Nicolosi, Jr.	Samuel J. Nicolosi, Jr.	1990	601
24	14 8/16	9 8/16	Koyuk River, AK	Thomas A. Vaughn	Thomas A. Vaughn	1990	601
24	15 1/16	8 15/16	Bastille Creek, BC	Robert Learie	Robert Learie	1991	601
24	14 13/16	9 3/16	Talik Ridge, AK	William J. Papineau	William J. Papineau	1991	601
24	15	9	Caribou Creek, AK	Lee M. Wahlund	Lee M. Wahlund	1991	601
24	14 12/16	9 4/16	Toklat River, AK	James W. Rodgers	James W. Rodgers	1993	601
24	14 14/16	9 2/16	Mt. Bendeleben, AK	Chad Farley	Chad Farley	1999	601
24	15 4/16	8 12/16	Quekilok Creek, AK	Mike McDonald	Mike McDonald	2001	601
24	14 12/16	9 4/16	Ungalik River, AK	Theodore D. James III	Theodore D. James III	2002	601
24	15 3/16	8 13/16	Preston Lake, AB	Travis S. Peterson	Travis S. Peterson	2003	601
26 6/16*	16 5/16	10 1/16	Iron Creek, AK	Scott Dunavin	Scott Dunavin	1998	601

* Final score is subject to revision by additional verifying measurements.

CATEGORY
GRIZZLY BEAR

SCORE
26-3/16

HUNTER
DANIEL S. BOLEK

LOCATION
OTTER CREEK, ALASKA

DATE OF KILL
SEPTEMBER 2001

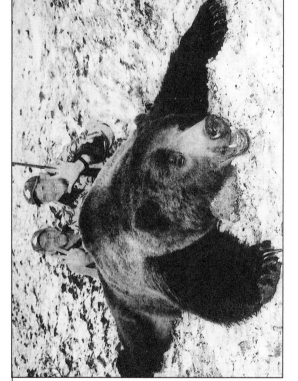

CATEGORY
GRIZZLY BEAR

SCORE
24-9/16

HUNTER
KENT DELIGANS

LOCATION
TAKU RIVER,
BRITISH COLUMBIA

DATE OF KILL
MAY 2003

CATEGORY
GRIZZLY BEAR

SCORE
24-2/16

HUNTER
MARK A. NUCCI

LOCATION
CHALCO CREEK,
BRITISH COLUMBIA

DATE OF KILL
MAY 1999

183

CATEGORY
GRIZZLY BEAR

SCORE
24-8/16

HUNTER
HOLLY E. OLIVER II

LOCATION
KOYUK RIVER, ALASKA

DATE OF KILL
MAY 2001

CATEGORY
GRIZZLY BEAR

SCORE
26-7/16

HUNTER
JON D. SEIFERT

LOCATION
LONE MOUNTAIN, ALASKA

DATE OF KILL
SEPTEMBER 2000

CATEGORY
GRIZZLY BEAR

SCORE
24-11/16

HUNTER
CHUCK R. SCHLINDWEIN

LOCATION
CHEENEETNUK RIVER, ALASKA

DATE OF KILL
SEPTEMBER 1999

CATEGORY
GRIZZLY BEAR

SCORE
24

HUNTER
MIKE MCDONALD

LOCATION
QUEKILOK CREEK,
ALASKA

DATE OF KILL
MAY 2001

CATEGORY
GRIZZLY BEAR

SCORE
24-2/16

HUNTER
THOMAS C. BROWN

LOCATION
KANTISHNA RIVER,
ALASKA

DATE OF KILL
APRIL 2002

ALASKA BROWN BEAR
WORLD'S RECORD

RANK
World's Record

SCORE
30 $^{12/16}$

LOCATION
Kodiak Island, AK

HUNTER
Roy Lindsley

OWNER
Los Angeles County
Museum

DATE KILLED
1952

Alaska's Kodiak Island, just below Cook Inlet, supports the largest land-based carnivores in the world. The World's Record for the Alaska brown bear (*Ursus arctos middendorffi*) continues to hold with a score at 30-12/16 after being taken in late May, 1952, near Karluk Lake, Kodiak Island. This immense bear was collected by a scientific expedition headed by Melville N. Lincoln and was sponsored by a habitat group affiliated with the Los Angeles County Museum. The actual shot was made by Roy R. Lindsley, an employee of the U.S. Fish and Wildlife Service in Kodiak, who was working in cooperation with the scientists. Lindsley, who had never before shot an Alaska brown bear, had many years of experience working among these intelligent giants. Technically, the Alaska brown bear and grizzly bear are classified as the same species, *Ursus arctos*. The Alaska brown bears that have been genetically and physically isolated on Kodiak Island have slightly varied skull proportions, claw shape, and dentition that have set them apart from browns found elsewhere in Alaska, and are therefore classified as a separate subspecies. A mature boar can weigh as much as 1,500 pounds after feeding on Coho salmon during the autumn season, and when he rises upright from the river bank to test the coastal winds, may stand well over nine feet tall. As a seasoned observer, Lindsley knew that he would need a heavy bullet that could deliver sufficient force in order to make a clean kill and prevent the possibility of the bear charging or running away. He took down the record-sized male brown bear using the 180-grain bullet in a .30-06 rifle. Lindsley's bear skull measures 17-15/16" long and 12-13/16" wide for a final score of 30-12/16. It was declared a World's Record at the Sixth Competition held at the American Museum of Natural History, New York City, New York, in 1954. ■

250 Station Drive
Missoula, MT 59801
(406) 542-1888

BOONE AND CROCKETT CLUB®

OFFICIAL SCORING SYSTEM FOR NORTH AMERICAN BIG GAME TROPHIES

BEAR

	MINIMUM SCORES	
	AWARDS	ALL-TIME
black bear	20	21
grizzly bear	23	24
Alaska brown bear	26	28
polar bear	27	27

KIND OF BEAR (check one)
- ☐ black bear
- ☐ grizzly
- ■ Alaska brown bear
- ☐ polar bear

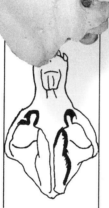

A

SEE OTHER SIDE FOR INSTRUCTIONS

	MEASUREMENTS
A. Greatest Length Without Lower Jaw	17 15/16
B. Greatest Width	12 13/16
FINAL SCORE	30 12/16

Exact Locality Where Killed: **Kodiak Island, AK**

Date Killed: **May 23, 1952**   Hunter: **Roy Lindsley**

Owner: **Los Angeles County Museum**

Owner's Address: Telephone #:

Guide's Name and Address:

Remarks: (Mention Any Abnormalities or Unique Qualities)

I, __**Grancel Fitz**__ , certify that I have measured this trophy on __**03/11/1953**__
PRINT NAME   MM/DD/YYYY

at **5 Tudor City Place**   **New York**   **NY**
STREET ADDRESS   CITY   STATE/PROVINCE

and that these measurements and data are, to the best of my knowledge and belief, made in accordance with the instructions given.

Witness: __**Samuel B. Webb**__   Signature: __**Grancel Fitz**__   I.D. Number ☐
                                                                   B&C OFFICIAL MEASURER

COPYRIGHT © 1999 BY BOONE AND CROCKETT CLUB®

ALASKA BROWN BEAR
WORLD'S RECORD SCORE CHART

187

ALASKA BROWN BEAR

Ursus arctos middendorffi and certain related subspecies

Score	Greatest Length of Skull Without Lower Jaw	Greatest Width of Skull	Locality	Hunter	Owner	Date Killed	Rank
30 12/16	17 15/16	12 13/16	Kodiak Island, AK	Roy Lindsley	Los Angeles Co. Mus.	1952	1
30 11/16	18 10/16	12 1/16	Kodiak Island, AK	Erling Hansen	Erling Hansen	1961	2
30 9/16	18 7/16	12 2/16	Kodiak Island, AK	Fred A. Henton	Los Angeles Co. Mus.	1938	3
30 8/16	18 12/16	11 12/16	Bear River, AK	Cap Wagner	Univ. of CA Museum	PR 1908	4
30 8/16	18	12 12/16	Kodiak Island, AK	W.S. Brophy, Jr. & W.E. McClure	William S. Brophy III	1966	4
30 7/16	19 13/16	10 10/16	Port Heiden, AK	Herschel A. Lamb	Herschel A. Lamb	1961	6
30 5/16	18	12 5/16	Deadman Bay, AK	Grancel Fitz	Mrs. Grancel Fitz	1955	7
30 4/16	18 12/16	11 8/16	Kodiak Island, AK	Donald S. Hopkins	Unknown	1940	8
30 4/16	18 12/16	11 8/16	Kodiak Island, AK	Jack Roach	Jack Roach	1947	8
30 4/16	18	11 8/16	Kodiak Island, AK	T.H. McGregor	T.H. McGregor	1960	8
30 4/16	18 5/16	11 15/16	Kodiak Island, AK	Will Gay	Will Gay	1997	8
30 3/16	18 2/16	12 1/16	Kodiak Island, AK	W.J. Fisher	U.S. Natl. Museum	PR 1904	12
30 3/16	18	12 3/16	Kodiak Island, AK	Oliver L. Durbin	Ben Hurtado	1952	12
30 3/16	18 12/16	11 7/16	Kodiak Island, AK	A.L. Hooker	A.L. Hooker	1958	12
30 3/16	18 5/16	11 14/16	Aliulik Pen., AK	Michael L. Ward	Michael L. Ward	1999	12
30 2/16	18 7/16	12 2/16	Uyak Bay, AK	Walter H. White	B&C National Collection	1954	16
30 2/16	18 7/16	11 11/16	Kodiak Island, AK	Dave Connor	Dave Connor	1957	16
30 1/16	18 1/16	12	Kodiak Island, AK	Seymour P. Smith	U.S. Natl. Museum	1927	18
30 1/16	18 3/16	11 14/16	Kodiak Island, AK	John M. Tait	John M. Tait	1957	18
30 1/16	18 2/16	11 15/16	Alinchak Bay, AK	Clarence R. Scott	Clarence R. Scott	1961	18
30 1/16	18 12/16	11 5/16	Cold Bay, AK	Randy J. Cain	Randy J. Cain	1992	18
29 15/16	18 6/16	11 9/16	Kodiak Island, AK	Donald S. Hopkins	Unknown	1939	22
29 15/16	18 6/16	11 9/16	Kodiak Island, AK	Samuel Atkinson	S. & F. Atkinson	1953	22
29 14/16	18 2/16	11 12/16	Unimak Island, AK	Fred W. Shield	Fred W. Shield	1950	24
29 14/16	18	11 14/16	Kodiak Island, AK	Unknown	Kim Clark	1958	24
29 14/16	17 15/16	11 15/16	Kodiak Island, AK	H.F. Primosch	H.F. Primosch	1959	24
29 14/16	18	11 14/16	Aliulik Pen., AK	Cindy L. Rhodes	Cindy L. Rhodes	1997	24
29 14/16	18 6/16	12 4/16	Uyak Bay, AK	John E. Schuchart	John E. Schuchart	1998	24
29 13/16	17 12/16	12 4/16	Nelson Lagoon, AK	Unknown	Harry H. Webb	1946	29
29 13/16	**18 5/16**	**11 8/16**	**Cold Bay, AK**	**Robert C. Reeve**	**Am. Mus. Nat. Hist.**	**1948**	**29**
29 13/16	18 6/16	11 7/16	Alaska Pen., AK	Lud W. Rettig	Denver Mus. Nat. Hist.	1955	29
29 13/16	18 5/16	11 8/16	Alaska Pen., AK	Don Johnson	Don Johnson	1962	29
29 13/16	17 14/16	11 15/16	Sturgeon River, AK	W. Ted Burger	W. Ted Burger	1985	29
29 12/16	17 13/16	11 15/16	Kodiak Island, AK	William D. Holmes	William D. Holmes	1957	34
29 12/16	18 11/16	11 1/16	Alaska Pen., AK	Russell J. Uhl	Russell J. Uhl	1963	34
29 11/16	17 13/16	11 14/16	Kodiak Island, AK	Herman Gibson	Herman Gibson	1951	36
29 11/16	17 9/16	12 2/16	Kodiak Island, AK	James H. Nash	James H. Nash	1954	36
29 11/16	17 12/16	11 15/16	Kodiak Island, AK	A.J. Taylor & E.A. Chappell	Allen J. Taylor	1976	36

Score			Locality	Hunter	Owner	Date	Rank
29 10/16	17 13/16	11 13/16	Kodiak Island, AK	Eddie W. Stinnett	Eddie W. Stinnett	1974	39
29 9/16	19 1/16	10 8/16	Unimak Island, AK	A.C. Gilbert	A.C. Gilbert	1950	40
29 9/16	17 7/16	12 2/16	Kodiak, AK	Peter W. Bading	Peter W. Bading	1964	40
29 8/16	17 14/16	11 8/16	Kodiak Island, AK	E.M. & H. Rusten	Elmer M. Rusten	1941	42
29 8/16	18 14/16	10 10/16	Mother Goose Lake, AK	Tom Moore	Chicago Nat. Hist. Mus.	1947	42
29 8/16	17 13/16	11 11/16	Kodiak Island, AK	F.W. Crail	F.W. Crail	1950	42
29 8/16	17 10/16	11 14/16	Kodiak Island, AK	W.H. Cothrum	W.H. Cothrum	1953	42
29 8/16	18 6/16	11 2/16	Cold Bay, AK	W.P. Waltz	W.P. Waltz	1953	42
29 8/16	17 12/16	11 12/16	Kodiak Island, AK	Carlos Alden	Carlos Alden	1956	42
29 8/16	18 4/16	11 4/16	Alaska Pen., AK	Charles C. Gates	Charles C. Gates	1960	42
29 8/16	18	11 8/16	Alaska Pen., AK	Sam Pancotto	Sam Pancotto	1963	42
29 8/16	18 2/16	11 6/16	Port Heiden, AK	Robert J. Miller	Robert J. Miller	1971	42
29 8/16	17 12/16	11 12/16	Sturgeon River, AK	Anthony Gioffre	Anthony Gioffre	1984	42
29 8/16	18 1/16	11 7/16	Kaiuguak Bay, AK	Martin H. Shaft	Martin H. Shaft	1990	42
29 7/16	17 10/16	11 13/16	Kodiak Island, AK	Robert R. Snodgrass	Robert R. Snodgrass	1949	53
29 7/16	17 8/16	11 15/16	Deadman Bay, AK	Ira M. Piper	Ira M. Piper	1954	53
29 7/16	17 11/16	11 12/16	Kodiak Island, AK	Keith Chisholm	Keith Chisholm	1956	53
29 7/16	17 13/16	11 10/16	Kodiak Island, AK	Richard Van Dyke	Richard Van Dyke	1957	53
29 7/16	17 13/16	11 10/16	Kodiak Island, AK	H.I.H. Prince Abdorreza Pahlavi	H.I.H. Prince Abdorreza Pahlavi	1967	53
29 7/16	17 15/16	11 8/16	Cold Bay, AK	Jiro Miyamoto	Jiro Miyamoto	1992	53
29 6/16	18 2/16	11 4/16	Pavlof Bay, AK	Willie Pavlof	U.S. Natl. Museum	1897	59
29 6/16	17 13/16	11 9/16	Belkofski Bay, AK	Laurenti Kuzakin	U.S. Natl. Museum	1897	59
29 6/16	17 15/16	11 7/16	Pavlof Bay, AK	H. Cutting	U.S. Natl. Museum	1917	59
29 6/16	18	11 6/16	Cold Bay, AK	Ira A. Minnick	U.S. Natl. Museum	1923	59
29 6/16	18 5/16	11 1/16	Alaska Pen., AK	E.I. Garrett	Am. Mus. Nat. Hist.	1926	59
29 6/16	17 9/16	11 13/16	Kodiak Island, AK	John S. Day	John S. Day	1953	59
29 6/16	17 8/16	12	Amook Island, AK	Albert C. Bledsoe	Albert C. Bledsoe	1959	59
29 6/16	18 3/16	11 3/16	Kodiak Island, AK	Herb Klein	Dallas Mus. of Natl. Hist.	1965	59
29 6/16	18 6/16	11	Stepovak Bay, AK	Roy Fencl	Roy Fencl	1966	59
29 5/16	18 7/16	10 14/16	Cold Bay, AK	Edwin Mallinkrodt, Jr.	U.S. Natl. Museum	1920	68
29 5/16	17 12/16	11 9/16	Sand Lake, AK	William A. Fisher	William A. Fisher	1953	68
29 5/16	17 13/16	11 8/16	Kodiak Island, AK	Picked Up	Am. Mus. Nat. Hist.	PR 1957	68
29 5/16	18 1/16	11 4/16	Braided Creek, AK	Robert L. Coleman	Robert L. Coleman	1991	68
29 5/16	17 12/16	11 9/16	Kodiak Island, AK	Jerry D. Johnson	Jerry D. Johnson	1996	68
29 5/16	18 6/16	10 15/16	Seal Islands, AK	Larry G. Collinson	Larry G. Collinson	1999	68
29 4/16	17 14/16	11 6/16	Kodiak Island, AK	A.C. Skinner, Jr.	A.C. Skinner, Jr.	1951	74
29 4/16	17 15/16	11 14/16	Kodiak Island, AK	H.R. Eavey & H. Wright	Harry R. Eavey	1960	74
29 4/16	18 2/16	11 5/16	Alaska Pen., AK	Johnnie White	Horns of Hunter Tr. Post	1962	74
29 4/16	18 4/16	11 2/16	Alaska Pen., AK	H.S. Kamil	H.S. Kamil	1963	74
29 4/16	18	11	Port Heiden, AK	Ashley C. Sanders	Ashley C. Sanders	1965	74
29 4/16	17 11/16	11 9/16	Deadman Bay, AK	George W. Aldredge	George W. Aldredge	1996	74
29 4/16	17 9/16	11 11/16	Spiridon Lake, AK	Dennis S. Boyer	Dennis S. Boyer	1997	74
29 4/16	18 10/16	10 12/16	Alaska Pen., AK	Peter K. Berga	Peter K. Berga	2000	74
29 3/16	18 10/16	11 4/16	Alaska Pen., AK	J.A. Atkinson	Am. Mus. Nat. Hist.	1948	82
29 3/16	17 15/16	11 4/16	Port Moller Bay, AK	A.M. Harper	A.M. Harper	1949	82
29 3/16	17 10/16	11 9/16	Kodiak Island, AK	Fred B. Hawk	Fred B. Hawk	1959	82
29 3/16	17 13/16	11 6/16	Kodiak Island, AK	William H. Sleith	Lutz Junior Museum	1966	82

ALASKA BROWN BEAR

Ursus arctos middendorffi and certain related subspecies

Score	Greatest Length of Skull Without Lower Jaw	Greatest Width of Skull	Locality	Hunter	Owner	Date Killed	Rank
29 3/16	17 15/16	11 4/16	Port Heiden, AK	Ralph E. Smith	Ralph E. Smith	1966	82
29 3/16	18 9/16	10 10/16	Mother Goose Lake, AK	Robert Denis	Robert Denis	1967	82
29 3/16	18	11 3/16	Alaska Pen., AK	Peter Ma	Peter Ma	1990	82
29 3/16	18 5/16	10 14/16	Alaska Pen., AK	T. Michael McMahon	T. Michael McMahon	1994	82
29 3/16	17 9/16	11 10/16	Deadman Bay, AK	Robert M. Ortiz	Robert M. Ortiz	2001	82
29 3/16	18 10/16	10 9/16	Cold Bay, AK	Gene White	Gene White	2001	82
29 3/16	18 11/16	10 8/16	Egegik Bay, AK	Steve Rakes	Steve Rakes	2003	82
29 2/16	17 10/16	11 8/16	Kodiak Island, AK	Mrs. J. Watson Webb	Mrs. J. Watson Webb	1948	93
29 2/16	17 14/16	11 4/16	Alaska Pen., AK	Mrs. John J. Louis, Jr.	Mrs. John J. Louis, Jr.	1955	93
29 2/16	17 15/16	11 3/16	Kodiak Island, AK	Alan O. Hickok	Alan O. Hickok	1957	93
29 2/16	17 11/16	11 7/16	Port Moller, AK	Milton L. Knapp	Milton L. Knapp	1960	93
29 2/16	17 10/16	11 8/16	Kodiak Island, AK	Edward F. Pedersen, Jr.	Edward F. Pedersen, Jr.	1961	93
29 2/16	18 3/16	10 15/16	Alaska Pen., AK	Kenneth Richmond	Kenneth Richmond	1962	93
29 2/16	17 10/16	11 8/16	Alaska Pen., AK	Wesley Pollock	Wesley Pollock	1964	93
29 2/16	18 3/16	10 15/16	Ugashik, AK	Joseph K. Link	Buffalo Mus. of Sci.	1966	93
29 2/16	18 2/16	11	Alaska Pen., AK	Richard Hodous	Richard Hodous	1966	93
29 2/16	17 7/16	11 11/16	Kodiak Island, AK	John F. Ries	John F. Ries	1967	93
29 2/16	18 10/16	10 8/16	Balboa Bay, AK	William C. LeMasters	William C. LeMasters	1994	93
29 1/16	17 8/16	11 9/16	Kodiak Island, AK	John C. Ayres	Signa J. Byers	1934	104
29 1/16	17 10/16	11 7/16	Kodiak Island, AK	H.H. Kissinger	H.H. Kissinger	1961	104
29 1/16	17 11/16	11 6/16	Port Heiden, AK	Marshall Carr	Marshall Carr	1963	104
29 1/16	17 11/16	11 6/16	Ugashik Lakes, AK	George Purdie	George Purdie	1963	104
29 1/16	18 2/16	10 15/16	Port Moller, AK	Russell H. Underdahl	Russell H. Underdahl	1967	104
29 1/16	17 15/16	11 2/16	Cold Bay, AK	George Caswell	George Caswell	1984	104
29 1/16	17 12/16	11 5/16	Fraser Lake, AK	Randy D. Klingenmeyer	Randy D. Klingenmeyer	1991	104
29	17 10/16	11 6/16	Kodiak Island, AK	John Fox	John Fox	1959	111
29	17 14/16	11 2/16	Kodiak Island, AK	Raymond C. Boystel	Raymond C. Boystel	1963	111
29	18 2/16	10 14/16	Cold Bay, AK	Jack S. Parker	Jack S. Parker	1964	111
29	17 12/16	11 4/16	Cold Bay, AK	Fritz A. Nachant	Fritz A. Nachant	1965	111
29	18 6/16	10 10/16	Yakutat, AK	Jack DeWald	Jack DeWald	1973	111
29	17 1/16	11 1/16	Kodiak Island, AK	Creig M. Sharp	Creig M. Sharp	1977	111
29	18 3/16	10 13/16	Alaska Pen., AK	Johnnie R. Lowe	Johnnie R. Lowe	1979	111
29	17 12/16	11 4/16	Shearwater Bay, AK	Chester E. Chellman	Chester E. Chellman	1987	111
29	17 12/16	11 4/16	Kiavak Bay, AK	John L. Largura	John L. Largura	1987	111
29	17 14/16	11 2/16	Amber Bay, AK	Richard M. Welch	Richard M. Welch	1988	111
29	17 7/16	11 8/16	Middle Bay, AK	Royal V. Large, Jr.	Royal V. Large, Jr.	1990	111
29	17 5/16	11 11/16	Kodiak Island, AK	James D. Nyce	James D. Nyce	1990	111
29	18 3/16	10 13/16	Karluk Lake, AK	Robert W. Stevens	Robert W. Stevens	1990	111

			Location	Name	Year	Rank
28 15/16	17 11/16	11 4/16	Port Moller Bay, AK	C.A. Stenger	1951	124
28 15/16	17 13/16	11 2/16	Alaska Pen., AK	G.W. Folta	1954	124
28 15/16	17 6/16	11 9/16	Kodiak Island, AK	Robert T. Leever	1959	124
28 15/16	17 12/16	11 3/16	Kodiak Island, AK	H.T. Hilderbrandt	1961	124
28 15/16	17 15/16	11	Sand Lake, AK	J.J. Stallone	1962	124
28 15/16	17 14/16	11 1/16	Port Moller, AK	Andrew S. Allen	1963	124
28 15/16	17 8/16	11 7/16	Kodiak Island, AK	Stephen A. Mihal	1969	124
28 15/16	17 11/16	11 4/16	Alaska Pen., AK	James A. Johnson	1970	124
28 15/16	17 4/16	11 11/16	Kodiak Island, AK	Robert E. Pippen	1975	124
28 15/16	18 1/16	10 14/16	Mother Goose Lake, AK	John H. Buckman	1976	124
28 15/16	17 7/16	11 8/16	Kiliuda Bay, AK	Dean J. Walden	1980	124
28 15/16	18 4/16	10 11/16	Stepovak Bay, AK	Kurt A. Haskin	1986	124
28 15/16	18 7/16	10 8/16	Alaska Pen., AK	Ron D. King	1988	124
28 15/16	17 8/16	11 7/16	Olga Bay, AK	Alan O'Neil	1988	124
28 15/16	17 5/16	11 10/16	Kodiak Island, AK	Geoffrey H.S. House	1989	124
28 15/16	17 6/16	11 9/16	Dog Salmon River, AK	John H. Sholtiss	1989	124
28 15/16	17 14/16	11 1/16	Kodiak Island, AK	George Pappas	1992	124
28 15/16	17 10/16	11 5/16	Terror Bay, AK	Terry A. Monson	2003	124
28 14/16	17 13/16	11 1/16	Yakataga Beach, AK	Melvin Grindel	1933	142
28 14/16	16 12/16	12 2/16	Kodiak Island, AK	A.J. Casper	1936	142
28 14/16	17 7/16	11 7/16	Kodiak Island, AK	Jack Honhart	1952	142
28 14/16	18 5/16	10 9/16	Alaska Pen., AK	Herb Elliott	1960	142
28 14/16	18 6/16	10 8/16	Kodiak Island, AK	Maurice S. Ireland	1961	142
28 14/16	18 5/16	10 9/16	Alaska Pen., AK	Ethel Prine	1964	142
28 14/16	18	10 14/16	Alaska Pen., AK	Richard Kilbane	1965	142
28 14/16	17 5/16	11 9/16	Kodiak Island, AK	William B. Valen	1965	142
28 14/16	17 14/16	11	Skwentna River, AK	Gerald N. Felando	1971	142
28 14/16	17 12/16	11 2/16	Alaska Pen., AK	Richard N. Von	1975	142
28 14/16	17 6/16	11 8/16	Kodiak Island, AK	Robert A. Wainscott	1978	142
28 14/16	17 3/16	11 11/16	Olga Bay, AK	William G. James	1989	142
28 14/16	18 5/16	10 9/16	Muddy River, AK	Chung C. Huang	1990	142
28 14/16	17 12/16	11 2/16	Meshik River, AK	R. Jackson Willingham	1990	142
28 14/16	18 11/16	10 3/16	Cold Bay, AK	Dick A. Jacobs	1991	142
28 14/16	17 5/16	11 9/16	Zachar Bay, AK	Richard E. Metzger	1992	142
28 14/16	17 8/16	11 6/16	Olga Bay, AK	Harvey R. Carson	1993	142
28 14/16	17 9/16	11 5/16	Aliulik Pen., AK	Annemarie Rome	1993	142
28 14/16	17 11/16	11 3/16	Afognak Island, AK	Ricardo E. Longoria	2001	142
28 14/16	18	10 14/16	Pumice Creek, AK	Larry F. O'Brian	2001	142
28 14/16	17 12/16	11 2/16	Meshik River, AK	Doyle D. Patterson	2001	142
28 13/16	18 2/16	10 11/16	Hoodoo Lake, AK	A.C. Gilbert	1950	163
28 13/16	17 4/16	11 9/16	Port Heiden, AK	John Du Puy	1951	163
28 13/16	17 12/16	11 1/16	Fraser Lake, AK	Rupert Chisholm	1956	163
28 13/16	17 15/16	10 14/16	Alaska Pen., AK	Elgin T. Gates	1960	163
28 13/16	17 13/16	11	Kodiak Island, AK	Charles Daniels	1962	163
28 13/16	17 6/16	11 7/16	Kodiak, AK	Hal Waugh	1964	163
28 13/16	17 12/16	11 1/16	Alaska Pen., AK	Ernest Rush, Jr.	1966	163
28 13/16	17 10/16	11 3/16	Deadman Bay, AK	Michael R. Anderson	1971	163
28 13/16	17 8/16	11 5/16	Herring Bay, AK	Michael F. Short	1983	163

ALASKA BROWN BEAR

Ursus arctos middendorffi and certain related subspecies

Score	Greatest Length of Skull Without Lower Jaw	Greatest Width of Skull	Locality	Hunter	Owner	Date Killed	Rank
28 13/16	17 14/16	10 15/16	Beaver Bay, AK	Jesse T. Kirk	Jesse T. Kirk	1988	163
28 13/16	17 13/16	11	Kejulik River, AK	Yuko Sato	Yuko Sato	1993	163
28 13/16	17 8/16	11 5/16	Uganik Bay, AK	R. Dale Ziegler	R. Dale Ziegler	1998	163
28 13/16	17 15/16	10 14/16	Mt. Veniaminof, AK	Roger L. McCosker	Roger L. McCosker	2001	163
28 12/16	18	10 12/16	Sand Lake, AK	A.C. Gilbert	A.C. Gilbert	1939	176
28 12/16	18 2/16	10 10/16	Sand Lake, AK	Jules V. Lane	Jules V. Lane	1939	176
28 12/16	18 4/16	10 8/16	Pavlof Bay, AK	Robert R. Stewart	Robert R. Stewart	1949	176
28 12/16	18 2/16	10 10/16	Alaska Pen., AK	Harry H. Webb	Harry H. Webb	1952	176
28 12/16	17 5/16	11 7/16	Kodiak Island, AK	Robert D. Boone	Robert D. Boone	1960	176
28 12/16	17 1/16	11 11/16	Alaska Pen., AK	Bert Klineburger	Bert Klineburger	1961	176
28 12/16	17 12/16	11	Alaska Pen., AK	Hans O. Meissner	Hans O. Meissner	1961	176
28 12/16	17 11/16	11 1/16	Karluk Lake, AK	Alberto F. Ruiloha	Alberto F Ruiloha	1962	176
28 12/16	16 14/16	11 14/16	Kodiak Island, AK	Vernon C. Jensen	Vernon C. Jensen	1963	176
28 12/16	17 2/16	11 10/16	Alaska Pen., AK	Bert Klineburger	Bert Klineburger	1964	176
28 12/16	17 9/16	11 3/16	Kodiak Island, AK	Joe M. Floyd, Jr.	Joe M. Floyd, Jr.	1966	176
28 12/16	17 15/16	10 13/16	Kodiak Island, AK	Clyde Ormond	Clyde Ormond	1968	176
28 12/16	18 2/16	10 10/16	Cold Bay, AK	Ted J. Forsi	Ted J. Forsi	1975	176
28 12/16	17 4/16	11 8/16	Kodiak Island, AK	Roy H. Tyler	Roy H. Tyler	1977	176
28 12/16	17 4/16	11 8/16	Kaiugnak Bay, AK	Dale E. Machacek	Dale E. Machacek	1984	176
28 12/16	17 5/16	11 7/16	Red Lake, AK	Joe B. Brewster	Joe B. Brewster	1985	176
28 12/16	17 14/16	10 14/16	Lilly Lake, AK	Darryl W. Indvik	Darryl W. Indvik	1987	176
28 12/16	17 3/16	11 9/16	Deadman Bay, AK	Marvin Shick	Marvin Shick	1989	176
28 12/16	17 8/16	11 4/16	Uganik Bay, AK	George M. Schmidt	George M. Schmidt	1992	176
28 12/16	17 12/16	11	Dog Salmon Creek, AK	Gene J. Brzek	Gene J. Brzek	1995	176
28 11/16	18 4/16	10 7/16	Cinder River, AK	George W. Vaughan	George W. Vaughan	1951	196
28 11/16	17 6/16	11 5/16	Kodiak Island, AK	John Treillet	John Treillet	1953	196
28 11/16	17 6/16	11 5/16	Kodiak Island, AK	Harold J. Ahrendt	Harold J. Ahrendt	1957	196
28 11/16	18 7/16	10 4/16	Alaska Pen., AK	Edward R. Crooks	Edward R. Crooks	1958	196
28 11/16	17 3/16	11 8/16	Kodiak Island, AK	Anthony A. Calderone	Anthony A. Calderone	1962	196
28 11/16	18 2/16	10 9/16	Alaska Pen., AK	Basil C. Bradbury	Basil C. Bradbury	1963	196
28 11/16	17 15/16	10 12/16	Afognak Island, AK	Clyde Gett	Clyde Gett	1969	196
28 11/16	17 6/16	11 6/16	Afognak Island, AK	Charles Hettman	Don Kimbrough, Jr.	1969	196
28 11/16	17 7/16	11 4/16	Afognak Island, AK	William A. Bardot	William A. Bardot	1972	196
28 11/16	18 6/16	10 5/16	Bear Lake, AK	Leon A. Naccarato	Leon A. Naccarato	1980	196
28 11/16	17 3/16	11 8/16	Deadman Bay, AK	James S. Fogel	James S. Fogel	1982	196
28 11/16	17 8/16	11 3/16	Kodiak Island, AK	Terry M. Webb	Terry M. Webb	1986	196
28 11/16	17 13/16	10 14/16	Cold Bay, AK	Simon Aragi	Simon Aragi	1988	196
28 11/16	17 12/16	10 15/16	Cold Bay, AK	John F. Bermen, Jr.	John F. Bermen, Jr.	1988	196

Score	Length	Width	Locality	Hunter	Date	Rank
28 11/16	18 3/16	10 8/16	Littlejohn Lagoon, AK	Anthony C. Henry	1990	196
28 11/16	17 6/16	11 5/16	Kodiak Island, AK	John T. Dembowiak	1992	196
28 11/16	17 5/16	11 5/16	Deadman Bay, AK	Raymond L. Holmes	1993	196
28 11/16	18 1/16	10 10/16	Olga Bay, AK	Melvin F. Hendricks	1996	196
28 11/16	16 14/16	11 13/16	Uganic Bay, AK	Paul G. Mater	2001	196
28 10/16	18 6/16	10 4/16	Pavlof Bay, AK	R.H. Rockwell	1921	215
28 10/16	18 2/16	10 8/16	Alaska Pen., AK	U.S. Natl. Museum	1952	215
28 10/16	17 11/16	10 15/16	Alaska Pen., AK	Harry H. Webb	1953	215
28 10/16	17 3/16	11 3/16	Kodiak Island, AK	Arthur C. Popham, Jr.	1954	215
28 10/16	17 9/16	11 9/16	Kodiak Island, AK	Kenneth D. Landes	1959	215
28 10/16	17 4/16	11 6/16	Alaska Pen., AK	Pat Soderburg	1959	215
28 10/16	18 1/16	10 9/16	Alaska Pen., AK	Selmer Torrison	1960	215
28 10/16	17 4/16	11 6/16	Cordova, AK	Win Condict	1962	215
28 10/16	17 12/16	10 14/16	Kodiak Island, AK	Wallace Fields	1962	215
28 10/16	17 8/16	11 8/16	Alaska Pen., AK	Alfonso Pasquel	1963	215
28 10/16	17 3/16	11 7/16	Kodiak, AK	Frederick O. Kielmam	1964	215
28 10/16	17 9/16	11 1/16	Alaska Pen., AK	Michael Friedland	1964	215
28 10/16	17 5/16	11 5/16	Kodiak Island, AK	Ed Shapiro	1965	215
28 10/16	17 8/16	11 2/16	Pavlof Bay, AK	John E. Crook	1965	215
28 10/16	17 10/16	11	Kodiak Island, AK	William M. Kessner	1965	215
28 10/16	17 8/16	11 2/16	Alaska Pen., AK	Alex W. McCoy III	1965	215
28 10/16	17 12/16	10 14/16	Port Gravina, AK	C.J. McElroy	1967	215
28 10/16	17 1/16	11 9/16	Kodiak Island, AK	Norton T. Montague	1972	215
28 10/16	17 4/16	11 6/16	Olga Bay, AK	Louis R. Kaminsky	1980	215
28 10/16	17 14/16	10 12/16	Long Bay, AK	Doug Latimer	1984	215
28 10/16	17 5/16	11 5/16	Kaguyak Bay, AK	Delbert E. Starr	1984	215
28 10/16	17	11 10/16	Kodiak Island, AK	Larry L. Stephens	1989	215
28 10/16	17 10/16	11 8/16	Alaska Pen., AK	Robert W. Bundtzen	1989	215
28 10/16	17 8/16	10 12/16	Aniakchak River, AK	John D. Powers	1990	215
28 10/16	17 14/16	10 8/16	Hoodoo Lake, AK	James L. Kedrowski	1992	215
28 10/16	18 2/16	10 12/16	Sunday Creek, AK	Jeffrey D. Lapp	1994	215
28 10/16	17 14/16	10 14/16	Kejulik River, AK	Jerry B. Cotner	1996	215
28 10/16	17 12/16	11	Alaska Pen., AK	Neil D. McKenzie	1999	215
28 10/16	17	10 10/16	Alaska Pen., AK	Robert D. Gibbs	2002	215
28 9/16	18	11 1/16	Kodiak Island, AK	John A. Dolan	1922	244
28 9/16	17 8/16	10 14/16	Alaska Pen., AK	Camp Fire Club of America	1962	244
28 9/16	17 11/16	11 2/16	Kodiak Island, AK	Peggy M. Noles	1963	244
28 9/16	17 7/16	11 3/16	Kodiak Island, AK	Charles Askins	1964	244
28 9/16	17 6/16	10 13/16	Becharof Lake, AK	Robert J. Brocker	1964	244
28 9/16	17 12/16	11 5/16	Cordova, AK	Marvin Kocurek	1966	244
28 9/16	17 4/16	10 9/16	Alaska Pen., AK	Robert L. Helms	1966	244
28 9/16	18	11	Alaska Pen., AK	George H. Landreth	1973	244
28 9/16	17 9/16	11 3/16	Chichagof Island, AK	Stewart N. Shaft	1975	244
28 9/16	17 2/16	11 7/16	Alaska Pen., AK	James B. Lindahl	1987	244
28 9/16	17 2/16	11 2/16	Talkeetna Mts., AK	Max C. Schwab	1989	244
28 9/16	17 6/16	11 7/16	Sitkalidak Island, AK	Travis L. Barber	1991	244
28 9/16	17 3/16	11 3/16	Kodiak Island, AK	Robert K. Deligans	1991	244
28 9/16	17	11	Spiridon Bay, AK	Michael H. Bolo	1992	244

ALASKA BROWN BEAR

Ursus arctos middendorffi and certain related subspecies

Score	Greatest Length of Skull Without Lower Jaw	Greatest Width of Skull	Locality	Hunter	Owner	Date Killed	Rank
28 9/16	17 4/16	11 5/16	Uganik Bay, AK	Jay M. Haverstick	Jay M. Haverstick	1993	244
28 9/16	16 12/16	11 13/16	Olga Bay, AK	John B. Martin	John B. Martin	1994	244
28 9/16	17 3/16	11 6/16	Dog Salmon Creek, AK	Gary R. Ploeckelmann	Gary R. Ploeckelmann	1994	244
28 9/16	17 5/16	11 4/16	Kodiak Island, AK	Richard E. Bennett	Richard E. Bennett	2000	244
28 9/16	17 5/16	11 4/16	Olga Bay, AK	Michael E. Kuglitsch	Michael E. Kuglitsch	2000	244
28 8/16	17 8/16	11	Kodiak Island, AK	Mrs. Donald S. Hopkins	Unknown	1939	262
28 8/16	18	10 8/16	Herendeen Bay, AK	Arthur Johnson	Univ. of Alaska	1950	262
28 8/16	17 2/16	11 6/16	Caribou Lake, AK	W.A. Heldt	W.A. Heldt	1956	262
28 8/16	16 10/16	11 14/16	Kodiak Island, AK	Gloria T. Zerega	Gloria T. Zerega	1956	262
28 8/16	17 4/16	11 4/16	Kodiak Island, AK	W.M. Hollinger	W.M. Hollinger	1958	262
28 8/16	17	11 8/16	Kodiak Island, AK	Ross Beach	Ross Beach	1963	262
28 8/16	17 12/16	10 12/16	Port Heiden, AK	Chic Kawahara	Chic Kawahara	1963	262
28 8/16	17 14/16	10 10/16	Alaska Pen., AK	W.H. Picher	W.H. Picher	1964	262
28 8/16	17 4/16	11 4/16	Unimak Island, AK	Richard A. Guthrie	Richard A. Guthrie	1974	262
28 8/16	17 9/16	11 2/16	Deadman Bay, AK	Frank Alabiso	Frank Alabiso	1976	262
28 8/16	17 10/16	10 14/16	Pavlof Bay, AK	Melvin B. Gillis	Melvin B. Gillis	1976	262
28 8/16	17 10/16	10 14/16	Karluk Lake, AK	Paul W. Hansen	Paul W. Hansen	1983	262
28 8/16	17 4/16	11 4/16	Kiavak Bay, AK	Robert J. Welsh, Jr.	Robert J. Welsh, Jr.	1987	262
28 8/16	17 12/16	10 12/16	Ash Creek, AK	Phil N. Alward	Phil N. Alward	1988	262
28 8/16	17 4/16	11 4/16	Viekoda Bay, AK	Houston Smith	Houston Smith	1989	262
28 8/16	17 8/16	11 4/16	Kodiak Island, AK	Andrew J. Fierro	Andrew J. Fierro	1991	262
28 8/16	16 15/16	11 9/16	Deadman Bay, AK	John L. Spencer	John L. Spencer	1991	262
28 8/16	17 14/16	10 10/16	Cold Bay, AK	Charles W. Drechsel III	Charles W. Drechsel III	1992	262
28 8/16	17 4/16	11 4/16	Malina Bay, AK	Ron T. Schmitz	Ron T. Schmitz	1994	262
28 8/16	18 2/16	10 6/16	Cinder River, AK	A.J. Foyt III	A.J. Foyt III	1995	262
28 8/16	17 2/16	11 6/16	Muklung Hills, AK	Phillip T. Stringer	Phillip T. Stringer	1998	262
28 8/16	17 8/16	11	Sturgeon River, AK	Bill C. Sapa	Bill C. Sapa	1999	262
28 8/16	18 1/16	10 7/16	Cold Bay, AK	Robert B. Johnson	Robert B. Johnson	2000	262
28 7/16	17 1/16	11 1/16	Alaska Pen., AK	William Ronning	Lloyd Ronning	1958	285
28 7/16	16 12/16	11 11/16	Kodiak Island, AK	Bill Polland	Bill Polland	1959	285
28 7/16	17 15/16	10 8/16	Cold Bay, AK	Virgil Brill	Virgil Brill	1960	285
28 7/16	17 10/16	10 13/16	Alaska Pen., AK	Milton L. Knapp	Milton L. Knapp	1961	285
28 7/16	17 2/16	11 5/16	Kodiak Island, AK	Edward F. Pedersen, Jr.	Edward F. Pedersen, Jr.	1961	285
28 7/16	17 2/16	11 2/16	Kodiak Island, AK	Frank H. Rogers	Frank H. Rogers	1961	285
28 7/16	17 9/16	10 14/16	Alaska Pen., AK	Kenneth Golden	Kenneth Golden	1962	285
28 7/16	17 7/16	11	Afognak Island, AK	Robert Munger	Robert Munger	1962	285
28 7/16	17 13/16	10 10/16	Alaska Pen., AK	Sam Pancotto	Sam Pancotto	1962	285
28 7/16	17 13/16	10 10/16	Alaska Pen., AK	Dennis Burke	Dennis Burke	1964	285

Score	Length	Width	Locality	Hunter	Owner	Rank	Date
28 7/16	17 10/16	10 13/16	Ugashik Lakes, AK	James E. Egger	James E. Egger	285	1966
28 7/16	17 11/16	10 12/16	Kodiak Island, AK	William A. Ross, Jr.	William A. Ross, Jr.	285	1968
28 7/16	17 2/16	11 5/16	Kodiak Island, AK	M.H. Brock	M.H. Brock	285	1971
28 7/16	17 11/16	10 12/16	Alaska Pen., AK	James E. Otto	James E. Otto	285	1973
28 7/16	17 4/16	11 3/16	Kodiak Island, AK	Virgil J. Sheppard	Virgil J. Sheppard	285	1978
28 7/16	17 8/16	10 15/16	Uganik River, AK	Donald W. Baxter	Donald W. Baxter	285	1985
28 7/16	17 8/16	10 15/16	Uganik Bay, AK	Mark T. Jacobson	Mark T. Jacobson	285	1989
28 7/16	18	10 7/16	Cold Bay, AK	George A. Bettas	George A. Bettas	285	1990
28 7/16	17 14/16	10 9/16	Karluk Lake, AK	Stanley N. Kaneshiro	Stanley N. Kaneshiro	285	1990
28 7/16	17 4/16	11 3/16	Uganik Island, AK	James J. Brooks	David S. Collett-Paule	285	1991
28 7/16	17 8/16	10 15/16	Unimak Island, AK	Danny V. Grangaard	Danny V. Grangaard	285	1991
28 7/16	17 9/16	10 14/16	Sandy River, AK	Lawrence W. Frisoli	Lawrence W. Frisoli	285	1992
28 7/16	17	11 7/16	Kodiak Island, AK	Kelly McClain	Kelly McClain	285	1993
28 7/16	17 1/16	11 6/16	Seven Rivers, AK	Karen H. Parks	Karen H. Parks	285	1993
28 7/16	16 10/16	11 13/16	Kodiak Island, AK	Gary F. Bogner	Gary F. Bogner	285	1994
28 7/16	17 13/16	10 10/16	Alaska Pen., AK	Stephen C. Walker	Stephen C. Walker	285	1994
28 7/16	17 3/16	11 4/16	Dog Salmon River, AK	Bell Mus. of Natl. Hist.	Wesley J. Streed	285	1996
28 7/16	17 11/16	10 12/16	Uyak Bay, AK	William E. Wilson	William E. Wilson	285	1996
28 7/16	17 15/16	10 8/16	David River, AK	Charles J. Watkins	Charles J. Watkins	285	1997
28 7/16	17 10/16	10 13/16	Halibut Bay, AK	Richard B. Sapa	Richard Sapa	285	1998
28 7/16	18 1/16	10 6/16	Unimak Island, AK	A. Timothy Toth	A. Timothy Toth	285	2000
28 7/16	17 6/16	11 1/16	Pavlof Bay, AK	Gordon L. Dorn	Gordon L. Dorn	285	2001
28 6/16	17 15/16	10 7/16	Moroski Bay, AK	U.S. Natl. Museum	Ivan Katchinof	317	1897
28 6/16	17 14/16	10 8/16	Sand Lake, AK	Mrs. J. Watson Webb	Mrs. J. Watson Webb	317	1939
28 6/16	17 9/16	10 13/16	Kodiak Island, AK	Martin J. Coyne	Martin J. Coyne	317	1960
28 6/16	17 11/16	10 11/16	Alaska Pen., AK	Alberto Pipia	Alberto Pipia	317	1965
28 6/16	17 7/16	10 15/16	Alaska Pen., AK	John F. Ault	John F. Ault	317	1967
28 6/16	17 4/16	11 2/16	Prince William Sound, AK	Ron Kacsmaryk	Ron Kacsmaryk	317	1970
28 6/16	16 12/16	11 10/16	Kodiak Island, AK	Earl Hahn	Darrel Williams	317	1976
28 6/16	17 14/16	10 8/16	Port Heiden, AK	Jack M. Holland, Jr.	Jack M. Holland, Jr.	317	1976
28 6/16	17 4/16	11 2/16	Port Heiden, AK	Russ McLennan	Russ McLennan	317	1980
28 6/16	17 2/16	11 4/16	Larsen Bay, AK	Sherron G. Perry	Sherron G. Perry	317	1983
28 6/16	17	11 6/16	Olga Bay, AK	David B. Colclough	David B. Colclough	317	1989
28 6/16	17 15/16	10 7/16	Pavlof Bay, AK	John R. Sullivan	John R. Sullivan	317	1989
28 6/16	17 2/16	11 4/16	Karluk River, AK	Terry J. Leffler	Terry J. Leffler	317	1990
28 6/16	17 2/16	11 4/16	Alaska Pen., AK	Robert W. Orzechowski	Robert W. Orzechowski	317	1991
28 6/16	17 3/16	11 3/16	Kodiak Island, AK	Thomas W. Triplett	Thomas W. Triplett	317	1997
28 6/16	16 15/16	11 7/16	Deadman Bay, AK	Isidro Lopez del Bosque	Isidro Lopez del Bosque	317	1998
28 6/16	17 8/16	10 14/16	Unimak Island, AK	Rusty Hall	Rusty Hall	317	1999
28 6/16	17 6/16	11	Sandy Cove, AK	Brian D. Hayes	Brian D. Hayes	317	1999
28 6/16	16 9/16	11 13/16	Black Point, AK	Richard E. Hunnewell	Richard E. Hunnewell	317	2000
28 6/16	17 12/16	10 10/16	Caribou River, AK	Ronald S. Schmidt	Ronald S. Schmidt	317	2001
28 6/16	17 9/16	10 13/16	Aliulik Pen., AK	Charles W. Stevens	Charles W. Stevens	317	2001
28 5/16	17 14/16	10 7/16	Pavlof Bay, AK	U.S. Natl. Museum	Peter Ruppi	338	1897
28 5/16	17 4/16	11 1/16	Captain Harbor, AK	MI State Univ. Mus.	Tarleton F. Smith	338	1949
28 5/16	17 4/16	11 1/16	Cold Bay, AK	L.S. Kuter	L.S. Kuter	338	1952
28 5/16	16 14/16	11 7/16	Kodiak Island, AK	C.D. Fuller & F.C. Miller	C.D. Fuller & F.C. Miller	338	1959

ALASKA BROWN BEAR

Ursus arctos middendorffi and certain related subspecies

Score	Greatest Length of Skull Without Lower Jaw	Greatest Width of Skull	Locality	Hunter	Owner	Date Killed	Rank
28 5/16	16 14/16	11 7/16	Kodiak Island, AK	J.D. Roebuck	J.D. Roebuck	1960	338
28 5/16	17 14/16	10 7/16	Port Heiden, AK	John S. Cochran, Jr.	John S. Cochran, Jr.	1964	338
28 5/16	17 9/16	10 12/16	Alaska Pen., AK	J.B. Kerley	J.B. Kerley	1964	338
28 5/16	17 8/16	10 13/16	Mother Goose Lake, AK	H.T. Sliger	H.T. Sliger	1964	338
28 5/16	17 3/16	11 2/16	Kodiak Island, AK	Jerry Coon	Jerry Coon	1965	338
28 5/16	18	10 5/16	Port Heiden, AK	Leonard W. Bruns	Leonard W. Bruns	1967	338
28 5/16	17	11 5/16	Kodiak Island, AK	Chris Klineburger	Chris Klineburger	1967	338
28 5/16	16 15/16	11 6/16	Kodiak Island, AK	King Mahendra of Nepal	King Mahendra of Nepal	1967	338
28 5/16	17 6/16	10 15/16	Kodiak Island, AK	Theodore J. Schorsch, Sr.	Theodore J. Schorsch, Sr.	1968	338
28 5/16	18	10 5/16	Alaska Pen., AK	Keith W. Bates	Keith W. Bates	1976	338
28 5/16	17 3/16	11 2/16	Dog Salmon Creek, AK	John D. Valle	John D. Valle	1981	338
28 5/16	18	10 5/16	Foot Bay, AK	Larry A. McComb	Larry A. McComb	1982	338
28 5/16	17 9/16	10 12/16	Cold Bay, AK	Kenneth C. Hayden	Kenneth C. Hayden	1984	338
28 5/16	17 13/16	10 8/16	Cold Bay, AK	Timothy Orton	Timothy Orton	1984	338
28 5/16	17 7/16	10 14/16	Stuyahok River, AK	William S. Greene, Jr.	William S. Greene, Jr.	1985	338
28 5/16	16 12/16	11 9/16	Kodiak Island, AK	Roy F. Bain	Roy F. Bain	1988	338
28 5/16	17	11 5/16	Kaguyak Bay, AK	Arnold F. Thibault	Arnold F. Thibault	1989	338
28 5/16	17 4/16	11 1/16	Kodiak Island, AK	J. Dorsey Smith	J. Dorsey Smith	1990	338
28 5/16	17 1/16	11 4/16	Kiliuda Bay, AK	Teresa I. Ramos	Teresa I. Ramos	1993	338
28 5/16	17 12/16	10 9/16	Cinder River, AK	Scott M. Ackleson	Scott M. Ackleson	1994	338
28 5/16	18 8/16	9 13/16	Mt. Veniaminof, AK	Steve D. Adams	Steve D. Adams	1996	338
28 5/16	17 8/16	10 13/16	Afognak Island, AK	Daniel M. Vogel	Daniel M. Vogel	1997	338
28 5/16	17 8/16	10 13/16	Cold Bay, AK	Charles B. Edwards	Charles B. Edwards	1999	338
28 5/16	17 13/16	10 8/16	Port Heiden, AK	Picked Up	Shawn R. Andres	2001	338
28 5/16	17 11/16	10 10/16	Cold Bay, AK	Richard W. Van Valkenburg	Richard W. Van Valkenburg	2001	338
28 5/16	17 4/16	11 1/16	Kodiak Island, AK	Steven Gauvin	Steven Gauvin	2002	338
28 4/16	17 12/16	10 8/16	Port Moller, AK	Harry H. Webb	Harry H. Webb	1953	368
28 4/16	17	11 4/16	Kodiak Island, AK	T.E. Shillingburg	T.E. Shillingburg	1954	368
28 4/16	17 4/16	11	Afognak Island, AK	Edward M. Simko	Edward M. Simko	1957	368
28 4/16	17 8/16	10 12/16	Kodiak Island, AK	Willie D. Payton	Willie D. Payton	1959	368
28 4/16	17 9/16	10 11/16	Alaska Pen., AK	Jeffrey G. Burmeister	Jeffrey G. Burmeister	1960	368
28 4/16	18 4/16	10	Alaska Pen., AK	Jean Branson	Jean Branson	1962	368
28 4/16	17	11 4/16	Uganik Bay, AK	Jerry Coker	J. Coker & J. Meagher	1963	368
28 4/16	17 3/16	11 1/16	Kodiak Island, AK	Roy M. Champayne	Roy M. Champayne	1965	368
28 4/16	16 12/16	11 8/16	Kodiak Island, AK	Keith Honhart	Keith Honhart	1965	368
28 4/16	16 15/16	11 5/16	Kodiak Island, AK	James E. Nelson	James E. Nelson	1979	368
28 4/16	17 4/16	11	Olga Bay, AK	Allan E. Bergland	Allan E. Bergland	1981	368
28 4/16	17 12/16	10 8/16	Cinder River, AK	Javier Zubia	Javier Zubia	1981	368

Score	Length	Width	Locality	Owner	By Whom Killed	Date Killed	Rank
28 4/16	17 9/16	10 11/16	Unimak Island, AK	John D. Frost	John D. Frost	1985	368
28 4/16	17 5/16	10 15/16	Alaska Pen., AK	H. Blake Allen	H. Blake Allen	1986	368
28 4/16	17 1/16	11 3/16	Kiavak Bay, AK	Garry V. Woodman	Garry V. Woodman	1992	368
28 4/16	17 6/16	10 14/16	Funny River, AK	Brian L. Larion	Brian L. Larion	1993	368
28 4/16	17	11 4/16	Kodiak Island, AK	Sam A. Francis	Sam A. Francis	1997	368
28 4/16	17 10/16	10 10/16	Herendeen Bay, AK	J. Wayne Heaton	J. Wayne Heaton	1998	368
28 4/16	17 4/16	11	Sturgeon River, AK	Mark Freshwaters	Mark Freshwaters	1999	368
28 4/16	17 4/16	11	Frazer Lake, AK	Terry L. Christiansen	Terry L. Christiansen	2000	368
28 4/16	18 4/16	10	Meshik River, AK	Stan W. Newding	Stan W. Newding	2000	368
28 3/16	17 4/16	10 15/16	Aniakchak Bay, AK	Francis J. Fabick	Francis J. Fabick	1949	389
28 3/16	17 1/16	11 2/16	Kodiak Island, AK	Raymond A. Du Four	Raymond A. Du Four	1959	389
28 3/16	17 14/16	10 5/16	Alaska Pen., AK	Kenneth Holland	Kenneth Holland	1959	389
28 3/16	17 5/16	11 1/16	Kodiak Island, AK	William Offenheim	William Offenheim	1960	389
28 3/16	17 7/16	10 12/16	Alaska Pen., AK	Elmer Graham	Elmer Graham	1961	389
28 3/16	16 15/16	11 4/16	Kodiak Island, AK	Frank Hollendonner	Frank Hollendonner	1961	389
28 3/16	18	10 3/16	Port Moller, AK	John D. Phillips	John D. Phillips	1961	389
28 3/16	17 4/16	10 15/16	Port Heiden, AK	Michael Ferrell	Michael Ferrell	1964	389
28 3/16	18 4/16	9 15/16	Port Moller, AK	Ray Eyler	Ray Eyler	1966	389
28 3/16	16 6/16	11 13/16	Talkeetna Mts., AK	Robert W. Holladay	Robert W. Holladay	1966	389
28 3/16	16 15/16	11 5/16	Kodiak Island, AK	T. Kimball Hill	T. Kimball Hill	1967	389
28 3/16	17 5/16	10 14/16	Cathedral Valley, AK	J.M. Norton	J.M. Norton	1982	389
28 3/16	17 13/16	10 6/16	Volcano Bay, AK	L. Clark Kiser	L. Clark Kiser	1984	389
28 3/16	17 1/16	11 2/16	Red Lake, AK	Richard H. Neville	Richard H. Neville	1984	389
28 3/16	16 13/16	11 6/16	Kaguyak Bay, AK	Jack D. Revelle	Jack D. Revelle	1984	389
28 3/16	17 15/16	10 4/16	Cold Bay, AK	Carlos F.S. Schutz	Carlos F.S. Schutz	1990	389
28 3/16	17 2/16	11	Chekok Creek, AK	Dana L. Timaeus	Dana L. Timaeus	1995	389
28 3/16	17 3/16	11 1/16	Foul Bay, AK	Robert L. Hales	Robert L. Hales	1997	389
28 3/16	17	11 2/16	Sandy River, AK	J.V. Lattimore III	J.V. Lattimore III	1998	389
28 3/16	16 11/16	11 3/16	Kodiak Island, AK	John W. Wilson	John W. Wilson	2000	389
28 2/16	17 12/16	11 7/16	Kodiak Island, AK	J. Watson Webb	J. Watson Webb	1948	409
28 2/16	18 1/16	10 6/16	Alaska Pen., AK	J.D. Jones	J.D. Jones	1954	409
28 2/16	17	10 2/16	Cold Bay, AK	Lewis E. Yearout	Lewis E. Yearout	1956	409
28 2/16	17 8/16	10 10/16	Kodiak Island, AK	Merril R. Reller	Merril R. Reller	1958	409
28 2/16	17 1/16	11 1/16	Cinder River, AK	Russell C. Cutter	Russell C. Cutter	1960	409
28 2/16	17 10/16	10 8/16	Kodiak Island, AK	Jim Alexander	Jim Alexander	PR 1961	409
28 2/16	17 12/16	10 6/16	Port Heiden, AK	Herman Kuchanek	Herman Kuchanek	1961	409
28 2/16	17 9/16	10 10/16	Alaska Pen., AK	Mrs. Sam Pancotto	Mrs. Sam Pancotto	1962	409
28 2/16	16 9/16	11 9/16	Alaska Pen., AK	Charles L. Ball, Jr.	Charles L. Ball, Jr.	1964	409
28 2/16	17 8/16	10 10/16	Kodiak Island, AK	Gordon G. Maclean	Gordon G. Maclean	1964	409
28 2/16	17 12/16	10 6/16	Unimak Island, AK	Don Burk	Don Burk	1966	409
28 2/16	16 8/16	11 10/16	Cold Bay, AK	Robert Hansen	Robert Hansen	1966	409
28 2/16	17 10/16	10 8/16	Eagle Harbor, AK	James T. Harrell	James T. Harrell	1966	409
28 2/16	17 5/16	10 13/16	Cold Bay, AK	John D. Jones	John D. Jones	1966	409
28 2/16	17 5/16	10 13/16	Alaska Pen., AK	Francis S. Levien	Francis S. Levien	1968	409
28 2/16	16 9/16	11 9/16	Afognak Island, AK	Laszlo Lemhenyi-Hanko	Laszlo Lemhenyi-Hanko	1970	409
28 2/16	17 5/16	10 13/16	Kodiak Island, AK	Dwight Hildebrandt	Dwight Hildebrandt	1971	409
28 2/16	16 9/16	11 9/16	Kodiak Island, AK	Bart D'Averso	Bart D'Averso	1974	409

Ursus arctos middendorffi and certain related subspecies

Score	Greatest Length of Skull Without Lower Jaw	Greatest Width of Skull	Locality	Hunter	Owner	Date Killed	Rank
28 2/16	17 3/16	10 15/16	Great Salmon Lake, AK	Siegfried Kube	Siegfried Kube	1974	409
28 2/16	17 2/16	11	Afognak Island, AK	Picked Up	David L. Lazer	PR 1976	409
28 2/16	17 4/16	10 14/16	Kodiak Island, AK	Charles A. Goldenberg	Charles A. Goldenberg	1978	409
28 2/16	17	10 2/16	Spiridon Lake, AK	Chris T. Hinchey	Bear Arms	1983	409
28 2/16	17 7/16	10 11/16	Cold Bay, AK	Lonnie W. McCurry, Sr.	Lonnie W. McCurry, Sr.	1984	409
28 2/16	17 1/16	11 1/16	Afognak Island, AK	Donald E. Peterson	Donald E. Peterson	1984	409
28 2/16	17 10/16	10 8/16	Cold Bay, AK	George A. Bettas	George A. Bettas	1986	409
28 2/16	17 12/16	10 6/16	Kiavak Bay, AK	Wayne E. Clark	Wayne E. Clark	1987	409
28 2/16	17 5/16	10 13/16	Pumice Creek, AK	Tony E. Jorgenson	Tony E. Jorgenson	1988	409
28 2/16	17 12/16	10 6/16	Meshik Lake, AK	Richard L. DeFelice	Richard L. DeFelice	1989	409
28 2/16	16 6/16	11 12/16	Uyak Bay, AK	Picked Up	Randy C. Arsenault	PR 1990	409
28 2/16	16 15/16	11 3/16	Karluk Lake, AK	Robert W. Stevens III	Robert W. Stevens III	1990	409
28 2/16	17 5/16	10 13/16	Port Heiden, AK	Florentino G. Escobedo	Florentino G. Escobedo	1991	409
28 2/16	17 4/16	10 14/16	Akwe River, AK	Roger R. Reck	Roger R. Reck	1991	409
28 2/16	17 2/16	11	Kodiak Island, AK	Michael P. Horstman	Michael P. Horstman	1992	409
28 2/16	17 6/16	10 12/16	Wildman Lake, AK	William M. Sumner	William M. Sumner	1993	409
28 2/16	16 13/16	11 5/16	Traders Mt., AK	Phillip D. Wagner	Phillip D. Wagner	1993	409
28 2/16	17 10/16	10 8/16	Glacier Bay, AK	Robert M. Daggett	Robert M. Daggett	1995	409
28 2/16	16 12/16	11 6/16	Uganik Bay, AK	William N. Adkins	William N. Adkins	1996	409
28 2/16	17 4/16	10 14/16	Rude River, AK	Karl Strenger	Karl Strenger	1997	409
28 2/16	17 10/16	10 8/16	Cold Bay, AK	Foster Yancey	Foster V. Yancey	1998	409
28 2/16	16 14/16	11 4/16	Lake Rose Tead, AK	Scott K. Parcell	Scott K. Parcell	1999	409
28 2/16	17 1/16	11 1/16	Kodiak Island, AK	Michael P. Horstman	Michael P. Horstman	2000	409
28 2/16	17 7/16	10 11/16	Alinchak Bay, AK	Matthew M. Perman	Matthew M. Perman	2000	409
28 2/16	17 8/16	10 10/16	Shotgun Hills, AK	Curt L. Bradford	Curt L. Bradford	2001	409
28 1/16	16 15/16	11 2/16	Port Moller, AK	Enos A. Axtell	Enos A. Axtell	1950	452
28 1/16	18	10 1/16	Alaska Pen., AK	R.H. Blum	R.H. Blum	1954	452
28 1/16	16 12/16	11 5/16	Kodiak Island, AK	Richard O. Daniels	Richard O. Daniels	1958	452
28 1/16	17	11 1/16	Kodiak Island, AK	Joe Maxwell	Joe Maxwell	1959	452
28 1/16	17 4/16	10 13/16	Kodiak Island, AK	L.W. Zeug	L.W. Zeug	1959	452
28 1/16	17 4/16	10 13/16	Alaska Pen., AK	Roscoe S. Mosiman	Roscoe S. Mosiman	1960	452
28 1/16	17 10/16	10 7/16	Cold Bay, AK	Keith C. Brown	Keith C. Brown	1962	452
28 1/16	17 11/16	10 6/16	Alaska Pen., AK	Bill Boone	Bill Boone	1964	452
28 1/16	17	11 2/16	Kodiak Island, AK	Dan G. Brown	Dan G. Brown	1967	452
28 1/16	16 15/16	11 2/16	Kodiak Island, AK	Cary E. Weldon	Cary E. Weldon	1968	452
28 1/16	17 8/16	10 9/16	Kodiak Island, AK	Bill Ulich	Bill Ulich	1976	452
28 1/16	17	11 1/16	Kenai Pen., AK	Charles Steele	AK Dept. of Fish & Game	1980	452
28 1/16	17 9/16	10 8/16	Olga Bay, AK	Robert N. Wainscott	Robert N. Wainscott	1982	452

Score	Length	Width	Locality	Hunter	Owner	Date Killed	Rank
28 1/16	18	10 1/16	Port Heiden, AK	William H.F. Wiltshire	William H.F. Wiltshire	1984	452
28 1/16	18	10 1/16	Alaska Pen., AK	Kurt R. Clark	Kurt R. Clark	1986	452
28 1/16	17 5/16	10 12/16	Sturgeon River, AK	Michael R. Dullen	Michael R. Dullen	1987	452
28 1/16	17 9/16	10 8/16	Canoe Bay, AK	John E. Hoye	John E. Hoye	1987	452
28 1/16	17 6/16	10 11/16	Kodiak Island, AK	Bruce T. Berger	Bruce T. Berger	1988	452
28 1/16	17 12/16	10 5/16	Cinder River, AK	Keith Pilz	Keith Pilz	1989	452
28 1/16	17 11/16	10 6/16	Stepovak Bay, AK	Martin G. Glover	Martin G. Glover	1990	452
28 1/16	16 8/16	10 14/16	Afognak Island, AK	Gary M. Allen	Gary M. Allen	1993	452
28 1/16	17 3/16	10 3/16	Uganik Bay, AK	Edwin E. Orr	Edwin E. Orr	1993	452
28 1/16	17	11 1/16	Olga Bay, AK	James Azevedo	James Azevedo	1994	452
28 1/16	17	11 1/16	Afognak Island, AK	John P. Burke	John P. Burke	1997	452
28 1/16	17 4/16	10 13/16	Deadman Bay, AK	Javier Lopez del Bosque	Javier Lopez del Bosque	1997	452
28 1/16	17 6/16	10 11/16	Olga Lake, AK	Brian A. Marang	Brian A. Marang	1998	452
28 1/16	17 6/16	10 11/16	Karluk Lake, AK	Buck Siler	Buck Siler	1999	452
28 1/16	17 14/16	10 3/16	Cold Bay, AK	Phillip R. Barker	Phillip R. Barker	2001	452
28 1/16	17 10/16	10 7/16	Big Creek, AK	Nicholas J.H. Borchert	Nicholas J.H. Borchert	2002	452
28 1/16	17 14/16	10 3/16	Cinder River, AK	Ronald V. Hunter	Ronald V. Hunter	2002	452
28 1/16	17 1/16	11	Aliulik Pen., AK	Tony Paden	Tony Paden	2002	452
28	17 11/16	10 6/16		Ronald G. Skloss	Ronald G. Skloss		484
28	17 2/16	10 14/16	Nelson Lagoon, AK	Harold Dugdale	Harold Dugdale	1954	484
28	17 10/16	10 6/16	Alaska Pen., AK	Robert D. Jones, Jr.	Robert D. Jones, Jr.	1955	484
28	17	11	Alaska Pen., AK	Harry F. Weyher	Harry F. Weyher	1958	484
28	17 15/16	10 1/16	Kodiak Island, AK	Fred Bear	Fred Bear	1960	484
28	17 12/16	10 12/16	Alaska Pen., AK	Wendell S. Fletcher	Wendell S. Fletcher	1960	484
28	17 7/16	10 9/16	Alaska Pen., AK	W.T. Yoshimoto	W.T. Yoshimoto	1961	484
28	17 3/16	10 13/16	Alaska Pen., AK	Gilbert Elton	B&C National Collection	1962	484
28	17 12/16	10 4/16	Port Moller, AK	Harry J. Armitage	Harry J. Armitage	1963	484
28	17 3/16	10 13/16	Kodiak Island, AK	Dean Herring	Dean Herring	1963	484
28	17 9/16	10 7/16	Alaska Pen., AK	James D. Smith	James D. Smith	1967	484
28	18	10	Alaska Pen., AK	Peter Santin	Peter Santin	1968	484
28	17 14/16	10 2/16	Alaska Pen., AK	Rudy Tuten	Rudy Tuten	1968	484
28	17	11	Alaska Pen., AK	James J. Fraioli	James J. Fraioli	1969	484
28	17 12/16	10 4/16	Alaska Pen., AK	Larry Lassley	Larry Lassley	1970	484
28	18	10	Chilkat River, AK	Philip L. Nare	Philip L. Nare	1975	484
28	16 10/16	11 6/16	Ugak Bay, AK	Arnie Gutenkauf	Arnie Gutenkauf	1981	484
28	17 12/16	10 12/16	Windy Bay, AK	Archie H. Stevens, Sr.	Archie H. Stevens, Sr.	1982	484
28	16 15/16	10 15/16	Skilak Glacier, AK	Richard W. Carlock	Richard W. Carlock	1983	484
28	17 4/16	10 12/16	Afognak Lake, AK	Leon A. Metz	Picked Up	1984	484
28	17 5/16	10 11/16	Copper River, AK	Roger R. Card	Roger R. Card	1985	484
28	17 9/16	10 7/16	Cold Bay, AK	John D. Teeter	John D. Teeter	1988	484
28	17	11	Sulna Bay, AK	Theodore A. Mallett	Theodore A. Mallett	1989	484
28	17	11	Uganik Bay, AK	Donald M. Sitton	Donald M. Sitton	1990	484
28	17 1/16	10 15/16	Pedro Bay, AK	Fred W. Amyotte	Fred W. Amyotte	1991	484
28	16 12/16	10 4/16	Uganik Bay, AK	Gene J. Brzek	Gene J. Brzek	1991	484
28	17 4/16	10 12/16	Kiliuda Bay, AK	Theodore A. Mallett	Theodore A. Mallett	1994	484
28	17 7/16	10 9/16	Upper Ugashik Lake, AK	Michael A. Telles	Michael A. Telles	1994	484
28	17 2/16	10 14/16	Grayback Mt., AK	David L. Bathke	David L. Bathke	1998	484

ALASKA BROWN BEAR

Ursus arctos middendorffi and certain related subspecies

Score	Greatest Length of Skull Without Lower Jaw	Greatest Width of Skull	Locality	Hunter	Owner	Date Killed	Rank
28	17 9/16	10 7/16	Unimak Island, AK	Jon A. Shiesl	Jon A. Shiesl	1999	484
28	17 1/16	10 15/16	Karluk Lake, AK	Joseph H. Snyder	Dana M. Snyder	1999	484
28	16 15/16	11 1/16	Ugak Bay, AK	Harry V. Fitzpatrick	Harry V. Fitzpatrick	2001	484
28	16 7/16	11 9/16	Port Lions, AK	Thomas E. Gannon	Thomas E. Gannon	2001	484
28 14/16*	17 13/16	11 1/16	Hinchinbrook Island, AK	Theodore A. Winnen	Theodore A. Winnen	2001	484

* Final score is subject to revision by additional verifying measurements.

CATEGORY
ALASKA BROWN BEAR

SCORE
28-8/16

HUNTER
BILL C. SAPA

LOCATION
STURGEON RIVER, ALASKA

DATE OF KILL
APRIL 1999

CATEGORY
ALASKA BROWN BEAR

SCORE
28-14/16

HUNTER
LARRY F. O'BRIAN (LEFT)

LOCATION
PUMICE CREEK, ALASKA

DATE OF KILL
OCTOBER 2001

SCORE
29-5/16

HUNTER
LARRY G. COLLINSON
(BELOW)

LOCATION
SEAL ISLANDS, ALASKA

DATE OF KILL
OCTOBER 1999

CATEGORY
ALASKA BROWN BEAR

SCORE
28-2/16

HUNTER
KARL STRENGER

LOCATION
RUDE RIVER, ALASKA

DATE OF KILL
MAY 1997

CATEGORY
ALASKA BROWN BEAR

SCORE
28-5/16

HUNTER
STEVEN GAUVIN

LOCATION
KODIAK ISLAND, ALASKA

DATE OF KILL
2002

CATEGORY
ALASKA BROWN BEAR

SCORE
28

HUNTER
HARRY V. FITZPATRICK

LOCATION
UGAK BAY, ALASKA

DATE OF KILL
APRIL 2001

CATEGORY
ALASKA BROWN BEAR

SCORE
28-8/16

HUNTER
PHILLIP T. STRINGER

LOCATION
MUKLUNG HILLS, ALASKA

DATE OF KILL
APRIL 1998

THEODORE ROOSEVELT 1858-1919

By Jack Reneau

Theodore Roosevelt did more for conservation of our natural resources and the preservation of sport hunting than any other person in the history of our nation. He showed a keen interest in nature with his first publication at the age of 20 in 1877 on summer birds in Franklin Co., New York. His experiences in the mid-1880s in the South Dakota badlands gave him a first-hand view of the problems associated with westward expansion, unregulated hunting, and the effects of market hunting. In 1887, he and his closest friends founded the Boone and Crockett Club – the nation's first conservation organization. He was the Club's first president and an active member until his death in 1919. Under his direction as Club president and president of the United States, numerous laws and legislative actions protecting wildlife and our natural resources were enacted. The creation of the U.S. Forest Service, National Wildlife Refuge System, and the National Park Service, which are among his most notable achievements, paved the way to ultimately set aside tens of millions of acres for the benefit of wildlife, our nation, and future generations. Theodore Roosevelt was the right person at the right time. ■

203

POLAR BEAR
WORLD'S RECORD

The polar bear (*Ursus maritimus*) taken by Shelby Longoria of Matamoros, Mexico, continues to hold the World's Record. In the spring of 1963, Longoria headed from his home south of the border toward the far north, embarking on what would become a harrowing yet rewarding adventure. Choosing from outfitters who operated out of Cape Lisburne, Point Hope, and as far north as Point Barrow, Longoria made a decision to hunt out of Kotzebue, Alaska. Spring in the North American Arctic can be an ideal window for hunting as warm flickers of light provide a pleasing contrast to the dark tones of winter. However, unlike the polar bears that are partially insulated by their long, shaggy coats, it is possible for a man to die from exposure within a matter of minutes if he should plunge into the cold polar seas. This was only one of many dangers that lingered as Longoria and his guides searched the windswept and wave-sculpted ice fields near the Bering Strait and Chukchi Sea for the grandest bear they could find.

Nearly a hundred miles offshore, the hunting expedition located a promising ivory-white bear wandering against a treacherous background pocketed with bulging mounds of splintered ice. Utilizing powerful hindquarters and long legs with partially webbed feet, "bears of the sea" have been spotted swimming up to 300 miles from shore and are capable of bounding completely out of the water onto an ice floe. After undertaking a contrastingly dangerous landing on the sea ice, Longoria continued to stalk his prey through the frozen maze before eventually bagging the impressive polar bear. Scoring 29-15/16, Longoria's trophy topped the former record held by Tom Bolack. It should be noted that polar bears are extremely capable hunters due to their nearly exclusive carnivorous diet. As a result of this adaptation to their environment, these bears typically have longer, narrower skulls than the Alaska brown bear. ∎

204

POLAR BEAR
WORLD'S RECORD SCORE CHART

Records of
North American
Big Game

250 Station Drive
Missoula, MT 59801
(406) 542-1888

BOONE AND CROCKETT CLUB®
OFFICIAL SCORING SYSTEM FOR NORTH AMERICAN BIG GAME TROPHIES

BEAR

	MINIMUM SCORES	
	AWARDS	ALL-TIME
black bear	20	21
grizzly bear	23	24
Alaska brown bear	26	28
polar bear	27	27

KIND OF BEAR (check one)
- ☐ black bear
- ☐ grizzly
- ☐ Alaska brown bear
- ■ polar

B

A

SEE OTHER SIDE FOR INSTRUCTIONS

	MEASUREMENTS
A. Greatest Length Without Lower Jaw	18 8/16
B. Greatest Width	11 7/16
FINAL SCORE	29 15/16

Exact Locality Where Killed: Kotzebue, AK

Date Killed: April 11, 1963   Hunter: Shelby Longoria

Owner: Shelby Longoria

Owner's Address:

Guide's Name and Address:

Remarks: (Mention Any Abnormalities or Unique

I, __Elgin T. Gates__ , certify that I have measured
                PRINT NAME

at __Carnegie Museum__   __Pittsburgh__
       STREET ADDRESS   CITY   PROVINCE

and that these measurements and data are, to the best of my knowledge and belief, made in   is given.

Witness: __John H. Batten__   Signature: __Elgin T. G__
                                                      B&C OFFICIAL

COPYRIGHT © 1999 BY BOONE AND CROC

POLAR BEAR
Ursus maritimus

MINIMUM SCORE 27

Score	Greatest Length of Skull Without Lower Jaw	Greatest Width of Skull	Locality	Hunter	Owner	Date Killed	Rank
29 15/16	18 8/16	11 7/16	Kotzebue, AK	Shelby Longoria	Shelby Longoria	1963	1
29 1/16	18 2/16	10 15/16	Kotzebue, AK	Louis Mussatto	Louis Mussatto	1965	2
28 12/16	17 13/16	10 15/16	Point Hope, AK	Tom F. Bolack	Tom F. Bolack	1958	3
28 12/16	17 11/16	11 1/16	Kotzebue, AK	Bill Nottley	Bill Nottley	1967	3
28 10/16	18	10 10/16	Little Diomede Island, AK	Richard G. Van Vorst	Richard G. Van Vorst	1963	5
28 10/16	17 8/16	11 2/16	Chukchi Sea, AK	Jack D. Putnam	Jack D. Putnam	1965	5
28 9/16	17 6/16	11 3/16	Kotzebue, AK	E.A. McCracken	E.A. McCracken	1966	7
28 8/16	17 6/16	11 2/16	Kotzebue, AK	Curtis S. Williams, Jr.	Curtis S. Williams, Jr.	1967	8
28 8/16	17 10/16	10 14/16	Kotzebue, AK	Winfred L. English	Winfred L. English	1968	8
28 7/16	17 5/16	11 2/16	Point Hope, AK	Rodney Lincoln	J.A. Columbus	1954	10
28 6/16	17 6/16	11	St. Lawrence Island, AK	H.B. Collins, Jr.	U.S. Natl. Museum	1929	11
28 6/16	17 8/16	10 14/16	Point Hope, AK	Clifford Thom	Clifford Thom	1964	11
28 6/16	17 3/16	11 3/16	Diomede Islands, AK	Stephen Pyle III	Stephen Pyle III	1965	11
28 5/16	17 10/16	10 11/16	Teller, AK	Walter Simas	Walter Simas	1966	14
28 4/16	18 2/16	10 2/16	Kotzebue, AK	Peter W. Bading	Peter W. Bading	1960	15
28 4/16	17 9/16	10 11/16	Big Diomede Island, AK	Vance A. Halverson	Vance A. Halverson	1963	15
28 4/16	17 7/16	10 13/16	Teller, AK	Jack C. Phillips	Jack C. Phillips	1964	15
28 3/16	17 9/16	10 10/16	Diomede Islands, AK	Louis F. Kincaid	Louis F. Kincaid	1955	18
28 3/16	17 15/16	10 4/16	Kotzebue, AK	Finis G. Cooper	Los Angeles Co. Museum	1959	18
28 3/16	17 12/16	10 7/16	Kotzebue, AK	S.D. Slaughter	S.D. Slaughter	1962	18
28 3/16	17 6/16	10 13/16	Kotzebue, AK	Harold Trulin	Harold Trulin	1962	18
28 3/16	17 6/16	10 13/16	Kotzebue, AK	C.J. McElroy	C.J. McElroy	1965	18
28 2/16	17 3/16	10 15/16	Big Diomede Island, AK	Francis Bogon	Francis Bogon	1957	23
28 2/16	17 6/16	10 12/16	Point Hope, AK	Pete Kesselring	Pete Kesselring	1957	23
28 2/16	17 1/16	11 1/16	Chukchi Sea, AK	Horace Steele	Horace Steele	1963	23
28 1/16	18 1/16	10	St. Paul Island, AK	C.H. Townsend	U.S. Natl. Museum	1875	26
28 1/16	17 6/16	10 11/16	Kotzebue, AK	Don Jahns	Don Jahns	1961	26
28	17 8/16	10 8/16	Point Hope, AK	Tommy Thompson	Pablo B. Romero	1958	28
28	17 7/16	10 9/16	Kotzebue, AK	Rupert Chisholm	Rupert Chisholm	1959	28
28	17 6/16	10 10/16	Point Hope, AK	William Stevenson	William Stevenson	1959	28
28	17 10/16	10 6/16	Kotzebue, AK	W.H. Hagenmeyer	W.H. Hagenmeyer	1961	28
28	17 5/16	10 11/16	Kotzebue, AK	Alberto Pipia	Alberto Pipia	1964	28
28	17 8/16	10 8/16	Diomede Islands, AK	Leonard W. Bruns	Leonard W. Bruns	1966	28
27 15/16	17 6/16	10 9/16	Kotzebue, AK	Russell C. Cutter	Russell C. Cutter	1960	34
27 15/16	17 8/16	10 7/16	Kotzebue, AK	Blair Truitt	Blair Truitt	1960	34
27 15/16	17 9/16	10 6/16	Kotzebue, AK	Jess L. Ferguson	Jess L. Ferguson	1961	34
27 15/16	17 4/16	10 11/16	Kotzebue, AK	William H. Smith, Jr.	William H. Smith, Jr.	1961	34
27 15/16	17 9/16	10 6/16	Kotzebue, AK	James S. Martin	James S. Martin	1962	34

Score	Length of Skull	Width of Skull	Locality	By	Owner	Date Killed	Rank
27 15/16	17 11/16	10 4/16	Teller, AK	R. Lynn Ross	R. Lynn Ross	1966	34
27 14/16	17 4/16	10 10/16	Point Barrow, AK	James W. Brooks	Univ. of Alaska	1952	40
27 14/16	17 10/16	10 4/16	Kotzebue, AK	Roy E. Weatherby	Roy E. Weatherby	1959	40
27 14/16	17 2/16	10 12/16	Kotzebue, AK	Don R. Downey	Don R. Downey	1960	40
27 14/16	17 5/16	10 9/16	Chukchi Sea, AK	C.D. Dofflemyer	C.D. Dofflemyer	1961	40
27 14/16	17 2/16	10 12/16	Kotzebue, AK	Nikolaus Koenig	Nikolaus Koenig	1966	40
27 13/16	17 13/16	10	Point Hope, AK	Hugh J. O'Dower	Hugh J. O'Dower	1959	45
27 13/16	17 7/16	10 6/16	Point Hope, AK	William P. Boone	William P. Boone	1960	45
27 13/16	17 8/16	10 5/16	Kotzebue, AK	Helen Burnett	Helen Burnett	1962	45
27 13/16	17 3/16	10 10/16	Cape Lisburne, AK	Charles Renaud	Charles Renaud	1963	45
27 13/16	16 15/16	10 14/16	Kotzebue, AK	Dale H. Wolff	Dale H. Wolff	1963	45
27 13/16	17 4/16	10 9/16	Alaska Coast	Lowell M. Cooke	Lowell M. Cooke	1965	45
27 13/16	17 7/16	10 6/16	Chukchi Sea, AK	Robert M. Mallett	Robert M. Mallett	1967	45
27 12/16	17 5/16	10 7/16	Cape Lisburne, AK	Edward M. Simko	Edward M. Simko	1956	52
27 12/16	17 5/16	10 7/16	Kotzebue, AK	J.E. Ottoviano	J.E. Ottoviano	1958	52
27 12/16	17 6/16	10 6/16	Little Diomede Island, AK	D.V. Merrick	D.V. Merrick	1959	52
27 12/16	17 8/16	10 4/16	Kotzebue, AK	Owen K. Murphy	Owen K. Murphy	1959	52
27 12/16	17	10 12/16	Point Hope, AK	A.H. Woodward, Jr.	A.H. Woodward, Jr.	1959	52
27 12/16	17 2/16	10 10/16	Kotzebue, AK	Arthur W. Clark	Arthur W. Clark	1963	52
27 12/16	17 5/16	10 7/16	Kotzebue, AK	Louis Menegas	Louis Menegas	1963	52
27 11/16	17 3/16	10 8/16	Teller, AK	Earl W. Nystrom	Earl W. Nystrom	1965	61
27 11/16	17	10 11/16	Teller, AK	William M. Kessner	William M. Kessner	1965	61
27 11/16	16 11/16	11	Kotzebue, AK	Arthur W. Smith	Arthur W. Smith	1960	61
27 10/16	17 6/16	10 4/16	Kotzebue, AK	Andrew S. Allen	Andrew S. Allen	1962	64
27 10/16	17 4/16	10 6/16	Kotzebue, AK	Patricia T. Bergstrom	Patricia T. Bergstrom	1962	64
27 10/16	17	10 10/16	Kotzebue, AK	Joe Foss	Joe Foss	1962	64
27 10/16	17 6/16	10 4/16	Kotzebue, AK	C.T. Kraftmeyer	C.T. Kraftmeyer	1963	64
27 10/16	16 11/16	10 15/16	Little Diomede Island, AK	Willard R. Skousen	Willard R. Skousen	1963	64
27 10/16	17 2/16	10 8/16	Kotzebue, AK	George P. Whittington	George P. Whittington	1966	64
27 9/16	17 6/16	10 3/16	Kotzebue, AK	Kenneth W. Vaughn	Kenneth W. Vaughn	1957	71
27 9/16	17 3/16	10 6/16	Point Hope, AK	Norma Wahrer	Norma Wahrer	1959	71
27 9/16	17 3/16	10 6/16	Kotzebue, AK	Robert L. Cohen	Robert L. Cohen	1963	71
27 9/16	16 15/16	10 10/16	Point Hope, AK	T.E. Shillingburg	T.E. Shillingburg	1964	71
27 9/16	17 5/16	10 4/16	Cape Thompson, AK	Daniel H. Cuddy	Daniel H. Cuddy	1964	71
27 8/16	17 2/16	10 6/16	Chukchi Sea, AK	Angelo Alessio	Angelo Alessio	1961	76
27 8/16	17 1/16	10 7/16	Point Hope, AK	Pat Auld Appersen	Pat Auld Appersen	1963	76
27 8/16	17 2/16	10 6/16	Diomede Islands, AK	Tony Oney	Tony Oney	1963	76
27 8/16	17 5/16	10 3/16	Kotzebue, AK	Harry D. Tousley	Harry D. Tousley	1965	76
27 8/16	17 5/16	10 3/16	Cape Lisburne, AK	Willard E. Flynn	Willard E. Flynn	1965	76
27 8/16	17	10 8/16	Point Hope, AK	Edward Frecker	Edward Frecker	1965	76
27 8/16	17 1/16	10 7/16	Kotzebue, AK	Ted Lick	Ted Lick	1965	76
27 8/16	17	10 8/16	Kotzebue, AK	Russell J. Uhl	Russell J. Uhl	1965	76
27 7/16	17 1/16	10 6/16	Pond Inlet, NU	Thomas H. Viuf	Thomas H. Viuf	1996	82
27 7/16	16 9/16	10 14/16	Kotzebue, AK	Mahlon T. Everhart	Mahlon T. Everhart	1959	82
27 7/16	17 6/16	10 1/16	Little Diomede Island, AK	Herb Klein	Dallas Mus. of Natl. Hist.	1960	82
27 7/16	17 5/16	10 2/16	Kotzebue, AK	Gregory E. Koshell	Gregory E. Koshell	1961	82
27 7/16	16 15/16	10 8/16	Polar Circle, AK	Aurelio Caccomo	Aurelio Caccomo	1965	82

POLAR BEAR
Ursus maritimus

Score	Greatest Length of Skull Without Lower Jaw	Greatest Width of Skull	Locality	Hunter	Owner	Date Killed	Rank
27 7/16	17 7/16	10	Kotzebue, AK	Andrew De Matteo	Andrew De Matteo	1965	82
27 6/16	16 11/16	10 11/16	Wales, AK	Eskimo	Univ. of Alaska	1956	87
27 6/16	16 15/16	10 7/16	Cape Lisburne, AK	Joseph S. Lichtenfels	Joseph S. Lichtenfels	1957	87
27 6/16	17	10 6/16	Kotzebue, AK	W.H. Cato, Jr.	W.H. Cato, Jr.	1960	87
27 6/16	17 5/16	10 1/16	Kotzebue, AK	Gene Klineburger	Gene Klineburger	1963	87
27 6/16	17 3/16	10 3/16	Teller, AK	James O. Campbell	James O. Campbell	1964	87
27 6/16	17	10 6/16	Little Diomede Island, AK	Bob Payne	Bob Payne	1964	87
27 6/16	16 10/16	10 12/16	Kotzebue, AK	Glen E. Park	Glen E. Park	1965	87
27 6/16	16 13/16	10 9/16	Chukchi Sea, AK	Terry Kennedy	Terry Kennedy	1967	87
27 6/16	17	10 6/16	Kotzebue, AK	Harry Daum	Harry Daum	1971	87
27 6/16	17 1/16	10 5/16	Home Bay, NU	Antonius Rensing	Antonius Rensing	2000	87
27 5/16	16 13/16	10 8/16	Kotzebue, AK	W.L. Coleman	W.L. Coleman	1961	97
27 5/16	16 15/16	10 6/16	Point Barrow, AK	Bert Klineburger	Bert Klineburger	1963	97
27 5/16	17 1/16	10 4/16	Point Hope, AK	Charles A. McKinsey	Charles A. McKinsey	1963	97
27 5/16	17 1/16	10 4/16	Point Hope, AK	Sherman R. Whitmore	Sherman R. Whitmore	1963	97
27 5/16	16 9/16	10 12/16	Big Diomede Island, AK	Basil C. Bradbury	Basil C. Bradbury	1964	97
27 5/16	17 1/16	10 4/16	Bering Strait, AK	William D. Backman, Jr	William D. Backman, Jr.	1965	97
27 5/16	16 12/16	10 9/16	Kotzebue, AK	Lewis Figone	Lewis Figone	1965	97
27 5/16	16 12/16	10 9/16	Point Barrow, AK	James Senn	James Senn	1965	97
27 5/16	17 2/16	10 3/16	Point Hope, AK	Richard K. Siller	Richard K. Siller	1965	97
27 5/16	16 15/16	10 6/16	Kotzebue, AK	Gene Barrow	Gene Barrow	1966	97
27 5/16	17 4/16	10 1/16	Point Hope, AK	E.F. Simon	E.F. Simon	1968	97
27 4/16	16 13/16	10 7/16	Wales, AK	Eldon Brant	Univ. of Alaska	1957	108
27 4/16	17	10 4/16	Point Hope, AK	Charles A. Brauch	Charles A. Brauch	1960	108
27 4/16	16 12/16	10 8/16	Cape Lisburne, AK	Richard Hanks	Richard Hanks	1962	108
27 4/16	17 1/16	10 3/16	Point Hope, AK	C. Sam Sparks	C. Sam Sparks	1962	108
27 4/16	16 14/16	10 6/16	Kotzebue, AK	Ralph Lenheim	Ralph Lenheim	1964	108
27 4/16	16 15/16	10 5/16	Kotzebue, AK	Bill Taylor	Bill Taylor	1964	108
27 4/16	16 14/16	10 6/16	Teller, AK	Joseph O. Porter, Sr.	Joseph O. Porter, Sr.	1965	108
27 4/16	17	10 4/16	Kotzebue, AK	Russell H. Underdahl	Russell H. Underdahl	1965	108
27 3/16	17 5/16	9 14/16	Nome, AK	J.H. Rogers	J.H. Rogers	1956	116
27 3/16	17 5/16	9 14/16	Bering Strait, AK	Henry S. Budney	Henry S. Budney	1959	116
27 3/16	16 11/16	10 8/16	Kotzebue, AK	Bud Lotstedt	Bud Lotstedt	1959	116
27 3/16	16 13/16	10 6/16	Point Hope, AK	Kenneth Holland	Kenneth Holland	1960	116
27 3/16	17 4/16	9 15/16	Point Hope, AK	Bert Klineburger	Bert Klineburger	1961	116
27 3/16	16 12/16	10 7/16	Point Hope, AK	Richard Hanks	Richard Hanks	1962	116
27 3/16	16 13/16	10 6/16	Chukchi Sea, AK	Charles P. Adkins	Charles P. Adkins	1964	116
27 3/16	17 3/16	10	Kotzebue, AK	Barbara Sjoden	Barbara Sjoden	1966	116

Score	Length	Width	Locality	Owner	By Whom Killed	Date	Rank
27 3/16	17 1/16	10 2/16	Kotzebue, AK	Bernard Domries	Bernard Domries	1970	116
27 3/16	16 8/16	10 11/16	Banks Island, NT	James R. Gall	James R. Gall	1997	116
27 3/16	16 13/16	10 6/16	Banks Island, NT	Robert B. Nancarrow	Robert B. Nancarrow	1997	116
27 2/16	16 11/16	10 7/16	Point Hope, AK	Finis Gilbert	Finis Gilbert	1959	127
27 2/16	17 4/16	9 14/16	Point Hope, AK	C.C. Irving	C.C. Irving	1960	127
27 2/16	16 13/16	10 5/16	Kotzebue, AK	John F. Meyer	John F. Meyer	1960	127
27 2/16	16 15/16	10 3/16	Kotzebue, AK	W.T. Yoshimoto	W.T. Yoshimoto	1962	127
27 2/16	16 12/16	10 6/16	Point Barrow, AK	Frank Bydalek	Frank Bydalek	1963	127
27 2/16	17	10 2/16	Kotzebue, AK	Ernest B. Schur	Ernest B. Schur	1964	127
27 2/16	16 14/16	10 4/16	Chuckchi Sea, AK	R.G. Howlett	R.G. Howlett	1965	127
27 2/16	16 12/16	10 6/16	Shishmaref, AK	R.V. Hoyt & W.H. Otis	R.V. Hoyt & W.H. Otis	1965	127
27 1/16	16 15/16	10 2/16	Cape Lisburne, AK	Howard W. Pollock	Howard W. Pollock	1957	135
27 1/16	16 13/16	10 4/16	Kotzebue, AK	Glenn B. Walker	Glenn B. Walker	1959	135
27 1/16	17 7/16	9 10/16	Kotzebue, AK	True Davis	True Davis	1961	135
27 1/16	16 13/16	10 4/16	Point Hope, AK	Bill Ellis	Bill Ellis	1962	135
27 1/16	16 12/16	10 5/16	Diomede Islands, AK	Flavy Davis	Flavy Davis	1963	135
27 1/16	16 11/16	10 6/16	Little Diomede Island, AK	Tony Oney	Tony Oney	1963	135
27 1/16	16 10/16	10 7/16	Kotzebue, AK	Fritz Worster	Fritz Worster	1963	135
27 1/16	16 14/16	10 6/16	Kotzebue, AK	Marshall Johnson	Marshall Johnson	1965	135
27 1/16	16 15/16	10 3/16	Kotzebue, AK	George W. Roberts	George W. Roberts	1965	135
27	17 2/16	10 1/16	Point Barrow, AK	U.S. Natl. Museum	T.L. Richardson	1917	144
27	16 7/16	9 14/16	Kotzebue, AK	Dick Drew	Unknown	1959	144
27	16 14/16	10 9/16	Point Hope, AK	Theodore A. Warren	Theodore A. Warren	1959	144
27	16 12/16	10 2/16	Point Barrow, AK	Clifford H. Dietz	Clifford H. Dietz	1960	144
27	16 12/16	10 4/16	Kotzebue, AK	Henry Blackford	Henry Blackford	1961	144
27	16 8/16	10 4/16	Kotzebue, AK	Cincinnati Mus. of Nat. Hist.	James T. Byrnes	1963	144
27	16 14/16	10 8/16	Kotzebue, AK	William A. Bond	William A. Bond	1964	144
27	16 9/16	10 2/16	Kotzebue, AK	Norman W. Garwood	Norman W. Garwood	1964	144
27		10 7/16	Kotzebue, AK	Charles E. Shedd	Charles E. Shedd	1964	144
27			Shishmaref, AK	Howard R. Driskell	Howard R. Driskell	1972	144

CATEGORY
POLAR BEAR

SCORE
27-6/16

HUNTER
ANTONIUS RENSING

LOCATION
HOME BAY, NUNAVUT

DATE OF KILL
MAY 2000

JAGUAR
WORLD'S RECORD

In 1965, C.J. McElroy returned from the jungle of Sinaloa, Mexico, with a World's Record jaguar (*Felis onca*) scoring 18-7/16.

Hunting under the cover of night, McElroy adapted himself to the methods of this formidable predator, enduring oppressive heat, foul smelling swamps, ticks, chiggers and snakes, which jaguars prey on as regular reptile killers. It was a hunting experience that would remain with McElroy. Two years after taking the trophy, McElroy gave a hair-raising account of his encounter in an article for *Outdoor Life*. It reveals that at one point during the chase, the hunter became the hunted.

"The tigre was bleeding heavily, and his trail led us out of the grass and into thick jungle. About 100 yards farther, Hugo made a discovery that shook us. The trail of blood circled, and we were crossing the cat's original trail. There was some conversation in Spanish that I didn't understand. Then Hugo looked at me grimly.

"The tigre is behind us!' he said.

"Hugo's words hit me with full impact. I knew that a wounded animal considering attack often doubles back to ambush the trackers from the rear. I still was confident in my ability with a rifle, and I believed I could kill the cat quickly if I had any chance at all."

Even though McElroy was shooting a light 100 grain bullet, his ability with a Winchester .270 saved his hide from the potentially fatal impact of the jaguar's teeth. The hunter and his guides emerged from a long night in the bush with what they knew was a magnificent trophy. On May 4, 1966, at the Club's 12th Biennial Awards dinner at the Carnegie Museum, in Pittsburgh, Pennsylvania, McElroy's jaguar was officially recognized as the best taken in North America. McElroy's estimated 270 pound jaguar beat Jack Funk's 1924 record that scored 18-5/16 points and was killed in Cibecue, Arizona. Sadly for hunters, the joint pressures of agriculture and development drove the last jaguars from the U.S. in the 1940s and continue to lead to the loss of habitat for the largest North American cat. ∎

Records of North American Big Game

BOONE AND CROCKETT CLUB®

OFFICIAL SCORING SYSTEM FOR NORTH AMERICAN BIG GAME TROPHIES

COUGAR AND JAGUAR

250 Station Drive
Missoula, MT 59801
(406) 542-1888

MINIMUM SCORES

	AWARDS	ALL-TIME
cougar	15	14 - 4/16
jaguar	14 - 4/16	14 - 4/16

KIND OF CAT (check one)
☐ cougar
☑ jaguar

A.
B.

SEE OTHER SIDE FOR INSTRUCTIONS	MEASUREMENTS
A. Greatest Length Without Lower Jaw	10 15/16
B. Greatest Width	7 8/16
FINAL SCORE	18 7/16

Exact Locality Where Killed: Sinaloa, MX

Date Killed: March 24, 1965 **Hunter:** C.J. McElroy

Owner: C.J. McElroy **Telephone #:**

Owner's Address:

Guide's Name and Address:

Remarks: (Mention Any Abnormalities or Unique Qualities)

I, ___**John E. Hammett**___ , certify that I have measured this trophy on ___**02/28/1966**___
        PRINT NAME   MM/DD/YYYY

at ___**Carnegie Museum**___   ___**Pittsburgh**___   ___**PA**___
     STREET ADDRESS   CITY   STATE/PROVINCE

and that these measurements and data are, to the best of my knowledge and belief, made in accordance with the instructions given.

Signature: ___**John E. Hammett**___   I.D. Number ☐☐☐☐
                  B&C OFFICIAL MEASURER

Witness: ___**John H. Batten**___

COPYRIGHT © 1999 BY BOONE AND CROCKETT CLUB®

211

JAGUAR

Felis onca hernandesii and related subspecies

Score	Greatest Length of Skull Without Lower Jaw	Greatest Width of Skull	Locality	Hunter	Owner	Date Killed	Rank
18 7/16	10 15/16	7 8/16	Sinaloa, MX	C.J. McElroy	C.J. McElroy	1965	1
18 5/16	10 14/16	7 7/16	Cibecue, AZ	Jack Funk	U.S. Natl. Museum	1924	2
18 3/16	10 15/16	7 4/16	Nogales, AZ	Fred Ott	U.S. Natl. Museum	1926	3
18 2/16	11	7 2/16	Vera Cruz, MX	E.W. Nelson & E.A. Goldman	U.S. Natl. Museum	1894	4
17 15/16	10 9/16	7 6/16	Tehuantepec, MX	Francis Sumuchrast	U.S. Natl. Museum	PR 1869	5
17 13/16	10 9/16	7 4/16	Guadalajara, MX	Elgin T. Gates	Elgin T. Gates	1954	6
17 11/16	10 11/16	7	Campeche, MX	Jacinta S. Dorantes	Squire Haskins	1960	7
17 10/16	10 9/16	7 1/16	Chiapas, MX	E.W. Nelson & E.A. Goldman	U.S. Natl. Museum	1900	8
17 8/16	10 6/16	7 2/16	Tamaulipas, MX	Henderson Coquat	M. Nowotny	1940	9
17 8/16	10 8/16	7	Campeche, MX	Alex Hudson III	Alex Hudson III	1962	9
17 7/16	10 7/16	7	Tamaulipas, MX	Unknown	Bond Carroll	1959	11
17 6/16	10 7/16	6 15/16	Nayarit, MX	Aldegundo Garza de Leon	Aldegundo Garza de Leon	1969	12
17 2/16	10 6/16	6 12/16	Mills Co., TX	H.D. Attwater	U.S. Natl. Museum	1903	13
17 2/16	10 5/16	6 13/16	Nayarit, MX	P. Mueller & D.O. Rudin	P. Mueller & D.O. Rudin	1959	13
17	10 4/16	6 12/16	Nayarit, MX	Graciano Guichard	Graciano Guichard	1969	15
16 15/16	10 4/16	6 11/16	Tamaulipas, MX	Squire Haskins	Dallas Mus. Nat. Hist.	1957	16
16 14/16	10 2/16	6 12/16	Helvetia, AZ	E.J. O'Doherty	U.S. Natl. Museum	1917	17
16 14/16	10 5/16	6 5/16	Sonora, MX	Frank C. Hibben	Frank C. Hibben	1934	17
16 14/16	10 5/16	6 5/16	Sonora, MX	Frank C. Hibben	Frank C. Hibben	1934	17
16 14/16	10 4/16	6 10/16	Nayarit, MX	J.F. Brinkley	J.F. Brinkley	1959	17
16 14/16	9 12/16	7 2/16	Tampico, MX	Hector Elizondo	Hector Elizondo	1962	17
16 13/16	10 5/16	6 6/16	Nayarit, MX	G. Hooker & L. Stephens	George W. Hooker	1957	22
16 13/16	10 4/16	6 5/16	Tabasco, MX	W.T. Yoshimoto	W.T. Yoshimoto	1971	22
16 12/16	10 1/16	6 11/16	Nayarit, MX	Herb Klein	Dallas Mus. of Natl. Hist.	1955	24
16 12/16	10 3/16	6 6/16	Nayarit, MX	Picked Up	Lawson E. Miller, Jr.	1959	24
16 11/16	9 15/16	6 12/16	Oaxaca, MX	Charles Oertel	U.S. Natl. Museum	1899	26
16 11/16	9 14/16	6 13/16	Sonora, MX	Dick Wooddell	Dick Wooddell	1955	26
16 11/16	10 1/16	6 10/16	Ft. Apache Res., AZ	Russell Culbreath	U.S. Natl. Museum	1964	26
16 10/16	9 11/16	6 15/16	Nayarit, MX	John Ryan	John Ryan	1962	29
16 10/16	9 14/16	6 12/16	Nayarit, MX	Morton J. Greene	Morton J. Greene	1965	29
16 9/16	9 14/16	6 11/16	Vera Cruz, MX	A. Wetmore & J. Canela	U.S. Natl. Museum	1939	31
16 9/16	9 15/16	6 10/16	Tamaulipas, MX	Juan Lebeira	Juan Lebeira	1965	31
16 6/16	9 14/16	6 6/16	Tamaulipas, MX	Alex Hudson III	Alex Hudson III	1964	33
16 6/16	9 14/16	6 6/16	Nayarit, MX	William J. Campbell	William J. Campbell	1970	33
16 5/16	9 14/16	6 7/16	Nayarit, MX	George H. Hodges, Jr.	George H. Hodges, Jr.	1960	35
16 5/16	9 12/16	6 5/16	Nayarit, MX	O.J. Fletcher	O.J. Fletcher	1964	35
16 4/16	9 11/16	6 6/16	Nayarit, MX	Charles Binney II	443rd Hunting Club	1965	37
16 3/16	9 11/16	6 5/16	Nayarit, MX	Ventura G. Cosio	Ventura G. Cosio	1965	38

			Locality			Year	
16 ²/₁₆	9 ⁹/₁₆	6 ⁹/₁₆	Arizona	Arvid F. Benson	Arvid F. Benson	1961	39
16 ²/₁₆	9 ¹¹/₁₆	6 ⁷/₁₆	Tamaulipas, MX	Juan A. Saenz, Jr.	Juan A. Saenz, Jr.	1970	39
16 ¹/₁₆	9 ⁹/₁₆	6 ⁸/₁₆	Tamaulipas, MX	A.D. Stenger	A.D. Stenger	1957	41
16	9 ²/₁₆	6 ¹⁴/₁₆	Tamaulipas, MX	Frank R. Denman	Frank R. Denman	1966	42
15 ¹⁵/₁₆	9 ⁶/₁₆	6 ⁹/₁₆	Tamaulipas, MX	Patrick W. Frederick	Patrick W. Frederick	1983	43
15 ¹³/₁₆	9 ¹⁰/₁₆	6 ³/₁₆	Tamaulipas, MX	Winfred L. English	Winfred L. English	1966	44
15 ⁸/₁₆	9 ⁵/₁₆	6 ³/₁₆	Nayarit, MX	Roy E. Cooper	Roy E. Cooper	1960	45
15 ⁸/₁₆	9 ⁵/₁₆	6 ⁵/₁₆	Nayarit, MX	Gene Biddle	Gene Biddle	1961	45
15 ⁸/₁₆	8 ¹⁴/₁₆	6 ¹⁰/₁₆	Tamaulipas, MX	O.A. Washburn	O.A. Washburn	1964	45
15 ⁶/₁₆	9 ¹/₁₆	6 ⁵/₁₆	Patagonia Mts., AZ	Laurence L. McGee	Univ. of AZ	1965	48
15 ⁵/₁₆	9 ¹/₁₆	6 ⁴/₁₆	Nayarit, MX	Jimmie Underwood	Steve M. Matthes	1963	49
15 ²/₁₆	9 ²/₁₆	6	Nayarit, MX	James G. Shirley, Jr.	James G. Shirley, Jr.	1959	50
15 ¹/₁₆	9	6 ¹/₁₆	Big Lake, AZ	Terry D. Penrod	Terry D. Penrod	1963	51
14 ¹⁵/₁₆	9	5 ¹⁵/₁₆	Nayarit, MX	E.W. Ennis, Jr.	E.W. Ennis, Jr.	1956	52
14 ¹⁴/₁₆	8 ¹¹/₁₆	6 ³/₁₆	Nogales, AZ	John F. Nutt	John F. Nutt	1958	53
14 ¹⁴/₁₆	9	5 ¹⁴/₁₆	Nayarit, MX	Glenn W. Slade, Jr.	Glenn W. Slade, Jr.	1960	53
14 ¹²/₁₆	8 ¹⁵/₁₆	5 ¹³/₁₆	Nayarit, MX	Cecil M. Hopper	Cecil M. Hopper	1971	55
14 ⁹/₁₆	8 ¹⁴/₁₆	5 ¹¹/₁₆	Santa Cruz Co., AZ	Ed Scarla	Ed Scarla	1959	56

COUGAR
WORLD'S RECORD

The World's Record for a cougar (*Felis concolor*) has held for two decades with a score of 16-4/16. Currently owned by Charles M. Travers, this cougar was taken by Douglas E. Schuk on the wintry afternoon of February 12, 1979. Schuk's hounds trailed the big tom through 32 inches of snow that had blanketed Tatlayoko Lake, British Columbia. At 3:00 p.m., Schuk's dogs closed in as the sun descended toward the far coastal mountains. Usually hunters recognize when a cat has been brought to bay as the excited tone of their dogs is answered by the shrill whistle of the cornered prey. Though cougars are generally tremulous in such circumstances, cats that can weigh up to 227 pounds are quite capable of taking out a hound with the rake of their powerful paws. Having taken a considerable amount of time and dedication to train his fine pack of dogs, Schuk knew he had to make a clean kill or there might be a very real risk of injury to his four-legged hunting companions. Using his .308, Schuk assuredly took down the impressive, snow-speckled cat.

Charles Travers later acquired the skull of the tom. When he had it measured, it was hard to believe. The entry measurement was well above the long standing 1964 record of 16 taken by Garth Roberts in Garfield County, Utah. As a potential record, it had to come before the Final Awards Judges Panel. They too found it to score better than the record and confirmed it as the new World's Record for the category. Since it

was no longer owned by the hunter, it was eligible only for a Certificate of Merit.

Schuk's World's Record cougar was nearly matched by a cougar taken in Idaho's Selway-Bitterroot Wilderness by Gene R. Alford of Kamiah, Idaho. Alford's cougar, taken on a solo month-long wilderness hunt in 1988 missed the World's Record by 1/16 of an inch. Alford's cougar was awarded the Sagamore Hill Award for the uniqueness of the hunt and the manner in which Alford's pursuit of this magnificent cat epitomized the essence of the Boone and Crockett Club's fair chase ethic.

The original World's Record was taken by President Theodore Roosevelt in 1901 near Meeker, Colorado, and scored at 15-12/16. Predominately gray in their northern range, Theodore Roosevelt shot both slate-gray and red pumas in Colorado, thus revealing that there is a considerable variation in the color of this American wild cat. ■

TROPHY INFO

RANK
World's Record

SCORE
16 4/16

LOCATION
Tatlayoko Lake, BC

HUNTER
Douglas E. Schuk

OWNER
Charles M. Travers

DATE KILLED
1979

Records of
North American
Big Game

250 Station Drive
Missoula, MT 59801
(406) 542-1888

BOONE AND CROCKETT CLUB®

OFFICIAL SCORING SYSTEM FOR NORTH AMERICAN BIG GAME TROPHIES

COUGAR AND JAGUAR

MINIMUM SCORES	AWARDS	ALL-TIME
cougar	14 - 8/16	15
jaguar	14 - 8/16	14 - 8/16

KIND OF CAT (check one)
■ cougar
☐ jaguar

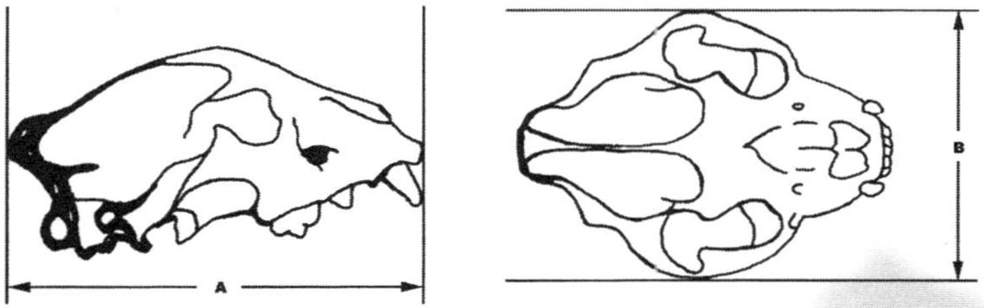

SEE OTHER SIDE FOR INSTRUCTIONS

	MEASUREMENTS
A. Greatest Length Without Lower Jaw	9 9/16
B. Greatest Width	6 11/16
FINAL SCORE	16 4/16

Exact Locality Where Killed: Tatlayoko Lake, BC

Date Killed: Feb. 12, 1979   Hunter: Douglas E. Schuk

Owner: Charles M. Travers   Telephone #:

Owner's Address:

Guide's Name and Address:

Remarks: (Mention Any Abnormalities or Unique Qualities)

I, ___Ed Williamson___ , certify that I have measured this trophy on ___06/20/1983___
PRINT NAME   MM/DD/YYYY

at ___Dallas Museum of Natural History___   ___Dallas___   ___TX___
STREET ADDRESS   CITY   STATE/PROVINCE

and that these measurements and data are, to the best of my knowledge and belief, made in accordance with the instructions given.

Witness: ___Frank Cook___   Signature: ___Ed Williamson___   I.D. Number
B&C OFFICIAL MEASURER

COPYRIGHT © 1999 BY BOONE AND CROCKETT CLUB®

215

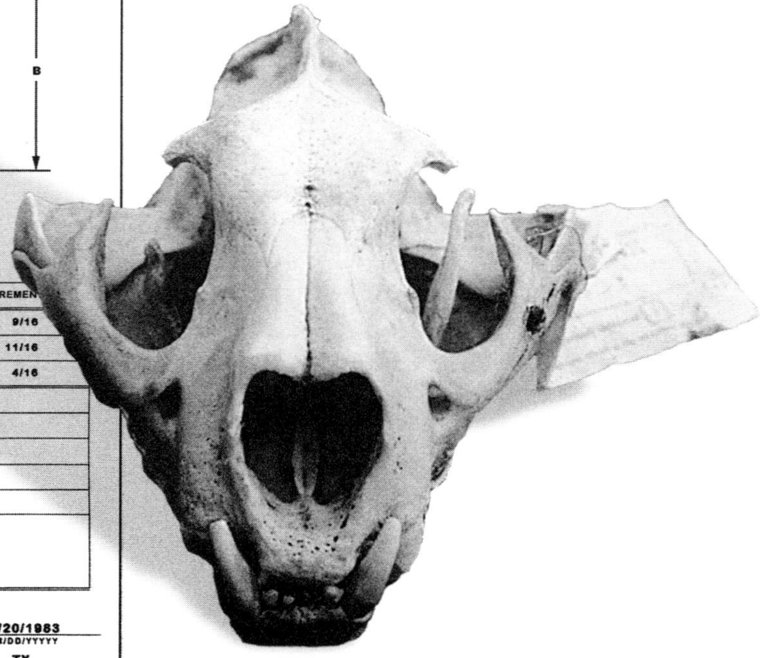

Felis concolor hippolestes and related subspecies

MINIMUM SCORE 15

Score	Greatest Length of Skull Without Lower Jaw	Greatest Width of Skull	Locality	Hunter	Owner	Date Killed	Rank
16 4/16	9 9/16	6 11/16	Tatlayoko Lake, BC	Douglas E. Schuk	Charles M. Travers	1979	1
16 3/16	**9 8/16**	**6 11/16**	**Idaho Co., ID**	**Gene R. Alford**	**B&C National Collection**	**1988**	**2**
16 1/16	9 7/16	6 10/16	Park Co., WY	Scott M. Moore	Scott M. Moore	1993	3
16	9 4/16	6 12/16	Garfield Co., UT	Garth Roberts	R. Scott Jarvie	1964	4
16	9 7/16	6 9/16	Tongue Creek, AB	T. Klassen & J.D. Gordon	T. Klassen & J.D. Gordon	1999	4
16	9 4/16	6 12/16	Archuleta Co., CO	Brian K. Williams	Brian K. Williams	2001	4
15 15/16	9 1/16	6 14/16	Clearwater River, AB	Walter R. Weller	Walter R. Weller	1973	7
15 15/16	9 5/16	6 10/16	Hinton, AB	Roy LePage	Roy LePage	1999	7
15 14/16	9 2/16	6 12/16	Walla Walla Co., WA	Robert A. Klicker	Robert A. Klicker	1988	9
15 14/16	9 3/16	6 11/16	Canim Lake, BC	Alejandro Vidaurreta	Alejandro Vidaurreta	1992	9
15 13/16	9 4/16	6 9/16	Carbon Co., UT	Anthony J. Berardi	Anthony J. Berardi	1999	11
15 13/16	9 5/16	6 8/16	Jefferson Co., WA	David Medley	David Medley	2002	11
15 12/16	9 5/16	6 7/16	Meeker Co., CO	Theodore Roosevelt	U.S. Natl. Museum	1901	13
15 12/16	9 2/16	6 10/16	Dutch Creek, AB	Edward D. Burton	Edward D. Burton	1954	13
15 12/16	9 1/16	6 11/16	Okanagan Lake, BC	Ted Razook	Ted Razook	1973	13
15 12/16	9 5/16	6 7/16	Mesa Co., CO	Robert R. Meyer	Robert R. Meyer	1978	13
15 12/16	9 3/16	6 5/16	Idaho Co., ID	Dave Hiatt	Dave Hiatt	1994	13
15 12/16	9 4/16	6 8/16	Lincoln Co., MT	Stan D. Stamey	Stan D. Stamey	1994	13
15 11/16	9 4/16	6 8/16	Darby, CO	Lowell Hayes	Sherman L. Hayes	1953	19
15 11/16	9 3/16	6 8/16	Selway River, ID	Gene R. Alford	Gene R. Alford	1961	19
15 11/16	9	6 11/16	Selway River, ID	Gene R. Alford	Gene R. Alford	1961	19
15 11/16	9 3/16	6 8/16	Valley Co., ID	Louis Rebillet	Louis Rebillet	1961	19
15 11/16	9 3/16	6 8/16	Fisher Creek, AB	John E. Cassidy	John E. Cassidy	1985	19
15 11/16	9 2/16	6 7/16	Okanagan Lake, BC	D. Cooper & M. Hubbard	Dusty R. Cooper	1985	19
15 11/16	9 4/16	6 6/16	Idaho Co., ID	Richard C. Farthing	Richard C. Farthing	1988	19
15 11/16	9 4/16	6 7/16	Eagle Co., CO	Layne K. Wing	Layne K. Wing	1990	19
15 11/16	9 3/16	6 7/16	Catherine Creek, OR	Ron Lay	Ron Lay	1966	27
15 10/16	9	6 10/16	Tatla Lake, BC	Harold J. Coult	Harold J. Coult	1986	27
15 10/16	9 3/16	6 7/16	Shoshone Co., ID	Henry L. Chandler	Henry L. Chandler	1992	27
15 10/16	9 1/16	6 7/16	Garfield Co., UT	Robin Siegfried	Robin Siegfried	1992	27
15 10/16	9 2/16	6 8/16	Idaho Co., ID	Bill Daugherty	Bill Daugherty	1998	27
15 9/16	9 2/16	6 7/16	Carbon Co., UT	H. Alan Foster	H. Alan Foster	1959	32
15 9/16	9 3/16	6 6/16	Okanogan Co., WA	Mike Lynch	Mike Lynch	1964	32
15 9/16	9 2/16	6 7/16	Salmon River, ID	Doug Kittredge	Doug Kittredge	1971	32
15 9/16	9	6 9/16	Gallatin Co., MT	Tracy J. Peterson	Tracy J. Peterson	1984	32
15 9/16	9 2/16	6 7/16	Carbon Co., UT	Robert F. McLawhorn	Robert F. McLawhorn	1985	32
15 9/16	9 2/16	6 7/16	Elko Co., NV	Joel C. Brown	Joel C. Brown	1986	32
15 9/16	9 2/16	6 7/16	Flathead Co., MT	Rusby Seabaugh	Brad Seabaugh	1986	32

Score			Locality	Hunter	Owner	Date	Rank
15 9/16	9 2/16	6 7/16	Idaho Co., ID	Randy L. Waddell	Randy L. Waddell	1990	32
15 9/16	9 1/16	6 8/16	Umatilla Co., OR	David L. Bradshaw	David L. Bradshaw	1994	32
15 9/16	9 3/16	6 6/16	Rio Arriba Co., NM	Robert J. Seeds	Robert J. Seeds	1995	32
15 9/16	9 3/16	6 6/16	Pondera Co., MT	Daneil L. Swanson	Daneil L. Swanson	1996	32
15 9/16	9 1/16	6 8/16	Idaho Co., ID	Dave Hiatt	Dave Hiatt	1997	32
15 9/16	9 1/16	6 8/16	Mesa Co., CO	Darryl Powell	Darryl Powell	1997	32
15 9/16	8 15/16	6 10/16	Lincoln Co., MT	Hershel E. Landon, Jr.	Hershel E. Landon, Jr.	1999	32
15 8/16	9 2/16	6 6/16	Cottonwood Co., NV	Berkley Hunt	Berkley Hunt	1962	46
15 8/16	9	6 8/16	Porcupine Hills, AB	Edward D. Burton	Edward D. Burton	1965	46
15 8/16	9 2/16	6	Huerfano Co., CO	J.D. Dodge	J.D. Dodge	1971	46
15 8/16	9 8/16	6 6/16	Priest Lake, ID	Ron Book	Ron Book	1972	46
15 8/16	9 1/16	6	Lincoln Co., MT	Gary Grenfell	Robert Fleshman	1975	46
15 8/16	9	6 7/16	Loblaw Creek, AB	John A. Jorgensen	John A. Jorgensen	1977	46
15 8/16	9	6 7/16	Idaho Co., ID	Jerry J. James	Jerry J. James	1982	46
15 8/16	9 2/16	6 8/16	Bannock Co., ID	Frank N. Hough	Frank N. Hough	1985	46
15 8/16	9 3/16	6	Rio Blanco Co., CO	Robert L. Raley	Robert L. Raley	1985	46
15 8/16	9	6	Rio Arriba Co., NM	Dick Ray	Dick Ray	1985	46
15 8/16	9 3/16	6 2/16	Wallowa Co., OR	Robin D. Dickenson	Robin D. Dickenson	1987	46
15 8/16	9 4/16	6 3/16	Robbins Range, BC	Robert J. Petrie	R.J. Petrie & G. Schweitzer	1987	46
15 8/16	9 4/16	6	Montrose Co., CO	Kendall Hamilton	Kendall Hamilton	1988	46
15 8/16	9 2/16	6 8/16	Boise Co., ID	Ron E. Romig	Ron E. Romig	1988	46
15 8/16	8 15/16	6 5/16	Clallam Co., WA	John M. Rawlings	John M. Rawlings	1990	46
15 8/16	9 1/16	6 4/16	Gila Co., AZ	Stephen D. Hornady	Stephen D. Hornady	1991	46
15 8/16	9 2/16	6 6/16	Bragg Creek, AB	Drew Ramsay	Drew Ramsay	1991	46
15 8/16	9	6 2/16	Grant Co., OR	Joe L. West	Joe L. West	1992	46
15 8/16	9 3/16	6 9/16	Sanders Co., MT	Wayne M. Foley	Wayne M. Foley	1993	46
15 8/16	9 4/16	6 7/16	Lemhi Co., ID	Michael A. Judas	Michael A. Judas	1995	46
15 8/16	9 3/16	6 6/16	Mount Skinner, BC	Jeff S. Ashe	Jeff S. Ashe	1997	46
15 8/16	9 2/16	6	Flat Creek, AB	A. Paul Kroshko	A. Paul Kroshko	1998	46
15 8/16	9 3/16	6 3/16	Rio Arriba Co., NM	Robert J. Seeds	Robert J. Seeds	1999	46
15 8/16	9	6 4/16	Tamaulipas, MX	Carlos A. Del Valle	Carlos A. Del Valle	2001	46
15 8/16	9 4/16	6 8/16	Rio Arriba Co., NM	Max D. Martinez	Max D. Martinez	2001	46
15 8/16	8 15/16	6 3/16	Mora Co., NM	Robert M. Ortiz	Robert M. Ortiz	2002	46
15 8/16	9 3/16	6 4/16	Elmore Co., ID	Daniel C. Weber	Daniel C. Weber	2002	46
15 7/16	9 1/16	6 3/16	Coleman, AB	H. Freeman & D. Girardi	H. Freeman & D. Girardi	1963	73
15 7/16	9 1/16	6 6/16	Kootenay, BC	Melvin E. Almas	Melvin E. Almas	1965	73
15 7/16	9 2/16	6 3/16	Coal Canyon, CO	Larry Bamford	Larry Bamford	1967	73
15 7/16	9	6 3/16	Lewis & Clark Co., MT	R. Jenkins & J. Lee	Ron Jenkins	1967	73
15 7/16	9 4/16	6	Rio Blanco Co., NM	Ronald D. Vincent	Ronald D. Vincent	1970	73
15 7/16	9	6 10/16	Columbia Co., WA	William R. Randall	William R. Randall	1972	73
15 7/16	8 13/16	6 5/16	Gold Creek, BC	Donovan W. Ellis	Donovan W. Ellis	1981	73
15 7/16	9 2/16	6 6/16	Lemhi Co., ID	David W. Thompson	David W. Thompson	1983	73
15 7/16	9	6 6/16	Columbia Co., WA	Curtis D. Neal	Curtis D. Neal	1986	73
15 7/16	9 1/16	6 5/16	Lewis & Clark Co., MT	M. Barthelmess & D. Wilson	Mike Barthelmess	1987	73
15 7/16	9 2/16	6 6/16	Idaho Co., ID	Harold A. Kottre	Harold A. Kottre	1988	73
15 7/16	9 1/16	6 8/16	Pend Oreille Co., WA	Wesley M. Kreiger	Wesley M. Kreiger	1988	73
15 7/16	8 15/16	6 8/16	Ferry Co., WA	John P. Peruchini	John P. Peruchini	1989	73

COUGAR

Felis concolor hippolestes and related subspecies

Score	Greatest Length of Skull Without Lower Jaw	Greatest Width of Skull	Locality	Hunter	Owner	Date Killed	Rank
15 7/16	9 4/16	6 3/16	Colfax Co., NM	Robert M. Werley	Robert M. Werley	1989	73
15 7/16	9 2/16	6 5/16	Gila Co., AZ	Antonio E. Ornes	Antonio E. Ornes	1991	73
15 7/16	9	6 7/16	Ravalli Co., MT	Paul R. Begins	Paul R. Begins	1992	73
15 7/16	9	6 7/16	Clearwater Co., ID	Dennis L. Butler	Dennis L. Butler	1992	73
15 7/16	8 15/16	6 8/16	Wallowa Co., OR	Benjamin D. Grote	Benjamin D. Grote	1992	73
15 7/16	9 3/16	6 4/16	Colfax Co., NM	Donald P. Travis	Donald P. Travis	1994	73
15 7/16	8 15/16	6 8/16	Williams Lake, BC	Dennis R. Beebe	Dennis R. Beebe	1995	73
15 7/16	8 14/16	6 9/16	Yahk River, BC	Gerry Tames	Gerry Tames	1995	73
15 7/16	8 14/16	6 9/16	Union Co., OR	Michael C. Bennett	Michael C. Bennett	1996	73
15 7/16	9 5/16	6 2/16	Twin Lakes, BC	T. Philcox & G. Thomas	Tim Philcox	1996	73
15 7/16	9 1/16	6 6/16	Latah Co., ID	Don Scoles	Tyson Scoles	1996	73
15 7/16	9 1/16	6 6/16	Madison Co., MT	Cody Stemler	Cody Stemler	1996	73
15 7/16	8 15/16	6 8/16	Bryant Creek, AB	Roger G. Nitzsche	Roger G. Nitzsche	1999	73
15 7/16	9 3/16	6 4/16	Navajo Co., AZ	Fred Peters	Fred Peters	2000	73
15 7/16	9	6 7/16	Idaho Co., ID	Daniel R. Helterline	Daniel R. Helterline	2001	73
15 7/16	9 3/16	6 4/16	King Co., WA	Roy B. Hisler	Roy B. Hisler	2002	73
15 6/16	9 1/16	6 5/16	Wind River Mts., WY	M. Abbott Frazier	U.S. Natl. Museum	1892	102
15 6/16	8 14/16	6 8/16	Okanogan Co., WA	Merle Hooshagen	Merle Hooshagen	1957	102
15 6/16	8 14/16	6 8/16	Young Co., AZ	Ed Scarla	Ed Scarla	1958	102
15 6/16	9 4/16	6 2/16	Sedalia, CO	Walt Paulk	Walt Paulk	1961	102
15 6/16	8 13/16	6 9/16	Fernie, BC	Oscar Jansen	Oscar Jansen	1964	102
15 6/16	9 2/16	6 4/16	West Salt Creek, CO	Hartle V. Morris	Hartle V. Morris	1964	102
15 6/16	8 14/16	6 8/16	Mineral Co., MT	Richard Ramberg	Richard Ramberg	1964	102
15 6/16	8 13/16	6 9/16	Natal, BC	Dick Ritco	Dick Ritco	1964	102
15 6/16	9	6 6/16	Missoula Co., MT	Jim Zeiler	William W. Zeiler	1966	102
15 6/16	9	6 6/16	Sanders Co., MT	Lloyd F. Behling	Lloyd F. Behling	1969	102
15 6/16	9	6 5/16	Bull River, BC	Henry Fercho	Henry Fercho	1976	102
15 6/16	9 1/16	6 4/16	Colfax Co., NM	Marta S. Burnside	Marta S. Burnside	1977	102
15 6/16	9 2/16	6 4/16	Mesa Co., CO	Jack Harrison	Jack Harrison	1980	102
15 6/16	9 1/16	6 5/16	Taos Co., NM	George P. Mann	George P. Mann	1981	102
15 6/16	8 11/16	6 14/16	Lewis & Clark Co., MT	Wayne L. Beach	Wayne L. Beach	1983	102
15 6/16	8 14/16	6 8/16	Socorro Co., NM	Edwin E. Finkbeiner	Edwin E. Finkbeiner	1984	102
15 6/16	9 5/16	6 1/16	Benewah Co., ID	Kurt R. Morris	Kurt R. Morris	1984	102
15 6/16	9 1/16	6 5/16	Missoula Co., MT	Bruce E. Parker	Bruce E. Parker	1984	102
15 6/16	9	6 6/16	Clearwater Co., ID	Daniel J. Greve	Daniel J. Greve	1985	102
15 6/16	9 1/16	6 4/16	Idaho Co., ID	Ralph L. Hatter	Ralph L. Hatter	1987	102
15 6/16	9	6 7/16	Mineral Co., MT	James E. Miller III	James E. Miller III	1988	102
15 6/16	8 14/16	6 8/16	James River, AB	Susan M. Geduhn	S. Geduhn & F. Geduhn	1989	102

		Locality	By Whom Killed	Owner	Date	Rank
15 6/16	9	Rio Arriba Co., NM	James E. Kapuscinski	James E. Kapuscinski	1989	102
15 6/16	9	Highwood River, AB	G. Burton & J.D. Gordon	G. Burton & J.D. Gordon	1990	102
15 6/16	8 15/16	Nez Perce Co., ID	Rob Courville	Rob Courville	1990	102
15 6/16	8 14/16	Coldstream Creek, BC	Christopher P. Barker	Christopher P. Barker	1992	102
15 6/16	9 4/16	Mora Co., NM	Andrew J. Ortega	Andrew J. Ortega	1992	102
15 6/16	9	Elmore Co., ID	Kelly Dougherty	Kelly Dougherty	1993	102
15 6/16	9	Idaho Co., ID	Mark L. Dunham	Mark L. Dunham	1994	102
15 6/16	9 1/16	Flathead Co., MT	Sidney E. Taylor	Sidney E. Taylor	1995	102
15 6/16	9 3/16	N. Saskatchewan River, AB	Lyle G. Andersen	Lyle G. Andersen	1996	102
15 6/16	9	Columbia Co., WA	Brian W. Hergert	Brian W. Hergert	1996	102
15 6/16	9 2/16	Mineral Co., MT	Michael R. Borden	Michael R. Borden	1997	102
15 6/16	9 3/16	Lemhi Co., ID	Robert Barningham	Robert G. Barningham	1998	102
15 6/16	9 3/16	Lemhi Co., ID	Larry Ward	Larry Ward	1999	102
15 6/16	8 14/16	Washington Co., UT	Eugene E. Hafen	Eugene E. Hafen	2000	102
15 5/16	8 12/16	Hamilton Co., MT	Lloyd Thompson	U.S. Natl. Museum	1922	138
15 5/16	8 13/16	Clearwater River, AB	William A. Schutte	William A. Schutte	1935	138
15 5/16	8 15/16	Missoula Co., MT	Ronald Thompson	U.S. Natl. Museum	1936	138
15 5/16	8 15/16	East Kootenay, BC	Martin Marigeau	C. Garrett	1940	138
15 5/16	8 15/16	Clearwater Co., ID	Andy Eatmon	H.H. Schnettler	1953	138
15 5/16	8 13/16	Spanish Fork Canyon, UT	R. Jones & G. Pierce	Ronald Jones	1954	138
15 5/16	8 15/16	Granite Co., MT	Oscar E. Nelson	Oscar E. Nelson	1961	138
15 5/16	8 15/16	Idaho Co., ID	W. & D. England	Wayne England	1962	138
15 5/16	8 3/16	Eagle Nest, NM	Hal Vaught	Hal Vaught	1963	138
15 5/16	9 2/16	Lake Quinault, WA	C.A. Heppe	C.A. Heppe	1964	138
15 5/16	8 13/16	Okanogan Co., WA	Clyde A. Paul	Clyde A. Paul	1965	138
15 5/16	9 1/16	Lac La Hache, BC	Andy Hagberg	Andy Hagberg	1967	138
15 5/16	8 15/16	Elk City, ID	W. Goodwin & D. Baldwin	David Baldwin	1969	138
15 5/16	9 4/16	Grand Junction, CO	John Lamicq, Jr.	John Lamicq, Jr.	1969	138
15 5/16	9	Elko Co., NV	Kenneth A. Johnson	Kenneth A. Johnson	1974	138
15 5/16	8 13/16	Okanogan Co., WA	Joel N. Hughes	Joel N. Hughes	1975	138
15 5/16	8 15/16	Osoyoos, BC	Alvin L. Reiff	Alvin L. Reiff	1975	138
15 5/16	9	Lemhi Co., ID	Larry L. Schweitzer	Larry L. Schweitzer	1976	138
15 5/16	9	Hardesty Creek, AB	John T. Shillingburg	John T. Shillingburg	1977	138
15 5/16	8 15/16	Custer Co., ID	Florence Buxton	Florence Buxton	1978	138
15 5/16	8 15/16	Jumpingpound Creek, AB	Max W. Good	Max W. Good	1979	138
15 5/16	8 15/16	Mineral Co., MT	Dennis E. Moos	Dennis E. Moos	1980	138
15 5/16	9	Wallowa Co., OR	Duane E. Neuschwander	Duane E. Neuschwander	1981	138
15 5/16	8 15/16	Pend Oreille Co., WA	Jack Schulte	Jack Schulte	1987	138
15 5/16	9 1/16	Rio Blanco Co., CO	Rocky O. Alburtis	Rocky O. Alburtis	1987	138
15 5/16	8 15/16	Beaverhead Co., MT	R.C. Carlson & O.D. Perala	R.C. Carlson & O.D. Perala	1988	138
15 5/16	9 2/16	Dutch Creek, AB	Darryl C. Naslund	Darryl C. Naslund	1988	138
15 5/16	8 15/16	Ravalli Co., MT	Edward J. Pines III	Edward J. Pines III	1991	138
15 5/16	9 1/16	Lewis & Clark Co., MT	Clyde S. Lankford	Clyde S. Lankford	1991	138
15 5/16	8 15/16	Boise Co., ID	Donald G. Thurston	Donald G. Thurston	1992	138
15 5/16	9 1/16	Ravalli Co., MT	Dean Irwin	Dean Irwin	1994	138
15 5/16	8 15/16	Flathead Co., MT	James L. Bates	James L. Bates	1994	138
15 5/16	9	Albany Co., WY	Dennis D. Church	Dennis D. Church	1994	138

COUGAR

Felis concolor hippolestes and related subspecies

Score	Greatest Length of Skull Without Lower Jaw	Greatest Width of Skull	Locality	Hunter	Owner	Date Killed	Rank
15 5/16	9	6 5/16	Duchesne Co., UT	Ferdell K. Day	Ferdell K. Day	1994	138
15 5/16	9	6 5/16	Las Animas Co., CO	Picked Up	Phillip L. Ehrlich	PR 1994	138
15 5/16	8 14/16	6 7/16	Shoshone Co., ID	Peter J. Gardner	Peter J. Gardner	1994	138
15 5/16	9	6 5/16	Delta Co., CO	Willaim E. Kallister	William E. Kallister	1995	138
15 5/16	9 1/16	6 4/16	Lemhi Co., ID	Mike B. Woltering	Mike B. Woltering	1995	138
15 5/16	9	6 5/16	Clearwater Co., ID	Donald W. Jacklin	Donald W. Jacklin	1997	138
15 5/16	8 15/16	6 6/16	Idaho Co., ID	Arthur W. Swanstrom	Arthur W. Swanstrom	1997	138
15 5/16	9	6 5/16	Granite Co., MT	Luke J. Bergey	Luke J. Bergey	1998	138
15 5/16	8 15/16	6 6/16	Idaho Co., ID	Bruce A. Peletier	Bruce A. Peletier	1999	138
15 5/16	8 15/16	6 6/16	Costilla Co., CO	Edward D. Eckes	Edward D. Eckes	2000	138
15 5/16	9 2/16	6 3/16	Pearson Ridge, BC	Joseph F. Kenny III	Joseph F. Kenny III	2000	138
15 5/16	9 3/16	6 2/16	Colfax Co., NM	Patrick H. Lyons	Patrick H. Lyons	2001	138
15 5/16	9 3/16	6 2/16	Washoe Co., NV	John D. McCollum, Jr.	John D. McCollum, Jr.	2001	138
15 5/16	9 1/16	6 4/16	Idaho Co., ID	George R. Naugle	George R. Naugle	2002	138
15 4/16		6 4/16	Okanogan Co., WA	Merle Hooshagen	Merle Hooshagen	1956	185
15 4/16	8 13/16	6 7/16	Wells Gray Park, BC	Colin Mann	Colin Mann	1960	185
15 4/16	8 13/16	6 7/16	Union Co., OR	Don Haefer	W.H. Miller	1961	185
15 4/16	8 15/16	6 5/16	Motoqua, UT	Basil C. Bradbury	Basil C. Bradbury	1963	185
15 4/16	9	6 4/16	Missoula Co., MT	Richard Ramberg	Maurice Hornocker	1964	185
15 4/16	8 14/16	6 6/16	Canim Lake, BC	H.C. Nickelsen	H.C. Nickelsen	1964	185
15 4/16	9	6 4/16	Salmon River, ID	Aaron U. Jones	Aaron U. Jones	1967	185
15 4/16	9	6 4/16	Missoula Co., MT	B. Stanley & C. Johnson	Bob Stanley	1967	185
15 4/16	9	6 4/16	Snake River, ID	Dee M. Cannon	Dee M. Cannon	1968	185
15 4/16	8 15/16	6 5/16	Okanogan Co., WA	Louis J. Ayers	Louis J. Ayers	1969	185
15 4/16	8 13/16	6 7/16	Sandpoint, ID	George C. Taft	George C. Taft	1969	185
15 4/16	9 3/16	6 4/16	Sanders Co., MT	Edna Hill	Edna Hill	1970	185
15 4/16	8 15/16	6 5/16	Beaver Creek, AB	Oscar Markle	Oscar Markle	1970	185
15 4/16	9	6 5/16	Vernal, UT	Harold Schneider	Harold Schneider	1970	185
15 4/16	9 2/16	6 2/16	Ravalli Co., MT	Larry A. Rose	Larry A. Rose	1973	185
15 4/16	8 15/16	6 5/16	Nakusp, BC	Glen Olson	Glen Olson	1974	185
15 4/16	9	6 4/16	Lincoln Co., MT	Wayne B. Hunt	Wayne B. Hunt	1975	185
15 4/16	8 15/16	6 5/16	Mineral Co., MT	Irving H. Ratnour	Irving H. Ratnour	1975	185
15 4/16	8 14/16	6 6/16	Meldrum Creek, BC	Walter A. Riemer	Walter A. Riemer	1977	185
15 4/16	8 14/16	6 4/16	Oliver, BC	Walter Snoke	Walter Snoke	1977	185
15 4/16	9	6 6/16	Rio Arriba Co., NM	Anderson Bakewell	Anderson Bakewell	1978	185
15 4/16	8 14/16	6 4/16	Threepoint Creek, AB	Robert C. Dickson	R.C. Dickson & R.J. Dickson, Jr.	1978	185
15 4/16	9	6 5/16	Idaho Co., ID	Ralph E. Close	Ralph E. Close	1980	185
15 4/16	8 14/16	6 6/16	Baker Co., OR	Joe J. Lay	Joe J. Lay	1981	185

Score	Owner	Hunter	Locality	Skull W	Skull L	Total	Date
185	Ray Toombs	Ray Toombs	Broadwater Co., MT	6 6/16	8 14/16	15 4/16	1982
185	Ronald G. Troyer	Ronald G. Troyer	Colfax Co., NM	6 2/16	9 2/16	15 4/16	1982
185	Donna Lancaster	Donna Lancaster	Wallowa Co., OR	6 7/16	8 13/16	15 4/16	1983
185	Robert A. Soukkala	Robert A. Soukkala	Lewis & Clark Co., MT	6 5/16	8 15/16	15 4/16	1983
185	Warren Burton	Warren Burton	Mill Creek, AB	6 2/16	9 2/16	15 4/16	1984
185	Bruce Nay	Bruce Nay	Dolores Co., CO	6 6/16	8 14/16	15 4/16	1984
185	Louie Profazi	L. Profazi & R. Troyer	Colfax Co., NM	6 2/16	9 2/16	15 4/16	1984
185	Gregg A. Thurston	Gregg A. Thurston	Coconino Co., AZ	6 4/16	9	15 4/16	1984
185	John R. Blanton	John R. Blanton	Sevier Co., UT	6 4/16	9	15 4/16	1985
185	Ray B. Bailey	Ray B. Bailey	Rio Arriba Co., NM	6 4/16	9	15 4/16	1986
185	Stephen P. Connell	Stephen P. Connell	Madison Co., MT	6 4/16	9	15 4/16	1986
185	Albert L. Farace	Albert L. Farace	Uintah Co., UT	6 4/16	9	15 4/16	1986
185	Gregory P. Leid	Gregory P. Leid	Columbia Co., WA	6 4/16	9	15 4/16	1987
185	Lyle Czember	Lyle Czember	Porcupine Hills, AB	6 3/16	9 1/16	15 4/16	1988
185	Charles W. Eagleson	Charles W. Eagleson	Cassia Co., ID	6 5/16	8 15/16	15 4/16	1988
185	Mark D. Armstrong	Mark D. Armstrong	Wallowa Co., OR	6 3/16	9 1/16	15 4/16	1989
185	William E. Pipes III	William E. Pipes III	Rio Blanco Co., CO	6 6/16	8 14/16	15 4/16	1989
185	Darrell G. Holmquist	Darrell G. Holmquist	Shoshone Co., ID	6 7/16	8 13/16	15 4/16	1990
185	Tracy L. Skay	Picked Up	Shoshone Co., ID	6 5/16	8 15/16	15 4/16	1990
185	Sally A. Kloosterman	Sally A. Kloosterman	Whaleback Ridge, AB	6 7/16	8 13/16	15 4/16	1991
185	Fred Schrader	Fred Schrader	Jumping Pond, AB	6 3/16	9 1/16	15 4/16	1991
185	Robert J. Barnett	Robert J. Barnett	Clearwater Co., ID	6 2/16	9 2/16	15 4/16	1992
185	Mark Jenkins	Mark Jenkins	Columbia Co., WA	6 4/16	9	15 4/16	1992
185	Walter R. Willey, Jr.	Walter R. Willey, Jr.	Ravalli Co., MT	6 5/16	8 15/16	15 4/16	1992
185	Benjamin D. Grote	Benjamin D. Grote	Wallowa Co., OR	6 5/16	8 15/16	15 4/16	1993
185	Dave Hiatt	Dave Hiatt	Idaho Co., ID	6 4/16	9	15 4/16	1993
185	Kenny E. Leo	Kenny E. Leo	Carbon Co., UT	6 4/16	9	15 4/16	1993
185	Bob Kaid	Bob Kaid	Utah Co., UT	6	9 4/16	15 4/16	1994
185	Shawn P. Price	Shawn P. Price	Flathead Co., MT	6 8/16	8 12/16	15 4/16	1994
185	Robert J. Seeds	Robert J. Seeds	Rio Arriba Co., NM	6 2/16	9 2/16	15 4/16	1994
185	James Dunigan	James Dunigan	Likely, BC	6 4/16	9	15 4/16	1996
185	Marc Simard	Marc Simard	Monte Lake, BC	6 3/16	9 1/16	15 4/16	1996
185	Robert Faiers	Robert Faiers	Moyie Lake, BC	6 6/16	8 14/16	15 4/16	1997
185	Douglas G. Jones	Douglas G. Jones	Cartier Creek, AB	6 5/16	8 15/16	15 4/16	1997
185	Kevin D. Harms	Kevin Harms	Broadwater Co., MT	6 3/16	9 1/16	15 4/16	1998
185	Carleton L. Mocabee	Carleton L. Mocabee	Flathead Co., MT	6 5/16	8 15/16	15 4/16	1998
185	Thomas J. Schank	Thomas J. Schank	Idaho Co., ID	6 5/16	8 15/16	15 4/16	1998
185	Robert E. Darmitzel	Robert E. Darmitzel	Colfax Co., NM	6	9 4/16	15 4/16	1999
185	Roland M. Larrabee	Roland Larrabee	Andreen Creek, BC	6 8/16	8 12/16	15 4/16	1999
185	Travis M. Schiller	Travis M. Schiller	Revelstoke Lake, BC	6 6/16	8 14/16	15 4/16	1999
185	Jay J. Fuller	Jay J. Fuller	Jumpingpound Creek, AB	6 6/16	8 14/16	15 4/16	2000
185	Gene White	Gene White	Silver Bow Co., MT	6 4/16	9	15 4/16	2000
185	Jonathan A. Adams	Jonathan A. Adams	Thurston Co., WA	6 2/16	9 2/16	15 4/16	2003
252	C. Garrett	Martin Marigeau	East Kootenay, BC	6 4/16	8 15/16	15 3/16	1940
252	Warren C. Johnston	Warren C. Johnston	Ventura Co., CA	6 6/16	8 13/16	15 3/16	1953
252	J.R. Aitchison	J.R. Aitchison	Churn Creek, BC	6 5/16	8 14/16	15 3/16	1956
252	Univ. of BC	R.A. Rutherglen	Nelson, BC	6 2/16	9 1/16	15 3/16	1956

Felis concolor hippolestes and related subspecies

Score	Greatest Length of Skull Without Lower Jaw	Greatest Width of Skull	Locality	Hunter	Owner	Date Killed	Rank
15 3/16	8 14/16	6 5/16	Saratoga Co., WY	Win Condict	Win Condict	1961	252
15 3/16	8 14/16	6 5/16	Pincher Creek, AB	Harry R. Freeman	Harry R. Freeman	1961	252
15 3/16	8 14/16	6 5/16	Trout Creek, AB	Kenny McRae	Kenny McRae	1961	252
15 3/16	8 14/16	6 5/16	McGregor Lake, AB	Gus Daley	A.C. Wilson	1962	252
15 3/16	8 14/16	6 5/16	Oliver, BC	Allan Nichol	Allan Nichol	1963	252
15 3/16	8 14/16	6 5/16	Okanogan Co., WA	Mike Lynch	Mike Lynch	1964	252
15 3/16	9	6 3/16	Tatlayoko Lake, BC	C.L. Anderson	C.L. Anderson	1967	252
15 3/16	8 15/16	6 4/16	Oroville, WA	L. Fleming & J. Lemaster	Leon Fleming	1967	252
15 3/16	8 11/16	6 3/16	Whitecourt, AB	K.J. Stanton	K.J. Stanton	1967	252
15 3/16	9 3/16	6	Meeker Co., CO	Jack Cadario	Jack Cadario	1968	252
15 3/16	8 15/16	6 4/16	Orofino, ID	Fairly Bonner	Fairly Bonner	1969	252
15 3/16	8 14/16	6 5/16	Falkland, BC	Earl Carlson	Wildl. Tax. Studios	1974	252
15 3/16	8 15/16	6 4/16	Prouton Lakes, BC	G.C. Ridley & R. Gillespie	G.C. Ridley & R. Gillespie	1976	252
15 3/16	9 2/16	6	Emery Co., UT	Dan Scartezina	Dan Scartezina	1976	252
15 3/16	9 2/16	6 1/16	Garfield Co., UT	William A. Coats	William A. Coats	1978	252
15 3/16	8 15/16	6 4/16	Mt. Evans, BC	Larry N. Dent	Larry N. Dent	1980	252
15 3/16	8 14/16	6 5/16	Stevens Co., WA	William K. Bean	William K. Bean	1981	252
15 3/16	8 10/16	6 9/16	Ferry Co., WA	Richard A. Bonander	Richard A. Bonander	1981	252
15 3/16	8 13/16	6 6/16	Silver Creek, AB	John E. Cassidy	John E. Cassidy	1981	252
15 3/16	8 14/16	6 5/16	Rio Blanco Co., CO	Robert L. Raley	Robert L. Raley	1983	252
15 3/16	8 13/16	6 6/16	Nez Perce Co., ID	Steavon C. Hornbeck	Steavon C. Hornbeck	1984	252
15 3/16	8 14/16	6 5/16	Plumbob Mt., BC	Andreas Felber	Andreas Felber	1985	252
15 3/16	8 14/16	6 5/16	Hot Springs Co., WY	Dan B. Artery	Dan B. Artery	1986	252
15 3/16	8 14/16	6 5/16	Idaho Co., ID	Steve C. Ryan	Richard C. Farthing	1987	252
15 3/16	8 13/16	6 6/16	Clearwater Co., ID	Michael T. McCain	Michael T. McCain	1988	252
15 3/16	8 14/16	6 5/16	Lincoln Co., MT	Jon G. Clark	Jon G. Clark	1989	252
15 3/16	9 1/16	6 2/16	Mt. Thynne, BC	Cliff C. Cory	Cliff C. Cory	1989	252
15 3/16	8 13/16	6 6/16	Porcupine Hills, AB	Sidney Websdale	Sidney Websdale	1989	252
15 3/16	8 15/16	6 4/16	Idaho Co., ID	Stephan D. Galles	Stephan D. Galles	1990	252
15 3/16	8 15/16	6 4/16	Larimer Co., CO	Peter A. Larson	Peter A. Larson	1990	252
15 3/16	8 11/16	6 8/16	San Miguel Co., NM	Robert J. Seeds	Robert J. Seeds	1990	252
15 3/16	9 2/16	6 1/16	Archuleta Co., CO	Charles T. Ames	Charles T. Ames	1991	252
15 3/16	8 15/16	6 4/16	Clearwater Co., ID	Donald K. Cooper	Donald K. Cooper	1991	252
15 3/16	8 14/16	6 5/16	Moffat Co., CO	Robert W. Dager	Robert W. Dager	1991	252
15 3/16	9 1/16	6 2/16	Coleman, AB	Jerry Fisher	Jerry Fisher	1991	252
15 3/16	8 14/16	6 5/16	Boundary Co., ID	Ron R. Frederickson	Ron R. Frederickson	1991	252
15 3/16	8 14/16	6 5/16	Elk River, BC	Jim Musil	Jim Musil	1991	252
15 3/16	9 1/16	6 2/16	Eagle Co., CO	Jeffrey S. Shoaf	Jeffrey S. Shoaf	1991	252

Score	Length	Width	Locality	By Whom Killed	Owner	Date	Rank
15 3/16	8 15/16	6 4/16	Whiskey Creek, AE	Dennis Watson	Dennis Watson	1991	252
15 3/16	8 13/16	6 6/16	Bannock Co., ID	Brad Hough	Brad Hough	1992	252
15 3/16	9 1/16	6 2/16	Gila Co., AZ	Fred Peters	Fred Peters	1992	252
15 3/16	8 15/16	6 4/16	Ram Mt., AB	Stanley D. Simpson	Stanley D. Simpson	1992	252
15 3/16	8 15/16	6 4/16	San Miguel Co., NM	Paul W. Brown	Paul W. Brown	1993	252
15 3/16	8 13/16	6 4/16	Boundary Co., ID	Tom D. Neuburg	Tom D. Neuburg	1993	252
15 3/16	9 1/16	6 2/16	Barkshanty Creek, BC	Daryl Donald	Daryl Donald	1994	252
15 3/16	8 13/16	6 6/16	Rio Arriba Co., NM	Robert J. Seeds	Robert J. Seeds	1994	252
15 3/16	8 15/16	6 4/16	McGregor Lake, AB	Frederick S. Fish	Frederick S. Fish	1995	252
15 3/16	8 14/16	6 5/16	Ravalli Co., MT	Gregory Sketas	Gregory Sketas	1995	252
15 3/16	8 15/16	6 4/16	Garfield Co., WA	DeWayne L. Straube	DeWayne L. Straube	1995	252
15 3/16	9 1/16	6 4/16	Echo Lake, BC	Terry S. Wasylyszyn	Terry Wasylyszyn	1996	252
15 3/16	8 14/16	6 5/16	Tooele Co., UT	Ed R. Sheets	Ed R. Sheets	1996	252
15 3/16	8 15/16	6 4/16	Garfield Co., CO	Daryl G. Speck	Daryl G. Speck	1996	252
15 3/16	9 1/16	6 4/16	Jefferson Co., WA	Willie Nation	J. Stevens & J. Rankin	1997	252
15 3/16	8 15/16	6 2/16	Benewah Co., ID	Kurt R. Morris	Kurt R. Morris	1997	252
15 3/16	9 4/16	6 4/16	Maze Lake, BC	Eric Petosa	Eric Petosa	1998	252
15 3/16	8 14/16	5 15/16	Idaho Co., ID	Jesse J. Higgins	Jesse J. Higgins	1998	252
15 3/16	8 11/16	6 5/16	Tooele Co., UT	Kevin J. Hunt	Kevin J. Hunt	1998	252
15 3/16	8 11/16	6 8/16	Valley Co., ID	Kenneth Leavitt	Kenneth Leavitt	1998	252
15 3/16	8 15/16	6 8/16	Hinton, AB	Danny Ljubsa	Danny Ljubsa	1998	252
15 3/16	8 13/16	6 4/16	Carbon Co., MT	Lynn R. McKittrick	Lynn R. McKittrick	1998	252
15 3/16	8 15/16	6 6/16	Rio Arriba Co., NM	Robert J. Seeds	Robert J. Seeds	1999	252
15 3/16	8 14/16	6 4/16	Clearwater Co., ID	James J. Backman	James J. Backman	1999	252
15 3/16	9 1/16	6 5/16	Lake Co., MT	Robert C. Hartwig	Robert C. Hartwig	1999	252
15 3/16	8 12/16	6 2/16	McLean Creek, AB	Neil G. Johnson	Neil G. Johnson	2000	252
15 3/16	8 15/16	6 7/16	Bullock Creek, BC	John A. Dolan	John A. Dolan	2000	252
15 3/16	8 14/16	6 4/16	Hawkins Creek, BC	Gary R. McMillan	Gary R. McMillan	2000	252
15 3/16	8 13/16	6 5/16	Willowbank Mt., BC	Gilles M. Rondeau	Gilles M. Rondeau	2000	252
15 3/16	9	6 4/16	James River, AB	Donald E. Taylor	Donald E. Taylor	2001	252
15 3/16	8 15/16	6 3/16	Flathead Co., MT	Ronald C. Gronitz	Ronald C. Gronitz	2002	252
15 3/16	8 13/16	6 4/16	Tsuniah Lake, BC	Adam W.J. Boehm	William C. Boehm	2002	252
15 3/16	8 12/16	6 6/16	Summit Co., UT	Jared L. Brown	Jared L. Brown	2002	252
15 3/16	8 14/16	6 6/16	Taos Co., NM	Albert R. Teupell	Albert R. Teupell	2002	252
15 2/16	9 1/16	6 1/16	East Kootenay, BC	C. Garrett	Martin Marigeau	1940	328
15 2/16	8 14/16	6 3/16	Benewah Co., ID	Karl Paulson	Karl Paulson	1945	328
15 2/16	9 1/16	6 4/16	Salmon River, ID	Bob Hagel	Bob Hagel	1950	328
15 2/16	9	6 1/16	Strawberry, AZ	Irene Morden	Irene Morden	1958	328
15 2/16	8 12/16	6 2/16	Pine Co., AZ	C.J. Prock	C.J. Prock	1958	328
15 2/16	8 11/16	6 6/16	New Harmony, UT	Art Coates	Art Coates	1962	328
15 2/16	8 14/16	6 7/16	Allison, CO	Georgianna Etheridge	Georgianna Etheridge	1962	328
15 2/16	8 14/16	6 4/16	Coleman, AB	T. & C. Michalsky	T. & C. Michalsky	1962	328
15 2/16	8 15/16	6 4/16	Lendrum Creek, AE	Gary G. Giese	Gary G. Giese	1964	328
15 2/16	8 12/16	6 3/16	Parowan, UT	William P. Mastrangel	William P. Mastrangel	1964	328
15 2/16	8 14/16	6 4/16	Reserve, NM	Wilmer C. Hansen	Wilmer C. Hansen	1966	328
15 2/16	8 15/16	6 3/16	Saratoga Co., WY	Win Condict	Win Condict	1967	328
15 2/16	8 12/16	6 6/16	Little Fort, BC	Earl E. Hill	Earl E. Hill	1968	328

COUGAR

Felis concolor hippolestes and related subspecies

Score	Greatest Length of Skull Without Lower Jaw	Greatest Width of Skull	Locality	Hunter	Owner	Date Killed	Rank
15 2/16	8 15/16	6 3/16	Duchesne Co., UT	Clyde C. Edwards	Clyde C. Edwards	1969	328
15 2/16	8 12/16	6 6/16	Okanogan Valley, WA	Patrick M. Davis	Patrick M. Davis	1970	328
15 2/16	8 14/16	6 4/16	Manzano Mts., NM	C.J. McElroy	C.J. McElroy	1970	328
15 2/16	9	6 2/16	Graveyard Creek, BC	Rod G. Hardie	Rod G. Hardie	1972	328
15 2/16	8 14/16	6 4/16	Duchesne Co., UT	Richard B. Sydnor, Jr.	Richard B. Sydnor, Jr.	1972	328
15 2/16	8 14/16	6 4/16	Stevens Co., WA	Leroy W. Kindsvogel	WA State U. Alumni Assoc.	1972	328
15 2/16	8 12/16	6 6/16	Ferry Co., WA	Paul L. Watts	Paul L. Watts	1972	328
15 2/16	8 13/16	6 5/16	Lincoln Co., MT	Katherine Kimberlin	Katherine Kimberlin	1973	328
15 2/16	9	6 2/16	Carbon Co., UT	L.A. Grelling	L.A. Grelling	1974	328
15 2/16	9	6 2/16	Pend Oreille Co., WA	Robert J. Robertson	Robert J. Robertson	1974	328
15 2/16	8 11/16	6 7/16	Granby River, BC	Everett B. Pannkuk, Jr.	Everett B. Pannkuk, Jr.	1977	328
15 2/16	8 12/16	6 6/16	Idaho Co., ID	Lawrence L. Seiler	Lawrence L. Seiler	1977	328
15 2/16	8 15/16	6 3/16	Uintah Co., UT	Dale Larson	Dale Larson	1978	328
15 2/16	8 13/16	6 5/16	Cascade Range, BC	Dennis C. Roach	Dennis C. Roach	1978	328
15 2/16	8 14/16	6 4/16	Mt. Roderick, BC	Gail W. Holderman	Gail W. Holderman	1979	328
15 2/16	9 1/16	6 1/16	Colfax Co., NM	Philip H. Whitley	Philip H. Whitley	1980	328
15 2/16	8 14/16	6 4/16	Stevens Co., WA	Fritz G. Nagel	Fritz G. Nagel	1981	328
15 2/16	8 13/16	6 5/16	Archuleta Co., CO	Judd Cooney	Judd Cooney	1982	328
15 2/16	8 14/16	6 4/16	Adams Co., ID	Warren J. Masson	Warren J. Masson	1982	328
15 2/16	8 12/16	6 6/16	Garfield Co., CO	Leslie H. Brewster	Leslie H. Brewster	1983	328
15 2/16	8 14/16	6 4/16	Sanders Co., MT	Conrad P. Anderson	Conrad P. Anderson	1984	328
15 2/16	8 12/16	6 6/16	Wallowa Co., OR	Samuel E. Briscoe	Samuel E. Briscoe	1984	328
15 2/16	8 11/16	6 7/16	Gallatin Co., MT	David M. Tofte	David M. Tofte	1984	328
15 2/16	8 13/16	6 5/16	Pondera Co., MT	Felix W. Parks	Felix W. Parks	1985	328
15 2/16	8 12/16	6 6/16	Little White Mt., BC	Thomas M. Lavelle	Thomas M. Lavelle	1986	328
15 2/16	8 13/16	6 5/16	Latah Co., ID	Terry L. Watkins	Terry L. Watkins	1986	328
15 2/16	8 15/16	6 3/16	Clearwater Co., ID	Michael J. Kennedy	Michael J. Kennedy	1987	328
15 2/16	8 13/16	6 5/16	Union Co., OR	F. Gale Culver	F. Gale Culver	1988	328
15 2/16	8 13/16	6 5/16	Castle River, AB	Duane B. Schultz	Duane B. Schultz	1988	328
15 2/16	8 13/16	6 5/16	Utah Co., UT	Brent M. Taylor	Brent M. Taylor	1988	328
15 2/16	8 12/16	6 6/16	Lake Co., MT	Kevin J. Warning	Kevin J. Warning	1989	328
15 2/16	9 1/16	6 1/16	Woods Lake, BC	S. MacKenzie & B.A. Jaeger	Sean MacKenzie	1990	328
15 2/16	9	6 2/16	Taos Co., NM	William L. Porteous	William L. Porteous	1990	328
15 2/16	8 15/16	6 3/16	Park Co., CO	Jack P. Van Vianen	Jack P. Van Vianen	1990	328
15 2/16	8 12/16	6 6/16	San Miguel Co., CO	Charles M. Karp	Charles M. Karp	1991	328
15 2/16	8 13/16	6 5/16	Missoula Co., MT	Kenneth P. Schoening	Kenneth P. Schoening	1991	328
15 2/16	8 15/16	6 3/16	Missoula Co., MT	Steve B. Tenold	Steve B. Tenold	1991	328
15 2/16	8 15/16	6 3/16	Duchesne Co., UT	Jet C. Abegglen	Jet C. Abegglen	1992	328

Score			Locality	Hunter	Owner	Date	Rank
15 2/16	8 13/16	6 5/16	Chimney Peak, AB	Derek A. Burdeny	Derek A. Burdeny	1992	328
15 2/16	8 10/16	6 8/16	Lincoln Co., MT	James R. Eff	James R. Eff	1992	328
15 2/16	9	6 2/16	Idaho Co., ID	William D. Ketcham II	Ben F. Ketcham	1992	328
15 2/16	8 15/16	6 3/16	Mineral Co., MT	Luke Cowan	Luke Cowan	1993	328
15 2/16	8 15/16	6 3/16	Shoshone Co., ID	Randy L. Fort	Randy L. Fort	1993	328
15 2/16	8 11/16	6 7/16	Kootenay Lake, BC	Robert Kuny	Robert Kuny	1993	328
15 2/16	9	6 2/16	Stevens Co., WA	William D. McWhinney	William D. McWhinney	1993	328
15 2/16	8 12/16	6 6/16	Park Co., MT	Primo Scapin	Primo Scapin	1993	328
15 2/16	8 15/16	6 3/16	Kootenay River, BC	Brian Schuck	Brian Schuck	1993	328
15 2/16	9 1/16	6 1/16	Okanogan Co., WA	David J. Burdulis	David J. Burdulis	1994	328
15 2/16	9 1/16	6 1/16	Uintah Co., UT	Shawn A. Labrum	Shawn A. Labrum	1994	328
15 2/16	8 14/16	6 4/16	Gold Creek, BC	Dean W. Hogaboam	Dean W. Hogaboam	1995	328
15 2/16	8 15/16	6 3/16	Idaho Co., ID	Allen D. Jones	Allen D. Jones	1995	328
15 2/16	9	6 2/16	Okanagan, BC	Jose L. Perez	Jose L. Perez	1995	328
15 2/16	9	6 2/16	Gila Co., AZ	Felix E. Sanchez	Felix E. Sanchez	1995	328
15 2/16	8 15/16	6 3/16	Flathead Co., MT	Curtis B. Stene	Curtis B. Stene	1996	328
15 2/16	8 14/16	6 4/16	Clallam Co., WA	Richard L. Deane	Richard L. Deane	1996	328
15 2/16	8 15/16	6 3/16	Elko Co., NV	Kazushige Harada	Kazushige Harada	1996	328
15 2/16	9 1/16	6 1/16	Kobau Mt., BC	James E. Riley	James E. Riley	1996	328
15 2/16	8 12/16	6 6/16	Rio Arriba Co., NM	Robert J. Seeds	Robert J. Seeds	1996	328
15 2/16	9	6 2/16	Archuleta Co., CO	Dolores E. Adams	Dolores E. Adams	1997	328
15 2/16	8 11/16	6 7/16	Kootenai Co., ID	Lawrence L. Booher	Lawrence L. Booher	1997	328
15 2/16	8 14/16	6 4/16	Mineral Co., MT	Timothy R. Brant	Timothy R. Brant	1997	328
15 2/16	8 9/16	6 9/16	Monroe Lake, BC	Terry Faiers	Terry Faiers	1997	328
15 2/16	9	6 2/16	Bonner Co., ID	Don P. Miller II	Don P. Miller II	1997	328
15 2/16	8 14/16	6 4/16	Rocky Mountain House, AB	Dennis J. Tucker	Dennis J. Tucker	1997	328
15 2/16	8 15/16	6 3/16	Chelan Co., WA	John A. Barnes	John A. Barnes	1998	328
15 2/16	8 15/16	6 3/16	Chain Lakes, AB	Tom Foss	Tom Foss	1998	328
15 2/16	8 13/16	6 5/16	Dry Lake, BC	David L. Hartin	David L. Hartin	1998	328
15 2/16	8 13/16	6 5/16	Cynthia, AB	Martin Lang	Martin Lang	1998	328
15 2/16	8 14/16	6 4/16	La Plata Co., CO	Brad F. Pfeffer	Brad F. Pfeffer	1998	328
15 2/16	8 14/16	6 4/16	Montezuma Co., CO	Terry D. Amrine	Terry D. Amrine	1999	328
15 2/16	8 13/16	6 5/16	Mineral Co., MT	Darren Crusch	Darren Crusch	1999	328
15 2/16	9	6 2/16	Lemhi Co., ID	Henry K. Leworthy	Henry K. Leworthy	1999	328
15 2/16	8 13/16	6 5/16	Montrose Co., CO	Steven R. Hickok	Steven R. Hickok	2000	328
15 2/16	9	6 2/16	Navajo Co., AZ	Fred Peters	Fred Peters	2001	328
15 2/16	8 14/16	6 4/16	Elko Co., NV	Michael A. Algerio	Michael A. Algerio	2002	328
15 2/16	9 1/16	6 1/16	Missoula Co., MT	Anthony Knuchel	Anthony Knuchel	2002	328
15 2/16	8 14/16	6 4/16	Park Co., CO	Michael F. Kwak	Michael F. Kwak	2002	328
15 2/16	8 13/16	6 4/16	Fraser River, BC	Tom & Mary Sword	Tom L. Sword	2002	328
15 1/16	8 13/16	6 4/16	Princeton, BC	C.F. Gigot	Alan Gill	1948	419
15 1/16	8 13/16	6 4/16	Okanogan Co., WA	Francis Randall	Francis Randall	1948	419
15 1/16	8 15/16	6 2/16	Saratoga Co., WY	Win Condict	Win Condict	1954	419
15 1/16	8 9/16	6 8/16	Ferris Mts., WY	Win Condict	W. Condict & E. Levasseur	1959	419
15 1/16	8 14/16	6 1/16	Cat Creek, AB	Hyrum R. Baker	Hyrum R. Baker	1960	419
15 1/16	9	6 1/16	Wild Horse Basin, WY	Win Condict	Win Condict	1961	419
15 1/16	8 13/16	6 4/16	Custer Co., ID	Joe Blackburn	Joe Blackburn	1962	419

COUGAR

Felis concolor hippolestes and related subspecies

Score	Greatest Length of Skull Without Lower Jaw	Greatest Width of Skull	Locality	Hunter	Owner	Date Killed	Rank
15 1/16	8 14/16	6 1/16	Oliver, BC	Allan Nichol	Allan Nichol	1963	419
15 1/16	9	6 1/16	Clearwater River, ID	Ted Hall	Ted Hall	1964	419
15 1/16	8 12/16	6 5/16	Idaho Co., ID	Elliot V. Nelson	Elliot V. Nelson	1965	419
15 1/16	8 14/16	6 3/16	Mineral Co., MT	Richard Ramberg	R. & N. Ramberg	1966	419
15 1/16	8 12/16	6 5/16	Missoula Co., MT	William W. Zeiler	William W. Zeiler	1966	419
15 1/16	8 14/16	6 3/16	Clearwater Co., ID	Robert W. Haskin	Robert W. Haskin	1967	419
15 1/16	8 13/16	6 4/16	Lincoln Co., MT	H.M. Johnston	H.M. Johnston	1967	419
15 1/16	8 13/16	6 4/16	S. Castle River, AB	James F. Simpson	James F. Simpson	1967	419
15 1/16	9 1/16	6	Price Co., UT	Robert H. Elder	Robert H. Elder	1968	419
15 1/16	8 13/16	6 4/16	Little Fort, BC	Earl E. Hill	Earl E. Hill	1968	419
15 1/16	8 15/16	6 2/16	Oroville, WA	Dan Lynch	Dan Lynch	1968	419
15 1/16	8 14/16	6 3/16	Douglas Co., CO	C.R. Anderson & E.H. Brown	Charles R. Anderson	1969	419
15 1/16	9 1/16	6	Sunflower Co., AZ	John C. Shaw	John C. Shaw	1969	419
15 1/16	8 12/16	6 5/16	Mineral Co., MT	William E. Bullock	William E. Bullock	1971	419
15 1/16	9 1/16	6	Gunlock, UT	L. Dean Taylor	L. Dean Taylor	1971	419
15 1/16	8 14/16	6 3/16	Pima Co., AZ	George W. Parker	George W. Parker	1972	419
15 1/16	9	6 1/16	Superior, MT	James L. Schaeffer	James L. Schaeffer	1972	419
15 1/16	8 13/16	6 4/16	Uintah Co., UT	Brent L. Winchester	Brent L. Winchester	1972	419
15 1/16	8 13/16	6 4/16	Emery Co., UT	Sharon A. Burkett	Sharon A. Burkett	1973	419
15 1/16	8 15/16	6 2/16	Granite Co., MT	James A. Raikos	James A. Raikos	1973	419
15 1/16	8 14/16	6 3/16	Idaho Co., ID	Chester D. Haight	Chester D. Haight	1975	419
15 1/16	8 15/16	6 2/16	Lake Co., MT	J.E. McCreedy & R.E. Seabaugh	James McCreedy	1977	419
15 1/16	8 13/16	6 4/16	Pend Oreille Co., WA	William M. Day	William M. Day	1978	419
15 1/16	8 15/16	6 2/16	Pimainus Hills, BC	Norman W. Dougan	Norman W. Dougan	1978	419
15 1/16	8 15/16	6 2/16	Wallowa Co., OR	Rollie Mattson	Rollie Mattson	1978	419
15 1/16	8 12/16	6 5/16	Nez Perce Co., ID	Pete M. Baughman, Jr.	Pete M. Baughman, Jr.	1979	419
15 1/16	9 1/16	6	Piute Co., UT	Fred J. Markley	Fred J. Markley	1979	419
15 1/16	8 14/16	6 3/16	Mill Creek, AB	Richard C. Davidson	Richard C. Davidson	1980	419
15 1/16	8 15/16	6 2/16	Rio Arriba Co., NM	Joseph Strasser, Jr.	Joseph Strasser, Jr.	1980	419
15 1/16	9	6 1/16	Wallowa Co., OR	William E. Hosford	William E. Hosford	1982	419
15 1/16	8 13/16	6 4/16	Erickson Creek, BC	R. John Kovak	R. John Kovak	1982	419
15 1/16	8 14/16	6 3/16	Idaho Co., ID	Roy M. Schumacher	Roy M. Schumacher	1984	419
15 1/16	8 13/16	6 4/16	Garfield Co., CO	Jay H. Kneasel	Jay H. Kneasel	1985	419
15 1/16	8 13/16	6 4/16	Whitney Creek, AB	Bryne J. Lengyel	Bryne J. Lengyel	1985	419
15 1/16	9 1/16	6	Lincoln Co., MT	Gary C. Cargill	Gary C. Cargill	1986	419
15 1/16	8 13/16	6 4/16	Newington Creek, BC	James W. Anderson	James W. Anderson	1987	419
15 1/16	8 14/16	6 3/16	Garfield Co., CO	Joseph S. Arrain	Joseph S. Arrain	1987	419
15 1/16	8 13/16	6 4/16	Idaho Co., ID	Ronald R. Feist	Ronald R. Feist	1987	419

Score	Length of Skull	Width of Skull	Locality	Hunter	Owner	Date Killed	Rank
15 1/16	8 15/16	6 2/16	Clearwater Co., ID	Charles C. Smith	Charles C. Smith	1987	419
15 1/16	8 11/16	6 6/16	Shoshone Co., ID	David K. Mueller	David K. Mueller	1988	419
15 1/16	8 14/16	6 3/16	Apache Co., AZ	Fred Peters	Fred Peters	1988	419
15 1/16	9	6 1/16	Missoula Co., MT	Kenneth P. Schoening	Kenneth P. Schoening	1989	419
15 1/16	8 13/16	6 1/16	Clallam Co., WA	John R. Franz	John R. Franz	1989	419
15 1/16	8 12/16	6 4/16	Hinton, AB	Rodney M. Janz	Rodney M. Janz	1990	419
15 1/16	8 14/16	6 3/16	Daggett Co., UT	T.C. Benson & L.V. Massey	Todd C. Benson	1990	419
15 1/16	8 14/16	6 5/16	Flathead Co., MT	Robert D. Boutang	Robert D. Boutang	1990	419
15 1/16	8 12/16	6 6/16	Utah Co., UT	Mary L. Brooks	Mary L. Brooks	1990	419
15 1/16	8 11/16	6 3/16	Rio Blanco Co., CO	Gerald L. Dowling	Gerald L. Dowling	1990	419
15 1/16	8 14/16	6 1/16	Millard Co., UT	Edwin A. Lewis	Edwin A. Lewis	1990	419
15 1/16	9	6 3/16	Bragg Creek, AB	Drew Ramsay	Drew Ramsay	1991	419
15 1/16	8 14/16	6 4/16	Dolores Co., CO	Anthony S. Wagner	Anthony S. Wagner	1991	419
15 1/16	8 13/16	6 3/16	Bonner Co., ID	Paul R. Allen	Paul R. Allen	1991	419
15 1/16	8 14/16	6 4/16	Latah Co., ID	Stephan D. Galles	Stephan D. Galles	1992	419
15 1/16	8 12/16	6 5/16	Cross River, BC	Mike J. McBride	Mike J. McBride	1992	419
15 1/16	8 15/16	6 2/16	Missoula Co., MT	John F. Haviland	John F. Haviland	1992	419
15 1/16	8 15/16	6 2/16	Missoula Co., MT	Robert J. Matye	Robert J. Matye	1992	419
15 1/16	9	6 1/16	Sanders Co., MT	Phillip J. Taylor	Phillip J. Taylor	1992	419
15 1/16	8 14/16	6 3/16	Chelan Co., WA	Douglas W. Thies	Douglas W. Thies	1993	419
15 1/16	8 10/16	6 7/16	Lincoln Co., MT	William R. Vyvyan	William R. Vyvyan	1993	419
15 1/16	9	6 1/16	Carbon Co., UT	Ray T. Bridge	Ray T. Bridge	1993	419
15 1/16	8 13/16	6 4/16	Shoshone Co., ID	Shawn Frederickson	Shawn Frederickson	1993	419
15 1/16	9	6 1/16	Montrose Co., CO	Kevin W. Smith	Kevin W. Smith	1994	419
15 1/16	8 14/16	6 3/16	Douglas Co., OR	Greg A. Thomas	Greg A. Thomas	1994	419
15 1/16	8 11/16	6 6/16	Boundary Co., ID	Ronald R. Frederickson	Ronald R. Frederickson	1994	419
15 1/16	8 14/16	6 4/16	Sanders Co., MT	Dennis J. Gripp	Dennis J. Gripp	1994	419
15 1/16	8 14/16	6 3/16	Teton Co., MT	Ivan L. Irwin	Ivan L. Irwin	1994	419
15 1/16	8 14/16	6 3/16	San Miguel Co., NM	James O. Pittman, Jr.	James O. Pittman, Jr.	1994	419
15 1/16	8 15/16	6 3/16	Missoula Co., MT	Picked Up	Dale A. Rivers	PR 1994	419
15 1/16	8 14/16	6 2/16	Wallowa Co., OR	Robert J. Seeds	Robert J. Seeds	1994	419
15 1/16	8 13/16	6 3/16	Rio Arriba Co., NM	Stephen Dyke	Stephen Dyke	1995	419
15 1/16	9	6 3/16	Whiskey Creek, AB	Brad R. Tacke	Brad R. Tacke	1995	419
15 1/16	8 14/16	6 1/16	Missoula Co., MT	John D. Devitt	John D. Devitt	1996	419
15 1/16	9	6 3/16	Stillwater Co., MT	Thomas G. Dunlap	Thomas G. Dunlap	1996	419
15 1/16	8 14/16	6 3/16	Summit Co., UT	Ken A. Krien	Ken A. Krien	1996	419
15 1/16	8 14/16	6 1/16	Grand Co., CO	Norman R. Noe	Norman R. Noe	1996	419
15 1/16	9	6 1/16	Las Animas Co., CO	Joe Roberts	Joe Roberts	1996	419
15 1/16	8 12/16	6 4/16	St. Mary River, BC	William D. Bradley	William D. Bradley	1997	419
15 1/16	8 13/16	6 2/16	Park Co., MT	Richard F. Karbowski	Richard F. Karbowski	1997	419
15 1/16	8 15/16	6 3/16	Grand Co., CO	Brian K. Mortz	Brian K. Mortz	1997	419
15 1/16	8 14/16	6	Penticton, BC	Arthur E. Ashcraft	Arthur E. Ashcraft	1999	419
15 1/16	9 1/16	6 7/16	Union Co., NM	Paul T. Jones	Paul T. Jones	1999	419
15 1/16	8 10/16	6 2/16	Grand Co., CO	James E. Vance	James E. Vance	1999	419
15 1/16	8 15/16	6 6/16	Rio Arriba Co., NM	W. Justin McCormick	W. Justin McCormick	2000	419
15 1/16	8 11/16	6 4/16	Mill Creek, AB	Luke Semenoff	Luke Semenoff	2000	419

Felis concolor hippolestes and related subspecies

Score	Greatest Length of Skull Without Lower Jaw	Greatest Width of Skull	Locality	Hunter	Owner	Date Killed	Rank
15 1/16	8 12/16	6 5/16	Missoula Co., MT	Gary L. Zabel	Gary L. Zabel	2000	419
15 1/16	8 15/16	6 2/16	Rio Arriba Co., NM	Dean McInnis	Dean McInnis	2001	419
15 1/16	8 14/16	6 3/16	Archuleta Co., CO	Kenneth D. Smith	Kenneth D. Smith	2002	419
15 1/16	8 12/16	6 5/16	Lake Koocanusa, BC	Joseph Kotlarz	Joseph Kotlarz	2003	419
15 1/16	8 12/16	6 5/16	Rio Arriba Co., NM	Michael J. Leonard	Michael J. Leonard	2003	419
15 1/16	8 12/16	6 5/16	Castle River, AB	Flint J. Simpson	Flint J. Simpson	2003	419
15	9	6	Columbia River, WA	J.K. Townsend	Acad. Nat. Sci., Phil.	1834	517
15	9	6	Dotsero, CO	J.T. Meirer	Univ. of KS Museum	1887	517
15	8 12/16	6 4/16	Lincoln Co., MT	Frank Haacke	Philip L. Wright Zool. Mus.	1950	517
15	8 15/16	6 1/16	Salmon River, ID	Bob Hagel	Bob Hagel	1953	517
15	8 13/16	6 3/16	Iron Co., UT	James A. Worthen	James A. Worthen	1958	517
15	8 11/16	6 5/16	Elko Co., NV	Earl Dudley	Earl Dudley	1959	517
15	8 15/16	6 1/16	Invermere, BC	R.A. Merkner	R.A. Merkner	1959	517
15	8 14/16	6 2/16	Salmon River, ID	Roy Tumilsen	Roy Tumilsen	1959	517
15	8 13/16	6 3/16	Flat Creek, AB	Hyrum R. Baker	Hyrum R. Baker	1960	517
15	8 8/16	6 8/16	Magdalena Mts., NM	Frank C. Hibben	Frank C. Hibben	1960	517
15	8 13/16	6 3/16	Cranbrook, BC	Unknown	Aasland Taxidermy	1961	517
15	8 12/16	6 4/16	Onyx, CA	Ray Mallory	Larry Mansfield	1961	517
15	8 12/16	6 4/16	Powell Co., MT	Copenhaver Bros.	Norris Pratt	1961	517
15	8 14/16	6 2/16	Lumby, BC	Ronald Catt	Ronald Catt	1962	517
15	9	6	Jesmond, BC	Charlie Coldwell	Charlie Coldwell	1963	517
15	8 10/16	6 6/16	Socorro Co., NM	Hugh Olney	Hugh Olney	1964	517
15	8 12/16	6 4/16	Mesa Co., CO	John Adams	John Adams	1965	517
15	9	6	Grass Valley, OR	Danny Henderson	Danny Henderson	1965	517
15	8 13/16	6 3/16	Grand Forks, BC	Clarence C. Bahr	Clarence C. Bahr	1966	517
15	8 12/16	6 4/16	West Kootenay, BC	M.E. Goddard	M.E. Goddard	1966	517
15	8 11/16	6 5/16	Darfield, BC	Ted Scott	Ted Scott	1966	517
15	8 12/16	6 4/16	Idaho Co., ID	Jack D. Sheppard	Jack D. Sheppard	1966	517
15	8 13/16	6 3/16	Selway River, ID	Ken Wolfinbarger	Ken Wolfinbarger	1966	517
15	8 12/16	6 4/16	Fisher Creek, AB	Perry Jacobson	Perry Jacobson	1967	517
15	8 14/16	6 2/16	Hanksville, UT	Eddie D. Scheinost	Eddie D. Scheinost	1967	517
15	8 12/16	6 4/16	Ferndale, MT	Loren R. Wittrock	Loren R. Wittrock	1967	517
15	8 14/16	6 2/16	Wolf Creek, MT	Gus R. Wolfe	G.R. Wolfe & J. Lee	1968	517
15	8 11/16	6 5/16	Alpine Co., CA	Jeffrey A. Brent	Jeffrey A. Brent	1968	517
15	8 13/16	6 3/16	Spanish Fork Canyon, UT	Richard C. Smith	Richard C. Smith	1968	517
15	8 11/16	6 5/16	Mizzezula Mts., BC	Bengt G. Bjalme	Bengt G. Bjalme	1969	517
15	8 15/16	6 1/16	Canon City, CO	Dale R. Leonard	Dale R. Leonard	1969	517
15	8 10/16	6 6/16	Ferry Co., WA	John D. Mercer	John D. Mercer	1969	517

Score	Greatest Length of Skull	Greatest Width of Skull	Locality	Killed By	Owner	Date Killed	Rank
15	8 14/16	6 2/16	Lucile, ID	Carl P. Bentz	Mrs. W.H. Prescott, Jr.	1969	517
15	8 12/16	6 4/16	Stevens Co., WA	N. Willey & L. Hedrick	N. Willey & L. Hedrick	1969	517
15	8 12/16	6 4/16	Wells Co., NV	Marvin Johnson	Marvin Johnson	1970	517
15	8 13/16	6 3/16	Canon City, CO	Glen Rosengarten	Glen Rosengarten	1970	517
15	8 13/16	6 3/16	Kootenai Co., ID	George H. Daly	George H. Daly	1971	517
15	9	6	Antelope Pass, CO	Phil Nichols	Phil Nichols	1971	517
15	8 12/16	6 4/16	Stevens Co., WA	Roger Lofts	Roger Lofts	1974	517
15	8 14/16	6 2/16	Las Animas Co., CO	Marion M. Snyder	Mike Powell	1974	517
15	8 12/16	6 4/16	Millard Co., UT	Picked Up	UT Div. of Wildl. Resc.	1974	517
15	8 14/16	6 2/16	Ashcroft, BC	Ken Kilback	Ken Kilback	1975	517
15	8 13/16	6 3/16	Huerfano Co., CO	Sheila D. Bisgard	Sheila D. Bisgard	1977	517
15	8 14/16	6 2/16	Latah Co., ID	Earl Landrus	Earl Landrus	1977	517
15	8 13/16	6 3/16	Prouton Lakes, BC	G.C. Ridley	G.C. Ridley & R. Gillespie	1977	517
15	8 12/16	6 4/16	Union Co., OR	Brian Spencer	Brian Spencer	1979	517
15	8 11/16	6 5/16	Stevens Co., WA	Roger A. Rasching	Roger A. Rasching	1979	517
15	8 15/16	6 1/16	Skokumchuck Creek, BC	Jack Walkley, Jr.	Jack Walkley, Jr.	1980	517
15	8 11/16	6 5/16	Nine Mile Creek, BC	Raymond Carry	Raymond Carry	1980	517
15	8 14/16	6 2/16	Madison Co., MT	George A. Dieruf	George A. Dieruf	1980	517
15	9	6	Washington Co., UT	J. Phil Goodson	J. Phil Goodson	1981	517
15	8 11/16	6 5/16	San Miguel Co., CO	James N. McHolme	James N. McHolme	1982	517
15	8 15/16	6 1/16	Millard Co., UT	William J. Alldredge	William J. Alldredge	1982	517
15	8 12/16	6 4/16	Rio Arriba Co., NM	Michael Ray	Michael Ray	1982	517
15	8 10/16	6 6/16	Teton Co., MT	Richard Klick	John F. Sulik	1983	517
15	8 14/16	6 2/16	Gila Co., AZ	William T. Haney	William T. Haney	1984	517
15	8 10/16	6 6/16	Wallowa Co., OR	Edward C. Cranston	Edward C. Cranston	1985	517
15	8 15/16	6 1/16	Ashnola River, BC	Bill Bryant	Bill Bryant	1985	517
15	8 13/16	6 3/16	Mesa Co., CO	Lawrence C. Glass	Lawrence C. Glass	1986	517
15	8 13/16	6 3/16	San Miguel Co., CO	Jerry J. Jergins	Jerry J. Jergins	1986	517
15	8 15/16	6 1/16	Dolores Co., CO	Ray E. Ables	Ray E. Ables	1986	517
15	9	6	Rio Grande Co., CO	Richard J. Dugas	Richard J. Dugas	1987	517
15	8 14/16	6 2/16	Idaho Co., ID	John G. Klauss	John G. Klauss	1987	517
15	8 15/16	6 1/16	Lewis & Clark Co., MT	Jim Foster	Jim Foster	1987	517
15	8 12/16	6 4/16	Dolores Co., CO	Richard S. Inman	Richard S. Inman	1988	517
15	8 14/16	6 2/16	Deadeye Creek, BC	Claude W. Rohrbaugh	Claude W. Rohrbaugh	1988	517
15	8 11/16	6 5/16	Columbia Co., WA	David N. Bowen	David N. Bowen	1988	517
15	8 13/16	6 3/16	Ferry Co., WA	Arthur E. Crate	Arthur E. Crate	1988	517
15	8 12/16	6 4/16	Big Horn Co., WY	Brant Z. Hilman	Brant Z. Hilman	1989	517
15	8 13/16	6 3/16	Summers Creek, BC	Jack Sprayberry	Jack Sprayberry	1989	517
15	8 14/16	6 2/16	Clear Creek Co., CO	Garry E. Fry	Garry E. Fry	1989	517
15	8 13/16	6 3/16	Pillow Lake, BC	K.T. Michie & T. Wasylyszyn	Kent T. Michie	1989	517
15	8 12/16	6 4/16	Porcupine Hills, AB	Dennis M. Olson	Dennis M. Olson	1989	517
15	8 14/16	6 2/16	Rio Arriba Co., NM	Robert J. Seeds	Robert J. Seeds	1989	517
15	9	6	Elmore Co., ID	Ed J. Strayhorn	Ed J. Strayhorn	1989	517
15	8 11/16	6 5/16	Cotton Creek, BC	Ed Swanson, Jr.	Ed Swanson, Jr.	1989	517
15	8 11/16	6 5/16	Bob Creek, AB	Tom Ellis	Tom Ellis	1990	517
15	8 15/16	6 1/16	Grand Co., UT	Darin King	Darin King	1990	517
15	8 14/16	6 2/16	Carbon Co., UT	Roy Wheeler, Jr.	Roy Wheeler, Jr.	1990	517

COUGAR

Felis concolor hippolestes and related subspecies

Score	Greatest Length of Skull Without Lower Jaw	Greatest Width of Skull	Locality	Hunter	Owner	Date Killed	Rank
15	8 12/16	6 4/16	Kane Co., UT	Robert A. Carlson	Robert A. Carlson	1991	517
15	8 10/16	6 6/16	Granite Co., MT	Hal W. Johnson	Hal W. Johnson	1991	517
15	8 13/16	6 3/16	Eagle Co., CO	James R. Johnston	James R. Johnston	1991	517
15	8 12/16	6 4/16	Spokane Co., WA	Colin F. MacRae	Colin F. MacRae	1991	517
15	8 15/16	6 1/16	Duchesne Co., UT	Lonnie L. Ritchey	Lonnie L. Ritchey	1991	517
15	8 11/16	6 5/16	Wallowa Co., OR	Sharron K. Tarter	Sharron K. Tarter	1991	517
15	8 11/16	6 5/16	Fergus Co., MT	Charles R. Taylor	Charles R. Taylor	1991	517
15	8 11/16	6 5/16	Columbia Co., WA	Paul R. Becker	Paul R. Becker	1992	517
15	8 14/16	6 2/16	Garfield Co., UT	Gregory A. Nixon	Gregory A. Nixon	1992	517
15	8 11/16	6 5/16	Eagle Co., CO	Dwain Spray	Dwain Spray	1992	517
15	9	6	Las Animas Co., CO	Rick E. Tenreiro	Rick E. Tenreiro	1992	517
15	9	6	Lander Co., NV	Travis S. Edgar	Travis S. Edgar	1993	517
15	8 14/16	6 2/16	Utah Co., UT	Jerome F. Heckman, Jr.	Jerome F. Heckman, Jr.	1993	517
15	8 13/16	6 3/16	Wallowa Co., OR	Dwayne E. Heikes	Dwayne E. Heikes	1993	517
15	8 13/16	6 3/16	Clallam Co., WA	Michael A. Reaves	Michael A. Reaves	1993	517
15	8 14/16	6 2/16	Okanogan Co., WA	Harlan R. Tverberg	Harlan R. Tverberg	1993	517
15	8 11/16	6 5/16	Park Co., WY	Jack E. Potter	Jack E. Potter	1994	517
15	8 13/16	6 3/16	Ram River, AB	John M. Straughan	John M. Straughan	1994	517
15	8 13/16	6 3/16	Hawkins Creek, BC	Ross S. Priest	Ross S. Priest	1995	517
15	8 3/16	6 13/16	Powell Co., MT	David F. Skaw	David F. Skaw	1995	517
15	8 13/16	6 3/16	Flathead Co., MT	Larry D. Dahlke	Larry D. Dahlke	1996	517
15	8 12/16	6 4/16	Duchesne Co., UT	Gary A. Durfee	Gary A. Durfee	1996	517
15	8 10/16	6 6/16	Stillwater Co., MT	Darrell G. Holmquist	Darrell G. Holmquist	1996	517
15	8 13/16	6 3/16	Rio Blanco Co., CO	Lyle R. Sigg	Lyle R. Sigg	1996	517
15	8 14/16	6 2/16	Idaho Co., ID	Garold J. Skluzacek	Garold J. Skluzacek	1996	517
15	8 12/16	6 4/16	Routt Co., CO	Bob Barnes	Bob Barnes	1997	517
15	8 12/16	6 4/16	Bonner Co., ID	Shawn Frederickson	Shawn Frederickson	1997	517
15	8 12/16	6 4/16	Bonner Co., ID	W. David Howton	W. David Howton	1997	517
15	8 15/16	6 1/16	Catron Co., NM	Kenneth E. Justus	Kenneth E. Justus	1997	517
15	8 13/16	6 3/16	Invermere, BC	Dave Lougheed	Dave Lougheed	1997	517
15	9 1/16	5 15/16	Routt Co., CO	Tavis D. Rogers	Tavis D. Rogers	1997	517
15	8 14/16	6 2/16	Missoula Co., MT	Mick T. Waletzko	Mick T. Waletzko	1997	517
15	8 14/16	6 2/16	Wallowa Co., OR	John M. Chung	John M. Chung	1998	517
15	8 13/16	6 3/16	Clearwater River, AB	Mark S. Coles	Mark S. Coles	1998	517
15	8 12/16	6 4/16	Crowsnest Pass, AB	Jeff Davis	Jeff B. Davis	1998	517
15	8 13/16	6 3/16	Benewah Co., ID	Donald L. Houk	Donald L. Houk	1998	517
15	8 12/16	6 4/16	Las Animas Co., CO	Barry G. Hasten	Barry G. Hasten	1999	517
15	8 14/16	6 2/16	Archuleta Co., CO	Harry M. Hocker	Harry M. Hocker	1999	517

Score			Hunter	Location	Owner	Date	Rank
15	8 $^{15/16}$	6 $^{1/16}$	Gary E. Huff	San Juan Co., UT	Gary E. Huff	1999	517
15	8 $^{9/16}$	6 $^{7/16}$	Joe R. Kuzmic	Flathead Co., MT	Joe R. Kuzmic	1999	517
15	8 $^{13/16}$	6 $^{3/16}$	Michael L. Lieffring	Lincoln Co., MT	Michael L. Lieffring	1999	517
15	8 $^{12/16}$	6 $^{4/16}$	Robert A. Marod	Ravalli Co., MT	Robert A. Marod	1999	517
15	8 $^{12/16}$	6 $^{4/16}$	Jody T. Nordin	Carbon Co., WY	Jody T. Nordin	2000	517
15	8 $^{13/16}$	6 $^{3/16}$	Bruce E. Young	Rio Arriba Co., NM	Bruce E. Young	2000	517
15	9	6	Jay D. Roche	Custer Co., ID	Jay D. Roche	2001	517
15	8 $^{15/16}$	6 $^{1/16}$	R.L. & M. Anderson	Okanogan Co., WA	Randy L. Anderson	2002	517
15	9	6	Joseph A. Borgna	Bull River, BC	Joseph A. Borgna	2002	517
15	8 $^{10/16}$	6 $^{6/16}$	Gary A. Sholund	Carbon Co., UT	Gary A. Sholund	2002	
15 $^{14/16}$*	9 $^{6/16}$	6 $^{8/16}$	John Rhoden	Wheeler Co., OR	John Rhoden	1996	
15 $^{12/16}$*	9 $^{5/16}$	6 $^{7/16}$	Jesse Dutchik	Lesueur Creek, AB	Jesse Dutchik	1999	
15 $^{10/16}$*	9 $^{3/16}$	6 $^{7/16}$	Richard J. Howden	Sibbald Flat, AB	Richard J. Howden	2002	
15 $^{9/16}$*	9 $^{2/16}$	6 $^{7/16}$	Frank Popson	Heath Creek, AB	F. & K. Popson	2001	

* Final score is subject to revision by additional verifying measurements.

CATEGORY
COUGAR

SCORE
15

HUNTER
GARY E. HUFF

LOCATION
SAN JUAN COUNTY, UTAH

DATE OF KILL
DECEMBER 1999

CATEGORY
COUGAR

SCORE
15-3/16

HUNTER
WILLIAM C. BOEHM (ABOVE LEFT)

OWNER
ADAM W.J. BOEHM (ABOVE RIGHT)

LOCATION
TSUNIAH LAKE,
BRITISH COLUMBIA

DATE OF KILL
DECEMBER 2002

SCORE
15

HUNTER
JOSEPH A. BORGNA (LEFT)

LOCATION
BULL RIVER,
BRITISH COLUMBIA

DATE OF KILL
DECEMBER 2002

CATEGORY
COUGAR

SCORE
15

HUNTER
BARRY G. HASTEN (ABOVE)

LOCATION
LAS ANIMAS COUNTY, COLORADO

DATE OF KILL
DECEMBER 1999

Mr. Akeley filming the climax of a lion hunt. The lion is surrounded by the native spear-throwers who are closing in from all sides.
Photo Courtesy World's Work

Carl Akeley at work on one of his specimens in the American Museum of Natural History, New York. He is here completing one of his celebrated elephant groups.
Photo Courtesy World's Work

CARL E. AKELEY
1864-1926
By Leonard H. Wurman

Carl Akeley gained famed as an innovative museum taxidermist working for Chicago's Field Museum of Natural History and later the American Museum of Natural History in New York City. No longer simply stuffing animal skins, Akeley sculpted forms upon which the skins were mounted, and then set the mount in a diorama that emphasized an interrelation with the natural environment. Akeley led numerous African Safaris collecting specimens. For these, he invented a movie camera that was also used for years in Hollywood. While hunting lowland gorillas, Akeley was impressed by both their ferocity and the gentility, and led the fight to establish a mountain gorilla sanctuary in central Africa. He died studying and filming the gorillas, and is buried there on the slopes of Mt. Mikeno. ■

233

ATLANTIC WALRUS
WORLD'S RECORD

TROPHY INFO

RANK
World's Record

SCORE
118 6/8

LOCATION
Greenland

HUNTER
Unknown

OWNER
Unknown

DATE KILLED
Prior to 1955

The story surrounding this big game World's Record cannot be traced much further back than the 1950s. It was at this time that Roy Vail of Warwick, New York, came across a unique find, the tremendous tusks of an Atlantic walrus (*Odobenus rosmarus rosmarus*). Vail, an importer-exporter of fine hunting supplies, purchased the loose tusks from a G.I. who had brought them back from his tour in Greenland. Having a good eye and genuine interest, Vail had a feeling that the tusks may just measure up as a Boone and Crockett record. On January 14, 1955, the trophy became the new World's Record at 118-6/8 and was generously donated to the National Collection of Heads and Horns.

The immensity of these ivory tusks sparks the imagination. The size of this Atlantic walrus may very well have been 12 feet long and weighed over 3,000 pounds. Tusks such as these would have indicated a superior social rank, providing ample protection during aggressive encounters with rivals as well as natural predators such as polar bears and killer whales. While diving for food, the walrus may have used the tusks to stir up clams and other shellfish along the sea bottom, and after resurfacing, as hooks to climb out of the water or to break up an ice floe for breathing holes.

Following Vail's donation, the record tusks became an educational tool that exhibited an insight into this incredible animal's behavior as well as the way of life of an ancient people. For thousands of years, the walrus has been hunted by the Inuit of Greenland for food and fuel, as well as for making tools, sleds, boats, shelter, and clothing. However, there are others that value the ivory tusks of the walrus merely for their monetary worth. This could very well have been the malicious intent underlying their theft from the National Collection of Heads and Horns at the Bronx Zoo, New York City, in 1974. ■

BOUNDARY FOR ATLANTIC WALRUS

The geographical boundary for Atlantic walrus is basically the Arctic and Atlantic coasts south to Massachusetts. More specifically the Atlantic walrus boundary in Canada extends westward to Mould Bay of Prince Patrick Island, to just east of Cape George Richards of Melville Island and to Taloyoak, Nunavut Province (formerly known as Spence Bay, Northwest Territories); and eastward to include trophies taken in Greenland.

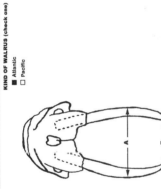

ATLANTIC WALRUS
WORLD'S RECORD SCORE CHART

BOUNDARY FOR ATLANTIC WALRUS

The geographical boundary for Atlantic walrus is basically the Arctic and Atlantic coasts south to Massachusetts. More specifically the Atlantic walrus boundary in Canada extends westward to Mould Bay of Prince Patrick Island, to just east of Cape George Richards of Melville Island and to Taloyoak, Nunavut Province (formerly known as Spence Bay, Northwest Territories); and eastward to include trophies taken in Greenland.

Records of
North American
Big Game

BOONE AND CROCKETT CLUB®

OFFICIAL SCORING SYSTEM FOR NORTH AMERICAN BIG GAME TROPHIES

WALRUS

250 Station Drive
Missoula, MT 59801
(406) 542-1888

MINIMUM SCORES

	AWARDS	ALL-TIME
Atlantic	95	95
Pacific	100	100

KIND OF WALRUS (check one)
■ Atlantic
☐ Pacific

SEE OTHER SIDE FOR INSTRUCTIONS

	COLUMN 1 Right Tusk	COLUMN 2 Left Tusk	COLUMN 3 Difference
A. Greatest Spread (if possible)	--		
B. Tip to Tip Spread (if possible)	--		
C. Entire Length of Loose Tusk	30 5/8	30 3/8	2/8
D-1. Circumference of Base	8 3/8	8 4/8	1/8
D-2. Circumference at First Quarter	8 2/8	8 3/8	1/8
D-3. Circumference at Second Quarter	7	7 2/8	2/8
D-4. Circumference at Third Quarter	5 3/8	5 3/8	0
TOTALS	59 5/8	59 7/8	

ADD	Column 1	59 5/8	Exact Locality Where Killed: Greenland
	Column 2	59 7/8	Date Killed: Prior to 1955
	Subtotal	119 4/8	Owner: Unknown
SUBTRACT Column 3		6/8	Owner's Address:
FINAL SCORE		118 6/8	Guide's Name and Address:

Hunter: Jlft of Roy Vail to N.C.H.M.

Telephone #:

Remarks: (Mention Any Abnormalities or Unique Qualities)

I, _____ **Samuel B. Webb** _____, certify that I hav
PRINT NAME

at **5 Tudor City Place**
STREET ADDRESS

and that these measurements and data are, to the best of my knowledge and b

Witness: ____ **Betty Fitz** ____   Signature: ____ **Samuel B** ____
BAC OFF

COPYRIGHT © 2005 BY BOONE AND CRO

COPYRIGHT © 2005 BY BOONE AND CRO

Atlantic walrus photograph courtesy of Jim Shockey

235

ATLANTIC WALRUS
Odobenus rosmarus rosmarus

MINIMUM SCORE 95

Score	Entire Length of Loose Tusk R	L	Circumference of Base R	L	Circumference at Third Quarter R	L	Locality	Hunter	Owner	Date Killed	Rank
118 6/8	30 5/8	30 3/8	8 3/8	8 4/8	5 3/8	5 3/8	Greenland	Gift of Roy Vail to NCHH	Unknown	PR 1955	1
117 6/8	27 1/8	26 3/8	9 2/8	9 2/8	5 6/8	5 7/8	Greenland, GR	Unknown	Zool. Mus., Copenhagen	PR 1951	2
116 6/8	29 3/8	29 3/8	7 3/8	7 4/8	6	5 7/8	Greenland, GR	Unknown	Zool. Mus., Copenhagen	PR 1951	3
114	28 6/8	28	7 4/8	7 1/8	6	5 7/8	Greenland, GR	Unknown	Zool. Mus., Copenhagen	PR 1951	4
105	25	25	7	7	5 4/8	5 4/8	Greenland, GR	Unknown	Demarest Memorial Mus.	1909	5
103 4/8	24 6/8	25	7 4/8	7 7/8	5 2/8	5	Crockerland, GR	D.B. MacMillan	Am. Mus. Nat. Hist.	PR 1916	6
100 6/8	23 7/8	23 5/8	7 4/8	7 2/8	5 2/8	5 3/8	Unknown	Unknown	Zool. Mus., Copenhagen	PR 1951	7
98 4/8	22 3/8	20 7/8	8 2/8	8 3/8	4 7/8	4 5/8	Arctic Ocean	Gift of Peary Arctic Club	Am. Mus. Nat. Hist.	PR 1899	8
98 4/8	24 4/8	24	6 7/8	6 7/8	5 2/8	5 1/8	Crockerland, GR	D.B. MacMillan	Am. Mus. Nat. Hist.	PR 1916	8
95 6/8	24 4/8	25 1/8	6 6/8	6 4/8	4 3/8	4 3/8	Foxe Basin, NU	Porter Hicks	B&C National Collection	2001	10
95 4/8	22	22 2/8	6 5/8	6 7/8	5 1/8	5 2/8	Foxe Basin, NU	Archie J. Nesbitt	Archie J. Nesbitt	1996	11
95 2/8	22 4/8	22 1/8	7 2/8	7 1/8	4 6/8	4 3/8	Foxe Basin, NU	Ralph F. Merkley	Ralph F. Merkley	2002	12
98 2/8*	24	23 1/8	7 2/8	6 6/8	5	5 2/8	Bencas Island, NU	James A. Bush, Jr.	James A. Bush, Jr.	1997	

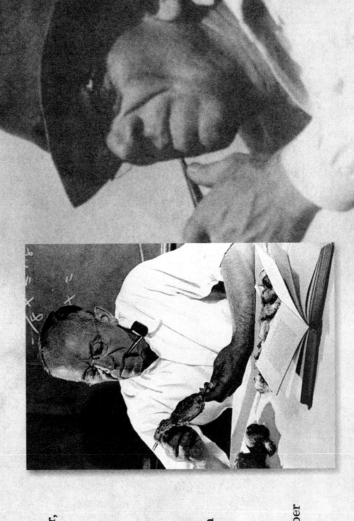

ALDO LEOPOLD
1887-1948
By H. Hudson DeCray

He is considered the father of wildlife ecology. A renowned scientist and scholar, exceptional teacher and philosopher, he was considered conservation's most influential advocate. As a gifted writer, he is best known for his book, *A Sand County Almanac*, often acclaimed as this century's literary landmark in conservation. Born in Iowa, he earned a degree in forestry at Yale and then joined the U.S. Forest Service, serving in the Arizona Territories. His cornerstone book, *Game Management*, defined the fundamental skills and techniques for managing and restoring wildlife populations. He was a professional member of the Boone and Crockett Club. ■

PACIFIC WALRUS
WORLD'S RECORD

TROPHY INFO

RANK
World's Record

SCORE
147 4/8

LOCATION
Bristol Bay, AK

HUNTER
Picked Up

OWNER
Ralph Young

DATE PICKED UP
1997

Searching the shores of Bristol Bay, Alaska, in 1997, Ralph Young picked up a big game World's Record — the colossal tusks of a Pacific walrus (*Odobenus rosmarus divergens*).

Young, who is Commodore of the Naknek Yacht Club, uses his pilot boat to guide barges en route to the salmon canneries along the interior of Bristol Bay. As a man of the sea, an avid hunter, and a pilot who uses his plane to beachcomb "Alaska style," Young has a zest for exploring the Alaskan frontier. He is well aware that the sea deposits many of its treasures in the area, having found Japanese glass ball floats and several walrus and whales. This was particularly evident following a large storm that swept the coast for several days leaving behind a wealth of debris washed upon the shores.

"On July 5th, the engine of my Super Cub coughed and soon settled into its normal steady hum over the muddy salmon-filled waters of Bristol Bay. The wind was gusty and soon the far shore came into view. The tide had reached its lowest point as vast expanses of wet mud and sand became dominant. Alaska is said to be twice the size of Texas, but at low tide, Alaska seems three times the size of Texas. Up ahead on the beach, I spotted a gray oblong form washed up on the sand. As I flew over, two white, ivory tusks could be seen against the contrasting sand. There was a small strip of gravel near the high tide breaker line and the Cub gently alighted on the mark. An axe made the removal of the ivory and mask from the mountain of walrus an easy task. Soon the little Cub was up and heading for the area of Cape Constantine. I spotted

another giant monarch up ahead, close to some hard-pack sand. The tusks seemed to be thicker than others, as I worked to remove them."

Aware that the Pacific walrus may not be hunted by non-native people and may only be possessed in compliance with the 1972 Marine Mammals Protection Act, Young took the find to the Alaska Department of Fish and Game and had them sealed and registered.

"Upon my friend's arrival, he was excited at the size of the tusks, but said they had to be removed from the skull to determine their true size. We took them down to the boat yard and boiled them. After four hours of boiling water filling the air with a unique scent, they were ready to be removed. Heavy gloves gripped the hot tusks as they were slammed down on a 2x12, held in a vise to break them loose. The tape showed each tusk in excess of 36 inches long and nearly 10 inches around each base."

Scored at 147-4/8, the tusks became a highlight of Young's years of beachcombing. ■

PACIFIC WALRUS
WORLD'S RECORD SCORE CHART

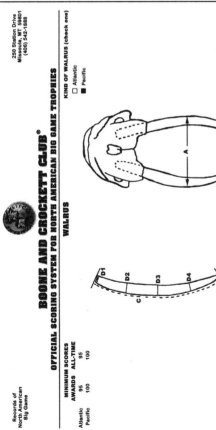

Records of
North American
Big Game

250 Station Drive
Missoula, MT 59801
(406) 542-1888

BOONE AND CROCKETT CLUB®
OFFICIAL SCORING SYSTEM FOR NORTH AMERICAN BIG GAME TROPHIES

	MINIMUM SCORES	
	AWARDS	ALL-TIME
Atlantic	95	95
Pacific	100	100

WALRUS

KIND OF WALRUS (check one)
☐ Atlantic
■ Pacific

SEE OTHER SIDE FOR INSTRUCTIONS		COLUMN 1	COLUMN 2	COLUMN 3
		Right Tusk	Left Tusk	Difference
A. Greatest Spread (if possible)	13 7/8			
B. Tip to Tip Spread (if possible)	11 1/8			
C. Entire Length of Loose Tusk		37 7/8	36 7/8	1
D-1. Circumference of Base		9 7/8	9 7/8	0
D-2. Circumference at First Quarter		10 5/8	10 6/8	1/8
D-3. Circumference at Second Quarter		9 4/8	9 2/8	2/8
D-4. Circumference at Third Quarter		7 1/8	7 1/8	0
TOTALS		75	73 7/8	1 3/8

		Exact Locality Where Killed: Bristol Bay, AK
ADD	Column 1	75	Date Killed: 1997	Hunter: Picked Up
	Column 2	73 7/8	Owner: Ralph Young	Telephone #:
	Subtotal	148 7/8	Owner's Address:
SUBTRACT Column 3	1 3/8	Guide's Name and Address:
FINAL SCORE	147 4/8	Remarks: (Mention Any Abnormalities or Unique Qualities)

I, _____George Tsukamoto_____ , certify that I have measured this trophy on __04/27/1998__
     PRINT NAME   MM/DD/YYYY

at __1080 Icehouse Ave.__ , __Sparks__ , __NV__
   STREET ADDRESS   CITY   STATE/PROVINCE

and that these measurements and data are, to the best of my knowledge and belief, made in accordance with the instructions given.

Witness: __Gerard Beaulieu__   Signature: __George Tsukamoto__   I.D. Number _____
                                        B&C OFFICIAL MEASURER

COPYRIGHT © 2005 BY BOONE AND CROCKETT CLUB®

BOUNDARY FOR PACIFIC WALRUS

That portion of the Bering Sea east of the International Dateline; south along coastal Alaska, including the Pribilof Islands and Bristol Bay; extending eastward into Canada to the southwest coasts of Banks and Victoria Islands and the mouth of Bathurst Inlet in Nunavut Province (formerly the northwest portion of Northwest Territories).

PACIFIC WALRUS
Odobenus rosmarus divergens

MINIMUM SCORE 100

Score	Entire Length of Loose Tusk		Circumference of Base		Circumference at Third Quarter		Locality	Hunter	Owner	Date Killed	Rank
	R	L	R	L	R	L					
147 4/8	37 7/8	36 7/8	9 7/8	9 7/8	7 1/8	7 1/8	Bristol Bay, AK	Picked Up	Ralph Young	1997	1
145 6/8	32 2/8	32 1/8	12 2/8	13	7 2/8	7 1/8	Point Hope, AK	Eskimo	Jonas Bros. of Seattle	1957	2
142 2/8	40 1/8	39 6/8	9 5/8	9 4/8	5 4/8	5 5/8	Bering Sea, AK	Bill Foster	Foster's Bighorn Rest.	1940	3
138 4/8	35 2/8	35 1/8	9 3/8	9 2/8	6 6/8	6 2/8	St. Lawrence Island, AK	Valentin De Madariaga	Valentin De Madariaga	1976	4
137 2/8	36 2/8	36 2/8	9 7/8	10 2/8	6	6 1/8	Alaska	Gift of N.A. Caesar to NCHH	Unknown	PR 1910	5
137	37 1/8	36 4/8	8 4/8	8 3/8	6 4/8	6 4/8	Port Moller, AK	Picked Up	Jim Miller	1999	6
136 4/8	32 6/8	32 4/8	9 5/8	9 3/8	7 4/8	7 2/8	Port Moller, AK	Picked Up	Larry R. Rivers	1981	7
136 2/8	35 6/8	35	9 5/8	9 3/8	6 3/8	6	Bristol Bay, AK	Eskimo	James W. Brooks	1955	8
135	38	36 3/8	9	9 4/8	5 6/8	5 6/8	Unknown	Picked Up	Paul Umlauf	1970	9
134 6/8	34	34 2/8	9 3/8	9 4/8	6	6	Wainwright, AK	Helen Burnett	Helen Burnett	1964	10
133 6/8	32 2/8	32 6/8	9 4/8	9 4/8	6 6/8	6 7/8	Diomede Islands, AK	Eskimo	Univ. of IA Museum	1893	11
133 6/8	34 4/8	36 3/8	8 7/8	8 5/8	6 4/8	6 4/8	Togiak Bay, AK	Picked Up	William W. Renfrew	1949	11
133 6/8	32 6/8	32	9 1/8	9 1/8	7 2/8	7 1/8	Port Heiden, AK	Picked Up	John T. Taylor	1980	11
133 4/8	37 3/8	37 2/8	7 4/8	7 5/8	6 1/8	6 3/8	Cape Seniavin, AK	Picked Up	Patrick C. Martin	1985	14
133	35	35 2/8	8 4/8	8 4/8	6	6	St. Lawrence Island, AK	Eskimo	Eugene E. Saxton	1956	15
132 6/8	36 2/8	37 3/8	8 1/8	8	6 2/8	6	Port Moller, AK	Picked Up	R. Hammack & J. Hammack	1984	16
132 4/8	38 1/8	37 6/8	8 5/8	8 6/8	5 4/8	5 5/8	Alaska	Unknown	Harvard Univ. Mus.	1870	17
132 4/8	37 6/8	35 3/8	8 6/8	8 6/8	6 2/8	5 5/8	St. Lawrence Island, AK	Eskimo	Adventurers Club of N.Y.	1964	17
132 4/8	34 1/8	34	10 3/8	9 3/8	6 2/8	5 7/8	Hazen Bay, AK	Daniel B. Moore	Daniel B. Moore	1979	17
132 4/8	31 5/8	31 6/8	9	9	7 6/8	7 1/8	Goodnews Bay, AK	Picked Up	Jim Riggle	2000	17
132 2/8	33 6/8	32 5/8	9 2/8	9	6 5/8	6 4/8	St. Lawrence Island, AK	Robert F. Hurford	Robert F. Hurford	PR 1971	21
132 2/8	33 2/8	33 6/8	8 6/8	9	6 6/8	7	Bering Sea, AK	Unknown	R. & C. Ballow	1959	21
132	35 2/8	34	9 4/8	8 7/8	7 1/8	5 7/8	Savoonga, AK	Unknown	Victor Rovier	1967	23
132	29	28 6/8	10 4/8	10 5/8	7 3/8	6 7/8	Savoonga, AK	Gordon Iya	C. Vernon Humble	1977	23
131 4/8	36 3/8	35 2/8	8 4/8	8 4/8	5 5/8	5 5/8	Bering Sea, AK	Gift of W.H. White	Am. Mus. Nat. Hist.	1916	25
131 2/8	33 1/8	33 4/8	8 4/8	8 4/8	6 4/8	6 4/8	Wainwright, AK	Eskimo	Ken Armstrong	PR 1946	26
131 2/8	34 3/8	34 6/8	8 6/8	9	5 7/8	5 7/8	Togiak Bay, AK	Picked Up	Clifford H. Driskell	1968	26
131 2/8	31 5/8	31 6/8	9 1/8	9 4/8	6 6/8	6 4/8	Savoonga, AK	Robert M. Vinovich	Robert M. Vinovich	1976	26
131	33 5/8	32 3/8	8 5/8	8 5/8	6 2/8	6 2/8	Hagemeister Island, AK	Picked Up	Frank M. Thomason	1964	29
130 6/8	33 5/8	32 4/8	8 7/8	9 1/8	6 3/8	6 4/8	St. Lawrence Island, AK	Peter W. Bading	Peter W. Bading	1960	30
130 6/8	31 6/8	32 4/8	8 7/8	9 1/8	6 7/8	7	Port Moller, AK	Picked Up	John Sarvis	1980	30
130 4/8	34 7/8	34 4/8	8 2/8	8	6 3/8	6 1/8	St. Lawrence Island, AK	Unknown	Univ. of Alaska	PR 1939	32
130 4/8	36 4/8	35 7/8	8 4/8	8	6 3/8	5 6/8	St. Lawrence Island, AK	George H. Landreth	George H. Landreth	1967	32
130 2/8	34 6/8	35	9	8	5 6/8	5 4/8	Point Barrow, AK	Eskimo	William E. Moss	1952	34
130 2/8	31 2/8	32	8 7/8	8 7/8	7 2/8	7 1/8	St. Lawrence Island, AK	Grancel Fitz	Mrs. Grancel Fitz	1957	34
129 4/8	34 6/8	33 4/8	8 3/8	8 3/8	6 4/8	6 1/8	Bering Sea, AK	Joseph J. Cafmeyer	Joseph J. Cafmeyer	1976	36
129 4/8	32	32	9	8 6/8	6 7/8	6 4/8	Izembek Lagoon, AK	Picked Up	John Sarvis	1981	36
129 4/8	32 5/8	32 7/8	8 5/8	8 5/8	6 2/8	6 3/8	Port Heiden, AK	Picked Up	Donald R. Warren	1982	36

Score	(1)	(2)	(3)	(4)	(5)	(6)	Locality	By Whom Killed	Owner	Date	Rank
129 4/8	36 5/8	34 6/8	7 6/8	7 4/8	6 1/8	6 4/8	Cape Seniavin, AK	Picked Up	Herman C. Meyer	1993	36
128 4/8	36	35 4/8	8	7 7/8	5 4/8	5 4/8	Goodnews Bay, AK	Picked Up	David S. Haeg	1994	40
128 2/8	32 2/8	32 2/8	9	9	9 1/8	9 1/8	St. Lawrence Island, AK	C. Pelowook	Charles A. LeKites	1968	41
128	30 6/8	30 4/8	9 2/8	9 2/8	7 1/8	7	Nome, AK	William M. Wheless III	William M. Wheless III	1977	42
127 6/8	32 7/8	33	8 7/8	9	6	5 5/8	St. Lawrence Island, AK	Charles F. Kleptz	Charles F. Kleptz	1978	43
127 4/8	35 6/8	34 4/8	8 2/8	8 5/8	5 4/8	5 2/8	Port Heiden, AK	Chris Klineburger	Chris Klineburger	1961	44
127 4/8	32 2/8	30 3/8	8 6/8	9	6 6/8	6 6/8	Wainwright, AK	Picked Up	Larry R. Rivers	1981	44
127 2/8	33 7/8	34 6/8	8 3/8	8 1/8	5 4/8	5 4/8	Point Barrow, AK	J. Richard Reuter III	J. Richard Reuter III	1970	46
127	32 4/8	32 4/8	8 3/8	8 3/8	6 1/8	6 1/8	St. Lawrence Island, AK	Karl W. Opryshek	Karl W. Opryshek	1965	47
127	33	33	9	8 5/8	5 6/8	6	St. Lawrence Island, AK	Norman W. Garwood	Norman W. Garwood	1976	47
127	32 4/8	32 5/8	9	8 5/8	6	6 2/8	Cape Pierce, AK	Dick Ullery	Dick Ullery	1976	47
127	34 2/8	34 2/8	7 5/8	8 4/8	6	6 1/8	Gambell, AK	Picked Up	David S. Haeg	1992	47
126 4/8	31 6/8	31 6/8	8 7/8	8 6/8	6 1/8	6 1/8	St. Lawrence Island, AK	Eskimo	Mike W. Millar	1982	51
126 2/8	32 3/8	32 7/8	8 4/8	8 5/8	6 2/8	6 2/8	Point Barrow, AK	Martin J. Foerster	Martin J. Foerster	1958	52
126 2/8	31 6/8	31 1/8	8 6/8	9	5 3/8	5 3/8	Savoonga, AK	Eskimo	Walter O. Sinn	1958	52
126 2/8	34 3/8	34 4/8	8 1/8	9	5 6/8	5 6/8	Alaska Pen., AK	Unknown	Wayne S. Weiler	1978	52
126	33 4/8	33	8	8	6 1/8	6 1/8	Bering Sea, AK	Unknown	Sam Pancotto	1962	55
126	31 1/8	31 3/8	8 3/8	8 4/8	6 6/8	6 7/8	St. Lawrence Island, AK	Wakon I. Redbird	Wakon I. Redbird	1977	55
125 6/8	34 2/8	34 5/8	7 6/8	7 6/8	5 6/8	5 6/8	Bering Sea, AK	Eskimo	Sidney T. Shore	1950	57
125 6/8	30 4/8	30 4/8	9 3/8	9 5/8	6 1/8	6 1/8	Gambell, AK	F.J. Bremer	F.J. Bremer	1971	57
125 4/8	35	34 4/8	8 5/8	9 1/8	4 7/8	4 7/8	Bering Sea, AK	Manfred O. Schroeder	Manfred O. Schroeder	1977	59
125	30 7/8	30 6/8	9 4/8	8 6/8	5 7/8	5 7/8	St. Lawrence Island, AK	Charles H.L. McLaughlin	Charles H.L. McLaughlin	1978	60
124 6/8	33 6/8	33 5/8	8 3/8	8 2/8	5 2/8	5 2/8	Bering Sea, AK	Henry A. Snow	Snow Museum	1923	61
124 6/8	30 7/8	32	9 4/8	8 6/8	5 3/8	5 3/8	St. Lawrence Island, AK	Bert Klineburger	Bert Klineburger	1962	61
124 6/8	31 3/8	31	8 6/8	8 2/8	5 7/8	5 7/8	Cape Seniavin, AK	Unknown	R. & C. Ballow	PR 1971	61
124 6/8	31 7/8	31 5/8	8 2/8	8 7/8	5 7/8	5 7/8	St. Lawrence Island, AK	Picked Up	James A. Atkins	1990	61
124 4/8	32 4/8	32 4/8	8 2/8	8 2/8	5 3/8	5 3/8	Pilot Point, AK	Tim Gollorgeren	George H. Landreth	1966	65
124 4/8	32 7/8	32 7/8	8 4/8	7 5/8	5 6/8	5 6/8	Nunivak Island, AK	Picked Up	Dick Gunlogson	PR 1969	65
124 4/8	36 2/8	35 6/8	7 1/8	7	5 3/8	5 3/8	Hagemeister Island, AK	Terry Yager	Terry Yager	1977	65
124 2/8	31 2/8	30 4/8	8 3/8	8 3/8	6 3/8	6 2/8	Port Moller, AK	Picked Up	Lloyd D. Friend	1979	65
124 2/8	31 5/8	31 6/8	7 7/8	8	6 2/8	6 2/8	Bering Sea, AK	F.E. Klinesmith	Daniel W. Wray	1995	65
124	32 6/8	32 6/8	8 4/8	8	5 6/8	5 6/8	St. Lawrence Island, AK	Bert Klineburger	Am. Mus. Nat. Hist.	PR 1951	70
123 6/8	35	33 6/8	7 5/8	7 3/8	5 6/8	5 5/8	St. Lawrence Island, AK	Eskimo	Bert Klineburger	1969	71
123 6/8	34 7/8	33 4/8	7 6/8	7 6/8	5 1/8	5 2/8	Little Diomede Island, AK	Eskimo	James W. Brooks	1953	72
123 4/8	33 7/8	33 3/8	8	8 3/8	6 2/8	6 3/8	Bering Sea, AK	Dick Salemi	Dick Salemi	1978	72
123 4/8	29 3/8	29 1/8	8 6/8	9	5 6/8	5 7/8	St. Lawrence Island, AK	C.J. McElroy	C.J. McElroy	1968	74
123 2/8	31 5/8	31 5/8	8 1/8	9	5 6/8	5 6/8	Bering Sea, AK	Dan H. Brainard	Dan H. Brainard	1977	74
123 2/8	30	29 7/8	9 4/8	8 1/8	6 1/8	5 6/8	Bering Sea, AK	Arthur H. Bullerdick	Arthur H. Bullerdick	1978	74
123 2/8	34	31 7/8	8 4/8	8 4/8	6 2/8	6 1/8	Alaskan Arctic	Eskimo	Robert C. Reeve	PR 1955	77
123 2/8	32 3/8	32 2/8	7 4/8	7 4/8	6 3/8	6 2/8	Nakuck, AK	Unknown	Leonard Schwah	1964	77
123	28 5/8	28 2/8	9 7/8	9 7/8	6 3/8	6 3/8	Teller, AK	W.J. Glunt	W.J. Glunt	1965	77
123	32 5/8	32 1/8	7 4/8	7 4/8	6	6	Cape Constantine, AK	Picked Up	Ray Tremblay	1960	80
123	31	32 5/8	8	7 5/8	5 5/8	6	St. Lawrence Island, AK	F. Phillips Williamson	F. Phillips Williamson	1961	80
122 6/8	33	31 2/8	7 6/8	8	6 4/8	6	Nunivak Island, AK	Arvid F. Benson	Arvid F. Benson	1970	80
122 6/8	32 3/8	31 6/8	8 1/8	8 1/8	5 6/8	5 6/8	Alaska	George Wright	Acad. Nat. Sci., Phil.	1960	83
122 4/8	32 5/8	31 4/8	8 3/8	8 4/8	5 7/8	5 7/8	Savoonga, AK	Lynn M. Castle	Lynn M. Castle	1971	83
122 4/8	32 1/8						St. Lawrence Island, AK	Herb Klein	Dallas Mus. of Natl. Hist.	1959	85

PACIFIC WALRUS
Odobenus rosmarus divergens

MINIMUM SCORE 100

Score	Entire Length of Loose Tusk R	L	Circumference of Base R	L	Circumference at Third Quarter R	L	Locality	Hunter	Owner	Date Killed	Rank
122 4/8	32 2/8	32 5/8	8 2/8	8	5 4/8	5 5/8	Savoonga, AK	William W. Garrison	William W. Garrison	1971	85
122 2/8	30	32 2/8	8 2/8	8 2/8	6 3/8	6 2/8	Walrus Island, AK	Unknown	Robert C. Reeve	1962	87
122 2/8	30 5/8	31 4/8	8 5/8	8 7/8	5 6/8	5 6/8	Alaska	Unknown	R. & C. Ballow	1996	87
122	27 2/8	28 6/8	10 2/8	10 2/8	5 7/8	6	Diomede Islands, AK	Tony Oney	Tony Oney	1964	89
122	31 4/8	31	9 1/8	9 2/8	5 3/8	5 3/8	St. Lawrence Island, AK	Ted Lick	Ted Lick	1970	89
121 6/8	31 7/8	32 6/8	8 1/8	8 6/8	5 3/8	5 4/8	Diomede Islands, AK	Jim Harrower	Tony Oney	1964	91
121 4/8	31 6/8	31	8 4/8	8 4/8	5 4/8	5 4/8	Savoonga, AK	Gerald G. Balciar	Gerald G. Balciar	1971	92
121 2/8	31 3/8	31 2/8	8 3/8	8 4/8	5 3/8	5 6/8	Savoonga, AK	Lowell C. Hansen II	Lowell C. Hansen II	1978	93
121 2/8	33 7/8	29 3/8	8 2/8	8 1/8	6 7/8	6 5/8	Alaska Pen., AK	Picked Up	Richard A. Pulley	1994	93
121	33 2/8	34 1/8	7 6/8	7 5/8	5 5/8	5 3/8	Bering Sea, AK	Eskimo	Elmer Keith	1956	95
121	28	28 5/8	11 2/8	9 6/8	5 6/8	5 7/8	Little Diomede Island, AK	William H. Picher	William H. Picher	1966	95
121	29 4/8	29 4/8	8 2/8	8 2/8	6 3/8	6	Nunivak Island, AK	C. Vernon Humble	C. Vernon Humble	1977	95
120 6/8	29	29 1/8	8 4/8	8 3/8	6 3/8	5 7/8	Little Diomede Island, AK	Robert Curtis	Robert Curtis	1963	98
120 6/8	33 6/8	34	6 7/8	7	5 3/8	5 4/8	Point Hope, AK	Don Johnson	Don Johnson	1963	98
120 6/8	29 7/8	30 4/8	8 4/8	8 7/8	6	6	Cape Thompson, AK	Eskimo	Nick Petropolis	PR 1965	98
120 6/8	29	30 1/8	9	9	5 7/8	5 6/8	Gambell, AK	L. Keith Mortensen	L. Keith Mortensen	1978	98
120 4/8	33 4/8	33 4/8	7	7 1/8	5 2/8	5 3/8	Alaska	S.R. Caldwell	Acad. Nat. Sci., Phil.	1902	102
120 2/8	28 7/8	29 1/8	9	9 1/8	5 4/8	5 4/8	Savoonga, AK	Werner-Rolf Muno	Werner-Rolf Muno	1971	103
120 2/8	30 2/8	29 4/8	8 4/8	8 3/8	5 7/8	5 7/8	Hazen Bay, AK	Richard D. Dimick	Richard D. Dimick	1979	103
120	29	27 5/8	9 1/8	9 3/8	6 1/8	6	Bristol Bay, AK	Eskimo	Foster H. Thompson	PR 1959	105
120	33	30 6/8	8 4/8	8 4/8	5 2/8	6	St. Lawrence Island, AK	Sarkis Atamian	Sarkis Atamian	1968	105
120	31 6/8	28 1/8	8 7/8	8 4/8	5 6/8	6	Bering Sea, AK	George L. Hall	George L. Hall	1977	105
119 6/8	28	33 1/8	9 3/8	8 7/8	6 5/8	6 5/8	Savoonga, AK	Edwin L. Cox, Jr.	Edwin L. Cox, Jr.	1977	108
119 6/8	31 6/8	33 1/8	7 1/8	7 1/8	6 3/8	6 1/8	Bristol Bay, AK	Picked Up	Eddie Clark	1990	108
119 2/8	31 1/8	31 2/8	7 6/8	8	5 4/8	5 4/8	Bering Sea, AK	Unknown	Gary Babcock	PR 1975	110
119 2/8	31 5/8	30 3/8	8	8	5 7/8	5 7/8	Port Moller, AK	Douglas E. Miller	Douglas E. Miller	1976	110
119	31 4/8	30 2/8	9 1/8	8 4/8	5 5/8	5 1/8	Diomede Islands, AK	Picked Up	Bob Stokes	1961	112
118 4/8	28 3/8	28 6/8	8 2/8	8 4/8	6 2/8	5 7/8	St. Lawrence Island, AK	Harry J. Armitage	Harry J. Armitage	1965	113
118 4/8	29 3/8	28 7/8	8 7/8	8 3/8	6 1/8	5 7/8	St. Lawrence Island, AK	Alice J. Landreth	Alice J. Landreth	1967	113
118 4/8	29 2/8	28 2/8	8 4/8	8 7/8	6 6/8	5 6/8	St. Lawrence Island, AK	Wilbur L. Leworthy	Wilbur L. Leworthy	1970	113
118 4/8	31 4/8	32	7 4/8	7 4/8	5 1/8	5 2/8	St. Lawrence Island, AK	Clifford Patz	Clifford Patz	1979	113
118 2/8	30 4/8	28 7/8	7 7/8	8	5 5/8	5 5/8	Savoonga, AK	Jack Schwabland	Jack Schwabland	1978	117
117 2/8	29	28 4/8	8	7 6/8	6	5 7/8	Little Diomede Island, AK	Robert Curtis	Robert Curtis	1963	118
117 2/8	28	30 1/8	8 5/8	8 2/8	6 4/8	5 7/8	St. Lawrence Island, AK	C. Pitt Sanders	C. Pitt Sanders	1978	118
116 6/8	28 6/8	26 7/8	8 6/8	9	6	6	Little Diomede Island, AK	Eskimo	Tony Oney	1962	120
116 4/8	28 6/8	27 2/8	8 7/8	8 5/8	6	6	Savoonga, AK	Arnold Carlson	Arnold Carlson	1971	121
116 4/8	28 4/8	29	8 4/8	8	6	6	Nunivak Island, AK	Darrell D. Wells	Darrell D. Wells	1978	121
116 2/8	29	29 3/8	8	8	5 7/8	5 7/8	Savoonga, AK	Unknown	R. & C. Ballow	PR 1994	123
116	28	28	8 3/8	8 3/8	5 6/8	5 5/8	Point Hope, AK	Picked Up	William C. Penttila	1965	124

Score	Length R	Length L	Base Cir. R	Base Cir. L	3rd Qtr Cir. R	3rd Qtr Cir. L	Locality	By Whom Collected	Owner	Date	Rank
116	30 3/8	29 6/8	8 6/8	8 2/8	5 1/8	5	Bering Sea, AK	Hugh L. Nichols, Jr.	Hugh L. Nichols, Jr.	1972	124
115 6/8	28 7/8	29	7 6/8	8 2/8	5 7/8	5 6/8	St. Lawrence Island, AK	Hugh H. Logan	U.S. Natl. Museum	1962	126
115 6/8	27 3/8	31 4/8	8 1/8	8	6 3/8	6	Savoonga, AK	Peter A. Bossart	Peter A. Bossart	1972	126
115 6/8	30 5/8	29 6/8	8	7 7/8	5 3/8	5 3/8	St. Lawrence Island, AK	Gerald L. Warnock	Gerald L. Warnock	1977	126
115 4/8	30 2/8	30 1/8	7 6/8	7 4/8	5 4/8	5 3/8	Diomede Islands, AK	Unknown	Univ. of Alaska	1953	129
115 4/8	27 2/8	25 2/8	9 2/8	9 2/8	6 1/8	6 1/8	St. Lawrence Island, AK	W.T. Yoshimoto	W.T. Yoshimoto	1962	129
115 4/8	28 1/8	28 2/8	7 6/8	7 6/8	6 2/8	6 2/8	Little Diomede Island, AK	Basil C. Bradbury	Basil C. Bradbury	1964	129
115 2/8	30 4/8	31	7 2/8	7 4/8	5 1/8	5 3/8	Little Diomede Island, AK	Jack D. Putnam	Jack D. Putnam	1965	132
115 2/8	27 6/8	31 6/8	8 6/8	8 7/8	5 5/8	5 2/8	Nunivak Island, AK	Lloyd B. Ward, Jr.	Lloyd B. Ward, Jr.	1971	132
115 2/8	28 5/8	28	7 7/8	8	5 4/8	5 6/8	Port Heiden, AK	Picked Up	Shawn R. Andres	1997	132
115	32 2/8	31 5/8	6 6/8	6 7/8	5 4/8	5 4/8	St. Lawrence Island, AK	Unknown	P.J. Londo	2001	136
114 6/8	31 1/8	30 7/8	6 7/8	7	5 4/8	5 6/8	Savoonga, AK	John L. Estes	John L. Estes	1978	137
114 6/8	29 6/8	29 4/8	7 6/8	7 6/8	5 3/8	5	Point Hope, AK	Eskimo	Jonas Bros. of Alaska	1958	137
114 4/8	29	29 5/8	7 6/8	7 5/8	5 6/8	5 6/8	Kigluaik Mts., AK	Russell H. Underdahl	Russell H. Underdahl	1978	139
114	29 3/8	29 4/8	8 2/8	8 2/8	5 1/8	5 1/8	Savoonga, AK	Richard G. Van Vorst	Richard G. Van Vorst	1976	140
113 6/8	26 4/8	26 6/8	9 6/8	9 5/8	5 2/8	5 2/8	Kotzebue, AK	E.B. Rhodes	E.B. Rhodes	1964	141
113 6/8	28 7/8	26 6/8	9	9	5 1/8	5	St. Lawrence Island, AK	Maitland Armstrong	Maitland Armstrong	1961	141
113 6/8	26	26 1/8	8 2/8	8 1/8	5 1/8	5 2/8	Point Hope, AK	Glenn W. Slade, Jr.	Glenn W. Slade, Jr.	1961	141
113 6/8	29	29 5/8	7 5/8	7 6/8	5 2/8	5 3/8	Point Hope, AK	Eskimo	John W. Elmore	1966	141
113 6/8	29 4/8	28 2/8	7 3/8	7 3/8	5 6/8	5 5/8	St. Lawrence Island, AK	Denver D. Coleman	Denver D. Coleman	1968	141
113 6/8	28 4/8	28 5/8	7 5/8	7 5/8	5 6/8	5 4/8	St. Lawrence Island, AK	Dick Davis	Dick Davis	1976	141
113 4/8	31 3/8	30 5/8	7 3/8	7 2/8	5 1/8	5 1/8	Savoonga, AK	Warren K. Parker	Warren K. Parker	1979	147
113 2/8	28 7/8	28 5/8	7 5/8	7 4/8	5 4/8	5 4/8	Savoonga, AK	Tom Andersen	Tom Andersen	1978	148
113 2/8	27 5/8	27 2/8	8 6/8	8 3/8	5 3/8	5 3/8	St. Lawrence Island, AK	W. Brandon Macomber	W. Brandon Macomber	1965	148
113 2/8	28 1/8	28 3/8	8 2/8	8 3/8	5	5	Nunivak Island, AK	C.R. Feazell	C.R. Feazell	1972	148
113	27 5/8	27 5/8	7 5/8	7 5/8	6 2/8	5 7/8	Bering Sea, AK	Jack M. Holland, Jr.	Jack M. Holland, Jr.	1978	151
113	29 5/8	29 1/8	8 1/8	8	5	5	St. Lawrence Island, AK	Jim Roe	Jim Roe	1969	151
113	30 4/8	29 1/8	7 7/8	7 3/8	5 4/8	5 4/8	St. Lawrence Island, AK	I.D. Shapiro	I.D. Shapiro	1970	151
113	28	27	8 3/8	8	5 5/8	5 5/8	Bering Sea, AK	Gail W. Holderman	Gail W. Holderman	1976	151
112 6/8	27 1/8	26	8 1/8	8	6	5 1/8	St. Lawrence Island, AK	Jon E. Holland	Jon E. Holland	1978	156
112 4/8	31 7/8	31	6 6/8	6 6/8	4 6/8	4 6/8	Bering Sea, AK	G.A. Treschow	G.A. Treschow	1979	157
112 4/8	27 7/8	27 6/8	8 2/8	8 1/8	5 1/8	5 3/8	St. Lawrence Island, AK	Alfred F. Corwin	Alfred F. Corwin	1964	157
112 4/8	28 1/8	27 7/8	7 7/8	7 4/8	5 3/8	5 2/8	St. Lawrence Island, AK	Henry K. Leworthy	Henry K. Leworthy	1970	157
112 4/8	27 7/8	27 6/8	8 2/8	8 2/8	5 4/8	5 4/8	Togiak Bay, AK	Picked Up	Lloyd E. Zeman	PR 1970	157
112 2/8	28 6/8	27 5/8	7 5/8	7 4/8	5 5/8	5 5/8	Savoonga, AK	Harm De Boer	Harm De Boer	1972	161
111 6/8	25	23 6/8	8 6/8	8 5/8	6 4/8	6 6/8	Nunivak Island, AK	William K. Leech	William K. Leech	1966	162
111 4/8	29 4/8	28 7/8	7 4/8	7 6/8	5 1/8	5	St. Lawrence Island, AK	Eskimo	George H. Landreth	1968	162
111 4/8	27 4/8	32 1/8	8 6/8	8 4/8	4 4/8	6	Point Hope, AK	Gary D'Aigle	Gary D'Aigle	1968	162
111	30 4/8	26 4/8	8 1/8	8 1/8	5 7/8	5 2/8	St. Lawrence Island, AK	Don L. Corley	Don L. Corley	1977	165
111	30 4/8	29 5/8	6 7/8	6 7/8	5 3/8	5 5/8	Strogonof Point, AK	Picked Up	Brian G. Oldfield	1993	165
110 6/8	28 3/8	28 1/8	7	7	5 5/8	5 5/8	Savoonga, AK	Robert E. Speegle	Robert E. Speegle	1972	167
110 4/8	28 5/8	30	7 7/8	7 7/8	4 5/8	4 7/8	St. Lawrence Island, AK	Don B. Skidmore	Don B. Skidmore	1977	168
110 2/8	29 1/8	30 1/8	7 6/8	7 6/8	4 6/8	4 6/8	Savoonga, AK	John M. Blair	John M. Blair	1971	169
110 2/8	29 7/8	27 5/8	6 3/8	6 3/8	5 6/8	5 7/8	St. Lawrence Island, AK	Hugh H. Logan	Los Angeles Co. Mus.	1962	169
110 2/8	27 4/8	27 4/8	8	8	5 4/8	5 1/8	St. Lawrence Island, AK	Robert Rood	Robert Rood	1966	169
110 2/8	27	26 4/8	8 1/8	8 1/8	5 4/8	5 3/8	Kuskokwim Bay, AK	James Lewis	Steve R. Bayless	1969	169
110 2/8	30 4/8	30 3/8	6 5/8	6 5/8	4 7/8	4 6/8	Nunivak Island, AK	Arthur LaCapria	Arthur LaCapria	1971	169

PACIFIC WALRUS
Odobenus rosmarus divergens

Score	Entire Length of Loose Tusk		Circumference of Base		Circumference at Third Quarter		Locality	Hunter	Owner	Date Killed	Rank
	R	L	R	L	R	L					
110 2/8	27 6/8	28	7 6/8	7 7/8	5	5	Point Barrow, AK	Cecil M. Hopper	Cecil M. Hopper	1972	169
110 2/8	28 6/8	28 6/8	7 3/8	7 2/8	5 1/8	4 7/8	St. Lawrence Island, AK	Wayne S. Weiler	Wayne S. Weiler	1972	169
110 2/8	28 3/8	28 2/8	7 2/8	7 2/8	5 2/8	5 2/8	St. Lawrence Island, AK	James A. Bush, Jr.	James A. Bush, Jr.	1979	169
110 2/8	29 7/8	29 1/8	7 3/8	7 3/8	4 7/8	4 6/8	St. Lawrence Island, AK	Eskimo	Val Tibbetts	1979	169
110	27 6/8	28 6/8	7 1/8	7 4/8	5 2/8	5 2/8	Nelson Island, AK	Picked Up	Brent R. Akers	1987	176
109 6/8	28 1/8	28 2/8	7 3/8	7 4/8	5	5	Point Franklin, AK	Michael R. Bogan	Michael R. Bogan	1978	177
109 4/8	26 4/8	26 2/8	8 2/8	8 2/8	5	5 2/8	Savoonga, AK	Richard A. Furniss	Richard A. Furniss	1972	178
109 4/8	27 6/8	27 5/8	8	8	4 7/8	5 3/8	St. Lawrence Island, AK	Mahlon T. White	Mahlon T. White	1977	178
108 6/8	28 6/8	27 1/8	7 7/8	7 2/8	5 6/8	5 3/8	St. Lawrence Island, AK	T.E. Shillingburg	T.E. Shillingburg	1961	180
108 6/8	24 6/8	24 5/8	8 3/8	8 6/8	5 6/8	5 7/8	Naknek, AK	Picked Up	Dean Collins	1982	180
108 6/8	30 6/8	30 7/8	7	6 7/8	4 4/8	5 4/8	Wainwright, AK	Delano J. Lietzau	Delano J. Lietzau	1978	182
108 4/8	27	30	7 3/8	7 1/8	5 1/8	5 1/8	Little Diomede Island, AK	Barrie White	Barrie White	1963	183
108 2/8	26 5/8	28 4/8	7 6/8	7 6/8	4 6/8	4 7/8	Bering Sea, AK	Gary Boychuk	Gary Boychuk	1977	184
107 2/8	27 2/8	27 5/8	7 2/8	7 2/8	5 1/8	5 1/8	St. Lawrence Island, AK	William A. Bond	William A. Bond	1964	185
107	26 5/8	26	7 3/8	7 2/8	5 4/8	5 1/8	Savoonga, AK	Jon G. Koshell	Jon G. Koshell	1972	186
106	23 3/8	23 3/8	7 1/8	7 1/8	6 2/8	6 2/8	St. Lawrence Island, AK	L.M. Cole	L.M. Cole	1964	187
104 4/8	26 4/8	26 7/8	7 5/8	7 4/8	4 6/8	4 5/8	Bering Sea, AK	Rudolf Sand	Rudolf Sand	1971	187
104 4/8	26 4/8	26 4/8	7 4/8	7 7/8	4 7/8	5	Savoonga, AK	Andrew A. Samuels, Jr.	Andrew A. Samuels, Jr.	1979	190
104	24 7/8	26	8	8	5	5 2/8	St. Lawrence Island, AK	Norman S. MacPhee	B&C National Collection	1978	190
104	27 7/8	26 3/8	6 4/8	6 4/8	5 1/8	5 4/8	Wainwright, AK	Donald R. Theophilus	Donald R. Theophilus	1978	192
103 2/8	26	26 1/8	6 7/8	6 6/8	4 7/8	5	Point Barrow, AK	Glenn W. Slade, Jr.	Glenn W. Slade, Jr.	1968	192
103 2/8	27 3/8	27 4/8	6 3/8	6 2/8	5 1/8	4 5/8	St. Lawrence Island, AK	Gunther Matschke	Gunther Matschke	1972	194
102 6/8	28 2/8	25 4/8	6 5/8	6 3/8	5 5/8	5 4/8	Port Moller, AK	Picked Up	Dan Lynch	1966	194
102	25 3/8	25 3/8	7 2/8	7 4/8	4 5/8	4 5/8	St. Lawrence Island, AK	Dalton Foster	Dalton Foster	1961	195
102	24 6/8	25	7 4/8	7 5/8	4 5/8	4 6/8	Savoonga, AK	Robert J. Bartlett	Robert J. Bartlett	1979	195
101 2/8	26 7/8	27 5/8	6 7/8	7	4 2/8	4 6/8	St. Lawrence Island, AK	Eskimo	Steve Fowler	1967	197

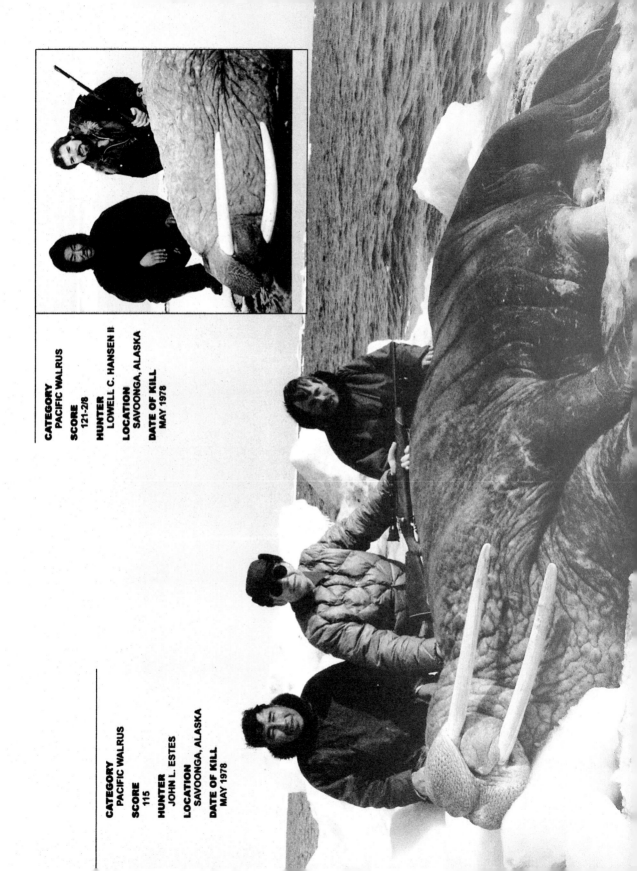

CATEGORY
PACIFIC WALRUS

SCORE
121-2/8

HUNTER
LOWELL C. HANSEN II

LOCATION
SAVOONGA, ALASKA

DATE OF KILL
MAY 1978

CATEGORY
PACIFIC WALRUS

SCORE
115

HUNTER
JOHN L. ESTES

LOCATION
SAVOONGA, ALASKA

DATE OF KILL
MAY 1978

AMERICAN ELK - TYPICAL ANTLERS
WORLD'S RECORD

RANK
World's Record

SCORE
442 5/8

LOCATION
White Mountains, AZ

HUNTER
Alonzo Winters

OWNER
Alan C. Ellsworth

DATE KILLED
1968

Growing up in the White Mountains of eastern Arizona has given Alan C. Ellsworth the opportunity to see some great elk. However, he never would have imagined what was going to take place on February 28, 1995.

"Being a local antler buyer, I was leaving my home to pick up some antlers. As I was waiting at the intersection to pull onto Main Street, a blue Dodge pickup loaded with a washer and dryer, along with a great elk rack, drove by. As I pulled onto Main, behind the truck, I was in awe of the faded elk rack. It was turned upside down, straddling the dryer. My first thought was, 'There's a 400 point bull!' I followed the truck for about a mile, guessing the 6x6 would score about 420 points. The truck turned into a local restaurant, and I had to see the bull up close, so I turned in as well.

"To make the story short, I was able to purchase the elk. I took the rack back home, quickly put a tape to it, and came up with a score of 438 points. Telling my wife, Debby, that we may have a new state record, I hurried out the door to get back to my antler business. While I was gone I kept thinking, 'I must have made a mistake on my score.' I didn't think it was that big. When I returned home that night, I re-measured the huge rack, this time a lot slower! After double checking everything I came up with a score of 445-4/8. Now I was really excited, but also in disbelief! Could I possibly have a new World's Record?"

Backtracking, Ellsworth traced the story to the previous owner's brother, Alonzo (Lon) Winters of Globe, Arizona. Winters, since deceased, was a second generation cattle rancher

who grew up enjoying the great outdoors of Arizona. Riding through the White Mountains during the fall of 1968, Winters and close friend, Bill Vogt, spotted the magnificent animal near the Black River. Winters took the elk down using his Savage Model 99 .308, and avoiding incident, the hunters headed out of the canyon with their prize packed on their horses. Later though, Ellsworth noted one minor dilemma Winters had to overcome.

"Tagging his elk presented a problem. In 1968, the Arizona Game and Fish game tags were a metal band. Lon was unable to fit this tag on the large elk, so he notched the bull's antler between the G-4 and G-5 points, so he could properly tag his elk. His children can remember eating elk burger that winter, and the rack was stored for years in the garage. Friends and relatives remember how proud Lon was when he showed them his trophy."

Nearly 30 years later, Ellsworth must have felt similar pride as he concluded the fine elk hunting story with a triumphant ending, a new World's Record scoring 442-5/8 points. ∎

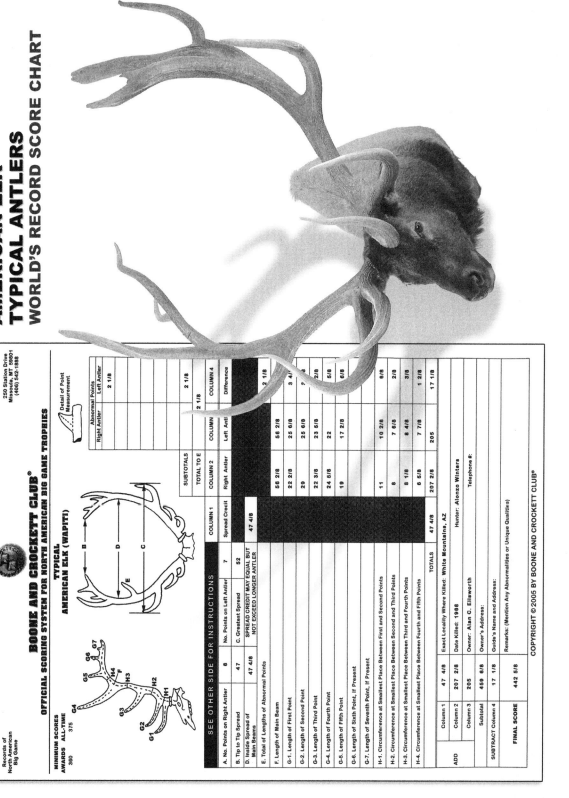

BOONE AND CROCKETT CLUB®

OFFICIAL SCORING SYSTEM FOR NORTH AMERICAN BIG GAME TROPHIES

TYPICAL AMERICAN ELK (WAPITI)

Records of
North American
Big Game

250 Station Drive
Missoula, MT 59801
(406) 542-1888

MINIMUM SCORES
AWARDS ALL-TIME
360   375

Detail of Point Measurement

Abnormal Points	Right Antler	Left Antler
		2 1/8
SUBTOTALS		2 1/8
TOTAL TO E		2 1/8

SEE OTHER SIDE FOR INSTRUCTIONS	COLUMN 1	COLUMN 2	COLUMN 3	COLUMN 4
		Right Antler	Left Antler	Difference
A. No. Points on Right Antler 8 No. Points on Left Antler 7	Spread Credit			
B. Tip to Tip Spread 47				
C. Greatest Spread 52				
D. Inside Spread of Main Beams 47 4/8	SPREAD CREDIT MAY EQUAL BUT NOT EXCEED LONGER ANTLER 47 4/8			2 1/8
E. Total of Lengths of Abnormal Points				2 1/8
F. Length of Main Beam		56 2/8	56 2/8	
G-1. Length of First Point		22 2/8	25 6/8	3 4/8
G-2. Length of Second Point		29	25 6/8	? ?
G-3. Length of Third Point		22 3/8	23 5/8	2/8
G-4. Length of Fourth Point		24 5/8	22	5/8
G-5. Length of Fifth Point		19	17 2/8	6/8
G-6. Length of Sixth Point, If Present				
G-7. Length of Seventh Point, If Present				
H-1. Circumference at Smallest Place Between First and Second Points		11	10 2/8	6/8
H-2. Circumference at Smallest Place Between Second and Third Points		8	7 6/8	2/8
H-3. Circumference at Smallest Place Between Third and Fourth Points		8 1/8	8 4/8	3/8
H-4. Circumference at Smallest Place Between Fourth and Fifth Points		6 5/8	7 7/8	1 2/8
TOTALS	47 4/8	207 2/8	205	17 1/8

	Column 1	47 4/8	Exact Locality Where Killed: White Mountains, AZ
ADD	Column 2	207 2/8	Date Killed: 1968 Hunter: Alonzo Winters
	Column 3	205	Owner: Alan C. Ellsworth Telephone #:
	Subtotal	459 6/8	Owner's Address:
SUBTRACT Column 4		17 1/8	Guide's Name and Address:
FINAL SCORE		442 5/8	Remarks: (Mention Any Abnormalities or Unique Qualities)

COPYRIGHT © 2005 BY BOONE AND CROCKETT CLUB®

247

NUMBER 2 — 442-3/8 POINTS
JOHN PLUTE — 1899

NUMBER 3 — 441-6/8 POINTS
UNKNOWN — 1890

NUMBER 1 — 442-5/8 POINTS
ALONZO WINTERS — 1968

NUMBER 4 — 425-3/8 POINTS
JERRY McKOEN — 1999

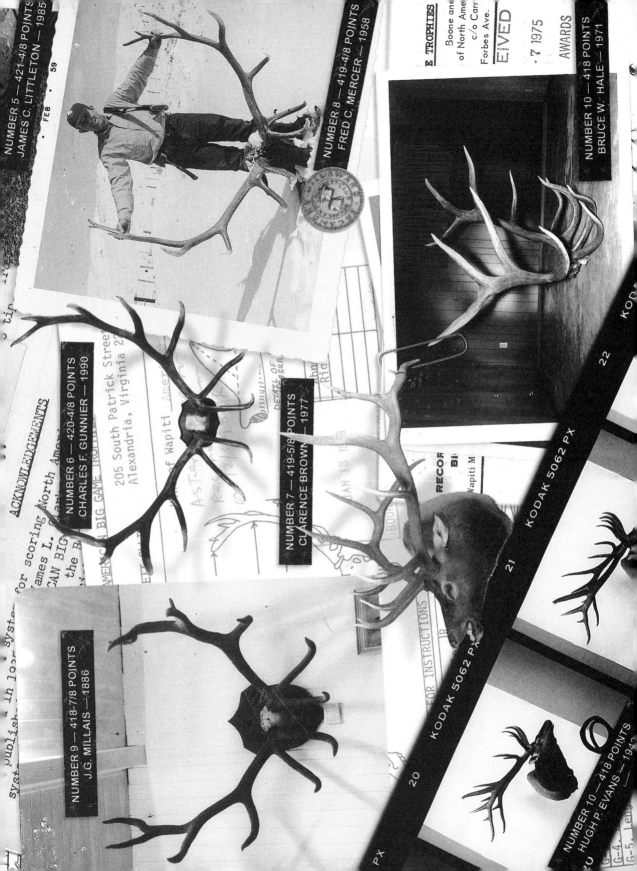

NUMBER 5 — 421-4/8 POINTS
JAMES C. LITTLETON — 1985

NUMBER 8 — 419-4/8 POINTS
FRED C. MERCER — 1958

NUMBER 10 — 418 POINTS
BRUCE W. HALE — 1971

NUMBER 6 — 420-4/8 POINTS
CHARLES F. GUNNIER — 1990

NUMBER 7 — 419-5/8 POINTS
CLARENCE BROWN — 1977

NUMBER 9 — 418-7/8 POINTS
J.G. MILLAIS — 1886

NUMBER 10 — 418 POINTS
HUGH P. EVANS — 19

AMERICAN ELK - TYPICAL ANTLERS

Cervus elaphus nelsoni and related subspecies

MINIMUM SCORE 375

Score	Length of Main Beam R	L	Inside Spread	Circumference at Smallest Place Between First and Second Points R	L	Number of Points R	L	Locality	Hunter	Owner	Date Killed	Rank
442 5/8	56 2/8	56 4/8	47 4/8	11	10 2/8	6	7	White Mts., AZ	Alonzo Winters	Alan C. Ellsworth	1968	1
442 3/8	55 5/8	59 5/8	45 4/8	12 1/8	11 2/8	8	7	Dark Canyon, CO	John Plute	Ed Rozman	1899	2
441 6/8	61 4/8	61 2/8	47	10 2/8	9 7/8	8	7	Big Horn Mts., WY	Unknown	Jackson Hole Museum	1890	3
425 3/8	56 7/8	60 2/8	54 6/8	10 3/8	10 7/8	6	7	Nye Co., NV	Jerry McKoen	Jerry McKoen	1999	4
421 4/8	55 4/8	58 2/8	39	11 2/8	10 6/8	7	7	Gila Co., AZ	James C. Littleton	James C. Littleton	1985	5
420 4/8	56 4/8	56 2/8	45 6/8	9	9 2/8	6	8	Yakima Co., WA	Charles F. Gunnier	Charles F. Gunnier	1990	6
419 5/8	62 3/8	62 2/8	49 2/8	10 3/8	10 3/8	6	7	Panther River, AB	Clarence Brown	Clarence Brown	1977	7
419 4/8	59 7/8	60 1/8	53	9 2/8	9 3/8	7	7	Madison Co., MT	Fred C. Mercer	Fred C. Mercer	1958	8
418 7/8	58	55	43 1/8	10 5/8	11 3/8	6	7	Wyoming	J.G. Millais	G. Kenneth Whitehead	1886	9
418	63 2/8	64 2/8	38 2/8	10 1/8	9 6/8	7	7	Crook Co., OR	Hugh P. Evans	Joseph S. Jessel, Jr.	1942	10
418	54 1/8	50 4/8	44 2/8	8 4/8	8 4/8	6	6	Muddywater River, AB	Bruce W. Hale	Bruce W. Hale	1971	10
417 3/8	62	59 4/8	47 3/8	9 2/8	9 3/8	8	7	Park Co., WY	Merwin D. Martin	Loaned to B&C Natl. Coll.	1991	12
412 5/8	51 6/8	51 1/8	42 5/8	10	9 1/8	9	8	Adams Co., ID	Elmer Bacus	Elmer Bacus	1954	13
412 3/8	55 5/8	56 5/8	52 3/8	9 6/8	9 5/8	6	7	Rosebud Co., MT	Chuck Adams	Chuck Adams	2000	14
411 3/8	56 5/8	61 1/8	45 6/8	10 2/8	9 2/8	6	7	Coconino Co., AZ	Thomas J. Wagner	Thomas J. Wagner	1999	15
411 2/8	61 4/8	59	41 1/8	8 6/8	8 4/8	7	8	Routt Co., CO	Henry Staats	Cabela's, Inc.	1879	16
410 5/8	59 2/8	59	44 2/8	8 6/8	8 1/8	7	8	Unknown	Picked Up	Neil R. Hinton	1943	17
410	56	53 4/8	43	8 6/8	9 1/8	6	6	Carbon Co., WY	Picked Up	Clarence D. Heinrich	1999	18
407 4/8	52	54 6/8	43 4/8	9 1/8	9 1/8	8	8	Summit Co., CO	Robert G. Young	Robert G. Young	1967	19
407	56 7/8	56 6/8	49 3/8	8 6/8	8 4/8	6	7	Duck Mt., MB	Herb Andres	Larry L. Huffman	1980	20
406 7/8	52 7/8	52 6/8	44 6/8	8 5/8	8 5/8	6	8	Ft. Apache Res., AZ	Roy R. Blythe	Roy R. Blythe	1970	21
405 7/8	53 4/8	55 5/8	47 2/8	9 5/8	9 1/8	8	7	Mineral Co., MT	Carl B. Snyder	Warren G. Stone	1959	22
404 6/8	58 6/8	57	41 6/8	8 2/8	8 1/8	6	6	Gila Co., AZ	William H. Tilley	William H. Tilley	1998	23
404	63 3/8	61 2/8	44 1/8	9 1/8	8 5/8	7	7	Red Deer River, AB	Henry Folkman	Henry Folkman	1946	24
401 7/8	59 1/8	59 6/8	45 3/8	9 4/8	9 4/8	6	6	Kootenay Lake, BC	Picked Up	Rick D. Armstrong	1986	25
401 7/8	55 3/8	54 4/8	42 4/8	8 4/8	9 2/8	6	7	Apache Co., AZ	Bruce R. Keller	Bruce R. Keller	1987	25
401 7/8	57 4/8	58 4/8	39 3/8	8 5/8	8 6/8	6	6	White Mtn. Indian Res., AZ	Picked Up	Cabela's, Inc.	1991	25
401 6/8	58 3/8	57 5/8	47 2/8	7 7/8	8	6	6	Teton Co., WY	Douglas Spicer	Douglas Spicer	1972	28
401 4/8	53 1/8	55 1/8	44 4/8	7 7/8	8 1/8	7	7	Park Co., MT	Wayne A. Hertzler	Wayne A. Hertzler	1977	29
401 3/8	60 4/8	64 5/8	43 7/8	9 3/8	9	6	7	Grant Co., OR	James T. Sproul	James T. Sproul	1972	30
401 1/8	59 3/8	59 3/8	47 5/8	8 4/8	8 2/8	7	7	Rock Lake, AB	Ray Hindmarsh	Ray Hindmarsh	1963	31
400 7/8	59 2/8	64 3/8	50	8 2/8	8 2/8	8	8	Navajo Co., AZ	Marvin W. Wuertz	Marvin W. Wuertz	1993	31
400 4/8	59 4/8	61	48 4/8	8 4/8	8 2/8	8	7	Routt Co., CO	Lewis Fredrickson	Jay Scott	1953	33
400 4/8	59 1/8	60 1/8	42 6/8	9 3/8	10	7	7	Owyhee Co., ID	Cecil R. Coonts	Cecil R. Coonts	1965	33
400 4/8	59 1/8	58 5/8	47 4/8	11 2/8	10	6	6	Lincoln Co., NV	W. Steve Perry	W. Steve Perry	1999	33
400 2/8	56	55 2/8	46	8 2/8	8 4/8	7	7	Jackson Hole, WY	C. Atkins & O. Maynard	Thomas Myers	1947	36

Score	Length R	Length L	Inside Spread	Circ. R	Circ. L	Pts R	Pts L	Locality	By Whom Killed	Owner	Date	Rank
400	56 2/8	57	49	9 1/8	9 1/8	7	7	Crook Co., OR	Picked Up	Randall L. Ryerse	1984	37
399 3/8	58 3/8	58	49 3/8	9 2/8	9 1/8	6	6	Coconino Co., AZ	Terry J. Rice	Terry J. Rice	1979	38
399 2/8	59 5/8	57 4/8	47 3/8	7 7/8	7 5/8	8	7	Ram River, AB	Ralph A. Fry	Ralph A. Fry	1952	39
398 7/8	56 4/8	56 4/8	39 5/8	9 6/8	10 3/8	8	6	Navajo Co., AZ	Terry C. Hickson	Terry C. Hickson	1997	40
398 5/8	57 2/8	53 4/8	40 5/8	9	9 2/8	8	8	Lewis & Clark Co., MT	Richard Mosher	J.A. Iverson	1953	41
398	50 5/8	50 7/8	39 4/8	10 5/8	11	7	7	Mora Co., NM	Bernabe Alcon	Cabela's, Inc.	1963	42
398	50 3/8	53 5/8	46 6/8	8 4/8	8 4/8	6	6	Pincher Creek, AB	Monty F. Adams	Pat Adams	1977	42
398	52	55 1/8	52 1/8	8 1/8	7 6/8	7	7	Sublette Co., WY	Ray Daugherty	Aldon L. Hale	1950	44
397 7/8	53	53	44 2/8	8 7/8	9	8	8	Cascade Co., MT	John W. Campbell	John W. Campbell	1955	45
397 5/8	57 2/8	57 2/8	62 2/8	9 2/8	9 2/8	6	6	Socorro Co., NM	Richard E. Westwood	Richard E. Westwood	1998	46
397 3/8	57 3/8	58 6/8	48 3/8	8 4/8	8 6/8	7	7	Coconino Co., AZ	Lonzo H. Shields	Lonzo H. Shields	1998	47
397 2/8	50 2/8	50 6/8	45 2/8	9 6/8	9 5/8	8	8	Gunnison Co., CO	John R. Burritt	John R. Burritt	1970	48
397 1/8	51 7/8	51 7/8	33 7/8	10 1/8	10 5/8	7	5	Lincoln Co., NV	Michael A. Trousdale	Michael A. Trousdale	1994	49
396 7/8	51 1/8	49 5/8	33 3/8	8 6/8	8 4/8	6	5	Catron Co., NM	Picked Up	Robert J. Seeds	2002	50
396 6/8	56 1/8	56 3/8	43 4/8	9 7/8	10 6/8	6	5	Volunteer Canyon, AZ	Lamar Haines	Lamar Haines	1960	51
396 4/8	59 6/8	57 6/8	44	8 1/8	7 6/8	6	5	Coconino Co., AZ	Aaron M. Lowry	Aaron M. Lowry	1995	51
396 2/8	53 2/8	53 2/8	37 4/8	9 2/8	9 1/8	7	5	Gila Co., AZ	Dan J. Agnew	Dan J. Agnew	1997	53
396 1/8	48	50 4/8	32 4/8	10	9 4/8	7	7	Duck Mt., MB	Paul Kirkowich	Paul Kirkowich	1960	54
396	56 6/8	56 7/8	39 5/8	8 2/8	8 2/8	7	7	Moffat Co., CO	Ron Moser	Cabela's, Inc.	PR 1958	55
395 4/8	58 5/8	59 6/8	45 2/8	9 2/8	8 4/8	6	5	Billings Co., ND	Paige M. Burian	Paige M. Burian	1997	56
395 4/8	57 5/8	60 1/8	47	8 1/8	8 6/8	6	5	Fremont Co., WY	Roger Linnell	Roger Linnell	1955	57
395 4/8	56 2/8	51 2/8	43 6/8	10 2/8	9 5/8	6	5	Silver Bow Co., MT	Wayne Estep	Wayne Estep	1966	57
395 1/8	50 2/8	51 4/8	49 6/8	10	10 3/8	7	5	Millard Co., UT	Philip K. Tuttle	Philip K. Tuttle	1999	57
395	52	51 4/8	41 3/8	9 2/8	9 2/8	6	5	Coconino Co., AZ	Picked Up	John C. McClendon	1995	60
395	56 2/8	56 2/8	48 7/8	8 7/8	8 7/8	7	7	Salmon Natl. For., ID	Fred W. Thomson	Randy Clark	1964	61
395	59 4/8	59	44 6/8	7 7/8	7 7/8	7	7	Apache Co., AZ	R. Steve Bass	R. Steve Bass	1993	61
394 6/8	56 4/8	54 3/8	39 4/8	9 5/8	9 4/8	6	6	Childs Lake, MB	Irvin Funk	Irvin Funk	1998	61
394 4/8	54 2/8	60 7/8	47 2/8	8 4/8	8 4/8	6	5	Jefferson Co., MT	John Willard	John Willard	1953	64
394 4/8	55	57 5/8	52 4/8	10	9 4/8	7	7	Beaverhead Co., MT	Gwyn Brown	Gwyn Brown	1944	65
394 4/8	53 4/8	53 2/8	46 4/8	8 7/8	8 7/8	6	6	Idaho Co., ID	L.M. White	L.M. White	1977	65
394 4/8	55 4/8	54 6/8	37	10	10	6	6	Duck Mt., MB	Melvin J. Podaima	Melvin J. Podaima	1991	65
394 2/8	56 7/8	57 2/8	42 6/8	7 6/8	9 2/8	6	6	Panther River, AB	Picked Up	George Browne	1938	68
394 2/8	53 2/8	56 2/8	41 2/8	8 3/8	9 2/8	6	6	Hoback Rim, WY	Clyde Robbins	George Franz	1940	68
394 2/8	53 1/8	55 3/8	45 2/8	8 3/8	9 4/8	6	6	Elkwater, AB	Roy Crawford	Roy Crawford	1976	68
394 2/8	54 2/8	51 4/8	47 7/8	9 1/8	9 2/8	7	7	Baca Co., UT	David B. Martin	David B. Martin	1994	68
394 2/8	52 3/8	52 1/8	49	9 2/8	9 2/8	7	7	Utah Co., UT	Lynn O. Grant	Lynn O. Grant	2003	68
394 1/8	58	58 4/8	46 7/8	8 6/8	10 2/8	6	6	Lincoln Co., WY	Roland Smith	Leon C. Smith	1930	73
393 7/8	57 1/8	58	43 7/8	9 6/8	8	6	6	Apache Co., AZ	T.R. Tidwell	T.R. Tidwell	1983	74
393 5/8	54 7/8	53 5/8	40	9 6/8	9	6	6	Greenlee Co., AZ	R. Alan Pennington	R. Alan Pennington	1999	75
393 4/8	56 2/8	52 4/8	42 5/8	9 4/8	9 4/8	7	7	Elmore Co., ID	Picked Up	Joe Adams	PR 1955	76
393 4/8	50	51 3/8	40 4/8	8 1/8	7 6/8	7	7	White Pine Co., NV	Paul Green	Paul Green	1993	77
393 2/8	57	56	46 6/8	9 7/8	9 2/8	6	6	Blaine Co., ID	Darren K. Spiers	Darren K. Spiers	2000	77
393 2/8	53 5/8	51 6/8	46 2/8	10 2/8	10	6	6	Big Horn Co., WY	Edwin Shaffer	Edwin Shaffer	1946	79
393 2/8	55 2/8	54 4/8	51 4/8	8 3/8	8 2/8	6	6	Winchester, ID	Alan Foster	Alan Foster	1952	79
393 2/8	58 6/8	52 1/8	45 2/8	9 1/8	9 4/8	6	6	Socorro Co., NM	Doyle Shriver	Doyle Shriver	1954	79
393 2/8	63 1/8	64 4/8	44 2/8	9 2/8	9 6/8	7	7	Catron Co., NM	Floyd R. Owens	Floyd R. Owens	1977	79
393 2/8	55 2/8	56 2/8	43 2/8	9 6/8	8 6/8	6	6	Socorro Co., NM	Robert M. Miller	Robert M. Miller	1997	79
393 2/8	51 4/8	53	43 6/8	9	7 4/8	6	6	Sanders Co., MT	Kenneth R. Groh	Kenneth R. Groh	2000	79

AMERICAN ELK - TYPICAL ANTLERS
Cervus elaphus nelsoni and related subspecies

Score	Length of Main Beam R	L	Inside Spread	Circumference at Smallest Place Between First and Second Points R	L	Number of Points R	L	Locality	Hunter	Owner	Date Killed	Rank
393 1/8	56 3/8	59 2/8	47 1/8	8 6/8	8 6/8	6	6	Kittitas Co., WA	Paul Anderson	Paul Anderson	1927	85
392 5/8	58 7/8	58 4/8	48 5/8	8 7/8	9	7	7	Panther River, AB	Bill Brooks	Bill Brooks	1955	86
392 4/8	51 3/8	51 1/8	42 3/8	7 7/8	7 7/8	7	7	Buford, CO	Picked Up	Robert T. Fulton	PR 1967	87
392 4/8	51 5/8	57 1/8	44 2/8	8 6/8	9	6	7	Gallatin Co., MT	Christopher R. Hann	Christopher R. Hann	2000	87
392 3/8	53 4/8	54 4/8	46 3/8	8 3/8	8 6/8	6	6	Umatilla Co., OR	Picked Up	Robert L. Brown	1982	89
392 3/8	54	54 6/8	41 7/8	9 4/8	10	6	6	Apache Co., AZ	McLean Bowman	McLean Bowman	1989	89
392 1/8	58 6/8	59 5/8	53 4/8	7 4/8	7 6/8	6	8	Coconino Co., AZ	Calvin Newmann	Cabela's, Inc.	1993	91
392	54 6/8	56 6/8	45 2/8	10	10 4/8	7	6	Jackson Co., CO	James A. Baller	North Park State Bank	1969	92
392	52 4/8	53 3/8	36 4/8	10 3/8	10 4/8	7	6	Campbell Co., WY	Paul E. Wollenman	Paul E. Wollenman	1996	92
392	55	57 2/8	42	9 5/8	9 4/8	7	7	White Pine Co., NV	Thomas M. Brunson	Thomas M. Brunson	2001	92
392	55 7/8	55 7/8	49 6/8	10 4/8	10	6	7	El Paso Co., CO	Fred Long	Cabela's, Inc.	1903	95
391 6/8	52 6/8	53 6/8	35 6/8	7 7/8	7 7/8	6	6	Slater, CO	W.J. Bracken	W.J. Bracken	1963	95
391 6/8	63 6/8	62	45 3/8	9 4/8	8 7/8	7	7	Jefferson Co., OR	Unknown	Chuck Hoyt	PR 1940	97
391 5/8	59 2/8	59 7/8	54 7/8	9 7/8	9	7	7	Tooele Co., UT	James A. Cook	James A. Cook	1999	97
391 5/8	54 5/8	56 3/8	43 2/8	9 1/8	9	6	6	Mt. Evans, CO	Unknown	Frank Brady	1874	99
391 4/8	52 2/8	52 7/8	51 2/8	8 5/8	8 2/8	7	7	Big Horn Mts., WY	Robert K. Hamilton	Robert K. Hamilton	1954	99
391 3/8	55 7/8	50 3/8	39 3/8	7 2/8	8 2/8	7	6	Grand Lake, CO	John Holzwarth	John Holzwarth	1949	101
391 2/8	57 4/8	59 7/8	47 4/8	8 6/8	8 5/8	6	6	Montana	Doug Dawson	Cabela's, Inc.	1939	102
390 6/8	53 5/8	54 3/8	49 6/8	9 3/8	9 5/8	7	7	Clearwater River, AB	Bob Dial	Bob Dial	1955	103
390 6/8	59 6/8	58	42	8 7/8	9	6	6	Caribou Co., ID	Ken Homer	Ken Homer	1963	103
390 6/8	57 3/8	57 2/8	51 2/8	8 6/8	8 4/8	6	6	Apache Co., AZ	Robert M. Brittingham	Robert M. Brittingham	1990	103
390 6/8	53 6/8	53 5/8	47 6/8	8 2/8	8 1/8	6	6	Cibola Co., NM	Lee A. Schawe	Lee A. Schawe	2001	103
390 5/8	58	61	44 3/8	9 4/8	9	7	7	Catron Co., NM	Picked Up	Robert J. Seeds	2001	107
390 3/8	57 1/8	54 1/8	40 1/8	9 2/8	9 1/8	6	6	Hoback Canyon, WY	Picked Up	Spanky Greenville	1977	108
390 3/8	57	60 2/8	42 7/8	9 1/8	9 1/8	7	7	Cibola Co., NM	Sam S. Jaksick, Jr.	Sam S. Jaksick, Jr.	1997	108
390 2/8	55	55 4/8	49 2/8	8 6/8	8 6/8	6	6	Hood River Co., OR	Bill Tensen	Bill Tensen	1980	110
390 2/8	51 1/8	52 1/8	49	9 2/8	8 7/8	7	7	Las Animas Co., CO	Robert A. Schnee	Robert A. Schnee	1993	110
389 7/8	64 4/8	64 4/8	42 7/8	8 1/8	8 7/8	6	6	Chelan Co., WA	Unknown	RMEF - Colockum Chapter	1947	112
389 7/8	54 1/8	55 5/8	48 7/8	9 4/8	9 3/8	6	6	Sevier Co., UT	O. Howard Shattuck	O. Howard Shattuck	2002	112
389 6/8	56 3/8	55 7/8	39 4/8	8 5/8	8 5/8	6	7	Navajo Co., AZ	R. Fred Fortier	R. Fred Fortier	1985	114
389 6/8	50 2/8	53	50 3/8	8	7 6/8	7	7	Park Co., MT	Thomas B. Adams	Jack Adams	1932	115
389 5/8	56 5/8	52 5/8	52 5/8	9 2/8	9 2/8	6	6	Fort a la Corne, SK	Jim Crozier	Jim Crozier	1955	115
389 5/8	55 1/8	54	45 7/8	7 7/8	8 1/8	7	7	Park Co., MT	Butch Kuflak	Butch Kuflak	1990	115
389 4/8	55 4/8	56 2/8	45	10 5/8	10	6	6	Helena, MT	Picked Up	Robert L. Smith	1964	118
389 4/8	57 3/8	55 2/8	42	8	8	6	6	Bitterroot Area, MT	Unknown	John Le Blanc	1965	118
389 4/8	53 7/8	54 7/8	46	8 7/8	8 7/8	6	6	Big Horn Co., WY	Floyd A. Clark	Floyd A. Clark	1976	118

Score	Length R	Length L	Inside Spread	Circ. R	Circ. L	Pts. R	Pts. L	Locality	Hunter	Owner	Date	Rank
389 4/8	49 5/8	48 5/8	49	8 4/8	8 6/8	6	6	Morgan Co, UT	Robert Farrell	Robert Farrell	1999	118
389 3/8	56 5/8	60 5/8	43 7/8	8 3/8	8 2/8	6	6	Salmon River, ID	Unknown	John M. Anderson	1915	122
389 3/8	60 3/8	63 4/8	48 3/8	11 5/8	11 5/8	5	5	Modoc Co, CA	Kasey M. Criss	Kasey M. Criss	2003	122
389 2/8	49 4/8	51 1/8	42 6/8	12 3/8	12 3/8	7	6	Nez Perce Co, ID	Picked Up	Michael Throckmorton	1949	124
389 2/8	49 7/8	48 1/8	40	10 7/8	10 3/8	6	6	Saskatchewan	Unknown	B.P.O.E. Lodge	PR 1956	124
389	51	48 3/8	41 6/8	8 2/8	8 2/8	6	6	Meacham, OR	H.M. Bailey	H.M. Bailey	1963	126
389	56 2/8	54 5/8	36 2/8	10 3/8	10 6/8	6	6	Otero Co, NM	Larry Stifflemire	Larry Stifflemire	1999	126
388 7/8	56	55 4/8	46 3/8	9 6/8	8 6/8	6	7	Jackson Hole, WY	Unknown	William Sonnenburg	PR 1912	128
388 6/8	50 6/8	47 2/8	45 6/8	9 4/8	9 4/8	6	6	Larimer Co, CO	John Zimmerman	Fort Collins Museum	PR 1890	129
388 6/8	56 1/8	55 1/8	41 3/8	10	10 3/8	7	8	Graham Co, AZ	Hans Veit Toerring	Hans Veit Toerring	1994	129
388 4/8	55 6/8	56 1/8	44 4/8	9 5/8	9 4/8	6	6	Platte Co, WY	Mike C. Boughton	Mike C. Boughton	1995	131
388 3/8	53 5/8	55	47 1/8	9 3/8	9	6	7	Coconino Co, AZ	Picked Up	Timothy M. Cotten	PR 1982	132
388 2/8	62 4/8	63 5/8	49 2/8	9 1/8	9 3/8	9	7	Unknown	Unknown	Carnegie Museum	PR 1966	133
388 2/8	52 5/8	51 3/8	39	10 1/8	10 1/8	6	6	Gila Co, AZ	Fred B. Dickey	Fred B. Dickey	1984	133
388 2/8	56 1/8	54 7/8	40	9 2/8	9 7/8	7	7	Sentinel Mt., BC	Martin Braun	Martin Braun	1986	133
388 1/8	59 1/8	59	54	7 6/8	7 5/8	6	6	Cutoff Creek, AB	Joseph A. Riveira	Joseph A. Riveira	1986	137
388	56 3/8	56 4/8	46 4/8	8 4/8	8 3/8	8	7	Slocan River, BC	Trevor W. Stetsko	Trevor W. Stetsko	1991	138
388	57 1/8	55 1/8	55	8 1/8	8 6/8	7	8	Medicine Lodge Creek, ID	D.W. Marshall & E.J. Stacy	D.W. Marshall & E.J. Stacy	1961	138
388	53 2/8	53 6/8	48 2/8	9 3/8	9	6	6	Madison Co, MT	Terry Carlson	Christine Mullikin	1965	138
388	55 4/8	54 4/8	50 2/8	9	8 4/8	9	8	Converse Co, WY	Jerry F. Cook	J.F. Cook & Mrs. P. Muchmore		138
388	54 6/8	54	41 6/8	9 2/8	9 1/8	7	6	Beaver Co, UT	Daniel Carter	Daniel Carter	1998	138
387 7/8	54 4/8	55 5/8	44 5/8	9 6/8	9 5/8	7	6	Kelly, WY	Roger Penney	Bernard Bronk	1963	142
387 7/8	55 3/8	57	37 2/8	10	9 5/8	7	6	Grant Co, OR	Arnold Troph	Arnold Troph	1966	142
387 7/8	52 1/8	53	44 5/8	7 7/8	8	6	6	Lincoln Co, WY	Dexter R. Gardner	Dexter R. Gardner	1967	142
387 6/8	57 6/8	56 4/8	51	8	7 7/8	7	6	Big Horn Mts, WY	Elgin T. Gates	Elgin T. Gates	1954	145
387 6/8	50 2/8	51 7/8	43 2/8	8 5/8	10 2/8	7	7	Fremont Co, ID	Charles A. Preston	Charles A. Preston	1963	145
387 6/8	52 7/8	52 5/8	39 4/8	8 3/8	8 3/8	6	6	Apache Co, AZ	John A. Cardwell	John A. Cardwell	1998	145
387 5/8	60 2/8	60	42 7/8	9	8 7/8	7	7	Cherokee Co, IA	C.A. Stiles	Jim Hass	1970	148
387 5/8	58 1/8	56	39 1/8	8 7/8	9 1/8	7	7	Yarrow Creek, AB	D. Belyea	D. Belyea	1994	148
387 5/8	50 7/8	51 6/8	41 5/8	8 3/8	8 5/8	6	6	Washington Co, ID	Rick H. Moser	Michael R. Damery	1999	148
387 4/8	53 5/8	55 4/8	39 7/8	8 3/8	10 3/8	7	7	Douglas Co, CO	Picked Up	CO Div. of Wildl.	1959	152
387 4/8	49 1/8	49 1/8	41 7/8	8 7/8	8 7/8	7	7	Grant Co, OR	Andy L. Chambers	Andy L. Chambers	1970	152
387 3/8	56 5/8	58 2/8	44 2/8	9	9	6	7	Sage Creek, MT	Joseph A. Vogel	Joseph A. Vogel	1978	154
387 3/8	52 2/8	52 3/8	47 3/8	8 1/8	8 1/8	6	6	Park Co, MT	Lawrence P. Deering	Lawrence P. Deering	1996	154
387 3/8	50 4/8	52 3/8	46 3/8	9 7/8	9 6/8	6	6	Johnson Co, WY	Wallace D. Ramsbottom	Wallace D. Ramsbottom	1995	154
387 2/8	54 7/8	54 7/8	39	8 4/8	8 1/8	7	8	Navajo Co, AZ	Leo W. Mack, Jr.	Leo W. Mack, Jr.	1971	156
387 1/8	54 6/8	58 1/8	46	9 5/8	9 5/8	7	8	Meagher Co, MT	B. McLees & H. Zehntner	Bud McLees	PR 1900	157
387	55	55 4/8	54 4/8	8 7/8	8 2/8	3	3	Chama, NM	Herb Klein	Dallas Mus. of Natl. Hist.	1952	158
387	58 2/8	59 3/8	41	10 3/8	10 2/8	5	7	Ouray Co, CO	Eugene D. Guilaroff	Cabela's, Inc.	1973	158
387	60 4/8	60 1/8	38 2/8	7 1/8	7 3/8	5	5	Apache Co, AZ	Picked Up	Donald H. McBride	1998	158
386 7/8	48 6/8	47 2/8	41 6/8	9 4/8	8 5/8	3	3	Powell Co, MT	Mildred Eder	Mildred Eder	1969	161
386 7/8	58 4/8	61 6/8	41 7/8	8 7/8	8 7/8	5	5	Otero Co, NM	Picked Up	William M. Wheless III	1981	161
386 6/8	52 2/8	51 5/8	34 4/8	10 3/8	10 2/8	5	5	Powell Co, MT	Unknown	Thomas W. Moen	1960	163
386 6/8	61 6/8	61 7/8	47 4/8	8 7/8	9 1/8	7	7	Flathead Co, MT	Floyd L. Jackson	Floyd L. Jackson	1976	163
386 5/8	59 3/8	60	52 1/8	9 1/8	9 1/8	7	7	Panther River, AB	Leonard L. Hengen	Leonard L. Hengen	1977	165
386 4/8	59	57	45	9	9	5	5	Cache Co, UT	Greg Nielsen	L. Dwight Israelsen	1937	166
386 4/8	49 2/8	50 3/8	39 6/8	9	8 6/8	7	7	Nez Perce Co, ID	H.H. Schnettler & J. Hanna	H.H. Schnettler	1957	166

AMERICAN ELK - TYPICAL ANTLERS
Cervus elaphus nelsoni and related subspecies

Score	Length of Main Beam		Inside Spread	Circumference at Smallest Place Between First and Second Points		Number of Points		Locality	Hunter	Owner	Date Killed	Rank
	R	L		R	L	R	L					
386 4/8	55 6/8	55 5/8	42	10	9 2/8	7	7	Smoky River, AB	Stephen Trulik	Stephen Trulik	1963	166
386 4/8	56 2/8	54 6/8	44	8 5/8	8 6/8	6	6	Coconino Co., AZ	Lee Clemson	Lee Clemson	1974	166
386 4/8	49 2/8	50 6/8	39	10 4/8	11 2/8	7	6	Navajo Co., AZ	Johnny Bliznak	Johnny Bliznak	1998	166
386 2/8	56 3/8	57 4/8	46 6/8	9 3/8	8 6/8	6	6	Carbon Co., UT	Edward C. Jessen	Edward C. Jessen	1961	171
386 2/8	52 4/8	54 1/8	48	8 7/8	9 1/8	6	6	Delta Co., CO	Bert Johnson	Bert Johnson	1974	171
386 2/8	59 6/8	60 4/8	47 4/8	9 7/8	9 6/8	6	7	Benewah Co., ID	Lee C. Mowreader	Lee C. Mowreader	1992	171
386 1/8	57 6/8	57 1/8	48 5/8	7 7/8	8 5/8	6	6	Forest Gate Store, SK	Edwin L. Roberts	Edwin L. Roberts	1962	174
386 1/8	59 1/8	58	36 5/8	10 3/8	9 4/8	6	6	Mescalero Apache Res., NM	Larry W. Bailey, Sr.	Larry W. Bailey, Sr.	1974	174
386 1/8	55 1/8	54 2/8	53 1/8	7 3/8	7 1/8	6	6	Apache Co., AZ	Don K. Callahan	Don K. Callahan	1993	174
386 1/8	58 2/8	58 3/8	45 1/8	8 3/8	8 2/8	7	7	Powder River Co., MT	Darrell L. Brabec	Darrell L. Brabec	1999	174
386	53 7/8	55 4/8	51	9 6/8	9 6/8	6	6	Valley Co., ID	Denny Young	Kenny Poe	1957	178
386	52 4/8	53	48 2/8	8 4/8	8 4/8	6	7	Big Horn Mts., WY	Unknown	Fred Gray	1966	178
385 7/8	49 1/8	51 7/8	44 3/8	7 7/8	7 7/8	6	6	Shoshone Co., ID	Jerry Nearing	Jerry Nearing	1976	180
385 6/8	56 7/8	56 1/8	40 4/8	7 7/8	8	6	6	Big Smoky River, AB	Fred T. Huntington, Jr.	Fred T. Huntington, Jr.	1961	181
385 6/8	52 4/8	56	41 3/8	9	8 4/8	7	8	Apache Co., AZ	Jay A. Kellett	Jay A. Kellett	1993	181
385 6/8	54 7/8	53 2/8	44 6/8	9 5/8	8 3/8	7	7	Billings Co., ND	James A. Feser	James A. Feser	1998	181
385 6/8	55 3/8	55 6/8	50	8 5/8	8 4/8	7	7	Beaverhead Co., MT	Raymond F. Ford, Jr.	Raymond F. Ford, Jr.	1998	181
385 6/8	53 3/8	59 2/8	40 4/8	8 6/8	9	6	6	Graham Co., AZ	Dwayne E. Heikes	Dwayne E. Heikes	2003	181
385 5/8	59 6/8	56 6/8	41 2/8	8 7/8	9 3/8	7	8	Ft. Apache Res., AZ	Glen Daly	Glen Daly	1957	186
385 5/8	53 2/8	53	40 3/8	8 4/8	8 1/8	6	6	Kootenai Co., ID	Arth Day	Arth Day	1971	186
385 5/8	52 7/8	54 7/8	46 7/8	9 3/8	9 1/8	6	6	Wheeler Co., OR	Ronny E. Rhoden	Ronny E. Rhoden	1986	186
385 4/8	56 2/8	57 3/8	37 4/8	8 2/8	8 2/8	6	6	Emery Co., UT	Neville L. Wimmer	Russell N. Wimmer	1939	189
385 3/8	55 4/8	55 2/8	47 3/8	10 1/8	10 5/8	6	6	Teton Co., WY	Gene J. Riordan	Timothy G. Riordan	1960	190
385 3/8	57 2/8	55 1/8	42 5/8	8	9	6	6	Sanders Co., MT	George R. Johnson	George R. Johnson	1977	190
385 3/8	51 1/8	54 2/8	41 5/8	10 7/8	10 5/8	6	6	Otero Co., NM	Gregory C. Saunders	Gregory C. Saunders	1985	190
385 3/8	51	51 5/8	36 1/8	9 6/8	10 1/8	7	6	Park Co., WY	Don W. Rogers	Don W. Rogers	2001	190
385 3/8	51 7/8	52 1/8	40 7/8	10 7/8	10 2/8	7	7	Garfield Co., UT	Raymond D. Fowler	Raymond D. Fowler	2003	190
385 2/8	53 3/8	52 2/8	41 1/8	10 1/8	9 7/8	6	6	Apache Co., AZ	Herman C. Meyer	Herman C. Meyer	1991	195
385 2/8	57 1/8	57	44	9 4/8	10 3/8	7	6	Park Co., WY	Brian R. Morency	Brian R. Morency	2000	195
385 1/8	48 5/8	49 3/8	34 7/8	8 3/8	8 6/8	6	6	Trappers Lake, CO	Byron W. Kneff	Byron W. Kneff	1954	197
385 1/8	51	52 4/8	48 4/8	11	11 4/8	8	8	Grande Cache Lake, AB	Kenneth A. Evans	Kenneth A. Evans	1966	197
385 1/8	56 7/8	56 4/8	46 5/8	8 3/8	10	7	7	Bozeman, MT	Robert B. McKnight	Robert B. McKnight	1966	197
385 1/8	46	48 2/8	44 3/8	7 6/8	8 2/8	6	6	Lincoln Co., WY	Ken Clark	Ken Clark	1979	197
385	54 7/8	53 3/8	46 6/8	8	8 3/8	6	6	Madison Co., MT	Boyd J. VanFleet	Boyd J. VanFleet	1991	201
385	52 4/8	51 4/8	41 4/8	8 5/8	9 6/8	6	6	Jefferson Co., CO	Thomas E. Tietz	Thomas E. Tietz	1997	201
385	56 4/8	59 4/8	47	9	9 4/8	6	6	Park Co., WY	Kelly Preuit	Kelly Preuit	1999	201

Score	Main Beam R	Main Beam L	Inside Spread	Tine R	Tine L	Pts R	Pts L	Locality	Hunter	Owner	Date	Rank
384 7/8	56 6/8	57 2/8	43 7/8	9 3/8	8 7/8	7	6	Sanders Co., MT	Brett M. Fisher	Brett M. Fisher	1994	204
384 6/8	55 3/8	54 3/8	36 4/8	9 2/8	9	6	6	Clearwater River, AB	William Lenz	William Lenz	1966	205
384 6/8	56 2/8	58 4/8	44	9 4/8	9 6/8	6	6	Ft. Apache Res., AZ	Jim P. Caires	Jim P. Caires	1978	205
384 6/8	60	60 2/8	44 3/8	9 5/8	10	7	7	Apache Co., AZ	Herman C. Meyer	H.C. Meyer & J.T. Caid	1982	205
384 6/8	55 5/8	56 2/8	42 4/8	9	8	6	6	Sublette Co., WY	Jerry W. Cover	Jerry W. Cover	2000	205
384 5/8	55 3/8	54 6/8	47 1/8	8 4/8	8 7/8	6	6	Ram River, AB	Joe Kramer	Joe Kramer	1966	209
384 5/8	57 6/8	56 6/8	40 5/8	8 7/8	9 3/8	7	6	Graham Co., AZ	Laura R. Williams	Laura R. Williams	1986	209
384 4/8	57	57	43 4/8	9 5/8	8 2/8	7	7	Bonneville Co., ID	David W. Anderson	David W. Anderson	1967	211
384 4/8	53 2/8	53 7/8	43	8 5/8	7 5/8	7	7	Bonneville Co., ID	Keith W. Hadley	Keith W. Hadley	1972	211
384 3/8	59 3/8	59 2/8	49 1/8	7 6/8	9 3/8	6	6	Jackson Hole, WY	Francis X. Bouchard	Francis X. Bouchard	1956	213
384 3/8	59	59	46 3/8	10 5/8	9 4/8	6	6	Beaverhead Co., MT	Phil Matovich	Phil Matovich	1960	213
384 3/8	54 5/8	54 5/8	50 7/8	9 7/8	12 6/8	6	7	Clear Creek Co., CO	John Wallace	John Wallace	1973	213
384 3/8	56 4/8	53 3/8	36 6/8	11 4/8	9 2/8	7	6	Apache Co., AZ	John A. Cardwell	John A. Cardwell	2001	213
384 3/8	53 4/8	54 4/8	52 5/8	9 3/8	10 4/8	6	7	Beaver Co., UT	Greg D. Myers	Greg D. Myers	2002	213
384 2/8	61 7/8	64 6/8	40 6/8	11	8 3/8	8	8	Ft. Apache Res., AZ	Ralph C. Winkler, Jr.	Ralph C. Winkler, Jr.	1977	218
384 2/8	58 1/8	60 6/8	49 3/8	10	7 7/8	6	7	Apache Co., AZ	Roy W. Baker	Roy W. Baker	1980	218
384 2/8	58	58	43	8	9 3/8	6	6	Catron Co., NM	Robert J. Seeds	Robert J. Seeds	1996	218
384 1/8	55 7/8	56 7/8	48 1/8	9 1/8	9 7/8	7	6	Gilpin Co., CO	James W. Wheeler	William C. Wheeler	1850	221
384 1/8	—	—	32 4/8	9 5/8	9 1/8	7	7	Navajo Co., AZ	Dennis K. Frandsen	Dennis K. Frandsen	1994	221
384	—	—	—	—	8 2/8	—	—	Willow Creek, MT	Mike Miles	Mike Miles	1958	223
384	57 2/8	57 2/8	44	9 7/8	8 1/8	7	7	Meagher Co., MT	Frank W. Fuller	Frank W. Fuller	1963	223
384	58 7/8	60	48 3/8	9 1/8	11 1/8	6	6	Costilla Co., CO	William E. Carl	William E. Carl	1967	223
384	58 1/8	56 6/8	47	8 5/8	9 6/8	6	6	Otero Co., NM	Robert McCasland	Robert McCasland	1992	223
384	53 2/8	54	41 1/8	7 6/8	8 6/8	6	6	Otero Co., NM	George R. Sellers	George R. Sellers	1992	223
383 7/8	56 3/8	51 5/8	41 4/8	11 4/8	9 5/8	6	6	Apache Co., AZ	Jerry Wascom	Jerry Wascom	2001	228
383 6/8	53 6/8	55 3/8	43 4/8	9 5/8	9	6	7	Unknown	S. Side Cody Elk Club	Unknown	1939	229
383 6/8	54	51 3/8	46	8 5/8	8 7/8	6	6	Las Animas Co., CO	Michael W. Marbach	Michael W. Marbach	1993	229
383 5/8	54 6/8	55	54 4/8	9 4/8	8 3/8	6	6	Apache Co., AZ	Randall S. Ulmer	Randall S. Ulmer	1987	231
383 4/8	51 3/8	52 4/8	48 4/8	8 7/8	9 5/8	6	6	Unknown	N. Side Cody Elk Club	Unknown	PR 1967	232
383 3/8	53 5/8	58	50 1/8	8 2/8	8	6	6	Maycroft, AB	Steve Kubasek	Steve Kubasek	1957	233
383 2/8	52 2/8	54 4/8	41 6/8	9 5/8	9 2/8	6	6	Nez Perce Co., ID	Thenton L. Todd	Thenton L. Todd	1956	234
383 2/8	55 5/8	55	45	8 2/8	10 5/8	7	7	Coconino Co., AZ	Jay E. Elmer	Jay E. Elmer	1979	234
383 2/8	57 6/8	55	39 6/8	9 4/8	8 4/8	6	6	Otero Co., NM	Larry Stifflemire	Larry Stifflemire	2001	234
383 1/8	58 1/8	52 3/8	53 1/8	10 3/8	9 6/8	6	6	Snowy Range, WY	Kermit Platt	Kermit Platt	1961	237
383	55	52	52 2/8	8 4/8	8 6/8	8	8	Coconino Co., AZ	Gene Bird	Gene Bird	1972	238
383	52 1/8	53 4/8	51 4/8	9	9	6	6	Panther River, AB	Echoglen Taxidermy	Thomas Coupland	1984	238
383	53 4/8	52	44 6/8	9 3/8	8 2/8	6	6	Garfield Co., UT	Jeffery H. Starr	Jeffery H. Starr	1998	238
382 7/8	54 3/8	51 4/8	47 4/8	9 5/8	10 2/8	7	8	Blacktail Creek, MT	Floyd E. Winn	Floyd E. Winn	1959	241
382 7/8	59 6/8	52 7/8	43 5/8	8 1/8	8 5/8	6	6	Castle River, AB	Albert Truant	Albert Truant	1970	241
382 6/8	56 1/8	59 6/8	42 5/8	9 7/8	8 6/8	6	6	Graham Co., AZ	Mark R. Herfort	Mark R. Herfort	1994	241
382 6/8	52 3/8	54 5/8	41 5/8	8 6/8	10 2/8	7	6	Rattlesnake Mt., WY	Bob Edgar	Bob Edgar	1966	244
382 5/8	52 3/8	56 7/8	48	9 3/8	10 5/8	6	6	Apache Co., AZ	William E. Moss	William E. Moss	1985	244
382 5/8	52	52 3/8	36 5/8	9 2/8	9	7	6	Kootenai Co., ID	Terry Cozad	Terry Cozad	1968	246
382 5/8	55 4/8	52	38 1/8	8 6/8	9 2/8	6	7	Butte Co., ID	Kirk Drussel	Paul E. Harrell	1997	246
382 5/8	52 5/8	57 4/8	38 4/8	9 5/8	8 7/8	6	6	San Juan Co., UT	Kirk E. Winward	Kirk E. Winward	1997	246
382 5/8	53 7/8	52 5/8	37 1/8	10 4/8	10 5/8	7	7	Dolores Co., CO	Andrea Holley	Andrea Holley	2000	246
382 5/8	49 6/8	53 3/8	44	9 4/8	9 3/8	6	7	Rich Co., UT	Thomas C. Hodges	Thomas C. Hodges	2003	246
382 4/8	—	48	32 7/8	14 4/8	13	9	7	Elbow River, AB	Harold F. Mailman	Harold F. Mailman	1964	251

AMERICAN ELK - TYPICAL ANTLERS

Cervus elaphus nelsoni and related subspecies

Score	Length of Main Beam R	L	Inside Spread	Circumference at Smallest Place Between First and Second Points R	L	Number of Points R	L	Locality	Hunter	Owner	Date Killed	Rank
382 4/8	56 6/8	56 7/8	41 3/8	8 7/8	9 2/8	6	7	Summit Co., CO	Marshall Sherman	Marshall Sherman	1966	251
382 4/8	49	48 5/8	36 5/8	8 5/8	8 6/8	6	6	Teton Co., WY	Randy Johnston	Randy Johnston	1970	251
382 4/8	54	55 1/8	40 5/8	8 4/8	9 1/8	7	7	Cascade Co., MT	Robert J. Gliko	Robert J. Gliko	1983	251
382 3/8	53 3/8	54	50 5/8	8 4/8	8 4/8	7	7	Sublette Co., WY	Frank Dew	Frank Dew	1931	255
382 3/8	49 6/8	52 1/8	35 5/8	11	10 1/8	6	6	Mormon Lake, AZ	Wayne A. Barry	John E. Rhea	1965	255
382 3/8	53 7/8	56 2/8	41 7/8	9 2/8	8 6/8	6	6	Klickitat Co., WA	Johnny T. Walker	Johnny T. Walker	1965	255
382 3/8	58	58 3/8	43 5/8	8 3/8	8 4/8	6	6	Cibola Co., NM	J.R. Dienst	J.R. Dienst	1998	255
382 3/8	55 4/8	55	47 4/8	7 4/8	7 2/8	6	6	Gallatin Co., MT	Henry Lambert	Charles F. Miller	1923	259
382 2/8	58 4/8	62 6/8	48	8	7 4/8	6	6	Williams Co., MT	Oscar B. Skaggs	Oscar B. Skaggs	1954	259
382 2/8	54 2/8	56 6/8	44 2/8	9	8 4/8	7	7	Clark Co., ID	John A. Larick, Jr.	John A. Larick, Jr.	1963	259
382 2/8	55 7/8	53 3/8	39 2/8	9 2/8	9 1/8	7	7	Grant Co., OR	Drake J. Davis	Drake J. Davis	1981	259
382 2/8	48	49 5/8	39 2/8	8 6/8	8 2/8	7	7	Apache Co., AZ	R. Steve Bass	R. Steve Bass	1992	259
382 2/8	50 5/8	49 1/8	50	8	7 5/8	6	6	Colfax Co., NM	Claude W. Hudson III	Claude W. Hudson III	1994	259
382 2/8	57 6/8	56 3/8	38 4/8	8 7/8	9 2/8	7	7	Apache Co., AZ	Alan D. Hamberlin	Alan D. Hamberlin	2000	259
382 2/8	50 2/8	50 7/8	42 4/8	9 5/8	9 5/8	6	6	Rich Co., UT	Marty Halpern	Marty Halpern	2002	259
382 1/8	57 3/8	55 7/8	44 3/8	8 1/8	8 2/8	7	7	Bob Marshall Wilder, MT	Gene E. Trenary	Gene E. Trenary	1958	267
382 1/8	54 3/8	54 6/8	45 7/8	8	8 2/8	6	6	Gallatin Co., MT	A. Francis Bailey	A. Francis Bailey	1966	267
382	52 2/8	51 1/8	47 2/8	9 2/8	8 6/8	8	7	Missoula Co., MT	Fritz Frey	Clifford Frey	1943	269
382	53 2/8	51 1/8	48	8 7/8	9 1/8	6	6	Little Cimmaron, CO	Newell Beauchamp	Bud Lovato	1957	269
382	58	56 7/8	50 4/8	7 7/8	8	6	6	Iron Co., UT	Douglas Ellett	Douglas Ellett	1998	269
381 7/8	59 5/8	58	52 1/8	7 6/8	7 5/8	7	7	Gallatin Co., MT	H.K. Shields	H.K. Shields	1958	272
381 7/8	57 1/8	56 6/8	40 7/8	9 7/8	10	8	8	Idaho Co., ID	Charles E. Carver	Charles E. Carver	1998	272
381 6/8	52 2/8	52	49 7/8	10 2/8	9 3/8	6	7	Beaverhead Co., MT	C.L. Jensen	C.L. Jensen	1960	274
381 6/8	55 2/8	57 1/8	41	9 6/8	9 6/8	7	7	Red Deer River, AB	Allan E. Brown	Allan E. Brown	1980	274
381 6/8	50 3/8	49 7/8	42	9 1/8	8 7/8	8	7	Madison Co., MT	Allan L. Mintken	Allan L. Mintken	1986	274
381 6/8	56 1/8	55	44 4/8	9 1/8	8 5/8	7	7	Waterton River, AB	Keith A. Keeler	Keith A. Keeler	1989	274
381 6/8	54 3/8	52 5/8	38 4/8	9 2/8	10	7	7	Otero Co., NM	David U. Inge	David U. Inge	1990	274
381 5/8	54 7/8	56 3/8	40 1/8	9 3/8	8	7	6	Rich Co., UT	Walter R. Moore	Kirk W. Moore	1935	279
381 5/8	56 2/8	56 2/8	41 5/8	10 4/8	10 1/8	6	6	Granite Co., MT	Jeff Conn	Jeff Conn	1971	279
381 5/8	59 6/8	58	39 7/8	9 5/8	9 2/8	6	6	Coconino Co., AZ	George E. Long	George E. Long	1985	279
381 5/8	58 2/8	57 2/8	39 5/8	9 7/8	10 1/8	6	6	Apache Co., AZ	McLean Bowman	McLean Bowman	1990	279
381 5/8	52	52 4/8	41 7/8	10 4/8	10 2/8	7	7	Platte Co., WY	James L. Brown	James L. Brown	1995	279
381 5/8	60 7/8	60 5/8	38 3/8	9 3/8	9 1/8	6	6	White Pine Co., NV	Zane D. Terry	Zane D. Terry	2002	279
381 4/8	56 4/8	57 2/8	42 4/8	8 7/8	9 2/8	6	6	Fremont Co., WY	John S. Maxson	John S. Maxson	1954	285
381 4/8	51 7/8	50 6/8	40 4/8	10 2/8	10 4/8	7	7	Fergus Co., MT	Joe R. Odom	Joe R. Odom	1994	285
381 3/8	57 2/8	57 7/8	41 1/8	9 6/8	9 4/8	7	6	Park Co., MT	Edward F. Skillman	Edward F. Skillman	1968	287

Score	Main Beam R	Main Beam L	Inside Spread	Circ. R	Circ. L	Points	Locality	Owner	Hunter	Date	Rank
381 3/8	55 3/8	54 5/8	37 4/8	9 6/8	9 1/8	7	Larimer Co., CO	Earl L. Erbes	Earl L. Erbes	1972	287
381 3/8	53 4/8	53 7/8	43 7/8	9 5/8	8 5/8	6	White Pine Co., NV	Michael N. Kalafatic	Michael N. Kalafatic	1985	287
381 3/8	56 4/8	56 6/8	34 7/8	10 3/8	9 4/8	6	Catron Co., NM	Gary F. Jamieson	Gary F. Jamieson	1993	287
381 2/8	57	55 4/8	44 2/8	9	8 6/8	6	Kittitas Co., WA	Clinton W. Morrow	Clinton W. Morrow	1957	291
381 2/8	55 1/8	55 1/8	50	9	9 1/8	8	Mora Co., NM	Andrew J. Ortega	Andrew J. Ortega	1989	291
381 2/8	50 6/8	49 2/8	41	9 5/8	9 2/8	7	Apache Co., AZ	Gerald Tenigieth	David Moore	1996	291
381 1/8	61 6/8	61	51 2/8	9 3/8	8	6	Coconino Co., AZ	Bernie Smits	Bernie Smits	2001	295
381 1/8	57 5/8	56 1/8	45 1/8	8	7 3/8	6	Laramie Peak, WY	Lawrence Prager	Lawrence Prager	1958	295
381 1/8	49 6/8	51 4/8	39 7/8	8 6/8	9	7	Flathead Co., MT	Earl Weaver, Jr.	Earl Weaver, Jr.	1962	295
381 1/8	50 1/8	51 5/8	43 1/8	8 6/8	8 3/8	7	Gila Co., AZ	Steve J. Rico	Steve J. Rico	1999	295
381	56 3/8	54 6/8	48 4/8	8 2/8	8 2/8	6	Gallatin Co., MT	Jack Bauer	Jack Bauer	1961	298
381	51 2/8	50 5/8	43 6/8	8	7 5/8	7	Big Horn Co., MT	Jerry Barnes	Jerry Barnes	1962	298
381	48	54 4/8	40 4/8	8 5/8	7 6/8	8	Bonneville Co., ID	Mrs. E. LaRene Smith	Mrs. E. LaRene Smith	1966	298
381	54	53 4/8	48 6/8	8	10	6	Gallatin Co., MT	Gerald Schroeder	Gerald Schroeder	1977	298
381	59 1/8	61	38 6/8	10 3/8	8 4/8	7	Garfield Co., UT	Joseph T. Jantorno	Joseph T. Jantorno	2000	298
380 7/8	56 2/8	55 2/8	38 3/8	8 5/8	8 4/8	7	Navajo Co., AZ	Thomas D. Friedkin	Thomas D. Friedkin	2003	303
380 6/8	51 7/8	51	43 6/8	10	9 7/8	7	Park Co., MT	John Caputo, Sr.	John Caputo, Sr.	1968	304
380 6/8	56 2/8	56 2/8	40	8 3/8	7 7/8	6	Unknown	Unknown	Bill Lyons, Jr.	PR 1990	304
380 6/8	57	57	47 2/8	7 5/8	7 3/8	7	Coconino Co., AZ	John C. McClendon	John C. McClendon	1995	304
380 5/8	50 6/8	54 3/8	47 5/8	9 4/8	9 7/8	6	Hayden, CO	Mike Holliday	Mike Holliday	1966	307
380 5/8	57 4/8	54 6/8	43 7/8	8 5/8	8 7/8	6	Sevier Co., UT	Miles A. Anderson	Miles A. Anderson	1970	307
380 5/8	54 2/8	57 7/8	51 3/8	7 7/8	7 4/8	8	Chaffee Co., CO	Anton Purkat	Anton Purkat	1972	307
380 5/8	62 4/8	55	49	8 5/8	8 5/8	6	Custer Co., ID	Mark Williams	Cabela's, Inc.	1976	307
380 5/8	54 3/8	53 4/8	42 3/8	10 2/8	9 3/8	6	Apache Co., AZ	Don L. Corley	Don L. Corley	1984	307
380 5/8	56 5/8	57	44 3/8	8	8 1/8	6	Apache Co., AZ	Pat C. Beaird	Pat C. Beaird	1995	307
380 4/8	52 4/8	52 6/8	41	9	8 6/8	6	Payson, AZ	Harold Foard	Harold Foard	1947	313
380 4/8	57 2/8	57 7/8	42 6/8	8 7/8	9 5/8	7	Grant Co., NM	Ryhan I. Peralta	Ryhan I. Peralta	2001	313
380 3/8	62 7/8	63 2/8	47 1/8	8 6/8	8 6/8	8	Harney Co., OR	Pat L. Wheeler	Pat L. Wheeler	1967	315
380 3/8	56 3/8	58	44 1/8	7 5/8	7 5/8	6	Catron Co., NM	Don J. Parks, Jr.	Don J. Parks, Jr.	1988	315
380 3/8	53 4/8	53 2/8	51 7/8	8 1/8	8 5/8	7	Rich Co., UT	Fahy S. Robinson, Jr.	Fahy S. Robinson, Jr.	1988	315
380 3/8	57 7/8	57 4/8	47 7/8	8 5/8	8 4/8	6	Grant Co., NM	Ken D. Lewis	Ken D. Lewis	1995	315
380 3/8	57	58	34 5/8	8 4/8	8 6/8	6	Millard Co., UT	Pam Smith	Pam Smith	1999	315
380 2/8	58	58	49 4/8	8 1/8	8 3/8	6	Madison Co., MT	Phil Hensel	Phil Hensel	1959	320
380 2/8	56 1/8	57 2/8	46 4/8	8 4/8	8 5/8	7	Lewis Co., WA	Charles Rudolph	Charles Rudolph	1973	320
380 2/8	57 4/8	57 3/8	45	9 4/8	8 7/8	6	Coconino Co., AZ	Doug Kittredge	Doug Kittredge	1975	320
380 2/8	56 2/8	54 1/8	42 2/8	9 6/8	8 6/8	6	Granite Co., MT	Richard Shoner	Richard Shoner	1977	320
380 2/8	58 7/8	58 3/8	55 6/8	7 6/8	9 7/8	7	Las Animas Co., CO	Picked Up	Crawford Ranch	1987	320
380 1/8	53 2/8	55 6/8	50 5/8	7 7/8	7 3/8	6	Beaverhead Co., MT	Edward Konda	Edward Konda	1947	325
380 1/8	59 1/8	58 2/8	41 5/8	7 7/8	8 5/8	6	Yavapai Co., AZ	Chris J. Dunn	Chris J. Dunn	1997	325
380 1/8	59 6/8	59 3/8	41 3/8	8 7/8	9 4/8	7	Coconino Co., AZ	Gerald Berkel	Gerald J. Berkel	1998	325
380 1/8	48 2/8	48 7/8	41 7/8	10 5/8	10 3/8	6	Moffat Co., CO	Dale L. Harthan	Dale L. Harthan	1998	325
380	49 1/8	51 1/8	48 2/8	8 7/8	8 4/8	6	Spring Creek, AB	Alva C. Bair	Alva C. Bair	1948	329
380	54	54	50 3/8	10 3/8	9 7/8	7	Ft. Apache Res., AZ	George E. Crosby	George E. Crosby	1957	329
380	53 2/8	56 2/8	35	7 6/8	8 3/8	6	Duck Mt., MB	G.N. Burton	G.N. Burton	1965	329
380	51 5/8	51 6/8	43 6/8	8	8 2/8	7	Navajo Co., AZ	Gerry J. Tod	Gerry J. Tod	1990	329
380	50 4/8	50 3/8	47 3/8	7 4/8	7 3/8	6	Blaine Co., ID	Howard W. Holmes	Howard W. Holmes	2001	329
379 7/8	53 1/8	54	42	9 1/8	8 4/8	6	Routt Co., CO	Walter R. Ducey	Walter R. Ducey	1961	334
379 7/8	58 6/8	56 2/8		8 1/8	8 4/8	6	Graham Co., AZ	Gerald Williams	Gerald Williams	1985	334

AMERICAN ELK - TYPICAL ANTLERS
Cervus elaphus nelsoni and related subspecies

Score	Length of Main Beam R	L	Inside Spread	Circumference at Smallest Place Between First and Second Points R	L	Number of Points R	L	Locality	Hunter	Owner	Date Killed	Rank
379 7/8	51 5/8	47 2/8	36 7/8	8 3/8	8 3/8	6	6	Apache Co., AZ	Thomas G. Kempken	Thomas G. Kempken	1994	334
379 6/8	58 3/8	58 4/8	45 2/8	9 2/8	9 6/8	6	6	Ruby Mts., MT	Jack Ballard	Jack Ballard	1960	337
379 6/8	50 2/8	51 4/8	45 4/8	9 4/8	9 4/8	6	6	Rock Lake, AB	Jim Soneff	Jim Soneff	1961	337
379 6/8	57 2/8	57 2/8	40 4/8	7 6/8	7 6/8	6	6	Big Horn Co., MT	George F. Gamble	George F. Gamble	1968	337
379 6/8	54	54 6/8	45 6/8	7 7/8	8 1/8	6	6	Daisy Pass, MT	Larry R. Price	Larry R. Price	1971	337
379 6/8	52	51 6/8	36 2/8	10	10	9	8	Adams Co., ID	William V. Baker	William V. Baker	1976	337
379 6/8	58 2/8	58 4/8	46 6/8	8 6/8	8 6/8	7	7	Grant Co., NM	Tony R. Grijalva	Tony R. Grijalva	1983	337
379 6/8	51 2/8	53 6/8	45 6/8	9 2/8	9 5/8	7	7	Park Co., WY	Timothy D. Metzler	Timothy D. Metzler	1994	337
379 6/8	54 7/8	56 6/8	41 2/8	9	8 7/8	6	6	Cibola Co., NM	Picked Up	Robert J. Seeds	1997	337
379 6/8	51 7/8	53 1/8	38 4/8	9 5/8	8 5/8	6	6	Millard Co., UT	Darwin B. Johnson	Darwin B. Johnson	2000	337
379 6/8	56 3/8	54	47	11 5/8	9 5/8	6	6	Carbon Co., UT	Paul J. Barton	Paul J. Barton	2002	337
379 5/8	57	53 1/8	48 1/8	9 2/8	9 2/8	6	6	Big Horn Mts., WY	Unknown	L.M. Brownell	1956	347
379 5/8	53 7/8	48 2/8	55	8 2/8	8 4/8	7	7	Valley Co., ID	Joe Gisler	Joe Gisler	1961	347
379 5/8	54 5/8	52 3/8	40 1/8	9 2/8	9 5/8	7	6	Gila Co., AZ	Bennie J. Rossetto	Bennie J. Rossetto	2001	347
379 4/8	51 7/8	52 3/8	39	9 7/8	9 7/8	6	6	Madison Co., MT	LeRoy Schweitzer	LeRoy Schweitzer	1964	350
379 4/8	58 1/8	58 4/8	41 6/8	8 2/8	7 5/8	7	7	Coconino Co., AZ	Dwight Crump	Dwight Crump	1997	350
379 4/8	59 2/8	61	39 6/8	7 5/8	7 5/8	6	6	King Co., WA	M. Sayers & L. Read	Michael L. Sayers	2003	350
379 3/8	54	52 6/8	42 3/8	8	7 4/8	6	6	Unknown	Gift of Arch. Rogers to NCHH	Unknown	PR 1951	353
379 3/8	60 1/8	61 1/8	45 5/8	8 7/8	8 3/8	6	6	Coconino Co., AZ	Tammy J. Otero	Tammy J. Otero	1984	353
379 3/8	51 2/8	47	42 3/8	9 4/8	9 7/8	6	6	Otero Co., NM	Hubert R. Kennedy	Hubert R. Kennedy	1985	353
379 3/8	52 4/8	53 6/8	40 1/8	11 1/8	12	6	6	Sierra Co., NM	James D. Wagner	James D. Wagner	1986	353
379 3/8	50	55 1/8	36 5/8	9 6/8	9 5/8	7	7	Red Deer River, SK	Emile Casavant	Emile Casavant	1997	353
379 2/8	55 7/8	56 1/8	44 4/8	9	8 7/8	6	6	Bozeman, MT	K.L. Berry	K.L. Berry	1959	358
379 2/8	58 3/8	57 2/8	41 6/8	9	9 4/8	6	6	Sierra Blanca Lake, AZ	Joseph A. Rozum	Joseph A. Rozum	1965	358
379 2/8	54 4/8	56 4/8	40 4/8	8 2/8	8 1/8	6	6	Sanders Co., MT	Robert L. Coates	Robert L. Coates	1974	358
379 2/8	57 1/8	55 5/8	41 6/8	8 1/8	8	6	6	Fremont Co., WY	Larry C. Nicholas	Frank J. Vrablic	1976	358
379 2/8	53 4/8	52 2/8	44	8	8 4/8	6	6	Yakima Co., WA	Donald G. Stein	Donald G. Stein	1985	358
379 2/8	53 4/8	53 4/8	41 4/8	8 5/8	8 7/8	6	6	Whirlpool River, MB	Rudy R. Usick	Rudy R. Usick	1989	358
379 2/8	56 3/8	57 1/8	53 2/8	8 6/8	8 3/8	6	6	Coconino Co., AZ	Fred Williams	Fred Williams	1990	358
379 2/8	54 5/8	53 5/8	41 2/8	9 4/8	9 6/8	6	6	Millard Co., UT	Timothy D. Park	Timothy D. Park	1996	358
379 1/8	56	57 4/8	33 7/8	8 6/8	9 1/8	6	6	Duvernay Bridge, AB	Alec Mitchell	Alec Mitchell	1917	366
379 1/8	56 6/8	56 1/8	45 5/8	9 5/8	9 3/8	6	7	Coconino Co., AZ	Charles M. Krieger	Charles M. Krieger	1992	366
379	50 4/8	51 1/8	40 6/8	9	8 6/8	6	6	Big Creek, ID	Picked Up	George Dovel	1963	368
379	49	50 4/8	39	10 1/8	10 1/8	8	8	Teton Park, WY	S.M. Vilven	S.M. Vilven	1964	368
379	50 7/8	51	44 4/8	9 7/8	10 2/8	6	6	Petroleum Co., MT	Lana J. Sluggett	Lana J. Sluggett	1984	368

258

Score	Main Beam R	Main Beam L	Inside Spread	Circ. R	Circ. L	Pts R	Pts L	Locality	Hunter	Owner	Date	Rank
379	52 4/8	53 2/8	40 6/8	8 2/8	8 3/8	7	7	Albany Co., WY	Carl G. Gross	Carl G. Gross	1995	368
379	57 3/8	56 5/8	44 6/8	10 2/8	10 4/8	6	6	Moffat Co., CO	Rod B. Morrison	Rod B. Morrison	1996	368
378 7/8	57 5/8	58 6/8	47 1/8	8 2/8	8 2/8	6	6	Carbon Co., WY	Donal F. Mueller	Donal F. Mueller	1964	373
378 7/8	56 6/8	56 1/8	46 5/8	8 4/8	8	6	6	Wildhay River, AB	Richard Clouthier	Richard Clouthier	1973	373
378 7/8	51 7/8	50 5/8	45 7/8	8 6/8	8 6/8	6	7	Grant Co., NM	Picked Up	David Palmer	1986	373
378 7/8	56 7/8	56 1/8	45 5/8	9 4/8	9 1/8	6	6	Elko Co., NV	Roger T. Mering	Roger T. Mering	1999	373
378 7/8	59 5/8	57 6/8	47 6/8	9 6/8	8 6/8	7	7	Millard Co., UT	Michael T. Kinney	Michael T. Kinney	2000	373
378 6/8	55	54 4/8	45	8	7 4/8	6	6	Gallatin Co., MT	Ted Shook	Ted Shook	1966	378
378 6/8	54 6/8	52 7/8	44 3/8	9 7/8	9 6/8	5	6	Otter Lake, MB	Walter Giesbrecht	Walter Giesbrecht	1989	378
378 5/8	52	55 2/8	44 7/8	8 7/8	8 6/8	6	6	Dutch Creek, AB	Harold King	Harold King	1951	380
378 5/8	50 7/8	53 3/8	44 7/8	8 4/8	8 4/8	7	7	White Pine Co., NV	George N. DeLong	George N. DeLong	2001	380
378 4/8	52 7/8	54 5/8	42 4/8	9 3/8	10	7	6	Park Co., WY	Kenneth Smith	Kenneth Smith	1954	382
378 4/8	54 3/8	55 3/8	45 2/8	8 6/8	8 6/8	6	6	Shoshone Co., ID	Edward L. Bradford	Edward L. Bradford	1963	382
378 4/8	58 3/8	56 3/8	43 6/8	8 4/8	8 3/8	6	6	Beaverhead Co., MT	Milton F. Steele	Milton F. Steele	1963	382
378 4/8	51 3/8	49 6/8	40 3/8	9 3/8	9 1/8	6	6	Park Co., MT	M.J. Young	M.J. Young	1967	382
378 4/8	50 1/8	50 3/8	36 2/8	11 5/8	11 1/8	6	8	Idaho Co., ID	Johnny Bliznak	Johnny Bliznak	1990	382
378 4/8	56 3/8	57 3/8	50 6/8	10 1/8	9 1/8	6	6	Apache Co., AZ	Robert E. Sterling	Robert E. Sterling	1991	382
378 4/8	52 4/8	52 4/8	43 6/8	8 5/8	9 3/8	7	7	Catron Co., NM	Terry K. Miller	Terry K. Miller	1997	382
378 4/8	53 4/8	51 6/8	38 4/8	9 4/8	9 4/8	6	6	Johnson Co., WY	Richard G. Pallister	Richard G. Pallister	1998	382
378 3/8	56	54 5/8	50 7/8	7 5/8	8 1/8	6	7	Panther River, AB	Allen Meyer	Allen A. Meyer	1993	390
378 3/8	49 5/8	49 7/8	42 7/8	8 4/8	8 5/8	6	7	San Juan Co., UT	Jeffery B. Booey	Jeffery B. Booey	1997	390
378 2/8	51 4/8	52 6/8	50	9 2/8	9 1/8	7	6	White River, CO	Art Wright	Art Wright	1953	392
378 1/8	60 5/8	58 1/8	47 5/8	8 3/8	8 3/8	6	7	Walla Walla Co., WA	Warren Robison	Kathy Lilya	1955	393
378 1/8	53 4/8	54 7/8	52 5/8	7 5/8	7 5/8	7	7	Navajo Co., AZ	Stanford H. Atwood, Jr.	Stanford H. Atwood, Jr.	1987	393
378 1/8	52 4/8	53 2/8	39 7/8	7 1/8	6 7/8	7	7	Langill Lake, BC	Gary D. Fodor	Gary D. Fodor	1989	393
378	49 3/8	50 2/8	39 5/8	8 1/8	8 6/8	7	8	Richard's Peak, MT	Albert Sales	Richard Eastman	1931	396
378	56 1/8	56 7/8	44 2/8	7 6/8	7 6/8	6	7	Gunnison Co., CO	Ed Lattimore, Jr.	Ed Lattimore, Jr.	1966	396
378	55	54 1/8	46 7/8	8 4/8	9 2/8	8	8	Catron Co., NM	Jayson W. Lucero	Jayson W. Lucero	1997	396
378	57 3/8	53 7/8	40 4/8	9 2/8	9 4/8	7	7	Teton Co., WY	Jessica L. Hedges	Jessica L. Hedges	2000	396
378	52 6/8	51 7/8	42 2/8	8 2/8	8 1/8	7	7	Cache Co., UT	Cory L. Jensen	Cory L. Jensen	2001	396
378	50	50 5/8	40	8 5/8	8 6/8	6	6	Johnson Co., WY	Richard A. Paradis	Richard A. Paradis	2001	396
378	55 3/8	50 7/8	46 2/8	9 5/8	9	6	6	Otero Co., NM	Scott M. Spangler	Scott M. Spangler	2003	396
377 7/8	56 2/8	56	46 2/8	8 3/8	8 2/8	6	6	Piute Co., UT	Michael G. Burr	Michael G. Burr	1961	404
377 7/8	52 7/8	53 6/8	47 1/8	8 4/8	9 4/8	7	7	Baker Co., OR	Donald B. Martin	Donald B. Martin	2002	404
377 7/8	52	51 6/8	41 5/8	8 1/8	9	6	6	Millard Co., UT	Reed Mellor	Reed Mellor	1959	406
377 6/8	51 3/8	52 3/8	45	8	8 3/8	7	7	Routt Co., CO	Tom Nidey	Tom Nidey	1973	406
377 6/8	56 6/8	55 6/8	41 6/8	8 2/8	8 2/8	10	9	Sanders Co., MT	Steve Barnes	Steve Barnes	1973	406
377 5/8	53 4/8	53 4/8	41 6/8	9 5/8	9	9	9	Mistatin, SK	Peter Hrbachek	Peter Hrbachek	1984	406
377 5/8	54 2/8	54 5/8	40 6/8	8 1/8	8 6/8	7	6	Apache Co., AZ	A.C. Goodell	A.C. Goodell	1963	409
377 5/8	53 7/8	53 7/8	51 7/8	9 1/8	9	6	7	Beaverhead Co., MT	Edmund J. Giebel	Edmund J. Giebel	1981	409
377 4/8	56 7/8	54 3/8	46 2/8	8 6/8	8 6/8	6	6	Jefferson Co., MT	Paul H. Temple	Gary L. Temple	1927	411
377 4/8	54 3/8	54 3/8	45 5/8	8 1/8	8 6/8	7	6	Granite Co., MT	Tom Villeneue	Tom Villeneue	1966	411
377 4/8	52 2/8	53 1/8	42 2/8	8 4/8	8 5/8	6	6	Ft. Apache Res., AZ	Picked Up	Gary Marsh	1971	411
377 4/8	47 5/8	47 2/8	45	8 5/8	8 4/8	6	7	Gunnison Co., CO	Leo Welch	Leo Welch	1972	411
377 4/8	57 4/8	55 1/8	37 4/8	9 3/8	9 5/8	6	6	Idaho	Unknown	Dale S. Rasmus	1973	411
377 3/8	52 2/8	52 2/8	41 4/8	8 3/8	8 6/8	7	7	Park Co., WY	Jon M. Mekeal	Jon M. Mekeal	1984	411
377 3/8	59	55	39 3/8	9 7/8	9 7/8	6	6	Teton Co., WY	Walter V. Solinski	Walter V. Solinski	1962	417
377 3/8	60	58	41 7/8	8 4/8	8 5/8	6	6	Sanders Co., MT	Allen White	Allen White	1968	417

AMERICAN ELK - TYPICAL ANTLERS
Cervus elaphus nelsoni and related subspecies

Score	Length of Main Beam R	L	Inside Spread	Circumference at Smallest Place Between First and Second Points R	L	Number of Points R	L	Locality	Hunter	Owner	Date Killed	Rank
377 3/8	53 1/8	52	46 1/3	8 4/8	9 1/8	6	6	Missoula Co., MT	Tom Schenarts	Tom Schenarts	1970	417
377 3/8	53 6/8	53 6/8	45 7/8	9 1/8	9 2/8	6	6	Lawrence Co., SD	Larry Miller	Larry Miller	1980	417
377 3/8	49 3/8	49 7/8	40 3/3	11 2/8	10 2/8	6	6	Petroleum Co., MT	Jack Atcheson, Jr.	Jack Atcheson, Jr.	1990	417
377 2/8	53 5/8	53 6/8	49 2/3	8 2/8	8 2/8	6	7	Gallatin Range, MT	E. Dehart, Sr., P. Van Beek, & H. Prestine	Earl Dehart, Sr.	1960	422
377 2/8	55 4/8	60 1/8	50 6/8	9 7/8	10 3/8	6	6	Show Low, AZ	Michael Pew	Michael Pew	1964	422
377 2/8	56	55 2/8	40 2/3	11 1/8	11	6	6	Park Co., WY	Mary J. Rickman	M.J. Rickman & E.R. Rickman, Jr.	1965	422
377 2/8	54 2/8	54 2/8	44 2/8	8 2/8	8 1/8	7	7	Apache Co., AZ	Donald E. Franklin	Donald E. Franklin	1981	422
377 1/8	53	51 6/8	45 4/8	9	8 5/8	6	8	Sublette Co., WY	Ted Dew	Ted Dew	1928	426
377	54 6/8	54 1/8	47 2/8	9 2/8	8 5/8	7	6	Brazeau River, AB	Ted Loblaw	Ted Loblaw	1960	427
377	45 6/8	46 4/8	42 2/8	7 4/8	7 2/8	7	7	Navajo Co., AZ	Melvin Nolte, Jr.	Melvin Nolte, Jr.	1983	427
377	49 4/8	48 1/8	39	7 1/8	7 4/8	7	7	Clearwater River, AB	Don H. Grimes	Don H. Grimes	1985	427
377	58 5/8	56 4/8	47 4/8	8 6/8	8 1/8	7	7	Benton Co., WA	Daniel J. Bishop	Daniel J. Bishop	1988	427
377	57 2/8	57 5/8	41 2/8	9 3/8	9 5/8	6	7	San Juan Co., UT	Bob Mitchell	Bob W. Mitchell	1998	427
377	52 5/8	54 6/8	38 3/8	9 2/8	9 3/8	7	7	Dawes Co., NE	John Walker	John Walker	1998	427
376 7/8	55	55 6/8	38 3/8	9 5/8	10 2/8	7	6	Jackson Hole, WY	H.M. Hanna	M.H. Haskell	PR 1890	433
376 7/8	56 4/8	57 2/8	52 2/8	7 3/8	7 7/8	6	6	Park Co., WY	Warren C. Cubbage	Warren C. Cubbage	1957	433
376 7/8	54 4/8	54 5/8	57 3/8	6 6/8	6 7/8	6	6	Routt Co., CO	J.L. Bailey	J.L. Bailey	1963	433
376 7/8	46 6/8	45 6/8	42 6/8	10	9 6/8	7	6	Flotten Lake, SK	Garry G. Ronald	Garry G. Ronald	1987	433
376 7/8	50 2/8	51 3/8	44 3/8	9 6/8	9 5/8	6	6	Red Deer River, AB	Donald E. Charlton	Donald E. Charlton	1999	433
376 6/8	56 5/8	54 4/8	44 6/8	9 4/8	9 3/8	7	7	Big Horn Mts., WY	Unknown	A.W. Hendershot	1912	438
376 6/8	51 3/8	52 4/8	48 2/8	8 4/8	8 3/8	8	7	Lewis & Clark Co., MT	Cameron G. Mielke	Cameron G. Mielke	1964	438
376 6/8	61	58 7/8	51	8 3/8	7 3/8	8	7	Teton Co., WY	Ward Keevert	Ward Keevert	1968	438
376 6/8	59 3/8	59 7/8	45 4/8	10	9 2/8	8	7	Crook Co., OR	Picked Up	Larry E. Miller	1983	438
376 6/8	51 1/8	51 6/8	40	8 1/8	8 1/8	8	7	Fremont Co., ID	Phil S. Borresen	Phil S. Borresen	1996	438
376 5/8	58 6/8	56 3/8	48 1/8	7 6/8	7 6/8	7	6	Granby, CO	Melvin Van Lewen	CO Div. of Wildl.	1961	443
376 5/8	48	50 1/8	39 3/8	8 5/8	8 7/8	6	7	Teton Co., ID	Edwin E. Schiess	Tim Schiess	1966	443
376 5/8	51 3/8	52 3/8	43 3/8	8 2/8	7 6/8	6	6	Unknown	Unknown	Charles F. Seibold	PR 1978	443
376 5/8	54 6/8	56 2/8	45 3/8	9 4/8	9 4/8	6	6	Coconino Co., AZ	Brent V. Trumbo	Brent V. Trumbo	1999	443
376 4/8	56 5/8	57	39 4/8	9 3/8	9 5/8	7	7	Highwood River, AB	Leonard Edwards	Ralph Seitz	1956	447
376 4/8	55 1/8	53 4/8	49 6/8	8 2/8	8 5/8	8	7	Albany Co., WY	Jerry F. Cook	Jerry F. Cook	1965	447
376 3/8	48 4/8	49 2/8	40 3/8	8	8 1/8	8	7	White River, CO	Ron Vance	Ronald Crawford	1957	449
376 3/8	49 3/8	49 7/8	41 5/8	7 7/8	7 4/8	6	6	Radium, CO	Bill Mercer	Bill Mercer	1964	449
376 3/8	54 2/8	55 5/8	43 3/8	9	9 1/8	6	6	Rocky Mt. House, AB	George P. Ebl	George P. Ebl	1966	449
376 3/8	55 5/8	55	30 2/8	8 6/8	8 4/8	7	6	Valley Co., ID	Ron Gastelecutto	Ron Gastelecutto	1985	449

Score	Main Beam R	Main Beam L	Inside Spread	Circ. R	Circ. L	Pts R	Pts L	Locality	Hunter	Owner	Date	Rank
376 3/8	55 5/8	55 4/8	39 1/8	9	9	6	6	Gunnison Co., CO	Gerald J. Obertino	Gerald J. Obertino	1986	449
376 3/8	53 2/8	53 1/8	53 5/8	8 6/8	8 5/8	8	7	White Pine Co., NV	William R. Balsi, Jr.	William R. Balsi, Jr.	1999	449
376 2/8	52 4/8	52 4/8	46 2/8	10 1/8	10	7	7	Juab Co., UT	Andrea McPherson	Andrea McPherson	2003	455
376 1/8	56 4/8	58 3/8	42 1/8	8 4/8	8 2/8	6	6	Lincoln Co., NM	Jim C. Carter	Jim C. Carter	1981	456
376 1/8	54 6/8	55 4/8	38 1/8	8 2/8	8 2/8	6	6	White Pine Co., NV	Robert A. Jackson	Robert A. Jackson	1994	456
376 1/8	54	55 6/8	47 3/8	8 4/8	9	6	7	Albany Co., WY	Dean D. Dick	Dean D. Dick	1996	456
376 1/8	57 3/8	55 4/8	49 1/8	9 7/8	9	6	6	Cibola Co., NM	Bruce T. Berger	Bruce T. Berger	1997	456
376 1/8	51 2/8	51	42 1/8	8 4/8	9	6	6	Bear Lake Co., ID	Gary J. Christensen	Gary J. Christensen	2002	456
376	51	49 6/8	39 2/8	8 5/8	9	6	6	Clark Co., ID	Darrell D. Riste	Bud Gifford	1951	461
376	59	60 4/8	44 4/8	8	9	6	6	Almont, CO	John Schwartz	John Schwartz	1961	461
376	54 1/8	55	42	9 1/8	7 5/8	6	6	Dormer River, AB	D.C. Thomas	D.C. Thomas	1978	461
376	50 1/8	47 5/8	48 6/8	10 1/8	9 3/8	6	6	Apache Co., AZ	William C. Moore	William C. Moore	1983	461
376	54 6/8	53 3/8	43	7 5/8	7 4/8	7	8	Unknown	Raymond A. Hanken	Unknown	PR 1999	461
375 7/8	54 4/8	54 6/8	43 5/8	8 5/8	8 4/8	8	8	Flathead Co., MT	Pat Roth	Pat Roth	1966	466
375 7/8	52	52	37 3/8	8 5/8	9	6	6	Apache Co., AZ	McLean Bowman	McLean Bowman	1986	466
375 7/8	55 1/8	55 2/8	52 5/8	8 1/8	8 1/8	6	6	Morgan Co., UT	Vernon A. Ridd	Vernon A. Ridd	1995	466
375 6/8	50 4/8	50 4/8	43	8 2/8	8 4/8	6	6	Big Horn Mts., WY	Robert F. Retzlaff	Robert F. Retzlaff	1957	469
375 6/8	57 2/8	57 7/8	43	7 3/8	7 2/8	6	6	Buck Creek, WY	Andrew W. Heard, Jr.	Andrew W. Heard, Jr.	1958	469
375 6/8	50 6/8	50 6/8	40 4/8	10 4/8	9 4/8	6	6	Crow Valley, CO	Dale R. Leonard	Dale R. Leonard	1961	469
375 6/8	54 4/8	55 1/8	39 4/8	8 2/8	8 7/8	6	6	North Fall Creek, WY	Bob G. Penny	Picked Up	1981	469
375 6/8	52 1/8	52 1/8	37 2/8	7 7/8	8 4/8	7	7	Shoshone Co., ID	Ralph H. Brandvold, Jr.	Ralph H. Brandvold, Jr.	1983	469
375 6/8	49 3/8	49 6/8	38	9 4/8	9 6/8	6	6	Glenboro, MB	Peter Sawatzky	Peter Sawatzky	1992	469
375 6/8	53 4/8	56 5/8	47 2/8	8	7 5/8	6	6	Coconino Co., AZ	Randy S. Ulmer	Randy S. Ulmer	1997	469
375 6/8	58	58	40 3/8	10 4/8	10 2/8	7	7	Unknown	Demarest Mem. Mus.	Unknown	PR 1952	469
375 6/8	53	53	43 7/8	9 1/8	9	7	7	Madison River, MT	Dale A. Hancock	Dale A. Hancock	1967	469
375 5/8	54 3/8	54 1/8	43 7/8	8 3/8	8 2/8	6	6	Sanders Co., MT	Tony B. Cox	Tony B. Cox	1980	476
375 5/8	48	51 6/8	46 7/8	8 2/8	8 5/8	6	6	Rich Co., UT	Bill L. Shupe	Bill L. Shupe	1996	476
375 5/8	55 6/8	57 6/8	41 7/8	9 4/8	9 3/8	6	6	Billings Co., ND	Monte Hoggarth	Monte Hoggarth	2000	476
375 4/8	57 6/8	55 2/8	48 4/8	8 1/8	8 7/8	6	6	Jefferson Co., MT	Ralph J. Huckaba	Ralph J. Huckaba	1949	476
375 4/8	50	53 2/8	48 4/8	9 1/8	8 7/8	6	6	Fremont Co., WY	Edward J Patik	Edward J Patik	1962	481
375 4/8	52 6/8	52 6/8	34 1/8	8 1/8	8 4/8	8	8	Powell Co., MT	Allan F. Kruse	Allan F. Kruse	1977	481
375 4/8	47 6/8	47 6/8	42 4/8	9	9	6	6	Skamania Co., WA	Kevin Schmid	Kevin Schmid	1990	481
375 4/8	54	54	38 6/8	8 1/8	7 6/8	7	6	Broadwater Co., MT	Joel S. Taylor	Joel S. Taylor	2001	481
375 4/8	53 1/8	53 1/8	43 6/8	10 1/8	9 2/8	6	7	Jefferson Co., MT	Mrs. Lou Sweet	Mrs. Lou Sweet	1924	481
375 3/8	52	52	44 7/8	8 2/8	7 6/8	7	6	Teton Co., WY	Nathan E. Hindman	Unknown	PR 1950	481
375 3/8	52	52	43 1/8	9 1/8	8 3/8	7	6	Snake River, WY	W.H. Robinson	W.H. Robinson	1957	486
375 3/8	51 1/8	51 1/8	44 5/8	9	9	6	6	Park Co., MT	Bruce Brown	Bruce Brown	1967	486
375 3/8	58 7/8	58 7/8	39 7/8	7 5/8	7 5/8	6	6	Beaverhead Co., MT	Harold F. Krieger, Jr.	Harold F. Krieger, Jr.	1970	486
375 3/8	52 6/8	52 6/8	37 3/8	8 6/8	8 4/8	6	6	Apache Co., AZ	Howard J. Corbin	Picked Up	1989	486
375 3/8	49	49	45 3/8	8 5/8	8 7/8	7	7	Apache Co., AZ	Michael S. Muhlbauer	Michael S. Muhlbauer	1989	486
375 3/8	58 1/8	59 1/8	40 1/8	9	9	6	6	Sevier Co., UT	Lee M. Bass	Lee M. Bass	1995	486
375 3/8	59 3/8	59 3/8	55 6/8	10	9 5/8	6	6	Jackson Co., WY	Lannce Sudweeks	Lannce Sudweeks	1999	486
375 3/8	52 7/8	52 7/8	49	9 6/8	9 3/8	7	7	Ten Sleep, WY	Cliff Smith	Bill Blanchard	1954	486
375 2/8	54 5/8	54 7/8	36 2/8	7 4/8	7 7/8	7	7	Craig Co., CO	Kenneth Hadland	Kenneth Hadland	1959	495
375 2/8	54 4/8	51 4/8	47 7/8	8 7/8	8 7/8	8	8	Natrona Co., WY	Kenneth W. Cramer	Kenneth W. Cramer	1960	495
375 2/8	51 1/8	52	41	10 4/8	10	7	8	Colfax Co., NM	Victor R. Jackson	Victor R. Jackson	1976	495
375 2/8	55 2/8	55 3/8	41 2/8	8 3/8	8 3/8	6	6	Albany Co., WY	Margaret M. Lindley	Slim Pickens	1981	495
375 2/8	53	56	38	8 4/8	8 4/8	6	6	Albany Co., WY	Don Stewart	Don Stewart	1981	495

AMERICAN ELK - TYPICAL ANTLERS

Cervus elaphus nelsoni and related subspecies

Score	Length of Main Beam R	L	Inside Spread	Circumference at Smallest Place Between First and Second Points R	L	Number of Points R	L	Locality	Hunter	Owner	Date Killed	Rank
375 2/8	58 2/8	57 6/8	43 2/8	9 1/8	9 4/8	6	6	Broadwater Co., MT	James Davies	James A. Davies	1998	495
375 2/8	54 4/8	54	47 2/8	8 3/8	8	6	6	Multnomah Co., OR	Charles E. Feldhacker	Charles E. Feldhacker	2001	495
375 2/8	55 2/8	55 6/8	49	8 6/8	8 1/8	6	6	Coconino Co., AZ	John H. Noble III	John H. Noble III	2003	495
375 1/8	52	53 4/8	39 3/8	9	10	6	6	Prince Albert, SK	Unknown	Lucky Lake Sask. Elks	1926	504
375 1/8	58 4/8	58 5/8	37 3/8	10 2/8	9 7/8	7	7	Tonto Lake, AZ	Louise F. Campbell	Louise F. Campbell	1967	504
375	57 1/8	54	38	8	8	7	7	Denton Co., TX	O.Z. Finley	Joe B. Finley, Jr.	1934	506
375	52 6/8	52 5/8	47 4/8	8 6/8	9	6	6	Fremont Co., ID	Eva Calonge	Eva Calonge	1960	506
375	57 3/8	54 4/8	41 2/8	9 3/8	9 5/8	7	7	Park Co., MT	Robert M. Brogan	Robert M. Brogan	1972	506
375	59	58 6/8	42 2/8	9 7/8	9 2/8	6	6	Lewis & Clark Co., MT	James Bollinger	James Bollinger	1982	506
375	57 1/8	58 1/8	42 6/8	9 1/8	8 6/8	6	6	Wheeler Co., OR	William K. Bartlett	William K. Bartlett	1986	506
375	57 5/8	57 5/8	49 4/8	6 7/8	7 3/8	6	6	Coconino Co., AZ	Arthur D. Ortiz	Arthur D. Ortiz	1993	506
375	48 2/8	50 2/8	46 4/8	8 1/8	8 4/8	6	6	Wyoming	Unknown	Randy Clark	1994	506
375	59 4/8	58	42	8 6/8	9	8	7	Cibola Co., NM	Archie J. Nesbitt	Archie J. Nesbitt	1997	506
402 4/8*	56 3/8	58 4/8	44 6/8	10 1/8	10 6/8	6	6	Emery Co., UT	Brian J. Gilson	Brian J. Gilson	2003	
399 6/8*	51 3/8	52 2/8	36	9 6/8	9 4/8	7	6	White Pine Co., NV	Troy A. Means	Troy A. Means	2000	
396 7/8*	55 3/8	55 5/8	44 1/8	9 3/8	10 3/8	7	6	Garfield Co., UT	Ryan D. Brindley	Ryan D. Brindley	2003	

* Final score is subject to revision by additional verifying measurements.

CATEGORY
AMERICAN ELK - TYPICAL ANTLERS

SCORE
382-3/8

HUNTER
J.R. DIENST

LOCATION
CIBOLA COUNTY, NEW MEXICO

DATE OF KILL
SEPTEMBER 1998

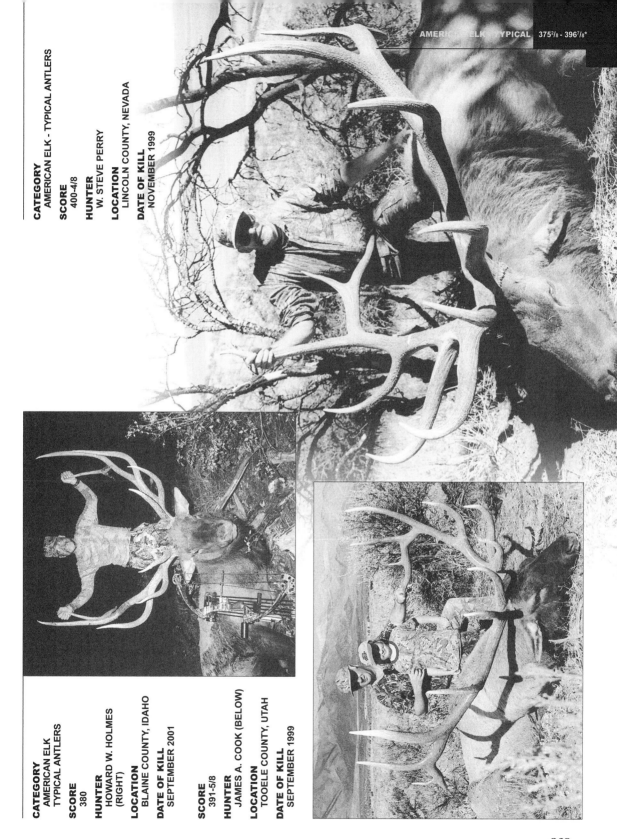

CATEGORY
AMERICAN ELK - TYPICAL ANTLERS

SCORE
400-4/8

HUNTER
W. STEVE PERRY

LOCATION
LINCOLN COUNTY, NEVADA

DATE OF KILL
NOVEMBER 1999

CATEGORY
AMERICAN ELK
TYPICAL ANTLERS

SCORE
380

HUNTER
HOWARD W. HOLMES
(RIGHT)

LOCATION
BLAINE COUNTY, IDAHO

DATE OF KILL
SEPTEMBER 2001

SCORE
391-5/8

HUNTER
JAMES A. COOK (BELOW)

LOCATION
TOOELE COUNTY, UTAH

DATE OF KILL
SEPTEMBER 1999

263

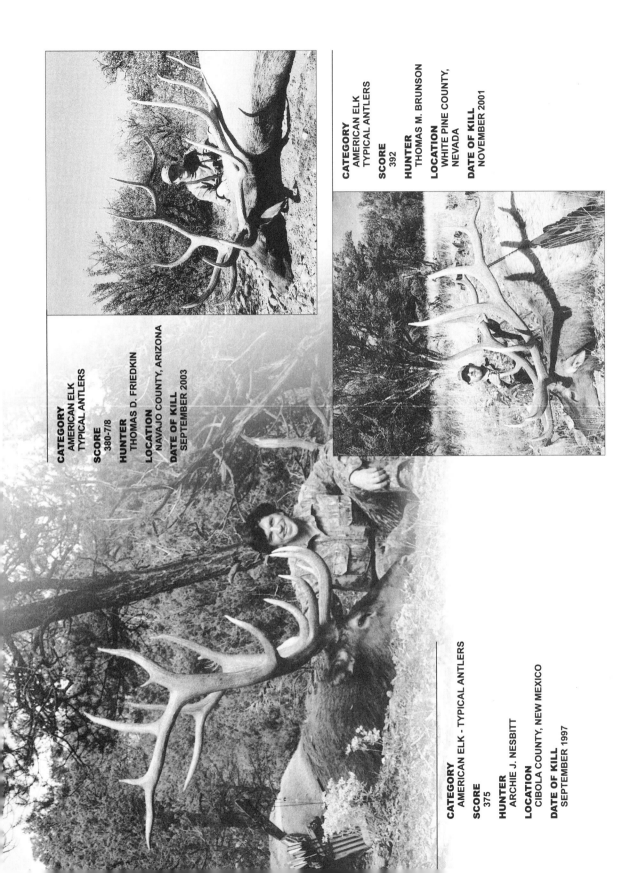

CATEGORY
AMERICAN ELK
TYPICAL ANTLERS

SCORE
380-7/8

HUNTER
THOMAS D. FRIEDKIN

LOCATION
NAVAJO COUNTY, ARIZONA

DATE OF KILL
SEPTEMBER 2003

CATEGORY
AMERICAN ELK
TYPICAL ANTLERS

SCORE
392

HUNTER
THOMAS M. BRUNSON

LOCATION
WHITE PINE COUNTY,
NEVADA

DATE OF KILL
NOVEMBER 2001

CATEGORY
AMERICAN ELK - TYPICAL ANTLERS

SCORE
375

HUNTER
ARCHIE J. NESBITT

LOCATION
CIBOLA COUNTY, NEW MEXICO

DATE OF KILL
SEPTEMBER 1997

B&C HISTORY

FREDERICK COURTENEY SELOUS
1851-1917

By H. Hudson DeCray

Perhaps the greatest of all African hunters, Selous was born in London, England, and educated at Rugby School. His dreams and ambitions took him to Southern Africa in 1871 where, at the age of 19, he undertook his legendary career as an elephant hunter and explorer. As a naturalist, his interests were diverse; he was ranked as one of the leading ornithologists of his day. He is credited with securing Mashonaland (later Rhodesia) for Britain in 1890. A gifted writer, he authored *A Hunter's Wanderings in Africa*, capturing the imagination of his native England. President Roosevelt considered him a hero and great friend, leading to his membership in the Boone and Crockett Club in 1907. He hunted throughout the American West and Canada. He returned to Africa to fight with the British in World War I and was killed in battle at Beho-Beho Ridge in Tanganyika on January 4, 1917. He was 65. ∎

AMERICAN ELK - NON-TYPICAL ANTLERS
WORLD'S RECORD

TROPHY INFO

RANK
World's Record

SCORE
465 2/8

LOCATION
Upper Arrow Lake, BC

HUNTER
Picked Up

OWNER
BC Environment

DATE PICKED UP
1994

On July 30, 1994, a huge elk was found floating in the Upper Arrow Lake of British Columbia. Conservation Officer, Jim Beck seized the salvaged antlers from a resident who had cut them from the rapidly decomposing body.

Though investigation into the cause of death would prove unsuccessful, Beck knew right off that this rack was deserving of a Boone and Crockett measurement. What he didn't know was the stir it was about to cause in an area of the Kootenays already known for its trophy bulls. With 9 and 11 points on the right and left antlers, respectively, the non-typical bull tallied an entry score of 456-3/8 points with a total of 47-3/8 inches of abnormal points. This was enough to potentially become the new World's Record.

Once the case was closed, the antlers were transferred to Rick Morley, Regional Fish and Wildlife Manager in Nelson, British Columbia. Officially measured at 465-2/8 points, the non-typical American elk was declared the new World's Record by the 23rd Awards Program Judges Panel. Interestingly, it was noted that the antlers were partially in velvet at the time of the bull's death and some of the main points had not fully hardened, indicating that they could have grown larger!

Elk management over the last 20 years in the Arrow Lakes portion of the Kootenays has deliberately aimed to produce trophy elk. Elk have gradually spread through this region from transplants in the 1950s and 1970s. Bull elk hunting, using a lottery permit system called Limited Entry Hunting (LEH), has been used since the early 1980s to control the harvest of bulls.

The management objective was to allow a significant number of bulls to reach 10 years of age or more, so they would have the body mass and condition to produce maximum growth. New populations were also given time to establish before very conservative hunts were initiated. Many of British Columbia's record elk antlers have resulted from this management strategy.

The Government of British Columbia plans to keep the antlers as a testimonial to the importance of elk in the Kootenay Region of British Columbia. Since 1995, the antlers have been treated by taxidermists, cleaned, stained, and put on a plaque for easier display. Efforts are being made to use the antlers to generate funds for elk management. These include the funds raised at Rocky Mountain Elk Foundation banquets and commissions on art work. Other means of generating funds for elk management, short of selling the antlers, will continue as well. ■

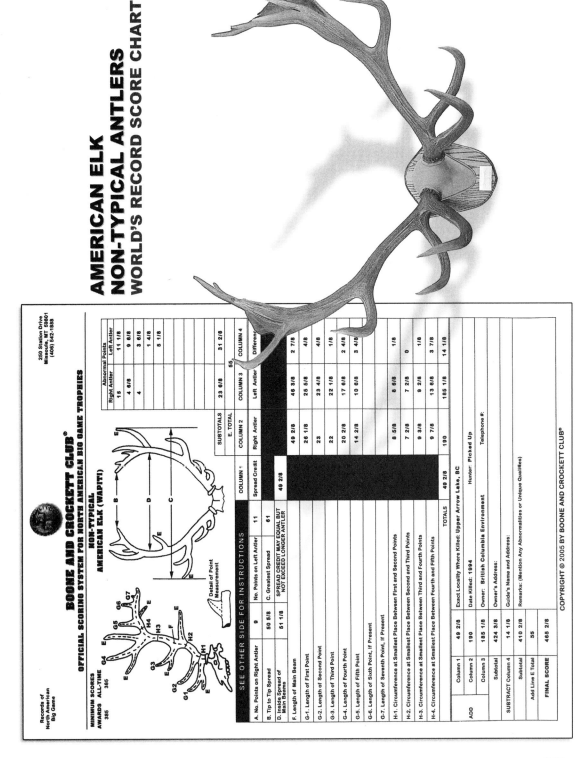

Records of North American Big Game

BOONE AND CROCKETT CLUB®

OFFICIAL SCORING SYSTEM FOR NORTH AMERICAN BIG GAME TROPHIES

250 Station Drive
Missoula, MT 59801
(406) 542-1888

NON-TYPICAL AMERICAN ELK (WAPITI)

AMERICAN ELK NON-TYPICAL ANTLERS WORLD'S RECORD SCORE CHART

MINIMUM SCORES
AWARDS 385
ALL-TIME 385

Detail of Point Measurement

SEE OTHER SIDE FOR INSTRUCTIONS

Abnormal Points	Right Antler	Left Antler
	15	11 1/8
	4 6/8	9 6/8
	4	3 6/8
		1 4/8
		5 1/8
SUBTOTALS	23 6/8	31 2/8
E. TOTAL		55

	COLUMN 1	COLUMN 2	COLUMN 3	COLUMN 4
A. No. Points on Right Antler 9 / No. Points on Left Antler 11	Spread Credit	Right Antler	Left Antler	Difference
B. Tip to Tip Spread 50 5/8				
C. Greatest Spread 61				
D. Inside Spread of Main Beams 51 1/8 / SPREAD CREDIT MAY EQUAL BUT NOT EXCEED LONGER ANTLER	49 2/8			
F. Length of Main Beam		49 2/8	46 3/8	2 7/8
G-1. Length of First Point		26 1/8	25 5/8	4/8
G-2. Length of Second Point		23	23 4/8	4/8
G-3. Length of Third Point		22	22 1/8	1/8
G-4. Length of Fourth Point		20 2/8	17 6/8	2 4/8
G-5. Length of Fifth Point		14 2/8	10 6/8	3 4/8
G-6. Length of Sixth Point, If Present				
G-7. Length of Seventh Point, If Present				
H-1. Circumference at Smallest Place Between First and Second Points		8 5/8	8 6/8	1/8
H-2. Circumference at Smallest Place Between Second and Third Points		7 2/8	7 2/8	0
H-3. Circumference at Smallest Place Between Third and Fourth Points		9 3/8	9 2/8	1/8
H-4. Circumference at Smallest Place Between Fourth and Fifth Points		9 7/8	13 6/8	3 7/8
TOTALS	49 2/8	190	185 1/8	14 1/8

ADD	Column 1	49 2/8
	Column 2	190
	Column 3	185 1/8
	Subtotal	424 3/8
SUBTRACT	Column 4	14 1/8
	Subtotal	410 2/8
	Add Line E Total	55
	FINAL SCORE	465 2/8

Exact Locality Where Killed: Upper Arrow Lake, BC

Date Killed: 1994   Hunter: Picked Up

Owner: British Columbia Environment   Telephone #:

Owner's Address:

Guide's Name and Address:

Remarks: (Mention Any Abnormalities or Unique Qualities)

KODAK 5062 PX

NUMBER 4 — 447-1/8 POINTS
JAMES R. BERRY — 1961

NUMBER 2 — 450-6/8 POINTS
ALAN D. HAMBERLIN — 1998

NUMBER 5 — 445-5/8 POINTS
JERRY J. DAVIS — 1984

NUMBER 1 — 465-2/8 POINTS
PICKED UP — 1994

NUMBER 3 — 449-7/8 POIN

NUMBER 6 — 444-4/8 POINTS
RONALD N. FRANKLIN — 2003

NUMBER 10 — 430-6/8 POINTS
BEN YOUNG — 1980

NUMBER 7 — 442-3/8 POINTS
DAN J. AGNEW — 2001

NUMBER 8 — 434-5/... — PRIOR TO ...
LAWRENCE SANCHEZ

NUMBER 9 — 432-5/8 POINTS
NATHANIEL BONI — 1994

269

AMERICAN ELK - NON-TYPICAL ANTLERS

Cervus elaphus nelsoni and related subspecies

MINIMUM SCORE 385

Score	Length of Main Beam R	L	Inside Spread	Circumference at Smallest Place Between First and Second Points R	L	Number of Points R	L	Locality	Hunter	Owner	Date Killed	Rank
465 2/8	49 2/8	46 3/8	51 1/8	8 5/8	8 6/8	9	11	Upper Arrow Lake, BC	Picked Up	B.C. Environment	1994	1
450 6/8	59	52 6/8	39 4/8	9 1/8	9 3/8	8	8	Apache Co., AZ	Alan D. Hamberlin	Alan D. Hamberlin	1998	2
449 7/8	55 1/8	53 7/8	44	8 7/8	9 4/8	8	7	Golden Valley Co., ND	Kevin D. Fugere	Kevin D. Fugere	1997	3
447 1/8	54 1/8	52 5/8	39 7/8	11	10 2/8	9	9	Gilbert Plains, MB	James R. Berry	D.J. Hollinger & B. Howard	1961	4
445 5/8	58	57 7/8	41 6/8	9 2/8	10	8	8	Apache Co., AZ	Jerry J. Davis	Jerry J. Davis	1984	5
444 4/8	54 6/8	52 6/8	52 2/8	9 4/8	9 4/8	9	10	Coconino Co., AZ	Ronald N. Franklin	Ronald N. Franklin	2003	6
442 3/8	53 7/8	49 7/8	44	8 7/8	9 2/8	7	8	Gila Co., AZ	Dan J. Agnew	Dan J. Agnew	2001	7
434 3/8	48 4/8	47	35 3/8	9 2/8	9 1/8	8	9	Colfax Co., NM	Lawrence Sanchez	Ed Sanchez	PR 1962	8
432 5/8	56 7/8	57 3/8	35 3/8	9 6/8	9 7/8	8	9	Gila Co., AZ	Nathaniel Boni	Alan C. Ellsworth	1994	9
430 6/8	46 5/8	51 5/8	45 3/8	8 6/8	9 4/8	10	8	Fraser River, BC	Ben Young	John Young	1980	10
430 2/8	56	55 7/8	49 7/8	7 7/8	8 2/8	8	9	Rio Blanco Co., CO	William D. Deweese	Royal Gorge Reg. Mus. & Hist.	1888	11
429 6/8	49 1/8	49 6/8	40	9 7/8	10 1/8	9	9	Navajo Co., AZ	Clay R. Heuett	Clay R. Heuett	2003	12
423 4/8	51 4/8	50 6/8	44 7/8	8 4/8	7 7/8	8	7	Granite Co., MT	Lee F. Tracy	Lee F. Tracy	1971	13
423	53 4/8	52 3/8	40	8 2/8	8 6/8	8	10	Coconino Co., AZ	James L. Ludvigson	James L. Ludvigson	1985	14
422 3/8	51 6/8	52 2/8	40 3/8	10	9 6/8	8	8	Navajo Co., AZ	John J. LoMonaco	John J. LoMonaco	1992	15
421 7/8	55	54	50 1/8	8 1/8	8 4/8	8	9	Kittitas Co., WA	Jeffrey G. Thorpe	Jeffrey G. Thorpe	2003	16
420 4/8	52	55 5/8	36 2/8	10 4/8	10 4/8	8	9	Kern Co., CA	Brad Peters	Brad Peters	2000	17
419 4/8	55 5/8	56	38 7/8	9 6/8	9 1/8	8	8	Yakima Co., WA	Jim R. Coe	James Walter	1932	18
417 6/8	58 1/8	52 1/8	47 4/8	9 3/8	9 2/8	7	9	Catron Co., NM	Martin D. Huggins	Martin D. Huggins	1992	19
417	57 5/8	56 5/8	48 4/8	10 6/8	9 6/8	7	6	Cibola Co., NM	Picked Up	Timothy A. Pender	1993	20
416 5/8	56 5/8	55 4/8	46	8 7/8	9 6/8	7	8	Navajo Co., AZ	Jack Mettler	Jack Mettler	2001	21
416 4/8	51 2/8	50 6/8	43 5/8	9 2/8	9 2/8	9	9	Navajo Co., AZ	John A. Gulius	John A. Gulius	1990	22
415 3/8	53 7/8	56 4/8	46 1/8	8 1/8	8 1/8	9	8	Steamboat Springs, CO	O.V. Johnson	Cabela's, Inc.	1952	23
415 2/8	54	55	42 6/8	8 7/8	9 4/8	8	8	Johnson Co., WY	Rod M. Odenbach	Rod M. Odenbach	1993	24
415 2/8	49 1/8	51 7/8	42	10 6/8	10 7/8	8	7	Apache Co., AZ	Thomas B. Anderson	Thomas B. Anderson	1999	24
414 6/8	49 4/8	54 2/8	45 3/8	9 5/8	10 3/8	8	8	Graham Co., AZ	Curley Bush, Jr.	Alan C. Ellsworth	1995	26
414 6/8	56 1/8	46 2/8	41	9 1/8	9 3/8	7	8	Navajo Co., AZ	James M. Cardwell	James M. Cardwell	2001	26
414 4/8	53 3/8	54 6/8	40 1/8	9 5/8	10 2/8	7	9	White Pine Co., NV	James A. Cook	James A. Cook	1996	28
414	43 6/8	44 7/8	34 5/8	10 2/8	11	9	10	Unknown	Unknown	Daniel F. Habjanetz	1858	29
414	48 2/8	48 2/8	46 7/8	7 3/8	6 5/8	9	10	Taos Co., NM	Lou A. DePaolis	Bass Pro Shops	1974	29
413 2/8	56	57	45 5/8	8 6/8	8 4/8	7	7	Coconino Co., AZ	Erik W. Swanson	Erik W. Swanson	2001	31
412 6/8	54 3/8	54 7/8	38 5/8	11 2/8	10 5/8	8	6	Apache Co., AZ	James P. Brooks	James P. Brooks	1997	32
412 1/8	55 4/8	60 7/8	46 7/8	7 7/8	8 1/8	8	6	Lewis & Clark Co., MT	Clinton N. Pierson	D.L. & R.O. Pierson	1935	33
412	53 4/8	53 4/8	44	11 5/8	11 1/8	7	8	Utah Co., UT	Jeffrey L. Didericksen	Jeffrey L. Didericksen	2002	34
411 6/8	52 7/8	50 4/8	49	9 6/8	9 2/8	9	7	Gallatin Co., MT	Unknown	Cabela's, Inc.	1965	35
411 1/8	55 4/8	55 3/8	41 2/8	10 3/8	9 7/8	10	8	Navajo Co., AZ	Dennis G. Hall	Dennis G. Hall	1996	36

Score	Main Beam R	Main Beam L	Inside Spread	Circ. R	Circ. L	Points R	Points L	Locality	By Whom Killed	Owner	Date Killed	Rank
410 3/8	48 3/8	52 5/8	45 1/8	10 6/8	11	7	8	Hill Co., MT	Brendan V. Burns	Brendan V. Burns	2000	37
410 1/8	46 3/8	47 1/8	50	9 4/8	9 3/8	11	10	Taos Co., NM	Picked Up	P.R. Ridilla & B. Adams	1993	38
410 1/8	54 6/8	53	45 3/8	9 3/8	8 7/8	7	7	White Pine Co., NV	George J. Brown	George J. Brown	1997	38
409 3/8	52 6/8	53	42 2/8	9 5/8	9 4/8	7	8	Coconino Co., AZ	Brent V. Trumbo	Brent V. Trumbo	2000	40
408 5/8	57 1/8	58 1/8	41	9 4/8	11 1/8	3	8	Apache Co., AZ	Herman C. Meyer	Herman C. Meyer	1992	41
408 5/8	53 2/8	52 3/8	45 6/8	8 5/8	9 4/8	3	6	Petroleum Co., MT	Riley T. McGiboney	Riley T. McGiboney	1998	41
408 4/8	50 7/8	47 1/8	41 5/8	10 2/8	9 5/8	9	9	Lincoln Co., MT	Picked Up	Grant Garcia	1995	43
408 3/8	57 4/8	58 2/8	46 7/8	7 7/8	8 6/8	9	9	Wallowa Co., OR	Lawton McDaniel	Doug McDaniel	1935	44
408	51 7/8	50 6/8	39 7/8	9	9 1/8	7	7	Sanders Co., MT	John Fitchett	John Fitchett	1980	45
408	53 5/8	53	40 6/8	9	8	7	7	Apache Co., AZ	J.G. Brittingham & W. Dale	Jack G. Brittingham	1987	45
407 6/8	54 6/8	54 2/8	46 4/8	8 5/8	7 6/8	8	8	Granite Co., MT	Scott Hicks	Scott Hicks	1971	47
407 3/8	54 6/8	52 6/8	40 3/8	9 7/8	9 1/8	8	8	Lincoln Co., MT	Terry V. Crooks	Terry V. Crooks	1996	48
407 2/8	53 7/8	47 2/8	48 7/8	8 2/8	7 4/8	8	9	Apache Co., AZ	Jay A. Kellett	Jay A. Kellett	2001	49
406 7/8	48 1/8	47 2/8	34 7/8	7 7/8	9 6/8	7	7	Apache Co., AZ	Joseph W. Carroll	Joseph W. Carroll	1982	50
406 6/8	43 4/8	47 3/8	40	9 6/8	7 1/8	9	9	Duck Mt., MB	John D. Harbarenko	Jerry McKoen	1973	51
406 4/8	53 6/8	54 2/8	42 2/8	7 5/8	10 5/8	10	10	King Co., WA	John Greiner	Alan C. Ellsworth	1953	52
406 4/8	53	53 3/8	39 6/8	10 5/8	9 3/8	8	8	Elko Co., NV	Randy Blackwell	Randy Blackwell	1999	52
406 3/8	55 5/8	51 2/8	49 6/8	9 5/8	9	7	7	Beaver Co., UT	Donald J. Willden	Donald J. Willden	2003	54
406 2/8	49 4/8	49 6/8	41 2/8	9	10 1/8	10	9	Fremont Co., WY	Unknown	Warren V. Spriggs, Sr.	PR 1952	55
406	57 2/8	54 2/8	40 4/8	10 2/8	8 5/8	8	9	Coconino Co., AZ	Clifford Happy	Clifford Happy	1994	56
405 5/8	53 1/8	50	38 4/8	9 4/8	9	8	7	Gila Co., AZ	R.J. Rick Smith	R.J. Rick Smith	2003	57
405 4/8	54 3/8	51 7/8	44	8 6/8	9 5/8	8	8	Granite Co., MT	Arthur W. Lundgren	Grace Lundgren	1946	58
405 3/8	54 2/8	54 7/8	46 5/8	10 4/8	8 2/8	7	8	Wallowa Co., OR	George Rogers	B.P.O.E., LaGrande Lodge 433	1933	59
405 3/8	59 4/8	58 1/8	40 2/8	8 4/8	9 6/8	8	7	Vermilion River, MB	Ernie M. Bernat	Ernie M. Bernat	1986	59
404 6/8	53 2/8	53 6/8	36 7/8	9 6/8	11 3/8	9	9	Juab Co., UT	David L. Naylor	David L. Naylor	2003	61
404 2/8	48	54	48 6/8	8 2/8	8 2/8	7	6	Flathead Indian Res., MT	Jimmie Walker	Cabela's, Inc.	PR 1991	62
404 2/8	54	54	50	10 1/8	10	7	7	Hualapai Indian Res., AZ	Tod Reichert	Tod Reichert	1975	63
404 1/8	51 6/8	52 5/8	37 2/8	9 7/8	10 1/8	7	7	Jefferson Co., CO	Chris White	Chris White	1993	64
403 7/8	46 5/8	52	32 4/8	10 3/8	10 6/8	8	8	Shoshone Co., ID	Fred S. Scott	D.J. Hollinger & B. Howard	1964	65
403 7/8	51 4/8	47 2/8	43 1/8	9 2/8	9	9	7	White Pine Co., NV	Geoffrey H.S. House	Geoffrey H.S. House	1994	65
403 6/8	50 1/8	63 6/8	40	9 4/8	7	6	8	Greenlee Co., AZ	Valentino J. Pugnea	Valentino J. Pugnea	1997	67
403 5/8	64 1/8	55 7/8	44 3/8	6 6/8	7 6/8	8	8	Catron Co., NM	Picked Up	Jack Diamond	1999	68
403 3/8	50 1/8	50 5/8	38 3/8	9 1/8	9 6/8	8	8	Coconino Co., AZ	Robert B. Krogh, Jr.	Robert B. Krogh, Jr.	1983	69
403 2/8	49 5/8	49 2/8	47 3/8	9 2/8	9 4/8	7	7	Yellowstone Co., MT	Charles A. Solem	Charles A. Solem	1995	69
403 1/8	57	59 3/8	47 4/8	8 6/8	9 2/8	6	9	Park Co., MT	Gary Beley	Gary Beley	1964	71
403	54 5/8	52 4/8	38 7/8	8 7/8	9 2/8	9	7	Big Horn Co., WY	Unknown	Steve Crossley	PR 1985	72
403	51 7/8	51 7/8	57 1/8	8 4/8	9 2/8	9	7	Uinta Co., WY	Steven W. Condos	Norman Heater	1967	73
403	52 5/8	52 3/8	43 6/8	8	8 4/8	8	10	Lincoln Co., MT	Delbert Bowe	Delbert Bowe	1992	73
402 7/8	48 2/8	49	31 6/8	10 5/8	10 4/8	8	8	Park Co., MT	Casey E. Turner	Casey E. Turner	2003	73
402 4/8	57 2/8	53 6/8	39	8 2/8	8 3/8	8	8	Powell Co., MT	Donald A. Roberson	Donald A. Roberson	1987	76
402 2/8	48 6/8	50	47 2/8	8 4/8	8 5/8	7	7	Selway River, ID	Unknown	Cabela's, Inc.	PR 1960	77
402 1/8	53 1/8	49 4/8	50 1/8	8 4/8	10 1/8	8	9	Dogrib Creek, AB	Robert H. Jochim	Robert H. Jochim	1984	78
402	55 6/8	55 7/8	41	11 5/8	11 7/8	7	8	Morton Co., KS	Jeff A. Newton	Jeff A. Newton	1988	79
401 7/8	48 5/8	49 2/8	38 3/8	8 6/8	8 2/8	8	9	Lundar, MB	Picked Up	Fred Thorkelson	1980	80
401 7/8	51 7/8	49	49 2/8	9 4/8	9 4/8	9	7	Beaverhead Co., MT	Ben C. Holland	Ben C. Holland	1953	81
401 6/8	54 3/8	51 6/8	46 3/8	9	10	7	8	Fergus Co., MT	Raymond J. Koch	Raymond J. Koch	2000	81
401 6/8	52 1/8	52	50 4/8	7 3/8	7 2/8	8	7	Rock Lake, AB	Harold R. Vaughn	Harold R. Vaughn	1968	83
401 5/8	53 5/8	55 5/8	43 3/8	7 7/8	7 4/8	8	7	Cowlitz Co., WA	Unknown	Steve Crossley	1959	84

AMERICAN ELK - NON-TYPICAL ANTLERS

Cervus elaphus nelsoni and related subspecies

Score	Length of Main Beam		Inside Spread	Circumference at Smallest Place Between First and Second Points		Number of Points		Locality	Hunter	Owner	Date Killed	Rank
	R	L		R	L	R	L					
401 4/8	48	45 1/8	39 1/8	11 5/8	11	8	11	Teton Co., WY	Douglas G. DeVivo	Douglas G. DeVivo	1992	85
401 4/8	48 6/8	47 7/8	32 6/8	9 1/8	9 7/8	7	10	Dauphin Lake, MB	Picked Up	Cabela's, Inc.	1998	85
401 1/8	51 3/8	51 3/8	47 6/8	9 1/8	9 4/8	8	6	Fremont Co., WY	Bud Cantleberry	Robert E. Cantleberry	1948	87
401	49 1/8	49 2/8	40 6/8	9 2/8	8 6/8	8	8	Cache Co., UT	Picked Up	L. Dwight Israelsen	1959	88
400 6/8	51 2/8	52	50 3/8	8 5/8	8 3/8	9	8	Madison Co., MT	Arthur A. Cooper	Arthur A. Cooper	1962	89
400 6/8	54 3/8	54	48 3/8	10 2/8	10 1/8	8	8	Mesa Co., CO	William C. Parrish	William C. Parrish	1994	89
400 6/8	55 1/8	55	50 5/8	7 6/8	7 7/8	7	8	Mesa Co., CO	Leland J. Cox	Leland J. Cox	2003	89
400 5/8	53 2/8	52 7/8	46 7/8	8 4/8	8 6/8	7	8	Montana	Unknown	William C. Perkins	PR 1870	92
400 4/8	54 7/8	54 6/8	40 5/8	7 4/8	7 2/8	10	8	Whipsaw Creek, BC	Harold Margerison	Harold Margerison	1899	93
400 2/8	52 7/8	52 3/8	42 1/8	8	7 6/8	8	7	Lemhi Co., ID	Bill Kelly	Bill Kelly	1967	94
400	55 3/8	53 4/8	42 2/8	9 7/8	9 5/8	6	7	Routt Co., CO	William E. Goosman	William E. Goosman	1939	95
400	55 1/8	53	41 6/8	9	10	12	8	Wallowa Co., OR	William L. Hamilton	William L. Hamilton	1982	95
400	56 5/8	51 3/8	43 2/8	8 5/8	8 7/8	8	7	Apache Co., AZ	Ben Hollingsworth, Jr.	Ben Hollingsworth, Jr.	1995	95
399 6/8	56 7/8	52	42 5/8	8 4/8	8 4/8	7	6	White Pine Co., NV	Stephanie C. Hull	Stephanie C. Hull	2000	98
399 3/8	59 3/8	60 4/8	43 3/8	9 2/8	10 2/8	7	7	Navajo Co., AZ	Marvin Brawley, Jr.	Pat E. Powell	2003	99
399 3/8	52	52 3/8	43 5/8	9 1/8	9 5/8	7	7	Pierce Co., WA	Larry N. Mohler	Larry N. Mohler	1991	100
398 5/8	52 7/8	51 3/8	42 3/8	10 1/8	10 1/8	7	9	Morton Co., KS	Camron Paxton	Camron Paxton	1987	101
398 3/8	52 2/8	51 1/8	37 6/8	8 7/8	9 3/8	8	9	Adams Co., ID	Unknown	Delvin L. Watkins	1955	102
398 3/8	48 2/8	47 7/8	37 3/8	8 3/8	8 3/8	10	9	Klickitat Co., WA	Ron Whitmire	Roger Kuhnhousen	1999	102
398 1/8	52 2/8	55	44 2/8	8 5/8	8 3/8	8	7	Park Co., MT	Picked Up	O. Cline Stelzig	1972	104
398 1/8	53 4/8	52 2/8	42 5/8	7 7/8	8 3/8	8	8	White Pine Co., NV	Brian D. Harwood	Brian D. Harwood	1998	104
398	49	53 4/8	38 1/8	9	9 6/8	8	9	Graham Co., AZ	George Harms	George R. Harms	1998	106
397 5/8	50 4/8	50 2/8	43	10	9 5/8	8	8	Greenlee Co., AZ	Gerald D. Spivey, Sr.	Gerald D. Spivey, Sr.	1997	107
397 4/8	47 7/8	51 6/8	35 2/8	8 5/8	8 1/8	8	7	Apache Co., AZ	McLean Bowman	McLean Bowman	1994	108
397 2/8	53 2/8	51 6/8	45 4/8	9 2/8	8 6/8	8	8	Powell Co., MT	Rex Sorenson	Philip L. Wright Zool. Mus.	1952	109
397 2/8	54 7/8	55	39 6/8	9 7/8	9 6/8	7	8	Billings Co., ND	Larry J. Fitterer	Larry J. Fitterer	1999	109
396 4/8	42 5/8	46 4/8	40 6/8	10 7/8	12 2/8	9	7	Tooele Co., UT	Jess Scott	Jess Scott	2003	111
396 3/8	54 7/8	54 3/8	54 4/8	11 1/8	10 4/8	8	6	Apache Co., AZ	Herman C. Meyer	Herman C. Meyer	1995	112
396 3/8	41 6/8	44	40 2/8	10 7/8	10 4/8	8	8	Pasqua Hills, SK	Wilfred Richer	Wilfred Richer	1998	112
396	52 7/8	51 4/8	38	9 4/8	9 2/8	7	6	Apache Co., AZ	Jay A. Kellett	Jay A. Kellett	1998	114
395 5/8	49 5/8	48	44 7/8	9 2/8	9 1/8	7	10	Fremont Co., ID	James E. Hoover	D.J. Hollinger & B. Howard	1976	115
395 3/8	51 5/8	50 7/8	40 4/8	8 7/8	9	7	7	Apache Co., AZ	Mark W. White, Jr.	Mark W. White, Jr.	1983	116
395 2/8	55 6/8	58 1/8	57	8 6/8	8 4/8	8	9	Coconino Co., AZ	Edward Boutonnet	Edward Boutonnet	1992	117
395 1/8	50 3/8	48 6/8	46 7/8	9 1/8	9	8	8	Hot Springs Co., WY	Unknown	Michael F. Conner	PR 1940	118
395	54	52 2/8	39 2/8	8 2/8	7 7/8	7	6	Unknown	Unknown	Cabela's, Inc.	PR 2001	119

Score	L.R	L.L	Inside Spread	Circ. R	Circ. L	Pts. R	Pts. L	Locality	Owner	By Whom Killed	Date	Rank
394 6/8	56	53 6/8	35 6/8	9	9 6/8	7	6	Otero Co., NM	Kelly R. Ginn	Kelly R. Ginn	1991	120
394 4/8	53	55 5/8	51 7/8	8 1/8	7 7/8	8	7	Sublette Co., WY	Charles R. Pennock	Charles R. Pennock	1942	121
394 4/8	47 4/8	50	41 4/8	8	7 5/8	7	7	Lytton Creek, BC	Cliff L. Loring	Cliff L. Loring	1984	121
394 4/8	31 6/8	30 3/8	33 2/8	10 4/8	10 2/8	10	12	Greenlee Co., AZ	Picked Up	Jaclyn M. Serfass	2002	121
394 3/8	46	47 2/8	35 1/8	11	10 1/8	9	9	Sandridge, MB	Joel Kayer	Joel Kayer	2003	125
394 3/8	55 5/8	49 7/8	42 5/8	9 7/8	9 6/8	8	7	Hill Co., MT	Picked Up	Gerald Small	1990	125
394 1/8	40 2/8	39 2/8	34 3/8	10 2/8	10	14	11	Carberry, MB	Brent Maxwell	Brent Maxwell	1991	127
393 6/8	58	56 6/8	44 6/8	8 7/8	8	6	8	Apache Co., AZ	Richard R. Childress	Richard R. Childress	1991	128
393 6/8	55 2/8	51 6/8	39 5/8	9 3/8	9 1/8	7	7	Yakima Co., WA	Jim Swanson	Cabela's, Inc.	PR 1963	128
393 3/8	54 5/8	55 6/8	46 6/8	7 5/8	7 4/8	7	8	Navajo Co., AZ	Larry G. Van Hassle	Burke Hudnall	1990	130
392 7/8	54 1/8	48 4/8	41 2/8	9 5/8	9 5/8	8	7	Shoshone Co., ID	Hugh M. Kitzmiller	John M. Kitzmiller	1974	131
392 7/8	55	56 4/8	41	8 5/8	8 4/8	9	8	Morkill River, BC	Picked Up	BC Mineral, Water, Land & Air	2003	131
392 5/8	56 3/8	54 1/8	45 3/8	8 7/8	9 1/8	7	7	Bowron River, BC	Greg Loring	Greg Loring	2003	133
392 4/8	46	56 1/8	46 7/8	7 7/8	8	6	8	Coconino Co., AZ	John L. Hontalas	John L. Hontalas	1990	134
392 2/8	54	47 5/8	41 6/8	12	12 1/8	7	8	Otero Co., NM	David U. Inge	David U. Inge	1989	135
392 2/8	56 1/8	55 2/8	47 2/8	9	8 1/8	8	8	Granite Co., MT	Robert E. Steffan	Robert E. Steffan	1956	135
392	54	56 1/8	39 5/8	10 6/8	10	8	6	Powder River Co., MT	Picked Up	Mark Kayser	1998	137
391 6/8	50 4/8	54	45 1/8	9 3/8	9 6/8	8	7	Mohave Co., AZ	Alfred L. McMicking	Alfred L. McMicking	1989	138
391 5/8	50 6/8	50 5/8	38 1/8	8 1/8	8 6/8	7	7	Columbia Co., WA	Ryan W. Block	Ryan W. Block	1999	139
391 3/8	47 1/8	51 1/8	37 6/8	9 2/8	9 6/8	9	7	Petroleum Co., MT	Russ Allen	Russ Allen	1995	140
391 3/8	46 4/8	55 2/8	42 6/8	10 2/8	10 4/8	8	7	Cibola Co., NM	Charlie Tamez, Jr.	Charlie Tamez, Jr.	1999	140
391 1/8	49	51 2/8	48 5/8	8 5/8	10 6/8	8	8	Gila Co., AZ	James P. Mellody, Jr.	James P. Mellody, Jr.	2001	142
390 7/8	52 5/8	45 4/8	46 3/8	9 3/8	9 6/8	8	10	Fergus Co., MT	Matthew D. McWilliams	Matthew D. McWilliams	1978	143
390 7/8	50 7/8	51 4/8	41	9 4/8	9 3/8	8	8	Apache Co., AZ	Theodore E. Dugey, Jr.	Theodore E. Dugey, Jr.	1993	143
390 5/8	55 4/8	51 1/8	46	9 7/8	9 2/8	7	7	Sublette Co., WY	Dale A. Shaklee	Dale A. Shaklee	1995	145
390 3/8	50 5/8	46 4/8	42 5/8	9 5/8	11	11	8	Apache Co., AZ	Hyland B. Erickson	Hyland B. Erickson	1900	146
390 2/8	51 6/8	49	55 3/8	9 1/8	9 3/8	8	7	Unknown	Unknown	W. Scott Smith	1995	147
389 7/8	50 2/8	52 5/8	38 2/8	8 3/8	8 1/8	10	11	Adams Co., ID	Robert F. Hughes	Robert F. Hughes	2001	148
389 7/8	50	49 7/8	43 3/8	8 6/8	8	7	7	Apache Co., AZ	Mark C. Harlow	Mark C. Harlow	2001	148
389	51 2/8	58 2/8	46 3/8	9 3/8	9 4/8	7	7	Albany Co., WY	Paul H. Reeder	Paul H. Reeder	1998	150
388 6/8	53	48 1/8	45	8 6/8	8 1/8	8	8	Juab Co., UT	Russell Jones	Russell Jones	1978	151
388 5/8	53	52	40 6/8	8 3/8	9 1/8	7	7	Shoshone Co., ID	Roger R. Davis	Aly M. Bruner	1998	152
388 4/8	53 3/8	50 5/8	42	9 4/8	9 1/8	8	8	White Pine Co., NV	Patrick J. Juhl	Patrick J. Juhl	2000	153
388 3/8	52 4/8	51 2/8	41 4/8	9	8 7/8	7	8	Saguache Co., CO	Anthony J. Heil	Anthony J. Heil	1990	154
388 3/8	50	50 4/8	53 6/8	10 7/8	11	7	8	Glacier Co., MT	John D. Fitzgerald	John D. Fitzgerald	1993	154
387 4/8	48 6/8	52 5/8	38 4/8	9 7/8	9 7/8	6	8	Platte Co., WY	Gary A. Pagel	Gary A. Pagel	1998	156
387 4/8	46 2/8	53 2/8	49 2/8	10 3/8	11 2/8	6	9	Lincoln Co., NV	Cory L. Lytle	Cory L. Lytle	1999	156
387 3/8	55 6/8	54 5/8	30 5/8	7 2/8	7 7/8	7	7	Coconino Co., AZ	James B. Herrick	James B. Herrick	2000	158
387 3/8	45 5/8	52 1/8	51 2/8	9 4/8	9 5/8	7	7	Pierce Co., WA	Wayne C. Milton	Craig S. Milton	2003	158
387 2/8	51 7/8	48 3/8	37 3/8	8 5/8	8 5/8	6	7	Garfield Co., UT	David R. Martin	David R. Martin	1992	160
387	50 6/8	44	43	9	8 6/8	8	7	Catron Co., NM	Robert J. Brooks	Cabela's, Inc.	2000	161
387	44 6/8	53 4/8	45 1/8	7	7 1/8	7	9	Crook Co., WY	Birch A. Negaard	Birch A. Negaard	2003	161
386 6/8	54 3/8	45 7/8	47 3/8	7 3/8	8 4/8	8	8	Navajo Co., AZ	Gary W. Crowe	Gary W. Crowe	2003	163
386 5/8	44 3/8	50 6/8	45 7/8	8 4/8	9 6/8	8	11	Unknown	Unknown	Donald F. Belker	PR 1981	164
386 4/8	50 2/8	46 1/8	38	9 6/8	9 6/8	5	7	Beaverhead Co., MT	Unknown	William H. Flesch	PR 1962	164
386 4/8	44 6/8	53 6/8	44	9	9	8	6	Gallatin Co., MT	Tom Satre	Tom Satre	1966	166
386 3/8	54 3/8	47 4/8	43 4/8	8 7/8	9	9	6	Apache Co., AZ	Alan Hamberlin	Alan Hamberlin	1994	166
386 2/8	44 3/8	47 4/8	43 4/8	8 7/8	9	9	6	Socorro Co., NM	Richard P. Gould	Richard P. Gould	1990	167

273

AMERICAN ELK - NON-TYPICAL ANTLERS
Cervus elaphus nelsoni and related subspecies

Score	Length of Main Beam R	L	Inside Spread	Circumference at Smallest Place Between First and Second Points R	L	Number of Points R	L	Locality	Hunter	Owner	Date Killed	Rank
386 2/8	50	50 1/8	41 4/8	8 6/8	8 4/8	7	7	Otero Co., NM	William M. Pitcher	William M. Pitcher	1992	167
386 1/8	56	54 1/8	39	10 2/8	10 3/8	7	6	Lincoln Co., NV	Jason House	Jason House	2001	169
385 6/8	51 6/8	51 7/8	38 6/8	8 7/8	9 2/8	8	8	Apache Co., AZ	R.G. Fraser, Sr. & M. Gatewood	Ronald G. Fraser, Sr.	1995	170
385 6/8	47 2/8	50	37	7 3/8	8 2/8	8	8	Socorro Co., NM	Kim C. Haberland	Kim C. Haberland	2002	170
385 5/8	50 4/8	49 7/8	35 4/8	9	9 7/8	8	7	Petroleum Co., MT	Gregory Herrin	Gregory A. Herrin	1997	172
385 2/8	56	55 5/8	43 5/8	11 7/8	11 6/8	7	8	Navajo Co., AZ	Truman Collins	Truman D. Collins	1998	173
385 1/8	50 5/8	48 6/8	40 4/8	7 5/8	7 4/8	9	8	Latah Co., ID	James A. Carpenter	James A. Carpenter	1985	174
385 1/8	63 2/8	63 6/8	49 7/8	8	7 4/8	7	7	Greenwater Lake Park, SK	Joseph C. Chernysh	Joseph C. Chernysh	1995	174
385 1/8	48 7/8	50	36 1/8	8 6/8	8	7	7	Clearwater Co., ID	Tim Papineau	Tim Papineau	1996	174
385	57 2/8	57 3/8	36 7/8	10 4/8	10 5/8	7	6	Navajo Co., AZ	David W. Baxter	David W. Baxter	1991	177
385	55 5/8	55 4/8	42 1/8	9 1/8	9 1/8	8	7	Navajo Co., AZ	Dennis K. Frandsen	Dennis K. Frandsen	1993	177
444 4/8*	56 5/8	54 2/8	40	9 1/8	11 4/8	8	13	Arm Lake, AB	John Almberg	John Almberg	1999	
434 1/8*	53 5/8	54 3/8	51	10 4/8	10 4/8	8	10	British Columbia	Picked Up	Neal Hutchinson	PR 1993	
424 6/8*	56 2/8	51 7/8	52 6/8	10 2/8	10 2/8	7	6	Lincoln Co., NV	Cindy S. Marques	Cindy S. Marques	2002	
423 4/8*	58	55 1/8	38 4/8	8 5/8	9 1/8	8	7	Yavapai Co., AZ	Lynn E. Munoz	Lynn E. Munoz	1998	
422 4/8*	55	56 1/8	39 4/8	11 7/8	10 7/8	7	8	Battle River, AB	Brent A. Kuntz	Brent A. Kuntz	2002	

* Final score is subject to revision by additional verifying measurements.

CATEGORY
AMERICAN ELK - NON-TYPICAL ANTLERS

SCORE
399-6/8

HUNTER
STEPHANIE C. HULL (ABOVE)

LOCATION
WHITE PINE COUNTY, NEVADA

DATE OF KILL
OCTOBER 2000

CATEGORY
AMERICAN ELK - NON-TYPICAL ANTLERS

SCORE
387

HUNTER
GARY W. CROWE (RIGHT)

LOCATION
NAVAJO COUNTY, ARIZONA

DATE OF KILL
OCTOBER 2003

SCORE
409-3/8

HUNTER
BRENT V. TRUMBO (BELOW)

LOCATION
COCONINO COUNTY, ARIZONA

DATE OF KILL
OCTOBER 2000

CATEGORY
AMERICAN ELK
NON-TYPICAL ANTLERS

SCORE
398-1/8

HUNTER
BRIAN D. HARWOOD

LOCATION
WHITE PINE COUNTY,
NEVADA

DATE OF KILL
SEPTEMBER 1998

CATEGORY
AMERICAN ELK
NON-TYPICAL ANTLERS

SCORE
412

HUNTER
JEFFREY L. DIDERICKSEN

LOCATION
UTAH COUNTY, UTAH

DATE OF KILL
DECEMBER 2002

CATEGORY
AMERICAN ELK - NON-TYPICAL ANTLERS

SCORE
416-5/8

HUNTER
JACK P. METTLER

LOCATION
CIBOLA COUNTY, NEW MEXICO

DATE OF KILL
OCTOBER 2001

CATEGORY
AMERICAN ELK - NON-TYPICAL ANTLERS

SCORE
391-3/8

HUNTER
JAMES P. MELLODY, JR.

LOCATION
GILA COUNTY, ARIZONA

DATE OF KILL
SEPTEMBER 2001

CATEGORY
AMERICAN ELK - NON-TYPICAL ANTLERS

SCORE
391-1/8

HUNTER
MATTHEW D. MCWILLIAMS

LOCATION
FERGUS COUNTY, MONTANA

DATE OF KILL
SEPTEMBER 2001

ROOSEVELT'S ELK
NEW WORLD'S RECORD

It was the summer of 2002, and Scott Ballard was enjoying the break from his high school shop teaching duties and working on a farm as a mechanic during the harvest. Ballard had drawn a Roosevelt's elk (*Cervus elaphus roosevelti*) tag for Western Oregon's Willamette Unit and was planning to hunt on the farm during the last of summer break.

A week before the start of the hunt, Ballard was approached by a co-worker, who said his dad had just seen five bulls in an un-thrashed ryegrass field on the property. They drove down to get a look, but the bulls had vanished into heavy cover before Ballard arrived. They walked the field and realized that the bulls had been in the area multiple times over the last few weeks. With large expanses of open field and difficult wind conditions, Ballard turned to his archery hunting tactics and decided to build a ground blind.

A dip in the landscape on the downwind side of the elk crossing offered an ideal location for the blind. Ballard marked the field in 100-yard increments out to 500 yards and practiced at these yardages to ensure accuracy.

The first few days of the hunt yielded close encounters with deer and varmints, but no elk were seen. On the ninth day of the hunt, however, Ballard's 7-year-old son, Benjamin, spotted what he described as "hay bales" moving in the field at about 400 yards. With eight minutes remaining until legal shooting light, they realized that the big "hay bales" were four massive bulls heading for the heavy brush. Ballard unsuccessfully attempted a stalk but by the time legal light arrived, the four bulls were 600-plus yards away and in the brush. Even from this distance, Ballard could see the two largest bulls were immense, and "Brutus" (the bigger of the two) was unlike anything he'd ever seen.

The next day, 12 minutes before shooting light, two six-point bulls and a third massive bull stepped out of the ash grove into the field at 450 yards. A few minutes later a tremendous 8x9 point bull appeared just inside the brush line—Brutus.

The bulls were within 100 yards of the property line, and Ballard knew time was of the essence. As the two six-point bulls sparred, the third bull watched on but Brutus stayed in the brush shredding trees. Concerned that the rising sun and commotion of battle would coach the group into the timber, Ballard decided to take the third bull instead of waiting for Brutus to step out.

Ballard found the bull broadside in the crosshairs, eased off the safety and adjusted himself on the rest. As he began to squeeze the trigger, the bull unexpectedly whirled and stared directly at Ballard. He put the safety back on and waited for the bull to turn back to broadside.

As time ran short, the fighting continued. With the third bull still glaring intently, Ballard saw Brutus ease into his field of view. Broadside at 450 yards, Ballard sent the bullet through the bull's shoulder and into his spine. Brutus, the new World's Record Roosevelt's elk, fell without another step. ∎

ROOSEVELT'S ELK
WORLD'S RECORD SCORE CHART

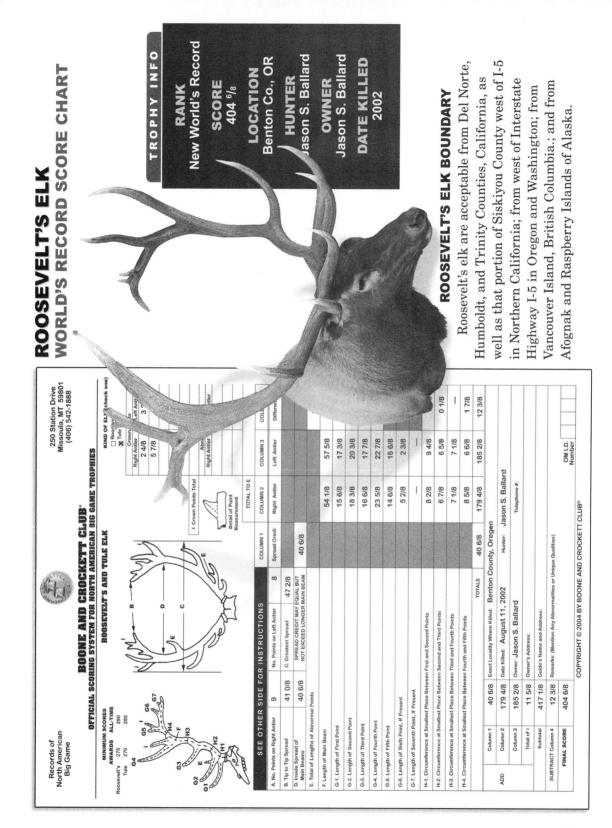

ROOSEVELT'S ELK BOUNDARY

Roosevelt's elk are acceptable from Del Norte, Humboldt, and Trinity Counties, California, as well as that portion of Siskiyou County west of I-5 in Northern California; from west of Interstate Highway I-5 in Oregon and Washington; from Vancouver Island, British Columbia.; and from Afognak and Raspberry Islands of Alaska.

Records of
North American
Big Game

250 Station Drive
Missoula, MT 59801
(406) 542-1888

BOONE AND CROCKETT CLUB®
OFFICIAL SCORING SYSTEM FOR NORTH AMERICAN BIG GAME TROPHIES
ROOSEVELT'S AND TULE ELK

MINIMUM SCORES	AWARDS	ALL-TIME
Roosevelt's	275	290
Tule	270	285

KIND OF ELK (check one)
☐ Roosevelt's
☒ Tule

	Crown Points	
	Right Antler	Left Antler
	2 4/8	3 7/8
	5 7/8	

E. Crown Points Total

Detail of Point Measurement

TOTAL TO E

SEE OTHER SIDE FOR INSTRUCTIONS		COLUMN 1	COLUMN 2	COLUMN 3	COLUMN 4
		Spread Credit	Right Antler	Left Antler	Difference
A. No. Points on Right Antler	9				
	No. Points on Left Antler	8			
B. Tip to Tip Spread	41 0/8				
C. Greatest Spread	47 2/8				
D. Inside Spread of Main Beams	40 6/8	SPREAD CREDIT MAY EQUAL BUT NOT EXCEED LONGER MAIN BEAM	40 6/8		
E. Total of Lengths of Abnormal Points					
F. Length of Main Beam			54 1/8	57 5/8	
G-1. Length of First Point			15 6/8	17 3/8	
G-2. Length of Second Point			18 3/8	20 3/8	
G-3. Length of Third Point			16 6/8	17 7/8	
G-4. Length of Fourth Point			23 5/8	22 7/8	
G-5. Length of Fifth Point			14 6/8	16 6/8	
G-6. Length of Sixth Point, If Present			5 2/8	2 3/8	
G-7. Length of Seventh Point, If Present			—	—	
H-1. Circumference at Smallest Place Between First and Second Points			8 2/8	9 4/8	
H-2. Circumference at Smallest Place Between Second and Third Points			6 7/8	6 5/8	0 1/8
H-3. Circumference at Smallest Place Between Third and Fourth Points			7 1/8	7 1/8	—
H-4. Circumference at Smallest Place Between Fourth and Fifth Points			8 5/8	6 6/8	1 7/8
	TOTALS		179 4/8	185 2/8	12 3/8

	Column 1	40 6/8	Exact Locality Where Killed: Benton County, Oregon
ADD	Column 2	179 4/8	Date Killed: August 11, 2002 Hunter: Jason S. Ballard
	Column 3	185 2/8	Owner: Jason S. Ballard
	Total of I	11 5/8	Owner's Address:
	Subtotal	417 1/8	Guide's Name and Address:
SUBTRACT Column 4	12 3/8		Remarks: (Mention Any Abnormalities or Unique Qualities)
FINAL SCORE	404 6/8		

Telephone #:

OM I.D. Number

COPYRIGHT © 2004 BY BOONE AND CROCKETT CLUB®

279

TOP 10 ROOSEVELT'S ELK

NUMBER 1 — 404-6/8 POINTS
JASON S. BALLARD — 2002

NUMBER 2 — 396-5/8 POINTS
KARL W. MINOR, SR. — 1997

NUMBER 3 — 388-3/8 POINTS
1989

NUMBER 4 — 384-3/8 POINTS
ROBERT SHARP — 1949

NUMBER 5 — 380-6/8 POINTS
SAM ARGO — 1983

Jason S. Ballard
Monroe
TROPHY: M2
KDAT:
KLOC:

KETT CLU
AMERICAN BIG GAME TROPHIE
TULE ELK

PAID
OCT 2 4 2002

Records
North Ame
Big Gam

MINI
AWAR
Roosevelt's 275
Tule 270

NUMBER 8 — 376-1/8 POINTS
NORMAN G. WILLIAMS — 1948

NUMBER 10 — 372-1/8 PQINTS
ROBERT H. GAYNOR — 2000

NUMBER 6 — 378-5/8 POINTS
FRED M. WILLIAMSON — 1947

NUMBER 7 — 376-3/8 POINTS
PICKED UP — 1912

NUMBER 9 — 374-3/8 POINTS
RONALD K. BRIDGE — 2002

ROOSEVELT'S ELK

Cervus elaphus roosevelti

MINIMUM SCORE 290

Score	Length of Main Beam R	L	Inside Spread	Circ. at Smallest Place Between First and Second Points R	L	Number of Points R	L	Locality	Hunter	Owner	Date Killed	Rank
404 6/8	54 1/8	57 5/8	40 6/8	8 2/8	9 4/8	9	8	Benton Co., OR	Jason S. Ballard	Jason S. Ballard	2002	1
396 5/8	46 3/8	46 7/8	32 3/8	8 7/8	9 5/8	10	9	Campbell River, BC	Karl W. Minor, Sr.	Karl W. Minor, Sr.	1997	2
388 3/8	44 2/8	46 7/8	36 1/8	11 2/8	11 2/8	11	8	Tsitika River, BC	Wayne Coe	Wayne Coe	1989	3
384 3/8	48 4/8	49	41 1/8	8 7/8	9 4/8	9	8	Clatsop Co., OR	Robert Sharp	Robert Sharp	1949	4
380 6/8	52 3/8	52 6/8	45 1/8	8 3/8	8 1/8	8	8	Jefferson Co., WA	Sam Argo	Sam Argo	1983	5
380 5/8	53 2/8	51 3/8	37	8 7/8	8 5/8	7	9	Clatsop Co., OR	Fred M. Williamson	Rusty Lindberg	1947	6
378 5/8	53 2/8	52 3/8	41 5/8	10 1/8	10 3/8	8	7	Clallam Co., WA	Picked Up	Roy C. Ewen	1912	7
376 3/8	51	49 1/8	38	10 1/8	10 3/8	8	7	Wahkiakum Co., WA	Norman G. Williams	Norman G. Williams	1948	8
376 1/8	50	47	42	9 2/8	8 5/8	8	8	Bonanza Lake, BC	Ronald K. Bridge	Ronald K. Bridge	2002	9
374 3/8	53 4/8	55 4/8	37 3/8	8 6/8	8 1/8	8	8	Del Norte Co., CA	Robert H. Gaynor	Loaned to B&C Natl. Coll.	2000	10
372 1/8	49 1/8	47 3/8	41	7 4/8	7 5/8	9	8	Columbia Co., OR	Picked Up	R.E. & T.D. Walker	PR 1940	11
372	47 4/8	49 5/8	34 5/8	8 6/8	8 4/8	8	8	Humboldt Co., CA	Scot A. Christiansen	Scot A. Christiansen	2000	11
372	53 4/8	54	39 5/8	8 7/8	8 2/8	7	9	Vancouver Island, BC	Lawrence A. Ondzik	Alf Spineto	1981	13
368	47 4/8	47 6/8	42 7/8	9 5/8	10	8	7	Woss Lake, BC	Johnny Bliznak	Johnny Bliznak	1992	14
367 6/8	50 3/8	53	37 4/8	9	8 5/8	7	7	Clatsop Co., OR	Pravomil Raichl	Cory D. Raichl	1959	15
367 5/8	43 5/8	46 7/8	39	9 2/8	9 6/8	9	8	Memekay River, BC	Armande Graham	Armande Graham	1994	16
367 3/8	51 6/8	51 4/8	43 2/8	9 6/8	9 6/8	6	6	Mason Co., WA	Unknown	George B. Putnam	1900	17
367	43	45 5/8	35 4/8	9	9 5/8	7	8	Columbia Co., OR	Floyd M. Lindberg	Floyd M. Lindberg	1962	18
366 5/8	46 6/8	46 5/8	43 4/8	9	9	7	8	Clatsop Co., OR	Oliver W. Dunsmoor	John R. Wall	PR 1938	19
363 1/8	46 6/8	45 5/8	37 4/8	9 4/8	9 1/8	7	7	Lincoln Co., OR	James H. Flescher	James H. Flescher	1955	20
362 6/8	45 7/8	45 4/8	38 5/8	9 2/8	9 2/8	8	8	Bonanza Lake, BC	Richard D. Smith	Richard D. Smith	1995	21
362 5/8	43 4/8	45 4/8	36	8 4/8	8 4/8	8	8	Clatsop Co., OR	Tod L. Reichert	Tod L. Reichert	2000	22
360 5/8	51 4/8	50 3/8	43 2/8	7	7 2/8	8	7	Clatsop Co., OR	Floyd Crandel	James C. Acock	PR 1960	23
359 7/8	49 2/8	53 5/8	43 2/8	9 6/8	10 2/8	7	7	Clatsop Co., OR	Donald A. Schoenborn	Eric Schoenborn	1939	24
358 6/8	51 4/8	51 4/8	42 2/8	9 5/8	8 7/8	7	8	Tillamook Co., OR	Albert Hoffarber	Ray Hoffarber	1940	25
358 5/8	55 4/8	53 4/8	42	8 6/8	8 5/8	8	8	Siskiyou Co., CA	Angela M. Cheula	Angela M. Cheula	2000	26
357 7/8	54 6/8	56 1/8	42 7/8	9 3/8	9 2/8	7	7	Davie River, BC	Larry A. Russak	Larry A. Russak	1999	27
356 4/8	48 4/8	49 7/8	35 2/8	9 2/8	9 6/8	8	7	Campbell River, BC	James L.M. Amos	James L.M. Amos	1998	28
356 2/8	48 5/8	50 7/8	38 1/8	9 7/8	10 7/8	6	7	Douglas Co., OR	Thomas B. Swanton	Thomas B. Swanton	1953	29
356	48 3/8	49 3/8	44 3/8	9 7/8	10	6	8	Vancouver Island, BC	Picked Up	Bruce Williamson	1955	30
355 4/8	50	52 1/8	42 1/8	9	9 2/8	8	8	Coos Co., OR	Hank Shields	Glenn Shields	1951	31
353 5/8	53 3/8	53	35 5/8	8 4/8	8 2/8	8	6	Coos Co., OR	Ken Wilson	Ken Wilson	1957	31
353 5/8	43 1/8	47 5/8	38 2/8	8 5/8	9 1/8	6	7	Washington Co., OR	Kenneth R. Adamson	Kenneth R. Adamson	1985	33
353 4/8	52	53 3/8	38 4/8	9 1/8	9 5/8	6	6	Bonanza Lake, BC	Wes Swain	Wes Swain	1996	34
353 1/8	51 1/8	51 3/8	36	9 1/8	9 5/8	7	7	Benton Co., OR	William Pitcher	William Pitcher	2003	34
352 5/8	53 2/8	50 5/8	40 7/8	7 7/8	7 6/8	8	9	Coos Co., OR	Bill Mattoon	Douglas County Mus.	PR 1907	36
351 7/8	49 2/8	49 4/8	46 6/8	9 4/8	9 4/8	8	7	Clatsop Co., OR	Steven E. Fick	Steven E. Fick	1995	37

Score	Length of Main Beam R	L	Inside Spread	Circumference R	L	Points R	L	Locality	Hunter	Owner	Date Killed	Rank
351 5/8	45	45 5/8	40 2/8	9 1/8	9 7/8	8	9	Menzies Bay, BC	Gordon J. Birgbauer, Jr.	Gordon J. Birgbauer, Jr.	1991	38
351 4/8	45 3/8	46 4/8	41 2/8	10	10 1/8	7	7	Sayward, BC	Ken Thulin	Ken Thulin	1996	39
350 3/8	47 6/8	47 4/8	35 7/8	11 1/8	11 7/8	7	7	Coos Co., OR	E.V. Schmidt	Steve Crossley	1948	40
349 3/8	48 2/8	46 2/8	40 3/8	9 3/8	9 3/8	7	7	Bonanza River, BC	Ted Brookman	Ted Brookman	2001	41
347 6/8	41 3/8	42 4/8	46 2/8	8 2/8	8	7	7	Tillamook Co., OR	Bud Davis	Herb W. Davis	1957	42
347	47 2/8	46 4/8	44 2/8	9 1/8	9 1/8	8	7	Columbia Co., OR	Al Glenn	Al Glenn	1955	43
347	51 5/8	51 3/8	40 5/8	11 1/8	11 1/8	6	7	Columbia Co., OR	Unknown	Harold E. Stepp	1962	44
345 6/8	54 1/8	54 3/8	35 2/8	8 7/8	9 4/8	7	7	Pacific Co., WA	Norman W. Scott	Raymond W. Scott	1971	44
345 6/8	47	47 2/8	41 2/8	9 5/8	8 6/8	7	6	Bonanza Lake, BC	Wanda LeBlanc	Wanda LeBlanc	1999	46
345 1/8	49 5/8	47 7/8	38 6/8	8 2/8	8 5/8	7	7	Campbell River, BC	James D. Verbrugge	James D. Verbrugge	1995	47
344 4/8	49 2/8	47 1/8	40	8 4/8	8 5/8	7	7	Jefferson Co., WA	Carroll E. Koenke	Carroll E. Koenke	1966	48
344 2/8	55	56 4/8	34 3/8	7 2/8	7 4/8	6	7	Humboldt Co., CA	Picked Up	Gary Backanen	1992	49
343 2/8	44	46 2/8	35 1/8	9 4/8	9 4/8	7	7	Memekay River, BC	David Todd	David H. Todd	1998	50
342 2/8	52	50 4/8	34 5/8	9 5/8	9 5/8	6	7	Jefferson Co., WA	Ralph Warren	Ralph Warren	1972	51
342 1/8	47 3/8	44 1/8	40 2/8	9 7/8	9 7/8	6	7	Vancouver Island, BC	Archie J. Nesbitt	Archie J. Nesbitt	1997	52
341 6/8	40 7/8	46 2/8	45	10 6/8	10 2/8	7	9	Grays Harbor Co., WA	Unknown	Jack Adams, Jr.	1997	53
341 4/8	45 1/8	42 4/8	44 6/8	9 6/8	9 2/8	7	8	Josephine Co., OR	Robert Veatch	Cass E. Raymond	PR 1890	54
341 2/8	45 1/8	45 2/8	33 5/8	10 3/8	9 3/8	8	8	Columbia Co., OR	Derl Roberts	Derl Roberts	1965	55
341	47	47	38 7/8	8 7/8	10	8	7	Lewis Co., WA	Keith A. Heldreth	Keith A. Heldreth	1988	55
341	45 5/8	44 7/8	35 1/8	9 3/8	8 7/8	6	8	Del Norte Co., CA	Monte D. Matheson	Monte D. Matheson	2000	57
340 7/8	46 1/8	45	36	9 3/8	8 5/8	7	7	Columbia Co., OR	Bud Holmes	Sam Woody	1962	58
340 4/8	47	47	36 7/8	9 2/8	9 2/8	7	8	Perry River, BC	Joseph S. Brannen	Joseph S. Brannen	2002	58
340 2/8	49	46 4/8	43 3/8	9 5/8	9 5/8	8	7	Clatsop Co., OR	Fain J. Little	Fain J. Little	1945	60
340 2/8	49 1/8	43 6/8	33 7/8	11 5/8	10	8	8	Benton Co., OR	Thomas R. Sherman	Thomas R. Sherman	2002	62
339 6/8	45 5/8	45 4/8	42 6/8	8 3/8	8	8	7	Gold River, BC	William H. Taylor	William H. Taylor	1987	63
338 7/8	49 6/8	50 4/8	43	8	7 4/8	7	7	Humboldt Co., CA	Paul E. Benoit	Paul E. Benoit	2000	64
338 1/8	54 4/8	49 1/8	32	7	8 1/8	8	8	Humboldt Co., CA	Ric Rhoades	Ric Rhoades	1984	65
338	43 4/8	44 4/8	41 1/8	9 7/8	9 7/8	7	7	Tillamook Co., OR	Tony W. Hancock	Tony W. Hancock	1985	65
337 5/8	50 7/8	48 3/8	36 2/8	9 6/8	9 6/8	8	6	Muchalat Lake, BC	Joshua Fyfe	Joshua D. Fyfe	1998	67
337 4/8	52 3/8	53 4/8	33 2/8	7 2/8	7 5/8	9	9	Humboldt Co., CA	Picked Up	Gary Backanen	1992	68
337 1/8	49 5/8	50 3/8	34 3/8	9	9	8	8	Greenstone Creek, BC	Gerald L. Warnock	Gerald L. Warnock	1989	69
337 1/8	46	52	30 2/8	9 1/8	8 4/8	7	9	Wahkiakum Co., WA	E.L. McKie & T. Faubian	E.L. McKie	1962	69
336 6/8	50 4/8	44 4/8	37 6/8	8 7/8	8 7/8	6	7	Jefferson Co., OR	Dave D. Godfrey	Dave D. Godfrey	1966	71
336 4/8	38	39 1/8	39	8	8	7	6	Tillamook Co., OR	Gary L. Cox	Gary L. Cox	1965	72
336 2/8	46 6/8	46 6/8	34 7/8	10 3/8	10 1/8	7	7	Jefferson Co., WA	L. & T. McClanahan	Larry McClanahan	1965	73
336	46	48 3/8	40 3/8	8 7/8	9 1/8	7	7	Oregon Coast Range, OR	Unknown	Richard Leach	PR 1981	74
335 7/8	46 3/8	46 3/8	39 6/8	8 3/8	9 1/8	7	7	Clallam Co., WA	Howard M. Cameron	Lawrence C. Cameron	1936	75
335 4/8	48 6/8	48 2/8	33 6/8	7 2/8	7 2/8	8	8	Humboldt Co., CA	Jeremy W. Flick	Jeremy W. Flick	2001	76
335 2/8	45 1/8	44 3/8	42	9	9	6	6	Union Bay, BC	Louis C. Podgorenko	Louis C. Podgorenko	1996	77
335 1/8	51 1/8	51 6/8	40 1/8	10 2/8	9	6	7	Clallam Co., WA	George R. Ames	George R. Ames	1956	78
335 1/8	47 2/8	49 4/8	46 3/8	11 3/8	10 3/8	7	8	Benton Co., OR	Gary W. Kinman	Gary W. Kinman	1997	79
335 1/8	51 2/8	51 7/8	42 1/8	9 4/8	9 1/8	8	6	Wahkiakum Co., WA	J.W. Robinson & W. Robinson	Jim W. Robinson	1966	79
334 7/8	48 3/8	48 5/8	39 3/8	10 1/8	10 3/8	7	6	Clatsop Co., OR	Picked Up	Andy Mendenhall, Jr.	1978	79
334 4/8	45	45 4/8	39 4/8	9	9 1/8	7	7	Humboldt Co., CA	Everett J. Goodale	Everett J. Goodale	2000	82
334 1/8	52	52 1/8	43 1/8	8 2/8	8 1/8	8	8	White River, BC	Sid D. Rajala	Sid D. Rajala	1994	83
333 3/8	49 1/8	47 6/8	35 6/8	9 4/8	11	8	7	Clallam Co., WA	Albert Clevenger	Albert Clevenger	1931	84
								Clatsop Co., OR	Charles L. Smith	Daniel L. Smith	1960	

ROOSEVELT'S ELK
Cervus elaphus roosevelti

Score	Length of Main Beam R	Length of Main Beam L	Inside Spread	Circumference at Smallest Place Between First and Second Points R	Circumference at Smallest Place Between First and Second Points L	Number of Points R	Number of Points L	Locality	Hunter	Owner	Date Killed	Rank
332 3/8	49	47 3/8	45	10 2/8	10 2/8	8	6	Jefferson Co., WA	Louis Ehlers	Donald G. Hyatt	PR 1954	85
332 2/8	51 6/8	51 4/8	41 2/8	8 6/8	9 1/8	8	6	Humboldt Co., CA	Picked Up	Leo Prshora	1955	86
332	49	48 4/8	45	8 1/8	8 5/8	7	6	Tillamook Co., OR	Robert B. Thornton	Dale R. Thornton	1964	87
331 5/8	49 6/8	44 6/8	40 6/8	8 4/8	9	7	6	Wahkiakum Co., WA	Kyle J. Parker	Kyle J. Parker	1996	88
330 5/8	53 2/8	55 1/8	38 2/8	7 1/8	7 7/8	6	6	Siskiyou Co., CA	William D. Johnson	William D. Johnson	1997	89
330	51	50 1/8	38 4/8	8 7/8	9	6	6	Nanaimo Lakes, BC	Picked Up	Eric D. Martin	1988	90
329 5/8	48 7/8	50 1/8	39 3/8	8 5/8	8 2/8	6	6	Tillamook Co., OR	Gary H. Purdy	Gary H. Purdy	1969	91
329	44 2/8	49	38 3/8	7 7/8	8	8	6	Clatsop Co., OR	David G. Bigsby	David G. Bigsby	1962	92
328 7/8	46 4/8	46 4/8	38 4/8	8 7/8	8 5/8	7	7	Vancouver Island, BC	Wayne H. Zaccarelli	Wayne H. Zaccarelli	1981	93
327 4/8	47 4/8	46	44 4/8	10 3/8	11	6	6	Clallam Co., WA	Daniel D. Hinchen	Daniel D. Hinchen	1976	94
327 3/8	48 5/8	50 5/8	42 3/8	8 3/8	8 1/8	8	7	Tillamook Co., OR	Picked Up	Dave Griffith	1958	95
327 2/8	50 5/8	50	40 5/8	8 7/8	9 1/8	7	6	Clatsop Co., OR	Billy L. Jasper	Billy L. Jasper	1946	96
327	49 4/8	50 5/8	38 4/8	9 4/8	9 7/8	6	6	Del Norte Co., CA	Patrick J. Papasergia	Patrick J. Papasergia	1996	97
326 4/8	48 1/8	51 2/8	42 3/8	7	7 2/8	6	6	Douglas Co., OR	Lawrence Smith	Jody Smith	1958	98
326 1/8	54 1/8	54 2/8	40	7 5/8	7 7/8	7	7	Pacific Co., WA	Donald Beasley	Donald Beasley	1963	98
325 7/8	49 6/8	49 2/8	33 6/8	8 1/8	8 1/8	7	7	Wahkiakum Co., WA	Otis E. Wright	Otis E. Wright	1966	100
325 5/8	48 4/8	48 2/8	33 5/8	7 5/8	8 1/8	6	8	Humboldt Co., CA	Kevin Atkinson	Kevin Atkinson	2001	101
325 3/8	47 3/8	47 6/8	43 2/8	7 2/8	8	7	8	Wahkiakum Co., WA	Robert B. Seaberg	Robert B. Seaberg	1958	102
325 2/8	50	49	43 6/8	9	9 6/8	8	7	Columbia Co., OR	Edgar J. Rea	Edgar J. Rea	1973	103
325 1/8	45 4/8	41 2/8	43 5/8	8 5/8	8 3/8	8	7	Del Norte Co., CA	Michael McCollum	Michael McCollum	1999	104
324 7/8	52 1/8	51	39 1/8	9 1/8	8 2/8	6	6	Siskiyou Co., CA	Jeremy W. Johnson	Jeremy W. Johnson	1997	105
324 4/8	50 1/8	47 4/8	36 5/8	8 7/8	8 6/8	7	7	Ucona River, BC	Norman W. Dougan	Norman W. Dougan	1986	106
324 4/8	43	43	43	10	10 5/8	7	5	Jefferson Co., WA	Vern Gedelman	Michael O'Dell	PR 1967	107
324 2/8	52 6/8	51	39 7/8	9 1/8	8 7/8	6	7	Polk Co., OR	Ronald Smith	Ronald G. Smith	1998	107
324 2/8	40 6/8	44 2/8	43 6/8	7 7/8	7 6/8	7	7	Jefferson Co., WA	Newton P. Morris	Newton P. Morris	1975	109
323 4/8	51 4/8	47 4/8	39 6/8	9 4/8	9 2/8	7	6	Vernon Lake, BC	George R. Banning	George R. Banning	1997	109
323 2/8	44	43 4/8	44	8 1/8	7 3/8	7	7	Jefferson Co., WA	Larry W. Haddock	Larry W. Haddock	1988	111
323	52	51 3/8	40	10 1/8	9 4/8	7	8	Clatsop Co., OR	David Tweedle	Scott A. Seppa	1938	112
323	45 5/8	47	37 7/8	7 2/8	7 1/8	7	7	Clatsop Co., OR	Clarence V. Jurhs	Clarence V. Jurhs	1958	113
322 7/8	53	51 5/8	42 5/8	9 4/8	9 2/8	8	6	Curry Co., OR	Dallas E. Ettinger	Dallas E. Ettinger	1993	114
322 3/8	47 6/8	44 5/8	38 1/8	8 7/8	9 2/8	8	7	Columbia Co., OR	William M. Curtis	Duane M. Bernard	1952	115
322 2/8	44 6/8	45 2/8	41 3/8	8 5/8	9 1/8	7	7	Lincoln Co., OR	James R. Goodwin	James R. Goodwin	1960	116
322 2/8	50	50 4/8	38 6/8	8	7 7/8	6	6	Benton Co., OR	Samuel R. Gray	Samuel R. Gray	2000	116
322 1/8	43 2/8	41	41 2/8	10 3/8	10 3/8	7	7	Clatsop Co., OR	Reed Holding	Reed Holding	1939	118
322 1/8	45 5/8	45 3/8	42 2/8	11 4/8	11	6	6	Polk Co., OR	R.L. Stamps	R.L. Stamps	1985	118
320 6/8	50	48 7/8	41	7 2/8	7 1/8	7	7	Humboldt Co., CA	Brian J. Noel	Brian J. Noel	2003	120

Score								Locality	Hunter	Owner	Date	Rank
320 4/8	47 1/8	51 1/8	32 5/8	8 6/8	8 6/8	7	6	Tillamook Co., OR	Stanley E. Kephart	Stanley E. Kephart	1964	121
320 2/8	44 5/8	44 5/8	29 3/8	7 5/8	8	8	6	Tillamook Co., OR	A. Wegler	Joseph Doerfler	PR 1950	122
320 2/8	49 6/8	48 2/8	42 4/8	8 4/8	8 1/8	6	6	Mason Co., WA	Tony J. Bogachus	Tony J. Bogachus	1955	122
320 1/8	43 1/8	43 5/8	47 1/8	8 1/8	8 2/8	7	7	Columbia Co., OR	Harry R. Olsen	Harry R. Olsen	1961	122
320 1/8	43 2/8	48 6/8	42 3/8	10 6/8	10 6/8	7	5	Clatsop Co., OR	Jack O. Bay	Jack O. Bay	1963	125
320 1/8	43 7/8	45 2/8	38 2/8	7 6/8	7 5/8	8	7	Columbia Co., OR	Larry G. Behrend	Howard C. Behrend	1973	125
319 5/8	49 4/8	47 6/8	39 7/8	6 6/8	6 7/8	7	6	Clatsop Co., OR	Picked Up	John T. Mee	1969	127
319 5/8	49 5/8	50 6/8	48	8 3/8	7 6/8	9	9	Curry Co., OR	Jamie L. White	Jamie L. White	1978	127
319 1/8	42 7/8	42	35 6/8	8 5/8	8 4/8	7	8	Grays Harbor Co., WA	Gary D. Schurr	Gary D. Schurr	1996	127
319 1/8	46 4/8	48	32	7 4/8	7 7/8	8	7	Humboldt Co., CA	Claire C. Hawkins	Claire C. Hawkins	2003	130
318 5/8	48	49 2/8	40	8	8 2/8	6	7	Del Norte Co., CA	Richard K. Armas	Richard K. Armas	1988	131
318 4/8	51 2/8	48 6/8	38 1/8	9 1/8	9 2/8	8	3	Conuma River, BC	Jason C. Hird	Jason C. Hird	2000	132
318 4/8	49 1/8	48	33 2/8	8 3/8	8 1/8	7	3	Coos Co., OR	Todd Freitag	Todd Freitag	2003	132
318 3/8	41 3/8	41 5/8	36 2/8	8 6/8	8 6/8	7	3	Grilise Creek, BC	Jack Foord	Jack Foord	1984	134
318	43 5/8	43 4/8	30 6/8	8 5/8	9	7	5	Sucwoa River, BC	Barry Naimark	Barry Naimark	1998	135
317 3/8	43 4/8	44 3/8	42 2/8	8 4/8	7 6/8	7	5	Tillamook Co., OR	Thomas G. Tompkins	Thomas G. Tompkins	1952	136
317 2/8	41 3/8	41 5/8	37 6/8	8 7/8	9	7	5	Columbia Co., OR	Max Oblack	Max Oblack	1967	137
316 6/8	51 3/8	49	39	9 7/8	8 6/8	7	5	Columbia Co., OR	Harry R. Olsen	Harry R. Olsen	1969	138
316 5/8	45 4/8	45 4/8	41 5/8	8 6/8	8 6/8	6	5	Lincoln Co., OR	Verlin H. Rhoades	Verlin H. Rhoades	1944	139
316 5/8	41 6/8	41 5/8	38 3/8	9 1/8	9 1/8	6	6	Clallam Co., WA	Daniel M. Hilt	Daniel M. Hilt	1982	139
316 5/8	44 5/8	46	36 7/8	10 1/8	9 7/8	6	6	Bonanza Lake, BC	Cameron W. Blacklock	Cameron W. Blacklock	1994	139
316 3/8	48	47 2/8	35	10 4/8	9 7/8	6	6	Del Norte Co., CA	Gary Towers	Gary Towers	2002	142
316 2/8	43 2/8	42 3/8	39 2/8	9 2/8	9 4/8	7	5	Columbia Co., CA	Everett Girt	James Girt	1951	143
316 1/8	48 6/8	48 3/8	32 5/8	8 1/8	8	6	5	Humboldt Co., CA	Tod O. Droege	Tod O. Droege	2003	144
316	47 3/8	46 5/8	43 1/8	10 1/8	10 3/8	6	6	Jefferson Co., WA	Hans Norbisrath	Hans Norbisrath	1966	145
315 4/8	48 2/8	47 7/8	42	9	9 4/8	6	6	Columbia Co., OR	William E. Curtis	Duane M. Bernard	1965	146
315 2/8	41 6/8	43	39 6/8	8 2/8	8 6/8	7	7	Columbia Co., OR	David A. Evenson	David A. Evenson	1998	147
314 6/8	46 6/8	46 6/8	42 2/8	8 5/8	8	8	8	Coos Co., OR	Picked Up	Harold E. Stepp	1962	148
314 4/8	52 1/8	49 2/8	36 3/8	9 3/8	9 5/8	6	6	Clatsop Co., OR	Robert D. Dunson	Robert D. Dunson	1982	149
314 3/8	45 7/8	46 1/8	42 3/8	8	8 4/8	7	7	Del Norte Co., CA	Robert L. Brown	Robert L. Brown	1966	150
313 5/8	50 3/8	50 3/8	41 3/8	9 5/8	9 6/8	7	6	Humboldt Co., CA	Richard L. Smith	Richard L. Smith	1998	151
313 3/8	47 6/8	48 6/8	31 2/8	7 7/8	8	7	6	Yamhill Co., OR	William Blunt	William Blunt	2002	152
313 2/8	43 5/8	45 1/8	50 1/8	9 1/8	9 1/8	7	6	Clallam Co., WA	Britt R. Madison	Britt R. Madison	2002	153
312 7/8	43 5/8	45 1/8	43 4/8	7 5/8	7 7/8	8	8	Columbia Co., WA	Donald W. Coman	Donald W. Coman	1981	154
312 6/8	41 7/8	43 4/8	33 5/8	8 1/8	7 7/8	8	9	Humboldt Co., OR	Glenn W. Bjorklund	Glenn W. Bjorklund	2002	155
312 4/8	45 7/8	44 2/8	39 4/8	8 3/8	8 2/8	6	6	Nimpkish River, BC	Noel J. Poux	Noel J. Poux	1993	156
312 1/8	48 5/8	46 5/8	34 3/8	8 2/8	8 5/8	7	6	Clallam Co., WA	Michael L. Fisher	Michael L. Fisher	1993	157
311 4/8	47 1/8	46 4/8	44 3/8	8 4/8	9 2/8	8	7	Clatsop Co., OR	Delmer A. Johnson	Casey Johnson	1957	158
311 2/8	47 6/8	46 4/8	32 2/8	9	9 3/8	9	7	Clatsop Co., OR	Don L. Twito	Don L. Twito	1956	159
311 2/8	43 4/8	40 3/8	41 2/8	8 6/8	8 6/8	8	7	Jefferson Co., OR	Walter L. Campbell	Walter L. Campbell	1987	159
310 5/8	44 6/8	44 6/8	38 2/8	7 3/8	7 7/8	7	7	Clallam Co., WA	Daniel M. Hilt	Daniel M. Hilt	1958	161
310 4/8	44 3/8	44	33 6/8	9 6/8	9 5/8	7	7	Clatsop Co., OR	Elman Petersen, Jr.	Elman Petersen, Jr.	1968	162
310 2/8	44 1/8	44 6/8	43 2/8	9 3/8	8 3/8	5	8	Clatsop Co., OR	Donald R. Chisholm	D.R. Chisholm & A. Holdridge	1957	163
310 1/8	44 5/8	44 4/8	34	9 3/8	10 2/8	7	7	Jefferson Co., WA	Howard L. Hill	Michael R. Raffaell	1969	164
309 6/8	43 1/8	48 1/8	31 6/8	9 4/8	9 2/8	7	7	Clatsop Co., OR	Terry E. Andrews	Terry E. Andrews	1984	165
309 1/8	47 3/8	43 7/8	37 7/8	8 7/8	9 2/8	6	6	Clatsop Co., OR	Valentine T. Mueller	John A. Mueller	1938	166

ROOSEVELT'S ELK
Cervus elaphus roosevelti

Score	Length of Main Beam R	L	Inside Spread	Circumference at Smallest Place Between First and Second Points R	L	Number of Points R	L	Locality	Hunter	Owner	Date Killed	Rank
308 5/8	49 1/8	47 4/8	37 7/8	12 1/8	11 2/8	6	5	Douglas Co., OR	George Kellis	Bob Wilkes	1952	167
308 4/8	46 1/8	44 6/8	36 2/8	6 5/8	6 6/8	7	7	Clatsop Co., OR	Earnest A. Stevens	Donald J. Stevens	PR 1964	168
308 3/8	48	48	41 5/8	9 7/8	9 2/8	6	7	Coos Co., OR	Dean Dunson	Dean Dunson	1986	169
308 3/8	46 4/8	45 7/8	35 3/8	9 5/8	9 6/8	7	8	Clatsop Co., OR	Brian D. Bonnell	Brian D. Bonnell	2000	169
308 3/8	49 2/8	44 2/8	41 4/8	7 4/8	7 6/8	6	6	Benton Co., OR	Mark Goracke	Mark Goracke	2002	169
307 6/8	44 5/8	46 4/8	35 4/8	8 7/8	8 6/8	6	6	Clallam Co., WA	David R. Hansen	David R. Hansen	1996	172
307 4/8	46 1/8	45 6/8	40 6/8	7 7/8	7 7/8	7	7	Tillamook Co., OR	John A. Wehinger	John A. Wehinger	1964	173
307 4/8	43 5/8	41 7/8	46 6/8	9 1/8	10 6/8	7	7	Clallam Co., WA	Kermit Guenkel	Kermit Guenkel	1972	173
307 4/8	49 7/8	48 1/8	34	10 1/8	11 7/8	7	7	Del Norte Co., OR	Richard L. Butler	Richard L. Butler	1998	173
307 2/8	48 1/8	45 7/8	39 7/8	9 1/8	8 2/8	7	7	Siskiyou Co., CA	Bill Kleaver	Bill Kleaver	1997	176
306 7/8	46 3/8	45 1/8	37 4/8	7 6/8	8 3/8	7	7	Memekay River, BC	Harold Ratushniak	Harold Ratushniak	1993	177
306 6/8	50 2/8	50 4/8	38 6/8	7 6/8	8	6	6	Polk Co., OR	James E. Wallen	James E. Wallen	1980	178
306 4/8	47	47 5/8	43 5/8	7 5/8	7 6/8	6	6	Humboldt Co., CA	Michael L. Johnson	Michael L. Johnson	1976	179
306	40 4/8	39 3/8	40 4/8	9 1/8	9 4/8	7	7	Washington Co., OR	Michael R. Jamieson	Michael R. Jamieson	1982	180
305 7/8	41 7/8	44	34 5/8	9 6/8	9	7	7	Gold River, BC	Cory C. Hanley	Cory C. Hanley	1998	181
305 7/8	44 7/8	46	38 7/8	9 2/8	9 2/8	7	6	Del Norte Co., CA	Steven Gauvin	Steven Gauvin	2003	181
305 4/8	47 2/8	47	37 3/8	7 6/8	7 2/8	6	6	Tillamook Co., OR	Patrick Windle	Patrick E. Windle	1995	183
305 2/8	43 2/8	43 6/8	35 2/8	8 4/8	8 5/8	7	7	Pacific Co., WA	Michael M. McHale	Michael M. McHale	1975	184
304 6/8	49	41 1/8	39 1/8	9 7/8	9 3/8	6	7	Clatsop Co., OR	William D. Mellinger	William D. Mellinger	1958	185
304 4/8	47 1/8	46	36 4/8	7 7/8	8 2/8	6	6	Jefferson Co., WA	Dennis Potter	Dennis Potter	1970	186
304 4/8	45	46 1/8	42 4/8	8 2/8	8 5/8	6	6	Muchalat Lake, BC	Michael H. Baturin	Michael H. Baturin	1994	186
304 3/8	46 2/8	46 3/8	47 1/8	10	9 5/8	6	6	Grays Harbor Co., WA	Richard B. Grinols	Richard B. Grinols	1992	188
304 3/8	45 2/8	49 2/8	42 1/8	9 2/8	9 1/8	6	6	Clallam Co., WA	Harry E. Reed	Harry E. Reed	1997	188
304 1/8	39 6/8	38 1/8	31 1/8	8	7 6/8	8	8	Yamhill Co., OR	Kevin E. Mishler	Kevin E. Mishler	1989	190
303 6/8	42 2/8	45 7/8	36 4/8	9 3/8	9 4/8	7	7	Gold River, BC	Abe J.N. Dougan	Abe J.N. Dougan	1988	191
303	47 4/8	47 6/8	42 2/8	9	8 6/8	7	5	Jefferson Co., WA	C.F. & C.H. Bernhardt	C.F. & C.H. Bernhardt	1972	192
303	46 6/8	44 3/8	35 3/8	7 4/8	7 5/8	7	7	Humboldt Co., CA	Walter M. Gibson	Walter M. Gibson	2002	192
302 6/8	50	50	36 7/8	7 3/8	7 7/8	6	6	Jefferson Co., CA	Gary Talley	Gary Talley	1981	194
302 6/8	45 6/8	44 3/8	37 3/8	8 6/8	9	6	6	Grays Harbor Co., WA	Donald M. Vestal	Dean Vestal	1981	194
302 6/8	49	49 1/8	38 4/8	7 7/8	7 7/8	6	6	Columbia Co., OR	Picked Up	Rick A. Hood	1991	194
302 5/8	41	39 6/8	44	9 7/8	9 5/8	9	6	Lincoln Co., OR	Michael Kosydar	Michael Kosydar	1985	197
302 1/8	41 3/8	41 7/8	37 5/8	8 2/8	8 4/8	6	6	Wahkiakum Co., WA	Kyle J. Parker	Kyle J. Parker	1990	198
301 7/8	48 3/8	48	34 5/8	7 6/8	8 2/8	6	7	Benton Co., OR	James R. Rice	James R. Rice	2003	199
301 6/8	43	43 7/8	36 2/8	8 6/8	9 4/8	8	8	Clatsop Co., OR	Pravomil Raichl	Pravomil Raichl	1963	200
301 6/8	39 5/8	40	33 2/8	8 5/8	8 2/8	7	8	Benton Co., OR	Scott Staten	Scott Staten	2000	200

Score	Length of Main Beam R	Length of Main Beam L	Inside Spread	Circumference R	Circumference L	Points R	Points L	Locality	Hunter	Owner	Date Killed	Rank
301 5/8	44 5/8	45 5/8	37 7/8	7 6/8	8 1/8	6	6	Columbia Co, OR	Bud Holmes	Bud Holmes	1949	202
301 5/8	44 3/8	48 2/8	37 2/8	9 6/8	9 2/8	6	6	Grays Harbor Co, WA	T. Franklin Stinchfield, Jr.	T. Franklin Stinchfield, Jr.	2001	202
301 4/8	48 2/8	49 3/8	35 7/8	8 6/8	8 5/8	6	7	Pacific Co, WA	Jeff D. Halsey	Jeff D. Halsey	2001	204
301 1/8	40 6/8	40 2/8	39	8 3/8	7 7/8	6	7	Jefferson Co, WA	Larry D. Hart	Larry D. Hart II	1969	205
301 1/8	46 5/8	44	34 2/8	8 5/8	8 2/8	7	8	Jefferson Co, WA	C.F. & C.H. Bernhardt	C.F. & C.H. Bernhardt	1973	205
301 1/8	47 4/8	45	35 5/8	9 2/8	9	7	7	Siskiyou Co, CA	Joseph B. Rightmier	Joseph B. Rightmier	2001	205
301	42 5/8	42 6/8	41	9	9 6/8	6	6	Coos Co, OR	Picked Up	William H. Flesch	1993	208
300 7/8	44	43 5/8	41	9 3/8	9 5/8	7	7	Vancouver Island, BC	William C. Holcombe	William C. Holcombe	1989	209
300 5/8	37 7/8	44	37 1/8	8 2/8	7 4/8	7	6	Mason Co, WA	David J. Beerbower	David J. Beerbower	1983	210
300 3/8	45 7/8	36 6/8	40 2/8	8 5/8	9 2/8	7	8	Lincoln Co.	Donald V. Miles	Donald V. Miles	1996	211
300 2/8	43	44 5/8	37 4/8	8 4/8	8 4/8	6	6	Columbia Co, OR	Harry R. Olsen	Harry R. Olsen	1963	212
300 2/8	40	40 6/8	33 2/8	8 1/8	9 2/8	7	7	Yamhill Co, OR	Timothy R. Bainter	Timothy R. Bainter	1997	212
300 1/8	47 3/8	39 5/8	34	8 3/8	8 4/8	6	6	Del Norte Co, CA	Paul H. Kunzler	Paul H. Kunzler	1999	214
299 6/8	48 7/8	48 6/8	37 2/8	9 1/8	7 7/8	6	7	Lincoln Co, OR	Jullian Smallwood	Gerald Smallwood	1945	215
299 4/8	41 1/8	49 1/8	33 6/8	9	9 5/8	6	6	Grays Harbor Co, WA	Robert Lentz	Robert Lentz	1948	216
299 3/8	42 2/8	42 1/8	39	8 2/8	7 7/8	7	7	Lincoln Co, OR	Gene Nyhus	Gene Nyhus	1950	217
299 2/8	43	40 7/8	36 4/8	7 5/8	7 2/8	7	7	Cowlitz Co, WA	Daniel L. Howe	Daniel L. Howe	1996	218
299	42 4/8	44 2/8	46 4/8	7 2/8	7 5/8	6	6	Columbia Co, OR	Charles H. Atkins	Charles H. Atkins	1964	219
298 6/8	47 6/8	41 6/8	33 3/8	8 6/8	7 7/8	6	6	Del Norte Co, CA	Glenn W. Ng	Glenn W. Ng	2000	220
298 5/8	47	46 2/8	38 6/8	9 1/8	7 7/8	6	7	Jefferson Co, WA	Douglas A. Smith	Douglas A. Smith	1989	221
298 5/8	46	47 6/8	33 1/8	8 4/8	8 6/8	8	8	Conuma River, BC	Monty A. Klein	Monty A. Klein	1998	221
298 3/8	45 6/8	41 2/8	39 6/8	8	8	8	8	Clatsop Co, OR	Harold O. Hundere	Harold O. Hundere	1943	223
298 2/8	48 1/8	45	38 3/8	8 1/8	7 4/8	6	6	White River, BC	Harvey J. King	Harvey J. King	1987	224
298	47 2/8	50 6/8	37 4/8	7 4/8	8 4/8	6	7	Columbia Co, OR	Nicholas A. Berg	Nicholas A. Berg	1963	225
298	43 1/8	44 1/8	40 6/8	8 7/8	8 4/8	7	8	Polk Co, OR	R.L. Stamps	R.L. Stamps	1981	225
298	46 6/8	44 3/8	40 5/8	9	9	6	6	Humboldt Co, CA	Eugene M. Boyd IV	Eugene M. Boyd IV	1988	225
297 6/8	44 3/8	43 1/8	34 5/8	7 4/8	7 2/8	6	6	Columbia Co, OR	Richard D. Banzer	Joseph D. Banzer	1959	228
297 5/8	44 4/8	43 1/8	42 7/8	7 3/8	7 3/8	6	6	Clallam Co, WA	Arnold J. LaGambina	Arnold J. LaGambina	1988	229
297 4/8	39	47 2/8	39 7/8	8 1/8	8 3/8	6	6	Del Norte Co, CA	Ronald F. Cibart	Ronald F. Cibart	2000	230
297 1/8	46	45 7/8	40 5/8	7 6/8	7 4/8	6	6	Siskiyou Co, CA	Michael R. Bell	Michael R. Bell	1996	231
296 6/8	44 3/8	44 6/8	36 7/8	9	9	7	7	Clallam Co, WA	Ronald W. Sanchez	Ronald W. Sanchez	1988	232
296 4/8	43 7/8	43 7/8	34 7/8	8 1/8	9 3/8	6	6	Clallam Co, WA	Randy F. Mesenbrink	Randy F. Mesenbrink	1977	233
296 4/8	39 7/8	39 3/8	47 6/8	7 4/8	8 4/8	6	5	Clallam Co, WA	Aubrey F. Taylor	Aubrey F. Taylor	1984	233
296 4/8	42 6/8	46 6/8	38 5/8	8 7/8	9 1/8	6	6	Coos Co, OR	Ryan K. Gardner	Ryan K. Gardner	2001	233
296 3/8	45 4/8	44 1/8	35 7/8	7 4/8	8 4/8	7	6	Douglas Co, WA	Matthew R. Fullerton	Matthew R. Fullerton	2000	236
296 1/8	46 5/8	45 1/8	35 2/8	9 2/8	8 2/8	7	7	Jefferson Co, WA	Max E. Graves	Max E. Graves	1970	237
296	46 4/8	41 6/8	36 6/8	8 5/8	7 7/8	7	7	Yamhill Co, OR	Steven E. Anderson	Steven E. Anderson	1983	238
295 7/8	46 1/8	43 5/8	41 5/8	9 1/8	7 5/8	7	7	Jefferson Co, WA	Newton P. Morris	Newton P. Morris	1970	239
295 4/8	43 5/8	45 4/8	34 7/8	8 4/8	8	6	6	Coos Co, OR	Wesley A. Plummer	Wesley A. Plummer	2001	240
295 2/8	44 1/8	46 1/8	41	8 3/8	8 2/8	6	6	Columbia Co, OR	Reed Holding	Reed Holding	1950	241
295 1/8	42 6/8	48 2/8	33 5/8	8 1/8	9 3/8	6	7	Washington Co, OR	Eric T. Sahnow	Eric T. Sahnow	1996	242
294 7/8	45 4/8	43 2/8	34 6/8	8 3/8	7 7/8	6	6	Clatsop Co, OR	Picked Up	Robert L. Brown	1965	243
294 5/8	45 4/8	43 6/8	43 1/8	9 1/8	9	6	6	Clatsop Co, OR	Nolen R. Schoenborn	Nolen R. Schoenborn	1944	244
294 4/8	46 1/8	42 2/8	34 7/8	7 1/8	8 4/8	6	6	Washington Co, OR	Chris Zurbrugg	Chris Zurbrugg	1996	245
294 1/8	48 2/8	44 1/8	45 2/8	8 2/8	8 2/8	8	6	Washington Co, OR	John A. Beavers, Jr.	John A. Beavers, Jr.	1976	246
293 7/8	43 2/8	43 6/8	36 7/8	7 5/8	7 6/8	6	6	Tillamook Co, OR	Steven F. Kellow	Steven F. Kellow	1979	247
293 4/8	44 1/8	42 2/8	39 7/8	8 4/8	8	8	8	Lincoln Co, OR	Timothy A. Landis	Timothy A. Landis	1993	248

ROOSEVELT'S ELK
Cervus elaphus roosevelti

Score	Length of Main Beam R	L	Inside Spread	Circumference at Smallest Place Between First and Second Points R	L	Number of Points R	L	Locality	Hunter	Owner	Date Killed	Rank
293 3/8	43 6/8	44 1/8	43 7/8	8 5/8	8 4/8	6	6	Coos Co., OR	Ken Wilson	Ken Wilson	2001	249
293 1/8	42	42 1/8	41 3/8	8 2/8	8 7/8	6	6	Jefferson Co., WA	William H. Boatman	William H. Boatman	1951	250
293 1/8	42 7/8	44	41 4/8	8	8 3/8	6	6	Douglas Co., OR	Bruce K. Moore	Tadd K. Moore	1998	250
292 7/8	44 1/8	47 4/8	36 4/8	8 4/8	8 4/8	6	7	Siskiyou Co., CA	Gearen L. Nugent	Gearen L. Nugent	2001	252
291 7/8	39 6/8	38	34 3/8	9 5/8	9 3/8	8	6	Wahkiakum Co., WA	Brian S. Boudreau	Brian S. Boudreau	2002	253
291 4/8	38 2/8	38 7/8	33 7/8	8 2/8	8 1/8	8	7	Tillamook Co., OR	Picked Up	Tim J. Christensen	1975	254
291 3/8	43 5/8	43 5/8	35 1/8	6 6/8	7	6	6	Clatsop Co., OR	Picked Up	Robert L. Brown	1979	255
291 3/8	43 5/8	43 7/8	37 3/8	8 7/8	9 1/8	6	7	Washington Co., OR	Matthew D. Schmidlin	Matthew D. Schmidlin	2001	255
291 1/8	41 6/8	40 4/8	43 6/8	6 7/8	6 6/8	6	6	Jefferson Co., WA	George R. Bernethy	George R. Bernethy	1956	257
290 7/8	45 6/8	44 1/8	37 4/8	9	9 3/8	6	6	Coos Co., OR	Gerald W. Hurst	Gerald W. Hurst	1979	258
290 7/8	44 1/8	44 3/8	42 5/8	7 7/8	8 6/8	6	6	Jefferson Co., WA	William A. Harrison	William A. Harrison	1984	258
290 5/8	43 7/8	43 2/8	34 3/8	8	8 7/8	7	8	Clatsop Co., OR	James H. Thrower	James H. Thrower	1998	260
290 5/8	42	41 4/8	37 3/8	8 4/8	9 4/8	6	7	Columbia Co., OR	Joseph D. Banzer	Joseph D. Banzer	2000	260
290 2/8	44 4/8	44 2/8	39 4/8	7 5/8	7 5/8	7	7	White River, BC	George A. Colegrave	George A. Colegrave	1994	262
290 1/8	42 4/8	42 1/8	37 6/8	8 1/8	8 3/8	7	7	Lincoln Co., OR	Terry W. Smith	Terry W. Smith	1997	263
290	43 7/8	44 3/8	39 6/8	7 7/8	8 2/8	6	6	Jefferson Co., WA	Elmer Loose	Elmer Loose	2000	264
369 *	50 5/8	48 2/8	40 4/8	7 2/8	7 4/8	8	7	Coos Co., OR	George J. Yost	Rudy A. Yost	1936	
367 1/8 *	49 5/8	49	39 4/8	7 6/8	8	7	8	Humboldt Co., CA	John J. Aboud	John J. Aboud	2003	
364 *	53 7/8	54 6/8	41 2/8	9	9	7	7	Adams River, BC	Michael R. Finnell	Michael R. Finnell	2000	

* Final score is subject to revision by additional verifying measurements.

CATEGORY
ROOSEVELT'S ELK

SCORE
300-1/8

HUNTER
PAUL H. KUNZLER

LOCATION
DEL NORTE COUNTY, CALIFORNIA

DATE OF KILL
SEPTEMBER 1999

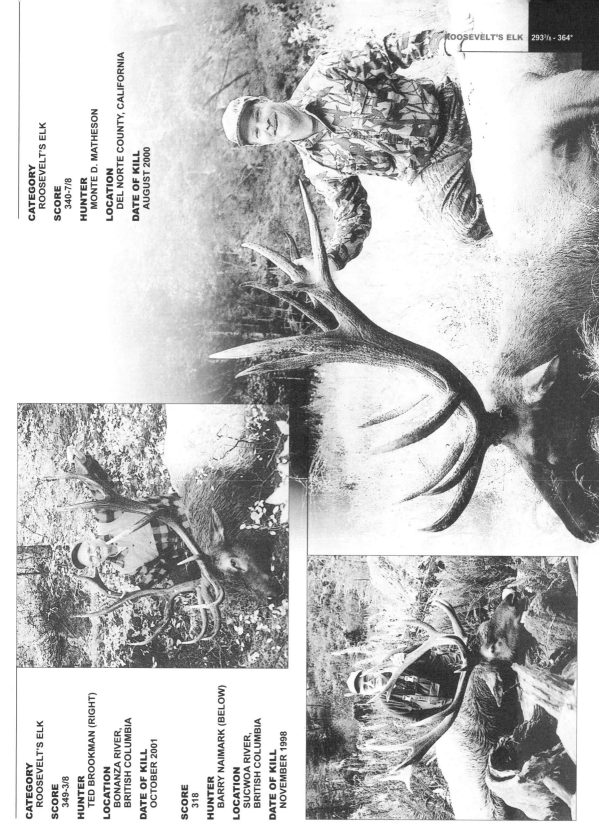

CATEGORY
ROOSEVELT'S ELK

SCORE
340-7/8

HUNTER
MONTE D. MATHESON

LOCATION
DEL NORTE COUNTY, CALIFORNIA

DATE OF KILL
AUGUST 2000

CATEGORY
ROOSEVELT'S ELK

SCORE
349-3/8

HUNTER
TED BROOKMAN (RIGHT)

LOCATION
BONANZA RIVER,
BRITISH COLUMBIA

DATE OF KILL
OCTOBER 2001

SCORE
318

HUNTER
BARRY NAIMARK (BELOW)

LOCATION
SUCWOA RIVER,
BRITISH COLUMBIA

DATE OF KILL
NOVEMBER 1998

TULE ELK
NEW WORLD'S RECORD

TROPHY INFO

RANK
New World's Record

SCORE
365

LOCATION
Solano Co., CA

HUNTER
Bryce Evans

OWNER
Bryce Evans

DATE KILLED
1997

California's tule elk are one of America's wildlife success stories, thanks to hunters and conservationists. Tule elk numbered near 550,000 before the settlement of California but totaled only a few animals in the mid-1850s. In 1874 two elk were located on a private ranch and, through aggressive rehabilitation efforts, they eventually became the start of the current population. As of 1990, the herds were large enough that hunting became a viable management tool. Two of these fortunate hunters were Bryce Evans and Duane Stroupe; both gentleman had come by their tags through fund-raising efforts, and both were happy to collaborate on this special opportunity.

Early opening morning found Duane and his guide Pat Gilligan watching a large 7x7 bull. At the same time, a short distance to the south, Bryce and his guide, Richard Cox, were looking over a 9x8. The plan was for Bryce to approach this bull first from the southeast, and if he could get the shot, he'd take it. Either way, the elk would retreat to the north where Duane and Pat were waiting.

By 9:00 a.m., Bryce and Richard were on a high point looking down at 65 head of elk, including the big 9x8. The elk had bedded down and, except for the occasional bugle, all was quiet. Bryce and Richard belly crawled until they were about 150 yards from the bull. With the wind blowing in their faces, Bryce and Richard studied the big bull to make sure none of his tines had broken off during the on-going rut.

Bryce laid down and got comfortable. He used a backpack for a rest and prepared for the shot. The bull was unaware he was being watched in the crosshairs, and stood to stretch. Bryce took the shot and the bull went down.

The other elk started moving out with the shot. With the cows scattering, the 7x7 stopped frequently to bugle, trying to lure the cows back. He bugled his way right into Duane's range, and the bull dropped at the report of his rifle.

The group field dressed the animals and prepared to green score the racks. As they scored Bryce's bull, they knew they had something special. When the math was verified, it appeared Bryce's bull could be a potential new World's Record.

To take two such remarkable bulls on the same day is a testament to the work of the California Department of Fish and Game management program headed by elk biologist Jon Fisher, and the Grizzly Island team of Dennis Becker and Jeff Cairn. ■

TULE ELK
WORLD'S RECORD SCORE CHART

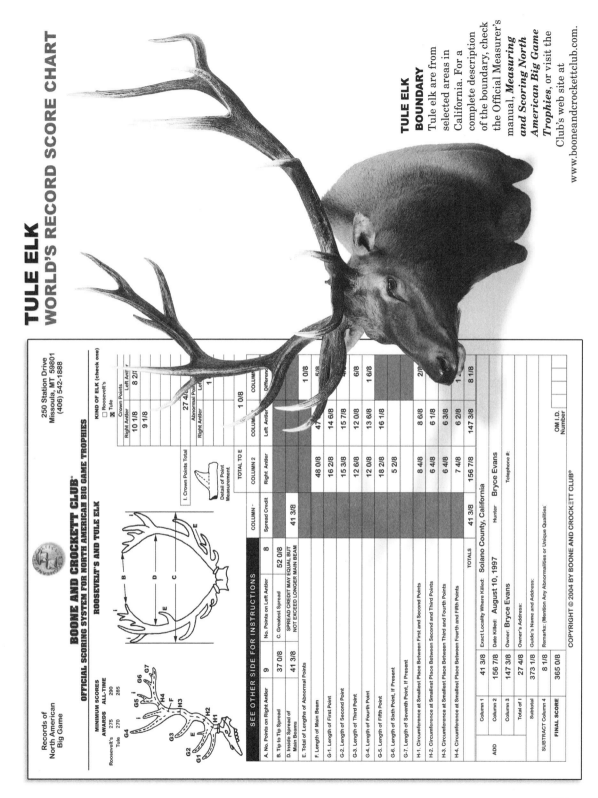

Records of
North American
Big Game

250 Station Drive
Missoula, MT 59801
(406) 542-1888

BOONE AND CROCKETT CLUB®
OFFICIAL SCORING SYSTEM FOR NORTH AMERICAN BIG GAME TROPHIES
ROOSEVELT'S AND TULE ELK

MINIMUM SCORES	AWARDS	ALL-TIME
Roosevelt's	275	290
Tule	270	285

KIND OF ELK (check one)
☐ Roosevelt's
☒ Tule

	Crown Points		
	Right Antler	Left Antler	r
	10 1/8	8 2/f
	9 1/8	1
		27 4/

	Abnormal Poi	Left
	Right Antler	
	1	

I. Crown Points Total

Detail of Point Measurement

TOTAL TO E

	COLUMN -	COLUMN 2	COLUMN 2	COLUMN
	Spread Credit	Right Antler	Left Antler	Difference
			1 0/8	
		48 0/8	47	1 0/8
				5/8
		16 2/8	14 6/8	
		15 3/8	15 7/8	
		12 6/8	12 0/8	6/8
		12 0/8	13 6/8	1 6/8
		18 2/8	16 1/8	
		5 2/8		
		8 4/8	8 6/8	2/8
		6 4/8	6 1/8	
		6 4/8	6 3/8	
		7 4/8	6 2/8	1
	41 3/8	156 7/8	147 3/8	8 1/8

SEE OTHER SIDE FOR INSTRUCTIONS			
A. No. Points on Right Antler	9	No. Points on Left Antler	8
B. Tip to Tip Spread	37 0/8	C. Greatest Spread	52 0/8
D. Inside Spread of Main Beams	41 3/8	SPREAD CREDIT MAY EQUAL BUT NOT EXCEED LONGER MAIN BEAM	41 3/8
E. Total of Lengths of Abnormal Points			
F. Length of Main Beam			48 0/8
G-1. Length of First Point			16 2/8
G-2. Length of Second Point			15 3/8
G-3. Length of Third Point			12 6/8
G-4. Length of Fourth Point			12 0/8
G-5. Length of Fifth Point			18 2/8
G-6. Length of Sixth Point, If Present			5 2/8
G-7. Length of Seventh Point, If Present			
H-1. Circumference at Smallest Place Between First and Second Points			8 4/8
H-2. Circumference at Smallest Place Between Second and Third Points			6 4/8
H-3. Circumference at Smallest Place Between Third and Fourth Points			6 4/8
H-4. Circumference at Smallest Place Between Fourth and Fifth Points			7 4/8
		TOTALS	156 7/8

ADD	Column 1	41 3/8	Exact Locality Where Killed: Solano County, California
	Column 2	156 7/8	Date Killed: August 10, 1997 Hunter: Bryce Evans
	Column 3	147 3/8	Owner: Bryce Evans
	Total of I	27 4/8	Owner's Address:
	Subtotal	373 1/8	Guide's Name and Address:
SUBTRACT Column 4		8 1/8	Remarks: (Mention Any Abnormalities or Unique Qualities
	FINAL SCORE	365 0/8	

Telephone #:

OM I.D. Number

COPYRIGHT © 2004 BY BOONE AND CROCKETT CLUB®

TULE ELK BOUNDARY

Tule elk are from selected areas in California. For a complete description of the boundary, check the Official Measurer's manual, *Measuring and Scoring North American Big Game Trophies,* or visit the Club's web site at www.booneandcrockettclub.com.

TOP 5 TULE ELK

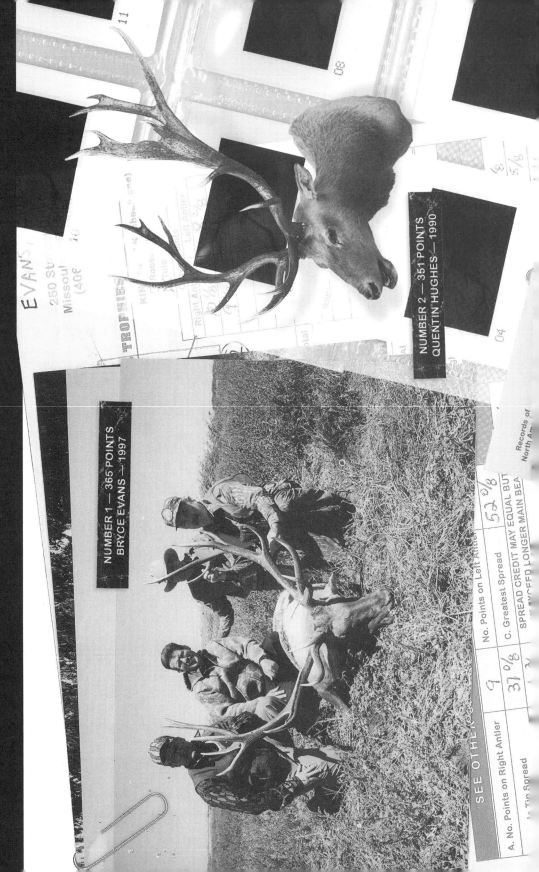

NUMBER 2 — 351 POINTS
QUENTIN HUGHES — 1990

NUMBER 1 — 365 POINTS
BRYCE EVANS — 1997

NUMBER 3 — 346-6/8 POINTS
CHRISTIAN WEISE — 1851

NUMBER 4 — 341-4/8 POINTS
ALVIN M. WALLEN — 1990

NUMBER 5 — 330-1/8 POINTS
TOD L. REICHERT — 1999

F. Lengt...

G-1. Length of First Point

G-2. Length of Second Point

G-3. Length of Third Point

G-4. Length of Fourth Point

G-5. Length of Fifth Point

G-6. Length of Sixth Point, If Present

G-7. Length of Seventh Point, If P...

293

TULE ELK
Cervus elaphus nannodes

MINIMUM SCORE 285

Score	Length of Main Beam R	L	Inside Spread	Circumference at Smallest Place Between First and Second Points R	L	Number of Points R	L	Locality	Hunter	Owner	Date Killed	Rank
365	48	47 3/8	41 3/8	8 4/8	8 6/8	9	8	Solano Co., CA	Bryce Evans	Bryce Evans	1997	1
351	48 6/8	47 4/8	51 3/8	7 1/8	6 4/8	9	9	Solano Co., CA	Quentin Hughes	B&C National Collection	1990	2
346 6/8	48	49 4/8	37 4/8	7 5/8	6 7/8	8	8	Sonoma Co., CA	Christian Weise	Harry Weise	1851	3
341 4/8	49 5/8	52 2/8	48 3/8	7 6/8	7 5/8	8	7	Solano Co., CA	Alvin M. Wallen	Alvin M. Wallen	1990	4
330 1/8	52 3/8	52 4/8	38 4/8	7 6/8	7 2/8	9	7	Solano Co., CA	Tod L. Reichert	Tod L. Reichert	1999	5
327	44 1/8	44 6/8	40 6/8	8 4/8	8 1/8	10	9	Solano Co., CA	David L. Newsom	David L. Newsom	1991	6
325	42 5/8	41 3/8	42	8 7/8	8	10	10	Solano Co., CA	Paul D. Osmond	Paul D. Osmond	1999	7
319 2/8	47 6/8	43	44 7/8	6 6/8	7 4/8	8	7	Solano Co., CA	H. James Tonkin, Jr.	H. James Tonkin, Jr.	1992	8
317 3/8	51 5/8	49 6/8	39 4/8	7 4/8	7 4/8	9	8	Solano Co., CA	Donald L. Potter	Donald L. Potter	1996	9
315 4/8	46 4/8	48 7/8	39 7/8	7 6/8	7 2/8	7	7	Solano Co., CA	David G. Paullin	David G. Paullin	1994	10
309 7/8	40 1/8	41 2/8	40 7/8	7 5/8	7 4/8	7	6	Monterey Co., CA	Chuck Adams	Chuck Adams	1990	11
308 6/8	40 4/8	42 4/8	52	8 1/8	8 1/8	8	6	San Luis Obispo Co., CA	Ray M. Tonkin	Ray M. Tonkin	1999	12
292	40 1/8	36 5/8	43 2/8	8 2/8	7 1/8	6	8	San Luis Obispo Co., CA	Lee M. Wahlund	Lee M. Wahlund	2003	13
289 2/8	42 5/8	43 7/8	43 6/8	7 5/8	7 3/8	8	6	Solano Co., CA	Dino W. Markette	Dino W. Markette	1990	14
287	38 6/8	39 2/8	38	7 4/8	7 5/8	7	8	San Luis Obispo Co., CA	Edward R. Frey	Kathleen A. Frey	2001	15
403 *	45 6/8	43 1/8	37 6/8	10 3/8	9 5/8	10	12	Solano Co., CA	Picked Up	CA Dept. of Fish & Game	1995	
342 6/8*	47 1/8	46 2/8	41 7/8	8 5/8	8 6/8	9	7	Solano Co., CA	Picked Up	Richard A. Cox	1996	
304 4/8*	41 4/8	43 4/8	45 3/8	7 7/8	8	8	8	Solano Co., CA	Patrick J. Gilligan	Patrick J. Gilligan	2003	
299 5/8*	40 6/8	46 4/8	44 2/8	7 3/8	8 4/8	10	8	Solano Co., CA	Patrick J. Gilligan	Patrick J. Gilligan	1991	

* Final score is subject to revision by additional verifying measurements.

CATEGORY
TULE ELK

SCORE
315-4/8

HUNTER
DAVID G. PAULLIN

LOCATION
SOLANO COUNTY, CALIFORNIA

DATE OF KILL
SEPTEMBER 1994

CATEGORY
TULE ELK

SCORE
287

HUNTER
EDWARD R. FREY

LOCATION
SOLANO COUNTY,
CALIFORNIA

DATE OF KILL
NOVEMBER 2001

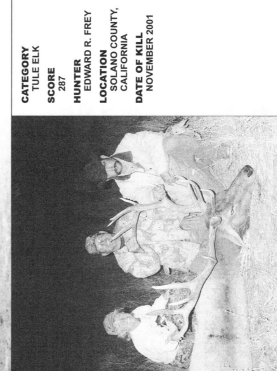

CATEGORY
TULE ELK

SCORE
319-2/8

HUNTER
H. JAMES TONKIN, JR.

LOCATION
SOLANO COUNTY, CALIFORNIA

DATE OF KILL
AUGUST 1992

MULE DEER - TYPICAL ANTLERS
WORLD'S RECORD

Doug Burris, Jr., began hunting the Dolores County area of Colorado in 1969. On his first three hunts, he took three nice bucks that any hunter would be proud to hang over their mantle. Little did Burris realize, however, that on his fourth trip he would shake the very foundation of the hunting community with a trophy that would surpass the World's Record.

On opening day of the 1972 season, Burris and his three companions, Jack Smith, Robbie Roe and Bruce Winters, piled into their Jeep before dawn and headed out. Working their way up one of the many mountain roads on the San Juan National Forest, Burris dropped the hunters off at regular intervals. Roe was the first, followed by Winters and then Smith. Burris continued on up the mountain. The day was rainy but all agreed to hunt until dark.

All the bucks the Texans saw that day were small and no one fired a shot. On the second day, Roe and Winters both took nice five-pointers, while Smith and Burris remained empty-handed. On the third day, Burris decided to go after a buck a friend had seen in Proven Canyon the day before. About mid-morning, Burris spotted two nice bucks feeding in a clearing about 500 yards away. While he watched these two bucks, a third one came into view.

Burris knew immediately that the latter buck had to be exceptional as he could see antlers even without the aid of binoculars. He decided to make the stalk. For the better part of an hour, Burris slowly and quietly worked his way through the oak brush. About the time he felt he had cut the distance in half, he nearly stepped on a doe bedded down in the underbrush. She exploded out of the brush, and the three bucks Burris was stalking scattered in different directions. Burris had time for one quick shot with his .264 Winchester Magnum, and the largest buck crumpled in mid stride.

Upon closer examination, Burris realized he had an unbelievable trophy. In 1974, at the 15th North American Big Game Awards Program held in Atlanta, Georgia, Burris' World's Record was confirmed. With a final score of 225-6/8 points, Burris' buck took the first place award for the typical mule deer category in addition to the coveted Sagamore Hill Award for the finest trophy taken during that Entry Period.

When the so-called "double-penalty" was dropped for excessive spread at a later date by the Club's Records Committee, the final score of Burris' buck increased by 6/8 of an inch to 226-4/8 points. ■

Reprinted with permission from Colorado's Biggest Bucks and Bulls

MULE DEER
TYPICAL ANTLERS
WORLD'S RECORD SCORE CHART

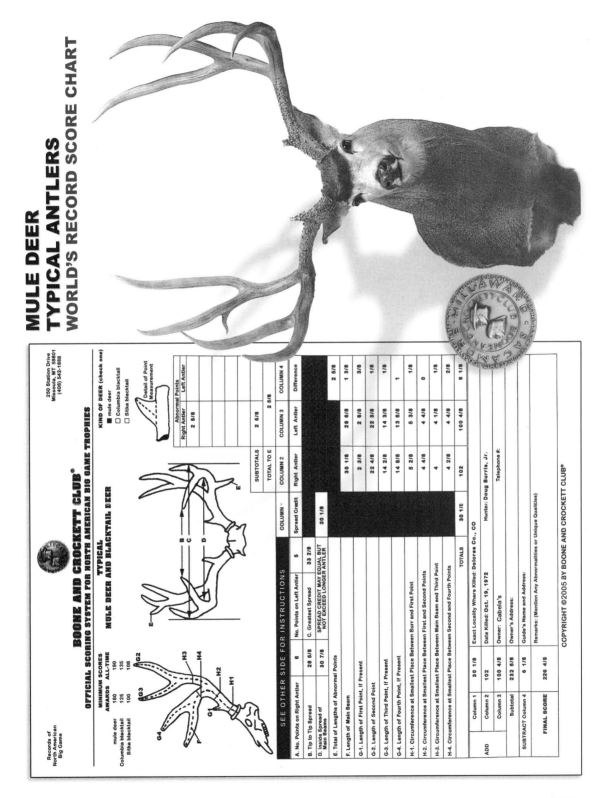

Records of
North American
Big Game

250 Station Drive
Missoula, MT 59801
(406) 542-1888

BOONE AND CROCKETT CLUB®
OFFICIAL SCORING SYSTEM FOR NORTH AMERICAN BIG GAME TROPHIES

TYPICAL MULE DEER AND BLACKTAIL DEER

	MINIMUM SCORES	
	AWARDS	ALL-TIME
mule deer	180	190
Columbia blacktail	125	135
Sitka blacktail	100	108

KIND OF DEER (check one)
- ☑ mule deer
- ☐ Columbia blacktail
- ☐ Sitka blacktail

Detail of Point Measurement

	Abnormal Points	
	Right Antler	Left Antler
	2 5/8	
		2 5/8
SUBTOTALS	2 6/8	2 5/8
TOTAL TO E		

SEE OTHER SIDE FOR INSTRUCTIONS

	COLUMN 1	COLUMN 2	COLUMN 3	COLUMN 4
	Spread Credit	Right Antler	Left Antler	Difference
A. No. Points on Right Antler	6			
No. Points on Left Antler	5			
B. Tip to Tip Spread	28 5/8			
C. Greatest Spread	33 2/8			
D. Inside Spread of Main Beams	30 7/8	SPREAD CREDIT MAY EQUAL BUT NOT EXCEED LONGER ANTLER	30 1/8	
E. Total of Lengths of Abnormal Points			2 6/8	2 5/8
F. Length of Main Beam		30 1/8	28 6/8	1 3/8
G-1. Length of First Point, If Present		2 3/8	2 6/8	3/8
G-2. Length of Second Point		22 4/8	22 3/8	1/8
G-3. Length of Third Point, If Present		14 2/8	14 3/8	1/8
G-4. Length of Fourth Point, If Present		14 6/8	13 6/8	1
H-1. Circumference at Smallest Place Between Burr and First Point		5 2/8	5 3/8	1/8
H-2. Circumference at Smallest Place Between First and Second Points		4 4/8	4 4/8	0
H-3. Circumference at Smallest Place Between Main Beam and Third Point		4	4 1/8	1/8
H-4. Circumference at Smallest Place Between Second and Fourth Points		4 2/8	4 4/8	2/8
TOTALS	30 1/8	102	100 4/8	6 1/8

ADD	Column 1	30 1/8	Exact Locality Where Killed: Dolores Co., CO
	Column 2	102	Date Killed: Oct. 19, 1972	Hunter: Doug Burris, Jr.
	Column 3	100 4/8	Owner: Cabela's	Telephone #:
	Subtotal	232 5/8	Owner's Address:
SUBTRACT	Column 4	6 1/8	Guide's Name and Address:
	FINAL SCORE	226 4/8	Remarks: (Mention Any Abnormalities or Unique Qualities)

COPYRIGHT ©2005 BY BOONE AND CROCKETT CLUB®

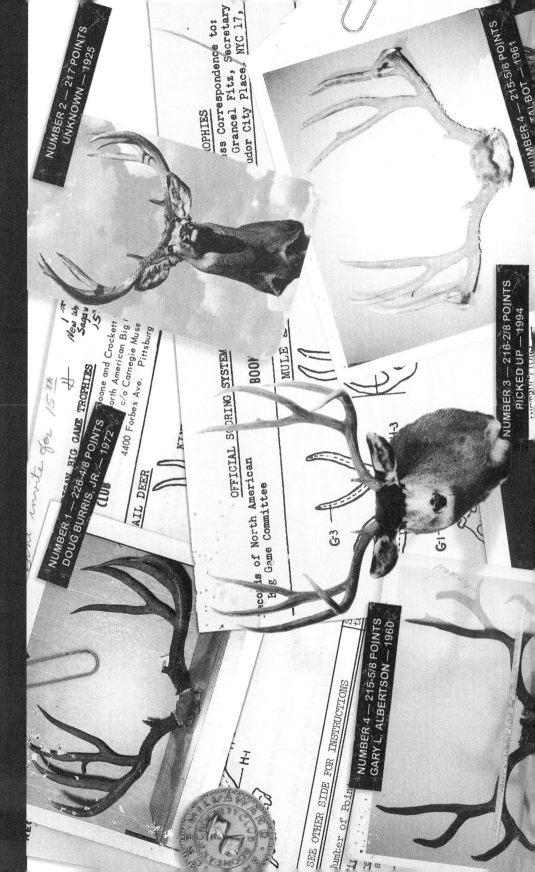

NUMBER 2 — 217 POINTS
UNKNOWN — 1925

NUMBER 4 — 215-5/8 POINTS
TALBOT — 1961

NUMBER 3 — 216-2/8 POINTS
PICKED UP — 1994

NUMBER 1 — 226-4/8 POINTS
DOUG BURRIS, JR. — 1972

NUMBER 4 — 215-5/8 POINTS
GARY L. ALBERTSON — 1960

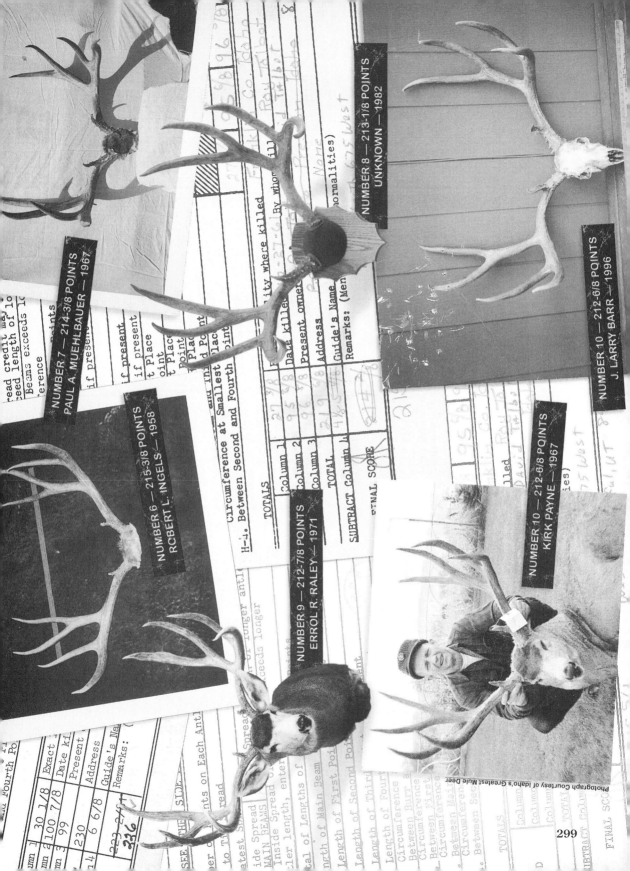

NUMBER 7 — 214-3/8 POINTS
PAUL A. MUEHLBAUER — 1967

NUMBER 6 — 215-3/8 POINTS
ROBERT L. INGELS — 1958

NUMBER 8 — 213-1/8 POINTS
UNKNOWN — 1982

NUMBER 10 — 212-6/8 POINTS
J. LARRY BARR — 1996

NUMBER 9 — 212-7/8 POINTS
ERROL R. RALEY — 1971

NUMBER 10 — 212-6/8 POINTS
KIRK PAYNE — 1967

MULE DEER - TYPICAL ANTLERS
Odocoileus hemionus hemionus and certain related subspecies

MINIMUM SCORE 190

Score	Length of Main Beam R	L	Inside Spread	Circumference at Smallest Place Between Burr and First Point R	L	Number of Points R	L	Locality	Hunter	Owner	Date Killed	Rank
226 4/8	30 1/8	28 6/8	30 7/8	5 2/8	5 3/8	6	5	Dolores Co., CO	Doug Burris, Jr.	Cabela's, Inc.	1972	1
217	28 4/8	28 2/8	26 6/8	5 5/8	5 6/8	6	6	Hoback Canyon, WY	Unknown	Jackson Hole Museum	1925	2
216 2/8	28 2/8	28 3/8	26 2/8	4 7/8	4 7/8	5	5	Coconino Co., AZ	Picked Up	B&C National Collection	1994	3
215 5/8	26 7/8	28 1/8	29 4/8	5 3/8	5 3/8	5	7	Uinta Co., WY	Gary L. Albertson	Cabela's, Inc.	1960	4
215 5/8	27 3/8	27 1/8	28 6/8	5 4/8	5 4/8	5	6	Franklin Co., ID	Ray Talbot	David Talbot	1961	4
215 3/8	29 6/8	30 1/8	28 6/8	5 4/8	5 3/8	5	5	Delta Co., CO	Robert L. Ingels	Fred Ferganchick	1958	6
214 3/8	27 5/8	27 4/8	31 3/8	4 7/8	4 7/8	5	5	Gypsum Creek, CO	Paul A. Muehlbauer	Paul A. Muehlbauer	1967	7
213 1/8	27 1/8	24 7/8	26	5	4 7/8	5	5	Moffat Co., CO	Unknown	David W. Blaker	1982	8
212 7/8	27 1/8	26 6/8	28 4/8	4 5/8	4 6/8	5	5	Garfield Co., CO	Errol R. Raley	Errol R. Raley	1971	9
212 6/8	26 6/8	26 7/8	25 4/8	5 2/8	5 2/8	5	5	Gem Co., ID	Kirk Payne	Kirk Payne	1967	10
212 6/8	28 1/8	28 2/8	26 4/8	4 6/8	5	6	5	Bonneville Co., ID	J. Larry Barr	J. Larry Barr	1996	10
212 1/8	26 3/8	26 6/8	26 4/8	6 1/8	6 1/8	8	6	San Juan Co., UT	V.R. Rayburn	V.R. Rayburn	1973	12
212 1/8	28 1/8	28 5/8	24 5/8	5 1/8	5	5	5	Idaho Co., ID	Urban H. Riener	Homer Saye	1979	12
212	29	28	21 4/8	5 4/8	5 4/8	5	5	Grand Co., CO	Wesley B. Brock	Wesley B. Brock	1963	14
211 7/8	28 6/8	28	27 6/8	6 5/8	6 5/8	5	6	Chama, NM	Joseph A. Garcia	Robert J. Seeds	1965	15
211 7/8	30 3/8	30 1/8	25 3/8	5	5	5	6	Adams Co., ID	Boyd W. Dennis	Boyd W. Dennis	1970	15
211 7/8	25 5/8	26 7/8	26 7/8	5 2/8	5 2/8	5	5	Park Co., WY	Picked Up	Cabela's, Inc.	1995	15
211 6/8	29 7/8	29 6/8	30 3/8	4 5/8	4 5/8	7	8	Teton Co., WY	Robert V. Parke	Cabela's, Inc.	1967	18
211 2/8	27 4/8	27 3/8	25 2/8	5	5 1/8	5	5	Bonneville Co., ID	Ike Ellis	Bass Pro Shops	1986	19
211 1/8	28 7/8	28 7/8	32 6/8	5 4/8	5 4/8	5	5	Cache Co., UT	Unknown	Cabela's, Inc.	PR 1950	20
210 4/8	27 3/8	28	19 4/8	5 7/8	5 7/8	5	6	Morgan Co., UT	K.P. Rafton	Cabela's, Inc.	1973	21
210 3/8	28	27 6/8	23 1/8	4 5/8	4 6/8	6	6	Madison Co., ID	Todd L. Landon	Todd L. Landon	1986	22
210 2/8	29 1/8	29 2/8	27	5 2/8	5 2/8	6	5	Southern Ute Res., CO	Jack D. Johnston	Jack D. Johnston	1963	23
210 2/8	27 7/8	27 4/8	31 4/8	5 1/8	5	5	6	Delta Co., CO	Tom Donaldson	Tom Donaldson	1972	23
210 1/8	28 3/8	28 7/8	30 4/8	4 7/8	4 6/8	6	6	Boulder Co., CO	Unknown	Cabela's, Inc.	PR 1965	25
210	26 2/8	26 4/8	25 4/8	5 2/8	5 1/8	6	6	Manti-Lasal Mts., UT	William Norton	William Norton	1970	26
209 5/8	29 7/8	29 2/8	29 2/8	5	5 2/8	5	7	Montrose Co., CO	Mike Thomas	Mike Thomas	1974	27
209 5/8	27 4/8	27 7/8	28 7/8	5 5/8	5 5/8	5	7	Rio Arriba Co., NM	Kelly Baird	Kelly Baird	1984	27
209 5/8	27 5/8	26 5/8	30 6/8	4 7/8	5 2/8	6	8	Coconino Co., AZ	Unknown	Cabela's, Inc.	PR 1985	27
209 4/8	28 7/8	29 6/8	28	5 7/8	5 7/8	6	8	Wallowa Co., OR	John C. Evans	Stan J. Neitling, Jr.	1920	30
209 3/8	26 4/8	25 6/8	23	5 1/8	5 2/8	8	5	Kansas	Brad Hughes	Cabela's, Inc.	1984	31
209 3/8	26 1/8	25 5/8	23 7/8	5	4 6/8	5	5	Lincoln Co., WY	L. Victor Clark	L. Victor Clark	1992	31
209 2/8	27 6/8	27 1/8	27 4/8	5 6/8	5 6/8	5	5	Amherst Mt., CO	Herbert Graham	Mrs. W.J. Graham	1963	33
209 2/8	28	29 4/8	28 4/8	4 7/8	4 6/8	5	5	Rich Co., UT	Dee Hildt	Dee Hildt	1968	33
209	24 4/8	25 4/8	24 1/8	6 1/8	6 2/8	5	7	Saguache Co., CO	William B. Pennington	William B. Pennington	1967	35
209	26 7/8	27	24 2/8	5 6/8	5 6/8	5	5	Boise Co., ID	Charles Root	Soron Root	1970	35

Score	L.M.B. R	L.M.B. L	Circ. R	Circ. L	Pts. R	Pts. L	Locality	Hunter	Owner	Date	Rank
208 6/8	27 6/8	26 7/8	5 1/8	5	6	5	North Kaibab, AZ	Horace T. Fowler	Aly M. Bruner	1938	37
208 6/8	24 4/8	17 4/8	5 3/8	5 3/8	6	6	Garfield Co., CO	George Shearer	Richard L. Baker	1952	37
208 6/8	26	26 4/8	5 2/8	5 2/8	4	5	Rio Arriba Co., NM	James R. Odiorne, Jr.	James R. Odiorne, Jr.	1978	37
208 5/8	26 7/8	27 2/8	5	5	5	5	Mesa Co., CO	Robert L. Zaina	Robert L. Zaina	1960	40
208	29	34 3/8	5 1/8	5 1/8	5	5	Utah Co., UT	Ned H. Losser	Ned H. Losser	1972	41
208	26 6/8	31 6/8	5 3/8	5 1/8	6	6	Franklin Co., ID	Herb Voyles, Jr.	Herb Voyles, Jr.	1972	41
207 6/8	26	23 2/8	4 7/8	5 1/8	6	6	Gem Co., ID	Thomas A. Sutton	Thomas A. Sutton	1991	43
207 5/8	25 3/8	31	5 1/8	5 2/8	6	6	Sonora, MX	Unknown	James E. Arias	1978	44
207 4/8	27 4/8	26	4 7/8	4 7/8	5	5	Washington Co., UT	John K. Frei	Cabela's, Inc.	1987	45
207 3/8	28 1/8	29 4/8	5 6/8	5 5/8	9	7	Mesa Co., CO	Wally Bruegman	Wally Bruegman	1972	46
207 2/8	28 5/8	28 1/8	6 5/8	6 4/8	6	6	Montrose Co., CO	Bill Crouch	Cabela's, Inc.	1974	47
207 1/8	26 6/8	24 1/8	5 6/8	5 4/8	6	5	Golden, CO	Harold B. Moser	Harold B. Moser	1967	48
207	31 6/8	27 4/8	7	7	6	6	Split Rock, WY	Herb Klein	Dallas Mus. of Natl. Hist.	1960	49
207	28	28 2/8	6	6	6	5	Montrose Co., CO	Warren S. Bachhofer	Warren S. Bachhofer	1966	49
207	26 7/8	29	5 3/8	5 3/8	5	6	Lincoln Co., WY	Al Firenze, Sr.	Al Firenze, Jr.	1969	49
207	25 2/8	28	6 2/8	6	4	6	Franklin Co., ID	Unknown	L. Dwight Israelsen	PR 1970	49
207	28 3/8	26 2/8	5 4/8	6	5	4	Kane Co., UT	Picked Up	John K. Springer	1986	49
206 7/8	29	29 3/8	5 3/8	5 4/8	6	7	Adams Co., ID	E. Jack Raby	E. Jack Raby	1968	54
206 7/8	26 1/8	21 3/8	4 6/8	4 7/8	5	5	Montrose Co., CO	W.L. Boynton	W.L. Boynton	1973	54
206 6/8	27 4/8	29 4/8	6 2/8	6 1/8	5	8	Pagosa Springs, CO	Richard V. Price	Richard V. Price	1962	56
206 6/8	25 6/8	28 2/8	5 1/8	4 7/8	6	5	Pagosa Springs, CO	Henry Trujillo, Jr.	Henry Trujillo, Jr.	1963	56
206 6/8	27 6/8	20 4/8	5	5 3/8	5	5	Rio Arriba Co., NM	Robert J. Seeds	Robert J. Seeds	1996	56
206 6/8	28 1/8	26	6 1/8	6 2/8	7	7	Sonora, MX	Jack Gurley	Jack Gurley	1998	56
206 5/8	27 4/8	28 3/8	4 6/8	4 6/8	6	6	Coconino Co., AZ	Lamell Ellsworth	Lamell Ellsworth	1971	60
206 4/8	28 7/8	28 5/8	5 2/8	5 1/8	7	7	New Mexico	Unknown	C. & J. Neill	PR 1956	61
206 3/8	27 2/8	27 7/8	5 1/8	5	5	5	Eagle Co., CO	Harold Taylor	Fred Palmer	1960	62
206 3/8	27 4/8	26 3/8	5 2/8	5 3/8	6	5	Rio Arriba Co., NM	Jim Roddie	Jim Roddie	1971	62
206 3/8	27 1/8	26 5/8	5 1/8	5 1/8	6	7	Coconino Co., AZ	Robert C. Kaufman	Robert C. Kaufman	1978	62
206 3/8	26 6/8	26 3/8	5	4 7/8	6	6	Coconino Co., AZ	Katie A. Norman	Katie A. Norman	1990	62
206 2/8	26	27 4/8	5 5/8	5 5/8	9	7	Rio Arriba Co., NM	Harley Hinds	Oran M. Roberts	1963	66
206 2/8	28 6/8	28 6/8	6	6	5	5	Montrose Co., CO	Patrick E. Courtin, Jr.	Patrick E. Courtin, Jr.	1972	66
206 2/8	26 5/8	27 5/8	5 5/8	5 7/8	6	5	Mesa Co., CO	Picked Up	Darryl Powell	1974	66
206 1/8	25 7/8	22 1/8	5 7/8	6	5	5	Coconino Co., AZ	Unknown	Danny Hopper	PR 1949	69
206 1/8	24	26 3/8	5 2/8	5 1/8	5	5	Peterson, UT	Picked Up	Paul Crittenden	PR 1965	69
206 1/8	27 6/8	25 2/8	5 1/8	5	5	5	Idaho Co., ID	William B. Joyner	William B. Joyner	1965	69
206 1/8	26 6/8	24 5/8	6 1/8	6 1/8	5	6	Summit Co., CO	Robb R. Rishor	Robb R. Rishor	2002	69
206	24 3/8	22 1/8	5 2/8	5 1/8	5	5	Eagle Co., CO	Harold L. Loesch	Harold L. Loesch	1967	73
206	28 4/8	31	5 2/8	5 4/8	7	5	Crooked Creek, AB	Chad J. Lyttle	Chad J. Lyttle	1996	73
205 6/8	27 6/8	25 2/8	5 4/8	5 3/8	5	5	Kanab, UT	Loyd A. Folkstad	Loyd A. Folkstad	1968	75
205 6/8	24 3/8	23 4/8	5 4/8	5 4/8	5	4	Eagle Co., CO	Mark A. McCormick	Mark A. McCormick	1981	75
205 5/8	28 7/8	27 2/8	5 3/8	5 2/8	5	5	Washington Co., UT	William C. Cloyd	William C. Cloyd	1994	77
205 4/8	27 3/8	22 7/8	5 1/8	5 6/8	5	6	Kremmling, CO	Larry Bell	Larry Bell	1962	78
205 4/8	25 3/8	25	5 2/8	5	6	6	Carbondale, CO	Richard Cobb	Richard Cobb	1962	78
205 4/8	29 1/8	28 4/8	5	4 6/8	4	5	Gunnison Co., CO	William T. Peacock	Ralph L. McKinley	1968	78
205 4/8	26 7/8	25 5/8	5 1/8	5 3/8	5	5	Lincoln Co., WY	John E. Myers	John E. Myers	1983	78
205 4/8	26 6/8	25 7/8	4 6/8	5 3/8	6	6	Lincoln Co., NV	Erich P. Burkhard	Erich P. Burkhard	1993	78
205 4/8	26 4/8	24 6/8	5 4/8	5	7	5	Rio Arriba Co., NM	Picked Up	Eudane Vicenti	1963	78
205 3/8	26 2/8	25 1/8	5 3/8	5 3/8	5	5	Starkey, OR	H.M. Bailey	H.M. Bailey	1963	84

MULE DEER - TYPICAL ANTLERS
Odocoileus hemionus hemionus and certain related subspecies

Score	Length of Main Beam R	L	Inside Spread	Circumference at Smallest Place Between Burr and First Point R	L	Number of Points R	L	Locality	Hunter	Owner	Date Killed	Rank
205 2/8	27 5/8	28	30 1/8	4 4/8	4 7/8	5	5	Montrose Co., CO	Joe M. Gardner	Zane G. Holland	1954	85
205 2/8	27 1/8	27 6/8	28 1/8	4 5/8	5	5	5	Carbon Co., WY	Shelly R. Risner	Shelly R. Risner	1986	85
205 1/8	26 3/8	25 6/8	25 5/8	4 4/8	4 4/8	5	5	Morgan Co., UT	Gale Allen	Gale Allen	1946	87
205 1/8	28 4/8	30	28 5/8	5	5	7	5	San Juan Co., NM	David A. Brooks	David A. Brooks	1995	87
204 7/8	27 2/8	27	23 5/8	5 5/8	5 4/8	6	5	Delta Co., CO	Frank Peterson	Frank Peterson	1956	89
204 7/8	26 4/8	26 1/8	26 3/8	5 2/8	5 2/8	5	5	Southern Ute Res., CO	Nolan Martins	Nolan Martins	1967	89
204 6/8	25 2/8	25	24 2/8	4 6/8	4 7/8	5	5	Colorado	Unknown	D.J. Hollinger & B. Howard	PR 1990	91
204 6/8	25	24 3/8	25 4/8	5 3/8	5 3/8	5	5	Colorado	Unknown	Cabela's, Inc.	PR 1992	91
204 5/8	25 5/8	26 1/8	24 6/8	4 7/8	4 7/8	6	5	Routt Co., CO	Paul Brenner	Craig Hoyer	1960	93
204 5/8	26 7/8	28 1/8	29 3/8	6 1/8	6 2/8	5	5	Adams Co., ID	Alvin Yantis	Alvin Yantis	1967	93
204 5/8	25 5/8	24 3/8	19 4/8	5 5/8	5 4/8	7	5	Eagle Co., CO	Robert V. Doerr	Robert V. Doerr	1982	93
204 4/8	27 6/8	26 6/8	28	4 5/8	4 5/8	6	5	Carbon Co., UT	Harold Wimmer	Tony Allred	1933	96
204 3/8	26 1/8	26 4/8	20 5/8	5 6/8	5 5/8	5	5	Grand Junction, CO	Charles M. Bentley	Michael N. Bentley	1962	97
204 3/8	29 2/8	30 1/8	35	4 4/8	4 5/8	5	5	Sonora, MX	David V. Collis	David V. Collis	1986	97
204 2/8	26	26 2/8	22 2/8	5 4/8	5 4/8	5	5	Garfield Co., UT	James D. Perkins	James D. Perkins	1969	99
204 1/8	28 6/8	30 4/8	24 1/8	4 5/8	4 7/8	6	5	Jicarilla Apache Res., NM	Juan Monarco	Juan Monarco	1960	100
204 1/8	27 5/8	26 1/8	25 1/8	5	5	5	5	Hinsdale Co., CO	Norman E. Ebbley	Jim Temple	1961	100
204 1/8	24 6/8	26	27 6/8	4 7/8	4 7/8	6	5	Morgan Co., UT	Kenneth R. Dickamore	Kenneth R. Dickamore	1967	100
204 1/8	27 2/8	27	25 7/8	5 2/8	5 2/8	6	5	Rio Arriba Co., NM	Waymon Burkhalter	Waymon Burkhalter	1992	100
204	27	27 3/8	24	5 4/8	5 3/8	5	5	Pitkin Co., CO	Jens O. Solberg	Jens O. Solberg	1950	104
204	28 3/8	28 4/8	23 7/8	5 4/8	5 6/8	6	5	Arizona	Unknown	Cabela's, Inc.	PR 1988	104
204	27 3/8	23 4/8	25	5 2/8	5 2/8	5	5	Kane Co., UT	Wade E. Ramsay	Wade E. Ramsay	1995	104
203 7/8	**24 5/8**	**26**	**24 4/8**	**5 7/8**	**5 6/8**	**6**	**6**	**North Park, CO**	**Edison A. Pillmore**	**Mrs. Edison A. Pillmore**	**1949**	**107**
203 7/8	26 3/8	27 5/8	26 3/8	5 2/8	5 3/8	6	6	Mesa Creek, CO	Ed Craig	Jerome Craig	1951	107
203 7/8	29 3/8	29 4/8	25 5/8	5 6/8	5 5/8	5	5	Jicarilla Apache Res., NM	Dick Wright	Dick Wright	1966	107
203 7/8	25 6/8	28 4/8	18 7/8	6 2/8	5 4/8	5	5	Apache Co., AZ	Picked Up	Mike A. Searles	1994	107
203 6/8	27	28 3/8	22 7/8	4 3/8	4 3/8	6	5	Montezuma Co., CO	Bob Meese	Cabela's, Inc.	1970	111
203 5/8	28 3/8	27 3/8	24 4/8	5 7/8	5 6/8	6	5	La Plata Co., CO	B.E. Gressett	B.E. Gressett	1950	112
203 5/8	24 5/8	25 5/8	25 6/8	4 5/8	4 6/8	5	5	Mesa Co., CO	William P. Burger	William P. Burger	1957	112
203 5/8	28 6/8	30 2/8	30 1/8	5	5	5	5	Grand Co., UT	Glen Dumas	S. Kim Bonnett	PR 1960	112
203 5/8	28 5/8	28 7/8	27 7/8	5 2/8	5 3/8	7	5	Caribou Co., ID	William E. Van Antwerp	William E. Van Antwerp	1992	112
203 4/8	25 7/8	29 5/8	27 6/8	5 4/8	5 3/8	5	5	Kaibab Natl. For., AZ	Herb Graham	Herb Graham	1939	116
203 4/8	27 2/8	24	24 2/8	5 4/8	5 3/8	5	5	Elko Co., NV	C.H. Wahl	C.H. Wahl	1953	116
203 4/8	26 5/8	27 3/8	25 2/8	5 4/8	5 4/8	5	7	Mohave Co., AZ	Nick Papac	Nick Papac	1964	116
203 4/8	27	28 1/8	24 4/8	5 4/8	5 4/8	6	5	Rio Arriba Co., NM	Arnold Wendt	John W. Hughes	1965	116
203 4/8	28	26 5/8	30 5/8	5 4/8	5 2/8	6	5	Adams Co., ID	Roy Eastlick	Roy Eastlick	1975	116

Score	Main Beam R	Main Beam L	Inside Spread	Circ. R	Circ. L	Pts R	Pts L	Locality	Hunter	Owner	Date	Rank
203 4/8	27 5/8	28 3/8	25	4 5/8	4 6/8	5	7	Garfield Co., CO	John T. Sewell	John T. Sewell	1985	116
203 4/8	28 6/8	28 1/8	29 4/8	5	5 1/8	6	5	Utah Co., UT	Carl B. Webb	Carl B. Webb	2000	116
203 2/8	25 7/8	28	22 4/8	4 4/8	4 4/8	6	5	White River, CO	Ron Vance	Ronald Crawford	1943	123
203 2/8	25 3/8	25 7/8	24 6/8	4 6/8	4 5/8	6	7	Crook Co., WY	Ora McGurn	Bob R. Butler	1957	123
203 2/8	28	28 4/8	29 6/8	5 2/8	5 2/8	5	5	De Beque, CO	Francis A. Moore	Francis A. Moore	1962	123
203 2/8	25 6/8	26 6/8	23 3/8	4 6/8	4 7/8	5	5	Garfield Co., UT	James D. Perkins	Mrs. James D. Perkins	1965	123
203 2/8	27 1/8	26 6/8	22 2/8	4 6/8	4 6/8	5	5	Collbran, CO	Joe R. Colingo	Joe R. Colingo	1973	123
203 2/8	26 5/8	26 5/8	22	5 2/8	5 2/8	5	6	McLeese Lake, BC	Dean Barlow	Dean Barlow	1980	123
203 1/8	26 2/8	26 6/8	27 1/8	5 6/8	5 6/8	6	5	North Kaibab, AZ	Monico Marquez	Monico Marquez	1957	129
203 1/8	22 5/8	22 7/8	27 6/8	5 3/8	6 3/8	5	6	Hayden, CO	M.W. Giboney	M.W. Giboney	1959	129
203 1/8	25 7/8	26 6/8	24	5	5 1/8	5	6	Fremont Co., ID	Michael W.G. Neff	Michael W.G. Neff	1990	129
203	25 5/8	23 5/8	25 5/8	5 3/8	5 3/8	6	6	Bonneville Co., ID	Jay Hoover	Cabela's, Inc.	1966	132
203	25	25 5/8	24	5 2/8	5 2/8	5	6	Mesa Co., CO	James K. Scott	James K. Scott	1966	132
203	26 3/8	24 5/8	27 1/8	5 4/8	5 6/8	5	5	Montrose Co., CO	Earl L. Markley	Aly M. Bruner	1968	132
203	24 2/8	26 3/8	23 5/8	4 6/8	4 6/8	9	8	Flathead Co., MT	Fran Cahoon	Cabela's, Inc.	1989	136
202 7/8	24 2/8	23	26 3/8	6	5 7/8	5	7	Adams Co., ID	James S. Denney	James S. Denney	1939	136
202 7/8	24 5/8	23 7/8	22 1/8	5 2/8	5 2/8	5	5	Lincoln Co., WY	Monte J. Brough	Monte J. Brough	1968	136
202 7/8	26 5/8	26	23 7/8	4 7/8	4 7/8	6	5	Idaho Co., ID	Myron L. Gilbert	Myron L. Gilbert	1975	136
202 6/8	25 3/8	24 7/8	19 2/8	6 6/8	6 7/8	5	5	Ouray Co., CO	Jewel E. Schottel	Jewel E. Schottel	1966	139
202 6/8	28 2/8	29 2/8	25 4/8	5 3/8	5 2/8	5	5	Rio Arriba Co., NM	James F. Leveritt, Jr.	James F. Leveritt, Jr.	1980	139
202 5/8	26 3/8	25 5/8	21 5/8	5 1/8	5	5	5	Ouray Co., CO	Louis V. Schlosser	Louis V. Schlosser	1965	141
202 5/8	27 1/8	26 1/8	25 1/8	5	5 1/8	5	5	Adams Co., ID	David J. Couch	David J. Couch	1970	141
202 4/8	26 1/8	26 2/8	28 2/8	4 7/8	4 7/8	5	5	Bear Lake Co., ID	Alan R. Crane	Alan R. Crane	1962	143
202 4/8	29 2/8	29	29 4/8	5 2/8	5 1/8	6	6	Park Co., WY	Paul M. Rothermel, Jr.	Paul M. Rothermel, Jr.	1962	143
202 4/8	27 4/8	27 6/8	21 2/8	6	5 7/8	7	4	Mesa Co., CO	Jack Thompson	Jack Thompson	1968	143
202 4/8	26 7/8	24 7/8	27	5 2/8	5 2/8	6	6	Rio Arriba Co., NM	Gerald J. Weber	Gerald J. Weber	1970	143
202 4/8	29 5/8	28 4/8	21 6/8	5	5	6	4	Garfield Co., CO	James S. Harden	Cabela's, Inc.	1982	143
202 3/8	25 6/8	26 1/8	30 3/8	5 1/8	5 1/8	4	6	Jicarilla Apache Res., NM	Theodore Serafin	Theodore Serafin	1959	148
202 3/8	26 3/8	27 1/8	23 5/8	5 3/8	5 3/8	5	6	Boulder Co., CO	Bob Wallace	Bob Wallace	1963	148
202 3/8	26 1/8	27 1/8	24 5/8	5 6/8	5 6/8	7	6	Baker Co., OR	Brett N. Haynes	Brett N. Haynes	1982	148
202 3/8	27 1/8	26	28 3/8	5 3/8	5 4/8	5	6	Sublette Co., WY	Derek L. Kendrick	Derek L. Kendrick	1992	148
202 3/8	23 7/8	25 2/8	21 4/8	5 6/8	6	5	5	Coconino Co., AZ	Steve B. Parizek	Steve B. Parizek	1993	148
202 2/8	25 6/8	26	24 5/8	5 3/8	5 6/8	5	6	Whitebear Lake, SK	Robert E. Code	Robert E. Code	2000	148
202 2/8	26 5/8	26	26 5/8	5 1/8	5	5	5	Pagosa Springs, CO	Allen R. Arnwine	Allen R. Arnwine	1960	154
202 2/8	27 2/8	28 1/8	31 3/8	5 2/8	5 2/8	7	7	Carbon Co., UT	Robert R. Henderson	Robert R. Henderson	1965	154
202 2/8	30 2/8	29 6/8	20 6/8	4 7/8	4 7/8	4	7	Archuleta Co., CO	Duane Yearwood	Duane Yearwood	1973	154
202	27 1/8	27 1/8	21 1/8	5 4/8	5 4/8	5	4	Deschutes Co., OR	Ray Cole	Ray Cole	1946	157
202	28	27	26	5 6/8	5 6/8	9	5	Bear Lake Co., ID	David L. Williams	Raymond L. Williams	1949	158
202	26 7/8	27 2/8	27 6/8	6 3/8	6 3/8	6	6	Lincoln Co., MT	William E. Hubbard	William E. Hubbard	1963	158
202	26 4/8	25 4/8	29 4/8	5 1/8	5 3/8	5	6	Gunnison Natl. For., CO	James M. Newsom	James M. Newsom	1963	158
202	27 2/8	27 1/8	24 2/8	5 2/8	5 1/8	5	6	Montrose Co., CO	Kenneth Klees	Kenneth Klees	1966 PR 1970	158
202	26	24 6/8	27 5/8	4 7/8	5 5/8	5	5	Chelan Co., WA	Unknown	James M. Brown	1976	158
202	26 1/8	26 4/8	27 4/8	5	4 7/8	5	5	Sweetwater Co., WY	Arnold A. Bethke	Arnold A. Bethke	1981	158
202	26 1/8	26 4/8	21 4/8	5	4 7/8	5	5	Idaho Co., ID	John H. Davis	John H. Davis	1982	158
202	26 1/8	27 7/8	25 6/8	5 1/8	5 3/8	5	5	Unknown	Picked Up	Dale Selby	1985	158
202	29	27 6/8	29	4 7/8	5	5	5	Hidalgo Co., NM	Matt Evans	Matt Evans	1985	158
202	27 4/8	27 3/8	25 6/8	5 2/8	5 2/8	5	5	Elko Co., NV	Arlo M. Hummell	Arlo M. Hummell	1989	158
202	27 1/8	26 1/8	26 6/8	5 4/8	5 4/8	5	5	Coconino Co., AZ	Donald Vanderwall	Donald Vanderwall	1992	158

MULE DEER - TYPICAL ANTLERS
Odocoileus hemionus hemionus and certain related subspecies

Score	Length of Main Beam R	L	Inside Spread	Circumference at Smallest Place Between Burr and First Point R	L	Number of Points R	L	Locality	Hunter	Owner	Date Killed	Rank
201 7/8	27 2/8	27 3/8	27 3/8	6 1/8	5 6/8	6	6	Daggett Co., UT	Earl Eldredge	Phil Brotherson	1940	169
201 7/8	26 5/8	27 2/8	26 3/8	4 6/8	4 5/8	6	5	Dolores Co., CO	Leonard J. Ashcraft	Leonard J. Ashcraft	1958	169
201 7/8	27	26	26 5/8	5 1/8	5 1/8	5	5	Union Co., OR	Brian M. Erwin	Brian M. Erwin	1991	169
201 6/8	26	26 5/8	21 2/8	5	5	5	4	Afton, WY	Bernard Domries	Bernard Domries	1967	172
201 6/8	25 7/8	26 1/8	26 4/8	6 1/8	6 4/8	6	6	Saddle Hills, AB	Dale Ophus	Dale Ophus	1989	172
201 6/8	26	26 3/8	27 1/8	5 2/8	5 2/8	6	5	Washoe Co., NV	Gordon Frazier	Ron W. Biggs	1991	172
201 6/8	26 6/8	26 1/8	25 2/8	5	4 7/8	5	6	Montrose Co., CO	Allan K. Slafter	Allan K. Slafter	1994	172
201 5/8	26 2/8	26 4/8	23 3/8	5 1/8	5	5	5	Gunnison Co., CO	Robert D. Rader	Robert D. Rader	1966	176
201 5/8	24 1/8	24 2/8	25 1/8	5 3/8	5 3/8	5	6	Cheyenne Co., KS	Jim Sutton	Cabela's, Inc.	PR 1972	176
201 5/8	26 6/8	25 6/8	28 4/8	5 2/8	5	6	6	Eagle Co., CO	Richard C. Bergquist	Richard C. Bergquist	1981	176
201 5/8	26 2/8	27 3/8	24 3/8	5 4/8	5 4/8	5	5	Baker Co., OR	Terry Williams	Terry Williams	1988	176
201 4/8	27	26	26	5	5	5	5	Garfield Co., CO	Unknown	Ronald E. McKinney	1954	180
201 4/8	27 4/8	24 6/8	25 1/8	5 4/8	5 4/8	5	6	Dolores Co., CO	James H. Becher	Jerry Schwaderer	1963	180
201 4/8	23	24	20	5 4/8	5 2/8	6	6	Moffat Co., CO	Carl E. Jacobson	Carl E. Jacobson	1967	180
201 4/8	26 6/8	24 7/8	28 4/8	6 3/8	6	5	5	Chama, NM	James W. Smith II	James W. Smith II	1969	180
201 4/8	26 3/8	25 3/8	24 2/8	5 3/8	5 2/8	5	5	Malheur Co., OR	David L. Bauer	David L. Bauer	1971	180
201 4/8	28 1/8	28 3/8	22 7/8	5 6/8	5 4/8	5	7	Ravalli Co., MT	Sherman L. Williams	Sherman L. Williams	1973	180
201 4/8	29 3/8	29 3/8	26 6/8	4 6/8	5	6	5	Washington Co., UT	Clyde Cannon	Troy T. Truman	1979	180
201 4/8	27 1/8	26 2/8	23 3/8	5 1/8	5 2/8	5	5	Adams Co., ID	Gary D. Lewis	Gary D. Lewis	1990	180
201 4/8	28 7/8	27 6/8	23 3/8	5 3/8	5 2/8	7	6	Mesa Co., CO	Michael W. Laws	Michael W. Laws	1996	180
201 4/8	29 2/8	28 5/8	28	5 6/8	5 4/8	9	6	Franklin Co., ID	Forrest Christensen	Forrest Christensen	2000	180
201 3/8	25 4/8	26 1/8	30 1/8	6 1/8	6	5	5	Archuleta Co., CO	Joe Moore	Joe Moore	1962	190
201 3/8	27 6/8	27 6/8	26 4/8	5 4/8	5 4/8	7	7	Blaine Co., ID	Brent Jones	Brent Jones	1965	190
201 3/8	25 5/8	26 4/8	25 3/8	5 4/8	5 4/8	5	5	Grand Junction, CO	William C. Byrd	William C. Byrd	1967	190
201 3/8	27 5/8	27	25 5/8	5 4/8	5 4/8	5	5	Idaho	Scott Rehn	D.J. Hollinger & B. Howard	1968	190
201 3/8	25 6/8	24 5/8	20 7/8	5 3/8	5 3/8	5	5	Unknown	Unknown	Matthew N. Davis	PR 1970	190
201 3/8	26 3/8	26 3/8	25 4/8	5 5/8	5 5/8	6	5	Rio Arriba Co., NM	Donald W. Johnson	Donald W. Johnson	1970	190
201 3/8	30 1/8	28 2/8	28 7/8	4 5/8	4 6/8	5	5	Wasatch Co., UT	Paul Probst	Paul Probst	1971	190
201 3/8	25 6/8	24 6/8	23 1/8	5 4/8	5 4/8	5	5	Montrose Co., CO	Grant Morlang	Grant Morlang	1972	190
201 3/8	28 3/8	29 7/8	34 2/8	5 3/8	5 6/8	4	5	Butte Co., ID	John A. Little	John A. Little	1981	190
201 3/8	26 5/8	25 7/8	23 3/8	5 2/8	5 2/8	6	7	Sublette Co., WY	Jerry C. Lopez	Jerry C. Lopez	1985	190
201 2/8	28	29	28	5	4 6/8	6	6	Bayfield Co., CO	D. Rockwell	D. Rockwell	1956	200
201 2/8	26 6/8	27 6/8	26 6/8	6	6	5	6	Jicarilla Apache Res., NM	Anthony Julian	Anthony Julian	1961	200
201 2/8	28 4/8	28 3/8	24	5 1/8	5 3/8	5	5	Chama, NM	Emitt W. Mundy	Emitt W. Mundy	1961	200
201 2/8	26	26	24 2/8	5 4/8	5 2/8	7	6	Lincoln Co., WY	Gavin S. Lovell	Gavin S. Lovell	2003	200
201 1/8	29 1/8	29 2/8	31	5 2/8	5 3/8	7	8	Sanpete Co., UT	Roger M. Allred	Roger M. Allred	1958	204

Score	Main Beam R	Main Beam L	Inside Spread	Circ. R	Circ. L	Pts. R	Pts. L	Locality	Hunter	Owner	Date	Rank
201 1/8	26 2/8	26 2/8	25 3/8	5	5	5	5	Cameo, CO	Thomas C. Krauss	Thomas C. Krauss	1962	204
201 1/8	27 2/8	26 4/8	26 6/8	6 3/8	6 5/8	7	5	Bayfield Co., CO	Les Patrick	Les Patrick	1966	204
201 1/8	25 6/8	25 6/8	26 4/8	5 1/8	5 4/8	6	5	Jicarilla Apache Res., NM	Arnold Cassador	Arnold Cassador	1967	204
201 1/8	27 5/8	26 5/8	25 2/8	5	5	6	6	Sonora, MX	Bruce K. Kidman	Bruce K. Kidman	1998	204
201	28 6/8	28 2/8	28 6/8	5 2/8	5	4	6	Summit Co., UT	Clinton A. Larson	Clinton A. Larson	1949	209
201	26 2/8	29	22 6/8	6 1/8	6 1/8	8	6	Grand Junction, CO	Ernest Mancuso	Ernest Mancuso	1954	209
201	25 4/8	25 4/8	25 6/8	4 7/8	5 1/8	5	5	Wallowa Co., OR	Ross Bennett	Ross Bennett	1959	209
201	26	24 7/8	23 1/8	5 1/8	5	5	6	Idaho	Unknown	Bruce D. Ringsmith	PR 1960	209
201	25 1/8	25	24 4/8	4 7/8	5	5	5	Dolores Co., CO	Mark Loverin	Mark Loverin	1978	209
201	26 2/8	26 2/8	23 6/8	5 1/8	5 1/8	5	5	La Plata Co., CO	Larry Pennington	Larry Pennington	1978	209
201	26 6/8	26 6/8	24 5/8	5 1/8	5 2/8	5	7	Idaho	Unknown	Rick Stover	PR 1990	209
201	24	23 2/8	23 1/8	5 2/8	5 3/8	8	7	Fremont Co., ID	Kenneth E. Stevens	Kenneth E. Stevens	1996	209
201	26	26	26 2/8	5 4/8	5 4/8	5	5	Elko Co., NV	Jerry D. Dye	Jerry D. Dye	2001	209
200 7/8	25 7/8	25 7/8	28 3/8	4 6/8	4 4/8	5	5	Colorado	Harry Ireland	Mrs. Harry Ireland	1919	218
200 7/8	26	26 5/8	26 3/8	5 6/8	5 4/8	6	6	Collbran, CO	Robert E. Lee, Jr.	Kent Lee	1956	218
200 7/8	28 4/8	28	25 4/8	5 2/8	5 2/8	6	5	Baker Co., OR	Homer O. Hartley	Homer O. Hartley	1962	218
200 7/8	27	27	26 7/8	5 4/8	5 6/8	5	5	Provo Canyon, UT	Hans C. Finke	Hans C. Finke	1998	218
200 6/8	26 3/8	26 7/8	23	4 6/8	4 7/8	5	5	Malheur Co., OR	Karl D. Zaugg	Karl D. Zaugg	1948	222
200 6/8	28	28	25 6/8	5 4/8	5 4/8	5	5	Eagle Co., CO	Raymond Duncan	Raymond Duncan	1949	222
200 6/8	27 1/8	27 7/8	22 4/8	5 7/8	5 6/8	5	5	Montrose Co., CO	John Robertson	John Robertson	1958	222
200 6/8	25 3/8	25 3/8	25 3/8	5 3/8	5 1/8	5	5	Southern Ute Res., CO	Dennis Carr	Dennis Carr	1963	222
200 6/8	24 7/8	25 1/8	26	5	5 4/8	5	6	Delta Co., CO	Jerry E. Morgan	Jerry E. Morgan	1965	222
200 6/8	25 1/8	24 7/8	23 4/8	5 6/8	5 2/8	7	5	Boise Co., ID	Emil Warber, Jr.	Emil Warber, Jr.	1966	222
200 6/8	26 4/8	26 4/8	26 7/8	5 2/8	5	7	8	Gunnison Co., CO	Delbert W. Crawford	Delbert W. Crawford	1969	222
200 6/8	25 2/8	25 2/8	23	5 5/8	5 6/8	5	5	Merritt, BC	James B. Holbrooks	James B. Holbrooks	1977	222
200 6/8	25 2/8	25 2/8	21 2/8	4 7/8	5 1/8	5	5	Eagle Creek, SK	Cory Christensen	Cory Christensen	1989	222
200 6/8	27	27 3/8	25	5	5 1/8	5	7	Caribou Co., ID	Ronald S. Cordes	Ronald S. Cordes	1998	222
200 6/8	25	26	25 3/8	4 6/8	5	6	6	Ogden, UT	Beaver Fillo	Beaver Fillo	2000	222
200 5/8	25 3/8	25 2/8	24 7/8	5	5 2/8	9	7	Lincoln Co., WY	Carl F. Worden	Carl F. Worden	1948	233
200 5/8	27	27	26 4/8	5	5 1/8	5	6	La Plata Co., CO	John E. Myers	John E. Myers	1973	233
200 5/8	26	25 2/8	25 2/8	5 3/8	4 6/8	5	5	Yavapai Co., AZ	Unknown	Ronald F. Lax	1979	233
200 5/8	25 2/8	25	26 5/8	5 5/8	5	5	5	Shoshone Co., ID	Joseph C. Pecha	Joseph C. Pecha	1983	233
200 5/8	28 4/8	28 5/8	22 5/8	5 3/8	5 3/8	6	5	Rio Arriba Co., NM	Jerry Madsen	Cabela's, Inc.	1989	233
200 5/8	27 2/8	27 2/8	27 5/8	5 5/8	5 4/8	7	6	Baker Co., OR	Larry L. Panzy	Larry L. Panzy	1998	233
200 4/8	27 1/8	27	27 2/8	5 5/8	5	6	6	Bear Lake Co., ID	Oliver D. Markle	Gene Markle	1924	239
200 4/8	26 3/8	28 6/8	27 6/8	5 1/8	5 4/8	6	5	Utah Co., UT	Frank Bidart	Frank Bidart	1965	239
200 4/8	28 6/8	27 5/8	28 2/8	4 7/8	5 2/8	5	4	Bear Lake Co., ID	Elroy A. Loveridge	Elroy A. Loveridge	1965	239
200 4/8	27 5/8	27	25 6/8	5 1/8	5 6/8	7	7	Bear Lake Co., ID	Lee Bridges	Lee Bridges	1966	239
200 4/8	27	26 4/8	23	5 3/8	5 1/8	5	5	Caribou Co., ID	Herb Voyles, Jr.	Herb Voyles, Jr.	1972	239
200 4/8	26 4/8	27 2/8	26 6/8	5 4/8	4 6/8	6	6	Adams Co., ID	Roy Eastlick	Roy Eastlick	1974	239
200 4/8	27 2/8	25	25	4 6/8	5	5	5	Eagle Co., CO	Jack Stevens	Jack Stevens	1975	239
200 4/8	31	27 4/8	30 5/8	5 5/8	5 4/8	5	5	Madison Co., MT	Glenn S. Shelton	Glenn S. Shelton	1976	239
200 4/8	27 4/8	24 6/8	24 3/8	4 6/8	5	6	6	Dolores Co., CO	James L. Horneck	James L. Horneck	1988	239
200 4/8	24	27	27	5	5	4	4	Rio Arriba Co., NM	Jay Walker	Jay Walker	1993	239
200 3/8	26 7/8	27 5/8	27 4/8	5 2/8	5 2/8	5	6	Okanogan Co., WA	E.R. Crooks	E.R. Crooks	1939	249
200 3/8	27 5/8	28 2/8	28 2/8	5 2/8	5 2/8	5	5	Modoc Co., CA	F.M. Huglin	Frank M. Huglin	1948	249
200 3/8	28 2/8	27 3/8	27 3/8	4 6/8	4 6/8	5	5	Ouray Co., CO	Ernest L. Veo	Ernest L. Veo	1961	249
200 3/8	27	27 4/8	26 1/8	5 4/8	5 3/8	7	7	Uncompahgre Natl. For., CO	Richard M. Holbrook	Richard M. Holbrook	1972	249

MULE DEER - TYPICAL ANTLERS

Odocoileus hemionus hemionus and certain related subspecies

Score	Length of Main Beam R	L	Inside Spread	Circumference at Smallest Place Between Burr and First Point R	L	Number of Points R	L	Locality	Hunter	Owner	Date Killed	Rank
200 3/8	26 7/8	29 1/8	24 4/8	5 1/8	5 1/8	5	7	Gypsum, CO	Gene D. Lintz	Gene D. Lintz	1974	249
200 3/8	25 7/8	25 7/8	20 1/8	5 2/8	5 1/8	5	6	Duchesne Co., UT	William E. Lewis	William E. Lewis	1980	249
200 2/8	25	25 1/8	22 4/8	5 6/8	5 6/8	6	6	Battle Mt., WY	Ron Vance	Ronald Crawford	1963	255
200 2/8	29 7/8	28 3/8	23 6/8	4 7/8	4 6/8	5	5	Southern Ute Res., CO	Arthur Burch	Steven Burch	1966	255
200 2/8	26 4/8	26	27	5 6/8	5 6/8	5	6	Mesa Co., CO	Mitchell J. Sacco	Mitchell J. Sacco	1966	255
200 2/8	27 4/8	27	26 7/8	5	4 7/8	6	5	Ouray Co., CO	Joseph T. Hollingshead	Joseph T. Hollingshead	1967	255
200 2/8	27 5/8	28 5/8	26	4 7/8	5	4	4	Asotin Co., WA	Grant E. Holcomb	Grant E. Holcomb	1975	255
200 2/8	25 7/8	24 1/8	19 6/8	4 6/8	4 5/8	5	5	Montrose Co., CO	Nelson Harding	Nelson Harding	1985	255
200 2/8	25 2/8	27 2/8	25 2/8	4 7/8	5	6	5	Sevier Co., UT	Mayben J. Crane	Mayben J. Crane	1987	255
200 2/8	23 6/8	24 5/8	19 3/8	5	4 7/8	5	6	Bonneville Co., ID	Richard A. Kelley	Richard A. Kelley	1990	255
200 2/8	26 3/8	27 1/8	19	4 6/8	4 6/8	5	5	Boise Co., ID	Richard L. Jakomeit	Richard L. Jakomeit	1992	255
200 1/8	27 3/8	27 6/8	27 3/8	5 3/8	5 4/8	5	5	Cashmere, WA	John F. Schurle	William H. Schott	1913	264
200 1/8	24 7/8	23 6/8	28 3/8	5 5/8	5 6/8	5	5	Ruby Mt., NV	Earl Frantzen	Earl Frantzen	1941	264
200 1/8	27 2/8	28 6/8	25 7/8	4 6/8	4 6/8	5	5	Mesa Co., CO	John M. Domingos	John M. Domingos	1965	264
200 1/8	24 4/8	25 4/8	26	5 2/8	5 3/8	7	6	Mohave Co., AZ	Jay M. Ogden	Jay M. Ogden	1990	264
200	26 1/8	27 4/8	29	4 6/8	4 6/8	4	4	Fremont Co., CO	W.E. Canterbury	Jerry E. Canterbury	1951	268
200	26 2/8	27	27	5 5/8	5 5/8	5	6	Summit Co., CO	Picked Up	Bill Knorr	1959	268
200	24 2/8	25 4/8	25 2/8	4 7/8	4 6/8	5	5	Piedra River, CO	Glenn A. Smith	Glenn A. Smith	1960	268
200	27	27 4/8	28 5/8	6 1/8	6 1/8	5	5	Silt, CO	George McCoy	George McCoy	1961	268
200	27 4/8	28 7/8	29 3/8	6 3/8	6 3/8	6	5	Garfield Co., CO	Picked Up	John F. Frost	1963	268
200	29 6/8	29 7/8	24 4/8	5 3/8	5 2/8	6	6	Mouqi, AZ	Tom Corey	Tom Corey	1964	268
200	28	27 5/8	21 6/8	5 7/8	6	6	5	Park Co., CO	Jim Fitzgerald	Rob Firth	1971	268
200	27 1/8	26	24 4/8	4 7/8	4 7/8	5	5	Eagle Co., CO	Dale R. Leonard	David P. Moore	1976	268
200	25 7/8	25 4/8	21 7/8	5 5/8	5 5/8	5	7	Hot Springs Co., WY	Basil C. Bradbury	Basil C. Bradbury	1977	268
200	24 7/8	26 2/8	25 4/8	5 3/8	5 2/8	6	6	Coconino Co., AZ	Adam R. Kowalski, Jr.	Adam R. Kowalski, Jr.	1995	268
199 7/8	22 6/8	23 2/8	22 6/8	5 1/8	5 1/8	7	6	Jackson Co., CO	G.B. Berger, Jr.	Denver Mus. Nat. Hist.	1934	278
199 7/8	24 4/8	25 3/8	26 1/8	5 6/8	5 6/8	5	5	Disappointment Creek, CO	Clifford Le Neve	Clifford Le Neve	1954	278
199 7/8	27 5/8	27 4/8	26 6/8	6	5 7/8	5	7	Jicarilla Apache Res., NM	Anthony Julian	Anthony Julian	1961	278
199 7/8	24 1/8	24 7/8	23 1/8	5	5 1/8	6	5	Uncompahgre Natl. For., CO	H.E. Gerhart	H.E. Gerhart	1963	278
199 7/8	26 1/8	25	20 1/8	4 6/8	4 5/8	6	6	Lincoln Co., WY	John D. Murphy	John D. Murphy	1963	278
199 7/8	25 3/8	24 6/8	25 1/8	5 4/8	5 4/8	5	5	Stillwater Co., MT	Basil C. Bradbury	Basil C. Bradbury	1965	278
199 7/8	26 4/8	26 4/8	24 4/8	4 7/8	4 7/8	6	6	Eagle Co., CO	George S. Burton	Betty Burton	1967	278
199 7/8	25 7/8	27 2/8	25 7/8	4 7/8	5	7	6	Coconino Co., AZ	John L. Johnson	John L. Johnson	1972	278
199 7/8	25 1/8	25 7/8	24 3/8	6 5/8	6 6/8	5	5	Wallowa Co., OR	Wilford E. Hingston	Wilford E. Hingston	1996	278
199 7/8	26	26 3/8	22 5/8	5 1/8	5 3/8	6	5	Pelletier Lake, SK	Tyson N. Faucher	Tyson N. Faucher	2003	278
199 6/8	29 7/8	29	21 5/8	5 2/8	5 2/8	6	8	Montrose Co., CO	James O. McCleary	John E. McCleary	1951	288

Score	Main Beam R	Main Beam L	Inside Spread	Circ. R	Circ. L	Pts. R	Pts. L	Locality	Owner	By Whom Killed	Date	Rank
199 6/8	27 4/8	29	24 7/8	4 6/8	4 6/8	6	6	Mesa Co., CO	Darryl Powell	Picked Up	PR 1975	288
199 6/8	25 3/8	25 1/8	25	5 1/8	5 1/8	5	5	Grant Co., OR	Steve M. Stevenson	Steve M. Stevenson	1982	288
199 6/8	25 4/8	26 6/8	24 5/8	5 3/8	5	6	5	Kane Co., UT	Gilbert T. Adams	Gilbert T. Adams	1993	288
199 6/8	27	26 5/8	20	5 4/8	5	4	4	Harney Co., OR	Chris Schweizer	Chris Schweizer	1995	288
199 6/8	25 6/8	24 5/8	22	5	5	6	6	Diefenbaker Lake, SK	Warren M. Heatherington	Warren M. Heatherington	1996	288
199 6/8	27 3/8	28 3/8	22 3/8	5 5/8	5 5/8	6	7	Unknown	Pat Powell	Unknown	PR 1950	288
199 5/8	29 5/8	30 5/8	27 5/8	5	5	6	5	Lake Co., OR	Bill Keene	B. Keene & D. Keene	1968	294
199 5/8	26	27 5/8	21 5/8	5 5/8	5 3/8	4	6	Princeton, BC	Buddy D. Baker	Buddy D. Baker	1979	294
199 5/8	25 4/8	27 5/8	26 4/8	5 2/8	6	6	5	Garfield Co., UT	Cabela's, Inc.	Picked Up	PR 1980	294
199 5/8	24 2/8	25 4/8	21 7/8	6 1/8	6	6	6	Humboldt Co., NV	Robert L. Swinney	Robert L. Swinney	1982	294
199 5/8	26 5/8	26 6/8	26 7/8	5	5	6	6	Archuleta Co., CO	Charles W. Pearson	Charles W. Pearson	1995	294
199 5/8	26 2/8	25 4/8	28 6/8	6 1/8	6 2/8	6	8	Highvale, AB	Gordon Kulak	Gordon Kulak	1997	294
199 4/8	27 3/8	28 2/8	27 3/8	4 6/8	4 6/8	7	7	Pagosa Springs, CO	Perry Dixon	Perry Dixon	1957	294
199 4/8	28 4/8	26 2/8	28 7/8	5 5/8	5 5/8	6	5	Salmon River, ID	C.A. Schwope	C.A. Schwope	1959	301
199 4/8	24 2/8	24 2/8	21 7/8	4 7/8	4 7/8	6	6	Bonneville Co., ID	Leonard J. Vella	Leonard J. Vella	1972	301
199 4/8	26 4/8	25 5/8	23 6/8	5	5	6	5	Sanpete Co., UT	Kevin P. Price	Kevin P. Price	1973	301
199 4/8	26	25	26	5	5	6	5	Dolores Co., CO	Kenneth L. Peters	Kenneth L. Peters	1976	301
199 4/8	27 3/8	26 7/8	27 3/8	5 6/8	5 6/8	5	4	Medicine Hat, AB	D. Baldie & K.W. McKenzie	Duncan Baldie	1981	301
199 4/8	24 7/8	25	25 6/8	6 2/8	6 4/8	7	7	Logan Co., KS	Stacy C. Hoeme	Stacy C. Hoeme	2001	301
199 4/8	26	26 2/8	22 1/8	5 4/8	5 2/8	5	5	Yuma Co., CO	Kerry G. Weed	Kerry G. Weed	2003	301
199 3/8	25 1/8	25 7/8	27 7/8	5 5/8	5 6/8	4	6	Uncompahgre Natl. For., CO	Jerome Burlingame	Floyd Whitner	PR 1933	309
199 3/8	26 4/8	26 5/8	23 4/8	5 2/8	5 2/8	6	6	Mesa Co., CO	Greg Duff	Picked Up	1949	309
199 3/8	25 1/8	27 3/8	25 5/8	5 4/8	5 4/8	4	4	Silt, CO	V.M. Spiller	V.M. Spiller	1961	309
199 3/8	26 3/8	25 5/8	25 1/8	4 5/8	5	5	5	San Miguel Co., NM	Robert Cordova	Frank Mata	1965	309
199 3/8	27 6/8	27	26 4/8	5 4/8	5 6/8	4	5	Rio Arriba Co., NM	John A. Farrell	John A. Farrell	1966	309
199 3/8	25 7/8	26 7/8	23 7/8	5 6/8	5 3/8	6	5	Rio Arriba Co., NM	Johnny L. Montgomery	Johnny L. Montgomery	1967	309
199 3/8	28 4/8	26 4/8	24 4/8	5 1/8	5 5/8	5	7	Harney Co., OR	John A. Echanis	John A. Echanis	1995	309
199 2/8	25 1/8	27 2/8	24 1/8	6 4/8	5 2/8	7	7	Mt. Blackstrap, SK	Gordon Kyler	Gordon Kyler	2001	317
199 2/8	27 2/8	25 2/8	25 7/8	5 4/8	5 1/8	7	5	Washoe Co., NV	Joseph N. Ruscigno	Joseph N. Ruscigno	1955	317
199 2/8	25 2/8	27 1/8	25	5	5	5	5	Beechy, SK	Marvin Taylor	Marvin Taylor	1961	317
199 2/8	25 3/8	25 3/8	21 5/8	5 6/8	5 6/8	5	8	Archuleta Co., CO	LeRoy C. Haug	Kenneth Hunter	1962	317
199 2/8	24 6/8	27 5/8	24 6/8	5 2/8	5 2/8	8	5	Strawberry, UT	Steve Payne	Steve Payne	1962	317
199 2/8	28	27 4/8	25 4/8	5 3/8	5 1/8	5	5	Eagle Co., CO	Howard Stoker	Howard Stoker	1965	317
199 2/8	26 1/8	26 1/8	26 4/8	5 2/8	5 6/8	5	6	Hidden Canyon, AZ	Milton Wyman	Milton Wyman	1972	317
199 2/8	25 1/8	26 4/8	24 1/8	5 1/8	5 6/8	6	5	Grand Co., UT	Jon P. Leatham	Picked Up	1976	317
199 2/8	26 4/8	26 6/8	27 4/8	5 6/8	5 3/8	7	6	Eagle Co., CO	Anthony W. DeToy	Anthony W. DeToy	1978	317
199 2/8	27 6/8	28 5/8	25 5/8	5 4/8	5 2/8	5	5	Garfield Co., CO	Gary W. Hartley	Gary W. Hartley	1978	317
199 2/8	26 3/8	26 6/8	25 1/8	5 2/8	5 4/8	5	6	Gable Mt., BC	Jack B. Quiring	Jack B. Quiring	1988	317
199 2/8	30 4/8	28 6/8	27 6/8	5 4/8	5 4/8	6	6	Great Sand Hills, SK	Howard Jackle	Howard Jackle	1991	317
199 2/8	25 1/8	25 1/8	25	5 3/8	5 7/8	6	9	Coconino Co., AZ	John R. Fogle	John R. Fogle	1992	317
199 1/8	28 3/8	28 3/8	25 3/8	5 7/8	5	9	8	Elmore Co., ID	Judi L. Williams	Picked Up	1998	330
199 1/8	27 2/8	25	27 2/8	6	5 6/8	8	6	Jicarilla Apache Res., NM	David L. Chandler	David L. Chandler	1961	330
199 1/8	24 3/8	27 6/8	24 3/8	5 6/8	5 5/8	6	6	San Juan Co., UT	Phyllis O. Crookston	Phyllis O. Crookston	1971	330
199 1/8	28 1/8	27	26 4/8	5 5/8	5 8/8	6	5	Adams Co., ID	Larry G. Averett	Wallace E. Averett	1976	330
199 1/8	26 2/8	26 2/8	27 2/8	5 4/8	6	5	5	Laramie Co., WY	David L. Shannon	David L. Shannon	1981	330
199 1/8	27 2/8	25 4/8	23 3/8	6	5 3/8	5	6	Morgan Co., UT	H. Ritman Jons	H. Ritman Jons	1987	330
199 1/8	28 3/8	27 6/8	27 6/8	5 3/8	5 3/8	5	5	Bonneville Co., ID	Scott B. Huntsman	Scott B. Huntsman	1992	330
199 1/8	26	27	29 3/8	5 2/8	5 2/8	6	6	Maple Bush, SK	Dallas E. Wilm	Dallas E. Wilm	1996	330

307

MULE DEER - TYPICAL ANTLERS
Odocoileus hemionus hemionus and certain related subspecies

Score	Length of Main Beam R	L	Inside Spread	Circumference at Smallest Place Between Burr and First Point R	L	Number of Points R	L	Locality	Hunter	Owner	Date Killed	Rank
199 1/8	24 3/8	24 7/8	23 5/8	4 4/8	4 4/8	5	5	Elmore Co., ID	Teresa R. Crone	Teresa R. Crone	2000	330
199	26 6/8	27 1/8	26 2/8	4 7/8	5 1/8	5	5	Echo, UT	Wilford Zaugg	Wilford Zaugg	1958	338
199	25 1/8	26 3/8	23 4/8	5 4/8	5 1/8	5	5	Park Co., WY	Lois M. Pelzel	Lois M. Pelzel	1965	338
199	24 2/8	24 2/8	21	5	5 2/8	5	6	Mohave Co., AZ	William M. Berger, Jr.	William M. Berger, Jr.	1973	338
199	24 7/8	23 6/8	23 3/8	4 7/8	4 6/8	6	5	Power Co., ID	Jim A. Rose	Jim A. Rose	1977	338
199	28 4/8	27 7/8	24 1/8	5 1/8	5 2/8	4	5	San Juan Co., UT	Bradley J. Young	Bradley J. Young	1991	338
199	25 5/8	25 4/8	23 1/8	5 4/8	5 2/8	5	7	Pondera Co., MT	Jim Luoma	Jim Luoma	2000	338
198 7/8	26 5/8	27 1/8	26 5/8	5 7/8	6	5	7	Jicarilla Apache Res., NM	Anthony Julian	Jicarilla Apache Res.	1961	344
198 7/8	26 4/8	24 2/8	19 3/8	5 7/8	5 7/8	7	5	Burns, CO	Charles D. Rush	Charles D. Rush	1967	344
198 7/8	26	25 7/8	21 3/8	5 1/8	5	5	5	Rio Arriba Co., NM	Ernest Petago	Ernest Petago	1994	344
198 7/8	28 7/8	28 3/8	26 2/8	4 5/8	4 6/8	6	6	S. Saskatchewan River, SK	Barry D. Miller	Barry D. Miller	2000	344
198 6/8	23 4/8	22 2/8	21 6/8	5 1/8	5 2/8	5	5	Hines Creek, AB	Charles Lundgard	Charles Lundgard	1960	348
198 6/8	32 7/8	32 4/8	25 3/8	6 3/8	7	7	6	Dulce, NM	Picked Up	Everett M. Vigil	1967	348
198 6/8	26	27 6/8	27 4/8	5	5 3/8	6	5	Mohave Co., AZ	William C. Cloyd	William C. Cloyd	1994	348
198 5/8	27 4/8	28 1/8	25 7/8	4 5/8	4 7/8	6	7	Colorado	Unknown	Cabela's, Inc.	PR 1960	351
198 5/8	26 2/8	27 2/8	24 5/8	5	5	6	7	Carbondale, CO	Ralph Clock	Ralph Clock	1961	351
198 5/8	26	25 3/8	28	5 4/8	5 7/8	5	7	Rio Arriba Co., NM	Stanley Davis	Stanley Davis	1965	351
198 5/8	24 4/8	24 7/8	24 1/8	5 3/8	5 5/8	6	6	Swan Valley, ID	Harry G. Brinkley, Jr.	Harry G. Brinkley, Jr.	1966	351
198 5/8	25 1/8	25 2/8	23 1/8	4 7/8	5	5	7	Carbon Co., WY	M. Gary Muske	M. Gary Muske	1968	351
198 5/8	25 6/8	27 4/8	25 5/8	4 4/8	4 7/8	5	5	Montezuma Co., CO	Mary Ann Ott	Mary Ann Ott	1968	351
198 5/8	25	24 7/8	23 5/8	4 7/8	4 6/8	5	5	Elmore Co., ID	William Hartwig	William Hartwig	1984	351
198 5/8	26 2/8	26 2/8	29 4/8	4 7/8	5 1/8	5	6	Pueblo Co., CO	James L. Bradley	James L. Bradley	1986	351
198 5/8	25 2/8	26 5/8	21 7/8	5 1/8	5 2/8	5	5	Rio Arriba Co., NM	Picked Up	Larry L. Panzy	1994	351
198 5/8	22 2/8	22 4/8	26 5/8	5 6/8	5 2/8	5	5	Sonora, MX	Jerry W. Willeford	Jerry W. Willeford	1998	351
198 5/8	26 5/8	28 6/8	28 2/8	4 5/8	4 5/8	6	6	Malheur Co., OR	Troy Cummins	Troy Cummins	2000	351
198 5/8	25 3/8	24 2/8	25 3/8	5	5	5	5	Rio Arriba Co., NM	Picked Up	Robert J. Seeds	2002	351
198 5/8	28	26 1/8	28 2/8	5 5/8	5 4/8	6	9	Kaibab Natl. For., AZ	W.O. Hart	W.O. Hart	1946	363
198 4/8	29	27 2/8	32 7/8	5	5	5	5	Del Norte Co., CO	Esequiel Trujillo	Esequiel Trujillo	1947	363
198 4/8	25 5/8	25 6/8	20 4/8	5	5	5	5	Tabiona, UT	Picked Up	H.A. Zumbrock	1957	363
198 4/8	27	26 2/8	28 6/8	6 1/8	5 6/8	5	5	North Kaibab, AZ	Simon C. Krevitsky	Simon C. Krevitsky	1963	363
198 4/8	26 4/8	27 6/8	29 2/8	5 3/8	5 2/8	5	6	San Juan Co., NM	Dan R. Anderson	Dan R. Anderson	1964	363
198 4/8	26	25 4/8	21 4/8	5 1/8	5 1/8	5	5	Routt Co., CO	Lloyd D. Kindsfater	Lloyd D. Kindsfater	1966	363
198 4/8	29	28 7/8	22 4/8	5 3/8	5 1/8	4	5	Dark Canyon, CO	O.P. McGuire	O.P. McGuire	1966	363
198 4/8	28 5/8	28 4/8	24 5/8	5 3/8	5 3/8	6	6	Afton, WY	Ray M. Vincent	Ray M. Vincent	1967	363
198 4/8	29 5/8	30	28 4/8	4 6/8	4 5/8	6	7	La Plata Co., CO	Pauline J. Bostic	Pauline J. Bostic	1971	363
198 4/8	27 5/8	26 2/8	27 2/8	6	5 6/8	5	6	Rio Arriba Co., NM	Lambert Callado	Lambert Callado	2003	363

Score	Length of Main Beam R.	Length of Main Beam L.	Inside Spread	Circ. R.	Circ. L.	Points R.	Points L.	Locality	Hunter	Owner	Date	Rank
198 3/8	26 6/8	26 5/8	28	5 2/8	5 2/8	6	6	Moffat Co., CO	Lucille Gooch	George Gooch	1951	373
198 3/8	25	25 5/8	26	6	5 7/8	6	6	Mt. Trumbull, AZ	E.O. Brown	E.O. Brown	1960	373
198 3/8	25	25 4/8	19 5/8	4 5/8	4 5/8	5	5	Bonneville Co., ID	Tony Dawson	Tony Dawson	1973	373
198 3/8	26 4/8	26 7/8	23 2/8	5 2/8	5 2/8	5	7	Montrose Co., CO	Allan K. Slafter	Allan K. Slafter	1989	373
198 3/8	27 3/8	26 7/8	28 7/8	4 6/8	4 7/8	6	5	Washoe Co., NV	Jerry W. Lowery	Jerry W. Lowery	1995	373
198 2/8	26 4/8	27 4/8	26 4/8	4 7/8	5	5	5	Summit Co., CO	Picked Up	Louis Ceriani	PR 1965	378
198 2/8	25 6/8	26 1/8	24 3/8	5 1/8	5 4/8	5	5	Sonora, MX	Heinz G. Holdorf	Heinz G. Holdorf	1966	378
198 2/8	24 4/8	26	26 6/8	5 2/8	4 7/8	5	5	Gunnison Co., CO	Bobby J. Watson	Bobby J. Watson	1975	378
198 2/8	28 2/8	25	26 3/8	5 1/8	5 3/8	5	7	Coconino Co., AZ	Dale C. Morse	Dale C. Morse	1977	378
198 2/8	27 1/8	27 4/8	27	5 4/8	5 7/8	6	6	Bonneville Co., ID	Thomas N. Thiel	Thomas N. Thiel	1987	378
198 2/8	27 1/8	24 6/8	24 7/8	5 7/8	5 1/8	5	5	Rio Arriba Co., NM	Charles Tapia	Charles Tapia	1991	378
198 2/8	25 3/8	26	27	5	5 4/8	5	5	Rio Arriba Co., NM	Robert J. Seeds	Robert J. Seeds	1992	378
198 1/8	25 5/8	25	25 2/8	5 6/8	5 2/8	5	5	Bonneville Co., ID	Chet Warwick	Chet Warwick	1959	385
198 1/8	25 3/8	26 1/8	26 1/8	5 1/8	5 7/8	5	6	Caribou Co., ID	Arlo T. Hopkins	Arlo T. Hopkins	1962	385
198 1/8	25	26 1/8	23 7/8	5 4/8	5 4/8	6	6	Bayfield Co., CO	C. Ben Boyd	C. Ben Boyd	1967	385
198 1/8	25 1/8	27 2/8	25 7/8	5 2/8	5	6	7	Routt Co., CO	William E. Goswick	William E. Goswick	1968	385
198 1/8	27 4/8	25 5/8	23 2/8	5 7/8	4 7/8	7	5	Montrose Co., CO	Robert A. Klatt	Robert A. Klatt	1975	385
198 1/8	26 5/8	26 1/8	25 5/8	5	5 2/8	5	5	Wallowa Co., OR	Dan L. Gober	Dan L. Gober	1980	385
198 1/8	25 4/8	27 5/8	26 1/8	4 6/8	5 1/8	5	5	Natrona Co., WY	Kerry J. Clegg	Kerry J. Clegg	1983	385
198 1/8	27 4/8	27 1/8	27 5/8	5 2/8	4 6/8	6	8	Colorado	Unknown	Richard A. Heitman	PR 1989	385
198 1/8	26 4/8	25 6/8	21	4 5/8	5 2/8	5	7	Swift Current, SK	Bryce Stan	Bryce Stan	2003	385
198	26 2/8	25 2/8	22 1/8	5 2/8	5	4	4	Unknown	Unknown	Lunds Wildlife Exhibit	1931	394
198	25 1/8	25 5/8	22 4/8	5 1/8	6	8	5	Davis Co., UT	Carl D. Craig	Jay D. Craig	1939	394
198	25 2/8	24 6/8	22 4/8	6 1/8	5 3/8	6	6	Garfield Co., CO	Leroy Failor	Leroy Failor	1944	394
198	25 4/8	25 4/8	25 1/8	5 4/8	4 7/8	7	7	Smithfield Canyon, UT	Stanley Richardson	Stanley Richardson	1961	394
198	23 7/8	27 7/8	27 1/8	4 7/8	5 6/8	6	5	Gunnison Co., CO	E.D. Palmer	E.D. Palmer	1962	394
198	25	24 7/8	22 4/8	5 6/8	5	5	5	Montpelier, ID	Charles R. Mann	Charles R. Mann	1973	394
198	28 5/8	26 1/8	30 6/8	5	5 6/8	6	6	Adams Co., ID	Allen Solterbeck	Ryan B. Hatfield	1975	394
198	24	23 7/8	22 4/8	6 1/8	5 3/8	7	7	Eagle Co., CO	Larry Schlasinger	Larry Schlasinger	1978	394
198	27	27	28 6/8	4 6/8	6	4	5	Hinsdale Co., CO	Alan L. VanDenBerg	Alan L. VanDenBerg	1978	394
198	24 2/8	25 1/8	26 2/8	6 1/8	4 7/8	5	5	Colorado	Unknown	D.J. Hollinger & B. Howard	PR 1980	394
197 7/8	27 7/8	27	27	5 2/8	5 3/8	6	8	Chaffee Co., CO	Marguerite Hill	Marguerite Hill	1956	404
197 7/8	25 2/8	25 7/8	24 5/8	4 6/8	5 1/8	5	6	Kaibab Natl. For., AZ	Eoans Pababla	Eoans Pababla	1957	404
197 7/8	27 6/8	27 7/8	28 5/8	5 1/8	5 4/8	6	6	San Miguel Co., CO	Everett Stutler	Everett Stutler	1965	404
197 7/8	26 1/8	27 4/8	24 1/8	4 7/8	5 5/8	5	5	Rio Blanco Co., CO	Gary L. Bicknell	D.J. Hollinger & B. Howard	1967	404
197 7/8	28 1/8	27 6/8	24 5/8	5 2/8	5 3/8	5	5	Rossland, BC	Robert Simm	Robert Simm	1968	404
197 7/8	28 6/8	26 5/8	25 6/8	5	5 3/8	6	5	Eagle Co., CO	Lee Frudden	Lee Frudden	1978	404
197 7/8	28 3/8	28 2/8	25 7/8	5 2/8	5 5/8	5	7	Elmore Co., ID	Bud Abele	Bud Abele	1981	404
197 7/8	25 7/8	25	21 7/8	5 6/8	5 1/8	7	5	Blaine Co., ID	James D. Scarrow	James D. Scarrow	1983	404
197 7/8	29 3/8	28 7/8	29 1/8	5 3/8	5 4/8	5	5	Malheur Co., OR	Gerald L. Warnock	Gerald L. Warnock	1996	404
197 7/8	27 6/8	26 3/8	25 3/8	5 4/8	5 5/8	5	5	Rio Arriba Co., NM	Picked Up	Robert J. Seeds	1999	404
197 7/8	25 4/8	28	25 2/8	4 6/8	4 6/8	5	5	Rio Arriba Co., NM	Aric DeJesus	Aric DeJesus	2000	404
197 6/8	25 4/8	26 7/8	23 6/8	5 2/8	5 2/8	6	6	Encampment, WY	Ralph E. Platt, Jr.	Ralph E. Platt, Jr.	1936	415
197 6/8	27 4/8	26 2/8	24 4/8	4 6/8	4 6/8	8	8	Elk Ridge, UT	Bill King	Joseph Fitting	1956	415
197 6/8	26 5/8	27 5/8	23 7/8	5 2/8	5 2/8	5	5	Jefferson Co., MT	James W. Rowe	James W. Rowe	1964	415
197 6/8	24 3/8	26 4/8	27 3/8	4 6/8	4 6/8	6	6	Teton Co., WY	John W. Farlow, Jr.	John W. Farlow, Jr.	1971	415
197 6/8	26 6/8	24 7/8	23 6/8	5	5	8	8	Bonneville Co., ID	Preston L. Winchell	Preston L. Winchell	1974	415
197 6/8	26 6/8	24 7/8	23 6/8	5 1/8	5 4/8	5	5	Botanie Lake, BC	Dennis R. Milton	Dennis R. Milton	1991	415

MULE DEER - TYPICAL ANTLERS
Odocoileus hemionus hemionus and certain related subspecies

Score	Length of Main Beam R	L	Inside Spread	Circumference at Smallest Place Between Burr and First Point R	L	Number of Points R	L	Locality	Hunter	Owner	Date Killed	Rank
197 5/8	25 1/8	25	27 5/8	5 1/8	5 3/8	8	6	Summit Co., UT	Wendell M. Smith	Nathan H. Smith	1954	421
197 5/8	24 3/8	24 1/8	24 7/8	4 7/8	5	5	5	Ashton, ID	Earl Johnson	O.M. Corbett	1959	421
197 5/8	22 7/8	22	22 1/8	4 5/8	4 4/8	5	5	Major, SK	Art Heintz	Art Heintz	1961	421
197 5/8	27	27	23 7/8	5 1/8	5 3/8	5	5	Unknown	Unknown	Robert E. Oldroyd	1963	421
197 5/8	27	26 6/8	22 7/8	5 7/8	5 5/8	6	6	San Miguel Co., CO	Virgil L. Burbridge	Jerry D. Burbridge	1964	421
197 5/8	23 5/8	29 5/8	21 3/8	5	5	5	5	Eagle Co., CO	Joseph Sokel, Jr.	Steve J. Sokel	1965	421
197 5/8	25 4/8	26 5/8	29 4/8	5 5/8	5 5/8	5	5	Elko Co., NV	Manfred E. Koska	Manfred E. Koska	1966	421
197 5/8	28 6/8	27 4/8	23 1/8	5 1/8	5 1/8	5	5	Kootenay River, BC	Raymond Carry	Raymond Carry	1982	421
197 5/8	25 6/8	26 1/8	19 5/8	5 2/8	5 2/8	5	5	Beechy, SK	Brett E. Seidle	Brett E. Seidle	1983	421
197 5/8	26 7/8	27 3/8	26	5	4 7/8	6	5	Uintah Co., UT	Robert C. Chapoose, Jr.	Robert C. Chapoose, Jr.	1987	421
197 5/8	26 7/8	26	27 6/8	5 2/8	5 2/8	7	6	S. Saskatchewan River, SK	Robert H. Boeschen	Robert H. Boeschen	1998	421
197 4/8	24	26	21 2/8	5 4/8	5 6/8	5	5	Moffat Co., CO	Russ H. Winslow	Russ H. Winslow	1967	432
197 4/8	26 3/8	25 7/8	24 7/8	4 6/8	4 7/8	5	6	Uinta Co., WY	Ken L. Vernon	Ken L. Vernon	1968	432
197 4/8	24 6/8	27	23 4/8	6	5 7/8	8	9	Routt Co., CO	William E. Goswick	William E. Goswick	1969	432
197 4/8	26	26 2/8	23 2/8	5 2/8	5 1/8	5	6	Rio Arriba Co., NM	Jerry Longenbaugh	Jerry Longenbaugh	1969	432
197 4/8	27	25 5/8	27	5 3/8	5 2/8	5	5	Rio Arriba Co., NM	Louis N. Burgess	Louis N. Burgess	1970	432
197 4/8	29 3/8	27 6/8	22 2/8	5 3/8	5 3/8	6	5	Grant Co., WA	Unknown	D.J. Hollinger & B. Howard	PR 1970	432
197 4/8	24 4/8	25 5/8	22 2/8	6	6 1/8	6	8	Routt Co., CO	John E. Simmons	John E. Simmons	1977	432
197 4/8	22 1/8	24	24	5 6/8	5 5/8	6	5	Gunnison Co., CO	Thomas Gray, Jr.	Thomas Gray, Jr.	1980	432
197 4/8	27 2/8	27 1/8	23 6/8	4 3/8	4 3/8	4	5	Bonneville Co., ID	LaDon Harriell	LaDon Harriell	1982	432
197 4/8	29	28 2/8	20 7/8	4 5/8	4 2/8	6	6	Idaho Co., ID	Marvin L. Lindquist	Marvin L. Lindquist	1988	432
197 4/8	28 4/8	27 3/8	26 1/8	5	5	9	5	Tompkins, SK	Edward J. Hardin	Edward J. Hardin	1994	432
197 4/8	28 3/8	28 7/8	26	5 4/8	5 3/8	7	5	Rio Arriba Co., NM	Travis Amarillo	Travis Amarillo	1999	432
197 4/8	24 1/8	24 4/8	26 1/8	5 2/8	5 2/8	5	5	Lincoln Co., WY	Douglas L. Stephens	Douglas L. Stephens	2001	432
197 3/8	27 4/8	26 1/8	23	4 7/8	5	6	6	Archuleta Co., CO	Lansing Kothmann	Lansing Kothmann	1957	445
197 3/8	26 7/8	26 5/8	24 5/8	5	5	5	6	Rio Blanco Co., CO	Picked Up	Jack Thompson	PR 1957	445
197 3/8	26 7/8	25	22 3/8	5 4/8	5 3/8	5	5	Currant Creek, UT	Morris Kidd	Morris Kidd	1960	445
197 3/8	27 1/8	27 4/8	24 2/8	5	5	5	7	Montrose Co., CO	H.R. Clark	H.R. Clark	1961	445
197 3/8	26 5/8	27 5/8	26 3/8	4 6/8	4 7/8	6	6	Fremont Co., ID	Stanley A. Gilgen	Stanley A. Gilgen	1964	445
197 3/8	26 6/8	26	25 4/8	5 2/8	5 2/8	5	6	Pagosa Springs, CO	John D. Guess	John D. Guess	1966	445
197 3/8	25 5/8	27 1/8	26 1/8	5 3/8	5 4/8	5	5	Apache Mesa, NM	Tom M. Martine	Tom M. Martine	1970	445
197 3/8	26	26 2/8	23 2/8	5 6/8	5 5/8	6	6	Gunnison Co., CO	Mark L. Hanna	Mark L. Hanna	1980	445
197 3/8	28 7/8	28 6/8	23 4/8	5 3/8	4 4/8	7	6	Garfield Co., UT	James R. McCourt	James R. McCourt	1985	445
197 3/8	24 7/8	24 5/8	27 2/8	4 5/8	4 4/8	5	4	Lincoln Co., WY	Kim L. King	Kim L. King	1990	445
197 2/8	26 4/8	26 4/8	21 6/8	7	6 6/8	7	5	Beechy, SK	Pete Perrin	Pete Perrin	1947	455
197 2/8	27 3/8	27 3/8	27 1/8	5 2/8	5 4/8	6	5	Afton, WY	Robert Williams	Robert Williams	1960	455

Score	Main Beam R	Main Beam L	Inside Spread	Circ. R	Circ. L	Pts R	Pts L	Locality	Hunter	Owner	Date	Rank
197 2/8	29 4/8	30 2/8	28 6/8	5 4/8	5 5/8	6	7	Harney Co., OR	Guy E. Osborne	Guy E. Osborne	1963	455
197 2/8	26 1/8	26 4/8	23 6/8	5 4/8	5 5/8	6	7	Custer Co., CO	Jerome L. DeGree	Jerome L. DeGree	1972	455
197 2/8	26 2/8	26 1/8	21 2/8	4 3/8	4 4/8	5	5	Weber Co., UT	Abe B. Murdock	Abe B. Murdock	1972	455
197 2/8	23	24	25	4 6/8	4 4/8	7	5	Elko Co., NV	John C. Burman	John C. Burman	1980	455
197 2/8	26 5/8	25 7/8	26 4/8	5 2/8	5 3/8	5	6	Blaine Co., ID	Bart Hofmann	Bart Hofmann	1980	455
197 2/8	24 4/8	24 6/8	23 2/8	4 6/8	4 6/8	5	6	Flathead Co., MT	James E. Betters	James E. Betters	1986	455
197 2/8	26 1/8	26 6/8	26	4 6/8	5 3/8	5	5	Shoshone Co., ID	Roger R. Davis	Aly M. Bruner	1987	455
197 2/8	24 5/8	23 4/8	24 2/8	5 3/8	4 3/8	5	5	Elbert Co., CO	Francis Wilson	Francis Wilson	1993	455
197 1/8	25 1/8	24 3/8	25 5/8	4 2/8	4 3/8	5	5	Morgan Co., UT	Gayle Allen	Gayle Allen	1948	465
197 1/8	27 1/8	26 7/8	29 7/8	6 1/8	6 4/8	5	5	Gunnison Co., CO	Ted Wolcott, Jr.	Ted Wolcott, Jr.	1961	465
197 1/8	26 5/8	27 6/8	26 3/8	5 2/8	5 1/8	5	5	Ashwood, OR	Harvey Rhoads	Harvey Rhoads	1962	465
197 1/8	27	28	28	5 3/8	5 3/8	7	5	Delta Co., CO	B. Allan Jones	B. Allan Jones	1977	465
197 1/8	28 1/8	27 3/8	22 7/8	5	4 7/8	5	7	Mesa Co., CO	Willis A. Kinsey	Willis A. Kinsey	1978	465
197 1/8	27 1/8	28 1/8	24 3/8	4 7/8	5 2/8	7	7	Colorado	Kenneth W. Knox	Kenneth W. Knox	PR 1980	465
197	27 4/8	28 4/8	25	4 6/8	5 6/8	5	7	Diefenbaker Lake, SK	Alvin Onofriechuck	Alvin Onofriechuck	2001	472
197	25 4/8	25 6/8	25	5 1/8	5 6/8	6	5	Sonora, MX	J.G. Cigarroa, Sr.	J.G. Cigarroa, Sr.	1957	472
197	27 4/8	26 3/8	29 3/8	5 4/8	5 4/8	5	6	Jackson Co., CO	Alvin Bush	Jerry Haldeman	1961	472
197	24 2/8	25 4/8	25 2/8	5 5/8	5 3/8	5	5	Grand Co., CO	Woodrow W. Dixon	Woodrow W. Dixon	1962	472
197	26 4/8	26	27 5/8	5 4/8	4 6/8	6	5	Rio Arriba Co., NM	Ross Lopez	Ross Lopez	1964	472
197	26 6/8	26	28 4/8	5 2/8	4 7/8	5	6	Archuleta Co., CO	Hugh W. Gardner	Hugh W. Gardner	1971	472
197	24 7/8	25 7/8	22	5 3/8	5	5	5	Franklin Co., ID	Robert C. Porter	Robert C. Porter	1972	472
197	25 2/8	24 1/8	25	4 7/8	4 6/8	5	5	Camas Co., ID	Bret C. Silver	Bret C. Silver	1980	472
197	25 3/8	27	22 3/8	5	5 3/8	6	5	Utah Co., UT	L. Doug Carlton	L. Doug Carlton	1982	472
197	25 1/8	26	25 2/8	4 7/8	5 2/8	7	5	Lincoln Co., MT	Darvin R. Chambliss	Darvin R. Chambliss	1986	472
197	25 7/8	26 4/8	21 7/8	5 2/8	5 2/8	5	6	Suffern Lake, SK	Picked Up	Macklin Wildl. Fed.	PR 1992	472
197	25 7/8	26	22 3/8	5 6/8	5 5/8	6	7	Grant Co., OR	Bruce J. Brothers	Bruce J. Brothers	1993	472
197	27 4/8	27 5/8	22 6/8	5 2/8	5 2/8	5	7	Rio Arriba Co., NM	Unknown	Robert M. Ortiz	1999	472
196 7/8	24	24 5/8	26 4/8	5 1/8	5 1/8	6	5	North Kaibab, AZ	Alex J. Haas	Alex J. Haas	1961	484
196 7/8	26 2/8	25 5/8	23 7/8	4 7/8	5 2/8	5	5	Mesa Co., CO	Carl England	James B. Sisco III	PR 1966	484
196 7/8	24 5/8	24 4/8	22 5/8	5 6/8	5 4/8	6	6	Boise Co., ID	Andrew T. Rogers	Andrew T. Rogers	1967	484
196 7/8	27	27 6/8	21 2/8	5 2/8	5 1/8	5	6	Teton Co., ID	Dennis Barker	Dennis Barker	1968	484
196 7/8	25 6/8	24	21 5/8	5 4/8	5	5	5	Lincoln Co., MT	Dennis J. Hauke	Dennis J. Hauke	1973	484
196 7/8	27 5/8	27	25 1/8	5 1/8	5	5	5	Scherf Creek, BC	Manuela Selby	Manuela Selby	1984	484
196 7/8	25 3/8	25 2/8	25 3/8	5	4 3/8	5	5	Lincoln Co., WY	William L. Lewis	William L. Lewis	1990	484
196 6/8	25 5/8	24 2/8	26 3/8	4 3/8	5 2/8	5	5	Rio Arriba Co., NM	Robert J. Seeds	Robert J. Seeds	1998	492
196 6/8	24 4/8	23 6/8	24 4/8	5 3/8	5 1/8	7	5	Bear Lake Co., ID	Nels H. Pehrson	Ralph V. Pehrson	1936	492
196 6/8	25 3/8	27 1/8	21 2/8	5 1/8	5 1/8	5	5	Montrose Co., CA	Howard S. Thrift	H.S. & B. Thrift	1962	492
196 6/8	27 1/8	27 7/8	26	5 2/8	5 2/8	7	7	Eagle Co., CO	Picked Up	Cabela's, Inc.	PR 1964	492
196 6/8	25 1/8	25 4/8	24 4/8	5 5/8	5	5	7	Delta Co., CO	Howard G. Reed	Howard G. Reed	1968	492
196 6/8	23 3/8	24 1/8	22 4/8	5 2/8	5	5	7	Bonneville Co., ID	William G. Pine	William G. Pine	1969	492
196 6/8	24 2/8	23 4/8	23 1/8	6 3/8	6 2/8	6	6	Garfield Co., CO	Walter C. Friauf	Walter C. Friauf	1970	492
196 6/8	26 1/8	26	26	5	5	5	5	San Juan Natl. For., CO	Wilford E. Seymour, Jr.	Wilford E. Seymour, Jr.	1974	492
196 6/8	25 4/8	24 4/8	22 2/8	5 1/8	4 6/8	5	5	Unknown	Picked Up	Curt M. Funk	1983	492
196 6/8	24	24 1/8	26 1/8	5 7/8	6 1/8	5	6	Coconino Co., AZ	James D. Wagner	James D. Wagner	1986	492
196 6/8	27 2/8	26 6/8	22 6/8	5 2/8	5 3/8	6	5	Malheur Co., OR	Dan Erwert	Dan L. Erwert	1992	492
196 6/8	24 4/8	23 4/8	22 6/8	5 5/8	5 6/8	5	5	Kane Co., UT	Sam S. Jaksick, Jr.	Sam S. Jaksick, Jr.	1995	492
196 5/8	26 6/8	26 6/8	25 6/8	6	6	6	6	Chelan Co., WA	George Bolton	Welcome Sauer	1930	503
196 5/8	24 7/8	24 7/8	23 7/8	5	5 1/8	6	5	Washington Co., ID	Phillip J. Wilson	Phillip J. Wilson	1958	503

MULE DEER - TYPICAL ANTLERS
Odocoileus hemionus hemionus and certain related subspecies

Score	Length of Main Beam		Inside Spread	Circumference at Smallest Place Between Burr and First Point		Number of Points		Locality	Hunter	Owner	Date Killed	Rank
	R	L		R	L	R	L					
196 5/8	26	26 6/8	24 1/8	4 4/8	4 6/8	5	5	Slater, CO	W.J. Bracken	W.J. Bracken	1959	503
196 5/8	26 2/8	26 7/8	23 3/8	6 5/8	5 3/8	8	8	Moffat Co., CO	Tran Canton	Tran Canton	1960	503
196 5/8	26	25 7/8	22 6/8	4 4/8	4 6/8	6	5	Dubois Co., WY	P.C. Alfred Dorow	P.C. Alfred Dorow	1960	503
196 5/8	27 6/8	24 2/8	22 5/8	5 4/8	5 4/8	5	5	Grand Mesa, CO	Marvin L. Shepard	Marvin L. Shepard	1960	503
196 5/8	26 5/8	26 4/8	27 2/8	4 7/8	4 7/8	6	6	Mesa Co., CO	Bill Styers	Bill Styers	1964	503
196 5/8	22	22 6/8	21 5/8	5	5 1/8	7	6	Lemhi Co., ID	Hubert M. Livingston	Cabela's, Inc.	1967	503
196 5/8	25 6/8	25 5/8	24 2/8	5	4 7/8	7	6	Summit Co., UT	Jerry L. Henriod	Jerry L. Henriod	1967	503
196 5/8	24 7/8	25	23 5/8	4 4/8	4 5/8	5	5	Maybell, CO	James W. Johnson	James W. Johnson	1968	503
196 5/8	23 7/8	24	22 5/8	4 6/8	4 7/8	5	5	Lincoln Co., WY	Chester P. Michalski	Chester P. Michalski	1974	503
196 5/8	24 4/8	24 7/8	25 5/8	4 7/8	4 7/8	7	5	Wyoming	Unknown	Richard C. Birch	PR 1980	503
196 5/8	26 5/8	27 5/8	22 5/8	5 1/8	5 1/8	5	5	Hayes Creek, BC	Dave Legg	Robert H. Legg	1982	503
196 5/8	28	26 7/8	31 2/8	5 3/8	5 1/8	6	6	Deschutes Co., OR	Robert Byrd	Robert E. Byrd	PR 1984	503
196 5/8	26 7/8	26 5/8	24 5/8	5 3/8	5 3/8	6	6	Eureka Co., NV	Michael G. Miller	Michael G. Miller	1995	503
196 5/8	26	25 6/8	21 3/8	4 7/8	4 7/8	5	5	Teton Co., ID	J. Scott Shipton	J. Scott Shipton	1995	503
196 5/8	27 3/8	27 6/8	24	5 4/8	5 1/8	7	7	Rio Arriba Co., NM	Picked Up	Elliot L. Vigil	1996	503
196 5/8	25	24 5/8	28 4/8	4 4/8	4 4/8	6	5	McKenzie Co., ND	Roy Mitten, Sr.	Roy Mitten, Jr.	1937	520
196 4/8	26 3/8	27 5/8	27 5/8	5	4 7/8	5	5	Missouri River, ND	Unknown	Robert L. Kliisares	PR 1958	520
196 4/8	24 5/8	25 5/8	25 1/8	5 2/8	5 1/8	5	5	Flathead River, MT	Stanley Rauscher	Stanley Rauscher	1959	520
196 4/8	23 2/8	22 6/8	19 6/8	5 1/8	5	5	5	Garfield Co., CO	Elmer Nelson	Elmer Nelson	1962	520
196 4/8	24 2/8	25 1/8	21	6 1/8	6 1/8	5	5	Vernal, UT	Selby G. Tanner	Selby G. Tanner	1966	520
196 4/8	22 1/8	22 2/8	23 5/8	5 3/8	5 4/8	5	6	Summit Co., CO	Steve Orecchio	Steve Orecchio	1967	520
196 4/8	26 2/8	26 1/8	25 2/8	5 2/8	5 6/8	6	5	Morgan Co., UT	Elwood Williams	Elwood Williams	1968	520
196 4/8	25 3/8	24 5/8	23	5 5/8	5 7/8	5	5	Southern Ute Res., CO	William C. Forsyth	William C. Forsyth	1974	520
196 4/8	23 5/8	23 5/8	23	5 2/8	5 2/8	5	4	Powell Co., MT	Raymond A. Fitzgerald	Raymond A. Fitzgerald	1983	520
196 4/8	24 7/8	26 2/8	27 5/8	5 4/8	5 4/8	7	7	Bonneville Co., ID	Michael Pinkham	Michael Pinkham	1985	520
196 4/8	25 7/8	26 6/8	25 1/8	5 2/8	5 4/8	7	5	Wasco Co., OR	Steven W. Forman	Steven W. Forman	1986	520
196 4/8	25 3/8	25 3/8	21 2/8	4 4/8	4 3/8	5	5	Park Co., WY	Thomas E. Ault	Thomas E. Ault	1991	520
196 4/8	24 4/8	25 1/8	24	4 5/8	4 5/8	7	5	Teton Co., WY	John C. Branca III	John C. Branca III	1991	520
196 4/8	25	25 4/8	23 2/8	4 7/8	5	5	5	Oneida Co., ID	Russell P. Roe	Russell P. Roe	1996	520
196 4/8	25 4/8	27	27	5 6/8	5 6/8	6	5	Park Co., WY	Keith G. Larsen	Keith G. Larsen	1997	520
196 4/8	24 3/8	26 7/8	24 2/8	4 7/8	4 7/8	5	5	Bonneville Co., ID	Louis H. Griffin	Louis H. Griffin	1998	520
196 4/8	26 4/8	26	24 1/8	5 3/8	5 4/8	7	6	Gooding Co., ID	Gary D. Loghry	Gary D. Loghry	1999	520
196 4/8	26 3/8	29 2/8	22 4/8	5 3/8	5 3/8	7	6	Rio Arriba Co., NM	Alan Vicenti	Alan Vicenti	1999	520
196 3/8	24 6/8	25 1/8	24 4/8	5 3/8	5 3/8	6	5	Powell Co., MT	Stanley F. Malcolm	Stanley F. Malcolm	1958	538
196 3/8	26 4/8	26	24 4/8	5 2/8	5 3/8	6	5	Durango, CO	Ronald Chitwood	Ronald Chitwood	1964	538
196 3/8	28 1/8	28 1/8	26 1/8	4 7/8	5	5	4	Uncompahgre Plateau, CO	Earl L. Markley	Earl L. Markley	1969	538

Score	L. R Beam	L. L Beam	Inside Spread	Circ. R	Circ. L	Pts R	Pts L	Locality	Hunter	Owner	Date	Rank
196 3/8	26 3/8	27 1/8	25 1/8	5 6/8	5 4/8	6	6	Sublette Co., WY	S. Kim Bonnett	S. Kim Bonnett	1978	538
196 3/8	28 3/8	28 4/8	23 5/8	5 3/8	5 4/8	5	6	Beaver Co., UT	Dawson Barnes	Dawson Barnes	1992	538
196 3/8	23 7/8	24 4/8	23 5/8	4 5/8	4 4/8	5	5	Hermosillo, MX	Glenn Bailey	Glenn Bailey	2001	538
196 3/8	25 1/8	27 5/8	23 3/8	5 1/8	5 3/8	5	6	Gunnison Co., CO	James A. Manuel	James A. Manuel	2002	538
196 3/8	25	27 7/8	28 1/8	6 4/8	6	5	6	Gunnison Co., CO	Leland J. Cox	Leland J. Cox	2003	538
196 2/8	27 1/8	27 1/8	27 3/8	5 6/8	5 3/8	5	5	Sonora, MX	Christopher T. Moser	Christopher T. Moser	2003	547
196 2/8	27 4/8	27 3/8	25 1/8	4 5/8	5 1/8	6	6	Lincoln Co., MT	Tommy Boothman	Tommy Boothman	1960	547
196 2/8	27 3/8	25 4/8	25 1/8	5 3/8	5 2/8	6	5	Sweetwater Co., WY	Donald H. Pabst	Donald H. Pabst	1962	547
196 2/8	25 6/8	22 5/8	25 4/8	5 3/8	5 4/8	6	5	Ravalli Co., MT	Gary Godfrey	Calvin D. Kluth	1965	547
196 2/8	22 5/8	23 7/8	22 5/8	5 3/8	5 3/8	7	5	Millard Co., UT	Burnell Washburn	Burnell Washburn	1967	547
196 2/8	26 1/8	26 4/8	23 7/8	6	5 7/8	5	6	Chama, NM	Laura Wilson	Laura Wilson	1967	547
196 2/8	26	25	26	5 4/8	5 4/8	5	5	Dawes Co., NE	Terry L. Sandstrom	Cabela's, Inc.	1968	547
196 2/8	24	27 1/8	20 6/8	4 2/8	4 5/8	5	5	Big Horn Mts., WY	Ruth Davis	Ruth Davis	1968	547
196 2/8	27	23 7/8	24 7/8	5 4/8	5 4/8	9	7	Rio Arriba Co., NM	B.D. Shipwash	B.D. Shipwash	1969	547
196 2/8	25 7/8	27 3/8	25 4/8	5 4/8	5 4/8	6	6	Idaho	Unknown	D.J. Hollinger & B. Howard	PR 1970	547
196 2/8	27 3/8	25 6/8	20 6/8	5 6/8	5 2/8	6	5	Meeker Co., CO	Mike Murphy	Mike Murphy	1971	547
196 2/8	25 4/8	25 4/8	22 4/8	5 2/8	5 3/8	6	5	Bingham Co., ID	Thomas D. Robison	Thomas D. Robison	1972	547
196 2/8	25 4/8	27 5/8	25 5/8	5	5 1/8	5	5	Meeker Co., CO	Max R. Zoeller	Max R. Zoeller	1972	547
196 2/8	27 1/8	26	26	5 2/8	5	5	6	Baker Co., OR	Vivian M. Zikmund	Vivian M. Zikmund	1986	547
196 2/8	25 6/8	26	28 4/8	5 4/8	5 3/8	4	5	San Juan Co., UT	John Rowley	John Rowley	1989	547
196 1/8	26 3/8	27 7/8	26 3/8	6	6 1/8	6	7	Jicarilla Apache Res., NM	Tim Vicenti	Tim Vicenti	1960	547
196 1/8	27 2/8	27 7/8	27	5 1/8	5 1/8	9	6	Chama, NM	Jerry Washburn	Jerry Washburn	1960	547
196 1/8	26	25	24 4/8	5 7/8	5 6/8	7	5	Boise Co., ID	H.L. Rice	H.L. Rice	1966	561
196 1/8	25 2/8	25 3/8	23 5/8	5 4/8	5 3/8	4	5	Uncompahgre Natl. For., CO	Harry L. Whitlock	Harry L. Whitlock	1968	561
196	25 5/8	27 4/8	25 5/8	4 6/8	4 7/8	5	5	Eagle Co., CO	Jeffery D. Harrison	Jeffery D. Harrison	1981	561
196	26 3/8	26 6/8	23 3/8	5 7/8	5 6/8	5	7	Blackwater River, BC	Dale Harrison	Dale Harrison	1998	561
196	27 5/8	26	26 6/8	5 3/8	5 3/8	6	5	Kaibab Natl. For., AZ	Graves Peeler	John E. Connor Museum	PR 1930	561
196	27 2/8	24 1/8	26	5	5 1/8	7	5	North Kaibab, AZ	John D. McNeley	John D. McNeley	1948	561
196	23 6/8	27 4/8	21 6/8	5 6/8	5 6/8	5	5	Kaibab Natl. For., AZ	Elgin T. Gates	Elgin T. Gates	1958	567
196	27 6/8	25 1/8	22 4/8	5	5 4/8	5	6	Huerfano Co., CO	Frank C. Hibben	Frank C. Hibben	1963	567
196	27 1/8	24 4/8	27 2/8	5 6/8	5	8	5	Delta Co., CO	Alvin T. Stivers	Alvin T. Stivers	1965	567
196	25	29 2/8	30 4/8	5 3/8	5 6/8	5	5	Corwin Springs, MT	Donald Strazzabosco	Donald Strazzabosco	1966	567
196	29 4/8	28	24	5	5 2/8	5	5	Jicarilla Apache Res., NM	Collins F. Kellogg	Collins F. Kellogg	1973	567
196	25 4/8	27 5/8	25 2/8	5 5/8	6	6	5	Franklin Co., ID	Larry W. Cross	Larry W. Cross	1974	567
196	25 5/8	25 4/8	23	5 7/8	4 6/8	5	5	Sevier Co., UT	Picked Up	Wade L. Eakle	1976	567
196	25 1/8	24 7/8	25 6/8	4 6/8	5 3/8	5	5	Ferry Co., WA	Owen R. Burgess	Owen R. Burgess	1982	567
196	25	28 2/8	21 6/8	5 2/8	4 7/8	5	5	Rio Arriba Co., NM	Picked Up	Steven C. Erquhart	1988	567
196	26 4/8	26 2/8	29 1/8	5 3/8	5	5	5	Elko Co., NV	Johnny W. Filippini	Johnny W. Filippini	1991	567
196	26 2/8	26 1/8	23 2/8	5 2/8	5	6	6	Fremont Co., WY	Peter R. Ardlen	Peter R. Ardlen	1992	567
196	26	25	22	5	5	5	5	Sounding Creek, AB	William F. Potosky	William F. Potosky	1998	567
196	25	24 7/8	27	4 6/8	4 6/8	5	5	Adams Co., ID	Jim Hostetler	Jim Hostetler	2001	567
195 7/8	27 6/8	25 7/8	26 4/8	4 7/8	4 7/8	7	5	Lassen Co., CA	Sulo E. Lakso	Tracy A. Jenkins	1943	567
195 7/8	25 4/8	25	22 5/8	5 3/8	5 4/8	6	5	Sioux Co., NE	Clarence Dout	Heath L. Serres	1949	582
195 7/8	27 4/8	26 6/8	25 7/8	5 6/8	5 6/8	5	6	Rio Blanco Co., CO	Randy Kruse	Randy Kruse	1951	582
195 7/8	26 2/8	25 7/8	26 5/8	5 4/8	5 4/8	7	5	Bannock Co., ID	William J. Barry	William J. Barry	1956	582
195 7/8	26 6/8	26 7/8	26 6/8	5 5/8	5 6/8	6	6	Southern Ute Res., CO	Richard Schmidt	Southern Ute Tribe	1960	582
195 7/8	25 3/8	23 5/8	20 3/8	5 5/8	5 6/8	5	6	Walla Walla Co., WA	Unknown	Rick H. Russo	1961	582
195 7/8	28 5/8	28	26 5/8	5 5/8	5 5/8	8	7	Cache Co., UT	Richard E. Reeder	Richard E. Reeder	1968	582

313

MULE DEER - TYPICAL ANTLERS

Odocoileus hemionus hemionus and certain related subspecies

Score	Length of Main Beam R	L	Inside Spread	Circumference at Smallest Place Between Burr and First Point R	L	Number of Points R	L	Locality	Hunter	Owner	Date Killed	Rank
195 7/8	27 4/8	26 5/8	24 7/8	5 5/8	5 5/8	5	5	San Miguel Co., CO	Jerry E. Albin	Jerry E. Albin	1972	582
195 7/8	27	28 4/8	28 4/8	5 3/8	5 4/8	7	7	Franklin Co., ID	Melvin S. Thomson	Melvin S. Thomson	1987	582
195 7/8	28	27 6/8	24 3/8	4 6/8	4 6/8	5	5	Teton Co., WY	Lewis E. Sharp	Lewis E. Sharp	1990	582
195 7/8	28	28	26 1/8	5 4/8	5 5/8	5	4	Rio Arriba Co., NM	Arlene Perea	Arlene Perea	1991	582
195 7/8	25 2/8	23 5/8	19 1/8	5 5/8	5 3/8	5	5	Teton Co., WY	Douglas L. Wynn	Douglas L. Wynn	1994	582
195 7/8	24	24 7/8	24 7/8	4 5/8	4 4/8	6	5	Teton Co., WY	Frank E. Baldwin	Frank E. Baldwin	1995	582
195 7/8	23 3/8	23 5/8	30 3/8	5 2/8	5 2/8	5	6	Sonora, MX	John L. Mussell	John L. Mussell	2002	582
195 6/8	27 3/8	28 2/8	26 3/8	5 4/8	5 5/8	7	6	Custer Co., ID	Sylvester Potaman	W. Douglas Lightfoot	1900	596
195 6/8	25 3/8	25 2/8	23 4/8	5 1/8	5	5	5	Jefferson Co., CO	Lloyd O. Rauchfuss	Lloyd O. Rauchfuss	1947	596
195 6/8	26 5/8	26 6/8	28 2/8	5 1/8	5 1/8	6	6	Eagle Co., CO	Orlo E. Park	Orlo E. Park	1954	596
195 6/8	27	23 7/8	24 2/8	5 2/8	5 1/8	5	6	Huerfano Co., CO	Mike Disert	Janet D. Wasson	1954	596
195 6/8	27 4/8	29	26 2/8	5 5/8	5 4/8	7	9	Keating, OR	Al Delepierre	Francis A. Delepierre	1966	596
195 6/8	25 2/8	26 4/8	24 6/8	4 6/8	4 6/8	5	5	Gunnison Co., CO	Randall R. Kieft	Randall R. Kieft	1967	596
195 6/8	28 7/8	28 4/8	28 4/8	5 1/8	5 3/8	5	5	Grant Co., OR	Larry Parlette	Larry Parlette	1967	596
195 6/8	26 4/8	27 2/8	23	5 1/8	5	6	5	Rio Arriba Co., NM	Herman A. Bennett	Herman A. Bennett	1968	596
195 6/8	24 6/8	25 2/8	22 6/8	5	5	5	7	Montrose Co., CO	Larry D. Bitta	Larry D. Bitta	1969	596
195 6/8	22 7/8	24 6/8	23 5/8	5 3/8	5 2/8	5	6	Gunnison Co., CO	George L. Hoffman, Jr.	George L. Hoffman, Jr.	1972	596
195 6/8	25 3/8	24 3/8	24 6/8	4 5/8	4 5/8	5	5	Teton Co., WY	Joel M. Leatham	Joel M. Leatham	1979	596
195 6/8	26	28	33	5 5/8	5 4/8	5	5	Grant Co., OR	Gordon E. Mitchell	Gordon E. Mitchell	1982	596
195 6/8	25 6/8	25 3/8	24 1/8	6 2/8	6 2/8	6	6	Eagle Co., CO	James B. Mesecke	James B. Mesecke	1985	596
195 6/8	24 5/8	26 1/8	24	5 1/8	5 1/8	5	5	Caribou Co., ID	John B. Kochever	John B. Kochever	1986	596
195 6/8	27	27	27 7/8	5 3/8	5 3/8	5	5	Kiskatinaw River, BC	Tim Roberts	Tim Roberts	1994	596
195 6/8	26 6/8	27	23	4 2/8	4 3/8	5	6	Potter Co., TX	Mickey G. VanHuss	Mickey G. VanHuss	1996	596
195 6/8	26 6/8	23 3/8	21 4/8	5 6/8	5 7/8	5	6	Rio Arriba Co., NM	Cevero Caramillo	Cevero Caramillo	2001	596
195 5/8	26 5/8	27 1/8	26 1/8	4 7/8	4 6/8	5	5	Ravalli Co., MT	William H. Cowan	William H. Cowan	1959	613
195 5/8	27 4/8	27 6/8	24 1/8	6	5 7/8	7	7	Slocan Valley, BC	John Braun	John Braun	1962	613
195 5/8	30 5/8	29	26 4/8	6 2/8	6 2/8	6	8	Jicarilla Apache Res., NM	Eldrid Vigil	Eldrid Vigil	1962	613
195 5/8	28	27 7/8	24 7/8	5 5/8	5 4/8	6	5	Lake Co., OR	Betty L. Morris	Betty L. Morris	1963	613
195 5/8	28 3/8	27	34 7/8	5	4 7/8	6	6	Idaho	Wayne Urdahl	Cabela's, Inc.	PR 1964	613
195 5/8	25 1/8	25 4/8	21 3/8	4 6/8	4 4/8	5	4	Pitkin Co., CO	William F. Kirby	William F. Kirby	1966	613
195 5/8	25 2/8	26 1/8	26 2/8	4 7/8	5	5	5	Garfield Co., CO	Jack A. Fitzgerald	Jack A. Fitzgerald	1967	613
195 5/8	27 5/8	25 3/8	20 5/8	4 7/8	4 6/8	5	5	Delta Co., CO	Royce J. Carville	Royce J. Carville	1974	613
195 5/8	25 3/8	25 4/8	21 3/8	5 2/8	5	6	6	Grand Co., CO	C. Jay Stout	C. Jay Stout	1981	613
195 5/8	26 1/8	26 1/8	24	5	5	5	6	Washington Co., UT	Scott M. Bulloch	Scott M. Bulloch	1985	613
195 5/8	26 5/8	27	24 3/8	5 2/8	5 2/8	9	5	Archuleta Co., CO	Matthew J. Arkins	Matthew J. Arkins	1986	613
195 5/8	24 7/8	24 4/8	22 3/8	5 4/8	5 4/8	5	5	Cibola Co., NM	Picked Up	Craig C. Sanchez	1988	613

Score	Length of Main Beam R	Length of Main Beam L	Inside Spread	Circumference R	Circumference L	Points R	Points L	Locality	By Whom Killed	Owner	Date Killed	Rank
195 5/8	25 3/8	25 3/8	26 3/8	5 3/8	5 5/8	5	5	Huerfano Co., CO	Hub R. Grounds	Hub R. Grounds	1989	613
195 5/8	25 6/8	25 7/8	26 2/8	5 4/8	5 2/8	5	5	Mesa Co., CO	John F. Stewart	John F. Stewart	1989	613
195 4/8	26 4/8	26 4/8	24 6/8	5 3/8	5 2/8	5	5	Princeton, BC	Glen Stadler	Glen Stadler	1958	627
195 4/8	25 1/8	25 4/8	22 6/8	5 2/8	5 2/8	5	5	Grover, UT	Vicki Davis	R.J. Davis	1959	627
195 4/8	26 3/8	25 1/8	26 2/8	5 3/8	5 2/8	5	5	Raton, NM	Unknown	John H. Steinle III	1963	627
195 4/8	24 2/8	24 7/8	24 2/8	5 2/8	5 2/8	7	7	Garfield Co., CO	Billy R. Babb	Billy R. Babb	1969	627
195 4/8	24 2/8	25	20 4/8	5 6/8	5 7/8	5	5	Montrose Co., CO	Tony L. Hill	Tony L. Hill	1969	627
195 4/8	25 2/8	27 1/8	27 2/8	5 4/8	5 4/8	6	6	Flathead Co., MT	Sharon M. Gaughan	B&C National Collection	1980	627
195 4/8	28 5/8	27 6/8	27 2/8	5 6/8	4 3/8	5	5	Gunnison Co., CO	Celso Rico	Celso Rico	1981	627
195 4/8	26 3/8	26 5/8	25 2/8	5 6/8	5 5/8	5	5	Sanders Co., MT	William B. Hart	William B. Hart	1984	627
195 4/8	26	26 1/8	25 4/8	5	5	6	5	Bear Lake Co., ID	Joseph R. Given	Joseph R. Given	1985	627
195 4/8	25 6/8	27 4/8	20 3/8	5 4/8	5 4/8	7	6	Harris Creek, BC	Al Hunt	Al Hunt	1986	627
195 3/8	27 3/8	26 6/8	25 7/8	5	5	7	7	Coconino Co., AZ	Bradford Eden	D.J. Hollinger & B. Howard	1949	637
195 3/8	25 4/8	24 2/8	25 4/8	5	5	8	7	Rio Arriba Co., NM	Robert W. Highfill	Robert W. Highfill	1964	637
195 3/8	28 7/8	27 5/8	25 5/8	5 2/8	5 2/8	4	4	Mohave Co., AZ	Bob B. Coker	Bob B. Coker	1972	637
195 3/8	27 5/8	27 3/8	30 7/8	4 3/8	4 4/8	7	5	Niobrara Co., WY	Unknown	Barry Dampman	1975	637
195 3/8	27 3/8	26 7/8	26 5/8	4 6/8	4 6/8	5	5	Natrona Co., WY	Dick Ullery	Dick Ullery	1977	637
195 3/8	26 4/8	25 7/8	26 3/8	5 1/8	5 1/8	5	5	Moffat Co., CO	Frank J. Kubin	Frank J. Kubin	1978	637
195 3/8	26 3/8	26	26 1/8	4 6/8	4 6/8	6	6	Frontier Co., NE	Brent S. Klein	Brent S. Klein	1984	637
195 3/8	25	25	25 1/8	4 6/8	4 6/8	5	5	Wallowa Co., OR	Michael R. Shirley	Michael R. Shirley	1986	637
195 3/8	25	25 5/8	25 5/8	5 2/8	5 3/8	6	5	Garfield Co., UT	John E. Braithwaite	John E. Braithwaite	1987	637
195 3/8	28 4/8	27 3/8	28 6/8	5 5/8	6	5	7	Apache Co., AZ	William D. Beck	William D. Beck	1991	637
195 2/8	29 1/8	27 7/8	25 7/8	5 4/8	5 3/8	7	7	Gunnison Co., CO	Herman F. Tomky	Russell J. Tomky	1937	647
195 2/8	24 4/8	24 3/8	24 6/8	4 6/8	4 5/8	5	5	Moffat Co., CO	Orville R. Meineke	Craig Sports	1964	647
195 2/8	26 4/8	27 1/8	27	5 7/8	5 5/8	7	7	Lewis & Clark Co., MT	Edward A. Ipser	Edward A. Ipser	1965	647
195 2/8	27 6/8	27 1/8	25 1/8	5 2/8	5 1/8	5	5	Marble, CO	Donald E. Alfson	Donald E. Alfson	1966	647
195 2/8	25 2/8	26 4/8	27 1/8	5 1/8	5 1/8	6	7	Davis Co., UT	David R. Allen	David R. Allen	1968	647
195 2/8	26 4/8	25	24 4/8	5 5/8	5 7/8	5	5	Niobrara Co., WY	Mitchell L. Cochran	Mitchell L. Cochran	1972	647
195 2/8	28 5/8	29 7/8	29	5 7/8	5 7/8	5	5	Antelope Lake, SK	David E. Pauna	David E. Pauna	1976	647
195 2/8	26 4/8	25 5/8	26 4/8	4 2/8	4 2/8	5	5	Sublette Co., WY	Doug Westergaard	Doug Westergaard	1977	647
195 2/8	23 3/8	24 6/8	21 4/8	5 1/8	5 1/8	5	5	Twin Falls Co., ID	John R. Birchett	John R. Birchett	1981	647
195 2/8	24 4/8	24 4/8	23 4/8	5 2/8	5 2/8	5	5	Nez Perce Co., ID	Alvin Tollini	Alvin Tollini	1990	647
195 2/8	26 4/8	24 3/8	25 1/8	4 6/8	4 6/8	7	7	Crook Co., OR	Patrick G. Sinclair	Patrick G. Sinclair	1991	647
195 2/8	27 6/8	28 1/8	24 2/8	4 3/8	4 4/8	6	6	Rio Arriba Co., NM	Leah D. Robertson	Leah D. Robertson	1995	647
195 2/8	25 2/8	27 7/8	22	4 4/8	4 3/8	5	4	Notukeu Creek, SK	Robert J. Seeds	Robert J. Seeds	1995	647
195 1/8	26 4/8	25 2/8	23 2/8	5 3/8	5 2/8	5	5	Gunnison Co., CO	Ron Boskill	Ron D. Button	2000	647
195 1/8	25 4/8	26 1/8	27 5/8	5 1/8	5 1/8	6	6	Elko Co., NV	Randy Clark	Randy Clark	2002	647
195 1/8	24 4/8	24 3/8	22 2/8	5 7/8	5 6/8	5	5	Utah	Donald G. Heidtman	Donald G. Heidtman	1954	662
195 1/8	25 4/8	24 2/8	24 1/8	5 1/8	5 1/8	6	5	Rio Arriba Co., NM	Unknown	R. Scott Jarvie	1959	662
195 1/8	26 3/8	26 1/8	24 1/8	5 6/8	5 6/8	5	5	Montrose Co., CO	Eddie W. Brieno, Jr.	Eddie W. Brieno, Jr.	1965	662
195 1/8	27	29 5/8	29 1/8	6	6	5	5	Fruitvale, BC	Eldon L. Webb	Eldon L. Webb	1968	662
195 1/8	25	22 4/8	22 4/8	5 7/8	6	8	8	Idaho Co., ID	Allan Endersby	Allan Endersby	1970	662
195 1/8	26 5/8	26 1/8	24 7/8	4 7/8	4 7/8	7	6	Coconino Co., AZ	Gary S. BeVan	Gary S. BeVan	1972	662
195 1/8	27 3/8	28 3/8	27 1/8	5 1/8	5 5/8	5	5	Kane Co., UT	Gary R. Clark	Gary R. Clark	1987	662
195 1/8	25 5/8	26 1/8	28 2/8	5 3/8	5 2/8	6	5	Rio Arriba Co., NM	Cecil Hunt	Cecil Hunt	1988	662
195 1/8	24	24 7/8	30	5 2/8	5 2/8	5	5	Sonora, MX	David Shadrick	David Shadrick	2002	662
195 1/8	27 1/8	27 4/8	21 4/8	4 4/8	4 4/8	5	5	Rio Arriba Co., NM	Grant A. Medlin	Grant A. Medlin	2002	662
195	27 1/8	27 4/8	21 4/8	4 4/8	4 4/8	5	5	Powder River Co., MT	Roy Dahlby	Michael R. Dahlby	1963	672

MULE DEER - TYPICAL ANTLERS
Odocoileus hemionus and certain related subspecies

Score	Length of Main Beam R	L	Inside Spread	Circumference at Smallest Place Between Burr and First Point R	L	Number of Points R	L	Locality	Hunter	Owner	Date Killed	Rank
195	27	25 6/8	28 1/8	5 5/8	5 7/8	6	6	Elko Co., NV	Steve Beneto, Sr.	Steve Beneto, Sr.	1966	672
195	27 1/8	26 1/8	22 4/8	5 6/8	5 6/8	5	5	Sun River, MT	Dick Lyman	Dick Lyman	1966	672
195	25 1/8	25 1/8	25	4 4/8	4 7/8	5	5	Rio Arriba Co., NM	Pat Wilson	John Lind, Jr.	1967	672
195	25 2/8	25 1/8	22 2/8	4 6/8	4 5/8	5	5	Beaver Co., UT	Unknown	Mark R. Dotson	1969	672
195	25 6/8	24 6/8	22	5 6/8	5 7/8	6	6	Mesa Co., CO	Paul Roddam, Jr.	Paul Roddam, Jr.	1972	672
195	26	25 5/8	23 4/8	4 5/8	5	5	5	Larimer Co., CO	Michael D. Blehm	Michael D. Blehm	1977	672
195	24 2/8	24 4/8	22 3/8	6 2/8	6 1/8	7	5	Sublette Co., WY	Norm Busselle	Norm Busselle	1977	672
195	24 6/8	24 7/8	22 4/8	5	5 1/8	5	5	Rio Blanco Co., CO	Gene Lawrence	Gene Lawrence	1988	672
195	27 1/8	26 5/8	27 1/8	5 3/8	5 2/8	5	7	Carbon Co., UT	Thomas E. Wilson	Thomas E. Wilson	1992	672
195	24 6/8	24	28	5	5 1/8	5	5	Blaine Co., ID	Donald G. Sams	Donald G. Sams	2001	672
195	28 1/8	27 5/8	25 4/8	5 1/8	5 1/8	6	5	Lincoln Co., WY	Randy S. Mixon	Randy S. Mixon	2001	672
195	27 5/8	27 4/8	24 5/8	5 7/8	6	5	6	Sonora, MX	Steven R. Huntley	Steven R. Huntley	2002	672
194 7/8	24 7/8	25 6/8	23 5/8	5 4/8	5 1/8	10	7	Mesa Co., CO	JoReva Wellborn	JoReva Wellborn	1949	685
194 7/8	28 3/8	28 2/8	21 1/8	5 4/8	6 1/8	5	5	Kamloops Lake, BC	Donald Meeks	Donald E. Meeks	PR 1987	685
194 7/8	26 4/8	26 5/8	21 2/8	5 3/8	5 3/8	5	7	Rio Arriba Co., NM	Elliot K. Vigil	Elliot K. Vigil	1997	685
194 7/8	25 1/8	24 3/8	22 7/8	5 5/8	5 5/8	5	5	Sublette Co., WY	Gil Winters	Gil Winters	1998	685
194 7/8	25 1/8	24 6/8	23 7/8	5 1/8	5 1/8	6	5	Tooele Co., UT	Wade L. Hanks	Wade L. Hanks	2002	685
194 7/8	25 4/8	24 6/8	23 1/8	4 3/8	4 3/8	6	5	Utah	Unknown	R. Scott Jarvie	1947	690
194 6/8	25 2/8	25 3/8	22 1/8	4 7/8	4 7/8	5	6	Adams Co., ID	Stanley Branstetter	Stanley Branstetter	1984	690
194 6/8	28	27 5/8	26 7/8	4 5/8	4 7/8	6	8	Grand Co., UT	Richard V. Beesley	Richard V. Beesley	1986	690
194 6/8	26	25 6/8	22 6/8	5 1/8	5 1/8	5	5	Rio Arriba Co., NM	Jordan Pearlman	Jordan Pearlman	1998	690
194 6/8	28 3/8	28 3/8	26 6/8	5 5/8	5 5/8	6	7	Duchesne Co., UT	Kate Hamilton	Raymond R. Cross	1948	694
194 5/8	27 1/8	26 6/8	31 5/8	5 1/8	5	6	7	Idaho	Harold R. Layher	Rod Stewardson	PR 1950	694
194 5/8	25 7/8	25 4/8	25 1/8	4 6/8	5 2/8	5	5	Weber River, UT	Desmond Shields	Desmond Shields	1960	694
194 5/8	26 7/8	26 7/8	23 5/8	4 7/8	4 6/8	5	6	Montezuma Co., CO	Tom G. Broderick	Tom G. Broderick	1990	694
194 5/8	24 7/8	25 2/8	21 3/8	4 5/8	4 5/8	6	6	Cabri Lake, SK	Dean R. Francis	Dean R. Francis	1991	694
194 5/8	26	28 2/8	25 7/8	5 4/8	5 4/8	7	7	Adams Co., CO	Daniel L. Kraft	Daniel L. Kraft	1995	694
194 5/8	27 5/8	24 4/8	24 4/8	4 6/8	4 5/8	6	6	Rio Arriba Co., NM	Patrick Notsinneh	Patrick Notsinneh	1984	694
194 5/8	25 6/8	25 2/8	23 2/8	5	5 1/8	5	5	Eagle Co., CO	William E. Pipes III	William E. Pipes III	1999	701
194 4/8	22 4/8	22 7/8	22 3/8	5 1/8	5 2/8	6	5	Kane Co., UT	Robert G. Ferrero	Robert G. Ferrero	1985	701
194 4/8	24 6/8	26	21 3/8	5	5	5	5	Grant Co., OR	Joey Wood	Joey Wood	2001	703
194 3/8	25	25 3/8	23 3/8	4 6/8	4 6/8	5	7	San Juan Co., UT	Roy T. Hume	Roy T. Hume	PR 2003	703
194 3/8	27 2/8	27 3/8	25 3/8	4 5/8	4 5/8	6	6	Unknown	Unknown	Cabela's, Inc.	PR 1950	703
194 3/8	24 2/8	25	25	5 5/8	5 5/8	5	5	Siskiyou Co., CA	Hap Hottenstein	Judy G. Cottini	1994	706
194 2/8	26	24 4/8	27 4/8	4 6/8	4 7/8	5	5	Grant Co., OR	Richard W. Erickson	Richard W. Erickson	1994	706
194 2/8	27 4/8	27 2/8	26 4/8	5 1/8	5 1/8	6	6	Mesa Co., CO	Frank J. Moore	Frank J. Moore	1999	706

Score	Length of Main Beam R	L	Inside Spread	Circumference R	L	Points R	L	Locality	Hunter	Owner	Date Killed	Rank
194 1/8	25 7/8	25	23 6/8	4 6/8	4 6/8	6	6	Hanksville, UT	Ernie Shirley	Ray Epps	1950	709
194 1/8	26	25 4/8	21	5	5	5	5	Delta Co., CO	Bill Rainer	Bill Rainer	1977	709
194 1/8	25 2/8	25	21 4/8	5	4 7/8	5	5	Petroleum Co., MT	Christopher G. Basham	Christopher G. Basham	1994	709
194 1/8	27 1/8	25 5/8	22 7/8	5 2/8	4 7/8	5	4	Rio Arriba Co., NM	Picked Up	Robert J. Seeds	1994	709
194 1/8	27 3/8	25 6/8	23 5/8	5	5 1/8	5	5	Bone Creek, SK	Kevin R. Whyte	Kevin R. Whyte	1998	709
194 1/8	22 4/8	23 7/8	22 1/8	5 4/8	5 3/8	5	6	Gooding Co., ID	Jeff L. Basterrechea	Jeff L. Basterrchea	1999	709
194	25 1/8	25 4/8	27 4/8	5 4/8	5 4/8	5	5	Rio Arriba Co., NM	C.J. McElroy	C.J. McElroy	1970	715
194	26 4/8	25 7/8	25	5	5	5	5	Lemhi Co., ID	Andrew W. Jones	Benjamin C. Jones	1979	715
194	23 3/8	25 1/8	22 4/8	4 6/8	4 7/8	5	5	Sublette Co., WY	James J. McBride	James J. McBride	1979	715
194	26 3/8	28 7/8	22 4/8	4 6/8	4 6/8	6	6	Grand Co., CO	Bill Britt	Larry Underwood	PR 1980	715
193 7/8	26 6/8	27 2/8	28 3/8	5 1/8	5 3/8	7	7	Madison Co., MT	Edgar Allard	R.G. Stroup	1948	719
193 7/8	25 5/8	27 2/8	26 7/8	5 2/8	5 2/8	5	5	S. Saskatchewan River, SK	Belinda M. Guckert	Belinda M. Guckert	1998	719
193 6/8	25 5/8	23 2/8	25 2/8	5	5 1/8	6	6	Unknown	Unknown	Paul Sides	PR 1960	721
193 6/8	27 6/8	27 2/8	29 4/8	5 5/8	5 3/8	6	6	Cimarron Co., CO	Reynolds L. Vanstrom	R.A. & E. Vanstrom	1960	721
193 6/8	25	26 2/8	22	4 4/8	4 5/8	5	5	Smoky River, AB	Jeffrey S. Reichert	Jeffrey S. Reichert	1989	721
193 6/8	26	26 6/8	27 1/8	4 2/8	4 1/8	6	6	Lander Co., NV	Picked Up	John W. Filippini	1992	721
193 6/8	24	24 1/8	22 6/8	5 1/8	5 4/8	6	5	Yuma Co., CO	John M. McAteer	John M. McAteer	1997	721
193 6/8	28 1/8	27 5/8	23 4/8	4 6/8	4 6/8	4	4	British Columbia	Picked Up	Cabela's, Inc.	PR 2001	721
193 6/8	24 4/8	25 4/8	21 6/8	4 5/8	4 6/8	5	5	Franklin Co., ID	Nicholas Q. Shumway	Nicholas Q. Shumway	2001	721
193 5/8	23 3/8	23 7/8	19 1/8	5	4 7/8	6	6	Sublette Co., WY	Paul Carter, Jr.	Paul Carter, Jr.	1966	728
193 5/8	25 7/8	25 7/8	22 2/8	4 7/8	4 6/8	5	5	Kane Co., UT	Jeffrey L. Janisch	Jeffrey L. Janisch	1993	728
193 5/8	27	25 3/8	26 1/8	5 4/8	5 5/8	6	5	Rio Arriba Co., NM	David W. DeMello	David W. DeMello	1994	728
193 5/8	23 3/8	23 2/8	23 6/8	5 5/8	5 4/8	6	5	Eagle Co., CO	William E. Pipes III	William E. Pipes III	1995	728
193 5/8	28 7/8	25 3/8	32 1/8	5 5/8	5 5/8	8	7	Adams Co., CO	Phillip E. Hupp	Phillip E. Hupp	2000	728
193 4/8	26 6/8	27 2/8	29 1/8	5 2/8	5 2/8	6	6	Iron Co., UT	Gordon Farnsworth	Gordon L. Farnsworth	1966	733
193 4/8	27 1/8	26 7/8	24 4/8	5 4/8	5 5/8	6	6	Garfield Co., CO	Marvin A. Meyers	Marvin A. Meyers	1982	733
193 4/8	24 5/8	25 4/8	20 3/8	5 1/8	5 1/8	5	5	Unknown	Unknown	Ron Boehm	1995	733
193 4/8	23 7/8	25	25 1/8	5	4 7/8	5	5	Gem Co., ID	David W. Bowman	David W. Bowman	1995	733
193 4/8	25 3/8	25 6/8	23	5 4/8	5 4/8	6	6	Sonora, MX	Gregory F. Lucero	Gregory F. Lucero	1996	733
193 4/8	25 7/8	25 5/8	22 2/8	4 4/8	4 3/8	6	6	Cassia Co., ID	Picked Up	David R. Harrow	1998	733
193 4/8	23 4/8	23 5/8	18 4/8	4 4/8	4 3/8	5	5	Utah Co., UT	Seth A. Poulson	Seth A. Poulson	2001	733
193 3/8	26 7/8	27 2/8	23 3/8	4 7/8	4 7/8	5	5	Washoe Co., NV	Barbara M. Conley	Barbara M. Conley	1987	740
193 3/8	25 3/8	24 2/8	22 6/8	5	5	6	6	Rio Arriba Co., NM	Edward C. Joseph	Edward C. Joseph	1995	740
193 3/8	28 2/8	28	24 7/8	5 1/8	5 1/8	6	6	Baker Co., OR	Anthony A. Myers	Anthony A. Myers	1996	740
193 3/8	25 5/8	24 4/8	18 5/8	5 2/8	5 3/8	6	6	Frenchman River, SK	Brian M. Irish	Brian M. Irish	1998	740
193 2/8	28 2/8	28 3/8	28 2/8	4 6/8	4 4/8	7	7	Eagle Co., CO	Robert D. Pape	Rory Pape	1959	744
193 2/8	26	26 7/8	25 2/8	6	6 1/8	5	5	Gunnison Co., CO	Bill Morrow	Nancy Morrow	1960	744
193 2/8	26 7/8	26 7/8	26 4/8	5 1/8	5	6	6	Delta Co., CO	Kenneth R. French	Kenneth R. French	1979	744
193 2/8	23 6/8	24	22 2/8	5 2/8	5 4/8	6	6	Franklin Co., ID	L. Munk & T. Braegger	Larry Munk	1990	744
193 2/8	23 7/8	24 4/8	22 4/8	5 1/8	5 1/8	4	4	Lincoln Co., WY	Greg E. Morris	Greg E. Morris	2000	744
193 2/8	23 7/8	25 5/8	21 6/8	5	5	5	5	Lincoln Co., WY	Michael J. Garrett	Michael J. Garrett	2001	744
193 2/8	26 5/8	26 4/8	21	4 7/8	4 7/8	6	6	Bear Lake Co., ID	Brad J. Michel	Brad J. Michel	2002	744
193 1/8	25	25 5/8	23 4/8	5 4/8	5 3/8	7	7	Sublette Co., WY	Edward E. Hall, Jr.	Edward E. Hall, Jr.	1958	751
193 1/8	26 7/8	26 2/8	27	5 2/8	5 1/8	6	6	Arizona	Unknown	Aly M. Bruner	PR 1970	751
193 1/8	28 4/8	28 5/8	23 1/8	5 5/8	5 4/8	6	6	Suffern Lake, SK	Dan C. McKinnon	Dan C. McKinnon	1998	751
193 1/8	24 3/8	24 3/8	22 2/8	5 4/8	5 4/8	8	8	Fraser River, BC	Kent Lawlor	Kent Lawlor	2000	751
193 1/8	27 7/8	27 1/8	23	5	4 7/8	5	5	Rio Arriba Co., NM	Picked Up	Lambert Callado	2001	751
193	26 7/8	24 1/8	23	5 4/8	5 4/8	5	5	Malheur Co., OR	LeRoy Zollo	Nick Spiropolos	1978	756

MULE DEER - TYPICAL ANTLERS

Odocoileus hemionus hemionus and certain related subspecies

Score	Length of Main Beam R	L	Inside Spread	Circumference at Smallest Place Between Burr and First Point R	L	Number of Points R	L	Locality	Hunter	Owner	Date Killed	Rank
193	27 4/8	27 7/8	24 6/8	4 6/8	4 6/8	5	5	Owyhee Co., ID	Bob Lambert	Cabela's, Inc.	PR 1980	756
193	25 2/8	27 6/8	29	5 4/8	5 5/8	7	6	Kane Co., UT	Unknown	D.J. Hollinger & B. Howard	PR 1983	756
193	25	25 6/8	22 2/8	4 6/8	5	5	7	Carbon Co., WY	Jeff Pfau	Jeff Pfau	1985	756
193	24 2/8	24 4/8	25 3/8	4 6/8	4 6/8	5	5	Uintah Co., UT	Unknown	D.R. & J. Harrow	PR 1986	756
193	25 5/8	23 7/8	21 4/8	5 1/8	5	5	5	Gem Co., ID	Blaine L. Hyde	Blaine L. Hyde	1995	756
193	24 4/8	24 5/8	22 3/8	5 6/8	5 4/8	4	4	Lincoln Co., WY	David K. Halverson	David K. Halverson	1997	756
192 7/8	25 1/8	26	20 3/8	4 6/8	4 6/8	5	5	Colorado	Unknown	D.J. Hollinger & B. Howard	1953	763
192 7/8	27 2/8	27	24 7/8	5 3/8	5	6	6	Bonneville Co., ID	Max L. Christensen	Terrel M. Christensen	1965	763
192 7/8	26 3/8	25 5/8	26 3/8	5 4/8	5 4/8	8	9	Rio Arriba Co., NM	J. Ed Morgan	J. Ed Morgan	1966	763
192 7/8	25 5/8	26 6/8	21 6/8	5	4 7/8	5	7	Cartier Creek, AB	Wayne Price	Wayne Price	1971	763
192 7/8	23 1/8	25 6/8	24 5/8	5	5	6	6	Swan Lake, BC	Jurgen Schulz	Jurgen Schulz	1995	763
192 6/8	26	25 6/8	21 2/8	5 4/8	5 5/8	6	5	Gunnison Co., CO	Stephen A. Mahurin	Stephen A. Mahurin	1968	768
192 6/8	27 1/8	27 1/8	28 3/8	5 4/8	5 4/8	5	6	Lincoln Co., WY	William D. Tate	William D. Tate	1981	768
192 6/8	24	23 6/8	24 5/8	5	5 6/8	7	5	Montezuma Co., CO	Jay N. Cruzan	Jay N. Cruzan	1988	768
192 6/8	26 2/8	26 6/8	24 2/8	5	5 1/8	5	5	Kane Co., UT	Steven A. Wilson	Steven A. Wilson	1991	768
192 6/8	24 2/8	25	23 7/8	5 5/8	5 4/8	6	6	Las Animas Co., CO	James S. Kent	James S. Kent	1995	768
192 6/8	26 7/8	26 4/8	22 4/8	5 3/8	5 3/8	6	5	Las Animas Co., CO	Fred D. Ruland	Fred D. Ruland	1997	768
192 6/8	24 6/8	25	22 1/8	4 7/8	5	6	7	Elbow, SK	Rick E. Hawkes	Rick E. Hawkes	1998	768
192 6/8	25 6/8	25 4/8	20 5/8	5 2/8	5 2/8	4	4	Grand Co., CO	Erwin R. Palmer	Erwin R. Palmer	1961	775
192 5/8	25	24 1/8	20 6/8	5 1/8	5 1/8	5	6	Park Co., WY	LaVerne M. Nelson	LaVerne M. Nelson	1992	775
192 5/8	23 6/8	24 3/8	21 3/8	4 4/8	4 6/8	5	5	Unknown	Unknown	Jerome E. Arledge	PR 1993	775
192 5/8	27 1/8	25 6/8	23	5 6/8	5 7/8	7	6	Montana	Unknown	James B. Sisco III	PR 1995	775
192 5/8	25 3/8	25	24 6/8	4 5/8	4 5/8	6	5	Lincoln Co., WY	James M. Snowden	James M. Snowden	2000	780
192 4/8	28 1/8	26 6/8	27 6/8	4 6/8	4 7/8	4	5	Mesa Co., CO	Lacy J. Harber	Lacy J. Harber	1963	780
192 4/8	24 4/8	25	20 1/8	5	5	6	6	Bear Lake Co., ID	Lee Bridges	Lee Bridges	1967	780
192 4/8	26 6/8	25 5/8	21 2/8	5 1/8	5 4/8	6	6	Idaho	Unknown	Alan C. Ellsworth	PR 1990	780
192 4/8	25 6/8	25 5/8	24	5 2/8	5 4/8	5	5	Apache Co., AZ	Bobby L. Beeman	Bobby L. Beeman	1991	780
192 4/8	28 2/8	26 3/8	27	6 1/8	6 2/8	5	5	Rio Arriba Co., NM	Charles Tapia	Charles Tapia	1993	780
192 4/8	29	27 7/8	28	5	5	4	4	Grant Co., OR	Don Messenger	Don Messenger	1994	780
192 4/8	24 3/8	24 2/8	19 6/8	4 4/8	4 6/8	6	5	Slope Co., ND	Jennifer A. Belland	Jennifer A. Belland	2000	780
192 4/8	24 1/8	24	23 7/8	4 7/8	5 5/8	6	5	Summit Co., UT	Boyd J. Pendleton	Boyd J. Pendleton	2000	780
192 4/8	26 3/8	25 4/8	21 3/8	5 6/8	5 5/8	5	6	Grizzly Creek, BC	Deller Watson	Deller Watson	2000	780
192 3/8	26 6/8	27	28 5/8	4 6/8	4 7/8	7	5	Klamath Co., OR	Douglas S. Golden	Douglas S. Golden	1955	789
192 3/8	25 6/8	25 7/8	27 6/8	4 4/8	4 4/8	5	5	Idaho	Unknown	Daniel Woodbridge	PR 1972	789
192 3/8	25 6/8	25 5/8	22 1/8	5 1/8	5	5	5	Grant Co., OR	Norman O. Peters	Norman O. Peters	1980	789
192 3/8	24 5/8	25 4/8	23	5 2/8	5 2/8	5	4	Kane Co., UT	Picked Up	Danny C. Stratton	1990	789

Score	Main Beam R	Main Beam L	Inside Spread	Circ. R	Circ. L	Pts. R	Pts. L	Locality	Hunter	Owner	Date	Rank
192 3/8	24 7/8	24 7/8	24 1/8	5 2/8	5 4/8	5	5	Platte Co, WY	Robby McAllister	Robby McAllister	1992	789
192 3/8	26 3/8	26 6/8	25 5/8	5 1/8	5 3/8	5	5	Williams Lake, BC	Evan D. Howarth	Evan D. Howarth	1994	789
192 3/8	24 6/8	25 5/8	23 3/8	5 1/8	5 1/8	5	5	Powder River Co, MT	Eric A. DeVuyst	Eric A. DeVuyst	1995	789
192 3/8	25	27	23 7/8	5	5 1/8	6	5	Rio Arriba Co, NM	Levi Pesata	Levi Pesata	1998	789
192 3/8	25	24 1/8	26 2/8	5 2/8	5 4/8	7	5	Camas Co, ID	Brian T. Storey	Brian T. Storey	1999	789
192 3/8	24 1/8	25	20 6/8	4 4/8	4 5/8	6	5	Teton Co, WY	Vance S. Welch	Vance S. Welch	2000	789
192 3/8	23 1/8	25 6/8	27 6/8	4 4/8	4 4/8	5	5	Unknown	Unknown	Cabela's, Inc.	PR 2001	789
192 3/8	25 6/8	23 6/8	27 5/8	5 2/8	5 2/8	5	5	Wilkie, SK	Melvin B. Gillis	Melvin B. Gillis	2001	789
192 3/8	23 6/8	23 6/8	21 7/8	4 5/8	4 5/8	5	5	Rio Arriba Co, NM	Eudane Vicenti	Eudane Vicenti	2002	789
192 3/8	28 1/8	27 7/8	25 1/8	4 7/8	5 1/8	5	6	Routt Co, CO	James S. Farleigh	James S. Farleigh	2003	789
192 2/8	26 4/8	26 5/8	25	4 7/8	4 7/8	5	6	Archuleta Co, CO	John Richardson	John Richardson	1965	803
192 2/8	26 3/8	25 7/8	24 3/8	5 4/8	5 3/8	6	6	Grant Co, OR	Paul D. Bennett	Paul D. Bennett	1968	803
192 2/8	25 3/8	26 1/8	19 5/8	4 7/8	4 7/8	5	5	Valley Co, ID	Bruce Myers	Bruce Myers	1976	803
192 2/8	27 3/8	27 5/8	28 3/8	5	5 1/8	10	6	Grant Co, OR	Larry T. Palmer	Larry T. Palmer	1990	803
192 2/8	25 7/8	26 2/8	21 6/8	4 4/8	4 5/8	6	5	San Juan Co, NM	Picked Up	Rogelio D. Couder, Jr.	1996	803
192 2/8	25 2/8	26 6/8	25 6/8	4 7/8	5	5	5	Eagle Co, CO	Ronald L. McCall	Ronald L. McCall	1996	803
192 2/8	26 4/8	27 3/8	22 6/8	6 3/8	5 1/8	7	6	Grizzly Bear Creek, AB	Andy P. Charchun	Andy P. Charchun	1998	803
192 2/8	25 2/8	25 2/8	24 6/8	5 1/8	4 7/8	6	5	Sonora, MX	Picked Up	Kirk Kelso	2003	803
192 1/8	25 4/8	27 4/8	27 6/8	5 5/8	5 3/8	5	7	Bonneville Co, ID	Glen M. Brown	Glen M. Brown	1949	811
192 1/8	25 4/8	25 2/8	23 3/8	4 7/8	4 7/8	7	8	Duchesne Co, UT	Dennis F. Mower	Dennis F. Mower	1969	811
192 1/8	24 2/8	26 1/8	27 6/8	5 1/8	5 1/8	5	5	Unknown	Unknown	Jeffrey W. Robinson	1970	811
192 1/8	25 6/8	24 4/8	21 5/8	5 1/8	5 1/8	5	5	Utah	Unknown	D.R. & J. Harrow	PR 1976	811
192 1/8	25 6/8	26 3/8	21 7/8	4 1/8	4 2/8	5	5	Great Sand Hills, SK	Richey Lane	Richey Lane	1983	811
192 1/8	27 3/8	26 1/8	28 6/8	5 1/8	5 2/8	5	5	Malheur Co, OR	William T. Monson	William T. Monson	1995	811
192 1/8	28 4/8	27 4/8	28 7/8	6	5 5/8	6	7	Dorothy, AB	David A. McIver	David A. McIver	1997	811
192 1/8	24 3/8	25 2/8	23 3/8	4 5/8	4 6/8	6	5	Duchesne Co, UT	Brandon K. Rowley	Brandon K. Rowley	2000	811
192 1/8	26 4/8	26 5/8	22 4/8	5 2/8	5	8	7	Delta Co, CO	James W. Arellano	James W. Arellano	1977	811
192	26 4/8	25 7/8	27 7/8	5 3/8	5 3/8	5	5	Larimer Co, CO	Picked Up	John R. Steffes, Sr.	PR 1990	819
192	23 3/8	24 6/8	22 4/8	5	5	5	5	Teton Co, WY	Steven G. Coy	Steven G. Coy	1992	819
192	25 6/8	26 2/8	25 6/8	4 7/8	4 7/8	5	5	Park Co, WY	Richard L. Kempka	Richard L. Kempka	1994	819
192	25 5/8	24 2/8	20 4/8	4 3/8	4 3/8	5	5	Wayne Co, UT	Ivan B. Henderson	Ivan B. Henderson	1996	819
192	23 3/8	23	21 4/8	5 4/8	5 6/8	7	6	Arapahoe Co, CO	Daniel R. Madajski	Daniel R. Madajski	1996	819
192	25 1/8	26 3/8	24 1/8	5	5 4/8	6	5	Wasco Co, OR	Jeffrey Davis	Jeffrey R. Davis	1998	819
191 7/8	24 4/8	24 4/8	24 7/8	5 4/8	5 5/8	5	5	Beaver Mt, BC	Earl Miller	Glenn Miller	1921	826
191 7/8	27	26 7/8	22 1/8	5	5	6	6	Dolores Co, CO	Jim Becher	Jerry Schwaderer	1961	826
191 7/8	26 4/8	27 3/8	27 3/8	5 1/8	5 1/8	6	6	Moffat Co, CO	Howard Hageman	Aly M. Bruner	1963	826
191 7/8	26 7/8	26	29 5/8	5 6/8	5 5/8	4	6	Unknown	Unknown	Thomas J. Lovrin	PR 1970	826
191 7/8	26 3/8	26 3/8	21 3/8	4 6/8	4 6/8	6	6	Carbondale River, AB	Michael Pearce	Michael Pearce	1992	826
191 6/8	25 1/8	23 5/8	23 5/8	4 7/8	5	5	5	Kane Co, UT	Scott S. Snyder	Scott S. Snyder	1995	833
191 6/8	28 4/8	22 7/8	27	5	5	5	7	Tooele Co, UT	Cody L. Warren	Cody L. Warren	2000	833
191 6/8	25 1/8	27	24 4/8	4 7/8	5	6	6	Teton Co, WY	Jesse Barker	Rex N. Barker	1963	833
191 6/8	26 7/8	26 7/8	20 6/8	5 3/8	5 5/8	5	5	Larimer Co, CO	N. Duane Wygant	N. Duane Wygant	1966	833
191 6/8	24 6/8	25 4/8	26 4/8	5 7/8	5 1/8	6	5	Mesa Co, CO	Thomas W. White	Thomas W. White	1972	833
191 6/8	26 6/8	25 7/8	24 1/8	5	5 4/8	5	6	Unknown	Unknown	Richard C. Birch	PR 1980	833
191 6/8	25 2/8	25 4/8	25 2/8	4 7/8	4 4/8	7	5	Unknown	Unknown	Gary P. Farley	PR 1993	833
191 6/8	28	25 2/8	25 4/8	5 6/8	5 4/8	5	6	Gooding Co, ID	Mark Moncrief	Mark E. Moncrief	1994	833
191 6/8	26 4/8	21 3/8	21 3/8	5 6/8	5 6/8	6	7	Rio Arriba Co, NM	Leroy TeCube	Leroy TeCube	1995	833
191 6/8	26	26	21 3/8	5 6/8	5 6/8	6	7	Kane Co, UT	Edward A. Tognetti	Edward A. Tognetti	1997	833

MULE DEER - TYPICAL ANTLERS

Odocoileus hemionus hemionus and certain related subspecies

Score	Length of Main Beam R	L	Inside Spread	Circumference at Smallest Place Between Burr and First Point R	L	Number of Points R	L	Locality	Hunter	Owner	Date Killed	Rank
191 5/8	25 2/8	26 2/8	21 3/8	5 4/8	5 6/8	5	5	Mesa Co., CO	Arlie Manship	Arlie Manship	1957	841
191 5/8	25	25 6/8	20 7/8	5 3/8	5 2/8	5	7	Power Co., ID	Stephen E. Wegner	Stephen E. Wegner	1965	841
191 5/8	27 5/8	27 6/8	24 7/8	5 2/8	5 2/8	5	5	Union Co., OR	Picked Up	Jon Anderson	1978	841
191 5/8	24 2/8	26	21	4 6/8	4 6/8	6	5	Kane Co., UT	James D. Delaney	James D. Delaney	1997	841
191 4/8	26 3/8	26 1/8	25 4/8	5 2/8	5	6	7	Coconino Co., AZ	Steven G. Mallory	Steven G. Mallory	1988	845
191 4/8	21 7/8	23	18 1/8	5	5	5	6	Fraser River, BC	Gerard Fournier	Gerard Fournier	1997	845
191 4/8	26 1/8	25 1/8	23 7/8	6 1/8	6	8	7	Kane Co., UT	Robert J. Pacini	Robert J. Pacini	1998	845
191 4/8	27 6/8	27 6/8	25 6/8	5 4/8	5 4/8	5	5	Rio Arriba Co., NM	Edward R. Frey	Kathleen A. Frey	2000	845
191 3/8	26	26	20 3/8	6	5 6/8	5	5	Cornwell Mt., BC	Don Bundus	John D. Bundus	1963	849
191 3/8	27 2/8	26 6/8	25 5/8	5 5/8	5 5/8	5	5	Rio Arriba Co., NM	Michael B. O'Banion	Michael B. O'Banion	1993	849
191 3/8	26 1/8	25 7/8	24 4/8	5 5/8	5 4/8	6	5	Forest Lake, BC	Gordon Simpson	Gordon Simpson	1994	849
191 3/8	24 7/8	24 1/8	27 6/8	4 7/8	4 5/8	5	5	Gooding Co., ID	Donald W. Larson	Donald W. Larson	2000	849
191 3/8	24 4/8	25 2/8	24 3/8	4 6/8	5 1/8	5	6	Carbon Co., WY	Kermit D. Russell	Patrick McKee	PR 2000	849
191 2/8	24 1/8	24 7/8	19 7/8	4 7/8	5 4/8	6	6	Lincoln Co., WY	Unknown	DeWayne A. Williams	1967	854
191 2/8	25 7/8	25 4/8	24 6/8	5	5	5	5	Gunnison Co., CO	Tim Hays	Tim Hays	1981	854
191 2/8	24 5/8	24 6/8	26	4 6/8	4 4/8	5	5	Morrow Co., OR	Russell D. Britt	Russell D. Britt	1990	854
191 2/8	27 4/8	27 6/8	22 2/8	4 3/8	4 3/8	5	5	Idaho	Unknown	Jerome E. Arledge	PR 1992	854
191 2/8	25 2/8	24	22 4/8	5 5/8	5 5/8	4	4	Rio Arriba Co., NM	D. Boone Kuersteiner	D. Boone Kuersteiner	1994	854
191 2/8	25 6/8	24 3/8	29 2/8	4 5/8	4 5/8	5	5	Gem Co., ID	Troy A. Gaskell	Troy A. Gaskell	1995	854
191 2/8	25 3/8	25 1/8	23	4 2/8	4 1/8	5	5	Lincoln Co., WY	Darin D. Kerr	Darin D. Kerr	2001	854
191 2/8	22 1/8	23 2/8	23	4 6/8	4 6/8	5	5	Larimer Co., CO	Albert Valles, Jr.	Albert Valles, Jr.	2001	854
191 2/8	25 3/8	24 3/8	25	4 2/8	4 1/8	5	5	Washoe Co., NV	Daniel A. Grayson	Daniel A. Grayson	2002	854
191 2/8	26 2/8	27 3/8	21 6/8	5 4/8	5 2/8	5	6	Malheur Co., OR	Tom Markle	Tom Markle	2002	854
191 2/8	26 3/8	25 7/8	22 4/8	5 2/8	5 2/8	6	5	Mesa Co., CO	Mark Blair	Mark Blair	2003	854
191 1/8	26 1/8	26 1/8	23 1/8	5	5	5	6	Moffat Co., CO	Len E. Mayfield	Len E. Mayfield	1959	865
191 1/8	27 7/8	27 3/8	22 4/8	5	5 1/8	6	6	Grand Co., CO	Lloyd A. Palmer	Lloyd A. Palmer	1959	865
191 1/8	27 1/8	27 4/8	22 1/8	5	4 6/8	5	6	Rich Co., UT	Carl Nelson	Brian C. Nelson	PR 1960	865
191 1/8	26 4/8	26 3/8	26 1/8	4 5/8	4 4/8	5	5	Washoe Co., NV	Jay Walker	Jay Walker	1967	865
191 1/8	25 5/8	24 1/8	22 2/8	4 6/8	4 6/8	6	5	Wallowa Co., OR	William Bruck	Robert P. Romine, Sr.	1976	865
191 1/8	26 4/8	26 7/8	24 7/8	4 7/8	4 7/8	6	5	Eagle Co., CO	Ralph L. Nygren	Ralph L. Nygren	1978	865
191 1/8	24	23 7/8	22	4 7/8	4 7/8	6	5	Washington Co., ID	Mike Meyer	Mike Meyer	1980	865
191 1/8	23 3/8	25 1/8	24 5/8	4 3/8	4 4/8	5	5	Grand Co., CO	Zane Palmer	Zane Palmer	1981	865
191 1/8	26 5/8	24 6/8	24 5/8	4 7/8	4 7/8	5	5	Uintah Co., UT	Robert B. Keel	Robert B. Keel	1986	865
191 1/8	28 2/8	28 1/8	26 5/8	4 4/8	4 5/8	4	5	Uinta Co., WY	Daniel T. Begley	Daniel T. Begley	1995	865
191 1/8	24 3/8	23 2/8	23 1/8	4 7/8	4 7/8	8	6	Sublette Co., WY	Gil Winters	Gil Winters	2001	865
191 1/8	25 4/8	26 1/8	27 5/8	5	5	5	4	Sonora, MX	Gerald P. McBride	Gerald P. McBride	2003	865

Score	Main Beam R	Main Beam L	Inside Spread	Circ. R	Circ. L	Pts R	Pts L	Locality	Hunter	Owner	Date	Rank
191	28 1/8	26 7/8	26 4/8	4 7/8	5	7	4	Colorado	Craig C. Christenson	Unknown	PR 1961	877
191	26 4/8	26 3/8	27 3/8	5 5/8	5 5/8	6	6	Teton Co., WY	Buck Taylor	Buck Taylor	1969	877
191	25 4/8	25 1/8	25 1/8	5 6/8	5 2/8	6	6	Kane Co., UT	Edward B. Franceschi, Jr.	Edward B. Franceschi, Jr.	1990	877
191	24 1/8	24 4/8	21 4/8	5	5	6	5	Lincoln Co., WY	Eric E. Andersen	Eric E. Andersen	1999	877
191	27 3/8	25 1/8	24 6/8	4 3/8	4 4/8	5	5	Montrose Co., CO	Johnny A. Grimes	Johnny A. Grimes	1999	877
191	26 6/8	26 6/8	24 4/8	5 1/8	5	6	5	Eagle Co., CO	Stephen V. Vallone	Stephen V. Vallone	2000	877
191	26	25 1/8	25 1/8	5	5 1/8	6	5	Rio Arriba Co., NM	Russell J. Jackson	Russell J. Jackson	2002	877
190 7/8	24	24 7/8	26	5 2/8	5 2/8	5	5	Dolores Co., CO	Henry A. Anderson	Unknown	1945	884
190 7/8	27 4/8	27 7/8	24 7/8	4 5/8	5	6	6	Elmore Co., ID	Michael H. Felton	Michael H. Felton	1980	884
190 7/8	24 6/8	24 6/8	27	5 7/8	5 5/8	8	8	Unknown		Cabela's, Inc.	PR 1986	884
190 7/8	28 3/8	28	25 6/8	5 2/8	5 2/8	5	5	Las Animas Co., CO	Robert D. Davidson	Robert D. Davidson	1995	884
190 7/8	24 6/8	25 5/8	27 7/8	5 2/8	5 3/8	5	5	Apache Co., AZ	Thomas B. Anderson	Thomas B. Anderson	1997	884
190 7/8	26 1/8	26 2/8	23 1/8	5 3/8	5 2/8	5	5	Riske Creek, BC	David Novak	David Novak	1997	884
190 7/8	26	25 7/8	20 5/8	5	4 7/8	4	4	Lincoln Co., NV	Dan Goff	Dan Goff	2001	884
190 7/8	27 7/8	27 6/8	20 5/8	4 7/8	4 7/8	5	4	Sonora, MX	Stan A. Hanes	Stan A. Hanes	2001	884
190 6/8	24 5/8	24 7/8	19 4/8	4 7/8	4 7/8	5	4	Garfield Co., UT	Arthur L. Holt	Tom E. Reese	1950	892
190 6/8	27	26 1/8	20 4/8	5 2/8	5 2/8	5	5	Fall River Co., SD	Art Thomsen	Art Thomsen	1953	892
190 6/8	26	25 1/8	25 2/8	4 6/8	4 6/8	5	5	Jackson Co., CO	Guy Amburgey	Guy Amburgey	1969	892
190 6/8	26 4/8	26 2/8	24 4/8	4 7/8	4 6/8	5	5	Dolores Co., CO	Jess Guynes	Jess Guynes	1974	892
190 6/8	25	25 2/8	28 4/8	5 1/8	5 3/8	5	5	Granite Co., MT	Larry Peterman	Larry Peterman	1976	892
190 6/8	24 4/8	24 2/8	20 2/8	5 4/8	5 3/8	5	5	Rio Arriba Co., NM	James G. Biela	James G. Biela	1977	892
190 6/8	26 2/8	25 4/8	20 1/8	4 6/8	4 7/8	6	6	Lincoln Co., WY	Dave Doney	Dave Doney	1986	892
190 6/8	22 6/8	22 7/8	20	4 5/8	4 5/8	5	5	Moyie River, BC	Robert C. Faiers	Robert C. Faiers	1998	892
190 6/8	24 1/8	26	20	4 6/8	4 4/8	5	5	Fly Hill, BC	Randy Bellows	Randy Bellows	1999	892
190 6/8	25 4/8	26 5/8	26 3/8	5 1/8	5 1/8	6	6	Lincoln Co., WY	Terry D. Goff	Terry D. Goff	2000	892
190 6/8	27 2/8	28 6/8	23 4/8	4 5/8	4 5/8	5	5	Klickitat Co., WA	Gary R. Hess	Gary R. Hess	2000	892
190 6/8	25 2/8	24 1/8	24	5 3/8	5 1/8	7	7	Rio Arriba Co., NM	Terry R. Chapman	Terry R. Chapman	2002	892
190 6/8	28 2/8	28 2/8	22 7/8	5 2/8	5	6	6	Carbon Co., WY	Archie P. Kirsch	Archie P. Kirsch	2002	892
190 5/8	26 2/8	27 2/8	25	5 7/8	5 7/8	7	7	Archuleta Co., CO	Lansing Kothmann	Lansing Kothmann	1958	905
190 5/8	26	25 3/8	21 4/8	5	5 1/8	7	7	Rock Creek, BC	Doug Killback	Herb Killback	1963	905
190 5/8	24 3/8	26 4/8	23 3/8	5 1/8	5 3/8	5	5	Nez Perce Co., ID	Richard A. Galles	Richard Galles	PR 1964	905
190 5/8	25 4/8	27	25 4/8	5 7/8	5 2/8	8	8	Elmore Co., ID	Robert Bentley	Robert Bentley	1970	905
190 5/8	24 6/8	23 6/8	22 4/8	6 2/8	5 6/8	6	6	Douglas Co., CO	Harold A. Weippert	Harold A. Weippert	1990	905
190 5/8	23 4/8	23 4/8	24	5	4 6/8	8	5	Boise Co., ID	Donald I. Mace	Donald I. Mace	1994	905
190 5/8	25 4/8	25 4/8	23 7/8	4 7/8	4 6/8	5	5	Twin Falls Co., ID	William L. McCall, Sr.	William L. McCall, Sr.	1994	905
190 5/8	25 6/8	26 1/8	22 5/8	5	5	6	6	Las Animas Co., CO	Mark W. Streissguth	Mark W. Streissguth	1997	905
190 5/8	27 3/8	26 4/8	27	4 6/8	4 6/8	5	4	Coconino Co., AZ	Stephen M. Milano	Stephen M. Milano	2000	905
190 5/8	22 7/8	23 3/8	22 7/8	4 7/8	5	7	5	Flathead Co., MT	Richard D. Clark	Richard D. Clark	2000	905
190 4/8	24	25 4/8	21 6/8	4 7/8	5 1/8	5	5	Arapahoe Co., CO	Michael D. Swanson	Ted Swanson	PR 1960	915
190 4/8	26	25 1/8	29 4/8	5 2/8	5 2/8	5	5	Garfield Co., CO	Dennis J. DaSilva	Donald M. Alburtus	1963	915
190 4/8	28 5/8	26	27	5 1/8	5 2/8	6	6	Okanogan Co., WA	John A. Propp	John A. Propp	1973	915
190 4/8	26 6/8	26 6/8	26 4/8	5 1/8	5 1/8	5	5	Garfield Co., CO	William D. Tate	William D. Tate	1978	915
190 4/8	25 1/8	25 4/8	21 7/8	5	5	5	5	Archuleta Co., CO	James M. Russell III	James M. Russell III	1985	915
190 4/8	23 1/8	23 7/8	25 7/8	4 7/8	4 6/8	6	6	Washoe Co., NV	Susan M. Ambrose	Susan M. Ambrose	1998	915
190 4/8	25 6/8	25 5/8	27 4/8	5 2/8	5 2/8	7	7	Colfax Co., NM	Campbell A. Griffin, Jr.	Campbell A. Griffin, Jr.	1999	915
190 4/8	25 4/8	25 6/8	31 3/8	4 6/8	4 6/8	6	6	Lincoln Co., WY	Gerald R. Tadina	Gerald R. Tadina	2000	915
190 3/8	25 6/8	25 6/8	25 6/8	4 6/8	4 6/8	6	6	Garfield Co., CO	Bert Jones	Bert Jones	1951	923
190 3/8	24 7/8	25 3/8	26	4 4/8	4 4/8	5	5	Mesa Co., CO	Robert W. Hill	Robert W. Hill	1963	923

Odocoileus hemionus hemionus and certain related subspecies

Score	Length of Main Beam R	L	Inside Spread	Circumference at Smallest Place Between Burr and First Point R	L	Number of Points R	L	Locality	Hunter	Owner	Date Killed	Rank
190 3/8	26	27 5/8	20 1/8	4 5/8	4 5/8	5	5	Lemhi Co., ID	Mac A. Hughes	Brad Sweeney	1978	923
190 3/8	25 1/8	26 3/8	26 3/8	5 4/8	5 5/8	7	6	Franklin Co., ID	Samuel L. Smith	Samuel L. Smith	1981	923
190 3/8	25 4/8	25 1/8	21 5/8	4 4/8	4 6/8	5	8	Lincoln Co., WY	Jerry A. McAllister	Jerry A. McAllister	1990	923
190 3/8	25 4/8	26 5/8	24 5/8	5	5 1/8	6	5	Yale, BC	Lewis B. Butcher	Lewis B. Butcher	1994	923
190 3/8	25 5/8	25 2/8	26 1/8	4 6/8	4 5/8	5	5	Deschutes Co., OR	Ronald J. Robinson, Jr.	Ronald J. Robinson, Jr.	1995	923
190 3/8	27 6/8	27 1/8	27 7/8	5 2/8	5 2/8	8	6	Delta Co., CO	Joe Alexander	Joe Alexander	1996	923
190 3/8	26 3/8	27 4/8	22 7/8	4 5/8	4 6/8	5	5	Kane Co., UT	Craig I. Haskell	Craig I. Haskell	1997	923
190 3/8	26 1/8	23	26 6/8	5	5 1/8	5	5	Coconino Co., AZ	Seth A. Brunsvold	Seth A. Brunsvold	1998	923
190 3/8	24 6/8	26 3/8	25 7/8	4 5/8	4 6/8	5	5	Rio Arriba Co., NM	Picked Up	Jicarilla Game & Fish	2002	923
190 2/8	21 3/8	23 3/8	21 7/8	4 3/8	4 6/8	6	5	Boise Co., ID	Rickey D. Addison	Rickey D. Addison	1984	934
190 2/8	25 2/8	25 1/8	23	5	4 7/8	5	5	Rich Co., UT	Troy Howard	Troy Howard	1992	934
190 2/8	24 4/8	23 6/8	21	4 6/8	4 5/8	5	7	Sounding Lake, AB	Brian J. Rehman	Brian J. Rehman	1992	934
190 2/8	22 6/8	23 2/8	24 3/8	4 6/8	4 6/8	5	5	Butte Co., ID	Keith G. Palmer	Keith G. Palmer	1995	934
190 2/8	22 4/8	23 5/8	20 4/8	4 5/8	4 5/8	5	5	Humboldt Co., NV	Daniel A. Hinz	Daniel A. Hinz	1997	934
190 2/8	27 6/8	26 7/8	21 6/8	5 4/8	5 1/8	7	6	Humboldt Co., NV	Kevin M. Budney	Kevin M. Budney	1999	934
190 2/8	24 4/8	25	19 2/8	4 7/8	4 7/8	5	6	Lincoln Co., WY	Picked Up	Marvin Fralich	2000	934
190 2/8	27 4/8	28 5/8	26	4 4/8	4 5/8	4	5	Malheur Co., OR	Alan E. Hebert	Alan E. Hebert	2000	934
190 2/8	27 1/8	26 5/8	29 6/8	5 3/8	5 4/8	5	6	French Creek, SK	Rod Roberts	Rod Roberts	2001	934
190 2/8	25 3/8	24 2/8	22 6/8	4 7/8	4 7/8	5	5	Rio Arriba Co., NM	Allan R. Cypert	Allan R. Cypert	2002	934
190 1/8	26 4/8	26 7/8	25 2/8	5	5 1/8	5	6	Rio Arriba Co., NM	Vernon R. Chapman	Vernon R. Chapman	1985	944
190 1/8	25 6/8	23 6/8	21 3/8	4 6/8	4 5/8	5	5	Lincoln Co., MT	Alfred A. Abrahamson	Alfred A. Abrahamson	1991	944
190 1/8	27 1/8	26 2/8	28 5/8	5	5 1/8	5	5	Unknown	Unknown	Timothy C. Sweeney	PR 1992	944
190 1/8	28	27 3/8	24 7/8	5 4/8	5 4/8	8	8	Archuleta Co., CO	John P. Parsons	John P. Parsons	1998	944
190 1/8	24 6/8	25 1/8	23 5/8	4 6/8	4 6/8	5	5	Rio Arriba Co., NM	Gary Rasche	Gary Rasche	1998	944
190 1/8	23 2/8	23 5/8	24 2/8	6 1/8	5 7/8	5	5	Lake Co., OR	Barbara K. Shaw	Barbara K. Shaw	1998	944
190 1/8	24 6/8	25	24 3/8	4 5/8	4 5/8	6	8	Custer Co., ID	Unknown	Aly M. Bruner	PR 1999	944
190 1/8	24 4/8	23 7/8	25 7/8	4 4/8	4 4/8	5	6	Lincoln Co., NV	Dan H. Gildner	Dan H. Gildner	1999	944
190 1/8	23 3/8	23 4/8	22 5/8	5 1/8	5	5	5	Lincoln Co., WY	Kenneth E. Brown	Kenneth E. Brown	2001	944
190 1/8	27 2/8	27 4/8	22	5 6/8	5 4/8	7	6	Ten Mile Lake, BC	Denis Hocevar	Denis Hocevar	2001	944
190	24	24 3/8	23 2/8	4 1/8	4 3/8	5	5	Stillwater Co., MT	Saschia Herman	S. Davies & G. Davies IV	PR 1953	954
190	27 2/8	26 3/8	21 6/8	4 7/8	4 7/8	7	7	Missoula Co., MT	James A. Schwartz	James A. Schwartz	1987	954
190	27 2/8	27 5/8	27 4/8	4 6/8	4 7/8	7	7	Carbon Co., WY	Stephen M. Murnan	Stephen M. Murnan	1990	954
190	24 1/8	24 2/8	19 5/8	5 2/8	5 1/8	5	6	Rich Co., UT	Ernie Davis	Ernie Davis	1992	954
190	24 6/8	27 2/8	25 4/8	5 1/8	5 1/8	6	5	Baker Co., OR	Mike Raney	Mike Raney	1996	954
190	26 6/8	26 6/8	25	4 5/8	4 6/8	6	6	Unknown	Unknown	Breck Johnson	PR 1997	954
190	24 2/8	25 7/8	26 5/8	5 4/8	5 2/8	5	6	Lassen Co., CA	Terry Schmitt	Terry M. Schmitt	1998	954

190	26 4/8	25 5/8	20 6/8	5 2/8	5 1/8	5	6	Rio Arriba Co., NM	Larry L. Panzy	Picked Up	1999	954
190	24	24 2/8	21 2/8	4 7/8	5	5	5	Fir Mt., SK	Randy J. Fehr	Randy J. Fehr	2000	954
218 4/8*	27 5/8	27 5/8	29 5/8	5 5/8	5 5/8	6	5	S. Saskatchewan River, SK	Larry Svenson	Lars Svenson	PR 1950	
205 7/8*	25 3/8	25 3/8	25 4/8	6 1/8	5 3/8	5	5	Luck Lake, SK	Douglas Erickson	Douglas Erickson	2001	
205 *	26	25 7/8	26 3/8	5 6/8	5 4/8	5	5	Sonora, MX	Russell G. Brice	Russell G. Brice	2003	
203 4/8*	27 3/8	26 7/8	21 3/8	5 1/8	5	8	7	Montezuma Co., CO	Olen J. Hicks	Olen J. Hicks	1999	

* Final score is subject to revision by additional verifying measurements.

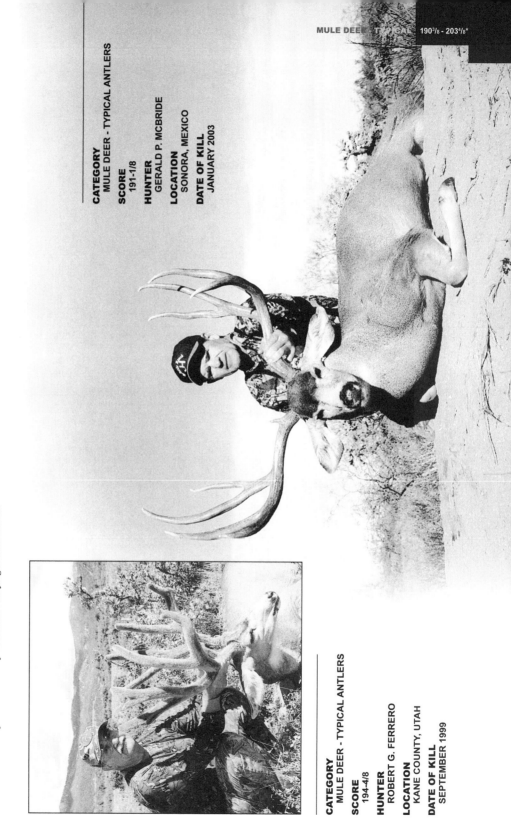

CATEGORY
MULE DEER - TYPICAL ANTLERS

SCORE
191-1/8

HUNTER
GERALD P. MCBRIDE

LOCATION
SONORA, MEXICO

DATE OF KILL
JANUARY 2003

CATEGORY
MULE DEER - TYPICAL ANTLERS

SCORE
194-4/8

HUNTER
ROBERT G. FERRERO

LOCATION
KANE COUNTY, UTAH

DATE OF KILL
SEPTEMBER 1999

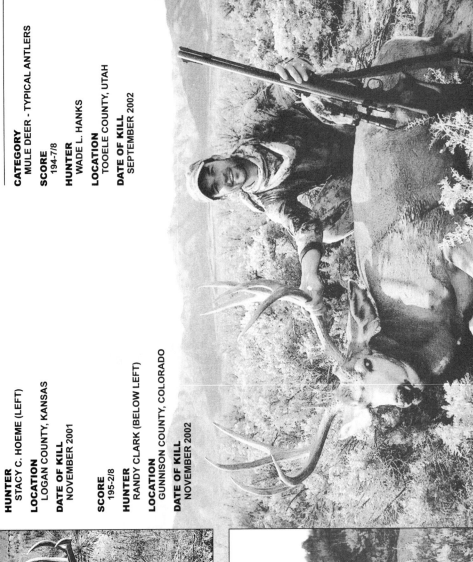

CATEGORY
MULE DEER - TYPICAL ANTLERS

SCORE
194-7/8

HUNTER
WADE L. HANKS

LOCATION
TOOELE COUNTY, UTAH

DATE OF KILL
SEPTEMBER 2002

CATEGORY
MULE DEER - TYPICAL ANTLERS

SCORE
199-4/8

HUNTER
STACY C. HOEME (LEFT)

LOCATION
LOGAN COUNTY, KANSAS

DATE OF KILL
NOVEMBER 2001

SCORE
195-2/8

HUNTER
RANDY CLARK (BELOW LEFT)

LOCATION
GUNNISON COUNTY, COLORADO

DATE OF KILL
NOVEMBER 2002

CATEGORY
MULE DEER - TYPICAL ANTLERS

SCORE
192-3/8

HUNTER
EUDANE VICENTI

LOCATION
RIO ARRIBA COUNTY,
NEW MEXICO

DATE OF KILL
OCTOBER 2002

CATEGORY
MULE DEER - TYPICAL ANTLERS

SCORE
190-5/8

HUNTER
RICHARD D. CLARK

LOCATION
FLATHEAD COUNTY, MONTANA

DATE OF KILL
NOVEMBER 2000

CATEGORY
MULE DEER -
TYPICAL ANTLERS

SCORE
192-5/8

HUNTER
JAMES M. SNOWDEN

LOCATION
LINCOLN COUNTY,
WYOMING

DATE OF KILL
SEPTEMBER 2000

MULE DEER - NON-TYPICAL ANTLERS
WORLD'S RECORD

Perhaps one of the most outstanding trophies ever recorded is the World's Record non-typical mule deer. This deer was taken in 1926 near Chip Lake, Alberta, by Ed Broder who gave a colorful account of his hunt.

"On November 25, 1926, I and two friends, driving an old 1914 Model T Ford, left Edmonton for Chip Lake, Alberta, a distance of approximately 100 miles. The weather was 20°F with a foot of soft snow. At a sawmill camp, near Chip Lake, we made arrangements to hire a team of horses and a sleigh to haul our gear and equipment. Finding a good cabin near the lake, we used this instead of putting up our tent.

"It was about 1 p.m. when I left camp and set out through some heavy timber and soon came across a large deer track. Following the deer tracks for a half mile, I found where he had bedded down. Knowing the deer could not be too far away, I tracked him off the timber ridge, through a jackpine swamp. There I found that two moose had crossed the deer's tracks. I had to make a decision as to whether to go after the moose or the deer. Through past experiences I knew moose would travel farther and faster than deer, and with only a short time before dark, I decided to carry on with the deer. Following these tracks through the swamp I came up onto a higher land with a clearing not too far off. In this clearing I spotted the deer; he was approximately, 200 yards away, standing and feeding with his back to me. So immediately I had to make a guess as to when and how to shoot. The distance was right but his position was wrong. I knew I had to select a rear shot. The shot would have to be placed high in the spine, so I pulled up my .32 Winchester Special to a firing position, waited for his head to rise so as to back up a high spine shot. I fired and the animal dropped; I had broken its spine. 'What a rack that one's got,' was the first thing I thought."

TROPHY INFO

RANK
World's Record

SCORE
355 2/8

LOCATION
Chip Lake, AB

HUNTER
Ed Broder

OWNER
Don Schaufler

DATE KILLED
1926

At 355-2/8, the final score replaced the former World's Record by over half as many points, but it was not officially scored until 1960. However, the rack was impressive enough that a drawing of it appeared in the 1939 edition of ***North American Big Game***. Broder acknowledged his record with the determined words of a true sportsman.

"I started hunting in the year 1909 and have never missed a season since; I am now 72 and in fair health. Who can tell, I may yet beat my old 1926 record!" ■

Records of
North American
Big Game

250 Station Drive
Missoula, MT 59801
(406) 542-1888

MULE DEER
NON-TYPICAL ANTLERS
WORLD'S RECORD SCORE CHART

BOONE AND CROCKETT CLUB®

OFFICIAL SCORING SYSTEM FOR NORTH AMERICAN BIG GAME TROPHIES

NON-TYPICAL MULE DEER

MINIMUM SCORES

	AWARDS	ALL-TIME
	215	230

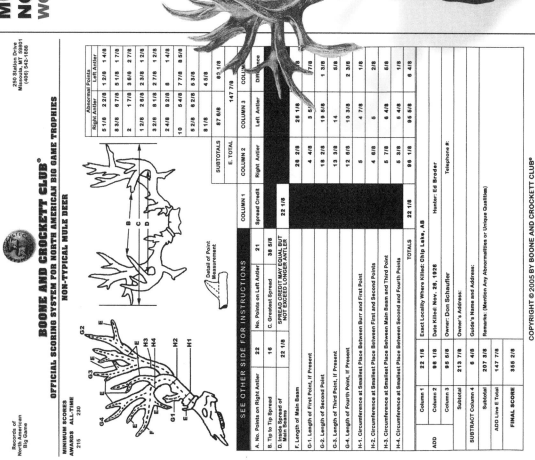

Detail of Point Measurement

Abnormal Points

Right Antler		Left Antler	
5 1/8	2 2/8	1 2/8	1 4/8
8 3/8	6 7/8	5 1/8	1 7/8
2	1 7/8	3 6/8	2 7/8
1 2/8	2 6/8	2 3/8	1 2/8
3 2/8	8 1/8	2 7/8	1 2/8
2 4/8	8 2/8	8	1 4/8
10	5 4/8	7 7/8	8 5/8
5 2/8	6 2/8	5 3/8	
8 1/8		4 5/8	

SUBTOTALS	87 6/8	80 1/8
E. TOTAL		**147 7/8**

SEE OTHER SIDE FOR INSTRUCTIONS	COLUMN 1	COLUMN 2	COLUMN 3	
		Right Antler	Left Antler	Difference
A. No. Points on Right Antler 22	No. Points on Left Antler 21	Spread Credit			
B. Tip to Tip Spread 16	C. Greatest Spread 38 5/8				
D. Inside Spread of Main Beams 22 1/8	SPREAD CREDIT MAY EQUAL BUT NOT EXCEED LONGER ANTLER	22 1/8			
F. Length of Main Beam			26 2/8	26 1/8	8
G-1. Length of First Point, If Present			4 4/8	3 5/8	7/8
G-2. Length of Second Point			18 2/8	19 5/8	1 3/8
G-3. Length of Third Point, If Present			13 3/8	14	5/8
G-4. Length of Fourth Point, If Present			12 5/8	10 3/8	2 3/8
H-1. Circumference at Smallest Place Between Burr and First Point			5	4 7/8	1/8
H-2. Circumference at Smallest Place Between First and Second Points			4 6/8	5	2/8
H-3. Circumference at Smallest Place Between Main Beam and Third Point			5 7/8	6 4/8	6/8
H-4. Circumference at Smallest Place Between Second and Fourth Points			5 3/8	6 4/8	1/8
TOTALS		22 1/8	96 1/8	95 5/8	6 4/8

	Column 1	22 1/8
ADD	Column 2	96 1/8
	Column 3	95 5/8
	Subtotal	213 7/8
SUBTRACT Column 4		6 4/8
	Subtotal	207 3/8
	ADD Line E Total	147 7/8
	FINAL SCORE	**355 2/8**

Exact Locality Where Killed: Chip Lake, AB

Date Killed: Nov. 26, 1926   Hunter: Ed Broder

Owner: Don Schauffer   Telephone #:

Owner's Address:

Guide's Name and Address:

Remarks: (Mention Any Abnormalities or Unique Qualities)

COPYRIGHT © 2005 BY BOONE AND CROCKETT CLUB®

TOP 10 MULE DEER – NON-TYPICAL

KODAK 5062 PX

NUMBER 2 — 339-2/8 POINTS
UNKNOWN — PRIOR TO 1890

NUMBER 5 — 324-1/8 POINTS
WILLIAM L. MURPHY — 1943

NUMBER 3 — 330-1/8 POINTS
ALTON HUNSAKER — 1943

NORTH AMERICAN BIG GAME TROPHIES
Address Correspondence to:
Grancel Fitz, Secretary
Vador City Place, NYC 17, N.Y.

NUMBER 1 — 355-2/8 POINTS
ED BRODER — 1926

NUMBER 4 — 325-6/8 POINTS
CLIFTON FAURIA — 1955

TEMPLE CITY NIMROD BAGS-NEAR-RECORD BUCK

TONOPAH, Nev. (P) Clifton Fauria of Temple City,
Cal. bagged one of the largest bucks ever reported killed
during a Nye county deer season.

Score: 195-45 = 240

328

NUMBER 7 — 320-4/8 POINT
GROVER BROWNING — 1960

NUMBER 10 — 307-6/8 POINTS
UNKNOWN — 1935

NUMBER 6 — 321-1/8 POINTS
ALBERT C. PETERSON — 1925

NUMBER 8 — 319-4/8 POINTS
HAROLD R. LAIRD — 1972

NUMBER 9 — 311-6/8 POINTS
VERNOR WILSON — 1941

329

MULE DEER - NON-TYPICAL ANTLERS

Odocoileus hemionus hemionus and certain related subspecies

MINIMUM SCORE 230

Score	Length of Main Beam R	L	Inside Spread	Circumference at Smallest Place Between Burr and First Point R	L	Number of Points R	L	Locality	Hunter	Owner	Date Killed	Rank
355 2/8	26 2/8	26 1/8	22 1/8	5	4 7/8	22	21	Chip Lake, AB	Ed Broder	Don Schaufler	1926	1
339 4/8	20 6/8	20 4/8	14 7/8	6 4/8	6 2/8	24	23	Okanagan, BC	Unknown	D.J. Hollinger & B. Howard	PR 1890	2
330 1/8	23 2/8	22	9 4/8	8 2/8	8 3/8	21	28	Box Elder Co., UT	Alton Hunsaker	D.J. Hollinger & B. Howard	1943	3
325 6/8	24 5/8	23 5/8	21 6/8	4 6/8	4 7/8	21	21	Nye Co., NV	Clifton Fauria	Cabela's, Inc.	1955	4
324 1/8	25 5/8	25 1/8	32 7/8	6 5/8	6 5/8	16	17	North Kaibab, AZ	William L. Murphy	Michael R. Karam	1943	5
321 1/8	28 1/8	25 4/8	26 5/8	6 7/8	6 7/8	17	25	Umatilla Co., OR	Albert C. Peterson	Cabela's, Inc.	1925	6
320 4/8	23 5/8	24 7/8	25	6	6 2/8	17	20	Madison Co., ID	Grover Browning	D.J. Hollinger & B. Howard	1960	7
319 4/8	24 2/8	24	23 5/8	7 7/8	7 1/8	27	23	Mariposa Co., CA	Harold R. Laird	Cabela's, Inc.	1972	8
311 6/8	26 7/8	24 7/8	24 1/8	6 1/8	6 5/8	22	21	Kaibab, AZ	Vernor Wilson	Cabela's, Inc.	1941	9
307 6/8	23 7/8	22 1/8	21 5/8	4 4/8	4 5/8	23	16	Idaho	Unknown	D.J. Hollinger & B. Howard	1935	10
306 7/8	30 3/8	30 5/8	24 3/8	5 2/8	5 4/8	16	18	Montezuma Co., CO	Lloyd Pyle	Cabela's, Inc.	1972	11
306 2/8	28 6/8	27 4/8	22 6/8	5 6/8	5 4/8	14	23	Norwood, CO	Steve H. Herndon	V.D. & D.F. Holleman	1954	12
306 2/8	29	28 5/8	28 7/8	5 4/8	5 5/8	18	18	Chama, NM	Joseph A. Garcia	Cabela's, Inc.	1963	12
305 6/8	23 7/8	24 1/8	21 3/8	6 1/8	6 4/8	17	17	Shasta Co., CA	Artie McGram	D.J. Hollinger & B. Howard	1987	14
305 3/8	25 1/8	26 4/8	22 2/8	4 6/8	4 5/8	13	17	Boise Co., ID	Babe Hansen	Cabela's, Inc.	1928	15
304 5/8	26 6/8	28 1/8	29 1/8	6 2/8	5 2/8	19	17	Elk Creek, CO	Andrew Daum	B&C National Collection	1886	16
303 6/8	26 4/8	26 7/8	24 3/8	5 2/8	5	13	11	Eagle Co., CO	James Austill	Cabela's, Inc.	1962	17
302 4/8	25 1/8	26 2/8	25 2/8	5 7/8	6 3/8	18	14	Paonia, CO	Louis H. Huntington, Jr.	Louis H. Huntington, Jr.	1965	18
302	26 7/8	26 2/8	21 5/8	6 3/8	6 5/8	21	15	Iron Co., UT	Darwin Hulett	Cabela's, Inc.	1950	19
300 7/8	24	22 6/8	29 4/8	5 5/8	5 3/8	17	16	Bonneville Co., ID	Brett J. Sauer	Cabela's, Inc.	1985	20
300	27	25 6/8	23 1/8	5 3/8	5 3/8	14	12	Mesa Co., CO	George Blackmon, Jr.	Cabela's, Inc.	1961	21
299 1/8	27 7/8	28 3/8	24 4/8	5 6/8	5 4/8	13	16	Eureka Co., NV	Dan Avery, Jr.	Cabela's, Inc.	1968	22
299	27 3/8	27 2/8	27 4/8	5 1/8	5 1/8	16	22	Lake Co., OR	Jack Aldredge	Cabela's, Inc.	1948	23
298 5/8	26 1/8	26	24 6/8	5 5/8	6	14	13	California	Unknown	D.J. Hollinger & B. Howard	1940	24
297 7/8	29 1/8	27 5/8	35 4/8	5 4/8	5 3/8	20	13	Malheur Co., OR	Bradley Barclay	Bradley Barclay	1971	25
297 5/8	26 1/8	26 3/8	26 5/8	6 4/8	6 6/8	17	15	Larimer Co., CO	Jack Autrey	Linda Guy	1941	26
296 2/8	30 1/8	30 2/8	26 5/8	5 7/8	5 7/8	12	14	Mesa Co., CO	Unknown	Cabela's, Inc.	PR 1981	27
294 4/8	25 2/8	24 2/8	21 6/8	6 1/8	5 5/8	15	11	Elmore Co., ID	Robert H. Arledge	Robert H. Arledge	1997	28
294 1/8	27 1/8	26 1/8	24 3/8	5 7/8	5 6/8	14	16	Coconino Co., AZ	Philip K. Coffeen	William A. Coffeen	1939	29
293 7/8	26 4/8	24 6/8	27 6/8	5 6/8	5 4/8	16	16	Wyoming	J.B. Marvin, Jr.	Unknown	PR 1924	30
293 6/8	26 7/8	26 3/8	27 3/8	5 3/8	5 5/8	12	17	Garfield Co., UT	Lloyd Barton	Lloyd Barton	1993	31
291 6/8	21 5/8	22 7/8	17 5/8	8 7/8	5 3/8	66	5	Linn Co., OR	Unknown	D.J. Hollinger & B. Howard	1992	32
288 7/8	26 3/8	26 5/8	28 5/8	4 6/8	4 2/8	16	12	Sweetwater Co., WY	Walter Boam	D.J. Hollinger & B. Howard	PR 1940	33
288 6/8	30 4/8	31 6/8	26 5/8	6 5/8	6 3/8	12	10	Chama, NM	Frank B. Maestas	Aly M. Bruner	1962	34
288 2/8	25	25 7/8	26	6	6	16	13	Blaine Co., ID	Robby Miller	Cabela's, Inc.	1969	35
287 6/8	21 1/8	19 7/8	18	6	6 1/8	14	24	Blaine Co., ID	Tim Weary	D.J. Hollinger & B. Howard	1942	36

Score	Inside Spread	R. Main Beam	L. Main Beam	R. Circ.	L. Circ.	R. Pts.	L. Pts.	Locality	Hunter	Owner	Date	Rank
287 5/8	28 6/8	29	29 5/8	4 7/8	4 7/8	15	16	Montezuma Co., CO	Travis Shippy	Cabela's, Inc.	1985	37
286 3/8	29 6/8	29 4/8	35 4/8	5 1/8	5 1/8	13	13	Eagle Co., CO	Albert L. Mulnix	Cabela's, Inc.	1928	38
286 1/8	22 7/8	21 2/8	20 6/8	4 4/8	4 5/8	14	21	Unknown	Walt Mednick	Ike Foster	PR 1940	39
286 1/8	26 6/8	27	26 4/8	5 3/8	5 2/8	12	20	Utah Co., UT	Joe Allen	Cabela's, Inc.	PR 1950	39
286 1/8	25	24 4/8	26 7/8	5	5	13	13	Elko Co., NV	Joseph W. Dooley	Raymond R. Cross	1954	39
285 7/8	27 6/8	27 1/8	26	6	6	19	16	Adams Co., ID	Picked Up	Raymond R. Cross	1967	42
284 3/8	24 3/8	27 4/8	24 1/8	5 1/8	5 2/8	15	15	Duchesne Co., UT	Clyde Lambert	Lucy L. Back	1935	43
284	26 3/8	25 7/8	28 3/8	5 2/8	5 4/8	15	15	Provo River, UT	Melvin T. Ashton	Cabela's, Inc.	1961	44
283 4/8	27 5/8	26 4/8	22 2/8	5	5	14	14	Lewis Co., WA	Quinten R. Grow	Desiree Gillingham	1943	45
283 1/8	28 3/8	28 5/8	24 3/8	5	5	14	13	Bonneville Co., ID	Picked Up	D.J. Hollinger & B. Howard	1990	46
283	28	28	29 4/8	8	7 7/8	14	16	Rose Creek, UT	Verl N. Creager	Verl N. Creager	1960	47
282 6/8	29 2/8	22 5/8	25 4/8	5 4/8	5 1/8	18	15	Cabri, SK	Robert Comba	Cabela's, Inc.	1962	48
282 3/8	21 3/8	22 2/8	22 1/8	4 6/8	5 1/8	17	13	North Kaibab, AZ	Robert C. Rantz	Robert C. Rantz	1969	49
282 2/8	25 6/8	25 3/8	24	7	6 2/8	14	13	Saskatchewan	William Olsen	Herman Cox	1947	50
281 6/8	27 4/8	27 2/8	22	5 3/8	5 3/8	13	11	Black Hills, SD	Unknown	Cabela's, Inc.	1944	51
281 6/8	27 6/8	28 6/8	21 2/8	5 6/8	5 6/8	19	22	Kaibab Natl. For., AZ	Unknown	Cabela's, Inc.	PR 1950	51
281 3/8	28 7/8	28 2/8	23 4/8	6	6	15	14	Idaho	Ronald S. Holbrook	Ronald S. Holbrook	PR 1950	53
280 4/8	26 6/8	27	26 4/8	6	6	10	15	Gem Co., ID	Unknown	Cabela's, Inc.	1982	54
280 2/8	24 4/8	25 7/8	24 2/8	5 1/8	5 4/8	11	16	Otthon, SK	Unknown	Marlen D. Murphy	1940	55
280 2/8	31 2/8	29	29 4/8	4 6/8	4 6/8	13	12	Coconino Co., AZ	Mr. Orr	L. Dwight Israelsen	1941	55
280 2/8	25 6/8	24 6/8	27 5/8	4 4/8	4 4/8	16	14	Cache Co., UT	Unknown	D.J. Hollinger & B. Howard	1969	55
279 6/8	24 2/8	24 6/8	21 6/8	6 4/8	6 4/8	18	10	Franklin Co., ID	M. Powell & D. Auld, Jr.	Milroy Powell	PR 1950	59
279 5/8	22 5/8	21 7/8	17 3/8	6 3/8	6 3/8	18	17	Kaibab Natl. For., AZ	Ed Martin	Ed Martin	1966	59
278 7/8	26	24 4/8	30 4/8	4 7/8	5 1/8	8	11	Adams Co., ID	Keith Thaute	Keith Thaute	1961	60
278 7/8	30	26 7/8	18	6 2/8	6 3/8	12	12	Montrose Co., CO	Dale L. Becker	Dale L. Becker	1978	61
278 3/8	28	27 2/8	24 6/8	5 2/8	5 2/8	11	13	Eagle Co., CO	Jack White	Cabela's, Inc.	1957	61
277 6/8	30	28 1/8	26	6 1/8	6 1/8	11	12	Bonneville Co., ID	James Duran	Robert J. Seeds	1959	63
277 2/8	25 1/8	23 6/8	26 4/8	5 2/8	5 2/8	11	10	Rio Arriba Co., NM	Jim Kilfoil	Gilbert Francis	1938	64
277 1/8	24 6/8	25 2/8	25 6/8	5 2/8	5 2/8	12	10	Morgan Co., UT	Native American	Charles McAden	1930	65
277 1/8	24 6/8	26 1/8	25 3/8	5 6/8	5 6/8	13	13	Colorado	Alice C. O'Brien	Cabela's, Inc.	1949	66
276 4/8	25	26 5/8	24 3/8	4 7/8	4 7/8	11	12	Bly, OR	Larry Prehm	Spanky Greenville	1967	66
275 7/8	25 4/8	29 2/8	23	5 5/8	5 6/8	16	13	Glenwood Springs, CO	Peter Zemljak, Sr.	Peter Zemljak	1962	68
275 6/8	26 3/8	25 4/8	34 3/8	5 2/8	5	20	16	Highland Mts., MT	Jim Hewitt	Jim Hewitt	1932	69
275 2/8	24 5/8	26 3/8	19 4/8	4 7/8	4 7/8	11	16	Dahlton, SK	K. Michael Weisbrod	K. Michael Weisbrod	1992	70
275 2/8	26 7/8	24 5/8	25 6/8	5 6/8	5 6/8	16	13	Red Deer River, SK	Unknown	Cabela's, Inc.	PR 1955	70
275 1/8	22 4/8	28 2/8	26 7/8	6	6	14	15	Rio Arriba Co., NM	Peter Zemljak	Peter Zemljak	1960	72
274 7/8	26 2/8	23 6/8	20 5/8	6 4/8	6 4/8	23	11	Ruby Mts., MT	Kenneth W. Plank	Cabela's, Inc.	1987	73
274 6/8	25 6/8	23 7/8	27	5 2/8	5 2/8	11	15	Morgan Co., CO	Robert G. Wilson	Robert G. Wilson	1989	74
274 6/8	23 6/8	27 3/8	23 6/8	5 3/8	5 3/8	14	13	Delta Co., CO	Picked Up	Carl D. Rey	1952	74
274 5/8	22 4/8	24 5/8	27 5/8	5 2/8	5 2/8	11	18	Unknown	Picked Up	Cabela's, Inc.	PR 2003	76
274 3/8	26	31 6/8	22 4/8	5 6/8	5 6/8	12	13	Washington	Unknown	Butler Ranch	1988	76
274 2/8	29 2/8	28 7/8	26	6 1/8	6	13	12	Pueblo Co., CO	Unknown	Buckhorn Mus. & Saloon, Ltd.	PR 1960	78
274 2/8	25	22 3/8	23 2/8	5 3/8	6	13	13	Sublett, ID	Mrs. Jack Keen	Mr. & Mrs. Jack Keen	1957	79
274 2/8	25 7/8	24 4/8	24 4/8	6 1/8	6	14	13	Fremont Co., ID	David L. Maurer	David L. Maurer	1979	80
274 2/8	25 3/8	25 7/8	25 3/8	6	6	15	12	Shackleton, SK	Glen A. Miller	Glen A. Miller	2003	80
274 1/8	28	28 3/8	23	5 4/8	5 4/8	10	4	Beaver Co., UT	Murray Bohn	Parowan Rod & Gun Club	1920	83
274 1/8	23 6/8	21 7/8	22 2/8	4 7/8	4 7/8	11	11	North Fork, ID	James D. Edwards	ID Dept. Fish & Game	1967	83

MULE DEER - NON-TYPICAL ANTLERS

Odocoileus hemionus hemionus and certain related subspecies

Score	Length of Main Beam R	L	Inside Spread	Circumference at Smallest Place Between Burr and First Point R	L	Number of Points R	L	Locality	Hunter	Owner	Date Killed	Rank
273 7/8	27 7/8	29 2/8	26 6/8	6 1/8	6	8	12	Kane Co., UT	Waldon Ballard	Alice Ballard	1950	85
273 6/8	23 2/8	24 2/8	23 3/8	5 4/8	5 6/8	15	15	Hayden, CO	Roy I. Roney	CO Div. of Wildl.	1930	86
273 6/8	26	26 4/8	26 1/8	5	5	15	18	Klamath Co., OR	J.J. McDaniels	J.J. McDaniels	1952	86
273 5/8	28 3/8	28 2/8	23 7/8	6	6 1/8	15	16	Morgan Co., UT	Harold B. Rollins	Harold B. Rollins	1944	88
273 4/8	25 4/8	24 2/8	22 2/8	5 7/8	5 2/8	20	19	Deschutes Co., OR	Picked Up	OR Dept. of Fish & Wildlife	1956	89
273 2/8	25 5/8	26 2/8	27 4/8	5 3/8	5 4/8	14	15	Richland Co., MT	Joe Berzel	Matthew Berzel	1955	90
273	21 7/8	20 5/8	24	6 6/8	7 4/8	23	18	Idaho	Unknown	Cabela's, Inc.	PR 1943	91
273	22 1/8	24	24	5 7/8	5 6/8	10	13	Madison Co., MT	Ray Ypma	Ray Ypma	1946	91
273	24 7/8	22 7/8	35 2/8	5 1/8	5	15	16	Cassia Co., ID	Donald Porter	Steven B. Curtis	1964	91
272 7/8	24 1/8	26 2/8	27 1/8	5 4/8	5 5/8	15	16	Caribou Co., ID	Picked Up	Cabela's, Inc.	1948	94
272 5/8	29	28	21 5/8	5 3/8	5 2/8	16	14	Glenwood Springs, CO	William L. Kurtz	William L. Kurtz	1967	95
272 4/8	28 3/8	27 2/8	21 2/8	6 3/8	6 2/8	19	17	Eagle Co., CO	Eddie Stephenson, Jr.	Eddie Stephenson, Jr.	1978	96
272 3/8	28 4/8	28 2/8	28 4/8	5 1/8	5 5/8	11	12	Albany Co., WY	S.A. Lawson	Acad. Nat. Sci., Phil.	1905	97
271 4/8	26	26 6/8	26 7/8	5 6/8	5 5/8	22	18	Colorado	Unknown	Cabela's, Inc.	PR 1985	98
271 2/8	24 3/8	24 4/8	20	4 6/8	5 1/8	13	14	East Canyon, UT	Joseph H. Greenig	Mrs. Joseph H. Greenig	1947	99
271 2/8	22 7/8	24 2/8	23 6/8	5 3/8	5	16	14	British Columbia	G.L. Popp	Cabela's, Inc.	PR 1960	99
270 7/8	25 6/8	26 7/8	23	5 2/8	5 2/8	12	11	Sanpete Co., UT	Preston Bown	Cabela's, Inc.	1963	101
270 6/8	23 2/8	24 6/8	23 4/8	5 3/8	5 3/8	10	13	Carbon Co., WY	Edward Vigil	Michelle Ferguson	PR 1950	102
270 6/8	26 6/8	26 3/8	20 1/8	5 4/8	5 4/8	13	11	Colorado	Floyd Hill	Cabela's, Inc.	1958	102
270 6/8	28 6/8	28 2/8	27 6/8	5 7/8	5 7/8	15	15	Crook Co., OR	C.F. Cheney	C.F. Cheney	1962	102
270 5/8	23 6/8	24 2/8	21 1/8	4 3/8	4 3/8	10	12	Big Horn Co., MT	R. Turnsback & J.V. Elsen	William Erdmann	1961	105
270 3/8	24	25	27 4/8	5 6/8	6	10	10	Kaibab Natl. For., AZ	Dean Naylor	D.B. Sanford	1948	106
270 3/8	23 7/8	25 4/8	27 5/8	5	4 6/8	11	13	Mesa Co., CO	Todd McKay	Todd McKay	1994	106
270 2/8	29 2/8	32 1/8	28	4 6/8	4 6/8	12	13	North Kaibab, AZ	Thomas M. Knoles, Jr.	Thomas M. Knoles, Jr.	1944	108
269 6/8	22 7/8	24 2/8	26	6 4/8	6 2/8	13	14	Morgan Co., CO	Picked Up	Aly M. Bruner	1987	109
269 4/8	28 3/8	28 7/8	25 7/8	5 5/8	6	14	13	Owyhee Co., ID	Frank Cogdill	Raymond R. Cross	1939	110
269 4/8	27 7/8	26 4/8	20 3/8	5 5/8	5 5/8	13	13	Unknown	Unknown	Ron Hall	PR 1987	110
269	25 4/8	26 5/8	17 4/8	5 4/8	5 4/8	13	14	Weston Co., WY	Lavonne M. Bucey-Bredehoeft	Lavonne M. Bucey-Bredehoeft	1961	112
268 6/8	28 3/8	28 4/8	24 6/8	5 5/8	5 5/8	12	13	Kaibab Natl. For., AZ	Milroy Powell	Milroy Powell	1952	113
268 5/8	24 2/8	22 7/8	27	6	6 3/8	14	15	Grant Co., OR	Lige Davis	Coy Johnston	1941	114
268 5/8	27	25 1/8	25 1/8	5	5 4/8	14	16	Leader, SK	Cocks Brothers	Richard Jensen	1954	114
268 4/8	21 3/8	23 6/8	17 4/8	6 5/8	6 5/8	17	16	Cascade Co., MT	Unknown	Kent Austin	PR 1980	116
268 3/8	25 4/8	27 5/8	23	6 1/8	6	17	11	Delta Co., CO	Shirley Smith	Shirley Smith	1962	117
268 1/8	24 6/8	23 7/8	25 7/8	5 1/8	4 7/8	12	11	Teton Co., ID	Picked Up	Cabela's, Inc.	1986	118
268 1/8	27 4/8	27 7/8	30 3/8	5 2/8	5 5/8	14	14	Elbow, SK	Allan J. Selzler	Cabela's, Inc.	1986	118

Score								Locality	Hunter	Owner	Date	Rank
268 1/8	29 6/8	27 7/8	26 2/8	5 3/8	5 2/8	10	10	Gallatin Co., MT	Michael O. Wold	Michael O. Wold	1992	118
268	28 1/8	31 2/8	26 3/8	5 5/8	5 4/8	14	9	Bonneville Co., ID	Picked Up	Picked Up	1979	121
268	27 6/8	26 7/8	22 5/8	4 7/8	5	17	12	Sherman Co., OR	James G. Petersen	James G. Petersen	1998	121
267 5/8	28 1/8	28 2/8	29 2/8	6	6 2/8	16	12	Wallowa Co., OR	Mark Thompson	Dale Potter	1924	123
267 5/8	26 4/8	25 7/8	26 3/8	4 7/8	4 6/8	13	18	Jicarilla Apache Res., NM	Byrd L. Minter, Jr.	Byrd L. Minter, Jr.	1961	123
267 5/8	23 2/8	23 3/8	23 5/8	4 7/8	4 6/8	18	16	Idaho Co., ID	Alan B. Hermann	Alan B. Hermann	1991	123
267 4/8	24	25 3/8	18 2/8	6 2/8	7 2/8	16	15	Mariposa Co., CA	Ray Douglas	John Douglas	1948	126
267 1/8	23 7/8	25 3/8	24 2/8	5 2/8	5 4/8	15	11	Eagle Co., CO	Josef P. Langegger	Josef P. Langegger	1969	127
266 7/8	26	25 1/8	24 4/8	6 4/8	6 1/8	13	15	Wyoming	J.L. Kemmerer	Am. Mus. Nat. Hist.	1905	128
266 7/8	22 5/8	22 7/8	18 6/8	5 1/8	5 1/8	8	8	Draper, UT	Glenn W. Furrow	Glenn W. Furrow	1962	128
266 6/8	25 5/8	22 7/8	20 6/8	5	5	13	11	Philip, SD	Clifford Ramsey	Clifford Ramsey	1959	130
266 2/8	24 4/8	24 7/8	21	5 3/8	5 4/8	12	18	Park Co., MT	Benton R. Venable	Benton R. Venable	1945	131
266 2/8	25 1/8	26	20 5/8	5 4/8	5 4/8	12	12	Williams Lake, BC	Robert R. Letts	D.J. Hollinger & B. Howard	1984	131
266 2/8	27	28 3/8	24 1/8	6 1/8	5 5/8	15	9	Mohave Co., AZ	Carl A. Luedeman	Carl A. Luedeman	1993	131
266 1/8	22 4/8	22 7/8	16 4/8	5 4/8	5 1/8	16	13	Stevens Co., WA	Joe C. Mally	Steve Mally	1933	134
266	25 3/8	24 2/8	27 7/8	5 6/8	5 6/8	16	20	Grant Co., OR	Harold T. Oathes	Harold T. Oathes	1965	135
266	29 3/8	27	22 7/8	5	5 2/8	11	12	Washington Co., ID	Ken McDaniel	Cabela's, Inc.	1969	135
265 7/8	25 5/8	26 4/8	27 6/8	5 4/8	5 6/8	8	12	Sidney, MT	Buster Dodson	F.P. Murray	1954	137
265 7/8	23 5/8	24 1/8	22 7/8	5 5/8	5 6/8	20	15	Powder River Co., MT	Michael A. Siewert	Michael A. Siewert	1987	137
265 6/8	25 6/8	25 6/8	24 1/8	5 1/8	5 4/8	11	13	Cache Co., UT	Jerry S. Wuthrich	Jerry S. Wuthrich	1966	139
265 5/8	24 7/8	26 7/8	27 2/8	6 7/8	6 5/8	16	14	Chama, NM	Stephanie D. Tartaglia	Stephanie D. Tartaglia	1966	140
265 3/8	26 6/8	27	23 4/8	5 3/8	5 2/8	21	16	Custer Co., ID	Merle Markle	D.J. Hollinger & B. Howard	1949	141
265 3/8	25 6/8	25 1/8	21 5/8	5 3/8	5 3/8	19	14	Tyaughton River, BC	Terry E. Crawford	Terry E. Crawford	1970	141
265 2/8	24 5/8	25 7/8	23 1/8	4 4/8	4 5/8	13	13	Beaver Co., UT	Blaine Blackett	Cabela's, Inc.	1938	143
265 2/8	25 5/8	24 5/8	24 5/8	6 2/8	5 6/8	14	13	Wheeler Co., NE	Leo Dwyer	Cabela's, Inc.	1959	143
265 1/8	25 6/8	24 4/8	18	5 6/8	5 2/8	22	18	Blue Mts., WA	Frank Henriksen	Frank Henriksen	1961	143
265 1/8	25	24 4/8	23	5	5	9	11	Sweetwater Co., WY	Unknown	John Cheese	PR 1940	146
265	26	25 2/8	20 6/8	4 6/8	4 5/8	10	10	Hayes Co., NE	Charles J. Hogeland	Charles J. Hogeland	1994	146
265	27 6/8	27	24 3/8	5	4 6/8	10	13	Fremont Co., ID	Dayle Sanderson	Cabela's, Inc.	1953	148
265	24	24 2/8	19 4/8	4 7/8	5	13	15	Custer Co., ID	John L. Simmons	John L. Simmons	1986	148
264 5/8	26	26 5/8	22 4/8	5 4/8	5 6/8	18	13	Bannock Co., ID	Jarel Neeser	Jarel Neeser	1974	150
264 4/8	28 5/8	26 5/8	29 5/8	4 7/8	5 1/8	16	12	Colorado	Unknown	Cabela's, Inc.	PR 1950	151
264 3/8	26	27 5/8	21 4/8	5 3/8	5 3/8	13	10	Gunnison Co., CO	Gordon E. Blay	Gorden E. Blay	1975	152
264 2/8	24 4/8	26 2/8	21	5 3/8	5 3/8	7	13	Southern Utah, UT	Unknown	Earl Mecham	1932	153
264 2/8	29 2/8	28 6/8	20 2/8	4 7/8	4 6/8	13	12	Utah	Garth Barrett	Cabela's, Inc.	PR 1978	153
264 1/8	22 2/8	22	22 7/8	4 5/8	4 5/8	14	9	Coconino Co., AZ	Gilbert T. Adams	Gilbert T. Adams	1989	155
264	25 5/8	26 1/8	22 7/8	6 2/8	5 7/8	13	14	Elko Co., NV	Jim Stichter	Jim Stichter	1965	156
263 6/8	27 6/8	28 1/8	25 7/8	5 7/8	5 4/8	10	13	Harney Co., OR	Dave Morris	Cabela's, Inc.	1960	157
263 6/8	26 5/8	26 5/8	22 2/8	5	5	16	10	Sanpete Co., UT	Wayne Dwyer	Raymond R. Cross	1974	157
263 4/8	26 5/8	26 4/8	23 6/8	5	5	12	14	Montrose Co., CO	Robert L. Price	Robert L. Price	1963	159
263 3/8	26	27 7/8	24 7/8	5 1/8	4 7/8	12	12	Lincoln Co., WY	Joe Welch	Cabela's, Inc.	1940	160
263 3/8	29 1/8	29 1/8	28 2/8	4 7/8	5	9	13	Rio Arriba Co., NM	Picked Up	Robert J. Seeds	1988	161
263 1/8	27 4/8	26 1/8	26 4/8	6 2/8	5	20	13	Blaine Co., ID	Robert C. Young	Robert C. Young	1956	162
263	26 3/8	27 5/8	25 4/8	5	5	12	13	Kaibab Natl. For., AZ	Unknown	Bob Housholder	1940	163
263	28 2/8	27 1/8	19	6	6	12	12	Kane Co., UT	Bob Talbott	Cabela's, Inc.	1958	164
262 7/8	27 1/8	27 5/8	25 1/8	4 7/8	4 7/8	14	14	Teton Co., WY	Thomas R. Ford	Thomas R. Ford	1984	164
262 5/8	24	24	23 7/8	4 6/8	4 6/8	14	13	Dawson Co., MT	Johnny Scheitlin	Bob Scheitlin	1949	166
262 4/8	28 2/8	29	28	5 4/8	5 4/8	14	12	Kaibab Natl. For., AZ	Jack Verner	Jack Verner	1947	167

MULE DEER - NON-TYPICAL ANTLERS

Odocoileus hemionus hemionus and certain related subspecies

Score	Length of Main Beam R	L	Inside Spread	Circumference at Smallest Place Between Burr and First Point R	L	Number of Points R	L	Locality	Hunter	Owner	Date Killed	Rank
262 3/8	30 2/8	27 6/8	28 6/8	6 2/8	6 4/8	10	15	Tierra Amarilla, NM	Pat Lovato, Jr.	Pat Lovato, Jr.	1966	168
262 3/8	30 7/8	29 3/8	29 4/8	5 3/8	5 6/8	10	11	Brush Creek, CO	Pete Taullie	Pete Taullie	1967	168
262 3/8	27 7/8	25 5/8	24 5/8	5 2/8	5 1/8	9	12	Cassia Co., ID	Ron Woodall	D.J. Hollinger & B. Howard	1984	168
262 2/8	22 5/8	28 2/8	24 1/8	4 3/8	4 5/8	8	9	Adams Co., ID	Carolyn Menichetti	Raymond R. Cross	1959	171
262 1/8	25 6/8	24 4/8	23 3/8	5 6/8	5 3/8	15	13	Franklin Co., ID	Lester Lowe	D.J. Hollinger & B. Howard	1933	172
262 1/8	26 5/8	26 2/8	29 3/8	5 2/8	4 7/8	17	12	Montana	Unknown	Keith Balfourd	PR 1943	172
262	24 2/8	24 6/8	16 6/8	4 6/8	4 7/8	14	16	John Day River, OR	Glen E. Park	Glen E. Park	1962	174
262	25 7/8	23 7/8	21	4 7/8	5	14	15	Utah Co., UT	Michael D. Atwood	Michael D. Atwood	1967	174
261 6/8	24 4/8	23 3/8	20 5/8	5 4/8	5 4/8	16	14	Gallatin Co., MT	Clifford B. Plum	Clifford R. Plum	1932	176
261 6/8	23 6/8	25 4/8	21 4/8	5 4/8	5 3/8	14	16	Montezuma Co., CO	Travis Shippy	Cabela's, Inc.	1986	176
261 5/8	25	26 3/8	23 6/8	4 7/8	5	10	12	Heber Mt., UT	DuWayne C. Bailey	DuWayne C. Bailey	1963	178
261 3/8	25 2/8	26 5/8	19 4/8	4 6/8	4 6/8	10	10	111 Mile House, BC	Picked Up	D.J. Hollinger & B. Howard	1998	179
261 2/8	25 2/8	26 2/8	24 3/8	4 6/8	5 1/8	13	19	Iron Creek, WA	Win Coultas	Win Coultas	1924	180
261 1/8	23	23 1/8	21 3/8	5 4/8	5 2/8	12	13	Rio Blanco Co., CO	L.C. Denny, Jr.	L.C. Denny, Jr.	1961	181
261	25 2/8	26 2/8	25 6/8	5	5 1/8	12	12	Kaibab Natl. For., AZ	Unknown	Larry Arndt	1930	182
260 6/8	29 4/8	27 7/8	28 6/8	5 4/8	5 7/8	10	14	Rooks Co., KS	Lee Odle	Lee Odle	1965	183
260 6/8	26 5/8	26 3/8	22 3/8	4 7/8	4 7/8	10	13	Boise Co., ID	Howard R. Cromwell	Raymond R. Cross	1975	183
260 4/8	25 5/8	27	26 6/8	5 7/8	5 7/8	13	14	Kaibab Natl. For., AZ	David Bevly	David Bevly	1949	185
260 2/8	23 1/8	24 3/8	25 4/8	5 7/8	6	15	17	Boise Co., ID	George M. Tweedy	George M. Tweedy	1946	186
260 2/8	26 7/8	25	21 2/8	4 6/8	4 5/8	12	13	Pinedale, WY	James H. Straley	Monte W. Straley	1965	186
260 1/8	26	27 2/8	24 3/8	4 6/8	5 1/8	16	20	Newcastle, UT	Unknown	UT Div. of Wildl. Resc.	1961	188
260	22 7/8	25	20	5	5	12	12	Caribou Co., ID	Arthur H. Summers	Arthur H. Summers	1966	189
260	27 2/8	25 6/8	32 6/8	5 6/8	6 2/8	13	11	Mohave Co., AZ	John W. Sokatch	John W. Sokatch	1978	189
259 7/8	25 7/8	24	24 6/8	4 7/8	4 6/8	11	13	Kanab, UT	Arthur Glover	Arthur Glover	1947	191
259 7/8	25 1/8	25 2/8	22 2/8	5	5	8	10	Caribou Co., ID	Jerry Hunt	Jerry Hunt	1966	191
259 7/8	19 3/8	31 1/8	25 6/8	5 3/8	5 2/8	15	19	Coconino Co., AZ	Picked Up	Alvin C. West	1967	191
259 7/8	28 4/8	27 4/8	29 4/8	5 7/8	5 5/8	12	15	Catron Co., NM	Jeff K. Gunnell	Jeff K. Gunnell	1981	191
259 6/8	24 2/8	25 4/8	21 3/8	5 3/8	5 3/8	13	13	Routt Co., CO	R.V. Rhoads	Cecil R. Weston	1949	195
259 6/8	25 7/8	24 7/8	29	6 3/8	5 7/8	15	14	Gooding Co., ID	Charles Hollingsworth	D.J. Hollinger & B. Howard	1970	195
259 5/8	27 2/8	26 6/8	24 1/8	5 2/8	5 2/8	12	13	Glendo, WY	Rudolph B. Johnson	Rudolph B. Johnson	1961	197
259 5/8	25 1/8	25 4/8	20 7/8	5 2/8	5 2/8	10	11	Sublette Co., WY	H. Duane Hermon	H. Duane Hermon	1973	197
259 4/8	24 3/8	24	25 3/8	5	5 2/8	13	15	Boise Co., ID	LeRoy Massey	LeRoy Massey	1959	199
259 3/8	27 3/8	29 2/8	24 6/8	5 6/8	5 4/8	13	13	Iron Co., UT	Mont Hunter	Mont Hunter	1939	200
259 3/8	23 4/8	23 4/8	21 6/8	5	5	15	16	Idaho Co., ID	Fred Warren	Raymond R. Cross	PR 1940	200
259 1/8	26 5/8	26 5/8	23 7/8	5 7/8	5 6/8	12	13	Otero Co., CO	John N. Lucero	John N. Lucero	1995	202
259	28 1/8	26 6/8	28 4/8	7 1/8	6 6/8	12	12	Coconino Co., AZ	Lue O. Nulliner	Lue O. Nulliner	1968	203

Score	Locality	Hunter	Owner	Date	Rank
258 7/8	North Kaibab, AZ	Marvin Fridenmaker	Marvin Fridenmaker	1968	204
258 6/8	Valley Co., ID	Larry Dwonch	Larry Dwonch	1972	205
258 6/8	Sweetwater Co., WY	John A. Fabian	John A. Fabian	1974	205
258 6/8	Washington Co., UT	Brian A. Bowler	Brian A. Bowler	1989	205
258 5/8	Decatur Co., KS	Lance W. Randolph	Lance W. Randolph	1996	205
258 5/8	Elko Co., NV	Edward J. Giauque	Edward J. Giauque	1960	209
258 4/8	Grand Co., UT	Vernon K. Heller	Vernon K. Heller	1971	210
258 3/8	Monte Vista, CO	Gus Nettlebeck	D.J. Hollinger & B. Howard	1956	211
258 2/8	Rock Creek, BC	George Whiting	BC Game Dept.	1909	212
258 1/8	Morgan Co., UT	Martin Harris	Rodney D. Layton	1935	213
258 1/8	Elmore Co., ID	Kenneth E. Potts	Cabela's, Inc.	1968	213
258	Sheridan Co., KS	John Simpson	Cabela's, Inc.	PR 1969	213
258	Cimarron Co., NM	Ralph L. Smith	William T. Parsons	1957	216
257 7/8	Coconino Co., AZ	William T. Parsons	Henry Callado	1967	216
257 7/8	Jicarilla Apache Res., NM	Henry Callado	Lamell Ellsworth	1961	218
257 5/8	Apache Co., AZ	Lamell Ellsworth	Ernest Fait	1992	218
257 5/8	Leclerc Creek, WA	Ernest Fait	John E. Connor Museum	1960	220
257 5/8	Kaibab Natl. For., AZ	Graves Peeler	David Mercier	1946	221
257 5/8	Manning, AB	Victor Mercier	John E. Connor Museum	1946	221
257 4/8	Kaibab Natl. For., AZ	Graves Peeler	D.L. DeMente	1947	221
257 4/8	Hell's Hole, AZ	D.L. DeMente	Rachael Palmer	1965	221
257 4/8	Rio Blanco Co., CO	Rachael Palmer	Mrs. Sam Whitney	1970	221
257 4/8	Encampment, WY	Sam Whitney	Dave Burgess	1946	226
257 3/8	Utah Co., UT	J. Clyde Burgess	Aly M. Bruner	1949	226
257 2/8	Colorado	Ed Hiler	Philip T. Homer	1957	226
257 1/8	Blaine Co., ID	Philip T. Homer	Dan J. Keller	1983	226
257	Sanpete Co., UT	Dan J. Keller	Dale McKinnon	1986	226
257	Coconino Co., AZ	Dale McKinnon	Sam S. Jaksick, Jr.	1995	226
257	Mohave Co., AZ	Sam S. Jaksick, Jr.	A.E. Hudson	1999	226
256 7/8	New Castle Co., CO	Unknown	D.J. Hollinger & B. Howard	1952	233
256 7/8	British Columbia	Carl Balantine	Nelson L. Jones	PR 1950	234
256 6/8	Juab Co., UT	P.I. Jones	Cabela's, Inc.	1949	235
256 6/8	Sevier Co., UT	Reed Hintze	Harold S. Shandrew	1939	236
256 6/8	Cache Co., UT	Harold S. Shandrew	D.J. Hollinger & B. Howard	1958	236
256 5/8	Madison Co., ID	Grover Browning	Cabela's, Inc.	1959	236
256 4/8	Lincoln Co., ID	Zach Shetler	Art Thomsen	2001	236
256 4/8	Chadron, NE	Art Thomsen	Paul Vetter	1960	240
256 4/8	Elmore Co., ID	Paul Vetter	Henry Thomas	1972	240
256 2/8	Moose Creek, AB	Henry Thomas	Buck Heide	1993	240
256 2/8	Hoback Basin, WY	Buck Heide	Cabela's, Inc.	1968	243
256 2/8	Bannock Co., ID	Unknown	Cabela's, Inc.	PR 1982	243
256	Jicarilla Apache Res., NM	Picked Up	S.L. Canterbury III	1967	245
256	Douglas Co., CO	Adolph A. Larsen	Cabela's, Inc.	1926	246
256	Summit Co., UT	Glen Holtman	Manuel C. Gonzales	1946	246
256	Portreeve, SK	Mike Spies	Mike Spies	1947	246
256	Baker Co., OR	Thomas M. Rousseau	Thomas M. Rousseau	1988	246
256 2/8	Mt. Trumbull, AZ	Ervin M. Schmutz	Ervin M. Schmutz	1965	250
256 2/8	Caribou Co., ID	Unknown	D.J. Hollinger & B. Howard	PR 1970	250

MULE DEER - NON-TYPICAL ANTLERS
Odocoileus hemionus hemionus and certain related subspecies

Score	Length of Main Beam		Inside Spread	Circumference at Smallest Place Between Burr and First Point		Number of Points		Locality	Hunter	Owner	Date Killed	Rank
	R	L		R	L	R	L					
256 2/8	24 6/8	24 1/8	21 6/8	4 5/8	4 4/8	12	11	Oneida Co., ID	S. Tracey Davis	S. Tracey Davis	1998	250
256 1/8	28 4/8	28 6/8	32 5/8	6 2/8	6 3/8	11	12	Missoula Co., MT	Leland Crow	Cabela's, Inc.	1952	253
256 1/8	23 7/8	24 7/8	25	4 7/8	5 1/8	12	13	East Zion, UT	Raymond Pocta	Raymond Pocta	1963	253
256 1/8	22 7/8	22 4/8	20 1/8	4 5/8	5	14	12	Irwin, ID	Hale K. Charlton	Hale K. Charlton	1966	253
256 1/8	26 2/8	27 4/8	21 6/8	4 6/8	4 5/8	15	13	Summit Lake, BC	Herald A. Friedenberger	Herald A. Friedenberger	1988	253
256	25 6/8	26	25	5	5 2/8	11	19	Jefferson Co., OR	Spencer Darrar	Gail McDougall	1953	257
256	24 4/8	26 7/8	25 1/8	5	4 6/8	13	10	Garfield Co., UT	James D. Perkins	James D. Perkins	1959	257
256	26 7/8	26 5/8	22 6/8	9 4/8	6 5/8	16	9	Gem Co., ID	Jay P. Baker	Jay P. Baker	1981	257
255 7/8	23	24 1/8	22 6/8	5 4/8	5	18	12	Unknown	Unknown	Buckhorn Mus. & Saloon, Ltd.	1901	260
255 6/8	26 5/8	26 7/8	26 5/8	5 2/8	5 2/8	11	9	Cache Co., UT	Roland Leishman	Roland Leishman	1980	261
255 5/8	25 2/8	25 7/8	24 3/8	4 5/8	4 4/8	12	12	Idaho	Unknown	D.J. Hollinger & B. Howard	PR 1948	262
255 4/8	23 3/8	23 5/8	25 5/8	5 6/8	5 7/8	12	12	Coconino Co., AZ	Glenn A. Hunt	Glenn A. Hunt	1985	263
255 3/8	26 3/8	28	23	5 4/8	5 6/8	10	11	Peace River, BC	C.C. Brandt	N. Peace Hist. Soc.	1930	264
255 2/8	28	27 3/8	28 2/8	5 7/8	5 5/8	14	12	Garfield Co., CO	Louis Lindauer	Louis Lindauer	1932	265
255 2/8	25 2/8	24 7/8	22 1/8	4 3/8	4 3/8	10	9	Eagle Co., CO	Lloyd Murphy	Cabela's, Inc.	1936	265
255 2/8	26	26 5/8	25 1/8	4 7/8	4 5/8	9	9	Rio Arriba Co., NM	Gene Garcia	Gene Garcia	1964	265
255 1/8	25 6/8	26 6/8	29 4/8	5 6/8	5 4/8	10	11	Nez Perce Co., ID	A. Frye & C. Chapman	Unknown	1948	268
255 1/8	25	25 7/8	26 5/8	4 7/8	5	7	9	Eagle Co., CO	Dennis Martinson	Dennis Martinson	1980	268
255	21 5/8	22 4/8	19 7/8	5 5/8	5 4/8	9	9	Dunkley Flat, CO	Richard A. Gorden	Richard A. Gorden	1966	270
255	26 6/8	25 4/8	23 4/8	4 6/8	4 6/8	8	8	Adams Co., ID	Fred Bain	Raymond R. Cross	1974	270
254 4/8	25 1/8	24	18 5/8	5 4/8	5 2/8	13	15	Maloy, AB	Otto Schmalzbauer	Otto Schmalzbauer	1930	272
254 4/8	25 1/8	24 1/8	21 1/8	4 6/8	4 6/8	16	12	Utah	Unknown	D.J. Hollinger & B. Howard	PR 1960	272
254 2/8	30	28 6/8	23 4/8	6 2/8	6 4/8	7	8	Columbine, CO	M.A. Story	M.A. Story	1955	274
254 1/8	24 4/8	25 2/8	23 7/8	4 5/8	4 6/8	9	10	Jefferson Co., CO	Larry J. Jones	Larry J. Jones	1994	275
254	26 7/8	26 5/8	21 5/8	6 1/8	6 3/8	13	9	Wyoming	Unknown	D.J. Hollinger & B. Howard	PR 1960	276
253 6/8	25	26 1/8	25 6/8	6 1/8	6 1/8	9	12	Mohave Co., AZ	Manuel Machado	Manuel Machado	1973	277
253 4/8	25 6/8	26 5/8	30 2/8	4 6/8	4 6/8	11	11	East End, SK	Henry Leroy	Henry Leroy	1960	278
253 4/8	24 6/8	25 1/8	25 6/8	6 2/8	5 1/8	11	10	Silt, CO	George McCoy	George McCoy	1961	278
253 3/8	25 3/8	23 4/8	26 1/8	5 4/8	5 4/8	13	17	Meeker Co., CO	George R. Howey	Robert L. Howey	1917	280
253 3/8	27 6/8	26 6/8	21	5 2/8	5 3/8	11	13	Georgetown Co., CO	George Lappin	Doug Grubbe	1947	280
253 3/8	24 4/8	24 3/8	20 4/8	5 3/8	5 3/8	11	11	Rawlins Co., WY	A.H. Henkel	A.H. Henkel	1952	280
253 3/8	20 1/8	22 1/8	22 6/8	5 2/8	5 3/8	15	22	Utah Co., UT	Paul H. Mitchell	Paul H. Mitchell	1953	280
253 2/8	24 3/8	25 2/8	20 5/8	5 2/8	5 5/8	15	17	Salmon, ID	Ben H. Quick	Ben H. Quick	1960	284
253 1/8	24 2/8	23 2/8	24 6/8	5 4/8	5 1/8	16	12	Sweetwater Co., WY	John C. Erickson	M. Painovich & J. Etcheverry	1932	285
253	26 1/8	25 1/8	23 2/8	5	5 1/8	10	13	Elko Co., NV	Joseph Souza	Joseph Souza	1953	286
253	25 5/8	25 4/8	25 2/8	5 6/8	6	11	11	Paonia, CO	F.F. Parham	F.F. Parham	1961	286

Score	Main Beam R	Main Beam L	Inside Spread	Circ. R	Circ. L	Pts R	Pts L	Locality	Hunter	Owner	Date	Rank
252 7/8	22 4/8	18 6/8	19 1/8	5 4/8	5 4/8	11	22	Boise Co., ID	Dennis D. Snider	Dennis D. Snider	1983	288
252 7/8	21 7/8	22 6/8	26 6/8	5 4/8	5 4/8	15	11	S. Saskatchewan River, SK	Glenn A. Vestre	Glenn A. Vestre	2001	288
252 6/8	25 2/8	24 3/8	22 4/8	5	4 7/8	12	17	Wyoming	Unknown	Cabela's, Inc.	PR 1970	290
252 6/8	25 6/8	24 4/8	22 4/8	4 7/8	4 7/8	14	12	Beaver Co., UT	Picked Up	Rance Rollins	1980	290
252 6/8	25 6/8	24 6/8	25 6/8	5 5/8	5 5/8	10	14	Fremont Co., ID	Trevor D. Larson	Trevor D. Larson	1990	290
252 5/8	26 7/8	28 7/8	29 1/8	5 3/8	5 3/8	13	13	Kaibab Natl. For., AZ	Graves Peeler	Graves Peeler	PR 1951	293
252 5/8	20 5/8	21 7/8	18 3/8	4 5/8	4 6/8	12	13	Boise Co., ID	Picked Up	Raymond R. Cross	PR 1989	293
252 4/8	23 1/8	26 4/8	21 1/8	5 4/8	5 4/8	12	12	Sonora, MX	Fredric W. Decker	Fredric W. Decker	1997	295
252 2/8	23 4/8	22	14 5/8	5 6/8	5 6/8	13	15	Glacier Co., MT	Bob Scriver	Philip Schlegel	1934	296
252 2/8	22	30	26 6/8	6	6	15	14	Garfield Co., CO	B.J. Slack	Aly M. Bruner	1973	296
252 1/8	30	24 1/8	21 5/8	4 6/8	4 7/8	15	10	Salina Canyon, UT	James C. Larsen	James C. Larsen	1969	298
252 1/8	25 1/8	27 3/8	24 4/8	5 5/8	5 3/8	11	11	Delta Co., CO	John W. Stockemer	John W. Stockemer	1969	298
252 1/8	27 3/8	28 6/8	28 3/8	5 4/8	5 4/8	11	10	Elmore Co., ID	Bud Abele	Bud Abele	1996	298
252	28 6/8	22 1/8	24 6/8	5 4/8	5 4/8	13	16	Grease Creek, AB	Jack McCallum	J.H. Fry	PR 1940	301
252	22 7/8	24 7/8	24 5/8	5	5	9	13	Eagle Co., CO	Richard G. Lundock	Richard G. Lundock	1945	301
252	24	26	20 3/8	4 6/8	4 6/8	14	14	Box Elder Co., UT	Mr. Selman	D.J. Hollinger & B. Howard	1951	301
251 7/8	26	22	17 1/8	5 1/8	4 5/8	13	10	Salem Co., UT	John Vincent	John Vincent	1956	304
251 6/8	22	24	20	5	5	13	14	Gem Co., ID	Archie K. England	Roscoe E. Ferris	1969	305
251 6/8	24	28 2/8	25 2/8	5 4/8	5 1/8	13	11	Ouray Co., CO	Bruce Phillips	T. Larry Pope	PR 1985	305
251 6/8	28 2/8	25 7/8	23	6	6	7	14	Washington Co., UT	Richard S. Mansker	Richard S. Mansker	1990	305
251 5/8	25 2/8	27 4/8	23 6/8	5 2/8	6 3/8	9	14	Gunnison Co., CO	John M. Ringler	John M. Ringler	1956	308
251 5/8	27 4/8	24 1/8	21	5 4/8	5 2/8	13	14	Roan Creek, CO	Anthony Morabito	Anthony Morabito	1965	308
251 4/8	24 1/8	26 4/8	23 2/8	5 4/8	5 1/8	13	13	Grand Co., UT	Picked Up	Joshua Gonzales	1976	310
251 4/8	26 4/8	28 2/8	22 1/8	5 5/8	5 2/8	14	9	Martha Creek, BC	Charles J. McKinney	Charles J. McKinney	1992	310
251 3/8	29 1/8	26	31 1/8	5 3/8	5 7/8	18	12	Wayne Co., UT	Chuck Simmons	Chuck Simmons	1988	312
251 2/8	26 7/8	27 1/8	24 1/8	6 1/8	5 5/8	10	15	Grant Co., OR	Edward Kock	Daniel E. Williams	1930	313
251 2/8	26 4/8	24 5/8	17 6/8	4 7/8	6 4/8	14	16	Tyee Lake, BC	Harold Bartha	Harold Bartha	1961	313
251 2/8	23 1/8	29	26 4/8	5 6/8	4 7/8	12	13	Wyoming	Unknown	D.J. Hollinger & B. Howard	PR 1970	313
251 2/8	29	25	25 6/8	5	5 2/8	10	9	Rosebud Co., MT	John P. Garner	Cabela's, Inc.	1978	313
251 1/8	25 1/8	25 7/8	25 7/8	5 2/8	5 3/8	10	9	Meeker Co., CO	Henry H. Zietz	Henry H. Zietz	1955	317
251 1/8	27 5/8	26 3/8	26 3/8	6	6 1/8	16	13	Iron Co., UT	James C. Howard	James C. Howard	1987	317
251	28 1/8	29 4/8	25 2/8	5 2/8	4 7/8	13	9	Crook Co., OR	Herrel C. Throop	Gerald L. Throop	1935	319
251	25 6/8	24 4/8	24 4/8	4 7/8	5	12	14	Washington	Unknown	D.J. Hollinger & B. Howard	1936	319
251	28 6/8	26 1/8	26 1/8	5 1/8	5 1/8	12	12	Adams Co., ID	Clarke Childers	Clarke Childers	1955	319
251	28 3/8	26 7/8	26 7/8	5 5/8	6 1/8	19	13	Cache Co., UT	John Reynolds	D. J. Hollinger & B. Howard	1960	319
250 7/8	26 4/8	24	24	6	5 4/8	12	14	Chelan Co., WA	Ben R. Williamson	Vera T. Williamson	1951	323
250 7/8	27 4/8	29 3/8	29 3/8	5 4/8	5 6/8	11	13	Unknown	Unknown	Buckhorn Mus. & Saloon, Ltd.	PR 1965	323
250 6/8	29	35 1/8	35 1/8	5 3/8	5 3/8	11	13	Pagosa Springs, CO	Thomas Jarrett	Thomas Jarrett	1962	325
250 6/8	29	28 3/8	28 3/8	5 2/8	5 2/8	11	11	Idaho	Unknown	D.J. Hollinger & B. Howard	PR 1970	325
250 6/8	30	28 7/8	28 7/8	6 2/8	6 2/8	13	12	Apache Co., AZ	Perry D. Null	Perry D. Null	1993	325
250 5/8	25 3/8	22 2/8	22 2/8	5 1/8	5 1/8	13	10	Millard Co., UT	Walter D. LeFevre	Walter D. LeFevre	1968	328
250 4/8	29 7/8	22 4/8	22 4/8	8	6 2/8	7	13	Bonneville Co., ID	Ralph D. Hogan	Ralph D. Hogan	1966	329
250 4/8	26 1/8	28 4/8	28 4/8	5	5 1/8	12	10	Washington	Unknown	Pat Redding	PR 1973	329
250 4/8	26	27 3/8	27 3/8	5 4/8	5 4/8	10	9	Quesnel, BC	Picked Up	Paul W. Stafford	1984	329
250 4/8	26 7/8	30 2/8	30 2/8	5 6/8	5 6/8	11	13	Shoshone Co., ID	Ron L. Purnell	Ron L. Purnell	1987	329
250 3/8	27 7/8	28 4/8	28 4/8	4 4/8	4 4/8	12	9	Grant Co., OR	Manford Pate	D.J. Hollinger & B. Howard	1946	333
250 3/8	29	27 4/8	27 4/8	5 1/8	4 6/8	10	12	Moffat Co., CO	Unknown	Aly M. Bruner	1960	333
250 3/8	26 2/8	24 7/8	25 4/8	5	5	10	10	Cedaredge, CO	E.K. Plante	E.K. Plante	1963	333

MULE DEER - NON-TYPICAL ANTLERS

Odocoileus hemionus hemionus and certain related subspecies

Score	Length of Main Beam R	L	Inside Spread	Circumference at Smallest Place Between Burr and First Point R	L	Number of Points R	L	Locality	Hunter	Owner	Date Killed	Rank
250 3/8	26 5/8	26 2/8	28 1/8	4 6/8	5	10	12	Petroleum Co., MT	Lawrence T. Keenan	Lawrence T. Keenan	1979	333
250 1/8	23 4/8	22 7/8	17 7/8	4 5/8	4 6/8	14	14	Sheridan Co., WY	Richard Legerski	Richard Legerski	1976	337
250 1/8	26	26	24	5 4/8	5 6/8	15	11	Montezuma Co., CO	Jack E. Reed	Jack E. Reed	1981	337
250	25 1/8	25	25 1/8	6 5/8	6 2/8	10	10	Elko Co., NV	Joseph Brodnik	J. & B. Brodnik	1965	339
250	29 5/8	28 4/8	28 4/8	4 6/8	4 2/8	11	10	Summit Co., UT	David Montoya	D.J. Hollinger & B. Howard	1976	339
250	25	27 1/8	21 4/8	6 5/8	6 4/8	14	14	Mohave Co., AZ	Douglas C. Mallory	Douglas C. Mallory	1980	339
249 6/8	23 3/8	21 6/8	23 3/8	6 2/8	5 7/8	12	12	Mt. Dellenbaugh, AZ	Ted Riggs	Cabela's, Inc.	1965	342
249 6/8	24 7/8	25 2/8	22	5	4 7/8	10	14	Red Willow Co., NE	Delman H. Tuller	Delman H. Tuller	1965	342
249 5/8	26 2/8	25 7/8	23	5	5 3/8	11	10	Colorado	Unknown	Cabela's, Inc.	PR 1960	344
249 3/8	25	24 2/8	19 6/8	5 4/8	5 3/8	12	9	Routt Co., CO	Howard Stoker	Howard Stoker	1958	345
249 3/8	27	27 4/8	27 5/8	6 1/8	6 2/8	7	11	Adams Co., ID	Howard E. Paradis	Howard E. Paradis	1966	345
249 3/8	25	24 6/8	22 6/8	5 4/8	5 4/8	18	16	Owyhee Co., ID	Tom Tomlinson	Raymond R. Cross	1968	345
249 2/8	26 1/8	28 4/8	29 1/8	5 6/8	6 1/8	14	10	Klamath Co., OR	Fred Teeny	Rick Teeny	1947	348
249 2/8	23 5/8	23 4/8	20 7/8	5	4 5/8	12	10	Mesa Co., CO	Gene Cavanagh	Gene Cavanagh	1967	348
249 2/8	26 7/8	26 5/8	21 4/8	6 6/8	6 4/8	21	22	Adams Co., ID	Henry Daniels	Raymond R. Cross	1975	348
249 2/8	24 3/8	23 5/8	27	4 6/8	4 6/8	10	10	Lincoln Co., WY	Robert J. Stallone	Robert J. Stallone	1986	348
249 1/8	25 3/8	23 4/8	19 2/8	5 4/8	5 5/8	13	16	Jackson Co., OR	Meryl Loy	Marvin M. Loy	1938	352
249 1/8	25 3/8	25 6/8	27 6/8	4 5/8	4 5/8	12	12	Shoshone Co., ID	Jim Brines	D.J. Hollinger & B. Howard	1962	352
249 1/8	25 4/8	26	25 1/8	5 1/8	5 1/8	8	11	Kaibab, AZ	Robert G. McDonald	Robert G. McDonald	1969	352
249	25 1/8	23 4/8	23 1/8	5 1/8	5	14	10	Minturn, CO	John F. Baldauf	Lin F. Nowotny	1941	355
249	27 1/8	29 7/8	25 6/8	5 3/8	5 1/8	11	8	Jemez Mts., NM	Max S. Jenson	Max S. Jenson	1962	355
249	26 7/8	26 7/8	26 7/8	5 1/8	5 1/8	8	10	New Castle Co., CO	William Wiedenfeld	William Wiedenfeld	1969	355
248 6/8	27	25 4/8	28	5 5/8	5 6/8	9	14	Okanogan Co., WA	Fred C. Heuer	Raymond R. Cross	1940	358
248 6/8	27 1/8	26 5/8	16 3/8	6	6	8	19	Adams Co., ID	Unknown	D.J. Hollinger & B. Howard	1962	358
248 6/8	22 2/8	25 6/8	23 3/8	5 4/8	6	10	8	Adams Co., CO	Picked Up	US Fish & Wildlife Service	1989	358
248 5/8	26 6/8	25 6/8	33 6/8	6 2/8	5 2/8	14	10	Franklin Co., ID	Joan Butterworth	Raymond R. Cross	1961	361
248 4/8	25 4/8	25 1/8	26	5 6/8	5 5/8	13	11	Kaibab Natl. For., AZ	H.W. Meisch	H.W. Meisch	1942	362
248 4/8	29 2/8	27 3/8	20 4/8	5 2/8	5 3/8	15	16	Baker Co., OR	Wally Hutton	R. Dwayne Wright	1964	362
248 4/8	27 3/8	26 4/8	29 2/8	6 2/8	6	13	13	Sevier Co., UT	Orson Lance	Orson Lance	1969	362
248 4/8	22 6/8	26 3/8	26 6/8	5 4/8	5	9	6	Lincoln Co., NV	Alan B. Shepherd	Alan B. Shepherd	2001	362
248 3/8	28	26 4/8	25 2/8	6 2/8	6 2/8	12	12	Okanogan Co., WA	William L. Tedford	Steve Nordness	1940	366
248 3/8	26 3/8	26 6/8	23 4/8	5 4/8	5 2/8	10	16	Kaibab Natl. For., AZ	O.M. Corbett	O.M. Corbett	1953	366
248 3/8	24 4/8	25 1/8	25 1/8	5 5/8	5 3/8	10	12	Mesa Co., CO	Edwin Baal	Edwin Baal	1988	366
248 3/8	29 3/8	27 6/8	27 2/8	6 1/8	6 2/8	10	9	Costilla Co., CO	Ronald E. Lewis	Ronald E. Lewis	1988	366
248 2/8	24	24 2/8	22 5/8	5 3/8	5 3/8	13	8	Elko Co., NV	Gary Murphy	Bart Druehl	PR 1947	370
248 2/8	25	25 3/8	26 7/8	6 6/8	7	12	12	Kaibab Natl. For., AZ	Graves Peeler	Graves Peeler	PR 1951	370

Score	Main Beam R	Main Beam L	Inside Spread	Pts R	Pts L	Circ. R	Circ. L	Locality	Hunter	Owner	Date	Rank
248 2/8	24 4/8	24 4/8	19 7/8	9	8	4 4/8	4 4/8	Colorado	Unknown	D.J. Hollinger & B. Howard	PR 1980	370
248 1/8	25 7/8	24 7/8	22 6/8	11	10	5	5 1/8	Rio Blanco Co., CO	Claude E. Shults	Claude E. Shults	1956	373
248 1/8	25 4/8	25	23	15	18	5 2/8	5	San Juan Natl. For., CO	Leland R. Tate	Leland R. Tate	1973	373
248	24	26	18 1/8	11	11	4 7/8	4 7/8	Treasure Co., MT	Orville Campbell	David E. Campbell	1948	375
248	23 3/8	22 4/8	23 2/8	22	14	5 6/8	5 6/8	Val Marie, SK	J. Milton Brown	J. Milton Brown	1958	375
248	26	27 1/8	22	11	9	5 2/8	5	Pinedale, WY	Lyle Rosendahl	Lyle Rosendahl	1960	375
248	25 5/8	26 4/8	24 7/8	13	10	4 4/8	5	Columbine, CO	Bobby McLaughlin	Bobby McLaughlin	1962	375
247 7/8	26 1/8	26	27 7/8	7	9	5 4/8	4 4/8	Uintah Co., UT	Mabel Henry	Cabela's, Inc.	1966	380
247 7/8	26	24	26	6	11	5 6/8	5 2/8	Idaho Co., ID	Howard Springston	Raymond R. Cross	1939	380
247 7/8	21 2/8	25 3/8	25	9	11	6	6	Norwood, CO	Walter L. Reisbeck	Walter L. Reisbeck	1951	380
247 7/8	25 6/8	26	24 6/8	19	10	5 4/8	6	Cabri, SK	Enos Mitchell, Jr.	Enos Mitchell, Jr.	1960	380
247 7/8	23 6/8	24	25 3/8	14	17	5 4/8	5 7/8	Weber Co., UT	John Lindsay	Robert R. Donaldson	1966	380
247 6/8	22 6/8	22 5/8	20 7/8	0	13	5	5 4/8	Asotin Co., WA	David G. Bennett	David G. Bennett	1971	385
247 5/8	24 7/8	24 7/8	19 2/8	11	13	4 3/8	5	Grand Co., UT	Bruce M. Turnbow	Bruce M. Turnbow	1967	385
247 5/8	28 4/8	28 4/8	22 2/8	10	16	5	5	Shoshone Co., ID	Gary J. Finney	Gary J. Finney	1983	387
247 5/8	26	28 1/8	23 5/8	0	13	6	5 1/8	Waterton Park, AB	Eric Westergreen	Eric Westergreen	1941	387
247 4/8	25 4/8	22 6/8	26 7/8	6	13	6 1/8	5 7/8	Hinsdale Co., CO	Fred Jardine	Fred Jardine	1966	387
247 4/8	22 6/8	24 1/8	26	2	20	6	6	Mohave Co., AZ	Brad L. Johnson	Brad L. Johnson	1986	390
247 4/8	24 3/8	23 4/8	25 4/8	4	16	6 2/8	6 6/8	Tooele Co., UT	Murray G. Loveless	Murray G. Loveless	1949	390
247 4/8	18 1/8	23 1/8	22 6/8	2	16	5 4/8	5 6/8	Bend, OR	L.M. Martinson	L.M. Martinson	1949	390
247 4/8	30 4/8	30 3/8	31 6/8	1	8	5 1/8	5 5/8	Sevier Co., UT	Unknown	D.J. Hollinger & B. Howard	PR 1960	390
247 3/8	25	25	24 3/8	9	10	6 1/8	5	Archuleta Co., CO	Vince Plaskett	Vince Plaskett	1970	394
247 3/8	28 3/8	27 7/8	23 1/8	0	12	5	6 4/8	Missoula Co., MT	Harold Wample	Ralph Raymond	1949	394
247 2/8	24 2/8	23 5/8	28 3/8	0	9	4 4/8	5	Eagle Co., CO	Earl M. Johnson	Earl M. Johnson	1966	394
247 2/8	25 7/8	25	33 6/8	1	9	5 3/8	4 4/8	Fremont Co., ID	Donald R. Craig	D.J. Hollinger & B. Howard	1982	394
247 2/8	29 7/8	28 6/8	25 2/8	3	10	4 7/8	5 5/8	Owyhee Co., ID	Elwin J. Saxton	Raymond R. Cross	1975	397
247 2/8	23 5/8	24 2/8	22 6/8	8	11	6 1/8	4 7/8	Elko Co., NV	Picked Up	Ron Druck	1980	397
247 1/8	25 5/8	23	24 1/8	1	11	4 6/8	6 2/8	Drummond, MT	Tom Brosovich	Tom Brosovich	1957	399
247 1/8	27 2/8	26 2/8	19 2/8	2	11	6 1/8	4 5/8	Whitebird, ID	Harold Gustin	Wayne Demaray	1965	399
247 1/8	24 6/8	21 3/8	28 3/8	0	9	5 2/8	6	San Miguel Co., CO	W.F. Grice	W.F. Grice	1978	399
247 1/8	23 4/8	24 4/8	27 2/8	1	15	5 6/8	5 1/8	Campbell Co., WY	Ron Fresuik	D.J. Hollinger & B. Howard	1979	399
247 1/8	24 7/8	21	25	7	13	6	5 4/8	Carbon Co., UT	Ralph A. Sanich	Ralph A. Sanich	1986	399
247	26 6/8	24 7/8	24 5/8	4	10	4 7/8	5 4/8	Elko Co., NV	Walter B. Hester	Walter B. Hester	1957	404
247	24 2/8	26 4/8	24 7/8	1	16	5 1/8	4 7/8	Montrose Co., CO	Thomas M. Bost	Thomas M. Bost	1967	404
246 7/8	25 3/8	23 3/8	21 1/8	0	8	5 2/8	5 1/8	Craig Co., CO	Fred E. Trouth	Fred E. Trouth	1960	406
246 7/8	25 5/8	25 6/8	26 4/8	4	7	5 4/8	5 5/8	Carbon Co., CO	Sherman R. Jensen, Jr.	Sherman R. Jensen, Jr.	1965	406
246 7/8	27 2/8	21 3/8	29 2/8	3	14	6 3/8	5 4/8	Needle Peak, ID	Michael G. Cameron	Michael G. Cameron	1966	406
246 7/8	24 6/8	24 4/8	21 3/8	0	10	4 6/8	6 4/8	Gallatin Co., MT	C. Martin Wood III	C. Martin Wood III	1994	406
246 6/8	23 4/8	21	26 3/8	0	14	4 7/8	4 6/8	Modoc Co., CA	Bill Foster	Foster's Bighorn Rest.	1930	410
246 6/8	24 7/8	24 7/8	24 6/8	3	15	5 2/8	4 7/8	Lawrence Co., SD	Unknown	Old Style Saloon	1945	410
246 6/8	26 6/8	26 4/8	20 7/8	9	11	5 3/8	5 2/8	Rio Blanco Co., CO	James A. Cook	James A. Cook	1963	410
246 6/8	24 2/8	24 2/8	25 1/8	1	17	5 6/8	5 5/8	Eagle Co., CO	William M. Nickels	William M. Nickels	1963	410
246 5/8	25 3/8	25 3/8	23	8	11	5	5 4/8	Empress, AB	George Servage	Richard Bonnett	PR 1987	414
246 3/8	25	25	26	2	14	5 4/8	5 4/8	Glenwood Springs, CO	Grady P. Lester	Grady P. Lester	1959	415
246 3/8	24 7/8	24 6/8	25 1/8	2	9	5 2/8	5 1/8	Kaibab Natl. For., AZ	Elgin T. Gates	Elgin T. Gates	1960	415
246 2/8	28 1/8	28 1/8	24 6/8	8	11	4 6/8	5 1/8	Eagle Co., CO	Charles H. Thornberg	Charles H. Thornberg	1949	417
246 2/8	23 4/8	24 1/8	26 1/8	2	14	5 1/8	5 1/8	Ravalli Co., MT	Lloyd G. Hunter	Lloyd G. Hunter	1963	417
246 1/8	26 6/8	25 4/8	25 4/8	2	10	5 3/8	5 3/8	Mesa Co., CO	Joseph J. Pitcherella	Joseph J. Pitcherella	1972	419

MULE DEER - NON-TYPICAL ANTLERS
Odocoileus hemionus hemionus and certain related subspecies

Score	Length of Main Beam R	L	Inside Spread	Circumference at Smallest Place Between Burr and First Point R	L	Number of Points R	L	Locality	Hunter	Owner	Date Killed	Rank
246 1/8	26 7/8	27 4/8	27 4/3	5 7/8	5 6/8	8	9	Twin Falls Co., ID	Jed Seamons	Jed Seamons	2000	419
246	26 7/8	25 3/8	26 4/3	5	4 6/8	9	13	Cherokee Co., IA	C.A. Stiles	Jim Hass	PR 1900	421
246	23 5/8	26 1/8	24 1/3	6 3/8	5 6/8	14	13	Mesa Co., CO	Harry A. Gay	Harry A. Gay	1962	421
246	27 1/8	26 5/8	31 6/3	5 5/8	5 5/8	8	8	Mohave Co., AZ	Bernard E. Anderson	Bernard E. Anderson	1969	421
246	29 6/8	31 1/8	23 4/3	6 7/8	6 6/8	9	11	Unknown	Unknown	D.J. Hollinger & B. Howard	PR 1993	421
246	24 3/8	24 6/8	27 3/3	5 3/8	5 4/8	15	13	Owyhee Co., ID	Douglas W. Pittman	Douglas W. Pittman	1998	421
245 7/8	24 4/8	25 6/8	22 4/3	5	5 1/8	18	15	Dolores Co., CO	Picked Up	Cabela's, Inc.	1984	426
245 6/8	27 1/8	28 2/8	24 4/3	5 6/8	5 7/8	11	9	Rio Arriba Co., NM	Kenneth W. Lee	Kenneth W. Lee	1971	427
245 5/8	27 5/8	28	23 3/3	5 1/8	5 2/8	13	11	Rio Blanco Co., CO	Charlie Grove	Dorothy Shults	1934	428
245 5/8	25 5/8	24 4/8	24	5 3/8	5 2/8	13	12	Latah Co., ID	Leonard Gunnerson	Michael R. Damery	PR 1944	428
245 5/8	26 4/8	26 6/8	22 2/3	5	5 3/8	10	10	Eagle Co., CO	Unknown	D.J. Hollinger & B. Howard	PR 1968	428
245 5/8	27 2/8	28 2/8	23 2/3	5 3/8	5 4/8	11	10	Montana	James Caraccioli	James Caraccioli	1978	428
245 3/8	24 1/8	24 6/8	21 7/3	5	5	10	7	Broadwater Co., MT	Harry Neafus	Dwayne Frandsen	PR 1870	432
245 2/8	28 2/8	24	31 6/3	5 1/8	5	10	12	Saguache Co., CO	Walter A. Larsen	Randy Clark	1962	432
245 2/8	23 6/8	24 6/8	24 3/3	5 1/8	5	18	10	Lac La Biche, AB	Julius Hagen	Olaf Hagen	1945	434
245 2/8	26 5/8	27 4/8	21 2/3	5 6/8	5 6/8	10	8	Jicarilla Apache Res., NM	Arthur Wanoskea	Arthur Wanoskea	1960	434
245 2/8	28	27 5/8	33 4/3	4 6/8	4 7/8	8	8	Fergus Co., MT	Unknown	Cabela's, Inc.	PR 1965	434
245 2/8	23 2/8	22 3/8	20 2/3	6 3/8	6 2/8	9	11	Rio Arriba Co., NM	Robert B. Loring	Robert B. Loring	1995	434
245 1/8	27 1/8	25 3/8	25 4/3	5 3/8	5 4/8	7	10	Coconino Co., AZ	Edward H. Abplanalp	Edward H. Abplanalp	1947	438
245 1/8	24	23 2/8	20 2/3	5 3/8	5 4/8	12	9	Power Co., ID	D.J. Hollinger & B. Howard	D.J. Hollinger & B. Howard	1984	438
245	24 6/8	22 5/8	18 5/8	6 5/8	7	12	14	Mt. Trumbull, AZ	Tony Stromei	Tony Stromei	1960	440
245	25 6/8	25 5/8	29 6/3	5 5/8	5 4/8	17	15	Bonner Co., ID	Dick Sherwood	Dick Sherwood	1963	440
245	26 5/8	26 7/8	24 1/3	5 3/8	5 2/8	12	12	Kane Co., UT	Koyle T. Cram	Koyle T. Cram	1966	440
245	30	26 3/8	27 5/8	5 2/8	5 2/8	6	11	Okanagan Valley, BC	Dan Osborne	Cabela's, Inc.	1969	440
244 7/8	28 3/8	28 5/8	25	5 5/8	6 4/8	9	11	Eagle Co., CO	Robert Rambo	Robert Rambo	1963	444
244 7/8	25 6/8	26 4/8	22 1/8	4 7/8	4 7/8	11	9	Lincoln Co., WY	Brian H. Suter	Brian H. Suter	1981	444
244 5/8	27 3/8	29 3/8	26 3/8	4 7/8	4 7/8	8	12	Summit Co., UT	Dewey R. Saxton	Dewey R. Saxton	1965	446
244 5/8	25 1/8	25 3/8	22 1/8	5 1/8	5 2/8	9	10	Park Co., MT	Unknown	Cabela's, Inc.	PR 1968	446
244 5/8	25 5/8	24 2/8	22 1/8	5 6/8	5 6/8	13	14	Teton Co., WY	Vern Shinkle	Vern Shinkle	1968	446
244 5/8	25 5/8	25 4/8	20 3/8	5 1/8	5 1/8	13	10	Delta Co., CO	Neil A. Briscoe, Jr.	Neil A. Briscoe, Jr.	1969	446
244 5/8	26	25	18 6/8	5 5/8	5 4/8	15	20	Rossland, BC	Victor Mattiazzi	Victor Mattiazzi	1970	446
244 5/8	23 7/8	22 4/8	20 5/8	5 3/8	5 1/8	8	9	Cibola Co., NM	Picked Up	D.J. Hollinger & B. Howard	1989	446
244 4/8	24 6/8	26 6/8	26	5	4 6/8	11	11	Kaibab Natl. For., AZ	C.M. Randal, Jr.	C.M. Randal, Jr.	1953	452
244 3/8	26 2/8	25 7/8	24 4/8	5 3/8	5 4/8	13	10	Lemhi Co., ID	Picked Up	Cabela's, Inc.	PR 1958	453
244 3/8	25 3/8	23 3/8	19 7/8	5 1/8	4 7/8	11	14	Wyoming	Unknown	D.J. Hollinger & B. Howard	PR 1990	453
244 2/8	25 1/8	24 5/8	22 5/8	5	5	12	13	Wasatch Co., UT	Unknown	Ted Clegg	1938	455

Score	Main Beam R	Main Beam L	Inside Spread	Circ. R	Circ. L	Points R	Points L	Locality	By	Owner	Date	Rank
244 2/8	24 4/8	26 2/8	28 4/8	5 6/8	5 5/8	8	9	Kaibab Natl. For., AZ	Ray Ramsey	Ray Ramsey	1952	455
244 2/8	24	24 6/8	20 6/8	6	6 1/8	16	16	British Columbia	Unknown	Douglas V. Grant	1958	455
244 2/8	28 4/8	28 7/8	30 1/8	5 2/8	5 4/8	8	9	Oak Creek, CO	Scott C. Hinkle	Scott C. Hinkle	1961	455
244 2/8	22 6/8	21 6/8	19 4/8	4 4/8	4 7/8	13	9	Fremont Co., WY	Warren V. Spriggs	Warren V. Spriggs	1962	455
244 2/8	25 6/8	26 3/8	22 7/8	5 2/8	5 4/8	13	12	San Juan Co., UT	Phil Acton	Phil Acton	1966	455
244 2/8	21 6/8	20 6/8	17 2/8	6	6	5	9	Mariposa Co., CA	Donald E. Nelson	Donald E. Nelson	1968	455
244 2/8	27 3/8	29 2/8	29 6/8	5 2/8	5 2/8	5	9	Montrose Co., CO	Jim Herndon	Mrs. Jim Herndon	1974	455
244 2/8	23 1/8	25	23 6/8	5 6/8	5 3/8	11	12	Mesa Co., CO	Thomas S. Hundley	Thomas S. Hundley	1986	455
244 1/8	25	26 2/8	29 2/8	5 5/8	5 6/8	12	11	Split Rock, WY	Herb Klein	Dallas Mus. of Natl. Hist.	1957	464
244 1/8	24 2/8	25 1/8	27	5 1/8	5 1/8	9	14	Mesa Co., CO	Edward B. Walsh	Mrs. Edward B. Walsh	1960	464
244 1/8	25 1/8	22 6/8	23 2/8	5 2/8	5 3/8	13	12	Grand Co., CO	Kenneth H. Newbury	Kenneth H. Newbury	1966	464
244 1/8	24 1/8	24 2/8	28	4 4/8	4 4/8	10	9	Big Horn Co., WY	Picked Up	Henry D. Frey	1978	464
244	26 4/8	27 1/8	24 6/8	4 6/8	4 6/8	10	9	East Canyon, UT	Ronald E. Coburn	Ronald E. Coburn	1961	468
244	25 6/8	25 6/8	28 7/8	5 1/8	5 1/8	10	9	Mohave Co., AZ	Eric P. McCormick	Eric P. McCormick	1998	468
243 7/8	23 6/8	23 7/8	26	5	4 6/8	11	10	Utah Co., UT	Zenneth K. Chamberlain	Zenneth K. Chamberlain	1956	470
243 7/8	24 1/8	27	24 6/8	4 6/8	4 4/8	12	18	St. Cyr Hills, SK	Raymond Jeancart	Raymond Jeancart	1963	470
243 7/8	26 7/8	27 2/8	26 3/8	4 4/8	5 3/8	13	10	Iron Co., UT	R. Kenneth Benson	Kendall L. Benson	1968	470
243 7/8	23 3/8	23 4/8	21 3/8	5	4 4/8	10	16	Malheur Co., OR	Larry L. Herron	Larry L. Herron	1983	470
243 6/8	24 1/8	27 3/8	27 3/8	4 3/8	5 5/8	18	10	Slave Lake, AB	R.W.H. Eben-Ebenau	R.W.H. Eben-Ebenau	1930	474
243 6/8	26	24 1/8	22 4/8	5 5/8	6 4/8	12	9	San Miguel Co., CO	Ben Crandell	Ben Crandell	1939	474
243 6/8	26 5/8	25 2/8	29 7/8	6 2/8	4 7/8	13	8	Apache Co., AZ	Jay M. Ogden	Jay M. Ogden	1991	474
243 6/8	25	24 6/8	22 3/8	4 7/8	5 3/8	11	12	Moose Creek, BC	Hartley Blatz	Hartley Blatz	1992	474
243 6/8	22 6/8	25 7/8	26 3/8	5 6/8	5 4/8	11	10	Montrose, SK	Gordon G. Pattison	Gordon G. Pattison	1992	474
243 6/8	24 2/8	23 6/8	22 7/8	5 4/8	4 7/8	9	7	Veteran, AB	Frank Geduhn	Frank Geduhn	1994	474
243 5/8	23 6/8	23 4/8	26 6/8	4 7/8	4 6/8	9	10	Cache Co., UT	Albert C. Steffenhagen	A. Ladell Atkinson	1924	480
243 5/8	25 6/8	25 6/8	23 3/8	4 6/8	5	11	10	Gunnison Co., CO	Unknown	D.J. Hollinger & B. Howard	PR 1970	480
243 4/8	23 6/8	22 7/8	21	5	5 5/8	13	14	Clear Creek Co., CO	Louis I. Kingsley	Louis I. Kingsley	1981	482
243 4/8	22 7/8	18 4/8	23 5/8	5 4/8	4 5/8	11	14	Cibola Co., NM	Fred R. Valdez, Jr.	Cabela's, Inc.	1986	482
243 4/8	24 4/8	28 1/8	21 6/8	4 6/8	4 7/8	11	11	Unknown	David Bicknell	D.J. Hollinger & B. Howard	PR 1986	482
243 3/8	25 4/8	28 3/8	25 5/8	5	5	10	8	Colorado	Unknown	Aly M. Bruner	1954	485
243 1/8	21 6/8	24 3/8	21 4/8	4 6/8	5 7/8	9	12	Harrison Gulch, CO	George R. Mattern	George R. Mattern	1958	486
243 1/8	25 7/8	23 4/8	25 1/8	5	5 5/8	7	8	Converse Co., WY	William E. Goswick	William E. Goswick	1968	486
243 1/8	27 3/8	24 4/8	21 5/8	5 4/8	5	11	11	Fremont Co., ID	Larry D. Hawker	Larry D. Hawker	1970	486
243 1/8	25	25 7/8	20	5 4/8	5 2/8	12	15	Mohave Co., AZ	Joe H. Heffelfinger	Joe H. Heffelfinger	1997	486
243	29 4/8	25	20 4/8	5	5 7/8	12	15	Crook Co., OR	Wes Mitts	Wes Mitts	1936	490
243	25 6/8	29 6/8	18	7 1/8	5 3/8	11	11	Winthrop, WA	Bruce Miller	Bruce Miller	1941	490
243	24 4/8	27 2/8	29	5 7/8	5	12	15	Oregon	Donald Mikkonen	Kevin J. Huserik	1950	490
243	29 6/8	24 1/8	22 6/8	5 3/8	5	10	10	Elko Co., NV	Paul Giuliani	Paul Giuliani	1971	490
242 7/8	22 6/8	30	28 4/8	4 7/8	5 4/8	11	12	Sheridan Co., WY	J.M. Blakeman	J.M. Blakeman	1952	494
242 7/8	24	23 7/8	26 4/8	5 1/8	5 1/8	8	10	Unknown	Unknown	Alan C. Ellsworth	PR 1960	494
242 7/8	26 4/8	25 6/8	22 7/8	5 4/8	5 7/8	12	18	Gem Co., ID	Roland Bright	Roland Bright	1965	494
242 7/8	26 3/8	26 3/8	22 3/8	5 1/8	5 6/8	13	11	Elko Co., NV	Edgar Meek	D.J. Hollinger & B. Howard	1971	494
242 5/8	25	26 3/8	18 3/8	6	6	16	14	Gem Co., ID	Cary G. Cada	Raymond R. Cross	1975	494
242 5/8	27 3/8	26 7/8	25 5/8	5 7/8	5 7/8	10	12	Idaho Co., ID	Daniel E. Osborne	Daniel E. Osborne	1959	499
242 5/8	27 3/8	27 3/8	27 3/8	4 6/8	4 6/8	9	13	Sanders Co., MT	Robert D. Frisk	Robert D. Frisk	1974	499
242 4/8	23 2/8	28 2/8	21 6/8	5 5/8	5 2/8	9	14	Camas Co., ID	Jeff M. Ashmead	Jeff M. Ashmead	1981	499
242 4/8	26 2/8	26 2/8	21 6/8	5	5	6		Sanders Co., MT	Ernest Butte	Roy Butte	1929	502
242 4/8	25 3/8	25 3/8	29 4/8	5	5	11	10	Blaine Co., ID	Roger A. Crowder	Roger A. Crowder	1957	502

MULE DEER - NON-TYPICAL ANTLERS
Odocoileus hemionus hemionus and certain related subspecies

Score	Length of Main Beam R	L	Inside Spread	Circumference at Smallest Place Between Burr and First Point R	L	Number of Points R	L	Locality	Hunter	Owner	Date Killed	Rank
242 4/8	27 4/8	27 5/8	25 4/8	6 1/8	5 6/8	9	8	Hinsdale Co., CO	Picked Up	Rick House	1991	502
242 4/8	26 4/8	26 7/8	24 7/8	5 3/8	5 1/8	10	10	Moffat Co., CO	Robert K. Kissling	Robert K. Kissling	2000	502
242 3/8	23 1/8	22 3/8	17 3/8	4 7/8	5	12	12	Arborfield, SK	Joseph Fournier	Joseph Fournier	1930	506
242 3/8	27 1/8	27 2/8	23 4/8	5	4 7/8	12	12	Sanpete Co., UT	Elwin Shelley	Cabela's, Inc.	1966	506
242 2/8	24 2/8	21 5/8	25 4/8	5 6/8	5 6/8	15	10	Iron Co., UT	Unknown	Cabela's, Inc.	PR 1958	508
242 2/8	23 2/8	23	20 2/8	5 3/8	5 6/8	12	17	Middle Park, CO	Picked Up	Karl H. Knorr	PR 1961	508
242 2/8	25 4/8	25 3/8	23 2/8	5	4 7/8	9	12	Rabbit Ears Pass, CO	Douglas Valentine	Douglas Valentine	1964	508
242 2/8	24	25 2/8	21	6	6	9	11	Rio Arriba Co., NM	Elvon DeVaney	Shannon DeVaney	1971	508
242 1/8	20 7/8	23 2/8	17 4/8	6	5 7/8	12	11	Cabri, SK	Gordon Millward	Gordon Millward	1960	512
242 1/8	28	27 6/8	22 1/8	6 1/8	6 1/8	9	11	Bear Lake Co., ID	Robert N. Gale	Robert N. Gale	1970	512
242 1/8	26	25 4/8	28	5 2/8	5 2/8	12	10	Hinsdale Co., CO	Bill Crose	Bill Crose	1973	512
242 1/8	25 6/8	25 5/8	23 2/8	5 4/8	5 4/8	10	14	S. Saskatchewan River, AB	Terry Lacey	Terry Lacey	1994	512
242 1/8	26 3/8	26 1/8	23 7/8	5 7/8	5 7/8	9	15	Clinton, BC	Jamie M. York	Jamie M. York	1995	512
242	26 2/8	26 6/8	28 1/8	5 4/8	5 4/8	10	8	Klamath Co., OR	Corinne Fields	Corinne Fields	1946	517
242	22 6/8	23 5/8	18 6/8	5 4/8	5 7/8	12	14	Garfield Co., CO	Daniel J. Stanek	Daniel J. Stanek	1981	517
242	25 7/8	25 6/8	26 2/8	5 2/8	5 1/8	14	8	Porcupine Ridge, BC	Richard C. Berreth	Richard C. Berreth	1985	517
241 7/8	25 4/8	24	24 3/8	5 4/8	5 4/8	7	13	Malheur Co., OR	Unknown	Daniel Woodbridge	PR 1938	520
241 7/8	24 5/8	24 2/8	25	5 2/8	5 2/8	11	19	Jefferson Co., OR	Spencer L. Darrar	Spencer L. Darrar	1953	520
241 7/8	22 5/8	20 2/8	20 2/8	5 1/8	5 1/8	9	10	Madison Co., ID	Grover Browning	D.J. Hollinger & B. Howard	1962	520
241 7/8	21	18	14 7/8	4 3/8	5 3/8	12	15	Sanders Co., MT	Buzz Faro	Buzz Faro	1963	520
241 7/8	24 2/8	25 6/8	24 5/8	5 3/8	5	10	11	Grand Co., CO	Ricky Dixon	D.J. Hollinger & B. Howard	1978	520
241 7/8	26 4/8	26 2/8	24	4 5/8	4 6/8	10	9	La Plata Co., CO	Randall N. Bostick	Randall N. Bostick	1984	520
241 7/8	24	25 4/8	30 6/8	5 7/8	6	14	11	Great Sand Hills, SK	A. Bruce LaRose	A. Bruce LaRose	1989	520
241 6/8	27 2/8	27 2/8	18 5/8	4 6/8	5	8	10	Bear Lake Co., ID	Len E. Mayfield	Len E. Mayfield	1972	527
241 6/8	25 6/8	26 3/8	26 6/8	5	5	11	9	Power Co., ID	Bryan Sprague	D.J. Hollinger & B. Howard	1981	527
241 6/8	24 7/8	23 5/8	31 1/8	5 6/8	6	17	19	Hot Springs Co., WY	Picked up	John A. Kotan, Jr.	1983	527
241 6/8	26	26	21 6/8	4	4 5/8	9	9	Park Co., WY	Troy A. Jones	Troy A. Jones	1997	527
241 5/8	27 1/8	27	23 4/8	5 3/8	5 3/8	13	10	Adams Co., ID	Joseph N. Ruscigno	Joseph N. Ruscigno	1960	531
241 5/8	23 4/8	22 3/8	21 7/8	6 2/8	6	15	16	Red Deer River, AB	Carl J. Peterson	Carl J. Peterson	1993	531
241 4/8	25 7/8	22 3/8	25 3/8	4 7/8	5 3/8	13	18	Park Co., MT	James H. Batzloff	James H. Batzloff	1959	533
241 4/8	26 4/8	27	27	5	5 3/8	8	7	Socorro Co., NM	James T. Everheart	James H. Everheart	1973	533
241 4/8	25 1/8	25 7/8	23 3/8	4 4/8	4 4/8	10	9	Summit Co., CO	Robert R. Ross	Robert R. Ross	1974	533
241 4/8	27 2/8	27	22 5/8	5 3/8	5 3/8	17	12	Douglas Co., CO	Donald E. Ditmars	Donald E. Ditmars	1994	533
241 4/8	27 6/8	28 1/8	22 3/8	6 4/8	6 6/8	8	13	Gooding Co., ID	Robert L. Fossceco	Robert L. Fossceco	1997	533
241 4/8	26 3/8	26 3/8	23 4/8	5 7/8	5 7/8	10	11	Colfax Co., NM	Andrew J. Ortega	Andrew J. Ortega	1998	533
241 3/8	22 3/8	23 7/8	20 4/8	5 1/8	5 2/8	10	12	Adams Co., ID	Peter Renberg	Peter Renberg	1963	539

Score								Locality	Hunter	Owner	Date	Rank
241 3/8	26 6/8	24 7/8	24 3/8	5	5 1/8	12	13	Salmon River, ID	Richard Shilling	Richard Shilling	1965	539
241 3/8	19	24 6/8	20	6 2/8	6 4/8	12	15	Nakusp, BC	Frank Vicen	Frank Vicen	1967	539
241 3/8	27 1/8	26 7/8	26 1/8	5 5/8	5 4/8	13	11	Kane Co., UT	Aivars O. Berkis	Aivars O. Berkis	1987	539
241 3/8	25 3/8	25 2/8	22 4/8	5 3/8	5 4/8	12	11	Unknown	Unknown	Aly M. Bruner	PR 1989	539
241 3/8	23 1/8	23 6/8	19 5/8	5 2/8	5 3/8	11	13	Sublette Co., WY	Larry G. Isley	Larry G. Isley	1999	539
241 2/8	23 3/8	24 3/8	21 2/8	5 5/8	5 6/8	12	11	Lumby, BC	Bill Shunter	Bill Shunter	1964	545
241 2/8	26 6/8	25 1/8	18 6/8	5	5	10	11	Oak Creek, CO	Richard J. Peltier	Richard J. Peltier	1967	545
241 1/8	24 3/8	24 5/8	24 6/8	5 7/8	5 7/8	16	13	Bloom Creek, BC	Ron Yerbury	Ron Yerbury	1992	547
241 1/8	27 1/8	26 1/8	26 6/8	6 3/8	6 1/8	11	12	Lincoln Co., WY	Mark C. Lafferty	Mark C. Lafferty	1994	547
241	26 6/8	25 7/8	26 7/8	6	5 5/8	9	10	Fremont Co., ID	Don Freeman	Don Freeman	1953	549
241	25 6/8	25 7/8	24 6/8	5	5 1/8	8	7	Colorado	Nolan Allen	Nolan Allen	PR 1969	549
241	26 2/8	25 4/8	26 3/8	4 6/8	4 6/8	11	11	Lewis & Clark Co., MT	Mike Filcher	Mike Filcher	1972	549
241	27	25 4/8	27 4/8	5 6/8	5 6/8	10	8	Colorado	Unknown	Cabela's, Inc.	PR 2001	549
241	24 5/8	25 7/8	23 4/8	5 5/8	5 1/8	12	11	Moffat Co., CO	Gary W. Christensen	Gary W. Christensen	2003	549
240 7/8	27	27 2/8	25 2/8	5 1/8	5 2/8	6	6	New Castle Co., CO	Harold F. Auld	Harold F. Auld	1960	554
240 7/8	27 7/8	27 5/8	29	5 1/8	5 3/8	7	9	Rio Arriba Co., NM	Douglas Bryant	Douglas Bryant	1988	554
240 7/8	27 4/8	28 2/8	22	6	5 7/8	7	12	Coconino Co., AZ	Robert B. Metzgus	Robert B. Metzgus	1993	554
240 6/8	26 3/8	25 6/8	23 6/8	5 5/8	5 5/8	9	11	Colorado	Unknown	Darryl Powell	PR 1970	557
240 6/8	27	25 6/8	27 1/8	5 7/8	5 1/8	10	8	Eagle Co., CO	Steve B. Humann	Steve B. Humann	1982	557
240 6/8	23	23 5/8	20 2/8	4 6/8	4 5/8	13	12	Norton Co., KS	Bill Bussen	Bill Bussen	1996	557
240 5/8	26 4/8	27 6/8	23 2/8	6	5 7/8	10	13	Kaibab Natl. For., AZ	Bert E. George	Bert E. George	1949	560
240 5/8	22	22	21	4 7/8	4 7/8	10	9	Elko Co., NV	George M. Boman	George M. Boman	1956	560
240 5/8	26	26 1/8	26 1/8	5 4/8	5 2/8	11	12	Lincoln Co., WY	Unknown	D.J. Hollinger & B. Howard	PR 1965	560
240 4/8	26 3/8	26 6/8	19	5 6/8	5 6/8	10	13	Montrose Co., CO	Albin C. Wood	Albin C. Wood	1961	563
240 4/8	26 4/8	27	21 4/8	6 2/8	6 2/8	10	9	Modoc Co., CA	Niilo Niemi	Niilo Niemi	1968	563
240 4/8	27 1/8	25 4/8	27 1/8	5 3/8	5 4/8	9	8	La Plata Co., CO	Cullen D. Wagoner	Cullen D. Wagoner	1976	563
240 4/8	23 6/8	22	22 6/8	5 1/8	5 4/8	10	11	Eagle Co., CO	James P. Hale	James P. Hale	1979	563
240 4/8	23 6/8	23 5/8	23 2/8	5 1/8	5 2/8	11	14	Morgan Co., UT	Pietro De Santis	Pietro De Santis	1982	563
240 4/8	23	24 4/8	21 5/8	5 2/8	5 2/8	15	14	Garfield Co., CO	James E. Powell, Jr.	James E. Powell, Jr.	1983	563
240 4/8	25 5/8	24 4/8	21 6/8	5 4/8	5 4/8	10	9	Great Sand Hills, SK	Emile T. Paradis	Emile T. Paradis	1989	563
240 4/8	22	22 3/8	17 4/8	4 4/8	4 4/8	13	11	Coconino Co., AZ	Craig R. Dunlap	Craig R. Dunlap	1993	563
240 3/8	22 3/8	24 5/8	21 2/8	5 6/8	5 7/8	13	12	Missoula Co., MT	Richard A. Gendrow	Richard A. Gendrow	1973	571
240 3/8	25 1/8	25 4/8	24 1/8	6 3/8	6	10	12	Unknown	Unknown	Terry L. Amos	PR 2000	571
240 2/8	27 3/8	27 1/8	21 7/8	5 2/8	5 2/8	11	11	Mt. Dellenbaugh, AZ	Edwin R. Riggs	Edwin R. Riggs	1964	573
240 2/8	25 4/8	25 4/8	19 4/8	4 7/8	4 7/8	9	9	Rio Arriba Co., NM	J.B. Meyers, Jr.	J.B. Meyers, Jr.	1971	573
240 2/8	28 4/8	28 1/8	23 1/8	5 1/8	5 1/8	9	8	Crook Co., OR	Charles H. Kies	Charles H. Kies	1995	573
240 2/8	27	26 4/8	22 2/8	6 3/8	6 4/8	13	7	Unknown	Unknown	Darryl Powell	PR 1995	573
240 1/8	22 7/8	22 6/8	24 5/8	5 2/8	5 2/8	9	11	Yuma Co., CO	Vernon E. Young	Vernon E. Young	1995	573
240 1/8	24 2/8	24	19 6/8	5 6/8	5 7/8	13	12	Harney Co., OR	R.G. Creager	R.G. Creager	1957	578
240 1/8	28 1/8	28 4/8	25 5/8	7 1/8	5 3/8	13	8	Caribou Co., ID	Roy M. McIntosh	Roy M. McIntosh	1967	578
240 1/8	23 4/8	23 1/8	25 5/8	5 6/8	5 5/8	12	12	Elmore Co., ID	Phillip K. Messer	Phillip K. Messer	1971	578
240 1/8	24 6/8	25 5/8	27 7/8	5 5/8	5 4/8	11	14	Sanpete Co., UT	Elwin Shelley	Elwin Shelley	1972	578
240	28 3/8	25	25	5 4/8	5 4/8	7	10	Kamloops, BC	Ralph McLean	Ralph McLean	1960	582
240	25 7/8	24 4/8	23 2/8	5 6/8	5 6/8	12	10	Grand Valley, CO	Ed Peters, Jr.	Ed Peters, Jr.	1962	582
240	26 1/8	28 5/8	27 1/8	4 7/8	4 7/8	9	8	San Juan Wilder., CO	Tommie Cornelius	Tommie Cornelius	1967	582
240	27 6/8	27 7/8	23 2/8	5 5/8	5 6/8	8	13	Frenchman River, SK	Edward J. Hardin	Edward J. Hardin	1992	582
239 7/8	26 6/8	24 5/8	21 4/8	5 7/8	5 7/8	11	10	Caribou Co., ID	Jack E. Detmer	Jack E. Detmer	1964	586
239 7/8	28 1/8	27 7/8	26 2/8	5 4/8	5 4/8	9	10	Blaine Co., ID	Unknown	D.J. Hollinger & B. Howard	PR 1975	586

Odocoileus hemionus hemionus and certain related subspecies

Score	Length of Main Beam R	L	Inside Spread	Circumference at Smallest Place Between Burr and First Point R	L	Number of Points R	L	Locality	Hunter	Owner	Date Killed	Rank
239 7/8	24 6/8	23 7/8	25	5	4 6/8	12	15	Diefenbaker Lake, SK	Anthony J. Pyette	Anthony J. Pyette	1996	586
239 6/8	27 6/8	26 6/8	27 4/8	5 2/8	5 1/8	13	13	La Plata Co., CO	David Blake	David Blake	1977	589
239 6/8	25	24 6/8	23	5 4/8	5 2/8	11	11	Carbon Co., UT	Michael R. Tryon	Michael R. Tryon	1998	589
239 4/8	25 1/8	25 5/8	19 2/8	5 3/8	5 2/8	14	13	Pondera Co., MT	Dan Mougeot	Dan Mougeot	1961	591
239 4/8	27 4/8	29 2/8	24 5/8	5 5/8	5 4/8	12	14	Washington Co., UT	Doug McKnight	Doug McKnight	1967	591
239 4/8	24 2/8	24 7/8	20 6/8	6	5 5/8	8	11	Teton Co., WY	Gary C. Livingston	Gary C. Livingston	1990	593
239 3/8	28 3/8	27 2/8	28 1/8	4 7/8	4 6/8	8	8	Grant Co., OR	Harry A. Dew	Derral A. Dew	1971	594
239 2/8	27 6/8	26 5/8	24	5 4/8	5 3/8	8	8	Mohave Co., AZ	Douglas B. Bundy	Douglas B. Bundy	1995	594
239 1/8	26 1/8	27 1/8	25	4 7/8	4 6/8	11	11	Summit Co., CO	Fred H. Palmer	Fred H. Palmer	1959	596
239 1/8	29	26 4/8	31 2/8	4 7/8	5 3/8	8	11	Lucky Lake, SK	Dan Mosley	Dan Mosley	1996	596
239 1/8	24 4/8	24	23 6/8	4 4/8	4 4/8	10	9	San Miguel Co., CO	Vodne O. Chapoose	Vodne O. Chapoose	2002	596
239	24 1/8	25 3/8	24 5/8	4 7/8	5	13	8	Wallace Co., KS	Rudolph A. Busen	Ralph L. McKinley	1993	599
238 7/8	24 1/8	27 5/8	29 2/8	5	5 1/8	8	12	Crook Co., OR	Derral A. Dew	Derral A. Dew	1969	600
238 7/8	24 4/8	26 6/8	29 5/8	5 4/8	5 6/8	9	8	Mohave Co., AZ	Rachelle Iverson	Rachelle Iverson	1997	600
238 6/8	26 2/8	26 3/8	28	4 7/8	4 6/8	11	9	Lincoln Co., WY	Waylon G. Beckstrom	Waylon G. Beckstrom	1997	602
238 5/8	26 4/8	25 2/8	19 5/8	5 3/8	5 2/8	10	12	Utah Co., UT	Jacob E. Coffman	Rick Brereton	1952	603
238 4/8	27	27 1/8	28 7/8	6 1/8	5 4/8	17	13	Pima Co., AZ	Richard M. Cordova	Richard M. Cordova	1989	604
238 4/8	26 2/8	25 6/8	23 7/8	5 1/8	5 2/8	11	13	Coconino Co., AZ	Gilbert T. Adams	Gilbert T. Adams	1992	604
238 2/8	27	26 3/8	21 7/8	6	5 7/8	12	8	Churn Creek, BC	Burt Collins	Corky Collins	PR 1920	606
238 2/8	23 6/8	24 1/8	26 5/8	5 1/8	5	16	11	Walsh, AB	Rick M. MacDonald	Rick M. MacDonald	1987	606
238	24 4/8	28 1/8	22 6/8	5 1/8	5 1/8	10	11	Fremont Co., WY	Hank Hammond	Ralph E. White	1943	608
238	26 3/8	26	26 4/8	5	5 1/8	12	10	Mesa Co., CO	James D. Greer	James D. Greer	1969	608
237 7/8	26 6/8	26 2/8	21 2/8	5 3/8	4 7/8	8	11	Gunnison Co., CO	Herbert Hild III	Herbert Hild III	1996	610
237 6/8	26 2/8	26 2/8	22 4/8	4 5/8	4 5/8	14	12	Carbon Co., WY	Terry L. Younce	Terry L. Younce	1969	611
237 6/8	25 3/8	25 2/8	25	4 5/8	4 5/8	9	11	Coconino Co., AZ	Ronald J. Wolosyn	Ronald J. Wolosyn	1992	611
237 6/8	23 7/8	23 1/8	20 1/8	5 5/8	5 4/8	13	10	Caribou Co., ID	Robert L. Rigby	Robert L. Rigby	1996	611
237 5/8	26 2/8	27 2/8	26	6 6/8	6 4/8	11	11	Pitkin Co., CO	Dennis G. Muth	Dennis G. Muth	1981	614
237 5/8	25 4/8	26	21 7/8	4 7/8	4 6/8	8	9	Lynx Creek, BC	J. Gregory Simmons	J. Gregory Simmons	1989	614
237 3/8	27 3/8	26 3/8	30 5/8	6 3/8	6	9	9	Harney Co., OR	Culver Page	Aly M. Bruner	1927	616
237 3/8	27 2/8	23 7/8	20 2/8	4 6/8	5 4/8	8	13	Lemhi Co., ID	Clifford Nealis	Dale Nealis	1960	616
237 3/8	25 4/8	24 1/8	22 4/8	5	5 1/8	12	10	Douglas Co., CO	Unknown	D.J. Hollinger & B. Howard	PR 1970	616
237 3/8	23 6/8	23 2/8	23 3/8	5 5/8	5 7/8	11	12	Bonneville Co., ID	Bert L. Freed	Bert L. Freed	1987	616
237 2/8	27 2/8	24 4/8	23 5/8	6	6 5/8	8	15	Chelan Co., WA	Louis Brown	Kim S. Scott	1940	620
237 2/8	25 5/8	24	21	4 2/8	4 3/8	15	9	Golden Valley Co., ND	Palmer Georgeson	Palmer Georgeson	1965	620
237 2/8	26 7/8	27 6/8	22 1/8	6 2/8	6 1/8	11	10	Colorado	Unknown	Aly M. Bruner	PR 1996	620
237	25 2/8	25 7/8	28 7/8	4 4/8	5 2/8	11	14	Colorado	Lillia Winkler	Mike Sheppeard	1982	623

Score	Main Beam R	Main Beam L	Inside Spread	Circ. R	Circ. L	Pts R	Pts L	Locality	Hunter	Owner	Date	Rank
236 7/8	24 5/8	24 4/8	23	5 1/8	5 4/8	9	12	Wallowa Co., OR	Unknown	Ken Moore	1940	624
236 7/8	26 2/8	27 2/8	30 4/8	4 4/8	4 5/8	9	9	Lincoln Co., WY	Terry Barton	D.J. Hollinger & B. Howard	1989	624
236 7/8	24 6/8	24	17 7/8	4 7/8	4 6/8	9	9	Fort St. John, BC	Jos Van Hage	Jos Van Hage	1994	624
236 7/8	24	24 7/8	22 3/8	4 4/8	4 5/8	10	8	Forty Mile Co., AB	Merle Klaudt	Merle Klaudt	1998	628
236 6/8	25 2/8	25 7/8	22 2/8	5	4 5/8	14	12	Opuntia Lake, SK	Tom D. Jiricka	Tom D. Jiricka	2003	629
236 5/8	25 6/8	26 5/8	25	5 5/8	6	12	11	Lincoln Co., NV	Ronald N. Anderson	Ronald N. Anderson	2001	630
236 3/8	25 3/8	24 6/8	17 7/8	5 3/8	5 6/8	10	12	Coconino Co., AZ	Johnny C. Parsons	Johnny C. Parsons	1997	631
236 2/8	25 1/8	23 6/8	23	6	6	10	10	Kane Co., UT	Ken Church	Cabela's, Inc.	1987	631
236 2/8	27 5/8	27 2/8	20 3/8	6 1/8	6	12	9	Rio Arriba Co., NM	Picked Up	Pat Powell	2000	633
236 1/8	26 3/8	26	21 2/8	5 7/8	6 1/8	16	12	Rio Arriba Co., NM	Shane Vigil	Shane Vigil	1997	634
236	26	27	28 1/8	5 4/8	5	11	10	Deschutes Co., OR	Ray Cole	Ray Cole	1951	634
236	26 5/8	29 1/8	27	5	4 6/8	10	10	Ravalli Co., MT	Daniel I. Cainan	B&C National Collection	1957	634
236	28 1/8	28 2/8	29 1/8	4 7/8	4 6/8	10	7	Summit Co., CO	Ray Alt	Ray Alt	1987	634
235 7/8	28 6/8	22	28 2/8	4 7/8	5 3/8	5	9	Antelope Lake, SK	Roland Joubert	Roland Joubert	1993	638
235 6/8	22 6/8	26 5/8	22	5 2/8	5 4/8	9	10	Nevada Co., CA	Unknown	Charles L. Leavell	1920	639
235 5/8	24	28 2/8	26 5/8	5 2/8	4 7/8	12	12	White Pine Co., NV	Roland J. DiSanza	Roland J. DiSanza	1968	639
235 5/8	27 4/8	24 4/8	27 3/8	4 7/8	5 3/8	14	10	Montezuma Co., CO	Picked Up	Tom G. Broderick	1992	641
235 5/8	23 6/8	24 5/8	30 2/8	5 4/8	5	10	8	Kane Co., UT	Rance Rollins	Rance Rollins	1965	641
235 4/8	24 6/8	24 6/8	28 2/8	5	4 5/8	11	10	Cypress Hills, SK	Margie R. Stabler	Margie R. Stabler	1994	643
235 3/8	24	24	23	4 6/8	5	13	12	Rio Arriba Co., NM	J.B. Meyers, Jr.	J.B. Meyers, Jr.	1969	644
235 3/8	25 1/8	25 1/8	21 1/8	5 2/8	5 4/8	9	12	Ferry Co., WA	Jack Ledgerwood	Kelly Ledgerwood	1938	644
235 3/8	27 4/8	27 4/8	20 3/8	5 3/8	5 6/8	10	10	Missoula Co., MT	Mitchel Rasmussen	Mitchel Rasmussen	1978	644
235 2/8	25 2/8	25 2/8	27 4/8	5 2/8	4 7/8	6	11	Cassia Co., ID	Picked Up	Keith G. Palmer	1996	647
235 2/8	24 7/8	24 3/8	24 6/8	4 7/8	5 4/8	7	13	Lincoln Co., WY	Steven M. James	Steven M. James	1991	647
235 1/8	23	23	27 7/8	5 4/8	5 2/8	8	11	Yuma Co., CO	Dusty T. Walters	Dusty T. Walters	1998	649
235	25 7/8	25 5/8	23 3/8	5 2/8	4 7/8	9	11	Clark Co., ID	James E. Gabettas	James E. Gabettas	1999	650
235	25 4/8	25 5/8	25 5/8	4 6/8	5 1/8	9	10	Garnier Lakes, AB	Arthur Gallagher	Richard C. Nelson	1936	650
235	25 2/8	25 2/8	25 5/8	5	5 3/8	10	10	Iron Co., UT	Don Higgins	Don C. Higgins	1988	650
234 6/8	28	29 2/8	22 4/8	5 2/8	5	9	11	Eagle Co., CO	Charles D. Elam	Charles D. Elam	2002	653
234 6/8	23 4/8	24 3/8	22	5 4/8	5 4/8	8	7	Modoc Co., CA	Unknown	D.J. Hollinger & B. Howard	1950	653
234 6/8	24 5/8	24 1/8	27 4/8	5 1/8	5 3/8	9	11	Lincoln Co., NV	George Brown	George J. Brown	1998	656
234 3/8	25 7/8	26	32 3/8	4 7/8	5	7	11	Salmon Arm, BC	Jeffrey M. Snow	Jeffrey M. Snow	2002	656
234 3/8	29	27 4/8	21	5 4/8	4 7/8	9	9	Fremont Co., WY	Gail E. Folston	Gail E. Folston	1968	656
234 2/8	25	25 2/8	22 4/8	5 1/8	5 2/8	9	12	Powell Co., MT	John D. Simons	John D. Simons	1978	659
234 2/8	28 7/8	29 1/8	26	5 2/8	6 4/8	8	8	Williams Lake, BC	Dean Mace	Dean Mace	1998	659
234 1/8	26 4/8	26	25 7/8	6 3/8	4 7/8	9	13	Boise Co., ID	Lowell B. Nosker	Lowell B. Nosker	1946	661
234 1/8	26 6/8	25 7/8	25 1/8	4 6/8	6	14	12	Delta Co., CO	Picked Up	Robert A. Kaufman	1980	661
234 1/8	23 1/8	22 7/8	28 2/8	6	5 2/8	8	6	Lake Co., OR	Unknown	Donnie J. Allen	1960	661
234	24 4/8	24 4/8	18 2/8	5 2/8	6	9	8	Gunnison Co., CO	Jack E. Moermond	Jack E. Moermond	1970	664
234	27 3/8	27 3/8	25	5 7/8	5 2/8	10	8	Larimer Co., CO	David R. Cheeseman	David R. Cheeseman	1986	664
233 7/8	23 5/8	23 5/8	28 7/8	6	5	9	11	Rio Arriba Co., NM	Alan Vicenti	Alan Vicenti	1994	666
233 7/8	26 3/8	26 3/8	26 6/8	5 2/8	5 5/8	9	9	Lincoln Co., NV	Jason G. Carter	Jason G. Carter	2003	666
233 6/8	23 2/8	24	25 7/8	6	4 7/8	13	10	Deschutes Co., OR	Mr. Matteson	Lisa I. Thomas	1960	666
233 6/8	29 3/8	24	25 6/8	4 6/8	5 4/8	13	9	Colorado	Unknown	Darryl Powell	PR 1992	668
233 4/8	25	26 7/8	22	4 4/8	5 2/8	12	10	Rio Blanco Co., CO	Robert E. Buckles	Robert E. Buckles	1960	669
233 3/8	20 7/8	24	25 5/8	5	5 5/8	11	9	Carbon Co., WY	William S. Nelson	William S. Nelson	1998	670
233 3/8	23 6/8	24	19 3/8	5 4/8	5	8	10	Blaine Co., ID	Art Richards	Kyle J. Kimball	1984	671
233 3/8	19 6/8	25	19 6/8	5	5 4/8	10	10	Cassia Co., ID	James J. Knoll	James J. Knoll	1986	671

Score	Length of Main Beam		Inside Spread	Circumference at Smallest Place Between Burr and First Point		Number of Points		Locality	Hunter	Owner	Date Killed	Rank
	R	L		R	L	R	L					
233 3/8	25	26 1/8	21 7/8	6 2/8	6 3/8	11	9	S. Saskatchewan River, AB	Kelvin J. Clary	Kelvin J. Clary	2003	671
233 2/8	26	25 4/8	22	5	4 7/8	9	9	Beaton River, BC	Dwayne Shawchek	Dwayne Shawchek	1992	673
233 2/8	26 1/8	28 1/8	26 2/8	5 2/8	5 2/8	8	7	Rio Arriba Co., NM	William J. Smith	William J. Smith	1998	673
233 2/8	25 6/8	25 6/8	24 4/8	6 2/8	6	11	12	San Juan Co., UT	Leon P. Rush, Jr.	Leon P. Rush, Jr.	2001	673
232 7/8	28 2/8	26 2/8	21 6/8	4 5/8	4 6/8	7	10	Arizona	Brian Quintero	D.J. Hollinger & B. Howard	1986	676
232 7/8	28 3/8	27 4/8	23 3/8	5 3/8	5 2/8	9	11	Caribou Co., ID	Michael H. Ferrera	Michael H. Ferrera	1992	676
232 6/8	23 6/8	22 4/8	28 5/8	4 6/8	4 7/8	13	11	Park Co., WY	Eddie Schwager	Bill Clark	1949	678
232 6/8	22 5/8	21	19 3/8	5 4/8	6	13	14	Scott Co., KS	Michael A. Kershner	Michael A. Kershner	1999	678
232 6/8	22 4/8	23 4/8	20 4/8	5 2/8	5 2/8	10	13	Hayes Co., NE	Delbert Fornoff	Christopher G. Fornoff	1959	680
232 5/8	24 4/8	25 7/8	17 5/8	4 3/8	4 3/8	13	10	Teton Co., WY	Bruce K. McRae	Bruce K. McRae	1986	680
232 4/8	25	24 2/8	20 3/8	5 4/8	5 1/8	10	10	Adams Co., ID	Allen Solterbeck	Ryan B. Hatfield	1973	682
232 3/8	27 2/8	26 5/8	22 2/8	5 3/8	5 5/8	14	9	Colorado	Unknown	Melvin A. Mitchell, Jr.	PR 1900	683
232 3/8	26 1/8	26	23 5/8	5 4/8	5 3/8	12	12	Eagle Co., CO	Joe W. Schmidt	D.J. Hollinger & B. Howard	PR 1960	683
232 3/8	27 2/8	25 7/8	25 3/8	5	5 2/8	11	13	Eagle Creek, SK	Joe W. Schmidt	Joe W. Schmidt	1997	683
232 2/8	25 4/8	25 6/8	25 6/8	4 5/8	4 7/8	9	8	Garfield Co., CO	Allen O. Downie, Jr.	Allen O. Downie, Jr.	2000	686
232 2/8	24 3/8	25 1/8	22 1/8	5	5	10	9	Elmore Co., ID	David R. Heck	David R. Heck	2002	686
232	24 6/8	26	21 3/8	6	5 7/8	10	10	Garfield Co., CO	Vern Williams	D.J. Hollinger & B. Howard	1961	688
232	23 1/8	24	18 3/8	5 3/8	5 3/8	10	10	Grand Co., CO	William L. Henry	William L. Henry	1986	688
232	26	25 2/8	23 1/8	4 7/8	5	8	9	Rio Arriba Co., NM	Picked Up	Robert J. Seeds	1998	688
231 7/8	26 5/8	26 6/8	25 1/8	4 4/8	4 6/8	11	12	Utah Co., UT	John Fast	Tony Mol	PR 1949	691
231 7/8	26	25 3/8	25	6 2/8	5 7/8	10	7	Lake Co., OR	Marion J. Rossiter	Marion J. Rossiter	1961	691
231 7/8	24 6/8	24 6/8	23 5/8	5 6/8	5 4/8	9	10	Bear Lake Co., ID	George L. Clifford	George L. Clifford	1966	691
231 7/8	25 5/8	30 2/8	25 2/8	5	4 7/8	11	9	Rio Arriba Co., NM	Dan F. Holleman	Vernon D. Holleman	1966	691
231 6/8	25 1/8	24 7/8	23 2/8	5 2/8	5 2/8	8	10	Yuma Co., CO	Gregg W. Stults	Gregg W. Stults	2000	695
231 4/8	26 5/8	25 7/8	30 2/8	5 5/8	5 5/8	5	9	Yuma Co., CO	I. Dwayne Bullock	I. Dwayne Bullock	1986	696
231 4/8	24 4/8	24 6/8	26 3/8	5 2/8	5 3/8	8	10	Elmore Co., ID	R.A. Thorpe & B. Wippel	Robert A. Thorpe	2000	696
231 3/8	28	28 1/8	35	5 5/8	5 6/8	10	10	Camas Co., ID	Jack Omohundro	Aly M. Bruner	1960	698
231 2/8	23 4/8	22 4/8	22	5 1/8	4 7/8	12	11	Bannock Co., ID	Kevin D. Linford	Kevin D. Linford	1982	699
231 2/8	21 1/8	21 3/8	20	5 4/8	5 2/8	7	8	Lincoln Co., NV	Leo W. Mack, Jr.	Leo W. Mack, Jr.	1995	699
231 1/8	24 4/8	25 6/8	16 4/8	5 1/8	5 3/8	9	6	Stevens Co., WA	David Kilmartin	David Kilmartin	1985	701
231 1/8	21	14 5/8	20 5/8	6 6/8	6 6/8	10	10	Cochrane, AB	Helmut Schock	Helmut Schock	1995	701
231 1/8	23 1/8	24 5/8	22 1/8	4 6/8	4 6/8	11	9	Eagle Co., CO	Mike Crites	Mike Crites	1996	701
231	23 7/8	26	19 3/8	5 7/8	5 4/8	7	13	Teton Co., ID	Unknown	D.J. Hollinger & B. Howard	1979	704
231	24 1/8	21 5/8	19 6/8	5 4/8	5 2/8	11	9	Coconino Co., AZ	Robert E. Anderson	Robert E. Anderson	1988	704
231	27 7/8	28 1/8	24 3/8	5	5 1/8	8	7	S. Saskatchewan River, SK	Sheldon C. McNabb	Sheldon C. McNabb	2001	704
230 7/8	21 7/8	21 3/8	16 3/8	5 4/8	5 7/8	12	9	Faulkland, BC	Unknown	D.J. Hollinger & B. Howard	PR 1960	707

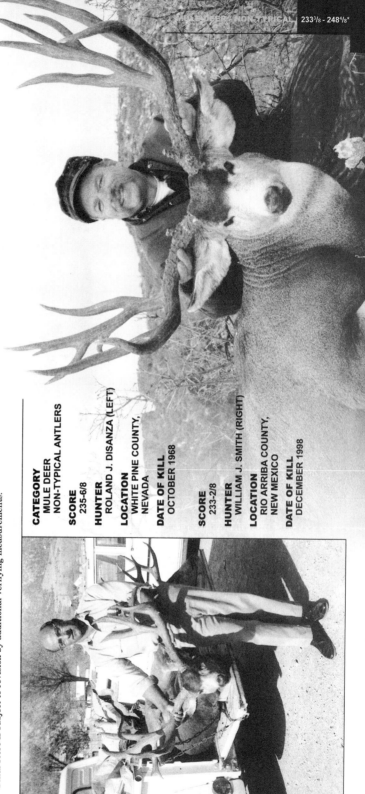

CATEGORY
MULE DEER
NON-TYPICAL ANTLERS

SCORE
235-6/8

HUNTER
ROLAND J. DiSANZA (LEFT)

LOCATION
WHITE PINE COUNTY, NEVADA

DATE OF KILL
OCTOBER 1968

SCORE
233-2/8

HUNTER
WILLIAM J. SMITH (RIGHT)

LOCATION
RIO ARRIBA COUNTY, NEW MEXICO

DATE OF KILL
DECEMBER 1998

Score								Owner	Location	Hunter	Year	Rank
230 5/8	24 1/8	25 2/8	27 4/8	5	5 4/8	7	10	Gregory S. Amaral	San Juan Co., UT	Gregory S. Amaral	1988	708
230 5/8	28 1/8	27 6/8	31 1/8	5 4/8	5 2/8	10	10	Ross A. Ray	Mohave Co., AZ	Ross A. Ray	1996	708
230 5/8	22 1/8	23 2/8	21 1/8	5 4/8	5 3/8	13	8	Jack W. Stewart	Salmon Arm, BC	Jack W. Stewart	2000	708
230 4/8	26 7/8	27 2/8	23 2/8	5 1/8	5 3/8	9	10	Mitch S. Crouser	Harney Co., OR	Mitch S. Crouser	1998	711
230 3/8	23 7/8	24 1/8	22 2/8	5 1/8	5	9	8	Ted R. Ramirez	Eagle Co., CO	Ted R. Ramirez	1996	712
230 1/8	27	25 2/8	22	5	4 5/8	11	12	Unknown	Baker Co., OR	D.J. Hollinger & B. Howard	PR 1970	713
230 1/8	27	26 7/8	27 4/8	4 5/8	4 5/8	11	8	Frank W. Penland	Delta Co., CO	Frank W. Penland	1978	713
230 1/8	25	24	24 5/8	4 4/8	5 5/8	3	12	Cloyd R. Ream	Wayne Co., UT	Cloyd R. Ream	1999	713
230 1/8	26	24 5/8	22 7/8	5 3/8	5 5/8	7	8	Shane Memmott	Mohave Co., AZ	Shane Memmott	2002	713
230	27 2/8	26 7/8	20 6/8	4 6/8	5	11	9	William Meyer	Buck Lake, AB	Bill Landals	PR 1910	717
230	23 3/8	22 7/8	22 6/8	5 1/8	5 1/8	11	11	Wayne W. Montgomery	Coconino Co., AZ	Virginia M. Reed	PR 1940	717
230	27 1/8	25 4/8	22 7/8	4 6/8	4 6/8	11	7	Unknown	Garfield Co., CO	Jack Thompson	PR 1978	717
230	25 7/8	25 5/8	20 1/8	5 4/8	5 4/8	11	8	Leland R. Nevill	Boise Co., ID	Leland R. Nevill	1986	717
230	24 4/8	23	25 4/8	5	5	12	12	Jason Langslet	Washoe Co., NV	Jason Langslet	1995	717
230	24 5/8	23 4/8	29 6/8	6 2/8	6 2/8	11	8	Joseph J. Stroh	Pitkin Co., CO	Joseph J. Stroh	2002	717
320 2/8*	25 2/8	24 4/8	16 3/8	7	6	23	25	Herb Bannister	Trinity Valley, BC	Charles Bannister	1943	717
248 4/8*	27 6/8	24 5/8	22 5/8	6	5	13	13	Aaron Q. Howell	Rio Arriba Co., NM	Aaron Q. Howell	2001	717

* Final score is subject to revision by additional verifying measurements.

CATEGORY
MULE DEER
NON-TYPICAL ANTLERS

SCORE
230-4/8

HUNTER
MITCH S. CROUSER (RIGHT)

LOCATION
HARNEY COUNTY, OREGON

DATE OF KILL
OCTOBER 1998

CATEGORY
MULE DEER
NON-TYPICAL ANTLERS

SCORE
234

HUNTER
JASON G. CARTER

LOCATION
LINCOLN COUNTY,
NEVADA

DATE OF KILL
OCTOBER 2003

CATEGORY
MULE DEER
NON-TYPICAL ANTLERS

SCORE
232-2/8

HUNTER
DAVID R. HECK

LOCATION
ELMORE COUNTY, IDAHO

DATE OF KILL
OCTOBER 2002

MULE DEER, COLUMBIA AND SITKA BLACKTAIL DEER BOUNDARIES

The problem of properly defining the boundary between the large antlered mule deer, which ranges widely over most of the western third of the United States and western Canada, and its smaller relatives, the Columbia and Sitka blacktails of the West Coast, has been difficult where the beginning of the records keeping. The three varieties belong to the same species and thus are able to interbreed readily where their ranges meet. The intent of the Club in drawing suitable boundary lines is to exclude intergrades from each of the three categories. These boundaries have been redrawn as necessary, as more details have become known about the precise ranges of these animals.

The current boundary for mule and Columbia blacktail deer is as follows:

British Columbia — Starting at the Washington-British Columbia border, blacktail deer range runs west of the height of land between the Skagit and and the Chilliwack Ranges, intersecting the Fraser River opposite the mouth of Ruby Creek, then west to and up Harrison Lake to and up Tipella Creek to the height of land in Garibaldi Park and northwesterly along this divide past Alta Lake, Mt. Dalgleish and Mt. Waddington, thence north to Bella Coola. From Bella Coola, the boundary continues north to the head of Dean Channel, Gardner Canal and Douglas Channel to the town of Anyox, then due west to the Alaska-British Columbia border, which is then followed south to open water. This boundary excludes the area west of the Klesilkwa River and the west side of the Lillooet River.

Washington — Beginning at the Washington-British Columbia border, the boundary line runs south along the west boundary of North Cascades National Park to the range line between R10E and R11E, Willamette Meridian, which is then followed directly south to its intersection with the township line between T18N and T17N, which is then followed westward until it connects with the north border of Mt. Rainier National Park, then along the north, west and south park boundaries until it intersects with the range line between R9E and R10E, Willamette Meridian, which is then followed directly south to the Columbia River near Cook.

Oregon — Beginning at Multnomah Falls on the Columbia River, the boundary runs south along the western boundary of the National Forest to Tiller in Douglas County, then south along Highway 227 to Highway 62 at Trail, then south following Highway 62 to Medford, from which the boundary follows the range line between R1W and R2W, Willamette Meridian, to the California border.

California — Beginning in Siskiyou County at the Oregon-California border, the boundary lies between townships R8W and R9W M.D.M., extending south to and along the Klamath River to Hamburg, then south along the road to Scott Bar, continuing south and then east on the unimproved road from Scott Bar to its intersection with the paved road to Mugginsville, then south through Mugginsville to State Highway 3, which is then followed to Douglas City in Trinity County, from which the line runs east on State Highway 299 to Interstate 5. The line follows Interstate 5 south to the area of Anderson, where the Sacramento River moves east of Interstate 5, following the Sacramento River until it joins with the San Joaquin River, which is followed to the south border of Stanislaus County. The line then runs west along this border to the east border of Santa Clara County. The east and south borders of Santa Clara County are then followed to the south border of Santa Cruz County, which is then followed to the edge of Monterey Bay.

On the Queen Charlotte Islands of British Columbia and along the coast of Alaska ranges another subspecies of mule deer, the Sitka blacktail. Accordingly, after a compilation of scores of the largest Sitka blacktail deer trophies from southern Alaska (including those from Kodiak Island where they have been transplanted), a separate trophy category was established for Sitka blacktail deer in 1984 with a minimum all-time records book entry score of 108.

Sitka blacktails have been transplanted to the Queen Charlotte Islands and are abundant there. Thus, the acceptable area for this category includes southeastern Alaska and the Queen Charlotte Islands of British Columbia. ∎

349

COLUMBIA BLACKTAIL DEER - TYPICAL ANTLERS
WORLD'S RECORD

On a dank October morning in 1953, Lester H. Miller found himself face to face with an extraordinary Columbia blacktail deer (*Odocoileus hemionus columbianus*). He had been waiting for this moment a long time.

From the very first day Miller saw this buck in 1950, he knew he had to have him, no matter the cost in time or effort. For almost four years Miller stalked, drove thickets, and took stands in the Upper Lincoln Creek Area of Lewis County, Washington, in pursuit of a near mythical buck that, except for an occasional sighting, eluded him and every hunter in the region.

"At Grange meetings, livestock auctions, and wherever people gathered in the nearby towns of Chehalis, Centralia, Fords Prairie, or Adna, it was not unusual to hear someone mention this majestic animal. Mostly, they would talk about his huge antlers, four points or bigger. Of course, the stories grew in the telling and soon he was almost a legend. Although I had twice jumped this deer out of his bed, and had seen him running down a runway on three or four different occasions, I still had never fired a shot at him, fearful that I might wound him and not make a clean kill."

Unhampered by the weight of his gun, Miller found himself spending the greater part of every day in the off-season cold-tracking, but occasionally hot on the trail of the Columbia blacktail. Gradually he began to familiarize himself with the deer's whereabouts hoping to catch an occasional glimpse in order to rid himself of the buck fever that was running so high.

He continued to keep tabs on the buck right up to that fateful October morning in 1953. Waiting in the final shadows of darkness, Miller's luck was about to change as the early autumn light signaled opening day of the season. After several false starts, Miller found himself on the right track following a muddy trail until he came across the ghostly figures of some deer disappearing into the alder trees. A huge four-pointer came into range, but Miller held back his instinct to shoot. It was not "The King." Miller continued on, making his way up the side of a ridge toward an opening in the timber.

"In the middle of the clearing, 80 yards away, stood my buck! He was quartering away from me, looking downhill right at me. I raised my gun and fired. The bullet struck him behind the shoulder and went into the heart. He went down in his tracks and never moved.

"I have killed many bull elk in my lifetime. But, no animal has ever had the impact on me that this huge buck had when I looked down on him as he lay there on the side of that ridge."

"The antlers were awesome to see with their spread, color, and symmetry. In addition, they were hanging heavy with moss and lichen that he had accumulated while feeding or "horning" the alders and willows along the creek."

Scored at 182-2/8, the story behind the World's Record Columbia blacktail would be retold by Miller for years as an endless stream of visitors came to see and admire his renowned trophy. ∎

COLUMBIA BLACKTAIL DEER
TYPICAL ANTLERS
WORLD'S RECORD SCORE CHART

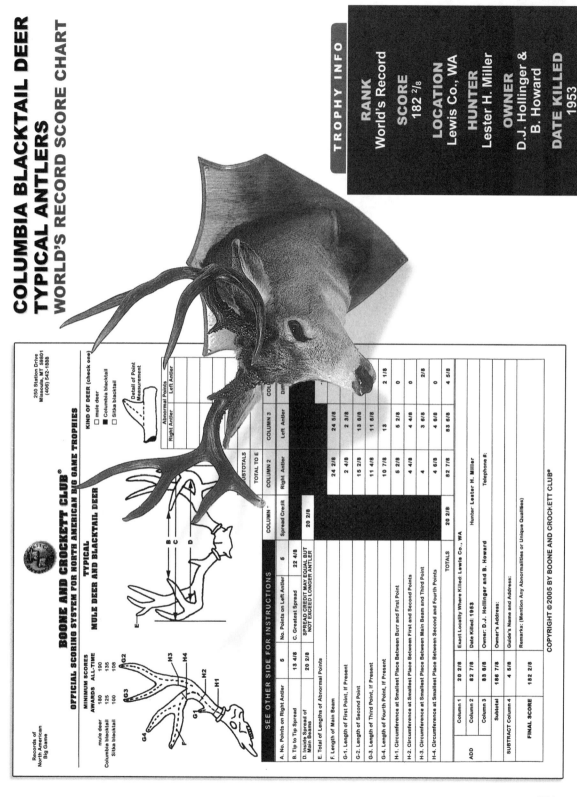

BOONE AND CROCKETT CLUB®

OFFICIAL SCORING SYSTEM FOR NORTH AMERICAN BIG GAME TROPHIES

TYPICAL
MULE DEER AND BLACKTAIL DEER

MINIMUM SCORES	AWARDS	ALL-TIME
mule deer	180	190
Columbia blacktail	125	135
Sitka blacktail	100	108

KIND OF DEER (check one)
☐ mule deer
■ Columbia blacktail
☐ Sitka blacktail

Detail of Point Measurement

Abnormal Points	
Right Antler	Left Antler

SEE OTHER SIDE FOR INSTRUCTIONS

	COLUMN 1	COLUMN 2	COLUMN 3	COLUMN
	Spread Credit	Right Antler	Left Antler	Diff
A. No. Points on Right Antler	5			
No. Points on Left Antler	5			
B. Tip to Tip Spread	13 4/8			
C. Greatest Spread	22 4/8			
D. Inside Spread of Main Beams	20 2/8	SPREAD CREDIT MAY EQUAL BUT NOT EXCEED LONGER ANTLER		
		20 2/8		
E. Total of Lengths of Abnormal Points				
F. Length of Main Beam		24 2/8	24 5/8	
G-1. Length of First Point, If Present		2 4/8	2 3/8	
G-2. Length of Second Point		15 2/8	13 6/8	
G-3. Length of Third Point, If Present		11 4/8	11 6/8	
G-4. Length of Fourth Point, If Present		10 7/8	13	2 1/8
H-1. Circumference at Smallest Place Between Burr and First Point		5 2/8	5 2/8	0
H-2. Circumference at Smallest Place Between First and Second Points		4 4/8	4 4/8	0
H-3. Circumference at Smallest Place Between Main Beam and Third Point		4	3 6/8	2/8
H-4. Circumference at Smallest Place Between Second and Fourth Points		4 6/8	4 6/8	0
TOTALS	20 2/8	82 7/8	83 6/8	4 5/8

SUBTOTALS

TOTAL TO E

Column 1	20 2/8	
ADD	Column 2	82 7/8
	Column 3	83 6/8
Subtotal	186 7/8	
SUBTRACT Column 4	4 5/8	
FINAL SCORE	182 2/8	

Exact Locality Where Killed: Lewis Co., WA

Date Killed: 1953   Hunter: Lester H. Miller

Owner: D.J. Hollinger and B. Howard   Telephone #:

Owner's Address:

Guide's Name and Address:

Remarks: (Mention Any Abnormalities or Unique Qualities)

TROPHY INFO

RANK
World's Record

SCORE
182 2/8

LOCATION
Lewis Co., WA

HUNTER
Lester H. Miller

OWNER
D.J. Hollinger &
B. Howard

DATE KILLED
1953

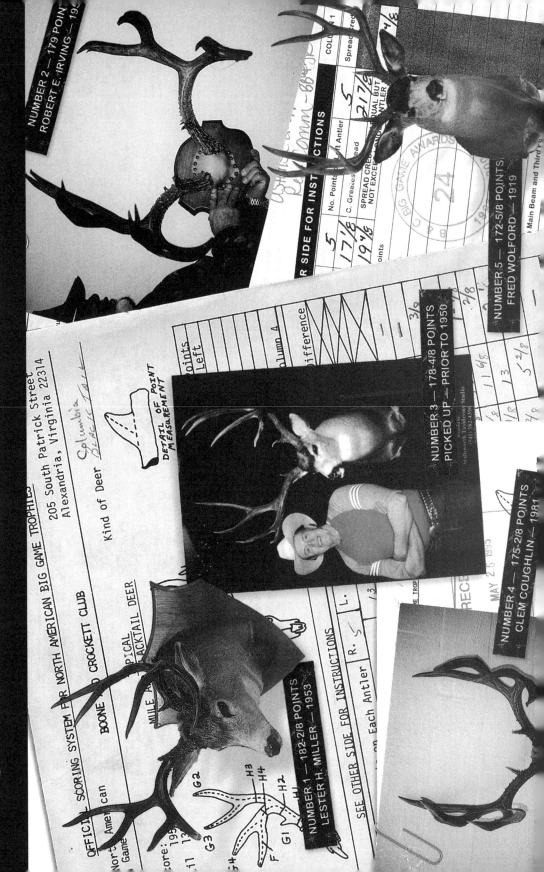

NUMBER 2 — 179 POINTS
ROBERT E. IRVING — 195_

NUMBER 5 — 172-5/8 POINTS
FRED WOLFORD — 1919

NUMBER 3 — 178-4/8 POINTS
PICKED UP — PRIOR TO 1950

NUMBER 4 — 175-2/8 POINTS
CLEM COUGHLIN — 1981

NUMBER 1 — 182-2/8 POINTS
LESTER H. MILLER — 1953

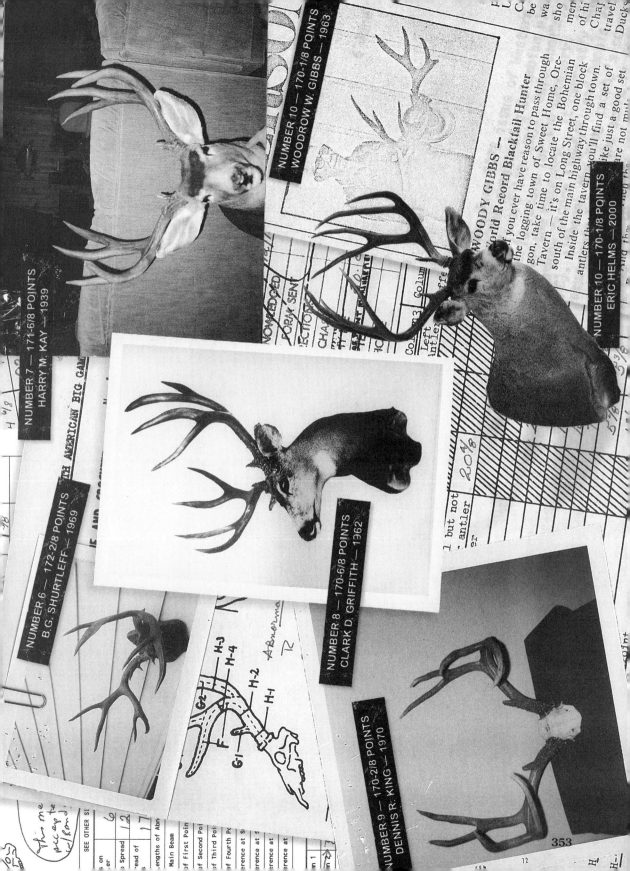

NUMBER 7 — 171-6/8 POINTS
HARRY M. KAY — 1939

NUMBER 10 — 170-1/8 POINTS
WOODROW W. GIBBS — 1963

WOODY GIBBS —
World Record Blacktail Hunter

If you ever have reason to pass through the logging town of Sweet Home, Oregon, take time to locate the Bohemian Tavern — it's on Long Street, one block south of the main highway through town.

Inside the tavern you'll find a set of antlers th...... ......like just a good set ....are not mu....

NUMBER 10 — 170-1/8 POINTS
ERIC HELMS — 2000

NUMBER 6 — 172-2/8 POINTS
B.G. SHURTLEFF — 1969

NUMBER 8 — 170-6/8 POINTS
CLARK D. GRIFFITH — 1962

NUMBER 9 — 170-2/8 POINTS
DENNIS R. KING — 1970

353

COLUMBIA BLACKTAIL DEER - TYPICAL ANTLERS
Odocoileus hemionus columbianus

MINIMUM SCORE 135

Score	Length of Main Beam R	L	Inside Spread	Circumference at Smallest Place Between Burr and First Point R	L	Number of Points R	L	Locality	Hunter	Owner	Date Killed	Rank
182 2/8	24 2/8	24 5/8	20 2/8	5 2/8	5 2/8	5	5	Lewis Co., WA	Lester H. Miller	D.J. Hollinger & B. Howard	1953	1
179	25	24 5/8	19 4/8	4 7/8	5 1/8	5	5	Coos Co., OR	Robert E. Irving	Robert E. Irving	1953	2
178 4/8	23	23 6/8	23 2/8	4 5/8	4 7/8	5	5	Jackson Co., OR	Picked Up	Mervyn R. Thomson	PR 1950	3
175 2/8	22 5/8	22	17 1/8	4 6/8	4 6/8	6	5	Mendocino Co., CA	Clem Coughlin	D.M. & J. Phillips	1981	4
172 5/8	23 6/8	23 1/8	21	4 7/8	4 6/8	6	5	Washington Co., OR	Fred Wolford	Gary A. French	1919	5
172 2/8	26 3/8	25 7/8	20 4/8	5 2/8	5 3/8	7	7	Marion Co., OR	B.G. Shurtleff	B.G. Shurtleff	1969	6
171 6/8	24 3/8	24 2/8	22 2/8	5 6/8	5 4/8	5	6	Skagit Co., WA	Harry M. Kay	Dan Heasley	1939	7
170 6/8	23 1/8	24	21 4/8	5 3/8	5 4/8	5	5	Elk City, OR	Clark D. Griffith	Clark D. Griffith	1962	8
170 2/8	25 6/8	25 5/8	20 2/8	4 5/8	4 6/8	5	5	Jackson Co., OR	Dennis R. King	King Tax. Studios	1970	9
170 1/8	23	22 6/8	19 5/8	5	4 6/8	5	5	Linn Co., OR	Woodrow W. Gibbs	Woodrow W. Gibbs	1963	10
170 1/8	26	24 5/8	17 2/8	4 4/8	4 4/8	5	6	Trinity Co., CA	Eric Helms	Eric Helms	2000	10
170	23 2/8	24	20 2/8	4 3/8	4 3/8	5	5	Jackson Co., OR	Wayne Despain	Wayne Despain	1989	12
169 3/8	23 2/8	22 7/8	18 3/8	5 7/8	6 1/8	6	6	Lewis Co., WA	Larry V. Taylor	Thomas Gogan	1941	13
168 3/8	24 5/8	23 6/8	19 1/8	4 5/8	4 6/8	5	5	Jackson Co., OR	Fred H. Bean	Riley F. Bean	1970	14
168 2/8	22 4/8	21 4/8	21 4/8	5 2/8	5 1/8	5	5	Lake Co., CA	Bob DeShields	D.M. & J. Phillips	1899	15
168	24 2/8	24 6/8	19	4 6/8	4 7/8	5	5	Jackson Co., OR	Fred H. Bean	Riley F. Bean	1951	16
167 4/8	24 3/8	24 3/8	19 4/8	4 7/8	5	5	6	Marion Co., OR	Robert L. Brown	Robert L. Brown	1980	17
167 2/8	24 3/8	26	16 1/8	6	6	7	6	Lewis Co., WA	Maurice D. Heldreth	Maurice D. Heldreth	1976	18
167	23	23	20	4 2/8	4 3/8	5	5	Jackson Co., OR	Riley F. Bean	Riley F. Bean	1958	19
166 2/8	23 2/8	24 3/8	26 5/8	5 4/8	5 1/8	6	6	Glenn Co., CA	Peter Gerbo	Dennis P. Garcia	1949	20
166 2/8	25 5/8	25 3/8	21 6/8	4 2/8	4 1/8	5	5	Polk Co., OR	Earl Starks	Earl Starks	1959	20
165 6/8	22 6/8	23	20 6/8	4 6/8	4 6/8	5	5	Curry Co., OR	Si Pellow	Si Pellow	1988	22
165 4/8	23 6/8	24 5/8	21 6/8	5 1/8	5 1/8	4	4	Yamhill Co., OR	Jim McKinley	Jim McKinley	1971	23
165 1/8	21 4/8	21 7/8	18 5/8	4 4/8	4 4/8	5	5	Jackson Co., OR	Jay Walker	Jay Walker	1983	24
164 6/8	23 4/8	23 6/8	17 4/8	5 1/8	5 2/8	5	5	Clackamas Co., OR	Howard D. Bunnell	Howard D. Bunnell	2003	25
164 1/8	20 5/8	20 4/8	21 2/8	4 6/8	4 5/8	6	5	Cowlitz Co., WA	Harold Melland	Harold Melland	1962	26
164 1/8	21 2/8	20 2/8	17 5/8	4 4/8	4 4/8	5	5	Mendocino Co., CA	Mervin E. Lee	Mildred Lee	1995	26
163 7/8	21 7/8	21 7/8	19 5/8	4 4/8	4 4/8	5	5	Lincoln Co., OR	Picked Up	B. & S. Wales	1987	28
163 6/8	22 3/8	21 4/8	18	5	5	5	5	Jackson Co., OR	Donald G. Spence	Donald G. Spence	1982	29
163 5/8	21 6/8	22 1/8	20 3/8	4 3/8	4 3/8	4	5	Lake Co., CA	Bill L. Conn	B&C National Collection	1976	30
163 1/8	23 3/8	21 5/8	20 4/8	5	4 7/8	7	6	Siskiyou Co., CA	Frank Barago	Frank Barago	1945	31
163 1/8	21 3/8	21 5/8	19 1/8	5 1/8	5	5	5	Eugene, OR	Russell Thomas	Russell Thomas	1964	31
162 7/8	23 2/8	23 4/8	19 4/8	4 7/8	4 7/8	5	5	Josephine Co., OR	John E. Webb, Jr.	John E. Webb, Jr.	1973	33
162 6/8	25	25 2/8	23 2/8	4 5/8	4 6/8	7	7	Pierce Co., WA	Dick Allen	Craig Allen	1952	34
162 6/8	22 4/8	22 4/8	20 2/8	5 2/8	5 2/8	5	5	Jackson Co., OR	Ken Wilson	Ken Wilson	1979	34
162 3/8	22	22 1/8	18 1/8	4 4/8	4 4/8	5	5	Trinity Co., CA	Sidney A. Nystrom	Sidney A. Nystrom	1961	36

Score	R. Main Beam	L. Main Beam	Inside Spread	R. Circ.	L. Circ.	R. Pts	L. Pts	Locality	Hunter	Owner	Date	Rank
162 2/8	25 1/8	24 5/8	19 2/8	4 2/8	4 2/8	5	5	Glenn Co., CA	Roger L. Spencer	Roger L. Spencer	1956	37
162 2/8	24	25	19 1/8	4 4/8	4 6/8	6	5	Jackson Co., OR	Norman J. Shanklin	Norman J. Shanklin	1979	37
160 7/8	23 3/8	23 3/8	19 3/8	4 6/8	4 5/8	6	5	Jackson Co., OR	G. Scott Jennings	G. Scott Jennings	1972	39
160 5/8	21 4/8	20 5/8	16 5/8	4 5/8	4 5/8	4	4	Camas Valley, OR	Bernard L. Den	Bernard L. Den	1958	40
160 4/8	22 7/8	23	17 6/8	4 3/8	4 4/8	5	5	Siskiyou Co., CA	Tommy McCaw	John A. Crawford	1934	41
160 4/8	24 3/8	23 5/8	21	4 7/8	4 7/8	5	5	Siskiyou Co., CA	John L. Masters	John L. Masters	1967	41
160 3/8	23 5/8	23 1/8	26 5/8	4 2/8	4	6	6	Trinity Co., CA	A.H. Hilbert	Jack T. Brusatori	1929	43
160 3/8	23 1/8	22 7/8	17 7/8	5	4 1/8	5	5	Jackson Co., OR	Mickey C. Haynes	Travis J. Harvey	1989	43
160 1/8	24 7/8	25 1/8	24 7/8	4 7/8	5 5/8	5	4	Trinity Co., CA	Lorio Verzasconi	Lorio Verzasconi	1946	45
160 1/8	22 1/8	22 5/8	15 7/8	4	4 7/8	5	5	Chilliwack Lake, BC	Mike Tenbos	Mike Tenbos	2000	45
159 7/8	21 7/8	22 2/8	16 3/8	4 5/8	4 4/8	5	5	Siskiyou Co., CA	John C. Ley	E.R. Cummins	1937	47
159 7/8	22 3/8	22 5/8	21 7/8	4 6/8	4 4/8	6	6	Siskiyou Co., CA	Francis M. Sullivan	Francis M. Sullivan	1951	47
159 6/8	24 4/8	25 6/8	22 4/8	5 4/8	5 5/8	6	6	Jackson Co., OR	Frank Chapman	Frank Chapman	1965	49
159 6/8	21 1/8	21	12 3/8	4 5/8	4 6/8	5	8	Humboldt Co., CA	Picked Up	D.M. & J. Phillips	1968	49
159 6/8	24 1/8	24 3/8	16 1/8	4 5/8	4 4/8	5	6	Jackson Co., OR	Douglas L. Milburn	Douglas L. Milburn	1985	49
159 4/8	23 6/8	24 4/8	14 7/8	4 4/8	5 2/8	6	5	Mendocino Co., CA	Russ McLennan	Russ McLennan	1984	52
159 2/8	24	24 7/8	24 4/8	5 2/8	4 4/8	4	4	Whatcom Co., WA	Paul A. Braddock	Paul A. Braddock	1963	53
159 2/8	22 4/8	24 7/8	19 4/8	4 4/8	4 3/8	5	5	Josephine Co., OR	Wayne Despain	Wayne Despain	1979	53
159 2/8	20 7/8	22 4/8	18 2/8	4 3/8	4 6/8	5	6	Jackson Co., OR	Jeffrey S. Sedey	Jeffrey S. Sedey	1988	53
159 1/8	22 1/8	21 7/8	19 1/8	4 6/8	5 1/8	5	5	Trinity Co., CA	A.H. Hilbert	A.H. Hilbert	1939	56
159	22 2/8	22 4/8	18 6/8	5 2/8	4 4/8	6	5	Lewis Co., WA	Picked Up	Larry F. Smith	1996	57
158 6/8	20 7/8	21 3/8	17 6/8	4 4/8	4 4/8	5	5	Josephine Co., OR	Glen R. Wooldridge	Glen R. Wooldridge	PR 1950	58
158 6/8	22	22	17 4/8	4 3/8	4 5/8	6	6	Marion Co., OR	Bradley M. Brenden	Bradley M. Brenden	1973	58
158 4/8	24	24	22 5/8	4 5/8	4 5/8	5	5	Trinity Co., CA	David Phillips	David Phillips	1974	60
158 2/8	23 7/8	22 4/8	19 6/8	5 2/8	4 6/8	5	5	Josephine Co., OR	James E. Brierley	James E. Brierley	1983	61
158 2/8	22 6/8	22 6/8	18 6/8	4 6/8	4 6/8	5	5	Lewis Co., WA	Keith A. Heldreth	Keith A. Heldreth	1984	61
158 1/8	24 1/8	24 7/8	17	4 6/8	4 4/8	7	6	Campbell Creek, BC	Barry Thoen	Barry Thoen	1968	63
158	22 7/8	22 7/8	18 4/8	4 6/8	4 3/8	5	5	Camas Valley, OR	Frank Kinnan	Frank Kinnan	1968	64
158	21 7/8	21 7/8	18 2/8	4 4/8	4 2/8	5	7	Trinity Co., CA	Charles A. Strickland	Charles A. Strickland	1984	64
158	23 4/8	23 4/8	18 3/8	4 3/8	4 3/8	5	5	Siskiyou Co., CA	Robert J. Ayers	Robert J. Ayers	1996	64
157 7/8	23	23	17 7/8	4 2/8	5	7	5	Tillamook Co., OR	Oscar L. Scudder	Lloyd W. Scudder	1954	67
157 7/8	20 6/8	20 6/8	20 5/8	4 2/8	4 5/8	5	5	Mendocino Co., CA	William Torcato	William Torcato	1999	67
157 5/8	22 6/8	22 6/8	21 5/8	4 3/8	4 2/8	5	5	Shasta Co., CA	Richard L. Sobrato	Richard L. Sobrato	1969	69
157 4/8	21 2/8	21 2/8	17 2/8	4 7/8	5 2/8	5	5	Yamhill Co., OR	Henry Davenport	Henry Davenport	1932	70
157 1/8	22 1/8	20 6/8	20 7/8	4 5/8	3 6/8	7	6	Jackson Co., OR	Fred H. Bean	Riley F. Bean	1947	71
157 1/8	23	22 4/8	17 5/8	4 4/8	4 2/8	5	5	Jackson Co., OR	Marty Artoff	Marty Artoff	1980	71
157	24 7/8	24 7/8	24 1/8	5	4 5/8	5	7	Santa Clara Co., CA	Brud Eade	Brud Eade	1961	73
157	21 2/8	21 4/8	18 6/8	4 4/8	4 4/8	5	5	Alameda Co., CA	Ramona L. Torcato	Ramona L. Torcato	1997	73
156 6/8	22 7/8	23	25 1/8	4 6/8	5	5	5	Benton Co., OR	Donald G. Breese	Donald G. Breese	1951	75
156 6/8	22 2/8	22 2/8	20 2/8	4 5/8	4 4/8	5	6	Pierce Co., WA	Horst A. Vierthaler	Horst A. Vierthaler	1963	75
156 6/8	23 7/8	23	16 6/8	4 6/8	4 6/8	6	5	Trinity Co., CA	Picked Up	Charles Hageman	1994	75
156 4/8	22 4/8	20 6/8	18	5 3/8	5 2/8	7	6	Mendocino Co., CA	Picked Up	D.M. & J. Phillips	1958	78
156 4/8	21 6/8	22 4/8	17	4 3/8	4 2/8	5	5	King Co., WA	Byron Gusa	Byron Gusa	1980	78
156 4/8	19 7/8	19 6/8	16 6/8	4 3/8	4 5/8	5	5	Lincoln Co., OR	Bruce G. Wales	Bruce G. Wales	1985	78
156 3/8	25 6/8	25 6/8	21 7/8	4 5/8	4 4/8	5	4	Siskiyou Co., CA	Henry Klope	William T. Klope	PR 1939	81
156 1/8	22 2/8	22 2/8	20 2/8	4 4/8	4 4/8	5	6	Lincoln Co., OR	Robert G. Biron	Robert G. Biron	1963	82
156	23 2/8	25	21	4 4/8	4 4/8	6	5	Polk Co., OR	Wayne Bond	Wayne Bond	1965	83
155 7/8	23 7/8	23 1/8	16 2/8	4 6/8	4 7/8	5	6	Pierce Co., WA	J.L. Bennett & F. Duell	J.L. Bennett & F. Duell	1983	84

COLUMBIA BLACKTAIL DEER - TYPICAL ANTLERS
Odocoileus hemionus columbianus

Score	Length of Main Beam R	L	Inside Spread	Circumference at Smallest Place Between Burr and First Point R	L	Number of Points R	L	Locality	Hunter	Owner	Date Killed	Rank
155 7/8	23 1/8	23 1/8	17 3/8	4	4 2/8	5	5	Tehama Co., CA	George R. Chaffin	G.R. Chaffin & S. Bennett	1995	84
155 3/8	21 4/8	21	15 1/8	4 3/8	4 3/8	5	5	Tehama Co., CA	Carol F. Williams	Carol F. Williams	1899	86
155 3/8	26 2/8	25 7/8	25 7/8	4 4/8	4 4/8	7	7	Jackson Co., OR	Gary B. Christlieb	Gary B. Christlieb	1979	86
155 2/8	21 5/8	21 6/8	23 1/8	3 3/8	3 4/8	5	5	Trinity Co., CA	Fred Heider	Fred Heider	1927	88
155 2/8	21 7/8	20 2/8	17 6/8	4 2/8	4 2/8	5	5	King Co., WA	Horst A. Vierthaler	Horst A. Vierthaler	1960	88
155 2/8	22 3/8	23 1/8	20 6/8	5 3/8	5	4	5	Jackson Co., OR	L.M. Morgan & L. Miller	Lewis M. Morgan	1971	88
155 2/8	22 1/8	22 7/8	19 2/8	5 3/8	4 7/8	5	5	Mendocino Co., CA	Gary Land	Gary Land	1972	88
155 1/8	21	21 6/8	18 5/8	4 3/8	4 3/8	4	4	Shasta Co., CA	Vance Corrigan	Vance Corrigan	1956	92
155 1/8	24	23	21	4 4/8	4 1/8	6	5	Tehama Co., CA	Ben M. Youtsey	Ben M. Youtsey	1995	92
154 7/8	22 2/8	20 7/8	19 5/8	4	4	4	4	Linn Co., OR	Don L. Twito	Don L. Twito	1971	94
154 6/8	22 4/8	23 4/8	18	4 5/8	4 6/8	5	6	Cowlitz Co., WA	Bud Whittle	Bud Whittle	1957	95
154 6/8	20 4/8	20 3/8	20 4/8	4 5/8	4 5/8	4	4	Mendocino Co., CA	W.A. McAllister	W.A. McAllister	1968	95
154 6/8	21 1/8	21 3/8	18 1/8	4 2/8	4 2/8	6	6	Mendocino Co., CA	Andy Amerson	Andy Amerson	1993	95
154 5/8	24	22 7/8	23 3/8	4 3/8	4 4/8	5	5	Humboldt Co., CA	Phillip Brown	Phillip Brown	1962	98
154 5/8	24 7/8	24 3/8	21	4 7/8	4 6/8	6	7	Siskiyou Co., CA	Darrell R. Jones	Darrell R. Jones	1984	98
154 2/8	20 3/8	20 2/8	17 5/8	5	5 1/8	6	5	Jackson Co., OR	Mary L. Hannah	Mary L. Hannah	1988	100
154 1/8	20 4/8	20 4/8	18 1/8	4 4/8	4 4/8	5	5	Lane Co., OR	Eldon Lundy	Eldon Lundy	1943	101
154 1/8	21 6/8	22 2/8	18 6/8	4 6/8	4 7/8	6	7	Glenn Co., CA	Mitchell A. Thorson	B&C National Collection	1969	101
154	26 4/8	25 7/8	28 6/8	4 4/8	4 6/8	6	6	Trinity Co., CA	A.H. Hilbert	A.H. Hilbert	1930	103
154	23 4/8	24 3/8	23 2/8	4 2/8	4 2/8	8	7	Mendocino Co., CA	Ernest McKee	Ralph McKee, Jr.	1957	103
154	22 6/8	21	16	4 5/8	4 6/8	5	5	Trinity Co., CA	Robert E. Blanc	Robert E. Blanc	1984	103
154	24 4/8	24 3/8	19 5/8	4 7/8	4 4/8	5	5	Josephine Co., OR	Wayne H. Breeze	Wayne H. Breeze	1986	103
154	23 3/8	23 3/8	23 3/8	4 1/8	4 2/8	6	6	Josephine Co., OR	Ryan Kinghorn	Ryan Kinghorn	1989	103
153 7/8	22	22 1/8	17	4 5/8	4 5/8	6	5	Jefferson Co., WA	Picked Up	Wayne Brown	PR 1940	108
153 7/8	22 4/8	22 2/8	22 3/8	4 6/8	4 5/8	5	5	Jackson Co., OR	Mike J. Prohoroff	Mike J. Prohoroff	2000	108
153 6/8	22 5/8	23 1/8	17 7/8	5 4/8	5 5/8	6	5	Thurston Co., WA	Denise A. George	Denise A. George	1987	110
153 5/8	23 2/8	22 4/8	21 7/8	3 6/8	3 6/8	5	5	Jackson Co., OR	Ken Wilson	Ken Wilson	2000	111
153 4/8	21 3/8	20 7/8	17 6/8	4 6/8	4 7/8	5	5	Linn Co., OR	Greg L. Anderson	Greg L. Anderson	1983	112
153 3/8	21 5/8	20 5/8	19 1/8	5 2/8	5 2/8	6	7	Columbia Co., OR	J.H. Roberts	OR Fish & Wildl. Div.	1946	113
153 3/8	24 5/8	24 4/8	18 5/8	4 6/8	4 7/8	5	5	Clallam Co., WA	Picked Up	Lawrence J. Bourm	1949	113
153 3/8	21 2/8	21 5/8	17 4/8	5	5	6	5	Tehama Co., CA	James L. Carr	James L. Carr	1979	113
153 2/8	20 1/8	20 4/8	21 1/8	4 3/8	4 1/8	5	5	Pierce Co., WA	Brooks Carmichael	Brooks Carmichael	1971	116
153 1/8	22 4/8	22	19 7/8	5 1/8	5 2/8	6	6	Canton Creek, OR	Marell Abeene	Marell Abeene	1967	117
153 1/8	20 6/8	20	17 1/8	4 6/8	4 6/8	5	5	Humboldt Co., CA	Paul M. Mustain	Paul M. Mustain	1975	117
153	22 6/8	23 6/8	14 6/8	4 3/8	4 5/8	6	5	Siskiyou Co., CA	John Carmichael	J.A. Brose	1969	119
153	19 7/8	19 7/8	15 6/8	4 7/8	4 7/8	5	5	Douglas Co., OR	James W. Martin, Jr.	James W. Martin, Jr.	2001	119

Score	R. Beam	L. Beam	Spread	R. Circ.	L. Circ.	R. Pts.	L. Pts.	Locality	By	Owner	Year	Rank
152 6/8	21 6/8	21 7/8	21 1/8	4 6/8	4 3/8	8	7	Tehama Co., CA	Randy E. Reno	Randy E. Reno	1995	121
152 5/8	23 6/8	22 7/8	18 5/8	5	5 2/8	5	4	Trinity Co., CA	Allen Brownfield	Jason Brownfield	1979	122
152 5/8	22 7/8	22	19 5/8	4 4/8	4 3/8	5	5	Mendocino Co., CA	Harold D. Schneider	H.D. & M.J. Schneider	1979	122
152 4/8	21 7/8	20 4/8	20 5/8	4	4 5/8	5	5	Stanislaus Co., CA	Scott A. Wilkinson	Scott A. Wilkinson	1998	122
152 4/8	23	23	20	4	4	6	7	Tehama Co., CA	Don Strickler	Don Strickler	1979	125
152 4/8	22	21 2/8	18 4/8	5 1/8	5	6	6	Mendocino Co., CA	Richard C. Martin	Richard C. Martin	1990	125
152 2/8	20 7/8	21	20 2/8	4	4 1/8	4	4	Douglas Co., OR	Ronald L. Sherva	Ronald L. Sherva	1987	127
152 1/8	22 4/8	21 1/8	17 7/8	4 2/8	4 1/8	5	5	Trinity Co., CA	Robert V. Strickland	Robert V. Strickland	1966	128
152 1/8	20 4/8	21 1/8	17 4/8	5 5/8	5 7/8	7	6	Pemberton, BC	Jim Decker	Jim Decker	1968	128
152 1/8	22 2/8	21 4/8	22	4 3/8	4 3/8	6	6	Josephine Co., OR	Bob Ferreira	Bob Ferreira	1988	128
152	23 3/8	22 7/8	21 6/8	4 4/8	4 4/8	5	5	Yolo Co., CA	Herman Darneille	E.L. Gallup	1943	131
152	20 6/8	21 7/8	15 2/8	4 6/8	4 7/8	6	6	Clackamas Co., OR	Larry W. Peterson	Larry W. Peterson	1980	131
151 7/8	25	24 3/8	20 3/8	4 3/8	4 5/8	5	5	Jackson Co., OR	David Ellefson	David Ellefson	1972	133
151 7/8	21 6/8	22 4/8	20 1/8	5	5	6	5	Tehama Co., CA	Gerald R. Cardoza, Jr.	Gerald R. Cardoza, Jr.	1994	133
151 6/8	22 3/8	22 4/8	17 4/8	5 4/8	5 1/8	6	5	Glide, OR	William Cellers	William Cellers	1947	135
151 6/8	24 6/8	25	23 6/8	4 1/8	4 2/8	3	4	Stanislaus Co., CA	Picked Up	Scott A. Wilkinson	2000	135
151 5/8	20 3/8	20 1/8	22 4/8	4 5/8	4 4/8	5	5	Mendocino Co., CA	Bill L. Conn	Bill L. Conn	1969	137
151 5/8	22 1/8	21 7/8	22 5/8	4 6/8	4 6/8	5	5	Siskiyou Co., CA	Jim A. Turnbow	Jim A. Turnbow	1973	137
151 5/8	21	21 3/8	15 5/8	4 1/8	4	5	5	Trinity Co., CA	Dean Giordanella	Dean Giordanella	1994	137
151 4/8	20 3/8	19 1/8	16 4/8	4 5/8	4 7/8	6	5	Marion Co., OR	John Davenport	John Davenport	1958	140
151 4/8	22 7/8	21 3/8	17 5/8	5	5 1/8	6	5	Douglas Co., OR	Robert Shrode	Robert Shrode	1959	140
151 4/8	21 6/8	21 6/8	16	5 1/8	5 3/8	6	6	Whatcom Co., WA	Steve V. McIvor	Steve V. McIvor	1994	140
151 4/8	23 7/8	23 3/8	22 6/8	4 4/8	4 5/8	5	5	Mendocino Co., CA	Ely O. Sanderson	Ely O. Sanderson	2000	140
151 3/8	23 1/8	22 6/8	19 4/8	5	5	5	6	Josephine Co., OR	E.L. McKie & S.E. McKie	Ernie L. McKie	1977	144
151 3/8	20 7/8	20 3/8	14 1/8	4 4/8	4 4/8	5	5	Clackamas Co., OR	David Wolford	David Wolford	1999	144
151 3/8	24 3/8	24 6/8	20 4/8	4 2/8	4 2/8	4	4	Trinity Co., CA	Leonard C. Waterman	Leonard C. Waterman	2003	144
151 2/8	22	22 3/8	17 6/8	4 1/8	4 1/8	5	5	Clallam Co., WA	Joe Pavel	Patrick M. Lockhart	1962	147
151 2/8	23	22 4/8	19 2/8	5 2/8	5 2/8	5	5	Mendocino Co., CA	Tommy E. Thompson	Tommy E. Thompson	1994	147
151 1/8	21 5/8	22 5/8	16 1/8	4	4	4	4	Josephine Co., OR	James Wineteer	James Wineteer	1980	149
151 1/8	22 1/8	22 6/8	19 3/8	4 4/8	4 4/8	6	8	Marion Co., OR	Chad A. Richardson	Chad A. Richardson	1997	149
151	20 4/8	21 6/8	17 2/8	4 6/8	4 6/8	6	6	Lewis Co., WA	Norman Henspeter	Norman Henspeter	1941	151
151	23 6/8	21	19 2/8	4 2/8	4 1/8	5	5	Humboldt Co., CA	Elgin T. Gates	Elgin T. Gates	1952	151
151	23 7/8	24	17 4/8	5 3/8	3 7/8	7	7	Lewis Co., WA	Harold Gossard	Ronald B. Gossard	1962	151
150 7/8	21 7/8	22	19 5/8	4 4/8	4 5/8	5	5	Jackson Co., OR	Darrell Leek	Darrell Leek	1974	154
150 7/8	21	22 5/8	16 4/8	4 5/8	4 5/8	7	7	Jackson Co., OR	Andy Wilkins	Andy Wilkins	1998	154
150 6/8	22	21 4/8	17	4 2/8	4 2/8	5	5	Siskiyou Co., CA	Raymond Whittaker	Raymond Whittaker	1978	156
150 6/8	21 3/8	22 2/8	18 3/8	4 7/8	4 7/8	6	6	Santa Clara Co., CA	Robert L. Fellom	Robert L. Fellom	1997	156
150 6/8	23 6/8	23 6/8	18 1/8	5	5	6	6	Humboldt Co., CA	Jason R. McCanless	Jason R. McCanless	2001	156
150 6/8	22 6/8	22 6/8	21 4/8	4 6/8	4 6/8	5	5	Trinity Co., CA	Cameron L. Brown	Cameron L. Brown	2002	156
150 5/8	21 4/8	20 7/8	16 5/8	5 4/8	5 6/8	6	5	Yamhill Co., OR	Russell W. Byers	Russell W. Byers	1961	160
150 4/8	24 1/8	24 2/8	19 5/8	5 1/8	5	6	6	Trinity Co., CA	E.L. Brightenstine	E.L. Brightenstine	1978	161
150 1/8	20 3/8	21	14 1/8	5 2/8	5 2/8	5	5	Lewis Co., WA	Carroll H. Fenn	Carroll H. Fenn	1959	162
150 1/8	22 4/8	22	16 1/8	4 1/8	4 1/8	5	5	Napa Co., CA	Robert G. Wiley	Robert G. Wiley	1965	162
150 1/8	21	21	20 1/8	3 7/8	3 7/8	5	5	Trinity Co., CA	Thomas L. Hough	Thomas L. Hough	1969	162
150 1/8	22 7/8	23 1/8	19 3/8	4 6/8	4 7/8	6	6	Clackamas Co., OR	E. Clint Kuntz	E. Clint Kuntz	1981	162
150 1/8	21	22 2/8	17 7/8	4 6/8	4 6/8	5	5	Lane Co., OR	Gene C. Rolston	Gene C. Rolston	1983	162
150 1/8	22 7/8	22	24 4/8	4 6/8	4 3/8	5	6	Mendocino Co., CA	Brock B. Perry	Brock B. Perry	2000	162
150	24	25 1/8	24	4 5/8	4 4/8	4	4	Napa Co., CA	W.C. Lambert	W.C. Lambert	1957	168

COLUMBIA BLACKTAIL DEER - TYPICAL ANTLERS
Odocoileus hemionus columbianus

Score	Length of Main Beam R	L	Inside Spread	Circumference at Smallest Place Between Burr and First Point R	L	Number of Points R	L	Locality	Hunter	Owner	Date Killed	Rank
150	22 5/8	22 7/8	19 4/8	5 6/8	5 5/8	5	5	King Co., WA	Roscoe Rainey	Roscoe Rainey	1963	168
150	20 5/8	21 5/8	16 6/8	5	4 7/8	5	5	Douglas Co., OR	Norman Burnett	Norman Burnett	1967	168
150	20 7/8	20 2/8	20	5 3/8	5 3/8	4	4	Lake Co., CA	Bruce Strickler	Bruce Strickler	1970	168
150	20 4/8	21 7/8	16 6/8	4 2/8	4 2/8	5	5	Tehama Co., CA	Marion F. Foster	Barbara J. Foster	1971	168
150	21 5/8	21 4/8	21 2/8	4 2/8	4 2/8	5	5	Trinity Co., CA	Richard E. Keller	Richard E. Keller	1995	168
150	21 5/8	22	17	5 6/8	5 5/8	6	6	Mendocino Co., CA	Mark A. Pennacchio	Mark A. Pennacchio	2002	168
149 7/8	22 4/8	23 4/8	19 7/8	4 3/8	4 3/8	6	6	Lewis Co., WA	Elvon A. Self	Elvon A. Self	1966	175
149 7/8	23 2/8	22 5/8	17 3/8	4 2/8	4 1/8	6	5	Siskiyou Co., CA	John R. Adams	John R. Adams	1985	175
149 7/8	21 2/8	20 4/8	16 1/8	4 2/8	4 1/8	5	5	Trinity Co., CA	Steven E. Delaney	Steven E. Delaney	1992	175
149 7/8	22 4/8	21 7/8	16 1/8	4 4/8	4 4/8	5	5	Lane Co., OR	Robert P. Mann	Robert P. Mann	1995	175
149 6/8	22 7/8	22	18 7/8	5	5	5	6	Siskiyou Co., CA	Emit C. Jones	Emit C. Jones	1961	179
149 6/8	20	20 4/8	18 4/8	3 7/8	4	5	5	Mendocino Co., CA	Robert Whiting	Ted T. Daly, Jr.	PR 1988	179
149 6/8	22 3/8	22 3/8	19	4 4/8	4 7/8	5	5	Mendocino Co., CA	Redhawk R. Pallesen	Redhawk R. Pallesen	1996	179
149 5/8	24 2/8	23 1/8	17 5/8	5	4 7/8	6	5	Whatcom Co., WA	Bruce V. Seton	Bruce B. Seton	1942	182
149 5/8	20	21 3/8	17 7/8	4 4/8	4 4/8	5	5	Humboldt Co., CA	Robert C. Stephens	Robert C. Stephens	1961	182
149 5/8	22 7/8	22 4/8	17 1/8	4 3/8	4 5/8	5	5	Clackamas Co., OR	Ray W. Bunnell	Ray W. Bunnell	1970	182
149 5/8	20 2/8	20	16 1/8	4 7/8	5	5	5	Trinity Co., CA	Craig Brown	Craig Brown	2002	182
149 4/8	22 5/8	21	20 6/8	5 1/8	5 2/8	5	5	Glenn Co., CA	George F. Stewart, Jr.	George F. Stewart, Jr.	1957	186
149 4/8	23 7/8	22 6/8	15 3/8	5 1/8	5	5	6	Lewis Co., WA	Scotty Mullins	James Stafford	1977	186
149 4/8	21 1/8	21 4/8	23	5 1/8	5	5	5	Mendocino Co., CA	C.W. Bill King	C.W. Bill King	1993	186
149 3/8	20 5/8	22 5/8	17 5/8	5 2/8	5 4/8	5	5	Cowlitz Co., WA	Milton C. Gudgell	Milton C. Gudgell	1957	189
149 3/8	22 3/8	21 2/8	20 3/8	4 5/8	4 4/8	5	5	Trinity Co., CA	Lyle L. Johnson	Lyle L. Johnson	1979	189
149 3/8	23 7/8	26 5/8	20 5/8	4 4/8	4 4/8	5	5	Tehama Co., CA	Bill F. Stevenson	Bill F. Stevenson	1989	189
149 3/8	22 2/8	23 6/8	19 7/8	4 4/8	4 4/8	5	5	Clackamas Co., OR	David P. Prom	David P. Prom	1995	189
149 2/8	24 3/8	24 3/8	17 6/8	5 4/8	5 4/8	8	8	Trinity Co., CA	Lauren A. Johnson	Lauren A. Johnson	1964	193
149 2/8	20 2/8	20 3/8	14 6/8	4 2/8	4	5	5	Clackamas Co., OR	Lance V. Bentz	Lance V. Bentz	1980	193
149 2/8	21 6/8	22 6/8	19 4/8	4 4/8	4 2/8	5	5	Lane Co., OR	Richard C. MacKenzie	Richard C. MacKenzie	1983	193
149 1/8	21 4/8	22 7/8	16 1/8	5	4 7/8	5	5	Clallam Co., WA	Otis Dahman	E.A. Dahman	1943	196
148 7/8	22 1/8	21 3/8	18	4 7/8	4 7/8	6	5	Humboldt Co., CA	F. Joe Parker	F. Joe Parker	1946	197
148 6/8	24 5/8	24 2/8	20 2/8	5	5 1/8	5	5	Tillamook Co., OR	Fred Dick	Fred Dick	1948	198
148 6/8	22 5/8	22 6/8	15 6/8	4 6/8	4 6/8	5	5	Trinity Co., CA	Donald A. Dunn	Donald A. Dunn	1993	198
148 6/8	21 2/8	22 1/8	22 4/8	4 1/8	4 2/8	7	5	Trinity Co., CA	David E. Evanow	David E. Evanow	1998	198
148 5/8	21 3/8	21 5/8	18 5/8	3 7/8	4 1/8	5	5	Lane Co., OR	Bill Sparks	Bill Sparks	1970	201
148 5/8	20 6/8	20 2/8	17 3/8	3 6/8	4	6	6	Jackson Co., OR	Jay Walker	Jay Walker	1975	201
148 4/8	24 4/8	24 1/8	22 4/8	4 6/8	5	5	5	Washington Co., OR	Floyd Gray	Joe G. Papasadero	PR 1945	203
148 4/8	23 2/8	22 7/8	20 6/8	4 3/8	4 5/8	5	5	Mendocino Co., CA	N.D. Windbigler	N.D. Windbigler	1969	203

Score	R. Main Beam	L. Main Beam	Inside Spread	R. Circ.	L. Circ.	R. Pts.	L. Pts.	Locality	Hunter	Owner	Date	Rank
148 4/8	22 5/8	22 1/8	16 5/8	4 4/8	4 4/8	6	5	Skamania Co., WA	Alan D. Borroz	Alan D. Borroz	1978	203
148 4/8	21 6/8	22 5/8	15 6/8	5 3/8	5 6/8	5	5	Linn Co., OR	Marlin D. Brinkley	Marlin D. Brinkley	1982	203
148 3/8	21 2/8	21	19 5/8	4 3/8	4 2/8	5	5	Douglas Co., OR	Unknown	Bud Jackson	1929	207
148 3/8	18 6/8	18 6/8	15 3/8	5 2/8	5 4/8	6	5	Snohomish Co., WA	C.T. Hasler	C.T. Hasler	1955	207
148 3/8	21 7/8	21 1/8	18 6/8	4 2/8	4 1/8	5	10	Marion Co., OR	Mike Fenimore	Mike Fenimore	1961	207
148 3/8	23	22 5/8	19 5/8	4 6/8	4 6/8	6	5	Clallam Co., WA	Nick R.D. Henry	Les Henry	1992	207
148 2/8	22 4/8	23	17 6/8	5	5 1/8	6	6	Josephine Co., OR	Riley F. Bean	Riley F. Bean	1954	211
148 2/8	24	24 4/8	23 4/8	6 2/8	5 6/8	8	6	Shasta Co., CA	Jerry W. Sander	Jerry W. Sander	1977	211
148 1/8	21 6/8	22 1/8	18 6/8	5	5 1/8	6	7	Trinity Co., CA	Dean Tackette	Dean Tackette	1981	213
148 1/8	23 4/8	22 4/8	15 5/8	5 1/8	5 1/8	5	5	Clackamas Co., OR	Steven C. Oaks	Steven C. Oaks	1986	213
147 7/8	22	22 3/8	18 5/8	4 1/8	4 2/8	5	5	Glenn Co., CA	Emmet T. Frye	Emmet T. Frye	1937	215
147 7/8	20 6/8	20 7/8	21 6/8	5	4 7/8	6	6	Trinity Co., CA	Chauncy Wilburn	Chauncy Wilburn	1955	215
147 7/8	22 1/8	22 2/8	18 5/8	4 2/8	4 3/8	6	5	Humboldt Co., CA	Melvin H. Kadle	Melvin H. Kadle	1979	215
147 7/8	23 1/8	24 1/8	17	4 2/8	4 3/8	5	6	Josephine Co., OR	Ken Wilson	Ken Wilson	1995	215
147 5/8	23	23 6/8	19 5/8	4 4/8	4 3/8	5	4	Santa Clara Co., CA	Maitland Armstrong	Maitland Armstrong	1944	219
147 5/8	22 3/8	22 7/8	22 3/8	4 5/8	4 5/8	4	4	Mendocino Co., CA	Richard Sterling	Richard Sterling	1986	219
147 5/8	20 5/8	21 3/8	20 3/8	4 4/8	4 4/8	4	6	Siskiyou Co., CA	James A. Swortzel	James A. Swortzel	2000	219
147 4/8	21 4/8	22 1/8	16 4/8	4	4	5	5	Mendocino Co., CA	Picked Up	Eugene E. Rentsch	1995	222
147 4/8	21 4/8	23	18	4 4/8	4 5/8	6	6	Jackson Co., OR	Steve S. Richardson	Steve S. Richardson	1997	222
147 3/8	20 2/8	21 1/8	19 2/8	4 4/8	4 4/8	6	4	Humboldt Co., CA	Bill C. Byron	Bill C. Byron	1997	224
147 3/8	21 7/8	22 5/8	18 5/8	5	5	4	5	Mendocino Co., CA	Paul D. Osmond	Paul D. Osmond	1998	224
147 3/8	22 5/8	21 5/8	18 3/8	4 6/8	4 6/8	6	5	Linn Co., OR	Dean Bowers	Dean Bowers	1999	224
147 2/8	22 5/8	23 4/8	19 6/8	4 2/8	4 3/8	5	7	Jackson Co., OR	Mike Taylor	Mike Taylor	1969	227
147 1/8	20 3/8	20 5/8	21 6/8	3 4/8	3 3/8	5	7	Humboldt Co., CA	Jimmy Lennon	Kenneth W. Springer	1930	228
147 1/8	19 4/8	20 2/8	15	4 3/8	4 5/8	5	5	Siskiyou Co., CA	Lowell Wolfe	Larry R. Wolfe	1946	228
147 1/8	22 1/8	21 3/8	16 4/8	4 2/8	4 3/8	5	6	Trinity Co., CA	Picked Up	Bruce D. Ringsmith	1961	228
147 1/8	20	17 7/8	17 1/8	5 1/8	4 6/8	5	5	Lane Co., OR	Jeff Heater	Jeff Heater	1978	228
147 1/8	18	18 2/8	16 7/8	4 3/8	4 3/8	6	5	Trinity Co., CA	Craig L. Brown	C.L. & J.L. Brown	1980	228
147 1/8	22 2/8	22 3/8	21 7/8	4 3/8	4 5/8	5	4	Trinity Co., CA	Barry D. Keyes	Barry D. Keyes	1992	228
147 1/8	22 4/8	22 2/8	17 3/8	4 5/8	4 3/8	6	5	Jackson Co., CA	Robert J. Rhodes	Robert J. Rhodes	1995	228
147 1/8	20	20 4/8	18 7/8	4 3/8	4 7/8	5	5	Santa Clara Co., CA	Domenic V. Genco	Domenic V. Genco	2003	228
147	21 4/8	21 5/8	21 4/8	5	4 3/8	5	5	King Co., WA	Robert B. Gracey	Robert B. Gracey	1963	236
147	23 6/8	23 2/8	17	4 3/8	5	5	5	Siskiyou Co., CA	Ray Whittaker	Ray Whittaker	1966	236
147	21 6/8	21	19 6/8	4 3/8	4 3/8	5	5	Mendocino Co., CA	David W. Wilson	David W. Wilson	1993	236
146 7/8	20 1/8	20 2/8	15 1/8	5 3/8	5 3/8	5	5	Clallam Co., WA	Charles W. Lockhart	Charles W. Lockhart	1946	239
146 6/8	22 6/8	22 4/8	18 4/8	4 2/8	4 2/8	5	5	Siskiyou Co., CA	Richard Silva	Richard Silva	1958	240
146 6/8	21 4/8	21 2/8	18 4/8	4 7/8	4 7/8	6	6	Camas Valley, OR	Adam J. Hipp	Adam J. Hipp	1961	240
146 5/8	23 6/8	23 2/8	18 7/8	5 3/8	5 3/8	7	5	Pierce Co., WA	Roy E. Erickson	Dwayne R. Erickson	1942	242
146 5/8	21 6/8	21	16 3/8	4 3/8	4 5/8	5	5	Coos Co., OR	Peter Serafin	Peter Serafin	1968	242
146 5/8	20 1/8	20 2/8	18 1/8	4 2/8	4 5/8	5	5	Clackamas Co., OR	Stan K. Naylor	Stan K. Naylor	1990	242
146 5/8	17 4/8	17 4/8	17 4/8	3 6/8	4 5/8	6	7	Trinity Co., CA	Gary M. Ireland	Gary M. Ireland	1997	242
146 4/8	22 6/8	22	22	5 2/8	5 4/8	5	5	King Co., WA	Leo Klinkhammer	Leo Klinkhammer	1961	246
146 4/8	21 2/8	17 2/8	17 2/8	4 6/8	4 6/8	5	5	Glenn Co., CA	Lawrence E. Germeshausen	Lawrence E. Germeshausen	1983	246
146 4/8	19 7/8	19 4/8	19 4/8	4 6/8	4 6/8	5	6	Norrish Creek, BC	Cliff L. Loring	Cliff L. Loring	1990	246
146 3/8	23 4/8	24 6/8	24 6/8	4 5/8	4 5/8	5	5	Trinity Co., CA	Carroll E. Dow	Carroll E. Dow	1962	249
146 3/8	21 5/8	17 5/8	17 5/8	4 5/8	4 5/8	5	5	Trinity Co., CA	David J. Deininger	David J. Deininger	1992	249
146 2/8	24 2/8	17	17	5 2/8	5 2/8	6	7	Clallam Co., WA	Earl Stone	Patrick M. Lockhart	1946	251
146 2/8	20 7/8	21 4/8	14 2/8	4 4/8	4 4/8	5	5	Douglas Co., OR	Bernard H. Schum	Bernard H. Schum	1966	251

COLUMBIA BLACKTAIL DEER - TYPICAL ANTLERS
Odocoileus hemionus columbianus

Score	Length of Main Beam R	L	Inside Spread	Circumference at Smallest Place Between Burr and First Point R	L	Number of Points R	L	Locality	Hunter	Owner	Date Killed	Rank
146 2/8	21 6/8	22 3/8	13 6/8	5 6/8	5 6/8	5	5	Shasta Co., CA	William H. Taylor	William H. Taylor	1971	251
146 2/8	21 7/8	21 6/8	16 2/8	3 7/8	3 7/8	5	5	Humboldt Co., CA	Charles R. Jurin	Charles R. Jurin	1988	251
146 2/8	22 5/8	23 3/8	23 1/8	4 3/8	4 3/8	6	5	Trinity Co., CA	Craig L. Brown	C.L. & J.L. Brown	1993	251
146 2/8	25 3/8	24 5/8	16 2/8	5 1/8	5	8	7	Mason Co., WA	David D. Johnston	David D. Johnston	1996	251
146 1/8	23 1/8	23 5/8	19 1/8	4 5/8	4	4	4	Trinity Co., CA	Kenneth M. Brown	Kenneth M. Brown	1972	257
146 1/8	22 1/8	22 4/8	14 5/8	4 5/8	4 3/8	5	5	Lewis Co., WA	Keith A. Heldreth	Keith A. Heldreth	1988	257
146 1/8	22 2/8	23 4/8	19 1/8	3 7/8	4 2/8	4	5	Mendocino Co., CA	Brad B. Pitt	Brad B. Pitt	1994	257
146	20 2/8	20 7/8	15 2/8	5	5	5	5	Little Fall Creek, OR	Gene B. Johnson	Gene B. Johnson	1963	260
146	22 6/8	22 2/8	19 2/8	4 4/8	4 5/8	5	5	Mendocino Co., CA	Brian E. Hornberger	Brian E. Hornberger	1991	260
146	20 5/8	21 5/8	21 4/8	4 3/8	4 2/8	5	5	Mendocino Co., CA	Renaldo J. Marin	Renaldo J. Marin	1993	260
146	22	21	22	4 2/8	4 2/8	5	5	Mendocino Co., CA	Cliff E. Jacobson	Cliff E. Jacobson	1996	260
145 7/8	23 4/8	23 3/8	22	5 3/8	5 4/8	6	8	Lake Co., CA	Floyd Goodrich	Mrs. William Olson	1926	264
145 7/8	22 4/8	22	18 7/8	4 4/8	4 5/8	5	5	Glenn Co., CA	George W. Wiget	Kathleen W. Dunn	1939	264
145 7/8	22	23 5/8	16 3/8	4 5/8	4 7/8	5	5	Napa Co., CA	C.H.N. Dailey	Tony Stoer	1948	264
145 7/8	24 5/8	22 4/8	19	5 5/8	5 6/8	6	6	Linn Co., OR	Harold Tonkin	C. Vernon Humble	1954	264
145 7/8	22 6/8	22 6/8	21 7/8	4 3/8	4 5/8	5	5	Shasta Co., CA	Gary J. Miller	Gary J. Miller	1968	264
145 7/8	21 7/8	21	14 5/8	4 2/8	4 1/8	6	5	Yamhill Co., OR	Dwight A. Homestead	Dwight A. Homestead	1992	264
145 6/8	22 2/8	20 5/8	17	4 2/8	4 2/8	5	5	King Co., WA	Terry Flowers	Terry Flowers	1959	270
145 6/8	19 4/8	20 2/8	14 6/8	5 3/8	6	5	6	Whatcom Co., WA	Dennis Miller	Dennis Miller	1970	270
145 5/8	22 4/8	23	18 7/8	4 1/8	4 1/8	6	5	Humboldt Co., CA	Joe Dickerson	Jay Grunert	1962	272
145 5/8	21 2/8	21 1/8	19 5/8	3 7/8	4	6	6	Siskiyou Co., CA	Wallace D. Barlow	Wallace D. Barlow	1985	272
145 4/8	22	21 4/8	16 6/8	5 6/8	6 3/8	6	6	Lewis Co., WA	Adolph M. Borden	Glenn M. Borden	1939	274
145 4/8	20 1/8	20 4/8	14 2/8	4 2/8	4 1/8	6	5	Jackson Co., OR	Gary D. Kaiser	Gary D. Kaiser	1967	274
145 4/8	21 1/8	20	16 2/8	4 7/8	4 7/8	5	5	Douglas Co., OR	Daniel J. Fisher	Daniel J. Fisher	1973	274
145 4/8	21 3/8	21 1/8	21 3/8	4 5/8	4 7/8	5	6	Mendocino Co., CA	Kenneth A. Bovero	Kenneth A. Bovero	1993	274
145 3/8	21 2/8	22 4/8	19 6/8	4 4/8	4 4/8	6	6	Clallam Co., WA	Ernest Hanewell	Patrick M. Lockhart	1964	278
145 3/8	22 3/8	21	23 4/8	4 5/8	4 6/8	5	5	Mendocino Co., CA	Paul M. Holleman II	Paul M. Holleman II	1976	278
145 3/8	23 3/8	22	22 6/8	4 1/8	4	6	5	Trinity Co., CA	Donald A. Dunn	Donald A. Dunn	1992	278
145 2/8	22 5/8	17 5/8	17 3/8	4	4	4	4	Harrison Lake, BC	Lloyd L. Ward, Jr.	Lloyd L. Ward, Jr.	1947	281
145 2/8	22 4/8	21 2/8	16 2/8	4 4/8	4 7/8	5	5	Jackson Co., OR	Bill Hays	Bill Hays	1968	281
145 2/8	20 2/8	21	16 4/8	5 4/8	5 2/8	5	5	Marion Co., OR	James J. Edgell	James J. Edgell	1979	281
145 2/8	22 4/8	22 5/8	21	5 3/8	5 1/8	7	9	Tehama Co., CA	Clint Heiber	Clint Heiber	1979	281
145 2/8	23	23 6/8	22 7/8	4 3/8	4 4/8	5	5	Josephine Co., OR	Jim Breeze	Jim Breeze	1986	281
145 1/8	21 5/8	21 6/8	16	4 6/8	4 4/8	7	6	Lewis Co., WA	Wenzel Tauscher	John L. Tauscher	1946	286
145 1/8	23 5/8	23 4/8	23 3/8	5 1/8	5 2/8	5	5	Tehama Co., CA	Lamar G. Hanson	Lamar G. Hanson	1972	286
145 1/8	21 6/8	22 6/8	16 3/8	5	5 3/8	6	5	Pierce Co., WA	Robert L. Armstrong	Robert L. Armstrong	1978	286

Score								Locality	Owner	Hunter	Date Killed	Rank
145 1/8	19 6/8	19 5/8	15 1/8	4 6/8	4 5/8	5	5	Lane Co., OR	Boyd Iverson	Boyd Iverson	1982	286
145 1/8	21 7/8	21 2/8	16 7/8	4 3/8	4 3/8	5	5	Lane Co., OR	Kevin M. Albin	Kevin M. Albin	1990	286
145 1/8	21 4/8	20 7/8	19 4/8	4 3/8	4 3/8	6	5	Trinity Co., CA	Gene Shannon	Daniel M. Phillips	1990	286
145 1/8	19 7/8	20 1/8	20 1/8	4 4/8	4 4/8	5	5	Jefferson Co., WA	Bryan L. Bukovnik	Bryan L. Bukovnik	2001	286
145	19 6/8	21 7/8	17 1/8	4 7/8	5 1/8	6	6	Humboldt Co., CA	Marvin D. Stapp	Marvin D. Stapp	1899	293
145	19 2/8	19 2/8	19 2/8	4 5/8	5 1/8	5	6	Douglas Co., OR	Larry E. Waller	Larry E. Waller	1980	293
145	22 2/8	21 4/8	21 2/8	5 1/8	5 1/8	7	5	Mendocino Co., CA	Ralph I. Sibley	Ralph I. Sibley	1986	293
145	24 2/8	23 7/8	14 4/8	4 3/8	4 3/8	5	6	Whatcom Co., WA	Harry E. Williams	Harry E. Williams	1992	293
145	21 7/8	20 6/8	20	4 3/8	4 5/8	5	5	Trinity Co., CA	Dennis A. Nilsen	Dennis A. Nilsen	1997	293
145	20 5/8	20 1/8	17 1/8	5	5	7	5	Tehama Co., CA	Douglas R. Jost	Douglas R. Jost	2002	293
144 7/8	21 6/8	21 5/8	19 5/8	5 6/8	5 7/8	4	3	Grays Harbor Co., WA	Ken Frank	Mitch Myers	1935	299
144 7/8	20 6/8	20 4/8	13 3/8	4	4 1/8	5	5	Clatsop Co., OR	Pravomil Raichl	Pravomil Raichl	1959	299
144 7/8	22 1/8	23 1/8	22 7/8	4 1/8	4 1/8	5	5	Lane Co., OR	Clair R. Thomas	Clair R. Thomas	1959	299
144 7/8	25 4/8	25	21	5 1/8	5	4	4	Jackson Co., OR	Riley F. Bean	Riley F. Bean	1971	299
144 7/8	27	26 5/8	21 3/8	5 4/8	5 6/8	6	6	Marion Co., OR	James C. Tennimon	James C. Tennimon	1988	299
144 7/8	22 1/8	21 6/8	18 3/8	5 1/8	5 2/8	5	5	Skamania Co., WA	Fred W. Campbell	Fred W. Campbell	1992	299
144 6/8	22 7/8	22 7/8	16 5/8	4 4/8	4 4/8	6	5	Benton Co., OR	Martin C. Goracke	Thomas Goracke	PR 1950	305
144 6/8	20	20 4/8	19 4/8	3 4/8	3 4/8	5	6	King Co., WA	R. Walter Williams	R. Walter Williams	1956	305
144 6/8	22 4/8	22	16 4/8	4 2/8	4 2/8	4	5	Linn Co., OR	Angeline Fischer	Angeline Fischer	1968	305
144 6/8	22 2/8	22 4/8	22 4/8	4 4/8	4 4/8	5	5	Mendocino Co., CA	Richard Vannelli	Richard Vannelli	1970	305
144 6/8	21 3/8	22 4/8	19 5/8	6	6	4	5	Lincoln Co., OR	William D. Harmon	OR Fish & Wildl. Div.	1976	305
144 6/8	22 2/8	22 1/8	17 7/8	4 4/8	4 3/8	6	5	Skamania Co., WA	Melvin D. Robertson	Melvin D. Robertson	1983	305
144 6/8	20 7/8	21 4/8	22	4 3/8	4 2/8	5	5	Trinity Co., CA	Craig L. Brown	C.L. & J.L. Brown	1996	305
144 6/8	21	20	18	4	4	5	5	Santa Clara Co., CA	Dean P. Filice	Dean P. Filice	1996	305
144 6/8	21 6/8	21 3/8	18 7/8	4 7/8	4 7/8	5	5	Mendocino Co., CA	John Tuso	John D. Tuso	1998	305
144 6/8	23 1/8	22 2/8	19 7/8	4 7/8	4 7/8	5	5	Humboldt Co., CA	Kevin R. Hunt	Kevin R. Hunt	2002	305
144 5/8	22 6/8	22 4/8	21 5/8	4 4/8	4 4/8	5	5	Josephine Co., OR	Jerry C. Sparlin	Jerry C. Sparlin	1963	315
144 5/8	21	21 1/8	17 7/8	4 2/8	4 3/8	5	5	Lewis Co., WA	LeRoy F. Benge	LeRoy F. Benge	1974	315
144 5/8	20 1/8	20	18 1/8	4	4	5	5	Jackson Co., OR	Dean P. Pasche	Dean P. Pasche	1988	315
144 5/8	21 5/8	21 2/8	20	4 4/8	4 4/8	5	5	Benton Co., OR	Gerald L. Hibbs	Gerald L. Hibbs	1990	315
144 5/8	22 5/8	22 5/8	21 2/8	4 3/8	4 3/8	5	5	Linn Co., OR	Donald J. Semolke	Donald J. Semolke	1990	315
144 4/8	21 4/8	21 3/8	23 1/8	4 2/8	4 3/8	5	5	Shasta Co., CA	Ernie Young	Chet Young	1953	320
144 4/8	21 6/8	21 5/8	21 5/8	4 2/8	4 2/8	5	5	Clackamas Co., OR	John R. Vollmer, Jr.	John R. Vollmer, Jr.	1960	320
144 4/8	21 2/8	20 5/8	20 5/8	4 2/8	4 2/8	5	5	Powers, OR	Ray A. Davis	Ray A. Davis	1968	320
144 4/8	20 5/8	21 7/8	17	3 7/8	3 6/8	4	4	Snohomish Co., WA	Roy Shogren	Roy Shogren	1979	320
144 4/8	21	21	17 7/8	4 1/8	4 1/8	5	5	Benton Co., OR	Lance M. Holm	Lance M. Holm	1988	320
144 4/8	20 5/8	20 7/8	15 4/8	4 6/8	4 7/8	5	5	Clark Co., WA	Raymond M. Gibson	Raymond M. Gibson	1992	320
144 4/8	22 6/8	20 6/8	16 4/8	4 4/8	4 5/8	6	5	Clackamas Co., OR	Gregory A. Latimer	Gregory A. Latimer	1992	320
144 3/8	22 1/8	22 1/8	14 2/8	5 2/8	5 2/8	4	4	Santa Clara Co., CA	Maitland Armstrong	Maitland Armstrong	1946	327
144 3/8	23 3/8	23 3/8	21 3/8	4	4	5	5	Siskiyou Co., CA	Floyd B. Hoisington	Floyd B. Hoisington	1976	327
144 3/8	24 4/8	24 4/8	21 5/8	4 1/8	4 1/8	4	5	Humboldt Co., CA	Gerald Wescott	Gerald Wescott	1980	327
144 3/8	21	20 7/8	16 5/8	4 7/8	4 7/8	5	5	Humboldt Co., CA	Richard G. Van Vorst	Richard G. Van Vorst	1990	327
144 3/8	20 4/8	20 7/8	14 7/8	4 4/8	4 4/8	5	5	Alameda Co., CA	Anthony S. Webb	Anthony S. Webb	1990	327
144 3/8	20 1/8	22	19 1/8	4 4/8	4 4/8	6	6	Jefferson Co., WA	John E. Shultz	John E. Shultz	1991	327
144 3/8	22 3/8	24 4/8	18 3/8	5	5	4	4	Mendocino Co., CA	Jack J. Tuso	Jack J. Tuso	1997	327
144 2/8	23 3/8	23 6/8	20 5/8	3 7/8	3 7/8	5	5	Jackson Co., OR	Warren Pestka	Warren Pestka	1974	334
144 2/8	20 3/8	21 6/8	17 2/8	4 4/8	4 6/8	6	6	Josephine Co., OR	Clinton Moore	Clinton Moore	1975	334
144 2/8	19 6/8	21 3/8	15 6/8	3 6/8	4 6/8	6	5	Marion Co., OR	Arthur L. Schmidt	Arthur L. Schmidt	1978	334

COLUMBIA BLACKTAIL DEER - TYPICAL ANTLERS
Odocoileus hemionus columbianus

Score	Length of Main Beam R	L	Inside Spread	Circumference at Smallest Place Between Burr and First Point R	L	Number of Points R	L	Locality	Hunter	Owner	Date Killed	Rank
144 2/8	21	22 4/8	20 4/8	4 4/8	4 4/8	5	5	Mendocino Co., CA	Frank Kester	Frank Kester	1981	334
144 1/8	21 7/8	21 3/8	17 7/8	4 5/8	4 4/8	5	5	Siskiyou Natl. For., OR	Dennis E. Bourn	Dennis E. Bourn	1971	338
144 1/8	20 2/8	19 2/8	17 7/8	4 6/8	4 6/8	5	5	Humboldt Co., CA	Richard L. Barsanti	Richard L. Barsanti	2000	338
144 1/8	22	21 4/8	16 3/8	4 2/8	4 1/8	5	5	Lane Co., OR	John W. Wheeler	John W. Wheeler	2001	338
144	20 7/8	20 4/8	17 2/8	4 4/8	4 5/8	5	5	Skamania Co., WA	Wayne Crockford	Wayne Crockford	1960	341
144	21 2/8	21 5/8	17	4 7/8	5 1/8	5	5	Linn Co., OR	Ed A. Taylor	Ed A. Taylor	1981	341
144	21 3/8	21 2/8	18	4 3/8	4 3/8	6	6	Clackamas Co., OR	Picked Up	Bob K. Oka	1993	341
144	21 6/8	23 2/8	19 2/8	4	3 7/8	5	5	Jackson Co., OR	Robert D. Davidson	Robert D. Davidson	2000	341
143 7/8	21 7/8	23	20 6/8	5	4 5/8	6	6	Linn Co., OR	Clarence Howe	Clarence Howe	1941	345
143 7/8	23 4/8	22 7/8	21 3/8	5	4 6/8	5	5	Clackamas Co., OR	Richard G. Mathis	Richard G. Mathis	1965	345
143 7/8	20 5/8	19 5/8	20 3/8	5	5 1/8	5	5	Humboldt Co., CA	Lois C. Miller	Lois C. Miller	1986	345
143 7/8	20 3/8	20 2/8	18 1/8	4 4/8	4 3/8	5	5	Siskiyou Co., CA	Frank L. Galea	Frank L. Galea	1996	345
143 7/8	22 2/8	22 5/8	16	3 7/8	3 7/8	5	6	Siskiyou Co., CA	Dave E. Scheve	Dave E. Scheve	1996	345
143 7/8	19 3/8	20 2/8	16	4 6/8	4 7/8	5	5	Squamish, BC	B. Miller	B. Miller	1962	350
143 6/8	21 7/8	21 7/8	15 6/8	4 6/8	5	5	5	Linn Co., OR	Michael D. Owen	Michael D. Owen	1973	350
143 6/8	20 1/8	20 2/8	16 4/8	5	5	5	5	Lewis Co., WA	Bill W. Latimer	Bill W. Latimer	1974	350
143 6/8	20 5/8	20 2/8	19 7/8	5 2/8	5 2/8	6	6	Tehama Co., CA	Clint Heiber	Clint Heiber	1978	350
143 6/8	19 5/8	19 4/8	15 2/8	4 7/8	4 6/8	5	6	Mendocino Co., CA	Mark Ciancio	Mark Ciancio	1986	350
143 6/8	20 6/8	20 3/8	15 4/8	5 2/8	4 7/8	5	5	Humboldt Co., CA	Hartwell A. Burnett	Hartwell A. Burnett	1988	350
143 5/8	21 2/8	21 2/8	17 7/8	5 6/8	5 7/8	5	6	Grays Harbor Co., WA	E. & R. Dierick	E. & R. Dierick	1958	356
143 5/8	20 4/8	20 4/8	18 5/8	4 4/8	4 4/8	4	4	Siskiyou Co., CA	Emit C. Jones	Emit C. Jones	1960	356
143 5/8	20 5/8	19 3/8	18 5/8	4 1/8	4 2/8	5	5	Trinity Co., CA	Kenneth L. Cogle, Jr.	Kenneth L. Cogle, Jr.	1985	356
143 5/8	21 3/8	21 5/8	17 7/8	4 4/8	4 5/8	5	5	Jefferson Co., WA	Earl L. Woodley	Earl L. Woodley	1994	356
143 4/8	21 4/8	22 5/8	16 2/8	4 1/8	4 3/8	5	5	Clark Co., WA	A.W. Gerber	Earl Gerber	1929	360
143 4/8	21 4/8	21 1/8	21 4/8	4 4/8	4 4/8	5	4	Snoqualmie, WA	Milton L. James	Milton L. James	1964	360
143 4/8	21 3/8	20 7/8	16 6/8	4 5/8	4 5/8	5	5	Jackson Co., OR	Jay Walker	Jay Walker	1978	360
143 4/8	21	20 4/8	17	4 6/8	4	5	5	Trinity Co., CA	Barry Griffin	Barry Griffin	1983	360
143 4/8	22	23	16 4/8	3 7/8	4	5	5	Josephine Co., OR	Virgil Welch	Virgil Welch	1983	360
143 4/8	22 6/8	22 4/8	20	4 2/8	4 3/8	5	5	Humboldt Co., CA	Arnold E. Dado	Arnold E. Dado	1993	360
143 4/8	21 1/8	21 2/8	18	4 4/8	4 2/8	5	5	Trinity Co., CA	Dennis A. Nilsen	Dennis A. Nilsen	1994	360
143 4/8	21 7/8	21 7/8	18 2/8	4 1/8	4 3/8	4	5	Clackamas Co., OR	Richard L. Schwichtenberg	Richard L. Schwichtenberg	2002	360
143 3/8	20	20 1/8	15 3/8	4 7/8	4 7/8	5	5	Chehalis River, BC	Clair A. Howard	Clair A. Howard	1971	368
143 3/8	21 4/8	21 5/8	20 1/8	4 3/8	4 3/8	5	5	Shasta Co., CA	David E. Smith	David E. Smith	1977	368
143 3/8	19 2/8	18 7/8	18 3/8	3 4/8	3 4/8	5	5	Mendocino Co., CA	Larry G. Miller	Larry G. Miller	1978	368
143 3/8	21	19 6/8	17 1/8	4 7/8	4 6/8	5	5	Trinity Co., CA	Joy L. Brown	C. L. & J.L. Brown	1991	368

Score	L. Main Beam R	L. Main Beam L	Inside Spread	Circ. R	Circ. L	Pts R	Pts L	Locality	Hunter	Owner	Date	Rank
143 3/8	21 6/8	21 5/8	19	4 3/8	4 5/8	5	5	Linn Co., OR	Basil C. Bradbury	Unknown	1960	372
143 3/8	22 3/8	22 6/8	21 4/8	4 2/8	4 2/8	5	5	Lake Co., CA	Mario Sereni, Jr.	Mario Sereni, Jr.	1965	372
143 3/8	19 5/8	19 4/8	17 2/8	4	4	5	5	Humboldt Co., CA	Jack Stedman	Jack Stedman	1965	372
143 3/8	20 6/8	19 6/8	19	4 7/8	6 2/8	6	7	Jones Lake, BC	James Haslam	James Haslam	1967	372
143 3/8	20 2/8	20 4/8	18 6/8	4 5/8	4 5/8	5	5	Jackson Co., OR	Riley F. Bean	Riley F. Bean	1972	372
143 3/8	21 2/8	21 3/8	25	4 6/8	4 6/8	6	5	Mendocino Co., CA	George W. Rogers	George W. Rogers	1977	372
143 3/8	20	20 2/8	18 2/8	5 1/8	5 1/8	5	5	Josephine Co., OR	Jaime L. Torres	Jaime L. Torres	1990	372
143 3/8	22 4/8	22 6/8	15 6/8	4	4	5	5	Shasta Co., CA	Ben Brackett	Ben Brackett	1993	372
143 1/8	21 4/8	20 7/8	17 2/8	4 1/8	4 2/8	5	7	Polk Co., OR	S. Mike Jacobsen	S. Mike Jacobsen	2000	381
143 1/8	22	22 1/8	17 3/8	4 4/8	4 4/8	5	6	Benton Co., OR	A.C. Nelson	A.C. Nelson	1957	381
143 1/8	21 6/8	21 5/8	18 1/8	4 1/8	4	6	5	Humboldt Co., CA	Mitchell A. Thorson	Mitchell A. Thorson	1965	381
143 1/8	22 3/8	22 2/8	17 1/8	4 1/8	4 1/8	5	5	Coos Co., OR	Ken Wilson	Ken Wilson	1980	381
143	20 1/8	22 3/8	18	4 2/8	4 2/8	5	5	Humboldt Co., CA	Eddie L. Mendes	Eddie L. Mendes	1992	385
142 7/8	23 5/8	22	16 3/8	4	4	4	4	Josephine Co., OR	Riley F. Bean	Riley F. Bean	1956	386
142 7/8	23 1/8	23 6/8	21 1/8	5 1/8	5 6/8	4	4	Clackamas Co., OR	Larry R. Tracy	Larry R. Tracy	1965	386
142 7/8	21 7/8	23 1/8	17 3/8	4	4 2/8	6	5	Clackamas Co., OR	Ross A. Gordon	Ross A. Gordon	1989	386
142 6/8	23 2/8	21 7/8	19 4/8	4 6/8	5	5	5	Tehama Co., CA	Randy Croote	Randy Croote	1993	389
142 6/8	20 4/8	22	17 2/8	3 7/8	4	4	4	Linn Co., OR	R. Reid & D. Liles	R. Reid & D. Liles	1982	389
142 6/8	20 1/8	20 4/8	22	4 4/8	3 7/8	4	5	Linn Co., OR	Kenneth W. Wegner	Kenneth W. Wegner	1986	389
142 6/8	21 4/8	20 2/8	20 1/8	5 4/8	5 6/8	5	5	Josephine Co., OR	Reginald P. Breeze	Reginald P. Breeze	1996	389
142 6/8	22	21 4/8	20 2/8	4 4/8	4 2/8	5	5	Mendocino Co., CA	Steen C. Henriksen	Steen C. Henriksen	1998	389
142 5/8	20 2/8	23 1/8	21 4/8	4 2/8	4 1/8	5	5	Mendocino Co., CA	Thomas J. Fetzer	Thomas J. Fetzer	1950	394
142 5/8	22 5/8	23	22 3/8	4 6/8	4 6/8	5	5	Marion Co., OR	Robert E. Bochsler	Robert E. Bochsler	1959	394
142 5/8	21 4/8	20 6/8	17 1/8	4 1/8	4	5	5	Jackson Co., OR	Leonard B. Sequeira	Nancy Sequeira	PR 1966	394
142 5/8	23 1/8	19 4/8	16 5/8	4 2/8	4 2/8	4	4	Santa Clara Co., CA	Picked Up	R. & N. Haera	PR 1966	394
142 5/8	22	20 5/8	17 7/8	4 4/8	4 3/8	5	5	Santa Clara Co., CA	Picked Up	Russel Rasmussen	1979	394
142 5/8	20 6/8	20 4/8	16 5/8	4 6/8	4 7/8	4	4	Trinity Co., CA	Larry Brown	C.L. & J.L. Brown	1979	394
142 5/8	19 4/8	22 6/8	19 7/8	4 5/8	3 7/8	6	7	Tehama Co., CA	Kenneth R. Hall	Kenneth R. Hall	1989	394
142 5/8	21 6/8	23 1/8	19 7/8	4 3/8	4 1/8	5	5	Mendocino Co., CA	Warren F. Coffman	Warren F. Coffman	1991	394
142 4/8	20 1/8	22	20 1/8	4 2/8	4 3/8	5	5	Trinity Co., CA	Robert T. Edwards	Robert T. Edwards	1992	405
142 4/8	22 2/8	20 6/8	20 5/8	4 3/8	4 4/8	5	5	Chilliwack Lake, BC	Blair R. Houdayer	Blair R. Houdayer	1995	405
142 4/8	21 4/8	20 1/8	20	4 4/8	4	5	5	Lane Co., OR	Byron Hoeper	Byron J. Hoeper	1999	405
142 4/8	22	22 2/8	16 6/8	4 6/8	4 2/8	4	4	Alameda Co., CA	Dino W. Markette	Dino W. Markette	1965	405
142 4/8	22 6/8	22	21	4 5/8	4 6/8	5	5	Trinity Co., CA	Jace Comfort	Jace Comfort	1967	405
142 4/8	18 3/8	15	18 4/8	4 3/8	4 6/8	5	5	Chilliwack, BC	Frank Rosenauer	Frank Rosenauer	1970	405
142 3/8	22 4/8	16 6/8	15 4/8	3 7/8	4 3/8	5	5	Clackamas Co., OR	Henry A. Charriere	Henry A. Charriere	1980	411
142 3/8	23 4/8	21	17 3/8	3 4/8	3 7/8	5	4	Jackson Co., OR	Donald G. Spence	Donald G. Spence	1991	411
142 3/8	20 6/8	18 4/8	19 3/8	4 6/8	3 4/8	3	4	Jackson Co., OR	Brian V. Morris	D.M. & J. Phillips	1993	411
142 2/8	23	15 4/8	19 1/8	4 3/8	4 6/8	5	9	Mendocino Co., CA	Jerry C. Russell	Jerry C. Russell	1964	414
142 2/8	20 6/8	20 4/8	17	4	4 5/8	5	5	Laytonville, CA	Byron J. Rowland, Jr.	Byron J. Rowland, Jr.	1976	414
142 2/8	23 4/8	22	16 2/8	4 6/8	4 1/8	5	5	Humboldt Co., CA	Darol L. Damm	Darol L. Damm	1992	414
142 2/8	20 7/8	22 3/8	19 6/8	4 2/8	4 6/8	4	4	Humboldt Co., CA	James L. Sloan	James L. Sloan	1992	414
142 2/8	20 7/8	20 5/8	20 4/8	4 3/8	4	5	5	Mendocino Co., CA	James A. Shelton	James A. Shelton	1944	414
142 2/8	20 7/8	23 3/8	20 7/8	4	4 2/8	6	6	Jackson Co., OR	Eileen F. Damone	Eileen F. Damone	1976	414
142 2/8	21 4/8	20 4/8	21 4/8	4 2/8	4	6	6	Trinity Co., CA	Donald A. Dunn	Donald A. Dunn	1981	414
142 2/8	22 5/8	20 6/8	22	4 2/8	4 2/8	5	5	Trinity Co., CA	Derek W. Harrison	Derek W. Harrison	1997	414
142 2/8	22 7/8	21 4/8	21 6/8	4 2/8	4 2/8	5	5	Mendocino Co., CA	Michael D. Callahan	Michael D. Callahan	1998	414
142 2/8	22 3/8	22 3/8	22	4 4/8	4 4/8	4	5	Mendocino Co., CA	George A. Deffterios	George A. Deffterios	2000	414

COLUMBIA BLACKTAIL DEER - TYPICAL ANTLERS
Odocoileus hemionus columbianus

Score	Length of Main Beam R	L	Inside Spread	Circumference at Smallest Place Between Burr and First Point R	L	Number of Points R	L	Locality	Hunter	Owner	Date Killed	Rank
142 1/8	21 3/8	22 3/8	19 7/8	5 1/8	5 1/8	5	4	Shasta Co., CA	Richard R. Lowell	Richard R. Lowell	1953	420
142 1/8	23 5/8	22 2/8	16 7/8	4 5/8	4 4/8	5	5	Linn Co., OR	Bob L. Brazeale	Jack V. Logozzo	1972	420
142 1/8	21 3/8	21 3/8	16 3/8	4 4/8	4 3/8	5	5	Lane Co., OR	William Jordan	William Jordan	1982	420
142 1/8	20 4/8	19 5/8	15 5/8	4 4/8	4 3/8	5	5	Lewis Co., WA	Michael H. Carle	Michael H. Carle	1989	420
142 1/8	22	22	20 3/8	4 3/8	4 1/8	4	4	Siskiyou Co., CA	John T. Scheffler	John T. Scheffler	1992	420
142 1/8	20 4/8	20 2/8	15 3/8	4 2/8	4	5	8	Tehama Co., CA	Michael R. Weber	Michael R. Weber	1996	420
142 1/8	22 6/8	21 4/8	14 7/8	4 2/8	4 2/8	5	5	Knight Inlet, BC	Andrew M. Rippingale	Andrew M. Rippingale	1998	420
142	20 1/8	20 6/8	17	4 3/8	4 2/8	5	5	Cowlitz Co., WA	Harold C. Johnson	Harold C. Johnson	1947	427
142	21 6/8	22 5/8	20 2/8	4 5/8	4 6/8	6	5	Mt. Sheazer, WA	Joseph B. Wilcox	Joseph B. Wilcox	1953	427
142	23 6/8	23 2/8	20	5 4/8	5 3/8	8	6	Lewis Co., WA	Calvin Harris	Pete Harris	1963	427
142	24	23 5/8	16 7/8	5 1/8	5 6/8	8	5	Marion Co., OR	Hugh W. Gardner	Hugh W. Gardner	1966	427
142	21 3/8	24 6/8	17	5	5	4	5	Skamania Co., WA	Ted Howell	Ted Howell	1968	427
142	21 3/8	21 4/8	18	4 4/8	4 4/8	5	5	Jackson Co., OR	Riley F. Bean	Riley F. Bean	1970	427
142	25 3/8	24	18 3/8	7	6 4/8	7	4	Doty, WA	Leslie A. Lusk	Leslie A. Lusk	1973	427
142	23	20 7/8	21 4/8	4 4/8	4 4/8	5	5	Skamania Co., WA	Herbert P. Roberts	Herbert P. Roberts	1983	427
141 7/8	20 7/8	21 3/8	18 1/8	5 5/8	5 5/8	4	4	Whatcom Co., WA	Kjell A. Thompson	Kjell A. Thompson	1963	435
141 7/8	21 4/8	21 2/8	17 7/8	4 7/8	5	5	5	Trinity Co., CA	Pedro H. Henrich	Pedro H. Henrich	1977	435
141 7/8	21 4/8	21 4/8	16 5/8	4 2/8	4 1/8	5	5	Lincoln Co., OR	Roy A. Parks	Roy A. Parks	1984	435
141 7/8	21 6/8	21 4/8	17 6/8	3 7/8	4	6	5	Trinity Co., CA	Melvin M. Clair	Melvin M. Clair	1992	435
141 7/8	21 3/8	21 2/8	15	5	4 4/8	7	6	Lane Co., OR	Picked Up	Dana H. Clay	1995	435
141 6/8	22 7/8	22 2/8	17 5/8	4 5/8	4 6/8	6	7	Pierce Co., WA	Joseph Kominski	Joseph Kominski	1954	440
141 6/8	21 3/8	21 3/8	19 2/8	4 4/8	4 4/8	5	5	Lane Co., OR	Jerry Shepard	Jerry Shepard	1954	440
141 6/8	19 7/8	19 3/8	16 4/8	4 7/8	4 7/8	5	5	Hobart, WA	Donald R. Heinle	Donald R. Heinle	1958	440
141 6/8	20 2/8	20 7/8	18 2/8	4 5/8	4 4/8	5	5	Linn Co., OR	Eugene L. Wilson	Eugene L. Wilson	1982	440
141 6/8	20 2/8	19 6/8	15 4/8	4 5/8	4 6/8	5	5	Mendocino Co., CA	Dennis Bartolomei	Dennis Bartolomei	1996	440
141 5/8	19 7/8	19 6/8	20 3/8	4	4 2/8	5	5	Trinity Co., CA	A.H. Hilbert	A.H. Hilbert	PR 1955	445
141 5/8	23	22 5/8	15 7/8	5 2/8	4 7/8	5	5	Skamania Co., WA	E. Gerald Tikka	E. Gerald Tikka	1987	445
141 5/8	21 1/8	21 6/8	18 5/8	3 6/8	3 6/8	5	5	Mendocino Co., CA	Lanny G. King	Lanny G. King	1992	445
141 4/8	20 2/8	20 6/8	17 6/8	4 7/8	5	5	5	Morton Co., WA	Ralph W. Cournyer	Ralph W. Cournyer	1962	448
141 4/8	22	22 5/8	15 4/8	5 2/8	5 1/8	5	5	Pierce Co., WA	Ron Dick	Ron Dick	1965	448
141 4/8	21 2/8	21 1/8	16 2/8	4 2/8	4 2/8	5	5	Mendocino Co., CA	Greg Rocha	Greg Rocha	1985	448
141 4/8	21 2/8	22 4/8	15 5/8	4 5/8	4 4/8	6	7	Trinity Co., CA	Larry Brown	C.L. & J.L. Brown	1986	448
141 4/8	20 7/8	20 4/8	20	4 4/8	4 4/8	5	5	Del Norte Co., CA	Les Johnson	Les Johnson	1986	448
141 3/8	22 5/8	23 2/8	20	5 3/8	5 4/8	6	6	Pierce Co., WA	Delmer H. Stotler	Delmer H. Stotler	1957	453
141 3/8	19 6/8	19 7/8	17 6/8	4 7/8	4 6/8	7	6	Harrison Lake, BC	D. Harrison	D. Harrison	1963	453
141 3/8	22 1/8	21 5/8	18 7/8	4 7/8	4 5/8	5	4	Trinity Co., CA	Larry Brown	C.L. & J.L. Brown	1980	453

Score	Length R	Length L	Inside Spread	Circ. R	Circ. L	Pts R	Pts L	Locality	Name	Name	Date	Rank
141 3/8	21 2/8	21 7/8	16 7/8	4 3/8	4 1/8	5	5	Mendocino Co., CA	Gene V. Bradley	Gene V. Bradley	1988	453
141 2/8	25 6/8	25 3/8	21 5/8	5 4/8	5 6/8	6	6	Pierce Co., WA	John Streepy, Sr.	John Streepy, Sr.	1956	457
141 2/8	21 4/8	20 6/8	18 2/8	4 3/8	4 2/8	5	5	Marion Co., OR	Arthur L. Schmidt	Arthur L. Schmidt	1986	457
141 2/8	21 4/8	20 4/8	18	4 2/8	4 4/8	5	5	Trinity Co., CA	Barry D. Keyes	Barry D. Keyes	1989	457
141 2/8	21 5/8	21 4/8	16	3 6/8	4	5	5	Trinity Co., CA	Donald A. Dunn	Donald A. Dunn	1996	457
141 1/8	22 2/8	22 4/8	17 7/8	4 6/8	4 6/8	5	6	Pierce Co., WA	Jerry E. Burke	Jerry E. Burke	1980	461
141 1/8	23 3/8	23 2/8	17 5/8	4 2/8	4 4/8	6	6	Jackson Co., OR	Harold R. Embury	Harold R. Embury	1985	461
141 1/8	21	21	19 3/8	4 6/8	4 5/8	5	5	Clallam Co., WA	David P. Sanford	David P. Sanford	1989	461
141	18 4/8	18 6/8	13	4 4/8	4 3/8	5	5	Santa Clara Co., CA	Charles Nesler	Ben W. Mazzone	1957	464
141	21 1/8	21 1/8	17	3 7/8	4 1/8	5	4	Humboldt Co., CA	Allen Pierce, Jr.	Allen Pierce, Jr.	1959	464
141	19 6/8	19 6/8	14	4	4	4	5	Lane Co., OR	Richard Porter	Ruel Holt	1962	464
141	21	20 2/8	19 4/8	4 4/8	4	5	5	Mendocino Co., CA	Richard Vannelli	Richard Vannelli	1970	464
141	23	24 4/8	22	5 4/8	5 4/8	7	7	Mendocino Co., CA	Gerald W. Whitmire	Gerald W. Whitmire	1976	464
141	21	20 4/8	17 6/8	4 1/8	4 1/8	5	5	Jackson Co., OR	Philip W. Sandquist	Philip W. Sandquist	1993	464
141	22 4/8	21 3/8	20	4 3/8	3 6/8	4	5	Mendocino Co., CA	Richard L. Valladao	Richard L. Valladao	1993	464
141	22 6/8	22 2/8	16 6/8	4 2/8	4 3/8	5	5	Yamhill Co., OR	Danny J. Moen	Danny J. Moen	1997	464
140 7/8	22 7/8	22 6/8	17 3/8	4 3/8	4 3/8	4	4	Clallam Co., WA	Irving C. Hansen	Kurt C. Hansen	PR 1950	472
140 7/8	22 2/8	25 7/8	12 3/8	6 5/8	7 4/8	7	5	Clallam Co., WA	Frank Foldi	Steve Crossley	1958	472
140 7/8	21 1/8	20 1/8	21 1/8	4 3/8	4 4/8	5	5	Shasta Co., CA	Dave Swenson	Dave Swenson	1968	472
140 7/8	23 3/8	22	16 5/8	3 7/8	4	5	5	Mendocino Co., CA	Douglas W. Lim	Douglas W. Lim	1981	472
140 7/8	22	23 7/8	18 6/8	5	5	8	10	Polk Co., OR	Gale A. Draper	Gale A. Draper	1984	472
140 7/8	23 7/8	19 1/8	16 1/8	4 4/8	4 4/8	5	5	Mendocino Co., CA	John T. Corrigan	John T. Corrigan	1997	472
140 7/8	18	23 5/8	22 5/8	4 2/8	4 2/8	4	5	Colusa Co., CA	John H. Knight	John H. Knight	1998	472
140 6/8	24	19 4/8	16 3/8	4 5/8	4 5/8	5	5	Tehama Co., CA	Donald J. Giottonini, Jr.	Donald J. Giottonini, Jr.	2002	480
140 6/8	21 1/8	18 5/8	17 2/8	4 4/8	4 4/8	6	6	Lewis Co., WA	Nick Nilson	Nick Nilson	1944	480
140 6/8	17 6/8	22 2/8	20 6/8	4	4	5	5	Mendocino Co., CA	Bill L. Conn	Bill L. Conn	1968	480
140 6/8	21	23	18 6/8	4 6/8	5 1/8	4	5	Mendocino Co., CA	Robert Lynch	Robert Lynch	1971	480
140 6/8	23 4/8	22 4/8	20	5 4/8	5 4/8	5	6	Mendocino Co., CA	Jerry D. Smith	Jerry D. Smith	1978	480
140 6/8	23	22 1/8	16 1/8	5	5	7	6	Trinity Co., CA	H. James Tonkin, Jr.	H. James Tonkin, Jr.	1995	480
140 6/8	21 3/8	21 5/8	20 2/8	4 6/8	4 7/8	5	6	Clackamas Co., OR	Casey Johnson	Casey Johnson	1997	480
140 6/8	21 3/8	20 5/8	16 4/8	5 1/8	5 3/8	5	5	Trinity Co., CA	Russell A. Nickols	Russell A. Nickols	1999	480
140 6/8	19 7/8	23 6/8	20	5	5	5	5	Clallam Co., WA	Darrell J. Johnson	Darrell J. Johnson	2003	480
140 5/8	23 5/8	21 7/8	18 3/8	4 6/8	4 5/8	6	6	Shasta Co., CA	Luther Clements	R.H. Bernhardy	1944	488
140 5/8	23	21	18 6/8	4 6/8	4 6/8	5	6	Glacier Co., WA	John J.A. Weatherby	John J.A. Weatherby	1965	488
140 5/8	21	20 4/8	18 4/8	4 7/8	5	5	6	Clark Co., WA	Wayne G. Place	Wayne G. Place	1995	488
140 4/8	21	22 2/8	18 4/8	4 4/8	4 4/8	5	5	Mendocino Co., CA	Bill L. Conn	Bill L. Conn	1977	491
140 4/8	20 2/8	20	17 2/8	4 4/8	4 4/8	6	5	Trinity Co., CA	Loran G. August	Loran G. August	1980	491
140 4/8	19 4/8	20 7/8	18 2/8	4 7/8	4 6/8	4	6	Yamhill Co., OR	Richard Watts	Richard Watts	1981	491
140 4/8	21 1/8	21 3/8	14 2/8	4 1/8	4 1/8	5	6	Mendocino Co., CA	Jay M. Gates III	Jay M. Gates III	1986	491
140 4/8	20 5/8	22	15	4 1/8	4 2/8	5	6	Trinity Co., CA	Jerry R. Cardoza	Jerry R. Cardoza	1996	491
140 4/8	22	21 2/8	19 4/8	4 1/8	4 1/8	5	5	Mendocino Co., CA	Ronald L. Christensen	Ronald L. Christensen	2002	491
140 3/8	21 2/8	20 5/8	16 5/8	3 7/8	4 3/8	5	5	Humboldt Co., CA	George S. Johnson	Roy F. Johnson	1934	497
140 3/8	20 1/8	21	17 7/8	4	4	5	4	Siskiyou Co., CA	Rodney Irwin	Rodney Irwin	1966	497
140 3/8	22	24 2/8	19 5/8	4 7/8	4 6/8	5	4	Jackson Co., OR	John T. Mee	John T. Mee	1974	497
140 3/8	24 3/8	23 5/8	19 2/8	4 4/8	4 2/8	4	4	Clackamas Co., OR	Anthony W. Wood	Anthony W. Wood	1996	497
140 3/8	22 6/8	22 6/8	19 6/8	4 6/8	4 6/8	4	6	Jackson Co., OR	Dusty S. McGrorty	Dusty S. McGrorty	2000	497
140 2/8	23 1/8	20 7/8	19 6/8	5	4 6/8	6	5	Mendocino Co., CA	Harry S. Richardson	Harry S. Richardson	1899	502
140 2/8	21	21 4/8	19 6/8	3 7/8	3 7/8	5	5	Mendocino Co., CA	Earl E. Hamlow, Jr.	Earl E. Hamlow, Jr.	1977	502

Score	Length of Main Beam R	L	Inside Spread	Circumference at Smallest Place Between Burr and First Point R	L	Number of Points R	L	Locality	Hunter	Owner	Date Killed	Rank
140 2/8	20 4/8	21 3/8	16 2/8	4 7/8	4 5/8	5	5	Lewis Co., WA	Randy J. Brossard	Randy J. Brossard	1978	502
140 2/8	22	21 1/8	23 4/8	4 3/8	4 3/8	4	5	Trinity Co., CA	Charles E. Davy	Charles E. Davy	1983	502
140 1/8	21 2/8	21 5/8	15 6/8	4 2/8	4 2/8	5	7	Mendocino Co., CA	Clarence W. Nelson	Clarence W. Nelson	1948	506
140 1/8	23 7/8	22 7/8	18 1/8	5	4 4/8	6	6	Lewis Co., WA	George Nichols	George Nichols	1964	506
140 1/8	20 6/8	20 1/8	19 7/8	5	5	5	5	Lane Co., OR	Jacob S. Huck	Jacob S. Huck	1971	506
140 1/8	20 4/8	19 4/8	16 3/8	4 3/8	4 2/8	4	4	Santa Clara Co., CA	Dick Sullivan	Dick Sullivan	1977	506
140 1/8	20 7/8	22 1/8	16 5/8	4 3/8	4 3/8	5	5	Lincoln Co., OR	Darrel R. Grishaber	Darrel R. Grishaber	1984	506
140 1/8	19	19 6/8	16 5/8	4 5/8	4 6/8	5	5	Snohomish Co., WA	Kenneth A. Peterson	Kenneth A. Peterson	1985	506
140 1/8	21 4/8	21 4/8	20 2/8	4 6/8	4 6/8	5	6	Trinity Co., CA	Craig L. Brown	C.L. & J.L. Brown	1986	506
140 1/8	21 1/8	20 2/8	16 3/8	3 7/8	4	4	4	Siskiyou Co., CA	Rickford M. Fisher	Rickford M. Fisher	1986	506
140 1/8	21 6/8	21	17 1/8	4	4 4/8	5	6	Trinity Co., CA	Wayne Sorensen	C.W. Sorensen	1986	506
140 1/8	22	21 2/8	19 1/8	3 5/8	3 6/8	4	5	Jackson Co., OR	Ronald L. Sherva	Ronald L. Sherva	1989	506
140 1/8	18 4/8	18 1/8	17 3/8	4 2/8	4 3/8	5	5	Santa Clara Co., CA	Darin S. Filice	Darin S. Filice	1995	506
140 1/8	20 2/8	20 2/8	16	4 7/8	4 6/8	7	5	Mendocino Co., CA	Roy Bergstrom	Roy Bergstrom	1966	506
140	23 1/8	24 1/8	17 6/8	4	4	4	4	Jackson Co., OR	Riley F. Bean	Riley F. Bean	1967	517
140	22 4/8	22 2/8	18	5 5/8	5 2/8	5	5	Mendocino Co., CA	Nick Deffterios	Nick Deffterios	1970	517
140	21	20 1/8	17	5	4 6/8	6	8	Polk Co., OR	Harold E. Stepp	Harold E. Stepp	1970	517
140	22	21 3/8	17 6/8	4 1/8	4 1/8	5	5	Humboldt Co., CA	Carl A. Anderson	Carl A. Anderson	1980	517
140	21 5/8	22 1/8	19	3 7/8	4 2/8	4	5	Trinity Co., CA	William J. Olson	William J. Olson	1981	517
139 7/8	20 4/8	21 4/8	17 2/8	4	3 6/8	7	5	Siskiyou Co., CA	Doug Weinrich	Doug Weinrich	1993	524
139 7/8	20 7/8	20 1/8	18 7/8	5 2/8	5	5	5	Jackson Co., OR	Dale E. Hoskins	Dale E. Hoskins	1946	524
139 7/8	19	18 6/8	15 5/8	4	4	4	4	Siskiyou Co., CA	Roy Eastlick	Roy Eastlick	1954	524
139 7/8	22 1/8	20 7/8	21 3/8	5 1/8	4 6/8	4	5	Trinity Co., CA	Craig L. Brown	C.L. & J.L. Brown	1981	524
139 7/8	23 2/8	22 2/8	17 6/8	4 7/8	5	5	6	Pierce Co., WA	John E. Mowatt	John E. Mowatt	1994	524
139 7/8	21 4/8	22	18 1/8	4 1/8	4 1/8	5	5	Mendocino Co., CA	David A. Chandler	David A. Chandler	1997	524
139 7/8	20 5/8	20 2/8	17 5/8	6	5 5/8	6	8	Humboldt Co., CA	Jace Comfort	Jace Comfort	1997	524
139 7/8	21	21	20 1/8	4	3 6/8	5	5	Mendocino Co., CA	Howard H. Bowles	Howard H. Bowles	1998	524
139 6/8	21 1/8	21 3/8	18 6/8	5	4 6/8	5	6	Thurston Co., WA	Eric Anderson	Eric Anderson	1937	531
139 6/8	20 5/8	21 7/8	16 2/8	4 6/8	4 6/8	6	6	Linn Co., OR	Gregory E. France	Gregory E. France	1961	531
139 6/8	21 5/8	22 4/8	16	4 1/8	4 1/8	5	5	Shasta Co., CA	Warren Hunter	Warren Hunter	1964	531
139 6/8	20 6/8	19 6/8	18 1/8	4 4/8	4 2/8	5	6	Josephine Co., OR	Richard H. Caswell	Richard H. Caswell	1969	531
139 6/8	19 6/8	19 7/8	18 6/8	4	4	5	5	Lewis Co., WA	Keith A. Heldreth	Keith A. Heldreth	1989	531
139 6/8	22 2/8	22 5/8	21 4/8	3 3/8	3 5/8	5	5	Trinity Co., CA	Andrew C. Hiebert	Andrew C. Hiebert	1993	531
139 6/8	21 4/8	21 6/8	17	4	4	5	5	Douglas Co., OR	Robert L. Baumgardner	Robert L. Baumgardner	1994	531
139 5/8	21 2/8	21 2/8	14 4/8	4 2/8	4 2/8	6	5	Cowlitz Co., WA	David A. Martin	David A. Martin	1962	538
139 5/8	20 2/8	19 6/8	16 6/8	4 5/8	4 5/8	6	6	Yamhill Co., OR	Mark J. Plummer	Mark J. Plummer	1994	538

Score	L. R	L. L	Inside Spread	Circ. R	Circ. L	Pts R	Pts L	Locality	Hunter	Owner	Date	Rank
139 5/8	19 1/8	19 4/8	16 1/8	4 4/8	4 4/8	5	5	Yolo Co., CA	Paul S. Matsumura	Paul S. Matsumura	2001	538
139 5/8	21 7/8	21 5/8	20 4/8	4 1/8	4 2/8	5	5	Lane Co., OR	Gene Tinker	Gene Tinker	1955	541
139 4/8	21 7/8	21 1/8	17 2/8	3 4/8	3 4/8	5	7	Jackson Co., OR	Arthur A. Ekerson	Arthur A. Ekerson	1966	541
139 4/8	22 2/8	21 5/8	16	4 6/8	4 6/8	5	4	Lewis Co., WA	Kevin Pointer	Kevin Pointer	1972	541
139 4/8	20 7/8	22 3/8	19 4/8	4 7/8	4 5/8	7	6	Jackson Co., OR	Everett B. Music, Jr.	Everett B. Music, Jr.	1985	541
139 4/8	19 3/8	18 6/8	19	4 6/8	4 5/8	5	5	Mendocino Co., CA	Ronald G. Malvino	Ronald G. Malvino	1993	541
139 4/8	22	22 3/8	20	4 1/8	4 2/8	5	5	Humboldt Co., CA	Robert B. Feamster	Robert B. Feamster	1996	541
139 4/8	20 3/8	22	15 6/8	4 3/8	4 2/8	5	5	Mendocino Co., CA	Jack J. Tuso	Jack J. Tuso	1996	541
139 4/8	21 4/8	22 4/8	15	5 4/8	6	5	5	Trinity Co., CA	Wayne C. Evans	Wayne C. Evans	1997	541
139 3/8	19 4/8	19 5/8	20 6/8	4 2/8	4 2/8	6	5	Mendocino Co., CA	Walter R. Schubert	Walter R. Schubert	1952	549
139 3/8	20 1/8	20 2/8	15 5/8	4 2/8	4 1/8	5	5	Whatcom Co., WA	Kim S. Scott	Kim S. Scott	1959	549
139 3/8	24 5/8	23 3/8	21 5/8	4 7/8	4 7/8	5	5	Trinity Co., CA	Andy Burgess	Andy Burgess	1964	549
139 3/8	21 4/8	21 1/8	22 5/8	4 3/8	4 1/8	5	5	Siskiyou Co., CA	Loren L. Lutz	Loren L. Lutz	1964	549
139 3/8	21 4/8	21 1/8	17 7/8	4 3/8	4 4/8	5	5	Monmouth Co., OR	Roy W. Miller	Roy W. Miller	1967	549
139 3/8	19 2/8	19 5/8	19 5/8	3 6/8	3 6/8	5	5	Marion Co., OR	Robert W. Hickman	Randall W. Hickman	1974	549
139 3/8	20 7/8	20 6/8	19 5/8	4 6/8	4 5/8	5	5	Marion Co., OR	Richard A. Hart	Richard A. Hart	1982	549
139 3/8	21	21	19 1/8	4 5/8	4 7/8	5	5	Mendocino Co., CA	Richard L. Moore	Richard L. Moore	1992	549
139 3/8	21	21	16 7/8	5	5 2/8	5	5	San Mateo Co., CA	Daniel R. Caughey III	Daniel R. Caughey III	1995	549
139 3/8	20 3/8	20	17 1/8	3 6/8	4 4/8	5	5	Lake Co., CA	Steven K. Farr	Steven K. Farr	1997	549
139 2/8	18 7/8	19 4/8	14 6/8	3 6/8	3 6/8	4	4	Trinity Co., CA	Donald A. Dunn	Donald A. Dunn	1899	559
139 2/8	21 3/8	21 4/8	20 1/8	4 1/8	4 1/8	5	5	Humboldt Co., CA	Jeff Bryant	Jeff Bryant	1964	559
139 2/8	22 5/8	21 1/8	18 6/8	3 5/8	3 5/8	6	4	Trinity Co., CA	Gary L. Mayberry	Gary L. Mayberry	1968	559
139 2/8	21 5/8	22 5/8	19 2/8	4 6/8	4 3/8	3	5	Lane Co., OR	Hubert Simmions	Jeff Heater	1978	559
139 2/8	21 7/8	23 3/8	17 1/8	5 1/8	3 7/8	4	7	Josephine Co., OR	David L. Teasley	David L. Teasley	1986	559
139 2/8	21	21	16 7/8	3 7/8	4	6	5	Trinity Co., CA	Terry H. Walker	Terry H. Walker	1986	559
139 2/8	20 5/8	20 4/8	20	4 1/8	3 7/8	4	4	Humboldt Co., CA	Daniel D. Zent	Daniel D. Zent	1991	559
139 2/8	23 7/8	22 3/8	16 4/8	4	4	5	5	Douglas Co., OR	Ken Wilson	Ken Wilson	1992	559
139 2/8	22 4/8	22 1/8	22 3/8	5 1/8	5 3/8	6	6	Trinity Co., CA	Joy L. Brown	C.L. & J.L. Brown	1993	559
139 2/8	22	21 1/8	18 6/8	4 4/8	4 3/8	6	6	Siskiyou Co., CA	Thomas K. Higgs	Thomas K. Higgs	1993	559
139 2/8	22	22 2/8	16	4	4 1/8	5	6	Tehama Co., CA	Paul J. Carlisle, Jr.	Paul J. Carlisle, Jr.	2000	559
139 1/8	22 4/8	21 2/8	18 5/8	3 7/8	4 2/8	5	5	Florence Co., OR	Edwin C. Stevens	Warner Pinkney	1928	570
139 1/8	21 7/8	21 2/8	18 5/8	4 2/8	4 5/8	5	5	Humboldt Co., CA	George E. Watson	George E. Watson	1933	570
139 1/8	23 3/8	23 3/8	20 3/8	5 3/8	5 6/8	4	5	Santa Clara Co., CA	Jack G. James	William R. James	1945	570
139 1/8	22 1/8	22	17 5/8	4	4 5/8	5	4	Mendocino Co., CA	John Winn, Jr.	John Winn, Jr.	1972	570
139	21 1/8	22 3/8	16 2/8	4 5/8	4 4/8	5	5	Jefferson Co., WA	Picked Up	Aubrey F. Taylor	1947	574
139	20	20 5/8	16 4/8	4 6/8	4 3/8	6	5	Lewis Co., WA	Mike Cournyer	Mike Cournyer	1964	574
139	21 7/8	21 1/8	15 7/8	4 3/8	4	6	6	Lane Co., OR	Picked Up	Ruel Holt	1964	574
139	19 3/8	19 3/8	18 2/8	4 1/8	3 7/8	5	5	Douglas Co., OR	Richard Wigle	Richard Wigle	1968	574
139	21 3/8	21 3/8	16 4/8	3 7/8	4 1/8	5	4	Marion Co., OR	Gene Collier	Gene Collier	1983	574
139	22	22	17 2/8	4	5 1/8	4	5	Trinity Co., CA	Roger J. Scala	Roger J. Scala	1990	574
139	21 2/8	20 7/8	17 2/8	5	4 2/8	5	5	Polk Co., OR	Jimmy L. Smithey	Jimmy L. Smithey	1990	574
139	19 2/8	19 2/8	17 6/8	4 4/8	4 4/8	4	5	Mendocino Co., CA	Emilio Flores	Emilio Flores	2001	574
139	20	20 3/8	17 4/8	3 7/8	3 7/8	5	4	Trinity Co., CA	Summer L. Brown	Summer L. Brown	2003	574
138 7/8	19 7/8	19 7/8	15 7/8	4 4/8	4 4/8	5	5	Pacific Co., WA	Russell Case	Russell Case	1956	583
138 7/8	21	22 2/8	20 5/8	4 5/8	4 5/8	4	4	Siskiyou Co., CA	Darrell Nowdesha	Darrell Nowdesha	1961	583
138 7/8	23 7/8	24 2/8	18 4/8	4 4/8	4 4/8	4	4	Tiller, OR	Ronald Elliott	Ronald Elliott	1963	583
138 7/8	19 1/8	20 5/8	15 3/8	5	4 7/8	6	5	Trinity Co., CA	William O. Louderback	William O. Louderback	1963	583
138 7/8	20 4/8	20 5/8	16 5/8	4 2/8	4 2/8	5	5	Tillamook Co., OR	Henry Naegeli	Henry Naegeli	1970	583

COLUMBIA BLACKTAIL DEER - TYPICAL ANTLERS

Odocoileus hemionus columbianus

Score	Length of Main Beam R	L	Inside Spread	Circumference at Smallest Place Between Burr and First Point R	L	Number of Points R	L	Locality	Hunter	Owner	Date Killed	Rank
138 7/8	23	22 6/8	19 4/8	4 3/8	4 3/8	7	5	Josephine Co., OR	Picked Up	Bobby G. Farmer, Jr.	1979	583
138 7/8	21 3/8	21 7/8	19 5/8	4 3/8	4 5/8	4	5	Mendocino Co., CA	Donald W. Biggs	Donald W. Biggs	1992	583
138 7/8	21	22 3/8	16 5/8	5	5	5	5	Whatcom Co., WA	Michael D. Scott	Michael D. Scott	1994	583
138 7/8	20 2/8	18 4/8	18 7/8	4	3 7/8	5	5	Trinity Co., CA	Cameron L. Brown	C.L. & J.L. Brown	1995	583
138 7/8	22 6/8	21 1/8	17 2/8	6 1/8	6 3/8	6	7	Clark Co., WA	Thomas Holland	Thomas Holland	1997	583
138 6/8	20 2/8	21 3/8	15 5/8	5 1/8	5 2/8	6	7	Snohomish Co., WA	Walter J. Kau	Walter J. Kau	1950	593
138 6/8	23 3/8	23	15 6/8	4 4/8	4 5/8	5	6	Pierce Co., WA	James Latimer	James Latimer	1962	593
138 6/8	21 3/8	20 4/8	16	4	4 1/8	5	5	Humboldt Co., CA	Larry Bowermaster	Larry Bowermaster	1964	593
138 6/8	20 2/8	21 3/8	15 4/8	4 5/8	4 5/8	5	5	Chipmunk Creek, BC	Larri H. Woodrow	Larri H. Woodrow	1987	593
138 6/8	22 2/8	21 1/8	22 2/8	4 1/8	4	5	5	Mendocino Co., CA	Gordon O. Hanson	Gordon O. Hanson	1988	593
138 6/8	18 4/8	18	16 2/8	3 6/8	3 7/8	5	5	Mendocino Co., CA	Richard L. Moore	Richard L. Moore	1988	593
138 6/8	22 3/8	25 2/8	20 6/8	3 6/8	3 6/8	4	4	Mendocino Co., CA	Thomas R. Erasmy	Thomas R. Erasmy	1993	593
138 6/8	20 3/8	19 7/8	16 7/8	4 6/8	4 5/8	5	6	Clackamas Co., OR	Timothy P. Brown	Timothy P. Brown	2001	593
138 5/8	21	21	15 5/8	5 2/8	5	5	5	Clatsop Co., OR	Russell L. Hemphill	Russell L. Hemphill	1972	601
138 5/8	19 3/8	19 5/8	14 6/8	5	4 7/8	5	6	Linn Co., OR	Jeff B. Garber	Jeff B. Garber	1987	601
138 5/8	21 1/8	20 4/8	16 7/8	3 6/8	3 6/8	4	5	Lake Co., CA	Frank Bush	Frank J. Bush	1997	601
138 4/8	22 4/8	22 7/8	18 6/8	4 3/8	4	5	4	Mendocino Co., CA	Jess T. Jones	Jess T. Jones	1950	604
138 4/8	21 1/8	20	18 2/8	4	4	5	5	Siskiyou Co., CA	Bob Courts	Bob Courts	1965	604
138 4/8	19 4/8	19 4/8	17 2/8	4	4	5	6	Siskiyou Co., CA	John Carmichael	John Carmichael	1969	604
138 4/8	20 5/8	20 7/8	18	4 6/8	4 5/8	5	5	Mendocino Co., CA	John D. Tuso	John D. Tuso	1997	604
138 4/8	22 6/8	23 1/8	20 6/8	4 2/8	4 4/8	4	4	Tehama Co., CA	Dean A. Chambers	Dean A. Chambers	2002	604
138 3/8	22 5/8	22	20 5/8	4 7/8	4 5/8	5	5	Clackamas Co., OR	J.B. Mitts	Wes Mitts	1896	609
138 3/8	23 7/8	22 4/8	16 3/8	5 3/8	5 4/8	5	6	Pierce Co., WA	George W. Halcott	George W. Halcott	1966	609
138 3/8	22 4/8	22 2/8	18	4 4/8	4 1/8	5	5	Humboldt Co., CA	Garry Hughes	Garry Hughes	1968	609
138 3/8	20 4/8	20 1/8	18 5/8	4 1/8	4 3/8	4	5	Trinity Co., CA	Stanley A. Apuli	Stanley A. Apuli	1991	609
138 3/8	22	21 2/8	19 1/8	4 1/8	3 6/8	5	4	Mendocino Co., CA	Glenn A. Zane	Glenn A. Zane	1998	609
138 3/8	19	21 1/8	18 1/8	4 7/8	4 7/8	5	5	Mendocino Co., CA	Gus J. Kerry	Gus J. Kerry	2002	609
138 2/8	21 4/8	22	18 2/8	5 2/8	5 3/8	5	6	Trinity Co., CA	E.G. Palmrose	Daniel M. Phillips	1940	615
138 2/8	19 4/8	21	16 2/8	5 2/8	4 4/8	5	5	Snohomish Co., WA	James J. McCarthy	James J. McCarthy	1961	615
138 2/8	21 3/8	21	15 6/8	4	3 7/8	5	5	Tehama Co., CA	Robert L. Armanasco	Robert L. Armanasco	1968	615
138 2/8	21 5/8	22	17 6/8	3 6/8	3 6/8	5	5	Trinity Co., CA	Thomas A. Pettigrew, Jr.	Thomas A. Pettigrew, Jr.	1972	615
138 2/8	18 6/8	18 6/8	15 6/8	4 1/8	4 3/8	5	5	Marion Co., OR	Gene Collier	Gene Collier	1974	615
138 2/8	20 6/8	21	19 6/8	4	3 7/8	5	5	Shasta Co., CA	David E. Smith	David E. Smith	1979	615
138 2/8	21 1/8	21 2/8	17 4/8	5	5 1/8	5	4	Linn Co., OR	Douglas J. Morehead	Douglas J. Morehead	1984	615

Score	L. Main Beam R	L. Main Beam L	Inside Spread	Circ. R	Circ. L	Pts. R	Pts. L	Locality	By	Owner	Date Killed	Rank
138 2/8	18	18	14 4/8	4 4/8	4 1/8	5	5	Mendocino Co., CA	Kenzia L. Drake	Kenzia L. Drake	1985	615
138 2/8	19 5/8	20 4/8	16 2/8	4 3/8	4 3/8	5	5	Trinity Co., CA	Monte D. Matheson	Monte D. Matheson	1990	615
138 2/8	21 2/8	21 2/8	15 2/8	3 5/8	3 7/8	5	5	Coos Co., OR	Lynn A. Schrag	Lynn A. Schrag	1996	615
138 1/8	18 5/8	20 3/8	17 1/8	4 2/8	4 1/8	5	5	Columbia Co., OR	Virginia L. Brown	Steve Crossley	1981	625
138 1/8	21 2/8	21	16 3/8	4 2/8	4 2/8	5	5	Polk Co., OR	Douglas G. Ellis	Douglas G. Ellis	2000	625
138 1/8	19 7/8	19 7/8	19 1/8	3 6/8	4	5	5	Siskiyou Co., CA	Gary G. Pitt	Gary G. Pitt	2001	625
138 1/8	22 1/8	22 1/8	16 6/8	4	4	5	4	Humboldt Co., CA	Donald C. Miller	Donald C. Miller	2002	625
138	19 6/8	19 6/8	16 7/8	4 5/8	4 6/8	4	4	Douglas Co., OR	Will H. Brown	Will H. Brown	1948	629
138	20 4/8	20 2/8	14	4 1/8	4 1/8	5	5	Marion Co., OR	Lawrence Sowa	Tim Sowa	1960	629
138	19 3/8	20 1/8	15	4 7/8	4 7/8	5	5	Marion Co., OR	Frank C. Bersin	Frank C. Bersin	1977	629
138	22 3/8	21 7/8	21 1/8	5	5	5	5	Mendocino Co., CA	Brian K. Isaac	Brian K. Isaac	1985	629
138	19 7/8	20	20 1/8	3 6/8	3 7/8	4	4	Siskiyou Co., CA	Jeff Mitola	Jeff Mitola	1997	629
137 7/8	20 3/8	20 4/8	17	4 4/8	4 4/8	6	5	Yamhill Co., OR	Wallace Hill	Wallace Hill	1963	634
137 7/8	19 4/8	20 4/8	18 6/8	4	4	5	6	Shasta Co., CA	Paul G. Carter	Paul G. Carter	1964	634
137 7/8	17 5/8	18 4/8	17 3/8	4 5/8	4	6	6	Trinity Co., CA	Picked Up	North Coast Taxidermy	1965	634
137 7/8	20 5/8	18 5/8	16 6/8	4 6/8	4 5/8	6	6	Vancouver Island, BC	Gordie Simpson	Gordie Simpson	1966	634
137 7/8	18	22 1/8	18 5/8	5	5	4	4	Santa Clara Co., CA	Farber L. Johnston, Jr.	Farber L. Johnston, Jr.	1967	634
137 7/8	22 1/8	19 3/8	16 5/8	4 7/8	4 5/8	4	4	Douglas Co., OR	Pat Johnsrud	Pat Johnsrud	1973	634
137 7/8	19 3/8	21	16 1/8	4 5/8	4 5/8	5	5	Trinity Co., CA	Craig L. Brown	C.L. & J.L. Brown	1989	634
137 7/8	21	20 1/8	16	4 7/8	5	6	5	Trinity Co., CA	Daniel M. Phillips	Daniel M. Phillips	1993	634
137 7/8	20 1/8	20 5/8	19 6/8	4 4/8	4 3/8	6	6	Douglas Co., OR	Loran G. August	Loran G. August	2000	634
137 6/8	21 2/8	20 5/8	18 6/8	4 4/8	4	4	4	Siskiyou Co., CA	Charles A. Cantwell	Dave Cantwell	1962	643
137 6/8	19 1/8	19 1/8	19 6/8	4 6/8	4 6/8	5	5	Trinity Co., CA	Robert L. Miller	Robert L. Miller	1985	643
137 6/8	20 2/8	20 2/8	18 6/8	3 7/8	3 6/8	4	5	Douglas Co., OR	Kevin Clair	Kevin D. Clair	1986	643
137 6/8	20 5/8	20 7/8	14 2/8	3 5/8	3 5/8	5	5	Trinity Co., CA	Gary A. Bradford	Gary A. Bradford	1996	643
137 6/8	19 4/8	19 4/8	17 5/8	4 6/8	4 6/8	5	7	Douglas Co., OR	Barry Smith	Barry Smith	1998	643
137 5/8	19 5/8	19 7/8	19 7/8	4 5/8	4 4/8	5	5	Napa Co., CA	Bruce D. Ringsmith	Bruce D. Ringsmith	1899	648
137 5/8	21 1/8	21 1/8	15 6/8	4 6/8	4 6/8	5	6	Shasta Co., CA	Vern A. Ferguson	Vern E. Ferguson	PR 1960	648
137 5/8	20 4/8	20 4/8	17 7/8	4 5/8	4 4/8	4	4	Mendocino Co., CA	P.R. Borton	John R. Borton	1965	648
137 5/8	20 1/8	20 1/8	15 4/8	4 4/8	4 4/8	6	6	Lewis Co., WA	Larry L. Larson	Larry L. Larson	1978	648
137 5/8	19 5/8	19 6/8	17 7/8	4 4/8	4 7/8	6	4	Mendocino Co., CA	Ronald L. Christensen	Ronald L. Christensen	1992	648
137 5/8	22 2/8	20 6/8	15 4/8	4 7/8	4	5	4	Linn Co., OR	Robert E. Ryan	Robert E. Ryan	1993	648
137 5/8	23 2/8	23	20 7/8	4	4 5/8	4	4	Trinity Co., CA	Kenzia L. Drake	Kenzia L. Drake	1994	648
137 4/8	19 3/8	19	17 5/8	4 5/8	4 5/8	5	5	Jefferson Co., WA	Karl K. Stueve	Karl K. Stueve	1997	656
137 4/8	21 1/8	17	19	4 1/8	4 1/8	5	5	Trinity Co., CA	Philip Grunert	Philip Grunert	1967	656
137 4/8	21 1/8	21 1/8	19	4 3/8	4 1/8	5	5	Trinity Co., CA	Picked Up	C.L. & J.L. Brown	1982	656
137 4/8	22	19 2/8	19 2/8	4 4/8	4 4/8	5	5	Linn Co., OR	Manny M. Kurtz	Manny M. Kurtz	1993	656
137 4/8	20 3/8	20 2/8	20 2/8	4 5/8	4 4/8	4	4	Santa Clara Co., CA	Ray Le Deit	Ray Le Deit	1997	656
137 3/8	21 5/8	21 5/8	15 7/8	4 5/8	4 5/8	5	5	Marion Co., OR	John D. Lulay	John D. Lulay	2001	661
137 3/8	20 5/8	20 7/8	15 7/8	4 7/8	4 7/8	6	5	Coos Co., OR	Eli P. Mast	Glenn E. Sickels	1876	661
137 3/8	20 4/8	20 4/8	19 1/8	4 6/8	4 6/8	5	5	Trinity Co., CA	Donald A. Dunn	Donald A. Dunn	1977	661
137 3/8	20 3/8	20	21 5/8	3 6/8	3 4/8	5	5	Jackson Co., OR	Jay Walker	Jay Walker	1981	661
137 3/8	21 7/8	21 1/8	18 7/8	4 5/8	4 6/8	5	6	Mendocino Co., CA	Carlton C. White	Carlton C. White	1983	661
137 3/8	21 2/8	21 2/8	17 6/8	4 1/8	4 1/8	6	5	Trinity Co., CA	Robert E. Fulmer	Robert E. Fulmer	1993	661
137 2/8	20 6/8	20 7/8	16 5/8	4 3/8	4 3/8	5	5	Clackamas Co., OR	Timothy P. Brown	Timothy P. Brown	2000	661
137 2/8	19 3/8	18	18	4 2/8	4 2/8	5	5	Douglas Co., OR	Bernard L. Den	Bernard L. Den	1934	667
137 2/8	19 6/8	15	15	4 3/8	4 3/8	5	5	Douglas Co., OR	Francis R. Young	Francis R. Young	1972	667
137 2/8	20 5/8	21 4/8	17 6/8	5 2/8	4 7/8	5	8	Jackson Co., OR	Michael E. Earnest	Michael E. Earnest	1992	667

COLUMBIA BLACKTAIL DEER - TYPICAL ANTLERS
Odocoileus hemionus columbianus

Score	Length of Main Beam R	L	Inside Spread	Circumference at Smallest Place Between Burr and First Point R	L	Number of Points R	L	Locality	Hunter	Owner	Date Killed	Rank
137 2/8	21 7/8	21 6/8	16	3 7/8	3 5/8	5	4	Jackson Co., OR	Ernie MacKenzie	Ernie MacKenzie	1992	667
137 2/8	21 6/8	22 3/8	16 6/3	4 3/8	4 3/8	5	5	Lake Co., CA	Kevin R. Smith	Kevin R. Smith	1997	667
137 2/8	20 4/8	20 4/8	18 2/3	3 7/8	3 6/8	5	5	Mendocino Co., CA	Norman Brown, Jr.	Norman Brown, Jr.	2000	667
137 2/8	21 3/8	21 1/8	15 2/3	4 1/8	4 4/8	5	5	Lane Co., OR	Glen E. Butler	Glen E. Butler	2001	667
137 2/8	20	21 2/8	19 3/3	4 2/8	4 4/8	6	5	Mendocino Co., CA	Cliff E. Jacobson	Cliff E. Jacobson	2001	667
137 1/8	21 3/8	19 2/8	15 7/3	4 2/8	4 2/8	5	5	Douglas Co., OR	Peter Serafin	Peter Serafin	1932	675
137 1/8	20 4/8	20 1/8	15 5/3	4 5/8	4 6/8	5	5	Tillamook Co., OR	Iola M. Pfaff	Iola M. Pfaff	1940	675
137 1/8	20	20 5/8	23 2/3	4 3/8	4 3/8	5	6	Shasta Co., CA	Jack Floyd	Jack Floyd	1957	675
137 1/8	23	22 4/8	22 7/3	5	4 6/8	5	4	Tehama Co., CA	Clint Heiber	Clint Heiber	1977	675
137 1/8	19 4/8	20 1/8	16 5/3	4 5/8	4 6/8	5	5	King Co., WA	John A. Grosvenor	John A. Grosvenor	1983	675
137 1/8	20 4/8	21 1/8	19 2/3	4 4/8	4 4/8	5	7	Douglas Co., OR	Jerry A. Caster	Jerry A. Caster	1989	675
137 1/8	23 5/8	23 4/8	18 3/3	4 3/8	4 3/8	6	5	Jackson Co., OR	Peter Buist	Peter Buist	1995	675
137 1/8	20 7/8	20 7/8	14 1/3	3 5/8	3 6/8	4	4	Lewis Co., WA	Bill C. Boehm	Bill C. Boehm	1997	675
137	20 4/8	21	21 6/3	3 7/8	3 6/8	5	5	Siskiyou Co., CA	Shirley Eastlick	Shirley Eastlick	1962	683
137	24	23 6/8	21 2/3	4 3/8	4 3/8	4	5	King Co., WA	Douglas F. Dammarell	Douglas F. Dammarell	1974	683
137	20	19 5/8	15 6/3	4 6/8	4 6/8	5	5	Polk Co., OR	Ralph Cooper	Ralph Cooper	1978	683
137	22 6/8	22 2/8	15 4/3	4 5/8	4 6/8	5	5	Trinity Co., CA	Robert J. King	Robert J. King	1979	683
137	22	21 3/8	19 2/3	4 7/8	4 7/8	4	4	Mendocino Co., CA	Shelby Bagley	Shelby Bagley	1991	683
137	21 2/8	19 6/8	18	4 2/8	4 2/8	5	5	Clackamas Co., OR	Mark Perez	Mark Perez	1991	683
137	20 1/8	21 2/8	16 6/3	4 7/8	4 6/8	5	5	Pierce Co., WA	Glenn T. Litzau	Glenn T. Litzau	1992	683
137	19 4/8	18 1/8	18 4/3	3 6/8	3 5/8	5	5	Mendocino Co., CA	Robert Flanagan	Robert Flanagan	1994	683
136 7/8	21 3/8	20 7/8	17 5/3	4 2/8	4 4/8	4	4	Lewis Co., WA	Allen J. Roehrick	Allen J. Roehrick	1968	691
136 7/8	20 1/8	20 3/8	16 1/3	4	4	5	5	Humboldt Co., CA	Michael M. Golightly	Michael M. Golightly	1991	691
136 7/8	21 3/8	20 5/8	18 1/3	4 6/8	4 3/8	6	6	Linn Co., OR	Terry L. Moore	Terry L. Moore	1993	691
136 7/8	20 5/8	20 3/8	15 7/3	4 3/8	4 2/8	5	5	Lane Co., OR	Noah C. Hoiland	Noah C. Hoiland	2000	691
136 6/8	21 3/8	21	14	5 2/8	5 2/8	5	5	King Co., WA	Ed Lochus	George B. Johnson	1930	695
136 6/8	23 7/8	25	22	4 7/8	5 1/8	6	6	Josephine Co., OR	Roxie Smith	Aly M. Bruner	1940	695
136 6/8	21 6/8	23	18 2/3	4 7/8	4 6/8	4	4	Shasta Co., CA	Vance Corrigan	Vance Corrigan	1957	695
136 6/8	19 3/8	20	14 3/3	4 5/8	5	6	6	Lewis Co., WA	Mark G. Frohmader	Mark G. Frohmader	1969	695
136 6/8	20 5/8	21 1/8	16	4 1/8	4 1/8	5	5	Pierce Co., WA	Patrick M. Blackwell	Patrick M. Blackwell	1971	695
136 6/8	23 1/8	22 7/8	20 2/3	4 4/8	4 7/8	4	3	Linn Co., OR	Mike Martell	Mike Martell	1985	695
136 6/8	18 6/8	18 7/8	15 4/3	4	4	5	5	Clackamas Co., OR	Edward L. Farmer, Sr.	Edward L. Farmer, Sr.	1996	695
136 6/8	20 6/8	20 6/8	17 2/3	4 2/8	4 1/8	5	5	Jackson Co., OR	Scott L. Ruppel	Scott L. Ruppel	2002	695
136 5/8	21 5/8	22 1/8	19 5/3	4 5/8	4 6/8	5	5	Tillamook Co., OR	J.A. Aaron	J.A. Aaron	1943	703
136 5/8	21 4/8	22 3/8	19	5 6/8	5 2/8	5	4	Arlington Co., WA	Ernest J. Kaesther	Ernest J. Kaesther	1959	703
136 5/8	21 6/8	21 6/8	15 7/3	4 1/8	4	5	5	Marion Co., OR	Ronald A. Bersin	Ronald A. Bersin	1978	703

Score	Main Beam R	Main Beam L	Inside Spread	Locality	By Whom Killed	Owner	Date
136 5/8	22 4/8	21 1/8	20 1/8	Jackson Co., OR	Alberto L. Garcia	Alberto L. Garcia	1988
136 5/8	22 7/8	22	16 7/8	Lincoln Co., OR	Leonard L. Wilson	Leonard L. Wilson	1997
136 5/8	20 2/8	20	18 7/8	Trinity Co., CA	Autumn L. Brown	C.L. & J.L. Brown	2000
136 4/8	20 3/8	20	18 4/8	Grays Harbor Co., WA	Joseph S. Prohaska	Stephen H. Prohaska	1952
136 4/8	20 3/8	20 1/8	18	Ukiah, CA	Charles Tollini	Charles Tollini	1960
136 4/8	23 4/8	22 1/8	18 2/8	Lewis Co., WA	Larry F. Smith	Larry F. Smith	1964
136 4/8	22	22 1/8	18 4/8	Mendocino Co., CA	Jeff P. Leyden	Jeff P. Leyden	1993
136 4/8	22 1/8	21 7/8	18 4/8	Clackamas Co., OR	Stan K. Naylor	Stan K. Naylor	1994
136 4/8	21 5/8	21 7/8	18 1/8	Clallam Co., WA	Bill Wilder	V. Birkland & M. Lewis	1953
136 3/8	20 2/8	20 1/8	19 1/8	Douglas Co., OR	Gerry F. Edwards	Gerry F. Edwards	1971
136 3/8	20 2/8	19 7/8	15 7/8	Tillamook Co., OR	Guy L. Thompson	Guy L. Thompson	1983
136 3/8	21 4/8	21	15 3/8	Marion Co., OR	Albert F. Brundidge	Albert F. Brundidge	1990
136 3/8	21 4/8	21 3/8	19 1/8	Chehalis River, BC	A. Larry Kahl	A. Larry Kahl	2001
136 3/8	21 4/8	20 5/8	22 3/8	Jackson Co., OR	Martin S. Durbin	Ellis A. Jones	1921
136 3/8	20 6/8	21 3/8	20 5/8	Santa Clara Co., CA	Glenn D. Brem	Glenn D. Brem	1941
136 2/8	20 3/8	20 4/8	21 3/8	Covelo, CA	David G. Cox	David G. Cox	1967
136 2/8	21 6/8	21 3/8	20 2/8	Yamhill Co., OR	Monty Dickey	Monty Dickey	1977
136 2/8	19 1/8	22	21 3/8	Siskiyou Co., CA	Wayne G. Rose	Wayne G. Rose	1985
136 2/8	20 7/8	20 3/8	17	Coos Co., OR	Ken Wilson	Ken Wilson	1990
136 2/8	19 6/8	20 1/8	21 4/8	Clackamas Co., OR	Loren R. Schilperoort	Loren R. Schilperoort	1997
136 2/8	19	18 6/8	16	Mendocino Co., CA	Denyse C. Linde	Denyse C. Linde	1960
136 2/8	20 4/8	20	16 5/8	Whatcom Co., WA	Richard E. Vander Yacht	Richard E. Vander Yacht	1971
136 1/8	22 2/8	21 3/8	19 2/8	Jackson Co., OR	Nancy J. Eden	Nancy J. Eden	1982
136 1/8	18 5/8	18 5/8	14 5/8	Pierce Co., WA	Randy Fisk	Randy Fisk	2003
136 1/8	21 6/8	23	15 1/8	Humboldt Co., CA	Brian E. Hornberger	Brian E. Hornberger	1956
136	21 4/8	21	14 6/8	Santa Clara Co., CA	Mrs. Maitland Armstrong	Mrs. Maitland Armstrong	1966
136	21 4/8	21	14 5/8	Mendocino Natl. For., CA	Edward Q. Garayalde	Edward Q. Garayalde	1968
136	23 1/8	23	19	Tehama Co., CA	Robert L. Armanasco	Robert L. Armanasco	1973
136	20 4/8	19 2/8	17	San Mateo Co., CA	Dan Caughey, Sr.	Dan Caughey, Sr.	1973
136	20 4/8	19 6/8	19 2/8	Trinity Co., CA	Richard G. Shelton	Richard G. Shelton	1987
136	18 7/8	18 7/8	19 4/8	Trinity Co., CA	John P. Morton	John P. Morton	1996
135 7/8	22 1/8	21 7/8	18 6/8	Mendocino Co., CA	George A. Deffierios	George A. Deffierios	1996
135 7/8	21 1/8	19 1/8	19 4/8	Columbia Co., OR	Jasson Kyser	Jasson Kyser	1998
135 7/8	18 5/8	22 2/8	15 7/8	Mendocino Co., CA	Anthony J. Grech	Anthony J. Grech	1959
135 7/8	22 1/8	19 3/8	17 3/8	Langley, BC	Charles R. Yeomans	James G. Hill	1972
135 7/8	19 2/8	20 4/8	16 1/8	Jackson Co., OR	Mrs. Ila B. Bethany	Mrs. Ila B. Bethany	1982
135 7/8	20 1/8	21	16 7/8	Tehama Co., CA	John A. Crockett	John A. Crockett	1984
135 7/8	21 2/8	21 4/8	16 5/8	Snohomish Co., WA	Edmund L. Hurst	Edmund L. Hurst	1992
135 7/8	21 3/8	21	22 3/8	Lane Co., OR	Aaron D. Helfrich	Aaron D. Helfrich	2000
135 6/8	20 7/8	19 3/8	20 3/8	Trinity Co., CA	Gregory C. Koehler	Gregory C. Koehler	2002
135 6/8	21	21 1/8	14 5/8	San Mateo Co., CA	Robert Caughey	Robert Caughey	2002
135 6/8	19 3/8	20 1/8	19 1/8	Skamania Co., WA	Kevin J. Lueders	Kevin J. Lueders	2003
135 6/8	21 1/8	20 4/8	18 2/8	Mendocino Co., CA	Joseph B. Ricard	Joseph B. Ricard	1939
135 6/8	20 2/8	20 5/8	19 4/8	Powell River, BC	Paddy Price	Duncan Formby	1965
135 6/8	21 2/8	19 7/8	18	Trinity Co., CA	Roy J. Renner	Roy J. Renner	1966
135 6/8	20 5/8	19 1/8	15	Linn Co., OR	Gene Collier	Gene Collier	1969
135 6/8	18 4/8	19 1/8	16 4/8	Whatcom Co., WA	Jack R. Teeter	Jack R. Teeter	1977
135 6/8				Linn Co., OR	Joel B. Care	Joel B. Care	

COLUMBIA BLACKTAIL DEER - TYPICAL ANTLERS
Odocoileus hemionus columbianus

Score	Length of Main Beam R	L	Inside Spread	Circumference at Smallest Place Between Burr and First Point R	L	Number of Points R	L	Locality	Hunter	Owner	Date Killed	Rank
135 6/8	20	20 2/8	17 7/8	4 6/8	4 6/8	5	5	Cowlitz Co., WA	William R. Gottfryd	William R. Gottfryd	1986	749
135 6/8	16 4/8	20 6/8	16 3/8	5 1/8	5 1/8	6	5	Marion Co., OR	Joseph V. Pileggi	Joseph V. Pileggi	1988	749
135 6/8	20 4/8	20 1/8	16	4 2/8	4 1/8	5	5	Mendocino Co., CA	Phyllis W. Stevenson	Phyllis W. Stevenson	1992	749
135 6/8	19 4/8	20 1/8	14 4/8	3 7/8	3 7/8	5	5	Washington Co., OR	Joseph G. Jaquith	Joseph G. Jaquith	1994	749
135 6/8	20 3/8	20 6/8	15 4/8	4 1/8	4	5	5	Lane Co., OR	Robert J. McClory	Robert J. McClory	1994	749
135 6/8	19 7/8	20	17 6/8	4 2/8	4 1/8	5	5	Trinity Co., CA	Bill Baker	Bill Baker	2000	749
135 5/8	19 6/8	19 3/8	17 5/8	4 3/8	4 1/8	4	4	Clallam Co., WA	Gary L. Smith	Gary L. Smith	1956	760
135 5/8	22 4/8	23 2/8	20 1/8	4 4/8	4 3/8	4	4	Pierce Co., WA	Mark A. Dye	Mark A. Dye	1987	760
135 5/8	22 4/8	21 5/8	20 1/8	3 7/8	3 7/8	5	5	Trinity Co., WA	Richard H. August	Richard H. August	1988	760
135 5/8	20 2/8	21 2/8	15 1/8	4 1/8	4 1/8	5	5	Humboldt Co., CA	Michael M. Golightly	Michael M. Golightly	1990	760
135 5/8	23 7/8	23 6/8	20 4/8	4 7/8	4 4/8	4	5	Mendocino Co., CA	Ray D. MacDonald, Jr.	Ray D. MacDonald, Jr.	1990	760
135 5/8	21 1/8	21 1/8	17 1/8	4 7/8	4 5/8	5	5	Napa Co., CA	Daniel M. Geisinger	Daniel M. Geisinger	2000	760
135 4/8	22 7/8	22 3/8	17 2/8	4 2/8	3 4/8	5	4	Pierce Co., WA	Joseph G. Williams	Joseph G. Williams	1954	766
135 4/8	20 4/8	20 1/8	16 6/8	3 6/8	3 7/8	5	5	Lewis Co., WA	Oren Layton	Oren Layton	1977	766
135 4/8	20 1/8	20 6/8	17 4/8	4 3/8	4 3/8	5	5	Trinity Co., WA	Robert T. Hammaker	Robert T. Hammaker	1988	766
135 4/8	20	21 5/8	15 4/8	4 3/8	4 3/8	5	6	Benton Co., OR	Mark A. Morris	Mark A. Morris	1990	766
135 4/8	18 3/8	18 3/8	16	4 2/8	4 3/8	5	5	Mendocino Co., CA	Ricky Stoddard	Ricky Stoddard	1996	766
135 4/8	21 2/8	21 1/8	15 4/8	4 5/8	4 5/8	5	5	Humboldt Co., CA	Jace Comfort	Jace Comfort	1998	766
135 4/8	21 3/8	20 7/8	19 4/8	4 6/8	4 3/8	5	5	Glenn Co., CA	Charles W. Abbott	Charles W. Abbott	2000	766
135 4/8	20 3/8	19 2/8	16 2/8	4 1/8	4 1/8	5	6	Skamania Co., WA	Joseph J. Boggioni	Joseph J. Boggioni	2000	766
135 4/8	20 5/8	20 3/8	18 6/8	4 2/8	4 2/8	5	5	Mendocino Co., CA	Richard A. Rajeski	Richard A. Rajeski	2002	766
135 3/8	21 5/8	21 2/8	17 6/8	4 6/8	4 5/8	6	6	Clark Co., WA	Francis E. Gillette	Francis E. Gillette	1934	775
135 3/8	21 7/8	21 6/8	16 5/8	5 1/8	5	5	5	King Co., WA	Ernest Zwiefelhofer	Wayne Ferderer	1941	775
135 3/8	19 2/8	20	16 1/8	4 3/8	4 6/8	5	5	Mendocino Co., CA	Melvin J. Domko	Melvin J. Domko	1982	775
135 3/8	19 7/8	20	13 7/8	4 6/8	4 6/8	5	5	Sonoma Co., CA	William M. Somma	William M. Somma	2002	775
135 3/8	19 6/8	20	15	3 4/8	3 3/8	4	4	Trinity Co., CA	Andy Burgess	Andy Burgess	1959	779
135 2/8	19 1/8	19 4/8	13 2/8	3 4/8	3 4/8	4	4	Humboldt Co., CA	Christopher A. Umbertus	Christopher A. Umbertus	1981	779
135 2/8	23 1/8	22 5/8	14 6/8	4 5/8	4 3/8	5	5	Lincoln Co., OR	David K. Oleman, Jr.	David K. Oleman, Jr.	1990	779
135 2/8	21 6/8	21 4/8	14 3/8	4	4	6	5	Lane Co., OR	Lorrie A. Nyseth	Lorrie A. Nyseth	1992	779
135 2/8	21	21 1/8	18 6/8	4 2/8	4 2/8	5	5	Humboldt Co., CA	Richard J. Banko Jr.	Richard J. Banko Jr.	1996	779
135 2/8	19 3/8	19 4/8	16 2/8	4 2/8	4 3/8	5	5	Lane Co., OR	Bill A. Parsons	Bill A. Parsons	1996	779
135 2/8	19 4/8	19 4/8	17	4 1/8	4 1/8	5	5	Humboldt Co., CA	Kirk Younker	Kirk D. Younker	1998	779
135 2/8	21	20 6/8	17 2/8	5 1/8	5 1/8	4	4	Linn Co., CA	Dennis R. Middleton	Dennis R. Middleton	2000	779
135 2/8	19 4/8	20 1/8	15 6/8	4 1/8	4 4/8	5	5	Humboldt Co., CA	Scott S. Eskra	Scott S. Eskra	2002	779
135 1/8	19 5/8	19 4/8	15 5/8	4 2/8	4 2/8	5	5	Lewis Co., WA	William A. Logan	William A. Logan	1975	788
135 1/8	20 2/8	20 1/8	15 3/8	3 6/8	3 6/8	5	5	Jackson Co., OR	Valton G. Albert	Valton G. Albert	1991	788

Score	L. Main Beam R	L. Main Beam L	Inside Spread	Pts R	Pts L	Circ.	By Whom Killed	Locality	Owner	Date	Rank
135 1/8	19 3/8	18 2/8	15 5/8	5	5	3 4/8	James A. Swortzel	Humboldt Co., CA	James A. Swortzel	1996	788
135 1/8	21	20 7/8	17 1/8	5	5	4 6/8	Michael L. Rudick	Trinity Co., CA	Michael L. Rudick	1997	788
135 1/8	19 1/8	19 7/8	17 7/8	5	5	4	Bradley E. Nolan	Trinity Co., CA	Bradley E. Nolan	1998	788
135 1/8	20 6/8	21 6/8	19 1/8	5	5	3 7/8	Thomas W. Atterbury	Mendocino Co., CA	Thomas W. Atterbury	2002	788
135 1/8	22 1/8	21 4/8	22 4/8	5	4	4 2/8	Michael R. Williams	Sonoma Co., CA	Michael R. Williams	2002	788
135 1/8	22 1/8	21 3/8	20 1/8	5	6	5 6/8	Phillip A. Corral	Santa Clara Co., CA	Phillip A. Corral	2003	788
135	19	19 5/8	15 4/8	5	5	4 2/8	Edward F. Burgess	Humboldt Co., CA	Edward F. Burgess	1965	796
135	19 1/8	19 4/8	15 4/8	5	5	4 3/8	Ray W. Bunnell	Clackamas Co., OR	Ray W. Bunnell	1978	796
135	20	19 7/8	16 2/8	5	5	4 1/8	Dennis R. Beebe	Whatom Co., WA	Dennis R. Beebe	1981	796
135	18 6/8	18 6/8	15 6/8	4	4	4 2/8	Andrew M. Felt	Trinity Co., CA	Andrew M. Felt	1986	796
135	22 6/8	23 2/8	20	5	5	4 3/8	Rodney E. Carley	Mendocino Co., CA	Rodney E. Carley	1989	796
135	19 1/8	20	19	4	5	4 4/8	Picked Up	Mendocino Co., CA	Bruce D. Ringsmith	1990	796
135	20 7/8	21	17 4/8	5	5	3 7/8	Bill H. Henderson	Lincoln Co., OR	Bill H. Henderson	1995	796
135	20 3/8	20 5/8	15 6/8	5	5	4 1/8	Kevin G. Fay	Josephine Co., OR	Kevin G. Fay	1998	796
135	19 3/8	19 3/8	16 2/8	5	5	4 1/8	Kevin D. Clair	Trinity Co., CA	Kevin D. Clair	2001	796
135	21 7/8	22 3/8	17	6	5	3 5/8	Walt Metcalfe	Lane Co., OR	Walt Metcalfe	2002	796

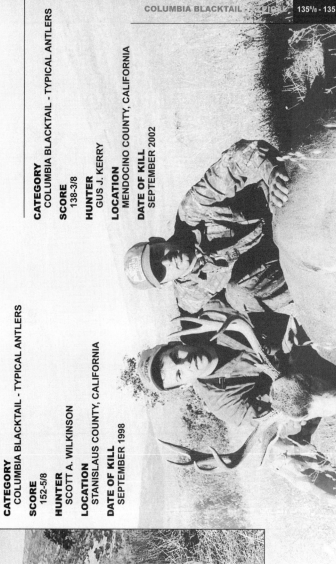

CATEGORY
COLUMBIA BLACKTAIL - TYPICAL ANTLERS

SCORE
138-3/8

HUNTER
GUS J. KERRY

LOCATION
MENDOCINO COUNTY, CALIFORNIA

DATE OF KILL
SEPTEMBER 2002

CATEGORY
COLUMBIA BLACKTAIL - TYPICAL ANTLERS

SCORE
152-5/8

HUNTER
SCOTT A. WILKINSON

LOCATION
STANISLAUS COUNTY, CALIFORNIA

DATE OF KILL
SEPTEMBER 1998

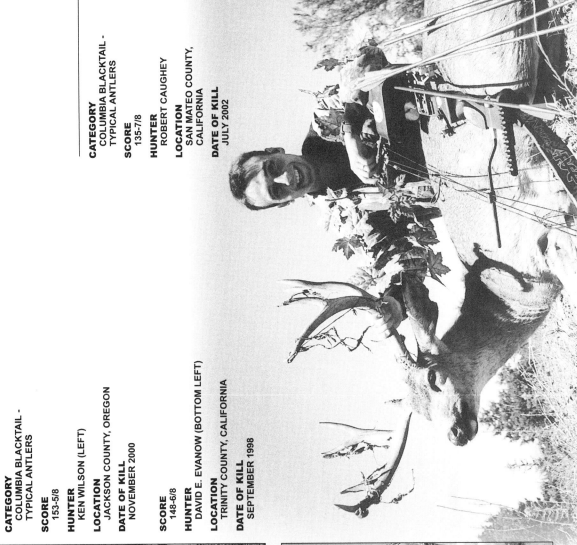

CATEGORY
COLUMBIA BLACKTAIL -
TYPICAL ANTLERS

SCORE
135-7/8

HUNTER
ROBERT CAUGHEY

LOCATION
SAN MATEO COUNTY,
CALIFORNIA

DATE OF KILL
JULY 2002

CATEGORY
COLUMBIA BLACKTAIL -
TYPICAL ANTLERS

SCORE
153-5/8

HUNTER
KEN WILSON (LEFT)

LOCATION
JACKSON COUNTY, OREGON

DATE OF KILL
NOVEMBER 2000

SCORE
148-6/8

HUNTER
DAVID E. EVANOW (BOTTOM LEFT)

LOCATION
TRINITY COUNTY, CALIFORNIA

DATE OF KILL
SEPTEMBER 1998

KERMIT ROOSEVELT
1889-1943

By Leonard H. Wurman

The spirit of adventure permeated all of Theodore Roosevelt's sons, but perhaps none more so that Kermit. At age 19, he took a year's leave from Harvard to accompany his father on his African safari. Four years later, the two explored the unknown course of Brazil's River of Doubt, where both struggled with illness, including malaria, and were given up for lost. Even before the U.S. entered WWI, Kermit served with British forces in the Middle East. He led a hunting expedition into Indo-China and western China, and was the first westerner to kill the now-endangered Giant Panda. Two years before the U.S. joined WWII, Kermit served with Finnish forces against Russia and later with the British in Norway fighting Germany. He was secretary of the Boone and Crockett Club from 1917-1918, president from 1937-1940, and "Honorary President for Life" until his death in 1943. ∎

KERMIT ROOSEVELT WITH
HIS FATHER DURING THEIR
1909-1910 AFRICAN SAFARI.

COLUMBIA BLACKTAIL DEER - NON-TYPICAL ANTLERS
NEW WORLD'S RECORD

RANK
New World's Record

SCORE
208 1/8

LOCATION
Polk Co., Oregon

HUNTER
Frank S. Foldi

OWNER
Bass Pro Shops

DATE KILLED
1962

I started hunting near a town called Valsetz in the Black Rock Mountain area when I first moved to Oregon from Washington. A logging friend of mine had hunted there for years, had always had success, and had taken some nice bucks. I hunted there the first year just to check it out. It was as as great as advertised.

The area was about an hour's drive, so I'd go down for the weekend. I went down three times the first season and always saw deer. I got a nice three-point the first year and saw a couple of dandies.

My second year was very stormy, but as it was the last part of the season, I hunted hard despite the weather. Even though the visibility was bad, I still hunted. I was mostly walking slowly on some fairly open deer trails.

After a while, I spotted a couple of does approximately 65 yards in front of me. They didn't see or scent me, so I knelt down to watch them. They seemed nervous. At first I thought it was because of me, but then I noticed they were looking uphill to the right. It must have been 10 or 15 minutes before they started moving away from me.

Almost immediately a tremendous buck came into view, walking down to the trail. It stopped, looked at the does, and that's when I shot. The buck walked the few yards to the trail and collapsed.

This deer is the biggest buck I have ever shot in approximately 50 years of hunting blacktail deer. I hung its rack on my garage for two or three years until someone told me that might not be wise. It has since been officially scored and is now the largest non-typical blacktail ever scored by Boone and Crockett. ∎

COLUMBIA BLACKTAIL DEER
NON-TYPICAL ANTLERS
WORLD'S RECORD SCORE CHART

Records of
North American
Big Game

250 Station Drive
Missoula, MT 59801
(406) 542-1888

BOONE AND CROCKETT CLUB®
OFFICIAL SCORING SYSTEM FOR NORTH AMERICAN BIG GAME TROPHIES
NON-TYPICAL
MULE DEER AND BLACKTAIL DEER

MINIMUM SCORES

	AWARDS	ALL-TIME
mule deer	215	230
Columbia blacktail	155	155
Sitka blacktail	118	118

KIND OF DEER (check one)
- ☐ mule deer
- ☒ Columbia blacktail
- ☐ Sitka blacktail

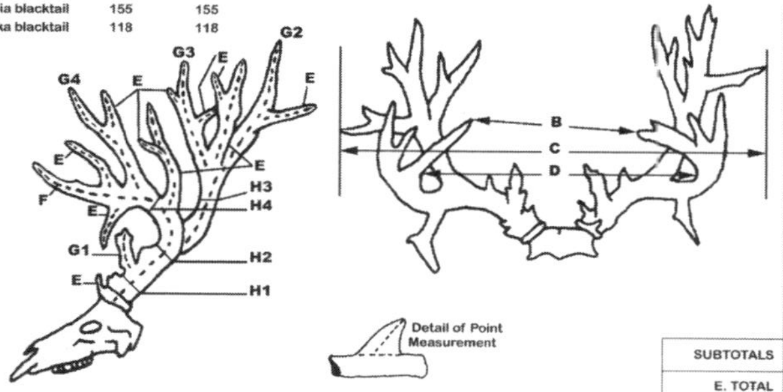

Abnormal Points

	Right Antler	Left Antler
	6 4/8	6 6/8
	2 4/8	3 1/8
	3 2/8	8
	5 1/8	6
		1 3/8
	20 4/8	4/8
	3 3/8	3/8
	12 2/8	5/8
	10 1/8	3/8
	12 1/8	1/8
	4 3/8	
	4 1/8	—
	3 3/8	
	4 6/8	1/8
SUBTOTALS	17 3/8	2
E. TOTAL	42 4/8	
	75 0/8	3 4/8

Detail of Point Measurement

SEE OTHER SIDE FOR INSTRUCTIONS		COLUMN 1	COLUMN 2	COLUMN 3	COLUMN 4
		Spread Credit	Right Antler	Left Antler	
A. No. Points on Right Antler	9				
No. Points on Left Antler	9				
B. Tip to Tip Spread	12 7/8				
C. Greatest Spread	25 6/8				
D. Inside Spread of Main Beams	17 5/8	SPREAD CREDIT MAY EQUAL BUT NOT EXCEED LONGER MAIN BEAM	17 5/8		
F. Length of Main Beam			21 7/8	20 4/8	
G-1. Length of First Point, If Present			2 7/8	3 3/8	
G-2. Length of Second Point			12 5/8	12 2/8	
G-3. Length of Third Point, If Present			10 6/8	10 1/8	
G-4. Length of Fourth Point, If Present			11 6/8	12 1/8	
H-1. Circumference at Smallest Place Between Burr and First Point			4 2/8	4 3/8	
H-2. Circumference at Smallest Place Between First and Second Points			4 1/8	4 1/8	
H-3. Circumference at Smallest Place Between Main Beam and Third Point			3 3/8	3 3/8	
H-4. Circumference at Smallest Place Between Second and Fourth Points			4 7/8	4 6/8	
	TOTALS	17 5/8	76 4/8	75 0/8	

ADD	Column 1	17 5/8
	Column 2	76 4/8
	Column 3	75 0/8
	Subtotal	169 1/8
SUBTRACT	Column 4	3 4/8
	Subtotal	165 5/8
	ADD Line E Total	42 4/8
	FINAL SCORE	**208 1/8**

Exact Locality Where Killed: Polk County, Oregon

Date Killed: October 1962   Hunter: Frank S. Foldi

Owner: Bass Pro Shops   Telephone #:

Owner's Address:

Guide's Name and Address:

Remarks: (Mention Any Abnormalities or Unique Qualifies)

OM I.D. Number

COPYRIGHT © 2004 BY BOONE AND CROCKETT CLUB®

377

NUMBER 2 — 197 4/8 POINTS
NEWT BOREN —1955

NUMBER 5 — 179 4/8 POINTS
RUSSEL F. ROACH — 2002

NUMBER 3 — 188 6/8 POINTS
BRAD E. WITTNER — 1981

NUMBER 1 — 208 1/8 POINTS
FRANK S. FOLDI — 1962

NUMBER 4 — 187 POINTS
ALVA J. FLOCK — 1967

BOONE AND CROCKETT CLUB
OFFICIAL SCORING SYSTEM FOR NORTH AMERICAN BIG GAME TROPHIES
NON-TYPICAL—MULE DEER

Records of
North American
Big Game

MINIMUM SCORES
AWARDS ALL-TIME
215

COLUMBIA BLACKTAIL DEER - NON-TYPICAL ANTLERS

Odocoileus hemionus columbianus

MINIMUM SCORE 155

Score	Length of Main Beam R	L	Inside Spread	Circumference at Smallest Place Between Burr and First Point R	L	Number of Points R	L	Locality	Hunter	Owner	Date Killed	Rank
208 1/8	21 7/8	20 4/8	17 5/8	4 2/8	4 3/8	9	9	Polk Co., OR	Frank S. Foldi	Bass Pro Shops	1962	1
197 4/8	23 7/8	22 6/8	19 1/8	4 1/8	4 1/8	11	11	Trinity Co., CA	Newt Boren	Richard Shepard	1955	2
188 6/8	23 4/8	19 7/8	17 4/8	4 3/8	5 1/8	7	9	Shasta Co., CA	Brad E. Wittner	Brad E. Wittner	1981	3
187	21 5/8	22 6/8	18 4/8	4 2/8	4 2/8	9	8	Douglas Co., OR	Alva J. Flock	Alva J. Flock	1967	4
179 4/8	24 1/8	23	22 1/8	5 2/8	5	6	12	Mendocino Co., CA	Russel F. Roach	Russel F. Roach	2002	5
177 4/8	22 7/8	23 5/8	17 2/8	4 6/8	4 7/8	6	6	Washington Co., OR	Randal P. Olsen	Randal P. Olsen	1954	6
176 5/8	20 4/8	20 3/8	13 4/8	4 7/8	4 6/8	8	10	Trinity Co., CA	Harland C. Moore, Sr.	James A. Swortzel	1947	7
176 5/8	21 4/8	22	16 5/8	4 2/8	4 3/8	8	8	Clackamas Co., OR	Ronald G. Searls	Ronald G. Searls	1970	7
173 7/8	20 6/8	21 3/8	18 6/8	5 2/8	5 1/8	6	8	Clark Co., WA	James D. Gipe	James D. Gipe	1976	9
171 6/8	20 3/8	20 4/8	15	4 6/8	4 7/8	8	7	Shasta Co., CA	Brad E. Wittner	Brad E. Wittner	1989	10
167 1/8	22 7/8	21 1/8	20 1/8	4 1/8	4 2/8	8	8	Jackson Co., OR	Richard Falls	Richard Falls	1971	11
167	22 4/8	22 3/8	16 2/8	4 4/8	4 4/8	7	7	Tehama Co., CA	Mark S. Swarsbrook	Mark S. Swarsbrook	1996	12
165	24	24 6/8	24 6/8	5 3/8	5 1/8	8	6	Clatsop Co., OR	Gerald E. Ryan	Gerald E. Ryan	1972	13
162	20 2/8	22 6/8	14	6 2/8	4 7/8	11	6	Benton Co., OR	David L. Barker	David L. Barker	1992	14
160 3/8	22 1/8	22 5/8	22 7/8	4 3/8	4 3/8	8	7	Linn Co., OR	Brian J. Cook	Brian J. Cook	2000	15
158	25 5/8	24 7/8	18 6/8	4 4/8	4 7/8	6	9	Siskiyou Co., CA	William H. Smith	William H. Smith	1966	16
155 6/8	20 5/8	21	16 6/8	5 2/8	5 2/8	6	8	San Mateo Co., CA	Robert Caughey	Robert Caughey	2002	17
201 3/8*	23 6/8	25 7/8	26 3/8	5 1/8	5 1/8	12	11	Jackson Co., OR	Merle Brainard	Vern Dollar	1936	

* Final score is subject to revision by additional verifying measurements.

SITKA BLACKTAIL DEER - TYPICAL ANTLERS
WORLD'S RECORD

TROPHY INFO

RANK
World's Record

SCORE
133

LOCATION
Juskatla, BC

HUNTER
Peter Bond

OWNER
D.J. Hollinger & B. Howard

DATE KILLED
1970

Bob Graham was visiting a shop in British Columbia when he spotted the captivating trophy of a Sitka blacktail (*Odocoileus hemionus sitkensis*). Graham offered to buy the rack, but Peter Bond turned the offer down. Upon hearing this conversation, Bond's son began to wonder what the story was behind the mount. After all, his father had always been a meat hunter and not a trophy hunter. The time had arrived for Peter Bond to recount the memorable evening of September 10, 1970.

"Graham Island, in the Queen Charlotte Island's chain, is the land of plenty for lovers of seafood and wild game. In the 1960s, a boat came once a week in good weather with our Woodwords Food or Sears order, and the mail. The only beef to be purchased was frozen New Zealand beef at a great cost, so we lived off the land. The blacktail deer had no predators except the occasional black bear and man. We were permitted to take 10 deer each year since the deer were small — 40 to 50 pounds dressed.

"On one hunt, I was by myself, on my way into camp in the evening, when I spotted several deer around a backline, but they were 600 yards away on a spur road. I decided to walk closer to get a good shot. When I closed to within 350 yards a couple of does got nervous, so I decided I had to shoot from there. As I put my trusty Weatherby 3x7 scope on each deer, looking for a buck, I ran into the biggest rack I had ever seen on the island.

"At first I thought it was a deer looking at me through a bush. I studied the buck for a while and when his head moved, looking away from me, I realized what I was looking at was all antler. I was still confused because the buck's body appeared too small for that rack size. All I could see was its head and the top of its back. I thought for a moment the buck was standing behind an old windfall or a dip in the ground. As I am never much on the chase of a wounded animal, I leveled my .300 Weatherby, 120 grain load on the top of his neck, just behind his rack, and let go.

"The buck instantly disappeared from sight, but I was sure he was hit. I climbed up the hill to find my buck had dropped where he stood. To my surprise it was a very large buck, the largest I had seen on the Charlottes. The buck dressed out at 110 pounds. Also, to my surprise, he had been lying down. That was why his body looked so small."

Having never been one to have his kills mounted, Bond made an exception with this buck. However, Bond never realized he had shot a World's Record. Luckily Graham's persistence and efforts to preserve the great buck prevailed. Now both the new owner and the old hunter can share a pride in the Certificate of Merit awarded by Boone and Crockett Club at the 23rd Awards Program in Reno, Nevada. ■

SITKA BLACKTAIL DEER
TYPICAL ANTLERS
WORLD'S RECORD SCORE CHART

Records of
North American
Big Game

250 Station Drive
Missoula, MT 59801
(406) 542-1888

BOONE AND CROCKETT CLUB®
OFFICIAL SCORING SYSTEM FOR NORTH AMERICAN BIG GAME TROPHIES
TYPICAL
MULE DEER AND BLACKTAIL DEER

MINIMUM SCORES	AWARDS	ALL-TIME
mule deer	180	190
Columbia blacktail	125	135
Sitka blacktail	100	108

KIND OF DEER (check one)
☐ mule deer
☐ Columbia blacktail
■ Sitka blacktail

	Abnormal Points	
Detail of Point Measurement	Right Antler	Left Antler

SEE OTHER SIDE FOR INSTRUCTIONS		COLUMN 1	COLUMN 2	COLUMN 3	COLUMN 4
		Spread Credit	Right Antler	Left Antler	Difference
A. No. Points on Right Antler	5				
No. Points on Left Antler	5				
B. Tip to Tip Spread	15 5/8				
C. Greatest Spread	23 2/8				
D. Inside Spread of Main Beams	19 6/8	SPREAD CREDIT MAY EQUAL BUT NOT EXCEED LONGER ANTLER	19 6/8			
E. Total of Lengths of Abnormal Points					--
F. Length of Main Beam			20 4/8	19 4/8	1
G-1. Length of First Point, If Present			2 4/8	1 7/8	5/8
G-2. Length of Second Point			9 4/8	9 3/8	1/8
G-3. Length of Third Point, If Present			5 2/8	5 4/8	2/8
G-4. Length of Fourth Point, If Present			6 7/8	8 2/8	1 3/8
H-1. Circumference at Smallest Place Between Burr and First Point			3 6/8	3 6/8	0
H-2. Circumference at Smallest Place Between First and Second Points			3 4/8	3 3/8	1/8
H-3. Circumference at Smallest Place Between Main Beam and Third Point			3	3 1/8	1/8
H-4. Circumference at Smallest Place Between Second and Fourth Points			3 6/8	3 5/8	0
TOTALS		19 6/8	58 5/8	58 3/8	3 6/8

		SUBTOTALS		
		TOTAL TO E		

Exact Locality Where Killed: Juskatla, BC

Date Killed: Sept. 10, 1970   Hunter: Peter Bond

Owner: D.J. Hollinger & B. Howard   Telephone #:

Owner's Address:

Guide's Name and Address:

Remarks: (Mention Any Abnormalities or Unique Qualities:)

ADD	Column 1	19 6/8	
	Column 2	58 5/8	
	Column 3	58 3/8	
	Subtotal	136 6/8	
SUBTRACT Column 4		3 6/8	
FINAL SCORE		133	

COPYRIGHT © 2005 BY BOONE AND CROCKETT CLUB®

TOP 10 SITKA BLACKTAIL – TYPICAL

KODAK PX 5062

NUMBER 2 — 128 POINTS
UNKNOWN — 1985

NUMBER 5 — 124 2/8 POINTS
DANIEL J. LEO — 1986

NUMBER 1 — 133 POINTS
PETER BOND — 1970

NUMBER 4 — 125 7/8 POINTS
DONALD E. THOMPSON — 1964

NUMBER 3 — 126 3/8 POINTS
HARRY R. HORNER — 1987

OFFICIAL SCORING SYSTEM

382

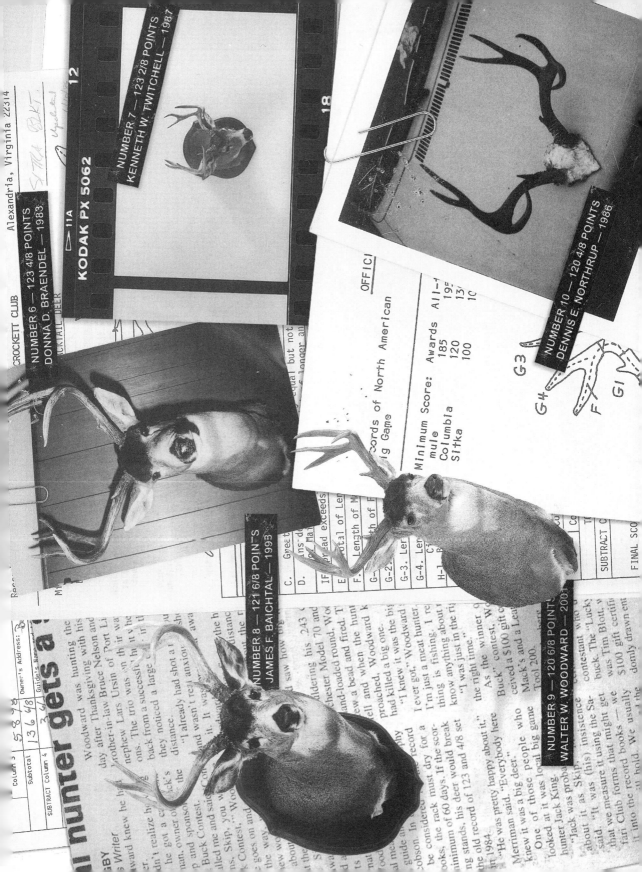

SITKA BLACKTAIL DEER - TYPICAL ANTLERS

Odocoileus hemionus sitkensis

MINIMUM SCORE 108

Score	Length of Main Beam R	L	Inside Spread	Circumference at Smallest Place Between Burr and First Point R	L	Number of Points R	L	Locality	Hunter	Owner	Date Killed	Rank
133	20 4/8	19 4/8	19 6/8	3 6/8	3 6/8	5	5	Juskatla, BC	Peter Bond	D.J. Hollinger & B. Howard	1970	1
128	19 6/8	19	19 4/8	4 7/8	4 1/8	5	5	Kodiak Island, AK	Unknown	Craig Allen	1985	2
126 3/8	18 5/8	19 4/8	14 5/8	4	4 1/8	5	4	Sunny Hay Mt., AK	Harry R. Horner	Harry R. Horner	1987	3
125 7/8	17 7/8	18 6/8	13 5/8	4	4	4	4	Tenakee Inlet, AK	Donald E. Thompson	Donald E. Thompson	1964	4
124 2/8	19 1/8	18 2/8	14 4/8	4 3/8	4	5	5	Exchange Cove, AK	Daniel J. Leo	Daniel J. Leo	1986	5
123 4/8	21 4/8	20 3/8	17 6/8	3 6/8	3 6/8	4	4	Uganik Bay, AK	Donna D. Braendel	Donna D. Braendel	1983	6
123 2/8	18 4/8	18 3/8	14 4/8	4 3/8	4 1/8	5	5	Prince of Wales Island, AK	Kenneth W. Twitchell	Kenneth W. Twitchell	1987	7
121 6/8	18 1/8	18 5/8	16	4 4/8	5	5	5	Dall Island, AK	James F. Baichtal	B&C National Collection	1998	8
120 6/8	18 7/8	18 2/8	15 4/8	3 6/8	4	6	6	Kizhuyak Bay, AK	Walter W. Woodward	Walter W. Woodward	2001	9
120 4/8	18 4/8	16 1/8	14 6/8	3 7/8	4 1/8	5	5	Cleveland Pen., AK	Dennis E. Northrup	Dennis E. Northrup	1986	10
120 1/8	17 6/8	17 6/8	16 3/8	4 5/8	4 4/8	5	5	Halibut Bay, AK	James W. Bickman, Jr.	James W. Bickman, Jr.	1987	11
118 5/8	17	16 6/8	15 1/8	3 7/8	3 7/8	5	5	Uganik Lake, AK	Larry D. Leuenberger	Larry D. Leuenberger	1985	12
118 3/8	19	17 1/8	14 7/8	4	4 1/8	5	5	Prince of Wales Island, AK	Johnnie R. Laird	Johnnie R. Laird	1987	13
117 4/8	17	16 6/8	15 2/8	3 7/8	3 7/8	5	5	Shrubby Island, AK	Alfred Oglend	Alfred Oglend	1986	14
117 1/8	16 4/8	16 4/8	13 1/8	4 1/8	4 2/8	5	6	Baird Peak, AK	William C. Dunham	William C. Dunham	1984	15
117 1/8	16 6/8	17 4/8	16 7/8	4 3/8	4 4/8	5	4	Mitkof Island, AK	Andrew Wright	Andrew Wright	1991	15
116 7/8	16 6/8	16 7/8	13 3/8	4 1/8	3 7/8	5	5	Prince of Wales Island, AK	James W. Bauers	James W. Bauers	2003	17
116 4/8	17 5/8	17 6/8	14 2/8	3 7/8	3 6/8	5	5	Kupreanof Island, AK	John N. Williams	John N. Williams	1995	18
116	17 2/8	16 5/8	16	4 1/8	3 6/8	5	5	Kiliuda Bay, AK	Timothy Tittle	Timothy Tittle	1984	19
115 6/8	18 6/8	18 6/8	17 2/8	4 2/8	4	5	5	Kodiak Island, AK	Daniel J. Folkman	Daniel J. Folkman	1991	20
115 6/8	18 4/8	18 2/8	13 4/8	4	4 1/8	5	5	Olga Bay, AK	Terry L. Wingert	Terry L. Wingert	1994	20
115 1/8	17 5/8	16 6/8	14 7/8	4 2/8	4 6/8	5	5	Thomas Bay, AK	Eli Lucas	Eli Lucas	1997	22
114 7/8	15 7/8	16 1/8	14 3/8	3 7/8	4	5	6	Control Lake, AK	Timothy C. Winsenberg	Timothy C. Winsenberg	1985	23
114 7/8	17 7/8	19 1/8	17 5/8	4 2/8	4	5	5	Dall Island, AK	Picked Up	Lynn W. Merrill	1987	23
114 6/8	17 2/8	17 2/8	13 4/8	4 2/8	4 2/8	5	5	Sharatin Bay, AK	H. Arthur Peck	H. Arthur Peck	1984	25
114 4/8	17 4/8	17	14 6/8	3 5/8	3 6/8	5	5	Kodiak Island, AK	Danny J. Lee	Danny J. Lee	2001	26
114 3/8	17 4/8	18 3/8	15 3/8	4 4/8	4 2/8	5	5	Hobart Bay, AK	Terry LaFrance	Terry LaFrance	1988	27
114	15 7/8	16	13 6/8	4	3 7/8	5	5	Olga Bay, AK	Frank E. Entsminger	Frank E. Entsminger	1986	28
113 6/8	17 5/8	19 1/8	16 2/8	3 2/8	3 2/8	4	4	Long Island, AK	Picked Up	Allan C. Merrill	1987	29
113 6/8	18	16 7/8	14 2/8	4 1/8	4 1/8	5	5	Kasaan Bay, AK	Charles Escoffon	Charles Escoffon	1994	29
113 5/8	17 4/8	17 7/8	14 7/8	4 1/8	4 2/8	5	5	Kodiak Island, AK	William C. Hayes	William C. Hayes	1991	31
113 4/8	18 4/8	18 1/8	15 4/8	3 5/8	3 4/8	4	4	Viekoda Bay, AK	Edward R. Hajdys	Edward R. Hajdys	1980	32
113 4/8	17	17 7/8	15	3 5/8	3 5/8	5	5	Tokeen Island, AK	Picked Up	Vaughn R. Ross	1986	32
113 1/8	17 5/8	18 7/8	16 1/8	3 6/8	3 7/8	5	5	Wadding Cove, AK	Kurt W. Kuehl	Kurt W. Kuehl	1984	34
113	16 1/8	16 4/8	13 6/8	4 3/8	4 2/8	5	5	Zarembo Island, AK	Scott D. Newman	Scott D. Newman	1993	35
112 7/8	17	18	15 1/8	3 6/8	3 6/8	5	5	Kodiak Island, AK	Gene Coughlin	Gene Coughlin	1984	36

Score	L. R	L. L	Inside Spread	Circ. R	Circ. L	Pts R	Pts L	Locality	By Whom Killed	Owner	Date Killed	Rank
112 4/8	16	15 7/8	15 6/8	3 4/8	3 5/8	5	5	Cumshewa Inlet, BC	Harold Larsen	Harold Larsen	1970	37
112 4/8	17 6/8	17 3/8	16	3 7/8	4 1/8	5	5	Prince of Wales Island, AK	William H. Welton	William H. Welton	1988	37
112 3/8	16 6/8	16 7/8	13 5/8	4	4 2/8	5	5	Kodiak Island, AK	Keith M. Nowell	Keith M. Nowell	1986	39
112 3/8	18 2/8	17 7/8	17 5/8	3 5/8	4	7	6	Alder Creek, AK	Richard L. Reeves	Richard L. Reeves	1988	39
112 3/8	19 4/8	19 7/8	17 5/8	4 1/8	4 1/8	4	4	Prince of Wales Island, AK	David L. Hahnes	David L. Hahnes	1990	39
112 2/8	17 5/8	17 2/8	16 4/8	4 1/8	3 7/8	5	5	Uganik Lake, AK	George W. Gozelski	George W. Gozelski	1983	42
112 2/8	19	19 2/8	16 4/8	4 2/8	4 3/8	5	4	Olga Bay, AK	John D. Frost	John D. Frost	1987	42
112 2/8	17 3/8	17	15 6/8	3 6/8	3 6/8	6	6	Big Salt Lake, AK	Roy Weatherford	Roy Weatherford	1988	42
112 1/8	17	16 2/8	15 5/8	4 1/8	4	6	5	Alitak Bay, AK	Dale J. Bunnage	Dale J. Bunnage	1988	45
112	17 1/8	16 7/8	15 2/8	4 3/8	4	5	5	Kaiugnak Bay, AK	Damian M. Baptiste	Damian M. Baptiste	1994	46
111 7/8	14 4/8	15 4/8	13 3/8	3 5/8	3 5/8	5	5	Prince of Wales Island, AK	Dick D. Hamlin	Dick D. Hamlin	1965	47
111 7/8	18 5/8	18 6/8	15 5/8	4 2/8	4 1/8	4	4	Uganik Bay, AK	Jeff A. Buffum	Jeff A. Buffum	1987	47
111 7/8	15 3/8	15	14 3/8	3 7/8	4	5	5	Kodiak Island, AK	Brad Holloway	Brad Holloway	1996	47
111 3/8	18	17 5/8	15 5/8	4 1/8	4	5	5	Uyak Bay, AK	Charlie W. Hastings	Charlie W. Hastings	1986	50
111 3/8	18	17 6/8	16 3/8	3 7/8	4	5	5	Spiridon Lake, AK	David H. Raskey	David H. Raskey	1986	50
111 3/8	18	18 1/8	15 5/8	3 7/8	3 7/8	4	4	Kodiak Island, AK	Craig T. Boddington	Craig T. Boddington	1992	50
111	16 3/8	16 5/8	14 2/8	3 6/8	3 6/8	5	5	Karluk Lake, AK	Ted H. Spraker	Ted H. Spraker	1983	53
110 7/8	17 4/8	17	15 7/8	3 4/8	3 4/8	5	5	Kodiak Island, AK	Ronnie L. Aldridge	Ronnie L. Aldridge	1989	54
110 7/8	17 6/8	17 6/8	12 3/8	3 7/8	3 7/8	5	5	Queen Charlotte Islands, BC	Gordon O. Tolman	Gordon O. Tolman	1990	54
110 6/8	16 4/8	16 4/8	14 6/8	3 6/8	3 6/8	5	5	Zarembo Island, AK	Helen G. Keller	Helen G. Keller	1993	56
110 5/8	19 1/8	18 2/8	15 5/8	3 7/8	3 7/8	4	4	Afognak Island, AK	Dale W. Grove	Dale W. Grove	1987	57
110 5/8	16 4/8	17 1/8	14 7/8	3 6/8	3 5/8	5	5	Amook Island, AK	Bob Price	Bob Price	1990	57
110 5/8	17 4/8	18 1/8	15 5/8	3 4/8	3 4/8	5	4	Prince of Wales Island, AK	Edward E. Toribio	Edward E. Toribio	1992	57
110 4/8	20 4/8	19	17 4/8	4 2/8	4 2/8	4	5	Klawock Lake, AK	Chris J. Blanc	Chris J. Blanc	1983	60
110 4/8	17 4/8	16 7/8	15 7/8	4 1/8	3 7/8	6	5	Kodiak Island, AK	William N. Krenz	William N. Krenz	1988	60
110 4/8	16 7/8	16 6/8	16 2/8	3 7/8	3 7/8	5	6	Zachar Bay, AK	Leslie Branson	Leslie Branson	1994	60
110 3/8	16 5/8	17	13 7/8	3 3/8	3 3/8	5	5	Hidden Basin, AK	Don J. Edwards	Don J. Edwards	1987	63
110 2/8	18 6/8	17 6/8	14 2/8	4 1/8	4	5	5	Kodiak Island, AK	R. Fred Fortier	R. Fred Fortier	1988	64
110 2/8	16 5/8	17 1/8	15	3 7/8	3 7/8	5	5	Halibut Bay, AK	Mike D. O'Malley	Mike D. O'Malley	1993	64
110 1/8	19	18 6/8	15 4/8	4 1/8	4 2/8	6	6	Outlet Cape, AK	Henry T. Hamelin	Henry T. Hamelin	1981	66
110 1/8	16 3/8	16 7/8	14 1/8	3 7/8	4 2/8	5	5	Ratz Harbor, AK	Gerald R. Hedges	Gerald R. Hedges	1985	66
110 1/8	18 1/8	17 6/8	15 5/8	4 1/8	3 7/8	6	6	Deadman Bay, AK	Donald W. Simmons	Donald W. Simmons	1989	66
110 1/8	18	17 3/8	15 3/8	4 6/8	4 5/8	4	4	Mitkof Island, AK	Joseph G. Doerr	Joseph G. Doerr	1992	66
110 1/8	16 6/8	16 1/8	14 1/8	3 5/8	3 4/8	5	5	Prince of Wales Island, AK	Jared Azure	Jared Azure	2002	66
110 1/8	17 2/8	16 4/8	13 7/8	3 7/8	3 7/8	5	5	Kosciusko Island, AK	Bob Ameen	Bob Ameen	2003	66
109 7/8	16 5/8	17 5/8	14 2/8	3 4/8	3 5/8	6	6	Kosciusko Island, AK	Michael C. Fezatte	Michael C. Fezatte	1983	72
109 6/8	17 7/8	17 3/8	14 4/8	4 3/8	4 4/8	5	5	Cleveland Pen., AK	Dennis E. Northrup	Dennis E. Northrup	1983	73
109 6/8	17 5/8	17 4/8	15 4/8	4	4	5	4	Kodiak Island, AK	Lonnie L. Ritchey	Lonnie L. Ritchey	2001	73
109 5/8	17 1/8	17	15 1/8	3 5/8	3 3/8	5	5	Terror Bay, AK	Christopher L. Linford	Christopher L. Linford	1987	75
109 5/8	18 2/8	18 2/8	14 7/8	3 6/8	3 6/8	5	4	Olga Bay, AK	Ronnie L. Aldridge	Ronnie L. Aldridge	1988	75
109 5/8	16 4/8	16 6/8	15 1/8	3 5/8	3 6/8	5	5	Thorne River, AK	James F. Baichtal	James F. Baichtal	1999	75
109 4/8	19	17 7/8	17 2/8	3 7/8	3 7/8	4	4	Uganik Bay, AK	Harvey D. Harms	Harvey D. Harms	1982	78
109 4/8	17 7/8	17 6/8	15 4/8	3 4/8	3 4/8	5	5	Elbow Mt., AK	Henry B. Lewandowski	Henry B. Lewandowski	1994	78
109 3/8	16 7/8	16 7/8	13 6/8	3 5/8	3 5/8	5	6	Prince of Wales Island, AK	Dick D. Hamlin	Dick D. Hamlin	PR 1960	80
109 3/8	18 1/8	18 1/8	15 5/8	3 6/8	3 6/8	5	5	Kodiak Island, AK	Gary L. McKay	Gary L. McKay	1991	80
109 3/8	18 4/8	19 1/8	15 1/8	4	4	5	5	Uganik Bay, AK	Remo Pizzagalli	Remo Pizzagalli	1991	80
109 2/8	16	18 4/8	15 2/8	3 6/8	3 6/8	6	6	Uyak Bay, AK	Bradley A. Pope	Bradley A. Pope	1986	83
109 2/8	18 2/8	18 2/8	15 2/8	4	4	4	4	Olga Bay, AK	David G. Kelleyhouse	David G. Kelleyhouse	1987	83

SITKA BLACKTAIL DEER - TYPICAL ANTLERS
Odocoileus hemionus sitkensis

Score	Length of Main Beam R	L	Inside Spread	Circumference at Smallest Place Between Burr and First Point R	L	Number of Points R	L	Locality	Hunter	Owner	Date Killed	Rank
109 1/8	18 4/8	18 7/8	14 7/8	3 7/8	3 7/8	5	5	Kupreanof Pen., AK	John B. Murray	John B. Murray	1982	85
109 1/8	18 3/8	18	16 7/8	4	3 6/8	5	5	Ugak Bay, AK	Donald H. Tetzlaff	Donald H. Tetzlaff	1984	85
109 1/8	16 4/8	17 4/8	13 5/8	3 6/8	3 4/8	5	5	Kizhuyak Bay, AK	Leonard J. Schwarz	Leonard J. Schwarz	1998	85
109	17 4/8	16 6/8	16 4/8	4	4	5	5	Uganik Bay, AK	Karl G. Braendel	Karl G. Braendel	1982	88
109	17	17 4/8	15 2/8	4	4	5	5	Kodiak Island, AK	D. Roger Liebner	D. Roger Liebner	1983	88
109	17 7/8	18	15	4 1/8	4	5	5	Dall Island, AK	Sharla L. Merrill	Sharla L. Merrill	1985	88
109	15 5/8	16	15 6/8	3 6/8	3 5/8	5	5	Terror Bay, AK	John R. Odom III	John R. Odom III	1985	88
108 7/8	17 5/8	17 5/8	15 7/8	3 7/8	3 7/8	5	5	Karluk Lake, AK	Wayne J. Jalbert	Wayne J. Jalbert	1993	92
108 7/8	17 3/8	17 5/8	14 7/8	3 7/8	3 6/8	5	5	Granite Mt., AK	Johnnie R. Laird	Johnnie R. Laird	1994	92
108 7/8	15 3/8	16	15 3/8	4	3 7/8	5	5	Red Bay, AK	Steve Geary	Steve Geary	1997	92
108 6/8	17 2/8	17 3/8	15 4/8	3 4/8	3 6/8	5	5	Barling Bay, AK	Guy C. Powell	Guy C. Powell	1984	95
108 6/8	17 7/8	17 4/8	14 4/8	3 3/8	3 3/8	5	5	Larsen Bay, AK	David Fischer	David Fischer	1994	95
108 6/8	18 2/8	18 1/8	15 4/8	3 7/8	3 7/8	4	5	Port Lyons, AK	Ronald W. Taylor	Ronald W. Taylor	1996	95
108 5/8	16 5/8	17 5/8	13 7/8	4	3 6/8	5	5	Uganik Bay, AK	Patrick M. Barwick	Patrick M. Barwick	1988	98
108 4/8	19 3/8	19 6/8	15	4	4	4	4	Cleveland Pen., AK	Dennis E. Northrup	Dennis E. Northrup	1985	99
108 4/8	16 4/8	15 6/8	15	3 6/8	3 5/8	5	5	Kodiak Island, AK	Chuck Adams	Chuck Adams	1986	99
108 4/8	16 4/8	15	15	4 5/8	4 6/8	5	6	Cape Uyak, AK	Richard H. Dykema	Richard H. Dykema	1986	99
108 4/8	15 5/8	16 2/8	11 6/8	3 6/8	3 5/8	5	5	Winter Harbor, AK	Rocky C. Littleton	Rocky C. Littleton	1988	99
108 4/8	17 3/8	17	15 2/8	4 1/8	4	5	5	Prince of Wales Island, AK	Brooke P. Drexler	Brooke P. Drexler	1994	99
108 2/8	18 7/8	19 2/8	15 7/8	4 4/8	4 7/8	7	5	Whale Passage, AK	Howard W. Honsey	Howard W. Honsey	1985	104
108 2/8	17 3/8	17 2/8	15 2/8	3 7/8	3 7/8	5	5	Kodiak Island, AK	Warren D. Winger	Warren D. Winger	1989	104
108 2/8	17 4/8	16 4/8	12 4/8	3 6/8	3 6/8	5	5	Uganik Bay, AK	John R. Primasing, Jr.	John R. Primasing, Jr.	1995	104
108 1/8	15 6/8	15 1/8	14 5/8	3 7/8	4	5	5	Kodiak Island, AK	Kenneth G. Gerg	Kenneth G. Gerg	1988	107
108 1/8	14 5/8	15	13 5/8	4 2/8	4	5	5	Spiridon Bay, AK	John T. Schloeder	John T. Schloeder	2001	107
108	16 6/8	17 3/8	14 4/8	3 6/8	3 6/8	5	5	Kizhuyak Bay, AK	Gene D. Carter	Gene D. Carter	1987	109
121 5/8*	19 3/8	19 2/8	16 6/8	4	4	6	6	Grassy Lake, AK	Picked Up	Janet B. Clark	1983	
121 2/8*	17 4/8	18 2/8	16 2/8	3 6/8	3 7/8	5	5	Prince of Wales Island, AK	Picked Up	Jack A. Adams	1989	
115 5/8*	18 1/8	18 3/8	14 3/8	3 6/8	3 6/8	5	5	Larsen Bay, AK	Stephen J. Dambacher	Stephen J. Dambacher	2001	
110 7/8*	18 2/8	16 2/8	14 3/8	3 5/8	3 7/8	5	5	Aliulik Pen., AK	Andrew R. Rios	Andrew R. Rios	1993	
110 3/8*	15 6/8	16 5/8	15 7/8	3 2/8	3 4/8	4	5	Three Saints Bay, AK	Louis Lashley	Louis Lashley	1997	

* Final score is subject to revision by additional verifying measurements.

CATEGORY
SITKA BLACKTAIL - TYPICAL ANTLERS

SCORE
121-6/8

HUNTER
JAMES F. BAICHTAL (BELOW)

LOCATION
DALL ISLAND, ALASKA

DATE OF KILL
AUGUST 1998

CATEGORY
SITKA BLACKTAIL - TYPICAL ANTLERS

SCORE
116-7/8

HUNTER
JAMES W. BAUERS (LEFT)

LOCATION
PRINCE OF WALES ISLAND, ALASKA

DATE OF KILL
AUGUST 2003

SCORE
110-1/8

HUNTER
BOB AMEEN (BOTTOM LEFT)

LOCATION
KOSCIUSKO ISLAND, ALASKA

DATE OF KILL
2003

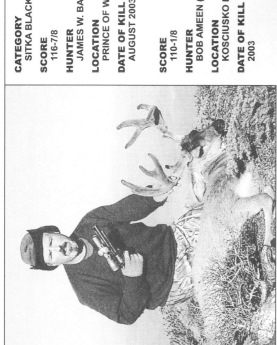

SITKA BLACKTAIL DEER - NON-TYPICAL ANTLERS
NEW WORLD'S RECORD

TROPHY INFO

RANK
New World's Record

SCORE
134

LOCATION
Control Lake, AK

HUNTER
William B. Steele, Jr.

OWNER
William B. Steele, Jr.

DATE KILLED
1987

It was 4 a.m. on a foggy Southeast Alaskan August morning in 1987 as William B. Steele drove the 20 miles of gravel road to reach his hunting area. He had chosen a large unnamed mountain, but the closer he got, the thicker the fog got. The weather was so bad he almost turned around several times during the mile-long hike to the top of the 1,500-foot ridge. An hour later William reached a pass on the ridge, and as he picked his way through the fog he jumped a few unseen deer and wondered why he was even there.

Overlooking a large bowl, William decided to take a break and do some glassing. As he ate a sandwich, he noticed a group of Sitka blacktail deer (*Odocoileus hemionus sitkensis*) 1,200 yards across the valley in a muskeg. Through streamers of fog, William picked out what looked to be a heavy-antlered deer. He decided to work his way across the bowl and try to get closer. He made a mental note of where the deer stood, took a compass bearing, and headed through the brush.

The wind was light and swirling, but mostly in his face as he started to creep through the timber toward where he had marked the deer. Eventually he ran out of cover and had to proceed across the open muskeg toward the next stand of timber.

Suddenly, in the wide open, William spotted two of the largest bucks he'd ever seen feeding through a group of pines 125 feet away. They were moving off to his right when he noticed a stiff-legged doe off to his left. Busted, he froze. The doe knew something was wrong, but wasn't sure what. Out of the corner of his eye he glanced at the bucks and one had fed nearly into view.

Knowing time was running out, William slowly started to raise his .30-06 and leaned to the right as far as he could without tipping over. He could see most of the buck past the tree so he put the crosshairs on its shoulder and squeezed the trigger. The buck jumped and then raced out of sight down through the muskeg, piling up no more than 150 feet away.

William was on his way home when a dump truck driver behind him signaled him to pull over. The driver got out and told him he had shot a deer the week before in the 125-point class, and he thought that William's looked to be as big. After the velvet was removed and the trophy dried, it was officially scored at 126-2/8 points.

Editor's Note: When William B. Steele's Sitka blacktail was originally measured, it was scored as a typical because there was no non-typical category. When the non-typical Sitka blacktail category was created at the beginning of the 25th Awards Period, the score on William B. Steele's great trophy was changed to 134 points. It now stands as the largest Sitka blacktail ever recorded. ■

SITKA BLACKTAIL DEER
NON-TYPICAL ANTLERS
WORLD'S RECORD SCORE CHART

Records of
North American
Big Game

250 Station Drive
Missoula, MT 59801
(406) 542-1888

BOONE AND CROCKETT CLUB®
OFFICIAL SCORING SYSTEM FOR NORTH AMERICAN BIG GAME TROPHIES
NON-TYPICAL
MULE DEER AND BLACKTAIL DEER

MINIMUM SCORES

	AWARDS	ALL-TIME
mule deer	215	230
Columbia blacktail	155	155
Sitka blacktail	118	118

KIND OF DEER (check one)
- ☐ mule deer
- ☐ Columbia blacktail
- ☒ Sitka blacktail

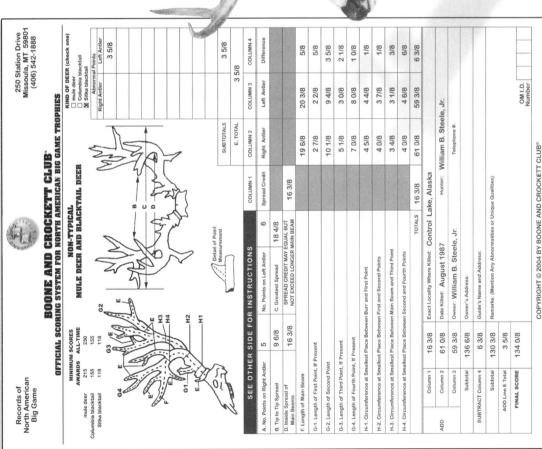

Detail of Point Measurement

Abnormal Points	
Right Antler	Left Antler
	3 5/8
SUBTOTALS	3 5/8
E. TOTAL	3 5/8

SEE OTHER SIDE FOR INSTRUCTIONS		COLUMN 1	COLUMN 2	COLUMN 3	COLUMN 4
		Spread Credit	Right Antler	Left Antler	Difference
A. No. Points on Right Antler	5				
No. Points on Left Antler	6				
B. Tip to Tip Spread	9 6/8				
C. Greatest Spread	18 4/8				
D. Inside Spread of Main Beams	16 3/8	SPREAD CREDIT MAY EQUAL BUT NOT EXCEED LONGER MAIN BEAM	16 3/8			
F. Length of Main Beam			19 6/8	20 3/8	5/8
G-1. Length of First Point, If Present			2 7/8	2 2/8	5/8
G-2. Length of Second Point			10 1/8	9 4/8	3 5/8
G-3. Length of Third Point, If Present			5 1/8	3 0/8	2 1/8
G-4. Length of Fourth Point, If Present			7 0/8	8 0/8	1 0/8
H-1. Circumference at Smallest Place Between Burr and First Point			4 5/8	4 4/8	1/8
H-2. Circumference at Smallest Place Between First and Second Points			4 0/8	3 7/8	1/8
H-3. Circumference at Smallest Place Between Main Beam and Third Point			3 4/8	3 1/8	3/8
H-4. Circumference at Smallest Place Between Second and Fourth Points			4 0/8	4 6/8	6/8
TOTALS		16 3/8	61 0/8	59 3/8	6 3/8

	Column 1	16 3/8	Exact Locality Where Killed: Control Lake, Alaska
ADD	Column 2	61 0/8	Date Killed: August 1987 Hunter: William B. Steele, Jr.
	Column 3	59 3/8	Owner: William B. Steele, Jr. Telephone #:
	Subtotal	136 6/8	Owner's Address:
SUBTRACT Column 4		6 3/8	Guide's Name and Address:
	Subtotal	130 3/8	Remarks: (Mention Any Abnormalities or Unique Qualities)
	ADD Line E Total	3 5/8	
	FINAL SCORE	**134 0/8**	

OM I.D. Number

COPYRIGHT © 2004 BY BOONE AND CROCKETT CLUB®

389

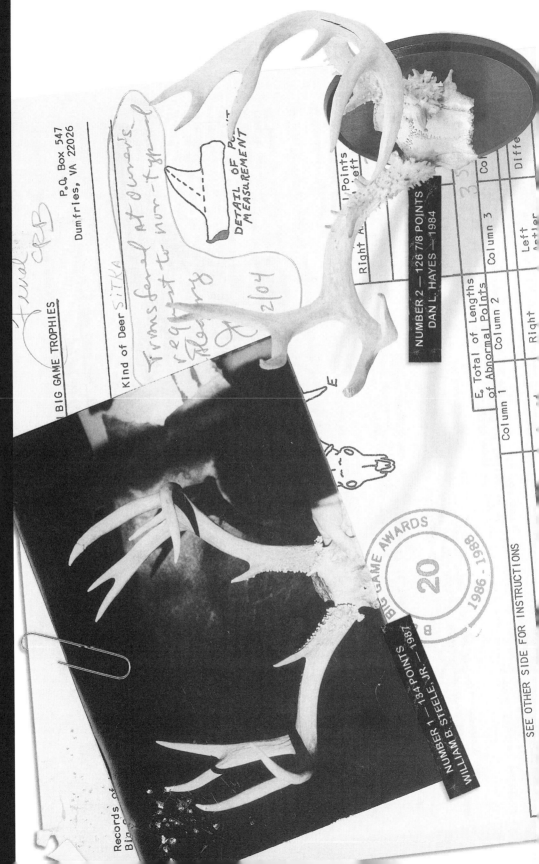

NUMBER 2 — 126 7/8 POINTS
DAN L. HAYES — 1984

NUMBER 1 — 134 POINTS — 1987
WILLIAM B. STEELE, JR.

SITKA BLACKTAIL DEER - NON-TYPICAL ANTLERS

Odocoileus hemionus sitkensis

MINIMUM SCORE 118

Score	Length of Main Beam R	L	Inside Spread	Circumference at Smallest Place Between Burr and First Point R	L	Number of Points R	L	Locality	Hunter	Owner	Date Killed	Rank
134	19 6/8	20 3/8	16 3/8	4 5/8	4 4/8	5	6	Control Lake, AK	William B. Steele, Jr.	William B. Steele, Jr.	1987	1
126 7/8	17	17 5/8	13 7/8	4 2/8	4 4/8	6	8	Prince of Wales Island, AK	Dan L. Hayes	B&C National Collection	1984	2
126 4/8*	18 7/8	20 3/8	17	4 3/8	4 2/8	6	5	Little Coal Bay, AK	Charles Escoffon	Charles Escoffon	1985	
120 1/8*	18 1/8	17 5/8	13 7/8	3 6/8	4 2/8	5	6	Revillagigedo Island, AK	Dick D. Hamlin	Dick D. Hamlin	PR 1970	

* Final score is subject to revision by additional verifying measurements.

WHITETAIL DEER - TYPICAL ANTLERS
WORLD'S RECORD

Working long days as a grain and cattle farmer in Biggar, Saskatchewan, Milo N. Hanson is not a man who has the time or money to hunt all over the continent, but then again he hasn't had to go that far. Hunting on his property in 1992, Hanson ended up reaping more from his fields than the usual autumn harvest.

"On the night of November 22, we had fresh snow, and I called the guys to plan our hunt.

"The next morning, I met my neighbor John Yaroshko and we drove to meet Walter Meger and Rene Igini. When we pulled up I knew something was happening because they were excited. They said they spotted the monster buck entering a willow run and not coming out.

"Rene walked the track while the rest of us surrounded the willows. I took a position that would keep the buck from running south onto nearby posted land. The buck bolted, giving me my first look at it. Believe me, my heart was pumping! We shot but missed it.

"Rene stayed on its tracks, and eventually lost the buck in a maze of other deer tracks because its tracks weren't large. Just when we were getting frustrated and ready to move on, the big buck ran out of an aspen bluff and headed into a willow run on my land. We posted ourselves around the willows, and Rene walked the buck's tracks. The buck ran flat out about 150 yards broadside from John and me. I think we both got buck fever this time! We fired several shots but missed the racing buck.

"We moved up to the next willow run, and when the buck ran out it turned straight away from me. I fired and the buck went down to its knees. 'You got him!' John hollered.

"The buck got up and ran into a nearby aspen bluff. I ran up the hill to where it disappeared, and saw it below me, standing still. I aimed through my 4-power scope and fired another shot with my .308 Winchester Model 88 lever-action. Down it went. I saw its head over a clump of willows. To ensure it stayed down, I fired another shot and the hunt ended.

"Shooting this buck gave me a feeling I will probably never experience again, even though I had no idea it would be declared the new Boone and Crockett Club World's Record in Dallas, Texas, at the 22nd Big Game Awards Program. I had never seen a bigger buck. The buck left me shaking."

Life on the farm took a turn. Following pre-preliminary measurements that put the whitetail in the running for the new World's Record, Hanson found his home under siege from journalists, promoters, collectors, and well-wishers. After the 60-day drying period, Norm Parchewsky, Robert Allemand, and Allan Holtvogt, all Boone and Crockett official measurers, scored the buck at 213-1/8 in a scoring ceremony attended by more than 400 people.

At the 22nd Big Game Awards Program, the Boone and Crockett Club Judges' Panel declared Hanson's buck the new World's Record typical whitetail with a final and official score of 213-5/8 points. ■

WHITETAIL DEER TYPICAL ANTLERS
WORLD'S RECORD SCORE CHART

TROPHY INFO

RANK
World's Record

SCORE
213 5/8

LOCATION
Biggar, SK

HUNTER
Milo N. Hanson

OWNER
Milo N. Hanson

DATE KILLED
1993

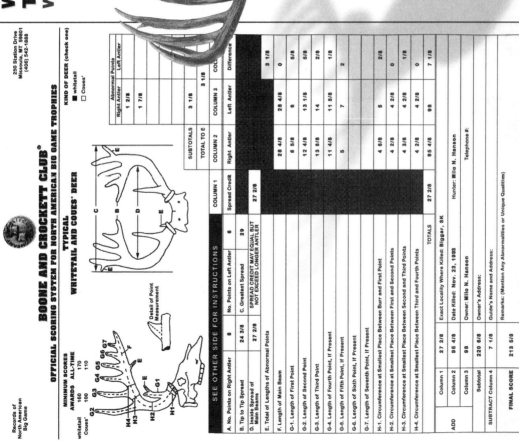

Records of
North American
Big Game

BOONE AND CROCKETT CLUB®
OFFICIAL SCORING SYSTEM FOR NORTH AMERICAN BIG GAME TROPHIES

250 Station Drive
Missoula, MT 59801
(406) 542-1888

TYPICAL
WHITETAIL AND COUES' DEER

MINIMUM SCORES

	AWARDS	ALL-TIME
whitetail	160	170
Coues'	100	110

KIND OF DEER (check one)
■ whitetail
☐ Coues'

Detail of Point Measurement

	Abnormal Points	
	Right Antler	Left Antler
	1 2/8	3 1/8
	1 7/8	
SUBTOTALS	3 1/8	3 1/8
TOTAL TO E		3 1/8

SEE OTHER SIDE FOR INSTRUCTIONS	COLUMN 1 Spread Credit	COLUMN 2 Right Antler	COLUMN 3 Left Antler	Difference
A. No. Points on Right Antler	8			
No. Points on Left Antler	8			
B. Tip to Tip Spread	24 3/8			
C. Greatest Spread	29			
D. Inside Spread of Main Beams	27 2/8			
SPREAD CREDIT MAY EQUAL BUT NOT EXCEED LONGER ANTLER	27 2/8			3 1/8
E. Total of Lengths of Abnormal Points				
F. Length of Main Beam		28 4/8	28 4/8	0
G-1. Length of First Point		6 5/8	6	5/8
G-2. Length of Second Point		12 4/8	13 1/8	5/8
G-3. Length of Third Point		13 6/8	14	2/8
G-4. Length of Fourth Point, If Present		11 4/8	11 5/8	1/8
G-5. Length of Fifth Point, If Present		5	7	2
G-6. Length of Sixth Point, If Present				
G-7. Length of Seventh Point, If Present				
H-1. Circumference at Smallest Place Between Burr and First Point		4 6/8	5	2/8
H-2. Circumference at Smallest Place Between First and Second Points		4 2/8	4 2/8	0
H-3. Circumference at Smallest Place Between Second and Third Points		4 3/8	4 2/8	1/8
H-4. Circumference at Smallest Place Between Third and Fourth Points		4 2/8	4 2/8	0
TOTALS	27 2/8	95 4/8	98	7 1/8

ADD	Column 1	27 2/8	Exact Locality Where Killed: Biggar, SK	
	Column 2	95 4/8	Date Killed: Nov. 23, 1993	Hunter: Milo N. Hanson
	Column 3	98	Owner: Milo N. Hanson	Telephone #:
	Subtotal	220 6/8	Owner's Address:	
SUBTRACT	Column 4	7 1/8	Guide's Name and Address:	
	FINAL SCORE	213 5/8	Remarks: (Mention Any Abnormalities or Unique Qualities)	

COPYRIGHT © 2005 BY BOONE AND CROCKETT CLUB®

TOP 10 WHITETAIL DEER – TYPICAL

NUMBER 2 — 206-1/8 POINTS
JAMES JORDAN — 1914

NUMBER 5 — 204-2/8 POINTS
STEPHEN JANSEN — 1967

NUMBER 3 — 205 POINTS
LARRY W. GIBSON — 1971

NUMBER 1 — 213-5/8 POINTS
MILO N. HANSON — 1993

NUMBER 4 — 204-4/8 POINTS
MEL J. JOHNSON — 1965

NUMBER 7 — 202-6/8 POINTS
BRUCE EWEN — 1992

NUMBER 10 — 201 POINTS
WAYNE G. STEWART — 1961

NUMBER 9 — 201-4/8 POINTS
WAYNE A. BILLS — 1974

NUMBER 6 — 203-3/8 POINTS
HUBERT COLLINS — 2003

NUMBER 8 — 202 POINTS
JOHN A. BREEN — 1918

WHITETAIL DEER - TYPICAL ANTLERS

Odocoileus virginianus virginianus and certain related subspecies

MINIMUM SCORE 170

Score	Length of Main Beam		Inside Spread	Circumference at Smallest Place Between Burr and First Point		Number of Points		Locality	Hunter	Owner	Date Killed	Rank
	R	L		R	L	R	L					
213 5/8	28 4/8	28 4/8	27 2/8	4 6/8	5	8	6	Biggar, SK	Milo N. Hanson	Milo N. Hanson	1993	1
206 1/8	30	30	20 1/8	6 2/8	6 1/8	5	5	Burnett Co., WI	James Jordan	Bass Pro Shops	1914	2
205	26 6/8	25 4/8	24 2/8	4 6/8	4 6/8	6	6	Randolph Co., MO	Larry W. Gibson	MO Show-Me Big Bucks Club	1971	3
204 4/8	27 5/8	26 6/8	23 5/8	6 1/8	6 2/8	7	6	Peoria Co., IL	Melvin J. Johnson	Bass Pro Shops	1965	4
204 2/8	26 4/8	22 6/8	25 1/8	5 1/8	5 1/8	7	10	Beaverdam Creek, AB	Stephen Jansen	Stephen Jansen	1967	5
203 3/8	25 7/8	27 2/8	19 3/8	5 7/8	5 5/8	6	6	Sturgeon River, SK	Hubert Collins	Hubert Collins	2003	6
202 6/8	28	27 1/8	21 2/8	5 3/8	5 3/8	9	8	Barrier Valley, SK	Bruce Ewen	Bass Pro Shops	1992	7
202	31 2/8	31	23 5/8	5 7/8	6	8	8	Beltrami Co., MN	John A. Breen	Bass Pro Shops	1918	8
201 4/8	27 5/8	29 1/8	23	5 7/8	5 2/8	6	6	Hamilton Co., IA	Wayne A. Bills	Bass Pro Shops	1974	9
201	26 2/8	26 2/8	15 5/8	4 5/8	4 7/8	8	6	Kittson Co., MN	Wayne G. Stewart	Wayne G. Stewart	1961	10
200 2/8	26 3/8	27 1/8	24	5	4 7/8	6	7	Whitkow, SK	Peter J. Swistun	Peter J. Swistun	1983	11
200 2/8	32	32 4/8	28 3/8	5 4/8	5 3/8	9	8	Macon Co., IL	Brian S. Damery	Bass Pro Shops	1993	11
199 5/8	30 1/8	28	29 1/8	5 3/8	5 3/8	6	6	Edmonton, AB	Don McGarvey	Don McGarvey	1991	13
199 4/8	27 2/8	26 2/8	20	5 4/8	5 1/8	6	5	Clark Co., MO	Jeffrey A. Brunk	Jeffrey A. Brunk	1969	14
199 3/8	27 3/8	27 4/8	22 3/8	4 4/8	4 6/8	6	7	Missoula Co., MT	Thomas H. Dellwo	Bass Pro Shops	1974	15
199 2/8	28 7/8	29	25 6/8	5	5 1/8	6	6	Lake of the Woods Co., MN	Vernon Jensen	Vernon Jensen	1954	16
199 2/8	27	27 1/8	21 4/8	5 2/8	5	5	5	Flathead Co., MT	Kent Petry	Bass Pro Shops	1966	16
199 2/8	27 2/8	27 1/8	21 3/8	6	5 7/8	6	7	Kansas	Picked Up	KS Dept. of Wildlife & Parks	1999	16
198 6/8	26 6/8	26 6/8	21 5/8	4 1/8	4 1/8	6	5	Lewis Co., MO	Daryl L. Blum	Daryl L. Blum	2002	19
198 3/8	29 5/8	29 4/8	18 1/8	4 6/8	4 6/8	6	8	Allegany Co., NY	Roosevelt Luckey	NY Dept. of Env. Cons.	1939	20
198 2/8	27 5/8	26 7/8	20 2/8	5	5	6	8	Nemaha Co., KS	Dennis P. Finger	Dennis P. Finger	1974	21
198 1/8	29 7/8	29 4/8	19 5/8	4 6/8	4 7/8	9	8	Decatur Co., IA	Kenneth Tilford	Bass Pro Shops	1985	22
198	29 2/8	29 4/8	20 2/8	5 2/8	5 1/8	9	7	Jackson Co., MI	Troy A. Stephens	MI Whitetail Hall of Fame Mus.	1996	23
197 7/8	27 4/8	27 2/8	19 4/8	4 6/8	4 6/8	8	9	Assiniboine River, MB	Larry H. MacDonald	Bass Pro Shops	1980	24
197 6/8	29 2/8	30	20 4/8	5 6/8	5 7/8	6	5	Wright Co., MN	Curtis F. Van Lith	Bass Pro Shops	1986	25
197 6/8	30	26 7/8	18 7/8	5 7/8	6	7	10	Kenosha Co., WI	Keith S. Brossard	Keith S. Brossard	1999	25
197 5/8	27 2/8	27 5/8	21 6/8	5 2/8	5 4/8	7	8	Wood Co., WI	Joe Haske	Goldie Haske	1945	27
197 3/8	29 1/8	29 7/8	21	5 1/8	5 2/8	9	7	Mann Lakes, AB	Lawrence J. Youngman	Lawrence J. Youngman	1992	28
197 2/8	25 4/8	27 2/8	32	5 2/8	5 3/8	6	7	Comanche Co., KS	Picked Up	H. James Reimer	1991	29
197 1/8	31	29 7/8	21 2/8	6 1/8	6 5/8	7	7	Macoupin Co., IL	Kevin L. Naugle	Bass Pro Shops	1988	30
196 6/8	29 6/8	29	21	5 2/8	5 6/8	6	8	Kane Co., IL	Ray Schremp	Ray Schremp	2000	31
196 4/8	28 6/8	27 5/8	24 2/8	4 6/8	4 6/8	8	6	Maverick Co., TX	Tom McCulloch	T. Dan Friedkin	1963	32
196 4/8	27	26 1/8	22 4/8	4 5/8	4 5/8	8	7	Des Moines Co., IA	Michael R. Edle	Michael R. Edle	1989	32
196 3/8	28 7/8	30 5/8	22 1/8	6 5/8	7	7	5	Plymouth Co., IA	Picked Up	H. James Reimer	1952	34
196 1/8	27 1/8	26 4/8	24 5/8	4 6/8	4 6/8	8	9	McMullen Co., TX	Milton P. George	John L. Stein	1906	35
195 7/8	26 4/8	27 1/8	21 1/8	4 1/8	4 1/8	6	6	Anoka Co., MN	Barry Peterson	Barry Peterson	1995	36

Score								Locality	By	Owner	Date	Rank
195 5/8	28 4/8	27 6/8	22 1/8	5 6/8	5 7/8	7	6	Marshall Co., MN	Robert Sands	Robert Sands	1960	37
195 5/8	29 4/8	27 5/8	18 7/8	4 6/8	4 7/8	8	6	Rock Island Co., IL	Kent E. Anderson	Kent E. Anderson	1999	37
195 4/8	25 3/8	25 7/8	19	4 7/8	4 7/8	6	6	Porcupine Plain, SK	Philip Philipowich	Philip Philipowich	1985	39
195 2/8	28 6/8	28 2/8	20 6/8	5 1/8	5 1/8	6	6	Pierce Co., ND	Kevin L. Bruner	Kevin L. Bruner	1994	40
195 1/8	28 6/8	28 4/8	20 3/8	4 7/8	5	5	5	Parke Co., ND	B. Dodd Porter	B. Dodd Porter	1985	41
195 1/8	25 6/8	28 1/8	19 6/8	5 2/8	5 2/8	8	8	Brightsand Lake, SK	Larry Pellerin	D.J. Hollinger & B. Howard	1993	41
194 7/8	26 7/8	27 2/8	23 1/8	6 1/8	5 6/8	7	7	Leavenworth Co., KS	William R. Mikijanis	William R. Mikijanis	1985	43
194 4/8	25 7/8	25 6/8	18 6/8	5 1/8	5 2/8	7	7	Monroe Co., IA	Lloyd Goad	Bass Pro Shops	1962	44
194 4/8	26 4/8	26	18 7/8	5 6/8	5 4/8	8	8	Nipawin, SK	Gerald Whitehead	Gerald Whitehead	1990	44
194 3/8	29 1/8	28 6/8	23 5/8	5 1/8	5 1/8	5	5	Warren Co., IA	Forest H. Richardson	Bass Pro Shops	1989	46
194 2/8	26 6/8	25	21	4 6/8	5	6	6	Jones Co., IA	Unknown	Bass Pro Shops	1977	47
194 2/8	30 6/8	30 3/8	24 7/8	5 3/8	5 2/8	9	7	Vigo Co., IN	D. Bates & S. Winkler	D. Bates & S. Winkler	1983	47
194 1/8	30	30 1/8	19 4/8	4 6/8	5	6	7	Dakota Co., NE	E. Keith Fahrenholz	E. Keith Fahrenholz	1966	49
194	28 4/8	28 6/8	22 2/8	5	5	6	6	Kent Co., MD	Kevin C. Miller	Kevin C. Miller	2002	50
193 7/8	25 3/8	25 2/8	21 5/8	4 7/8	4 7/8	7	7	Van Buren Co., IA	W. Eugene Zieglowsky	W. Eugene Zieglowsky	1997	51
193 6/8	24 5/8	24 4/8	18 1/8	5	5	7	7	Christopher Lake, SK	Jerry Thorson	Jerry Thorson	1959	52
193 6/8	29 5/8	30	23 1/8	5 4/8	5 3/8	6	6	Antigonish Co., NS	Kevin Boyle	Bass Pro Shops	1987	52
193 4/8	29	29 5/8	23 7/8	5 4/8	5 3/8	6	6	Linn Co., IA	Picked Up	Gary W. Bowen	1994	54
193 3/8	25 6/8	24 5/8	19 1/8	5 6/8	5 5/8	8	8	Witchekan Lake, SK	Marcel Tetreault	Marcel Tetreault	1998	55
193 3/8	27 7/8	29	25 4/8	5 3/8	5 5/8	7	5	Franklin Co., MA	Kajetan R. Sovinski	Kajetan R. Sovinski	2002	55
193 2/8	28 6/8	28 6/8	21 2/8	4 4/8	4 4/8	5	5	Itasca Co., MN	Picked Up	Paul M. Shaw	1935	57
193 2/8	26	25 6/8	22 2/8	5 6/8	5 6/8	5	5	Aroostook Co., ME	Ronnie Cox	Bass Pro Shops	1965	57
193 2/8	28 3/8	27 7/8	22 2/8	5 4/8	5 4/8	8	8	Jackson Co., MI	Craig Calderone	Bass Pro Shops	1986	57
193 2/8	29 4/8	29 1/8	24 6/8	5 2/8	5 2/8	7	7	Chitek Lake, SK	David L. Wilson	David L. Wilson	1992	57
193	25 6/8	26	25	5 3/8	5 5/8	6	6	South Dakota	Unknown	Eugene J. Lodermeier	1964	61
192 7/8	27 4/8	27 2/8	19 3/8	4 3/8	4 5/8	8	9	York Co., ME	Alphonse Chase	Earl Taylor	1920	62
192 7/8	28 1/8	28 1/8	19 7/8	5 7/8	6	7	7	Williamson Co., IL	A. & J. Albers	A. & J. Albers	1991	62
192 7/8	26 6/8	25 6/8	18 4/8	5 1/8	5 1/8	7	6	Wabatansik Creek, AB	Norman Trudeau	Norman Trudeau	1992	62
192 7/8	25 6/8	25 7/8	18 5/8	5 4/8	5 3/8	9	9	Makwa Lake, SK	Ken Brown	Ken Brown	1993	62
192 6/8	28 5/8	28 5/8	22	5 2/8	5 2/8	7	7	Mercer Co., IL	Jerry W. Whitmire	Cabela's, Inc.	2000	62
192 6/8	26	27	19 2/8	5 6/8	5 6/8	6	6	Washington Co., NE	Robert E. Wackel	Robert E. Wackel	1961	67
192 3/8	24 1/8	23 6/8	17 3/8	5	4 6/8	6	6	Monroe Co., IN	Donald L. Fritch	Donald L. Fritch	1992	68
192 3/8	28 4/8	28 4/8	19 4/8	5 7/8	5 4/8	9	9	Monroe Co., IA	Roy E. Allison	Roy E. Allison	1995	68
192 3/8	26 7/8	26 7/8	18 5/8	5 1/8	4 6/8	5	5	Jennings Co., IN	Walter M. Johnson	Walter M. Johnson	1997	68
192 2/8	27 3/8	27 3/8	22 6/8	4 4/8	4 2/8	6	6	Frio Co., TX	Basil Dailey	John L. Stein	1903	71
192 2/8	28 1/8	28 1/8	23 5/8	5 3/8	5 4/8	6	6	Pope Co., MN	Roger D. Syrstad	B&C National Collection	1989	71
192 2/8	26 7/8	26 7/8	18 4/8	5 4/8	5 4/8	5	5	Mills Co., IA	John Chase	John Chase	1997	71
192 2/8	29 1/8	27 7/8	21 4/8	5 7/8	5 7/8	6	5	Souris River, MB	T.K. Patterson & D. Dickson	T.K. Patterson & D. Dickson	2002	71
192	27 1/8	27 1/8	19	4 5/8	4 5/8	6	6	Pine Co., MN	Frank Worlickey	Robert Worlickey	1952	75
192	27 7/8	28	19 2/8	4 6/8	4 6/8	8	9	Lyman Co., SD	Bob Weidner	E.N. Eichler	1957	75
192	24 3/8	23 5/8	17	4 7/8	4 6/8	7	7	Clay Co., MN	Mark L. Peterson	Mark L. Peterson	1984	75
191 7/8	30 5/8	30 7/8	19 2/8	5	5 4/8	6	6	Charles Mix Co., SD	John Simon	John Simon	PR 1970	78
191 7/8	29	27	20 5/8	5 1/8	5 1/8	6	6	Monroe Co., IA	Picked Up	Troy Amoss	1986	78
191 7/8	29 5/8	30 1/8	20 4/8	5 7/8	5 7/8	9	8	Wayne Co., IL	Leo E. Elliott	Leo E. Elliott	1990	78
191 6/8	27	26	19 6/8	4 6/8	4 5/8	5	5	Hudson Bay, SK	George Chalus	Bass Pro Shops	1973	81
191 6/8	27 7/8	28	21	5	4 6/8	6	6	Union Co., IL	Everett F. Ellis	Everett F. Ellis	1994	81
191 5/8	26 2/8	26 2/8	19	5 1/8	5	7	6	Flathead Co., MT	Earl McMaster	Bass Pro Shops	1963	83
191 5/8	26	26 1/8	21 7/8	5	5 1/8	7	5	Goodhue Co., MN	David C. Klatt	Bass Pro Shops	1985	83

WHITETAIL DEER - TYPICAL ANTLERS

Odocoileus virginianus virginianus and certain related subspecies

Score	Length of Main Beam R	L	Inside Spread	Circumference at Smallest Place Between Burr and First Point R	L	Number of Points R	L	Locality	Hunter	Owner	Date Killed	Rank
191 5/8	25 5/8	25	22 7/8	4 3/8	4 4/8	5	6	Albany Co., WY	Robert D. Ross	Robert D. Ross	1986	83
191 5/8	31 1/8	29 4/8	21	5 2/8	4 6/8	8	8	Scioto Co., OH	Lowell E. Kinney	Lowell E. Kinney	2000	83
191 4/8	30 4/8	30 4/8	22 3/8	5 7/8	5 2/8	9	7	Monroe Co., GA	Buck Ashe	Buck Ashe	PR 1962	87
191 4/8	26 5/8	27 4/8	20	4 7/8	5	6	7	Chautauqua Co., KS	Michael A. Young	Michael A. Young	1973	87
191 4/8	28 5/8	28 5/8	21 2/8	4 6/8	4 6/8	5	5	Henry Co., IL	Keith Hamerlinck	Keith Hamerlinck	1999	87
191 3/8	31 6/8	31 1/8	27 5/8	6 1/8	6 1/8	5	6	Vilas Co., WI	Robert Hunter	May Docken	1910	90
191 3/8	24 6/8	25 1/8	25 5/8	4 7/8	5 1/8	5	5	Meade Co., KY	Picked Up	William N. Burrell	1977	90
191 2/8	29	28 6/8	23 6/8	4 7/8	4 7/8	5	5	Monroe Co., MI	Michael A. Kelly	MI Whitetail Hall of Fame Mus.	1997	92
191 2/8	28 1/8	27 1/8	20 2/8	5 7/8	5 7/8	5	6	Scott Co., IA	Jeffery L. Whisker	Bass Pro Shops	1993	93
191	27 6/8	28 3/8	19	5	5 3/8	5	5	Cass Co., MO	John D. Meyer	John D. Meyer	2001	93
190 7/8	26 3/8	26 1/8	19 5/8	4 4/8	4 6/8	7	6	Lyon Co., KS	Jamie Fowler	Jamie Fowler	1992	95
190 7/8	25 2/8	25 4/8	20 7/8	4 5/8	5	5	5	Geary Co., KS	Gary L. Taylor	Gary L. Taylor	1994	95
190 7/8	29 5/8	29 4/8	24 3/8	4 6/8	4 4/8	6	6	Leduc, AB	Robert J. Kowalyshyn	Robert J. Kowalyshyn	1997	95
190 6/8	26 6/8	26	20 4/8	4 4/8	4 3/8	6	5	Wayne Co., IA	Douglas M. Eldridge	Douglas M. Eldridge	2000	95
190 6/8	27 7/8	27 5/8	22 4/8	5 3/8	5 6/8	5	5	Pelly, SK	James R. Strelioff	James R. Strelioff	1980	99
190 6/8	30	30 2/8	20 6/8	5 1/8	5 2/8	7	7	Union Co., IN	John R. Ison, Jr.	John R. Ison, Jr.	1997	99
190 6/8	26 5/8	27	17 6/8	5 1/8	5	7	6	Whiteshell Prov. Park, MB	Darrin Murash	Cabela's, Inc.	1999	99
190 5/8	22 4/8	23 5/8	19 5/8	4 4/8	4 4/8	7	6	Buffalo Lake, AB	Eugene L. Boll	Eugene L. Boll	1969	102
190 5/8	28 6/8	28	17 6/8	5 6/8	6	5	7	Polk Co., IA	Richard B. Swim	Richard B. Swim	1981	102
190 5/8	29	28	19 4/8	5 6/8	5 6/8	5	7	Parke Co., IN	Tony A. Trotter	Tony A. Trotter	1992	102
190 5/8	27 6/8	29 2/8	20 1/8	4 6/8	5	5	5	Ogle Co., IL	Geoff Lester	Geoff Lester	2000	102
190 5/8	26 3/8	26 5/8	18 5/8	4 5/8	4 6/8	8	7	Hillsdale Co., MI	Gregory D. McCuiston	Gregory D. McCuiston	2001	102
190 4/8	27 3/8	27 6/8	22 3/8	5 1/8	5 2/8	6	6	Monona Co., IA	Jeffery D. Scott	Jeffery D. Scott	1996	107
190 4/8	28 2/8	29 1/8	24 3/8	5 5/8	5 5/8	8	8	Menard Co., IL	Dwaine E. Heyen	Dwaine E. Heyen	1997	107
190 3/8	27	26 7/8	20 4/8	4 5/8	4 5/8	6	7	Pettis Co., MO	Jesse A. Perry	Jesse A. Perry	1986	109
190 3/8	29 3/8	28 6/8	22 2/8	5 6/8	5 7/8	10	7	Republic Co., KS	John M. Nylund	John M. Nylund	1995	109
190 2/8	26 1/8	23 1/8	25 7/8	4 3/8	4 2/8	6	7	Shackelford Co., TX	Steven W. O'Carroll	John L. Stein	1991	111
190 2/8	25 6/8	26 2/8	21 3/8	5	4 5/8	13	13	Pike Co., IN	Vince Brock	Vince Brock	1993	111
190 1/8	26 4/8	27	18 4/8	6 1/8	5 7/8	9	7	Randolph Co., IL	Kevin Leemon	Kevin Leemon	1990	113
190	24 2/8	25 2/8	20 6/8	5	5	7	6	Dimmit Co., TX	C.P. Howard	C.P. Howard	1950	114
190	29 1/8	29	24 6/8	5 2/8	5 2/8	6	6	Fremont Co., IA	Randall D. Forney	Randall D. Forney	1971	114
190	29 2/8	31 1/8	23	5 1/8	5	6	6	Cherokee Co., IA	Dennis R. Vaudt	Dennis R. Vaudt	1974	114
190	26	24 6/8	21 1/8	6 2/8	6 4/8	6	9	Turtleford, SK	Dick Rooney	D.J. Hollinger & B. Howard	1989	114
190	27 5/8	26 6/8	19 4/8	5	4 7/8	5	5	Clinton Co., IA	Merwin E. Koch	Merwin E. Koch	1994	114
190	25	24 7/8	23 4/8	4 7/8	5	7	7	Callaway Co., MO	Ben Barks	Ben Barks	1995	114
190	31 2/8	31 2/8	24 6/8	5 4/8	5 2/8	5	5	Page Co., IA	Arlen D. Meyer	Arlen D. Meyer	1996	114

Score	Main Beam R	Main Beam L	Inside Spread	Circ. R	Circ. L	Pts R	Pts L	Locality	Hunter	Owner	Date	Rank
189 7/8	29 6/8	29 4/8	19 5/8	5	4 7/8	9	6	Trempealeau Co., WI	Emil Stelmach	Emil Stelmach	1959	121
189 7/8	26 6/8	26 1/8	22 1/8	4 7/8	5 1/8	6	6	Henry Co., IL	Reginald M. Anseeuw	Reginald M. Anseeuw	1992	121
189 7/8	25 5/8	26 4/8	23 2/8	5 7/8	6 1/8	6	6	Sangamon Co., IL	Leo J. Romanotto	Leo J. Romanotto	1994	121
189 5/8	29 2/8	29 3/8	21 4/8	4 7/8	4 6/8	5	6	Tabor, SD	Duane Graber	Sam Peterson	1954	124
189 5/8	26 3/8	27 3/8	25 1/8	6 2/8	6 7/8	9	7	Schuyler Co., IL	Picked Up	Bass Pro Shops	1990	124
189 5/8	28	28 3/8	21 6/8	4 5/8	4 7/8	6	7	Ministikwan Lake, SK	James L. Cohick	James L. Cohick	1992	124
189 5/8	26 4/8	26 1/8	18 3/8	4 7/8	4 6/8	6	5	Geary Co., KS	Ron Wolford	Cabela's, Inc.	2002	128
189 5/8	25 4/8	24 7/8	20	5	4 6/8	5	5	Monmouth Co., NJ	Scott W. Borden	Scott W. Borden	1995	129
189 4/8	28 3/8	28 2/8	20 1/8	4 1/8	4 1/8	6	7	McKenzie Co., ND	Gene Veeder	Legendary Whitetails	1972	129
189 3/8	25 7/8	25 5/8	23 1/8	6 2/8	6 2/8	6	6	Fillmore Co., MN	Tom Norby	Tom Norby	1975	129
189 3/8	24 6/8	24 6/8	23 6/8	5	4 7/8	7	6	Henry Co., IA	Lamonte A. Stark	Bass Pro Shops	1984	129
189 3/8	29 1/8	29 1/8	19 2/8	5 1/8	5 2/8	8	7	Union Co., IA	Christopher C. Jimerson	Christopher C. Jimerson	1995	129
189 3/8	25 5/8	26	18 1/8	5 3/8	5 2/8	7	7	Lewis Co., KY	Jim Cooper	Jim Cooper	1999	134
189 2/8	29 7/8	29	22 3/8	4 4/8	4 5/8	7	6	Hubbard Co., MN	Hans Lorentzen	Danny L. Cole	PR 1944	134
189 2/8	28 5/8	27 1/8	18 4/8	4 3/8	4 3/8	5	5	Buchanan Co., VA	Jerry L. James	Jerry L. James	1999	136
189 1/8	26	26 5/8	17 3/8	5 6/8	5 6/8	8	9	Douglas Co., WI	Bryan Lawler	Bass Pro Shops	1946	136
189 1/8	28	28 1/8	23 5/8	4 4/8	4 5/8	5	7	Blaine Co., MT	Kenneth Morehouse	Cabela's, Inc.	1959	136
189 1/8	27 5/8	27 5/8	25 7/8	5 1/8	5 2/8	6	5	Nuckolls Co., NE	Van Shotzman	Van Shotzman	1968	136
189 1/8	30 3/8	30 1/8	18 7/8	5 2/8	5 1/8	5	5	Washtenaw Co., MI	Mark C. Ritchie	MI Whitetail Hall of Fame Mus.	1984	136
189	27 6/8	28 3/8	20 1/8	5 3/8	5 3/8	6	6	Allamakee Co., IA	Randy L. Petersburg	Randy L. Petersburg	1996	141
189	26 6/8	26 5/8	20 2/8	5	4 4/8	6	6	Shelby Co., KY	Frank W. Kendall	Frank W. Kendall	1971	141
189	25 1/8	25 4/8	17 2/8	5 5/8	5 1/8	6	6	Crawford Co., AR	Tom Sparks, Jr.	Tom Sparks, Jr.	1975	141
188 7/8	25 4/8	25 4/8	23 2/8	4 5/8	5 1/8	8	8	Red Deer Lake, MB	Will Bigelow	Will Bigelow	1986	144
188 7/8	28 2/8	27 3/8	19 2/8	5 1/8	6 1/8	6	6	Shelby Co., IL	James M. Holley	James M. Holley	1995	144
188 6/8	28 7/8	28 7/8	19 4/8	5 1/8	5 3/8	6	6	Clark Co., IL	Larry Shaw	Larry Shaw	1998	146
188 6/8	25 3/8	25 3/8	16 2/8	6	5 3/8	6	5	Shenandoah Co., VA	Gene W. Wilson	Gene W. Wilson	1985	146
188 6/8	26 6/8	28 5/8	18 4/8	5 2/8	4 6/8	6	6	Shelby Co., IL	Elmer Agney	Elmer Agney	1992	146
188 6/8	29	29 2/8	22 2/8	5 3/8	4 7/8	5	6	Crawford Co., WI	Eli D. Randall	Eli D. Randall	1995	146
188 5/8	27 4/8	27 4/8	25	4 6/8	4 4/8	5	6	Stafford Co., KS	Robin L. Austin	Robin L. Austin	2002	146
188 4/8	27 2/8	27 2/8	19 7/8	4 7/8	5	6	6	Flathead Co., MT	Len E. Patterson	Len E. Patterson	1992	150
188 4/8	27 2/8	27 3/8	20 5/8	4 4/8	4 6/8	6	8	Lewis Co., KY	Ben C. Johnson	Ben C. Johnson	1993	150
188 4/8	22 2/8	22 2/8	22 5/8	5 6/8	5 5/8	8	7	Burstall, SK	W.P. Rolick	W.P. Rolick	1957	152
188 4/8	27 1/8	27 4/8	22 2/8	5	4 7/8	5	6	Metiskow, AB	Norman T. Salminen	Norman T. Salminen	1977	152
188 4/8	27 4/8	27 1/8	20 1/8	4 6/8	4 6/8	10	5	Riley Co., KS	Robert E. Luke	Brad Sowter	1984	152
188 4/8	30 3/8	30 6/8	17	6 6/8	6 4/8	5	8	Crawford Co., WI	Roger W. Salmon	Roger W. Salmon	1986	152
188 4/8	23	23 4/8	20 6/8	5 3/8	5 1/8	8	8	Souris River, MB	Wes Todoruk	Wes Todoruk	1986	152
188 4/8	27 4/8	27 3/8	21 3/8	5	5	7	5	Macon Co., MO	Eugene J. Bausch	Eugene J. Bausch	2001	152
188 4/8	24 2/8	24 2/8	18 6/8	5 3/8	5 5/8	7	7	Sandy Lake, MB	Darren L. Yanchycki	Darren L. Yanchycki	2001	152
188 3/8	26 4/8	26 4/8	18 3/8	5 4/8	5 4/8	6	6	Fulton Co., OH	Scott E. May	Scott E. May	2002	160
188 3/8	28 4/8	28 2/8	18 6/8	5 1/8	5 1/8	7	7	Sanford, MB	Picked Up	MB Wildl. Branch	1982	160
188 3/8	27 6/8	27 6/8	17 2/8	5	5	5	5	Red Deer, AB	Edwin Koberstein	Edwin Koberstein	1991	160
188 2/8	29 1/8	28 6/8	21 7/8	4 7/8	4 5/8	8	8	Peoria Co., IL	Jill M. Adcock	Jill M. Adcock	1993	160
188 2/8	28 1/8	28 1/8	22 4/8	4 4/8	5 2/8	7	7	Montgomery Co., IL	Travis L. Hartman	Travis L. Hartman	1999	164
188	27 1/8	27 6/8	25 7/8	5	6	10	10	Cowley Co., KS	Armand L. Hillier	Armand L. Hillier	1996	165
188	27 6/8	28 6/8	19	5 1/8	5 6/8	5	5	Marshall Co., MN	Paul J. Wolf	Cabela's, Inc.	1991	165
188	26 3/8	27 2/8	21 2/8	5 7/8	5 2/8	10	10	Chisago Co., MN	John B. Nelson	John B. Nelson	1992	165
188	28 4/8	27 2/8	19 1/8	5 2/8	5 2/8	7	7	N. Saskatchewan River, AB	Darrel J. Patera	Darrel J. Patera	1999	165
188	28 4/8	27 2/8	17 1/8	5 2/8	5 2/8	7	6	Williams Co., OH	Brad A. McNalley	Brad A. McNalley	2000	165

WHITETAIL DEER - TYPICAL ANTLERS

Odocoileus virginianus virginianus and certain related subspecies

Score	Length of Main Beam		Inside Spread	Circumference at Smallest Place Between Burr and First Point		Number of Points		Locality	Hunter	Owner	Date Killed	Rank
	R	L		R	L	R	L					
187 7/8	25 5/8	26 1/8	21 3/8	4 6/8	4 6/8	7	7	Zavala Co., TX	Donald Rutledge	Frank Rutledge	1946	169
187 7/8	28	28 3/8	21 2/8	5	5	7	8	Bayfield Co., WI	Simon Jacobs	Jon Jacobs	1951	169
187 7/8	27 4/8	28 7/8	19 5/8	5	5	6	5	Langlade Co., WI	Kory J. Schumacher	Kory J. Schumacher	1994	169
187 7/8	27 6/8	25 6/8	20 7/8	4 6/8	4 4/8	5	5	Schuyler Co., IL	Donald L. Smith	Donald L. Smith	2001	169
187 7/8	27 5/8	26 7/8	23 3/8	5 2/8	5	6	6	Whitesand Lake, SK	Stan Eskovich	Stan Eskovich	2002	169
187 6/8	27 4/8	27 7/8	25 2/8	5 2/8	5 3/8	6	6	Union Co., KY	Charles Meuth	Larry S. Melton	1964	174
187 6/8	28	28 4/8	20 6/8	5 6/8	6 1/8	6	5	Houston Co., MN	Donald M. Grant	Donald M. Grant	1978	174
187 6/8	25 5/8	26 4/8	19	4 6/8	5 1/8	5	5	Johnson Co., IA	Gregg R. Redlin	Gregg R. Redlin	1983	174
187 6/8	25 5/8	23 2/8	17 7/8	6	5 6/8	6	8	Mantagao Lake, MB	Picked Up	Mel Podaima	1988	174
187 6/8	29 7/8	29 6/8	21	5	5 1/8	5	6	Clinton Co., MO	Scott E. Looney	Scott E. Looney	1994	174
187 5/8	28 2/8	27 6/8	19 6/8	5	5	6	8	Starr Co., TX	Picked Up	Jack F. Quist	1945	179
187 5/8	25	25 2/8	20 1/8	5 2/8	5 2/8	6	6	Emmons Co., ND	Joseph F. Bosch	Joseph F. Bosch	1959	179
187 5/8	25 2/8	25 5/8	19 2/8	5 2/8	5 3/8	6	8	Winona Co., MN	Ken W. Koenig	Ken W. Koenig	1976	179
187 5/8	27	27 1/8	17	5 3/8	5 2/8	7	6	Bourbon Co., KS	Picked Up	George J. McLiney, Jr.	1990	179
187 5/8	27 1/8	27 2/8	20 5/8	5 5/8	5 4/8	5	5	Pickaway Co., OH	Jeffrey M. Bragg	Jeffrey M. Bragg	1999	179
187 5/8	28 2/8	29	23 3/8	5 4/8	5	6	8	Greene Co., IA	Chris Jones	Chris Jones	1999	179
187 5/8	27 2/8	28 1/8	22 2/8	4 5/8	4 6/8	7	7	Franklin Co., MO	Mickey R. Montee	Mickey R. Montee	2001	179
187 4/8	28 3/8	27	24 6/8	5 3/8	5 3/8	8	5	Winona Co., MN	Dan Groebner	Dan Groebner	1974	186
187 4/8	27	27 4/8	19 5/8	5 2/8	4 7/8	9	8	Brown Co., IL	Charles A. Howell	Charles A. Howell	1988	186
187 4/8	26 7/8	27 2/8	26 2/8	4 7/8	4 5/8	8	8	Zapata Co., TX	Phillip T. Stringer	Phillip T. Stringer	1992	186
187 4/8	28	28 1/8	21	4 7/8	5 3/8	5	5	Miami Co., OH	Dale L. Bevington	Dale L. Bevington	1996	186
187 4/8	26 6/8	26 7/8	21 3/8	5	5	7	6	Plunkett, SK	Myles Mann	Myles Mann	1996	186
187 4/8	25 4/8	27 4/8	25 4/8	4 2/8	4 4/8	7	6	Warren Co., MO	Gary D. Schuster	Gary D. Schuster	1998	186
187 3/8	24 7/8	25 2/8	23 3/8	5 3/8	5	6	7	St. Francis Co., AR	Andy Anderson	Andy Anderson	1998	192
187 3/8	26 7/8	26 4/8	19 7/8	5 3/8	5 4/8	6	7	Pine Creek, MB	C. Anne Reddon	C. Anne Reddon	2001	192
187 2/8	31 4/8	30 6/8	30 3/8	4 6/8	4 5/8	7	8	Warren Co., IA	Dwight E. Green	Dwight E. Green	1964	194
187 2/8	29	28 5/8	26 4/8	5 2/8	5 3/8	5	5	Lyon Co., MN	Lynn Jackson	Dick Rossum	1967	194
187 2/8	26	26 2/8	19 4/8	4 6/8	4 6/8	6	8	Scotland Co., MO	Robin Berhorst	Robin Berhorst	1971	194
187 2/8	26 3/8	25	18 6/8	5 1/8	5 1/8	7	7	McLean Co., ND	Frank O. Bauman	Donald Bauman	1986	194
187 2/8	27 1/8	26 4/8	24 2/8	5 2/8	5 3/8	6	6	Wandering River, AB	Jason L. Hayes	Jason L. Hayes	1999	194
187 1/8	26 4/8	26 5/8	19 4/8	4 4/8	4 5/8	6	7	Cooper Co., MO	Joe Ditto	Joe Ditto	1974	199
187 1/8	26 6/8	26 4/8	18 7/8	4 6/8	4 7/8	6	6	Pulaski Co., KY	Scott Abbott	Scott Abbott	1982	199
187 1/8	27 7/8	28 3/8	18 7/8	5 6/8	5 7/8	5	5	Mercer Co., MO	Picked Up	Bob Summers	1986	199
187 1/8	27 2/8	27 6/8	17 7/8	5	5	8	6	Montgomery Co., IN	Larry E. Lawson	Larry E. Lawson	1988	199
187 1/8	26 3/8	28 1/8	24 1/8	5 2/8	5 2/8	5	5	Rossburn, MB	G. Wayne Preston	G. Wayne Preston	1994	199
187 1/8	28	28 3/8	22 3/8	4 7/8	4 5/8	7	7	Hocking Co., OH	Stephen C. Corley	Stephen C. Corley	1995	199

Score	Main Beam R	Main Beam L	Inside Spread	Circ. R	Circ. L	Pts. R	Pts. L	Locality	By Whom Killed	Owner	Date	Rank
187	24 7/8	24 7/8	18 4/8	5 7/8	5 5/8	6	6	Unknown	Unknown	MI Whitetail Hall of Fame Mus.	1962	205
187	29 5/8	29	18	4 4/8	4 3/8	6	6	Warren Co., IL	John K. Poole	John K. Poole	1994	205
187	29 2/8	28	25 5/8	5 6/8	5 7/8	6	6	Geary Co., KS	Jack Swenson	Brad Sowter	1997	205
187	24 6/8	24 7/8	19	4 7/8	4 7/8	6	6	Swift Co., MN	George A. Piotter	George A. Piotter	2002	205
186 7/8	25 5/8	25 3/8	20 1/8	5	5	5	5	Arkansas Co., AR	Walter Spears	Cabela's, Inc.	1952	209
186 7/8	27 7/8	27 2/8	19 1/8	5 4/8	5 2/8	5	5	Atchison Co., MO	Mike Moody	Mike Moody	1968	209
186 7/8	26 3/8	26 7/8	20 5/8	5 2/8	5 3/8	5	5	Andrew Co., MO	Kenneth Till	Kenneth Till	1989	209
186 7/8	27 1/8	28 3/8	17 4/8	5 2/8	5	6	7	Adair Co., IA	Dennis J. Gruss	Dennis J. Gruss	1995	209
186 7/8	28 4/8	27 5/8	20 4/8	5 3/8	5 3/8	7	5	Lewis Co., KY	W. David Mains	Cabela's, Inc.	1996	209
186 7/8	30 4/8	29 2/8	20 7/8	4 7/8	4 7/8	5	8	Greene Co., OH	Dale A. Heathcook	Dale A. Heathcook	2001	209
186 6/8	26 7/8	26 4/8	19	5 5/8	5 5/8	7	6	St. Louis Co., MN	Unknown	George W. Flaim	PR 1983	215
186 6/8	29 1/8	29 7/8	23	4 6/8	4 6/8	5	5	Logan Co., OH	Bernard R. Hines	Bernard R. Hines	1990	215
186 6/8	27 7/8	28 5/8	19 6/8	4 5/8	4 6/8	5	5	Bullitt Co., KY	Troy Gentry	Troy Gentry	2002	215
186 5/8	24 4/8	24 7/8	16 7/8	4 7/8	4 7/8	10	6	Langlade Co., WI	Fred J. Hofmann	Fred J. Hofmann	1994	218
186 5/8	27	26 5/8	22 1/8	5 2/8	5 2/8	5	5	Kelvington, SK	David Martin	David Martin	1999	218
186 5/8	27 1/8	26 4/8	21 4/8	4 4/8	4 3/8	8	6	Buffalo Co., WI	Kenneth H. Shane	Kenneth H. Shane	2000	218
186 4/8	27 6/8	26	22	5 1/8	5 2/8	7	6	Becker Co., MN	Ilo Dugger	Jeff Dugger	1930	221
186 4/8	26 3/8	26 3/8	19 6/8	4 4/8	4 3/8	6	5	Pine Co., MN	Unknown	Ralph Blessum	PR 1970	221
186 4/8	29	28 4/8	20 2/8	4 5/8	4 4/8	5	5	Monroe Co., IA	Picked Up	H. James Reimer	1992	221
186 4/8	28 6/8	28	26 2/8	5 4/8	5 5/8	7	7	Coles Co., IL	Charles H. McElwee	Charles H. McElwee	1994	221
186 4/8	28 3/8	28 3/8	24 3/8	5 4/8	5 4/8	6	6	Appanoose Co., IA	Picked Up	Robert Walker	1998	221
186 3/8	27 5/8	27 1/8	20 4/8	6 1/8	5 6/8	5	5	Morris Co., KS	Garold D. Miller	Garold D. Miller	1969	226
186 3/8	30 2/8	29	22 5/8	4 4/8	4 5/8	7	8	Flathead Co., MT	Unknown	Wayne Williamson	1973	226
186 3/8	26 1/8	26 1/8	18 6/8	4 7/8	4 6/8	5	5	Otter Tail Co., MN	Robert Ames	David R. Brigan	1977	226
186 3/8	26 2/8	27 2/8	20 4/8	5 2/8	5 2/8	7	7	Ontonagon Co., MI	Unknown	Mac's Taxidermy	1980	226
186 3/8	28 5/8	28 5/8	20 7/8	5 3/8	5 1/8	5	5	Pike Co., IL	Merle L. Shull	Merle L. Shull	1985	226
186 3/8	28	28	23 1/8	4 6/8	4 6/8	6	6	Lee Co., AL	Picked Up	George P. Mann	1986	226
186 3/8	28	26 4/8	20	5 7/8	5 6/8	6	6	Monona Co., IA	Mark Maynard	Mark Maynard	1992	226
186 3/8	26 4/8	27 1/8	19 1/8	4 7/8	4 6/8	7	5	Greene Co., IL	Picked Up	Cory L. Walker	1992	226
186 3/8	27 1/8	25 3/8	21 7/8	5 4/8	5 4/8	5	8	Rocky Mt. House, AB	Wyndell A. Wroten	Wyndell A. Wroten	1992	226
186 3/8	25	24 6/8	18 4/8	5 6/8	5 6/8	8	6	Adams Co., CO	David A. McCracken	David A. McCracken	1996	226
186 2/8	25 4/8	25 6/8	21	4 6/8	4 6/8	6	5	La Salle Co., TX	Herman C. Schliesing	Herman C. Schliesing	1967	236
186 2/8	25 2/8	27 4/8	18	4 6/8	4 6/8	10	8	Kenedy Co., TX	Jack Van Cleve III	McGill Estate	1972	236
186 2/8	27 4/8	25 4/8	22 4/8	5	5 2/8	7	6	Laclede Co., MO	Larry Ogle	Larry Ogle	1972	236
186 2/8	25	28 6/8	19	5 2/8	5 1/8	5	5	Hancock Co., ME	Gerald C. Murray	Gerald C. Murray	1984	236
186 2/8	28 6/8	29 1/8	22	4 7/8	4 6/8	6	6	Carter Co., KY	Herman G. Holbrooks	Herman G. Holbrooks	1989	236
186 2/8	29 1/8	25 7/8	20 3/8	4 6/8	5	7	6	Bayfield Co., WI	Ken T. Johnson	Ken T. Johnson	1994	236
186 2/8	25 7/8	25 1/8	18	5 2/8	5 2/8	6	6	White Co., IN	Samuel T. Young	Samuel T. Young	1997	236
186 2/8	25 1/8	25 6/8	18	5 4/8	5 4/8	7	6	Adams Co., OH	Larry D. Napier	Larry D. Napier	2001	236
186 1/8	25 6/8	26 2/8	20 1/8	4 6/8	4 6/8	5	5	Roane Co., TN	W.A. Foster	W.A. Foster	1959	244
186 1/8	25 1/8	26 2/8	21 1/8	6	6 1/8	9	8	Waupaca Co., WI	Fred Penny	Dale Trinrud	1963	244
186 1/8	28	29 2/8	21	4 5/8	4 6/8	5	5	Zavala Co., TX	Picked Up	Paul W. Sanders, Jr.	1965	244
186 1/8	29 4/8	28 4/8	18 5/8	5 1/8	5	5	8	St. Louis Co., MN	Unknown	George W. Flaim	1980	244
186 1/8	28 4/8	27 4/8	20 7/8	4 6/8	5 6/8	6	6	St. Louis Co., MN	Mark O. DuLong	Mark O. DuLong	1988	244
186 1/8	27 4/8	26 2/8	22	5 5/8	6	5	6	Pope Co., IL	Picked Up	Jim Frailey	1990	244
186 1/8	26 2/8	26 2/8	19 4/8	5 2/8	5 3/8	7	6	Camrose, AB	Dale A. Broker	Dale A. Broker	1992	244
186 1/8	29 1/8	27 3/8	20 1/8	5 1/8	5 1/8	5	5	Buchanan Co., IA	Garry W. Rasmussen	Garry W. Rasmussen	1994	244
186 1/8	27 6/8	24 7/8	19 1/8	5	4 7/8	8	6	Columbia Co., OH	Jared T. MacNees	Jared T. MacNees	2000	244

WHITETAIL DEER - TYPICAL ANTLERS
Odocoileus virginianus virginianus and certain related subspecies

Score	Length of Main Beam		Inside Spread	Circumference at Smallest Place Between Burr and First Point		Number of Points		Locality	Hunter	Owner	Date Killed	Rank
	R	L		R	L	R	L					
186 1/8	29 2/8	28 2/8	20 3/8	4 6/8	4 5/8	7	7	Franklin Co., KS	Stephen P. Edwards	Stephen P. Edwards	2001	244
186	30 5/8	31 3/8	26 3/8	5 1/8	5	5	9	Itasca Co., MN	Knud W. Jensen	Bass Pro Shops	1955	254
186	25 1/8	25 3/8	19	4 3/8	4 3/8	6	6	Flathead Co., MT	Douglas G. Mefford	Douglas G. Mefford	1966	254
186	30	29 4/8	22	6	5 4/8	6	5	Warren Co., KY	Arnold M. Bush	Arnold M. Bush	1986	254
186	25 5/8	25 6/8	23	5 3/8	5 2/8	6	7	Union Co., IA	Christine A. Weeks	Christine A. Weeks	1991	254
186	26 6/8	27 6/8	16 2/8	6 1/8	6 3/8	5	5	Monona Co., IA	David L. Zima	David L. Zima	1996	254
186	28	27 7/8	19 1/8	5 4/8	5 4/8	6	6	Macoupin Co., IL	Picked Up	Darrell Baker	1998	254
185 7/8	28 5/8	28 3/8	20 5/8	5 2/8	5 2/8	5	5	Beltrami Co., MN	Picked Up	Jerome D. Erdahl	1987	260
185 7/8	29 7/8	30 1/8	19 5/8	5	5 1/8	6	6	Prairie Co., AR	Lonnie W. Copeland	Jack G. Brittingham	1992	260
185 7/8	28 2/8	27 7/8	23 7/8	4 4/8	4 5/8	5	5	Queen Anne's Co., MD	Walter Lachewitz	Walter J. Lachewitz	1998	260
185 6/8	26 3/8	26 2/8	20 7/8	5	5 2/8	8	8	Bryan Co., OK	Larry D. Luman	Larry D. Luman	1997	263
185 5/8	24 3/8	25	19 5/8	4 6/8	4 5/8	6	6	Nenzel, NE	Richard Kehr	Richard Kehr	1965	264
185 5/8	25 2/8	25 4/8	19 2/8	4 5/8	4 3/8	6	7	Dallas Co., MO	James E. Headings	James E. Headings	1986	264
185 5/8	26	27 5/8	19 5/8	6	5 4/8	5	5	Johnson Co., IN	Michael J. Arney	Michael J. Arney	1998	264
185 4/8	27 1/8	27 2/8	22 2/8	4 7/8	5	6	8	Brisco, BC	Baptiste Paul	Winston Wolfenden	1914	267
185 4/8	26 6/8	27 1/8	22	4 5/8	4 5/8	6	6	Otter Tail Co., MN	Orris T. Neirby	Orris T. Neirby	1942	267
185 4/8	27 7/8	25 6/8	18 7/8	5 3/8	5 5/8	8	7	Zapata Co., TX	Jesus Lopez	John L. Stein	1969	267
185 4/8	26 2/8	26 3/8	20 2/8	4 6/8	4 6/8	5	5	Sussex Co., DE	Herbert N. Milam	Herbert N. Milam	1978	267
185 4/8	29	28 1/8	24 6/8	5 2/8	5 3/8	5	6	Benton Co., MN	Clifford G. Knier	Clifford G. Knier	1992	267
185 3/8	26 4/8	27	19 4/8	5 1/8	5 2/8	7	10	Marshall Co., MN	Donald W. Wilkens	Donald W. Wilkens	1973	272
185 3/8	27 6/8	28	20 5/8	4 7/8	4 7/8	5	5	Canwood, SK	Clark Heimbechner	Clark Heimbechner	1984	272
185 3/8	29	28 1/8	23	4 7/8	4 7/8	9	8	Riley Co., KS	Robert L. Tully	Robert L. Tully	1988	272
185 3/8	27 7/8	27 7/8	21 5/8	5 1/8	5 1/8	5	5	Helene Lake, SK	Wayne A. Foster	Wayne A. Foster	1991	272
185 3/8	27 7/8	27 7/8	23 3/8	5	5 1/8	5	6	Woodlands, MB	Picked Up	Cabela's, Inc.	1994	272
185 3/8	26 3/8	27	19 5/8	4 2/8	4 3/8	6	6	Harrison Co., MO	John W. Rhea II	John W. Rhea II	1995	272
185 3/8	23 1/8	27 3/8	23 7/8	5 1/8	5 5/8	7	9	Morris Co., KS	Gregory A. Glasgow	Gregory A. Glasgow	1998	272
185 2/8	30	29 2/8	30 2/8	5 2/8	5 2/8	8	8	Todd Co., KY	C.W. Shelton	Bass Pro Shops	1964	279
185 2/8	26 4/8	24 3/8	17 2/8	4 5/8	4 6/8	6	7	Adair Co., MO	Ronald Lene	Bobby D. Lene	1976	279
185 2/8	24 7/8	27	23 2/8	5 7/8	5 3/8	6	5	Mercer Co., IL	Richard L. McCaw	Richard L. McCaw	1997	279
185 1/8	25 6/8	25 3/8	27	5	4 6/8	7	6	Webb Co., TX	Henderson Coquat	Henderson Coquat	1949	282
185 1/8	29 5/8	29 2/8	25 5/8	5	5 1/8	7	6	Warren Co., IA	Joyce McCormick	Joyce McCormick	1968	282
185 1/8	27 7/8	27 4/8	19 1/8	5 2/8	5	6	7	Harrison Co., IA	Marvin E. Tippery	Marvin E. Tippery	1971	282
185 1/8	26 2/8	27 4/8	23 1/8	4 5/8	5 1/8	6	7	Franklin Co., IN	Gayle Fritsch	Gayle Fritsch	1972	282
185 1/8	27 4/8	28	18 6/8	5	4 6/8	5	8	Porter Co., IN	Mathieu J. Price	Mathieu J. Price	1990	282
185 1/8	26 3/8	25 6/8	24 7/8	5 7/8	5 7/8	6	7	Bonnyville, AB	Richard A. Rhoden	Richard A. Rhoden	1996	282
185	25 2/8	25	19 2/8	4 6/8	4 6/8	6	6	Frio Co., TX	Loyd Nail	Steven L. Smith	1941	288

Score	Main Beam R	Main Beam L	Inside Spread	Circ. R	Circ. L	Pts. R	Pts. L	Locality	By	Owner	Date	Rank
185	26 6/8	26 7/8	18 6/8	5 1/8	5 1/8	6	6	Carter Co., MO	Richard N. Goggin	Richard N. Goggin	1963	288
185	29 1/8	28 5/8	18 6/8	4 3/8	4 4/8	5	5	Vernon Co., WI	Harold Christianson	Harold Christianson	1968	288
185	25 7/8	25 7/8	19	4 7/8	4 7/8	7	7	Winona Co., MN	Ronald Bunke	B., S., & B. Bunke	1973	288
185	27 4/8	27 2/8	18 6/8	5 4/8	5 3/8	8	6	Putnam Co., IN	Earl G. McCammack	Earl G. McCammack	1985	288
185	26 7/8	27	17 5/8	6	5 7/8	8	10	Seward Co., KS	Michael D. Gatlin	Michael D. Gatlin	1987	288
185	28	27 3/8	26 5/8	5 4/8	5 2/8	11	10	Lyon Co., KS	Ronald L. Sleisher	Ronald L. Sleisher	2001	288
184 7/8	26 5/8	26 6/8	27	5 7/8	5 7/8	7	6	Delaware Co., IA	R.E. Stewart	R.E. Stewart	1953	295
184 7/8	25 1/8	24 4/8	17 7/8	5 1/8	5 1/8	7	9	Yellowstone Co., MT	Picked Up	Dennis Helmey	1984	295
184 7/8	28	28	23 4/8	6	6	8	6	Vermilion, AB	C. Letawsky & B. Myshak	C. Letawsky & B. Myshak	1986	295
184 7/8	26 3/8	26 3/8	21	5 7/8	6	6	6	Baraga Co., MI	Louis J. Roy	Louis J. Roy	1987	295
184 7/8	24 4/8	23 5/8	17 3/8	5 5/8	5 6/8	7	6	Aitken Creek, BC	Guyle G. Cox	Guyle G. Cox	1990	295
184 7/8	25 2/8	25	18	5	4 7/8	7	5	Dallas Co., MO	Lynn Garner	Lynn Garner	1992	295
184 6/8	28 6/8	26 6/8	21 6/8	5 4/8	5 6/8	6	7	Madison Parish, LA	John Lee	Donald R. Broadway	1943	301
184 6/8	25 4/8	25 2/8	19 4/8	5 1/8	5 1/8	7	6	Morrison Co., MN	Mr. Holt	Michael J. Kampa	PR 1960	301
184 6/8	26 7/8	27	24 4/8	5 3/8	5 3/8	9	6	Desha Co., AR	Lee Perry	Walter Brock	1961	301
184 6/8	24 1/8	26 1/8	21 2/8	5 3/8	5 3/8	6	6	Dore Lake, SK	Garvis C. Coker	Garvis C. Coker	1971	301
184 6/8	26 3/8	26 2/8	24 2/8	4 6/8	4 6/8	6	6	Starr Co., TX	Harry Richardson, Jr.	Harry Richardson, Jr.	1973	301
184 6/8	26 7/8	26 4/8	20 6/8	4 5/8	4 5/8	6	6	Greene Co., PA	Ivan Parry	Ivan Parry	1974	301
184 6/8	27	26	27 4/8	6 1/8	6	5	6	Muskingum Co., OH	Dale Hartberger	Dale Hartberger	1981	301
184 6/8	26 6/8	25 2/8	19 4/8	5 4/8	5 5/8	5	6	Sauk Co., WI	Jeffrey J. Wilson	Jeffrey J. Wilson	1995	301
184 6/8	27	27	27 6/8	5	4 7/8	8	6	St. Brieux, SK	Ted Gaillard	Ted Gaillard	1996	301
184 5/8	26 6/8	25 2/8	22	4 4/8	4 5/8	7	6	Washington Co., ME	Unknown	Chuck P. Vose	1944	310
184 5/8	28 6/8	28 2/8	21 7/8	5 3/8	5 3/8	5	5	Polk Co., NE	Keith Houdersheldt	Keith Houdersheldt	1985	310
184 5/8	26	25 1/8	23 2/8	5 2/8	5 1/8	4	5	Nuevo Leon, MX	Charles H. Priess	Charles H. Priess	1985	310
184 5/8	28 2/8	29	19 3/8	5 4/8	5 3/8	5	5	Hudson Bay, SK	Picked Up	Wade Hersikorn	1986	310
184 5/8	24 7/8	24 4/8	15 7/8	5 3/8	5 4/8	5	6	Phelps Co., MO	Picked Up	Donald E. Davidson	1988	310
184 5/8	27	27	21 2/8	5 4/8	5	6	8	Paddle River, AB	Gregory D. Graff	Gregory D. Graff	1988	310
184 5/8	27 1/8	27 1/8	21	5 3/8	5 4/8	6	6	McDonough Co., IL	Louise Thompson	Louise Thompson	1991	310
184 5/8	26	25 2/8	19 1/8	6 1/8	6 1/8	6	7	Champaign Co., OH	Eric Coleman	Eric Coleman	2000	310
184 5/8	27	27	23 1/8	5 1/8	5 1/8	5	6	Birch Lake, SK	Michael G. Taylor	Michael G. Taylor	2000	310
184 5/8	26 7/8	26 5/8	20 7/8	5 2/8	5 2/8	5	6	Jasper Co., MO	Picked Up	Andy S. Johnson	2002	310
184 5/8	23 3/8	22 5/8	19 5/8	4 6/8	5 1/8	5	5	Walworth Co., WI	Scot Zajdel	Scot Zajdel	2002	310
184 4/8	25 7/8	26 6/8	22 5/8	5 1/8	5 1/8	8	10	Bandera Co., TX	Picked Up	Wyatt Birkner	1949	321
184 4/8	26 1/8	28 3/8	22 4/8	5 1/8	5 3/8	5	6	Bossier Parish, LA	Earnest O. McCoy	Lucille McCoy	1961	321
184 4/8	26 5/8	27 6/8	20 2/8	5 6/8	5 6/8	6	6	Ravalli Co., MT	Picked Up	Walter R. Willey	1978	321
184 4/8	28	23 4/8	17	5 3/8	5	7	7	Fayette Co., TN	Benny M. Johnson	Benny M. Johnson	1979	321
184 4/8	23 4/8	30 4/8	20 4/8	4 6/8	5	7	7	Chase Co., KS	Thomas D. Mosher	Thomas D. Mosher	1984	321
184 4/8	30 3/8	26 3/8	19 7/8	4 4/8	5 6/8	7	7	Missoula Co., MT	Jack M. Greenwood	Jack M. Greenwood	1985	321
184 4/8	26 7/8	26	19	5 1/8	5 3/8	6	6	Smoky Lake, AB	Brendon Rezewski	Brendon Rezewski	1995	321
184 4/8	26 4/8	26 4/8	20	4 7/8	5 2/8	6	6	Echo Lake, SK	Dale McKay	Dale McKay	1997	321
184 4/8	26 7/8	27 3/8	19 2/8	5 3/8	5 6/8	6	6	Eagle Creek, SK	Preston Haanen	Preston Haanen	1999	321
184 4/8	27 1/8	30 1/8	19 6/8	5 2/8	5 3/8	7	4	McHenry Co., IL	Russell A. Lovins	Russell A. Lovins	1999	321
184 3/8	27	26	17 7/8	4 6/8	4 6/8	5	5	St. Louis Co., MN	Unknown	Dick Rossum	1935	331
184 3/8	28 4/8	29	25 5/8	5 7/8	5 6/8	7	6	Kingsbury Co., SD	Rudy F. Weigel	Rudy F. Weigel	1960	331
184 3/8	26	26 6/8	20 6/8	5 6/8	5 6/8	6	8	Paulding Co., GA	Floyd Benson	Floyd Benson	1962	331
184 3/8	27 6/8	28	23	5 4/8	5 1/8	6	6	Reno Co., KS	Michael Denney	Michael Denney	1991	331
184 3/8	26 5/8	26	19	5	5	6	6	Keokuk Co., IA	Randy D. Schmidt	Randy D. Schmidt	1995	331
184 3/8	26 3/8	27 1/8	23 7/8	5 1/8	5 2/8	6	6	Porcupine Plain, SK	Lee Krantz	Lee Krantz	1998	331

WHITETAIL DEER - TYPICAL ANTLERS

Odocoileus virginianus virginianus and certain related subspecies

Score	Length of Main Beam R	L	Inside Spread	Circumference at Smallest Place Between Burr and First Point R	L	Number of Points R	L	Locality	Hunter	Owner	Date Killed	Rank
184 2/8	28 2/8	27 6/8	24	5	5 1/8	5	6	Franklin Parish, LA	H.B. Womble	Carey B. McCoy	1914	337
184 2/8	29 1/8	28 2/8	18 6/8	4 7/8	5	6	7	Hardin Co., IA	Robert D. Imsland	Robert D. Imsland	1985	337
184 2/8	25 5/8	24 7/8	17 5/8	5 2/8	5 1/8	6	6	Dooly Co., GA	Joe Morgan	Joe Morgan	1985	337
184 2/8	25 1/8	28 4/8	23 1/8	5	5	5	6	Dillberry Lake, AB	Scott M. Rowein	Scott M. Rowein	1992	337
184 2/8	29 5/8	27 3/8	21	5 6/8	5 6/8	5	6	Jackson Co., IA	Unknown	Charles E. Matthiesen	PR 1994	337
184 2/8	24 7/8	24 6/8	18 4/8	5 6/8	5 7/8	7	7	Meeting Lake, SK	Dennis Woloshyn	Dennis Woloshyn	1996	337
184 2/8	28 4/8	29 4/8	21 2/8	5	5	5	7	McLeod River, AB	Clifford L. Haddock	Clifford L. Haddock	1998	337
184 2/8	27	27 4/8	20 6/8	4 6/8	4 6/8	5	5	Shelby Co., TN	Picked Up	Sammy Beesinger	2001	337
184 1/8	26 7/8	27 6/8	21	5	5	8	7	Marshall Co., MN	Alvin C. Westerlund	Alvin C. Westerlund	1953	345
184 1/8	29	31	20 5/8	5 5/8	4 4/8	6	5	Vinton Co., OH	Dan F. Allison	Dan F. Allison	1965	345
184 1/8	31 3/8	29	24	6	6	8	8	Waldo Co., ME	Christopher Ramsey	Bass Pro Shops	1983	345
184 1/8	25 3/8	25 4/8	18 1/8	4 4/8	4 5/8	6	6	Carroll Co., OH	Timothy F. Treadway	Timothy F. Treadway	1989	345
184 1/8	26 3/8	26 6/8	17 3/8	5	5 1/8	6	7	Muhlenberg Co., KY	Chad Mathis	Chad Mathis	1995	345
184 1/8	31	30 2/8	22	5 6/8	5 7/8	7	7	Montgomery Co., OH	Glenn Parks	Glenn Parks	1999	345
184 1/8	28 3/8	27 5/8	20 3/8	4 5/8	4 5/8	6	7	Wapello Co., IA	Ryan W. Scott	Ryan W. Scott	2000	345
184 1/8	24 6/8	25 1/8	20 7/8	5 7/8	5 6/8	5	5	Allamakee Co., IA	Steve Heim	Steve Heim	2002	345
184	25 2/8	25 1/8	16 2/8	4 3/8	4 3/8	6	6	Arkansas Co., AR	Willard L. Harper	Delwyn E. Harper	1946	353
184	27 4/8	29 1/8	18 4/8	5	4 7/8	5	6	Newton Co., GA	Gene Almand	Duncan A. Dobie	1966	353
184	24 5/8	24 4/8	18 5/8	5 1/8	5 2/8	7	6	Menominee Co., WI	Keith Miller	Charles Loberg	1969	353
184	28 1/8	27 6/8	20 5/8	5 2/8	5 1/8	6	6	Saline Co., KS	James R. Bell	James R. Bell	1985	353
184	25	24 4/8	17 4/8	4 1/8	4	6	6	Hart Co., GA	Kenton L. Adams	Kenton L. Adams	1986	353
184	28 6/8	27 6/8	20 4/8	4 5/8	4 5/8	6	6	Grayson Co., KY	Floyd Stone	Floyd Stone	1987	353
184	28 4/8	29 1/8	24 7/8	5	5 1/8	7	9	Allamakee Co., IA	William P. Mitchell	W.P. Mitchell & J. Bakewell	1989	353
184	27 2/8	26	20 4/8	5 6/8	5 4/8	5	5	Wapello Co., IA	Raymond M. Todey	Raymond M. Todey	1993	353
184	27 6/8	25 6/8	24 6/8	4 6/8	4 6/8	6	6	Douglas Co., WI	David H. Johnson	David H. Johnson	1998	353
183 7/8	27 7/8	28 3/8	20 1/8	6 2/8	6 5/8	6	7	Taylor Co., IA	Wayne Swartz	Spanky Greenville	1953	362
183 7/8	28	27 1/8	19 6/8	5	4 7/8	7	5	Forest Co., WI	James M. Thayer	James M. Thayer	1980	362
183 7/8	26 6/8	27 6/8	23 2/8	4 3/8	4 3/8	6	5	White Co., AR	W.A. Harden & C. Craven	Wilburn A. Harden	1993	362
183 7/8	27 7/8	27 5/8	20 2/8	5 2/8	5 1/8	5	6	Muhlenberg Co., KY	James E. Brewer	James E. Brewer	1997	362
183 7/8	29 3/8	27 3/8	22 5/8	5 1/8	5 1/8	6	5	Washington Co., KS	Rick B. Novak	Rick B. Novak	1997	362
183 7/8	26 5/8	26 5/8	18 5/8	3 7/8	3 7/8	6	6	Adams Co., IA	Gregory L. Andrews	Gregory L. Andrews	2000	362
183 7/8	26	26 2/8	18 3/8	4 2/8	4 2/8	5	5	Angelina Co., TX	Jeffery T. Capps	Jeffery T. Capps	2000	362
183 7/8	24 2/8	24	20 6/8	4 6/8	5	9	7	Naramata Creek, BC	Al J. Thibodeau	Al J. Thibodeau	2002	362
183 7/8	27 2/8	27 4/8	20 5/8	5 3/8	5 4/8	6	5	Scott Co., IA	Marlon J. Vander Heiden	Marlon J. Vander Heiden	2003	362
183 6/8	26 7/8	25 1/8	18 6/8	5 4/8	5 4/8	7	7	Pepin Co., WI	LaVerne Anibas	LaVerne Anibas	1965	371
183 6/8	26 7/8	26 4/8	21 2/8	5 7/8	5 5/8	5	6	Winona Co., MN	Picked Up	Kevin J. Nelsen	1967	371

Score	Main Beam R	Main Beam L	Inside Spread	Circ. R	Circ. L	Points R	Points L	Locality	Hunter	Owner	Date Killed	Rank
183 6/8	26 6/8	27 6/8	19 2/8	4 3/8	4 4/8	6	6	Clinton Co., IN	Stuart C. Snodgrass	Stuart C. Snodgrass	1977	371
183 6/8	30 7/8	29 7/8	24	5 5/8	5 4/8	6	8	Morris Co., KS	Craig C. Johnson	Craig C. Johnson	1991	371
183 6/8	27 4/8	27 1/8	22 2/8	5 2/8	5 3/8	6	6	Franklin Co., KS	Picked Up	B&C National Collection	1994	371
183 6/8	28 7/8	29 1/8	19 4/8	4 4/8	4 4/8	5	5	Sumner Co., KS	Larry D. Bacon	Larry D. Bacon	1995	371
183 6/8	27 5/8	27 5/8	19	5 1/8	5 1/8	5	5	Soundng Lake, AB	David W. Higman	David W. Higman	2001	371
183 6/8	26 5/8	26 6/8	20 6/8	6	6	5	5	Bureau Co., IL	Rebecca Ratay	Rebecca Ratay	2002	371
183 5/8	27 1/8	26	23 2/8	4 6/8	4 6/8	7	7	Buffalo Co., WI	Lee F. Spittler	Mrs. Lee F. Spittler	1953	379
183 5/8	30	29 3/8	24 5/8	4 7/8	5 1/8	6	5	Clark Co., IN	Donald B. Minnich	Donald B. Minnich	1999	379
183 5/8	28 2/8	28 6/8	21 5/8	4 5/8	4 4/8	7	5	Qu'Appelle River, SK	Anthony Roberts	Anthony Roberts	2000	379
183 5/8	27 6/8	27 1/8	20 3/8	5 6/8	5 7/8	5	5	Guthrie Co., IA	Charles S. Callaway	Charles S. Callaway	2001	379
183 5/8	28 4/8	28 2/8	18 1/8	5	4 6/8	5	5	Clay Co., IL	Scott Fritschle	Scott Fritschle	2002	379
183 4/8	26 6/8	26 6/8	18 2/8	5 3/8	5 4/8	6	6	Sumner Co., MO	Marvin F. Lentz	Marvin F. Lentz	1968	384
183 4/8	29 7/8	29 3/8	23 7/8	5 4/8	5 6/8	8	8	Holmes River, BC	Randy Lloyd	Randy Lloyd	1991	384
183 4/8	26 5/8	26 4/8	24 7/8	6 6/8	6 2/8	7	7	Madison Co., IA	Roy P. Mikesell	Roy P. Mikesell	1995	384
183 4/8	26 4/8	27 1/8	24	4 6/8	4 7/8	7	7	Douglas Co., WI	Michael Head	Michael Head	1999	384
183 3/8	21 5/8	23 3/8	19 3/8	5 4/8	5 2/8	9	9	Flathead Co., MT	Unknown	Edwin M. Sager	1957	388
183 3/8	27 1/8	26 4/8	18 5/8	4 3/8	4 4/8	9	9	Dorchester Co., MD	John R. Seifert, Jr.	John R. Seifert, Jr.	1973	388
183 3/8	27 5/8	27 4/8	20 5/8	5 2/8	5 2/8	6	6	Drew Co., AR	Jimmy Monk	Jimmy Monk	1978	388
183 3/8	26 1/8	26 1/8	18 7/8	4 6/8	4 7/8	5	5	McLean Co., KY	Lawrence G. Porter	Lawrence G. Porter	1980	388
183 3/8	26 7/8	27 2/8	19 7/8	5 4/8	5 2/8	6	6	St. Louis Co., MN	Unknown	Real Boulanger	1982	388
183 3/8	28 5/8	29 5/8	18 5/8	5 4/8	5 3/8	6	5	Franklin Co., ME	Real Boulanger	George W. Flaim	1990	388
183 3/8	27 5/8	27 1/8	20 1/8	5 2/8	5 3/8	5	5	Talbot Co., MD	Petey L. Councell	Petey L. Councell	1994	388
183 3/8	27 2/8	25	21 5/8	5 4/8	5 3/8	5	5	La Salle Co., IL	Bernard Ernat	Bernard Ernat	1996	388
183 3/8	29 1/8	29 6/8	20 4/8	5	5	6	6	Coos Co., NH	Frank Thurston	Frank Thurston	1997	388
183 3/8	26 6/8	26 7/8	21 1/8	5	5 2/8	9	9	Nemaha Co., KS	Roy D. Rissky	Roy D. Rissky	1998	388
183 3/8	27 4/8	27 3/8	17	4 7/8	5	6	6	Wayne Co., OH	Lloyd K. Eshler	Lloyd K. Eshler	2000	388
183 3/8	28	28	19 1/8	5	5	6	6	Pulaski Co., KY	Billy M. Haynes	Billy M. Haynes	2000	388
183 3/8	27 4/8	27 3/8	19 7/8	4 5/8	4 6/8	7	5	Anderson Co., KS	Brian K. Hanes	Brian K. Hanes	2001	388
183 2/8	26 7/8	26 7/8	16	5 4/8	5 4/8	7	7	Ashland Co., WI	Unknown	Martin Bonack	1900	401
183 2/8	25 5/8	26	19	5	5	6	6	St. Louis Co., MN	Unknown	Kenneth Wilson	PR 1917	401
183 2/8	29 1/8	28 2/8	20 4/8	4 1/8	4 4/8	5	5	Shawnee Co., KS	Mark W. Young	Mark W. Young	1990	401
183 2/8	26 5/8	28 5/8	20 4/8	4 4/8	4 4/8	5	5	Custer Co., MT	Dennis Young	Dennis Young	1994	401
183 2/8	29 1/8	29 6/8	27	5	4 7/8	6	6	Whiteside Co., IL	Jacob A. Amesquita	Jacob A. Amesquita	1995	401
183 2/8	28 7/8	27 6/8	18 5/8	4 6/8	4 6/8	7	7	Knox Co., IL	Bradley A. Wunder	Bradley A. Wunder	1995	401
183 2/8	24 4/8	22 6/8	18 7/8	5 5/8	5 6/8	7	7	Invermay, SK	Trevor Jennings	Trevor Jennings	1996	401
183 1/8	29 5/8	30 5/8	22 1/8	5 6/8	5 6/8	6	6	Guthrie Co., IA	Don McCarty	Chad Redfern	1962	408
183 1/8	27 7/8	28 6/8	21 5/8	5	5	6	6	Duval Co., TX	Charles Drennan	Bill Carter	1973	408
183 1/8	25 3/8	26 1/8	21 5/8	5 4/8	5 4/8	8	7	Nuevo Leon, MX	Thomas D. Brittingham	Thomas D. Brittingham	1990	408
183 1/8	27 1/8	27 2/8	19 3/8	4 6/8	4 5/8	6	6	Crawford Co., WI	Ray Volkert	Cabela's, Inc.	1990	408
183 1/8	26 1/8	26 4/8	21 1/8	5	5 2/8	6	6	Wabash Co., IL	Dale E. Strockbine	Dale E. Strockbine	1994	408
183 1/8	26 3/8	25 6/8	22 1/8	4 6/8	4 6/8	7	7	Cass Co., MO	Gerald E. Lemmer	Gerald E. Lemmer	1997	408
183 1/8	26 2/8	26 5/8	20 3/8	5 4/8	5 4/8	6	6	Chisago Co., MN	Timothy L. Ryan	Timothy L. Ryan	2000	408
183	27 1/8	27 7/8	18 6/8	4 6/8	4 6/8	5	5	Desha Co., AR	R.J. Diekhoff	Franzen Bros.	1954	408
183	26 2/8	25	19 6/8	5	5	9	9	Piedmont Lake, OH	J. Rumbaugh & J. Ruyan	J. Rumbaugh & J. Ruyan	1958	415
183	25 6/8	26	21	4 6/8	4 5/8	5	5	Red Deer River, AB	Picked Up	Ovar Uggen	1966	415
183	26 3/8	25 3/8	23	4 6/8	4 4/8	5	5	Emmet Co., IA	Bill Walstead	Bill Walstead	1974	415
183	28 4/8	28 1/8	20 4/8	5 5/8	5 5/8	6	6	Union Co., IA	Randy G. Hall	Randy G. Hall	1986	415
183	26 1/8	26 1/8	19 3/8	5	5	8	8	Lorne, MB	Alain G. Comte	Alain G. Comte	1987	415

WHITETAIL DEER - TYPICAL ANTLERS
Odocoileus virginianus virginianus and certain related subspecies

Score	Length of Main Beam R	L	Inside Spread	Circumference at Smallest Place Between Burr and First Point R	L	Number of Points R	L	Locality	Hunter	Owner	Date Killed	Rank
183	26 6/8	28 4/8	18 5/8	5 5/8	5 5/8	5	7	Van Buren Co., IA	Picked Up	Timothy J. Wilson	1990	415
183	26	24 7/8	18 2/8	5 6/8	5 6/8	5	5	Lincoln Co., NE	Kevin L. Wood	Kevin L. Wood	1999	415
183	29 4/8	28 5/8	20 4/8	5 3/8	5 3/8	5	5	Sedgwick Co., CO	Glenn W. Vinton	Glenn W. Vinton	2000	415
182 7/8	27 7/8	28 1/8	21 1/8	4 7/8	4 7/8	5	5	Iosco Co., MI	Harvey H. Keast	Harvey H. Keast	1938	424
182 7/8	27 4/8	28 2/8	19 3/8	5 5/8	5 5/8	6	5	Hale Co., AL	James C. Bailey	James C. Bailey	1974	424
182 7/8	26 4/8	25 6/8	19 2/8	5 3/8	5 3/8	6	7	Lyon Co., MN	Jim Anderson	LuAnn Anderson	1975	424
182 7/8	28 5/8	28 5/8	19	5 6/8	6	6	6	Wayne Co., OH	Gary E. Landry	Gary E. Landry	1975	424
182 7/8	29 1/8	28 3/8	20 1/8	5 2/8	5 3/8	7	6	Oromocto River, NB	Bruce MacGougan	Bruce MacGougan	1984	424
182 7/8	27 7/8	27 3/8	19 2/8	5	5 3/8	7	7	Noxubee Co., MS	Glen D. Jourdon	Glen D. Jourdon	1986	424
182 7/8	22	23 1/8	19 5/8	5	4 7/8	8	7	Rock Island Co., IL	Clifton L. Webster	Clifton L. Webster	1986	424
182 7/8	26 3/8	27	19 3/8	5	4 7/8	6	6	Cross Co., AR	B. Jason Franklin	B. Jason Franklin	1995	424
182 7/8	28 3/8	27 7/8	23 5/8	5 1/8	5	6	5	Monroe Co., IA	Les A. Bateman	Les A. Bateman	2001	424
182 6/8	28 2/8	28	22 6/8	4 6/8	4 6/8	6	5	Vilas Co., WI	George Sparks	Mac's Taxidermy	1942	433
182 6/8	28 4/8	28 7/8	19 3/8	4 1/8	4 1/8	6	6	Osage Co., MO	Picked Up	Ralph Reynolds	1972	433
182 6/8	26	25 4/8	18	4 7/8	5	8	6	Webb Co., TX	George Strait	George Strait	1988	433
182 6/8	28 2/8	28 6/8	19	6 3/8	6 2/8	8	6	Labette Co., KS	David W. Steeby	Cabela's, Inc.	1989	433
182 6/8	27 5/8	28 4/8	19 4/8	4 6/8	4 4/8	9	7	Lee Co., IA	John L. Kite	John L. Kite	1990	433
182 6/8	25 3/8	25 1/8	22	4 3/8	4 3/8	6	6	Coahuila, MX	Manuel A. Flores Rojas	Manuel A. Flores Rojas	1990	433
182 6/8	24 5/8	24 3/8	20 6/8	5 2/8	5 1/8	8	7	Pembina River, AB	Curtis R. Siegfried	Curtis R. Siegfried	1991	433
182 6/8	28 6/8	28 3/8	22 6/8	5	4 7/8	5	5	La Salle Co., TX	Daniel A. Herson	Daniel A. Herson	1995	433
182 6/8	29 7/8	29 4/8	20 1/8	4 3/8	4 5/8	7	9	Wayne Co., IA	Donald P. Greenlee	Donald P. Greenlee	1997	433
182 6/8	26	26	18 4/8	4 4/8	4 5/8	6	5	Kelvington, SK	Roger D. Bibee	Roger D. Bibee	1999	433
182 6/8	26 7/8	26 1/8	19	4 6/8	4 6/8	5	5	Roanoke Co., VA	Dwayne E. Webster	Dwayne E. Webster	1999	433
182 5/8	27 6/8	28 4/8	21 5/8	5 6/8	5 5/8	6	8	Virden, MB	Darryl Gray	Darryl Gray	1957	444
182 5/8	23 6/8	24 3/8	19 4/8	5 5/8	5 7/8	6	8	Yuma Co., CO	Ivan W. Rhodes	Ivan W. Rhodes	1978	444
182 5/8	28 3/8	28 4/8	24 1/8	5 2/8	5 1/8	5	6	Jefferson Co., IA	William J. Waugh	William J. Waugh	1985	444
182 5/8	24 6/8	26 3/8	18 1/8	5	5 1/8	5	5	Jones Co., SD	Richard A. Gordon	Richard A. Gordon	1989	444
182 5/8	24	23 4/8	21 6/8	6 6/8	6 5/8	8	7	Crawford Creek, SK	Dale C. Conacher	Dale C. Conacher	1991	444
182 5/8	21 5/8	21 3/8	14 2/8	5 5/8	5 4/8	8	7	Noble Co., OH	William J. Estadt	William J. Estadt	1993	444
182 5/8	24	23 7/8	20 1/8	5 4/8	5 3/8	5	5	Boundary Co., ID	Aaron M. McNall	Aaron M. McNall	1993	444
182 5/8	24 4/8	23 5/8	20 5/8	4 6/8	4 6/8	6	7	Mantagao Lake, MB	Stephen Obelnicki	Stephen Obelnicki	1993	444
182 5/8	25 4/8	26 4/8	20 1/8	5 7/8	5 7/8	8	6	Jefferson Co., IL	Jerry R. Simmons	Jerry R. Simmons	1993	444
182 5/8	27 6/8	28 5/8	19 2/8	5 4/8	5 6/8	7	5	Republic Co., KS	Jody Hadachek	Jody Hadachek	1995	444
182 5/8	29 4/8	30 4/8	27 1/8	5 3/8	5 3/8	4	5	Viking, AB	Charles D. Dobbs	Charles D. Dobbs	2001	444
182 4/8	28 5/8	29	23 6/8	5 3/8	5 1/8	6	6	Carrot River, SK	Lori Lonson	J.D. Andrews	1960	455
182 4/8	27	26 6/8	18 4/8	5 3/8	5 3/8	7	5	Warren Co., MO	Donald L. Tanner	Donald L. Tanner	1968	455

Score	Main Beam R	Main Beam L	Inside Spread	Circ. R	Circ. L	Points R	Points L	Locality	Hunter	Owner	Date	Rank
182 4/8	28 3/8	27 1/8	23 4/8	5 5/8	5 5/8	7	7	Kanabec Co., MN	Steven R. Berg	Steven R. Berg	1973	455
182 4/8	26 3/8	26 4/8	15 4/8	5	5 4/8	6	6	Jackson Co., IN	Rocky Deakin	Rocky Deakin	1985	455
182 4/8	27	28 4/8	19 2/8	4 2/8	4 2/8	6	6	Franklin Co., IL	Tim Broy	Tim Broy	1997	455
182 4/8	25 5/8	25 7/8	18 4/8	4 5/8	4 6/8	6	6	Maverick Co., TX	Christopher J. Roswell	Christopher J. Roswell	1997	455
182 4/8	26 3/8	26 5/8	24 6/8	5 3/8	5 2/8	6	6	Wells Co., IN	Matt Roush	Matt Roush	1999	455
182 3/8	28 1/8	27 3/8	20 5/8	5 4/8	5 4/8	5	5	Itasca Co., MN	Harry Haug	Harry Haug	1959	462
182 3/8	28 2/8	27 2/8	17 1/8	5 2/8	5 2/8	6	6	St. Louis Co., MN	Unknown	John R. Steffes, Sr.	PR 1960	462
182 3/8	27	26 5/8	23 1/8	5 7/8	5 7/8	6	6	Waubaunsee, KS	Norman Anderson	Norman Anderson	1966	462
182 3/8	25 5/8	25 1/8	18 1/8	4 6/8	4 6/8	6	6	Marshall Co., IA	Barbara Daniel	Terry Daniel	1967	462
182 3/8	25 4/8	25 6/8	21 3/8	6	6	5	5	Freeborn Co., MN	Robert H. Dowd	Robert H. Dowd	1969	462
182 3/8	28 1/8	27 1/8	21 5/8	4 4/8	4 5/8	6	6	Braxton Co., WV	William D. Given	William D. Given	1976	462
182 3/8	28 3/8	27 3/8	19 1/8	4 3/8	4 4/8	6	6	Buffalo Co., WI	Anthony F. Wolfe	Anthony F. Wolfe	1984	462
182 3/8	26 5/8	26 7/8	15 6/8	5 5/8	5 6/8	6	6	Unknown	Unknown	Rick Stover	PR 1993	462
182 3/8	26 4/8	25 5/8	22	5 6/8	6	7	7	Derwent, AB	Michael A. Miller	Michael A. Miller	1994	462
182 3/8	25 5/8	26	19 7/8	4 2/8	4 3/8	6	6	S. Saskatchewan River, SK	Jim Clary	Jim Clary	1996	462
182 3/8	27 7/8	26 6/8	23 4/8	5 5/8	5 7/8	5	5	Monroe Co., IA	Elisha G. Hugen	Elisha G. Hugen	1996	462
182 3/8	26 2/8	26 5/8	17 7/8	5	5	7	7	McPherson Co., NE	Leonard Bergantzel	Leonard Bergantzel	1999	462
182 3/8	29 6/8	27 6/8	18 3/8	5 1/8	5 1/8	7	7	Polk Co., MN	Benjamin D. Faldet	Benjamin D. Faldet	2000	462
182 2/8	27	27	20 4/8	5	4 7/8	5	5	Sullivan Co., PA	Floyd Reibson	Maynard Reibson	1930	475
182 2/8	27 1/8	26 4/8	19 6/8	5 1/8	5 2/8	5	5	Claiborne Co., MS	R.L. Bobo	R.L. Bobo	1955	475
182 2/8	27 1/8	26 6/8	19 3/8	4 7/8	5 1/8	6	6	Nicollet Co., MN	T.J. Merkley	T.J. Merkley	1966	475
182 2/8	26	26 4/8	18 1/8	5 2/8	5 1/8	5	5	Park Co., MT	Jim Whitt	Jim Whitt	1983	475
182 2/8	28 1/8	27	20	5 3/8	5 5/8	6	6	Champaign Co., IL	Tom Babb	Tom Babb	1985	475
182 2/8	29 3/8	29	19 4/8	5 7/8	6	6	6	Forest Co., WI	Richard J. Moore	Richard J. Moore	1987	475
182 2/8	24 4/8	25 4/8	17 2/8	5 4/8	5 4/8	6	6	Stearns Co., MN	Michael G. Maki	Michael G. Maki	1988	475
182 2/8	27 1/8	25 6/8	23 4/8	5 3/8	5 1/8	5	5	Hancock Co., IL	Robert A. Reed	Robert A. Reed	1988	475
182 2/8	29	25 7/8	18 7/8	5 2/8	5	6	6	Bonnyville, AB	Jim Baik	Jim Baik	1998	475
182 2/8	30 1/8	30	19 2/8	4 5/8	4 5/8	5	5	Hancock Co., IL	Jeffrey L. Akers	Jeffrey L. Akers	2000	475
182 2/8	27 2/8	28 6/8	20 1/8	5 5/8	5 7/8	8	8	Muskingum Co., OH	Charles E. Goldsmith	Charles E. Goldsmith	2001	475
182 1/8	25 6/8	25 2/8	22 7/8	5 6/8	5 5/8	5	5	Round Lake, SK	Jesse Bates	Jesse Bates	1984	486
182 1/8	27 4/8	26 6/8	24	5	5 1/8	6	6	Frontier Co., NE	Robert G. Bortner	Robert G. Bortner	1985	486
182 1/8	27	26 7/8	22 1/8	5 2/8	5 1/8	5	5	Lincoln Co., MO	David L. Mudd	David L. Mudd	1988	486
182 1/8	28	27 4/8	25 4/8	6	6 2/8	7	7	MacCafferty Lake, AB	Alan S. Bell	Alan S. Bell	1990	486
182 1/8	28	28 1/8	22	5	5	6	5	Hardin Co., OH	Tim Campbell	Tim Campbell	1991	486
182 1/8	29 5/8	30 5/8	24	5	5	7	6	Clark Co., IN	William F. Mills II	William F. Mills II	1995	486
182 1/8	28 2/8	27 4/8	23 1/8	4 7/8	4 6/8	8	7	Adair Co., MO	Selby Lusher	Selby Lusher	1996	486
182 1/8	27 4/8	28 5/8	20 3/8	5 1/8	5 1/8	6	6	Richland Co., OH	Bruce L. King	Bruce L. King	2000	486
182 1/8	29 1/8	27 4/8	19 5/8	4 6/8	4 7/8	5	5	Jackson Co., MI	Brian T. Kessman	Brian T. Kessman	2002	486
182	24 4/8	25	23	4	4 3/8	7	7	Zap, ND	Wally Duckwitz	Sioux Sporting Goods	1962	495
182	28 1/8	28 4/8	22 6/8	4 5/8	4 4/8	5	5	St. Louis Co., MN	Unknown	George W. Flaim	1975	495
182	27	26 5/8	21 2/8	5	5	5	5	Unknown	Bernie Benson	Kenneth W. Springer	1976	495
182	24 7/8	24 5/8	18 4/8	5 4/8	5 6/8	7	5	Polk Co., MN	E. Norgaard, M. Sorenson, D. Sorenson & K. Oraskovich	E. Norgaard, M. Sorenson & D. Sorenson	1986	495
182	27 7/8	28 4/8	21 4/8	5 1/8	5 1/8	6	6	Monona Co., IA	Jerry W. Conover	Jerry W. Conover	1990	495
182	23	25	19	5 3/8	5 3/8	6	6	Crawford Co., WI	Andrew D. Marg	Andrew D. Marg	1995	495
182	25	24 1/8	22 6/8	5 7/8	5 7/8	5	5	Henderson Co., IL	Nicky J. Clark, Jr.	Nicky J. Clark, Jr.	1999	495
182	24 1/8	23 3/8	22 3/8	5 4/8	5 5/8	6	6	Henderson Co., IL	Jeffrey A. Bloise	Jeffrey A. Bloise	2000	495

WHITETAIL DEER - TYPICAL ANTLERS

Odocoileus virginianus virginianus and certain related subspecies

Score	Length of Main Beam R	L	Inside Spread	Circumference at Smallest Place Between Burr and First Point R	L	Number of Points R	L	Locality	Hunter	Owner	Date Killed	Rank
182	27 7/8	28 1/8	23 7/8	4 5/8	5 1/8	7	7	Hancock Co., OH	Larry G. Rader	Larry G. Rader	2000	495
182	27 1/8	27 1/8	25	5	5	5	6	Peoria Co., IL	Thomas Missen	Thomas Missen	2001	495
181 7/8	26 3/8	26 3/8	21 1/8	5	4 7/8	6	6	Jackson Co., IA	Ambrose Beck	Ambrose Beck	1963	505
181 7/8	26 7/8	27 1/8	23 3/8	5 4/8	5 3/8	8	7	Cottonwood Co., MN	Picked Up	MN Div. of Fish & Wildl.	1963	505
181 7/8	24 5/8	25 1/8	26 5/8	5 7/8	5 3/8	7	7	Todd Co., MN	Alvin Tvrdik	Alvin Tvrdik	1965	505
181 7/8	24 4/8	24 4/8	15 5/8	4 3/8	4 4/8	6	6	McMullen Co., TX	Oscar Hassette	Bill Carter	1971	505
181 7/8	26 2/8	26 2/8	21 3/8	4 6/8	4 6/8	5	5	Hotchkiss, AB	Andy G. Petkus	Andy G. Petkus	1984	505
181 7/8	26 5/8	27 3/8	21 5/8	4 4/8	4 4/8	5	5	Clearwater Co., ID	Richard E. Carver	Richard E. Carver	1985	505
181 7/8	27 4/8	27 5/8	20 5/8	4 4/8	4 4/8	5	6	Whitman Co., WA	George A. Cook III	George A. Cook III	1985	505
181 7/8	24 6/8	25 2/8	17 1/8	5 4/8	5 4/8	7	7	Lesser Slave Lake, AB	Picked Up	Jerry Napier	1985	505
181 7/8	28 5/8	27 4/8	22 1/8	4 6/8	4 6/8	5	5	Coahuila, MX	German L. Flores	German L. Flores	1986	505
181 7/8	25 3/8	25 4/8	23 5/8	5 3/8	5	5	5	Guilford Co., NC	Terry E. Daffron	Terry E. Daffron	1987	505
181 7/8	25 4/8	26 3/8	21 1/8	5 2/8	5 2/8	5	5	Alice Lake, AB	Dave S. Seitz	Dave S. Seitz	1989	505
181 7/8	27	24 7/8	22 1/8	4 7/8	5	6	7	Wright Co., MN	Craig S. Hansen	Craig S. Hansen	1992	505
181 7/8	25 1/8	27 2/8	23 6/8	4 7/8	5	8	9	Ghost River, AB	Dean Lee	Dean Lee	1995	505
181 7/8	26 5/8	26 5/8	20 4/8	5 2/8	5 2/8	7	7	Washington Co., MN	Daniel F. Gallagher	Daniel F. Gallagher	2001	505
181 6/8	23 6/8	23 3/8	20 6/8	5 3/8	5 2/8	5	5	Lyon Co., KS	Kenneth C. Haynes	Kenneth C. Haynes	1969	519
181 6/8	26 1/8	26 4/8	17 6/8	6	6 1/8	5	5	Wabasha Co., MN	Lee G. Partington	Lee G. Partington	1971	519
181 6/8	25 5/8	25 5/8	24	4 6/8	4 6/8	6	7	Nuevo Leon, MX	J.P. Davis	J.P. Davis	1985	519
181 6/8	25 5/8	26 6/8	23 6/8	5	4 7/8	6	7	Montgomery Co., MD	Gary F. Menso	Gary F. Menso	1985	519
181 6/8	27 5/8	27 7/8	21 4/8	4 4/8	4 3/8	5	5	Sussex Co., DE	Donald L. Betts	Donald L. Betts	1989	519
181 6/8	27 5/8	28 3/8	21 2/8	4 6/8	5 3/8	6	6	Bourbon Co., KS	Larry Daly	Larry Daly	1990	519
181 6/8	27 7/8	28 4/8	18 4/8	5	5 2/8	7	6	Davis Co., IA	Craig S. Heaverlo	Craig S. Heaverlo	1994	519
181 6/8	28 7/8	30 4/8	24	5 6/8	5 6/8	5	5	Cando, SK	Karl Oliver	Karl Oliver	1998	519
181 5/8	27 6/8	27 6/8	21 5/8	5 2/8	5 2/8	6	6	Ionia Co., MI	Lester Bowen	Richard Bowen	1947	527
181 5/8	24 1/8	25	21 3/8	4 4/8	4 6/8	6	6	La Salle Co., TX	Buck Turman	Lawson W. Walden	1947	527
181 5/8	28 2/8	27 2/8	19 7/8	3 7/8	4 1/8	6	6	Pierce Co., WI	Raymond G. Miller, Sr.	Raymond G. Miller, Sr.	1960	527
181 5/8	25 5/8	25 7/8	19 7/8	5 4/8	5 4/8	6	7	Wilkinson Co., MS	Ronnie P. Whitaker	Ronnie P. Whitaker	1981	527
181 5/8	26 4/8	27 6/8	21 5/8	6 1/8	6 3/8	6	6	Wabash Co., IL	Mike Drone	Mike Drone	1987	527
181 5/8	28	27 5/8	25 3/8	4 6/8	4 6/8	5	5	Blaine Co., MT	David A. Sprinkle	David A. Sprinkle	1989	527
181 5/8	27 2/8	27 3/8	22 1/8	6 7/8	6 7/8	6	6	Porcupine Hills, SK	Brian R. Anderson	Brian R. Anderson	1993	527
181 5/8	27	27 7/8	17 5/8	4 6/8	4 6/8	5	5	Pike Co., IL	George R. Metcalf	George R. Metcalf	1995	527
181 5/8	28 5/8	28	19 3/8	5 4/8	5 2/8	5	5	Des Moines Co., IA	Joseph J. Birkenstock	Joseph J. Birkenstock	1996	527
181 5/8	26 5/8	25 7/8	24 1/8	4 5/8	4 5/8	7	6	Nipawin, SK	Steve Clifford	Steve Clifford	1996	527
181 5/8	24 7/8	25 6/8	24 1/8	5 1/8	5 3/8	6	5	Racine Co., WI	Andrae D'Acquisto	Andrae D'Acquisto	1996	527
181 5/8	25 2/8	25 2/8	16 6/8	5 5/8	5 4/8	6	6	Sawyer Co., WI	Picked Up	Teresa Kleutsch	1996	527

Score								Locality	Hunter	Owner	Date	Rank
181 5/8	24 1/8	24	17 7/8	5	5 1/8	5	5	Fulton Co., IL	George S. Hadsall	George S. Hadsall	1999	527
181 5/8	25 7/8	25 5/8	19 7/8	7	7	9	5	Dixon Co., NE	Kirk C. Kneifl	Kirk C. Kneifl	1999	527
181 5/8	26 7/8	27 7/8	22 3/8	5 1/8	5 1/8	5	5	Berrien Co., MI	Steven E. Coleman	Steven E. Coleman	2000	527
181 5/8	24	26 5/8	19	5 2/8	5 2/8	8	6	Edgar Co., IL	Christopher L. Newhart	Christopher L. Newhart	2001	527
181 4/8	29	28 5/8	23 5/8	4 5/8	4 5/8	5	7	Oxford Co., ME	Dean W. Peaco	Dean W. Peaco	1953	543
181 4/8	25 2/8	25 6/8	22 7/8	5 7/8	5 7/8	7	7	Licking Co., OH	Arlee McCullough	Arlee McCullough	1962	543
181 4/8	28 4/8	27 7/8	22	5 3/8	5 3/8	5	5	Wadena Co., MN	Lester Zentner, Jr.	E.E. Patson	1962	543
181 4/8	26	28 5/8	18 6/8	5 2/8	5 2/8	9	9	Canton, IL	Arnold C. Hegele	Arnold C. Hegele	1968	543
181 4/8	25 4/8	27	22 6/8	5 6/8	5 6/8	6	6	Pine Lake, AB	Robert Crosby	Robert Crosby	1977	543
181 4/8	26 1/8	27 2/8	20 2/8	4 6/8	4 6/8	7	6	Trempealeau Co., WI	Randy A. Hoff	Randy A. Hoff	1987	543
181 4/8	26 6/8	26	18 2/8	5	5	7	7	Will Co., IL	James J.A. O'Keefe	James J.A. O'Keefe	1989	543
181 4/8	26 7/8	26 5/8	21	4 4/8	4 4/8	5	5	Wayne Co., IA	Picked Up	Ron King	1990	543
181 4/8	29 1/8	29	21	5	5 1/8	5	5	Grant Co., WI	Charles P. Fralick	Charles P. Fralick	1996	543
181 4/8	25 6/8	25 4/8	20	5 4/8	5 4/8	6	6	Valley Lake, AB	Terry O. Hobbs	Terry O. Hobbs	2000	543
181 4/8	28 4/8	28 4/8	20 1/8	4 7/8	4 7/8	9	9	Cole Co., MO	Douglas S. Middleton	Douglas S. Middleton	2000	543
181 4/8	26 1/8	26 6/8	18	5 3/8	5 3/8	6	6	Vernon Co., WI	Timothy T. Nordengren	Timothy T. Nordengren	2001	543
181 3/8	26 3/8	26 3/8	20 3/8	4 4/8	4 4/8	7	7	Bureau Co., IL	William J. Calbow, Jr.	William J. Calbow, Jr.	2002	556
181 3/8	27 4/8	27 5/8	20 6/8	4 4/8	4 4/8	6	7	Portage Co., OH	Robert M. Smith	Robert M. Smith	1953	556
181 3/8	25 2/8	24 3/8	21 2/8	5 6/8	5 6/8	7	7	Southey, SK	A.K. Flaman	Sam Peterson	1955	556
181 3/8	24 7/8	27 4/8	18 1/8	5	5	6	6	Orange Co., NY	Roy Vail	Roy Vail	1960	556
181 3/8	24 5/8	24 5/8	18 5/8	6 2/8	6 2/8	6	6	Pope Co., IL	Jack A. Higgs	Jack A. Higgs	1963	556
181 3/8	28	26 6/8	18 5/8	4 6/8	4 5/8	6	6	Polk Co., IA	Bob Boydston	Kevin Freymiller	1972	556
181 3/8	26 2/8	27 6/8	19 3/8	5	5	5	5	Houston Co., MN	Picked Up	Robert A. Morken	1980	556
181 3/8	26	25	17 5/8	4 5/8	4 5/8	5	6	Winona Co., MN	Kenneth W. Schreiber	Kenneth W. Schreiber	1980	556
181 3/8	24 1/8	24	20 4/8	5 3/8	5 3/8	8	7	Harding Co., SD	Cregg Else	Cregg Else	1985	556
181 3/8	26 7/8	26 7/8	18 4/8	4 7/8	5 1/8	5	6	Warren Co., IN	Todd J. Hemke	Todd J. Hemke	1987	556
181 3/8	24 6/8	26 3/8	19 7/8	5 5/8	4 7/8	6	6	Adair Co., IA	Gale D. Johnston	Gale D. Johnston	1995	556
181 3/8	28 2/8	29 3/8	21 2/8	5 1/8	5 5/8	8	8	Stafford Co., KS	Aaron W. King	Aaron W. King	1995	556
181 3/8	26 3/8	26 3/8	19 7/8	5 1/8	5 1/8	7	7	Meadow Lake, SK	Freeman R. Bell	Freeman R. Bell	1997	556
181 3/8	27	27	17 6/8	6 4/8	6 4/8	8	5	Lawrence Co., IL	Charles Morehead	Charles Morehead	2002	556
181 2/8	27	27 4/8	21 2/8	5 3/8	5 3/8	7	7	Sheridan Co., MT	Arthur M. Hagan, Sr.	Ken Hagan	1957	569
181 2/8	26	26	25 7/8	5 4/8	5 4/8	7	6	Hardin Co., KY	Thomas L. House	Thomas L. House	1963	569
181 2/8	25 7/8	25 7/8	20	4 3/8	4 3/8	6	5	Pike Co., IL	Stephen J. Smith	Stephen J. Smith	1973	569
181 2/8	30	30 1/8	21	4 3/8	4 3/8	5	6	Lafayette Co., WI	Michael H. Morrissey	Michael H. Morrissey	1982	569
181 2/8	25	25 2/8	20 6/8	5 2/8	5 2/8	6	6	Scotland Co., MO	Jerry Kennedy	Jerry Kennedy	1989	569
181 2/8	27 7/8	28 2/8	19 5/8	5	5	6	5	McBride Lake, SK	Bryan Rothenburger	Bryan Rothenburger	1993	569
181 2/8	25 6/8	27	23 6/8	4 7/8	4 7/8	6	6	Sangamon Co., IL	Jack D. Davis	Jack D. Davis	1995	569
181 2/8	28 2/8	28 2/8	22 2/8	4 7/8	4 7/8	5	5	Will Co., IL	Jozef H. Skubisz	Jozef H. Skubisz	1996	569
181 2/8	26 2/8	25 2/8	18	5	5	5	5	Sangamon Co., IL	Sean Shymansky	Sean Shymansky	1997	569
181 2/8	28 4/8	26 5/8	19 7/8	5 5/8	5 5/8	8	8	Fawcett Lake, AB	Robert Neimor	Robert Neimor	1998	569
181 2/8	28 3/8	26 3/8	23 2/8	6 1/8	6 3/8	5	5	Morrison Co., MN	Scott A. Shonka	Scott A. Shonka	2000	569
181 1/8	26 5/8	27 1/8	21 6/8	5 2/8	5 2/8	7	6	Elk River, MN	John E. Bush	Bass Pro Shops	1870	580
181 1/8	27 1/8	28	20 7/8	5 2/8	5 2/8	6	6	Polk Co., MN	Henry Cook	Steven D. Cook	1938	580
181 1/8	28	26 2/8	17 3/8	5 4/8	5 4/8	5	7	Waldo Co., ME	Clarendon Pomeroy	Larry C. Pomeroy	1946	580
181 1/8	27 6/8	26 1/8	18 5/8	5	5	6	5	Frio Co., TX	Warren Smith	Roy Hindes	PR 1950	580
181 1/8	26 1/8	27 6/8	20 7/8	6 2/8	6 2/8	7	10	Empress, SK	Don Leach	Don Leach	1960	580
181 1/8	27 3/8	25 1/8	20 5/8	5 3/8	5 3/8	7	7	Wood River, SK	Jeremy Egan	Jeremy Egan	1990	580
181 1/8	24 5/8	25 6/8	20	5 1/8	5	7	7	Crawford Co., WI	Randall E. Kreuscher	Randall E. Kreuscher	1992	580

WHITETAIL DEER - TYPICAL ANTLERS
Odocoileus virginianus virginianus and certain related subspecies

Score	Length of Main Beam R	L	Inside Spread	Circumference at Smallest Place Between Burr and First Point R	L	Number of Points R	L	Locality	Hunter	Owner	Date Killed	Rank
181 1/8	27 4/8	27 1/8	19	5 7/8	6	7	6	Henry Co., MO	William C. Buckner	William C. Buckner	1997	580
181 1/8	26 4/8	27 1/8	19 3/8	5 4/8	5 3/8	6	5	Avoyelles Parish, LA	Donald A. Riviere	Donald A. Riviere	1998	580
181 1/8	29 5/8	28 5/8	18 4/8	5 7/8	5 7/8	5	6	St. Clair Co., IL	Dean R. Billhartz	Dean R. Billhartz	1999	580
181 1/8	25 7/8	25 6/8	20 1/8	5 5/8	5 4/8	8	6	Manitowoc Co., WI	Ronald R. Rieth	Ronald R. Rieth	1999	580
181 1/8	30 1/8	29 1/8	22 3/8	5 1/8	5 3/8	8	6	Waushara Co., WI	Kenneth G. Wilson	Kenneth G. Wilson	2001	580
181	25 7/8	24 6/8	22 3/8	4 7/8	5 3/8	6	8	Beltrami Co., MN	Robert C. Shaw	Robert C. Shaw	1910	592
181	26 3/8	26 2/8	20 2/8	4 7/8	5	6	5	Ransom Co., ND	Gerald V. Sweet	Gerald V. Sweet	1959	592
181	25 6/8	26 5/8	19	5 6/8	5	5	5	Langlade Co., WI	Elroy W. Timm	Elroy W. Timm	1959	592
181	27	26 5/8	20	5 7/8	5 7/8	5	6	Stettler, AB	Archie Smith	Archie Smith	1962	592
181	29 3/8	29 1/8	18	5 6/8	5 4/8	5	5	Rutland Co., VT	Picked Up	Gary E. Merrill	1971	592
181	28 3/8	28 4/8	20	4 4/8	4 4/8	5	5	Wood Co., WI	James D. Wyman	James D. Wyman	1977	592
181	26 5/8	26 2/8	21 2/8	6 2/8	6 3/8	7	8	Lac qui Parle Co., MN	Mary A. Barvels	Mary A. Barvels	1978	592
181	27 7/8	27	20 3/8	5 2/8	5 1/8	8	8	Gallatin Co., KY	Kenneth D. Hoffman	Kenneth D. Hoffman	1979	592
181	27 1/8	27 2/8	20 7/8	5 2/8	5 2/8	7	8	Foam Lake, SK	Ray Howe	Ray Howe	1991	592
181	27 6/8	26 6/8	20 6/8	5 3/8	5 4/8	9	7	Adair Co., MO	Michael D. Hill	Michael D. Hill	1992	592
181	26 4/8	27 6/8	20 2/8	4 7/8	5	7	7	Saskatchewan	Unknown	Tom Eustace	1999	592
180 7/8	26 5/8	28	17 3/8	4 4/8	4 4/8	5	5	Marinette Co., WI	Albert Giese	Kenneth J. Giese	1938	603
180 7/8	29	29 6/8	20 4/8	5 2/8	5 2/8	7	6	Jones Co., GA	James H.C. Kitchens	James H.C. Kitchens	1957	603
180 7/8	22 1/8	23 1/8	16 7/8	5 3/8	5 1/8	7	7	Chicot Co., AR	Lee R. Mathews	Henry Mathews	1963	603
180 7/8	29 6/8	29 2/8	24 1/8	5 2/8	5	6	5	Keya Paha Co., NE	Steve R. Pecsenye	Steve R. Pecsenye	1966	603
180 7/8	25 7/8	25 3/8	17 7/8	5 1/8	5 1/8	8	7	Castor, AB	Norman D. Stienwand	Norman D. Stienwand	1981	603
180 7/8	28 5/8	27 7/8	22 1/8	5 2/8	5 3/8	6	6	Polk Co., MN	Daniel Omdahl	Daniel Omdahl	1987	603
180 7/8	26 4/8	26 6/8	22	5 2/8	5	5	5	Wayne Co., IA	Richard L. Spencer	Richard L. Spencer	1990	603
180 7/8	27 1/8	26	18 1/8	6 4/8	6 1/8	7	7	Monona Co., IA	Picked Up	David E. Fender	1991	603
180 7/8	26 7/8	26 5/8	22 1/8	5 3/8	5 3/8	7	5	Cedar Co., IA	Glenn U. Farrington	Glenn U. Farrington	1994	603
180 7/8	27	25 6/8	19 7/8	5 2/8	5 2/8	5	5	Adair Co., IA	Picked Up	Jerry Funke	1995	603
180 7/8	27 2/8	26 6/8	21 5/8	5 2/8	5 4/8	5	5	Rush Co., IN	Cain M. Grocox	Cain M. Grocox	1995	603
180 7/8	26 6/8	25 7/8	19	5 4/8	5 2/8	8	8	Dafoe, SK	Jamin Bolt	Jamin Bolt	1996	603
180 7/8	27 6/8	25 4/8	18 7/8	4 5/8	4 4/8	6	7	Audubon Co., IA	Michael M. Miller	Keith E. Brock	1996	603
180 7/8	25 5/8	26	21 1/8	5 1/8	5	8	7	Clayton Co., IA	Robert M. Hefel	Robert M. Hefel	1998	603
180 6/8	30	29 4/8	23 4/8	5 6/8	5 6/8	6	6	Hancock Co., ME	Cyrus H. Whitaker	Orrin W. Whitaker	1912	617
180 6/8	31 6/8	31 2/8	19 4/8	6	5 5/8	8	8	New Brunswick	Unknown	Acad. Nat. Sci., Phil.	1937	617
180 6/8	26 6/8	26	25	5	4 4/8	6	9	Dimmit Co., TX	Edward Gardner	Edward Gardner	1937	617
180 6/8	26 3/8	26 1/8	18 2/8	5 5/8	5 5/8	6	6	Jefferson Co., IA	James J. Hoskins	James J. Hoskins	1982	617
180 6/8	25 4/8	25 7/8	19	5 2/8	5 1/8	5	5	Marshall Co., MN	Scott T. Rabehl	Scott T. Rabehl	1987	617
180 6/8	27 2/8	28 3/8	22	4 7/8	5	6	7	Pike Lake, SK	Roger Ireland	Roger Ireland	1990	617

Score	Main Beam R	Main Beam L	Inside Spread	Circ. R	Circ. L	Pts R	Pts L	Locality	Hunter	Owner	Date	Rank
180 6/8	27 6/8	27 6/8	26	5 1/8	5 1/8	5	5	Sounding Lake, AB	Morris Thompson	Morris Thompson	1993	617
180 6/8	27 2/8	26 5/8	17 6/8	4 7/8	5	5	5	Anne Arundel Co., MD	Paul H. Anderson, Jr.	Paul H. Anderson, Jr.	1995	617
180 6/8	28 3/8	28 5/8	16 4/8	5 4/8	5 4/8	6	8	Linn Co., MO	Picked Up	Doug D. Davis	1998	617
180 6/8	29 6/8	27 1/8	22 5/8	4 6/8	4 5/8	5	5	Horse Lake, SK	Cheryl Kaban	Cheryl Kaban	1999	617
180 6/8	23 4/8	25 2/8	24 6/8	5 4/8	5 6/8	6	6	Drayton Valley, AB	Peter Underwood	Peter Underwood	1999	617
180 5/8	25	27 4/8	20	4 4/8	4 4/8	6	6	Iosco Co., MI	Zack T. Shellenbarger	Zack T. Shellenbarger	2000	629
180 5/8	24 7/8	23 4/8	19 7/8	4 7/8	4 6/8	7	7	Maverick Co., TX	Jim Webb	Richard H. Bennett	1912	629
180 5/8	25	25 1/8	18 3/8	5 3/8	5 3/8	7	6	Treasure Co., MT	Jack Welch	Jack Welch	1958	629
180 5/8	25	23 6/8	23 3/8	4 7/8	5	6	7	Cheat Mt., WV	Joseph V. Volitis	Bass Pro Shops	1969	629
180 5/8	28 3/8	25	18 7/8	4 4/8	4 4/8	5	8	St. Landry Parish, LA	Shawn P. Ortego	Shawn P. Ortego	1975	629
180 5/8	29 6/8	29 3/8	22 5/8	4 5/8	4 3/8	5	5	Adams Co., IL	Kenneth E. Klauser	Kenneth E. Klauser	1990	629
180 5/8	25 6/8	24 7/8	19 3/8	6 2/8	6 4/8	6	5	Jim Hogg Co., TX	Michael L. Vickers	Michael L. Vickers	1991	629
180 5/8	26	26 3/8	21 3/8	5 4/8	5 4/8	6	6	Tuscarawas Co., OH	Thomas K. Winters	Thomas K. Winters	1991	629
180 5/8	27 6/8	27 2/8	23 3/8	5 1/8	5	8	6	Good Spirit Lake, SK	Grant Landstad	Grant Landstad	1993	629
180 5/8	26 3/8	26 2/8	18 3/8	4 1/8	4 1/8	6	6	Turner Co., SD	Nicklaus J. Schrag	Nicklaus J. Schrag	1996	629
180 5/8	23	23 7/8	19 3/8	5 3/8	5 3/8	7	5	Waterhen, MB	Craig R. Zmijewski	Craig R. Zmijewski	1996	629
180 5/8	25 1/8	25 2/8	18 1/8	5 3/8	4 5/8	6	7	Coles Co., IL	H. Lee Adams	H. Lee Adams	1999	629
180 5/8	28 3/8	28 3/8	17 3/8	4 5/8	4 4/8	7	6	Ashe Co., NC	William Price	William Price	1999	629
180 5/8	27 3/8	27 4/8	17 5/8	4 3/8	5 1/8	5	5	Wabasha Co., MN	Bradley S. Kreofsky	Bradley S. Kreofsky	2000	629
180 4/8	24 5/8	23 4/8	19 1/8	5 1/8	4 6/8	6	6	Saline Co., MO	Alvin Croka	Alvin Croka	2001	643
180 4/8	29 2/8	28 4/8	20 6/8	4 7/8	5 2/8	5	6	Iron Co., MI	John Schmidt	Robert E. Schmidt	1927	643
180 4/8	28	26 2/8	20	4 6/8	4 6/8	7	7	Jim Hogg Co., TX	Roy L. Henry	Roy L. Henry	1958	643
180 4/8	27 6/8	26 6/8	16 6/8	6	5	7	6	Madison Parish, LA	Buford Perry	Buford Perry	1961	643
180 4/8	27 1/8	26 4/8	17 2/8	5 2/8	4 7/8	6	6	Adams Co., IA	Dale D. Blazek	Dale D. Blazek	1962	643
180 4/8	23 5/8	24 4/8	22 7/8	5	5	5	5	Andrew Co., MO	Virgil M. Ashley	Virgil M. Ashley	1967	643
180 4/8	28	27	19	5 1/8	5 1/8	6	6	Leflore Co., MS	W.F. Smith	W.F. Smith	1968	643
180 4/8	26 7/8	25 5/8	18 6/8	5 1/8	5 1/8	6	6	Clay Co., SD	James E. Olson	James E. Olson	1975	643
180 4/8	26 5/8	26 3/8	24 5/8	5 4/8	5 3/8	6	5	Dawson Co., NE	Jerry Lauby	Jerry Lauby	1983	643
180 4/8	30	29 1/8	17 4/8	4 7/8	5	5	5	Okanogan Co., WA	Joe Peone	Joe Peone	1983	643
180 4/8	25 6/8	26 2/8	20	4 3/8	4 7/8	8	8	Carver Co., MN	Stephen M. Polston	Stephen M. Polston	1985	643
180 4/8	27 3/8	27 5/8	22 2/8	4 4/8	4 4/8	6	6	Portage Co., OH	Michael J. Simons	Michael J. Simons	1990	643
180 4/8	25 6/8	25 7/8	21	5 1/8	5 1/8	5	5	Livingston Co., MO	Jack Hampton	Jack Hampton	1991	643
180 4/8	24 7/8	26 4/8	22 2/8	5 3/8	5 2/8	5	5	Henry Co., IA	Jeff L. Weigert	Jeff L. Weigert	1991	643
180 4/8	27 7/8	27 5/8	21 1/8	5 2/8	5 4/8	10	9	Holt Co., NE	Fred L. Kubik	Fred L. Kubik	1994	643
180 3/8	27	26 6/8	19 2/8	5 4/8	5 6/8	6	6	Dubois Co., IN	Kenneth R. Hasenour	Kenneth R. Hasenour	1995	662
180 3/8	26 4/8	27	22 5/8	5 4/8	5 3/8	5	6	Washburn Co., WI	Timothy J. Clare	Timothy J. Clare	1998	662
180 3/8	25 5/8	25 5/8	21 3/8	5	5	6	6	Olmsted Co., MN	Thomas C. Kroening	Thomas C. Kroening	1998	662
180 3/8	28 6/8	26 5/8	20 1/8	5 3/8	5 3/8	7	7	Pottawatomie Co., KS	Picked Up	Cabela's, Inc.	2001	662
180 3/8	27 1/8	26 6/8	16 3/8	5 1/8	5 1/8	6	7	Rock Island Co., IL	Douglas J. Hood	Douglas J. Hood	2002	662
180 3/8	26 5/8	26 5/8	23 1/8	5 4/8	5 4/8	7	8	Minnesota	Unknown	Isaak Walton League	PR 1901	662
180 3/8	30 2/8	30 2/8	20 2/8	5 2/8	5 2/8	8	8	Livingston Co., NY	Edward Beare	Edward Beare	1943	662
180 3/8	26 4/8	26 4/8	19 1/8	4 6/8	4 6/8	6	7	Sheboygan Co., WI	Unknown	James K. Lawton	1955	662
180 3/8	27	27	21 5/8	5	5	8	6	Ovando, MT	Clinton Berry	Clinton Berry	1957	662
180 3/8	24 4/8	24 4/8	20 1/8	6 3/8	6 2/8	7	6	Stoughton, SK	Joe Zbeetnoff	Joe Zbeetnoff	1961	662
180 3/8	25 6/8	26 3/8	21 5/8	4 5/8	4 5/8	6	5	Aitkin Co., MN	Donald J. Sorenson	Donald J. Sorenson	1963	662
180 3/8	26 6/8	26 6/8	22 3/8	5 7/8	5 7/8	5	5	Antler Lake, AB	German Wagenseil	German Wagenseil	1964	662
180 3/8	27 5/8	26	22 3/8	5	5	5	5	Hand Co., SD	Vernon Winter	J.D. Andrews	1965	662
180 3/8	28 3/8	28 2/8	22 5/8	4 7/8	5	5	5	Dodge Co., WI	Herman Pautsch	Brian E. Neitzel	1965	662

WHITETAIL DEER - TYPICAL ANTLERS
Odocoileus virginianus virginianus and certain related subspecies

Score	Length of Main Beam R	L	Inside Spread	Circumference at Smallest Place Between Burr and First Point R	L	Number of Points R	L	Locality	Hunter	Owner	Date Killed	Rank
180 3/8	30	29 5/8	22 3/8	4 5/8	4 5/8	6	8	Meeker Co., MN	Stanley M. Messner	Stanley M. Messner	1981	662
180 3/8	27	28 1/8	17 6/8	4 5/8	4 5/8	9	6	Huron Co., MI	Picked Up	Raymond W. Hatfield	1985	662
180 3/8	25 1/8	24 7/8	17 2/8	4 7/8	4 5/8	7	6	Story Co., IA	Richard L. Borton	Richard L. Borton	1987	662
180 3/8	25 1/8	24 4/8	20 1/8	5	5	6	6	St. Louis Co., MN	Unknown	George W. Flaim	PR 1992	662
180 3/8	22 7/8	23 6/8	19 7/8	5	4 7/8	7	6	Nuevo Leon, MX	Melbourn Shillings	Melbourn Shillings	1992	662
180 3/8	28 1/8	28	19 6/8	5 5/8	5 3/8	6	4	Menard Co., IL	Ronald J. Wadsworth	Ronald J. Wadsworth	1993	662
180 3/8	26 5/8	27 3/8	21 1/8	5 1/8	5 2/8	5	5	Crane Lake, SK	Darron J. Corfield	Darron J. Corfield	1994	662
180 3/8	27 1/8	27 1/8	19 5/8	4 4/8	4 3/8	7	8	Dakota Co., MN	William E. Urbaniak	William E. Urbaniak	1996	662
180 3/8	25 4/8	23 6/8	21 1/8	5 5/8	5 5/8	6	5	Wapiti River, AB	Terry D. Hagman	Terry D. Hagman	1997	662
180 3/8	30 7/8	28 5/8	21 4/8	4 6/8	4 7/8	6	8	Westchester Co., NY	Richard L. Johnson	Richard L. Johnson	1998	662
180 3/8	32 6/8	32 4/8	22 3/8	5 2/8	5 3/8	4	4	Hillsdale Co., MI	Victor L. Bulliner	Victor L. Bulliner	2001	662
180 3/8	25 7/8	24 5/8	17 1/8	4 6/8	4 6/8	8	7	Allamakee Co., IA	James Sinclair	James Sinclair	2001	662
180 3/8	27 6/8	28 1/8	19 7/8	5 1/8	5 3/8	7	6	Mountain Lake, SK	Joseph Lieb	Joseph Lieb	2002	662
180 2/8	28 2/8	27 7/8	20 2/8	4 7/8	4 7/8	6	6	Texas	Alfred Schroeder	John E. Hamilton	PR 1926	684
180 2/8	26 4/8	25	22 5/8	5 4/8	5 2/8	7	7	Lumsden, SK	Mike Lukas	E.M. Gazda	1959	684
180 2/8	26 7/8	26 6/8	18 7/8	4 7/8	4 7/8	6	6	Wayne Co., KY	Green Hamlin	Green Hamlin	1966	684
180 2/8	28 1/8	28 4/8	18 4/8	4 6/8	4 6/8	5	5	Newton Co., GA	David Moon	David Moon	1972	684
180 2/8	24 1/8	26 6/8	19 1/8	5	4 6/8	6	6	Madison Co., IA	Carl W. Schroder	Carl W. Schroder	1977	684
180 2/8	26 3/8	26 3/8	18 2/8	4 5/8	4 5/8	6	6	Eau Claire Co., WI	Dennis B. Bryan	Dennis B. Bryan	1979	684
180 2/8	27 1/8	27 1/8	19 4/8	4 4/8	4 4/8	5	5	Iowa	Unknown	Tom Williams	PR 1984	684
180 2/8	25 1/8	25 3/8	20 4/8	4 4/8	4 3/8	5	5	Yuma Co., CO	Jeff L. Mekelburg	Jeff L. Mekelburg	1989	684
180 2/8	26 5/8	27 5/8	21 1/8	5 1/8	5 1/8	6	6	Drew Co., AR	Terry Tackette	Terry Tackette	1989	684
180 2/8	26 6/8	27 4/8	22 4/8	5	4 6/8	6	7	Polk Co., IA	Jeff P. Susic	Jeff P. Susic	1990	684
180 2/8	30	28 3/8	23 4/8	5	5	6	6	Pepin Co., WI	William J. Bates	William J. Bates	1991	684
180 2/8	25 2/8	25 7/8	20 4/8	4 7/8	4 6/8	5	5	Monroe Co., IA	Michael R. Maddy	Michael R. Maddy	1992	684
180 2/8	28 1/8	26 1/8	21 4/8	4 6/8	4 7/8	7	8	Cowley Co., KS	Thomas W. Jackson	Thomas W. Jackson	1994	684
180 2/8	28 4/8	27 6/8	21 1/8	5	5 2/8	6	8	Allamakee Co., IA	David L. Goedert	David L. Goedert	1995	684
180 2/8	25 3/8	25 6/8	20 1/8	4 7/8	4 6/8	8	7	Jefferson Co., WI	Randy Latsch	Randy Latsch	1995	684
180 2/8	26 7/8	28 5/8	19 4/8	5 2/8	5 1/8	5	6	Madison Co., MS	Stephen C. Greer	Stephen C. Greer	1996	684
180 2/8	27	26 6/8	20 2/8	5 4/8	5 3/8	5	5	Clinton Co., MI	John L. Benedict	John L. Benedict	2002	684
180 2/8	25 5/8	25 7/8	17 4/8	5	4 5/8	7	7	Rock Island Co., IL	Andrew K. Crippen	Andrew K. Crippen	2002	684
180 1/8	23 3/8	23 5/8	17 5/8	5 2/8	5 2/8	5	6	Maryfield, SK	Donald Cook	Richard J. Christoforo	1956	702
180 1/8	25 4/8	26 6/8	17 3/8	4 7/8	4 6/8	7	6	Ashland Co., WI	Audrey Kundinger	Audrey Kundinger	1961	702
180 1/8	26 4/8	26 5/8	20 1/8	4 4/8	4 5/8	6	6	Phelps Co., MO	William A. Hagenhoff	William A. Hagenhoff	1973	702
180 1/8	24	24 4/8	19 1/8	4 7/8	5	7	6	Vermilion, AB	Ralph M. McDonald	Ralph M. McDonald	1975	702
180 1/8	25 1/8	24 4/8	26 7/8	5 6/8	5 4/8	6	7	Hardisty, AB	George R. Walker	George R. Walker	1977	702
180 1/8	27	26	15 7/8	4 7/8	4 6/8	6	5	Chariton Co., MO	Ricky Pearman	Ricky Pearman	1982	702

Score	R. Beam	L. Beam	Spread	Circ. R	Circ. L	Pts. R	Pts. L	Locality	Hunter	Owner	Year	Rank
180 1/8	25 1/8	25 2/8	19 1/8	5 2/8	5 2/8	6	6	Cottonwood Co., MN	Charles C. Burnham	Charles C. Burnham	1983	702
180 1/8	24	24 7/8	19 4/8	5	5 1/8	7	7	Hubbard Co., MN	Larry D. Dierks	Larry D. Dierks	1984	702
180 1/8	29 7/8	28 6/8	25 1/8	5 3/8	5 1/8	5	5	Caroline Co., MD	Unknown	Charles D. Anderson	1987	702
180 1/8	26 1/8	25 4/8	20 1/8	5 2/8	5 2/8	5	5	Jackson Co., SD	Timothy J. Kelley	Timothy J. Kelley	1988	702
180 1/8	25 6/8	25 4/8	22 1/8	4 2/8	4 3/8	6	6	Parry, SK	Doug Hennie	Doug Hennie	1993	702
180 1/8	26 4/8	26 1/8	20	4 6/8	4 7/8	6	6	Montgomery Co., TN	Lonnie Hulse	Lonnie Hulse	1995	702
180 1/8	27 2/8	24 4/8	15 3/8	4 7/8	4 6/8	6	5	Macon Co., MO	M.F. Rickwa & S.M. Rickwa	M.F. Rickwa & S.M. Rickwa	1995	702
180 1/8	26 7/8	25 5/8	18 4/8	4 6/8	4 3/8	5	5	Rice Co., MN	Picked Up	Stephen L. Albers	1998	702
180 1/8	27 3/8	28	22 7/8	4 5/8	4	5	5	Medina Co., OH	Stephen F. DeMeulenaere	Stephen F. DeMeulenaere	1998	702
180 1/8	28 2/8	27 1/8	19 6/8	4 5/8	4 5/8	7	7	Boone Co., MO	Benjamin K. Betz	Benjamin K. Betz	1999	702
180 1/8	28 7/8	28 5/8	20 2/8	4 5/8	4 5/8	6	6	Ohio Co., KY	Anthony Goff	Anthony Goff	2000	702
180 1/8	30 2/8	29 1/8	23 5/8	5 2/8	5 4/8	8	8	Waukesha Co., WI	Kevin A. McNeven	Kevin A. McNeven	2000	702
180 1/8	25	25 3/8	23 4/8	4 5/8	4 6/8	7	7	Clark Co., IN	Matthew D. Miller	Matthew D. Miller	2000	702
180	27 5/8	27 6/8	20	5	5	5	5	Oneida Co., WI	Milo K. Fields	Milo K. Fields	1938	721
180	26 6/8	26 5/8	19 6/8	4 4/8	4 4/8	6	6	Desha Co., AR	Turner Neal	Turner Neal	1962	721
180	26	25 7/8	19	4 7/8	4 7/8	5	5	Zavala Co., TX	Mrs. Richard King III	Mrs. Richard King III	1966	721
180	25 7/8	25 5/8	19 4/8	6 1/8	6 1/8	10	7	Big Horn Co., MT	Clair W. Jensen	Clair W. Jensen	1967	721
180	26 7/8	26 1/8	20 4/8	5 7/8	5 7/8	6	8	Castor, AB	Kenneth Larson	Kenneth Larson	1969	721
180	26 4/8	27 1/8	18 2/8	5 3/8	4 7/8	5	7	Edwards Co., KS	David R. Cross	David R. Cross	1985	721
180	25 3/8	25 6/8	22 7/8	4 5/8	5 5/8	6	8	Pulaski Co., IL	Picked Up	Pat Kearny	1988	721
180	26 7/8	28	19 4/8	4 4/8	4 4/8	6	6	Florence Co., WI	Dale E. Samsa	Dale E. Samsa	1988	721
180	25 6/8	25 4/8	20	4 5/8	5 6/8	5	5	Dawson Creek, BC	H. Peter Bruhs	H. Peter Bruhs	1989	721
180	25 4/8	25 6/8	19 4/8	5 1/8	5 1/8	10	7	Pembina River, AB	Joe Jandl	Joe Jandl	1989	721
180	23 5/8	25 2/8	19 5/8	5 2/8	5 3/8	7	7	Torch River, SK	David Matchett	David Matchett	1991	721
180	24 5/8	24 5/8	22 6/8	5	5	5	5	Helene Lake, SK	Kevin R. Garner	Kevin R. Garner	1993	721
180	24 4/8	25 3/8	23 3/8	7	7	7	6	Boone Co., IA	Loren H. Phipps	Loren H. Phipps	1993	721
180	25 7/8	26	20 2/8	5 3/8	5 1/8	5	5	Brown Co., IL	Rocco Gibala	Rocco Gibala	1995	721
180	23 3/8	22 7/8	17 4/8	6	6	5	7	Moose Mt. Prov. Park, SK	Robin Hilts	Robin Hilts	1997	721
180	26	26	19	5	5 1/8	5	5	Redberry Lake, SK	Steven Hupaelo	Steven Hupaelo	1998	721
180	26 5/8	26 5/8	18 2/8	5 1/8	4 7/8	6	6	Winona Co., MN	James R. Walkes	James R. Walkes	1998	721
180	25 3/8	27 1/8	19	5 1/8	5	9	9	Hancock Co., ME	Butler B. Dunn	Butler B. Dunn	2001	721
179 7/8	27 6/8	26 6/8	19 7/8	5 4/8	5 4/8	6	5	Hamiota, MB	Alan J. Sheridan	Alan J. Sheridan	1930	738
179 7/8	26 1/8	26 3/8	19 4/8	5 3/8	5 3/8	5	5	Nicollet Co., MN	Joe Welter	Joe Welter	1984	738
179 7/8	26 2/8	26 3/8	19 5/8	5 1/8	5 1/8	6	6	Tensas Parish, LA	Anthony Guice	Anthony Guice	1987	738
179 7/8	28 4/8	27 7/8	23 7/8	4 7/8	4 6/8	6	6	Valley Co., NE	Leonard L. Krason	Leonard L. Krason	1995	738
179 7/8	25 4/8	27 5/8	21 2/8	5 6/8	5 5/8	7	9	Pasquia Hills, SK	Jeffrey S. Metzler	Jeffrey S. Metzler	1998	738
179 7/8	26 7/8	26 7/8	21 3/8	4 6/8	4 3/8	6	7	Beltrami Co., MN	Richard L. Dickinson	Richard L. Dickinson	1998	738
179 6/8	28 5/8	28 3/8	20 4/8	4 6/8	4 7/8	5	6	Hancock Co., ME	M. Don Betts	Larry Snell	2001	738
179 6/8	27 1/8	29 3/8	21 3/8	4 7/8	5	7	5	Steele Co., MN	Elmer Janning	Elmer Janning	1884	745
179 6/8	28 1/8	26 4/8	22 2/8	4 6/8	4 6/8	6	5	Aitkin Co., MN	Harland A. Kern	Harland A. Kern	1972	745
179 6/8	29 1/8	28	21	5 5/8	5 5/8	7	6	Longview, AB	Eldred Umbach	Eldred Umbach	1973	745
179 6/8	26 7/8	26 5/8	21 4/8	4 4/8	4 4/8	7	7	Woodbury Co., IA	Harlan L. Allison	Harlan L. Allison	1977	745
179 6/8	26 3/8	26 2/8	19 6/8	4 5/8	4 5/8	6	6	Jim Hogg Co., TX	William B. Van Fleet	William B. Van Fleet	1979	745
179 6/8	25 6/8	26 6/8	21 5/8	5 3/8	5 3/8	7	7	Penobscot Co., ME	Dale Rustin	Dale Rustin	1979	745
179 6/8	27	26 6/8	15 6/8	4 4/8	4 4/8	7	8	Clark Co., IL	Robert E. Sweitzer	Robert E. Sweitzer	1984	745
179 6/8	25 1/8	24 7/8	20	4 6/8	4 6/8	6	6	Valhalla Centre, AB	Terry D. Hagman	Terry D. Hagman	1994	745
179 6/8	25 3/8	26	19 1/8	5 3/8	5 4/8	7	7	Decatur Co., IA	Wayne W. Owens	Wayne W. Owens	1995	745
179 6/8	25 2/8	25 3/8	22 3/8	5 5/8	5 4/8	7	5	Plamondon, AB	Edmond Bourassa	Edmond Bourassa	1998	745

413

WHITETAIL DEER - TYPICAL ANTLERS

Odocoileus virginianus virginianus and certain related subspecies

Score	Length of Main Beam		Inside Spread	Circumference at Smallest Place Between Burr and First Point		Number of Points		Locality	Hunter	Owner	Date Killed	Rank
	R	L		R	L	R	L					
179 6/8	26 4/8	25 4/8	21 2/8	5	4 7/8	6	6	Warren Co., OH	Rex A. Gill	Rex A. Gill	1998	745
179 6/8	25 6/8	26 6/8	21	6 1/8	5 5/8	7	5	Osage Co., KS	Ronald D. Fine	Ronald D. Fine	1999	745
179 6/8	26 7/8	27 7/8	19 6/8	4 6/8	5 2/8	8	6	Madison Co., OH	Robert E. Hunter II	Robert E. Hunter II	1999	745
179 6/8	24 5/8	24 4/8	20 4/8	5	5	6	6	Red Deer River, SK	Robert Abbott	Robert Abbott	2001	745
179 6/8	26 4/8	26 4/8	22 1/8	5 5/8	5 6/8	6	6	Cutarm Creek, SK	Rick Schuster	Rick Schuster	2001	745
179 6/8	28 4/8	28	21	4 7/8	4 6/8	5	5	Porter Co., IN	Herbert R. Smith	Herbert R. Smith	2001	745
179 6/8	26 5/8	28 2/8	22 1/8	5	5	5	8	Lawrence Co., IL	Donald E. Stangle	Donald E. Stangle	2001	745
179 5/8	25 4/8	25 7/8	19 5/8	6	6	6	6	Rumsey, AB	Arley Harder	Arley Harder	1969	763
179 5/8	28 6/8	27 6/8	21	4 6/8	5	6	5	Putnam Co., MO	Wes A. Seaton	Wes A. Seaton	1992	763
179 5/8	29 6/8	29	21 3/8	4 6/8	4 7/8	5	5	Houghton Co., MI	Matthew R. Usitalo	Matthew R. Usitalo	1992	763
179 5/8	25 5/8	25 3/8	20 6/8	4 3/8	4 3/8	5	6	Handhill Lakes, AB	D. Troutman & G. Amendt	Dave Troutman	1996	763
179 5/8	26 3/8	25 6/8	19 3/8	5 1/8	5 1/8	6	6	Pike Co., IL	Dale B. Karns	Dale B. Karns	2002	763
179 4/8	23 4/8	23 5/8	19 2/8	4 6/8	4 5/8	6	6	Coronation, AB	Harold McKnight	Harold McKnight	1969	768
179 4/8	26 5/8	26 6/8	20	5 3/8	5 2/8	5	5	Sandridge, MB	Robert Anderson	Robert Anderson	1971	768
179 4/8	24 1/8	24 2/8	19 2/8	5 2/8	5 1/8	7	6	Spokane Co., WA	Bert E. Smith	Bert E. Smith	1972	768
179 4/8	27 3/8	27 3/8	19 7/8	5	5	6	6	Elk Co., KS	Lowell E. Howell	Lowell E. Howell	1973	768
179 4/8	27 3/8	28 4/8	20 1/8	5 3/8	5 5/8	6	5	Pawnee Co., NE	Kenneth C. Mort	Kenneth C. Mort	1975	768
179 4/8	24 1/8	25 3/8	19 5/8	5	4 7/8	7	8	Chouteau Co., MT	Richard L. Charlson	Richard L. Charlson	1977	768
179 4/8	26 3/8	26 5/8	22 3/8	4 2/8	4 3/8	5	6	Grant Co., WI	Rick L. Parker	Rick L. Parker	1982	768
179 4/8	26 2/8	26 2/8	19 5/8	5 6/8	5 3/8	6	5	Whitemud River, MB	L. Greg Fehr	L. Greg Fehr	1985	768
179 4/8	27 3/8	27 2/8	20 2/8	4 7/8	5	6	6	Cremona, AB	E. Roger Jackson	E. Roger Jackson	1985	768
179 4/8	28 3/8	28 5/8	21	4 4/8	4 4/8	5	6	Collingsworth Co., TX	Picked Up	F. Gus Reinarz	1987	768
179 4/8	28 1/8	28 1/8	19 6/8	6	6 1/8	6	6	Clarke Co., IA	Rodney D. Hommer	Cabela's, Inc.	1990	768
179 4/8	24 6/8	24 1/8	22	5 4/8	5 3/8	6	5	Yankee Lake, SK	Leo Stieb	Leo Stieb	1990	768
179 4/8	30 1/8	29 2/8	23	4 6/8	5	5	5	Litchfield Co., CT	Garry J. Lovrin	Garry J. Lovrin	1993	768
179 4/8	25 2/8	25 2/8	19 4/8	5 2/8	5 6/8	5	5	Macoupin Co., IL	Kurt A. Bohl	Kurt A. Bohl	1997	768
179 4/8	25	24 7/8	21	4 7/8	5	7	6	Maverick Co., TX	Lee M. Bass	Lee M. Bass	1998	768
179 4/8	26 5/8	25 3/8	22	5 4/8	5 2/8	6	6	Barber Co., KS	Picked Up	Bill J. Timms	1999	768
179 3/8	29	29 2/8	19 7/8	4 6/8	4 5/8	10	8	Essex Co., NY	Herbert Jaquish	Herbert Jaquish	1953	784
179 3/8	28 5/8	28	20 7/8	5 6/8	5 6/8	5	5	Parkman, SK	Harold Larsen	Sam Peterson	1958	784
179 3/8	26 1/8	26 2/8	17 7/8	4 7/8	4 6/8	6	6	Vernon Co., WI	Alois V. Schendel	Alois V. Schendel	1966	784
179 3/8	26	26 2/8	17 3/8	6	5 5/8	6	6	Oberon, MB	Arnold W. Poole	Arnold W. Poole	1968	784
179 3/8	26 1/8	26	22 5/8	4 5/8	4 6/8	7	7	Pelican Mt., AB	Harold B. Biggs	Harold B. Biggs	1993	784
179 3/8	26 3/8	25 7/8	22 1/8	5	5	6	7	Allamakee Co., IA	Picked Up	David Gordon	1994	784
179 3/8	27 6/8	26 4/8	18 3/8	5 5/8	5 5/8	6	6	Sherman Co., NE	Richard McCauley, Jr.	Richard McCauley, Jr.	1994	784
179 3/8	25 3/8	27 7/8	21	5 3/8	5 4/8	6	7	Jennings Co., IN	Dennis L. Day	Dennis L. Day	1995	784

Score	L. Beam	R. Beam	Spread	Circ.	Circ.	Pts.	Pts.	Locality	Hunter	Owner	Date	Rank
179 3/8	25	24 4/8	18 3/8	5 2/8	5 3/8	5	6	Lincoln Co., MO	Alfred W. Masterson	Alfred W. Masterson	1995	784
179 3/8	26 7/8	27 5/8	19 5/8	4 2/8	4 2/8	5	5	St. Lawrence Co., NY	Craig A. Morrill	Craig A. Morrill	1995	784
179 3/8	25	25 4/8	19 5/8	4 4/8	4 6/8	8	7	Priddis, AB	Jeffrey C. Dunn	Jeffrey C. Dunn	1996	784
179 3/8	26 1/8	26 6/8	22	4 6/8	4 6/8	8	6	Anoka Co., MN	Thomas M. Evertz	Thomas M. Evertz	1996	784
179 3/8	24 6/8	24 6/8	20 3/8	5 7/8	6	8	7	High Prairie, AB	Walter J. Malysh	Walter J. Malysh	1997	784
179 3/8	26 5/8	25 7/8	18 7/8	6 1/8	5 2/8	5	8	Warren Co., IN	Steven B. Childress	Steven B. Childress	1999	784
179 2/8	27 2/8	27 1/8	23 3/8	5	5 2/8	3	11	Prairie Co., AR	Charles Newsom	Charles Newsom	1962	798
179 2/8	28 5/8	28 5/8	20 6/8	5 2/8	5 3/8	3	5	Koochiching Co., MN	Ted Davis	Marc M. Jackson	1963	798
179 2/8	27 6/8	27	20	5 4/8	5 6/8	9	9	Cypress Hills, SK	Raymond McCrea	Raymond McCrea	1964	798
179 2/8	25 4/8	24 6/8	21 3/8	4 5/8	4 6/8	7	7	Lamar Co., GA	Gary Littlejohn	Gary Littlejohn	1968	798
179 2/8	26 5/8	25 5/8	17 7/8	5	5	7	7	Worth Co., IA	John Janssen	John Janssen	1976	798
179 2/8	26 7/8	28	16	4 4/8	4 3/8	6	5	Ashland Co., WI	Jack D. Hultman	Jack D. Hultman	1981	798
179 2/8	28 1/8	28 1/8	25 2/8	4 5/8	4 5/8	6	5	Webster Co., IA	Douglas W. Baedke	Douglas W. Baedke	1982	798
179 2/8	24 2/8	24 2/8	19 4/8	4 4/8	4 5/8	6	6	Dimmit Co., TX	William M. Knolle	William M. Knolle	1982	798
179 2/8	23 6/8	25 1/8	19 3/8	5 5/8	5 5/8	7	7	Buffalo Co., WI	Jerome Kulig	Jerome Kulig	1984	798
179 2/8	25 4/8	25 6/8	20 6/8	4 7/8	5	6	7	Hinds Co., MS	Marlon Stokes	Marlon Stokes	1988	798
179 2/8	28 7/8	27 1/8	23 2/8	5 3/8	5 3/8	5	5	Peoria Co., IL	Christopher M. McNulty	Christopher M. McNulty	1994	798
179 2/8	25 4/8	25 6/8	21	5 1/8	5 2/8	9	9	Unknown	Picked Up	David Gheen	1995	798
179 2/8	27 6/8	27 7/8	19 4/8	4 7/8	4 7/8	6	6	Henry Co., VA	Tony E. Meade	Tony E. Meade	1995	798
179 2/8	25 7/8	24 2/8	19 4/8	5 2/8	5 1/8	6	7	Vernon Lake, AB	Del Kirchmayer	Del Kirchmayer	1997	798
179 2/8	28	27 7/8	20 7/8	4 5/8	4 5/8	6	6	Blaine Co., OK	Matt Parker	Matt Parker	1999	798
179 2/8	27 5/8	26 1/8	20 7/8	5 4/8	5 5/8	8	8	Kalamazoo Co., MI	Steve J. Williams	Steve J. Williams	2000	798
179 2/8	25 1/8	25	19 4/8	4 5/8	4 4/8	7	7	St. Landry Parish, LA	Shannon R. Deville	Shannon R. Deville	2001	798
179 1/8	28 6/8	28 2/8	18 2/8	4 6/8	4 6/8	6	6	Twiggs Co., GA	Cy Smith	Duncan A. Dobie	1970	815
179 1/8	24 6/8	25 1/8	19 3/8	5 7/8	5 7/8	6	6	Fulton Co., IL	Jerry D. Manning	Jerry D. Manning	1977	815
179 1/8	27 3/8	27 7/8	21 3/8	4 7/8	4 7/8	5	6	Renville Co., MN	Todd Swartz	Todd Swartz	1984	815
179 1/8	24 5/8	25 4/8	15 7/8	4 4/8	4 4/8	7	7	Dallas Co., IA	Steven W. Hick	Steven W. Hick	1992	815
179 1/8	28 4/8	28 1/8	21 3/8	5	5	6	6	Butler Co., KS	Donald B. Williamson	Donald B. Williamson	1994	815
179 1/8	25 6/8	25 6/8	16 3/8	5 1/8	4 4/8	7	7	Macoupin Co., IL	William T. Wiser, Sr.	William T. Wiser, Sr.	1994	815
179 1/8	27	27 2/8	19 3/8	4 6/8	4 6/8	5	5	Bremer Co., IA	Blaine A. Davis	Blaine A. Davis	2000	815
179 1/8	25 7/8	25 7/8	17 4/8	6 1/8	6 2/8	6	6	N. Saskatchewan River, SK	Miles A. Johnson	Miles A. Johnson	2003	815
179	25	25	18 2/8	5 2/8	5 3/8	9	9	Chippewa Co., WI	John F. Kukuska	John F. Kukuska	1931	823
179	23	23 7/8	16 5/8	3 5/8	3 5/8	8	9	La Salle Co., TX	Charles Duffy	Emory C. Thompson	PR 1941	823
179	27 1/8	25 5/8	19 4/8	5 5/8	5 4/8	6	7	Sherburne Co., MN	Victor Nagel	Victor Nagel	1956	823
179	26 6/8	26 2/8	21 4/8	4 6/8	4 4/8	6	6	Jasper Co., GA	Hubert R. Moody	Hubert R. Moody	1957	823
179	25 6/8	25 6/8	19 3/8	5	5	5	5	Waldersee, MB	W. Wutke	W. Wutke	1959	823
179	28 4/8	28 5/8	20 6/8	4 5/8	4 6/8	6	6	Dooly Co., GA	Shannon Akin	Shannon Akin	1981	823
179	27 4/8	29 4/8	20 2/8	4 6/8	5	5	5	Logan Co., OH	Gregory K. Snyder	Greta J. Snyder	1982	823
179	27 6/8	29 1/8	20 7/8	5 6/8	5 6/8	7	7	Perry Co., IL	Roy A. Smith	Roy A. Smith	1987	823
179	26 2/8	26 5/8	21	4 7/8	4 7/8	8	8	Monroe Co., MO	Tommy Garnett	Tommy Garnett	1988	823
179	27 2/8	26 4/8	19 1/8	5 1/8	5	11	11	Pictou Co., NS	Earl Perry	Earl Perry	1990	823
179	27 6/8	27 6/8	17 4/8	4 4/8	4 3/8	5	5	Benton Co., MN	Michael A. Gapinski	Michael A. Gapinski	1991	823
179	27 7/8	29 1/8	21 4/8	5 2/8	5 4/8	6	6	Union Co., IA	Richard Reed	Richard Reed	1996	823
179	29 2/8	29 1/8	19 6/8	5 1/8	5	7	6	McLean Co., IL	Ryan B. Bottles	Ryan B. Bottles	1999	823
179	26 3/8	26 3/8	18 2/8	5 2/8	5 3/8	5	5	St. Croix Co., WI	Kelly A. Geraghty	Kelly A. Geraghty	1999	823
179	26	26	16	5 3/8	5 6/8	6	6	Dauphin Lake, MB	Maurice Theoret	Maurice Theoret	2001	823
178 7/8	24 3/8	28	21 7/8	5 3/8	5 3/8	7	7	Monroe Co., OH	Roger E. Schumacher	Roger E. Schumacher	1958	838
178 7/8	28 1/8	26 2/8	19 5/8	4 6/8	4 6/8	6	6	Van Buren Co., IA	Noel E. Harlan	Noel E. Harlan	1984	838

WHITETAIL DEER - TYPICAL ANTLERS
Odocoileus virginianus virginianus and certain related subspecies

Score	Length of Main Beam R	L	Inside Spread	Circumference at Smallest Place Between Burr and First Point R	L	Number of Points R	L	Locality	Hunter	Owner	Date Killed	Rank
178 7/8	28 3/8	28 3/8	19 1/8	4 6/8	5	5	5	Pierce Lake, SK	Edwin Johnson	Edwin Johnson	1984	838
178 7/8	28 3/8	27 6/8	22	5	5 1/8	6	5	Brown Co., IL	Joseph V. Barnett	Joseph V. Barnett	1988	838
178 7/8	30	29 4/8	18 1/8	5	5	5	5	Whiteside Co., IL	Bernard J. Higley, Jr.	Bernard J. Higley, Jr.	1990	838
178 7/8	26 4/8	26 4/8	22 7/8	4 5/8	4 5/8	5	5	Coahuila, MX	Donald R. Summers	Donald R. Summers	1990	838
178 7/8	30	28 5/8	21 1/8	5	5 4/8	5	5	Scioto Co., OH	Craig D. Smith	Craig D. Smith	1991	838
178 6/8	27 3/8	27 5/8	20 7/8	4	4 1/8	9	8	Texas	Unknown	Buckhorn Mus. & Saloon, Ltd.	PR 1920	845
178 6/8	26	25	22 7/8	5 2/8	5 1/8	6	6	Elkhorn, MB	Jerry May	Jerry May	1959	845
178 6/8	27 6/8	27 6/8	25 4/8	5 3/8	5 4/8	6	5	Windthorst, SK	Clarence E. Genest	Clarence E. Genest	1965	845
178 6/8	26	26 5/8	21 2/8	5 2/8	5 2/8	6	8	McPherson Co., KS	Larry D. Daniel	Larry D. Daniel	1967	845
178 6/8	27	24 4/8	22 1/8	5 7/8	5 7/8	7	7	Breton, AB	George Clark	George Clark	1981	845
178 6/8	26 2/8	27 2/8	20 6/8	5	5	6	6	Aroostook Co., ME	John R. Hardy	John R. Hardy	1983	845
178 6/8	28 1/8	27 3/8	21 3/8	4 2/8	4 4/8	6	5	Corson Co., SD	Dean Little Dog	Dick Rossum	1984	845
178 6/8	27	27	19 2/8	4 6/8	4 5/8	6	6	Vilna, AB	M.J. Satcher	M.J. Satcher	1987	845
178 6/8	25 7/8	26 4/8	22 2/8	4 6/8	4 7/8	6	7	Shawano Co., WI	M.M. Berrien, Jr.	M.M. Berrien, Jr.	1990	845
178 6/8	26	25 7/8	16	4 6/8	4 5/8	6	6	Hancock Co., IL	Gregory L. Teske	Gregory L. Teske	1991	845
178 6/8	29 2/8	27 6/8	21 5/8	5 3/8	5 5/8	5	6	Bolivar Co., MS	Carl A. Lee	Carl A. Lee	1996	845
178 5/8	25 6/8	27 2/8	20 2/8	5 4/8	5 4/8	6	5	Beechy, SK	Grady Robertson	Merigold Hunting Club	1951	856
178 5/8	28 7/8	27	24	5 1/8	5 1/8	7	7	Harlan Co., NE	Archie D. McRae	Archie D. McRae	1957	856
178 5/8	27	26 4/8	20 4/8	4 3/8	4 3/8	6	6	St. Louis Co., MN	Don Tripe	Don Tripe	1961	856
178 5/8	28 4/8	28 1/8	16 7/8	5 4/8	5 3/8	6	6	Debden, SK	Picked Up	Jerome L. Schaller	1962	856
178 5/8	27 7/8	29 2/8	26 3/8	5 2/8	5 2/8	6	7	Thomas Co., GA	Henry Rydde	Henry Rydde	1966	856
178 5/8	28 5/8	26 3/8	20	5 2/8	5 1/8	6	5	Pincher Creek, AB	Clyde E. Anderson	Clyde E. Anderson	1969	856
178 5/8	24 1/8	24 7/8	20 4/8	4 7/8	5 1/8	6	7	St. Louis Co., MN	Unknown	H. Bruce Freeman	1973	856
178 5/8	27 2/8	26 4/8	21 5/8	4 7/8	5	6	6	Scott Co., TN	John Nordenstam	George W. Flaim	1977	856
178 5/8	27	26 4/8	21 1/8	5 3/8	5 3/8	5	5	Itasca Co., MN	Charles H. Smith	Charles H. Smith	1978	856
178 5/8	25 4/8	25 5/8	22 7/8	4 4/8	4 4/8	5	5	Crawford Co., WI	Gino P. Maccario	Gino P. Maccario	1980	856
178 5/8	27 3/8	27 1/8	24 1/8	5	5 2/8	6	5	Grant Co., WI	Dale Check, Jr.	Dale Check, Jr.	1985	856
178 5/8	24 7/8	25 1/8	18 1/8	5	4 7/8	6	6	Caldwell Co., MO	I. James Meng	I. James Meng	1985	856
178 5/8	25 4/8	26 1/8	20 1/8	5 4/8	5 3/8	7	7	Flat Lake, AB	Jack L. Murray	Jack L. Murray	1986	856
178 5/8	25 2/8	24 7/8	21 3/8	5	5	5	6	Grundy Co., IL	Paul Franchuk	Paul Franchuk	1987	856
178 5/8	25 7/8	23 7/8	18 7/8	5 1/8	5 1/8	8	7	Jones Co., IA	Charles H. Frantini	Charles H. Frantini	1987	856
178 5/8	26	26 2/8	19 5/8	5 4/8	5 6/8	8	6	Riley Co., KS	Dennis Boots	Dennis Boots	1988	856
178 5/8	27 1/8	27 5/8	20 3/8	4 6/8	4 6/8	8	8	Roseau Co., MN	Colt Knutson	Colt Knutson	1989	856
178 5/8	25 5/8	26 1/8	20 1/8	4 5/8	4 5/8	8	8	Saskatoon, SK	Jeffrey Benson	Jeffrey Benson	1991	856
178 5/8	28 3/8	28 1/8	18 6/8	4 5/8	4 4/8	6	6	Saskatoon, SK	Patrick D. Shendruk	Patrick D. Shendruk	1992	856
178 5/8	25 7/8	25 3/8	17 7/8	4 5/8	4 5/8	6	7	Monroe Co., NY	David P. Ives	David P. Ives	1993	856

Score	L.R	L.L	Spread	Circ.R	Circ.L	Pts.R	Pts.L	Locality	Hunter	Owner	Date	Rank
178 5/8	23 2/8	23 2/8	21 7/8	4 2/8	4 2/8	6	7	Crittenden Co., KY	Mendel Davidson	Mendel Davidson	1994	856
178 5/8	26 4/8	26 1/8	20 7/8	5 5/8	5 4/8	7	7	La Salle Co., IL	Larry G. Simmons	Larry G. Simmons	1995	856
178 5/8	26 6/8	26 7/8	17 3/8	4 5/8	4 6/8	5	5	Taylor Co., GA	W. Michael Layfield	W. Michael Layfield	1997	856
178 5/8	25 4/8	25	17 5/8	4 4/8	4 5/8	6	6	Blueberry Creek, AB	Dennis Wolney	Mark E. Wolney	1997	856
178 5/8	27 1/8	27 1/8	22 7/8	5 4/8	5 3/8	6	5	Peoria Co., IL	Steven M. DeSmet	Steven M. DeSmet	1998	856
178 5/8	26	26 2/8	20 3/8	5 1/8	5 3/8	6	6	Cedar Co., IA	Michael M. Hatzky	Michael M. Hatzky	1999	856
178 5/8	26 2/8	26 4/8	19 3/8	4 4/8	5 1/8	6	5	Macon Co., GA	Brent McCarty	Brent McCarty	1999	856
178 5/8	26 4/8	25 2/8	18 2/8	5	5	6	5	Hemphill Co., TX	Cliff Norris	Cliff Norris	1999	856
178 5/8	25 6/8	25 5/8	22 1/8	5 2/8	5 1/8	5	5	Franklin Co., NE	Robert L. Lennemann	Robert L. Lennemann	2000	856
178 5/8	25	24 7/8	17 1/8	5 5/8	5 5/8	6	6	Noble Co., IN	William M. Hart, Jr.	William M. Hart, Jr.	2001	856
178 5/8	28 2/8	28	22 6/8	4 2/8	4 7/8	5	5	Lincoln Co., WA	Gary H. Wilcox	Melvin Scheuss	1951	856
178 4/8	26 6/8	26 1/8	28 2/8	5	5	7	7	Beltrami Co., MN	Arthur A. Hill	Arthur I. Hill	1957	886
178 4/8	23 7/8	24 6/8	21 3/8	4 3/8	4 3/8	5	5	Addy, WA	Irving Naff	Irving Naff	1954	886
178 4/8	25 2/8	25	23 2/8	5 4/8	5 4/8	5	5	McMullen Co., TX	D.H. Waldron	D.H. Waldron	1957	886
178 4/8	25 1/8	25 3/8	16 1/8	5 2/8	5 2/8	6	6	Yuma Co., CO	Terry M. Scheidecker	Terry M. Scheidecker	1964	886
178 4/8	27 3/8	27 3/8	18 6/8	4 7/8	4 5/8	6	6	Cumberland Co., ME	Patrick D. Wescott	Patrick D. Wescott	1979	886
178 4/8	24 2/8	25 2/8	18 1/8	5 5/8	5 5/8	5	5	St. Clair Co., IL	Emil W. Kromat	Emil W. Kromat	1980	886
178 4/8	26 2/8	26 1/8	21	5 3/8	5 3/8	5	5	Scotland Co., MO	Roland E. Meyer	Picked Up	1981	886
178 4/8	26 1/8	27 3/8	22 6/8	4 3/8	4 4/8	6	6	Edmonson Co., KY	Joseph G. Saling	Picked Up	1984	886
178 4/8	27 6/8	28 4/8	18 4/8	4 7/8	4 6/8	5	5	Fulton Co., IL	Locie L. Murphy	Locie L. Murphy	1984	886
178 4/8	28 2/8	29	19 4/8	5 3/8	5 3/8	5	5	Firdale, MB	Randall J. Bean	Randall J. Bean	1985	886
178 4/8	25 2/8	25 2/8	18 2/8	6 2/8	5 6/8	8	10	Nance Co., NE	Robert J. Ziemba	Robert J. Ziemba	1988	886
178 4/8	25 1/8	26 1/8	19 6/8	5 3/8	5 3/8	8	6	Blue Earth Co., MN	Harry J. Baker	Harry J. Baker	1988	886
178 4/8	26 7/8	26 1/8	22 4/8	4 7/8	5 1/8	5	5	Iosco Co., MI	Frederic J. Latta	Frederic J. Latta	1991	886
178 4/8	27	26 7/8	23	4 6/8	4 6/8	6	6	Jack Fish Lake, SK	Michael J. Frawley	Michael J. Frawley	1991	886
178 4/8	26 5/8	26 3/8	20 6/8	5 7/8	5 7/8	7	9	Cass Co., IA	Mark A. Funk	Mark A. Funk	1997	886
178 4/8	25 2/8	25 2/8	21 4/8	5 1/8	5 1/8	5	5	Jo Daviess Co., IL	Jack R. Herman	Jack R. Herman	1997	886
178 4/8	27 2/8	27 3/8	19 1/8	4 4/8	4 6/8	6	8	Buffalo Co., WI	Edward P. Brannen	Edward P. Brannen	2000	886
178 4/8	25 3/8	23 2/8	21 1/8	4 5/8	4 7/8	6	8	Clinton Co., IL	Richard V. Spihlmann	Richard V. Spihlmann	2001	886
178 3/8	28 4/8	26	24 3/8	5 4/8	5 2/8	6	5	Aitkin Co., MN	George E. Jenks	George E. Jenks	1961	904
178 3/8	27	26 7/8	17 5/8	4 3/8	4 4/8	5	7	Queens Co., NB	Bert Bourque	Bert Bourque	1969	904
178 3/8	26 5/8	26 3/8	19 7/8	5 3/8	5 2/8	5	5	Fillmore Co., MN	Alanson W. Hamernik, Jr.	Alanson W. Hamernik, Jr.	1970	904
178 3/8	25 2/8	23 2/8	19 1/8	5 2/8	5 1/8	7	6	Phillips Co., KS	Robert C. Dusin	Harold Dusin	1973	904
178 3/8	27 2/8	26	17 1/8	5	5 2/8	7	8	Carroll Co., AR	Roy F. Bartlett	Roy F. Bartlett	1975	904
178 3/8	25 3/8	28 1/8	20	5 4/8	5 5/8	7	6	Allamakee Co., IA	Stanley L. Jarosh	Stanley L. Jarosh	1976	904
178 3/8	28 4/8	28 7/8	23 7/8	5 2/8	5 1/8	7	8	Lincoln Co., MN	Larry Lustfield	Larry Lustfield	1978	904
178 3/8	28 7/8	27 7/8	17 1/8	4 7/8	4 7/8	6	6	Dubuque Co., IA	Clay W. Gronen	Clay W. Gronen	1980	904
178 3/8	23 1/8	24 2/8	25	5 6/8	6	7	6	Gregory Co., SD	Ronald L. Larson	Ronald L. Larson	1981	904
178 3/8	27 2/8	26 4/8	18 5/8	4 6/8	4 6/8	6	6	Goochland Co., VA	Edward W. Fielder	Edward W. Fielder	1986	904
178 3/8	26 4/8	25	19	4 7/8	4 7/8	6	7	Jo Daviess Co., IL	Gary J. Flynn	Gary J. Flynn	1993	904
178 3/8	27 6/8	27 3/8	22 4/8	5 3/8	5 3/8	6	6	Phillips Co., AR	Christopher Warren	Christopher Warren	1994	904
178 3/8	26 7/8	26 5/8	16 7/8	5 2/8	5 1/8	6	7	Keya Paha Co., NE	Joseph V. Bauer	Joseph V. Bauer	1994	904
178 3/8	25 5/8	26	22 1/8	6 2/8	6	7	6	Tippecanoe Co., IN	Robert Whitus	Robert Whitus	1994	904
178 3/8	29 4/8	30 2/8	18 4/8	5 5/8	5 5/8	7	6	Bourbon Co., KS	Ronald D. Pfeiffer	Ronald D. Pfeiffer	1995	904
178 3/8	24 4/8	26 1/8	18 5/8	4 2/8	4 2/8	5	5	Fayette Co., IA	Richard A. Wulfekuhle	Richard A. Wulfekuhle	1995	904
178 3/8	29 4/8	29 7/8	19 5/8	5 2/8	5 2/8	6	6	Mitchell Co., GA	Ricky C. Dowis	Ricky C. Dowis	1997	904
178 3/8	29 1/8	29 7/8	17 4/8	4 3/8	4 3/8	7	7	De Kalb Co., MO	Merrill Hall	Merrill Hall	1997	904
178 3/8	24 7/8	25	19 1/8	5 2/8	5 2/8	6	5	Marion Co., IA	Lyle E. Palmer	Lyle E. Palmer	1998	904

Score	Length of Main Beam R	L	Inside Spread	Circumference at Smallest Place Between Burr and First Point R	L	Number of Points R	L	Locality	Hunter	Owner	Date Killed	Rank
178 3/8	25 2/8	24 3/8	19 5/8	4 3/8	4 4/8	6	6	Crawford Co., IA	Clark A. Corbin	Clark A. Corbin	2000	904
178 3/8	24 3/8	24 2/8	25 3/8	5 4/8	5 3/8	5	6	Fillmore Co., NE	Jan Rischling	Jan Rischling	2000	904
178 3/8	27 3/8	27 4/8	18 6/8	5 1/8	5 1/8	5	7	Perry Co., KY	Henry Sizemore	Henry Sizemore	2001	904
178 3/8	27 2/8	26 4/8	21 3/8	4 6/8	4 6/8	5	5	Morgan Co., IL	Allen Gerberding	Allen Gerberding	2002	904
178 3/8	25 1/8	25 6/8	18 1/8	4 5/8	4 6/8	6	6	Kleberg Co., TX	Eugene Werlin, Jr.	Eugene Werlin, Jr.	2002	904
178 2/8	25 4/8	26 1/8	18 4/8	4 7/8	4 7/8	5	5	Shawano Co., WI	Picked Up	Ray T. Charles	1953	929
178 2/8	26 5/8	26 1/8	20 6/8	4 6/8	4 6/8	5	5	Pawnee Co., NE	Picked Up	Gale Sup	1960	929
178 2/8	25 7/8	25	23	5 5/8	5 5/8	7	5	Pope Co., MN	Greg Kobbermann	Greg Kobbermann	1976	929
178 2/8	27 6/8	28 3/8	19 4/8	4 4/8	4 4/8	5	5	Crawford Co., WI	Lance Bangen	Brant J. Mueller	PR 1980	929
178 2/8	27 6/8	27 3/8	24 6/8	4 3/8	4 3/8	6	6	Wallowa Co., OR	Sterling K. Shaver	Sterling K. Shaver	1982	929
178 2/8	27 4/8	27	19 6/8	4 3/8	4 4/8	5	5	Tuscarawas Co., OH	Raymond D. Gerber, Jr.	Raymond D. Gerber, Jr.	1983	929
178 2/8	26 6/8	28 1/8	19 6/8	5 4/8	5 4/8	7	7	Ohio Co., KY	Earl R. Trogden	Earl R. Trogden	1986	929
178 2/8	28	25 7/8	21 2/8	5 1/8	5 3/8	5	5	Lawrence Co., IL	Brian M. Dining	Brian M. Dining	1987	929
178 2/8	28 5/8	27 5/8	21	4 4/8	4 4/8	7	6	Richland Co., ND	Jeffrey D. Krabbenhoft	Jeffrey D. Krabbenhoft	1993	929
178 2/8	26 7/8	25 7/8	21 6/8	4 5/8	4 5/8	7	6	Clay Co., MN	Darrin D. Tonsfeldt	Darrin D. Tonsfeldt	1993	929
178 2/8	26 7/8	25 1/8	18 6/8	6 1/8	6 3/8	5	5	Union Co., IL	K. Kent Treece	K. Kent Treece	1997	929
178 2/8	28 3/8	28 7/8	19 4/8	5 3/8	5 4/8	8	7	Kanabec Co., MN	Lennie L. Henning	Lennie L. Henning	1999	929
178 2/8	27 6/8	27 1/8	21 5/8	5 6/8	5 4/8	8	9	Warren Co., IL	Picked Up	Tory Mills	1999	929
178 2/8	28 7/8	28 7/8	21 6/8	4 7/8	5	4	4	Yorkton, SK	Wayde Morley	Wayde Morley	1999	929
178 2/8	25	25	22 1/8	4 3/8	4 4/8	5	6	Greene Co., VA	Clyde E. Eppard, Sr.	Clyde E. Eppard, Sr.	2000	929
178 1/8	24 1/8	23 5/8	19 1/8	4 4/8	4 5/8	8	8	Dismal River, NE	Gift of G.B. Grinnell to NCHH	Unknown	PR 1909	944
178 1/8	28 3/8	26 7/8	18 7/8	4 7/8	5	5	7	Concrete, ND	Lawrence E. Vandal	Lawrence E. Vandal	1947	944
178 1/8	24 6/8	25 5/8	25 6/8	4 3/8	4 3/8	6	6	Kent Co., MD	Herman Gravatt	Donald P. Travis	1955	944
178 1/8	27 5/8	27 4/8	17 4/8	4 7/8	4 7/8	8	7	Iron Co., WI	DuWayne A. Weichel	Robert G. Steidtmann	1957	944
178 1/8	28 1/8	28 1/8	18 1/8	4 6/8	4 6/8	5	5	Iron Co., MI	James Locke	Cabela's, Inc.	1960	944
178 1/8	29 1/8	28 4/8	18 4/8	4 7/8	4 7/8	7	7	Harlan Co., NE	Duane E. Johnson	Duane E. Johnson	1967	944
178 1/8	26 5/8	26 5/8	20 4/8	4 2/8	4 3/8	5	6	Vonda, SK	Orest Hilkewich	Orest Hilkewich	1980	944
178 1/8	27 4/8	27 4/8	21 1/8	5 5/8	5 4/8	5	5	Price Co., WI	Terry Staroba	Terry Staroba	1983	944
178 1/8	28 5/8	29	21 7/8	5 5/8	5 5/8	5	5	Aroostook Co., ME	Gary G. Saucier	Gary G. Saucier	1987	944
178 1/8	24	23 3/8	16 3/8	4 4/8	4 4/8	5	6	Teton Co., MT	Ivan F. Holland	Ivan F. Holland	1991	944
178 1/8	29 1/8	28	19 5/8	4 3/8	4 3/8	7	7	Arkansas Co., AR	Roger Hansell	Roger Hansell	1992	944
178 1/8	26 7/8	26 2/8	20 7/8	5 1/8	5 1/8	5	5	Coteau Hills, SK	Trevor A. Broom	Trevor A. Broom	1997	944
178 1/8	26 6/8	26 6/8	25 3/8	5 3/8	5 3/8	5	6	Cass Co., MN	Robert C. Palmer, Jr.	Robert C. Palmer, Jr.	1997	944
178 1/8	25 5/8	25 3/8	19 5/8	6 1/8	5 6/8	6	6	De Kalb Co., MO	Kendall J. Weigand	Kendall J. Weigand	1998	944
178 1/8	26 7/8	27	21 3/8	4 2/8	4 2/8	5	6	Morgan Co., IL	Clark K. Dirden	Clark K. Dirden	1999	944

Score	Main Beam R	Main Beam L	Inside Spread	Circ. R	Circ. L	Pts R	Pts L	Locality	Hunter	Owner	Date	Rank
178 1/8	28 2/8	28 6/8	22 3/8	5 2/8	5 2/8	7	7	Wheeler Co., NE	Raymond M. Gay	Raymond M. Gay	1999	944
178 1/8	25 5/8	25 5/8	19 6/8	5 5/8	5 5/8	6	6	Johnson Co., IL	Jordan R. Lewis	Jordan R. Lewis	2000	944
178	27	27 2/8	17 4/8	5	4 6/8	7	6	Price Co., WI	Emery Swan	Emery Swan	1949	961
178	26 7/8	27 2/8	21 6/8	4 3/8	4 3/8	6	6	Clark Co., MO	Allen L. Courtney	Allen L. Courtney	1966	961
178	24 1/8	25 3/8	16 6/8	4 7/8	4 6/8	6	6	Hillsdale Co., MI	Dudley N. Spade	Dudley N. Spade	1972	961
178	25	24 6/8	17 2/8	4 5/8	4 6/8	6	7	Washington Co., IA	Brad Gardner	Vaughn Wilkins	1978	961
178	27 5/8	27 2/8	20	5 2/8	5 1/8	7	6	Price Co., WI	John E. Martinson	John E. Martinson	1981	961
178	25 1/8	26 2/8	22 6/8	6	6	5	5	Union Co., KY	Gary L. Gibson	Gary L. Gibson	1983	961
178	29	30 2/8	25	5 1/8	5	7	9	Appanoose Co., IA	Steve G. Huff	Steve G. Huff	1988	961
178	25 4/8	25 1/8	18 5/8	4 1/8	4 1/8	5	7	Caswell Co., NC	Picked Up	Jimmy Koger	1988	961
178	28 2/8	26 5/8	18 2/8	5	4 5/8	7	5	Crawford Co., WI	Picked Up	Cabela's, Inc.	1992	961
178	29 5/8	28 2/8	21	5 3/8	5 2/8	5	5	Macon Co., MO	Charles L. Harrington	Charles L. Harrington	1992	961
178	28 2/8	28 2/8	19 3/8	5 2/8	5 1/8	5	6	Shell Lake, SK	Brent Brewer	Brent Brewer	1994	961
178	25 7/8	26 2/8	18 1/8	5 1/8	5 2/8	6	6	Decatur Co., IA	Picked Up	Jeffrey R. Danner	1995	961
178	28	28 6/8	19 2/8	4 4/8	4 4/8	5	6	Sweet Grass, SK	Leo J. Lefevre	Leo J. Lefevre	1999	961
178	28 1/8	28 2/8	21 6/8	5 1/8	5 2/8	5	5	Chariton Co., MO	G. Duane Gunn	G. Duane Gunn	2001	961
177 7/8	29 2/8	29 5/8	18 2/8	5 5/8	5 3/8	7	5	Burnett Co., WI	John Backlund	Lester Thor	1916	975
177 7/8	27	28 4/8	20 3/8	4 6/8	4 6/8	6	7	Chicot Co., AR	George Matthews	W.T. Haynes	1923	975
177 7/8	28	27 4/8	20	5 6/8	5 6/8	5	6	Iron Co., MI	Felix Brzoznowski	Joseph Brzoznowski	1939	975
177 7/8	26 4/8	25 4/8	22 5/8	5	5	6	6	Houston Co., MN	Oscar W. Bernsdorf	Roger Bernsdorf	1959	975
177 7/8	24 2/8	23 7/8	19 3/8	4 4/8	4 6/8	7	7	Ymir, BC	Frank Gowing	Frank Gowing	1961	975
177 7/8	25 7/8	25 1/8	24 3/8	5 1/8	5	5	5	Wibaux Co., MT	Dan Amunrud	David Welliever	1967	975
177 7/8	26 3/8	26 6/8	22 1/8	5 2/8	5 2/8	6	6	Christian Co., IL	Rodney J. Gorden	Rodney J. Gorden	1974	975
177 7/8	27 6/8	26 1/8	18 5/8	5 3/8	5	5	5	Haralson Co., GA	Picked Up	Alfred Wright	1982	975
177 7/8	26 4/8	26 6/8	23	5	5	9	9	Jefferson Co., MT	Tracy Forcella	Tracy Forcella	1983	975
177 7/8	26 6/8	26 6/8	18 2/8	4 3/8	4 3/8	6	6	Penobscot Co., ME	Andrew B. Alexander	Andrew B. Alexander	1985	975
177 7/8	22 4/8	22 4/8	17 4/8	5 2/8	5 2/8	7	7	Cass Co., ND	Joe D. Chesley	Joe D. Chesley	1987	975
177 7/8	25	25	17	5 1/8	5	8	6	Vilas Co., WI	Dean A. Casper	Dean A. Casper	1990	975
177 7/8	28 6/8	26 5/8	23 7/8	5 3/8	5 4/8	7	7	St. Mary's Co., MD	Timothy B. Moore	Timothy B. Moore	1990	975
177 7/8	24 3/8	24	19 5/8	4 5/8	4 6/8	10	5	Harper Co., OK	Scott Davis	Scott Davis	1993	975
177 7/8	27	27 7/8	19 5/8	5 4/8	5 3/8	6	6	Rosieisle, MB	Richard A. Fay	Richard A. Fay	1995	975
177 7/8	27 4/8	27 2/8	18 7/8	5 3/8	5 4/8	6	7	Bates Co., MO	Daniel P. White	Daniel P. White	1995	975
177 7/8	25 5/8	22	19 5/8	4 2/8	4 4/8	7	8	Ontario Co., NY	Stephen E. McAllister	Stephen E. McAllister	1996	975
177 7/8	25 1/8	25 3/8	18 5/8	5	5	5	5	Pettis Co., MO	Michael J. Macaffree	Michael J. Macaffree	1997	975
177 7/8	25 2/8	26 5/8	18 1/8	5 3/8	5 1/8	6	6	Jefferson Co., IA	John J. Oberhaus	John J. Oberhaus	1997	975
177 7/8	24 2/8	24 7/8	19 7/8	4 4/8	4 5/8	6	5	Sioux Narrows, ON	Michael Christopher	Michael Christopher	1999	975
177 7/8	27 1/8	24 5/8	23 5/8	5 1/8	4 7/8	6	5	Morgan Co., IL	Clint A. Rhea	Clint A. Rhea	2002	975
177 6/8	24 5/8	24 7/8	19	4 6/8	4 5/8	6	6	Paxton, NE	Ole Herstedt	Ole Herstedt	1956	996
177 6/8	24	24	22	4 4/8	4 4/8	6	6	Kleberg Co., TX	Elaine A. O'Brien	Patrick O'Brien	1972	996
177 6/8	26 6/8	25 4/8	22 6/8	5	5	6	5	Atoka Co., OK	Skip Rowell	Skip Rowell	1972	996
177 6/8	23 4/8	24	24	4 6/8	4 5/8	6	6	Duval Co., TX	Harry Heimer	Harry Heimer	1974	996
177 6/8	26 5/8	27 4/8	23 4/8	4 4/8	4 4/8	5	5	Stearns Co., MN	Robert G. Schwarz	Robert G. Schwarz	1975	996
177 6/8	26 4/8	24 4/8	18 2/8	5 1/8	5	7	9	Shaunavon, SK	Stan J. Crawford	Stan J. Crawford	1979	996
177 6/8	24 3/8	23 5/8	19	4 6/8	4 6/8	5	5	Clark Co., MO	Billie G. Noble	Billie G. Noble	1985	996
177 6/8	25 7/8	26 4/8	18	4 2/8	4 3/8	6	7	Kankakee Co., IL	Robert R. Tolmer, Jr.	Robert R. Tolmer, Jr.	1987	996
177 6/8	25 4/8	26 3/8	20	5 1/8	5 1/8	6	6	Pendleton Co., KY	Daniel Michalski	Daniel Michalski	1988	996
177 6/8	26 2/8	27 2/8	18 2/8	5 4/8	5 4/8	6	6	Antler River, SK	Larry Sterling	Larry Sterling	1989	996
177 6/8	27 6/8	28 1/8	19 1/8	4 4/8	4 3/8	8	7	Anderson Co., KS	Randall R. West	Randall R. West	1990	996

WHITETAIL DEER - TYPICAL ANTLERS
Odocoileus virginianus virginianus and certain related subspecies

Score	Length of Main Beam		Inside Spread	Circumference at Smallest Place Between Burr and First Point		Number of Points		Locality	Hunter	Owner	Date Killed	Rank
	R	L		R	L	R	L					
177 6/8	26 4/8	26 5/8	20 7/8	4 6/8	4 4/8	5	6	Lincoln Co., MT	Bernard B. White	Bernard B. White	1990	996
177 6/8	31	29	23	5	5	5	7	Washington Co., ME	Edward S. Welsh, Jr.	Edward S. Welsh, Jr.	1992	996
177 6/8	29	27 7/8	20	5 2/8	5 2/8	6	5	St. Louis Co., MN	Ronald R. Anderson	Ronald R. Anderson	1994	996
177 6/8	26 5/8	27 4/8	19 6/8	4 6/8	4 6/8	5	5	Sumner Co., KS	Alan K. Boyle	Alan K. Boyle	1995	996
177 6/8	25 3/8	25 2/8	20 2/8	5 1/8	5	5	5	Vernon Co., MO	Darrell Chapman	Darrell Chapman	1997	996
177 6/8	26 5/8	25 5/8	19 7/8	5 1/8	5	6	5	Crow Wing Co., MN	Gil Atwater	Donald McNevin	1926	1012
177 5/8	24 6/8	23 3/8	24 7/8	5 1/8	5 2/8	7	6	Dimmit Co., TX	Carter Younts	Carter Younts	1963	1012
177 5/8	25 5/8	26 2/8	19 1/8	5 4/8	5 3/8	5	5	Endeavour, SK	Terry L. Halgrimson	Terry L. Halgrimson	1971	1012
177 5/8	26 2/8	26 6/8	22 6/8	4 7/8	4 7/8	7	6	Wabasha Co., MN	Bruce J. Hall	Bruce J. Hall	1972	1012
177 5/8	25	24 3/8	17 6/8	4 1/8	4 1/8	6	8	Macon Co., GA	James W. Athon	Mike's Gun Shop	1976	1012
177 5/8	25	25 4/8	17 5/8	5	5 2/8	6	6	Macon Co., GA	Dalton H. Cannon	Dalton H. Cannon	1977	1012
177 5/8	24 4/8	25 3/8	18 3/8	5 1/8	5 1/8	6	7	Jim Hogg Co., TX	Howard Sturgess	Lawson W. Walden	PR 1982	1012
177 5/8	29	28 2/8	22	4 4/8	4 4/8	7	8	Harrison Co., OH	Mark Dulkoski	Mark Dulkoski	1984	1012
177 5/8	25 5/8	25 5/8	19 5/8	5 3/8	5 3/8	5	5	Washburn Co., WI	Patrick Henk	Patrick Henk	1984	1012
177 5/8	26	25 6/8	21 3/8	4 5/8	4 5/8	5	5	Idaho Co., ID	Donna M. Knight	Donna M. Knight	1986	1012
177 5/8	27 6/8	28 5/8	18	5 5/8	5 4/8	6	6	Colquitt Co., GA	Timothy Carter	Timothy Carter	1990	1012
177 5/8	23 4/8	25 7/8	20 7/8	5 1/8	5 4/8	7	9	Morrison Co., MN	Jeanne Backowski-Jensen	Jeanne Backowski-Jensen	1991	1012
177 5/8	27 7/8	27	19 2/8	6 3/8	6 5/8	9	9	Marshall Co., KS	Terre J. Carter	Terre J. Carter	1992	1012
177 5/8	25 7/8	27	18 1/8	4 6/8	4 6/8	7	6	Kittson Co., MN	Picked Up	Cabela's, Inc.	1993	1012
177 5/8	26 5/8	25	17 7/8	5 1/8	5 1/8	5	6	Nemaha Co., KS	Stephen C. Damron	Stephen C. Damron	1995	1012
177 5/8	26 1/8	26 1/8	22 3/8	5 6/8	5 5/8	5	5	Winneshiek Co., IA	Glen J. Gienau	Glen J. Gienau	1995	1012
177 5/8	28 5/8	28 2/8	20 1/8	4 4/8	4 4/8	6	5	Berkshire Co., MA	William E. Tatro	William E. Tatro	1995	1012
177 5/8	28	28 2/8	21 3/8	5 1/8	5 1/8	5	5	Concordia Parish, LA	John W. King	John W. King	1996	1012
177 5/8	26 4/8	26 6/8	18 4/8	5 1/8	4 5/8	5	6	Schuyler Co., IL	Archie D. Stagner	Archie D. Stagner	1997	1012
177 5/8	26 2/8	25 4/8	20 1/8	4 3/8	5 4/8	6	5	Buffalo Co., WI	Mark T. Gleiter	Mark T. Gleiter	1998	1012
177 5/8	26 3/8	26	15 6/8	4 7/8	5	7	5	Roger Mills Co., OK	Dusty W. Davis	Dusty W. Davis	2000	1012
177 5/8	25 5/8	27 1/8	21 5/8	4 3/8	4 3/8	5	6	Frio Co., TX	Guy S. Perkins	Guy S. Perkins	2001	1012
177 5/8	25 7/8	25 3/8	18 6/8	5 7/8	6	6	7	Fulton Co., IL	Justin Hillman	Justin Hillman	2002	1012
177 5/8	28 1/8	30	20 3/8	5	4 6/8	4	4	Warren Co., IL	Matthew J. Lovdahl	Matthew J. Lovdahl	2002	1012
177 5/8	23	24 3/8	21 1/8	5 5/8	5 4/8	6	6	Pierce Co., WI	Robert H. Zich	Robert H. Zich	2002	1012
177 4/8	26	26 4/8	21 5/8	4 5/8	4 4/8	8	6	Oneida Co., WI	Elmer Ahlborn	Gene Ahlborn	1926	1037
177 4/8	27 6/8	27 4/8	23 4/8	5	5	6	5	Dimmit Co., TX	Tom Brady	McLean Bowman	1926	1037
177 4/8	27 2/8	27 7/8	20	4 6/8	4 5/8	7	5	Marinette Co., WI	Henry L. Hoffman	Henry L. Hoffman	1942	1037
177 4/8	25	24 4/8	21 1/8	5 2/8	5 4/8	5	6	Dundurn, SK	L.B. Galbraith	L.B. Galbraith	1956	1037
177 4/8	26 1/8	26	21	4	4 1/8	5	5	Bedford Co., PA	Raymond Miller	Raymond Miller	1957	1037
177 4/8	28 5/8	29 2/8	18 3/8	5 5/8	5 5/8	6	9	Cass Co., MN	Larry K. Sherman	Larry K. Sherman	1964	1037

Score								Locality			Date	Rank
177 4/8	28 2/8	28 3/8	22 4/8	5 6/8	5 6/8	5	6	Beltrami Co., MN	Sheldon M. Stockdale	Sheldon M. Stockdale	1968	1037
177 4/8	25 7/8	26 2/8	16 4/8	4 7/8	4 5/8	6	7	Wisconsin	Unknown	Brant J. Mueller	PR 1975	1037
177 4/8	26	26 4/8	24	5	5	6	6	Montana	Unknown	Unknown	1983	1037
177 4/8	28 3/8	28 4/8	23 5/8	4 4/8	4 3/8	8	5	Otter Tail Co., MN	Robert J. Perszyk	Robert J. Perszyk	1985	1037
177 4/8	26	28	21 6/8	5 6/8	5 3/8	7	6	Krydor, SK	Julian Shewchuk	Julian Shewchuk	1985	1037
177 4/8	29 7/8	28 6/8	21 6/8	4 6/8	4 7/8	5	6	Grayson Co., KY	David W. Mercer	David W. Mercer	1986	1037
177 4/8	28 3/8	28	25	5 3/8	5 2/8	8	7	Simpson Co., KY	Mickel J. Norris	Mickel J. Norris	1992	1037
177 4/8	26 3/8	26 2/8	20 4/8	5	5	6	5	Swan River, MB	Myles T. Keller	Myles T. Keller	1994	1037
177 4/8	26 3/8	25 6/8	17	4 6/8	4 6/8	6	6	Torquay, SK	Wayne Daae	Wayne Daae	1996	1037
177 4/8	28 6/8	28 5/8	19 2/8	4 5/8	4 5/8	6	6	St. Lawrence Co., NY	Timothy B. Lucas	Timothy B. Lucas	1997	1037
177 4/8	27 6/8	26 5/8	18 6/8	4 4/8	4 4/8	9	6	Arborfield, SK	Tyler Johnson	Terry L. Amos	1998	1037
177 4/8	26 6/8	26 6/8	20 5/8	5	5 1/8	6	5	Pike Co., IL	Chad S. Lankford	Chad S. Lankford	2001	1037
177 4/8	28 6/8	27 2/8	20	5 2/8	5 3/8	5	7	Meeting Lake, SK	Carl C. Sankey	Carl C. Sankey	2001	1037
177 3/8	25 4/8	25 4/8	18	6	6 2/8	6	5	Hall Co., NE	Charles R. Babel	C.P. Medore	1969	1056
177 3/8	27	26 2/8	23 1/8	5	5 1/8	5	5	Menominee Co., WI	William Matchopatow, Sr.	William Matchopatow, Sr.	1981	1056
177 3/8	26	26	20 2/8	5 3/8	5 2/8	6	5	Rusk Co., WI	David A. Reichel	David A. Reichel	1981	1056
177 3/8	27 1/8	26 3/8	20 3/8	5 4/8	5 2/8	5	5	Greene Co., IA	Roger V. Carlson	Roger V. Carlson	1983	1056
177 3/8	27 3/8	28	16 5/8	5	5 1/8	5	5	Claiborne Parish, LA	Steven L. Morton	Steven L. Morton	1986	1056
177 3/8	29 1/8	30 1/8	24 7/8	6 4/8	6 2/8	9	9	Menominee Co., WI	Jeff N. Dixon	Jeff N. Dixon	1987	1056
177 3/8	25 4/8	27 1/8	22 3/8	5 1/8	5 4/8	6	6	Chautauqua Co., KS	Wesley D. Coldren	Wesley D. Coldren	1991	1056
177 3/8	27 3/8	27 1/8	18 6/8	5 4/8	5 5/8	9	9	Weasel Creek, AB	Ray M. Fels	Ray M. Fels	1991	1056
177 3/8	26	25 7/8	20 3/8	4 5/8	4 6/8	6	6	Vermilion River, AB	Larry Flaata	Larry Flaata	1995	1056
177 3/8	26 1/8	25	20	5 1/8	5 1/8	7	6	Jefferson Co., WI	John L. Hausz	John L. Hausz	1996	1056
177 3/8	26 6/8	26 5/8	18 7/8	5 2/8	5 1/8	5	7	Gove Co., KS	Daniel L. Arndt	Daniel L. Arndt	1997	1056
177 3/8	28 3/8	29 5/8	23 7/8	4 5/8	4 6/8	5	5	Madison Co., IL	Joseph S. Cannon	Joseph S. Cannon	1998	1056
177 3/8	27 7/8	28 2/8	23 1/8	5 3/8	5 2/8	5	5	Woodson Co., KS	Terry S. Wells	Terry S. Wells	1998	1056
177 3/8	26	25 2/8	18 5/8	5 3/8	5 3/8	5	6	Lee Co., IL	Picked Up	Paul A. Harmon	2002	1056
177 2/8	26 6/8	25 3/8	26 2/8	5 1/8	5 1/8	7	7	Webb Co., TX	Unknown	Eugene Roberts	1924	1070
177 2/8	27 5/8	27 1/8	19 4/8	4 6/8	4 6/8	7	5	Pine Co., MN	C. Foster & E. Kepler	Lois Youngbauer	1930	1070
177 2/8	29 4/8	24 1/8	22 2/8	4 2/8	4 1/8	7	5	La Salle Co., TX	T.H. Barker	Michael R. Barker	1939	1070
177 2/8	29 1/8	24 5/8	21	4 5/8	4 5/8	5	5	Buffalo Co., WI	George W. Kees	George W. Kees	1957	1070
177 2/8	28 1/8	29 2/8	20 6/8	4 6/8	4 6/8	5	5	Augusta Co., VA	Donald W. Houser	Donald W. Houser	1963	1070
177 2/8	25 3/8	28	21 5/8	4 1/8	4 1/8	8	9	Golden Valley Co., ND	Allen Goltz	Allen Goltz	1964	1070
177 2/8	26 5/8	24 3/8	22	4 4/8	4 4/8	7	7	Guthrie Co., IA	Picked Up	Dalton H. Hoover	1970	1070
177 2/8	27 4/8	27 3/8	21 2/8	5 1/8	5 1/8	5	5	Rainy River, ON	Lynn Wilson	Lynn Wilson	1972	1070
177 2/8	29 4/8	30 2/8	18 2/8	6 3/8	6 5/8	6	6	Geary Co., KS	Kelly D. Gulker	Kelly D. Gulker	1982	1070
177 2/8	25 5/8	25 7/8	18 2/8	4 6/8	4 6/8	6	6	Richland Co., WI	Dewitt S. Pulham	Dewitt S. Pulham	1982	1070
177 2/8	27 5/8	29	21 7/8	6	6	6	5	Litchfield Co., CT	Picked Up	Rickey A. Vincent	1984	1070
177 2/8	27 5/8	26 3/8	17 3/8	4 4/8	4 6/8	8	7	Montgomery Co., KY	Bobby M. Dale	Bobby M. Dale	1986	1070
177 2/8	27	27 4/8	20 6/8	5	5	5	5	Belmont Co., OH	Kevin A. Grimes	Kevin A. Grimes	1987	1070
177 2/8	29 4/8	28 3/8	18 6/8	4 5/8	4 5/8	7	7	Clarke Co., IA	Richard Bassett	Richard Bassett	1989	1070
177 2/8	24 2/8	23 4/8	20 2/8	5	5	6	6	Sawyer Co., ME	William H. Laney	William H. Laney	1991	1070
177 2/8	27	25 6/8	19 4/8	5 4/8	5 4/8	6	6	Somerset Co., ME	Richard D. Hagerty	Richard D. Hagerty	1993	1070
177 2/8	25 4/8	25	16 7/8	4 7/8	4 7/8	6	6	Pushmataha Co., OK	Herbert W. Savage	Herbert W. Savage	1994	1070
177 2/8	26	27	19 4/8	5 4/8	5 4/8	5	5	Mills Co., IA	James Roberts	James H. Roberts	1998	1070
177 2/8	25 6/8	24 2/8	20 2/8	4 7/8	4 7/8	6	6	Webb Co., TX	Gordon Still	Gordon Still	1999	1070
177 2/8	28 7/8	28 2/8	18 7/8	5 4/8	5 4/8	6	5	Pendleton Co., KY	John C. Bowers	John C. Bowers	2000	1070
177 2/8	30	29 4/8	20 6/8	5 1/8	5	5	6	Monroe Co., WI	Mark A. Schmitz	Mark A. Schmitz	2000	1070

WHITETAIL DEER - TYPICAL ANTLERS

Odocoileus virginianus virginianus and certain related subspecies

Score	Length of Main Beam R	L	Inside Spread	Circumference at Smallest Place Between Burr and First Point R	L	Number of Points R	L	Locality	Hunter	Owner	Date Killed	Rank
177 2/8	28 7/8	29 2/8	22 6/8	5 1/8	5 1/8	5	4	Page Co., IA	Darrel L. Vogel	Darrel L. Vogel	2000	1070
177 2/8	25 4/8	25 7/8	18 6/8	5 6/8	5 7/8	5	5	Stockholm, SK	Justin Banga	Justin Banga	2001	1070
177 2/8	25 4/8	24 6/8	21 6/8	4 6/8	4 7/8	5	5	Grundy Co., IL	Brandon Smith	Brandon Smith	2001	1070
177 2/8	25	25 1/8	20 4/8	5 5/8	5 4/8	6	5	Allamakee Co., IA	Mark E. Walleser	Mark E. Walleser	2002	1070
177 1/8	25 5/8	26 1/8	19	5 1/8	5 2/8	7	10	Newcastle, WY	H.W. Julien	John W. Julien	1954	1095
177 1/8	25 2/8	25 4/8	21 1/8	4 5/8	4 3/8	7	7	Marshall Co., MN	Dennis W. Severson	Dennis W. Severson	1954	1095
177 1/8	27	27	18 1/8	4 6/8	4 7/8	6	5	Gregory Co., SD	Harold Deering	Harold Deering	1969	1095
177 1/8	26 7/8	27 1/8	22 1/8	5	4 7/8	5	6	Harrison Co., KY	Picked Up	George Simpson	1978	1095
177 1/8	26 3/8	25 5/8	21 6/8	5 2/8	5 3/8	6	8	Calhoun Co., IL	Paul V. Stumpf	Paul V. Stumpf	1979	1095
177 1/8	27 2/8	27	21 7/8	4 4/8	4 4/8	5	5	Walworth Co., WI	Daniel J. Brede	Daniel J. Brede	1984	1095
177 1/8	28 4/8	26 6/8	20 3/8	5 1/8	5	6	7	Washington Co., IA	Ernest Aronson	Ernest Aronson	1985	1095
177 1/8	25 5/8	25 5/8	22 3/8	4 5/8	4 6/8	6	5	Thorsby, AB	Adam Tomaszewski	Adam Tomaszewski	1985	1095
177 1/8	28	26 7/8	21 1/8	5 7/8	5 7/8	5	5	Kittson Co., MN	Unknown	George W. Flaim	1987	1095
177 1/8	25 7/8	25 3/8	18 5/8	4 5/8	4 4/8	8	6	Forest Co., WI	Carl S. Ernst	Carl S. Ernst	1990	1095
177 1/8	27 1/8	28 6/8	21 2/8	4 6/8	4 6/8	7	5	St. Croix Co., WI	Phillip R. Hovde	Phillip R. Hovde	1990	1095
177 1/8	26 4/8	27	19 4/8	4 6/8	4 7/8	5	6	Cass Co., IA	Cleve H. Powell	Cleve H. Powell	1990	1095
177 1/8	27 7/8	26 3/8	18 4/8	5 5/8	5 6/8	6	7	Wolf Lake, AB	Keith W. Hamilton	Keith W. Hamilton	1992	1095
177 1/8	25 2/8	24 7/8	20 5/8	5	5	7	5	Ogle Co., IL	Daniel L. Bouton	Daniel L. Bouton	1993	1095
177 1/8	26 6/8	27 1/8	20 7/8	5 1/8	5 2/8	6	5	Toole Co., MT	Anthony W. Enos	Anthony W. Enos	1994	1095
177 1/8	25 7/8	25 7/8	18 1/8	4 7/8	4 6/8	5	5	Davis Co., IA	Michael G. White	Michael G. White	1995	1095
177 1/8	26 6/8	26 6/8	25 1/8	5 3/8	5 3/8	8	7	Golden City Lake, ON	Beverly E. Bennett	Beverly E. Bennett	1995	1095
177 1/8	25 5/8	25 7/8	23 5/8	4 7/8	4 7/8	6	7	Clay Co., IA	Jeff D. Tiefenthaler	Jeff D. Tiefenthaler	2001	1095
177	28 1/8	28	17 2/8	4 6/8	4 6/8	6	7	Bayfield Co., WI	Elof E. Sjostrom	Mrs. Elof E. Sjostrom	1932	1113
177	25 1/8	25 3/8	17 2/8	5	5 1/8	7	7	Rainey River, ON	Robert K. Hayes	Robert K. Hayes	1949	1113
177	26 2/8	25 6/8	19 7/8	5	5 1/8	8	10	Kandiyohi Co., MN	Dale E. Nelson	Scott Nelson	1949	1113
177	23 4/8	24 2/8	16 6/8	4 7/8	5	6	7	St. Louis Co., MN	Chuck Perkins	Chuck Perkins	1964	1113
177	25	26	19 1/8	6	5 7/8	6	5	Gage Co., NE	Art Wallman	Art Wallman	1968	1113
177	26 2/8	27 6/8	18 4/8	4 4/8	4 6/8	5	5	Cass Co., IN	Herbert R. Frushour	Herbert R. Frushour	1974	1113
177	28 7/8	28 6/8	22 3/8	4 1/8	4	6	5	Jasper Co., IN	Dan Haskins	Douglas R. Plourde	1975	1113
177	28 1/8	26 1/8	20 7/8	5 4/8	5 6/8	7	6	Innisfree, AB	Donald M. Baranec	Donald M. Baranec	1984	1113
177	24 7/8	25	16 2/8	5 1/8	5 1/8	8	9	Daly, MB	Bruce A. Crofton	Bruce A. Crofton	1984	1113
177	23 7/8	25 1/8	14 3/8	5 2/8	5 1/8	11	7	Lundar, MB	Fred Thorkelson	Fred Thorkelson	1986	1113
177	26 2/8	26 1/8	20 4/8	4 3/8	4 5/8	6	6	Muscatine Co., IA	Jack Van Nice	Jack Van Nice	1986	1113
177	23 4/8	22 1/8	16 4/8	4 6/8	4 6/8	6	5	Harrison Co., IA	Craig D. Mitchell	Craig D. Mitchell	1988	1113
177	28 2/8	28 1/8	18 3/8	5	5	8	6	Baltimore Co., MD	Richard B. Traband	Richard B. Traband	1990	1113
177	26 1/8	25 1/8	19 6/8	4 3/8	4 3/8	6	6	Macon Co., MO	Wilbert R. Freeman	Wilbert R. Freeman	1991	1113

Score	Main Beam R	Main Beam L	Spread	Circ. R	Circ. L	Pts R	Pts L	Locality	By Whom Killed	By Whom Owned	Date	Rank
177	26	27 3/8	21 6/8	5 3/8	5	6	10	Lewis Co., KY	David E. Henderson	David E. Henderson	1994	1113
177	25 5/8	26 2/8	18 4/8	4 3/8	4 5/8	5	5	Rapides Parish, LA	H. Glenn Feazell	H. Glenn Feazell	1997	1113
177	29 2/8	27 6/8	19 2/8	5 2/8	5 2/8	6	6	Nicholas Co., KY	Jim D. Whisman	Jim D. Whisman	1998	1113
177	25 4/8	25 1/8	18	4 3/8	4 3/8	8	6	Union Co., IA	Michael A. Herrick	Michael A. Herrick	2000	1113
177	27 7/8	28 1/8	26 2/8	4 5/8	4 7/8	8	8	Lake Co., OH	Thomas A. Lasko	Thomas A. Lasko	2000	1113
177	28 3/8	26 6/8	17 6/8	4 7/8	4 6/8	5	5	Casey Co., KY	Jeff Bastin	Jeff Bastin	2001	1113
176 7/8	25 5/8	25 5/8	22 4/8	5	5 1/8	6	9	Prince George Co., VA	Fred W. Collins	Fred W. Collins	1949	1133
176 7/8	28	26 7/8	16 2/8	3 7/8	3 6/8	7	5	Day Co., SD	William B. Davis	William B. Davis	1959	1133
176 7/8	27 2/8	28 4/8	24 2/8	4 4/8	4 4/8	6	6	Lincoln Co., WI	Edmond H. Pay	Edmond H. Pay	1959	1133
176 7/8	25 4/8	26	19 7/8	5 5/8	5 4/8	6	6	Pierson, MB	Bud Smith	Bud Smith	1960	1133
176 7/8	27 3/8	27 3/8	23	4 6/8	5 7/8	6	6	Logan Co., OH	David Sutherly	David Sutherly	1975	1133
176 7/8	25 6/8	25 5/8	22 1/8	4 5/8	4 6/8	5	5	Butler Co., KS	Craig D. Waltman	Craig D. Waltman	1982	1133
176 7/8	27 4/8	27 4/8	20 3/8	4 5/8	4 5/8	5	5	Pierce Co., WI	John M. Oelke	John M. Oelke	1984	1133
176 7/8	27 1/8	28	18 1/8	5 6/8	4 7/8	7	7	McDonough Co., IL	Richard F. Krohe	Richard F. Krohe	1986	1133
176 7/8	30	28	25 3/8	4 4/8	5 6/8	5	5	Marion Co., OH	Thomas A. Bridenstine	Thomas A. Bridenstine	1987	1133
176 7/8	27 4/8	27 5/8	18 5/8	5 4/8	4 5/8	5	5	Cass Co., IL	Mark A. Kluckman	Mark A. Kluckman	1988	1133
176 7/8	26 7/8	26 6/8	29 5/8	4 4/8	5 4/8	4	4	Unknown	Unknown	R. Rogers and R. Scott	PR 1988	1133
176 7/8	24 1/8	25 7/8	21 1/8	5 5/8	4 4/8	5	5	Warren Co., OH	Richard M. Barhorst	Richard M. Barhorst	1990	1133
176 7/8	28 1/8	28 6/8	21 3/8	5 1/8	5 4/8	5	5	Saline Co., IL	Edward L. Brown	Edward L. Brown	1991	1133
176 7/8	27 1/8	27 1/8	20 7/8	4 7/8	5	6	6	Jackson Co., MI	David M. Lindeman	David M. Lindeman	1991	1133
176 7/8	25 3/8	25 3/8	19 1/8	5 5/8	4 7/8	5	5	Qu'Appelle River, SK	W. Leo Bumphrey	W. Leo Bumphrey	1992	1133
176 7/8	25 6/8	25 6/8	21 6/8	5	5 4/8	5	5	Medina Co., OH	Bradley K. Shafer	Bradley K. Shafer	1994	1133
176 7/8	27 1/8	25 6/8	17 4/8	6 5/8	6 7/8	5	5	Sullivan Co., IN	Larry A. Nash	Larry A. Nash	1995	1133
176 7/8	27 3/8	25 6/8	20 1/8	5 2/8	5 2/8	4	4	Harrison Co., IA	Jay D. Jensen	Jay D. Jensen	2000	1133
176 6/8	27 1/8	26	20 7/8	5 3/8	5 4/8	6	6	Vilas Co., WI	Porter Dean	Safari North Tax.	1938	1151
176 6/8	26 3/8	25	19	5 7/8	5 1/8	6	6	Langlade Co., WI	Jack Ryan	Ray T. Charles	1950	1151
176 6/8	25 5/8	27 3/8	20 6/8	4 4/8	4 4/8	6	6	Clinton Co., MI	Ray Sadler	Ray Sadler	1963	1151
176 6/8	26 3/8	26	19 2/8	4 6/8	4 8/8	6	6	Winona Co., MN	Harry M. Timm	Harry M. Timm	1964	1151
176 6/8	26 2/8	26 2/8	18 4/8	5 2/8	5 3/8	11	12	Knox Co., NE	Alvin Zimmerman	Spanky Greenville	1966	1151
176 6/8	25	25	23 4/8	4 6/8	4 1/8	5	5	Frankfort, KS	Ray A. Mosher	Ray A. Mosher	1966	1151
176 6/8	26 5/8	26 4/8	21 4/8	5 2/8	5 4/8	6	6	Pine Co., MN	Kim Shira	Kim Shira	1977	1151
176 6/8	26 4/8	25 6/8	20 2/8	4 7/8	4 6/8	6	6	Muscatine Co., IA	Donald L. McCullough	Donald L. McCullough	1980	1151
176 6/8	27	27 7/8	22 2/8	5 7/8	5 7/8	5	5	Buffalo Co., WI	Dean Broberg	Dean Broberg	1985	1151
176 6/8	24 4/8	24 5/8	19 4/8	5	5 3/8	5	5	Miami Co., KS	Richard T. Hale	Richard T. Hale	1985	1151
176 6/8	22 3/8	23 6/8	16 2/8	4 1/8	4 1/8	7	7	Idaho Co., ID	Edward D. Moore	Edward D. Moore	1986	1151
176 6/8	23 6/8	23 6/8	19 2/8	5 4/8	5 2/8	9	8	Saskatchewan	Unknown	D. Ross Sayrs	1986	1151
176 6/8	26 1/8	25	20 5/8	6 2/8	5 7/8	6	6	Adams Co., WI	Mark R. Faber	Mark R. Faber	1987	1151
176 6/8	26 5/8	25 6/8	17	5 2/8	5 1/8	7	7	Idaho Co., ID	Frank J. Loughran	Frank J. Loughran	1987	1151
176 6/8	23 7/8	26 1/8	20 3/8	5 3/8	5 4/8	5	5	Linn Co., IA	Douglas D. Kriegel	Douglas D. Kriegel	1988	1151
176 6/8	26	26	22 7/8	4 5/8	5 1/8	6	6	McHenry Co., IL	Eugene Melby	Eugene Melby	1988	1151
176 6/8	27 4/8	27 4/8	23	5	4 7/8	6	6	Sturgeon River, AB	Michael G. Schmermund	Michael G. Schmermund	1990	1151
176 6/8	26 2/8	25 1/8	21 4/8	4 6/8	4 5/8	6	6	Kane Co., IL	Mark O. DuLong	Mark O. DuLong	1991	1151
176 6/8	24 6/8	23 7/8	17 6/8	4 4/8	4 4/8	9	9	Moose Mt., SK	Dwight C. Tonn	Dwight C. Tonn	1991	1151
176 6/8	28 1/8	28 6/8	24 6/8	5 1/8	5 1/8	4	4	Saskatchewan	Jim McCrea	D.J. Hollinger & B. Howard	1992	1151
176 6/8	26 5/8	27	18 3/8	4 2/8	4 2/8	5	5	Rusk Co., WI	Kent E. Lund	Kent E. Lund	1992	1151
176 6/8	28 3/8	27 6/8	17 6/8	5 1/8	5 3/8	8	8	Morris Co., KS	Nathan D. Muncy	Nathan D. Muncy	1995	1151
176 6/8	25 1/8	25 1/8	17 6/8	5 6/8	5 6/8	6	6	Van Buren Co., IA	Bruce C. Spiller	Bruce C. Spiller	1995	1151
176 6/8	25 4/8	25 4/8	21 1/8	4 6/8	4 6/8	6	6	Bureau Co., IL	John Binz	John Binz	1996	1151

WHITETAIL DEER - TYPICAL ANTLERS
Odocoileus virginianus virginianus and certain related subspecies

Score	Length of Main Beam R	L	Inside Spread	Circumference at Smallest Place Between Burr and First Point R	L	Number of Points R	L	Locality	Hunter	Owner	Date Killed	Rank
176 6/8	26 7/8	26 3/8	23 6/8	6 2/8	5 5/8	6	7	Jefferson Co., IL	Steve S. Shields	Steve S. Shields	1996	1151
176 6/8	29 1/8	28 5/8	20	4 6/8	4 7/8	6	5	Jackson Co., MO	Charles H. Williams	Charles H. Williams	1996	1151
176 6/8	27	26	22 2/8	5 3/8	5 3/8	6	5	Mozart, SK	Frank Prisciak	Frank Prisciak	1997	1151
176 6/8	26 5/8	26 2/8	19 4/8	5 2/8	5 2/8	5	5	River Glade, NB	Dennis Halliday	Dennis Halliday	1998	1151
176 6/8	28 6/8	28	19 6/8	5 2/8	5 1/8	5	5	Cottonwood Co., MN	Cory S. Paplow	Cory S. Paplow	1999	1151
176 6/8	26 2/8	25 6/8	19 6/8	5	4 7/8	7	5	Little Quill Lake, SK	Jonathan Rorquist	Jonathan Rorquist	1999	1151
176 6/8	25 4/8	24 7/8	20 4/8	5 7/8	6 1/8	5	5	Athabasca, AB	Nikki G. Wescott Haley	Nikki G. Wescott Haley	2000	1151
176 6/8	26 1/8	25 1/8	19 6/8	4 4/8	4 4/8	6	7	Jasper Co., IL	Marty A. Draves	Marty A. Draves	2001	1151
176 6/8	26 5/8	28	18 4/8	4 5/8	4 4/8	8	6	Washtenaw Co., MI	Walter J. Kempher	Walter J. Kempher	2002	1151
176 5/8	24 6/8	26 2/8	27 2/8	4 6/8	5	5	6	Hays Co., TX	Bill Kuykendall	Bill Kuykendall	1925	1184
176 5/8	24 2/8	23 3/8	16 7/8	4 3/8	4 3/8	9	9	Webb Co., TX	Antonio Gonzalez	Edmundo R. Gonzalez, Jr.	1929	1184
176 5/8	30	28	21 5/8	4 6/8	4 4/8	6	7	Mifflin Co., PA	John Zerba	Kenneth Zerba	1936	1184
176 5/8	25 4/8	25 4/8	21 7/8	4 5/8	4 7/8	5	5	Bolivar Co., MS	Sidney D. Sessions	Sidney D. Sessions	1952	1184
176 5/8	24 1/8	24 2/8	17 6/8	5	5 1/8	8	8	Washington	Unknown	Jonas Bros. of Seattle	PR 1953	1184
176 5/8	27 4/8	27 2/8	20 5/8	5 1/8	5 1/8	5	5	Winona Co., MN	Robert J. Haessig	Robert J. Haessig	1961	1184
176 5/8	25	25	23 2/8	5	5	6	5	Roberts Co., SD	Fred Kuehl	J.D. Andrews	1964	1184
176 5/8	23 2/8	26 1/8	21 1/8	5 1/8	5	7	7	Rusk Co., WI	Ercel Dustin	Ercel Dustin	1966	1184
176 5/8	26 5/8	25 6/8	17 3/8	4 2/8	4 2/8	5	5	Meade Co., SD	Jerry Humble	Jerry Humble	1970	1184
176 5/8	26 1/8	25 7/8	18 7/8	4 6/8	4 6/8	6	6	St. Louis Co., MN	Unknown	Allen Valley	PR 1970	1184
176 5/8	26 1/8	25 7/8	21 1/8	6 1/8	6 1/8	6	5	Buffalo, AB	Bob Fraleigh	Bob Fraleigh	1978	1184
176 5/8	24 6/8	28 6/8	19 1/8	5 2/8	5 3/8	7	6	Dickinson Co., KS	Robert L. Aldrich	Robert L. Aldrich	1986	1184
176 5/8	24 6/8	25	19 6/8	5 7/8	5 7/8	7	7	Pigeon Lake, AB	Milton Fawcett	Milton Fawcett	1991	1184
176 5/8	26 6/8	25 5/8	18 5/8	4 4/8	4 6/8	6	6	Henderson Co., IL	Quinton R. Koch	Quinton R. Koch	1991	1184
176 5/8	28	27 5/8	20 5/8	5 5/8	5 6/8	9	5	McHenry Co., IL	David J. Binz	David J. Binz	1992	1184
176 5/8	26 3/8	25 7/8	22 3/8	5 3/8	5 3/8	7	9	Kleberg Co., TX	Donald M. Brock, Jr.	Donald M. Brock, Jr.	1993	1184
176 5/8	25 2/8	25 2/8	18 3/8	5 6/8	5 5/8	5	5	Grant Co., MN	W.R. Freeburg & C. Adams	William R. Freeburg	1993	1184
176 5/8	26	25 3/8	23 5/8	4 7/8	4 5/8	5	5	La Porte Co., IN	Alicia Boguslawski	Alicia Boguslawski	1995	1184
176 5/8	26	26	17 1/8	5 2/8	5 3/8	8	7	White Co., AR	Dickie P. Duke	Dickie P. Duke	1996	1184
176 5/8	27	27 5/8	22 6/8	5 1/8	5 3/8	7	6	Fairfield Co., OH	Harold R. McCafferty	Harold R. McCafferty	1996	1184
176 5/8	25 7/8	26 3/8	20 5/8	5 5/8	5 4/8	6	5	Wilbarger Co., TX	Owen P. Carpenter III	Owen P. Carpenter III	1999	1184
176 5/8	25 2/8	25 2/8	18 3/8	4 1/8	4 2/8	6	6	Linn Co., MO	Joel Head	Joel Head	2000	1184
176 5/8	23	22 6/8	20 1/8	4 7/8	5	6	6	Saunders Co., NE	John I. Kunert	John I. Kunert	2000	1184
176 5/8	25 1/8	25	15 4/8	5 5/8	5 4/8	5	5	Carrot River, SK	Larry K. Trout	Larry K. Trout	2001	1184
176 5/8	23 1/8	22 7/8	17 1/8	4 5/8	4 5/8	6	8	Buffalo Co., WI	Michael A. Ward	Michael A. Ward	2001	1184
176 4/8	24 6/8	24 5/8	19 4/8	4 5/8	4 5/8	6	7	Charlotte Co., NB	Albert E. Dewar	Albert E. Dewar	1960	1209
176 4/8	23 3/8	23 4/8	22	5 3/8	5 5/8	6	5	Esterhazy, SK	Albert Kristoff	Albert Kristoff	1960	1209

Score	Main Beam	Inside Spread	Circ. R	Circ. L	Pts. R	Pts. L	Locality	Owner	Hunter	Date	Rank
176 4/8	26 6/8	18 4/8	5 1/8	5 1/8	6	6	Itasca Co., MN	Jim Soukup	Jim Soukup	1960	1209
176 4/8	23 5/8	17 4/8	5 3/8	5 4/8	5	5	St. Louis Co., MN	Michael J. Nielsen	Michael J. Stroud	1962	1209
176 4/8	25 2/8	19	4 1/8	3 7/8	6	6	Shackelford Co., TX	H.V. Stroud	H.V. Stroud	1964	1209
176 4/8	23	16 4/8	4 2/8	4 4/8	7	9	Carrizo Springs, TX	Lin F. Nowotny	Lin F. Nowotny	1966	1209
176 4/8	25	19 4/8	4 4/8	4 4/8	6	7	Crawford Co., WI	Louis Franks	Louis Franks	1969	1209
176 4/8	26 6/8	26 6/8	4 2/8	4 3/8	6	6	Houston Co., MN	James L. Reinhart	James L. Reinhart	1971	1209
176 4/8	27 3/8	21 2/8	4 3/8	4 6/8	5	5	Sanders Co., MT	Dallas J.C. Nelson	Dallas J.C. Nelson	1983	1209
176 4/8	25 1/8	19 2/8	4 6/8	6	8	7	Jim Hogg Co., TX	Eduardo M. Garza	Picked Up	1990	1209
176 4/8	25 7/8	21 4/8	6	5 4/8	10	10	Davis Co., IA	Jeffrey A. Getz	Jeffrey A. Getz	1991	1209
176 4/8	26 1/8	23 6/8	5 4/8	5 3/8	6	5	Todd Co., MN	Walter Zastrow	Walter Zastrow	1991	1209
176 4/8	22 6/8	17 6/8	5 3/8	5	6	6	Turtle Mt., MB	David Murray	David Murray	1992	1209
176 4/8	26 6/8	20 3/8	5	5 5/8	5	6	Linn Co., IA	David E. Heck	David E. Heck	1994	1209
176 4/8	28 6/8	21 3/8	5 5/8	5 3/8	7	8	Chisholm, AB	Paul Murray	Paul Murray	1994	1209
176 4/8	26 4/8	18 4/8	5 3/8	4 6/8	6	5	Duck Mt., MB	Kevin E. Scott	Kevin E. Scott	1996	1209
176 4/8	28 3/8	18 3/8	4 6/8	4 2/8	10	7	Muscatine Co., IA	Tim S. Kroul	Tim S. Kroul	1997	1209
176 4/8	26 2/8	22 4/8	4 2/8	5 3/8	6	5	Refugio Co., TX	William M. Murphy IV	William M. Murphy IV	1997	1209
176 4/8	22 5/8	19 2/8	5 3/8	5 4/8	7	5	Oldman Lake, AB	John Proud	John Proud	1997	1209
176 4/8	28 7/8	18 5/8	5 4/8	4 7/8	6	6	Columbiana Co., OH	Blane A. Wade	Blane A. Wade	1998	1209
176 4/8	30 1/8	25 2/8	4 7/8	5 1/8	6	5	Long Sault, ON	Robert Archambault, Jr.	Robert Archambault, Jr.	1999	1209
176 4/8	27 2/8	20 7/8	5 1/8	5 7/8	8	7	Saline Co., IL	John D. Jackson	John D. Jackson	1999	1209
176 4/8	28 5/8	22 4/8	4 1/8	5 4/8	5	6	Ashland Co., WI	Thomas J. Warren	Thomas J. Warren	2000	1209
176 4/8	26	23 1/8	5 7/8	5 7/8	7	6	Todd Co., SD	Richard B. Carlsen	Richard B. Carlsen	2002	1209
176 4/8	27 2/8	20 6/8	5 4/8	5 6/8	5	7	Kingman Co., KS	Jonathon C. Henning	Jonathon C. Henning		1209
176 4/8	26	20 5/8	5 6/8	5 1/8	6	6	Baraga Co., MI	Paul Korhonen	Paul Korhonen		1209
176 3/8	26 1/8	22 4/8	5 1/8	4 7/8	7	6	Koochiching Co., MN	James R. Smith	Picked Up		1209
176 3/8	28 1/8	19 6/8	4 7/8	4 6/8	6	6	St. Louis Co., MN	Howard Maki	Howard Maki	1945	1234
176 3/8	27 7/8	18 5/8	4 7/8	5 2/8	7	7	Cherokee Co., IA	Bob Roberts	Bob Roberts	1957	1234
176 3/8	27 2/8	21 1/8	4 6/8	4 7/8	6	6	Otter Tail Co., MN	Steven C. Stinar	Steven C. Stinar	1958	1234
176 3/8	24 3/8	17 3/8	5 2/8	5 3/8	7	8	Pope Co., MN	Richard M. Thompson	Richard M. Thompson	1963	1234
176 3/8	25	17 5/8	4 5/8	5 2/8	6	6	Stockton, MB	Robert R. Blain	Robert R. Blain	1968	1234
176 3/8	28	20 2/8	5 1/8	5 1/8	6	5	Montgomery Co., IA	Stanley D. Means	Stanley D. Means	1976	1234
176 3/8	25 1/8	20 2/8	5 3/8	5	7	5	Wright Co., MO	Mike Napier	Mike Napier	1977	1234
176 3/8	26 6/8	18 7/8	4 4/8	4 7/8	7	5	Fremont Co., IA	Scott J. Carnes	Scott J. Carnes	1986	1234
176 3/8	25 6/8	20 1/8	5 1/8	5 2/8	6	6	Logan Co., OH	Larry D. Hyzer	Larry D. Hyzer	1987	1234
176 3/8	22 3/8	21 7/8	5 2/8	5 1/8	4	4	Champaign Co., OH	David A. Owen	David A. Owen	1987	1234
176 3/8	28	20 5/8	4 7/8	4 7/8	6	5	Boulder Co., CO	Michael J. Scrivner	Picked Up	1988	1234
176 3/8	24 5/8	17 1/8	5 3/8	4 7/8	6	5	Round Lake, SK	Randy Tulloch	Randy Tulloch	1989	1234
176 3/8	27 3/8	21 6/8	5 2/8	5 3/8	6	10	Hamilton Co., IL	Dennis W. Woolard, Jr.	Dennis W. Woolard, Jr.	1989	1234
176 3/8	27 3/8	23 3/8	5 1/8	5 2/8	10	8	Cypress Hills, SK	Dwight W. Dobson	Dwight W. Dobson	1990	1234
176 3/8	25 4/8	18 1/8	5	5 1/8	6	6	Fremont, SK	Earl M. Gilles	Earl M. Gilles	1992	1234
176 3/8	24 2/8	21 4/8	5 2/8	5	6	5	Craven, SK	Steven G. Ries	Steven G. Ries	1993	1234
176 3/8	28 3/8	21 3/8	5 7/8	5 7/8	9	5	Geary Co., KS	Donald J. Ereth	Donald J. Ereth	1994	1234
176 3/8	27 4/8	22 3/8	5 1/8	5 1/8	6	4	Marion Co., OH	David B. Lafferty	David B. Lafferty	1994	1234
176 3/8	28 4/8	20 5/8	4 6/8	4 6/8	5	5	Rock Island Co., IL	Douglas J. Grudzinski	Douglas J. Grudzinski	1995	1234
176 3/8	27 7/8	16 1/8	5 3/8	5 3/8	5	6	Knox Co., IL	Jason McCulloch	Jason McCulloch	1996	1234
176 3/8	24 3/8	21 2/8	5	5	6	5	Juneau Co., WI	Paul F. Beall	Paul F. Beall	1997	1234
176 3/8	27 5/8	18 1/8	5	5	6	6	Adams Co., IL	Lawrence Walton	Lawrence Walton	1997	1234
176 3/8	25 7/8	21 6/8	4 3/8	4 5/8	9	7	Lanigan, SK	Derek Fisher	Derek Fisher	2000	1234

WHITETAIL DEER - TYPICAL ANTLERS
Odocoileus virginianus virginianus and certain related subspecies

Score	Length of Main Beam R	L	Inside Spread	Circumference at Smallest Place Between Burr and First Point R	L	Number of Points R	L	Locality	Hunter	Owner	Date Killed	Rank
176 3/8	25 4/8	26 1/8	17 4/8	5 6/8	5 6/8	6	6	S. Saskatchewan River, SK	Cory M. Schommer	Cory M. Schommer	2000	1234
176 3/8	25 2/8	26 2/8	17 7/8	4 7/8	5	6	5	Van Buren Co., IA	Bruce C. Spiller	Bruce C. Spiller	2000	1234
176 2/8	24 7/8	26 1/8	21	4 1/8	4	6	6	Karnes Co., TX	Gideon Pace	Steve Mansfield	PR 1905	1261
176 2/8	25 6/8	28 6/8	25 4/8	4 7/8	5	5	5	Erie Co., NY	Wesley H. Iulg	Wesley H. Iulg	1944	1261
176 2/8	24	23 6/8	15 6/8	5	5 2/8	5	5	Jefferson Co., AR	Arthur Hubbard	Charles Burnett	1953	1261
176 2/8	25 6/8	25 7/8	20 3/8	5 4/8	5 4/8	7	6	Rappahannock Co., VA	George W. Beahm	George W. Beahm	1959	1261
176 2/8	23	25 5/8	18 6/8	5	4 7/8	5	5	Swanson, SK	L.S. Wood	L.S. Wood	1959	1261
176 2/8	25 2/8	26 4/8	22 2/8	5	5	6	6	Des Moines Co., IA	Virgil Landrum	Virgil Landrum	1960	1261
176 2/8	24 4/8	26 4/8	17 1/8	5 4/8	5 4/8	8	7	Warren Co., NY	Frank Dagles	Frank Dagles	1961	1261
176 2/8	28 4/8	27 4/8	25	5 4/8	5 4/8	5	4	Washington Co., NE	Albert Ohrt	Spanky Greenville	1962	1261
176 2/8	28 4/8	29 2/8	20 6/8	5 4/8	5 4/8	5	5	Richland Parish, LA	Willard Roberson	Willard Roberson	1968	1261
176 2/8	26 1/8	28 5/8	23 2/8	4 3/8	4 3/8	5	5	Houston Co., MN	Harold Kruse	Cabela's, Inc.	1975	1261
176 2/8	30	28 2/8	23	6 1/8	6 1/8	7	6	Coshocton Co., OH	James R. Gardner	James R. Gardner	1976	1261
176 2/8	26 7/8	27 4/8	21 6/8	4 4/8	4 5/8	5	5	St. Louis Co., MN	Picked Up	George W. Flaim	1978	1261
176 2/8	28	26 4/8	21	5 4/8	5 4/8	8	7	Macon Co., GA	Charles M. Wilson	Charles M. Wilson	1981	1261
176 2/8	28 2/8	27 5/8	21	4 7/8	4 6/8	7	5	Houston Co., MN	John W. Zahrte	John W. Zahrte	1981	1261
176 2/8	24 7/8	25 4/8	20 6/8	4 5/8	4 7/8	6	6	Troup Co., GA	Claude A. McKibben, Jr.	James E. Lasater	1984	1261
176 2/8	26 2/8	26 3/8	20 4/8	4 6/8	5	5	7	Litchfield Co., CT	Frederick H. Clymer	Frederick H. Clymer	1987	1261
176 2/8	28 3/8	29 4/8	23 2/8	5 2/8	5 1/8	6	6	Aroostook Co., ME	Daniel T. Geary	Daniel T. Geary	1989	1261
176 2/8	24 5/8	23 1/8	15 6/8	6	6 2/8	7	7	Converse Co., WY	Basil C. Bradbury	Basil C. Bradbury	1990	1261
176 2/8	27	27	21 4/8	4 6/8	4 6/8	5	5	Dauphin, MB	Unknown	Wayne Selby	PR 1990	1261
176 2/8	25 5/8	27 4/8	18	5 2/8	5 4/8	7	7	Bon Homme Co., SD	Lonnie L. Huber	Lonnie L. Huber	1991	1261
176 2/8	26 2/8	25 5/8	18 4/8	4 7/8	4 7/8	6	8	Brown Co., IL	Picked Up	William S. Boyd	PR 1992	1261
176 2/8	25 6/8	26 2/8	20 6/8	5 4/8	5 6/8	5	5	Lucas Co., IA	Corey E. Gwinn	Corey E. Gwinn	1992	1261
176 2/8	28	26	24 2/8	5 6/8	5 6/8	6	5	Nuckolls Co., NE	Tim Brewster	Tim Brewster	1993	1261
176 2/8	26 6/8	26 3/8	20 3/8	5 5/8	5 5/8	8	6	Moose Creek, SK	Joseph Romer	Joseph Romer	1993	1261
176 2/8	23 6/8	23 3/8	19 4/8	5 3/8	5 2/8	8	7	Walworth Co., WI	Thomas G. Senft	Thomas G. Senft	1993	1261
176 2/8	24 7/8	24 1/8	15 6/8	4 5/8	4 5/8	6	7	St. Louis Co., MN	Brian J. Keating	Brian J. Keating	1995	1261
176 2/8	27 1/8	26 2/8	24	5	5	5	6	Washington Co., KS	Roger W. Novak	Roger W. Novak	1995	1261
176 2/8	24 3/8	25 4/8	18 2/8	4 3/8	4 2/8	5	9	Monroe Co., IN	Chad A. DeGolyer	Chad A. DeGolyer	1996	1261
176 2/8	25 5/8	25 5/8	20 6/8	4 6/8	4 6/8	5	6	Vermilion River, AB	Edwin J. Bowman	Edwin J. Bowman	1997	1261
176 2/8	28 5/8	30 3/8	20 4/8	4 7/8	4 5/8	7	7	Wayne Co., IL	Kent A. Ochs	Kent A. Ochs	1997	1261
176 2/8	29 4/8	29	15 5/8	5 6/8	5 5/8	5	6	Aitkokan, ON	Robert G. Schlingmann	Robert G. Schlingmann	1998	1261
176 2/8	25 5/8	26 4/8	18 7/8	4 5/8	4 6/8	6	6	Meyers Lake, SK	Trent Derkatz	Trent Derkatz	1999	1261
176 2/8	27 2/8	27 1/8	19 1/8	4 6/8	4 7/8	7	5	Foam Lake, SK	Stanley Kaban	Stanley Kaban	1999	1261
176 2/8	26 2/8	25 7/8	20	5	5	5	5	Worth Co., MO	David Shipman	David Shipman	1999	1261

Score	Main Beam R	Main Beam L	Inside Spread	Circ. R	Circ. L	Pts R	Pts L	Locality	Hunter	Owner	Date	Rank
176 2/8	27 4/8	27 2/8	21 2/8	4 4/8	4 4/8	6	7	Nueva Leon, MX	Al Mendoza	Al Mendoza	2000	1261
176 1/8	28	27 4/8	21 2/8	5 4/8	5 4/8	6	5	Florence Co., WI	Theron A. Meyer, Sr.	Theron A. Meyer, Sr.	1943	1296
176 1/8	25 3/8	24 5/8	19 7/8	6 7/8	6 6/8	7	7	Goodhue Co., MN	David Anderson	David Anderson	1960	1296
176 1/8	26 4/8	27 3/8	24 3/8	5	5 1/8	5	5	Monroe Co., MS	J.D. Hood	Michael D. Steadman	1972	1296
176 1/8	25 6/8	26 1/8	20 5/8	5 7/8	5 6/8	5	5	Door Co., WI	Unknown	Steve Pluff	PR 1973	1296
176 1/8	25 7/8	23 7/8	24 1/8	5 5/8	5 5/8	5	6	Assiniboine River, MB	G.G. Graham	G.G. Graham	1984	1296
176 1/8	25 7/8	25 5/8	21 1/8	4 4/8	4 4/8	5	6	Grunthal, MB	Edwin Froese	Edwin Froese	1986	1296
176 1/8	23 4/8	25 4/8	19 5/8	5 3/8	5 2/8	9	8	Pierce Lake, SK	Edwin Johnson	Edwin Johnson	1989	1296
176 1/8	24 1/8	25 4/8	24 1/8	4 7/8	4 7/8	5	5	Jackson Co., IA	Roy O. Lindemier	Roy O. Lindemier	1990	1296
176 1/8	27 1/8	27 4/8	19 5/8	5 4/8	4 7/8	6	5	Johnson Co., MO	James A. Stephens	James A. Stephens	1990	1296
176 1/8	28 4/8	26	23 6/8	4 7/8	5	5	5	Randolph Co., GA	Jeff Hill	Jeff Hill	1991	1296
176 1/8	25 7/8	25 6/8	18 5/8	5 1/8	5 1/8	6	6	Brown Co., KS	Dennis P. Finger	Dennis P. Finger	1992	1296
176 1/8	26 6/8	26 5/8	19 5/8	5 2/8	5 2/8	6	6	Jackson Co., IL	Aaron E. Harsy	Aaron E. Harsy	1994	1296
176 1/8	30 4/8	29 6/8	20 6/8	5 5/8	5 5/8	6	5	Lucas Co., IA	Justin J. Adams	Justin J. Adams	1995	1296
176 1/8	25 4/8	27	19 1/8	4 6/8	4 7/8	5	5	Southampton Co., VA	Samuel B. Drewry, Jr.	Samuel B. Drewry, Jr.	1997	1296
176 1/8	24 2/8	23 2/8	17 1/8	4 7/8	4 7/8	6	7	Webb Co., TX	Robert L. Hixson, Jr.	Robert L. Hixson, Jr.	1997	1296
176 1/8	27 7/8	27 7/8	20 6/8	4 1/8	4 2/8	6	6	Maverick Co., TX	Steve E. Holloway	Steve E. Holloway	1997	1296
176 1/8	28 6/8	28 1/8	20 2/8	4 6/8	4 5/8	6	7	Linn Co., IA	Rudolph Ashbacher	Rudolph C. Ashbacher	1998	1296
176 1/8	25 7/8	26 4/8	24 2/8	5	5	7	8	Lenore Lake, SK	Emile Creurer	Emile Creurer	1998	1296
176 1/8	24 3/8	24	17 7/8	4 7/8	4 6/8	6	6	Adams Co., IL	Thomas M. Foote	Thomas M. Foote	1998	1296
176 1/8	25 1/8	24 5/8	16 7/8	5 1/8	5	7	8	Gentry Co., MO	Frank L. Thomas	Frank L. Thomas	1998	1296
176 1/8	24 3/8	26 3/8	20 3/8	4 7/8	5 1/8	6	6	Pike Co., MO	Christopher C. Clamors	Christopher C. Clamors	1999	1296
176 1/8	25 4/8	24 4/8	21 5/8	5 1/8	4 6/8	6	6	Solberg Lake, SK	Dale W. Brinkman	Dale W. Brinkman	2001	1296
176 1/8	27	27 4/8	21 2/8	5 1/8	5	8	8	Jefferson Co., IA	Dale E. Manor	Dale E. Manor	2001	1296
176 1/8	28 5/8	29 6/8	19 7/8	5 3/8	5 3/8	8	6	Hillsborough Co., NH	Phillip J. Marrotte	Phillip J. Marrotte	2002	1296
176	24 4/8	24 7/8	17 5/8	4	3 7/8	8	7	Florence Co., WI	John G. Kozicki	Vernon J. Kozicki	1936	1320
176	28 3/8	29	17 4/8	5 3/8	5 1/8	8	6	Bradford Co., PA	Clyde H. Rinehuls	Clyde H. Rinehuls	1944	1320
176	28 3/8	28 3/8	17 6/8	4 4/8	4 4/8	5	5	Koochiching Co., MN	John A. Lind	John M. Lind	1956	1320
176	27	25 4/8	20 4/8	5 2/8	5 6/8	5	5	Dawson Co., NE	Unknown	Spanky Greenville	1957	1320
176	23 7/8	25 4/8	19 3/8	5 6/8	5 6/8	5	7	Lyon Co., IA	Duane K. Rohde	Duane K. Rohde	1964	1320
176	26	26 3/8	20	5 4/8	5 3/8	8	5	Veblen, SD	John W. Cimburek	John W. Cimburek	1966	1320
176	24 5/8	25 6/8	21 6/8	4 7/8	4 7/8	5	5	Russell Co., KS	Don Mai	Don Mai	1981	1320
176	26	26	18 4/8	6 2/8	5 7/8	5	5	Racine Co., WI	Daniel P. Cramer	Daniel P. Cramer	1985	1320
176	26 4/8	27	18 4/8	4 6/8	4 7/8	5	7	Nemaha Co., KS	Joseph L. Schmelzle	Joseph L. Schmelzle	1985	1320
176	26 3/8	27 2/8	20	5 1/8	5 1/8	5	6	Goodhue Co., MN	Martin H. Bollum	Martin H. Bollum	1986	1320
176	23 7/8	28 5/8	16	4 4/8	4 4/8	5	6	Ghost Lake, AB	Viktor Nill	Viktor Nill	1989	1320
176	27 3/8	27	19 7/8	5 3/8	5 4/8	7	5	Duck Lake, SK	Larry Attig	Larry Attig	1993	1320
176	26 7/8	28 4/8	20 6/8	4 7/8	4 7/8	7	6	Redwater, AB	Tim T. Bourne	Tim T. Bourne	1993	1320
176	30	29 5/8	20 7/8	5 1/8	5	4	6	Butler Co., OH	Chris Allen	Chris Allen	1994	1320
176	27 2/8	27 2/8	21 2/8	4 6/8	4 7/8	5	5	Pickens Co., SC	William C. Wyatt	William C. Wyatt	1994	1320
176	26 6/8	26 6/8	18 7/8	4 2/8	4 2/8	7	6	Buffalo Co., WI	Guy A. Hansen	Guy A. Hansen	1995	1320
176	27 2/8	28 5/8	19	5 6/8	5 3/8	6	6	Butler Co., OH	Rick Sizemore	Rick Sizemore	1995	1320
176	27	19	24 5/8	4 6/8	4 3/8	7	8	Montgomery Co., MO	Dave Knoepflein	Dave Knoepflein	1996	1320
176	26 4/8	26	20 6/8	4 2/8	4 2/8	5	7	Green Lake Co., WI	Timothy S. Judas	Timothy S. Judas	1997	1320
176	25 5/8	25 5/8	20 7/8	4 3/8	4 1/8	6	7	Monroe Co., MO	David J. Godat	David J. Godat	2000	1320
176	27 6/8	27 2/8	17 6/8	5	5	4	5	Penobscot Co., ME	David R. Morrison	David R. Morrison	2001	1320
175 7/8	23 3/8	24 3/8	26 4/8	4 4/8	4 3/8	5	6	Kinney Co., TX	Walter Griener	John L. Stein	1935	1341
175 7/8	26 1/8	26 4/8	20 3/8	4 3/8	4 3/8	7	7	Lewis Co., NY	Andrew Lustyik	Andrew F. Lustyik	1942	1341

WHITETAIL DEER - TYPICAL ANTLERS

Odocoileus virginianus virginianus and certain related subspecies

Score	Length of Main Beam		Inside Spread	Circumference at Smallest Place Between Burr and First Point		Number of Points		Locality	Hunter	Owner	Date Killed	Rank
	R	L		R	L	R	L					
175 7/8	23	23 1/8	16 7/8	5 1/8	5 1/8	5	5	Hanley, SK	G. Koyl & W. King	Gavin Koyl	1964	1341
175 7/8	24 6/8	25 6/8	17 4/8	4 5/8	4 4/8	5	5	Logan Co., CO	Picked Up	Marvin Gardner	1971	1341
175 7/8	26 3/8	26 3/8	17 1/8	4 6/8	4 6/8	6	7	Brooks Co., GA	Joseph J. Freeman	Joseph J. Freeman	1978	1341
175 7/8	26 5/8	27	21 7/8	4 3/8	4 3/8	5	6	Swift Co., MN	Kim Manska	Kim Manska	1982	1341
175 7/8	27	26 6/8	22 5/8	4 4/8	4 4/8	5	5	Sundre, AB	Russell D. Holmes	Russell D. Holmes	1984	1341
175 7/8	27 5/8	27 1/8	22 5/8	6 5/8	6 2/8	9	7	Pouce Coupe River, BC	Dale Callahan	Dale Callahan	1986	1341
175 7/8	25 6/8	25 5/8	21 2/8	6	5 6/8	6	6	Hardin Co., OH	Royal R. Chisholm	Royal R. Chisholm	1988	1341
175 7/8	25 2/8	25 1/8	16 3/8	5	5 2/8	5	5	Barrhead, AB	Hugh L. Schmaus	Hugh L. Schmaus	1990	1341
175 7/8	28 3/8	27 7/8	22 5/8	5	4 6/8	6	6	Washburn Co., WI	Terry A. Severson	Terry A. Severson	1991	1341
175 7/8	26 1/8	26 4/8	19 5/8	5 3/8	5 2/8	6	6	Huron Co., OH	Donald W. Howard	Donald W. Howard	1992	1341
175 7/8	23 4/8	25	17 1/8	5 2/8	5 2/8	6	5	Johnson Co., IL	Thomas F. Byrne	Thomas F. Byrne	1993	1341
175 7/8	24 4/8	25 1/8	17 5/8	5 1/8	5 1/8	5	5	Putnam Co., IN	Picked Up	Terry Outcalt	1993	1341
175 7/8	24 7/8	25 2/8	19 2/8	5 4/8	5 2/8	9	6	Bennett Lake, ON	Randy M. Love	Randy M. Love	1994	1341
175 7/8	24 3/8	27	18	4 5/8	4 5/8	5	6	Buffalo Co., WI	Larry L. Bloom	Larry L. Bloom	1995	1341
175 7/8	26 2/8	24 6/8	19 1/8	4 6/8	5 2/8	5	6	Boone Co., IA	Monte A. Carlson	Monte A. Carlson	1995	1341
175 7/8	26 1/8	25 1/8	20 7/8	4 5/8	4 6/8	5	8	Pulaski Co., AR	Charles L. Marcum, Jr.	Charles L. Marcum, Jr.	1996	1341
175 7/8	26 7/8	26 3/8	16 5/8	5 2/8	4 7/8	8	10	Brown Co., IL	Mark W. West	Mark W. West	1997	1341
175 7/8	25 7/8	25 6/8	20	5 4/8	5 4/8	6	5	Shipman, SK	William L. Cox	William L. Cox	1998	1341
175 7/8	28 1/8	28 2/8	21 3/8	3 7/8	3 7/8	5	6	Iowa Co., IA	Chris Adams	Chris Adams	2000	1341
175 7/8	28 6/8	29 4/8	18 5/8	4 2/8	4 3/8	6	6	Switzerland Co., IN	Dale A. Dixon, Jr.	Dale A. Dixon, Jr.	2000	1341
175 7/8	24 5/8	23 1/8	18 7/8	5 1/8	5	6	6	Nez Perce Co., ID	Rusty P. Kirtley	Rusty P. Kirtley	2000	1341
175 6/8	25 6/8	26	20 7/8	4	4	6	6	Webb Co., TX	William Bretthauer, Sr.	George H. Glass	1915	1364
175 6/8	21 6/8	23 2/8	18	4 4/8	4 5/8	6	6	St. Onge, SD	Don Ridley	Don Ridley	1957	1364
175 6/8	25 3/8	26 1/8	19 6/8	5 3/8	5 3/8	5	5	Southey, SK	J.A. Maier	J.A. Maier	1958	1364
175 6/8	26 4/8	25 3/8	16 7/8	5 4/8	5 4/8	8	6	Cuming Co., NE	Herman Blankenau	Herman Blankenau	1963	1364
175 6/8	22 6/8	24 5/8	20	5	5	6	6	Burleigh Co., ND	Earl Haakenson	Earl Haakenson	1963	1364
175 6/8	29 3/8	29 5/8	28 4/8	6	6	6	5	Randolph Co., IL	Picked Up	Bass Pro Shops	1965	1364
175 6/8	26 5/8	27 2/8	19 6/8	4 6/8	4 7/8	6	7	Cypress River, MB	Murray Jones	Murray Jones	1973	1364
175 6/8	26 4/8	27 6/8	20 2/8	5 2/8	5 2/8	6	5	Nine Mile Brook, NB	Leopold Leblanc	Jim Oickle	1973	1364
175 6/8	24 6/8	24 5/8	17 7/8	6 2/8	6 3/8	8	10	Marshall Co., MN	Ell-Kay B. Foss	Ell-Kay B. Foss	1974	1364
175 6/8	27 2/8	26 7/8	22 5/8	5 4/8	5	7	6	Webb Co., TX	Norman Frede	John L. Stein	1978	1364
175 6/8	25 4/8	26 4/8	20	5 3/8	5 2/8	6	6	Dinmit Co., TX	George E. Light III	George E. Light III	1979	1364
175 6/8	26 2/8	25	22 4/8	5 1/8	5	5	6	Pope Co., IL	Picked Up	James W. Seets	PR 1982	1364
175 6/8	26 3/8	24 5/8	21 4/8	5 4/8	5 5/8	6	6	Crawford Co., WI	David R. Kluesner	David R. Kluesner	1985	1364
175 6/8	25	24 5/8	19 6/8	5 5/8	5 7/8	5	6	Nemaha Co., KS	Kevin L. Kramer	Kevin L. Kramer	1988	1364
175 6/8	28 6/8	29 1/8	21 4/8	5 7/8	5 5/8	8	8	Williamson Co., IL	Timothy S. Holmes	Timothy S. Holmes	1991	1364

Score	Length R	Length L	Inside Spread	Circ. R	Circ. L	Pts R	Pts L	Locality	Hunter	Owner	Date	Rank
175 6/8	29 2/8	28 6/8	21 3/8	4 6/8	5 1/8	6	5	Brown Co., OH	Robert W. Young	Robert W. Young	1991	1364
175 6/8	29 5/8	28 6/8	21	5 3/8	5 3/8	5	5	Kent Co., MI	Ronald L. Visser	Ronald L. Visser	1992	1364
175 6/8	30	27 5/8	18 5/8	5 7/8	6	6	6	Montgomery Co., IA	Randy L. Wienhold	Randy L. Wienhold	1992	1364
175 6/8	26	25 4/8	21	4 4/8	6	6	6	Faribault Co., MN	Lyle D. Ihle	Lyle D. Ihle	1995	1364
175 6/8	26 3/8	27 3/8	22	5 2/8	5 3/8	5	5	Davis Co., IA	Kendall M. Palmer	Kendall M. Palmer	1997	1364
175 6/8	25 2/8	25 3/8	18 3/8	5 3/8	5 2/8	6	6	Hart Co., KY	Patrick Devore	Patrick Devore	2000	1364
175 6/8	27	27 4/8	19 4/8	5 2/8	5 2/8	8	5	Wayne Co., IN	Brent E. Ferguson	Brent E. Ferguson	2000	1364
175 6/8	24 1/8	24 2/8	21 1/8	5 7/8	5 7/8	5	5	Logan Co., CO	Thomas P. Grainger	Thomas P. Grainger	2000	1364
175 6/8	25 5/8	24 6/8	19	4 7/8	4 7/8	6	7	Allen Co., KS	Gary L. Cleaver	Gary L. Cleaver	2002	1364
175 6/8	26 1/8	26 4/8	24 1/8	5 5/8	5 5/8	5	5	Itasca Co., MN	Art R. Swanson	LeRoy R. Swanson	1945	1388
175 5/8	26 5/8	26 7/8	18 5/8	4 6/8	4 5/8	5	5	Rock Co., WI	Neil Laube	Neil Laube	1965	1388
175 5/8	26 5/8	25 6/8	17 5/8	5 1/8	5 1/8	5	5	Mellette Co., SD	Ben Krogman	Ben Krogman	1969	1388
175 5/8	27 6/8	27 3/8	19 5/8	4 6/8	4 7/8	5	6	Goodhue Co., MN	Ellsworth Ramseier	Chuck Ramseier	1972	1388
175 5/8	24 7/8	25 2/8	25 1/8	4 7/8	4 4/8	7	7	Lake Co., MT	Kenneth D. Johnson	Kenneth D. Johnson	1974	1388
175 5/8	26	27 4/8	18 1/8	4 4/8	4 4/8	6	6	Allegany Co., NY	William L. Damon	William L. Damon	1981	1388
175 5/8	25 4/8	25	17 7/8	4 5/8	4 5/8	7	7	Benewah Co., ID	Carl Groth	Carl Groth	1982	1388
175 5/8	24 2/8	26	17 1/8	5 1/8	5 1/8	5	5	Unknown	Unknown	Brad Lewis	PR 1985	1388
175 5/8	26 6/8	26	20 6/8	4 5/8	4 5/8	6	6	Warren Co., IA	Art L. Daniels	Art L. Daniels	1986	1388
175 5/8	24 1/8	23 4/8	17 3/8	4 6/8	4 7/8	7	7	Woodbury Co., IA	Paul Feddersen	Paul Feddersen	1988	1388
175 5/8	25 5/8	25 6/8	19 3/8	4	4 1/8	7	7	Lucas Co., IA	Dean E. Chandler	Dean E. Chandler	1991	1388
175 5/8	28	28 2/8	21 4/8	5	5	9	6	Morgan Co., OH	John E. Hite	John E. Hite	1991	1388
175 5/8	25 3/8	26 3/8	22	4 6/8	5 1/8	5	6	Sullivan Co., IN	Steven L. Hobbs	Steven L. Hobbs	1991	1388
175 5/8	26 4/8	26	20 5/8	4 6/8	4 6/8	7	7	Big Horn Co., MT	Darell R. Webber	Darell R. Webber	1992	1388
175 5/8	24 6/8	24 6/8	17 5/8	4 5/8	4 6/8	5	5	Pottawatomie Co., KS	Orten L. Dodds	Orten L. Dodds	1992	1388
175 5/8	26 5/8	26 3/8	24 5/8	5 6/8	5 6/8	7	6	Randolph Co., IL	Larry A. Ruebke	Larry A. Ruebke	1993	1388
175 5/8	28 4/8	25 7/8	20 5/8	5 4/8	5 4/8	8	8	Bayfield Co., WI	Lorry A. Hagstrom	Lorry A. Hagstrom	1994	1388
175 5/8	30 5/8	28 6/8	23 3/8	6 1/8	5 5/8	5	5	Bucks Co., PA	Albert J. Muntz	Albert J. Muntz	1995	1388
175 5/8	26 3/8	25 6/8	18 5/8	5	4 7/8	6	7	Leoville, SK	Frank Tucek	Frank Tucek	1998	1388
175 5/8	28 4/8	27 7/8	18 2/8	5 2/8	5 2/8	5	6	Sullivan Co., NH	Robert Lucas, Jr.	Robert Lucas, Jr.	2002	1388
175 4/8	25 5/8	25	21 2/8	5 2/8	5 2/8	6	6	McKean Co., PA	Arthur Young	C.R. Studholme	1830	1408
175 4/8	25 6/8	27	21 2/8	5 1/8	5 1/8	5	5	Pepin Co., WI	Carl E. Frick	Carl E. Frick	1954	1408
175 4/8	25 6/8	25 4/8	21 2/8	6 1/8	5 5/8	5	5	Corning, MO	Orrie L. Schaeffer	Orrie L. Schaeffer	1962	1408
175 4/8	25 5/8	27	20 4/8	4 4/8	4 4/8	5	5	Dodge Co., NE	Leroy W. Ahrndt	Leroy W. Ahrndt	1963	1408
175 4/8	30 2/8	29	22 3/8	5 7/8	5 6/8	8	7	Jo Daviess Co., IL	J.O. Engebretson	J.O. Engebretson	1963	1408
175 4/8	29	27 1/8	20 2/8	5 3/8	5 2/8	6	6	Trigg Co., KY	Picked Up	L.J. Hendon	1967	1408
175 4/8	26 5/8	28	21	5 1/8	5	6	6	Mille Lacs Co., MN	John Krol	Ronald D. Evensen	1973	1408
175 4/8	26 3/8	27 7/8	21 2/8	5 1/8	5 1/8	5	5	Renville Co., MN	Larry D. Youngs	Larry D. Youngs	1973	1408
175 4/8	26 3/8	25 7/8	20 1/8	4 7/8	5 1/8	5	5	Winnebago Co., IA	Joel Kingland	Joel Kingland	1975	1408
175 4/8	25 5/8	25 5/8	16 5/8	4 7/8	4 7/8	6	5	Buffalo Co., WI	Picked Up	Charles G. Dienger	1983	1408
175 4/8	26 2/8	26 3/8	16 2/8	5 3/8	5 3/8	7	5	Canaan, NB	Marcel Poirier	Marcel Poirier	1985	1408
175 4/8	24 5/8	26 7/8	22 3/8	5 2/8	4 7/8	7	8	Macon Co., GA	Charles W. Haynie	Charles W. Haynie	1987	1408
175 4/8	25 7/8	26 3/8	19 6/8	5 1/8	5 2/8	6	10	Wabasha Co., MN	Ronald V. Hurlburt	Ronald V. Hurlburt	1987	1408
175 4/8	22 4/8	26 4/8	21 6/8	5 1/8	5 1/8	6	6	Maine	Unknown	Richard P. Arsenault	PR 1989	1408
175 4/8	27 5/8	27 3/8	22 6/8	5	4 6/8	5	5	Jo Daviess Co., IL	Richard J. McCartin, Sr.	Richard J. McCartin, Sr.	1991	1408
175 4/8	26	26 4/8	22 3/8	5 2/8	5 2/8	6	7	Logan Co., KY	Mark H. Hall	Mark H. Hall	1992	1408
175 4/8	26 5/8	26 7/8	21 2/8	4 7/8	4 7/8	5	5	Wayne Co., IN	Michael H. Baker	Michael H. Baker	1993	1408
175 4/8	25 1/8	25 2/8	23 4/8	4 4/8	4 5/8	5	5	Houston Co., MN	Wesley Lapham	Wesley Lapham	1993	1408
175 4/8	30 1/8	30 4/8	23 4/8	5	5 4/8	5	9	Wayne Co., IL	Donald L. Sutton	Donald L. Sutton	1994	1408

WHITETAIL DEER - TYPICAL ANTLERS

Odocoileus virginianus virginianus and certain related subspecies

Score	Length of Main Beam R	L	Inside Spread	Circumference at Smallest Place Between Burr and First Point R	L	Number of Points R	L	Locality	Hunter	Owner	Date Killed	Rank
175 4/8	28 4/8	28 4/8	22 2/8	4 3/8	4 3/8	5	5	Allamakee Co., IA	William Moody	William Moody	1997	1408
175 4/8	24 6/8	24 3/8	20 2/8	5 5/8	5 6/8	5	7	Meyers Lake, SK	Picked Up	Chad Nickeson	1997	1408
175 4/8	28 3/8	27 4/8	21 2/8	5 3/8	5 1/8	6	5	Hart Co., KY	Randy Ray	Randy Ray	1998	1408
175 4/8	26 2/8	25	15 2/8	4 7/8	4 7/8	5	5	Kaposvar Creek, SK	Scott W. Soyka	Scott W. Soyka	1999	1408
175 4/8	27 1/8	26 3/8	19 3/8	4 6/8	4 6/8	7	6	Preble Co., OH	Jerry W. Jones	Jerry W. Jones	2000	1408
175 4/8	26 6/8	26 1/8	17 7/8	5 1/8	5 1/8	6	5	Grant Co., WI	Picked Up	Andrew J. Nelson	2000	1408
175 3/8	26 5/8	26 5/8	19 3/8	4 5/8	4 6/8	6	6	Endeavour, SK	Alfred Norman	Terry L. Amos	1954	1433
175 3/8	26 1/8	25 4/8	23 3/8	5 1/8	5 2/8	5	5	Bridgeford, SK	Elgin T. Gates	Elgin T. Gates	1958	1433
175 3/8	27 1/8	26 6/8	18 4/8	5 5/8	5 5/8	6	5	Worth Co., GA	Picked Up	L. Edwin Massey	1962	1433
175 3/8	25 4/8	25 4/8	20 1/8	5 2/8	5 2/8	5	5	Gallia Co., OH	Jack Auxier	Jack Auxier	1969	1433
175 3/8	24 5/8	25 2/8	20 4/8	5 6/8	5 5/8	5	6	Williamson Co., IL	Lewis F. Simon	Lewis F. Simon	1973	1433
175 3/8	24	22 2/8	19 4/8	4 7/8	4 7/8	6	8	Monroe Co., OH	David Mancano	David Mancano	1976	1433
175 3/8	29 1/8	28 7/8	21 4/8	5 2/8	5 2/8	6	5	Wright Co., IA	Picked Up	Ron Schaumburg	1976	1433
175 3/8	25	25	18 1/8	4 2/8	4 1/8	6	6	Dimmit Co., TX	Betsy Campbell	Betsy Campbell	1978	1433
175 3/8	29 6/8	28	22 3/8	4 6/8	4 4/8	6	5	Todd Co., KY	Gary W. Crafton	Gary W. Crafton	1981	1433
175 3/8	28 3/8	28 5/8	17 6/8	4 6/8	4 4/8	6	7	Carroll Co., IA	Edward L. Golay	Edward L. Golay	1984	1433
175 3/8	22 4/8	23 2/8	16 3/8	4 1/8	4 2/8	6	6	White Co., AR	Jerry Parish	Jerry Parish	1984	1433
175 3/8	26	25 4/8	17 7/8	5 1/8	5 3/8	5	6	Clark Co., IL	Gary L. Lovell	Gary L. Lovell	1986	1433
175 3/8	26	25 5/8	18 7/8	5 6/8	5 7/8	5	5	Carberry, MB	H.E. & B. Calvert	H.E. & B. Calvert	1987	1433
175 3/8	25 6/8	26 1/8	22 3/8	4 7/8	5 1/8	6	7	Collingsworth Co., TX	Eugene Hanna	John L. Stein	1988	1433
175 3/8	27 1/8	25 7/8	19 5/8	5 3/8	5 2/8	6	6	Satellite Hill, BC	Bill Shunter	Bill Shunter	1990	1433
175 3/8	27	26 6/8	16 6/8	4 7/8	4 7/8	6	6	Boone Co., IA	James D. Champion	James D. Champion	1991	1433
175 3/8	27 7/8	26 4/8	21 2/8	4 6/8	4 5/8	8	9	Fayette Co., IA	Donald Massman	Phyllis Massman	1991	1433
175 3/8	27 2/8	27 2/8	19 3/8	5	4 7/8	6	6	Worcester Co., MA	Thomas W. Bombard	Thomas W. Bombard	1992	1433
175 3/8	28 4/8	29 2/8	20 5/8	4 6/8	4 6/8	5	5	Mississippi Co., AR	Luther Gifford	Luther Gifford	1994	1433
175 3/8	25 4/8	25	21	4 6/8	4 5/8	6	8	Linn Co., KS	Lloyd L. Wilson III	Lloyd L. Wilson III	1995	1433
175 3/8	25 5/8	25 5/8	20 1/8	5	5 1/8	5	5	Basin Lake, SK	Kurt R. Moorman	Kurt R. Moorman	1996	1433
175 3/8	25 2/8	26 1/8	20 6/8	6	6 2/8	8	7	Shelby Co., IN	Timothy D. Taggart	Timothy D. Taggart	1999	1433
175 3/8	26 6/8	26 6/8	20 1/8	6 1/8	5 7/8	6	6	Chickasaw Co., IA	Dennis P. Troyna	Dennis P. Troyna	1999	1433
175 3/8	27	27	18 6/8	6 2/8	5 6/8	8	7	Richland Co., WI	Vince L. Fairchild	Vince L. Fairchild	2000	1433
175 3/8	26 4/8	26 6/8	22 1/8	5 2/8	5 1/8	5	6	Jefferson Co., ID	Daniel R. Merrill	Daniel R. Merrill	2001	1433
175 2/8	25 5/8	25 5/8	19 4/8	4 6/8	4 6/8	6	5	Bayfield Co., WI	Bill Holiday	Douglas R. Plourde	PR 1920	1458
175 2/8	22 7/8	22 7/8	19	4 4/8	4 5/8	6	6	Encinal, TX	W.S. Benson, Sr.	W.S. Benson III	1928	1458
175 2/8	26 4/8	26 3/8	21 6/8	4 5/8	4 5/8	6	6	Lake Co., MN	John Brassill	Lorraine Brassill	1951	1458
175 2/8	27 2/8	27 3/8	15 4/8	5 2/8	6	6	8	Cherokee Co., IA	Unknown	H. James Reimer	1954	1458
175 2/8	24 2/8	24 6/8	20	4 2/8	4 2/8	6	6	Aitkin Co., MN	Terry Kullhem	Terry Kullhem	1958	1458

Score	Main Beam R	Main Beam L	Inside Spread	Circ. R	Circ. L	Pts. R	Pts. L	Locality	Hunter	Owner	Date	Rank
175 2/8	27 3/8	27 7/8	22 4/8	5 1/8	5	7	6	Kittson Co., MN	Fred Bloomquist	Gordon Johnson	1962	1458
175 2/8	24	23 6/8	19 6/8	5 4/8	5 5/8	5	6	Qu'Appelle, SK	Douglas Garden	Douglas Garden	1965	1458
175 2/8	30 3/8	22 6/8	21 2/8	5 2/8	5 1/8	5	7	Clinton Co., IN	William W. Cripe	William W. Cripe	1974	1458
175 2/8	26 2/8	26 2/8	21	4 4/8	4 3/8	6	6	Texas	Elmo Wilson	Joe B. Wilson	PR 1975	1458
175 2/8	28 1/8	28 6/8	17 6/8	5 2/8	5 2/8	6	5	Val Marie, SK	Leon Perrault	Leon Perrault	1977	1458
175 2/8	26 1/8	25 6/8	21 1/8	5 1/8	5 2/8	6	8	Wilkinson Co., MS	Johnnie J. Leake, Jr.	Johnnie J. Leake, Jr.	1978	1458
175 2/8	28 2/8	28 3/8	19 6/8	5 1/8	5 2/8	5	7	Fulton Co., IN	Larry A. Croxton	Larry A. Croxton	1984	1458
175 2/8	27 1/8	27	19	6	6 1/8	5	5	Union Co., IL	Randy Edmonds	Randy Edmonds	1984	1458
175 2/8	25	24 4/8	17	4 7/8	5	6	6	Russell, MB	Emile DeCorby	Emile DeCorby	1986	1458
175 2/8	25 3/8	26 3/8	23 4/8	5 5/8	5 7/8	6	6	Krydor, SK	Lorne M. Shewchuk	Lorne M. Shewchuk	1986	1458
175 2/8	23 2/8	24 1/8	19 6/8	4 7/8	4 5/8	5	6	Mayerthorpe, AB	Gregory Graff	Gregory Graff	1987	1458
175 2/8	28 3/8	27 4/8	21 2/8	4 6/8	4 3/8	5	5	Henderson Co., KY	Donald K. White	Donald K. White	1987	1458
175 2/8	25	25 1/8	18 6/8	5	5	5	5	Aitkin Co., MN	Picked Up	Steven M. Landrus	1988	1458
175 2/8	30	28 3/8	22	6 1/8	6 1/8	7	8	Schuyler Co., IL	Rodney C. Chute	Rodney C. Chute	1989	1458
175 2/8	26 6/8	27 4/8	23	5 1/8	5 3/8	6	5	Henry Co., IL	Bradley DeMay	Bradley DeMay	1989	1458
175 2/8	28 6/8	30 7/8	19 2/8	4 7/8	4 7/8	5	5	Van Buren Co., MI	Daryl D. Kovach	Daryl D. Kovach	1989	1458
175 2/8	25 6/8	26 2/8	19 5/8	4 3/8	4 4/8	7	5	Jo Daviess Co., IL	Michael J. Traum	Michael J. Traum	1989	1458
175 2/8	25 2/8	26 1/8	20 2/8	5 4/8	5 2/8	5	5	Ohio Co., KY	James B. Wettstain	James B. Wettstain	1989	1458
175 2/8	27 1/8	27 2/8	21 1/8	5 4/8	5 4/8	5	5	Greene Co., IL	Picked Up	Mark B. Thompson	1991	1458
175 2/8	25 6/8	26 7/8	15 2/8	4 4/8	4 4/8	9	6	Frio Co., TX	India N. Shackelford	India N. Shackelford	1992	1458
175 2/8	24 2/8	23 5/8	18 1/8	5 3/8	5 4/8	6	7	Pembina River, AB	Curtis R. Siegfried	Curtis R. Siegfried	1992	1458
175 2/8	26 3/8	25 4/8	19 5/8	5 1/8	5 3/8	8	8	Meadow Lake, SK	Joseph V. Caccamo, Jr.	Joseph V. Caccamo, Jr.	1995	1458
175 2/8	27 7/8	28 4/8	18 4/8	4 6/8	5 2/8	7	7	Meade Co., KY	David M. Jupin	David M. Jupin	1995	1458
175 2/8	26 5/8	28 3/8	21 4/8	5 2/8	5 2/8	5	5	Clayton Co., IA	Thomas J. Shea	Thomas J. Shea	1995	1458
175 2/8	27 4/8	26 7/8	21 7/8	5 3/8	5 4/8	6	6	Richland Co., IL	Cory A. Ristvedt	Cory A. Ristvedt	1997	1458
175 2/8	26 7/8	27 2/8	21	4 7/8	4 7/8	5	5	Jersey Co., IL	Jacob J. Laramee	Jacob J. Laramee	1998	1458
175 2/8	25 3/8	25 4/8	20 4/8	4 7/8	4 6/8	6	5	Johnson Co., IA	George J. Hebl	George J. Hebl	1999	1458
175 2/8	25 4/8	25 4/8	22 6/8	4 6/8	4 6/8	5	6	Piatt Co., IL	Jerry Rudisill	Jerry Rudisill	1999	1458
175 2/8	30 1/8	30 4/8	22 5/8	5 1/8	5 1/8	7	5	Hardin Co., OH	Tracey H. Seiler	Tracey H. Seiler	1999	1458
175 2/8	28 7/8	27 6/8	19 4/8	4 5/8	4 7/8	6	5	Pike Co., IL	Lewis W. Henry, Jr.	Lewis W. Henry, Jr.	2000	1458
175 2/8	26	28 3/8	21 3/8	5	5	5	8	Logan Co., OH	Larry E. Pooler	Larry E. Pooler	2000	1458
175 2/8	28 6/8	28 5/8	19	5 6/8	5 6/8	5	6	Neshoba Co., MS	Charlie G. Wilson II	Charlie G. Wilson II	2001	1458
175 2/8	24 6/8	24 2/8	16	5	5	4	7	Lucas Co., IA	Larry L. Davis	Larry L. Davis	2002	1458
175 1/8	28	28 3/8	20 3/8	5 5/8	5	6	5	Lake Co., IN	Matthew A. Kelnhofer	Matthew A. Kelnhofer	2002	1458
175 1/8	28	27 6/8	25	4 7/8	4 6/8	8	8	Waldo Co., ME	Unknown	Kenneth T. Winters	1924	1497
175 1/8	25 7/8	27 2/8	19 5/8	4 4/8	4 4/8	7	5	Alger Co., MI	Warren Beebe	Donald J. Docking	1936	1497
175 1/8	26 2/8	25 7/8	17 4/8	5 1/8	5 1/8	5	5	Taylor Co., WI	Jack L. Dittrich	Jack L. Dittrich	1945	1497
175 1/8	23 5/8	22 7/8	22 3/8	5 6/8	5 6/8	6	5	Chedderville, AB	Larry Trimble	Larry Trimble	1963	1497
175 1/8	25 5/8	25 5/8	22 1/8	4 5/8	4 5/8	5	5	Gerald, SK	Ken Cherewka	Ken Cherewka	1964	1497
175 1/8	27 4/8	28 5/8	22 3/8	4 6/8	4 6/8	7	5	Roberts Co., SD	Rudy Duwenhoeger, Jr.	Rudy Duwenhoeger, Jr.	1966	1497
175 1/8	25 6/8	27	20 3/8	5	5	7	8	Menominee Co., WI	Gerald Ponfil	Gerald Ponfil	1968	1497
175 1/8	25 2/8	25 6/8	16 7/8	5 3/8	5 3/8	6	6	Howard Co., IA	Russell L. Stevenson, Jr.	Russell L. Stevenson, Jr.	1971	1497
175 1/8	25 7/8	26 5/8	22 4/8	5 1/8	5 1/8	6	5	Sac Co., IA	Randy J. Bentsen	Randy J. Bentsen	1973	1497
175 1/8	25 5/8	25 1/8	24 4/8	4 7/8	4 7/8	6	6	Lincoln Co., MN	Robert R. Bushman	Robert R. Bushman	1973	1497
175 1/8	27 1/8	25 5/8	18 3/8	5	5	5	6	Houston Co., MN	Craig F. Swenson	Craig F. Swenson	1976	1497
175 1/8	24 7/8	26 1/8	20 7/8	4 4/8	4 4/8	7	6	Lac qui Parle Co., MN	Harold Kittelson	Harold Kittelson	1976	1497
175 1/8	22 7/8	23 6/8	19 7/8	4 7/8	4 7/8	6	7	Dimmit Co., TX	Ray Perry	Ray Perry	1976	1497
175 1/8	25 4/8	24 5/8	19 7/8	5 2/8	5 1/8	5	6	Shaunavon, SK	Richard Klink	Richard Klink	1981	1497

WHITETAIL DEER - TYPICAL ANTLERS
Odocoileus virginianus virginianus and certain related subspecies

Score	Length of Main Beam R	L	Inside Spread	Circumference at Smallest Place Between Burr and First Point R	L	Number of Points R	L	Locality	Hunter	Owner	Date Killed	Rank
175 1/8	22 1/8	22 7/8	20 5/8	5	5 5/8	6	6	Marinette Co., WI	John Nielson	John Nielson	1983	1497
175 1/8	27 3/8	27 1/8	21 2/8	5 7/8	6	6	5	Wetzel Co., WV	Matthew Scheibelhood	Matthew Scheibelhood	1984	1497
175 1/8	23 7/8	24 4/8	17 3/8	4 5/8	4 4/8	6	6	Kings Co., NB	Wayne F. Anderson	Wayne F. Anderson	1987	1497
175 1/8	27 5/8	27 1/8	19 6/8	5 3/8	5 5/8	7	6	Marquette Co., MI	Andrew E. Cook II	Andrew E. Cook II	1987	1497
175 1/8	27 3/8	27 6/8	20 7/8	5 5/8	5 4/8	7	7	Des Moines Co., IA	Gordon F. Rorebeck	Gordon F. Rorebeck	1987	1497
175 1/8	24 5/8	25 4/8	17 5/8	5 4/8	5 4/8	5	5	Witchekan Lake, SK	Brent A. Smith	Brent A. Smith	1989	1497
175 1/8	27 5/8	26 4/8	17 2/8	4 6/8	4 4/8	7	8	Crawford Co., IA	Kermit Greenstreet	Kermit Greenstreet	1989	1497
175 1/8	25 1/8	24 5/8	23 7/8	6 2/8	6 2/8	5	6	Otero Co., CO	Kenny D. Mills	Kenny D. Mills	1992	1497
175 1/8	23	23 7/8	17 1/8	5 1/8	5	9	9	Loon Lake, SK	Thomas P. Shields	Thomas P. Shields	1992	1497
175 1/8	26 3/8	26 2/8	19 7/8	5 2/8	5 1/8	6	7	Butler Co., KS	Paul E. Kemp	Paul E. Kemp	1993	1497
175 1/8	27 1/8	28 2/8	24 3/8	4 3/8	4 2/8	9	5	Penobscot Co., ME	Peter A. Duncombe	Peter A. Duncombe	1994	1497
175 1/8	26 6/8	29	19 7/8	5	5	6	7	Cole Co., MO	Brian L. Bruemmer	Brian L. Bruemmer	1995	1497
175 1/8	27	26 7/8	20 1/8	5 7/8	5 6/8	6	6	Scott Co., IA	Jeffrey R. Coonts	Jeffrey R. Coonts	1996	1497
175 1/8	26 4/8	25 5/8	17 3/8	5 1/8	5	6	5	Jackfish Lake, SK	Dan Fitch	Dan Fitch	1996	1497
175 1/8	28 7/8	29 3/8	19 5/8	4 3/8	4 3/8	5	5	Wells Co., IN	Ryan C. Howard	Ryan C. Howard	1996	1497
175 1/8	29	27 7/8	19 1/8	5	5	5	5	Hardin Co., OH	Donald O. Braun	Donald O. Braun	1997	1497
175 1/8	26 2/8	28 4/8	23 6/8	5 1/8	5	6	6	Huron Co., OH	Keith B. Keysor	Keith B. Keysor	1999	1497
175 1/8	25 7/8	27 1/8	19 5/8	4 2/8	4 1/8	6	7	Spokane Co., WA	Michael G. McBride	Michael G. McBride	1999	1497
175 1/8	26 6/8	28	19 5/8	4 1/8	4 5/8	6	5	Lac St. Anne, AB	Shane A. Thue	Shane A. Thue	2002	1497
175	26 2/8	26	18 4/8	4 5/8	4 4/8	6	6	Webb Co., TX	Leslie G. Fisher	Leslie G. Fisher, Jr.	1935	1530
175	28	27 1/8	18 6/8	5	4 6/8	7	7	Minnesota	Floyd Baade	Maverick Russell	1944	1530
175	28 6/8	29 3/8	22 2/8	5 2/8	5 1/8	6	5	Pope Co., MN	Picked Up	R. Benson & K. Wick	1957	1530
175	25 6/8	25 1/8	21	4 4/8	3 7/8	5	5	New Salem, ND	John T. Cartwright	John T. Cartwright	1957	1530
175	24 3/8	22 2/8	18 6/8	4 7/8	4 7/8	7	7	La Salle Co., TX	Leonard W. Bouldin	Leonard W. Bouldin	1972	1530
175	28 4/8	28 3/8	18 2/8	4 4/8	4 4/8	6	6	La Salle Co., TX	Phil Lyne	Phil Lyne	1972	1530
175	23 2/8	24	19 6/8	5 1/8	5 2/8	5	5	Harrison Co., MO	Carl J. Graham	Carl J. Graham	1973	1530
175	28 2/8	27 5/8	18 1/8	5	4 7/8	6	5	Louisa Co., IA	Glen D. Brandt	Glen D. Brandt	1974	1530
175	28 5/8	29 1/8	21 5/8	5 1/8	5	7	5	Henry Co., IA	Richard Doggett	Richard Doggett	1975	1530
175	28 2/8	28 7/8	20 2/8	5 6/8	5 6/8	7	6	Peace River, BC	Unknown	Shane Pallister	PR 1980	1530
175	24	24	18 6/8	5 2/8	5 3/8	6	6	Ohio Co., IN	Rick T. Henry	Rick T. Henry	1981	1530
175	25 3/8	25 4/8	19 2/8	5 4/8	5 4/8	5	5	Itasca Co., MN	David A. Frandsen	David A. Frandsen	1982	1530
175	31 3/8	31	23 2/8	4 7/8	5	6	8	Mower Co., MN	Scott R. Lau	Scott R. Lau	1983	1530
175	26	27 4/8	21	5 1/8	5 1/8	5	6	Jim Hogg Co., TX	Carl D. Ellis	Lee H. Lytton, Jr.	1984	1530
175	25 3/8	24 3/8	17 5/8	5 4/8	5 7/8	7	7	Hardin Co., OH	Roger E. Titus	Roger E. Titus	1988	1530
175	27	27	21	5 2/8	5 2/8	5	5	Riverdale, MB	David Hofer, Jr.	David Hofer, Jr.	1989	1530
175	27 6/8	28 6/8	19	4 3/8	4 1/8	6	6	Lee Co., IA	Stephen D. McKeehan, Jr.	Stephen D. McKeehan, Jr.	1989	1530

Score	Main Beam R	Main Beam L	Inside Spread	Circ. R	Circ. L	R	L	Locality	Hunter	Owner	Date	Rank
175	26 3/8	25 4/8	17	4 7/8	4 6/8	5	5	Bureau Co., IL	Paul S. Cobane III	Paul S. Cobane III	1990	1530
175	26 5/8	27	19 2/8	5 3/8	5 3/8	6	7	Rochester, AB	Terry Hill	Terry Hill	1991	1530
175	27	26 2/8	21	4 5/8	4 5/8	7	5	Dubuque Co., IA	Lawrence E. Blatz	Lawrence E. Blatz	1992	1530
175	27 4/8	27 7/8	21	5 1/8	5	9	7	Stearns Co., MN	Gregory M.J. Gunnerson	Gregory M.J. Gunnerson	1992	1530
175	26 2/8	28 2/8	22	5	5	5	5	Bjork Lake, SK	Don C. Wright	James E. Nelson	1992	1530
175	25 2/8	25 2/8	18 2/8	5 4/8	5 3/8	8	7	McKenzie Co., ND	Larry D. Schultz	Larry D. Schultz	1992	1530
175	24 6/8	25 1/8	19 6/8	4 4/8	4 3/8	6	6	Maverick Co., TX	William M. Wheless III	William M. Wheless III	1992	1530
175	25 3/8	25 4/8	17 4/8	4	4 1/8	7	5	Schuyler Co., IL	Gary L. Braun	Gary L. Braun	1993	1530
175	28 3/8	28 5/8	21	5 4/8	5 3/8	6	6	Gregory Co., SD	Marc S. Anthony	Marc S. Anthony	1993	1530
175	27 7/8	27 4/8	19 3/8	4 6/8	4 7/8	7	6	Clayton Co., IA	Ken Dooley	Ken Dooley	1995	1530
175	27 6/8	26 6/8	21 2/8	4 6/8	4 6/8	6	6	Crittenden Co., KY	Clifton L. Kauffman	Clifton L. Kauffman	1996	1530
175	26 2/8	26	23 2/8	5	5	6	5	Lac La Biche, AB	Steve L. Clark	Steve L. Clark	1996	1530
175	28 1/8	27 1/8	22 4/8	4 7/8	5 2/8	6	6	Lake Co., IL	Ronald N. Carpenter	Ronald N. Carpenter	1997	1530
175	26 5/8	28 2/8	21 4/8	5 1/8	5 1/8	5	6	Butler Co., KY	Picked Up	Nancy L. Egbert	1998	1530
175	27	27 3/8	18 3/8	5 1/8	5	6	6	Echo Lake, SK	Stevie Henderson	Stevie Henderson	1998	1530
175	26 6/8	26 4/8	21 4/8	5 3/8	5 1/8	5	6	Union Co., IA	Kelvin E. Karpinski	Kelvin E. Karpinski	1998	1530
175	27 2/8	26 1/8	19	5 1/8	5 3/8	6	6	Maverick Co., TX	Luke A. Bradley	Luke A. Bradley	1998	1530
175	26 6/8	28 3/8	21 6/8	5 2/8	5 3/8	8	6	Washington Co., NE	John A. Cardwell	John A. Cardwell	1999	1530
175	27	26 5/8	22 4/8	4 6/8	4 6/8	5	6	Torch River, SK	Allan K. Wical	Allan K. Wical	1999	1530
175	26 2/8	25 3/8	21 3/8	5 3/8	5 3/8	6	5	Cooper Co., MO	Leo L. Arcand	Leo L. Arcand	1999	1530
175	22 7/8	23 5/8	18 3/8	4 3/8	4 7/8	6	6	Lac La Biche, AB	Bradley M. Baker	Bradley M. Baker	2000	1530
175	24 4/8	24 2/8	19	5 2/8	5 1/8	5	5	Sheridan Co., KS	Tony J. Mitchell	Tony J. Mitchell	2000	1530
175	27 6/8	28 1/8	18 6/8	5	5	5	5	Knox Co., IL	Les S. Brown	Les S. Brown	2001	1530
175	24 3/8	24 2/8	20 2/8	5 2/8	5 3/8	6	6	Leavenworth Co., KS	Joel P. Catlin	Joel P. Catlin	2001	1530
175	26 5/8	25	21 2/8	4 6/8	4 7/8	6	5	Ottawa Co., OH	Dennis L. Yarnell	Dennis L. Yarnell	2001	1530
175	27 6/8	28 1/8	23 4/8	5 7/8	5 6/8	5	6	Delta Co., MI	John L. Biggert, Sr.	John L. Biggert, Sr.	2002	1530
174 7/8	24 3/8	24 2/8	23 6/8	4 7/8	4 7/8	7	6	Rivers, MB	Will Wellman	Delor J. Wellman	1930	1573
174 7/8	26 5/8	25	22 6/8	5 3/8	5 4/8	9	6	Decatur Co., IA	N. Manchur	N. Manchur	1954	1573
174 7/8	25	25 2/8	18 7/8	4 3/8	4 4/8	5	5	Burnett Co., WI	Mike Boswell	Mike Boswell	1976	1573
174 7/8	28 1/8	28 1/8	21 3/8	5	5	6	5	Fillmore Co., MN	Myles T. Keller	Myles T. Keller	1977	1573
174 7/8	25 5/8	25 5/8	16 5/8	4 4/8	5	6	6	Jo Daviess Co., IL	Daniel M. Hansen	Daniel M. Hansen	1979	1573
174 7/8	25 5/8	25 6/8	21 3/8	4 7/8	4 6/8	6	6	Polk Co., TX	W.V. Patrick	Jerry Patrick	1983	1573
174 7/8	25 1/8	25 1/8	20 6/8	4 1/8	4 3/8	7	8	Stevens Co., WA	Charlie L. Albertson	Charlie L. Albertson	1984	1573
174 7/8	26 1/8	26 1/8	18 4/8	5 1/8	5 1/8	6	7	Dent Co., MO	Clifton W. Hamilton	Clifton W. Hamilton	1990	1573
174 7/8	23 3/8	23 5/8	16 7/8	4 3/8	4 4/8	5	6	Clinton Co., IL	Thomas P. Wylie	Thomas P. Wylie	1990	1573
174 7/8	27 5/8	27 5/8	20 1/8	4 4/8	4 3/8	5	6	Warren Co., IA	Mark A. Porter	Mark A. Porter	1991	1573
174 7/8	28 3/8	28 6/8	18 7/8	4 7/8	4 3/8	5	5	Washtenaw Co., MI	Picked Up	John I. Kunert	PR 1992	1573
174 7/8	25 7/8	26 4/8	19 2/8	5 1/8	4 7/8	6	6	Scott Co., IN	Michael F. Burger	Michael F. Burger	1993	1573
174 7/8	25 3/8	25 1/8	17 5/8	5 3/8	5 2/8	6	5	Woods Co., OK	Henry E. Reynolds	Henry E. Reynolds	1994	1573
174 7/8	26 1/8	25 7/8	19 5/8	5 1/8	5 2/8	5	5	Langbank, SK	Eddie Mustard	Eddie Mustard	1995	1573
174 7/8	22	22 3/8	18 5/8	5 3/8	5 4/8	4	6	St. Louis Co., MN	Allan Brehaut	Allan Brehaut	1996	1573
174 7/8	27 6/8	27 3/8	20 2/8	5 5/8	5 4/8	5	6	Goodsoil, SK	Randy Fredlund	Randy Fredlund	1999	1573
174 7/8	25 4/8	26 6/8	18 1/8	4 4/8	4 4/8	6	5	Elbow River, AB	Richard C. Moulton	Richard C. Moulton	2000	1573
174 7/8	25 7/8	25 2/8	17 4/8	4 7/8	5	6	5	Pipestone River, SK	James W. Taylor	James W. Taylor	2000	1573
174 7/8	23	24 1/8	17 7/8	4 6/8	4 7/8	6	5	Door Co., WI	Brent M. Urschel	Brent M. Urschel	2000	1573
174 7/8	28 1/8	27 5/8	23 5/8	4 4/8	4 4/8	5	6	Clayton Co., IA	Keith N. Bink	Keith N. Bink	2001	1573
174 7/8	28 6/8	27 5/8	21 3/8	5 3/8	5 3/8	7	7	Decatur Co., IA	Scott D. Geater	Scott D. Geater	2001	1573
174 7/8	24 3/8	25 4/8	20 7/8	4 7/8	4 7/8	7	5	Decatur Co., IA	Thomas G. Krikke	Thomas G. Krikke	2001	1573

Odocoileus virginianus and certain related subspecies

Score	Length of Main Beam R	L	Inside Spread	Circumference at Smallest Place Between Burr and First Point R	L	Number of Points R	L	Locality	Hunter	Owner	Date Killed	Rank
174 7/8	24 1/8	24 1/8	18 1/8	5	4 7/8	7	6	Barron Co., WI	Wayne Phillips	Wayne Phillips	2001	1573
174 6/8	26 2/8	27 4/8	21	5 6/8	5 6/8	8	6	Hayward, WI	Bill Metcalf	John Metcalf	1924	1596
174 6/8	27 2/8	29 1/8	21 2/8	5 1/8	5	5	5	Coahoma Co., MS	O.P. Gilbert	O.P. Gilbert	1960	1596
174 6/8	23 6/8	24 4/8	17 5/8	6	5 6/8	6	7	Lancaster Co., NE	Vaughn Wright	Phillip Wright	1960	1596
174 6/8	28 4/8	29	18 6/8	5 2/8	5 2/8	7	7	Essex Co., NY	Richard Olcott	Richard Olcott	1967	1596
174 6/8	24 6/8	24 2/8	18 2/8	4 4/8	4 4/8	6	6	Isanti Co., MN	Larry Roos	Larry Roos	1971	1596
174 6/8	28 3/8	27 6/8	21	4 6/8	4 5/8	5	6	Maine	Unknown	Warren H. Delaware	PR 1977	1596
174 6/8	24 4/8	24 3/8	19 4/8	5 2/8	5 1/8	9	9	Unknown	Unknown	Gerald Hillman	PR 1978	1596
174 6/8	27 2/8	27 2/8	21 2/8	5 1/8	5 1/8	8	7	Clayton Co., IA	James Trappe	James Trappe	1980	1596
174 6/8	26 5/8	26 1/8	20 1/8	4 4/8	4 6/8	6	5	Talbot Co., GA	Harold Cole, Sr.	Harold Cole, Sr.	1985	1596
174 6/8	27 4/8	28	19 4/8	5 2/8	5 3/8	6	5	Lake William, NS	Neil G. Oickle	Neil G. Oickle	1985	1596
174 6/8	25 5/8	24	18	4 7/8	5	6	6	Fisher Branch, MB	Paul Sanduliak	Paul Sanduliak	1985	1596
174 6/8	24 6/8	26 3/8	21 3/8	5 2/8	5 2/8	5	6	Shannon Co., MO	Picked Up	Scott D. Lindsey	1992	1596
174 6/8	23 3/8	24 4/8	23	5 3/8	5 2/8	5	5	Lincoln Co., MT	Daniel P. Murray	Daniel P. Murray	1993	1596
174 6/8	26 6/8	26	20 6/8	4 6/8	4 5/8	6	5	Jo Daviess Co., IL	Steven C. Rosenthal	Steven C. Rosenthal	1993	1596
174 6/8	23 3/8	23 7/8	16	4 7/8	4 7/8	6	6	Coahuila, MX	Gustavo Garza	Gustavo Garza	1994	1596
174 6/8	26 7/8	26 7/8	20	5	5	5	5	Fayette Co., IA	Gerald E. Gress	Gerald E. Gress	1995	1596
174 6/8	28 7/8	26 3/8	20 3/8	4 6/8	4 7/8	6	7	Medina Co., OH	Charles M. Hummel	Charles M. Hummel	1996	1596
174 6/8	27 2/8	26 7/8	17	4 3/8	4 4/8	6	7	Allamakee Co., IA	Dave Moritz, Jr.	Dave Moritz, Jr.	1996	1596
174 6/8	28	28	18 6/8	6	5 6/8	5	5	Adams Co., MS	Jeremy E. Boelte	Jeremy E. Boelte	1997	1596
174 6/8	27 7/8	27 6/8	18 6/8	4 5/8	4 6/8	5	5	Union Co., IL	Dirk A. Hernandez	Dirk A. Hernandez	1997	1596
174 6/8	25 3/8	25 7/8	21 2/8	4 5/8	4 5/8	6	6	Franchere, AB	Franklin B. Janz	Franklin B. Janz	1997	1596
174 6/8	27	27	20 2/8	4 1/8	4 2/8	5	5	Ray Co., MO	Douglas Kirk	Douglas Kirk	1997	1596
174 6/8	25 7/8	27 1/8	24 4/8	4 6/8	4 5/8	6	6	Winnebago Co., IL	Charles P. Lanzendorf	Brian S. Anderson	1998	1596
174 6/8	26 3/8	26 6/8	19	5 2/8	5 3/8	6	6	Desha Co., AR	James F. Finch	James F. Finch	1999	1596
174 6/8	25 1/8	24 6/8	18 3/8	4 7/8	4 6/8	7	7	Leavenworth Co., KS	Mark R. Wegner	Mark R. Wegner	1999	1596
174 6/8	23 3/8	23 5/8	15 4/8	4 4/8	4 3/8	6	6	Jefferson Co., WI	Ronald Jongetjez	Ronald Jongetjez	2000	1596
174 6/8	26 4/8	26 4/8	19 6/8	4 4/8	4 3/8	6	6	Oneida Co., WI	Michael J. Krueger	Michael J. Krueger	2000	1596
174 6/8	27 1/8	25	19 2/8	4 6/8	4 7/8	5	5	Vermilion Co., IL	Chris W. Magrini	Chris W. Magrini	2000	1596
174 6/8	25 5/8	27 6/8	18 6/8	5 4/8	5 4/8	6	6	Avoyelles Parish, LA	Allen J. Gaspard	Allen J. Gaspard	2003	1596
174 5/8	27 1/8	27 2/8	20 3/8	4 3/8	4 5/8	5	7	Isanti Co., MN	Unknown	Pete Thiry	PR 1940	1625
174 5/8	25	25 2/8	24 3/8	4 3/8	4 2/8	7	7	Kleberg Co., TX	C.T. Burris	Darrel Pitts	1959	1625
174 5/8	24 2/8	24 3/8	19 6/8	5 5/8	5 4/8	7	6	Manitoba	C.S. Browning	C.S. Browning	1960	1625
174 5/8	23	23 2/8	17 7/8	4 7/8	5	8	7	Lincoln Co., MO	William Ziegelmeyer	Ronald Ziegelmeyer, Sr.	1968	1625
174 5/8	25 2/8	26 1/8	18 3/8	5 1/8	4 7/8	5	6	Butler Co., IA	Vernon Simon	Vernon Simon	1972	1625
174 5/8	22 4/8	21 4/8	17 1/8	5	5	7	6	Jefferson Co., KS	Keith D. Hendrix	Keith D. Hendrix	1973	1625

Score	Main Beam R	Main Beam L	Inside Spread	Pts R	Pts L	Circ R	Circ L	Locality	Hunter	Owner	Date	Rank
174 5/8	24	22 5/8	18 3/8	5	5	4 5/8	4 4/8	Meeker Co., MN	James L. Mattson	James L. Mattson	1973	1625
174 5/8	29 4/8	28 1/8	21 7/8	9	6	6	6	Otter Tail Co., MN	James C. Vorderbruggen	James C. Vorderbruggen	1976	1625
174 5/8	26	26 2/8	21 1/8	6	5	5 3/8	5 3/8	Baldonnel, BC	D. Ian Williams	D. Ian Williams	1978	1625
174 5/8	26	25 4/8	19 5/8	5	8	5 1/8	4 6/8	Des Moines Co., IA	Gene L. McAlister	Gene L. McAlister	1980	1625
174 5/8	27 5/8	26 4/8	18 1/8	5	5	4 6/8	5 2/8	Jasper Co., IL	Harold L. Ochs	Harold L. Ochs	1982	1625
174 5/8	25 1/8	27 5/8	18 3/8	6	6	5 2/8	5 3/8	Door Co., WI	Patrick D. Madden	Patrick D. Madden	1984	1625
174 5/8	28 2/8	25	16 5/8	5	5	5 1/8	5 3/8	Livingston Co., MI	Nicholas S. Converse	Nicholas S. Converse	1987	1625
174 5/8	26	28	22 5/8	5	5	5 3/8	5 3/8	Johnson Co., MO	Thomas E. White	Thomas E. White	1990	1625
174 5/8	28 6/8	25 3/8	22 3/8	8	8	6 7/8	6 5/8	Beaver Co., OK	Tanner Alexander	Tanner Alexander	1990	1625
174 5/8	24	28	20 4/8	6	6	5 5/8	5 4/8	Ray Co., MO	Dennis B. Bales	Dennis B. Bales	1990	1625
174 5/8	28 2/8	25 3/8	21 5/8	9	5	5 6/8	5 4/8	Jackson Co., MI	Louise S. Klarr	Louise S. Klarr	1990	1625
174 5/8	26 2/8	28 1/8	19 1/8	5	5	5 4/8	5 4/8	Delaware Co., OH	Robert J. Miller	Robert J. Miller	1990	1625
174 5/8	25 1/8	25 3/8	18 7/8	6	6	5 2/8	4 4/8	Buffalo Co., WI	Daniel L. Scharmer	Daniel L. Scharmer	1990	1625
174 5/8	30 4/8	25 5/8	30 4/8	5	5	4 5/8	4 4/8	Larimer Co., CO	George S. Sumter, Jr.	George S. Sumter, Jr.	1990	1625
174 5/8	27 5/8	27 5/8	20 1/8	5	6	4 4/8	4 4/8	Jefferson Co., OH	Walter R. Sutton	Walter R. Sutton	1991	1625
174 5/8	29 2/8	26 6/8	20 3/8	6	6	4 7/8	5 1/8	Jackson Co., IA	Ronald J. Casel	Ronald J. Casel	1992	1625
174 5/8	27 3/8	27 3/8	19 3/8	8	8	5	5	Jefferson Co., IL	Brian G. Pierce	Brian G. Pierce	1992	1625
174 5/8	27 1/8	26 4/8	20 3/8	5	5	4 4/8	4 4/8	Webb Co., TX	Edward O. Radke	Edward O. Radke	1992	1625
174 5/8	26 5/8	25	20 7/8	8	7	4 6/8	4 6/8	St. Louis Co., MN	Unknown	George W. Flaim	PR 1993	1625
174 5/8	26 3/8	25 2/8	17 5/8	7	5	5 5/8	5 3/8	Lodgepole, AB	Frank Spilak	Frank Spilak	1995	1625
174 5/8	25 6/8	25 3/8	16 7/8	5	5	6 2/8	6 2/8	St. Francis Co., AR	J.S. & J.R. Cook	J.S. & J.R. Cook	1996	1625
174 5/8	25 6/8	26 2/8	20 3/8	5	5	4 5/8	4 6/8	Saskatoon, SK	Kelly D. Day	Kelly D. Day	1996	1625
174 5/8	24	24 7/8	18 1/8	5	5	5	4 7/8	Lyon Co., KS	Joshua W. Koch	Joshua W. Koch	1997	1625
174 5/8	26 2/8	25 4/8	20 7/8	6	5	4 4/8	4 4/8	Jumping Deer Creek, SK	Doug Blaha	Doug Blaha	1998	1625
174 5/8	25 4/8	24 6/8	19 3/8	6	5	6 1/8	5 2/8	Webb Co., TX	Alan W. Saralecos	Alan W. Saralecos	2000	1625
174 5/8	24 7/8	24 3/8	21 5/8	6	5	4 6/8	4 5/8	Lyman Co., SD	Leeman E. Moore, Jr.	Leeman E. Moore, Jr.	2002	1625
174 5/8	25 6/8	26	16 7/8	6	6	4 5/8	4 6/8	Maverick Co., TX	Frank A. Wojtek	Frank A. Wojtek	2002	1625
174 4/8	22 5/8	24 1/8	16 6/8	5	5	5 1/8	5 2/8	Marquette Co., MI	Henry L. Terres	Bass Pro Shops	1944	1658
174 4/8	26 4/8	25 2/8	16 7/8	5	6	4 6/8	4 3/8	Koochiching Co., MN	Unknown	Michael Murphy	PR 1950	1658
174 4/8	27 3/8	23 2/8	19 4/8	6	6	6	6	Fort Steele, BC	John Lum	John Lum	1958	1658
174 4/8	22 2/8	23 3/8	20 4/8	7	7	5 1/8	5 7/8	Buffalo Co., WI	Unknown	Douglas R. Plourde	1961	1658
174 4/8	22 6/8	24 6/8	19 5/8	6	5	4 6/8	5 2/8	Butler Co., KY	Lonnie D. Hardin	Lonnie D. Hardin	1966	1658
174 4/8	24 6/8	26 3/8	18	7	5	4 3/8	5	Powell Co., MT	Dave Rittenhouse	Dave Rittenhouse	1973	1658
174 4/8	26 3/8	27 4/8	20 2/8	6	6	5 2/8	5	McKenzie Co., ND	Ben Dekker	Ben Dekker	1976	1658
174 4/8	27 4/8	27 4/8	19 1/8	5	5	5 2/8	5 6/8	Jensen Reservoir, AB	Gary Stanford	Gary Stanford	1976	1658
174 4/8	28 2/8	27 3/8	21	6	5	4 2/8	4	Charlotte Co., VA	Jerry C. Claybrook	Jerry C. Claybrook	1977	1658
174 4/8	24 7/8	27 4/8	17	5	5	5 3/8	5 2/8	Knox Co., ME	Robert E. Young	Robert E. Young	1979	1658
174 4/8	27 2/8	28 2/8	20 6/8	5	5	4 5/8	4 5/8	Boone Co., IA	Curtis A. Lind	Curtis A. Lind	1982	1658
174 4/8	27 3/8	26 3/8	18 3/8	5	6	4 6/8	5 2/8	La Salle Co., TX	H.C. Eppright	H.C. Sims	1982	1658
174 4/8	29	27 6/8	18	8	7	5 1/8	5	Lee Co., IL	Fred L. Schimel	Fred L. Schimel	1988	1658
174 4/8	28 2/8	29 5/8	19 7/8	5	5	5 3/8	5 1/8	Calhoun Co., IL	Michael L. Moore	Michael L. Moore	1989	1658
174 4/8	27 3/8	27 5/8	16	6	6	5 4/8	5 2/8	McDonough Co., IL	Gary Shelley	Gary Shelley	1991	1658
174 4/8	25 6/8	24 1/8	24 7/8	6	5	4 1/8	4 1/8	Washington Co., IN	Michael L. Bledsoe	Michael L. Bledsoe	1992	1658
174 4/8	24 2/8	26 2/8	17 6/8	5	5	5 2/8	5 2/8	Nicollet Co., MN	Ambrose R. McCabe	Ambrose R. McCabe	1992	1658
174 4/8	26 2/8	24 2/8	23 4/8	8	7	5 5/8	5 1/8	Wolfe Co., KY	Toy E. Hazenfield	Toy E. Hazenfield	1993	1658
174 4/8	27 2/8	25 3/8	17 5/8	9	8	5 3/8	5 4/8	Glaslyn, SK	Roger D. Matheny	Roger D. Matheny	1993	1658
174 4/8	—	26 2/8	16 1/8	6	5	5 4/8	5	Hamilton Co., IA	Todd L. Darling	Todd L. Darling	1994	1658
174 4/8	—	27 2/8	—	6	5	4 6/8	5	Stafford Co., KS	Darin J. Brummer	Darin J. Brummer	1995	1658

WHITETAIL DEER - TYPICAL ANTLERS
Odocoileus virginianus virginianus and certain related subspecies

Score	Length of Main Beam		Inside Spread	Circumference at Smallest Place Between Burr and First Point		Number of Points		Locality	Hunter	Owner	Date Killed	Rank
	R	L		R	L	R	L					
174 4/8	25 5/8	26 2/8	19 7/8	5 2/8	5 4/8	6	5	Wright Co., MN	Michael J. Buennich	Michael J. Buennich	1995	1658
174 4/8	27 3/8	28 3/8	23 2/8	5 2/8	5 1/8	8	7	Massac Co., IL	Josh A. Bowman	Josh A. Bowman	1997	1658
174 4/8	29 2/8	29	28 3/8	5 2/8	5 6/8	7	7	Unknown	Unknown	Aly M. Bruner	PR 1997	1658
174 4/8	30 1/8	28 6/8	22 5/8	5 2/8	5 3/8	7	6	Randolph Co., IL	William S. Simmons	William S. Simmons	1998	1658
174 4/8	27 3/8	27 7/8	22 4/8	5	4 6/8	5	5	Jackson Co., IA	Ted B. Howell	Ted B. Howell	1999	1658
174 4/8	26 5/8	25 1/8	20 6/8	4 7/8	4 6/8	6	6	Polk Co., MN	Steven R. Cornell	Steven R. Cornell	2000	1658
174 4/8	26 1/8	25 4/8	18 6/8	4 6/8	4 6/8	5	5	Gull Lake, AB	Robert Meredith	Robert Meredith	2001	1658
174 4/8	28	27 2/8	20 5/8	5	4 7/8	6	6	Jackson Co., IA	Randy P. Steines	Randy P. Steines	2002	1658
174 3/8	27 1/8	27 2/8	15 5/8	4 4/8	4 3/8	7	7	Texas	Unknown	Buckhorn Mus. & Saloon, Ltd.	PR 1956	1687
174 3/8	27 6/8	27 6/8	21 5/8	5 5/8	5 2/8	7	8	Guthrie Co., IA	Larry R. Belding	Larry R. Belding	1965	1687
174 3/8	24 7/8	23 6/8	17 7/8	5 5/8	5 1/8	5	5	Aitkin Co., MN	Christopher W. Steinke	Christopher W. Steinke	1969	1687
174 3/8	28 1/8	26 7/8	23 5/8	5 3/8	5 4/8	6	5	Knox Co., MO	Jon Simmons	Jon Simmons	1972	1687
174 3/8	25 4/8	26 3/8	18 3/8	4 6/8	5	9	8	Marshall Co., KS	Michael J. Krogman	Michael J. Krogman	1981	1687
174 3/8	26 2/8	25 2/8	20 5/8	4 4/8	4 2/8	5	5	McCreary Co., KY	Richmond Keeton	Ruby Keeton	1982	1687
174 3/8	27 2/8	25 2/8	23 6/8	5 1/8	5	7	7	Geary Co., KS	James Brethour	James Brethour	1984	1687
174 3/8	25 2/8	25 3/8	20 1/8	4 5/8	4 6/8	5	5	Goshen Co., WY	Casey L. Hunter	Casey L. Hunter	1984	1687
174 3/8	24	24	17 4/8	5 4/8	5 4/8	8	7	Sawyer Co., WI	Patrick E. Jasper	Patrick E. Jasper	1985	1687
174 3/8	28	28 4/8	21 2/8	4 6/8	4 7/8	5	6	La Crosse Co., WI	Kevin M. Kastenschmidt	Kevin M. Kastenschmidt	1986	1687
174 3/8	26 4/8	26 4/8	23 2/8	5 2/8	5 2/8	6	7	Trempealeau Co., WI	Laverne Killian, Jr.	Laverne Killian, Jr.	1986	1687
174 3/8	27 1/8	27 1/8	21 3/8	6 2/8	5 2/8	5	5	Itasca Co., MN	Mark O. DuLong	Mark O. DuLong	1987	1687
174 3/8	28 3/8	26 2/8	23 1/8	4 3/8	4 4/8	7	7	Dimmit Co., TX	Steven W. Vaughn	Steven W. Vaughn	1987	1687
174 3/8	28 3/8	25	17 3/8	5 2/8	5 7/8	6	5	N. Saskatchewan River, AB	James S. Romanchuk	James S. Romanchuk	1988	1687
174 3/8	25 4/8	25 4/8	19 5/8	4 2/8	4 3/8	5	5	Jackson Co., IN	Max E. Gambrel	Max E. Gambrel	1989	1687
174 3/8	26	26 6/8	21 7/8	5 4/8	5 4/8	5	5	Hardin Co., OH	Ron Hamilton	Ron Hamilton	1989	1687
174 3/8	27	27 6/8	22 7/8	5 2/8	5 2/8	8	7	Warren Co., IA	Craig O. Carpenter	Craig O. Carpenter	1990	1687
174 3/8	27 7/8	28	28	5 3/8	5 3/8	5	5	Washtenaw Co., MI	Picked Up	Comm. Bucks of Mich.	1991	1687
174 3/8	24 4/8	24 2/8	17 1/8	4 7/8	5 1/8	7	7	Roddick Lake, SK	Peter J. Laroque	Peter J. Laroque	1993	1687
174 3/8	28 5/8	28 5/8	21 2/8	5 2/8	5 3/8	6	7	Barber Co., KS	James B. Talbott	James B. Talbott	1993	1687
174 3/8	26 1/8	25 6/8	15 6/8	5	4 7/8	6	5	Bayfield Co., WI	Steven W. Schilthelm	Steven W. Schilthelm	1994	1687
174 3/8	26 1/8	25 5/8	16 3/8	4 5/8	4 4/8	6	6	Newton Co., MO	Scott Wolfe	Scott Wolfe	1994	1687
174 3/8	23 4/8	23 4/8	19 3/8	5 2/8	5 3/8	6	6	Marion Co., KS	Matt E. Vaughn	Matt E. Vaughn	1995	1687
174 3/8	27 6/8	27 3/8	22 3/8	5 1/8	5 1/8	5	5	Osage Co., KS	Evans Woehlecke	Evans Woehlecke	1997	1687
174 3/8	24 4/8	24	22 7/8	4 6/8	4 5/8	6	7	Cynthia, AB	Camillo J. Baratto	Camillo J. Baratto	1998	1687
174 3/8	25 2/8	25 3/8	16 1/8	4 1/8	4 2/8	6	6	Outagamie Co., WI	Alan B. Conger	Alan B. Conger	1998	1687
174 3/8	26 7/8	26 7/8	18 5/8	4 7/8	5	6	7	Sullivan Co., NY	Domenick DeMaria	Domenick A. DeMaria	1998	1687
174 3/8	26	26	22	5 5/8	5 7/8	7	5	Allamakee Co., IA	Clinton C. Mohn	Clinton C. Mohn	1999	1687

Score	Main Beam R	Main Beam L	Inside Spread	Circ. R	Circ. L	Pts R	Pts L	Locality	Hunter	Owner	Date	Rank
174 3/8	26	25 1/8	20 2/8	5 2/8	5 6/8	5	7	Fulton Co., IL	Robert V. Stevenson, Jr.	Robert V. Stevenson, Jr.	1999	1687
174 3/8	28 6/8	27 2/8	20 5/8	5 1/8	5	5	5	Otter Tail Co., MN	Picked Up	Frank Virchow	1999	1687
174 3/8	27	27 2/8	20 1/8	5 6/8	5 3/8	8	9	Jackson Co., MO	Mark A. Trowbridge	Mark A. Trowbridge	2000	1687
174 3/8	24 1/8	24 4/8	16 1/8	4 4/8	4 5/8	7	6	Mineral Co., MT	Dan Woodson	Dan Woodson	2000	1687
174 3/8	26	26	20 1/8	5 2/8	4 6/8	6	7	Genesee Co., NY	Jeffrey A. Mullin	Jeffrey A. Mullin	2002	1687
174 2/8	28 2/8	27 3/8	25 2/8	4 4/8	5 4/8	4	4	Cerralvo, MX	Unknown	Antonio G. Gonzalez	1900	1720
174 2/8	25 4/8	26	20	4 5/8	4 4/8	6	8	Zavala Co., TX	Ernest Holdsworth	E.M. Holdsworth	1908	1720
174 2/8	25 3/8	26 3/8	22	4 6/8	4 6/8	5	5	Livingston Co., NY	Kenneth Bowen	Kenneth Bowen	1941	1720
174 2/8	24 6/8	24 2/8	22	4 6/8	4 6/8	6	6	Dimmit Co., TX	Red Tollet	McLean Bowman	1958	1720
174 2/8	27 2/8	28 1/8	20 2/8	5 4/8	5 3/8	5	5	Langlade Co., WI	Lyman Aderman	Ray T. Charles	PR 1963	1720
174 2/8	21 4/8	22	17	4 6/8	4 5/8	6	6	Cass Co., TX	R.J. Perkins	John D. Small	1963	1720
174 2/8	23 3/8	28 2/8	22 2/8	5 4/8	5 4/8	4	4	Cass Co., IA	Cecil Erickson	Cecil Erickson	1975	1720
174 2/8	26 1/8	23 6/8	15 6/8	4 4/8	4 5/8	10	9	La Salle Co., TX	Walter L. Taylor	Walter L. Taylor	1979	1720
174 2/8	27 7/8	27	22 6/8	5	5 1/8	5	6	Clearwater Co., ID	Douglas B. Crockett	Douglas B. Crockett	1983	1720
174 2/8	27 6/8	26 5/8	21 2/8	5 2/8	6 1/8	5	5	Ashland Co., WI	Kelly J. McClaire	Kelly J. McClaire	1986	1720
174 2/8	27 6/8	25 7/8	19 4/8	5 2/8	4 6/8	5	5	Butler Co., PA	Ralph Stoltenberg, Jr.	Ralph Stoltenberg, Jr.	1986	1720
174 2/8	27 5/8	27 1/8	19 5/8	4 7/8	4 6/8	7	7	Monona Co., IA	Larry R. Petersen	Larry R. Petersen	1990	1720
174 2/8	25 3/8	25 3/8	23 4/8	4 6/8	4 1/8	5	5	Dimmit Co., TX	Picked Up	John I. Kunert	PR 1991	1720
174 2/8	25 3/8	25	21	4	4	7	7	Mt. Pleasant, NS	Garth Hirtle	Garth Hirtle	1993	1720
174 2/8	25 4/8	24 2/8	22 2/8	6 1/8	5 4/8	8	8	Leask, SK	Brian Brad	Brian Brad	1994	1720
174 2/8	27 5/8	27 4/8	17 2/8	5 2/8	5 2/8	8	8	St. Francis Co., AR	Brice Fletcher II	Brice Fletcher II	1995	1720
174 2/8	27 3/8	27 2/8	20 3/8	5	4 6/8	6	5	Highland Co., OH	Jeffrey A. Cooper	Jeffrey A. Cooper	1996	1720
174 2/8	28 1/8	27 5/8	19 4/8	4 5/8	5 1/8	5	5	Sussex Co., DE	J.R. Cropper	J.R. Cropper	1997	1720
174 2/8	26 6/8	26 1/8	23 1/8	5 3/8	4 4/8	8	8	Jefferson Co., IA	James W. Ferguson	James W. Ferguson	1997	1720
174 2/8	25 5/8	26	23 5/8	5 6/8	5 2/8	5	5	Pulaski Co., KY	Ishmael R. Helton	Ishmael R. Helton	1998	1720
174 2/8	23 3/8	23 5/8	21 6/8	4 6/8	5 4/8	7	7	Lake of the Prairies, MB	Stephen Davies	Stephen Davies	1999	1720
174 2/8	24 1/8	24	18	4 6/8	4 6/8	6	6	Montgomery Co., MO	S. Douglas Lensing	S. Douglas Lensing	1999	1720
174 2/8	25 4/8	27 3/8	16 4/8	4 6/8	4 6/8	7	6	Moosomin, SK	Jim Toth	Jim Toth	1999	1720
174 2/8	26 3/8	26 3/8	18 6/8	4 4/8	4 6/8	8	7	Saline Co., KS	Robert L. Darrow	Cabela's, Inc.	2000	1720
174 2/8	26 1/8	26 1/8	22 2/8	6	5 7/8	5	5	Richland Co., WI	Mitch Shewchuk	Mitch Shewchuk	2000	1720
174 2/8	24 5/8	24 5/8	19 7/8	4 4/8	4 4/8	6	6	Hudson Bay, SK	Norman Belchamber	Norman Belchamber	2001	1720
174 2/8	28 3/8	28	20 4/8	6 3/8	5 1/8	4	4	Brown Co., IL	David A. Bowen	David A. Bowen	2002	1720
174 2/8	24 4/8	26	25 6/8	5 6/8	4 6/8	8	7	Knox Co., IL	Bradley M. Nelson	Bradley M. Nelson	2002	1720
174 2/8	27	26 1/8	19 5/8	4 3/8	4 7/8	7	7	Fish Lake, AB	Aldo B. Zanon	Aldo B. Zanon	2002	1720
174 1/8	27 3/8	27 3/8	21 1/8	5 1/8	5 2/8	6	7	Aroostook Co., ME	Unknown	Vern Black	1930	1749
174 1/8	27 1/8	28 1/8	16 7/8	5 4/8	4 3/8	7	6	Essex Co., NY	Denny Mitchell	Lewis P. Evans	1933	1749
174 1/8	25 3/8	25 5/8	24 7/8	4 5/8	5 1/8	6	6	Mahnomen Co., MN	Rolland Agnew	James Frazee	1941	1749
174 1/8	27	26 5/8	19 2/8	4 7/8	5 4/8	5	5	Pierson, MB	Art Minshull	Brad Minshull	PR 1950	1749
174 1/8	25	25	18 4/8	5 4/8	4 5/8	6	6	Buffalo Co., WI	Apolinary Sonsalla	Apolinary Sonsalla	1959	1749
174 1/8	24 5/8	23 5/8	16 6/8	5 1/8	5 4/8	8	7	Callaway Co., MO	Jac LaFon	Jac LaFon	1968	1749
174 1/8	25 2/8	25 2/8	19 5/8	5 4/8	5 1/8	5	5	Blackfoot, AB	Thomas J. Slager	Thomas J. Slager	1969	1749
174 1/8	26	26	23 3/8	5 1/8	5	6	6	Renville Co., MN	Galen Kodet	Galen Kodet	1970	1749
174 1/8	26 4/8	26 3/8	18 5/8	4 6/8	4 6/8	6	6	Iowa Co., IA	Ronald L. Brecht	Ronald L. Brecht	1973	1749
174 1/8	23 2/8	24 5/8	20	5 1/8	5 1/8	5	6	Anarchist Mt., BC	George Urban	George Urban	1980	1749
174 1/8	27	26 1/8	20 6/8	5 1/8	5 2/8	5	5	Johnson Co., KS	Ralph E. Schlagel	Ralph E. Schlagel	1984	1749
174 1/8	25 6/8	25 5/8	20 7/8	6 4/8	6 7/8	7	6	Tuscarawas Co., OH	Dennis J. May, Jr.	Dennis J. May, Jr.	1985	1749
174 1/8	27 3/8	26 4/8	19 6/8	6 7/8	4 7/8	6	6	McDonough Co., IL	Jack C. Icenogle	Jack C. Icenogle	1986	1749
174 1/8	26	25 4/8	18 1/8	5	5 4/8	5	6	Clarke Co., IA	Lee R. Lundstrom	Lee R. Lundstrom	1987	1749

WHITETAIL DEER - TYPICAL ANTLERS

Odocoileus virginianus virginianus and certain related subspecies

Score	Length of Main Beam R	L	Inside Spread	Circumference at Smallest Place Between Burr and First Point R	L	Number of Points R	L	Locality	Hunter	Owner	Date Killed	Rank
174 1/8	26 3/8	26 4/8	20 7/8	4 7/8	4 7/8	5	5	Amherstview, ON	Tony H. Stranak	Tony H. Stranak	1987	1749
174 1/8	23 7/8	23 5/8	19 7/8	5	5	5	5	Goodhue Co., MN	Tom Nesseth	Tom Nesseth	1988	1749
174 1/8	25	25 4/8	18 1/8	5	5	5	5	Mason Co., KY	Rocky L. Hamm	Rocky L. Hamm	1989	1749
174 1/8	24 3/8	25 4/8	19 2/8	5 3/8	5 4/8	7	6	Day Co., SD	Vernon L. Skoba	Vernon L. Skoba	1989	1749
174 1/8	25 5/8	25 6/8	20 7/8	4 2/8	4 2/8	6	6	Seneca Co., OH	Patrick J. Gillig	Patrick J. Gillig	1990	1749
174 1/8	28 4/8	28 3/8	22 3/8	5 1/8	5 6/8	5	6	Wright Co., MN	William J. Stuhr	William J. Stuhr	1990	1749
174 1/8	26	24 4/8	18 7/8	5 1/8	5 1/8	6	5	Stockholm, SK	Rienhold S. Kulcsar	Rienhold S. Kulcsar	1991	1749
174 1/8	27 2/8	25 4/8	20 6/8	5 3/8	5 4/8	6	6	Freeborn Co., MN	Charles D. Stadheim	Charles D. Stadheim	1991	1749
174 1/8	25 2/8	27	21 3/8	5	5	5	5	Chisago Co., MN	Richard A. Townsend	Richard A. Townsend	1991	1749
174 1/8	25 3/8	25 2/8	18 4/8	4 5/8	4 6/8	6	6	Brown Co., NE	Marvin D. Hart	Cabela's, Inc.	1993	1749
174 1/8	26 2/8	27	20	4 7/8	5 1/8	7	5	Adams Co., IL	Robert Daly	Robert Daly	1993	1749
174 1/8	28	27 2/8	25	5 4/8	5 6/8	6	5	Montgomery Co., IL	Justin K. Arndt	Justin K. Arndt	1994	1749
174 1/8	24 7/8	24 7/8	17 1/8	4	3 7/8	6	6	Archer Co., TX	Wade G. Schreiber	Wade G. Schreiber	1994	1749
174 1/8	27 4/8	26	16 1/8	4 5/8	4 6/8	5	5	Livingston Co., MI	Dolores E. Kassuba	Dolores E. Kassuba	1995	1749
174 1/8	25 7/8	26 5/8	22 1/8	5 2/8	5 1/8	5	7	Coahoma Co., MS	William L. Walters	William L. Walters	1995	1749
174 1/8	24 5/8	24 5/8	21 5/8	5 1/8	5 1/8	6	5	Dubuque Co., IA	James E. Beecher	James E. Beecher	1998	1749
174 1/8	26 4/8	25 7/8	18 1/8	5 2/8	5 3/8	7	7	Allamakee Co., IA	Hugh E. Conway	Hugh E. Conway	1998	1749
174 1/8	26 5/8	26 3/8	19 5/8	5 3/8	5 4/8	5	5	Allamakee Co., IA	Picked Up	IA Dept. of Natl. Resc.	1998	1749
174 1/8	25 5/8	25	18 4/8	4 7/8	4 7/8	7	8	Johnson Co., NE	Fred Leuenberger	Fred Leuenberger	1998	1749
174 1/8	25 7/8	25 2/8	16 4/8	4 7/8	5	6	5	Clayton Co., IA	Milo Rolfe	Milo Rolfe	1998	1749
174 1/8	27 1/8	27 4/8	20 1/8	4 5/8	4 4/8	5	5	Coahuila, MX	Wayne Glover	Wayne Glover	1999	1749
174 1/8	24 1/8	23 4/8	19 1/8	5	5 2/8	7	5	Dallas Co., MO	Otis Villines	Otis Villines	1999	1749
174 1/8	26	25 6/8	22 7/8	5 1/8	5	6	8	Summit Co., OH	Robert E. Faber	Robert E. Faber	2000	1749
174 1/8	25	25 3/8	21 1/8	4 6/8	5	9	7	Starke Co., IN	Charles W. Via	Charles W. Via	2000	1749
174 1/8	26 3/8	25	19 5/8	5	5	8	6	Franklin Co., IN	Clarence G. Hupfer	Clarence G. Hupfer	2001	1749
174 1/8	26 2/8	25 2/8	17 2/8	6 1/8	6 3/8	8	7	Cass Co., IL	Christopher C. Gosset	Christopher C. Gosset	2002	1749
174 1/8	28 4/8	29	21	5 2/8	5 2/8	7	5	Clark Co., IL	Barry Howe	Barry Howe	2002	1749
174 1/8	26 4/8	27 1/8	19	4 7/8	4 7/8	7	6	Hocking Co., OH	David C. Jones	David C. Jones	2002	1749
174 1/8	24 6/8	25 4/8	20 1/8	4 4/8	4 3/8	6	7	Blaine Lake, SK	James Skarpinsky	James Skarpinsky	2002	1749
174	28	27 6/8	24 7/8	5 1/8	5	6	6	La Salle Co., TX	Unknown	Lawson W. Walden	1949	1792
174	26 1/8	26 2/8	20 4/8	5	4 6/8	7	7	Bulyea, SK	W.H. Dodsworth	Edward B. Shaw	1961	1792
174	25 6/8	26	19 6/8	4 3/8	4 3/8	5	5	Desha Co., AR	David Wren	Maurice Abowitz	1962	1792
174	26 4/8	26	17 5/8	4 4/8	4 5/8	7	5	Jefferson Co., WI	Gary A. Coates	Gary A. Coates	1970	1792
174	29 2/8	28	21 2/8	5 2/8	5	5	5	Fayette Co., IA	Charles Schott	Charles Schott	1982	1792
174	26 4/8	25 6/8	18 2/8	5 7/8	5 4/8	8	5	Eaton Co., MI	Rodney S. Brown	Connie Brown	1984	1792
174	25 5/8	24 6/8	17 2/8	4 1/8	4 1/8	6	5	Christian Co., KY	Christopher Cundiff	Christopher Cundiff	1985	1792

Score	Length of Main Beam R	Length of Main Beam L	Inside Spread	Circumference R	Circumference L	Points R	Points L	Locality	By Whom Killed	Owner	Date Killed	Rank
174	27 5/8	28	24	5	4 7/8	5	5	Mills Co., IA	Rick W. Elliott	Rick W. Elliott	1987	1792
174	29 1/8	28 3/8	17	5 2/8	5 1/8	5	5	Jefferson Co., NY	James S. Hoar	James S. Hoar	1988	1792
174	27 6/8	28 4/8	19 6/8	4 3/8	4 4/8	5	5	Whitley Co., KY	Edward S. Pittman	Edward S. Pittman	1988	1792
174	26 3/8	26 2/8	17 6/8	4 2/8	4 2/8	6	6	Harrison Co., IA	Ricky G. Seydel	Ricky G. Seydel	1989	1792
174	26 5/8	26 5/8	18 3/8	5 4/8	5 4/8	6	6	Swan River, MB	Picked Up	Clint Martin	1991	1792
174	21 6/8	21 3/8	15 4/8	4 3/8	4 4/8	6	7	Dawson Co., MT	Clayton L. Verke	Clayton L. Verke	1991	1792
174	24 1/8	24 2/8	18	5 1/8	4 7/8	6	6	Chase Co., NE	Kent E. Wasieleski	Kent E. Wasieleski	1993	1792
174	27	18	16 6/8	4 6/8	4 6/8	6	6	Lake of the Prairies, SK	Brian Wonitowy	Brian Wonitowy	1994	1792
174	27	25 7/8	21	4 7/8	5 1/8	6	6	Brown Co., SD	John F. Culp	John F. Culp	1995	1792
174	25 7/8	28 1/8	23	5 1/8	5 1/8	8	5	Vermilion Co., IL	Alex L. Ramm	Alex L. Ramm	1995	1792
174	26 4/8	26 3/8	18	6	6	5	5	La Salle Co., IL	Michael Armstrong	Michael Armstrong	1996	1792
174	29 3/8	26 4/8	19	4 6/8	5	4	5	Johnson Co., KS	Kevin M. Hancock	Kevin M. Hancock	1996	1792
174	27 6/8	29 7/8	18	4 6/8	4 6/8	5	4	Marion Co., KS	Gerald W. Lock	Gerald W. Lock	1997	1792
174	27 7/8	26	23	5 3/8	5 3/8	4	5	Allen Co., IN	James L. Harden	James L. Harden	1998	1792
174	25 6/8	28	20 2/8	5 3/8	5 2/8	6	5	Lake Co., IN	Picked Up	Howard Munson	1998	1792
174	24 1/8	26 1/8	23 5/8	4 3/8	4 4/8	6	6	Battle River, AB	Jeff White	Jeff White	1998	1792
174	23 6/8	25	16	4 4/8	4 3/8	7	8	Pierce Lake, SK	James W. Beresford	James W. Beresford	1999	1792
174	25 4/8	21 7/8	20 2/8	4 4/8	4 3/8	5	6	Saginaw Co., MI	Orrin R. Nothelfer	Orrin R. Nothelfer	2000	1792
174	27 2/8	25 4/8	20 5/8	4 4/8	4 4/8	5	5	Otter Tail Co., MN	John D. Thorson	John D. Thorson	2000	1792
174	25 5/8	26 1/8	22 5/8	5 4/8	5 4/8	6	6	Van Buren Co., MI	Mark A. Meulendyk	Mark A. Meulendyk	2002	1792
174	21 6/8	21	18 6/8	4 5/8	4 4/8	7	8	Tuscarawas Co., OH	Wes S. McMillen	Wes S. McMillen	2003	1792
173 7/8	24 5/8	23 7/8	23 3/8	5 1/8	4 7/8	8	7	Dundurn, SK	Herb Wilson	Herb Wilson	1960	1820
173 7/8	25 4/8	26	19 3/8	5	5	6	6	Starr Co., TX	Leonard A. Schwarz	Leonard A. Schwarz	1965	1820
173 7/8	25 7/8	25 7/8	20 7/8	5 1/8	4 7/8	5	5	Floyd Co., IA	James R. Lines	James R. Lines	1968	1820
173 7/8	26 1/8	26 1/8	19 3/8	5 6/8	5 6/8	6	5	Henry Co., IA	Marion L. Shappell	Marion L. Shappell	1970	1820
173 7/8	25 6/8	24 2/8	20 1/8	5 1/8	5 2/8	7	6	Ohio Co., KY	Rolly Tichenor	Rolly Tichenor	1982	1820
173 7/8	28 6/8	27 5/8	18 5/8	5 3/8	5 3/8	6	7	Penobscot Co., ME	Gregory A. York	Gregory A. York	1986	1820
173 7/8	25 7/8	25	19 1/8	4 6/8	4 6/8	5	5	Wadena Co., MN	Picked Up	Kelly C. Marshall	1987	1820
173 7/8	23 6/8	24 4/8	17 5/8	4	3 7/8	6	6	Allamakee Co., IA	Richard Gaunitz	Richard Gaunitz	1990	1820
173 7/8	26 1/8	26	18	4 6/8	5	6	8	Barrhead, AB	C.J. Fuller	C.J. Fuller	1992	1820
173 7/8	24 3/8	23 1/8	18 2/8	4 7/8	4 7/8	5	7	Esterhazy, SK	Garry Hawcutt	Garry Hawcutt	1992	1820
173 7/8	24	24 1/8	22 3/8	6 4/8	6 2/8	5	6	Ralls Co., MO	Nicholas D. Mudd	Nicholas D. Mudd	1992	1820
173 7/8	27 3/8	27 2/8	19	4 5/8	4 5/8	5	5	Meigs Co., OH	Roger L. Hoffman	Roger L. Hoffman	1993	1820
173 7/8	27	26 7/8	16 4/8	5	5	6	5	Rocky Mt. House, AB	Daniel F. Breton	Daniel F. Breton	1994	1820
173 7/8	26 3/8	27 7/8	21 4/8	6 1/8	5 7/8	6	6	Will Co., IL	Harry D. Hammock	Harry D. Hammock	1995	1820
173 7/8	25 3/8	26 2/8	20 2/8	4 2/8	4 7/8	7	7	Blue Earth Co., MN	Jeffery L. Zimmerman	Jeffery L. Zimmerman	1995	1820
173 7/8	28	28	17 3/8	4 5/8	4	5	5	Drew Co., AR	Ronald E. Pearce	Ronald E. Pearce	1996	1820
173 7/8	29 2/8	30 1/8	24 3/8	4 6/8	4 5/8	6	6	Appanoose Co., IA	Tim G. Anderson	Tim G. Anderson	1997	1820
173 7/8	26 1/8	26 1/8	21 7/8	4 2/8	4 6/8	6	6	Webster Co., KY	Glenn R. Cummings	Glenn R. Cummings	1997	1820
173 7/8	27 6/8	26 6/8	18 4/8	5 6/8	5 6/8	4	4	Wilbarger Co., TX	John T. Wright	John T. Wright	1998	1820
173 7/8	24 1/8	23 2/8	22 5/8	5 3/8	4	5	5		Unknown	Terry L. Amos	PR 1999	1820
173 7/8	28 3/8	28 6/8	24 5/8	4 3/8	4 7/8	7	7	Grant Parish, LA	Dwayne H. Robertson	Dwayne H. Robertson	1999	1820
173 7/8	29 5/8	28 6/8	22 3/8	4 7/8	5 1/8	5	5	Union Co., IA	David Wetsch	David Wetsch	1999	1820
173 7/8	25 4/8	25 5/8	18 7/8	4 7/8	4 7/8	5	5	Appanoose Co., IA	Joel V. Ash	Joel V. Ash	2001	1820
173 7/8	28 7/8	28 3/8	17 3/8	5 3/8	5 3/8	6	6	Pittsylvania Co., VA	Picked Up	David Baker	2001	1820
173 7/8	26 1/8	26 4/8	16 4/8	5 3/8	5 6/8	6	6	Pike Co., MO	Marty Niffen	Marty Niffen	2001	1820
173 7/8	26	27 4/8	17 2/8	5 6/8	5 6/8	6	6	Franklin Co., OH	Casey M. Murphy, Jr.	Casey M. Murphy, Jr.	2002	1820
173 6/8	27 1/8	26 1/8	19 4/8	5 2/8	5 3/8	6	7	Florence Co., WI	Walter Knutson	Mark Shaw	1902	1846

WHITETAIL DEER - TYPICAL ANTLERS
Odocoileus virginianus virginianus and certain related subspecies

Score	Length of Main Beam R	L	Inside Spread	Circumference at Smallest Place Between Burr and First Point R	L	Number of Points R	L	Locality	Hunter	Owner	Date Killed	Rank
173 6/8	26 6/8	27 1/8	19 7/8	5 5/8	5 3/8	7	5	Mercer Co., IL	Floyd A. Clark	Floyd A. Clark	1961	1846
173 6/8	26	26	18 6/8	5 7/8	6 1/8	6	5	Colfax Co., NE	Leonard Bowman	Leonard Bowman	1962	1846
173 6/8	24 3/8	23 6/8	18 3/8	4 6/8	4 4/8	6	7	Lucas Co., IA	James E. Wolfe	James E. Wolfe	1964	1846
173 6/8	27	26 6/8	21 4/8	5	5	7	9	Bullitt Co., KY	George W. Owens	George W. Owens	1965	1846
173 6/8	26 6/8	27 6/8	20 3/8	5 7/8	5 4/8	9	6	Bonner Co., ID	Robert L. Campbell	Robert L. Campbell	1967	1846
173 6/8	25	25 3/8	22 4/8	5 1/8	5	5	5	McAuley, MB	Alex D. Vallance	Alex D. Vallance	1967	1846
173 6/8	25 1/8	25 5/8	18 6/8	5 3/8	5 4/8	7	6	Knox Co., NE	Paul H. Klawitter	Paul H. Klawitter	1970	1846
173 6/8	23 7/8	24	19 6/8	4 6/8	4 6/8	6	6	Dimmit Co., TX	Booth W. Petry	Booth W. Petry	1970	1846
173 6/8	25 6/8	25 6/8	19 6/8	4 1/8	4 4/8	5	5	Pulaski Co., IL	Rose M. Blanchard	Rose M. Blanchard	1973	1846
173 6/8	28 1/8	28 1/8	20 6/8	5 1/8	5 2/8	6	6	Bayfield Co., WI	Henry Pajtash	Henry Pajtash	1978	1846
173 6/8	25 5/8	26 1/8	22 1/8	4 7/8	4 7/8	6	5	Des Moines Co., IA	Richard R. Hassell	Richard R. Hassell	1979	1846
173 6/8	25 6/8	25 6/8	18 4/8	4 3/8	4 3/8	6	6	Livingston Co., MI	Terry J. Kemp	Terry J. Kemp	1979	1846
173 6/8	26 6/8	26 6/8	19 1/8	4 7/8	4 7/8	5	7	Minburn, AB	Joseph R. McGillis	Joseph R. McGillis	1981	1846
173 6/8	24 1/8	24 1/8	17 6/8	4 6/8	4 6/8	6	6	Regina, SK	Don Wolk	Don Wolk	1982	1846
173 6/8	25 4/8	25 3/8	18 2/8	4 3/8	4 4/8	7	7	Carroll Co., GA	Ken Yearta	Ken Yearta	1983	1846
173 6/8	24	24 4/8	18	4 4/8	4 4/8	6	6	Marshall Co., MN	Neil Jacobson	Neil Jacobson	1984	1846
173 6/8	24 5/8	24 4/8	23 4/8	5 2/8	5 4/8	5	5	Hart Creek, BC	Greg Lamontange	Greg Lamontange	1984	1846
173 6/8	26 1/8	25	21 5/8	4 4/8	4 4/8	6	5	Winneshiek Co., IA	Herbert I. Amundson	Herbert I. Amundson	1985	1846
173 6/8	26 4/8	25 4/8	18 6/8	4 2/8	4 2/8	7	6	Stephens Co., TX	Robert L. Murphy	Robert L. Murphy	1986	1846
173 6/8	26 1/8	26 2/8	18 7/8	5 3/8	5 3/8	6	8	Schoolcraft Co., MI	Thomas J. Haas	Thomas J. Haas	1987	1846
173 6/8	25 5/8	25 1/8	18 4/8	5 6/8	5 6/8	5	5	Lincoln Co., NE	Raymond E. Blede	Raymond E. Blede	1988	1846
173 6/8	29 3/8	28 4/8	20 6/8	5 5/8	5 4/8	6	5	Mahaska Co., IA	Gareth P. VandeKieft	Gareth P. VandeKieft	1988	1846
173 6/8	25 3/8	26 6/8	19 3/8	4 5/8	4 5/8	6	5	Warren Co., IA	Wayne E. Bueltel	Wayne E. Bueltel	1989	1846
173 6/8	25 6/8	26 6/8	20	4 5/8	4 3/8	5	5	Dawson Co., NE	Michael L. Seaman	Michael L. Seaman	1989	1846
173 6/8	26 4/8	25 2/8	21 4/8	5 2/8	5 3/8	6	5	Mercer Co., IL	Clarence R. Howard	Clarence R. Howard	1990	1846
173 6/8	23 6/8	24 5/8	22	4 3/8	4 2/8	7	7	Grant Co., NE	Barry Leach	Barry Leach	1991	1846
173 6/8	27 1/8	26 4/8	20	5	5 2/8	5	7	Clinton Co., IA	Picked Up	Wayne Fowler	1992	1846
173 6/8	24 7/8	24 6/8	18 2/8	4 6/8	4 7/8	6	6	Jasper Co., IA	Danny E. Keuning	Danny E. Keuning	1992	1846
173 6/8	26 6/8	26	20 4/8	4 2/8	4 1/8	5	5	Vermillion Co., IN	Brian W. Meeker	Brian W. Meeker	1992	1846
173 6/8	27 1/8	27 3/8	23 3/8	4 5/8	4 5/8	7	7	Dolcy Lake, AB	Joseph P. Baker	Joseph P. Baker	1993	1846
173 6/8	28 6/8	26	23 6/8	4 6/8	4 7/8	6	6	St. Lina, AB	Don Felts	Don Felts	1993	1846
173 6/8	25	23 6/8	22 3/8	6	6	7	5	Sublette, KS	Neal Heaton	Neal Heaton	1993	1846
173 6/8	26 5/8	26 5/8	19	4 6/8	5	7	6	Meadow Lake, SK	Ike Rainey	Ike Rainey	1993	1846
173 6/8	25 5/8	26	21	5 6/8	5 6/8	5	5	Menominee Co., WI	Picked Up	Ray T. Charles	1994	1846
173 6/8	28 3/8	27 7/8	20 7/8	5 1/8	4 7/8	6	6	Louisa Co., IA	Todd J. Parsons	Todd J. Parsons	1994	1846
173 6/8	30 6/8	31 2/8	19 6/8	5 2/8	5 3/8	7	7	Union Co., KY	Robert C. Caudill	Robert C. Caudill	1995	1846

Score	R. Beam	L. Beam	Spread	R. Circ.	L. Circ.	R. Pts	L. Pts	Locality	Hunter	Owner	Date	Rank
173 6/8	25 2/8	24 2/8	19 4/8	5 2/8	5 4/8	6	6	Owen Co., IN	Troy C. Denney	Troy C. Denney	1995	1846
173 6/8	24 2/8	25 3/8	19 5/8	4 4/8	4 4/8	8	8	Webb Co., TX	Hunter McGrath	Hunter McGrath	1995	1846
173 6/8	28 2/8	27 7/8	20 6/8	5	5	4	4	Atchison Co., MO	Robert B. Tussing	Robert B. Tussing	1995	1846
173 6/8	25	24 5/8	24 4/8	5 2/8	5 1/8	5	5	Clinton Co., IA	Patrick J. Hall	Patrick J. Hall	1996	1846
173 6/8	28 4/8	28	25	5 2/8	5 1/8	6	6	Green Lake Co., WI	Steven J. Coda	Steven J. Coda	1997	1846
173 6/8	27 2/8	28	19 2/8	4 4/8	4 4/8	5	5	Reno Co., KS	James E. Dye	James E. Dye	1997	1846
173 6/8	24 4/8	25	17 4/8	4 3/8	4 1/8	5	5	Allen Co., KS	Dewey L. Lewis	Dewey L. Lewis	1997	1846
173 6/8	27 1/8	27	24 4/8	5	5	6	6	McHenry Co., IL	Richard E. Pope	Richard E. Pope	1997	1846
173 6/8	27 4/8	26 4/8	21 2/8	5 1/8	5 2/8	6	5	Brown Co., IL	Michael P. Postema	Michael P. Postema	1997	1846
173 6/8	26 5/8	26 5/8	20 7/8	5	5	7	7	Allamakee Co., IA	Joseph Lieb	Joseph Lieb	1998	1846
173 6/8	26 1/8	26 5/8	21 3/8	5 6/8	5 6/8	7	6	Cherokee Co., IA	Robert L. Lundquist	Robert L. Lundquist	1998	1846
173 6/8	24	24 3/8	21	5 2/8	5 3/8	5	5	Good Spirit Lake, SK	Blair Sawka	Blair Sawka	1998	1846
173 6/8	24 1/8	26 6/8	25 3/8	5 5/8	5 5/8	7	7	Ribstone Creek, AB	Morgan J. Williams	Morgan J. Williams	2000	1846
173 6/8	26	25 4/8	20	5	5	9	9	Montgomery Co., IN	Andrew A. Horning	Andrew A. Horning	2001	1846
173 6/8	25 6/8	25 6/8	21 4/8	5 2/8	5 2/8	5	5	Comanche Co., KS	Kenneth W. Williams	Kenneth W. Williams	2001	1846
173 6/8	25	26	18 4/8	3 7/8	3 7/8	5	5	Stokes Co., NC	Buddie Adkins	Buddie Adkins	2002	1846
173 6/8	27 5/8	26 7/8	21 4/8	5 2/8	5 2/8	5	5	Adams Co., OH	Stacey E. Blevins	Stacey E. Blevins	2002	1846
173 6/8	26 5/8	26 3/8	20 1/8	5 6/8	5 4/8	8	8	Sedgwick Co., KS	Mary A. Fuller	Mary A. Fuller	2002	1846
173 6/8	30 1/8	29 5/8	20 5/8	5 3/8	5 4/8	6	6	Erie Co., OH	James W. Zimmerman	James W. Zimmerman	2002	1846
173 5/8	26 6/8	26 6/8	17 5/8	4 4/8	4 4/8	5	5	Sawyer Co., WI	Maurice Peterson	Mac's Taxidermy	1940	1902
173 5/8	26 2/8	26 4/8	22 5/8	5 2/8	5 2/8	6	5	Alberta	Frank Lind	Frank Lind	1952	1902
173 5/8	27 4/8	27	19 7/8	4 2/8	4 2/8	6	6	Winona Co., MN	John W. Brand	John W. Brand	1969	1902
173 5/8	25 4/8	25 4/8	18 3/8	5	5	6	6	Gentry Co., MO	William F. Oberbeck	William F. Oberbeck	1969	1902
173 5/8	26 6/8	26 6/8	19 1/8	4 6/8	4 6/8	6	6	Webb, SK	Roger R. Zimmer	Roger R. Zimmer	PR 1976	1902
173 5/8	22 6/8	21 7/8	20 5/8	4 7/8	4 7/8	6	6	Valley Co., MT	Scott Fossum	Scott Fossum	1978	1902
173 5/8	25	25 6/8	22 5/8	4 4/8	4 4/8	6	6	Lowndes Co., MS	Geraline Holliman	Geraline Holliman	1982	1902
173 5/8	27 5/8	28 1/8	22 6/8	5 3/8	5 3/8	7	4	Woods Co., OK	Jack Clover	Jack Clover	1983	1902
173 5/8	28 3/8	28 5/8	20 7/8	5 2/8	5 4/8	6	6	Flathead Co., MT	Mike J. Beaty	Mike J. Beaty	1984	1902
173 5/8	24	22 2/8	19 1/8	5	5	5	5	Morris Co., KS	Wayne Kasten	Wayne Kasten	1985	1902
173 5/8	25 3/8	26	18 5/8	4 7/8	4 7/8	6	6	Plymouth Co., IA	Pat Kenaley	Pat Kenaley	1986	1902
173 5/8	28	26 4/8	20 3/8	4 4/8	4 4/8	5	5	Fillmore Co., MN	Kelly J. McQuay	Kelly J. McQuay	1986	1902
173 5/8	25 5/8	27 2/8	18 1/8	4 5/8	4 6/8	6	6	Roseau Co., MN	David A. Harmon	David A. Harmon	1987	1902
173 5/8	27 3/8	27 7/8	18 7/8	5 5/8	6 4/8	7	7	Pike Co., IL	Jimmy Howard	Jimmy Howard	1989	1902
173 5/8	25 1/8	25 1/8	19 7/8	4 5/8	4 6/8	8	8	Duck Creek, SK	Barry Marquette	Barry Marquette	1991	1902
173 5/8	27 4/8	26 5/8	18 6/8	4 6/8	4 6/8	8	8	Bottineau Co., ND	Alvin A. Hall	Alvin A. Hall	1993	1902
173 5/8	28 7/8	28 1/8	23 3/8	4 1/8	4 2/8	6	5	Unknown	Unknown	Rick Stover	PR 1993	1902
173 5/8	27 5/8	26 6/8	25 1/8	4 4/8	4 6/8	8	8	Will Co., IL	Jeremy L. Johnson	Jeremy L. Johnson	1994	1902
173 5/8	23 1/8	22 3/8	22 3/8	5 1/8	5 1/8	6	6	Renville Co., ND	Shawna R. Atwood	Shawna R. Atwood	1995	1902
173 5/8	24 2/8	23 5/8	17 6/8	5 3/8	5 1/8	9	8	Otter Tail Co., MN	Terry D. Krumwiede	Terry D. Krumwiede	1995	1902
173 5/8	30 1/8	30	25 3/8	5	5 2/8	8	8	Jackson Co., MO	Michael J. Sytkowski	Michael J. Sytkowski	1995	1902
173 5/8	25 3/8	25 1/8	19 4/8	4 7/8	4 7/8	8	7	Buffalo Co., WI	James R. Gabrick	James R. Gabrick	1996	1902
173 5/8	25 3/8	25 1/8	19 1/8	4 7/8	5	7	6	Atwater, SK	Gary Griffith	Gary Griffith	1996	1902
173 5/8	26 6/8	26 2/8	17 4/8	4 6/8	4 6/8	7	7	Morgan Co., OH	Daniel Clemens	Daniel Clemens	1997	1902
173 5/8	26 1/8	26	20 1/8	4 5/8	5 1/8	6	7	La Salle Co., TX	Jeff S. Golbow	Jeff S. Golbow	1997	1902
173 5/8	26 4/8	26 4/8	20	4 6/8	4 5/8	8	8	Kankakee Co., IL	Tim Lynch	Tim Lynch	1999	1902
173 5/8	27 4/8	25 7/8	19 2/8	5 7/8	5	6	6	Adams Co., IL	Mike L. Melton	Mike L. Melton	2000	1902
173 5/8	25 5/8	25 5/8	19 7/8	4 3/8	4 2/8	5	5	Jo Daviess Co., IL	William B. Bland	William B. Bland	2001	1902
173 5/8	26 2/8	26 7/8	21 5/8	5	5	6	5	Hubbard Co., MN	Justin Sandmeyer	Justin Sandmeyer	2001	1902

WHITETAIL DEER - TYPICAL ANTLERS
Odocoileus virginianus virginianus and certain related subspecies

Score	Length of Main Beam R	L	Inside Spread	Circumference at Smallest Place Between Burr and First Point R	L	Number of Points R	L	Locality	Hunter	Owner	Date Killed	Rank
173 4/8	26 6/8	27 1/8	16	4 7/8	4 7/8	5	5	Zavala Co., TX	Roger Morris	Alvin Morris	1931	1931
173 4/8	28	27 6/8	18 2/8	5	5	5	5	Winona Co., MN	Raymond A. Manion	Raymond A. Manion	1950	1931
173 4/8	26 4/8	27	20 6/8	4 4/8	4 6/8	7	8	Augusta Co., VA	David H. Wolfe	David H. Wolfe	1957	1931
173 4/8	28 3/8	29 7/8	18	4 4/8	4 3/8	5	6	Livingston Co., MI	Paul M. Peckens	Paul M. Peckens	1959	1931
173 4/8	28 4/8	28 3/8	20 5/8	5	5	7	5	St. Louis Co., MN	Clarence Lindstrom	Donald A. Fondrick	1960	1931
173 4/8	23 6/8	23 7/8	18 6/8	4 6/8	4 6/8	6	6	Shelby Co., TN	John J. Heirigs	John J. Heirigs	1962	1931
173 4/8	24 7/8	23 6/8	17	5 6/8	5 7/8	7	6	Clover Leaf, MB	Walter Lucko	Walter Lucko	1962	1931
173 4/8	24 3/8	25	20 1/8	5 2/8	5 3/8	5	6	Tuffnell, SK	Ed Mattson	Ed Mattson	1964	1931
173 4/8	30 5/8	29 6/8	20 7/8	5 2/8	5 3/8	7	5	Todd Co., KY	Troy L. Harris	Troy L. Harris	1965	1931
173 4/8	28	27 4/8	21 6/8	4 7/8	5 1/8	5	5	Union Co., IA	Danny E. Abbott	Danny E. Abbott	1966	1931
173 4/8	26	26	21	5 3/8	5 1/8	5	5	Vilas Co., WI	Unknown	Donald Krueger	1967	1931
173 4/8	28 4/8	27 1/8	22 1/8	5 6/8	5 2/8	5	5	Ellsworth Co., KS	Monte Hudson	Monte Hudson	1986	1931
173 4/8	24 3/8	24 2/8	20 2/8	4 7/8	4 7/8	7	7	Tamaulipas, MX	John F. Sontag, Jr.	John F. Sontag, Jr.	1987	1931
173 4/8	25 7/8	27	23	5	5 1/8	5	5	McHenry Co., IL	Gordon R. Sunderlage	Gordon R. Sunderlage	1987	1931
173 4/8	25 5/8	25 3/8	18	5	5	6	6	Barber Co., KS	James R. Schreiner	James R. Schreiner	1990	1931
173 4/8	24 7/8	25 6/8	22 4/8	4 7/8	4 7/8	5	5	Maverick Co., TX	Clifton F. Douglass III	Clifton F. Douglass III	1991	1931
173 4/8	24 5/8	25 5/8	21 4/8	4 6/8	4 6/8	7	9	Rogers Co., OK	Marc Thompson	Marc Thompson	1991	1931
173 4/8	24 7/8	24 7/8	18	5 1/8	5 2/8	5	5	Allen Co., IN	Douglas R. Hill	Douglas R. Hill	1993	1931
173 4/8	25 3/8	25 2/8	20	4 1/8	4 5/8	5	5	Seneca Co., OH	Peter Lammers	Peter Lammers	1993	1931
173 4/8	25 6/8	25	19 2/8	4 4/8	4 3/8	7	6	Coahuila, MX	Fernando G. Fuentes	Fernando G. Fuentes	1994	1931
173 4/8	27 2/8	28	18 6/8	4 2/8	4 3/8	5	5	Flathead Co., MT	Ed M. Peter, Jr.	Ed M. Peter, Jr.	1994	1931
173 4/8	25 1/8	25 2/8	19 2/8	4 5/8	4 5/8	6	6	Porcupine Plain, SK	Picked Up	Terry L. Amos	PR 1997	1931
173 4/8	25 7/8	25 6/8	18 4/8	4 1/8	4 4/8	5	5	La Salle Co., TX	James K. Haney	James K. Haney	1997	1931
173 4/8	26	26 1/8	17 1/8	4 3/8	4 3/8	5	5	Rusk Co., WI	Jody Lebal	Jody Lebal	1998	1931
173 4/8	24 6/8	25	15 2/8	6	6	5	6	Sweet Grass, SK	Steven Riley	Steven Riley	1998	1931
173 4/8	27 6/8	27 6/8	22	4 6/8	4 5/8	6	7	Logan Co., KY	Jesse Wolf	Jesse Wolf	1998	1931
173 4/8	27 4/8	29 3/8	22	4 5/8	4 4/8	5	5	Appanoose Co., IA	Randy Andreini	Randy Andreini	1999	1931
173 4/8	25 2/8	25 5/8	17 7/8	5	5	7	7	St. Louis Co., MN	Gerald R. Fausone	Gerald R. Fausone	1999	1931
173 4/8	30	28 4/8	23 2/8	4 7/8	4 7/8	6	5	Monroe Co., IA	Glen A. McElroy	Glen A. McElroy	1999	1931
173 4/8	28 1/8	27 4/8	21	4 2/8	4 1/8	5	6	Chisago Co., MN	Robert C. Palmer	Robert C. Palmer	1999	1931
173 4/8	26 6/8	25 6/8	22	6 1/8	6 2/8	5	5	Decatur Co., IA	Picked Up	Bill J. Timms	1999	1931
173 4/8	25 1/8	24 3/8	18 6/8	5 3/8	5 4/8	5	5	Adams Co., IL	Wayne A Brinkley	Wayne A Brinkley	2000	1931
173 4/8	26 4/8	27 3/8	18 4/8	5 5/8	5 5/8	7	6	Meadow Lake, SK	David A. Holmes	David A. Holmes	2000	1931
173 4/8	26 2/8	26 3/8	20 5/8	4 7/8	4 5/8	5	6	Torch River, SK	Picked Up	Kurt Rempel	2000	1931
173 4/8	25 4/8	25 4/8	19 4/8	4 7/8	4 6/8	5	5	Trempealeau Co., WI	Ross P. Lambert	Ross P. Lambert	2001	1931
173 4/8	26	26 5/8	20 6/8	4 4/8	4 2/8	7	6	Greene Co., IL	Ryan M. Swearingin	Ryan M. Swearingin	2001	1931

Score	L. R	L. L	Spread	Circ. R	Circ. L	Pts. R	Pts. L	Locality	Hunter	Owner	Killed	Ranked
173 3/8	28 5/8	29 3/8	23 2/8	6 3/8	6 2/8	7	8	Ontario Co., NY	Martin Solway	NY Dept. of Env. Cons.	1946	1967
173 3/8	27 6/8	28 1/8	20 1/8	4 5/8	4 5/8	5	6	Clarion Co., PA	Mead R. Kiefer	Mead R. Kiefer	1947	1967
173 3/8	26 3/8	26 3/8	19 1/8	5 3/8	5 3/8	7	7	Arkansas Co., AR	Jimmy Hanson	Jimmy Hanson	1948	1967
173 3/8	25 6/8	25 7/8	17 5/8	4 4/8	4 4/8	5	5	Clarion Co., PA	Picked Up	Fred Gallagher	1954	1967
173 3/8	25 6/8	26 2/8	19 2/8	4 7/8	5	8	7	St. Louis Co., MN	Picked Up	William E. Clink	1960	1967
173 3/8	26 4/8	26 6/8	20 1/8	5	4 7/8	6	5	St. George, NB	Gilbert L. Leavitt	Gilbert L. Leavitt	1962	1967
173 3/8	27	27 2/8	21 4/8	5 2/8	5 4/8	5	5	Lewis Co., KY	Darrell Tully	Darrell Tully	1968	1967
173 3/8	23 3/8	23 3/8	23 3/8	5 1/8	5 1/8	5	5	Rosebud Co., MT	Ted Millhollin	Ted Millhollin	1975	1967
173 3/8	24 4/8	25	16 7/8	5 1/8	5 1/8	5	5	Valley Co., MT	Steve K. Sukut	Steve K. Sukut	1978	1967
173 3/8	26 1/8	27 4/8	18 6/8	5	5	5	5	Keya Paha Co., NE	Gene F. Pool	Gene F. Pool	1980	1967
173 3/8	27 4/8	27 4/8	17 1/8	4 5/8	4 6/8	7	5	Clay Co., KS	Charles A. Hammons	Charles A. Hammons	1984	1967
173 3/8	28 7/8	28 1/8	19 1/8	4 7/8	5 2/8	5	5	Monona Co., IA	Steve D. Maher	Steve D. Maher	1986	1967
173 3/8	27 3/8	27 3/8	19 3/8	4 6/8	4 6/8	6	6	Pend Oreille Co., WA	Thomas R. Lentz	Thomas R. Lentz	1987	1967
173 3/8	26 6/8	26 6/8	24 2/8	4 4/8	4 5/8	5	5	Bullitt Co., KY	Leon R. Allen	Leon R. Allen	1988	1967
173 3/8	26 5/8	26 1/8	18 7/8	4 6/8	4 5/8	7	9	Montgomery Co., IL	Douglas C. Furtwengler	Douglas C. Furtwengler	1988	1967
173 3/8	26 3/8	26 6/8	25 7/8	4 5/8	4 5/8	6	5	Riley Co., KS	Russell B. Santo	Russell B. Santo	1989	1967
173 3/8	23 3/8	26 7/8	18 6/8	5 3/8	5 4/8	7	5	Coles Co., IL	Thomas D. Simmering	Thomas D. Simmering	1989	1967
173 3/8	26	26	18 1/8	4 1/8	4 3/8	6	5	Chautauqua Co., KS	Wesley D. Coldren	Wesley D. Coldren	1992	1967
173 3/8	24 6/8	25 1/8	21 1/8	4 6/8	4 7/8	5	5	Pembina River, AB	Adrian Marr	Adrian Marr	1993	1967
173 3/8	26 3/8	25	17 5/8	5 1/8	5	7	6	Coahoma Co., MS	Richard D. Powell	Richard D. Powell	1994	1967
173 3/8	25	25	16 5/8	5 6/8	5 1/8	6	6	Bent Co., CO	Rick J. Tokarski	Rick J. Tokarski	1994	1967
173 3/8	27 2/8	27	28 7/8	5	5 6/8	5	6	Kane Co., IL	James Meyer	James Meyer	1995	1967
173 3/8	27 5/8	27 2/8	20 7/8	5 5/8	5 3/8	8	6	Fayette Co., WV	Richard L. Schoolcraft	Richard L. Schoolcraft	1995	1967
173 3/8	30 4/8	30 6/8	21 4/8	4 7/8	4 6/8	6	6	Miami Co., OH	Mike Newman	Mike Newman	1996	1967
173 3/8	26 6/8	26 5/8	17 5/8	5 4/8	5 3/8	5	5	Grant Parish, LA	Michael G. Hicks	Michael G. Hicks	1997	1967
173 3/8	26 1/8	26 4/8	23	5 1/8	5 2/8	5	8	Linn Co., KS	Vernon L. Morrell, Jr.	Vernon L. Morrell, Jr.	1997	1967
173 3/8	26 1/8	26 3/8	20 1/8	5 6/8	5 6/8	5	5	Prowers Co., CO	Les F. Ohlhauser	Les F. Ohlhauser	1997	1967
173 3/8	25 7/8	27 2/8	21 5/8	5	4 7/8	5	5	Jones Co., IA	Todd J. Rollinger	Todd J. Rollinger	1997	1967
173 3/8	27 4/8	26 4/8	20 3/8	5	5 1/8	7	6	Noble Co., OH	David W. Heeter	David W. Heeter	1998	1967
173 3/8	26 3/8	26 7/8	19 7/8	5 1/8	6 2/8	6	6	Gage Co., NE	Harold G. McPheron	Harold G. McPheron	1998	1967
173 3/8	26 4/8	26 4/8	20 7/8	6 2/8	5 7/8	5	5	Clay Co., IN	Rex A. Treadway	Rex A. Treadway	2001	1967
173 3/8	25 7/8	25 7/8	18 3/8	5 6/8	4 1/8	6	6	Schuyler Co., IL	Ken J. Shaw	Ken J. Shaw	2002	1967
173 2/8	30 3/8	29 6/8	19	5 2/8	5 7/8	6	8	Texas	Unknown	Marvin Schwarz	PR 1940	1999
173 2/8	25 6/8	24 2/8	21 1/8	5	5 1/8	8	6	Chicot Co., AR	Yan Sturdivant	Bruce Sturdivant	1951	1999
173 2/8	24 3/8	25 3/8	25 2/8	5 4/8	4 6/8	7	6	Price Co., WI	Clarence Parmelee	J.D. Andrews	1959	1999
173 2/8	25 2/8	24 4/8	20 6/8	4 5/8	5 3/8	5	5	Bemersyde, SK	R.L. McCullough	R.L. McCullough	1959	1999
173 2/8	26 6/8	26 6/8	21 2/8	5 4/8	4	8	6	Unknown	Unknown	Neal T. Rietveld	PR 1960	1999
173 2/8	25 5/8	25 6/8	20	4	4	6	5	Lincoln Co., AR	Billy McGriff	Billy McGriff	1962	1999
173 2/8	26 7/8	24 3/8	21	5 2/8	5 6/8	8	5	Whitewood, SK	L. Reichel	L. Reichel	1964	1999
173 2/8	29	29 4/8	20 6/8	5 1/8	5	5	5	Antler, SK	Elmer Lowry	Elmer Lowry	1966	1999
173 2/8	27 3/8	25 3/8	20	4 1/8	5 2/8	6	6	Furnas Co., NE	Marvin F Wieland	Marvin F. Wieland	1969	1999
173 2/8	25 3/8	28 4/8	18 4/8	4 3/8	4 1/8	6	6	Decatur Co., TN	Glen D. Odle	Glen D. Odle	1972	1999
173 2/8	28	28 4/8	21 6/8	4 4/8	4 4/8	5	8	Lyman Co., SD	William G. Psychos	William G. Psychos	1972	1999
173 2/8	26 7/8	26	20 5/8	5 2/8	5 2/8	9	6	Allen Co., KY	Terry W. Sims	Terry W. Sims	1979	1999
173 2/8	24 7/8	24 3/8	23 5/8	4 4/8	4 4/8	6	6	Warren Co., MO	Jerome E. Ley	Jerome E. Ley	1980	1999
173 2/8	25 5/8	25 3/8	17 6/8	4 3/8	4 2/8	6	6	Kent Co., DE	William R. Conner	William R. Conner	1984	1999
173 2/8	24 4/8	22 5/8	19	4 6/8	4 6/8	5	5	Battle River, AB	Steven M. Cooper	Steven M. Cooper	1984	1999
173 2/8			19 4/8	5	5 5/8	6	8	Eagle Creek, SK	Perry Haanen	Perry Haanen	1984	1999

WHITETAIL DEER - TYPICAL ANTLERS
Odocoileus virginianus virginianus and certain related subspecies

Score	Length of Main Beam R	L	Inside Spread	Circumference at Smallest Place Between Burr and First Point R	L	Number of Points R	L	Locality	Hunter	Owner	Date Killed	Rank
173 2/8	26 4/8	26 5/8	19	4 1/8	4	5	5	Chisago Co., MN	Roger A. Peterson	Roger A. Peterson	1984	1999
173 2/8	25 3/8	25 4/8	21 2/8	5 3/8	5 2/8	6	8	Webb Co., TX	Frank J. Sitterle	Frank J. Sitterle	1987	1999
173 2/8	30 1/8	27 5/8	20 6/8	5	5	6	6	Calhoun Co., IL	Picked Up	Dean Diaz	1990	1999
173 2/8	26 3/8	26 6/8	17 4/8	5 2/8	5 2/8	5	5	Woodbury Co., IA	Jim C. Jepsen	Jim C. Jepsen	1990	1999
173 2/8	26	24 6/8	19	4 2/8	4 2/8	5	5	Chicot Co., AR	James W. Brown	James W. Brown	1991	1999
173 2/8	27 2/8	25 5/8	22	4 6/8	4 5/8	5	5	La Salle Co., TX	Wayne W. Webb	Wayne W. Webb	1992	1999
173 2/8	25 7/8	25 6/8	20 3/8	5 2/8	5 4/8	8	9	Cass Co., MN	Picked Up	Robert Johnson	1993	1999
173 2/8	22 2/8	21 5/8	17 2/8	5	5	5	5	Loon Lake, SK	J. Ronnie Ray	J. Ronnie Ray	1993	1999
173 2/8	27 1/8	28 1/8	19 3/8	5 2/8	5 1/8	6	4	Sangamon Co., IL	Brian Daily	Brian Daily	1995	1999
173 2/8	25 7/8	25 5/8	18	4 5/8	4 6/8	5	5	Delaware Co., OH	John W. Hill, Jr.	John W. Hill, Jr.	1996	1999
173 2/8	26 6/8	26 5/8	18 2/8	4 7/8	5	5	6	Jackson Co., IA	Pat J. Schilling	Pat J. Schilling	1996	1999
173 2/8	24 2/8	25	19	5	5 2/8	5	5	Butler Co., MO	Marcus O. Milligan	Marcus O. Milligan	1997	1999
173 2/8	26 5/8	26 5/8	24 6/8	4 1/8	4 3/8	5	5	Pickaway Co., OH	Timothy S. Ritchie	Timothy S. Ritchie	1997	1999
173 2/8	21 3/8	22 4/8	15	5 1/8	5 2/8	6	5	Pope Co., IL	James W. Sanderson	James W. Sanderson	1998	1999
173 2/8	25 2/8	24 3/8	23 2/8	5	5	5	5	Marion Co., IA	Joseph C. Laird	Joseph C. Laird	1998	1999
173 2/8	24 1/8	24 1/8	17 2/8	4 4/8	4 4/8	6	6	Chautauqua Co., NY	Brian Whalen	Brian Whalen	1998	1999
173 2/8	28 3/8	27 3/8	21 2/8	5 3/8	5 2/8	5	5	Pike Co., OH	Kathleen E. Kellough	Kathleen E. Kellough	1999	1999
173 2/8	26 2/8	26 6/8	22	5	5	7	7	Preble Co., OH	Gary H. Vest	Gary H. Vest	1999	1999
173 2/8	24 3/8	24 4/8	24 4/8	5 2/8	5 2/8	6	8	Henderson Co., IL	David L. Alberts	David L. Alberts	2000	1999
173 2/8	26 2/8	26 2/8	19 3/8	4 5/8	4 5/8	7	6	Hyde Co., SD	Dillon K. Baloun	Dillon K. Baloun	2001	1999
173 2/8	26 3/8	25 1/8	20 1/8	5	5 1/8	6	6	Harrison Co., IA	Troy Rath	Troy Rath	2001	1999
173 2/8	24 5/8	25	18 2/8	4 7/8	4 6/8	6	6	Beaver Co., PA	Robert E. Davenport	Robert E. Davenport	2002	1999
173 2/8	27 1/8	26 7/8	21 6/8	5 3/8	5	4	4	Adams Co., OH	Doug N. Ruehl	Doug N. Ruehl	2002	1999
173 1/8	27 4/8	26 3/8	21 7/8	5 5/8	5 3/8	5	5	St. Louis Co., MN	Unknown	George W. Flaim	1934	2038
173 1/8	23 6/8	24 1/8	20 3/8	5	5	6	7	Marie, SK	King Trew	King Trew	1957	2038
173 1/8	25 5/8	24 7/8	19 2/8	5	4	7	5	Estuary, SK	Melvin J. Anderson	Melvin J. Anderson	1962	2038
173 1/8	23 3/8	23 6/8	18 3/8	4	4	6	6	Slope Co., ND	Robert L. Stroup	Robert L. Stroup	1967	2038
173 1/8	28 5/8	28 6/8	22 2/8	5 4/8	5 7/8	6	6	Wabaunsee Co., KS	James D. Downey	James D. Downey	1970	2038
173 1/8	26 1/8	24 6/8	21 1/8	4 7/8	4 6/8	5	5	Lake Co., MT	Darrell Brist	Darrell Brist	1971	2038
173 1/8	25 6/8	25 6/8	17 6/8	5 2/8	5 3/8	7	7	Union Co., AR	James O. Cox	Arkansas County Seed	1973	2038
173 1/8	29 3/8	28 7/8	25 1/8	5 2/8	5 1/8	4	4	Fillmore Co., MN	Gerry D. Arnold	Gerry D. Arnold	1973	2038
173 1/8	26	26 6/8	18 5/8	4 1/8	3 7/8	6	6	White Co., TN	Sam H. Langford	Sam H. Langford	1980	2038
173 1/8	26 5/8	27 6/8	19 5/8	4 4/8	4 5/8	7	6	Shelby Co., MO	William A. Light, Jr.	William A. Light, Jr.	1981	2038
173 1/8	24 4/8	25 3/8	16 3/8	4 3/8	4 3/8	5	5	Big Muddy Valley, SK	Lyndon T. Ross	Lyndon T. Ross	1984	2038
173 1/8	26 2/8	26 6/8	20 5/8	4 2/8	4 3/8	5	5	Adams Co., OH	Mark N. Barnes	Mark N. Barnes	1986	2038
173 1/8	28	28 2/8	21 5/8	4 6/8	4 6/8	7	7	Dunn Co., WI	Jack K. Dodge	Jack K. Dodge	1987	2038

Score	Main Beam R	Main Beam L	Inside Spread	Circ. R	Circ. L	Points R	Points L	Locality	By Whom Killed	Owner	Date Killed	Rank
173 1/8	27 4/8	27 1/8	20 2/8	4 6/8	4 5/8	4	5	Ralls Co., MO	Picked Up	Les James	1988	2038
173 1/8	27 7/8	27 3/8	20 3/8	4 4/8	4 2/8	5	5	Allegan Co., MI	Charles O. Hooper	Charles O. Hooper	1990	2038
173 1/8	26 4/8	26 2/8	20 1/8	4 6/8	4 4/8	5	5	Pottawatomie Co., KS	Donald L. Smith	Donald L. Smith	1990	2038
173 1/8	25 1/8	26	18 1/8	4 5/8	4 6/8	8	5	Latah Co., ID	John D. Kauffman	John D. Kauffman	1991	2038
173 1/8	25 5/8	26 2/8	19 1/8	4 6/8	4 7/8	6	6	Mahaska Co., IA	Ted Smith	Ted Smith	1991	2038
173 1/8	27 3/8	26 2/8	21 4/8	4 4/8	4 6/8	7	5	Buffalo Co., WI	Dale M. Komro	Dale M. Komro	1992	2038
173 1/8	26	25 6/8	17	4 5/8	4 6/8	6	7	Lincoln Co., MO	Daniel A. Narup	Daniel A. Narup	1992	2038
173 1/8	24 4/8	25 6/8	20 3/8	4 7/8	4 7/8	5	5	Crawford Co., OH	Roger C. Rothhaar	Roger C. Rothhaar	1992	2038
173 1/8	24 7/8	24 6/8	16 2/8	5 1/8	5 1/8	6	5	Dodge Co., GA	Paul W. Smith	Paul W. Smith	1993	2038
173 1/8	24 6/8	26 2/8	21 5/8	4 4/8	4 4/8	5	7	Jackson Co., IN	Sean C. Ashley	Sean C. Ashley	1994	2038
173 1/8	25	24 6/8	17 7/8	5	4 7/8	5	5	Greene Co., IN	J.D. Holtsclaw & K.J. Hobson	J.D. Holtsclaw & K.J. Hobson	1994	2038
173 1/8	26 6/8	26 7/8	19 6/8	5 3/8	5 3/8	6	6	Gibbons, AB	Thomas Kampjes	Thomas Kampjes	1994	2038
173 1/8	30	30 5/8	23	5 1/8	5 2/8	7	7	Brown Co., OH	Michael P. Nunnelley	Michael P. Nunnelley	1995	2038
173 1/8	25 5/8	25	21 1/8	4 2/8	4 2/8	6	7	Kansas	Unknown	James B. Sisco III	PR 1995	2038
173 1/8	24	24 4/8	21 1/8	5	5 2/8	5	5	Winneshiek Co., IA	Kenny J White	Kenny J. White	1995	2038
173 1/8	26 2/8	25 6/8	18	4 4/8	4 3/8	7	6	White Co., AR	Ricky S. Cantrell	Ricky S. Cantrell	1996	2038
173 1/8	26 2/8	26 2/8	19 5/8	5 4/8	5 3/8	5	5	Macon Co., IL	Stuart A. Wolken	Stuart A. Wolken	1996	2038
173 1/8	27 3/8	27	22 1/8	5	4 7/8	6	5	Williamson Co., IL	Jay Johns	Jay Johns	1997	2038
173 1/8	25	24 2/8	23 3/8	4 3/8	4 3/8	5	5	Buffalo Co., WI	Thomas J. Johnson	Thomas J. Johnson	1997	2038
173 1/8	26 4/8	26 7/8	19 7/8	5 3/8	5 5/8	5	5	Unknown	Unknown	Terry L. Amos	1998	2038
173 1/8	27 6/8	22 4/8	16 1/8	4 6/8	4 5/8	9	7	Custer Co., NE	Mitch W. Hickey	Mitch W. Hickey	1999	2038
173 1/8	26 7/8	24 1/8	13 7/8	4 4/8	4 6/8	6	6	Torch River, SK	Debbie Karle	Debbie Karle	1999	2038
173 1/8	26 5/8	26 6/8	18 1/8	5 1/8	5 1/8	5	5	Jackson Co., WI	David R. Stalheim	David R. Stalheim	1999	2038
173 1/8	28	25 3/8	19 1/8	4 7/8	5	5	5	Clermont Co., OH	Alton L. Cornett	Alton L. Cornett	2000	2038
173 1/8	29 1/8	26	17 7/8	4 5/8	4 5/8	5	5	Saline Co., MO	Jesse H. Little	Jesse H. Little	2000	2038
173 1/8	25 7/8	28 2/8	20	6	6	6	5	Coles Co., IL	Ron Osborne	Ron Osborne	2000	2038
173 1/8	28 7/8	26 3/8	20 3/8	4 5/8	4 6/8	5	5	Clayton Co., IA	Alan E. Troester	Alan E. Troester	2000	2038
173	25 5/8	25 6/8	20	5 4/8	5 2/8	5	5	Becker Co., MN	Cliff C. Wessels	Cliff C. Wessels	2001	2080
173	28 2/8	28 5/8	23	4 6/8	4 6/8	5	5	Porter Co., IN	Joseph J. Marlow	Joseph J. Marlow	PR 1930	2080
173	28 3/8	28 5/8	21	4 7/8	5 1/8	8	6	Bayfield Co., WI	Unknown	Eagle Knob Lodge	PR 1960	2080
173	26	28 5/8	22	4 6/8	4 7/8	8	8	Pope Co., MN	Unknown	Tom Hammer	1963	2080
173	24 4/8	28 4/8	17 2/8	4 5/8	4 5/8	7	8	Mellette Co., SD	Calvin R. Joy	Calvin R. Joy	1967	2080
173	27	25 5/8	25 3/8	5 6/8	5 7/8	5	6	Pawnee Co., NE	Gary G. Habegger	Gary G. Habegger	1969	2080
173	23 2/8	28 2/8	21 2/8	5 5/8	5 6/8	6	6	Oconto Co., WI	Donald P. Wimmer	Donald P. Wimmer	PR 1974	2080
173	24 7/8	27	21	4 6/8	4 6/8	7	7	Koochiching Co., MN	Unknown	Marc M. Jackson	1975	2080
173	28	27 4/8	20 4/8	4 5/8	4 6/8	6	6	Sandusky Co., OH	Harold M. Chalfin	Harold M. Chalfin	1978	2080
173	28	28 7/8	21 7/8	5 3/8	5 3/8	5	5	Howard Co., MO	Thomas R. Banning	Thomas R. Banning	1978	2080
173	26 5/8	28 2/8	19 4/8	5 1/8	5 1/8	7	7	Owen Co., KY	Roger Breeden	Roger Breeden	1979	2080
173	28 4/8	25 3/8	25	4 2/8	4 2/8	6	6	Dimmit Co., TX	George Light IV	George Light IV	1979	2080
173	25 2/8	28 2/8	21 7/8	4 5/8	4 5/8	7	9	Hidalgo Co., TX	William L. Turk	William L. Turk	1980	2080
173	27 1/8	24 2/8	21 6/8	4 5/8	4 6/8	6	5	Cook Co., MN	Wesley A. Nelson	Wesley A. Nelson	1981	2080
173	26	27 2/8	21	4 6/8	4 6/8	6	6	Somerset Co., ME	Charles A. Moulton	Charles A. Moulton	1983	2080
173	24 4/8	26	16 7/8	4 5/8	3 6/8	6	6	Trinity Co., TX	Don Knight	Don Knight	1983	2080
173	27	25 5/8	23 5/8	5 7/8	6 1/8	6	7	Doniphan Co., KS	Charles A. Staudenmaier	Charles A. Staudenmaier	1983	2080
173	23 2/8	27 2/8	19 5/8	4 6/8	4 6/8	7	8	Bunder Lake, AB	Steve Swinhoe	Steve Swinhoe	1984	2080
173	24 7/8	25 5/8	16 4/8	5 2/8	5 2/8	8	5	Bonnyville, AB	Lionel P. Tercier	Lionel P. Tercier		2080
173	25 4/8	25 1/8	19 4/8	4 5/8	4 5/8	5	5	Sullivan Co., TN	C. Alan Altizer	C. Alan Altizer		2080

WHITETAIL DEER - TYPICAL ANTLERS
Odocoileus virginianus virginianus and certain related subspecies

Score	Length of Main Beam R	L	Inside Spread	Circumference at Smallest Place Between Burr and First Point R	L	Number of Points R	L	Locality	Hunter	Owner	Date Killed	Rank
173	27 3/8	27	21 3/8	4 5/8	4 3/8	5	7	Jim Hogg Co., TX	Eliverto Cantu	Eddie M. Garza	1985	2080
173	26 4/8	25 7/8	18 4/8	4 6/8	4 6/8	5	6	Becker Co., MN	Albert E. Jahnke	Albert E. Jahnke	1985	2080
173	28 1/8	29 4/8	24 4/8	4 6/8	4 6/8	5	6	Jefferson Co., OH	Adam Firm	Adam Firm	1987	2080
173	25 1/8	24 7/8	18 6/8	5 1/8	4 7/8	6	5	Fairfield Co., OH	James Carmichael	James Carmichael	1988	2080
173	27 1/8	27 1/8	21 3/8	5 1/8	5 1/8	5	7	Shawnee Co., KS	Frank R. Murray	Frank R. Murray	1989	2080
173	27	26	20 1/8	4 1/8	4 2/8	6	6	Big Horn Co., WY	Daniel D. Wood	Daniel D. Wood	1989	2080
173	25 4/8	26 2/8	21 6/8	4 7/8	4 6/8	6	5	Pepin Co., WI	William A. Gray	William A. Gray	1990	2080
173	24	25 2/8	18 6/8	4 6/8	4 5/8	5	6	Sheridan Co., WY	Robert G. Green	Robert G. Green	1991	2080
173	27 1/8	27	21 1/8	5 2/8	5 2/8	7	6	Monroe Co., IA	Richard A. Bishop	Richard A. Bishop	1992	2080
173	23 6/8	24	19	4 6/8	4 7/8	6	5	Westlock, AB	Billy W. Kothmann	Billy W. Kothmann	1992	2080
173	26 5/8	26 6/8	17	5 1/8	5 1/8	6	6	Davis Co., IA	James E. Pierceall	James E. Pierceall	1992	2080
173	27 5/8	28	19	4 3/8	4 1/8	7	6	Flathead Co., MT	Derek Schulz	Derek Schulz	1992	2080
173	28 6/8	29 3/8	21 6/8	5 4/8	5 6/8	4	4	Caroline Co., MD	Jay Downes, Jr.	Jay Downes, Jr.	1993	2080
173	26 2/8	26 6/8	17 6/8	5 2/8	5 1/8	6	6	Muhlenberg Co., KY	Larry Vincent	Larry Vincent	1993	2080
173	27	27 6/8	18 2/8	4 4/8	4 3/8	8	7	Johnson Co., NE	Kent Hippen	Kent Hippen	1994	2080
173	24	25 7/8	18 4/8	4 5/8	4 6/8	5	5	Crawford Co., IA	Picked Up	IA Dept. of Natl. Resc.	1994	2080
173	24 3/8	24 7/8	20	5 5/8	5 3/8	5	5	St. Croix Co., WI	James A. O'Keefe	James A. O'Keefe	1994	2080
173	25 7/8	25 3/8	16 7/8	5 4/8	5 4/8	6	8	Adair Co., OK	Louis C. Mattler	Louis C. Mattler	1995	2080
173	23 5/8	23 7/8	19 2/8	5	5 7/8	7	7	Whitewood Lake, SK	Geordie D. McKay	Geordie D. McKay	1995	2080
173	26 6/8	26 5/8	17 6/8	4 4/8	4 4/8	8	6	Macoupin Co., IL	Dickie A. Spurgeon	Dickie A. Spurgeon	1995	2080
173	25 4/8	27 1/8	19 4/8	5 2/8	5	9	8	Clay Co., MO	Neal B. Breshears	Neal B. Breshears	1996	2080
173	27	26	20 4/8	5 2/8	5 1/8	7	9	Harrison Co., IA	Dell C. Wohlers	Dell C. Wohlers	1996	2080
173	27 1/8	26 5/8	23 4/8	5	5 1/8	6	8	Christian Co., KY	Mark C. Morris	Mark C. Morris	1997	2080
173	25 6/8	25 2/8	19 6/8	4 7/8	4 7/8	6	6	Allamakee Co., IA	Thomas E. Peters	Thomas E. Peters	1997	2080
173	24 3/8	24 5/8	18	4 2/8	4 2/8	6	6	St. Marie Lake, QC	Philippe Gratton	Philippe Gratton	1998	2080
173	28 6/8	29 3/8	16 5/8	5 7/8	5 6/8	5	7	Itasca Co., MN	Robert W. Bourman	Robert W. Bourman	1999	2080
173	27 7/8	28 2/8	19 6/8	4 6/8	4 6/8	7	5	Preble Co., OH	Jeffery T. Haeseker	Jeffery T. Haeseker	1999	2080
173	26 3/8	25 1/8	19 3/8	4 4/8	4 6/8	8	6	Jo Daviess Co., IL	Jim Bielema	Jim Bielema	2000	2080
173	24 4/8	24 7/8	18 3/8	4 5/8	4 5/8	7	7	Douglas Co., WI	Raymond J. Dolsen	Raymond J. Dolsen	2000	2080
173	26	25 7/8	21 6/8	4 7/8	4 5/8	6	6	McHenry Co., IL	Chase M. Ziller	Chase M. Ziller	2001	2080
173	27 5/8	26 4/8	24 6/8	4 6/8	4 6/8	4	4	Botetourt Co., VA	James E. Broughman, Jr.	James E. Broughman, Jr.	2002	2080
173	27 7/8	27 3/8	19 6/8	4 6/8	4 4/8	5	7	Webb Co., TX	Betty C. Robison	Betty C. Robison	2002	2080
172 7/8	25 6/8	25 5/8	22 5/8	4 7/8	5	6	6	Windthorst, SK	Jack Glover	Jack Glover	1951	2130
172 7/8	25 3/8	25	20 2/8	4 3/8	4 2/8	7	7	McHenry Co., ND	David Medalen	David Medalen	1959	2130
172 7/8	24 6/8	24 3/8	20 1/8	5 4/8	5 3/8	5	5	Ashland Co., WI	Einar Sein	Rick Iacono	1965	2130
172 7/8	26 4/8	26 1/8	16 7/8	4 2/8	4 1/8	6	6	Olmsted Co., MN	Wesley W. Holtz	Wesley W. Holtz	1966	2130

Score	Main Beam R	Main Beam L	Inside Spread	Circ. R	Circ. L	Pts. R	Pts. L	Locality	By	Owner	Date	Rank
172 7/8	26 1/8	27	18	5 3/8	5 3/8	6	7	Newton Co., GA	L.W. Shirley, Jr.	L.W. Shirley, Jr.	1967	2130
172 7/8	27	26 2/8	21 7/8	4 7/8	5 5/8	6	5	Seneca Co., NY	Martin J. Way	Martin J. Way	1968	2130
172 7/8	25 4/8	26 5/8	19 7/8	5 4/8	4 5/8	5	6	Williamson Co., IL	Picked Up	John L. Roseberry	1975	2130
172 7/8	24 3/8	25 1/8	21 1/8	4 4/8	5 2/8	6	8	Cascade Co., MT	Skip Halmes	Skip Halmes	1976	2130
172 7/8	28 7/8	28 2/8	18 7/8	5 1/8	4 3/8	5	6	Granville Co., NC	James M. Wilkerson	James M. Wilkerson	1981	2130
172 7/8	22 3/8	23	20	4 3/8	4 4/8	5	8	Dallas Co., IA	Gordon Cochran	Gordon Cochran	1982	2130
172 7/8	26	27 3/8	22 5/8	4 4/8	4 6/8	6	10	Heard Co., GA	Keith McCullough	Keith McCullough	1982	2130
172 7/8	25 7/8	26 5/8	20 6/8	4 6/8	4	6	6	Pike Co., IL	Robert L. Hubbell	Robert L. Hubbell	1987	2130
172 7/8	26 6/8	27 3/8	19 6/8	4 2/8	5 3/8	5	6	Jefferson Co., IN	Chet A. Nolan	Chet A. Nolan	1987	2130
172 7/8	27 6/8	27 1/8	18 5/8	5 2/8	4 7/8	5	4	Vermilion Co., IL	Edwin B. Gudgel	Edwin B. Gudgel	1988	2130
172 7/8	29 3/8	28 4/8	24 7/8	4 7/8	4 6/8	5	6	Jackson Co., IA	Picked Up	Roy Rathje	1989	2130
172 7/8	25 1/8	23 3/8	16 5/8	4 5/8	5 1/8	5	5	McMullen Co., TX	Steve Best	Steve Best	1991	2130
172 7/8	29	27 5/8	20 5/8	5 1/8	4 2/8	5	7	Sullivan Co., NH	Gordon E. Adams	Gordon E. Adams	1992	2130
172 7/8	25 2/8	24 3/8	18	4 1/8	5 5/8	8	8	Kootenai Co., ID	Kevin L. Lundblad	Kevin L. Lundblad	1992	2130
172 7/8	27 4/8	28 2/8	18 3/8	5 7/8	4 7/8	8	7	Schoolcraft Co., MI	Lanny D. Higley	Lanny D. Higley	1994	2130
172 7/8	27	27	21 7/8	4 7/8	5	7	6	Huron Co., OH	James A. McMorrow	James A. McMorrow	1994	2130
172 7/8	26 7/8	27	19	5	4 5/8	6	5	Fillmore Co., MN	Susan M. LeGare-Gulden	Susan M. LeGare-Gulden	1996	2130
172 7/8	25	26	18 3/8	4 5/8	4 5/8	5	5	Estevan, SK	Brent Barreth	Brent Barreth	1998	2130
172 7/8	25 2/8	24 2/8	19 1/8	4 5/8	5	6	5	Jackson Co., WI	Donald R. Anderson	Donald R. Anderson	1999	2130
172 7/8	28 3/8	27 6/8	29	5 2/8	5 4/8	6	7	Donley Co., TX	Barrett W. Thorne	Barrett W. Thorne	1999	2130
172 7/8	29 1/8	29 1/8	19 7/8	6	5 7/8	6	5	Buffalo Co., WI	Robert H. Becker	Robert H. Becker	2000	2130
172 7/8	25 5/8	26 5/8	21 5/8	4 7/8	4 5/8	6	5	Minnehaha Co., SD	Daniel D. Anderson	Daniel D. Anderson	2001	2130
172 7/8	28 2/8	27 7/8	21 3/8	5 4/8	4 2/8	6	5	Scott Co., IL	Josh L. Roach	Josh L. Roach	2001	2130
172 7/8	28 6/8	29	20 7/8	5 4/8	4 6/8	6	6	Kent Co., MI	Matthew Sikma	Matthew Sikma	2002	2130
172 6/8	27	26	18 6/8	4 2/8	4 6/8	6	5	Woodruff Co., WI	Unknown	Mac's Taxidermy	PR 1918	2158
172 6/8	25 4/8	27 4/8	23 4/8	4 6/8	4 2/8	5	5	Texas	Unknown	Thomas P. Kosub	PR 1945	2158
172 6/8	27	25 1/8	19	4 6/8	4 6/8	5	7	Somerset Co., PA	Edward B. Stutzman	Edward B. Stutzman, Jr.	1945	2158
172 6/8	28 2/8	24 1/8	21 4/8	4 6/8	4 6/8	5	6	Trempealeau Co., WI	Henry M. Hoff	Henry M. Hoff	1956	2158
172 6/8	24 1/8	24 3/8	24	5	5	5	5	Waldo Co., ME	Wallace Humphrey	Arthur Humphrey	1963	2158
172 6/8	24 3/8	27 5/8	20 2/8	4 7/8	4 6/8	5	5	Pope Co., IL	George Koderhandt, Sr.	David Koderhandt	1963	2158
172 6/8	26 5/8	28 2/8	22 4/8	4 4/8	4 4/8	5	5	Webb Co., TX	B.A. Vineyard	B.A. Vineyard	1964	2158
172 6/8	23 4/8	26 3/8	15 4/8	5 6/8	5 5/8	6	5	Vilas Co., WI	James Homan	Cabela's, Inc.	1967	2158
172 6/8	27 2/8	25 1/8	22 4/8	4 4/8	5 3/8	6	7	Spokane Co., WA	Maurice Robinette	Maurice Robinette	1968	2158
172 6/8	24 5/8	27 4/8	23 7/8	6 4/8	4 7/8	7	4	Custer Co., MT	Picked Up	George A. Bettas	1974	2158
172 6/8	27 6/8	27 6/8	20 4/8	5 3/8	6	4	6	Louisa Co., IA	Merrill Flake	Monna B. Flake	1974	2158
172 6/8	25 4/8	23 2/8	20 3/8	6	5	5	5	Boone Co., IA	Lonne L. Tracy	Lonne L. Tracy	1975	2158
172 6/8	24 4/8	27 7/8	22 2/8	4 7/8	3 7/8	6	6	Allamakee Co., IA	Picked Up	Tom Kerndt, Sr.	1976	2158
172 6/8	26 1/8	24 4/8	21 2/8	5 2/8	5 3/8	6	5	Dimmit Co., TX	David R. Park	David R. Park, Jr.	1978	2158
172 6/8	24 3/8	27 2/8	16 5/8	5	5 1/8	5	5	Edgerton, AB	Richard T. Abbott	Richard T. Abbott	1980	2158
172 6/8	27 2/8	25 1/8	17 6/8	5	5 4/8	5	5	Mitchell Co., IA	Dan A. Block	Dan A. Block	1981	2158
172 6/8	24 5/8	27 6/8	22	3 7/8	5	6	6	Surry Co., VA	Edward B. Jones	Edward B. Jones	1984	2158
172 6/8	27 6/8	25 4/8	20 2/8	5 5/8	4 7/8	6	6	Fayette Co., IA	Greg P. Bordignon	Greg P. Bordignon	1987	2158
172 6/8	25 4/8	21	18	6 2/8	4 3/8	5	5	Ashland Co., WI	Picked Up	David Sanborn	PR 1987	2158
172 6/8	24 4/8	26	22	5	5 4/8	4	5	Stafford Co., KS	Donald G. Fisher	Donald G. Fisher	1989	2158
172 6/8	25 5/8	26 2/8	18 6/8	5 4/8	4 7/8	5	5	Biggar, SK	Roy Polsfut	Roy Polsfut	1989	2158
172 6/8	26 2/8	27 8/8	18 7/8	4 4/8	4 3/8	6	5	Bee Co., TX	John W. Galloway	John W. Galloway	1990	2158
172 6/8	27 1/8	27 1/8	18 4/8	4 2/8	4 3/8	4	5	Pike Co., OH	James W. Howard	James W. Howard	1990	2158
172 6/8	27 1/8	27 1/8	21 1/8	4 3/8	4 4/8	6	7	Renville Co., MN	Elroy E. Kuglin	Elroy E. Kuglin	1990	2158

WHITETAIL DEER - TYPICAL ANTLERS

Odocoileus virginianus virginianus and certain related subspecies

Score	Length of Main Beam R	L	Inside Spread	Circumference at Smallest Place Between Burr and First Point R	L	Number of Points R	L	Locality	Hunter	Owner	Date Killed	Rank
172 6/8	26 4/8	27 3/8	20	4 6/8	4 6/8	6	5	Crawford Creek, SK	Scott Macnab	Scott Macnab	1990	2158
172 6/8	27 1/8	27 7/8	17 4/8	6 1/8	5 1/8	5	5	Mitchell Co., GA	Al Collins	Al Collins	1991	2158
172 6/8	29 4/8	26 2/8	22 6/8	6 1/8	6 2/8	7	6	Richland Co., IL	Donald L. Ginder	Donald L. Ginder	1991	2158
172 6/8	26 5/8	27	22 3/8	5 3/8	5 2/8	6	8	Cheshire Co., NH	Peter J. Krochunas	Peter J. Krochunas	1991	2158
172 6/8	28	28 7/8	19 2/8	5 1/8	5 1/8	6	5	Moultrie Co., IL	Joseph D. Nelson	Joseph D. Nelson	1991	2158
172 6/8	25 3/8	24 7/8	18 2/8	4 1/8	4 2/8	6	6	Johnson Co., NE	Dan Hollatz	Dan Hollatz	1992	2158
172 6/8	26 5/8	26 4/8	18 6/8	4 5/8	4 5/8	5	5	Manitowoc Co., WI	Stephen J. Kortens	Stephen J. Kortens	1992	2158
172 6/8	26 5/8	25 2/8	20 4/8	4 6/8	4 4/8	5	5	Horsehide Creek, SK	Gene Markowsky	Gene Markowsky	1992	2158
172 6/8	26	24 1/8	22 7/8	4 5/8	4 5/8	6	6	Seminole Co., OK	Lester H. Reich	Lester H. Reich	1994	2158
172 6/8	27	26 4/8	21 5/8	5 3/8	5 6/8	5	9	Menominee Co., WI	Marvin R. Ninham	Marvin R. Ninham	1995	2158
172 6/8	26 1/8	25 3/8	17 4/8	4 5/8	4 6/8	7	6	Cass Co., IL	Tom M. Roberts	Tom M. Roberts	1995	2158
172 6/8	25 4/8	25 4/8	17 4/8	4 6/8	4 5/8	6	7	Keokuk Co., IA	Michael A. Veres	Michael A. Veres	1995	2158
172 6/8	26	26 4/8	18	5 5/8	5 5/8	6	6	Washington Co., KS	Todd Jueneman	Todd Jueneman	1996	2158
172 6/8	27 2/8	27 7/8	20 3/8	4 1/8	5 1/8	6	9	Washington Co., PA	Ronald J. LaBrosse, Jr.	Ronald J. LaBrosse, Jr.	1996	2158
172 6/8	28	28 1/8	24 4/8	4 1/8	4 2/8	5	5	Russell Co., KS	Mark A. Heinz	Mark A. Heinz	1997	2158
172 6/8	27 2/8	28 2/8	23 4/8	4 6/8	4 5/8	5	5	Franklin Co., ME	Michael W. Auger	Michael W. Auger	1998	2158
172 6/8	25	25 6/8	19 1/8	6 3/8	6 3/8	5	8	McLean Co., IL	Picked Up	Matt Cheever	1998	2158
172 6/8	27 5/8	28 3/8	22 2/8	5 6/8	5 6/8	7	6	Morrison Co., MN	Leroy R. Zimmerman	Leroy R. Zimmerman	1998	2158
172 6/8	24 7/8	25 7/8	18 4/8	5 4/8	5 2/8	7	7	Northampton Co., NC	L. Thomas Baird	L. Thomas Baird	1999	2158
172 6/8	25 4/8	25 2/8	18 1/8	5 7/8	5 5/8	7	7	Lost Bay, ON	Peter Marciuk	Peter Marciuk	1999	2158
172 6/8	26 3/8	26 4/8	20	4 2/8	4 2/8	5	5	Anne Arundel Co., MD	Gus Andujar	Gus Andujar	2000	2158
172 6/8	29 3/8	27 7/8	18 6/8	4 6/8	5	6	6	Elk Co., KS	Michael E. Benge	Michael E. Benge	2000	2158
172 6/8	25 6/8	24 6/8	18	4 6/8	4 6/8	5	6	Mercer Co., PA	Michael D. Heckathorn	Michael D. Heckathorn	2001	2158
172 6/8	25 6/8	26	17	5 1/8	5 1/8	5	5	N. Battleford, SK	Chris G. Gilmer	Chris G. Gilmer	2002	2158
172 6/8	22 1/8	22 2/8	15 5/8	4 5/8	4 7/8	9	8	Jefferson Co., IL	Picked Up	Randy Banes	PR 1940	2158
172 5/8	24 2/8	24 4/8	21 1/8	5 2/8	5	6	6	Frio Co., TX	Unknown	Roy Hindes	PR 1940	2207
172 5/8	25 4/8	26 3/8	20 5/8	4 3/8	4 4/8	5	6	Greene Co., AR	Unknown	Harry Willcockson	1960	2207
172 5/8	25 4/8	26	22 6/8	4 3/8	4 5/8	6	5	Esterhazy, SK	J. Weise	J. Weise	1967	2207
172 5/8	24	24 3/8	23 5/8	4 3/8	4 3/8	7	7	San Patricio Co., TX	Mary L. Edwards	Mary L. Edwards	1967	2207
172 5/8	25 1/8	24 5/8	19 1/8	5 7/8	5 6/8	7	5	Shoal Lake, MB	Gary Phillips	Gary Phillips	1971	2207
172 5/8	26 7/8	25 5/8	18 4/8	5 4/8	5 3/8	6	6	Cass Co., MI	Ben R. Williams	Ben R. Williams	1972	2207
172 5/8	24 1/8	23	18 1/8	4 3/8	4 3/8	5	6	Tuscarawas Co., OH	Charles Kerns	Charles Kerns	1974	2207
172 5/8	25	25	17 2/8	4 5/8	4 7/8	9	6	Knox Co., ME	Willis A. Moody, Jr.	Willis A. Moody, Jr.	PR 1977	2207
172 5/8	27 6/8	28 1/8	22 3/8	4 7/8	4 6/8	5	5	Koochiching Co., MN	Unknown	Marc M. Jackson	1979	2207
172 5/8	26 3/8	26 4/8	21 3/8	4 7/8	4 7/8	5	7	Highland Co., OH	Wilbur D. Rhoads	Wilbur D. Rhoads	1983	2207
172 5/8	28 4/8	28	22	6 2/8	6 3/8	8	8	Adams Co., MS	Adrian L. Stallone	Adrian L. Stallone	1983	2207

Score	R Beam	L Beam	Spread	Circ R	Circ L	Pts R	Pts L	Locality	Hunter	Owner	Date	Rank
172 5/8	24 7/8	25 7/8	25 1/8	4 7/8	4 7/8	5	5	Barren Co., KY	Billy N. Short	Billy N. Short	1984	2207
172 5/8	25 3/8	25 6/8	18 3/8	5	5 2/8	6	5	Sauk Co., WI	Terry A. Diske	Terry A. Diske	1987	2207
172 5/8	25 1/8	27	20 1/8	5 6/8	5 2/8	5	6	Surry Co., VA	Picked Up	Virginia L. Logan	1987	2207
172 5/8	22 5/8	23 3/8	19 7/8	4 5/8	4 4/8	6	6	Short Creek, SK	Neil Fornwald	Neil Fornwald	1989	2207
172 5/8	26 7/8	27 1/8	18 7/8	5 2/8	5 4/8	5	5	Rosebud Co., MT	Michael E. Gayheart	Michael E. Gayheart	1989	2207
172 5/8	26 2/8	25 6/8	18 6/8	5 3/8	5 5/8	7	6	Douglas Co., MO	Virgil Churchill	Virgil Churchill	1990	2207
172 5/8	26 7/8	27 1/8	19 2/8	4 4/8	4 4/8	6	5	Lyon Co., KS	Dale L. Hellman	Dale L. Hellman	1990	2207
172 5/8	26 6/8	27 1/8	22 3/8	5 1/8	5 2/8	4	4	Jackson Co., IA	Robert R. Morehead	Robert R. Morehead	1990	2207
172 5/8	26 4/8	26 1/8	17 1/8	4 2/8	4 1/8	5	5	Wayne Co., KY	Ronald G. Sexton	Ronald G. Sexton	1991	2207
172 5/8	27 1/8	26 4/8	21 2/8	4 7/8	5 2/8	5	5	Marshall Co., IL	Oscar C. Weber	Oscar C. Weber	1992	2207
172 5/8	25 1/8	25 2/8	16 5/8	4 4/8	4 4/8	6	6	Stewart Co., TN	Thomas M. Bowers	Thomas M. Bowers	1992	2207
172 5/8	23 4/8	23 1/8	20 1/8	5	5 2/8	7	6	Dawson Creek, BC	J. Grant Bowie	J. Grant Bowie	1992	2207
172 5/8	25 2/8	25 1/8	20 4/8	6 2/8	6	6	6	Crawford Co., IA	Picked Up	S.L. Reetz & J. Shumate	1992	2207
172 5/8	26 5/8	24 5/8	18 6/8	5 4/8	5 4/8	5	5	Buffalo Lake, SK	Garth Sander	Garth Sander	1994	2207
172 5/8	25 6/8	25 6/8	20 7/8	5	4 7/8	5	5	Holmes Co., OH	Sam Anderson	Sam Anderson	1994	2207
172 5/8	25 7/8	27	18 3/8	4 3/8	4 2/8	5	5	Ringgold Co., IA	Herbert J. Weigel	Herbert J. Weigel	1995	2207
172 5/8	26 1/8	26	19 6/8	4 6/8	4 6/8	5	5	Long Lake, AB	Gerald Bodner	Gerald Bodner	1995	2207
172 5/8	25 5/8	24 7/8	18 2/8	5 3/8	5 1/8	7	7	N. Saskatchewan River, SK	Blaine LaRose	Blaine LaRose	1995	2207
172 5/8	26 2/8	25 7/8	17 7/8	4 5/8	4 4/8	5	5	Eastland Co., TX	Kevin L. Reed	Kevin L. Reed	1996	2207
172 5/8	25 1/8	25 6/8	17	4 7/8	4 7/8	6	6	Menard Co., IL	Jeffrey M. Balding	Jeffrey M. Balding	1996	2207
172 5/8	26 2/8	25	24 1/8	5 1/8	5 2/8	5	5	Acton-Vale, QC	Guy Cusson	Guy Cusson	1996	2207
172 5/8	27 5/8	26 6/8	19 7/8	5 4/8	5 4/8	5	4	Coles Co., IL	Shane D. Duzan	Shane D. Duzan	1996	2207
172 5/8	25 4/8	26	20 1/8	5	4 7/8	6	6	Fayette Co., IL	Joseph M. Kirk	Joseph M. Kirk	1996	2207
172 5/8	26 1/8	26	20 7/8	4 6/8	4 6/8	5	5	Kootenai Co., ID	Shane Moyer	Shane Moyer	1996	2207
172 5/8	30 4/8	28 5/8	18 7/8	4 7/8	5	4	5	Jones Co., IA	Johnny S. Cook	Johnny S. Cook	1997	2207
172 5/8	26	26 1/8	22 3/8	5	5 1/8	6	6	Smith Co., KS	Jonathan D. Weavers	Jonathan D. Weavers	1998	2207
172 5/8	24 3/8	22 5/8	18 3/8	5 1/8	4 7/8	7	7	Treasure Co., MT	Picked Up	Ted K. Welchlin	1998	2207
172 5/8	24 5/8	25 1/8	25 1/8	4 5/8	4 5/8	5	5	Adams Co., WI	Vernon J. Williams, Jr.	Vernon J. Williams, Jr.	1998	2207
172 5/8	25 5/8	27	21 1/8	4 6/8	4 6/8	6	5	Kipling, SK	Tim Davies	Tim Davies	1999	2207
172 5/8	26 1/8	26 3/8	17 7/8	4 3/8	4 3/8	6	6	Stafford Co., KS	David Carlton	David Carlton	2000	2207
172 5/8	27 1/8	27 7/8	22 5/8	5	4 7/8	6	6	Long Island Lake, AB	David G. McGraw	David G. McGraw	2000	2207
172 5/8	26 6/8	28 5/8	19 1/8	5 1/8	5 2/8	5	5	Porcupine Plain, SK	Ron Daunheimer	Ron Daunheimer	2001	2207
172 5/8	26 2/8	25 6/8	19 3/8	4 3/8	4 4/8	5	5	Grant Co., WI	Pete W. Glassmaker	Pete W. Glassmaker	2001	2207
172 5/8	28 7/8	28 5/8	19 3/8	5	4 7/8	6	6	Stafford Co., KS	Trenton L. Teager	Trenton L. Teager	2003	2207
172 5/8	26 5/8	25 6/8	20 2/8	4 4/8	4 6/8	9	8	Mason Co., TX	Allen Family	Earl E. Allen	PR 1926	2252
172 4/8	25 6/8	27	20 2/8	5 2/8	5	6	6	Cotulla, TX	George E. Light III	George E. Light III	1959	2252
172 4/8	24 4/8	24 4/8	18 4/8	4 4/8	4 4/8	6	6	Webb Co., TX	A.M. Russell	A.M. Russell	1961	2252
172 4/8	27 3/8	26 7/8	22 5/8	5 1/8	4 6/8	5	5	Laird, SK	A.E. Nikkel	A.E. Nikkel	1963	2252
172 4/8	27 3/8	26 6/8	21 2/8	4	4	5	5	Zavala Co., TX	Gaston F. Maurin	Clint Arnold	1964	2252
172 4/8	26 4/8	27 2/8	24	4 3/8	5 3/8	5	5	Fort Knox, KY	E.G. Christian	E.G. Christian	1966	2252
172 4/8	27 5/8	27	23 3/8	5 3/8	5 1/8	7	5	Dougherty Co., GA	J.P. Flournoy	J.P. Flournoy	1969	2252
172 4/8	24 4/8	24 3/8	20	5	5	6	6	Chauvin, AB	Ron D. Jakimchuk	Ron D. Jakimchuk	1971	2252
172 4/8	26 7/8	25 2/8	19	4 6/8	4 5/8	5	5	Randolph Co., GA	Robert D. Bell	Robert D. Bell	1979	2252
172 4/8	24 3/8	25 2/8	23 4/8	5 6/8	5 4/8	8	7	Muhlenberg Co., KY	Dennis Nolen	Dennis Nolen	1982	2252
172 4/8	26 4/8	26 2/8	21 7/8	5 2/8	5 2/8	6	6	Muskingum Co., OH	Michael Wilson	Michael Wilson	1982	2252
172 4/8	23 5/8	25 2/8	20	6 1/8	5 7/8	6	6	Franklin Co., IL	Joseph S. Smothers	Joseph S. Smothers	1984	2252
172 4/8	29 4/8	28 6/8	20	5 3/8	5 2/8	5	5	Iron Co., WI	Dale D. Tuszke	Dale D. Tuszke	1987	2252
172 4/8	22	25 5/8	23 7/8	4 7/8	4 6/8	7	7	Smoky River, AB	Bevar C. Rose	Bevar C. Rose	1988	2252

WHITETAIL DEER - TYPICAL ANTLERS
Odocoileus virginianus virginianus and certain related subspecies

Score	Length of Main Beam R	L	Inside Spread	Circumference at Smallest Place Between Burr and First Point R	L	Number of Points R	L	Locality	Hunter	Owner	Date Killed	Rank
172 4/8	26 2/8	26 4/8	20 4/8	5 1/8	5	5	5	Fulton Co., IL	Marcus E. Christensen	Marcus E. Christensen	1990	2252
172 4/8	25 4/8	25 2/8	17	4 5/8	4 6/8	6	6	Stevens Co., WA	Don Ledbeter	Don Ledbeter	1990	2252
172 4/8	24	23 6/8	20 4/8	5 3/8	5 4/8	6	7	Battle River, SK	Ronald Bexfield	Ronald Bexfield	1991	2252
172 4/8	25 4/8	25 2/8	18	5 5/8	6	6	6	Hillsdale Co., MI	Turley G. Crisp	Turley G. Crisp	1991	2252
172 4/8	27 5/8	27 3/8	20 2/8	4 7/8	4 6/8	8	9	Marion Co., IL	Michele Hanks	Michele Hanks	1991	2252
172 4/8	26 2/8	25 4/8	17 6/8	4 5/8	4 5/8	6	8	Ringgold Co., IA	Edward D. Miller	Edward D. Miller	1991	2252
172 4/8	22 2/8	22 3/8	18 1/8	4 4/8	4 3/8	7	6	Dawson Co., NE	Kim L. Farnstrom	Kim L. Farnstrom	1992	2252
172 4/8	29 1/8	27 5/8	19 2/8	5	5	5	5	Guilford Co., NC	Rodney D. Summers	Rodney D. Summers	1993	2252
172 4/8	26 2/8	26 5/8	21	4 6/8	4 6/8	5	5	Lucas Co., IA	Perry L. Klages, Jr.	Perry L. Klages, Jr.	1994	2252
172 4/8	27 7/8	28 4/8	16 2/8	5	5	5	6	Stafford Co., KS	Alan Baldwin	Alan Baldwin	1995	2252
172 4/8	24 5/8	26 2/8	16 6/8	4 2/8	4 3/8	5	5	Bond Co., IL	William G. Brown	William G. Brown	1995	2252
172 4/8	25 4/8	25 4/8	18 2/8	5 6/8	5 4/8	5	5	McLennan, AB	Gordon Ristow	Gordon Ristow	1995	2252
172 4/8	26 5/8	27 4/8	17 2/8	4 4/8	4 5/8	5	5	Colquitt Co., GA	Alan Whitaker	Alan Whitaker	1996	2252
172 4/8	27 1/8	27 2/8	24	4 6/8	4 6/8	5	5	Muscatine Co., IA	John D. Russell	John D. Russell	1997	2252
172 4/8	22 4/8	23 2/8	16 6/8	5 1/8	5 1/8	7	6	Athabasca, AB	Christopher Sawchyn	Christopher Sawchyn	1997	2252
172 4/8	26 6/8	25 7/8	18 4/8	4 7/8	5	6	6	Evansburg, AB	Dana Baksa	Dana Baksa	1998	2252
172 4/8	26 2/8	25	17 6/8	5 2/8	5 4/8	6	6	St. Clair Co., MI	Djura Drazic	Djura Drazic	1998	2252
172 4/8	25 6/8	25 1/8	20	5	4 7/8	6	5	Fir River, SK	Andrew Dyess	Andrew Dyess	1998	2252
172 4/8	28	26 3/8	19 3/8	4 7/8	4 7/8	6	9	Piscataquis Co., ME	James A. Nicols	James A. Nicols	1998	2252
172 4/8	28 4/8	28 2/8	19 5/8	4 2/8	4 1/8	6	6	Fayette Co., IA	Rick L. Taylor	Rick L. Taylor	1998	2252
172 4/8	28	27 7/8	20	5 4/8	5 5/8	9	8	Putnam Co., IN	M.R. Abner & C. Yates	M.R. Abner & C. Yates	1999	2252
172 4/8	24 5/8	25 4/8	21 1/8	5	5	7	5	Dubuque Co., IA	Steven W. Berkley	Steven W. Berkley	1999	2252
172 2/8	27 2/8	26	19	4 7/8	4 7/8	6	7	Adair Co., MO	Eldon L. Grissom, Sr.	Eldon L. Grissom, Sr.	1999	2252
172 4/8	27 5/8	28 6/8	21 5/8	4 3/8	4 2/8	6	6	Haywood Co., TN	Mark S. Powell	Mark S. Powell	1999	2252
172 4/8	23 5/8	24 3/8	19 6/8	5 1/8	5 1/8	5	5	Marion Co., IA	Richard P. Johnson	Richard P. Johnson	2000	2252
172 4/8	24 4/8	24 7/8	23 6/8	4 5/8	4 5/8	5	5	Keokuk Co., IA	Michael D. Wells	Michael D. Wells	2000	2252
172 4/8	26	27 6/8	21	5	5 1/8	5	5	Harrison Co., MO	Bill Cook	Bill Cook	2001	2252
172 4/8	26 6/8	26 4/8	21 6/8	5 7/8	5 7/8	5	5	Mozart, SK	Wesley M. Spuzak	Wesley M. Spuzak	2001	2252
172 4/8	25 4/8	25 6/8	18 6/8	4 7/8	5	5	5	Anselmo, AB	Robert J. Wegner	Robert J. Wegner	2001	2252
172 4/8	21 4/8	23 4/8	25	4 7/8	5	6	6	Polk Co., AR	Lonnie Cecil	Lonnie Cecil	2002	2252
172 3/8	26 6/8	26 7/8	19 2/8	4 6/8	5	7	7	Taylor Co., WI	Karl Raatz	Kathleen Powell	1939	2296
172 3/8	27	28	23 6/8	4 6/8	4 6/8	7	8	Rainy Lake, ON	Floyd Kielczewski	Floyd Kielczewski	1953	2296
172 3/8	27	26	21	5 2/8	5 3/8	7	5	Hamilton Co., NY	Unknown	Donald K. Hamilton	1956	2296
172 3/8	27 4/8	27 2/8	20 4/8	6	6 1/8	5	6	Brookings Co., SD	Paul W. Back	Paul W. Back	1967	2296
172 3/8	26	26 2/8	19 5/8	4 6/8	4 6/8	6	5	Monroe Co., MO	Clark E. Bray	Clark E. Bray	1967	2296
172 3/8	29 5/8	29 1/8	20 3/8	4 2/8	4 4/8	5	6	Snider Mt., NB	Jack W. Brown	Jack W. Brown	1975	2296

Score	Length of Main Beam R	L	Inside Spread	Circumference R	L	Points R	L	Locality	Hunter	Owner	Date	Rank
172 3/8	26 5/8	27 6/8	17 1/8	4 3/8	4 4/8	8	5	Kanabec Co., MN	Gregory L. Schultz	Gregory L. Schultz	1976	2296
172 3/8	27 6/8	28 2/8	17 2/8	4 6/8	4 5/8	6	5	Decatur Co., TN	Danny Pope	Danny Pope	1982	2296
172 3/8	24 5/8	24 3/8	18	4 6/8	4 7/8	8	7	Rusk Co., WI	Randy A. Jochem	Randy A. Jochem	1984	2296
172 3/8	30 1/8	30 3/8	22 3/8	5 4/8	5 4/8	9	9	Porcupine Plain, SK	Kim Mikkonen	Kim Mikkonen	1985	2296
172 3/8	28 1/8	28 4/8	22 5/8	4 3/8	4 3/8	5	5	Fulton Co., GA	Michael Gregory	Lee E. Johnson	1986	2296
172 3/8	27 6/8	26 5/8	16	4 6/8	4 6/8	5	6	Dane Co., WI	Randy L. Letlebo	Randy L. Letlebo	1987	2296
172 3/8	26 4/8	26 7/8	16 2/8	5	5 2/8	7	7	Mercer Co., MO	Jarin J. Simpson	Jarin J. Simpson	1988	2296
172 3/8	27 6/8	26 1/8	18	5 6/8	4 7/8	6	5	Boone Co., IA	Kevin A. Anderson	Kevin A. Anderson	1989	2296
172 3/8	26 3/8	26 3/8	19 1/8	4 6/8	4 3/8	6	5	Monona Co., IA	Larry Hieber	Larry Hieber	1989	2296
172 3/8	24 6/8	24 6/8	17 5/8	4 3/8	4 7/8	5	5	Dearborn Co., IN	Walter C. Drake	Walter C. Drake	1990	2296
172 3/8	27	26 7/8	19 1/8	5	5 3/8	5	6	Johnson Co., KS	David T. Reed	David T. Reed	1990	2296
172 3/8	27	27 3/8	23 5/8	5 3/8	4 7/8	6	6	McHenry Co., IL	Kevin Rubow	Kevin Rubow	1990	2296
172 3/8	26 3/8	26 6/8	22 1/8	4 7/8	5	5	6	Harrison Co., KY	Charles B. Burgess	Charles B. Burgess	1993	2296
172 3/8	29 6/8	30 2/8	21 2/8	4 5/8	4 3/8	4	6	Prince George's Co., MD	Lance D. Canter	Lance D. Canter	1993	2296
172 3/8	28 3/8	27 5/8	21 1/8	4 4/8	4 3/8	5	5	Bedford Co., VA	Robert A. McGann	Robert A. McGann	1993	2296
172 3/8	28	28	18 3/8	4 2/8	5	5	5	Jackson Co., WI	J. Esanbock & M. Finch	J. Esanbock & M. Finch	1994	2296
172 3/8	26 5/8	27 5/8	18 7/8	5	4 7/8	5	5	La Salle Co., IL	William J. Keith	William J. Keith	1994	2296
172 3/8	23 5/8	24	16 2/8	4 7/8	5	8	8	Sheridan Co., MT	Kent G. Unhjem	Kent G. Unhjem	1994	2296
172 3/8	24 5/8	25 6/8	16 6/8	5	4 6/8	6	5	Queen Anne's Co., MD	Paul A. Pletzer	Paul A. Pletzer	1995	2296
172 3/8	24	24 1/8	17 3/8	4 5/8	4 5/8	6	6	Sounding Lake, AB	Neil Scammell	Neil Scammell	1995	2296
172 3/8	26 7/8	27 4/8	18 3/8	4 6/8	4 7/8	5	5	Greeley Co., NE	Alan D. Vanosdall	Alan D. Vanosdall	1995	2296
172 3/8	25	25 2/8	22 5/8	5	5 6/8	6	6	Des Moines Co., IA	Colin J. Gerst	Colin J. Gerst	1997	2296
172 3/8	25 6/8	27 4/8	19 3/8	5 6/8	4 7/8	7	6	Monroe Co., NY	Picked Up	Joseph Masci	1997	2296
172 3/8	28	27 5/8	22 2/8	5	4 6/8	5	6	Iowa Co., WI	Bruce E. Schuelke	Bruce E. Schuelke	1997	2296
172 3/8	26 7/8	25 7/8	17 7/8	4 7/8	5 2/8	5	5	Hart Co., KY	Terry Avery	Terry Avery	1999	2296
172 3/8	23 4/8	23 3/8	18 5/8	5 2/8	5 5/8	6	5	Washington Co., KY	Gordon S. Adam	Gordon S. Adam	2000	2296
172 3/8	26	24 6/8	24 5/8	5 4/8	6 2/8	5	5	Walworth Co., WI	Daniel Miller	Daniel Miller	2000	2296
172 3/8	25 6/8	26 3/8	17	6 3/8	5 2/8	5	9	Morgan Co., GA	Jeff L. Banks	Jeff L. Banks	2001	2296
172 3/8	26 4/8	26 6/8	17 1/8	5	5	7	6	Credit River, ON	Eugene Bulizo	Eugene Bulizo	2001	2296
172 3/8	25 6/8	25 7/8	16 2/8	4 5/8	4 5/8	6	7	Grundy Co., MO	Wayne A. Moore, Jr.	Wayne A. Moore, Jr.	2001	2296
172 3/8	26 4/8	26 4/8	17 3/8	4 7/8	4 7/8	5	5	Fayette Co., IL	Lisa A. Tarvin	Lisa A. Tarvin	2001	2296
172 3/8	25 6/8	25 6/8	20 3/8	4 6/8	4 5/8	4	4	Crawford Co., IL	W. Dave Johnson	W. Dave Johnson	2002	2296
172 2/8	27 7/8	28	20	4 4/8	4 5/8	5	6	Lincoln Co., WI	Alfred Theilig	Ronald F. Lax	1928	2334
172 2/8	24 6/8	24 3/8	18	4 5/8	4 3/8	6	6	Vilas Co., WI	Ray Hermanson	J. James Froelich	1936	2334
172 2/8	26 7/8	27	20 6/8	4 1/8	5 6/8	5	5	St. Louis Co., MN	Everett Larson	George W. Flaim	1942	2334
172 2/8	28 6/8	26 4/8	21 5/8	6	5 1/8	6	6	Bedford Co., PA	John F. Sharpe	John F. Sharpe	1942	2334
172 2/8	26 4/8	25 6/8	20	5 1/8	4 6/8	7	7	Weyburn, SK	Wilfred LaValley	Wilfred LaValley	1958	2334
172 2/8	25 6/8	26 3/8	20	5	5 1/8	5	5	Jones Co., SD	Walter Prahl	J.D. Andrews	1960	2334
172 2/8	27 4/8	26 4/8	19 4/8	4 7/8	5 1/8	6	8	Manor, SK	Albert McConnell	Albert McConnell	1962	2334
172 2/8	25 4/8	25 2/8	23 5/8	4 7/8	5	5	7	Flathead Co., MT	Lonny Hanson	Lonny Hanson	1963	2334
172 2/8	23	23	19	5	4 5/8	6	7	Adams Co., WI	W.R. Ingraham	W.R. Ingraham	1965	2334
172 2/8	31 4/8	30 7/8	23 5/8	4 5/8	4 7/8	6	5	Perry Co., IL	Raymond E. Haertling	Raymond E. Haertling	1968	2334
172 2/8	25 4/8	24 4/8	23 3/8	5 2/8	4 5/8	7	6	Perry Co., IL	Ralph J. Przygoda, Jr.	Ralph J. Przygoda, Jr.	1978	2334
172 2/8	25 6/8	24 2/8	20	4 4/8	5 1/8	5	8	Perkins Co., SD	Randy G. Swenson	Randy G. Swenson	1979	2334
172 2/8	24 6/8	25 3/8	18 2/8	5	5 1/8	5	5	Trego Co., KS	Alan Baldwin	Alan Baldwin	1982	2334
172 2/8	25 7/8	25 6/8	20 2/8	5	4 4/8	5	5	Cattaraugus Co., NY	Thomas J. Hinchey	Thomas J. Hinchey	1982	2334
172 2/8	26 2/8	25 1/8	22	5	5	7	7	Pendleton Co., KY	Kevin L. Galloway	Kevin L. Galloway	1983	2334
172 2/8	24 7/8	25	18 2/8	4 7/8	5	5	5	Putnam Co., GA	Spunky Thornton	Spunky Thornton	1983	2334

WHITETAIL DEER - TYPICAL ANTLERS
Odocoileus virginianus virginianus and certain related subspecies

Score	Length of Main Beam R	L	Inside Spread	Circumference at Smallest Place Between Burr and First Point R	L	Number of Points R	L	Locality	Hunter	Owner	Date Killed	Rank
172 2/8	26 2/8	25	18 7/8	5	5	6	6	Stewart Co., TN	Joe K. Sanders	Joe K. Sanders	1984	2334
172 2/8	27 6/8	30	20 4/8	5 4/8	5 4/8	8	7	Minnedosa River, MB	Eric W.C. Abel	Eric W.C. Abel	1986	2334
172 2/8	27 1/8	27	22	5 3/8	5	5	5	Jefferson Co., IA	Paul Hagist, Jr.	Paul Hagist, Jr.	1986	2334
172 2/8	26 7/8	27 6/8	26 2/8	4 2/8	4 3/8	6	5	Saunders Co., NE	John I. Kunert	John I. Kunert	1986	2334
172 2/8	24 2/8	25	18 1/8	4 2/8	4 3/8	8	5	Minnesota	Unknown	Jeff A. Puhl	PR 1987	2334
172 2/8	26 2/8	25 5/8	23 4/8	4 4/8	4 4/8	6	6	Scott Co., MN	Kenneth J. Scherer	Kenneth J. Scherer	1987	2334
172 2/8	22 7/8	27 1/8	16 3/8	5 3/8	5 4/8	8	7	Rainy Lake, ON	Andrew Brigham	Andrew Brigham	1989	2334
172 2/8	26 1/8	26 6/8	21	5 2/8	5 2/8	8	8	Norman Co., MN	Corey Hoseth	Corey Hoseth	1989	2334
172 2/8	26	26	22	5 4/8	5	5	5	Washtenaw Co., MI	Guy A. Miller	Guy A. Miller	1989	2334
172 2/8	25 1/8	25	18	5 2/8	5	6	6	Union Co., IL	Richard A. Sotiropoulos	Richard A. Sotiropoulos	1990	2334
172 2/8	26 3/8	25	21 2/8	5	4 6/8	6	5	Coahuila, MX	G. Rone Allen	G. Rone Allen	1992	2334
172 2/8	27 2/8	26	20	5 3/8	5 3/8	5	5	Miami Co., OH	Donald J. Boehmer, Jr.	Donald J. Boehmer, Jr.	1992	2334
172 2/8	27 4/8	27 3/8	20	4 6/8	5	6	5	Christian Co., KY	Randall G. Joiner	Randall G. Joiner	1992	2334
172 2/8	26 3/8	25 5/8	19 5/8	5	5 1/8	6	7	Sussex Co., DE	David T. Murray	David T. Murray	1992	2334
172 2/8	24 2/8	25 4/8	18	4	4 3/8	6	6	Mercer Co., MO	Brad Holt	Brad Holt	1993	2334
172 2/8	27 3/8	27 6/8	21 3/8	5 5/8	5 6/8	8	8	Norton Co., KS	Jim Keenan	Jim Keenan	1993	2334
172 2/8	27 3/8	27 6/8	19 4/8	4	4 2/8	5	5	Scott Co., IA	Patrick D. Willhoite	Patrick D. Willhoite	1994	2334
172 2/8	26 2/8	26	22 4/8	4 6/8	4 7/8	6	5	Clayton Co., IA	Scott L. Doerring	Scott L. Doerring	1995	2334
172 2/8	26	25 7/8	19 7/8	5	5	7	5	Lee Co., IA	Chris L. Schiller	Chris L. Schiller	1995	2334
172 2/8	25 5/8	25 2/8	18	5	4 7/8	7	5	Brandon, MB	Robert W. Jonasson	Robert W. Jonasson	1996	2334
172 2/8	29 2/8	28 6/8	17 6/8	4 7/8	4 7/8	5	5	St. Louis Co., MN	Picked Up	Jerome L. Schaller	1996	2334
172 2/8	27 6/8	26 5/8	20 2/8	4 4/8	4 4/8	6	5	Ashland Co., WI	Arnold D. Miller	Arnold D. Miller	1997	2334
172 2/8	27 2/8	27 2/8	19 6/8	4 5/8	4 6/8	5	5	Randolph Co., MO	Edward L. Sneed	Edward L. Sneed	1997	2334
172 2/8	27 4/8	27 4/8	22 6/8	4 7/8	4 6/8	7	6	Wabasha Co., MN	John K. Gusa	John K. Gusa	1998	2334
172 2/8	28 4/8	28 1/8	18 6/8	4 5/8	4 7/8	7	5	Talbot Co., MD	Jack W. Jones	Jack W. Jones	1998	2334
172 2/8	26 1/8	25	20	5	5	6	6	Knox Co., OH	David K. Palmer	David K. Palmer	1998	2334
172 2/8	28 3/8	28 2/8	19 6/8	4 4/8	4 4/8	4	4	Frio Co., TX	Thomas W. Burell	Thomas W. Burell	1999	2334
172 2/8	27 4/8	28	20 2/8	4 7/8	5 1/8	6	6	Peoria Co., IL	Heye H. Peters, Jr.	Heye H. Peters, Jr.	1999	2334
172 2/8	26 5/8	26 1/8	19 6/8	5 1/8	4 7/8	5	5	Vernon Co., WI	Ronald J. Stilwell	Ronald J. Stilwell	1999	2334
172 2/8	25 7/8	26	18	4 7/8	5	5	5	Berrien Co., MI	Mike C. Payne	Mike C. Payne	2000	2334
172 2/8	26	26 6/8	19 2/8	5 1/8	5 2/8	5	6	Martin Co., KY	Julius Jude	Julius Jude	2001	2334
172 2/8	25 6/8	25 2/8	25 2/8	4 4/8	4 4/8	5	5	Perkins Co., NE	G. Michael Martin	G. Michael Martin	2001	2334
172 2/8	23 3/8	22 6/8	17	5 3/8	5 3/8	6	6	Bartholomew Co., IN	Dustin G. Prewitt	Dustin G. Prewitt	2001	2334
172 2/8	20 2/8	24	18 4/8	4 7/8	4 7/8	5	5	Tamaulipas, MX	William W. Gouldin	William W. Gouldin	2002	2334
172 1/8	24 2/8	24 7/8	19 5/8	4 3/8	4 3/8	5	6	Wyandotte Co., KS	Earl A. Cooksey	Earl A. Cooksey	1922	2384
172 1/8	26	25 5/8	18	4 3/8	4 6/8	6	5	Baraga Co., MI	Gust Varlen	Bass Pro Shops	1945	2384

Score	Main Beam R	Main Beam L	Inside Spread	Circ. R	Circ. L	Pts. R	Pts. L	Locality	Hunter	Owner	Date	Rank
172 1/8	25 6/8	25 5/8	19 3/8	5 4/8	5 2/8	5	5	Juneau Co., WI	Clark G. Gallup	Unknown	1949	2384
172 1/8	26 1/8	26 2/8	19 3/8	4 4/8	4 4/8	6	5	St. Louis Co., MN	Ted Schoeppner	Luke Schoeppner	1955	2384
172 1/8	28 3/8	28 1/8	25 5/8	5	5 2/8	5	5	Morson, ON	Almer Godin	Almer Godin	1957	2384
172 1/8	30 2/8	30 1/8	20 7/8	5 1/8	4 7/8	5	6	Fillmore Co., MN	Charles J. Semmen	C.J. Semmen & G. Lea	1961	2384
172 1/8	26 3/8	26 4/8	21 5/8	4 6/8	5 3/8	5	5	Pickens Co., AL	Walter Jaynes	Walter Jaynes	1968	2384
172 1/8	27	27 3/8	23 2/8	4 6/8	4 4/8	7	8	Hughes Co., SD	Mark Lilevjen	Mark Lilevjen	1971	2384
172 1/8	28 5/8	28 3/8	19 2/8	4 6/8	5	7	6	Coshocton Co., OH	Virgil E. Carpenter	Virgil E. Carpenter	1972	2384
172 1/8	27 2/8	26 5/8	18 6/8	5 1/8	4 6/8	5	6	Queen Anne's Co., MD	James R. Spies, Jr.	James R. Spies, Jr.	1976	2384
172 1/8	24	24 4/8	20 6/8	4 3/8	5 1/8	7	8	Fillmore Co., MN	Murrel Mathison	Murrel Mathison	1977	2384
172 1/8	25 3/8	24 2/8	17 5/8	4 7/8	4 2/8	6	6	Wabasha Co., MN	Timothy R. Pries	Timothy R. Pries	1977	2384
172 1/8	25 1/8	25 5/8	16 4/8	4 1/8	4 7/8	6	6	Winona Co., MN	Robert J. Cordie	Robert J. Cordie	1979	2384
172 1/8	26 7/8	25 3/8	16	5 5/8	4	6	5	Price Co., NE	Greg K. Young	Picked Up	1981	2384
172 1/8	26 1/8	25	18 5/8	4 6/8	5 5/8	7	8	Clinton Co., IA	R. Dean Grimes	R. Dean Grimes	1984	2384
172 1/8	24 7/8	24	18 6/8	4 5/8	4 6/8	7	6	Clinton Co., IL	James D. Rueter	James D. Rueter	1984	2384
172 1/8	27 6/8	27 1/8	19 4/8	4 4/8	4 3/8	6	7	Granville Co., NC	Dudley Barnes	Dudley Barnes	1985	2384
172 1/8	25 1/8	25 5/8	19 1/8	4 2/8	4 3/8	6	6	Rock Island Co., IL	Keith Hogan	Ron Baum	1985	2384
172 1/8	27 1/8	25 7/8	20 3/8	5 3/8	5 3/8	5	5	Buffalo Co., WI	Aaron Comero	Aaron Comero	1986	2384
172 1/8	24 1/8	24 5/8	19 6/8	5 4/8	5 5/8	7	7	Louisa Co., IA	John Bloomer	John Bloomer	1987	2384
172 1/8	25	25 5/8	18 3/8	5 6/8	5 6/8	6	5	Lac Emilien, AB	Dennis Ewanec	Dennis Ewanec	1987	2384
172 1/8	27 2/8	26 7/8	21 1/8	5 5/8	5 5/8	4	4	Chase Co., KS	Darwin Bailey	Picked Up	1989	2384
172 1/8	26 2/8	26 4/8	20 1/8	5 7/8	5 7/8	7	8	Jennings Co., IN	Gerald G. Powers	Gerald G. Powers	1989	2384
172 1/8	25 1/8	24 6/8	20 5/8	4 3/8	4 1/8	8	8	Lake Co., IL	Mark J. Kramer	Mark J. Kramer	1990	2384
172 1/8	27 6/8	27 4/8	17 5/8	5 4/8	5 5/8	6	6	Dooly Co., GA	Marty T. McNulty	Marty T. McNulty	1990	2384
172 1/8	22 7/8	22 6/8	17 5/8	5 5/8	5 3/8	6	4	Smoky River, AB	Lawrence Zawacki	Lawrence Zawacki	1990	2384
172 1/8	27 3/8	27 3/8	22 3/8	4 6/8	4 6/8	4	5	Goose Lake, SK	Joe W. Schmidt	Joe W. Schmidt	1991	2384
172 1/8	25 4/8	25 4/8	19 3/8	4 7/8	4 7/8	5	6	Genesee Co., MI	David C. Bastion	David C. Bastion	1992	2384
172 1/8	25 2/8	26 3/8	19 3/8	6	4 4/8	6	6	Miller Co., MO	Jim L. Bell	Jim L. Bell	1992	2384
172 1/8	24 2/8	23 7/8	18 1/8	4 5/8	5 7/8	6	6	Harrison Co., IA	Chad M. Kuhns	Picked Up	1994	2384
172 1/8	27 1/8	23 7/8	20 6/8	6	4 6/8	6	6	Butler Co., KY	Bradley D. Cardwell	Bradley D. Cardwell	1995	2384
172 1/8	24 4/8	30 2/8	18 5/8	5	4 4/8	6	7	Kenedy Co., TX	Lee M. Bass	Lee M. Bass	1996	2384
172 1/8	29 3/8	26 7/8	21	5 1/8	5 2/8	8	7	Rock Co., WI	Steven W. Kravick	Steven W. Kravick	1996	2384
172 1/8	27 2/8	26 1/8	21	5	5 3/8	5	6	Jefferson Co., IA	Joe F. Arndt	Joe F. Arndt	1997	2384
172 1/8	26 3/8	25 2/8	20 1/8	4 1/8	4 2/8	5	5	Keokuk Co., IA	Ric L. Bishop	Ric L. Bishop	1997	2384
172 1/8	25 2/8	25 4/8	17 2/8	4 5/8	4 5/8	6	6	Wabasha Co., MN	Michael R. Klagge	Michael R. Klagge	1997	2384
172 1/8	27 2/8	27	24	5	5	6	6	Pipestone Creek, SK	Clayton Roberts	Clayton Roberts	1998	2384
172 1/8	25 5/8	24 1/8	18 4/8	4 4/8	4 4/8	6	6	Todd Co., MN	Kenneth J. Ostendorf	Kenneth J. Ostendorf	1999	2384
172 1/8	27 5/8	27 5/8	22 5/8	5 2/8	5 1/8	6	8	Monroe Co., IA	Jeffrey A. Butler	Jeffrey A. Butler	1999	2384
172 1/8	28 4/8	25 7/8	20	5 3/8	4 6/8	7	4	Kankakee Co., IL	Darrel L. Duby	Darrel L. Duby	1999	2384
172 1/8	26 2/8	25 6/8	17 5/8	4 4/8	4 5/8	5	5	Crooked Lake, SK	Gil Mountney	Gil Mountney	2000	2384
172 1/8	24 5/8	25 4/8	22 7/8	5 2/8	5 4/8	5	5	Lake Co., IL	Derrell W. Listhartke	Derrell W. Listhartke	2000	2384
172 1/8	25 6/8	25 6/8	18 5/8	5 7/8	5 6/8	5	5	Buffalo Co., WI	David G. Lyga	David G. Lyga	2001	2384
172 1/8	28 4/8	28	22 3/8	5 2/8	5 3/8	5	5	Van Buren Co., IA	Bob McWilliams	Picked Up	2001	2384
172	26 4/8	25 2/8	19 4/8	4 7/8	4 6/8	6	5	Carlton Co., MN	John R. Steffes, Sr.	Picked Up	1937	2428
172	25 4/8	26 3/8	19 1/8	5 2/8	4 4/8	5	5	Oconto Co., WI	Henry J. Bredael	Henry J. Bredael	1939	2428
172	24 4/8	23 6/8	19 6/8	5 2/8	5 2/8	5	5	Sauk Co., WI	Philip J. Rouse III	Rudy Lehnherr	1946	2428
172	25 6/8	26 7/8	17	5 3/8	5 1/8	6	6	Neepawa, MB	Jim Sinclair	Jim Sinclair	1947	2428
172	25 2/8	25 6/8	24 2/8	5 1/8	5 2/8	6	5	Woodbury Co., IA	Harold Horsley	Harold Horsley	1956	2428
172	25 6/8	25 2/8	18 4/8	5 2/8	5 3/8	7	5	Henderson Co., IL	Harry M. Carner	Harry M. Carner	1959	2428

WHITETAIL DEER - TYPICAL ANTLERS
Odocoileus virginianus virginianus and certain related subspecies

Score	Length of Main Beam R	L	Inside Spread	Circumference at Smallest Place Between Burr and First Point R	L	Number of Points R	L	Locality	Hunter	Owner	Date Killed	Rank
172	26 2/8	27 2/8	18 5/8	5 5/8	5 5/8	9	8	Wadena, SK	Edgar Smale	Edgar Smale	1959	2428
172	26 2/8	23	21 4/8	4 6/8	4 6/8	5	6	Buffalo Co., WI	Ralph Duellman	Ralph Duellman	1960	2428
172	24 3/8	24	17 7/8	5 2/8	5 2/8	5	6	N. Battleford, SK	Dick Napastuk	Dick Napastuk	1962	2428
172	26 1/8	25	24 2/8	4 5/8	4 4/8	5	5	Bearden, AR	Buddy Wise	Buddy Wise	1962	2428
172	24 1/8	24 1/8	20 2/8	6 5/8	6 4/8	8	7	Butts Co., GA	Jack Hammond	Jack Hammond	1963	2428
172	25	26 4/8	21 4/8	5 1/8	5 2/8	5	5	Parkman, SK	A.T. Mair	A.T. Mair	1963	2428
172	24 6/8	24 6/8	17 2/8	4 3/8	4 4/8	6	5	Joseph Plains, ID	Jim Felton	Jim Felton	1965	2428
172	23 7/8	23 4/8	18 6/8	4 4/8	4 4/8	5	5	Fergus Co., MT	Bill Scott	Martin J. Killham, Jr.	1973	2428
172	25 5/8	24 5/8	25 6/8	5 1/8	5 4/8	5	5	Perry Co., OH	William J. Pargeon	William J. Pargeon	1976	2428
172	25	25 2/8	18 6/8	5 2/8	5 2/8	6	6	Adams Co., MS	Nan F. New	Nan F. New	1977	2428
172	25 1/8	26	19 3/8	5 2/8	4 7/8	7	5	Furnas Co., NE	Marvin A. Briegel	Marvin A. Briegel	1980	2428
172	26	25 6/8	22 3/8	4 4/8	4 3/8	6	7	Muskingum Co., OH	David R. Hatfield	David R. Hatfield	1980	2428
172	27 3/8	27 1/8	19 3/8	4 4/8	4 4/8	5	6	Marshall Co., MN	Keith D. Anderson	Keith D. Anderson	1982	2428
172	24 6/8	25 6/8	22 6/8	5 3/8	5 3/8	5	6	Miami Co., KS	Dan R. Moore	Dan R. Moore	1982	2428
172	24	25 7/8	18	4 2/8	4 2/8	6	5	Tift Co., GA	Mayo Tucker	Mayo Tucker	1982	2428
172	27 3/8	28 3/8	18 2/8	5	5 1/8	5	5	Westmoreland Co., NB	Edgar Cormier	Edgar Cormier	1983	2428
172	25 7/8	25 2/8	19	4 5/8	4 5/8	5	5	Waukesha Co., WI	Donald R. Friedlein	Donald R. Friedlein	1983	2428
172	29 5/8	29 4/8	22 2/8	5 4/8	5 4/8	4	4	Edwards Co., IL	Picked Up	George W. Flaim	1985	2428
172	26 1/8	26 3/8	17 4/8	5	4 6/8	5	6	Dodge Co., WI	Dennis E. Schulteis	Dennis E. Schulteis	1985	2428
172	27	27	17 1/8	4 6/8	5 2/8	6	5	Caroline Co., MD	Garey N. Brown	Garey N. Brown	1986	2428
172	25 4/8	25 4/8	17 4/8	4 6/8	4 4/8	6	6	Coahuila, MX	Picked Up	Carl Kallina	1986	2428
172	28	28 2/8	19 5/8	4 7/8	4 7/8	9	10	Otter Tail Co., MN	Paul W. Wagner	Paul W. Wagner	1987	2428
172	25 6/8	26 4/8	21 6/8	4 4/8	4 4/8	6	6	Henderson Co., KY	Gary Hancock	Gary Hancock	1990	2428
172	23 7/8	23 5/8	15 6/8	4 2/8	4	5	5	Callaway Co., MO	Picked Up	Larry W. Quick	1990	2428
172	24 4/8	25 3/8	18	4 6/8	4 6/8	6	7	Harrison Co., MO	Timothy E. Black	Timothy E. Black	1991	2428
172	24 2/8	24 7/8	19 5/8	4 7/8	4 7/8	10	5	De Kalb Co., MO	Dean Davis	Dean Davis	1991	2428
172	26 3/8	24 6/8	19 7/8	5 1/8	5 1/8	5	9	Battle River, SK	Robert J. Bullock	Robert J. Bullock	1992	2428
172	24 5/8	22 7/8	18 5/8	4 6/8	4 4/8	6	5	Daviess Co., MO	David K. DeWeese	David K. DeWeese	1992	2428
172	27 5/8	28	23 5/8	5 5/8	6	6	6	Greene Co., IL	B. David McCarthy	B. David McCarthy	1992	2428
172	22 2/8	22	16 2/8	5	5	7	8	Ebel Creek, SK	Cory Zastrizny	Cory Zastrizny	1992	2428
172	26	26 3/8	19 5/8	5 7/8	5 4/8	5	6	Buffalo Co., WI	James L. Sturz	James L. Sturz	1994	2428
172	25 7/8	26 3/8	20 4/8	5 4/8	6 1/8	6	7	Hillsdale Co., MI	Art P. Toney	Art P. Toney	1994	2428
172	26 2/8	26 2/8	20	4 5/8	4 4/8	7	5	Fayette Co., IA	Robert Goad	Robert Goad	1996	2428
172	26 2/8	26	20 7/8	5 3/8	5 3/8	5	6	Arkansas Co., AR	Donald R. Sweetin	Donald R. Sweetin	1996	2428
172	26 3/8	26 5/8	20 7/8	5 2/8	5 4/8	7	6	Kenedy Co., TX	Lee M. Bass	Lee M. Bass	1997	2428
172	26 2/8	26 2/8	19 3/8	4 6/8	4 6/8	5	5	Delaware Co., IA	Charles E. Fessler	Charles E. Fessler	1997	2428

Score	R. Main Beam	L. Main Beam	Inside Spread	R. Points	L. Points	R. Circ.	L. Circ.	Location	Owner	Hunter	Date	Rank
172	24 4/8	26	18 4/8	5	5	4 7/8	5	Avoyelles Parish, LA	Richard J. Dupuy, Jr.	Richard J. Dupuy, Jr.	1998	2428
172	23 3/8	23 3/8	19 4/8	5	5	5 6/8	5 6/8	Little Red River, SK	Peter LoPiccolo	Peter LoPiccolo	1998	2428
172	25 5/8	25 4/8	20 4/8	9	7	5 4/8	5 4/8	Jefferson Co., IA	Brandon Slaubaugh	Brandon Slaubaugh	1998	2428
172	26 1/8	25 6/8	19	5	5	6	6 1/8	Jackson Co., MI	Justin D. Wright	Justin D. Wright	1998	2428
172	27 5/8	29 6/8	21 2/8	5	6	5 1/8	4 7/8	Pasquia Hills, SK	Easton C. Kapeller	Easton C. Kapeller	1999	2428
172	26 3/8	28 1/8	27 4/8	6	6	5 1/8	4 7/8	Crawford Co., OH	William E. Crall	William E. Crall	2000	2428
172	25 7/8	26	18 4/8	5	5	5	5	Govan, SK	James J. King	James J. King	2000	2428
172	25 3/8	24 6/8	17 4/8	6	7	4 5/8	4 5/8	Pike Co., MO	Randall E. Pilliard	Randall E. Pilliard	2000	2428
172	26 5/8	28 3/8	17 7/8	7	6	4 6/8	4 6/8	Pettis Co., MO	James R. Ellison	James R. Ellison	2001	2428
172	27 1/8	26	24 2/8	5	6	4 7/8	5 1/8	Jennings Co., IN	Guy Euler	Guy Euler	2001	2428
172	27 2/8	27 1/8	20 7/8	5	5	5 1/8	4 7/8	St. Clair Co., IL	James R. Smith	James R. Smith	2001	2428
172	25 4/8	25 1/8	20 4/8	5	5	4 2/8	4	Shelby Co., KY	Frank L. Walker	Frank L. Walker	2002	2428
172	26 2/8	26 2/8	16	5	5	5 3/8	5 4/8	Yazoo Co., MS	Barry S. Barnes	Barry S. Barnes	2003	2428
171 7/8	27 6/8	27 2/8	20 1/8	5	8	5	5	Madison Parish, LA	David D. Arnold	M.L. Arnold	1941	2483
171 7/8	25 4/8	25 4/8	16 4/8	7	6	5 7/8	5 7/8	Scotch Bay, MB	W.J. Harker	W.J. Harker	1951	2483
171 7/8	27	27	21 4/8	6	6	6 5/8	6 3/8	Fillmore Co., MN	Maynard Howe	Maynard Howe	1957	2483
171 7/8	26 1/8	26 1/8	20 5/8	5	5	4 6/8	4 6/8	Houston Co., MN	Donald R. Sobolik	Donald R. Sobolik	1958	2483
171 7/8	25 6/8	25 6/8	20 1/8	7	7	5 2/8	5 1/8	Aroostook Co., ME	Julian B. Perry	Julian B. Perry	1962	2483
171 7/8	25 3/8	25 3/8	18 2/8	8	7	5 1/8	4 7/8	Prairie Co., AR	C.L. Vanhouten	C.L. Vanhouten	1964	2483
171 7/8	24 6/8	24 6/8	17 2/8	7	7	4 1/8	4 2/8	Duval Co., TX	Mike Pillow	Dan Harrison	1969	2483
171 7/8	25 4/8	25 4/8	18 4/8	6	6	5 3/8	5	Union Co., IA	Darrell M. Gutz	Darrell M. Gutz	1973	2483
171 7/8	26 4/8	26 4/8	17 4/8	6	6	6	5 7/8	Menominee Co., MI	Bass Pro Shops	Karl Schwartz	1974	2483
171 7/8	26 6/8	26 6/8	21 4/8	7	6	5 5/8	5 5/8	Jackson Co., KY	Tony Mahaffey	Jessie Mahaffey	1979	2483
171 7/8	25 7/8	26 1/8	21 1/8	5	5	4 4/8	4 2/8	Oxford Co., ME	Francis Ontengco	Picked Up	1980	2483
171 7/8	25	24 4/8	20	5	5	5	5	Washington Co., OH	Thomas E. Burnette	Thomas E. Burnette	1982	2483
171 7/8	26 2/8	26 4/8	24 1/8	5	5	4 4/8	4 4/8	Scotland Co., MO	David R. Smith	David R. Smith	1984	2483
171 7/8	27 7/8	26 6/8	22 7/8	5	5	4 5/8	4 3/8	Putnam Co., IL	Robert D. Koeppel	Robert D. Koeppel	1985	2483
171 7/8	25 2/8	25 7/8	18 5/8	6	5	4 7/8	4 7/8	Lafayette Co., AR	Billy D. Bland, Jr.	Billy D. Bland, Jr.	1986	2483
171 7/8	26	26 1/8	20 3/8	6	6	5	5 1/8	Clayton Co., IA	Michael A. Roussel	Michael A. Roussel	1986	2483
171 7/8	26 5/8	27	19	6	6	4 6/8	4 6/8	Grundy Co., TN	Wilson W. Weaver	Wilson W. Weaver	1987	2483
171 7/8	27 5/8	26 6/8	21 5/8	5	5	4 3/8	4 4/8	Lucas Co., IA	Tim M. Whitlatch	Tim M. Whitlatch	1989	2483
171 7/8	24 7/8	25 5/8	21 7/8	5	5	5 1/8	5 1/8	Todd Co., MN	Del Halverson	Picked Up	1991	2483
171 7/8	24 3/8	23 4/8	18 2/8	6	6	5 2/8	5 2/8	Dunn Co., ND	Doug L. Martin	Doug L. Martin	1991	2483
171 7/8	27 7/8	27 6/8	20 5/8	5	6	4 7/8	4 7/8	Whiteside Co., IL	Ann M. Ryan	Ann M. Ryan	1991	2483
171 7/8	27 6/8	27 7/8	22 2/8	4	5	5 1/8	5 1/8	Cross Co., AR	Mark C. Taylor	Mark C. Taylor	1992	2483
171 7/8	25 5/8	24 6/8	16 5/8	6	5	4 6/8	4 6/8	Winneshiek Co., IA	Richard A. Bollman	Richard A. Bollman	1993	2483
171 7/8	29 6/8	30 3/8	21 3/8	6	5	4 5/8	4 5/8	Jones Co., IA	Michael L. First	Michael L. First	1993	2483
171 7/8	27 4/8	26 7/8	20 7/8	6	6	4 6/8	4 6/8	Jo Daviess Co., IL	Donald W. Hansen, Jr.	Donald W. Hansen, Jr.	1994	2483
171 7/8	27 4/8	28 2/8	17 7/8	5	5	4 6/8	4 6/8	Pulaski Co., AR	Charles L. Marcum, Jr.	Charles L. Marcum, Jr.	1994	2483
171 7/8	25 7/8	26 1/8	19 4/8	5	5	4 4/8	4 5/8	Portage Co., WI	Lawrence P. Wierzba	Lawrence P. Wierzba	1994	2483
171 7/8	28 1/8	28	17 7/8	5	5	5 3/8	5 2/8	Almonte, ON	Scott K. Camp	Scott K. Camp	1995	2483
171 7/8	26 3/8	25 4/8	21 3/8	5	6	5 1/8	5	Henderson Co., KY	Aaron D. Parrish	Aaron D. Parrish	1995	2483
171 7/8	26 6/8	26 7/8	19 7/8	7	5	4 7/8	5	Muhlenberg Co., KY	Creighton Spurlock	Creighton Spurlock	1995	2483
171 7/8	24 2/8	25 6/8	22 7/8	8	7	5 3/8	5 2/8	Peoria Co., IL	Richard W. Winship	Richard W. Winship	1996	2483
171 7/8	25 3/8	25 3/8	20 5/8	6	8	5 6/8	5 6/8	Meigs Co., OH	Raymond G. Golden	Raymond G. Golden	1997	2483
171 7/8	24 4/8	24 4/8	17 5/8	5	6	4 4/8	4 4/8	Maverick Co., TX	William H. Whitley	William H. Whitley	1997	2483
171 7/8	25 5/8	25 2/8	18 3/8	6	5	5	5	Romance, SK	Cameron Kirzinger	Cameron Kirzinger	1999	2483
171 7/8	27 1/8	26 7/8	19 6/8	5	6	5 5/8	5 4/8	Essex Co., MA	Michael G. Prescott	Michael G. Prescott	1999	2483

WHITETAIL DEER - TYPICAL ANTLERS
Odocoileus virginianus virginianus and certain related subspecies

Score	Length of Main Beam R	L	Inside Spread	Circumference at Smallest Place Between Burr and First Point R	L	Number of Points R	L	Locality	Hunter	Owner	Date Killed	Rank
171 7/8	26 7/8	25 5/8	19 5/8	5 3/8	5 4/8	5	6	Moniteau Co., MO	Randy Wilson	Randy Wilson	1999	2483
171 7/8	27 3/8	27 4/8	22 3/8	4 6/8	4 5/8	7	6	Caldwell Co., MO	Robert T. Lobb	Robert T. Lobb	2001	2483
171 7/8	27 7/8	27 4/8	21 1/8	4	4 1/8	5	6	Larue Co., KY	Gary Polly	Gary Polly	2001	2483
171 7/8	26 1/8	28 3/8	21 3/8	5 3/8	5 2/8	8	5	Wayne Co., IL	Donald E. Riley	Donald E. Riley	2002	2483
171 7/8	26 1/8	26 2/8	16 7/8	4 6/8	4 6/8	6	6	W. Feliciana Parish, LA	James A. Jackson	James A. Jackson	2003	2483
171 7/8	26 5/8	26 4/8	18	4 6/8	4 6/8	5	5	Niagara Co., WI	Francis H. Van Ginkel	David Watson	1945	2523
171 6/8	26	27	18 4/8	6 2/8	6 2/8	5	5	St. Louis Co., MN	Paul S. Paulson	Paul S. Paulson	1946	2523
171 6/8	25	24 6/8	22	4 6/8	4 6/8	7	6	Maverick Co., TX	Harry Garner	Harry Garner	1962	2523
171 6/8	24 6/8	24 6/8	19	5 2/8	5 1/8	5	5	Turtle Mt., MB	Roy Hainsworth	Roy Hainsworth	1963	2523
171 6/8	27 1/8	26 5/8	21 5/8	4 6/8	5 2/8	6	9	Asquith, SK	M.S. Vanin	M.S. Vanin	1963	2523
171 6/8	25 6/8	25 6/8	18 2/8	4 4/8	4 5/8	5	5	Maple Creek, SK	G.J. Burch	G.J. Burch	1967	2523
171 6/8	24 4/8	24 3/8	17 1/8	4 1/8	4 1/8	8	8	Muscatine Co., IA	Larry Dipple	Larry Dipple	1967	2523
171 6/8	26 3/8	26 1/8	20 5/8	5 6/8	5 5/8	6	6	St. Louis Co., MN	Unknown	David G. Gagnon	PR 1970	2523
171 6/8	28 4/8	27 2/8	19 3/8	5 3/8	5 3/8	4	4	Buffalo Co., WI	Richard Schultz	Richard Schultz	1973	2523
171 6/8	25 1/8	24 6/8	18 4/8	4 7/8	4 7/8	5	5	Dawes Co., NE	Tim Morava	Tim Morava	1974	2523
171 6/8	27 3/8	26 2/8	21	4 5/8	4 4/8	6	5	Adams Co., IL	R.C. Stephens	R.C. Stephens	1975	2523
171 6/8	25 5/8	25 6/8	24 1/8	5 6/8	5 6/8	6	6	Clinton Co., NY	William J. Branch	William J. Branch	1982	2523
171 6/8	26 6/8	26 3/8	19 7/8	5 3/8	5 3/8	7	10	Perry Co., IL	Daniel P. Hollenkamp	Daniel P. Hollenkamp	1982	2523
171 6/8	24 4/8	23 2/8	19 4/8	4 5/8	4 5/8	10	8	Gray Creek, BC	Ross Oliver	Ross Oliver	1982	2523
171 6/8	26 3/8	26 3/8	20 4/8	4 5/8	4 6/8	4	5	Van Buren Co., MI	Ronald E. Eldred	Ronald E. Eldred	1983	2523
171 6/8	28 3/8	29 2/8	23 7/8	6	6	8	8	Taylor Co., GA	Picked Up	Charles L. Childree	1985	2523
171 6/8	25 5/8	25 6/8	16	5 3/8	5 3/8	5	5	Peace River, AB	Austin V. Cowan, Jr.	Austin V. Cowan, Jr.	1988	2523
171 6/8	26 2/8	26	21 6/8	4 6/8	4 7/8	5	5	Garden Co., NE	Doreen R. Lawrence	Doreen R. Lawrence	1989	2523
171 6/8	24 5/8	24 7/8	19 7/8	4 7/8	5 1/8	6	6	Tunica Co., MS	Delton D. Davis	Delton D. Davis	1990	2523
171 6/8	24 6/8	23 4/8	20 6/8	4 6/8	4 6/8	5	5	Dunn Co., WI	James W. Belmore	James W. Belmore	1991	2523
171 6/8	26 5/8	25 3/8	21 6/8	5 1/8	5 1/8	6	6	Webb Co., TX	David W. Bivins	David W. Bivins	1992	2523
171 6/8	27 5/8	25 3/8	18	5 1/8	5 2/8	9	8	Miami Co., KS	Garth S. Davis	Garth S. Davis	1992	2523
171 6/8	28 1/8	29	19	5	5 2/8	7	6	Campbell Creek, AB	K. Ryan & B. Winters	Ken Ryan	1992	2523
171 6/8	28	25 4/8	19 1/8	5	5 3/8	7	9	Endeavour, SK	Jeffery A. Duckworth	Jeffery A. Duckworth	1993	2523
171 6/8	27 7/8	29 3/8	22 6/8	5 5/8	5 5/8	7	6	Hancock Co., IL	Garold E. McConnull	Garold E. McConnull	1993	2523
171 6/8	26 6/8	27 3/8	20 2/8	4 4/8	4 4/8	5	6	Telfair Co., GA	Craig Walker	Craig Walker	1993	2523
171 6/8	27 3/8	27 5/8	18 5/8	4 3/8	4 3/8	7	7	Juneau Co., WI	Thomas J. Brien	Thomas J. Brien	1994	2523
171 6/8	26 3/8	26 1/8	19 6/8	4 6/8	4 6/8	5	5	Lone Rock, SK	Keith R. Fournier	Keith R. Fournier	1994	2523
171 6/8	26 3/8	25 7/8	14 6/8	4 3/8	4 3/8	5	6	Grayson Co., KY	Jurl Huffman	Jurl Huffman	1994	2523
171 6/8	28 5/8	27 1/8	19 2/8	4 5/8	4 6/8	5	7	Washtenaw Co., MI	Richard J. Degrand	Richard J. Degrand	1995	2523
171 6/8	26 4/8	26 5/8	19	5 2/8	5 5/8	5	5	Osage Co., OK	Don Gaddis	Don Gaddis	1995	2523

Score	Length R	Length L	Inside Spread	Circ. R	Circ. L	Pts R	Pts L	Locality	Hunter	Owner	Date	Rank
171 6/8	28 1/8	28 1/8	22 1/8	5 2/8	5 1/8	6	5	Jackson Co., IA	Rodger L. Johnson	Rodger L. Johnson	1995	2523
171 6/8	28 4/8	28 4/8	24 4/8	5	5 1/8	7	9	Allamakee Co., IA	Gregg N. Klein	Gregg N. Klein	1995	2523
171 6/8	23 4/8	22 6/8	16 2/8	5 2/8	5 6/8	6	6	Grande Prairie, AB	Theodore H. Stegman	Theodore H. Stegman	1995	2523
171 6/8	27	27	16 2/8	4 3/8	4 5/8	5	5	Linn Co., IA	Picked Up	IA Dept. of Natl. Resc.	1996	2523
171 6/8	23 5/8	24 4/8	16 7/8	4 5/8	4 5/8	6	5	Chinook, AB	Ian Proudfoot	Ian Proudfoot	1996	2523
171 6/8	26 5/8	26 5/8	18 6/8	3 6/8	3 6/8	7	7	Anderson Co., KS	Gary Shields	Gary Shields	1996	2523
171 6/8	27 3/8	28	21 7/8	6 2/8	5 7/8	5	5	Hamilton Co., OH	Donald R. Johnson	Donald R. Johnson	1997	2523
171 6/8	28 6/8	28 3/8	20 4/8	4 3/8	4 3/8	8	8	S. Saskatchewan River, SK	Garry Kennon	Garry Kennon	1997	2523
171 6/8	23 6/8	24	20	5 4/8	5 4/8	5	5	Big Horn Co., WY	Thomas D. Dixon	Thomas D. Dixon	1998	2523
171 6/8	26 2/8	24 4/8	23	4 6/8	4 6/8	5	5	Tamarack Lake, MB	John L. Duncan	John L. Duncan	1998	2523
171 6/8	25 3/8	25 2/8	17 6/8	5 2/8	5 2/8	7	7	Winona Co., MN	James J. Heberlein	James J. Heberlein	1998	2523
171 6/8	26	25	16 3/8	5 3/8	5 3/8	6	8	Dakota Co., MN	Vincent A. LaCroix	Vincent A. LaCroix	1998	2523
171 6/8	25 7/8	26 2/8	19 4/8	5 6/8	5 6/8	5	5	Hart Co., KY	Paul A. Miller	Paul A. Miller	1998	2523
171 6/8	25 6/8	25 1/8	16 2/8	4 7/8	4 6/8	5	5	Dunn Co., WI	David J. Tuschl, Sr.	David J. Tuschl, Sr.	1998	2523
171 6/8	25 3/8	25 7/8	18 5/8	5 1/8	5 1/8	6	5	Cookson, SK	Bry Loyd	Bry Loyd	1999	2523
171 6/8	26 3/8	24 7/8	17 2/8	4 7/8	4 6/8	5	5	Greene Co., IN	Barry A. Stoner	Barry A. Stoner	1999	2523
171 6/8	26 5/8	26 5/8	21 6/8	4 2/8	4	5	5	Unknown	Unknown	Bill J. Timms	PR 1999	2523
171 6/8	28 2/8	27 1/8	21 1/8	5	5	6	8	Monroe Co., OH	Terry L. Bartrug	Terry L. Bartrug	2000	2523
171 6/8	25 7/8	24 7/8	20 1/8	5 6/8	6 3/8	6	10	Adams Co., OH	Larry D. Napier	Larry D. Napier	2000	2523
171 6/8	24 2/8	24 2/8	19 4/8	4 2/8	4 2/8	6	5	Throckmorton Co., TX	D. David Teague	D. David Teague	2000	2523
171 6/8	27 1/8	27 3/8	18 7/8	5 3/8	5 4/8	6	6	Kenton Co., KY	Mike White	Mike White	2000	2523
171 6/8	28 4/8	29 3/8	21 6/8	4 4/8	4 4/8	6	4	Linn Co., IA	Gerald R. Peters	Gerald R. Peters	2001	2523
171 6/8	25 2/8	23 6/8	20 2/8	4 4/8	4 4/8	6	7	Jumping Deer Creek, SK	Keegan Benko	Keegan Benko	2002	2523
171 6/8	27 1/8	27	21 4/8	5	5	5	5	Waukesha Co., WI	Ryan Bischop	Ryan Bischop	2002	2523
171 6/8	28 5/8	28	17 5/8	4 6/8	4 6/8	5	6	Scott Co., IA	Ray Garvin	Greg Garvin	2002	2523
171 6/8	28 2/8	26 5/8	20	4 4/8	4 3/8	8	7	McPherson Co., KS	Ronald R. Myers	Ronald R. Myers	2002	2523
171 5/8	25	25 5/8	16 2/8	4 3/8	4 3/8	6	6	Koochiching Co., MN	Ray W. Bastin	Ray W. Bastin	1930	2580
171 5/8	24 4/8	24 6/8	19 4/8	5	5	9	10	Morton Co., ND	Dick Eastman	Sioux Sporting Goods	1955	2580
171 5/8	23	23	19	5 2/8	5 4/8	7	6	Tensas Parish, LA	Jim Keahey	Gerald P. Begnaud, Jr.	1960	2580
171 5/8	25 6/8	26 4/8	20 6/8	5 1/8	5 1/8	6	7	Hanley, SK	L.R. Libke	L.R. Libke	1961	2580
171 5/8	26	26	24 4/8	4 7/8	4 6/8	7	8	Langbank, SK	Thomas K. Grimm	Thomas K. Grimm	1968	2580
171 5/8	26 4/8	28 4/8	20 1/8	5	4 6/8	5	6	Meeker Co., MN	Ronald E. Meeker	Ronald E. Lampi	1973	2580
171 5/8	27 2/8	27	17 6/8	4 4/8	4 6/8	6	6	Willowbrook, SK	William Hrebenik	William Hrebenik	1976	2580
171 5/8	25 1/8	26 1/8	16 7/8	4	4	6	7	Baldwin Co., GA	E. Donald Graham	Picked Up	1977	2580
171 5/8	27	25 5/8	18 2/8	5 2/8	5 2/8	6	6	Otter Tail Co., MN	Carl D. Hill	Carl D. Hill	1977	2580
171 5/8	27 5/8	27 3/8	19 3/8	4 2/8	4 1/8	6	6	Todd Co., MN	Harlan D. Hinzmann	Harlan D. Hinzmann	1978	2580
171 5/8	25 3/8	24 7/8	18 3/8	4 6/8	4 5/8	6	6	Grant Co., MN	Gary P. Kollman	Gary P. Kollman	1980	2580
171 5/8	27 3/8	27 4/8	18 3/8	5	4 6/8	6	5	Riley Co., KS	Mick McCallister	Mick McCallister	1980	2580
171 5/8	26	25 6/8	17 3/8	4 3/8	4 3/8	6	5	Crawford Co., MO	Chris Glaser	Fred Glaser	1982	2580
171 5/8	27 1/8	25 7/8	20	4 7/8	5	6	5	Pocahontas Co., IA	Larry G. Almond	Larry G. Almond	1983	2580
171 5/8	25 4/8	26 5/8	19 3/8	5 5/8	5 6/8	6	7	Bonnell Brook, NB	Steve R. McCutcheon	Steve R. McCutcheon	1984	2580
171 5/8	24 2/8	23 2/8	16 1/8	4 6/8	4 6/8	6	6	Carlton Co., MN	Charles T. Ditmarsen	Charles T. Ditmarsen	1985	2580
171 5/8	26 3/8	25 5/8	19 3/8	5 2/8	5 2/8	6	5	Logan Co., KY	Alan M. Scott	Alan M. Scott	1987	2580
171 5/8	25 5/8	24 6/8	21 6/8	4 6/8	4 6/8	6	5	Mercer Co., OH	Daniel J. Garman	Daniel J. Garman	1988	2580
171 5/8	26 3/8	26 4/8	18 3/8	5 4/8	5 5/8	8	9	Anderson Co., KY	Blaine K. Price	Blaine K. Price	1990	2580
171 5/8	23 6/8	24 1/8	19 7/8	4 7/8	4 6/8	6	6	La Salle Co., TX	Harvey N. Bouldin, Jr.	Harvey N. Bouldin, Jr.	1992	2580
171 5/8	27 3/8	27 7/8	17 3/8	4 2/8	4 2/8	5	5	Trempealeau Co., WI	Scott D. Schank	Scott D. Schank	1993	2580
171 5/8	29 2/8	28	22 1/8	5 1/8	5 2/8	7	6	Warren Co., MO	Scott Parker	Scott Parker	1994	2580

WHITETAIL DEER - TYPICAL ANTLERS
Odocoileus virginianus virginianus and certain related subspecies

Score	Length of Main Beam R	L	Inside Spread	Circumference at Smallest Place Between Burr and First Point R	L	Number of Points R	L	Locality	Hunter	Owner	Date Killed	Rank
171 5/8	26 5/8	26 7/8	18 1/8	4 2/8	4 2/8	6	5	Penobscot Co., ME	David Nadeau	David Nadeau	1995	2580
171 5/8	27 4/8	27 7/8	18 1/8	4 7/8	4 5/8	5	5	Lucas Co., IA	Picked Up	Harry Nicholson	1995	2580
171 5/8	21 7/8	25 7/8	18 3/8	5 2/8	5 2/8	5	5	Douglas Co., KS	Jerry S. Pippen	Jerry S. Pippen	1995	2580
171 5/8	25 2/8	26	22 5/8	5 5/8	5 4/8	5	5	Fremont Co., IA	Ryan T. Knapp	Ryan T. Knapp	1996	2580
171 5/8	26	27 1/8	21 6/8	4 4/8	4 7/8	6	6	Turtle Lake, SK	Andrew M. Milanowski	Andrew M. Milanowski	1996	2580
171 5/8	26 5/8	24 5/8	18 4/8	5	5 2/8	7	6	Clayton Co., IA	Chris M. Borcherding	Chris M. Borcherding	1997	2580
171 5/8	27 6/8	27 6/8	20 4/8	6 1/8	6 2/8	6	6	Pottawatomie Co., KS	Kevin P. Devader	Kevin P. Devader	1997	2580
171 5/8	26	26 5/8	19 5/8	4 6/8	4 6/8	5	5	Grundy Co., IL	Joseph A. Gray	Joseph A. Gray	1997	2580
171 5/8	23 3/8	23 6/8	15 4/8	5 2/8	5 4/8	6	6	Strasbourg, SK	Donald A. Williamson	Donald A. Williamson	1998	2580
171 5/8	26 5/8	26 6/8	17 4/8	5 2/8	5 2/8	6	5	Swan Lake, MB	John Gidney	John Gidney	1999	2580
171 5/8	28 7/8	28	20 1/8	5	5 4/8	5	5	Atchison Co., MO	Frank Hackworth	Frank Hackworth	1999	2580
171 5/8	25 5/8	27 1/8	18 5/8	5	5	5	5	Marion Co., KY	Francis M. Hutchins	Francis M. Hutchins	1999	2580
171 5/8	28 3/8	27 2/8	19 5/8	5 4/8	5 4/8	7	6	Paradise Valley, AB	Dale Luedtke	Dale Luedtke	1999	2580
171 5/8	25	25 4/8	18 5/8	4 5/8	4 3/8	7	6	Larue Co., KY	Robert L. Bachuss	Robert L. Bachuss	2000	2580
171 5/8	26 3/8	27 3/8	19 1/8	4 3/8	4 3/8	5	5	Sherburne Co., MN	Jeffrey C. Cox	Jeffrey C. Cox	2000	2580
171 5/8	23 4/8	24	24 4/8	4 4/8	4 5/8	7	5	Putnam Co., IN	Sharon K. Lepper	Sharon K. Lepper	2000	2580
171 5/8	26 7/8	26 3/8	21 7/8	5 1/8	5	5	5	Allamakee Co., IA	John E. Wood	John E. Wood	2000	2580
171 5/8	24 7/8	24 7/8	20 4/8	5 3/8	5 3/8	5	5	Todd Co., KY	Roger Cherry	Roger Cherry	2001	2580
171 5/8	27	26 6/8	18 4/8	4 5/8	4 5/8	7	7	Vermilion Co., IL	Jeff Dodd	Jeff Dodd	2001	2580
171 5/8	25 6/8	26 2/8	21 5/8	4 6/8	4 7/8	5	5	Dewitt Co., IL	William A. Steward	William A. Steward	2001	2580
171 5/8	26 5/8	24 4/8	21 4/8	4 5/8	4 4/8	7	7	Webb Co., TX	Xavier Villasenor, Jr.	Xavier Villasenor, Jr.	2001	2580
171 5/8	26 3/8	25 4/8	21 7/8	4 6/8	4 6/8	8	6	Adams Co., OH	Mark A. Garman	Mark A. Garman	2002	2580
171 5/8	25 6/8	25 6/8	19 7/8	4 6/8	4 4/8	6	6	Vinton Co., OH	Brian Huff	Brian Huff	2002	2580
171 5/8	28 4/8	28 2/8	18 7/8	5	5 1/8	5	5	Washington Co., OH	Kenneth G. Kidder	Kenneth G. Kidder	2002	2580
171 4/8	25 5/8	24	17 4/8	5 2/8	5 2/8	7	7	Wood Co., WI	Unknown	Joe Hutwagner	1918	2626
171 4/8	25 1/8	25 6/8	20 4/8	4 5/8	4 7/8	6	6	Delta Co., MI	Lawrence Charles	Bass Pro Shops	PR 1941	2626
171 4/8	24 6/8	26 1/8	19 2/8	5 2/8	5 1/8	5	5	Hayter, AB	H.D.L. Loucks	H.D.L. Loucks	1953	2626
171 4/8	26	26 3/8	21 6/8	5	4 7/8	11	6	Woodlands Dist., MB	Bill Rutherford	Bill Rutherford	1961	2626
171 4/8	26 3/8	27 2/8	23 6/8	5 6/8	5 7/8	7	9	Clay Co., MN	Clint Foslien	Clint Foslien	1965	2626
171 4/8	26	26	23 2/8	4 7/8	4 3/8	5	5	Essex Co., NY	Richard E. Johndrow	Richard E. Johndrow	1968	2626
171 4/8	24 7/8	25 2/8	22 3/8	5	5	5	6	Cass Co., NE	Alvin H. Baller	Alvin H. Baller	1971	2626
171 4/8	28 6/8	28 7/8	22 7/8	5 1/8	5 1/8	5	5	Hamilton Co., IA	Picked Up	Jerry Price	1972	2626
171 4/8	25 3/8	26 6/8	22	5 2/8	5 1/8	8	8	Lac qui Parle Co., MN	Wayne A. Hegland	Wayne A. Hegland	1977	2626
171 4/8	26	26 6/8	22 6/8	4 6/8	4 7/8	5	6	Southampton Co., VA	Sam J. Pope, Jr.	Davis-Ridley Hunt Club	1978	2626
171 4/8	25	25	18 2/8	4 6/8	4 7/8	6	6	Steele Co., MN	Craig Evans	Craig Evans	1978	2626
171 4/8	25 6/8	24 5/8	19 6/8	4 4/8	4 3/8	6	5	Clearwater Co., MN	Peter Tranby	Peter Tranby	1978	2626

Score								Locality	Hunter	Owner	Date	Rank
171 4/8	5	5	4 5/8	4 6/8	19 2/8	25 4/8	25	Cherry Co., NE	Jim R. Monnier	Jim R. Monnier	1981	2626
171 4/8	4	4	5 2/8	5 3/8	27 2/8	30 3/8	30 1/8	Union Co., KY	Wayne Gibson	Wayne Gibson	1982	2626
171 4/8	6	6	4 4/8	4 3/8	20 4/8	24 4/8	25	Rusk Co., WI	Luke Dernovsek III	Luke Dernovsek III	1983	2626
171 4/8	6	8	4 5/8	4 5/8	18 6/8	26 7/8	27 1/8	Becker Co., MN	Kraig J. Ketter	Kraig J. Ketter	1983	2626
171 4/8	6	6	5	5	21 3/8	21 7/8	24 5/8	Crooked Lake, AB	Bruce J. Ferguson	Bruce J. Ferguson	1984	2626
171 4/8	8	8	5 2/8	4 7/8	19 4/8	25 2/8	24 7/8	Latah Co., ID	Darwin L. Baker	Darwin L. Baker	1986	2626
171 4/8	6	6	4 5/8	4 4/8	20 1/8	26	26 1/8	Rocky Mt. House, AB	Lloyd Cadrain	Lloyd Cadrain	1987	2626
171 4/8	6	6	5	4 7/8	17 2/8	26 7/8	25 6/8	Unknown	Unknown	Jerry L. Johnson	PR 1987	2626
171 4/8	5	5	4 6/8	4 6/8	19 6/8	25 2/8	26 6/8	Licking Co., OH	Michael E. Fleitz	Michael E. Fleitz	1988	2626
171 4/8	5	5	4 5/8	4 6/8	23 6/8	25 5/8	25 1/8	Washtenaw Co., MI	Michael C. Lamirand	Michael C. Lamirand	1988	2626
171 4/8	6	6	5 3/8	5 2/8	17	26 7/8	26	Kankakee Co., IL	Dennis Schneider	Dennis Schneider	1988	2626
171 4/8	8	6	4 7/8	4 7/8	18	25 7/8	25 5/8	Bollinger Co., MO	Darrell L. Bostic	Darrell L. Bostic	1989	2626
171 4/8	5	6	4 5/8	4 6/8	21	27 5/8	28 2/8	Ballard Co., KY	Howard P. Gardner	Howard P. Gardner	1989	2626
171 4/8	5	5	5 3/8	5 4/8	17 6/8	27 5/8	26 7/8	Lenawee Co., MI	Robert E. Knight	Robert E. Knight	1989	2626
171 4/8	6	5	4 4/8	4 4/8	17 5/8	26 3/8	26 3/8	Clay Co., KS	Eldyn W. Peck	Eldyn W. Peck	1989	2626
171 4/8	5	5	4 5/8	4 5/8	18 6/8	25 2/8	26 4/8	Scotland Co., MO	Harry Robeson	Harry Robeson	1989	2626
171 4/8	6	6	5 1/8	5 1/8	21	24 3/8	25 3/8	Rock Island Co., IL	David Parchert	David Parchert	1990	2626
171 4/8	5	5	5 2/8	5 4/8	21 2/8	26 4/8	27	Greene Co., IN	Jason B. Anderson	Jason B. Anderson	1991	2626
171 4/8	6	6	4 5/8	4 6/8	18 4/8	24 5/8	24 1/8	Sangamon Co., IL	Michael R. Vincent	Michael R. Vincent	1991	2626
171 4/8	6	6	5 1/8	4 6/8	21 4/8	26 2/8	26 3/8	Whiteside Co., IL	William D. Kruse	William D. Kruse	1992	2626
171 4/8	6	6	5	5	22 6/8	26 6/8	27	Jasper Co., IL	Rick N. Strole	Rick N. Strole	1992	2626
171 4/8	6	5	4 6/8	5 1/8	21	26 6/8	26 7/8	Harrison Co., KY	Ronald Daugherty	Ronald Daugherty	1994	2626
171 4/8	5	5	5 1/8	4 7/8	17	23 7/8	24	Thunder Hill, SK	James R. Riddick	James R. Riddick	1994	2626
171 4/8	5	5	4 7/8	4 6/8	21 7/8	26 7/8	26 5/8	Treesbank, MB	Tom J. Gross	Tom J. Gross	1995	2626
171 4/8	9	5	4 1/8	4 1/8	21 1/8	28 1/8	28	Buffalo Pound Lake, SK	Troy E. Riche	Troy E. Riche	1995	2626
171 4/8	5	6	4 2/8	4 6/8	18 5/8	26	25 1/8	Jefferson Co., WI	Bradley J. Hering	Bradley J. Hering	1996	2626
171 4/8	6	6	4 4/8	4 6/8	20	27 4/8	28 2/8	Carlton Co., MN	Vincent A. Mullen, Sr.	Vincent A. Mullen, Sr.	1996	2626
171 4/8	6	6	4 6/8	4 5/8	25 4/8	24 6/8	25 2/8	Thickwood Hills, SK	Brian C. Sankey	Brian C. Sankey	1996	2626
171 4/8	5	5	4 4/8	4 4/8	20 6/8	28 5/8	28 1/8	Dimmit Co., TX	Kenneth P. Crawford	Kenneth P. Crawford	1997	2626
171 4/8	5	5	4 6/8	4 6/8	16 4/8	27 1/8	27 4/8	Pierceland, SK	Stacer Helton	Stacer Helton	1997	2626
171 4/8	6	6	5 6/8	5 5/8	19 1/8	26	25 3/8	Talbot Co., MD	William D. Collison	William D. Collison	1998	2626
171 4/8	5	5	5	4 7/8	21 4/8	26 1/8	25 5/8	Scott Co., IA	William H. Fahrenkrog	William H. Fahrenkrog	1998	2626
171 4/8	5	5	5 1/8	5 2/8	21	25 1/8	26	Edson, AB	Ted E. Mortimer	Ted E. Mortimer	1998	2626
171 4/8	5	6	4 3/8	4 6/8	22 2/8	27 5/8	26 2/8	Raleigh Co., WV	Omar O. Burns	Omar O. Burns	1999	2626
171 4/8	6	6	6 3/8	6 3/8	17 6/8	24 5/8	24 6/8	Tallahatchie Co., MS	Ricky Lee	Ricky Lee	1999	2626
171 4/8	5	5	4 5/8	4 5/8	22	24 7/8	24 7/8	Webb Co., TX	Willie H. Esse, Jr.	Willie H. Esse, Jr.	2000	2626
171 4/8	5	5	4 7/8	4 7/8	19	27 2/8	27 2/8	St. Croix Co., WI	Picked Up	Mike Kessler	2000	2626
171 4/8	5	5	4 1/8	4	18 2/8	25 4/8	24 4/8	Jackson Co., IA	Picked Up	Alan Andreson	2001	2626
171 4/8	7	8	4 1/8	4 1/8	18 6/8	25 5/8	26 1/8	Cumberland Co., NC	Lucas J. Hinerman	Lucas J. Hinerman	2001	2626
171 4/8	6	8	5 3/8	5 2/8	20	27 3/8	26 3/8	Wabigoon Lake, ON	James H. Trapp	James H. Trapp	2001	2626
171 4/8	5	5	5	5	19	26 6/8	27 2/8	Pike Co., OH	Terry L. Waits	Terry L. Waits	2001	2626
171 4/8	7	5	4 2/8	4 2/8	21	25 4/8	25	Red River Co., TX	Clint L. Jackson	Clint L. Jackson	2002	2626
171 4/8	5	7	4 4/8	4 4/8	17	24 7/8	24 6/8	White Co., AR	Dennis Needham	Dennis Needham	2002	2626
171 4/8	7	6	4 5/8	4 5/8	23 4/8	25 1/8	25 6/8	Jefferson Co., OH	Frank J. Rozic	Frank J. Rozic	2002	2626
171 3/8	6	5	5 5/8	5 1/8	18 3/8	25 1/8	26	Morgan Co., IN	David L. Wolford	David L. Wolford	2002	2683
171 3/8	7	8	5 1/8	4 4/8	21 5/8	26 6/8	26 5/8	Juneau Co., WI	Fay Hammersley	Fay Hammersley	1938	2683
171 3/8	7	5	4 4/8	4 4/8	17 6/8	26 3/8	26	Herkimer Co., NY	John Christie	John Christie	1957	2683
171 3/8	6	5	5 2/8	5 1/8	26 3/8	25 3/8	25 3/8	Whatshan Lake, BC	Ernest Roberts	Ernest Roberts	1957	2683

WHITETAIL DEER - TYPICAL ANTLERS

Odocoileus virginianus virginianus and certain related subspecies

Score	Length of Main Beam R	L	Inside Spread	Circumference at Smallest Place Between Burr and First Point R	L	Number of Points R	L	Locality	Hunter	Owner	Date Killed	Rank
171 3/8	31 1/8	29	16	5	5	7	9	Frio Co., TX	Leonard Van Horn	Leonard Van Horn	1962	2683
171 3/8	24 3/8	24 3/8	18 5/8	4 3/8	4 3/8	6	6	Parker Co., TX	Velton L. Ford	Velton L. Ford	1963	2683
171 3/8	26	24 1/8	15 1/8	4 3/8	4	5	6	La Salle Co., TX	Charles D. Johnson	Charles D. Johnson	1964	2683
171 3/8	22 5/8	22 4/8	18	5 3/8	5 3/8	7	6	Grenfell, SK	George DeMontigny	George DeMontigny	1965	2683
171 3/8	25 2/8	25 2/8	19 3/8	4 2/8	4 3/8	6	6	Oceana Co., MI	Delos Highland	Delos Highland	1967	2683
171 3/8	25 3/8	26 6/8	18 5/8	5 3/8	5 2/8	5	7	Forest Co., WI	Chester Cox, Jr.	Chester Cox, Jr.	1969	2683
171 3/8	22 3/8	23 1/8	14 5/8	5	5	7	6	Metaline Falls, WA	Scott Hicks	Scott Hicks	1970	2683
171 3/8	23 4/8	24 2/8	23 1/8	4 7/8	4 7/8	5	5	Kandiyohi Co., MN	Werner B. Reining	Werner B. Reining	1974	2683
171 3/8	25 2/8	24 5/8	22 5/8	5	5	7	6	Pope Co., MN	Corbin G. Corson	Corbin G. Corson	1975	2683
171 3/8	25 2/8	25 3/8	25 2/8	4 3/8	4 4/8	7	6	Bennett Co., SD	David Risse	David Risse	1975	2683
171 3/8	24 4/8	23 6/8	21 5/8	4 4/8	4 4/8	5	5	Athabasca River, AB	Ron J. Holm	Ron J. Holm	1977	2683
171 3/8	25 3/8	26 2/8	16 2/8	4 6/8	4 6/8	6	7	Pike Co., IL	John C. Shover	John C. Shover	1979	2683
171 3/8	26 1/8	26 2/8	23 2/8	5 4/8	5 5/8	5	6	Buffalo Co., WI	Donald C. Neitzel	Donald C. Neitzel	1981	2683
171 3/8	27 2/8	27 2/8	21 2/8	5	4 7/8	7	6	Boyd Co., NE	Scott A. Sperling	Scott A. Sperling	1982	2683
171 3/8	28	27 1/8	18 4/8	4 4/8	4 7/8	5	6	Kalamazoo Co., MI	Harvey B. Braden	Harvey B. Braden	1984	2683
171 3/8	25 7/8	26 3/8	21 3/8	5 1/8	5 1/8	8	10	Douglas Co., MN	Gregory A. Dropik	Gregory A. Dropik	1984	2683
171 3/8	27 2/8	28 2/8	18 1/8	4 4/8	4 4/8	5	5	Sumner Co., KS	Jeff D. Ehlers	Jeff D. Ehlers	1984	2683
171 3/8	26 7/8	26 6/8	17 7/8	4 7/8	4 6/8	8	6	Turner Co., GA	Jerry S. Cook	Jerry S. Cook	1986	2683
171 3/8	20 4/8	22	19 1/8	4 7/8	5 1/8	8	6	Webb Co., TX	Robert K. Deligans	Robert K. Deligans	1986	2683
171 3/8	23 1/8	23	18	5	5	6	5	Washington Co., MO	Jerry D. Bouse	Jerry D. Bouse	1987	2683
171 3/8	23 3/8	23 6/8	18 3/8	4 5/8	4 5/8	5	5	Stonewall Co., TX	Jay W. Knorr	Jay W. Knorr	1988	2683
171 3/8	25 1/8	25 2/8	18 7/8	4 6/8	4 6/8	5	5	Washington Co., KY	Robert F. Medley	Robert F. Medley	1988	2683
171 3/8	26 5/8	25 5/8	19 6/8	5	5	6	5	Washington Co., WI	Joseph E. Kohler	Joseph E. Kohler	1989	2683
171 3/8	27	26 6/8	21 2/8	4 3/8	4 3/8	7	7	Custer Co., NE	Larry C. Beitel	Larry C. Beitel	1990	2683
171 3/8	23 7/8	24 5/8	18 7/8	5	5 2/8	6	6	Wabamun, AB	Greg Crain	Greg Crain	1992	2683
171 3/8	24 3/8	24 7/8	21 1/8	5	4 7/8	5	5	Jersey Co., IL	Louis E. Johnson	Louis E. Johnson	1992	2683
171 3/8	26 4/8	26 6/8	18 5/8	5 3/8	5 2/8	7	7	Howard Co., MO	Derrick Powell	Derrick Powell	1992	2683
171 3/8	26 1/8	27	20 7/8	5 6/8	6	6	7	Washburn Co., WI	Dale M. Swan	Dale M. Swan	1992	2683
171 3/8	27 2/8	27 4/8	19 2/8	4 5/8	4 6/8	7	8	Madison Co., IL	Keith T. Probst	Keith T. Probst	1993	2683
171 3/8	24 6/8	24 7/8	17 1/8	4 5/8	4 6/8	6	6	Dimmit Co., TX	Robert E. Zaiglin	Robert E. Zaiglin	1993	2683
171 3/8	29 2/8	27 4/8	21 2/8	4 6/8	4 7/8	6	5	Clark Co., OH	David A. Arrington	David A. Arrington	1994	2683
171 3/8	27 2/8	27 2/8	19 5/8	5 6/8	6	7	7	Crooked Lake, SK	John Duryba	John Duryba	1994	2683
171 3/8	27 3/8	26 5/8	19 5/8	4 7/8	4 7/8	7	8	Biggar, SK	Milo N. Hanson	Milo N. Hanson	1994	2683
171 3/8	27 2/8	27 4/8	20 7/8	4 4/8	4 6/8	7	5	Labette Co., KS	Dorothea L. Ludwig	Dorothea L. Ludwig	1994	2683
171 3/8	26 6/8	26 7/8	22 5/8	4 5/8	4 5/8	5	7	Dorchester Co., MD	Mark S. Bronder	Mark S. Bronder	1995	2683
171 3/8	27	27 6/8	21 3/8	5	5	6	6	Washington Co., WI	Daniel J. Hanrahan	Daniel J. Hanrahan	1995	2683

Score	L.R	L.L	Spread	Circ. R	Circ. L	Pts R	Pts L	Locality	Hunter	Owner	Date	Rank
171 3/8	21 5/8	22 6/8	17 3/8	5	5	6	10	N. Saskatchewan River, AB	Picked Up	Dale Loosemore	1995	2683
171 3/8	27 4/8	26 2/8	20 5/8	4 7/8	5	6	5	Bayne, SK	William Matsalla	William Matsalla	1995	2683
171 3/8	24 3/8	24 4/8	17 5/8	5 1/8	5 1/8	7	5	Boundary Co., ID	Donald B. Vickaryous	Donald B. Vickaryous	1995	2683
171 3/8	27 4/8	25 5/8	19 6/8	5 3/8	5 5/8	9	5	Glaslyn, SK	Brian Huscroft	Brian Huscroft	1996	2683
171 3/8	26 3/8	25 5/8	18 3/8	4 4/8	4 4/8	5	5	Buffalo Co., WI	Dave K. Kitzman	Dave K. Kitzman	1996	2683
171 3/8	28 5/8	27 3/8	21 3/8	5 3/8	5 1/8	4	4	Oregon Co., MO	Dale Conner	Scott D. Lindsey	1996	2683
171 3/8	26 6/8	27 3/8	19 7/8	5	5	5	5	Trempealeau Co., WI	Heidi A. Daffinson	Heidi A. Daffinson	1997	2683
171 3/8	26	26 3/8	20 1/8	4 6/8	4 4/8	6	5	Monroe Co., IA	Michael L. DeMoss	Michael L. DeMoss	1997	2683
171 3/8	27 2/8	27 4/8	22 5/8	5 1/8	5 1/8	5	6	Parke Co., IN	Ronald A. Keys	Ronald A. Keys	1997	2683
171 3/8	27 2/8	27	17 7/8	4 7/8	4 7/8	5	5	Charles Co., MD	Patrick E. Langley	Patrick E. Langley	1997	2683
171 3/8	24 6/8	26 2/8	25 5/8	5 2/8	5 4/8	6	5	Wayne Co., OH	Ivan R. Schlabach	Ivan R. Schlabach	1997	2683
171 3/8	27 7/8	26 4/8	18 2/8	4 1/8	4	6	6	Nemaha Co., KS	Paul L. Steinlage	Paul L. Steinlage	1997	2683
171 3/8	24 4/8	24 2/8	17 4/8	5	5	8	6	Hamilton Twp., ON	Peter Francis	Peter Francis	1998	2683
171 3/8	27	26 7/8	20	5 7/8	6	6	5	Breathitt Co., KY	Kenneth J. Minks	Kenneth J. Minks	1998	2683
171 3/8	27 2/8	27	20 1/8	4 7/8	4 7/8	6	5	Little Manitou Lake, SK	Bruce Soderberg	Bruce Soderberg	1998	2683
171 3/8	27 4/8	27 4/8	19 3/8	5 1/8	5 1/8	5	6	Monroe Co., MO	Shelton Wheelan	Shelton Wheelan	1999	2683
171 3/8	26 2/8	26 4/8	18 1/8	4 4/8	4 3/8	6	5	Adair Co., MO	Karen White	Karen White	2000	2683
171 3/8	27 3/8	27	17 5/8	5	5	6	5	Sangamon Co., IL	James V. Holdenried	James V. Holdenried	2001	2683
171 3/8	25 7/8	25 7/8	18 1/8	4 3/8	4 7/8	5	5	Dearborn Co., IN	Nick T. Lobenstein	Nick T. Lobenstein	2001	2683
171 3/8	26	26	24 1/8	5 1/8	5 1/8	5	6	St. Francois Co., MO	Edward A. Peterson	Edward A. Peterson	2002	2683
171 3/8	25 3/8	25 6/8	28	5 2/8	5 1/8	6	5	Twin Lakes, AB	Shaun P.W. Proulx	Shaun P.W. Proulx	2002	2683
171 3/8	27 2/8	27 2/8	21 1/8	5 7/8	4 4/8	7	5	Appanoose Co., IA	Kris A. Shondel	Kris A. Shondel	2002	2683
171 3/8	27 2/8	27 2/8	19 2/8	5 4/8	5	5	6	Randolph Co., IL	James E. Mraz	James E. Mraz	2003	2683
171 3/8	28 2/8	28 3/8	21 3/8	4 4/8	5 1/8	9	8	Somerset Co., PA	Paul E. Walker	Paul E. Walker	2003	2683
171 2/8	26 6/8	26 6/8	19 4/8	5 1/8	5 1/8	8	6	Alger Co., MI	John Peterson	Bass Pro Shops	1941	2745
171 2/8	29 2/8	28 6/8	21 4/8	5	4 4/8	6	9	Arkansas Co., AR	Wilbur Stephens	Wilbur Stephens	1948	2745
171 2/8	25 6/8	25 7/8	22 4/8	5 2/8	4 6/8	5	5	Gregory Co., SD	Leonard L. Nespor	Leonard L. Nespor	1953	2745
171 2/8	25 6/8	25 6/8	19 4/8	4 6/8	5	5	6	Bayfield Co., WI	Lawrence Stumo	Lawrence Stumo	1956	2745
171 2/8	27	27	18 2/8	5	5	6	6	Waldo Co., ME	Paul K. Nickerson	Paul K. Nickerson	1956	2745
171 2/8	26 2/8	25	18	5 6/8	5 3/8	6	6	Macintosh, ON	Richard Kouhi	Richard Kouhi	1957	2745
171 2/8	25 4/8	25 4/8	16 7/8	5 1/8	5 6/8	5	5	Webb Co., TX	Ernie Pavlas	Ernie Pavlas	1967	2745
171 2/8	26 7/8	26 7/8	19 4/8	5 2/8	5 2/8	5	5	Beltrami Co., MN	Mickey Ewing	Mickey Ewing	1970	2745
171 2/8	26	26	16 6/8	5 1/8	5 5/8	6	6	Lucas Co., IA	James L. Barlow	James L. Barlow	1981	2745
171 2/8	26	26	18 6/8	5 5/8	5 1/8	7	5	Yuma Co., CO	John O. Cletcher, Jr.	John O. Cletcher, Jr.	1985	2745
171 2/8	21 1/8	21	21	5 1/8	5 4/8	5	6	Pembina Co., ND	Lee A. Einarson	Lee A. Einarson	1985	2745
171 2/8	24	23 7/8	22 4/8	5 4/8	4 2/8	5	5	Lake Co., MT	Del A. Niemeyer	Del A. Niemeyer	1985	2745
171 2/8	23 1/8	24	21 2/8	4 2/8	4 4/8	5	5	Oyen, AB	Daryl Peers	Daryl Peers	1986	2745
171 2/8	26 3/8	26 3/8	20 6/8	4 5/8	4 5/8	6	5	Randolph Co., IL	Steven R. Thompson	Steven R. Thompson	1986	2745
171 2/8	27	27	20 4/8	4 6/8	4 6/8	5	5	Ringgold Co., IA	John H. Good	John H. Good	1986	2745
171 2/8	27 4/8	27 4/8	19 1/8	5 2/8	5	6	5	Marshall Co., IA	Dale E. Smith	Dale E. Smith	1988	2745
171 2/8	26 1/8	26 1/8	18 1/8	5 7/8	5 7/8	6	5	Adams Co., IA	Gary D. Maatsch	Gary D. Maatsch	1988	2745
171 2/8	25 1/8	23 2/8	19 6/8	4 1/8	4 1/8	6	5	Missoula Co., MT	James R. Zullo	James R. Zullo	1990	2745
171 2/8	26 6/8	27 3/8	17 2/8	5 1/8	5 1/8	7	6	Henry Co., IL	Kevin P. Casteel	Kevin P. Casteel	1992	2745
171 2/8	27 5/8	27 5/8	20	5	5	6	7	Duck Lake, SK	Colin P. Laroque	Colin P. Laroque	1992	2745
171 2/8	26	26	19 5/8	4 6/8	4 6/8	6	6	Linn Co., MO	Bryan H. Mueller	Bryan H. Mueller	1992	2745
171 2/8	25	25	17 2/8	4 2/8	4 3/8	6	6	Lincoln Co., MO	F. Neil Norton	F. Neil Norton	1992	2745
171 2/8	24	23 5/8	20	5	5 1/8	5	6	Racine Co., WI	Charles Michna	Charles Michna	1993	2745
171 2/8	27 6/8	27 5/8	19 6/8	4 5/8	4 4/8	5	5	Todd Co., SD	Timothy E. Guerue	Timothy E. Guerue	1994	2745

WHITETAIL DEER - TYPICAL ANTLERS
Odocoileus virginianus virginianus and certain related subspecies

Score	Length of Main Beam		Inside Spread	Circumference at Smallest Place Between Burr and First Point		Number of Points		Locality	Hunter	Owner	Date Killed	Rank
	R	L		R	L	R	L					
171 2/8	25 5/8	26	17 2/8	4 5/8	4 5/8	5	5	Pepin Co., WI	Sharon M. Bauer	Sharon M. Bauer	1995	2745
171 2/8	25 7/8	26 7/8	18 4/8	5	5	5	5	Saline Co., MO	Jeffrey E. Edwards	Jeffrey E. Edwards	1995	2745
171 2/8	25 5/8	25 5/8	20 2/8	5	4 5/8	5	5	Bartholomew Co., IN	Gary B. Owsley	Gary B. Owsley	1995	2745
171 2/8	26 1/8	26	21	5	5 1/8	6	7	Warren Co., IL	R. Craig Akers	R. Craig Akers	1996	2745
171 2/8	25	26 3/8	20 6/8	4 4/8	4 4/8	5	5	Union Co., IA	Trevor Paulus	Trevor Paulus	1996	2745
171 2/8	27 1/8	27 3/8	20 2/8	5 4/8	5 2/8	6	5	Coshocton Co., OH	Michael H. Wills	Michael H. Wills	1996	2745
171 2/8	26 3/8	25 5/8	19 5/8	6	5 7/8	6	6	S. Saskatchewan River, SK	Cheri Boeschen	Cheri Boeschen	1997	2745
171 2/8	27 6/8	26 4/8	20 4/8	4 5/8	4 6/8	6	5	Logan Co., IL	Brian M. Laubenstein	Brian M. Laubenstein	1997	2745
171 2/8	25 6/8	24 5/8	18 2/8	5 1/8	4 7/8	5	5	Benton Co., IA	Timothy McLaud	Timothy McLaud	1997	2745
171 2/8	23 3/8	24 4/8	18 6/8	5 2/8	5	5	5	Cowan, MB	Scott P. Nigbor	Scott P. Nigbor	1998	2745
171 2/8	24 6/8	25 4/8	18	4 3/8	4 3/8	5	5	Ashtabula Co., OH	Gene E. Clemens	Gene E. Clemens	1999	2745
171 2/8	26 1/8	26 5/8	21	5 5/8	5 7/8	6	6	Green Lake Co., WI	Richard Waters	Richard Waters	1999	2745
171 2/8	24 7/8	27	19 6/8	4 2/8	4 4/8	6	6	Warren Co., MO	Billy DeCoster	Billy DeCoster	2000	2745
171 2/8	27 1/8	28 7/8	22	5 1/8	5 5/8	7	7	Madison Co., OH	Bartly D. Howerton	Bartly D. Howerton	2000	2745
171 2/8	25 4/8	25 4/8	16 6/8	4 3/8	4 3/8	6	6	Onondaga Co., NY	Kenneth L. Lamb	Kenneth L. Lamb	2000	2745
171 2/8	27 2/8	26 5/8	22 1/8	5 5/8	5 2/8	6	7	Warren Co., IA	David G.J. Milby	David G.J. Milby	2000	2745
171 2/8	27 1/8	27 6/8	20 6/8	5	5 1/8	6	8	Rainy Lake, ON	John N. Nelson	John N. Nelson	2000	2745
171 2/8	25	26 4/8	18 2/8	5 6/8	5 7/8	6	6	Meigs Co., TN	James E. Rose	James E. Rose	2000	2745
171 2/8	24 7/8	25 2/8	21 5/8	5 6/8	5 4/8	6	6	Lee Co., IA	Jim D. Wages	Doyle M. Jarrell	2001	2745
171 2/8	23 2/8	25 2/8	24 4/8	4 7/8	4 6/8	6	7	Scott Co., IA	Jeffrey R. Coonts	Jeffrey R. Coonts	2002	2745
171 2/8	23 6/8	25 1/8	21 4/8	5 5/8	5 6/8	6	5	Bulyea, SK	Fred Hansen	Fred Hansen	2002	2745
171 2/8	28 2/8	28 4/8	21	5 1/8	5 3/8	6	6	Jefferson Co., WI	Daniel J. Marks	Daniel J. Marks	2002	2745
171 1/8	24 7/8	25 3/8	21 1/8	4 6/8	4 4/8	5	7	Sanders Co., MT	William Brox	Henry C. Bennett	1948	2792
171 1/8	27 4/8	27 4/8	21 1/8	4 2/8	4 2/8	5	5	Charlevoix Co., MI	Noel Thomson	Ivan Thomson	1957	2792
171 1/8	22 6/8	21	18 5/8	5 1/8	5 2/8	6	6	Medicine Hat, AB	Frank Chevalier	Marcel Houle	1958	2792
171 1/8	24 7/8	25	20 6/8	6	6	6	5	Penobscot Co., ME	Kenneth Scott	Kenneth W. Bennett	1960	2792
171 1/8	26	26 7/8	16 7/8	5 6/8	5 6/8	5	5	Douglas Co., MN	James M. Bircher	James M. Bircher	1962	2792
171 1/8	27 2/8	27 1/8	18	4 4/8	4 4/8	8	7	Alger Co., MI	Shirley L. Robare	Shirley L. Robare	1963	2792
171 1/8	23 2/8	23 1/8	20 6/8	5	5 2/8	5	6	Whitewood, SK	W. Cook	W. Cook	1966	2792
171 1/8	27	27	20 3/8	4 7/8	4 6/8	6	6	Polk Co., WI	Harold Dau	Harold Dau	1966	2792
171 1/8	23 6/8	24 7/8	15 7/8	4	4	7	7	Jackson Co., SD	Dale Jarman	Dale Jarman	1966	2792
171 1/8	25 5/8	26 7/8	16 1/8	4 3/8	4 4/8	7	7	Menominee Co., WI	Vyron N. Dixon, Sr.	Vyron N. Dixon, Sr.	1968	2792
171 1/8	26 7/8	27	18 7/8	5	5 1/8	5	7	Lafayette Co., AR	Picked Up	John Upton	1975	2792
171 1/8	26	24 7/8	16 5/8	4 2/8	4 2/8	5	5	Koochiching Co., MN	Picked Up	Marc M. Jackson	1977	2792
171 1/8	23 4/8	23 4/8	18 3/8	7 2/8	6 3/8	5	5	Bayfield Co., WI	James A. Peters	James A. Peters	1979	2792
171 1/8	26 4/8	25 3/8	17 4/8	4 2/8	4 2/8	6	6	La Salle Co., TX	Unknown	Lex Cottle	PR 1980	2792

Score	Main Beam R	Main Beam L	Inside Spread	Circ. R	Circ. L	Pts. R	Pts. L	Locality	Hunter	Owner	Date	Rank
171 1/8	26 6/8	26 6/8	19 3/8	4 2/8	4 4/8	5	5	Unknown	Unknown	Keith Spencer	PR 1981	2792
171 1/8	23 7/8	23 5/8	17 1/8	5 6/8	5 1/8	8	8	Otter Tail Co., MN	Thomas E. Berger	Thomas E. Berger	1985	2792
171 1/8	27 2/8	27 3/8	21 5/8	5 6/8	5 4/8	4	6	Fulton Co., NY	Kenneth R. Mowrey, Jr.	Kenneth R. Mowrey, Jr.	1985	2792
171 1/8	26	25 7/8	19 2/8	4 7/8	4 7/8	5	6	Nuevo Leon, MX	Jose L. Flores	Jose L. Flores	1986	2792
171 1/8	25 5/8	25 2/8	19 5/8	5 4/8	5 5/8	6	6	Howard Brook, NB	Ralph L. Orser	Ralph L. Orser	1986	2792
171 1/8	28 5/8	26 6/8	20 1/8	5	5	6	6	Livingston Co., MO	Richard L. West	Richard L. West	1986	2792
171 1/8	25 2/8	25	17 6/8	4 7/8	5	8	5	Hubbard Co., MN	Merald D. Folkestad	Merald D. Folkestad	1987	2792
171 1/8	26 1/8	26 2/8	22 7/8	5 6/8	6 4/8	5	5	Van Buren Co., IA	Walter S. Church	Walter S. Church	1988	2792
171 1/8	25 3/8	25 2/8	20 1/8	5 2/8	5 3/8	5	7	Clark Co., OH	Lafayette Boggs III	Lafayette Boggs III	1991	2792
171 1/8	25 5/8	25 6/8	19 2/8	4 4/8	4 5/8	7	7	Pike Co., IL	Jarrod Kirk	Jarrod Kirk	1991	2792
171 1/8	25 3/8	26	21 4/8	6	5 6/8	6	6	Jersey Co., IL	Allen E. Conrad	Allen E. Conrad	1992	2792
171 1/8	26 4/8	26 3/8	20 7/8	5 7/8	5 6/8	9	9	Coffey Co., KS	Gerald L. Garrett	Gerald L. Garrett	1992	2792
171 1/8	28 1/8	27 1/8	24 6/8	6 5/8	6 2/8	7	7	Perth, ON	Robert J. Moir	Robert J. Moir	1992	2792
171 1/8	24 6/8	25 1/8	17 4/8	4 4/8	4 7/8	5	5	Flathead Co., MT	Gary Packer	Gary Packer	1992	2792
171 1/8	25 3/8	24 7/8	16 2/8	4 5/8	4 6/8	6	6	Dunn Co., WI	Jamie W. Mitlestadt	Jamie W. Mitlestadt	1993	2792
171 1/8	24 5/8	24 5/8	18 4/8	4 6/8	4 6/8	7	6	Huard Lake, SK	Garner H. Travelpiece	Garner H. Travelpiece	1994	2792
171 1/8	28 4/8	28	18 6/8	4 6/8	5 5/8	8	8	Franklin Co., ME	Michael J. Zubiate	Michael J. Zubiate	1994	2792
171 1/8	27 4/8	25 6/8	22 3/8	5 5/8	5 4/8	5	5	Buffalo Co., WI	George Clausen	George Clausen	1995	2792
171 1/8	26 5/8	27 1/8	17 3/8	4 6/8	4 4/8	5	6	Dane Co., WI	Miles Weaver	Miles Weaver	1996	2792
171 1/8	25 4/8	25 4/8	17 3/8	4 4/8	5 1/8	5	5	Scotland Co., MO	Joseph Frye	Joseph Frye	1997	2792
171 1/8	23 7/8	23 7/8	19 3/8	5 1/8	5 4/8	5	5	Ringgold Co., IA	Darren Martin	Darren Martin	1998	2792
171 1/8	25 2/8	24 6/8	18 4/8	5	5	8	7	Sauk Co., WI	David K. Zimmerman	David K. Zimmerman	1999	2792
171 1/8	26 6/8	28	21 3/8	4 5/8	4 5/8	5	5	Menominee Co., WI	Robert L. Boyd	Robert L. Boyd	2000	2792
171 1/8	25 2/8	24 7/8	19 1/8	4 3/8	4 3/8	5	6	Polk Co., WI	Jack G. Fleming	Jack G. Fleming	2000	2792
171 1/8	24 6/8	25 1/8	18 7/8	5	5 1/8	5	5	Shawano Co., WI	Leo M. McDonald	Leo M. McDonald	2000	2792
171 1/8	26 2/8	27 2/8	20 5/8	5 3/8	5 4/8	5	5	Stafford Co., KS	Michael E. Read	Michael E. Read	2000	2792
171 1/8	28 1/8	27	23 3/8	4 6/8	4 5/8	6	7	Fayette Co., IA	Gerald D. Miller	Gerald D. Miller	2001	2792
171 1/8	25 7/8	28 1/8	18 4/8	5 7/8	5 5/8	7	5	Lamar Co., AL	Richard L. Moore	Richard L. Moore	2001	2792
171 1/8	30 5/8	28 3/8	20 4/8	5 2/8	4 6/8	8	7	Kenton Co., KY	Mike White	Mike White	2001	2792
171 1/8	26	26 1/8	21 7/8	5	5 1/8	5	5	Kenton Co., KY	Jim Bezold	Jim Bezold	2002	2792
171 1/8	25 6/8	26 6/8	23 7/8	4 7/8	5 4/8	7	5	Clark Co., KS	Cullen R. Spitzer	Cullen R. Spitzer	2002	2792
171 1/8	28 6/8	28 5/8	20	5 2/8	5	5	5	Windsor Co., VT	Picked Up	Alfred A. Durkee	1935	2837
171 1/8	26 4/8	26 4/8	19 1/8	5	4 5/8	6	6	Sherwood, ND	Roy Foss	Roy Foss	1947	2837
171 1/8	27 1/8	26 3/8	19 4/8	4 4/8	4 3/8	5	5	Hampshire Co., WV	Conda L. Shanholtz	Conda L. Shanholtz	1958	2837
171 1/8	28 2/8	25 6/8	24 2/8	5 4/8	5 1/8	5	5	Brown Co., SD	Anthony B. Goldade	Anthony B. Goldade	1960	2837
171 1/8	23 5/8	26	19 2/8	5 1/8	5 2/8	6	6	Windthorst, SK	Thomas Dovell	Thomas Dovell	1961	2837
171 1/8	28 5/8	27 7/8	20 4/8	5 2/8	5 1/8	5	5	Perkins Co., SD	Ethel Schrader	Ethel Schrader	1963	2837
171 1/8	22 6/8	20 4/8	19 5/8	5 7/8	5 7/8	6	7	Antelope Co., NE	Leo M. Beelart	Leo M. Beelart	1964	2837
171 1/8	26 2/8	25 6/8	20 5/8	4 1/8	4 1/8	6	6	Buffalo Co., WI	Clarence H. Castleberg, Jr.	Clarence H. Castleberg, Jr.	1964	2837
171 1/8	26	24 4/8	19 6/8	5 2/8	5 2/8	5	5	Wabasha Co., MN	John W. Mussell	John W. Mussell	1966	2837
171 1/8	24 4/8	25 2/8	17 2/8	4 2/8	4 2/8	5	5	Ray Co., MO	Darle R. Siegel	Darle R. Siegel	1966	2837
171 1/8	24 5/8	23 6/8	21	5	5	5	5	Seven Persons, AB	Haven Lane	Haven Lane	1968	2837
171 1/8	28 1/8	26 7/8	21	4 6/8	4 6/8	8	7	Speers, SK	Charles E. Strautman	Charles E. Strautman	1969	2837
171 1/8	26 2/8	24 4/8	18 3/8	4 6/8	4 6/8	7	6	Lyman Co., SD	Art Zimbelmann	Art Zimbelmann	1973	2837
171 1/8	27	26 5/8	26 2/8	5 2/8	5 3/8	8	7	Otter Tail Co., MN	Lawrence J. Anderson	Lawrence J. Anderson	1974	2837
171 1/8	26 1/8	26 1/8	17 2/8	5 3/8	5 2/8	6	6	Pierce Co., WI	Picked Up	Roger Hines	1975	2837
171 1/8	26	26	20	4 6/8	5	5	5	Aroostook Co., ME	Roland L. Demers	Roland L. Demers	1983	2837
171 1/8	25 2/8	24	15 6/8	5 1/8	5 2/8	5	5	Christian Co., MO	Melba J. Herndon	Melba J. Herndon	1983	2837

WHITETAIL DEER - TYPICAL ANTLERS

Odocoileus virginianus virginianus and certain related subspecies

Score	Length of Main Beam R	L	Inside Spread	Circumference at Smallest Place Between Burr and First Point R	L	Number of Points R	L	Locality	Hunter	Owner	Date Killed	Rank
171	25 2/8	25 4/8	19 2/8	4 7/8	4 7/8	5	6	Okanagan Range, BC	Picked Up	Dennis A. Dorholt	1984	2837
171	28 5/8	30 4/8	22 5/8	5 2/8	5 1/8	7	4	Penobscot Co., ME	Samuel C. Hands	Samuel C. Hands	1985	2837
171	27	26 5/8	20 2/8	4 3/8	4 3/8	6	6	Delaware Co., IA	G. Covington & A. Schnitjer	Greg Covington	1986	2837
171	23 3/8	24 3/8	19	4 3/8	4 4/8	7	8	Independence Co., AR	Frankie Felton	Frankie Felton	1986	2837
171	25 7/8	26 2/8	20 2/8	5	5 1/8	7	7	Comanche Co., KS	C. Robert Jensen	C. Robert Jensen	1986	2837
171	24 3/8	23 7/8	20 6/8	5	4 4/8	6	6	Pike Co., IN	Philip L. Lemond	Philip L. Lemond	1986	2837
171	24 2/8	23 4/8	17 1/8	4 1/8	4 1/8	5	7	Boone Co., IN	Kevin L. Albert	Kevin L. Albert	1988	2837
171	26 2/8	25 4/8	21 6/8	4 4/8	4 7/8	5	5	Williamson Co., IL	Ronnie G. Fletcher	Ronnie G. Fletcher	1988	2837
171	26 2/8	25 4/8	21 4/8	5 4/8	5 4/8	5	5	Okemasis Lake, SK	Rick Galloway	Rick Galloway	1989	2837
171	25 7/8	26 2/8	19 3/8	5 1/8	5	6	5	Wabasha Co., MN	Thomas J. Mullenbach	Thomas J. Mullenbach	1989	2837
171	26	26 2/8	21 2/8	5 1/8	5 3/8	5	6	Nuevo Leon, MX	Farryl Holub	Farryl Holub	1991	2837
171	27 2/8	26 4/8	23 4/8	5 2/8	5 4/8	5	5	Davis Co., IA	Picked Up	IA Dept. of Natl. Resc.	1991	2837
171	24 6/8	25	18 6/8	4 4/8	4 5/8	6	6	Peoria Co., IL	Leslie G. Shipp	Leslie G. Shipp	1991	2837
171	24 5/8	23 7/8	20	4 7/8	4 6/8	5	4	La Porte Co., IN	Picked Up	Josh Skalka	1991	2837
171	25 2/8	24	17 2/8	5 3/8	5 2/8	6	6	Lincoln Co., KY	Clell T. Gooch, Jr.	Clell T. Gooch, Jr.	1992	2837
171	24 4/8	24 7/8	20 4/8	5 2/8	5 4/8	5	5	Livingston Co., IL	Lloyd D. Kemnetz, Jr.	Lloyd D. Kemnetz, Jr.	1992	2837
171	26 4/8	27 2/8	20 2/8	4 4/8	4 4/8	5	5	Marshall Hill, NB	Michael J. Maxwell	Michael J. Maxwell	1992	2837
171	27 5/8	27	19 2/8	4 6/8	4 6/8	7	7	Nez Perce Co., ID	Paul A. Eke	Paul A. Eke	1993	2837
171	25	25 4/8	20 3/8	4 2/8	4 2/8	5	6	Marinette Co., WI	Roger W. Gusick	Roger W. Gusick	1993	2837
171	26 1/8	25 4/8	17 2/8	4 4/8	4 5/8	5	5	Vernon Co., WI	Larry C. Hooverson	Larry C. Hooverson	1993	2837
171	25	25 2/8	18 4/8	5 7/8	5 5/8	5	5	Fisher Branch, MB	Garth J. Lagimodiere	Garth J. Lagimodiere	1993	2837
171	24 7/8	24 7/8	21 1/8	4 4/8	4 7/8	7	7	Kleberg Co., TX	Darwin D. Baucum	Darwin D. Baucum	1994	2837
171	24	24 1/8	23 2/8	4 6/8	4 6/8	5	5	Lac La Biche, AB	Ken Harris	Ken Harris	1994	2837
171	25	25	16 6/8	4 5/8	4 4/8	6	6	Clinton Co., IA	Thomas J. Straka	Thomas J. Straka	1994	2837
171	27 5/8	26 6/8	20 4/8	5 1/8	5 1/8	6	5	Somerset Co., MD	Lloyd B. Bloodsworth	Lloyd B. Bloodsworth	1995	2837
171	24	24	23 3/8	4 3/8	4 3/8	7	7	Pipestone Co., MN	Scott A. Crawford	Scott A. Crawford	1995	2837
171	29 4/8	27 7/8	26 4/8	6	6	4	6	Alexander Co., IL	Robert A. Kaufman	Robert A. Kaufman	1995	2837
171	29	29 1/8	23 5/8	4 7/8	5	5	6	Sedgwick Co., KS	John E. McMurry	John E. McMurry	1995	2837
171	26 4/8	27 1/8	22 4/8	5 1/8	5 1/8	6	5	St. Clair Co., MI	John Pierce	John Pierce	1995	2837
171	25 6/8	26	18	5 1/8	5 1/8	5	5	Blue Earth Co., MN	Robert E. Richards	Robert E. Richards	1995	2837
171	24 6/8	25 2/8	18 2/8	6 2/8	6 3/8	6	5	Crittenden Co., KY	Marshall Tennison	Marshall Tennison	1995	2837
171	25 3/8	24 3/8	18 5/8	4 4/8	4 4/8	6	6	Union Co., IA	Steven A. Wearmouth	Steven A. Wearmouth	1995	2837
171	26 5/8	26 5/8	18 4/8	3 7/8	3 7/8	5	5	Minnehaha Co., SD	Carl L. Murra	Carl L. Murra	1996	2837
171	26 5/8	25 5/8	19 1/8	5 3/8	5 4/8	7	7	Lawrence Co., IL	Picked Up	Michael E. Neikiek	1996	2837
171	27 7/8	27 5/8	18 5/8	6 1/8	6 2/8	8	6	Wadena Co., MN	Terry L. Thurstin	Terry L. Thurstin	1996	2837
171	25 5/8	26 1/8	21 2/8	5 3/8	5 2/8	8	7	Knox Co., MO	Herbert J. Wedemeier	Herbert J. Wedemeier	1997	2837

Score	Main Beam R	Main Beam L	Inside Spread	Circ. R	Circ. L	Pts R	Pts L	Locality	Hunter	Owner	Date	Rank
171	28 5/8	28	21	5	5 1/8	7	8	Palo Alto Co., IA	Paul R. Demiter	Paul R. Demiter	1998	2837
171	26 4/8	27	19	4 6/8	4 5/8	6	7	Becker Co., MN	Jeff D. Holmer	Jeff D. Holmer	1998	2837
171	25 7/8	26 2/8	19	4 6/8	4 6/8	7	6	St. Clair Co., MI	James R. Hurd, Jr.	James R. Hurd, Jr.	1998	2837
171	25 5/8	26	20 4/8	4 5/8	4 4/8	6	6	Washington Co., ME	William S. Lawrence	William S. Lawrence	1998	2837
171	28 2/8	28 7/8	22 4/8	4 7/8	4 6/8	6	4	Clark Co., OH	Louis J. Graham	Louis J. Graham	1999	2837
171	24 2/8	23 7/8	17 6/8	4 1/8	4	6	7	Gooseberry Lake, SK	Terry R. McGillicky	Terry R. McGillicky	1999	2837
171	26 2/8	26 6/8	16 5/8	4 6/8	4 5/8	7	7	Callaway Co., MO	Jeff M. Sumpter	Jeff M. Sumpter	1999	2837
171	25 2/8	25 3/8	17 2/8	5 2/8	5	5	8	Bulyea, SK	Tracy K. Hubick	Tracy K. Hubick	2000	2837
171	27 1/8	27	19 2/8	4 5/8	4 5/8	5	6	Maverick Co., TX	William A. Jordan III	William A. Jordan III	2001	2837
171	26 4/8	26 4/8	20	4 6/8	4 6/8	5	6	Albemarle, VA	Eddie W. Snow	Eddie W. Snow	2001	2837
171	26 4/8	29 5/8	19 6/8	4 4/8	4 4/8	5	7	Casey Co., KY	Larry Haggard	Larry Haggard	2002	2837
171	25 1/8	25 1/8	18 4/8	6 3/8	5 7/8	5	5	Queenie Creek, AB	Barton F. Toporowski	Barton F. Toporowski	2002	2837
171	24 6/8	25 1/8	21	4 1/8	4 1/8	5	5	Lake of the Rivers, SK	Bryan Bogdan	Bryan Bogdan	2003	2837
170 7/8	29	29	20 1/8	4 6/8	4 4/8	8	3	Marinette Co., WI	Charles Rader	Thomas W. Goddard	1909	2903
170 7/8	28 1/8	27 1/8	19 2/8	5	5	4	5	Issaquena Co., MS	Warren A. Miller	Alford M. Cooley	1920	2903
170 7/8	26 3/8	26	21 5/8	5 2/8	5 3/8	6	5	Cass Co., MN	Orland Weekley	George W. Flaim	1929	2903
170 7/8	26 4/8	25 7/8	17 6/8	5	5	7	7	Frio Co., TX	Lex Stewart	Lex Stewart	1930	2903
170 7/8	24 5/8	24 3/8	16 6/8	5 4/8	5 4/8	5	5	Delta Co., MI	Jim Lawson	Mary J. Wellman	1939	2903
170 7/8	26 2/8	25 7/8	19 1/8	4 6/8	4 6/8	5	5	Bath Co., VA	Maurice Smith	Maurice Smith	1953	2903
170 7/8	27 1/8	26 3/8	20 3/8	4 1/8	4	7	5	Bayfield Co., WI	John Kavajecz	John Kavajecz	1964	2903
170 7/8	26 3/8	27 1/8	20 4/8	5 1/8	5	7	5	Beltrami Co., MN	Kenneth Slechta	Kenneth Slechta	1965	2903
170 7/8	30	30	20 2/8	5	5	8	5	Des Moines Co., IA	Craig A. Field	Craig A. Field	1967	2903
170 7/8	30 4/8	26 7/8	22 4/8	4 1/8	4 3/8	7	7	Texas	Unknown	Larry Bollier	PR 1970	2903
170 7/8	26	27 4/8	21 1/8	5 2/8	5 6/8	5	5	Kingman, AB	Robert D. Kozack	Robert D. Kozack	1971	2903
170 7/8	27 4/8	27 1/8	21 2/8	5 2/8	5 2/8	7	5	Holmes Co., OH	Ken Taylor	Ken Taylor	1975	2903
170 7/8	26 7/8	24 5/8	18 3/8	5 7/8	5 6/8	7	3	Tippecanoe Co., IN	Harold A. Anthrop	Harold A. Anthrop	1976	2903
170 7/8	25 3/8	27	23 1/8	5	4 7/8	6	5	Steuben Co., NY	Duane L. Horton	Duane L. Horton	1976	2903
170 7/8	27	26 5/8	17 5/8	5	5	5	5	McDonald Lake, NS	Frederick Zwarum	Frederick Zwarum	1976	2903
170 7/8	25 2/8	25 4/8	17 7/8	4 1/8	4 2/8	6	5	Sherburne Co., MN	Merlin F. Kittelson	Merlin F. Kittelson	1977	2903
170 7/8	26	25 5/8	17 5/8	5 4/8	5 4/8	5	5	Washington Co., ME	Merle G. Michaud	Merle G. Michaud	1979	2903
170 7/8	26 4/8	25 7/8	22	5 1/8	5 1/8	7	7	Henry Co., IA	Lewis E. Dallmeyer	Lewis E. Dallmeyer	1981	2903
170 7/8	28 5/8	26 5/8	22 2/8	5 2/8	5 2/8	6	3	Warren Co., IA	Gary L. Johnson	Gary L. Johnson	1981	2903
170 7/8	26 2/8	24 6/8	22 5/8	5 7/8	5 7/8	7	6	Burleigh Co., ND	Ronald C. Wagner	Ronald C. Wagner	1982	2903
170 7/8	26 4/8	29 3/8	21 5/8	4 2/8	6 3/8	5	4	Shelby Co., IL	Paul C. Marley, Sr.	Paul C. Marley, Sr.	1985	2903
170 7/8	24	30 2/8	24 7/8	4 5/8	4 2/8	5	5	Alexander Co., IL	Kenneth L. Karhliker	Kenneth L. Karhliker	1986	2903
170 7/8	25 7/8	26	16 3/8	4 5/8	4 5/8	8	7	Grundy Co., MO	Bill Zang	Bill Zang	1986	2903
170 7/8	27 4/8	28 4/8	21 4/8	5	4 7/8	7	6	Leavenworth Co., KS	Jacob W. Dragieff	Jacob W. Dragieff	1987	2903
170 7/8	28 1/8	23 5/8	18 7/8	4 6/8	4 6/8	6	6	Polk Co., WI	Timothy J. Droher	Timothy J. Droher	1988	2903
170 7/8	25 2/8	26 3/8	17 3/8	4 3/8	4 3/8	6	5	Crawford Co., WI	Dale M. Hanson	Dale M. Hanson	1988	2903
170 7/8	26	25 5/8	21 1/8	4 2/8	4 2/8	6	6	Eau Claire Co., WI	John F. Prissel	John F. Prissel	1988	2903
170 7/8	26 4/8	25 7/8	17 1/8	5 2/8	5 2/8	5	5	Houston Co., MN	Tony S. Rostad	Tony S. Rostad	1988	2903
170 7/8	28 5/8	28 6/8	26 2/8	5 3/8	5 3/8	5	6	Jackson Co., IA	Clarence E. Gartman	Clarence E. Gartman	1989	2903
170 7/8	26 2/8	26 2/8	18 6/8	5 2/8	5 2/8	6	5	Lamont, AB	Allen C. Johnston	Allen C. Johnston	1989	2903
170 7/8	26 4/8	25 7/8	19 2/8	5 1/8	5 1/8	5	5	Monona Co., IA	Byron S. Mesenbrink	Byron S. Mesenbrink	1989	2903
170 7/8	24	25 6/8	20 1/8	4 7/8	4 7/8	6	7	Knox Co., IL	Carl A. Swanson	Carl A. Swanson	1990	2903
170 7/8	25 7/8	26 1/8	16 6/8	4 3/8	4 4/8	6	6	Monroe Co., AR	William E. Bartlett	William E. Bartlett	1990	2903
170 7/8	27 4/8	26 5/8	21 5/8	5	5	5	6	Wapello Co., IA	Ray L. Schafer	Ray L. Schafer	1991	2903
170 7/8	28 1/8	27	21 5/8	4 7/8	4 6/8	8	5	Polk Co., WI	Dennis R. Measner	Dennis R. Measner	1991	2903

Odocoileus virginianus virginianus and certain related subspecies

Score	Length of Main Beam R	L	Inside Spread	Circ. at Smallest Place Between Burr and First Point R	L	Number of Points R	L	Locality	Hunter	Owner	Date Killed	Rank
170 7/8	26 1/8	25 6/8	20 7/8	4 5/8	4 5/8	7	5	Sumner Co., KS	Hiram Tucker, Jr.	Hiram Tucker, Jr.	1992	2903
170 7/8	26 3/8	26 5/8	20 5/8	4 6/8	4 6/8	5	5	Des Moines Co., IA	Timothy Verhey	Timothy Verhey	1992	2903
170 7/8	24	23 6/8	17 7/8	5 3/8	5 2/8	5	5	Jones Creek, SK	Andre Verville	Andre Verville	1992	2903
170 7/8	24 5/8	24 7/8	19 1/8	5	4 7/8	6	6	Christian Co., KY	Nicholas J. Gresham	Nicholas J. Gresham	1993	2903
170 7/8	26 4/8	27 7/8	19 1/8	4 3/8	4 4/8	6	6	St. Clair Co., IL	Donald F. Mehrtens	Donald F. Mehrtens	1993	2903
170 7/8	25 5/8	25 7/8	21 5/8	5 2/8	5 1/8	5	5	Wabasha Co., MN	Terry P. Ryan	Terry P. Ryan	1993	2903
170 7/8	26 1/8	23 5/8	21 1/8	5 4/8	5 1/8	5	6	Van Buren Co., MI	Donald J. Hamilton, Jr.	Donald J. Hamilton, Jr.	1994	2903
170 7/8	26	26	17 3/8	5 2/8	5	6	6	Vinton Co., OH	Mark Nusbaum	Mark Nusbaum	1994	2903
170 7/8	25 4/8	25 4/8	23 5/8	4 5/8	4 4/8	5	5	Price Co., WI	David A. Pritzl	David A. Pritzl	1994	2903
170 7/8	24 4/8	24 5/8	21 1/8	5	5	5	5	Ostenfeld, MB	Karl E. Mistelbacher	Karl E. Mistelbacher	1995	2903
170 7/8	27 3/8	27 6/8	19 5/8	4 4/8	4 3/8	6	7	Montgomery Co., OH	Lee H. White	Lee H. White	1995	2903
170 7/8	28 7/8	27 4/8	25 1/8	4 7/8	4 5/8	5	5	Charles Co., MD	Richard L. Albright	Richard L. Albright	1997	2903
170 7/8	27 5/8	28 1/8	21 3/8	5	4 7/8	6	6	Dane Co., WI	Alison J. Baake	Alison J. Baake	1997	2903
170 7/8	25 1/8	25 3/8	21 1/8	5 1/8	5 2/8	5	5	Hamilton Co., NE	Clint J. Ochsner	Clint J. Ochsner	1997	2903
170 7/8	25 5/8	26	22 5/8	4 6/8	4 6/8	6	5	Worth Co., MO	Duane Hostikka	Duane Hostikka	1998	2903
170 7/8	23 3/8	23 3/8	18 1/8	5	5	7	6	Shelby Co., IL	Robert A. Howell	Robert A. Howell	1998	2903
170 7/8	26 7/8	26 3/8	19 7/8	4 7/8	4 7/8	5	5	Parry Sound, ON	Gary Jackson	Gary Jackson	1998	2903
170 7/8	25 3/8	25 4/8	19 4/8	4 6/8	4 6/8	5	5	Loon Lake, SK	James D. Schatz	James D. Schatz	1998	2903
170 7/8	24	24 3/8	15 5/8	4 4/8	4 5/8	6	6	Spencer Co., IN	Jamie L. Waninger	Jamie L. Waninger	1999	2903
170 7/8	25	25 5/8	18 6/8	5 6/8	5 5/8	6	5	Porcupine Plain, SK	Edward H. Marinelli	Edward H. Marinelli	2000	2903
170 7/8	24 5/8	24 4/8	22	5 1/8	5	7	6	Qu'Appelle River, SK	Mel Tuck	Mel Tuck	2000	2903
170 7/8	27 4/8	26 4/8	22 5/8	5	5	5	7	Boyle Co., KY	Wilburn Turner	Wilburn Turner	2000	2903
170 7/8	23 4/8	21 6/8	16 3/8	5 2/8	5 3/8	6	8	Timeu Creek, AB	Tom A. Wong	Tom A. Wong	2000	2903
170 7/8	26 5/8	27 4/8	22 3/8	6 3/8	6 5/8	5	4	Lewis Co., KY	Phillip R. Hall	Phillip R. Hall	2001	2903
170 7/8	26 3/8	26 5/8	21	4 6/8	4 6/8	5	7	Perry Co., OH	Ron D. Nash	Ron D. Nash	2001	2903
170 7/8	25 7/8	25 4/8	20 6/8	5	5 2/8	6	7	Pierce Co., WI	Donald G. Frandrup	Donald G. Frandrup	2002	2903
170 7/8	26 6/8	26 3/8	18 3/8	4 7/8	5	6	6	Oakland Co., MI	Rick L. Holderbaum	Rick L. Holderbaum	2002	2903
170 7/8	23 7/8	25 6/8	19 2/8	4 7/8	5 4/8	5	5	Spink Co., SD	William D. Mitchell	William D. Mitchell	2002	2903
170 6/8	28 4/8	28 1/8	24 6/8	4 2/8	4 1/8	6	8	Zapata Co., TX	G.O. Elliff	Michael Elliff	1926	2966
170 6/8	27	26 2/8	18	4 4/8	4 3/8	6	5	Eau Claire Co., WI	Kenneth W. Kling	Mrs. Kenneth W. Kling	1938	2966
170 6/8	24 6/8	23 4/8	19 2/8	5 6/8	6 5/8	5	5	Aitkin Co., MN	Unknown	George W. Flaim	PR 1947	2966
170 6/8	28 6/8	28 4/8	27 1/8	5 2/8	4 7/8	6	6	Shoshone Co., ID	Clarence Hagerman	Robert D. Myers	1947	2966
170 6/8	26 3/8	27 2/8	19 4/8	4 4/8	4 5/8	6	6	Kasshabog Lake, ON	Clarence Holdcroft	Jim Holdcroft	PR 1948	2966
170 6/8	25 6/8	26 7/8	19 1/8	4 6/8	4 5/8	6	6	Bayfield Co., WI	Sigurd A. Sandstrom	Sigurd A. Sandstrom	1955	2966
170 6/8	26	26	21	5 4/8	5 2/8	5	5	Dimmit Co., TX	J.H. Hixon	J.H. Hixon	1958	2966
170 6/8	25 2/8	24 2/8	24 2/8	4 5/8	4 6/8	6	5	Elbow, SK	W.H. Crossman	W.H. Crossman	1959	2966

Score	L. Main Beam R	L. Main Beam L	Inside Spread	Circ. R	Circ. L	Pts R	Pts L	Locality	Hunter	Owner	Date	Rank
170 6/8	25 3/8	25 1/8	19 4/8	5 3/8	5 3/8	7	6	Gerald, SK	Jerry Norek	Jerry Norek	1959	2966
170 6/8	27 4/8	26 4/8	18	5	5 2/8	6	7	Chicot Co., AR	Mrs. L.M. Hamilton	Mrs. L.M. Hamilton	1960	2966
170 6/8	24	24	21 2/8	4 6/8	5 1/8	6	6	Arnes, MB	T. Litwin	T. Litwin	1963	2966
170 6/8	25 7/8	25 3/8	16 4/8	4 7/8	4 4/8	5	5	Union Co., AR	Chester New	Chester New	1968	2966
170 6/8	24 6/8	25 6/8	19	4 6/8	4 5/8	5	5	Guysborough Co., NS	Roy B. Simpson	Roy B. Simpson	1968	2966
170 6/8	25 7/8	25 6/8	20	4 2/8	4 6/8	5	5	Carroll Co., MD	Wes McKenzie	Wes McKenzie	1971	2966
170 6/8	27 2/8	27 1/8	18 4/8	5 3/8	4 4/8	6	6	Kent Co., MD	Thomas C. Duff, Jr.	Thomas C. Duff, Jr.	1973	2966
170 6/8	28	28	21 3/8	4 4/8	5 3/8	6	5	Penobscot Co., ME	William Stratton	William Stratton	1974	2966
170 6/8	27 7/8	26 4/8	20	4 7/8	4 4/8	5	6	Howell Co., MO	Roy W. Woodson	Roy W. Woodson	1974	2966
170 6/8	26	26 1/8	19 2/8	4 6/8	5	5	5	Seneca Co., OH	Cheyenne Bloom	Cheyenne Bloom	1980	2966
170 6/8	23 7/8	23 4/8	19 2/8	4 6/8	4 6/8	5	5	Winn Parish, LA	William C. Erwin	William C. Erwin	1980	2966
170 6/8	24 4/8	24 1/8	16 4/8	4	4	7	7	Harris Co., GA	Gorman S. Riley	Gorman S. Riley	1983	2966
170 6/8	23 3/8	23 6/8	19 5/8	5	4 6/8	5	5	Great Sand Hills, SK	Ralph L. Cervo	Ralph L. Cervo	1984	2966
170 6/8	26 2/8	25 6/8	19	5 1/8	5 1/8	6	6	Coles Co., IL	Jeff D. Shrader	Jeff D. Shrader	1990	2966
170 6/8	23 3/8	23 3/8	18	4 1/8	4 1/8	6	6	Chisago Co., MN	Gary Thomas	Gary Thomas	1990	2966
170 6/8	24 5/8	23 5/8	14 6/8	4 3/8	4 3/8	7	7	Jackson Co., MI	Richard J. Galicki	Richard J. Galicki	1991	2966
170 6/8	25 1/8	25 1/8	20	4 7/8	4 7/8	6	6	Richland Co., OH	Curt McBride	Curt McBride	1991	2966
170 6/8	28 5/8	29 1/8	20 4/8	5 2/8	5 2/8	5	5	Laurens Co., GA	Darrell Evans	Darrell Evans	1992	2966
170 6/8	27 3/8	29 3/8	28 7/8	5	5	6	6	Calling Lake, AB	Fred J. Rein	Fred J. Rein	1993	2966
170 6/8	26 4/8	26 1/8	21 4/8	4 3/8	4 4/8	5	5	Natchitoches Parish, LA	Randy K. Ward	Randy K. Ward	1993	2966
170 6/8	27 4/8	26 7/8	18 5/8	4 7/8	4 7/8	6	6	Putnam Co., IN	Mark L. Goodpaster	Mark L. Goodpaster	1995	2966
170 6/8	28 4/8	26 7/8	18 7/8	4 3/8	4 3/8	5	5	Tazewell Co., IL	Steve R. Larimore	Steve R. Larimore	1995	2966
170 6/8	28 2/8	26 3/8	19 2/8	4 7/8	5 5/8	6	5	Saskatchewan	Unknown	James B. Sisco III	PR 1995	2966
170 6/8	25 7/8	24 6/8	24 4/8	5 5/8	4 6/8	5	5	Kenedy Co., TX	John A. Cardwell	John A. Cardwell	1996	2966
170 6/8	25 4/8	24 7/8	18 6/8	4 6/8	4 6/8	5	7	Derwent, AB	Vincent D. Charchun	Vincent D. Charchun	1996	2966
170 6/8	28 6/8	28 2/8	19 2/8	4 5/8	4 6/8	6	6	Phelps Co., MO	Dave Gabel	Dave Gabel	1996	2966
170 6/8	30	29	25 6/8	5 2/8	5 2/8	4	4	Grant Co., WI	Randall J. Ertz	Randall J. Ertz	1997	2966
170 6/8	26	25	19 6/8	5 4/8	5 4/8	5	5	Montgomery Co., IA	Steve Philby	Steve Philby	1997	2966
170 6/8	26 4/8	25 7/8	20 7/8	4 6/8	4 7/8	6	6	Sullivan Co., MO	Rodney A. Raley	Rodney A. Raley	1997	2966
170 6/8	27 1/8	27 3/8	18 6/8	5 4/8	5 4/8	5	5	Adams Co., IL	Steven A. Schwartz	Steven A. Schwartz	1997	2966
170 6/8	27	25 3/8	20 4/8	5 1/8	5 1/8	5	5	Rock Co., WI	Dan Davis	Dan Davis	1998	2966
170 6/8	26 5/8	26 6/8	18	4 6/8	5	6	7	Waukesha Co., WI	Jonathan A. Denk	Jonathan A. Denk	1998	2966
170 6/8	22 7/8	21 7/8	17	4 4/8	4 4/8	6	6	Waskesiu Lake, SK	Edwin W. Ehler	Edwin W. Ehler	1999	2966
170 6/8	25 3/8	24 2/8	19 6/8	5 6/8	5 3/8	5	5	Columbia Co., WI	Robert J. Kau	Robert J. Kau	1999	2966
170 6/8	23	22 4/8	17 5/8	5 5/8	6 1/8	6	5	Isle of Wight Co., VA	Picked Up	David A. Reece	1999	2966
170 6/8	26 1/8	26	18 2/8	4 7/8	4 7/8	5	5	Moore Co., NC	Jason A. Cole	Jason A. Cole	2000	2966
170 6/8	29 4/8	29 7/8	27 7/8	4 6/8	4 5/8	6	6	Hart Co., KY	Darryl L. Shelby	Darryl L. Shelby	2000	2966
170 6/8	23 4/8	23 4/8	18	5	4 4/8	7	6	Torch River, SK	William H. Worley, Jr.	William H. Worley, Jr.	2001	2966
170 6/8	25 3/8	24 3/8	20 2/8	4 6/8	4 5/8	6	5	Labette Co., KS	Stefan S. Smith	Stefan S. Smith	2001	2966
170 6/8	28	25 7/8	20 6/8	4 5/8	4 4/8	6	6	Greene Co., IN	Jesse D. Yeryar	Jesse D. Smith	2002	2966
170 6/8	26 5/8	23 5/8	18 4/8	4 4/8	5 1/8	6	6	Franklin Co., MO	Daryl J. Klekamp	Daryl J. Klekamp		2966
170 6/8	23 6/8	24 3/8	17 5/8	5 1/8	4 5/8	6	6	Kinney Co., TX	Don T. Barksdale	Marshall E. Kuykendall	1925	2966
170 5/8	25 3/8	21 7/8	20 5/8	4 5/8	5 2/8	10	10	Pennington Co., SD	Glen Wilson	Dick Rossum	1948	3015
170 5/8	21 5/8	27 2/8	15 3/8	5 3/8	4 6/8	6	6	Allegan Co., MI	William Caywood	William Caywood	1959	3015
170 5/8	27 2/8	25 5/8	20 4/8	5 2/8	5 3/8	8	8	Sawyer Co., WI	Virgil A. Scanlon	Virgil A. Scanlon	1960	3015
170 5/8	25 5/8	26 5/8	18 3/8	4 6/8	4 6/8	6	6	Lake Co., MN	Unknown	George W. Flaim	1961	3015
170 5/8	26 1/8	27 1/8	19 3/8	4 5/8	5	6	6	Jasper Co., GA	Gordon W. Cown	Gordon W. Cown	1962	3015
170 5/8	23 2/8	23 2/8	17 7/8	5	4 7/8	5	5	St. Charles Co., MO	Oscar Mallinckrodt	Oscar Mallinckrodt		3015

WHITETAIL DEER - TYPICAL ANTLERS
Odocoileus virginianus virginianus and certain related subspecies

Score	Length of Main Beam		Inside Spread	Circumference at Smallest Place Between Burr and First Point		Number of Points		Locality	Hunter	Owner	Date Killed	Rank
	R	L		R	L	R	L					
170 5/8	27 5/8	26 5/8	19 3/8	4 6/8	4 6/8	7	7	Douglas Co., WI	George Pettingill	George Pettingill	1963	3015
170 5/8	25 2/8	26 1/8	18 5/8	5	5 1/8	5	5	Wawota, SK	Benjamin F. Kregel	Benjamin F. Kregel	1965	3015
170 5/8	27 2/8	27 2/8	21 6/8	5 4/8	5 2/8	5	7	Sherburne Co., MN	Sylvester Zormeier	Sylvester Zormeier	1967	3015
170 5/8	26 6/8	27 2/8	18 3/8	5 4/8	5 4/8	6	8	Price Co., WI	Nyle H. Rodman	Nyle H. Rodman	1970	3015
170 5/8	26 2/8	26 2/8	18 1/8	4 3/8	4 3/8	6	6	Shannon Co., MO	Garry Bland	Garry Bland	1971	3015
170 5/8	26 1/8	25 4/8	19 3/8	4 2/8	4 2/8	5	6	Boyd Co., NE	Leonard Reiser	Leonard Reiser	1973	3015
170 5/8	28 1/8	27 1/8	24 5/8	5 2/8	5 1/8	6	7	Cedar Co., IA	Robert G. Grunder	Robert G. Grunder	1974	3015
170 5/8	29 3/8	29 4/8	21	4 6/8	4 6/8	5	6	Christian Co., KY	Henry J. Oliver	Henry J. Oliver	1978	3015
170 5/8	27	26 7/8	19 5/8	5	5 1/8	5	5	St. Louis Co., MN	Unknown	George W. Flaim	PR 1979	3015
170 5/8	26 2/8	26 6/8	20 5/8	5	5	5	5	Clayton Co., IA	Todd A. Moon	Todd A. Moon	1979	3015
170 5/8	24 3/8	26 4/8	17 3/8	5 1/8	4 7/8	5	5	St. Mary's Co., MD	Brian M. Boteler	Brian M. Boteler	1980	3015
170 5/8	26 7/8	25 4/8	18 2/8	5 4/8	5 2/8	5	5	Atchison Co., MO	Roy E. Munsey	Roy E. Munsey	1980	3015
170 5/8	25 5/8	26	20 3/8	4 4/8	4 5/8	6	6	Berrien Co., MI	G. Steven Abdoe	G. Steven Abdoe	1982	3015
170 5/8	28 7/8	28 2/8	19 5/8	4 6/8	4 6/8	7	7	Lowndes Co., GA	Jack L. Garrison	Jack L. Garrison	1983	3015
170 5/8	26 5/8	27 2/8	21	6	5 3/8	6	7	Lyon Co., KS	Bill D. Hollond	Bill D. Hollond	1984	3015
170 5/8	22 4/8	24 6/8	16 6/8	4 6/8	4 6/8	7	7	Webster Parish, LA	Henry G. Gregory	Henry G. Gregory	1985	3015
170 5/8	25 2/8	27 1/8	16	4 7/8	4 7/8	7	6	Big Stone Co., MN	Jeffrey A. Thielke	Jeffrey A. Thielke	1985	3015
170 5/8	24 1/8	24 6/8	16 7/8	4 5/8	4 5/8	5	5	Kings Co., NB	Allen A. MacDonald	Allen A. MacDonald	1986	3015
170 5/8	25 2/8	26 6/8	20 2/8	6	5 7/8	7	6	Prowers Co., CO	Douglas W. Kuhns	Douglas W. Kuhns	1987	3015
170 5/8	24 6/8	25 1/8	20 6/8	4 5/8	4 4/8	7	8	Henry Co., IA	Michael S. Mathews	Michael S. Mathews	1988	3015
170 5/8	27 3/8	27 7/8	18 5/8	5 4/8	5 4/8	5	6	Grundy Co., MO	Michael C. Weathers	Michael C. Weathers	1988	3015
170 5/8	27 6/8	29 4/8	23 3/8	5 4/8	5 3/8	7	8	Sawyer Co., WI	Thorvald Skar	James M. Skar	PR 1990	3015
170 5/8	28 1/8	28 4/8	23 3/8	5 6/8	5 5/8	4	5	Polk Co., MN	D. Keith Thunem, Jr.	D. Keith Thunem, Jr.	1990	3015
170 5/8	26 2/8	26 5/8	18	4 6/8	4 7/8	5	8	Mervin, SK	Terry Brett	Terry Brett	1991	3015
170 5/8	24 2/8	24 3/8	17 4/8	5 4/8	5 4/8	6	6	Rocky Mt. House, AB	Robin L. McDonald	Robin L. McDonald	1991	3015
170 5/8	24 2/8	23 6/8	23 3/8	3 7/8	3 7/8	6	5	Crook Co., WY	Rick Shannon	Rick Shannon	1991	3015
170 5/8	26	25	20 2/8	4 7/8	4 7/8	6	6	Lee Co., GA	Stan R. Steiner	Stan R. Steiner	1991	3015
170 5/8	24 6/8	25 3/8	19 4/8	5 5/8	5 5/8	6	7	Aroostook Co., ME	Douglas P. Legasse	Douglas P. Legasse	1993	3015
170 5/8	26 4/8	27 2/8	17 3/8	5 4/8	5 2/8	7	7	Spokane Co., WA	Laura M. Kaiser	Laura M. Kaiser	1994	3015
170 5/8	25 5/8	25 1/8	17 6/8	5 6/8	5 5/8	7	7	St. Anne Lake, AB	Allen T. Carstairs	Allen T. Carstairs	1995	3015
170 5/8	26 7/8	25 7/8	18 5/8	5 1/8	5 1/8	6	6	Warren Co., IA	Martin L. Gehringer	Martin L. Gehringer	1995	3015
170 5/8	27 4/8	27 7/8	22	5 2/8	5 1/8	8	7	Eagle Creek, SK	Perry Haanen	Perry Haanen	1995	3015
170 5/8	25 1/8	25 7/8	21 2/8	5 5/8	5 5/8	5	7	Melfort, SK	Dave Parfitt	Dave Parfitt	1995	3015
170 5/8	26 4/8	25 3/8	18 2/8	6	5 6/8	6	6	Spruce Lake, SK	Shawn Bleakney	Shawn Bleakney	1996	3015
170 5/8	26 2/8	27 6/8	23 6/8	5 2/8	5 1/8	8	6	Paddle River, AB	Dwayne C. Moore	Dwayne C. Moore	1997	3015
170 5/8	24 2/8	25 3/8	17 3/8	4 5/8	4 5/8	6	6	Washington Co., ME	David Shaffner	David Shaffner	1997	3015

Score	Main Beam R	Main Beam L	Inside Spread	Circ. R	Circ. L	Pts R	Pts L	Locality	Hunter	Owner	Date	Rank
170 5/8	26 6/8	27 5/8	20 1/8	5 3/8	5 3/8	6	5	Williamsburg Co., SC	A. Hugh Gaskins	A. Hugh Gaskins	1998	3015
170 5/8	27 7/8	26 4/8	19 3/8	5	5 5/8	5	5	Highland Co., OH	Harold D. Jewett	Harold D. Jewett	1998	3015
170 5/8	29	27 4/8	21 1/8	5 1/8	5 1/8	5	5	Adams Co., IL	Randy J. Kurz	Randy J. Kurz	1998	3015
170 5/8	25 7/8	25 6/8	23 1/8	4 7/8	4 5/8	5	5	Clayton Co., IA	Jerry E. Morris	Jerry E. Morris	1998	3015
170 5/8	25 7/8	26	23 1/8	5 2/8	5 2/8	5	5	Kenosha Co., WI	Gary Schaetten	Gary Schaetten	1999	3015
170 5/8	26 2/8	25 5/8	20 6/8	5	5	5	5	Toole Co., MT	Cody P. Voermans	Cody P. Voermans	1999	3015
170 5/8	26 1/8	26 2/8	21 2/8	4 4/8	4 4/8	8	7	Pike Co., OH	Jesse H. Brubacher	Jesse H. Brubacher	2000	3015
170 5/8	25 7/8	26 2/8	17 4/8	5 1/8	5 1/8	7	7	Decatur Co., KS	H. Robert Foster	H. Robert Foster	2000	3015
170 5/8	26 1/8	25 4/8	16 7/8	5	4 7/8	9	6	Lawrence Co., IL	Tim Golden	Tim Golden	2000	3015
170 5/8	27 3/8	27 7/8	18 1/8	4 7/8	5 2/8	5	5	Fond du Lac Co., WI	Victor J. Ketchpaw	Victor J. Ketchpaw	2000	3015
170 5/8	22 7/8	26 4/8	18 2/8	4 6/8	4 6/8	6	6	Meadow Lake, SK	John W. Stoothoff, Jr.	John W. Stoothoff, Jr.	2000	3015
170 5/8	26 1/8	26 4/8	19 5/8	4 5/8	4 5/8	7	6	Mason Co., IL	Randall E. Ballard	Randall E. Ballard	2001	3015
170 5/8	25 2/8	25	20 7/8	5 3/8	5 2/8	6	6	S. Saskatchewan River, SK	Jack Clary	Jack Clary	2001	3015
170 5/8	25 6/8	26 1/8	19 1/8	5 4/8	5 3/8	5	5	Union Co., KY	Craig Nally	Craig Nally	2002	3015
170 4/8	26 1/8	25 4/8	20 4/8	4 5/8	4 6/8	6	6	Beltrami Co., MN	Hank Sandland	Hank Sandland	1931	3072
170 4/8	25 7/8	25 7/8	18	4 4/8	4 4/8	5	5	Pend Oreille Co., WA	Picked Up	Eugene M. Bailey	1944	3072
170 4/8	26	25 2/8	18 6/8	4 4/8	4 4/8	6	6	Douglas Co., MN	August P.J. Nelson	Roger M. Holmes	1946	3072
170 4/8	27	27 2/8	20 6/8	5 2/8	5 2/8	6	6	Desha Co., AR	Bob Norris	Bob Norris	1948	3072
170 4/8	23 5/8	26 1/8	22 4/8	5 7/8	5 6/8	5	5	Kittson Co., MN	Unknown	George W. Flaim	PR 1950	3072
170 4/8	25 3/8	25 4/8	18 3/8	5 2/8	5 2/8	6	6	Monroe Co., GA	T.E. Land	Jerry Moseley	1958	3072
170 4/8	25 4/8	24 5/8	19 1/8	4 7/8	4 7/8	8	7	Craven, SK	Ted Paterson	Ted Paterson	1960	3072
170 4/8	21	22 6/8	17 3/8	5 3/8	5 2/8	7	5	Great Sand Hills, SK	Picked Up	Frank Yeast	PR 1960	3072
170 4/8	24 2/8	24	20 6/8	5 6/8	5 5/8	6	5	Preeceville, SK	Vernon Hoffman	Vernon Hoffman	1965	3072
170 4/8	25 4/8	25 1/8	16 7/8	5 5/8	5 3/8	5	6	Marengo Co., AL	Frank W. Gardner	Frank W. Gardner	1967	3072
170 4/8	26	25 3/8	19	4 2/8	4 2/8	6	6	Henry Co., IA	Gerald Bailey	Gerald Bailey	1970	3072
170 4/8	27 2/8	28 5/8	21 2/8	5 1/8	5 1/8	5	5	Bedford Co., VA	W. Bane Bowyer	W. Bane Bowyer	1972	3072
170 4/8	27 4/8	27 2/8	20 2/8	5 4/8	5 3/8	6	5	St. Louis Co., MN	Unknown	Cabela's, Inc.	1974	3072
170 4/8	24 2/8	25 2/8	17	5 3/8	4 4/8	5	5	La Salle Co., TX	Jerome Knebel	Jerome Knebel	1974	3072
170 4/8	26 4/8	25	17 7/8	5 1/8	5 1/8	6	6	Winona Co., MN	Sam Nottleman	Sam Nottleman	1977	3072
170 4/8	27	27 4/8	23 4/8	4 2/8	4 2/8	5	5	Webb Co., TX	R.W. Mann	R.W. Mann	1979	3072
170 4/8	29 6/8	29 2/8	21 2/8	4 6/8	4 6/8	7	8	Sherburne Co., MN	Curtis G. Nelson	Curtis G. Nelson	1981	3072
170 4/8	25 1/8	25 1/8	19	4 4/8	3 7/8	6	6	Sullivan Co., MO	Randy Tucker	Randy Tucker	1981	3072
170 4/8	25 2/8	24 2/8	16 4/8	5	5	7	7	Oneida Co., WI	Leonard E. Westberg	Leonard E. Westberg	1981	3072
170 4/8	26 1/8	25 4/8	18	4 4/8	4 4/8	5	5	Marshall Co., IN	Alan R. Collins	Alan R. Collins	1982	3072
170 4/8	24	24 2/8	18 2/8	4 6/8	4 6/8	5	5	Day Co., SD	Credan Ewalt	Credan Ewalt	1982	3072
170 4/8	28 5/8	28	20	5	5	8	8	Todd Co., MN	Freddie H. Peterson	Freddie H. Peterson	1982	3072
170 4/8	26 6/8	26 3/8	17 3/8	4	4	5	5	Houston Co., MN	Kenneth Carlson	Kenneth Carlson	1983	3072
170 4/8	25 2/8	25 2/8	17	4 5/8	4 6/8	6	6	Madison Co., IA	Merle Allen	Merle Allen	1984	3072
170 4/8	24 7/8	24 1/8	21	4 7/8	4 7/8	5	5	Chippewa Co., MI	Paul Slawski	Paul Slawski	1984	3072
170 4/8	26 2/8	25 4/8	18 4/8	5 3/8	4 7/8	9	9	Keya Paha Co., NE	Michael L. LeZotte	Michael L. LeZotte	1984	3072
170 4/8	26 3/8	26 3/8	22 4/8	5 3/8	5 3/8	5	5	Oak Mts., NB	Michael E. Mertz	Michael E. Mertz	1986	3072
170 4/8	23 4/8	24 1/8	18 4/8	4 4/8	4 5/8	5	5	Logan Co., ND	Jon M. Midthun	Jon M. Midthun	1986	3072
170 4/8	25 4/8	25 3/8	18 2/8	5 1/8	5 1/8	6	7	Lesser Slave Lake, AB	Adriaan Mik	Adriaan Mik	1986	3072
170 4/8	25 2/8	24 7/8	17 6/8	5	5	5	5	Taylor Co., IA	Picked Up	Jim Haas	1986	3072
170 4/8	27 2/8	26 5/8	20 2/8	4 3/8	4 3/8	5	5	Buffalo Co., WI	Stephen F. Lang	Stephen F. Lang	1987	3072
170 4/8	26 1/8	26 5/8	20 5/8	4 5/8	4 5/8	5	5	Des Moines Co., IA	Lewis Mehaffy	Lewis Mehaffy	1987	3072
170 4/8	28 1/8	29	21 4/8	5	4 5/8	7	5	Rockingham Co., NC	Lindsey H. Watkins	Lindsey H. Watkins	1987	3072
170 4/8	27 1/8	26 7/8	21 6/8	4 5/8	4 5/8	5	5	Washington Co., MN	Peter J. Mogren	Peter J. Mogren	1988	3072

WHITETAIL DEER - TYPICAL ANTLERS
Odocoileus virginianus virginianus and certain related subspecies

Score	Length of Main Beam R	L	Inside Spread	Circumference at Smallest Place Between Burr and First Point R	L	Number of Points R	L	Locality	Hunter	Owner	Date Killed	Rank
170 4/8	24 7/8	25 4/8	20 6/8	4 2/8	4 2/8	5	5	Clay Co., NE	James R. Vaughn	James R. Vaughn	1988	3072
170 4/8	23 6/8	23 3/8	18 4/8	4 2/8	4 3/8	6	6	Bradley Co., AR	Joe Hairston	Joe Hairston	1989	3072
170 4/8	26 4/8	28	18 5/8	4 3/8	4 3/8	6	6	Clinton Co., IA	Scott Jacobsen	Scott Jacobsen	1989	3072
170 4/8	25 3/8	24 7/8	20	5 2/8	5 3/8	6	6	Vilas Co., WI	Rick R. Lax	Rick R. Lax	1990	3072
170 4/8	26 3/8	26	19 6/8	4 2/8	4 2/8	5	5	Rock Island Co., IL	Joseph V. De Schepper	Joseph V. De Schepper	1991	3072
170 4/8	26 6/8	26 2/8	21 2/8	5 3/8	5 3/8	7	6	Jasper Co., IL	Joseph W. McIntyre	Joseph W. McIntyre	1991	3072
170 4/8	24 6/8	24 5/8	18	4 7/8	4 7/8	7	7	Pawnee Co., NE	Kenneth C. Mort	Kenneth C. Mort	1991	3072
170 4/8	25 4/8	24 7/8	22 2/8	5 1/8	5 1/8	5	5	Pike Co., IL	Donald E. Stefancic, Sr.	Donald E. Stefancic, Sr.	1991	3072
170 4/8	23 7/8	26	19 6/8	5 5/8	5 2/8	5	5	Chitek Lake, SK	Timothy E. Baxley	Timothy E. Baxley	1992	3072
170 4/8	26 3/8	23 1/8	20 6/8	4 6/8	4 5/8	5	6	Muskingum Co., OH	Kevin A. Berton	Kevin A. Berton	1992	3072
170 4/8	25 5/8	25 3/8	19 6/8	5 2/8	5 2/8	7	6	Appanoose Co., IA	John M. Aiello	John M. Aiello	1994	3072
170 4/8	25 4/8	26	19 2/8	4 1/8	4 2/8	6	5	Atascosa Co., TX	James C. Coffman	James C. Coffman	1994	3072
170 4/8	26 1/8	26 5/8	21 5/8	4 6/8	4 7/8	6	8	Livingston Co., IL	Alan E. Gray	Alan E. Gray	1994	3072
170 4/8	24 6/8	24 4/8	21	4 6/8	4 6/8	5	5	Carroll Co., KY	Tracey D. Kelley	Tracey D. Kelley	1994	3072
170 4/8	24 2/8	23 3/8	21	5 6/8	5 6/8	8	8	Swan Plain, SK	Chris Halsey	Chris Halsey	1997	3072
170 4/8	28 7/8	27 7/8	19	5 6/8	5 5/8	7	6	Hopkins Co., KY	Luther T. Mincy, Jr.	Luther T. Mincy, Jr.	1997	3072
170 4/8	28 1/8	28	22 2/8	5 2/8	5 3/8	5	5	Lucas Co., IA	Rick L. Mitchell	Rick L. Mitchell	1997	3072
170 4/8	24 2/8	23 7/8	19 3/8	5 2/8	5 3/8	6	6	Marion Co., IL	Louis P. Williams, Jr.	Louis P. Williams, Jr.	1997	3072
170 4/8	28 2/8	28 4/8	22 6/8	4 4/8	4 4/8	6	6	Dimmit Co., TX	Joe E. Coleman	Joe E. Coleman	1998	3072
170 4/8	25 7/8	26	19 2/8	4 5/8	4 7/8	7	6	Rooks Co., KS	Shawn Sammons	Shawn Sammons	1998	3072
170 4/8	28 1/8	26 4/8	19 2/8	5 2/8	5 3/8	5	6	Dunn Co., WI	Richard H. Damro	Richard H. Damro	1999	3072
170 4/8	26 6/8	27 1/8	21 7/8	5 2/8	5	6	6	Marinette Co., WI	Randy J. Willms	Randy J. Willms	1999	3072
170 4/8	25 3/8	25 4/8	18 5/8	5 6/8	5 6/8	7	5	Warren Co., IA	George H. Eckstrom II	George H. Eckstrom II	2000	3072
170 4/8	23 2/8	23 5/8	19	5	5 1/8	5	5	Etomami River, SK	William K. Batty	William K. Batty	2001	3072
170 4/8	26 5/8	26 4/8	19 4/8	5 7/8	5 6/8	5	6	Posey Co., IN	Steve Reed, Jr.	Steve Reed, Jr.	2001	3072
170 4/8	23 1/8	21 5/8	18 4/8	4 6/8	4 6/8	6	6	Mercer Co., MO	Jason T Goforth	Jason T. Goforth	2002	3072
170 4/8	26 5/8	26 2/8	21 1/8	5 3/8	5 6/8	6	5	Oneida Co., NY	Tjaart A. Kruger	Tjaart A. Kruger	2002	3072
170 4/8	25 5/8	25 6/8	17	4 3/8	4 4/8	5	5	Ottawa Co., OH	Donald S. Loucks	Donald S. Loucks	2002	3072
170 4/8	27 6/8	28 7/8	19 4/8	5	5	7	6	Licking Co., OH	Mark E. McCoy	Mark E. McCoy	2002	3072
170 4/8	26 5/8	27 6/8	19 1/8	5	5	5	6	Vermilion Co., IL	Ryan D. Sparling	Ryan D. Sparling	2002	3072
170 3/8	25 2/8	25 3/8	17	4 5/8	4 5/8	5	6	Madison Co., IN	George Groff	Larry Shannon	PR 1900	3136
170 3/8	25 5/8	25 1/8	16 4/8	4 7/8	5	9	9	Price Co., WI	N.J Groelle	Melvin Guenther	1905	3136
170 3/8	25 6/8	25 1/8	22 2/8	3 7/8	3 7/8	6	6	Travis Co., TX	W.A. Brown	W.A. Brown	1922	3136
170 3/8	24 2/8	25	24 4/8	6	6	6	6	Madison Parish, LA	Stephens M. White, Sr.	Stephens M. White, Jr.	1945	3136
170 3/8	26	26	19 1/8	5 3/8	5 3/8	6	5	Woodruff Co., AR	R.L. Taylor	R.L. Taylor	1960	3136
170 3/8	27 3/8	26 2/8	25 6/8	5 4/8	5 5/8	5	5	Fort Qu'Appelle, SK	L.A. Magnuson	L.A. Magnuson	1962	3136

Score								Locality	Hunter	Owner	Date	Rank
170 3/8	28 5/8	28 2/8	21 6/8	4 6/8	4 6/8	6	4	Hall Co., NE	Gust Bergman	Gust Bergman	1965	3136
170 3/8	25 2/8	25 4/8	23 3/8	5 2/8	5 2/8	6	5	Grant Co., SD	James Boerger	James Boerger	1965	3136
170 3/8	28 1/8	25 2/8	25 7/8	5	5	4	4	Saline Co., IL	Jack Crain	Jack Crain	1966	3136
170 3/8	26 2/8	25	21 4/8	4 7/8	4 7/8	5	8	Webb Co., TX	Clarence Zieschang	Clarence Zieschang	1966	3136
170 3/8	26 3/8	26	20 3/8	5 2/8	5 2/8	5	5	Portage La Prairie, MB	Robert Boyachek	Robert Boyachek	1967	3136
170 3/8	24 4/8	23 4/8	22	5	5 2/8	7	5	Duval Co., TX	R.L. Kruger	R.L. Kruger	1968	3136
170 3/8	28 5/8	28 4/8	23 4/8	5 1/8	5 1/8	8	8	Kingsbury Co., SD	Jerry Ellingson	Jerry Ellingson	1969	3136
170 3/8	26 1/8	26 1/8	21 1/8	4 7/8	4 7/8	8	7	Buffalo Co., WI	Lee E. Lang	Lee E. Lang	1969	3136
170 3/8	24 2/8	24 2/8	19 7/8	5	5	7	5	Buffalo Co., WI	Ralph Pella	Cabela's, Inc.	1970	3136
170 3/8	25 2/8	25 2/8	22 6/8	5 2/8	5 4/8	5	5	Lac qui Parle Co., MN	Paul W. Hill	Paul W. Hill	1974	3136
170 3/8	29 4/8	28 7/8	17 7/8	4 2/8	4 4/8	8	8	Muskingum Co., OH	John H. O'Flaherty	John H. O'Flaherty	1976	3136
170 3/8	25 6/8	26 1/8	18 5/8	4 7/8	5	5	5	Newaygo Co., MI	Dennis A. Carlson	Dennis A. Carlson	1978	3136
170 3/8	26 6/8	26 3/8	17 3/8	4 3/8	4 2/8	7	6	Coweta Co., GA	Douglas R. Freeman	Douglas R. Freeman	1978	3136
170 3/8	29 5/8	29 3/8	26	5 3/8	5 1/8	5	6	Dimmit Co., TX	McLean Bowman	McLean Bowman	1981	3136
170 3/8	23 6/8	24 3/8	15 7/8	4 4/8	4 4/8	6	5	Wilcox Co., GA	Scott H. Urguhart	Scott H. Urguhart	1981	3136
170 3/8	27 4/8	25 4/8	21 1/8	6 4/8	6 4/8	4	4	Franklin Co., KS	Fran E. Wiederholt	Judy E. Wiederholt	1981	3136
170 3/8	25 5/8	26 3/8	17 7/8	4 4/8	4 7/8	5	5	Decatur Co., IA	Julian J. Toney	Julian J. Toney	1982	3136
170 3/8	25 2/8	25 4/8	18 6/8	5 2/8	4 7/8	6	6	Wilkinson Co., GA	James W. Whitaker	James W. Whitaker	1982	3136
170 3/8	28 1/8	26 4/8	18 5/8	5 5/8	5 5/8	6	6	Jackson Co., IA	Steven Morehead	Unknown	1983	3136
170 3/8	25 7/8	26 1/8	18 7/8	5 1/8	5 2/8	6	6	Beltrami Co., MN	Floyd Hlucny	Floyd Hlucny	1985	3136
170 3/8	26 1/8	26 4/8	19 5/8	4 4/8	4 2/8	6	6	Haskell Co., OK	Loyd Long	Loyd Long	1985	3136
170 3/8	23 1/8	23 2/8	19 5/8	4 6/8	4 5/8	6	7	Niobrara Co., WY	Joseph A. Perry III	Joseph A. Perry III	1985	3136
170 3/8	23 7/8	23 7/8	19 7/8	4 4/8	4 5/8	5	6	Emmet Co., MI	Jeffery A. Phillips	Jeffery A. Phillips	1985	3136
170 3/8	25 2/8	24	16 4/8	4 5/8	4 4/8	9	8	Cow Lake, AB	Edward J. Burns	Edward J. Burns	1986	3136
170 3/8	25 6/8	25 3/8	15 7/8	4 5/8	4 5/8	5	7	Baraga Co., MI	Howard D. Musick	Howard D. Musick	1987	3136
170 3/8	23 2/8	24 2/8	17	4 1/8	4 2/8	5	6	Marshall Co., MN	John R. O'Donnell	John R. O'Donnell	1988	3136
170 3/8	25	22 6/8	18 1/8	4 5/8	4 5/8	5	5	Pottawatomie Co., KS	Larry C. Schroeder	Larry C. Schroeder	1988	3136
170 3/8	27 4/8	27 5/8	23 1/8	5	5	5	6	Orange Co., IN	John W. Matthew	John W. Matthew	1989	3136
170 3/8	25	25 1/8	18 3/8	5 2/8	5	5	5	Griffin, SK	Leonard Mitchell	Leonard Mitchell	1989	3136
170 3/8	27 5/8	27 3/8	17 7/8	5	5	6	5	Montcalm Co., MI	Michael R. Nelson	Michael R. Nelson	1989	3136
170 3/8	27	26 4/8	19 7/8	4 2/8	4 3/8	5	5	Bruton, ON	Mark Vesters	Mark Vesters	1989	3136
170 3/8	27 1/8	27 5/8	20 1/8	5 1/8	4 7/8	5	5	Warren Co., IA	Lanny Caligiuri	Lanny Caligiuri	1990	3136
170 3/8	28 3/8	28 1/8	21 5/8	4 6/8	4 5/8	6	6	Dubuque Co., IA	Richard S. Hillard	Richard S. Hillard	1990	3136
170 3/8	25 2/8	25 3/8	21 5/8	5 4/8	5 4/8	7	7	Mercer Co., MO	Robert W. Vasey	Robert W. Vasey	1990	3136
170 3/8	26 6/8	26 6/8	17 7/8	4 6/8	4 6/8	5	5	McCook Co., SD	Sam A. Wilson	Unknown	PR 1990	3136
170 3/8	26	25 5/8	18 7/8	5 6/8	5 4/8	5	5	Coffey Co., KS	Glen R. Freeman	Glen R. Freeman	1991	3136
170 3/8	26 1/8	26 1/8	17 3/8	5	5 4/8	7	5	Harrison Co., MO	Glen D. Gentry	Glen D. Gentry	1991	3136
170 3/8	27 3/8	28 4/8	18 5/8	4 6/8	4 5/8	5	5	Howard Co., IA	Clarence Mincks	Clarence Mincks	1991	3136
170 3/8	26 6/8	26 5/8	18	5 1/8	5 1/8	7	6	Ziebach Co., SD	James S. Nelson IV	James S. Nelson IV	1992	3136
170 3/8	27 3/8	27	22 1/8	4 4/8	4 4/8	6	5	Grafton Co., NH	William M. Gordon	William M. Gordon	1993	3136
170 3/8	26	25 5/8	18 7/8	5	5	5	5	Lake Rosseau, ON	Philip Giroday	Picked Up	PR 1994	3136
170 3/8	23 6/8	24	17 7/8	4 1/8	4	6	6	Maverick Co., TX	Jay C. Harmon	Jay C. Harmon	1994	3136
170 3/8	26 1/8	27 6/8	20 6/8	4 6/8	4 5/8	5	5	Warren Co., IA	Bruce L. Hupke	Bruce L. Hupke	1994	3136
170 3/8	27 1/8	27 1/8	19 2/8	5 1/8	5 1/8	6	6	Le Sueur Co., MN	Roy H. Krohn	Roy H. Krohn	1994	3136
170 3/8	27 5/8	27 5/8	21 5/8	5	4 7/8	5	5	Jasper Co., IL	Skip Moore	Skip Moore	1994	3136
170 3/8	27 4/8	22 2/8	22 2/8	5 2/8	5 2/8	6	6	Crawford Co., KS	David E. Onelio	David E. Onelio	1994	3136
170 3/8	25 5/8	27 5/8	23 5/8	5 4/8	5 4/8	5	5	Shelby Co., OH	Buck Siler	Buck Siler	1994	3136
170 3/8	23 6/8	24 3/8	18 5/8	4 4/8	4 5/8	5	5	Meagher Co., MT	Randy L. Kunkle	Randy L. Kunkle	1995	3136

WHITETAIL DEER - TYPICAL ANTLERS
Odocoileus virginianus virginianus and certain related subspecies

Score	Length of Main Beam R	L	Inside Spread	Circumference at Smallest Place Between Burr and First Point R	L	Number of Points R	L	Locality	Hunter	Owner	Date Killed	Rank
170 3/8	28 4/8	27 1/8	23 2/8	5 6/8	5 6/8	5	8	Carroll Co., OH	Myron L. Miller	Myron L. Miller	1995	3136
170 3/8	26 5/8	26 4/8	19 6/8	5 1/8	5 1/8	6	7	Grundy Co., IL	Robert Alfonso, Jr.	Robert Alfonso, Jr.	1996	3136
170 3/8	24 6/8	24 4/8	16 7/8	5	4 7/8	6	6	Juneau Co., WI	Gaylord J. Downing	Gaylord J. Downing	1996	3136
170 3/8	23	23 2/8	17 3/8	5 6/8	5 7/8	6	6	McHenry Co., IL	Donald E. Hoey	Donald E. Hoey	1996	3136
170 3/8	25 4/8	25 3/8	19 3/8	4 2/8	4 2/8	6	5	St. Croix Co., WI	Earl L. Neumann	Earl L. Neumann	1996	3136
170 3/8	23 2/8	23 4/8	21 5/8	4 7/8	4 7/8	7	6	Smeaton, SK	Samuel D. Singer	Samuel D. Singer	1997	3136
170 3/8	24 7/8	24 6/8	17 5/8	4 2/8	4 1/8	5	5	Throckmorton Co., TX	Ken W. Youngblood	Ken W. Youngblood	1997	3136
170 3/8	26 1/8	25 5/8	21 3/8	5 2/8	5 2/8	5	5	Whiteside Co., IL	Mark Trent	David Billman	1998	3136
170 3/8	25 2/8	25	20 2/8	4 7/8	5 2/8	8	6	Wayne Co., KY	Kelvin Casada	Kelvin Casada	1998	3136
170 3/8	26 6/8	27 2/8	22 4/8	6	5 5/8	6	6	Jo Daviess Co., IL	Cliff Perry	Cliff Perry	1998	3136
170 3/8	26	25 6/8	18 7/8	5 5/8	5 6/8	6	6	E. Carroll Parish, LA	David L. Roselle	David L. Roselle	1998	3136
170 3/8	23 7/8	23 3/8	21 3/8	5 6/8	5 7/8	5	5	Turtleford, SK	Gordon E. Janz	Gordon E. Janz	1999	3136
170 3/8	28 6/8	27 6/8	19 7/8	4 7/8	4 7/8	7	6	Houston Co., MN	Picked Up	MN Dept. of Natl. Resc.	1999	3136
170 3/8	25 3/8	24 6/8	18 7/8	5 3/8	5 2/8	6	7	Quill Lake, SK	Eddy Korolchuk	Eddy Korolchuk	2000	3136
170 3/8	27 7/8	26 4/8	17 5/8	4 6/8	4 6/8	5	5	Penobscot Co., ME	Lawrence L. Lord	Lawrence L. Lord	2000	3136
170 3/8	24 2/8	24 1/8	21 2/8	4 6/8	4 6/8	5	6	Scott Co., MN	Joe Shotliff	Joe Shotliff	2000	3136
170 3/8	25 2/8	25 6/8	18 1/8	4 4/8	4 3/8	6	6	Dimmit Co., TX	Robert E. Zaiglin	Robert E. Zaiglin	2001	3136
170 3/8	26 2/8	25 3/8	17 7/8	5	5 1/8	5	6	Idaho	Unknown	Larry Haines	PR 2002	3136
170 3/8	25 7/8	25 4/8	22 3/8	4 6/8	4 7/8	6	5	Concordia Parish, LA	Ronnie L. Wilkinson	Ronnie L. Wilkinson	2002	3136
170 2/8	26 7/8	26 4/8	20 1/8	5 1/8	5 1/8	6	5	Shawano Co., WI	Jule Vandergate	Don E. Smith	1932	3209
170 2/8	27 1/8	26 7/8	18 6/8	5 1/8	5 2/8	6	6	Florence Co., WI	Unknown	David G. Mueller	1940	3209
170 2/8	24 2/8	25 5/8	17 2/8	4 4/8	4 3/8	6	7	Marinette Co., WI	Phillip Marquis	Phillip Marquis	1944	3209
170 2/8	24 6/8	23 6/8	18	4 3/8	4 3/8	6	8	Polk Co., WI	Robert G. Overman	Robert G. Overman	1945	3209
170 2/8	27	27 1/8	19 2/8	4 3/8	4 4/8	5	7	Webb Co., TX	Roy C. Rice	Roy C. Rice	1948	3209
170 2/8	24 3/8	25 2/8	16 6/8	5 2/8	5 3/8	5	5	Carlton Co., MN	Unknown	George W. Flaim	1950	3209
170 2/8	27 2/8	26 6/8	20	5	5 1/8	5	5	Dafoe, SK	A. Linder	A. Linder	1959	3209
170 2/8	25 3/8	26 3/8	19 4/8	5 2/8	5 2/8	5	5	Calhoun Co., AR	George M. Gorman	George M. Gorman	1961	3209
170 2/8	24 4/8	24	19 4/8	4 6/8	4 6/8	6	5	McMullen Co., TX	Earl Welch	Earl Welch	1964	3209
170 2/8	26 2/8	25 7/8	22	5 1/8	5 2/8	7	6	Lestock, SK	Zoltan Blaskovich	Zoltan Blaskovich	1965	3209
170 2/8	24 3/8	24 7/8	21 6/8	4 3/8	4 3/8	6	6	Avonlea, SK	Doug English	Doug English	1965	3209
170 2/8	28 6/8	29 1/8	19 5/8	4 5/8	4 4/8	9	5	Blue Earth Co., MN	Roland Bode	Roland Bode	1967	3209
170 2/8	24 6/8	24 3/8	19 5/8	4 5/8	4 5/8	8	7	Jim Hogg Co., TX	Tom P. Hayes	Tom P. Hayes	1968	3209
170 2/8	23 2/8	24 2/8	15	4 4/8	4 4/8	8	7	Spokane Co., WA	Edward A. Floch, Jr.	Edward A. Floch, Jr.	1970	3209
170 2/8	23 6/8	26 4/8	18 2/8	5 2/8	5 4/8	5	5	Oglethorpe Co., GA	H.D. Cannon	H.D. Cannon	1971	3209
170 2/8	27 4/8	25 5/8	18	4 6/8	4 6/8	6	5	Houston Co., MN	Randy J. Benson	Randy J. Benson	1972	3209
170 2/8	27 4/8	27 5/8	19 7/8	4 6/8	4 4/8	7	6	Jefferson Co., OH	James S. Pratt	James S. Pratt	1976	3209

Score	Main Beam R	Main Beam L	Inside Spread	Circ. R	Circ. L	Pts. R	Pts. L	Locality	Hunter	Owner	Date	Rank
170 2/8	23 7/8	22 4/8	17 4/8	4 4/8	4 6/8	5	5	Hopkins Co., KY	Michael E. Dillingham	Michael E. Dillingham	1977	3209
170 2/8	25 2/8	24 6/8	19 4/8	5 1/8	5 2/8	6	6	Bradley Co., AR	Brad J. Davis	Brad J. Davis	1979	3209
170 2/8	27 1/8	27 2/8	21	5 3/8	5 3/8	4	4	Lee Co., AL	George P. Mann	George P. Mann	1980	3209
170 2/8	25 6/8	25	16 6/8	4 3/8	4 4/8	5	6	Olmsted Co., MN	James L. Miller	James L. Miller	1981	3209
170 2/8	26 6/8	26 7/8	22 2/8	5 6/8	5 6/8	5	6	Riley Co., KS	Paul K. Byarlay	Paul K. Byarlay	1983	3209
170 2/8	25 1/8	26	20 4/8	6 7/8	6 7/8	5	6	Ribstone Creek, AB	David H. Crum	David H. Crum	1984	3209
170 2/8	25 3/8	25 5/8	18 4/8	4 5/8	4 4/8	5	5	Adair Co., IA	Gale D. Johnston	Gale D. Johnston	1984	3209
170 2/8	24 6/8	26 1/8	18	5	5	5	5	Pembina River, MB	Bernie Thiessen	Bernie Thiessen	1987	3209
170 2/8	24 7/8	24 7/8	19 6/8	5	4 7/8	5	5	Winneshiek Co., IA	David Hageman	David Hageman	1988	3209
170 2/8	24 2/8	24 2/8	18	5	4 7/8	5	5	Pend Oreille Co., WA	George T. Law	George T. Law	1988	3209
170 2/8	26 3/8	25 5/8	19 6/8	4 7/8	4 7/8	8	7	Whitley Co., KY	Shevelery C. Sturgill	Shevelery C. Sturgill	1988	3209
170 2/8	26 1/8	26 1/8	25 2/8	4 3/8	4 3/8	5	5	Houston Co., MN	Omer M. Wangen	Omer M. Wangen	1988	3209
170 2/8	25 4/8	26 1/8	19 1/8	5 4/8	5 5/8	7	7	Clayton Co., IA	Myles T. Keller	Myles T. Keller	1989	3209
170 2/8	24 4/8	25 4/8	19 2/8	4 1/8	4 1/8	6	5	Jackson Co., OH	Roger K. Saltsman	Roger K. Saltsman	1989	3209
170 2/8	28 4/8	26	20 2/8	4 7/8	4 7/8	5	7	Adams Co., OH	R. Scott Boschert	R. Scott Boschert	1990	3209
170 2/8	26	25 6/8	26 6/8	4 4/8	4 4/8	4	5	Washington Co., ME	Phillip R. Dobbins	Phillip R. Dobbins	1990	3209
170 2/8	26 2/8	25 5/8	22 6/8	4 7/8	4 6/8	5	5	Lafayette Co., WI	Everett E. Mau	Everett E. Mau	1990	3209
170 2/8	27 6/8	26 2/8	22 6/8	5 6/8	6	7	7	Knox Co., OH	Ralph D. Wiley	Ralph D. Wiley	1991	3209
170 2/8	27	27 2/8	17	4 5/8	4 5/8	5	5	Macon Co., MO	Renee L. DeWeese	Renee L. DeWeese	1991	3209
170 2/8	25 4/8	25 6/8	18	4 2/8	4 1/8	5	5	Meade Co., MO	Paul E. Ice	Paul E. Ice	1991	3209
170 2/8	24 4/8	25 6/8	26	5 2/8	5 2/8	8	6	Washtenaw Co., MI	Tod G. Jaggi	Tod G. Jaggi	1991	3209
170 2/8	25 5/8	25 7/8	19 1/8	4 5/8	4 5/8	6	6	Fillmore Co., MN	Terry L. Rasmussen	Terry L. Rasmussen	1992	3209
170 2/8	26 3/8	27	20 4/8	5 1/8	5 2/8	5	5	Lincoln Co., CO	Joseph C. Fox	Joseph C. Fox	1992	3209
170 2/8	24 4/8	25 4/8	17	5 3/8	5 3/8	5	6	Ogle Co., IL	Dick V. Lalowski	Dick V. Lalowski	1992	3209
170 2/8	25 7/8	26	18 6/8	4 3/8	4 3/8	6	6	Dimmit Co., TX	Glenn H. Lau	Glenn H. Lau	1992	3209
170 2/8	27 4/8	26	18 6/8	5 2/8	5 1/8	6	7	Aroostook Co., ME	Peter C. Pedro	Peter C. Pedro	1992	3209
170 2/8	25	24 3/8	18 2/8	5	5	5	5	Platte Co., WY	Johnny Wehrmann	Johnny Wehrmann	1992	3209
170 2/8	25 3/8	25 3/8	20 6/8	4 5/8	4 6/8	6	6	Tippecanoe Co., IN	Jimmy M. Crites	Jimmy M. Crites	1993	3209
170 2/8	27 4/8	27 4/8	22 2/8	4 7/8	4 6/8	5	4	Page Co., IA	Arlen D. Meyer	Arlen D. Meyer	1993	3209
170 2/8	27 1/8	26 2/8	22 2/8	5	5	5	5	Chisago Co., MN	John B. Nelson	John B. Nelson	1993	3209
170 2/8	26 2/8	26 2/8	21 2/8	4 7/8	4 7/8	4	4	St. Louis Co., MN	Charles R. Wagaman	Charles R. Wagaman	1993	3209
170 2/8	30 2/8	26 4/8	19 7/8	4 3/8	4 5/8	6	6	Van Buren Co., IA	Dennis R. Besick	Dennis R. Besick	1994	3209
170 2/8	26 3/8	26 3/8	23 6/8	5	5 3/8	7	7	Madison Co., MS	David G. McAdory	David G. McAdory	1994	3209
170 2/8	27 5/8	26 6/8	20	5 2/8	5 2/8	6	6	Hennepin Co., MN	Picked Up	Charles G. Nordstrom	1994	3209
170 2/8	26 6/8	25 7/8	19 2/8	4 4/8	4 4/8	5	5	Boone Co., IL	Matthew L. Schaller	Matthew L. Schaller	1994	3209
170 2/8	26 2/8	25 7/8	17 1/8	4 7/8	4 6/8	8	5	Logan Co., KY	Jim F. Sweeney	Jim F. Sweeney	1994	3209
170 2/8	25 2/8	26 3/8	21 4/8	5	5 1/8	8	11	St. Charles Co., MO	Leroy H. Vehige	Leroy H. Vehige	1994	3209
170 2/8	27	25 5/8	19 4/8	5	5	7	6	Jackson Co., SD	Jean Amiotte	Jean Amiotte	1995	3209
170 2/8	26 6/8	28	21 3/8	5 5/8	5 6/8	6	6	Hardisty, AB	David W. Higman	David W. Higman	1995	3209
170 2/8	28 1/8	27 4/8	22 6/8	5 3/8	4 6/8	7	7	Edgar Co., IL	Sharon McDaniel	Sharon McDaniel	1995	3209
170 2/8	25 4/8	27 1/8	20 5/8	5 2/8	5 3/8	6	6	Clay Co., IL	Jeremy D. Current	Jeremy D. Current	1996	3209
170 2/8	26 6/8	26 2/8	19 4/8	4 5/8	4 7/8	5	5	Scotts Bluff Co., NE	Russel C. McKeehan II	Russel C. McKeehan II	1996	3209
170 2/8	24 3/8	24 5/8	23	4 6/8	4 7/8	6	5	Pike Co., IL	Michael E. Kennedy	Michael E. Kennedy	1997	3209
170 2/8	27 7/8	27 4/8	25 6/8	5 1/8	5 6/8	5	5	Jackson Co., IA	Nathan Kilburg	Picked Up	1997	3209
170 2/8	27	27 4/8	19 7/8	5 5/8	5 6/8	5	5	Rusk Co., WI	Fredrick J. Marcon	Fredrick J. Marcon	1997	3209
170 2/8	26 7/8	26 3/8	19 3/8	4 7/8	5 2/8	7	7	Clayton Co., IA	Randy D. Reck	Randy D. Reck	1997	3209
170 2/8	24	24 5/8	18 6/8	4 3/8	4 4/8	6	6	Davis Co., IA	Richard C. Riggenbach	Richard C. Riggenbach	1997	3209
170 2/8	24 7/8	28	21 4/8	4 6/8	4 6/8	6	6	Hamilton Co., IN	James P. Tomasik	James P. Tomasik	1997	3209

WHITETAIL DEER - TYPICAL ANTLERS
Odocoileus virginianus virginianus and certain related subspecies

Score	Length of Main Beam R	L	Inside Spread	Circumference at Smallest Place Between Burr and First Point R	L	Number of Points R	L	Locality	Hunter	Owner	Date Killed	Rank
170 2/8	24 7/8	25	20	4 7/8	4 7/8	5	6	Esterhazy, SK	Sidney W. Golling	Sidney W. Golling	1998	3209
170 2/8	26 3/8	26 1/8	18 4/8	5 1/8	5 3/8	8	8	Hubbard Co., MN	Michael E. Greetan	Michael E. Greetan	1998	3209
170 2/8	25 6/8	25	17 2/8	4 6/8	4 6/8	5	5	Washington Co., MO	William M. Hazer	William M. Hazer	1998	3209
170 2/8	28 1/8	27	21 6/8	5 3/8	5 3/8	7	4	Hancock Co., IL	James E. Lenix	James E. Lenix	1998	3209
170 2/8	27 3/8	27 6/8	20	4 6/8	4 7/8	5	5	Tobin Lake, SK	Trevor Rehaluk	Trevor Rehaluk	1998	3209
170 2/8	27 7/8	27 1/8	19 2/8	4 6/8	4 5/8	4	5	Walworth Co., WI	Dale Wilson	Dale Wilson	1998	3209
170 2/8	28 1/8	27 6/8	20 4/8	5 7/8	5 6/8	6	5	Battle River, AB	Jeff Golka	Jeff Golka	1999	3209
170 2/8	26 3/8	26 2/8	24	4 3/8	4 2/8	5	5	George Lake, AB	Susan G. Isaacs	Susan G. Isaacs	1999	3209
170 2/8	24 6/8	25 4/8	18 4/8	4 3/8	4 6/8	6	6	Langlade Co., WI	Jay P. Konetzke	Jay P. Konetzke	1999	3209
170 2/8	24	25	21	4 4/8	4 5/8	5	5	Clark Co., KS	Ray Morais	Ray Morais	1999	3209
170 2/8	25	25 1/8	19 2/8	5 6/8	5 3/8	5	5	Unknown	Unknown	Manuel F. Nunez	PR 1999	3209
170 2/8	26	25 5/8	16 4/8	5 5/8	5 1/8	7	5	Christian Co., KY	Brian K. Oatts	Brian K. Oatts	1999	3209
170 2/8	28 2/8	29 4/8	23 7/8	5 6/8	5 6/8	5	5	Clythe Creek, ON	Bill T. Henshall	Bill T. Henshall	2000	3209
170 2/8	29 6/8	27 3/8	17 3/8	5 5/8	6 2/8	8	6	Bedford Co., VA	Picked Up	Michael T. Ingram	2000	3209
170 2/8	27 6/8	28 5/8	20 6/8	4 4/8	4 3/8	6	4	Crane Lake, SK	Jeff M. Slabik	Jeff M. Slabik	2000	3209
170 2/8	25 5/8	25 3/8	20 1/8	4 6/8	4 7/8	7	6	Monroe Co., IA	Vince L. Feehan	Vince L. Feehan	2001	3209
170 2/8	28 1/8	29 2/8	20 4/8	5 6/8	5 4/8	9	7	Clinton Co., IA	Kiner Giddings	Kiner Giddings	2001	3209
170 2/8	21 2/8	21 2/8	15	4 4/8	4 3/8	7	8	Maverick Co., TX	Steve E. Holloway	Steve E. Holloway	2001	3209
170 2/8	23 4/8	23 7/8	17 2/8	4 6/8	4 7/8	6	6	Lake Co., IL	Jeffrey B. Keller	Jeffrey B. Keller	2002	3209
170 1/8	25 7/8	27 6/8	19	5 2/8	5 2/8	5	6	Minnesota	Unknown	Cabela's, Inc.	PR 1950	3293
170 1/8	26 5/8	27	19 3/8	5 7/8	5 7/8	8	9	Massanutton Mt., VA	Lloyd Lam	Lloyd Lam	1955	3293
170 1/8	28 5/8	29	23 3/8	4 2/8	4 3/8	4	5	Faribault Co., MN	Harlan Francis	Harlan Francis	1956	3293
170 1/8	25 3/8	24 6/8	16 5/8	4 7/8	5	6	7	St. Louis Co., MN	Allan Ramstad	Allan Ramstad	1959	3293
170 1/8	30	27 5/8	23 1/8	4 2/8	4 2/8	6	6	Bayfield Co., WI	Roy Jacobson	David R. Jacobson	1960	3293
170 1/8	23 7/8	22 7/8	16 1/8	5 5/8	5 5/8	7	7	Swift Current, SK	Brian Baumann	Brian Baumann	1966	3293
170 1/8	28 4/8	27	15 1/8	4 3/8	4 3/8	5	5	Jasper Co., GA	Glenn Owens	James E. Owens	1967	3293
170 1/8	27 6/8	24 7/8	20 7/8	4 7/8	4 7/8	6	6	Jackson Co., OH	Theodore R. Yates	Theodore R. Yates	1967	3293
170 1/8	23 6/8	25 6/8	20 5/8	4 2/8	4 3/8	6	6	Marinette Co., WI	Leonard Schartner	Leonard Schartner	1968	3293
170 1/8	26 1/8	26	21 1/8	4 6/8	4 6/8	6	6	Lake Co., MN	Ed Gregorich	George W. Flaim	1969	3293
170 1/8	24 3/8	24 2/8	18 1/8	4 4/8	4 2/8	5	5	Pincher Creek, AB	Dave Simpson	Dave Simpson	1971	3293
170 1/8	28 3/8	28 3/8	21 5/8	4 6/8	5	6	6	White Co., AR	Ernest W. Stephenson	Ernest W. Stephenson	1971	3293
170 1/8	24 2/8	25 4/8	15 3/8	6	5 7/8	5	5	Iowa Co., IA	Edward E. Best	Edward E. Best	1972	3293
170 1/8	25 3/8	24 5/8	17 1/8	4 4/8	4 5/8	6	6	Putnam Co., MO	Ralph J. Shoultz	Otteline Shoultz	1973	3293
170 1/8	24 5/8	25 4/8	19	5 5/8	4 4/8	7	5	Warren Co., IA	Arnold J. Hoch	Arnold J. Hoch	1975	3293
170 1/8	23 7/8	24 7/8	18 3/8	4 7/8	4 6/8	5	5	Oglethorpe Co., GA	Robert C. Thaxton	Robert C. Thaxton	1978	3293
170 1/8	22 4/8	25 5/8	20 5/8	4 6/8	4 5/8	6	6	Logan Co., IL	Gary L. Humbert	Gary L. Humbert	1979	3293

Score	Main Beam	Main Beam	Inside Spread	Circ.	Circ.	Pts.	Pts.	Locality	Hunter	Owner	Date Killed	Rank
170 1/8	22 3/8	24 3/8	16 1/8	4 7/8	4 7/8	6	7	Morehouse Parish, LA	Johnnie Kovac	Johnnie Kovac, Jr.	1979	3293
170 1/8	20 6/8	21 4/8	16 7/8	4 5/8	4 5/8	5	6	Smoky River, AB	Bernie Reiswig	Bernie Reiswig	1980	3293
170 1/8	25 4/8	25 7/8	22 2/8	4 5/8	4 3/8	7	6	Winona Co., MN	Roger J. Traxler	Roger J. Traxler	1980	3293
170 1/8	26 7/8	27	19 5/8	5 1/8	5 4/8	7	7	Breckinridge Co., KY	Thomas F. Dean	Thomas F. Dean	1982	3293
170 1/8	27	27 1/8	19	4 6/8	4 6/8	6	7	Cook Co., MN	William Bohnen	William Bohnen	1984	3293
170 1/8	24 3/8	22 6/8	18 3/8	5	5 1/8	6	8	Sanders Co., MT	Richard Lukes	Richard Lukes	1984	3293
170 1/8	25 6/8	25 2/8	21 3/8	4 4/8	4 5/8	6	6	Mower Co., MN	Robert D. Plumb	Robert D. Plumb	1984	3293
170 1/8	25 7/8	25 7/8	21 5/8	4 4/8	4 5/8	5	5	Pulaski Co., MO	Chuck Adkins	Chuck Adkins	1986	3293
170 1/8	27 1/8	27 2/8	20 3/8	5 6/8	5 6/8	5	5	Essex Co., VT	Kevin A. Brockney	Kevin A. Brockney	1986	3293
170 1/8	27 1/8	22 3/8	15 5/8	5 3/8	5 2/8	7	5	Greene Co., IA	Charles Gunn	Charles Gunn	1986	3293
170 1/8	22 3/8	27	20 3/8	4 6/8	4 7/8	7	7	Vermilion River, AB	Vince V. Philipps	Vince V. Philipps	1987	3293
170 1/8	26 4/8	28 1/8	23	5	5	6	7	Winona Co., MN	Gary L. Bornfleth	Picked Up	1987	3293
170 1/8	28 6/8	26	20 7/8	4 6/8	4 6/8	6	6	Harford Co., MD	Edward C. Garrison	Edward C. Garrison	1987	3293
170 1/8	26 7/8	25 6/8	17 5/8	5 5/8	5 5/8	5	5	Comal Co., TX	Lyman Skolaut	Lyman Skolaut	1988	3293
170 1/8	25 6/8	25 1/8	23 1/8	5	5	6	5	Lycoming Co., PA	Richard C. Tebbs, Jr.	Richard C. Tebbs, Jr.	1988	3293
170 1/8	25 4/8	25 3/8	22 1/8	4 7/8	4 7/8	5	5	Coahuila, MX	Rodolfo F. Barrera	Rodolfo F. Barrera	1988	3293
170 1/8	27 3/8	26	18 7/8	5 4/8	5 1/8	6	7	Montgomery Co., MO	Kenneth B. Maskey	Kenneth B. Maskey	1989	3293
170 1/8	27 7/8	26 4/8	23 7/8	5 1/8	4 6/8	5	6	Douglas Co., KS	Frank Virchow	Picked Up	1990	3293
170 1/8	28 1/8	29 4/8	20 5/8	4 6/8	4 7/8	5	6	Racine Co., WI	Michael H. Poeschel	Michael H. Poeschel	1990	3293
170 1/8	23 3/8	27 4/8	17 6/8	4 7/8	5 6/8	6	6	Saginaw Co., MI	Scott M. Hutchins	Scott M. Hutchins	1991	3293
170 1/8	25 2/8	26 5/8	15 3/8	5 6/8	4 6/8	6	7	Webb Co., TX	Gerald W. Rentz, Jr.	Gerald W. Rentz, Jr.	1991	3293
170 1/8	23 6/8	23 1/8	20 1/8	4 6/8	5 3/8	7	5	Perry Co., IL	Stephen E. Brand	Stephen E. Brand	1992	3293
170 1/8	26	25 5/8	24 2/8	5 3/8	5 1/8	5	6	La Crosse Co., WI	Scott R. Wavra	Scott R. Wavra	1993	3293
170 1/8	26 6/8	26 4/8	22 1/8	5	5 6/8	5	5	Lake Co., IL	John W. Schnider, Jr.	John W. Schnider, Jr.	1993	3293
170 1/8	28 2/8	27 4/8	17 1/8	4 6/8	4 7/8	6	6	Butler Co., KY	David W. Alford	David W. Alford	1993	3293
170 1/8	25 2/8	25 6/8	20 3/8	5 6/8	6 1/8	6	5	Webb Co., TX	William O. Carter	Picked Up	1993	3293
170 1/8	26 3/8	26 1/8	23 1/8	5	5 5/8	5	5	Iroquois Co., IL	Michael L. Krumweide	Michael L. Krumweide	1993	3293
170 1/8	26 7/8	25	21 5/8	5 5/8	5 2/8	4	5	Elk Co., KS	Terry L. Tindle	Terry L. Tindle	1993	3293
170 1/8	25	29	21 6/8	5 1/8	5 2/8	5	8	Jim Hogg Co., TX	Frances Weil	Frances Weil	1994	3293
170 1/8	30	24 3/8	18	5 2/8	4 7/8	6	6	Pine Creek, AB	Daniel W. LaPierre	Daniel W. LaPierre	1994	3293
170 1/8	25 3/8	25 5/8	21 2/8	4 7/8	4 3/8	6	4	Muhlenberg Co., KY	Jamie G. Noble	Jamie G. Noble	1994	3293
170 1/8	26 5/8	30 1/8	18 6/8	4 3/8	5 4/8	5	6	Adams Co., IL	Jeffrey J. Rakers	Jeffrey J. Rakers	1994	3293
170 1/8	28 4/8	25 3/8	22 7/8	5 4/8	4 6/8	6	6	Sullivan Co., IN	Troy J. Rambis	Troy J. Rambis	1994	3293
170 1/8	26 7/8	27	18 5/8	4 6/8	4 5/8	6	9	Allamakee Co., IA	Cabela's, Inc.	Eric W. Thorstenson	1995	3293
170 1/8	25 4/8	26	17	5	4 6/8	7	7	Athabasca River, AB	Patrick S. Casey	Patrick S. Casey	1995	3293
170 1/8	24 7/8	24 4/8	21 3/8	5 1/8	4 7/8	8	8	Douglas Co., WI	Duane Christiansen	Duane Christiansen	1995	3293
170 1/8	26 7/8	26 7/8	18 4/8	5	5	5	5	Hooker Co., NE	Jan J. Finley	Jan J. Finley	1995	3293
170 1/8	25 4/8	23 7/8	26 1/8	4 2/8	4 3/8	5	5	Dunn Co., WI	Clarence P. Janota	Clarence P. Janota	1995	3293
170 1/8	25 3/8	27 2/8	19 5/8	4 5/8	5 2/8	5	6	Otter Tail Co., MN	Randle R. Litke	Randle R. Litke	1995	3293
170 1/8	24 6/8	24 2/8	22 7/8	5	4 6/8	6	7	Hubbard, SK	Lionel Rokosh	Lionel Rokosh	1995	3293
170 1/8	25 3/8	25 7/8	19 3/8	4 2/8	4 5/8	5	5	Branch Co., MI	Jeffrey M. Stauffer	Jeffrey M. Stauffer	1996	3293
170 1/8	28 7/8	29 4/8	19 5/8	4 1/8	4 7/8	5	5	Clayton Co., IA	Thomas G. Baumgartner	Thomas G. Baumgartner	1996	3293
170 1/8	26 4/8	26 1/8	18 4/8	5 2/8	5	6	6	Alberta Beach, AB	Rodney M. Janz	Rodney M. Janz	1996	3293
170 1/8	27	25 5/8	20 1/8	5 6/8	5 2/8	6	6	Clark Co., IN	Daniel H. Lenfert	Daniel H. Lenfert	1996	3293
170 1/8	24 2/8	25 2/8	21 1/8	4 5/8	4 7/8	8	5	Ashland Co., OH	Steven J. Orchard	Steven J. Orchard	1996	3293
170 1/8	25 4/8	24 3/8		5 2/8	5 6/8			Cowley Co., KS	Mitchell D. Payne	Mitchell D. Payne	1996	3293
170 1/8	24 4/8	24 4/8		6 2/8				Roseau Co., MN	Rodney E. Putney	R.E. Putney & F. Walker	1996	3293
170 1/8	26 5/8	27 6/8		4 7/8				Nuevo Laredo, MX	John F. Taylor	John F. Taylor	1996	3293

WHITETAIL DEER - TYPICAL ANTLERS

Odocoileus virginianus virginianus and certain related subspecies

Score	Length of Main Beam R	L	Inside Spread	Circumference at Smallest Place Between Burr and First Point R	L	Number of Points R	L	Locality	Hunter	Owner	Date Killed	Rank
170 1/8	22 7/8	22 7/8	17 5/8	4 1/8	4 1/8	5	5	Maverick Co., TX	Donald Gann	Donald Gann	1997	3293
170 1/8	23 4/8	23 2/8	17 7/8	5	5 3/8	7	6	Cochin, SK	John M. Hanger II	John M. Hanger II	1997	3293
170 1/8	27 2/8	26 5/8	19 2/8	4 2/8	4 1/8	7	7	Kleberg Co., TX	Robert Nichols III	Robert Nichols III	1997	3293
170 1/8	26 1/8	26 4/8	17 1/8	4 2/8	4 2/8	7	6	Gates Co., NC	William W. Parker	William W. Parker	1997	3293
170 1/8	28 5/8	29 1/8	22 3/8	5 1/8	5 3/8	4	5	Hart Co., KY	Paul B. Wilson	Paul B. Wilson	1997	3293
170 1/8	26 2/8	26 6/8	16 1/8	5 4/8	5 4/8	6	6	Brown Co., IL	Todd D. Carlton	Todd D. Carlton	1998	3293
170 1/8	28 1/8	28 3/8	20 5/8	4 4/8	4 4/8	5	6	Hart Co., KY	Doug Fields	Doug Fields	1998	3293
170 1/8	24 6/8	23 6/8	18 1/8	4 5/8	4 5/8	6	6	Kenedy Co., TX	Jarred W. Peeples	Jarred W. Peeples	1998	3293
170 1/8	28 4/8	28 1/8	17 2/8	4 2/8	4 4/8	6	6	Taylor Co., GA	Joseph J. Ryals	Joseph J. Ryals	1998	3293
170 1/8	27	27 1/8	22 7/8	5	5	5	5	Keya Paha Co., NE	Picked Up	Teresa A. Bammerlin	1999	3293
170 1/8	23 7/8	23 4/8	18 3/8	4 4/8	4 4/8	5	5	Unknown	Unknown	Martin E. Cahoon	PR 1999	3293
170 1/8	28 5/8	28 2/8	19 1/8	5 5/8	5 6/8	6	6	Saginaw Co., MI	Mario VanderMeulen	Mario VanderMeulen	1999	3293
170 1/8	29	29 1/8	19 4/8	5	4 7/8	8	6	Allamakee Co., IA	Gary W. Anfinson	Gary W. Anfinson	2000	3293
170 1/8	25 4/8	25 3/8	21 2/8	5 6/8	6	7	6	Little Quill Lake, SK	Bennie Buttram	Bennie Buttram	2000	3293
170 1/8	25 4/8	26	21 7/8	4 6/8	5	5	6	Buffalo Co., WI	Dan Folkedahl	Dan Folkedahl	2000	3293
170 1/8	25 7/8	26 4/8	16 7/8	4 2/8	4 2/8	6	7	Lake of the Woods Co., MN	Kevin L. Olson	Kevin L. Olson	2000	3293
170 1/8	25	25 6/8	22 1/8	4 2/8	4 2/8	7	7	La Salle Co., TX	Weldon L. Nichols	Weldon L. Nichols	2001	3293
170 1/8	26 3/8	26 7/8	19 3/8	4 6/8	4 7/8	6	6	Tomahawk Creek, AB	Jim W. Robertson	Jim W. Robertson	2001	3293
170 1/8	26 7/8	26 3/8	22 3/8	5 2/8	5 1/8	5	9	Iron Co., WI	Randy D. Szukalski	Randy D. Szukalski	2001	3293
170 1/8	26 6/8	26 2/8	20 1/8	5	4 7/8	5	5	Boone Co., IA	Paul K. Adix	Paul K. Adix	2002	3293
170 1/8	23 7/8	23 6/8	17 5/8	4 5/8	4 4/8	6	6	Unknown	Unknown	Cabela's, Inc.	PR 2002	3293
170 1/8	27 6/8	27 6/8	19 1/8	4 5/8	4 4/8	4	4	Geary Co., KS	Picked Up	Carlos Navarro	2002	3293
170 1/8	25 6/8	26 4/8	20 1/8	5	4 7/8	6	6	Fairfield Co., OH	Kirk H. Smith	Kirk H. Smith	2002	3293
170	26	26 6/8	17 5/8	4 1/8	4 1/8	7	6	Schoolcraft Co., MI	Harold P. Dixner	J. Kenneth Dixner	PR 1918	3381
170	24 7/8	26 5/8	21 6/8	4 3/8	4 4/8	5	5	Oneida Co., WI	Felix Holewinski, Sr.	Ray T. Charles	1928	3381
170	24 2/8	24 2/8	18 4/8	4 1/8	4 1/8	6	7	Oiltown, TX	L.D. Roberts	L.D. Roberts	1941	3381
170	25 5/8	24 1/8	21 6/8	4 4/8	4 6/8	10	10	Blair Co., PA	Claude Feathers	Claude Feathers	1943	3381
170	26 4/8	27	23	6 4/8	6 4/8	5	5	Virden, MB	Jessie Byer	Jessie Byer	1951	3381
170	28 2/8	27 4/8	19 2/8	5	5 2/8	6	6	Clayton Co., IA	Kenneth D. Gossman	Darlene Gossman	1955	3381
170	27	28	22 4/8	4 4/8	4 4/8	5	5	Webb Co., TX	Herbert Zieschang	Herbert Zieschang	1957	3381
170	28 7/8	27 5/8	20	5 1/8	5 1/8	6	5	Chippewa Co., WI	John J. Scheidler	Jim Falls Lions Club	1959	3381
170	27 4/8	27 6/8	23 1/8	6 5/8	6 7/8	6	6	Fullerton, NE	Truman Lauterback	Truman Lauterback	1959	3381
170	26 2/8	25 2/8	21	5 4/8	5 4/8	5	5	W. Feliciana Parish, LA	Jerry Loper	Jerry Loper	1960	3381
170	23 2/8	26	19 6/8	5 1/8	5 2/8	7	6	Henderson Co., IL	Donald R. Vaughn	Donald R. Vaughn	1960	3381
170	27 5/8	26 5/8	24 1/8	4 1/8	4	6	8	Atascosa Co., TX	Ben H. Moore, Jr.	Ben H. Moore, Jr.	1961	3381
170	26 1/8	24 5/8	17 7/8	4 4/8	4 4/8	6	6	Flathead Co., MT	Dave Delap	Dave Delap	1966	3381

Score	Main Beam R	Main Beam L	Inside Spread	Points R	Points L	Circ. R	Circ. L	Locality	Hunter	Owner	Date Killed	Rank
170	22 7/8	22 4/8	18 4/8	6	5	4 6/8	4 7/8	Stevens Co., WA	Clair Kelso	Clair Kelso	1966	3381
170	26 4/8	26 5/8	17 4/8	5	7	4 6/8	4 7/8	Bates Co., MO	Gary Rosier	Gary Rosier	1969	3381
170	28 3/8	25 6/8	21 1/8	7	6	5 2/8	5 3/8	Hancock Co., IL	Henry F. Collins	Henry F. Collins	1973	3381
170	26 3/8	24 5/8	19 6/8	5	5	5 2/8	5 1/8	Shelby Co., MO	Rusty D. Gander	Rusty D. Gander	1973	3381
170	26 4/8	25 5/8	19 5/8	6	5	4 5/8	4 4/8	York Co., ME	Aubin Huertas	Aubin Huertas	1973	3381
170	28 4/8	27 3/8	21 4/8	7	8	4 7/8	5	Latah Co., ID	Lewis L. Turcott	Lewis L. Turcott	1974	3381
170	24 3/8	23 2/8	20 6/8	5	5	5	4 6/8	Scotland Co., MO	Chester J. Young	Chester J. Young	1974	3381
170	26	26	21	6	7	4 4/8	4 3/8	Dunn Co., WI	James W. Seehaver	James W. Seehaver	1976	3381
170	25 3/8	25 2/8	18	6	7	4 5/8	4 5/8	Ballard Co., KY	Rudolf Koranchan, Jr.	Rudolf Koranchan, Jr.	1977	3381
170	28 3/8	27 4/8	21	6	4	4 6/8	5	Androscoggin Co., ME	Ricky D. Cavers	Ricky D. Cavers	1981	3381
170	25 3/8	26 7/8	19 3/8	6	5	4 7/8	4 5/8	Des Moines Co., IA	Dean A. Dravis	Dean A. Dravis	1983	3381
170	26 2/8	26 6/8	20 2/8	7	5	4 7/8	5	Wapello Co., IA	George C. Ellis	George C. Ellis	1984	3381
170	25 6/8	25 6/8	16 5/8	8	5	5 4/8	5	Harrison Co., IA	Rodney P. Stahlnecker	Rodney P. Stahlnecker	1984	3381
170	29 1/8	27 7/8	23 4/8	6	6	4 7/8	5 4/8	Penobscot Co., ME	Picked Up	Tad D. Proudlove	1985	3381
170	27	26 7/8	19 2/8	5	7	4 7/8	5	Emo, ON	Jack Booth	Jack Booth	PR 1986	3381
170	27 7/8	27 6/8	21 6/8	7	7	4 6/8	4 6/8	Putnam Co., MO	Unknown	Terry L. Gates	1987	3381
170	27 5/8	27 5/8	20 4/8	5	5	5 5/8	5 2/8	Jefferson Co., WI	Robert L. Becker	Robert L. Becker	1988	3381
170	26 7/8	27 2/8	18 5/8	5	5	5 4/8	5 6/8	Jones Co., IA	James L. Coyle	James L. Coyle	1989	3381
170	28	28 1/8	20	7	8	4 4/8	4 4/8	Dane Co., WI	Patrick D. Anderson	Patrick D. Anderson	1989	3381
170	28 4/8	26 7/8	19 2/8	5	5	4 2/8	4 2/8	Madison Co., IA	Terry L. Snyder	Terry L. Snyder	1990	3381
170	26	26 1/8	19 4/8	7	7	4 6/8	4 7/8	Webster Co., IA	Picked Up	Clare E. Bailey	1990	3381
170	27	27	21	6	6	4 5/8	4 6/8	Jackson Co., MI	Michael D. Fitzgerald	Michael D. Fitzgerald	1990	3381
170	29 3/8	27 5/8	18 2/8	5	5	3 7/8	3 7/8	Sounding Lake, AB	Bill Kostenuk	Bill Kostenuk	1990	3381
170	24 2/8	24 2/8	23	5	8	5 1/8	5 2/8	Hyde Co., SD	Matthew Kusser	Matthew Kusser	1990	3381
170	27 1/8	26 5/8	16 1/8	7	5	5 4/8	5 3/8	Wabamun Lake, AB	John Nagtegaal	John Nagtegaal	1990	3381
170	25 6/8	25 4/8	17 4/8	6	7	4 1/8	4	Tift Co., GA	Alan Parrish	Alan Parrish	1991	3381
170	28 3/8	27 4/8	16 3/8	6	6	4 4/8	4 4/8	Worth Co., GA	Travis Strength	Travis Strength	1991	3381
170	25 7/8	26 1/8	21 3/8	7	7	5 5/8	5 6/8	Boone Co., MO	Norman M. Barrows	Norman M. Barrows	1991	3381
170	28 1/8	27 3/8	20 3/8	9	9	5 1/8	5 2/8	Bond Co., IL	Mark A. Carr	Mark A. Carr	1991	3381
170	25 2/8	26 2/8	18 2/8	7	6	5 2/8	6	Montgomery Co., IA	Jerry A. Foote	Jerry A. Foote	1991	3381
170	23 7/8	23 7/8	23 7/8	7	6	6	5 4/8	Marion Co., IA	Helen Hall	Helen Hall	1992	3381
170	28 1/8	28 2/8	18 2/8	6	7	5 2/8	5 4/8	Ripley Co., IN	Robert N. Hughes	Robert N. Hughes	1992	3381
170	27	26 1/8	23 4/8	5	5	5 4/8	6	Davis Co., IA	Picked Up	IA Dept. of Natl. Resc.	PR 1992	3381
170	28 7/8	27 3/8	20 1/8	6	6	4 2/8	4 2/8	McHenry Co., IL	Daniel L. Doherty	Daniel L. Doherty	1993	3381
170	25 6/8	24 5/8	20 6/8	6	7	6	4 6/8	Buffalo Co., WI	Gary G. Ruff	Gary G. Ruff	1993	3381
170	26 1/8	26 3/8	17 4/8	7	6	4 6/8	4 7/8	Crow Wing Co., MN	Unknown	Calvin L. Seguin	1993	3381
170	27 1/8	27 2/8	18 2/8	6	5	4 7/8	5	Bottineau Co., ND	Ryan M. Bernstein	Ryan M. Bernstein	1993	3381
170	24 7/8	24 4/8	18 2/8	5	5	5	5 5/8	Porcupine Forest, SK	Jeff B. Brigham	Jeff B. Brigham	1993	3381
170	25 4/8	25 1/8	20 2/8	5	6	5 6/8	5 1/8	McHenry Co., IL	Mike R. Fischer	Mike R. Fischer	1994	3381
170	25	24 6/8	25 1/8	6	6	5 1/8	5 3/8	De Witt Co., IL	Charles A. Leimbach	Charles A. Leimbach	1994	3381
170	27 1/8	27 1/8	21 6/8	6	4	5 3/8	5 2/8	Desha Co., AR	Ben J. Miller	Ben J. Miller	1994	3381
170	25 6/8	25 6/8	22 2/8	4	7	5	5	Brown Co., AR	Paul I. Reid	Paul I. Reid	1994	3381
170	23 7/8	23 3/8	16 6/8	6	5	4 7/8	4 6/8	Harrison Co., IN	Phillip L. Whiteman	Phillip L. Whiteman	1994	3381
170	27 5/8	26 3/8	19 6/8	5	6	4 6/8	4 2/8	Wayne Co., KY	Danny Phillips	Danny Phillips	1995	3381
170	24 4/8	25	17 6/8	6	5	4 3/8	4 1/8	Porcupine Plain, SK	Picked Up	Terry L. Amos	1996	3381
170	25	27 2/8	21 6/8	5	5	4 1/8	4 3/8	Cross Co., AR	Clay C. Bassham	Clay C. Bassham	1996	3381
170	28 4/8	25 4/8	18	6	6	4 3/8	4 3/8	Washington Co., OH	Robert L. Clark, Jr.	Robert L. Clark, Jr.	1996	3381
170	24 1/8	25 2/8	20 5/8	5	8	6 2/8	6 2/8	Pike Co., IL	Perry Stanley	Perry Stanley	1996	3381

WHITETAIL DEER - TYPICAL ANTLERS
Odocoileus virginianus virginianus and certain related subspecies

Score	Length of Main Beam		Inside Spread	Circumference at Smallest Place Between Burr and First Point		Number of Points		Locality	Hunter	Owner	Date Killed	Rank
	R	L		R	L	R	L					
170	26 4/8	25 4/8	22 2/8	4 6/8	4 6/8	5	5	Washington Co., WI	Alan R. Gehl	Alan R. Gehl	1997	3381
170	24 4/8	23 7/8	17	4 2/8	4 2/8	5	5	Allamakee Co., IA	Lloyd O. Griffith	Lloyd O. Griffith	1998	3381
170	27 1/8	25 1/8	19	4 6/8	4 7/8	5	5	Whiteside Co., IL	Arlyn D. Hamstra	Arlyn D. Hamstra	1998	3381
170	24 6/8	25 4/8	19 3/8	5	4 7/8	5	5	Kane Co., IL	Bradley J. Lundsteen	Bradley J. Lundsteen	1998	3381
170	26 5/8	27 3/8	20 5/8	4 6/8	4 4/8	5	6	Cherokee Co., IA	Ben R. Puttmann	Ben R. Puttmann	1998	3381
170	25 6/8	24 5/8	20 2/8	4 5/8	4 5/8	5	5	Wakaw Lake, SK	Nolan Balone	Nolan Balone	1999	3381
170	25 1/8	25 1/8	20 7/8	5 3/8	5 3/8	7	5	Cedar Co., IA	Ronald R. Cain	Ronald R. Cain	1999	3381
170	25 2/8	25 2/8	18 2/8	4 4/8	4 5/8	7	7	Wabasha Co., MN	Chad R. Collins	Chad R. Collins	1999	3381
170	26 2/8	26 6/8	20 2/8	4 7/8	4 7/8	7	5	Pratt Co., KS	Ronald R. George	Ronald R. George	1999	3381
170	29 3/8	28 6/8	18	4 6/8	4 7/8	6	6	Neosho Co., KS	Frank L. Pechacek	Frank L. Pechacek	1999	3381
170	27 2/8	25 7/8	22	4 7/8	4 6/8	5	5	Fowler Lake, SK	Stuart J. Bishop	Stuart J. Bishop	2000	3381
170	26 2/8	26 1/8	18 6/8	4 6/8	4 6/8	7	7	Otsego Co., MI	Robert M. Cannon	Robert M. Cannon	2000	3381
170	27	26 2/8	18 2/8	5	4 4/8	6	5	Tazewell Co., IL	Picked Up	Melissa A. Chirello	2000	3381
170	26 3/8	25 7/8	15 4/8	4 7/8	5	5	5	Crawford Co., WI	Joel B. Oppriecht	Joel B. Oppriecht	2000	3381
170	26 6/8	27 6/8	21 6/8	4 6/8	4 7/8	5	5	Oxford Co., ME	Kenneth A. Zerbst	Kenneth A. Zerbst	2000	3381
170	26	24 5/8	20	5	5	5	6	Logan Co., OH	Randy D. Longshore	Randy D. Longshore	2001	3381
170	26 6/8	27	20 6/8	5	4 7/8	5	6	Edgar Co., IL	K. David Neal	K. David Neal	2001	3381
170	29	27 1/8	21 4/8	4 7/8	4 7/8	5	5	Erie Co., OH	John A. Smith	John A. Smith	2001	3381
170	25 4/8	25 3/8	24 4/8	5 1/8	5 3/8	7	7	Buffalo Co., WI	Gilbert A. Arnoldy	Gilbert A. Arnoldy	2002	3381
204 2/8*	30 2/8	29 6/8	20 4/8	4 5/8	4 5/8	6	5	Pendleton Co., KY	Robert W. Smith	Robert W. Smith	2000	
198 7/8*	24 6/8	25 3/8	18 1/8	5	5	6	6	Moose Mountain Lake, SK	Mark Hordeski	Cabela's, Inc.	1999	
195 6/8*	26 2/8	26 4/8	20	5	4 6/8	6	6	Parker View, SK	Carl L. Sawchuk, Sr.	Carl A. Sawchuk, Jr.	1954	

* Final score is subject to revision by additional verifying measurements.

CATEGORY
WHITETAIL DEER -
TYPICAL ANTLERS

SCORE
179-2/8

HUNTER
DEL KIRCHMAYER

LOCATION
VERNON LAKE, ALBERTA

DATE OF KILL
NOVEMBER 1997

CATEGORY
WHITETAIL DEER -
TYPICAL ANTLERS

SCORE
170-5/8

HUNTER
JOHN W. STOOTHOFF, JR.

LOCATION
MEADOW LAKE,
SASKATCHEWAN

DATE OF KILL
NOVEMBER 2000

CATEGORY
WHITETAIL DEER -
TYPICAL ANTLERS

SCORE
180-1/8

HUNTER
MATTHEW D. MILLER

LOCATION
CLARK COUNTY,
INDIANA

DATE OF KILL
NOVEMBER 2000

CATEGORY
WHITETAIL DEER - TYPICAL ANTLERS

SCORE
180-1/8

HUNTER
STEPHEN F. DEMEULENAERE

LOCATION
MEDINA COUNTY, OHIO

DATE OF KILL
DECEMBER 1998

CATEGORY
WHITETAIL DEER -
TYPICAL ANTLERS

SCORE
180-4/8

HUNTER
THOMAS C. KROENING

LOCATION
OLMSTED COUNTY,
MINNESOTA

DATE OF KILL
NOVEMBER 1998

CATEGORY
WHITETAIL DEER -
TYPICAL ANTLERS

SCORE
179-6/8

HUNTER
RICK SCHUSTER

LOCATION
CUTARM CREEK,
SASKATCHEWAN

DATE OF KILL
NOVEMBER 2001

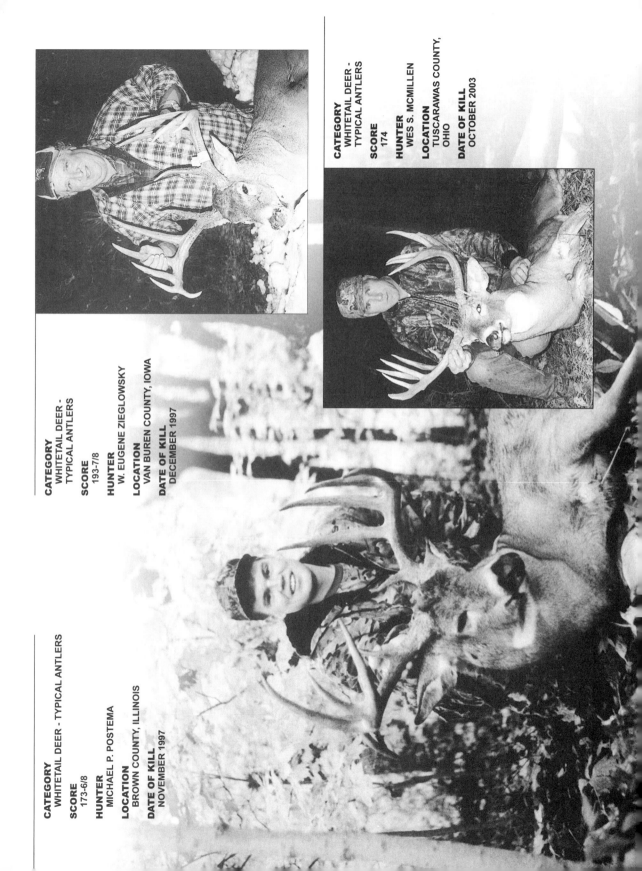

CATEGORY
WHITETAIL DEER -
TYPICAL ANTLERS

SCORE
193-7/8

HUNTER
W. EUGENE ZIEGLOWSKY

LOCATION
VAN BUREN COUNTY, IOWA

DATE OF KILL
DECEMBER 1997

CATEGORY
WHITETAIL DEER -
TYPICAL ANTLERS

SCORE
174

HUNTER
WES S. MCMILLEN

LOCATION
TUSCARAWAS COUNTY,
OHIO

DATE OF KILL
OCTOBER 2003

CATEGORY
WHITETAIL DEER - TYPICAL ANTLERS

SCORE
173-6/8

HUNTER
MICHAEL P. POSTEMA

LOCATION
BROWN COUNTY, ILLINOIS

DATE OF KILL
NOVEMBER 1997

CATEGORY
WHITETAIL DEER -
TYPICAL ANTLERS

SCORE
176-5/8

HUNTER
LARRY K. TROUT

LOCATION
CARROT RIVER,
SASKATCHEWAN

DATE OF KILL
NOVMEBER 2001

CATEGORY
WHITETAIL DEER -
TYPICAL ANTLERS

SCORE
171-3/8

HUNTER
JAMES V. HOLDENRIED

LOCATION
SANGAMON COUNTY,
ILLINOIS

DATE OF KILL
DECEMBER 2001

CATEGORY
WHITETAIL DEER - TYPICAL ANTLERS

SCORE
170-7/8

HUNTER
DONALD G. FRANDRUP

LOCATION
PIERCE COUNTY, WISCONSIN

DATE OF KILL
2002

Mary J. La General Sun City.

RIGHT: DING BECAME THE "FATHER OF THE FEDERAL 'DUCK STAMP'" ON MARCH 16, 1934, WHEN CONGRESS PASSED, AND PRESIDENT FRANKLIN ROOSEVELT SIGNED, THE MIGRATORY BIRD HUNTING STAMP ACT.

ABOVE: DING, A POLITICAL CARTOONIST FOR THE DES MOINES REGISTER, WAS KNOWN FOR HIS BITING SATIRES.

JAY N. "DING" DARLING
1876-1962

By H. Hudson DeCray

He was a newspaper reporter, author, and cartoonist. He was also the 1924 winner of the Pulitzer Prize for the "best cartoon" published in any American newspaper during the preceding year. He was a leading conservationist with a deep and abiding interest in wildlife. As such, he was probably the first to draw attention to the plight of the Florida Key Deer in the late 1950s. Ding designed the first Federal Duck Stamp in 1934. The Boone and Crockett Club bestowed him with an Honorary Life Membership in 1959. ∎

483

WHITETAIL DEER - NON-TYPICAL ANTLERS
WORLD'S RECORD

RANK
World's Record

SCORE
333 7/8

LOCATION
St. Louis Co., MO

HUNTER
Picked Up

OWNER
MO Dept. of Cons.

DATE KILLED
1981

Although several all-time typical whitetail trophies have been from Missouri, it was not until the fall of 1981 that this state acquired the bragging rights to the World's Record non-typical whitetail deer (Odocoileus virginianus).

On November 15, 1981, David Beckman met Conservation Agent Michael Helland along a road in northern St. Louis County, Missouri. Beckman had killed a deer and he asked Helland to officially check and seal it, to save the drive to an official check station.

They talked for a few minutes after sealing the deer, and then Beckman drove away. Not long after leaving Helland, Beckman saw a dead buck with a very large rack lying inside a fence along the road. Knowing that the deer was on private property and that he would not be able to retrieve it, Beckman decided to find Helland and tell him of his discovery.

Agent Helland obtained permission of the landowner to recover the carcass. With the help of friends, he skinned the deer and removed the rack that weighed over 11 pounds. It was estimated that the deer weighed over 250 pounds. Examination of the teeth revealed that the monstrously large deer was only 5-1/2 years old. Cause of death could not be determined, but it did not appear to have been shot.

Winter is a busy time of year for conservation agents. The rack was forgotten until after the first of the year when Helland took the cape and rack to a taxidermist friend. The taxidermist to whom he took it recognized its outstanding trophy character. Helland arranged to have the trophy scored by Dean Murphy, a Boone and Crockett Club official measurer. With the help of Wayne Porath, deer biologist for the Missouri Department of Conservation, Murphy scored the trophy for entry into the 18th Awards Entry Period at 325-7/8. Later it was officially scored at 333-7/8, and became the new World's Record non-typical whitetail.

All persons involved agreed that a trophy of this stature should be held in public ownership and on public display for everyone to enjoy. Accordingly, the Missouri Department of Conservation was assumed possession of the marvelous antlers. ■

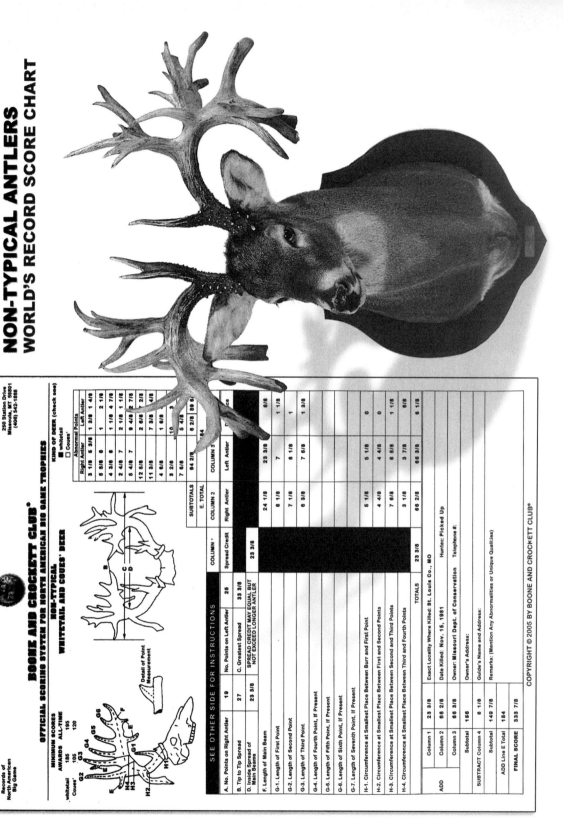

WHITETAIL DEER NON-TYPICAL ANTLERS WORLD'S RECORD SCORE CHART

Records of North American Big Game

250 Station Drive
Missoula, MT 59801
(406) 542-1888

BOONE AND CROCKETT CLUB®

OFFICIAL SCORING SYSTEM FOR NORTH AMERICAN BIG GAME TROPHIES

NON-TYPICAL WHITETAIL AND COUES' DEER

MINIMUM SCORES

	AWARDS	ALL-TIME
Whitetail	185	195
Coues'	105	120

KIND OF DEER (check one)
- ☑ whitetail
- ☐ Coues'

Abnormal Points

Right Antler		Left Antler	
3 1/8	5 3/8	1 3/8	1 4/8
5 6/8	6	1	2 1/8
4 3/8	8	1 1/8	4 7/8
2 4/8	7	2 1/8	1 1/8
5 4/8	7	9 4/8	2 7/8
12 5/8		2 6/8	2/8
11 3/8		7 3/8	4/8
4 6/8		1 6/8	
3 2/8		10	3
7 6/8		5 4/8	
SUBTOTALS 94 2/8		6 2/8	89 0/8

E. TOTAL 184

SEE OTHER SIDE FOR INSTRUCTIONS

		COLUMN 1	COLUMN 2	COLUMN 3
		Spread Credit	Right Antler	Left Antler
A. No. Points on Right Antler	19			
No. Points on Left Antler	25			
B. Tip to Tip Spread	27			
C. Greatest Spread	33 3/8			
D. Inside Spread of Main Beams	23 3/8			
SPREAD CREDIT MAY EQUAL BUT NOT EXCEED LONGER ANTLER		23 3/8		
F. Length of Main Beam			24 1/8	23 3/8
G-1. Length of First Point			8 1/8	7
G-2. Length of Second Point			7 1/8	6 1/8
G-3. Length of Third Point			6 3/8	7 6/8
G-4. Length of Fourth Point, If Present				
G-5. Length of Fifth Point, If Present				
G-6. Length of Sixth Point, If Present				
G-7. Length of Seventh Point, If Present				
H-1. Circumference at Smallest Place Between Burr and First Point			5 1/8	5 1/8
H-2. Circumference at Smallest Place Between First and Second Points			4 4/8	4 4/8
H-3. Circumference at Smallest Place Between Second and Third Points			7 6/8	6 5/8
H-4. Circumference at Smallest Place Between Third and Fourth Points			3 1/8	3 7/8
TOTALS		23 3/8	66 2/8	66 3/8

ADD	Column 1	23 3/8
	Column 2	66 2/8
	Column 3	66 3/8
	Subtotal	156
SUBTRACT	Column 4	6 1/8
	Subtotal	149 7/8
	ADD Line E Total	184
	FINAL SCORE	333 7/8

Exact Locality Where Killed: St. Louis Co., MO
Date Killed: Nov. 15, 1981   Hunter: Picked Up
Owner: Missouri Dept. of Conservation   Telephone #:
Owner's Address:
Guide's Name and Address:
Remarks: (Mention Any Abnormalities or Unique Qualities)

Detail of Point Measurement

COPYRIGHT © 2005 BY BOONE AND CROCKETT CLUB®

485

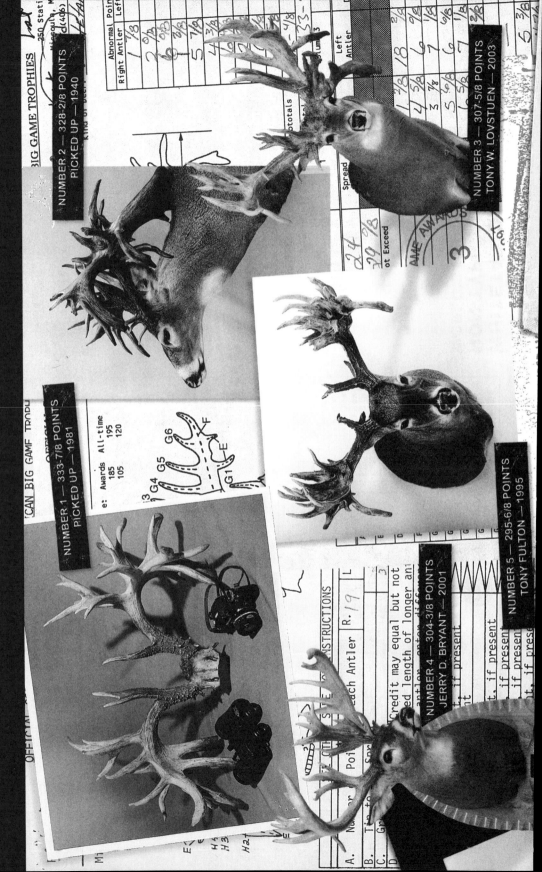

NUMBER 7 — 282 POINTS
LARRY RAVELING — 1973

NUMBER 10 — 279-6/8 POINTS
NEIL J. MORIN — 1991

NUMBER 6 — 284-3/8 POINTS
UNKNOWN — 1892

NUMBER 9 — 280-4/8 POINTS
JOSEPH H. WATERS — 1987

NUMBER 8 — 281-6/8 POINTS
JAMES H. McMURRAY — 1994

WHITETAIL DEER - NON-TYPICAL ANTLERS

Odocoileus virginianus virginianus and certain related subspecies

MINIMUM SCORE 195

Score	Length of Main Beam		Inside Spread	Circumference at Smallest Place Between Burr and First Point		Number of Points		Locality	Hunter	Owner	Date Killed	Rank
	R	L		R	L	R	L					
333 7/8	24 1/8	23 3/8	23 3/8	5 1/8	5 1/8	19	25	St. Louis Co., MO	Picked Up	MO Dept. of Cons.	1981	1
328 2/8	25 5/8	24 4/8	24 3/8	6 2/8	5 6/8	23	22	Portage Co., OH	Picked Up	Bass Pro Shops	1940	2
307 5/8	26 3/8	23 5/8	22	8	6 4/8	21	17	Monroe Co., IA	Tony W. Lovstuen	Bass Pro Shops	2003	3
304 3/8	27 3/8	27 2/8	23 1/8	5 1/8	5 7/8	17	20	Fulton Co., IL	Jerry D. Bryant	Jerry D. Bryant	2001	4
295 6/8	21 2/8	18 2/8	22 3/8	5 5/8	5 3/8	21	24	Winston Co., MS	Tony Fulton	Tony Fulton	1995	5
284 3/8	21 4/8	19 6/8	16 2/8	4 4/8	4 4/8	21	26	McCulloch Co., TX	Unknown	Buckhorn Mus. & Saloon, Ltd.	1892	6
282	26 1/8	27	24 3/8	6 5/8	6 2/8	15	14	Clay Co., IA	Larry Raveling	Bass Pro Shops	1973	7
281 6/8	22 1/8	20 6/8	17 6/8	5 2/8	5	16	13	Tensas Parish, LA	James H. McMurray	James H. McMurray	1994	8
280 4/8	25 3/8	25 2/8	19 6/8	6 1/8	6 4/8	16	13	Shawnee Co., KS	Joseph H. Waters	Brad Gsell	1987	9
279 6/8	27 6/8	26	21 6/8	6	6	13	14	Whitemud Creek, AB	Neil J. Morin	Brad Gsell	1991	10
277 5/8	27 5/8	28 4/8	24 6/8	6	6 1/8	17	16	Hardisty, AB	Doug Klinger	Doug Klinger	1976	11
277 3/8	28 1/8	28 3/8	21 1/8	6 5/8	6 7/8	19	18	Hall Co., NE	Del Austin	Bass Pro Shops	1962	12
273 6/8	27 3/8	27 5/8	20 6/8	6	6	19	16	West Afton River, NS	Alexander C. MacDonald	Bass Pro Shops	1960	13
272	23 7/8	25	17 5/8	6 2/8	5 6/8	23	16	Junction, TX	Picked Up	Fred Mudge	1925	14
268 5/8	20 6/8	24 6/8	14 2/8	6 4/8	5 3/8	20	21	Norman Co., MN	Mitchell A. Vakoch	Bass Pro Shops	1974	15
267 7/8	25	24 4/8	22 6/8	6 1/8	6 2/8	20	18	Shoal Lake, AB	Jerry Froma	Jerry Froma	1984	16
267 4/8	26 6/8	27 6/8	29 1/8	5 1/8	5 6/8	16	23	Idaho	Unknown	Jack G. Brittingham	PR 1923	17
267 3/8	25 4/8	28 2/8	20	6 5/8	6 3/8	18	7	Peoria Co., IL	Richard A. Pauli	Richard A. Pauli	1983	18
267	26 2/8	25 4/8	24	5 7/8	5 7/8	12	16	Pike Co., OH	Chester T. Veach	Brad Gsell	1971	19
266 1/8	26 6/8	27	20 4/8	6 4/8	7 1/8	17	16	Pike Co., MO	Randy J. Simonitch	Randy J. Simonitch	2000	20
265 3/8	25 7/8	26	18 3/8	6 6/8	6 5/8	16	17	White Fox, SK	Elburn Kohler	Bass Pro Shops	1957	21
262 1/8	24 1/8	25 2/8	20	6 2/8	6 4/8	14	13	Ross Co., OH	Jay Pfankuch	D.J. Hollinger & B. Howard	1995	22
261 5/8	25 6/8	23	21 5/8	5 7/8	6	16	15	Park Co., WY	Bobby L. Beeman	Bobby L. Beeman	1998	23
260 1/8	24 1/8	24 1/8	23 4/8	5 5/8	5 5/8	18	17	Garrard Co., KY	Benjamin J. Brogle	Bass Pro Shops	2002	24
259 7/8	27	28 4/8	22 1/8	5	5 6/8	27	9	Perry Co., AL	Jon G. Moss	Jon G. Moss	1989	25
259 5/8	26 7/8	26 7/8	20 3/8	6	5 4/8	14	13	Chariton Co., MO	Duane R. Linscott	Bass Pro Shops	1985	26
259 2/8	24 4/8	23 3/8	21 7/8	5 3/8	5 6/8	12	14	Souris River, MB	Howard G. Pauls	Bass Pro Shops	2000	27
259	25 4/8	26 7/8	19 5/8	6 1/8	5 7/8	15	16	Washington Co., ME	Hill Gould	Bass Pro Shops	1910	28
259	16 2/8	15 3/8	15 6/8	5 4/8	5 3/8	16	11	Frio Co., TX	William B. Brown	Bettie B. Brown	PR 1967	28
258 6/8	22 4/8	26 2/8	23 6/8	6 4/8	6	17	15	Republic Co., KS	John O. Band	Bass Pro Shops	1965	30
258 6/8	24 3/8	25 4/8	22 7/8	5 4/8	5 5/8	15	15	Edgar Co., IL	Ernest R. Hires	Bass Pro Shops	1994	30
258 4/8	27 3/8	29	19 5/8	5 7/8	6	16	19	Steep Rock, MB	John DeLorme	Bass Pro Shops	1973	32
258 2/8	27	26 6/8	19 5/8	4 7/8	4 6/8	17	17	Becker Co., MN	J.J. Matter	J.J. Matter	1973	33
258 2/8	28 5/8	28 1/8	24 1/8	7	6 7/8	10	14	Louisa Co., IA	Lyle E. Spitznogle	Bass Pro Shops	1982	33
258 2/8	23	23	16 2/8	6 4/8	6 1/8	14	15	Cheyenne Co., CO	Michael J. Okray	Bass Pro Shops	1992	33
258 1/8	23 1/8	24 4/8	18 3/8	5 3/8	5 4/8	17	12	Cedar Co., IA	Picked Up	Bass Pro Shops	1988	36

Score	Main Beam R	Main Beam L	Inside Spread	Circ. R	Circ. L	Points R	Points L	Locality	By Whom Killed	Owner	Date Killed	Rank
257 6/8	24 3/8	22 1/8	22 1/8	5	6 3/8	9	17	Nez Perce Co., ID	John D. Powers, Jr.	Bass Pro Shops	1983	37
257 4/8	29 1/8	28 2/8	21	5 5/8	5 3/8	15	15	Warren Co., VA	James W. Smith	James W. Smith	1992	38
257 3/8	25 5/8	23 5/8	16 2/8	4 6/8	4 4/8	21	17	Elkhorn, MB	Harvey Olsen	Harvey Olsen	1973	39
257 1/8	29 4/8	27 4/8	23 6/8	6 2/8	5 6/8	20	14	Marion Co., KS	Jamie L. Remmers	Bass Pro Shops	1997	40
256 7/8	28 3/8	27 6/8	21	5 1/8	5 4/8	18	17	Jackson Co., IA	David B. Manderscheid	Bass Pro Shops	1977	41
256 5/8	29 1/8	27 7/8	24 6/8	6 5/8	6 1/8	14	16	Holmes Co., OH	Picked Up	OH Dept. of Natl. Resc.	1975	42
256 2/8	28 7/8	28 7/8	20 4/8	6 5/8	6 4/8	11	13	Monona Co., IA	Carroll E. Johnson	Carroll E. Johnson	1968	43
256 1/8	28 7/8	26 5/8	23 3/8	7 5/8	7 2/8	18	16	Marshall Co., SD	Francis Fink	Cabela's, Inc.	1948	44
256 1/8	30 1/8	29	21 7/8	5 3/8	5 5/8	11	15	McDonough Co., IL	Brian E. Bice	Bass Pro Shops	1992	44
255 4/8	23 2/8	21 7/8	18 1/8	5 6/8	5 5/8	18	17	Pigeon Lake, AB	Leo Eklund	Leo Eklund	1973	46
254 6/8	23 3/8	22 7/8	20 2/8	5 2/8	5	14	13	Stanley Co., ND	Roger Ritchie	Roger Ritchie	1968	47
254 3/8	29 1/8	27	24 2/8	4 3/8	4 4/8	13	15	McHenry Co., ND	Austin Dugan	James K. Dugan	1940	48
254 2/8	28	27 2/8	21 3/8	6 1/8	6 2/8	16	15	Caroline, AB	Mike Chrustawka	Cabela's, Inc.	1991	49
253	29 7/8	28	21 4/8	5 5/8	5 6/8	14	26	Goldenville, NS	Neil MacDonald	Bass Pro Shops	1945	50
253	23 4/8	29 7/8	24	5 3/8	5 4/8	12	12	Miami Co., KS	Kenneth R. Cartwright	Bass Pro Shops	1994	50
252 2/8	25	25	21 3/8	4 7/8	5 1/8	17	18	Concordia Parish, LA	J.D. Shields	J. Logan Sewell	1948	52
252 1/8	28 3/8	28 3/8	19 5/8	5 7/8	5 6/8	9	9	Hill Co., MT	Frank A. Pleskac	Dick Idol	1968	53
252	24 3/8	24 3/8	19 1/8	5 4/8	5 4/8	11	16	Lee Co., IA	Carl Wenke	Bass Pro Shops	1972	54
251 4/8	26 3/8	27 5/8	22 7/8	6 6/8	5 3/8	17	14	Beltrami Co., MN	Rodney Rhineberger	Bass Pro Shops	1976	55
251 4/8	27 3/8	22 1/8	19 3/8	6	6 5/8	15	14	Hendricks Co., IN	Timothy J. Goode	Bass Pro Shops	1980	55
251 4/8	26 5/8	26 6/8	22 6/8	5 5/8	5 6/8	13	10	Meeting Lake, SK	Greg Brataschuk	Brad Gsell	1987	55
251 1/8	28 2/8	28	19	5 4/8	5 5/8	12	13	Mitchell Co., KS	Theron E. Wilson	Theron E. Wilson	1974	58
250 6/8	25 3/8	25 4/8	15 1/8	5 5/8	5 3/8	19	19	South Dakota	Howard Eaton	Jack G. Brittingham	1870	59
250 6/8	27 2/8	27 2/8	23 4/8	7 1/8	5 2/8	12	12	Richland Co., OH	David D. Dull	David D. Dull	1987	59
250 4/8	29 6/8	29 7/8	20 5/8	5 7/8	5 7/8	13	9	Alexander Co., IL	Andrew French III	Andrew French III	2000	61
250 2/8	24 5/8	24 5/8	16 1/8	6 2/8	7	16	12	Washington Co., KS	Picked Up	Gale Sup	1988	62
250 1/8	27 3/8	27 3/8	19	4 1/8	6 1/8	16	17	Rainy Lake, ON	Grant Gustafson	Grant Gustafson	1995	63
250	29 5/8	30 1/8	23 4/8	5 1/8	6 1/8	15	13	Clearwater Co., MN	Ernest Sauer	Duane O. Bagley Wildl. Mus.	1931	64
249 7/8	26 5/8	25 6/8	23 2/8	5 2/8	4 2/8	12	22	Kings Co., NB	Ronald Martin	Bass Pro Shops	1946	65
249 3/8	26 3/8	26 3/8	25 3/8	6 4/8	5	14	14	Rockingham Co., VA	Jeffery W. Hensley	Jeffery W. Hensley	1990	66
249 3/8	29 6/8	28 7/8	21 3/8	5 7/8	5 2/8	10	14	Fillmore Co., MN	Dallas R. Henn	Bass Pro Shops	1961	67
249 1/8	26 2/8	26 7/8	19 2/8	6	6 2/8	12	20	Lily, SD	Jerry Roitsch	J.D. Andrews	1965	68
248 7/8	27 6/8	27 2/8	20 1/8	5 1/8	5 7/8	8	10	Greenwood Co., KS	Clifford G. Pickell	Bass Pro Shops	1968	69
248 6/8	27 4/8	28 1/8	20 5/8	7 7/8	5 7/8	18	19	Warren Co., IA	Larry J. Caldwell	Larry J. Caldwell	1990	70
248 6/8	25	24	20 5/8	6 1/8	6	16	12	Snowy Mts., MT	Unknown	McLean Bowman	PR 1980	71
248 4/8	24 3/8	24 3/8	22	6	5 1/8	15	11	Moose Mt. Park, SK	Walter Bartko	George Hooey	1964	72
248 4/8	28	27 4/8	23 5/8	5 4/8	7 4/8	16	13	Fulton Co., IN	Robert S. Sears	Bass Pro Shops	1990	72
248 4/8	26 5/8	26 1/8	18 1/8	7 2/8	5 7/8	12	19	Millet, AB	Donald Mayer	D.J. Hollinger & B. Howard	1995	72
248 1/8	26 1/8	26 3/8	22 3/8	5 4/8	6	15	14	Wellwood, MB	Paul A. Adriaansen	Paul A. Adriaansen	1999	72
248 1/8	31 1/8	32 1/8	22 6/8	5 3/8	5 4/8	12	15	Penobscot Co., ME	Unknown	James L. Mason, Sr.	1945	76
247 7/8	27 5/8	27 5/8	20 2/8	5 5/8	7 2/8	13	12	Crawford Co., KS	Bruce Jameson	Bass Pro Shops	1989	76
247 3/8	26 1/8	26	19 5/8	5 1/8	5 4/8	12	17	Frio Co., TX	Raul Rodriquez II	Raul Rodriquez II	1966	78
247 2/8	23 5/8	24 7/8	24 6/8	5 5/8	5 3/8	16	13	Vernon Co., WI	Arnold N. Stalsberg	Arnold N. Stalsberg	1998	79
246 3/8	25 4/8	25 3/8	24 6/8	5 1/8	5 5/8	9	14	Johnston Co., OK	Bill M. Foster	Bill M. Foster	1970	80
245 7/8	27 7/8	27 7/8	29 3/8	5 5/8	5 1/8	11	14	Anderson Co., KS	Richard T. Stahl	Bass Pro Shops	1992	81
245 6/8	31 2/8	27 6/8	25 3/8	5 1/8	5 6/8	13	14	Elk River, BC	James I. Brewster	James I. Brewster	1905	82
245 6/8	24 1/8	24 3/8	18 7/8	5 5/8	5 6/8	12	13	Souris River, MB	Richard D. Pauls	Richard D. Pauls	2000	83
245 5/8	25 5/8	25 2/8	24 2/8	5 2/8	5 3/8	12	12	Itasca Co., MN	Peter Rutkowski	Bass Pro Shops	1942	84

WHITETAIL DEER - NON-TYPICAL ANTLERS

Odocoileus virginianus virginianus and certain related subspecies

Score	Length of Main Beam R	L	Inside Spread	Circumference at Smallest Place Between Burr and First Point R	L	Number of Points R	L	Locality	Hunter	Owner	Date Killed	Rank
245 5/8	28 2/8	26 6/8	18 5/8	6 2/8	6 4/8	13	15	Kankakee Co., IL	Lawrence G. Ekhoff	Lawrence G. Ekhoff	1999	84
245 4/8	24 6/8	21 5/8	16 5/8	5 3/8	5	18	12	Carrot River, SK	Picked Up	Ken Halloway	1962	86
245 4/8	27 7/8	27 5/8	18 6/8	6 1/8	6 2/8	16	15	Kittson Co., MN	Lyndon K. Westerberg	Lyndon K. Westerberg	1990	86
245 3/8	24	24 4/8	17 4/8	5 7/8	6 1/8	14	14	Itasca Co., MN	Mike Hammer	Bass Pro Shops	1956	88
245 3/8	28	25 7/8	18 4/8	4 6/8	4 7/8	17	16	Marshall Co., IA	Don L. Boucher	Don L. Boucher	1996	88
245	27 4/8	27	20 6/8	5 3/8	5 4/8	15	15	Buffalo Co., WI	Elmer F. Gotz	Elmer F. Gotz	1973	90
244 6/8	25 4/8	28	17 4/8	5 3/8	5 2/8	18	13	Monroe Co., IA	Robert N. Wonderlich	Bass Pro Shops	1970	91
244 3/8	22 1/8	23 1/8	17 4/8	5 4/8	4 7/8	25	24	Sumner Co., TN	David K. Wachtel III	David K. Wachtel III	2000	92
244 2/8	27	27 2/8	16 5/8	5 6/8	5 5/8	13	13	Allegany Co., NY	Homer Boylan	Harry J. Boylan	1939	93
244 2/8	20 7/8	20	16 1/8	4 7/8	4 2/8	18	14	Zavala Co., TX	John R. Campbell	John L. Stein	1947	93
244 1/8	25 6/8	23 1/8	20	4 7/8	5 6/8	10	15	Kenton, MB	Frank Smart	Cabela's, Inc.	1949	95
244 1/8	27 4/8	28	20 6/8	5	4 6/8	11	11	Sangamon Co., IL	William E. Hood	William E. Hood	1991	95
244	25 4/8	30 3/8	20 2/8	5 5/8	5 4/8	8	10	Becker Co., MN	James Saurdoff	Bass Pro Shops	1985	97
244	28 7/8	28 3/8	20 1/8	7	6 4/8	15	11	Morris Co., KS	Burt Nichols	Cabela's, Inc.	1997	97
243 7/8	26 7/8	26 3/8	16 2/8	8 2/8	8 2/8	18	15	Wirral, NB	H. Glenn Johnston	Arnold Alward	1962	99
243 7/8	26 3/8	26 5/8	20 4/8	6 5/8	7 1/8	14	13	Cook Co., IL	Picked Up	Jeffrey A. DeVroy	1995	99
243 5/8	24 1/8	24 1/8	22 2/8	5 1/8	5	11	15	Govan, SK	A.W. Davis	Bass Pro Shops	1951	101
243 3/8	27 7/8	29 7/8	17 7/8	4 5/8	4 6/8	11	9	Mahoning Co., OH	David L. Klemm	Bass Pro Shops	1980	102
242 7/8	18 1/8	17 2/8	15 7/8	4 7/8	5 2/8	21	21	Pope Co., IL	William E. Henderson	William E. Henderson	1991	103
242 6/8	24	24 4/8	18 6/8	6 2/8	6	22	18	Bedford Co., VA	Walter Hatcher	Walter Hatcher	1993	104
242 5/8	27 2/8	26 1/8	17 2/8	6	5 4/8	13	16	Nance Co., NE	Robert E. Snyder	Bass Pro Shops	1961	105
242 4/8	26 4/8	27	20 6/8	5 1/8	5 1/8	10	12	S. Saskatchewan River, SK	Earl W. Green	Bass Pro Shops	1993	106
242 2/8	24 3/8	21 5/8	20 5/8	6 1/8	6 5/8	18	14	Auburnville, NB	John L. MacKenzie	Arnold Alward	1958	107
242	24 6/8	25	22 5/8	6 6/8	6 1/8	14	12	McDonough Co., IL	Picked Up	Danny L. Powell	2002	108
241 7/8	26 1/8	25 2/8	20 1/8	4 5/8	5	14	19	Flathead Co., MT	George Woldstad	George Woldstad	1960	109
241 7/8	22 2/8	28 3/8	19	5 3/8	5	15	11	Lyon Co., KS	Picked Up	D.J. Hollinger & B. Howard	1996	109
241 7/8	28	27 2/8	21 2/8	6 3/8	6 4/8	10	9	Henry Co., IL	Andy S. Carlson	Andy S. Carlson	2002	109
241 6/8	25 7/8	26 1/8	19 3/8	5 6/8	5 3/8	11	10	Des Moines Co., IA	Picked Up	IA Dept. of Natl. Resc.	1999	112
241 5/8	25	24 4/8	21 3/8	6 2/8	6 2/8	19	18	Manitoba	Unknown	Jack G. Brittingham	1984	113
241 3/8	29 2/8	25 7/8	19 3/8	5 2/8	5	9	11	Wisconsin	Unknown	Robert Kietzman	1940	114
241 3/8	23 5/8	23 2/8	20 7/8	6 5/8	6 7/8	13	8	Putnam Co., IL	Michael D. Ublish	Michael D. Ublish	2001	114
241 1/8	26 4/8	26 1/8	18 1/8	6 1/8	6	19	18	Bighill Creek, AB	Donald D. Dwernychuk	Donald D. Dwernychuk	1984	116
240 7/8	28	28 6/8	20 2/8	6 3/8	6 2/8	13	10	Lewis Co., KY	Anthony D. Mefford	Cabela's, Inc.	1996	117
240 6/8	25 5/8	26 2/8	17 2/8	5 2/8	5 1/8	17	20	St. Louis Co., MN	John Cesarek	John Cesarek	1964	118
240 6/8	26 2/8	25 7/8	20 7/8	7 4/8	7 2/8	13	13	Clay Co., KS	Picked Up	H. James Reimer	1989	118
240 6/8	28 3/8	28 6/8	19 1/8	5 2/8	5 2/8	10	15	Wapello Co., IA	Picked Up	IA Dept. of Natl. Resc.	1991	118

Score	L. Main Beam R	L	Inside Spread	Circ. R	Circ. L	Pts R	Pts L	Locality	By Whom Killed	Owner	Date	Rank
240 4/8	24 5/8	24 4/8	18 7/8	6 3/8	6 3/8	12	18	Tisdale, SK	John Law	John Law	1988	121
240 4/8	26 4/8	27 7/8	20 7/8	5	5 1/8	13	15	Allamakee Co., IA	David Gordon	David Gordon	2000	121
240 3/8	24 6/8	24 2/8	18 5/8	7 2/8	7 2/8	18	20	Monroe Co., GA	John L. Hatton, Jr.	John L. Hatton, Jr.	1973	123
240 3/8	28 2/8	28 7/8	20 4/8	5	5	13	13	Pine Lake, AB	Edwin R. Pick	Edwin R. Pick	1997	123
240 2/8	20	20 1/8	22 1/8	4 5/8	4 6/8	15	12	Hunt Co., TX	Tom Cole	John L. Stein	1997	125
240 2/8	28 4/8	28 4/8	22 4/8	6 1/8	6 1/8	15	11	Warren Co., IA	Rick L. Dye	Rick L. Dye	2000	125
240	26	26 4/8	21 5/8	5 4/8	5 4/8	15	11	Kerr Co., TX	Walter R. Schreiner	Charles Schreiner III	1905	127
240	27 5/8	28 5/8	17	5 1/8	5 2/8	10	11	Allen Co., KS	Doug Whitcomb	Cabela's, Inc.	1987	127
239 4/8	25 6/8	25 7/8	17 2/8	4 4/8	4 4/8	10	12	Meeker Co., MN	Michael D. Dick	Michael D. Dick	1994	129
239 4/8	25 7/8	26 1/8	19 6/8	6 5/8	6 5/8	13	12	Glasyn, SK	Mark Schumlick	Cabela's, Inc.	1997	129
239 4/8	25 1/8	26 6/8	19 4/8	5 1/8	5	13	13	Kleberg Co., TX	Adan Alvarez	Adan Alvarez	1998	129
239 3/8	26 6/8	27 7/8	20 2/8	6 2/8	6 2/8	12	13	White Co., IL	Reed T. Rountree	Reed T. Rountree	2002	132
239 2/8	26 4/8	25 5/8	22 4/8	7 1/8	6 6/8	13	9	Prowers Co., CO	Scott M. Tenold	Scott M. Tenold	1997	133
239 1/8	29 2/8	31 1/8	22 1/8	5 7/8	5 4/8	9	11	Illinois	William Seidel	D.J. Hollinger & B. Howard	1987	134
239	29 2/8	28	22 3/8	5 7/8	5 7/8	13	13	Lyon Co., KS	Don E. Roberts	Bass Pro Shops	1987	135
239	27 1/8	26 2/8	16 3/8	5 3/8	5 3/8	11	8	Montgomery Co., KS	Picked Up	Cabela's, Inc.	1992	135
239	25 1/8	25 3/8	17	5 6/8	5 3/8	16	12	Pawnee Co., NE	Danny C. Boliver	Danny C. Boliver	1996	135
238 7/8	21 6/8	22 4/8	18 1/8	5 2/8	5	17	15	Crook Co., WY	Picked Up	J.D. Andrews	1962	138
238 6/8	22 2/8	22 6/8	18 3/8	5 2/8	5	18	15	Mahoning Co., OH	Ronald K. Osborne	Bass Pro Shops	1986	139
238 6/8	25 3/8	26 2/8	20 5/8	6 7/8	7 2/8	11	12	Fulton Co., IL	Neil M. Booth	Cabela's, Inc.	1988	139
238 4/8	18 6/8	25 4/8	21	6 5/8	6 3/8	13	15	Schuyler Co., IL	Kenneth B. Robertson	Kenneth B. Robertson	1997	139
238 3/8	28 6/8	28 3/8	15 6/8	5 2/8	5 2/8	9	9	Piscataquis Co., ME	Christian B. Oberholser, Jr.	Christian B. Oberholser, Jr.	1996	142
238 2/8	26 6/8	28	22 7/8	6	6	15	10	Assiniboine River, MB	Doug Hawkins	Doug Hawkins	1981	143
238 2/8	23 2/8	24 2/8	13 2/8	5 6/8	5 6/8	12	15	Prairie Co., AR	William Dooley	William Dooley	1999	143
238 2/8	25 2/8	24 3/8	22 6/8	6 2/8	7 4/8	10	11	Potter Co., SD	Larry Nylander	Donna Nylander	1963	145
238 1/8	26 2/8	27 1/8	21 4/8	5 5/8	5 7/8	12	17	Bay Co., MI	Paul M. Mickey	Paul M. Mickey	1976	145
238 1/8	28 1/8	27 6/8	19 6/8	6 3/8	6 2/8	15	17	Barren Co., KY	Picked Up	Ed Rigdon	1995	145
238	21 7/8	24 2/8	22	5 2/8	5 2/8	13	15	Whitewood, SK	Jack Davidge	Jack Davidge	1967	148
237 6/8	27 5/8	21 7/8	27	5 6/8	5 6/8	13	17	Madison Co., IL	Joe Bardill	Patrick Bardill	1985	148
237 6/8	28 4/8	26 4/8	21	6 1/8	6 1/8	10	17	Lewis Co., KY	Tom D. Fetters, Sr.	Cabela's, Inc.	1998	148
237 6/8	31	31	23 6/8	5 6/8	5 7/8	12	8	Keya Paha Co., NE	Donald B. Phipps	Donald B. Phipps	1969	151
237 5/8	23 3/8	26 4/8	15	6	6	15	12	Henderson Co., IL	Robert E. Todd	Robert E. Todd	1978	152
237 4/8	27 6/8	23 4/8	19 5/8	5 4/8	5 4/8	14	17	Meadow Lake, SK	Picked Up	Darrell Roney	1996	152
237 3/8	26 3/8	27 2/8	25	5 6/8	5 5/8	9	13	Des Moines Co., IA	Harlan Swehla	Harlan Swehla	2002	152
237 3/8	25	26 3/8	20 2/8	6	6	18	16	Cross Co., AR	Picked Up	Kevin Ward	1994	155
237 1/8	24 2/8	25	23 2/8	5 4/8	5 4/8	12	11	Whiteshell, MB	Angus McVicar	Angus McVicar	1925	156
237	23 7/8	22 7/8	17 6/8	6 2/8	6 3/8	14	15	Wayne Co., IA	Picked Up	Cabela's, Inc.	1998	156
237	24 6/8	24 2/8	16 3/8	5 1/8	5 1/8	17	10	Delaware Co., OK	Charles A. Tullis	Charles A. Tullis	1998	156
237	28 1/8	23 7/8	17 1/8	6	6 1/8	13	11	Monroe Co., IA	Larry V. Zach	Larry V. Zach	2000	156
236 7/8	26 6/8	28 3/8	21 1/8	6 7/8	6 7/8	10	16	Wayne Co., KY	Jessie D. Fulton	Cabela's, Inc.	2000	160
236 7/8	25 6/8	25	22 4/8	5 5/8	5 5/8	14	11	Barber Co., KS	Ronald D. Wilt	Cleon Almond	1986	161
236 7/8	25 4/8	24 7/8	23	6 3/8	6 3/8	16	9	Madison Co., IA	Picked Up	IA Dept. of Natl. Resc.	PR 1989	161
236 5/8	26 3/8	28 3/8	25 3/8	5 3/8	5 4/8	11	10	Douglas Co., KS	Terry D. Mayle	Terry D. Mayle	1994	161
236 5/8	27	27 5/8	18 6/8	5 7/8	5 7/8	13	12	Dallas Co., IA	Russ A. Clarken	Russ A. Clarken	1994	164
236 5/8	26 4/8	24 4/8	18 2/8	5 1/8	5 1/8	18	12	Preble Co., OH	Bruce A. Turner	Bruce A. Turner	1994	164
236 5/8	24 7/8	28	21 3/8	4 6/8	4 6/8	14	17	Beltrami Co., MN	Edwin C. Moe	Edwin C. Moe	1995	164
236 5/8	26	24 2/8	21 3/8	5 2/8	5 2/8	18	14	Pend Oreille Co., WA	George Gretener	John E. Gretener	PR 1931	167
236 5/8	26 3/8	24 7/8	21 4/8	6 1/8	6	12	14	Pope Co., MN	Douglas D. Vesledahl	Douglas D. Vesledahl	1961	167

WHITETAIL DEER - NON-TYPICAL ANTLERS

Odocoileus virginianus virginianus and certain related subspecies

Score	Length of Main Beam R	L	Inside Spread	Circumference at Smallest Place Between Burr and First Point R	L	Number of Points R	L	Locality	Hunter	Owner	Date Killed	Rank
236 5/8	27 2/8	26 1/8	20 1/8	7 1/8	6 6/8	11	9	Pike Co., IL	Floyd Pursley	Floyd Pursley	1987	167
236 4/8	24 6/8	25	20 5/8	5 4/8	5 6/8	17	12	Reserve, SK	Harry Nightingale	D.J. Hollinger & B. Howard	1959	170
236 3/8	25 7/8	23 6/8	20 3/8	5 4/8	5 4/8	14	16	Union Co., KY	Wilbur E. Buchanan	Wilbur E. Buchanan	1970	171
236 3/8	25 6/8	25 6/8	18 4/8	5 6/8	5 6/8	9	13	Bayfield Co., WI	Unknown	Jean B. Schultz	1998	171
236 1/8	27	27 2/8	20 4/8	4 3/8	4 2/8	15	15	St. Joseph Co., MI	Picked Up	Kenneth L. Moore, Jr.	1995	173
236	22 3/8	24 6/8	19 5/8	5 4/8	5 1/8	11	12	Winona Co., MN	Francis A. Pries	Bass Pro Shops	1964	174
235 5/8	30 7/8	29 7/8	21 4/8	5 4/8	5 7/8	17	13	Nemaha Co., KS	Picked Up	James R. Matlock	PR 1998	175
235 4/8	29 2/8	27 1/8	22 7/8	5 7/8	5 6/8	11	13	Ashtabula Co., OH	James L. Clark	Bass Pro Shops	1957	176
235 4/8	25 4/8	24 5/8	19 6/8	5 4/8	5 7/8	9	20	Pipestone Valley, SK	E.J. Marshall	E.J. Marshall	1958	176
235 3/8	21 7/8	22 6/8	21 6/8	6 2/8	6	13	10	Harding Co., SD	J.H. Krueger & R. Keeton	Bass Pro Shops	1965	178
235 1/8	24	23 7/8	21 2/8	5	4 7/8	14	15	Frio Co., TX	C.J. Stolle	John F. Stolle	1919	179
235	25 5/8	24 3/8	22 2/8	4 7/8	4 7/8	13	14	Daviess Co., MO	Justin K. Moore	Justin K. Moore	1997	180
234 7/8	27 3/8	22 3/8	20 7/8	5 3/8	5 7/8	8	13	Coffey Co., KS	Danny L. Hawkins	Cabela's, Inc.	1999	181
234 5/8	23 5/8	24	19 4/8	5 7/8	6 1/8	15	12	Nebraska	Picked Up	L.B. Philips	PR 1972	182
234 5/8	28 6/8	23 3/8	17 1/8	4 7/8	6 4/8	9	9	Round Lake, ON	Picked Up	Harry Jones	1990	182
234 5/8	27	28	25	6 2/8	6 2/8	8	7	Gallatin Co., IL	Scott G. Bosaw	Scott G. Bosaw	1994	182
234 4/8	29	28 2/8	20 7/8	5 3/8	5 6/8	14	16	Stevens Co., WA	Larry G. Gardner	Legendary Whitetails	1953	185
234 4/8	27 1/8	26 3/8	24 2/8	5 7/8	5 7/8	14	11	Knox Co., IL	James R. Hensley, Jr.	James R. Hensley, Jr.	2000	185
234 4/8	24	23 4/8	17 4/8	5 6/8	5 6/8	9	9	Peterson, SK	Murray A. Pulvermacher	Murray A. Pulvermacher	2002	185
234 2/8	27 3/8	26 5/8	20 1/8	7	7 1/8	10	12	Alfalfa Co., OK	Loren Tarrant	Loren Tarrant	1984	188
234 1/8	25 7/8	27 4/8	17 2/8	4 5/8	4 2/8	6	10	Glacier Co., MT	Unknown	Larry W. Lander	PR 1968	189
234 1/8	26 7/8	26 3/8	20 2/8	5 5/8	6 2/8	16	14	Minnesota	Unknown	Gale Sup	PR 1985	189
234 1/8	26 1/8	26 4/8	21 1/8	6	6 2/8	11	14	Hamilton Co., IL	Mark A. Potts	Mark A. Potts	1995	189
234 1/8	29 6/8	29 2/8	19 7/8	4 7/8	4 6/8	13	10	Lewis Co., KY	Joey Smith	Cabela's, Inc.	1997	189
234	26 7/8	26 2/8	18 5/8	6 6/8	6 6/8	14	12	Lac qui Parle Co., MN	Clifford A. Estlie	Wayne Williamson	1991	193
233 7/8	27	26 7/8	21 4/8	5 5/8	5 3/8	16	16	Loraine, WI	Homer Pearson	Bass Pro Shops	1937	194
233 7/8	23 6/8	22 4/8	16 5/8	6	5 7/8	9	14	Tompkins, SK	Don Stueck	McLean Bowman	1961	194
233 7/8	27 6/8	30 1/8	21 4/8	5 6/8	5 6/8	10	13	Blueberry Mt., AB	William Shumaker	William Shumaker	1994	194
233 7/8	26	27 2/8	18	5 4/8	5 2/8	14	16	Carroll Co., IN	James R. Houston, Jr.	James R. Houston, Jr.	1995	194
233 6/8	26 2/8	26	22	4 7/8	4 6/8	14	13	Thompson Creek, WA	George Sly, Jr.	D.J. Hollinger & B. Howard	1964	198
233 6/8	28 2/8	27	21 1/8	5	5 4/8	13	13	Custer Co., NE	Lonnie E. Poland	Lonnie E. Poland	1986	198
233 5/8	30 5/8	30 6/8	21 2/8	5	5	11	13	Morrow Co., OH	Religh D. Martin	Religh D. Martin	1995	198
233 5/8	27 4/8	28 1/8	19 3/8	4 7/8	4 6/8	11	17	Chippewa Co., WI	Russell W. Jones	Russell W. Jones	2000	201
233 4/8	21 1/8	26	18 5/8	5 4/8	5	14	10	Saskatchewan	Unknown	Cabela's, Inc.	2001	202
233 3/8	25 3/8	29 7/8	19 4/8	5 6/8	5 3/8	12	8	Carlton Co., MN	Peter Antonson	Roy Ober	PR 1938	203
233 3/8	27	26 4/8	18 3/8	5 3/8	5 6/8	13	12	Pueblo Co., CO	Raymond A. Vertovec	Raymond A. Vertovec	1994	203

Score	L. R	L. L	Spread	Circ R	Circ L	Pts R	Pts L	Locality	Hunter	Owner	Date	Rank
233 2/8	27 2/8	25 5/8	18 6/8	4 7/8	4 7/8	9	11	Switzerland Co., IN	Henry Mitchell	Bass Pro Shops	1972	205
233 1/8	26 7/8	26 2/8	24 6/8	4 5/8	4 3/8	9	9	Acadia Valley, AB	James J. Niwa	James J. Niwa	1973	205
233 1/8	29 2/8	29	20 4/8	5 6/8	5 6/8	14	9	Condon Lakes, NS	Don McDonnell	Don McDonnell	1987	207
233	20 2/8	23 4/8	19 6/8	5 2/8	5	12	7	Punnichy, SK	Steve Kapay	Gale Sup	1968	208
232 7/8	25 7/8	26	18 7/8	5	5 1/8	13	11	Montana	Unknown	Raymond R. Cross	PR 1950	209
232 7/8	29 1/8	28 1/8	26 7/8	5 4/8	5 4/8	10	12	Montgomery Co., IA	Picked Up	Dirk M. Paul	1988	209
232 7/8	21 2/8	20 3/8	15 6/8	4	4	18	19	Haywood Co., TN	Justin K. Samples	Justin K. Samples	2001	209
232 5/8	28 3/8	29	23 6/8	5 3/8	5 2/8	9	9	Wabasha Co., MN	Robert R. Friese	Robert R. Friese	1948	212
232 5/8	23 2/8	23 7/8	18 2/8	6 5/8	7	15	11	Winfield, AB	Harry O. Hueppelshevser	Harry O. Hueppelshevser	1986	212
232 5/8	23 7/8	24 1/8	18 2/8	6	7	12	13	Fulton Co., IL	Carl B. Brown	Carl B. Brown	1997	212
232 4/8	29 2/8	28 6/8	18 7/8	7 2/8	5 4/8	14	18	Buckingham Co., VA	James R. Shumaker	James R. Shumaker	1986	215
232 3/8	26 3/8	19 6/8	23 2/8	5 4/8	4 4/8	11	12	Breathitt Co., KY	Delmar R. Hounshell	Delmar R. Hounshell	1990	216
232 3/8	25 2/8	24 2/8	19 6/8	5 3/8	6 7/8	12	11	Glendon, AB	John Diedrich	John Diedrich	1995	216
232 3/8	28	27 1/8	17	5 5/8	5 4/8	10	11	Glass Lake, SK	Karpo S. Stokalko	Karpo S. Stokalko	2001	216
232 2/8	23 3/8	22 7/8	17 2/8	5 6/8	5 4/8	12	18	Thorsby, AB	Robert G. MacRae	Robert G. MacRae	1987	219
232 1/8	24 5/8	24 5/8	16 4/8	4 7/8	4 6/8	11	11	McLean Co., ND	Olaf P. Anderson	Bass Pro Shops	1886	220
232	25 6/8	25	17	6	6	18	11	Waukesha Co., WI	John Herr, Sr.	Mac's Taxidermy	1955	221
232	30 1/8	30 7/8	18 7/8	5 3/8	5 4/8	11	11	Barron Co., WI	Wayne F. Lindemans	Cabela's, Inc.	1988	221
232	17 4/8	16 6/8	18 3/8	4 4/8	4 4/8	26	8	Monroe Co., AR	Picked Up	Kirk Brann	2000	221
231 7/8	24	22 2/8	18	5 5/8	5 4/8	10	20	Harris, SK	Herman Cox	R.M. Burnett	1954	224
231 6/8	26 1/8	25 3/8	23 2/8	6	6 1/8	11	13	Peace River, AB	Terry Doll	Terry Doll	1978	225
231 5/8	28 1/8	26 5/8	19 2/8	5 1/8	5 1/8	11	11	Dane Co., WI	Dennis D. Shanks	Dennis D. Shanks	1979	226
231 5/8	26 1/8	26	20 3/8	5 4/8	5 2/8	16	11	Wayne Co., WV	Charles I. McLaughlin	D.J. Hollinger & B. Howard	1997	226
231 5/8	26 6/8	27 5/8	23	6 1/8	6 1/8	10	9	Battle River, SK	Kevin Rowswell	Kevin Rowswell	1998	226
231 5/8	27 3/8	26 6/8	18 4/8	6 2/8	6 1/8	11	11	Porter Co., IN	Robert J. Johannsen	Robert J. Johannsen	2002	226
231 4/8	29 4/8	29 4/8	18 6/8	6 1/8	6 2/8	14	13	Perry Co., IN	Unknown	Bass Pro Shops	1968	230
231 4/8	25 7/8	26 4/8	27 3/8	6 2/8	6 2/8	11	14	Logan Co., IL	Donald D. Stiner	Donald D. Stiner	1993	230
231 3/8	29 3/8	27 4/8	23 1/8	4 3/8	4 3/8	9	10	Licking Co., OH	Norman L. Myers	Norman L. Myers	1964	232
231 3/8	28	28 4/8	26 1/8	6 3/8	6 6/8	9	9	Holland, MB	W. Ireland	Wayne Williamson	1968	232
231 2/8	25 6/8	26 3/8	18 4/8	4 7/8	5	17	13	Forest Co., WI	Robert Jacobson	Robert Jacobson	1958	234
231 2/8	26 1/8	30 4/8	20 6/8	5 2/8	5 2/8	10	10	Renville Co., MN	James L. Rath	Bass Pro Shops	1977	234
231 2/8	30	30	22 5/8	5	5	9	11	Nebraska	Unknown	Cabela's, Inc.	PR 1993	234
231 2/8	25	25 2/8	17 5/8	8 1/8	5 7/8	21	12	Muscogee Co., GA	Blakely H. Voltz	Blakely H. Voltz	1997	234
231 1/8	19 5/8	22 3/8	20 4/8	6	5 7/8	12	12	Lac qui Parle Co., MN	Willard Evans	Paul Evans	1951	238
231 1/8	28 3/8	28 4/8	24 2/8	5 1/8	5 3/8	12	9	Winona Co., MN	Robert E. Bains	Robert E. Bains	1973	238
231 1/8	25 3/8	25 7/8	21 4/8	5 6/8	5 6/8	14	12	Henry Co., IA	Wendell R. Prottsman	Wendell R. Prottsman	1988	238
231	26	25 7/8	18	5	5	12	12	Stevens Co., WA	Joe Bussano	Joe Bussano	1946	241
231	27 5/8	28	21 2/8	5 2/8	5 1/8	8	7	Cass Co., MN	L.S. Hanson	Cabela's, Inc.	1970	241
230 7/8	26 2/8	28 4/8	19 7/8	5	5 1/8	12	13	West Kootenay, BC	Karl H. Kast	Karl H. Kast	1940	243
230 7/8	25 4/8	25 2/8	21 5/8	5 1/8	5 1/8	12	14	Provost, AB	Richard C. Nelson	Richard C. Nelson	1990	243
230 6/8	27 2/8	27 2/8	19 3/8	6	5 7/8	14	16	Red Deer, AB	Delmer E. Johnson	Bass Pro Shops	1973	245
230 6/8	22 3/8	23 3/8	19 7/8	5 4/8	4 4/8	13	10	Peoria Co., IL	Picked Up	David T. Lockhart	2000	245
230 5/8	25 1/8	25 1/8	28 4/8	6 1/8	6 3/8	14	13	Iron Co., MI	Carl Runyan	Bass Pro Shops	1942	247
230 5/8	24 7/8	24 6/8	17 4/8	6 3/8	5 2/8	11	11	Okfuskee Co., OK	Joe A. Green	Johnny J. Green	1971	247
230 2/8	26 1/8	26	19 1/8	5	5 1/8	11	11	Todd Co., MN	John Berscheit	John Berscheit	1976	249
230 2/8	30	30	23 7/8	5 6/8	5 5/8	9	13	Walworth Co., WI	F. Dan Dinelli	F. Dan Dinelli	1992	249
230 2/8	24 4/8	25 1/8	15 5/8	5 7/8	5 7/8	17	20	Lawrence Co., PA	Michael D. Ambrosia	Michael D. Ambrosia	2001	249
230 1/8	27 2/8	27 1/8	18	5 3/8	5 3/8	15	11	Pope Co., MN	Harvey J. Erickson	Harvey J. Erickson	1974	252

WHITETAIL DEER - NON-TYPICAL ANTLERS

Odocoileus virginianus virginianus and certain related subspecies

Score	Length of Main Beam R	L	Inside Spread	Circumference at Smallest Place Between Burr and First Point R	L	Number of Points R	L	Locality	Hunter	Owner	Date Killed	Rank
230 1/8	25 6/8	24 7/8	18 5/8	4 6/8	4 7/8	12	11	Guthrie Co., IA	Todd A. Hawley	Todd A. Hawley	1982	252
230	26 6/8	26	22 2/8	6 3/8	6 1/8	13	12	Schoolcraft Co., MI	Bill Ogle	MI Whitetail Hall of Fame Mus.	1943	254
230	25 1/8	25 2/8	23 7/8	5 5/8	5 4/8	14	16	Bayfield Co., WI	Picked Up	Cabela's, Inc.	1958	254
230	27 1/8	28 1/8	19 7/8	5	5	11	8	Houston Co., MN	Winnie Papenfuss	Winnie Papenfuss	1973	254
230	24 5/8	24 2/8	21 7/8	4 7/8	4 6/8	14	13	Clayton Co., IA	Fredrick A. Becker	Cabela's, Inc.	1993	254
229 7/8	27 4/8	26 7/8	19 7/8	6 4/8	6 2/8	13	13	Jackson Co., IN	Larry E. Deaton	Larry E. Deaton	1990	258
229 6/8	26 1/8	26	21 5/8	5 1/8	5 1/8	12	13	Decatur Co., IA	Edgar Shields	Edgar Shields	1986	259
229 5/8	31 7/8	26	23 7/8	5	5	12	13	Scioto Co., OH	Ron Vastine	Ron Vastine	2002	260
229 4/8	28 5/8	28 4/8	20 4/8	5 3/8	5 3/8	9	8	Dewey Co., OK	Ricky C. Watt	Ricky C. Watt	1987	261
229 4/8	24 2/8	24 5/8	19 3/8	5	4 7/8	10	10	Marshall Co., IL	Daniel R. Ferguson	Daniel R. Ferguson	1994	261
229 4/8	27 5/8	26 2/8	21 3/8	6 7/8	6 6/8	13	9	Polk Co., IA	Terry M. Long	Terry M. Long	1995	261
229 3/8	27 7/8	26 6/8	23 6/8	5 3/8	5 4/8	8	8	Wapello Co., IA	Robert D. Harding	Robert D. Harding	1985	264
229 3/8	26 2/8	26 3/8	19 3/8	5 6/8	5 5/8	13	9	Montgomery Co., IL	Lee A. Heldebrandt	Lee A. Heldebrandt	1996	264
229 2/8	27	28 5/8	21 1/8	6 2/8	7	8	15	Linn Co., KS	Merle C. Beckman	Merle C. Beckman	1984	266
229 2/8	21 4/8	21 4/8	16 3/8	5 5/8	5 4/8	15	13	Flathead Co., MT	Carl E. Goetsch	Carl E. Goetsch	1992	266
229 2/8	26 4/8	26 3/8	22 2/8	4 2/8	4 3/8	11	12	Lincoln Co., MT	Picked Up	Steve Crossley	1994	266
229	27 1/8	27 4/8	16 2/8	6 7/8	6 2/8	8	9	Lake Co., IL	Rodney J. Rasmussen	Rodney J. Rasmussen	1995	269
228 7/8	28 2/8	27 4/8	18 5/8	5 7/8	6	11	10	Cherryfield, ME	Flora Campbell	Dick Idol	1953	270
228 7/8	28 1/8	27 4/8	22 5/8	5 7/8	5 6/8	13	11	W. Feliciana Parish, LA	Tommy Rice	Tommy Rice	1998	270
228 6/8	27 7/8	28 5/8	22 2/8	5 6/8	6 2/8	9	10	Unknown	Unknown	Steven Miller	PR 1972	272
228 6/8	24 3/8	24 5/8	18 1/8	6	5 6/8	18	14	Fulton Co., OH	Bernard Williamson III	Bernard Williamson III	1989	272
228 6/8	27 1/8	29 1/8	21 7/8	6	5 6/8	11	7	Frenchman Butte, SK	Dan Fedirko	Cabela's, Inc.	1998	272
228 6/8	28 3/8	26 4/8	17 1/8	5 1/8	5	9	14	Perry Co., IN	Richard L. Hubert	Richard L. Hubert	2002	272
228 4/8	24	26	20 6/8	5 2/8	5 2/8	10	13	Montgomery Co., MD	John W. Poole	John W. Poole	1987	276
228 4/8	28 3/8	26 2/8	19 5/8	6 2/8	6	14	11	Lake Co., MN	Lisa A. Baxter	Lisa A. Baxter	1991	276
228 4/8	26 7/8	26 2/8	19 1/8	6	5 3/8	12	11	Person Co., NC	Don C. Rockett	Don C. Rockett	1998	276
228 3/8	26 6/8	26 4/8	23	5 3/8	5 4/8	13	11	Kiowa Co., KS	Lance P. Ringler	Lance P. Ringler	1993	279
228 3/8	24 5/8	26 5/8	15 4/8	6 5/8	5 6/8	13	10	Randolph Co., IL	Aaron L. Eggemeyer	Aaron L. Eggemeyer	2001	279
228 2/8	26 6/8	29 2/8	21	5 2/8	5 2/8	13	10	Cable, WI	Charles Berg	Eva M. Fisher	1910	281
228 2/8	28 3/8	28 2/8	19 1/8	6 4/8	6 3/8	7	8	Dubuque Co., IA	Arthur D. Wille	Arthur D. Wille	2000	281
228 2/8	24 5/8	26 1/8	20 4/8	6 4/8	6 4/8	15	12	Weld Co., CO	Ronald E. Kammerzell	Ronald E. Kammerzell	2001	281
228 1/8	28 7/8	29	20 1/8	5 6/8	6	13	14	Maine	Henry A. Caesar	Unknown	PR 1911	284
228 1/8	28 4/8	27	21 6/8	5 1/8	5 5/8	11	13	Bureau Co., IL	Keith F. VanderMeersch	Keith F. VanderMeersch	1992	284
228	23 2/8	23 3/8	18 1/8	5 5/8	5 6/8	13	12	Las Animas Co., CO	Brad C. Hardin	Brad C. Hardin	1998	286
228	27 3/8	26 4/8	21 3/8	6 1/8	5 7/8	11	14	Manitoba	Unknown	Gale Sup	PR 1998	286
227 6/8	21 6/8	25	17	6 4/8	6	13	10	Des Moines Co., IA	Edgar J. Steward	Edgar J. Steward	1990	288

Score								Locality	Hunter	Owner	Date	Rank
227 6/8	24 5/8	25 3/8	18 6/8	4 6/8	4 5/8	13	13	Sumner Co., KS	Matthew L. Dalton	Matthew L. Dalton	2001	288
227 5/8	23 6/8	24 4/8	15 6/8	5 3/8	5 2/8	10	10	Pike Co., IL	Gavin Risley	Gavin Risley	2002	290
227 4/8	25 3/8	25 2/8	18 4/8	6 4/8	6 4/8	16	17	Bayfield Co., WI	Earl Holt	Mrs. Earl Holt	1934	291
227 4/8	27 1/8	26 2/8	20 2/8	5 2/8	5 2/8	12	9	Pullman, WA	Glenn C. Paulson	Glenn C. Paulson	1965	291
227 4/8	22 6/8	23 6/8	24	4 7/8	4 7/8	17	12	Fannin Co., TX	Joe P. Moore, Jr.	Joe P. Moore, Jr.	2001	294
227 3/8	27 2/8	26 5/8	17 1/8	5 4/8	5 5/8	7	10	Madison Co., IA	Jerry L. Wells	Jerry L. Wells	2001	294
227 2/8	26 4/8	26 4/8	29	6	6 1/8	11	8	Pembina River, AB	Joe Oleksiw	Joe Oleksiw	1992	295
227 1/8	26	27 3/8	16 3/8	4 6/8	4 6/8	8	10	Clark Co., WI	Edward W. Schoen	Edward W. Schoen	1955	296
227 1/8	24	23 5/8	21 4/8	4 4/8	4 4/8	8	9	Dimmit Co., TX	Stuart W. Stedman	Stuart W. Stedman	1990	296
227 1/8	24 7/8	26 6/8	18 6/8	5 1/8	4 7/8	11	14	Sang Lake, AB	V. Lynn Steeves	V. Lynn Steeves	1992	296
227 1/8	22	23 4/8	19	6	5 1/8	15	13	Dunn Co., WI	David D. Dewey	David D. Dewey	1999	296
227	26	26 2/8	21 4/8	6 1/8	6 2/8	19	14	Concordia Parish, LA	Picked Up	Sandra Leger	1969	300
227	25 7/8	26 6/8	24 1/8	7 2/8	7 4/8	12	10	Miami Co., KS	Gary A. Smith	Bass Pro Shops	1970	300
227	26 5/8	26 1/8	17 7/8	5 1/8	5	13	11	Jackson Co., MO	Picked Up	H. James Reimer	1989	300
227	26 1/8	25 3/8	18	5 6/8	6	9	12	Lucas Co., IA	Picked Up	H. James Reimer	1992	300
227	29 4/8	30 4/8	23 1/8	6 2/8	6 6/8	10	11	Decatur Co., IA	Jack J. Schuler, Jr.	Jack J. Schuler, Jr.	1995	300
226 7/8	30 2/8	28 1/8	20 2/8	5	5	13	10	Dimmit Co., TX	Lake Webb	Warren N. Webb	1937	305
226 6/8	28 4/8	27 4/8	15 5/8	4 7/8	5 2/8	22	25	Rusk Co., WI	Joe Michalets	John R. Michalets	1911	306
226 6/8	28 4/8	28 2/8	22 1/8	5 4/8	5 5/8	10	12	Manor, SK	Stan Balkwill	Cabela's, Inc.	1960	306
226 6/8	24 4/8	22 3/8	19 7/8	5 2/8	5 4/8	13	12	Polk Co., IA	Picked Up	IA Dept. of Natl. Resc.	1998	306
226 6/8	27 3/8	27 2/8	21 2/8	6 2/8	6 1/8	10	9	Piatt Co., IL	Mark Wimpy	Mark Wimpy	2000	306
226 5/8	26 5/8	26	18 7/8	6 1/8	6	15	12	Shell Lake, SK	Marcel Proulx	D.J. Hollinger & B. Howard	1984	310
226 5/8	26 6/8	26	18 7/8	6	5 6/8	7	9	Pulaski Co., KY	H.C. Sumpter	H.C. Sumpter	1984	310
226 5/8	29	28 4/8	18 1/8	5 3/8	5 2/8	13	13	Licking Co., OH	John S. Blythe	John S. Blythe	1999	310
226 4/8	26	26 4/8	24 7/8	4 7/8	4 5/8	11	12	La Salle Co., TX	A.L. Lipscomb, Sr.	John L. Stein	1909	313
226 4/8	21 3/8	22 2/8	19 2/8	4 6/8	4 5/8	13	11	Muskingum Co., OH	Rex A. Thompson	Rex A. Thompson	1981	313
226 4/8	26 1/8	24 3/8	22	6 7/8	6 5/8	12	10	Linn Co., KS	Jerry O. Hampton	Bass Pro Shops	1988	313
226 4/8	27 4/8	27 4/8	20 3/8	4 7/8	4 7/8	11	12	Plymouth Co., IA	Ronald H. Junck	Ronald H. Junck	1995	313
226 3/8	25 7/8	27 3/8	18 2/8	5 5/8	5 3/8	10	8	Nez Perce Co., ID	Mrs. Ralph Bond	Mrs. Ralph Bond	1964	317
226 3/8	27 2/8	26 2/8	22 7/8	5 4/8	5 4/8	8	10	Clark Co., IN	Robert L. Bromm, Sr.	Robert L. Bromm, Sr.	1985	317
226 2/8	26 6/8	25 3/8	24 5/8	6	6	10	11	Warren Co., OH	Daniel H. Detrick	Daniel H. Detrick	1989	319
226 2/8	27 2/8	28 3/8	22 7/8	5 6/8	5 6/8	11	10	Amherst Co., VA	Picked Up	Brent W. Campbell	1994	319
226 2/8	27 7/8	28 3/8	19 6/8	5 2/8	5 2/8	11	13	Fulton Co., IL	Picked Up	David L. Lidwell	1996	319
226 1/8	25 3/8	24 7/8	22 3/8	5	5	12	14	Kimble Co., TX	Coke R. Stevenson	Marguerite K. Stevenson	1934	322
226 1/8	25 1/8	26 3/8	20 3/8	4 7/8	4 7/8	10	10	Trumbull Co., OH	Paul E. Lehman	Paul E. Lehman	1948	322
226 1/8	25 1/8	22 3/8	14 6/8	6	6	8	15	Iowa Co., WI	Robert Odey	Robert Odey	2002	322
226	28 1/8	27	20 4/8	4 7/8	5 2/8	17	17	Morgan Co., MO	Art Sousley	Cabela's, Inc.	1962	325
226	23 4/8	25 2/8	26 4/8	5	5	11	11	Winona Co., MN	Terry D. Masso	Terry D. Masso	1991	325
225 7/8	24 5/8	24 3/8	18	5 2/8	5 2/8	10	8	Linn Co., KS	Douglas L. Below	Douglas L. Below	2001	327
225 7/8	22 5/8	19 4/8	17 4/8	4 7/8	4 7/8	13	13	Grayson Co., TX	Jeffery L. Duncan	Jeffery L. Duncan	2001	327
225 6/8	27 3/8	26 3/8	26 3/8	4 4/8	4 2/8	7	9	La Porte Co., IN	David Grundy	Bass Pro Shops	1987	329
225 5/8	24 5/8	24 5/8	21 5/8	5 2/8	5 2/8	9	8	Yellow Medicine Co., MN	Glen Bullick	Glen Bullick	1989	329
225 5/8	25 3/8	25 4/8	16 4/8	5 6/8	5 6/8	11	14	Laclede Co., MO	Picked Up	Brad Sowter	PR 1993	331
225 4/8	23 7/8	26 5/8	19 4/8	7	7	10	18	Greene Co., OH	Alan J. Meade	Alan J. Meade	1999	332
225 3/8	26	26 2/8	19 2/8	5 5/8	5 4/8	12	13	Chitek Lake, SK	Wade L. Higgins	Wade L. Higgins	2003	333
225 2/8	29 1/8	29 2/8	23 4/8	6 1/8	6 2/8	9	8	St. Louis Co., MN	Elmer H. Sellin	Bass Pro Shops	1938	334
225 2/8	23 2/8	23 5/8	16 7/8	6 3/8	6 1/8	13	10	Fayette Co., IA	Duane J. Cahoy	Duane J. Cahoy	1975	334
225 2/8	24 7/8	26 2/8	24 3/8	5 2/8	5	12	13	St. Lawrence Co., NY	Kenneth M. Locy	Kenneth M. Locy	1992	334

WHITETAIL DEER - NON-TYPICAL ANTLERS
Odocoileus virginianus virginianus and certain related subspecies

Score	Length of Main Beam		Inside Spread	Circumference at Smallest Place Between Burr and First Point		Number of Points		Locality	Hunter	Owner	Date Killed	Rank
	R	L		R	L	R	L					
225 2/8	24 5/8	21 6/8	24	5 2/8	5 3/8	9	13	Scott Co., IA	Rick Porske	Rick Porske	1996	334
225 1/8	22 4/8	22 6/8	17 1/8	4 7/8	5	10	13	Burnet Co., TX	Mr. Stevens	Mclean Bowman	1938	338
225 1/8	28 3/8	28 1/8	20 2/8	6	6	8	9	Winona Co., MN	Jeffrey S. Wilder	Jeffrey S. Wilder	1977	338
225 1/8	27 7/8	27 4/8	22 6/8	5 2/8	5	8	9	Comanche Co., OK	Michael C. Apoka	Michael C. Apoka	1993	338
225 1/8	27	26 1/8	18 4/8	5 2/8	5 6/8	11	14	Holmes Co., OH	Chris G. Hider	Chris G. Hider	1998	338
225	28 7/8	26 6/8	20 3/8	5 7/8	5 7/8	10	13	Barber Co., KS	Picked Up	Bass Pro Shops	1979	342
225	24 1/8	24 7/8	24 7/8	4 7/8	5	11	9	Lowndes Co., MS	Richard Herring	Richard Herring	1988	342
225	25 6/8	24 5/8	23	5	4 7/8	12	14	Alameda Dam, SK	Duane Gervais	Duane Gervais	1992	342
224 7/8	20 2/8	24 2/8	17	8	5 5/8	19	11	Kinney Co., TX	Unknown	Joe L. Collins	1900	345
224 6/8	27	26 7/8	27 1/8	5 2/8	5 2/8	11	10	Mills Co., IA	James C. Reed	James C. Reed	1988	346
224 6/8	22 5/8	24 2/8	15 1/8	5 4/8	5 2/8	16	15	La Salle Co., TX	Minnie D.B. Haynes	Minnie D.B. Haynes	1992	346
224 6/8	28 2/8	28 2/8	20 4/8	5 5/8	5 7/8	9	9	Ross Co., OH	Richard F. Barnett	Richard F. Barnett	1995	346
224 5/8	24 6/8	27 1/8	25 1/8	5 7/8	5 4/8	15	7	Perry Co., AL	Robert E. Royster	Robert E. Royster	1976	349
224 5/8	25 7/8	27 4/8	19 3/8	5 2/8	5 2/8	10	8	Mercer Co., IL	Roger R. Roy	Roger R. Roy	1999	349
224 5/8	26 6/8	27 1/8	14 2/8	5 1/8	5 3/8	17	15	Hart Co., KY	Picked Up	S. Colvin & J. Coe	2003	349
224 4/8	25 3/8	27 6/8	20 2/8	5 5/8	5 4/8	9	8	Cass Co., MN	Roy K. Blowers, Sr.	Roy K. Blowers, Sr.	1947	352
224 4/8	26	26 3/8	25 6/8	5 6/8	5 6/8	11	14	Rock Co., WI	Joseph T. Fisher	Joseph T. Fisher	1988	352
224 4/8	25 7/8	26 5/8	21 3/8	6	6	20	13	Unknown	Rick Stover	Rick Stover	PR 1993	352
224 4/8	27 7/8	27 7/8	26 3/8	5 4/8	6	8	12	Marshall Co., IL	Frank A. McKean	Frank A. McKean	2000	352
224 3/8	26 7/8	27	21 2/8	5 1/8	5 2/8	8	7	Lac qui Parle Co., MN	Mike Unzen	Mike Unzen	1969	356
224 3/8	30 5/8	30 1/8	21 2/8	4 7/8	4 5/8	11	8	Chisago Co., MN	Nathan Stimson	Nathan Stimson	2001	356
224 2/8	26 4/8	27 6/8	20 5/8	5	5 1/8	11	11	Salmon River, NB	Ford Fulton	Legendary Whitetails	1966	358
224 2/8	23 2/8	23 2/8	22	5 3/8	5 2/8	18	15	Pine Co., MN	Greg S. Blom	Greg S. Blom	1980	358
224 1/8	25	24 7/8	19 6/8	4 5/8	4 3/8	12	13	Crook Co., WY	John S. Mahoney	John S. Mahoney	1947	360
224 1/8	25 6/8	26 7/8	28 3/8	6 5/8	6 2/8	9	8	Monona Co., IA	David Freihage	Bass Pro Shops	1991	360
224 1/8	19 7/8	21 7/8	18 3/8	6 4/8	6	13	10	Rose Prairie, BC	Rob White	Rob White	2000	360
224	29 4/8	29 2/8	20	6 2/8	5 4/8	15	13	Minnesota	Unknown	Harvard Univ. Mus.	1890	363
224	23 1/8	24	17 6/8	4 6/8	5	16	12	Lincoln Co., MT	Ray Baenen	Ed Boyes	1935	363
224	31	31 2/8	19 2/8	5 3/8	5 2/8	11	11	Hancock Co., IL	Ronald A. Paul	Bass Pro Shops	1968	363
224	29 2/8	29 2/8	27	5 2/8	5 3/8	7	14	Hancock Co., ME	Picked Up	Wesley B. Starn	PR 1975	363
224	24 4/8	24 2/8	16 6/8	6	6 1/8	13	10	Torch River, SK	Gus Fomradas	Helmut Fomradas	1993	363
224	27 6/8	27 4/8	23 5/8	6 4/8	6 3/8	10	8	Will Co., IL	Picked Up	Rita O. Luedtke	2002	363
223 6/8	28	28	25 5/8	7 1/8	6 4/8	10	11	Greene Co., IL	Terry L. Walters	Terry L. Walters	1982	369
223 6/8	25 1/8	24 2/8	16 3/8	4 3/8	4 3/8	10	13	Nuevo Leon, MX	Ron Kolpin	Ron Kolpin	1983	369
223 6/8	24	26 4/8	18 5/8	5	5 2/8	11	11	Jasper Co., IA	Picked Up	Bruce A. Sanburn	1997	369
223 5/8	28	28 3/8	18 7/8	4 7/8	4 7/8	10	12	Woods Co., OK	Monty E. Pfleider	Monty E. Pfleider	1987	372

Score								Locality	Hunter	Owner	Date Killed	Rank
223 5/8	25 5/8	24 4/8	19 5/8	5 6/8	5 6/8	13	16	Manitoba	Unknown	Wayne Selby	PR 1987	372
223 5/8	24 6/8	24 6/8	24 2/8	6	6 2/8	8	14	Wabash Co., IL	Tim W. Stout	Bass Pro Shops	1988	372
223 5/8	23 6/8	24 5/8	17	5 5/8	5 4/8	10	12	Stevens Co., WA	Mike W. Naff	Mike W. Naff	1992	372
223 5/8	26 2/8	26 3/8	19 6/8	5 1/8	5 1/8	12	11	St. Francis Co., AR	Tony Gore	Tony Gore	1999	372
223 4/8	23 7/8	21 1/8	17	5 1/8	5 1/8	18	13	Richland Co., MT	Verner King	Verner King	1960	377
223 4/8	21 3/8	23	23 4/8	4 1/8	4 2/8	19	11	Hawkins Co., TN	Luther E. Fuller	Luther E. Fuller	1984	377
223 4/8	26 3/8	27 4/8	23 2/8	6 4/8	6 4/8	8	13	Turtle Lake, SK	Blaine LaRose	Blaine LaRose	1996	377
223 4/8	25 5/8	26 3/8	20 2/8	5 5/8	6	16	16	Dickenson Co., VA	Picked Up	James A. Cox	1998	377
223 3/8	28 2/8	27 5/8	24 1/8	5 4/8	5 4/8	10	11	Maine	Frank Maxwell	David G. Cordray	1900	381
223 3/8	20 7/8	24 5/8	19	5 5/8	5 5/8	19	12	Cochin, SK	Vic Pearsall	D.J. Hollinger & B. Howard	1960	381
223 3/8	22 5/8	20 5/8	12 5/8	8 1/8	8 7/8	12	12	Madison Co., IA	Duane Fick	Duane Fick	1972	381
223 3/8	24 7/8	26 1/8	20 2/8	5 5/8	5 5/8	11	15	Jefferson Co., KS	David P. Haeusler	David P. Haeusler	1990	381
223 3/8	30 1/8	29 2/8	24	5 5/8	5 5/8	12	12	Iron Co., WI	Parker E. Milewski	Parker E. Milewski	1994	381
223 2/8	24 3/8	27 3/8	25	4 4/8	4 5/8	12	12	Madison Co., TX	B.C. Bienek	B.C. Bienek	1967	386
223 2/8	29 6/8	32 4/8	22 1/8	6 5/8	5 7/8	7	13	Fulton Co., IL	Lyle Mason	Lyle Mason	2000	386
223 1/8	23 7/8	24 5/8	15	6	5 6/8	21	12	Sumter Co., AL	James L. Spidle, Sr.	Elizabeth McCormick	PR 1942	388
223 1/8	23 6/8	24 1/8	18 3/8	5 3/8	5 4/8	21	14	McCreary Co., KY	James H. Sanders	James H. Sanders	1957	388
223 1/8	29 7/8	29 5/8	21 1/8	4 3/8	4 3/8	12	8	Wyandotte Co., KS	Randy W. Tillery	Randy W. Tillery	1988	388
223 1/8	26 4/8	25 1/8	25 1/8	5 2/8	5 4/8	10	9	Republic Co., KS	Roy C. Wilson	Roy C. Wilson	1995	388
223 1/8	28 6/8	23 6/8	18	5 6/8	5 7/8	13	13	Wilson Co., KS	John Bowser	Cabela's, Inc.	2002	388
223	19 7/8	19 2/8	18 2/8	7 6/8	8 2/8	6	10	Van Buren Co., IA	Picked Up	Wade Roberts	1979	393
223	28 1/8	27 5/8	20 1/8	5 5/8	5 6/8	11	11	Jefferson Co., IN	Sam O. Leverett, Jr.	Sam O. Leverett, Jr.	1997	393
223	24 5/8	22 6/8	14 3/8	6 6/8	6 5/8	14	17	Callaway Co., MO	Herman D. Stiefferman, Jr.	Herman D. Stiefferman, Jr.	2000	393
222 7/8	26 6/8	31 2/8	19 7/8	5 7/8	5 7/8	12	12	Murray Co., MN	Clyde Robbins	David C. Robbins	1964	396
222 7/8	27 5/8	28 1/8	18 6/8	5	5	9	7	Coles Co., IL	Kim L. Boes	Bass Pro Shops	1989	396
222 7/8	29 7/8	30 1/8	21 6/8	5	5	15	9	Morgan Co., KY	Denzil C. Potter	Denzil C. Potter	1999	396
222 6/8	24 4/8	23 4/8	17 7/8	5 4/8	5 6/8	8	8	Rusk Co., WI	Raymond Charlevois	Philip Schlegel	1936	399
222 6/8	21 4/8	22 7/8	16 1/8	5 7/8	5 3/8	11	10	Itasca Co., MN	Picked Up	James R. Smith	1936	399
222 5/8	27	25 5/8	19 2/8	5 7/8	5 7/8	9	12	Mair, SK	R.A. McGill	Mr. & Mrs. M. Melom	1952	401
222 5/8	24 6/8	23 7/8	18 5/8	5 1/8	5 5/8	9	9	Edgerton, AB	Nick Leskow	Russell Thornberry	1964	401
222 5/8	31 7/8	31 2/8	19 1/8	5 5/8	5 4/8	8	10	Nodaway Co., MO	Ken Barcus	Bass Pro Shops	1982	401
222 5/8	25 4/8	26 6/8	22 1/8	6 5/8	6	11	11	Henderson Co., KY	Ronnie D. Stacy	Ronnie D. Stacy	1992	401
222 5/8	24 4/8	24 2/8	20 7/8	5 6/8	5 4/8	10	10	Clark Co., IL	David E. Morris	David E. Morris	1997	401
222 4/8	24 2/8	25 6/8	20 6/8	5 3/8	5 6/8	16	10	Ostrea Lake, NS	Verden M. Baker	John L. Stein	1949	406
222 4/8	25 4/8	23 6/8	21 1/8	5 3/8	5 2/8	14	11	Richland Co., WI	Janice K. Beranek	Janice K. Beranek	1983	406
222 4/8	25 1/8	24 1/8	18 2/8	6 1/8	6 2/8	10	13	Davis Co., IA	James L. Fine	James L. Fine	1987	406
222 4/8	25	24 2/8	25 2/8	6 4/8	6 3/8	12	12	Barber Co., KS	Michel M. Letourneau	Michel M. Letourneau	1999	406
222 4/8	24 3/8	29 3/8	20 6/8	4 7/8	4 7/8	12	9	Richland Co., IL	Lloyd E. Lemke	Lloyd E. Lemke	2000	406
222 4/8	26	26 1/8	18 5/8	6 3/8	5 5/8	11	11	Clinton Co., OH	Jonathan K. Hale	Jonathan K. Hale	2001	406
222 3/8	25 2/8	25 6/8	19 1/8	5 6/8	5 6/8	14	12	Itasca Co., MN	Lumie Jackson	Rick Ferguson	1942	412
222 3/8	24 1/8	23 3/8	18	4 3/8	4 2/8	15	14	Ashley Co., AR	Picked Up	Cabela's, Inc.	1959	412
222 3/8	29 3/8	28 1/8	19 7/8	5 7/8	5 5/8	9	12	Van Buren Co., IA	Le Roy G. Everhart	Grundy Co. Cons. Center	1969	412
222 3/8	27 5/8	27 5/8	22 3/8	6 7/8	6 5/8	9	7	Stearns Co., MN	Richard E. Sand	Richard E. Sand	1988	412
222 3/8	27 6/8	27 3/8	18 1/8	6	6 5/8	9	14	Macoupin Co., IL	Paul Luttmann	Lewis F. Smith	1993	412
222 3/8	25 4/8	25	17 4/8	5	5	11	10	Dallas Co., IA	Chris S. Wilson	Chris S. Wilson	1996	412
222 3/8	28 1/8	27	18 4/8	6 3/8	6 6/8	12	11	Pickaway Co., OH	C. Joseph Schneider	C. Joseph Schneider	1998	412
222 3/8	26 2/8	25 3/8	23 5/8	5 4/8	5 4/8	11	12	Hancock Co., IL	James E. Bowdish	James E. Bowdish	2000	412
222 3/8	29 1/8	27 7/8	16 4/8	7	6 4/8	13	9	Wilson Co., KS	Kent Marr	Kent Marr	2003	412

WHITETAIL DEER - NON-TYPICAL ANTLERS
Odocoileus virginianus virginianus and certain related subspecies

Score	Length of Main Beam R	L	Inside Spread	Circumference at Smallest Place Between Burr and First Point R	L	Number of Points R	L	Locality	Hunter	Owner	Date Killed	Rank
222 1/8	26 2/8	25 7/8	17 3/8	4 5/8	4 4/8	14	12	Hancock Co., IA	Jerry M. Monson	Bass Pro Shops	1977	421
222 1/8	27 1/8	28 1/8	22 3/8	4 6/8	4 7/8	12	10	Cass Co., MN	Marvel R. Utke	Marvel R. Utke	1977	421
222 1/8	26 5/8	26 1/8	22 2/8	5 4/8	5 1/8	11	11	Latah Co., ID	Randy L. Clemenhagen	Randy L. Clemenhagen	1995	421
222 1/8	22 3/8	24 2/8	14 3/8	4 2/8	4 4/8	11	13	Ellis Co., TX	David Krajca	David Krajca	2001	421
221 7/8	26 6/8	26	21 3/8	5	5 1/8	11	11	Tama Co., IA	Charles Upah	Richard Upah	1959	425
221 7/8	25 4/8	26 4/8	16 4/8	5 6/8	5 4/8	12	14	Trigg Co., KY	Bill McWhirter	Bill McWhirter	1982	425
221 7/8	28 2/8	28	25 7/8	4 3/8	4 3/8	9	13	Texas	Unknown	Lawson W. Walden	PR 1988	425
221 7/8	27 1/8	27 1/8	21	5 7/8	5 6/8	10	10	Jefferson Co., IA	Jared L. Rebling	Jared L. Rebling	2000	425
221 6/8	23 2/8	25 7/8	21 5/8	5 5/8	5 6/8	13	10	Snipe Lake, AB	Robert Dickson, Sr.	Robert Dickson, Sr.	1984	429
221 5/8	25 2/8	24 6/8	23 7/8	5	5	10	11	Clearwater Co., MN	Kevin Crane	Kevin Crane	1994	430
221 4/8	27 4/8	27 5/8	15 5/8	5 4/8	5 4/8	12	12	Michigan	Unknown	MI Whitetail Hall of Fame Mus.	PR 1964	431
221 4/8	30	29 2/8	23 3/8	6 2/8	6 2/8	12	12	Humboldt Co., IA	Donald Crossley	Donald Crossley	1971	431
221 4/8	25	20 7/8	21 2/8	6 3/8	6 1/8	12	21	Hancock Co., IL	Neal C. Meyer	Neal C. Meyer	1987	431
221 4/8	27 4/8	27 5/8	20 3/8	5 4/8	5 4/8	10	10	Pike Co., MO	Billy J. Schanks	Cabela's, Inc.	1991	431
221 4/8	26 2/8	24 2/8	22	5	5 2/8	11	16	Comanche Co., OK	Ted M. Evans	Ted M. Evans	2001	431
221 3/8	29 3/8	29 5/8	19	5 5/8	5 4/8	11	10	Dewey Co., SD	Leo Fischer	Leo Fischer	1958	436
221 3/8	21 6/8	19 4/8	17 1/8	10	10	12	13	Anne Arundel Co., MD	Unknown	Frederick H. Horn	1979	436
221 3/8	26 3/8	25	19 2/8	6 3/8	7 7/8	11	13	Louisa Co., VA	Picked Up	James T. Rapalee	1981	436
221 2/8	22 5/8	23 6/8	17 1/8	4 5/8	4 4/8	16	19	Itasca Co., MN	Richard I. Goble	Richard I. Goble	1955	439
221 2/8	20 5/8	23 6/8	19 2/8	4 7/8	5	13	19	Holmes Co., MS	Milton Parrish	Milton Parrish	1970	439
221 2/8	28 5/8	28 7/8	22 3/8	5 5/8	5 4/8	10	11	Franklin Co., KS	Marvin R. Smith	Brad Sowter	1988	439
221 2/8	25 7/8	26 2/8	18 1/8	4 5/8	4 5/8	15	11	Lapeer Co., MI	Picked Up	William Schmidt, Jr.	1993	439
221 2/8	25 5/8	25 6/8	19 1/8	5 1/8	5 2/8	11	11	Muhlenberg Co., KY	Mark A. Smith	Mark A. Smith	1998	439
221 2/8	25 6/8	26 7/8	20 1/8	5	5	10	9	Jersey Co., IL	Ross A. Eggebrecht	Ross A. Eggebrecht	2002	439
221 1/8	27 2/8	29 4/8	22 6/8	5 5/8	5 4/8	15	14	Jefferson Co., IA	Daniel R. Thurman	Daniel R. Thurman	1979	445
221	29 1/8	29	23 4/8	4 5/8	4 4/8	9	9	Pike Co., IL	Frank C. Skelton	Frank C. Skelton	1987	446
220 7/8	23 1/8	23 7/8	14 4/8	6 7/8	6 6/8	17	12	Pembina Co., ND	Gary F. Bourbanis	Gary F. Bourbanis	1985	447
220 7/8	27 6/8	27 7/8	22 6/8	5 6/8	5 7/8	9	11	Sauk Co., WI	Bryan J. McGann	Bryan J. McGann	1986	447
220 7/8	26 1/8	27 1/8	19 6/8	5 2/8	5 3/8	11	8	Ross Co., OH	Tommy E. Dailey	Tommy E. Dailey	1993	447
220 7/8	26 4/8	26 4/8	22 4/8	5 6/8	5 6/8	10	9	Trego Co., KS	John M. Benewiat	John M. Benewiat	1999	447
220 6/8	26 4/8	25 6/8	19 6/8	6 1/8	6 3/8	12	15	Anoka Co., MN	Donald Torgerson	Bass Pro Shops	1946	451
220 6/8	26 4/8	27 2/8	27 7/8	5 2/8	5 1/8	10	9	Dallas Co., IA	Picked Up	Gale Sup	1992	451
220 6/8	27 4/8	22 6/8	18	5 4/8	6 4/8	9	15	Crawford Co., IA	Picked Up	Raymond H. Schulte	2000	451
220 5/8	22 1/8	23 6/8	16 6/8	4 3/8	4 3/8	10	15	Halfway River, BC	Bill Miller	Deb Fleet	PR 1934	454
220 5/8	29 1/8	28 2/8	20 6/8	5 4/8	5 6/8	13	12	Kittson Co., MN	Todd J. Porter	Dick Rossum	1986	454
220 5/8	28	28	21 3/8	6 2/8	6 2/8	12	8	Jefferson Co., IA	Mike Laux	Bass Pro Shops	1990	454

Score	Main Beam R	Main Beam L	Inside Spread	Circ. R	Circ. L	Points R	Points L	Locality	Hunter	Owner	Date	Rank
220 5/8	25 3/8	24 7/8	23 1/8	5 7/8	5 7/8	8	12	Berrien Co., MI	Robert C. Sexton	Robert C. Sexton	2002	454
220 4/8	28 6/8	28 7/8	20 2/8	5 6/8	5 6/8	9	8	Dixon Co., NE	Otto D. Kneifl	Otto D. Kneifl	1964	458
220 4/8	30	30 6/8	20 5/8	4 7/8	5 1/8	12	8	Mercer Co., IL	Roger D. Hultgren	Roger D. Hultgren	1970	458
220 4/8	29 2/8	29 2/8	20 2/8	5 1/8	4 6/8	8	8	Knox Co., OH	Richard E. Boyd	Richard E. Boyd	1995	458
220 4/8	27 4/8	26 3/8	20 3/8	4 5/8	5	14	14	Chitek Lake, SK	Douglas Falone	Douglas Falone	1998	458
220 3/8	25 1/8	25 6/8	18 6/8	5	5	13	13	Olmsted Co., MN	E.E. Comartin III	E.E. Comartin, Jr.	1963	462
220 3/8	26 2/8	26 7/8	21	5 5/8	5 4/8	10	10	Oktibbeha Co., MS	Dean E. Jones	Dean E. Jones	1976	462
220 3/8	27 1/8	27	19 7/8	5 6/8	5 5/8	12	12	Todd Co., MN	Gary V. Martin	Gary V. Martin	1992	462
220 2/8	28 2/8	28 4/8	21	5	5	8	8	Zavala Co., TX	Jerry D. Jarratt	Jerry D. Jarratt	1930	465
220 2/8	25	26 4/8	19 1/8	5 4/8	5 4/8	9	12	Union Co., IA	George L. Foster	George L. Foster	1968	465
220 2/8	27 4/8	27 1/8	19	5 1/8	5 1/8	13	13	Caldwell Co., KY	Loyd Holt	Loyd Holt	1984	465
220 2/8	29 4/8	31 2/8	22 4/8	5 7/8	5 7/8	14	14	Prince George's Co., MD	Robert Y. Clagett, Jr.	Robert Y. Clagett, Jr.	1995	465
220 1/8	26 6/8	27 5/8	20 2/8	4 7/8	4 6/8	8	8	Lewis Co., ID	Steavon C. Hornbeck	Steavon C. Hornbeck	2000	465
220 2/8	27 4/8	27 5/8	24 3/8	4 7/8	4 6/8	9	9	Redvers, SK	Ira E. Sampson	Ira E. Sampson	1969	470
220 2/8	23 6/8	26 7/8	18 4/8	5 2/8	5 2/8	12	12	Iroquois Co., IL	John P. Boshears	John P. Boshears	1998	470
220 1/8	27	26 5/8	22 1/8	6 6/8	6	13	10	Ashland Co., OH	Jeffrey J. Spreng	Jeffrey J. Spreng	2002	470
220	28 1/8	28 6/8	18 5/8	4 7/8	4 7/8	13	9	Wayne Co., IA	Dallas Patterson	Dallas Patterson	1975	473
220	30 3/8	28 6/8	17 4/8	6 6/8	6 6/8	8	15	Allen Co., KS	Merril R. Lamb	Merril R. Lamb	1999	473
220	26 3/8	26 2/8	18 7/8	4 4/8	4 4/8	16	13	Scott Co., AR	Daniel Boyd	Daniel Boyd	2001	473
220	29 1/8	27 4/8	20 4/8	5	5	8	7	Fayette Co., WV	Jess E. Kelly	Jess E. Kelly	2002	473
219 7/8	27 2/8	27 6/8	19 7/8	6	6	10	10	Genesee Co., NY	Robert Wood	Robert Wood	1944	477
219 7/8	25 4/8	25 7/8	20 4/8	5 3/8	5 3/8	10	10	Clearwater Co., ID	Kipling D. Manfull	Kipling D. Manfull	1989	477
219 7/8	23 4/8	26 1/8	23 2/8	5 2/8	5 5/8	11	8	Saskatchewan River, SK	Don Thorimbert	Don Thorimbert	1996	477
219 6/8	19 1/8	23 1/8	18 4/8	4 4/8	4 6/8	11	8	Caddo Parish, LA	William D. Ethredge, Jr.	William D. Ethredge, Jr.	1988	480
219 6/8	25	27 7/8	21 1/8	5 4/8	5 5/8	15	15	N. Saskatchewan River, SK	Terry D. Redpath	Terry D. Redpath	1993	480
219 6/8	25 4/8	26 2/8	23 7/8	5 1/8	5 1/8	10	10	Christian Co., IL	Eric D. Garrett	Eric D. Garrett	1994	480
219 6/8	24 6/8	26	21 2/8	5 3/8	5 5/8	9	11	Cass Co., MI	Bruce C. Heslet II	Bruce C. Heslet II	2000	480
219 5/8	24 5/8	25 1/8	21 1/8	6 3/8	6 3/8	13	12	Warren Co., MO	James E. Williams	James E. Williams	1959	484
219 5/8	22 7/8	24 2/8	16 5/8	4 4/8	4 5/8	13	13	Black Hawk, ON	Picked Up	Marc M. Jackson	1990	484
219 5/8	28 4/8	24 2/8	20	5 2/8	4 7/8	9	10	Meeting Lake, SK	Earl Braun	Earl Braun	2002	484
219 4/8	27	27 2/8	24 2/8	5 6/8	5 6/8	11	11	Lake of the Woods Co., MN	Thomas Barden	Robert V. Ellenson	PR 1951	487
219 4/8	26 5/8	26 1/8	21 2/8	5	5	11	11	Sumner Co., KS	Picked Up	Greg L. Hill	1987	487
219 3/8	27 4/8	27 4/8	20	5 2/8	5 2/8	11	8	Webb Co., TX	Richard O. Rivera	John L. Stein	1972	489
219 3/8	28 1/8	28 1/8	20 5/8	4 4/8	4 4/8	11	10	Webster Co., IA	David Propst	David Propst	1987	489
219 3/8	25 2/8	24	17 4/8	5 4/8	5 4/8	12	17	Maine	Unknown	Gale Sup	PR 1988	489
219 3/8	26 7/8	26 2/8	18	6	6	9	9	Fulton Co., IL	Christopher W. Schweigert	Christopher W. Schweigert	1998	489
219 3/8	26 2/8	26 5/8	18 4/8	5 3/8	5 3/8	10	10	Schuyler Co., IL	James R. Lehman	James R. Lehman	2000	489
219 2/8	26	30 5/8	19 2/8	6 2/8	6 2/8	13	11	Buffalo Co., WI	Glenn Lehman	Glenn Lehman	1958	494
219 2/8	23 6/8	23 6/8	23 2/8	4 5/8	4 6/8	12	12	Mud Creek, AB	Hank Stainbrook	Caroline Supplies Ltd.	1971	494
219 2/8	24 6/8	24 6/8	21 6/8	5 4/8	5 4/8	9	9	Aroostook Co., ME	Harold C. Kitchin	Harold C. Kitchin	1973	494
219 2/8	26 2/8	26 6/8	22 3/8	4 7/8	5	11	11	Midway, BC	Gordon Kamigochi	Gordon Kamigochi	1980	494
219 1/8	27 3/8	27	17	5 1/8	4 7/8	8	8	Hinds Co., MS	Matt M. Woods	Matt M. Woods	1998	494
219 1/8	27	27	18 2/8	5 4/8	5 1/8	9	10	Flathead Co., MT	R.C. Garrett	R.C. Garrett	1962	494
219 1/8	22 5/8	22 5/8	18 4/8	5 1/8	5 4/8	17	15	Pontotoc Co., OK	Timothy F. Harris	Timothy F. Harris	1996	499
219 1/8	27 6/8	27 6/8	18 7/8	5 3/8	5 1/8	15	17	Bell Co., KY	Jeff D. Jackson	Jeff D. Jackson	1999	499
219 1/8	26 6/8	26 3/8	19 1/8	5 3/8	5 3/8	13	9	Porter Co., IN	John S. Biggs, Jr.	John S. Biggs, Jr.	2000	499
219 1/8	24 6/8	24 6/8	17 4/8	4 5/8	4 5/8	10	12	S. Saskatchewan River, SK	Picked Up	Thad W. Karwandy	2000	499
219	24 1/8	24 6/8	21	4 4/8	4 4/8	11	9	Van Buren Co., IA	James E. Garrels	Wayne G. Nevar	1988	504

WHITETAIL DEER - NON-TYPICAL ANTLERS
Odocoileus virginianus virginianus and certain related subspecies

Score	Length of Main Beam R	L	Inside Spread	Circumference at Smallest Place Between Burr and First Point R	L	Number of Points R	L	Locality	Hunter	Owner	Date Killed	Rank
219	27 3/8	27	17 6/8	5 6/8	5 7/8	8	11	Morrison Co., MN	Michael R. Langin	Michael R. Langin	1992	504
218 7/8	28 1/8	27 7/8	20	5 2/8	4 7/8	12	11	Florence Co., WI	W.C. Gotstein	Bass Pro Shops	1914	506
218 7/8	29 2/8	28 6/8	21	5 4/8	5 4/8	6	8	Waldo Co., ME	Roy C. Guse	J. Bruce Probert	1957	506
218 7/8	22 6/8	23 3/8	15 4/8	7 3/8	7 1/8	16	11	Bay of Fundy, NS	Basil S. Lewis	Basil S. Lewis	1983	506
218 7/8	25 3/8	22 4/8	18 7/8	4 5/8	4 7/8	12	12	Marshall Co., IA	Picked Up	Charles E. Lewis	1989	506
218 7/8	26 6/8	25 5/8	20 3/8	6	6	8	12	St. Joseph Co., MI	Picked Up	Rex A. Mayer	PR 1989	506
218 6/8	23 5/8	24 7/8	19 2/8	6 2/8	5 4/8	14	7	Morrison Co., MN	Wilfred LeBlanc	George W. Flaim	1938	511
218 6/8	29 4/8	29 3/8	23 3/8	6	6	11	9	Williamson Co., IL	Carl W. Norris	Carl W. Norris	1994	511
218 6/8	26	27 7/8	21 7/8	7 3/8	7 4/8	10	8	Cass Co., IL	Stanley E. Walker	Stanley E. Walker	1998	511
218 5/8	25	25 2/8	14 4/8	5 1/8	5 1/8	13	15	Itasca Co., MN	John W. Pierson, Sr.	John W. Pierson, Sr.	1945	514
218 5/8	26 2/8	25 6/8	18 4/8	4 4/8	4 4/8	9	11	Chariton Co., MO	Stanley McSparren	Stanley McSparren	1979	514
218 5/8	28 6/8	27 4/8	20	6 1/8	6	14	11	St. Louis Co., MN	Unknown	George W. Flaim	PR 1983	514
218 5/8	25 3/8	24 6/8	18	6 7/8	6 3/8	17	13	Otter Tail Co., MN	Gerald P. Lucas	Gerald P. Lucas	1985	514
218 5/8	24 5/8	27	18 5/8	5 7/8	5 6/8	11	9	Page Co., IA	John L. Novy	John L. Novy	1989	514
218 5/8	23 5/8	24 6/8	17 1/8	4 7/8	4 5/8	7	10	Dawson Creek, BC	John D. Todd	John D. Todd	1992	514
218 5/8	29 5/8	30	21 5/8	5	5	11	7	Kansas	Unknown	Larry D. Bollier	PR 1997	514
218 4/8	27	26 3/8	18 7/8	5 2/8	5 3/8	12	12	Sawyer Co., WI	Walter Kittleson	Walter Kittleson	1920	521
218 4/8	26 2/8	26 3/8	17 2/8	5 5/8	5 3/8	8	8	St. Martin Parish, LA	Drew Ware	Gary S. Crnko	1941	521
218 4/8	23 1/8	22 7/8	20 5/8	7 5/8	7 1/8	9	12	Logan Co., KY	Robert L. Schrader, Jr.	Robert L. Schrader, Jr.	1987	521
218 3/8	27	24 3/8	17	5 7/8	5 5/8	9	11	La Crosse Co., WI	Daniel P. Cavadini	D.J. Hollinger & B. Howard	1951	524
218 3/8	20 7/8	24 3/8	19 3/8	4 6/8	5	13	15	South Goodeve, SK	Fred Bohay	Fred Bohay	1958	524
218 3/8	24 7/8	25 5/8	23 2/8	5 2/8	5 2/8	10	11	Keweenaw Co., MI	Bernard J. Murn	Bernard J. Murn	1980	524
218 3/8	23	26	16 7/8	5 4/8	5 4/8	15	11	Itasca Co., MN	Unknown	George W. Flaim	1983	524
218 3/8	29 2/8	29 5/8	19 5/8	5 1/8	4 7/8	12	10	Fillmore Co., MN	Darrel R. Highum	Darrel R. Highum	1989	524
218 2/8	29 3/8	29 7/8	23 4/8	5 3/8	5 3/8	7	7	Allamakee Co., IA	Bernard Rank	Bass Pro Shops	1963	529
218 2/8	27	26 7/8	18 6/8	5 4/8	5 6/8	8	7	Waukesha Co., WI	Picked Up	WI Dept. of Natl. Resc.	1986	529
218 1/8	27 2/8	27 1/8	15	5 7/8	5 7/8	13	8	Iron Co., MI	Carl Mattson	Mary J. Wellman	1945	531
218	25 4/8	25 3/8	19	5 4/8	5 3/8	11	15	Otter Tail Co., MN	Dennis A. Pearson	Dennis A. Pearson	1977	532
217 7/8	23 4/8	23 4/8	19 4/8	4 5/8	4 5/8	11	10	Dimmit Co., TX	Unknown	McLean Bowman	1920	533
217 7/8	27 7/8	28 2/8	21 3/8	5 4/8	5 7/8	10	16	Maries Co., MO	Gerald R. Dake	Gerald R. Dake	1974	533
217 7/8	24 4/8	26 5/8	20	6 1/8	5 4/8	18	14	Cherokee Co., KS	Craig E. Ruddick	Craig E. Ruddick	1983	533
217 7/8	24	22 4/8	21 1/8	5 3/8	7 6/8	8	20	Washakie Co., WY	Kenneth A. Fossum	Kenneth A. Fossum	1991	533
217 7/8	25 6/8	25 1/8	16 4/8	5 7/8	5 5/8	13	7	Jefferson Co., IL	Steve Gum	Steve Gum	2002	533
217 6/8	26 2/8	28 5/8	18 6/8	5 1/8	5	12	12	Macoupin Co., IL	Albert Grichnik	Albert Grichnik	1966	538
217 6/8	27 6/8	24	20 3/8	4 7/8	6	8	11	Otoe Co., NE	Douglas E. Gregg	Douglas E. Gregg	1994	538
217 6/8	28 4/8	28 7/8	20 5/8	6 1/8	6	11	9	Clark Co., IL	David P. Mosley	David P. Mosley	1995	538

Score								Locality	Hunter	Owner	Date	Rank
217 5/8	27 3/8	24 6/8	23	4 6/8	5 3/8	14	14	Carroll Co., MS	Mark T. Hathcock	Mark T. Hathcock	1978	541
217 5/8	28 6/8	27 7/8	14 6/8	6	6	13	15	Hardin Co., KY	Michael F. Meredith	Michael F. Meredith	1980	541
217 5/8	26	23 2/8	18 5/8	5 1/8	5 5/8	9	16	Flagstaff, AB	Craig A. Miller	Craig A. Miller	1990	541
217 5/8	24 4/8	24 3/8	17 3/8	4 5/8	4 4/8	11	16	Tobin Lake, SK	Picked Up	SK Parks & Renew. Resc.	1991	541
217 5/8	25 4/8	26 1/8	19 3/8	5 5/8	5 3/8	16	14	Butler Co., KS	Trent A. Busenitz	Trent A. Busenitz	2002	541
217 4/8	25 5/8	25	19 4/8	6 2/8	6 3/8	11	12	Aitkin Co., MN	Fred C. Melichar	Fred C. Melichar	1973	546
217 4/8	24 2/8	26 1/8	20 3/8	5	5 2/8	8	7	Allamakee Co., IA	George A. Smith	George A. Smith	1991	546
217 4/8	27 4/8	27 6/8	23 5/8	5 3/8	5 3/8	8	8	Bethune, SK	Ronald N. Riche	Ronald N. Riche	1998	546
217 3/8	28 1/8	25 2/8	21 2/8	5 7/8	6 4/8	11	8	Douglas Co., WI	Unknown	Ross A. Manthey	1939	549
217 3/8	22 7/8	23 6/8	13	4 6/8	4 6/8	10	11	Weston Co., WY	Harry Phillips	Harry Phillips	1957	549
217 3/8	27	28 5/8	18 3/8	5 2/8	5 4/8	12	15	Meeker Co., MN	Steven R. Turck	Steven R. Turck	1982	549
217 3/8	30 4/8	29	28 4/8	5	5	8	8	Cross Co., AR	Randal Harris	Randal Harris	1986	549
217 3/8	27 5/8	29 2/8	18 7/8	4 2/8	4 3/8	9	11	Dewer River, NS	Alan Fahey	Alan Fahey	1989	549
217 2/8	29 2/8	29 4/8	20	5 6/8	5 6/8	12	9	St. Louis Co., MN	Unknown	George W. Flaim	1957	554
217 2/8	23 3/8	23 1/8	19	5 3/8	5 2/8	11	11	Sprucehome, SK	Tom Pillar	Tom Pillar	1957	554
217 2/8	22	20	20	4 5/8	4 5/8	13	12	Talbot Co., MD	Vincent L. Jordan, Sr.	Vincent L. Jordan, Sr.	1974	554
217 2/8	29 6/8	29 6/8	25 3/8	5 2/8	5 2/8	8	7	Mills Co., IA	Rick W. Elliott	Rick W. Elliott	1976	554
217 2/8	28 6/8	28 5/8	21 6/8	4 7/8	5 2/8	11	8	Clark Co., MO	Lawrence L. Paul	Lawrence L. Paul	1977	554
217 2/8	23 6/8	24 3/8	19	5 4/8	5 4/8	13	10	Hudson Bay, SK	Ron Kenyon	Ron Kenyon	1987	554
217 2/8	30	29 3/8	21 2/8	4 6/8	5	6	12	Kandiyohi Co., MN	Picked Up	Dean Salzl	1988	554
217 2/8	24 5/8	24 2/8	17 4/8	5 5/8	6 3/8	5	14	Dallas Co., AL	Robert Tate	Robert Tate	1988	554
217 2/8	19	24 4/8	16 5/8	7 4/8	6 2/8	16	10	Benewah Co., ID	Daniel Dodd	Cabela's, Inc.	1996	554
217 1/8	25 2/8	27 6/8	20 6/8	6	5 7/8	12	8	Sturgeon River, SK	Francis Rask	Francis Rask	1995	563
217 1/8	27 3/8	27 5/8	21 1/8	6 2/8	5 6/8	13	13	Butler Co., KY	Merle Raymer	Merle Raymer	1999	563
217	23 6/8	23 6/8	17 1/8	4 4/8	4 6/8	13	12	Unknown	Charles H. Reames	Ronald L. Christensen	PR 1872	565
217	23	25 4/8	25 7/8	5 7/8	5 6/8	11	11	Isle of Wight Co., VA	Peter F. Crocker, Jr.	Peter F. Crocker, Jr.	1963	565
217	29	27 4/8	19 4/8	5 4/8	5 4/8	10	9	Fulton Co., IL	Picked Up	IL Dept. of Nat. Resources	1990	565
217	30 7/8	28 6/8	18 4/8	5 2/8	5	9	10	Dearborn Co., IN	Jerry L. Irvine	Jerry L. Irvine	1990	565
217	23 2/8	22 1/8	20 2/8	4 7/8	4 6/8	15	10	Love Co., OK	Greg French	Greg French	1996	565
216 7/8	26 7/8	24 7/8	17 2/8	6	5 7/8	12	17	Concordia Parish, LA	Richard Dale	Richard Dale	1956	570
216 7/8	19 2/8	21 1/8	13 7/8	7	6 5/8	12	15	Brown Co., SD	Francis Shattuck	D.J. Hollinger & B. Howard	1960	570
216 7/8	27 3/8	28 7/8	21 6/8	5 2/8	5 1/8	12	12	Wilson Co., KS	Gilbert J. McGee	Gilbert J. McGee	1988	570
216 7/8	25 3/8	28 1/8	19 7/8	6	5 5/8	13	10	Howard Co., IN	Jason E. Young	Jason E. Young	1995	570
216 7/8	25 4/8	25 7/8	21	4 6/8	5	10	11	Lee Co., IL	Clifford L. Walter	Clifford L. Walter	1997	570
216 6/8	25 4/8	27 1/8	22 3/8	5 5/8	5 4/8	12	7	Wayne Co., IL	Kenneth L. Tucker	Kenneth L. Tucker	2000	570
216 6/8	26	24 4/8	22 3/8	5 2/8	5 1/8	11	13	Kathryn, ND	Gerald R. Elsner	Gerald R. Elsner	1963	576
216 6/8	25 1/8	25 4/8	18 2/8	6 3/8	6 4/8	10	13	Barber Co., KS	Robert L. Rose	Robert L. Rose	1972	576
216 6/8	24 4/8	24 1/8	17	7	7 1/8	11	11	Lake of the Woods Co., MN	Andy Streiff	Andy Streiff	1974	576
216 6/8	26 3/8	26 1/8	25 1/8	5	5 4/8	7	11	Brown Co., IL	David R. Herschelman	David R. Herschelman	1991	576
216 6/8	29	27 3/8	22 7/8	6 2/8	6 4/8	13	13	Charles Co., MD	Brian G. Klaas	Brian G. Klaas	1993	576
216 6/8	25	25	18	5 6/8	5 7/8	12	14	Menard Co., IL	Randy Boyle	Randy Boyle	1995	576
216 5/8	24 4/8	23 5/8	17 2/8	5 2/8	5 3/8	12	13	Dickinson Co., MI	Earl Wilt	Richard H. Wilt	1943	582
216 4/8	25 2/8	27 1/8	23	5	5	12	10	Surry Co., VA	Stanley M. Hall	Stanley M. Hall	1986	583
216 4/8	18	18	17	5 4/8	5 6/8	14	13	Macon Co., AL	George B. Bulls	George B. Bulls	1995	583
216 4/8	27 6/8	26 1/8	19 2/8	5	5 4/8	9	10	Jefferson Co., MO	Picked Up	Jeff L. Vaughan	1995	583
216 3/8	26	24 4/8	18 6/8	5 3/8	5 6/8	14	17	Comanche Co., OK	Dwight O. Allen	Dwight O. Allen	1962	586
216 3/8	26	25 5/8	17 4/8	5 4/8	5 4/8	10	9	Clay Co., IA	Blaine Salzkorn	Blaine Salzkorn	1970	586
216 3/8	26 3/8	26 3/8	20 3/8	4 7/8	5	9	10	Powhatan Co., VA	William E. Schaefer	William E. Schaefer	1970	586

WHITETAIL DEER - NON-TYPICAL ANTLERS

Odocoileus virginianus virginianus and certain related subspecies

Score	Length of Main Beam R	L	Inside Spread	Circumference at Smallest Place Between Burr and First Point R	L	Number of Points R	L	Locality	Hunter	Owner	Date Killed	Rank
216 3/8	29 2/8	27 1/8	17 5/8	6 2/8	7 1/8	8	10	Jersey Co., IL	Walter L. Baker	Walter L. Baker	1998	586
216 3/8	29 1/8	28 3/8	26 3/8	4 4/8	4 4/8	9	8	Christian Co., IL	John R. Reese	John R. Reese	1998	586
216 3/8	26 3/8	27 1/8	19 2/8	6 3/8	6 4/8	12	12	Woodbury Co., IA	Picked Up	Helen Peterson	1999	586
216 2/8	30	28 2/8	23	5 7/8	5 5/8	7	9	Blue Earth Co., MN	Marion Abbas	Harold Abbas	1961	592
216 2/8	23 5/8	24	18 4/8	4 4/8	4 4/8	10	8	Buchanan, SK	Mike Spezrivka	Linda Christoforo	1961	592
216 2/8	26 5/8	27 5/8	20 3/8	5 6/8	5 7/8	10	14	Richland Co., MT	Joseph P. Culbertson	Joseph P. Culbertson	1972	592
216 2/8	25	24 3/8	19	6 7/8	7	10	11	Porter Co., IN	Lester W. Fornshell	Lester W. Fornshell	1994	592
216 2/8	28 7/8	26 7/8	23 3/8	4 7/8	5 1/8	10	9	Floyd Co., VA	Ronnie T. Perdue	Ronnie T. Perdue	1996	592
216 2/8	26 6/8	26 3/8	20	4 6/8	5 5/8	8	11	Lyon Co., KS	Rodney D. Watson	Rodney D. Watson	2000	592
216 1/8	25 2/8	23 4/8	19 6/8	4 4/8	4 3/8	13	12	Gillespie Co., TX	J.C. Park	John L. Stein	1932	598
216 1/8	23 1/8	19 4/8	15 2/8	5 3/8	6 1/8	15	16	Itasca Co., MN	Thomas Thurstin	Thomas Thurstin	1977	598
216 1/8	27	27 6/8	17 7/8	5 6/8	5 7/8	10	11	Stephenson Co., IL	Steven M. Knopes	Steven M. Knopes	1999	598
216 1/8	26	26 6/8	22 2/8	6 3/8	6 3/8	9	10	Grundy Co., IL	Steven E. Claypool	Steven E. Claypool	2001	598
216	29 4/8	29 4/8	19 1/8	5 2/8	5 2/8	11	10	Prairie Co., AR	Cecil M. Miller	Cecil M. Miller	1973	602
216	24 1/8	24 1/8	19 3/8	5 1/8	4 6/8	14	9	Manitoba	Unknown	Robert J. Winnekens	1990	602
216	25 3/8	25 6/8	19 2/8	5 3/8	5 2/8	11	9	Jackson Co., IA	Picked Up	Douglas J. Horst	1992	602
216	24 6/8	22 1/8	16 2/8	4	4 4/8	13	12	Kiowa Co., KS	Ray L. Magby	Ray L. Magby	2001	602
215 7/8	25	24 4/8	24 3/8	6 6/8	6	11	12	Long Pine, NE	Picked Up	Duane Lotspeich	1964	606
215 7/8	29 6/8	27 7/8	16 7/8	6 1/8	6 4/8	13	13	Putnam Co., GA	Thomas H. Cooper	Thomas H. Cooper	1974	606
215 7/8	27 1/8	26 5/8	27 7/8	6	5 2/8	9	6	Schuyler Co., IL	Donald E. Ziegenbein	Donald E. Ziegenbein	1981	606
215 7/8	27 7/8	26	24 1/8	6 1/8	6 2/8	10	10	Taney Co., MO	Roy S. Smith	Ronald L. Smith	1986	606
215 7/8	27 1/8	27 5/8	22 2/8	5 5/8	5 6/8	9	13	Wabasha Co., MN	Leroy Goranson	Leroy Goranson	1990	606
215 7/8	26 2/8	26 7/8	21 4/8	6	5 5/8	10	10	Eau Claire Co., WI	Dale G. Planert	Dale G. Planert	1997	606
215 7/8	28	25 1/8	21 2/8	5 5/8	5 6/8	9	11	Trego Co., KS	Stephen G. Chaffee	Stephen G. Chaffee	2000	606
215 6/8	25 1/8	25 3/8	21	4 4/8	5 4/8	12	10	Idaho	Leroy Shaffer	D.J. Hollinger & B. Howard	1968	613
215 6/8	24 4/8	24 4/8	23 3/8	6 2/8	7 4/8	10	12	Chippewa Co., MN	Micheal Allickson	Micheal Allickson	1974	613
215 6/8	26	25 1/8	24 2/8	4 3/8	5 2/8	6	11	Macoupin Co., IL	Allen E. McKee	Allen E. McKee	1992	613
215 6/8	28 1/8	28 1/8	26 2/8	6 6/8	6 1/8	10	9	Mayerthorpe, AB	Gary F. Jamieson	Gary F. Jamieson	1998	613
215 5/8	26	25 6/8	20	5 5/8	5 6/8	16	12	Iron Co., MI	C. & R. Lester	C. & R. Lester	1970	617
215 5/8	28	28	20 2/8	5 2/8	5 1/8	10	9	Worth Co., MO	B. Miller & R. Nonneman	B. Miller & R. Nonneman	1974	617
215 5/8	28 2/8	29 2/8	18 6/8	4 6/8	4 5/8	9	11	Wise Co., VA	Edison Holcomb	Edison Holcomb	1987	617
215 5/8	24 4/8	21 3/8	17 6/8	5 3/8	6	11	13	Huron Co., MI	Patrick L. Flanagan, Jr.	Patrick L. Flanagan, Jr.	1990	617
215 5/8	21 6/8	22	15	5 7/8	6 2/8	14	15	Medicine Hat, AB	Dave Moore	Dave Moore	1998	617
215 4/8	26 7/8	26 6/8	19 3/8	5 3/8	5 3/8	10	9	Morrison Co., MN	James P. Poser	James P. Poser	1978	622
215 4/8	29 1/8	29 4/8	23 2/8	6 1/8	6 2/8	11	13	Wayne Co., IN	Clyde L. Day	Clyde L. Day	1986	622
215 4/8	23	24 3/8	21 7/8	6 3/8	5 1/8	11	8	Schuyler Co., IL	Raymond Shouse	Raymond Shouse	1993	622

Score	Main Beam R	Main Beam L	Inside Spread	Circ. R	Circ. L	Points	Points	Locality	Owner	Hunter	Date	Rank
215 4/8	24 3/8	28 2/8	24 5/8	6 4/8	6 3/8	9	11	Fulton Co., IL	Roger H. Mann	Roger H. Mann	1994	622
215 4/8	25	24 6/8	20 3/8	4 7/8	5 1/8	10	11	Drayton Valley, AB	Mitch B. Reimer	Mitch B. Reimer	2002	622
215 3/8	21	23 4/8	15	7 2/8	6 6/8	12	15	Trinity Co., TX	Earl Smith	Lawson W. Walden	1965	627
215 3/8	29 4/8	28 6/8	23 7/8	5 6/8	5 6/8	8	8	Lafayette Co., WI	Roger Vickers	Roger Vickers	1969	627
215 2/8	24 3/8	27 1/8	18 2/8	5 3/8	5 3/8	9	9	Fillmore Co., MN	George E. Holets	George E. Holets	1960	629
215 2/8	21	19	24	4	4	12	16	Parker Co., TX	Pleasant Mitchell	Pleasant Mitchell	1982	629
215 2/8	23 3/8	23 1/8	17 7/8	7 1/8	7 2/8	11	12	Henderson Co., KY	Gary E. Boucherie	Gary E. Boucherie	1991	629
215 2/8	25 6/8	25 1/8	16 6/8	5 6/8	5 5/8	11	14	La Crosse Co., WI	Mark R. Thorn	Mark R. Thorn	2000	633
215 1/8	26 5/8	25 6/8	21 6/8	6	6	11	9	Cass Co., IL	David G. Bolletto	David G. Bolletto	1988	633
215 1/8	25 3/8	24	22 1/8	6 7/8	6 4/8	11	10	Winnebago Co., IL	Dennis F. Shipler	Dennis F. Shipler	1990	633
215 1/8	25 5/8	25 3/8	23 4/8	5 2/8	5 2/8	11	11	Jefferson Co., NE	Gary A. Hellbusch	Gary A. Hellbusch	1994	633
215 1/8	29 2/8	28 1/8	21 7/8	5 4/8	5 4/8	13	11	Rusagonis River, NB	Art Appleby	Art Appleby	1998	633
215 1/8	24 4/8	26 2/8	19 3/8	6 7/8	7 2/8	17	13	Racine Co., WI	Mike T. Thelen	Mike T. Thelen	2001	638
215	23 3/8	25 6/8	15 5/8	5 6/8	5 4/8	13	13	Fergus Co., MT	Robert D. Fleherty	Robert D. Fleherty	1958	638
215	26 3/8	25 6/8	15 6/8	5 2/8	5 2/8	11	12	Fillmore Co., MN	Picked Up	Jeffrey S. Mackey	1968	638
215	25 4/8	25 6/8	21 6/8	5	5	10	8	Stevens Co., WA	Unknown	Dick Rossum	PR 1989	638
215	30 3/8	30	22 7/8	4 4/8	5 7/8	11	15	Allen Co., KS	James W. Baker	James W. Baker	1992	638
215	25 1/8	25 1/8	18 1/8	5 3/8	4 5/8	8	10	Wood River, SK	Scott Cowie	Scott Cowie	1997	638
215	24 3/8	23 3/8	22 2/8	6 7/8	5 2/8	8	10	Caldwell Co., KY	C.J. Brummett	C.J. Brummett	1998	638
214 7/8	28 1/8	27 5/8	19 5/8	6 7/8	7 2/8	7	11	Todd Co., MN	Picked Up	Tom Kendall	2000	645
214 7/8	27 6/8	27	20 1/8	4 6/8	7	9	12	Concordia Parish, LA	W.E. Beazley	Mike Harper	1938	645
214 7/8	25 3/8	24 3/8	24 3/8	5 1/8	4 6/8	9	13	Aweme, MB	Criddle Bros.	Criddle Bros.	1954	645
214 7/8	26 3/8	26 6/8	21 1/8	5 2/8	6 4/8	15	12	Cass Co., MN	Glen W. Slagle, Sr.	Glen W. Slagle, Sr.	1959	645
214 7/8	24 6/8	23 1/8	17	4 6/8	5 1/8	12	10	St. John Co., NB	T. Emery	New Brunswick Museum	1968	650
214 6/8	21 3/8	26 7/8	12 4/8	4 3/8	4 6/8	13	12	Big Horn Co., WY	Michael K. Smith	Michael K. Smith	1987	650
214 6/8	24 7/8	27 6/8	23 1/8	7 2/8	6	13	9	Quinlan Creek, NS	Fred Doucette	Fred Doucette	1962	650
214 6/8	25 6/8	28	22 2/8	5	4 7/8	9	7	Hitchcock Co., NE	David W. Oates	David W. Oates	1985	650
214 6/8	26 6/8	26 3/8	21 6/8	5 5/8	5 5/8	10	8	Decatur Co., IA	Dean D. Grimm	Dean D. Grimm	1988	655
214 5/8	27	27	17 2/8	4 7/8	4 7/8	11	11	Roseau River, MB	Darcy J. Stewart	Darcy J. Stewart	1990	655
214 5/8	27 1/8	26 1/8	16 4/8	5	5	15	8	Audrain Co., MO	John D. Burgher	Cabela's, Inc.	2002	655
214 5/8	25 5/8	25 5/8	16 5/8	5 7/8	5 1/8	13	14	Koochiching Co., MN	Unknown	Wilbur Tilander	1956	658
214 4/8	24 6/8	24 5/8	18	5 2/8	5 6/8	9	12	Turtle Lake, SK	Scott Macnab	Scott Macnab	1993	658
214 4/8	28	28 5/8	23	5 1/8	5 1/8	11	8	Pike Co., IL	David B. Crown	David B. Crown	1995	658
214 4/8	26 6/8	26 4/8	20 1/8	5 2/8	5 2/8	12	9	Swift Co., MN	Leonard N. Kanuit	Leonard N. Kanuit	1972	658
214 4/8	25 4/8	25 4/8	22 2/8	5	5	15	9	Clearwater Co., ID	Don L. Twito	Don L. Twito	1975	662
214 3/8	23 4/8	20 7/8	28 6/8	5 7/8	5 5/8	11	12	De Witt Co., IL	Kelly E. Riggs	Kelly E. Riggs	1996	662
214 3/8	26 7/8	26 6/8	26 6/8	5 6/8	5 6/8	11	15	Payne Co., OK	Chad Hane	Chad Hane	2003	662
214 3/8	25	25 1/8	15 3/8	5 2/8	5 3/8	14	10	Price Co., WI	Henry J. Copt	James A. Copt	1926	662
214 3/8	23 2/8	24	14 2/8	5 1/8	5 2/8	11	10	Missoula Co., MT	Lyle Pettit	Lyle Pettit	1962	662
214 3/8	24 1/8	26	17 3/8	5	5	14	11	Bayfield Co., WI	Clarence Lauer	Mrs. Clarence Lauer	1963	662
214 3/8	24 3/8	26 2/8	18 3/8	5 1/8	5 2/8	11	14	Roseau Co., MN	Warren Tveit	Warren Tveit	1976	662
214 3/8	30 2/8	29	22 7/8	5	5 1/8	10	11	Washington Co., ME	E. Colson Fales	E. Colson Fales	1999	670
214 2/8	27 3/8	26 4/8	23 3/8	5 5/8	5 5/8	8	12	Macoupin Co., IL	Clifford Bressler	Clifford Fales	2002	670
214 2/8	26 1/8	23 7/8	14 6/8	5 7/8	5 7/8	10	9	Wicomico Co., MD	Michael D. Lawhorn	Michael D. Lawhorn	2002	670
214 2/8	27 4/8	25 3/8	23	5 4/8	5 3/8	8	14	McDonough Co., IL	Neil A. Twidwell	Neil A. Twidwell	2002	
214 2/8	24 6/8	25 3/8	20 4/8	6 4/8	6 2/8	9	9	Crook Co., WY	Clinton Berry	Clinton Berry	1953	
214 2/8	22 5/8	22 5/8	16 5/8	4 5/8	4 6/8	8	8	Unknown	Unknown	Bass Pro Shops	PR 1991	
214 2/8	23 4/8	24 7/8	17 1/8	6 2/8	5 6/8	13	15	Monona Co., IA	Brian R. Hebb	Brian R. Hebb	1996	

WHITETAIL DEER - NON-TYPICAL ANTLERS

Odocoileus virginianus virginianus and certain related subspecies

Score	Length of Main Beam R	L	Inside Spread	Circumference at Smallest Place Between Burr and First Point R	L	Number of Points R	L	Locality	Hunter	Owner	Date Killed	Rank
214 2/8	23 3/8	22 3/8	15 6/8	4 4/8	4 2/8	12	16	Pickett Co., TN	Ronnie D. Perry, Jr.	Ronnie D. Perry, Jr.	2001	670
214 2/8	27 2/8	27 2/8	20	4 5/8	4 5/8	6	10	Little Fishing Lake, SK	Larry R. Kobsar	Larry R. Kobsar	2003	670
214 1/8	25 5/8	27	15 4/8	4 4/8	4 4/8	10	9	Michigan	Unknown	MI Whitetail Hall of Fame Mus.	1934	675
214 1/8	28	28 3/8	21 4/8	6 1/8	6 2/8	7	9	Van Buren Co., IA	Douglas W. Farrell	Douglas W. Farrell	2001	675
214	23 6/8	24 5/8	17 3/8	5 4/8	5 6/8	13	14	Atchison Co., MO	Warren E. Davis	Warren E. Davis	1983	677
214	28 7/8	28 6/8	23 1/8	4 5/8	4 4/8	10	9	Clay Co., MN	Dean Klemetson	Dean Klemetson	1984	677
214	26 7/8	26 3/8	21	5 4/8	5 2/8	14	9	Hamilton Co., IA	Picked Up	Bass Pro Shops	1987	677
214	24 3/8	20 5/8	19 7/8	6	7 3/8	9	12	Scott Co., IL	James K. Garrett	James K. Garrett	1994	677
214	24 1/8	25 3/8	19	6 3/8	6	10	13	Madison Co., IA	Merle Allen	Merle Allen	1998	677
214	25 2/8	26 1/8	19	5	5 2/8	9	6	Hancock Co., IL	Steven Guedesse	Steven Guedesse	1999	677
213 7/8	25	25 3/8	18	5 5/8	5 7/8	17	12	Sawyer Co., WI	Charles Ross	Charles Ross	1949	683
213 7/8	27 3/8	25 3/8	16 5/8	5 3/8	5 3/8	12	8	Bresaylor, SK	Barry Braun	Barry Braun	1966	683
213 7/8	28 5/8	28 5/8	19 3/8	5 1/8	4 7/8	9	10	Pottawatomie Co., KS	Picked Up	Tim Wanklyn	1974	683
213 7/8	29 1/8	29 2/8	19 3/8	5 3/8	5 5/8	8	9	Bonner Co., ID	Fred B. Post	Michael R. Damery	1978	683
213 7/8	22 5/8	25 2/8	18 2/8	5 2/8	5 2/8	10	10	Botetourt Co., VA	Craig A. Brogan	Craig A. Brogan	1989	683
213 7/8	23 3/8	28 4/8	20 7/8	6 3/8	6 6/8	15	11	Athabasca River, AB	Todd Armstrong	Todd Armstrong	1990	683
213 7/8	25 6/8	27 5/8	20 7/8	6 1/8	6 6/8	7	9	Pope Co., IL	Jason B. Potts	Jason B. Potts	1995	683
213 7/8	29 7/8	28 6/8	20	6 5/8	6 2/8	11	9	Greene Co., IL	Adam T. Hoene	Adam T. Hoene	1999	683
213 7/8	24 5/8	25 2/8	18 5/8	5 7/8	5 6/8	10	8	S. Saskatchewan River, SK	Keith A. Graves	Keith A. Graves	2000	683
213 6/8	26 5/8	26 3/8	26 5/8	5 3/8	5 4/8	10	10	Lycoming Co., PA	Al Prouty	Al Prouty	1949	692
213 6/8	23 7/8	24 4/8	18 6/8	4 6/8	5	10	11	Webb Co., TX	Unknown	John B. Collier, IV	1961	692
213 6/8	30 2/8	30 6/8	26 5/8	4 6/8	4 7/8	10	9	Fayette Co., IL	Sammy D. Diveley	Sammy D. Diveley	1990	692
213 6/8	26 1/8	26 7/8	19 6/8	5 4/8	5 6/8	14	13	Adams Co., IL	Michelle L. Hunter	Michelle L. Hunter	1991	692
213 6/8	28 4/8	27 2/8	20	5 6/8	5 4/8	12	14	Cass Co., IL	Vince C. Brewer	Vince C. Brewer	1993	692
213 5/8	24 2/8	24 2/8	17 1/8	5 6/8	5 5/8	12	6	Beltrami Co., MN	Jim Smith	Jim Smith	PR 1924	697
213 5/8	22 7/8	22 6/8	13 5/8	3 6/8	3 7/8	9	18	Webb Co., TX	Unknown	McLean Bowman	PR 1950	697
213 5/8	29 3/8	29 6/8	21 4/8	5 7/8	5 7/8	7	9	Guthrie Co., IA	Merle Shirbrown	Sherrill Shirbrown	1963	697
213 5/8	23	23 7/8	16 2/8	6	6 1/8	10	12	Buffalo Co., WI	Norman C. Ratz	Ed Klink	1968	697
213 5/8	27 1/8	24 6/8	23 6/8	5 4/8	7	9	9	Bonner Co., ID	Rodney Thurlow	Rodney Thurlow	1968	697
213 5/8	18 5/8	18 1/8	17 5/8	4 1/8	4	14	15	Washington Co., TX	Thomas N. Holle	Thomas N. Holle	1987	697
213 5/8	24 7/8	25 6/8	19 7/8	6 2/8	6 2/8	12	13	Ogle Co., IL	Jerome F. Bruns	Jerome F. Bruns	1994	697
213 5/8	27 4/8	26 2/8	20 1/8	5 4/8	5 6/8	11	11	Ogle Co., IL	Jeffrey R. Breen	Jeffrey R. Breen	1995	697
213 4/8	22 1/8	23 1/8	19 2/8	5	5	15	15	Texas	Unknown	Buckhorn Mus. & Saloon, Ltd.	PR 1950	705
213 4/8	26 3/8	23 2/8	18 6/8	6 1/8	6 4/8	12	11	Rochester, AB	Lamar A. Windberg	Lamar A. Windberg	1973	705
213 4/8	25 4/8	26	22	6 2/8	6 1/8	11	13	Pike Co., IL	Donald L. Roseberry	Michael R. Roseberry	1984	705
213 3/8	25 4/8	24 5/8	18 5/8	4 7/8	4 7/8	9	10	Midale, SK	Picked Up	Dick Rossum	1969	708

Score	Main Beam R	Main Beam L	Inside Spread	Circ. R	Circ. L	Pts R	Pts L	Locality	By	Owner	Date	Rank
213 3/8	27 6/8	31 1/8	18 6/8	5 5/8	6 6/8	11	13	Cumberland Co., VA	Jimmy E. Dedmond	Jimmy E. Dedmond	1995	708
213 3/8	27 1/8	27 2/8	18 5/8	5	5 1/8	7	8	Fillmore Co., MN	Steven A. Johnson	Steven A. Johnson	1988	708
213 2/8	26 2/8	26 4/8	20 2/8	5 2/8	5 3/8	13	13	Cold Lake, AB	John F. Koreman	John F. Koreman	1991	710
213 2/8	24 4/8	24	16 4/8	5 5/8	5 3/8	11	10	Washington Co., KS	Lance D. Black	Lance D. Black	2002 PR	710
213 2/8	28 6/8	28 7/8	19	4 7/8	4 7/8	10	7	Michigan	Unknown	Keith H. Lundberg	1941	710
213 1/8	28	30 1/8	23 5/8	4 6/8	4 6/8	7	10	Kimble Co., TX	Henry B. Allsup	Frederica Wyatt	1950	713
213 1/8	22	22	17	5 1/8	5 1/8	10	7	Havre, MT	Unknown	Frank English	1988	713
213 1/8	25	25	20 6/8	5 6/8	6 2/8	9	10	Milwaukee Co., WI	Picked Up	WI Dept. of Natl. Resc.	1997	713
213 1/8	24 4/8	24 7/8	19	7 4/8	8 1/8	10	9	Schuyler Co., IL	Todd A. Ritchey	Todd A. Ritchey	2000	713
213 1/8	25 4/8	24 7/8	21 2/8	6 3/8	6	8	10	Buffalo Co., WI	Picked Up	Byron H. Hoch	2001	713
213 1/8	27 3/8	28 4/8	20 7/8	5 3/8	5 3/8	10	12	Leech Lake, AB	Greg J. Gilbertson	Greg J. Gilbertson	1935	713
213 1/8	24 6/8	24 5/8	15 5/8	4 6/8	4 5/8	14	10	St. Louis Co., MN	Walfred Olson	Erling H. Olson	1960	713
213	27	27 7/8	17 5/8	4 7/8	4 5/8	10	15	Kinney Co., TX	Rankin F. O'Neill	John L. Stein	1966	720
213	24	24	20 6/8	5 4/8	5 6/8	5	9	Rush Lake, SK	Jim Runzer	Murray Bromley	1973	720
213	25 7/8	24 1/8	17 6/8	4 6/8	4 6/8	9	12	Boone Co., IA	Orlin Sorber	Ron Sorber	1976	720
212 7/8	24 4/8	22 5/8	21 1/8	5 2/8	5	7	13	Waukesha Co., WI	Max Mollgaard	Max Mollgaard	1985	723
212 7/8	30	23 3/8	20 6/8	5 3/8	5 2/8	10	10	Otter Tail Co., MN	Harold L. Collins	Harold L. Collins	2002	723
212 7/8	25 5/8	29 1/8	17 4/8	5 3/8	5 5/8	10	16	Carroll Co., MO	John L. Crose	John L. Crose	1952	723
212 7/8	25 6/8	25 2/8	18 1/8	5 2/8	5 2/8	14	9	Lewis & Clark Co., MT	Mr. LeFleur	L.S. Kuter	1988	723
212 6/8	26 7/8	26 7/8	19 5/8	4 4/8	4 4/8	14	6	McCurtain Co., OK	Robert H. Crenshaw	Robert H. Crenshaw	1989	727
212 6/8	24 3/8	24 3/8	28 3/8	5 1/8	5	11	14	Illinois	Picked Up	John Brewer	1995	727
212 6/8	24 6/8	26 2/8	24 6/8	4 7/8	5 1/8	8	8	Fremont Co., IA	Picked Up	Jeffrey S. Haning	1996	727
212 6/8	25 3/8	26 3/8	24 1/8	5 4/8	5 3/8	10	9	Long Lake, AB	Philip H. Preisel	Philip H. Preisel	1973	727
212 6/8	25 4/8	25 4/8	22 7/8	4 7/8	5 1/8	11	11	Shell Lake, SK	Robert Barlow	Robert Barlow	1975	727
212 6/8	25 3/8	25 4/8	23 6/8	4 2/8	4 4/8	10	9	Lincoln Co., MT	Charles F. Woods, Jr.	Charles F. Woods, Jr.	1975	727
212 5/8	29 6/8	28 2/8	23 7/8	5 7/8	5 7/8	14	16	Lake Co., MT	Dennis Courville	Dennis Courville	1980	733
212 5/8	21 3/8	20 1/8	16 5/8	4	4	12	12	Brooks Co., TX	Ken Smith	Lawson W. Walden	1984	733
212 5/8	23 7/8	23 5/8	18 3/8	6 1/8	6 3/8	14	13	Alberta	Picked Up	D.J. Hollinger & B. Howard	1991	733
212 5/8	23 7/8	25 2/8	17 6/8	5	5	11	9	Glentworth, SK	Garnet Fortnum	Garnet Fortnum	1993	733
212 5/8	24 6/8	24 5/8	29 1/8	5 4/8	5 4/8	10	9	Appanoose Co., IA	Picked Up	IA Dept. of Natl. Resc.	1993	733
212 5/8	23 5/8	26 4/8	21 3/8	5 4/8	5 4/8	11	13	Pelican River, AB	John Kozyra	John Kozyra	1995	733
212 5/8	29 1/8	25 1/8	19 7/8	4 7/8	5 1/8	13	10	Madison Co., IN	Michael A. Wallace	Michael A. Wallace	1998	733
212 5/8	25 1/8	24 2/8	21 6/8	4 2/8	4 4/8	6	10	Page Co., IA	Kevin L. Reints	Kevin L. Reints	1998	733
212 5/8	27 6/8	27 6/8	19 5/8	5 5/8	5 4/8	9	9	Greenwood Co., KS	Picked Up	B&C National Collection	2001	733
212 5/8	24 6/8	23 1/8	19 6/8	6 1/8	6 7/8	12	12	Marshall Co., IL	Picked Up	Carl H. Kimble	1997	733
212 5/8	27 4/8	27 4/8	20 3/8	5	4 4/8	12	11	Licking Co., OH	J. Chris Lepley	J. Chris Lepley	2000	733
212 5/8	23 4/8	23 4/8	19 6/8	4 7/8	4 6/8	10	8	Swan Lake, MB	William A. Riel	William A. Riel	1934	733
212 4/8	25	25 4/8	21	5 2/8	6 3/8	10	11	Randolph Co., IL	Mark E. Houba	Mark E. Houba	1959	745
212 4/8	24 6/8	23 6/8	18 3/8	5	5	11	10	Alger Co., MI	Karl Beck	Rick Johnson	1979	745
212 3/8	29	28 4/8	24 3/8	5 6/8	5 5/8	10	11	Hershey, NE	Ray Liles	Spanky Greenville	2000	747
212 3/8	23 4/8	23 2/8	18 4/8	4 7/8	5	10	14	Rosebud Co., MT	Picked Up	Art F. Hayes III	1949	747
212 3/8	25 2/8	22 7/8	22 2/8	6 2/8	6 1/8	17	13	Brown Co., IL	Martin L. Brobst	Martin L. Brobst	1977	747
212 3/8	25	25	19 4/8	5 2/8	5 2/8	11	13	Webb Co., TX	Claude W. King	Claude W. King	1983	747
212 2/8	26 6/8	26 1/8	23 6/8	4 6/8	5 3/8	9	7	Houston Co., MN	Alfred C. Pieper	Alfred C. Pieper	1984	751
212 2/8	23 1/8	20 3/8	20 3/8	5 1/8	5	11	10	Gregory Co., SD	Picked Up	J.D. Andrews	1993	751
212 2/8	28 2/8	28 6/8	24 4/8	5 3/8	5	9	8	Madison Co., IA	Larry D. Bain	Larry D. Bain	1994	751
212 2/8	27 4/8	27 2/8	20 2/8	7 4/8	6	10	9	Van Buren Co., IA	Chris E. Clingan	Chris E. Clingan	1993	751
212 2/8	29 7/8	27 7/8	21 4/8	5 2/8	5	13	8	Lane Co., KS	Picked Up	R. & A. Johnson	1994	751

Odocoileus virginianus virginianus and certain related subspecies

Score	Length of Main Beam		Inside Spread	Circumference at Smallest Place Between Burr and First Point		Number of Points		Locality	Hunter	Owner	Date Killed	Rank
	R	L		R	L	R	L					
212 2/8	25 3/8	27 1/8	22 5/8	5 5/8	5 5/8	9	9	Langenburg, SK	Hartley Biley	Hartley Biley	1996	751
212 2/8	26 1/8	26 3/8	25 7/8	5 7/8	5 7/8	9	10	Two Hills, AB	Wesley I. Nikiforuk	Wesley I. Nikiforuk	1999	751
212 1/8	24	24 3/8	20 1/8	5 1/8	5	16	13	Minnesota	Unknown	John R. Steffes, Sr.	PR 1960	759
212 1/8	26 5/8	25 6/8	20	4 7/8	5	9	8	Stevens Co., MN	Ronald J. Mohr	Ronald J. Mohr	1963	759
212 1/8	28 1/8	28 1/8	21 6/8	5 3/8	6	8	10	Woodbury Co., IA	Harold M. Leonard	Harold M. Leonard	1965	759
212 1/8	23 3/8	23	20 3/8	5	5 2/8	8	7	Minnedosa, MB	Albert Pfau	Albert Pfau	1966	759
212 1/8	27	27 2/8	19 6/8	5 2/8	5 3/8	14	16	St. Louis Co., MN	Robert J. LaPine	Robert J. LaPine	1968	759
212 1/8	28 1/8	28	18 1/8	5 4/8	5 4/8	9	8	Winona Co., MN	Donald J. Mehren	Donald J. Mehren	1985	759
212 1/8	26	25 7/8	21 4/8	6 1/8	5 7/8	12	11	Clinton Co., MI	Kenneth V. Montgomery	Kenneth V. Montgomery	1997	759
212 1/8	27	28 5/8	18 5/8	5 6/8	6 2/8	11	1	Koochiching Co., MN	Tom Sutch	Tom Sutch	2000	759
212	26 7/8	25	16 7/8	4 7/8	5 1/8	14	13	Becker Co., MN	Unknown	Unknown	1922	767
212	29	27 4/8	23 6/8	6 7/8	6 5/8	8	9	Iron Co., MI	Ben Komblevicz	Duaine K. Wenzel	1942	767
212	20 5/8	20 7/8	16 5/8	6 2/8	6 3/8	11	12	Wibaux Co., MT	Roy Berg	Daniel Burnosky	PR 1963	767
212	28 3/8	28 3/8	20 4/8	5 6/8	6	6	9	Greene Co., IA	Don Buswell	Don Buswell	1973	767
212	28 4/8	27 7/8	24 5/8	6	6 1/8	7	8	Big Stone Co., MN	Picked Up	Danny L. Cole	1993	767
212	29 4/8	26 3/8	19 1/8	5 1/8	5 1/8	10	10	Vermilion, AB	Derry Heathcote	Derry Heathcote	1995	767
212	23 5/8	23	14 5/8	6 3/8	5 6/8	11	14	Madison Co., MS	Richard W. Parker	Richard W. Parker	1999	767
212	26 4/8	25 7/8	22 6/8	6 2/8	6	11	11	Kankakee Co., IL	Thomas Miller	Thomas Miller	2002	767
211 7/8	25 6/8	26 3/8	24 1/8	6	5 7/8	14	11	Raymore, SK	Adolf Wulff	Adolf Wulff	1951	775
211 7/8	25	25 4/8	20 2/8	4 6/8	4 6/8	10	12	Rockingham Co., VA	Dorsey O. Breeden	Dorsey O. Breeden	1966	775
211 7/8	22	23 2/8	21 4/8	4 4/8	4 4/8	15	15	Crook Co., WY	Curtis U. Nelson	Curtis U. Nelson	1971	775
211 7/8	24 1/8	24 4/8	19 5/8	4 7/8	4 7/8	11	8	Van Buren Co., IA	Loras R. Ernzen	Loras R. Ernzen	1988	775
211 7/8	27 6/8	27	18 6/8	5 5/8	5 6/8	12	8	Waukesha Co., WI	Patrick F. Cherone III	Patrick F. Cherone III	1989	775
211 6/8	26 3/8	26	24 7/8	5 3/8	5 2/8	11	6	Marion Co., IA	Paul J. Pearson	Paul J. Pearson	1964	780
211 6/8	22 3/8	25 5/8	21	5	5	10	11	Cottonwood Co., MN	James A. Sykora	James A. Sykora	1981	780
211 6/8	26 5/8	27 7/8	18 4/8	5 1/8	4 6/8	12	12	Roseau Co., MN	Edward L. Quiring	Edward L. Quiring	1988	780
211 6/8	26 4/8	26 5/8	18 3/8	5	5	10	8	Green Co., WI	Kevin W. Bouers	Kevin W. Bouers	1999	780
211 6/8	27 1/8	26 4/8	23 5/8	6 4/8	6 2/8	10	9	Clark Co., KS	Cullen R. Spitzer	Cullen R. Spitzer	2001	780
211 5/8	23 1/8	22 5/8	13 4/8	7	5 4/8	18	11	Alda, NE	Donald Knuth	Donald Knuth	1964	785
211 5/8	28 2/8	28 4/8	23	5 7/8	6	11	11	Glaslyn, SK	Carl R. Frohaug	Carl R. Frohaug	1981	785
211 5/8	26 3/8	23 3/8	20 2/8	5 1/8	6 1/8	9	12	Adams Co., OH	William J. DeCamp	William J. DeCamp	1987	785
211 5/8	23 2/8	23 2/8	16	4 7/8	4 5/8	13	14	Rains Co., TX	Tommy Couch	Lawson W. Walden	PR 1988	785
211 5/8	27 3/8	26 6/8	26 2/8	5 2/8	5 1/8	12	7	Adair Co., IA	Bob Garside	Bob C. Garside	1998	785
211 4/8	26 4/8	27	20 3/8	6 1/8	6 2/8	13	11	Hillsborough Co., NH	Curtiss Whipple	Herman Whipple	1947	790
211 4/8	27 2/8	25 6/8	20 2/8	5 3/8	5 3/8	10	9	Minnesota	Picked Up	David Cater	1960	790
211 4/8	25 3/8	25	18 3/8	5 1/8	4 7/8	14	17	St. Louis Co., MN	John E. Peterson, Jr.	John E. Peterson, Jr.	1963	790

Score	Main Beam R	Main Beam L	Inside Spread	Circ.	Circ.	Circ.	R	L	Locality	By Whom Killed	Owner	Date Killed	Rank
211 4/8	24 6/8	22 4/8	18 6/8	5 5/8	5 5/8	5 4/8	10	11	Saskatchewan	Vernon Nokinsky	D.J. Hollinger & B. Howard	1976	790
211 4/8	23 2/8	23 3/8	13 6/8	6 2/8	6 2/8	5 6/8	12	10	Dodge Co., WI	Michael A. Koehler	Michael A. Koehler	1984	790
211 4/8	23 3/8	23	18 6/8	5	4 7/8	5	13	14	Worth Co., GA	Wade Patterson	Wade Patterson	1988	790
211 4/8	24 5/8	24 4/8	18 3/8	5 5/8	5 5/8	6 2/8	10	12	Washington Co., WI	LeRoy Neu	LeRoy Neu	1999	790
211 3/8	27 3/8	24 4/8	20 3/8	4 7/8	4 5/8	5 6/8	12	12	Dimmit Co., TX	L.C. Wright	H.R. Wright	1927	797
211 3/8	24 7/8	25 2/8	16 6/8	5 6/8	5 2/8	5 3/8	11	10	Borden, SK	Leonard Verishine	Leonard Verishine	1972	797
211 3/8	25 2/8	26 6/8	23 4/8	5 2/8	5 4/8	5 6/8	10	9	Polk Co., IA	Picked Up	IA Dept. of Natl. Resc.	1993	797
211 3/8	26 2/8	27 5/8	22 2/8	5 4/8	5 2/8	5 3/8	10	9	Scotland Co., MO	Gary L. Childress	Gary L. Childress	1998	797
211 3/8	27 3/8	27 6/8	20 5/8	5 7/8	5 4/8	6	10	9	Chase Co., KS	Picked Up	Tom Crump	1998	797
211 3/8	29 2/8	27 1/8	18 1/8	6 4/8	6	6 4/8	7	10	Fayette Co., IL	Greg A. Raterman	Greg A. Raterman	2000	797
211 3/8	27 3/8	26 2/8	19 7/8	4 6/8	5 1/8	5 1/8	9	8	Perry Co., IL	Richard W. Murphy	Richard W. Murphy	2002	797
211 3/8	27 6/8	27	14 7/8	6	6 2/8	6 2/8	9	8	Kitson Co., MN	Picked Up	Floyd R. Nelson	1942	797
211 3/8	24 5/8	24 4/8	19 3/8	6 2/8	6	6 4/8	10	9	Marshall Co., MN	Robert Sands	Robert Sands	1959	797
211 2/8	27 7/8	25 5/8	16 6/8	5 7/8	6	5 1/8	9	9	Hughenden, AB	Morris Sather	Morris Sather	1966	804
211 2/8	23 2/8	23 4/8	19 4/8	4 2/8	4 6/8	6 2/8	9	9	Stearns Co., MN	Ronald Steil	Ronald Steil	1983	804
211 2/8	26 1/8	29	19 5/8	5 4/8	5 4/8	5 6/8	9	7	Spokane Co., WA	Cary C. Janson	Cary C. Janson	1992	804
211 2/8	24 2/8	29 2/8	24	5 1/8	5 1/8	5 3/8	7	8	Athabasca, AB	Tim M. Shmigelsky	Tim M. Shmigelsky	1995	804
211 2/8	29 2/8	26 2/8	26 2/8	4 7/8	4 7/8	4 7/8	9	7	Pigeon Lake, AB	Jeff Strandquist	Jeff Strandquist	1997	804
211 2/8	25	25	18 4/8	5 7/8	5 7/8	5 4/8	7	7	Breathitt Co., KY	Michael D. Johnson	Michael D. Johnson	2000	804
211 2/8	27 5/8	24 2/8	18 6/8	5 6/8	5 6/8	5 6/8	8	9	Itasca Co., MN	Glen V. Jones	Mark W. Jones	PR 1948	804
211 1/8	24 5/8	24 5/8	23	4 7/8	4 7/8	4 6/8	9	10	Wells Co., ND	Robert Newman	Robert Newman	1961	812
211 1/8	26 5/8	26	22 4/8	5 1/8	5 1/8	5	9	9	Clarke Co., IA	Randy J. Showers	Randy J. Showers	1991	812
211 1/8	26 5/8	26 1/8	21 3/8	5 4/8	5 4/8	5 4/8	9	9	Rich Lake, AB	Sammy J. Schrimsher	Sammy J. Schrimsher	1994	812
211 1/8	24 2/8	24 6/8	24 6/8	5 1/8	5 1/8	5 1/8	15	11	Houston Co., MN	Daniel P. Gade	Daniel P. Gade	1998	812
211 1/8	28 5/8	28 5/8	20 4/8	6	6	6 2/8	11	11	Grady Co., OK	Bon D. Lentz	Bon D. Lentz	1999	812
211	23 6/8	23 4/8	16 3/8	6	6	6	12	13	Dimmit Co., TX	D.V. Day	McLean Bowman	1948	818
211	29 1/8	29 1/8	19 1/8	5 2/8	5 4/8	5 4/8	13	6	Allen Co., KY	Danny R. Towe	Ben & Seth Towe	1987	818
211	27 3/8	27 3/8	22 2/8	6 4/8	6 4/8	6 3/8	10	11	Rock Co., WI	Kevin C. Viken	Kevin C. Viken	1990	818
211	27 1/8	26	20 1/8	6 6/8	6 6/8	6 6/8	9	13	Monroe Co., IA	Picked Up	IA Dept. of Natl. Resc.	1991	818
211	29	29 6/8	20 1/8	6 6/8	5 6/8	5 6/8	7	8	Gallia Co., OH	Robert D. Wallis	Robert D. Wallis	1992	818
211	21 4/8	21 4/8	15 3/8	4	4	4	9	11	Mercer Co., MO	Treve A. Gray	Treve A. Gray	1995	818
211	27	26 4/8	19 3/8	4 4/8	4 4/8	4 4/8	10	10	Lenawee Co., MI	Paul T. Kintner	Paul T. Kintner	1996	818
210 7/8	27 4/8	25 7/8	20 6/8	5 6/8	5 6/8	5 3/8	9	10	Dearborn Co., IN	Chad M. Hornberger	Chad M. Hornberger	1997	827
210 7/8	27 3/8	24 1/8	25	5 1/8	5 1/8	5 1/8	11	8	Christian Co., IL	Jeffery Tumiati	Jeffery Tumiati	1997	827
210 7/8	24 2/8	22 6/8	18 1/8	5 2/8	5 2/8	5 2/8	11	9	Stevens Co., WA	Charles Tucker	Charles Tucker	1966	827
210 7/8	23 1/8	27	20 1/8	4 6/8	4 6/8	4 6/8	9	11	Patience Lake, SK	Rick Schindel	Rick Schindel	1990	827
210 7/8	25 3/8	26	19 5/8	6 2/8	6 2/8	6 2/8	12	9	Peoria Co., IL	Picked Up	Randy L. Isbell	1995	827
210 7/8	26 7/8	19 4/8	15 5/8	6 3/8	6 3/8	7 2/8	11	10	Lac La Biche, AB	Render L. Crowder, Sr.	Render L. Crowder, Sr.	1998	827
210 7/8	23 4/8	27 4/8	20 6/8	5 3/8	5 3/8	5 7/8	10	11	Winona Co., MN	Donald D. Zenk	Donald D. Zenk	1998	827
210 7/8	27 5/8	25 4/8	22	5 4/8	5 4/8	5	11	12	Wayne Co., IA	Jack J. Pershy	Jack J. Pershy	2001	827
210 6/8	25 4/8	22	20 4/8	5	5	5	11	8	Coahuila, MX	Picked Up	John L. Stein	1981	833
210 6/8	26 7/8	20 4/8	23 6/8	5 5/8	5 4/8	5 4/8	12	9	Todd Co., MN	Paul E. Berscheit	Paul E. Berscheit	1990	833
210 6/8	25	25	17 4/8	5 3/8	5 3/8	5 4/8	10	13	Grafton Co., NH	David C. Braley	David C. Braley	1991	833
210 6/8	26 2/8	26 2/8	23 6/8	5 3/8	5 3/8	5 4/8	14	11	N. Saskatchewan River, SK	Brent La Clare	Brent La Clare	1998	833
210 6/8	25 2/8	25 4/8	26 2/8	6	6	5 7/8	11	13	Unknown	Unknown	Charles J. Kramer	2001	833
210 5/8	26 2/8	26 2/8	23 3/8	5	5	5	8	9	Lincoln Co., MT	Glen Savage	Patrick W. Savage	1934	838
210 5/8	28 5/8	26	24 6/8	6	6 4/8	6 4/8	8	8	Walworth Co., SD	H.F. McClellan, Sr.	H.F. McClellan, Sr.	1952	838
210 5/8	24 7/8	25 7/8	18 6/8	5 6/8	5 5/8	5 5/8	14	10	Renville Co., ND	Glen Southam	Glen Southam	1978	838

WHITETAIL DEER - NON-TYPICAL ANTLERS
Odocoileus virginianus virginianus and certain related subspecies

Score	Length of Main Beam R	L	Inside Spread	Circumference at Smallest Place Between Burr and First Point R	L	Number of Points R	L	Locality	Hunter	Owner	Date Killed	Rank
210 5/8	25 7/8	27 1/8	20 3/8	6	5 4/8	7	7	Waukesha Co., WI	Gerald J. Roethle, Jr.	Gerald J. Roethle, Jr.	1991	838
210 5/8	26 6/8	27 2/8	22 1/8	6	6	9	8	Ogle Co., IL	Daniel M. Pierce	Daniel M. Pierce	1994	838
210 5/8	23 7/8	23 7/8	19 3/8	5 4/8	5 2/8	13	14	Wapello Co., IA	Picked Up	IA Dept. of Natl. Resc.	1996	838
210 5/8	21 7/8	21 1/8	18 2/8	5 6/8	6	9	11	Dawson Creek, BC	Kenn F. Chysyk	Nick Trenke	1999	838
210 5/8	25 5/8	25 5/8	21 6/8	6 2/8	6 4/8	8	12	Fork River, MB	Jimmy D. Blaine	Jimmy D. Blaine	2000	838
210 5/8	25 2/8	22 5/8	20 4/8	5 3/8	5 1/8	10	10	Qu'Appelle Valley, SK	Bryce Burns	Bryce Burns	2000	838
210 4/8	26 7/8	25 6/8	20	5 1/8	5 1/8	12	11	Dane Co., WI	LaVerne W. Marten	LaVerne W. Marten	1970	847
210 4/8	26 1/8	26	21 7/8	5 1/8	5 2/8	14	11	Stearns Co., MN	Kim C. Kirckof	Kim C. Kirckof	1992	847
210 4/8	27 2/8	27 5/8	23 5/8	4 3/8	4 3/8	10	8	Pope Co., MN	Scott G. Finn	Scott G. Finn	1993	847
210 4/8	25 6/8	26 3/8	19 6/8	6 1/8	6 1/8	10	12	Wabaunsee Co., KS	Ron E. Pletcher	Ron E. Pletcher	1994	847
210 4/8	31	29 2/8	21	6	5 5/8	10	11	Allegan Co., MI	Bruce A. Maurer	Bruce A. Maurer	1997	847
210 4/8	25	25 2/8	20 4/8	5 5/8	5	11	9	Mason Co., IL	Jesse Stinauer	Jesse Stinauer	2002	847
210 3/8	24 3/8	24 1/8	16	4 7/8	5	9	9	Adams Co., IL	Unknown	Chuck House	1897	853
210 3/8	28 4/8	27 4/8	21 4/8	5	5 1/8	9	10	Marinette Co., WI	George E. Bierstaker	Mrs. G.E. Bierstaker	1947	853
210 3/8	25 1/8	25 1/8	20 6/8	5 2/8	5	10	9	White Co., AR	Chester Weathers, Sr.	Chester Weathers, Jr.	1973	853
210 3/8	24 3/8	25	19 2/8	5	5	13	12	Lyon Co., KY	Roy D. Lee	Roy D. Lee	1975	853
210 3/8	30 4/8	29 2/8	24 4/8	5 4/8	5 2/8	8	9	Calhoun Co., IL	Timothy A. Moore	Timothy A. Moore	1999	853
210 3/8	24	19 5/8	16 2/8	6	8 4/8	7	10	Morgan Co., IL	Frankie Wildhagen	Frankie Wildhagen	1999	853
210 3/8	27 7/8	26 7/8	19 3/8	6 4/8	6 4/8	9	8	Linn Co., KS	Randall W. Hinde	Randall W. Hinde	2001	860
210 2/8	26 4/8	25 2/8	21 4/8	5 3/8	5 3/8	8	9	Columbiana Co., OH	Harold L. Hawkins	Harold L. Hawkins	1981	860
210 2/8	25 3/8	26	26 6/8	8 2/8	5 4/8	13	7	Fremont Co., IA	Mike Moody	Mike Moody	1990	860
210 2/8	29	27	19 1/8	5 1/8	5	10	11	Grayson Co., KY	Adam Pence	Adam Pence	1994	863
210 1/8	26 7/8	26 6/8	20	5 1/8	4 6/8	10	7	Crawford Co., GA	Walter Keel	Grace Stinson	1971	863
210 1/8	23 4/8	24	18 5/8	4 6/8	5	9	7	Harris, SK	Kenneth M. Lepp	Kenneth M. Lepp	1985	863
210 1/8	24 1/8	24 7/8	21 5/8	5 4/8	5	14	12	Chain Lakes, AB	Jim Chapman	Jim Chapman	1989	863
210 1/8	23 6/8	24 1/8	20 2/8	5 4/8	5 1/8	9	10	Macomb Co., MI	Bob H. Dismuke	Bob H. Dismuke	1992	863
210 1/8	24	26	20 2/8	6 1/8	5 4/8	8	9	Leoville, SK	Ray J. Guarisco	Ray J. Guarisco	1994	863
210 1/8	26 4/8	23 3/8	20 6/8	5 3/8	5 4/8	15	16	Madison Co., IA	Andy A. Ross	Andy A. Ross	1994	863
210 1/8	24 6/8	25 1/8	19	5 5/8	6 1/8	8	12	Lac La Biche, AB	Otis W. Cowles	Otis W. Cowles	1998	863
210 1/8	22 6/8	23	19 2/8	5 1/8	5 1/8	9	7	St. Paul, AB	Richard C. Nelson	Richard C. Nelson	1999	863
210	26 5/8	27 2/8	17 5/8	5 6/8	5 6/8	13	9	Vilas Co., WI	Elmer T. Reise	John A. Kellett	1940	871
210	26	26 1/8	18	5 5/8	5 4/8	10	9	Glenewen, SK	H. Frew	H. Frew	1955	871
210	27 5/8	25	24 2/8	5 2/8	5 2/8	9	7	Lee Co., IA	Picked Up	Mike Conger	1978	871
210	23 4/8	23 6/8	20 3/8	5 7/8	6 2/8	9	8	Gregory Co., SD	Richard C. Berte	Richard C. Berte	1982	871
210	28 3/8	26	26 5/8	4 7/8	4 7/8	7	13	Calvert Co., MD	Robert E. Barnett	Robert E. Barnett	1984	871
210	22	24	13 5/8	4 4/8	5 3/8	10	8	Jefferson Co., IA	Jared L. Rebling	Jared L. Rebling	1998	871

Score	R. Main Beam	L. Main Beam	Inside Spread	R. Circ.	L. Circ.	R. Pts.	L. Pts.	Locality	Hunter	Owner	Date
210	29 4/8	27 5/8	31	5 7/8	5 6/8	12	15	Kingman Co., KS	Picked Up	Odie Sudbeck	1998
210	23 1/8	23 5/8	17 3/8	5 4/8	5 4/8	10	12	Wright Co., MN	Picked Up	John R. Thole	1998
209 7/8	25 3/8	24 1/8	22 4/8	4 5/8	4 5/8	9	9	Maryfield, SK	W.W. Nichol	W.W. Nichol	1967
209 7/8	25 6/8	25 4/8	18 1/8	4 5/8	4 6/8	15	10	Pine Co., MN	Scott A. Miller	Scott A. Miller	1980
209 7/8	20 6/8	28 2/8	19 6/8	4 7/8	5 3/8	11	13	Hawkins Co., TN	Johnny W. Byington	Johnny W. Byington	1982
209 7/8	29	27	18 4/8	5 4/8	5 4/8	8	10	Todd Co., KY	Kenny V. Wilson	Kenny V. Wilson	1990
209 7/8	25 7/8	24 2/8	21 1/8	4 6/8	4 4/8	8	12	Adams Co., IA	Gregory L. Andrews	Gregory L. Andrews	1998
209 7/8	24 6/8	27 2/8	18 2/8	4 4/8	5 1/8	13	11	Waupaca Co., WI	Ryan A. Thiel	Ryan A. Thiel	1999
209 6/8	27	24 2/8	17 1/8	5 1/8	5 3/8	10	11	Koochiching Co., MN	Harry Van Keuren	Louis E. Muench	1929
209 6/8	24 6/8	24 1/8	20 7/8	5 6/8	4 6/8	11	10	Franklin Co., MS	Ronnie Strickland	Ronnie Strickland	1981
209 6/8	23 2/8	25 2/8	22 6/8	4 6/8	5 6/8	11	8	Edwards Co., KS	Tim C. Schaller	Tim C. Schaller	1984
209 6/8	25 5/8	25	16	5 6/8	5 6/8	9	14	Oak Lake, MB	Michael W. Leochko	Michael W. Leochko	1985
209 6/8	25 6/8	26 7/8	19 5/8	4 5/8	4 5/8	18	12	Pulaski Co., KY	Alan Sidwell	Alan Sidwell	1988
209 6/8	26 4/8	27 5/8	18 1/8	6	6	10	9	Union Co., IN	Billy G. Finch	Billy G. Finch	1989
209 6/8	26 5/8	19 7/8	20 7/8	5 5/8	5 3/8	8	9	Sangamon Co., IL	Mark A. Rademaker	Mark A. Rademaker	1994
209 6/8	23 4/8	25 3/8	15 5/8	5 6/8	5 6/8	14	13	Morton, MB	Charles C. Dixon	Charles C. Dixon	1996
209 6/8	25 6/8	25 3/8	17 7/8	5 1/8	5 1/8	7	10	Sullivan Co., MO	Curt E. Richardson	Curt E. Richardson	1997
209 6/8	25 1/8	25 3/8	16 5/8	5 3/8	5 2/8	12	13	Jefferson Co., AR	Kenneth Colson	Kenneth Colson	1968
209 5/8	24 4/8	26 4/8	22 4/8	5	4 6/8	11	13	Butler Co., KY	Dean A. Hannold	Dean A. Hannold	1979
209 5/8	26 4/8	25 3/8	16 7/8	5 1/8	5 1/8	12	11	McCreary Co., KY	Picked Up	Johnny Farmer	1983
209 5/8	25 4/8	25 3/8	21 5/8	5 3/8	5 3/8	8	9	Franklin Co., VA	Timothy J. Wright	Timothy J. Wright	1989
209 5/8	25 2/8	27 4/8	21 1/8	5	5	11	9	Harrison Co., IA	James A. Spelman	James A. Spelman	1991
209 5/8	23 3/8	23 3/8	18 2/8	4 2/8	4 1/8	14	9	Logan Co., IL	Clint M. Awe	Clint M. Awe	1997
209 5/8	27 3/8	28	21 3/8	5	5 1/8	10	10	Van Buren Co., IA	Allen C. Funk	Allen C. Funk	2000
209 5/8	24 4/8	25 3/8	21	5 1/8	5 1/8	10	8	Livingston Co., MI	Michel A. LaFountain	Michel A. LaFountain	2000
209 5/8	24 3/8	22 5/8	16 4/8	5 7/8	5 7/8	14	11	Jasper Co., IL	Chris Rush	Chris Rush	2002
209 4/8	23 3/8	23 1/8	22 5/8	4 5/8	4 5/8	14	10	Webb Co., TX	A. Holden	McLean Bowman	1940
209 4/8	25	25	19 2/8	4 1/8	4 2/8	9	13	Sterling Co., TX	Sam E. Kapavik	Sam E. Kapavik	1973
209 4/8	28 3/8	27 5/8	22 5/8	5	5	8	11	White Co., IL	David J. South	David J. South	1991
209 4/8	26 3/8	25 4/8	17 7/8	5	5	12	10	Manitou Lake, SK	Dustin Elchyson	Dustin Elchyson	2001
209 3/8	26 1/8	26 1/8	21	5 1/8	5 1/8	9	13	La Salle Co., TX	Unknown	E.T Reilly	1931
209 3/8	24 2/8	24 2/8	17 1/8	4 4/8	4 4/8	10	11	Crook Co., WY	Roy H. Lubbert	Murphy's Tavern	1967
209 3/8	23 5/8	22	16 6/8	4 4/8	4 3/8	10	9	Grant Co., WI	Tim Yanna	Tim Yanna	1982
209 3/8	28 3/8	26	24 4/8	5 4/8	5	11	10	Jefferson Co., IN	Tim L. Brawner	Tim L. Brawner	1989
209 3/8	27 6/8	26 7/8	22 7/8	5 1/8	5 1/8	9	8	Keokuk Co., IA	Michael D. Hoover	Michael D. Hoover	1991
209 3/8	26 4/8	26 7/8	22 7/8	5 6/8	5 6/8	7	8	Pittsburg Co., OK	Unknown	William R. Starry	PR 1994
209 3/8	24 6/8	26 6/8	20 1/8	5	5	8	15	Racine Co., WI	Lon M. Swatek	Lon M. Swatek	1994
209 3/8	24 5/8	24 3/8	19 6/8	6 5/8	6 4/8	11	9	Macon Co., MO	Bryan Dickbernd	Bryan Dickbernd	2002
209 2/8	23 7/8	23 1/8	16 4/8	6 2/8	6 2/8	9	10	Clarke Co., IA	James C. Reed	James C. Reed	1988
209 2/8	25 1/8	22	19 1/8	5	5	6	8	Person Co., NC	Stuart E. Gentry	Stuart E. Gentry	1996
209 2/8	25 6/8	22 2/8	20 4/8	5 3/8	5 2/8	13	8	De Witt Co., IL	Ronald L. Willmore	Ronald L. Willmore	1997
209 2/8	26 3/8	27 1/8	18 7/8	5 5/8	5 7/8	8	12	Crawford Co., KS	Jason C. Ball	Jason C. Ball	2000
209 1/8	26	26 3/8	19 1/8	5 4/8	5 4/8	9	8	Keweenaw Co., MI	Nathan E. Ruonavaara	Nathan E. Ruonavaara	1946
209 1/8	26	26 2/8	19 3/8	4 7/8	5	8	13	Clinton Co., IA	Gregory Stewart	Gregory Stewart	1963
209 1/8	23 4/8	27 7/8	28 5/8	5 5/8	4 3/8	6	10	N. Saskatchewan River, SK	Gerald Hamel	Gerald Hamel	1986
209 1/8	26	24 4/8	16 6/8	4 2/8	4 3/8	12	14	Kenedy Co., TX	Dick Roberts	Dick Roberts	1988
209 1/8	22 4/8	25 7/8	22 4/8	5	5	9	8	Monroe Co., IA	Kelly J. Willis	Kelly J. Willis	1988
209 1/8	27 6/8	30 5/8	19 6/8	6 3/8	6 3/8	8	10	Monona Co., IA	Vincent P. Jauron	Vincent P. Jauron	1990

Odocoileus virginianus virginianus and certain related subspecies

Score	Length of Main Beam R	Length of Main Beam L	Inside Spread	Circumference at Smallest Place Between Burr and First Point R	Circumference at Smallest Place Between Burr and First Point L	Number of Points R	Number of Points L	Locality	Hunter	Owner	Date Killed	Rank
209 1/8	23 4/8	22 7/8	17 3/8	5 6/8	5 4/8	10	12	Riley Co., KS	Jerry P. McIntyre	Jerry P. McIntyre	1994	919
209 1/8	25 4/8	26	26	6	5 7/8	11	9	Prowers Co., CO	Paul D. Mirley	Paul D. Mirley	1997	919
209 1/8	24 1/8	24	17 3/8	5 4/8	6	9	17	Waupaca Co., WI	Vince Burns II	Vince Burns II	1999	919
209 1/8	28	24 4/8	17 1/8	5 7/8	6	10	11	Butler Co., OH	Ronald N. Fields	Ronald N. Fields	2001	919
209	26 7/8	28 2/8	23 6/8	5 4/8	5 4/8	8	9	Lee Co., IA	Glenn L. Carter II	Glenn L. Carter II	1984	929
209	26 4/8	25 6/8	20 5/8	4 7/8	5	11	10	Hughes Co., OK	Lane Grimes	Lane Grimes	1987	929
209	24 6/8	24 4/8	17	6 1/8	6	12	6	Saskatchewan	Unknown	Aly M. Bruner	PR 1996	929
209	28 7/8	29 5/8	17 4/8	6 1/8	6 3/8	10	14	Crawford Co., KS	Steven R. Burt	Steven R. Burt	1999	929
209	23 3/8	22 2/8	22 2/8	5 6/8	6 2/8	9	14	Highland Co., OH	Eddie Hunter, Sr.	Eddie Hunter, Sr.	2000	929
208 7/8	25 1/8	26	21 6/8	5	4 7/8	11	16	Atchison Co., MO	Kenneth W. Lee	Kenneth W. Lee	1964	934
208 7/8	24 5/8	23 3/8	18 4/8	4 2/8	4 2/8	14	10	Bradley Co., AR	Carthel Forte	Carthel Forte	1971	934
208 7/8	29 4/8	27 5/8	18 4/8	4 6/8	4 6/8	10	8	Washington Co., ME	Robert E. Cooke	Robert E. Cooke	1972	934
208 7/8	26 7/8	26 7/8	26 6/8	5 3/8	5 3/8	11	13	Charles Co., MD	Robert A. Boarman	Robert A. Boarman	1984	934
208 7/8	27 1/8	27	23 5/8	6 3/8	6	8	7	Rideau River, ON	Harry Rathwell	Harry Rathwell	1988	934
208 7/8	24 1/8	25 3/8	19 2/8	5	4 7/8	7	10	Anoka Co., MN	Picked Up	Becky Wozney	1998	934
208 6/8	27 1/8	26 6/8	20 4/8	5 3/8	5 1/8	13	12	Crook Co., WY	Joe Engelhaupt	Joe Engelhaupt	1956	940
208 6/8	24	24 2/8	19 2/8	5	5 1/8	7	6	McCreary Co., KY	Richard G. Lohre	Richard G. Lohre	1968	940
208 6/8	24 4/8	25	21 5/8	4 2/8	4 3/8	9	8	Idaho	Unknown	Richard J. Dorchuck	PR 1975	940
208 6/8	26 3/8	27 4/8	21 7/8	5 3/8	5 4/8	12	7	Unknown	Unknown	David A. Boys	PR 1982	940
208 6/8	22 3/8	25 3/8	19 1/8	6 7/8	5 3/8	10	14	Bartholomew Co., IN	Randy E. Cash	Randy E. Cash	1997	940
208 6/8	25 2/8	22 2/8	15 7/8	4 1/8	4 1/8	10	8	Haskell Co., OK	Michael B. Vail	Michael B. Vail	1999	940
208 5/8	27 4/8	28	22	6	5 7/8	11	10	Taylor Co., WI	Unknown	Mac's Taxidermy	PR 1945	946
208 5/8	19 6/8	23 4/8	18 4/8	5	5	10	12	Beaufort Co., SC	John M. Wood	John M. Wood	1971	946
208 5/8	26 2/8	24 3/8	20 4/8	6 3/8	7 1/8	7	7	Woodbury Co., IA	Ronald J. Eickholt	Ronald J. Eickholt	1977	946
208 5/8	27	26 1/8	24 2/8	6 5/8	6 2/8	16	14	Red River, MB	Unknown	Jeffrey Gustafson	1977	946
208 5/8	25 1/8	25	17 6/8	4 7/8	5	8	8	Unknown	Unknown	Darryl Powell	PR 1980	946
208 5/8	27	26 1/8	20 4/8	5 1/8	5 1/8	9	12	Dunn Co., WI	Milburn Fleege	Brant J. Mueller	1986	946
208 5/8	27 4/8	26 5/8	22 4/8	4 6/8	5	16	13	St. Francis Co., AR	George W. Hobson	George W. Hobson	1987	946
208 5/8	22 2/8	22 2/8	13 4/8	4 5/8	4 5/8	8	8	Pontotoc Co., OK	S. Chris Snell	S. Chris Snell	1997	946
208 4/8	26 6/8	27 3/8	21 6/8	6	6 1/8	7	9	Itasca Co., MN	Unknown	William L. Achman	1945	954
208 4/8	30 5/8	29 2/8	17 3/8	5 1/8	5 1/8	11	10	Day Co., SD	Unknown	J.D. Andrews	PR 1950	954
208 4/8	28	27 1/8	23 5/8	6 2/8	6 1/8	12	13	Dixon Co., NE	Dan Greeny	Dan Greeny	1969	954
208 4/8	22	21 4/8	17 4/8	5	5	7	8	Webb Co., TX	Travis D. Kelly	Travis D. Kelly	1978	954
208 4/8	30 5/8	30 2/8	20 6/8	5 5/8	5 4/8	10	13	Ford Co., KS	Picked Up	Bass Pro Shops	1985	954
208 4/8	25 1/8	25 3/8	17 5/8	5 4/8	5 5/8	10	9	Fulton Co., IL	Jeffrey C. Warmath	Jeffrey C. Warmath	1995	954
208 4/8	28 3/8	29 2/8	22 5/8	5 4/8	5 4/8	10	9	Grenfell, SK	Clayton Roberts	Clayton Roberts	1998	954

Score	Main Beam R	Main Beam L	Inside Spread	Circ. R	Circ. L	Pts R	Pts L	Locality	Hunter	Owner	Rank	Date
208 4/8	24 4/8	26 3/8	20 2/8	7 6/8	7 4/8	12	12	Lee Co., IA	Dennis L. Case	Dennis L. Case	954	1999
208 4/8	23 4/8	23 1/8	19 7/8	4 2/8	4 2/8	17	10	Pope Co., AR	Danny L. Reed	Danny L. Reed	954	1999
208 4/8	24 3/8	24 7/8	14 7/8	5 2/8	4 5/8	12	10	Pike Co., IL	Brian M. Rennecker	Brian M. Rennecker	954	1999
208 3/8	25 4/8	25 6/8	19 1/8	5 5/8	5 6/8	13	10	Mille Lacs Co., MN	Picked Up	Louis J. Los	954	PR 2002
208 3/8	25 2/8	28 2/8	18 7/8	5 1/8	5 1/8	13	10	St. Louis Co., MN	Unknown	George W. Flaim	965	PR 1940
208 3/8	26 2/8	28 6/8	19 3/8	4 7/8	4 4/8	10	6	St. Louis Co., MN	Kenneth Anderson	Thomas S. Anderson	965	1959
208 3/8	27 5/8	28 1/8	21 7/8	5	4 7/8	11	7	Okanogan Co., WA	James L. Darley	James L. Darley	965	1964
208 3/8	21 6/8	23 7/8	24 1/8	5	4 7/8	8	8	Decatur Co., GA	Charles Danielson	J.D. Andrews	965	1969
208 3/8	24 4/8	24 4/8	17 7/8	4 3/8	4 5/8	13	10	Prairie Co., MT	Richard C. Hansen	Richard C. Hansen	965	1995
208 2/8	27	26 2/8	27	5 4/8	5 4/8	10	7	Frio Co., TX	Unknown	Roy Hindes	970	PR 1950
208 2/8	27	26 1/8	20 4/8	4 7/8	4 7/8	11	11	St. Louis Co., MN	Walter H. Enzenauer	Walter H. Enzenauer	970	1961
208 2/8	26 5/8	26	22 2/8	5 3/8	5 4/8	7	10	St. Louis Co., MN	Ed Mikulich	Terry Mikulich	970	1964
208 2/8	24 3/8	19 3/8	19 3/8	7 3/8	5 3/8	10	10	Chauvin, AB	Picked Up	Shane Hansen	970	1981
208 2/8	24 3/8	23 4/8	19	5	5	11	7	Monona Co., IA	Rob L. Cadwallader	Rob L. Cadwallader	970	1984
208 2/8	28 6/8	24 6/8	21 4/8	5 4/8	5 4/8	13	9	Price Co., WI	Robin J. Manning	Robin J. Manning	970	1993
208 2/8	25	25 5/8	17	4 4/8	4 5/8	12	11	Van Buren Co., TN	A. Duane Hodges	A. Duane Hodges	970	1994
208 2/8	25 7/8	22 2/8	17 3/8	6	6 1/8	13	10	Washington Co., OH	Robert R. Zimmerman	Robert R. Zimmerman	970	1995
208 2/8	28 4/8	29 1/8	22 6/8	5 2/8	5 2/8	12	10	Saline Co., IL	Mark A. Sheldon	Mark A. Sheldon	970	1999
208 2/8	27 1/8	23 4/8	23	6	5 6/8	13	7	Rockingham Co., NH	Glenn R. Townsend	Glenn R. Townsend	970	2000
208 2/8	25 6/8	24	21 1/8	4 6/8	4 6/8	11	8	Guthrie Co., IA	Jay Miller	Jay Miller	970	2002
208 1/8	30	31 2/8	23 6/8	5 4/8	5 3/8	8	8	Hancock Co., ME	Hollis Staples	Doug Scott	981	1922
208 1/8	25 4/8	24 5/8	19 6/8	4 6/8	4 6/8	8	8	Griswold, MB	J.V. Parker	J.V. Parker	981	1946
208 1/8	26 3/8	24 2/8	18 2/8	4 4/8	4 6/8	12	12	Mexico	Unknown	William M. Day	981	1959
208 1/8	28 1/8	25 2/8	20 2/8	4 7/8	4 7/8	13	8	Antelope Co., NE	Leon McCoy	Leon McCoy	981	1965
208 1/8	22	24 1/8	24 2/8	5	6 2/8	8	8	Atkinson Hwy., NE	Russell Angus	Russell Angus	981	1966
208 1/8	28 1/8	30 1/8	24 3/8	4 7/8	4 7/8	9	9	Beaverhill Lake, AB	Dean Hrehirchuk	Dean Hrehirchuk	981	1989
208 1/8	25 2/8	26 1/8	19 6/8	5 4/8	5 3/8	11	9	Brown Co., IL	Mark V. Piazza	Mark V. Piazza	981	1989
208 1/8	26 6/8	26 5/8	18 3/8	4 6/8	4 6/8	11	8	Peterson, SK	Albert Huber	Albert Huber	981	1993
208	25 1/8	25 5/8	19 4/8	5 3/8	4 6/8	10	11	Monroe Co., AR	Picked Up	Donald Barkley	981	2000
208	23 5/8	24 2/8	21	6 2/8	5 3/8	10	10	Rainy River, ON	Leroy Berglund	Marc M. Jackson	990	PR 1930
208	27	26	21 5/8	4 7/8	4 5/8	9	10	Chesaw, WA	Charles Eder	Charles Eder	990	1967
208	25 4/8	25	19 6/8	4 5/8	4 5/8	9	10	Buena Vista Co., IA	Robert L. Vierow	Robert L. Vierow	990	1982
208	26 3/8	26	15	4 1/8	4 1/8	14	10	Lucas Co., IA	Mitch W. Hosler	Mitch W. Hosler	990	1991
208	28 1/8	30	22	5 2/8	5 2/8	8	8	Olmsted Co., MN	Glen E. Leighton	Glen E. Leighton	990	1991
208	22	22 2/8	22 2/8	6 1/8	6 1/8	11	8	Bath Co., KY	William Shields	William Shields	990	1993
208	21 2/8	24 5/8	17 4/8	4 7/8	4 7/8	15	6	Wayne Co., AR	George M. Tonelli	George M. Tonelli	990	1999
208	24 4/8	26 2/8	19 1/8	4 6/8	4 6/8	8	10	Sangamon Co., IL	Daniel R. Lusardi	Daniel R. Lusardi	990	2001
207 7/8	29	27 1/8	22 2/8	5 3/8	5 3/8	11	13	Pinehurst Lake, AB	Steve Onciul	Steve Onciul	990	—
207 7/8	27 5/8	27 5/8	21 3/8	5 4/8	5 5/8	9	11	McMullen Co., TX	Robert L. Hodges	William D. Connally	999	1924
207 7/8	24 6/8	25 4/8	15 5/8	4 2/8	4 2/8	7	9	Suffolk Co., NY	George Hackal	Gary C. Boyer	999	1950
207 7/8	23 7/8	23 5/8	23 3/8	4 7/8	4 7/8	13	19	Juniata Co., PA	C. Ralph Landis	Ruth V. Landis	999	1951
207 7/8	29 5/8	31 1/8	24 4/8	5 5/8	5 5/8	11	19	Union Co., AR	Unknown	Travis Worthington	999	PR 1952
207 7/8	28 3/8	28 4/8	18 4/8	5 1/8	5 3/8	14	8	Fond du Lac Co., WI	Henry Theisen	Henry Theisen	999	1956
207 7/8	24 4/8	23 6/8	20 3/8	5 3/8	5 1/8	12	12	Perkins Co., SD	W.E. Brown	Dick Rossum	999	1957
207 7/8	24 4/8	19	19	5 1/8	5 7/8	11	14	Monona Co., IA	Robert V. Dean	Vernon R. Dean	999	1968
207 7/8	23 7/8	22 2/8	22 2/8	5 6/8	5 1/8	11	11	Fort Sill, OK	R.B. Robertson	Jessie L. Salisbury	999	1968
207 7/8	25 2/8	24 5/8	17 6/8	5	6 1/8	10	11	Monitor, AB	Raymond Worobo	Raymond Worobo	999	1979
207 7/8	26 5/8	26	24 7/8	5 2/8	5 3/8	7	12	Assiniboine River, MB	Terry L. Simcox	Terry L. Simcox	999	1987

Odocoileus virginianus virginianus and certain related subspecies

Score	Length of Main Beam		Inside Spread	Circumference at Smallest Place Between Burr and First Point		Number of Points		Locality	Hunter	Owner	Date Killed	Rank
	R	L		R	L	R	L					
207 7/8	30 3/8	31 3/8	23 7/8	6 2/8	6 1/8	9	9	Ribstone Creek, AB	Trevor C. Thorpe	Trevor C. Thorpe	1992	999
207 7/8	23 6/8	24 4/8	15 6/8	5	5	9	9	Breckinridge Co., KY	Joseph T. Smith	Joseph T. Smith	1993	999
207 7/8	25 3/8	25 7/8	25 2/8	7	6 7/8	8	7	Lee Co., IA	Timothy A. Miller	Timothy A. Miller	1994	999
207 7/8	29 5/8	29 1/8	21 1/8	5 3/8	5 1/8	7	7	Warren Co., IA	Michael J. King	Michael J. King	1995	999
207 6/8	22 2/8	20 1/8	15 4/8	5	5	14	16	Kleberg Co., TX	Unknown	King Ranch	1940	1013
207 6/8	27	27 5/8	25 4/8	6 6/8	6 4/8	9	9	Aroostook Co., ME	Alfred Wardwell	Alfred Wardwell	1945	1013
207 6/8	29	28 4/8	28 2/8	6 1/8	6	8	7	Henry Co., IL	Richard Vyneman	Richard Vyneman	1992	1013
207 6/8	22 4/8	24 6/8	24 3/8	5	5 2/8	9	9	MacNutt, SK	Delwin Andres	Delwin Andres	1993	1013
207 6/8	24 4/8	25 1/8	22 6/8	6 6/8	6 6/8	10	9	Edgeley, SK	Ian G. Gilchrist	Ian G. Gilchrist	1995	1013
207 6/8	18	18 1/8	16 4/8	5	5	14	13	Cross Co., AR	Picked Up	Aaron Mauldin	PR 1996	1013
207 5/8	29 3/8	28 6/8	19 3/8	5 1/8	4 7/8	10	11	Ashland Co., WI	Carl W. Moebius, Sr.	Eric Moebius	1934	1019
207 5/8	25 4/8	25 4/8	15 4/8	4 7/8	5	11	7	Argenteuil Co., QC	R. Desjardins & A. Dobie	R. Desjardins & R. Morrison	1959	1019
207 5/8	27 1/8	26 5/8	22 2/8	6 6/8	7	11	9	Lincoln Co., MN	Joe Ness	Joe Ness	1961	1019
207 5/8	24 2/8	23 6/8	17 5/8	5 6/8	5 4/8	7	8	Moosomin, SK	Leslie Hanson	Sam Peterson	1961	1019
207 5/8	25	20 5/8	19 6/8	6	6	10	17	Seward Co., NE	Ladislav Dolezal	Ladislav Dolezal	1964	1019
207 5/8	25 4/8	25 4/8	21 2/8	6	6	11	7	Keephills, AB	Unknown	William J. Greenhough	PR 1970	1019
207 5/8	30 1/8	29 3/8	20 4/8	5 1/8	5 2/8	10	9	Webster Co., IA	Larry E. Iles	Larry E. Iles	1979	1019
207 5/8	24	23 6/8	23 6/8	6 3/8	6 2/8	10	8	Buffalo Co., WI	Dennis M. Eberhardt	Dennis M. Eberhardt	1984	1019
207 5/8	25 3/8	25	20 3/8	4 7/8	4 6/8	8	14	Gentry Co., MO	Eric D. Sybert	Eric D. Sybert	1990	1019
207 5/8	27 3/8	28 3/8	23 2/8	6 1/8	5 6/8	12	11	Penobscot Co., ME	Picked Up	Randall Madden	1995	1019
207 5/8	26 7/8	27 6/8	21	5 2/8	5 6/8	6	9	Dane Co., WI	William L. Myhre, Jr.	William L. Myhre, Jr.	1997	1019
207 5/8	25 6/8	25 3/8	18 5/8	5 7/8	6 2/8	11	11	Fulton Co., IL	Jack L. Link	Jack L. Link	1999	1019
207 4/8	28 7/8	27 6/8	19 5/8	4 7/8	4 4/8	10	9	Barron Co., WI	Charles Slayton	Gordon Lee	PR 1920	1031
207 4/8	25 2/8	24 6/8	16 2/8	5 2/8	5 2/8	12	11	Burnett Co., WI	Harold Miller	Mac's Taxidermy	1938	1031
207 4/8	23 4/8	22 1/8	18 5/8	5 3/8	6	9	10	Lawrence Co., SD	Ernest C. Larive	J.D. Andrews	1957	1031
207 4/8	26 4/8	26 4/8	29 1/8	6	6	7	10	Portageville, NY	Howard W. Smith	Howard W. Smith	1959	1031
207 4/8	26 5/8	25 5/8	18 7/8	5 2/8	5 2/8	8	14	Comanche Co., KS	Picked Up	Bass Pro Shops	1984	1031
207 4/8	27	26 3/8	17 7/8	5 2/8	5 1/8	8	9	Macoupin Co., IL	John D. Carey	John D. Carey	1991	1031
207 4/8	26 7/8	26 4/8	19	5 2/8	5 2/8	10	8	Lewis Co., MO	Leonard G. Grant	Leonard G. Grant	1999	1031
207 4/8	27 7/8	27 7/8	17 3/8	5 4/8	5 4/8	12	8	Winona Co., MN	Picked Up	Ray T. Charles	2001	1031
207 3/8	25 4/8	25 6/8	20 4/8	4 1/8	4 3/8	8	12	Langlade Co., WI	Henry L. Schewe	John R. Konkel	1907	1039
207 3/8	25 3/8	26	26 3/8	5 2/8	5 3/8	8	11	Aitkin Co., MN	Viola Scott	Viola S. Weimer	1954	1039
207 3/8	28 7/8	29 1/8	18 5/8	6 5/8	6 2/8	10	10	Lincoln Co., MO	Melvin Zumwalt	Melvin Zumwalt	1955	1039
207 3/8	24 3/8	25 3/8	21 3/8	5	5 2/8	9	15	Throckmorton Co., TX	Jack Carlile	Watt R. Matthews	1960	1039
207 3/8	28 3/8	27 6/8	21 3/8	5 6/8	5 7/8	10	11	Roberts Co., SD	Delbert Lackey	Delbert Lackey	1975	1039
207 3/8	25 7/8	25 4/8	20 3/8	4 4/8	4 4/8	10	8	Zapata Co., TX	Romeo H. Garcia	Romeo H. Garcia	1977	1039

Score	L. Main Beam R	L. Main Beam L	Inside Spread	Circ. R	Circ. L	Pts. R	Pts. L	Locality	Hunter	Owner	Date	Rank
207 3/8	25 7/8	26 3/8	17 4/8	6 2/8	6 1/8	12	9	Dane Co., WI	Todd J. DeForest	Todd J. DeForest	1989	1039
207 3/8	25 6/8	25 6/8	17 6/8	5	5	8	8	Lee Co., IA	Donald L. Butler	Donald L. Butler	1999	1039
207 3/8	18 5/8	12 1/8	17 1/8	4	4 1/8	15	14	Madison Co., MS	Kenneth L. Reece	Kenneth L. Reece	2001	1039
207 2/8	24 4/8	19 5/8	11 7/8	5 6/8	5 5/8	11	17	Oroville, WA	Victor E. Moss	Victor E. Moss	1967	1048
207 2/8	27 1/8	26 5/8	18 3/8	5 2/8	5 1/8	7	10	Drayton Valley, AB	Hassib Halabi	Hassib Halabi	1977	1048
207 2/8	23 4/8	24 4/8	19	5	5 1/8	12	8	Unknown	Unknown	Unknown	PR 1979	1048
207 2/8	30 1/8	29 5/8	21	5 5/8	5 4/8	8	7	Andrew Co., MO	Frank Kelso	Delores C. Kelso	1981	1048
207 2/8	26 2/8	22 7/8	18 2/8	6	6 5/8	9	11	Brown Co., NE	Terry J. Graff	Terry J. Graff	1987	1048
207 2/8	26 2/8	25 5/8	18 7/8	5 3/8	5 3/8	7	7	Adair Co., MO	Kevin Elsea	Kevin Elsea	1988	1048
207 2/8	23 4/8	23 7/8	20 2/8	6 1/8	6 3/8	15	10	Swan Plain, SK	Gary A. Markofer	Gary A. Markofer	1991	1048
207 2/8	26 3/8	24 6/8	19 5/8	5 2/8	5 4/8	7	13	Crawford Co., WI	Brent Swiggum	Brent Swiggum	1991	1048
207 2/8	29 5/8	28 2/8	22 1/8	5 5/8	5 7/8	9	8	Clark Co., IL	Richard D. Ellington	Richard D. Ellington	1997	1048
207 2/8	27 3/8	26 2/8	20 6/8	5 3/8	5 5/8	12	10	Pulaski Co., KY	Mark Jones	Mark Jones	1998	1048
207 1/8	27 7/8	27	20 6/8	6	5 5/8	11	9	Wilkin Co., MN	Richard K. Christopher	Richard K. Christopher	1999	1059
207 1/8	28 5/8	28 4/8	18 4/8	5 5/8	5 5/8	10	10	St. Louis Co., MO	Unknown	Kent Austin	1958	1059
207 1/8	25 5/8	26 7/8	17 3/8	6	5 1/8	12	9	Clay Co., IA	Rodney W. Dean	Rodney W. Dean	1973	1059
207 1/8	25 7/8	24 3/8	20 6/8	5 5/8	5 2/8	9	10	Provost, AB	Michael D. Kerley	Michael D. Kerley	1977	1059
207 1/8	22	23 7/8	22	5 1/8	8	14	13	Buffalo Co., NE	Unknown	Unknown	PR 1978	1059
207 1/8	27 5/8	27 1/8	15 6/8	8	4 6/8	11	8	Traverse Co., MN	Joel E. Kuschel	Joel E. Kuschel	1996	1059
207 1/8	27 4/8	27 7/8	23 4/8	5 4/8	5 7/8	10	10	Montgomery Co., IA	Raymond E. Crouch	Raymond E. Crouch	1997	1059
207 1/8	29 3/8	28 4/8	16 6/8	4 6/8	5	9	11	Ohio Co., KY	Rick Daugherty	Rick Daugherty	1997	1059
207 1/8	27 3/8	27 1/8	25 4/8	5 5/8	5 4/8	8	7	Page Co., IA	Jeremy Williams	Jeremy Williams	1997	1059
207 1/8	27	26 3/8	20 2/8	4 6/8	4 7/8	8	9	Waseca Co., MN	Scott Schaible	Scott Schaible	1998	1059
207	24 4/8	23 3/8	16 1/8	4 7/8	5 1/8	10	12	Montgomery Co., IN	Michael R. Davis	Michael R. Davis	2000	1070
207	23 4/8	23 1/8	18 4/8	6	6	12	16	Linn Co., KS	Charles E. Jasper	Charles E. Jasper	2000	1070
207	26 6/8	26	19 1/8	5 6/8	6 4/8	16	9	Bayfield Co., WI	Francis F. Zifko	Francis F. Zifko	1954	1070
207	26 4/8	27 1/8	25	5 4/8	5 7/8	9	10	Cowley Co., KS	Joyce Williams	Joyce Williams	1983	1070
207	22 7/8	23 3/8	20	5 5/8	5 2/8	10	8	Stark Co., OH	Tad E. Crawford	Tad E. Crawford	1987	1070
207	22 7/8	23 4/8	18 6/8	6 4/8	5 6/8	7	10	Eagle Creek, SK	Perry Haanen	Perry Haanen	1993	1070
206 7/8	24 3/8	23 6/8	18 4/8	6 2/8	6 2/8	9	11	Davis Co., IA	David L. Johnson	David L. Johnson	1994	1076
206 7/8	25	24 1/8	16 5/8	5	5	12	9	Walworth Co., WI	Kurt Mohrbacher	Kurt Mohrbacher	1997	1076
206 7/8	23 4/8	25 5/8	18	5 3/8	5 2/8	14	12	Oneida Co., WI	Clarence Staudenmayer	Clarence Staudenmayer	1942	1076
206 7/8	28 6/8	30 3/8	18 4/8	4 7/8	5 3/8	10	14	Loup Co., NE	T.A. Brandenburg	Picked Up	1963	1076
206 7/8	25 4/8	25 6/8	23 4/8	5 6/8	4 7/8	11	10	Horicon Marsh, WI	Picked Up	Ronald A. Lillge	1966	1076
206 7/8	26 2/8	29 5/8	21 6/8	5 1/8	5 6/8	10	9	Claiborne Parish, LA	J.H. Thurmon	J.H. Thurmon	1970	1076
206 7/8	25 5/8	27 1/8	22 4/8	5 2/8	5 4/8	10	9	Pine Lake, AB	Richard D. Doan	Leila R. Doan	1979	1076
206 7/8	20 4/8	21 3/8	14 5/8	5 1/8	4 6/8	11	8	Wright Co., MN	Richard A. Erickson	Richard A. Erickson	1983	1076
206 7/8	26	26	17 4/8	5 1/8	5	8	9	Maple Creek, SK	Theodore Reierson	Theodore Reierson	1984	1076
206 7/8	28 3/8	27 7/8	20 1/8	5 1/8	5 1/8	9	8	Whitemouth River, MB	Tom Clark, Jr.	Tom Clark, Jr.	1987	1076
206 7/8	24 7/8	24 6/8	21 4/8	5 2/8	5 1/8	9	6	St. Louis, SK	Kelvin Tate	D.J. Hollinger & B. Howard	1987	1076
206 7/8	28 1/8	27 1/8	18 6/8	5 3/8	5	13	12	Stearns Co., MN	Steven J. Sperl	Steven J. Sperl	1987	1076
206 7/8	25	22 5/8	21 6/8	5 4/8	5	12	14	Baxter Lake, AB	Terry F. Ermel	Terry F. Ermel	1988	1076
206 7/8	22 5/8	29 3/8	17 2/8	4 7/8	4 7/8	9	11	Dodge Co., WI	Steven J. Schultz	Steven J. Schultz	1989	1076
206 7/8	29 3/8	25	21 6/8	5 1/8	5 1/8	8	9	Deserters Creek, AB	Duane Paisley	Duane Paisley	1992	1076
206 7/8	26 3/8	26 3/8	17 2/8	5 7/8	5 7/8	11	8	McPherson Co., KS	Dennis G. Bordner	Dennis G. Bordner	1994	1076
206 7/8	23 7/8	25	19 6/8	5 3/8	5 3/8	10	9	Hamilton Co., OH	Mickey E. Lotz	Mickey E. Lotz	1995	1076
206 7/8	23 7/8	25	19 5/8	5 4/8	5 3/8	10	10	Douglas Co., WI	Neil R. Hagen	Neil R. Hagen	1996	1076
206 7/8	27 1/8	27 7/8	19 5/8	5 2/8	5 2/8	10	10	Jo Daviess Co., IL	Picked Up	Doug D. Jones	1998	1076

Score	Length of Main Beam R	L	Inside Spread	Circumference at Smallest Place Between Burr and First Point R	L	Number of Points R	L	Locality	Hunter	Owner	Date Killed	Rank
206 7/8	26 7/8	26 5/8	18 6/8	5 1/8	5 1/8	7	13	Crawford Co., WI	Thomas Oppriecht	Thomas Oppriecht	2001	1076
206 7/8	24 6/8	22 5/8	15 5/8	5 4/8	5 3/8	9	12	Adair Co., MO	Mearl Janes	Scott Janes	2002	1076
206 6/8	25 4/8	25 4/8	24	5 4/8	5 4/8	7	11	Beechy, SK	Harold Penner	Spanky Greenville	1959	1095
206 6/8	26	26 2/8	19 2/8	5 1/8	5	8	9	Fulton Co., IN	Lewis Polk	Robert E. VanMeter III	1960	1095
206 6/8	25 4/8	26 4/8	17 2/8	5 4/8	5 4/8	8	10	Grant Parish, LA	Richard D. Ellison, Jr.	Richard D. Ellison, Jr.	1969	1095
206 6/8	25 6/8	23 3/8	23 7/8	5 4/8	5 5/8	12	9	Somerset Co., ME	Mark T. Lary	Mark T. Lary	1979	1095
206 6/8	26 7/8	27	20 1/8	5	5	7	10	Buffalo Co., WI	Monte R. Nichols	Monte R. Nichols	1996	1095
206 6/8	27 5/8	24 1/8	16 6/8	6 4/8	6	6	14	N. Saskatchewan River, SK	David C. Pezderic	David C. Pezderic	1997	1095
206 6/8	30 2/8	29 5/8	20 6/8	5 5/8	5 3/8	8	13	Hart Co., KY	Daniel Behr	Daniel Behr	1998	1095
206 6/8	23 7/8	27	23 1/8	5 6/8	5 4/8	12	11	Vermilion Co., IL	Ronald Weddle	Ronald Weddle	2001	1095
206 5/8	26 5/8	25 2/8	19 7/8	5 1/8	5	11	9	Outlook, SK	Unknown	Dick Rossum	1971	1103
206 5/8	26	24 2/8	19 6/8	5 3/8	5 2/8	7	12	Chase Co., KS	Jay A. Talkington	Jay A. Talkington	1983	1103
206 5/8	26	25 5/8	20 1/8	5 5/8	5 4/8	9	7	Iowa Co., IA	Picked Up	Ralph McBride	1990	1103
206 5/8	24 5/8	24 3/8	19 6/8	6	6 1/8	8	11	Kevisville, AB	Brian R. McKain	Brian R. McKain	1990	1103
206 5/8	24	23 3/8	23	4 5/8	4 4/8	9	12	Marshall Co., KY	Perry Beyer, Jr.	Perry Beyer, Jr.	1996	1103
206 5/8	26	25 7/8	20 1/8	6	6 3/8	11	11	Guthrie Co., IA	Terry R. Adams	Terry R. Adams	1998	1103
206 5/8	22	22 3/8	18 1/8	4 4/8	4 5/8	10	12	Stevens Co., WA	Dick E. Jones	Dick E. Jones	1998	1103
206 5/8	24 4/8	24 4/8	14 6/8	7 1/8	6	13	11	Penobscot Co., ME	Jay L. McLellan	Jay L. McLellan	2001	1103
206 4/8	21 1/8	21 1/8	16 6/8	5 7/8	5 7/8	10	12	Chippewa Co., MI	John Nevins	Bass Pro Shops	PR 1904	1111
206 4/8	22 2/8	22 2/8	19 4/8	5	5	10	13	Brooks Co., TX	John E. Wilson	James M. Hancock, Jr.	1947	1111
206 4/8	23 2/8	23 1/8	16 4/8	5 4/8	5 4/8	14	8	Norman Co., MN	Unknown	Tom Williams	1950	1111
206 4/8	25 4/8	24 7/8	17 7/8	6 6/8	6 4/8	12	9	Yankton Co., SD	William Sees	William Sees	1973	1111
206 4/8	26	26 1/8	19 2/8	6 3/8	6 1/8	11	6	Lac qui Parle Co., MN	Steven J. Karels	Steven J. Karels	1974	1111
206 4/8	28 4/8	26 7/8	20 5/8	5 1/8	5 3/8	10	9	Lawrence Co., IL	Shirley Lewis	Shirley Lewis	1976	1111
206 4/8	16 5/8	18 7/8	15 7/8	4 5/8	5	15	13	Madison Co., GA	Picked Up	GA Dept. of Natl. Resc.	1993	1111
206 4/8	24 6/8	23 7/8	18 1/8	5 3/8	5 3/8	9	13	Chippewa Co., WI	Richard C. Bennesch	Richard C. Bennesch	2000	1111
206 3/8	22 7/8	23 2/8	19	4 7/8	4 5/8	11	11	Webb Co., TX	Willard V. Brenizer	Gerry Elliff	1942	1119
206 3/8	24 6/8	20 6/8	18 3/8	5	5	12	12	Menard Co., IL	Frank C. Pickett	Frank C. Pickett	1985	1119
206 3/8	26 7/8	26 7/8	19	5 2/8	5 3/8	10	9	Clay Co., IN	Jason S. Shaw	Jason S. Shaw	1989	1119
206 3/8	29 6/8	28 5/8	22 2/8	5 4/8	5 5/8	12	10	Adams Co., OH	James M. Wilson	James M. Wilson	1989	1119
206 3/8	24 6/8	24 7/8	14	5 4/8	4 6/8	9	9	Colquitt Co., GA	Picked Up	GA Dept. of Natl. Resc.	1990	1119
206 3/8	27 4/8	27 7/8	20	4 6/8	4 7/8	7	8	Cass Co., IA	Rodney A. Watson	Rodney A. Watson	1993	1119
206 3/8	25	24 7/8	18 6/8	6	5 7/8	9	11	Kuroki, SK	Picked Up	K. Ian Cooper	1995	1119
206 3/8	26 6/8	26 5/8	21 6/8	5 7/8	5 4/8	9	8	St. Louis Co., MN	Picked Up	Paul Coughlin	2002	1119
206 2/8	28 4/8	28 5/8	25	5 5/8	5 6/8	9	11	Cortland Co., NY	Hank Hayes	Interlaken Sportsmans Club	1947	1127
206 2/8	25 4/8	25	16 6/8	5	5	7	9	Cotulla, TX	George E. Light III	George E. Light III	1950	1127

Score	L. Main Beam R	L. Main Beam L	Inside Spread	Circ. R	Circ. L	Pts R	Pts L	Locality	By Whom Killed	Owner	Date Killed	Rank
206 7/8	31 1/8	31	22 7/8	6	5 3/8	7	3	Piscataquis Co., ME	Ralph E. Dow	Ralph E. Dow	1964	1127
206 6/8	24 4/8	24 1/8	19	6	5 3/8	13	13	Lincoln Co., MT	Larry H. Beller	Larry H. Beller	1985	1128
206 6/8	31 5/8	29 3/8	23 4/8	4 6/8	4 4/8	9	3	Benton Co., MN	Kenneth R. Nodo	Kenneth R. Nodo	1987	1128
206 6/8	26 5/8	26 4/8	19 7/8	5 4/8	5 1/8	8	9	McLennan, AB	Gordon E. Ristow	Gordon E. Ristow	1993	1128
206 6/8	29 3/8	28 6/8	20 5/8	5 1/8	5 7/8	8	6	Adair Co., MO	Charles M. Zeman	Charles M. Zeman	1997	1128
206 6/8	26 6/8	27 5/8	23 3/8	5 6/8	5 4/8	12	10	Henry Co., IL	Jon R. Wolf	Jon R. Wolf	2000	1128
206 6/8	26 7/8	27 6/8	20 6/8	5 1/8	5 5/8	9	10	Gull Lake, AB	Jack K. Mulder	Jack K. Mulder	2001	1128
206 6/8	24 6/8	24 1/8	24 1/8	5	6 2/8	13	8	Jefferson Co., KS	Michael J. Navrat, Jr.	Michael J. Navrat, Jr.	2001	1128
206 6/8	26 2/8	26 2/8	19	4 5/8	5	13	9	Pike Co., IN	William J. Goeppner	William J. Goeppner	2003	1128
206 1/8	22	20 6/8	20 7/8	5 4/8	4 6/8	10	10	Loon Lake, WA	Bill Quirt	Jeffrey Gustafson	1955	1138
206 1/8	22 4/8	22 5/8	22	5 4/8	5 1/8	10	15	Kisbey, SK	J. Harrison	J. Harrison	1956	1138
206 1/8	23 2/8	23 3/8	18 4/8	6	5 4/8	9	10	Lincoln Co., WI	Picked Up	Louis Pond	PR 1974	1138
206 1/8	25 4/8	25 3/8	22	5 4/8	5 1/8	9	9	Dunn Co., ND	Kenneth E. DeLap	Kenneth E. DeLap	1982	1138
206 1/8	26 3/8	26 2/8	18 1/8	5 2/8	6	12	12	Osage Co., OK	Wesley D. Coldren	Wesley D. Coldren	1986	1138
206 1/8	25 1/8	26 1/8	17 4/8	4 6/8	5 5/8	12	10	Lake of the Woods Co., MN	Keith D. Yahnke	Keith D. Yahnke	1987	1138
206 1/8	23 5/8	23	19 7/8	5 3/8	5 1/8	9	7	Union Co., OH	Henry W. Leistritz	Henry W. Leistritz	1989	1138
206	26 5/8	25 4/8	21	4 6/8	4 6/8	11	11	Cameron Co., PA	William P. Rhines	David Rhines	1910	1145
206	26 4/8	24 6/8	18 6/8	5 3/8	5 3/8	8	8	McMullen Co., TX	Robert L. Hodges	Robert L. Connally	1925	1145
206	25 6/8	24 5/8	16 6/8	4 7/8	4 7/8	10	10	St. Louis Co., MN	Earl Skarp	George W. Flaim	1938	1145
206	25	24 3/8	15 6/8	5 6/8	5	14	8	Queen Anne's Co., MD	Kenneth J. Houtz	Kenneth J. Houtz	1992	1145
206	24 1/8	25 1/8	24 3/8	5	5 3/8	7	8	Shoshone Co., ID	Marion G. Macaluso	Marion G. Macaluso	1993	1145
206	25 3/8	25 4/8	17 5/8	6 1/8	5 4/8	11	13	Lincoln Co., MO	Robert J. Leacock	Robert J. Leacock	2002	1145
205 7/8	24 4/8	27 4/8	17 1/8	4 6/8	5 4/8	13	5	Steuben Co., NY	Fred J. Kelley	Fred J. Kelley	1938	1151
205 7/8	23 4/8	23 4/8	19 3/8	4 4/8	5 7/8	17	9	Swift Co., MN	A.P. Vander Weyst	A.P. Vander Weyst	1954	1151
205 7/8	25 5/8	25 5/8	20 6/8	5 6/8	5 2/8	8	10	Franklin Co., MO	Alfred Osborn	Jack E. Osborn	1957	1151
205 7/8	25 4/8	25 6/8	20 6/8	6	4 3/8	16	10	Houston Co., TX	Gary Rogers	Gary Rogers	1969	1151
205 7/8	27 3/8	26 2/8	18 1/8	5	5 7/8	10	13	Todd Co., MN	Ben Sadlovsky	Matthew K. Sadlovsky	1973	1151
205 7/8	25	25	20 2/8	6 3/8	6	10	10	Missoula Co., MT	Unknown	Unknown	1973	1151
205 7/8	27 4/8	28 6/8	19 4/8	5 2/8	5 1/8	12	14	Switzerland Co., IN	Paul J. Graf	Paul J. Graf	1981	1151
205 7/8	23 3/8	23 3/8	17 5/8	4 5/8	5 4/8	8	11	Clark Co., MO	Allen L. Courtney	Allen L. Courtney	1983	1151
205 7/8	24 7/8	24 7/8	20	4 4/8	6	11	9	Battle River, AB	Bryan Champagne	Bryan Champagne	1987	1151
205 7/8	28 1/8	28	25 4/8	5 7/8	6 6/8	9	5	Atchison Co., MO	Larry Poppa	Larry Poppa	1990	1151
205 7/8	28 2/8	27 4/8	23 2/8	5 4/8	5 6/8	11	8	Breckinridge Co., KY	Bruce Parris	Bruce Parris	1991	1151
205 7/8	25	25 6/8	21 6/8	5 6/8	6	9	10	Greene Co., IL	Ronald R. Okonek	Ronald R. Okonek	1998	1151
205 7/8	31 3/8	31 4/8	22 5/8	6 3/8	6 3/8	7	7	McPherson Co., KS	Chad Doughman	Chad Doughman	1999	1151
205 7/8	26 6/8	26 6/8	19 7/8	5 2/8	5 2/8	11	11	Lawrence Co., AL	Ronald R. Laymon	Ronald R. Laymon	2000	1151
205 6/8	26 6/8	25 1/8	18 1/8	5 1/8	4 4/8	9	9	Minnesota	Unknown	Greg Jensen	1965	1165
205 6/8	25 3/8	23 1/8	21	5 3/8	4 7/8	12	12	Lowndes Co., MS	Joe W. Shurden	Joe W. Shurden	1976	1165
205 6/8	23 1/8	24 3/8	21	5 6/8	5 2/8	9	9	Ritchie Co., WV	Charles E. Bailey, Jr.	Charles E. Bailey, Jr.	1979	1165
205 6/8	24 3/8	24	15 6/8	5 7/8	6	14	14	Koochiching Co., MN	Unknown	Marc M. Jackson	PR 1979	1165
205 6/8	26 3/8	25 2/8	20 3/8	5 4/8	5 7/8	10	8	Cloud Co., KS	Gary G. Pingel	Gary G. Pingel	1982	1165
205 6/8	23 5/8	23	19 2/8	5 6/8	5 4/8	8	8	Lucas Co., IA	William F. Bingaman	William F. Bingaman	1991	1165
205 6/8	26 2/8	26 6/8	20	5 3/8	5 3/8	8	10	Hickman Co., KY	Jerry M. Evans	Jerry M. Evans	1998	1165
205 6/8	23 7/8	25 7/8	16 6/8	5 3/8	5 6/8	11	9	Trimble Co., KY	Billy A. Riddell, Jr.	Billy A. Riddell, Jr.	2001	1165
205 5/8	26 4/8	24 2/8	20 6/8	5 6/8	5 7/8	10	15	Orange Co., NY	Unknown	Victor T. Zarnock	PR 1944	1173
205 5/8	23 3/8	26	21 2/8	5 7/8	6 3/8	15	14	Cottonwood Co., MN	Larry G. Gravley	Larry G. Gravley	1975	1173
205 5/8	26	25 2/8	18 6/8	6 3/8	5	14	10	Spencer Co., KY	Phillip W. Lawson	Phillip W. Lawson	1989	1173
205 5/8	28	25	21 4/8	5 1/8	5	12	14	Fellers Heights, BC	Billy L. Franks	Billy L. Franks	1995	1173

Score	Length of Main Beam		Inside Spread	Circumference at Smallest Place Between Burr and First Point		Number of Points		Locality	Hunter	Owner	Date Killed	Rank
	R	L		R	L	R	L					
205 5/8	29 1/8	27 7/8	21 4/8	5 3/8	5 1/8	11	8	Doniphan Co., KS	Fran E. Wiederholt	Fran E. Wiederholt	1996	1173
205 4/8	27 2/8	25 4/8	22 4/8	5 5/8	5 6/8	9	9	Roseau Co., MN	Erwin Klaassen	Erwin Klaassen	1955	1178
205 4/8	25 4/8	25 4/8	17 7/8	4 7/8	5 1/8	9	12	Charlotte Co., NB	Clayton Tatton	J.D. Andrews	1959	1178
205 4/8	25	25 6/8	19 4/8	6 1/8	5 6/8	11	7	Adams Co., IL	Eldon K. Dagley	Eldon K. Dagley	1981	1178
205 4/8	23 5/8	23	19 6/8	5 5/8	5 6/8	12	16	St. Louis Co., MN	Picked Up	George W. Flaim	1985	1178
205 4/8	26	25 7/8	20 2/8	5 4/8	5 6/8	8	8	Washington Co., MN	Lonnie J. Diethert	Lonnie J. Diethert	1987	1178
205 4/8	25 4/8	26 1/8	23 3/8	4 6/8	4 6/8	8	6	Ram River, AB	William Howard	William Howard	1988	1178
205 4/8	21	21 3/8	17 3/8	5 1/8	5 1/8	18	16	Edgefield Co., SC	Bradley E. Means	Bradley E. Means	1994	1178
205 4/8	23 5/8	22 7/8	19	4 1/8	4 1/8	9	11	Armit River, SK	Marvin B. Borsa	Marvin B. Borsa	1995	1178
205 4/8	26 6/8	26 4/8	19 6/8	6 3/8	6 2/8	11	8	Dodge Co., WI	John Steckling	John Steckling	1998	1178
205 4/8	23 5/8	22	18 2/8	5 7/8	5 6/8	10	12	Adams Co., IL	Mike Theuil	Bruce Bruening	2002	1178
205 4/8	28 6/8	28 4/8	22 1/8	4 5/8	4 6/8	9	7	Geauga Co., OH	R. Chris Harris	R. Chris Harris	2002	1178
205 3/8	23 3/8	21 7/8	18 7/8	4 7/8	5	6	12	Kelvington, SK	D. Minor	D. Minor	1954	1189
205 3/8	25 3/8	27 1/8	22 2/8	4 1/8	4 1/8	10	9	Trempealeau Co., WI	Dennis L. Ulberg	Dennis L. Ulberg	1968	1189
205 3/8	22 4/8	23 2/8	17	6	6	10	12	Todd Co., MN	Mark A. Miksche	Mark A. Miksche	1979	1189
205 3/8	27 1/8	25 7/8	21	6 2/8	6	8	12	Louisa Co., IA	Daniel Kaufman	Daniel Kaufman	1984	1189
205 3/8	24 7/8	24 1/8	17 4/8	4 5/8	4 6/8	10	9	Wadena Co., MN	Donald R. Brockob	Donald R. Brockob	1990	1189
205 3/8	25 1/8	24	15	6	7 3/8	8	12	Beltrami Co., MN	Matt E. Stone	Matt E. Stone	1990	1189
205 3/8	28 4/8	28	20 2/8	4 7/8	5	7	8	Allamakee Co., IA	Picked Up	Frank Miller	1993	1189
205 3/8	26 3/8	24 6/8	16 4/8	4 5/8	4 5/8	10	9	Duval Co., TX	Daniel A. Pedrotti	Daniel A. Pedrotti	1995	1189
205 3/8	20 4/8	23 1/8	20 6/8	5 4/8	5 3/8	9	9	St. Anne Lake, AB	Allen H. Wilkie	Allen H. Wilkie	1995	1189
205 3/8	25 5/8	23 6/8	18 4/8	5 6/8	5 4/8	10	8	Dallas Co., IA	Picked Up	Jeff Kempf	PR 1996	1189
205 3/8	26	26 1/8	19 1/8	5 3/8	5 4/8	10	10	Freeborn Co., MN	Picked Up	Kevin J. Nelsen	1997	1189
205 3/8	19 7/8	23 4/8	20	5 6/8	4 7/8	12	7	White Co., AR	Charles L. Marcum, Jr.	Charles L. Marcum, Jr.	1998	1189
205 3/8	25	25 3/8	19 2/8	4 7/8	5 2/8	7	13	Winona Co., MN	James D. Vitcenda	James D. Vitcenda	1998	1189
205 3/8	26 3/8	23 2/8	23 1/8	4 7/8	4 6/8	14	9	Henderson Co., KY	Stephen L. Arend	Stephen L. Arend	2000	1189
205 3/8	24 4/8	26 2/8	21	8 4/8	8	12	11	Kansas	Picked Up	Keith A. Baird	2000	1189
205 2/8	24	23 5/8	27	5 4/8	5 4/8	11	8	Hungry Hollow, SK	K.W. Henderson	K.W. Henderson	1954	1204
205 2/8	25 6/8	27	21 2/8	5	5	9	9	Richland Co., MT	Loyd Salsbury	Marlo Salsbury	PR 1958	1204
205 2/8	28 6/8	29 2/8	18 7/8	4 3/8	4 4/8	10	11	Effingham Co., IL	Allen K. Bandelow	Allen K. Bandelow	1991	1204
205 2/8	27 5/8	27 1/8	19 4/8	5	5	7	11	Cross Co., AR	Gordon R. Banton	Gordon R. Banton	1992	1204
205 2/8	25	25 2/8	16 3/8	5 1/8	5 3/8	14	11	Willow Brook, SK	Alvie Warcomika	Alvie Warcomika	1993	1204
205 2/8	26 6/8	27 2/8	22 1/8	4 6/8	4 7/8	9	9	Bollinger Co., MO	Linda K. Peters	Linda K. Peters	1998	1204
205 2/8	25 6/8	25 1/8	19 7/8	6 2/8	6 2/8	8	8	Morgan Co., IL	Shawn R. Keegan	Shawn R. Keegan	2000	1204
205 1/8	26 4/8	24 4/8	20 3/8	4 7/8	5	10	9	Leross, SK	R. Weger	R. Weger	1961	1211
205 1/8	26 6/8	25 4/8	20 3/8	5 4/8	5 4/8	11	9	Rat River, MB	Ken L. Maxymowich	Ken L. Maxymowich	1987	1211

Score	Main Beam R	Main Beam L	Inside Spread	Points R	Points L	Circ. R	Circ. L	Locality	Owner	Hunter	Date	Rank
205 1/8	24 5/8	24 4/8	20 2/8	13	11	5	4 7/8	Antler, SK	Regina K.V. Ross	Regina K.V. Ross	1987	1211
205 1/8	21	22 2/8	14 6/8	12	13	5	5	Bonner Co., ID	Clinton M. Hackney	Clinton M. Hackney	1990	1211
205 1/8	28 7/8	29	24 1/8	9	8	5	4 6/8	Erie Co., NY	Mark C. Surdi	Mark C. Surdi	1996	1211
205 1/8	25 7/8	25 7/8	25 3/8	8	9	4 6/8	4 6/8	Moose Mountain Creek, SK	Darrell Arndt	Darrell Arndt	1999	1211
205	21	25 1/8	18	14	5	4 1/8	4 4/8	Boundary Co., ID	Lee Mahler	Lee Mahler	1961	1217
205	26 3/8	26 4/8	16 7/8	12	11	6 1/8	5 7/8	St. Louis Co., MN	Ed Nelson	George W. Flaim	1964	1217
205	25 5/8	24 5/8	22 1/8	7	10	6	5 5/8	Jo Daviess Co., IL	David L. Virtue	David L. Virtue	1990	1217
205	25 3/8	25	24 1/8	9	10	5 4/8	3 7/8	Peoria Co., IL	Picked Up	Dick Rossum	1991	1217
205	25 4/8	25 4/8	18 7/8	12	11	4	5 5/8	Marathon Co., WI	Joshua J. Erdman	Joshua J. Erdman	1994	1217
205	24 2/8	22 4/8	18	9	11	5 5/8	4 5/8	Carroll Co., IL	Robert D. Guenzler	Robert D. Guenzler	1994	1217
205	27 3/8	27 1/8	19 3/8	9	11	4 7/8	5 1/8	Guthrie Co., IA	James C. Long	James C. Long	1994	1217
205	24 2/8	22 1/8	17 6/8	12	13	5 3/8	5 7/8	Union Co., IA	Jeff J. Tussey	Jeff J. Tussey	1995	1217
205	26 3/8	24 4/8	18	9	9	6 2/8	4 4/8	White Fox, SK	Richard N. Kimball	Richard N. Kimball	1997	1217
205	27 4/8	26 2/8	22 4/8	3	9	4 5/8	5 7/8	Warren Co., IL	Jason A. Schwass	Jason A. Schwass	1997	1217
205	24 2/8	25 6/8	21 6/8	10	8	5 7/8	4 5/8	Fulton Co., IL	Picked Up	Robert E. Burgard	1998	1217
205	27 3/8	26 5/8	15 6/8	10	9	4 6/8	5 1/8	Grady Co., OK	Rickie L. Jenkins	Rickie L. Jenkins	2001	1217
204 7/8	23 3/8	23 1/8	17 6/8	3	11	5 1/8	4 5/8	Warren Co., IL	Brad Wike	Brad Wike	2002	1230
204 7/8	26 3/8	26 4/8	22 7/8	10	8	4 7/8	4 6/8	Minnesota	Steve Scholl	Steve Scholl	1941	1230
204 7/8	25 2/8	25 2/8	21 4/8	6	12	4 5/8	5 3/8	Trempealeau Co., WI	Ralph Klimek	Ralph Klimek	1960	1230
204 7/8	25 4/8	26 3/8	21 7/8	13	9	5	5 4/8	Roseau Co., MN	Andy Streiff	Andy Streiff	1967	1230
204 7/8	26	24 5/8	21 2/8	13	12	5 5/8	4 6/8	Bentley, AB	Stanley A. Anderson	Stanley A. Anderson	1968	1230
204 7/8	27 2/8	22 2/8	18 5/8	9	8	4 5/8	5 1/8	Winona Co., MN	Picked Up	Gary L. Bornfleth	1979	1230
204 7/8	21 2/8	21 2/8	23 6/8	7	11	5 1/8	4 5/8	Battle River, SK	Corey M. Young	Corey M. Young	1992	1230
204 7/8	26 3/8	24 6/8	18 5/8	11	9	4 5/8	5 2/8	Anson Co., NC	Keith M. Reese	Keith M. Reese	1994	1230
204 7/8	23 3/8	23 3/8	20 2/8	9	12	5 2/8	5 1/8	Yankton Co., SD	Daniel M. Rederick	Daniel M. Rederick	1998	1230
204 7/8	22 7/8	22 7/8	21 2/8	12	10	5 3/8	4 7/8	Ogle Co., IL	Troy W. O'Brien	Troy W. O'Brien	2001	1230
204 7/8	23 4/8	24 1/8	21 2/8	7	14	5	6 6/8	Koochiching Co., MN	H.T. Hanson	Kevin Blomer	1920	1230
204 6/8	25 4/8	22 6/8	15 2/8	9	10	5 2/8	5 4/8	Moose Jaw, SK	Earl Sears	Earl Sears	1958	1239
204 6/8	28 4/8	26 5/8	19 6/8	10	9	5 2/8	5 7/8	Lowndes Co., MS	Picked Up	Thomas B. Yeatman	1959	1239
204 6/8	23 1/8	21 7/8	21 7/8	8	12	5 7/8	5 6/8	Gilmer Co., WV	Brooks Reed	Brooks Reed	1960	1239
204 6/8	28 4/8	26 3/8	26 1/8	8	12	5 6/8	4 5/8	Saskatchewan River, MB	Dieter Boehner	Dieter Boehner	1973	1239
204 6/8	26 7/8	27 6/8	21 1/8	6	7	4 4/8	5	Stearns Co., MN	Curt Fettig	Curt Fettig	1975	1239
204 6/8	26 3/8	26 4/8	19 2/8	6	8	5 1/8	5 3/8	Innisfree, AB	Donald M. Baranec	Donald M. Baranec	1977	1239
204 6/8	24 1/8	24	18 3/8	11	8	5 4/8	5 4/8	Washington Co., IN	David Souder	David Souder	1988	1239
204 6/8	27 4/8	22 6/8	19 1/8	11	16	5 2/8	6 1/8	Clay Co., AR	Rob W. Boling	Rob W. Boling	1996	1239
204 6/8	23 4/8	23	19 1/8	9	10	6	5 4/8	St. Anne Lake, AB	Todd K. Kirk	Todd K. Kirk	1996	1239
204 6/8	25 4/8	25 5/8	19 4/8	6	9	5 4/8	7 4/8	Harris Co., GA	Lauren C. Atwell	Lauren C. Atwell	2002	1239
204 6/8	26	26	22 4/8	12	12	5 6/8	4 4/8	Warren Co., OH	Rex A. Gill	Rex A. Gill	2002	1239
204 5/8	27 2/8	27 3/8	19 7/8	11	12	4 4/8	5 2/8	Bandera Co., TX	August Dienger	Larry L. Stahl	1906	1251
204 5/8	26 5/8	26 1/8	17 4/8	5	8	5 2/8	5 6/8	Unknown	Unknown	John A. Jarosz	PR 1930	1251
204 5/8	23 4/8	26 1/8	20 4/8	8	10	5 4/8	5 4/8	Richland Co., MT	Harold R. Moran	Harold R. Moran	1956	1251
204 5/8	27 1/8	25 7/8	19 7/8	8	12	4 7/8	4 7/8	Okanogan Co., WA	Matthew B. King	Matthew B. King	1992	1251
204 5/8	29 5/8	30 4/8	16 1/8	11	10	6 4/8	6 4/8	Bull River, BC	Gary Nonis	Gary Nonis	1994	1251
204 5/8	30	28 6/8	21 6/8	8	10	5 4/8	5 7/8	Cloud Co., KS	Darrell L. Zimmerman	Darrell L. Zimmerman	1994	1251
204 5/8	22 2/8	21 6/8	20 3/8	6	11	4 4/8	4 4/8	Spruce Grove, AB	Darryl Legge	Darryl Legge	1999	1251
204 4/8	27 1/8	25 7/8	21 1/8	7	6	4 7/8	5 2/8	Calhoun Co., IL	Chad Strickland	Chad Strickland	1999	1251
204 4/8	25 4/8	24 6/8	16 3/8	10	12	5 2/8	4 7/8	Jackson Co., OH	Bernard Tennant	Bernard Tennant	1960	1259
204 4/8	22 2/8	21 6/8	15 6/8	10	11	5 1/8	5	Love Co., OK	William B. Heller	William B. Heller	1970	1259

WHITETAIL DEER - NON-TYPICAL ANTLERS
Odocoileus virginianus virginianus and certain related subspecies

Score	Length of Main Beam		Inside Spread	Circumference at Smallest Place Between Burr and First Point		Number of Points		Locality	Hunter	Owner	Date Killed	Rank
	R	L		R	L	R	L					
204 4/8	28 6/8	29	20 4/8	4 6/8	5 1/8	10	7	Monroe Co., MO	Rogelio L. Bautista	Rogelio L. Bautista	1996	1259
204 4/8	25 3/8	25 1/8	20 1/8	5 5/8	5 5/8	12	10	Fisher Co., TX	Keith H. Prince	Keith H. Prince	1997	1259
204 4/8	21 4/8	22 1/8	22 6/8	5 1/8	5 3/8	9	8	Dogpound Creek, AB	Patrick F. Kinch	Patrick F. Kinch	2002	1259
204 3/8	27 2/8	28	20 1/8	4 4/8	4 4/8	7	9	Dimmit Co., TX	Knox Miller	Clayton R. Johnson	1938	1264
204 3/8	26 7/8	26 4/8	21 2/8	5 2/8	5 5/8	7	12	Valley City, ND	William F. Cruff	George W. Flaim	1955	1264
204 3/8	26	24 4/8	18 3/8	4 7/8	5 2/8	11	12	Newport Co., WA	David R. Buchite	David R. Buchite	1960	1264
204 3/8	27 3/8	27 3/8	20 3/8	5 5/8	5 4/8	13	8	Harrison Co., IA	Raymond McDaniel	Raymond McDaniel	1970	1264
204 3/8	23 4/8	24	20 4/8	5 5/8	5 6/8	10	12	Waukesha Co., WI	Unknown	Mac's Taxidermy	PR 1975	1264
204 3/8	25	25 6/8	14 7/8	5 1/8	5 2/8	10	10	Clearwater Co., MN	Gilbert Oien	Vance R. Norgaard	1976	1264
204 3/8	24 5/8	25 6/8	19 3/8	5 3/8	5 3/8	10	8	Nanton, AB	Barry Flipping	Barry Flipping	1986	1264
204 3/8	27 1/8	26 6/8	18 7/8	5 3/8	5 4/8	13	11	Rock Island Co., IL	Jeff B. Davis	Jeff B. Davis	1990	1264
204 3/8	25 4/8	25 2/8	16 7/8	5 4/8	5 7/8	9	9	Jefferson Co., KS	Michael D. Wright	Michael D. Wright	1995	1264
204 3/8	26 1/8	26 3/8	17 2/8	5 6/8	5 6/8	9	9	Montgomery Creek, SK	Don L. Davey	Don L. Davey	1997	1264
204 3/8	27	24 3/8	16 2/8	5 1/8	4 7/8	11	10	Doniphan Co., KS	Robby L. Buford	Robby L. Buford	1998	1264
204 3/8	23 5/8	23 6/8	18 5/8	5 4/8	6 2/8	8	10	Waushara Co., WI	Debra A. Schmalzer	Debra A. Schmalzer	1998	1264
204 3/8	23 1/8	25	17 2/8	6 1/8	5 2/8	9	6	Lincoln Co., NE	Clyde L. Albers	Clyde L. Albers	2000	1264
204 3/8	24 3/8	25	19 6/8	4 1/8	4 1/8	10	10	Assiniboine River, SK	Karen R. Seginak	Karen R. Seginak	2000	1264
204 3/8	26 2/8	26 2/8	17 2/8	5 2/8	4 5/8	12	7	Otter Tail Co., MN	John L. Sabbin	John L. Sabbin	2001	1264
204 3/8	27 5/8	28 2/8	25 4/8	5 3/8	5 4/8	6	8	Allen Co., IN	Charles E. Dennis	Charles E. Dennis	2002	1264
204 2/8	23	23	17 2/8	4 6/8	4 4/8	11	15	Crook Co., WY	David Sipe	David Sipe	1956	1280
204 2/8	23 2/8	23 7/8	17 2/8	5 6/8	5 3/8	12	12	Rainy Lake, ON	Rod Hebert	Rod Hebert	1969	1280
204 2/8	25 2/8	25 5/8	23 2/8	6 5/8	6 4/8	9	10	Meeker Co., MN	Walter J. Tintes	Walter J. Tintes	1975	1280
204 2/8	25 5/8	23 1/8	17 1/8	5 1/8	5 4/8	7	15	Silver Lake, AB	Edwin Nelson	Gary Padleski	1980	1280
204 2/8	26 2/8	26 4/8	22 2/8	4 6/8	4 6/8	5	8	Boone Co., MO	Calvin E. Brown	Calvin E. Brown	1985	1280
204 2/8	27 3/8	27 7/8	21 4/8	6 2/8	6	6	11	Yuma Co., CO	Jeff L. Mekelburg	Jeff L. Mekelburg	1986	1280
204 2/8	30	27 6/8	21 2/8	6 3/8	6 4/8	6	11	Cass Co., IL	J. David Bartels	J. David Bartels	1989	1280
204 2/8	29 1/8	27 7/8	23 3/8	6 2/8	6	4	4	Ashland Co., OH	Keith A. Beringo	Keith A. Beringo	1991	1280
204 2/8	25 6/8	25 3/8	18 2/8	5 1/8	5 3/8	10	12	Livingston Co., IL	Michael T. Schopp	Michael T. Schopp	1996	1280
204 2/8	25 7/8	25 4/8	19 3/8	5 5/8	5 7/8	13	12	Winneshiek Co., IA	Benjamin Christopher	Benjamin Christopher	1999	1280
204 2/8	28 3/8	28 1/8	18 4/8	4 7/8	5	11	11	Grant Co., WI	Michael M. White	Michael M. White	2001	1280
204 1/8	28 1/8	27 2/8	22 3/8	6	5 4/8	10	12	Lyon Co., MN	Ray Evans	David C. Johnson	1940	1291
204 1/8	29 1/8	28 4/8	22 1/8	6 2/8	6 1/8	10	9	O'Brien Co., IA	Roy Jalas	Delores Jalas	1961	1291
204 1/8	28	27 3/8	24 5/8	5 2/8	5 2/8	8	11	Pope Co., MN	LeRoy D. Hausmann	LeRoy D. Hausmann	1967	1291
204 1/8	25 6/8	25 7/8	18 6/8	3 4/8	3 5/8	9	8	Dodge Co., WI	Wesley F. Braunschweig	Wesley F. Braunschweig	1976	1291
204 1/8	28 5/8	25 7/8	22 2/8	5 7/8	6 1/8	12	9	Charlotte Co., NB	Gary L. Lister	Gary L. Lister	1984	1291
204 1/8	26 5/8	26 2/8	22	5	4 7/8	7	9	Dubuque Co., IA	Joe J. Rettenmeier	Joe J. Rettenmeier	1987	1291

Score								Locality	Hunter	Owner	Date	Rank
204 1/8	25 2/8	26 1/8	18 3/8	5 5/8	5 5/8	14	11	Douglas Co., MN	Samuel Knapp	Samuel Knapp	1993	1291
204 1/8	27 1/8	26 6/8	21	6 2/8	5 6/8	7	9	Crawford Co., WI	Francis J. Manning	Francis J. Manning	1994	1291
204 1/8	25 4/8	26 3/8	19 5/8	5 2/8	5 2/8	11	10	Pike Co., MO	Robert J. Jeffries	Robert J. Jeffries	1995	1291
204 1/8	25 4/8	25 1/8	19 7/8	5 5/8	4 6/8	12	11	Van Buren Co., IA	Geoffrey N. Phillips	Geoffrey N. Phillips	1995	1291
204 1/8	26	26	19 7/8	4 5/8	4 5/8	9	11	Jefferson Co., OH	Ronald J. Ault	Ronald J. Ault	2002	1291
204	27 6/8	27 3/8	21 1/8	5 1/8	5 1/8	10	14	Sutton Co., TX	L.H. McMillan	L.H. McMillan	1961	1302
204	26 1/8	27 3/8	16 2/8	4 7/8	5 3/8	7	11	Carlton Co., MN	Erick Zack	Glen Van Guilder	1964	1302
204	27 2/8	25 2/8	21 7/8	5 1/8	5 3/8	13	12	Sheep River, AB	Walter L. Brown	Walter L. Brown	1966	1302
204	26 1/8	26 1/8	18 6/8	5 2/8	5 2/8	13	10	Grant Co., MN	Douglas S. Olson	Douglas S. Olson	1977	1302
204	23 5/8	23 6/8	18 3/8	5 7/8	5 6/8	13	14	Holbein, SK	Jesse Bates	Jesse Bates	1981	1302
204	26 6/8	27 1/8	21 7/8	5 1/8	5 4/8	11	11	Webster Co., KY	Jeff Robinson	Jeff Robinson	1982	1302
204	24 3/8	23 2/8	19 2/8	4 4/8	4	13	8	Hardin Co., KY	Picked Up	Dennis J. Haberkorn	1990	1302
204	26 3/8	26 7/8	17 4/8	5 1/8	5	8	9	Beltrami Co., MN	Terence C. Derosier	Terence C. Derosier	1991	1302
204	28 2/8	28 3/8	23 3/8	5 1/8	5 1/8	8	8	Rockbridge Co., VA	Michael J. Shifflett	Michael J. Shifflett	1993	1302
204	27 1/8	25 2/8	16 6/8	5 4/8	5 6/8	14	12	Webster Co., MS	William D. Eshee III	William D. Eshee III	1996	1302
204	26 2/8	26 4/8	22 6/8	5	5	12	8	Warren Co., IA	Jack J. Schuler, Jr.	Jack J. Schuler, Jr.	1997	1302
204	25	26 6/8	22 6/8	4 6/8	5	9	11	Buffalo Pound Lake, SK	Jim Weatherall	Jim Weatherall	1997	1302
204	29	28 7/8	20 7/8	5 7/8	6 3/8	10	9	McHenry Co., IL	Rick Lagerhausen	Rick Lagerhausen	2002	1302
203 7/8	25	25 6/8	20 5/8	5 4/8	5 3/8	14	9	Carver Co., MN	Peter Kamann	Eugene L. Kamann	1900	1315
203 7/8	25	27 4/8	17 4/8	4 6/8	4 6/8	11	8	Eastland Co., TX	Picked Up	William B. Wright, Jr.	1920	1315
203 7/8	27 4/8	25 4/8	18	4 7/8	4 6/8	8	11	McMullen Co., TX	Bruce Phillips	Jeffery C. Phillips	1941	1315
203 7/8	25	22 5/8	19	5 1/8	5 1/8	10	10	Pope Co., MN	Irwin E. Stangeland	Irwin E. Stangeland	1980	1315
203 7/8	22	18 7/8	16 2/8	4 3/8	4 4/8	11	14	Eaton Co., MI	Mark R. Janousek	Mark R. Janousek	1991	1315
203 7/8	23	25 5/8	22 6/8	4 7/8	5 1/8	6	9	Portage Co., OH	Lee C. Morris	Lee C. Morris	1994	1315
203 7/8	24 4/8	25 5/8	24 1/8	6 7/8	6 5/8	7	10	Greene Co., IN	Robert J. Cornwell	Robert J. Cornwell	2000	1315
203 7/8	25 2/8	27 3/8	20	5 1/8	5 3/8	7	10	George Lake, NB	Henry Kirk	Ronald Kirk	1903	1322
203 6/8	28	28	14 5/8	5 1/8	4 7/8	11	8	Dickinson Co., MI	Harold Eskil	Bass Pro Shops	1929	1322
203 6/8	23 6/8	24 6/8	16 5/8	4	3 7/8	8	8	Maverick Co., TX	Picked Up	Richard H. Bennett	1941	1322
203 6/8	24 2/8	24 2/8	19 7/8	4 7/8	4 7/8	10	9	Phillips Co., AR	Dolph Horton	N.V. Hyde, Jr.	1948	1322
203 6/8	27 1/8	27 1/8	28	4 4/8	4 4/8	9	8	McCurtain Co., OK	Gary L. Birge	Gary L. Birge	1981	1322
203 6/8	25	25	26 2/8	5 7/8	5 7/8	11	12	Pike Co., IL	Randall B. Long	Randall B. Long	1987	1322
203 6/8	23	23	22 4/8	5 5/8	5 5/8	16	7	Washtenaw Co., MI	Picked Up	Terry Melvin	1992	1322
203 6/8	25 6/8	25 6/8	27 3/8	5 4/8	5 4/8	10	8	Kendall Co., IL	Ronald R. Chabot	Ronald R. Chabot	1996	1322
203 6/8	23 6/8	24 6/8	24 6/8	6 1/8	6 1/8	6	14	Neosho Co., KS	Brian Carlson	Brian Carlson	1998	1322
203 6/8	25 1/8	26 5/8	23 2/8	5 6/8	5 6/8	10	12	Calloway Co., KY	Michael J. Hentzen	Michael J. Hentzen	1999	1322
203 6/8	23 6/8	23 7/8	17 7/8	5 3/8	5 4/8	15	14	Chariton Co., MO	John D. Morgan	John D. Morgan	1999	1322
203 5/8	26 4/8	28	15 5/8	5 7/8	6	18	13	Meigs Co., OH	Vernon Sower	Vernon Sower	1953	1333
203 5/8	23 2/8	25 2/8	15	6 6/8	6 6/8	8	14	Grand Forks Co., ND	Wesley Gilkey	Wesley Gilkey	1970	1333
203 5/8	26 6/8	30 6/8	17 3/8	6	6 6/8	10	9	Page Co., IA	Thomas G. Bernotas	Thomas G. Bernotas	1975	1333
203 5/8	23	25 2/8	17 5/8	5 6/8	5 7/8	14	9	Sabine Co., TX	Picked Up	Rodney S. Brooks	1981	1333
203 5/8	23 2/8	28	15 7/8	6 2/8	5 7/8	13	9	St. Louis Co., MN	Marvin E. Dickerson	Joe R. Dickerson	1981	1333
203 5/8	28	23 3/8	21 7/8	4 5/8	4 7/8	12	11	Warren Co., IA	Picked Up	Phillip A. Roalstad	1981	1333
203 5/8	24	24	21 7/8	5	5	11	11	Monona Co., IA	Ted Miller	Ted Miller	1986	1333
203 5/8	24 3/8	25 1/8	17 5/8	5 2/8	5 3/8	9	11	Spokane Co., WA	Robert S. Jensen	Robert S. Jensen	1991	1333
203 5/8	25 1/8	27 4/8	21 3/8	5 2/8	6 1/8	9	10	Chariton Co., MO	Jeff Whitman	Jeff Whitman	1992	1333
203 5/8	30 4/8	26 6/8	20 4/8	6 4/8	6	9	10	Buffalo Co., WI	Kevin R. Stroup	Ann Walton	1995	1333
203 5/8	26 6/8	23 6/8	15 2/8	5 1/8	6	10	10	Buffalo Co., WI	Ronald J. Jilot	Ronald J. Jilot	1997	1333
203 4/8	25	25 1/8	22	4 6/8	4 5/8	13	12	Live Oak Co., TX	Alec Coker	Henderson Coquat	1916	1344

Score	Length of Main Beam R	L	Inside Spread	Circumference at Smallest Place Between Burr and First Point R	L	Number of Points R	L	Locality	Hunter	Owner	Date Killed	Rank
203 4/8	24 4/8	25 2/8	16 4/8	5 6/8	5 5/8	9	13	Kootenai Co., ID	A.P. Hegge	Kevin L. Lundblad	1929	1344
203 4/8	28	27 5/8	23 3/8	5 2/8	4 7/8	9	8	Jones Co., GA	Curtis F. Long	Mrs. Curtis F. Long	1965	1344
203 4/8	24	22 1/8	18 6/8	5 1/8	5 2/8	9	9	Lincoln Co., MT	Sean M. Blackley	Sean M. Blackley	1990	1344
203 4/8	27	27 7/8	19 6/8	4 6/8	4 7/8	8	11	Upper Cutbank, BC	William E. Eckert	William E. Eckert	1990	1344
203 4/8	24 6/8	25 3/8	19 1/8	5 2/8	5 4/8	9	10	Appanoose Co., IA	Clem A. Herman	Clem A. Herman	1990	1344
203 4/8	22 5/8	24	16 5/8	6 4/8	6	14	12	Putnam Co., MO	Casey R. Hartlip	Casey R. Hartlip	1993	1344
203 4/8	28	28 3/8	23 5/8	6 4/8	6	9	7	Prince George's Co., MD	Charles C. Blankenship, Jr.	Charles C. Blankenship, Jr.	1995	1344
203 4/8	24 6/8	24 2/8	16	5 6/8	6	7	11	Lincoln Co., NE	Truman A. Burch III	Truman A. Burch III	1996	1344
203 4/8	27 2/8	26 5/8	24	5 5/8	5 6/8	9	9	Ford Co., IL	Gary G. Tessdale	Gary G. Tessdale	1997	1344
203 4/8	25 3/8	23 1/8	18 6/8	5 6/8	6	12	12	Clearwater Co., MN	Craig Maxwell	Craig Maxwell	1998	1344
203 4/8	22 3/8	21 3/8	22 6/8	4 6/8	4 6/8	12	15	Hardin Co., KY	Odell Chambers	Odell Chambers	1999	1344
203 4/8	28 4/8	29	22 3/8	4 7/8	5 1/8	6	7	Greene Co., IL	Greg L. Griswold	Greg L. Griswold	2001	1344
203 3/8	27 4/8	26 4/8	16	5 4/8	5 5/8	8	9	St. Louis Co., MN	Eino W. Nurmi	Eino W. Nurmi	1934	1357
203 3/8	25 2/8	25 2/8	21 5/8	5	5	10	8	Okanogan Co., WA	Michael A. Anderson	Michael A. Anderson	1961	1357
203 3/8	25 1/8	24 1/8	21	5 4/8	5 3/8	8	10	Olmsted Co., MN	Logan Behrens	Logan Behrens	1961	1357
203 3/8	22 4/8	23 3/8	19 2/8	6	6 1/8	8	8	Piapot, SK	Frank Kelly	John R. Steffes, Sr.	1966	1357
203 3/8	26 2/8	26 1/8	17 6/8	5 4/8	5 4/8	8	10	Olmsted Co., MN	Daniel J. Bernard	Daniel J. Bernard	1967	1357
203 3/8	25	24 2/8	19	5 1/8	4 7/8	10	13	Marquette Co., WI	Joseph E. Bell	Jeffrey L. Morgan	1969	1357
203 3/8	24 6/8	20 1/8	18 3/8	6 4/8	7 3/8	9	11	Van Buren Co., IA	Robert R. McWilliams	Robert R. McWilliams	1981	1357
203 3/8	23	24 1/8	20 2/8	6 4/8	6 2/8	10	13	Dunn Co., WI	Terry J. Evenson	Terry J. Evenson	1987	1357
203 3/8	27 2/8	27 7/8	21 4/8	5	5 2/8	7	10	Fayette Co., IA	Steve M. Loban	Steve M. Loban	1995	1357
203 3/8	28 2/8	29	22 2/8	5 5/8	5 6/8	8	7	Fulton Co., IL	Russell G. White	Russell G. White	1996	1357
203 3/8	29 3/8	28 4/8	21 3/8	6 3/8	6 3/8	10	7	Gallia Co., OH	Hoyle S. Foy, Sr.	Hoyle S. Foy, Sr.	1998	1357
203 3/8	26	23 2/8	17 1/8	5 4/8	5 6/8	12	11	Red Pheasant Indian Res., SK	Douglas A. Salomon	Douglas A. Salomon	1998	1357
203 3/8	22 3/8	21 2/8	18 2/8	4 4/8	4 3/8	10	13	Cumberland Co., NJ	Darrell T. Capps	Darrell T. Capps	2000	1357
203 3/8	22 4/8	23 3/8	20 4/8	4 4/8	4 4/8	10	9	Candle Lake, SK	Joseph R. Conard	Joseph R. Conard	2001	1357
203 3/8	22 3/8	24 1/8	17 5/8	4 3/8	4 4/8	11	10	Monroe Co., WI	Darrell G. Schultz	Darrell G. Schultz	2001	1357
203 2/8	25 2/8	25 1/8	21 6/8	4 1/8	4 2/8	7	8	Marshall Co., MN	Andrew Anderson	Elmer Anderson	1947	1372
203 2/8	28	27 7/8	21	4 7/8	4 5/8	9	10	Preston Co., WV	Unknown	L. Keith Casteel	1952	1372
203 2/8	23 7/8	23 3/8	17 2/8	5 1/8	5 3/8	13	13	Esterhazy, SK	Walter Tucker	Walter Tucker	1966	1372
203 2/8	27 1/8	26 6/8	16 6/8	5 6/8	5 6/8	10	10	Marinette Co., WI	Marvin E. Holmgren	Marvin E. Holmgren	1986	1372
203 2/8	24 6/8	25 1/8	18 7/8	5 3/8	5 1/8	12	11	McHenry Co., ND	Garry L. Heizelman	Garry L. Heizelman	1987	1372
203 2/8	25 2/8	25 5/8	16 1/8	5 1/8	5 1/8	13	9	Scott Co., IA	Marv A. Schmidt, Jr.	Marv A. Schmidt, Jr.	1987	1372
203 2/8	24	23 2/8	19 6/8	6 1/8	7 6/8	7	14	Ross Co., OH	Scott Zurmehly	Scott Zurmehly	1987	1372
203 2/8	23 6/8	23 6/8	15 5/8	5 3/8	5 3/8	11	12	Churchbridge, SK	Kevin W. Prince	Kevin W. Prince	1991	1372
203 2/8	24 4/8	25 2/8	21 7/8	4 5/8	5 1/8	10	12	Sanders Co., MT	Donald W. Heerdt	Donald W. Heerdt	1992	1372

Score							Locality	Owner	Hunter	Year	Rank
203 3/8	25 6/8	26 2/8	18 4/8	5 7/8	9	11	McLeod Co., MN	William Sandman	William Sandman	1994	1372
203 3/8	29	28 4/8	23	5 7/8	10	13	W. Feliciana Parish, LA	Estus S. Sykes	Estus S. Sykes	1994	1372
203 3/8	26	27 2/8	21 5/8	5 1/8	12	13	Decatur Co., IA	Kenneth R. Jones	Kenneth R. Jones	1995	1372
203 3/8	26 7/8	26 7/8	22 2/8	7 1/8	13	7	Andrew Co., MO	James C. Schweizer	James C. Schweizer	1995	1372
203 3/8	23 3/8	23 5/8	22	5	10	9	Open Creek, AB	David Serhan	David Serhan	1996	1372
203 3/8	23 7/8	24 1/8	20 4/8	5 3/8	9	9	Jefferson Co., NE	Greg D. Hansmire	Greg D. Hansmire	1996	1372
203 3/8	26 2/8	25 1/8	24 4/8	5 7/8	6	6	Logan Co., CO	Wade D. Shults	Wade D. Shults	2000	1372
203 2/8	22 2/8	21 3/8	15 4/8	4 7/8	9	6	Pike Co., IL	J. Brett Evans	J. Brett Evans	2001	1372
203 2/8	25 7/8	27 2/8	19	5 6/8	8	10	Iroquois Co., IL	Michael A. Lucht	Michael A. Lucht	2002	1372
203 1/8	23 5/8	25 5/8	16	4 6/8	11	8	Koochiching Co., MN	Unknown	George W. Flaim	1934	1390
203 1/8	23 7/8	24 3/8	17 6/8	4 6/8	13	9	Kootenai Co., ID	William M. Ziegler	William M. Ziegler	1965	1390
203 1/8	28 1/8	27 5/8	21	4 6/8	9	7	Pawnee Co., NE	Virgil J. Fisher	Virgil J. Fisher	1970	1390
203 1/8	23 7/8	24 4/8	19 6/8	5 4/8	10	12	Wetzel Co., WV	Tom Kirkhart	Tom Kirkhart	1981	1390
203 1/8	23 5/8	23 2/8	16 6/8	5 2/8	10	12	Roosevelt Co., MT	Jerry L. Altland	Jerry L. Altland	1991	1390
203 1/8	22 4/8	19 1/8	14 3/8	4 4/8	10	13	Campbell Co., WY	Picked Up	John P. Riley	1992	1390
203 1/8	29 2/8	28 2/8	19 3/8	5 3/8	11	8	Swan River, SK	Edwin E. Orr	Edwin E. Orr	1993	1390
203 1/8	24 6/8	24	21 4/8	6 6/8	8	12	Greenwood Co., KS	Paul E. Bunyard	Paul E. Bunyard	1994	1390
203 1/8	26 2/8	26	19 4/8	5	8	10	Lafayette Co., WI	Vernus Larson	Bass Pro Shops	1995	1390
203 1/8	25 7/8	26 1/8	24 5/8	5 2/8	8	8	N. Saskatchewan River, SK	Barrie Taylor	Barrie Taylor	1997	1390
203 1/8	24 4/8	23 5/8	19 2/8	4 6/8	9	7	St. Clair Co., IL	Gary W. White	Gary W. White	1997	1390
203 1/8	24 5/8	26 1/8	24	5 5/8	10	7	Bureau Co., IL	Jack E. Davis	Jack E. Davis	2001	1390
203	26 2/8	26 1/8	15	5 2/8	9	11	Hancock Co., IL	S.E. Brockschmidt	S.E. Brockschmidt	1958	1402
203	26 3/8	25 4/8	18 4/8	4 5/8	9	8	Madison Co., IA	Joe Bruns	Tim Bruns	1967	1402
203	28 4/8	27 3/8	21 7/8	5 5/8	9	8	Guthrie Co., IA	Ronald R. Hoyt	Ronald R. Hoyt	1974	1402
203	27	23 6/8	18 1/8	5 4/8	8	9	Lee Co., IA	Wayne L. McClain	Wayne L. McClain	1980	1402
203	26 1/8	27 6/8	17 4/8	4 5/8	9	8	Jefferson Co., KS	Dale Heston	Dale Heston	1982	1402
203	24	23 6/8	15	4 7/8	9	12	Wayne Co., KY	Jack L. Keith	Jack L. Keith	1990	1402
203	28 6/8	26 4/8	25 2/8	6 1/8	7	7	Coles Co., IL	Richard A. Miller	Richard A. Miller	1991	1402
203	25 6/8	26 2/8	21 2/8	4 5/8	7	10	Du Page, IL	Kevin J. Moran	Kevin J. Moran	1995	1402
203	29 1/8	27 6/8	22 2/8	6	10	10	Lake of the Prairies, SK	Eldon Conrad	Eldon Conrad	2000	1402
203	26 3/8	26 5/8	16 2/8	5 1/8	6	11	Cooper Co., MO	Tim Folmer	Tim Folmer	2000	1402
202 7/8	25 1/8	24 4/8	23 7/8	5	7	10	Marinette Co., WI	Theodore Maes	Theodore Maes	1932	1412
202 7/8	27 7/8	26 2/8	18	5 3/8	12	7	Du Page, IL	Picked Up	E. Dolf Pfefferkorn	1962	1412
202 7/8	24 4/8	24 2/8	19	5 7/8	10	10	Kingman Co., KS	Picked Up	Michael L. Piaskowski	1966	1412
202 7/8	30 1/8	29 6/8	21	6	8	7	Houston Co., MN	John B. Broers	John B. Broers	1991	1412
202 7/8	25 3/8	26 7/8	20 1/8	5 3/8	11	12	Decatur Co., IA	Kevin J. Anderson	Kevin J. Anderson	1992	1412
202 7/8	27 2/8	28 3/8	22 6/8	5 4/8	10	8	Brown Co., IL	Sylvan Purcell, Jr.	Sylvan Purcell, Jr.	1992	1412
202 7/8	26	26	19 1/8	5 2/8	10	10	Clearwater Co., MN	Donald E. Holm	Donald E. Holm	1993	1412
202 7/8	25 2/8	24 4/8	18 2/8	6 3/8	10	11	Saline Co., IL	Lindy R. Potts	Lindy R. Potts	1995	1412
202 7/8	21 5/8	21 7/8	16 3/8	4	10	13	Fergus Co., MT	Daniel N. Balster	Daniel N. Balster	1998	1412
202 7/8	26	27	17 6/8	5 1/8	8	6	Sioux Co., IA	Jason W. Davelaar	Jason W. Davelaar	1999	1412
202 7/8	25 5/8	27	20 2/8	5 2/8	11	12	Adams Co., IA	Ben H. Myers	Ben H. Myers	1999	1412
202 6/8	27 6/8	27 6/8	20 6/8	5 1/8	8	7	Cutarm River, SK	Charles Bassingthwaite	Charles Bassingthwaite	2001	1412
202 6/8	22 3/8	22	18	5 6/8	7	14	Garrison, ND	Clarence Hummel	Clarence Hummel	1961	1424
202 6/8	25 1/8	24 5/8	20 7/8	5 7/8	8	13	Warren Co., IA	Leland Cortum	Leland Cortum	1969	1424
202 6/8	25 6/8	25 3/8	18 4/8	5 3/8	8	10	Fayette Co., IA	John M. McMillen	John M. McMillen	1983	1424
202 6/8	25	25 1/8	17 2/8	5 3/8	8	10	Chautauqua Co., KS	John L. Brown	John L. Brown	1990	1424
202 6/8	24 7/8	22 6/8	15 5/8	4 4/8	12	10	Kenedy Co., TX	Alex Hixon	Alex Hixon	1993	1424

WHITETAIL DEER - NON-TYPICAL ANTLERS

Odocoileus virginianus virginianus and certain related subspecies

Score	Length of Main Beam R	L	Inside Spread	Circumference at Smallest Place Between Burr and First Point R	L	Number of Points R	L	Locality	Hunter	Owner	Date Killed	Rank
202 6/8	24 6/8	22	20	5 4/8	5 1/8	10	8	Hamilton Co., OH	Vernon Smith	Vernon Smith	1993	1424
202 6/8	27 2/8	27 6/8	22	5 5/8	5 5/8	7	6	McHenry Co., IL	Jim Kunde	Jim Kunde	2001	1424
202 6/8	25	24 7/8	19	5 2/8	4 7/8	12	7	Sullivan Co., IN	Tate R. Graves	Tate R. Graves	2002	1424
202 5/8	26 7/8	26 7/8	23 1/8	4 5/8	4 5/8	9	10	Kleberg Co., TX	Richard J. Mills	Richard J. Mills	1926	1432
202 5/8	26 3/8	23 6/8	18 6/8	4 7/8	5	9	11	Grafton Co., NH	Picked Up	Robert Hoffman	PR 1945	1432
202 5/8	22 5/8	23 4/8	18 4/8	4 6/8	4 6/8	16	9	Carroll Co., MS	George Galey	Terry Galey	1960	1432
202 5/8	29	29 3/8	20 6/8	4 7/8	4 7/8	10	9	Dane Co., WI	Ray S. Outhouse	Ray S. Outhouse	1964	1432
202 5/8	23	24	14 7/8	5 6/8	5 4/8	9	9	Unknown	Unknown	Ralph W. Jones	PR 1984	1432
202 5/8	26 2/8	26 2/8	19	4 6/8	4 6/8	8	11	Columbia Co., WI	William M. Bletsch	William M. Bletsch	1992	1432
202 5/8	25 1/8	25 6/8	18 7/8	5 3/8	4 7/8	9	9	Pike Co., IL	Brian M. Hill	Brian M. Hill	1994	1432
202 5/8	21	23	17 4/8	5 1/8	4 7/8	13	11	St. Louis Co., MN	Timothy Rosendahl	Timothy Rosendahl	1995	1432
202 5/8	24 5/8	24 7/8	17 4/8	4 1/8	4 1/8	9	10	Ripley Co., IN	James A. Leveille	James A. Leveille	1999	1432
202 5/8	29	28 2/8	20 5/8	4 7/8	4 7/8	7	8	Weld Co., CO	Picked Up	Matt Yocam	1999	1432
202 5/8	24 3/8	24 5/8	16 4/8	5 2/8	6	7	13	Johnson Co., IL	Timothy J. Boyle	Timothy J. Boyle	2001	1432
202 5/8	26	26 4/8	22 3/8	5 4/8	5 4/8	9	10	Spiritwood, SK	Donald J. Chamberlain	Donald J. Chamberlain	2001	1432
202 5/8	28 5/8	27 4/8	17 6/8	5 1/8	5 1/8	11	9	Muskingum Co., OH	Gil W. Gard II	Gil W. Gard II	2002	1432
202 4/8	24 7/8	24 6/8	23 6/8	4 7/8	5	10	11	Texas	Unknown	Buckhorn Mus. & Saloon, Ltd.	PR 1920	1445
202 4/8	24 4/8	24 6/8	16 4/8	5	4 7/8	13	12	Missoula Co., MT	Unknown	Robert A. Bracken	1962	1445
202 4/8	26 2/8	25 3/8	22 1/8	5 1/8	5 2/8	9	8	Spokane Co., WA	Unknown	Dick Rossum	PR 1989	1445
202 4/8	22 4/8	25 4/8	19 4/8	6 3/8	5 2/8	11	9	Boundary Co., ID	Picked Up	Steve Crossley	1990	1445
202 4/8	27 5/8	29 7/8	22 4/8	5 7/8	6 1/8	7	6	St. Louis Co., MN	Jeff P. Marczak	Jeff P. Marczak	1991	1445
202 4/8	26 5/8	27 1/8	20 6/8	6	6 1/8	8	9	Fond du Lac Co., WI	Warren Miller	Warren Miller	2000	1445
202 4/8	23 3/8	24 2/8	19 5/8	5 6/8	5 3/8	10	8	Pontotoc Co., MS	William H. Westmoreland	William H. Westmoreland	2001	1445
202 3/8	26	24 5/8	21 2/8	5 4/8	5 4/8	11	12	Koochiching Co., MN	George A. Balaski	George A. Balaski	1955	1452
202 3/8	26 4/8	26 1/8	17 5/8	4 7/8	5 2/8	8	9	Lac qui Parle Co., MN	Donald M. Nygaard	Donald M. Nygaard	1958	1452
202 3/8	26 1/8	27	20 7/8	5	5 1/8	10	10	Aitkin Co., MN	Joe Clarke	Joe Clarke	1960	1452
202 3/8	23 5/8	25 3/8	16 5/8	4 5/8	4 5/8	11	6	Crook Co., WY	Marshall Miller	Marshall Miller	1968	1452
202 3/8	26 2/8	25 4/8	18 1/8	4 7/8	4 6/8	10	7	Cass Co., MN	Hollace Brockoff	Hollace Brockoff	1976	1452
202 3/8	25 7/8	24 6/8	22 7/8	5 6/8	6	9	13	Delaware Co., OH	Duane E. Robinson	Duane E. Robinson	1980	1452
202 3/8	26 1/8	26 6/8	26 1/8	5 7/8	6 4/8	13	13	Washington Co., IL	Richard C. Keller	Richard C. Keller	1986	1452
202 3/8	23 1/8	26 3/8	20 1/8	6	5 7/8	11	6	Lake Co., MN	Lawrence J. Simonich	Lawrence J. Simonich	1987	1452
202 3/8	26 7/8	28 2/8	22 7/8	6 1/8	6 2/8	10	9	Douglas Co., MN	Timothy C. Sukke	Timothy C. Sukke	1988	1452
202 3/8	26 4/8	26 1/8	19	4 5/8	4 5/8	9	8	Thomas Co., GA	Rolf Kauka	Rolf Kauka	1991	1452
202 3/8	27 5/8	27 2/8	24 1/8	5	5 1/8	9	7	Bond Co., IL	Douglas E. Hays	Douglas E. Hays	1992	1452
202 3/8	26 7/8	26 3/8	25 2/8	4 3/8	4 7/8	8	9	Chisago Co., MN	John W. Holmblad	John W. Holmblad	1992	1452
202 3/8	25 2/8	24 2/8	19 5/8	4 6/8	4 7/8	13	12	Allen Co., KS	John F. Pfeiffer	John F. Pfeiffer	1998	1452

Score	Main Beam R	Main Beam L	Inside Spread	Circ. R	Circ. L	Points R	Points L	Locality	Hunter	Owner	Date Killed	Rank
202 3/8	24	25 7/8	18 3/8	4 4/8	4 4/8	9	8	Houston Co., TX	Clint M. Croft	Clint M. Croft	1999	1452
202 3/8	27 2/8	27 5/8	22 4/8	5	5	11	15	Keweenaw Co., MI	Bernard J. Jackovich	Bernard J. Jackovich	2000	1452
202 2/8	21 6/8	22 4/8	22	5 1/8	4 6/8	12	9	Fergus Co., MT	Harold K. Stewart	Harold K. Stewart	1948	1467
202 2/8	25 1/8	24 7/8	19 2/8	4 7/8	5 2/8	9	9	East Kooteney, BC	Andrew W. Rosicky	Andrew W. Rosicky	1956	1467
202 2/8	26 1/8	23 1/8	26 6/8	5 2/8	6 2/8	8	10	Waldo Co., ME	James A. Tripp, Sr.	James A. Tripp, Sr.	1959	1467
202 2/8	28 4/8	28 3/8	20 1/8	5 7/8	5 6/8	12	7	Oglethorpe Co., GA	J. Richard Mocko	J. Richard Mocko	1983	1467
202 2/8	27 6/8	26 2/8	19 3/8	5 7/8	5 1/8	9	9	Louisa Co., IA	Robert L. McFadden	Robert L. McFadden	1986	1467
202 2/8	25 4/8	24 3/8	17 5/8	5 1/8	5	13	9	Lenawee Co., MI	Fredrick M. Hood, Jr.	Fredrick M. Hood, Jr.	1988	1467
202 2/8	25 5/8	25 3/8	17	6 3/8	6	9	8	Pike Co., IL	Picked Up	George R. Metcalf	1996	1467
202 2/8	22 5/8	22 2/8	13 6/8	5 5/8	5 7/8	8	6	Crow Wing Co., MN	Michael L. Daly	Michael L. Daly	2000	1467
202 2/8	25	25 4/8	18 6/8	5 2/8	5 3/8	11	6	Audrain Co., MO	Barbara L. Blackmore	Barbara L. Blackmore	2001	1467
202 2/8	25 5/8	25 2/8	19 5/8	5 1/8	5	9	11	Mitchell Co., GA	Tommy S. Burford	Tommy S. Burford	2001	1467
202 1/8	25 1/8	26 4/8	22 6/8	5	4 7/8	8	9	Zehner, SK	Lee Danison	Lee Danison	1958	1477
202 1/8	26 1/8	25 4/8	19 3/8	6 2/8	6 1/8	10	8	Gary, SD	Dennis Cole	Dennis Cole	1960	1477
202 1/8	25 4/8	25 4/8	19 1/8	4 6/8	4 5/8	15	9	Pennington Co., MN	R. Scott Sorvig	R. Scott Sorvig	1980	1477
202 1/8	28 7/8	28 1/8	16 7/8	5 4/8	5 6/8	7	7	Oktibbeha Co., MS	Oliver H. Lindig	Oliver H. Lindig	1983	1477
202 1/8	27 5/8	27 2/8	15	6 2/8	6 1/8	9	11	Peoria Co., IL	Leonard A. Asbell	Leonard A. Asbell	1993	1477
202 1/8	27 7/8	27	21 6/8	4 7/8	4 7/8	12	11	Holt Co., MO	Gary F. Hoeper	Gary F. Hoeper	1997	1477
202 1/8	26	26 3/8	20	5 3/8	5 3/8	8	10	Whitefish Lake, AB	Bill Yaceyko	Bill Yaceyko	1997	1477
202 1/8	26 7/8	26 7/8	24 4/8	6 4/8	6 5/8	11	11	Jewell Co., KS	Rex A. Morgan	Rex A. Morgan	1998	1477
202 1/8	23 7/8	24 4/8	19 3/8	6 4/8	6 5/8	9	9	Wright Co., MN	Picked Up	Jacob Burley	1999	1477
202 1/8	29 3/8	28	25	5 2/8	5 3/8	9	10	Wood Co., OH	Wynn A. Brinker	Wynn A. Brinker	2001	1477
202 1/8	26 3/8	27	22 5/8	6 1/8	6 1/8	6	9	Bayfield Co., WI	Native American	Bass Pro Shops	1960	1477
202	28 6/8	27 3/8	15 5/8	6	5 6/8	12	7	Nodaway Co., MO	Richard L. Stewart	Richard L. Stewart	1972	1487
202	26 7/8	27	23 4/8	5 2/8	5 2/8	13	10	Powell Co., KY	Hershel Ingram	Hershel Ingram	1980	1487
202	26 6/8	28 6/8	26 6/8	5	5	8	10	Knox Co., ME	Skip Black	Skip Black	1981	1487
202	25 3/8	19 6/8	18 3/8	6 3/8	5 5/8	10	9	Monona Co., IA	Gary W. Anfinson	Gary W. Anfinson	1988	1487
202	24	24 3/8	19 2/8	5 4/8	5 4/8	12	12	Roberts Co., SD	Ronnie A. Bucklin	Ronnie A. Bucklin	1988	1487
202	25	24 6/8	14 7/8	7 2/8	6 6/8	8	15	Platte Co., MO	Steven Richardson	Steven Richardson	1991	1487
202	23 6/8	24 1/8	23 5/8	5 2/8	5 1/8	9	8	Manito Lake, SK	Barry Manchester	Barry Manchester	1992	1487
202	24 1/8	23 5/8	18	4 7/8	5 7/8	16	10	Pushmataha Co., OK	Lucas Young	Lucas Young	1993	1487
202	20 4/8	22 4/8	17 4/8	6 1/8	6	12	8	Macon Co., MO	Larry Allen	Bill J. Timms	1994	1487
202	26 1/8	26 1/8	22 7/8	5 2/8	5 1/8	9	8	Guthrie Co., IA	Donald E. Jensen	Ronald E. Jensen	1995	1487
202	26 4/8	26 4/8	18 5/8	5	4 4/8	8	9	Callaway Co., MO	Marc E. Meng	Marc E. Meng	1995	1487
202	27 4/8	27 1/8	20	6	6	8	7	Tippecanoe Co., IN	Stephen L. Burkhalter	Stephen L. Burkhalter	1997	1487
202	28 4/8	28 3/8	20 5/8	4 4/8	4 5/8	11	8	Roseau Co., MN	Picked Up	Phillip C. Larson	1999	1487
202	26 1/8	25 7/8	17 7/8	5 7/8	5 7/8	8	7	Falls Co., TX	Rudy Garcia	Rudy Garcia	2000	1487
201 7/8	25	24 1/8	14 5/8	4 4/8	4 4/8	12	8	Itasca Co., MN	Lewis Rocco, Sr.	Lewis R. Rocco, Jr.	1944	1502
201 7/8	27	26 5/8	21	5 6/8	5 6/8	9	8	Michigan	Unknown	Steve Crossley	1945	1502
201 7/8	25 4/8	28	19 7/8	5 4/8	5 4/8	9	7	Winnebago Co., IA	Unknown	Peter G. Weiss	PR 1957	1502
201 7/8	28	23 3/8	23 4/8	5 4/8	5 6/8	11	8	Burmis, AB	Joe Tapay	Joe Tapay	1964	1502
201 7/8	24 2/8	24 2/8	22	6	6	11	11	Todd Co., KY	Russell E. Carver	Russell E. Carver	1966	1502
201 7/8	29 4/8	24 2/8	17 2/8	5 1/8	5 1/8	11	7	Itasca Co., IA	Picked Up	J. Gorden & G. Dopp	1981	1502
201 7/8	28 2/8	27	17 4/8	5 5/8	5 3/8	7	7	Louisa Co., IA	Jason Gapinski	Jason Gapinski	1987	1502
201 7/8	27	25 2/8	20 1/8	5 1/8	5	9	8	Anderson Co., KS	Arthur O. Bell	Arthur O. Bell	1990	1502
201 7/8	26 1/8	25 3/8	20 2/8	4 6/8	4 6/8	8	7	Kiowa Co., KS	Jimmie L. Spencer	Jimmie L. Spencer	1991	1502
201 7/8	27 4/8	25 5/8	16	6 1/8	6 1/8	7	8	Pembina River, AB	Gordon Modanese	Gordon Modanese	1995	1502
201 7/8	28 4/8	26 3/8	24	5 2/8	5 1/8	13	9	New London Co., CT	Henry M. Konow, Jr.	Henry M. Konow, Jr.	2000	1502

WHITETAIL DEER - NON-TYPICAL ANTLERS
Odocoileus virginianus virginianus and certain related subspecies

Score	Length of Main Beam R	L	Inside Spread	Circumference at Smallest Place Between Burr and First Point R	L	Number of Points R	L	Locality	Hunter	Owner	Date Killed	Rank
201 6/8	24 1/8	24 6/8	19 3/8	4 2/8	4 1/8	12	12	Texas	Unknown	Buckhorn Mus. & Saloon, Ltd.	PR 1920	1513
201 6/8	23 3/8	23 4/8	19 7/8	4 6/8	4 4/8	10	10	Custer Co., SD	Unknown	Kenny Spring	PR 1940	1513
201 6/8	25 7/8	24 4/8	16 3/8	6 5/8	6 7/8	9	18	Unknown	Unknown	Ray Panaro	PR 1960	1513
201 6/8	25 1/8	25	19 4/8	5 2/8	5 4/8	7	8	Minnesota	Unknown	Larry D. Bollier	1969	1513
201 6/8	24	24	17 6/8	6	6	17	15	Wilkinson Co., MS	Jimmy Ashley	Jimmy Ashley	1985	1513
201 6/8	25 2/8	24 6/8	18 7/8	5 7/8	5 6/8	8	7	Van Buren Co., IA	Randy Kramer	Randy Kramer	1989	1513
201 6/8	29	25 6/8	25	5 5/8	5 7/8	8	11	Plamondon, AB	Steve K. Swinhoe	Steve K. Swinhoe	1996	1513
201 5/8	25 5/8	24 3/8	17 2/8	4 3/8	4 4/8	9	9	Cass Co., MN	Guy Chisholm	Charles F. Green	1945	1520
201 5/8	24 2/8	24 7/8	21	5	5	8	8	Brown Co., SD	Wallace Labisky	D.J. Hollinger & B. Howard	1962	1520
201 5/8	27 6/8	22 3/8	20 5/8	5 6/8	5 5/8	8	12	Sisseton, SD	Truman M. Nelson	Truman M. Nelson	1967	1520
201 5/8	27	26 6/8	18	5 6/8	5 6/8	15	16	Charlevoix Co., MI	Robert V. Doerr	Robert V. Doerr	1973	1520
201 5/8	25	24 7/8	17 1/8	5 2/8	5 1/8	10	8	Ohaton, AB	Curtis R. Siegfried	Curtis R. Siegfried	1976	1520
201 5/8	25 1/8	24 7/8	19 7/8	6 3/8	6 1/8	7	8	Baraga Co., MI	Dennis D. Bess	Dennis D. Bess	1981	1520
201 5/8	27	26	18 3/8	5 5/8	5 6/8	7	10	Johnson Co., IA	Duane E. Papke	Duane E. Papke	1981	1520
201 5/8	25 2/8	26 6/8	21 6/8	4 7/8	5	10	10	Howard Co., MO	Gregory A. O'Brian	Gregory A. O'Brian	1983	1520
201 5/8	26 4/8	26 2/8	24 7/8	5 1/8	5	8	8	Clinton Co., MO	David E. Eads	David E. Eads	1989	1520
201 5/8	24 2/8	24 6/8	16 6/8	5 6/8	5 5/8	15	9	Kane Co., IL	Keith R. Kampert	Keith R. Kampert	1991	1520
201 5/8	23 5/8	22 7/8	20 3/8	4 6/8	4 6/8	11	11	Candle Lake, SK	Brian F. Prior	Brian F. Prior	1993	1520
201 5/8	29 6/8	28 2/8	22	5 6/8	5 4/8	10	9	Madison Co., IA	Raymond Dawson	Raymond Dawson	1994	1520
201 5/8	26 1/8	25 3/8	21 1/8	5 2/8	5 4/8	6	10	Roanoke Co., VA	James D. Scott	James D. Scott	1994	1520
201 5/8	25 6/8	26 3/8	19 7/8	5 1/8	5 1/8	13	8	Sheboygan Co., WI	Darren T. Winter	Darren T. Winter	1995	1520
201 5/8	28 6/8	28 4/8	19 1/8	4 7/8	4 7/8	10	10	Sumner Co., KS	Jeremy A. Schroeder	Jeremy A. Schroeder	1996	1520
201 5/8	26 3/8	25 7/8	16 2/8	5 7/8	5 7/8	9	13	Tama Co., IA	Rod L. Waschkat	Rod L. Waschkat	2001	1520
201 4/8	22 3/8	23 3/8	16 5/8	4 1/8	4 2/8	9	8	Campbell Co., SD	Edward J. Torigian	J.D. Andrews	1957	1536
201 4/8	22 5/8	23	15 4/8	4 3/8	4 4/8	8	8	Monroe Co., AR	Hugh Erwin	Randy Erwin	1962	1536
201 4/8	25 2/8	23 1/8	16 6/8	4 5/8	5 2/8	14	13	Stevens Co., WA	Robert W. Newell	Robert W. Newell	1963	1536
201 4/8	28 5/8	28 1/8	22 1/8	5 3/8	5 1/8	8	9	Brown Co., NE	R.L. Tinkham	R.L. Tinkham	1965	1536
201 4/8	29 7/8	28 5/8	19 7/8	5 2/8	5 4/8	10	10	Hubbard Co., MN	Duane G. Lorsung	Duane G. Lorsung	1973	1536
201 4/8	22	29 3/8	23 3/8	6 7/8	6	9	8	Barber Co., KS	Joe Ash	Joe Ash	1975	1536
201 4/8	28 5/8	25 6/8	18 3/8	6 7/8	6 7/8	7	7	Flathead Co., MT	Barry L. Wensel	Barry L. Wensel	1976	1536
201 4/8	28 3/8	27 6/8	17 7/8	4 6/8	4 7/8	7	8	Clayton Co., IA	Paul C. Crawford	Paul C. Crawford	1987	1536
201 4/8	24 7/8	26 1/8	20 2/8	6 6/8	6 3/8	8	8	Allamakee Co., IA	Daniel J. Gallagher	Daniel J. Gallagher	1989	1536
201 4/8	22 4/8	21 2/8	14	5 2/8	5 6/8	13	13	Wayne Co., MO	David L. Hays	David L. Hays	1992	1536
201 4/8	25 6/8	25	21 4/8	5 5/8	5 5/8	10	9	Douglas Co., MN	Gerald F. Hoppe	Gerald F. Hoppe	1992	1536
201 4/8	25 4/8	25 5/8	19 3/8	4 7/8	5	9	9	Ebel Creek, SK	Barry D. Koshman	Barry D. Koshman	1992	1536
201 4/8	25 5/8	24 4/8	19 6/8	5 7/8	6	11	13	Fulton Co., IL	John R. Rosas	John R. Rosas	1994	1536

Score	Main Beam R	Main Beam L	Inside Spread	Circ. R	Circ. L	Points R	Points L	Locality	Hunter	Owner	Date
201 4/8	25 7/8	25 1/8	18 7/8	5 7/8	6 4/8	7	9	Sumner Co., KS	Bradley A. Smith	Bradley A. Smith	1994
201 4/8	29	28 4/8	21 1/8	6	5 7/8	8	9	Dane Co., WI	Susan Clack	Picked Up	1995
201 4/8	23 3/8	22 6/8	21 1/8	5 2/8	5 2/8	14	9	Athabasca, AB	Aldo B. Zanon	Aldo B. Zanon	1995
201 4/8	29 7/8	28 7/8	22	7	6 2/8	12	10	Shawnee Co., KS	J.S. Smith	J.S. Smith	1999
201 4/8	28	26 7/8	20 2/8	5 6/8	5 6/8	13	11	Jackson Co., IL	Mark D. Ralph	Mark D. Ralph	2000
201 4/8	25	25 7/8	23 4/8	5 4/8	5 2/8	9	14	Jefferson Co., PA	James D. Rowles	James D. Rowles	2000
201 4/8	27 1/8	27 7/8	18	5 4/8	5	9	9	Dauphin Co., PA	Darron A. Erdman	Darron A. Erdman	2002
201 3/8	23 1/8	23 1/8	20 2/8	5 3/8	5	13	13	Monroe Co., AR	Jerry Griggs	Jerry Griggs	2002
201 3/8	23 5/8	24 1/8	17 3/8	5 4/8	5 3/8	11	14	Wakulla Co., FL	Clark Durrance	Clark Durrance	1941
201 3/8	24 1/8	24 6/8	18 1/8	4 5/8	4 6/8	12	10	Dickinson Co., MI	Mary J. Wellman	Ludvic Riihimaki	1948
201 3/8	26 5/8	26 3/8	18 4/8	5 2/8	5 2/8	10	8	St. Louis Co., MN	Andrew G. Groen	Andrew G. Groen	1958
201 3/8	25 7/8	25 7/8	21 3/8	4 6/8	4 6/8	16	11	Bonner Co., ID	Leroy Coleman	Leroy Coleman	1960
201 3/8	21 1/8	21 6/8	18 5/8	5 6/8	5 5/8	11	9	Concordia Parish, LA	G.O. McGuffee	G.O. McGuffee	1963
201 3/8	26 4/8	26 4/8	19 3/8	5 3/8	5 3/8	13	9	Swift Co., MN	Joel T. Schmidt	Joel T. Schmidt	1973
201 3/8	26 6/8	26 6/8	15 7/8	5 6/8	5 2/8	15	17	Pushmataha Co., OK	Maurice Jackson	Maurice Jackson	1975
201 3/8	24 5/8	24 5/8	19	5 2/8	5 2/8	12	10	Queen Anne's Co., MD	Franklin E. Jewell	Franklin E. Jewell	1978
201 3/8	24 7/8	24 7/8	15	4 7/8	4 6/8	6	11	Monona Co., IA	Thomas R. Flynn	Thomas R. Flynn	1989
201 3/8	28 2/8	28 2/8	20	5 4/8	5 5/8	9	9	Kiowa Co., CO	Dale A. Dilulo	Dale A. Dilulo	1991
201 3/8	29	29 3/8	20 4/8	5 6/8	4 5/8	9	9	Donovan, SK	Glen E. Kristoff	Glen E. Kristoff	1992
201 3/8	26 6/8	26 6/8	20 2/8	5 2/8	4 6/8	14	12	Grayson Co., TX	Donnie M. Brewer	Donnie M. Brewer	1995
201 3/8	25 5/8	25 2/8	16 7/8	5	5	9	8	Morton Co., ND	Paul R. Shannon	Paul R. Shannon	1995
201 3/8	24 4/8	24 6/8	21 6/8	5 4/8	5 4/8	10	7	Greene Co., OH	Richard D. Steen	Richard D. Steen	1996
201 3/8	24 6/8	25	18 4/8	5 7/8	5 3/8	9	9	De Kalb Co., MO	Charles F. Christensen	Charles F. Christensen	1998
201 3/8	30 4/8	30 6/8	20 7/8	6 4/8	6 2/8	6	9	Mitchell Co., KS	Terry L. Fiala	Terry L. Fiala	1998
201 3/8	25 4/8	25 3/8	18 6/8	5 3/8	5 2/8	9	9	Le Flore Co., OK	William M. Russell	William M. Russell	2001
201 3/8	25 7/8	25 1/8	22 6/8	4 2/8	4 1/8	9	12	Washington Co., MS	Shelby R. Barrett, Jr.	Shelby R. Barrett, Jr.	2002
201 3/8	24 5/8	24 5/8	21	5	5 1/8	13	10	Licking Co., OH	Ty L. Yoho	Ty L. Yoho	2002
201 2/8	26 7/8	26 7/8	16	5 7/8	5 4/8	17	14	Pennington Co., MN	Glenn Tasa	Glenn Tasa	1940
201 2/8	25 1/8	24 6/8	18 1/8	5 5/8	5 3/8	12	10	Dickinson Co., MI	Gene R. Barlament	Unknown	1948
201 2/8	26 7/8	23 4/8	22 4/8	4 5/8	4 6/8	13	13	San Saba Co., TX	Ted J. Bode	Ted J. Bode	1965
201 2/8	24 6/8	25 2/8	17 5/8	4 2/8	4 2/8	8	7	Cumberland Co., KY	Ewing Groce	Ewing Groce	1968
201 2/8	23 4/8	28	16 5/8	4 7/8	4 7/8	10	7	Itasca Co., MN	Cecil L. Johnson	Cecil L. Johnson	1976
201 2/8	30 6/8	26 3/8	23 1/8	5 4/8	4 6/8	11	10	Coshocton Co., OH	Lou L. Rogers	Lou L. Rogers	1979
201 2/8	26 3/8	28 5/8	16 2/8	4 7/8	5 5/8	12	9	McLeod River, AB	Roy Schueler	Roy Schueler	1992
201 2/8	28 5/8	21 1/8	19 5/8	5 5/8	5 4/8	10	9	High Prairie, AB	Leo Morawski	Leo Morawski	1997
201 2/8	21 1/8	24 7/8	18 6/8	5 4/8	5	8	8	Dawes Co., NE	Cole Emmett	Cole Emmett	1998
201 2/8	24 7/8	24 1/8	21 4/8	5	5 4/8	12	5	Lorain Co., OH	D. Cody Kelch	D. Cody Kelch	1999
201 2/8	24 1/8	23 6/8	18 6/8	5 3/8	5 1/8	8	11	Jefferson Co., IL	Dwight N. Pfeiffer	Dwight N. Pfeiffer	1999
201 1/8	23 6/8	25 7/8	16 5/8	5 2/8	5 1/8	8	9	Arkansas Co., AR	Daniel B. Bullock	Daniel B. Bullock	1953
201 1/8	25 7/8	28 2/8	21 2/8	4 6/8	4 5/8	9	9	Unknown	Larry D. Bollier	Unknown	PR 1957
201 1/8	28 2/8	29 2/8	16 3/8	5 2/8	5 2/8	9	11	Slope Co., ND	J.D. Andrews	Arthur Hegge	1961
201 1/8	29 2/8	23	14 5/8	5 1/8	4 6/8	13	16	Westmoreland Co., PA	Richard K. Mellon	Richard K. Mellon	1966
201 1/8	21 6/8	25	20 4/8	6 4/8	6 1/8	10	12	Freeborn Co., MN	Jim Palmer	Jim Palmer	1972
201 1/8	23	25 3/8	18 2/8	4 7/8	5	8	7	Butler Co., NE	James L. Sklenar	James L. Sklenar	1973
201 1/8	25	20 3/8	20 3/8	4 2/8	4	10	9	Lincoln Co., AR	H.R. Morgan, Jr.	H.R. Morgan, Jr.	1977
201 1/8	25 3/8	26 1/8	20 1/8	5 1/8	5 1/8	9	9	Jackson Co., MI	Steven G. Crocker	Steven G. Crocker	1989
201 1/8	19 3/8	28	20 6/8	5 7/8	5 6/8	3	10	Carroll Co., IL	Mel Landwehr	Mel Landwehr	1991
201 1/8	20 3/8	26 7/8	16 5/8	4 2/8	4 2/8	11	9	King Edward Lake, BC	Reiny Lippert	Reiny Lippert	1994

Score	Length of Main Beam R	L	Inside Spread	Circumference at Smallest Place Between Burr and First Point R	L	Number of Points R	L	Locality	Hunter	Owner	Date Killed	Rank
201 1/8	23 6/8	23 2/8	15 5/8	6 1/8	6 3/8	11	11	Jackson Co., IL	Allen S. Casten	Allen S. Casten	1996	1587
201 1/8	27 5/8	25 5/8	21 1/8	5 2/8	5 2/8	7	9	Coffey Co., KS	Lance W. Jacob	Cabela's, Inc.	2000	1587
201	22 4/8	22 7/8	15 2/8	5 3/8	5 3/8	14	12	Delta Co., MI	Ernest B. Fosterling	Ernest B. Fosterling	1953	1599
201	28 5/8	26 4/8	18 4/8	4 7/8	5	11	10	Becker Co., MN	Gill S. Gigstead, Jr.	Gill S. Gigstead, Jr.	1964	1599
201	25 7/8	26 4/8	20 3/8	4 4/8	4 5/8	9	13	Cessford, AB	Russell C. Chapman	Russell C. Chapman	1966	1599
201	27 1/8	27 6/8	21 4/8	5 4/8	5 5/8	11	8	Mercer Co., IL	Gerald L. Olson	Gerald L. Olson	1972	1599
201	28	27	21 3/8	4 7/8	5	11	8	Empress, AB	David Booker	David Booker	1979	1599
201	26 1/8	25	22 5/8	4 6/8	4 6/8	10	7	Crawford Co., WI	Lloyd C. Rickleff	Lloyd C. Rickleff	1989	1599
201	25 4/8	26 1/8	22 2/8	5 7/8	5 7/8	9	9	Wilkinson Co., GA	E. Dwaine Davis	E. Dwaine Davis	1990	1599
201	22 1/8	25 6/8	15 4/8	5 1/8	7 2/8	6	13	Jasper Co., MO	Picked Up	Richard Morris	1991	1599
201	24 7/8	25 5/8	17 3/8	6 4/8	6 1/8	9	9	Guthrie Co., IA	Patrick Thompson	Patrick N. Thompson	1996	1599
201	22 6/8	27 4/8	20 5/8	5 3/8	5 6/8	16	13	Delaware Co., OH	Charles W. Henderson	Charles W. Henderson	1997	1599
201	25 7/8	26 4/8	22 1/8	4 5/8	4 4/8	11	13	Cooke Co., TX	Michael W. Lang	Michael W. Lang	1997	1599
201	24 2/8	24	16 5/8	6	5 6/8	12	9	Republic Co., KS	Bucky D. Barber	Bucky D. Barber	2000	1599
201	27	26 2/8	20 4/8	5 7/8	5 5/8	9	12	Pottawatomie Co., KS	M. Evan Porterfield	M. Evan Porterfield	2002	1599
200 7/8	22 5/8	28 4/8	18 6/8	4 5/8	4 6/8	10	9	Lawrence Co., AR	E.B. Ivie	Jimmy Huskey	1928	1612
200 7/8	26 7/8	24 5/8	15 6/8	4 2/8	4 6/8	9	13	Unknown	Unknown	Robert J. Werner	PR 1940	1612
200 7/8	23 4/8	24 5/8	20 1/8	5 3/8	5 2/8	9	8	Mandan, ND	Virgil Chadwick	Peter Voigt	1957	1612
200 7/8	23	23 7/8	19	4 7/8	4 6/8	11	9	Rusk Co., WI	Gerald Cleven	Gerald Cleven	1963	1612
200 7/8	26 1/8	26 4/8	18	5 2/8	5 1/8	10	11	Desha Co., AR	Edgar Farmer	Harold Farmer	1963	1612
200 7/8	23 4/8	24 3/8	21	4 4/8	4 5/8	11	10	Kleberg Co., TX	Picked Up	John A. Larkin	1982	1612
200 7/8	24	22 5/8	22 1/8	5 1/8	6 3/8	8	7	Davis Co., IA	R.G. Pettit & W. Van Mersberger	Roger G. Pettit	1988	1612
200 7/8	25 3/8	25 1/8	20	5 1/8	5 2/8	10	12	Morgan Co., KY	Gregory Powers	Gregory Powers	1989	1612
200 7/8	26 1/8	22 7/8	18 3/8	4 7/8	5 1/8	8	13	Davison Co., SD	Louis W. Cooper	Louis W. Cooper	1990	1612
200 7/8	23 6/8	19 4/8	20	4 5/8	4 5/8	13	14	Pulaski Co., AR	Lyle K. Sinkey	Lyle K. Sinkey	1994	1612
200 7/8	27 1/8	25 4/8	23 6/8	5 5/8	5 4/8	7	8	Muscatine Co., IA	William L. Brockert	William L. Brockert	1998	1612
200 7/8	23 1/8	23 7/8	19 6/8	4 4/8	4 2/8	11	9	Langlade Co., WI	Jordan Halverson	Jordan Halverson	1998	1612
200 7/8	28	29 7/8	19	5	4 7/8	11	9	Cochrane, AB	Terry L. Raymond	Terry L. Raymond	2001	1612
200 6/8	24 1/8	24 3/8	17 6/8	5	5	11	9	Juneau Co., WI	Anchor Nelson	Bass Pro Shops	1946	1625
200 6/8	28	28 1/8	22	5 6/8	5 5/8	15	12	Clay Co., MN	Unknown	Richard L. Meyer	1975	1625
200 6/8	24 4/8	24	18 2/8	5 1/8	5	10	8	Morrison Co., MN	Elmer J. Hollenkamp	Elmer J. Hollenkamp	1977	1625
200 6/8	24 7/8	25 7/8	25 1/8	6 4/8	6 6/8	9	11	Wapello Co., IA	Rod A. McKelvey	Rod A. McKelvey	1983	1625
200 6/8	25 1/8	26	13 7/8	6 5/8	6 5/8	8	10	Saskatchewan	Picked Up	Ron Lavoie	1989	1625
200 6/8	27 1/8	26 2/8	17 1/8	4 4/8	4 3/8	11	9	Coahuila, MX	M.S. Mac Collum	M.S. Mac Collum	1992	1625
200 6/8	25 6/8	24 4/8	18	4 7/8	4 6/8	16	12	Okanogan Co., WA	Fred R. Miller	Fred R. Miller	1993	1625

Score	Main Beam R	Main Beam L	Inside Spread	Circ. R	Circ. L	Points R	Points L	Locality	Hunter	Owner	Date Killed	Rank
200 6/8	25 2/8	25 7/8	22 3/8	6	6 1/8	7	10	Oktibbeha Co., MS	Pamela Reid-Rhoades	Will Sanders	1993	1625
200 6/8	26 5/8	25	16 7/8	4 6/8	4 6/8	8	8	Wapello Co., IA	Michael W. Garber	Michael W. Garber	1996	1625
200 6/8	28	26 2/8	19 3/8	6	6	9	10	Sarpy Co., NE	Mark A. Dillon	Mark A. Dillon	2001	1625
200 6/8	23 6/8	23 6/8	16 3/8	4 6/8	4 4/8	11	9	Uvalde Co., TX	James R. Schroeder	James R. Schroeder	2003	1625
200 5/8	28	27 6/8	22 1/8	5 6/8	5 2/8	8	7	Jackson Co., OH	Glenn McCall	Glenn McCall	1970	1636
200 5/8	26 2/8	26 7/8	18 6/8	5 7/8	5 6/8	10	7	Washington Co., IA	Bruce Guy	Bruce Guy	1973	1636
200 5/8	26 6/8	26 1/8	18 7/8	4 5/8	4 7/8	7	9	Clayton Co., IA	Dorrance Arnold	Dorrance Arnold	1977	1636
200 5/8	24 6/8	26 2/8	14	5 4/8	5 5/8	6	9	Texas Co., OK	Jeffery T. Wright	Jeffery T. Wright	1987	1636
200 5/8	26 5/8	24 6/8	22 2/8	5 5/8	5 5/8	10	9	Harper Co., KS	Robert A. Thomas	Robert A. Thomas	1990	1636
200 5/8	24 5/8	25 3/8	20 3/8	5 5/8	5 3/8	11	9	Mitchell Co., IA	Dean A. Beyer	Dean A. Beyer	1991	1636
200 5/8	26 2/8	23 5/8	19 5/8	5 4/8	5 2/8	8	9	Pembina Valley, MB	Claude R.J. Chappellaz	Claude R.J. Chappellaz	1992	1636
200 5/8	23 4/8	25 2/8	18 3/8	5 2/8	4 6/8	8	11	Madison Co., IA	Steve A. Marsh	Steve A. Marsh	1994	1636
200 5/8	27 2/8	24 1/8	18 4/8	5 4/8	5 2/8	7	8	Grayson Co., TX	Forrest L. Robertson	Forrest L. Robertson	1995	1636
200 5/8	25 5/8	25 5/8	20 6/8	4 7/8	5	10	10	Iowa Co., IA	Michael L. Ealy	Michael L. Ealy	1998	1636
200 5/8	25 5/8	25 3/8	19 6/8	5	5	14	8	Woods Co., OK	Aaron R. Sheik	Aaron R. Sheik	1998	1636
200 5/8	22 1/8	26 2/8	17 1/8	5	5 1/8	16	10	Adams Co., IL	Edward B. Tucker	Edward B. Tucker	1999	1636
200 5/8	29 6/8	23 5/8	16 1/8	5 3/8	5 4/8	9	10	Lewis Co., MO	Bennett E. Nation	Bennett E. Nation	2000	1636
200 5/8	23 5/8	29 7/8	18 6/8	5 5/8	6	8	9	Clinton Co., OH	Robert C. Sargent	Robert C. Sargent	2002	1636
200 5/8	25 2/8	23 2/8	19 6/8	5 7/8	4 4/8	8	6	Barber Co., KS	Rick Behrends	Rick Behrends	2003	1636
200 4/8	25 1/8	28	21 1/8	4 5/8	6 1/8	9	9	Uvalde Co., TX	W.S. Gordon	1st State Bank of Uvalde	1923	1651
200 4/8	24 5/8	23 5/8	23	6 1/8	6	10	6	Brentford, SD	S.C. Mitchell	S.C. Mitchell	1948	1651
200 4/8	26 2/8	28	19 6/8	6	5 4/8	12	10	Wainwright, AB	Paul Pryor	Paul Pryor	1968	1651
200 4/8	27	26 2/8	19 7/8	5 4/8	4 2/8	8	10	Geauga Co., OH	Rudy C. Grecar	Rudy C. Grecar	1969	1651
200 4/8	25 5/8	27 1/8	19 6/8	4 1/8	5 7/8	8	8	Kleberg Co., TX	Charles Hoge	Charles Hoge	1976	1651
200 4/8	23 1/8	24 6/8	22	5 5/8	4 5/8	10	8	Clearwater Co., MN	Ronald O. Halvorson	Ronald O. Halvorson	1987	1651
200 4/8	27 4/8	24	16 6/8	4 5/8	4 7/8	11	7	Howard Co., IA	Victor J. Buresh	Victor J. Buresh	1990	1651
200 4/8	25 6/8	27	19 2/8	5 3/8	5 5/8	9	9	Clinton Co., MO	R. Rea Norton	R. Rea Norton	1991	1651
200 4/8	26	23 5/8	21 1/8	5 5/8	5 5/8	7	6	Sawyer Co., WI	Gary A. Haus	Gary A. Haus	2000	1651
200 4/8	27 3/8	23 6/8	17 7/8	5 4/8	4 4/8	13	9	Allamakee Co., IL	Bruce L. Schuttemeier	Bruce L. Schuttemeier	2000	1651
200 4/8	24 6/8	26	16	4 4/8	5 5/8	8	11	Menominee Co., WI	Michael G. Firgens	Michael G. Firgens	2001	1651
200 4/8	24	27 3/8	20 4/8	5 1/8	5 3/8	8	7	Webb Co., TX	James Robison	James Robison	2003	1651
200 3/8	27	27 2/8	18	5 5/8	4 4/8	10	10	Crook Co., WY	Paul L. Wolz	Paul L. Wolz	1967	1663
200 3/8	25	22 1/8	18 6/8	5	4 6/8	8	8	Lake of the Woods Co., MN	Mark H. Hagen	Mark H. Hagen	1974	1663
200 3/8	25 3/8	27	19 1/8	4 3/8	5	11	10	Tuscarawas Co., OH	Michael D. Korns, Sr.	Michael D. Korns, Sr.	1978	1663
200 3/8	25 6/8	25	24 5/8	4 6/8	4 7/8	9	7	Knox Co., OH	Albert Hall	Albert Hall	1983	1663
200 3/8	29 1/8	28	17 4/8	6 4/8	5 1/8	6	8	Nez Perce Co., ID	Tim C. Baldwin	Tim C. Baldwin	1987	1663
200 3/8	20 1/8	25 5/8	21 4/8	5 2/8	5 3/8	8	10	Fremont Co., WY	Wallace M. Oldman	Wallace M. Oldman	1989	1663
200 3/8	22 1/8	25 3/8	20 4/8	4 6/8	5 5/8	7	8	Logan Co., CO	Picked Up	Dennis D. Reid	1994	1663
200 3/8	24 7/8	25 6/8	20 3/8	5 1/8	5 6/8	13	11	Branch Co., MI	Mitchell S. Brock	Mitchell S. Brock	1995	1663
200 3/8	24 4/8	29 1/8	21 3/8	5 3/8	5 6/8	6	10	Marion Co., IA	Louis L. Floden	Louis L. Floden	1996	1663
200 3/8	24 7/8	20 1/8	13 4/8	4 4/8	4 4/8	9	9	Powder River Co., MT	Levi Mitchell	Levi Mitchell	1996	1663
200 3/8	23 6/8	21 4/8	21 5/8	5 4/8	6 6/8	10	9	Keya Paha Co., NE	Charles V. Stroud	Charles V. Stroud	1998	1663
200 3/8	26 2/8	20 1/8	15 3/8	4 6/8	4 7/8	7	11	Boone Co., MO	Kevin B. Sample	Kevin B. Sample	1999	1663
200 3/8	24 4/8	24 7/8	20 7/8	6 6/8	5 6/8	8	7	Lancaster Co., NE	Tyler Fountain	Tyler Fountain	2000	1663
200 3/8	24 7/8	24 2/8	19 3/8	4 7/8	5 4/8	11	9	Washington Co., NE	Elton O. Jones	Elton O. Jones	2002	1663
200 3/8	23 6/8	24 4/8	18 5/8	5 6/8	7 6/8	13	10	Sauk Co., WI	Rob Horton	Rob Horton	2003	1663
200 2/8	25	25 7/8	21 5/8	5 6/8	4 7/8	10	11	Swift Co., MN	George Piotter	George Piotter	1983	1678
200 2/8	26	26 2/8	19	5 2/8	5 2/8	13	14	Delaware Co., OH	Franklin D. Ronk	Franklin D. Ronk	1990	1678

WHITETAIL DEER - NON-TYPICAL ANTLERS
Odocoileus virginianus virginianus and certain related subspecies

Score	Length of Main Beam		Inside Spread	Circumference at Smallest Place Between Burr and First Point		Number of Points		Locality	Hunter	Owner	Date Killed	Rank
	R	L		R	L	R	L					
200 2/8	26 7/8	27 4/8	20 2/8	5 5/8	5 5/8	8	8	Wyandot Co., OH	Anthony Gentile	Anthony Gentile	1991	1678
200 2/8	26 4/8	26 2/8	25	4 5/8	4 4/8	9	9	Live Oak Co., TX	E.W. Douglass	E.W. Douglass	1993	1678
200 2/8	24 4/8	24 5/8	19 5/8	4 5/8	4 4/8	12	11	Koochiching Co., MN	Jack Karsnia	Jack Karsnia	1994	1678
200 2/8	28	28 5/8	25 3/8	5 6/8	5 6/8	7	7	La Salle Co., IL	James A. Carr	James A. Carr	1999	1678
200 2/8	25 6/8	26 4/8	22 5/8	5 2/8	5 2/8	6	8	Athabasca, AB	John M. Gibbs	John M. Gibbs	2000	1678
200 2/8	26 6/8	26 7/8	21 6/8	4 5/8	4 5/8	8	7	Greenup Co., KY	Eric E. Sparks	Eric E. Sparks	2000	1678
200 2/8	26 1/8	26 3/8	18 1/8	5 5/8	5 4/8	8	10	Isanti Co., MN	Michael W. Shattuck	Michael W. Shattuck	2001	1678
200 2/8	29 2/8	29 1/8	23 7/8	5 7/8	5 3/8	8	9	Marion Co., KY	Chris Lyvers	Chris Lyvers	2002	1678
200 1/8	27	26 4/8	21 7/8	5 6/8	5 5/8	9	9	Itasca Co., MN	Clyde Sucher	James Davidson	1926	1688
200 1/8	26	24 2/8	23	6	6	11	12	Parrsboro, NS	Allison Smith	Edward B. Shaw	1960	1688
200 1/8	27 3/8	26 6/8	21 2/8	4 7/8	5 1/8	12	12	Kandiyohi Co., MN	Robert J. Custer	Robert J. Custer	1966	1688
200 1/8	24 3/8	24 5/8	20 4/8	5	5	9	8	Blaine Co., NE	Pauline C. Sander	Pauline C. Sander	1983	1688
200 1/8	24 3/8	25 4/8	18 2/8	5 1/8	5 2/8	12	7	Dallas Co., AL	H. Lloyd Morris	H. Lloyd Morris	1989	1688
200 1/8	27 1/8	27 4/8	23	6 2/8	6 4/8	7	11	Smoky Lake, AB	Brent Weber	Brent Weber	1991	1688
200 1/8	23 5/8	24 1/8	17	5 6/8	5 5/8	10	8	Parke Co., IN	Chris Ebersole	Chris Ebersole	1992	1688
200 1/8	25 4/8	26 3/8	20 3/8	5 2/8	5	8	9	Indian Lake, SK	Glen Lantz	Glen Lantz	1992	1688
200 1/8	25	28 3/8	23 5/8	5 3/8	5 4/8	8	9	Macoupin Co., IL	John M. Ragusa	John M. Ragusa	1992	1688
200 1/8	26 3/8	26 7/8	20 7/8	5 2/8	5 1/8	11	9	St. Louis Co., MN	Picked Up	John R. Steffes, Sr.	1992	1688
200 1/8	28 5/8	27	19 3/8	5 1/8	5 3/8	12	7	Ogle Co., IL	Theodore H. Hysell	Theodore H. Hysell	1993	1688
200 1/8	31	30	22 2/8	4 6/8	4 5/8	8	9	Coshocton Co., OH	Edward J. Page	Edward J. Page	1993	1688
200 1/8	26 2/8	24 4/8	19 3/8	4 6/8	4 6/8	10	13	Holt Co., MO	Bruce Copsey	Bruce Copsey	1994	1688
200 1/8	29 5/8	29	18 5/8	5 4/8	5 3/8	10	7	Dallas Co., IA	Andy J. Lounsbury	Andy J. Lounsbury	1996	1688
200 1/8	27 1/8	27 2/8	23 2/8	6	6 3/8	11	9	Marion Co., OH	Brent E. Dorfe	Brent E. Dorfe	1999	1688
200 1/8	24 3/8	24 3/8	19 5/8	5 3/8	5 4/8	8	11	Marion Co., IA	Boyd L. Mathes	Boyd L. Mathes	2002	1688
200 1/8	28 3/8	28 6/8	18 7/8	4 5/8	4 5/8	8	8	Colquitt Co., GA	Jacky R. Stanfill	Jacky R. Stanfill	2002	1688
200	25 1/8	25 4/8	18 4/8	4 7/8	4 5/8	11	10	Outlook, SK	Earl B. Schmitt	Earl B. Schmitt	1966	1705
200	26 2/8	25 2/8	21 7/8	5 4/8	5 7/8	12	12	Todd Co., MN	James J. Carr	James J. Carr	1978	1705
200	25 3/8	26	19	4 6/8	4 7/8	11	10	Clay Co., IA	Picked Up	IA Dept. of Natl. Resc.	1987	1705
200	19 5/8	18 1/8	17 1/8	4 7/8	5 1/8	6	11	Crook Co., WY	Ralph R. Van Beck	Ralph R. Van Beck	1989	1705
200	27	25 6/8	22 3/8	5 4/8	5 2/8	11	12	Boone Co., IN	John E. Wright	John E. Wright	1989	1705
200	24 6/8	25	20 5/8	5 4/8	5 4/8	9	10	Monona Co., IA	Picked Up	Timothy C. Ashley	PR 1990	1705
200	25 5/8	26 1/8	18 2/8	4 6/8	4 6/8	9	7	Stearns Co., MN	David L. LaVoi	David L. LaVoi	1990	1705
200	22 5/8	18 7/8	20 1/8	5 5/8	5 5/8	12	6	Stevens Co., WA	Ronald F. Barber	Ronald F. Barber	1991	1705
200	26 6/8	25 6/8	17 5/8	5 4/8	5 3/8	10	8	Baca Co., CO	David Sanford	David Sanford	1996	1705
200	26 3/8	26 3/8	20 3/8	5 7/8	6	6	8	Otter Tail Co., MN	Timothy J. Kapphahn	Timothy J. Kapphahn	1998	1705
200	26 3/8	26 3/8	21 2/8	4 7/8	4 7/8	10	8	Nance Co., NE	Gale Sup	Gale Sup	1998	1705

Score	Length R	Length L	Inside Spread	Circ. R	Circ. L	Pts R	Pts L	Locality	Hunter	Owner	Date	Rank
200	25 2/8	24 4/8	18 2/8	4 7/8	5 1/8	10	7	James River, AB	Picked Up	Chad Lenz	1999	1705
200	23 3/8	24 1/8	23 1/8	5	5	8	9	Lake of the Prairies, SK	Phil Olshewski	Phil Olshewski	1999	1705
200	21 6/8	22 7/8	18 4/8	5	4 7/8	10	12	Buffalo Co., WI	John E. Blanchar	John E. Blanchar	2000	1705
200	28 6/8	30 2/8	19 5/8	5 4/8	5 4/8	9	8	Breckenridge, KY	James Bowles	James Bowles	2000	1705
200	27	26 4/8	23 4/8	5 7/8	5 6/8	8	10	Clayton Co., IA	Michael A. Hinzman	Michael A. Hinzman	2000	1705
200	27 7/8	27 1/8	22 5/8	5 1/8	5 4/8	8	10	Lake Co., IN	John E. Quinlan	John E. Quinlan	2002	1705
199 7/8	20 1/8	20 1/8	19	6	5	6	14	Queens Lake, NB	George Lacey	Wendell Lacey	1915	1722
199 7/8	28 5/8	28 1/8	19 1/8	5 1/8	6	7	8	Hickory Co., MO	Darwin L. Stogsdill	Darwin L. Stogsdill	1971	1722
199 7/8	27	27	19 7/8	6	5	8	8	Peesane, SK	Pete Prosofsky	Pete Prosofsky	1982	1722
199 7/8	24 5/8	24 5/8	19 7/8	5 2/8	5 4/8	8	11	Knox Co., IL	Rodney G. Eklund	Rodney G. Eklund	1990	1722
199 7/8	28 6/8	28 6/8	16 6/8	6 4/8	6 4/8	10	12	Vernon Co., WI	D. & K.D. McClurg	D. & K.D. McClurg	2001	1722
199 7/8	27 2/8	26 5/8	19 2/8	5 2/8	4 2/8	7	8	Meigs Co., OH	Cody R. Boothe	Cody R. Boothe	1970	1722
199 6/8	24	23 4/8	18 5/8	5 1/8	5 3/8	9	7	Harris Co., GA	Kenneth H. Brown	Kenneth H. Brown	1974	1727
199 6/8	23 3/8	23 3/8	17 4/8	5 1/8	6	9	9	Rochester, AB	James Weismantel	James Weismantel	1979	1727
199 6/8	25 2/8	25 2/8	15 5/8	6 3/8	5 2/8	13	12	Duck Mt., MB	Picked Up	Jim Whitt	PR 1986	1727
199 6/8	24 7/8	24 6/8	27	5 3/8	5 3/8	11	9	Musquodoboit River, NS	David W. Brown	David W. Brown	1993	1727
199 6/8	27 5/8	27 5/8	22 5/8	5 6/8	4 6/8	10	6	Edgar Co., IL	Brad Davis	Brad Davis	1996	1727
199 6/8	26 2/8	26 7/8	20 2/8	4 5/8	5 2/8	11	9	Crawford Co., WI	John M. Kane	John M. Kane	1996	1727
199 6/8	24	26 7/8	24	5	6	8	11	Red River Parish, LA	Jason I. Dupree	Jason I. Dupree	2001	1727
199 6/8	27 5/8	27 3/8	18 6/8	5 6/8	5 7/8	8	10	Licking Co., OH	Terry L. Garee	Terry L. Garee	2002	1727
199 6/8	23 5/8	24 7/8	21 2/8	6	5 1/8	8	7	Baraga Co., MI	William Simula	Kenneth J. Harjala	1925	1727
199 6/8	30 6/8	30	23	4 7/8	6 1/8	6	10	Jasper Co., GA	Hugh Barber	Donald A. Barber	1959	1727
199 5/8	27 7/8	29	19 4/8	6 3/8	4 6/8	8	6	Jefferson Co., WI	Jerome Stockheimer	Jerome Stockheimer	1968	1736
199 5/8	27 4/8	27 4/8	20 7/8	4 5/8	6 2/8	9	11	Hopkins Co., KY	Dwight L. Mason	Dwight L. Mason	1979	1736
199 5/8	22	25 2/8	18 4/8	6 2/8	5 4/8	9	12	Clinton Co., KS	Arlo M. Ketelsen	Arlo M. Ketelsen	1985	1736
199 5/8	27 3/8	27 7/8	23 2/8	5 2/8	4 7/8	8	9	Labette Co., KS	John L. Bryant	John L. Bryant	1987	1736
199 5/8	30 1/8	30 1/8	20 4/8	5	5 1/8	10	7	Hopkins Co., KY	Picked Up	James D. Spurlock	1988	1736
199 5/8	25 6/8	25 6/8	24 6/8	4 5/8	4 3/8	8	12	Pend Oreille Co., WA	John C. Kroker	John C. Kroker	1989	1736
199 5/8	24 6/8	24 6/8	19 4/8	4 1/8	5 6/8	10	8	Dinmit Co., TX	John T. Brannan III	John T. Brannan III	1992	1736
199 5/8	27 6/8	27 6/8	19 3/8	5 3/8	5 6/8	7	9	Jackson Co., OH	Jerry W. Butcher	Jerry W. Butcher	1992	1736
199 5/8	29 3/8	29 1/8	21	5 5/8	5 5/8	11	9	Douglas Co., MT	Timothy J. Hoel	Timothy J. Hoel	1999	1736
199 5/8	26 4/8	26 4/8	19 2/8	6 2/8	7 2/8	9	10	Unknown	Unknown	Harley L. Johnson	PR 2000	1736
199 5/8	27 2/8	27 3/8	19 7/8	6 4/8	5 4/8	10	20	Gregory Co., SD	Fred Gnirk	Adeline Gnirk	1958	1736
199 4/8	26 1/8	25 7/8	20 6/8	5 1/8	5 4/8	8	8	Aitkin Co., MN	Sanford Patrick	Sanford Patrick	1963	1748
199 4/8	25 2/8	25 2/8	17 6/8	5 4/8	5 3/8	10	10	St. Francois Co., MO	Unknown	Tom Williams	PR 1980	1748
199 4/8	23 6/8	23 6/8	17 5/8	5	5 1/8	13	11	Linn Co., IA	Henry A. Hull	Henry A. Hull	1984	1748
199 4/8	26 2/8	26 2/8	22 2/8	5 1/8	5	8	8	Sangamon Co., IL	Don J. Jilovec	Don J. Jilovec	1988	1748
199 4/8	28	28	21 6/8	5 1/8	6 1/8	10	6	Cross Co., AR	Kenneth J. Barlow	Kenneth J. Barlow	1991	1748
199 4/8	28 3/8	28 4/8	22 4/8	5 1/8	5 4/8	9	15	Columbia Co., WI	Picked Up	William Loyd, Jr.	1992	1748
199 4/8	26 2/8	26 2/8	21 2/8	5	5 6/8	9	7	Seneca Co., OH	Cameron L. Gramse	Cameron L. Gramse	2001	1748
199 4/8	25 3/8	25 3/8	19 3/8	6	6	6	10	Chisago Co., MN	Gerald D. Terry	Gerald D. Terry	2002	1748
199 3/8	27 2/8	27 2/8	20 4/8	5 6/8	4 7/8	8	9	Clark Co., MO	Helmer Benson	Jeff Benson	1965	1757
199 3/8	28	28	21 6/8	6	4 5/8	10	8	Morgan Co., IL	Bob Arnold	Bob Arnold	1973	1757
199 3/8	26 4/8	26 4/8	20 1/8	4 7/8	5 3/8	11	9	Van Buren Co., MI	David W. Roehrs	David W. Roehrs	1979	1757
199 3/8	22 3/8	28	18 5/8	4 5/8	5 1/8	17	12		Michael A. DeRosa	Michael A. DeRosa	1989	1757
199 3/8	17 1/8	22 7/8	21 3/8	5 3/8	5 3/8	10	7	Iowa	Unknown	Charles E. Matthiesen	PR 1995	1757
199 3/8	24 7/8	20	17 3/8	5 2/8	5 2/8	9	8	Houston Co., MN	Picked Up	MN Dept. of Natl. Resc.	1997	1757
199 3/8	23 4/8	27 1/8	19 1/8	5 1/8	5 1/8	9	11	Penobscot Co., ME	Robert Raymond	Robert Raymond	1997	1757

Score	Length of Main Beam		Inside Spread	Circumference at Smallest Place Between Burr and First Point		Number of Points		Locality	Hunter	Owner	Date Killed	Rank
	R	L		R	L	R	L					
199 3/8	24 6/8	24 3/8	16	5	5	11	8	Logan Co., KY	Michael D. Forrest	Michael D. Forrest	1998	1757
199 3/8	24 1/8	24 1/8	28 1/8	5 1/8	5 2/8	8	9	Charette Lake, SK	Chris J. Weinkauf	Chris J. Weinkauf	1998	1757
199 3/8	20 6/8	22 2/8	15	6 6/8	6	13	9	Talbot Co., MD	William H. Shields	William H. Shields	2001	1757
199 2/8	24 6/8	25 4/8	14	5 2/8	5 1/8	13	9	Richland Co., MT	Aron Schmierer	Raymond Schmierer	1952	1767
199 2/8	21 4/8	21 5/8	20 6/8	5 6/8	5 6/8	8	8	Jasmin, SK	Richard Gill	Richard Gill	1958	1767
199 2/8	29 1/8	28 1/8	21 3/8	5	5	7	8	Todd Co., MN	Wayne V. Jensen	Wayne V. Jensen	1965	1767
199 2/8	28 7/8	27 3/8	23 5/8	5 2/8	5 2/8	7	9	Winston Co., AL	James W. Huckbay	James W. Huckbay	1973	1767
199 2/8	27 7/8	26 7/8	24 7/8	5 4/8	5 5/8	9	9	Delta Co., MI	Derwood Moore	Michael Waldvogel	1977	1767
199 2/8	28 3/8	28	18 5/8	6 3/8	6 3/8	8	8	Fountain Co., IN	Ken S. Harmeson	Ken S. Harmeson	1989	1767
199 2/8	26 3/8	25 5/8	19 7/8	5	4 7/8	8	10	Trigg Co., KY	Picked Up	Michael Shelton	1990	1767
199 2/8	25 3/8	25 1/8	23 4/8	5 7/8	7 1/8	7	8	Shannon Co., MO	Charles Martin	Doug Masner	1996	1767
199 2/8	26 1/8	26 3/8	18 1/8	5 2/8	5 3/8	11	11	Washtenaw Co., MI	Donald W. Bollinger	Donald W. Bollinger	1998	1767
199 2/8	26 1/8	26 4/8	19 4/8	5 3/8	5 2/8	7	8	Clayton Co., IA	Shane M. Hass	Shane M. Hass	2001	1767
199 2/8	23 4/8	22 3/8	15 5/8	4 6/8	4 4/8	14	13	Johnson Co., KY	Gary L. Music	Gary L. Music	2002	1767
199 1/8	26	26 4/8	19 5/8	6	6 2/8	7	9	Nodaway Co., MO	Sandra K. Gillenwater	Sandra K. Gillenwater	2002	1779
199 1/8	23 5/8	24 1/8	24 4/8	4 6/8	4 7/8	11	10	Billings Co., ND	Jake Braun	Jake Braun	1949	1779
199 1/8	26 3/8	26	24 1/8	5 4/8	5 2/8	11	11	Meade Co., SD	Donald Trohkimoinen	Donald Trohkimoinen	1966	1779
199 1/8	21 7/8	24 6/8	20	4 6/8	4 7/8	12	10	Clinton Co., NY	Unknown	William F. Mathieson	PR 1971	1779
199 1/8	25 2/8	25 7/8	17 4/8	5 1/8	5 2/8	10	13	St. Louis Co., MN	Orville Schultz	Orville Schultz	1978	1779
199 1/8	23 2/8	23 2/8	22 5/8	5 5/8	5 6/8	9	8	Smoky Lake, AB	Helmuth Ritter	Helmuth Ritter	1992	1779
199 1/8	28 3/8	26 6/8	21 3/8	6	5 7/8	10	8	Macoupin Co., IL	Jerry A. Dittmer	Jerry A. Dittmer	1994	1779
199 1/8	25 2/8	24 3/8	19 4/8	5	5	8	8	Morgan Co., CO	Michael L. Furolow	Michael L. Furolow	1997	1788
199 1/8	25 1/8	25 7/8	17 5/8	5 3/8	4 6/8	11	7	Lucas Co., IA	J.J. Keller & J.R. Keller	J.J. Keller & J.R. Keller	2000	1788
199 1/8	26 6/8	26 6/8	19 2/8	5 2/8	5 2/8	11	10	Richland Co., IL	Picked Up	Roy A. Albertson	2001	1788
199	22 7/8	21	17 7/8	5 3/8	5	13	7	Clark Co., WI	George Mashin	Douglas Wampole	1946	1788
199	23 2/8	22 4/8	15 2/8	5	5	10	9	Harrison Co., IA	Chester R. Hilton	Chester R. Hilton	1958	1788
199	25 1/8	26	19 2/8	5 5/8	5 6/8	9	6	Grattan Creek, AB	Torleif A. Larson	Torleif A. Larson	1968	1788
199	24 2/8	24 7/8	19 4/8	5	5 1/8	13	8	Penobscot Co., ME	Picked Up	Todd Affricano	1971	1788
199	25	24 6/8	16 3/8	5 3/8	5 6/8	9	8	Cottonwood Co., MN	Lane L. Horn	Lane L. Horn	1972	1788
199	27 6/8	27 1/8	22 3/8	5 2/8	5 3/8	8	8	Adams Co., IL	Jerry Schaller	Jerry Schaller	1974	1788
199	26 3/8	27 2/8	19 1/8	5 1/8	5	10	8	Yellow Medicine Co., MN	William A. Botten	William A. Botten	1976	1788
199	26 1/8	23 1/8	19 5/8	5 4/8	5 4/8	10	8	Jackson Co., IA	John T. Kremer	John T. Kremer	1983	1788
199	24 7/8	24 7/8	19 7/8	5	5	8	7	Westaskiwin, AB	John Miller	John Miller	1984	1788
199	23 7/8	23 7/8	18	4 4/8	4 3/8	8	9	Crawford Co., WI	Jeff Sheckler	Jeff Sheckler	1989	1788
199	29 6/8	28 4/8	20	7	6 6/8	8	10	Lake Co., IL	Steven Hysell	Steven Hysell	1994	1788
199	26 1/8	25 7/8	19 7/8	4 5/8	4 4/8	6	8	Vernon Co., WI	Manuel M. Bahr	Manuel M. Bahr	1995	1788

Score	Main Beam R	Main Beam L	Spread	Circ. R	Circ. L	Pts. R	Pts. L	Locality	Hunter	Owner	Date	Rank
199	27 7/8	27 2/8	18 4/8	5	4 6/8	7	7	Macoupin Co., IL	Jon D. DeNeef	Jon D. DeNeef	1995	1788
199	24 4/8	26	20	5 1/8	5	9	9	Harrison Co., IN	Timothy P. Uhl	Timothy P. Uhl	1995	1788
199	28 4/8	26 2/8	26 3/8	4 7/8	4 7/8	6	9	La Salle Co., IL	Hank J. Walsh III	Hank J. Walsh III	1995	1788
199	25 5/8	24 2/8	17 1/8	5 1/8	6	8	8	Qu'Apelle River, SK	Gilbert Brule	Gilbert Brule	1998	1788
199	25 2/8	24 5/8	21 2/8	6	5 3/8	9	10	Hancock Co., ME	Dale Henderson	Dale Henderson	1998	1788
199	25 5/8	24 1/8	18 5/8	5 6/8	5 3/8	13	13	Harrison Co., IA	Kody Wohlers	Kody Wohlers	1998	1788
198 7/8	24 4/8	24 7/8	24 7/8	5 3/8	7 3/8	7	9	Unknown	Unknown	Max E. Chittick	1900	1806
198 7/8	25	23 2/8	16 5/8	5 1/8	5 4/8	11	11	Weston Co., WY	G. Huls & B.L. Arfmann	Chester S. Jones	1973	1806
198 7/8	26 7/8	25 6/8	21 4/8	5 2/8	5 4/8	10	7	Chippewa Co., MN	Ray N. Strand	Ray N. Strand	1976	1806
198 7/8	29 2/8	28 3/8	24 6/8	4 7/8	4 6/8	3	7	Ripley Co., IN	William L. Wagner	William L. Wagner	1982	1806
198 7/8	24	24	22 3/8	5 6/8	5 4/8	9	7	Morse River, AB	Leo M. Schmaus	Leo M. Schmaus	1985	1806
198 7/8	27	27	17 7/8	4 6/8	4 6/8	11	13	Logan Co., KY	Oscar Howard	Oscar Howard	1989	1806
198 7/8	24 2/8	24 3/8	18 2/8	6 2/8	6 2/8	7	7	Pembina River, AB	Thomas Free	Thomas Free	1992	1806
198 7/8	28 5/8	28 4/8	21 1/8	6 2/8	4 7/8	5	5	Bollinger Co., MO	Picked Up	Michael W. Welker	1992	1806
198 7/8	25 4/8	25 4/8	18 4/8	4 7/8	5 2/8	13	10	Greene Co., IL	James M. Bowker	James M. Bowker	1995	1806
198 7/8	28 1/8	28 1/8	20 3/8	5 6/8	5 6/8	10	8	Richardson Co., NE	Kenneth L. Harmon	Kenneth L. Harmon	1995	1806
198 7/8	25 6/8	25 1/8	17 2/8	5 7/8	5 1/8	7	7	Pike Co., IL	James Kruczynski	James Kruczynski	1998	1806
198 7/8	25 2/8	25 1/8	19 6/8	5	6	6	13	Fulton Co., IL	Todd L. DeGroot	Todd L. DeGroot	1999	1806
198 7/8	26 7/8	24 4/8	18 6/8	6 7/8	5 4/8	11	14	Knox Co., OH	James T. Hlay	James T. Hlay	2002	1806
198 7/8	26 2/8	27 4/8	19 4/8	5 3/8	5 4/8	9	11	Randolph Co., IL	Mark E. Houba	Mark E. Houba	2002	1806
198 6/8	25 6/8	25 2/8	18 4/8	5 2/8	5 4/8	9	9	Aitkin Co., MN	John Baker	Don Anderson	1910	1820
198 6/8	28 4/8	25 4/8	21 4/8	4 3/8	4 3/8	8	9	Crow Wing Co., MN	Unknown	George W. Flaim	1965	1820
198 6/8	29 7/8	27 1/8	15 7/8	5 3/8	5 3/8	11	7	Fillmore Co., MN	Phillip S. Hansen	Phillip S. Hansen	1973	1820
198 6/8	24 6/8	25 3/8	24	6 2/8	5 7/8	5	9	Lake of the Woods Co., MN	Gerald K. Sorenson	Gerald K. Sorenson	1977	1820
198 6/8	28 6/8	28 4/8	23 2/8	5 6/8	5	9	5	Gallatin Co., KY	Thomas K. Ernst	Thomas K. Ernst	1978	1820
198 6/8	25 1/8	27 4/8	15 4/8	5	6 1/8	10	8	Buffalo Co., WI	Rod Buck	Rod Buck	1984	1820
198 6/8	26 2/8	26 2/8	17 3/8	6 1/8	6 2/8	10	8	James River, AB	Hans Van Vlaanderen	Hans Van Vlaanderen	1986	1820
198 6/8	25 4/8	24 7/8	19 2/8	6 2/8	4 3/8	11	13	Rappahannock Co., VA	Chris K. Foster	Chris K. Foster	1989	1820
198 6/8	25 5/8	24 7/8	19 3/8	4 7/8	5 1/8	10	8	Jefferson Co., WI	Picked Up	Wayne Perry	1989	1820
198 6/8	22 5/8	24 5/8	15	6 5/8	4 4/8	11	10	Peoria Co., IL	Roger Woodcock	Roger Woodcock	1989	1820
198 6/8	23 7/8	25 4/8	19 6/8	4 4/8	4 6/8	10	9	Randolph Co., IL	John A. Brown	John A. Brown	1992	1820
198 6/8	26 5/8	26 3/8	20	5 6/8	5 3/8	10	10	Buffalo Co., WI	Brady Weiss	Brady Weiss	1993	1820
198 6/8	23 3/8	23 1/8	17 3/8	4	6 1/8	12	11	Cherokee Co., TX	Randall L. Chandler	Randall L. Chandler	1994	1820
198 6/8	28 3/8	27 4/8	23 4/8	6 2/8	4 3/8	7	7	Rock Co., WI	Robert D. Adamson	Robert D. Adamson	1995	1820
198 6/8	20	20 6/8	17 4/8	4 3/8	5 1/8	9	9	Angelina Co., TX	B. Tyler Fenley	Daniel Fenley	1999	1820
198 6/8	26	24	16 7/8	5	5	19	9	Story Co., IA	Jarod J. Pedersen	Jarod J. Pedersen	1999	1820
198 6/8	26 7/8	26 4/8	17 7/8	4 6/8	4 6/8	12	11	Butler Co., IA	Harlan Schmadeke	Harlan Schmadeke	1999	1820
198 6/8	25	25	14 6/8	4 6/8	5 3/8	12	9	Greenwater Lake, SK	Picked Up	Don Kjelshus	2000	1820
198 6/8	28 3/8	22 2/8	15 1/8	5 3/8	5 4/8	11	9	Madison Co., IL	Eric W. Barach	Eric W. Barach	2001	1820
198 5/8	24 2/8	24 2/8	17 7/8	6 4/8	5 4/8	7	11	Hayward, WI	Unknown	Harold Burrows	PR 1920	1839
198 5/8	26 7/8	26 1/8	18 3/8	5 5/8	5 5/8	13	11	Iron Co., MI	Eino Macki	Bass Pro Shops	1930	1839
198 5/8	27 2/8	25 7/8	22 4/8	5 4/8	5 7/8	11	8	Morton Co., ND	Grant C. Starck	Grant C. Starck	1952	1839
198 5/8	26 1/8	26 6/8	22 2/8	5 7/8	6 7/8	10	6	Concordia Parish, LA	Raymond Cowan	Raymond Cowan	1961	1839
198 5/8	26 1/8	26 6/8	22 4/8	5 5/8	5	8	8	Webb Co., TX	Larry Bickham	Larry Bickham	1962	1839
198 5/8	26 2/8	25 2/8	17 4/8	4 7/8	5 2/8	7	6	Jackson Co., OH	Stanley Elam	Stanley Elam	1962	1839
198 5/8	25 3/8	22 2/8	23 2/8	5 4/8	5	6	10	Oconto Co., WI	Paul M. Krueger	Paul M. Krueger	1977	1839
198 5/8	23 6/8	22 2/8	17 7/8	5	4 6/8	10	14	Will Co., IL	William H. Rutledge	William H. Rutledge	1977	1839
198 5/8	25 6/8	25 6/8	21 3/8	5 7/8	5 5/8	12	9	Hamilton Co., IL	Thomas D. Flannigan	Thomas D. Flannigan	1989	1839

Score	Length of Main Beam R	L	Inside Spread	Circumference at Smallest Place Between Burr and First Point R	L	Number of Points R	L	Locality	Hunter	Owner	Date Killed	Rank
198 5/8	28 5/8	27 2/8	22 1/8	5 5/8	6 2/8	6	8	Franklin Co., IL	Freddie Cooper	Freddie Cooper	1990	1839
198 5/8	22	22	20 2/8	4 6/8	4 5/8	9	9	Dawson Creek, BC	Philip D. Springer	Philip D. Springer	1990	1839
198 5/8	25 4/8	23 5/8	18 2/8	6 3/8	6 2/8	7	9	Pleasantdale, SK	Picked Up	Don Kjelshus	PR 1992	1839
198 5/8	24 3/8	22 5/8	21 3/8	5 7/8	6 2/8	12	11	Otter Tail Co., MN	Roger A. LeBrun	Roger A. LeBrun	1992	1839
198 5/8	28 7/8	29 2/8	19 4/8	6 2/8	5 6/8	7	7	Ray Co., MO	Stephen D. Kirk	Stephen D. Kirk	1997	1839
198 5/8	24 6/8	24 1/8	15 6/8	3 7/8	3 7/8	8	9	Clay Co., TX	Glenn M. Lucas	Glenn M. Lucas	1997	1839
198 5/8	26 6/8	27	17 2/8	4 5/8	4 5/8	8	8	Jackson Co., IA	James M. Ruggeberg	James M. Ruggeberg	1997	1839
198 5/8	25 4/8	24 4/8	20 5/8	4 5/8	4 7/8	12	15	Oktibbeha Co., MS	Timothy P. Watson	Timothy P. Watson	1997	1839
198 5/8	26 6/8	27 6/8	20 4/8	7 2/8	6	10	8	Des Moines Co., IA	Craig R. Belknap	Craig R. Belknap	1998	1839
198 5/8	22	23 1/8	20 4/8	5 6/8	5 1/8	8	8	N. Saskatchewan River, SK	Robin McLean	Robin McLean	1998	1839
198 5/8	23 7/8	24 1/8	22 1/8	5	5	9	7	Turtle Mt., MB	Charles C. Dixon	Charles C. Dixon	1999	1839
198 5/8	23 7/8	24 6/8	20 2/8	4 6/8	4 6/8	10	10	Pulaski Co., MO	Donald R. McGraw	Donald R. McGraw	1999	1839
198 5/8	27 2/8	27	22 2/8	5 3/8	5 1/8	6	9	Kanabec Co., MN	Unknown	David G. Gagnon	1927	1860
198 4/8	25 2/8	25 6/8	19 2/8	4 5/8	4 6/8	10	11	Cheboygan Co., MI	Maurice G. Fullerton	Robert G. Fullerton	1943	1860
198 4/8	26 4/8	22 5/8	18 7/8	5 6/8	5 5/8	9	10	Clay Co., MN	F.W. Kolle	Kolle Farms, Inc.	1946	1860
198 4/8	26	26 4/8	21	4 4/8	4 6/8	13	9	Forest Co., WI	John Lehner	Eric Lehner	1946	1860
198 4/8	24 2/8	23 1/8	18	5 2/8	5 4/8	13	12	Cow Creek, WY	Thelma Martens	Thelma Martens	1951	1860
198 4/8	24	23 5/8	19	5 5/8	5 6/8	11	11	Itasca Co., MN	Wayne W. Blesi, Jr.	Wayne W. Blesi, Jr.	1968	1860
198 4/8	23 7/8	23 5/8	17 7/8	4 6/8	4 7/8	8	9	Iroquois Co., IL	Charles E. Crow	Charles E. Crow	1974	1860
198 4/8	26 2/8	24 2/8	21 5/8	4 7/8	4 6/8	7	8	Lincoln Co., MN	Dennis G. Geiken	Dennis G. Geiken	1980	1860
198 4/8	28 1/8	27 3/8	19 7/8	4 6/8	4 6/8	10	9	Madison Co., IA	Elvin H. Dickinson	Elvin H. Dickinson	1982	1860
198 4/8	22 6/8	26	21 1/8	5 2/8	4 5/8	12	8	Wheeler Co., GA	David Frost	David Frost	1983	1860
198 4/8	25	26 2/8	23 6/8	4 6/8	4 6/8	7	8	Webb Co., TX	Alvin C. Santleben, Jr.	Alvin C. Santleben, Jr.	1983	1860
198 4/8	26 1/8	26 2/8	22 5/8	6	5 4/8	8	8	Perry Co., OH	Donald J. Griggs	Donald J. Griggs	1988	1860
198 4/8	26 3/8	26 6/8	19 7/8	4 6/8	4 4/8	10	9	Arborfield, SK	Terry G. Haugo	Terry G. Haugo	1989	1860
198 4/8	24	23 7/8	21 2/8	4 5/8	4 3/8	8	7	Lake Co., MT	Mike Gouge	Jim G. Ferguson III	1990	1860
198 4/8	29	29 4/8	23 4/8	5	5 1/8	9	5	Missisquoi, QC	Mario L. Quintin	Mario L. Quintin	1990	1860
198 4/8	22 3/8	17 4/8	13 6/8	5 2/8	5 1/8	15	14	Hamilton Co., TX	Randy L. Wright	Randy L. Wright	1992	1860
198 4/8	21 6/8	25 2/8	15	7 2/8	7	13	8	Adams Co., IL	Rick L. Dormire	Rick L. Dormire	1993	1860
198 4/8	26 5/8	26 4/8	20 5/8	5 5/8	5 4/8	8	10	Meacham, SK	Darren B. Maroniuk	Darren B. Maroniuk	1993	1860
198 4/8	26 7/8	24 1/8	19 2/8	5 2/8	5 1/8	7	10	Wallace Co., KS	Kent E. Rains	Kent E. Rains	1993	1860
198 4/8	25 3/8	24 6/8	17 4/8	4 2/8	4 4/8	14	9	Kleberg Co., TX	Glenn Thurman	Glenn Thurman	1994	1860
198 4/8	25 5/8	25 2/8	17	5 3/8	5 2/8	11	8	Chautauqua Co., KS	Mark A. Shull	Mark A. Shull	1998	1860
198 4/8	29 4/8	29 5/8	24 6/8	5 4/8	5 6/8	10	7	Macoupin Co., IL	Brett E. Bridgewater	Brett E. Bridgewater	1999	1860
198 4/8	25 1/8	22 5/8	19 1/8	5 6/8	5 7/8	10	5	Smoky River, AB	Jim Boland	Jim Boland	2000	1860
198 4/8	26 1/8	25 3/8	19 6/8	5 6/8	6	8	7	Pottawattamie Co., IA	Picked Up	IA Dept. of Natl. Resc.	2000	1860

Score	Main Beam R	Main Beam L	Inside Spread	Circ. R	Circ. L	Points R	Points L	Locality	Hunter	Owner	Date Killed	Rank
198 4/8	28 2/8	27 4/8	19 4/8	6 7/8	6 4/8	11	10	Issaquena Co., MS	John T. Campbell	John T. Campbell	2001	1860
198 4/8	21 5/8	23	17 5/8	4 4/8	4 3/8	7	9	Rapides Parish, LA	William A. Jordan, Jr.	William A. Jordan, Jr.	2001	1860
198 3/8	25 7/8	27	20 3/8	5	5 1/8	9	8	Uvalde Co., TX	George Judson, Jr.	George Judson, Jr.	1958	1886
198 3/8	25 7/8	26 6/8	19 5/8	4 6/8	5	9	9	Rappahannock Co., VA	Collis W. Dodson, Jr.	Collis W. Dodson, Jr.	1966	1886
198 3/8	26 2/8	26 1/8	17 5/8	4 2/8	4 2/8	8	10	Montgomery Co., TN	Clarence McElhaney	Clarence McElhaney	1978	1886
198 3/8	25	24 5/8	22 4/8	5 2/8	5 1/8	8	9	Adams Co., IL	Eldie J. Miller	Eldie J. Miller	1980	1886
198 3/8	20 7/8	22 2/8	17 5/8	4 4/8	4 7/8	10	10	Nez Perce Co., ID	Milton R. Wilson	G. & J. Reed	1983	1886
198 3/8	27	25 6/8	21 6/8	5	4 7/8	10	9	Clark's Brook, NB	Bernard V. Sharp	Bernard V. Sharp	1985	1886
198 3/8	23 6/8	23 3/8	19 7/8	5 2/8	5 2/8	9	7	Pottawattamie Co., IA	Rodney P. Stahlnecker	Rodney P. Stahlnecker	1991	1886
198 3/8	25 3/8	24 4/8	18 1/8	5 2/8	5 2/8	7	10	Pike Lake, SK	Robert J. MacDonald	Robert J. MacDonald	1992	1886
198 3/8	24 4/8	24 4/8	20 5/8	5	5	9	6	Sherburne Co., MN	David J. Valerius	David J. Valerius	1997	1886
198 2/8	23 2/8	23 2/8	17 5/8	6 6/8	6 4/8	6	8	Pasqua Lake, SK	Trent Mattick	Trent Mattick	1998	1886
198 2/8	23 3/8	22 5/8	21 6/8	4 1/8	4 2/8	9	12	Crow Wing Co., MN	Harold B. Stotts	Harold B. Stotts	1941	1896
198 2/8	27 3/8	27 4/8	22 2/8	5	5	5	8	Raymore, SK	William Kobzey	Cabela's, Inc.	1958	1896
198 2/8	23 5/8	23 1/8	19 4/8	6 1/8	6 3/8	8	8	Rock Co., NE	Gerald M. Lewis	Gerald M. Lewis	1966	1896
198 2/8	27	26 2/8	21	5 7/8	5 7/8	8	9	Cass Co., MN	Timothy L. Anderson	Timothy L. Anderson	1987	1896
198 2/8	26 4/8	26 6/8	17 6/8	4 7/8	4 5/8	7	8	Madison Co., IA	Dan L. Bush	Dan L. Bush	1987	1896
198 2/8	24 6/8	24 6/8	16 3/8	4 6/8	5 1/8	10	15	Rock Co., NE	Picked Up	Dan L. Sandall	1987	1896
198 2/8	26 7/8	26 5/8	19 7/8	5 4/8	5 7/8	9	8	Decatur Co., IA	Julian J. Toney	Julian J. Toney	1991	1896
198 2/8	25 4/8	25	16 5/8	5 1/8	5 2/8	12	9	Osage Co., KS	Jerry L. Sand	Jerry L. Sand	1992	1896
198 2/8	25 4/8	26 1/8	21 6/8	6	5 2/8	12	11	Wayne Co., IA	Dan L. Bishop	Dan L. Bishop	1993	1896
198 2/8	25 4/8	24 7/8	20 6/8	4 6/8	6 2/8	9	8	Rochester, AB	Vern E. Alton	Vern E. Alton	1995	1896
198 2/8	27 2/8	28 7/8	21 3/8	5 6/8	5	8	9	Geauga Co., OH	Greg Raudenbush	Greg Raudenbush	1997	1896
198 1/8	25 5/8	25 5/8	16 6/8	5 2/8	5 7/8	11	10	Marinette Co., WI	Stephen R. Couveau	Stephen R. Couveau	2001	1896
198 1/8	22 5/8	21 7/8	16 6/8	5 2/8	5 3/8	9	9	Dogpound Creek, AK	Steve K. Thompson	Steve K. Thompson	2001	1896
198 2/8	27	28 1/8	19 1/8	5 1/8	4 5/8	9	7	Lewis Co., KY	Phillip R. Hall	Phillip R. Hall	2002	1896
198 2/8	27 3/8	28 3/8	23 3/8	6	5 3/8	8	8	Fairfield Co., OH	Rodney A. McManus	Rodney A. McManus	2002	1896
198 1/8	21 7/8	21 2/8	17	4 7/8	5	13	12	Nelway, BC	Edward John	Edward John	1935	1911
198 1/8	27 6/8	28 2/8	22 4/8	4 6/8	4 6/8	7	9	Harrison Co., OH	Roy Hines	Roy Hines	1959	1911
198 1/8	25 3/8	25	23	5 1/8	5 1/8	10	10	Koochiching Co., MN	Maris Stolcers	Maris Stolcers	1963	1911
198 1/8	27	27	20 2/8	5	5 4/8	10	7	Hocking Co., OH	Hugh Cox	Hugh Cox	1964	1911
198 1/8	24 6/8	24 3/8	19 6/8	5 5/8	5 4/8	10	9	Kootenai Co., ID	Frank J. Cheney	ID Dept. Fish & Game	1967	1911
198 1/8	26 3/8	26 6/8	22 6/8	5 3/8	4 6/8	10	10	Iron Co., WI	Ben Benzine	Timothy C. Ashley	1968	1911
198 1/8	25 6/8	26 2/8	20 2/8	4 6/8	5 5/8	12	8	Carrot River, SK	Wayne W. Karlin	Wayne W. Karlin	1989	1911
198 1/8	25	24 1/8	24 4/8	5 3/8	4 3/8	10	6	Unknown	Unknown	Rick Stover	PR 1990	1911
198 1/8	26 3/8	26 3/8	22 5/8	5 4/8	4 6/8	6	10	Lawrence Co., OH	Eugene Baisden	Eugene Baisden	1991	1911
198 1/8	30 1/8	29 5/8	22 4/8	5 6/8	5	8	8	Jefferson Co., OH	William H. Ferguson III	William H. Ferguson III	1992	1911
198 1/8	22 3/8	21 6/8	18	4 3/8	5 2/8	8	12	Calhoun Co., MI	William D. Vickers	William D. Vickers	1994	1911
198 1/8	29	28 5/8	18 5/8	4 6/8	5 5/8	9	13	Itasca Co., MN	Dennis C. Campbell	Dennis C. Campbell	1995	1911
198 1/8	28 3/8	26 5/8	20 5/8	5	5	12	14	Chippewa Co., MI	Timothy Spence	Timothy Spence	1995	1911
198 1/8	27 3/8	27 3/8	22 1/8	4 2/8	5	10	5	Kingman Co., KS	Harold W. Hellman	Harold W. Hellman	1997	1911
198 1/8	25 1/8	25 1/8	19 1/8	5 4/8	4 2/8	12	9	Kootenai Co., ID	Luke Finney	Luke D. Finney	1998	1911
198 1/8	25 2/8	25 2/8	16 4/8	5 4/8	5 4/8	11	8	Pike Co., IL	Picked Up	Sam Moore	1998	1911
198	27 5/8	26 5/8	21	6 1/8	6	8	9	Jefferson Co., WI	Charles E. Emery	Charles E. Emery	2001	1928
198	26 1/8	24 4/8	23	7 4/8	6 2/8	7	7	Valley Co., NE	Ivan Masher	Ivan Masher	1961	1928
198	25 5/8	25 2/8	17 5/8	6 2/8	6 4/8	9	9	Osage Co., KS	Joe A. Rose, Jr.	Joe A. Rose, Jr.	1977	1928
198	25 6/8	25 3/8	20 6/8	5 2/8	6 2/8	9	10	Mercer Co., OH	Werner H. Schmiesing	Werner H. Schmiesing	1979	1928
198	25 7/8	23 4/8	17 5/8	5	5	8	8	Assiniboine River, MB	James A. Roberts	James A. Roberts	1980	1928

WHITETAIL DEER - NON-TYPICAL ANTLERS

Odocoileus virginianus virginianus and certain related subspecies

Score	Length of Main Beam R	L	Inside Spread	Circumference at Smallest Place Between Burr and First Point R	L	Number of Points R	L	Locality	Hunter	Owner	Date Killed	Rank
198	28 6/8	27 3/8	21 7/8	5 2/8	5 4/8	8	10	Christian Co., IL	Jack B. Hartwig	Jack B. Hartwig	1987	1928
198	28 3/8	26 2/8	18 3/8	5 6/8	5 3/8	9	10	Edgar Co., IL	Aaron C. Bishop	Aaron C. Bishop	1990	1928
198	26	26 2/8	20	5	4 6/8	7	11	McLeod Co., MN	Owen L. Knacke	Owen L. Knacke	1990	1928
198	27	27 4/8	20 4/8	5 6/8	5 7/8	10	9	Jo Daviess Co., IL	Victor W. Rogers	Victor W. Rogers	1990	1928
198	25 4/8	22 3/8	20 5/8	5	5 1/8	9	12	Kipling, SK	Robert Lyons	Robert Lyons	1993	1928
198	24 3/8	24 1/8	13 5/8	5 4/8	6 2/8	11	12	Brown Co., SD	Paul J. Hill	Paul J. Hill	1994	1928
198	26 5/8	26 5/8	19 4/8	5 3/8	5 1/8	12	8	Meigs Co., OH	Jack Satterfield, Jr.	Jack Satterfield, Jr.	2000	1928
198	27 5/8	26 7/8	22 4/8	5	4 7/8	7	9	Holt Co., NE	Randy D. Sell	Randy D. Sell	2000	1928
198	27 1/8	25 5/8	17 3/8	5 5/8	6 3/8	9	7	Jefferson Co., IA	Jesse Rebling	Jesse Rebling	2001	1928
198	25 5/8	27 5/8	18 7/8	4 7/8	4 6/8	8	9	Jackson Co., IA	Jesse H. Smith	Jesse H. Smith	2001	1928
197 7/8	25 4/8	25	18 1/8	5	5	10	9	Clearwater Co., MN	Unknown	Danny L. Cole	PR 1975	1942
197 7/8	27 4/8	28 1/8	25	5 4/8	5 2/8	9	8	Cheyenne Co., NE	Reid Block	Reid Block	1984	1942
197 7/8	24 4/8	25	17 2/8	5	5	9	10	Keokuk Co., IA	Bradley J. Messenger	Bradley J. Messenger	1988	1942
197 7/8	25	25 5/8	25 1/8	5 3/8	5 4/8	12	11	St. John River, NB	James A. Perruso	James A. Perruso	1988	1942
197 7/8	24 7/8	24 6/8	19 6/8	5 4/8	5	10	9	Riley Co., KS	Gary L. Schroller	Gary L. Schroller	1990	1942
197 7/8	26 5/8	25 5/8	23 2/8	5 6/8	6	7	9	Eagle Creek, SK	Preston Haanen	Preston Haanen	1992	1942
197 7/8	22 2/8	23	19 2/8	5 1/8	5 1/8	8	12	Latah Co., ID	Dean C. Weyen	Dean C. Weyen	1992	1942
197 7/8	22 5/8	25 7/8	29 7/8	4 7/8	4 7/8	10	10	Cross Co., AR	Picked Up	Jimmy W. Rhodes	1993	1942
197 7/8	23 7/8	22 5/8	18	4 2/8	4 3/8	8	13	Hunt Co., TX	Wade Grimes	Wade Grimes	1994	1942
197 7/8	24 6/8	25 1/8	16 2/8	4 7/8	5	11	11	Great Sand Hills, SK	Craig Schwengler	Craig Schwengler	1996	1942
197 7/8	26 3/8	27	20 4/8	4 6/8	4 6/8	10	7	Madison Co., IA	Scott R. Busch	Scott R. Busch	1997	1942
197 7/8	26 2/8	27 2/8	19 6/8	7 1/8	6 1/8	10	7	Woods Co., OK	Steve Purviance	Steve Purviance	1997	1942
197 7/8	25	24 7/8	18 6/8	5 2/8	5 2/8	10	8	Aitkin Co., MN	Thomas N. Sauro	Thomas N. Sauro	1998	1942
197 7/8	26 2/8	26 3/8	17 7/8	5 6/8	5 5/8	7	6	Fishing Lake, SK	Nicole Hrycak	Nicole Hrycak	1999	1942
197 7/8	24 1/8	23 2/8	17 6/8	4 5/8	4 6/8	6	7	Willacy Co., TX	Clifton L. Smith	Garcia Estate	2000	1942
197 7/8	26 7/8	25 3/8	22	4 1/8	4 5/8	1	8	Richland Co., OH	James C. Carpenter	James C. Carpenter	2001	1942
197 7/8	28 7/8	27	21 2/8	5 2/8	4 5/8	8	6	Hardin Co., KY	Ellis E. Givens	Ellis E. Givens	2001	1942
197 6/8	23 5/8	26 2/8	20 2/8	5 2/8	5	10	8	Hunters, WA	Rachel Mally	Rachel Mally	1961	1959
197 6/8	25 6/8	26 4/8	17	5 3/8	5	9	11	Riceville, MT	James R. Eastman	James R. Eastman	1965	1959
197 6/8	24	24 4/8	18 4/8	5 1/8	5 4/8	10	7	Langham, SK	Leonard Waldner	Leonard Waldner	1967	1959
197 6/8	27 2/8	26 3/8	18 2/8	5	4 6/8	6	8	Harrison Co., MO	Rod L. Shain	Rod L. Shain	1985	1959
197 6/8	24 5/8	24 6/8	13 4/8	4 6/8	4 4/8	11	9	Prowers Co., CO	Samuel S. Pattillo	Samuel S. Pattillo	1988	1959
197 6/8	26	26 1/8	19 3/8	4 2/8	4 2/8	7	5	Box Elder Creek, SK	David A. Thomson	David A. Thomson	1991	1959
197 6/8	24 3/8	26 7/8	16	5 2/8	4 7/8	12	10	York Co., PA	Kevin R. Brumgard	Kevin R. Brumgard	1992	1959
197 6/8	26 7/8	27 7/8	16 6/8	4 5/8	4 6/8	8	12	Edmonson Co., KY	Picked Up	Rex Hurt	1992	1959
197 6/8	26 2/8	25 2/8	19 4/8	4 2/8	4 4/8	8	9	Dimmit Co., TX	Michael H. Oldfather	Michael H. Oldfather	1992	1959

Score	L. R	L. L	Inside Spread	Circ. R	Circ. L	Pts R	Pts L	Locality	Hunter	Owner	Date Killed	Date
197 6/8	23 6/8	23 5/8	20 6/8	5 3/8	5 5/8	9	10	Spy Hill, SK	William Gilchuk	William Gilchuk	1996	1959
197 6/8	31 4/8	30 4/8	23	5 3/8	5 4/8	11	9	Fairfield Co., OH	Bob Sink	Bob Sink	1997	1959
197 6/8	25 6/8	27 1/8	19 4/8	5 2/8	5 5/8	7	9	Fayette Co., IN	Boyd L. Lunsford	Boyd L. Lunsford	1998	1959
197 6/8	27 3/8	28	20 4/8	5 5/8	5 7/8	6	10	Preble Co., OH	Larry E. Hickman	Larry E. Hickman	1999	1959
197 6/8	27 4/8	27 1/8	21 1/8	4 7/8	5	9	9	Foam Lake, SK	Tom Taylor	Tom Taylor	1999	1959
197 6/8	24 5/8	22 6/8	18	4 5/8	4 5/8	21	16	Barber Co., KS	Barte G. Miller	Barte G. Miller	2002	1959
197 5/8	20	24	18	8 4/8	4 7/8	12	8	Luce Co., MI	Sid Jones	Jim Deavereaux	1917	1974
197 5/8	22 7/8	25 4/8	17 7/8	4 6/8	4 6/8	11	8	Sawyer Co., WI	Unknown	Brant J. Mueller	1940	1974
197 5/8	24 4/8	24 1/8	20 3/8	6 2/8	5 1/8	7	11	Sawyer Co., WI	James P. Borman	James P. Borman	1945	1974
197 5/8	23 3/8	23 4/8	15 6/8	5 7/8	5 6/8	10	9	Marathon Co., WI	Boots Greiner	Todd Rheinschmidt	1951	1974
197 5/8	31 5/8	32 3/8	25 2/8	5 1/8	5 1/8	5	6	Geauga Co., OH	Edward Dooner	Edward Dooner	1956	1974
197 5/8	24	24	17 5/8	5 2/8	4 6/8	7	7	Pennington Co., SD	Lynn Williams	Dick Rossum	1958	1974
197 5/8	28	28 2/8	21	5 7/8	5 6/8	10	7	Jo Daviess Co., IL	David H. Carpenter	David H. Carpenter	1962	1974
197 5/8	25 1/8	24 6/8	22 4/8	5 4/8	5 4/8	10	8	Blue Earth Co., MN	Daniel R. Nelson	Daniel R. Nelson	1981	1974
197 5/8	26 5/8	27 3/8	20 5/8	5	5	8	9	Monona Co., IA	Picked Up	Larry Koch	1987	1974
197 5/8	28	25 2/8	21 5/8	5 5/8	5 6/8	9	11	Adams Co., IL	Daniel J. Schlosser	Daniel J. Schlosser	1987	1974
197 5/8	28 4/8	29 3/8	22 5/8	5 1/8	4 5/8	10	8	Stephenson Co., IL	Richard M. Keller	Richard M. Keller	1988	1974
197 5/8	28 2/8	27 1/8	19	5 3/8	5 4/8	7	7	Thurston Co., NE	Picked Up	Rudy Reichelt	1989	1974
197 5/8	24 7/8	24 7/8	16 7/8	4 5/8	4 7/8	7	9	McDonough Co., IL	Jeffery W. Foxall	Jeffery W. Foxall	1990	1974
197 5/8	26	25 1/8	21 5/8	5 6/8	5 6/8	10	8	Morris Co., KS	John H. Payne	John H. Payne	1992	1974
197 5/8	26 5/8	27	20 5/8	5 2/8	5 2/8	10	8	Pierce Co., WI	Charles L. Wilkinson	Marilyn Wilkinson	1993	1974
197 5/8	24	24 6/8	16 4/8	4 7/8	5 1/8	9	8	Monroe Co., IA	Raymond F. Hinkel	Raymond F. Hinkel	1995	1974
197 5/8	25 2/8	26 2/8	22 6/8	5 2/8	5	9	10	Waldo Co., ME	Ronald A. Edwards	Ronald A. Edwards	1998	1974
197 5/8	26 5/8	23 1/8	17 1/8	5 1/8	5 1/8	9	10	McDonough Co., IL	Thad E. Powell	Thad E. Powell	1998	1974
197 5/8	26 3/8	23 1/8	22 4/8	4 7/8	4 6/8	9	11	Appanoose Co., IA	Bill R. Clark	Bill R. Clark	2001	1974
197 4/8	25	25 6/8	25	5 4/8	5 4/8	10	9	Pope Co., IL	Joe C. Schwegman	Joe C. Schwegman	1961	1993
197 4/8	25 5/8	26 4/8	25 5/8	5 1/8	5 3/8	11	7	Wainwright, AB	George Bauman	George Bauman	1967	1993
197 4/8	25	23 7/8	22 2/8	5	5 4/8	7	7	Johnson Co., IA	Dennis R. Ballard	Dennis R. Ballard	1971	1993
197 4/8	24 4/8	24 6/8	21 6/8	5 3/8	7	8	10	Chippewa Co., MN	Dean D. Anspach	Dean D. Anspach	1973	1993
197 4/8	25 7/8	25 5/8	20 1/8	6 1/8	6 1/8	8	10	Garfield Co., OK	Derald D. Crissup	Derald D. Crissup	1980	1993
197 4/8	25 3/8	26 3/8	16 7/8	5 3/8	5 1/8	6	8	Lyon Co., KS	John R. Clifton	John R. Clifton	1984	1993
197 4/8	27 3/8	26 3/8	18	4 6/8	4 7/8	10	8	Dooly Co., GA	Wayne Griffin	Wayne Griffin	1984	1993
197 4/8	26 3/8	26 3/8	19 6/8	5 1/8	5 3/8	7	7	Clay Co., SD	Curtis Gregg	Curtis Gregg	1988	1993
197 4/8	27	24 2/8	17 4/8	5 7/8	5 7/8	7	8	Comanche Co., KS	Allan Prasser	Brant J. Mueller	1989	1993
197 4/8	27 1/8	27	20 1/8	5 3/8	5 2/8	9	9	Boone Co., IA	Grant E. Saunders	Grant E. Saunders	1990	1993
197 4/8	26 6/8	26 4/8	19 1/8	5 1/8	4 6/8	10	8	Independence Co., AR	Terry L. Pease	Terry L. Pease	1993	1993
197 4/8	23 3/8	23	19 1/8	4 6/8	4 7/8	8	8	Lee Co., IA	Carl A. Bell	Carl A. Bell	1995	1993
197 4/8	26 5/8	25	19 6/8	5 5/8	6 3/8	9	8	Buffalo Co., WI	Dennis L. Mackeben	Dennis L. Mackeben	1995	1993
197 4/8	25 3/8	26 3/8	22 6/8	5 2/8	5 2/8	8	9	Tuscarawas Co., OH	Michael W. McKenzie	Michael W. McKenzie	1996	1993
197 4/8	29	29 5/8	27 2/8	5 4/8	5 4/8	9	9	Pike Co., IL	Donald Reynolds	Donald Reynolds	1997	1993
197 4/8	26	27	19 5/8	6 4/8	6 3/8	8	7	Vermilion Co., IL	Alan D. Hingson	Alan D. Hingson	1997	1993
197 4/8	27 3/8	25	17 5/8	4 3/8	4 4/8	10	9	Willow Creek, SK	Arie Vandertweel	Arie Vandertweel	1998	1993
197 4/8	25 6/8	27 3/8	20 5/8	5 3/8	5 4/8	8	8	Dore Lake, SK	Erwin W. Brown	Erwin W. Brown	2002	1993
197 4/8	26 1/8	26 2/8	21 3/8	4 2/8	4 3/8	11	12	Aroostook Co., ME	Robert W. Cameron, Jr.	Robert W. Cameron, Jr.	2002	1993
197 3/8	25 1/8	23 7/8	17 3/8	5 5/8	5 6/8	8	7	Iowa Co., WI	Roger S. Venden	Roger S. Venden	2002	1993
197 3/8	23 3/8	26 1/8	17 1/8	5 7/8	5 5/8	12	9	Harrison Co., MO	William M. White	William M. White	1948	1993
197 3/8	26	26	17 4/8	5 5/8	5 5/8	10	11	Stevens Co., WA	Coulston W. Drummond	Coulston W. Drummond	1948	2014
197 3/8	24 4/8	22 4/8	18 6/8	6 2/8	5 7/8	9	12	Buffalo Co., WI	Walter Mengelt	Timothy W. Trones	1957	2014

WHITETAIL DEER - NON-TYPICAL ANTLERS
Odocoileus virginianus virginianus and certain related subspecies

Score	Length of Main Beam R	L	Inside Spread	Circumference at Smallest Place Between Burr and First Point R	L	Number of Points R	L	Locality	Hunter	Owner	Date Killed	Rank
197 3/8	24	26 5/8	16 4/8	5 6/8	5 6/8	9	10	Newton Co., GA	R.H. Bumbalough	R.H. Bumbalough	1969	2014
197 3/8	27 3/8	26 3/8	20 4/8	5 2/8	5 2/8	8	9	Faribault Co., MN	Randy L. Sandt	Randy L. Sandt	1982	2014
197 3/8	22 2/8	23 7/8	21 6/8	5 6/8	5 1/8	14	10	Marshall Co., KS	Lloyd Wenzl	Lloyd Wenzl	1983	2014
197 3/8	26 5/8	27 2/8	16 5/8	5 1/8	5 1/8	8	14	Kittson Co., MN	Unknown	George W. Flaim	PR 1988	2014
197 3/8	26 3/8	26 7/8	17 3/8	5 1/8	5 2/8	10	12	Douglas Co., WI	Unknown	Wayne G. Nevar	PR 1988	2014
197 3/8	29 1/8	27 2/8	18	4 7/8	5 3/8	8	11	Anoka Co., MN	Dale M. Zimmerman	Dale M. Zimmerman	1990	2014
197 3/8	23 7/8	21 7/8	24	5 2/8	6	7	10	Gallia Co., OH	Jimmy W. Brumfield	Jimmy W. Brumfield	1992	2014
197 3/8	24 6/8	24 3/8	16 2/8	4 4/8	4 4/8	9	9	Cold Lake, SK	Anthony Clemenza, Jr.	Anthony Clemenza, Jr.	1994	2014
197 3/8	24 3/8	24 4/8	20 1/8	5 2/8	5 3/8	8	7	Clark Co., SD	Steven R. Frank	Steven R. Frank	1995	2014
197 3/8	24 6/8	24 6/8	16	6 6/8	7	8	17	Perry Co., IL	Dwayne Rogers	Dwayne Rogers	1996	2014
197 3/8	22	21 4/8	17 6/8	3 6/8	3 6/8	11	10	Hopkins Co., KY	Tim Capps	Brian Capps	1998	2014
197 3/8	23 5/8	24 2/8	18 2/8	5 5/8	5 5/8	10	12	Iowa Co., WI	Luke J. Leiterman	Luke J. Leiterman	1998	2014
197 3/8	21 4/8	20 5/8	18 5/8	4 7/8	5 3/8	12	11	Athabasca, AB	Clinton Peredery	Clinton Peredery	1999	2014
197 3/8	22 1/8	21	17 5/8	4 4/8	4 4/8	16	14	Mifflin Co., PA	Garry L. Forgy	Garry L. Forgy	2000	2014
197 3/8	28 5/8	27 6/8	21 6/8	6 4/8	5 2/8	16	14	Suffolk Co., NY	John E. Hansen	John E. Hansen	2001	2014
197 3/8	24 5/8	24 2/8	21 1/8	6 3/8	6 4/8	10	9	Black Hawk Co., IA	Michael R. Lichty	Michael R. Lichty	2002	2014
197 2/8	25 5/8	26 7/8	19	5 2/8	5 1/8	14	9	Washington Co., MN	Albert J. Cotton	Margie Barnett	1930	2032
197 2/8	26 2/8	26 6/8	20	5 2/8	5 1/8	10	7	Iron Co., WI	Unknown	Henry C. Gilbertson	PR 1940	2032
197 2/8	23 5/8	23 7/8	23 1/8	5 2/8	5	14	9	Vilas Co., WI	Unknown	Ross A. Manthey	1943	2032
197 2/8	27 4/8	26 5/8	21	5	5	8	9	Hancock Co., ME	Hollis Patterson	Reginald R. Clark	PR 1950	2032
197 2/8	22 6/8	23 1/8	20	6 2/8	5 6/8	13	10	Koochiching Co., MN	John Erickson	Marc M. Jackson	1951	2032
197 2/8	23 2/8	26 1/8	17 1/8	5 4/8	6 1/8	10	9	Stanton Co., NE	Peter Bartman III	Peter Bartman III	1963	2032
197 2/8	29 7/8	30	21 1/8	5 5/8	5 4/8	6	8	Douglas Co., MN	David S. Paulson	David S. Paulson	1966	2032
197 2/8	23	24	20	6 2/8	5 6/8	12	8	Chouteau Co., MT	J. Burton Long	J. Burton Long	1975	2032
197 2/8	27 4/8	26 3/8	20	5	5	10	11	Tiudish River, NS	Clayton Ward	Clayton Ward	1982	2032
197 2/8	24 5/8	24 3/8	18 5/8	4 4/8	4 3/8	9	14	Redvers, SK	Eugene M. Gazda	Eugene M. Gazda	1984	2032
197 2/8	23 4/8	24 4/8	23 4/8	4 5/8	4 7/8	10	11	Scott Co., IN	Wilson D. Barger	Wilson D. Barger	1991	2032
197 2/8	27	27 2/8	17 1/8	4 1/8	4 3/8	11	8	McCreary Co., KY	Curtis Morrow	Curtis Morrow	1996	2032
197 2/8	27 6/8	25 1/8	21	5 4/8	5 3/8	9	8	Sangamon Co., IL	Robert W. Penwell	Robert W. Penwell	1996	2032
197 2/8	23 7/8	23 5/8	15 5/8	4 7/8	4 6/8	15	14	Starr Co., TX	Matthew J. Arnold	Matthew J. Arnold	1997	2032
197 2/8	26 3/8	26 2/8	22 1/8	4 6/8	4 4/8	10	11	Winneshiek Co., IA	Richard M. Blaess	Richard M. Blaess	1997	2032
197 2/8	24 5/8	25	17 5/8	5	4 7/8	12	10	Stephens Co., OK	Bryan C. Walker	Bryan C. Walker	1997	2032
197 2/8	28 2/8	28 6/8	20 6/8	5 7/8	5 7/8	8	6	Piscataquis Co., ME	Penny Demar	Penny Demar	1998	2032
197 2/8	25 2/8	23 3/8	15	5 6/8	5 6/8	9	12	Casey Co., KY	Ryan Elmore	Ryan Elmore	1998	2032
197 2/8	27 7/8	26 5/8	19 2/8	5 6/8	5 6/8	11	9	Sanilac Co., MI	Charles E. Goodfellow	Charles E. Goodfellow	1998	2032
197 2/8	28 6/8	28 2/8	22 4/8	5 3/8	5 3/8	9	14	Noxubee Co., MS	Edward A. Halfacre	Edward A. Halfacre	1998	2032

Score	Main Beam R	Main Beam L	Inside Spread	Circ. R	Circ. L	Pts. R	Pts. L	Locality	Hunter	Owner	Date	Rank
197 2/8	24 3/8	26	23 4/8	5 4/8	4 6/8	9	7	Marion Co., IA	Larry J. Lautenbach	Larry J. Lautenbach	1998	2032
197 2/8	27 6/8	29 4/8	19 7/8	5 2/8	5 2/8	9	8	Fayette Co., IL	Todd L. Hodson	Todd L. Hodson	2000	2032
197 2/8	25	23 7/8	19 5/8	5 5/8	5 6/8	7	8	Fulton Co., IL	Nicholas P. McElroy	Nicholas P. McElroy	2000	2032
197 2/8	23 1/8	22 7/8	20 3/8	5 5/8	5 3/8	10	10	Van Buren Co., MI	John Pierson	John Pierson	2000	2032
197 1/8	27 5/8	27 2/8	21 4/8	4 5/8	4 7/8	9	9	Becker Co., MN	Unknown	George W. Flaim	1924	2056
197 1/8	24 3/8	24 1/8	18 3/8	5 6/8	5 6/8	17	14	Edmonson Co., KY	Leroy Wilson	Leroy Wilson	1963	2056
197 1/8	20 6/8	20 1/8	18 4/8	5 1/8	4 6/8	13	17	Kenedy Co., TX	Manuel Amaya	Arturo R. Amaya	1969	2056
197 1/8	23	22 7/8	17 7/8	5	5	13	9	Noble Co., OK	Kenneth R. Bright	Kenneth R. Bright	1982	2056
197 1/8	28 2/8	26 6/8	18 7/8	5 1/8	5 7/8	3	11	Worth Co., MO	Gary G. Kinder	Gary G. Kinder	1982	2056
197 1/8	25 3/8	25 2/8	21	5 2/8	4 6/8	11	10	Jefferson Co., IL	Unknown	Jeff Sartaine	1983	2056
197 1/8	26 1/8	26 3/8	17 3/8	4 6/8	4 5/8	3	7	Jackson Co., MO	Jim Martin	Jim Martin	1984	2056
197 1/8	27 4/8	27 3/8	18 3/8	4 5/8	4 5/8	3	9	Clay Co., TX	Dale L. Coleman	Dale L. Coleman	1988	2056
197 1/8	22 6/8	22 4/8	17 3/8	6 3/8	5	3	6	Caldwell Co., MO	James B. Nickles	James B. Nickles	1990	2056
197 1/8	26 6/8	26 3/8	19 3/8	5	5 3/8	11	11	Franklin Co., KS	Ron R. Rumford	Ron R. Rumford	1992	2056
197 1/8	26 2/8	25	18 3/8	5 3/8	5 6/8	6	7	Preeceville, SK	Dale Prestie	Dale Prestie	1996	2056
197 1/8	27 5/8	27 7/8	18 3/8	5 3/8	6	9	10	Rocky Mountain House, AB	Robin L. McDonald	Robin L. McDonald	1998	2056
197 1/8	25 6/8	25 4/8	18	5 7/8	5 7/8	9	13	Bartholomew Co., IN	C. Greg Caudill	C. Greg Caudill	1999	2056
197 1/8	23 6/8	23 4/8	20 2/8	5 6/8	5 4/8	11	11	Clark Co., SD	Marlin Maynard	Marlin Maynard	1999	2056
197 1/8	24	23 3/8	17 3/8	5	5 6/8	7	9	S. Saskatchewan River, SK	Barry D. Miller	Barry D. Miller	1999	2056
197 1/8	26	25 5/8	24 1/8	5	5	8	9	Caddo Co., OK	Jerid C. Avery	Jerid C. Avery	2000	2056
197	23 4/8	24 2/8	19 4/8	5	4 5/8	7	13	Oak River, MB	Sam Henry	J.J. Henry	1946	2072
197	27 2/8	26 3/8	20 4/8	4 4/8	5 3/8	8	14	Cook Co., MN	Edwin F. Niemeyer	Helen Niemeyer	1947	2072
197	27 5/8	27 6/8	22 7/8	5 1/8	6	6	11	Houghton Co., MI	Edward Heinonen	Bass Pro Shops	1970	2072
197	28 2/8	26 5/8	22 1/8	5 3/8	5 1/8	6	8	Fayette Co., IA	Stanley E. Harrison	Stanley E. Harrison	1973	2072
197	24 2/8	26 4/8	25 3/8	5 1/8	5	9	9	Kootenai Co., ID	D.L. Whatcott & R.C. Carlson	D.L. Whatcott & R.C. Carlson	1980	2072
197	29 3/8	29 4/8	21	5 2/8	4 4/8	13	14	Bedford Co., VA	John P. Kirby, Sr.	John P. Kirby, Sr.	1981	2072
197	21 4/8	22 1/8	20 6/8	5 4/8	5	11	11	Rosebud Co., MT	Mark D. Holmes	Mark D. Holmes	1983	2072
197	24 1/8	24 1/8	23 2/8	6 2/8	6	7	8	Souris River, MB	Picked Up	T. Allan Good	1986	2072
197	23 6/8	22 3/8	18 5/8	4 3/8	4 6/8	9	14	Barber Co., KS	Lewis M. Mull	Lewis M. Mull	1986	2072
197	22	28 2/8	19 5/8	5 6/8	5 4/8	13	11	Montgomery Co., IA	Picked Up	M. & S. Philby	1988	2072
197	28 2/8	26 4/8	21	5	5	7	7	Bayfield Co., WI	Larry M. Nyhus	Larry M. Nyhus	1997	2072
196 7/8	26 4/8	27 1/8	20 6/8	5 1/8	5 1/8	8	9	La Salle Co., IL	Ken Sparks, Jr.	Ken Sparks, Jr.	2002	2084
196 7/8	26 2/8	23 4/8	23 2/8	4 7/8	5 2/8	11	12	St. Louis Co., MN	James A. Guist	James A. Guist	1963	2084
196 7/8	27 1/8	24 6/8	18 5/8	5 2/8	4 7/8	10	5	Macon Co., GA	Major Beard	Major Brannon	1972	2084
196 7/8	27 2/8	26 3/8	19	4 7/8	5	12	13	Caddo Parish, LA	Robert W. Anderson	Robert W. Anderson	1983	2084
196 7/8	22 6/8	24 2/8	19 2/8	5	5	10	8	Edmunds Co., SD	Melvin Borkirchert	Melvin Borkirchert	1983	2084
196 7/8	24 6/8	22 1/8	22 6/8	5 1/8	5 3/8	7	7	Pepin Co., WI	Jerry R. Breitung	Jerry R. Breitung	1985	2084
196 7/8	26 5/8	23 1/8	17 1/8	4 5/8	4 4/8	7	9	Wayne Co., IA	Marshall V. Ruble	Marshall V. Ruble	1986	2084
196 7/8	24 1/8	25 1/8	23 1/8	4 4/8	4 4/8	11	9	Trigg Co., KY	Homer Stevens, Jr.	Homer Stevens, Jr.	1986	2084
196 7/8	22 6/8	27	18 5/8	4 2/8	6	8	11	Yazoo Co., MS	Eddie J. Alias, Jr.	Eddie J. Alias, Jr.	1989	2084
196 7/8	23	26	21 5/8	6	4 6/8	11	10	Jackson Co., MI	Herb C. Miller, Jr.	Herb C. Miller, Jr.	1993	2084
196 7/8	25 1/8	27 1/8	18	4 4/8	4 7/8	8	9	Bureau Co., IL	Steve M. Mazurek	Steve M. Mazurek	1995	2084
196 7/8	27	18	17 6/8	5 4/8	4 2/8	8	10	McLean Co., KY	John D. Greenfield	John D. Greenfield	1996	2084
196 7/8	27 1/8	17 6/8	22	4 2/8	5 2/8	8	11	Linn Co., IA	James L. Newman	James L. Newman	1996	2084
196 7/8	21 6/8	22	21 7/8	5 2/8	6 1/8	7	5	Winneshiek Co., IA	David G. Baumler	David G. Baumler	1997	2084
196 7/8	28	21 7/8	20 6/8	6 1/8	5 3/8	10	8	Chipman, AB	Don F. MacLean	Don F. MacLean	1997	2084
196 7/8	25 6/8	20 6/8	20 6/8	5 4/8	6 5/8	7	8	Becker Co., MN	James A. Henderson	James A. Henderson	1998	2084

WHITETAIL DEER - NON-TYPICAL ANTLERS
Odocoileus virginianus virginianus and certain related subspecies

Score	Length of Main Beam R	L	Inside Spread	Circumference at Smallest Place Between Burr and First Point R	L	Number of Points R	L	Locality	Hunter	Owner	Date Killed	Rank
196 7/8	27 5/8	28 4/8	24 1/8	5 2/8	5 7/8	8	8	Shawano Co., WI	Robert D. Little	Robert D. Little	1998	2084
196 7/8	24 6/8	24 5/8	16	4 3/8	4 5/8	13	14	Allegheny Co., PA	Charles E. Main	Charles E. Main	2000	2084
196 7/8	23 6/8	23	22 4/8	5 3/8	5 3/8	12	11	Hart Co., KY	John L. Seymour	John L. Seymour	1934	2084
196 6/8	22 2/8	22 5/8	17 5/8	5	5	8	8	Vilas Co., WI	Joe Wilfer	Rick Iacono	1949	2102
196 6/8	26 2/8	25 5/8	18 2/8	5 6/8	5 5/8	9	8	Perry Co., PA	Kenneth Reisinger	Kenneth Reisinger	1972	2102
196 6/8	25	25	19 1/8	4 6/8	5	9	10	Unicoi Co., TN	Elmer Payne	Elmer Payne	PR 1984	2102
196 6/8	26 7/8	27 6/8	21 4/8	5 2/8	5 3/8	13	10	Lake Co., MN	Unknown	George W. Flaim	1989	2102
196 6/8	28 2/8	28	21	5 2/8	5 3/8	7	8	McHenry Co., IL	Timothy A. Schulze	Timothy A. Schulze	1994	2102
196 6/8	24 5/8	22 7/8	20 3/8	5 4/8	5 3/8	7	9	Athabasca, AB	Robert Camarillo	Robert Camarillo	1994	2102
196 6/8	25 4/8	27 5/8	20	6	5 6/8	9	6	Licking Co., OH	Michael E. Evans, Sr.	Michael E. Evans, Sr.	1994	2102
196 6/8	27	28 2/8	18 6/8	4 4/8	4 4/8	9	9	Clinton Co., IA	Robert W. Franks	Robert W. Franks	1994	2102
196 6/8	24 1/8	24 2/8	20	5 3/8	5 3/8	10	12	Birch Lake, SK	Brent V. Trumbo	Brent V. Trumbo	1995	2102
196 6/8	19 4/8	21 5/8	19	4 2/8	4 2/8	16	14	Stephens Co., TX	Thomas N. Clark	Lawson W. Walden	1996	2102
196 6/8	26 2/8	26 4/8	25 1/8	6 1/8	6 1/8	8	6	Jackson Co., IA	James L. Beetem	James L. Beetem	1996	2102
196 6/8	23 7/8	26 4/8	22 4/8	5 2/8	5 2/8	12	13	Porcupine Plain, SK	Picked Up	Terry L. Amos	PR 1997	2102
196 6/8	25 2/8	25 2/8	18 2/8	4 7/8	5 1/8	8	12	Latimer Co., OK	Brian K. Paul	Brian K. Paul	1998	2102
196 6/8	24 2/8	24	25 6/8	4 7/8	4 7/8	9	10	Whitefish Bay, ON	Matthew R. Rydberg	Matthew R. Rydberg	1998	2102
196 6/8	21 2/8	20 6/8	18 2/8	4 4/8	4 3/8	10	11	Butler Co., IA	Edwin T. Blanchard	Edwin T. Blanchard	2000	2102
196 6/8	25 7/8	26	21 2/8	5	4 5/8	10	8	Lewis Co., MO	Kenneth W. Brocksmith	Kenneth W. Brocksmith	2000	2102
196 6/8	27 2/8	26 2/8	21 2/8	5	5	10	9	Pike Co., IL	Larry D. Grant	Larry D. Grant	2001	2102
196 6/8	24 3/8	23 2/8	16 3/8	5 3/8	6 3/8	11	11	Jackson Co., IA	Wayne M. Harvey	Wayne M. Harvey	2002	2102
196 6/8	25 5/8	24 5/8	15	5 1/8	5 1/8	9	8	Dakota Co., NE	David J. Miller	David J. Miller	2002	2102
196 6/8	26 5/8	25 7/8	23 6/8	5 5/8	5 7/8	10	10	Buffalo Co., WI	Bill Black, Sr.	Tom Black	1956	2121
196 6/8	26 3/8	27 3/8	15 5/8	5 6/8	5 6/8	11	11	Delta Co., MI	Frans Kuula	Bass Pro Shops	1967	2121
196 5/8	28 7/8	25 4/8	22	5 4/8	4 6/8	10	12	Westchester Co., NY	Picked Up	John J. Vitale	1968	2121
196 5/8	21 2/8	20 5/8	19 4/8	4 7/8	4 7/8	9	12	Wilkinson Co., MS	Robert D. Sullivan	Robert D. Sullivan	1982	2121
196 5/8	25 6/8	25 1/8	20 6/8	5 7/8	5 5/8	9	8	Van Buren Co., IA	Kenneth R. Barker	Kenneth R. Barker	1984	2121
196 5/8	30 2/8	30 3/8	20 5/8	5 6/8	5 6/8	9	7	Langlade Co., WI	Thomas G. Jahnke	Thomas G. Jahnke	1990	2121
196 5/8	26 4/8	27 6/8	20 6/8	4 7/8	4 6/8	8	6	Scott Co., IL	Michael G. Schildman	Michael G. Schildman	1992	2121
196 5/8	19 2/8	18	18 4/8	5 1/8	5 1/8	15	13	Comanche Co., OK	R. Dewayne High	R. Dewayne High	1998	2121
196 5/8	25	25 1/8	17 5/8	5 7/8	5 5/8	12	10	Henry Co., IA	Troy M. Matter	Troy M. Matter	1998	2121
196 5/8	27 7/8	27 5/8	20 6/8	6 3/8	6 3/8	9	9	Nottawasaga River, ON	James P. Baird	James P. Baird	2000	2121
196 5/8	23 1/8	23 2/8	19 3/8	4 7/8	4 5/8	9	11	Rabbit Lake, SK	Jim Clary	Jim Clary	2000	2121
196 5/8	29 2/8	28 5/8	19 1/8	6 2/8	5 6/8	7	9	Winnipeg River, MB	Mark S. Ilijanic	Mark S. Ilijanic	2000	2121
196 5/8	26 7/8	26 5/8	20 2/8	5	4 7/8	9	9	Kayosuar Creek, SK	Kelly Schuster	Kelly Schuster	2000	2121
196 5/8	27	27 2/8	19 4/8	7	7	9	10	Bates Co., MO	Joseph E. Favre	Joseph E. Favre	2002	2121

Score	Beam R	Beam L	Inside Spread	Circ. R	Circ. L	Pts R	Pts L	Locality	Hunter	Owner	Date	Rank
196 4/8	26 6/8	28 5/8	19	5	4 7/8	8	8	Desha Co., AR	Turner Neal	Turner Neal	1955	2135
196 4/8	24 1/8	23 3/8	18 2/8	5 1/8	5 2/8	9	8	Trigg Co., KY	Jeffery Taylor	Jeffery Taylor	1983	2135
196 4/8	27	27 7/8	23 6/8	5 1/8	5	10	10	Garland Co., AR	Eldon G. Sisney	Eldon G. Sisney	1986	2135
196 4/8	26 4/8	25 6/8	18 5/8	4 7/8	4 6/8	8	11	Lucas Co., IA	Steve Shanks	Steve Shanks	1987	2135
196 4/8	28 1/8	26 4/8	25 3/8	4 2/8	4 2/8	6	8	Jackson Co., OH	Francis L. Ray	Francis L. Ray	1988	2135
196 4/8	27	27	19 7/8	4 4/8	4 6/8	11	8	Buffalo Co., WI	Scott T. Beach	Scott T. Beach	1996	2135
196 4/8	25 1/8	24 2/8	19 2/8	4 7/8	4 6/8	15	17	Franklin Co., IN	Cory A. Rogers	Cory A. Rogers	1996	2135
196 4/8	26 4/8	24 2/8	20 7/8	5 4/8	5 3/8	8	8	Charlotte Co., VA	Paul S. Wray	Paul S. Wray	1997	2135
196 4/8	24 1/8	25 6/8	17 1/8	5 4/8	5	12	10	Page Co., IA	Michael L. Hughes	Michael L. Hughes	1999	2135
196 4/8	24 4/8	25 1/8	19 6/8	5 1/8	6 2/8	8	10	Wayne Co., NY	Jonathan S. Countryman	Jonathan S. Countryman	2001	2135
196 4/8	22 4/8	24 2/8	18 6/8	6	6	8	10	Crystal Lakes, SK	Andrew Gazdewich	Andrew Gazdewich	2001	2135
196 3/8	23 6/8	23	23 6/8	6 3/8	4 7/8	10	11	Dunn Co., WI	Unknown	Cabela's, Inc.	PR 1940	2146
196 3/8	23 6/8	24 4/8	20 2/8	4 4/8	4 6/8	7	7	Texas	Unknown	Roy Hindes	PR 1950	2146
196 3/8	25 1/8	25 2/8	17 6/8	4 5/8	5 2/8	6	6	Webb Co., TX	R. Blair James	R. Blair James	1954	2146
196 3/8	25 6/8	24 4/8	22 7/8	5	5	7	9	Prairie River, SK	Herb Kopperud	Herb Kopperud	1959	2146
196 3/8	26	25 7/8	21	4 7/8	5 3/8	8	10	Baldwin Co., AL	Carl Raley	Kyle Ferguson	1962	2146
196 3/8	24 3/8	18 6/8	24	5 4/8	4 7/8	9	10	Clark Co., IL	Mary K. Le Crone	Mary K. Le Crone	1982	2146
196 3/8	24 7/8	25 2/8	15 3/8	4 6/8	4 3/8	10	12	Lee Co., IA	Douglas W. Hopp	Douglas W. Hopp	1984	2146
196 3/8	26 3/8	26 6/8	20 7/8	4 4/8	4 5/8	7	9	Spokane Co., WA	Eric Friesen	Eric Friesen	1986	2146
196 3/8	26 2/8	25 7/8	18 3/8	4 4/8	6 1/8	11	8	Price Co., WI	John R. Lemke	John R. Lemke	1986	2146
196 3/8	25 4/8	26 5/8	20 1/8	6	5 6/8	12	11	Magaguadowic Lake, NB	Albert Fawcett	Albert Fawcett	1988	2146
196 3/8	27	26 1/8	17 7/8	5 7/8	4 4/8	8	7	Houghton Co., MI	Robert L. Marr	Robert L. Marr	1990	2146
196 3/8	22 5/8	22 5/8	17 3/8	5 1/8	5 1/8	8	6	Coahuila, MX	Jeanie D. Willard	Jeanie D. Willard	1993	2146
196 3/8	23 2/8	23 3/8	23 5/8	5 1/8	5	8	7	Pierceland, SK	Robert B. Rhyne	Robert B. Rhyne	1994	2146
196 3/8	28 4/8	27	21 3/8	4 6/8	5 4/8	9	7	Ringgold Co., IA	Frank J. Scovel	Frank J. Scovel	1994	2146
196 3/8	25 6/8	24 4/8	19 1/8	5 6/8	6	10	8	Ellis Co., KS	Douglas W. Carmichael	Douglas W. Carmichael	1996	2146
196 3/8	28 3/8	25 6/8	21 1/8	6	6	8	10	Belmont Co., OH	Brian R. Elston	Brian R. Elston	1999	2146
196 3/8	22 5/8	23 7/8	18 5/8	5 2/8	5 3/8	11	8	Gregory Co., SD	Michael O. Jacobsen	Michael O. Jacobsen	1999	2146
196 3/8	23 1/8	23 2/8	20 3/8	5 6/8	5 6/8	11	7	Clayton Co., IA	David D. Sadewasser	David D. Sadewasser	2000	2146
196 3/8	24 4/8	23 5/8	22 3/8	5 5/8	5 5/8	10	7	Franklin Co., KY	Gene C. Brown	Gene C. Brown	2001	2146
196 3/8	24 5/8	24 3/8	14 3/8	6 4/8	7 3/8	7	11	St. Mary's Co., MD	Terry L. Starr	Terry L. Starr	PR 1951	2146
196 2/8	22 4/8	24 6/8	20 4/8	4 6/8	4 6/8	14	12	Delta Co., MI	William H. Johnson	Bass Pro Shops	1951	2166
196 2/8	23 2/8	23 1/8	17 5/8	5 2/8	4 7/8	11	7	Lake of the Woods Co., MN	Ralph Rehder	Ralph Rehder	1958	2166
196 2/8	24	24 5/8	18 5/8	5 3/8	5 5/8	11	10	Crook Co., WY	Donald W. Clements	Colleen B. Clements	1965	2166
196 2/8	28 4/8	27 5/8	22	4 7/8	4 7/8	6	6	Henry Co., KY	Picked Up	Michael L. Roberts	1975	2166
196 2/8	29 3/8	29 2/8	22 4/8	6	5 1/8	10	6	Crow Wing Co., MN	LeRoy E. Pelarski	LeRoy E. Pelarski	1979	2166
196 2/8	27	27	27	6	6	7	7	Dorchester Co., MD	Kevin R. Coulbourne	Kevin R. Coulbourne	1987	2166
196 2/8	23 7/8	23 2/8	17 3/8	6 3/8	6 1/8	10	14	Otter Tail Co., MN	William J. Klyve	William J. Klyve	1987	2166
196 2/8	25 6/8	26 6/8	22 3/8	5 5/8	6	11	8	Webster Co., KY	Timothy J. Shelton	Timothy J. Shelton	1993	2166
196 2/8	26 6/8	26 7/8	22 4/8	5 3/8	5 4/8	6	9	Butler Co., KY	Bradley S. Pharris	Bradley S. Pharris	1996	2166
196 2/8	27 6/8	24 3/8	18 1/8	3 7/8	4 2/8	11	8	Edwards Co., IL	David Broster	David Broster	1996	2166
196 2/8	24 7/8	24 6/8	18 4/8	5 2/8	5 4/8	8	11	Louisa Co., IA	Tony Thomas	Tony Thomas	1997	2166
196 2/8	29 3/8	27	19 3/8	6 1/8	6 2/8	11	7	Pratt Co., KS	Travis D. Kolm	Travis D. Kolm	1999	2166
196 2/8	27 5/8	25 2/8	17 7/8	5 5/8	6 6/8	11	12	Bourbon Co., KS	Picked Up	Odie Sudbeck	2000	2166
196 2/8	25	25 7/8	24	4 7/8	5 2/8	12	16	Putnam Co., IN	Todd G. Barnes	Todd G. Barnes	2000	2166
196 2/8	25 4/8	25	25 4/8	5 2/8	6 3/8	5	8	Henderson Co., KY	Nathan A. Peak	Nathan A. Peak	2001	2166
196 2/8	23 4/8	24 3/8	16 4/8	6 1/8	5 6/8	7	14	Pierce Co., WI	Mark P. Dolan	Mark P. Dolan	2001	2166
196 1/8	24 3/8	24 1/8	19 3/8	5 4/8	5 6/8	8	9	Nemaha Co., NE	Picked Up	Gale Sup	1975	2182

Odocoileus virginianus virginianus and certain related subspecies

Score	Length of Main Beam		Inside Spread	Circumference at Smallest Place Between Burr and First Point		Number of Points		Locality	Hunter	Owner	Date Killed	Rank
	R	L		R	L	R	L					
196 1/8	24 4/8	26	17 2/8	5 7/8	5 6/8	11	10	McCreary Co., KY	Jack W. Bailey	Jack W. Bailey	1976	2182
196 1/8	25 5/8	24 4/8	16 7/8	5	4 7/8	11	10	Wyoming Co., NY	Eric D. Baney	Eric D. Baney	1985	2182
196 1/8	26 4/8	21 7/8	21 3/8	5 5/8	5 5/8	9	7	Henderson Co., IL	Bruce Keever	Bruce Keever	1992	2182
196 1/8	27 3/8	27 2/8	21 3/8	5 6/8	7 2/8	10	10	Leduc, AB	Gordon Gulick	Gordon Gulick	1993	2182
196 1/8	25 2/8	25 1/8	20 2/8	5 1/8	5 2/8	7	7	Ketchen, SK	Vernon C. Hoffman	Vernon C. Hoffman	1993	2182
196 1/8	28	27 1/8	18 7/8	4 1/8	4 4/8	9	7	Guthrie Co., IA	Terry D. Danielson	Terry D. Danielson	1995	2182
196 1/8	23 4/8	23 4/8	18 1/8	5 4/8	5 4/8	9	9	Jefferson Co., IN	Bill A. Knoblock	Bill A. Knoblock	1996	2182
196 1/8	22 6/8	24 5/8	19 4/8	5 3/8	5 4/8	14	8	Rumsey, AB	Greg Smith	Greg Smith	1996	2182
196 1/8	23 5/8	25 4/8	18 1/8	6	5 6/8	11	9	Pontotoc Co., OK	Bruce A. Hall	Bruce A. Hall	1999	2182
196 1/8	25 4/8	26 2/8	18 6/8	4 6/8	4 6/8	7	8	Frio Co., TX	Orville W. Simmang, Sr.	Orville W. Simmang, Sr.	1999	2182
196 1/8	25 2/8	24 4/8	17 3/8	5 7/8	5 2/8	8	7	Lyon Co., KS	A. Scott Ritchie	A. Scott Ritchie	2000	2182
196 1/8	26 1/8	25 7/8	13 6/8	6 1/8	5 7/8	9	9	Whitley Co., KY	Douglas Angel	Douglas Angel	2001	2182
196 1/8	21 6/8	19 5/8	21	4 5/8	4 5/8	20	13	Montgomery Co., NC	Roger D. Hunt	Roger D. Hunt	2001	2182
196 1/8	25 2/8	25	19 3/8	5 6/8	5 5/8	8	8	Wabasha Co., MN	Angela Reinhardt	Angela Reinhardt	2002	2182
196 1/8	23 5/8	23 6/8	18 4/8	4 3/8	4 2/8	13	9	Lincoln Co., OK	Joshua A. Shade	Joshua A. Shade	2002	2182
196	25	24 2/8	20	4 6/8	4 6/8	8	8	Forest Co., WI	Aaron E. Huettl	Aaron E. Huettl	1939	2198
196	27 7/8	26 2/8	15 4/8	5 2/8	5 2/8	12	15	Marinette Co., WI	Joseph Braun	Brant J. Mueller	1940	2198
196	22 3/8	24 5/8	16 5/8	5 1/8	5 2/8	13	10	Luce Co., MI	Herbert Miller, Sr.	Bass Pro Shops	1945	2198
196	25 5/8	25 1/8	16 1/8	5 1/8	5 4/8	7	12	Westmoreland Co., PA	Edward G. Ligus	Edward G. Ligus	1956	2198
196	25 1/8	25 5/8	16 1/8	4 1/8	4 4/8	11	11	Jasper Co., GA	Frank M. Pritchard	Frank M. Pritchard	1968	2198
196	26 4/8	25 6/8	18 7/8	5	5 2/8	6	7	Buffalo Co., WI	William A. Gatzlaff	William A. Gatzlaff	1970	2198
196	28 7/8	30 4/8	25 1/8	5 4/8	5 2/8	12	10	Annapolis Valley, NS	David Cabral	David Cabral	1984	2198
196	25 2/8	25 4/8	19 6/8	4 6/8	4 6/8	13	9	Dubuque Co., IA	James D. Pladson	James D. Pladson	1987	2198
196	26 5/8	24 7/8	17 2/8	5 3/8	5 4/8	10	9	Richland Co., WI	Terry D. Freese	Terry D. Freese	1990	2198
196	24	24 4/8	18 5/8	4 6/8	4 5/8	10	7	McNairy Co., TN	Picked Up	Jeff DuCharme	1992	2198
196	20 6/8	24 6/8	16 2/8	4	4	8	12	Muscatine Co., IA	Bradley S. Koeppel	Bradley S. Koeppel	1993	2198
196	21 5/8	22	13 2/8	5 6/8	6 2/8	8	9	Harlan Co., KY	James D. Evans	James D. Evans	1995	2198
196	28 1/8	28 3/8	22 2/8	5 2/8	5 4/8	5	9	Cumberland Co., IL	Lester S. Whitehead	Lester S. Whitehead	1996	2198
196	26 6/8	23 3/8	15 5/8	7 1/8	7	9	9	Washington Co., KS	Jeff A. Light	Jeff A. Light	1997	2198
196	27 6/8	28 3/8	23 6/8	5 3/8	5 4/8	7	7	Fayette Co., OH	Jeff W. Novak	Jeff W. Novak	1998	2198
196	27 5/8	26 3/8	19 1/8	6	6 1/8	6	9	Mercer Co., MO	Sean C. Huff	Sean C. Huff	1999	2198
196	24 6/8	26 2/8	20 4/8	5 3/8	5 4/8	9	12	Franklin Co., IN	James W. Berryman	James W. Berryman	2001	2198
196	24 4/8	25 6/8	19 7/8	4 7/8	5 4/8	9	7	Webb Co., TX	John D. Burkhart	John D. Burkhart	2002	2198
195 7/8	24 6/8	25	23 6/8	3 6/8	3 6/8	8	6	Beltrami Co., MN	Charles J. Schelper, Sr.	Vernon L. Watson	1930	2216
195 7/8	26 3/8	26 5/8	19 2/8	6	6	10	7	Florence Co., WI	Ollie Jamtaas	James Gorden	1938	2216
195 7/8	26	27	20 4/8	5 2/8	5 2/8	10	8	Florence Co., WI	E.J. Nichols	Barbara R. Bowman	PR 1940	2216

Score			Spread			Points		Locality	Hunter	Owner	Date	Rank
195 7/8	25 4/8	25 1/8	18 6/8	4 7/8	5 5/8	7	8	Allamakee Co., IA	John L. Cahalan	John L. Cahalan	1953	2216
195 7/8	21 4/8	21 6/8	20 6/8	4 4/8	4 4/8	9	10	La Salle Co., TX	Steve A. Meyer	Steve A. Meyer	1968	2216
195 7/8	27 1/8	25 2/8	20 2/8	5 2/8	5 2/8	11	10	Grant Co., WI	Roger Derrickson	Roger Derrickson	1973	2216
195 7/8	29 1/8	21 7/8	21 6/8	4 7/8	5	3	8	Perry Co., OH	Pearl R. Wiseman	Pearl R. Wiseman	1976	2216
195 7/8	30	30 1/8	21 4/8	4 7/8	5	7	8	Jackson Co., MI	Ronald D. Murphy	Picked Up	1984	2216
195 7/8	28	27 6/8	21 2/8	5 5/8	5	6	10	Meade Co., KY	J. Mark Stull	J. Mark Stull	1984	2216
195 7/8	24 5/8	23 7/8	18 2/8	6	5 5/8	7	7	Monroe Co., MS	Kenneth A. Dye	Kenneth A. Dye	1986	2216
195 7/8	23 1/8	23 4/8	19	4 7/8	4 5/8	9	9	Latah Co., ID	Cecil H. Cameron	Cecil H. Cameron	1989	2216
195 7/8	25 6/8	25 4/8	15 1/8	5	5	9	11	Webster Parish, LA	Shannon Stanley	Shannon Stanley	1991	2216
195 7/8	26 6/8	26 4/8	23 6/8	5 1/8	5 2/8	8	6	Webb Co., TX	Marko T. Barrett	Marko T. Barrett	1993	2216
195 7/8	24 3/8	24 4/8	18 5/8	4 2/8	4 3/8	9	9	Kenedy Co., TX	Michael D. Fain	Michael D. Fain	1993	2216
195 7/8	28	28 5/8	20 1/8	5	4 7/8	8	8	Wayne Co., IA	Michael S. Perkins	Michael S. Perkins	1995	2216
195 7/8	25 2/8	27 6/8	20 6/8	4 6/8	5	11	7	Marshall Co., MN	Vernon Blazejewski	Vernon Blazejewski	1997	2216
195 7/8	23	22 6/8	15 6/8	5 3/8	5 5/8	10	9	Unknown	Larry Bollier	Unknown	PR 1998	2216
195 7/8	26 7/8	27 5/8	18 3/8	5	4 7/8	11	11	Blueberry River, BC	Ernie Kuehne	Ernie Kuehne	2000	2238
195 7/8	23 3/8	23 6/8	15 6/8	6 5/8	6 6/8	12	15	Thorhild, AB	Picked Up	Picked Up	2000	2238
195 7/8	26 4/8	27	19 2/8	4 7/8	5 6/8	9	6	Webb Co., TX	Jimmie L. Speake	Jimmie L. Speake	2000	2238
195 7/8	24 7/8	24	18 2/8	4 4/8	4 4/8	11	7	Kleberg Co., TX	Allyn Archer	Allyn Archer	2002	2238
195 7/8	25 3/8	27	20	6 2/8	6 3/8	7	9	Peoria Co., IL	Stanley E. Goard	Stanley E. Goard	2002	2238
195 6/8	24 1/8	24 4/8	15 6/8	6 1/8	5 6/8	7	11	Ontonagon Co., MI	Andrew Pietila	Bass Pro Shops	PR 1920	2238
195 6/8	28 6/8	30 2/8	22	5 7/8	6	7	8	Illinois	Unknown	Unknown	1945	2238
195 6/8	26 4/8	27 4/8	19 6/8	5 3/8	5 3/8	11	10	Moosomin, SK	Tom Ryan	Tom Ryan	1961	2238
195 6/8	25 6/8	25	20 2/8	5 3/8	5 2/8	7	7	St. Louis Co., MN	Mike Desanto	Mike Desanto	1963	2238
195 6/8	28 2/8	29 5/8	16 4/8	5 4/8	5 6/8	7	8	Douglas Co., WI	Buckhorn of Gordon, Inc.	Unknown	PR 1970	2238
195 6/8	24 2/8	24 6/8	18 3/8	5 1/8	5	7	7	Wetaskiwin, AB	Lewis D. Callies	Lewis D. Callies	1972	2238
195 6/8	25 4/8	26 5/8	19 5/8	6 5/8	7	11	12	Roseau Co., MN	George H. Tepley	George H. Tepley	1984	2238
195 6/8	21 7/8	25 7/8	27 6/8	6 3/8	5 2/8	14	8	Greenwater Creek, SK	Edward R. Mielke	Picked Up	1988	2238
195 6/8	26 2/8	24 4/8	17 6/8	4 3/8	4 4/8	8	10	Coal Co., OK	Todd Tobey	Todd Tobey	1988	2238
195 6/8	21 6/8	24 6/8	20 7/8	4 2/8	4 2/8	15	12	Ashland Co., OH	Michael R. Dull	Michael R. Dull	1992	2238
195 6/8	25 7/8	25 6/8	20 5/8	4 7/8	4 5/8	10	8	Howard Co., MO	Daniel A. Larkin	Daniel A. Larkin	1993	2238
195 6/8	23	23	17	4 1/8	4	9	8	Bonner Co., ID	Brian T. Farley	Picked Up	PR 1994	2238
195 6/8	24	24	20	4 5/8	4 5/8	8	9	Missoula Co., MT	Eugene L. Tripp, Sr.	Eugene L. Tripp, Sr.	1994	2238
195 6/8	25 4/8	25	17 4/8	5 1/8	5 1/8	6	9	Washington Co., ME	James H. Guertin	James H. Guertin	1995	2238
195 6/8	24 4/8	25 2/8	19 4/8	5 6/8	5 4/8	8	10	Lee Co., IA	Jesse W. Logan	Jesse W. Logan	1996	2238
195 6/8	23 6/8	25	18 2/8	5 4/8	5 4/8	12	8	Vernon Co., WI	William T. Newman	William T. Newman	1997	2238
195 6/8	29 1/8	29	21 3/8	4 7/8	4 7/8	7	8	Pierce Co., WI	Jody M. Anderson	Jody M. Anderson	1998	2238
195 6/8	24 3/8	24 3/8	16 7/8	5 3/8	5 4/8	16	10	Putnam Co., MO	Douglas E. Gadberry	Douglas E. Gadberry	1998	2238
195 6/8	24 4/8	23 5/8	21 3/8	4 4/8	4 5/8	8	7	Lake Co., MN	Corey A. Swartout	Corey A. Swartout	1998	2238
195 6/8	21	19 6/8	15	4 5/8	4 6/8	8	12	Park Co., MT	Larry R. Faust	Larry R. Faust	2001	2238
195 6/8	25 6/8	25 7/8	18	5 1/8	5 1/8	10	9	Little Moose Lake, SK	Carl Grundman	Carl Grundman	2001	2238
195 6/8	25	24 2/8	20 7/8	5 2/8	5 2/8	9	10	Madison Co., IL	James M. Hoefert	James M. Hoefert	2002	2238
195 5/8	24 2/8	25 2/8	14	5 5/8	5 4/8	8	9	Johnston Co., OK	Rhonda L. Upchurch	Rhonda L. Upchurch	2002	2238
195 5/8	23 6/8	22 6/8	19 2/8	4 4/8	4 4/8	12	10	Florence Co., WI	Joseph R. Szczepanski, Jr.	Terry J. Baranczyk	PR 1945	2261
195 5/8	25 4/8	25 6/8	19	6 1/8	6	10	10	Parkman, SK	H.E. Kennett	H.E. Kennett	1949	2261
195 5/8	25 5/8	24 2/8	19 1/8	5 4/8	5 4/8	8	8	Carlton Co., MN	Nick Rukovina	George W. Flaim	1960	2261
195 5/8	24 6/8	25 3/8	21 3/8	5 5/8	5 5/8	11	9	Jackson Co., MN	Allan Amundson	Allan Amundson	1973	2261
195 5/8	25 6/8	25 6/8	19 1/8	5 2/8	5	8	8	Duffield, AB	Robert A. Schaefer	Robert A. Schaefer	1980	2261
195 5/8	23 7/8	24 2/8	13	5 2/8	5	14	10	Adams Co., MS	Kathleen McGehee	Kathleen McGehee	1981	2261

541

Score	Length of Main Beam		Inside Spread	Circumference at Smallest Place Between Burr and First Point		Number of Points		Locality	Hunter	Owner	Date Killed	Rank
	R	L		R	L	R	L					
195 5/8	26 2/8	26 1/8	21 3/8	5 3/8	5 2/8	8	7	Story Co., IA	Jordan L. Larson	Jordan L. Larson	1983	2261
195 5/8	21 1/8	22 4/8	16 7/8	4 4/8	4 4/8	11	14	Menard Co., TX	Don N. Jones, Jr.	Lawson W. Walden	1987	2261
195 5/8	24 6/8	24 7/8	19 2/8	5 2/8	5	10	9	Nez Perce Co., ID	Paul S. Snider	Paul S. Snider	1989	2261
195 5/8	27	25 7/8	19 7/8	4 6/8	5 1/8	10	8	Winneshiek Co., IA	Picked Up	Milan Kumlin	1990	2261
195 5/8	25 6/8	26 6/8	19 5/8	5 3/8	5 2/8	6	10	Unknown	Unknown	C.J. Fuller	PR 1993	2261
195 5/8	24 2/8	24 3/8	13 7/8	5 3/8	5 6/8	8	9	Appanoose Co., IA	Brent Carlson	Brent Carlson	1994	2261
195 5/8	28 1/8	27 5/8	21 4/8	5 3/8	5 4/8	8	7	Brown Co., IL	Brian Matsko	Brian Matsko	1994	2261
195 5/8	27 3/8	27 3/8	19 7/8	5 2/8	5 2/8	9	10	Allamakee Co., IA	Gary L. Mezera	Gary L. Mezera	1994	2261
195 5/8	20 6/8	21 4/8	17 3/8	5 7/8	5 3/8	12	9	Stafford Co., KS	Kenneth R. Van Winkle	Kenneth R. Van Winkle	1994	2261
195 5/8	24 1/8	21 7/8	21 7/8	4 4/8	4 2/8	7	11	Livingston Co., MI	Patrick M. Harris	Patrick M. Harris	1995	2261
195 5/8	26 3/8	26	18 1/8	4 7/8	5 1/8	7	8	Platte Co., MO	Lincoln A. Godfrey	Lincoln A. Godfrey	1999	2261
195 5/8	28	21	21	4 4/8	4 6/8	9	10	Schuyler Co., MO	Jason McCartney	Jason McCartney	1999	2261
195 5/8	24 3/8	24	18 3/8	4 2/8	4	7	7	Madison Co., MS	Damon C. Saik	Damon C. Saik	2001	2261
195 5/8	29 2/8	28 3/8	22 4/8	5 5/8	5 3/8	8	6	Pike Co., MO	Zachary E. Sutter	Zachary E. Sutter	2002	2261
195 5/8	24	23 5/8	21 2/8	4 7/8	5 1/8	14	9	Wisconsin	Unknown	Brant J. Mueller	PR 1942	2281
195 4/8	28	27 7/8	24 3/8	4 4/8	4 4/8	9	11	La Salle Co., TX	Unknown	John C. Korbell	1952	2281
195 4/8	24 7/8	25 1/8	20	5 1/8	4 7/8	10	10	Eau Claire Co., WI	Sylvester Champa	Sylvester Champa	1959	2281
195 4/8	24 5/8	24 1/8	17 6/8	4 4/8	4 2/8	9	9	Maverick Co., TX	Ronald K. Hudson	Ronald K. Hudson	1971	2281
195 4/8	28 5/8	27 3/8	21 2/8	4	4	8	7	Fillmore Co., MN	Jim Sletten	Mrs. Jim Sletten	1974	2281
195 4/8	26	25 3/8	16 6/8	4 7/8	4 6/8	10	7	Winona Co., MN	Patrick Bartholomew	Patrick Bartholomew	1976	2281
195 4/8	25 6/8	16 2/8	20 6/8	6	6	7	7	Bureau Co., IL	Picked Up	John Cotter	1976	2281
195 4/8	26 3/8	27 2/8	20 2/8	5 1/8	4 7/8	11	9	Kanabec Co., MN	Kenneth L. Smith	Kenneth L. Smith	1976	2281
195 4/8	27	26	20 3/8	5 6/8	5 6/8	7	9	Dorchester Co., MD	Charles D. Anderson	Charles D. Anderson	1978	2281
195 4/8	21 3/8	22 4/8	17 2/8	5	5	10	8	Carlisle Co., KY	William H. Deane IV	William H. Deane IV	1979	2281
195 4/8	25 3/8	24 3/8	21 6/8	4 3/8	4 4/8	7	10	Worth Co., GA	Shane Calhoun	Shane Calhoun	1985	2281
195 4/8	28 6/8	27 5/8	18 2/8	4 7/8	5 3/8	10	15	Hamilton Co., IL	Douglas P. Collins	Douglas P. Collins	1985	2281
195 4/8	21 6/8	23 7/8	22 1/8	4 7/8	5 2/8	9	13	St. Louis Co., MN	LeRoy N. Nelson	LeRoy N. Nelson	1987	2281
195 4/8	26 2/8	27 6/8	17 4/8	5	5	10	8	Peoria Co., IL	Jerry T. Wyatt	Jerry T. Wyatt	1989	2281
195 4/8	21 4/8	23 4/8	15 2/8	6 1/8	4 2/8	11	8	Jessamine Co., KY	Tony W. Drury	Tony W. Drury	1991	2281
195 4/8	24	23 7/8	20	5	5	9	8	Red Deer River, SK	Glen Gulka	Glen Gulka	1993	2281
195 4/8	25 6/8	24	15 3/8	4 3/8	4 3/8	11	9	Allegan Co., MI	Jason A. Newman	Jason A. Newman	1994	2281
195 4/8	24 2/8	23 7/8	19 7/8	5 4/8	5 2/8	9	10	Angus Brook, NS	John Breslin, Jr.	John Breslin, Jr.	1995	2281
195 4/8	23 5/8	24 5/8	20 7/8	4 5/8	4 7/8	9	10	Uvalde Co., TX	Gary G. Patterson	Gary G. Patterson	1996	2281
195 4/8	24	22	18 1/8	4 6/8	4 6/8	6	9	Lincoln Co., MO	David M. Thiemet	David M. Thiemet	1996	2281
195 4/8	28	27 3/8	20 3/8	5 2/8	5 2/8	8	8	Jo Daviess Co., IL	Glen M. Volk	Glen M. Volk	1997	2281
195 4/8	25 1/8	25 1/8	15 3/8	5 2/8	4 6/8	17	11	Natrona Co., WY	Picked Up	Ann Ginder	1998	2281

Score	Beam R	Beam L	Spread	Circ R	Circ L	Pts R	Pts L	Locality	Hunter	Owner	Date	Rank
195 4/8	23 3/8	23 3/8	23 3/8	5 4/8	5 3/8	8	9	Winneshiek Co., IA	Clair R. Malanaphy	Clair R. Malanaphy	1998	2281
195 4/8	25 3/8	26 2/8	18 5/8	5 1/8	5 3/8	9	8	Grenfell, SK	Anthony Roberts	Anthony Roberts	1998	2281
195 4/8	23	22 6/8	26 5/8	4 2/8	4 1/8	8	11	Hughes Co., OK	Mike K. Williams	Mike K. Williams	1998	2281
195 4/8	25 5/8	24 6/8	23 4/8	5	5 1/8	11	8	Suffolk Co., NY	Eric Kowalski	Eric Kowalski	1999	2281
195 4/8	25 5/8	25 2/8	18 4/8	6 6/8	6 3/8	13	7	Anderson Co., KS	H.C. Stokes	H.C. Stokes	1999	2281
195 4/8	25 2/8	22 4/8	17 6/8	4 7/8	4 6/8	12	10	Comanche Co., OK	Jerry L. Timmons	Jerry L. Timmons	2000	2281
195 4/8	22 3/8	24 4/8	16 6/8	6 3/8	6 1/8	8	9	Boone Co., IA	Joe R. Busch	Joe R. Busch	2001	2281
195 4/8	24 4/8	25 3/8	20 4/8	5 1/8	5 2/8	11	10	Livingston Co., MO	Wayne D. Cunningham	Wayne D. Cunningham	2002	2281
195 4/8	24 5/8	24 4/8	18 4/8	4 6/8	4 6/8	10	9	Door Co., WI	Robert F. Meingast	Robert F. Meingast	2002	2281
195 3/8	24 2/8	24 1/8	18 4/8	4 3/8	4 3/8	11	11	Pope Co., MN	Kenneth M. Besonen	Kenneth M. Besonen	2002	2281
195 3/8	23 7/8	24 2/8	20 5/8	6	5 4/8	6	7	Colquitt Co., GA	Olen P. Ross	Olen P. Ross	1975	2312
195 3/8	27 3/8	20 5/8	16 2/8	7 3/8	7 5/8	10	12	Beltrami Co., MN	John G. Binsfeld	John G. Binsfeld	1976	2312
195 3/8	20 1/8	22 4/8	20 1/8	5 3/8	5 2/8	11	8	Grassland, AB	Frederick Neumann	Frederick Neumann	1980	2312
195 3/8	25 2/8	26 3/8	22 4/8	5	4 6/8	9	12	Webb Co., TX	Sidney A. Lindsay, Jr.	Sidney A. Lindsay, Jr.	1983	2312
195 3/8	25 4/8	25 4/8	20 2/8	6	5 7/8	9	8	Scott Co., IA	Jeffrey Rasche	Jeffrey Rasche	1989	2312
195 3/8	26 3/8	26	23	5 1/8	5 2/8	9	11	N. Saskatchewan River, AB	Thomas J. Procinsky	Thomas J. Procinsky	1990	2312
195 3/8	26	23	22 7/8	4 4/8	4 5/8	9	10	Jackson Co., IL	Robert L. Koehn	Robert L. Koehn	1991	2312
195 3/8	24 2/8	24 2/8	26 1/8	6 4/8	6 3/8	11	10	Hart Co., KY	Robbie Toms	Robbie Toms	1991	2312
195 3/8	26 5/8	26 1/8	14 6/8	5	4 6/8	10	7	Henry Co., IN	Donn W. Duncan	Donn W. Duncan	1994	2312
195 3/8	25 6/8	25 4/8	19 3/8	4 6/8	4 5/8	9	7	Pottawatomie Co., KS	Thomas G. Holthaus	Thomas G. Holthaus	1994	2312
195 3/8	27 1/8	26 4/8	19 5/8	5	5 1/8	7	6	Dane Co., WI	Gaylord N. Denner	Gaylord N. Denner	1995	2312
195 3/8	27 4/8	28 4/8	22 3/8	5 1/8	4 6/8	7	7	Rock Co., WI	Dennis A. Losey	Dennis A. Losey	1995	2312
195 3/8	27 4/8	26 7/8	19 7/8	4 6/8	4 2/8	7	8	Lewis Co., KY	Chris McCane	Picked Up	1996	2312
195 3/8	26 7/8	25 2/8	19 3/8	4 2/8	5 3/8	8	12	Allamakee Co., IA	Douglas A. Bartz	Douglas A. Bartz	1998	2312
195 3/8	25 2/8	25 2/8	17	5 3/8	5 1/8	9	10	Souris River, SK	Corinne Biette	Corinne Biette	1998	2312
195 3/8	25 6/8	25 7/8	18 5/8	5 1/8	4 6/8	7	8	Pike Co., IL	Ray Yates	Picked Up	1998	2312
195 3/8	25 1/8	25 1/8	19 7/8	4 5/8	4 1/8	9	15	Johnson Co., GA	Jackie Bailey	Picked Up	1999	2312
195 3/8	26 3/8	27 4/8	21 4/8	4 1/8	4 2/8	8	8	Pierce Co., WI	Jesse W. Sullivan	Jesse W. Sullivan	1999	2312
195 3/8	21 1/8	21 4/8	19 7/8	5 4/8	5 3/8	8	7	Hopkins Co., KY	Brad Nelson	Picked Up	2000	2312
195 3/8	28 2/8	27 2/8	22 1/8	5 1/8	5 2/8	7	11	Outagamie Co., WI	Michael S. Schernick	Michael S. Schernick	2000	2312
195 3/8	25 5/8	26 1/8	18	5 2/8	5 1/8	14	6	Vermilion River, MB	Greg O'Hare	Greg O'Hare	2001	2312
195 3/8	26 1/8	24 2/8	18 3/8	6 6/8	6 3/8	10	9	Stephens Co., OK	David J. Vassella	David J. Vassella	2001	2312
195 3/8	24 2/8	25 2/8	20 7/8	6 3/8	6 3/8	7	6	Marion Co., OH	Douglas S. Campbell	Douglas S. Campbell	2002	2312
195 2/8	24 5/8	24 7/8	20 5/8	6 2/8	6 2/8	9	9	Rusk Co., WI	Roger King	Alexander King	1890	2336
195 2/8	23	28 4/8	19 2/8	4 6/8	4 7/8	11	8	Du Charme Coulee, WI	Eugene E. Morovitz	Eugene E. Morovitz	1959	2336
195 2/8	28 7/8	26	20 5/8	4 5/8	4 5/8	11	11	Pottawattamie Co., IA	Ted Houser	Ted Houser	1968	2336
195 2/8	26	25	18 4/8	5 3/8	5 4/8	10	11	Brooks Co., TX	Latrelle D. Burkholder	Donald K. Duren	1970	2336
195 2/8	28 4/8	31 6/8	21 5/8	5	5	9	9	Kenedy Co., TX	Don E. Harrison	Don E. Harrison	1975	2336
195 2/8	27 2/8	24 4/8	17 3/8	4 7/8	4 3/8	12	10	Stevens Co., WA	Floyd E. Newell	Floyd E. Newell	1981	2336
195 2/8	23 4/8	25 3/8	22 2/8	4 2/8	5 3/8	12	13	Somerset Co., ME	David A. McAllister	David A. McAllister	1985	2336
195 2/8	31	28 3/8	21	5 3/8	5 4/8	9	8	Chitek Lake, SK	Charles E. Gambino	Charles E. Gambino	1990	2336
195 2/8	24 4/8	24 4/8	21	5 4/8	6	8	8	Grimes Co., TX	Walter Schroeder, Jr.	Walter Schroeder, Jr.	1990	2336
195 2/8	25 3/8	12 4/8	20	5	5 1/8	21	16	Witchekan Lake, SK	Kim Tiringer	Kim Tiringer	1990	2336
195 2/8	28 3/8	23 4/8	16 7/8	4	4 1/8	8	8	Adams Co., IL	Thomas D. Stice	Thomas D. Stice	1991	2336
195 2/8	24	20	17 5/8	4 5/8	4 5/8	8	8	Lily Lake, AB	Richard J. Leclercq	Richard J. Leclercq	1993	2336
195 2/8	11 4/8	26	15 7/8	5 3/8	5 6/8	12	10	Dakota Co., MN	Mark A. LeMay	Mark A. LeMay	1993	2336
195 2/8	23 2/8	24 3/8	22 7/8	5	5	10	9	Grady Co., OK	Robert J. Rempe	Robert J. Rempe	1994	2336
195 2/8	20	22 2/8	17 3/8	5 3/8	4 6/8	11	11	Copiah Co., MS	Bill Kimble	Bill Kimble	1995	2336

Score	Length of Main Beam R	L	Inside Spread	Circumference at Smallest Place Between Burr and First Point R	L	Number of Points R	L	Locality	Hunter	Owner	Date Killed	Rank
195 2/8	26 2/8	24 6/8	18 1/8	5 7/8	5 4/8	6	9	Warren Co., OH	Ronald E. Lay	Ronald E. Lay	1995	2336
195 2/8	24 4/8	23 5/8	16 6/8	5 6/8	5 7/8	8	9	Christian Co., KY	George Hilton, Jr.	George Hilton, Jr.	1997	2336
195 2/8	24 2/8	24 4/8	19 6/8	4 2/8	4 3/8	7	8	Major Co., OK	Hoot M. Patterson	Hoot M. Patterson	1999	2336
195 2/8	23 7/8	24 4/8	16 3/8	5	5	17	13	Dodge Co., WI	Michael Peirick	Michael Peirick	2000	2336
195 2/8	28 3/8	28 6/8	20 5/8	6	5 6/8	9	6	Jefferson Co., IL	William C. Bell	William C. Bell	2000	2336
195 2/8	29 1/8	30 1/8	19	5 2/8	5 2/8	9	10	Licking Co., OH	Roger J. Holbrook	Roger J. Holbrook	2001	2336
195 2/8	23 3/8	23 5/8	21 2/8	5	5	8	8	Dimmit Co., TX	Guinn D. Crousen	Guinn D. Crousen	2001	2336
195 2/8	24 6/8	23	20 4/8	5 3/8	5 4/8	6	11	Tunica Co., MS	Leland N. Dye, Jr.	Leland N. Dye, Jr.	2001	2336
195 2/8	20 3/8	20	15 5/8	4 3/8	5 4/8	6	17	Carlton Co., MN	Unknown	George W. Flaim	1910	2359
195 1/8	25 5/8	23 4/8	18	4 3/8	4 4/8	15	13	Bonner Co., ID	George B. Hatley	George B. Hatley	1939	2359
195 1/8	27 2/8	27 6/8	20 7/8	5 5/8	5 2/8	7	7	Buffalo Co., WI	Maynard Trones	Maynard Trones	1958	2359
195 1/8	24 7/8	24 3/8	17 5/8	5 5/8	5 4/8	8	8	Merrick Co., NE	Robert K. Betts	Robert K. Betts	1962	2359
195 1/8	23 2/8	28 6/8	15	4 4/8	5 1/8	15	14	Washington Co., ME	M. Chandler Stith	M. Chandler Stith	1963	2359
195 1/8	26	25 7/8	21	4 4/8	4 6/8	9	9	Zapata Co., TX	Corando Mirelez	Corando Mirelez	1966	2359
195 1/8	27	26	18 6/8	5 2/8	5 2/8	6	8	Dorchester Co., MD	Carroll R. Seegard	Charles D. Anderson	1974	2359
195 1/8	24 2/8	23 4/8	23 2/8	4 5/8	5 2/8	10	9	Whitman Co., WA	R. & R. Boyer	R. & R. Boyer	1975	2359
195 1/8	23 1/8	23 5/8	15 3/8	5	4 7/8	8	8	Macon Co., GA	Wesley E. Jones	Wesley E. Jones	1986	2359
195 1/8	26 7/8	27 4/8	19 4/8	5 2/8	5	8	10	Holmes Co., OH	Randy Strohminger	Randy Strohminger	1987	2359
195 1/8	26 7/8	25 5/8	20 5/8	5 1/8	5 1/8	8	7	Otter Tail Co., MN	Kent Sommer	Kent Sommer	1989	2359
195 1/8	25 3/8	25 5/8	21 3/8	6	6 1/8	9	9	Otter Tail Co., MN	Thomas E. Joseph, Jr.	Thomas E. Joseph, Jr.	1992	2359
195 1/8	26	27	21 5/8	4 5/8	4 6/8	8	7	Polk Co., MN	Michael J. Wilson	Michael J. Wilson	1992	2359
195 1/8	25 4/8	26	17 3/8	4 4/8	4 4/8	7	8	Lucas Co., IA	Picked Up	Don Jessop	1993	2359
195 1/8	22 7/8	22 2/8	12 4/8	5 2/8	5 4/8	8	10	Newton Co., MO	W.P. & J.R. Pritchard	W.P. & J.R. Pritchard	1993	2359
195 1/8	27	26 5/8	17 3/8	5 4/8	5 6/8	7	8	Ashland Co., WI	Jerry M. Anderson	Jerry M. Anderson	1995	2359
195 1/8	25 1/8	26 4/8	17 1/8	5 2/8	5 4/8	7	9	Otter Tail Co., MN	Allen Antonsen	Allen Antonsen	1995	2359
195 1/8	27	25 7/8	15 5/8	4 6/8	7 2/8	9	9	Cecil Co., MD	Charles M. Crouse	Charles M. Crouse	1995	2359
195 1/8	25 3/8	24 6/8	19 1/8	4 2/8	4 2/8	10	9	Lonoke Co., AR	John W. Henderson	John W. Henderson	1995	2359
195 1/8	26 1/8	25 3/8	20	4 5/8	4 3/8	7	10	Bath Co., VA	Joe W. Bond	Joe W. Bond	1996	2359
195 1/8	23 4/8	23 4/8	16 6/8	5	4 6/8	8	8	Crook Co., WY	John P. Barrows	John P. Barrows	1998	2359
195 1/8	25 5/8	25 7/8	19 1/8	5 6/8	5 6/8	10	13	Parke Co., IN	Todd D. Farris	Todd D. Farris	1998	2359
195 1/8	23 3/8	25 3/8	22 2/8	6 2/8	6	14	7	Buffalo Co., WI	Michael J. Barstad	Michael J. Barstad	1999	2359
195 1/8	24 3/8	23 1/8	17	5 4/8	5 3/8	7	9	Sylvan Lake, AB	Les Diehl	Les Diehl	1999	2359
195 1/8	20 5/8	23 3/8	14 2/8	6 3/8	5 7/8	11	13	Dukes Co., MA	Picked Up	Daniel C. Feeney	1999	2359
195 1/8	23 6/8	23 2/8	16 6/8	5 1/8	5 1/8	10	8	Woods Co., OK	Stephen C. Elias	Stephen C. Elias	2000	2359
195 1/8	26 2/8	26 3/8	23	5 1/8	5	10	8	Maury Co., TN	Chris Hagan	Chris Hagan	2002	2359
195 1/8	26 7/8	26	24	4 5/8	4 5/8	7	8	Washington Co., IL	Leo M. Suchomski	Leo M. Suchomski	2002	2359

Score								Locality	Hunter	Owner	Date	Rank
195	26 3/8	25 3/8	20 2/8	5	5	7	8	Dickinson Co., MI	Ed Hogberg	Michael Waldvogel	PR 1921	2387
195	24 6/8	24 4/8	18 3/8	5 6/8	5 5/8	6	13	Dome Creek, BC	John Hale	John Charters	PR 1960	2387
195	27 2/8	25 5/8	21 5/8	5 3/8	5 4/8	9	7	Windham Co., CT	Harold Tanner	Warren W. Rogers	1970	2387
195	25 6/8	27 5/8	20 3/8	5 4/8	5 3/8	11	13	Guthrie Co., IA	Tom C. Klever	Tom C. Klever	1982	2387
195	22 4/8	23 4/8	18 6/8	5 4/8	5 2/8	8	9	Calhoun Co., IL	Roger F. Becker	Roger F. Becker	1983	2387
195	25 4/8	25	20	4 5/8	4 5/8	10	9	Clarke Co., IA	Picked Up	Jeff Jorgenson	1985	2387
195	27 5/8	27 1/8	17 1/8	5	5	9	8	Montgomery Co., IA	Mark L. King	Mark L. King	1985	2387
195	23 1/8	21 4/8	17	4 4/8	4 4/8	9	10	Kenedy Co., TX	Phil Lyne	Phil Lyne	1986	2387
195	25 6/8	26 1/8	22 5/8	4 3/8	4 3/8	11	7	Goodhue Co., MN	Darrin L. Goplen	Darrin L. Goplen	1990	2387
195	27 7/8	28 1/8	20 2/8	5 6/8	5 6/8	7	9	Lac du Bonnet, MB	Brad Ehinger	Brad Ehinger	1993	2387
195	24	24	15 7/8	4 7/8	4 6/8	9	8	Rusk Co., WI	Jon R. Lane	Jon R. Lane	1993	2387
195	24 1/8	23 5/8	19 5/8	5	5 2/8	7	9	Bayfield Co., WI	Bradley A. Kuhnert	Bradley A. Kuhnert	1994	2387
195	24 7/8	24 4/8	20 2/8	5 5/8	5 1/8	9	8	Marquette Co., WI	Donald E. Voskuil	Donald E. Voskuil	1994	2387
195	27 4/8	27 7/8	20 1/8	4 6/8	5 2/8	9	10	Jersey Co., IL	Glenn A. Wilson	Glenn A. Wilson	1994	2387
195	25 6/8	27 2/8	22	5 1/8	5	11	9	Westmoreland Co., PA	Eugene W. Livingston	Eugene W. Livingston	1995	2387
195	26 1/8	26 1/8	18 5/8	5 6/8	5 6/8	7	11	Darke Co., OH	Bob Spitler	Bob Spitler	1995	2387
195	25 4/8	26 1/8	23 6/8	5 4/8	5 3/8	8	9	McLean Co., IL	Frank G. Bartels	Frank G. Bartels	1996	2387
195	27 3/8	27	20 6/8	5 1/8	5 1/8	7	8	Guthrie Co., IL	Chad Laabs	Chad Laabs	1996	2387
195	24 4/8	24 4/8	18 7/8	3 7/8	3 7/8	7	8	St. Francis Co., AR	John H. Parker	John H. Parker	1996	2387
195	25 3/8	25 3/8	23 1/8	4 6/8	4 7/8	8	10	Jasper Co., IA	Ronald D. Steenhoek	Ronald D. Steenhoek	1998	2387
195	25	25 4/8	19 6/8	5	5 1/8	8	9	Mitchell Creek, AB	Gord Moreau	Gord Moreau	1998	2387
195	27 1/8	27 6/8	20	5 3/8	5 4/8	7	7	Lenawee Co., MI	Craig Rodosalewicz	Craig Rodosalewicz	1998	2387
195	25 2/8	27 2/8	19 3/8	4 3/8	4 5/8	7	10	Dimmit Co., TX	J. Marvin Smith IV	J. Marvin Smith IV	1999	2387
195	22 6/8	26 6/8	19 3/8	5 3/8	5 7/8	10	8	Shawnee Co., KS	Mark E. Conaway	Mark E. Conaway	1999	2387
195	21 7/8	21 7/8	15 2/8	5 4/8	5 4/8	12	14	Carter Co., OK	William A. Crosby	William A. Crosby	2000	2387
195	26 6/8	26 6/8	19 1/8	5 5/8	5 5/8	8	7	Delaware Co., IA	Joseph D. Hoeger	Joseph D. Hoeger	2000	2387
195	26	25 4/8		4 5/8	4 5/8	9	7	Shell River, MB	Wayne Todoschuk	Wayne Todoschuk	2000	2387
195	26 4/8	26 1/8		5 6/8	5 6/8	7	7	Dubuque Co., IA	Adam W. Anglin	Adam W. Anglin	2001	2387
254 2/8*	26 3/8	25 1/8	19 1/8	5 6/8	5 6/8	13	11	Frenchman Butte, SK	Dwayne Erb	Cabela's, Inc.	1999	
252 6/8*	27 1/8	24 5/8	17 1/8	5 7/8	5 7/8	9	15	Sandy Lake, AB	Donald Brenneman	Donald Brenneman	1998	
251 6/8*	30 4/8	31 6/8	25 2/8	5 5/8	5 3/8	12	13	Fulton Co., IL	William K. Brown	William K. Brown	1999	
251 2/8*	27 2/8	27 5/8	22 1/8	6 3/8	6 5/8	10	13	Lorain Co., OH	Kirk W. Gott	Kirk W. Gott	2000	

* Final score is subject to revision by additional verifying measurements.

CATEGORY
WHITETAIL DEER -
NON-TYPICAL ANTLERS

SCORE
198-7/8

HUNTER
MARK E. HOUBA

LOCATION
RANDOLPH COUNTY,
ILLINOIS

DATE OF KILL
NOVEMBER 2002

CATEGORY
WHITETAIL DEER -
NON-TYPICAL ANTLERS

SCORE
196-5/8

HUNTER
MARK S. ILIJANIC

LOCATION
WINNIPEG RIVER,
MANITOBA

DATE OF KILL
NOVEMBER 2000

CATEGORY
WHITETAIL DEER - NON-TYPICAL ANTLERS

SCORE
195-6/8

HUNTER
LARRY R. FAUST

LOCATION
PARK COUNTY, MONTANA

DATE OF KILL
NOVEMBER 2001

CATEGORY
WHITETAIL DEER -
NON-TYPICAL ANTLERS

SCORE
245-6/8

HUNTER
RICHARD D. PAULS (BELOW)

LOCATION
SOURIS RIVER, MANITOBA

DATE OF KILL
OCTOBER 2000

CATEGORY
WHITETAIL DEER - NON-TYPICAL ANTLERS

SCORE
226-1/8

HUNTER
ROBERT ODEY (LEFT)

LOCATION
IOWA COUNTY, WISCONSIN

DATE OF KILL
NOVEMBER 2002

SCORE
204-4/8

HUNTER
PATRICK F. KINCH (BELOW LEFT)

LOCATION
DOGPOUND CREEK, ALBERTA

DATE OF KILL
NOVEMBER 2002

547

CATEGORY
WHITETAIL DEER -
NON-TYPICAL ANTLERS

SCORE
220-1/8

HUNTER
JEFFREY J. SPRENG

LOCATION
ASHLAND COUNTY, OHIO

DATE OF KILL
NOVEMBER 2002

CATEGORY
WHITETAIL DEER -
NON-TYPICAL ANTLERS

SCORE
231-5/8

HUNTER
ROBERT J. JOHANNSEN

LOCATION
PORTER COUNTY, INDIANA

DATE OF KILL
NOVEMBER 2002

CATEGORY
WHITETAIL DEER - NON-TYPICAL ANTLERS

SCORE
207-1/8

HUNTER
MICHAEL R. DAVIS

LOCATION
MONTGOMERY COUNTY, INDIANA

DATE OF KILL
NOVEMBER 2000

B&C HISTORY

GEORGE BIRD GRINNELL
1849-1938

By H. Hudson DeCray

Together with Theodore Roosevelt, George Bird Grinnell was one of the founding members of the Boone and Crockett Club in December of 1887. He served as its president from 1918 to 1927. He founded the Audubon Society in 1886. The establishment of Glacier National Park in 1910 came about largely due to the efforts of Dr. Grinnell. He developed a great interest in the Plains Indians and was considered the leading authority on the Blackfoot, Cheyenne, and Pawnee Nations. He was editor-in-chief of *Forest and Stream* magazine, the leading outdoor magazine of its time. He is considered one of the preeminent conservationists in the early history of the movement. ■

COUES' WHITETAIL DEER - TYPICAL ANTLERS
WORLD'S RECORD

RANK
World's Record

SCORE
144 1/8

LOCATION
Pima Co., Az

HUNTER
Ed Stockwell

OWNER
Barbara Stockwell

DATE KILLED
1953

As trophy measurements were reviewed for the 1955 Competition, judges were startled by a Coues' whitetail deer entry from Ed Stockwell of Pima County, Arizona. Stockwell had also added an equally amazing account of his hunt.

"In 1958, after hunting all morning in the Santa Rita Mountains of southern Arizona, my partner and I were heading back to camp. There was a low but very rugged mountain to one side, and we decided to hunt around it. I began a slanting climb along the slope. My buddy took a lower route. There were lots of big rocks and impassable bluffs. Angling around them, I kept working upward until suddenly I was on top, and then, while going through the rocky terrain toward the smoother eastern slope, I jumped a big buck that had a small spike with him.

"As only the big antlers showed up behind a rocky ridge, I ran to get a better view. The big buck disappeared. Just as I was giving him up, he moved from behind a large oak tree and started down the slope, giving me a clear shot. I dropped him at about 60 yards. Evidently I had come up the side of the mountain that he used as his sneak exit, and it was probably due to this that I got such a good chance at him. My rifle was a .300 Savage, without a scope."

Scored at no less than 143, Ed Stockwell's trophy initially raised a few doubts in regard to its classification. The situation called for a careful examination of this head to make sure that it hadn't come from one of the larger whitetail subspecies, even though the Coues' whitetail deer range is not known to touch that of the bigger whitetails. By getting most of its water from cactus, this species has adapted to the dry country where most whitetails are incapable of surviving. After only a brief study of this rack it was verified that it had every characteristic of Coues' deer conformation. Although the antler beams were a trifle shorter than those of the 1952 leader, what set the official new World's Record apart at 144-1/8 was a massiveness that Coues' deer antlers very rarely show. ■

COUES' WHITETAIL DEER
TYPICAL ANTLERS
WORLD'S RECORD SCORE CHART

Photograph by Eldon L. "Buck" Buckner

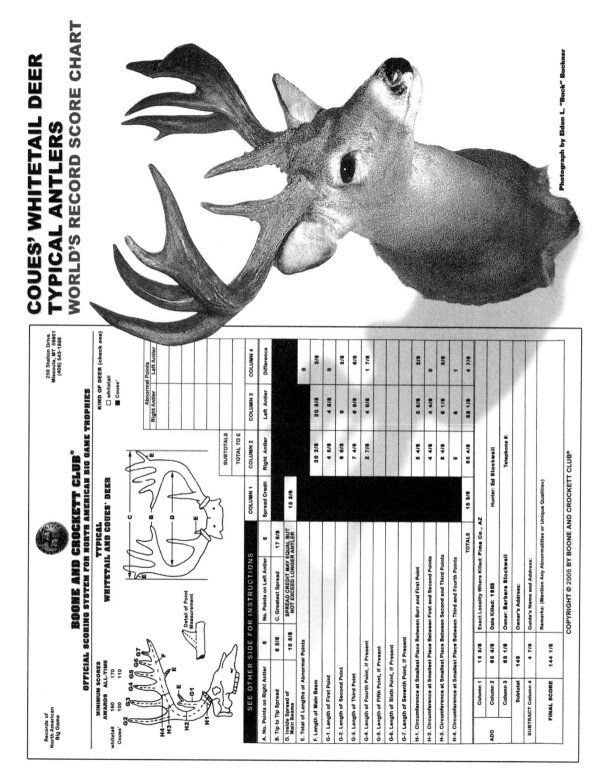

Records of North American Big Game

250 Station Drive
Missoula, MT 59801
(406) 542-1888

BOONE AND CROCKETT CLUB®
OFFICIAL SCORING SYSTEM FOR NORTH AMERICAN BIG GAME TROPHIES

TYPICAL
WHITETAIL AND COUES' DEER

MINIMUM SCORES

	AWARDS	ALL-TIME
whitetail	160	170
Coues	100	110

KIND OF DEER (check one)
☐ whitetail
☑ Coues'

Detail of Point Measurement

SEE OTHER SIDE FOR INSTRUCTIONS

			Abnormal Points	
			Right Antler	Left Antler

SUBTOTALS
TOTAL TO E

		COLUMN 1 Spread Credit	COLUMN 2 Right Antler	COLUMN 3 Left Antler	COLUMN 4 Difference
A. No. Points on Right Antler	5				
No. Points on Left Antler	5				
B. Tip to Tip Spread	6 3/8				
C. Greatest Spread	17 6/8				
D. Inside Spread of Main Beams	15 3/8	SPREAD CREDIT MAY EQUAL BUT NOT EXCEED LONGER ANTLER	15 3/8			
E. Total of Lengths of Abnormal Points					
F. Length of Main Beam				20 2/8	20 5/8	3/8
G-1. Length of First Point				4 6/8	4 6/8	0
G-2. Length of Second Point				8 6/8	6 6/8	2/8
G-3. Length of Third Point				7 4/8	6 6/8	6/8
G-4. Length of Fourth Point, If Present				2 7/8	4 6/8	1 7/8
G-5. Length of Fifth Point, If Present						
G-6. Length of Sixth Point, If Present						
G-7. Length of Seventh Point, If Present						
H-1. Circumference at Smallest Place Between Burr and First Point				5 4/8	5 6/8	2/8
H-2. Circumference at Smallest Place Between First and Second Points				4 4/8	4 4/8	0
H-3. Circumference at Smallest Place Between Second and Third Points				6 4/8	6 1/8	3/8
H-4. Circumference at Smallest Place Between Third and Fourth Points				5	6	1
TOTALS			15 3/8	65 4/8	65 1/8	4 7/8

ADD	Column 1	15 3/8	Exact Locality Where Killed: Pima Co., AZ
	Column 2	65 4/8	Date Killed: 1953 — Hunter: Ed Stockwell
	Column 3	65 1/8	Owner: Barbara Stockwell — Telephone #:
	Subtotal	149	Owner's Address:
SUBTRACT	Column 4	4 7/8	Guide's Name and Address:
	FINAL SCORE	144 1/8	Remarks: (Mention Any Abnormalities or Unique Qualities)

COPYRIGHT © 2005 BY BOONE AND CROCKETT CLUB®

TOP 10 COUES' WHITETAIL – TYPICAL

NUMBER 1 — 144-1/8 POINTS
ED STOCKWELL — 1953

NUMBER 2 — 143 POINTS
LARRY JOHNSON — 1995

NUMBER 3 — 134-4/8 POINTS
VICTOR P. GIACOLETTI, JR. — 1981

NUMBER 4 — 133 POINTS
MICHAEL E. DUPERRET — 1990

NUMBER 5 — 131-7/8 POINTS
GEORGE W. KOUTS — 1935

552

NUMBER 7 — 130-4/8 POINTS
KIM J. POULIN — 1981

SEE OTHER SIDE FOR INST...

NUMBER 10 — 127-4/8 PQINTS
PICKED UP — PRIOR TO 2003

A.
B. Tip to Tip Sp...
C. Greatest S...
D. Inside Sp...
    of Main B...
E   E Spread exceed...
    Total of Le...
F. Total of Len...
G-1. Length of Ma...
G-2. Length of Fir...
G-3. Length of Seco...
G-4. Length of Third...
G-5. Length of Fourth...
G-6. Length of Fifth P...
G-7. Length of Sixth P...
     Length of Seventh P...
H-1. Between Burr and Fir...
H-2. Circumference at Sma...
     Between First and Se...
H-3. Circumference at Smalle...
     Between Second and Third...
H-4. Circumference at Smallest...
     and Fourth Points (see ba...

TOTALS

ADD | Column 1 | | Exac...
    | Column 2 | 15-4/8 |
    | Column 3 | 64 |
    | Total | |
SUBTRACT Column 4 | |

FINAL SCORE | 12A-4/ |

Guide's N...
Remarks...

G-1. Length of First Point...
G-2. Length of Second Point
G-3. Length of Third Point
G-4. Length of Fourth Point, if present
G-5. Length of Fifth Point, if present
G-6 ...th Point, if present
G-7 ...if present
Circumference at ...ce
H-1. Between Burr and Fil...
Circumference at Smallest...
H-2. Between First and Second Point
Circumference at Smallest Place
H-3. Between Second and Third Points
H-4. Between Sec...

Circumfere...
Fourth Poi...
Beam Tip...

NUMBER 6 — 130-5/8 POINTS
WAYNE KLEINMAN — 1958

NUMBER 9 — 128-POINTS
RAMON C. BORREGO — 1988

X...g...

NUMBER 8 — 128-3/8 POINTS
PICKED-UP — 2002

TOTA...
...Co...

ADD

SUBTRA...
FINAL S...

553

COUES' WHITETAIL DEER - TYPICAL ANTLERS
Odocoileus virginianus couesi

MINIMUM SCORE 110

Score	Length of Main Beam R	L	Inside Spread	Circumference at Smallest Place Between Burr and First Point R	L	Number of Points R	L	Locality	Hunter	Owner	Date Killed	Rank
144 1/8	20 2/8	20 5/8	15 3/8	5 4/8	5 6/8	5	5	Pima Co., AZ	Ed Stockwell	Barbara Stockwell	1953	1
143	19 7/8	20 3/8	13 2/8	4 6/8	4 6/8	5	5	Navajo Co., AZ	Larry Johnson	Alan C. Ellsworth	1995	2
134 4/8	20 5/8	21 1/8	16	4 5/8	4 3/8	5	5	Grant Co., NM	Victor P. Giacoletti, Jr.	Victor P. Giacoletti, Jr.	1981	3
133	20 6/8	19 7/8	18	3 7/8	3 7/8	6	6	Pima Co., AZ	Michael E. Duperret	M.E. Duperret & J.K. Volk	1990	4
131 7/8	19 6/8	19 2/8	16 1/8	4 2/8	4 2/8	5	5	Cochise Co., AZ	George W. Kouts	George W. Kouts	1935	5
130 5/8	20 5/8	19 3/8	14 5/8	3 2/8	3 2/8	5	5	Chihuahua, MX	Wayne Kleinman	Wayne Kleinman	1958	6
130 4/8	20 6/8	20 6/8	15 6/8	4 6/8	4 5/8	8	6	Pima Co., AZ	Kim J. Poulin	Kim J. Poulin	1981	7
130 1/8	20 6/8	21	15	3 7/8	4	5	6	Santa Cruz Co., AZ	Sergio Orozco	Sergio Orozco	2001	8
128 3/8	20 1/8	20 3/8	16 7/8	4 1/8	4 1/8	5	5	Sonora, MX	Picked Up	Kirk Kelso	2002	9
128	21 1/8	20	19 2/8	4 6/8	4 4/8	4	4	Grant Co., NM	Ramon C. Borrego	Ramon C. Borrego	1988	10
127 4/8	19 5/8	20 3/8	12 6/8	3 6/8	4	6	5	Sonora, MX	Picked Up	Kirk Kelso	PR 2003	11
126 6/8	20	18 7/8	17 6/8	4 7/8	5 1/8	5	5	Yavapai Co., AZ	Picked Up	Joshua E. Epperson	1999	12
126 5/8	21 6/8	19 6/8	14	4	4 2/8	6	5	Cochise Co., AZ	Mike Kasun	Mike Kasun, Jr.	1959	13
126 5/8	19 4/8	18 6/8	11 1/8	4 5/8	4 3/8	5	6	Pima Co., AZ	DeWayne M. Hanna	DeWayne M. Hanna	1977	13
126 1/8	19 5/8	19 7/8	16 2/8	3 7/8	4	6	6	Pima Co., AZ	Robert G. McDonald	Robert G. McDonald	1986	15
125 4/8	18 6/8	19	16 2/8	3 7/8	3 6/8	5	5	Arivaca, AZ	Gerald Harris	Gerald Harris	1953	16
125	19 6/8	19 7/8	15 4/8	4 1/8	4 1/8	5	5	Ft. Apache Res., AZ	Picked Up	Jerry S. Pippen	PR 1969	17
125	21	20 6/8	16 2/8	4 3/8	4 4/8	4	5	Sonora, MX	Enrique Barrett	Enrique Barrett	1995	17
125	19 6/8	19 5/8	15 4/8	4 1/8	4 3/8	7	6	Graham Co., AZ	Bradley Johns	Bradley Johns	2000	17
124 7/8	18 4/8	18 5/8	12 6/8	4 4/8	4 5/8	6	6	Hidalgo Co., NM	Martha M. Montes	Martha M. Montes	1994	20
124 7/8	20 6/8	20 5/8	14 3/8	4 3/8	4 3/8	5	4	Santa Cruz Co., AZ	Kirk Kelso	Kirk Kelso	2001	20
124 6/8	16 7/8	17 1/8	15 1/8	3 7/8	4 1/8	7	6	Gila Co., AZ	Tommy T. Zienka	Tommy T. Zienka	1998	22
124 5/8	19 6/8	19	14 1/8	4	4 1/8	6	6	Rincon Mts., AZ	James Pfersdorf	Mrs. J.E. Pfersdorf, Sr.	1936	23
124 5/8	18 2/8	18 7/8	13 5/8	3 6/8	3 6/8	5	5	Sonora, MX	Enrique Lares	Enrique Lares	1959	23
124	19 1/8	19 1/8	16 6/8	3 7/8	3 7/8	5	5	Greenlee Co., AZ	Ronald H. Gerdes	Ronald H. Gerdes	1993	25
124	18 7/8	18 6/8	15	3 4/8	3 4/8	6	5	Sonora, MX	Joseph P. Kalt	Joseph P. Kalt	1998	25
123 7/8	17 2/8	17 3/8	13 7/8	4 3/8	4 3/8	6	6	Gila Co., AZ	Stephen P. Hayes	Stephen P. Hayes	1965	27
123 7/8	21 3/8	19 5/8	15 3/8	4 2/8	4 1/8	5	4	Pima Co., AZ	Kenneth R. Murray	Kenneth R. Murray	1996	27
123 6/8	18 2/8	17 7/8	14 2/8	4 4/8	4 4/8	6	6	Cochise Co., AZ	Larry Vance, Jr.	Larry Vance, Jr.	1985	29
123 6/8	19 7/8	19 6/8	14 4/8	3 7/8	3 7/8	5	4	Sonora, MX	William J. Mills	William J. Mills	2002	29
123 3/8	20 2/8	20 5/8	16 1/8	4	4	4	4	Pima Co., AZ	Picked Up	Brian A. Rimsza	2002	31
122 7/8	18 7/8	18 2/8	14 1/8	4 1/8	4 1/8	5	6	Chiricahua Mts., AZ	Roger Becksted	Roger Becksted	1960	32
122 5/8	20 5/8	20	15	4 4/8	4 4/8	5	5	Chihuahua, MX	Kirk Kelso	Kirk Kelso	1997	33
122 4/8	22	20 4/8	15 2/8	3 1/8	3 2/8	5	5	Sonora, MX	Lloyd L. Ward, Jr.	Lloyd L. Ward, Jr.	1945	34
122 1/8	19 6/8	20 6/8	16 7/8	4 2/8	4	4	4	Sonora, MX	J. Marvin Smith III	J. Marvin Smith III	1990	35
121 5/8	20 1/8	19 3/8	15 5/8	4 2/8	4	4	4	Pima Co., AZ	Joe Fanning	Joe Fanning	1964	36

Score	Main Beam R	Main Beam L	Spread	Circ. R	Circ. L	Pts. R	Pts. L	By Whom Killed	Owner	Locality	Date	Rank
121 4/8	19	17 6/8	14 1/8	4	3 6/8	6	6	Max E. Wilson	Max E. Wilson	Santa Rita Mts., AZ	1965	37
121 3/8	16 1/8	17	10 7/8	3 4/8	3 4/8	6	6	George Shaar	George Shaar	Santa Rita Mts., AZ	1964	38
121 3/8	21	20	15 3/8	4 2/8	4 3/8	4	4	Picked Up	Kirk Kelso	Sonora, MX	2003	38
121 1/8	19 5/8	19 2/8	15 7/8	3 7/8	3 7/8	5	5	T. Reed Scott	T. Reed Scott	Pima Co., AZ	1975	40
121	20 3/8	19 5/8	13	3 7/8	3 7/8	5	5	Herb Klein	Dallas Mus. of Natl. Hist.	Sierra Madre Mts., MX	1965	41
121	20 6/8	20 7/8	16	4	4 1/8	6	5	Picked Up	Kirk Kelso	Sonora, MX	2003	41
120 7/8	19 4/8	19 4/8	14 4/8	4	4	5	5	Harold Lyons	Harold Lyons	Santa Rita Mts., AZ	1956	43
120 6/8	19	18 2/8	12 1/8	4 2/8	4 4/8	5	4	Manuel A. Caravantez	Manuel A. Caravantez	Sonora, MX	1960	44
120 5/8	20 1/8	19 2/8	12 4/8	3 5/8	3 6/8	4	4	George W. Parker	George W. Parker	Sonora, MX	1969	45
120 5/8	17 6/8	19 2/8	16 3/8	4	4	6	5	Becki D. Goffrier	Becki D. Goffrier	Cochise Co., AZ	1984	45
120 4/8	18	18 3/8	13	4	4	4	4	Diego G. Sada	Diego G. Sada	Sonora, MX	1969	47
120 1/8	18 5/8	18 5/8	13 5/8	4 2/8	4 6/8	5	4	Homer R. Edds	Homer R. Edds	Baboquivari Mts., AZ	1961	48
120	20 7/8	17 7/8	14 2/8	4 1/8	3 7/8	4	4	Picked Up	Kirk Kelso	Sonora, MX	2000	49
119 7/8	20 2/8	20 7/8	17 5/8	4 4/8	4	5	4	Tom Connolly	Tom Connolly	Gila Co., AZ	1960	50
119 7/8	20 1/8	20 4/8	15 1/8	4	4 1/8	4	4	Picked Up	George W. Parker	Sonora, MX	1960	50
119 6/8	19	19	12 2/8	4	4 4/8	4	4	George W. Parker	George W. Parker	Canelo Hills, AZ	1960	52
119 6/8	19 3/8	19 4/8	13 2/8	3 7/8	4 6/8	4	4	Frank L. Riley	Frank L. Riley	Hidalgo Co., NM	1990	52
119 4/8	19 7/8	19 7/8	15 4/8	4 2/8	4 1/8	5	5	James A. Hall	James A. Hall	Cochise Co., AZ	1991	54
119 4/8	18 4/8	18 2/8	16 4/8	4 1/8	3 7/8	4	5	Allen J. Anspach	Allen J. Anspach	Gila Co., AZ	1992	54
119 3/8	19 6/8	20 1/8	12	3 7/8	4	6	4	A.R. Anglen	A.R. Anglen	Canelo Hills, AZ	1967	56
119 2/8	16 7/8	16 7/8	15	4	4 1/8	6	7	Bert M. Pringle	Mrs. Bert M. Pringle	Gila Co., AZ	1952	57
119 2/8	18	18	15 4/8	3 7/8	5 3/8	4	4	Michael Lonuzzi	Michael Lonuzzi	Sonora, MX	1996	57
119 1/8	18	18	10 5/8	5 3/8	3 3/8	6	6	Monte L. Colvin	Monte L. Colvin	Santa Rita Mts., AZ	1965	59
119 1/8	19 2/8	19 2/8	14 3/8	3 3/8	3 7/8	4	4	James A. Leiendecker	James A. Leiendecker	Cochise Co., AZ	1986	59
119 1/8	19	19	15 3/8	3 7/8	3 5/8	4	4	Scott Davis	Scott Davis	Pima Co., AZ	1995	59
119	18	18	13 6/8	3 4/8	4 3/8	6	7	Jesse E. Williams	Jesse E. Williams	Hidalgo Co., NM	1971	62
118 6/8	17 7/8	17 7/8	16 4/8	3 7/8	4	5	5	Alberto Trousselle	Alberto Trousselle	Chihuahua, MX	1996	63
118 5/8	18	18	14 5/8	4 4/8	4 5/8	4	4	Ward Becksted	Ward Becksted	Chiricahua Mts., AZ	1958	64
118 3/8	19 5/8	19 5/8	13 7/8	4 5/8	3 6/8	4	4	Michael E. Duperret	M.E. Duperret & J.K. Volk	Hidalgo Co., NM	1993	65
118 1/8	18 1/8	18 7/8	15 1/8	3 6/8	3 7/8	5	5	David W. Ahnell	David W. Ahnell	Santa Cruz Co., AZ	1977	66
118	17 1/8	17 1/8	14 1/8	3 7/8	4 2/8	8	7	Ralph Vaga	Ralph Vaga	Washington Co., AZ	1962	67
118	16 6/8	16 5/8	16 6/8	4 1/8	3 7/8	4	4	Michael L. Valenzuela	Michael L. Valenzuela	Santa Cruz Co., AZ	1982	67
118	18 2/8	19 2/8	12 6/8	3 5/8	3 5/8	7	7	Larry C. Dixon	Larry C. Dixon	Pima Co., AZ	1995	67
117 7/8	17 7/8	18 1/8	13	4	4	4	4	Picked Up	H.L. Russell	Rincon Mts., AZ	1963	70
117 7/8	19	18 1/8	16 5/8	4 1/8	3 7/8	4	4	George Shaar	George Shaar	Santa Rita Mts., AZ	1965	70
117 6/8	19 5/8	19	12 3/8	3 5/8	3 5/8	6	6	Raymond J Kassler	Raymond J Kassler	Canelo Hills, AZ	1958	72
117 5/8	18 6/8	19 4/8	14	4 2/8	4 5/8	4	4	Abe R. Hughes	Abe R. Hughes	Libertad, MX	1967	73
117 4/8	20 3/8	18 6/8	18 5/8	4 6/8	4 2/8	4	4	Steven J. Stayner	Steven J. Stayner	Graham Co., AZ	1993	74
117 4/8	17 7/8	17 1/8	14 4/8	4 3/8	4 3/8	4	4	Harry Neff	Harry Neff	Apache Co., AZ	1995	74
117 3/8	18 1/8	18	15 6/8	3 6/8	3 6/8	4	4	F.O. Haskell	F.O. Haskell	Atasco Mts., AZ	1939	76
117 3/8	17 4/8	17 4/8	14 3/8	3 6/8	3 6/8	5	5	George S. Tsaguris	George S. Tsaguris	Sicritta Mts., AZ	1958	76
117 3/8	17 2/8	17 2/8	12 5/8	4 4/8	4 4/8	6	6	Charles B. Leonard	Charles B. Leonard	Sonora, MX	1974	76
117 2/8	19 2/8	19 3/8	16 3/8	4 7/8	4 2/8	6	6	George L. Garlits	George L. Garlits	Santa Rita Mts., AZ	1957	79
117 2/8	19	19 3/8	11 6/8	4 4/8	3 4/8	8	7	Picked Up	Warren A. Cartier	Chiricahua Mts., AZ	1963	79
117 2/8	19 3/8	18 2/8	17 5/8	3 5/8	4 1/8	4	4	Charles H. Pennington	Charles H. Pennington	Tumacacori Mts., AZ	1968	79
117	18 2/8	18	12	4 1/8	3 6/8	5	5	W.R. Tanner	Fred Tanner	Cochise Co., AZ	1941	82
117	18 7/8	18 7/8	14 2/8	3 6/8	3 6/8	7	6	Arthur L. Butler	Arthur L. Butler	Pima Co., AZ	1974	82
116 7/8	18 1/8	17 3/8	13 1/8	3 6/8	3 6/8	5	5	Seymour H. Levy	Seymour H. Levy	Santa Cruz Co., AZ	1967	84

Odocoileus virginianus couesi

Score	Length of Main Beam R	L	Inside Spread	Circumference at Smallest Place Between Burr and First Point R	L	Number of Points R	L	Locality	Hunter	Owner	Date Killed	Rank
116 7/8	19	19 6/8	16 3/8	4	3 6/8	5	5	Pima Co., AZ	Arcenio G. Valdez	Arcenio G. Valdez	1971	84
116 6/8	17 7/8	18 3/8	14	4 7/8	5	4	4	Coconino Co., AZ	Clay McDonald	Clay McDonald	1985	86
116 6/8	18 2/8	18 1/8	15 4/8	4 5/8	4 3/8	5	5	Yavapai Co., AZ	Kevin S. Stimple	Kevin S. Stimple	1992	86
116 6/8	19 2/8	19 2/8	14 2/8	4 2/8	4 1/8	4	4	Sonora, MX	Len H. Guldman	Len H. Guldman	2003	86
116 5/8	17 5/8	19	14 3/8	4	4	5	5	Santa Rita Mts., AZ	Mike Holloran	Mike Holloran	1962	89
116 5/8	17 2/8	17 3/8	14 7/8	4 6/8	4 5/8	4	4	Gila Co., AZ	Richard A. Thom	Richard A. Thom	1978	89
116 5/8	20 7/8	19 6/8	17 7/8	4 3/8	4 3/8	6	6	Greenlee Co., AZ	John R. Primasing, Jr.	John R. Primasing, Jr.	1997	89
116 4/8	19 5/8	20 2/8	14 5/8	3 7/8	3 6/8	5	5	Gila Co., AZ	Nathan Ellison	Nathan Ellison	1950	92
116 3/8	19 2/8	19	14 7/8	4 1/8	4 2/8	5	5	Blue River, AZ	Earl H. Harris	Earl H. Harris	1965	93
116 2/8	15 2/8	16 4/8	13 4/8	4 3/8	4 3/8	6	6	Chiricahua Mts., AZ	Freeman Neal	R.M. Woods	1947	94
116 2/8	16 2/8	16 5/8	14	4	4	5	5	Graham Co., AZ	Dale J. Holladay	Dale J. Holladay	1984	94
116 1/8	19 4/8	19 5/8	12 7/8	3 6/8	3 6/8	4	5	Greenlee Co., AZ	Richard A. Benson	Richard A. Benson	1991	96
116	17 4/8	17 3/8	13 2/8	4 6/8	4 7/8	4	4	Santa Cruz Co., AZ	Ben Richardson	Ben Richardson	1978	97
116	19	18 7/8	14	3 5/8	3 5/8	4	4	Santa Cruz Co., AZ	Jeffrey C. Lichtenwalter	Jeffrey C. Lichtenwalter	1982	97
115 7/8	18 6/8	16 7/8	14 3/8	4 6/8	4 6/8	5	7	Sonora, MX	Berry B. Brooks	Berry B. Brooks	1954	99
115 7/8	19 2/8	18 6/8	14 1/8	4	4	5	5	Yavapai Co., AZ	Robert W. Gaylor	Robert W. Gaylor	1987	99
115 6/8	20	19 5/8	16	4	3 7/8	4	6	Sonora, MX	Richard G. Bailey	Richard G. Bailey	2003	101
115 5/8	18 5/8	18 4/8	14 3/8	3 6/8	3 7/8	4	5	Breadpan Mt., AZ	Mitchell R. Holder	Mitchell R. Holder	1966	102
115 4/8	15 6/8	16 6/8	13	4	4 2/8	5	4	Santa Rita Mts., AZ	Picked Up	James Bramhall	PR 1963	103
115 4/8	18 6/8	18 2/8	15	4	4	5	4	Cochise Co., AZ	Bill F. Byrd	Bill F. Byrd	1983	103
115 4/8	18	17 1/8	15 4/8	4 2/8	4 2/8	5	4	Gila Co., AZ	Doug J. Althoff	Doug J. Althoff	1985	103
115 4/8	21 3/8	22 4/8	18	4	4	4	3	Sonora, MX	Picked Up	Kirk Kelso	2003	103
115 3/8	19 1/8	19 5/8	19 5/8	3 7/8	3 6/8	4	4	Pima Co., AZ	William H. Taylor	William H. Taylor	1986	107
115 2/8	17 2/8	17	13 4/8	5	4 7/8	5	4	Santa Rita Mts., AZ	Denis Wolstenholme	Denis Wolstenholme	1958	108
115 2/8	18	20 1/8	15	4	4	5	4	Cerro Colo. Mts., AZ	Manuel V. Guillen	Manuel V. Guillen	1962	108
115 2/8	20 4/8	19 4/8	12 6/8	4 2/8	4 3/8	5	5	Santa Rita Mts., AZ	Bill J. Ford	Bill J. Ford	1965	108
115 2/8	20 1/8	19	16 4/8	4 2/8	4 3/8	5	5	Catalina Mts., AZ	Jim Stough	Jim Stough	1972	108
115 1/8	18 3/8	18 1/8	13 1/8	4	4	5	5	Pima Co., AZ	Robert A. Finelli	Robert A. Finelli	1997	112
115	19 5/8	19 5/8	17 6/8	4 2/8	4 1/8	4	4	Baboquivari Mts., AZ	Karl G. Ronstadt	Karl G. Ronstadt	1967	113
115	19 6/8	20 1/8	18 2/8	4	4	5	4	Coconino Co., AZ	Picked Up	Jerry C. Walters	PR 1970	113
115	18 4/8	18 1/8	16 6/8	4	4	5	5	Pima Co., AZ	Glen A. Elmer	Glen A. Elmer	1980	113
115	18 6/8	18	17 2/8	4 2/8	4 2/8	5	5	Pinal Co., AZ	George Martin	George Martin	1983	113
114 7/8	18 2/8	18 6/8	12 3/8	4 7/8	4 7/8	4	4	Ruby, AZ	Richard McDaniel	Richard McDaniel	1963	117
114 7/8	20	19 4/8	16 1/8	3 6/8	3 6/8	5	5	Santa Rita Mts., AZ	John H. Lake	John H. Lake	1965	117
114 7/8	18	19	13 1/8	4 3/8	4 2/8	5	4	Sonora, MX	Carlos G. Hermosillo	Carlos G. Hermosillo	1995	117
114 6/8	16 6/8	16 6/8	13 6/8	4 1/8	4 1/8	5	5	Chihuahua, MX	Tom Jones	Richard Rhoades	1932	120

Score	Main Beam R	Main Beam L	Inside Spread	Circ. R	Circ. L	Pts. R	Pts. L	Locality	By Whom Killed	Owner	Date Killed	Rank
114 6/8	19 5/8	19 3/8	14 5/8	4 4/8	4 5/8	6	8	Chiricahua Mts., AZ	John Miller	John Miller	1949	120
114 6/8	17 4/8	16	15 2/8	4 5/8	4 4/8	4	5	Santa Rita Mts., AZ	Art Pollard	Art Pollard	1951	120
114 6/8	17 2/8	17 4/8	16 2/8	4 2/8	4	4	4	Cochise Co., AZ	Rudy Alvarez	Rudy Alvarez	1960	120
114 6/8	18 3/8	18	15 1/8	4	3 7/8	6	5	Canelo Hills, AZ	Guy Perry	Guy Perry	1960	120
114 6/8	16 6/8	16 4/8	11	4 2/8	4 3/8	5	7	Santa Rita Mts., AZ	John Bessett	John Bessett	1965	120
114 6/8	17 5/8	17 5/8	14 4/8	4 1/8	4 1/8	5	5	Nogales, AZ	Arthur N. Lindsey	Arthur N. Lindsey	1967	120
114 5/8	18 6/8	18 2/8	15 5/8	3 5/8	3 6/8	4	5	Pima Co., AZ	James A. Reynolds	James A. Reynolds	1984	127
114 5/8	15 2/8	14 7/8	14 3/8	3 4/8	3 5/8	5	5	Gila Co., AZ	J. Bradley Johns	J. Bradley Johns	1992	127
114 4/8	19 3/8	20 4/8	15	4 2/8	4 4/8	4	4	Graham Mts., AZ	Robert R. Stonoff	Robert R. Stonoff	1962	129
114 4/8	15 6/8	16 1/8	12 4/8	3 7/8	4 1/8	6	4	Patagonia Mts., AZ	Verna Conlisk	Verna Conlisk	1964	129
114 4/8	17 5/8	17 1/8	13 7/8	3 5/8	3 5/8	6	5	Cherry Creek, AZ	Alan G. Adams	Alan G. Adams	1968	129
114 4/8	15 6/8	15 4/8	14 2/8	3 6/8	3 5/8	5	5	Chiricahua Mts., MX	Elgin T. Gates	Elgin T. Gates	1968	129
114 4/8	19 6/8	18 3/8	14 4/8	3 6/8	3 6/8	4	4	Pima Co., AZ	James M. Machac	James M. Machac	1985	129
114 4/8	17 5/8	17 5/8	14 4/8	4 1/8	4	4	5	Hidalgo Co., NM	W.B. Darnell	Travis Darnell	1986	129
114 4/8	18	17 5/8	15	4 2/8	4 1/8	4	4	Gila Co., AZ	Dallas J. Duhamell, Jr.	Dallas J. Duhamell, Jr.	1990	129
114 3/8	18	18 3/8	12 5/8	4	3 7/8	4	4	Atasco Mts., AZ	Antonio Lopez	Antonio Lopez	1961	136
114 3/8	17 2/8	18 5/8	13 3/8	3 7/8	4	5	4	Pima Co., AZ	James A. Reynolds	James A. Reynolds	1980	136
114 2/8	18 4/8	18 1/8	15 2/8	4 3/8	4 2/8	5	5	Catalina Mts., AZ	Wayne L. Heckler	Wayne L. Heckler	1958	138
114 2/8	18 5/8	18 3/8	11 5/8	4 2/8	3 6/8	5	6	Canelo, AZ	Earl Stillson	Earl Stillson	1967	138
114 2/8	18 4/8	17 6/8	14 2/8	4 2/8	3 4/8	5	5	Grant Co., NM	Picked Up	Victor P. Giacoletti, Jr.	1985	138
114 2/8	20 1/8	19 7/8	17	4 2/8	4 2/8	5	5	Pima Co., AZ	Steven E. Shooks	Steven E. Shooks	1998	138
114 1/8	19	18 7/8	13 6/8	4 1/8	4 2/8	4	4	Sonora, MX	Unknown	Bill Quimby	PR 1965	142
114 1/8	17	16 1/8	14 1/8	4 4/8	4 2/8	5	5	Yavapai Co., AZ	Jim D. Snodgrass	Jim D. Snodgrass	1983	142
114	17 3/8	17 2/8	16 7/8	3 4/8	3 4/8	4	4	Animas Mts., NM	Frank C. Hibben	Frank C. Hibben	1955	144
114	19 6/8	18 1/8	10 4/8	3 6/8	3 7/8	4	6	Pima Co., AZ	Jeffrey K. Volk	Michael E. Duperret	2001	144
114	18 1/8	18 3/8	13	3 4/8	4 1/8	5	5	Galiuro Mts., AZ	Clifford Kouts	Clifford Kouts	1964	144
113 7/8	18 2/8	17 6/8	14 2/8	3 5/8	4 2/8	4	5	Santa Rita Mts., AZ	Joe M. Moore, Jr.	Joe M. Moore, Jr.	1968	146
113 7/8	15 4/8	14 3/8	14 3/8	3 3/8	4 1/8	4	4	Pima Co., AZ	James A. Reynolds	James A. Reynolds	1985	146
113 7/8	17 3/8	16 7/8	14 5/8	3 6/8	3 5/8	5	6	Sonora, MX	James W. Hutcheson	James W. Hutcheson	1996	146
113 7/8	16	16 1/8	15 5/8	3 7/8	3 6/8	5	5	Pinal Co., AZ	James L. Boyd	James L. Boyd	1997	146
113 7/8	18	18	14 3/8	4	3 7/8	5	5	Santa Cruz Co., AZ	Picked Up	Craig T. Boddington	1999	146
113 7/8	18 4/8	18 1/8	12 1/8	4 2/8	4 5/8	6	6	Sonora, MX	Craig T. Boddington	Dallas Mus. of Natl. Hist.	2000	146
113 6/8	19	17 7/8	13 4/8	4	4	8	8	Chihuahua, MX	Herb Klein	Herb Klein	1957	153
113 6/8	19	18 2/8	13 6/8	4 2/8	4	5	5	Mt. Graham, AZ	Bill Sizer	Bill Sizer	1963	153
113 6/8	19	18 4/8	13 5/8	4 5/8	4 2/8	6	7	Galiuro Mts., AZ	Doran V. Porter	Doran V. Porter	1966	153
113 6/8	19 2/8	19	13 2/8	4	3 6/8	4	4	Pima Co., AZ	Richard N. Huber	Richard N. Huber	1979	153
113 5/8	16 7/8	18	16 5/8	4	4 1/8	5	5	Pima Co., AZ	Andy A. Ramirez	Andy A. Ramirez	1979	153
113 5/8	19 6/8	19	17 1/8	3 7/8	4 1/8	4	4	Graham Mts., AZ	J.H. Hunt	J.H. Hunt	1962	158
113 5/8	17 4/8	17 1/8	14 7/8	3 6/8	3 5/8	4	4	Pinal Co., AZ	Randall E. Martin	Randall E. Martin	1992	158
113 4/8	16	16 3/8	15	3 7/8	3 6/8	4	4	Socorro Co., NM	Gerad Montoya	Gerad Montoya	1999	158
113 4/8	17 3/8	19 2/8	12 4/8	3 7/8	3 7/8	6	6	Sonora, MX	George W. Parker	George W. Parker	1947	161
113 4/8	18	16 2/8	14 2/8	4 5/8	4 4/8	4	4	Santa Rita Mts., AZ	Jack Englet	Jack Englet	1962	161
113 4/8	16 5/8	19	12 2/8	4	4 1/8	6	7	Santa Rita Mts., AZ	George W. Parker	George W. Parker	1962	161
113 3/8	17 4/8	17 1/8	12 2/8	4 5/8	4 1/8	5	5	Santa Cruz Co., AZ	Robert A. Smith	Robert A. Smith	1985	161
113 3/8	16	16 3/8	12 5/8	4 4/8	4	4	4	Santa Teresa Mts., AZ	D.B. Sanford	D.B. Sanford	1950	165
113 3/8	17 3/8	16 7/8	13 3/8	4 2/8	4	4	4	Tumacacori Mts., AZ	Tom W. Caid	Tom W. Caid	1958	165
113 3/8	18	17	14 3/8	4	4 2/8	4	4	Four Peaks Mt., AZ	Carl J. Slagel	Carl J. Slagel	1963	165
113 3/8	16 5/8	16 4/8	12 3/8	4 4/8	4 4/8	6	5	Pima Co., AZ	Sam E. Harrison, Jr.	Sam E. Harrison, Jr.	1969	165

COUES' WHITETAIL DEER - TYPICAL ANTLERS
Odocoileus virginianus couesi

Score	Length of Main Beam		Inside Spread	Circumference at Smallest Place Between Burr and First Point		Number of Points		Locality	Hunter	Owner	Date Killed	Rank
	R	L		R	L	R	L					
113 3/8	17 2/8	18 2/8	15 3/8	4 1/8	4 1/8	4	4	Navajo Co., AZ	Picked Up	Harry Neff	1997	165
113 3/8	16 7/8	17 6/8	15 4/8	3 6/8	3 6/8	5	5	Santa Rita Mts., AZ	Donna Greene	Donna Greene	1958	170
113 3/8	18 7/8	17 5/8	14 4/8	4	4	5	5	Tumacacori Mts., AZ	Carlos G. Touche	Carlos G. Touche	1961	170
113 2/8	18	17	14 2/8	4 1/8	4 1/8	4	5	Santa Cruz Co., AZ	Hector Guglielmo	Hector Guglielmo	1984	170
113 2/8	19 3/8	18 5/8	16	4 3/8	4 4/8	4	4	Gila Co., AZ	David W. Miller, Jr.	David W. Miller, Jr.	1984	170
113 2/8	18 3/8	18 1/8	14 2/8	4	4	5	5	Pima Co., AZ	James A. Reynolds	James A. Reynolds	1995	170
113 2/8	17 4/8	17 5/8	12 2/8	3 7/8	3 6/8	5	5	Sonora, MX	Betsy S. Grainger	Betsy S. Grainger	2001	170
113 3/8	19 5/8	19 3/8	14 6/8	3 7/8	3 7/8	4	4	Sonora, MX	Brian K. Murray	Brian K. Murray	2001	170
113 1/8	20 1/8	19 6/8	19	4	4 1/8	5	6	Chiricahua Mts., AZ	Ralph Hopkins	Fred Tanner	1928	177
113 1/8	15 6/8	16 2/8	13 7/8	4 4/8	4 5/8	5	5	Grant Co., NM	Andrew A. Musacchio	Andrew A. Musacchio	1985	177
113	18 1/8	18	15 4/8	4 2/8	4 2/8	4	4	Canelo Hills, AZ	Carlos Ochoa	Carlos Ochoa	1955	179
113	18 2/8	18 3/8	11 4/8	4 3/8	4 3/8	5	5	Pima Co., AZ	Frank C. Benvenuto	Frank C. Benvenuto	1967	179
113	19	18 7/8	12 2/8	3 6/8	3 6/8	5	5	Tumacacori Mts., AZ	Basil C. Bradbury	Unknown	1968	179
113	18 1/8	18 4/8	15 4/8	3 7/8	3 7/8	5	5	Pima Co., AZ	Jeffrey K. Volk	M.E. Duperret & J.K. Volk	1998	179
112 7/8	17	17 1/8	14 5/8	4 2/8	4 2/8	4	4	Ruby, AZ	Roger Scott	Roger Scott	1962	183
112 7/8	18 3/8	17 6/8	14 5/8	3 4/8	3 4/8	4	4	Catron Co., NM	Picked Up	Mark Barboa	1994	183
112 7/8	17 5/8	18 2/8	13 1/8	3 6/8	4 1/8	6	6	Gila Co., AZ	James J. Zanzot	James J. Zanzot	1995	183
112 6/8	17 5/8	18 4/8	14 4/8	5 1/8	4 6/8	6	6	Baboquivari Mts., AZ	Charles R. Whitfield	Charles R. Whitfield	1969	186
112 6/8	17 4/8	18 6/8	15 7/8	4 7/8	4 6/8	6	6	Cochise Co., AZ	Mike York	Mike York	1973	186
112 6/8	16 3/8	17	10 6/8	3 7/8	3 6/8	4	4	Sonora, MX	Lee Christmas	Lee Christmas	1999	186
112 5/8	18 1/8	17 2/8	14 1/8	4	3 7/8	4	4	Sonora, MX	Henry Lares	Henry Lares	1959	189
112 5/8	18 6/8	19 1/8	13 1/8	3 4/8	3 5/8	5	6	Sonora, MX	William W. Sharp	William W. Sharp	1968	189
112 5/8	17 6/8	17 4/8	15 3/8	5	4 7/8	4	4	Greenlee Co., AZ	John W. Barber	John W. Barber	1985	189
112 5/8	17 7/8	18 2/8	10 3/8	4 1/8	4 1/8	5	5	Sonora, MX	Michael C. Cupell	Michael C. Cupell	2000	189
112 4/8	17 3/8	17 3/8	15	4 2/8	4 3/8	5	5	Gila Co., AZ	R.T Beach & L.A. Mossinger	Ronald T. Beach	1974	193
112 4/8	14 6/8	15 6/8	13	3 5/8	3 4/8	6	5	Pima Co., AZ	Gary D. Ramirez	Gary D. Ramirez	1993	193
112 4/8	19 6/8	19 1/8	12 6/8	4	4	4	4	Pima Co., AZ	Donald H. McBride	Donald H. McBride	1999	193
112 4/8	17 2/8	16 7/8	13 6/8	4 1/8	4 1/8	4	5	Sonora, MX	Kirk Kelso	Kirk Kelso	2001	193
112 3/8	17 3/8	17	15 5/8	4 1/8	4 2/8	4	4	White Mts., AZ	Dennis E. Nolen	Dennis E. Nolen	1961	197
112 3/8	19	19 5/8	13 3/8	4 2/8	4 4/8	5	5	Santa Cruz Co., AZ	W.C. Grant	W.C. Grant	1973	197
112 3/8	17 2/8	17 3/8	15 7/8	3 4/8	3 3/8	4	4	Pima Co., AZ	Robert H. Conway	Robert H. Conway	1998	197
112 3/8	17 3/8	16 3/8	12 3/8	3 4/8	3 6/8	5	5	Sonora, MX	Michael M. Golightly	Michael M. Golightly	2001	197
112 2/8	19 6/8	19 1/8	11 6/8	3 4/8	3 5/8	5	5	Sonora, MX	George W. Parker	George W. Parker	1960	201
112 2/8	18	17 6/8	17	4	3 7/8	5	5	Maricopa Co., AZ	Gary D. Nichols	Gary D. Nichols	1980	201
112 2/8	16 2/8	16	13 2/8	4 6/8	4 6/8	4	5	Pima Co., AZ	William W. Sharp	William W. Sharp	1981	201
112 2/8	18 2/8	17 5/8	15	4 4/8	4 2/8	4	4	Pima Co., AZ	Angel J. Yslas	Angel J. Yslas	1994	201

Score	R. Beam	L. Beam	Spread	R. Circ.	L. Circ.	Pts. R	Pts. L	Locality	Hunter	Owner	Date	Rank
112 ²/₈	17 ³/₈	18 ⁶/₈	14 ⁴/₈	3 ⁷/₈	3 ⁷/₈	6	5	Cochise Co., AZ	Edwin L. Hawkins	Edwin L. Hawkins	1977	205
112 ²/₈	18 ²/₈	17 ¹/₈	10 ⁷/₈	3 ⁷/₈	3 ⁷/₈	5	5	Pima Co., AZ	David J. Vancas	David J. Vancas	1985	205
112 ²/₈	17 ²/₈	18 ²/₈	17 ¹/₈	4 ³/₈	4 ⁴/₈	4	5	Pima Co., AZ	Travis D. Robbins	Travis D. Robbins	1992	205
112 ²/₈	18 ⁶/₈	19	13 ⁶/₈	3 ⁶/₈	3 ⁶/₈	5	4	Sonora, MX	Kerry L. Mailloux	Kerry L. Mailloux	1996	205
112	19 ¹/₈	19 ³/₈	16 ⁵/₈	4	4 ¹/₈	6	5	Grant Co., NM	Charles Arendt	Bud Arendt	1924	209
112	18 ³/₈	18 ⁷/₈	14 ²/₈	3 ⁶/₈	3 ⁶/₈	5	5	Bartlett Mts., AZ	Keith Robbins	Keith Robbins	1957	209
112	17 ²/₈	15 ⁶/₈	13 ⁶/₈	4	3 ⁷/₈	5	5	Baboquivari Mts., AZ	Jesse Genin	Jesse Genin	1961	209
112	15 ⁴/₈	18	12 ⁴/₈	3 ⁶/₈	3 ⁴/₈	5	5	Greenlee Co., AZ	Jerald S. Wager	Jerald S. Wager	1982	209
111 ⁷/₈	18	17 ⁶/₈	12 ⁴/₈	3 ⁴/₈	4	4	4	Sonora, MX	Mark G. Mills	Mark G. Mills	1998	214
111 ⁷/₈	18 ⁶/₈	20 ⁵/₈	13 ⁷/₈	4	4	6	4	Canelo Hills, AZ	Walter G. Sheets	Walter G. Sheets	1959	214
111 ⁶/₈	20 ⁵/₈	16 ⁴/₈	15 ³/₈	4	4	5	5	Greenlee Co., AZ	Ronald H. Gerdes	Ronald H. Gerdes	1992	216
111 ⁶/₈	17 ¹/₈	17	13 ²/₈	3 ²/₈	3 ²/₈	5	5	Gila Co., AZ	Karl J. Payne	Karl J. Payne	1955	216
111 ⁶/₈	17	17	11 ⁶/₈	3 ⁵/₈	3 ⁵/₈	5	5	Catron Co., NM	Charles Tapia	Charles Tapia	1959	216
111 ⁶/₈	18 ⁶/₈	19 ⁵/₈	14 ¹/₈	3 ⁷/₈	4 ⁵/₈	5	5	Patagonia Mts., AZ	Norval L. Wesson	Norval L. Wesson	1967	216
111 ⁶/₈	18 ²/₈	18 ⁵/₈	14 ⁴/₈	3 ⁴/₈	3 ⁵/₈	5	5	Baboquivari Mts., AZ	Stanley W. Gaines	Stanley W. Gaines	1971	216
111 ⁶/₈	17 ¹/₈	16 ⁵/₈	14	3 ⁷/₈	3 ⁷/₈	4	4	Pima Co., AZ	George V. Borquez	George V. Borquez	1979	216
111 ⁶/₈	16 ⁵/₈	16 ⁶/₈	12 ³/₈	4 ⁴/₈	4 ⁴/₈	8	5	Cochise Co., AZ	Gregory F. Lucero	Gregory F. Lucero	1991	216
111 ⁵/₈	19 ²/₈	19 ⁶/₈	11 ⁴/₈	3 ⁷/₈	3 ⁷/₈	5	4	Sonora, MX	Lynn H. Stinson	Lynn H. Stinson	2000	223
111 ⁵/₈	18 ⁷/₈	19	14 ⁶/₈	3 ⁴/₈	3 ⁴/₈	5	5	Santa Rita Mts., AZ	Rick Detwiler	Rick Detwiler	1968	223
111 ⁴/₈	17 ²/₈	18 ²/₈	13 ⁷/₈	3 ⁶/₈	3 ⁶/₈	5	5	Pima Co., AZ	Kevin T. Murray	Kevin T. Murray	1996	225
111 ⁴/₈	20 ¹/₈	19 ⁵/₈	14 ²/₈	3 ⁷/₈	4	4	4	Sonora, MX	George W. Parker	George W. Parker	1926	225
111 ⁴/₈	17 ⁴/₈	18	15	4	3 ⁶/₈	5	5	Santa Rita Mts., AZ	Tom L. Swanson	Tom L. Swanson	1965	225
111 ⁴/₈	17 ⁶/₈	17 ⁷/₈	15 ⁴/₈	4 ⁴/₈	4 ⁴/₈	4	5	Coconino Co., AZ	Picked Up	Dennis L. Campbell	1987	225
111 ³/₈	18 ²/₈	17 ⁷/₈	17 ⁶/₈	4 ¹/₈	4 ²/₈	4	5	Graham Co., AZ	Robert L. Osborn	Robert L. Osborn	1993	229
111 ³/₈	20 ⁶/₈	21 ²/₈	12 ³/₈	3 ⁴/₈	3 ⁴/₈	5	5	Sierra Madre Mts., MX	Herb Klein	Dallas Mus. of Natl. Hist.	1965	229
111 ³/₈	18 ⁶/₈	18 ⁶/₈	12 ⁵/₈	3 ⁶/₈	3 ⁶/₈	4	4	Pima Co., AZ	Unknown	Ruel Holt	PR 1974	229
111 ³/₈	17 ⁶/₈	18 ⁵/₈	16 ⁵/₈	4 ¹/₈	4 ¹/₈	4	4	Santa Cruz Co., AZ	Frank Yubeta III	Frank Yubeta III	1983	229
111 ³/₈	17 ⁴/₈	17 ⁴/₈	14 ¹/₈	4	3 ⁷/₈	4	4	Sonora, MX	Larry J. Kruse	Larry J. Kruse	1999	229
111 ²/₈	17 ⁶/₈	17	15 ²/₈	4	4	4	4	Graham Co., AZ	C.R. Hale	C.R. Hale	1958	233
111 ²/₈	18 ⁷/₈	19 ⁵/₈	11 ⁶/₈	3 ⁴/₈	3 ⁴/₈	5	5	Sonora, MX	George W. Parker	George W. Parker	1960	233
111 ²/₈	19 ²/₈	19 ⁴/₈	16 ⁶/₈	4 ³/₈	4 ²/₈	6	6	Graham Mts., AZ	Bill Barney	Bill Barney	1962	233
111 ²/₈	19 ¹/₈	19	15 ⁶/₈	4 ²/₈	4 ³/₈	6	6	Atascosa Mt., AZ	Henry B. Carrillo	Henry B. Carrillo	1964	233
111 ²/₈	17 ⁵/₈	17 ³/₈	15 ²/₈	3 ⁶/₈	4 ¹/₈	5	5	Santa Rita Mts., AZ	Lon E. Bothwell	Lon E. Bothwell	1969	233
111 ²/₈	16 ⁴/₈	16 ⁴/₈	12 ³/₈	3 ⁴/₈	4 ¹/₈	6	5	Santa Cruz Co., AZ	Robert L. Rabb	Robert L. Rabb	1977	233
111 ²/₈	16 ²/₈	15 ⁵/₈	16	4	4	6	5	Hidalgo Co., NM	Jess T. Jones	Jess T. Jones	1993	233
111 ¹/₈	17 ⁵/₈	17 ⁶/₈	14 ⁵/₈	4	3 ⁷/₈	6	5	Sonora, MX	Joe Daneker, Jr.	Joe Daneker, Jr.	1973	240
111 ¹/₈	17 ⁴/₈	17 ⁴/₈	14 ⁵/₈	3 ⁷/₈	4 ¹/₈	5	5	Cochise Co., AZ	Harvey G. Ward, Jr.	Harvey G. Ward, Jr.	1988	240
111 ¹/₈	18	17	18	3 ⁷/₈	3 ⁷/₈	5	5	Pinal Co., AZ	John P. Garcia	John P. Garcia	1991	240
111 ¹/₈	18 ⁵/₈	18 ⁴/₈	14 ²/₈	4	4	4	5	Sonora, MX	David J. Lechel	David J. Lechel	2001	240
111	17 ⁶/₈	17 ⁶/₈	17 ⁶/₈	3 ⁷/₈	3 ⁷/₈	5	5	Pima Co., AZ	William G. Roberts	William G. Roberts	1992	244
111	18 ⁶/₈	17 ²/₈	15	4	4 ¹/₈	4	4	Pima Co., AZ	Michael W. Lynch	Michael W. Lynch	1996	244
111	17	18 ⁶/₈	11 ³/₈	4 ²/₈	4 ¹/₈	4	5	Sonora, MX	Jack Atcheson, Jr.	Jack Atcheson, Jr.	1998	244
111	19 ⁴/₈	19 ⁴/₈	14 ⁶/₈	4 ¹/₈	4 ¹/₈	5	5	Santa Cruz Co., AZ	David M. Yearin	David M. Yearin	1999	244
110 ⁷/₈	17 ²/₈	18 ⁶/₈	13 ¹/₈	3 ⁶/₈	3 ⁶/₈	4	4	Chiricahua Mts., AZ	Wayne A. Dirst	Wayne A. Dirst	1954	248
110 ⁷/₈	19 ³/₈	19	11 ²/₈	4 ¹/₈	4	5	5	Canelo Hills, AZ	Bill Fidelo	Bill Fidelo	1958	248
110 ⁷/₈	16 ⁶/₈	16 ⁶/₈	15 ⁷/₈	3 ⁵/₈	3 ⁶/₈	5	6	Rincon Mts., AZ	Ollie O. Barney, Jr.	Ollie O. Barney, Jr.	1961	248
110 ⁷/₈	18 ⁶/₈	19 ²/₈	13 ¹/₈	4	4	6	5	Pima Co., AZ	William W. Sharp	William W. Sharp	1974	248
110 ⁷/₈			15 ⁶/₈	4 ³/₈	4 ²/₈	4	5	Gila Co., AZ	Kristin M. Currie	Kristin M. Currie	1994	248

COUES' WHITETAIL DEER - TYPICAL ANTLERS

Odocoileus virginianus couesi

Score	Length of Main Beam R	L	Inside Spread	Circumference at Smallest Place Between Burr and First Point R	L	Number of Points R	L	Locality	Hunter	Owner	Date Killed	Rank
110 6/8	18	18 2/8	13 4/8	3 6/8	3 6/8	4	5	Catalina Mts., AZ	H.C. Ruff	H.C. Ruff	1959	253
110 6/8	18 5/8	18 2/8	15 6/8	4	4	4	4	Santa Rita Mts., AZ	John S. McFarling	John S. McFarling	1965	253
110 6/8	17 2/8	16 2/8	14 2/8	4 4/8	4 1/8	4	4	Pima Co., AZ	Rudolph B. Aguilar	Rudolph B. Aguilar	1998	253
110 6/8	17 4/8	17 5/8	13 1/8	4 2/8	4	5	4	Santa Cruz Co., AZ	Julie L. Hopkins	Julie L. Hopkins	1998	253
110 6/8	17	17	12 6/8	3 3/8	3 3/8	5	5	Santa Cruz Co., AZ	Andrew M. Lopez	Andrew M. Lopez	2000	253
110 6/8	17 2/8	17 2/8	13 4/8	4	4 1/8	5	4	Sonora, MX	Travis J. Adams	Travis J. Adams	2001	253
110 6/8	16	15 6/8	11	3 4/8	3 5/8	5	6	Sonora, MX	Joe McDowell	Joe McDowell	2003	253
110 5/8	19 5/8	19 2/8	16 1/8	3 7/8	4	5	4	Pinal Co., AZ	Chuck Adams	Chuck Adams	1989	260
110 5/8	18 5/8	18 4/8	15	3 2/8	3 5/8	5	4	Pima Co., AZ	David E. Furnas	David E. Furnas	1990	260
110 5/8	17 5/8	17 2/8	18	3 5/8	3 5/8	4	4	Pima Co., AZ	James E. Hatcher	James E. Hatcher	1993	260
110 4/8	16 7/8	17 6/8	14 2/8	4 4/8	4 4/8	4	4	Canelo Hills, AZ	Otto L. Fritz	Otto L. Fritz	1947	263
110 4/8	16 7/8	16 6/8	14 2/8	4 1/8	4	5	5	Tumacacori Mts., AZ	John N. Doyle	John N. Doyle	1966	263
110 4/8	18	18 4/8	14 2/8	3 3/8	3 2/8	4	4	Sonora, MX	Ricardo A. Andrade	Ricardo A. Andrade	1988	263
110 4/8	18 6/8	18 3/8	14 6/8	4 2/8	4 2/8	4	5	Pima Co., AZ	William T. Crutchley	William T. Crutchley	1992	263
110 4/8	17 2/8	17 2/8	13 6/8	3 5/8	3 6/8	4	4	Sonora, MX	Lynn H. Stinson	Lynn H. Stinson	2001	263
110 3/8	17 7/8	17 7/8	13 7/8	4 1/8	4	4	4	Santa Rita Mts., AZ	Edward L. Blixt	Edward L. Blixt	1946	268
110 3/8	18 7/8	18 4/8	12 6/8	3 7/8	3 4/8	4	4	Santa Rita Mts., AZ	Lyle K. Sowls	Lyle K. Sowls	1956	268
110 3/8	17 6/8	18 6/8	15 7/8	3 6/8	3 4/8	4	5	Hidalgo Co., NM	Ronald M. Gerdes	Ronald M. Gerdes	1979	268
110 3/8	18 2/8	18 2/8	13 5/8	3 7/8	4	4	4	Sonora, MX	Michael G. Adams	Michael G. Adams	1998	268
110 3/8	18 4/8	18 7/8	13 5/8	3 3/8	3 4/8	4	4	Santa Cruz Co., AZ	Benjamin H. Richardson	Benjamin H. Richardson	2000	268
110 2/8	17	16 3/8	14	4 6/8	4 6/8	5	5	Gila Co., AZ	William P. Hampton, Jr.	William P. Hampton, Jr.	1976	273
110 2/8	16	15 4/8	15 4/8	3 6/8	4	5	4	Hidalgo Co., NM	Jay M. Gates III	Jay M. Gates III	1981	273
110 2/8	18 6/8	18	16	4 1/8	4	4	5	Pima Co., AZ	David G. Mattausch	David G. Mattausch	1984	273
110 2/8	19 1/8	17 5/8	16	3 7/8	3 6/8	5	5	Yavapai Co., AZ	Fred J. Nobbe, Jr.	Fred J. Nobbe, Jr.	1994	273
110 2/8	15	16 7/8	13 6/8	4	4	5	5	Pima Co., AZ	Kurt J. Kreutz	Kurt J. Kreutz	2000	273
110 1/8	16 7/8	16 3/8	15 7/8	4 4/8	4 6/8	4	4	Payson, AZ	Picked Up	Richard Noonan	PR 1963	278
110 1/8	16 1/8	16 3/8	11 5/8	4 4/8	4 3/8	4	4	Hidalgo Co., NM	Neuman Sanford	Neuman Sanford	1981	278
110 1/8	16 4/8	17	12 3/8	4 7/8	4 4/8	4	4	Pima Co., AZ	Andy C. Strebe	Andy C. Strebe	1981	278
110 1/8	18 2/8	17 6/8	16 4/8	4 5/8	4 6/8	5	5	Cochise Co., AZ	Richard T. Ziehmer	Richard T. Ziehmer	1995	278
110 1/8	16 6/8	18 4/8	13 5/8	4	4	5	5	Sonora, MX	Picked Up	Kirk Kelso	2003	278
110	19 4/8	18 6/8	14 2/8	4 2/8	4 3/8	5	5	Sonora, MX	Enrique C. Cicero	Enrique C. Cicero	1966	283
110	18 1/8	17 6/8	14 5/8	4 6/8	5	4	6	Cochise Co., AZ	Bill Saathoff	Bill Saathoff	1987	283
110	18 1/8	18 2/8	18 1/8	3 6/8	4	5	4	Pima Co., AZ	David E. Furnas	David E. Furnas	1991	283
110	15 5/8	15 7/8	13	4 3/8	4 2/8	5	6	Maricopa Co., AZ	Picked Up	L. Pangerl & B. Johnson	1998	283

CATEGORY
COUES' WHITETAIL DEER -
TYPICAL ANTLERS

SCORE
110-6/8

HUNTER
TRAVIS J. ADAMS

LOCATION
SONORA, MEXICO

DATE OF KILL
JANUARY 2001

CATEGORY
COUES' WHITETAIL DEER -
TYPICAL ANTLERS

SCORE
113-7/8

HUNTER
CRAIG T. BODDINGTON (BELOW)

LOCATION
SONORA, MEXICO

DATE OF KILL
DECEMBER 2000

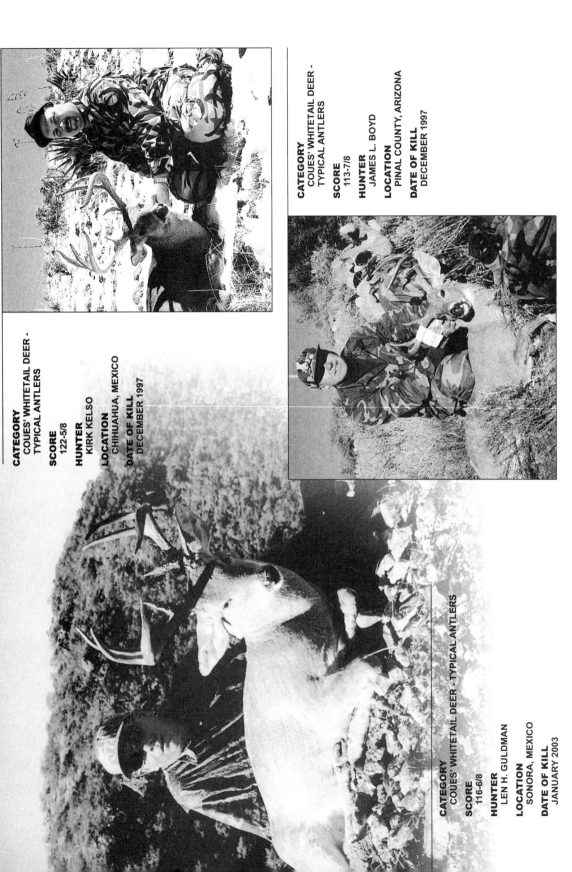

CATEGORY
COUES' WHITETAIL DEER -
TYPICAL ANTLERS

SCORE
122-5/8

HUNTER
KIRK KELSO

LOCATION
CHIHUAHUA, MEXICO

DATE OF KILL
DECEMBER 1997

CATEGORY
COUES' WHITETAIL DEER -
TYPICAL ANTLERS

SCORE
113-7/8

HUNTER
JAMES L. BOYD

LOCATION
PINAL COUNTY, ARIZONA

DATE OF KILL
DECEMBER 1997

CATEGORY
COUES' WHITETAIL DEER - TYPICAL ANTLERS

SCORE
116-6/8

HUNTER
LEN H. GULDMAN

LOCATION
SONORA, MEXICO

DATE OF KILL
JANUARY 2003

IRA GABRIELSON
1889-1977

By Leonard H. Wurman

Gabrielson joined the U.S. Biological Survey in 1915 to study economic ornithology. Three years later, he switched to rodent control for the Survey, and in 1930 became the head of its Division of Wildlife Research. In 1934, he was appointed Chief of the Survey. Under his leadership, the Federal Aid to Wildlife (Pittman-Robertson) Act was passed. In 1940, when the Biological Survey was combined with the Bureau of Fisheries to form the U.S. Fish and Wildlife Service, Gabrielson was named its first chief, a position he held until 1940. He strongly advocated stringent waterfowl regulations and refuge creation in order to increase the depleted duck populations. Gabrielson was President of the Wildlife Management Institute form 1946 until 1970, and then chairman of the board for another seven years. Much of the success of the WMI's North American Wildlife and Natural Resources Conference was due to his leadership. ■

GABRIELSON RELEASES A WILD PACIFIC COAST MALLARD, CAUGHT A DAY EARLIER IN SAN FRANCISCO, AT ROACHES RUN NEAR WASHINGTON, D.C., ON MARCH 8, 1940. THE RELEASE WAS A TEST OF THE THE BIOLOGICAL SURVEY'S ABILITY TO TRACK BANDED DUCKS VIA GOLD-PLATED, NUMBERED LEG BANDS.

COUES' WHITETAIL - NON-TYPICAL ANTLERS
NEW WORLD'S RECORD

RANK
New World's Record

SCORE
196 $^2/_8$

LOCATION
Graham Co., AZ

HUNTER
Native American

OWNER
D.J. Hollinger and
B. Howard

DATE KILLED
Prior to 1971

Not much is known about the circumstances of the hunt on the day that the largest-ever recorded Coues' deer was taken. That information passed away with the now deceased hunter. Undoubtedly, he must have been in awe of his tremendous trophy.

This phenomenal deer was taken in the late 1960s on the San Carlos Indian Reservation by a tribal member. It was taken south of Highway 70, possibly in the Mt. Turnbull area.

The 11x15 rack sports a 152-3/8 typical frame and an incredible 43 7/8" worth of non-typical points. This outstanding Coues' deer was originally sold to an antler dealer many years ago. It is now owned by Dana J. Hollinger and Bob Howard. ■

COUES' WHITETAIL DEER NON-TYPICAL ANTLERS WORLD'S RECORD SCORE CHART

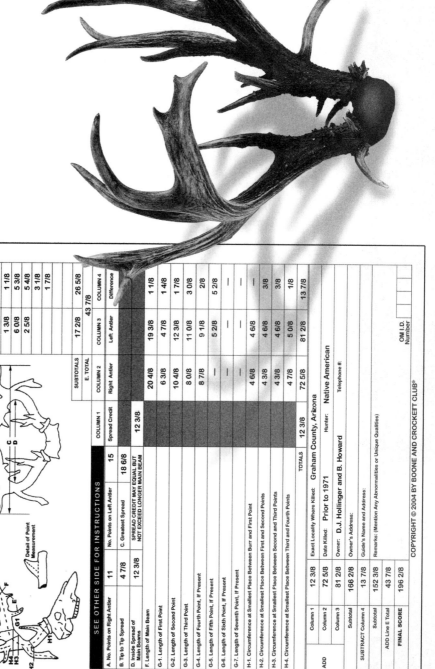

Records of North American Big Game

250 Station Drive
Missoula, MT 59801
(406) 542-1888

BOONE AND CROCKETT CLUB®
OFFICIAL SCORING SYSTEM FOR NORTH AMERICAN BIG GAME TROPHIES

NON-TYPICAL WHITETAIL AND COUES' DEER

MINIMUM SCORES

	AWARDS	ALL-TIME
whitetail	185	195
Coues'	105	120

Detail of Point Measurement

KIND OF DEER (check one)
☐ whitetail
☒ Coues'

Abnormal Points

Right Antler	Left Antler
4 3/8	1 0/8
1 6/8	2 0/8
1 1/8	1 1/8
1 3/8	5 3/8
6 0/8	5 4/8
2 5/8	3 1/8
	1 7/8

SUBTOTALS	17 2/8	26 5/8
E. TOTAL		43 7/8

SEE OTHER SIDE FOR INSTRUCTIONS		COLUMN 1	COLUMN 2	COLUMN 3	COLUMN 4
		Spread Credit	Right Antler	Left Antler	Difference
A. No. Points on Right Antler	11				
B. Tip to Tip Spread	4 7/8				
C. Greatest Spread	15				
No. Points on Left Antler	15				
D. Inside Spread of Main Beams	12 3/8	12 3/8	SPREAD CREDIT MAY EQUAL BUT NOT EXCEED LONGER MAIN BEAM		
F. Length of Main Beam	18 6/8		20 4/8	19 3/8	1 1/8
G-1. Length of First Point			6 3/8	4 7/8	1 4/8
G-2. Length of Second Point			10 4/8	12 3/8	1 7/8
G-3. Length of Third Point			8 0/8	11 0/8	3 0/8
G-4. Length of Fourth Point, If Present			8 7/8	9 1/8	2/8
G-5. Length of Fifth Point, If Present			—	5 2/8	5 2/8
G-6. Length of Sixth Point, If Present			—	—	—
G-7. Length of Seventh Point, If Present			—	—	—
H-1. Circumference at Smallest Place Between Burr and First Point			4 6/8	4 6/8	—
H-2. Circumference at Smallest Place Between First and Second Points			4 3/8	4 6/8	3/8
H-3. Circumference at Smallest Place Between Second and Third Points			4 3/8	4 6/8	3/8
H-4. Circumference at Smallest Place Between Third and Fourth Points			4 7/8	5 0/8	1/8
	TOTALS	12 3/8	72 5/8	81 2/8	13 7/8

ADD	Column 1	12 3/8
	Column 2	72 5/8
	Column 3	81 2/8
	Subtotal	166 2/8
SUBTRACT	Column 4	13 7/8
	Subtotal	152 3/8
ADD	Line E Total	43 7/8
	FINAL SCORE	196 2/8

Exact Locality Where Killed: Graham County, Arizona

Date Killed: Prior to 1971   Hunter: Native American

Owner: D.J. Hollinger and B. Howard   Telephone #:

Owner's Address:

Guide's Name and Address:

Remarks: (Mention Any Abnormalities or Unique Qualities)

OM I.D. Number

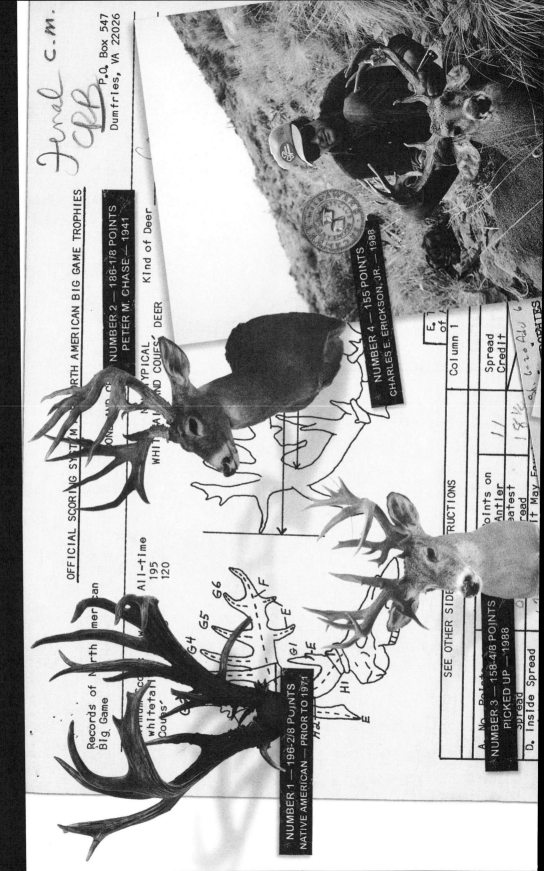

NUMBER 1 — 196-2/8 POINTS
NATIVE AMERICAN — PRIOR TO 1971

NUMBER 2 — 186-1/8 POINTS
PETER M. CHASE — 1941

NUMBER 3 — 158-4/8 POINTS
PICKED UP — 1988

NUMBER 4 — 155 POINTS
CHARLES E. ERICKSON, JR. — 1988

NUMBER 5 — 151-3/8 POINTS
PICKED UP — 1997

NUMBER 10 — 148-6/8 POINTS
CLAY E. GOLDMAN — 1993

NUMBER 8 — 150-3/8 POINTS
JEFFREY K. VOLK — 1992

NUMBER 6 — 150-5/8 POINTS (not pictured)
ROBERT RABB — 1954

NUMBER 6 — 150-5/8 POINTS
CHARLES C. MABRY — 1929

NUMBER 9 — 149-7/8 POINTS
MARVIN R. HARDIN — 1950

COUES' WHITETAIL DEER - NON-TYPICAL ANTLERS

Odocoileus virginianus couesi

MINIMUM SCORE 120

Score	Length of Main Beam R	L	Inside Spread	Circumference at Smallest Place Between Burr and First Point R	L	Number of Points R	L	Locality	Hunter	Owner	Date Killed	Rank
196 2/8	20 4/8	19 3/8	12 3/8	4 6/8	4 6/8	11	15	Graham Co., AZ	Native American	D.J. Hollinger & B. Howard	PR 1971	1
186 1/8	17 6/8	16 5/8	18 2/8	4 5/8	4 6/8	8	8	Hidalgo Co., NM	Peter M. Chase	W.B. Darnell	1941	2
158 4/8	17 1/8	16 7/8	12 6/8	3 7/8	4 1/8	11	11	Santa Cruz Co., AZ	Picked Up	B&C National Collection	1988	3
155	**19**	**20**	**16 6/8**	**4 7/8**	**4 5/8**	**9**	**8**	**Gila Co., AZ**	**Charles E. Erickson, Jr.**	**Charles E. Erickson, Jr.**	**1988**	**4**
151 3/8	19 6/8	19 7/8	15 3/8	4 3/8	4 4/8	7	8	Pima Co., AZ	Picked Up	Patrick H. Taylor	1997	5
150 5/8	18 4/8	18 5/8	15 6/8	5 4/8	5 4/8	9	8	Cochise Co., AZ	Charles C. Mabry	Cabela's, Inc.	1929	6
150 5/8	18 4/8	19	12 5/8	4 3/8	4 4/8	8	7	Sasabe, AZ	Robert Rabb	Robert Rabb	1954	6
150 3/8	18 3/8	18	15 2/8	4 3/8	4 3/8	8	7	Pima Co., AZ	Jeffrey S. Volk	J.K. Volk & M.E. Duperret	1992	8
149 7/8	17 2/8	18 5/8	13 3/8	4 6/8	4 2/8	10	8	Chiricahua Mts., AZ	Marvin R. Hardin	Marvin R. Hardin	1950	9
148 6/8	16 3/8	15 7/8	18 4/8	4 6/8	4 4/8	12	8	Gila Co., AZ	Clay E. Goldman	Clay E. Goldman	1993	10
147	18 6/8	19 6/8	16 6/8	5	4 5/8	10	7	Pima Co., AZ	James A. Reynolds	James A. Reynolds	1991	11
143 6/8	17 3/8	16 5/8	14 5/8	4 2/8	5	6	9	Pima Co., AZ	Oscar C. Truex	Oscar C. Truex	1983	12
142 7/8	20 4/8	18 7/8	13 3/8	4 4/8	4 5/8	9	7	Apache Indian Res., AZ	Native American	AZ Game & Fish Dept.	1950	13
142 6/8	17 6/8	17 1/8	14 2/8	4 6/8	4 5/8	8	8	Pinal Mts., AZ	Phil Rothengatter	Phil Rothengatter	1967	14
141	21 6/8	22	15 3/8	4 6/8	4 5/8	5	6	Sonora, MX	Picked Up	Jorge Camou	2001	15
140 7/8	17	18	14	4 4/8	4 2/8	10	7	Santa Cruz Co., AZ	Randal W. Reaves	Randal W. Reaves	1998	16
139 7/8	18 3/8	18 3/8	15	4 7/8	4 7/8	8	6	Patagonia Mts., AZ	Howard W. Drake	Howard W. Drake	1968	17
138 5/8	16 6/8	16 6/8	11 5/8	4 3/8	4 3/8	9	6	Sonora, MX	Glenn Hall	Glenn Hall	2000	18
137 6/8	19 4/8	19 2/8	14 5/8	4 4/8	4 4/8	6	7	Patagonia Mts., AZ	Ivan J. Buttram	Ivan J. Buttram	1969	19
137 3/8	16 6/8	16 7/8	13 6/8	4 5/8	4 5/8	8	8	Gila Co., AZ	Cal W. Bryant	Cal W. Bryant	1991	20
134 3/8	21 3/8	21	16 6/8	4 5/8	4 4/8	8	5	Cochise Co., AZ	Brian Childers	Brian Childers	1990	21
134 2/8	20 6/8	20 4/8	13 5/8	4 2/8	4 3/8	7	8	Yavapai Co., AZ	William B. Bullock	William B. Bullock	1986	22
134 2/8	17 7/8	16 5/8	13 1/8	4 5/8	4 5/8	6	7	Sonora, MX	Unknown	Ronald D. Hyatt	PR 1986	22
133 4/8	19 4/8	19 5/8	15 3/8	3 2/8	3 3/8	5	7	Gila Co., AZ	Picked Up	Kirk Kelso	2002	24
132 3/8	17 4/8	17 1/8	14 7/8	5	5	5	7	Sonora, MX	Dale J. Little	Dale J. Little	1989	25
132	20	19 7/8	19 7/8	3 6/8	5	5	5	Sonora, MX	Picked Up	Harry P. Samarin	PR 1988	26
131 5/8	18 2/8	18 1/8	13	4 6/8	4 6/8	8	5	Cochise Co., AZ	Phil M. Krentz	Phil M. Krentz	1991	27
131 3/8	19 1/8	18 1/8	14 7/8	3 7/8	4 1/8	6	6	Cochise Co., AZ	Erik M. Thorsrud	Erik M. Thorsrud	1986	28
131 2/8	16 1/8	18	13 5/8	6 6/8	5	9	8	Gila Co., AZ	Nathan E. Ellison	Nathan E. Ellison	1958	29
131 2/8	20 1/8	19 7/8	13 3/8	4 3/8	4 5/8	7	5	Pima Co., AZ	William A. Ball	William A. Ball	1999	29
131	18 7/8	19 2/8	18 2/8	4 4/8	4	9	7	Greenlee Co., AZ	Linda A. Reese	Dee Charles	1993	31
130 3/8	17 2/8	17 5/8	17 5/8	4 2/8	4 2/8	9	9	Santa Cruz Co., AZ	Jack Everhart	Fred Baker	1946	32
130 2/8	14 5/8	15 7/8	10 1/8	5	5	10	8	Rincon Mts., AZ	Velton Clark	Velton Clark	1962	33
130 1/8	17	18 3/8	14 5/8	4 3/8	4 5/8	8	4	Yavapai Co., AZ	David K. Moore	David K. Moore	1988	34
130	17 3/8	16 2/8	13 7/8	5 2/8	5 2/8	6	11	Whetstone Range, AZ	Unknown	Roger Clyne	PR 1967	35
129 7/8	20 6/8	20 5/8	17 3/8	4	4	5	7	Apache Co., AZ	Picked Up	Donald H. McBride	1999	36

Score	R	L	Spread	Circ. R	Circ. L	Pts R	Pts L	Locality	Hunter	Owner	Date	Rank
129 5/8	19 6/8	19 7/8	16 6/8	3 4/8	3 5/8	7	8	Cochise Co., AZ	James C. Cornelius	James C. Cornelius	1994	37
128 3/8	17 6/8	17 4/8	15 1/8	4 2/8	4 1/8	5	7	Pima Co., AZ	Gary D. Gorsuch	Gary D. Gorsuch	1992	38
128	19 1/8	18 6/8	16 2/8	5 2/8	4 3/8	5	8	Santa Cruz Co., AZ	Carlos G. Touche	Carlos G. Touche	1968	39
127 7/8	20 2/8	20 2/8	15 4/8	4 1/8	4	5	8	Grant Co., NM	Unknown	Mike W. Leonard	PR 1960	40
127 6/8	17 2/8	17 3/8	13 4/8	4 1/8	4 2/8	6	8	Hidalgo Co., NM	Michael C. Finley	Michael C. Finley	1983	41
127 5/8	20	18 2/8	18	4 7/8	4 7/8	6	6	Pima Co., AZ	Robert E. Pierce	R.E. Pierce & D. May	1993	42
127 1/8	19 4/8	19 5/8	13 3/8	4 2/8	4 2/8	5	5	Sonora, MX	Picked Up	D.J. Hollinger & B. Howard	1993	43
126 5/8	17 6/8	17 5/8	13 3/8	4	4	5	6	Gila Co., AZ	Paul A. Stewart	Paul A. Stewart	1992	44
126 2/8	17	16 3/8	15 6/8	5	5	8	6	Graham Co., AZ	Steve T. Letcher	Steve T. Letcher	2001	45
126 1/8	14 7/8	15 2/8	11 2/8	4 6/8	4 5/8	6	8	Pima Co., AZ	William F. Crull	William F. Crull	1979	46
125 7/8	16 7/8	16 2/8	13 4/8	4 2/8	4 4/8	6	6	Pima Co., AZ	Fred W. Havens	Fred W. Havens	1966	47
125 3/8	18 7/8	17 7/8	12 1/8	4	4	6	8	Arizona	Picked Up	Michael J. Tamboli	PR 1976	47
125 1/8	15 3/8	16 4/8	13 6/8	4 3/8	4 2/8	9	6	Sonora, MX	Enrique C. Cicero	Enrique C. Cicero	1967	49
124 7/8	16 3/8	16 4/8	12	3 6/8	3 4/8	8	8	Santa Cruz Co., AZ	Lee E. Sullivan	Lee E. Sullivan	1996	50
124 5/8	15 3/8	17 1/8	11 3/8	4 7/8	4 6/8	8	5	Las Guijas Mts., AZ	Aubrey F. Powell	Aubrey F. Powell	1966	51
124 4/8	20	18 4/8	17 2/8	4	3 7/8	6	6	Pinal Co., AZ	C.J. Adair	C.J. Adair	1966	52
124 3/8	17 4/8	19	15	4 4/8	4 3/8	6	6	Yavapai Co., AZ	James W.P. Roe	James W.P. Roe	1971	53
124 2/8	19 4/8	19 5/8	16 2/8	4 1/8	4 3/8	5	5	Arizona	C. Touche	Alan C. Ellsworth	1977	54
123 5/8	17 1/8	17	15 5/8	5 2/8	5 5/8	4	4	Gila Co., AZ	Denny L. Hunsaker	Denny L. Hunsaker	1997	55
123 1/8	19 5/8	17 6/8	15 4/8	4 4/8	4 4/8	7	7	Cochise Co., AZ	William H. Nollsch	William H. Nollsch	1994	56
122 7/8	16 6/8	18 5/8	14 3/8	4	4	6	6	Pima Co., AZ	Doug Field	Doug Field	2001	57
122 6/8	16 2/8	15 1/8	11 5/8	4	4	5	5	Sonora, MX	Edwin L. Robinson	Edwin L. Robinson	1992	58
122 4/8	16 7/8	16 6/8	12 4/8	4 2/8	4 2/8	6	6	Hidalgo Co., NM	Jack Samson	Jack Samson	1984	59
122 4/8	15 7/8	16 7/8	12	4	4 1/8	9	9	Cochise Co., AZ	Randy D. Goll	Randy D. Goll	1984	60
122 2/8	19 2/8	19 4/8	15 5/8	4 1/8	4	7	7	Sonora, MX	Robert P. Ellingson III	Robert P. Ellingson III	1997	60
121 7/8	19 1/8	18	15 2/8	4	3 7/8	4	4	Sonora, MX	Michael L. Braegelmann	Michael L. Braegelmann	2002	60
121 6/8	18	16 5/8	15 2/8	4	4	7	7	Santa Cruz Co., AZ	Clifton E. Cox	Clifton E. Cox	1980	63
121 5/8	17 2/8	16 5/8	13 4/8	4 4/8	4 4/8	5	5	Gila Co., AZ	Ken Ashley	Ken Ashley	1988	64
121 2/8	18 5/8	18 5/8	13 6/8	4 6/8	4 5/8	7	7	Pima Co., AZ	Rene E. Rodriguez	Rene E. Rodriguez	1998	65
121 1/8	15 7/8	14 1/8	14 1/8	4 3/8	4 2/8	6	6	Pima Co., AZ	James A. Reynolds	James A. Reynolds	1979	66
121	17 2/8	16 1/8	15 2/8	4	4	6	6	Graham Co., AZ	Stuart Hancock	Stuart Hancock	2001	66
120 7/8	19	19 2/8	13	3 3/8	3 3/8	8	7	Apache Co., AZ	Picked Up	Harry Neff	1998	68
120 7/8	16 6/8	16 5/8	14	3 5/8	3 5/8	6	8	Sonora, MX	Michael L. Braegelmann	Michael L. Braegelmann	2000	69
120 5/8	16 7/8	17	13 3/8	4 6/8	4 4/8	6	6	Gila Co., AZ	James E. Stinson	James E. Stinson	1983	70
120 2/8	17 2/8	17 6/8	13 4/8	5 1/8	4 7/8	6	6	Pima Co., AZ	Carl E. Fasel	Carl E. Fasel	1981	71
120 1/8	20 7/8	20	13 4/8	3 7/8	4	6	6	Gila Co., AZ	David M. Conrad	David M. Conrad	1982	71
120 1/8	14 4/8	17 5/8	11 5/8	4 3/8	4 3/8	8	8	Santa Cruz Co., AZ	Jerry M. Myers	Jerry M. Myers	1970	73
120	18 5/8	19	13 6/8	4 1/8	4 1/8	8	8	Pima Co., AZ	Unknown	Mike Yeager	PR 1966	74
120 1/8	19	17 6/8	15	3 4/8	3 6/8	7	7	Santa Cruz Co., AZ	Gerald M. Kluzik	Gerald M. Kluzik	1981	75
120 1/8	17 2/8	17 4/8	13 7/8	4 2/8	4 2/8	5	5	Santa Cruz Co., AZ	Eugene S. Robinson	Eugene S. Robinson	1985	75
120	18 4/8	18 1/8	13 7/8	3 5/8	3 5/8	6	6	Apache Co., AZ	Picked Up	Harry Neff	1998	77
120	15 6/8	15 6/8	15 6/8	4 1/8	4	5	5	Pima Co., AZ	William A. Keebler	William A. Keebler	2001	77
159 *	17 4/8	17 4/8	17 4/8	7 6/8	5	7	7	Sonora, MX	Daniel D. King	SCI International Wildlife Mus.	1991	
154 1/8 *	18 1/8	18 1/8	15 6/8	4 2/8	4 1/8	7	7	Pima Co., AZ	Picked Up	Jorge Camou	2001	
152 *	20	20 2/8	17 4/8	4 4/8	4 4/8	8	8	Sonora, MX	Picked Up	Mike Sullivan	1971	

* Final score is subject to revision by additional verifying measurements.

CATEGORY
COUES' WHITETAIL DEER -
NON-TYPICAL ANTLERS

SCORE
120

HUNTER
WILLIAM A. KEEBLER

LOCATION
SONORA, MEXICO

DATE OF KILL
JANUARY 2001

CATEGORY
COUES' WHITETAIL DEER -
NON-TYPICAL ANTLERS

SCORE
126-2/8

HUNTER
STEVE T. LETCHER

LOCATION
GRAHAM COUNTY, ARIZONA

DATE OF KILL
JANUARY 2001

B&C HISTORY

WILLIAM T. HORNADAY
1854-1937

By H. Hudson DeCray

Born in 1854, this Indiana farm boy was to become one of the Nation's most eloquent leaders in the protection of wildlife. His early interest was in scientific taxidermy. He founded the National Society of American Taxidermists in New York in 1880. He was appointed chief taxidermist of the U.S. National Museum in Washington, D.C. Later, as director of the New York Zoological Society, he supervised the building and administration of the Bronx Zoo. He wrote hundreds of newspaper and magazine articles and over 20 books in the field of conservation. He was a leading influence in the passage of the Migratory Bird Treaty Act and the 1911 Fur Seal Treaty. But his greatest victory was probably his successful fight to preserve the American bison from extermination. ■

HORNADAY, BELOW LEFT, PREPARES A SHIPMENT OF BISON FROM THE BRONX ZOO TO WICHITA KANSAS — CIRCA 1907

571

CANADA MOOSE
WORLD'S RECORD

TROPHY INFO

RANK
World's Record

SCORE
242

LOCATION
Grayling River, BC

HUNTER
Michael E. Laub

OWNER
Michael E. Laub

DATE KILLED
1980

In the fall of 1980, Michael E. Laub left the gentle hills of Pennsylvania for the rough terrain of British Columbia in pursuit of a "childhood dream," a big-game wilderness hunt. Laub's consequential encounter with an enormous Canada moose (*Alces alces americana*) became a story for the records book.

Accompanying friends Sal Casino and Angelo Brocatello, the hunting party landed in a small plane in the outback of Vizer Creek, British Columbia. Gil Weins and three of his guides met the hunters, and the next morning they mounted up and began a long search for moose and grizzly bear.

"On October 19th, after a couple of days of fly-camping, we were pretty demoralized. We hadn't even seen a rabbit. I was able to call my wife Carol via shortwave radio to tell her of our misfortune.

"After I spoke to my wife, Sal and I went out again with our guides. We had lunch around a lake, and then we split up. My guide, George, was on the trail of a moose. We got to the top of a mountain and looked down. To my surprise I saw a bull just grazing with his antlers glittering in the sun. The moose was at least 400 yards away, so we began the descent on our horses.

"I was so excited; but, I didn't realize how big the bull was because I had never seen a moose before. We kept moving down the mountain and I stopped to shoot, but missed. The moose took off into the brush, and we continued down the mountain. I then saw the moose standing, his back toward me in the thick, high grass at about 250 yards, when I shot.

He went down, got up again, and moved off. We got on our horses and galloped through the brush. We were behind and above the moose, the sun to our back. I was now 25 feet from my moose. I grabbed my rifle out of its scabbard and downed him with my last bullet.

"George was so excited that he jumped up and down like a little boy. He knew what I didn't, that this was a World's Record-sized moose."

Shot near Grayling River, British Columbia, Laub's trophy was officially scored at 242, and thus became the new World's Record for a Canada moose. ∎

BOUNDARY FOR CANADA MOOSE

Canada moose includes trophies from Canada (except for the Yukon and Northwest Territories), Minnesota, Maine, New Hampshire, North Dakota, and Vermont.

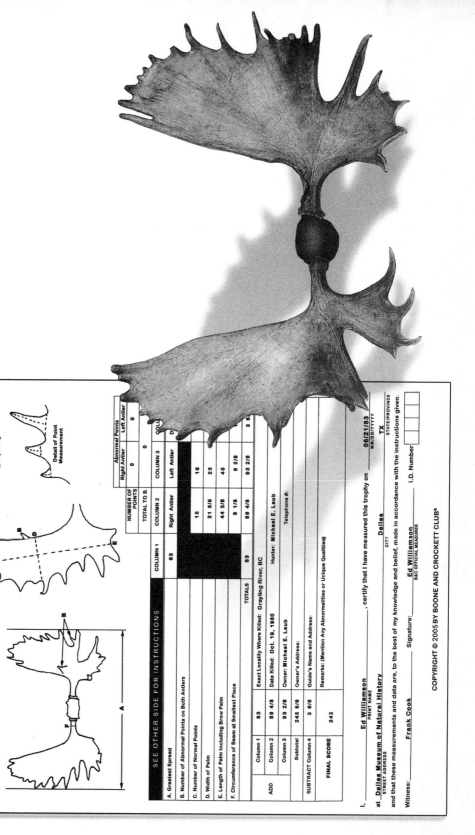

CANADA MOOSE
WORLD'S RECORD SCORE CHART

Records of North American Big Game

250 Station Drive
Missoula, MT 59801
(406) 542-1888

BOONE AND CROCKETT CLUB®
OFFICIAL SCORING SYSTEM FOR NORTH AMERICAN BIG GAME TROPHIES

MOOSE

MINIMUM SCORES	AWARDS	ALL-TIME
Canada	185	195
Alaska-Yukon	210	224
Wyoming	140	155

KIND OF MOOSE (check one)
■ Canada
□ Alaska-Yukon
□ Wyoming

Detail of Point Measurement

Abnormal Points	Right Antler	Left Antler
	0	0

NUMBER OF POINTS	Right Antler	Left Antler
	0	0

TOTAL TO B.

SEE OTHER SIDE FOR INSTRUCTIONS	COLUMN 1	COLUMN 2 Right Antler	COLUMN 3 Left Antler	COLUMN 4
A. Greatest Spread	63			
B. Number of Abnormal Points on Both Antlers				
C. Number of Normal Points		15	16	
D. Width of Palm		21 6/8	23	
E. Length of Palm Including Brow Palm		44 5/8	45	
F. Circumference of Beam at Smallest Place		8 1/8	9 2/8	
TOTALS	63	89 4/8	93 2/8	3 6/8

Exact Locality Where Killed: Grayling River, BC
Date Killed: Oct. 19, 1980   Hunter: Michael E. Laub
Owner: Michael E. Laub   Telephone #:
Owner's Address:
Guide's Name and Address:
Remarks: (Mention Any Abnormalities or Unique Qualities)

ADD	Column 1	63
	Column 2	89 4/8
	Column 3	93 2/8
	Subtotal	245 6/8
SUBTRACT	Column 4	3 6/8
FINAL SCORE		242

I, Ed Williamson , certify that I have measured this trophy on 06/21/83
PRINT NAME   MM/DD/YYYY

at Dallas Museum of Natural History , Dallas , TX
STREET ADDRESS   CITY   STATE/PROVINCE

and that these measurements and data are, to the best of my knowledge and belief, made in accordance with the instructions given.

Witness: Frank Cook   Signature: Ed Williamson   I.D. Number
B&C OFFICIAL MEASURER

COPYRIGHT © 2005 BY BOONE AND CROCKETT CLUB®

573

TOP 10 CANADA MOOSE

NUMBER 2 — 240-6/8 POINTS
DOUG E. FRANK — 2002

NUMBER 5 — 228-6/8 POINTS
BRENTON HOLLAND — 1997

NUMBER 3 — 240-2/8 POINTS
ALBERTONI FERRUCCIO — 1982

NUMBER 1 — 242 POINTS
MICHAEL E. LAUB — 1980

NUMBER 4 — 238-5/8 POINTS
SILAS H. WITHERBEE — 1914

DETAIL OF
POINT MEASUREME

574

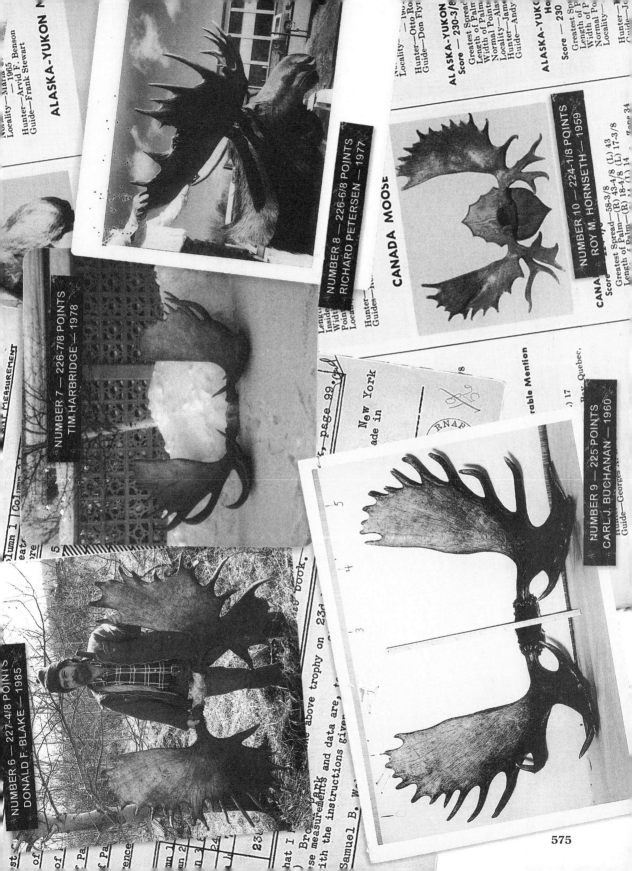

CANADA MOOSE

Alces alces americana and *Alces alces andersoni*

MINIMUM SCORE 195

Score	Greatest Spread	Length of Palm R	Length of Palm L	Width of Palm R	Width of Palm L	Circumference of Beam at Smallest Place R	Circumference of Beam at Smallest Place L	Number of Normal Points R	Number of Normal Points L	Locality	Hunter	Owner	Date Killed	Rank
242	63	44 5/8	45	21 6/8	23	8 1/8	9 2/8	15	16	Grayling River, BC	Michael E. Laub	Michael E. Laub	1980	1
240 6/8	63 4/8	48 7/8	47 2/8	18	19 4/8	7 7/8	8	16	16	Kinaskan Lake, BC	Doug E. Frank	Doug E. Frank	2002	2
240 2/8	66 6/8	46 3/8	45 4/8	19	18 6/8	7 4/8	7 7/8	15	15	Teslin River, BC	Albertoni Ferruccio	Albertoni Ferruccio	1982	3
238 5/8	65 5/8	44 6/8	43 1/8	21	18 6/8	7 5/8	7 7/8	18	19	Bear Lake, QC	Silas H. Witherbee	B&C National Collection	1914	4
228 6/8	70	39 6/8	42 2/8	16 4/8	17 5/8	8 1/8	8 3/8	17	15	MacEachern Lake, NS	Brenton Holland	Glenwood Holland	1997	5
227 4/8	58 4/8	44	43 4/8	17 3/8	17 5/8	7 6/8	7 5/8	19	16	Cook Co., MN	Donald F. Blake	Donald F. Blake	1985	6
226 7/8	63 1/8	48 5/8	47	16 4/8	16 4/8	8 4/8	8 3/8	11	10	Whitecourt, AB	Tim Harbridge	Tim Harbridge	1978	7
226 6/8	63	44 3/8	42 2/8	18 1/8	18 7/8	7	7	15	15	Halfway River, BC	Richard Petersen	Richard Petersen	1977	8
225	60	45 7/8	46 1/8	14 6/8	14 3/8	7 4/8	7 2/8	17	15	Driftwood River, AB	Carl J. Buchanan	Carl J. Buchanan	1960	9
224 1/8	58 3/8	43 4/8	43	18 4/8	17 3/8	8 4/8	8 4/8	14	14	Nipawin, SK	Roy M. Hornseth	Roy M. Hornseth	1959	10
223 7/8	60 5/8	47 5/8	46	16 7/8	14 5/8	7 3/8	7	17	14	Buffalo Lake, MB	Pierre A. Lachance	Pierre A. Lachance	1985	11
223 5/8	64 7/8	46 1/8	47 1/8	17 4/8	14	7 4/8	7 2/8	12	12	Island Lake, MB	Native American	Jack E. Dunn	1980	12
223	56 2/8	48 4/8	48 2/8	13 6/8	14 5/8	7 6/8	7 3/8	15	14	Stikine River, BC	Donald G. Allen	Donald G. Allen	1995	13
223	59	46	47 1/8	14 3/8	14	7 6/8	7 4/8	15	14	Clearwater River, AB	Manuel Dominguez	Manuel Dominguez	1947	14
222	63 5/8	47 7/8	45 6/8	13 2/8	13 7/8	8 1/8	8 2/8	13	12	Goat Creek, BC	Roland Wilz	Roland Wilz	1971	15
221 7/8	64 4/8	48 6/8	47 7/8	15 2/8	11	8 6/8	8 7/8	14	11	Arborfield, SK	Ed Lutz	Ed Lutz	1959	16
221 4/8	66	40 1/8	41	15 7/8	15	7 5/8	8 1/8	16	15	Logan Mt., QC	Charles R. Roy	C.R. Roy & R. Roy	1988	17
220 3/8	67 5/8	41 6/8	46 6/8	17 2/8	15 6/8	8 2/8	7 7/8	11	13	Cassiar, BC	Unknown	Luxton Museum	PR 1954	18
220 3/8	61 3/8	43 7/8	43 4/8	14 4/8	17 3/8	7 4/8	8 1/8	16	14	Hancock Co., ME	James T. Robertson	James T. Robertson	2002	18
219 7/8	65 5/8	40 1/8	44 2/8	16 4/8	16 4/8	7 4/8	7 6/8	16	13	East West Lake, ON	Kurt Skalitzky	Kurt Skalitzky	1989	20
219 6/8	61 2/8	46 6/8	45	15 7/8	16	7 3/8	7 5/8	13	11	Kinaskan Lake, BC	Thomas E. Farmer	Thomas E. Farmer	1998	21
219 2/8	62 2/8	40 5/8	39 6/8	18 7/8	15 2/8	7 5/8	7 4/8	17	19	Canada	Gift of W.B.O. Field to NCHH	Unknown	1924	22
219 1/8	64 1/8	45	43 1/8	15 5/8	13 7/8	7 6/8	7 4/8	14	13	Cold Fish Lake, BC	G. & P. Halvorson	G. & P. Halvorson	1974	23
218 6/8	58 2/8	42 6/8	40 4/8	15	15 4/8	8 7/8	8 6/8	16	16	Kennicott Lake, BC	Mike Popoff	Mike Popoff	1984	24
218 1/8	61 7/8	44 3/8	42 5/8	15	15	7 4/8	7 5/8	13	13	Chuchinra River, BC	Friedbert Prill	Friedbert Prill	1973	25
218	58 4/8	43 2/8	43 3/8	17	16 4/8	7	7 1/8	13	15	Wellman Lake, MB	Clifford S. Henderson	Bernie P. Nemetchek	1964	26
217 6/8	64 4/8	44 1/8	47 2/8	15	15	7 6/8	7 4/8	10	12	Cassiar Mts., BC	J. Barry Dyar	J. Barry Dyar	1977	27
217 6/8	63 6/8	40 6/8	39 6/8	17 4/8	18 7/8	7 7/8	7 6/8	12	16	Meat Cove, NS	Picked Up	Shawn Hadley	1995	27
217 5/8	64 3/8	44 3/8	42 7/8	16 3/8	15 4/8	7 6/8	7 2/8	11	16	Buffalo River, AB	Abe Teichroeb	Abe Teichroeb	2001	29
217 4/8	63 2/8	42 1/8	44	19 4/8	15 2/8	7 6/8	7 6/8	17	12	Hart Mt., BC	Donna Loewenstein	Donna Loewenstein	1966	30
217 2/8	63 6/8	42 2/8	39 5/8	17 5/8	15 3/8	7	6 6/8	15	15	Firebag River, AB	Frank Baldwin	Carlysle Baldwin	1977	31
217 1/8	63 1/8	40 4/8	43 6/8	14 3/8	15	8 2/8	8 1/8	14	15	Liard River, BC	Wayne E. Dalgleish	Wayne E. Dalgleish	1984	32
217	61 6/8	42 6/8	47 7/8	14 3/8	18 4/8	6 4/8	6 7/8	14	18	Franklin Co., ME	Clifford H. Damon	Clifford H. Damon	1997	33
216 7/8	59 3/8	41 6/8	44 2/8	17 2/8	15 4/8	7 4/8	7 4/8	17	14	Prophet River, BC	John G. Oltmanns	John G. Oltmanns	1971	34
216 3/8	58 5/8	43 6/8	46 2/8	14 6/8	15 3/8	8 3/8	8 4/8	16	12	Cassiar Mts., BC	Ross Ferguson	Ross Ferguson	1978	35
216 2/8	62 4/8	46 7/8	43 6/8	14 4/8	13 4/8	7 7/8	7 5/8	15	12	Cassiar Mts., BC	Don L. Corley	Don L. Corley	1984	36
216 1/8	71 5/8	38 1/8	37	14 1/8	14 4/8	7 5/8	8	14	14	Maine	H.M. Boice	Everhart Museum	1900	37

Score	Greatest Spread	Length of Palm R	Length of Palm L	Width of Palm R	Width of Palm L	Circ. R	Circ. L	Points R	Points L	Locality	Hunter	Owner	Date Killed	Rank
216 1/8	58 1/8	41 4/8	42 4/8	18 4/8	19 4/8	7	7 2/8	17	12	Dease Lake, BC	George A. Sinclair	George A. Sinclair	1981	37
215 4/8	64	41 4/8	42	13 4/8	13 4/8	6 7/8	6 6/8	14	15	Maine	Albert Bierstadt	Unknown	1880	39
215 3/8	53 1/8	43 7/8	43 4/8	18	14	7 6/8	7 5/8	16	20	Meekwap Lake, AB	Russell S. Watts, Sr.	Russell G. Watts, Jr.	1960	40
215 3/8	54 7/8	39 4/8	38 6/8	17 3/8	17 3/8	7 1/8	7 1/8	17	20	Latornell River, AB	Artie G. Brown	Artie G. Brown	1971	40
215 3/8	60 3/8	43 6/8	45 3/8	13 4/8	14 2/8	8 2/8	8 4/8	12	12	Kearl Lake, AB	Leo D. Paquin	Leo D. Paquin	1998	40
215 2/8	60 4/8	44 2/8	45 2/8	12 7/8	13 1/8	7 6/8	7 6/8	12	13	Cassiar Mts., BC	Milton J. Duffin	Milton J. Duffin	1976	43
215 1/8	62 3/8	44 1/8	44 1/8	14 4/8	13 3/8	7 2/8	7 2/8	13	13	Dease Lake, BC	Bert Klineburger	Bert Klineburger	1960	44
215 1/8	66 3/8	41 2/8	41	13 2/8	14 2/8	7 1/8	7 2/8	13	14	Prairie River, SK	John Horvath	John Horvath	1987	44
215	57 4/8	43	45 1/8	15 5/8	14	7 6/8	7 6/8	15	14	Ice Mt., BC	David H. Hilsberg	David H. Hilsberg	1985	46
215	70	42 2/8	38 6/8	15 2/8	15 4/8	7 4/8	7 4/8	11	12	Teslin Lake, BC	Steven D. Kellesvig	Steven D. Kellesvig	1997	46
214 6/8	53 6/8	44 2/8	44 2/8	16	13 4/8	7 6/8	7 6/8	16	15	Narraway River, AB	Karl Weber	Karl Weber	1956	48
214 6/8	68	39 5/8	39 3/8	16 4/8	15	8 4/8	8 4/8	13	13	Dease River, BC	Herb Klein	Dallas Mus. of Natl. Hist.	1960	48
214 6/8	56 2/8	45 5/8	42 3/8	17 4/8	19 4/8	7 3/8	7 4/8	14	12	Kennicott Lake, BC	Robert G. Burkhouse	Robert G. Burkhouse	1988	48
214 6/8	57	46 2/8	41 7/8	15 1/8	15 3/8	7 7/8	7 7/8	14	14	Red Lake, ON	Dan K. Brumm	D.K. Brumm & J. Krizsan	1991	48
214 4/8	62	42 2/8	38 6/8	15 7/8	17	7 5/8	7 5/8	15	16	Piscataquis Co., ME	Desmond Harvey	Desmond Harvey	1984	52
214 2/8	62 4/8	48 5/8	45	14	14 4/8	7 7/8	7 7/8	14	9	Nipekamew Lake, SK	Greg Cochran	Greg Cochran	1999	53
214 1/8	60 7/8	44 5/8	42 5/8	17 3/8	14 5/8	7 3/8	7 5/8	12	12	Teslin River, BC	John P. Costello II	John P. Costello II	1976	54
214	62 6/8	43	43 5/8	13 2/8	13 1/8	7	7	13	14	Alaska Hwy, Mile 100, BC	Karl Fritzsche	Karl Fritzsche	1968	55
214	62	41 2/8	38 5/8	17 3/8	17 2/8	7 2/8	7 1/8	15	13	North Brook, NL	Unknown	Sidney J. LeLuan, Sr.	1988 PR	55
213 6/8	58 6/8	39 7/8	41 6/8	18 4/8	19 1/8	8	7 5/8	13	17	Lesser Slave Lake, AB	Herbert R. Dobson	Herbert R. Dobson	1993	57
213 5/8	60 7/8	44 3/8	45 3/8	15 3/8	13 6/8	7 2/8	7 4/8	13	11	Prophet River, BC	Daniel T. Applebaker	Daniel T. Applebaker	1972	58
213 4/8	62 4/8	47 3/8	44 3/8	13 5/8	13 4/8	8	7 5/8	11	10	Tatshenshini River, BC	James C. Ranck	James C. Ranck	1998	59
213 2/8	51 4/8	44	44	19	17 4/8	7 5/8	7 5/8	12	12	Atlin, BC	Ewald Krentz	Ewald Krentz	1971	60
213	63 2/8	41 4/8	39 6/8	15 4/8	15 2/8	7 7/8	7 7/8	12	12	Hines Creek, AB	Elwood Baird	Elwood Baird	1975	61
213	62 2/8	45 1/8	42 4/8	14 3/8	11 5/8	8 3/8	8 2/8	14	13	Stikine River, BC	Sam Sanders, Jr.	Sam Sanders, Jr.	1975	61
213	52	45	46 5/8	15	15 7/8	7 4/8	7 4/8	14	13	Liard River, BC	Hayden O. Woods, Sr.	Hayden O. Woods, Sr.	1976	61
213	59	42	41 7/8	15	14 3/8	7 2/8	7 3/8	14	14	Candle Lake, SK	Roger F. Mann	Roger F. Mann	1989	61
213	61 2/8	42 6/8	44	16 1/8	14	7 6/8	7 5/8	12	14	Gladys Lake, BC	Ronald A. Landree	Ronald A. Landree	1997	61
213	61 4/8	40 1/8	41	14	13 3/8	8 3/8	8 3/8	14	14	Thunder Bay, ON	Claude R. Vincent	Claude R. Vincent	2001	61
212 6/8	61	42 5/8	42 6/8	13 1/8	14 4/8	7 6/8	7 5/8	14	13	Love, SK	Robert J. Rogers	Robert J. Rogers	1966	67
212 6/8	60 6/8	41 4/8	38	16 4/8	17 4/8	8 1/8	8	16	18	Sikanni Chief River, BC	David B. Willis	David B. Willis	1977	67
212 5/8	60 6/8	41 7/8	43 5/8	13 6/8	15 4/8	8	8	14	14	Slave Lake, AB	R.W.H. Eben-Ebenau	R.W.H. Eben-Ebenau	1937	69
212 5/8	55 7/8	38 2/8	44 2/8	13 3/8	12 7/8	7 2/8	7 2/8	15	15	Marion Lake, BC	J. Clifton Jensen	J. Clifton Jensen	1974	69
212 3/8	63 1/8	40	39 2/8	18	17 6/8	7 4/8	7	12	16	Lake Co., MN	Randall J. Wise	Randall J. Wise	1998	69
212 1/8	56 3/8	43 2/8	43 4/8	14 4/8	14 4/8	8	7 3/8	17	15	Cassiar Mts., BC	Dean A. Bloomfield	Dean A. Bloomfield	1979	72
212 1/8	59 1/8	47 6/8	42 1/8	13 2/8	14 4/8	8 2/8	8 2/8	14	16	Fort Nelson River, BC	Glen S. Huntley	Glen S. Huntley	1995	73
212	54	42	45	18 6/8	18 7/8	8 4/8	8 5/8	16	18	Grayling River, BC	Arnold E. Dado	Arnold E. Dado	1984	74
212	58 4/8	41 7/8	43 5/8	12 2/8	12 4/8	7 6/8	7 4/8	14	14	Taku River, BC	William A. Van Alstine	William A. Van Alstine	1990	74
211 7/8	65 3/8	38 2/8	44 2/8	11 7/8	13 7/8	7 2/8	7 1/8	15	15	Pasquia Hills, SK	William H. Schweitzer	William H. Schweitzer	1978	76
211 6/8	56 6/8	40	39 2/8	13 4/8	17 4/8	7 1/8	7	15	17	Ft. St. John, BC	Jack Fries	Jack Fries	1977	77
211 6/8	58 6/8	43 2/8	43 4/8	14 4/8	14 1/8	7	7 6/8	11	11	Teslin River, BC	Ron Harris	Ron Harris	1994	77
211 5/8	61 7/8	46	46	14 4/8	18 7/8	8 3/8	8 6/8	12	10	Powell Lake, ON	Jerry R. Brocksmith	Jerry R. Brocksmith	1969	79
211 4/8	65	40 6/8	40 2/8	12 2/8	12 4/8	7 6/8	8 4/8	14	13	Pine Lake, QC	Walter Geismar	Walter Geismar	1949	80
211 4/8	64 6/8	41 7/8	43	11 7/8	12 7/8	7 5/8	7 5/8	12	17	Atlin, BC	William L. Frederick	William L. Frederick	1969	80
211 4/8	54	45 1/8	44 7/8	13 4/8	13 1/8	8 3/8	7 6/8	15	13	Sheslay River, BC	Daniel E. Gorecki	Daniel E. Gorecki	1989	80
211 3/8	63 6/8	36 2/8	37 4/8	15 7/8	16 4/8	7 6/8	7 6/8	15	14	Lake Madeleine, QC	Clement Chouinard	Michel Miouse	1992	80
211 3/8	60 2/8	39 6/8	40 6/8	18 5/8	14 5/8	7 2/8	7 2/8	14	16	Ptarmigan Lake, BC	Jack W. Ahart, Sr.	Jack W. Ahart, Sr.	2002	80
211 3/8	54 1/8	40 1/8	40	18 1/8	15 1/8	7 1/8	7 1/8	17	16	Tochieka Range, BC	C. Thomas Manier	C. Thomas Manier	1978	85

CANADA MOOSE

Alces alces americana and Alces alces andersoni

Score	Greatest Spread	Length of Palm		Width of Palm		Circumference of Beam at Smallest Place		Number of Normal Points		Locality	Hunter	Owner	Date Killed	Rank
		R	L	R	L	R	L	R	L					
211 1/8	57 7/8	41 7/8	41	13 4/8	14 4/8	7 1/8	7 3/8	15	15	Rabbit River, BC	Richard A. Jacobs	Richard A. Jacobs	1995	86
211	49	43 6/8	43 4/8	16 2/8	14 4/8	8 1/8	8	15	15	Grande Prairie, AB	Lester C. Hearn	Lester C. Hearn	1972	87
211	59 6/8	40 6/8	38 7/8	15 5/8	15 4/8	8 6/8	8 2/8	15	13	Mojikit Lake, ON	Charles R. Salfer	Charles R. Salfer	1987	87
211	63 2/8	41 1/8	42 2/8	18 5/8	15 6/8	7 6/8	7 4/8	16	10	Red Earth Creek, AB	M. Nathan Sabo	M. Nathan Sabo	2000	87
210 7/8	70 1/8	40	40 2/8	15 7/8	11 3/8	8	8 1/8	11	12	Round Lake, ON	M.A. Kennedy	Royal Ontario Mus.	1912	90
210 7/8	60 1/8	40 2/8	44 2/8	15 7/8	14 6/8	7 6/8	7 3/8	15	13	Clova, QC	R. Theriault & J.P. Lavoie	R. Theriault & J.P. Lavoie	2002	90
210 6/8	63 2/8	45 4/8	44 2/8	13 7/8	13 4/8	7	7 1/8	11	9	Sikanni Chief River, BC	Gerald Stecklein	Gerald Stecklein	1965	92
210 6/8	61	43 3/8	43	14 6/8	14 6/8	7 2/8	7 1/8	10	11	Toad River, BC	Jerry D. Bechard	Jerry D. Bechard	2001	92
210 5/8	58 5/8	43	42 6/8	14 6/8	15	7 4/8	7 5/8	16	11	Billard Lake, MB	Kendall J. Bauer	Kendall J. Bauer	1998	94
210 1/8	62 1/8	42 7/8	42 2/8	12 5/8	11 2/8	7 4/8	7 4/8	13	13	Sheep Creek, AB	R.V.D. Goltz	R.V.D. Goltz	1964	95
210	59 2/8	41 4/8	40 1/8	15 4/8	14 3/8	6 7/8	6 7/8	14	16	Sheep River, AB	Elton Boggs	Elton Boggs	1956	96
210	54 6/8	44 5/8	47 4/8	14 1/8	13 4/8	7 6/8	7 6/8	12	14	Cassiar Mts., BC	Richard J. Wristen	Richard J. Wristen	1978	96
210	53 4/8	42 3/8	39 2/8	19	18 4/8	7 4/8	7 5/8	13	15	Cold Fish Lake, BC	Glenroy G. Livingston	Glenroy G. Livingston	1990	96
209 7/8	53 3/8	43 1/8	43 5/8	12 7/8	12 6/8	7 4/8	7 3/8	15	15	Kakwa River, AB	Rolf Koelblinger	Rolf Koelblinger	1969	99
209 7/8	53 3/8	44 5/8	45 7/8	12 5/8	12 6/8	7 3/8	7	15	14	Cutbank River, AB	Alan D. Taylor	Alan D. Taylor	1970	99
209 7/8	54 3/8	45 3/8	42 2/8	15 3/8	15 2/8	7 2/8	7 2/8	13	13	Turnagain River, BC	Gordon R. Cole	Gordon R. Cole	1974	99
209 7/8	58 5/8	42	40 4/8	14	14 6/8	7 2/8	7 1/8	14	14	Cassiar Mts., BC	William M. Silva	William M. Silva	1976	99
209 7/8	57 5/8	44 3/8	41	16 6/8	14 7/8	7 4/8	7 2/8	13	15	Dease Mts., BC	Michael D. Rochette	Michael D. Rochette	1988	99
209 6/8	64 6/8	39 4/8	44	12	13 5/8	7	7 2/8	14	14	Oba Lake, ON	Bruce McPherson	Bruce McPherson	1963	104
209 6/8	60 6/8	43 4/8	43 7/8	14	15 3/8	7	7 1/8	10	10	Jennings Lake, BC	Collins F. Kellogg	Collins F. Kellogg	1969	104
209 5/8	59 1/8	41 5/8	41 3/8	13 5/8	17 2/8	8 2/8	8 6/8	12	15	Malone Lake, QC	Harvey A. Kipp	Harvey A. Kipp	1953	106
209 5/8	68 3/8	41	41	13 3/8	13 4/8	7 7/8	7 7/8	10	9	Liard River, BC	Ronald B. Barker	Ronald B. Barker	1990	106
209 5/8	58 1/8	42 3/8	43 6/8	14 5/8	14 4/8	7 7/8	8	11	11	Dover River, AB	Allan M. Fenerty	Allan M. Fenerty	2001	106
209 4/8	57 4/8	40 3/8	42 2/8	16 1/8	15	7 5/8	7 5/8	13	13	Hasler Creek, BC	Mike Nussbaumer	Mike Nussbaumer	1984	109
209 4/8	57	41 2/8	40 4/8	14 6/8	13 6/8	7 1/8	7 5/8	15	16	Hayes Peak, BC	Richard Kling	Richard Kling	2000	109
209 3/8	59 3/8	42 5/8	42 1/8	15 3/8	16 3/8	7 6/8	7 4/8	10	10	Cassiar Mts., BC	Hurnie H. Whitehead	Hurnie H. Whitehead	1978	111
209 2/8	59	44	50 4/8	12 5/8	12 5/8	7 4/8	7 5/8	12	11	Smoky River, AB	William R. Farmer	William R. Farmer	1970	112
209 1/8	55 5/8	40 6/8	41 4/8	13	13	7	7 2/8	16	16	Kenora, ON	David O. Moreton	David O. Moreton	1970	113
209 1/8	53 7/8	43 2/8	43 4/8	13	11 4/8	6 7/8	7	16	17	Red Earth Creek, AB	Gabriel J. Plamondon	Gabriel J. Plamondon	1997	113
209	63	39 4/8	39	15	17 6/8	8	8	11	11	Manawaki, QC	George A. Krikory	George A. Krikory	1953	115
208 7/8	56 5/8	39 2/8	43 4/8	15 7/8	15	6 7/8	7 2/8	15	15	Hudson Bay, SK	Don Hendricks	Don Hendricks	1961	116
208 7/8	60 7/8	39 7/8	41 7/8	15	13 4/8	7 5/8	7 5/8	13	14	Sheslay River, BC	T.T. Stroup	T.T. Stroup	1968	116
208 7/8	54 3/8	43	43 2/8	13 7/8	13 4/8	6 6/8	6 6/8	14	14	Hivon Lake, AB	R. George Crooker	R. George Crooker	1997	116
208 6/8	63 2/8	43	44 6/8	15 3/8	16 4/8	6 7/8	7 2/8	11	15	The Pas, MB	Denver M. Wright	Denver M. Wright	1950	119
208 6/8	61 6/8	41	41 5/8	17 3/8	15 6/8	7 6/8	8	9	12	Hudson Bay, SK	Frank B. Miller	Frank B. Miller	1967	119
208 6/8	61	41 7/8	40 1/8	16 3/8	14	6 6/8	6 6/8	14	13	Ft. St. John, BC	Richard O. Vycital	Richard O. Vycital	1967	119
208 6/8	57 2/8	42 6/8	41 1/8	13 6/8	13 4/8	7 1/8	7 2/8	14	14	Catagua River, BC	Dominic Arone	Dominic Arone	1969	119
208 6/8	56	43 6/8	47 6/8	12 5/8	14 2/8	7 1/8	7 4/8	14	16	Pepaw Lake, SK	Maurice R. LaRose	Maurice R. LaRose	1976	119

Score	Greatest Spread	Length of Palm R	Length of Palm L	Width of Palm R	Width of Palm L	Circ. of Beam R	Circ. of Beam L	Points R	Points L	Locality	Hunter	Owner	Date	Rank
208 6/8	61	41 2/8	41 1/8	14 7/8	14 5/8	7 1/8	7 2/8	13	11	Ketchum Lake, BC	Gailand K. Hann	Gailand K. Hann	1985	119
208 6/8	65 2/8	42 6/8	40 7/8	13 6/8	11 6/8	8 1/8	8 4/8	11	12	Coos Co., NH	Norma J. Taplin	Norma J. Taplin	1999	119
208 5/8	58 5/8	43 4/8	44 6/8	15 1/8	13 1/8	7 4/8	7 3/8	11	12	Muskwa River, BC	Gary D. Linsinbigler	Gary D. Linsinbigler	1969	126
208 4/8	52 2/8	46 4/8	45 5/8	16 4/8	12 4/8	8	8	12	14	Prophet River, BC	Vollrad J. von Berg	Vollrad J. von Berg	1967	127
208 4/8	61 4/8	42 6/8	41 5/8	16 4/8	19 5/8	7 3/8	7 4/8	8	10	Trutch Mt., BC	Charles H. Veasey	Charles H. Veasey	1976	127
208 4/8	56 2/8	43 4/8	40 1/8	13 3/8	14 4/8	7 5/8	8 2/8	15	15	Notikewin, AB	Bruce Friedel	Bruce Friedel	1994	127
208 3/8	58 7/8	43 4/8	44 4/8	14	15 3/8	7 2/8	7 2/8	19	12	Taku River, BC	Robert J. Matyas	Robert J. Matyas	1989	130
208 3/8	60 1/8	40 2/8	40 5/8	15	15 1/8	7	6 7/8	13	13	Hall Lake, BC	Theodore G. Yerasimides	Theodore G. Yerasimides	1991	130
208 3/8	53 5/8	45 4/8	44 5/8	14 5/8	12 2/8	8 4/8	8 5/8	12	14	Snowdon Range, BC	Ronald E. Gartner	Ronald E. Gartner	1997	130
208 2/8	61 2/8	40 1/8	40 7/8	11 6/8	13 5/8	7 5/8	7 6/8	14	13	Chetwynd, BC	Louis Carriere	Louis Carriere	1976	133
208 2/8	61 4/8	40 4/8	40 1/8	15 2/8	12	8 3/8	8 4/8	12	12	Coos Co., NH	Charles A. Covey, Sr.	Charles A. Covey, Sr.	1990	133
208 2/8	64 4/8	41 2/8	38 6/8	14	13 6/8	8 3/8	8 4/8	11	11	Beatty Creek, BC	Duane A. Enders	Duane A. Enders	1997	133
208 1/8	59 5/8	39 2/8	40 2/8	15 4/8	17 4/8	6 4/8	6 7/8	13	13	Halfway River, BC	Eugene F. Konopaski	Eugene F. Konopaski	1967	136
208 1/8	61 3/8	42 2/8	40	16 3/8	17 1/8	7	7 3/8	10	12	Cadomin, AB	Picked Up	E.F. Madole	1977	136
208 1/8	51 3/8	44 1/8	42	13 7/8	15 3/8	7 5/8	7 4/8	17	16	Elk Lake, ON	Florien Buch	Florien Buch	1991	136
208	58 2/8	41 7/8	40 7/8	14 1/8	12 3/8	7 7/8	7 5/8	16	14	Muskwa River, BC	William D. Phifer	William D. Phifer	1969	139
208	61 4/8	41 2/8	42 7/8	16	13 3/8	7 7/8	7 5/8	11	12	Legend Lake, AB	Reginald R. Berry	Reginald R. Berry	1977	139
208	62	40 7/8	40 5/8	13 4/8	11 6/8	7 6/8	7 6/8	13	15	Hotchkiss River, AB	Andy G. Petkus	Andy G. Petkus	1985	139
208	62	40 6/8	43	12 3/8	12	6 2/8	6 2/8	15	14	Thorhild, AB	Ross F. Lyons	Ross F. Lyons	2001	139
207 7/8	56 1/8	43 2/8	43	13 2/8	13 4/8	7 5/8	7 5/8	12	14	Hudson Bay, SK	Harold Read	Philip Schlegel	1956	143
207 7/8	52 3/8	47 3/8	46 3/8	14 2/8	16	7 3/8	7 1/8	10	11	Neaves Creek, BC	Mrs. George A. Strom, Jr.	Mrs. George A. Strom, Jr.	1960	143
207 7/8	62 5/8	40 1/8	40 2/8	14 1/8	15	8 2/8	8 2/8	15	11	Aroostook Co., ME	Michael C. Hall	Michael C. Hall	1991	143
207 7/8	56 7/8	42 6/8	42 3/8	13 5/8	11 7/8	7 2/8	7 3/8	14	16	Buckley Lake, BC	John F. Abbott	John F. Abbott	1996	143
207 6/8	71 4/8	41 6/8	42 6/8	13 6/8	12 5/8	7 3/8	7 7/8	10	11	Moccasin Lake, ON	Charles W. Reiley	Charles W. Reiley	1961	147
207 6/8	62	41 1/8	38 1/8	13 3/8	13 3/8	7 7/8	7 5/8	11	13	Bocquene Lake, AB	John M. Damberger	John M. Damberger	1998	147
207 5/8	52 7/8	44 2/8	41 3/8	15 7/8	13 6/8	7 5/8	7 1/8	12	16	Ash Mt., BC	Robert E. Rabon	Robert E. Rabon	1984	149
207 5/8	54 7/8	40 4/8	44	16	15 6/8	7 2/8	7 5/8	13	13	Dease Lake, BC	Robert T. Ryan	Robert T. Ryan	1997	149
207 5/8	56 6/8	42 4/8	41 6/8	12 4/8	14	7 3/8	7 5/8	13	14	Long Lake, AB	Garry A. Debienne	Garry A. Debienne	1975	151
207 4/8	60 4/8	42 4/8	48	16 4/8	15 4/8	7 4/8	7 4/8	16	12	Sulphur Creek, AB	Willard L. Gamin	Willard L. Gamin	1980	151
207 4/8	51 2/8	38 4/8	40 3/8	14 1/8	14 4/8	7	7	15	16	Prophet River, BC	Arvin Harrell	Arvin Harrell	1981	151
207 4/8	70 1/8	31	43	15	16	7 7/8	7 5/8	15	15	Alberta	Unknown	Acad. Nat. Sci., Phil.	1905	151
207 3/8	59 3/8	39 3/8	40 3/8	14 6/8	14	7 6/8	7 5/8	13	14	Smoky River, AB	Robert L. Carmichael, Jr.	Robert L. Carmichael, Jr.	1974	154
207 3/8	53 5/8	40 5/8	41 5/8	15 3/8	16	6 7/8	7 5/8	14	13	Birch Mts., AB	Leo F. Neuls	Leo F. Neuls	1992	154
207 3/8	59 4/8	43	40 3/8	13 6/8	13 6/8	7 6/8	7 6/8	12	14	Hudson Bay, SK	A.L. Moore	A.L. Moore	1961	154
207 2/8	61 4/8	39 5/8	39 1/8	13 4/8	15 6/8	7 5/8	7 5/8	14	13	Indian Brook, NS	Claude Langley	Claude Langley	1994	157
207 2/8	56 4/8	38 4/8	39 4/8	14 4/8	14 4/8	7 3/8	7 6/8	13	13	Rock Lake, BC	Timothy J. Koll	Timothy J. Koll	1999	157
207 1/8	60 3/8	40 4/8	39 7/8	13 2/8	15	7 2/8	7 2/8	13	15	Manning, AB	Gary Cumming	Gary Cumming	1971	157
207	61 6/8	43 4/8	45 7/8	12 4/8	15	7 5/8	7 5/8	12	9	Goose River, AB	O.D. Evans	O.D. Evans	1960	160
207	58 6/8	42 2/8	44 4/8	13 2/8	14 3/8	8	8	14	12	Nipisi Lake, AB	J.M. Kirkpatrick	J.M. Kirkpatrick	1966	161
207	60	47	43	12	12	7 4/8	7 4/8	12	11	Atlin, BC	Gerald Larsen	Gerald Larsen	1996	161
207	53 4/8	41	40 4/8	15 4/8	16 4/8	6 6/8	6 6/8	16	14	Tabor Lake, BC	Carolynn Quamme	Carolynn Quamme	2000	161
207	62 5/8	41	40 3/8	13 3/8	13 2/8	7 4/8	7 4/8	13	11	Somerset Co., ME	Stephen D. Cole	Stephen D. Cole	1984	161
206 7/8	61 7/8	44 5/8	40 7/8	14 7/8	16	7 6/8	7 6/8	11	13	Notikewin River, AB	Denis Drainville	Denis Drainville	1987	165
206 7/8	60 2/8	39 1/8	39 1/8	14	14 4/8	7 6/8	7 6/8	13	17	Smithers, BC	W.G. Reed	Louis Calder	1951	165
206 7/8	60 2/8	37 4/8	38 5/8	16 1/8	13 4/8	7 6/8	7 6/8	17	15	Black Sturgeon Lake, ON	Joseph J. Casey	Joseph J. Casey	1967	167
206 6/8	61 6/8	43 4/8	40 6/8	15 6/8	14 5/8	7 1/8	7 1/8	10	10	Gordondale, AB	Chuck LeDuc	Chuck LeDuc	1975	167
206 6/8	68	39	35 4/8	14 2/8	16 4/8	7 6/8	7 6/8	12	12	Cook Co., MN	R.J. Parent, J. Parent, & R. Parent	Rick J. Parent	2000	167

Alces alces americana and Alces alces andersoni

Score	Greatest Spread	Length of Palm		Width of Palm		Circumference of Beam at Smallest Place		Number of Normal Points		Locality	Hunter	Owner	Date Killed	Rank
		R	L	R	L	R	L	R	L					
206 5/8	57 3/8	43 7/8	44 3/8	13	12 4/8	7 2/8	7 4/8	11	11	Assiniboine River, SK	Francis Peecock	Francis Peecock	1976	171
206 5/8	59 5/8	41 1/8	43 4/8	14 3/8	15 2/8	8	8	10	12	Peerless Lake, AB	Janet E. Spinks	Jonathan Spinks	1989	171
206 4/8	60	40 2/8	35 3/8	16	17 2/8	8 3/8	9 2/8	14	14	White River, ON	Ronald L. Porter	Ronald L. Porter	1975	173
206 4/8	56 2/8	41 3/8	41 6/8	13 3/8	14 4/8	7 3/8	7 4/8	15	13	Horseranch Mts., BC	Bill McCoy	Bill McCoy	1976	173
206 3/8	56 3/8	46 1/8	49	15	15	7 5/8	7 6/8	9	9	Windfall Creek, AB	Brian Richardson	Brian Richardson	1978	175
206 3/8	59 3/8	44 1/8	42 3/8	15 5/8	15	7 1/8	7 2/8	9	13	Hyland Lake, BC	John B. Barnhardt	John B. Barnhardt	1996	175
206 2/8	55 4/8	41 2/8	42 2/8	13 4/8	13	8 1/8	8 2/8	13	13	Trutch, BC	Richard M. Wilkey	Richard M. Wilkey	1976	177
206 2/8	61 2/8	44 2/8	40 4/8	13 6/8	14 1/8	8 4/8	8 7/8	10	13	Piscataquis Co., ME	Vernon Knott	Vernon Knott	1987	177
206 2/8	66 4/8	38 7/8	41 6/8	13 6/8	13 6/8	8 5/8	8 2/8	12	9	Manning, AB	Nick Denecky	Nick Denecky	1988	177
206 1/8	59 1/8	40 2/8	39 6/8	18 3/8	16 3/8	6 3/8	6 4/8	11	12	Brule, AB	Steven L. Rose	Steven L. Rose	1969	180
206 1/8	59 1/8	42 4/8	42 4/8	14 3/8	15 3/8	7 1/8	7 1/8	12	11	Klappan River, BC	Bert Varkonyi	J. & N. Varkonyi	1979	180
206 1/8	61 7/8	37 3/8	37 4/8	16 6/8	15 5/8	7 1/8	7 1/8	12	14	Aroostook Co., ME	Shawn LeClair	Shawn LeClair	1993	180
206 1/8	59 7/8	42 4/8	42	12 6/8	12 7/8	7 3/8	7 3/8	12	11	Gladys River, BC	Rory Kuchenbecker	Rory Kuchenbecker	1994	180
206	52 4/8	41 6/8	41 2/8	16 2/8	21 2/8	7 2/8	7 4/8	12	13	Trimble Lake, BC	Clifford E. Palmer	Clifford E. Palmer	1962	184
206	59 4/8	38 7/8	42 1/8	15 4/8	13 4/8	7 7/8	7 7/8	13	13	Moose Call Lake, BC	W.W. Harvie	W.W. Harvie	1965	184
206	54 4/8	40 3/8	40 3/8	16 3/8	15 2/8	7 3/8	7 1/8	13	14	Muskwa River, BC	C. Dale Hippensteel	C. Dale Hippensteel	1968	184
206	59 4/8	40 1/8	39 4/8	14 1/8	15 1/8	6 5/8	6 6/8	13	13	Halfway River, BC	Robert Lordahl	Robert Lordahl	1993	184
206	54 2/8	42 4/8	41 1/8	13 2/8	14 6/8	7 4/8	7 5/8	14	15	Gem Lake, BC	John H. Hoppe III	John H. Hoppe III	1997	184
206	61 2/8	42	38 5/8	13 3/8	16 1/8	8 5/8	8 4/8	13	12	Oxford Co., ME	Gerard L. Roy	Gerard L. Roy	2000	184
205 7/8	64 3/8	41 2/8	38 6/8	12 4/8	14 4/8	6 4/8	6 5/8	13	16	Cook Co., MN	H. Chapman, C. Chapman, M. Chapman & J. Anderson	H. Chapman, C. Chapman, M. Chapman & J. Anderson	1987	190
205 7/8	59 5/8	41	37 3/8	15 4/8	15	8	7 6/8	14	13	Dease Lake, BC	Gordon E. Janz	Gordon E. Janz	1997	190
205 6/8	56	41 5/8	40 4/8	12 4/8	14 4/8	6 7/8	7 1/8	15	17	Sheep Creek, AB	Rudiger Schwarz	Rudiger Schwarz	1959	192
205 6/8	55	42	41 7/8	14 3/8	16 5/8	8 2/8	8 1/8	12	11	Kechika River, BC	Len Eklund	Len Eklund	1968	192
205 6/8	54 2/8	42	41 4/8	14 1/8	16 6/8	7 6/8	7 5/8	14	13	Turnagain River, BC	Audrey E. Crabtree	Audrey E. Crabtree	1984	192
205 6/8	56 4/8	39	42 6/8	15 4/8	15 6/8	7 1/8	7 2/8	15	13	Badman Point, BC	K. James Malady III	K. James Malady III	1995	192
205 6/8	62 4/8	42 5/8	44	18 4/8	11 7/8	8 1/8	8 1/8	16	9	Piscataquis Co., ME	Steve Heath	Brian Ross	1997	192
205 5/8	65 3/8	45	40	14 1/8	14 6/8	7 5/8	7 3/8	13	8	Vice Lake, ON	A.W. Winchester	A.W. Winchester	1959	197
205 5/8	55 3/8	43 3/8	43 4/8	13 7/8	12 4/8	7 4/8	7 2/8	12	13	Simonette River, AB	John G. Stelfox	John G. Stelfox	1965	197
205 5/8	54 1/8	41 1/8	41	12	17 6/8	8 1/8	7 6/8	15	17	Cassiar Mts., BC	Richard Trapp	Richard Trapp	1972	197
205 5/8	65 1/8	38 2/8	39 7/8	13 4/8	13 4/8	7 4/8	7 6/8	11	13	Bottineau Co., ND	Lloyd E. Burgard	Lloyd E. Burgard	1985	197
205 4/8	66 2/8	40 2/8	43 4/8	13 4/8	11 1/8	7 2/8	7 2/8	12	11	Bay Tree, AB	A. Iverson	Wally's Sporting Goods	1926	201
205 4/8	61 6/8	39 6/8	40 6/8	16 7/8	17	7 6/8	7 6/8	9	8	Kedahla Lake, BC	Jack Perisits, Jr.	Jack Perisits, Jr.	1970	201
205 3/8	62 5/8	44 2/8	37 6/8	14 7/8	13 3/8	8 2/8	8 4/8	13	12	Kleena Kleene, BC	Roger Dane	Roger Dane	1965	203
205 3/8	59 7/8	38 5/8	44 2/8	15 5/8	16 3/8	7 4/8	7 5/8	11	15	Liard Plateau, BC	Charles W. Melton	Charles W. Melton	1971	203
205 3/8	60 7/8	43 4/8	42 6/8	13 4/8	15 4/8	7	7 4/8	9	11	Cassiar Mts., BC	George R. Weeks	George R. Weeks	1985	203
205 2/8	57 2/8	39 4/8	39 7/8	13 4/8	14 3/8	7 3/8	7 2/8	17	14	Stikine Plateau, BC	Mike Papac	Mike Papac	1977	206

Score								Location	Hunter	Owner	Date	Rank
205 2/8	61 4/8	41	40 5/8	16	16 3/8	9	8	Serpentine River, NL	Picked Up	Gerard Beaulieu	1989	206
205 2/8	60	41	42 4/8	13 3/8	13 4/8	11	12	Charlie Lake, BC	Thomas C. Bieberle	Thomas C. Bieberle	2001	206
205 1/8	53 5/8	43 3/8	42	13 3/8	14 7/8	13	12	Cold Fish Lake, BC	Armin O. Baltensweiler	Armin O. Baltensweiler	1965	209
205 1/8	56 1/8	40 1/8	38 3/8	14	13 6/8	18	15	Atlin, BC	Joey H. Longpre	Joey H. Longpre	1994	209
205 1/8	58 1/8	43	43	14 4/8	24 3/8	8	10	Eddies Cove, NL	Floyd Lawless	F. & I. Lawless	1999	209
205	57 4/8	36 2/8	35 4/8	17 2/8	19 4/8	16	14	Prophet River, BC	John E. Hammett, Jr.	John E. Hammett, Jr.	1944	212
205	56	42 7/8	42 6/8	11 6/8	12	14	16	Moose Lake, MB	Leif R. Langsjoen	Leif R. Langsjoen	1960	212
205	57 4/8	43 2/8	42 6/8	11 4/8	12	12	13	Cassiar, BC	James H. Bryant	James H. Bryant	1965	212
205	60 4/8	41	43	12	12	11	13	Cassiar Mts., BC	Earl I. Jones	Earl I. Jones	1978	212
205	58 2/8	42 6/8	42	15 1/8	15 1/8	9	9	Letain Lake, BC	Jesse Mengler	Jesse Mengler	1995	212
205	59	41 5/8	42	15	13 2/8	13	11	Dease Creek, BC	Bert Berry	Bert Berry	1997	212
205	61	37 4/8	41 2/8	13 5/8	17	13	13	Long Lake, ON	Randy H. Shell	Randy H. Shell	1998	212
204 7/8	62 3/8	38 1/8	40 2/8	14 4/8	14 3/8	15	11	Prophet River, BC	Lewis M. Morgan	Lewis M. Morgan	1970	219
204 7/8	59 1/8	42	42 4/8	14 5/8	14 4/8	10	12	Thorpe Creek, BC	Gary W. Cunningham	Gary W. Cunningham	2001	219
204 6/8	56 2/8	46 6/8	43 6/8	15 1/8	15 7/8	8	8	Hudson Bay, SK	Fred Smorodin	Fred Smorodin	1957	221
204 6/8	57	45 4/8	43 6/8	13 4/8	13 2/8	9	10	Heart Mts., BC	Timothy E. Walters	Timothy E. Walters	1995	221
204 6/8	64 6/8	42 7/8	45	11 6/8	10 2/8	10	11	Cassiar Mts., BC	Douglas Rehbein	Douglas Rehbein	1998	221
204 6/8	64	38 3/8	38 6/8	14 2/8	14	12	10	Aroostook Co., ME	Michael G. Mele	Michael G. Mele	2003	221
204 4/8	54 4/8	40 3/8	40 2/8	13 5/8	12 2/8	16	16	Cassiar, BC	Unknown	BC Game Dept.	PR 1918	225
204 4/8	51 6/8	45 3/8	44 2/8	15	14 3/8	13	11	Germansen Mts., BC	Edward A. McLarney	Edward A. McLarney	1978	225
204 3/8	57 7/8	40 6/8	39 7/8	14	13 7/8	12	13	Prophet River, BC	W.T. Yoshimoto	W.T. Yoshimoto	1966	227
204 3/8	55 7/8	42 3/8	41 6/8	16 6/8	14 4/8	11	10	Summit Lake, BC	R. A. Schweitzer	R.A. Schweitzer	1970	227
204 3/8	56 5/8	43	41	15 2/8	14 4/8	16	11	Prophet River, BC	Daniel L. Rafferty	Daniel L. Rafferty	1986	227
204 2/8	52 4/8	36 3/8	38 3/8	16 1/8	16 7/8	16	16	Buckinghorse, BC	John C. Belcher	John C. Belcher	1955	230
204 2/8	60	37 4/8	38 4/8	16 2/8	14 2/8	14	13	The Pas, MB	Eddy Burkhartsmeir	Eddy Burkhartsmeir	1960	230
204 2/8	62	37 4/8	38 2/8	15 3/8	16 6/8	10	10	Duti Lake, BC	John M. Haugen	John M. Haugen	1966	230
204 2/8	62 2/8	41 1/8	41 1/8	16 6/8	14 5/8	8	9	Ice Mt., BC	Jerry E. Mason	Jerry E. Mason	1966	230
204 2/8	55 4/8	44 7/8	39 4/8	15 7/8	14 3/8	13	14	Muskwa River, BC	James C. Kolbe	James C. Kolbe	1969	230
204 2/8	58 6/8	36 3/8	41 7/8	19 1/8	18 4/8	11	16	Wawa, ON	Edward A. Hall	Edward A. Hall	1970	230
204 2/8	56 6/8	45	44 2/8	11 4/8	12 4/8	12	11	Tetsa River, BC	Alex Nesterenko	Alex Nesterenko	1973	230
204 2/8	65	41 6/8	39 5/8	15 1/8	13	11	10	Peace River, AB	Wilbur C. Savage	Wilbur C. Savage	1984	230
204 1/8	55 1/8	41 3/8	46 2/8	15	13 5/8	13	16	Ft. St. James, BC	Ed Cornish	Ed Cornish	1964	238
204 1/8	62 1/8	36	38 2/8	16 5/8	15 5/8	12	12	Cassiar Mts., BC	Roger B. Donahue, Jr.	Roger B. Donahue, Jr.	1995	238
204 1/8	63 1/8	40 3/8	40 7/8	13	13	11	10	Eight Mile Creek, BC	Leroy C. Mooney	Leroy C. Mooney	1995	238
204	68 4/8	35	33 6/8	15 2/8	13	13	13	Elderslay, SK	R.E. McKenzie	R.E. McKenzie	1930	241
204	55	40 7/8	41 2/8	13 5/8	13 5/8	15	14	Lake Nipigon, ON	Gary C. Jacobson	Gary C. Jacobson	1965	241
204	57 6/8	42 6/8	43 6/8	13 4/8	13 4/8	11	10	Tachilta Lakes, BC	Karen White	Karen White	1997	241
204	58	39 4/8	39 4/8	15 7/8	15 3/8	12	12	Dease Lake, BC	Robert L. Hudman	Robert L. Hudman	1998	241
203 7/8	63 3/8	41 3/8	39 6/8	10 7/8	11 6/8	13	12	Lodge, SK	F. Foarie	F. Foarie	1962	245
203 7/8	52 3/8	41 6/8	41 5/8	13 5/8	14 7/8	13	14	Kakwa River, AB	Dean A. Estes	Dean A. Estes	1987	245
203 7/8	53 1/8	40 3/8	42 2/8	18 2/8	15 4/8	13	12	Somerset Co., ME	Gary T. Brown	Gary T. Brown	1994	245
203 7/8	58 1/8	37 7/8	39 1/8	13 6/8	14	15	14	Glundebery Creek, BC	Ronald K. Pettit	Ronald K. Pettit	2003	245
203 6/8	55	38 1/8	39	15 2/8	15 3/8	14	15	Jackfish Lake, AB	A. Stopson	A. Stopson	1955	249
203 6/8	59 4/8	42 6/8	41 2/8	10 5/8	12 4/8	13	12	Hudson Bay, SK	Abraham Hassen	Abraham Hassen	1959	249
203 6/8	60	38 1/8	41 1/8	13	14	13	15	Rabbit River, BC	Bob V. Kelley	Bob V. Kelley	1969	249
203 6/8	58 4/8	39 1/8	39	12 2/8	12 5/8	13	14	Pink Mt., BC	Garth C. Hardy	Garth C. Hardy	1973	249
203 6/8	52 2/8	43	43 4/8	13 4/8	12 1/8	13	13	Turnagain River, BC	Larry Zilinski	Larry Zilinski	1986	249
203 6/8	58 4/8	41 5/8	42	11 6/8	12 2/8	12	13	Rhuda Lake, QC	Richard Cordes	Richard Cordes	1994	249

Score	Greatest Spread	Length of Palm R	L	Width of Palm R	L	Circumference of Beam at Smallest Place R	L	Number of Normal Points R	L	Locality	Hunter	Owner	Date Killed	Rank
203 6/8	61 4/8	41 4/8	41	11 5/8	16 2/8	8 4/8	8 4/8	10	14	Somerset Co., ME	Fanado J. Pelotte	Fanado J. Pelotte	1998	249
203 6/8	63 2/8	41	40 5/8	13	12 5/8	7 1/8	7	10	11	Muskwa River, BC	Martin W. Lowe	Martin W. Lowe	2001	249
203 5/8	53 3/8	43 4/8	43 3/8	11 4/8	12 2/8	7 2/8	7 3/8	14	13	Overflowing River, MB	Lester Ochsner	Lester Ochsner	1957	257
203 5/8	56 3/8	43 1/8	45	13 1/8	13 2/8	7 4/8	7 3/8	16	10	Surmont Lake, AB	Daryl Goodine	Daryl Goodine	1984	257
203 5/8	59 5/8	39 2/8	41 7/8	13 5/8	13 1/8	7 5/8	7 6/8	12	12	Gladys Lake, BC	Harry Hoeft	Harry Hoeft	1984	257
203 5/8	55 6/8	38 4/8	40	13 2/8	13 2/8	8 1/8	8 4/8	14	15	Pink Mt., BC	John L. London	John L. London	1966	260
203 4/8	61	39 7/8	39 6/8	13 2/8	14 5/8	7 2/8	7 3/8	13	11	Graham River, BC	R.M. Frye	R.M. Frye	1970	260
203 4/8	55 2/8	43 4/8	41	14 1/8	14 1/8	7	7 1/8	13	12	Dease Lake, BC	John W. Goodwin	John W. Goodwin	1986	260
203 4/8	56 4/8	42	41 6/8	16 1/8	14	7 6/8	8	13	10	Otter Lake, BC	Melissa J. Lawrence	Melissa J. Lawrence	2001	260
203 3/8	64 7/8	41	36 3/8	15 4/8	14	7 7/8	8 2/8	11	11	Leaf Lake, SK	Tom Skoretz	Tom Skoretz	1959	264
203 3/8	55 3/8	42	48 6/8	12 6/8	14 2/8	7 2/8	7 3/8	12	13	Hudson Bay Junct., SK	Murray Griffin	Murray Griffin	1965	264
203 3/8	53 3/8	40 6/8	42	17 6/8	16 2/8	7 5/8	7 4/8	11	17	Big Smoky River, AB	Ross D. Carrick	Ross D. Carrick	1971	264
203 3/8	58 3/8	39 1/8	40	17 6/8	16 2/8	7 1/8	7 4/8	10	10	Muskwa River, BC	John A. Kolman	John A. Kolman	1975	264
203 3/8	64 5/8	36 5/8	33 3/8	17 7/8	17 6/8	7 6/8	6 6/8	12	13	Ruggles Lake, ON	Alvin D. Chapman	Alvin D. Chapman	1983	264
203 3/8	59 3/8	38 6/8	38 3/8	12 4/8	13 5/8	7 1/8	7 1/8	14	17	Teslin Lake, BC	Russ LaFreniere	Russ LaFreniere	1988	264
203 2/8	69 2/8	32 7/8	32 6/8	17	16 1/8	7 1/8	7 1/8	11	11	Kvass Creek, AB	Frank C. Hibben	Frank C. Hibben	1958	270
203 2/8	59 6/8	39 3/8	38 3/8	13 4/8	15 7/8	8	7 7/8	12	12	Wapiti River, AB	David L. Savage	David L. Savage	1984	270
203 2/8	60 4/8	39 4/8	40 4/8	11 6/8	13 1/8	8 1/8	8 3/8	12	14	Bigstone River, MB	Corbett P. Smith	Corbett P. Smith	1994	270
203 2/8	60	42	44	14 6/8	15 2/8	6 7/8	7	8	11	Little Rancheria River, BC	G.E. & R.G. Lueck	George E. Lueck	1999	270
203 2/8	54	40 2/8	41 1/8	15 4/8	15 4/8	8 2/8	7 7/8	12	11	Halfway River, BC	Dan P. Adams	Dan P. Adams	2002	270
203 1/8	56 1/8	37 4/8	37 6/8	14 4/8	15	7 6/8	7 6/8	15	14	Scoop Lake, BC	Dwight E. Farr, Jr.	Dwight E. Farr, Jr.	1980	275
203 1/8	52 3/8	43	42 2/8	14 4/8	13	7 3/8	7 1/8	14	13	Birch Mts., AB	Charles N. Johns	Charles N. Johns	1997	275
203 1/8	49 3/8	40 5/8	41	13 6/8	13 6/8	7 4/8	7 6/8	15	16	Hatin Lake, BC	Werner Wistuba	Werner Wistuba	1998	275
🅑 203	55	39	40	15 2/8	14	7	9 2/8	14	15	Fawcett, AB	A. Juckli	Mrs. A. Juckli	PR 1933	278
203	58 2/8	42	41 4/8	11	12 5/8	6 7/8	6 7/8	14	13	Cassiar, BC	Tom Lindahl	Tom Lindahl	1961	278
203	57 2/8	38 6/8	39 1/8	15 6/8	14	7 2/8	7 1/8	13	14	Cassiar, BC	Arvid F. Benson	Arvid F. Benson	1965	278
203	58 2/8	41 1/8	38 5/8	12 5/8	13 1/8	7 1/8	7 2/8	16	14	Pink Mt., BC	T.C. Britt, Jr.	T. C. Britt, Jr.	1966	278
203	61 2/8	39 1/8	42	14 2/8	15 3/8	7 6/8	7 4/8	13	10	Manning, AB	James Harbick	James Harbick	1967	278
203	55	43 1/8	44 2/8	13 2/8	12 1/8	7 6/8	7 6/8	13	11	Robb Lake, BC	Jerome Metcalfe	Jerome Metcalfe	1967	278
203	62	39 2/8	44 7/8	11 7/8	12 5/8	7 3/8	7 3/8	12	12	Graham River, BC	Harold L. Sperfslage	Harold L. Sperfslage	1975	278
203	67	42 2/8	38 1/8	13 4/8	14 6/8	7 3/8	7 4/8	9	10	Coast Range, BC	Picked Up	Neal Coleman	PR 1980	278
203	59	42 2/8	44	12 6/8	12 2/8	7	7	11	11	Bloodvein River, MB	R. Stearns, R. Sigurdson, R. Blowers & L. Walters	R. Stearns, R. Sigurdson, R. Blowers & L. Walters	1988	278
🅑 203	53 2/8	43 3/8	42 6/8	12 2/8	13 1/8	7 7/8	8 1/8	12	13	Gladys River, BC	Spencer J. Vaa	Spencer J. Vaa	1998	278
202 7/8	60 3/8	42	47 2/8	13 1/8	14 3/8	7 1/8	7 5/8	9	9	Prophet River, BC	Elbert Stiles	Elbert Stiles	1960	288
202 7/8	55 3/8	39 3/8	39 4/8	17 1/8	16	7 2/8	7 2/8	11	11	Atlin, BC	Robert H. Morgan	Robert H. Morgan	1973	288
202 7/8	57 1/8	43 4/8	46 3/8	15	11 5/8	8 1/8	7 6/8	10	11	Lower Manitou Lake, ON	Donald R. Anderson	Donald R. Anderson	1979	288
202 7/8	56 1/8	41 6/8	46 1/8	18 6/8	13 6/8	8 1/8	7 7/8	13	10	Frog River, BC	Malcom D. Dinges, Jr.	Malcom D. Dinges, Jr.	1980	288

Score	Greatest Spread	Length of Palm R	Length of Palm L	Width of Palm R	Width of Palm L	Circ. R	Circ. L	Pts. R	Pts. L	Locality	Hunter	Owner	Date	Rank
202 6/8	58	43 1/8	40 3/8	11 4/8	11 7/8	7 4/8	7 4/8	14	13	Bee Peak, BC	Dennis J. Eakin	Dennis J. Eakin	1984	292
202 6/8	60 4/8	42	43 1/8	12	12 3/8	7 1/8	7 1/8	12	11	Chinchaga River, AB	Oliver Travers	Oliver Travers	1985	292
202 6/8	58 2/8	41 1/8	38 4/8	15	16 7/8	8	7 6/8	11	13	Tommy Lakes, BC	David G. Clary	David G. Clary	2001	292
202 5/8	59 7/8	43 1/8	43 7/8	12	14	7 2/8	7 2/8	9	13	Alder Flats, AB	Fred J. Simpson	Carnegie Museum	1966	295
202 5/8	56 1/8	39 3/8	40 5/8	13 7/8	13 5/8	7 2/8	7 4/8	13	14	Harmon Lake, ON	Dale C. Curtis	Dale C. Curtis	1969	295
202 5/8	55 1/8	40	40 6/8	14 5/8	13 5/8	7 4/8	7 1/8	13	13	High Prairie, AB	Dean L. Walker	Dean L. Walker	1973	295
202 4/8	57	39 5/8	38 7/8	14 7/8	15 7/8	8	8 1/8	11	13	Chelan, SK	Picked Up	Harold Bergman	1955	298
202 4/8	58 2/8	41 2/8	41 7/8	13 6/8	13 4/8	8	7 7/8	10	10	Watson Lake, BC	Lloyd Nosler	Lloyd Nosler	1964	298
202 4/8	61 6/8	41	40 2/8	14 3/8	15 6/8	7 6/8	7 7/8	8	10	Prophet River, BC	Lyle Nosler	Lyle Nosler	1964	298
202 4/8	62 4/8	43 6/8	40 2/8	13 4/8	14	7 2/8	7 3/8	9	10	Stewart Lake, BC	Keith Wilson	Keith Wilson	1980	298
202 4/8	58	38 1/8	35 5/8	15 4/8	17 7/8	7 1/8	7 3/8	14	15	Margaree Valley, NS	Leo C. Horne	Leo C. Horne	1986	298
202 4/8	60 2/8	43	46 4/8	11 6/8	13 3/8	7 3/8	7 1/8	9	14	Glundebery Creek, BC	Neil Lawson	Neil Lawson	1988	298
202 3/8	59 1/8	39 3/8	40 4/8	13	15 1/8	7 3/8	7 6/8	12	14	Cassiar, BC	Unknown	BC Game Dept.	PR 1918	304
202 3/8	53 5/8	43	43	19	16 2/8	7 6/8	7 5/8	13	12	Swan Hills, AB	Harold R. Wiese	Harold R. Wiese	1967	304
202 3/8	62 3/8	41	41	12 3/8	11 2/8	8 2/8	7 2/8	11	12	Grovedale, AB	Douglas R. Morris	Douglas R. Morris	1974	304
202 2/8	55 2/8	42	43 4/8	15	14	7 4/8	7 4/8	10	11	Cormorant, MB	Howard J. Lang	Howard J. Lang	1950	307
202 2/8	60 6/8	42 3/8	41 3/8	12 7/8	16 2/8	7 6/8	7 6/8	12	9	Goose Mt., AB	Fred Bartel	Fred Bartel	1956	307
202 2/8	56 4/8	40 4/8	44 5/8	12 7/8	13 5/8	7 4/8	7 4/8	13	13	Hines Creek, AB	Ralph Jumago	Ralph Jumago	1960	307
202 2/8	61 4/8	41	41	10 3/8	12 4/8	7 4/8	7 5/8	13	13	Turcotte Lake, QC	S.B. Fredenburgh, Jr.	S.B. Fredenburgh, Jr.	1962	307
202 2/8	59 2/8	36 4/8	38 3/8	16	17 6/8	6 6/8	6 6/8	12	13	Telegraph Creek, BC	George D. Young	George D. Young	1962	307
202 2/8	59	40 1/8	44 2/8	13 1/8	14 4/8	7 4/8	7 4/8	11	11	Atlin, BC	J.D. Kethley	J.D. Kethley	1966	307
202 2/8	59 4/8	38 1/8	37 4/8	12 4/8	15 4/8	7 3/8	7 3/8	14	14	King Brook, NB	Glen Gilks	Glen Gilks	1972	307
202 2/8	63 2/8	38	37	13	13 6/8	7 4/8	7 4/8	12	12	Wreck Cove Lakes, NS	Donald J. Sauveur	Donald J. Sauveur	1988	307
202 2/8	57 2/8	41 2/8	41 1/8	15	17 2/8	7 7/8	7 7/8	11	11	Swift River, BC	Jean Sirois	Jean Sirois	1991	307
202 2/8	58	40 1/8	44 7/8	14	13	7 3/8	8	15	12	Somerset Co., ME	John A. Albee	John A. Albee	1998	307
202 2/8	54 2/8	44 5/8	46 3/8	12	12 3/8	8	7 7/8	14	14	Milo Lake, BC	Lisa K. Allen	Lisa K. Allen	2001	307
202 2/8	53	43 3/8	39 3/8	11 6/8	12 4/8	7 2/8	7 2/8	11	15	Mitch Lake, AB	John Maryanski	John Maryanski	2001	307
202 1/8	66 4/8	44 2/8	42 6/8	13 1/8	13 4/8	7 1/8	7 5/8	9	8	Kawdy Mt., BC	Herman Kirn	Herman Kirn	1981	319
202 1/8	51 5/8	40 7/8	41 1/8	13 5/8	14	7	6 7/8	14	12	Graham River, BC	Thomas H. Morrison	Thomas H. Morrison	1981	319
202 1/8	54 3/8	39 6/8	40 3/8	14 6/8	15 3/8	7 2/8	7 2/8	11	11	Halfway River, BC	M. Toby Hodek	M. Toby Hodek	1990	319
202 1/8	57 1/8	37	37 2/8	13	13 3/8	6 6/8	7 1/8	13	14	Franklin Co., ME	Byron Beauregard	Byron Beauregard	1994	319
202	58	39 2/8	42	14	16 4/8	7	7 2/8	14	15	St. Jovite, QC	Ed Schmeller	Ed Schmeller	1942	323
202	61	41 6/8	38 7/8	14	15	7 3/8	7 4/8	10	10	Muskwa River, BC	Gordon C. Arndt	Gordon C. Arndt	1976	323
202	62 6/8	39 7/8	41 6/8	17 1/8	14 6/8	8	7 4/8	9	9	Tumbler Ridge, BC	Dale R. Duperreault	Dale R. Duperreault	1993	323
202	54 4/8	40 4/8	39 7/8	16	15 1/8	7 5/8	7 2/8	12	12	Dease Lake, BC	Dan Franzen	Dan Franzen	2003	323
201 7/8	51 1/8	40 5/8	39 7/8	13 5/8	14 5/8	7 4/8	7 5/8	15	17	Saskatchewan	Gordon Lund	Gordon Lund	PR 1954	327
201 7/8	56 3/8	37 5/8	40 4/8	15	12 6/8	7 7/8	7 4/8	15	12	Cassiar Mts., BC	Clark A. Goetzmann	Clark A. Goetzmann	1968	327
201 7/8	56 5/8	39	43 7/8	15 2/8	12	7 2/8	7 2/8	15	16	Ft. St. John, BC	William J. Heiman	William J. Heiman	1969	327
201 7/8	57 5/8	38 7/8	41 2/8	14 6/8	13 3/8	7 5/8	7 5/8	14	11	Lake Co., MN	Dustin J. Benes	Dustin J. Benes	1994	327
201 7/8	55 7/8	41 4/8	40 3/8	17 1/8	15 2/8	8 1/8	7 6/8	10	10	Turnagain River, BC	Rodney S. Marcum	Rodney S. Marcum	1997	327
201 7/8	60 2/8	41 1/8	40	15 4/8	16	7 5/8	7 5/8	10	14	Kechika Range, BC	Norman Lougheed	Norman Lougheed	1964	327
201 6/8	57 2/8	39 5/8	40 3/8	14 5/8	14	7 4/8	7 4/8	17	12	Colt Lake, BC	James C. Wood	James C. Wood	1965	332
201 6/8	59 4/8	38 7/8	39 6/8	15	16 3/8	7 3/8	7 3/8	10	15	Pink Mt., BC	John P. Blanchard	John P. Blanchard	1970	332
201 6/8	55 2/8	41 1/8	42	13 4/8	13 2/8	7 6/8	7 6/8	11	12	Cabin Lake, BC	Donald F. Gould	Donald F. Gould	1974	332
201 6/8	54 6/8	41 1/8	40 2/8	13 2/8	12	7 4/8	7 4/8	14	15	Toad River, BC	Dennis R. Gustafson	Dennis R. Gustafson	1982	332
201 6/8	59 6/8	39 5/8	36 7/8	13 6/8	16	7 2/8	7 3/8	13	18	Wapiti River, BC	Picked Up	Peter Christie	1989	332
201 6/8	54	39 5/8	43 3/8	17 1/8	18	7 3/8	7 3/8	12	13	Lake Co., MN	Dick, Bill, Ron & Joe Klesk	Joe Klesk	1993	332
201 6/8	56	43 3/8	42 1/8	12	13 1/8	6 7/8	6 7/8	12	14	Chukachida River, BC	Nelson T. Offutt	Nelson T. Offutt	1993	332

CANADA MOOSE

Alces alces americana and Alces alces andersoni

Score	Greatest Spread	Length of Palm R	L	Width of Palm R	L	Circumference of Beam at Smallest Place R	L	Number of Normal Points R	L	Locality	Hunter	Owner	Date Killed	Rank
201 5/8	53 5/8	37	39	18	20	7	7 2/8	12	12	Omineca Mt., BC	C.L. Burnette	C.L. Burnette	1973	340
201 5/8	57 5/8	43 4/8	40 7/8	12 3/8	12 4/8	7 2/8	7 2/8	12	12	Calata Lake, BC	Klaus Schmidt	Klaus Schmidt	1994	340
201 5/8	56 7/8	42 6/8	41 2/8	16 1/8	14 7/8	8 2/8	7 6/8	9	9	Rainbow Lake, BC	Kelly D. Voigt	Kelly D. Voigt	1997	340
201 4/8	49 2/8	42 7/8	42 3/8	15 2/8	13 3/8	7 3/8	7 3/8	15	13	Cold Fish Lake, BC	Charles E. Wilson, Jr.	Charles E. Wilson, Jr.	1957	343
201 4/8	56	36 6/8	34 5/8	18	19 2/8	7 1/8	7 2/8	17	13	Island Lake, QC	Silvene Bracalente	Silvene Bracalente	1962	343
201 4/8	54 4/8	43 5/8	42 1/8	16 1/8	15 5/8	7 2/8	7 3/8	10	10	Ospika River, BC	William E. Goosman	William E. Goosman	1964	343
201 4/8	55 2/8	46 6/8	42 6/8	12 4/8	11 4/8	7 3/8	7 3/8	12	12	Mt. Lady Laurier, BC	Peter L. Halbig	Peter L. Halbig	1968	343
201 4/8	56 6/8	41 4/8	44	12 4/8	14 1/8	6 7/8	6 7/8	12	15	Bougie Mt., BC	Dennis R. Mitchell	Dennis R. Mitchell	1987	343
201 4/8	56 6/8	42 1/8	43 3/8	12 4/8	14 1/8	7 6/8	8	10	14	Denetiah Lake, BC	Lee Frudden	Lee Frudden	1995	343
201 4/8	55	40 5/8	43 6/8	12 4/8	14	7 1/8	7 3/8	13	15	Coos Co, NH	Ricky A. Matulaitis	Ricky A. Matulaitis	1997	343
201 3/8	57 1/8	40	40 4/8	13 1/8	13 3/8	7	7	14	12	Swan Hills, AB	Vale E. Wood	Earl C. Wood	1967	350
201 3/8	52 1/8	43 6/8	44 3/8	13 2/8	15 6/8	7 5/8	7 6/8	10	10	Peace River, AB	Kenneth R. Gray	Kenneth R. Gray	2001	350
201 2/8	56 2/8	41	40 6/8	13 2/8	14 4/8	7	7 2/8	12	13	Rocky Mt. House, AB	John B. Gibson	John B. Gibson	1955	352
201 2/8	62	40	43	11 2/8	13 2/8	7 3/8	7 6/8	11	12	Racing River, BC	Anthony Battaglia	Anthony Battaglia	1966	352
201 2/8	58	36 5/8	37 6/8	15	14 4/8	6 4/8	6 4/8	14	14	Upsala, ON	Daniel F. Volkmann	Daniel F. Volkmann	1969	352
201 2/8	63 6/8	34 6/8	34 1/8	15 3/8	15 1/8	7 7/8	7 4/8	13	12	Quebec	Diana Baglino	Diana Baglino	1971	352
201 2/8	53	40 7/8	38 4/8	13 1/8	13 7/8	7 4/8	7 5/8	15	15	Lesser Slave Lake, AB	B. Strain & B. Baergen	Bert Strain	1976	352
201 2/8	56 2/8	40 6/8	44	11	13 4/8	7 6/8	8 3/8	13	14	Crow River, QC	Richard P. Legare	Richard P. Legare	1994	352
201 2/8	55	41 3/8	42 5/8	13 4/8	16	7 2/8	7 2/8	11	11	Minaker River, BC	Marvin F. Mason	Marvin F. Mason	1996	352
201 1/8	53 5/8	39 6/8	42 4/8	15 7/8	15 7/8	7 5/8	8	11	11	Reserve, SK	O.A. Kjelshus	O.A. Kjelshus	1953	359
201 1/8	55 3/8	41 7/8	40	15 5/8	15	7 5/8	7 3/8	13	11	Big Sandy Lake, SK	John Longley	John Longley	1961	359
201 1/8	56 7/8	40 5/8	43	15 4/8	12 4/8	7 3/8	7	15	12	Slave Lake, AB	A.F. Harry	A.F. Harry	1967	359
201 1/8	60 5/8	38	40	13 1/8	14 1/8	7 3/8	7 1/8	13	12	Porcupine Forest, SK	Ted Yuzek	Robert Yuzek	1967	359
201 1/8	61 3/8	41	45	16 6/8	13 1/8	7 5/8	7 2/8	11	13	Skeena Mts., BC	Wayne A. Tri	Wayne A. Tri	1978	359
201 1/8	57 5/8	38 3/8	40 3/8	11 6/8	14 5/8	8 5/8	8 6/8	13	13	Piscataquis Co., ME	Walter V. Scott	Walter V. Scott	1980	359
201 1/8	61 3/8	40 1/8	39	11 4/8	12	8 3/8	9 2/8	11	14	Lost Lake, BC	Kenneth C. Adair, Jr.	Kenneth C. Adair, Jr.	1992	359
201	55 4/8	38 2/8	42	14 4/8	15 1/8	8	8 2/8	13	12	Muskwa River, BC	J.H. Blu	J.H. Blu	1972	366
201	55 2/8	39 7/8	41	14 7/8	13 2/8	7 4/8	7 2/8	13	13	Sipanok Channel, SK	Clarence Saretsky	Clarence Saretsky	1974	366
201	54 4/8	43 4/8	42	14	13 1/8	8 5/8	8 1/8	10	12	Toad River, BC	Steven Ronshausen	Steven Ronshausen	1981	366
201	53 4/8	44 4/8	42 4/8	15 4/8	14 4/8	7 6/8	8	10	9	Wallace River, BC	Victor R. Tessier	Victor R. Tessier	1985	366
201	60 6/8	38 4/8	43	12 6/8	15 6/8	6 7/8	7 1/8	12	12	Wolverine River, AB	Arlan C. Castner	Arlan C. Castner	2000	366
201	54 2/8	38 1/8	36 3/8	17 3/8	17 2/8	7 6/8	8	13	15	Aroostook Co, ME	Mark P. Olson	Mark P. Olson	2000	366
200 7/8	61 3/8	39 7/8	41 5/8	10 7/8	13 1/8	7 4/8	7 5/8	12	14	Grande Prairie, AB	John W. Benson	John W. Benson	1969	372
200 7/8	60 7/8	38 2/8	34 4/8	14 4/8	14 6/8	7 2/8	7	14	14	Spatsizi River, BC	G.C. Taylor	G.C. Taylor	1974	372
200 7/8	61 5/8	36 7/8	40 3/8	16 6/8	14 5/8	7 5/8	7 7/8	11	13	Muskwa River, BC	Stan Longyear	Stan Longyear	1984	372
200 7/8	56 5/8	41	38	12 3/8	16	7 6/8	7 7/8	15	14	Aroostook Co, ME	Ernest L. Leighton	Ernest L. Leighton	1988	372
200 7/8	63 3/8	42 7/8	39	13 3/8	14 7/8	7 7/8	8	9	9	Swan Lake, BC	Gary A. Markofer	Gary A. Markofer	1990	372
200 7/8	52 3/8	39 1/8	42 2/8	14 3/8	19 6/8	8	7 6/8	13	13	Muskwa River, BC	Teresa M. Mull	Teresa M. Mull	1995	372

Score	Spread	Length R	Length L	Width R	Width L	Circ. R	Circ. L	Pts. R	Pts. L	Locality	Hunter	Owner	Date	Rank
200 6/8	50 2/8	41 5/8	42	13 5/8	13 5/8	7	7	14	13	Goodwin Lake, BC	Bill R. Mooney	Bill R. Mooney	1974	378
200 6/8	56 6/8	39	38 5/8	15	14 4/8	6 7/8	7	12	15	Turnagain River, BC	Kenneth M. Brown	Kenneth M. Brown	1986	378
200 6/8	55 6/8	39 4/8	38 7/8	13 2/8	13 7/8	7 3/8	7 4/8	13	14	Cassiar Mts., BC	Gale B. Miller	Gale B. Miller	2000	378
200 5/8	61 4/8	37 5/8	37 4/8	12 7/8	14 3/8	7 2/8	7 2/8	12	14	Franklin Co., ME	Adam Tibbetts	Adam Tibbetts	2002	378
200 5/8	61 1/8	39 1/8	39	11 2/8	11 5/8	6 4/8	6 4/8	13	13	Prophet River, BC	Chauncey Everard	Chauncey Everard	1967	382
200 5/8	63 1/8	38 3/8	39	11 4/8	12	7 7/8	7 7/8	11	13	Alberta	Ray Pierson	Ray Pierson	1967	382
200 5/8	58 1/8	37 6/8	39 2/8	13	13 2/8	7 4/8	7 4/8	14	14	Fort Nelson, BC	Everett L. Ashley	Everett L. Ashley	1975	382
200 5/8	59 1/8	39 1/8	41 1/8	16 3/8	13	7 7/8	7 7/8	15	11	Cassiar Mts., BC	G.L. Garrett	G.L. Garrett	1977	382
200 5/8	59 5/8	40 2/8	41 6/8	14	13 2/8	8 2/8	8 2/8	9	14	Robb Lake, BC	Richard L. Bostrom	Richard L. Bostrom	1985	382
200 5/8	66 5/8	36	37 2/8	14 6/8	15 3/8	7 3/8	7 3/8	9	11	Low Fog Creek, BC	Delmar L. Achenbach	Delmar L. Achenbach	1989	382
200 4/8	61	39 3/8	41 6/8	15 2/8	13 5/8	6 6/8	6 6/8	10	12	Deadmans Lake, BC	John Caputo, Sr.	John Caputo, Sr.	1950	388
200 4/8	61 4/8	38 2/8	39 2/8	14 2/8	16 2/8	7	7	10	12	Watson Lake, BC	Dan E. O'Neal, Jr.	Dan E. O'Neal, Jr.	1968	388
200 4/8	52	40	41 7/8	15	15 4/8	7 2/8	7 2/8	14	12	Muskwa River, BC	William W. Veigel	William W. Veigel	1971	388
200 4/8	59 2/8	42 3/8	40 1/8	15 3/8	15 1/8	6 7/8	7 1/8	9	10	Cassiar Mts., BC	Calvin D. Boatwright	Calvin D. Boatwright	1976	388
200 4/8	60	39 4/8	40	14 2/8	12 5/8	7 4/8	7 4/8	11	11	Adsit Lake, BC	Morris R. Nadeau	Morris R. Nadeau	1986	388
200 4/8	57 6/8	38 3/8	38 3/8	14 4/8	15	8 4/8	8 4/8	10	10	Kedahda Lake, BC	Brian Bergen	Brian Bergen	1990	388
200 4/8	52	38 6/8	38 6/8	13 6/8	15 3/8	7 6/8	7 6/8	14	15	Halfway River, BC	Harold Schmidt	Harold Schmidt	1993	388
200 4/8	52 4/8	41 2/8	40 2/8	15 1/8	15 1/8	8	8	12	13	Aulneau Pen., ON	Donald F. Holland	Donald F. Holland	1994	388
200 3/8	58 1/8	36 3/8	39	15	15	7	6 7/8	13	13	English River, ON	Jack Radke	Jack Radke	1966	396
200 3/8	59 3/8	43 6/8	41 1/8	13 5/8	11 3/8	8 1/8	8 1/8	10	11	Peace River, BC	Walter W. Kassner	Walter W. Kassner	1968	396
200 3/8	51 7/8	41 7/8	43	14	13 5/8	6 6/8	6 6/8	12	12	Cassiar Mts., BC	Don Stallings	Don Stallings	1971	396
200 3/8	53 1/8	40 6/8	38 6/8	13 7/8	13 7/8	6 5/8	6 5/8	16	14	Cypress Creek, BC	Raymond A. Racette	Raymond A. Racette	1984	396
200 3/8	56 7/8	40 1/8	41 5/8	13	13	7 5/8	7 5/8	12	14	Hixon, BC	Scott Paterson	Scott Paterson	1996	396
200 3/8	53 1/8	38 4/8	38 6/8	13 7/8	13 4/8	7 2/8	7 2/8	16	14	Buffalo River, AB	Alan M. Jesse	Alan M. Jesse	2001	396
200 2/8	62	42	42	13 4/8	11 5/8	7 5/8	7 5/8	10	10	Atlin, BC	John Vigna	John Vigna	1965	402
200 2/8	56 6/8	36 6/8	37 4/8	14 5/8	15 4/8	7 3/8	7 3/8	14	13	Pink Mt., BC	Danny Taylor	Danny Taylor	1970	402
200 1/8	56 7/8	39 7/8	41 2/8	12 7/8	12 2/8	8	8	12	13	Turcotte Lake, QC	George Clark, Jr.	George Clark, Jr.	1960	404
200 1/8	55 1/8	41 4/8	39 6/8	14 7/8	13 2/8	7 5/8	7 4/8	14	12	Whitebeech, SK	John J. Kuzma	John J. Kuzma	1966	404
200 1/8	52 7/8	46 2/8	46 6/8	11 6/8	10 2/8	7 1/8	7 1/8	12	10	Red Fern Lake, BC	M. Steven Weaver	M. Steven Weaver	1966	404
200 1/8	49 3/8	47 2/8	47 5/8	15	13	8 2/8	8 2/8	8	7	Disella Lake, BC	Bryant Dunn	Bryant Dunn	1996	404
200 1/8	56 5/8	43 1/8	41 6/8	11	11 4/8	7	7	12	12	Ten Mile Lake, NL	David W. Chambers	David W. Chambers	1997	404
200	59	43	42 2/8	14 5/8	12 6/8	7	7	9	11	Cold Fish Lake, BC	G. Kenneth Whitehead	G. Kenneth Whitehead	1964	409
200	56 4/8	37 7/8	41 6/8	15 3/8	13 1/8	6 6/8	6 7/8	14	16	Lac Seul, ON	Robert B. Peregrine	Robert B. Peregrine	1966	409
200	59 2/8	40 3/8	41	14 1/8	14 1/8	7 4/8	7 4/8	11	14	Nass Lake, BC	Dan A. Pick	Dan A. Pick	1969	409
200	53	36 1/8	35 6/8	16	16 2/8	7 7/8	7 5/8	15	12	Muskwa River, BC	Roy V. Haskell	Roy V. Haskell	1978	409
200	59 2/8	44 3/8	41 2/8	11 2/8	11 4/8	7 7/8	7 6/8	10	11	Pelican Lake, AB	Terrance Krawec	Terrance Krawec	1993	409
199 7/8	62 3/8	32 6/8	33 2/8	16 6/8	16 6/8	7 6/8	7 6/8	15	15	Patapedia Lakes, QC	Frederick K. Barbour	William Darrow	1911	414
199 7/8	46 5/8	41 6/8	40 3/8	17 5/8	17	7 3/8	7 4/8	13	13	Vanderhoof, BC	William Ilnisky	William Ilnisky	1978	414
199 7/8	54 3/8	40 2/8	44 3/8	14 6/8	13 7/8	8 3/8	8 1/8	13	10	Chukachida River, BC	Gregory M. Pacacha	Gregory M. Pacacha	1991	414
199 6/8	61 4/8	36 6/8	36 1/8	12 7/8	13 7/8	7 4/8	7 3/8	12	12	Cutbank River, AB	Steve Kalischuk	Steve Kalischuk	1960	417
199 6/8	51 4/8	40 2/8	40 6/8	14 4/8	14 6/8	7 5/8	7 4/8	12	13	Halfway River, BC	Jack Taylor	Jack Taylor	1973	417
199 6/8	57	39 7/8	39 7/8	14	13 4/8	8 2/8	7 5/8	11	13	Kledo Creek, BC	Rick L. McGowan	Rick L. McGowan	1975	417
199 6/8	60 6/8	37 3/8	41	13	12 7/8	8 6/8	7 2/8	11	11	Lake Co., MN	L.D. Holtegaard, R. Smith, B. Nessler, & P. Nietz	L.D. Holtegaard	1981	417
199 6/8	59	37	36 1/8	14 3/8	13 2/8	7	7 4/8	14	14	Cassiar Mts., BC	James D. Hoekstra	James D. Hoekstra	1986	417
199 6/8	58 6/8	40 6/8	40 2/8	13 6/8	14 6/8	7 4/8	7 2/8	11	9	St. Louis Co., MN	Arlo Manzke	Arlo Manzke	1993	417
199 6/8	57 6/8	38 7/8	37 3/8	13 3/8	13 3/8	7 2/8	7 4/8	14	13	Bear Creek, BC	L. Scot Jenkins	L. Scot Jenkins	1997	417
199 6/8	55	38 6/8	39 5/8	13 2/8	12 6/8	8	7 7/8	14	13	Fort McMurray, AB	Thomas J. Skovron	Thomas J. Skovron	1997	417

CANADA MOOSE

Alces alces americana and Alces alces andersoni

Score	Greatest Spread	Length of Palm R	L	Width of Palm R	L	Circumference of Beam at Smallest Place R	L	Number of Normal Points R	L	Locality	Hunter	Owner	Date Killed	Rank
199 5/8	53 3/8	38 5/8	39 7/8	13 1/8	15 3/8	7 3/8	7 4/8	14	15	Greenbush, SK	Tom Flanagan	Tom Flanagan	1955	425
199 5/8	61 7/8	38 7/8	39 2/8	15 2/8	14	8	8	10	8	Prairie River, SK	Clarence Slater	Clarence Slater	1955	425
199 5/8	58 7/8	41 2/8	38 2/8	13 3/8	15 7/8	7	6 6/8	12	12	Tootsee Lake, BC	Robert E. Alexander	James L. Clark	1992	425
199 5/8	64 3/8	38 1/8	39 3/8	13 6/8	13 6/8	7 6/8	7 6/8	9	8	Big Sand Lake, MB	Ronald J. Zockle	Ronald J. Zockle	1992	425
199 5/8	56 3/8	41 6/8	40 7/8	13 3/8	14 5/8	7 4/8	7 3/8	10	16	Sawn Lake, AB	Dean V. Manz	Dean V. Manz	2003	425
199 4/8	59	41	42	9 4/8	11 7/8	7 6/8	7 6/8	12	14	Drayton Valley, AB	Ollie Fedorus	Ollie Fedorus	1962	430
199 4/8	60	37 7/8	39 6/8	12 1/8	13	6 6/8	6 7/8	13	13	Dease Lake, BC	Peter Hohorst	Peter Hohorst	1968	430
199 4/8	58 6/8	40 1/8	40 4/8	12 2/8	14 1/8	7	7	11	11	Aroostook Co., ME	Richard Neal	Richard Neal	1983	430
199 4/8	56 4/8	36 6/8	38 5/8	14 4/8	14	7 6/8	7 6/8	13	13	Biencourt Lake, QC	Rodier Dumont	Rodier Dumont	1987	430
199 4/8	64	37 7/8	37	12 5/8	12 5/8	7 1/8	7 3/8	12	17	Kechika River, BC	John R. Shotzberger	John R. Shotzberger	1990	430
199 4/8	59 4/8	38 2/8	38 3/8	14	14 1/8	8 2/8	8 3/8	10	12	Seine River, ON	Robert K. Reuther	Robert K. Reuther	1994	430
199 4/8	52 2/8	43 3/8	44	15	12	8 3/8	7 7/8	11	11	Dease River, BC	William J. Falcheck	William J. Falcheck	1999	430
199 4/8	61 6/8	35 7/8	38 3/8	11 7/8	11 3/8	7 6/8	7 5/8	14	14	Tutsingale Mt., BC	Keith Frederiksen	Keith Frederiksen	2001	430
199 3/8	49 7/8	43	45 1/8	13	12	7 6/8	7 6/8	12	14	Buckinghorse River, BC	Fain J. Little	Fain J. Little	1967	438
199 3/8	57 7/8	40 1/8	40 2/8	12 3/8	12 3/8	7 2/8	7 3/8	11	11	Sand River, AB	Douglas R. Lowe	Douglas R. Lowe	1977	438
199 3/8	69 3/8	33 7/8	34 6/8	12 3/8	14 3/8	7 6/8	7 6/8	11	13	Blanchard River, BC	James T. Walter	James T. Walter	1987	438
199 3/8	56 3/8	44 6/8	41 6/8	13 2/8	13	7 6/8	8 1/8	13	9	Kechika River, BC	Willy Tielen	Willy Tielen	1997	438
199 2/8	52 4/8	37 1/8	37 6/8	15 3/8	15 5/8	7 2/8	6 7/8	14	18	Glaslyn, SK	Allan Johnson	Allan Johnson	1956	442
199 2/8	57 4/8	41 5/8	43 7/8	11 3/8	12 2/8	6 7/8	7 1/8	11	11	Pasco Hills, SK	Mac B. Ford	Mac B. Ford	1969	442
199 2/8	63	38 7/8	37 1/8	14 1/8	15 1/8	7 3/8	7 3/8	10	14	English River, ON	Melvin Vetse	Melvin Vetse	1969	442
199 2/8	53 4/8	38 4/8	40	13 4/8	13	7 3/8	7 3/8	14	14	Kluayaz Lake, BC	William F. Jury	William F. Jury	1970	442
199 2/8	52 6/8	41 6/8	43 1/8	11 6/8	11 6/8	7 6/8	8 2/8	12	12	Cut Beaver Lake, SK	Don Thorimbert	Don Thorimbert	1979	442
199 2/8	54 2/8	40 7/8	43 5/8	13 6/8	13 5/8	7	7 2/8	11	14	Teslin Lake, BC	Douglas Schnabel	Douglas Schnabel	1994	442
199 2/8	55	37 6/8	36 4/8	14 6/8	14 6/8	6 7/8	7	15	14	McGraw Brook, NB	David A. McCrea	David A. McCrea	2000	442
199 1/8	55 3/8	39 5/8	37	12 2/8	12 6/8	7 5/8	7 5/8	15	15	Mayerthorpe, AB	Unknown	Bennie Ziemmer	PR 1965	449
199 1/8	57 3/8	37 6/8	36 4/8	13	12 7/8	7 4/8	7 7/8	14	14	Dixonville, AB	Edward W. Filpula	Edward W. Filpula	1977	449
199 1/8	52 3/8	43 5/8	43 4/8	12 4/8	11	8	7 7/8	11	12	Iskut, BC	Larry Zilinski	Larry Zilinski	1979	449
199 1/8	51 5/8	43 4/8	43 4/8	11 6/8	13 3/8	7 4/8	7 5/8	11	12	Coutts River, AB	George J. Thimer	George J. Thimer	1983	449
199 1/8	56 3/8	43 1/8	41 2/8	13	14	6 6/8	6 6/8	10	13	Victoria Creek, BC	Bradley Bowden	Bradley Bowden	1986	449
199 1/8	58 1/8	38 2/8	41 2/8	13 4/8	13 1/8	7 5/8	7 6/8	12	12	Fox Back Ridge, NS	Joseph MacIsaac	Joseph MacIsaac	1994	449
199 1/8	58 3/8	42 1/8	46 4/8	12 2/8	14 1/8	7	7 2/8	9	9	Cassiar Mts., BC	Edward D. Yates	Edward D. Yates	1997	449
199	58 6/8	38	35 4/8	16	17	7 5/8	7 6/8	12	11	Hornepayne, ON	Harry T. Young	Harry T. Young	1967	456
199	57 4/8	38 4/8	37 4/8	14 3/8	14	7 2/8	7 2/8	12	16	Stikine River, BC	Francis O.N. Morris	Francis O.N. Morris	1968	456
199	61 6/8	36 6/8	35 5/8	12	13 2/8	8	8	14	13	Timmins, ON	Domenic V. Ripepi	Domenic V. Ripepi	1968	456
199	51 4/8	41 6/8	44 1/8	17 6/8	15 3/8	7 5/8	7 7/8	14	9	Fox Creek, AB	Ken McDonald	Merv Zaddery	1969	456
199	53 4/8	41 3/8	41 1/8	14 1/8	13 3/8	7 2/8	7 2/8	15	11	Trout Lake, BC	William R. Lee	William R. Lee	1982	456
199	58 6/8	36 7/8	36 6/8	14 1/8	13 5/8	7 6/8	7 6/8	13	12	Otter Lake, MB	Horace R. Cockerill	Horace R. Cockerill	1985	456
199	62 4/8	39 4/8	40 4/8	13 2/8	14 2/8	8	7 6/8	9	8	Piscataquis Co., ME	Darlene M. Ross	Darlene M. Ross	1993	456

Score	Greatest Spread	Width of Palm R	Width of Palm L	Length of Palm R	Length of Palm L	Circ. Beam R	Circ. Beam L	Pts R	Pts L	Locality	By Whom Killed	Owner	Date Killed	Rank
199	53 6/8	40	42	14 4/8	14 5/8	7 1/8	7 1/8	11	13	Aconitum Lake, BC	Blair G. Fisher	Blair G. Fisher	1994	456
199	59 2/8	46 4/8	40 4/8	17 3/8	14	7 7/8	8	13	10	Coos Co., NH	Ross H. Marble	Ross H. Marble	1998	456
198 7/8	56 5/8	41 7/8	43	13 7/8	11 7/8	7 3/8	7 3/8	12	10	Hotchkiss, AB	R.A. Anderson	R.A. Anderson	1960	465
198 7/8	54 5/8	42 2/8	39 3/8	14 4/8	16 4/8	8 2/8	8 2/8	11	10	Monkman Pass, BC	A.E. Haddrell	A.E. Haddrell	1971	465
198 7/8	54 5/8	37 2/8	37 3/8	13	13 2/8	6 7/8	6 7/8	15	15	Manning, AB	Eugene G. McGee	Eugene G. McGee	1975	465
198 7/8	53 3/8	41 5/8	40	15	12	7 6/8	8 2/8	13	13	Coconino Creek, BC	Allan C. Endersby	Allan C. Endersby	1980	465
198 7/8	60 7/8	45 6/8	43 5/8	11 4/8	11 6/8	7 7/8	7 7/8	7	7	Copper River, BC	J. William Hofsink	J. William Hofsink	1985	465
198 6/8	52	40 6/8	39 4/8	14	13 1/8	6 6/8	7	14	15	Prophet River, BC	T.D. Braden	T.D. Braden	1973	470
198 6/8	53 4/8	40 6/8	40 7/8	13 6/8	17	7 3/8	7 1/8	11	11	Mt. Laurier, BC	Don Miller	Don Miller	1985	470
198 5/8	61 3/8	39 3/8	36	12 6/8	13 5/8	7 7/8	7 7/8	12	12	Stony Lake, BC	George Kalischuk	George Kalischuk	1962	472
198 5/8	57 1/8	40 3/8	40 3/8	16 4/8	16 3/8	8	8 5/8	9	6	Lake Nipigon, ON	Ohne L. Raasch	Ohne L. Raasch	1991	472
198 5/8	58 5/8	36 4/8	36 4/8	16 2/8	18 2/8	7 2/8	7 4/8	10	12	Penobscot Co., ME	James B. Crowley	James B. Crowley	2001	472
198 5/8	47 5/8	40 4/8	39 6/8	13 4/8	13 2/8	7 5/8	7 3/8	16	15	Scoop Lake, BC	Donnie Moffat	Donnie Moffat	2001	472
198 4/8	62 2/8	36 4/8	36 7/8	13 5/8	13	6 5/8	6 6/8	12	15	Serpentine Lake, BC	Randolph P. Wilson	Randolph P. Wilson	1976	476
198 4/8	58	39 2/8	40 2/8	13 7/8	16	7 3/8	7 1/8	10	13	Spatsizi Plateau, BC	Gordon J. Birgbauer, Jr.	Gordon J. Birgbauer, Jr.	1986	476
198 4/8	58 4/8	41 6/8	42 3/8	14 4/8	13	7 2/8	7 3/8	8	8	Nazcha Creek, BC	William H. Heafner	William H. Heafner	1994	476
198 4/8	51 6/8	39 2/8	39 3/8	14 2/8	14 5/8	6 7/8	7	13	14	Rainbow Lake, AB	David S. Stelter	David S. Stelter	1998	476
198 4/8	50 4/8	37 6/8	43 3/8	15	18 4/8	7 2/8	7 2/8	14	14	Carroll Co., NH	A. Jay Van Dyne	A. Jay Van Dyne	1973	476
198 3/8	53 5/8	43 3/8	39 6/8	17 4/8	18 5/8	7 1/8	7 1/8	8	11	Robb, BC	Bernholdt R. Nystrom	Bernholdt R. Nystrom	1977	481
198 3/8	60 3/8	40 3/8	43	10 5/8	12 7/8	7 2/8	7	11	12	Besa River, BC	Tommy D. Prance	Tommy D. Prance	1993	481
198 3/8	54 5/8	43	39 6/8	14 1/8	16 6/8	7	7	16	11	Tatshenshini River, BC	Wayne Patterson	Wayne Patterson	1996	481
198 3/8	58 3/8	37 4/8	37 4/8	12	14 2/8	7 4/8	7 5/8	13	16	Denetiah Lake, BC	Douglas J. Dee	Douglas J. Dee	1999	481
198 3/8	57 3/8	43 4/8	42 3/8	12 2/8	10 6/8	8	7 3/8	10	11	Aroostook Co., ME	George A. Pickel	George A. Pickel	1960	481
198 2/8	57 4/8	38	38	13 4/8	12	7	7 3/8	14	17	Whitecourt, AB	Richard Jensen	Glen Cox	1963	486
198 2/8	54 2/8	39 6/8	41 5/8	12 2/8	14	7	7	14	12	Beale Lake, BC	John O. Forster	John O. Forster	1967	486
198 2/8	53 4/8	43 6/8	42 2/8	17	12 6/8	6 7/8	7 1/8	11	11	Prairie River, BC	C.J. McElroy	C.J. McElroy	1973	486
198 2/8	59 4/8	36 5/8	41 5/8	11 4/8	15 6/8	7 1/8	7 1/8	11	14	Lake Co., MN	D.P. & H. Bradley	D.P. & H. Bradley	1989	486
198 2/8	57	40 7/8	38 6/8	15 4/8	12 7/8	7 3/8	7 3/8	11	13	Heart Mts., BC	Richard E. Radavich	Cabela's, Inc.	1994	486
198 2/8	51 2/8	38 7/8	44 6/8	14 2/8	14 5/8	8	8	13	11	Carp Lake, BC	Harvey G. Underwood	Harvey G. Underwood	1994	486
198 1/8	58 1/8	43 6/8	38 6/8	15	15	7	9 4/8	10	9	Crow Wing Co., MN	Mr. Gustetson	Bob Coborn	PR 1920	492
198 1/8	56 5/8	42	43 2/8	12 1/8	13 2/8	7 5/8	7 4/8	10	10	Saskatchewan	Neil Oliver	Neil Oliver	1954	492
198 1/8	56 3/8	40	40	12 7/8	11 6/8	7 2/8	7 1/8	13	12	Dore Lake, SK	O. Dore	O. Dore	1966	492
198 1/8	63 5/8	40 3/8	34	12 4/8	17	8 6/8	8 6/8	13	15	Chapleau, ON	Chester Anderegg	Chester Anderegg	1968	492
198 1/8	50 5/8	39 5/8	41	16	13 6/8	8 1/8	8 1/8	14	13	Fraser River, BC	J. Henry Scown	J. Henry Scown	1973	492
198 1/8	55 7/8	42 4/8	42 7/8	12	13 2/8	7 5/8	7 5/8	9	9	Hluey Lakes, BC	Dale Campbell	Dale Campbell	1982	492
198 1/8	61 3/8	39 3/8	38	13	11	8 5/8	8 3/8	12	11	Bolkow, ON	Terry Coutcher	Terry Coutcher	1998	492
198 1/8	57 3/8	44 4/8	38 2/8	12 5/8	12 5/8	6 5/8	6 4/8	13	13	Dease Lake, BC	Andres Garza-Tijerina	Andres Garza-Tijerina	2001	492
198 1/8	63 5/8	40 4/8	41 6/8	15	13 1/8	7 3/8	7 1/8	7	10	Windsor Co., VT	Picked Up	Eli Holmquist	2001	492
198	62 2/8	37 3/8	38 4/8	12 1/8	14 4/8	7	7	13	12	Cold Fish Lake, BC	Dan M. Edwards, Jr.	Dan M. Edwards, Jr.	1961	501
198	57	37	37 3/8	13	14 3/8	6 4/8	6 4/8	14	15	Hardwood Lake, ON	Weston Cook	Weston Cook	1963	501
198	56 4/8	38 3/8	36 3/8	15 7/8	14 6/8	7 6/8	7 5/8	12	14	Crooked Lake, BC	J.W. Cornwall	J.W. Cornwall	1977	501
198	63 6/8	37	37	14 2/8	15	6 7/8	7	10	11	Upper Besa River, BC	Lloyd Schoenauer	Lloyd Schoenauer	1977	501
198	54 2/8	39 4/8	42 6/8	16 2/8	17	7 2/8	7 1/8	11	9	Pink Mt., BC	Wallace E. Anderson	Wallace E. Anderson	1982	501
197 7/8	55 7/8	44 1/8	40 6/8	11 5/8	13 3/8	7 5/8	7 6/8	11	11	Prophet River, BC	Paul W. Sharp	Paul W. Sharp	1963	506
197 7/8	59 7/8	39 6/8	40 1/8	11 4/8	11 4/8	7 6/8	7 6/8	11	11	Pink Mt., BC	Robert H. Ruth	Robert H. Ruth	1964	506
197 7/8	62 5/8	39	39	11 6/8	10 5/8	8 1/8	8	10	10	Swan Plain, SK	Gene Petryshyn	Gene Petryshyn	1971	506
197 7/8	56 3/8	40 2/8	40 7/8	14	15	7 4/8	7 5/8	12	9	Sikanni Chief River, BC	Nicholas M. Esposito	Nicholas M. Esposito	1974	506
197 7/8	49 7/8	42 7/8	43	13 6/8	13 6/8	7 5/8	7 3/8	9	10	Fish Lake, BC	Richard E. Glenz	Richard E. Glenz	1993	506

CANADA MOOSE

Alces alces americana and Alces alces andersoni

Score	Greatest Spread	Length of Palm R	L	Width of Palm R	L	Circumference of Beam at Smallest Place R	L	Number of Normal Points R	L	Locality	Hunter	Owner	Date Killed	Rank
197 7/8	55 5/8	44 4/8	45 4/8	14 3/8	11 4/8	7 2/8	7 1/8	8	8	Somerset Co., ME	Richard G. Bernier	Richard G. Bernier	1999	506
197 7/8	58 1/8	45	42 3/8	16	12 5/8	6 7/8	6 7/8	15	8	Jennings River, BC	Dean L. Rehbein	Dean L. Rehbein	2003	506
197 6/8	63 6/8	38 7/8	41 7/8	10 4/8	10 3/8	6 7/8	6 6/8	12	11	Willow Creek, AB	Helmut Vollmer	Helmut Vollmer	1960	513
197 6/8	52	37 2/8	39 3/8	14 2/8	13 4/8	7 1/8	7 1/8	15	15	Marion Lake, BC	Virgil W. Binkley	Virgil W. Binkley	1964	513
197 6/8	59 6/8	34 5/8	36 6/8	14 4/8	12 4/8	7	6 7/8	15	16	Pipestone River, ON	Howard E. Bennett	Howard E. Bennett	1973	513
197 5/8	56 7/8	42 1/8	38 2/8	13 1/8	13 2/8	7 2/8	7	12	12	Glaslyn, SK	Ernest Noble	Ernest Noble	1960	516
197 5/8	67 1/8	39	36	10 5/8	10 7/8	7 5/8	8	11	11	Smuts Lake, ON	Ronald S. Regan	Ronald S. Regan	1981	516
197 5/8	57 5/8	44	43 2/8	14 1/8	11 6/8	7 4/8	7 4/8	12	9	Simeon Lake, ON	Craig L. Chandonnet	Craig L. Chandonnet	1986	516
197 5/8	56 5/8	41 1/8	39 1/8	14 2/8	14 6/8	7 1/8	7 2/8	11	13	Stikine River, BC	Chad Clayburg	Chad Clayburg	1989	516
197 5/8	52 5/8	39 3/8	39 5/8	13 2/8	13 5/8	7 7/8	7 7/8	13	12	Peace River, AB	Angela Wolansky	Angela Wolansky	1993	516
197 5/8	56 1/8	44 4/8	42 6/8	12 2/8	14	6 6/8	6 7/8	9	11	Cassiar Mts., BC	Dennis D. Brust	Dennis D. Brust	1995	516
197 4/8	57 2/8	42 5/8	41 5/8	10 4/8	14 1/8	7	7	11	15	Telegraph Creek, BC	Gordon Best	Gordon Best	1968	522
197 4/8	51 4/8	36 4/8	37 1/8	16 4/8	17 2/8	8	8	12	15	Cassiar Mts., BC	Russell H. Underdahl	Russell H. Underdahl	1968	522
197 4/8	56 2/8	39 3/8	39 4/8	13 6/8	13	7 2/8	7 3/8	14	11	Atlin, BC	John Konrad	John Konrad	1973	522
197 4/8	54 4/8	41	42 4/8	12 2/8	12	7 4/8	7 6/8	11	13	Dease River, BC	Terry Jackson	Terry Jackson	1975	522
197 4/8	50 6/8	43 4/8	41 4/8	13 4/8	13 3/8	7 4/8	7 4/8	11	11	Kelly Creek, BC	Leonard O. Farlow	Leonard O. Farlow	1980	522
197 4/8	63 2/8	39 5/8	38 5/8	15	15 2/8	7	7	10	8	Cassiar Mts., BC	Michael J. Jacobson	Michael J. Jacobson	1986	522
197 4/8	49 4/8	40 3/8	41 3/8	13 2/8	13 5/8	7 3/8	8 1/8	14	13	Albany River, ON	Lee H. Monge	Lee H. Monge	1986	522
197 4/8	47 6/8	40 2/8	47 6/8	13 1/8	14 6/8	7 4/8	8 1/8	14	16	Inverness River, AB	Steve C. Klask	Steve C. Klask	1988	522
197 4/8	58	37 3/8	41 1/8	13 2/8	13 2/8	7 5/8	7 1/8	12	13	Porcupine Mts., MB	Sidney G. Humphries	Sidney G. Humphries	2001	522
197 4/8	62 2/8	40 3/8	42	9 4/8	12 4/8	6 6/8	6 6/8	11	11	Gnat Creek, BC	Jody J. Marcks	Jody J. Marcks	2003	522
197 3/8	58 1/8	40 1/8	41 7/8	13 7/8	13 4/8	8	8	11	8	Sikanni Chief River, BC	Leslie Bowling	Leslie Bowling	1962	532
197 3/8	48 3/8	43 4/8	47 4/8	13	11 2/8	7 6/8	7 6/8	12	12	Cabin Lake, BC	W. Harrison	W. Harrison	1964	532
197 3/8	57 5/8	41 3/8	38 3/8	13 2/8	16 1/8	7 2/8	7 2/8	11	15	Firth Lake, BC	Gordon J. Pengelly	Gordon J. Pengelly	1973	532
197 3/8	50 1/8	39 7/8	39 5/8	13	13 2/8	7 1/8	7	14	14	Fleming Lake, BC	Peter Holland	Peter Holland	1976	532
197 3/8	55 3/8	40 7/8	43 4/8	11 5/8	14	7 4/8	7 7/8	11	11	Coos Co., NH	Armand L. Hebert	Armand L. Hebert	1998	532
197 3/8	51 3/8	42	42 7/8	13 4/8	12 5/8	7 4/8	7 3/8	12	11	Atlin Lake, BC	James R. Gall	James R. Gall	1999	532
197 2/8	58 4/8	39 1/8	37 4/8	17 4/8	17 2/8	6 5/8	6 6/8	8	8	St. Louis Co., MN	Paul W. Anthony	MN Dept. of Natl. Resc.	1906	538
197 2/8	56 4/8	37 6/8	38 4/8	10 6/8	12 2/8	7 7/8	8 2/8	14	15	Jackfish Lake, AB	Unknown	Ovar Uggen	1955	538
197 2/8	50 4/8	40 5/8	43 4/8	13	16 2/8	7 6/8	7 6/8	12	15	Terminus Mt., BC	Basil C. Bradbury	Basil C. Bradbury	1962	538
197 2/8	50	44	43 5/8	14 4/8	17 4/8	7 4/8	7 4/8	8	8	Liard Plateau, BC	George Roberts	George Roberts	1970	538
197 2/8	59 4/8	36 3/8	34 5/8	15 5/8	14	7 3/8	7 2/8	13	13	Hayes River, BC	John R. Schleicher	John R. Schleicher	1990	538
197 2/8	59 6/8	38 4/8	36 1/8	13 6/8	14	6 7/8	6 7/8	14	12	Penobscot Co., ME	Tabitha S. Dudley	Tabitha S. Dudley	1996	538
197 1/8	56 5/8	40 4/8	38 1/8	13 4/8	13 3/8	7 6/8	7 7/8	11	13	Tisdale, SK	Bill Hrechka	Bill Hrechka	1960	544
197 1/8	54 7/8	38 4/8	43 2/8	12 7/8	15 4/8	6 6/8	6 6/8	13	14	Pink Mt., BC	Allison R. Smith	Allison R. Smith	1963	544
197 1/8	53 3/8	38 5/8	39 7/8	13	14 6/8	8	8	11	12	Fir River, SK	Harold Kriger	Harold Kriger	1994	544
197	57 6/8	38	38 4/8	11 2/8	11 2/8	7 3/8	7 4/8	13	13	Cold Fish Lake, BC	George W. Hale	George W. Hale	1967	547
197	54 2/8	40	39 1/8	17 4/8	15 3/8	7 2/8	6 7/8	11	10	Brothers Lake, BC	William D. Phifer	William D. Phifer	1971	547

Score	Greatest Spread	Length of Palm R	Length of Palm L	Width of Palm R	Width of Palm L	Circumference R	Circumference L	Points R	Points L	Locality	Hunter	Owner	Date Killed	Rank
197	60 6/8	39 3/8	37 4/8	12 6/8	12 1/8	7 5/8	7 4/8	11	13	Swan Lake, BC	Carl E. Larson	Carl E. Larson	1975	547
197	48 4/8	40 4/8	41 2/8	14 2/8	13 6/8	7	7 2/8	16	13	Turnagain River, BC	Jack W. Lester, Jr.	Jack W. Lester, Jr.	1982	547
197	58	42 6/8	40 5/8	12	13 1/8	8	7 7/8	9	13	Chinchaga River, AB	Glen Mulzet	Glen Mulzet	1986	547
197	61 6/8	41 3/8	40 5/8	14 6/8	12 4/8	7 4/8	7 5/8	7	9	Level Mt. Range, BC	Thomas R. Conrardy	Thomas R. Conrardy	2000	547
197	51 2/8	39 4/8	39 2/8	15 6/8	15 1/8	7	7 4/8	11	12	Piscataquis Co., ME	Dieter Tiarks	Dieter Tiarks	2002	547
196 7/8	58 7/8	36 3/8	38 5/8	13 5/8	12 5/8	7 4/8	7 5/8	13	14	Weeks, SK	Ken Holloway	Ken Holloway	1961	554
196 7/8	54 1/8	39 5/8	39 4/8	14 7/8	13 3/8	7	7 4/8	11	13	Slave Lake, AB	Kathleen Wickersham	Ernest Wickersham	1967	554
196 7/8	50 7/8	38 3/8	41 2/8	20 4/8	13 7/8	7 4/8	7 3/8	13	13	Cassiar Mts., BC	Larry Herwick	Larry Herwick	1979	554
196 7/8	62 3/8	38 3/8	43	13 6/8	12	7 4/8	7 2/8	14	10	Pink Mt., BC	Tony J. Farace	Tony J. Farace	1984	554
196 7/8	55 7/8	40 2/8	40 1/8	12 2/8	13 7/8	7 1/8	6 7/8	11	11	Polk Co., MN	William H. Vollbrecht, Jr.	William H. Vollbrecht, Jr.	1985	554
196 7/8	50 1/8	42 2/8	40 2/8	14 4/8	14 2/8	7	7 1/8	12	14	Christina Falls, BC	David V. Collis	David V. Collis	1987	554
196 7/8	59 7/8	36 2/8	35 7/8	13 6/8	12 4/8	7 1/8	7 1/8	13	13	Lake Dumoine, QC	Claude Lapointe	Claude Lapointe	1993	554
196 7/8	59 5/8	36 5/8	36 5/8	15 3/8	14 4/8	6 5/8	6 4/8	11	12	Cook Co., MN	M. Groven, M. Groven, R. Anderson, & P. Anderson	M. Groven, M. Groven, R. Anderson, & P. Anderson	1999	554
196 6/8	49 6/8	43	44	14 6/8	12 6/8	6 7/8	6 6/8	15	11	Hines Creek, AB	Harry Kashuba	Harry Kashuba	1959	562
196 6/8	57	40 7/8	39 4/8	13 7/8	14 1/8	7 7/8	7 4/8	9	11	Atlin, BC	Dennis Downton	Dennis Downton	1969	562
196 6/8	57 6/8	36	38 2/8	16 4/8	16 3/8	7 3/8	7 1/8	10	12	Wapiti River, AB	John J. Seeliger	John J. Seeliger	1985	562
196 6/8	56	41 2/8	38	14 5/8	14 5/8	6 7/8	6 6/8	12	14	Scoop Lake, BC	Mark S. Coles	Mark S. Coles	1996	562
196 6/8	48 2/8	37 1/8	37 1/8	17 5/8	16 6/8	7	7	14	10	Moberly Lake, BC	Stephen Gilles	Picked Up	1997	562
196 5/8	58 6/8	41 4/8	40 1/8	11 7/8	12 3/8	7 2/8	7 2/8	13	11	Stony Lake, BC	George Kalischuk	George Kalischuk	1963	567
196 5/8	53 3/8	42 3/8	43 7/8	12	11 6/8	7 4/8	7 2/8	10	11	Atlin, BC	Ernest Wilfong	Ernest Wilfong	1965	567
196 5/8	50 3/8	42 1/8	40 3/8	15 1/8	13 5/8	8 2/8	8 3/8	13	13	Cassiar, BC	Richard Pain	Richard Pain	1967	567
196 5/8	53 3/8	42 3/8	40 3/8	11 4/8	14 4/8	6 6/8	6 5/8	11	11	Medicine Lake, AB	Stan Reiser	Stan Reiser	1967	567
196 5/8	57 7/8	41	39 4/8	13 6/8	11 3/8	7 4/8	7 4/8	12	11	Telegraph Creek, BC	Paul Inzanti, Jr.	Paul Inzanti, Jr.	1969	567
196 5/8	62 5/8	42 5/8	39 3/8	11 5/8	11 7/8	7	7	11	9	Adsit Creek, BC	Loren D. Bliss	Loren D. Bliss	1980	567
196 5/8	53 7/8	38 2/8	36 7/8	16 7/8	16 4/8	7	7	14	12	Lake Co., MN	Brian S. Agnoli	Brian S. Agnoli	1981	567
196 5/8	61 5/8	42 6/8	36 6/8	13 2/8	13 1/8	8	8	13	10	Aroostook Co., ME	Marcie M. Shoulders	Marcie M. Shoulders	2002	567
196 4/8	46 6/8	37	37 4/8	18 1/8	14	7 6/8	7 6/8	12	13	Belcourt Lake, BC	Robert Agnello	Robert Agnello	1965	575
196 4/8	50 4/8	39 6/8	43 2/8	14	12 5/8	7 3/8	7 3/8	13	12	Perrault Falls, ON	A.H. Nettleship	A.H. Nettleship	1967	575
196 4/8	56 6/8	38 2/8	41 3/8	12	12 1/8	7 5/8	7 5/8	12	12	Sikanni Chief River, BC	W.C. Spencer	W.C. Spencer	1970	575
196 4/8	56 6/8	39 2/8	39 4/8	11 3/8	14 6/8	7 3/8	7 2/8	14	12	Kula Tan Tan River, BC	Arnold J. Kaslon	Arnold J. Kaslon	1972	575
196 4/8	53 3/8	43 2/8	38 6/8	14 6/8	13 1/8	7 1/8	7 1/8	11	13	Turnagain River, BC	George H. Biddle	George H. Biddle	1973	575
196 4/8	45 6/8	42 1/8	44 5/8	13 1/8	16 5/8	7 1/8	7 1/8	13	13	Pink Mt., BC	Gary Bloxham	Gary Bloxham	1973	575
196 4/8	60	36 2/8	36 6/8	16 3/8	17 7/8	7 5/8	7 5/8	9	8	Lake Co., MN	Roy H. Anderson	Roy H. Anderson	1977	575
196 4/8	57 4/8	41	42 6/8	13 6/8	10 6/8	7 6/8	7 6/8	10	13	Swan Lake, BC	Patricia Markofer	Patricia Markofer	1989	575
196 3/8	59 3/8	38 4/8	41 6/8	12 3/8	12 3/8	7 4/8	7 4/8	12	12	Abitibi Canyon, ON	Pelham Glasier	Pelham Glasier	1951	583
196 3/8	52 1/8	38 2/8	43 3/8	15 4/8	15 4/8	8 3/8	8 3/8	11	11	Green Lake, SK	Mike Spies	Mike Spies	1959	583
196 3/8	58 1/8	38 2/8	37 4/8	14 1/8	12 1/8	7 4/8	7 4/8	10	11	Cassiar Mts., BC	E. David Slye	E. David Slye	1967	583
196 3/8	55 7/8	43 2/8	43 1/8	10 2/8	15 2/8	7 3/8	7 3/8	12	12	Blackfox Mt., BC	Robert P. O'Connor	Robert P. O'Connor	1999	583
196 3/8	52 7/8	42 1/8	41 2/8	14 2/8	14 4/8	7 3/8	7 2/8	9	10	Ft. McMurray, AB	Bruce A. Friedel	Bruce A. Friedel	2001	583
196 3/8	51 3/8	40 3/8	41 2/8	14 4/8	14 4/8	7 5/8	7 5/8	12	9	Somerset Co., ME	Jared Mitchell	Jared Mitchell	2001	583
196 2/8	59	39 4/8	39 4/8	12 2/8	16 3/8	6 7/8	6 7/8	10	10	Jack Pine, ON	William Picht	William Picht	1963	589
196 2/8	55 2/8	43	45 4/8	13 6/8	12 4/8	7	7	10	10	Anguille Mts., NL	Robert D. Smith	Robert D. Smith	1963	589
196 2/8	55 4/8	39 7/8	37 7/8	16 2/8	15 4/8	7 1/8	7 1/8	10	12	Cassiar Mts., BC	Bryan Upchurch	Bryan Upchurch	1975	589
196 2/8	56 6/8	35 4/8	37	14	13 7/8	7 3/8	7 3/8	14	13	Aroostook Co., ME	R.E. Gatchell & C. Dole	Robert E. Gatchell	1982	589
196 2/8	54	41 4/8	41 2/8	12 5/8	14 3/8	8 3/8	8 3/8	11	9	Pleasant Bay, NS	Richard M. Bouchard	Richard M. Bouchard	1992	589
196 2/8	52 2/8	43	42 6/8	14	12	7 4/8	7 5/8	10	9	Gardner Lake, AB	Edward Capes, Jr.	Edward Capes, Jr.	1992	589

CANADA MOOSE

Alces alces americana and Alces alces andersoni

Score	Greatest Spread	Length of Palm R	L	Width of Palm R	L	Circumference of Beam at Smallest Place R	L	Number of Normal Points R	L	Locality	Hunter	Owner	Date Killed	Rank
196 2/8	54 2/8	42 1/8	41 2/8	12 5/8	12 7/8	7 2/8	7 1/8	13	11	Cassiar Mts., BC	Alan C. Cole	Alan C. Cole	1993	589
196 2/8	56 2/8	41 7/8	42 5/8	13	10 7/8	7 3/8	7 2/8	10	11	Meikle River, AB	Robert Kramer	R. Kramer & B. Friedel	1993	589
196 2/8	62 6/8	35 1/8	37	15 1/8	12 6/8	7 2/8	6 7/8	12	12	Essex Co., VT	Dale E. Potter	Dale E. Potter	1996	589
196 2/8	60 6/8	41 6/8	37 2/8	13 3/8	13 4/8	10 1/8	10 5/8	11	9	Ottawa Lake, QC	Robert Durocher	Robert Durocher	1998	589
196 2/8	63	36 6/8	38 3/8	13 3/8	11 6/8	7 1/8	7 1/8	11	11	McGregor River, BC	Kevin D. Gull	Kevin D. Gull	1999	589
196 2/8	57	37 5/8	38 7/8	13 6/8	14 5/8	7 2/8	7 3/8	13	11	French Creek, BC	Wes Peters	Wes Peters	1999	589
196 1/8	55 5/8	36 6/8	37	15 2/8	16 6/8	7 2/8	7 6/8	11	13	Endeavour, SK	G.N. Galbraith	G.N. Galbraith	1955	601
196 1/8	55 7/8	42 2/8	39 2/8	13 4/8	13 7/8	7 3/8	7 4/8	10	16	Jack Pine River, ON	M.H. Brown	M.H. Brown	1962	601
196 1/8	56 1/8	38	38 2/8	13 2/8	12 7/8	6 6/8	6 6/8	13	14	Atlin, BC	Cliff Schmidt	Cliff Schmidt	1966	601
196 1/8	49 1/8	42 2/8	42 2/8	11 3/8	11 2/8	7 1/8	7	13	13	Atlin, BC	H.J. Schwegler	H.J. Schwegler	1967	601
196 1/8	52 3/8	41 5/8	40 1/8	15 4/8	14 2/8	7 4/8	7 4/8	10	12	Frog River, BC	Robert McMurray	Robert McMurray	1968	601
196 1/8	51 5/8	38 2/8	37 4/8	14 1/8	12 3/8	7 3/8	7 3/8	15	16	Ft. St. John, BC	Kanton R. Flemming	Kanton R. Flemming	1975	601
196 1/8	51 1/8	41 2/8	42 4/8	12 4/8	12 3/8	8 1/8	7 7/8	13	11	Penobscot Co., ME	Richard A. Record	Richard A. Record	1982	601
196 1/8	59 5/8	38 3/8	40 4/8	12 5/8	13 4/8	7 2/8	7 2/8	13	10	Fort Nelson, BC	Don C. Hurlbut	Don C. Hurlbut	1996	601
196 1/8	58 5/8	40 2/8	41 1/8	12	14 1/8	7 4/8	7 4/8	15	9	Cree Lake, SK	Greg G. Darby	Greg G. Darby	1998	601
196 1/8	54 5/8	41 2/8	39	11 3/8	13 4/8	7 3/8	7 3/8	13	13	Kearl Lake, AB	Robert Paquin	Robert Paquin	1999	601
196	56 2/8	38 7/8	39 6/8	13 3/8	14 6/8	8	7 5/8	11	13	Pelican River, AB	Douglas A. Stoller	Douglas A. Stoller	1971	611
196	54 6/8	43 7/8	40 4/8	10 5/8	12 2/8	7	7	13	14	Tatuk Lake, BC	Erling E. Gull	Erling E. Gull	1980	611
196	53 6/8	39 2/8	40 3/8	13 1/8	15 5/8	6 7/8	6 7/8	12	12	Wollaston Lake, SK	Daryl V. Johannesen	Daryl V. Johannesen	1982	611
196	49 6/8	41	40 4/8	13 3/8	14 3/8	7 2/8	7 4/8	12	15	Birchwood Creek, AB	Gert B. Nielsen	Gert B. Nielsen	1990	611
196	57	38	38 4/8	15 5/8	12	7 6/8	7 4/8	13	12	Somerset Co., ME	Carol A. Hepfner	Carol A. Hepfner	1994	611
196	53 4/8	40 7/8	37 6/8	14 6/8	14	7 6/8	7 6/8	12	12	Franklin Co., ME	Richmond E. Yorke, Jr.	Richmond E. Yorke, Jr.	1994	611
196	60 4/8	39 6/8	40 7/8	11 5/8	12 6/8	7 3/8	7 6/8	9	13	Big Sand Lake, MB	Ronald F. Mancl	Ronald F. Mancl	1999	611
195 7/8	56 3/8	37 4/8	40 3/8	12 6/8	13 5/8	7 6/8	7 4/8	13	12	Cassiar, BC	Donald F. Conway	Donald F. Conway	1965	618
195 7/8	54 1/8	37	41 7/8	14	13 6/8	7 1/8	7 2/8	13	13	Sheep Creek, AB	S.J. Blaupot Ten Cate	S.J. Blaupot Ten Cate	1966	618
195 7/8	54 5/8	40	40	12 7/8	12 6/8	7 7/8	8 1/8	10	12	Franklin Co., ME	Matthew Duguay	Matthew Duguay	1998	618
195 7/8	56 7/8	46 6/8	44	11 6/8	11 6/8	7 6/8	7 6/8	6	7	Nipigon Bay, ON	David L. Keith	David L. Keith	2002	618
195 6/8	56	38 6/8	38	11 3/8	11 3/8	8 4/8	8 4/8	15	12	Prophet River, BC	Earl Mumaw	Earl Mumaw	1957	622
195 6/8	53 4/8	38 2/8	39 1/8	12 7/8	13 6/8	7 2/8	7	13	14	Hudson Bay, SK	Charles Hamilton	Charles Hamilton	1964	622
195 6/8	59	44	43 2/8	13 1/8	13 2/8	7	7 1/8	10	14	Smoky River, AB	Ken G. Johnson	Ken G. Johnson	1966	622
195 6/8	56 2/8	42 6/8	39 4/8	12 2/8	12	7 2/8	7 2/8	11	12	Ft. St. John, BC	Louis M. Soetebeer	Louis M. Soetebeer	1969	622
195 6/8	48 6/8	42 4/8	42 3/8	12	13 7/8	8 1/8	8 2/8	11	16	Pasquia Hills, SK	Ray Eros	Ray Eros	1985	622
195 6/8	52 6/8	40 1/8	42 3/8	13 7/8	13 1/8	7 2/8	7 3/8	11	15	Denetiah Lake, BC	Scott S. Snyder	Scott S. Snyder	1995	622
195 6/8	59 4/8	36	37 3/8	13 2/8	12 7/8	7 3/8	7 2/8	12	12	Deadwood Lake, BC	J. George Williams	J. George Williams	2003	622
195 5/8	57 7/8	36 6/8	40 6/8	12 5/8	16 4/8	7 4/8	7 7/8	12	13	Pink Mt., BC	Michael H. LaViolette	Michael H. LaViolette	1989	629
195 5/8	57 3/8	38 4/8	39 5/8	12 7/8	12 6/8	6 7/8	7	11	13	Uslika Lake, BC	Brad K. Smith	Brad K. Smith	1993	629
195 5/8	56 6/8	40	41 6/8	11 2/8	10 3/8	7 1/8	7 1/8	12	12	Kechika River, BC	Don Pedersen	Don Pedersen	1999	629
195 4/8	58	37 2/8	37 2/8	15 1/8	15	7 4/8	7 4/8	9	13	Pasquia Hills, SK	Henry Dyck	Henry Dyck	1955	632

Score	Greatest Spread	Length of Palm R	Length of Palm L	Width of Palm R	Width of Palm L	Circ. R	Circ. L	Points R	Points L	Locality	Hunter	Owner	Date	Rank
195 4/8	65 2/8	39	40 2/8	11 4/8	10	7 1/8	7 2/8	9	9	Sheep Creek, AB	H.C. Early	H.C. Early	1957	632
195 4/8	57 6/8	38 4/8	39 2/8	12 4/8	13 3/8	8	7 7/8	11	10	Blanchard River, BC	William E. Lauffer	William E. Lauffer	1969	632
195 4/8	61	37 5/8	36 3/8	13 2/8	13 3/8	7 6/8	7 6/8	10	13	Whitecourt, AB	John E. Esslinger	John E. Esslinger	1971	632
195 4/8	54 6/8	38 7/8	39 4/8	13 4/8	13 6/8	8 1/8	8	13	10	Stikine River, BC	Manfred Beier	Manfred Beier	1976	632
195 4/8	57 4/8	37 7/8	40 6/8	11 3/8	16	7 3/8	7 2/8	13	13	Somerset Co., ME	Frank White	Frank White	1983	632
195 4/8	55 4/8	41 4/8	41 7/8	14 2/8	12 6/8	6 6/8	6 6/8	9	9	Turnagain Lake, BC	Fenton C. Carter	Fenton C. Carter	1985	632
195 4/8	52 2/8	39	39 4/8	12 6/8	13 1/8	6 5/8	6 5/8	13	13	Spatsizi Wilderness, BC	J.D. O'Rear	J.D. O'Rear	1985	632
195 4/8	52 4/8	43 4/8	39 5/8	12 1/8	12 1/8	7	6 6/8	16	16	Smoky River, AB	Thomas F. Wood	Thomas F. Wood	1996	632
195 4/8	57 6/8	39	38 2/8	14 3/8	14	7 5/8	7 6/8	10	9	McKenzie Lake, ON	Larry N. Cornellier, Sr.	Larry N. Cornellier, Sr.	1997	632
195 4/8	59 2/8	40 2/8	39	12 4/8	17 2/8	7 2/8	7 1/8	11	10	Port au Port Bay, NL	Paul R. Pearsall	Paul R. Pearsall	2000	632
195 4/8	63 3/8	36 2/8	37 1/8	14 3/8	13 5/8	7 2/8	7 1/8	9	9	Trembleur Lake, BC	Harry McCarter	Harry McCarter	1965	632
195 3/8	57 3/8	38 7/8	39 5/8	13	12 7/8	7 7/8	7 5/8	10	10	Atlin, BC	Jerome A. Ree	Jerome A. Ree	1965	643
195 3/8	52 5/8	39 5/8	38 7/8	12 5/8	12 5/8	6 7/8	7	13	13	Prophet River, BC	Ronald B. Sorensen	Ronald B. Sorensen	1967	643
195 3/8	54 1/8	38 2/8	40 1/8	13 7/8	12 7/8	7 6/8	7 6/8	12	12	Kechika Range, BC	Frank S. Kohar	Frank S. Kohar	1968	643
195 3/8	55 7/8	39 1/8	43 6/8	15	13 7/8	6 6/8	7	10	10	Chip Lake, AB	Elon Johnson	Elon Johnson	1984	643
195 3/8	55 7/8	39	37 1/8	16	15 6/8	6 7/8	6 7/8	10	11	Metsantan Lake, BC	Dwight L. Boettcher	Dwight L. Boettcher	1986	643
195 3/8	61 5/8	36 2/8	37	12 3/8	13 2/8	7 2/8	7 4/8	12	13	Duck Mt., MB	Nick Malchuk	Nick Malchuk	1994	643
195 3/8	60	37	39 2/8	12 7/8	11 1/8	7 3/8	7 2/8	10	13	Atlin, BC	Wilbert Hoffman	Wildl. Tax. Studios	1966	643
195 2/8	57 4/8	39 4/8	42 7/8	10 3/8	13 5/8	7 4/8	7 5/8	9	14	British Columbia	Len Anderson	Len Anderson	1966	650
195 2/8	56 2/8	39 7/8	40	14 5/8	19 5/8	7 1/8	7 4/8	12	15	Blanchard River, BC	Pat Archibald	Pat Archibald	1967	650
195 2/8	60	41 6/8	39 2/8	14 5/8	14 3/8	7 3/8	7 4/8	12	13	Ignace, ON	Ervey W. Smith	Ervey W. Smith	1969	650
195 2/8	59 2/8	38 1/8	40	13	14 4/8	8 4/8	8 4/8	7	13	Lake Nipigon, BC	Danny E. Breivogel	Danny E. Breivogel	1974	650
195 2/8	54	37 4/8	39	13 4/8	13 5/8	7 1/8	7 3/8	13	15	Turnagain River, BC	Donald E. Franklin	Donald E. Franklin	1977	650
195 2/8	52	39 6/8	41 5/8	15 2/8	15 6/8	7 3/8	7 3/8	11	17	Ospika River, BC	John L. Fullmer	John L. Fullmer	1977	650
195 2/8	54 4/8	35	42	12	14	7 1/8	7 2/8	13	13	Piscataquis Co., ME	William H. Gagnon, Jr.	W.H. Gagnon, Jr. & R.R. Gagnon	1980	650
195 2/8	57 2/8	41 6/8	42	12	12 3/8	7 3/8	7 2/8	8	8	Nuthinaw Mt., BC	Robert S. Curtis	Robert S. Curtis	1984	650
195 2/8	63	35 1/8	32	12 6/8	13 4/8	7 4/8	7 3/8	14	14	Penobscot Co., ME	Kati J. Deane	Kati J. Deane	2001	650
195 2/8	51 2/8	43	38 4/8	13 3/8	13 5/8	8 1/8	8 6/8	14	12	Wapiti River, AB	Kevin D. Wojciechowski	Kevin D. Wojciechowski	2001	650
195 2/8	55 1/8	40	42 6/8	11 6/8	12 2/8	7 7/8	7 6/8	10	14	Berland River, AB	W.C. Kadatz	W.C. Kadatz	1962	650
195 1/8	55 3/8	39 5/8	39 1/8	13 7/8	11 6/8	8 1/8	7 5/8	12	11	Hudson Bay, SK	Walter Sukkau	Walter Sukkau	1964	661
195 1/8	56 3/8	38 5/8	36 5/8	15 3/8	13 7/8	7	6 7/8	11	12	British Columbia	Charles Waugaman	Charles Waugaman	1969	661
195 1/8	56 1/8	36	36 5/8	14 1/8	16	7 1/8	7 1/8	13	14	Muskwa River, BC	Buck Heide	Buck Heide	1979	661
195 1/8	61 5/8	39	34 2/8	11 5/8	15 3/8	6 4/8	5 7/8	11	14	Terminus Mt., BC	Modesta S. Williams	Modesta S. Williams	1982	661
195 1/8	58 7/8	38 3/8	38 2/8	12 4/8	14 1/8	7 2/8	7 3/8	14	11	Ash Mt., BC	H. Frank Grainger	H. Frank Grainger	1984	661
195 1/8	55 3/8	36 7/8	36 1/8	12 6/8	11 5/8	7 2/8	7 4/8	14	14	Goodwin Lake, BC	Delmar W. Welch	Delmar W. Welch	1986	661
195 1/8	54 1/8	38 7/8	38 7/8	14 1/8	12 4/8	7 3/8	7 2/8	12	13	Piscataquis Co., ME	Frank M. Harris	Frank M. Harris	1991	661
195 1/8	56 5/8	39 2/8	39 4/8	14 5/8	12 3/8	7 2/8	7 2/8	12	12	Ludwig Creek, BC	John M. Hinkle, Jr.	John M. Hinkle, Jr.	1998	661
195 1/8	57 6/8	34 3/8	38 2/8	11 5/8	12 6/8	7 6/8	7 6/8	15	15	Little Codroy Pond, NL	J. Russell Allison	J. Russell Allison	1957	661
195	57 4/8	37 6/8	38 2/8	13 1/8	14 5/8	6 3/8	6 5/8	14	14	Turner Valley, AB	Bart Rockwell	Bart Rockwell	1958	670
195	58	37 3/8	42 1/8	14	11 5/8	7 2/8	7 3/8	13	13	Pontiac Co., QC	Roger Cashdollar	Roger Cashdollar	1966	670
195	52	41 5/8	40	15	12 7/8	7 4/8	8	11	10	Houston, BC	R. Starnes	R. Starnes	1966	670
195	54 6/8	38	37 2/8	14	13 1/8	8	7 1/8	13	13	Piscataquis Co., ME	Keith B. Gould	Keith B. Gould	1980	670
195	54 2/8	39	38 2/8	12 4/8	14	7 1/8	7 3/8	11	11	Lake Co., MN	Lewis N. Hostrawser	Lewis N. Hostrawser	1981	670
195	53 4/8	40 1/8	40	16 7/8	15	7 3/8	7 2/8	11	11	Piscataquis Co., ME	Lester Whitten	Cecile D. Therrien	1982	670
195	61 1/8	37 4/8	36 6/8	12	14	7 2/8	8	11	11	Aroostook Co., ME	Sterling W. Waterman	Sterling W. Waterman	1982	670
195	59	42 2/8	39 4/8	12	12 4/8	7 5/8	7 7/8	9	8	Loune Lake, ON	Douglas H. Campbell	Douglas H. Campbell	1998	670
195	54 6/8	40 2/8	42	12	12	8 3/8	6 7/8	11	13	Keily Creek, BC	Dennis D. Church	Dennis D. Church	1999	670

CANADA MOOSE

Alces alces americana and Alces alces andersoni

Score	Greatest Spread	Length of Palm		Width of Palm		Circumference of Beam at Smallest Place		Number of Normal Points		Locality	Hunter	Owner	Date Killed	Rank
		R	L	R	L	R	L	R	L					
195	56 2/8	41 3/8	40 2/8	12 4/8	12 2/8	7	6 7/8	10	11	Kakwa River, AB	David J. Gochenaur	David J. Gochenaur	1999	670
228 5/8*	68 5/8	44 1/8	44 2/8	16 7/8	16 1/8	7 6/8	8 2/8	12	12	Parton River, BC	Randy E. Miller	Randy E. Miller	2001	
220 6/8*	60 4/8	43 2/8	43 3/8	14 1/8	14 4/8	7 6/8	8 2/8	15	16	Aroostook Co., ME	Cynthia M. Higgins	Cynthia M. Higgins	2000	
219 3/8*	59 5/8	48 2/8	44 6/8	15 4/8	14 3/8	8	7 6/8	15	13	Kahntah River, BC	Michael Green	Michael Green	2001	
216 *	61 4/8	37 5/8	43 3/8	17 6/8	17 4/8	8 1/8	8 6/8	16	14	Oxford Co., ME	Brian A. Martin	Brian A. Martin	1998	

Final score is subject to revision by additional verifying measurements.

CATEGORY
CANADA MOOSE

SCORE
197-3/8

HUNTER
JAMES R. GALL (RIGHT)

LOCATION
ATLIN LAKE, BRITISH COLUMBIA

DATE OF KILL
OCTOBER 1999

SCORE
198-3/8

HUNTER
GEORGE A. PICKEL (LEFT)

LOCATION
AROOSTOOK COUNTY, MAINE

DATE OF KILL
OCTOBER 1999

CATEGORY
CANADA MOOSE

SCORE
203

HUNTER
SPENCER J. VAA

LOCATION
GLADYS RIVER, BRITISH COLUMBIA

DATE OF KILL
OCTOBER 1998

CATEGORY
CANADA MOOSE

SCORE
203-1/8

HUNTER
WERNER WISTUBA (RIGHT)

LOCATION
HATIN LAKE, BRITISH COLUMBIA

DATE OF KILL
SEPTEMBER 1998

SCORE
197

HUNTER
THOMAS R. CONRARDY (BELOW)

LOCATION
LEVEL MOUNTAIN RANGE,
BRITISH COLUMBIA

DATE OF KILL
SEPTEMBER 2000

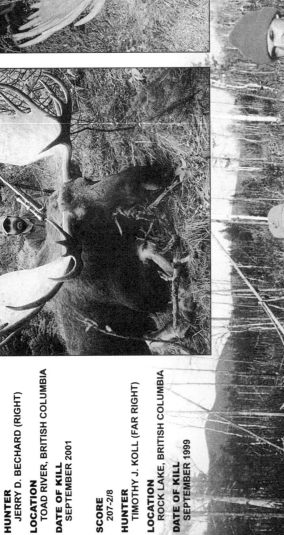

CATEGORY
CANADA MOOSE

SCORE
210-6/8

HUNTER
JERRY D. BECHARD (RIGHT)

LOCATION
TOAD RIVER, BRITISH COLUMBIA

DATE OF KILL
SEPTEMBER 2001

SCORE
207-2/8

HUNTER
TIMOTHY J. KOLL (FAR RIGHT)

LOCATION
ROCK LAKE, BRITISH COLUMBIA

DATE OF KILL
SEPTEMBER 1999

CATEGORY
CANADA MOOSE

SCORE
202-2/8

HUNTER
JOHN A. ALBEE

LOCATION
SOMERSET COUNTY, MAINE

DATE OF KILL
OCTOBER 1998

594

GIFFORD PINCHOT
1865-1946

By H. Hudson DeCray

He was the first American professional forester, and served as the first Chief of the U.S. Forest Service. He was an early leader in crusading for the conservation of this nation's natural resources. He worked closely with President Theodore Roosevelt to engage the governors of the states and the leaders of both Canada and Mexico in long-range planning to conserve the continent's resources. He served as Governor of Pennsylvania for two terms: 1923-27 and 1931-35. ∎

GIFFORD PINCHOT, THE HEAD OF THE U.S. FOREST SERVICE AT THE TURN OF THE LAST CENTURY, WITH PRESIDENT THEODORE ROOSEVELT.

595

ALASKA-YUKON MOOSE
WORLD'S RECORD

It was during the late summer of 1994 that John A. Crouse caught the reflection of antlers belonging to an Alaska-Yukon moose near Fortymile River, Alaska.

"Suddenly, the bull stood up broadside to me and turned its head in our direction. My heart pounded. A slight breeze in our faces confirmed the bull didn't smell our scent. Could it have heard me whispering? I got back down over my scope. The bull stared at me. Ragged threads of velvet dangled from its front brow tines, and gunny sack-size pieces draped from each palm.

"I tried to put the cross hairs behind its front shoulder, but a branch blocked a clean shot. The bull stood as I inched to my right. My sights found the spot, and I squeezed the trigger. I heard the 'whump' of a solid hit and watched the bull leap into the air, whirl, and run 180 feet before dropping to the ground. I chambered another round into my .270 Winchester and again found the bull in my scope.

"The bull stood its ground as I watched it for several seconds. I decided I didn't want the moose getting any farther from our camp. The second shot rocked the bull. In a final effort it tried to leap forward but its hind legs collapsed. The bull toppled over backwards, plowing its antlers into the soft earth."

Crouse and hunting partners, Dennis and Doug Chester, spent the remainder of that memorable September day, plus another full day and a half, butchering and packing the meat and the antlers back to their camp. Crouse knew the moose's rack was big -- more than 60 inches wide. What he didn't figure was just how those antlers might fit into a Cessna.

When Charlie and Ron arrived with their Cubs, they were impressed with the rack. Charlie commented that it was the biggest set of antlers he had ever seen. Ron worried that we might not be able to get the antlers out with the small planes. He feared the wide palms might cause too much drag.

"I suggested we split the skull and put the antlers inside the airplane rather than tying them to the wing strut, but Charlie said, 'No way.' He said he wanted them scored by a Boone and Crockett Club Official Measurer. Charlie knew that trophies with split skulls are not eligible for entry in Boone and Crockett.

"The tips of the antlers were just a few short inches from the ground as they hung from the wing strut of Charlie's Cub. He decided to try and hop them over a few miles to an abandoned mine where they could land a larger plane to ferry them the rest of the way back to Tok. The plane, with its cumbersome load, quickly lifted off the ground and disappeared after a few minutes.

"I returned to Cordova just as the antlers arrived. The antlers did not fit into a Cessna 185, so a Cessna 206 with double cargo doors was flown out to retrieve them. A truck driver, on his route to Anchorage, brought them to Doug for storage. At the end of the 60-day drying period, Doug made the arrangements to have the antlers officially measured."

Upon receiving the news in late November, Crouse couldn't believe what he was told. Scored at 261-5/8, his trophy had set a new World's Record for Alaska-Yukon moose. ■

ALASKA-YUKON MOOSE
WORLD'S RECORD SCORE CHART

RANK
World's Record

SCORE
261 5/8

LOCATION
Fortymile River, AK

HUNTER
John A. Crouse

OWNER
John A. Crouse

DATE KILLED
1994

BOUNDARY FOR ALASKA-YUKON MOOSE

Alaska-Yukon moose includes trophies from Alaska, Yukon Territory, and Northwest Territories.

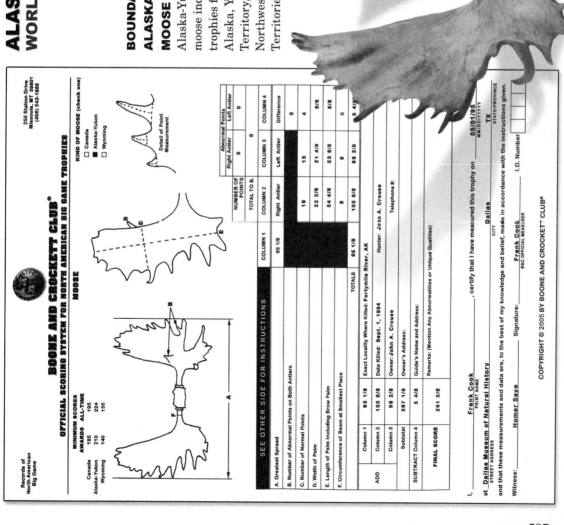

Records of
North American
Big Game

250 Station Drive
Missoula, MT 59801
(406) 542-1888

BOONE AND CROCKETT CLUB®
OFFICIAL SCORING SYSTEM FOR NORTH AMERICAN BIG GAME TROPHIES

MOOSE

MINIMUM SCORES	AWARDS	ALL-TIME
Canada	185	195
Alaska-Yukon	210	224
Wyoming	140	155

KIND OF MOOSE (check one)
☐ Canada
■ Alaska-Yukon
☐ Wyoming

Detail of Point Measurement

	NUMBER OF POINTS	Right Antler	Left Antler
		0	0

Abnormal Points
	Right Antler	Left Antler
TOTAL TO B.	0	

SEE OTHER SIDE FOR INSTRUCTIONS	COLUMN 1	COLUMN 2 Right Antler	COLUMN 3 Left Antler	COLUMN 4 Difference
A. Greatest Spread	65 1/8			
B. Number of Abnormal Points on Both Antlers				0
C. Number of Normal Points		19	15	4
D. Width of Palm		22 2/8	21 4/8	6/8
E. Length of Palm Including Brow Palm		54 4/8	53 6/8	6/8
F. Circumference of Beam at Smallest Place		8	8	0
TOTALS	65 1/8	103 6/8	98 2/8	5 4/8

	Column 1	65 1/8	Exact Locality Where Killed: Fortymile River, AK	
ADD	Column 2	103 6/8	Date Killed: Sept. 1, 1994	Hunter: Joan A. Crouse
	Column 3	98 2/8	Owner: John A. Crouse	Telephone #:
	Subtotal	267 1/8	Owner's Address:	
SUBTRACT Column 4		5 4/8	Guide's Name and Address:	
FINAL SCORE		261 5/8	Remarks: (Mention Any Abnormalities or Unique Qualities)	

I, **Frank Cook** , certify that I have measured this trophy on **05/01/95**
PRINT NAME MM/DD/YYYY

at **Dallas Museum of Natural History** **Dallas** **TX**
STREET ADDRESS CITY STATE/PROVINCE

and that these measurements and data are, to the best of my knowledge and belief, made in accordance with the instructions given.

Witness: **Homer Saye** Signature: **Frank Cook** I.D. Number
B&C OFFICIAL MEASURER

COPYRIGHT © 2005 BY BOONE AND CROCKETT CLUB®

TOP 10 ALASKA-YUKON MOOSE

NUMBER 2 — 256-6/8 POINTS
WILLIAM G. NELSON — 1997

NUMBER 5 — 250-3/8 POINTS
DYTON A. GILLILAND — 1947

NUMBER 1 — 261-5/8 POINTS
JOHN A. CROUSE — 1994

DETAIL OF POINT
MEASUREMENT

NUMBER 3 — 255 POINTS
KENNETH BEST — 1978

NUMBER 4 — 251 POINTS
BERT KLINEBURGER — 1961

NUMBER 6 — 249-6/8 POINTS
JOSEF WELLE — 1967

NUMBER 10 — 248-7/8 POINTS
LOREN G. HAMMER — 1967

NUMBER 8 — 249-2/8 POINTS
HENRY S. BUDNEY — 1967

NUMBER 7 — 249-3/8 POINTS
JOHN R. JOHNSON — 1995

NUMBER 9 — 249-1/8 POINTS
DAVID B. PARENT — 1982

KODAK PX 5062

DETAIL OF POINT MEAS

Column 2 | Column 3
Right | Left
Antler | Antler

Exact locality
Date killed
Present owner
Address
Guide's
Remarks: (Menti

ALASKA-YUKON MOOSE
Alces alces gigas

MINIMUM SCORE 224

Score	Greatest Spread	Length of Palm R	Length of Palm L	Width of Palm R	Width of Palm L	Circumference of Beam at Smallest Place R	Circ. L	Number of Normal Points R	Points L	Locality	Hunter	Owner	Date Killed	Rank
261 5/8	65 1/8	54 4/8	53 6/8	22 2/8	21 4/8	8	8	19	15	Fortymile River, AK	John A. Crouse	John A. Crouse	1994	1
256 6/8	78 2/8	49 6/8	50 5/8	17 3/8	18 2/8	7 5/8	7 6/8	16	15	Beluga River, AK	William G. Nelson	William G. Nelson	1997	2
255	77	49 5/8	49 6/8	20 6/8	15 6/8	7 7/8	7 5/8	18	16	McGrath, AK	Kenneth Best	Kenneth Best	1978	3
251	77 4/8	46 3/8	51	17	20	7 7/8	8 1/8	18	17	Mt. Susitna, AK	Bert Klineburger	Bert Klineburger	1961	4
250 3/8	65 1/8	55 2/8	49 2/8	21 1/8	20	8 3/8	8 3/8	18	16	Kenai Pen., AK	Dyton A. Gilliland	Unknown	1947	5
249 6/8	67	47 7/8	48 2/8	22 1/8	21 1/8	7 3/8	7 5/8	15	15	Mother Goose Lake, AK	Josef Welle	Josef Welle	1967	6
249 3/8	75 3/8	51 6/8	53 1/8	17	18 6/8	7 2/8	7 2/8	11	12	Tikchik Lake, AK	John R. Johnson	John R. Johnson	1995	7
249 2/8	72	48 4/8	49 6/8	19 2/8	17	8 1/8	8 6/8	15	16	Alaska Range, AK	Henry S. Budney	Henry S. Budney	1967	8
249 1/8	69 5/8	46 6/8	43 2/8	21 2/8	22	8 2/8	8 4/8	22	17	Granite Mt., AK	David B. Parent	Earl D. Hahn	1982	9
248 7/8	73 1/8	47 4/8	47 4/8	20	19 2/8	7 4/8	7 4/8	14	19	Farewell Lake, AK	Loren G. Hammer	Loren G. Hammer	1967	10
248 5/8	68 7/8	54 3/8	46 5/8	19 6/8	19 5/8	7 5/8	8	17	16	Kenai Pen., AK	Bill Foster	Foster's Bighorn Rest.	1912	11
248 3/8	68 5/8	49 7/8	50 4/8	17 2/8	17 4/8	7 6/8	7 6/8	15	17	Natla River, NT	Myron A. Peterson	Myron A. Peterson	1988	12
248 1/8	77 5/8	47 5/8	48 5/8	18 3/8	18 6/8	8 2/8	8 3/8	13	16	Mulchatna River, AK	Bruce B. Hodson	Bruce B. Hodson	1970	13
247 7/8	80 3/8	45 6/8	46 2/8	21 2/8	21 2/8	8 3/8	9 3/8	11	11	Rapid Creek, AK	Mark S. Rose	Mark S. Rose	2003	14
247 5/8	73 1/8	46	46 1/8	19 6/8	21 4/8	9 4/8	9	15	15	Bering River, AK	Vol S. Davis, Jr.	Vol S. Davis, Jr.	1984	15
247 4/8	79 6/8	45 7/8	46 1/8	22 1/8	22 6/8	9	8 7/8	10	7	Iliamna Lake, AK	Gale L. Galloway	Gale L. Galloway	1970	16
247 2/8	66 4/8	48	48	18 4/8	19	7 7/8	7 7/8	17	16	Mackenzie Mts., NT	Harry Rogers	Harry Rogers	1978	17
247 2/8	70 4/8	50 6/8	52 4/8	18	16 5/8	9	9	12	12	Alagnak River, AK	Robert L. Marvin	Robert L. Marvin	1981	17
247 2/8	71	48 2/8	49 2/8	20 2/8	21 7/8	8 2/8	8 1/8	17	12	Ogilvie Mts., YT	Dennis C. Campbell	Dennis C. Campbell	1998	17
246 5/8	77 5/8	48 7/8	48 4/8	16	17 6/8	7 5/8	7 4/8	13	15	Melozitna River, AK	Elmer Raphael	D.J. Hollinger & B. Howard	1978	20
246 3/8	67 5/8	44 5/8	49 5/8	22 2/8	22	10 2/8	9 3/8	19	16	Kenai Pen., AK	Henry Hope	Henry Hope	1957	21
246 3/8	67 7/8	51 2/8	52 2/8	18 5/8	16 7/8	8 1/8	9 1/8	13	13	Redoubt Bay, AK	T.J. Hinkle	T.J. Hinkle	1993	21
245 6/8	75 3/8	48	46 2/8	18 6/8	19 5/8	8 3/8	8 5/8	12	16	Alaska Range, AK	Ralph Davies	Ralph Davies	1970	23
245 3/8	72 2/8	46 3/8	46 3/8	17	17 4/8	7 3/8	7 4/8	16	17	Wrangell Mts., AK	Philip S. Davidson	Philip S. Davidson	1970	24
245 3/8	73 3/8	49 3/8	51 3/8	16	15 4/8	8 5/8	9 5/8	14	13	Wien Lake, AK	Travis D. Thorniley	Travis D. Thorniley	1994	25
245 3/8	70 4/8	46 4/8	44 4/8	22 2/8	19	8 1/8	7 7/8	16	16	Ruby Creek, AK	James W. Gelhaus	James W. Gelhaus	1997	26
245 1/8	63 3/8	49 4/8	49 4/8	17 5/8	18 5/8	7 6/8	7 7/8	16	17	Kuskokwim River, AK	Ronald H. Barenz	Ronald H. Barenz	1995	27
244 6/8	64	52 1/8	52 4/8	18 4/8	15 4/8	8	7 6/8	16	15	Ogilvie Mts., YT	John F. Bruce	John F. Bruce	1995	28
244 4/8	67 4/8	51 2/8	49 1/8	20	18 2/8	8 6/8	8 5/8	13	14	Talkeetna Mts., AK	William H. Moore	Michael C. Horasanian	1953	29
244 3/8	72 3/8	48 6/8	47 2/8	19 4/8	19 7/8	7 2/8	7 3/8	12	12	Long Lake, AK	William F. Rae, Jr.	William F. Rae, Jr.	1973	30
244 2/8	71	48 4/8	48 4/8	15 4/8	16 6/8	7 5/8	7 5/8	15	15	Holy Cross, AK	Frank W. Dutton	Frank W. Dutton	1995	31
243 6/8	71 6/8	49 4/8	48 4/8	14 4/8	17 2/8	7 6/8	7 4/8	16	17	Mayo, YT	Carl Straub	Carl Straub	1971	32
243 6/8	69 4/8	49 6/8	50 6/8	15 6/8	21 1/8	8 1/8	7 5/8	17	14	Wrangell Mts., AK	John Ringstad	Loren St. Amand	1977	32
243	70	47 2/8	50 5/8	19 5/8	20 2/8	7 6/8	7 5/8	15	12	Kenai Pen., AK	D. Thompson & F. Walunga	Denny Thompson	1958	34
242 7/8	61 7/8	50 6/8	50 7/8	17 4/8	19 4/8	8 6/8	8 6/8	15	18	McGrath, AK	Leonard H. Wurman	Leonard H. Wurman	1995	35
242 6/8	63 6/8	51 4/8	50 4/8	16 7/8	16 7/8	8	7 5/8	16	15	Alaska	Unknown	Jonas Bros. Of Seattle	1954	36
242 6/8	65 6/8	45 6/8	46 1/8	16 6/8	18 4/8	8	8	18	18	Keele Range, AK	Spike Jorgensen	B. & T. Jorgensen	1994	36

Score	Greatest Spread	Length of Palm R	Length of Palm L	Width of Palm R	Width of Palm L	Circumference of Beam	Points R	Points L	Locality	By Whom Killed	Owner	Date Killed	Rank
242 4/8	69 2/8	49 2/8	46 7/8	15 6/8	15 6/8	8 6/8	16	17	Upper Susitna, AK	Helen S. Rusten	Carnegie Mus.	1948	38
242 4/8	76	44 7/8	45 7/8	17 1/8	17 1/8	7 2/8	14	18	Nuyakuk River, AK	Ron D. DeRoest	Ron D. DeRoest	1995	38
242 3/8	67 3/8	46 2/8	46 6/8	19 3/8	21	7 5/8	15	15	Iliamna Lake, AK	Charles C. Parsons	Charles C. Parsons	1997	40
242 1/8	78 7/8	44	44 4/8	19 4/8	21 7/8	8 1/8	11	11	Alaska Pen., AK	H.S. Kamil	H.S. Kamil	1963	41
242	73 6/8	45 5/8	48 5/8	19 6/8	19 6/8	8	15	11	Homer, AK	Dan Jones	Dan Jones	1957	42
242	68	48 5/8	49 2/8	19 4/8	19 4/8	7 6/8	14	16	Grass Lakes, YT	Melvin R. Spohn	Melvin R. Spohn	1981	42
241 5/8	72 5/8	49 6/8	46 7/8	16 7/8	16 7/8	8 5/8	12	16	Neresna, AK	Lorene Ellis	Lorene Ellis	1962	44
241 5/8	67 5/8	46 5/8	46 7/8	19 1/8	19 1/8	8 2/8	16	16	Dawson City, YT	Ray C. Dillman	Ray C. Dillman	1971	44
241 5/8	72 1/8	48 1/8	47 7/8	19 6/8	20 6/8	8	12	16	Lower Ugashik Lake, AK	Bert A. McLay	John H. McLay	1986	44
241 4/8	76 6/8	47	47 2/8	16 4/8	15 3/8	7 1/8	10	10	King Salmon, AK	O.O. Parker & B. Bradley	O.O. Parker & B. Bradley	1960	47
241	74 2/8	47 3/8	42 7/8	18	20	8 2/8	12	12	Anvil Range, YT	Dawson H. Colby, Jr.	Cabela's, Inc.	2000	48
240 7/8	72 5/8	48 1/8	42 7/8	17 7/8	21 7/8	7 6/8	13	13	Kenai Pen., AK	A.S. Reed	B&C National Collection	1900	49
240 5/8	80 5/8	43 4/8	43 2/8	18 6/8	16 2/8	8	12	15	Redoubt Bay, AK	Glenn B. Walker	Glenn B. Walker	1958	50
240 4/8	71 4/8	43 6/8	51 3/8	21 6/8	20 7/8	8 4/8	15	11	Ugashik Lakes, AK	Gene Buckles	Gene Buckles	1973	51
240 4/8	73 6/8	43 6/8	45	17	17	9	16	18	Alaska Pen., AK	Gregory C. McCann	Gregory C. McCann	1990	51
240 3/8	73 1/8	46 5/8	50 2/8	16 4/8	16 6/8	7 7/8	13	15	Huslia River, AK	Bradley J. Drake	Bradley J. Drake	1993	53
240 2/8	70 4/8	43 5/8	43 5/8	17 4/8	17 4/8	7 5/8	17	17	Yukon River, YT	Unknown	G. Kenneth Whitehead	PR 1899	54
240 2/8	64 6/8	48 4/8	42 5/8	20 5/8	17 4/8	7 7/8	21	21	Noatak River, AK	J. & M. Jacobson	J. & M. Jacobson	1974	54
240 1/8	66 3/8	49 6/8	41 2/8	18 4/8	15 4/8	9	16	16	Wrangell Mts., AK	Forest Bigelow	Forest Bigelow	1973	56
240 1/8	70 3/8	44 4/8	42 6/8	20 4/8	20 4/8	7 6/8	16	17	Martin River, AK	Eugene B. Desjarlais	Eugene B. Desjarlais	1992	56
240 1/8	75 3/8	53 2/8	49 3/8	20	16 5/8	7 5/8	15	16	Koyukuk River, AK	Mark V. Cuppetilli	Mark V. Cuppetilli	1997	56
240	62 4/8	48 4/8	45 2/8	16 5/8	16 5/8	8 2/8	18	16	Beluga Mt., AK	Walter Renz	Walter Renz	1976	59
239 6/8	66 6/8	47 3/8	43 4/8	21	21 6/8	8 1/8	16	18	Rainy Pass, AK	Mrs. J Watson Webb	Mrs. J Watson Webb	1935	60
239 6/8	75 4/8	44 5/8	47 6/8	14 7/8	14 7/8	8 2/8	18	12	Mayo, YT	Dave Moses	Yukon Hist. Society	1950	60
239 6/8	70	52 7/8	56	18 3/8	19	7 3/8	14	15	Alaska Range, AK	James E. Egger	James E. Egger	1965	60
239 6/8	66 2/8	46 5/8	45 2/8	16 6/8	14 6/8	8 2/8	12	12	Yukon Territory	Nick Engles	Don C. Kirkpatrick	1967	60
239 6/8	74 2/8	47 4/8	48 1/8	14 7/8	14 7/8	7 4/8	14	15	Tustumena Lake, AK	Richard R. Sawyer	Richard R. Sawyer	1988	60
239 5/8	75 7/8	45 2/8	42	19	20 2/8	9 2/8	11	13	Gold King, AK	Billy J. Morris	Billy J. Morris	1971	65
239 4/8	62 4/8	53 4/8	56	20 4/8	16 1/8	8 7/8	11	11	Alaska Pen., AK	Lars Degefors	Lars Degefors	1967	66
239 4/8	74	44 7/8	45 2/8	17 3/8	16 7/8	8	14	14	Bonnet Plume Range, YT	Tafford E. Oltz	Tafford E. Oltz	1978	66
239 3/8	65 7/8	47 4/8	45 2/8	20 6/8	14 6/8	8 7/8	17	18	Alaska Pen., AK	J. Paul Dittrich	J. Paul Dittrich	1962	68
239 2/8	67	45 1/8	48 1/8	12 5/8	14 7/8	8	14	14	Beluga Lake, AK	Peter W. Bading	Peter W. Bading	1961	69
239 2/8	74	51 2/8	50 4/8	15	13 7/8	8 7/8	10	13	Alaska Pen., AK	George J. Markham	George J. Markham	1967	69
239 2/8	73 4/8	49 6/8	52 4/8	16 7/8	14 6/8	8 6/8	12	12	Ugashik, AK	Alois A. Mauracher	Alois A. Mauracher	1973	69
239 2/8	69	49 4/8	50 2/8	15 5/8	16 1/8	8 1/8	14	14	Ladue River, AK	Tim N. Hand	Tim N. Hand	1997	69
239 1/8	64 1/8	49	50 7/8	18 4/8	17 5/8	7 7/8	14	14	Rabideux Creek, AK	Derrick G. Bell	Derrick G. Bell	1997	73
239	67	46 1/8	48 4/8	18 3/8	16 4/8	8 3/8	14	13	Mackenzie Mts., NT	Burl A. Jones	Burl A. Jones	1973	74
238 4/8	69 2/8	47 4/8	48 4/8	15 6/8	14 4/8	8 1/8	14	15	Nushagak River, AK	Ira L. Kruger	Ira L. Kruger	1994	75
238 3/8	71 1/8	44	48	19 3/8	17 6/8	7 7/8	11	14	Lake Clark, AK	Frits Kielman	Frits Kielman	1973	76
238 2/8	72 4/8	46 3/8	45 6/8	18	22 1/8	8 1/8	13	11	Alaska Range, AK	Jeff Sievers	Jeff Sievers	1963	77
238 2/8	63 6/8	44	43 2/8	19 7/8	20 5/8	8 3/8	17	16	Anvil Range, YT	James F. Byers	James F. Byers	1977	77
238 1/8	74 5/8	43 5/8	47	21 4/8	25	8 5/8	16	9	Iliamna, AK	Joseph C. Anzalone	Joseph C. Anzalone	1972	79
238	69	48 4/8	47	17 6/8	17 6/8	9	15	11	Copper River, AK	Howard E. Thilenius II	Howard E. Thilenius II	1973	80
238	70 6/8	46 4/8	44 6/8	16 1/8	16	7 7/8	15	15	Mulchatna River, AK	Gary A. Smith	Gary A. Smith	1974	80
238	70 4/8	49 2/8	46 4/8	15 4/8	15 4/8	8 3/8	16	14	Kenai Pen., AK	Richard K. Mayer	Richard K. Mayer	2002	80
238	65 4/8	51 7/8	51	20 3/8	17 3/8	7 7/8	10	13	Dennison Creek, AK	Lynda S. Donahoe	Michael L. Cronk	2003	80
237 7/8	77 1/8	45 3/8	42 3/8	19 6/8	19 6/8	9	12	11	Dog Salmon River, AK	Peter Von Kap-Herr	Peter Von Kap-Herr	1971	84
237 6/8	71 4/8	47 6/8	48 7/8	16 3/8	15 5/8	7 7/8	11	12	Selwyn Mts., YT	William J. Weaver	William J. Weaver	1970	85

ALASKA-YUKON MOOSE
Alces alces gigas

Score	Greatest Spread	Length of Palm R	L	Width of Palm R	L	Circumference of Beam at Smallest Place R	L	Number of Normal Points R	L	Locality	Hunter	Owner	Date Killed	Rank
237 6/8	72	44 2/8	50	18 3/8	21 6/8	7 6/8	8 2/8	13	16	Melozitna River, AK	Darrell C. Aplanalp	Darrell C. Aplanalp	1998	85
237 6/8	75 2/8	47 1/8	43 1/8	24 6/8	19 2/8	9	8 7/8	12	13	Timberline Lake, AK	Dan K. Presley	Dan K. Presley	2002	85
237 6/8	67	50 6/8	49 5/8	14 3/8	13 1/8	8 5/8	8 6/8	14	14	Kenai Pen., AK	Robert M. Stacy	Robert M. Stacy	2003	85
237 5/8	68 1/8	46 6/8	44 6/8	17 6/8	22 4/8	7 7/8	8 1/8	14	20	Birch Lakes, AK	Kassem Meiss	Kassem Meiss	2002	89
237 3/8	67 1/8	46	48 2/8	18 3/8	18 1/8	8	8	17	13	Kenai Pen., AK	Leslie Maff	Temple Bros. Tax.	PR 1958	90
237 2/8	68 4/8	49	53 1/8	17 4/8	18	7 3/8	7 4/8	12	11	Tikchik River, AK	Mark T. Rule	Mark T. Rule	1999	91
237	69 2/8	49 1/8	47 7/8	15 4/8	15 6/8	8 4/8	8 4/8	13	12	Talkeetna Mts., AK	Merle C. LaFortune	Merle C. LaFortune	1970	92
237	71 6/8	48 7/8	51 4/8	14 5/8	16 5/8	7 7/8	7 5/8	12	16	Koyukuk River, AK	Picked Up	Jay Wattenbarger	1994	92
237	64 4/8	45 2/8	48 3/8	16 5/8	16 6/8	8 7/8	8 3/8	17	16	Mid. Fork Twitya River, NT	James L. Chase	James L. Chase	1996	92
236 7/8	68 1/8	48 1/8	48 3/8	14 2/8	14 1/8	8 2/8	8 1/8	14	14	Beluga Mt., AK	Albert W. Erickson	Albert W. Erickson	1961	95
236 7/8	67 5/8	46 3/8	47 6/8	15 6/8	18 7/8	8 4/8	9	14	15	Talkeetna Mts., AK	Mario Pasquel	Mario Pasquel	1961	95
236 7/8	67 5/8	42 4/8	43	22	21 1/8	8	8 2/8	15	13	Koyukuk River, AK	Harry B. Markoskie	Harry B. Markoskie	1969	95
236 7/8	62 7/8	45 6/8	46 4/8	22 3/8	21 1/8	7 2/8	7 1/8	14	13	Kiana Lake, AK	Lane H. Drury	Lane H. Drury	1977	95
236 5/8	65 1/8	49 1/8	51 2/8	19 4/8	16 4/8	8 3/8	8 1/8	13	12	Farewell Lake, AK	Steven S. Bruggeman	Steven S. Bruggeman	1994	99
236 5/8	73 3/8	49 6/8	47 6/8	15 7/8	15 1/8	7 6/8	7 7/8	11	11	Buckstock River, AK	Thomas R. Drake	Thomas R. Drake	2000	99
236 4/8	72 2/8	47 2/8	48 3/8	15 5/8	17 5/8	8 2/8	8 4/8	11	11	Blueberry Creek, AK	Heinrich Klimaszewski-Blettner	Heinrich Klimaszewski-Blettner	1991	101
236 3/8	68 1/8	46 4/8	49 3/8	16 4/8	17 7/8	8 2/8	8 1/8	14	13	Wood River, AK	Ronald Long	Ronald Long	1963	102
236 3/8	70 5/8	44 6/8	45 2/8	16 4/8	17 1/8	7 5/8	7 1/8	14	18	Lake Clark, AK	Gordon F. Wentzel	Gordon F. Wentzel	1973	102
236 2/8	68 4/8	46 4/8	52 2/8	18 3/8	16 6/8	8 1/8	8 6/8	16	16	Brusha Kama River, AK	Robert Harnish	Robert Harnish	1953	104
236 2/8	72	47	41 4/8	16 4/8	18 1/8	8 1/8	8 1/8	16	17	Upper Kiana Lake, AK	Marvin A. Henriksen	Marvin A. Henriksen	1964	104
236 2/8	73 6/8	41 6/8	42 1/8	23 1/8	22 6/8	8 3/8	8 2/8	9	14	Muddy River, AK	Richard J. Tomany	Richard J. Tomany	1993	104
236 2/8	65 4/8	48 4/8	49	15 6/8	15 5/8	7 2/8	7 4/8	14	14	Lake Clark, AK	Robert J. Salome	Robert J. Salome	1998	104
236 1/8	66 7/8	44 3/8	43 5/8	16 3/8	18 4/8	8 1/8	8 1/8	17	20	Birch Creek, AK	D.T. Sharp	D.T. Sharp	1962	108
236 1/8	70 7/8	47 4/8	48	14 4/8	15 3/8	7 6/8	7 5/8	14	13	Black Lake, AK	Robert B. Ryan	Robert B. Ryan	1969	108
236 1/8	68 3/8	50	49 5/8	16 7/8	17 1/8	8 3/8	8 7/8	13	9	Alaska Range, AK	Dennis R. Johnson	Dennis R. Johnson	1980	108
236 1/8	67 5/8	45 3/8	48	18	21 2/8	8	8 2/8	13	14	Chikuminuk Lake, AK	Walter A. Brown	Walter A. Brown	1994	108
236	68 6/8	48 6/8	54 2/8	13 4/8	17 4/8	7 7/8	7 7/8	14	14	Cook Inlet, AK	Robert L. Godwin	Robert L. Godwin	2000	112
235 7/8	73 5/8	50 5/8	46 4/8	16 4/8	17 4/8	8 1/8	8 1/8	10	10	Dog Salmon River, AK	Gary R. Swanson	Gary R. Swanson	1966	113
235 7/8	69 3/8	50	50 2/8	17 4/8	15 6/8	7 5/8	7 4/8	11	10	Farewell Lake, AK	Wilhelm H. Koehler	Wilhelm H. Koehler	1974	113
235 6/8	74	44 3/8	46 2/8	15 7/8	16 2/8	8 1/8	8 1/8	13	13	Alaska	Frank Alexander	Univ. of Alaska	1952	115
235 6/8	65 2/8	46 4/8	51 6/8	20 4/8	16 2/8	9 2/8	8 2/8	15	10	Kenai Pen., AK	J.D. Rasmusson	J.D. Rasmusson	1959	115
235 4/8	69 1/8	46 3/8	47 4/8	14 6/8	15 6/8	7 1/8	7 3/8	13	15	Nowitna River, AK	Brian C. Ziegenfuss	Brian C. Ziegenfuss	1988	117
235 4/8	63 2/8	47 3/8	47 4/8	16 5/8	17 2/8	8 2/8	8 1/8	14	14	Tanana River, AK	Kenneth J. Dooley	Kenneth J. Dooley	1992	118
235 4/8	66 4/8	46 4/8	45	20 3/8	19 2/8	8 4/8	8 4/8	13	12	Farewell Lake, AK	James M. Moore	James M. Moore	2000	118
235 2/8	71 4/8	50 6/8	50 2/8	14 1/8	14 4/8	8 4/8	8 4/8	9	10	Rainy Pass, AK	Ralph Vogel	Ralph Vogel	1956	120
235 2/8	66 6/8	51 6/8	49	17 7/8	16 2/8	7 5/8	7 4/8	12	12	Post Lake, AK	Charles Bradley	Charles Bradley	1978	120
235 2/8	68	48 4/8	46 4/8	15 3/8	17	8	7 6/8	13	13	Iditarod River, AK	Glen D. Keil	Glen D. Keil	1992	120

Score	Greatest Spread	Length of Palm R	Length of Palm L	Width of Palm R	Width of Palm L	Circ. of Beam R	Circ. of Beam L	Pts R	Pts L	Locality	Hunter	Owner	Date Killed	Rank
235 1/8	67 3/8	47 2/8	46 3/8	15 5/8	15 6/8	8 4/8	7 7/8	15	16	Kantishna River, AK	James L. Munsell	James L. Munsell	2000	123
235	71	47	45	14	15 5/8	8	8 3/8	15	16	Alaska Pen., AK	Otis Chandler	Otis Chandler	1964	124
235	74	45 2/8	45 1/8	15 4/8	14 3/8	8	8	15	13	Yellow River, AK	Peter Apokedak	Peter Apokedak	1966	124
235	71	47	46	16	17	8	8	12	14	Kateel River, AK	Ronald S. Peterson	Ronald S. Peterson	1976	124
234 6/8	74 4/8	50 7/8	49 1/8	16 7/8	16 3/8	8 1/8	7 5/8	12	8	Hewitt Lake, AK	W.L. Braun	W.L. Braun	1951	127
234 6/8	66 2/8	46 6/8	45 5/8	18 5/8	19 7/8	7 4/8	7 7/8	13	13	Alaska Range, AK	Bill Brown, Jr.	Bill Brown, Jr.	1987	127
234 6/8	74 6/8	46 6/8	46 1/8	15 7/8	20 5/8	8	8 3/8	10	13	Alaska Range, AK	Lon O. Willer	Lon O. Willer	1991	127
234 6/8	67 4/8	47 1/8	47 3/8	18 1/8	18	7 4/8	7 4/8	11	15	Mackenzie Mts., NT	Thomas M. Roles	Thomas M. Roles	2002	127
234 4/8	62 4/8	48 3/8	45 2/8	16 4/8	17 1/8	8 2/8	8 3/8	18	16	Mayo Landing, YT	Edwin Edger	J.H. McEvoy	1962	131
234 4/8	70 6/8	43	42 6/8	18 3/8	17 4/8	7 5/8	7 6/8	14	16	Alaska Pen., AK	Herb Klein	Dallas Mus. of Natl. Hist.	1967	131
234 4/8	69	47 1/8	48	18 2/8	17 5/8	8	8 1/8	11	12	Alaska Pen., AK	Robert P. Bliss	Robert P. Bliss	1969	131
234 4/8	66 6/8	47 6/8	44 4/8	17 4/8	16 6/8	8 4/8	7 7/8	16	15	Alaska	L.M. Hanson	L.M. Hanson	1969	131
234 4/8	71 4/8	47 6/8	49 2/8	14 2/8	15 6/8	8 6/8	8 4/8	11	11	Council, AK	Arden L. Peterson	Arden L. Peterson	1979	131
234 4/8	65 2/8	47 6/8	47 6/8	18 3/8	17 4/8	7 3/8	7 6/8	12	13	Teslin, YT	Bernard M. Stehelin	Bernard M. Stehelin	1995	131
234 4/8	68 4/8	46 1/8	46	18 7/8	18 1/8	7 7/8	8 2/8	11	15	Mt. Susitna, AK	Richard M. Young	Richard M. Young	1999	131
234 2/8	58	52 6/8	51 6/8	16 7/8	16 6/8	8 5/8	8 5/8	15	11	Alaska Range, AK	Wakon I. Redbird	Wakon I. Redbird	1969	138
234 2/8	71 2/8	45 4/8	44 7/8	16 7/8	16 7/8	7 3/8	7 2/8	14	15	Fortymile River, AK	Orval R. Evans	Orval R. Evans	1973	138
234 2/8	70 4/8	45 2/8	46 1/8	17 5/8	17 5/8	8 1/8	8	12	11	Koyukuk River, AK	Oren Johnson	Oren Johnson	1975	138
234 2/8	71 4/8	49 2/8	47 6/8	14 7/8	14 7/8	7 7/8	7 6/8	12	14	Beluga Lake, AK	Eugene J. Smart	Eugene J. Smart	1989	138
234 2/8	66 6/8	47 7/8	45 4/8	16 1/8	15	7 6/8	8 3/8	15	17	Salcha River, AK	Robert C. Lang	Robert C. Lang	1991	138
234 1/8	65 3/8	51 1/8	51 7/8	15	14 7/8	7 3/8	7 5/8	11	13	Alaska	Unknown	Ronald F. Lax	1972	143
234 1/8	71 3/8	41 4/8	43 2/8	19 2/8	18 1/8	7 6/8	7 6/8	16	14	Galena, AK	Michael J. Stowell	Michael J. Stowell	1977	143
234 1/8	68 5/8	44 2/8	46 4/8	17 2/8	17 2/8	7 4/8	7 2/8	14	16	Ditna River, AK	Richard C. Thompson	Richard C. Thompson	1992	143
234	68 4/8	46 4/8	43 3/8	18 6/8	17 3/8	8	8 1/8	14	16	Ugashik Lakes, AK	Richard C. Rubin	Richard C. Rubin	1968	146
234	75 4/8	49 2/8	48 5/8	14 4/8	14 4/8	7 6/8	8	10	11	King Salmon, AK	Larry R. Price	Larry R. Price	1971	146
233 7/8	68 3/8	53 4/8	50 4/8	15 4/8	15 5/8	8 4/8	7 6/8	9	12	Kuskokwim River, AK	Brian G. Mangold	Brian G. Mangold	2001	148
233 6/8	71 4/8	43 3/8	41	17 1/8	16 3/8	7 6/8	7 7/8	17	16	Kenai Pen., AK	A.S. Reed	Unknown	1900	149
233 6/8	76	42 2/8	50 2/8	20 5/8	20 5/8	7 2/8	8	10	12	Kenai Pen., AK	Otto Rohm	Otto Rohm	1964	149
233 6/8	63	50 5/8	49 2/8	20 3/8	20 3/8	7 3/8	7 3/8	13	14	Wrangell Mts., AK	Dan L. Quen	Dan L. Quen	1965	149
233 6/8	67 6/8	50 2/8	49 1/8	15	15 6/8	7	6 7/8	12	18	Galena, AK	Picked Up	Richard M. Reynolds	1995	149
233 5/8	77 5/8	41	44 1/8	14 5/8	18 3/8	7	7	15	13	Kenai Pen., AK	Picked Up	Am. Mus. Nat. Hist.	1938	153
233 5/8	65 7/8	46 3/8	45 1/8	18	20 6/8	7 6/8	7 6/8	14	13	Alaska Pen., AK	Jack S. Parker	Jack S. Parker	1968	153
233 5/8	71 3/8	45 4/8	50	15 4/8	18 2/8	8 5/8	8 5/8	11	17	Iliamna Lake, AK	Wayne Rattray	Wayne Rattray	1972	153
233 5/8	71 7/8	46 1/8	48 4/8	18 1/8	16 2/8	8 1/8	8	13	13	McGrath, AK	Art Beattie	Linda Beattie	1978	153
233 5/8	70 3/8	43 4/8	46 6/8	17 4/8	17 4/8	7 6/8	7 6/8	11	14	Telaquanna Lake, AK	Alvin A. Pierce	Alvin A. Pierce	1996	153
233 5/8	74 6/8	43 4/8	42 4/8	16 2/8	16 2/8	7 5/8	7 5/8	13	17	Kenai Pen., AK	Unknown	Gift of C.H. Mackay to NCHH	PR 1939	153
233 4/8	72 6/8	40 6/8	47 4/8	25 5/8	25 2/8	8	7 7/8	11	9	Kenai Pen., AK	Picked Up	Shawn T. Brown	PR 1972	159
233 4/8	70 4/8	50	45 5/8	16 4/8	15 7/8	8 3/8	8	14	12	Koyukuk River, AK	Arnold K. Wolf	Arnold K. Wolf	1993	159
233 3/8	66 1/8	48	48	15 6/8	16 3/8	8 7/8	8 7/8	12	11	Worm Lake, YT	James E. Nelson	James E. Nelson	1985	161
233 2/8	69 4/8	46 7/8	48 7/8	16 5/8	16 6/8	7 3/8	7 3/8	11	16	Chulitna River, AK	Joe L. Aprill	Elizabeth D. Aprill	1970	162
233 2/8	70 4/8	49 1/8	47 1/8	17 1/8	17 1/8	8 4/8	8 6/8	13	13	Koyukuk River, AK	Scott A. Shipman	Scott A. Shipman	1998	162
233 1/8	66 7/8	46 6/8	47 7/8	16	16 2/8	7 3/8	7 4/8	15	13	Yuki River, AK	Steven B. Spaulding	Steven B. Spaulding	1998	164
233	69	48 1/8	46 6/8	15 4/8	13 1/8	8	8 1/8	14	14	Merrill Pass, AK	Andrew F. Bjorge	Andrew F. Bjorge	1963	165
233	73 4/8	49 5/8	48	15 1/8	14 3/8	7 5/8	7 6/8	11	12	Dillinger River, AK	James N. McHolme	James N. McHolme	1976	165
232 7/8	67 1/8	50 1/8	48	15 7/8	15	8 3/8	8 4/8	13	12	Post Lake, AK	Andrew P. Schultze	Andrew P. Schultze	1996	167
232 6/8	65 6/8	46 1/8	42 7/8	15 6/8	18 7/8	7 7/8	7 7/8	15	17	Port Heiden, AK	Don C. Killom	Don C. Killom	1965	168
232 6/8	75	45 3/8	44 3/8	19 6/8	17 1/8	8 5/8	8 3/8	10	9	Port Heiden, AK	Gerald L. Lavenstein	Gerald L. Lavenstein	1967	168

ALASKA-YUKON MOOSE
Alces alces gigas

Score	Greatest Spread	Length of Palm R	L	Width of Palm R	L	Circumference of Beam at Smallest Place R	L	Number of Normal Points R	L	Locality	Hunter	Owner	Date Killed	Rank
232 6/8	74 2/8	48 2/8	48 1/8	13 4/8	15 4/8	7 2/8	7 1/8	11	13	Koyukuk River, AK	Chris M. Kendrick	Chris M. Kendrick	1994	168
232 5/8	65 1/8	43 3/8	45 4/8	18 1/8	18 6/8	8 2/8	8 3/8	15	14	Swede Lake, AK	Paul Bierdeman	Paul Bierdeman	1956	171
232 5/8	70 5/8	46 2/8	47 7/8	18 1/8	15 3/8	7 3/8	7 4/8	12	12	Ugashik Lakes, AK	Jack A. Shane, Sr.	Jack A. Shane, Sr.	1967	171
232 5/8	69 7/8	47 3/8	48 7/8	18 1/8	17	8	8	9	10	Lake Clark, AK	Wyatt B. Peek	Wyatt B. Peek	1987	171
232 5/8	67 1/8	49 6/8	49 6/8	17	16 6/8	7 3/8	7 2/8	10	9	Pilot Point, AK	Dennis M. Wick	Dennis M. Wick	1993	171
232 5/8	68 1/8	51 1/8	49 1/8	13 3/8	14	7 7/8	7 6/8	14	12	Lachbuna Lake, AK	Lavern W. Kind	Lavern W. Kind	2002	171
232 4/8	69 6/8	45	45	18 3/8	17 5/8	6 6/8	6 6/8	13	12	Talkeetna, AK	Ole Dahl	Boston Mus. of Science	1950	176
232 4/8	67 4/8	47 7/8	48 3/8	15 1/8	17 1/8	7 4/8	8	12	15	Stewart River, YT	Patrick Seaman	Patrick Seaman	1968	176
232 4/8	68	45 2/8	46 7/8	17 4/8	17 1/8	7 7/8	8 1/8	12	12	Teklanika River, AK	Richard O. Cook	Richard O. Cook	1976	176
232 4/8	70 6/8	48	49 6/8	14 6/8	14 6/8	8 2/8	8 1/8	12	13	Matanuska Valley, AK	Jim Sakaguchi	Wendy Kleker	1979	176
232 4/8	63 4/8	46 1/8	48 2/8	19 5/8	17	7 5/8	7 3/8	14	14	Tok River, AK	Kenneth L. Klawunder	Kenneth L. Klawunder	1992	176
232 4/8	69 4/8	44 5/8	46 2/8	16 7/8	16 7/8	8 2/8	8	14	12	Tuck Creek, AK	Thomas J. O'Neill	Thomas J. O'Neill	2001	176
232 2/8	71	43	43 1/8	20 1/8	17	8 5/8	8 6/8	14	12	Alaska Pen., AK	Stewart G. Richards	Stewart G. Richards	1968	182
232 2/8	66 2/8	50 4/8	49 4/8	16 4/8	14 6/8	7 6/8	7 6/8	12	11	Wien Lake, AK	James E. Guist	James E. Guist	1988	182
232 1/8	67 3/8	45 7/8	45 2/8	17	16 7/8	8 7/8	8 6/8	12	12	Amos Lakes, AK	Buddy R. Donaldson	Buddy R. Donaldson	1990	184
232 1/8	69 5/8	47 5/8	47 4/8	14 7/8	14 2/8	7 5/8	7 4/8	12	12	Mackenzie Mts., NT	J.L. Madden	J.L. Madden	1994	184
232	66 6/8	47 3/8	50 7/8	17 4/8	18 3/8	7 6/8	7 7/8	10	11	Alaska Pen., AK	A.R. Buckles	A.R. Buckles	1967	186
232	63	55	55 3/8	14	14 5/8	7 4/8	7 4/8	8	9	Alaska Pen., AK	L.W. Bailey, Jr.	L.W. Bailey, Jr.	1969	186
232	65	47 5/8	46	17	15	9 4/8	9 6/8	15	13	King Salmon, AK	P.J. Grady	J. Michael Conoyer	1979	186
231 7/8	63 1/8	50 6/8	49 7/8	12	12 2/8	8 4/8	8 4/8	15	14	Talkeetna Mts., AK	T.A. Miller	T.A. Miller	1959	189
231 7/8	69 1/8	43 6/8	44	22 4/8	18	8 2/8	8 1/8	13	15	Red Paint Creek, AK	Larry D. Kropf	Larry D. Kropf	1983	189
231 7/8	69 5/8	45 7/8	49 7/8	16 5/8	17 3/8	8 2/8	8 1/8	11	13	Wood River, AK	Robert Kennedy	Robert Kennedy	1989	189
231 7/8	68 5/8	42	46 7/8	17 4/8	17 7/8	7 1/8	7 2/8	15	16	Allen River, AK	Gordon L. Stewart	Gordon L. Stewart	2003	189
231 6/8	76	44 6/8	44 5/8	12 6/8	15 4/8	8 4/8	8 4/8	12	14	Kenai Pen., AK	Gift of C.H. MacKay to NCHH	Unknown	PR 1939	193
231 6/8	64 2/8	45 2/8	51 4/8	16 2/8	18	8 2/8	9	14	15	Lake Louise, AK	Paul Kunning	Paul Kunning	1966	193
231 6/8	65	45 5/8	46 6/8	18 5/8	18 4/8	7 6/8	8	13	12	Koyukuk River, AK	Don N. Bunker	Don N. Bunker	1990	193
231 6/8	59 6/8	48 5/8	48 6/8	17	18 1/8	8	7 7/8	12	13	Koyukuk River, AK	John W. Griffin	John W. Griffin	1996	193
231 5/8	73 1/8	48 6/8	44 4/8	15 4/8	15 4/8	7 6/8	7 7/8	12	16	Alaska Range, AK	Cecil M. Hopper	Cecil M. Hopper	1969	197
231 4/8	67 4/8	42 4/8	45 5/8	20 6/8	26 4/8	9 4/8	8 6/8	10	12	Alaska Pen., AK	George H. Landreth	George H. Landreth	1967	198
231 4/8	69 2/8	43 1/8	46 2/8	17	16 5/8	6 7/8	7 1/8	18	15	Steese Hwy., AK	Denver Perry	Denver Perry	1968	198
231 4/8	62 6/8	44	44 7/8	17 2/8	16 7/8	7 5/8	7 4/8	16	17	Alaska Range, AK	Peter J. Cassinelli	Peter J. Cassinelli	1977	198
231 4/8	67 4/8	46	44 4/8	17 2/8	17	7 5/8	7 4/8	13	15	Wood River, AK	H. Peter Blount	H. Peter Blount	1989	198
231 3/8	64 2/8	45 4/8	47 2/8	16 3/8	17	7 6/8	7 7/8	14	14	Ogilvie Mts., YT	Ken Taylor	Ken Taylor	1997	198
231 3/8	66 3/8	47 7/8	49 5/8	21 2/8	19 2/8	8 3/8	8 4/8	9	13	Kenai Mts., AK	Paula Rak	Paula Rak	1987	203
231 2/8	67	47 1/8	47 3/8	16 2/8	16	8	8	13	11	Brooks Range, AK	Lezlie D. Fickes	Lezlie D. Fickes	1972	204
231 1/8	66 5/8	49 3/8	49 6/8	15 4/8	14 1/8	7 6/8	7 6/8	12	11	Alaska Pen., AK	Frank N. Rome	Frank N. Rome	1976	205
231	67 6/8	42 7/8	45 5/8	18 1/8	17 4/8	7 2/8	7 3/8	14	17	Tazlina Glacier, AK	Stanley B. Hoagland	Stanley B. Hoagland	1963	206

Score	Greatest Spread	Length of Palm R	Length of Palm L	Width of Palm R	Width of Palm L	Circ. of Beam R	Circ. of Beam L	No. Points R	No. Points L	Locality	By whom killed	Owner	Date Killed	Rank
231	67 2/8	45 6/8	46 3/8	17 3/8	19	7 6/8	8 1/8	11	12	Amber Bay, AK	Charles E. Guess	Charles E. Guess	1974	206
231	68	45 6/8	47 5/8	13 4/8	14 4/8	8 2/8	8 3/8	14	14	Kuskokwim River, AK	Larry S. Lewis	Larry S. Lewis	1994	206
231	61	47 2/8	48 1/8	14 1/8	17 1/8	7 5/8	8 1/8	16	16	Chisana River, AK	Steven J. DeRicco	Steven J. DeRicco	1995	206
230 6/8	67 6/8	48 6/8	46 6/8	16 2/8	17 6/8	7 4/8	7 4/8	11	13	Petersville, AK	Johnny Lamb	Johnny Lamb	1969	210
230 6/8	67 4/8	53 5/8	52 6/8	13 1/8	14 2/8	7 7/8	7 6/8	9	8	Innoko River, AK	Leslie R. Hunter	Leslie R. Hunter	1983	210
230 6/8	67 6/8	54 4/8	45	19 1/8	15 7/8	9	8 4/8	14	14	Deadlock Mt., AK	Vernon W. Van Wyk	Vernon W. Van Wyk	1995	210
230 5/8	68 7/8	47 4/8	53 2/8	15	14 5/8	7 2/8	9	6	6	Cordova, AK	John B. Pecel	John B. Pecel	1969	213
230 5/8	65 5/8	43 4/8	47	16 2/8	16 2/8	7 3/8	8	12	12	Port Heiden, AK	Brent Greenburg	Brent Greenburg	1972	213
230 5/8	71 5/8	46 7/8	44 2/8	17	14 6/8	7 2/8	8	22	14	Bonnet Plume Lake, YT	Walter P. Griffin	Walter P. Griffin	1978	213
230 5/8	64 1/8	50	48 2/8	15 3/8	16 4/8	8 2/8	8	13	14	Alaska Pen., AK	Lucky Christoph	Lucky Christoph	1981	213
230 5/8	60 1/8	49 7/8	47 4/8	13 7/8	14 4/8	7 6/8	7 5/8	16	16	Hart River, YT	Charles H. Menzer	Charles H. Menzer	1988	213
230 4/8	70 3/8	50	50	15 2/8	19 5/8	7 5/8	7 7/8	12	12	Talkeetna River, AK	Wayne DiSarro	Wayne DiSarro	1989	219
230 4/8	61	48 7/8	49 4/8	14 4/8	15 5/8	8 7/8	8 1/8	9	14	Alaska Pen., AK	Louis Stojanovich	Louis Stojanovich	1993	219
230 4/8	69 4/8	45 4/8	47	17 4/8	17 4/8	8 1/8	7 6/8	13	17	Tazimina River, AK	Gary L. Jacobs II	Gary L. Jacobs II	1998	219
230 3/8	63	49	47 1/8	15 1/8	18 3/8	8 5/8	8 3/8	10	15	Melozitna River, AK	Dennis M. Fuller	Dennis M. Fuller	1999	222
230 3/8	69 1/8	42 6/8	46 5/8	19	22 2/8	7 4/8	7 4/8	10	16	Alaska Pen., AK	James H. Lieffers	James H. Lieffers	1963	222
230 2/8	66 7/8	45 1/8	47	15 6/8	16	8 2/8	8 2/8	14	15	Innoko River, AK	Keith W. Arnold	Keith W. Arnold	1987	224
230 2/8	66 4/8	40 1/8	39 5/8	18 7/8	17	8	8	13	11	Chelatna Lake, AK	G.O. Wiegner	G.O. Wiegner	1969	224
230 2/8	81 4/8	46 5/8	46 2/8	17 1/8	17 2/8	8 3/8	8 1/8	9	11	Iliamna Lake, AK	Peter Zipperle	Peter Zipperle	1972	224
230 2/8	70 2/8	44 5/8	45 6/8	16 6/8	17 6/8	7	6 7/8	10	12	Alaska Range, AK	Earl R. Hossman	Earl R. Hossman	1975	224
230 2/8	70 4/8	46	48 2/8	19 4/8	16	9 2/8	9	11	14	Lakina River, AK	Don W. Noah	Don W. Noah	1977	224
230 1/8	73 6/8	45 7/8	47 4/8	18 5/8	25	8	7 7/8	11	12	Branch River, AK	Robert E. Farone	Robert E. Farone	2002	229
230	66 2/8	43 5/8	45	18 7/8	19 7/8	7 3/8	7 6/8	12	10	Alaska Pen., AK	Walter Pfisterer	Walter Pfisterer	1960	230
230	65 3/8	44 2/8	44 3/8	14 4/8	14 6/8	7 6/8	7 4/8	12	12	Port Heiden, AK	Norman W. Garwood	Norman W. Garwood	1964	230
230	70 4/8	44 7/8	45 2/8	16 4/8	16 2/8	8	7 6/8	12	10	Miner River, YT	Gary L. Knepp	Gary L. Knepp	1979	230
230	73	44 4/8	47 2/8	15 7/8	16 3/8	8	7 4/8	12	10	Maclaren River, AK	Ronald D. Hocking	Ronald D. Hocking	1988	230
230	72	43 1/8	45 6/8	16 5/8	19 5/8	7 5/8	7 7/8	12	13	Ugashik River, AK	Angelo Poliseno	Angelo Poliseno	1991	230
230	66	46 4/8	47 2/8	15 4/8	16 4/8	8 4/8	7 4/8	13	15	Yellow River, AK	Patrick L. Kirsch	Patrick L. Kirsch	1993	230
230	70	43 3/8	46 4/8	18 1/8	16 4/8	7 4/8	7 6/8	11	11	Sleetmute, AK	Todd A. Horner	Todd A. Horner	1996	230
229 7/8	70	42 4/8	41 5/8	17 6/8	17 1/8	7 7/8	7 7/8	18	15	Ogilvie River, YT	Dean L. Benner	Dean L. Benner	2002	237
229 7/8	65 2/8	46	46 2/8	19 2/8	20 7/8	8 6/8	8 5/8	17	17	Wood River, AK	Bert Klineburger	Bert Klineburger	1964	237
229 7/8	66 7/8	45 7/8	46 5/8	16 3/8	14	7 6/8	7 6/8	8	13	King Salmon River, AK	Wilfred von Brand	Wilfred von Brand	1966	237
229 6/8	66 1/8	48 4/8	51	17	18	8 1/8	8 1/8	12	12	Kokwok River, AK	Patrick L. McDonald	Patrick L. McDonald	1990	240
229 6/8	70 5/8	47	45	17	19 6/8	8 2/8	8 2/8	11	12	Alaska Pen., AK	Robert H. Stewart	Robert H. Stewart	1963	240
229 6/8	64 7/8	45 6/8	45 4/8	17 2/8	17 2/8	7 4/8	7 4/8	12	12	Kenai Pen., AK	Barjona Meek	Barjona Meek	1973	240
229 6/8	60 4/8	43 1/8	45 4/8	16 6/8	16 6/8	7 3/8	3 4/8	11	12	Anvil Range, YT	Fritz Kemper	Fritz Kemper	1978	240
229 6/8	67 6/8	48 3/8	49 6/8	16 2/8	18	8 7/8	7 6/8	17	20	Yanert Fort, AK	Marvin H. Breitkreutz	Marvin H. Breitkreutz	1988	240
229 5/8	64 6/8	45 4/8	45 4/8	16 2/8	16 3/8	7 1/8	3	15	12	Kuskokwim River, AK	Theodore L. Hetrick, Jr.	Theodore L. Hetrick, Jr.	1999	245
229 5/8	61 6/8	45	48 1/8	15	15	8 7/8	7 6/8	14	15	McGrath, AK	Fred M. Poorman	Fred M. Poorman	1958	245
229 5/8	58 6/8	42	43	21	21	7 7/8	8 3/8	12	10	Kuichack River, AK	C.J. McElroy	C.J. McElroy	1966	245
229 4/8	64 7/8	45 6/8	46 2/8	15 1/8	18 6/8	7 6/8	3 2/8	10	12	Alaska Pen., AK	W.M. Ellis	W.M. Ellis	1963	247
229 4/8	68 7/8	44 4/8	46 6/8	16 7/8	17 1/8	8 3/8	3	12	13	Alaska Pen., AK	Arnold H. Craine	Arnold H. Craine	1968	247
229 4/8	63 4/8	46 1/8	47	16 4/8	16 4/8	3 2/8	3 1/8	10	11	Ogilvie Mts., YT	Johnny Bunsen	Johnny Bunsen	1996	247
229 4/8	72 2/8	43 5/8	43	17 4/8	15 7/8	3	3	10	11	Bear Creek, AK	J. Arden Meyer	J. Arden Meyer	1999	247
229 2/8	66 6/8	45	45 1/8	14 6/8	15	3 1/8	3 1/8	14	16	Fortymile River, AK	Brian E. Yamamoto	Brian E. Yamamoto	1988	251
229 2/8	69 6/8	45 2/8	47 1/8	13 1/8	14 2/8	8 2/8	8 2/8	15	15	Fortymile River, AK	Chuck Thorsrud	Chuck Thorsrud	1998	251
229 2/8	73	47 1/8	48 7/8	14 2/8	13 1/8	8	7 7/8	15	12	Pilot Mt., AK	Todd L. Johnson	Todd L. Johnson	2002	251
229 1/8	65 6/8	47 7/8	48 7/8	16 4/8	13 4/8	8	8	12	13	Mosquito Mt., AK	Gary L. Hebbert	Gary L. Hebbert	2000	254

ALASKA-YUKON MOOSE
Alces alces gigas

Score	Greatest Spread	Length of Palm R	Length of Palm L	Width of Palm R	Width of Palm L	Circ. of Beam at Smallest Place R	Circ. of Beam at Smallest Place L	Normal Points R	Normal Points L	Locality	Hunter	Owner	Date Killed	Rank
229 1/8	70 1/8	45 5/8	47 2/8	15	14 7/8	8	8 3/8	11	11	Coleen River, AK	Rick J. Schikora	Rick J. Schikora	2002	254
229	72 2/8	44 7/8	43 4/8	13 1/8	13 6/8	7 6/8	8	15	14	Wood River, AK	A. Knutson	A. Knutson	1957	256
229	62 4/8	47	45	19 3/8	20 1/8	7 4/8	6 7/8	12	13	Shaw Creek Flats, AK	William Bugh	William Bugh	1962	256
229	69	44	42 6/8	22 5/8	24	7 5/8	8	8	13	Mother Goose Lake, AK	Paul R. Sharick	Paul R. Sharick	1966	256
229	65 2/8	44 2/8	44 4/8	14	13 6/8	8	7 7/8	16	16	Wind River, YT	William G. Latimer	William G. Latimer	1973	256
229	67 2/8	47 2/8	43 7/8	16 5/8	17 2/8	7 3/8	7 5/8	14	13	Nushagak River, AK	Gary D. Myers	Gary D. Myers	1995	256
229	75 4/8	47 2/8	44 4/8	18 6/8	16	8 5/8	8 2/8	10	13	Mulchatna River, AK	Charles A. LeKites	Charles A. LeKites	1999	256
229	65 6/8	43 3/8	44 5/8	15 7/8	15 7/8	7 3/8	7 4/8	15	15	Lake Clark, AK	Ronald W. Rogers	Ronald W. Rogers	2000	256
229	70 2/8	44 4/8	42 6/8	15 2/8	15 2/8	8 3/8	8 4/8	13	14	Old Womens Mountain, AK	Ralph L. Ivanoff	Ralph L. Ivanoff	2003	256
228 7/8	65 7/8	47 3/8	44 4/8	17 4/8	16 5/8	8 6/8	8 3/8	15	13	Wood River, AK	Berry B. Brooks	Berry B. Brooks	1958	264
228 7/8	63 7/8	48 6/8	48 4/8	13 5/8	13 6/8	8 3/8	8 4/8	12	12	Talkeetna Mts., AK	David F. Bremner, Jr.	David F. Bremner, Jr.	1959	264
228 7/8	70 7/8	42 1/8	45 2/8	22 1/8	15 5/8	8 2/8	8 2/8	13	13	Cantwell, AK	Ray L. Aldridge	Ray L. Aldridge	1964	264
228 7/8	70 1/8	46 3/8	42 2/8	20 2/8	18 4/8	8 5/8	9 2/8	12	10	Ugashik Lakes, AK	Russell Matthes	Russell Matthes	1969	264
228 7/8	70 5/8	45 4/8	45 3/8	15 2/8	16 2/8	7 5/8	7 4/8	11	12	Mackenzie Mts., NT	Thomas N. Osso	Thomas N. Osso	2000	264
228 7/8	70 3/8	46 3/8	46 4/8	15	14 4/8	7 7/8	7 3/8	12	11	Tazimina River, AK	Samuel P. Albanese, Jr.	Samuel P. Albanese, Jr.	2001	264
228 6/8	65 6/8	47 5/8	44	17 4/8	18 1/8	8 1/8	8	12	13	Mulchatna River, AK	R.D. Eichenour	R.D. Eichenour	1968	270
228 6/8	72 6/8	43 6/8	48 6/8	14	16	8 2/8	8 4/8	13	12	Holitna River, AK	E.L. Dosdall	E.L. Dosdall	1975	270
228 6/8	63 4/8	47 2/8	44 7/8	15 5/8	15 3/8	7	6 7/8	19	16	Koyukuk River, AK	Scott R. Sexson	Scott R. Sexson	1978	270
228 6/8	69	49 4/8	47 6/8	14 2/8	13 2/8	7 7/8	8 1/8	13	11	Alganak River, AK	David W. Doner	David W. Doner	1988	270
228 6/8	70	44 6/8	43 7/8	15 5/8	19 5/8	8 3/8	7 7/8	12	12	Kenai Pen., AK	John T. Jondal	John T. Jondal	1992	270
228 5/8	78 3/8	42 4/8	40 2/8	22 2/8	20 1/8	8 2/8	8 2/8	11	15	Ugashik Bay, AK	Dale R. Wood	Dale R. Wood	1960	275
228 5/8	54 3/8	48 4/8	48 4/8	16 4/8	18 4/8	8 1/8	9	15	14	Kijik River, AK	Max Fugler	Max Fugler	1966	275
228 5/8	69 1/8	47 6/8	47 4/8	14	16	7 2/8	7 3/8	11	14	Wood River, AK	Edward A. Kneeland	Edward A. Kneeland	1970	275
228 5/8	72 1/8	42	46 1/8	15 6/8	15 4/8	8	7 6/8	14	13	Brooks Range, AK	Larry B. Jamison	Larry B. Jamison	1979	275
228 5/8	68 3/8	45	47 5/8	15 3/8	16	7 6/8	8 2/8	12	16	Bear Lake, AK	Robert L. Nelson	Robert L. Nelson	1981	275
228 5/8	61 3/8	47	47 4/8	13 5/8	15	8	8	15	15	Wrangell Mts., AK	William E. Pipes III	William E. Pipes III	1994	275
228 4/8	58	47	45 4/8	16 2/8	21 2/8	8 4/8	8 5/8	19	15	Bonnet Plume Lake, YT	G.W. Berry	G.W. Berry	1960	281
228 4/8	65 6/8	43 5/8	45 2/8	15 5/8	15 6/8	8 4/8	8 1/8	14	15	Alaska Pen., AK	Ted T. Dabrowski	Ted T. Dabrowski	1965	281
228 4/8	70	45 6/8	44 7/8	17 2/8	16 3/8	8	8 1/8	10	13	Wernecke Mts., YT	Tom W. Degefors	Tom W. Degefors	1967	281
228 4/8	65 4/8	45 1/8	45 6/8	14 1/8	13 5/8	7 6/8	8 2/8	17	15		Hugh Beasley	Hugh Beasley	1968	281
228 4/8	57 4/8	48 6/8	50	18 1/8	16 2/8	8 4/8	8 5/8	12	13	Emerald Lake, YT	J. George Williams	J. George Williams	1979	281
228 4/8	71	47 3/8	47 3/8	15 4/8	15 1/8	7 3/8	7 5/8	12	10	Tagagawik River, AK	Jesse C. Sprague	Jesse C. Sprague	1983	281
228 4/8	68 4/8	47 1/8	47 5/8	15 2/8	15 3/8	7 5/8	7 5/8	10	10	Flattop Mt., AK	John F. Walchli	John F. Walchli	1991	281
228 4/8	63 4/8	49 4/8	48 4/8	14	14 6/8	7	7 1/8	13	14	Fuller Mt., AK	Richard S. Edelen	Richard S. Edelen	2002	281
228 3/8	70 7/8	47 5/8	46 3/8	15 4/8	15 3/8	7	7	13	10	Paxson Lake, AK	Vern Mahoney	Vern Mahoney	1953	289
228 3/8	73 7/8	43 7/8	44 4/8	12	15 4/8	7 3/8	7 4/8	14	16	Nushagak River, AK	William C. Thorp	William C. Thorp	2003	289
228 2/8	66 6/8	44 1/8	44	16 3/8	15 4/8	8 5/8	8 1/8	15	14	Blair Lakes, AK	Jerry D. Redick	Jerry D. Redick	1979	291
228 2/8	66	49 2/8	48	14 1/8	14 5/8	8	8 1/8	11	14	Shotgun Creek, AK	James D. Chambers	James D. Chambers	1993	291
228 2/8	69 4/8	44 4/8	43 1/8	17 4/8	17 1/8	7 7/8	7 5/8	12	12	Kateel River, AK	Thomas O. Sandsmark	Thomas O. Sandsmark	2002	291

Score	Greatest Spread	Length of Palm R	Length of Palm L	Width of Palm R	Width of Palm L	Circ. R	Circ. L	Points R	Points L	Locality	Hunter	Owner	Date Killed	Rank
228 1/8	71 7/8	40 5/8	41 4/8	18 1/8	19 3/8	8 3/8	8 4/8	12	11	Mother Goose Lake, AK	Bert Klineburger	Bert Klineburger	1967	294
228 1/8	65 5/8	46	45 6/8	15 2/8	15	8 1/8	8	13	15	Rainy Pass, AK	W.J. Brule	W.J. Brule	1968	294
228 1/8	74 7/8	49 4/8	52	13	14 5/8	7 5/8	7 6/8	9	13	Jones River, AK	Dale J. Martin	Dale J. Martin	2000	294
228 1/8	64 7/8	44 7/8	47	17 7/8	20 6/8	7 3/8	7 3/8	12	13	Tay River, YT	William L. Cox	William L. Cox	2001	294
228	69 6/8	45	44	17	18	7 2/8	7 1/8	17	15	Rainy Pass, AK	J.W. Dixon	J.W. Dixon	1949	298
228	69 4/8	42 2/8	44 2/8	14 6/8	15 2/8	8 2/8	8 2/8	16	14	Talkeetna Mts., AK	Wayne C. Eubank	Wayne C. Eubank	1957	298
228	62 2/8	46 5/8	45 7/8	15 2/8	15 7/8	7 6/8	7 6/8	14	14	Alaska Pen., AK	M.E. Davis, Jr.	M.E. Davis, Jr.	1958	298
228	69	41 2/8	43 1/8	16 4/8	16 1/8	8 3/8	8 1/8	17	14	Mt. Susitna, AK	Peter W. Bading	Peter W. Bading	1963	298
228	67	47	45 4/8	15 6/8	20	7 6/8	8	12	12	Tonzona River, AK	Glen Miller	Glen Miller	1971	298
228	63 2/8	47 3/8	46 5/8	15 2/8	14 4/8	7 4/8	7 2/8	16	14	Koyukuk River, AK	Michael J. Harlin	Michael J. Harlin	1988	298
228	64 4/8	53 4/8	48 3/8	15 3/8	15	8 4/8	8 5/8	10	11	Cinder River, AK	John S. Pangborn	John S. Pangborn	1990	298
227 7/8	65 3/8	42 6/8	42 5/8	14 2/8	15	7 3/8	7 4/8	17	17	Savage River, AK	Jack V. Morkal	Thomas V. Scrivner	1966	305
227 7/8	65 3/8	46 2/8	49 1/8	17 1/8	18 2/8	7 7/8	8 2/8	10	10	Dog Salmon River, AK	John C. Davis	John C. Davis	1984	305
227 7/8	69 1/8	46	44 6/8	14 1/8	15	9	9 1/8	13	12	Koyuk River, AK	James R. Ryffel	James R. Ryffel	1986	305
227 7/8	71 1/8	44 5/8	46 4/8	13 3/8	13 1/8	8 3/8	8 1/8	14	13	Tonzona River, AK	Jim Fuchs	Jim Fuchs	1995	305
227 6/8	62 2/8	44 2/8	44 3/8	14	13 4/8	7	7 2/8	18	21	Soslota Creek, AK	Alex Cox	Alex Cox	1957	309
227 6/8	72 4/8	42	43	17	16 4/8	8 5/8	8 1/8	11	12	Nikabuna Lake, AK	James E. Curley	James E. Curley	1968	309
227 6/8	73 2/8	50 2/8	42 5/8	16 1/8	17 1/8	7 4/8	8 4/8	12	16	Martin River, AK	Jim Goodfellow, Jr.	Jim Goodfellow, Jr.	1977	309
227 6/8	61 2/8	49 3/8	45 2/8	17 6/8	22	9 5/8	9 2/8	11	11	Seward Pen., AK	Andrew Pellessier	Homer Westmark	1990	309
227 6/8	70 4/8	41 6/8	41 2/8	15 7/8	19 4/8	7 2/8	7	15	16	Kotzbue, AK	Hugh S. Wilson	Hugh S. Wilson	1992	309
227 6/8	66 6/8	48 6/8	49	15 3/8	14 2/8	8 4/8	8 4/8	9	10	Chekok Lake, AK	Don W. Noah	Don W. Noah	2000	309
227 6/8	61 6/8	45 7/8	46 3/8	15 3/8	15 7/8	8 6/8	8 6/8	13	15	Koyukuk River, AK	Ted R. Ramirez	Ted R. Ramirez	2001	309
227 5/8	72 1/8	41 4/8	41 1/8	18 4/8	18 2/8	8 4/8	8	11	10	Livengood, AK	James W. Keasling	James W. Keasling	1973	316
227 5/8	67 3/8	47 3/8	47 5/8	15 1/8	19 2/8	7 5/8	7 5/8	10	12	Alaska Pen., AK	Floyd F. Marrs	Floyd F. Marrs	1977	316
227 5/8	67 7/8	45	46 3/8	14 5/8	17 5/8	7 2/8	8	13	13	Susitna River, AK	Darryl G. Sanford	Darryl G. Sanford	1981	316
227 5/8	63 1/8	47 1/8	43 4/8	15 4/8	17 1/8	7 2/8	7 2/8	16	22	Divide Lake, NT	Joseph L. Bell	Joseph L. Bell	1986	316
227 5/8	74 5/8	43 3/8	43 4/8	18 7/8	17	8 3/8	8 2/8	9	8	Big River, AK	Adolf Hnup	Adolf Hnup	1994	316
227 5/8	64 3/8	44 5/8	50 3/8	15 3/8	15 3/8	7 6/8	7 7/8	14	16	Discovery Creek, AK	Joseph R. Weber	Joseph R. Weber	1998	316
227 4/8	75 4/8	39 6/8	45 4/8	17 4/8	20 4/8	7 6/8	8 2/8	12	11	Cinder River, AK	John Humphreys	John Humphreys	1963	322
227 4/8	56 2/8	48 4/8	46 6/8	21 4/8	19 2/8	8 6/8	8 5/8	13	11	Alaska Pen., AK	R.H. Platt	R.H. Platt	1965	322
227 4/8	71 2/8	51 4/8	46 4/8	14 5/8	14 1/8	8 4/8	8 4/8	10	9	Iliamna Lake, AK	Robert L. Hammond	Robert L. Hammond	1968	322
227 4/8	63	46	46 5/8	17	16 4/8	8 6/8	8 6/8	11	12	Kluane Lake, YT	Richard C. Wolff	Richard C. Wolff	1971	322
227 4/8	66	44 2/8	42 5/8	16 3/8	16 1/8	9 2/8	7 5/8	15	15	Elliott Lake, YT	Paul E. Wollenman	Paul E. Wollenman	1984	322
227 4/8	68 6/8	45 6/8	42 2/8	16 6/8	16 1/8	7 4/8	7 3/8	16	13	Harvey Lake, AK	David A. Coray	David A. Coray	1993	322
227 4/8	61 2/8	46 2/8	45 6/8	14 4/8	14 3/8	7 7/8	8	11	15	Granite Mt., AK	Michael A. Mendenhall	Michael A. Mendenhall	1998	322
227 4/8	69	49	44 3/8	15 4/8	16 6/8	9 4/8	9 5/8	15	16	Wheeler Creek, AK	Stephen R. Vogler	Stephen R. Vogler	1999	322
227 4/8	68 6/8	42 4/8	45 4/8	14 2/8	14	7 5/8	7 6/8	13	13	Squirrel River, AK	James E. Wolfe	James E. Wolfe	2000	322
227 3/8	69 6/8	47 4/8	44 4/8	13 6/8	16 6/8	8 1/8	8 2/8	13	16	Canyon Creek, AK	Jeremy S. Davis	Jeremy S. Davis	2002	322
227 3/8	69 1/8	44 2/8	44 6/8	15	14	8	7 7/8	12	14	Tok River, AK	Walter W. Kellogg	Walter W. Kellogg	1967	332
227 3/8	72 1/8	41 2/8	41 4/8	13 7/8	15 5/8	8 4/8	8	14	14	Big River, AK	Ronald W. Le Beaumont	Ronald W. Le Beaumont	1996	332
227 2/8	69 6/8	44 6/8	44 1/8	16	15 7/8	8 5/8	8 4/8	11	12	Salana River, AK	Jules R. Ashlock	Jules R. Ashlock	1961	334
227 2/8	68 2/8	44 4/8	44 4/8	20	15 1/8	7 2/8	8 1/8	10	12	Port Heiden, AK	Pressley R. Rankin, Jr.	Pressley R. Rankin, Jr.	1966	334
227 2/8	70 4/8	41 7/8	41 6/8	14 7/8	15 1/8	7 6/8	7 6/8	14	15	Aniak River, AK	Donn W. Ulrich	Donn W. Ulrich	1980	334
227 2/8	67 6/8	48	49 5/8	17	13 2/8	8 4/8	8 4/8	13	10	Bonnet Plume Lake, YT	A.H. Clise	A.H. Clise	1982	334
227 2/8	62 6/8	46 2/8	46 7/8	14 5/8	15 2/8	8 1/8	7 7/8	14	17	Kuskokwim River, AK	Dennis Harms	Dennis Harms	1994	334
227 1/8	74 3/8	46 1/8	44 4/8	14	15 1/8	8 1/8	8 1/8	10	11	Aniak Lake, AK	Michael L. Caverly	Michael L. Caverly	1982	339
227 1/8	61 1/8	51 5/8	49 5/8	14	15 1/8	7 4/8	7 3/8	13	12	Mulchatna River, AK	Brett L. Foster	Brett L. Foster	1997	339

ALASKA-YUKON MOOSE

Alces alces gigas

Score	Greatest Spread	Length of Palm R	L	Width of Palm R	L	Circumference of Beam at Smallest Place R	L	Number of Normal Points R	L	Locality	Hunter	Owner	Date Killed	Rank
227	69	47 2/8	45 3/8	15 2/8	14 1/8	8 5/8	8 4/8	11	12	Rainy Pass, AK	John A. Mueller	John A. Mueller	1966	341
227	67 4/8	45 1/8	44 3/8	16 3/8	16 1/8	8 3/8	8 2/8	11	11	Ugashik Lakes, AK	Robert Loch	Robert Loch	1967	341
227	68 2/8	48 4/8	46 6/8	15 6/8	18	8 1/8	7 7/8	9	12	Ugashik Lakes, AK	Emil Underberg	Emil Underberg	1967	341
227	64 4/8	52	46	15 4/8	14 7/8	7 3/8	7 4/8	13	13	Ketchumstuk, AK	C.O. Tweedy, J. Albright & W. Burnette, Sr.	C.O. Tweedy, Sr.	1968	341
227	66 2/8	44 4/8	44 7/8	20 7/8	17	7 7/8	8	14	11	Farewell Lake, AK	Duke of Penaranda	Duke of Penaranda	1969	341
227	62 4/8	47 6/8	47 4/8	14 4/8	14 5/8	7 2/8	7 3/8	13	13	South Macmillan River, YT	Louis T. Hill	Louis T. Hill	1973	341
227	69 2/8	48 4/8	43 1/8	14 5/8	14 6/8	8 1/8	8 1/8	13	15	Susitna River, AK	L.E. Wold & W.A. Vollendorf	L.E. Wold	1978	341
227	66 2/8	43	41 1/8	16 1/8	17	8 1/8	8 1/8	15	19	Wood River, AK	Wayne G. Elwood	Wayne G. Elwood	1986	341
227	67 4/8	45 2/8	45 4/8	14 5/8	17 6/8	7 7/8	8 7/8	12	14	Iliamna River, AK	David S. Haeg	David S. Haeg	1987	341
227	74 2/8	44 6/8	48 4/8	15 1/8	17 3/8	8 4/8	8 4/8	8	14	Alaska Pen., AK	John A. Schumacher	John A. Schumacher	1987	341
226 7/8	63 5/8	47 3/8	46 2/8	13 2/8	12	7 4/8	7 3/8	16	16	Wood River, AK	M.D. Gilchrist	M.D. Gilchrist	1958	351
226 7/8	63 7/8	41	43	17 7/8	17 2/8	8 2/8	8 7/8	16	15	Yakutat, AK	Ray E. Buckwalter	Ray E. Buckwalter	1963	351
226 7/8	61 7/8	47 3/8	44 7/8	16 7/8	16 4/8	7 3/8	7 3/8	16	14	Nessling Range, YT	Eric Pilkington	Eric Pilkington	1965	351
226 7/8	63 3/8	43 3/8	47	16 5/8	16 7/8	7 6/8	8	14	14	Eagle, AK	David G. Martini	David G. Martini	1969	351
226 7/8	67 7/8	48 4/8	43 2/8	12 2/8	16 6/8	7 4/8	7 4/8	18	17	Ray River, AK	William A. Galster	William A. Galster	1972	351
226 7/8	58 3/8	52 5/8	50 7/8	13 6/8	15 1/8	7 5/8	7 5/8	14	12	Camp Creek, AK	Michael E. Carter	Michael E. Carter	1982	351
226 7/8	66 5/8	47	48	15 3/8	19	7 6/8	7 5/8	10	11	Alaska Pen., AK	Michael Z. Abrams	Michael Z. Abrams	1989	351
226 6/8	67	41 2/8	49	20 6/8	19 1/8	9	7 4/8	13	12	Alaska Pen., AK	George A. Waldriff	George A. Waldriff	1962	358
226 6/8	68	45 6/8	46 6/8	14	15 3/8	9 6/8	9 5/8	12	10	Nabesna River, AK	Ross L. Phillippi, Jr.	Ross L. Phillippi, Jr.	1968	358
226 6/8	70 4/8	45 4/8	41 1/8	18	17 4/8	7 4/8	7 6/8	12	12	Alaska Pen., AK	Gerald F. McNamara	Mac's Taxidermy	1979	358
226 6/8	71 2/8	44 4/8	43	15 4/8	14 4/8	7 5/8	7 5/8	12	12	McGrath, AK	Bryan T. Patterson	Bryan T. Patterson	1999	358
226 5/8	61 3/8	44	44 4/8	16 4/8	17	8 1/8	8 1/8	15	14	Talkeetna Mts., AK	Lino F. Vannelli	Lino F. Vannelli	1979	362
226 5/8	68 5/8	44 5/8	46 1/8	13 4/8	13 4/8	8	7 7/8	14	13	Talkeetna Mts., AK	Wolfgang Porsche	Wolfgang Porsche	1981	362
226 5/8	72 5/8	46 4/8	43 5/8	16	15 5/8	7 6/8	8	13	10	King Salmon River, AK	Daniel E. Farr	Daniel E. Farr	1986	362
226 5/8	72 5/8	41	41 1/8	19	19 6/8	7 2/8	7	10	15	Fifteen Mile River, YT	Tammy L. Wagner	Tammy L. Wagner	1996	362
226 5/8	65 5/8	42 3/8	46 2/8	16 2/8	15 4/8	8 5/8	8 5/8	14	14	Manley Hot Springs, AK	Robert J. Fowler	Robert J. Fowler	1999	362
226 4/8	70 6/8	44 2/8	44 6/8	15 4/8	14 4/8	7 1/8	7 3/8	12	12	Wood River, AK	Dan Auld, Jr.	Dan Auld, Jr.	1949	367
226 4/8	68	43 7/8	54 3/8	11 4/8	12 2/8	7 7/8	8	16	17	Charley River, AK	G.P. Nehrbas	AK Natl. Bank	1951	367
226 4/8	63	45 4/8	47	15	14 2/8	8	7 7/8	14	15	Rainy Pass, AK	W.B. Macomber	W.B. Macomber	1953	367
226 4/8	62 6/8	46	43 7/8	18 3/8	16 2/8	7 5/8	7 7/8	12	13	Paxson Lake, AK	L.M. Cole	L.M. Cole	1958	367
226 4/8	65 4/8	46	44 2/8	16 6/8	15 2/8	8	8	13	14	Chugach Mts., AK	R.E. Kelley	R.E. Kelley	1961	367
226 4/8	64 2/8	48 3/8	49	15 7/8	15	7 6/8	7 6/8	12	10	Talkeetna Mts., AK	Harold Froehle	Harold Froehle	1965	367
226 4/8	60 6/8	48	50 1/8	15 6/8	16	7 1/8	7 2/8	12	12	Dog Salmon River, AK	H.H. Ahlemann	H.H. Ahlemann	1968	367
226 4/8	73 2/8	45 3/8	42 7/8	16 6/8	17 7/8	8	8 4/8	9	10	Koyukuk River, AK	Paul H. Ruesch	Paul H. Ruesch	1990	367
226 4/8	67 6/8	44	46 5/8	14 5/8	16 2/8	7 7/8	7 6/8	13	13	Nisling River, YT	Harmon D. Maxson	Harmon D. Maxson	1994	367
226 4/8	71 4/8	43	43	17 4/8	17 5/8	7	7	13	10	Alaska Pen., AK	Ben E. Meyers	Ben E. Meyers	1994	367

Score	Greatest Spread	Length of Palm R	Length of Palm L	Width of Palm R	Width of Palm L	Circ. Beam R	Circ. Beam L	Points R	Points L	Locality	Hunter	Owner	Date	Rank
226 4/8	68 2/8	42 7/8	46	15 6/8	17 5/8	7 4/8	7 4/8	13	14	Kuskokwim River, AK	Andrew R. Domas III	Andrew R. Domas III	1996	367
226 4/8	65	46	47 2/8	14 4/8	14 7/8	8 2/8	8 2/8	12	12	Fortymile River, AK	Alan Jubenville	Alan Jubenville	1998	367
226 3/8	69 5/8	46	41 2/8	21	19 4/8	7 6/8	7 5/8	10	14	Lake Louise, AK	H.C. Ragsdale II	H.C. Ragsdale II	1958	379
226 3/8	65 5/8	45 4/8	45 4/8	20 6/8	17 1/8	7 6/8	8 2/8	11	10	Alaska Pen., AK	Lit Ng	Lit Ng	1967	379
226 3/8	65 1/8	42 6/8	47	18	18	8 4/8	8 3/8	13	14	Naknek, AK	Noel Thompson	Noel Thompson	1971	379
226 3/8	71 1/8	43 6/8	42 2/8	18 2/8	17 6/8	6 5/8	7 1/8	11	11	Big River, AK	Karl L. Strecker	Karl L. Strecker	1996	379
226 3/8	61 5/8	41 6/8	42 6/8	15 3/8	17 5/8	7 3/8	7 2/8	18	19	Shale Lake, NT	Jerold B. Millendorf	Jerold B. Millendorf	1997	379
226 3/8	74 5/8	41 5/8	43 2/8	17 1/8	16 2/8	8	8 1/8	10	10	Tikchik Mt., AK	Norman D. Abell	Norman D. Abell	2003	379
226 2/8	69	48 3/8	44 6/8	13 6/8	12 7/8	7 4/8	7 7/8	16	14	Talkeetna Mts., AK	Toddie L. Wynne, Jr.	Toddie L. Wynne, Jr.	1958	385
226 2/8	68	47 1/8	44 5/8	16 3/8	13	7 5/8	7 4/8	14	14	Kenai Pen., AK	Ottokar J. Skal	Ottokar J. Skal	1963	385
226 2/8	65 6/8	44	43	14 4/8	14 4/8	8	8	15	15	Bonnet Plume Lake, YT	Ted T. Dabrowski	Ted T. Dabrowski	1965	385
226 2/8	67 6/8	45	43 7/8	12 7/8	13 5/8	8 4/8	8 4/8	14	14	Elliott Lake, YT	Collins F. Kellogg, Sr.	Collins F. Kellogg, Sr.	1992	385
226 2/8	68 2/8	40 7/8	41 2/8	16 3/8	18 5/8	6 6/8	6 7/8	15	18	Koyukuk River, AK	Mel J. Tenneson	Mel J. Tenneson	1993	385
226 1/8	70 7/8	44 4/8	46 4/8	14 2/8	14 6/8	7 7/8	8	11	12	King Salmon Creek, AK	Tiney Mitchell	Tiney Mitchell	1971	390
226	67 5/8	52	45	16 3/8	16 2/8	8	8 2/8	10	13	Talkeetna Mts., AK	Duane E. Stroupe	Duane E. Stroupe	1982	390
226	66	46	48 5/8	17 4/8	16	8	8	11	11	Alaska Pen., AK	Robert L. Wesner	Robert L. Wesner	1963	392
226	67 2/8	46 6/8	44 1/8	17 4/8	20 7/8	7 2/8	7 4/8	11	14	Fort Greely, AK	Jerry L. Bailey	Jerry L. Bailey	1970	392
226	58 2/8	46 5/8	46 3/8	18 6/8	18 4/8	8	8	11	11	Black Lake, AK	John M. Behan	John M. Behan	1972	392
226	64 4/8	47	45 4/8	14 4/8	16 6/8	7 6/8	7 6/8	13	14	Dillinger River, AK	Jerry E. Romanowski	Jerry E. Romanowski	1976	392
226	65	44 4/8	47 3/8	13 4/8	14 1/8	8	8 1/8	15	17	Alagnak River, AK	John H. Webster	John H. Webster	1985	392
226	60 2/8	48 6/8	46 4/8	16 3/8	17 1/8	8 2/8	8 1/8	13	13	Ketchumstuk Mt., AK	Donald P. Chase	Donald P. Chase	1993	392
226	63 2/8	47 6/8	45 4/8	13 2/8	18 2/8	8 5/8	8 4/8	11	13	Tsiu River, AK	Frank L. Fackovec	Frank L. Fackovec	1994	392
226	68 2/8	44	48 2/8	13 2/8	14 4/8	7 5/8	7 6/8	15	14	Willow Handle Lake, NT	M.R. James	M.R. James	1995	392
226	57	48 2/8	48	15 7/8	14 7/8	8 6/8	8 6/8	13	13	Koyukuk River, AK	Jack L. Brickner	Jack L. Brickner	1999	392
226	67	44 1/8	47 6/8	16	18 6/8	7 3/8	7 5/8	12	14	Innoko River, AK	John J. Cronin III	John J. Cronin III	1999	392
226	65	49	49 4/8	15 1/8	17 3/8	8 4/8	8 3/8	9	10	Cantwell, AK	Monson Nicklie, Jr.	Monson Nicklie, Jr.	2001	392
225 7/8	68 5/8	44 4/8	43 1/8	15 1/8	13 2/8	8 2/8	8 4/8	14	14	Wrangell Mts., AK	Lee Chambers	Lee Chambers	1969	403
225 7/8	68 1/8	50 7/8	45 2/8	14 1/8	14 4/8	7 6/8	8	12	11	Melozitna River, AK	John E. Stenehjem	John E. Stenehjem	1985	403
225 7/8	66 1/8	46 1/8	47	19 1/8	15 3/8	7 1/8	7 1/8	12	12	White Mts., AK	Vince A. Osborne	Vince A. Osborne	2002	403
225 6/8	76 6/8	46 2/8	44 1/8	14 2/8	14 2/8	8	8 1/8	10	9	Alaska Pen., AK	Bill Rappley	Herman J. Kulhanek	1961	406
225 6/8	66 4/8	46 4/8	43 5/8	13 3/8	16	9 4/8	8 4/8	15	14	Alaska Range, AK	Don Johnson	Don Johnson	1963	406
225 6/8	63 4/8	46 6/8	45 6/8	18 7/8	18 2/8	7 3/8	7 2/8	12	10	Alaska Range, AK	J.B. Copeland, Jr.	J.B. Copeland, Jr.	1968	406
225 6/8	57 6/8	46 6/8	47 6/8	14 2/8	16 4/8	8 2/8	8 3/8	18	18	St. George Creek, AK	Joseph G. Gaillard	Joseph G. Gaillard	1968	406
225 6/8	70 2/8	46 4/8	45	15 5/8	15 7/8	8 1/8	8 2/8	10	10	Farewell Station, AK	Daniel M. DiBenedetto, Sr.	Daniel M. DiBenedetto, Sr.	1973	406
225 6/8	75 2/8	43 2/8	38 5/8	14 3/8	15 2/8	8 2/8	7 1/8	14	14	Kenai Pen., AK	Willi Hilpert	Willi Hilpert	1973	406
225 6/8	66	46 7/8	46	13 4/8	16	8 3/8	8	12	10	Upper Mulchatna River, AK	O.B. Beard III	O.B. Beard III	1974	406
225 6/8	65 4/8	40 1/8	41	21 4/8	18 2/8	7 3/8	7 2/8	15	17	Spring Creek, AK	William D. Phifer	William D. Phifer	1975	406
225 6/8	67 2/8	43 4/8	42	15 4/8	16	8 6/8	8 6/8	13	13	Glennallen, AK	Eugene E. Wheeler	Eugene E. Wheeler	1981	406
225 6/8	67 2/8	43 4/8	44 4/8	17 2/8	18 2/8	8 4/8	8 4/8	10	12	Kugururok River, AK	H.I.H. Prince Abdorreza Pahlavi	Abdorreza Pahlavi	1988	406
225 6/8	65	44 4/8	43 5/8	16 1/8	16 4/8	7 6/8	7 5/8	13	17	Ogilvie Mts., YT	George F. Dennis, Jr.	George F. Dennis, Jr.	1997	406
225 6/8	67 2/8	46 6/8	45 2/8	13 1/8	12 7/8	8 1/8	8 1/8	15	13	White River, AK	Dave L. Hanson	Dave Hanson	1998	406
225 5/8	66 7/8	45	42 5/8	15 1/8	18 6/8	8 2/8	8 2/8	14	14	Unknown	Unknown	Gift of C.H. Mackay to NCHH	PR 1951	418
225 5/8	72 3/8	44	43 4/8	16	21 2/8	7 1/8	7 1/8	11	10	Port Heiden, AK	Harold Sill	Harold Sill	1964	418
225 5/8	65 5/8	45 4/8	46 4/8	16 2/8	14 7/8	7 5/8	7 5/8	13	12	High Lake, AK	Glen E. Park	Glen E. Park	1965	418
225 5/8	70 1/8	41 1/8	43	19 1/8	17 1/8	8	8 1/8	13	13	Alaska Range, AK	Robert Pinamont	R. Pinamont & J. Albright	1972	418

ALASKA-YUKON MOOSE
Alces alces gigas

Score	Greatest Spread	Length of Palm R	L	Width of Palm R	L	Circumference of Beam at Smallest Place R	L	Number of Normal Points R	L	Locality	Hunter	Owner	Date Killed	Rank
225 5/8	69 3/8	44 7/8	41 6/8	17 7/8	20 3/8	8	8 5/8	11	11	Farewell, AK	G. Jack Tankersley	G. Jack Tankersley	1975	418
225 5/8	66 3/8	44	49 1/8	15 2/8	13 6/8	8 3/8	8 3/8	14	14	Chandalar River, AK	William O. Dudley	William O. Dudley	1980	418
225 5/8	66 5/8	44 3/8	47 7/8	16	15 5/8	8	8 1/8	14	12	Koyukuk River, AK	Michael S. Berg	Michael S. Berg	1997	418
225 5/8	65 5/8	46 2/8	44 5/8	15 5/8	15 2/8	8 1/8	9	15	12	Moody Creek, AK	Robert J. Kaseta	Robert J. Kaseta	1997	418
225 5/8	69 3/8	45 6/8	46 5/8	15 1/8	17 3/8	7 7/8	7 6/8	10	12	Koyukuk River, AK	Paul B. Cochran	Paul B. Cochran	2003	418
225 4/8	68 4/8	41 4/8	41	15 4/8	18 4/8	8	8	14	15	Alaska Pen., AK	Dolores F. Jones	Dolores F. Jones	1958	427
225 4/8	71	44 2/8	46 6/8	15 4/8	18 3/8	7 4/8	7 7/8	10	10	Stony River, AK	Leland R. McFarland	Leland R. McFarland	1969	427
225 4/8	66 6/8	47 2/8	48 3/8	14 1/8	16 1/8	8 2/8	8	10	14	Blackstone River, YT	Marc Korting	Marc Korting	1970	427
225 4/8	66 4/8	42 6/8	43 1/8	14 6/8	13 4/8	7 5/8	7 2/8	18	16	Cub Lake, AK	William McNamara	William McNamara	1979	427
225 4/8	65 6/8	42 5/8	43 1/8	16 1/8	16 5/8	7 1/8	7 2/8	15	14	Caribou Hills, AK	Bill H. Baucum	Bill Baucum	1996	427
225 4/8	60 6/8	44 2/8	48 5/8	16 4/8	15 5/8	8 4/8	8 7/8	14	16	MacMillan River, YT	Warren L. Strickland	Warren L. Strickland	1998	427
225 3/8	70 3/8	45	45	16 3/8	16 4/8	7 5/8	8	10	10	Lake Clark, AK	George W. Robinson	George W. Robinson	1965	433
225 3/8	65 3/8	43 3/8	41 4/8	15	15 7/8	7 6/8	7 4/8	18	16	Tustumena Lake, AK	Harley E. Johnson	Harley E. Johnson	1983	433
225 3/8	69 7/8	43 1/8	43 1/8	15	15 4/8	6 5/8	6 6/8	13	14	Stony River, AK	David S. Haeg	David S. Haeg	1997	433
225 3/8	66 3/8	45 1/8	44	14 7/8	14 7/8	7 5/8	7 7/8	13	15	Rainy Pass, AK	Michael Rivard	Michael H. Rivard	1997	433
225 3/8	68 1/8	45 6/8	43 6/8	15 6/8	13 6/8	8 2/8	8 1/8	13	13	Teklanika River, AK	Roger D. Speer	Roger D. Speer	2000	433
225 3/8	70 1/8	40 7/8	44	15 4/8	14 4/8	7 7/8	8	11	11	Selawik Hills, AK	Daniel A. Marks	Daniel A. Marks	2001	433
225 2/8	66 2/8	43 5/8	43	17	16 2/8	8 4/8	8 2/8	12	12	Wernecke Mt., YT	David V. Collis	David V. Collis	1984	439
225 2/8	65	39 6/8	43 4/8	22 1/8	19 2/8	9 1/8	10 7/8	16	12	Dog Salmon River, AK	Marvin D. Fuller	Marvin D. Fuller	1988	439
225 2/8	63	48	45 3/8	19 4/8	18 3/8	8 3/8	8 3/8	9	12	King Salmon, AK	Bob L. Chain, Jr.	Bob L. Chain, Jr.	1995	439
225 2/8	66 6/8	46	43 5/8	15 6/8	16 4/8	8 3/8	8 3/8	12	12	Yanert, AK	Christopher J. Davis	Christopher J. Davis	1997	439
225 1/8	64 7/8	48 3/8	46 3/8	16 1/8	17 5/8	7 5/8	7 5/8	10	10	Alaska Pen., AK	James A. Ford	James A. Ford	1970	443
225 1/8	69 3/8	40 7/8	44	14 6/8	13 6/8	8 2/8	8 3/8	15	16	Alaska Range, AK	Richard C. Beall	Richard C. Beall	1978	443
225 1/8	73 1/8	43 4/8	44 5/8	17 4/8	15 6/8	8 4/8	8 2/8	12	11	Alagnak River, AK	J. & J. Hertel	J & J Hertel	1987	443
225 1/8	61 5/8	47 6/8	47 2/8	15 4/8	15 7/8	7	7	12	13	June Lake, NT	Bertha E. Thompson	Bertha E. Thompson	1987	443
225 1/8	62 5/8	46 2/8	53 5/8	17 7/8	18 4/8	8 1/8	8 2/8	9	10	King Salmon River, AK	Michaelangelo P. Ripepi	Michaelangelo P. Ripepi	1989	443
225 1/8	67 5/8	48	46 3/8	13 6/8	15 4/8	7 5/8	7 6/8	11	14	Aniak River, AK	Michael Williams	Michael Williams	1999	443
225	66 4/8	45 6/8	43 5/8	15 2/8	13	8 6/8	8 5/8	14	15	Kenai Pen., AK	Walter R. Peterson	Walter R. Peterson	1935	449
225	74	41	41 2/8	17	18 2/8	7 7/8	7 4/8	17	11	Livengood, AK	Bill Thomas	Univ. of Alaska	1952	449
225	65 2/8	40 7/8	41 2/8	15 4/8	17 4/8	8	8 1/8	16	20	Nelchina, AK	Jack D. Putnam	Denver Mus. Nat. Hist.	1961	449
225	65 4/8	50	49	15	14 7/8	7 7/8	7 7/8	8	9	Alaska Range, AK	Basil C. Bradbury	Basil C. Bradbury	1963	449
225	72	45	47 5/8	14	16 1/8	7 4/8	7 6/8	10	15	Farewell Lake, AK	Lyman Strong	Lyman Strong	1965	449
225	58	47 4/8	45 7/8	14 4/8	17 5/8	8 3/8	8 5/8	14	17	Tok, AK	Bruce Dodson	Bruce Dodson	1974	449
225	70	44	44 1/8	13 1/8	15 2/8	8 7/8	10 2/8	12	14	Talkeetna Mts., AK	Eberhart Herzog	Eberhart Herzog	1981	449
225	61 2/8	46 2/8	46 1/8	15 3/8	15 7/8	7 4/8	7 3/8	12	17	Pelly River, YT	Glen H. Taylor	Glen H. Taylor	1985	449
225	64 2/8	44 4/8	46 4/8	19	16 4/8	7 3/8	7 3/8	12	13	Koyukuk River, AK	Alan L. Earnest	Alan L. Earnest	1998	449
225	68	46 2/8	46	15 5/8	15	7 6/8	7 4/8	11	10	Squirrel River, AK	David F. Witmer	David F. Witmer	2000	449
224 7/8	71 5/8	48 1/8	42 2/8	16	17 3/8	7 3/8	7 3/8	12	11	Mt. Katmai, AK	Morris Roberts	Morris Roberts	1951	459

Score	Spread							Points		Locality	Hunter	Owner	Date	Rank
224 7/8	61 7/8	48 1/8	47 7/8	14 6/8	14 1/8	7 5/8	7 4/8	12	13	Ugashik Narrows, AK	Wayne Ewing	Wayne Ewing	1966	459
224 7/8	67 3/8	45 6/8	45 3/8	17 1/8	16 6/8	7 5/8	7 5/8	9	12	King Salmon, AK	Albert B. Fay	Albert B. Fay	1969	459
224 7/8	67 1/8	45 2/8	46 7/8	14 3/8	14 6/8	8 4/8	8 2/8	11	13	Koyukuk River, AK	Dennis E. Reiner	Dennis E. Reiner	1973	459
224 7/8	68 5/8	42 6/8	43 2/8	14 4/8	14 4/8	8 1/8	7 7/8	13	17	Wind River, YT	Chris P. Morton	Chris P. Morton	1997	459
224 6/8	70 2/8	41 4/8	45	17 4/8	18 4/8	7 4/8	7 4/8	14	11	Farewell Lake, AK	Gust Pabst	Gust Pabst	1963	464
224 6/8	74 2/8	41 6/8	42 6/8	19 2/8	16 2/8	7 5/8	7 3/8	12	13	Alaska Pen., AK	Charles Bonnici	Charles Bonnici	1969	464
224 6/8	58 6/8	46	47	15	15	8 4/8	8 5/8	14	14	Cantwell, AK	Gene Sivell	Gene Sivell	1970	464
224 6/8	61 6/8	46 4/8	44 2/8	20 1/8	20 1/8	9 5/8	9 1/8	9	9	Lower Ugashik Lake, AK	Hugo Klinger	Hugo Klinger	1972	464
224 6/8	69 4/8	44 1/8	44 1/8	16 6/8	16 6/8	8 4/8	8 4/8	12	11	Little Tok River, AK	Edward J. Janus	Edward J. Janus	1974	464
224 6/8	62 6/8	47 3/8	46	19	15 4/8	7 4/8	7 4/8	13	14	Earn Lake, YT	Julian D. Weiant	Julian D. Weiant	1978	464
224 6/8	64 6/8	45 6/8	48 6/8	15	15 6/8	8 2/8	8 2/8	11	11	Stony River, AK	Bradford W. Reddick	Bradford W. Reddick	1993	464
224 6/8	64 4/8	47 4/8	45 5/8	15 1/8	15 2/8	7 4/8	7 3/8	12	12	Blackstone River, YT	Jerry Stefanitsis	Jerry Stefanitsis	1993	464
224 6/8	68 4/8	46 5/8	43 6/8	17 5/8	15 6/8	7 5/8	7 5/8	16	16	Koyukuk River, AK	Beattie J. Smith	Beattie J. Smith	1994	464
224 6/8	62 6/8	45 4/8	45 5/8	15 6/8	15 4/8	7 7/8	8	13	13	Post Lake, AK	Leonard H. Wurman	Leonard H. Wurman	1994	464
224 6/8	71	43 2/8	43 6/8	15 4/8	16 2/8	8 3/8	8 1/8	11	10	Koktuli River, AK	Alfred J. Ogella	Alfred J. Ogella	1994	464
224 6/8	67 6/8	47 4/8	48 1/8	20 4/8	13 5/8	7 3/8	8 3/8	13	11	Chilchitna River, AK	Mike Henry	Mike Henry	1996	464
224 6/8	68 1/8	45 1/8	47 2/8	16 4/8	18 7/8	9 1/8	8 5/8	13	13	Port Heiden, AK	Jon G. Koshell	Jon G. Koshell	1999	464
224 5/8	67 7/8	45 5/8	41 6/8	19 3/8	17 4/8	8 2/8	8 2/8	8	13	Fifteenmile River, YT	Joel B. Benner	Joel B. Benner	1964	476
224 5/8	72 1/8	40	38 1/8	17 4/8	20 4/8	6 7/8	6 5/8	14	12	Yuki River, AK	Steven B. Spaulding	Steven B. Spaulding	1986	476
224 5/8	65 1/8	44 4/8	40 3/8	20 6/8	23 2/8	8 3/8	7 7/8	12	13	Kandik River, YT	Charles W. Brammer	Charles W. Brammer	1986	476
224 5/8	66 6/8	40 4/8	50 4/8	23 2/8	15 3/8	8 2/8	8 3/8	7	11	Bering Glacier, AK	Steven L. Folkman	Steven L. Folkman	1988	476
224 5/8	68 3/8	44 5/8	46 5/8	15 2/8	14 2/8	8 2/8	8 2/8	11	13	Iliamna Lake, AK	William F. Rode	William F. Rode	1991	476
224 5/8	65 6/8	45 3/8	45	14 2/8	15 5/8	7 2/8	7 3/8	13	12	Bonnet Plume Lake, YT	Chris Brewer	Chris Brewer	1993	476
224 5/8	62 5/8	47 3/8	47	15 5/8	13 4/8	8 4/8	8	11	11	Bonnet Plume Lake, YT	Jerry E. Mason	Jerry E. Mason	1994	476
224 5/8	63 6/8	49 6/8	48 5/8	13 4/8	16 2/8	8 5/8	8 3/8	13	13	Mountain River, NT	Jerome N. Ida	Jerome N. Ida	2001	476
224 5/8	68 4/8	45	45	16 2/8	17 6/8	8 1/8	7 7/8	10	13	Aishihik Lake, YT	C. Don Steepleton	C. Don Steepleton	2002	476
224 4/8	67	46 3/8	44 5/8	17 6/8	14 6/8	8 3/8	8 5/8	9	11	Cook's Inlet, AK	Dall Dew	Colorado Outdoor Journal	PR 1898	486
224 4/8	67	43 6/8	44 2/8	14 2/8	15	7 6/8	7 6/8	15	14	Unknown	Unknown	Buckhorn Mus. & Saloon, Ltd.	PR 1957	486
224 4/8	62	44 3/8	44 3/8	15	15 6/8	7 7/8	7 7/8	14	16	Fog Lakes, AK	C.A. Schwope	C.A. Schwope	1960	486
224 4/8	68 2/8	45 1/8	43 7/8	18	14 2/8	8 1/8	8	14	12	Alaska Pen., AK	James E. McFarland	James E. McFarland	1967	486
224 4/8	71 4/8	41 6/8	46 4/8	19 5/8	18 4/8	7 3/8	7 2/8	9	9	Alaska Range, AK	William M. Harrington	William M. Harrington	1970	486
224 4/8	66 6/8	46 5/8	48 5/8	16 2/8	18 4/8	7 4/8	7 4/8	9	14	Koyukuk River, AK	Philip C. Wahlbom	Philip C. Wahlbom	1976	486
224 4/8	63 6/8	45 2/8	45	16 4/8	16 2/8	7 7/8	7 1/8	12	13	Hess River, YT	Richard B. Limbach	Richard B. Limbach	1985	486
224 4/8	65 6/8	44 4/8	47	17 3/8	16 7/8	8	8	13	10	Iliamna Lake, AK	Norbert A. Prokosch	Norbert A. Prokosch	1986	486
224 4/8	57	45 7/8	46 5/8	19 4/8	20	7 7/8	8	10	15	Caribou Hills, AK	Dan K. Presley	Dan K. Presley	2001	486
224 4/8	67 5/8	48 3/8	49 5/8	12 2/8	12 2/8	8	8	10	12	Nowitna River, AK	Jeffrey H. Bushke	Jeffrey H. Bushke	2003	486
224 3/8	58 1/8	44 3/8	48 7/8	13 1/8	16 5/8	8 1/8	8 1/8	14	19	Kenai Pen., AK	Carole Colclasure	Carole Colclasure	1962	496
224 3/8	71 7/8	47 6/8	43 2/8	19 6/8	16	8 4/8	8 4/8	12	11	Alaska Pen., AK	Alice J. Landreth	Alice J. Landreth	1967	496
224 3/8	61 5/8	47 3/8	46 4/8	18 4/8	14 6/8	8 2/8	8 2/8	14	15	Kenai Pen., AK	Gloria Reiter	Gloria Reiter	1969	496
224 3/8	67 7/8	44 4/8	44 7/8	13 5/8	13 5/8	8	7 3/8	12	11	Farewell Lake, AK	Arthur W. Dages	Arthur W. Dages	1993	496
224 2/8	70 4/8	45	46 6/8	14 7/8	15	7 3/8	7 1/8	11	10	Alligator Lake, YT	Arthur C. Popham, Jr.	Arthur C. Popham, Jr.	1950	496
224 2/8	63 6/8	43 3/8	43 5/8	17 4/8	14 3/8	8 6/8	8 7/8	14	16	Yukon	J.R. Gray	J.R. Gray	1951	500
224 2/8	61 3/8	48 1/8	48 6/8	13 3/8	13 6/8	8 1/8	8	12	12	Susitna River, AK	Donald E. Wicks	Donald E. Wicks	1963	500
224 2/8	60 7/8	42 6/8	46 2/8	16 4/8	13 6/8	7 6/8	7 6/8	15	12	Post Lake, AK	Wulf Nosofsky	Wulf Nosofsky	1965	500
224 2/8	58	49 4/8	49 4/8	17 3/8	17 3/8	8 7/8	8 6/8	11	12	Wood River Mts., AK	F. Jay Riley	F. Jay Riley	1987	500
224 2/8	62 2/8	48 4/8	47	16 1/8	15 5/8	7 7/8	7 3/8	13	13	Tatonduk River, YT	Thomas Covert	Thomas Covert	1992	500
224 2/8	69 4/8	45 4/8	42 3/8	15 1/8	15 6/8	8 1/8	7 7/8	12	14	Koyukuk River, AK	Mary S. Hubbard McIsaac	Mary S. Hubbard McIsaac	1995	500

ALASKA-YUKON MOOSE
Alces alces gigas

Score	Greatest Spread	Length of Palm R	L	Width of Palm R	L	Circumference of Beam at Smallest Place R	L	Number of Normal Points R	L	Locality	Hunter	Owner	Date Killed	Rank
224 2/8	68 4/8	43 6/8	48 3/8	18 2/8	16 3/8	7 6/8	7 7/8	10	15	Ogilvie Mts, YT	Edwin A. Lewis	Edwin A. Lewis	1996	500
224 2/8	63 4/8	49 6/8	49 3/8	14 4/8	13 5/8	7 3/8	7 5/8	11	10	Iliamna Lake, AK	Craig L. Halstead	Craig L. Halstead	1997	500
224 2/8	62	46 2/8	45 5/8	17	18 5/8	8 5/8	8 4/8	11	10	Koyukuk River, AK	Steven C. Tressler	Steven C. Tressler	1997	500
224 1/8	70 4/8	46 6/8	48 1/8	13 6/8	16	7 4/8	7 3/8	9	12	Alaska Pen., AK	Gary J. Pals	Gary J. Pals	2001	500
224 1/8	67 3/8	44 6/8	46 6/8	18 7/8	15 6/8	8 4/8	7 7/8	10	10	Telaquana Lake, AK	Paul G. Curren	Paul G. Curren	1960	511
224 1/8	68 7/8	47 2/8	44	14 7/8	15 2/8	7 7/8	7 6/8	11	12	Port Salmon, AK	Graf Scheel-Plessen	Graf Scheel-Plessen	1965	511
224 1/8	68 7/8	45 4/8	44 6/8	15 2/8	13 1/8	7 6/8	7 6/8	14	12	Bear Lake, AK	Earl K. Wahl, Jr.	Earl K. Wahl, Jr.	1987	511
224 1/8	61 7/8	49 3/8	48 7/8	12 6/8	13	7 4/8	7 5/8	12	12	Fifteenmile River, YT	Larry Lee	Larry Lee	1990	511
224 1/8	55 7/8	45 6/8	47 4/8	15 4/8	15 4/8	7 7/8	7 7/8	16	15	Mulchatna River, AK	Timothy D. Smithen	Timothy D. Smithen	1995	511
224	65 6/8	43 2/8	47 1/8	18 5/8	17 1/8	7 6/8	7 6/8	11	13	Alaska Range, AK	L.J. Pfeifer	L.J. Pfeifer	1977	516
224	66 6/8	42 6/8	44 4/8	15 6/8	14 5/8	7 2/8	7 3/8	15	14	Franklin Creek, AK	Vernon K. Lucas	Vernon K. Lucas	1994	516
224	65 4/8	45 3/8	53	14 7/8	14 2/8	7 5/8	7 7/8	12	12	Iliamna Lake, AK	Zane Streater	Zane Streater	1995	516
224	70 2/8	42 3/8	47	15 5/8	17	9 1/8	8 7/8	14	10	Aniak, AK	Larry W. Goehring	Larry W. Goehring	1997	516
244 6/8*	78 2/8	45 3/8	46	16 1/8	17 4/8	7 6/8	8	14	15	Tsiu River, AK	John T. Portemont	John T. Portemont	1998	
240 6/8*	72 4/8	44 6/8	46 5/8	19 4/8	16 4/8	7 7/8	8 2/8	17	15	Ogilvie River, YT	John L. Croft	John L. Croft	2002	
240 6/8*	70 6/8	48 2/8	48 7/8	18 6/8	19 4/8	8	8 3/8	10	10	Becharof Lake, AK	Chad A. Reel	Chad A. Reel	2002	

* Final score is subject to revision by additional verifying measurements.

CATEGORY
ALASKA-YUKON MOOSE

SCORE
244-6/8

HUNTER
JOHN T. PORTEMONT

LOCATION
TSIU RIVER, ALASKA

DATE OF KILL
SEPTEMBER 1998

CATEGORY
ALASKA-YUKON MOOSE

SCORE
241

HUNTER
DAWSON H. COLBY, JR.

LOCATION
ANVIL RANGE,
YUKON TERRITORY

DATE OF KILL
AUGUST 2000

CATEGORY
ALASKA-YUKON MOOSE

SCORE
237-6/8

HUNTER
ROBERT M. STACY (LEFT)

LOCATION
KENAI PENINSULA, ALASKA

DATE OF KILL
SEPTEMBER 2003

SCORE
225-1/8

HUNTER
MICHAEL WILLLIAMS
(BELOW LEFT)

LOCATION
ANIAK RIVER, ALASKA

DATE OF KILL
SEPTEMBER 1999

613

CATEGORY
ALASKA-YUKON MOOSE

SCORE
228-2/8

HUNTER
THOMAS O. SANDSMARK

LOCATION
KATEEL RIVER, ALASKA

DATE OF KILL
SEPTEMBER 2002

CATEGORY
ALASKA-YUKON MOOSE

SCORE
225-3/8

HUNTER
DANIEL A. MARKS

LOCATION
SELAWIK HILLS, ALASKA

DATE OF KILL
SEPTEMBER 2001

CATEGORY
ALASKA-YUKON MOOSE

SCORE
225-3/8

HUNTER
MICHAEL H. RIVARD

LOCATION
RAINY PASS, ALASKA

DATE OF KILL
SEPTEMBER 1997

SCORE
225-2/8

HUNTER
CHRISTOPHER J. DAVIS
(BELOW)

LOCATION
YANERT, ALASKA

DATE OF KILL
SEPTEMBER 1997

CATEGORY
ALASKA-YUKON MOOSE

SCORE
230

HUNTER
DEAN L. BENNER (ABOVE)

LOCATION
OGILVIE RIVER, YUKON TERRITORY

DATE OF KILL
OCTOBER 2002

SHIRAS MOOSE
WORLD'S RECORD

TROPHY INFO

RANK
World's Record

SCORE
205 4/8

LOCATION
Green River Lake, WY

HUNTER
John M. Oakley

OWNER
Jackson Hole Museum

DATE KILLED
1952

The World's Record Shiras moose (*Alces alces shirasi*) was taken by John M. Oakley of Cheyenne. Shot during the 1952 season near Green River Lake, Wyoming, this specimen scored 205-4/8 at the national competition.

This Shiras moose was most likely stripping the delicate leaves from willow tips when Oakley spotted the reflection of the antlers as he made his way into the Gypsum Creek area of the Wind River Range. Because it can be difficult to judge the size of antlers against the immensity of a bull, Oakley did not know right off that the rack was of record size.

Having lived in Wyoming, Oakley had a healthy respect for the unpredictability of this animal, which is capable of moving extremely quickly. Bull's have been known to utilize their antlers as weapons, as well as symbols of intimidation.

Moose do not have strong vision but do possess extraordinary senses of smell and hearing. Making his stalk, Oakley had to be weary of the unpredictable gusts of wind that rush through the surrounding mountains.

Although they are the largest big game animal in North America, moose are usually taken down without too much difficulty. However, the bone in a moose's shoulder blade is heavy enough to deflect a bullet. Oakley had to shoot the powerful moose four times with 180-grain Speer bullets in .270 caliber hand loads.

The outcome was a new World's Record that edged ahead of the former record, taken by A.E. Chandler of Casper, by the narrow margin of 3/8 of a point. Mounted and initially owned by J.L. Nevins and H.A. Yocum of Frontier Taxidermists, the prized moose was later sold to the Jackson Hole Museum, Jackson, Wyoming. ■

BOUNDARY FOR SHIRAS MOOSE

Shiras moose includes trophies taken in Colorado, Idaho, Montana, Utah, Washington, and Wyoming.

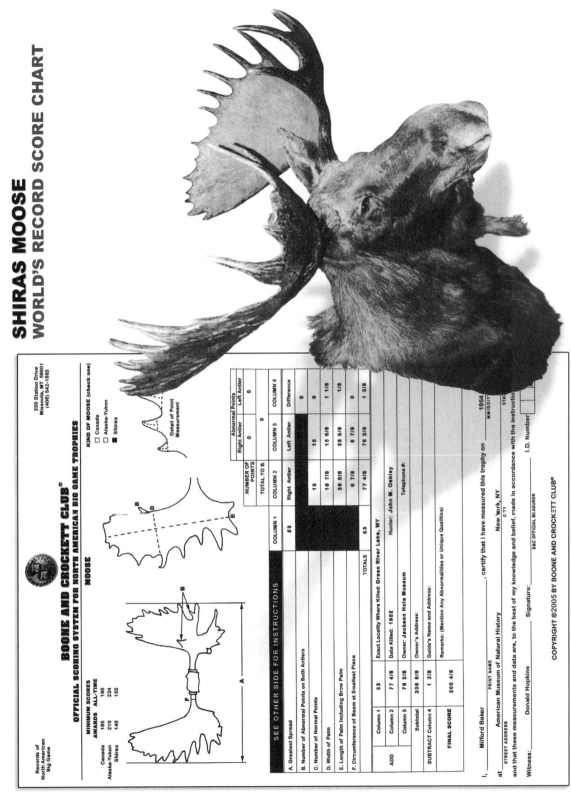

Records of North American Big Game

BOONE AND CROCKETT CLUB®

250 Station Drive
Missoula, MT 59801
(406) 542-1888

OFFICIAL SCORING SYSTEM FOR NORTH AMERICAN BIG GAME TROPHIES

MOOSE

MINIMUM SCORES

	AWARDS	ALL-TIME
Canada	185	195
Alaska-Yukon	210	224
Shiras	140	155

KIND OF MOOSE (check one)
- ☐ Canada
- ☐ Alaska-Yukon
- ■ Shiras

Detail of Point Measurement

		Abnormal Points	
		Right Antler	Left Antler
		0	0

	NUMBER OF POINTS		
	TOTAL TO B.		0

SEE OTHER SIDE FOR INSTRUCTIONS	COLUMN 1	COLUMN 2	COLUMN 3	COLUMN 4
		Right Antler	Left Antler	Difference
A. Greatest Spread	53			
B. Number of Abnormal Points on Both Antlers			0	0
C. Number of Normal Points		15	15	0
D. Width of Palm		16 7/8	15 6/8	1 1/8
E. Length of Palm Including Brow Palm		38 6/8	38 5/8	1/8
F. Circumference of Beam at Smallest Place		8 7/8	8 7/8	0
TOTALS	53	77 4/8	76 2/8	1 2/8

ADD	Column 1	53
	Column 2	77 4/8
	Column 3	76 2/8
	Subtotal	206 6/8
SUBTRACT Column 4		1 2/8
	FINAL SCORE	**205 4/8**

Exact Locality Where Killed: **Green River Lake, WY**

Date Killed: **1952**   Hunter: **John M. Oakley**

Owner: **Jackson Hole Museum**   Telephone #:

Owner's Address:

Guide's Name and Address:

Remarks: (Mention Any Abnormalities or Unique Qualities)

I, **Milford Baker** , certify that I have measured this trophy on **1954**
    PRINT NAME   MM/DD/Y

at **American Museum of Natural History**   **New York, NY**   STA
  STREET ADDRESS   CITY

and that these measurements and data are, to the best of my knowledge and belief, made in accordance with the instructio

Witness: **Donald Hopkins**   Signature: B&C OFFICIAL MEASURER   I.D. Number

COPYRIGHT ©2005 BY BOONE AND CROCKETT CLUB®

NUMBER 2 — 205-1/8 POINTS
ARTHUR E. CHANDLER — 1946

NUMBER 5 — 199 POINTS
AMOS E. HAND — 1946

NUMBER 3 — 200-3/8 POINTS
ALDON L. HALE — 1981

NUMBER 1 — 205-4/8 POINTS
JOHN M. OAKLEY — 1952

NUMBER 4 — 199-3/8 POINTS
REED T. FISHER — 1957

618

NUMBER 6 — 196-5/8 POINTS
BRAD B. SCHWINDT — 1997

NUMBER 7 — 195-5/8 POINTS
ALFRED C. BEROL — 1933
PHOTO NOT AVAILABLE

NUMBER 10 — 193 POINTS
RICHARD K. SMITH — 2000

NUMBER 8 — 195-1/8 POINTS
C.M. SCHMAUCH — 1952

NUMBER 9 — 194-4/8 POINTS
JACK A. ANDERSON — 1995

DETAIL OF POINT MEASUREMENT

Column 2
Left
Antler

Column
Right
Antler

MONTANA STATE REC
WYOMING

Photograph courtesy of C.M. Schmauch.

E.

F. Circumference 0

TOTALS

SHIRAS MOOSE
Alces alces shirasi

MINIMUM SCORE 155

Score	Greatest Spread	Length of Palm R	Length of Palm L	Width of Palm R	Width of Palm L	Circumference of Beam at Smallest Place R	Circumference of Beam at Smallest Place L	Number of Normal Points R	Number of Normal Points L	Locality	Hunter	Owner	Date Killed	Rank
205 4/8	53	38 6/8	38 5/8	16 7/8	15 6/8	6 7/8	6 7/8	15	15	Green River Lake, WY	John M. Oakley	Jackson Hole Museum	1952	1
205 1/8	56 5/8	40	40	13 3/8	14 2/8	7 7/8	7 7/8	13	13	Fremont Co., WY	Arthur E. Chandler	Arthur E. Chandler	1944	2
200 3/8	55 7/8	38 4/8	36 6/8	13 1/8	13 4/8	7	6 3/8	16	17	Lincoln Co., WY	Aldon L. Hale	Aldon L. Hale	1981	3
199 3/8	62 3/8	38 1/8	36 2/8	12 5/8	16 4/8	7 5/8	8 5/8	12	15	Elk City, ID	Reed T. Fisher	Reed T. Fisher	1957	4
199	48 4/8	40 4/8	42 1/8	12 1/8	11	7 7/8	7 6/8	17	16	Teton Co., WY	Amos M. Hand	B.W. & M. Smith	1946	5
196 5/8	53 1/8	39 6/8	40 4/8	14 5/8	14 2/8	6 6/8	6 6/8	13	11	Larimer Co., CO	Brad B. Schwindt	Brad B. Schwindt	1997	6
195 5/8	52 1/8	41 4/8	40	13	11	7	6 6/8	14	15	Atlantic Creek, WY	Alfred C. Berol	Alfred C. Berol	1933	7
195 1/8	55 7/8	43 1/8	35 6/8	15 1/8	14 5/8	7 3/8	7 2/8	14	14	Beaverhead Co., MT	C.M. Schmauch	C.M. Schmauch	1952	8
194 4/8	58 4/8	39	40	13 5/8	13	7 1/8	7	11	9	Jackson Co., CO	Jack A. Anderson	Jack A. Anderson	1995	9
193	51	40 4/8	42 2/8	14 1/8	11 7/8	7	6 5/8	12	14	Bingham Co., ID	Richard K. Smith	Richard K. Smith	2000	10
188 4/8	50 2/8	34 3/8	36 4/8	15	15 3/8	6 6/8	6 7/8	13	13	Madison Co., ID	Vicki Grover	Vicki Grover	1976	11
187 3/8	50 3/8	42 4/8	42 7/8	12 7/8	12 4/8	6 5/8	6 4/8	13	7	Bonneville Co., ID	Robin R. Pearson	Robin R. Pearson	2000	12
186 3/8	56 7/8	37 1/8	38 3/8	11 3/8	11 6/8	7 3/8	7	18	10	Sublette Co., WY	Curt Mann	Curt Mann	1972	13
186 1/8	58 1/8	41 4/8	37 5/8	12 3/8	12 5/8	7 5/8	7	8	7	Ravalli Co., MT	Picked Up	George Beechwood	1957	14
185 6/8	54	42 2/8	42	9 3/8	8 4/8	7 5/8	7	8	11	Sheridan Co., WY	Richard E. Jones, Jr.	Richard E. Jones, Jr.	1987	15
185 4/8	48 5/8	35 4/8	36 3/8	13 6/8	14 7/8	6 2/8	6 3/8	13	14	Bonneville Co., ID	Mary A. Isbell	Mary A. Isbell	2000	16
185 1/8	56 2/8	41 4/8	40	10 6/8	12 2/8	6 7/8	7	7	9	Sublette Co., WY	Robert C. Neely	Robert C. Neely	1959	17
185	47 1/8	38	36 2/8	14 2/8	14	7	6 6/8	12	14	Cache Co., UT	Lloyd E. Lish, Jr.	Lloyd E. Lish, Jr.	1993	18
185	52 2/8	37 1/8	36 1/8	12 2/8	11	6 7/8	6 6/8	13	15	Teton Co., WY	Isabelle Perry	Isabelle Perry	1961	19
184 7/8	56 3/8	33 7/8	33 6/8	13 1/8	14 1/8	7 7/8	7 3/8	11	10	Green River Lake, WY	Vern A. Bapst	Charles E. Jamieson	1961	20
184 6/8	48 2/8	35 7/8	34 7/8	13 6/8	14	6 5/8	6 6/8	13	14	Bonneville Co., ID	Jacque J. Steele	Jacque J. Steele	1989	21
184 4/8	49	42 1/8	40 4/8	10 2/8	11	7	7	10	10	Fremont Co., WY	Jack C. Dow	Jack C. Dow	1948	22
183 4/8	57 2/8	36 7/8	35 4/8	11 5/8	14 4/8	7	7	9	13	Sublette Co., WY	Norb Voerding	Loaned to B&C Natl. Coll.	1940	23
183 3/8	56 7/8	35 4/8	37 7/8	13 4/8	12 2/8	7	7	12	9	Teton Co., WY	George E. Long	George E. Long	1993	24
183 2/8	45 6/8	37 5/8	38	13	13 6/8	6 1/8	6 2/8	12	15	Bear Lake Co., ID	Claudia R. Howell	Claudia R. Howell	1977	25
182 6/8	50	35 7/8	38	11 7/8	13	6 5/8	6 5/8	12	13	Other Location Co., ID	Charles A. Oswald	Charles A. Oswald	1957	26
182 6/8	48 2/8	34 6/8	38 3/8	12 4/8	13	6 6/8	6	14	15	Caribou Co., ID	Patricia A. Wood	Patricia A. Wood	1983	26
182 2/8	55 6/8	35 6/8	36 4/8	11 6/8	12 1/8	6 6/8	6 7/8	10	9	Teton Co., WY	Dick Gaudern	Dick Gaudern	1946	28
182	45 2/8	37 3/8	38 1/8	11 4/8	11 1/8	6 7/8	6 7/8	15	13	Sublette Co., WY	James R. Brougham	James R. Brougham	1969	29
182	51 2/8	36	34	14 2/8	11 6/8	6 6/8	6 5/8	16	13	Sheridan Co., WY	Picked Up	William E. Trapp	PR 1993	29
181 5/8	51 7/8	38 6/8	38 4/8	8 7/8	9 7/8	6 4/8	6 4/8	11	12	Bear River, UT	John W. Way	UT Div. of Wildl. Resc.	1958	31
181 2/8	53 6/8	39 1/8	40 3/8	12 6/8	10 6/8	8	7 3/8	12	7	Clearwater Co., ID	Thad L. Gilkey	Thad L. Gilkey	1997	32
181	52 4/8	35 4/8	35 6/8	11 3/8	11 6/8	6 3/8	6 5/8	11	12	Jackson Co., CO	Dennis Pahlisch	Dennis Pahlisch	2001	33
180 7/8	48 3/8	37 2/8	37 1/8	12 4/8	10 2/8	6 7/8	6 7/8	15	12	Sublette Co., WY	Glen W. Beane	Glen W. Beane	1957	34
180 7/8	53 1/8	39 3/8	41	10 6/8	10 6/8	6 6/8	6 7/8	8	7	Sublette Co., WY	Donald Irwin	Donald Irwin	1976	34
180 7/8	58 7/8	32 3/8	32 6/8	11 2/8	10 5/8	6	6	12	14	Missoula Co., MT	Picked Up	MT Dept. of Fish, Wildl. & Parks	1997	34
180 3/8	49 3/8	32 6/8	32	13 5/8	14 6/8	6	5 7/8	14	16	Caribou Co., ID	Thomas R. McKenna	Thomas R. McKenna	1994	37

Score	Greatest Spread	Length of Palm R	Length of Palm L	Width of Palm R	Width of Palm L	Circ. of Beam R	Circ. of Beam L	Points R	Points L	Locality	Hunter	Owner	Date Killed	Rank
180 2/8	51 2/8	35 1/8	34 3/8	13 5/8	14 4/8	6 4/8	6 5/8	11	10	Weber Co, UT	Robert S. Mastronardi	Robert S. Mastronardi	1981	38
180	45 4/8	40 1/8	38 5/8	10 7/8	9 4/8	7 2/8	7 1/8	13	12	Green River, WY	L.W. Isaacs	L.W. Isaacs	1948	39
180	47	33 5/8	34 6/8	11 7/8	12 4/8	6 6/8	6 5/8	15	16	Pinedale, WY	Stuart W. Shepherd	Stuart W. Shepherd	1966	39
179 7/8	51 1/8	32 1/8	35 6/8	12 6/8	12 4/8	6 6/8	6 7/8	13	14	Gallatin Co, MT	John Williams	Powderhorn Sportsman Supply	1930	41
179 6/8	49 2/8	36 2/8	34 5/8	12 1/8	12 7/8	6 4/8	6 6/8	12	14	Grey's River, WY	Serena Malech	Serena Malech	1972	42
179 6/8	52	35 2/8	38	12 7/8	14 3/8	6 6/8	6 7/8	9	10	Flathead Co, MT	Michael Clanton	Michael Clanton	1988	42
179 4/8	47 2/8	38 4/8	38 1/8	11 4/8	12 7/8	6 4/8	6 7/8	10	11	Teton Co, WY	John D. Seifert	John D. Seifert	1976	44
179 1/8	45 1/8	35 5/8	34 6/8	14 6/8	11 4/8	6 6/8	6 6/8	14	14	Nalley, WY	Stephen S. Fisher	Stephen S. Fisher	1964	45
179 1/8	49 7/8	36	38 4/8	11 6/8	11	6 5/8	6 6/8	12	11	Teton Co, WY	Marion J. Fonville	Marion J. Fonville	1987	45
178 7/8	52 5/8	38 5/8	37 1/8	9 7/8	10 1/8	6 1/8	6 2/8	11	10	Eagle Creek, WY	Loren L. Lutz	Loren L. Lutz	1956	47
178 7/8	48 3/8	42	36 3/8	14 4/8	12 6/8	7 2/8	7 1/8	15	9	Granite Co, MT	Jack A. Wilkinson	Jack A. Wilkinson	1994	47
178 6/8	55 2/8	33 4/8	31 3/8	10 4/8	13 3/8	6	5 7/8	14	16	Upper Hoback River, WY	Daniel T. Burch	Daniel T. Burch	1967	49
178 6/8	48 4/8	36 3/8	37 1/8	10 3/8	10 3/8	6 3/8	6 3/8	12	14	Sublette Co, WY	Charles Thornton	Charles Thornton	1973	49
178 6/8	46 3/8	33 5/8	31 2/8	16 6/8	14 6/8	6 1/8	6 1/8	20	14	Cache Co, UT	Barton R. Critchlow	Barton R. Critchlow	1985	49
178 5/8	47 7/8	34 3/8	38 3/8	12 7/8	13	7 4/8	7 1/8	12	11	Sheridan Co, WY	Jack A. Wilkinson	Jack A. Wilkinson	1991	51
178 5/8	58 5/8	35 4/8	36 6/8	9 3/8	9 3/8	6 7/8	6 7/8	11	9	Sublette Co, WY	Robert Dennis	Robert Dennis	1969	51
178 3/8	42 5/8	37 1/8	36	12 6/8	13 1/8	7 3/8	7 3/8	12	13	Sublette Co, WY	Christopher W. Doak	Christopher W. Doak	2002	53
178 3/8	49 4/8	32 4/8	32 1/8	13 6/8	15 4/8	6 4/8	6 4/8	15	12	Buffalo Park, WY	Ross J. Berlin	Ross J. Berlin	1972	53
178 2/8	50 3/8	35	36 5/8	15 1/8	11 4/8	6 6/8	6 6/8	11	12	Teton Co, WY	Walter Russell	Walter Russell	1956	55
178 1/8	49 7/8	37	37	10 6/8	12 6/8	6 4/8	6 4/8	10	9	Madison Co, ID	Harold L. Roby	Garvice E. Roby	1961	56
178 1/8	51 2/8	36 1/8	33 1/8	10 2/8	9 5/8	7	7 1/8	11	12	Thorofare River, WY	Kevin W. Nichols	Kevin W. Nichols	1987	56
178	50 2/8	37 2/8	34 3/8	13 3/8	12 5/8	7	7	11	11	Big Piney, WY	Earl Brahler	H.E. Wolfe	1959	58
177 6/8	49	37	37 7/8	14 7/8	14 7/8	6 1/8	6 2/8	9	13	Green River, WY	George F. Stewart, Jr.	George F. Stewart, Jr.	1965	59
177 5/8	52 3/8	35	34 2/8	13 7/8	14	6 5/8	6 5/8	12	14	Teton Co, WY	Walter C. Motta, Sr.	Walter C. Motta, Sr.	1956	59
177 5/8	51 7/8	30 1/8	32	11 5/8	11 5/8	6 6/8	6 6/8	10	12	Park Co, MT	John R. Blanton	John R. Blanton	1985	61
177 2/8	51 4/8	38 1/8	37 7/8	11 4/8	11 2/8	6 4/8	6 1/8	12	11	Jackson Co, CO	Lawrence A. Allestad	Lawrence A. Allestad	1961	61
177 2/8	42 4/8	33 3/8	37 6/8	10 7/8	11 4/8	6 7/8	6 7/8	14	12	Shoshone Co, ID	Steven P. Kugler	Steven P. Kugler	1995	63
177 2/8	54 2/8	41 1/8	35 4/8	12	9 5/8	6 3/8	6 4/8	8	14	Big Piney, WY	April H. Preston	April H. Preston	1999	63
177 1/8	50 3/8	35 6/8	36 4/8	11 1/8	11 3/8	6 1/8	6 7/8	13	8	Teton Co, WY	Mrs. Robert R. Jamieson	Mrs. Robert R. Jamieson	1966	63
177	53	35	33 5/8	12 5/8	11 4/8	6 7/8	6 3/8	14	12	Teton Co, WY	Elgin T. Gates	Elgin T. Gates	1947	66
177	54 2/8	32 4/8	35	10 7/8	11 6/8	7 3/8	5 7/8	8	14	Teton Co, WY	James E. Jones	James E. Jones	2000	67
177	50 5/8	36 4/8	38 1/8	11	11 7/8	7 2/8	7 2/8	10	7	Beaverhead Co, MT	Jack G. Binkley	Jack G. Binkley	1977	67
176 7/8	48 4/8	36 4/8	33 5/8	11 4/8	10 4/8	6 2/8	6 1/8	12	10	Caribou Co, ID	Charles L. Walters	Charles L. Walters	1966	69
176 6/8	49 5/8	35	35	11 2/8	11	6 5/8	6 7/8	11	12	Bonneville Co, ID	Justin P. Jones	Justin P. Jones	1995	70
176 5/8	50 6/8	35 1/8	31 1/8	11 2/8	10 7/8	6 1/8	6 4/8	11	11	Madison Co, ID	Diggs Lewis	Diggs Lewis	1972	71
176 4/8	47	35 4/8	36 4/8	12 6/8	12	7 3/8	7 3/8	13	12	Morgan Co, UT	Robert L. Johnston	Robert L. Johnston	1994	72
176 4/8	43 6/8	35 1/8	36 4/8	11 6/8	11 6/8	7 3/8	6 3/8	10	13	Bingham Co, ID	Gerald D. Madsen	Gerald D. Madsen	1998	72
176 4/8	51 6/8	40	39	10	13 6/8	7 1/8	7 1/8	9	12	Bonneville Co, ID	Larry R. Brower	Larry R. Brower	2003	72
176 3/8	53 1/8	36 4/8	33 5/8	11 6/8	11 4/8	6 1/8	6 1/8	11	10	Cache Co, UT	Michael B. Messick	Michael B. Messick	1988	76
176 2/8	50 4/8	33	35	11 4/8	12 1/8	6 3/8	6 3/8	12	14	Teton Co, WY	Steven A. Barnard	Steven A. Barnard	1985	77
176 2/8	50 5/8	33 3/8	34 3/8	12 1/8	12 3/8	6 2/8	6 2/8	14	11	Uinta Co, WY	Richard E. Green	Richard E. Green	1988	78
176	39 6/8	31 4/8	35 7/8	13	13	6 7/8	6 6/8	11	14	Weber Co, UT	Romaine L. Marshall	Romaine L. Marshall	1992	79
175 7/8	50 7/8	36 4/8	40 2/8	10 6/8	10 6/8	6 2/8	6 2/8	14	9	Uinta Co, WY	Kurt P. Argyle	Kurt P. Argyle	2000	80
175 6/8	41 6/8	34 4/8	34 4/8	13 3/8	13 2/8	6 3/8	6 3/8	11	13	Weber Co, UT	Robert A. Cox	Robert A. Cox	1973	81
175 5/8	45 5/8	41 1/8	35 7/8	14 3/8	12 6/8	6 4/8	6 4/8	14	9	Caribou Co, ID	Robert V. Kimball	Robert V. Kimball	1987	82
175 3/8	62 5/8	29 2/8	29 5/8	10 5/8	10	7 1/8	7 1/8	10	13	Spokane Co, WA	Picked Up	B&C National Collection	1992	83
175 2/8	50	31 6/8	34 6/8	12 5/8	11 6/8	7 1/8	7 2/8	12	13	Lincoln Co, WY	Leon Gordon	Leon Gordon	1967	84

SHIRAS MOOSE
Alces alces shirasi

Score	Greatest Spread	Length of Palm		Width of Palm		Circumference of Beam at Smallest Place		Number of Normal Points		Locality	Hunter	Owner	Date Killed	Rank
		R	L	R	L	R	L	R	L					
175 2/8	47 4/8	35 4/8	38 4/8	11 4/8	11 2/8	7 1/8	7 1/8	11	10	Jackson Co., CO	Virgil A. Lair	Virgil A. Lair	1996	84
175 2/8	50 4/8	32 5/8	36 3/8	13 6/8	14 2/8	6 3/8	6 4/8	10	11	Larimer Co., CO	Thomas A. Thorson	Thomas A. Thorson	2000	84
175 1/8	48 3/8	36 3/8	35 6/8	12 2/8	11 4/8	6 2/8	6 1/8	10	14	Hoback River, WY	George Tolan	George Tolan	1964	87
175 1/8	46 7/8	33 7/8	37 4/8	12 1/8	11 7/8	6 3/8	6 4/8	12	15	Squaw Creek, WY	Denton C. Barker	Triangle C Ranch	1969	87
175	54 4/8	34	34	11 2/8	10	6 2/8	6 2/8	10	11	Park Co., MT	Thomas J. Radoumis	D.J. Hollinger & B. Howard	1974	89
175	51 4/8	38 2/8	33 4/8	12	10 2/8	7 2/8	7	13	11	Lewis & Clark Co., MT	James C. Johnson	James C. Johnson	1999	89
174 7/8	45 3/8	35 4/8	36 3/8	11 1/8	11 1/8	7 2/8	7 1/8	11	13	Teton Co., WY	John W. Whalen, Jr.	John W. Whalen, Jr.	1988	91
174 7/8	49 5/8	37 1/8	35 7/8	13 7/8	12 6/8	7 4/8	7 4/8	8	7	Idaho Co., ID	Unknown	Brad Davis	PR 1995	91
174 7/8	45 7/8	34 6/8	32 6/8	13 3/8	13 4/8	6 3/8	7 2/8	14	12	Teton Co., WY	William T. Jones	William T. Jones	2000	91
174 7/8	48 5/8	38 6/8	34 3/8	9 5/8	10 4/8	7	6 4/8	12	13	Sublette Co., WY	Christopher S. Dauphin	Christopher S. Dauphin	2001	91
174 6/8	50 2/8	33 1/8	34 3/8	11 5/8	13	6 4/8	6 4/8	11	14	Livingston Co., MT	Bill Cutler	Bill Cutler	1964	95
174 6/8	50 6/8	36	36 5/8	9 5/8	10 4/8	6 3/8	6 7/8	10	11	Park Co., MT	Picked Up	Duane A. Ferrell	1973	95
174 6/8	48	33 5/8	36 1/8	11	14 3/8	6 6/8	6 6/8	12	12	Gallatin Co., MT	Loring C. Hulslander	L.C. Hulslander & K. Bennet	1981	95
174 4/8	45 4/8	37 2/8	36 3/8	10 1/8	11 5/8	7	7 1/8	11	13	Teton Co., WY	John F. Cross	John F. Cross	1965	98
174 4/8	46	35 1/8	33 2/8	11	11 4/8	7	7	13	13	Park Co., WY	Walter L. Gale	Walter L. Gale	1983	98
174 4/8	50 6/8	36 3/8	34 1/8	9 2/8	9 7/8	7 4/8	7 5/8	11	12	Lincoln Co., MT	Unknown	Mike Kropp	PR 1987	98
174 3/8	58 1/8	32 4/8	29 3/8	12 5/8	12 5/8	6 2/8	6 1/8	13	10	Idaho Co., ID	Paul L. White	Paul L. White	1981	101
174 3/8	51 5/8	34 7/8	33 4/8	10 1/8	9 6/8	6 1/8	6 1/8	12	12	Caribou Co., ID	Leo E. Lish	Leo E. Lish	2000	101
174 2/8	46	32 2/8	32 1/8	14 3/8	13 3/8	6 5/8	6 5/8	12	14	Teton Co., WY	John R. Harju	John R. Harju	1980	103
173 7/8	46 5/8	37 3/8	36 7/8	9 6/8	10 3/8	7	7 4/8	10	11	Gallatin Co., MT	Rolf S. Dull	Rolf S. Dull	1988	104
173 6/8	50 4/8	30 6/8	34 4/8	13 7/8	13 3/8	7 4/8	7 4/8	10	12	Atlantic Creek, WY	Clyde Ormond	Clyde Ormond	1955	105
173 6/8	58	35 2/8	32 5/8	10 4/8	12 2/8	6 6/8	7	11	8	Teton Co., WY	David A. Yearsley	David A. Yearsley	1994	105
173 5/8	47 7/8	40 1/8	35 6/8	11 7/8	10 6/8	7 3/8	7 5/8	12	9	Weber Co., UT	C. Brent Morgan	C. Brent Morgan	1985	107
173 4/8	45 2/8	37 2/8	39 4/8	11 1/8	11 2/8	6 6/8	6 7/8	9	9	Sheridan Co., WY	Picked Up	R.R. Smith & D.V. Collis	1987	108
173 3/8	54 5/8	32 5/8	31 2/8	10 6/8	10 3/8	7 6/8	7 6/8	10	10	Flathead Co., MT	Tom Scheer	Tom Scheer	1976	109
173 2/8	58 4/8	34 4/8	34 1/8	8 4/8	10 4/8	6 6/8	6 6/8	8	10	Fremont Co., ID	Lula O. Jackson	Lula O. Jackson	1994	110
173 2/8	50 4/8	35 4/8	34	11 3/8	9 3/8	7	7	12	11	Lincoln Co., WY	David W. Whitesell	David W. Whitesell	2000	110
173 1/8	48 3/8	34 6/8	38	8 4/8	10	7	7 1/8	12	12	Madison Co., MT	Thomas L. Carter	Thomas L. Carter	1955	112
173 1/8	52 1/8	32 6/8	34 4/8	11 6/8	11 6/8	6	6	10	12	Sublette Co., WY	John C. Eklund	John C. Eklund	1970	112
173 1/8	48 3/8	35 5/8	35 2/8	11 6/8	10	6 1/8	6 1/8	11	11	Teton Co., WY	Raymond E. Pittman	Raymond E. Pittman	1995	112
173 1/8	45 1/8	38 1/8	38	10	13 4/8	7	7 2/8	10	9	Larimer Co., CO	Picked Up	Dustin H. Bailey	2003	112
173	49 4/8	33 1/8	35 3/8	11 2/8	12	6 4/8	6 3/8	11	13	Buffalo River, WY	Robert L. Hitch	Robert L. Hitch	1951	116
173	46	33 4/8	34	12 3/8	13	6 5/8	6 6/8	11	11	Cache Co., UT	Michael C. Leonhardt	Michael C. Leonhardt	1987	116
173	47 6/8	35 4/8	36 2/8	11	11 4/8	6 1/8	6 2/8	11	10	Flathead Co., MT	David A. Rose	David A. Rose	1991	116
173	53 6/8	33 4/8	31 1/8	13	11 4/8	6	6	11	12	Lincoln Co., MT	Ronald R. Higgins	Ronald R. Higgins	1994	116
172 6/8	41	35 1/8	35	11 3/8	11 3/8	6 4/8	6 4/8	13	13	Bridger Natl. For., WY	J.D. Bradley	J.D. Bradley	1970	120
172 4/8	42	35 4/8	33 1/8	12 4/8	14 4/8	6 5/8	6 6/8	13	17	Lincoln Co., MT	Tom DeShazer	Tom DeShazer	1956	121
172 4/8	50	32 3/8	36 4/8	10 1/8	10 5/8	6 6/8	6 6/8	12	12	Kilgore Creek, WY	Bill Jhun	Bill Jhun	1967	121

Score	Greatest Spread	Length of Palm R	Length of Palm L	Width of Palm R	Width of Palm L	Circ. Beam R	Circ. Beam L	Pts. R	Pts. L	Locality	Hunter	Owner	Date	Rank
172 3/8	44 1/8	37 1/8	38 6/8	12	10 7/8	6 1/8	6 2/8	10	10	Pinedale, WY	Basil C. Bradbury	Basil C. Bradbury	1969	123
172 3/8	43 3/8	36	37	11	11 1/8	7 4/8	7 4/8	10	8	Silver Bow Co., MT	Derrold O. Paige	Derrold O. Paige	1995	123
172 1/8	51 5/8	35	35	11 2/8	10 7/8	6 3/8	6 6/8	8	8	Summit Co., UT	David R. Gualazzi	David R. Gualazzi	2002	125
172	51	36 6/8	38 4/8	8 7/8	9 6/8	6 7/8	6 7/8	8	8	Sublette Co., WY	William D. Stewart	William D. Stewart	1954	126
172	46 2/8	35 7/8	38 5/8	9 3/8	10	6 5/8	6 5/8	11	11	Teton Co., WY	Holland C. McHenry	Holland C. McHenry	1980	126
171 7/8	58 3/8	30	33 5/8	9 5/8	9 5/8	6 1/8	6 1/8	11	11	Weber Co., UT	Kent G. Yearsley	Kent G. Yearsley	1981	128
171 7/8	52 3/8	33 2/8	33 6/8	11 1/8	9 7/8	6 7/8	6 5/8	13	10	Jackson Co., CO	Nancy A. Sommer	Nancy A. Sommer	1994	128
171 6/8	56 4/8	33 1/8	35 7/8	9 2/8	10	7 2/8	7 3/8	11	8	Grand Co., CO	Kenneth S. Gates	Kenneth S. Gates	2001	130
171 5/8	49 1/8	32 1/8	31 6/8	12 5/8	12 2/8	7 2/8	8	9	10	Fremont Co., ID	Rodney Chandler	Rodney Chandler	1967	131
171 5/8	49 3/8	36 2/8	32 2/8	12	12 4/8	6 7/8	7	11	10	Beaverhead Co., MT	George J. Wood	George J. Wood	2000	131
171 3/8	51 5/8	37 7/8	37 2/8	9 5/8	10	7	7	10	10	Cache Co., UT	Picked Up	Bennie J. Rossetto	PR 1975	133
171 2/8	50	34 4/8	37 5/8	10 6/8	10 3/8	6 6/8	6 6/8	6	8	Silver Bow Co., MT	Martin E. Carlson	Martin E. Carlson	1980	134
171 2/8	56	32 1/8	31 4/8	11 2/8	12 2/8	6 3/8	6 5/8	9	9	Teton Co., WY	Scott N. Carter	Scott N. Carter	2001	134
171 2/8	49 2/8	36 7/8	33 5/8	13 5/8	11 1/8	7 1/8	6 2/8	9	13	Larimer Co., CO	Billy Havens	Billy Havens	2002	134
171	45 7/8	34 5/8	33 5/8	10 6/8	10 3/8	7	7 1/8	8	11	Lincoln Co., MT	Keith H. Hanson	Keith H. Hanson	1972	137
170 7/8	47 7/8	37 2/8	38 3/8	10 2/8	8 4/8	7 4/8	7 1/8	11	13	Sublette Co., WY	Bruce C. Todd	Bruce C. Todd	1982	138
170 7/8	50 2/8	35 4/8	34 4/8	10 4/8	11 7/8	6 1/8	7 4/8	12	12	Bridger Natl. For., WY	Don L. Corley	Don L. Corley	1983	138
170 6/8	47 6/8	35 6/8	34 2/8	8 7/8	11 6/8	7 4/8	6 1/8	9	9	Sublette Co., WY	Unknown	Neil Blair	1965	140
170 6/8	54 2/8	38 1/8	35 1/8	9 7/8	11 2/8	6 6/8	7 5/8	12	11	Cache Co., UT	Kenneth E. Myers	Kenneth E. Myers	1968	140
170 6/8	46 6/8	39	29 6/8	11 6/8	9 7/8	7 6/8	6 2/8	12	13	Warm Spring Creek, WY	Jim Vanderbeek	Jim Vanderbeek	1990	140
170 4/8	45 4/8	34 3/8	34 3/8	9 7/8	12 6/8	5 6/8	7 5/8	13	13	Flathead Co., MT	Herbert L. Palmer	Herbert L. Palmer	1951	143
170 4/8	49 2/8	32 4/8	31	13 5/8	10 3/8	6 4/8	5 6/8	11	11	Teton Co., WY	Arthur M. Nelson	Arthur M. Nelson	1987	143
170 4/8	51 2/8	35 5/8	34 6/8	11 3/8	12 7/8	6 5/8	6 4/8	10	10	Madison Co., MT	W.R. Titterington	W.R. Titterington	1989	143
170 4/8	39 7/8	33 7/8	34	9 3/8	12 2/8	6 4/8	6 5/8	13	13	Lincoln Co., MT	Michael W. Gallagher	Michael W. Gallagher	1996	143
170 3/8	48 4/8	34 7/8	35 5/8	10 7/8	11 5/8	6 5/8	6 5/8	9	9	Bonneville Co., ID	Picked Up	Wayne Lundberg	1974	147
170	44 2/8	35 4/8	35	10 6/8	10 3/8	7	6 4/8	11	10	Teton Co., WY	Dean L. Brown	Dean L. Brown	1987	148
170	47 1/8	34 6/8	35 4/8	11 6/8	11 2/8	7 2/8	6 5/8	11	11	Lincoln Co., MT	Hazer K. Bulkley	Hazer K. Bulkley	1994	148
169 7/8	50 1/8	33 1/8	33 2/8	10 6/8	10 5/8	6 4/8	6 6/8	10	11	Weber Co., UT	William A. Stevens	William A. Stevens	1967	150
169 7/8	54 4/8	32 7/8	32 2/8	10 7/8	11 1/8	7	6 6/8	15	15	Wilson Co., WY	Riley A. Bushman	Riley A. Bushman	1969	150
169 6/8	52 5/8	30 4/8	27 6/8	10 6/8	11 3/8	6 2/8	6 2/8	10	13	Merna, WY	Howard Bennage	Howard Bennage	1958	152
169 6/8	40 6/8	35	32 1/8	12 3/8	11 4/8	7 1/8	6 7/8	11	10	Dubois Co., WY	C. Von De Graaff	C. Von De Graaff	1959	152
169 5/8	42 3/8	42 3/8	35 2/8	12 1/8	11 7/8	5 7/8	7	15	15	Lincoln Co., WY	Albert Wagner, Jr.	Albert Wagner, Jr.	1962	154
169 3/8	53 3/8	30 7/8	34	12	11 4/8	6 4/8	5 1/8	11	11	Lincoln Co., WY	Vannetta Marshinsky	Vannetta Marshinsky	1968	155
169 3/8	53 6/8	34 6/8	30 4/8	9 4/8	11 7/8	6 2/8	7 1/8	8	10	Freemont, ID	W.H. Mitchell & R.F. Henry	W.H. Mitchell & R.F. Henry	2001	155
169 3/8	53	33 2/8	34 7/8	10 5/8	10 5/8	5 7/8	5 1/8	9	9	Lincoln Co., MT	Picked Up	Frank J. O'Connor	1982	155
169 2/8	54 5/8	31 6/8	33 5/8	10 7/8	11 7/8	6 4/8	5 5/8	10	12	Park Co., MT	Sam A. Terakedis	Sam A. Terakedis	1995	158
169 1/8	48 1/8	31 4/8	31 4/8	9 4/8	9 4/8	6 2/8	5 2/8	12	10	Clark Co., ID	Carolyn Karvinen	Carolyn Karvinen	1966	159
169 1/8	47 3/8	34 1/8	33 4/8	12	13 1/8	6 4/8	5 4/8	11	9	Bonneville Co., ID	Picked Up	Michael J. Zwicker	1986	159
169 1/8	52	33 3/8	33 2/8	11 1/8	12 5/8	6 6/8	5 5/8	12	9	Flathead Co., MT	Frank J. Telling	Frank J. Telling	1994	159
169	46 4/8	36	33 2/8	8 6/8	8 7/8	7 3/8	7 3/8	9	10	Jackson Hole, WY	Shirley Straley	Shirley Straley	1963	162
169	47 4/8	31 4/8	33 5/8	11 4/8	12 7/8	6 2/8	6 1/8	10	11	Caribou Co., ID	Richard M. Hydzik	Richard M. Hydzik	1988	162
169	50 6/8	30 6/8	33 2/8	11 7/8	12 4/8	6 3/8	5 3/8	11	11	Madison Co., ID	Ronald K. Farris	Ronald K. Farris	2000	162
169	58	30 4/8	31 2/8	11 5/8	9 5/8	7	7 1/8	13	13	Jackson Co., CO	George Whisenhunt	George Whisenhunt	2001	162
168 6/8	48 2/8	36 3/8	30	11 6/8	11 7/8	6 5/8	6 5/8	8	7	Park Co., WY	John A. Mahoney, Jr.	John A. Mahoney, Jr.	1957	166
168 6/8	51 6/8	31 5/8	34 2/8	10 2/8	10 3/8	6 6/8	7 2/8	12	10	Sublette Co., WY	Larry Petersen	Larry Petersen	1964	166
168 6/8	50	33 5/8	37 2/8	9 7/8	10	7	7 2/8	10	9	Sheridan Co., WY	James W. Owens	James W. Owens	1987	166
168 6/8	50	33 7/8	33 7/8	10 6/8	10 3/8	6 4/8	6 3/8	9	9	Park Co., MT	Jerry R. Blaquiere	Jerry R. Blaquiere	1992	166

SHIRAS MOOSE
Alces alces shirasi

Score	Greatest Spread	Length of Palm R	L	Width of Palm R	L	Circumference of Beam at Smallest Place R	L	Number of Normal Points R	L	Locality	Hunter	Owner	Date Killed	Rank
168 5/8	52 1/8	33 4/8	34 4/8	9 2/8	9 6/8	6 5/8	6 4/8	9	11	Bonneville Co., ID	Michael L. Adams	Michael L. Adams	1999	170
168 5/8	48 1/8	41 4/8	35 4/8	10 3/8	10 2/8	6 4/8	6 5/8	8	13	Summit Co., UT	Brandon E. Haws	Brandon E. Haws	2000	170
168 4/8	50 4/8	31 3/8	31 5/8	11 5/8	12 6/8	6	6	10	11	Wyoming	Unknown	Bill H. McCabe	1958	172
168 3/8	43 3/8	36 2/8	39 6/8	13 2/8	12 4/8	6 7/8	6 6/8	13	7	Park Co., MT	Victoria L. Miller	Victoria L. Miller	1977	173
168 3/8	47 3/8	34 4/8	35 7/8	9 4/8	9 7/8	6 4/8	6 4/8	11	11	Teton Co., WY	Clyde E. Harnden	Clyde E. Harnden	1991	173
168 3/8	47 3/8	35 5/8	35 4/8	10 4/8	10 5/8	6 4/8	6 4/8	8	9	Fremont Co., CO	Alfred C. Deshaw	Alfred C. Deshaw	2000	173
168 2/8	46 4/8	36 5/8	34 2/8	14	14 3/8	6 1/8	6 1/8	14	7	Bonneville Co., ID	Norman E. Stanley	Norman E. Stanley	1991	176
167 7/8	43 5/8	39 4/8	33 2/8	10 5/8	11	6 2/8	6 4/8	13	12	Gros Ventre, WY	Bonita Young	Bonita Young	1960	177
167 6/8	51	34 2/8	33 6/8	8 3/8	9 4/8	6 2/8	6 2/8	10	11	Teton Co., WY	Roger Wilmot	Roger Wilmot	1972	178
167 6/8	44	33 7/8	37	12 7/8	11 6/8	6 4/8	6 2/8	10	12	Beaverhead Co., MT	Peter A. Parini	Peter A. Parini	1981	178
167 4/8	47 4/8	34 6/8	32 4/8	11	11	6 4/8	6 4/8	10	10	Park Co., WY	Leo C. Chapel	Leo C. Chapel	1967	180
167 4/8	52	31 1/8	31 6/8	10 6/8	10	6 5/8	6 5/8	11	10	Summit Co., UT	L. Irvin Barnhart	L. Irvin Barnhart	1985	180
167 4/8	44 6/8	32	30 4/8	14 4/8	13 4/8	6 3/8	6 3/8	11	11	Morgan Co., UT	Roger L. Gregg	Roger L. Gregg	1991	180
167 4/8	46 6/8	34 6/8	37 2/8	9 4/8	10 6/8	6 5/8	6 1/8	10	12	Bear Lake Co., ID	Tony Lloyd	Tony Lloyd	1992	180
167 4/8	44 2/8	34 4/8	35 2/8	11 6/8	13 2/8	6 3/8	6 4/8	9	9	Uinta Co., WY	David W. Black	David W. Black	1999	180
167 3/8	53 2/8	33 7/8	33	10 4/8	10	6 1/8	6 2/8	8	9	Teton Co., WY	Richard A. Hlavnicka	Richard A. Hlavnicka	2000	180
167 3/8	43 7/8	37 5/8	33 7/8	11 6/8	10 1/8	6 6/8	6 6/8	12	11	Lincoln Co., WY	Timothy G. Coulson	Timothy G. Coulson	1974	186
167 3/8	49 1/8	36 5/8	30 5/8	12	12	6 4/8	6 4/8	12	10	Bonneville Co., ID	John K. Ryan	John K. Ryan	1984	186
167 3/8	52 5/8	33 4/8	37	11 5/8	12 6/8	6 2/8	6 4/8	6	9	Idaho Co., ID	Antony Forrer	Antony G. Forrer	1998	186
167 2/8	50	34 1/8	34 1/8	11 3/8	12	6 1/8	6 1/8	8	7	Uinta Co., WY	Vanessa A. Bair	Vanessa A. Bair	2000	189
167 2/8	48	33	33	9 4/8	12 6/8	7 1/8	7 1/8	10	10	Sheridan Co., WY	Bill E. Hitt	Bill E. Hitt	2001	189
167 2/8	49 2/8	36 4/8	36 6/8	8 6/8	11 1/8	6 4/8	6 4/8	10	12	Sheridan Co., WY	Mark B. Steffen	Mark B. Steffen	2003	189
167 1/8	45 1/8	32 6/8	34	11 7/8	10 6/8	6 5/8	6 4/8	11	11	Teton Co., WY	L. Stanley	L. Stanley	1964	192
167 1/8	48 1/8	32 7/8	30 7/8	10 7/8	11	6 6/8	6 7/8	11	11	Sublette Co., WY	Bob Housholder	Bob Housholder	1968	192
167 1/8	48 3/8	32 7/8	36 1/8	10	9 6/8	7 2/8	6 6/8	11	10	Caribou Co., ID	Ernest Saxton	Ernest Saxton	1969	192
167 1/8	46 7/8	30 5/8	31 3/8	12 1/8	12 4/8	6 3/8	6 4/8	11	12	Clearwater Co., ID	Richard E. Hardy	Richard E. Hardy	1987	192
167 1/8	51 7/8	33 6/8	30 2/8	10 6/8	10 6/8	6 5/8	6 5/8	12	11	Boundary Co., ID	Robbie A. Piehl	Robbie A. Piehl	1998	192
167	46 6/8	35 4/8	35 4/8	8 7/8	12 1/8	6 6/8	6 7/8	9	12	Sublette Co., WY	Picked Up	Robert Dory	1976	197
167	46 2/8	38 6/8	34 2/8	9 5/8	10 5/8	6 5/8	6 4/8	13	10	Fremont Co., WY	LeRoy Castagno	LeRoy Castagno	1977	197
167	44 6/8	33 5/8	32 5/8	11 1/8	11 6/8	6 3/8	6 3/8	11	12	Lincoln Co., MT	Jeff Wisehart	Jeff Wisehart	1983	197
167	44 2/8	35 1/8	35 2/8	12 3/8	10 5/8	6 5/8	6 5/8	12	9	Sheridan Co., WY	David V. Collis	David V. Collis	1987	197
167	45 4/8	35 4/8	34 5/8	10 4/8	10 7/8	6 2/8	6 1/8	10	10	Broadwater Co., MT	Mac Vosbeck	Mac Vosbeck	1996	197
166 7/8	51 1/8	33 5/8	33 7/8	9 7/8	10	6 3/8	6 3/8	10	8	Gallatin Co., MT	Rodney R. Richardson	Rodney R. Richardson	1979	202
166 7/8	48 3/8	32 7/8	32 6/8	10 1/8	9	6 5/8	6 4/8	11	11	Gallatin Co., MT	Albert D. Williams	Albert D. Williams	1986	202
166 7/8	53 5/8	31 5/8	32 2/8	9 1/8	10 1/8	6 7/8	7	12	9	Bonneville Co., ID	Craig A. McBride	Craig A. McBride	1993	202
166 6/8	47 2/8	33	32 7/8	13 5/8	12 2/8	6 5/8	6 5/8	8	8	Lincoln Co., WY	Nancy J. Combs	Nancy J. Combs	1986	205
166 6/8	46 2/8	36 2/8	37 6/8	9 1/8	10	5 7/8	5 7/8	9	9	Weber Co., UT	George V. Aalberg	George V. Aalberg	1991	205
166 6/8	49 2/8	29 5/8	30 1/8	12	13 2/8	6 1/8	6 1/8	11	12	Bonneville Co., ID	LeRoy C. Meyer	LeRoy C. Meyer	1995	205

Score										Locality	Owner	Hunter	Date	Rank
166 6/8	45 4/8	34 3/8	35 1/8	9 3/8	9 7/8	11	11	6 1/8	6	Sublette Co., WY	Dianne Boroff	Picked Up	1997	205
166 5/8	48 7/8	34 4/8	36	7 5/8	10 3/8	10	11	7	7 4/8	Teton Co., WY	R.G. De Graff	R.G. De Graff	1963	209
166 5/8	46 7/8	34 3/8	33 6/8	10 2/8	11 4/8	9	10	6 7/8	7 1/8	Lincoln Co., WY	James A. Grivet, Jr.	James A. Grivet, Jr.	1993	209
166 4/8	50	28 5/8	28 4/8	13 4/8	15 4/8	11	10	6 2/8	6 4/8	Bonneville Co., ID	Daniel J. Duggan	Daniel J. Duggan	1982	211
166 4/8	51 2/8	30 3/8	33 2/8	13 1/8	13 2/8	8	11	6 1/8	6 3/8	Caribou Co., ID	Diane G. Hall	Diane G. Hall	1985	211
166 3/8	50 1/8	34 2/8	32 4/8	8 7/8	9 7/8	10	10	6 6/8	6 6/8	Teton Co., WY	Terry Nilsen	Terry Nilsen	1970	213
166 3/8	48 5/8	37	35 2/8	11 6/8	9 6/8	11	8	6	5 7/8	Bonner Co., ID	Brian T. Farley	Brian T. Farley	1977	213
166 3/8	50 3/8	35 2/8	33 5/8	10 6/8	9 2/8	9	9	6 2/8	6 1/8	Lincoln Co., WY	T. Jefferson Cook	T. Jefferson Cook	1988	213
166 3/8	49 3/8	35 4/8	33	11 2/8	10	7	9	6 1/8	6	Boundary Co., ID	Ronald R. Frederickson	Ronald R. Frederickson	2001	213
166 2/8	43 4/8	31 2/8	32 4/8	14 1/8	15 1/8	11	10	6	6 3/8	Morgan Co., UT	Michael F. Gleason	Michael F. Gleason	1990	217
166 1/8	46 3/8	34 4/8	29 7/8	13 6/8	13	11	11	6 2/8	6	Caribou Co., ID	Robert L. Christophersen	Robert L. Christophersen	1995	218
166	48 4/8	35 4/8	32 4/8	9 3/8	10	10	10	6 7/8	7	Tosi Creek, WY	Roscoe O. McKeehan	Roscoe O. McKeehan	1960	219
166	47	30	31	12	11 4/8	11	11	7	7	Glade Creek, WY	E.E. Hosafros	E.E. Hosafros	1961	219
166	48 4/8	34 1/8	33 5/8	14 7/8	9 7/8	10	9	6 2/8	6 3/8	Bonneville Co., ID	E. Ray Robinson	E. Ray Robinson	1977	219
166	42 6/8	39 6/8	38 2/8	8 7/8	9 1/8	9	9	6 5/8	6 7/8	Flathead Co., MT	Kathy A. Nagel	Kathy A. Nagel	1988	219
165 7/8	52 6/8	29 4/8	29 4/8	11	11	11	11	7 2/8	7 1/8	Clark Co., ID	Elden L. Perry	Elden L. Perry	1975	223
165 7/8	50 3/8	34 2/8	30 4/8	11 3/8	11 5/8	13	13	6 7/8	6 7/8	Morgan Co., UT	Alfred E. Cornelison	Alfred E. Cornelison	2003	223
165 6/8	48 4/8	32	30 2/8	13 2/8	13 3/8	8	9	7 2/8	7 1/8	Bridger Lake, WY	Hugh W. Mildren	Larry Arndt	1959	225
165 6/8	48 4/8	33	33 5/8	11	11	9	8	6 5/8	6 6/8	Sublette Co., WY	Ray Snow	Don Boyer	1959	225
165 5/8	45	34 3/8	33 1/8	12 3/8	13 5/8	12	12	6	5 7/8	Weber Co., UT	Wayne J. Yamashita	Wayne J. Yamashita	1985	225
165 5/8	47 3/8	36	32	10 6/8	12 1/8	9	9	7 3/8	7 4/8	Carbon Co., WY	Tana E. Sullivan	Tana E. Sullivan	2000	228
165 4/8	46 6/8	32 4/8	36 2/8	9 3/8	11 2/8	11	11	6 6/8	7	Sublette Co., WY	Paul A. Graham	Paul A. Graham	1970	229
165 4/8	51 2/8	32 3/8	33 5/8	9 5/8	9 2/8	12	12	6 4/8	6 5/8	Sheridan Co., WY	Jerry K. Hutchinson	Jerry K. Hutchinson	1993	229
165 4/8	50 6/8	31 4/8	31 4/8	11 3/8	11	11	11	5 7/8	5 7/8	Gallatin Co., MT	Jerry D. Johnson	Jerry D. Johnson	1994	229
165 3/8	53 7/8	39 3/8	33 6/8	8 6/8	7 4/8	11	11	6 4/8	6 6/8	Lincoln Co., WY	Brad H. Jacobs	Brad H. Jacobs	1990	232
165 2/8	43 6/8	32 2/8	32 6/8	10 4/8	12 4/8	12	12	6 4/8	6	Buffalo River, WY	Jock H. White	Jock H. White	1953	233
165 2/8	47 6/8	32 4/8	32 4/8	12	12 6/8	8	10	6 5/8	6 4/8	Fremont Co., ID	Harvey W. Lewis	Harvey W. Lewis	1964	233
165 2/8	45 4/8	27 7/8	28 4/8	14 2/8	14 4/8	12	12	5 6/8	5 7/8	Lincoln Co., WY	Ryley Z. Dawson	Ryley Z. Dawson	1969	233
165 2/8	43 6/8	33 3/8	32 1/8	11 6/8	10	14	14	6 5/8	6 5/8	Dubois Co., WY	Vernon Limbach	Vernon Limbach	1969	233
165 2/8	47 6/8	32	31 4/8	11 1/8	11 2/8	10	11	6 4/8	6 1/8	Lincoln Co., MT	Roger L. Haas	Roger L. Haas	1997	233
165 2/8	48 6/8	30	31 5/8	11 6/8	12 3/8	10	10	6 6/8	6 4/8	Lincoln Co., MT	Chad M. Place	Chad M. Place	1998	233
165 1/8	44 6/8	31 4/8	31 4/8	12 4/8	13 2/8	11	10	6 2/8	6 2/8	Granite Co., MT	Larry E. Clark	Larry E. Clark	2001	233
165 1/8	47 1/8	34	35 4/8	9	9 2/8	9	9	7	7 2/8	Lincoln Co., WY	Bern Whittaker	Bern Whittaker	1964	240
165 1/8	45 1/8	29 7/8	31	10 4/8	11	14	14	5 5/8	5 5/8	Teton Co., WY	Joseph M. Griset	Joseph M. Griset	1969	240
165 1/8	48 7/8	32	36	9 5/8	11 2/8	11	10	6 4/8	6 4/8	Lincoln Co., WY	Kenneth Madsen	Kenneth Madsen	1974	240
165	46 4/8	36 6/8	38 6/8	10 1/8	11 3/8	7	7	6 2/8	6 3/8	Gallatin Co., MT	Ray E. Brooks	Picked Up	1961	243
165	51 6/8	35	32	9 7/8	11 6/8	9	8	7 5/8	7 4/8	Fremont Co., WY	Charles A. Boyle	Charles A. Boyle	1965	243
164 7/8	52 1/8	30 2/8	34 1/8	9 7/8	11 6/8	10	9	6 4/8	6 4/8	Sublette Co., WY	Edmund J. Giebel	Edmund J. Giebel	1971	245
164 7/8	45 1/8	33 4/8	37 3/8	10	11 4/8	10	10	7 3/8	7 4/8	Fremont Co., WY	Eugene H. Putnam	David F. Burk	1973	245
164 7/8	47 3/8	38 1/8	31 4/8	11 3/8	11	9	9	7 2/8	7 3/8	Sheridan Co., WY	John D. Frost	John D. Frost	1988	245
164 7/8	54 3/8	33	28 2/8	12 6/8	11 3/8	11	11	6 6/8	6 5/8	Salt Lake Co., UT	Elizabeth Burrows	Elizabeth Burrows	1995	245
164 7/8	42 7/8	33 2/8	34 2/8	10 2/8	11 6/8	11	11	6 4/8	6 6/8	Teton Co., WY	Roger L. Roraff	Roger L. Roraff	1997	245
164 7/8	52 1/8	31 6/8	33	11 4/8	11 6/8	12	12	6 2/8	6 3/8	Shoshone Co., ID	John L. Amistoso	John L. Amistoso	2001	245
164 6/8	41	33 3/8	34 6/8	12 4/8	10 6/8	7	11	7	7	Bonneville Co., ID	Stanley M. Grover	Stanley M. Grover	1996	251
164 5/8	50 3/8	34 1/8	32 7/8	8 6/8	9 1/8	13	9	6 4/8	6 4/8	Pinedale, WY	Clifford G. McConnell	Clifford G. McConnell	1959	252
164 5/8	47 5/8	29 7/8	32 1/8	10 4/8	10 5/8	9	9	6 2/8	6 1/8	Teton Co., WY	Ernest L. Cummings	Ernest L. Cummings	1960	252
164 5/8	50 7/8	33	33 4/8	9 6/8	8 4/8	12	16	6 3/8	6 4/8	Lincoln Co., WY	Vernal J. Larsen	Vernal J. Larsen	1973	252
164 5/8	52 5/8	29	29	10 7/8	11 1/8	9	10	6 1/8	6 2/8	Bonneville Co., ID	Robert Martineau	Robert Martineau	2000	252

SHIRAS MOOSE
Alces alces shirasi

Score	Greatest Spread	Length of Palm R	L	Width of Palm R	L	Circumference of Beam at Smallest Place R	L	Number of Normal Points R	L	Locality	Hunter	Owner	Date Killed	Rank
164 5/8	44 1/8	33 3/8	32 2/8	9 5/8	11 3/8	6 3/8	6 3/8	12	14	Caribou Co., ID	Wendel E. Hetzler	Wendel E. Hetzler	2002	252
164 4/8	51 6/8	30 6/8	30 1/8	9 6/8	11 7/8	5 4/8	5 4/8	11	11	Flathead Co., MT	Picked Up	John Castles	PR 1954	257
164 4/8	51 4/8	32	30 4/8	10 4/8	10 1/8	6 4/8	6 3/8	11	10	Cache Co., UT	Bruce N. Moss	Bruce N. Moss	1977	257
164 4/8	49	32 7/8	32	11 2/8	13	6 4/8	6 7/8	8	9	Morgan Co., UT	Craig S. Engelke	Craig S. Engelke	1987	257
164 4/8	40 4/8	32 6/8	32 4/8	10 7/8	11	6 5/8	6 5/8	12	12	Sheridan Co., WY	Warren D. Mischke	Warren D. Mischke	1991	257
164 4/8	49 4/8	34	34	9 2/8	10 3/8	6 2/8	6 3/8	8	10	Summit Co., UT	Roger P. Deschaine	Roger P. Deschaine	1994	257
164 3/8	48 5/8	31	36 1/8	9 5/8	10	6 3/8	7	11	12	Uinta Co., WY	Richard J. Gilmore	Richard J. Gilmore	1986	262
164 3/8	48 5/8	30 4/8	31 5/8	10 3/8	13	9 1/8	7	10	11	Cache Co., UT	Robert L. Jacobsen	Robert L. Jacobsen	1994	262
164 2/8	48 4/8	34	34 2/8	8 3/8	11	6 4/8	6 7/8	9	10	Spread Creek, WY	George Malouf	George Malouf	1966	264
164 2/8	51 4/8	34	34 6/8	7 7/8	7 7/8	6 4/8	6 6/8	8	9	Park Co., WY	Burton H. Ward	Burton H. Ward	1984	264
164 2/8	40	35 7/8	37 6/8	10 2/8	10 7/8	6 5/8	6 7/8	9	10	Teton Co., WY	Don L. Corley	Don L. Corley	1985	264
164 2/8	41 6/8	34 4/8	38 2/8	11 5/8	10 7/8	6 7/8	7	9	10	Morgan Co., UT	S. Kim Bonnett	S. Kim Bonnett	1986	264
164 2/8	51 6/8	32 3/8	30	10 3/8	11 3/8	6 7/8	7	9	10	Cache Co., UT	Karl E. Engelke	Karl E. Engelke	1987	264
164 2/8	43 6/8	34 2/8	33 5/8	9	10 3/8	6 5/8	6 5/8	12	11	Sublette Co., WY	Kenneth D. Rupp	Kenneth D. Rupp	1988	264
164 2/8	54 6/8	32 1/8	34 1/8	7 1/8	8 7/8	7	7	9	9	Teton Co., WY	Rick L. Parish	Rick L. Parish	1996	264
164 1/8	52 5/8	31 1/8	28 5/8	10 1/8	8 6/8	6 4/8	6 3/8	11	12	Skull Crack, UT	Blaine E. Worthen	Blaine E. Worthen	1975	271
164	55	26 3/8	29 3/8	10 6/8	11	6 3/8	6 7/8	11	11	Wilson Co., WY	V. Tullis & A. Van Noye	Victor Tullis	1955	272
164	43 4/8	30 4/8	31 3/8	11 4/8	13 7/8	6 2/8	6 3/8	12	12	Teton Co., WY	Clifford H. Rockhold	Clifford H. Rockhold	1984	272
164	53 4/8	30 5/8	33 7/8	9 4/8	9 6/8	6 1/8	6 3/8	9	9	Beaverhead Co., MT	Glenn M. Smith	Glenn M. Smith	1998	272
164	47 2/8	32 3/8	37 2/8	11	11 6/8	6	6 1/8	9	10	Teton Co., ID	Picked Up	Ken V. Beard	2001	272
163 7/8	49 7/8	31 2/8	34 5/8	10 3/8	11 3/8	6 3/8	6 3/8	11	9	Park Co., MT	William D. West	William D. West	1990	276
163 7/8	50 1/8	34	33	9 4/8	11 2/8	6 3/8	6	11	12	Summit Co., UT	Wade Wilde	Wade Wilde	2001	276
163 6/8	45 2/8	32 4/8	30 4/8	11 6/8	12	6	6	11	11	Teton Co., WY	Robert D. Rice	Robert D. Rice	1982	278
163 6/8	45 6/8	31 6/8	33	11	11 2/8	6 2/8	6 4/8	10	11	Grand Co., CO	Steve R. Countway	Steve R. Countway	1992	278
163 6/8	49 2/8	37 6/8	35 1/8	8 5/8	9	6 4/8	6 4/8	7	9	Lincoln Co., MT	Trent W. Warness	Trent W. Warness	1993	278
163 6/8	48 4/8	30 4/8	31 4/8	10 5/8	9 4/8	6 5/8	6 6/8	12	12	Madison Co., MT	Steven L. Blank	Steven L. Blank	1994	278
163 6/8	60	35 6/8	27	10 6/8	10 3/8	6 5/8	6 4/8	10	8	Carbon Co., WY	Rodney B. Weinman	Rodney B. Weinman	2000	278
163 5/8	49 5/8	34	34 3/8	8 1/8	9 4/8	6 7/8	7	8	8	Bear Canyon, MT	John Olsen	John Olsen	1962	283
163 5/8	51 5/8	33 2/8	33 6/8	9 4/8	10 1/8	6 3/8	6 2/8	7	8	Teton Co., WY	Gordon Hay	Gordon Hay	1970	283
163 5/8	47 3/8	33 2/8	36 1/8	11 7/8	12 2/8	6	6 1/8	7	12	Teton Co., WY	Michael S. Greenwald	Michael S. Greenwald	1978	283
163 5/8	51 5/8	30 2/8	35 6/8	11 6/8	10 4/8	6 2/8	6 4/8	10	10	Lincoln Co., MT	Alfred E. Journey	Alfred E. Journey	1983	283
163 5/8	46 7/8	29 4/8	32 2/8	9 4/8	9 5/8	7 3/8	7 4/8	12	12	Madison Co., MT	Danny L. Johnerson	Danny L. Johnerson	1992	283
163 4/8	50	34	32	10 4/8	11	6 2/8	6 2/8	10	8	West Yellowstone, MT	Pete Hansen	Forest B. Fenn	1948	288
163 4/8	43 6/8	35 4/8	37	9 1/8	10	6 2/8	6 4/8	9	10	Teton Co., WY	Bruce C. Liddle	Bruce C. Liddle	1974	288
163 4/8	44 6/8	37 1/8	35 6/8	11 7/8	11 3/8	6 6/8	6 6/8	6	10	Bonneville Co., ID	Gerald E. Hill	Gerald E. Hill	1981	288
163 2/8	48 4/8	31 2/8	32 6/8	11 7/8	14 2/8	6 2/8	6 4/8	8	9	Lincoln Co., ID	Russell J. Smuin	Russell J. Smuin	1976	291
163 2/8	41 6/8	40 2/8	38 1/8	9 2/8	7 1/8	6 4/8	6 4/8	9	10	Fremont Co., ID	Lavonne A. Crews	Lavonne A. Crews	1985	291
163 2/8	46 6/8	33 7/8	32 7/8	9 3/8	10	6 7/8	6 6/8	10	10	Bonneville Co., ID	Judith A. Gordon	Judith A. Gordon	1988	291

Score	Greatest Spread	Length of Palm R	Length of Palm L	Width of Palm R	Width of Palm L	Circ. R	Circ. L	Points R	Points L	Locality	Hunter	Owner	Date	Rank
163 1/8	44 3/8	31 3/8	32 4/8	10 2/8	10 2/8	6 6/8	6 6/8	11	11	Jackson Co., WY	Richard Butts	Richard Butts	1968	294
163 1/8	49 7/8	31 3/8	29 7/8	11 2/8	13 2/8	6 4/8	6 6/8	9	9	Sublette Co., WY	Gerald A. Hoefner	Gerald A. Hoefner	1974	294
163 1/8	48 1/8	31 5/8	29 7/8	10 6/8	11 3/8	6 1/8	5 7/8	11	11	Weber Co., UT	Randy K. Allen	Randy K. Allen	1992	294
163 1/8	52 7/8	29 4/8	29 5/8	10 1/8	10	6 6/8	6 6/8	9	10	Summit Co., UT	Brent V. Buhler	Brent V. Buhler	1994	294
163 1/8	51 1/8	34 6/8	31	10 1/8	10 1/8	5 7/8	5 7/8	11	9	Bear Lake Co., ID	Toni R. Walo	Toni R. Walo	2000	294
163	44 4/8	32	31 6/8	11 3/8	9 6/8	6	6	12	12	Morgan Co., UT	Archie J. Nesbitt	Archie J. Nesbitt	1987	299
163	46 6/8	37 4/8	33 4/8	10 2/8	9 1/8	6 4/8	6 4/8	10	9	Lincoln Co., MT	Bob L. Summerfield	Bob L. Summerfield	1992	299
163	43	33 6/8	31 4/8	12 4/8	12 4/8	6 2/8	6	10	10	Morgan Co., UT	Lynn L. Wilcox	Lynn L. Wilcox	1992	299
162 7/8	48 5/8	30 4/8	30	10 2/8	10 2/8	6 2/8	6 7/8	11	10	Hot Springs Co., WY	Kenneth J. Kucera	Kenneth Kucera	1998	302
162 6/8	49 4/8	34 3/8	33 2/8	9 7/8	9 1/8	6 7/8	6 5/8	11	11	Mineral Co., MT	Shawn R. Andres	Shawn R. Andres	1991	303
162 6/8	51 6/8	35 3/8	34 1/8	8 7/8	7	6 3/8	6 3/8	9	8	Uintah Co., UT	Mitchell S. Bastian	Mitchell S. Bastian	1995	303
162 4/8	42	32 1/8	31 5/8	11 4/8	12 6/8	6 1/8	6 1/8	8	13	Lincoln Co., WY	Gayle E. Hubert	Gayle E. Hubert	1987	305
162 4/8	51 2/8	29	28 4/8	10 3/8	11 4/8	5 7/8	5 6/8	13	12	Lincoln Co., MT	Lance K. Parks	Lance K. Parks	1991	305
162 4/8	49	33 3/8	36 3/8	10	11 7/8	6 3/8	6 3/8	12	7	Lincoln Co., MT	Kurt Spencer	Kurt Spencer	1991	305
162 4/8	44	36 4/8	32	10 2/8	10 3/8	6 1/8	6 1/8	7	11	Bingham Co., ID	Larry D. Jaeger	Larry Jaeger	1998	305
162 3/8	46 7/8	30 6/8	31 1/8	13 2/8	11 3/8	6 5/8	6 5/8	11	9	Sublette Co., WY	Donald K. Irvine	Donald K. Irvine	1969	309
162 3/8	46 7/8	35 6/8	36 6/8	8 6/8	9 4/8	6 3/8	6 2/8	9	7	Bonner Co., ID	Chris Culbertson	Chris Culbertson	2001	309
162 3/8	46 5/8	35 1/8	34	11 3/8	9 2/8	6 5/8	6 5/8	8	8	Idaho Co., ID	Gerhardt L. Phillips III	Gerhardt L. Phillips III	2003	309
162 1/8	44 5/8	31 4/8	31 4/8	10 4/8	9 6/8	6 4/8	6 7/8	12	11	Teton Co., WY	Patrick L. Shanahan	Patrick L. Shanahan	1966	312
162	44 4/8	33 6/8	32 3/8	11 2/8	12 5/8	6 1/8	6 4/8	9	9	Upper Hoback, WY	Walter L. Flint	Walter L. Flint	1951	313
162	48 6/8	29 6/8	34	10 3/8	11 5/8	6 7/8	6 2/8	11	10	Lincoln Co., WY	Joan Burnett	Dee J. Burnett	1963	313
162	42	33	34 4/8	9 6/8	9 6/8	6 2/8	6 2/8	13	11	Madison Co., MT	Joseph M. Aanes	Joseph M. Aanes	1984	313
162	53 4/8	29 5/8	29 3/8	12 6/8	12 1/8	6 6/8	7 3/8	6	6	Jackson Co., CO	Dennis W. Macy	Dennis W. Macy	1991	313
162	45 2/8	33 3/8	36	10 5/8	10	7	7	10	8	Flathead Co., MT	Wendell L. Ellsworth, Jr.	Wendell L. Ellsworth, Jr.	1992	313
162	51	32	32 7/8	9 6/8	9 3/8	7 3/8	7 1/8	7	8	Weber Co., UT	Joseph E. Ricca	Joseph E. Ricca	1994	313
162	49	31 5/8	32 4/8	10 7/8	9	6 7/8	6 4/8	9	9	Jackson Co., CO	Michael R. Tucker	Michael R. Tucker	1998	313
161 7/8	48 7/8	31 7/8	31 2/8	10 7/8	10 7/8	6 2/8	6 1/8	10	9	Teton Co., ID	James Suitts	James Suitts	1992	320
161 7/8	45 5/8	34	33 5/8	9 4/8	11 4/8	6	6	9	9	Weber Co., UT	Michael R. Pribbanow	Michael R. Pribbanow	2000	320
161 7/8	51 1/8	33 6/8	31 2/8	11 5/8	9 6/8	6	5 7/8	12	9	Bonner Co., ID	Troy L. Black	Troy L. Black	2001	320
161 7/8	47 1/8	32 6/8	31 4/8	9 7/8	13 2/8	6	6	10	10	Carbon Co., MT	Stephen Tylinski	Stephen Tylinski	2001	320
161 6/8	51	30 6/8	32	9 6/8	10 4/8	5 7/8	6	10	9	Fremont Co., WY	Robert E. Novotny	Ernest R. Novotny	1944	324
161 6/8	46 6/8	33 2/8	32	10 2/8	10 4/8	6 1/8	6 2/8	9	11	Teton Co., WY	Bob G. Penny	Bob G. Penny	1989	324
161 6/8	45 6/8	35 1/8	36 1/8	9 3/8	9 3/8	6 4/8	6 5/8	7	7	Sublette Co., WY	Robert W. Skorcz	Robert W. Skorcz	1996	324
161 5/8	46 3/8	28 6/8	29 7/8	11 6/8	12 2/8	6 2/8	6 1/8	10	10	Flathead Co., MT	Sharon L. Chase	Sharon L. Chase	1979	327
161 5/8	51 3/8	30 5/8	32 2/8	10 3/8	9 4/8	6 1/8	6	11	9	Cache Co., UT	Kenneth Hamilton	Kenneth Hamilton	1980	327
161 5/8	49 3/8	29 2/8	27 6/8	10 1/8	10 1/8	6 2/8	6 2/8	12	12	Cache Co., UT	Lloyd M. Owens	Lloyd M. Owens	1987	327
161 5/8	52 3/8	31 4/8	31	8 4/8	9 2/8	8 2/8	7 1/8	9	8	Sublette Co., WY	David S. Luzmoor	David S. Luzmoor	1993	327
161 5/8	51 3/8	32	35 1/8	8 1/8	10 1/8	6 4/8	6	9	9	Pend Oreille Co., WA	Seth Greenhaw, Jr.	Seth Greenhaw, Jr.	2000	327
161 5/8	48 5/8	30 6/8	32	9 4/8	10 6/8	6 2/8	6 2/8	11	11	Cache Co., UT	Richard E. Reeder	Richard E. Reeder	2001	327
161 4/8	51	32 4/8	28 3/8	10 1/8	10 6/8	6 6/8	6 6/8	10	10	Teton Co., WY	Don M. Sheaffer	Don M. Sheaffer	1958	333
161 4/8	52 6/8	29	35 3/8	11 7/8	9 4/8	6 4/8	6 3/8	10	11	Jackson Co., WY	Robert D. Lynn	Robert D. Lynn	1969	333
161 4/8	40 2/8	34 3/8	34 6/8	12 7/8	12 6/8	6 4/8	6 4/8	9	8	Teton Co., WY	Lynn C. Hill	Oliver Hill	1979	333
161 4/8	40 4/8	36 1/8	30 4/8	12 7/8	11 7/8	6 1/8	6 3/8	12	12	Bonneville Co., ID	Joe M. Coelho III	Joe M. Coelho III	1982	333
161 4/8	46	32 6/8	36 2/8	8 5/8	8 7/8	6 2/8	6 3/8	11	11	Bonneville Co., ID	Richard H. Meservey	Richard H. Meservey	1989	333
161 4/8	51 2/8	30 1/8	32 6/8	10 6/8	10 4/8	6 4/8	6 5/8	10	10	Teton Co., WY	Archie J. Nesbitt	Archie Nesbitt	1992	333
161 4/8	53	30 3/8	28 5/8	9 5/8	9 4/8	7 2/8	7 2/8	9	9	Park Co., MT	Spence J. Jahner	Spence J. Jahner	1994	333
161 4/8	47 2/8	31 6/8	31 6/8	11 3/8	10	5 7/8	5 7/8	10	10	Madison Co., ID	Archie Moe	Archie Moe	1998	333
161 3/8	51 7/8	30 4/8	31 2/8	10 3/8	10 4/8	5 7/8	5 7/8	11	8	Teton Co., WY	Dean Collins	Dean Collins	2000	341

SHIRAS MOOSE
Alces alces shirasi

Score	Greatest Spread	Length of Palm R	L	Width of Palm R	L	Circumference of Beam at Smallest Place R	L	Number of Normal Points R	L	Locality	Hunter	Owner	Date Killed	Rank
161 2/8	50	34 4/8	27 4/8	11 3/8	11 4/8	6 6/8	6 6/8	11	10	Lincoln Co., MT	Stanley J. Evans	Stanley J. Evans	1982	342
161 2/8	50 6/8	32	33 6/8	8 6/8	9 3/8	6 4/8	6 4/8	8	11	Sheridan Co., WY	Danny R. Hart	Danny R. Hart	1996	342
161 2/8	50 6/8	27 7/8	27 1/8	12	11 3/8	7	6 6/8	10	11	Jackson Co., CO	Wayne R. Kroft	Wayne R. Kroft	1999	342
161 2/8	56	31 1/8	25 4/8	12 4/8	12	6 5/8	6 5/8	10	9	Teton Co., WY	Jerrie L. Eaton	Jerrie L. Eaton	2000	342
161 2/8	50	29 4/8	32 7/8	10 2/8	11 2/8	7	6 7/8	9	9	Pend Oreille Co., WA	Eric B. Walker	Eric B. Walker	2001	342
161 1/8	43 1/8	35 4/8	30 6/8	13 4/8	11 6/8	5 4/8	5 5/8	11	11	Teton Co., WY	Patrick J. Baumann	Patrick J. Baumann	2001	347
161	51 4/8	31 6/8	33 4/8	8 4/8	10 3/8	6 4/8	6 4/8	11	8	Rich Co., UT	Picked Up	Robert G. Petersen	1984	348
161	37 2/8	34 3/8	33 1/8	10 4/8	12 1/8	6 2/8	6 4/8	12	13	Lincoln Co., MT	Charles M. Miller	Charles M. Miller	1990	348
161	50 6/8	29 7/8	29 7/8	9 6/8	13 6/8	6	6 2/8	10	14	Weber Co., UT	Paul J. Rivas	Paul J. Rivas	1992	348
161	48 6/8	38 1/8	33 3/8	8 1/8	9 2/8	6 5/8	7 2/8	8	9	Boundary Co., ID	Lon E. Merrifield	Lon E. Merrifield	2000	348
160 7/8	43 5/8	32 4/8	32 7/8	10 2/8	10 6/8	6 7/8	7 2/8	9	10	Park Co., MT	Wes Synness	Wes Synness	1970	352
160 7/8	46 1/8	30	30 2/8	10 3/8	10 6/8	6	6	12	11	Lincoln Co., WY	Hugh E. Taylor	Hugh E. Taylor	1976	352
160 7/8	40 5/8	34	32 6/8	11 7/8	11 1/8	7 3/8	7 2/8	9	9	Lincoln Co., WY	Julian E. Sjostrom	Julian E. Sjostrom	1990	352
160 7/8	50 3/8	31 4/8	29 4/8	10 6/8	9 7/8	7 7/8	7 1/8	8	8	Cache Co., UT	Obert L. Haines	Obert L. Haines	1992	352
160 7/8	46 7/8	30 2/8	30 2/8	12 1/8	10 5/8	6 1/8	6 2/8	10	11	Bonneville Co., ID	Terry M. Jensen	Terry M. Jensen	1993	352
160 7/8	48 1/8	32 5/8	30	13	12 1/8	6 5/8	6 2/8	11	8	Wasatch Co., UT	Susan S. Willis	Susan S. Willis	1997	352
160 7/8	45 3/8	33 4/8	33 5/8	9 6/8	7 7/8	6 5/8	6 3/8	10	10	Madison Co., ID	Lisa M. Sherick	Lisa M. Sherick	1998	352
160 6/8	49	32 1/8	34 4/8	8 6/8	9 4/8	6	6 2/8	9	12	Pend Oreille Co., WA	Archie D. Wyles	Archie D. Wyles	1977	359
160 6/8	43 4/8	32	33 7/8	11	11	6 5/8	7 3/8	10	9	Sanders Co., MT	Ray E. Wolff	Ray E. Wolff	1987	359
160 6/8	40 4/8	33 3/8	33	10 5/8	10 7/8	6 4/8	6 4/8	11	10	Jackson Co., CO	Robert T. Goettl	Robert T. Goettl	1994	359
160 6/8	57	32 3/8	32	9 2/8	10 3/8	6 5/8	6 6/8	4	6	Mineral Co., MT	Dennis E. Althoff	Dennis E. Althoff	1995	359
160 6/8	47 2/8	30 2/8	30	10 2/8	9 4/8	7 3/8	7 2/8	10	10	Jackson Co., CO	Bill Dalley	Bill Dalley	2001	359
160 6/8	38 6/8	35 2/8	36 4/8	11 6/8	9 7/8	5 7/8	6 1/8	12	10	Summit Co., UT	Catherine D. Mower	Catherine D. Mower	2002	359
160 6/8	50	32 3/8	31 5/8	9 4/8	9	5 7/8	5 6/8	9	9	Flathead Co., MT	Shawn P. Price	Shawn P. Price	2003	359
160 5/8	53 7/8	30 2/8	35 6/8	9	12 7/8	6 1/8	6 1/8	8	10	Caribou Co., ID	Dale E. Lindstrom	Dale E. Lindstrom	1988	366
160 5/8	49 5/8	31 2/8	31 1/8	7 6/8	10 6/8	6 5/8	6 5/8	11	11	Bonneville Co., ID	Gary L. Sant	Gary L. Sant	1991	366
160 4/8	48	29 2/8	30 4/8	11 4/8	11 1/8	6 7/8	7	10	9	Lincoln Co., WY	Vic Dana	Fred's Taxidermy	1971	368
160 4/8	43 2/8	31 7/8	31 2/8	11 2/8	11	7 4/8	7 3/8	10	9	Beaverhead Co., MT	Morton L. Arkava	Morton L. Arkava	1980	368
160 4/8	47 6/8	31 6/8	32 6/8	7 4/8	10 4/8	7 1/8	7 2/8	10	10	Sheridan Co., WY	Don D. Morrison	Don D. Morrison	1993	368
160 4/8	50 4/8	30 3/8	29 2/8	11	9 5/8	6 2/8	6 2/8	10	10	Jackson Co., CO	Ronald W. Madsen	Ronald W. Madsen	1996	368
160 4/8	45 6/8	35	37 2/8	9 2/8	10 3/8	6 1/8	6 1/8	7	9	Clark Co., ID	David L. Denny	David L. Denny	2002	368
160 3/8	45 3/8	30 2/8	31 2/8	11 7/8	12 7/8	7 3/8	7 6/8	11	8	Madison Co., MT	Tom Bugni	Tom Bugni	1959	373
160 3/8	45 1/8	31 3/8	34 2/8	9 6/8	12 4/8	6 4/8	6 6/8	10	14	Jackson Hole, WY	Jack Griset	Jack Griset	1967	373
160 3/8	49 3/8	29 6/8	31 4/8	9 4/8	11 6/8	6 2/8	6 2/8	10	12	Lincoln Co., WY	Eugene Heap	Eugene Heap	1970	373
160 3/8	50 1/8	29 4/8	29 4/8	10 2/8	10 1/8	5 4/8	5 4/8	10	10	Teton Co., WY	Joy L. Gage	Joy L. Gage	1981	373
160 3/8	50 1/8	33 2/8	32 4/8	9 4/8	11 1/8	6 1/8	6 1/8	7	9	Bonner Co., ID	Frederick Veltri	Frederick Veltri	1992	373
160 2/8	59 6/8	29	38	8 7/8	8 7/8	6 3/8	6 3/8	6	7	Lower Hoback, WY	Obby Agins	Obby Agins	1966	378
160 1/8	46 5/8	32 4/8	32 2/8	9 6/8	11 2/8	5 6/8	5 6/8	9	11	Sublette Co., WY	Nancy Burstad	Nancy Burstad	1996	379

Score	Spread	Length R	Length L	Width R	Width L	Circ R	Circ L	Pts R	Pts L	Locality	Hunter	Owner	Date	Rank
159 6/8	49	32 4/8	31 3/8	7 3/8	8 3/8	6 5/8	6 7/8	10	11	Madison Co., ID	Max Bosworth	Max Bosworth	1985	380
159 6/8	45 2/8	33 2/8	32 6/8	9 6/8	10 3/8	6 6/8	6 6/8	8	11	Summit Co., UT	Dal Eyre	Dal Eyre	1991	380
159 6/8	36 2/8	33 3/8	35 1/8	9 2/8	9 4/8	7 2/8	7 1/8	12	12	Sheridan Co., WY	Jerry D. Blakeman	Jerry D. Blakeman	1992	380
159 6/8	49 4/8	28 3/8	31 2/8	10 5/8	10 2/8	6 4/8	6 5/8	11	10	Sanders Co., MT	Robert A. Parker	Robert A. Parker	1997	380
159 6/8	43 6/8	33 4/8	33 3/8	10	13 4/8	6 5/8	6 5/8	8	10	Bonneville Co., ID	Eric P. Horman	Eric P. Horman	2001	380
159 5/8	49 5/8	32 5/8	31 6/8	10 1/8	9 4/8	6	6	8	8	Caribou Co., ID	Douglas C. Hall	Douglas C. Hall	1994	385
159 4/8	49 2/8	31 4/8	31 6/8	9 4/8	8 6/8	6 6/8	6 7/8	8	10	Teton Co., WY	Willis McAmis	Willis McAmis	1972	386
159 4/8	46	32	32 4/8	10 3/8	7 6/8	6 1/8	6	9	10	Fremont Co., ID	Lennard C. Bradley	Lennard C. Bradley	1983	386
159 4/8	45 6/8	33 1/8	32 6/8	10 2/8	10 4/8	6 7/8	7 1/8	7	12	Jackson Co., CO	Donald I. Poeschl	Donald I. Poeschl	1987	386
159 4/8	42 6/8	30 2/8	30 6/8	11 6/8	9 4/8	6 3/8	6 5/8	12	10	Weber Co., UT	Neal W. Darby	Neal W. Darby	1989	386
159 4/8	47	33 4/8	32	12 5/8	14	6 3/8	6 2/8	11	9	Jackson Co., CO	Steven M. Weinberg	Steven M. Weinberg	1998	386
159 4/8	48 4/8	30 2/8	36 3/8	15	9	6 3/8	6 2/8	5	5	Boundary Co., ID	Marcus Byler	Marcus Byler	1999	386
159 3/8	45 3/8	26 4/8	29 5/8	10 5/8	11 2/8	5 6/8	5 6/8	9	10	Pinedale, WY	C.J. McElroy	C.J. McElroy	1969	392
159 3/8	55 3/8	30 7/8	28	10	10 7/8	6 6/8	6 6/8	11	11	Idaho Co., ID	Rick E. Kramer	Rick E. Kramer	1980	392
159 3/8	41 5/8	31 7/8	30 6/8	10 7/8	10 5/8	6 4/8	6 5/8	10	13	Weber Co., UT	Carl O. Berube	Carl O. Berube	1983	392
159 3/8	46 7/8	31 1/8	31 7/8	11 4/8	11 6/8	6 5/8	6 2/8	8	9	Teton Co., WY	Tony D. Poulos	Tony D. Poulos	1983	392
159 3/8	49 7/8	31 1/8	29	11 5/8	9 2/8	6 2/8	6 1/8	9	8	Clearwater Co., ID	Jeffrey D. Dunbar	Jeffrey D. Dunbar	1997	392
159 3/8	49 5/8	29 4/8	29 4/8	10 4/8	11 4/8	6 3/8	6 2/8	9	9	Teton Co., WY	Warren J. Hatton	Warren J. Hatton	2000	392
159 3/8	44 3/8	31 1/8	30 4/8	11	9 6/8	6 6/8	6 3/8	11	9	Teton Co., WY	Scott L. Ray	Scott L. Ray	2001	392
159 2/8	53 4/8	34 1/8	30 2/8	11 4/8	11 4/8	7	6	6	10	Pine Creek, WY	Bud Toliver	Bud Toliver	1971	399
159 2/8	52 4/8	31 4/8	31	7 6/8	9 4/8	6 5/8	6 5/8	8	9	Lincoln Co., WY	Orlando J. Bernardi	Orlando J. Bernardi	1979	399
159 2/8	53 6/8	33 7/8	33 2/8	9	7 4/8	6	6 6/8	6	8	Pend Oreille Co., WA	Eric F. Rebitzer	Eric F. Rebitzer	2000	399
159 1/8	51 1/8	33 3/8	29	8 7/8	8 6/8	7 2/8	7 2/8	9	7	Sublette Co., WY	Robert W. Sievers	Mrs. R.B. McCullough	1967	402
159 1/8	47 3/8	33	30 2/8	12 6/8	14	5 7/8	5 7/8	9	9	Teton Co., WY	Eugene E. Hafen	Eugene E. Hafen	1989	402
159 1/8	54 1/8	30 2/8	33 1/8	10 1/8	8 6/8	5 4/8	5 4/8	9	8	Boundary Co., ID	Todd W. Egland	Todd W. Egland	1994	402
159 1/8	47 7/8	27 1/8	29 4/8	11 7/8	11 4/8	6	6	11	11	Grand Co., CO	Gerry A. Adair	Gerry A. Adair	1997	402
159 1/8	48 3/8	32	32	9 2/8	7 6/8	6 5/8	6 5/8	9	9	Bonneville Co., ID	Richard F. Karbowski	Richard F. Karbowski	1998	402
159 1/8	45 1/8	32	34 7/8	11 2/8	9 4/8	6 5/8	6 4/8	12	12	Jackson Co., WY	Brian G. Edgerton	Brian G. Edgerton	2000	402
159	48 4/8	33 4/8	35 3/8	13 2/8	11 6/8	6 4/8	6	10	12	Green River, WY	Earl F. Hayes	Earl F. Hayes	1953	408
159	41 2/8	35 1/8	32 5/8	9 4/8	10 6/8	6	6 7/8	8	7	Sheridan Co., WY	W.M. Hightower	W.M. Hightower	1962	408
159	48	32 4/8	33	9 4/8	9 5/8	7	6 7/8	10	12	Teton Co., WY	Bradley C. Wichman	Bradley C. Wichman	1990	408
159	47 3/8	28 2/8	30 5/8	11 2/8	11 2/8	6 2/8	6 2/8	12	12	Caribou Co., ID	James A. Fanning	James A. Fanning	1992	408
159	44 6/8	31 3/8	34 1/8	11	12 1/8	6 3/8	5 7/8	11	11	Weber Co., UT	Kenneth W. Logue	Kenneth W. Logue	2002	408
158 7/8	47 1/8	29 4/8	32 6/8	9 2/8	9 2/8	6 3/8	6 2/8	9	9	Teton Co., WY	Donald E. Franklin	Donald E. Franklin	1985	413
158 7/8	48 3/8	32 3/8	34 3/8	10 2/8	11	6 5/8	6 4/8	9	9	Madison Co., MT	Robert E. Bergquist	Robert E. Bergquist	1998	413
158 7/8	49 1/8	27 3/8	33 2/8	13 6/8	14 6/8	6 1/8	6	13	13	Gallatin Co., MT	Paul A. Pernak	Paul A. Pernak	2001	413
158 6/8	40 6/8	36 1/8	33 2/8	9 6/8	9 4/8	6 4/8	6 2/8	8	8	N. Hoback, WY	Fred Moger	Lance F. Hossack	1951	416
158 6/8	45 2/8	35	35 3/8	9 5/8	10 2/8	6 2/8	6 2/8	7	7	Johnson Co., WY	Geo. W. Hundley	Geo. W. Hundley	1970	416
158 6/8	42 6/8	32	32 5/8	11 1/8	12 4/8	6 4/8	6 2/8	6	6	Idaho Co., ID	Brian G. Griffin	Brian G. Griffin	1996	416
158 6/8	51	33	33	9 6/8	9 4/8	7 2/8	7 2/8	8	8	Trail Creek, WY	Loren R. Alley	Loren R. Alley	2003	416
158 5/8	44 5/8	35 6/8	33	11 7/8	12 1/8	6 4/8	6 4/8	10	10	Teton Co., WY	John J. Huseas	John J. Huseas	1953	420
158 5/8	47 3/8	30 7/8	30 5/8	10 5/8	10 5/8	5	5	12	13	Lincoln Co., WY	Albert Pantelis	Albert Pantelis	1967	420
158 5/8	40 1/8	35 2/8	34 1/8	11 1/8	12 2/8	6	6	7	8	Park Co., MT	Caroline Nare	Caroline Nare	1979	420
158 5/8	42 1/8	28 7/8	28 6/8	11 6/8	14 6/8	6 1/8	3 1/8	11	11	New Fork River, WY	Anthony W. Pollari	Anthony W. Pollari	1994	420
158 4/8	43 2/8	32	34	11 2/8	9 6/8	6 1/8	5	8	8	Teton Co., WY	Oscar Boyd	Oscar Boyd	1966	424
158 4/8	47	33 1/8	29	11 2/8	8 4/8	6 1/8	5	9	9	Teton Co., WY	Roy G. Hoover	Roy G. Hoover	1966	424
158 3/8	51 1/8	33 1/8	31 6/8	11 2/8	8 4/8	8 3/8	7 5/8	9	9	Teton Co., WY	Clyde E. Harnden	Clyde E. Harnden	1986	426
158 3/8	46 7/8	31 6/8	35 4/8	8 5/8	11 7/8	6 3/8	3 5/8	10	10	Fremont Co., ID	Rance B. Dye	Rance B. Dye	1998	426

SHIRAS MOOSE
Alces alces shirasi

Score	Greatest Spread	Length of Palm R	L	Width of Palm R	L	Circumference of Beam at Smallest Place R	L	Number of Normal Points R	L	Locality	Hunter	Owner	Date Killed	Rank
158 3/8	42 3/8	36	31 1/8	11	11 5/8	7 3/8	6 7/8	9	10	Latah Co., ID	Dustin L. Thomas	Dustin L. Thomas	1998	426
158 3/8	50 6/8	26	26 7/8	10 2/8	10 6/8	6 4/8	6 5/8	11	12	Pinedale, WY	Donald C. Rehwaldt	Donald C. Rehwaldt	1966	429
158 2/8	51	30 5/8	26 3/8	11 1/8	11 1/8	7 2/8	7 1/8	10	9	Clark Co., ID	Harold Vietz	Harold Vietz	1968	429
158 2/8	46 2/8	33 1/8	31 6/8	10 7/8	10 1/8	6 2/8	6 1/8	10	8	Cache Co., UT	Scott W. Crosbie	Scott W. Crosbie	1987	429
158 2/8	56	26 4/8	28	10 7/8	10 6/8	7	6 5/8	8	8	Summit Co., UT	Picked Up	Ralph E. Swiss	1991	429
158 2/8	46 4/8	31 7/8	33 3/8	10 6/8	9	6	6	10	9	Summit Co., UT	Thomas A. Von Hatten	Thomas A. Von Hatten	1995	429
158 2/8	45	34 6/8	34 6/8	9 6/8	9 7/8	6 1/8	6 2/8	7	6	Pend Oreille Co., WA	Carl T. Bach	Carl T. Bach	1998	429
158 2/8	44	34 4/8	32	11 1/8	13 4/8	6	6	8	11	Idaho Co., ID	Ray Brown	Ray Brown	2001	429
158 2/8	46	34 2/8	32 4/8	9 6/8	9	6 6/8	6 5/8	8	8	Albany Co., WY	J. Darroll Bennett	J. Darroll Bennett	2002	429
158 1/8	42 5/8	33 4/8	35 6/8	11 6/8	11 6/8	6 5/8	6 4/8	9	6	Gravel Mt., WY	W.A. Kalkofen	W.A. Kalkofen	1966	437
158 1/8	46 3/8	30 4/8	31 7/8	8 7/8	10 3/8	6 4/8	6 4/8	10	10	Teton Co., WY	Fred L. Eales	Fred L. Eales	1984	437
158 1/8	47 7/8	32 2/8	31 3/8	11	11 2/8	6 6/8	6 7/8	6	7	Grand Co., CO	Ronald R. Pomeroy	Ronald R. Pomeroy	1993	437
158 1/8	44 3/8	29 2/8	28 5/8	11 6/8	11 3/8	6 7/8	6 7/8	11	10	Jackson Co., CO	Bill L. Olson	Bill L. Olson	1994	437
158 1/8	47 3/8	30 3/8	35 3/8	11 5/8	11 6/8	6 3/8	6 5/8	12	7	Summit Co., UT	Stephen W. Davis	Stephen W. Davis	1995	437
158 1/8	47 5/8	33 3/8	30 1/8	11	10 3/8	6	5 6/8	9	10	Shoshone Co., ID	John L. Pongrac	John L. Pongrac	1997	437
158	46 2/8	30 3/8	30 4/8	10 1/8	9 7/8	5 6/8	5 5/8	10	14	Bonneville Co., ID	Michael P. Dome	Michael P. Dome	1992	443
158	45 2/8	32 6/8	33 3/8	8 7/8	10 4/8	6 6/8	7	8	9	Bonneville Co., ID	Larry T. Evens	Larry T. Evens	1997	443
158	47	30 7/8	33 6/8	9	9 4/8	5 5/8	5 5/8	10	10	Boundary Co., ID	John P. Thomas	John P. Thomas	2000	443
158	48 4/8	33 6/8	32 4/8	9	9	6 2/8	6 2/8	7	7	Sublette Co., WY	Maureen Montgomery	Maureen Montgomery	2001	443
157 7/8	43 7/8	31 6/8	31 6/8	9 4/8	8 4/8	6 6/8	6 7/8	10	10	Teton Co., WY	Willard H. Leedy	Willard H. Leedy	1982	447
157 7/8	43 5/8	34 4/8	33 4/8	9 5/8	13 2/8	6	6	8	13	Flathead Co., MT	James M. Milligan	James M. Milligan	1982	447
157 7/8	52 3/8	32	30 3/8	8 4/8	10 6/8	5 7/8	6 1/8	8	8	Lincoln Co., WY	Patrick H. Roberts	Patrick H. Roberts	1988	447
157 7/8	47 1/8	33 3/8	29 1/8	11 4/8	10 7/8	6 3/8	6 4/8	9	10	Lincoln Co., MT	John K. Curry	John K. Curry	1997	447
157 7/8	50 5/8	29 2/8	30 2/8	9 7/8	10 3/8	6 5/8	6 4/8	9	12	Flathead Co., MT	Tom Ritzdorf	Tom L. Ritzdorf	1998	447
157 6/8	47 2/8	27	29	13 2/8	12 2/8	6 1/8	6	10	12	Cache Co., UT	David W. Jensen	David W. Jensen	1977	452
157 6/8	47 3/8	35 4/8	33	8 4/8	9 7/8	6 6/8	6 6/8	7	8	Sublette Co., WY	Mrs. Kenneth Fortuna	Mrs. Kenneth Fortuna	1984	452
157 6/8	46 4/8	29 2/8	31 2/8	10	10 7/8	6 4/8	6 3/8	10	14	Morgan Co., UT	John L. Estes	John L. Estes	1987	452
157 6/8	43 4/8	32 2/8	32 6/8	10 2/8	10 2/8	6 7/8	7 2/8	8	8	Beaverhead Co., MT	Louis A. Kluesner	Louis A. Kluesner	1997	452
157 6/8	46 6/8	29 1/8	29 5/8	10 2/8	10 6/8	6 1/8	6 2/8	10	10	Weber Co., UT	Andreas Boehlendorf	Andreas Boehlendorf	2000	452
157 6/8	51 2/8	28 7/8	31 6/8	10 1/8	9 4/8	5 7/8	5 7/8	9	12	Carbon Co., MT	Mark Theroux	Mark Theroux	2001	452
157 5/8	41 5/8	33 2/8	34 1/8	10 2/8	9 5/8	6 1/8	6 1/8	9	12	Madison Co., ID	Lawrence Buckland	Lawrence Buckland	1987	458
157 5/8	44 5/8	29 7/8	32 4/8	10 1/8	12 6/8	6 4/8	6 5/8	12	10	Summit Co., UT	Robert C. Chidester	Robert C. Chidester	1999	458
157 4/8	50 2/8	28 1/8	26 2/8	10 6/8	11 1/8	6 5/8	6 5/8	11	10	Grey's River, WY	Mary B. Mikalis	Mary B. Mikalis	1969	460
157 4/8	42 6/8	30 5/8	30 5/8	10 1/8	9 1/8	5 5/8	5 5/8	12	12	Flathead Co., MT	Scott L. Davis	Scott L. Davis	1991	460
157 3/8	51 1/8	31 2/8	28	10	9 5/8	6 4/8	6 4/8	9	9	Sublette Co., WY	Teressa Ennis	Teressa Ennis	1983	462
157 3/8	41 3/8	28 6/8	28 6/8	12 2/8	12	6 2/8	6 2/8	12	11	Idaho Co., ID	Norman R. Fuchs	Norman R. Fuchs	1984	462
157 3/8	49 7/8	37 5/8	25 5/8	13 6/8	14	6 7/8	7	11	8	Bonneville Co., ID	George L. Vivian	George L. Vivian	1987	462
157 3/8	50 1/8	28 6/8	31	9 4/8	10	6 3/8	6 4/8	9	11	Teton Co., ID	Wenda W. Jones	Wenda W. Jones	1995	462

Score	Greatest Spread	Length of Palm R	Length of Palm L	Width of Palm R	Width of Palm L	Circumference of Beam R	Circumference of Beam L	Points R	Points L	Locality	Hunter	Owner	Date	Rank
157 3/8	46 1/8	29 2/8	31 6/8	11 3/8	10 4/8	6 7/8	6 7/8	9	10	Weber Co., UT	Scott George	Scott George	1998	462
157 3/8	44 3/8	31 4/8	33 5/8	10 6/8	12 3/8	6 3/8	6 2/8	8	13	Carbon Co., WY	Chad D. Blake	Chad D. Blake	2002	462
157 2/8	45 4/8	33	37 4/8	10 3/8	9 7/8	6	6	7	8	Lincoln Co., MT	Bob Stafford	Bob Stafford	1963	468
157 2/8	43 6/8	30 3/8	30 2/8	10 4/8	11 4/8	6 4/8	6 4/8	12	10	Teton Co., WY	Thomas L. Buller	Thomas L. Buller	2000	468
157 2/8	49 6/8	32 6/8	30 5/8	7 6/8	8 3/8	6 3/8	6 4/8	10	9	Jackson Co., CO	James E. Schmid	James E. Schmid	2001	468
157 1/8	53 3/8	29 2/8	29 2/8	9	9 4/8	5 5/8	5 5/8	8	8	Pend Oreille Co., WA	William C. Phifer	William C. Phifer	1994	471
157 1/8	46 7/8	30 4/8	36 3/8	9 3/8	12 1/8	6 2/8	6 3/8	9	11	Teton Co., WY	Gary J. Amrine	Gary J. Amrine	2000	471
157 1/8	53 1/8	29 3/8	34 4/8	9 5/8	13 2/8	6 1/8	6	7	12	Flathead Co., MT	Larry A. Fenster	Larry A. Fenster	1962	471
157	47 4/8	29 6/8	31 3/8	9 6/8	12 2/8	6 4/8	6 2/8	10	9	Fremont Co., WY	Fred S. Finley	Fred S. Finley	1986	474
157	47 2/8	29 1/8	26 7/8	11 6/8	11 6/8	6 2/8	6 3/8	10	10	Beaverhead Co., MT	Jason W. Roylance	Jason W. Roylance	1994	474
157	43 6/8	35 1/8	29 1/8	10 3/8	9 6/8	6 6/8	6 2/8	11	11	Teton Co., WY	Steven C. Rudd	Steven C. Rudd	1994	474
157	57	30 4/8	32 1/8	5 2/8	7	6 3/8	6 2/8	8	11	Ruby Mts., MT	Thomas E. Tillman	Thomas E. Tillman	1960	474
156 7/8	46 1/8	29 6/8	28	14 7/8	14 6/8	7 1/8	6 5/8	6	9	Madison Co., MT	Milton Burdick	Milton Burdick	1971	478
156 7/8	38 7/8	30 3/8	31	11 3/8	12 3/8	6 2/8	6 3/8	11	13	Deer Lodge Co., MT	Mike Munson	Mike Munson	1952	478
156 6/8	45 2/8	33 1/8	31 6/8	10 4/8	9	7 3/8	7	9	8	Teton Co., WY	Palmer Hegge	Palmer Hegge	1967	480
156 6/8	37	34	36	11 2/8	13 2/8	6 5/8	6 5/8	8	9	Devil's Basin, WY	Charlotte Bruce	Charlotte Bruce	1979	480
156 6/8	46 2/8	33 7/8	31 3/8	11	11 1/8	5 7/8	5 7/8	9	7	Sublette Co., WY	Richard A. Bonander	Richard A. Bonander	1985	480
156 6/8	43 2/8	31	29 4/8	10 4/8	11	5 6/8	6 7/8	10	10	Fremont Co., WY	Jan Liggett	J. Liggett & L. Liggett	1989	480
156 6/8	45 6/8	34 2/8	34 4/8	10	9 2/8	5	6 3/8	6	7	Lincoln Co., WY	Bryan Dexter	Bryan Dexter	1994	480
156 6/8	46 4/8	28	30 3/8	10 4/8	10 4/8	3 5/8	6 6/8	10	13	Cache Co., UT	Darin Seamons	Darin Seamons	1997	480
156 6/8	43 6/8	32 2/8	32	9 2/8	9 4/8	3 2/8	6 2/8	9	10	Flathead Co., MT	Charles J. Fritz	Charles J. Fritz	2001	480
156 6/8	44 6/8	35 4/8	32 6/8	11	10	3 4/8	6 4/8	8	8	Sublette Co., WY	Dianna L. Trapp	Dianna L. Trapp	1977	480
156 5/8	42 3/8	29 5/8	31 7/8	11 3/8	11 6/8	7 4/8	7	9	9	Teton Co., WY	George A. Nevills	George A. Nevills	1999	488
156 5/8	41 7/8	32	32	11 1/8	10 2/8	3 2/8	6 5/8	11	10	Power Co., ID	Wesley T. Port	Wesley T. Port	2000	488
156 5/8	49 3/8	34 4/8	34 1/8	7 2/8	10 4/8	3 2/8	6 2/8	6	10	Bonneville Co., ID	Daniel J. Branagan	Daniel J. Branagan	2002	488
156 5/8	53 1/8	27 1/8	26 2/8	11 4/8	11 3/8	5 1/8	6 2/8	8	9	Jackson Co., CO	Frank S. Noska IV	Frank S. Noska IV	1960	488
156 4/8	42 6/8	32 3/8	34 5/8	12 2/8	12 4/8	5 2/8	6 2/8	6	6	Gallatin River, MT	Paul Mako	Paul Mako	1966	492
156 4/8	51 2/8	29	32	8 6/8	9	5 7/8	6 7/8	8	9	Buffalo Horn Lake, MT	Vincent De Stefano	Vincent De Stefano	1973	492
156 4/8	49 6/8	30	30	10 2/8	9 5/8	5 7/8	5 7/8	11	12	Thorofare River, WY	Dean Johnson	Dean Johnson	1991	492
156 4/8	42 2/8	30 6/8	28 5/8	10 2/8	9 7/8	6 1/8	6 4/8	11	11	Caribou Co., ID	Reuben R. Barzee	Raelene Barzee	2001	492
156 4/8	42 6/8	30 1/8	30 5/8	11 1/8	10 4/8	6 4/8	6 6/8	10	8	Beaverhead Co., MT	Dan Alzheimer	Dan Alzheimer	1986	492
156 4/8	48 1/8	33 1/8	30 5/8	11	10 1/8	6 6/8	7	6	10	Idaho Co., ID	Max D. Hunsaker	Max D. Hunsaker	1993	497
156 3/8	39 3/8	33 1/8	32 3/8	10 3/8	9 6/8	6 6/8	6 6/8	9	9	Lincoln Co., MT	Arthur H. Baker	Arthur H. Baker	1997	497
156 3/8	43 7/8	34 4/8	34 4/8	8 7/8	8 2/8	6 2/8	6 2/8	7	9	Lincoln Co., MT	Thomas A. Steenberg	Thomas A. Steenberg	1999	497
156 3/8	52 3/8	30 6/8	30 6/8	7 7/8	8 4/8	6 3/8	6 3/8	7	8	Morgan Co., UT	Robert O. Calvert	Robert O. Calvert	1970	501
156 2/8	43	40 7/8	31 4/8	10 2/8	10 1/8	7	7	9	10	Teton Co., WY	Gerda Prince	Gerda Prince	1980	501
156 2/8	46 6/8	31 4/8	30 5/8	8	9 5/8	6 1/8	6 1/8	10	11	Summit Co., UT	John G. Allred	John G. Allred	1988	501
156 2/8	41 6/8	32	32	10 4/8	9 7/8	6 3/8	6 4/8	11	10	Teton Co., WY	James A. Kent	James A. Kent	1990	501
156 2/8	42 4/8	31 4/8	31 3/8	10 1/8	10 4/8	7 3/8	7 5/8	10	8	Beaverhead Co., MT	Todd M. Gilstrap	Todd M. Gilstrap	2000	501
156 2/8	51 6/8	29 4/8	30 2/8	7 7/8	9 1/8	5 7/8	6 2/8	9	10	Lincoln Co., MT	Gay M. Osler-Cook	Gay M. Osler-Cook	2002	501
156 1/8	47 2/8	31 2/8	31 4/8	8 4/8	9 6/8	5 6/8	5 6/8	10	9	Beaverhead Co., MT	Lori J. Ginn	Lori J. Ginn	1967	507
156 1/8	47 3/8	31 5/8	34 4/8	9 6/8	7 6/8	6 1/8	6 4/8	9	9	Lewis Creek, WY	Donald J. Krist	Donald J. Krist	1973	507
156 1/8	45 7/8	30 3/8	31 1/8	11	10 2/8	6 4/8	6 5/8	8	7	Glade Creek, WY	Joseph A. Merrill, Jr.	Joseph A. Merrill, Jr.	1986	507
156	40 1/8	33 4/8	31 4/8	12 3/8	13 6/8	6 2/8	6	7	8	Idaho Co., ID	John R. Lewinski	John R. Lewinski	1957	510
156	45 4/8	32 4/8	29 1/8	8 4/8	8	6 6/8	7	11	9	Missoula Co., MT	W.L. Rohrer	W.L. Rohrer	1990	510
156	43 4/8	31 2/8	29 2/8	11 6/8	11 6/8	6 2/8	6 2/8	13	11	Bonneville Co., ID	Bruce J. Thomson	Bruce J. Thomson	1997	510
156	50 2/8	29	30 2/8	9 6/8	10 3/8	6 1/8	6 1/8	8	10	Sublette Co., WY	Allen C. Capes	Allen C. Capes	1997	510
156	44	29	27 4/8	11	11	6 4/8	6 4/8	12	11	Sublette Co., WY	James M. Cody	James M. Cody	1998	510

SHIRAS MOOSE
Alces alces shirasi

Score	Greatest Spread	Length of Palm R	L	Width of Palm R	L	Circumference of Beam at Smallest Place R	L	Number of Normal Points R	L	Locality	Hunter	Owner	Date Killed	Rank
156	39 2/8	34	33 1/8	10 1/8	10	6 2/8	6 4/8	10	9	Idaho Co., ID	Matthew J. Herbek	Matthew J. Herbek	1998	510
156	42 4/8	32	30	10 6/8	11 1/8	6	6 4/8	10	9	Teton Co., WY	Thomas Covert	Thomas Covert	2001	510
155 7/8	52 3/8	29 4/8	30 4/8	7 2/8	9 1/8	6	6	9	9	Ashton, ID	Robert H. Thomas	Robert H. Thomas	1972	516
155 7/8	44 5/8	34 7/8	34 4/8	11 1/8	9 3/8	6 6/8	6 6/8	5	10	Jackson Co., CO	Thomas A. Yukman	Thomas A. Yukman	1992	516
155 6/8	46	31 4/8	31 2/8	8 4/8	7 4/8	7 1/8	7 2/8	10	9	Jackson Hole, WY	Don Phillips	Don Phillips	1956	518
155 6/8	48 6/8	27 4/8	27 6/8	10 4/8	11 6/8	6 4/8	7	9	10	Jackson Hole, WY	Ralph Brumbaugh	Ralph Brumbaugh	1960	518
155 6/8	39 4/8	28	28 1/8	13	16 7/8	6 2/8	6 1/8	11	12	Upper Hoback, WY	Stephen N. Bean	Stephen N. Bean	1969	518
155 6/8	52 2/8	36 4/8	33 6/8	7 3/8	6 2/8	5 6/8	5 7/8	8	6	Summit Co., UT	Monika M. Anderson	Monika M. Anderson	1982	518
155 6/8	44 6/8	30	37 7/8	10 1/8	9 3/8	6 1/8	6 2/8	10	10	Lake Co., MT	Kenneth E. Trickey	Kenneth E. Trickey	1993	518
155 6/8	46	29 7/8	27 6/8	11	11 1/8	6 1/8	6 2/8	12	10	Fremont Co., ID	Debra L. Borresen	Debra L. Borresen	1994	518
155 5/8	41 5/8	30	31 4/8	11 3/8	11 3/8	5 5/8	6	10	11	Lincoln Co., MT	Robert D. Nolin	Robert D. Nolin	1979	524
155 5/8	52 7/8	29 4/8	31 2/8	8	8	5 7/8	5 7/8	10	8	Summit Co., UT	Michelle R. Liechty	Michelle R. Liechty	1989	524
155 5/8	48 1/8	30 5/8	30 3/8	9 4/8	10 5/8	5 7/8	6	8	9	Lincoln Co., WY	Robert B. Williams	Robert B. Williams	1994	524
155 5/8	42 1/8	30 4/8	30 5/8	10 5/8	12	6 6/8	6 5/8	10	9	Beaverhead Co., MT	Larry G. Marshall	Larry G. Marshall	1999	524
155 4/8	51 2/8	30 7/8	31 2/8	11 1/8	8 7/8	6 2/8	6 3/8	9	7	Green River, WY	H.S. Jackman	H.S. Jackman	1964	528
155 4/8	46	27 1/8	31	12 6/8	11 4/8	6	6 1/8	11	10	Jackson Co., WY	Bud Weaver	Bud Weaver	1968	528
155 4/8	42 2/8	29	29	10 6/8	10 5/8	6	6	11	11	Lincoln Co., WY	Ralph Wood	Ralph Wood	1977	528
155 4/8	48 4/8	31	31 7/8	12 6/8	9 1/8	5 5/8	5 3/8	9	8	Lincoln Co., MT	H.E. Thompson, Jr.	H.E. Thompson, Jr.	1984	528
155 4/8	47 6/8	30 2/8	31 4/8	9 3/8	10 1/8	6 2/8	6 4/8	8	10	Morgan Co., UT	Michael C. Allen	Michael C. Allen	1987	528
155 4/8	43 6/8	31	30 5/8	9 2/8	9 3/8	6 1/8	5 7/8	10	10	Lincoln Co., WY	Rhonda S. Crank	Rhonda S. Crank	1989	528
155 4/8	48 2/8	27 1/8	30 6/8	9 5/8	10 6/8	5 7/8	6 2/8	11	12	Gallatin Co., MT	Mark A. Davidson	Mark A. Davidson	1992	528
155 4/8	38	31 3/8	30 6/8	12 7/8	13 3/8	6 1/8	6 3/8	10	10	Madison Co., ID	Jeffrey L. Griffith	Jeffrey L. Griffith	1994	528
155 4/8	46 2/8	28 3/8	30 7/8	10 3/8	10	6 2/8	6 1/8	10	10	Teton Co., WY	Richard W. Woodfin	Richard W. Woodfin	1998	528
155 4/8	47 6/8	31 4/8	31 2/8	8 7/8	8 4/8	6 1/8	5 1/8	8	8	Caribou Co., ID	J. George Williams	J. George Williams	2001	528
155 4/8	49 2/8	29 1/8	31 1/8	9 3/8	8 7/8	5 2/8	6 6/8	10	8	Teton Co., WY	Bruce Dodson	Bruce Dodson	2002	528
155 3/8	52 3/8	28	27 4/8	9 7/8	9 2/8	6 6/8	6 1/8	8	8	Upper Yellowstone, WY	Harold E. Anthony	Am. Mus. Nat. Hist.	1934	539
155 3/8	49 5/8	30 5/8	30 2/8	8 5/8	9 5/8	6	7	8	9	Spread Creek, WY	Marty Fiorello	Marty Fiorello	1963	539
155 3/8	43 3/8	33 4/8	30	10 2/8	10 6/8	6 6/8	6 5/8	9	10	Sublette Co., WY	Tom J. Schwindt	Tom J. Schwindt	1973	539
155 3/8	49 5/8	23 4/8	29	13 3/8	14 7/8	6 4/8	6 5/8	10	11	Pend Oreille Co., WA	Thomas F. Kneeshaw	Thomas F. Kneeshaw	1983	539
155 3/8	48 5/8	30 2/8	28 7/8	10 3/8	9 4/8	6 5/8	6 5/8	9	9	Clark Co., ID	Louis E. Beardall	Louis E. Beardall	1994	539
155 2/8	47	28 3/8	29 4/8	10	9 4/8	6 2/8	6 2/8	11	10	Teton Co., WY	Clarence Harris	David M. Clark	1947	544
155 2/8	51 7/8	28 2/8	25 2/8	10 1/8	10 3/8	6 5/8	6 5/8	11	11	Dubois Co., WY	Clyde Thompson	Clyde Thompson	1954	544
155 2/8	46	29 2/8	30 2/8	9 4/8	8 6/8	6 5/8	6 2/8	10	10	Lolo Creek, MT	Edward Churchwell	Virgil Fite	1955	544
155 2/8	41 4/8	32 7/8	30 4/8	11 1/8	11 2/8	6 2/8	6 4/8	9	10	Teton Co., WY	Thomas F. Smith	Thomas F. Smith	1973	544
155 2/8	42 4/8	31 6/8	34 7/8	9 1/8	9 5/8	6 4/8	6 2/8	10	9	Weber Co., UT	David I. Dashnaw	David I. Dashnaw	1992	544
155 2/8	46 6/8	27 4/8	31	11	10 2/8	6 6/8	6 4/8	10	11	Sheridan Co., WY	Vicki M. Stites	Vicki M. Stites	1994	544
155 2/8	40 4/8	33 1/8	29 2/8	11 7/8	13 2/8	7 2/8	7 3/8	11	9	Cache Co., UT	William F. Kneer, Jr.	William F. Kneer	2003	544
155 1/8	40 3/8	33 4/8	30 7/8	11	11	5 4/8	5 5/8	10	14	Yellowstone River, WY	T. Robert Johnson	T. Robert Johnson	1974	551

Score										Owner	Location	Hunter	Date Killed	Rank
155 1/8	45 3/8	30 7/8	31	9 6/8	10 1/8	6 4/8	6 2/8	10	8	Shawn G. Stewart	Madison Co., MT	Shawn G. Stewart	1987	551
155 1/8	48 5/8	31 6/8	33 2/8	8 6/8	9 4/8	6 6/8	6 7/8	6	9	John J. King	Teton Co., WY	John J. King	1988	551
155 1/8	43 3/8	31 4/8	28 3/8	11 2/8	12 3/8	6 2/8	6 2/8	11	10	Brian R. Nosker	Cache Co., UT	Brian R. Nosker	1988	551
155 1/8	45 3/8	32 5/8	32 6/8	8 5/8	8	6 3/8	6 3/8	8	9	Katharine F. Heffner	Beaverhead Co., MT	Katharine F. Heffner	1990	551
155 1/8	51 5/8	29 4/8	30	8 3/8	9 7/8	6	5 7/8	10	8	Mike R. Coyle	Spokane Co., WA	Mike R. Coyle	2001	551
155	46 6/8	29 6/8	30	9	9 4/8	6 4/8	6	9	9	Vernon Williams, Jr.	Jackson Hole, WY	Vernon Williams, Jr.	1969	557
155	48 2/8	31 4/8	29 5/8	10 6/8	10 6/8	6 3/8	6	8	7	Leonard J. Kosirog	Teton Co., WY	Leonard J. Kosirog	2001	557
183 7/8*	49 7/8	36 4/8	36 4/8	13 3/8	14 4/8	7 3/8	7 1/8	12	10	Scott A. Wodahl	Johnson Co., WY	Scott A. Wodahl	2002	
180 4/8*	54 4/8	35 1/8	34 5/8	11 4/8	10 2/8	6 1/8	6 1/8	12	12	Jon H. Phillips	Duchesne Co., UT	Jon H. Phillips	2003	
178 2/8*	50	39 5/8	43 5/8	9 7/8	11 3/8	6 7/8	6 5/8	10	8	Edward M. Jungers	Missoula Co., MT	Edward M. Jungers	2000	
177 7/8*	57 3/8	35 3/8	37 3/8	11 1/8	10 3/8	6 5/8	6 4/8	8	11	Shaun Rees	Teton Co., WY	Shaun Rees	1999	

* Final score is subject to revision by additional verifying measurements.

CATEGORY
SHIRAS MOOSE

SCORE
177-2/8

HUNTER
APRIL H. PRESTON (LEFT)

LOCATION
SHOSHONE COUNTY, IDAHO

DATE OF KILL
OCTOBER 1999

SCORE
187-3/8

HUNTER
ROBIN R. PEARSON (RIGHT)

LOCATION
BONNEVILLE COUNTY, IDAHO

DATE OF KILL
OCTOBER 2000

CATEGORY
SHIRAS MOOSE

SCORE
185-5/8

HUNTER
MARY A. ISBELL (ABOVE)

LOCATION
BONNEVILLE COUNTY, IDAHO

DATE OF KILL
AUGUST 2000

CATEGORY
SHIRAS MOOSE

SCORE
164

HUNTER
GLENN M. SMITH (BELOW)

LOCATION
BEAVERHEAD COUNTY, MONTANA

DATE OF KILL
SEPTEMBER 1998

CATEGORY
SHIRAS MOOSE

SCORE
176-4/8

HUNTER
GERALD D. MADSEN (LEFT)

LOCATION
MADISON COUNTY, IDAHO

DATE OF KILL
OCTOBER 1998

SCORE
161-2/8

HUNTER
DANNY R. HART (BELOW)

LOCATION
SHERIDAN COUNTY, WYOMING

DATE OF KILL
SEPTEMBER 1996

CATEGORY
SHIRAS MOOSE

SCORE
176-4/8

HUNTER
LARRY R. BROWER (ABOVE)

LOCATION
MORGAN COUNTY, UTAH

DATE OF KILL
OCTOBER 2003

CARIBOU BOUNDARIES

The various varieties of caribou, which vary widely in size and antler configuration, have required subdivision of the species into five different trophy categories: mountain, woodland, barren ground, Central Canada barren ground, and Quebec-Labrador. Prior to 1960, the classification of the different species and subspecies of the world was in disarray. At that time, Frank Banfield (a Canadian wildlife biologist) reviewed all of the available museum specimens of the world's caribou and reduced the number of valid subspecies. Among his conclusions were that the new world caribou and the old world reindeer should all be classified as one species, but that northern barren ground caribou differ from the more southerly distributed woodland caribou, both in Eurasia and in North America.

The largest antlered caribou from North America are the Grant's variety from Alaska and northern Yukon Territory. These caribou, called barren ground caribou for records-keeping purposes, have long, rounded main beams with very long top points. They also have the highest all-time records book minimum entry score of 400 points. (See below also for description of boundary between barren ground caribou and mountain caribou in Yukon Territory.)

The so-called mountain caribou, now regarded as a variety of woodland caribou, is found in British Columbia, Alberta, southern Yukon Territory, and the Mackenzie Mountains of Northwest Territories. In Yukon Territory, the boundary (see map below) begins at the intersection of the Yukon River with the boundary between Yukon Territory and the state of Alaska. The boundary runs southeasterly following the Yukon River upstream to Dawson; then easterly and southerly along the Klondike Highway to Stewart Crossing; then easterly following the road to Mayo; then northeasterly following the road to McQuesten Lake; then easterly following the south shore of McQuesten Lake and then upstream following the main drainage to the divide leading to Scougale Creek to its confluence with the Beaver River; then south following the Beaver River downstream to its confluence with the Rackla River; then southeasterly following the Rackla River downstream to its confluence with the Stewart River; then northeasterly following the Stewart River upstream to its confluence with the North Stewart River to the boundary between Yukon Territory and Northwest Territories. North of this line caribou are classified as barren ground caribou for records-keeping purposes, while those specimens taken south of this line are considered mountain caribou.

Central Canada barren ground caribou occur on Baffin Island and the mainland of Northwest Territories and Nunavut, as well as in northern Manitoba. The geographic boundaries in the mainland of Northwest Territories are: the Mackenzie River to the west; the north edge of the continent to the north

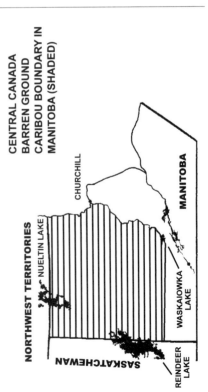

**CENTRAL CANADA
BARREN GROUND
CARIBOU BOUNDARY IN
MANITOBA (SHADED)**

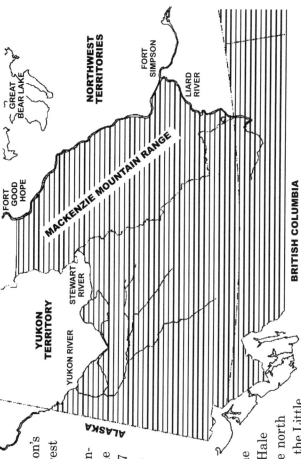

NORTHERN
BOUNDARY FOR MOUN-
TAIN CARIBOU (SHADED)

(excluding any islands except Baffin Island); Hudson's Bay to the east; and the southern boundary of Northwest Territories to the south.

The boundary (see map above) for Central Canada barren ground caribou in Manitoba begins at the point of intersection of the south limit of township 87 with the provincial boundary between the provinces of Manitoba and Saskatchewan. The boundary then follows this township line east to the point of confluence with Waskaiowka Lake. From there it proceeds in a northeasterly direction along the high-water mark of the north shore of the aforementioned lake following the sinuosities of the shoreline to the point of intersection with the water connection to Hale Lake. From this point, the high-water mark of the north shoreline is followed to the point of intersection with the Little Churchill River. Henceforth, it follows the high-water mark of the north or westerly shore of the Little Churchill River including expansions of the river into lakes to the point of confluence with the Churchill River. From there the boundary crosses the mouth of the Little Churchill River and follows the high-water mark on the south or easterly shore of the Churchill River to the community of Churchill located on Hudson Bay.

Caribou taken in Manitoba north of the above described boundary are now classified as Central Canada barren ground caribou.

The Quebec-Labrador caribou category was established in 1968. This large woodland caribou has very wide, long-beamed antlers with almost universally palmated bez formations. To have left these animals in competition with the woodland cari-

bou of Newfoundland would have resulted in a complete swamping of the smaller-antlered woodland caribou from Newfoundland. Boundaries for Quebec-Labrador caribou are just as the name implies, Quebec and the Labrador region of Newfoundland.

Woodland caribou are eligible for entry from Nova Scotia, Newfoundland and New Brunswick. Woodland caribou occur sparingly all the way across Canada to southern British Columbia. Although there may be some open seasons in these provinces, they are not taken in large numbers anywhere. It would seem inappropriate to place such animals in competition with those from Newfoundland where they have been regularly hunted for more than 100 years. ∎

MOUNTAIN CARIBOU
NEW WORLD'S RECORD

When Candler Hunt made the decision to hunt Dall's sheep in Yukon Territory, he had no intention of hunting mountain caribou (*Rangifer tarandus montanus*). Although earlier in his life he'd hunted elk, bear, and whitetail, sheep hunting was now his passion. Candler had no idea that this sheep hunt would net him a new World's Record mountain caribou.

Candler's sheep hunt in September of 1998 had been a wonderful experience. At home in Madison, Georgia, Candler had spent countless hours researching and checking outfitter references. He had chosen to hunt with outfitter Tim Mervin in an area northwest of Whitehorse. For days, Candler and his 24-year old guide, Jake Gunson, had been riding, walking, and glassing. Candler took his Dall's sheep on the fourth day of the hunt.

It was a nice ram, and Candler was thrilled to add it to his collection. As far as he was concerned, his hunt was over; he had harvested the animal he wanted. Jake asked Candler whether he wanted to hunt caribou on the way back to the airstrip. "Caribou really don't turn me on," admitted Candler, "but I'm having so much fun, I'll give it a try."

For three days, Candler, Jake, and a young wrangler named Bradley Malfair, saw only a few cows and calves as they moved toward the airstrip. On the fourth day, a thunderstorm kept the men in camp until early evening when they rode to a high point from which to glass. "I think I see a caribou about a mile away," Bradley said. As he continued peering through his binoculars, Bradley changed his mind. "No, I'm sorry; it's a moose." Candler and Jake had seen sign of moose, and decided to get a better look. They put a spotting scope on the animal, and immediately determined this was a big caribou. Candler and Jake mounted their horses, leaving Bradley on the top of the ridge to tell them, with hand signals, if the bull started to move.

They rode for 45 minutes through thick cover and across a large creek. At the base of the ridge, they tethered the horses and quietly hiked up the ridge. As they neared the top, they saw the bull at 300 yards. There was little cover, so they stayed on their bellies, crawling a few more yards to get as close as they could without spooking the bull.

Candler placed the animal in the crosshairs of his Ruger Model 77 featherweight .270. "Don't look at the antlers," cautioned Jake, "and stay calm."

Jake's advice was well taken. This bull was much bigger than anything they had anticipated and Candler was having a hard time controlling his excitement. Finally, after five minutes, the bull moved and presented him with a broadside shot.

After the antlers had dried for 60 days, a Boone and Crockett Club Official Measurer scored Candler's mountain caribou. It was given an entry score of 453-4/8 points. The 24th Awards Judges' Panel gave the bull an official score of 453 points making it the new World's Record mountain caribou. ■

MOUNTAIN CARIBOU
WORLD'S RECORD SCORE CHART

TROPHY INFO

RANK
New World's Record

SCORE
453

LOCATION
Prospector Mt., YT

HUNTER
C. Candler Hunt

OWNER
C. Candler Hunt

DATE KILLED
1998

BOUNDARY FOR MOUNTAIN CARIBOU

Mountain caribou includes trophies from Alberta, British Columbia, southern Yukon Territory, and the Mackenzie Mountains of Northwest Territories.

Records of North American Big Game

250 Station Drive
Missoula, MT 59801
(406) 542-1888

BOONE AND CROCKETT CLUB®

OFFICIAL SCORING SYSTEM FOR NORTH AMERICAN BIG GAME TROPHIES

CARIBOU

MINIMUM SCORES

	AWARDS	ALL-TIME
mountain	360	390
woodland	265	295
barren ground	375	400
Central Canada barren ground	345	360
Quebec-Labrador	365	375

Detail of Point Measurement

KIND OF CARIBOU (check one)
- ☒ mountain
- ☐ woodland
- ☐ barren ground
- ☐ Central Canada barren ground
- ☐ Quebec-Labrador

SEE OTHER SIDE FOR INSTRUCTIONS

	COLUMN 1	COLUMN 2	COLUMN 3	COLUMN 4
	Spread Credit	Right Antler	Left Antler	Difference
A. Tip to Tip Spread		35 5/8		
B. Greatest Spread		48 5/8		
C. Inside Spread of Main Beams	45 6/8	SPREAD CREDIT MAY EQUAL BUT NOT EXCEED LONGER MAIN BEAM	45 6/8	
D. Number of Points on Each Antler Excluding Brows		16	19	3
Number of Points on Each Brow		7	2	2
E. Length of Main Beam		48 2/8	49 5/8	1 3/8
F-1. Length of Brow Palm or First Point		20 0/8	17 1/8	2 1/8
F-2. Length of Bez or Second Point		25 2/8	27 3/8	2 1/8
F-3. Length of Rear Point, If Present		5 6/8	4 6/8	1 0/8
F-4. Length of Second Longest Top Point		18 1/8	18 6/8	5/8
F-5. Length of Longest Top Point		25 2/8	24 2/8	1 0/8
G-1. Width of Brow Palm		13 1/8	4 0/8	1 2/8
G-2. Width of Top Palm		5 4/8	6 6/8	1 2/8
H-1. Circumference at Smallest Place Between Brow and Bez Point		6 3/8	6 5/8	2/8
H-2. Circumference at Smallest Place Between Bez and Rear Point		6 4/8	6 1/8	3/8
H-3. Circumference at Smallest Place Between Rear Point and First Top Point		6 7/8	7 0/8	1/8
H-4. Circumference at Smallest Place Between Two Longest Top Palm Points		10 4/8	11 4/8	1 0/8
TOTALS		214 4/8	204 7/8	12 4/8

ADD	Column 1	45 6/8	Exact Locality Where Killed: Prospector Mountain, Yukon Territory
	Column 2	214 4/8	Date Killed: August 1998 — Hunter: C. Candler Hunt
	Column 3	204 7/8	Owner: C. Candler Hunt — Telephone #:
	Subtotal	465 1/8	Owner's Address:
SUBTRACT	Column 4	12 4/8	Guide's Name and Address:
	FINAL SCORE	**453**	Remarks: (Mention Any Abnormalities or Unique Qualities.)

OM I.D. Number

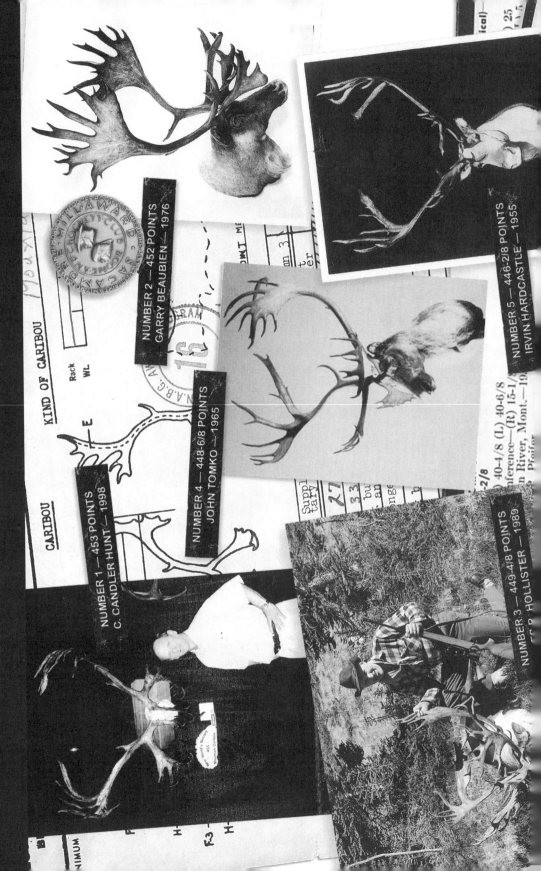

TOP 10 MOUNTAIN CARIBOU

NUMBER 1 — 453 POINTS
C. CANDLER HUNT — 1998

NUMBER 2 — 452 POINTS
GARRY BEAUBIEN — 1976

NUMBER 3 — 449-4/8 POINTS
HOLLISTER — 1989

NUMBER 4 — 448-6/8 POINTS
JOHN TOMKO — 1965

NUMBER 5 — 446-2/8 POINTS
IRVIN HARDCASTLE — 1955

NUMBER 10 — 442-7/8 PQINTS
JAY. L. BRASHER — 1984

NUMBER 7 (TIE) — 444 PQINTS
JOHN A. KOLAR — 1984

OUNTAIN CARIBOU—1st Prize
445-3/8

NUMBER 7 (TIE) — 444 PQINTS
JAMES C. JOHNSON — 1988

(R) 19 (L) 20
—Cold Fish Lake, B. C.—1
John I. Moore
—Ray Henyu

1958–19

NUMBER 6 — 445-3/8 POINTS
JOHN I. MOORE — 1958

NUMBER 7 (TIE) — 444 PQINTS
RUSS MERCER — 1965

Circumfe
H-1. Between
Circumfe
H-2. Between B
Circumfere
H-3. Before F
Circumfer
H-4. Between
TOTALS

D'ALENE, IDAHO, FRIDAY, OCTOBER 8, 1965

en Bright   Co
Here Tops $3 M

641

MOUNTAIN CARIBOU
Rangifer tarandus caribou

MINIMUM SCORE 390

Score	Length of Main Beam R	L	Inside Spread	Circumference at Smallest Place Between Brow and Bez Points R	L	Length of Brow Points R	L	Width of Brow Points R	L	Number of Points R	L	Locality	Hunter	Owner	Date Killed	Rank
453	48 2/8	49 5/8	45 6/8	6 3/8	6 5/8	20	17 1/8	13 1/8	4	23	21	Prospector Mt., YT	C. Candler Hunt	C. Candler Hunt	1998	1
452	**43 1/8**	**42 2/8**	**30 3/8**	**7 3/8**	**7 5/8**	**16 4/8**	**16 1/8**	**11 2/8**	**5**	**22**	**19**	**Turnagain River, BC**	**Garry Beaubien**	**Garry Beaubien**	**1976**	**2**
449 4/8	37 2/8	37 4/8	30 2/8	5 7/8	5 7/8	17 5/8	13 6/8	10 6/8	9 3/8	40	33	Fire Lake, YT	James R. Hollister	James R. Hollister	1989	3
448 4/8	51 3/8	51 5/8	40 2/8	6 6/8	6 6/8	18	4	10 6/8	1	24	20	Great Salmon Lake, YT	John Tomko	John Tomko	1965	4
446 6/8	55	53 5/8	40 2/8	7 5/8	7 2/8	14 7/8	13 2/8	9 3/8	5	20	14	Atlin, BC	Irvin Hardcastle	Loaned to B&C Natl. Coll.	1955	5
445 3/8	48 7/8	46 2/8	27 4/8	6 2/8	5 7/8	17 6/8	20 2/8	4 5/8	17 6/8	19	20	Cold Fish Lake, BC	John I. Moore	Buckhorn Mus. & Saloon, Ltd.	1958	6
444	44 2/8	45 2/8	36 1/8	6 6/8	6 6/8	13 7/8	20 4/8	4	15 6/8	17	21	Quiet Lake, YT	Russ Mercer	Robert A. VanSkyock	1965	7
444	52	52 1/8	38 2/8	6	6 1/8	8 6/8	20 2/8	1/8	15 7/8	16	25	Mountain River, NT	John A. Kolar	John A. Kolar	1984	7
444	42	43 1/8	35	6 4/8	6 1/8	15 6/8	17	8 1/8	7 3/8	20	23	Kechika Range, BC	James C. Johnson	James C. Johnson	1988	7
442 7/8	44 2/8	46 2/8	37 2/8	7	6 7/8	15 6/8	17 1/8	11 6/8	4 6/8	23	23	Spatsizi Plateau, BC	Jay L. Brasher	Jay L. Brasher	1984	10
442 4/8	44 4/8	45 5/8	38 3/8	8 3/8	8 2/8	14	15 6/8	8 2/8	7 3/8	19	25	Fortin Lake, YT	Kim Runions	Kim Runions	1994	11
441 5/8	49 4/8	46 2/8	33 1/8	7	6 7/8	19 2/8	21	15 3/8	4 7/8	24	19	Cold Fish Lake, BC	Drew W. Getgen	Carnegie Museum	1961	12
440 7/8	57 2/8	55 3/8	42 6/8	6 4/8	6	20 2/8	18 1/8	11 2/8	9	16	16	Nisling River, YT	Larry D. Merillat	Larry D. Merillat	2003	13
440	55 7/8	55 3/8	46 2/8	6	5 5/8	21	21	5 4/8	3 4/8	17	17	Carcajou River, NT	David P. McBrayer	David P. McBrayer	1990	14
438 4/8	43	42 2/8	33 2/8	7 1/8	6 6/8	19 4/8	18 1/8	14 3/8	5 2/8	25	24	Divide Lake, NT	Monte Sorgard	Monte Sorgard	1988	15
437 6/8	50 2/8	46	39 4/8	7 3/8	7 1/8	19	18 5/8	14 4/8	11 5/8	17	17	Willow Handle Lake, NT	M.R. James	M.R. James	1995	16
436 3/8	57	54 4/8	46 4/8	6 5/8	6 2/8	20 2/8	16 7/8	10 2/8	8	17	14	St. Cyr Range, YT	Randall W. Lawton	Randall W. Lawton	1985	17
436 1/8	43	43 3/8	34 4/8	6 2/8	6 1/8	19 4/8	18 1/8	13 6/8	5	24	23	June Lake, NT	Ronald K. Pettit	Ronald K. Pettit	1993	18
430 7/8	44 2/8	42	40 2/8	7 2/8	7 2/8	20 2/8	9 5/8	16 1/8	3 5/8	25	20	Ludwig Lake, BC	Gary D. Lloyd	Gary D. Lloyd	1987	19
428 5/8	42 5/8	47 2/8	35 2/8	7 4/8	7 4/8	17 1/8	16 1/8	12 3/8	10 4/8	21	22	Atlin, BC	Rafael Garcia Cano	Cascade Lodge	1968	20
428 4/8	56 6/8	55	37	7 4/8	7 4/8	15 4/8	15	17	15 6/8	19	19	Dease Lake, BC	Fred G. Kelly	Fred G. Kelly	1964	21
428 1/8	40 2/8	43 3/8	34 4/8	6 7/8	6 6/8	19 6/8	18 1/8	14 4/8	1/8	19	14	Ross River, YT	Picked Up	Jack R. Cook	1991	22
427 3/8	56 7/8	59	44 4/8	7 4/8	7 3/8	6	15 4/8	10 2/8	14 6/8	10	15	Atlin, BC	Anna Chabara	Anna Chabara	1960	23
426 4/8	48 4/8	51 6/8	38 2/8	6 7/8	7	15 2/8	14 5/8	8	10	17	18	Pelly Mts., YT	Knut Wittfoth	Knut Wittfoth	1989	24
425 6/8	52 6/8	54 5/8	47	6 4/8	6 4/8	18 4/8	21 1/8	2 5/8	16	13	15	Kechika Range, BC	Victor E. Moss	Victor E. Moss	1988	25
425 1/8	55 3/8	52 2/8	34	7 3/8	7 7/8	10	20 2/8	1/8	17 6/8	12	25	Dease Lake, BC	Unknown	B&C National Collection	1917	26
424 3/8	47 7/8	49 5/8	43 5/8	6 7/8	7	16 6/8	16 2/8	10 7/8	8 5/8	22	22	Cold Fish Lake, BC	A.H. Clise	A.H. Clise	1968	27
424 2/8	47	46 4/8	37 3/8	6 1/8	6 2/8	15 2/8	15 2/8	9 7/8	7 2/8	20	19	Cold Fish Lake, BC	Howard Keeler	Howard Keeler	1954	28
423 7/8	46 2/8	45 2/8	34 6/8	7	6 5/8	14 5/8	14	10 3/8	4 3/8	19	16	Cold Fish Lake, BC	Edward E. Wilson	Edward E. Wilson	1963	29
423 6/8	42	40 5/8	33 1/8	6 3/8	6 4/8	17 6/8	16 3/8	13 4/8	6	21	23	Stikine Plateau, BC	Dwight Lewis	Dwight Lewis	1970	30
423 4/8	47 1/8	47 1/8	48 5/8	6 2/8	6 2/8	14 2/8	16	1 6/8	12 1/8	19	25	Cassiar, BC	Arvid F. Benson	Arvid F. Benson	1967	31
423 4/8	55 5/8	53 6/8	41 5/8	7	7 1/8	19 2/8	17 2/8	10 1/8	1 6/8	15	16	Divide Lake, NT	Les Jacobson	Les Jacobson	1988	31
423 1/8	51 6/8	50 6/8	32 3/8	7 1/8	7 1/8	20 7/8	17 2/8	6 3/8	11 2/8	16	18	Twitya River, NT	Carol S. Kraft	Carol S. Kraft	1987	33
422 7/8	45 4/8	44 7/8	36 5/8	7 1/8	7	15 4/8	19 3/8	1/8	13 2/8	17	20	Watson Lake, YT	Gary Lundstrom	Gary Lundstrom	1980	34
422 3/8	53 2/8	54 3/8	46	5 7/8	6 1/8	18 3/8	19 7/8	1/8	16 4/8	14	22	Keele Park, YT	Donald P. Smith, Jr.	Donald P. Smith, Jr.	1954	35
422 3/8	50 5/8	52	50	5 7/8	6	21 5/8	20 1/8	6 1/8	13 4/8	16	15	Little Dal Lake, NT	Dale L. Martin	Dale L. Martin	1976	35

Score											Locality	Hunter	Owner	Date	Rank
422 2/8	65 1/8	62 2/8	50 5/8	8 3/8	9 6/8	15 4/8	7	7	22	14	Cassiar, BC	D.W. Bell	Acad. Nat. Sci., Phil.	1923	37
422 2/8	50 6/8	52 2/8	28 3/8	18 6/8	17 4/8	22 4/8	6 1/8	6 7/8	23	14	Mountain River, NT	Leroy A. Schommer	Leroy A. Schommer	1985	37
421 6/8	50 1/8	54 6/8	39 1/8	7 6/8	18	14 1/8	6 7/8	6 7/8	15	18	Arctic Red River, NT	Jerrell Coburn	Jerrell Coburn	1995	39
421 5/8	54	52 5/8	35 5/8	12 3/8	18	18 2/8	6 3/8	6 5/8	20	19	Aishihik Lake, YT	A.W. Fees, Jr.	A.W. Fees, Jr.	1971	40
421 4/8	42 5/8	40 2/8	25 6/8	7 6/8	13 5/8	15 4/8	6 2/8	6 2/8	25	22	Netson Lake, BC	Charlie D. Todd	Charlie D. Todd	1985	41
421 1/8	49 3/8	43 4/8	41 4/8	16 1/8	3 3/8	18 2/8	6 2/8	6 2/8	27	20	Taku Lake, YT	Lloyd Walker	Lloyd Walker	1961	42
420 5/8	45 1/8	43 6/8	40 4/8	13 3/8	19 2/8	15 4/8	6 2/8	6	27	17	Cold Fish Lake, BC	Maurice C. Perkins	Maurice C. Perkins	1961	43
420	59 6/8	62 3/8	44 3/8	20 2/8	8 4/8	22 7/8	5 7/8	6	21	15	Mackenzie Mts., NT	Martin C. Ernest	Martin C. Ernest	1978	44
420	51 3/8	52	42	9 7/8	12 6/8	15 2/8	6 7/8	6 7/8	17	16	Mountain River, NT	John D. Todd	John D. Todd	1985	44
419 6/8	52 2/8	50 2/8	42 2/8	13 4/8	11	19 5/8	7 4/8	7 4/8	21	18	Atlin Lake, BC	John Haefeli, Jr.	John Haefeli, Jr.	1964	46
419 5/8	50	50 3/8	37 1/8	15 1/8	16 1/8	18 4/8	8 2/8	6 5/8	21	16	Livingstone, YT	Charlie L. Bertani	Charlie L. Bertani	1977	47
419 3/8	51 2/8	49 5/8	40 7/8	15 1/8	1/8	18 1/8	7 2/8	7 2/8	20	13	Mt. Mye, YT	Clark A. Johnson	Clark A. Johnson	1981	48
417 7/8	47 4/8	50	36 4/8	20 5/8	13	6 5/8	6 4/8	7 1/8	13	21	Gladstone River, YT	Herman Peterson	Herman Peterson	1960	49
417 6/8	51	51 2/8	29 4/8	17 5/8	1/8	15 7/8	6 5/8	6 4/8	13	16	Fire Lake, YT	Marvin E. Egger	Marvin E. Egger	1986	50
417 4/8	43 7/8	43 2/8	30 3/8	20 1/8	12 2/8	18 7/8	6 1/8	6 1/8	15	21	Cassiar, BC	Elgin T. Gates	Elgin T. Gates	1953	51
417 4/8	51 5/8	49 4/8	42 4/8	12 1/8	4 1/8	18 7/8	6 4/8	6 7/8	24	15	Cold Fish Lake, BC	John E. Rhea	John E. Rhea	1959	51
417 1/8	49 5/8	49 5/8	40 6/8	12 6/8	6	21 1/8	6 4/8	6 4/8	15	16	Connally Lake, YT	Marlin P. Alt	Marlin P. Alt	1973	53
416 7/8	51	50 3/8	38 7/8	1/8	14	11 6/8	7 2/8	6 7/8	15	19	Arctic Red River, NT	E. Royce Gunter, Jr.	E. Royce Gunter, Jr.	1999	54
416 7/8	50 3/8	49 6/8	45 2/8	1 5/8	14 3/8	18 1/8	6 2/8	6 2/8	20	13	Arctic Red River, NT	Garth W. Peterson	Garth W. Peterson	2002	54
416 6/8	53 1/8	52 1/8	38 7/8	13 2/8	1/8	17 1/8	6 6/8	5 5/8	14	20	Little Dal Lake, NT	Patricia M. Dreeszen	Patricia M. Dreeszen	1984	56
416 4/8	50 1/8	47 2/8	46	10 3/8	5	15 2/8	5 5/8	7 3/8	14	18	Redstone River, NT	David D. Hill	David D. Hill	1980	57
416 3/8	42 4/8	40 2/8	31 5/8	11 1/8	14 5/8	14 7/8	6 3/8	6 4/8	24	26	Cold Fish Lake, BC	Charles E. Wilson, Jr.	Charles E. Wilson, Jr.	1970	58
416 3/8	52 6/8	51 2/8	47 6/8	2 3/8	11 3/8	17 6/8	7 4/8	8 3/8	11	12	Mountain Lake, NT	Stewart N. Shaft	Stewart N. Shaft	1985	58
416 1/8	50 2/8	50	42	8 2/8	9 5/8	18 3/8	6 1/8	6 1/8	20	13	Cold Fish Lake, BC	Clyde Williams	Clyde Williams	1966	60
416	57 1/8	53 5/8	45 2/8	6	14 3/8	16 5/8	7 3/8	7 1/8	16	13	Atlin, BC	R.W. Johnson	R.W. Johnson	1956	61
416	37 5/8	38	37 7/8	12	11 3/8	16 5/8	7 4/8	6 7/8	15	28	Little Rancheria River, BC	Brian T. Pelczar	Brian T. Pelczar	1996	61
415 3/8	58 1/8	54 1/8	40 5/8	7 4/8	1/8	11 3/8	6 6/8	6 7/8	17	15	Pelly River, YT	Lee F. Olsen	Lee F. Olsen	1950	63
415 3/8	46 4/8	49	40 2/8	7 2/8	1 1/8	14 6/8	7 2/8	6 7/8	20	21	Cassiar, BC	James Keegan	James Keegan	1971	63
415 3/8	48 2/8	44 7/8	33 4/8	7 1/8	1 1/8	15	6 5/8	6 7/8	18	23	Mackenzie Mts., NT	Gerald Schroeder	Gerald Schroeder	1974	63
415 3/8	42 2/8	43 5/8	31	11 7/8	13	16 3/8	7 3/8	7 2/8	23	23	Lawson Lake, BC	Daniel E. Kelly	Daniel E. Kelly	1997	63
414 4/8	48 4/8	43 5/8	34	13 6/8	10	16 1/8	7 4/8	7 2/8	14	17	Arrowhead Lake, YT	Robert L. Pagel	Robert L. Pagel	1973	67
414 3/8	50 7/8	47 2/8	41 4/8	11	14	19 3/8	5 5/8	5 5/8	19	12	Watson Lake, BC	John H. Myaard	John H. Myaard	1971	68
414 3/8	48 3/8	48 2/8	40 2/8	1 7/8	11	3 1/8	7 1/8	7 1/8	17	21	Hoole River, YT	Kris M. Gustafson	Kris M. Gustafson	1984	68
414 1/8	54	53 4/8	28 2/8	1 7/8	11 7/8	15	7 3/8	7 7/8	16	19	Tweedsmuir Park, BC	Gary J. Deleenheer	Gary J. Deleenheer	1966	70
414 1/8	44 1/8	47	37 3/8	11 7/8	10	20 6/8	6 7/8	6 7/8	15	17	Kawdy Plateau, BC	Dan S. Muchow	Dan S. Muchow	1997	70
413 6/8	49 5/8	51 2/8	26	11 7/8	10	15 5/8	6 5/8	6 4/8	16	18	Cold Fish Lake, BC	D.W. Thiem	D.W. Thiem	1956	72
413 6/8	55	54 6/8	42 6/8	10	14 3/8	12 7/8	6 4/8	6 2/8	13	18	Johiah Lake, BC	Harold G. Vriend	Harold G. Vriend	1990	72
413 5/8	47 7/8	49	35 7/8	8 1/8	1 1/8	17 4/8	6 2/8	6 2/8	20	14	Dease Lake, BC	Bert Klineburger	Bert Klineburger	1960	74
413 5/8	49	49	36 4/8	11 6/8	2	20 2/8	6 6/8	6 6/8	17	15	Cassiar Mts., BC	Ira Jones	Ira Jones	1963	74
413 5/8	47 4/8	46	39 1/8	9 6/8	7 2/8	16 3/8	6 6/8	6 6/8	18	15	Divide Lake, NT	Chuck Adams	Chuck Adams	1995	74
413 5/8	50 5/8	52 1/8	34 1/8	16 7/8	2 5/8	20 7/8	6 3/8	6 2/8	26	17	Ethel Lake, YT	Russel Tait	Russel Tait	1999	74
413 4/8	53 4/8	51 3/8	45 6/8	8	14 2/8	1	7	7	15	27	Atlin, BC	Mrs. R.S. Marvin, Jr.	Mrs. R.S. Marvin, Jr.	1956	78
413 3/8	42 3/8	39 6/8	35 1/8	18 4/8	1 1/8	18 3/8	6 7/8	7 1/8	18	27	Livingstone Creek, YT	Lawrence W. Dossman	Lawrence W. Dossman	1984	79
413 2/8	51 4/8	55	39 2/8	10 6/8	11 1/8	16	7 1/8	7 1/8	15	10	Atlin, BC	Mrs. Ramon Somavia	Mrs. Ramon Somavia	1955	80
413 2/8	41	44 1/8	40 3/8	13 6/8	6	15 6/8	8 7/8	7 5/8	19	20	Nisutlin Lake, YT	James V. Bosco, Sr.	James V. Bosco, Jr.	1935	81
413 2/8	44 1/8	49	31 6/8	7 2/8	9 6/8	18 4/8	7 1/8	7 2/8	16	14	Livingstone, YT	Lawrence W. Dossman	Lawrence W. Dossman	1975	81
413 2/8	43	46 7/8	25 7/8	7 5/8	1	17 1/8	7 5/8	7 1/8	22	26	Livingstone, YT	Mike J. Chirpich	Mike J. Chirpich	1977	81
413	51 4/8	53 7/8	43	8 5/8	7 4/8	15 4/8	6 5/8	6 5/8	14	18	Drury Lake, YT	James H. Russell	James H. Russell	1971	84

643

MOUNTAIN CARIBOU
Rangifer tarandus caribou

Score	Length of Main Beam R	L	Inside Spread	Circumference at Smallest Place Between Brow and Bez Points R	L	Length of Brow Points R	L	Width of Brow Points R	L	Number of Points R	L	Locality	Hunter	Owner	Date Killed	Rank
413	51 3/8	50 7/8	49 2/8	7 2/8	7 1/8	18 2/8	2 2/8	11 7/8	1/8	15	16	Kechika Range, BC	John J. Ottman	John J. Ottman	1988	84
412 6/8	50 3/8	53 6/8	47 3/8	6 2/8	6 3/8	18 1/8	2 6/8	12 3/8	1/8	18	18	Cassiar Mts., BC	John R. Rinkevich	John R. Rinkevich	1968	86
412 6/8	48	47	47	7 3/8	7 2/8	16 5/8	17 4/8	10 6/8	10 3/8	14	18	Grass Lakes, YT	Carol A. Domes	Carol A. Domes	1987	86
412 6/8	42 1/8	45 1/8	30 7/8	6 4/8	6	16 3/8	16 3/8	14 2/8	12 1/8	20	17	Black Fox Creek, BC	Norman L. Meints	Norman L. Meints	1987	86
412 6/8	51 2/8	50 7/8	40 6/8	6 4/8	6 4/8	21 6/8	5 6/8	19 1/8	1/8	25	15	Kechika Range, BC	Tom Andres	Tom Andres	1991	86
412 5/8	49 7/8	50 2/8	38 5/8	6 6/8	6 5/8	15 6/8	17 6/8	10 2/8	9 6/8	21	23	Cassiar Mts., BC	Nolan Martins	Nolan Martins	1967	90
412 4/8	55 6/8	57 4/8	26	6 6/8	6 2/8	12 4/8	12 2/8	6	11	20	22	Telegraph Creek, BC	James F. Clarke	James F. Clarke	1929	91
412 4/8	48 1/8	51 3/8	33 3/8	7 3/8	6 7/8	19 4/8	14 1/8	14 2/8	8 2/8	18	15	Cassiar Mts., BC	Leon Mazzeo	Leon Mazzeo	1971	91
412 4/8	51 6/8	50	37 2/8	7 4/8	7 2/8	14 7/8	21 7/8	4 2/8	15 6/8	16	17	Ross River, YT	Barry E. Enders	Barry E. Enders	1984	91
412 3/8	49 2/8	48	36 3/8	6 3/8	6 3/8	18 2/8	12 2/8	14 5/8	3 7/8	16	16	Fort Nelson, BC	Elmer T. Newman	Gary F. Silc	1970	94
412 3/8	50 6/8	49 6/8	38 3/8	6 4/8	6 4/8	17 3/8	18	1/8	12 2/8	16	18	Mackenzie Mts., NT	James F. Willoughby	James F. Willoughby	1988	94
412	47 2/8	47 4/8	33 2/8	6 1/8	6 1/8	14	14	11 2/8	7 2/8	26	25	Dease River, BC	Herb Klein	Dallas Mus. of Natl. Hist.	1960	96
412	43	47	37 2/8	7 3/8	7 3/8	11 6/8	16 4/8	1/8	11 3/8	21	19	Livingstone, YT	Arvo W. Kannisto	Arvo W. Kannisto	1974	96
412	47 7/8	52 4/8	40	6 5/8	6 7/8	17 6/8	16 1/8	12 4/8	5 1/8	14	18	Cassiar Mts., BC	Peter E. Paulos	Peter E. Paulos	1988	96
411 7/8	40 1/8	43 3/8	39 1/8	7 4/8	8 1/8	18	13 6/8	13 1/8	8 5/8	21	23	Fire Lake, YT	James C. Wondzell	James C. Wondzell	1991	99
411 4/8	48 3/8	49 4/8	29 6/8	6 7/8	7	15 5/8	20	13 4/8	12 5/8	18	21	Cassiar Mts., BC	Jeffery T. Redfearn	Jeffery T. Redfearn	1998	100
411 2/8	49 2/8	49 1/8	30 7/8	6	6 2/8	17 2/8	18 3/8	11 6/8	11 2/8	20	21	Watson Lake, YT	John Csepp	John Csepp	1988	101
411 1/8	48 6/8	49 4/8	43	6 4/3	6 5/8	18 1/8	10	13 3/8	1/8	22	13	Norman Wells, NT	Elmer R. Kochans	Elmer R. Kochans	1981	102
411	39 5/8	40 5/8	31 6/8	7 5/8	7 5/8	20	1 7/8	14	10	17	15	Nisling Range, YT	Jack Odor	Jack Odor	1977	103
410 6/8	57 2/8	57 7/8	42 5/8	7	6 4/8	18 3/8	1 7/8	12 4/8	1/8	17	17	Keele Lake, YT	Robert L. Gilkey	Robert L. Gilkey	1986	104
410 6/8	54 5/8	55 6/8	43 1/8	6 1/3	5 6/8	20 3/8	20	11 5/8	6 7/8	12	11	Prospector Mt., YT	Allen Gunson	Allen Gunson	1998	104
410 3/8	48 5/8	47 7/8	34	6 6/8	6 2/8	17 3/8	5 4/8	16 1/8	1/8	27	19	Level Mts., BC	Stephen Sipes, Jr.	Stephen Sipes, Jr.	1985	106
410 1/8	53	53 2/8	41 2/8	7 1/8	7 1/8	16 7/8	18 7/8	9	5 7/8	14	18	Atlin, BC	Dale L. McCord	Dale L. McCord	1966	107
410 1/8	55 4/8	54 2/8	30 7/8	6 6/8	7 6/8	17 6/8	17 6/8	9 2/8	5 4/8	15	12	Cassiar Mts., BC	Charles J. Woodruff	Charles J. Woodruff	1970	107
410 1/8	52 4/8	53 7/8	39	7 4/3	7 3/8	19 5/8	18 1/8	16	10 1/8	22	21	Ram River, NT	Michael N. Andersen	Michael N. Andersen	1979	107
410	44 2/8	45 4/8	22 3/8	6 4/8	6 4/8	18 2/8	14 7/8	15 6/8	2 2/8	26	23	Deadwood Lake, BC	James W. Reilly	James W. Reilly	1968	110
410	47	49 6/8	37 6/8	6 2/3	6 4/8	18 2/8	18 1/8	11 5/8	1 6/8	14	10	Deadwood Lake, BC	Joseph Mannino	Joseph Mannino	1986	110
409 7/8	46	45	44	7	7 5/8	20	18 6/8	9 3/8	15 6/8	17	20	Atlin, BC	Cliff Schmidt	Cliff Schmidt	1966	112
409 7/8	51 7/8	51 7/8	40 1/8	6 1/5	6 2/8	16 3/8	17 1/8	4	9 2/8	19	16	Divide Lake, NT	Eldon L. Thompson	Eldon L. Thompson	1986	112
409 3/8	41 4/8	42	36 4/8	7 7/8	7 1/8	20 4/8	7 2/8	15	3 1/8	17	13	Dease Lake, BC	Wilf Klingsat	Wilf Klingsat	1974	114
409 1/8	51 2/8	52 5/8	30 6/8	6 3/8	6 4/8	20	14 3/8	13 6/8	12 4/8	22	22	Ice Mt., BC	David M. George	David M. George	1966	115
409 1/8	45 3/8	46	30 6/8	7 2/8	7 4/8	14 4/8	14 4/8	10 6/8	1/8	22	24	Johanson Lake, BC	George L. Seifert	George L. Seifert	1968	115
409	48 2/8	44	48 2/8	8 1/8	7 7/8	18 6/8	11 4/8	14 1/8	12 4/8	18	14	Level Mts., BC	Larry A. Zullo	Larry A. Zullo	1978	117
408 7/8	43	43 7/8	34 1/8	6 1/8	6	14	15 2/8	6	8 4/8	18	16	Skeena River, BC	Gordon Baird	Gordon Baird	1966	118
408 5/8	50 7/8	50 6/8	42 3/8	7 1/8	6 2/8	18 2/8	19	14 6/8	10 2/8	15	14	Ramparts River, NT	Robert Gruszecki	Robert Gruszecki	1999	119
408 4/8	48 6/8	47 6/8	35 6/8	6 7/8	6 7/8	14 7/8	16 4/8	1/8	6 2/8	16	16	Atlin, BC	Bradford O'Connor	Bradford O'Connor	1951	120

Score	Locality	Hunter	Owner	Date Killed	Rank
408 4/8	Mackenzie Mts., NT	Janet R. Johnson	Janet R. Johnson	1987	120
408 2/8	Spatsizi Plateau, BC	Michael M. Golightly	Michael M. Golightly	1985	122
408 2/8	Mt. Pike, YT	John T. Woloszyn	John T. Woloszyn	1994	122
408 2/8	Tsichu River, NT	Kristan Lashmore	Kristan Lashmore	1997	125
407 6/8	Cassiar Mts., YT	H.R. Safford III	H.R. Safford III	1968	125
407 5/8	Mackenzie Mts., NT	John K. Miller	John K. Miller	1989	127
407 5/8	Finlayson Lake, YT	Ken N. Booker	Ken N. Booker	1985	127
407 5/8	Tummel River, YT	William F. Calcagno, Jr.	William F. Calcagno, Jr.	1996	129
407 4/8	Buttle Creek, YT	Roy McLeod	Kerry Wagantall	1991	130
407 3/8	Keele River, NT	Roland Schwengler	Roland Schwengler	1984	130
407 3/8	Mackenzie Mts., NT	Tod L. Reichert	Tod L. Reichert	1996	132
407 1/8	Lower Post, BC	Jack Jordon	Jack Jordon	1960	133
407	Watson Lake, BC	Len Anderson	Len Anderson	1967	133
407	Norman Wells, NT	Thomas P. Warner	Thomas P. Warner	1980	135
406 7/8	Tatlatui Lake, BC	Winston P. Woodman	Winston P. Woodman	1966	136
406 5/8	Mountain River, NT	Grover F. Glasner	Grover F. Glasner	1985	136
406 5/8	Ruby Range, NT	Bill Strange	Bill Strange	1986	136
406 4/8	Tay Lake, YT	Ray J. Dennehy	Ray J. Dennehy	1988	139
406 3/8	Dawson Range, BC	Harold Ramberg	Harold Ramberg	1995	140
406 3/8	Kechika Range, BC	Basil C. Bradbury	B&C National Collection	1962	140
406 2/8	Drury Lake, YT	Robert T. Sanders	Robert T. Sanders	1997	142
406 1/8	Ross River, YT	Terrance D. Ferguson	Brian Hoffert	1994	143
406	Cassiar Mts., BC	Arvid F. Benson	Arvid F. Benson	1965	144
406	Tweedsmuir Park, BC	Bob Stewart	Bob Stewart	1964	144
406	Dawson Range, YT	John M. Domingos	John M. Domingos	1980	144
405 6/8	Jennings River, YT	R.D. Thomas, Jr.	R.D. Thomas, Jr.	1986	147
405 1/8	Watson Lake, BC	M.L. Walker	Marvin Walker	1968	148
404 4/8	Mackenzie Mts., NT	Robert J. Begeny	Robert J. Begeny	1976	149
404 1/8	Cassiar Mts., BC	Robert H. Cobun	Robert H. Cobun	1998	150
404 1/8	Cold Fish Lake, BC	O.A. Campbell	O.A. Campbell	1959	151
404	Hess River, YT	Stanley W. Scruggs	Stanley W. Scruggs	1994	152
404	June Lake, NT	Myron A. Peterson	Myron A. Peterson	1980	152
404	Kawdy Mt., BC	Mark Drake	Mark Drake	2002	155
404 3/8	Nisling River, YT	Richard R. Anspaugh	Richard R. Anspaugh	2003	155
404 3/8	Cassiar Mts., BC	Francis B. Wadelton	Francis B. Wadelton	1969	157
404 2/8	Mackenzie River, NT	Michael B. Murphy	Michael B. Murphy	1991	157
404 1/8	White River, YT	Perry Shankle	Perry Shankle	1955	159
404 1/8	Keele Peak, YT	Robert L. Gilkey	Robert L. Gilkey	1987	159
404	Teslin Lake, BC	Peter Hohn	Peter Hohn	1988	159
404	French Range, BC	Mike Harvella	Mike Harvella	2000	162
403 4/8	Mountain River, NT	Carles A. Webb	Carles A. Webb	2003	162
403 4/8	Keele River, NT	T.C. Britt, Jr.	T.C. Britt, Jr.	1968	162
403 3/8	Gem Lake, BC	Johann Gerdenits	Johann Gerdenits	1976	165
403 3/8	Carcajou River, NT	Julian B. White, Jr.	Julian B. White, Jr.	1988	165
403 3/8	Cassiar Mts., BC	Mrs. G.L. Gibbons	Mrs. G.L. Gibbons	1964	168
403 3/8	Gataga River, BC	Laurel E. Brown	Laurel E. Brown	1970	
403 2/8	Ross River, BC	Gail W. Holderman	Gail W. Holderman	1989	
403 2/8	Pelly Mts., YT	B.F. Briggs	B.F. Briggs	1963	

645

MOUNTAIN CARIBOU
Rangifer tarandus caribou

Score	Length of Main Beam R	L	Inside Spread	Circumference at Smallest Place Between Brow and Bez Points R	L	Length of Brow Points R	L	Width of Brow Points R	L	Number of Points R	L	Locality	Hunter	Owner	Date Killed	Rank
403 2/8	45 3/8	43 4/8	34 5/8	7 6/8	8 2/8	19 2/8	21 1/8	10 4/8	14	13	16	Drury Lake, YT	Henry Macagni	Henry Macagni	1963	168
403 2/8	52 3/8	50 6/8	31	9	8 5/8	13 5/8	16 6/8	7 7/8	8 4/8	18	24	Ketchum Lake, NT	Andy Proksch	Andy Proksch	1978	168
403 2/8	50	52 2/8	41 5/8	7 3/8	7 2/8	20 1/8	17 7/8	12 6/8	11 1/8	16	14	Mountain River, NT	Reginald Zebedee	Reginald Zebedee	1986	168
402 7/8	47 1/8	48 3/8	36 6/8	5 2/8	5 2/8	10 1/8	18 5/8	12 6/8	15	18	24	Twitya River, NT	Percy Pyra	Percy Pyra	1984	172
402 7/8	46 1/8	47 7/8	28 4/8	7 1/8	6 5/8	18 4/8	15 2/8	14 4/8	1/8	20	14	Tootsee River, BC	David Unruh	David Unruh	2000	172
402 6/8	49 5/8	51 4/8	37 5/8	6 3/8	6 4/8	20 5/8	6	14 7/8	1/8	18	14	Caesar Lakes, YT	Gladys M. Jamieson	Gladys M. Jamieson	1994	174
402 6/8	51 1/8	53 2/8	48 7/8	8 2/8	7 1/8	13 3/8	20 3/8	1 2/8	12 3/8	13	13	Glenlyon Range, YT	C. Kelly Farmer	C. Kelly Farmer	1997	174
402 4/8	48 3/8	50 2/8	41 2/8	6 7/8	6 5/8	11 3/8	19 2/8	1	14 2/8	17	27	Level Mts., BC	Phillip Neuweiler	Phillip Neuweiler	1956	176
402 4/8	50 2/8	49 6/8	40 5/8	6 3/8	6 1/8	17 1/8	16 7/8	1	13 4/8	13	21	Mountain Mts., NT	Charles J. Gagliano	Charles J. Gagliano	1988	176
402 3/8	45 1/8	47	40 5/8	6 4/8	6 7/8	16 7/8	20 5/8	12	12 7/8	15	13	Dease Lake, BC	G.C.F. Dalziel	G.C.F. Dalziel	1958	178
402 1/8	41 6/8	47	39 4/8	7 1/8	7	13	7 5/8	8 1/8	1/8	19	15	Cottonwood Lake, BC	Collins F. Kellogg	Collins F. Kellogg	1969	179
402 1/8	45	43 1/8	40 1/8	6 5/8	7 3/8	12 6/8	16 2/8	7 6/8	9	20	25	Glenlyon Range, YT	Louis A. Rupp	Louis A. Rupp	1985	179
402	42 7/8	42 4/8	35 6/8	7 1/8	6 5/8	18 4/8	12 7/8	11 4/8	1/8	19	14	Tuya Lake, BC	Robert G. Frew	Robert G. Frew	1988	181
401 7/8	50 4/8	51 4/8	39 6/8	7 1/8	5 4/8	20	16 7/8	17 1/8	1 3/8	19	13	Mackenzie Mts., NT	Thomas E. South	Thomas E. South	1976	182
401 6/8	50 6/8	48 6/8	41 7/8	5 6/8	6 4/8	15 2/8	13 1/8	10	6 4/8	20	20	Mackenzie Mts., NT	Larry C. Fisher	Larry C. Fisher	1992	183
401 4/8	43 7/8	46 6/8	32 1/8	6 2/8	5 7/8	8 1/8	10 4/8	8 7/8	10 3/8	19	19	Dease Lake, BC	Hugh Bennett	Hugh Bennett	1961	184
401 3/8	47 3/8	47 2/8	38 2/8	7 4/8	7 2/8	15 2/8	2	11 7/8	4/8	23	15	Arctic Red River, NT	Timothy F. McGinn	Timothy F. McGinn	2000	185
401 3/8	54 3/8	52 4/8	45 4/8	6 6/8	6 4/8	5 7/8	21 4/8	1/8	17 3/8	12	14	Cassiar Mts., BC	Tim D. Caldwell	Tim D. Caldwell	2001	185
401 2/8	46 7/8	46 6/8	41 6/8	7	7 2/8	15 7/8	15 7/8	1/8	11 1/8	14	15	Cassiar Mts., BC	Bernard W. McNamara	Bernard W. McNamara	1958	187
401 1/8	41 4/8	40	36 4/8	6 6/8	6 3/8	17	4 6/8	13 5/8	1 2/8	23	15	Cold Fish Lake, BC	P. Walsh	P. Walsh	1970	188
401 1/8	48	47 2/8	37 5/8	6 4/8	6 4/8	10 4/8	17 7/8	1/8	14	12	18	Arctic Red River, NT	Picked Up	L.M. Schmaus & S. Bowick	1986	188
401	42	41 6/8	36 4/8	8 4/8	8 5/8	16 1/8	11 6/8	11 2/8	1/8	15	15	Kechika Range, BC	H.I.H. Prince Abdorreza Pahlavi	H.I.H. Prince Abdorreza Pahlavi	1960	190
401	47 5/8	48 4/8	28 6/8	7	6 4/8	20 4/8	18 4/8	19 5/8	3 5/8	22	18	Mackenzie Mts., NT	James O. White	James O. White	1988	190
400 6/8	42 2/8	43 7/8	33 2/8	6 6/8	7	19	7 3/8	15 4/8	1/8	25	22	Aishihik Lake, YT	Armando J. Garcia	Armando J. Garcia	1987	192
400 5/8	44 6/8	44 6/8	34 4/8	6	6 3/8	17 3/8	19 3/8	11 6/8	13 1/8	14	18	Cassiar Mts., BC	Jack Fleishman, Jr.	Jack Fleishman, Jr.	1965	193
400 5/8	54 7/8	54 5/8	36 1/8	7 2/8	7 4/8	16 4/8	2 3/8	10	7/8	19	22	Nascha Creek, BC	W.A.K. Seale	W.A.K. Seale	1968	193
400 3/8	47 2/8	47	39 4/8	7	8 6/8	19	3 1/8	14 4/8	4/8	21	17	Cold Fish Lake, BC	Juan Brittingham	Juan Brittingham	1961	195
400 3/8	41 7/8	42 5/8	28 5/8	7 6/8	6 7/8	18 5/8	18 3/8	6 2/8	9 2/8	16	17	Caribou Mt., YT	Charles B. Heuring	Charles B. Heuring	1984	195
400 2/8	58 5/8	57 6/8	39 5/8	8	8 1/8	20 5/8	2 3/8	13 3/8	6/8	14	11	Dease Lake, BC	Stanley A. Chase	Stanley A. Chase	1973	197
400	37 1/8	39	31 1/8	6 5/8	6 4/8	13 7/8	13 2/8	9 6/8	7	19	22	Cold Fish Lake, BC	Charles P. Yarn, Jr.	Charles P. Yarn, Jr.	1965	198
400	54	53 6/8	37 4/8	6 4/8	6 4/8	17	14 4/8	6 4/8	5 4/8	18	14	Nahanni River, NT	Kevin Davidson	Kevin Davidson	1977	198
400	42 1/8	41	29	7	7 1/8	16 1/8	14 2/8	10 4/8	6 1/8	22	17	Little Rancheria River, BC	Allan Edwards	Allan Edwards	1988	198
400	50 2/8	45 4/8	36 3/8	7	7 1/8	19 5/8	1 6/8	14 1/8	1/8	24	24	Boya Lake, YT	Dale Selby	Dale Selby	1995	198
400	43	41 7/8	36 6/8	8 5/8	8 1/8	16 6/8	16 4/8	9	9	18	21	Fire Lake, YT	Jonathan Thornberry	Jonathan Thornberry	1998	198
400	43 2/8	41 1/8	33 4/8	6 2/8	6 6/8	15 2/8	19 2/8	4 2/8	14 4/8	19	22	Pine Lake, YT	William Watson	William Watson	2001	198

Score	Main Beam R	Main Beam L	Inside Spread	4	5	6	7	8	9	Pts R	Pts L	Locality	By Whom Killed	Owner	Date	Rank
399 7/8	49 5/8	50 2/8	32 4/8	6 1/8	6 1/8	3 3/8	17 4/8	5/8	8 7/8	16	22	Eaglenest Range, BC	Robert J. Stevens	Robert J. Stevens	1967	204
399 7/8	43 2/8	41	37 5/8	6 5/8	7 1/8	18 3/8	18 6/8	12 3/8	16 3/8	15	16	Mackenzie Mts., NT	James J. McBride	James J. McBride	1989	204
399 7/8	46	44	37 1/8	5 6/8	5 6/8	18 5/8	17 6/8	13 6/8	6 5/8	26	18	Mackenzie Mts., NT	John E. Monek	John E. Monek	1994	204
399 6/8	47 2/8	49 2/8	33 2/8	8 4/8	8 6/8	14 4/8	17 3/8	3	14 3/8	20	27	Divide Lake, NT	Brooks Carmichael	Brooks Carmichael	1984	207
399 4/8	46 5/8	48	34 1/8	6 7/8	6 6/8	17 1/8	17 6/8	4	12 2/8	21	17	Cassiar Mts., BC	William R. Franklin	William R. Franklin	1969	208
399 4/8	45 1/8	45 1/8	38 1/8	5 6/8	5 7/8	15 1/8	3 1/8	8 2/8	1/8	19	16	Turnagain River, BC	Gerald L. Simpson	Gerald L. Simpson	1984	208
399 4/8	49 5/8	53 2/8	33	6 6/8	5 7/8	15 3/8	16 6/8	14 2/8	4 1/8	23	16	Mackenzie Mts., NT	Lawrence T. Keenan	Lawrence T. Keenan	1994	208
399 4/8	51 4/8	50 1/8	39 7/8	6 3/8	6 4/8	17 1/8	19 5/8	11 4/8	7 5/8	19	14	Mackenzie Mts., NT	Ilynn R. Schwartzberg	Ilynn R. Schwartzberg	1994	208
399 3/8	48 5/8	48 7/8	39	6 7/8	8	16	16	11 4/8	8 2/8	17	18	Ice Lakes, YT	F. David Thornberry	F. David Thornberry	1996	212
399 3/8	45 4/8	45 4/8	47	6 5/8	7	18 3/8	17 3/8	12 3/8	8	17	14	Teslin River, BC	Abe J.N. Dougan	Abe J.N. Dougan	1998	212
399	49 7/8	51 5/8	40 2/8	6 6/8	6 4/8	18	10 5/8	15 1/8	3	14	13	Cassiar Mts., BC	Joseph C. Hinderman	Joseph C. Hinderman	1997	214
398 7/8	51 6/8	49	34 6/8	6 6/8	5 7/8	14 5/8	20	1 3/8	13 5/8	16	18	Cold Fish Lake, BC	George W. Hooker	George W. Hooker	1956	215
398 7/8	48 5/8	52 1/8	40 4/8	5 7/8	5 7/8	6 5/8	15 6/8	1/8	12 5/8	17	19	Mackenzie Mts., NT	Craig R. Johnson	Craig R. Johnson	1987	215
398 7/8	46 1/8	44 5/8	37 4/8	6 4/8	6 5/8	8	17 4/8	1/8	12 4/8	17	22	Mackenzie Mts., NT	James Markle	James Markle	1992	215
398 7/8	52 4/8	53 2/8	31 1/8	6 1/8	5 5/8	18 3/8	19 7/8	6 2/8	8	16	16	Telegraph Creek, BC	James J. Kass	James J. Kass	2002	215
398 6/8	44 7/8	42	34	6 6/8	6 4/8	19 4/8	18	11	12 6/8	21	26	Cassiar Mts., BC	John W. Zomer	John W. Zomer	1995	219
398 3/8	45 3/8	46 5/8	36 6/8	6 1/8	6	18 7/8	18 7/8	15	1/8	28	13	Divide Lake, NT	Udo Kerber	Udo Kerber	1995	220
398 2/8	54 4/8	56	38 6/8	7 1/8	6 7/8	19	11 1/8	14 3/8	1	18	14	Spatsizi Plateau, BC	Warren Page	Warren Page	1970	221
398 2/8	47	47 5/8	43 5/8	6 2/8	6 7/8	9 4/8	18	14 3/8	6 8/8	22	16	Tuya Lake, BC	Jack Clary	Jack Clary	1999	221
398	47 1/8	49 4/8	39 1/8	7 7/8	6	15 5/8	18 6/8	10 2/8	12 6/8	13	18	Pelly Mts., YT	Michael F. Short	Michael F. Short	1982	223
398	47 1/8	49 4/8	39 1/8	7 1/8	6	15 5/8	18 6/8	11 1/8	9 5/8	22	12	Arctic Red River, NT	William J. Ostrom	William J. Ostrom	1994	223
398	50 2/8	48 2/8	32 7/8	7 7/8	8	18 3/8	15	15 2/8	5/8	20	16	Cassiar Mts., BC	Troy Cummins	Troy Cummins	1999	223
397 6/8	46 4/8	47	29 4/8	5 7/8	5 7/8	4 7/8	16 7/8	14 2/8	5/8	17	23	Muncho Lake, BC	Bob Landis	Tom Mould	1960	226
397 4/8	46 1/8	43	34 1/8	6 4/8	6 6/8	14 6/8	14 5/8	7 6/8	11 5/8	17	20	Mountain River, NT	Kenn M. Haugen	Kenn M. Haugen	1993	227
397 4/8	42 4/8	40 7/8	30 1/8	5 6/8	6 5/8	16 6/8	15 3/8	16 3/8	14 1/8	21	20	June Lake, NT	Katherine A. Pyra	Katherine A. Pyra	1995	227
397 3/8	50	49	35	6 7/8	6 5/8	17	17 3/8	11 6/8	8 5/8	17	17	Mackenzie Mts., NT	Robert L. Donnelly	Robert L. Donnelly	1988	229
397 2/8	47	49	39 6/8	8 3/8	7 7/8	17 4/8	18 1/8	12	10 1/8	11	13	Glacier Lake, BC	Helmuth Katz	Helmuth Katz	1967	230
397 2/8	52 7/8	51 2/8	42 4/8	7 3/8	7 6/8	16 4/8	15 6/8	10 4/8	4	11	14	Mackenzie Mts., NT	William J. Chronister	William J. Chronister	1978	230
397 1/8	45 2/8	47 2/8	37 7/8	6 2/8	5 6/8	15 6/8	15	7 1/8	8 5/8	20	18	Little Cottonwood Lake, BC	William J. Kuehn	William J. Kuehn	2001	232
396 6/8	44 1/8	43 5/8	35 3/8	6 7/8	6 7/8	17	15 1/8	3 3/8	12 5/8	15	21	Divide Lake, NT	Delbert E. Rieckers	Delbert E. Rieckers	1990	233
396 4/8	46 4/8	47 6/8	34 4/8	7 1/8	6 7/8	18 4/8	20 4/8	13 1/8	13 3/8	18	15	Mackenzie Mts., NT	Mark Cook	Mark Cook	1988	234
396 3/8	46 2/8	44 4/8	29 4/8	7 1/8	7 1/8	19 5/8	17 1/8	2	2 1/8	14	15	Cold Fish Lake, BC	L.W. Zimmerman	L.W. Zimmerman	1960	235
396 3/8	47 3/8	46 2/8	38 2/8	6 6/8	6 7/8	17 3/8	17 1/8	10 3/8	11	12	13	Mackenzie Mts., NT	Kirk M. Cavanaugh	Kirk M. Cavanaugh	2001	235
396 2/8	49 4/8	48 7/8	40 1/8	6 1/8	5 7/8	20 1/8	18 7/8	9	15 3/8	19	14	Pelly Mts., YT	Ken Taylor	Ken Taylor	2002	237
396 1/8	47 3/8	46 3/8	31 1/8	8 6/8	6 5/8	16	15 1/8	7 7/8	7 7/8	19	19	Telegraph Creek, BC	John H. Johnson	Roger S. Johnson	1952	238
396 1/8	54 2/8	58 4/8	44 7/8	7	7 1/8	18 4/8	15 2/8	1 4/8	9	19	12	Cassiar Mts., BC	Peter C. Jurs	Peter C. Jurs	1964	238
396 1/8	47 2/8	44 3/8	38	7	6 2/8	20 1/8	2 6/8	13 3/8	6 4/8	15	14	Dease Lake, BC	David A. Smith	David A. Smith	1987	238
396	52 7/8	52 7/8	41 5/8	6	6 2/8	19 5/8	9 6/8	14 4/8	1/8	18	16	Drury Lake, YT	Ostell G. Penner	Ostell G. Penner	1985	241
395 7/8	52 5/8	54 3/8	36 1/8	5 5/8	5 4/8	17 5/8	16 4/8	4	5 6/8	15	17	Arctic Red River, NT	Hal Wheeler	Hal Wheeler	1993	242
395 6/8	46	42 4/8	40 5/8	6 7/8	6 7/8	4	19	1/8	15 7/8	18	21	Ice Lakes, YT	Tadeus S. Konieczka	Tadeus S. Konieczka	1982	243
395 6/8	48 3/8	48 4/8	37 6/8	8 1/8	8 1/8	15 2/8	17 4/8	10 3/8	10 4/8	15	17	O'Grady Lake, NT	Ralph Fleegle	R. Fleegle & D. Fleegle	1988	243
395 6/8	50	47 7/8	31 7/8	7 1/8	6 5/8	18 4/8	17	12 5/8	10 3/8	16	18	Mackenzie Mts., NT	Connie Blaszczak	Connie Blaszczak	1990	243
395 4/8	51 3/8	53 1/8	42 5/8	6 2/8	6 1/8	17 4/8	17 4/8	10 7/8	9	16	13	Atlin, BC	Ray Foerster	Ray Foerster	1960	246
395 4/8	52 4/8	54 6/8	30 6/8	5 5/8	6 1/8	15 3/8	21 3/8	16 5/8	9	16	22	Mackenzie Mts., NT	Carl V. Hancock, Jr.	Carl V. Hancock, Jr.	1997	246
395 3/8	52 4/8	53 2/8	37 5/8	6 6/8	6 4/8	20 7/8	16 7/8	10 2/8	2	17	13	Willow Creek, NT	Dwayne Moore	Dwayne Moore	1996	248
395 2/8	47 4/8	47 3/8	36 4/8	6 5/8	6 2/8	20 7/8	20 7/8	3 3/8	17 3/8	20	14	Cold Fish Lake, BC	D.A. Boyd	D.A. Boyd	1963	249
395 2/8	43 4/8	42 1/8	34 2/8	6 6/8	6 6/8	14 7/8	13 1/8	2 6/8	9	17	15	Dease Lake, BC	George H. Glass	George H. Glass	1963	249

647

MOUNTAIN CARIBOU
Rangifer tarandus caribou

Score	Length of Main Beam R	L	Inside Spread	Circumference at Smallest Place Between Brow and Bez Points R	L	Length of Brow Points R	L	Width of Brow Points R	L	Number of Points R	L	Locality	Hunter	Owner	Date Killed	Rank
395 2/8	42 2/8	39 3/8	32 5/8	7	6 6/8	18 6/8	9 5/8	14 5/8	7 5/8	23	19	Keele River, NT	George H. Fisher	George H. Fisher	1993	249
395 1/8	48	48 2/8	29 6/8	7 1/8	7 1/8	2 2/8	14	1/8	10 4/8	15	21	Prophet River, BC	V.B. Seigel	V.B. Seigel	1961	252
395	56 5/8	54 7/8	46 7/8	5 6/8	5 7/8	19 5/8	15 5/8	18 1/8	1 4/8	17	9	Mountain River, NT	Robert L. Williamson	Robert L. Williamson	1983	253
394 7/8	47 1/8	45 7/8	37 6/8	6 7/8	6 5/8	14 7/8	14	8 7/8	12 3/8	17	18	Wolf Creek, BC	Riley N. Ferguson	Riley N. Ferguson	1991	254
394 6/8	42 4/8	43	39 3/8	6 7/8	7 5/8	18 6/8	17 7/8	9	11 6/8	15	15	Cassiar, BC	Arcadio Guerra	Arcadio Guerra	1957	255
394 6/8	52 2/8	48 5/8	39 2/8	6 2/8	6 2/8	22 1/8	7 2/8	20	1/8	12	14	Divide Lake, NT	Richard A. Belotti	Richard A. Belotti	1987	255
394 6/8	45 4/8	46 2/8	36 4/8	6 4/8	6 4/8	17 2/8	16 1/8	6 3/8	14 4/8	15	16	Keele River, NT	Anthony T. Brazil	Anthony T. Brazil	1991	255
394 4/8	44 4/8	44 5/8	39 1/8	5 7/8	6 1/8	18 2/8	9 1/8	10 1/8	1/8	20	14	Ruby Range, YT	John R. Bloise	John R. Bloise	1985	258
394 3/8	37 3/8	39 3/8	24 3/8	7 6/8	7 5/8	14 6/8	14 1/8	10 1/8	2 4/8	28	22	Muncho Lake, BC	H.W. Julien	John W. Julien	1965	259
394 3/8	44	46 7/8	30 2/8	7 3/8	7 1/8	9 1/8	16 4/8	1 1/8	8 5/8	17	19	Cassiar Mts., BC	Raymond A. Schneider	Raymond A. Schneider	1968	259
394 3/8	48 3/8	51 1/8	35 2/8	6 2/8	6 6/8	21 4/8	18 6/8	7 6/8	13	15	16	Selwyn Valley, YT	Hans Berg	Hans Berg	1991	259
394 2/8	51 2/8	54 5/8	39 3/8	6 6/8	6 6/8	14 6/8	19 1/8	2 7/8	11 4/8	14	18	Niven Creek, BC	Jamie Gunn	Jamie Gunn	2002	262
394 1/8	51 1/8	52	41 6/8	7 2/8	7 6/8	10 5/8	19 3/8	1/8	13 2/8	13	21	Cry Lake, BC	Ritchey Elliott	Catherine Mulvahill	1987	263
394	56 6/8	56 7/8	51 4/8	6 4/8	7	18 2/8	5 6/8	13 3/8	13 7/8	11	18	Turnagain River, BC	Robert E. Miller	Robert E. Miller	1968	264
393 7/8	54	51 6/8	49 3/8	7 4/8	6 7/8	19 5/8	8 2/8	13 7/8	1/8	23	13	Pelly Mts., YT	Thomas J. Grogan	Thomas J. Grogan	2000	265
393 6/8	45 6/8	42 2/8	38 5/8	7	6 7/8	14 6/8	2 2/8	8 7/8	12	16	17	Redstone River, NT	William E. Pipes III	William E. Pipes III	1974	266
393 6/8	45 4/8	43 4/8	39	7 6/8	6 7/8	15 7/8	2 2/8	8 7/8	1/8	17	16	Mackenzie Mts., NT	Steven S. Bruggeman	Steven S. Bruggeman	1988	266
393 6/8	47 3/8	42 6/8	38 2/8	6 6/8	6 6/8	15 4/8	17	11 1/8	10 3/8	18	15	Arctic Red River, NT	James K. McCasland	James K. McCasland	1988	266
393 6/8	49 5/8	51 3/8	36 7/8	6 7/8	7	18 3/8	3 2/8	12 1/8	1/8	13	13	Ross River, BC	Greg Kushnak	Greg Kushnak	1997	266
393 6/8	42 3/8	46	41 6/8	6 6/8	6 7/8	17 4/8	10 6/8	11	1 5/8	19	13	Blanchet Lake, BC	Rick E. Abbott	Rick E. Abbott	2000	266
393 3/8	47 1/8	50 4/8	30 2/8	5 3/8	5 4/8	18 3/8	13 6/8	12 3/8	2 4/8	18	16	Mackenzie Mts., NT	Lonnie L. Ritchey	Lonnie L. Ritchey	1990	271
393 2/8	38	37 6/8	30 2/8	8 1/8	8 4/8	2 4/8	17 2/8	1/8	14 1/8	18	21	Tweedsmuir Park, BC	Harold Daye	Harold Daye	1960	272
393 2/8	49 7/8	51 7/8	39 4/8	6 4/8	6 2/8	11 4/8	20 4/8	1	10	14	17	Cassiar Dist., BC	Robert E. Miller	Robert E. Miller	1966	272
393 1/8	54 4/8	54 2/8	33 7/8	6 4/8	6 2/8	18 7/8	16 7/8	4	12 2/8	13	18	Grass Lakes, YT	Melvin R. Spohn	Melvin R. Spohn	1981	274
393	52 4/8	50 5/8	39 2/8	5 4/8	5 6/8	16 7/8	18 7/8	7 1/8	11	13	17	Mt. Thule, BC	William L. Searle	William L. Searle	1963	275
393	42 2/8	43 4/8	34 6/8	7 1/8	6 7/8	10 5/8	18 4/8	3 5/8	12 6/8	12	19	Ross River, BC	Robert C. Stephens	Robert C. Stephens	1993	275
393	47 1/8	47 2/8	34 4/8	6 3/8	6 1/8	18 4/8	15	4 4/8	11 1/8	14	15	Tay River, YT	Mark R. Zimmerman	Mark R. Zimmerman	1998	275
392 7/8	47 6/8	49 6/8	37 6/8	6 3/8	6 7/8	16 2/8	16 2/8	6/8	1 3/8	16	16	Cassiar Mts., BC	Charles F. Haas	Charles F. Haas	1959	278
392 7/8	41 2/8	42 4/8	36	6 6/8	6 6/8	14 4/8	3 1/8	9 6/8	1/8	21	17	Atlin, BC	Earl H. Carlson	Wildl. Tax. Studios	1966	278
392 6/8	45 6/8	45 1/8	40 1/8	7 3/8	7 4/8	16 7/8	7 4/8	13 1/8	1/8	22	17	W. Toad River, BC	Daniel R. Bond	Daniel R. Bond	1966	280
392 6/8	46 3/8	44 3/8	36	6 7/8	6 7/8	17 4/8	7 4/8	9 7/8	5	18	20	Little Dal Lake, NT	Douglas M. Dreeszen	Douglas M. Dreeszen	1984	280
392 5/8	39 6/8	39 3/8	33 4/8	5 5/8	5 5/8	7 4/8	16 7/8	1/8	10 6/8	22	34	Cold Fish Lake, BC	Richard G. Van Vorst	Richard G. Van Vorst	1974	282
392 5/8	46 7/8	48 4/8	30 6/8	7 1/8	7 3/8	7 4/8	2 4/8	1/8	14 2/8	21	23	Arctic Red River, NT	Leo M. Schmaus	Leo M. Schmaus	1986	282
392 3/8	46 3/8	48 7/8	32	6 2/8	6 5/8	16 6/8	16 1/8	6	12	12	14	Kechika Range, BC	H.I.H. Prince Abdorreza Pahlavi	Game Council of Iran	1960	284
392 3/8	48 6/8	52 2/8	43 5/8	6 1/8	6 1/8	19 2/8	15 3/8	1/8	15 4/8	10	17	Ice Mt., BC	Jerry E. Mason	Jerry E. Mason	1966	284

Score	Main Beam R	Main Beam L	Inside Spread	Circ. R	Circ. L	Brow Palm L/R	Brow Palm	Width R	Width L	Pts R	Pts L	Locality	Hunter	Owner	Date	Rank
392 3/8	47 7/8	45 4/8	32 4/8	6 3/8	6 6/8	16 6/8	17 2/8	9 7/8	6	15	12	Logan Mts., YT	Gordon R. Graham	Gordon R. Graham	1978	284
392 3/8	44 7/8	44	34 7/8	6 3/8	6 3/8	16 4/8	17 2/8	10 7/8	6 5/8	18	16	Dease Lake, BC	Ross H. Mann	Ross H. Mann	1984	284
392 2/8	45 6/8	43 1/8	30 7/8	5 2/8	5 2/8	16 3/8	17	8 7/8	11 6/8	18	22	Keele River, NT	Dale R. Hill	Dale R. Hill	1980	288
392 2/8	41 1/8	46	29 6/8	7 5/8	6 7/8	3 6/8	16 3/8	/8	13	14	20	Fire Lake, YT	Michael L. Haydock	Michael L. Haydock	1989	288
392 1/8	39 4/8	46 2/8	38	7 4/8	7 2/8	17 4/8	17	7 7/8	7 1/8	17	13	Rabbit River, BC	Bob C. Jones	Bob C. Jones	1969	290
392	42 4/8	47 4/8	32 4/8	5 6/8	6 4/8	19 2/8	16 4/8	13 7/8	1	19	15	Twopete Mt., YT	David H. Crum	David H. Crum	1984	291
392	47 5/8	45 6/8	40 6/8	7	7	16 4/8	15 7/8	5 2/8	4 1/8	21	17	Cassiar Mts., BC	H. Ross Mann	H. Ross Mann	2000	291
391 7/8	43 4/8	45 5/8	42 3/8	6 5/8	6 1/8	15 5/8	16 1/8	5 5/8	11	11	19	Cassiar, BC	Dorothy N. Benson	Dorothy N. Benson	1967	293
391 7/8	53 3/8	53	40 3/8	6 1/8	6 4/8	17 5/8	15 7/8	5 4/8	9	24	11	Glacier Lake, BC	Lowell C. Hansen II	Lowell C. Hansen II	1970	293
391 7/8	44 6/8	44 4/8	30 2/8	6 3/8	6 4/8	15 1/8	15 6/8	7 4/8	19	19	11	Mt. Rognaas, BC	Michael D. Miklosi	Michael D. Miklosi	1983	293
391 7/8	48 2/8	44 7/8	36 4/8	6 4/8	6	18 6/8	12 7/8	15 4/8	1/8	20	13	Keele River, NT	Dean Miller	Dean Miller	1994	293
391 5/8	46 3/8	43 7/8	34	5 7/8	5 7/8	19	21 2/8	19 6/8	17 6/8	18	21	Cassiar, BC	E.F. Ardourel	E.F. Ardourel	1960	297
391 3/8	48	46 2/8	37 6/8	6 6/8	6 3/8	19	18 3/8	6	6	15	16	Cassiar Mts., BC	Stan McKay	Stan McKay	1990	298
391 3/8	53 3/8	54 1/8	36 6/8	6 4/8	6 7/8	3 2/8	14 5/8	10 1/8	10 1/8	12	17	Tuya Lake, BC	John D. Frost	John D. Frost	1995	299
391 3/8	47 1/8	49	34 7/8	6 1/8	7 5/8	13 7/8	15	6 1/8	8	18	14	Mackenzie Mts., NT	William G. James	William G. James	1995	299
391 3/8	49 4/8	48 7/8	35 7/8	6 6/8	6 5/8	16 7/8	13 7/8	17 3/8	1/8	12	19	Dick Lake, BC	James R. Colosimo	James R. Colosimo	1996	299
391 2/8	50 2/8	50	37 4/8	6 2/8	5 7/8	17 3/8	16 1/8	4 7/8	10 7/8	14	18	Drury Lake, YT	Nick Spiropolos	Nick Spiropolos	1970	302
391 1/8	49	52 5/8	40 4/8	5 6/8	5 5/8	22	21 2/8	5 5/8	11 3/8	13	13	Ruby Range, YT	William K. Hilton	William K. Hilton	1985	302
391 1/8	49 4/8	49 4/8	44 1/8	6 7/8	6 6/8	18 5/8	21 2/8	6 6/8	5 4/8	13	16	Twitya River, NT	Melvin E. Kraft	Melvin E. Kraft	1987	302
391 1/8	46 1/8	44 1/8	38 4/8	6 7/8	6 6/8	3	18 4/8	13	13	16	17	Atlin, BC	Bob Reinhold	Bob Reinhold	1963	305
391	49 1/8	47	36 4/8	6 7/8	6 6/8	14 6/8	13 3/8	8 7/8	15 4/8	15	15	Lonesome Creek, NT	Frank J. Kukurin	Frank J. Kukurin	1989	305
391	49 6/8	50 7/8	42 7/8	6 3/8	6 3/8	16 2/8	15 2/8	4 7/8	10 4/8	19	20	Blue River, BC	Aldo Guglielmini	Aldo Guglielmini	1976	307
391	38 5/8	39 4/8	37 7/8	7	7	7 4/8	7 1/8	11 7/8	23	23	17	Tuya Range, BC	Robert L. Gilkey	Robert L. Gilkey	1978	307
390 7/8	40 3/8	39	34 1/8	6 2/8	6 2/8	15 6/8	2 7/8	1/8	10	23	23	Tuya Lake, BC	John H. Epstein	John H. Epstein	1953	309
390 6/8	46	46 6/8	34	5 7/8	5 7/8	2 4/8	16 3/8	14	24	22	Snake River, BC	J.W.L. Monaghan	J.W.L. Monaghan	1963	309
390 6/8	46 6/8	46 2/8	44 2/8	6 6/8	6 2/8	15 4/8	4 7/8	13 3/8	25	12	Mackenzie Mts., NT	Scott S. Snyder	Scott S. Snyder	1991	311
390 6/8	42 3/8	45 4/8	44 4/8	6 2/8	6 2/8	15	14 2/8	13 3/8	13 3/8	12	17	Redstone River, NT	H. Hudson DeCray	H. Hudson DeCray	1995	311
390 5/8	51 7/8	48 1/8	45 1/8	7 1/8	6 6/8	6 6/8	15	3 4/8	20	20	12	Atlin, BC	Vern Cox	Vern Cox	1962	313
390 5/8	50 4/8	51 7/8	43	6 6/8	6 6/8	5	18 3/8	9 6/8	17	20	Semenot Hills, YT	Thomas F. Jeffcote	Thomas F. Jeffcote	1975	313
390 5/8	43 2/8	39 4/8	27 5/8	6 2/8	6 2/8	16 3/8	15 6/8	9 4/8	8	20	17	Drury Lake, YT	Robert D. Day	Robert D. Day	1986	313
390 5/8	44 4/8	45 7/8	35 3/8	5 6/8	6 6/8	15 3/8	15 3/8	9 2/8	9	23	18	Arctic Red River, NT	Arthur J. Bayer	Arthur J. Bayer	1994	313
390 4/8	39 2/8	39 3/8	36	5 7/8	6 2/8	16	16 2/8	7 5/8	11 7/8	20	18	Muncho Lake, BC	Dennis Dean	Dennis Dean	1963	317
390 4/8	37 4/8	38 5/8	37 5/8	7 4/8	7 4/8	18 2/8	17 4/8	13 4/8	17 4/8	19	17	Cassiar Mts., BC	Milo L. Blickenstaff	Milo L. Blickenstaff	1965	317
390 4/8	36 1/8	37 2/8	29 4/8	7 2/8	7 2/8	17 4/8	15 1/8	12 4/8	11 3/8	20	17	Halfway River, BC	Steven L. Rose	R. Lynn Ross	1965	317
390 4/8	57 3/8	57 6/8	42 1/8	5 7/8	5 4/8	2 4/8	15 1/8	1	1	15	17	Mountain River, NT	Jack R. Cook	Jack R. Cook	1981	317
390 3/8	54 2/8	54 6/8	37 2/8	7	6 6/8	17	2 4/8	11 4/8	1	15	14	Level Mts., BC	Donald S. Hopkins	Unknown	1928	321
390 3/8	55	56 6/8	37 2/8	7 4/8	6 6/8	18 2/8	17	8 7/8	16 5/8	12	12	Cassiar, BC	Orlando Bodeau	Orlando Bodeau	1953	321
390 2/8	41 7/8	41 3/8	34 7/8	5 6/8	8 1/8	16 6/8	1	14 3/8	4 5/8	16 6/8	19	18	Ice Lakes, YT	J. Michael Thornberry II	J. Michael Thornberry II	1996	323
390 2/8	44 4/8	43 7/8	31 2/8	5 7/8	5 6/8	11 1/8	19	17 5/8	16	11 1/8	19	12	Mackenzie Mts., NT	Charles M. Mendenhall	Charles M. Mendenhall	1997	323
390 1/8	47 1/8	50	40 4/8	6 7/8	6 3/8	17 1/8	6	14 7/8	1/8	6	21	Dease Lake, BC	W.A. Tharp	W.A. Tharp	1962	325
390 1/8	55 2/8	51 6/8	34 1/8	6 3/8	6 2/8	17 6/8	18 4/8	12 4/8	2 3/8	18 4/8	15	Firesteel Lake, BC	Melvin K. Wolf	Melvin K. Wolf	1970	325
390	56 7/8	58 3/8	44 7/8	6 4/8	6 3/8	18 6/8	18 6/8	11	1/8	18 6/8	18	Mackenzie Mts., NT	John R. Young	John R. Young	1985	327
390	46 1/8	47	30 4/8	6 4/8	6 1/8	18 3/8	10 1/8	17	10 1/8	18 5/8	21	Teslin River, BC	Dan Stacey	Dan Stacey	1998	327
390	51 2/8	48 3/8	48 3/8	6 2/8	5 7/8	16 4/8	17	7 7/8	14 3/8	19 5/8	12	Mountain River, NT	Gary Nehring	Gary Nehring	2002	327
441 *	49 3/8	48 3/8	48 2/8	6 2/8	5 7/8	19 5/8	19 7/8	7 7/8	11 3/8	19 7/8	18	Gana River, NT	Allen A. Meyer	Allen A. Meyer	2001	
438 1/8*	51 5/8	52 7/8	37 5/8	7 5/8	7 3/8	17 5/8	17 5/8	5 7/8	11 6/8	17 5/8	20	Mackenzie Mts., NT	Mark J. Sheridan	Mark J. Sheridan	2002	
419 6/8*	48 5/8	48 6/8	37 5/8	6 4/8	6 4/8	18 3/8	10 6/8	4 /8	10 6/8	18 3/8	17	Calata Lake, BC	Terry A. Street	Terry A. Street	2002	
417 4/8*	49 7/8	49 6/8	37	6 1/8	6 2/8	16 4/8	15 6/8	11 7/8	10 4/8	16 4/8	18	Mountain River, NT	William E. Hosford	William E. Hosford	2000	

* Final score is subject to revision by additional verifying measurements.

CATEGORY
MOUNTAIN CARIBOU

SCORE
410-6/8

HUNTER
ALLEN GUNSON (BELOW)

LOCATION
PROSPECTOR MOUNTAIN,
YUKON TERRITORY

DATE OF KILL
SEPTEMBER 1998

CATEGORY
MOUNTAIN CARIBOU

SCORE
416-7/8

HUNTER
E. ROYCE GUNTER, JR. (LEFT)

LOCATION
ARCTIC RED RIVER,
NORTHWEST TERRITORIES

DATE OF KILL
SEPTEMBER 1999

CATEGORY
MOUNTAIN CARIBOU

SCORE
398

HUNTER
TROY CUMMINS

LOCATION
CASSIAR MOUNTAINS,
BRITISH COLUMBIA

DATE OF KILL
SEPTEMBER 1999

CATEGORY
MOUNTAIN CARIBOU

SCORE
441*

HUNTER
ALLEN A. MEYER (BELOW)

LOCATION
GANA RIVER, NORTHWEST TERRITORIES

DATE OF KILL
AUGUST 2001

CATEGORY
MOUNTAIN CARIBOU

SCORE
393-6/8

HUNTER
RICK E. ABBOTT (LEFT)

LOCATION
BLANCHET LAKE, BRITISH COLUMBIA

DATE OF KILL
OCTOBER 2000

SCORE
390

HUNTER
GARY NEHRING
(BOTTOM LEFT)

LOCATION
MOUNTAIN RIVER,
NORTHWEST TERRITORIES

DATE OF KILL
SPETEMBER 2002

WOODLAND CARIBOU
WORLD'S RECORD

TROPHY INFO

RANK
World's Record

SCORE
419 5/8

LOCATION
Newfoundland

HUNTER
Gift of
H. Casmir de Rham

OWNER
B&C National Collection

DATE KILLED
Prior to 1910

Continuing to stand as the oldest World's Record, the top woodland caribou (*Rangifer tarandus caribou*) was shot in Newfoundland before 1910 and donated to the National Collection of Heads and Horns by the late Casimir de Rham.

The hunter who obtained the impressive mahogany-colored antlers probably took his shot just before the rut in late summer, early fall when the animal's antlers had become fully developed and hardened. Newfoundland is considered the best hunting grounds for woodland trophies. Weighing upwards of 500 pounds, a particularly impressive woodland caribou will have a rack with as many as 40 tines. However, these are extremely difficult to count in the field, and other criteria must be considered such as rarer double shovels, as well as the size of the rack in proportion to the body.

Woodland caribou sometimes merely shift locally, and would have not moved much further than the southern part of the island during the autumn rut. Therefore, this trophy would have been hunted without too much concern for timing. If the animal was with the herd it would not have been overly difficult to track as the herd will leave a dark, obvious path on the delicate surface of the barrens. It is this soft terrain that allows them to be heard grazing from afar or clicking their ankles as they move, and on a chilly, dank morning the hunter may even have spotted the rising vapor from the herd. Cover on the tundra is minimum, the ubiq-

uitous bogs often make a stalk a cumbersome and wet task, and the wind is always a consideration. As the woodland caribou lowered his head to graze upon the barrens for birch leaves or their mainstay, lichens, it would have proved difficult for the hunter to pick out the largest trophy without spooking the herd, which can suddenly move at 30 miles an hour.

Balancing all of these factors, this enormous woodland caribou was taken in a fair chase manner and exemplifies decades of Boone and Crockett's achievement in recording big game records. ■

BOUNDARY FOR WOODLAND CARIBOU

Woodland caribou includes trophies from Nova Scotia, New Brunswick, and Newfoundland.

WOODLAND CARIBOU
WORLD'S RECORD SCORE CHART

Records of North American Big Game

BOONE AND CROCKETT CLUB®

250 Station Drive
Missoula, MT 59801
(406) 542-1888

OFFICIAL SCORING SYSTEM FOR NORTH AMERICAN BIG GAME TROPHIES

CARIBOU

KIND OF CARIBOU (check one)
- ☐ mountain
- ☑ woodland
- ☐ barren ground
- ☐ Central Canada barren ground
- ☐ Quebec-Labrador

MINIMUM SCORES

	AWARDS	ALL-TIME
mountain	360	390
woodland	265	295
barren ground	375	400
Central Canada barren ground	345	360
Quebec-Labrador	365	375

Detail of Point Measurement

SEE OTHER SIDE FOR INSTRUCTIONS		COLUMN 1	COLUMN 2	COLUMN 3	COLUMN 4
		Spread Credit	Right Antler	Antler	Difference
A. Tip to Tip Spread	36 4/8				
B. Greatest Spread	44 3/8				
C. Inside Spread of Main Beams	43 2/8	SPREAD CREDIT MAY EQUAL BUT NOT EXCEED LONGER ANTLER	43 2/8			
D. Number of Points on Each Antler Excluding Brows			12		2
Number of Points on Each Brow			7		
E. Length of Main Beam			50 1/8	4	2 6/8
F-1. Length of Brow Palm or First Point			20	17	1 4/8
F-2. Length of Bez or Second Point			22 7/8	21 3/8	1 4/8
F-3. Length of Rear Point, If Present			5 4/8	5 6/8	2/8
F-4. Length of Second Longest Top Point			13 7/8	14 1/8	2/8
F-5. Length of Longest Top Point			18	18 4/8	2
G-1. Width of Brow Palm			17 6/8	12 2/8	2 2/8
G-2. Width of Top Palm			8 6/8	6 4/8	2 2/8
H-1. Circumference at Smallest Place Between Brow and Bez Point			6 1/8	6 5/8	4/8
H-2. Circumference at Smallest Place Between Bez and Rear Point			6 3/8	7 4/8	1 1/8
H-3. Circumference at Smallest Place Between Rear Point and First Top Point			6 6/8	5 6/8	7/8
H-4. Circumference at Smallest Place Between Two Longest Top Palm Points			8	7 7/8	1/8
TOTALS		43 2/8	201	189 4/8	14 1/8

	Column 1	43 2/8	Exact Locality Where Killed: Newfoundland
ADD	Column 2	201	Date Killed: Prior to 1910 Hunter: Gift of H. Casmir de Rham
	Column 3	189 4/8	Owner: National Collection of Heads and Horns Telephone #:
	Subtotal	433 6/8	Owner's Address:
SUBTRACT	Column 4	14 1/8	Guide's Name and Address:
	FINAL SCORE	419 5/8	Remarks: (Mention Any Abnormalities or Unique Qualities)

COPYRIGHT © 2005 BY BOONE AND CROCKETT CLUB®

TOP 10 WOODLAND CARIBOU

NUMBER 3 — 405-1/8 POINTS
ROBERT V. KNUTSON — 1966

NUMBER 5 — 375-3/8 POINTS
PICKED UP — 1999

NUMBER 2 — 405-4/8 POINTS
GEORGE H. LESSER — 1951

NUMBER 4 — 380-2/8 POINTS
UNKNOWN — 1935

NUMBER 1 — 419-5/8 POINTS
GIFT OF H. CASMIR DE RHAM — Prior to 1910

NUMBER 10 — 356-7/8 POINTS
F.W. AYER — 1899
PHOTOGRAPH NOT AVAILABLE

J. WOODLAND

crockett Club
can Big Game Co
egie Museum
Pittsburgh, Pa.

NUMBER 6 — 373-6/8 POINTS
GIFT OF J.B. MARVIN, JR. – Prior to 1924.

FRONT VIEW
WOODLAND CARIBOU
NEWFOUNDLAND
KILLED BY
GEO. H. LESSER
Johnstown, N.Y.
Sept 22-1937

NUMBER 8 — 357-6/8 POINTS
PICKED UP — 1988

NUMBER 7 — 359-2/8 POINTS
PICKED UP (locked antlers) — 1996

OFFICIAL
RTH AMER
RE   US
GAME COMMITTE

MUM SCOR
RIBOU: Barre
Mountain
Woodland

NUMBER 9 — 357-4/8 PO
PICKED UP — 1968

655

WOODLAND CARIBOU
Rangifer tarandus caribou

MINIMUM SCORE 295

Score	Length of Main Beam R	L	Inside Spread	Circumference at Smallest Place Between Brow and Bez Points R	L	Length of Brow Points R	L	Width of Brow Points R	L	Number of Points R	L	Locality	Hunter	Owner	Date Killed	Rank
419 5/8	50 1/8	47 3/8	43 2/8	6 1/8	6 5/8	20	17 7/8	17 6/8	12 2/8	19	18	Newfoundland	Gift of H. Casmir de Rham	B&C National Collection	PR 1910	1
405 4/8	**45**	**44**	**30 3/8**	**5 6/8**	**5 6/8**	**20 1/8**	**20 1/8**	**19 4/8**	**19 5/8**	**22**	**21**	**Gander River, NL**	**George H. Lesser**	**Harold Pelley**	**1951**	**2**
405 1/8	38	39 6/8	34	5 4/8	6 1/8	21 7/8	20 3/8	18 7/8	18 4/8	22	25	Millertown, NL	Robert V. Knutson	Robert V. Knutson	1966	3
380 2/8	47 7/8	45 7/8	36 7/8	5 6/8	5 6/8	21 7/8	22	17 4/8	16 6/8	22	18	Bonavista Bay, NL	Unknown	Crow's Nest Officers Club	1935	4
375 3/8	42 1/8	43 3/8	37	6 5/8	5 7/8	17 1/8	15 5/8	15 2/8	13 5/8	16	15	Ten Mile Lake, NL	Picked Up	Baxter N. House	1999	5
373 3/8	39 7/8	43	22 1/8	5 2/8	5 4/8	24 4/8	22 3/8	20	21	21	22	Newfoundland	Gift of J.B. Marvin, Jr.	Unknown	PR 1924	6
359 2/8	40 1/8	42 3/8	34 3/8	6 6/8	6 2/8	16 2/8	14	11 1/8	11 2/8	18	13	Main Brook, NL	Picked Up	Gerard R. Beaulieu	1996	7
357 6/8	39 4/8	41 7/8	46 3/8	5 4/8	5 2/8	16	17 2/8	1 6/8	12 7/8	13	15	Gull River, NL	Picked Up	Gerard R. Beaulieu	1988	8
357 4/8	43 4/8	43 6/8	45 2/8	5	4 7/8	19 7/8	12 2/8	17 1/8	3 2/8	23	15	Mt. Peyton, NL	Picked Up	Harold Pelley	1968	9
356 7/8	42 5/8	43 7/8	31 6/8	5 2/8	5 4/8	19 3/8	19 2/8	17 2/8	16 4/8	15	18	Serpentine Lake, NB	F.W. Ayer	Carnegie Museum	1899	10
352 2/8	40	43 5/8	23 1/8	5 2/8	6 1/8	20 1/8	19 3/8	15 2/8	15 5/8	12	13	Deer Pond, NL	John McTurk, Jr.	John McTurk, Jr.	1996	11
351 2/8	45 7/8	46 1/8	45 2/8	6 1/8	5 4/8	17 2/8	17 1/8	14 4/8	7 4/8	14	11	St. Anthony, NL	Thomas D. Lund	Thomas D. Lund	1998	12
350 3/8	44 4/8	41 7/8	30 5/8	5 6/8	5 4/8	21 5/8	19 5/8	11 5/8		21	16	Louse Lake, NL	William J. Chasko	William J. Chasko	1963	13
350 1/8	39 3/8	44	39 4/8	5 6/8	6 3/8	15 2/8	14 6/8	22	17 2/8	20	18	Gander, NL	Robert M. Lee	Robert M. Lee	1951	14
347 7/8	41 3/8	39 7/8	33 3/8	6 2/8	5 7/8	14	19	14	5 5/8	20	20	Gander River, NL	E.B. Warner	E.B. Warner	1951	15
347	45 3/8	43 1/8	35 2/8	5 5/8	5 4/8	15 1/8	15 6/8	13 1/8	3	15	12	Rocky Pond, NL	Gordon J. Birgbauer, Jr.	Gordon J. Birgbauer, Jr.	1984	16
346 6/8	39 2/8	39 2/8	32	6 3/8	6	14	14 7/8	10	12 5/8	17	17	Deer Pond, NL	Buck Taylor	Buck Taylor	1991	17
345 5/8	42 3/8	43	35 2/8	7 1/8	6 5/8	17 3/8	16 5/8	15 4/8	1 2/8	23	14	Lake Kaegudeck, NL	J.J. Veteto	J.J. Veteto	1968	18
345 2/8	39 7/8	39 7/8	28 2/8	6 6/8	6 7/8	16 4/8	18 4/8	15 7/8	16 3/8	18	19	Newfoundland	Wilson Potter	Unknown	1909	19
341 2/8	37 6/8	38 1/8	31	5 3/8	5 3/8	17	17 1/8	11	17	15	20	Grey River, NL	Karl Dore	Karl Dore	1984	20
341 2/8	38 7/8	38 6/8	38 1/8	5 6/8	6 1/8	15 2/8	16 4/8	7 4/8	13 2/8	13	15	Barachois Brook, NL	Harry L. Gunter	Harry L. Gunter	1986	20
340 7/8	38 6/8	40 3/8	31	5 4/8	5 6/8	17 2/8	17 2/8	12 3/8	10 2/8	19	17	Shanadithit Brook, NL	Gene Manion	Gene Manion	1964	22
340 2/8	46	44 6/8	27 2/8	5 6/8	6 1/8	16 1/8	17	15 1/8	10 6/8	15	16	Victoria River, NL	Dempsey Cape	Dempsey Cape	1966	23
340 2/8	40 3/8	41 1/8	35 3/8	5 1/8	4 7/8	1 3/8	16 3/8	13 4/8	10 2/8	17	17	Wall's Pond, NL	Jeff Lawton	Jeff Lawton	1971	23
339 7/8	50 6/8	50	30 5/8	8 6/8	8 6/8	16 3/8	13 5/8	1/8	13 2/8	10	20	New Gander, NL	Elgin T. Gates	Elgin T. Gates	1962	25
339 1/8	37 4/8	38 4/8	38 2/8	6 1/8	5 7/8	13 5/8	14 7/8	11 5/8	8 7/8	18	14	Watsons Brook, NL	Harold E. Coons	Harold E. Coons	1998	26
338 3/8	37 7/8	41 3/8	35	4 7/8	5 1/8	14 7/8	18	13 1/8	12 3/8	17	12	Avalon Pen., NL	Picked Up	Gerard Beaulieu	PR 1970	27
337	40 4/8	41	42 7/8	6 3/8	6 1/8	17	16 3/8	8 3/8	12 3/8	11	10	Gander, NL	Michael Savino	Michael Savino	1969	28
336 1/8	40 6/8	40 6/8	26 7/8	5 3/8	5 3/8	16 3/8	18 3/8	19 4/8	1/8	15	9	Barachois Brook, NL	Thomas W. Triplett	Thomas W. Triplett	1986	29
335 3/8	42	40	40	6	5 1/8	18 3/8	15 4/8	15 7/8	6 2/8	18	14	Main Brook, NL	George R. Stoner	George R. Stoner	1999	30
334 6/8	39 5/8	40 1/8	28 5/8	5 2/8	5 1/8	13 7/8	13 7/8	12 5/8	14 5/8	18	16	North Arm, NL	Dennis C. Frederick	Dennis C. Frederick	1999	31
334 6/8	36 2/8	35 3/8	33 6/8	4 6/8	4 6/8	15 2/8	15 7/8	12 7/8	14	23	24	Adies Pond, NL	Gerard R. Beaulieu	Gerard R. Beaulieu	2000	31
334 1/8	39 6/8	39 6/8	31	5 1/8	4 7/8	17 2/8	16 7/8	17 4/8	16	15	18	King George Lake, NL	John R. Blanton	John R. Blanton	1984	33
334	34 4/8	37 5/8	29 4/8	5 6/8	5 6/8	14 7/8	14 1/8	10 6/8	12 4/8	25	16	Red Indian Lake, NL	Grancel Fitz	Mrs. Grancel Fitz	1960	34
333 2/8	39 6/8	40 3/8	33 3/8	4 7/8	5	17 4/8	16 5/8	15 4/8	8	12	13	Cat Arm River, NL	William R. Reed	William R. Reed	1998	35

332 7/8	46 6/8	43 5/8	28 6/8	5	5 1/8	15 2/8	15 3/8	14 3/8	11 5/8	20	19	La Poile, NL	Donald A. Piombo	Donald A. Piombo	1979	36
332 6/8	30 4/8	28 3/8	26 3/8	4 7/8	5	15 5/8	16 6/8	12 5/8	15 3/8	14	19	Robinson Brook, NL	Picked Up	Harold Pelley	1990	37
332 3/8	38 3/8	35 2/8	31 4/8	5 7/8	6 6/8	15 1/8	13 3/8	13 6/8	10 1/8	19	20	Daniel's Harbour, NL	Shawn D. Perry	Shawn D. Perry	1996	38
332 2/8	35 6/8	36	27 6/8	6 2/8	6 2/8	17 2/8	16 3/8	16 2/8	13 3/8	23	18	Newfoundland	Gift of J.B. Marvin to NCHH	Unknown	PR 1924	39
332 2/8	35 5/8	36 7/8	28	6	6 2/8	16 1/8	15	13 5/8	13 6/8	25	21	Newfoundland	Gift of Grover Asmus to NCHH	Unknown	1932	39
331 3/8	37 4/8	37	29	5 2/8	5 1/8	17 7/8	16 5/8	12 6/8	12 1/8	17	16	Gander River, NL	David W. Schrody	David W. Schrody	2000	41
331 2/8	46 2/8	48	40 6/8	5 6/8	5 6/8	17 2/8	18 4/8	11	14	11	11	Newfoundland	Frederick Brooks	Harvard Univ. Mus.	1881	42
331 1/8	39 1/8	35	28 3/8	5 7/8	6 3/8	16	15 2/8	9 4/8	13 2/8	20	18	Alexander Pond, NL	Charles M. Bloom	Charles M. Bloom	1999	43
330 5/8	31 2/8	34 2/8	26 6/8	5 5/8	5 4/8	15 4/8	15 3/8	13 4/8	11	22	23	New Brunswick	R.W. Gelbach	M.C. McQueen	1900	44
330 5/8	41 2/8	42 3/8	33 3/8	5 5/8	5 6/8	14 1/8	16 2/8	13 4/8	14 3/8	18	19	Meelpaeg, NL	Alex Kariotakis	Alex Kariotakis	1969	44
330 3/8	37 1/8	38 6/8	38 6/8	5 3/8	5 5/8	17 1/8	16 6/8	7	13 4/8	17	20	Deer Lake, NL	Picked Up	Gerard R. Beaulieu	1997	46
329 4/8	37 6/8	38 6/8	26 2/8	5	5 1/8	15 2/8	16	11 5/8	7 7/8	17	16	Robinsons River, NL	Timothy E. Fiedler	Timothy E. Fiedler	1980	47
329 2/8	40 1/8	44 2/8	32 1/8	5 4/8	5 4/8	16 6/8	14 5/8	12 2/8	10 2/8	15	14	Long Range Mts., NL	Thomas Robarts	Thomas Robarts	1991	48
329 2/8	34 6/8	35 2/8	26 6/8	6	6 2/8	15	16 6/8	11 3/8	17 5/8	19	21	Eddy's Cove, NL	Annie Larkin	Gerard R. Beaulieu	1999	48
329 2/8	40 3/8	40 2/8	40 7/8	5	5	16 5/8	17 6/8	13 3/8	11 1/8	10	13	Parsons Pond, NL	Donald L. Strickler	Donald L. Strickler	2000	48
328 7/8	39	36 3/8	19 5/8	6	6 6/8	13 5/8	14 2/8	13 1/8	8 2/8	14	16	Harbour Deep, NL	Drew E. Kline	Drew E. Kline	1998	51
328 2/8	35 4/8	38	31 1/8	5 4/8	5 1/8	15 4/8	17	12 5/8	13 6/8	18	17	Gulp Pond, NL	Michael E. Lombardo	Michael E. Lombardo	1968	52
327 7/8	44 2/8	44 3/8	32 1/8	5 6/8	5 5/8	14 5/8	12 7/8	13 5/8	11 3/8	18	17	Princes Pond, NL	Dermod O. Sullivan	Dermod O. Sullivan	1967	53
327 5/8	43 1/8	40 6/8	38 7/8	6 1/8	6 1/8	10 3/8	14 4/8	1/8	11 2/8	12	15	South Branch, NL	Mark L. Johansen	Mark L. Johansen	1986	54
327 3/8	39 3/8	39 3/8	27	4 6/8	4 5/8	16 1/8	17 3/8	6 4/8	14 3/8	18	18	Caribou Lake, NL	Conrad R. Bragg	Conrad R. Bragg	1962	55
327 3/8	33 5/8	36 3/8	32 3/8	6	5 4/8	13 7/8	17 7/8	12 2/8	13 6/8	19	18	Caribou Lake, NL	Robert Sparks	Robert Sparks	2002	55
326 7/8	35 1/8	37 7/8	32 6/8	5 3/8	5 3/8	15 7/8	15 4/8	10 1/8	9 3/8	17	15	Cat Arm River, NL	Steven R. Vande Giessen	Steven R. Vande Giessen	1997	57
326 7/8	37 2/8	37 4/8	32 1/8	6	7 2/8	16	13 3/8	14 4/8	10 7/8	17	20	Long Pond, NL	Lawrence J. Nolan	Lawrence J. Nolan	1999	57
326 3/8	41 2/8	40 4/8	31 1/8	6	5 7/8	14 1/8	15 7/8	11 3/8	9 7/8	21	23	Avalon Pen., NL	Harrold Clarke	Harrold Clarke	1971	59
326 2/8	39 5/8	41 1/8	31 7/8	5 5/8	5 6/8	15 5/8	12 4/8	9	8 2/8	13	17	Rocky Pond, NL	Thomas E. Phillippe, Jr.	Thomas E. Phillippe, Jr.	1975	60
325 6/8	40 2/8	38	27	5 3/8	5 4/8	16	14	10 2/8	12 4/8	19	17	Ten Mile Brook, NL	Bruce G. Miles	Bruce G. Miles	1999	61
325 4/8	42 4/8	41	36 1/8	5 4/8	5 2/8	17	17 5/8	10 7/8	10 7/8	11	12	Caribou Lake, NL	Lyle M. Paro	Lyle M. Paro	1981	62
325 3/8	43 5/8	45 2/8	34 3/8	6 1/8	6 1/8	13 3/8	13 2/8	12 1/8	7 4/8	18	15	Dashwoods Pond, NL	Daniel P. Amatuzzo	Daniel P. Amatuzzo	1983	63
325	45 7/8	44 5/8	42 6/8	6 2/8	6 2/8	12 6/8	2	16 5/8	1/8	17	14	Bear Pond, NL	Stanley T. Beers	Stanley T. Beers	1970	64
324 7/8	40 5/8	41 3/8	30 6/8	5 6/8	5 5/8	14 2/8	13 3/8	10 4/8	8 4/8	17	16	Rocky Point, NL	Richard N. Gubler	Richard N. Gubler	2000	65
324 7/8	39 6/8	38 7/8	38 5/8	6 2/8	6 2/8	16 2/8	16 4/8	11 6/8	15 4/8	13	17	Gander River, NL	Robert P. Meyers, Jr.	Robert P. Meyers, Jr.	2002	65
324 3/8	36 5/8	39 4/8	36 4/8	5 7/8	5 4/8	13 3/8	18 6/8	9	14 6/8	13	15	Conne River, NL	John B. Bazile	John B. Bazile	1996	67
324 3/8	39 6/8	40 3/8	33 3/8	5 4/8	5 3/8	18 4/8	17 2/8	13 1/8	13 3/8	18	13	Belle Isle, NL	Aaron D. Coomer	Aaron D. Coomer	2002	67
323 6/8	43 5/8	42 5/8	50 2/8	5 4/8	5 2/8	16 4/8	16 2/8	11 7/8	10 2/8	13	10	Hynes Lake, NL	Martin W. Nasadowski	Martin W. Nasadowski	1969	69
323 6/8	39 6/8	41 3/8	31 2/8	5 7/8	5 4/8	14 5/8	7	12 4/8	1/8	15	13	West River, NL	Thomas L. Nederveld	Thomas L. Nederveld	2002	69
322 6/8	40 7/8	41 6/8	33 3/8	5 6/8	5 6/8	2 5/8	16 1/8	1/8	12 2/8	10	18	Rocky Pond, NL	Wayne W. Karlin	Wayne W. Karlin	1988	71
322 5/8	37 5/8	36 7/8	37 1/8	5 7/8	6 1/8	14 7/8	15 1/8	14 3/8	10 7/8	14	14	Avalon Pen., NL	Richard F. Lewis	Richard F. Lewis	1977	72
322 3/8	40 2/8	38 1/8	35 1/8	4 5/8	5	13 2/8	15 3/8	8 3/8	9 6/8	12	20	Avalon Pen., NL	Angus J. Chafe	Angus J. Chafe	1969	73
322 2/8	40	40 4/8	25	5 6/8	5 6/8	15	14 7/8	13 5/8	14	15	16	Lloyds River, NL	Richard P. Navas	Richard P. Navas	1980	74
322 1/8	42 4/8	41 6/8	34 2/8	5 7/8	5 6/8	14 4/8	14 1/8	4 4/8	11	13	15	Cappahayden, NL	T.E. Best, Jr. & H.A. Chafe	Thomas E. Best, Jr.	1982	75
322 1/8	40 2/8	42 5/8	30 4/8	6	6 1/8	18	14 7/8	14 6/8	10 2/8	15	12	Avalon Pen., NL	Unknown	Gerard Beaulieu	PR 1991	75
322 1/8	47 3/8	40 5/8	38 5/8	5 5/8	6 1/8	16 2/8	17 5/8	12 7/8	17 2/8	13	16	Bay du Nord River, NL	Joby Quann	Myrtle Quann	1992	75
322	38 6/8	39 3/8	31 1/8	4 7/8	5	15	14 5/8	9 2/8	10 2/8	14	20	Gull Lake, NL	Michael J. Berenz	Michael J. Berenz	1999	78
321 6/8	42 2/8	43 6/8	35 6/8	6 1/8	6 1/8	13 2/8	17 2/8	6 5/8	15 1/8	11	16	Princes Pond, NL	Henry Bondesen	Henry Bondesen	1966	79

WOODLAND CARIBOU
Rangifer tarandus caribou

Score	Length of Main Beam R	L	Inside Spread	Circ. at Smallest Place Between Brow and Bez Points R	L	Length of Brow Points R	L	Width of Brow Points R	L	Number of Points R	L	Locality	Hunter	Owner	Date Killed	Rank
321 2/8	44 4/8	41 7/8	35	6 4/8	6 3/8	14 4/8	16 5/8	9	11 5/8	12	16	Hare Bay, NL	William P. Bleckley	William P. Bleckley	1999	80
320 7/8	37 4/8	40 6/8	34 4/8	5 5/8	6	15 3/8	16 4/8	8 5/8	11 7/8	15	17	La Poile, NL	David J. Coleman	David J. Coleman	1974	81
320 6/8	38 1/8	38 1/8	30 6/8	4 5/8	6	16 5/8	15 3/8	14 7/8	10 7/8	20	19	Long Range Mts., NL	Gary L. Benner	Gary L. Benner	1983	82
320 6/8	38	35	25 7/8	4 5/8	4 7/8	18 1/8	18 1/8	16 7/8	14	17	14	Crabbes River, NL	Joseph R. Levy	Joseph R. Levy	1983	82
320 6/8	45	39 6/8	36 3/8	5 6/8	6 3/8	5 4/8	15 4/8	1/8	12 6/8	11	15	Owl Pond, NL	Michael J. Kennedy	Michael J. Kennedy	2000	82
320 4/8	43 4/8	43 3/8	31 2/8	4 7/8	5	17 3/8	15 5/8	15 1/8	4 1/8	17	14	Gander River, NL	M.R. James	M.R. James	1999	85
320 2/8	39 4/8	39 4/8	34	4 6/8	5 1/8	15 5/8	17 3/8	12	6 4/8	12	17	Top Pond, NL	Donald F. Senter	Donald F. Senter	1984	86
319 5/8	40 3/8	39	38 3/8	5 2/8	5 4/8	15 4/8	15 5/8	11 5/8	3 1/8	17	15	Conne River, NL	Lloyd W. McClelland	Lloyd W. McClelland	1970	87
319 4/8	40 6/8	37 1/8	30 6/8	6	5 6/8	11 4/8	11 7/8	8 4/8	1 1/8	21	16	Long Range Mts., NL	William H. Taylor	William H. Taylor	1983	88
319 4/8	39 4/8	37 1/8	23 7/8	4 7/8	4 7/8	14 3/8	13 6/8	9	8 2/8	18	17	Leander Lake, NL	James J. Dietz, Jr.	James J. Dietz, Jr.	1997	88
319	32 4/8	32 2/8	27 4/8	4 6/8	5	11 5/8	12 7/8	8 6/8	10 4/8	18	24	Fishels Brook, NL	Fred Waite	Fred Waite	1986	90
318 7/8	37 6/8	38 3/8	29 5/8	4 7/8	5 1/8	15 2/8	15 7/8	12 5/8	9 6/8	20	20	Deer Lake, NL	Alexander Thane	Alexander Thane	1951	91
318 7/8	38 7/8	39 4/8	27	5	4 7/8	13 4/8	14 2/8	11 2/8	13 3/8	16	17	Lake Margaret, NL	Edward J. Bugden	Edward J. Bugden	1973	91
318 7/8	37 7/8	41	34 4/8	4 6/8	5	14 3/8	12 6/8	11 4/8	15	15	16	Medonnegonix Lake, NL	Buck Taylor	Buck Taylor	1993	91
318 6/8	39 5/8	39 3/8	25 1/8	5 2/8	5 1/8	12 6/8	12 5/8	13 6/8	19	15	16	Mouse Pond, NL	C.T. Barnett	C.T. Barnett	1987	94
318 5/8	39 5/8	34 3/8	27 6/8	5 4/8	5 1/8	16 6/8	16 6/8	12 4/8	10 3/8	16	15	Island Pond, NL	Collins F. Kellogg, Sr.	Collins F. Kellogg, Sr.	1997	95
318 5/8	38 4/8	36 3/8	34 1/8	5 7/8	6	14 4/8	16 2/8	5 6/8	15	14	15	Portland Creek, NL	Picked Up	Gerard R. Beaulieu	1998	95
318 4/8	38 7/8	38 5/8	34 1/8	5 4/8	5 4/8	18 5/8	17	15 5/8	4 5/8	12	9	Great Rattling Brook, NL	Picked Up	Henry D. Frey	1970	97
318 3/8	40	41 5/8	26 2/8	5 3/8	5 4/8	13 6/8	12 2/8	11 6/8	6 3/8	12	16	La Poile, NL	Van R. Johnson	Van R. Johnson	1977	98
318 2/8	40 2/8	37	38 4/8	5 4/8	5 4/8	12 1/8	16	10 4/8	2 3/8	22	16	Gander River, NL	W.H. Wilson	W.H. Wilson	1955	99
317 7/8	32	34 1/8	31 3/8	5 1/8	5 4/8	13	13 4/8	11 4/8	10	20	18	Walls Pond, NL	Laurence Brown	Laurence Brown	1967	100
317 6/8	45 2/8	45 2/8	30 7/8	5 4/8	5 4/8	18 2/8	17	1/8	15 5/8	18	18	Doyles, NL	Franklin H. Burns	Franklin H. Burns	1956	101
317 4/8	41 1/8	45	33 6/8	5 5/8	5 4/8	17 4/8	6/8	14 4/8	4/8	9	15	Eclipse Lake, NL	Matthew L. Wiskowski	Matthew L. Wiskowski	1998	102
316 7/8	30 4/8	32 4/8	32 2/8	5	5 1/8	14 3/8	14 6/8	11 5/8	12 5/8	13	16	Hinds Lake, NL	Daniel C. McNeill	Daniel C. McNeill	1998	103
316 4/8	35 5/8	35	26 6/8	5 3/8	5 2/8	18 6/8	18 7/8	14 6/8	7 1/8	20	16	Parson's Pond, NL	Frederick L. Gers, Jr.	Frederick L. Gers, Jr.	1999	104
316 4/8	37 4/8	36 3/8	34 4/8	5 2/8	4 7/8	16 5/8	16 4/8	13 4/8	7 4/8	15	16	Middle Ridge, NL	Kenneth J. Miller	Kenneth J. Miller	2002	104
316 3/8	40 7/8	42	33 1/8	5 6/8	5 5/8	18	16 4/8	11 3/8	16 5/8	12	21	Sandy Pond Barrens, NL	George L. Harrison	Acad. Nat. Sci., Phil.	1897	106
315 7/8	43 3/8	46 1/8	33 5/8	4 7/8	5 2/8	14 2/8	16 4/8	11 3/8	11 1/8	16	16	Newton Lake, NL	W.H. Wilson	W.H. Wilson	1957	107
315 6/8	43 1/8	42 1/8	33 4/8	6 1/8	5 7/8	12 4/8	12	7 3/8	6 1/8	10	14	Sitdown Pond, NL	H.R. Wambold	H.R. Wambold	1966	108
315 6/8	40 4/8	39 5/8	34 4/8	5 1/8	4 7/8	14 5/8	14 7/8	5 1/8	11 1/8	13	13	Jubilee Lake, NL	James W. Beitler	James W. Beitler	1994	108
315 1/8	39 1/8	36	33 6/8	5 2/8	5	15 2/8	15 1/8	12 7/8	10 1/8	15	13	Hinds Plains, NL	Picked Up	Gerard Beaulieu	1977	110
314 7/8	42 4/8	42 4/8	34 2/8	5 2/8	5 2/8	14 7/8	14 6/8	9 6/8	3	16	12	Long Range Mts., NL	James J. McBride	James J. McBride	1982	111
314 2/8	47 2/8	47 3/8	24 7/8	5 7/8	5 7/8	13 1/8	12 1/8	9 7/8	3	13	13	Mt. Howley, NL	Picked Up	Tom Rose	1988	112
314	36 3/8	35	34 1/8	6 1/8	6	14 6/8	14	11 6/8	12 5/8	14	16	Rainy Lake, NL	Arnold H. Craine	Arnold H. Craine	1967	113
314	34 1/8	34 6/8	29 4/8	5 1/8	4 7/8	14 2/8	14 5/8	13 1/8	12 2/8	10	21	Long Range Mts., NL	Gordon J. Birgbauer, Jr.	Gordon J. Birgbauer, Jr.	1986	113
313 4/8	36 1/8	35	24 7/8	4 3/8	4 5/8	16 6/8	16	14 7/8	14 6/8	16	17	Cormacks Lake, NL	John Wirth, Jr.	John Wirth, Jr.	1993	115

Score	Main Beam R	Main Beam L	Inside Spread	Circ. R	Circ. L	Width R	Width L	Pts R	Length R	Length L	Pts L	Locality	Hunter	Owner	Date Killed	Rank
313 4/8	35 4/8	35 4/8	30 4/8	5 2/8	5	16 7/8	19 5/8	14	7 1/8	11 5/8	12	Cat Arm River, NL	Michael P. Jones	Michael P. Jones	1999	115
313 3/8	40	42 1/8	25	5 3/8	5 3/8	15 5/8	14 2/8	18	11 4/8	9 4/8	17	Rainy Lake, NL	Jon Santangelo	Jon Santangelo	1971	117
313 3/8	33 3/8	32 2/8	29 5/8	5 7/8	5	12 3/8	10 5/8	20	9	11 2/8	17	Buchans Plateau, NL	Robert R. Kampstra	Robert R. Kampstra	1980	117
313 3/8	37 4/8	34 7/8	30 7/8	5 1/8	5 1/8	17 7/8	15 4/8	23	7 1/8	9	13	Hinds Lake, NL	William D. Graham	William D. Graham	2002	117
312 7/8	39 3/8	40 5/8	40 6/8	5 3/8	5 2/8	16 1/8	16 6/8	13	15 6/8	11 7/8	14	Crooked Lake, NL	Vernon L. Hanlin	Vernon L. Hanlin	1967	120
312 6/8	31 7/8	33 1/8	35 5/8	5 6/8	5 7/8	15 2/8	14 4/8	17	2 4/8	11 7/8	15	Victoria Lake, NL	Gordon T. Casey	Gordon T. Casey	1992	121
312 3/8	36 1/8	36 4/8	29 6/8	6 6/8	6 4/8	12 7/8	14 5/8	20	6 6/8	9 7/8	15	Stag Pond, NL	Max Meister	Max Meister	1976	122
312 1/8	35 5/8	35 5/8	29	5 4/8	5 2/8	15 3/8	15 4/8	18	13 5/8	11 7/8	17	Stag Lake, NL	James T. Kovac	James T. Kovac	1996	123
312 1/8	38 6/8	35 6/8	28 7/8	5 3/8	5	15 5/8	14 2/8	19	12 2/8	11 1/8	20	Sandy Lake, NL	Cecil S. Reaser, Jr.	Cecil S. Reaser, Jr.	1998	123
311 6/8	40 5/8	43 6/8	40 4/8	5 1/8	5 2/8	13 3/8	15 7/8	17	14	4 6/8	14	Buchans Plateau, NL	Basil C. Bradbury	Basil C. Bradbury	1971	125
311 6/8	35 5/8	40 4/8	28	5 7/8	5 5/8	19 5/8	18 3/8	19	8	6 4/8	14	Grey River, NL	Edward R. Janas	Edward R. Janas	1986	125
310 3/8	42	42	29 6/8	5 4/8	5 5/8	12 3/8	12	13	8 7/8	9 3/8	14	Port aux Basques, NL	George C. Thompson, Jr.	George C. Thompson, Jr.	1987	127
310 2/8	37 4/8	35 5/8	38	5 7/8	5 4/8	12 3/8	13 5/8	14	9 1/8	8 5/8	16	Third Pond, NL	Keith C. Halstead	Keith C. Halstead	2002	128
310	40 5/8	40 2/8	37	5 3/8	5 5/8	8 1/8	13	17	2 3/8	9	17	Hinds Lake, NL	David P. Weber	David P. Weber	1999	129
309 7/8	40 7/8	40	28 1/8	5 6/8	5 4/8	12	20 3/8	9	17 7/8	1/8	21	Adies Pond, NL	Dan J. Chaisson	Dan J. Chaisson	1999	130
309 5/8	35 4/8	38 5/8	28	5 6/8	5 6/8	16 2/8	13 4/8	18	10 4/8	8 1/8	13	Main River, NL	John V. D'Ambro, Jr.	John V. D'Ambro, Jr.	1998	131
309 4/8	38	36	34 2/8	5 5/8	5 5/8	16	15 2/8	15	13 6/8	5 6/8	12	Neola Paul Brook, NL	Ted Dreimans	Ted Dreimans	1962	132
309 3/8	43	43 3/8	33	5 5/8	5 2/8	16	15	15	13 3/8	13 3/8	15	Rainy Lake, NL	A.L. Levenseler	A.L. Levenseler	1967	133
309 2/8	40 2/8	36 5/8	36 5/8	5 2/8	5 6/8	14 7/8	18 3/8	16	11 4/8	9 4/8	19	Island Pond, NL	David J. DuFlo	David J. DuFlo	1996	134
309	39	44	30	6 5/8	5 3/8	3 1/8	2 1/8	13	1/8	17 5/8	15	Corner Brook, NL	Gilbert J. Heuer	Gilbert J. Heuer	1970	135
309	42 3/8	43 7/8	38 7/8	5 1/8	5 6/8	16 2/8	13	13	9 1/8	9 1/8	13	Alex Lake, NL	James E. Conklin	James E. Conklin	1981	135
308 7/8	46 3/8	40	29	4 7/8	5 1/8	14	14	16	10 5/8	10	12	Caribou Creek, NL	Remo Pizzagalli	Remo Pizzagalli	1994	137
308 4/8	38 5/8	36 2/8	31 6/8	5 3/8	5 5/8	15 3/8	14 7/8	12	13 4/8	11 2/8	15	Deer Pond, NL	George S. Walker III	George S. Walker III	1998	138
308 4/8	35 7/8	39	35	5 5/8	5 5/8	12	13 1/8	17	12 2/8	8 1/8	15	River of Ponds, NL	Roger B. Donahue, Jr.	Roger B. Donahue, Jr.	1999	138
308 3/8	39	42	29 6/8	5	5 1/8	1	14 6/8	15	10 2/8	5	16	Harbour Deep, NL	Mike Olmstead	Mike Olmstead	1996	140
308 1/8	40 2/8	39 3/8	39 7/8	5 2/8	5 3/8	15 2/8	3	11	11	15 2/8	15	Kitty's Brook, NL	H. Glen Dodd	H. Glen Dodd	1999	140
308 1/8	39 3/8	37 2/8	31 3/8	5 5/8	5 5/8	12 4/8	12 2/8	19	10 2/8	8 3/8	11	Gaff Topsail, NL	Warren L. Miller	Warren L. Miller	1993	142
308	29 3/8	37 1/8	25 7/8	5 7/8	5 7/8	16 1/8	16 1/8	19	9	13 7/8	16	Northern Pen., NL	George M. Jerry	George M. Jerry	1999	142
308	39	40 5/8	35 2/8	5 1/8	4 7/8	13 6/8	13 7/8	14	5 7/8	10 2/8	15	Shanadithit Brook, NL	L. Ben Hull	L. Ben Hull	1969	144
307 7/8	38 2/8	38 2/8	34 5/8	5 2/8	5 2/8	15 2/8	13 7/8	12	11 6/8	2 2/8	16	Meelpaeg, NL	Richard M. Moorehead	Richard M. Moorehead	1969	144
307 7/8	39 6/8	41 2/8	31 4/8	5 1/8	5 1/8	14 1/8	15 3/8	13	11 1/8	10 2/8	13	Grey River, NL	Roy S. Bowers	Roy S. Bowers	1993	146
307 6/8	41 2/8	41	30 4/8	4 7/8	4 7/8	16 7/8	14 2/8	18	9 7/8	10 4/8	12	Crabbs River, NL	Robert D. Bostater	Robert D. Bostater	1995	146
307 5/8	34 5/8	35	34 5/8	5 1/8	5	16	14 6/8	14	10 5/8	14 6/8	17	Whites River, NL	Lawrence E. Kirby	Lawrence E. Kirby	1999	148
307 5/8	39 2/8	39 3/8	30 4/8	5 2/8	5 5/8	16 7/8	17 1/8	17	13 6/8	13	19	White Bear Bay, NL	John K. Howard	John K. Howard	1938	149
307 5/8	38 3/8	39 5/8	34 5/8	5 4/8	5 4/8	16 4/8	15 4/8	19	16	15	13	West River, NL	Timothy S. Nederveld	Timothy S. Nederveld	2002	149
307 1/8	37	38 3/8	29 1/8	5 6/8	5 3/8	13 5/8	16 4/8	12	2 4/8	2 2/8	19	Buchans Plateau, NL	Gary A. Laatsch	Gary A. Laatsch	1986	151
307 1/8	38	37 2/8	30 5/8	5 2/8	5 3/8	17 1/8	14 1/8	16	13 5/8	11 5/8	17	Conne River, NL	Michael J. Park	Michael J. Park	1987	151
306 7/8	35 4/8	37 1/8	29 1/8	4 7/8	5 1/8	12 4/8	10 5/8	13	14 1/8	11 2/8	11	Long Range Mts., NL	Kenneth W. Shafer, Jr.	Kenneth W. Shafer, Jr.	1997	151
306 6/8	39 6/8	40 5/8	31 7/8	5 1/8	4 7/8	16 1/8	16 1/8	11	6 2/8	10 3/8	16	Parsons Pond, NL	Gerard R. Beaulieu	Gerard R. Beaulieu	1992	154
306 6/8	39 6/8	42 4/8	23	5 4/8	5 4/8	17 1/8	16 7/8	15	12 2/8	15 2/8	10	Greenwood Brook, NL	Harold Pelley	Unknown	1988	155
306 4/8	31 5/8	31 5/8	28 7/8	8 6/8	5 4/8	15 4/8	14	13	12 1/8	12 7/8	17	White Hills, NL	Donald Z. Detwiler	Donald Z. Detwiler	2000	155
306 4/8	39 5/8	42 7/8	34 6/8	5 6/8	5 5/8	13 6/8	14 7/8	10	14 5/8	9 1/8	14	Grand Lake, NL	Theodore Greenwood	Theodore Greenwood	1983	157
306 3/8	37 1/8	42 2/8	29	5 1/8	5 1/8	14 7/8	14 1/8	11	10 4/8	10 4/8	11	Harbour Deep, NL	Jack S. Zuidema	Jack S. Zuidema	1997	157
306 3/8	34 3/8	32 3/8	28 2/8	6	6 1/8	14 6/8	16 1/8	18	14 6/8	13	18	Millertown, NL	Gerhart H. Huber	Gerhart H. Huber	1966	159
306 3/8	39	39	29 1/8	4 7/8	4 7/8	13 1/8	13 1/8	13	12 5/8	12 3/8	13	Portage Lake, NL	Arnold Tonn	Arnold Tonn	1967	161
305 7/8	41 3/8	39 3/8	37 3/8	5	5	13 1/8	12 5/8	10	9 1/8	10 3/8	20	Grey River, NL	Jeffrey J. Eichhorst	Jeffrey J. Eichhorst	1980	161
305 5/8	38 1/8	39 7/8	32 3/8	5	4 6/8	2	16 1/8	11	14 5/8	1/8	18	Long Range Mts., NL	Collins F. Kellogg, Sr.	Collins F. Kellogg, Sr.	1989	162
305 5/8	36 4/8	33	25 5/8	4 5/8	4 5/8	13 1/8	13	13	10 6/8	11 7/8	17	Cerf River, NL	Pat Genell	Pat Genell	1999	162

WOODLAND CARIBOU
Rangifer tarandus caribou

Score	Length of Main Beam R	L	Inside Spread	Circumference at Smallest Place Between Brow and Bez Points R	L	Length of Brow Points R	L	Width of Brow Points R	L	Number of Points R	L	Locality	Hunter	Owner	Date Killed	Rank
305 1/8	37 4/8	36 5/8	28 2/8	5	5 2/8	11 5/8	13 5/8	10 2/8	11 7/8	17	19	Buchans Plateau, NL	Raymond M. Cappelli	Raymond M. Cappelli	1981	164
304 6/8	44 6/8	48 2/8	26 5/8	5 4/8	5 3/8	18 7/8	20 7/8	1 2/8	18 1/8	9	15	Middle Ridge, NL	Nat Levenson	Nat Levenson	1950	165
304 6/8	39 4/8	35 4/8	34 5/8	5 6/8	5 4/8	15 5/8	14 3/8	11 4/8	10 1/8	15	13	Deer Lake, NL	John F. Babler	John F. Babler	2002	165
304 3/8	41 3/8	42 2/8	30 3/8	5 1/8	5 4/8	15	13	11 4/8	6	12	10	Hynes Cove, NL	David J. Sullivan, Jr.	David J. Sullivan, Jr.	1997	167
304 1/8	33	31 1/8	20 3/8	5 4/8	5 2/8	16 6/8	14 4/8	14 6/8	6 2/8	22	16	Island Pond, NL	John P. Polinski	John P. Polinski	2000	168
304	38	40	33 5/8	5 1/8	5 2/8	12 1/8	12 2/8	4 4/8	10 6/8	13	14	Avalon Pen., NL	Unknown	Gerard Beaulieu	PR 1991	169
303 7/8	44	45	33 4/8	4 6/8	5 1/8	16 6/8	16 3/8	9	10 4/8	12	12	Blue Hills, NL	Charlie D. Todd	Charlie D. Todd	1986	170
303 4/8	44 1/8	46 3/8	38 2/8	5 2/8	5 2/8	12 7/8	13 7/8	1 7/8	10 7/8	11	14	Parsons Pond, NL	Donald L. Strickler	Donald L. Strickler	1998	171
302 7/8	51 1/8	50 5/8	29 1/8	6	6	18 4/8	11 3/8	16 4/8	1/8	14	10	Newfoundland	Gift of H.C. de Rham to NCHH	Unknown	PR 1910	172
302 5/8	40 6/8	41 3/8	29 5/8	5 4/8	5 4/8	15 5/8	15	9 4/8	11 3/8	11	11	La Poile, NL	L. Dale Gaugler	L. Dale Gaugler	1986	173
302 4/8	39 4/8	36	26 5/8	5 5/8	5 1/8	16 6/8	14 2/8	9 2/8	14 1/8	17	17	Rocky Ridge Pond, NL	Randal E. Daley	Randal E. Daley	1999	174
302	38 4/8	36 2/8	29 7/8	5 4/8	5 2/8	16 2/8	16 3/8	15	13 6/8	15	16	River of Ponds, NL	Harold L. Nyce	Harold L. Nyce	1998	175
301 3/8	29 3/8	31 5/8	32 4/8	5	5	11 3/8	11 2/8	7 6/8	6 1/8	15	13	Buchans Plateau, NL	Robert C. Kaufman	Robert C. Kaufman	1988	176
301 1/8	38	39 6/8	27 4/8	5 2/8	5	13 6/8	15 2/8	12 2/8	9 3/8	14	13	Eastern Pond, NL	H.W. Doyle	H.W. Doyle	1953	177
301 1/8	39 5/8	40 6/8	29 1/8	5 3/8	5	13 3/8	13 3/8	8 3/8	12 5/8	11	14	Parsons Pond, NL	Gerard Beaulieu	Gerard Beaulieu	1991	177
301	39 4/8	40 6/8	27	5	5	16 5/8	16 7/8	12 7/8	11 5/8	15	14	Long Range Mts., NL	Michael E. Wegner	Michael E. Wegner	1998	179
300 5/8	41 3/8	40	37 7/8	6 1/8	5 3/8	11 4/8	18	2 4/8	14 6/8	15	14	Long Range Mts., NL	John L. Van Horn	John L. Van Horn	1983	180
300 3/8	33 1/8	31 4/8	31 6/8	5 2/8	5 1/8	13 1/8	12 7/8	11	9 3/8	22	13	St. Johns Co., NL	Craig A. LaBelle	Craig A. LaBelle	1991	181
300 3/8	37 5/8	38	25 5/8	6	5 7/8	14 1/8	18 6/8	2 4/8	13 2/8	13	11	Deer Lake, NL	William L. Cochran	William L. Cochran	2001	181
300 1/8	38 7/8	36 7/8	34 6/8	5	4 7/8	16 4/8	16 3/8	2 4/8	13 6/8	13	13	Buchans Plateau, NL	Ernest J. Morgan	Ernest J. Morgan	1979	183
300 1/8	37 2/8	38 2/8	36 4/8	5	4 7/8	16 4/8	15 6/8	2 7/8	14	14	15	Terra Nova, NL	George Satterfield	George Satterfield	1996	183
299 7/8	43 7/8	42 3/8	36 2/8	5 2/8	5 3/8	12 1/8	12 3/8	9 3/8	8 2/8	12	14	Long Range Mts., NL	Edwin J. Tichy, Jr.	Edwin J. Tichy, Jr.	1985	185
299 7/8	42	41 7/8	29 2/8	5 6/8	5 4/8	8 7/8	17 7/8	1/8	15 6/8	11	18	Loon Lake, NL	Collins F. Kellogg, Sr.	Collins F. Kellogg, Sr.	1994	185
299 7/8	41 5/8	44 6/8	28 6/8	5	4 7/8	15 5/8	16 7/8	11 4/8	13 3/8	16	12	Deer Lake, NL	Kevin S. Peterson	Kevin S. Peterson	1994	185
299 4/8	37 5/8	35 5/8	28 5/8	5 3/8	4 7/8	13 6/8	14 4/8	6 3/8	9 6/8	14	17	La Poile, NL	W.T. Yoshimoto	W.T. Yoshimoto	1973	188
299 2/8	35 7/8	36 6/8	28 2/8	5 5/8	5 7/8	12 7/8	14 1/8	10	11 4/8	17	14	SW Gander River, NL	Anthony C. Crowell	Anthony C. Crowell	2002	189
299	36 3/8	37 4/8	35 1/8	4 4/8	4 5/8	12 7/8	10 6/8	9	9 7/8	15	15	La Poile, NL	Newton F. Moyer	Newton F. Moyer	1986	190
299	38 3/8	39 3/8	34 7/8	5 7/8	6	15 2/8	13 4/8	12	7 3/8	16	13	Main Brook, NL	Picked Up	Gerard R. Beaulieu	1996	190
298 6/8	33 5/8	35 5/8	34 2/8	5 6/8	5 5/8	13	15 2/8	1/8	10 5/8	15	17	Koskaecodde Lake, NL	Joseph A. Strick	Joseph A. Strick	1999	192
298 5/8	40 2/8	41 5/8	31 6/8	5 4/8	5 5/8	15	16 3/8	16 3/8	12 3/8	14	11	Pasadena, NL	C.J. McElroy	C.J. McElroy	1968	193
298 4/8	40 6/8	37 3/8	33 5/8	4 6/8	5	17 2/8	14 6/8	9 2/8	7 3/8	11	13	Lloyds River, NL	William A. Shaw	William A. Shaw	1987	194
298 4/8	33 2/8	35 1/8	25	5 3/8	5 6/8	14 3/8	15	9 2/8	12 3/8	14	15	Andrew Pond, NL	Roy K. McCollum	Roy K. McCollum	1994	194
298 4/8	39 4/8	37 5/8	33 3/8	4 7/8	4 7/8	17 4/8	19	13 1/8	9 2/8	18	14	Gander River, NL	John S. Griesinger	John S. Griesinger	1999	194
298 4/8	35 6/8	37 2/8	28 7/8	4 6/8	4 6/8	13 4/8	15 5/8	7 4/8	11 2/8	12	11	Western Brook Pond, NL	Norbert D. Bremer	Norbert D. Bremer	2003	194
298 2/8	37 4/8	35 7/8	30 2/8	6 1/8	5 6/8	15 1/8	15 5/8	9 4/8	7 6/8	15	11	Upper Humber River, NL	Picked Up	Gerard R. Beaulieu	1992	198

Score												Location	Hunter		Rank
298	42 4/8	39 6/8	35	5 3/8	5 2/8	17	15 7/8	7 2/8	11 3/8	9	10	Buchans Plateau, NL	Stewart N. Shaft	1982	199
298	37 4/8	36 4/8	31 4/8	5 4/8	5 1/8	15 1/8	14 5/8	11 5/8	11 5/8	13	12	Conne River, NL	Donald H. Reuter	1993	199
297 7/8	38 2/8	38 6/8	37 3/8	5 5/8	5 4/8	14 6/8	9	9 5/8	1/8	15	10	Princes Pond, NL	Richard C. Desjardins	1996	201
297 5/8	32 4/8	33 3/8	29 7/8	5 5/8	5 4/8	13 4/8	12 5/8	9 4/8	6 4/8	17	14	Buchans Plateau, NL	Morton J. Greene	1983	202
296 7/8	34 2/8	34 7/8	29 1/8	4 5/8	6	13	15	6 2/8	10	13	15	Loon Lake, NL	Lanny C. Fields	1999	203
296 1/8	33 6/8	33	31 7/8	5 2/8	5 2/8	15 2/8	16 6/8	13 2/8	6	13	13	Goose Lake, NL	L. Reed Williams	1993	204
295 6/8	37 6/8	37 5/8	29 6/8	5 1/8	5 1/8	15 5/8	15 7/8	13	13	18	17	Burnt Pond, NL	Richard C. Desjardins	1999	205
295 4/8	40 4/8	38 1/8	26 7/8	5	5	16 5/8	15 6/8	9 5/8	14	16	17	Top Pond, NL	Robert L. Rex	1966	206
295 4/8	41 5/8	41 1/8	28	5 2/8	5	16 5/8	14 5/8	12 2/8	9 6/8	18	14	South Branch, NL	Victor Pelletier	1967	206
295 3/8	37 5/8	40 5/8	22 6/8	4 4/8	4 5/8	16 3/8	15 6/8	12 2/8	8 6/8	16	15	North Lake, NL	Douglas S. Kennedy	1998	208
295	40 6/8	38 6/8	29 6/8	5 5/8	5 4/8	12 1/8	11 1/8	8 4/8	6 7/8	13	16	Parsons Pond, NL	Gerard R. Beaulieu	PR 1994	209
333 6/8*	40 1/8	38 6/8	31 3/8	6 1/8	6 7/8	16	16	16 6/8	9 1/8	20	22	Caribou Lake, NL	Picked Up	Jason P. Keber	2000
332 6/8*	40 6/8	40 5/8	38	5 2/8	5 4/8	16 6/8	15 2/8	13	2 6/8	17	15	Great Harbour Deep, NL	Rolland G. Bohm	2000

* Final score is subject to revision by additional verifying measurements.

CATEGORY
WOODLAND CARIBOU

SCORE
331-3/8

HUNTER
DAVID W. SCHRODY (RIGHT)
HAROLD PELLEY (GUIDE - LEFT)

LOCATION
GANDER RIVER, NEWFOUNDLAND

DATE OF KILL
SEPTEMBER 2000

CATEGORY
WOODLAND CARIBOU

SCORE
322

HUNTER
MICHAEL J. BERENZ (LEFT)

LOCATION
GULL LAKE, NEWFOUNDLAND

DATE OF KILL
OCTOBER 1999

SCORE
320-4/8

HUNTER
M.R. JAMES (RIGHT)

LOCATION
GANDER RIVER, NEWFOUNDLAND

DATE OF KILL
AUGUST 1999

SCORE
320-6/8

HUNTER
MICHAEL J. KENNEDY
(LEFT)

LOCATION
OWL POND, NEWFOUNDLAND

DATE OF KILL
OCTOBER 2000

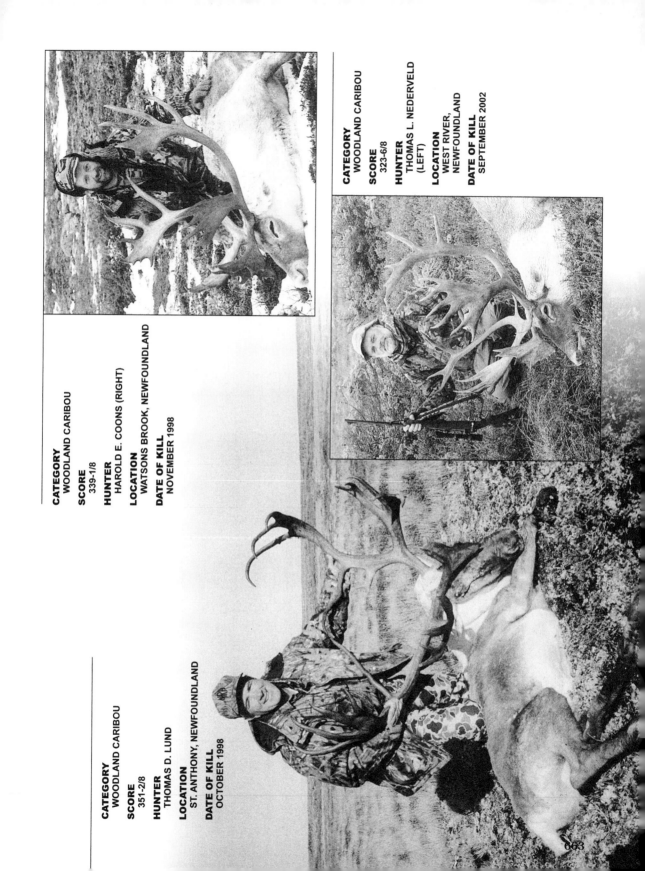

CATEGORY
WOODLAND CARIBOU

SCORE
339-1/8

HUNTER
HAROLD E. COONS (RIGHT)

LOCATION
WATSONS BROOK, NEWFOUNDLAND

DATE OF KILL
NOVEMBER 1998

CATEGORY
WOODLAND CARIBOU

SCORE
323-6/8

HUNTER
THOMAS L. NEDERVELD (LEFT)

LOCATION
WEST RIVER, NEWFOUNDLAND

DATE OF KILL
SEPTEMBER 2002

CATEGORY
WOODLAND CARIBOU

SCORE
351-2/8

HUNTER
THOMAS D. LUND

LOCATION
ST. ANTHONY, NEWFOUNDLAND

DATE OF KILL
OCTOBER 1998

663

BARREN GROUND CARIBOU
NEW WORLD'S RECORD

Dan Dobbs' only desire was to take a ten-foot Alaska brown bear. But in the end, he had so much more—a new World's Record barren ground caribou (*Rangifer tarandus*) to be exact. Dan had dreamed of shooting a really big bear nearly all his life. He had already set aside a place in his trophy room for the mount. He hadn't thought much about caribou until he signed up for an Alaska brown bear hunt that included caribou.

On September 16, 1999, Dan flew to Iliamna Lake on the Alaska Peninsula, before boarding a floatplane to the Rainbow River Lodge to begin bear hunting on September 18th—the opening day of the season. As luck would have it, Dan shot a nice, but not enormous bear the second day of the season. Happy but a little disappointed, Dan told himself that the hunt was not over, and he vowed to "make up for it with a big caribou." Little did he know what the future had in store.

Dan and assistant guide Mark Freshwaters traveled by floatplane for about 45 minutes to a small lake and set up a comfortable spike camp. They were hunting caribou from the Alaska Peninsula North herd, and the rut was just beginning to get them moving. For several days Dan and Mark didn't see any caribou, other than a small group at the camp when they landed. The cold and windy weather only added discomfort to disappointment.

The morning of the fourth day, Dan and Mark walked from camp to the top of a hill they had been us-

ing as a vantage point. From there, they had a good view of the draw and the broad valley where the caribou were traveling. To get a better look, they moved to yet another hill, when after a few minutes of glassing, Mark cried, "There is your caribou!" The bull he spotted was a little less than a mile away but on the move. In order to get a shot, the men sprinted back to the top of the original hill three-quarters of a mile away, arriving just moments before the bull arrived.

The bull was following a ravine, and they could see the tips of his antlers just above the hill's crest. As he moved, more and more of his antlers became visible, and Dan's excitement mounted. At 90 yards, the bull stepped into full view. Dan squeezed the trigger, driving the bullet into his front shoulder.

"This caribou will make the Boone and Crockett records book," Mark announced as the men admired the magnificent animal. "No way!" Dan responded, silently hoping Mark really knew what he was talking about. Dan's caribou was officially scored at 477 points by the 24th Awards Program Judges Panel in Springfield, Missouri, making it the new World's Record barren ground caribou and the largest caribou ever taken out of the five species recognized by the Boone and Crockett Club. ∎

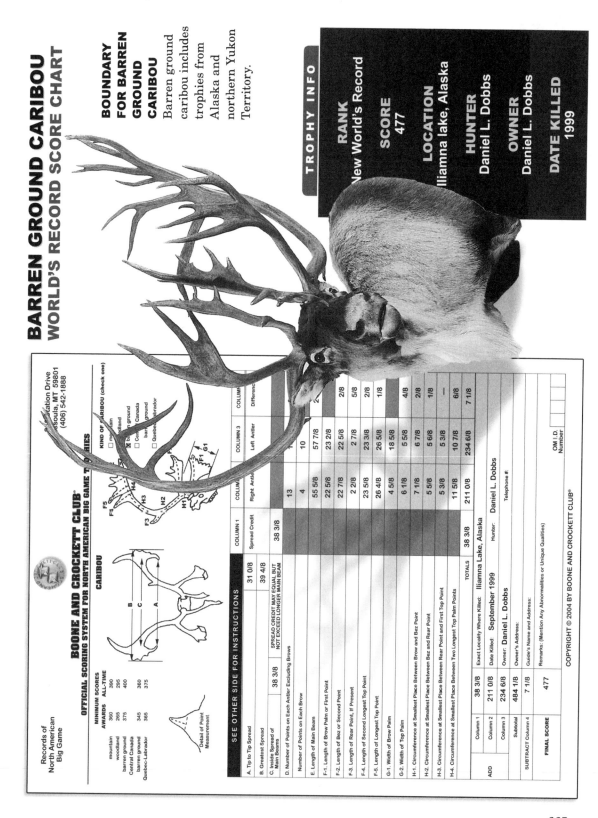

BARREN GROUND CARIBOU
WORLD'S RECORD SCORE CHART

BOUNDARY FOR BARREN GROUND CARIBOU

Barren ground caribou includes trophies from Alaska and northern Yukon Territory.

TROPHY INFO

RANK
New World's Record

SCORE
477

LOCATION
Iliamna lake, Alaska

HUNTER
Daniel L. Dobbs

OWNER
Daniel L. Dobbs

DATE KILLED
1999

Records of North American Big Game

BOONE AND CROCKETT CLUB
OFFICIAL SCORING SYSTEM FOR NORTH AMERICAN BIG GAME TROPHIES

...dation Drive
...soula, MT 59801
(406) 542-1888

CARIBOU

MINIMUM SCORES	AWARDS	ALL-TIME
mountain	360	390
woodland	265	295
barren ground	375	400
Central Canada		
barren ground	345	360
Quebec-Labrador	365	375

KIND OF CARIBOU (check one)
- ☐ mountain
- ☐ woodland
- ☒ barren ground
- ☐ Central Canada barren ground
- ☐ Quebec-Labrador

SEE OTHER SIDE FOR INSTRUCTIONS

	COLUMN 1	COLUMN 2 Right Antler	COLUMN 3 Left Antler	COLUMN Difference
A. Tip to Tip Spread	31 0/8			
B. Greatest Spread	39 4/8			
C. Inside Spread of Main Beams	38 3/8	SPREAD CREDIT MAY EQUAL BUT NOT EXCEED LONGER MAIN BEAM		
		38 3/8		
D. Number of Points on Each Antler Excluding Brows		13	10	
Number of Points on Each Brow		4		
E. Length of Main Beam		55 5/8	57 7/8	2
F-1. Length of Brow Palm or First Point		22 5/8	23 2/8	
F-2. Length of Bez or Second Point		22 7/8	22 5/8	2/8
F-3. Length of Rear Point, If Present		2 2/8	2 7/8	5/8
F-4. Length of Second Longest Top Point		23 5/8	23 3/8	2/8
F-5. Length of Longest Top Point		26 4/8	26 5/8	1/8
G-1. Width of Brow Palm		4 5/8	18 5/8	
G-2. Width of Top Palm		6 1/8	5 5/8	4/8
H-1. Circumference at Smallest Place Between Brow and Bez Point		7 1/8	6 7/8	2/8
H-2. Circumference at Smallest Place Between Bez and Rear Point		5 5/8	5 6/8	1/8
H-3. Circumference at Smallest Place Between Rear Point and First Top Point		5 3/8	5 3/8	—
H-4. Circumference at Smallest Place Between Two Longest Top Palm Points		11 5/8	10 7/8	6/8
TOTALS	38 3/8	211 0/8	234 6/8	7 1/8

ADD	Column 1	38 3/8	Exact Locality Where Killed: Iliamna Lake, Alaska
	Column 2	211 0/8	Date Killed: September 1999 Hunter: Daniel L. Dobbs
	Column 3	234 6/8	Owner: Daniel L. Dobbs Telephone #:
Subtotal		484 1/8	Owner's Address:
SUBTRACT Column 4		7 1/8	Guide's Name and Address:
FINAL SCORE		**477**	Remarks: (Mention Any Abnormalities or Unique Qualities)

OM I.D. Number

Detail of Point Measurement.

NUMBER 2 — 465-1/8 POINTS
ROGER HEDGECOCK — 1987

NUMBER 5 — 461-4/8 POINTS
BUCK D. MANTSCH — 1994

NUMBER 4 — 461-6/8 POINTS
JOHN V. POTTER, JR. — 1976

NUMBER 1 — 477 POINTS
DANIEL L. DOBBS — 1999

NUMBER 3 — 463-6/8 POINTS
RAY LOESCHE — 1967

NUMBER 7 — 459-3/8 POINTS
FRANK LOBITZ — 1988

BOONE AND CROCKETT CLU

CARIBOU

NUMBER 10 (tie) — 458-1/8 POINTS
BOBBY E. ROBINSON — 1963
Photograph not available.

NUMBER 10 (tie) — 458-1/8 POINTS
W.J. KRAUSE — 1953

NUMBER 8 — 458-6/8 POINTS
JOSEPH SHOAF — 1968

NUMBER 9 — 458-2/8 POINTS
JOSEF MERAN — 1967

NUMBER 6 — 459-6/8 POINTS
FLOYD A. BLICK — 1954

BARREN GROUND CARIBOU
Rangifer tarandus granti

Score	Length of Main Beam R	L	Inside Spread	Circumference at Smallest Place Between Brow and Bez Points R	L	Length of Brow Points R	L	Width of Brow Points R	L	Number of Points R	L	Locality	Hunter	Owner	Date Killed	Rank
477	55 5/8	57 7/8	38 3/8	7 1/8	6 7/8	22 5/8	23 2/8	4 5/8	18 5/8	17	25	Iliamna Lake, AK	Daniel L. Dobbs	Daniel L. Dobbs	1999	1
465 1/8	50 6/8	49 7/8	40 1/8	7	7	19	20 4/8	9 7/8	14 5/8	24	23	Mosquito Creek, AK	Roger Hedgecock	Loaned to B&C Natl. Coll.	1987	2
463 6/8	51 2/8	51 5/8	46 7/8	5 7/8	6 1/8	18 2/8	24 6/8	12 7/8	21 4/8	22	23	Ugashik Lakes, AK	Ray Loesche	Ray Loesche	1967	3
461 6/8	53 2/8	55 3/8	35	8 6/8	8 4/8	20	18 2/8	16 4/8	12 4/8	29	21	Post River, AK	John V. Potter, Jr.	John V. Potter, Jr.	1976	4
461 4/8	59 1/8	61 4/8	44 4/8	7 2/8	7 2/8	22 5/8	21 1/8	15	6	19	15	Kenai Pen., AK	Buck D. Mantsch	Buck D. Mantsch	1994	5
459 6/8	58	59 3/8	40 6/8	7 1/8	7	19 4/8	18 3/8	16 5/8	4	30	17	Slana, AK	Floyd A. Blick	Floyd A. Blick	1954	6
459 3/8	53 5/8	55 3/8	33 3/8	7 5/8	6 4/8	19 5/8	19 3/8	8 5/8	13 3/8	19	17	Sharp Mt., AK	Frank Lobitz	Bass Pro Shops	1988	7
458 6/8	68 2/8	68 6/8	41 6/8	6 1/8	5 6/8	18 6/8	15 7/8	9	2 3/8	21	17	Alaska Pen., AK	Joseph Shoaf	Joseph Shoaf	1968	8
458 2/8	55 2/8	54 4/8	45 3/8	5 4/8	5 6/8	20 6/8	20 5/8	10 6/8	15 2/8	15	21	Cinder River, AK	Josef Meran	Josef Meran	1967	9
458 1/8	54 1/8	56	38 6/8	6 6/8	7 2/8	15 1/8	20 5/8	1/8	20 6/8	21	29	Gulkana River, AK	W.J. Krause	W.J. Krause	1953	10
458 1/8	49 7/8	50	31 1/8	7 3/8	7 3/8	17 6/8	15 2/8	13 2/8	8 7/8	18	17	Alaska Range, AK	Bobbie E. Robinson	Bobbie E. Robinson	1963	10
457 6/8	50 4/8	50 2/8	38 3/8	5 7/8	7 2/8	18 2/8	19 1/8	8 5/8	15 3/8	27	28	Aniak River, AK	Timothy K. Kanady	Timothy K. Kanady	1994	12
456 3/8	53 1/8	55	43 5/8	7	7	9 4/8	19 3/8	1/8	16 6/8	27	31	Mulchatna River, AK	Dan Bottrell	Dan Bottrell	1965	13
456 1/8	63 3/8	59 7/8	48	6 7/8	6 7/8	23 1/8	25 6/8	8 3/8	13 1/8	22	21	Alaska Pen., AK	Kenneth R. Best	Bavarian Builders, Inc.	1978	14
455 6/8	49 6/8	48 6/8	41 1/8	7 3/8	7 3/8	21 1/8	19	10 5/8	15 3/8	22	26	Alaska Pen., AK	Fred H. Blatt, Jr.	Fred H. Blatt, Jr.	1979	15
454 3/8	57 3/8	58 1/8	44 6/8	9 4/8	7 4/8	22 6/8	21 4/8	19 2/8	2 3/8	19	17	Wrangell Mts., AK	Mary Brisbin	Mary Brisbin	1959	16
454 3/8	46 5/8	46 6/8	38 2/8	6 7/8	6 6/8	17	18 4/8	10 4/8	5 7/8	23	21	Tangle Lakes, AK	Mrs. Robert Dosdall	Mrs. Robert Dosdall	1955	17
453 1/8	50 6/8	51 3/8	35 5/8	11	6 5/8	20 6/8	15 7/8	20 6/8	5 2/8	36	18	Alaska Pen., AK	Ken Higginbotham	Ken Higginbotham	1984	18
453	50 6/8	57 2/8	56 6/8	6 3/8	6 2/8	5 1/8	20 6/8	1/8	14 4/8	17	22	Becharof Lake, AK	Gordon G. Chittick	Gordon G. Chittick	1983	19
452 6/8	60 1/8	57 7/8	31 2/8	7 3/8	7 5/8	19 4/8	18 6/8	13 4/8	9 4/8	23	22	Alaska Range, AK	Mrs. Leah Clemmons	Mrs. Leah Clemmons	1956	20
451 6/8	54 7/8	54 1/8	47 7/8	7 3/8	6 3/8	19 4/8	8 1/8	14 5/8	1/8	22	13	Wood River, AK	Q. Odell Robinson	Q. Odell Robinson	1980	21
451 4/8	51 3/8	52 6/8	47 1/8	6 1/8	6 3/8	20	21 6/8	11 5/8	11 4/8	22	16	Bonanza Hills, AK	David A. Fulbright	David A. Fulbright	1987	22
450 6/8	58 1/8	59 4/8	55 5/8	6 5/8	6 1/8	19 4/8	22 2/8	7 4/8	10 4/8	16	18	Alaska Pen., AK	Phillip D. Wagner	Phillip D. Wagner	1977	23
450 4/8	64 7/8	61	44 3/8	6 5/8	8 3/8	19 2/8	20 7/8	17	8 5/8	25	23	Lake Clark, AK	Dennis Burdick	Dennis Burdick	1984	24
449 6/8	49 7/8	47 7/8	40 3/8	9 5/8	6 3/8	17 1/8	19 1/8	11 5/8	12 7/8	19	23	Ugashik Lakes, AK	Frank Knies	Frank Knies	1965	25
449 4/8	50	47 5/8	46	6 3/8	5 7/8	20 6/8	23 2/8	1/8	16 5/8	18	24	Alaska Pen., AK	Eddie L. House	Eddie L. House	1979	26
449 1/8	45 3/8	43 5/8	42 5/8	5 6/8	5 7/8	17	16 2/8	13 5/8	4 3/8	20	24	Talkeetna Mts., AK	George L. Clark	George L. Clark	1960	27
449	47 7/8	48 5/8	36 6/8	7 3/8	6 5/8	20	13 3/8	15 1/8	7 5/8	22	24	Little Mulchatna Lake, AK	Morton P. Donohue	Morton P. Donohue	1968	28
448 6/8	50 5/8	51 1/8	40 5/8	8 4/8	7 3/8											
448 3/8	56 5/8	59	45 3/8	6 5/8	6 2/8	20 3/8	20 5/8	8 1/8	14 1/8	15	19	Stony River, AK	Picked Up	William O. West	1987	29
448 2/8	60 2/8	56 5/8	41	5 7/8	6 1/8	21 7/8	15	17 6/8	1/8	23	15	Ogilvie River, YT	Glen E. Christman	Glen E. Christman	1997	30
448 1/8	54 7/8	56 4/8	42	6 5/8	6 3/8	16 7/8	24 2/8	4 2/8	21 4/8	18	20	Dog Salmon River, AK	Picked Up	Butch Hautanen	1982	31
447 7/8	59 4/8	58 5/8	49	7 5/8	6 5/8	20	23 4/8	4 6/8	14 3/8	18	19	Alaska Pen., AK	A.D. Heetderks	A.D. Heetderks	1966	32
447 5/8	54 4/8	57 1/8	48 5/8	6 1/8	6	17 2/8		13	14 4/8	24	22	Denali Hwy., AK	K.K. Anton	K.K. Anton	1957	33
447 5/8	52 3/8	50 3/8	42 5/8	6 6/8	6	19	18 5/8	15 6/8	16 7/8	26	21	Ugashik Lakes, AK	Neil C. McLaughlin	Neil C. McLaughlin	1971	33
447 5/8	52 4/8	52 4/8	48 5/8	7 4/8	6 7/8	17 1/8	17 1/8	14 4/8	13 5/8	26	22	Alaska Range, AK	Richard K. Tollison	Sandra L. Tollison	1978	33

Score											Locality	Hunter	Owner	Date Killed	Rank
447 4/8	58 3/8	59 5/8	52 7/8	5	17 1/8	19 5/8	11 4/8	12 1/8	20	24	Nelchina, AK	Bert Klineburger	Bert Klineburger	1964	36
446 6/8	58 2/8	55 5/8	48 5/8	5 7/8	20 5/8	23 6/8	17 5/8	17 5/8	15	19	Cinder River, AK	Clifford Thom	Clifford Thom	1966	37
446 3/8	56	58 1/8	45 1/8	6	12 2/8	3 6/8	/8	11	15	18	Stuyahok River, AK	Marc C. Phillips	Marc C. Phillips	1993	38
444 5/8	44 6/8	46 4/8	51 2/8	7	18 2/8	3 3/8	14 7/8	/8	25	17	Port Heiden, AK	Marshall Carr	Marshall Carr	1963	39
444 4/8	60 6/8	57 6/8	59	6 3/8	24 2/8	21 5/8	17 7/8	1/8	18	13	Mother Goose Lake, AK	S.W. Terry	S.W. Terry	1967	40
444 4/8	47 4/8	51	41 4/8	6	21 3/8	20 1/8	19 7/8	16 7/8	21	22	King Salmon River, AK	John C. Belcher	John C. Belcher	1967	41
444 1/8	51 6/8	50 3/8	45 1/8	6 5/8	22	19 4/8	3 /8	15 7/8	19	21	Wrangell Mts., AK	A.E. Bruggeman	A.E. Bruggeman	1962	42
443 7/8	46 6/8	49 6/8	39 7/8	5 7/8	15 6/8	19 1/8	9 7/8	15 2/8	16	21	Denali Hwy., AK	Stephen Vacula	Stephen Vacula	1967	43
443 1/8	53 4/8	41	41	6	17 5/8	22	13 7/8	11 4/8	20	22	Kobuk River, AK	Ralph G. Colas	Ralph G. Colas	1988	43
443 1/8	60 6/8	60 6/8	50 4/8	5 6/8	20 2/8	16 6/8	8 7/8	7 6/8	14	24	Copper Creek, AK	Walter C. Dallis	Park A. Dallis	1994	43
443 1/8	57 1/8	57 6/8	51 7/8	6 3/8	10	21	1	16 1/8	20	15	Denali Hwy., AK	C.W. Hilbish	C.W. Hilbish	1958	46
443	50 7/8	50 5/8	37	8	17 4/8	19 6/8	12	14 4/8	12	18	Lime Village, AK	William R. Ellis III	William R. Ellis III	1978	46
443	62 6/8	62 7/8	41 4/8	6 7/8	24 2/8	7 2/8	20 /8	1/8	22	23	Wood River, AK	Charles M. Bentley	Michael N. Bentley	1960	48
442 6/8	52 7/8	51 6/8	52 7/8	7	24 2/8	23 6/8	14 7/8	5 6/8	21	14	Kvichak River, AK	Todd C. Jacobson	Todd C. Jacobson	1996	48
442 2/8	45	50	48 7/8	6 5/8	26 5/8	23 4/8	6	/8	22	18	Talkeetna Mts., AK	Jack C. Robb	Cabela's, Inc.	1958	50
442 2/8	51 5/8	53 7/8	38 2/8	7 4/8	15 3/8	14 4/8	7 4/8	17 5/8	22	26	Alaska Pen., AK	George A. Waldriff	George A. Waldriff	1962	51
441 6/8	51 5/8	53 7/8	47	6 3/8	22 3/8	5 3/8	16 7/8	1 3/8	17	13	Healy, AK	G.H. Gunn	G.H. Gunn	1968	52
441 4/8	55 6/8	53 3/8	37 2/8	5 7/8	20	15 1/8	14 1/8	/8	20	15	Pilot Point, AK	Clifford H. Driskell	Clifford H. Driskell	1970	53
441 3/8	51 3/8	52 3/8	52 7/8	5 2/8	16	18 6/8	/8	14 1/8	17	20	Tonzona River, AK	Dean W. Coffman	Dean W. Coffman	1964	54
441 1/8	43 3/8	46 6/8	41 1/8	6 7/8	19 2/8	21 7/8	1	15 4/8	15	23	Snowshoe Lake, AK	Ray A. Winchester	Demarest Memorial Mus.	1953	55
440 7/8	59 6/8	56 4/8	44 2/8	7 1/8	24 2/8	22 2/8	17 2/8	17 2/8	17	15	Lake Clark, AK	James W. Vorhease	James W. Vorhease	1988	56
440 3/8	54 2/8	56 5/8	38 5/8	6 5/8	13 6/8	13 6/8	14 6/8	4 6/8	11	19	Blue Berry Creek, AK	Ed Shapiro	Ed Shapiro	1964	57
440 2/8	54 2/8	58 1/8	44 2/8	7 3/8	15 3/8	14 4/8	11 7/8	7 6/8	23	28	Kenai, AK	Picked Up	Marcia L. King	1972	57
440 2/8	54 4/8	55 1/8	40 4/8	7	9 1/8	20 7/8	/8	16 5/8	19	17	Wood River, AK	David A. Schuller	David A. Schuller	1982	59
440 1/8	55 3/8	57	48 1/8	6 2/8	20 4/8	18 2/8	10 4/8	11	18	17	Mulchatna River, AK	Ted J. Forsi, Jr.	Ted J. Forsi, Jr.	1988	60
440	54	57	41 3/8	6 1/8	18 3/8	17 7/8	12 6/8	9 2/8	18	30	Talkeetna Mts., AK	Chris Klineburger	Chris Klineburger	1961	61
440	50	50 1/8	40 6/8	6 5/8	17 5/8	16 1/8	12 5/8	10 6/8	23	12	Egegik River, AK	Norman Tibbetts	Norman Tibbetts	1959	62
439 5/8	60 5/8	61 3/8	45 2/8	6 5/8	7 2/8	7 3/8	12 1/8	1/8	16	33	Iliamna Lake, AK	Edward L. Fuchs	Edward L. Fuchs	1955	63
439 3/8	45 7/8	36 1/8	38 4/8	7 2/8	23 4/8	19 3/8	16	13 6/8	25	15	Twin Lakes, AK	Thomas H. Lutsey	Thomas H. Lutsey	1955	63
439 1/8	53 4/8	53 4/8	45 6/8	6 4/8	22 5/8	21 4/8	16 2/8	3 3/8	23	22	Port Moller, AK	Joseph H. Johnson	Joseph H. Johnson	1976	65
439 1/8	59 4/8	59	46	7	2 4/8	18 4/8	16 2/8	10 4/8	12	15	Three Arm Bay, AK	Heber Simmons, Jr.	Heber Simmons, Jr.	2000	66
439	62 5/8	60 2/8	53 4/8	5 7/8	21 1/8	15 3/8	16 6/8	9 6/8	19	22	Nushagak River, AK	Vincent P. Sullivan	Vincent P. Sullivan	1992	67
438 7/8	51 3/8	50 6/8	47 3/8	6 7/8	23 4/8	6 1/8	1 7/8	14 1/8	19	15	Maclaren River, AK	Donald W. Bunselmeier	Donald W. Bunselmeier	1981	68
438 6/8	50 4/8	47	45 2/8	5	19 3/8	18	14 6/8	14 6/8	27	23	Iliamna Lake, AK	Jerry L. Peterson	Jerry L. Peterson	1986	69
438 1/8	52 4/8	51 6/8	41 5/8	6 3/8	17 4/8	15 2/8	8 1/8	8 1/8	21	19	Ugashik Lakes, AK	Norman W. Gilmore	Norman W. Gilmore	1967	70
438	58 2/8	58 6/8	53 6/8	6 4/8	23 6/8	23	7 6/8	2 2/8	16	12	Lower Ugashik Lake, AK	Bert A. McLay	Bert A. McLay	1981	70
438	60 6/8	55 4/8	40 7/8	8 6/8	21 4/8	6 2/8	17	/8	18	16	Alaska Pen., AK	Herb Klein	Dallas Mus. of Natl. Hist.	1967	72
438	53 7/8	49	47	5 2/8	19 4/8	14	15	7 4/8	20	18	Nelchina River, AK	Don Flynn	Don Flynn	1959	73
437 7/8	46 2/8	51	38 2/8	6 3/8	21 4/8	16 7/8	14 4/8	9 4/8	20	14	Tangle Lakes, AK	Dennis Weston	Dennis Weston	1964	74
437 4/8	61 6/8	61 3/8	37 2/8	6 1/8	21 4/8	23 3/8	5 1/8	9 1/8	15	25	Port Heiden, AK	Joyce A. Houston	Joyce A. Houston	1987	74
437 4/8	48 1/8	48 1/8	38 6/8	7 2/8	5 1/8	5	14 4/8	18 5/8	22	22	Naknek, AK	C.J. McElroy	C.J. McElroy	1966	76
437 3/8	48 5/8	50 7/8	37 1/8	6	21 4/8	21 6/8	18 4/8	16 5/8	18	16	Mulchatna River, AK	Lyle W. Bentzen	Lyle W. Bentzen	1974	77
437 2/8	60	61 2/8	50 5/8	6 7/8	13 6/8	19 5/8	1 4/8	12 3/8	15	19	Crescent Lake, AK	Joseph C. Tennison	Joseph C. Tennison	1991	77
437 2/8	59 3/8	57 2/8	43 5/8	6 3/8	20 1/8	19 4/8	5	12 6/8	19	23	Chisana River, AK	Terry Overly	Terry Overly	1976	79
436 2/8	60 6/8	58 2/8	39 6/8	7 1/8	20 3/8	17 3/8	16	10 2/8	23	21	Nabesna, AK	Bill Ellis	Bill Ellis	1964	80
436 2/8	52 2/8	53	48	6 2/8	16 6/8	20 6/8	12 6/8	10 6/8	21	16	Alaska Pen., AK	A.R. Buckles	A.R. Buckles	1967	80
436 1/8	54 4/8	53 1/8	41 6/8	6	19 1/8	19 5/8	15 7/8	15 7/8	16	18	Port Moller, AK	Marvin L. Fergastad	Marvin L. Fergastad	1962	82
436 1/8	55 3/8	55	47 3/8	7 7/8	21 4/8	6 3/8	15 1/8	1/8	15	19	Iliamna Lake, AK	Robert S. Marvin	Robert S. Marvin	1987	82

BARREN GROUND CARIBOU
Rangifer tarandus granti

Score	Length of Main Beam R	L	Inside Spread	Circ. Between Brow and Bez Points R	L	Length of Brow Points R	L	Width of Brow Points R	L	Number of Points R	L	Locality	Hunter	Owner	Date Killed	Rank
435 7/8	56 2/8	54	44 3/8	6 3/8	7	18 1/8	3	16	1/8	23	16	McClaren Ridge, AK	Peter W. Bading	Peter W. Bading	1959	84
435 7/8	55 2/8	51 5/8	39 4/8	6 7/8	8 3/8	10 3/8	17 4/8	10	5 2/8	23	33	Wrangell Mts., AK	Fred Williams	Fred Williams	1964	84
435 6/8	48 2/8	52 2/8	43	8 1/8	8 6/8	14 1/8	13 6/8	11 3/8	10	22	19	Farewell, AK	Henry Budny	Henry Budny	1960	86
435 6/8	53 1/8	53	41	6 2/8	5 7/8	4 3/8	17 4/8	1/8	11 4/8	17	24	Talkeetna Mts., AK	John M. Killian	John M. Killian	1960	86
435 6/8	53 6/8	54 3/8	37	6 7/8	6 7/8	18 4/8	20 6/8	11 1/8	14 4/8	22	19	Talkeetna Mts., AK	Mrs. Arnt Antonsen	Mrs. Arnt Antonsen	1960	88
435 5/8	51 2/8	50 3/8	41 7/8	7 7/8	7	23 7/8	12 1/8	18 1/8	2 7/8	19	13	Ugashik Lakes, AK	Robert E. Sass	Robert E. Sass	1963	89
435 3/8	54 1/8	52 4/8	48 6/8	6 3/8	6 2/8	3 1/8	20 6/8	1/8	11 7/8	14	13	Funny River, AK	David M. Bowen	David M. Bowen	1994	89
435 2/8	52 2/8	49 6/8	32 2/8	9 2/8	9 5/8	19 7/8	18 7/8	9 5/8	6 5/8	19	19	Naknek River, AK	Chris M. Kendrick	Chris M. Kendrick	1977	91
435 2/8	53 1/8	55 4/8	30 2/8	5 6/8	5 3/8	22 3/8	18 7/8	11 5/8	12 3/8	25	19	Alaska Range, AK	Kermit G. Johnson	Kermit G. Johnson	1970	92
435 1/8	53 1/8	55 1/8	55 1/8	6 1/8	6 2/8	22 5/8	20 7/8	3 4/8	12 6/8	15	23	King Salmon, AK	Warren F. Phillips	Warren F. Phillips	1983	93
435	51 1/8	51 5/8	35 2/8	6	6 2/8	24 6/8	11 4/8	14 7/8	1/8	30	16	Alinchak Bay, AK	Rodney R. Havens	Rodney R. Havens	1991	94
434 7/8	53 2/8	51 5/8	42 4/8	6 2/8	6	17 7/8	17 2/8	11 4/8	9	22	22	Tangle Lakes, AK	Bryant Flynn	Bryant Flynn	1953	95
434 3/8	58 4/8	57 5/8	45 6/8	5 2/8	5 3/8	18 2/8	18 4/8	5 7/8	12 4/8	23	18	Nushagak River, AK	John N. Pritchard	John N. Pritchard	1993	95
434 1/8	42 3/8	45 4/8	35 2/8	4 4/8	6 5/8	16	17 4/8	7 5/8	12 4/8	21	22	Tazlina, AK	Chuck Sutter	Chuck Sutter	1958	97
434	61 3/8	60	40 4/8	6 4/8	6 2/8	19 3/8	19 7/8	11 4/8	6 4/8	14	18	Little Nelchina River, AK	Joseph Brisco, Jr.	Joseph Brisco, Jr.	1955	98
434	51 6/8	48 6/8	44 3/8	6 1/8	6 1/8	20 1/8	19 4/8	15 4/8	14 2/8	21	16	King Salmon, AK	Roger W. Seiler	Roger W. Seiler	1959	98
433 7/8	51	52 4/8	28 6/8	5 7/8	6	19	19 4/8	7	15 3/8	34	34	Taylor Mt., AK	James C. Davis	James C. Davis	1993	100
433 6/8	59 2/8	56 7/8	41 2/8	6 4/8	6 2/8	15 5/8	20 4/8	10 1/8	15	25	21	Port Moller, AK	Paul M. Sweezey	Paul M. Sweezey	1968	101
433 6/8	59 4/8	59 7/8	57 2/8	6 3/8	6 1/8	23	8 4/8	18 2/8	1	22	13	Alaska Pen., AK	Herb Klein	Dallas Mus. of Natl. Hist.	1964	102
433 4/8	50 2/8	50 2/8	33 5/8	6 6/8	6 1/8	19 1/8	22 7/8	10	14 5/8	16	21	Seventy Mile River, AK	Bronk Jorgensen	Bronk Jorgensen	1989	102
433 3/8	59 3/8	56	33 5/8	5 6/8	6	3 6/8	19 7/8	5/8	14 6/8	16	21	Port Heiden, AK	D.R. Klein	D.R. Klein	1966	104
433 1/8	54	56 4/8	32 1/8	6 5/8	6 2/8	26	10 6/8	19 1/8	1/8	17	12	Killey River, AK	Timothy D. Evans	Timothy D. Evans	1994	105
432 7/8	52 1/8	52 6/8	48 4/8	6 5/8	6 1/8	5 5/8	23 7/8	4	16 5/8	15	19	Black Lake, AK	John T. Swiss	John T. Swiss	1967	106
432 7/8	50 2/8	48 4/8	39 1/8	9	12 4/8	14 2/8	15 1/8	1/8	8 4/8	16	21	Healy River, AK	Anitra Talerico	Frank H. Talerico	1982	106
432 5/8	55 6/8	55 4/8	48 1/8	5 5/8	5 4/8	7	21 1/8	17 2/8	1/8	23	15	Hick Creek, AK	Justin D. Hall	Justin D. Hall	1984	108
432 4/8	58 3/8	50 3/8	50	7 1/8	6 1/8	5 4/8	22	1	16 2/8	15	18	King Salmon, AK	Dan E. McCarty	Dan E. McCarty	1967	109
432 2/8	52 4/8	56	48 1/8	6	6 7/8	19	17 3/8	9 6/8	10 6/8	19	18	Iliamna Lake, AK	Thomas R. Reed, Jr.	Thomas R. Reed, Jr.	1988	110
432 1/8	54	53 3/8	49 7/8	6	5 7/8	10 1/8	22 3/8	1/8	15 5/8	15	25	Wide Bay, AK	Roy C. Jablonski	Roy C. Jablonski	1990	111
432	49 2/8	49 4/8	37 6/8	6 3/8	5 5/8	18 3/8	15 5/8	11 7/8	1/8	18	19	Upper Susitna River, AK	Theodore A. Warren	Theodore A. Warren	1955	112
432	52 1/8	51 5/8	42 4/8	7	7	10 1/8	15	4 6/8	12 1/8	21	22	Lake Louise, AK	Mike Walganski	Mike Walganski	1961	112
431 7/8	48	53 5/8	37 6/8	5 6/8	6	17 4/8	17 2/8	11 3/8	11	18	21	Nondalton, AK	Gordon S. Swift	Gordon S. Swift	1981	114
431 7/8	58 3/8	60 7/8	34 7/8	6 3/8	7	18	22 2/8	8 3/8	14 1/8	15	20	Egegik River, AK	David L. Dargis	David L. Dargis	1992	114
431 6/8	49 2/8	45 6/8	33 3/8	7 1/8	7	18	19 2/8		16 5/8	20	29	Clarence Lake, AK	Jack Hill	Jack Hill	1964	116
431 3/8	54 3/8	54 7/8	41 6/8	6 3/8	6 6/8	18 7/8	18 7/8	1 3/8	10 7/8	15	17	Talkeetna Mts., AK	Joseph R. Good	Joseph R. Good	1956	117
431 3/8	49	52 4/8	36 4/8	6 7/8	6 5/8	15 6/8	13 3/8	14	5 6/8	28	24	Cold Bay, AK	Gary D'Aigle	Gary D'Aigle	1973	117
431 3/8	54 1/8	51 7/8	35 4/8	6 7/8	7 3/8	18 4/8	18 7/8	14 1/8	10 7/8	20	20	Lake Clark, AK	William R. Lykken	William R. Lykken	1976	117

Score	Length R	Length L	Inside Spread	Brow R	Brow L	Bez R	Bez L	Circ. R	Circ. L	Pts R	Pts L	Locality	Hunter	Owner	Date Killed	Rank
431 3/8	53 5/8	54 2/8	43	6 5/8	7 1/8	16 7/8	17 5/8	6 3/8	11 4/8	20	19	Mulchatna River, AK	Valerie E. King	Valerie E. King	1984	117
431	50 6/8	54 2/8	39	6 6/8	6 5/8	21	21	13 3/8	14 5/8	20	21	Port Heiden, AK	Ray B. Nienhaus	Ray B. Nienhaus	1966	121
430 7/8	49	48 3/8	40 2/8	7 4/8	7 2/8	14	15 5/8	8	7 6/8	18	19	Susitna River, AK	James I. Roland	James I. Roland	1983	122
430 7/8	51 2/8	49 4/8	36 6/8	7 2/8	7 1/8	18 2/8	16 4/8	6 3/8	11	12	15	Mulchatna River, AK	Ted M. Labedz	Ted M. Labedz	1987	122
430 6/8	50 7/8	49 6/8	32 3/8	5 6/8	6	16 6/8	17 4/8	10 6/8	10 5/8	20	26	Talkeetna Mts., AK	Nelson Spencer	Nelson Spencer	1962	124
430 3/8	47	49 6/8	35 6/8	6 6/8	6	13 4/8	22	10 6/8	8 4/8	24	24	Gulkana River, AK	Troy Bogard	Troy Bogard	1954	125
430 3/8	57	54 1/8	46 4/8	8	8 5/8	6 1/8	17 3/8	8 4/8	14 1/8	22	24	Alaska Pen., AK	Michaux Nash, Jr.	Michaux Nash, Jr.	1968	125
430 2/8	57 7/8	53 6/8	44 5/8	6 2/8	6 4/8	16 6/8	18 3/8	9 5/8	10 6/8	23	16	Mother Goose Lake, AK	R.C. Parker	R.C. Parker	1959	127
430 2/8	53 1/8	54 3/8	44 1/8	6 1/8	5 6/8	22 4/8	22 4/8	15 2/8	10 6/8	15	20	Alaska Pen., AK	Ernest Milani	Ernest Milani	1961	127
430	52 4/8	56	36 4/8	6 6/8	6 7/8	24 4/8	21 6/8	2 6/8	17 3/8	15	17	Alaska Pen., AK	Richard A. Vozzi	Richard A. Vozzi	1991	129
429 6/8	51 1/8	49 7/8	40 3/8	8 6/8	8 1/8	14 6/8	14 3/8	22 1/8	9 1/8	20	16	Mulchatna River, AK	William S. Leffingwell	William S. Leffingwell	1990	130
429 5/8	56 5/8	48 4/8	39 5/8	8	7 5/8	11 7/8	18 6/8	10 6/8	5 4/8	17	14	Mulchatna River, AK	Jerry D. Downing	Jerry D. Downing	1986	131
429 4/8	51 5/8	51 5/8	30 7/8	5 3/8	5 7/8	19 2/8	15 7/8	15 7/8	12 6/8	21	24	Bonnet Plume, YT	R.G. Studemann	R.G. Studemann	1963	132
429 4/8	54 2/8	54 4/8	42 6/8	5 7/8	6	15 6/8	17 6/8	10 2/8	7	17	17	Mulchatna River, AK	Bruce C. Wassom	Bruce C. Wassom	1991	132
429 4/8	48 1/8	56 6/8	41 6/8	8 3/8	9 5/8	22 4/8	23	21 3/8	19 3/8	19	22	Alaska Pen., AK	Charles C. Parsons	Charles C. Parsons	1993	132
429 3/8	53 6/8	59	42 6/8	7 6/8	7	15 6/8	15 6/8	11 3/8		24	17	Mulchatna River, AK	Lem Crofton	Lem Crofton	1978	135
429 3/8	56	54 7/8	31 5/8	7	6	18 6/8	18 6/8	1 7/8	16 7/8	19	26	Juneau Lake, AK	Don Nickel	Don Nickel	1993	135
429 1/8	58	58	35	6 6/8	6	15	15	19	19	22	15	Alaska Range, AK	Harvard Univ. Mus.	J.C. Phillips	1928	137
429 1/8	49	48 3/8	43 6/8	9 3/8	7	16 6/8	17 3/8	8 7/8	8 7/8	21	19	Tyone Lake, AK	Ralph Marshall	Ralph Marshall	1960	137
429	50 3/8	51 6/8	48 6/8	5 4/8	6	18 6/8	18 6/8	8 6/8	10 3/8	18	24	Pinochle Creek, AK	William B. Ripley	William B. Ripley	1989	139
429	57	54 1/8	41	6 4/8	6 6/8	19 1/8	19 1/8	13 5/8	11 1/8	23	12	Mulchatna River, AK	Picked Up	Darryl Sanford	1999	139
428 5/8	62 6/8	62	49 1/8	6 3/8	6 5/8	7	21 6/8	16 6/8	1/8	20	12	Iliamna Lake, AK	Linda J. Corley	Linda J. Corley	1983	141
428 1/8	53	55 3/8	38 1/8	6 2/8	6 1/8	11 4/8	23 1/8	14 6/8	1/8	12	9	Mulchatna River, AK	Ricky A. Beauchamp	Ricky A. Beauchamp	1987	142
428 1/8	54 5/8	54 3/8	44 2/8	5 7/8	5 7/8	19 7/8	19 4/8	3 7/8	12 4/8	19	20	Ivishak River, AK	Joseph A. Renfrow, Jr.	Joseph A. Renfrow, Jr.	1987	142
428 1/8	56 3/8	59 2/8	44 1/8	5 2/8	5 4/8	20 1/8	20 1/8	13 3/8	14 4/8	16	11	Tutna Lake, AK	Robert W. Roessel	Robert W. Roessel	1987	142
427 5/8	57 2/8	53 7/8	42 2/8	7 4/8	7 3/8	19 6/8	18 4/8	13 7/8	1/8	19	17	Talkeetna Mts., AK	Donald Parker	Donald Parker	1969	145
427 4/8	49	46	40 5/8	6 1/8	6 1/8	18 2/8	21 2/8	10 6/8	10 4/8	17	25	Aniak River, AK	Lad R. Neilson	Lad R. Neilson	1991	146
426 7/8	52 4/8	53 1/8	45 1/8	6 1/8	6	21 7/8	16	9 2/8	11 1/8	22	17	Cinder River, AK	John G. Merry, Jr.	John G. Merry, Jr.	1968	147
426 6/8	52 3/8	52 6/8	52 6/8	8 3/8	8	16	15 2/8	17 3/8	1/8	25	20	Anchorage, AK	Peter W. Bading	Peter W. Bading	1963	148
426 6/8	52 6/8	54 4/8	54 4/8	8	8	15 2/8	3 2/8	1/8	1/8	17	17	Alaska Range, AK	Dan Parker	Dan Parker	1971	148
426 6/8	51 6/8	51 6/8	39 4/8	7 6/8	7 6/8	20	24	13 6/8	15 2/8	20	20	King Salmon, AK	Donald E. Twa	Donald E. Twa	1993	148
426 6/8	54	58 1/8	47 5/8	5 5/8	5 5/8	16 6/8	1 6/8	1/8	11 4/8	18	19	Smelt Creek, AK	Chris Pickering	Chris Pickering	1996	148
426 6/8	55 3/8	54 2/8	34 1/8	7	8 4/8	13 7/8	19 4/8	5 7/8	14 2/8	14	16	Shagak Bay, AK	James A. McIntosh	James A. McIntosh	2002	148
426 3/8	59	56 6/8	44 5/8	6 1/8	6 1/8	19 3/8	18	6 4/8	9 2/8	19	16	Alaska Pen., AK	John S. Rohrer	John S. Rohrer	1987	153
426 2/8	52 6/8	54 6/8	37 6/8	6 5/8	7 4/8	15	21 4/8	13	1 7/8	20	16	Eureka, AK	C.C. Grey	C.C. Grey	1953	154
426 2/8	52 3/8	48 7/8	40 5/8	5 6/8	6 3/8	18 1/8	18 1/8	3 2/8	15 5/8	15	22	Wrangell Mts., AK	Richard Conroy	Richard Conroy	1961	154
426 2/8	53 2/8	54 4/8	44 3/8	8 3/8	7 1/8	17	17	1/8	11 3/8	17	22	Black Lake, AK	Lester W. Miller, Jr.	Lester W. Miller, Jr.	1963	154
426 2/8	50 3/8	56 4/8	56 4/8	8	6 6/8	24	13 6/8	1/8		19	22	Lake Clark, AK	Mark E. Carda	Mark E. Carda	1986	154
426 1/8	56 2/8	60 3/8	41 6/8	6 1/8	7 6/8	13	1 6/8	15 3/8	1/8	18	15	White River, YT	Unknown	F.C. Havemeyer	1912	158
426 1/8	48 5/8	47 5/8	43 4/8	5 7/8	6 1/8	18 5/8	19 4/8	4 7/8	8 2/8	17	23	Pumice Creek, AK	Raymond F. Fogarty	Raymond F. Fogarty	1991	158
426 1/8	55 4/8	55 5/8	47 6/8	6 3/8	6 5/8	7 3/8	17 3/8	9 5/8	1/8	18	20	Nushagak River, AK	John R. Herr, Jr.	John R. Herr, Jr.	1991	158
426	48 3/8	50 6/8	37	7	6 7/8	19 4/8	19 1/8	9 4/8	14 6/8	20	17	Coal Creek, AK	Dustin L. Sikes	Dustin L. Sikes	1993	161
425 7/8	53 5/8	52 6/8	42 1/8	6 5/8	6 7/8	19 1/8	19 1/8	8 4/8	11 1/8	20	22	Fog Lakes, AK	Larry F. Grout	Larry F. Grout	1981	162
425 7/8	54 2/8	58 2/8	40 6/8	5 6/8	5 4/8	18	2 7/8	1/8	13 6/8	18	27	Bear Creek, AK	Douglas E. Christiansen	Douglas E. Christiansen	1988	162
425 7/8	52 3/8	53	36 2/8	7 1/8	6 6/8	16 1/8	16 1/8	11 5/8	1/8	25	20	Hart River, YT	Peter C. Elarde, Jr.	Peter C. Elarde, Jr.	1990	162
425 6/8	45 4/8	49 4/8	32 2/8	6	6	19 3/8	17 7/8	11 4/8	18 6/8	18	18	Denali Hwy., AK	Sam Pancotto	Sam Pancotto	1960	165
425 6/8	53 2/8	55 2/8	39 4/8	7 4/8	7 4/8	14	3 2/8	1/8	10 1/8	15	19	Nabesna, AK	Frank Martin, Jr.	Frank Martin, Jr.	1965	165
425 5/8	52 6/8	48	31	7 2/8	7 2/8	19	13	1/8	13 4/8	14	19	Iliamna Lake, AK	Donald R. Barnes	Donald R. Barnes	1973	167

BARREN GROUND CARIBOU
Rangifer tarandus granti

Score	Length of Main Beam R	L	Inside Spread	Circumference at Smallest Place Between Brow and Bez Points R	L	Length of Brow Points R	L	Width of Brow Points R	L	Number of Points R	L	Locality	Hunter	Owner	Date Killed	Rank
425 5/8	48 1/8	47 5/8	46 7/8	5 5/8	5 4/8	20 5/8	19	4 3/8	14 6/8	17	21	Becharof Lake, AK	Lavon L. Chittick	Lavon L. Chittick	1981	167
425 5/8	50 3/8	50	35	7 1/8	6 7/8	22 1/8	19 2/8	14 5/8	17 3/8	15	15	Igiugig, AK	William F. Peot	William F. Peot	1995	167
425 3/8	56 4/8	59	43 2/8	7 1/8	7	20 6/8	19 6/8	8	10 3/8	20	14	Iliamna Lake, AK	A.A. Bishop	A.A. Bishop	1982	170
425 3/8	55 6/8	56 2/8	41	6 6/8	7 2/8	17 7/8	18 2/8	5 4/8	9 6/8	17	17	Moody Creek, AK	Ervin Hostetler	Ervin Hostetler	1983	170
425 3/8	49 4/8	50 3/8	39 2/8	5 6/8	5 3/8	19 4/8	16 1/8	6 5/8	9 5/8	16	15	Taylor Mts., AK	Val B. Jones	Val B. Jones	1990	170
425 3/8	57 3/8	55 7/8	52 6/8	5	5	19 1/8	14	11 6/8	1 4/8	18	13	Alaska Pen., AK	James T. Hartley	James T. Hartley	1996	174
425 2/8	46 7/8	48 2/8	35 2/8	6 4/8	6 5/8	16	17 2/8	7 5/8	12 3/8	20	21	McClaren Ridge, AK	Peter W. Bading	Peter W. Bading	1959	174
425	52 2/8	52 6/8	40 5/8	6 1/8	6 3/8	17 5/8	9 3/8	12 2/8	7 5/8	23	17	Susitna, AK	Elmer M. Rusten	Elmer M. Rusten	1952	175
425	45 1/8	45 2/8	36 7/8	5 6/8	5 3/8	20 3/8	21 6/8	15 1/8	7 7/8	22	22	Talkeetna Mts., AK	Thorne Donnelley	Thorne Donnelley	1959	175
425	47 1/8	52 4/8	36	7	6 3/8	8	23	1 3/8	18 5/8	18	32	Lake Louise, AK	H.E. O'Neal	H.E. O'Neal	1964	175
424 7/8	52 5/8	58 5/8	43 3/8	7 6/8	8 1/8	15 6/8	14 4/8	5 4/8	9	19	16	Denali Hwy., AK	Moyer Johnstone	Moyer Johnstone	1958	178
424 7/8	53 3/8	53 5/8	36 7/8	6 7/8	6 4/8	21 1/8	2 3/8	16 1/8	1/8	18	20	Alaska Range, AK	Dennis R. Johnson	Dennis R. Johnson	1980	178
424 7/8	58 3/8	54 5/8	45 4/8	6 4/8	6 4/8	3 7/8	25 2/8	1/8	18 5/8	14	14	Ugashik Lakes, AK	Robert C. Jones	Robert C. Jones	1981	178
424 7/8	53 7/8	54 6/8	41 6/8	7	6 7/8	21 7/8	18 7/8	11	13 7/8	13	14	Post River, AK	Roger E. Austin	Roger E. Austin	1988	178
424 6/8	50 5/8	53 6/8	39 2/8	7	7 3/8	16 6/8	20 7/8	1 3/8	14 2/8	19	17	Swan River, AK	Kenneth G. Rogowski	Kenneth G. Rogowski	1992	182
424 6/8	44 5/8	45 2/8	38 4/8	6 6/8	7 3/8	19 3/8	19 1/8	15 2/8	13 4/8	29	33	Nushagak River, AK	A. Mark Horvat	A. Mark Horvat	1995	182
424 6/8	48	46 5/8	34 5/8	5 6/8	6 5/8	24	1 5/8	1	19 2/8	13	30	Shotgun Hills, AK	Clinton E. Hanson, Jr.	Clinton E. Hanson, Jr.	2003	182
424 4/8	51 4/8	47 4/8	43 6/8	6 5/8	6 4/8	17	17	11 3/8	8 1/8	18	20	Talkeetna Mts., AK	Wayne C. Eubank	Wayne C. Eubank	1959	185
424 4/8	55	52 5/8	47 5/8	7 1/8	7 6/8	17 1/8	19 5/8	14 2/8	1 6/8	18	13	Talkeetna Mts., AK	Karl Weber	Karl Weber	1959	185
424 4/8	57 7/8	55 4/8	42 4/8	7 2/8	6 3/8	16 4/8	1 2/8	8 3/8	4/8	17	16	Funny River, AK	Ted H. Spraker	Ted H. Spraker	1994	185
424 3/8	61	59	46	5 5/8	5 5/8	19 6/8	14 6/8	13	4 5/8	17	13	Lake Louise, AK	Picked Up	Dick Luckow	1959	188
424 3/8	51 7/8	52 1/8	48	6 2/8	6 1/8	12 2/8	22 4/8	1	17 7/8	16	23	Post River, AK	Guntram Rhomberg	Guntram Rhomberg	1966	188
424 2/8	51 1/8	46 1/8	43 3/8	6 5/8	7 4/8	20 1/8	19 7/8	7 4/8	16	18	26	Summit, AK	Morris Spencer	Morris Spencer	1962	190
424 2/8	50	49	38 4/8	5 3/8	5 4/8	15 5/8	19 1/8	10 4/8	15 6/8	17	19	Talkeetna Mts., AK	Myron Bethel	Myron Bethel	1976	190
424 2/8	57 2/8	58 2/8	40 2/8	6 2/8	5 4/8	17 6/8	19 4/8	9 1/8	4 6/8	16	17	King Salmon, AK	Samuel C. Johnson	Samuel C. Johnson	1978	190
424 1/8	52 5/8	52 4/8	46 6/8	6 2/8	6 2/8	16	1 7/8	13 4/8	5 4/8	37	24	Wrangell Mts., AK	Lyle E. Reynolds	Lyle E. Reynolds	1960	193
424 1/8	52 4/8	43 4/8	32 7/8	6 7/8	6 2/8	11 4/8	19 3/8	1/8	17 2/8	17	23	Mulchatna River, AK	Dan G. Best	Dan G. Best	1961	193
423 7/8	57 1/8	57	41 5/8	6 1/8	5 6/8	18 4/8	14 2/8	12 5/8	1 4/8	16	12	Alaska Pen., AK	Monte R. Ford	Monte R. Ford	1988	195
423 6/8	56 5/8	55 1/8	40 7/8	6 4/8	6 6/8	1 7/8	15 1/8	1/8	10 4/8	19	23	King Salmon River, AK	Rex Hancock	Rex Hancock	1961	196
423 6/8	52 7/8	50 6/8	40 3/8	5 2/8	5 3/8	17 2/8	10 7/8	11 3/8	3 2/8	25	23	Cinder River, AK	Henry N. Warren	Henry N. Warren	1978	196
423 6/8	55	54 7/8	47	5 6/8	5 6/8	18 4/8	18 4/8	8 1/8	14 4/8	18	22	Port Heiden, AK	Gary F. Romaniw	Gary F. Romaniw	1981	196
423 6/8	53 4/8	52 1/8	39 3/8	6 2/8	6 4/8	18 4/8	20 4/8	7 7/8	13 1/8	16	18	Hook Creek, AK	James A. Prince, Jr.	James A. Prince, Jr.	1988	196
423 4/8	52 6/8	52 4/8	37 6/8	5 4/8	5 5/8	19 2/8	19	8	16 2/8	17	21		D. Alan Shreves	D. Alan Shreves	1996	196
423 3/8	53 3/8	59 4/8	41 1/8	6 6/8	6 4/8	19	17	11 4/8	10 5/8	24	23	Ferry, AK	Roy Maxwell	Roy Maxwell	1965	201
423 3/8	53 2/8	53 1/8	43 2/8	6 6/8	8 3/8	17	18 3/8	10 5/8	11 3/8	17	23	Maka Creek, AK	Julian B. White, Jr.	Julian B. White, Jr.	1993	201
423 2/8	51 1/8	50	45 7/8	7 2/8	7 3/8	18 3/8	15 6/8	13 5/8	11 3/8	19	16	Killey River, AK	Dennis H. Johns	Dennis H. Johns	1997	203

Score												Locality	Hunter	Owner	Date	Rank
423 1/8	44 6/8	44	32 4/8	19 3/8	7 1/8	6 7/8	20 3/8	9 1/8	17	18	24	Tyone River, AK	Alva H. Rich	Alva H. Rich	1961	204
423	53 1/8	55 2/8	44 1/8	16	6 7/8	6 7/8	15 3/8	6 2/8	9 4/8	13	15	Gulkana River, AK	Lewis E. Yearout	Lewis E. Yearout	1956	205
423	43 5/8	43 7/8	40	6 7/8	7 2/8	5 6/8	16 7/8	3	11	14	15	Port Heiden, AK	Robert D. Jones	Robert D. Jones	1981	205
423	47 6/8	50	48	18 2/8	6 3/8	6 4/8	16 3/8	9 2/8	8 7/8	15	16	Panorama Mt., AK	Ronald R. Minard	Ronald R. Minard	1985	205
422 7/8	50 6/8	51 5/8	37	21 1/8	6 2/8	6 2/8	20 2/8	9 1/8	8 7/8	20	21	Rainy Pass, AK	L. Arthur Cushman, Jr.	L. Arthur Cushman, Jr.	1961	208
422 6/8	49 2/8	48 6/8	47 3/8	16 4/8	6 3/8	6 3/8	14 5/8	11 2/8	6 6/8	19	13	Slana River, AK	Kirby Kiltz	Kirby Kiltz	1959	209
422 6/8	46 6/8	51 7/8	37	16 4/8	6 1/8	5 7/8	17	12 4/8	3 6/8	18	17	Matanuska River, AK	Stephen E. Skaggs	Stephen E. Skaggs	1978	209
422 6/8	55 4/8	55 6/8	45 4/8	19 6/8	7 1/8	6 3/8	18 6/8	4 4/8	15 6/8	16	18	Mother Goose Lake, AK	James B. Bloomer	James B. Bloomer	1987	209
422 6/8	51 3/8	51 4/8	41 7/8	20 6/8	6 3/8	7 1/8	19 3/8	4 4/8	3 4/8	23	16	Becharof Lake, AK	Richard-Salim F. Farah	Richard-Salim F. Farah	1993	209
422 5/8	50 4/8	45 4/8	34 4/8	22 4/8	6 3/8	6 2/8	17	17 4/8	5 5/8	16	19	Mt. Sanford, AK	John J. Heidel	John J. Heidel	1982	213
422 5/8	44 2/8	44 6/8	35 4/8	20 2/8	9 4/8	6 6/8	17	15	1 2/8	23	16	Snipe Lake, AK	Steven S. Lambe	Steven S. Lambe	1983	213
422 5/8	53 3/8	54 7/8	42 4/8	22	6 2/8	5 7/8	22	13 6/8	5 5/8	16	22	Alaska Pen., AK	Kirk D. Atter	Kirk D. Atter	1992	213
422 4/8	52 1/8	47 4/8	45 4/8	16 1/8	6 2/8	5 4/8	20 7/8	1/8	17 7/8	17	20	Iliamna Lake, AK	Bill Sims	Bill Sims	1973	216
422 3/8	49 2/8	49 3/8	37 4/8	21 4/8	6 3/8	6 2/8	18	4 2/8	11 7/8	22	20	Tangle Lakes, AK	Leroy G. Bohuslor	Leroy G. Bohuslor	1952	217
422 3/8	47	52 3/8	49	17 3/8	7 3/8	6	19 3/8	13 4/8	11 7/8	27	16	Hoholitna River, AK	Bradley A. Finch	Bradley A. Finch	1990	217
422 3/8	51	51 6/8	30 6/8	15 4/8	5 6/8	5 6/8	15 4/8	14 6/8	11 4/8	24	25	Hart River, YT	Steven B. Curtis	Steven B. Curtis	1996	217
422 1/8	42 3/8	45 7/8	37	16 3/8	6 5/8	6 5/8	13	15 2/8	11	27	21	Susitna River, AK	Warren Jones	Warren Jones	1961	220
422 1/8	57 3/8	59 3/8	54 4/8	16 5/8	6 1/8	6 3/8	1 4/8	17 4/8	1/8	21	14	King Salmon, AK	Jerry R. Jones	Jerry R. Jones	1981	220
422 1/8	49	49 2/8	36 1/8	22 2/8	6 6/8	6 6/8	17 6/8	16 7/8	14	22	21	Mulchatna River, AK	Thomas N. Govin	Thomas N. Govin	1987	220
422	53 5/8	51 5/8	40 6/8	20 1/8	6 6/8	6 7/8	20 1/8	15	15	22	22	Alaska Pen., AK	Debbie D. Burfiend	Debbie D. Burfiend	1993	223
421 7/8	55 5/8	48	33 6/8	17 5/8	7 3/8	7	17 5/8	16 5/8	10 7/8	22	21	Farewell Lake, AK	Richard K. Siller	Richard K. Siller	1958	224
421 7/8	50 1/8	50 5/8	36 6/8	16 5/8	6 5/8	7 5/8	16 5/8	11 3/8	1 4/8	20	15	Mosquito Creek, AK	Thomas L. Teague	Thomas L. Teague	1989	224
421 6/8	64 5/8	59 3/8	57	22 1/8	7 5/8	7 1/8	2 6/8	16 5/8	1	18	12	King Salmon, AK	Edwin W. Seiler	Edwin W. Seiler	1958	226
421 6/8	50 4/8	50 4/8	38 2/8	3 5/8	5 7/8	5 7/8	3 5/8	1	14 3/8	12	21	Cinder River, AK	Jerry A. Wilkinson	Jerry A. Wilkinson	1972	226
421 5/8	51 4/8	50	36 3/8	18 4/8	8 7/8	7 4/8	18 4/8	9	14	17	23	Port Moller, AK	John S. Clark	John S. Clark	1966	228
421 5/8	56 7/8	55 5/8	56	18 6/8	5 5/8	5 5/8	18	12 5/8	14	14	9	Upper Ugashik Lake, AK	Barry Barbour	Barry Barbour	1969	228
421 4/8	55 3/8	54 6/8	42 6/8	20 3/8	7 2/8	6 7/8	20 3/8	12 2/8	15 5/8	17	16	Denali Hwy., AK	D.G. Skagerberg	D.G. Skagerberg	1956	230
421 4/8	55	53 4/8	43	16 3/8	5 4/8	5 4/8	16 3/8	10	9 2/8	18	18	Denali Hwy., AK	John Schmidel	John Schmidel	1961	230
421 4/8	55 1/8	54 2/8	45 5/8	15 5/8	5 4/8	5 4/8	15 5/8	10	17	17	26	Twin Lakes, AK	Paul O'Hollaren	Paul O'Hollaren	1964	230
421 4/8	58 1/8	58 1/8	44 6/8	19	8 4/8	7 1/8	2 4/8	12 3/8	4 5/8	17	12	Kuskokwim River, AK	Dennis Harms	Dennis Harms	1967	230
421 4/8	47	51 4/8	32	18 7/8	6 3/8	6 2/8	22 2/8	1 6/8	18 4/8	15	22	Becharof Lake, AK	Ronnie L. Smith	Ronnie L. Smith	1993	230
421 2/8	58 7/8	57 3/8	37 1/8	19 2/8	6 2/8	6 2/8	12 7/8	12 7/8	11 6/8	22	19	Alaska	Jonas Bros. of Seattle	Unknown	1953	235
421 2/8	47 2/8	48 6/8	43 4/8	11 6/8	6	7	11 6/8	8 3/8	11 4/8	19	22	Cantwell, AK	Richard L. Miller	Richard L. Miller	1979	235
421 2/8	52 6/8	50 5/8	43 2/8	4 3/8	6 4/8	6 4/8	4 3/8	1/8	16 7/8	14	20	Boulder Creek, AK	Neal E. Osgood	Neal E. Osgood	1986	235
421 2/8	61 6/8	58	43 4/8	20 6/8	6 3/8	6 3/8	20 6/8	16 6/8	1/8	15	13	Lake Clark, AK	Ben C. Shafsky	Ben C. Shafsky	1993	235
421 2/8	53 4/8	54 3/8	38 1/8	19 1/8	5 6/8	5 5/8	19 1/8	3 6/8	11 5/8	24	23	Funny River, AK	Robert W. Nelson	Robert W. Nelson	1995	235
421 1/8	47	51 4/8	37 3/8	19	7 4/8	7 3/8	18 2/8	10 5/8	10 5/8	24	21	Lake Louise, AK	Orel O. Parker	Orel O. Parker	1959	240
421 1/8	58 7/8	57 3/8	45 6/8	19 2/8	5 6/8	5 5/8	19	10 5/8	10 5/8	19	12	Ugashik Lakes, AK	Jack A. Shane, Sr.	Jack A. Shane, Sr.	1967	240
421 1/8	47 2/8	48 6/8	43 6/8	19 6/8	6	6	19 6/8	14 1/8	14 6/8	19	17	Alaska Pen., AK	Alice J. Landreth	Alice J. Landreth	1968	240
421 1/8	57 4/8	54 6/8	35 1/8	19	7 3/8	6 7/8	4 1/8	1/8	14 4/8	16	23	Maka Creek, AK	Larry G. Berry	Larry G. Berry	1994	240
421	56 4/8	58 4/8	49 1/8	20 4/8	5 4/8	7 1/8	20 3/8	15 5/8	14 1/8	13	19	Alaska Pen., AK	Lloyd W. Birdwell	Lloyd W. Birdwell	1970	244
421	55 5/8	57	44 7/8	9 7/8	7 1/8	6 4/8	18	10 7/8	1/8	20	14	Ugashik Lakes, AK	J. Mark Hanger	J. Mark Hanger	1988	244
420 7/8	56 2/8	57	45 3/8	23 6/8	5 5/8	5 6/8	2 4/8	21 4/8	4/8	16	14	Port Heiden, AK	Otis Chandler	Otis Chandler	1964	246
420 7/8	54 1/8	54 7/8	38 4/8	20 1/8	7 7/8	6 3/8	9 1/8	14 6/8	4/8	22	15	Farewell, AK	Vern G. Smith	Vern G. Smith	1967	246
420 6/8	45 5/8	47 4/8	36 4/8	16	6	6 3/8	20 1/8	10 2/8	5	27	21	Becharof Lake, AK	Glenn E. Anderson	Glenn E. Anderson	1982	248
420 6/8	56 4/8	57 4/8	46 1/8	20 1/8	5 4/8	6 7/8	18 1/8	5 2/8	5	18	14	Becharof Lake, AK	Steven H. Schaust	Steven H. Schaust	1983	248
420 5/8	53 7/8	49 1/8	40 2/8	18 1/8	6 1/8	5 7/8	18 1/8	11 3/8	11 2/8	12	13	Mulchatna River, AK	Ronald K. Hodges	Ronald K. Hodges	1986	250
420 4/8	59 1/8	57 4/8	42 4/8	12	8 6/8	8 5/8	12	1	17 7/8	11	16	Tangle Lakes, AK	J.W. Latham	J.W. Latham	1961	251

BARREN GROUND CARIBOU
Rangifer tarandus granti

Score	Length of Main Beam R	L	Inside Spread	Circumference at Smallest Place Between Brow and Bez Points R	L	Length of Brow Points R	L	Width of Brow Points R	L	Number of Points R	L	Locality	Hunter	Owner	Date Killed	Rank
420 4/8	46 4/8	48	39 5/8	6 1/8	6 2/8	18 1/8	18 3/8	3 3/8	13 2/8	19	24	Dog Salmon River, AK	Gary R. Swanson	Gary R. Swanson	1966	251
420 4/8	55 5/8	58 4/8	46 4/8	6 3/8	6 3/8	18 2/8	18 2/8	12 5/8	7 3/8	21	14	Kaskanak Creek, AK	Robert J. Priewe	Robert J. Priewe	1991	251
420 4/8	55 5/8	55 5/8	46 2/8	6	7	1	21 3/8	1/8	14 4/8	17	19	Wolf Lake, AK	Thompson L. Reed	Thompson L. Reed	1994	251
420 3/8	55	52 4/8	40 4/8	5 4/8	5 4/8	23	15 3/8	17 4/8	3	19	12	Alaska Pen., AK	W.M. Ellis	W.M. Ellis	1963	255
420 3/8	45 2/8	46 1/8	37 3/8	6 2/8	6	10 3/8	17	1/8	14 2/8	16	23	Cranberry Creek, AK	Robert A. Black	Robert A. Black	1994	255
420 2/8	48 1/8	46 4/8	35	7 5/8	6 7/8	19 4/8	18 2/8	12 6/8	12	26	25	Mulchatna River, AK	Bradley E. Groves	Bradley E. Groves	1994	257
420 1/8	59 2/8	57 2/8	40 4/8	6 2/8	6 3/8	22 7/8	22 6/8	5 4/8	17 4/8	15	19	Iliamna Lake, AK	A.E. Wilson	A.E. Wilson	1955	258
420 1/8	50 5/8	55 3/8	41 2/8	6 6/8	6 4/8	20	21	16 1/8	18	14	20	King Salmon River, AK	Frank N. Rome	Frank N. Rome	1983	258
420 1/8	56 1/8	54 2/8	37 6/8	7 3/8	7 3/8	20	17 6/8	13 4/8	1/8	18	15	Yanert Fork, AK	Michael H. Werner	Michael H. Werner	1984	258
420	50 2/8	50 5/8	42	7 1/8	7 7/8	17 2/8	13	13 1/8	1/8	20	17	Chisana, AK	John S. Newkam, Jr.	John S. Newkam, Jr.	1960	261
419 7/8	44	46 1/8	46 2/8	6 7/8	7 7/8	14 4/8	15 5/8	1/8	12 2/8	15	22	Aleutian Range, AK	Fred Dykema	Fred Dykema	1973	262
419 7/8	49 7/8	49 2/8	37 3/8	6 5/8	6 4/8	14 7/8	18 5/8	1 4/8	14 2/8	16	23	Alaska Pen., AK	Kenneth E. Hess	Kenneth E. Hess	1987	262
419 6/8	54 6/8	50 5/8	47 3/8	7 4/8	6 5/8	17 1/8	16 4/8	9 4/8	10 2/8	15	16	Dog Salmon River, AK	Ralph H. Eisaman	Ralph H. Eisaman	1971	264
419 6/8	53 7/8	51 3/8	41	6 1/8	6 1/8	16 3/8	15 4/8	9 4/8	12 4/8	18	21	Mulchatna River, AK	Robert P. Colson	Robert P. Colson	1993	264
419 5/8	43 6/8	45 3/8	29 7/8	7 2/8	7 5/8	14	15 4/8	8 7/8	10 7/8	22	22	Chisana, AK	Thomas F. Esper	Thomas F. Esper	1965	266
419 5/8	51 1/8	50 1/8	35 6/8	6 2/8	6 1/8	16 5/8	15 7/8	9 5/8	12 4/8	22	23	Mt. Drum, AK	Jerald T. Waite	Jerald T. Waite	1966	266
419 5/8	53 3/8	53 5/8	39 4/8	6 6/8	6 5/8	16 4/8	20 4/8	14 7/8	10 2/8	16	16	Nabesna, AK	Bernard Kendall	Bernard Kendall	1969	266
419 4/8	50	51 7/8	45 3/8	7 2/8	7	6 4/8	19 3/8	1/8	12 3/8	13	21	Rainy Pass, AK	Warren Page	Warren Page	1956	269
419 4/8	46 2/8	47 2/8	32	7	6 4/8	16 5/8	15 2/8	8 1/8	8 4/8	20	20	Talkeetna, AK	Dale Westenbarger	Dale Westenbarger	1965	269
419 4/8	57 3/8	57 3/8	46 6/8	6 4/8	6 1/8	15 3/8	19 3/8	9 6/8	1 2/8	26	16	King Salmon, AK	David C. Smith	David C. Smith	1987	269
419 3/8	45	45 4/8	35 5/8	7 4/8	8 1/8	18	18	13 1/8	1 6/8	26	21	Fairbanks, AK	Unknown	Ladd Air Force Base	PR 1953	272
419 3/8	54	52 3/8	37	7	7	19 3/8	19 3/8	7 7/8	11 7/8	14	17	Alaska Pen., AK	C. Driskell	C. Driskell	1965	272
419 3/8	53 1/8	53 1/8	40 5/8	7 4/8	8 4/8	18 7/8	3 6/8	17	1/8	18	15	Kenai River, AK	Allison L. Darsey	David A. Darsey	1992	272
419 3/8	52 2/8	52	42 5/8	6 1/8	6 1/8	14	19 6/8	4	12 2/8	12	17	Iliamna Lake, AK	Scott King	Scott King	1993	272
419 2/8	49 7/8	49 4/8	35 6/8	6 6/8	6 6/8	22 4/8	21 5/8	15 1/8	4 6/8	15	11	Iliamna Lake, AK	Roy F. Smith	Roy F. Smith	1987	276
419 2/8	53 5/8	55 3/8	37 2/8	6 3/8	6 3/8	19 1/8	15 1/8	12 6/8	5 7/8	19	16	Polly Creek, AK	Mark W. Linebarger	Mark W. Linebarger	1993	276
419 1/8	49 6/8	48	48	5 7/8	5 7/8	15	15 1/8	5 7/8	11 6/8	19	22	Cinder River, AK	Al E. Neether	Al E. Neether	1972	278
419 1/8	44 3/8	44 4/8	31 6/8	7 4/8	6 6/8	20	20 3/8	5	13	19	25	Ugashik River, AK	Ronald W. Madsen	Ronald W. Madsen	1987	278
419	45 2/8	44 2/8	35 5/8	7 4/8	7 4/8	15 7/8	14 1/8	8 2/8	9 1/8	18	19	Becharof Lake, AK	Ron L. Lerch	Ron L. Lerch	1966	280
419	42 3/8	46 5/8	35 3/8	6 4/8	6 4/8	11 6/8	17 4/8	1/8	11 4/8	24	17	Iliamna Lake, AK	Michael Clanton	Michael Clanton	1994	280
418 7/8	49 5/8	50	43	6	5 6/8	18	1 4/8	12	1/8	28	20	Nabesna River Valley, AK	Wayne Platt	Wayne Platt	1958	282
418 7/8	52 6/8	53 1/8	40 1/8	5 5/8	5 6/8	19 2/8	22 6/8	9	8 4/8	10	15	Mother Goose Lake, AK	Robert A. Epperson	Robert A. Epperson	1963	282
418 7/8	54 1/8	50 5/8	40 6/8	7	6 2/8	15 3/8	17	10 6/8	11 4/8	17	19	Hoholitna River, AK	O.B. Beard III	O.B. Beard III	1974	282
418 7/8	49 4/8	49 3/8	44	5 6/8	5 6/8	17 2/8	18 2/8	12 4/8	11 1/8	20	19	Cold Bay, AK	James E. Carson	James E. Carson	1974	282
418 7/8	48 7/8	54 1/8	38 2/8	6 4/8	7	17 3/8	18 3/8	5 7/8	13 2/8	15	15	Iliamna Lake, AK	Richard L. Deane	Richard L. Deane	1993	282
418 7/8	50 4/8	51 5/8	38	9 4/8	7 1/8	18 2/8	18 7/8	8	15 6/8	16	18	Nishlik Lake, AK	Kirby S. Kulbeck	Kirby S. Kulbeck	1994	282

674

Score	L. Main Beam R	L. Main Beam L	Inside Spread	M4	M5	M6	M7	M8	M9	M10	Pts R	Pts L	Locality	Hunter	Owner	Date Killed	Rank
418 6/8	59 6/8	60	53 1/8	6 6/8	6 6/8	6 7/8	19 7/8	17 2/8	12 5/8	3 3/8	12	15	Eureka, AK	William Curtis	F.A. Harrington	1949	288
418 6/8	59	55 5/8	34 4/8	6 4/8	5 7/8	6 1/8	14	22 3/8	1 1/8	6 1/8	17	21	Alaska Pen., AK	Otis Chandler	Otis Chandler	1964	288
418 6/8	55 5/8	53 4/8	40 7/8	6	5 6/8	6 1/8	20 6/8	15 1/8	7/8	6 1/8	11	18	Groundhog Mt., AK	Lloyd H. Richardson	Lloyd H. Richardson	1993	288
418 6/8	53 4/8	55 2/8	42 5/8	6 1/8	6 5/8	6 5/8	19 4/8	6 4/8			15	14	Alaska Pen., AK	V. Leland Richins	V. Leland Richins	1996	288
418 6/8	57 6/8	52 7/8	28 1/8	5 4/8	5 4/8	5 3/8	18 6/8	20 3/8	6 4/8	11	20	17	Slate Creek, AK	John S. Wylie	John S. Wylie	1999	288
418 5/8	50 6/8	49 5/8	32 7/8	5 6/8	5 7/8	5 3/8	19 6/8	20 3/8	28 1/8	27	15	17	Hicks Creek, AK	Charles Brumbelow	Charles Brumbelow	1956	293
418 5/8	50 4/8	49 3/8	37 6/8	5 7/8	5 3/8	6 4/8	20 7/8	19 7/8	12 7/8		15	17	Kenai Mts., AK	Randall Yost	Randall Yost	1996	293
418 4/8	49 5/8	55	38 6/8	7 2/8	7 3/8	5 3/8	20 7/8	19 7/8	5 5/8	14 2/8	15	17	Ivishak River, AK	William O. Dudley	William O. Dudley	1979	295
418 3/8	54 5/8	55	38 6/8	7 3/8	7 2/8	6 3/8	2 3/8	18	7/8	13 4/8	17	19	Chistochina, AK	James H. Lahey	James H. Lahey	1961	296
418 3/8	52 6/8	51 5/8	50 4/8	6 2/8	5 6/8	5 6/8	18 7/8	19	5 5/8	8 2/8	12	13	Rainy Pass, AK	Aaron Saenz, Jr.	Aaron Saenz, Jr.	1964	296
418 3/8	52 7/8	52 5/8	45 5/8	5 6/8	5 6/8	6 7/8	18 7/8	19	5 5/8	9 3/8	15	17	High Lake, AK	Glen E. Park	Glen E. Park	1965	296
418 3/8	47 1/8	46 5/8	39 6/8	7 3/8	7 3/8	6 1/8	12 1/8	19 1/8	1 5/8	15 7/8	15	12	Aleutian Range, AK	Wayne Patton	Wayne Patton	1968	296
418 3/8	53	56	38 7/8	6 6/8	6 5/8	8	19 3/8	11 4/8	1	14 1/8	21	23	Agenuk Mt., AK	James L. Johnson	James L. Johnson	2000	296
418 3/8	50 4/8	51 1/8	37 7/8	5 7/8	5 1/8	20	17 4/8	15 1/8	8 1/8		20	18	Big Susitna, AK	Forrest Boyce	Jack Dustin	1957	296
418 2/8	52 2/8	54 4/8	43 1/8	6 4/8	6	20 5/8	21 2/8	4	15 4/8		14	20	Denali Hwy., AK	Jerry Shepard	Jerry Shepard	1961	301
418 1/8	50 5/8	48 4/8	34 7/8	6	6	18 2/8	16 5/8	16 1/8	8		24	19	Caribou Creek, AK	Gary Joll	Gary Joll	1963	302
418 1/8	53 3/8	50 7/8	39 7/8	7	6 4/8	20	10 5/8	18 4/8	7		23	13	Chistochina, AK	Delbert H. Bullock	Delbert H. Bullock	1964	302
418 1/8	50 2/8	53 2/8	45 3/8	6 3/8	6 2/8	13 6/8	17	2 4/8	14 6/8	5 1/8	22	23	Becharof Lake, AK	William M. Beyl	William M. Beyl	1981	302
418 1/8	57 5/8	55 3/8	41 5/8	6	5 6/8	22	19	9 3/8	5 1/8		11	11	Alaska Range, AK	Richard L. McClellan	Richard L. McClellan	1978	302
418	54 2/8	54	42 7/8	6 3/8	6 1/8	19 7/8	14 1/8	15 7/8	1/8	5 5/8	18	15	Alaska Range, AK	Gary L. Zerbe	Gary L. Zerbe	1981	306
418	54 6/8	53 6/8	47 3/8	7 5/8	7 6/8	17	20 4/8	1/8	14 4/8		12	17	Kenai, AK	Robert D. Lewallen	Robert D. Lewallen	1989	306
417 7/8	48	47 2/8	39 4/8	5 5/8	5 2/8	15 2/8	1 5/8	4 5/8	14 1/8		17	21	Becharof Lake, AK	Fred T. Hecox	Fred T. Hecox	1983	306
417 7/8	50 1/8	54 2/8	38 6/8	5 5/8	7 3/8	19 1/8	1 4/8	17	1 5/8		20	14	Tonzona River, AK	Edward D. Hull	Quint Hull	1987	309
417 7/8	56 6/8	58 5/8	45 4/8	6 1/8	6 3/8	19 1/8	10 7/8	18 5/8	1/8		11	10	Tyone River, AK	Norman C. Wilslef	Norman C. Wilslef	1989	309
417 6/8	52 6/8	54 5/8	45 5/8	6 4/8	5 7/8	16 4/8	20 6/8	13 7/8	20 6/8		23	17	Shotgun Creek, AK	Mrs. Roscoe S. Mosiman	Mrs. Roscoe S. Mosiman	1958	309
417 6/8	51 7/8	50 1/8	42 1/8	6 5/8	6 1/8		16 4/8	12 4/8			13	19	Talkeetna Mts., AK	William J. Miller	William J. Miller	1967	312
417 6/8	55 2/8	60 4/8	46 2/8	5 5/8	6 1/8	15 7/8	21 7/8	13 6/8	9		15	19	Alaska Pen., AK	John M. Glover	John M. Glover	1988	312
417 5/8	57 4/8	57	50 1/8	6 2/8	6 4/8	18 5/8	16 4/8	7 7/8	11 5/8		16	13	Nushagak River, AK	Fred Packer	Fred Packer	1955	312
417 5/8	51 3/8	51 2/8	38 4/8	6 2/8	6 7/8	15 6/8	13 7/8	11 7/8	1/8		15	16	Wrangell Mts., AK	Richard K. Mellon	Richard K. Mellon	1959	315
417 5/8	48 7/8	49 2/8	27 3/8	6 4/8	6 4/8	21 7/8	13 2/8	17 7/8	17		25	26	Alaska Range, AK	Kurt C. Dunn	Kurt C. Dunn	1981	315
417 4/8	56 4/8	56 4/8	38 1/8	5 7/8	6 1/8	19 2/8	4 7/8	11	18		11	14	Tangle Lakes, AK	R.D. Eichenour	R.D. Eichenour	1968	315
417 4/8	48 4/8	48 2/8	41 7/8	7 4/8	7 1/8	17 6/8	18 1/8	12 4/8	13 1/8		19	21	Mulchatna River, AK	Bradley P. Anderson	Bradley P. Anderson	1993	318
417 4/8	47 2/8	50 6/8	38 7/8	5 4/8	5 4/8	18 3/8	18 3/8	12 4/8	13 1/8		17	13	Mulchatna River, AK	Gerald H. Nolen	Peter S. Nolen	1993	318
417 3/8	50 6/8	50 4/8	43	6 1/8	5 6/8	17 4/8	18 1/8	6 1/8	12		12	13	Lake Clark, AK	Samuel B. Webb, Jr.	Samuel B. Webb, Jr.	1960	318
417 3/8	54 2/8	52 3/8	35 2/8	7 6/8	6 3/8	14 6/8	19	7 7/8	15		14	17	Twin Lakes, AK	Herb Klein	Dallas Mus. of Natl. Hist.	1964	321
417 3/8	47 4/8	49 4/8	45 4/8	6 3/8	5 5/8	24 5/8	18 6/8	12 5/8	11 1/8		26	16	Alaska Pen., AK	Tyson Nichols	Tyson Nichols	1979	321
417 3/8	48 4/8	48 2/8	41 7/8	7 6/8	6 3/8	18 4/8	17	12 1/8	3 1/8		17	17	Alaska Pen., AK	L. Irvin Barnhart	L. Irvin Barnhart	1983	321
417 3/8	50 6/8	50 4/8	38 7/8	6 1/8	6 2/8	19 5/8	19	16 1/8	5 5/8		23	21	Fracture Creek, AK	Dennis Brieske	Dennis Brieske	1984	321
417 1/8	54 2/8	52 3/8	36 1/8	6 4/8	6	17 5/8	16 4/8	6	12 5/8		19	22	Mt. Sanford, AK	Gary L. Todd	Gary L. Todd	1984	321
417	47 4/8	48 6/8	40 4/8	6 3/8	6 5/8	20 1/8	3 6/8	15 5/8	1/8		18	13	White River, AK	Roger O. Wyant	Roger O. Wyant	1989	326
417	50 5/8	52 3/8	40 3/8	7 4/8	6 2/8	16 3/8	17 4/8	12 5/8	12		22	19	Chanuk Creek, AK	Sigurd Jensen	Sigurd Jensen	1956	328
417	50	48 6/8	25 3/8	7 6/8	6 2/8	19 5/8	17 1/8	5	11		16	19	Rainy Pass, AK	Fred Bear	Fred Bear	1959	329
417	50 5/8	52 3/8	33 6/8	8 3/8	9 1/8	20	15 4/8	10 4/8	9 5/8		13	17	Little Delta River, AK	Mark H. Young	Mark H. Young	1987	329
417	59 6/8	60 7/8	38 3/8	6 3/8	6 2/8	17 5/8	23 4/8	13 4/8	9		14	16	Mulchatna River, AK	Richard A. Bergman	Richard A. Bergman	1991	329
417	55 1/8	61 5/8	42 5/8	6	5 6/8	21 4/8	17 7/8	11 1/8	10 4/8		18	15	Bonanza Hills, AK	Thomas D. Hess	Thomas D. Hess	1992	329
417	51 5/8	57	39	6 2/8	6 5/8	21 4/8	19 3/8	16 3/8	5 6/8		17	14	Iliamna Lake, AK	Lowell N. Wacker	Lowell N. Wacker	1996	329
416 7/8	51	48	37 2/8	6 4/8	6 5/8	20 6/8	21 4/8	14 4/8	13		21	16	Dillingham, AK	James K. Harrower	James K. Harrower	1961	334
416 7/8	61 3/8	61 4/8	40 1/8	6 3/8	6 3/8	11 1/8	20 2/8	1	14 7/8		13	22	Clarence Lake, AK	James K. Harrower	James K. Harrower	1961	334
416 7/8	61 3/8	60 2/8	42 6/8	5 6/8	6	2 1/8	17 4/8	4/8	12 2/8		13	20	Mulchatna River, AK	Q.D. Edwards	Q.D. Edwards	1987	334

BARREN GROUND CARIBOU
Rangifer tarandus granti

Score	Length of Main Beam R	L	Inside Spread	Circumference at Smallest Place Between Brow and Bez Points R	L	Length of Brow Points R	L	Width of Brow Points R	L	Number of Points R	L	Locality	Hunter	Owner	Date Killed	Rank
416 7/8	52 3/8	55	39 3/8	6 5/8	6 2/8	9 5/8	19 3/8	1/8	15 1/8	12	16	Windy Fork River, AK	William G. Hagerty	William G. Hagerty	1993	334
416 7/8	47 3/8	45 6/8	32 3/8	6	6 1/8	21 1/8	23 1/8	17 1/8	7 1/8	19	22	Nushagak River, AK	Robert D. Henderson	Robert D. Henderson	1994	334
416 6/8	54 3/8	51 7/8	43	8	8	21 1/8	18 5/8	1/8	15 1/8	17	20	Wood River, AK	A. Knutson	A. Knutson	1957	338
416 6/8	59 6/8	57 5/8	45 6/8	5 4/8	5 4/8	4 2/8	21 3/8	1/8	17	11	17	King Salmon, AK	F. Robert Bell	F. Robert Bell	1983	338
416 5/8	56 4/8	58 4/8	41	7	6 6/8	12 2/8	19 3/8	1	14 6/8	15	16	Mulchatna River, AK	R.D. Eichenour	R.D. Eichenour	1968	340
416 5/8	51 2/8	51 4/8	36 4/8	6 4/8	6 5/8	17 7/8	4 5/8	12 3/8	1 4/8	31	21	Alaska Pen., AK	James A. Ford	James A. Ford	1970	340
416 5/8	53 1/8	51 1/8	52	6 5/8	6 5/8	21	14	17	1/8	23	14	Black Lake, AK	Merle L. Schreiner	Merle L. Schreiner	1993	340
416 4/8	56	54	37 5/8	7 4/8	7 6/8	13 6/8	16 2/8	7 3/8	13 2/8	15	21	Rainy Pass, AK	J. Watson Webb, Jr.	J. Watson Webb, Jr.	1934	343
416 4/8	45 1/8	45 7/8	41 4/8	8 4/8	7 6/8	20 7/8	18 6/8	5 1/8	14 4/8	17	21	Upper Ugashik Lake, AK	Russell Matthes	Russell Matthes	1969	343
416 4/8	56 7/8	54 2/8	48 6/8	5 6/8	6	15	19 6/8	3 6/8	10 4/8	13	18	Mulchatna River, AK	Willard L. Hubbard	Willard L. Hubbard	1983	343
416 4/8	49 3/8	52	44 3/8	6 4/8	6 3/8	16 7/8	17 6/8	12	10	18	20	American Pass, AK	Brett G. Alexander	Brett G. Alexander	1984	343
416 4/8	52 3/8	51 6/8	45 1/8	6	6 2/8	1 6/8	17 6/8	1/8	11 2/8	15	20	Lake Clark, AK	James E. Schoudel	James E. Schoudel	1993	343
416 4/8	50 6/8	51	34	7 2/8	6	17 1/8	18	10 3/8	13 6/8	22	21	Iliamna, AK	Tony L. Spriggs	Tony L. Spriggs	1995	343
416 3/8	52 1/8	51 3/8	44 2/8	7 5/8	7 4/8	15 4/8	17 4/8	9	8 3/8	13	17	Talkeetna Mts., AK	Karris Keirn	Karris Keirn	1958	349
416 3/8	53 4/8	52 7/8	38 3/8	6 2/8	5 6/8	18 6/8	19	16 1/8	14 5/8	24	18	Post Clark, AK	Gerald Scheuerman	Gerald Scheuerman	1961	349
416 3/8	58 1/8	59 7/8	46	7 5/8	8 2/8	20 7/8	10 1/8	13 2/8	1/8	13	11	Iliamna Lake, AK	Michael J. Ryan, Sr.	Michael J. Ryan, Sr.	1973	349
416 3/8	49 2/8	49 1/8	43 3/8	6 4/8	6 6/8	13 3/8	16 7/8	1 1/8	9 1/8	17	19	Port Heiden, AK	Charlie Martin	Charlie Martin	1981	349
416 3/8	56 6/8	56 7/8	35 1/8	5 3/8	5 4/8	20 1/8	19	6 3/8	14 6/8	13	18	Blackstone River, YT	Ken Vickerman	Ken Vickerman	1983	349
416 2/8	45 7/8	42 6/8	41 3/8	6 6/8	6 5/8	19 3/8	19 3/8	13 6/8	3 5/8	19	17	Kenakuchuk Creek, AK	Ed I. Zavadlov	Ed I. Zavadlov	1996	354
416 2/8	54 4/8	54 3/8	46 1/8	7 6/8	7	19 3/8	21	13 3/8	4 3/8	17	17	Nushagak River, AK	Shawn L. Wagner	Shawn L. Wagner	1997	354
416 1/8	52 6/8	52 7/8	37 5/8	6 2/8	6 2/8	15 3/8	19 1/8	1 2/8	15 2/8	11	20	Wrangell Mts., AK	William H. Warrick	William H. Warrick	1961	356
416 1/8	54 2/8	56 6/8	46 1/8	7	7	24	20 2/8	16		11	20	Farewell Lake, AK	K.T. Miller	K.T. Miller	1962	356
416 1/8	49 2/8	49 2/8	38 2/8	6 3/8	6 5/8	17 7/8	17 7/8	17 4/8	4 4/8	16	14	Crooked Creek, AK	Bill E. Slone	Bill E. Slone	1964	356
416 1/8	51 2/8	50 4/8	35	5 7/8	5 6/8	19	18 5/8	15	12 2/8	20	22	Little Mulchatna River, AK	M.E. Kulik	M.E. Kulik	1967	356
416 1/8	54 1/8	54 7/8	37 3/8	7 3/8	6 3/8	5	19 2/8	1/8	14 1/8	21	24	Becharof Lake, AK	Todd Rice	Todd Rice	1987	356
416 1/8	50	46	39 2/8	5 5/8	6 2/8	18 3/8	17	14	13 4/8	21	16	Lake Clark, AK	Rainer H. Unger	Rainer H. Unger	1987	356
416 1/8	57 4/8	57 4/8	34 5/8	6 1/8	5 7/8	21 5/8	19	17 4/8	9 7/8	17	16	Blackstone River, YT	Jack Franklin	Jack Franklin	1994	356
416	57 3/8	56 7/8	39 6/8	6 1/8	6 2/8	21 2/8	3 1/8	17 3/8	6/8	17	14	Ugashik, AK	Richard S. Farr	Richard S. Farr	1966	363
416	50 2/8	51 5/8	48	5 5/8	5 4/8	18 1/8	17 6/8	13 5/8	10	19	22	Alaska Pen., AK	Bill E. Hodson	Bill E. Hodson	1978	363
416	50 7/8	50 7/8	40 4/8	9 7/8	7 4/8	18 6/8	6 3/8	15 4/8	1/8	19	16	Stony River, AK	Charles F. Nadler	Charles F. Nadler	1985	363
416	55 2/8	53 5/8	45 3/8	6 3/8	6 3/8	16	16 7/8	10 5/8	10 2/8	25	25	Steese Hwy., AK	Howard Hill	Howard Hill	1958	366
415 7/8	51 2/8	52 6/8	40 3/8	6 1/8	6 2/8	18 2/8	12 6/8	12 7/8	2	14	14	Alaska Pen., AK	Richard A. Bengraff	Richard A. Bengraff	1981	366
415 7/8	64	63 1/8	45 4/8	6 1/8	7 3/8	21 4/8	17 4/8	8	10 7/8	19	12	Becharof Lake, AK	Alfred T. Bachman	Alfred T. Bachman	1989	366
415 7/8	51 5/8	53 2/8	38 2/8	6 7/8	7 1/8	17 2/8	17 6/8	13	11 3/8	21	17	Stuyahok River, AK	Barry N. Zimdars	Barry N. Zimdars	1992	366
415 6/8	50 6/8	47 5/8	40 7/8	5 1/8	5 1/8	19 4/8	16 6/8	13 5/8	12 2/8	19	19	Monsoon Lake, AK	Paul A. Szopa	Paul A. Szopa	1983	370

Score	Locality	Hunter	Owner	Date
415 6/8	Becharof Lake, AK	Paul G. Forslund	Paul G. Forslund	1995
415 5/8	King Salmon River, AK	Robert G. Barta	Robert G. Barta	1978
415 5/8	Whitefish Lake, AK	Jeffrey S. Sorg	Jeffrey S. Sorg	1982
415 4/8	Tyone River, AK	E.H. Miller	E.H. Miller	1956
415 4/8	Egegik River, AK	George J. Markham	George J. Markham	1967
415 4/8	Becharof Lake, AK	Max E. Chittick	Max E. Chittick	1980
415 4/8	Watana Lake, AK	Kurt K. Knutson	Kurt K. Knutson	1981
415 4/8	Hoholitna River, AK	Franklin E. Phillips	Franklin E. Phillips	1997
415 3/8	Nenana River, AK	James H. Hunt	James H. Hunt	1983
415 3/8	Colville River, AK	Edward A. Rabalais	Edward A. Rabalais	1993
415 3/8	Portage Creek, AK	Harry P. Samarin	Harry P. Samarin	1998
415 3/8	Becharof Lake, AK	L. Keith Mortensen	L. Keith Mortensen	1980
415 1/8	Alaska Pen., AK	Picked Up	William P. Bredesen, Jr.	1974
415	Alaska Pen., AK	Herb Klein	Dallas Mus. of Natl. Hist.	1967
414 7/8	Denali Hwy., AK	Paul Patz	Paul Patz	1965
414 6/8	Yanert Fork, AK	Russell W. McInnis	Russell W. McInnis	1988
414 6/8	Post River, AK	Shawn A. Lar	Shawn A. Lar	1998
414 5/8	Rainy Pass, AK	Mahlon T. White	Mahlon T. White	1969
414 5/8	Miner River, YT	Gary L. Selig	Gary L. Selig	1979
414 5/8	Dog Salmon River, AK	Robert G. Good	Robert G. Good	1994
414 4/8	Shotgun Hills, AK	Douglas J. Aikin	Douglas J. Aikin	1995
414 3/8	Iliamna Lake, AK	Timothy F. McGinn	Timothy F. McGinn	1995
414 3/8	Naknek, AK	C.J. McElroy	C.J. McElroy	1966
414 3/8	Denali Hwy., AK	C.W. Hilbish	C.W. Hilbish	1958
414 3/8	Talkeetna Mts., AK	G.W. Berry	G.W. Berry	1960
414 3/8	Alaska Pen., AK	George H. Landreth	George H. Landreth	1967
414 2/8	Alaska Pen., AK	Robert Wessner	Robert Wessner	1969
414 2/8	Lake Clark, AK	Stanley J. Leger	Stanley J. Leger	1986
414 2/8	Tutna Lake, AK	James S. Campbell	James S. Campbell	1987
414 2/8	Nushagak Hills, AK	Robert D. Jones	Robert D. Jones	1991
414 1/8	Taylor Mts., AK	Robert J. Allen	Robert J. Allen	1989
414 1/8	Little Mulchatna River, AK	David B. Nielsen	David B. Nielsen	1992
414 1/8	Kvichak River, AK	Lee R. Nieman	Lee R. Nieman	1998
414 1/8	Clarence Lake, AK	Jack Hill	Jack Hill	1964
414 1/8	Snake River, YT	Leslie Kish	Leslie Kish	1985
414 1/8	Iliamna Lake, AK	Richard J. Sands	Richard J. Sands	1989
414	Koktuli River, AK	Mark B. Nielsen	Mark B. Nielsen	1993
414	Beluga Lake, AK	Ted A. Clark	Ted A. Clark	1997
414	Indian Mt., AK	Jeffrey D. Lapp	Jeffrey D. Lapp	1998
414	Upper Susitna, AK	Harold Gould	Harold Gould	1953
414	Little Nelchina River, AK	Picked Up	Temple Bros. Taxidermy	1954
413 7/8	Johnson River, AK	Donald W. Bunselmeier	Donald W. Bunselmeier	1988
413 6/8	Hart Lake, YT	Curt Curtis	Curt Curtis	1996
413 6/8	Nishlik Lake, AK	Nick J. Helterline	Nick J. Helterline	1994
413 6/8	Alaska Pen., AK	Ira Swartz	Ira Swartz	1967
413 6/8	Wrangell Mts., AK	Robert Reed	Robert Reed	1968
413 6/8	Alaska Pen., AK	Robert A. Patzer	Robert A. Patzer	1992

BARREN GROUND CARIBOU
Rangifer tarandus granti

Score	Length of Main Beam R	L	Inside Spread	Circumference at Smallest Place Between Brow and Bez Points R	L	Length of Brow Points R	L	Width of Brow Points R	L	Number of Points R	L	Locality	Hunter	Owner	Date Killed	Rank
413 5/8	47 6/8	47 5/8	44 6/8	7 4/8	6 6/8	22 6/8	2 7/8	6/8	17 2/8	17	20	King Salmon River, AK	Basil C. Bradbury	B&C National Collection	1967	418
413 5/8	48 4/8	52	33 4/8	5 7/8	5 7/8	16 5/8	17 2/8	13 1/8	15 5/8	22	18	Kuskokwim River, AK	Walther Schmitz	Walther Schmitz	1969	418
413 4/8	50 4/8	50 4/8	38	7	7	18	18	1	16 4/8	19	29	Talkeetna Mts., AK	Louis Mussatto	Louis Mussatto	1964	420
413 4/8	52 1/8	53 2/8	37 4/8	5 5/8	5 2/8	19 2/8	1 6/8	14 3/8	1/8	13	8	Iliamna Lake, AK	Wright W. Allen	Wright W. Allen	1993	420
413 4/8	53 4/8	52 4/8	41 6/8	5 7/8	5 2/8	17 5/8	20 1/8	14 2/8	11	18	20	Grayling Creek, AK	Jack W. McElmurry	Jack W. McElmurry	2002	420
413 3/8	52 3/8	53	44	6	5 6/8	20 4/8	19 6/8	13	1/8	15	12	Denali Hwy., AK	Albert E. Greer	Albert E. Greer	1963	423
413 2/8	55 6/8	57 2/8	44 5/8	6 7/8	6 5/8	18	5 7/8	13 6/8	1/8	19	14	Whitefish Lake, AK	Larry D. Domson	Larry D. Domson	1984	424
413 2/8	53 3/8	54 1/8	39 5/8	6 2/8	6 1/8	4 4/8	19 3/8	1/8	15 5/8	17	19	Dry Tok Creek, AK	Todd A. Brewer	Todd A. Brewer	1994	424
413 1/8	59 3/8	57 3/8	40 5/8	5 5/8	5 7/8	20 5/8	16 6/8	8 7/8	7 6/8	14	14	Tyone River, AK	Walter Elam	Walter Elam	1959	426
413 1/8	50 1/8	49 6/8	37 5/8	6 3/8	7	18 4/8	18 7/8	9 7/8	14 6/8	15	18	Kuskokwim River, AK	Dewey F. Gibson	Dewey F. Gibson	1996	426
413 1/8	52 6/8	54 1/8	36 2/8	6 1/8	6	19 7/8	15	12 6/8	9 2/8	22	18	Lake Clark, AK	Edward W. Threlkeld	Edward W. Threlkeld	1996	426
413	38 6/8	41 7/8	40 2/8	7	6 4/8	16 1/8	17 3/8	12 5/8	8 5/8	17	18	Tangle Lakes, AK	David J. Morlock	David J. Morlock	1956	429
413	61 4/8	60 4/8	45 4/8	6 2/8	6	17 7/8	20 6/8	7 4/8	11 6/8	17	25	Aniakchak Crater, AK	M.G. Johnson	M.G. Johnson	1964	429
413	49 7/8	49 5/8	40 2/8	8 2/8	6 2/8	17 7/8	19	15 6/8	14 7/8	16	20	Mad Creek, AK	Larry G. Hurst	Larry G. Hurst	1992	429
412 7/8	51 2/8	48 7/8	31 6/8	8 6/8	7 5/8	11 6/8	14 4/8	2 5/8	9 6/8	20	28	Rainy Pass, AK	Ernst Von Hake	Ernst Von Hake	1963	432
412 7/8	56 2/8	56 2/8	41	5 6/8	6 3/8	16 2/8	14 6/8	10	7 5/8	18	16	Lake Clark, AK	William F. Rae, Jr.	William F. Rae, Jr.	1968	432
412 7/8	58 5/8	58 3/8	47 2/8	5 5/8	5 7/8	16 4/8	10 7/8	12 1/8	1/8	28	20	Tutna Lake, AK	Ernest C. Noble	Ernest C. Noble	1987	432
412 7/8	46 6/8	46 5/8	37	6 3/8	7 1/8	7 7/8	21 3/8	5 1/8	14 1/8	24	26	Hoholitna River, AK	Dale H. Maass	Dale H. Maass	1992	432
412 6/8	56 4/8	58	47	6 2/8	6 2/8	17	20 4/8	4 2/8	14 5/8	12	15	Alaska Pen., AK	John P. Nelson, Jr.	John P. Nelson, Jr.	1961	436
412 6/8	50 3/8	46 3/8	38 6/8	5 1/8	5 2/8	17 6/8	18 4/8	12 3/8	17 1/8	19	23	Port Moller, AK	Billy W. Green	Billy W. Green	1983	436
412 5/8	47 3/8	53 7/8	33 6/8	8 4/8	9	17 4/8	18 4/8	4 4/8	11 5/8	16	15	Nishlik Lake, AK	Randy L. Jansma	Randy L. Jansma	2003	438
412 4/8	50 3/8	53 7/8	42 2/8	5	5	21 2/8	18 2/8	9 2/8	13 2/8	15	16	Eli River, AK	David R. Lautner	David R. Lautner	1992	439
412 4/8	49 7/8	49	42 3/8	6	6	14 5/8	20 3/8	1/8	10	13	20	Becharof Lake, AK	Terry M. Dittrich	Terry M. Dittrich	1997	439
412 3/8	50 6/8	55 5/8	41 3/8	6 1/8	6	20 6/8	14 6/8	15 4/8	8 6/8	18	13	Twin Lakes, AK	Inge Hill, Jr.	Inge Hill, Jr.	1965	441
412 3/8	61 5/8	62 5/8	50 1/8	5 5/8	5 5/8	22 6/8	8 7/8	14	1/8	18	11	King Salmon, AK	Larry Spiva	Larry Spiva	1983	441
412 3/8	59	60 2/8	40 5/8	5 6/8	5 6/8	21 4/8	23 2/8	15	7 6/8	15	13	Dog Salmon River, AK	John S. Alley	John S. Alley	1987	441
412 3/8	44 2/8	44 5/8	30 3/8	4 7/8	5 7/8	17 2/8	19	4 6/8	17 4/8	20	21	Squirrel River, AK	Jack D. Adams	Jack D. Adams	1991	441
412 3/8	54 4/8	54 6/8	43	5 7/8	6 1/8	21	2 2/8	15 2/8	1/8	18	14	Iliamna Lake, AK	Richard R. Lefler	Richard R. Lefler	1993	441
412 3/8	56 4/8	57	48 5/8	6	6 4/8	4 5/8	18 6/8	1/8	15	14	20	Killey River, AK	Brett A. Aldridge	Brett A. Aldridge	1998	441
412 2/8	59 5/8	58 6/8	24 7/8	8 6/8	8 7/8	19	18 3/8	13 4/8	7	15	13	Slana, AK	William Kiltz	William Kiltz	1959	447
412 2/8	51 5/8	51 6/8	38 4/8	7 7/8	7 4/8	15 4/8	14 6/8	11 1/8	8 2/8	18	18	Gulkana River, AK	Danny K. Shepherd	Danny K. Shepherd	1993	447
412 2/8	47 2/8	46 2/8	44 1/8	7 2/8	7 4/8	15 2/8	16 2/8	11 6/8	14 3/8	21	22	Lake Clark, AK	William E. Pipes III	William E. Pipes III	1995	447
412 1/8	46	46 7/8	25 3/8	7 1/8	6 5/8	17 4/8	17 2/8	5 7/8	13 3/8	18	17	Tay Lake, YT	Dan Newlon	Dan Newlon	1963	450
412 1/8	44	46	44	6 4/8	6 1/8	20 6/8	19 2/8	1/8	16 6/8	17	26	Hoholitna River, AK	Daniel E. Lunde	Daniel E. Lunde	1986	450
412 1/8	54 5/8	51 5/8	47	6 1/8	6 1/8	19 6/8	18 5/8	14 1/8	3 3/8	19	18	Mulchatna River, AK	Sid A. Richards	Sid A. Richards	1993	450
412	43 6/8	47 2/8	40	8	8 3/8	19 6/8	20	13	13 4/8	27	29	Alaska Pen., AK	Paul T. Hartman	Paul T. Hartman	1966	453
411 7/8	57	53 2/8	46 4/8	7 3/8	7	3 3/8	23 3/8	1/8	20	12	21	Talkeetna Mts., AK	Walter J. Wojciuk	Walter J. Wojciuk	1960	454

Score	Length of Main Beam R	Length of Main Beam L	Inside Spread	Locality	Hunter	Owner	Date Killed
411 7/8	59 7/8	60 2/8	49 1/8	Jimmy Lake, AK	Jack M. Matthews	Jack M. Matthews	1966
411 7/8	45 6/8	44 5/8	40	Dog Salmon River, AK	Benny B. Kerns	Benny B. Kerns	1983
411 7/8	53 2/8	55	41 2/8	Becharof Lake, AK	Douglas G. Bonetti	Douglas G. Bonetti	1987
411 7/8	53 6/8	51 1/8	39 1/8	Billy Creek, AK	David L. Richards	David L. Richards	1987
411 6/8	49 6/8	50 1/8	41	Becharof Lake, AK	Gary F. Silc	Gary F. Silc	1995
411 5/8	61 3/8	59 3/8	47	Alaska Pen., AK	H. Sagesser	Berne Mus. Nat. Hist.	1962
411 5/8	53 6/8	57 5/8	48	Big River, AK	Phillip D. Wagner	Phillip D. Wagner	1994
411 4/8	45 3/8	45 5/8	45 7/8	Lake Louise, AK	John Trautner	John Trautner	1960
411 4/8	49	45 7/8	34 1/8	Twin Lakes, AK	Richard R. Oberle	Richard R. Oberle	1973
411 4/8	56 4/8	57	42 2/8	Wood River, AK	Carol L. Schwabland	Carol L. Schwabland	1981
411 4/8	51 4/8	49 5/8	34 3/8	Hartman River, AK	Robert B. Hancock	Robert B. Hancock	1988
411 1/8	57 4/8	56 1/8	45 1/8	King Salmon River, AK	Gordon G. Chittick	Gordon G. Chittick	1994
411	53 3/8	55 5/8	46 4/8	Wood River, AK	Luther W. Palmer	Luther W. Palmer	1984
411	43	43 3/8	32 2/8	Healy, AK	Michael A. Couch	Michael A. Couch	1969
411	55 4/8	56 4/8	35 4/8	Wood River, AK	James C. Midcap	James C. Midcap	1970
410 7/8	59 6/8	55 7/8	54	Tutna Lake, AK	Joseph M. Negri	Joseph M. Negri	1986
410 7/8	53 1/8	49 6/8	36 4/8	Mt. Harper, AK	Gary L. Truitt	Gary L. Truitt	1987
410 7/8	53 5/8	52 4/8	32 7/8	Wrangell Mts., AK	John C. Belcher	John C. Belcher	1956
410 7/8	49 5/8	56 1/8	47 1/8	Talkeetna Mts., AK	Clifford F. Hood	Clifford F. Hood	1958
410 7/8	64 3/8	65 1/8	53 4/8	Becharof Lake, AK	Gordon G. Chittick	Gordon G. Chittick	1981
410 7/8	55 4/8	54 3/8	42 4/8	Ugashik Lake, AK	Christian Heyden	Christian Heyden	1995
410 6/8	60 6/8	58 4/8	47 3/8	Chandalar Lake, AK	L.A. Miller	L.A. Miller	1953
410 6/8	60 3/8	64 2/8	53	Talkeetna Mts., AK	Elgin T. Gates	Elgin T. Gates	1960
410 6/8	53 2/8	54 7/8	40 7/8	Denali Hwy., AK	Ray W. Holler	Ray W. Holler	1965
410 6/8	57 5/8	56 2/8	35	Alaska Pen., AK	Jim Keeler	Jim Keeler	1966
410 6/8	55 4/8	56 5/8	41 1/8	Talkeetna Mts., AK	Melissa A. Everett	Melissa A. Everett	1988
410 5/8	54 3/8	55 3/8	45 1/8	Denali Hwy., AK	J.W. Jett	J.W. Jett	1960
410 5/8	51 7/8	52 4/8	33 6/8	Tanana Valley, AK	Bob Hagel	Bob Hagel	1961
410 5/8	51 4/8	51 4/8	31 3/8	McKinley Nat. Park, AK	Joseph M. Messana	Joseph M. Messana	1968
410 5/8	58 3/8	56 7/8	33 7/8	Wrangell Mts., AK	Lee Chambers	Lee Chambers	1969
410 5/8	49 2/8	47 7/8	35	Hunt River, AK	James W. Styler	James W. Styler	1981
410 5/8	53 4/8	52	43 1/8	Haines Lake, AK	Len F. Onorato	Cabela's, Inc.	1987
410 5/8	57 2/8	57 5/8	48 3/8	Becharof Lake, AK	Marcus C. Deede	Marcus C. Deede	1987
410 4/8	55	53 4/8	36 5/8	Caribou Pass, AK	David E. Krompacky	David E. Krompacky	1997
410 3/8	48 6/8	49 6/8	36 5/8	Lake Clark, AK	Donald J. Hotter III	Donald J. Hotter III	1979
410 3/8	58 2/8	53 7/8	46 3/8	Becharof Lake, AK	Lavon L. Chittick	Lavon L. Chittick	1981
410 3/8	53 7/8	51 2/8	41 7/8	Shotgun Hills, AK	David W. Nelson	David W. Nelson	1995
410 2/8	57 6/8	56	41 4/8	Rainy Pass, AK	Mrs. J. Watson Webb	Mrs. J. Watson Webb	1934
410 2/8	55 2/8	57 4/8	55 1/8	King Salmon, AK	Richard J. Guthrie	Richard J. Guthrie	1979
410 2/8	50 7/8	51	43 3/8	Fog Lakes, AK	Squee Shore	Squee Shore	1958
410	53 6/8	54 7/8	40	Nenana River, AK	Tom Grady	Tom Grady	1961
410	47 5/8	51 7/8	43 6/8	Alaska Pen., AK	C.G. Suits	C.G. Suits	1965
410	54 2/8	59	44 3/8	White River, AK	Dirk E. Brinkman	Dirk E. Brinkman	1974
410	51 7/8	50 7/8	40 2/8	Cinder River, AK	Joe B. Owen	Joe B. Owen	1990
410	51 3/8	51 2/8	37 3/8	Mulchatna River, AK	Scott M. McDowell	Scott M. McDowell	1994
409 7/8	59 5/8	59 7/8	42 4/8	Post Lake, AK	Werner Frey	Werner Frey	1963
409 7/8	56 7/8	55	42 5/8	Mulchatna River, AK	Christine H. Bukowski	Christine H. Bukowski	1992
409 7/8	50	50	54 7/8	Mulchatna River, AK	Lana K. Glowcheski	Lana K. Glowcheski	1994

BARREN GROUND CARIBOU
Rangifer tarandus granti

Score	Length of Main Beam		Inside Spread	Circumference at Smallest Place Between Brow and Bez Points		Length of Brow Points		Width of Brow Points		Number of Points		Locality	Hunter	Owner	Date Killed	Rank
	R	L		R	L	R	L	R	L	R	L					
409 7/8	51	47 6/8	42 1/8	8 4/8	7 5/8	15	22	16 8/8		18	25	Nuyakuk Lake, AK	Roy S. Bowers	Roy S. Bowers	1995	500
409 6/8	54 6/8	52 7/8	27 5/8	6 3/8	6 5/8	15	15 3/8	5 7/8	10 7/8	19	21	Wood River, AK	Stuart L.G. Rees	Stuart L.G. Rees	1983	504
409 6/8	45 3/8	46	34	6 4/8	6	15 3/8	17	10 4/8	10 1/8	19	22	King Salmon, AK	Romaine L. Marshall	Romaine L. Marshall	1993	504
409 6/8	45	45 6/8	31 1/8	13	8 2/8	20	19 6/8	16 4/8	13 1/8	23	22	Becharof Lake, AK	David N. Reppen	David N. Reppen	1993	504
409 6/8	54 7/8	55 5/8	33 2/8	6 7/8	7 6/8	22 5/8	16	16 7/8	1/8	17	14	Tyone Lake, AK	Ralph Marshall	Ralph Marshall	1960	507
409 5/8	46 2/8	48 7/8	47 1/8	6 1/8	5 7/8	21	11	15 6/8	4/8	19	13	Point Moller, AK	John S. Clark	John S. Clark	1966	507
409 5/8	53 2/8	52 3/8	43	6 2/8	6 4/8	19 2/8	16 2/8	13 1/8	5 6/8	15	14	Iliamna Lake, AK	William R. Deiley	William R. Deiley	1984	507
409 5/8	46 2/8	47 1/8	46 6/8	6 3/8	6 3/8	13 7/8	17 1/8	4 6/8	9 3/8	13	15	Whitefish Lake, AK	Thomas M. Krueger	Thomas M. Krueger	1987	507
409 5/8	48	47 1/8	35 6/8	6 3/8	7 4/8	18 4/8	18 4/8	11 1/8	13 1/8	15	25	Alaska Range, AK	James C. Forrest	James C. Forrest	1988	507
409 5/8	44 5/8	48 1/8	28 1/8	6 3/8	6 1/8	17 6/8	17 7/8	14 7/8	9 2/8	23	23	Hicks Lake, AK	Raymond S. George	Raymond S. George	1990	507
409 5/8	49 1/8	51 5/8	36 5/8	6 3/8	6 1/8	17 6/8	14 4/8	6 6/8	10 4/8	14	18	Taylor Mts., AK	Lonnie R. Henriksen	Lonnie R. Henriksen	1995	507
409 4/8	54 6/8	53 6/8	42 4/8	6 6/8	6 6/8	18 2/8	18 3/8	10 3/8	2/8	17	14	Paxton Lake, AK	Gary J. Lundgren	James Lundgren	1950	514
409 4/8	57 3/8	58 2/8	41 1/8	5 7/8	5 7/8	16 2/8	15 7/8	13 2/8	7 7/8	17	17	Port Heiden, AK	Frank W. Ussery, Jr.	Frank W. Ussery, Jr.	1963	514
409 4/8	47 4/8	49 6/8	33 6/8	6 7/8	7 5/8	16 6/8	15 4/8	19 1/8	12 6/8	25	30	Mulchatna River, AK	L. John Sheppard	L. John Sheppard	1991	514
409 4/8	57	53 2/8	35 4/8	6	6	20 5/8	18 4/8	12	12 6/8	21	17	Becharof Lake, AK	Thomas L. Davidson	Thomas L. Davidson	1992	514
409 4/8	44 6/8	43 5/8	40 3/8	7	6 6/8	18 4/8	16 6/8	18 6/8	14 2/8	22	26	Whitefish Lake, AK	Charles E. Trojan	Charles E. Trojan	1992	514
409 3/8	54 5/8	54 7/8	38 3/8	6 3/8	6 3/8	12 1/8	12 5/8	15 3/8	1	20	13	King Salmon River, AK	Lit Ng	Lit Ng	1967	519
409 3/8	55 5/8	53 5/8	35 2/8	6 4/8	6 2/8	24 7/8	12 5/8	15 5/8	1/8	19	13	Alaska Range, AK	James W. Rehm	James W. Rehm	1978	519
409 3/8	45 6/8	47 2/8	28 7/8	9	8	20 3/8	13 2/8	7	5 2/8	28	20	Chisana, AK	James B. Higgins	James B. Higgins	1967	521
409 2/8	53 2/8	53	40 6/8	8	6 2/8	22	19 7/8	12 4/8	12	15	13	Alaska Pen., AK	Herb Klein	Dallas Mus. of Natl. Hist.	1950	521
409 2/8	47 2/8	46 6/8	46	5 5/8	5 5/8	21 3/8	16	15 7/8	1/8	20	24	Alaska Pen., AK	L.W. Bailey	L.W. Bailey	1967	521
409 2/8	51 3/8	56 7/8	39	6 2/8	6	16	17 4/8	14 2/8	1	22	13	King Salmon, AK	Jerry Ida	Jerry Ida	1969	521
409 2/8	52	50 5/8	35 5/8	6 1/8	6 5/8	29 1/8	6 6/8	1/8	14 2/8	15	21	Chulitna River, AK	Cynthia M. Buzby	Cynthia M. Buzby	1990	521
409 1/8	46 2/8	51 5/8	36 1/8	6 5/8	7 7/8	1	18 4/8	9 5/8	13 3/8	21	19	Alaska Pen., AK	Herb Klein	Dallas Mus. of Natl. Hist.	1996	526
409 1/8	51	51	47 2/8	8	7 1/8	16 1/8	18 1/8	15	12 2/8	20	21	King Salmon, AK	Robert E. Deis	Robert E. Deis	1968	526
409 1/8	56 6/8	60	44 4/8	6 5/8	6 5/8	18 2/8	19 7/8	12 2/8	1/8	18	21	Nikabuna Lakes, AK	Stephen E. Warner	Stephen E. Warner	1986	526
409 1/8	48 2/8	51 5/8	43 6/8	6 4/8	6 4/8	19 4/8	2	1/8	5 4/8	15	15	Iliamna Lake, AK	Picked Up	Richard A. Link	1990	526
409 1/8	48 6/8	46 3/8	35 2/8	6	6 1/8	18 5/8	19 1/8	15 6/8	12 4/8	19	17	Chisana Valley, AK	William Burns	William Burns	1963	526
409	55 1/8	54 3/8	41 1/8	11	11	17 7/8	16 7/8	8 4/8	18 1/8	23	21	Port Heiden, AK	D.J. Lehman	D.J. Lehman	1967	530
409	55 1/8	51 6/8	40 2/8	6 2/8	7 5/8	23	9 7/8	18 1/8	1/8	15	11	Kuskokwim River, AK	Thomas B. May	Thomas B. May	1987	530
409	52	51 5/8	40 3/8	7 5/8	7 7/8	19	13 2/8	9 7/8	9 5/8	12	11	Nushagak Hills, AK	David J. Allen	David J. Allen	1993	530
409	52 4/8	53 6/8	36 5/8	6	6	11	19 5/8	1/8	15 1/8	23	18	Muklung Hills, AK	James J. McBride	James J. McBride	1996	530
409	47 6/8	48 1/8	36 2/8	5 5/8	6 2/8	18 3/8	2 5/8	15 6/8	14 4/8	17	13	Funny River, AK	Kam P. St. John	Kam P. St. John	2002	530
409	55	53 7/8	45	6 6/8	5 5/8	18 5/8	17	14 4/8	8 1/8	19	16	Deadman Lake, AK	R.J. Brocker	R.J. Brocker	1950	530
408 7/8	41 6/8	42 7/8	37 5/8	6 6/8	6 6/8	16 1/8	16 1/8	6 5/8	9 7/8	19	19	Talkeetna Mts., AK	R.J. Brocker	R.J. Brocker	1950	536
408 7/8				8 6/8	8 5/8	15 6/8	12 2/8	11	1 1/8	18	16		H.I.H. Prince Abdorreza Pahlavi	H.I.H. Prince Abdorreza Pahlavi	1960	536
408 7/8	49 3/8	43 5/8	41 3/8	5 2/8	5 3/8	17 3/8	17 4/8	2 5/8		16	17	Hart River, YT	Gordon MacRae	Gordon MacRae	1999	536

Score	Main Beam L	Main Beam R	Spread	Circ.	Circ.	Brow/Bez	Brow/Bez	Width	Width	Pts R	Pts L	Locality	Hunter	Owner	Date	Rank
408 6/8	54 4/8	54 7/8	39 6/8	6 4/8	7 1/8	18 1/8	10 7/8	9 7/8	3 3/8	14	13	Ingersol Lake, AK	John A. Du Puis	John A. Du Puis	1973	539
408 6/8	52 1/8	53 7/8	34	8 4/8	7 3/8	17 6/8	17 4/8	12 4/8	4 2/8	18	17	David River, AK	W.K. Leech	W.K. Leech	1979	539
408 6/8	52 2/8	51	39 3/8	10	9 1/8	4	18 7/8	1	12 6/8	14	17	Red Paint Creek, AK	Larry D. Kropf	Larry D. Kropf	1983	539
408 5/8	46 4/8	46 5/8	40 1/8	7	7 4/8	5 6/8	19 4/8	7/8	19 7/8	20	23	Talkeetna Mts., AK	Bill Lachenmaier	Bill Lachenmaier	1961	542
408 5/8	55 5/8	56 2/8	37 3/8	6 2/8	6 4/8	18 4/8	12 6/8	13 5/8	1 3/8	18	14	Lake Clark, AK	J.G. Blow	J.G. Blow	1968	542
408 5/8	48 1/8	49 1/8	35 5/8	7 3/8	7 4/8	17 3/8	21 4/8	9	11 1/8	17	15	Iliamna Lake, AK	David L. Mastolier	David L. Mastolier	1994	545
408 4/8	52 5/8	51	40 3/8	6	6 6/8	12 6/8	18 6/8	1	15 1/8	16	25	Susitna River, AK	Richard G. Drew	Richard G. Drew	1961	545
408 4/8	54 3/8	56 2/8	38 5/8	6 1/8	6 1/8	17 5/8	19 4/8	8 3/8	10 6/8	18	22	Sandy River, AK	Mrs. Ken McConnell	Mrs. Ken McConnell	1966	545
408 4/8	56	49 4/8	40 3/8	6 1/8	5 6/8	3	17 7/8	6 7/8	9	13	15	Alaska Pen., AK	Robert E.L. Wright	Robert E.L. Wright	1978	548
408 3/8	52 3/8	53 6/8	44 3/8	5 5/8	5 5/8	15 6/8	22 5/8	1/8	16 2/8	15	22	Becharof Lake, AK	Pete M. Baughman, Jr.	Pete M. Baughman, Jr.	1984	548
408 3/8	48 5/8	50 6/8	38 4/8	5 7/8	5 7/8	20 7/8	18 6/8	6 2/8	14 3/8	18	23	Port Heiden, AK	Harold L. Moore, Jr.	Harold L. Moore, Jr.	1985	550
408 2/8	50 6/8	51 6/8	35 4/8	6 3/8	6 1/8	13	20 1/8	7 5/8	13 7/8	13	13	Rainy Pass, AK	John S. Howell	John S. Howell	1966	550
408 2/8	52 6/8	52 6/8	50	6	6	15 6/8	14 5/8	11 3/8	4	17	18	Alaska Pen., AK	Robert J. Nellett	Robert J. Nellett	1966	550
408 2/8	58 4/8	59 5/8	48 5/8	6 7/8	6 3/8	20 3/8	20 3/8	8 2/8	8 2/8	19	18	Dog Salmon River, AK	Arlington F. Svoboda	Arlington F. Svoboda	1983	550
408 2/8	52 1/8	51 1/8	37 7/8	7 1/8	6 2/8	15 2/8	18 6/8	7 4/8	9 1/8	14	18	Bruskasna Creek, AK	Rod Boertje	Rod Boertje	1984	550
408 1/8	52 6/8	54	36 4/8	7	7 1/8	21 4/8	16	15	1/8	17	13	Wood River, AK	Max Lukin	Max Lukin	1964	554
408 1/8	53 6/8	52 4/8	39 6/8	5 4/8	5 6/8	7	19 2/8	1/8	13 4/8	12	19	Smelt Creek, AK	Eddie Clark	Eddie Clark	1986	554
408	46 1/8	48 7/8	32 4/8	6 2/8	6 2/8	15 5/8	16 6/8	10	13 7/8	25	30	Aniak River, AK	Renn G. Neilson	Renn G. Neilson	1991	556
408	50 2/8	48 4/8	38	7 1/8	6 3/8	14 4/8	15 1/8	6	7 3/8	17	19	Becharof Lake, AK	James D. Knight	James D. Knight	1992	556
407 7/8	46 1/8	48	41 3/8	9	7 1/8	15 4/8	15 1/8	2 2/8	9 3/8	16	15	Caribou Creek, AK	Donald Kettlekamp	Donald Kettlekamp	1957	558
407 7/8	54 3/8	51	36 1/8	7 1/8	7 1/8	20 4/8	17 5/8	4 7/8	10 4/8	15	18	Alaska Pen., AK	Frank R. Fowler	Frank R. Fowler	1976	558
407 7/8	58 5/8	56	37 1/8	7 2/8	6 6/8	19 2/8	19 4/8	10 2/8	12 6/8	16	22	Kuskokwim River, AK	Robert Jacobsen	Robert Jacobsen	1982	558
407 7/8	49 6/8	54	42 2/8	6 2/8	6 3/8	7 6/8	18 6/8	1/8	14 4/8	15	17	Whitefish Lake, AK	Robert R. King	Robert R. King	1986	558
407 7/8	50 6/8	47 1/8	38 3/8	6 3/8	6 3/8	19 4/8	20 3/8	4 2/8	13 5/8	17	18	Post Lake, AK	Lyle D. Fett	Lyle D. Fett	1988	558
407 7/8	48 1/8	50 4/8	42 7/8	5 6/8	5 7/8	9 6/8	19 1/8	12 3/8	9 6/8	28	28	Mulchatna River, AK	Harold L. Biggs	Harold L. Biggs	1990	558
407 6/8	48 1/8	44 3/8	38 5/8	7 4/8	6 6/8	17 2/8	17 2/8	1/8	11 5/8	16	16	Shotgun Creek, AK	Roger O. Wyant	Roger O. Wyant	1994	558
407 6/8	43	43 7/8	29 4/8	7 3/8	6 2/8	17 7/8	17 7/8	9 6/8	15 4/8	25	22	Fern Lake, AK	Ralph B. Feriani	Ralph B. Feriani	1976	565
407 6/8	55 7/8	54 5/8	30 5/8	6	6 1/8	16 7/8	18 1/8	12 2/8	17 3/8	25	18	Old Man Creek, AK	Gary A. French	Gary A. French	1991	565
407 6/8	57 3/8	55 7/8	39 3/8	6 6/8	7	19 6/8	18	13	7 7/8	18	13	Big Creek, AK	Edwin Epps	Edwin Epps	1993	565
407 6/8	55 4/8	56 1/8	48 5/8	5 3/8	5 6/8	16 3/8	18 1/8	4 4/8	16 1/8	21	16	Noatak River, AK	Christopher J. Sawyer	Christopher J. Sawyer	2000	565
407 5/8	45	49 5/8	46 1/8	7	6 2/8	19 2/8	19	1 5/8	13 7/8	18	15	Butte Creek, AK	James H. Doolittle	James H. Doolittle	1956	569
407 5/8	50 2/8	49 7/8	44 1/8	5 6/8	5 7/8	6	20 7/8	6	3 4/8	15	13	Becharof Lake, AK	Max E. Chittick	Max E. Chittick	1981	569
407 5/8	55	52 4/8	40 3/8	6 7/8	6 7/8	17 4/8	13 4/8	6 6/8	6 6/8	15	16	Reindeer Lake, AK	Earl C. Christiansen	E.C. & D. Christiansen	1993	569
407 4/8	58 1/8	56 6/8	45 1/8	6 5/8	7 1/8	19	5	12 2/8	3/8	11	13	Alaska Pen., AK	Peter Serafin	Peter Serafin	1966	572
407 4/8	51 7/8	50 4/8	35 4/8	6 5/8	6 7/8	1 1/8	20 4/8	1/8	16	16	16	Adak Island, AK	Delbert R. Oney	Delbert R. Oney	2003	572
407 3/8	57	55 5/8	44 4/8	6	6	16 6/8	2 6/8	12 2/8	1/8	20	20	Tetlin River, AK	O.F. Goeke	O.F. Goeke	1954	574
407 3/8	50	47 3/8	34 1/8	6 2/8	5 6/8	14 4/8	14 4/8	3 3/8	10 2/8	14	20	Chisana, AK	Lewis S. Kunkel, Jr.	Lewis S. Kunkel, Jr.	1964	574
407 3/8	56 3/8	56 6/8	43 2/8	5 7/8	6 2/8	19 3/8	12 6/8	16	1	30	30	Ugashik Lakes, AK	Gary J. Gray	Gary J. Gray	1981	574
407 3/8	48 3/8	49 3/8	40 2/8	6 1/8	6 2/8	19 1/8	21 6/8	13 2/8	9 4/8	19	19	Wolf Lake, AK	R. Douglas Isbell	R. Douglas Isbell	1993	574
407 3/8	49 5/8	51	41 1/8	7	6 3/8	17 1/8	19 5/8	8 1/8	13 3/8	14	14	Mulchatna River, AK	Richard D. Larson	Richard D. Larson	1994	574
407 2/8	47	49	35 4/8	8 5/8	6 6/8	19	16 6/8	15 3/8	5 1/8	22	15	Snowshoe Lake, AK	John P. Hale	John P. Hale	1962	579
407 2/8	47 6/8	50	31 6/8	6 2/8	6 5/8	8 1/8	17	7/8	13 2/8	22	24	Chandler Lake, AK	Steve Scheidness	Steve Scheidness	1974	579
407 2/8	49 1/8	44 6/8	34 1/8	7	6 7/8	16 3/8	8 3/8	11	1/8	22	16	Lake Clark, AK	Arthur L. Patterson	Arthur L. Patterson	1978	579
407 2/8	62 4/8	58 7/8	45 5/8	5 6/8	6	8 7/8	15 5/8	5 6/8	12 6/8	12	12	Kanuti River, YT	Leslie A. Olson	Leslie A. Olson	1981	579
407 2/8	53 2/8	52 2/8	44 1/8	6 2/8	6 2/8	12 3/8	19 5/8	1/8	18 4/8	25	14	Brooks Range, AK	Carol Kilian	Carol Kilian	1987	579
407 1/8	55	57 3/8	38 6/8	6 3/8	6 1/8	22	9 3/8	15	1/8	18	14	Mulchatna River, AK	James E. Stenga	James E. Stenga	1997	585
407 1/8	53 4/8	51 4/8	38 1/8	6 1/8	5 6/8	20 4/8	16 3/8	14 5/8	1	22	18	Mt. Watana, AK	James A. Jana	James A. Jana	1966	585
407 1/8	51 2/8	55 4/8	33	7 7/8	7 2/8	19 3/8	6 4/8	14 3/8	1/8	23	14	Charley River, AK	John J. Holcomb	John J. Holcomb	1997	585

BARREN GROUND CARIBOU
Rangifer tarandus granti

Score	Length of Main Beam R	L	Inside Spread	Circumference at Smallest Place Between Brow and Bez Points R	L	Length of Brow Points R	L	Width of Brow Points R	L	Number of Points R	L	Locality	Hunter	Owner	Date Killed	Rank
407	52	54 2/8	35 4/8	6 4/8	6 1/8	21 4/8	19 1/8	13 5/8	5 6/8	18	16	Farewell Lake, AK	Ken Golden	Ken Golden	1962	587
407	51 3/8	49 2/8	42	5 6/3	6 1/8	20 5/8	19 3/8	11 3/8	13 3/8	13	16	Dog Salmon River, AK	Jack A. Wilkinson	Jack A. Wilkinson	1989	587
407	51 5/8	51 5/8	45	6	5 7/8	20 3/8	22	10	10 1/8	14	15	Becharof Lake, AK	Max E. Chittick	Max E. Chittick	1994	587
406 7/8	52	52 6/8	44 3/8	8 2/3	8	16 3/8	18 4/8	6 4/8	10 3/8	15	14	Cantwell, AK	W.F. Shoemaker	W.F. Shoemaker	1958	590
406 7/8	51 1/8	54	50 3/8	6 5/8	6 5/8	5 1/8	19 6/8	1/8	5 1/8	14	19	Hoholitna River, AK	Shawn T. Brown	Shawn T. Brown	1988	590
406 6/8	47 3/8	47 7/8	30	5 7/3	6 3/8	19	22 1/8	4 4/8	16 1/8	15	21	Hart River, YT	Daniel J. Galles	Daniel J. Galles	2002	592
406 4/8	46 2/8	47 1/8	41 3/8	7	7	16 1/8	14 4/8	4	8 2/8	21	20	Denali Hwy., AK	D.L. Lucas	D.L. Lucas	1957	593
406 4/8	48 7/8	52 6/8	32 7/8	5 6/8	6 1/8	15 3/8	23 1/8	1/8	18 4/8	15	18	King Salmon, AK	Joe B. Reynolds	Joe B. Reynolds	1981	593
406 4/8	53 7/8	54	34 1/8	5 2/8	6 1/8	20 5/8	21	14	6 4/8	18	14	Stony River, AK	William T. Mailer	William T. Mailer	1993	593
406 3/8	51 3/8	52 7/8	39 2/8	6 3/8	6 5/8	18 6/8	19 2/8	12 2/8	12 7/8	17	17	Matanuska Valley, AK	James W. Wright	Thomas J. Wright	1956	596
406 3/8	53 6/8	55 4/8	41 6/8	6	6	18	1	1/8	12 6/8	16	18	Kuskokwim River, AK	C. & D. Harms	Cheryl Harms	1967	596
406 3/8	65 4/8	59 2/8	57 4/8	6 6/8	6 6/8	1 4/8	17 4/8	1/8	12	17	22	Becharof Lake, AK	Gordon G. Chittick	Gordon G. Chittick	1980	596
406 3/8	49 5/8	50 6/8	50 6/8	6 2/8	5 5/8	18	7 3/8	13 2/8	5	23	17	Alaska Pen., AK	Harace R. Morgan	Harace R. Morgan	1980	596
406 3/8	49 7/8	50 2/8	50 3/8	7 4/8	7 4/8	17 6/8	19 2/8	2 3/8	15 2/8	14	13	Stuyahok River, AK	John C. Vickers	John C. Vickers	1991	596
406 2/8	51 7/8	53	28 6/8	6	6 2/8	24 4/8	18 6/8	10 1/8	8 5/8	14	13	Talkeetna Mts., AK	Herb Klein	Dallas Mus. of Natl. Hist.	1960	601
406 2/8	48	50	35 6/8	7 4/8	8	20 2/8	19 6/8	5 6/8	13	13	16	Lake Louise, AK	Eugene Fetzer	Eugene Fetzer	1961	601
406 2/8	54 1/8	50 6/8	43	5 5/8	6	19 6/8	20 3/8	8 2/8	12 3/8	13	16	Alaska Range, AK	Chuck A. Oeleis	Chuck A. Oeleis	2000	601
406 1/8	52 2/8	50	44 3/8	7 6/8	6 3/8	16 4/8	4 1/8	13 4/8	1/8	14	18	Moller Bay, AK	Harry H. Webb	Harry H. Webb	1953	604
406 1/8	50 2/8	52	45 7/8	5 6/8	5	21 4/8	17 2/8	17 4/8	13 2/8	20	16	Ugashik Lakes, AK	John A. Moody	John A. Moody	1983	604
406 1/8	56 5/8	56 5/8	51 2/8	6 2/8	5 5/8	19 1/8		15		16	16	Kvichak River, AK	John Jondal	John Jondal	1991	604
406 1/8	44 7/8	44	38	8 3/8	7 3/8	18 3/8			13	22	30	Big River, AK	Steven F. Lesikar	Steven F. Lesikar	1992	604
406 1/8	52 7/8	51 4/8	39 3/8	6 7/8	6 7/8	1 2/8	21 5/8	1/8	16 4/8	13	20	Killey River, AK	Roger H. Rosin	Roger H. Rosin	1997	604
406	50	49 7/8	30 5/8	7 7/8	5 6/8	6 4/8	19 5/8	1	15 2/8	14	19	Squaw Creek, AK	Elmo Strickland	Elmo Strickland	1960	609
406	50 4/8	47 3/8	36 1/8	7 4/8	7 2/8	23	11	18 3/8	1	17	12	Lake Louise, AK	C.J. Sullivan	C.J. Sullivan	1960	609
406	51 2/8	51 6/8	47 1/8	6 5/8	6 4/8	14	15 5/8	10 6/8	8	16	16	Fairbanks, AK	H.A. Cox, Jr.	H.A. Cox, Jr.	1968	609
406	58	53 1/8	46 6/8	6 6/8	6 6/8	16 7/8	15 4/8	12	1/8	13	10	Kenai, AK	Ernest A. Stirman	Ernest A. Stirman	1981	609
406	47 3/8	59 2/8	45	7 1/8	6 7/8	5 6/8	20 2/8	1 6/8	15	15	19	Black Lake, AK	William S. Lenz	William S. Lenz	1994	609
406	51 6/8	52	36	5 3/8	5 6/8	18 7/8	17 5/8	2 6/8	10 6/8	14	17	Hook Creek, AK	D. Alan Shreves	D. Alan Shreves	1996	609
405 7/8	57 2/8	58 4/8	57	6	6	19	11 6/8	11 6/8		15	16	Becharof Lake, AK	Max E. Chittick	Max E. Chittick	1983	615
405 7/8	47 4/8	43 2/8	39 1/8	7	6 2/8	18 2/8	18	12	3 2/8	15	17	Lake Clark, AK	Anthony Appel	Ronald Appel	1991	615
405 6/8	53 7/8	52	43	6 2/8	7 4/8	18 7/8	19	17 1/8	12	18	16	Taylor Mts., AK	John Burcham	John Burcham	1988	617
405 6/8	44 2/8	50 3/8	43 3/8	5 4/8	6 1/8	13	15 3/8	8 5/8	11 1/8	20	18	King Salmon, AK	Brett D. Mattson	Brett D. Mattson	1994	617
405 5/8	47 4/8	51 2/8	45 2/8	6 3/8	6 2/8	6 1/8	17 1/8	11 1/8	2/8	20	16	Paxton, AK	Maurice A. Stafford	Maurice A. Stafford	1956	619
405 5/8	47 7/8	48 7/8	36 4/8	5 6/8	5 6/8	17 3/8	19 6/8	2	16 6/8	17	24	Port Heiden, AK	James V. Pepa	James V. Pepa	1968	619
405 5/8	60 4/8	42 2/8	42 2/8	5 7/8	5 6/8	19 4/8	16 2/8	14 1/8	1 4/8	20	12	Joseph Creek, AK	Madeline M. Kelleyhouse	Madeline M. Kelleyhouse	1984	619
405 4/8	54 1/8	52 5/8	44 2/8	5 7/8	5 5/8	20 4/8	3	13	1	17	14	Denali Hwy., AK	Edna Conegys	Edna Conegys	1958	622

Score	Locality	Hunter	Owner	Date	Rank
405 4/8	Little Nelchina, AK	Simon Jensen	Simon Jensen	1960	622
405 4/8	Mesa Mt., AK	Robert E. Lieberum	Robert E. Lieberum	1988	622
405 3/8	Becharof Lake, AK	Roy Ruiz	Roy Ruiz	1987	625
405 3/8	Dog Salmon River, AK	Earl T. Sweig	Earl T. Sweig	1992	625
405 3/8	Stuyahok River, AK	A. Mark Horvat	A. Mark Horvat	1993	625
405 2/8	Ochetna River, AK	Elbert E. Husted	Elbert E. Husted	1962	628
405 2/8	Alaska Pen., AK	Jose Garcia	Jose Garcia	1971	628
405 2/8	Mulchatna River, AK	Thomas J. Gallo	Thomas J. Gallo	1983	628
405 2/8	Lake Clark, AK	Jeff LaBour	Jeff LaBour	1991	628
405 1/8	Wood River, AK	Herb Klein	Dallas Mus. of Natl. Hist.	1955	632
405 1/8	Denali Hwy., AK	W. Auckland	W. Auckland	1958	632
405 1/8	Rainy Pass, AK	W.D. Vogel	W.D. Vogel	1958	632
405 1/8	Talkeetna Mts., AK	Digvijay Sinh	Digvijay Sinh	1963	632
405 1/8	Bear Lake, AK	Ruth S. Kennedy	Ruth S. Kennedy	1983	632
405 1/8	Iliamna, AK	Fred W. Amyotte	Fred W. Amyotte	1987	632
405 1/8	Nushagak Hills, AK	Curtis C. Johnson	Curtis C. Johnson	1992	632
405 1/8	Swan Lake, AK	Tanya N. Dickinson	Tanya N. Dickinson	2003	632
405	Susitna Valley, AK	E. Michael Rusten	E. Michael Rusten	1948	640
405	Port Heiden, AK	Lee W. Richie	Lee W. Richie	1963	640
405	Wrangell Mts., AK	Roger H. Belke	Roger H. Belke	1974	640
405	Stevens Creek, AK	John T. Lunenschloss	John T. Lunenschloss	1987	640
405	Hoholitna River, AK	Eugene R. Lewis	Eugene R. Lewis	1993	640
405	Nishlik Lake, AK	Jim P. Manley	Jim P. Manley	1995	640
405	Nushagak River, AK	Kurt D. Voge	Kurt D. Voge	1996	640
405	Goodpastor River, AK	Allen E. Bird	Allen E. Bird	1997	640
404 7/8	Wrangell Mts., AK	J.D. Waring	J.D. Waring	1959	648
404 7/8	Iliamna Lake, AK	Myron E. Wackler	Myron E. Wackler	1990	648
404 7/8	Harris Creek, AK	Brian M. Winter	Brian M. Winter	1994	648
404 6/8	Alaska Pen., AK	W.T. Yoshimoto	W.T. Yoshimoto	1961	651
404 6/8	Alaska Pen., AK	M.C. Worster	M.C. Worster	1963	651
404 6/8	King Salmon, AK	Henry A. Elias	Henry A. Elias	1965	651
404 6/8	King Salmon, AK	Paul Hopkins	Paul Hopkins	1973	651
404 6/8	Lake Clark, AK	Douglas W. Butler	Douglas W. Butler	1980	651
404 6/8	Cathedral Valley, AK	Victor M. Koenig	Victor M. Koenig	1981	651
404 6/8	Becharof Lake, AK	Dan M. Rudanovich	Dan M. Rudanovich	1983	651
404 6/8	Mulchatna River, AK	Daryl Stanley	Daryl Stanley	1988	651
404 6/8	Taylor Mts., AK	Wayne W. Woods	Wayne W. Woods	1993	651
404 6/8	Taylor Hwy., AK	Charles C. Parsons	Charles C. Parsons	1950	651
404 6/8	Taylor Hwy., AK	John C. Howard	John C. Howard	1960	651
404 5/8	Talkeetna Mts., AK	J.W. Lawson	J.W. Lawson	1965	660
404 5/8	Wood River, AK	Robert D. Hancock, Jr.	Robert D. Hancock, Jr.	1983	660
404 5/8	Kobuk River, AK	Ron Herring	Ron Herring	2000	660
404 5/8	Wrangell Mts., AK	William B. Henley, Jr.	William B. Henley, Jr.	1962	660
404 4/8	Alaska Pen., AK	Peter Roemer	Camp Fire Club of America	1970	660
404 4/8	Black River, AK	Alfred E. Wochner	Alfred E. Wochner	1981	665
404 4/8	Becharof Lake, AK	William Cade	William Cade	1984	665
404 4/8	Moose Creek, AK	Dee Sanderson	Chuck J. Sanderson	1988	665
404 4/8	Chilchitna River, AK	Mark S. Woltanski	Mark S. Woltanski	1988	665

BARREN GROUND CARIBOU
Rangifer tarandus granti

Score	Length of Main Beam R	L	Inside Spread	Circumference at Smallest Place Between Brow and Bez Points R	L	Length of Brow Points R	L	Width of Brow Points R	L	Number of Points R	L	Locality	Hunter	Owner	Date Killed	Rank
404 4/8	54 2/8	51	41 6/8	6 1/8	7 1/8	15 5/8	15 4/8	12 6/8	1 6/8	14	16	Titnuk Creek, AK	David O. Tinlin	David O. Tinlin	1992	665
404 4/8	51	48 5/8	32 7/8	6 3/8	6 7/8	12 4/8	18 2/8	1/8	13 6/8	17	27	Mulchatna River, AK	Robert W. Stoeckmann	Robert W. Stoeckmann	1997	665
404 3/8	52 1/8	52 3/8	46 4/8	6 3/8	6 3/8	19	6/8	13 6/8	5/8	20	15	Wood River, AK	C.A. Stenger	C.A. Stenger	1968	673
404 3/8	50 5/8	51	47 1/8	4 7/8	4 7/8	14 1/8	13 4/8	14 1/8	6 6/8	25	14	Brooks Range, AK	Dwight C. Davis	Dwight C. Davis	1984	673
404 3/8	49 3/8	51 2/8	34 7/8	6	5 7/8	16 6/8	18 3/8	5	10 5/8	12	18	Grant River, AK	Clifford R. Caldwell	Clifford R. Caldwell	1995	673
404 3/8	46 7/8	45 6/8	37 3/8	6 3/8	6	14	15	2 5/8	9 1/8	20	24	Brooks Range, AK	Dale E. Helmbrecht	Dale E. Helmbrecht	2003	673
404 2/8	48	48	34 2/8	5 3/8	5 2/8	15 2/8	16 2/8	3 5/8	12 2/8	17	24	Upper Susitna, AK	Elmer M. Rusten	Elmer M. Rusten	1950	677
404 2/8	38 4/8	37	36 4/8	6	6 3/8	16 3/8	16 2/8	14 3/8	14 2/8	21	22	Talkeetna Mts., AK	Ken Oldhem	Ken Oldhem	1959	677
404 2/8	58 6/8	58 5/8	59 4/8	5 4/8	5 5/8	18 7/8	4 6/8	16 2/8	1/8	20	12	Port Heiden, AK	Jon B. Chaney	Jon B. Chaney	1962	677
404 2/8	52 1/8	52 6/8	38 6/8	7 2/8	7 3/8	22 5/8	16 4/8	7 3/8	10	15	16	Oshetna River, AK	Marven A. Henriksen	Marven A. Henriksen	1962	677
404 1/8	55	52 4/8	41	6 3/8	6 1/8	17 1/8	18	13 2/8	11 6/8	19	22	Nabesna, AK	B.C. Varner	B.C. Varner	1955	681
404 1/8	45 2/8	48	41	7	6 4/8	18 7/8	18 4/8	14 7/8	14 3/8	18	16	Wood River, AK	Berry B. Brooks	Berry B. Brooks	1958	681
404 1/8	53 5/8	51 6/8	39 6/8	7 3/8	6 7/8	15 4/8	18 1/8	1/8	15 5/8	19	24	Kvichak River, AK	John Jondal	John Jondal	1988	681
404 1/8	54 2/8	52 6/8	37 6/8	7 1/8	5 6/8	16 5/8	18 7/8	2 4/8	15 3/8	19	21	Nushagak Hills, AK	David W. Hanna	David W. Hanna	1993	681
404	52	55 2/8	36 2/8	8	8 4/8	19 5/8	17	9 4/8	13 1/8	17	15	Salmon Mts., YT	Earl Faas	Earl Faas	1960	685
403 7/8	52 1/8	52 4/8	32	5 5/8	6	3 5/8	16 6/8	1 1/8	11 7/8	22	22	Butte Creek, AK	John R. Copenhaver	John R. Copenhaver	1956	686
403 7/8	50 2/8	50 6/8	43 5/8	5 7/8	5 4/8	22 5/8	21 3/8	18	1 6/8	21	15	Port Moller, AK	Melvin Hetland	Melvin Hetland	1962	686
403 7/8	57 6/8	52 6/8	30	11	6 7/8	21 3/8	21	12	8	13	14	Cantwell, AK	Ben Bearse	Ben Bearse	1968	686
403 7/8	47 5/8	44 2/8	44	6	5 6/8	2 4/8	14 4/8	1/8	11 4/8	16	18	Halfway Mt., AK	Richard S. Hembroff	Richard S. Hembroff	1974	686
403 7/8	38 6/8	41 5/8	37 1/8	7 3/8	6 7/8	15	13 7/8	7	5 7/8	22	20	Holitna River, AK	Tony Weiss	Tony Weiss	1979	686
403 6/8	41 2/8	43 6/8	27 1/8	6 2/8	6 5/8	16 6/8	17 2/8	9 7/8	14 2/8	21	25	Talkeetna Mts., AK	Joe Nevins	Joe Nevins	1958	691
403 6/8	52 6/8	52 6/8	29 3/8	6 4/8	6 5/8	19 5/8	15 1/8	14 3/8	1	20	14	Denali Hwy., AK	Robert R. Opland	Robert R. Opland	1959	691
403 6/8	48 5/8	47 2/8	44 5/8	6 6/8	6 2/8	19	18	13	13 5/8	15	19	Denali Hwy., AK	Jim Carpenter	Jim Carpenter	1960	691
403 6/8	47 7/8	47 4/8	44 2/8	6 1/8	5 7/8	18 2/8	2 2/8	13 2/8	6/8	23	16	Port Heiden, AK	Gene Gall	Gene Gall	1967	691
403 6/8	52 7/8	52 1/8	34	6 7/8	7	20 1/8	17 5/8	10 2/8	9 2/8	16	13	Tyone River, AK	Frederick W. Fernelius	Frederick W. Fernelius	1981	691
403 6/8	51	49 6/8	46 3/8	6 2/8	6 6/8	16 5/8	18 4/8	7 2/8	8 4/8	15	19	Alaska Pen., AK	J. Leslie Rainey	J. Leslie Rainey	1989	691
403 6/8	54 1/8	53 2/8	40	5 3/8	5 2/8	17 4/8	13 4/8	16 3/8	5 1/8	21	19	Omar River, AK	S. Preston Kelley	S. Preston Kelley	1997	691
403 5/8	49 7/8	46 6/8	33 4/8	7 6/8	7 7/8	16 7/8	2 1/8	8 2/8	6	22	18	Tyone Lake, AK	Ralph Marshall	Ralph Marshall	1957	698
403 5/8	49 6/8	48 2/8	52 2/8	6 6/8	6 6/8	19	19	13	4/8	22	20	Talkeetna Mts., AK	Joe Van Daalwyk	Joe Van Daalwyk	1957	698
403 5/8	51 5/8	50 6/8	34 6/8	6 1/8	6 4/8	15	14	8 6/8	6 7/8	21	21	Lake Louise, AK	Marvin Kocurek	Marvin Kocurek	1961	698
403 5/8	57 6/8	57 2/8	46 3/8	5 6/8	6	20 4/8	19 7/8	11 2/8	14 5/8	15	15	King Salmon, AK	Gary A. Markofer	Gary A. Markofer	1986	698
403 5/8	44 5/8	45 1/8	27 4/8	6 7/8	6 7/8	19 6/8	3 3/8	14 2/8	2 2/8	15	12	Mulchatna River, AK	William H. Basil	William H. Basil	1987	698
403 5/8	47 4/8	50 7/8	37	7 6/8	6 7/8	13 6/8	13 6/8	10 1/8	13 2/8	18	20	New Stuyahok, AK	Lawrence E. Hodel	Lawrence E. Hodel	1996	698
403 4/8	43 5/8	42 7/8	29 6/8	7 4/8	7 4/8	26 4/8	21	15 4/8	5 2/8	18	14	Tazlina, AK	Harry L. Swank, Jr.	Mrs. Harry L. Swank, Jr.	1959	704
403 4/8	50 1/8	50 6/8	39 7/8	6 2/8	6 3/8	13	21	1/8	17 2/8	14	19	Port Heiden, AK	Mrs. Jon B. Chaney	Mrs. Jon B. Chaney	1962	704
403 4/8	53 5/8	55 3/8	49 6/8	5 7/8	6	15 5/8	17 1/8	11 6/8	11 4/8	14	17	Alaska Pen., AK	Gerald Roland Gold	Gerald Roland Gold	1977	704

Score	Length of Main Beam R	Length of Main Beam L	Inside Spread	Circ. R	Circ. L	Width R	Width L	Length R	Length L	Points R	Points L	Locality	Hunter	Owner	Date Killed	Rank
403 4/8	60 4/8	60 5/8	59 5/8	5 6/8	5 4/8	27 6/8	21 5/8	15	1/8	13	9	Becharof Lake, AK	Max E. Chittick	Max E. Chittick	1979	704
403 4/8	49 1/8	49 7/8	32 1/8	7	6 7/8	19 1/8	18 2/8	4 7/8	12 1/8	15	21	Kotsetna River, AK	Kevin J. Bores	Kevin J. Bores	1987	704
403 3/8	51	53 1/8	41	5 7/8	5 2/8	16 7/8	17 6/8	10 5/8	10 2/8	19	21	Nishlik Lake, AK	Adam J. Cummings	Adam J. Cummings	1994	709
403 3/8	49 4/8	49	35 4/8	6 7/8	6 1/8	18	18 3/8	13 5/8	8 2/8	23	20	Iliamna Lake, AK	Denton S. Haynes	Denton S. Haynes	1994	709
403 2/8	56 6/8	50	42 2/8	6 2/8	6	16 1/8	18 5/8	8	12 4/8	19	21	Deadman Lake, AK	Charles R. Green	Charles R. Green	1959	711
403 2/8	49 1/8	48 4/8	38 5/8	6 3/8	6 2/8	16 4/8	19 7/8	5 7/8	14 7/8	17	19	Eureka, AK	James S. Evans	James S. Evans	1960	711
403 2/8	59	59 3/8	42 4/8	5 1/8	5 1/8	20 7/8	22 3/8	13 4/8	8 3/8	16	14	Nusagagak River, AK	Karen L. Morris	Karen L. Morris	1991	711
403 2/8	48 2/8	47	48 5/8	7 4/8	5 1/8	16 7/8	20 7/8	9 4/8	4 5/8	19	18	Stuyahok River, AK	John M. Arkley	John M. Arkley	1994	711
403 2/8	51	45 7/8	42 2/8	6 7/8	6 4/8	18 1/8	17 1/8	11 4/8	6	15	12	King Salmon, AK	James L. Corriea	James L. Corriea	1996	711
403 1/8	49 1/8	49 2/8	37 7/8	5 4/8	5 3/8	20 4/8	8 7/8	16	1/8	27	19	Pear Lake, AK	William M. Sowers	William M. Sowers	1981	716
403 1/8	54 5/8	51 5/8	45 6/8	6	6	22 4/8	16 6/8	14 4/8	1 7/8	14	14	Becharof Lake, AK	Linda J. McBride	Linda J. McBride	1988	716
403 1/8	46 5/8	49 4/8	34 4/8	8 3/8	7 1/8	15 4/8	12 6/8	14	7 6/8	30	24	Lake Clark, AK	Michael L. Brandt	Michael L. Brandt	1994	716
403 1/8	49 5/8	48 7/8	41 3/8	5 6/8	5 4/8	16 5/8	14 5/8	8 7/8	11	17	16	Tunkaleshna Creek, AK	Michael E. Craig	Michael E. Craig	1997	716
403	53 2/8	50 2/8	43 6/8	6 1/8	6 1/8	14 5/8	4 2/8	1 7/8	8 1/8	13	10	Deadman Lake, AK	E.C. Lentz	E.C. Lentz	1955	720
403	56 4/8	54 7/8	39 1/8	7	7	18 6/8	14	14	1/8	20	10	Wood River, AK	Norman L. Akau, Jr.	Norman L. Akau, Jr.	1980	720
403	48 4/8	47 4/8	47 5/8	6 2/8	5 5/8	15 3/8	15 2/8	10 4/8	13 5/8	21	23	Brooks Range, AK	Jerry Imperial	Jerry Imperial	1985	720
403	62 5/8	63 3/8	37 6/8	5 7/8	6 1/8	16 2/8	19 5/8	3 4/8	10 1/8	12	16	Hoholitna River, AK	Patrick Meitin	Patrick Meitin	1993	720
402 7/8	48	46 4/8	28 6/8	8	8	11 7/8	11 7/8	0/8	17 1/8	17	25	Ogilvie Mts., YT	E.J. Miller	E.J. Miller	1956	724
402 7/8	54 5/8	54 6/8	41 3/8	5 2/8	5 2/8	19 4/8	19 6/8	14 7/8	11 7/8	18	17	Nelchina, AK	Chris Klineburger	Chris Klineburger	1957	724
402 7/8	53 1/8	56 6/8	37	6 3/8	6 6/8	13 4/8	13 4/8	16 4/8	11 7/8	19	19	Sheep Creek, AK	David J. Palonis	David J. Palonis	1987	724
402 7/8	44	45 1/8	43 4/8	5 6/8	5 4/8	19 4/8	6 3/8	14 1/8	14 1/8	22	20	Grant Lake, AK	Daniel P. Schilkey	Daniel P. Schilkey	1991	724
402 7/8	49	54	33	7 1/8	7	15 6/8	14 6/8	9	0/8	15	18	Rainy Pass, AK	Daniel P. Harrington	Daniel P. Harrington	1996	724
402 6/8	52	50 4/8	43 4/8	5	4 7/8	15 2/8	16	8 4/8	7 2/8	22	18	Ugashik Lakes, AK	William Sleith	William Sleith	1961	729
402 6/8	53 6/8	51 6/8	51	5 7/8	5 5/8	2 3/8	19 1/8	8 4/8	15 3/8	14	14	King Salmon, AK	Vincent T. Ciaburri	Vincent T. Ciaburri	1977	729
402 6/8	59 4/8	58 3/8	54 6/8	5 7/8	5 5/8	21 2/8	14 6/8	15 3/8	5 3/8	17	13	Egegik, AK	Daniel R. Nilles	Daniel R. Nilles	1985	729
402 6/8	46 2/8	47 1/8	34 4/8	5 4/8	5 4/8	16 3/8	15 4/8	1 4/8	13 5/8	19	26	Old Crow, YT	Michael D. Odegard	Michael D. Odegard	1985	729
402 5/8	48 4/8	52	42 1/8	5	5 1/8	17 4/8	20 1/8	14 2/8	14 2/8	12	15	Alaska Pen., AK	Otto W. Geist	Otto W. Geist	1958	733
402 5/8	53	54 2/8	41 3/8	6 2/8	6 4/8	5 6/8	17 3/8	4 6/8	4 6/8	19	21	Pilot Point, AK	Robert C. Kaufman	Robert C. Kaufman	1978	733
402 5/8	51 5/8	50 1/8	34 6/8	5 2/8	5 2/8	18 5/8	19 2/8	14 5/8	13	14	18	Lake Clark, AK	Joseph P. Sebo, Jr.	Joseph P. Sebo, Jr.	1987	733
402 5/8	46 3/8	47 2/8	39 4/8	7 4/8	7 4/8	15 3/8	16 1/8	6 1/8	13	15	16	Clarence Lake, AK	Gene Thoney	Gene Thoney	1987	733
402 4/8	58	54 4/8	34 6/8	6 5/8	6 2/8	16 1/8	19 3/8	6 1/8	10 5/8	13	16	Rainy Pass, AK	John C. Heck	John C. Heck	1951	737
402 4/8	49 2/8	49 3/8	30 2/8	6	7 3/8	16 2/8	15 5/8	13 4/8	1/8	23	17	Talkeetna Mts., AK	Mahlon T. White	Mahlon T. White	1954	737
402 4/8	56 4/8	56	43 4/8	6 5/8	6 2/8	19 3/8	19 7/8	10 5/8	7	11	10	Talkeetna Mts., AK	Arvid F. Benson	Arvid F. Benson	1956	737
402 4/8	53 4/8	53 3/8	36 2/8	7	7	22 2/8	21 6/8	18 1/8	2 1/8	14	11	Glen Hwy., AK	W.L. Miers	W.L. Miers	1959	737
402 4/8	45	48	34 7/8	8 3/8	11	18 4/8	17	10	12 4/8	20	21	Talkeetna Mts., AK	Walter Pfisterer	Walter Pfisterer	1959	737
402 4/8	52 4/8	51 2/8	41 2/8	7 2/8	7 2/8	16 6/8	16 6/8	1 3/8	13 1/8	13	24	Nelchina, AK	A. Sweat	A. Sweat	1959	737
402 4/8	59 4/8	49 6/8	37 5/8	5 6/8	6 1/8	19 2/8	23 1/8	1 7/8	17 1/8	13	12	Port Heiden, AK	Joseph Caputo	Joseph Caputo	1965	737
402 4/8	47 6/8	49 6/8	44 4/8	6 1/8	6 4/8	17 5/8	17 5/8	10 4/8	13	15	14	Moose Lake, AK	Walter R. Schubert	Walter R. Schubert	1991	737
402 4/8	53 5/8	52 5/8	47	7 1/8	7 7/8	15 3/8	18 1/8	4 4/8	4 4/8	14	14	Mulchatna River, AK	Walter R. Willey	Walter R. Willey	1996	737
402 3/8	43 6/8	44 7/8	33 7/8	8 2/8	7 6/8	15 7/8	14 7/8	7	13 2/8	18	20	Tyone Lake, AK	James S. FonFerek	James S. FonFerek	1959	747
402 3/8	51 2/8	55 7/8	44	6 4/8	6 2/8	7 1/8	7 1/8	3 3/8	14 4/8	15	20	Denali Hwy., AK	Leon J. Brochu	Leon J. Brochu	1961	747
402 3/8	53 2/8	53 4/8	44 4/8	5 7/8	5 7/8	18	18	9 5/8	2 4/8	16	25	White Fish Lake, AK	Jerry Shepard	Jerry Shepard	1981	747
402 2/8	52 6/8	52 7/8	35 2/8	6 6/8	7 6/8	20 7/8	20 7/8	16 6/8	16 6/8	12	18	Swan Lake, AK	Carol A. Rollings	Carol A. Rollings	1994	751
402 2/8	54 4/8	53 1/8	49 1/8	6 1/8	6 3/8	2 7/8	19 6/8	15 3/8	1/8	20	16	Ugashik Lakes, AK	Frank Gregersen	Frank Gregersen	1964	751
402 2/8	46	46	39	5 6/8	5 6/8	17	16	12 4/8	12 2/8	17	23	Alaska Pen., AK	John W. Elmore	John W. Elmore	1977	751
402 2/8	57 2/8	54 6/8	38 2/8	7 1/8	7	2 3/8	19 4/8	1/8	16 6/8	13	20	Post Lake, AK	William K. Leech	William K. Leech	1983	751
402 2/8	50 5/8	47 3/8	35 4/8	6 2/8	6 2/8	18 2/8	20	13	13	19	20	Cathedral Bluff, AK	John H. Harvey, Jr.	John H. Harvey, Jr.	1987	751

Score	Length of Main Beam R	L	Inside Spread	Circumference at Smallest Place Between Brow and Bez Points R	L	Length of Brow Points R	L	Width of Brow Points R	L	Number of Points R	L	Locality	Hunter	Owner	Date Killed	Rank
402 1/8	55 2/8	54	42 5/8	6 3/8	7	21 1/8	4 1/8	17 5/8	1/8	19	11	Twin Lakes, AK	Cecil Glessner	Cecil Glessner	1966	755
402 1/8	52 1/8	47	32 4/8	7	7	1 1/8	17 7/8	4/8	14 3/8	16	24	Rainy Pass, AK	George V. Lenher	George V. Lenher	1967	755
402 1/8	48	49 2/8	43 6/8	8 3/8	6 2/8	23 4/8		13 1/8		19	16	Susitna River, AK	Fredrick W. Thornton	Fredrick W. Thornton	1969	755
402 1/8	53 4/8	54 6/8	49 7/8	5 7/8	5 5/8	15 5/8	16 5/8	6	13 2/8	16	21	Dago Creek, AK	John M. Gillette	John M. Gillette	1987	755
402	48 4/8	55 4/8	41 5/8	7 3/8	7 3/8	19 6/8	23 3/8	11 6/8	11 6/8	12	12	Mulchatna River, AK	Phillip Miller	Phillip Miller	1972	759
402	51 6/8	52 2/8	43 1/8	4 7/8	5 1/8	22 5/8	23 2/8	12 5/8	9 3/8	14	17	Talkeetna Mts, AK	Clyde A. McLeod	Clyde A. McLeod	1983	759
402	51 4/8	57 3/8	45 6/8	5 2/8	5 1/8	5	18 3/8	1/8	15 4/8	17	25	Ivishak River, AK	Vernon D. Holleman	Vernon D. Holleman	1986	759
402	49	49 6/8	32 5/8	6	6 2/8	17 7/8	19	12 3/8	10 7/8	20	22	Tundra River, AK	Clyde A. James	Clyde A. James	1986	759
402	53 6/8	52 5/8	51 2/8	6 2/8	6	21 5/8	21	9 4/8	12 7/8	11	17	Groundhog Mt., AK	James B. Haynes III	J.B. Haynes & Q.T. Hardtner	1988	759
402	48 4/8	49 4/8	44 2/8	5 4/8	5 7/8	21 2/8	19 3/8	16	7 1/8	19	16	Alaska Pen., AK	Roger O. Wyant	Roger O. Wyant	1990	759
401 7/8	55 6/8	55 5/8	35 5/8	7 3/8	9 3/8	17 6/8	18 3/8	11 3/8	15 4/8	16	15	Tyone Lake, AK	Eileen Marshall	Eileen Marshall	1961	765
401 7/8	59 3/8	56 2/8	35 1/8	6 6/8	7 3/8	19	18 1/8	5 2/8	16 5/8	18	24	Nabesna, AK	Bill Copeland	Bill Copeland	1969	765
401 7/8	54 4/8	54 2/8	44 6/8	5 1/8	4 7/8	17 2/8	20 1/8	14	4 4/8	15	13	Alaska Range, AK	Glenn E. Allen	Glenn E. Allen	1979	765
401 7/8	53 7/8	50 4/8	36 4/8	5 5/8	5 6/8	18 1/8	4 2/8	11 7/8	3 5/8	22	18	Stony River, AK	Richard N. Berry	Richard N. Berry	1986	765
401 7/8	51 4/8	51 2/8	37 4/8	7 5/8	7	18 4/8	18	13 4/8	9 2/8	14	13	Whitefish Lake, AK	Wesley W. Siegrist	Michael S. Siegrist	1986	765
401 6/8	41 4/8	40 4/8	40 5/8	6 2/8	5 7/8	13 2/8	13 7/8	11 2/8	7 6/8	29	27	Tazlina, AK	Lloyd Ronning	Lloyd Ronning	1958	770
401 6/8	45 2/8	49 7/8	39 4/8	6 6/8	6 6/8	17 2/8	15 6/8	5 6/8	6 3/8	18	14	Talkeetna Mts., AK	David Maroney	David Maroney	1961	770
401 6/8	50 4/8	50 2/8	37 6/8	6 5/8	6 3/8	19	17 7/8	10 2/8	11 1/8	18	10	Totatlanika River, AK	Heinrich K. Springer	Heinrich K. Springer	1969	770
401 6/8	47 7/8	48 7/8	44 1/8	5 6/8	6 1/8	15 6/8	6 2/8	12 6/8	1/8	15	14	Mt. Sanford, AK	Harold R. Clark	Harold R. Clark	1981	770
401 6/8	50 1/8	52 2/8	32 3/8	6 5/8	6 5/8	14 5/8	18 6/8	5 6/8	11 6/8	14	21	Deadman Lake, AK	Richard W. Dean	Richard W. Dean	1986	770
401 6/8	53 7/8	54 2/8	41 5/8	6	6 6/8	19 1/8	18 7/8	7 1/8	11 4/8	14	14	West Lake, AK	Stephen J. McGrath	Stephen J. McGrath	1990	770
401 5/8	45 2/8	44 6/8	36 5/8	6 2/8	7 3/8	16 4/8	18 5/8	13	9 1/8	19	21	Lake Louise, AK	Dale A. Hillmer	Dale A. Hillmer	1961	776
401 5/8	50 2/8	51 4/8	30 2/8	6 7/8	7	13 6/8	20 4/8	7 3/8	15 2/8	17	24	Rainy Pass, AK	Reed Sandvig	Reed Sandvig	1964	776
401 5/8	45 4/8	46 7/8	41 6/8	7 1/8	7 1/8	5 3/8	17	7	8 1/8	17	20	Mulchatna River, AK	Don N. Brown	Don N. Brown	1994	776
401 4/8	50	54 2/8	35 2/8	7	7 4/8	17 6/8	18 6/8	9 1/8	11 2/8	13	18	Talkeetna River, AK	J. Donald Neill	J. Donald Neill	1961	779
401 4/8	52	53	32 5/8	5 2/8	5 3/8	14 3/8	14 1/8	10 7/8	8	20	18	Wrangell Mts., AK	Gerald F. McNamara	Gerald F. McNamara	1968	779
401 4/8	61 4/8	63 5/8	48 4/8	7 2/8	7 1/8	17 4/8	6	10 7/8	1/8	17	14	Stuyahok River, AK	Fred A. Wright	Fred A. Wright	1982	779
401 4/8	61 2/8	59 6/8	39 2/8	7 4/8	7	17 7/8	18 1/8	2 4/8	9 6/8	13	13	Little Delta River, AK	Danny R. Hart	Danny R. Hart	1983	779
401 4/8	49 3/8	49	38 4/8	5 6/8	5 4/8	19 5/8	20 7/8	16 4/8	6 6/8	23	17	Becharof Lake, AK	Bill D. Reed	Bill D. Reed	1983	779
401 3/8	51 2/8	52 5/8	26 3/8	7 2/8	8	19 6/8	19	11 3/8	15 7/8	15	13	Little Nelchina River, AK	Francis M. Thistle	Francis M. Thistle	1957	784
401 3/8	51 2/8	51 2/8	35 6/8	6 3/8	6 1/8	16 4/8	15 6/8	9 5/8	9 6/8	18	18	Denali Hwy., AK	Norman Smith	Norman Smith	1959	784
401 3/8	57 5/8	56 4/8	42 7/8	6 2/8	6 3/8	9 4/8	16 5/8	1/8	13	14	18	Wrangell Mts., AK	Ronald Bergstrom	Ronald Bergstrom	1965	784
401 3/8	51 3/8	51 4/8	51 1/8	6 4/8	6 1/8	5 7/8	18 4/8	1/8	10 2/8	13	18	Black Creek, AK	Lonnie L. Ritchey	Lonnie L. Ritchey	1995	784
401 3/8	55 6/8	54 4/8	40 2/8	6 4/8	6 7/8	17 1/8	6/8	11 7/8	1/8	25	19	Lake Clark, AK	Donald Kolasinski	Donald L. Kolasinski	1998	784
401 3/8	54 4/8	52 7/8	47 6/8	6 2/8	5 7/8	17 7/8	18 4/8	5 2/8	8 6/8	14	14	Swan Lake, AK	Loren B. Hollers	Loren B. Hollers	2001	784
401 2/8	48 6/8	43 5/8	34 6/8	6 5/8	8	16 5/8	13 6/8	13 1/8	9 2/8	18	17	Alaska Range, AK	Robert B. Boone	Robert B. Boone	1959	790

Score	Length of Main Beam R	Length of Main Beam L	Inside Spread	Circumference R	Circumference L	Length of Brow Palm R	Length of Brow Palm L	Number of Points R	Number of Points L	Locality	Hunter	Owner	Date Killed	Rank
401 2/8	50 5/8	54 2/8	42 4/8	6 6/8	6 4/8	17 2/8	11 6/8	16	14	Wood River, AK	William P. Ghiorso	William P. Ghiorso	1983	790
401 2/8	57 5/8	59 6/8	49 6/8	6 7/8	6 3/8	20 4/8	3 6/8	10	13	Mulchatna River, AK	Heidi J. Albrecht	Heidi J. Albrecht	1988	790
401 2/8	46	45 2/8	40 7/8	6 3/8	6 5/8	10 7/8	1	14	19	Iliamna Lake, AK	Jerome B. McElhannon	Jerome B. McElhannon	1992	790
401 2/8	49 1/8	51 4/8	31 4/8	5 5/8	5 4/8	20 6/8	12 7/8	18	19	Carin Mt., AK	Douglas D. Mosier	Douglas D. Mosier	1995	790
401 1/8	52	52 6/8	45 4/8	7 1/8	7 2/8	15 6/8	8 4/8	15	16	Nicholson Lake, AK	John P. Scribner	John P. Scribner	1956	795
401 1/8	53 4/8	54 4/8	40 5/8	6 1/8	6 6/8	6 2/8	1/8	11	21	Rainy Pass, AK	John Weirdsma	John Weirdsma	1961	795
401 1/8	61 5/8	57 2/8	47 3/8	5 6/8	7 4/8	22 4/8	9 2/8	13	10	Little Nelchina River, AK	Elton Aarestad	Elton Aarestad	1964	795
401 1/8	54 4/8	51	44	6 4/8	7	17	7 4/8	13	17	Nondalton, AK	Anton L. Cerro	Anton L. Cerro	1973	795
401 1/8	51 1/8	51 1/8	43 7/8	7 1/8	7	15 1/8	11 1/8	22	12	Big River, AK	Roger L. Gregg	Roger L. Gregg	1977	795
401 1/8	60 6/8	53 6/8	43 5/8	6 2/8	7	19 3/8	16 3/8	20	14	King Salmon, AK	Edward W. Ratcliff	Edward W. Ratcliff	1984	795
401 1/8	47 2/8	45 5/8	30 2/8	7 1/8	5 4/8	17 2/8	6 7/8	15	16	Mt. Harper, AK	John J. Auman	John J. Auman	1992	795
401 1/8	51 4/8	51 7/8	37 4/8	7 2/8	6 2/8	22 7/8	12 4/8	17	17	Nushagak River, AK	John R. Thodos	John R. Thodos	1995	795
401	58	58	46	7	7	20	8	19	19	Talkeetna Mts., AK	Louis Mussatto	Louis Mussatto	1964	803
401	55 2/8	56 2/8	37	8 6/8	7 3/8	18 3/8	11 7/8	14	14	Red Devil, AK	Joseph L. LaNou	Joseph L. LaNou	1984	803
401	53 6/8	56 5/8	46 7/8	5	5 2/8	20	10 2/8	17	16	Whitefish Lake, AK	Joe C. Simmons	Joe C. Simmons	1986	803
401	49 2/8	49 2/8	41 6/8	7 4/8	8 2/8	12 3/8	4 4/8	18	16	Iliamna Lake, AK	Thomas R. Reed III	Thomas R. Reed III	1988	803
400 7/8	56 5/8	56 3/8	39	6 3/8	6 4/8	14 4/8	6 3/8	13	14	Snake River, YT	William W. Goodridge	William W. Goodridge	2001	807
400 6/8	51 1/8	50 7/8	38	6 5/8	7 4/8	11 7/8	6 2/8	14	19	Chisana, AK	Harry L. Thompson	Harry L. Thompson	1966	808
400 5/8	57 6/8	57 7/8	38 1/8	5 5/8	5 5/8	8 2/8	1	12	22	Alaska Pen., AK	E.J. Hansen	E.J. Hansen	1964	809
400 5/8	54 5/8	51	47 4/8	5 6/8	5 5/8	25 4/8	18 2/8	13	12	Port Heiden, AK	H. Bruce Freeman	Picked Up	1984	809
400 5/8	57 3/8	58 3/8	44 3/8	6 4/8	7	4	14 7/8	15	21	Iliamna Lake, AK	K. James Malady III	K. James Malady III	1987	809
400 5/8	58	59	43 3/8	5 3/8	5	19 3/8	11 7/8	18	20	Cinder River, AK	Brian L. Peterson	Brian L. Peterson	1988	809
400 5/8	51 7/8	51 1/8	42 3/8	6	6 1/8	16 6/8	9	13	16	Whitefish Lake, AK	John E. Alexander	John E. Alexander	1990	809
400 5/8	49 7/8	49 6/8	36 1/8	8 3/8	8 5/8	15 6/8	10 7/8	17	21	Nishlik Lake, AK	Rollie J. Smith	Rollie J. Smith	2001	809
400 4/8	48 1/8	54	29 1/8	7	6 6/8	22 3/8	4 6/8	20	14	Fortymile River, AK	Arnold O. Burton	Arnold O. Burton	1985	815
400 4/8	54 1/8	54 1/8	39 1/8	6 2/8	6 2/8	16 3/8	1/8	13	15	Mulchatna River, AK	Darryl G. Sanford	Darryl G. Sanford	1996	815
400 4/8	58 6/8	58 2/8	45 4/8	7 4/8	7 1/8	17 1/8	9 6/8	18	16	Koliganek, AK	Jeffrey T. Mardis	Jeffrey T. Mardis	1997	815
400 4/8	58	56 7/8	40	6 3/8	6 5/8	14 6/8	11 2/8	20	17	Purcell Mt., AK	Chris G. Sanford	Chris G. Sanford	1998	815
400 4/8	57 3/8	58 3/8	45 4/8	7 6/8	6 5/8	17 3/8	9	15	13	Wood River, AK	Berry B. Brooks	Berry B. Brooks	1958	815
400 3/8	42 1/8	41 2/8	33 5/8	5 6/8	5 7/8	3 4/8	7	19	19	Talkeetna, AK	S.H. Sampson	S.H. Sampson	1959	819
400 3/8	52	35	42	7 5/8	5 5/8	18 1/8	16	19	15	Ingersoll Lake, AK	Peter H. Merlin	Peter H. Merlin	1970	819
400 3/8	49 2/8	49	42	5 7/8	5 7/8	16	9 7/8	19	14	Cinder River, AK	Mervin Bergstrom	Mervin Bergstrom	1975	819
400 3/8	49 5/8	47 6/8	39 4/8	6 1/8	6 5/8	17 2/8	15 3/8	19	26	Alaska Pen., AK	James Swartout	James Swartout	1978	819
400 3/8	59 6/8	58 3/8	43	6	6	19 4/8	1/8	16	10	Hook Lake, AK	James L. Horneck	James L. Horneck	1983	819
400 3/8	52 6/8	56 7/8	46	6 1/8	5 7/8	10 5/8	2/8	15	21	Painter Creek, AK	Stephen R. Hurt	Stephen R. Hurt	1987	819
400 3/8	57 7/8	54 7/8	50 3/8	5 7/8	6 2/8	7 3/8	1/8	10	13	Iliamna Lake, AK	Steven R. Crawford	Steven R. Crawford	1991	819
400 3/8	52 1/8	51	42 3/8	6 5/8	6 4/8	17 6/8	13 2/8	21	18	Nushagak River, AK	Stephen G. Jolley	Stephen G. Jolley	1991	819
400 3/8	58 1/8	57 2/8	46 6/8	5 1/8	5 6/8	3 3/8	1/8	19	16	Otter Lake, AK	George W. Swierkos	George W. Swierkos	1991	819
400 3/8	61 1/8	55 6/8	43 1/8	5 5/8	5 5/8	19	13 1/8	14	22	Kvichak River, AK	Larry Crnkovich	Larry Crnkovich	1993	819
400 2/8	60	60 4/8	50	7 2/8	9 4/8	5 3/8	10 1/8	15	19	King Salmon, AK	Richard O. Burns III	Richard O. Burns III	1982	830
400 1/8	51 3/8	50 3/8	42	6 7/8	6 3/8	18	1	17	16	Denali Hwy., AK	Wilbur T. Gamble	Wilbur T. Gamble	1963	831
400 1/8	59 3/8	59 5/8	43	5 6/8	5 5/8	16	7	18	18	Monahan Flats, AK	C.H. Dana, Jr.	C.H. Dana, Jr.	1965	831
400 1/8	48 6/8	55	31 1/8	5 7/8	5 7/8	16	12 1/8	17	14	Alaska Pen., AK	Lillie E. Kriss	Lillie E. Kriss	1972	831
400 1/8	56 4/8	55	41 5/8	6 5/8	7	20 4/8	9 3/8	17	17	Iliamna Lake, AK	David L. Pfiester	David L. Pfiester	1992	831
400 1/8	49 3/8	47 4/8	38 1/8	6 3/8	5 4/8	18 4/8	1/8	13	16	Naknek River, AK	Ronald L. Petersen, Jr.	Ronald L. Petersen, Jr.	1996	831
400	47 6/8	50 4/8	30 5/8	8 1/8	5 6/8	3	17	19	19	Anchorage, AK	C.C. Irving	C.C. Irving	1959	836
400	57 4/8	56 7/8	37 4/8	7 4/8	6	18 7/8	11 6/8	14	16	Alaska Pen., AK	Bert Klineburger	Bert Klineburger	1961	836
400	45	46 5/8	44 1/8	5	5	16 4/8	7/8	16	24	Nelchina, AK	Webb Hilgar	Webb Hilgar	1962	836

BARREN GROUND CARIBOU
Rangifer tarandus granti

Score	Length of Main Beam R	L	Inside Spread	Circumference at Smallest Place Between Brow and Bez Points R	L	Length of Brow Points R	L	Width of Brow Points R	L	Number of Points R	L	Locality	Hunter	Owner	Date Killed	Rank
400	53 1/8	53 1/8	37	5 5/8	5 5/8	20 2/8	21 2/8	1	14 4/8	9	19	Lake Louise, AK	George Moerlein	George Moerlein	1962	836
400	54 3/8	56 1/8	35 1/8	7 1/8	7 1/8	19 6/8	16 6/8	17 2/8	1/8	17	8	King Salmon, AK	G.O. Wiegner	G.O. Wiegner	1970	836
400	48	50	39 6/8	6 4/8	6	15 3/8	17 1/8	12	1 4/8	19	15	Caribou Lake, AK	Donald J. Giottonini, Jr.	Donald J. Giottonini, Jr.	1983	836
400	54 3/8	53 1/8	31 1/8	6 3/8	7	6	17	1/8	9	18	20	White Fish Lake, AK	Thomas K. Willard	Thomas K. Willard	1984	836
400	49 5/8	48 1/8	39 6/8	6 1/8	6 1/8	21 1/8	19 1/8	14 1/8	2 1/8	19	11	Lake Aleknagik, AK	Monty D. McCormick	Monty D. McCormick	1987	836
400	45 4/8	48 7/8	36 5/8	7	7 5/8	9 1/8	18 4/8	1/8	15 5/8	18	25	Mulchatna River, AK	Francis W. Rosendale	Francis W. Rosendale	1991	836
434 4/8*	53	54 2/8	49 1/8	6 4/8	6 4/8	16 3/8	13 7/8	9 7/8	5	21	18	Killey River, AK	Aaron Doshier	Aaron Doshier	1997	
431 3/8*	50 4/8	48	42 2/8	8 5/8	8 1/8	17 3/8		10 4/8		22	18	Chulitna River, AK	Harry E. Buzby III	Harry E. Buzby III	2001	
427 7/8*	56 6/8	56 7/8	40 3/8	6 1/8	7 1/8	19 6/8	17 1/8	15 3/8	7	24	16	Kipchuk River, AK	Charles F. Craft	Charles F. Craft	1992	
426 6/8*	54 3/8	51 4/8	43 6/8	6 5/8	7	17 4/8	7 6/8	10 1/8	1/8	14	14	Twin Lakes, AK	Paul A. Lautner	Paul A. Lautner	2002	
418 4/8*	48 2/8	49 1/8	24 3/8	7 4/8	7 6/8	1 5/8	23 2/8	1/8	19 1/8	16	22	Kenai Mts., AK	Jack C. Standiford	Jack C. Standiford	2001	

* Final score is subject to revision by additional verifying measurements.

CATEGORY
BARREN GROUND CARIBOU

SCORE
400-4/8

HUNTER
JEFFREY T. MARDIS (RIGHT)

LOCATION
KOLIGANEK, ALASKA

DATE OF KILL
SEPTEMBER 1997

CATEGORY
BARREN GROUND CARIBOU

SCORE
409

HUNTER
KAM P. ST. JOHN

LOCATION
FUNNY RIVER, ALASKA

DATE OF KILL
SEPTEMBER 2002

CATEGORY
BARREN GROUND CARIBOU

SCORE
426-6/8

HUNTER
JAMES A. McINTOSH (BELOW)

LOCATION
SHAGAK BAY, ALASKA

DATE OF KILL
2002

CATEGORY
BARREN GROUND CARIBOU

SCORE
411-4/8

HUNTER
GORDON G. CHITTICK (RIGHT)

LOCATION
KING SALMON RIVER, ALASKA

DATE OF KILL
SEPTEMBER 1994

SCORE
424-6/8

HUNTER
CLINTON E. HANSON (BELOW)

LOCATION
SHOTGUN HILLS, ALASKA

DATE OF KILL
SEPTEMBER 2003

CENTRAL CANADA BARREN GROUND CARIBOU
WORLD'S RECORD

Hunting Central Canada barren ground caribou (*Rangifer tarandus groelandicus*) in Northwest Territories during the late summer of 1994, Donald J. Hotter III was faced with the ultimate decision. "Is this the bull I want?" Taking heed from an experienced friend, Wes Vining, president of The Trophy Connection in Cody, Wyoming, Hotter's decision was narrowed to two potential trophies the hunters spotted near Humpy Lake on September 11.

"We saw lots of antlers through our binoculars. Two bulls were worth a closer look. We examined them for 20 to 30 minutes. 'The third bull from the left has fantastic bottoms, good tops and outstanding main beam length,' Wes said. I agreed.

"We asked Leon Wellin, our guide, how to get to the bulls. He suggested we go back to the boat, circle a ridge and climb above the caribou to relocate and intercept them. Everything worked perfectly, and our guide knew the ground like the back of his hand. After about 30 minutes, we were in place and found the caribou feeding at a fast walk up a valley, so we hurried ahead to intercept. Everything went as planned, and the bulls were feeding straight up the anticipated route.

"'Not that bull. I know the bull I was looking at had better palms,' I heard Wes whisper. 'Not that one. He's too narrow.'

"On it went with Wes' whisperings until the fifth bull stepped out and Wes said, 'That's the bull. Look at those palms and bezes!'

"I concentrated on this one bull as it slowly walked behind a ridge and out of sight. I rushed farther up the ridge and hoped to see the bull again. The other bulls saw my movement and became alert. I heard Wes say the bull was only 100 yards in front of me, but I still couldn't see it.

"I sneaked forward and saw the bull. I looked over my shoulder to ask Wes if this was the bull and could see by the excitement in his eyes that it was. I asked if I should shoot and he responded that if I didn't, he would shoot for me. My shot was an easy 100 yards downhill, standing, one-shot kill.

"I had killed the new World's Record Central Canada barren ground caribou by 10 a.m. on the first morning of the hunt. We all knew we had an exceptional bull, but we were hesitant to dream of the final score. We taped the antlers and thought we made a mistake. Back at camp, we measured and remeasured the antlers, each time getting a slightly different score. 'This is some kind of trophy,' Wes kept saying."

After packing out the prized caribou from Humpy Lake, the trophy was taken back to Cody where resident and Boone and Crockett Club Official Measurer, Bob Hanson, measured the caribou rack with a score of 428-1/8 points. The score beat the old World's Record by more than 15 points! Later in May of 1995, when the Judges' Panel officially measured the rack in Dallas, the final score would ascend even further to 433-4/8 points. ∎

CENTRAL CANADA BARREN GROUND CARIBOU
WORLD'S RECORD SCORE CHART

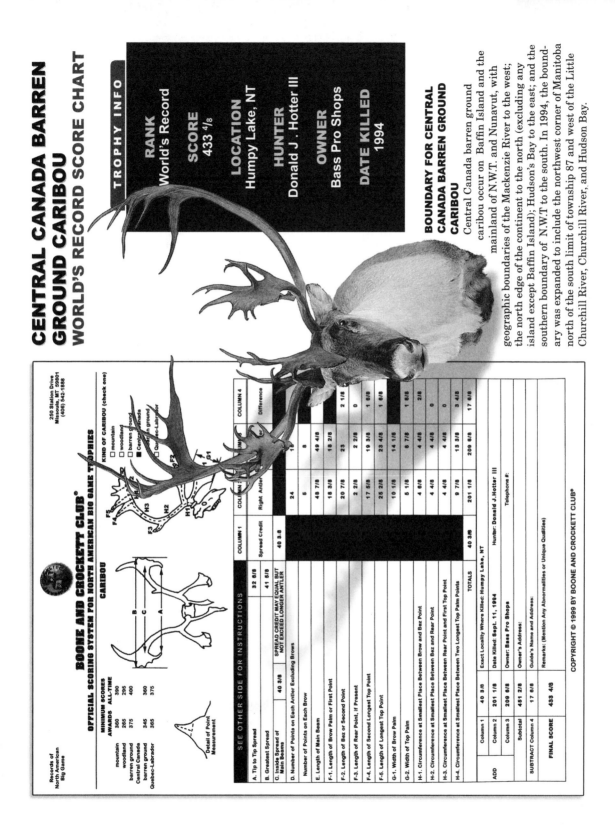

TROPHY INFO

RANK
World's Record

SCORE
433 4/8

LOCATION
Humpy Lake, NT

HUNTER
Donald J. Hotter III

OWNER
Bass Pro Shops

DATE KILLED
1994

BOUNDARY FOR CENTRAL CANADA BARREN GROUND CARIBOU

Central Canada barren ground caribou occur on Baffin Island and the mainland of N.W.T. and Nunavut, with geographic boundaries of the Mackenzie River to the west; the north edge of the continent to the north (excluding any island except Baffin Island); Hudson's Bay to the east; and the southern boundary of N.W.T to the south. In 1994, the boundary was expanded to include the northwest corner of Manitoba north of the south limit of township 87 and west of the Little Churchill River, Churchill River, and Hudson Bay.

Records of
North American
Big Game

250 Station Drive
Missoula, MT 59801
(406) 542-1888

BOONE AND CROCKETT CLUB®
OFFICIAL SCORING SYSTEM FOR NORTH AMERICAN BIG GAME TROPHIES

CARIBOU

	MINIMUM SCORES	
	AWARDS	ALL-TIME
mountain	360	390
woodland	265	295
barren ground	375	400
Central Canada barren ground	345	360
Quebec-Labrador	365	375

Detail of Point Measurement

KIND OF CARIBOU (check one)
- ☐ mountain
- ☐ woodland
- ☐ barren ground
- ■ Central Canada barren ground
- ☐ Quebec-Labrador

SEE OTHER SIDE FOR INSTRUCTIONS	COLUMN 1	COLUMN 2	COLUMN 3	COLUMN 4
	Spread Credit	Right Antler	Left Antler	Difference
A. Tip to Tip Spread	32 6/8			
B. Greatest Spread	41 5/8			
C. Inside Spread of Main Beams	40 3/8	SPREAD CREDIT MAY EQUAL BUT NOT EXCEED LONGER ANTLER		
D. Number of Points on Each Antler Excluding Brows		24	16	
Number of Points on Each Brow		5	8	
E. Length of Main Beam		48 7/8	49 4/8	
F-1. Length of Brow Palm or First Point		18 3/8	18 2/8	
F-2. Length of Bez or Second Point		20 7/8	23	2 1/8
F-3. Length of Rear Point, if Present		2 2/8	2 2/8	0
F-4. Length of Second Longest Top Point		17 5/8	19 3/8	1 6/8
F-5. Length of Longest Top Point		25 2/8	23 4/8	1 6/8
G-1. Width of Brow Palm		10 1/8	14 1/8	
G-2. Width of Top Palm		5 1/8	6 7/8	1 6/8
H-1. Circumference at Smallest Place Between Brow and Bez Point		4 6/8	4 4/8	2/8
H-2. Circumference at Smallest Place Between Bez and Rear Point		4 4/8	4 4/8	0
H-3. Circumference at Smallest Place Between Rear Point and First Top Point		4 4/8	4 4/8	0
H-4. Circumference at Smallest Place Between Two Longest Top Palm Points		9 7/8	13 3/8	3 4/8
TOTALS	40 3/8	201 1/8	209 6/8	17 6/8

ADD	Column 1	40 3/8	Exact Locality Where Killed: Humpy Lake, NT
	Column 2	201 1/8	Date Killed: Sept. 11, 1994 Hunter: Donald J. Hotter III
	Column 3	209 6/8	Owner: Bass Pro Shops Telephone #:
	Subtotal	451 2/8	Owner's Address:
SUBTRACT	Column 4	17 6/8	Guide's Name and Address:
	FINAL SCORE	**433 4/8**	Remarks: (Mention Any Abnormalities or Unique Qualities)

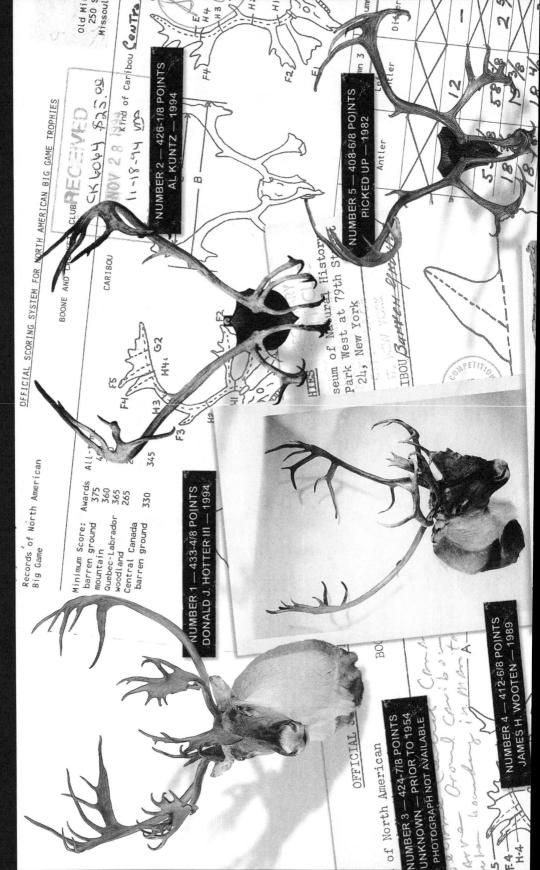

NUMBER 2 — 426-1/8 POINTS
AL KUNTZ — 1994

NUMBER 5 — 408-6/8 POINTS
PICKED UP — 1982

NUMBER 1 — 433-4/8 POINTS
DONALD J. HOTTER III — 1994

NUMBER 3 — 424-7/8 POINTS
PRIOR TO 1954
UNKNOWN — PRIOR TO 1954
PHOTOGRAPH NOT AVAILABLE

NUMBER 4 — 412-6/8 POINTS
JAMES H. WOOTEN — 1989

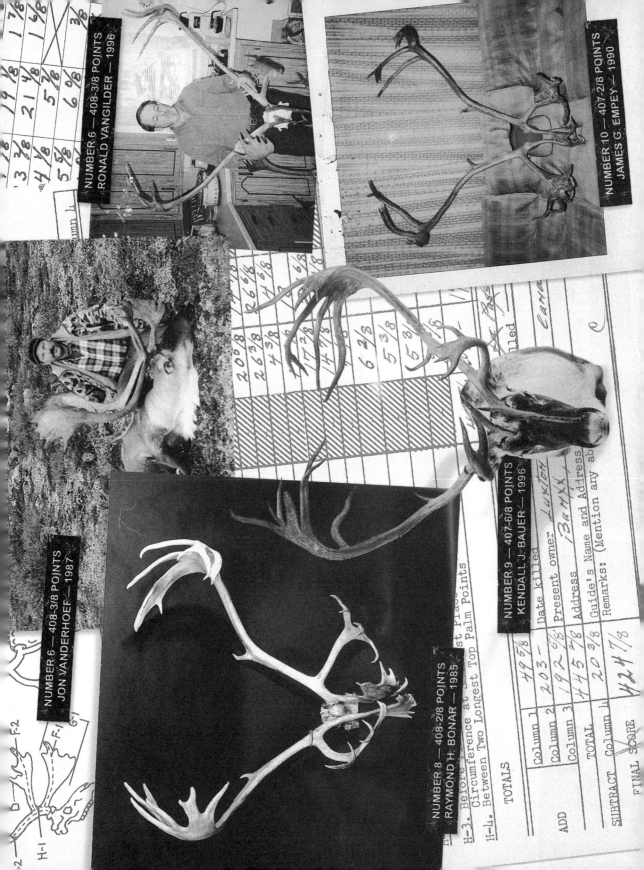

NUMBER 6 — 408-3/8 POINTS
RONALD VANGILDER — 1996

NUMBER 10 — 407-2/8 POINTS
JAMES G. EMPEY — 1990

NUMBER 6 — 408-3/8 POINTS
JON VANDERHOEF — 1987

NUMBER 8 — 408-2/8 POINTS
RAYMOND H. BONAR — 1985

NUMBER 9 — 407-6/8 POINTS
KENDALL J. BAUER — 1996

H-3. Before at
Circumference at Smallest Place
Between Two Longest Top Palm Points

H-4. Between

TOTALS			
	Column 1	49 5/8	
ADD	Column 2	203-	
	Column 3	192 6/8	
	TOTAL	445 7/8	
SUBTRACT	Column 4	20 3/8	
	FINAL SCORE	425 4/8	

Date killed
Present owner _Luxion_
Address _Banix_
Guide's Name and Address
Remarks: (Mention any ab

CENTRAL CANADA BARREN GROUND CARIBOU
Rangifer tarandus groenlandicus

MINIMUM SCORE 360

Score	Length of Main Beam R	L	Inside Spread	Circumference at Smallest Place Between Brow and Bez Points R	L	Length of Brow Points R	L	Width of Brow Points R	L	Number of Points R	L	Locality	Hunter	Owner	Date Killed	Rank
433 4/8	48 7/8	49 4/8	40 3/8	4 6/8	4 4/8	18 3/8	18 2/8	10 1/8	14 1/8	29	26	Humpy Lake, NT	Donald J. Hotter III	Bass Pro Shops	1994	1
426 1/8	55 5/8	58 2/8	38 1/8	6	7 1/8	18 3/8	15 3/8	14 1/8	5 7/8	19	15	Humpy Lake, NT	Al Kuntz	Al Kuntz	1994	2
424 7/8	57 1/8	54	49 5/8	6 2/8	6 5/8	20 5/8	14 4/8	14 7/8	1 4/8	18	16	Manitoba	Unknown	Luxton Museum	PR 1954	3
412 6/8	50 2/8	49 3/8	36 2/8	4 5/8	4 6/8	18 6/8	20	6 3/8	15 7/8	17	19	MacKay Lake, NT	James H. Wooten	James H. Wooten	1989	4
408 6/8	52 2/8	51 1/8	38 7/8	4 6/8	4 6/8	21 2/8	18 2/8	8 6/8	15 5/8	17	23	Rendez-vous Lake, NT	Picked Up	Tom W. Barry	1982	5
408 3/8	47 1/8	46 2/8	31 5/8	4 7/8	5 1/8	18 1/8	13 6/8	12 3/8	9	15	14	Courageous Lake, NT	Jon Vanderhoef	Jon Vanderhoef	1987	6
408 3/8	49 4/8	49 2/8	44 2/8	5 1/8	5 2/8	14 6/8	17 2/8	8 1/8	12 4/8	19	17	MacKay Lake, NT	Ronald VanGilder	Ronald VanGilder	1996	6
408 2/8	46 4/8	47	39 1/8	4 2/8	4 4/8	16 3/8	19	10 7/8	18 3/8	20	25	Courageous Lake, NT	Raymond H. Bonar	Raymond H. Bonar	1985	8
407 6/8	52 7/8	53 1/8	35 1/8	5 2/8	5 2/8	16 1/8	17 3/8	6 1/8	13 4/8	12	17	Repulse Bay, NT	Kendall J. Bauer	Kendall J. Bauer	1996	9
407 2/8	54 1/8	54 4/8	36 4/8	5 2/8	4 7/8	19 7/8	17 7/8	15	15 4/8	21	16	Kugaryuak River, NT	James G. Empey	James G. Empey	1990	10
407	55 6/8	55	35	5 2/8	5 4/8	11 5/8	15	16 2/8	1/8	23	18	MacKay Lake, NT	Daniel J. Gartner	Daniel J. Gartner	1997	11
406 2/8	45 6/8	47	35 2/8	5 2/8	4 6/8	18 3/8	15 3/8	2 4/8	11 7/8	22	24	Artillery Lake, NT	Michael J. Siegler	Michael J. Siegler	1998	12
404	51 3/8	54 2/8	42 7/8	5 2/8	4 6/8	21 4/8	19 2/8	1/8	15 3/8	12	16	Courageous Lake, NT	Gordon A. Welke	Doris Welke	2001	13
402 6/8	49 7/8	49 4/8	46 7/8	4 6/8	4 7/8	16 6/8	17	13 6/8	14 5/8	23	17	MacKay Lake, NT	Gordon Carpenter	Gordon Carpenter	2001	14
401 1/8	53	52 5/8	40	5 6/8	5 6/8	17	17 1/8	12	11	14	15	Courageous Lake, NT	Richard B. Limbach	Richard B. Limbach	1989	15
401	54 3/8	57 1/8	35 5/8	4 7/8	4 6/8	19 6/8	20 5/8	13	6 5/8	19	14	Courageous Lake, NT	John H. Smith	John H. Smith	1992	16
400 6/8	51 2/8	50	27 2/8	4 6/8	5 5/8	12 6/8	16 5/8	1/8	14 2/8	19	26	Rendez-vous Lake, NT	Dale L. Zeigler	Loaned to B&C Natl. Coll.	1986	17
400 6/8	56 5/8	56 7/8	37 3/8	5	5 3/8	16 6/8	16 6/8	14 3/8	14 1/8	28	19	Humpy Lake, NT	William G. Farley	William G. Farley	1996	17
400 3/8	53 6/8	57	40 6/8	5 7/8	5 4/8	21	19 1/8	19 1/8	6 7/8	18	17	Little Marten Lake, NT	Joel C. Garner	Joel C. Garner	2001	19
399 6/8	50 3/8	54 7/8	42 5/8	5 3/8	4 5/8	17 2/8	16 7/8	13	11	32	17	Nicholson Lake, MB	Francis N. George	Francis N. George	2001	20
398 6/8	48 6/8	50 2/8	38 2/8	6 6/8	5 6/8	16 3/8	16 4/8	6 5/8	12 2/8	20	25	Little Marten Lake, NT	William J. Mills	William J. Mills	1998	21
398 4/8	46 3/8	44 1/8	31 3/8	5 4/8	5 5/8	17 6/8	18 3/8	13 7/8	7 7/8	23	23	Rendez-vous Lake, NT	Robert M. Hazlewood	Robert M. Hazlewood	1986	22
398 2/8	47 7/8	45 3/8	31 7/8	5 4/8	5 4/8	18 1/8	18 4/8	3 2/8	13 6/8	26	25	Rendez-vous Lake, NT	Jim Moellman	Jim Moellman	1991	23
398 1/8	52 3/8	52 1/8	34 3/8	5	5	16 5/8	16 5/8	12 4/8	12 6/8	20	19	Lac de Gras, NT	Glen P. Rupe	Glen P. Rupe	1987	24
397 2/8	55 5/8	51 5/8	30 1/8	4 4/8	4 4/8	17 6/8	17	15 1/8	14	20	21	Humpy Lake, NT	Tracy A. Peterson	Tracy A. Peterson	2000	25
395 3/8	49 3/8	49 5/8	31 4/8	4 5/8	4 7/8	15 7/8	16 2/8	11 1/8	7 5/8	18	20	Courageous Lake, NT	George O. Poston	George O. Poston	1985	26
394 7/8	50 1/8	53 1/8	42 6/8	5	5	17	17 2/8	2 5/8	14	18	26	MacKay Lake, NT	Alfred E. Journey	Alfred E. Journey	1988	27
394 5/8	54 5/8	53 7/8	37 5/8	5	4 7/8	21 7/8	17 1/8	15	9	16	12	Schmok Lake, MB	Dennis A. Branfield	Dennis A. Branfield	2001	28
394 4/8	45 6/8	46 2/8	33 6/8	5 5/8	5 3/8	15	18 5/8	13 3/8	15 7/8	20	25	Courageous Lake, NT	Thomas E. Kriz	Thomas E. Kriz	2000	29
394 3/8	49 3/8	49 6/8	28 1/8	5 3/8	5 2/8	14 4/8	18 5/8	13 3/8	19 4/8	23	22	Rendez-vous Lake, NT	John P. Poston	John P. Poston	1986	30
394 3/8	54 3/8	52 2/8	35	5 3/8	5 3/8	19 5/8	16 6/8	8 4/8	18 4/8	20	21	Courageous Lake, NT	James R. Adams, Jr.	James R. Adams, Jr.	1997	30
393 7/8	47 3/8	48 3/8	24 6/8	5 4/8	5 3/8	19	21 3/8	4 2/8	18 7/8	19	25	Courageous Lake, NT	Robert G. Koffman	Robert G. Koffman	1987	32
391 7/8	54 2/8	52 6/8	41 4/8	5 5/8	6 1/8	16 6/8	17 7/8	2	15	14	17	Lake Providence, NT	Bert Varkonyi	Joey Varkonyi	1986	33
391 7/8	54 4/8	52 4/8	38 6/8	5 7/8	6 6/8	15 1/8	15 1/8	9 1/8	13 6/8	15	18	Courageous Lake, NT	Jack L. Odor	Jack L. Odor	1995	33
391 6/8	45 4/8	48 2/8	27	6	5 7/8	20 2/8	22 5/8	6 2/8	20 6/8	13	13	Rendez-vous Lake, NT	Diana L. Ross	Diana L. Ross	2003	33
391 1/8	47 1/8	50 6/8	25	5 4/8	5	16 7/8	16 7/8	11 2/8	11 2/8	27	23	MacKay Lake, NT	Grady E. Maggard, Jr.	Grady E. Maggard, Jr.	1988	36

Score	Main Beam R	Main Beam L	Inside Spread	Points	Locality	Hunter	Owner	Date	Rank
391	51 1/8	51	43 1/8	15	Humpy Lake, NT	Dennis C. Campbell	Dennis C. Campbell	1996	37
390 4/8	43 5/8	44 2/8	28	24	Courageous Lake, NT	Joseph Pinkas	Joseph Pinkas	1987	38
390 3/8	55 4/8	54 1/8	43 5/8	8	Courageous Lake, NT	Patrick H. Ackerman	Patrick H. Ackerman	1988	39
390 2/8	63	61 3/8	37	18	Little Marten Lake, NT	Daniel Butzler	Daniel Butzler	1989	40
390	53 5/8	54 7/8	35 2/8	17	Little Marten Lake, NT	Adolfo R. Gutierrez	Adolfo R. Gutierrez	2002	41
389 5/8	51 3/8	52 7/8	40 2/8	18	Point Lake, NT	George E. Kimmel	George E. Kimmel	1997	42
389 3/8	48 4/8	50 2/8	27 3/8	18	Courageous Lake, NT	William D. Backman, Jr.	William D. Backman, Jr.	1989	43
389 2/8	43 7/8	53 3/8	39 4/8	16	Destaffany Lake, NT	Gordon W. Russell	Mike Howden	1989	44
389 1/8	51 4/8	53	35 2/8	20	Little Marten Lake, NT	Stewart N. Shaft	Stewart N. Shaft	1995	45
388 6/8	51 7/8	49 7/8	30	21	Lynn Lake, MB	Carl E. Houghton	Carl E. Houghton	1996	46
388 5/8	54 1/8	53 4/8	35 2/8	18	Little Marten Lake, NT	Mike R. Coyle	Mike R. Coyle	1998	47
388 4/8	52 1/8	54	40 4/8	19	Point Lake, NT	Robert S. Everson	Robert S. Everson	1996	48
388 3/8	49 4/8	51 6/8	30 1/8	18	MacKay Lake, NT	John W. Scurfield	John W. Scurfield	1999	49
387 7/8	50 5/8	50 5/8	31 6/8	17	Rendez-vous Lake, NT	Michael Andres	Michael Andres	1994	50
387 5/8	47 3/8	49 5/8	38 6/8	21	Courageous Lake, NT	Brian L. Dam	Brian L. Dam	1995	51
387 4/8	50 2/8	49	23 3/8	21	Whitewolf Lake, NT	M. Joseph Brough	M. Joseph Brough	1999	51
387 1/8	46 1/8	43 4/8	30 2/8	20	MacKay Lake, NT	Johnny Bliznak	Johnny Bliznak	1998	53
387 1/8	47 4/8	49	38 5/8	23	Courageous Lake, NT	James J. McBride	James J. McBride	1987	54
386 7/8	49 1/8	47	30 7/8	20	Point Lake, NT	Blair C. Rumble	Blair C. Rumble	1996	54
386 6/8	47 6/8	47 2/8	40 1/8	19	Little Marten Lake, NT	Michael C. Jesch	Michael C. Jesch	1995	56
386 4/8	45 6/8	43 6/8	33 5/8	18	Jolly Lake, NT	James J. Hudson	James J. Hudson	2001	57
386 3/8	54 4/8	51 1/8	26 6/8	14	Rendez-vous Lake, NT	Victor E. Moss	Victor E. Moss	1993	58
386 3/8	52 4/8	52 1/8	28 2/8	25	Rendez-vous Lake, NT	Jerome T. Loendorf	Jerome T. Loendorf	1988	59
386 2/8	43 1/8	42 6/8	38	20	Tsoko Lake, NT	Picked Up	Roger A. Hansen	1989	59
386	54 1/8	56 6/8	41 5/8	13	Little Marten Lake, NT	Ken G. Wilson	Ken G. Wilson	1998	61
385 5/8	48 6/8	48 1/8	33 5/8	18	Parry Pen., NT	Bernard Sippin	Bernard Sippin	1988	62
385 5/8	54 7/8	55 1/8	40 2/8	14	Little Marten Lake, NT	C. Page Senn	C. Page Senn	1991	63
385 4/8	52 7/8	51 3/8	36 7/8	22	Munroe Lake, MB	Thomas A. Koepke	Thomas A. Koepke	1997	63
385 1/8	49 4/8	51 4/8	31 4/8	17	Rendez-vous Lake, NT	James S. Nelson IV	James S. Nelson IV	1997	65
384 7/8	57 5/8	57 4/8	41	11	Humpy Lake, NT	Paul Wisness	Paul Wisness	1987	66
384 4/8	51 7/8	49 5/8	21 3/8	20	Lake Providence, NT	Picked Up	Carol A. Mauch	1993	67
384 3/8	54	54 4/8	39 1/8	15	MacKay Lake, NT	Chris E. Brough	Chris E. Brough	1999	68
384 3/8	49	50 2/8	39	21	Whitewolf Lake, NT	John L. Branneky	John L. Branneky	1991	69
383 7/8	46	47 5/8	29 6/8	16	Lake Providence, NT	John S. Walkenhauer	J.S. & J. Walkenhauer	1994	69
383 7/8	50 4/8	50 2/8	31 4/8	28	Rendez-vous Lake, NT	Michael L. Chaffin	Michael L. Chaffin	1988	71
383 6/8	47	45 7/8	41 1/8	21	Rendez-vous Lake, NT	Michael A. Dahlheimer	Michael A. Dahlheimer	2003	71
383 4/8	50 2/8	50 3/8	40 7/8	17	Nejanilini Lake, MB	Shawn R. Andres	Shawn R. Andres	1991	73
383 1/8	51 5/8	51 7/8	34 6/8	14	Rendez-vous Lake, NT	James D. Nyce	James D. Nyce	1998	74
382 7/8	46 2/8	46 1/8	32 7/8	17	Providence Lake, NT	Kathleen N. Cook	Kathleen N. Cook	1999	75
382 7/8	55	54	36 2/8	12	Destaffany Lake, NT	Roger J. Larson	Roger J. Larson	1989	76
382 5/8	53 4/8	55 4/8	30 2/8	15	Little Marten Lake, NT	Steve MacKenzie	Steve MacKenzie	1989	77
382 4/8	42 1/8	41	32	23	Destaffany Lake, NT	Ken Weber	Ken Weber	2000	77
382 3/8	47 4/8	47 3/8	32 2/8	18	Courageous Lake, NT	James C. Johnson	James C. Johnson	1990	79
382 3/8	50 6/8	46 7/8	31 1/8	20	Rendez-vous Lake, NT	Seth R. Hootman	Lynn K. Richardson	1998	79
382 2/8	49 4/8	48 3/8	31 1/8	37	Humpy Lake, NT	Jerrold L. Nye	Jerrold L. Nye	2001	81
382	47 3/8	49 7/8	34 3/8	17	Little Marten Lake, NT	Ron Kerr	Ron Kerr	2001	82
382	49 7/8	44 6/8	31 3/8	26	MacKay Lake, NT	Patrick T. Stanosheck	Patrick T. Stanosheck	1989	83
382 2/8	56	56 1/8	37 1/8	15	Courageous Lake, NT	Earle H. Harder	Earle H. Harder	1985	84

CENTRAL CANADA BARREN GROUND CARIBOU

Rangifer tarandus groenlandicus

Score	Length of Main Beam R	L	Inside Spread	Circumference at Smallest Place Between Brow and Bez Points R	L	Length of Brow Points R	L	Width of Brow Points R	L	Number of Points R	L	Locality	Hunter	Owner	Date Killed	Rank
382 2/8	47 4/8	50 1/8	30 7/8	8 2/8	6 2/8	13 6/8	14 1/8	4 2/8	11 2/8	19	20	Paulatuk, NT	William H. Taylor	William H. Taylor	1986	84
382 1/8	51 5/8	50 5/8	32 2/8	5 1/8	5	16 1/8	17 4/8	13 1/8	14 7/8	19	16	Courageous Lake, NT	Kevin J. McCormick	Kevin J. McCormick	1983	86
381 3/8	51 4/8	52 7/8	33 3/8	5	5 2/8	17 4/8	19	1/8	16 1/8	17	22	Lake Providence, NT	Vicki L. St. Germaine	Vicki L. St. Germaine	1989	87
381 2/8	54 3/8	54 6/8	34 3/8	6	5 7/8	14 6/8	17 5/8	4 7/8	11 3/8	14	16	Point Lake, NT	Jim Anderson	Jim Anderson	1986	88
381 1/8	55	51 1/8	33	5 4/8	6 2/8	19	9 6/8	14 2/8	6	16	13	Little Marten Lake, NT	Brad S. Long	Brad S. Long	1996	89
381 1/8	50 3/8	54 1/8	35 4/8	5 5/8	5 4/8	15 2/8	20 4/8	9	6	23	14	MacKay Lake, NT	Tafford E. Oltz	Tafford E. Oltz	1997	89
381	52	47 6/8	33 5/8	6	6 2/8	15 6/8	19	11 1/8	15 7/8	15	17	Little Marten Lake, NT	Scott D. Fink	Scott D. Fink	1988	91
381	43 6/8	54 4/8	38 1/8	4 4/8	4 3/8	15	16 4/8	10 6/8	14 7/8	19	25	Little Marten Lake, NT	Anne Marie Freed	Anne Marie Freed	1995	91
381	54 6/8	49 1/8	34 5/8	5 4/8	5 5/8	21 7/8	12 4/8	17 7/8	1/8	18	12	Little Marten Lake, NT	Ken G. Wilson	Ken G. Wilson	1998	91
380 6/8	48 3/8	50 6/8	44 1/8	5	4 7/8	15 2/8	16	12 3/8	16 2/8	17	20	Courageous Lake, NT	Brian G. Edgerton	Brian G. Edgerton	1990	94
380 5/8	52 6/8	52 5/8	36 1/8	6	5 7/8	6 6/8	17 5/8	2 3/8	14 4/8	16	16	Courageous Lake, NT	Bernie L. Zimmerman	Bernie L. Zimmerman	2002	95
380 4/8	52 1/8	49 5/8	33 2/8	4 3/8	4 4/8	18 6/8	15 4/8	13 1/8	12	17	18	Lac de Gras, NT	James R. Crawford	James R. Crawford	1987	96
380 4/8	51 3/8	50 3/8	40	5 5/8	5	11 4/8	17 3/8	5	15 1/8	13	14	Rendez-vous Lake, NT	Brent W. Ross	Brent W. Ross	2003	96
380 2/8	49 1/8	54 6/8	37 6/8	6	6 2/8	18 6/8	16	15 1/8	3 1/8	13	13	MacKay Lake, NT	Richard B. Martin	Richard B. Martin	1990	98
379 2/8	54 2/8	50	36 3/8	5 7/8	6	15 3/8	13 7/8	13 3/8	7 3/8	19	15	Courageous Lake, NT	Wesley V. Hazen	Wesley V. Hazen	1992	99
379 1/8	51 4/8	49 6/8	35	5 1/8	5 1/8	19 4/8	18 6/8	16 6/8	13 2/8	18	15	Courageous Lake, NT	Gordon B. Knipe, Jr.	Gordon B. Knipe, Jr.	1989	100
379 1/8	53 1/8	51 2/8	30 2/8	5 1/8	6 1/8	18 1/8	16 7/8	15 2/8	7 3/8	16	16	Courageous Lake, NT	Lester I. Pearmine	Lester I. Pearmine	1989	100
379 1/8	51 7/8	49 5/8	33 6/8	5 4/8	4 7/8	20	19 4/8	16	5 1/8	16	14	Jolly Lake, NT	Gordon L. MacKinnon	Gordon L. MacKinnon	1998	100
378 7/8	54 6/8	49 5/8	34 5/8	6 1/8	4 6/8	17 6/8	17 2/8	12 4/8	13 1/8	23	17	Courageous Lake, NT	Ronald R. Ragan	Ronald R. Ragan	1996	103
378 3/8	48	49 5/8	38	6 3/8	5 6/8	16 5/8	13 1/8	15 3/8	6 3/8	25	17	Courageous Lake, NT	Robert J. Clifton	Robert J. Clifton	1998	104
378 3/8	46 2/8	47 3/8	38 2/8	5 1/8	5 1/8	18 6/8	18 4/8	14 6/8	7 7/8	20	16	Wolf Lake, NT	Harry H. Sanford	Harry H. Sanford	1999	104
378 2/8	50 4/8	52 4/8	35 6/8	5 2/8	5 1/8	15 4/8	14	9 3/8	9 1/8	12	17	Courageous Lake, NT	James A. Erickson	James A. Erickson	1989	106
377 7/8	56 2/8	56 3/8	31 2/8	5 1/8	5	16 1/8	18 5/8	14 2/8	13 5/8	17	19	Courageous Lake, NT	John C. Clumpner	John C. Clumpner	1994	107
377 5/8	47 4/8	48 6/8	41	5 5/8	5 2/8	17 3/8	18 5/8	12	16 7/8	17	18	Winter Lake, NT	Warren D. St. Germaine	Warren D. St. Germaine	1985	108
377 5/8	52 3/8	49	32 3/8	6 1/8	5 3/8	1 3/8	18 1/8	1/8	15	14	24	Humpy Lake, NT	Terry L. Miller	Terry L. Miller	1995	108
377 4/8	49 2/8	47 4/8	24 3/8	6 4/8	6 4/8	15 7/8	15 2/8	10 6/8	10 4/8	15	18	Whitewolf Lake, NT	Ray E. Stewart	Ray E. Stewart	1999	110
377 3/8	49 7/8	50 7/8	38 7/8	7	6 4/8	19 5/8	19	16 1/8	5 4/8	22	15	Desteffany Lake, NT	David W. Davison	David W. Davison	1998	111
377 2/8	54 7/8	54 5/8	38 2/8	5 3/8	4 7/8	16 6/8	16 6/8	8 2/8	11 7/8	16	12	Reid Lake, NT	Daryl Ouillette	Daryl Ouillette	1992	112
376 5/8	55 4/8	54	37 7/8	5 5/8	5 3/8	15 4/8	1 1/8	1/8	1/8	16	15	Snare Lake, NT	Gary L. Temple	Cabela's, Inc.	1987	113
376 4/8	48 5/8	46 6/8	29 4/8	6	6 2/8	4/8	15 7/8	11	11	16	19	MacKay Lake, NT	David Emken	David Emken	1990	114
376 3/8	49 7/8	47 5/8	31 6/8	6 2/8	5 4/8	6 3/8	13 4/8	1/8	11 5/8	16	21	Courageous Lake, NT	Dennis C. Ault	Dennis C. Ault	1991	115
376 3/8	45 7/8	47 5/8	42 5/8	4 3/8	5	4/8	15 7/8	1/8	11 5/8	17	19	Jolly Lake, NT	Frank Kacsinko	Frank Kacsinko	1997	115
376 3/8	50 7/8	51 5/8	32 4/8	5	5	17 4/8	16 4/8	7 7/8	10 5/8	17	16	Courageous Lake, NT	Gary Nehring	Gary Nehring	2001	115
376 1/8	54 3/8	52 4/8	35	4 5/8	4 3/8	19 3/8	17	7 7/8	10 5/8	11	19	Warburton Bay, NT	John L. Campbell	John L. Campbell	1995	118
375 6/8	55 2/8	53 6/8	43 4/8	4 7/8	4 6/8	19 1/8	14	13	1/8	20	9	Jolly Lake, NT	William L. Pederson	William L. Pederson	1996	119
375 4/8	52	53 1/8		5 2/8	5 1/8	3 2/8	17 1/8	1/8	13 6/8	14	22	Little Marten Lake, NT	Richard J. Wristen	Richard J. Wristen	1995	120

Score	Locality	Hunter	Owner	Date Killed	Rank
375 2/8	Dymond Lake, MB	Al Kuntz	Al Kuntz	2000	121
375	Courageous Lake, NT	Hal L. Shockey	Hal L. Shockey	1994	122
374 7/8	Little Marten Lake, NT	Scott D. Fink	Scott D. Fink	1988	123
374 6/8	Courageous Lake, NT	Anna Marie Pavlik	Anna Marie Pavlik	1995	124
374 5/8	Jolly Lake, NT	Bill LaSalle	Bill LaSalle	1996	125
374 2/8	Little Marten Lake, NT	Houston Smith	Houston Smith	1999	126
374 1/8	Warburton Bay, NT	J. Aaron Dillabough	J. Aaron Dillabough	2001	127
374	Jolly Lake, NT	Kim Aliprandini	Kim Aliprandini	1995	128
373 7/8	Little Marten Lake, NT	William Vaznis	William Vaznis	1989	129
373 7/8	MacKay Lake, NT	Ronald K. Serwa	Ronald K. Serwa	1999	129
373 6/8	Aylmer Lake, NT	James Holzberger	James Holzberger	2003	131
373 5/8	Courageous Lake, NT	Wayne H. Kingsley	Wayne H. Kingsley	1989	132
373 2/8	Granet Lake, NT	George R. Breiwa II	George R. Breiwa II	2000	133
373 1/8	Point Lake, NT	Gary A. Bingham	Gary A. Bingham	1989	134
373	Lake Providence, NT	Dean G. Fletcher	Dean G. Fletcher	1987	135
373	Rendez-vous Lake, NT	Joe Hocevar	Joe Hocevar	2002	135
372 7/8	Little Marten Lake, NT	Ronald V. Hurlburt	Ronald V. Hurlburt	1989	137
372 7/8	Point Lake, NT	John Durand	John Durand	1997	137
372 7/8	Rendez-vous Lake, NT	Charles H. Rohrer	Charles H. Rohrer	2001	137
372 5/8	Courageous Lake, NT	Charles L. Cleis	Charles L. Cleis	1990	140
372 5/8	Humpy Lake, NT	Calvin Conley	Calvin Conley	1998	140
372 4/8	Little Forehead Lake, NT	Thomas P. Grainger	Thomas P. Grainger	2003	143
372 2/8	Lac de Gras, NT	Raymond C. Hunt	Raymond C. Hunt	1987	144
371 7/8	MacKay Lake, NT	Ronald L. Chapman	Ronald L. Chapman	1990	144
371 7/8	Courageous Lake, NT	Robert C. Kaufman	Robert C. Kaufman	1984	145
371 6/8	Little Marten Lake, NT	David J. Richey, Sr.	David J. Richey, Sr.	1990	145
371 5/8	Courageous Lake, NT	Ken Weber	Ken Weber	2000	147
371 5/8	Humpy Lake, NT	David W. Baxter	David W. Baxter	1998	148
371 3/8	Jolly Lake, NT	Don LeCain	Don LeCain	1998	148
371 2/8	Lake Providence, NT	John C. Pitts	John C. Pitts	1993	150
371 1/8	Courageous Lake, NT	James M. Arnold	James M. Arnold	1992	151
371 1/8	MacKay Lake, NT	Bob J. Williams	Bob J. Williams	2001	151
371 1/8	Courageous Lake, NT	Jon R. Stephens	Jon R. Stephens	1984	153
371 1/8	MacKay Lake, NT	Daniel W. Brockman	Daniel W. Brockman	1990	153
371	MacKay Lake, NT	Phillip Henry	Phillip Henry	1988	155
371	Jolly Lake, NT	Ronald E. Kohler	Ronald E. Kohler	1995	155
370 7/8	MacKay Lake, NT	James D. Powless	James D. Powless	1997	157
370 6/8	Courageous Lake, NT	Francis J. Kelsch	Francis J. Kelsch	2000	158
370 5/8	Muskox Lake, NT	Neill A. Murphy	Fred Freidmeyer	1978	159
370 3/8	MacKay Lake, NT	A. Oscar Carlson	A. Oscar Carlson	1996	160
370 3/8	Rendez-vous Lake, NT	Donald J. Malisani	Donald J. Malisani	1999	160
370 2/8	Courageous Lake, NT	Victor E. Moss	Victor E. Moss	1989	162
370 1/8	Nichols Lake, MB	Marion G. Macaluso	Marion G. Macaluso	1999	163
370	Rendez-vous Lake, NT	Jeffrey W. Strain	Jeffrey W. Strain	1999	164
369 7/8	Caribou Lake, MB	Philip L. Wright	Hedwig Vogel-Wright	1986	165
369 7/8	Whitewolf Lake, MB	Warren Johnson	Warren Johnson	1992	165
369 6/8	Schmok Lake, MB	Aaron Levine	Aaron Levine	2001	165
369 6/8		Thomas W. Petry	Thomas W. Petry	2001	165

Rangifer tarandus groenlandicus

Score	Length of Main Beam R	L	Inside Spread	Circumference at Smallest Place Between Brow and Bez Points R	L	Length of Brow Points R	L	Width of Brow Points R	L	Number of Points R	L	Locality	Hunter	Owner	Date Killed	Rank
369 3/8	48 6/8	45 1/8	38 6/8	4 5/8	4 6/8	14 2/8	16 4/8	7	11 3/8	16	22	Lynn Lake, MB	Lloyd J. Fink	Lloyd J. Fink	1996	169
369 3/8	54 4/8	53 2/8	46 1/8	4 7/8	5	14 4/8	15 1/8	1 2/8	9 5/8	14	15	Humpy Lake, NT	Scott S. Snyder	Scott S. Snyder	2000	169
369 3/8	53 4/8	51 7/8	36 5/8	4 7/8	5 2/8	19 1/8	17 6/8	13 1/8	14 1/8	14	16	Whitewolf Lake, NT	David E. Combs	David E. Combs	1999	171
369 1/8	50 3/8	51 4/8	43	5	5 4/8	14 5/8	14 2/8	9	7 6/8	15	14	Seahorse Lake, NT	Barry D. Taylor	Barry D. Taylor	1985	172
369 1/8	48 3/8	48 3/8	29	5 6/8	5 6/8	14 1/8	15 2/8	12 2/8	11 6/8	26	24	Rendez-vous Lake, NT	Sherwood Mack	Sherwood Mack	2002	172
369	52 6/8	53	33 2/8	5 4/8	6 5/8	6 6/8	17	1/8	11 6/8	12	16	Desteffany Lake, NT	William J. Burwash	William J. Burwash	1991	174
368 7/8	56	56 4/8	43 7/8	5 6/8	6	1 2/8	16 5/8	1/8	13 6/8	16	17	Courageous Lake, NT	Kent T. Michaelson	Kent T. Michaelson	1988	175
368 7/8	58 4/8	56 1/8	36 4/8	5 2/8	5 3/8	18	17 3/8	12 3/8	14	16	17	Courageous Lake, NT	Richard Fitch	Richard Fitch	1989	175
368 5/8	55 7/8	56	41 6/8	5 4/8	5		14 7/8	3 2/8	9 4/8	15	17	Point Lake, NT	Douglas G. Kirchhoff	Douglas G. Kirchhoff	1987	177
368 5/8	46	48 2/8	36 5/8	5 3/8	5 2/8	11	15 3/8	15 3/8	2 2/8	17	19	Point Lake, NT	Robert S. Everson	Robert S. Everson	1996	177
368 4/8	47 5/8	48 6/8	25	5 1/8	5 2/8	16 2/8	17 2/8	1/8	13 6/8	21	16	Rocher Lake, NT	Henry C. Gilbertson	Henry C. Gilbertson	1997	179
368 4/8	48 4/8	51	31 2/8	5	4 7/8	10 1/8	16 1/8	11	10 6/8	14	16	MacKay Lake, NT	Kevin R. Williams	Kevin R. Williams	2001	179
368 3/8	48	49 4/8	29 4/8	10	7 1/8	17 6/8	14 3/8	13	8	12	15	Courageous Lake, NT	Kent T. Michaelson	Kent T. Michaelson	1988	181
368 2/8	54	55 4/8	39 7/8	5	4 5/8	15 3/8	15	13 5/8	11 5/8	15	11	Rendez-vous Lake, NT	David P. Jacobson	David P. Jacobson	1995	182
368 2/8	51 7/8	51 7/8	31 7/8	5	5 5/8	18 6/8	15 7/8	12 2/8	4 3/8	19	15	MacKay Lake, NT	Patrick M. Condie	Patrick M. Condie	1996	182
367 5/8	48 3/8	52	33 2/8	6 7/8	5 5/8	16 2/8	15 2/8	1/8	14 1/8	21	25	Little Marten Lake, NT	Allen R. Prince	Allen R. Prince	1989	184
367 1/8	51	49 4/8	35 7/8	5	5 6/8	9 3/8	18 4/8	9 2/8	8 3/8	19	17	MacKay Lake, NT	James L. White	James L. White	1997	185
367 1/8	53 7/8	52 6/8	30	6 1/8	5 2/8	19 5/8	15 5/8	15 4/8	8 7/8	12	16	Commonwealth Lake, MB	Robert R. Theer, Jr.	Robert R. Theer, Jr.	1995	186
366 7/8	50 4/8	51 6/8	36 2/8	5 3/8	5 1/8	18	15 2/8	14 5/8		13	12	MacKay Lake, NT	K.D. Schwanky	K.D. Schwanky	1995	187
366 4/8	52 1/8	53 6/8	34 1/8	5 2/8	5 3/8	20 1/8	5 4/8	1 3/8	18 2/8	17	12	Courageous Lake, NT	William H. Moyer	William H. Moyer	1993	188
366 2/8	54	54 1/8	38 7/8	4 7/8	4 6/8	18 1/8	23 1/8	8 7/8	7 6/8	18	11	Point Lake, NT	John O. Plahn	John O. Plahn	1997	189
366 2/8	51 2/8	52 1/8	35 5/8	4 2/8	4 3/8	13 2/8	10 4/8	13 2/8	8 2/8	10	18	Courageous Lake, NT	Brad White	Brad White	1987	189
366	45 4/8	47 1/8	32 5/8	4 5/8	4 4/8	16 3/8	14 2/8	11 4/8	9	18	23	Courageous Lake, NT	Arthur C. Peckham, Jr.	Arthur C. Peckham, Jr.	1989	191
365 7/8	54 2/8	52 2/8	32 4/8	5	5 1/8	15 5/8	16 6/8	8 6/8	11 3/8	15	14	Little Marten Lake, NT	Ralph Madden	Ralph Madden	1994	192
365 6/8	44 3/8	42 5/8	34 5/8	5 2/8	5 6/8	16 6/8	16	5 4/8		16	18	Lake Providence, NT	Jeffrey M. Farnsworth	Jeffrey M. Farnsworth	1996	193
365 6/8	54 4/8	53 5/8	36 1/8	5 2/8	5 1/8	15 6/8		1/8	10 6/8	15	12	Humpy Lake, NT	Garrett T. Bayrd	Garrett T. Bayrd	1975	193
365 5/8	48	47 2/8	31 1/8	9 3/8	8 2/8	2 1/8	16 5/8	1/8	10 4/8	14	12	Coppermine River, NT	David P. Jacobson	David P. Jacobson	1997	195
365 5/8	52 3/8	51 2/8	39	5	5 1/8	13 4/8	12 7/8	10 5/8	10 4/8	14	16	Courageous Lake, NT	Rob W. Shatzko	Rob W. Shatzko	1987	195
365 3/8	44 3/8	44 3/8	27 5/8	5 2/8	5 2/8	17 1/8		17 3/8		23	23	Courageous Lake, NT	Lilly Pinkas	Lilly Pinkas	1987	197
365 2/8	48	46 3/8	28 4/8	5 6/8	5 5/8		18 2/8			26	23	Snare River, NT	William M. Leitner	William M. Leitner	1987	198
365 1/8	47	49 4/8	32 1/8	5 2/8	5 1/8	14 7/8		11 4/8	15 4/8	16	20	Courageous Lake, NT	Frederick E. Haskell	Frederick E. Haskell	1987	199
365	50 7/8	48 4/8	36	5	5 1/8	10 3/8	17 7/8	1/8	10 4/8	15	12	Little Marten Lake, NT	Robin Bonner	Robin Bonner	1989	200
365	50 7/8	51 2/8	41	5 2/8	5 2/8	13	15 4/8	1/8	13 7/8	18	18	Providence Lake, NT	Linda A. Neifert	Linda A. Neifert	1998	200
364 7/8	46 3/8	44 6/8	34 6/8	5	4 6/8	15 7/8	13	6 6/8	11 1/8	12	13	Lake Providence, NT	Bert Varkonyi	Nini Varkonyi	1986	202
364 6/8	51 6/8	51 3/8	36 3/8	5 5/8	5 2/8	15 7/8		10		16	13	Point Lake, NT	Rodger E. Warwick	Rodger E. Warwick	1991	203
364 4/8	48	45	40 2/8	4 4/8	4 4/8	11 3/8	13 2/8	7 5/8	10 6/8	16	19	Little Marten Lake, NT	Robin Bonner	Robin Bonner	1989	204

Score	L. Main Beam R	L. Main Beam L	Inside Spread	Circ. R	Circ. L	Width Brow R	Width Brow L	Width Top R	Width Top L	Pts R	Pts L	Locality	Owner	Hunter	Date Killed	Rank
364 4/8	49	50 5/8	29 2/8	4 7/8	4 5/8	18 2/8	17 7/8	12 1/8	15 4/8	19	16	Courageous Lake, NT	John E. Howard	John E. Howard	1998	204
364 3/8	46 1/8	42 4/8	33 1/8	5 4/8	6 1/8	15 7/8	14 3/8	13 1/8	9 7/8	18	23	Pellatt Lake, NU	James D. Mierzwiak	James D. Mierzwiak	1996	206
364 3/8	51 4/8	50 5/8	32 4/8	6	5	18 7/8	17 2/8	14 7/8	6 1/8	15	14	Humpy Lake, NT	Robert M. Anderson	Robert M. Anderson	2001	206
364	46 2/8	45 1/8	32 3/8	5	4 6/8	15 6/8	14 7/8	11 5/8	8 5/8	17	21	Commonwealth Lake, MB	James F. Mervenne	James F. Mervenne	1996	208
364	48	47 5/8	34 6/8	5 5/8	5	15 2/8	18 4/8	8 2/8	14 4/8	17	14	Glover Lake, MB	Dean Toth	Dean Toth	1997	208
363 7/8	46 3/8	46 6/8	33 2/8	4 6/8	5 6/8	15	13 4/8	7 6/8	7 6/8	17	19	Humpy Lake, NT	Jeffrey M. Grab	Jeffrey M. Grab	1996	210
363 7/8	46 7/8	47 6/8	37 7/8	6 1/8	6 2/8	12 5/8	4 5/8	13 2/8	5 1/8	14	22	Little Marten Lake, NT	Buck Taylor	Buck Taylor	1999	210
363 6/8	47 6/8	47 5/8	29 3/8	4 7/8	4 5/8	14 5/8	15 2/8	10 5/8	10 6/8	22	16	MacKay Lake, NT	Gary A. Jackson	Gary A. Jackson	1988	212
363 5/8	47 4/8	47 2/8	32 4/8	4 7/8	4 7/8	17 1/8	15 4/8	13 4/8	10 4/8	20	22	MacKay Lake, NT	Robert J. Gribble	Robert J. Gribble	1995	213
363 5/8	48	47	33 7/8	4 6/8	5	14 7/8	16 3/8	6 3/8	10 1/8	18	21	Jolly Lake, NT	Ronald D. Zelewski	Ronald D. Zelewski	1998	214
363 3/8	47 6/8	48 7/8	31	7	6	13 4/8	14 1/8	11 7/8	12 3/8	25	14	Nueltin Lake, MB	John W. Brand	John W. Brand	1999	214
363 3/8	48 1/8	48 4/8	35	5 1/8	5 4/8	15 6/8	15 4/8	4 5/8	14 4/8	16	27	MacKay Lake, NT	Vincent J. Strickler	Vincent J. Strickler	2000	216
362 2/8	53 2/8	51 2/8	25 6/8	7	6 4/8	9 7/8	18 2/8	6 2/8	8	21	12	Courageous Lake, NT	John D. Frost	John D. Frost	1994	217
362 1/8	50 3/8	53 4/8	28 4/8	4 7/8	4 7/8	13 6/8	15 6/8	6 5/8	18 3/8	16	12	Rendez-vous Lake, NT	Victor E. Moss	Victor E. Moss	1989	218
362 1/8	47 1/8	49	37	4 6/8	4 7/8	8 2/8	22 1/8		13 6/8	16	13	Courageous Lake, NT	Larry H. Beller	Larry H. Beller	1991	218
362	53 4/8	54	36 4/8	6	5 5/8	19	16 4/8	14	15 1/8	18	13	Humpy Lake, NT	Robert W. Ehle	Robert W. Ehle	1997	218
362	51 6/8	53 2/8	35 2/8	5 2/8	5 7/8	11 2/8	20 3/8	1/8	14 6/8	22	15	Little Marten Lake, NT	William H. Oliver	William H. Oliver	1990	221
362	51 1/8	50 6/8	26 6/8	5 6/8	5 7/8	11 3/8	19 1/8	1/8	10 4/8	15	23	Rocher Lake, NT	John C. Marsh	John Marsh	1998	221
361 7/8	45 1/8	47 4/8	32 4/8	5 7/8	6 2/8	14 4/8	18 1/8	11 1/8	10 4/8	22	17	Point Lake, NT	Rick L. Clark	Rick L. Clark	1997	223
361 6/8	47 2/8	47 3/8	31 2/8	4 4/8	4	12	15 1/8	1 7/8	7 7/8	23	22	MacKay Lake, NT	Donald C. Norheim	Donald C. Norheim	2001	224
361 5/8	43	44 4/8	41 2/8	4 2/8	4 2/8	15 4/8	13 2/8	12 7/8	3	17	14	Courageous Lake, NT	Jack Lamb	Jack Lamb	1986	225
361 4/8	53 6/8	53 6/8	53 6/8	5 1/8	5 4/8	17 2/8	16 7/8	14 5/8	10 4/8	10	10	Lake Providence, NT	Grant M. St. Germaine	Grant M. St. Germaine	1988	226
361 2/8	47 4/8	50 1/8	29 4/8	5 4/8	5 4/8	18 7/8	18 6/8	15 7/8	7 4/8	13	18	Point Lake, NT	Neil Harles	Warren D. St. Germaine	1991	227
361 1/8	49 4/8	49 5/8	31 7/8	5 6/8	5 6/8	6 5/8	16 2/8	2 1/8	12	23	14	Rendez-vous Lake, NT	Barry Jacobson	Barry Jacobson	1994	227
361 1/8	51 2/8	51 5/8	31 5/8	5 7/8	5 7/8	17 6/8	13 7/8	13	15 3/8	11	17	Winter Lake, NT	Warren D. St. Germaine	Warren D. St. Germaine	1984	229
360 7/8	48 4/8	49 2/8	30 1/8	5 5/8	5 3/8	6	2 6/8	1/8	5 5/8	15	13	Courageous Lake, NT	Paul E. Opfermann	Paul E. Opfermann	1988	229
360 6/8	46 3/8	47 2/8	31 2/8	6 3/8	6 3/8	13 1/8	14 6/8	10 4/8	14 1/8	15	18	Humpy Lake, NT	John J. D'Alessandro	John J. D'Alessandro	2002	231
360 6/8	49 5/8	48 7/8	26 7/8	5 4/8	5 4/8	6 4/8	2 1/8	1/8	5 6/8	24	19	Cape Dorset, NU	Ronald E. Gray	Ronald E. Gray	1985	232
360 6/8	52 2/8	51 2/8	33 5/8	5 4/8	4	19 6/8	2 1/8	12	10 6/8	12	19	Little Marten Lake, NT	Allen R. Prince	Allen R. Prince	1996	232
360 5/8	50 3/8	51 5/8	27 3/8	4	4 4/8	2 1/8	18 1/8	15 3/8	18 3/8	17	15	MacKay Lake, NT	Johnny Bliznak	Johnny Bliznak	1998	232
360 5/8	54 4/8	53 4/8	39 7/8	4 7/8	5 1/8	18 1/8	16	12 2/8	11 7/8	14	19	Humpy Lake, NT	William Vaznis	William Vaznis	1994	235
360 3/8	49 4/8	50 4/8	37 4/8	5 2/8	5 1/8	16	19 6/8	10 4/8	1 6/8	16	13	MacKay Lake, NT	Michael J. Spence	Michael J. Spence	1995	235
360 3/8	49 1/8	45 1/8	38	5	5	18 2/8	15 2/8	14 4/8	14 4/8	15	14	Point Lake, NT	Sharon Ziegenhagen	Sharon Ziegenhagen	1988	237
360 3/8	52 7/8	52 2/8	39	4 7/8	4 7/8	4	14 5/8	11 2/8	6/8	12	13	Humpy Lake, NT	William Vaznis	William Vaznis	1993	237
360 3/8	54 4/8	56 6/8	36 3/8	4 7/8	4 6/8	15 4/8	17 2/8	1/8	13 7/8	13	21	Courageous Lake, NT	Robert J. Maslowski	Robert J. Maslowski	1996	237
360 3/8	45	43 4/8	27 7/8	4 7/8	5 3/8	15 4/8	2	2 2/8	10 6/8	21	20	Point Lake, NT	Gary L. Vogel	Gary L. Vogel	1996	237
360 2/8	52 4/8	53 2/8	33 5/8	5 1/8	5 1/8	17 2/8	19 1/8	7 7/8	10 7/8	13	27	Jolly Lake, NT	Ronald D. Zelewski	Ronald D. Zelewski	1998	237
360 1/8	48 4/8	48 1/8	27 3/8	5 1/8	5 6/8	15 2/8	14 7/8	6 3/8	10 7/8	15	18	Obstruction Rapids, NT	George Bishop	George Bishop	1989	242
360 1/8	52 4/8	49 5/8	31 4/8	7	6 3/8	14 7/8	6 5/8	10	10 7/8	22	23	Rocher Lake, NT	Jason C. Marsh	Jason Marsh	1998	243
417 5/8*	50 7/8	49 4/8	34 3/8	5	5 7/8	13 5/8	14 6/8	9 1/8		22	20	Pellatt Lake, NU	Bill Tait	Aaron P. Hassler	2001	
400 6/8*	46 7/8	49 4/8	34 3/8	5	5 7/8	13 5/8	14 6/8	9 1/8	10 7/8	20	27	Blevins Lake, MB	Ron Shykitka	Ron Shykitka	1998	
395 2/8*	54 3/8	56 3/8	37 7/8	4 5/8	4 4/8	18 6/8	19 5/8	13 1/8	10 7/8	22	23	Commonwealth Lake, MB	Michael Reimer	Michael Reimer	1996	

* Final score is subject to revision by additional verifying measurements.

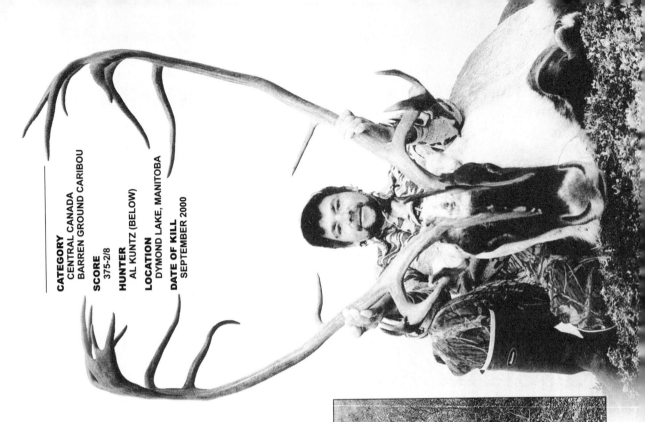

CATEGORY
CENTRAL CANADA
BARREN GROUND CARIBOU

SCORE
375-2/8

HUNTER
AL KUNTZ (BELOW)

LOCATION
DYMOND LAKE, MANITOBA

DATE OF KILL
SEPTEMBER 2000

CATEGORY
CENTRAL CANADA
BARREN GROUND CARIBOU

SCORE
368-4/8

HUNTER
KEVIN R. WILLIAMS (ABOVE)

LOCATION
MACKAY LAKE, NORTHWEST
TERRITORIES

DATE OF KILL
SEPTEMBER 2001

SCORE
387-5/8

HUNTER
M. JOSEPH BROUGH (RIGHT)

LOCATION
WHITEWOLF LAKE,
NORTHWEST TERRITORIES

DATE OF KILL
SEPTEMBER 1999

CATEGORY
CENTRAL CANADA
BARREN GROUND CARIBOU

SCORE
360-3/8

HUNTER
RONALD D. ZELEWSKI

LOCATION
JOLLY LAKE, NORTHWEST
TERRITORIES

DATE OF KILL
SEPTEMBER 1998

CATEGORY
CENTRAL CANADA
BARREN GROUND CARIBOU

SCORE
394-4/8

HUNTER
THOMAS E. KRIZ (LEFT)

LOCATION
COURAGEOUS LAKE,
NORTHWEST TERRITORIES

DATE OF KILL
SEPTEMBER 2000

SCORE
361-6/8

HUNTER
DONALD C. NORHEIM (BELOW)

LOCATION
MACKAY LAKE,
NORTHWEST TERRITORIES

DATE OF KILL
SEPTEMBER 2001

CATEGORY
CENTRAL CANADA
BARREN GROUND CARIBOU

SCORE
407

HUNTER
DANIEL J. GARTNER (RIGHT)

LOCATION
MACKAY LAKE, NORTHWEST
TERRITORIES

DATE OF KILL
SEPTEMBER 1997

SCORE
373

HUNTER
JOE HOCEVAR (TOP LEFT)

LOCATION
RENDEZ-VOUS LAKE,
NORTHWEST TERRITORIES

DATE OF KILL
SEPTEMBER 2002

SCORE
384-4/8

HUNTER
CHRIS E. BROUGH
(LEFT)

LOCATION
WHITEWOLF LAKE,
NORTHWEST
TERRITORIES

DATE OF KILL
SEPTEMBER 1999

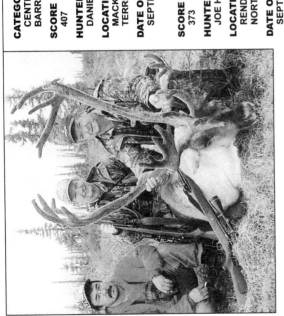

ROY CHAPMAN ANDREWS
1884-1960

By Leonard H. Wurman

Long considered the model and inspiration for Indiana Jones, Andrews was a scientist and adventurer best known for organizing and leading the Central Asiatic Expeditions. Like history's other great explorers, he undertook prodigious challenges with unwavering resolve at great personal risk. From 1922 through 1930, under the auspices of New York's American Museum of Natural History, Andrews led five complex expeditions into the Gobi Desert to study modern zoological life and to search for fossil evidence of prehistoric mammals and dinosaurs. Groups of scientists using motor vehicles functioned as independent working groups, and camel caravans were used to bring in supplies and take out specimens. The teams found enormous fossil deposits, including the first known dinosaur eggs. Andrews' charisma, courage, and resourcefulness secured the expeditions' successes despite the extreme political instability of the region and constant harassment by the armies of competing warlords. ■

ANDREWS IS SHOWN HERE WITH DINOSAUR EGGS FOUND ON ONE OF HIS MANY EXPEDITIONS IN ASIA.

QUEBEC-LABRADOR CARIBOU
WORLD'S RECORD

RANK
World's Record

SCORE
474 $^{6}/_{8}$

LOCATION
Nain, LB

HUNTER
Zack Elbow

OWNER
B&C National Collection

DATE KILLED
1931

This fine caribou trophy makes one wonder how many potential big game World's Records were already taken by the Inuit during their long tradition of hunting in North America. The trophy is one of the few specimens of the rare caribou race from Labrador. It was shot by Zack Elbow near Nain, Canada, during the winter of 1931 and later picked up by Charles Ray Peck who recorded an account of his find.

"During the summer of 1932, I was cruising home from Norway on a chartered Norwegian sealing vessel. When we reached Nain, a small village on the Labrador coast, we had our first sight of trees and of continental North America, so we decided to explore a fjord that ran inland for perhaps 50 miles to the northwest. As a sort of guide, we took along from the village an Eskimo named Zack Elbow for we had gathered that we might see some caribou and find some good trout fishing. We stayed at the head of the fjord for several days. While some of the party were enjoying the fishing, my friend Hoff Benjamin and I went caribou hunting with the Eskimo, who understood no English.

"Mosquitos were extremely bothersome, but the first day we saw two or three small caribou, which I did not shoot. This seemed to irritate the Eskimo. However, by the next day I had succeeded in conveying to him that I was hunting for 'big Tuktu.' So we proceeded overland, I would say about 12 miles, to a spot where Zack had shot a couple of bulls, for meat, during the previous winter. When he led

us to this place I could see two huge heads lying on the ground, 50 yards away. Foxes, of course, had eaten everything that Zack had left except the bones. We tossed a coin to see whether Hoff Benjamin or I would be the possessor of the larger head. I won."

This head, presented to the Boone and Crockett Club's National Collection of Heads and Horns by Peck in 1951, is the highest scoring caribou ever recorded. As the picture below shows, these Quebec-Labrador heads often differ markedly from those of the caribou races in the western part of the continent. ■

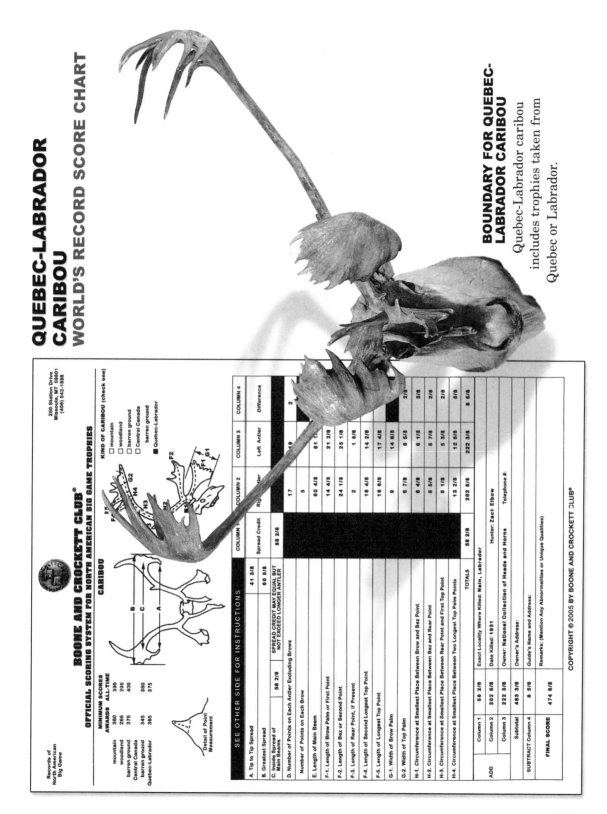

QUEBEC-LABRADOR CARIBOU
WORLD'S RECORD SCORE CHART

Records of
North American
Big Game

250 Station Drive
Missoula, MT 59801
(406) 542-1888

BOONE AND CROCKETT CLUB®
OFFICIAL SCORING SYSTEM FOR NORTH AMERICAN BIG GAME TROPHIES

CARIBOU

MINIMUM SCORES	AWARDS	ALL-TIME
mountain	360	390
woodland	265	295
barren ground	375	400
Central Canada barren ground	345	360
Quebec-Labrador	365	375

KIND OF CARIBOU (check one)
- ☐ mountain
- ☐ woodland
- ☐ barren ground
- ☐ Central Canada barren ground
- ■ Quebec-Labrador

Detail of Point Measurement

SEE OTHER SIDE FOR INSTRUCTIONS	COLUMN 1	COLUMN 2	COLUMN 3	COLUMN 4
		Right Antler	Left Antler	Difference
A. Tip to Tip Spread	41 3/8			
B. Greatest Spread	60 3/8			
C. Inside Spread of Main Beams	58 2/8	SPREAD CREDIT MAY EQUAL BUT NOT EXCEED LONGER ANTLER	Spread Credit	58 2/8
D. Number of Points on Each Antler Excluding Brows				
Number of Points on Each Brow		17	19	
E. Length of Main Beam		5	6	1
F-1. Length of Brow Palm or First Point		60 4/8	61 1	1
F-2. Length of Bez or Second Point		14 4/8	21 2/8	
F-3. Length of Rear Point, If Present		24 1/8	25 1/8	
F-4. Length of Second Longest Top Point		2	1 6/8	
F-5. Length of Longest Top Point		16 4/8	14 2/8	2
G-1. Width of Brow Palm		16 6/8	17 4/8	
G-2. Width of Top Palm		9	14 6/8	
H-1. Circumference at Smallest Place Between Brow and Bez Point		6 7/8	6 5/8	2/8
H-2. Circumference at Smallest Place Between Bez and Rear Point		6 4/8	6 1/8	3/8
H-3. Circumference at Smallest Place Between Rear Point and First Top Point		5 5/8	5 7/8	2/8
H-4. Circumference at Smallest Place Between Two Longest Top Palm Points		5 1/8	5 3/8	2/8
		13 2/8	12 5/8	5/8
TOTALS	58 2/8	202 6/8	222 3/8	8 5/8

	Column 1	58 2/8	Exact Locality Where Killed: Nain, Labrador
ADD	Column 2	202 6/8	Date Killed: 1931 — Hunter: Zack Elbow
	Column 3	222 3/8	Owner: National Collection of Heads and Horns
	Subtotal	483 3/8	Owner's Address:
SUBTRACT Column 4		8 5/8	Guide's Name and Address:
FINAL SCORE		474 6/8	Remarks: (Mention Any Abnormalities or Unique Qualities)

Telephone #:

COPYRIGHT © 2005 BY BOONE AND CROCKETT CLUB®

BOUNDARY FOR QUEBEC-LABRADOR CARIBOU

Quebec-Labrador caribou includes trophies taken from Quebec or Labrador.

TOP 10 QUEBEC-LABRADOR CARIBOU

NORTH AMERICAN BIG GAME TROPHY

KIND OF CA

CARIBOU

NUMBER 5 — 439-1/8 POINTS
DON TOMBERLIN — 1985

NUMBER 4 — 441-7/8 POINTS
LARRY R. WALDRON — 1993

NUMBER 2 — 464-4/8 POINTS
JAMES A. DELUCA — 1983
Centi
New York

NUMBER 1 — 474-6/8 POINTS
ZACK ELBOW — 1931

NUMBER 3 — 460-6/8 POINTS
LYNN D. MCLAUD — 1978

C. of MAIN BEAMS 58-2/8 exceed length of lor
of MAIN BEAMS of Main Beams exceeds l
C. IF Inside Spread of Main Beams exceeds l
antler length, enter difference
D. Number of Points on Each Antler excluding
antler length
D. Number of Points on Each Antler exclud
Number of Points on Each Brow

NUMBER 6 — 438-2/8 POINTS
RONALD R. RAGAN — 1975

NUMBER 10 — 431-6/8 POINTS
CAROL A. MAUCH — 1984

NUMBER 9 — 433-2/8 POINTS
ROBERT E. MCNEILL — 1986

NUMBER 8 — 433-3/8 POIN
DEWEY MARK — 1973

DON L. CORLEY — 1983

QUEBEC-LABRADOR CARIBOU

Rangifer tarandus

Score	Length of Main Beam R	L	Inside Spread	Circumference at Smallest Place Between Brow and Bez Points R	L	Length of Brow Points R	L	Width of Brow Points R	L	Number of Points R	L	Locality	Hunter	Owner	Date Killed	Rank
474 6/8	60 4/8	61 1/8	58 2/8	6 4/8	6 1/8	14 4/8	21 2/8	9	14 6/8	22	30	Nain, LB	Zack Elbow	B&C National Collection	1931	1
464 4/8	55 7/8	54 2/8	54 5/8	5 6/8	5 6/8	19 2/8	19 5/8	2 1/8	14 1/8	18	23	Tunulic River, QC	James A. DeLuca	James A. DeLuca	1983	2
460 6/8	59 4/8	56 5/8	49 2/8	5 1/8	5 2/8	16 6/8	21 4/8	13 6/8	18 4/8	22	24	Ungava Bay, QC	Lynn D. McLaud	Lynn D. McLaud	1978	3
441 7/8	52 3/8	51 7/8	44	5 6/8	5 7/8	16 6/8	21 6/8	6 7/8	14 5/8	23	23	Lake Arbique, QC	Larry R. Waldron	Larry R. Waldron	1993	4
439 4/8	56 6/8	59 1/8	42	6 7/8	5 7/8	17 7/8	20 2/8	12 3/8	13 7/8	11	22	Ungava Bay, QC	Don Tomberlin	Don Tomberlin	1985	5
438 2/8	59 3/8	55 4/8	52 7/8	5 3/8	5 3/8	8	21 1/8	1/8	19 1/8	17	25	Beach Camp, QC	Ronald R. Ragan	Ronald R. Ragan	1975	6
434 7/8	51 2/8	52	44 5/8	4 7/8	5 1/8	16 3/8	20 6/8	14 7/8	8 6/8	25	22	Mistinibi Lake, QC	Don L. Corley	Don L. Corley	1983	7
433 3/8	50 6/8	53 7/8	54	5 6/8	5 4/8	16 5/8	20 1/8	9 7/8	16 1/8	22	28	George River, QC	Dewey Mark	Dewey Mark	1973	8
433 2/8	46 5/8	44 2/8	41 1/8	5 1/8	5 6/8	20 1/8	20 1/8	14 5/8	17 4/8	22	24	Lake Otelnuk, QC	Robert E. McNeill	Robert E. McNeill	1986	9
431 6/8	53 4/8	56	46 1/8	5 4/8	5 6/8	16 5/8	20 5/8	3 6/8	15 1/8	19	18	Tunulik River, QC	Carol A. Mauch	Carol A. Mauch	1984	10
430 7/8	52 2/8	56 4/8	47	6 2/8	6 5/8	11	20 6/8	1 7/8	17 4/8	22	33	George River, QC	Larry Barnett	Larry Barnett	1978	11
429 6/8	55 1/8	59 1/8	50 1/8	5 6/8	5 5/8	21 6/8	2 1/8	19 1/8	1/8	15	12	Ford Lake, QC	George Shultz	George Shultz	1972	12
429 2/8	51 6/8	50 1/8	48 3/8	5 6/8	5 4/8	18 1/8	18 5/8	13 1/8	14 6/8	21	21	Mistinibi Lake, QC	Charles E. Wilson, Jr.	Charles E. Wilson, Jr.	1980	13
428 5/8	51 5/8	52 1/8	38 5/8	6	6	14 7/8	15 3/8	9 4/8	12	26	30	George River, QC	Cayetano G. Arriola, Jr.	Cayetano G. Arriola, Jr.	1975	14
427	56 1/8	57 6/8	48 2/8	6 4/8	6 6/8	16 6/8	14 7/8	14 4/8	2 7/8	21	13	Ungava Bay, QC	David Walker	David Walker	1984	15
425 7/8	52 5/8	51 4/8	41 3/8	5 5/8	6	21 5/8	17 1/8	18	12 2/8	19	15	Natuak Lake, QC	Patricio M. Sada	Patricio M. Sada	1993	16
424 1/8	55 2/8	55 3/8	47 6/8	6 2/8	5 6/8	16 2/8	18 3/8	9 4/8	14 6/8	18	22	Serigny River, QC	Brad Case	Brad Case	1989	17
423 6/8	50 4/8	49 1/8	52 5/8	5 7/8	6 1/8	15 4/8	21 4/8	7 4/8	16 2/8	26	24	Helluva Lake, QC	Jeff C. Wright	Jeff C. Wright	2001	18
421 4/8	52 7/8	54 4/8	53 5/8	5 7/8	5 3/8	17 2/8	5 6/8	12 2/8	1/8	20	16	George River, QC	Maurice Southmayd	Maurice Southmayd	1979	19
417	53 2/8	57 4/8	52 1/8	5 4/8	5 3/8	16 2/8	21 3/8	10 1/8	12 3/8	24	16	Caniapiscau River, QC	John A. Picard	John A. Picard	1994	20
416 7/8	48 7/8	48 5/8	38 4/8	6	5 4/8	14 5/8	18 4/8	11 4/8	16 4/8	23	24	Schefferville, QC	Michael L. Hoft	Michael L. Hoft	1997	21
416 1/8	45 3/8	47 7/8	47 4/8	4 7/8	4 7/8	13 1/8	16	6 4/8	11	28	27	George River, QC	Collins F. Kellogg	Collins F. Kellogg	1978	22
416 1/8	48	45 2/8	38 4/8	5 1/8	5 1/8	21 2/8	16 4/8	15 7/8	13 7/8	25	21	Lake Amichinatwayach, QC	Thomas R. Conrardy	Thomas R. Conrardy	1995	23
416	52	50 3/8	50	5 3/8	5 2/8	21 2/8	20 7/8	14	15 5/8	17	20	Lake Consigny, QC	Ricardo L. Garza	Ricardo L. Garza	1989	24
415 7/8	59 4/8	55 6/8	44	5 1/8	5	16 1/8	17 4/8	10 2/8	14 2/8	20	22	Minto Lake Island, QC	Curt M. Coleman	Curt M. Coleman	1999	25
415 5/8	54 6/8	52 4/8	46	5	5 2/8	17 3/8	18 2/8	8 2/8	16 6/8	15	21	George River, QC	George E. Poleshock	George E. Poleshock	1980	26
414 7/8	62 4/8	66	43 6/8	5 1/8	5 6/8	21 5/8	2 3/8	1/8	16 6/8	16	22	Schefferville, QC	Peggy A. Vallery	Peggy A. Vallery	1980	27
414	42 7/8	43 5/8	41	5 6/8	6	15 1/8	13 7/8	8 3/8	8 1/8	22	23	George River Lodge, QC	James E. McCarthy	James E. McCarthy	1974	28
412 2/8	53 6/8	52 2/8	45 5/8	6	6 4/8	17 7/8	16	13 1/8	11 1/8	16	22	Whale River, QC	Daniel E. Merrell	Daniel E. Merrell	1972	29
411 7/8	51	51 7/8	52 5/8	7	8 2/8	13 3/8	14	5 6/8	4 1/8	9	14	Mistinibi Lake, QC	Rudolf Sand	Rudolf Sand	1973	30
411 7/8	53 2/8	49 2/8	56 6/8	5 2/8	5 3/8	17 6/8	22 4/8	8 5/8	13	14	19	Tunulik River, QC	Leon Orzechowski	Leon Orzechowski	1978	30
411 1/8	61 4/8	63 4/8	48	5 7/8	6	16 7/8	3 2/8	17 7/8	1/8	19	18	Mistinibi Lake, QC	David H. Crum	David H. Crum	1980	32
410 7/8	50 7/8	51 2/8	54	5 1/8	5 6/8	19 5/8	17 5/8	13 5/8	13 4/8	19	23	Caniapiscau Lake, QC	Stephen C. Lockhart	Stephen C. Lockhart	1989	33
410 6/8	59 4/8	60 4/8	40 6/8	5 7/8	5 6/8	17 2/8	17 5/8	14	8 7/8	26	22	George River, QC	Kenneth E. Goslant	Kenneth E. Goslant	1974	34
410 6/8	44 5/8	42 4/8	46 4/8	6 1/8	5 7/8	13 4/8	13 4/8	14 6/8	13 7/8	25	24	George River, QC	Gail W. Holderman	Gail W. Holderman	1979	34

Score													Locality	Hunter	Owner	Date	Rank
410 4/8	52 4/8	51 6/8	48 6/8	18	6 2/8	6	16 5/8	18	12	10 7/8	18	20	Pons River, QC	Donald F. Young	Donald F. Young	1988	36
410	56	55 6/8	52 1/8	21 1/8	5	6 2/8	22 4/8	14	12 2/8	8	15	16	Lake Nachicapau, QC	Charles L. Buechel, Jr.	Charles L. Buechel, Jr.	1987	37
409 6/8	51 2/8	50 6/8	51 1/8	14	5 2/8	5 1/8	16 2/8	16	8 7/8	11	18	20	Mistinibi Lake, QC	George H. Fearons	George H. Fearons	1982	38
409 4/8	48 7/8	49 1/8	43	16	5 4/8	5 2/8	20 1/8	28	12 4/8	12 6/8	28	22	Tunulik Lake, QC	Robert F. Cook	Robert F. Cook	1979	39
408 4/8	57 2/8	47 6/8	45	21 6/8	5 3/8	5 3/8	15 4/8	15 4/8	12 2/8	1 7/8	19	14	Mistinibi Lake, QC	Lee Frudden	Lee Frudden	1980	40
408 4/8	53 2/8	55 1/8	46 1/8	18	6 7/8	6	13 4/8	13 4/8	12 2/8	6 6/8	19	19	Ungava Bay, QC	Richard H. Propp	Richard H. Propp	1985	40
408	55 2/8	56 3/8	44 6/8	18 3/8	5 3/8	5	19 1/8	18 3/8	17 2/8	16 6/8	20	23	Caniapiscau River, QC	Bernard W. Masino	Bernard W. Masino	1987	42
407 7/8	54 6/8	56 3/8	42 1/8	17 6/8	6 3/8	6 3/8	15 2/8	17 6/8	11 4/8	10	19	17	Tunulik Lake, QC	Robert L. Sprinkle, Jr.	Robert L. Sprinkle, Jr.	1979	43
407 5/8	50 3/8	50	45 3/8	17 3/8	5 6/8	5 6/8	18 7/8	17 3/8	13 4/8	11	18	21	Lake Moyer, QC	Jeffrey S. Baker	Jeffrey S. Baker	1988	44
406 3/8	58 5/8	59	46 3/8	9	8 6/8	8 6/8	21	9	13 5/8	11	15	18	Delay River, QC	Trevor H.S. Povah	Trevor H.S. Povah	1989	45
406 2/8	49	49	43 2/8	5 2/8	4 6/8	4 6/8	22 2/8	5 2/8	1/8	16 4/8	21	22	Caniapiscau River, QC	Michael R. Miggins	Michael R. Miggins	1987	46
406	45 4/8	44 3/8	48 7/8	16 3/8	4 5/8	4 6/8	17 5/8	18 4/8	14 3/8	15 4/8	25	18	Narcy Lake, QC	Thomas A. Rue	Thomas A. Rue	1988	47
405 4/8	55	56 1/8	51 3/8	18 4/8	5 7/8	5 4/8	22	16 6/8	12 3/8	11 2/8	19	19	Tunulik River, QC	Jerry Ippolito	Jerry Ippolito	1980	48
405 2/8	52	53	44 6/8	16 6/8	6	5 6/8	17	15 7/8	12 4/8	17 6/8	19	23	De Pas River, QC	Herbert J. Engelmann	Herbert J. Engelmann	1979	49
405 1/8	51 2/8	52	52	20	4 6/8	5 2/8	20 1/8	20	2 4/8	12 6/8	16	16	Nullualuk Lake, QC	Henry C. Gilbertson	Henry C. Gilbertson	1988	50
405	53 1/8	54 4/8	51 4/8	20 3/8	5 2/8	5	20 4/8	17 3/8	15 7/8	9 5/8	15	15	Knob Lake, QC	Chester Gluck	Chester Gluck	1964	51
404 6/8	46 4/8	46	40 4/8	17 3/8	6 1/8	6 4/8	18 2/8	15 2/8	10 7/8	19 2/8	14	14	Ungava Bay, QC	Daniel W. Inserra	Daniel W. Inserra	1979	52
404 5/8	53 4/8	57 6/8	42 6/8	19 4/8	5 2/8	5 2/8	18 2/8	17 3/8	9 6/8	10 7/8	15	15	Camp Tuktu, QC	Robert E. Prittinen	Robert E. Prittinen	1980	53
404 2/8	53 3/8	50 4/8	46	19 4/8	5 6/8	5 6/8	13 7/8	19 4/8	2	9 6/8	13	16	George River, QC	Paul Bambara	Paul Bambara	1985	54
404	49 5/8	50 4/8	51 7/8	16 5/8	5 4/8	5 3/8	17 3/8	16 5/8	14 7/8	8 5/8	20	17	Sagler Fiord, NL	Ernest W. Foster, Jr.	Ernest W. Foster, Jr.	1985	55
403 5/8	46 1/8	48 2/8	50 7/8	17 1/8	5 4/8	5 4/8	16 7/8	17 1/8	9 7/8	13 3/8	20	18	Schefferville, QC	L.C. Harold	L.C. Harold	1982	56
403 3/8	58 6/8	61	44 2/8	19 5/8	5 3/8	5	18 4/8	19 5/8	10 5/8	12 1/8	18	21	Ungava Bay, QC	John A. Gulius	John A. Gulius	1975	57
403 3/8	54 3/8	54 2/8	41 5/8	18 4/8	5 5/8	4 6/8	11 2/8	18 4/8	14 7/8	1/8	20	17	Caniapiscau River, QC	Bernard W. Masino	Bernard W. Masino	1987	58
403 2/8	47 3/8	50 2/8	43	20 7/8	5 3/8	6 1/8	11 1/8	20 7/8	16 4/8	1/8	28	28	Samuel Lake, QC	James R. Blankenheim	James R. Blankenheim	1989	58
403	51 2/8	51 1/8	48 1/8	18 2/8	5 2/8	5 7/8	19 1/8	18 2/8	13 4/8	11	15	16	Thibault Lake, QC	Ralph L. Cervo	Ralph L. Cervo	1983	60
403	47 7/8	54	35 2/8	11 6/8	5 2/8	5 2/8	17 4/8	11 6/8	14 6/8	3 4/8	21	28	Caniapiscau River, QC	Barbara A. Shuler	Barbara A. Shuler	1985	61
402 6/8	56 4/8	54	47	1	5	5	19 7/8	1	16 6/8	1/8	20	28	Kuujjuaq, QC	John T. Richards, Jr.	John T. Richards, Jr.	1986	62
402 6/8	56 5/8	53 4/8	45 5/8	18 4/8	5 1/8	4 7/8	17 1/8	18 4/8	15 5/8	13 6/8	22	21	Mollet Lake, QC	James C. Johnson	James C. Johnson	2001	62
402 2/8	60 2/8	57 3/8	44 2/8	16 6/8	4 6/8	6 1/8	15 3/8	16 6/8	8 2/8	11 4/8	19	16	George River, QC	Paul B. Brunner	Paul B. Brunner	1980	64
402	54 2/8	57 3/8	48 3/8	15 6/8	5 2/8	5 3/8	16	15 6/8	10 2/8	6 3/8	19	18	Mistinibi Lake, QC	Theodore Greenwood	Theodore Greenwood	1981	65
401 3/8	57 1/8	57 6/8	48 5/8	20	5 7/8	5 5/8	19	20	9 2/8	15 6/8	19	17	Koksoak River, QC	Arthur J. Pelon	Arthur J. Pelon	1986	66
401 3/8	49 4/8	45 1/8	49 4/8	10 7/8	4 4/8	6	18 6/8	10 7/8	13	1 6/8	16	22	Ungava Bay, QC	C. Gordon Demeritt	C. Gordon Demeritt	1988	66
401 2/8	57	58 3/8	48 1/8	18 6/8	5 1/8	5 1/8	16 4/8	18 6/8	8 7/8	9 6/8	17	15	Indian River, QC	Bruce Hartel	Bruce Hartel	1981	68
401 1/8	49 7/8	51	49 2/8	17 3/8	5 7/8	5 7/8	18 4/8	17 3/8	13 7/8	1 6/8	15	16	George River, QC	Claude E. Genet	Claude E. Genet	1966	69
401	51 2/8	52 7/8	44 4/8	18 5/8	6 1/8	6 6/8	19 4/8	18 5/8	16	10 4/8	20	24	George River, QC	Robert A. Krizek	Cabela's, Inc.	1979	70
400 5/8	52 4/8	52 6/8	37 7/8	6 6/8	5 5/8	5 5/8	13	6 6/8	15 2/8	16	17	22	Tunulic River, QC	M. Farrel Gosman	M. Farrel Gosman	1978	71
400 5/8	46	46 1/8	46 1/8	12 4/8	6	6	14 4/8	12 4/8	11 3/8	13 3/8	21	18	Mistinibi Lake, QC	Dennis E. Moos	Dennis E. Moos	1980	71
400 5/8	47 2/8	47 7/8	45 1/8	7 6/8	5 1/8	5 1/8	18 6/8	7 6/8	8 6/8	16 2/8	24	26	Marin Lake, QC	Wilhelm Hollstein	Wilhelm Hollstein	1995	71
400 4/8	54 5/8	56 2/8	52 5/8	6	5 4/8	5 3/8	23 4/8	6	17 4/8	1/8	15	11	George River, QC	Dale D. Wieand	Dale D. Wieand	1977	74
400 1/8	56 6/8	53 1/8	47 3/8	17 3/8	5 4/8	6	16 6/8	17 3/8	9 3/8	11	21	18	Pons River, QC	Charles E. Putt	Charles E. Putt	1988	75
400 1/8	51 1/8	51 1/8	51 1/8	18 5/8	5 5/8	5	19 2/8	18 5/8	15 5/8	15 7/8	22	22	Pons River, QC	Ronald L. Boucher	Ronald L. Boucher	1986	76
400	56 4/8	58 2/8	51 6/8	6 6/8	5 1/8	5 6/8	16 3/8	6 6/8	9 2/8	9 2/8	15	19	George River, QC	John C. Sullivan, Jr.	John C. Sullivan, Jr.	1978	77
400	53	50 4/8	54	12 4/8	5 3/8	5 2/8	18 4/8	12 4/8	13 7/8	1 4/8	11	21	Fort Chimo, QC	Elwood Larsen	Elwood Larsen	1986	77
399 7/8	55	56	58	7 6/8	5	4 7/8	18 5/8	7 6/8	12 2/8	1 4/8	13	14	George River, QC	David L. George	David L. George	1968	79
399 5/8	54 2/8	52 2/8	45	6	5 3/8	5	18 5/8	6	12 2/8	2 4/8	15	21	Desbergeres Lake, QC	William E. Johnson	William E. Johnson	1996	80
399 3/8	57 7/8	59 3/8	45 3/8	17 7/8	6	5 6/8	17 1/8	17 7/8	13 1/8	1 4/8	15	14	Dihourse Lake, QC	George E. Rommler	George E. Rommler	1980	81
399 3/8	55 7/8	53 5/8	53 5/8	17 7/8	6 4/8	6 1/8	15 7/8	17 7/8	5 7/8	4 4/8	27	20	Pons River, QC	Robert L. Smock	Gary R. Smock	1986	81
398 6/8	52 4/8	51 1/8	48 3/8	13 4/8	5 3/8	5 4/8	15 6/8	13 4/8	3 5/8	9 4/8	16	14	George River, QC	Bob Bates	Bob Bates	1980	83

QUEBEC-LABRADOR CARIBOU
Rangifer tarandus

Score	Length of Main Beam R	L	Inside Spread	Circumference at Smallest Place Between Brow and Bez Points R	L	Length of Brow Points R	L	Width of Brow Points R	L	Number of Points R	L	Locality	Hunter	Owner	Date Killed	Rank
398 4/8	52 7/8	51 6/8	45	6	6	16 4/8	16 5/8	12 2/8	11 3/8	14	14	Tunulik River, QC	Jack Schwabland	Jack Schwabland	1980	84
398 3/8	54 4/8	53	49	5 2/8	5 2/8	19 4/8	17 5/8	16 2/8	1 4/8	18	17	Tunulik River, QC	Anthony L. Pinnavaia, Sr.	Anthony L. Pinnavaia, Sr.	1987	85
398 1/8	54 3/8	55 7/8	52 4/8	4 7/8	4 7/8	10 4/8	20 2/8	1/8	15 6/8	15	14	Ford Lake, QC	George H. Fearons	George H. Fearons	1977	86
397 6/8	48 5/8	49 4/8	47	5 1/8	5	19 4/8	18	16	10 4/8	22	16	Lac Vallerenne, QC	Charles J. Spies	Charles J. Spies	1988	87
397 5/8	54 2/8	53	57 4/8	5 6/8	5 7/8	9 4/8	16 4/8	1/8	11 2/8	12	20	George River, QC	Stanley M. Boots	Stanley M. Boots	1983	88
397 5/8	53 1/8	54 4/8	49 4/8	5 4/8	5 6/8	16 7/8	18	14 3/8		14	21	Caniapiscau River, QC	John R. Connelly	John R. Connelly	1988	88
397 5/8	51 1/8	49 4/8	50 7/8	5 3/8	5 6/8	16 7/8	17 7/8	11 6/8	8	20	15	Lake Rigouville, QC	James M. Parker	James M. Parker	1998	88
397 4/8	48 1/8	51 2/8	38 7/8	5 6/8	5 7/8	19 2/8	15 4/8	12 6/8	10 7/8	22	19	Serigny River, QC	Gary A. Perin	Gary A. Perin	1987	91
397 3/8	43 2/8	45 6/8	42 3/8	5 7/8	5 6/8	18	16	15 7/8	4	23	20	Black Duck Bay, NL	Hal W. Johnson	Hal W. Johnson	1994	92
397 3/8	53	51 6/8	45 2/8	5 4/8	5 2/8	16	11 3/8	13		21	20	Fel Lake, QC	Roscoe Blaisdell	Roscoe Blaisdell	2001	92
397 2/8	43 5/8	47 7/8	46 2/8	6	5 6/8	2 1/8	17 1/8	1/8	12 7/8	21	18	Twin River Lodge, QC	Fred W. Sheaman, Jr.	Fred W. Sheaman, Jr.	1969	94
397 1/8	56 5/8	56 6/8	61 1/8	5 2/8	5 2/8	18 1/8	2	8 5/8	1/8	19	17	George River, QC	Morris Weinstein	Morris Weinstein	1972	95
397	54 2/8	54 2/8	40	5 1/8	5 1/8	15 1/8	15 4/8	14 1/8	15 4/8	21	22	Ungava Bay, QC	Charles T. Sheley	Charles T. Sheley	1979	96
396 5/8	46 7/8	47 7/8	39 3/8	5 7/8	5 6/8	19 4/8	16 2/8	1/8	15 3/8	21	23	Tunulik River, QC	Charles W. Dixon	Charles W. Dixon	1979	97
396 5/8	47 7/8	50 4/8	46 3/8	5 4/8	5 4/8	16 4/8	16 4/8	13 4/8	5 2/8	20	12	Innuksuak River, QC	Michel Labbe	Michel Labbe	2000	97
396 4/8	59 7/8	59 2/8	46 4/8	6	5 6/8	20 3/8	16 4/8	17 1/8	8 6/8	16	17	George River Lodge, QC	Robert S. Carroll	Robert S. Carroll	1974	99
396 4/8	45 2/8	46 7/8	40	5 5/8	5 7/8	14 3/8	16 7/8	11 4/8	13 6/8	24	21	Gerido Lake, QC	Jerry McDonald	Jerry McDonald	1992	99
396 3/8	53 1/8	52	38 7/8	5 1/8	5 1/8	19 3/8	16 3/8	14 2/8	1	21	18	Pons River, QC	Glenn M. Smith	Glenn M. Smith	1986	101
396 2/8	54 1/8	55 2/8	48 5/8	6 4/8	7 3/8	11 4/8	11 4/8	13 4/8	6 2/8	21	14	George River, QC	John E. Clark	John E. Clark	1980	102
396	55 2/8	57 2/8	42 5/8	5 3/8	5 1/8	21 5/8	21 3/8	8 3/8	16 2/8	17	20	Ungava Bay, QC	Edwin L. DeYoung	Edwin L. DeYoung	1989	103
396	53 4/8	50 5/8	40 2/8	5 3/8	5 5/8	18 6/8	17 1/8	16 4/8	12 5/8	19	16	Black Duck Bay, NL	Hal W. Johnson	Hal W. Johnson	1994	103
395 5/8	55 4/8	58 3/8	51	5 5/8	5 6/8	1	18 7/8	1/8	14 3/8	15	22	Ungava Bay, QC	Bruce S. Markham	Bruce S. Markham	1979	105
395	47 7/8	51 2/8	44 6/8	5 2/8	5 4/8	8 7/8	18	1/8	14 4/8	19	24	George River, QC	Kurt Roenspies	Kurt Roenspies	1990	106
394 7/8	41	40 5/8	37 3/8	5 2/8	5 2/8	16	5 7/8	12 4/8	1/8	27	24	Kamaywapakich Lake, QC	Michael R. Carlson	Michael R. Carlson	1994	107
394 6/8	54 6/8	52 2/8	48 5/8	4 6/8	5 6/8	17 3/8	5	13	12 1/8	15	17	Ungava Bay, QC	Norbert D. Bremer	Norbert D. Bremer	1989	108
394 4/8	51 4/8	48 4/8	42 7/8	5 1/8	4 6/8	19 4/8	17 7/8	2 6/8	11 4/8	17	17	De Pas River, QC	William A. O'Connor	William A. O'Connor	1980	109
394 4/8	44 1/8	44 2/8	38 2/8	5 7/8	6 2/8	13 5/8	17 6/8	10	13 5/8	22	21	Rogers Lake, QC	Gregg D. Dunkel	Gregg D. Dunkel	1988	109
394 3/8	47 2/8	47 1/8	43	4 6/8	4 5/8	19 2/8	20 1/8	16 2/8	11 4/8	30	25	Caniapiscau River, QC	Jerilyn K. Zwolinski	Jerilyn K. Zwolinski	2001	111
394 2/8	58 4/8	55 4/8	54 2/8	5 4/8	6	20 4/8	7 2/8	1/8	13 7/8	14	13	Fiddle Lake, QC	Robert E. Hammond	Robert E. Hammond	1967	112
394 2/8	49 1/8	50 6/8	41	5 6/8	5 7/8	18 5/8	1 1/8	12	1	13	16	Mistinibi Lake, QC	Paul E. Robey	Paul E. Robey	1981	112
394 1/8	52 6/8	52 6/8	46 5/8	4 2/8	4 2/8	19 3/8	4 4/8	4 4/8	13	16	19	Ungava Region, QC	James F. Tappan	James F. Tappan	1967	114
394 1/8	50 2/8	52 1/8	42 4/8	5 6/8	5 4/8	18 5/8	19 6/8	10 7/8	12 1/8	22	17	Lake Ballantyne, QC	Donald A. Cowe	Donald A. Cowe	1993	114
394	54 2/8	51 6/8	48	6	5 6/8	18	5	4/8	15 2/8	13	21	Ungava Bay, QC	Nancy J. Alward	Nancy J. Alward	1988	116
393 6/8	50 7/8	54 2/8	40 1/8	4 7/8	5	16 7/8	9 4/8	12 5/8	1/8	22	16	George River, QC	Dick Ullery	Dick Ullery	1975	117
393 6/8	50 4/8	48 2/8	52 5/8	5 6/8	5 5/8	3 4/8	15	1/8	11 5/8	16	22	Bourg Lake, QC	Fred F. Boyce	Fred F. Boyce	1997	117

Score	M1	M2	M3	M4	M5	M6	M7	M8	M9	M10	Pts R	Pts L	Locality	Hunter	Owner	Date Killed	Rank
393 5/8	55 6/8	50 3/8	52 4/8	53 5/8	5 1/8	5 3/8	17 4/8	15 5/8	4 3/8	9 7/8	12	14	Ungava Bay, QC	Arthur Bashore	Arthur Bashore	1971	119
393 5/8	59 2/8	57 4/8	53 5/8		6 2/8	6 1/8	17 5/8	11 3/8		11 3/8	17	13	George River, QC	Michael J. Merritt	Michael J. Merritt	1978	119
393 3/8	45 1/8	42 1/8	41 7/8	18 2/8	5 3/8	4 4/8	16 7/8	14 4/8	11 1/8	11 1/8	24	26	Caniapiscau River, QC	Donald J. Coughlin	Donald J. Coughlin	1995	119
393 3/8	47 7/8	49 5/8	30	18 7/8	5 1/8	5 7/8	16 2/8	15 4/8	1/8	9 7/8	27	22	Petite Baleine River, QC	Gary A. Borton	Gary A. Borton	1995	122
393 3/8	55 3/8	56 6/8	48 4/8	1	5 7/8	5 6/8	18 2/8	14	14	9 7/8	15	19	Lake Natuak, QC	Dale Stangl	Dale Stangl	1989	123
393 1/8	51 3/8	50 2/8	53 2/8	16 2/8	5 1/8	5 1/8	17 3/8	16 2/8	1/8	9 5/8	17	19	Lake Ptarmigan, QC	Robert L. Sobolisky	Robert L. Sobolisky	1998	124
392 7/8	48 6/8	44 5/8	47 4/8	17 3/8	4 7/8	5 1/8	17 1/8	9 5/8	10 1/8	10 1/8	21	17	Manereuille Lake, QC	David MacDonald	David MacDonald	1999	125
392 5/8	49 4/8	48 6/8	46 4/8	17	5	5 3/8	17 7/8	8 6/8	12 2/8	12 2/8	21	21	Mollet Lake, QC	Stephen M. Van Poucke	Stephen M. Van Poucke	2001	125
392 5/8	52 5/8	52 4/8	52 5/8	19 1/8	5 2/8	5 2/8	17 1/8	6 4/8	8 7/8	8 7/8	20	20	Lake Consigny, QC	Thomas L. Vaux	Thomas L. Vaux	1988	127
392 5/8	55	53 4/8	53 4/8	18 5/8	5 1/8	5 3/8	7 2/8	15 3/8	1/8	1/8	20	17	Schefferville, QC	Robert Henn	Robert Henn	1979	128
392 4/8	48	47	35 2/8	17 3/8	4 4/8	4 5/8	17 4/8	14	14	13 3/8	24	25	George River, QC	Kerry W. Blanton	Kerry W. Blanton	1983	129
392 4/8	52 4/8	53 4/8	44 7/8	18 5/8	5 2/8	5 2/8	17 3/8	12 2/8	1/8	1/8	16	14	Caniapiscau River, QC	Michael E. Ingold	Michael E. Ingold	1988	129
392 4/8	50 7/8	52 4/8	52 7/8	12	5 6/8	6	11 6/8	10 6/8	12 6/8	12 6/8	15	17	Nulluluak Lake, QC	Charles L. McConn	Charles L. McConn	1993	129
392 3/8	57 3/8	57 1/8	43 4/8	16 7/8	5 4/8	5 6/8	18 2/8	2 4/8	13	13	19	20	Ungava Region, QC	Frank J. Blaha, Jr.	Frank J. Blaha, Jr.	1978	132
392 3/8	51 4/8	51 2/8	51 2/8	1 4/8	4 6/8	5 4/8	14 6/8	1/8	1 4/8	1 4/8	19	19	Baleine River, QC	John D. Sheaffer	John D. Sheaffer	1988	132
392 3/8	51	50 5/8	46 1/8	23	4 6/8	4 7/8	21 5/8	12 4/8	1/8	5 7/8	16	19	Pons River, QC	Louis J. Lorenzo	Louis J. Lorenzo	1991	132
392 3/8	54 4/8	54 4/8	44 2/8	18	5 5/8	5 5/8	18 2/8	1/8	12 6/8	12 6/8	15	13	Caniapiscau Lake, QC	Matthew Christy	Matthew Christy	2001	132
392 2/8	53 6/8	47 2/8	43 4/8	16 4/8	5 6/8	6 1/8	15	13 2/8	1/8	1/8	22	16	Maki Lake, QC	Sharon M. Pack	Sharon M. Pack	2001	132
392 2/8	51 6/8	51 2/8	43 5/8	16 4/8	5 1/8	5 2/8	16 4/8	13 2/8	1/8	11 4/8	19	16	False River, QC	Serge Danis	Serge Danis	1998	137
392 1/8	56 6/8	55 2/8	40 5/8	16 4/8	4 6/8	5 2/8	20 4/8	11 5/8	15 6/8	15 6/8	15	23	Tunulik River, QC	Salvatore A. Gusmano	Salvatore A. Gusmano	1981	138
391 7/8	55	53 4/8	41	3 5/8	6 2/8	4 6/8	14 6/8	3 7/8	1/8	14	15	18	George River, QC	Donald F. Senter	Donald F. Senter	1983	138
391 4/8	56 3/8	56	51 3/8	16 3/8	6 2/8	6 1/8	19 6/8	1/8	16 3/8	16 3/8	15	15	George River, QC	Alex Kariotakis	Alex Kariotakis	1974	140
391 3/8	60 4/8	57	54 7/8	15	5 6/8	5 3/8	19 3/8	2 4/8	13 6/8	13 6/8	13	15	Tunulik River, QC	Kenneth J. Gerstung	Kenneth J. Gerstung	1979	141
391 2/8	44 4/8	44 2/8	45 6/8	16 7/8	7 1/8	6	17	12 4/8	11 4/8	11 4/8	24	16	Rose Lake, QC	Paul F. Frigault	Paul F. Frigault	1998	142
391 2/8	49 2/8	48 3/8	46 4/8	15 1/8	5 6/8	5 1/8	16 1/8	9 3/8	12 6/8	12 6/8	18	24	Kakiattukallak Lake, QC	Dale E. Toweill	Dale E. Toweill	1994	143
391 1/8	48 3/8	53 4/8	37 4/8	18 5/8	5 4/8	5 6/8	18 5/8	12	4 3/8	1/8	18	17	Mollet Lake, QC	William K. Herndon	William K. Herndon	2001	144
391	54	54 6/8	39 2/8	18 2/8	5 4/8	5 2/8	18 2/8	13 3/8	14 6/8	14 6/8	24	15	Wolf Lake, QC	Robert G. Burkhouse	Robert G. Burkhouse	1993	145
390 5/8	51 3/8	51 2/8	47 4/8	8	6 3/8	5 4/8	20	13 4/8	1/8	1/8	15	16	Mistinibi Lake, QC	Thomas J. Merkley	Thomas J. Merkley	1979	146
390 4/8	54	55 2/8	53 7/8	14 1/8	5 4/8	5 4/8	17	8	13 5/8	13 5/8	16	14	Agnew Lake, QC	Walter Brennen	Walter Brennen	1996	146
390 4/8	49 6/8	52 4/8	42 1/8	18 4/8	5 5/8	5 5/8	14 6/8	12	6 5/8	6 5/8	18	18	George River, QC	James E. Prevost	James E. Prevost	1979	148
390 4/8	54	52 4/8	48 5/8	17 2/8	4 7/8	4 7/8	10 7/8	10 2/8	1/8	12 5/8	14	17	Caniapiscau River, QC	John W. Flies	John W. Flies	1990	148
390 2/8	46 1/8	45 3/8	47 2/8	23	6 1/8	4 6/8	14 6/8	15 -/8	17 2/8	17 2/8	21	23	George River, QC	John Daniels	John Daniels	1972	150
390 1/8	45 1/8	43 2/8	38 7/8	19 5/8	4 6/8	4 6/8	21 1/8	4 6/8	14 6/8	14 6/8	16	15	Musset Lake, QC	Gerald C. Gilbert	Gerald C. Gilbert	2000	151
390	53	55	46 4/8	15 4/8	5 4/8	5 4/8	18 4/8	1 7/8	14	14	12	17	Lake Astree, QC	Peter W. Spear	Peter W. Spear	1994	152
389 7/8	54 2/8	56 3/8	48 7/8	15 6/8	5 7/8	5 7/8	12 4/8	9 5/8	1 5/8	1 5/8	18	16	Schefferville, QC	Samuel March, Jr.	Samuel March, Jr.	1972	153
389 6/8	56 5/8	55 4/8	46 4/8	13 3/8	5 2/8	5 3/8	18 4/8	1	15 1/8	15 1/8	13	21	Ford Lake, QC	Carl F. Gernold	Carl F. Gernold	1982	154
389 6/8	53 3/8	54 6/8	44	11 1/8	5 4/8	5 5/8	22 4/8	1/8	20 6/8	20 6/8	15	20	Echo Lake, QC	James T. Luxem	James T. Luxem	1989	155
389 5/8	50 4/8	49 6/8	42 1/8	14 3/8	5 6/8	5 6/8	17 6/8	9 4/8	16 1/8	16 1/8	19	21	Sardine Lake, QC	David L. Turner	David L. Turner	1997	155
389 5/8	48 7/8	49 5/8	46 1/8	2 5/8	4 7/8	4 6/8	16 6/8	1/8	16 6/8	16 6/8	14	20	Lake Ronald, QC	Christopher H. Kantianis	Christopher H. Kantianis	1993	157
389 4/8	48 3/8	51 5/8	39 6/8	20 1/8	5 3/8	5 3/8	19 5/8	2	17 6/8	17 6/8	21	20	Pons River, QC	Henry R. Binette	Henry R. Binette	1995	157
389 4/8	48 4/8	49 4/8	40 5/8	13 4/8	5 4/8	5	18 1/8	6 6/8	14	14	16	25	Ungava Region, QC	Eugene M. Decker	Eugene M. Decker	1973	159
389 3/8	53 1/8	58 4/8	41 7/8	17 7/8	5 7/8	5 7/8	17 7/8	5	11 6/8	11 6/8	12	16	Mistinibi Lake, QC	Don L. Corley	Don L. Corley	1983	159
389 3/8	57	56 7/8	51 5/8	19 3/8	5	4 7/8	19 3/8	15 7/8	15 7/8	15 7/8	25	14	Potier River, QC	Donald L. Sagner	Donald L. Sagner	1995	159
389 2/8	43	43	37 5/8	18	6 1/8	6 1/8	19 6/8	14 4/8	16 6/8	16 6/8	22	22	Dunphy Lake, QC	Robert M. Johnston	Robert M. Johnston	1998	162
389 1/8	51 2/8	50 6/8	40 4/8	18	7 4/8	6 7/8	14 2/8	1/8	10 5/8	10 5/8	16	16	Tunulic River, QC	Clarence M. Pitsch	Clarence M. Pitsch	1987	163
389 1/8	53 3/8	57 6/8	42	18 5/8	7 1/8	5 7/8	17 4/8	13 2/8	1 7/8	1 7/8	23	13	George River, QC	George Dempsey	George Dempsey	1990	164
388 6/8													George River, QC	Rodney A. Scott	Rodney A. Scott	1990	165

QUEBEC-LABRADOR CARIBOU
Rangifer tarandus

Score	Length of Main Beam R	L	Inside Spread	Circumference at Smallest Place Between Brow and Bez Points R	L	Length of Brow Points R	L	Width of Brow Points R	L	Number of Points R	L	Locality	Hunter	Owner	Date Killed	Rank
388 4/8	52 7/8	52 5/8	58 1/8	5 7/8	5 5/8	17 4/8	14 4/8	12 1/8	10	18	17	Koksoak River, QC	Charlie D. Todd	Charlie D. Todd	1987	166
388	55	54 5/8	53	5 2/8	5 2/8	21 5/8	18 3/8	6 5/8	1/8	15	12	Caniapiscau River, QC	Henry O. Fromm	Henry O. Fromm	1985	167
387 7/8	52 2/8	51 4/8	42 7/8	6 2/8	6 1/8	17 4/8	17 4/8	1	13 1/8	21	17	George River, QC	Michael Yeck	Michael Yeck	1985	168
387 7/8	53 2/8	52 1/8	55 1/8	5 3/8	5 3/8	2 5/8	15	1/8	17	17	22	George River, QC	John Downing	John Downing	1987	168
387 6/8	52 1/8	53 3/8	37 4/8	5 5/8	5 5/8	18	18 2/8	13	6 2/8	23	23	Ungava Bay, QC	Fred N. Huston, Sr.	Fred N. Huston, Sr.	1987	170
387 5/8	53 2/8	56	53	5 2/8	5 2/8	18	14 5/8	12 6/8		14	19	Ungava Bay, QC	Phil N. Alward	Phil N. Alward	1988	171
387 5/8	56 5/8	57 2/8	46 7/8	5 7/8	7 1/8	18 3/8	16 1/8	5 7/8	10 5/8	14	14	Ablonviak Fjord, QC	Frederick S. Fish	Frederick S. Fish	1989	171
387 4/8	42 2/8	39 5/8	47 7/8	5 4/8	5 4/8	15 5/8	17 2/8	11 7/8	13 2/8	27	18	Delay River, QC	Larry E. Smith	Larry E. Smith	1987	173
387 4/8	44 5/8	47 2/8	45 2/8	5 3/8	5 4/8	18 6/8	17 5/8	12	9 5/8	22	20	Whale River, QC	Michael J. Karboski	Michael J. Karboski	1988	173
387 3/8	54 2/8	53 4/8	61 1/8	5 5/8	5 4/8	17 5/8		14 6/8		17	12	Tunulik Lake, QC	Jay G. St. Charles	Jay G. St. Charles	1986	175
387 1/8	53 4/8	53 2/8	47	5 7/8	5 7/8	1	17	1/8	11 4/8	14	18	Tunulik River, QC	Larry Hoff	Larry Hoff	1984	176
387 1/8	54 2/8	53 7/8	51 4/8	4 6/8	4 5/8	18	17 4/8	10 7/8	6 6/8	15	14	Mollet Lake, QC	William M. Wheless III	William M. Wheless III	2002	176
387	51 2/8	50 3/8	40 6/8	6 1/8	5 7/8	14 6/8	20 2/8	7 7/8	16 7/8	20	19	Minto Lake, QC	Duane Armitage	Duane Armitage	2002	178
386 7/8	54 3/8	54 7/8	47 3/8	6 6/8	5 7/8	18 6/8	7	14 5/8	1/8	17	14	George River, QC	Arthur C. Sadowski	Arthur C. Sadowski	1979	179
386 7/8	56 2/8	52 4/8	50	4 6/8	4 4/8	19 6/8	18 6/8	17 1/8	15 7/8	15	16	Chapiteau Lake, QC	Matthew C. Ash	Matthew C. Ash	1999	179
386 3/8	55 2/8	54 1/8	43 7/8	5 6/8	5 7/8	17 5/8	19 5/8	11 5/8	11	15	15	Crossroads Lake, NL	Kenneth Mowerson, Jr.	Kenneth Mowerson, Jr.	1998	181
386 2/8	49 6/8	49 4/8	44 1/8	5	5 3/8	12 7/8	18 3/8	2 7/8	12 1/8	17	17	Mistinibi Lake, QC	W.T. Yoshimoto	W.T. Yoshimoto	1980	182
386 1/8	50 2/8	51 6/8	49 7/8	5 1/8	5	16 4/8	19	10 4/8	15 3/8	14	15	Massie Lake, QC	W.T. Garry Drummond	W.T. Garry Drummond	2001	183
386	52 1/8	53	53	5 4/8	5 2/8	12 1/8	17 2/8	1/8	13 5/8	14	15	Pons River, QC	George D. Berger	George D. Berger	1991	184
386	57 4/8	56 6/8	40 4/8	5 6/8	6 2/8	1 1/8	18 4/8	1/8	13 6/8	15	20	Horse Lake, NL	Ronald J. Bartels	Ronald J. Bartels	2001	185
385 7/8	52 4/8	54 7/8	46 1/8	5 3/8	5	15 6/8	19 3/8	11 5/8	15 6/8	15	17	Minto Lake, QC	Anthony A. Moles	Anthony A. Moles	1999	186
385 5/8	57	58 1/8	48 6/8	5	5 2/8	20 4/8	4 5/8	1/8	13 6/8	16	17	Koksoak River, QC	Donald E. Eberman	Donald E. Eberman	1990	187
385 5/8	46 4/8	48	48 1/8	5 4/8	5 1/8	19 3/8	18 2/8	10 3/8	11 7/8	20	14	George River, QC	David G. Noble	David G. Noble	1986	188
385 4/8	52 2/8	51 2/8	36 2/8	5 1/8	4 7/8	15 1/8	18 3/8	6 6/8	10 2/8	16	14	Fort-Chimo, QC	James E. Carroll	James E. Carroll	1998	189
385 3/8	51	49 7/8	47 1/8	6	5 6/8	20 1/8	15 3/8	12 1/8	10	14	20	George River, QC	James J. McBride	James J. McBride	1982	190
385 2/8	52 2/8	49 6/8	45 3/8	4 7/8	4 7/8	20 6/8	18 6/8	12 1/8	13 3/8	14	21	Minto Lake, QC	Randy Spedoske	Randy Spedoske	2001	190
385 1/8	57 4/8	56	42 3/8	5 1/3	5	16 1/8	20 7/8	6	5	13	15	George River, QC	Michael A. Pilchard	Michael A. Pilchard	1983	192
385	57 4/8	55 1/8	54 4/8	4 7/8	4 7/8	17 7/8	16 3/8	9 6/8	13 4/8	18	27	May Lake, QC	Dan E. Stimmell	Dan E. Stimmell	2001	192
384 7/8	46 1/8	45 7/8	42 3/8	4 6/8	4 7/8	16 1/8	19 3/8	12 3/8	11 5/8	24	19	Delay River, QC	George P. Mann	George P. Mann	1990	194
384 5/8	50	51	50 1/8	5 2/8	4 7/8	19 7/8	19 4/8	11 7/8	11 4/8	17	16	Pons Lake, QC	Arthur J. Petroff	Arthur J. Petroff	1994	195
384 5/8	45 4/8	44 1/8	46 2/8	4 7/8	5	21 5/8	14 5/8	16 5/8	1/8	20	13	Lake Demitte, QC	Ronald I. McDiarmid	Ronald I. McDiarmid	1991	196
384 4/8	53 4/8	52 1/8	46 6/8	5 7/8	6	23 2/8	18 6/8	19 2/8	1/8	29	17	Charlieu Lake, QC	Stewart N. Shaft	Stewart N. Shaft	1998	196
384 4/8	50 4/8	52 1/8	48	5 2/8	5 7/8	17 3/8	17 3/8	12 7/8		18	15	Mistinibi Lake, QC	Brian L. Dam	Brian L. Dam	1979	198
384 4/8	46 4/8	46 5/8	42 4/8	5 2/8	5	16	12 7/8	7	7 3/8	19	19	Ablonviak Fiord, QC	Elmer R. Luce, Jr.	Elmer R. Luce, Jr.	1986	198
384 3/8	46 4/8	45 6/8	42 4/8	4 7/8	4 8/8	17 5/8	17 5/8	7	10 5/8	18	19	Baleine River, QC	Louie Kitcoff	Louie Kitcoff	1987	198
384 3/8	48 3/8	45 6/8	36 3/8	4 5/8	4 4/8	20 3/8	17 2/8	4 5/8	11	14	15	Pons River, QC	Elmer R. Luce, Jr.	Elmer R. Luce, Jr.	1996	201
384 2/8	45 2/8	46 4/8	49	5 2/8	5	15 1/8	15 1/8	8 5/8		19	23	Baleine River, QC	Elmer R. Luce, Jr.	Elmer R. Luce, Jr.	1987	202

Score	Length of Main Beam R	Length of Main Beam L	Inside Spread	Circ. R	Circ. L	Top Point R	Top Point L	Brow	Pts R	Pts L	Locality	Hunter	Owner	Date	Rank
384 2/8	47 6/8	51 4/8	40 6/8	6	5 3/8	16 7/8	18	15 5/8	20	16	Pons Lake, QC	Jonathan S. Warke	Jonathan S. Warke	1991	202
384 2/8	54 4/8	55 5/8	47 7/8	5 1/8	5 5/8	18 3/8	20 4/8	9 1/8	18	15	Minto Lake, QC	Sandra K. Thorn	Sandra K. Thorn	2001	202
384 1/8	48 1/8	48 2/8	44 3/8	4 6/8	4 6/8	17 5/8	18 1/8	11 4/8	17	20	Mollet Lake, QC	William H. Taylor	William H. Taylor	2001	205
383 7/8	52 4/8	51 2/8	45 3/8	5 2/8	5	18 4/8	20 4/8	14	15	14	George River Lodge, QC	Clayton C. Dovey, Jr.	Clayton C. Dovey, Jr.	1969	206
383 7/8	47 3/8	49 5/8	46 7/8	4 6/8	5 1/8	15	19 3/8	13 4/8	18	23	Lake Loudin, QC	Roger M. Schmitt	Roger M. Schmitt	1988	206
383 5/8	51 4/8	52 2/8	53 6/8	5 1/8	5 3/8	18 5/8	15 7/8	13 4/8	16	20	Ungava Bay, QC	Fred S. DeHaan	Fred S. DeHaan	1986	208
383 5/8	47 6/8	45 4/8	41 6/8	4 4/8	5 6/8	17 3/8	19 3/8	4	21	12	Nastapoka River, QC	Robert W. DeVlieger II	Robert W. DeVlieger II	2002	208
383 4/8	51 4/8	50 7/8	55	5 5/8	5 6/8	19 1/8	17 7/8	12 5/8	12	12	Tunulic River, QC	Peter Smith	Peter Smith	1982	210
383 4/8	50 3/8	50	36 1/8	5 3/8	5 1/8	17 2/8	18 6/8	2	12	17	Caniapiscau River, QC	Roy Jebb, Jr.	Roy Jebb, Jr.	1984	210
383 4/8	46 2/8	43 6/8	40 2/8	5	5 6/8	18 2/8	18 6/8	11 6/8	15	23	Ungava Pen., QC	Jon D. Johnson	Jon D. Johnson	1995	210
383 3/8	50 2/8	50 7/8	50 1/8	5 7/8	5 1/8	16 1/8	16 1/8	13	16	19	Abloviak Fjord, QC	Steven N. Mitchell	Steven N. Mitchell	1991	213
383 2/8	48	50 1/8	43 6/8	5 1/8	6 1/8	14 3/8	5 4/8	1/8	16	14	Attikamagen Lake, NL	Barbara L. Cole	Barbara L. Cole	2001	214
383 1/8	51 6/8	53 3/8	42 6/8	6 6/8	6 2/8	17 3/8	6 7/8	12 4/8	25	23	George River, QC	Ralph Zampella	Ralph Zampella	1972	215
383 1/8	49 7/8	49 6/8	43	4 7/8	5 1/8	20 1/8	17 7/8	13	21	15	Glinel Lake, QC	Howard F. Lemon	Howard F. Lemon	1995	215
383 1/8	48 1/8	48 6/8	46 5/8	4 5/8	4 4/8	12 6/8	14 7/8	14 7/8	15	14	Nullualuk Lake, QC	Steve A. Rivet	Steve A. Rivet	1996	215
382 7/8	50 4/8	50 5/8	33	4 5/8	4 4/8	17 1/8	15 1/8	10 5/8	15	17	Lake Diane, QC	Wayne R. Martka	Wayne R. Martka	1990	218
382 7/8	53	56	39 6/8	5 5/8	4 4/8	23 1/8	16 3/8	7 2/8	13	22	Caniapiscau River, QC	Greg L. Farnworth	Greg L. Farnworth	1993	218
382 7/8	52 1/8	51 4/8	42 5/8	4 6/8	4 5/8	20 4/8	16 2/8	7	18	18	Bienville Lake, QC	L. Reed Breight	L. Reed Breight	1997	218
382 5/8	53 2/8	53 1/8	53 6/8	5 5/8	5 6/8	22	4 2/8	14 3/8	16	17	Mistinibi Lake, QC	W.T. Yoshimoto	W.T. Yoshimoto	1979	221
382 5/8	48 1/8	50 2/8	45 5/8	6 6/8	5 7/8	15 5/8	17 5/8	12 3/8	16	24	Wayne Lake, QC	Timothy D. Gildersleeve	Timothy D. Gildersleeve	1987	221
382 5/8	47 1/8	46 6/8	42 1/8	4 7/8	5 2/8	18 2/8	19 1/8	13 4/8	17	23	Lake Fremin, QC	Jon D. Upton	Jon D. Upton	1997	221
382 5/8	47 6/8	49 1/8	42 6/8	5 3/8	5 1/8	21 7/8	2	10 3/8	24	21	Lake Chabanel, QC	Ronald D. Britton	Ronald D. Britton	2003	221
382 3/8	59 3/8	59 1/8	54 4/8	5 4/8	6 2/8	18 4/8	16	5 7/8	19	25	Ungava Region, QC	John R. Oakes	John R. Oakes	1971	225
382 3/8	59	55 7/8	53 2/8	5 7/8	5 1/8	1 2/8	19 5/8	6 1/8	13	14	Nullualuk Lake, QC	Walter J. Manning	Walter J. Manning	1988	225
382 2/8	47 5/8	48 2/8	45 2/8	5 2/8	5 2/8	16 5/8	16 3/8	4 6/8	23	22	Indian Lake, QC	Donald A. Lawrence	Donald A. Lawrence	1987	227
382 2/8	51 2/8	51 1/8	41 6/8	5 1/8	6	18 5/8	14 2/8	11 4/8	19	18	Ungava Bay, QC	James B. Wessinger	James B. Wessinger	1987	227
382 2/8	53 7/8	51 2/8	42 2/8	4 6/8	5 2/8	18 2/8	15 4/8	15 1/8	15	13	Pons River, QC	Chris S. Marshall	Chris S. Marshall	1990	227
382 1/8	48 6/8	47 5/8	38 5/8	5	4 6/8	2	16 2/8	6 5/8	15	16	Kamaywapakich Lake, QC	Steve T. Bartolomucci	Steve T. Bartolomucci	1994	230
382	52	52 3/8	60	5 1/8	5	2 4/8	8 6/8	8 6/8	16	15	Ungava Bay, QC	Edward J. Pallay	Edward J. Pallay	1982	231
381 7/8	53 1/8	53 6/8	46	7	5	1 4/8	14 5/8	14 5/8	11	15	Kogaluk, NL	Basil C. Bradbury	Basil C. Bradbury	1949	232
381 7/8	51 6/8	54 4/8	45 4/8	5 4/8	7	20 6/8	1 4/8	4/8	15	19	Caniapiscau River, QC	Donald P. Travis	Donald P. Travis	1986	232
381 7/8	49 3/8	50 5/8	45 5/8	5 1/8	5 4/8	17 6/8	1	1/8	19	25	Wayne Lake, QC	Vincent P. Cina, Sr.	Vincent P. Cina, Sr.	1990	232
381 6/8	48 3/8	49 1/8	53 2/8	4 5/8	6 2/8	14 5/8	9 1/8	12 6/8	17	18	Tudor Lake, QC	Collins F. Kellogg, Jr.	Collins F. Kellogg, Jr.	1970	235
381 6/8	56	53 3/8	47 2/8	6	5 1/8	18 2/8	13 2/8	8 4/8	17	21	Koksoak River, QC	Arthur J. Pelon	Arthur J. Pelon	1984	235
381 4/8	53 5/8	55 2/8	48 6/8	5 5/8	5 6/8	19	2	13 4/8	14	15	Ungava Bay, QC	Jeff S. Koster	Jeff S. Koster	1990	237
381 4/8	52 7/8	50 3/8	45 6/8	6 2/8	5 1/8	18 4/8	16 4/8	10 3/8	18	13	Riviere Aux Feuilles, QC	Wayne F. Kilgore	Wayne F. Kilgore	1992	237
381 3/8	51 7/8	51 3/8	47 6/8	5	5 1/8	18 4/8	17 2/8	5 1/8	18	16	Tunulik River, QC	Joseph P. Toth	Joseph P. Toth	1986	239
381 2/8	45 3/8	45 3/8	44 4/8	5 3/8	5 6/8	15 1/8	14 4/8	12 7/8	16	18	Mistinibi Lake, QC	Paul F. Barnhart	Paul F. Barnhart	1980	240
381 2/8	48 1/8	51 1/8	41 4/8	4 7/8	6	14 7/8	13	13 5/8	14	18	Lake May, QC	Steven L. Fair	Steven L. Fair	1993	240
381	53 4/8	60 2/8	44 4/8	4 4/8	6	16 3/8	12 5/8	14 2/8	21	16	Fiddle Lake, QC	Herb Dittmar	Herb Dittmar	1966	242
381	58	58	41 1/8	5 4/8	6	22 4/8	16	8 4/8	15	17	Lake Gerido, QC	Dan D. Boy	Dan D. Boy	1987	242
381	55	55	44 4/8	5 5/8	6	11 3/8	17 3/8	13 4/8	17	16	Ungava Bay, QC	William G. Freed	William G. Freed	1992	242
381	53 4/8	50 3/8	48 6/8	5 1/8	7 2/8	15 4/8	8 2/8	1 2/8	11	24	Torngat Mts., NL	Robert G. Best	Robert G. Best	2001	242
380 6/8	53 4/8	51	39 6/8	7 2/8	6 2/8	16 2/8	16 7/8	16 2/8	20	17	Whale River, QC	John A. Yeager	John A. Yeager	1979	246
380 4/8	62 4/8	65	55 5/8	5 6/8	5 6/8	11 2/8	8	11 1/8	10	15	Pons River, QC	Ronald S. Newman	Ronald S. Newman	1990	246
380 2/8	53 4/8	51 7/8	48 6/8	6 2/8	5 1/8	17	13	13 4/8	16	15	Fort Chimo, QC	B.N. McCrum	B.N. McCrum	1967	248
380 2/8	53 4/8	55	39 6/8	6 2/8	6 2/8	14 4/8	16 7/8	11 1/8	20	16	George River, QC	Roger R. Card	Roger R. Card	1980	248
380 2/8	62 4/8	65	55 5/8	5 6/8	5 6/8	15 4/8	8	11 2/8	10	11	George River, QC	Randal L. Diehl	Randal L. Diehl	1980	248

QUEBEC-LABRADOR CARIBOU
Rangifer tarandus

Score	Length of Main Beam R	L	Inside Spread	Circumference at Smallest Place Between Brow and Bez Points R	L	Length of Brow Points R	L	Width of Brow Points R	L	Number of Points R	L	Locality	Hunter	Owner	Date Killed	Rank
379 7/8	49 7/8	46 5/8	44 2/8	5 1/8	5	14	18 3/8	13 7/8	1/8	11	17	Serigny River, QC	Gary A. Perin	Gary A. Perin	1987	251
379 7/8	49	50 2/8	50 2/8	5	5 1/8	3 7/8	17	1/8	11 3/8	16	17	Baleine River, QC	Michael C. Dysh	Michael C. Dysh	1990	251
379 6/8	42 7/8	47 2/8	41 6/8	5 7/8	6	14 6/8	15 5/8	9 6/8	8 5/8	20	21	Wade Lake, NL	Unknown	Gerard Beaulieu	1985	253
379 6/8	49 4/8	49 2/8	42 5/8	5 5/8	5 2/8	19 6/8	19 4/8	10	11 7/8	17	14	Long Lake, QC	Ted K. Jaycox	Ted K. Jaycox	1986	253
379 6/8	45 6/8	47	44 4/8	5 1/8	5 1/8	18 6/8	2 7/8	13	1/8	18	19	Caniapiscau River, QC	John W. Czerwinski	John W. Czerwinski	1987	253
379 6/8	45 7/8	50 1/8	48 2/8	4 7/8	4 6/8	18 4/8	15 6/8	13 5/8	13 1/8	25	28	Pons River, QC	Christopher J. Cass	Christopher J. Cass	1993	253
379 5/8	52 1/8	54 6/8	52 7/8	5 3/8	5 4/8	15 5/8	19	6 7/8	10	12	13	George River, QC	Frank R. Heller	Frank R. Heller	1978	257
379 3/8	60 2/8	59 7/8	50 6/8	5 4/8	5 7/8	5 5/8	20 5/8	4 7/8	15 3/8	13	14	Tunulik River, QC	Thomas L. Cash	Thomas L. Cash	1988	258
379 3/8	62 2/8	64 2/8	41	6	6	1 4/8	23 6/8	1/8	17 2/8	11	14	Ungava Bay, QC	Bruce E. Cepicky	Bruce E. Cepicky	1988	258
378 6/8	56	56 4/8	56 6/8	5 4/8	5 4/8	15 2/8	5/8	10 4/8	1/8	18	15	Ford River, QC	Vivian Sleight	Vivian Sleight	1973	260
378 6/8	54	52 4/8	40 4/8	4 5/8	4 5/8	17 3/8	15 1/8	7	9 2/8	15	14	Tunulliq Lake, QC	Scott M. Showalter	Scott M. Showalter	1982	260
378 4/8	49 7/8	49 1/8	49	5	5 1/8	21 1/8	6 1/8	13 7/8	1/8	21	15	May Lake, QC	D. Ross Sheridan	D. Ross Sheridan	1989	262
378 3/8	45 6/8	50 1/8	41	4 5/8	4 7/8	17 7/8	15 6/8	17 2/8	7 4/8	16	19	Wendell Lake, QC	Terry E. Lefever	Terry E. Lefever	1988	263
378 3/8	47 5/8	48 3/8	35 3/8	5 6/8	5 4/8	18	20	15	15	20	18	Amiskunipts Lakes, QC	Richard R. Hess	Richard R. Hess	2001	263
378 3/8	54 3/8	53 5/8	40	6	5 5/8	19	17 3/8	17 7/8	3 2/8	18	12	Ungava Bay, QC	James B. Wessinger	James B. Wessinger	1987	265
378 2/8	47 2/8	47 4/8	53 7/8	4 6/8	4 6/8	18 5/8	17 2/8	10 7/8	13	22	12	Martine Lake, QC	Robert A. Ritter	Robert A. Ritter	1991	265
378 2/8	52 5/8	52 5/8	62 3/8	5	5 5/8	15 1/8	4 1/8	8 2/8	1/8	13	15	Bobby Lake, QC	Stan L. Saxion	Stan L. Saxion	2002	265
378 1/8	46 5/8	44	49 6/8	6 4/8	6 2/8	14	13 7/8	9 6/8	1 3/8	16	16	Ungava Pen., QC	Theodore M. Schall	Theodore M. Schall	1985	268
378 1/8	45 2/8	45	36	5	4 5/8	14 1/8	13 7/8	12 2/8	11 5/8	29	25	Little Cedar Lake, QC	David G. Baker	David G. Baker	1998	268
378	53	51 2/8	49 6/8	5 2/8	4 7/8	2 1/8	18 1/8	10 7/8	13 1/8	15	17	George River, QC	Dick Ullery	Dick Ullery	1975	270
377 7/8	45 5/8	45 4/8	40 6/8	4 6/8	4 7/8	16 6/8	16 2/8	12 6/8	12 6/8	20	17	Lake Brisson, QC	David Read	David Read	1983	271
377 7/8	51	49 7/8	40 4/8	5 3/8	5 5/8	19 5/8	11 2/8	17 4/8	1 2/8	16	14	Ungava Bay, QC	Joseph Mannino	Joseph Mannino	1985	271
377 7/8	49 3/8	48	42 7/8	4 5/8	4 5/8	21 2/8	19 5/8	9	14 5/8	22	22	Maricourt Lake, QC	James O. Kingsley	James O. Kingsley	1992	271
377 7/8	45 3/8	45 7/8	40 6/8	5 1/8	5 7/8	16 5/8	14 4/8	13 4/8	10	21	22	Caniapiscau River, QC	Daniel C. Craft	Daniel C. Craft	1993	271
377 7/8	49 1/8	47 2/8	47 1/8	6	6 5/8	17 5/8	17 1/8	11 5/8	11 3/8	19	17	Kamaywapakich Lake, QC	Christopher Vozzo	Christopher Vozzo	1997	271
377 6/8	45 7/8	45 6/8	41 5/8	6 1/8	5 1/8	6 7/8	19	1/8	14 3/8	16	20	George River, QC	Normand Poulin	Normand Poulin	1976	276
377 6/8	50 1/8	50	37	5	5 1/8	4 1/8	17 6/8	15 4/8	17	17	14	Clear Water Lake, QC	Greg A. Abbas	Greg A. Abbas	2001	276
377 4/8	47	50 6/8	38 1/8	4 4/8	4 5/8	14 7/8	19	6	11	13	14	Kakiattualuk Lake, QC	Ronald C. Rockwell	Ronald C. Rockwell	2001	278
377 3/8	51 1/8	49 5/8	43 1/8	5 7/8	5 7/8	3 2/8	15 1/8	1/8	12 4/8	13	14	Ungava Bay, QC	Arlo J. Spiess	Arlo J. Spiess	1985	279
377 3/8	49 5/8	49 7/8	36 2/8	6 1/8	6 3/8	17 4/8	20 2/8	10 3/8	20 6/8	25	28	Minto Lake, QC	Charles F. Nopper	Charles F. Nopper	1997	279
377 3/8	47 4/8	45 3/8	43 6/8	5 4/8	5 5/8	3 2/8	16 5/8	1/8	10 1/8	19	27	Snow Lake, QC	John A. Irwin	John A. Irwin	1999	279
377 2/8	45 1/8	48 4/8	42 5/8	4 7/8	5 1/8	2 5/8	17 6/8	1/8	12 5/8	15	18	Lac du Rougemont, QC	Albert O. Toaldo	Albert O. Toaldo	1992	282
377 1/8	56 2/8	58 6/8	49 7/8	5 3/8	5 1/8	20 1/8	18 2/8	13 3/8	9 2/8	24	18	Mistinibi Lake, QC	James H. Meckes, Jr.	James H. Meckes, Jr.	1980	283
377 1/8	53 6/8	54 5/8	48	5 1/8	5 3/8	18 7/8	18 2/8	12 2/8	9 2/8	18	16	Rainbow Lake, QC	David J. Richey, Sr.	David J. Richey, Sr.	1990	283
377 1/8	43 2/8	44	47 7/8	5 6/8	5 3/8	14 4/8	14 1/8	6 1/8	10 1/8	20	18	Moyer Lake, QC	Ricky L. Gleeson	Ricky L. Gleeson	2002	283
377	53 5/8	55 6/8	49 4/8	5 6/8	5 5/8	18	18 4/8	4	16 4/8	12	11	George River, QC	Stanley R. Smith	Stanley R. Smith	1975	286

Score												Hunter	Owner	Location	Date Killed	Rank
376 7/8	48 1/8	49 6/8	51	4 7/8	4 7/8	20 1/8	4 3/8	1/8	16	18	27	Edward A. Mertins	Edward A. Mertins	Lake Lachine, QC	1990	287
376 7/8	48 4/8	46 4/8	38 4/8	5 4/8	5 3/8	13 6/8	20 5/8	4 1/8	9 3/8	24	17	John L. Guerra	John L. Guerra	Chailly Lake, QC	2000	287
376 6/8	51 5/8	53 5/8	52 5/8	5 2/8	5 2/8	18 6/8	14 7/8	1 7/8	17 7/8	21	24	C.J. McElroy	C.J. McElroy	George River, QC	1969	289
376 5/8	50 1/8	50 6/8	45 4/8	5 4/8	5 4/8	15 6/8	16 7/8	13 1/8	10 2/8	18	13	John D. Powers	John D. Powers	Ungava Bay, QC	1981	290
376 4/8	45 6/8	48 7/8	48	5 3/8	5 2/8	19 3/8	16 3/8	1/8	14 7/8	15	19	Carl J. Los	Carl J. Los	Schefferville, QC	1970	291
376 4/8	48 3/8	48 5/8	43 6/8	4 7/8	4 7/8	17 7/8	17 1/8	12 4/8	11 6/8	25	21	Richard A. Allen	Richard A. Allen	Pons River, QC	1999	291
376 4/8	52 6/8	43 6/8	36	4 7/8	5	16 6/8	16 2/8	14 3/8	10 4/8	18	20	Floyd E. Osterhoudt	Floyd E. Osterhoudt	Fremin Lake, QC	2001	291
376 3/8	40 1/8	42 4/8	28	4 4/8	4 7/8	20 4/8	11 3/8	1 3/8	18	21	27	Norman Clausen	Norman Clausen	George River, QC	1973	294
376 2/8	53	53 6/8	46 2/8	6	6 1/8	17 2/8	2 6/8	1/8	13 3/8	18	20	Don Peters	Don Peters	Ungava Region, QC	1969	295
376 1/8	49 5/8	50 4/8	47 6/8	6 2/8	6 3/8	12 4/8	13 2/8	8 3/8	9 7/8	17	15	Charles Lanzarone	Charles Lanzarone	Schefferville, QC	1980	296
376 1/8	46 7/8	46 5/8	50 4/8	5	5	18 6/8	17	13	13 4/8	21	20	Karam Guergis	Karam Guergis	Gordon Lake, QC	1999	296
376 1/8	47 6/8	48	41 3/8	5 2/8	5 2/8	17 3/8	16 3/8	12 2/8	11 5/8	17	17	Bob Taylor	Bob Taylor	Mollet Lake, QC	2002	296
376	50 3/8	50 3/8	44	5 4/8	5 4/8	16 6/8	18	13 7/8	6	19	15	Burnell R. Kauffman	Burnell R. Kauffman	Lake Patu, QC	1985	299
376	47 5/8	46 4/8	40	5	4 5/8	18	14	14	14 4/8	17	21	David A. Ogilvie	David A. Ogilvie	Dornon Lake, QC	2001	299
375 7/8	44 6/8	46 4/8	29 5/8	4 4/8	4 4/8	20 4/8	15 7/8	11 7/8	11	21	21	Brian J. Gorbutt	Brian J. Gorbutt	Eaton Canyon, QC	2000	301
375 6/8	49 4/8	49	46 2/8	4 7/8	5 1/8	13 2/8	15	7 4/8	7 4/8	12	15	Max Landers	Max Landers	Minto Lake, QC	1999	302
375 5/8	61 1/8	58 6/8	41	5 3/8	5 2/8	20 4/8	6 5/8	1/8	16 7/8	17	22	Arden Bancroft	Arden Bancroft	Du Gue River, QC	1989	303
375 4/8	55 7/8	54 1/8	55 5/8	5 1/8	5 1/8	10 3/8	19 5/8	12 5/8	2 7/8	15	12	Collins F. Kellogg	Collins F. Kellogg	North Tudor Lake, QC	1970	304
375 3/8	51 7/8	52 3/8	37 2/8	4 4/8	4 5/8	18 1/8	16 6/8	4 7/8	11 5/8	17	18	Gerald A. Gredell	Gerald A. Gredell	Caniapiscau River, QC	1987	305
375 2/8	50 2/8	52 2/8	55 3/8	7 2/8	7	14 4/8	19 1/8	14 1/8	1/8	16	13	Norma J. Laros	Norma J. Laros	George River, QC	1975	306
375 1/8	56 2/8	56 1/8	46 1/8	5 1/8	5 1/8	15 5/8	14 2/8	15 1/8	14 3/8	23	16	Ronald R. Pomeroy	Ronald R. Pomeroy	Ungava Bay, QC	1986	307
375	52 2/8	53 7/8	40	5 4/8	5 1/8	19	9 4/8	1/8	14 6/8	17	19	Donald A. Boyer	Donald A. Boyer	Fritz Lake, QC	1978	308
375	48 6/8	52 3/8	52 2/8	5 2/8	5	16 4/8	17	14 6/8	16	23	20	Glenn M. Smith	Glenn M. Smith	Ungava Bay, QC	1986	308
375	50 4/8	50 2/8	52 2/8	5 1/8	5 2/8	18 2/8	16 2/8	6 4/8	13 2/8	11	11	Ronald V. Hurlburt	Ronald V. Hurlburt	Caniapiscau River, QC	1987	308
375	53 4/8	52 3/8	36	5 1/8	5 1/8	19 1/8	12 4/8	1/8	16	15	18	Kenneth G. Straub	Kenneth G. Straub	Tunulik River, QC	1989	308
407 1/8*	55 1/8	55 7/8	47 7/8	4 7/8	4 7/8	18 7/8	17 6/8	6/8	13	21	22	George J. West	George J. West	Dulhut Lake, QC	1997	
405 2/8*	47 4/8	45 5/8	39 7/8	6	5 6/8	15 6/8	17 6/8	11 6/8	13 1/8	12	17	David A. Parish	David A. Parish	Bull Lake, QC	2002	
399 3/8*	46 7/8	46 1/8	44 1/8	5 4/8	5 6/8	21 5/8	20 2/8	7 6/8	19 7/8	20	28	Jack D. Stroud	Jack D. Stroud	Andrea Lake, NL	2001	
394 4/8*	47 3/8	47 3/8	44 3/8	5 2/8	5 2/8	18 3/8	16	11 4/8	15 5/8	15	18	Mark A. Brueggeman	Mark A. Brueggeman	Ungava Bay, QC	1996	

CATEGORY
QUEBEC-LABRADOR CARIBOU

SCORE
376

HUNTER
DAVID A. OGILVIE

LOCATION
DORNON LAKE, QUEBEC

DATE OF KILL
SEPTEMBER 2001

CATEGORY
QUEBEC-LABRADOR CARIBOU

SCORE
387-1/8

HUNTER
WILLIAM M. WHELESS III

LOCATION
MOLLET LAKE, QUEBEC

DATE OF KILL
OCTOBER 2002

CATEGORY
QUEBEC-LABRADOR CARIBOU

SCORE
405-2/8

HUNTER
DAVID A. PARISH (BELOW)

LOCATION
BULL LAKE, QUEBEC

DATE OF KILL
SEPTEMBER 2002

CATEGORY
QUEBEC-LABRADOR CARIBOU

SCORE
378-2/8

HUNTER
STAN SAXION (RIGHT)

LOCATION
BOBBY LAKE, QUEBEC

DATE OF KILL
SEPTEMBER 2002

DR. PHILIP L. WRIGHT 1914-1997

By Jack Reneau

Philip Wright was a dedicated family man, professor, and B&C member. His exemplary teaching career in the University of Montana's Department of Zoology extended from 1939 to 1985. During his tenure he influenced more nationally prominent wildlife biologists than any other professor. He became a Regular Member in 1971, after already serving 21 years as an Official Measurer. Phil was a member and/or chair of the Records Committee from 1971 to 1997. He served on eight Awards Program Judges Panels as judge, consultant, and/or chair. Phil also served the Club in many other capacities, including chair of the historical and grants-in-aids committees. In 1984, Phil was elected an Honorary Life Member of B&C. He was presented the Sagamore Hill Award in 1996 "For lifelong commitment to conservation; For dedication to the principles of fair chase and scientific integrity of the records program." Wright Rock in Rock Creek, Montana, was named in his honor. ∎

PRONGHORN
NEW WORLD'S RECORD (TIE)

Dylan Woods never expected to get drawn for the famous Arizona Unit 9 pronghorn tag. Two years earlier he had been lucky enough to draw a premium elk tag, and he figured his luck couldn't be that good. He had never hunted pronghorn (*Antilocapra americana*) before, so when news came that he had in fact drawn the tag, he set aside his college course work and started scouting.

Woods, along with friends Scott Ellis, his father Ken Ellis, and Nathan Schreiber, spent every weekend locating as many bucks as possible. None of them knew what a big buck looked like, so they compared them against each other for size. Finally, they located an area that was holding a few good bucks and formulated an opening-day plan.

They woke up extra early to be sure they were the first ones to their spot. The area they were hunting had a small hill that the bucks were hanging around in the mornings, so with Nathan and Ken watching from a distance, Scott and Woods snuck over the backside of the hill for the shot. It was a perfect set-up, spoiled only by the fact that someone had beaten them to the spot.

When they returned to the truck, Ken and Nathan reported that the other hunters had scared the pronghorns across the road. The hunt was back on!

Scott, Nathan, and Woods headed out after them while Ken stayed at the truck. By this time the sun was just coming up and the perfectly clear sky was already getting warm. The three men walked slowly, watching in front and keeping an eye on a series of small gullies to their left that were just deep enough to hide feeding pronghorn. Every few steps they would stop and look.

While glassing, Woods motioned to the others that he saw something: a single buck feeding 300 yards away. As soon as he saw horns through binoculars, he started to tremble. This buck was much bigger than any buck they'd seen.

The buck had no idea they were there, and cover was sparse. The 7mm Remington Magnum had no problem with the distance, but there was just enough of a rise between the men and the animal that Woods could only see the buck's head. He decided to wait the pronghorn out, realizing that if the buck moved he would get a shot. The wait was short.

Soon the massive buck came out of the depression and walked directly toward Woods. When he saw the buck's vitals, Woods put the trembling crosshairs on them and squeezed the trigger. Before the gun erupted, he knew he'd missed. Woods calmed and made a second shot that put the buck down.

After congratulatory high-fives and hugs, the four-some skinned and caped the buck, then attempted to measure it. Their initial measurement put the horn length at about 16 inches. They were way off.

After the 60-day drying period, Official Measurer Mike Cupell of Phoenix scored the pronghorn at 95 inches — surpassing the World's Record — while the right and left horns measured 19-3/8" and 18-5/8" long, respectively. ∎

PRONGHORN
WORLD'S RECORD SCORE CHART

RANK
New World's Record

SCORE
95

LOCATION
Coconino Co., AZ

HUNTER
Dylan M. Woods

OWNER
Dylan M. Woods

DATE KILLED
2000

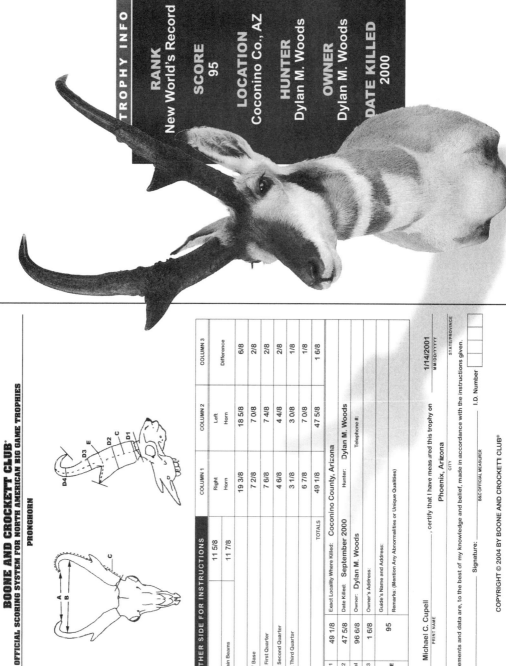

Records of
North American
Big Game

BOONE AND CROCKETT CLUB®

250 Station Drive
Missoula, MT 59801
(406) 542-1888

OFFICIAL SCORING SYSTEM FOR NORTH AMERICAN BIG GAME TROPHIES

PRONGHORN

MINIMUM SCORES	
AWARDS	ALL-TIME
80	82

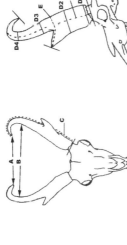

SEE OTHER SIDE FOR INSTRUCTIONS		COLUMN 1	COLUMN 2	COLUMN 3
		Right Horn	Left Horn	Difference
A. Tip to Tip Spread	11 5/8			
B. Inside Spread of Main Beams	11 7/8			
C. Length of Horn		19 3/8	18 5/8	6/8
D-1. Circumference of Base		7 2/8	7 0/8	2/8
D-2. Circumference at First Quarter		7 6/8	7 4/8	2/8
D-3. Circumference at Second Quarter		4 6/8	4 4/8	2/8
D-4. Circumference at Third Quarter		3 1/8	3 0/8	1/8
E. Length of Prong		6 7/8	7 0/8	1/8
TOTALS		49 1/8	47 5/8	1 6/8

ADD	Column 1	49 1/8
	Column 2	47 5/8
	Subtotal	96 6/8
SUBTRACT Column 3		1 6/8
FINAL SCORE		**95**

Exact Locality Where Killed: Coconino County, Arizona

Date Killed: September 2000   Hunter: Dylan M. Woods

Owner: Dylan M. Woods   Telephone #:

Owner's Address:

Guide's Name and Address:

Remarks: (Mention Any Abnormalities or Unique Qualities)

I, Michael C. Cupell , certify that I have measured this trophy on 1/14/2001
PRINT NAME   MM/DD/YYYY

at _____ Phoenix, Arizona _____
STREET ADDRESS   CITY   STATE/PROVINCE

and that these measurements and data are, to the best of my knowledge and belief, made in accordance with the instructions given.

Witness: _____   Signature: _____   I.D. Number _____
                                          B&C OFFICIAL MEASURER

719

PRONGHORN
NEW WORLD'S RECORD (TIE)

For David Meyer to be able to hunt at all in 2002 was miraculous; to be able to harvest a World's Record pronghorn was extraordinary. Several years earlier Meyer underwent very serious surgery to remove a large mass in his chest, followed by a long recovery period that kept him from even the slightest physical activity. During this time, Meyer began dreaming of a hunt for pronghorn (*Antilocapra americana*).

After securing a pronghorn tag at the Rocky Mountain Elk Foundation auction in the spring, Meyer heard of an exceptional pronghorn in Arizona's area 13B. After seeing film of this buck Meyer couldn't believe the estimated mass measurements of this antelope. With the home range of the buck established, there was great anticipation as the hunt approached.

Although able to locate the enormous buck without issue, the first day of the hunt, Meyer and his guide, John Caid, failed to get within range. The second day produced similar results, although several protracted stalks led to an off-hand shot. To hear Meyer tell the story:

"As it began to rain, we saw the movement of the lead doe over the next ridge where the group—including the large buck—had bedded down. It had now been 12 hours of stalking, and we felt we were close. We carefully moved to the next small ridge of elevation, and then the big buck was there, moving toward us!

"As it came closer and caught us by sight, its white rump elevated as the buck paced and turned slightly. I shot, and it disappeared into the sage. I knew I had missed."

Six more days of failed attempts led Meyer and Caid to consider a new approach. They worked their way through a series of serpentine-like washes, rising out of each in succession to glass the sagebrush plateau. After the fourth wash, Meyer spotted the movement of a smaller buck near a prominent bush. For close to an hour they watched the bush, until finally two huge ebony horns appeared above the clay, followed closely by the large buck.

Caid quietly ranged the buck at 178 yards. The buck suddenly stopped and stared in Meyer's direction, but it appeared to look beyond the concealed hunters. Before hearing the shot, the buck went down, and the bedded herd came to life and was gone.

Based on an incisor sent to the Arizona Game and Fish laboratory, the age of the animal was determined to be just under three-and-a-half years old. The buck had been trapped and transplanted as part of their genetic relocation program two years earlier. A Boone and Crockett Official Measurer scored the horns, and a Special Judges Panel was convened in May 2003, to verify the score and certify Meyer's trophy as a new World's Record pronghorn. ∎

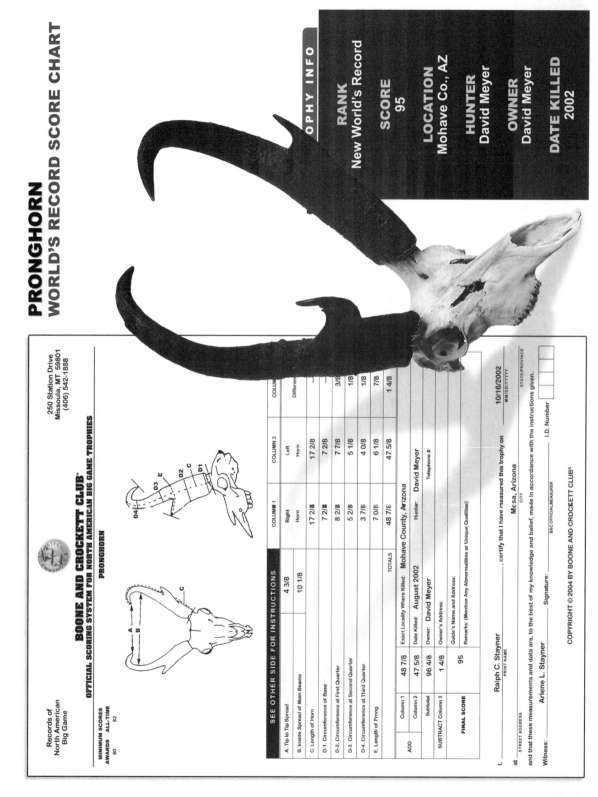

PRONGHORN
WORLD'S RECORD SCORE CHART

Records of
North American
Big Game

250 Station Drive
Missoula, MT 59801
(406) 542-1888

BOONE AND CROCKETT CLUB®
OFFICIAL SCORING SYSTEM FOR NORTH AMERICAN BIG GAME TROPHIES

PRONGHORN

MINIMUM SCORES
AWARDS	ALL-TIME
80	82

TROPHY INFO

RANK
New World's Record

SCORE
95

LOCATION
Mohave Co., AZ

HUNTER
David Meyer

OWNER
David Meyer

DATE KILLED
2002

SEE OTHER SIDE FOR INSTRUCTIONS		COLUMN 1	COLUMN 2	COLUMN
		Right Horn	Left Horn	Difference
A. Tip to Tip Spread	4 3/8			
B. Inside Spread of Main Beams	10 1/8			
C. Length of Horn		17 2/8	17 2/8	
D-1. Circumference of Base		7 2/8	7 2/8	
D-2. Circumference at First Quarter		8 2/8	7 7/8	3/8
D-3. Circumference at Second Quarter		5 2/8	5 1/8	1/8
D-4. Circumference at Third Quarter		3 7/8	4 0/8	1/8
E. Length of Prong		7 0/8	6 1/8	7/8
	TOTALS	48 7/8	47 5/8	1 4/8

ADD	Column 1	48 7/8
	Column 2	47 5/8
	Subtotal	96 4/8
SUBTRACT Column 3		1 4/8
FINAL SCORE		95

Exact Locality Where Killed: Mohave County, Arizona

Date Killed: August 2002   Hunter: David Meyer

Owner: David Meyer   Telephone #:

Owner's Address:

Guide's Name and Address:

Remarks: (Mention Any Abnormalities or Unique Qualities)

I, Ralph C. Stayner , certify that I have measured this trophy on 10/16/2002

PRINT NAME   MM/DD/YYYY

at   Mesa, Arizona

STREET ADDRESS   CITY   STATE/PROVINCE

and that these measurements and data are, to the best of my knowledge and belief, made in accordance with the instructions given.

Witness: _____ Signature: Arlene L. Stayner   I.D. Number

B&C OFFICIAL MEASURER

721

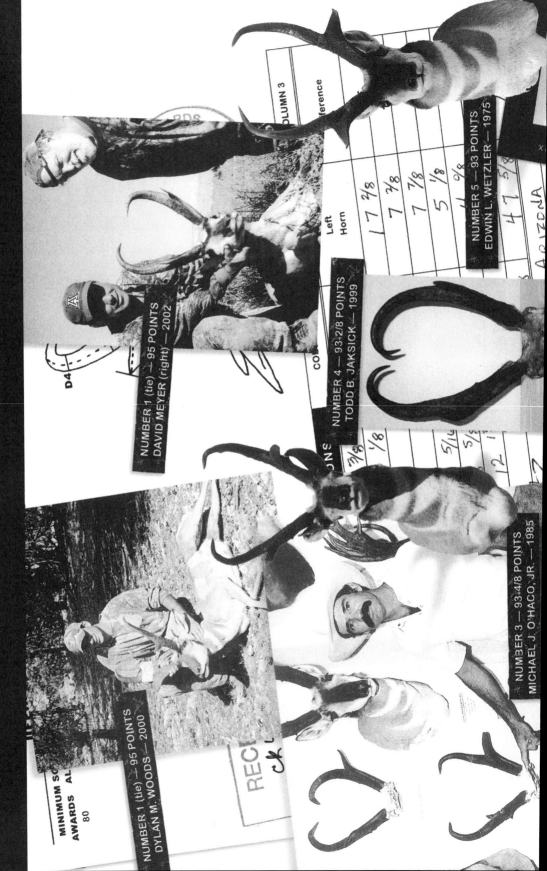

NUMBER 5 — 93 POINTS
EDWIN L. WETZLER — 1975

NUMBER 4 — 93-2/8 POINTS
TODD B. JAKSICK — 1999

NUMBER 1 (tie) — 95 POINTS
DAVID MEYER (right) — 2002

NUMBER 3 — 93-4/8 POINTS
MICHAEL J. O'HACO, JR. — 1985

NUMBER 1 (tie) — 95 POINTS
DYLAN M. WOODS — 2000

NUMBER 8 — 91-6/8 POINTS
STEVEN E. HOPKINS — 1992

NUMBER 9 (tie) — 91-4/8 POINTS
DONALD W. YATES — 1977

NUMBER 6 (tie) — 92-6/8 POINTS
SAM BARRY — 2000

NUMBER 6 (tie) — 92-6/8 POINTS
SAM S. JACKSICK, JR. — 1991

NUMBER 9 (tie) — 91-4/8 POINTS
WILSON POTTER — 1899

NUMBER 9 (tie) — 91-4/8 POINTS
BOB SCHNEIDMILLER — 1965

B&C OFFICIAL MEASURER

2000 BY BOONE AND

and that these

Signature:

Witness:

STREET ADD

KODAK 5062 PX

KODAK

32

32

31

RETURN
N.A.B.G. Aw
1600 Rhode
Washington

AMERICAN BIG GAME TROPHI

PRONGHORN

Length—(R) 10-1/8 (L) 10-1/8
Basal Circumference—(R) 3-7/8 (L) 3-
Locality—Colt Lake, B. C. 1965
Hunter—George P. Jackson, Jr.
Guide—Frank Cooke

COUGAR

Locality—St. Lawrence Island, Alaska — 1964
Hunter—Eskimo
Owner—Ed Shepherd

NEW WORLD'S RECORD

COUGAR — 1st Award
Score — 16

PRONGHORN — 1st Award

Score — 91-4/8
Length—(R) 15-1/8 (L) 15-2/8
Basal Circumference—(R) 7-7/8 (L) 7-7/8
Length of Prong—(R) 7-7/8

PRONGHORN

Antilocapra americana americana and related subspecies

MINIMUM SCORE 82

Score	Length of Horn R	L	Circumference of Base R	L	Circumference at Third Quarter R	L	Inside Spread	Tip to Tip Spread	Length of Prong R	L	Locality	Hunter	Owner	Date Killed	Rank
95	19 3/8	18 5/8	7 2/8	7	3 1/8	3	11 7/8	11 5/8	6 7/8	7	Coconino Co., AZ	Dylan M. Woods	Dylan M. Woods	2000	1
95	17 2/8	17 2/8	7 2/8	7 2/8	3 7/8	4	10 1/8	4 3/8	7	6 1/8	Mohave Co., AZ	David Meyer	David Meyer	2002	1
93 4/8	**17 6/8**	**17 4/8**	**6 7/8**	**7**	**3 1/8**	**3 2/8**	**12 5/8**	**8 2/8**	**8**	**8 2/8**	**Coconino Co., AZ**	**Michael J. O'Haco, Jr.**	**Michael J. O'Haco, Jr.**	**1985**	**3**
93 2/8	18 4/8	18 4/8	7 2/8	7 2/8	2 6/8	2 6/8	8 1/8	1	7	6 7/8	Humboldt Co., NV	Todd B. Jaksick	Todd B. Jaksick	1999	4
93	18 1/8	18 2/8	7 2/8	7	2 5/8	2 6/8	10 1/8	6 5/8	7 6/8	7 6/8	Yavapai Co., AZ	Edwin L. Wetzler	Loaned to B&C Natl. Coll.	1975	5
92 6/8	16 4/8	16 4/8	7 2/8	7 1/8	3 1/8	3 1/8	12 4/8	9 5/8	7 3/8	7 4/8	Coconino Co., AZ	Sam S. Jaksick, Jr.	Sam S. Jaksick, Jr.	1991	6
92 6/8	16 6/8	17 3/8	7 5/8	7 4/8	2 6/8	2 5/8	11 4/8	7	7 5/8	7 1/8	Harney Co., OR	Sam Barry	Sam Barry	2000	6
91 6/8	17 2/8	17 1/8	7 6/8	7 6/8	3 3/8	2 7/8	13 4/8	9	7 4/8	7 3/8	Coconino Co., AZ	Steven E. Hopkins	Steven E. Hopkins	1992	8
91 4/8	20 1/8	20	7	7	2 6/8	2 6/8	12	11 3/8	4 5/8	5 3/8	Arizona	Wilson Potter	Unknown	1899	9
91 4/8	15 1/8	15 2/8	7 7/8	7 7/8	3 4/8	3 4/8	10 4/8	9 4/8	7	7	Weld Co., CO	Bob Schneidmiller	Bob Schneidmiller	1965	9
91 4/8	17 1/8	17	7 3/8	7 1/8	3 3/8	3 2/8	13 5/8	10 1/8	4 7/8	4 7/8	Garfield Co., MT	Donald W. Yates	Donald W. Yates	1977	9
91 2/8	18 4/8	18 5/8	6 7/8	6 6/8	3	3	9	3 3/8	6 2/8	6 1/8	Lincoln Co., NM	Robert S. Guevara	Robert S. Guevara	1996	12
91	16 6/8	16 4/8	6 7/8	6 6/8	2 6/8	2 5/8	10 3/8	3 3/8	7 2/8	7 4/8	Carbon Co., WY	J. Ivan Kitch	J. Ivan Kitch	1964	13
91	16 2/8	15 6/8	7 1/8	7 1/8	3	3 1/8	14 1/8	11 7/8	5 6/8	5 5/8	Rawlins Co., WY	Fred Starling	Fred Starling	1967	13
91	17 7/8	17 5/8	6 7/8	6 7/8	2 5/8	2 5/8	14	8 2/8	7 1/8	7 3/8	Humboldt Co., NV	Steve W. Dustin	Steve W. Dustin	1990	13
90 6/8	16 2/8	16 4/8	7 4/8	7 4/8	3 4/8	3 4/8	17 2/8	15 3/8	7 5/8	7 5/8	Weston Co., WY	Allen Douglas	Richard J. Macy	1943	16
90 6/8	17 5/8	17 1/8	6 7/8	7	2 5/8	2 5/8	9 5/8	3 4/8	5 4/8	5 2/8	Catron Co., NM	John P. Grimmett	John P. Grimmett	1986	16
90 6/8	16 3/8	16 4/8	7	7 3/8	3 4/8	3 4/8	13 2/8	8 6/8	5 7/8	6 1/8	Natrona Co., WY	Richard J. Guthrie	Richard J. Guthrie	1989	16
90 4/8	18 1/8	18 3/8	6 5/8	6 5/8	2 6/8	2 7/8	10 3/8	2 7/8	7	6 4/8	Yavapai Co., AZ	Joe P. Fornara	Joe P. Fornara	1984	19
90 4/8	18 6/8	18 6/8	6 5/8	6 6/8	3	3	10 1/8	4	6	6	Hudspeth Co., TX	Walter O. Ford III	Walter O. Ford III	1994	19
90 4/8	16 1/8	16 2/8	7 1/8	7 1/8	3 5/8	3 5/8	14 3/8	10	7 3/8	7 1/8	Washakie Co., WY	Alden L. Curtis	Alden L. Curtis	1998	19
90 4/8	18 4/8	18 4/8	7 7/8	7 7/8	3	3	10 3/8	5 4/8	5	4 7/8	Big Horn Co., WY	Michael P. Dellos	Michael P. Dellos	1998	19
90 4/8	15 7/8	15 5/8	7 6/8	7 5/8	2 7/8	2 7/8	13 7/8	10 5/8	6 6/8	7	Pershing Co., NV	Mark R. Forsmark	Mark R. Forsmark	2001	19
90 4/8	16	17 4/8	7 3/8	7 2/8	3	2 5/8	7 2/8	4	7 7/8	7 3/8	Lincoln Co., NM	Dale Hislop	Dale Hislop	2003	19
90 2/8	17 3/8	17 4/8	6 4/8	6 4/8	2 7/8	2 7/8	10 3/8	6 7/8	7 2/8	7 1/8	Clark Co., ID	Randy Grover	Randy Grover	1997	25
90 2/8	17 3/8	17 2/8	6 7/8	6 7/8	2 6/8	2 4/8	12 1/8	9	7 2/8	7 1/8	Catron Co., NM	Robert N. Bushong	Robert N. Bushong	1998	25
90 2/8	15 6/8	15 7/8	7 6/8	7 4/8	3 1/8	3	11 2/8	10	6 2/8	6	Albany Co., WY	Gary W. Spiegelberg	Gary W. Spiegelberg	2001	25
90 2/8	17 2/8	17 1/8	6 2/8	6 3/8	2 5/8	2 5/8	13 5/8	10 2/8	8 5/8	8 5/8	Grant Co., NM	Lanny S. Rominger	Lanny S. Rominger	2002	25
90	19 4/8	19 5/8	6 6/8	6 6/8	2 7/8	2 7/8	10 1/8	8	4 7/8	4 6/8	Guano Creek, OR	E.C. Starr	E.C. Starr	1942	29
90	17	17 2/8	7	6 6/8	3 2/8	3 2/8	6	3 4/8	5 7/8	5 6/8	Yavapai Co., AZ	Marvin N. Zieser	Marvin N. Zieser	1995	29
90	18 4/8	19	6 6/8	6 6/8	3	3 1/8	11 2/8	2 6/8	5 1/8	5 1/8	Yavapai Co., AZ	Sam T. Aiton III	Sam T. Aiton III	1998	29
90	16 4/8	16 5/8	6 6/8	6 6/8	3 4/8	3 4/8	12 1/8	8 4/8	6 5/8	6 6/8	Socorro Co., NM	Len H. Guldman	Len H. Guldman	1999	29
90	16 4/8	16 4/8	7 2/8	7 4/8	2 3/8	2 4/8	11 5/8	11 5/8	7 2/8	7 4/8	Natrona Co., WY	Frank C. Kalasinsky	Frank C. Kalasinsky	2003	29
89 6/8	18 3/8	18	6 5/8	6 4/8	2 7/8	2 7/8	9 4/8	4	7 1/8	7 3/8	Seligman, AZ	J.W. Johnson	J.W. Johnson	1959	34
89 6/8	17 5/8	17 6/8	7 3/8	7	2 6/8	2 6/8	11 1/8	6 5/8	6 1/8	6 2/8	Rawlins Co., WY	Mary C. Kircher	Mary C. Kircher	1961	34
89 6/8	17 2/8	17 4/8	7	6 7/8	2 5/8	2 6/8	12 5/8	11 1/8	7 4/8	7 2/8	Rosebud Co., MT	Jim Ollom	Jim Ollom	1973	34
89 6/8	18 2/8	18	7	7	3	2 7/8	9 7/8	3 3/8	6 3/8	6 3/8	Coconino Co., AZ	James W. Barrett	James W. Barrett	1987	34
89 6/8	18 7/8	19	6 1/8	6	3	3	12 4/8	8	6	5 6/8	Colfax Co., NM	H. Hudson DeCray	B&C National Collection	1989	34

Score	L. Horn R	L. Horn L	Circ. Base R	Circ. Base L	Circ. 3rd Qtr R	Circ. 3rd Qtr L	Inside Spread	Tip to Tip	L. Prong	Hunter	Owner	Locality	Date	Rank
89 6/8	16 5/8	17	7 4/8	7 5/8	3 1/8	3 3/8	10 2/8	5 1/8	6 4/8	Sam S. Jaksick, Jr.	Sam S. Jaksick, Jr.	Coconino Co., AZ	1993	34
89 6/8	16 5/8	16 2/8	7 3/8	7 3/8	3 3/8	3 3/8	11 1/8	5 2/8	6 1/8	Sam S. Jaksick, Jr.	Sam S. Jaksick, Jr.	Yavapai Co., AZ	1996	34
89 6/8	16 4/8	16 2/8	7 3/8	7 3/8	3	3	9 7/8	4 4/8	6 5/8	Sam S. Jaksick, Jr.	Sam S. Jaksick, Jr.	Washoe Co., AZ	2000	34
89 6/8	17 2/8	17 2/8	6 6/8	6 7/8	3 3/8	3 4/8	11	5 1/8	6	James M. Machac	James M. Machac	Yavapai Co., AZ	2000	34
89 6/8	17 3/8	17 1/8	6 7/8	6 6/8	2 7/8	2 7/8	9 5/8	3 5/8	6 3/8	Debbie E. Cronin	Debbie E. Cronin	Harney Co., OR	2001	34
89 6/8	16 3/8	16 4/8	7 6/8	7 5/8	3	3 1/8	9 4/8	7 6/8	6	David A. Diede	David A. Diede	Washakie Co., WY	2003	34
89 4/8	16 5/8	15 7/8	7 3/8	7 1/8	3 4/8	2	12 7/8	7 1/8	6	Dennis J. Waitman	Dennis J. Waitman	Coconino Co., AZ	2003	46
89 4/8	17 6/8	17 6/8	7 1/8	7	3 2/8	3 2/8	10	3 2/8	6 1/8	John T. Peddy	John T. Peddy	Ferris, WY	1957	46
89 4/8	17 2/8	17 2/8	7	7 1/8	2 6/8	2 5/8	13 5/8	9 7/8	6 3/8	Roy Vail	Roy Vail	Laramie Co., WY	1958	46
89 4/8	16	15 4/8	7 4/8	7 4/8	2 7/8	3 2/8	12	8 5/8	6 1/8	Thomas V. Schrivner	P.K. Colquitt, Jr.	Sierra Co., NM	1961	46
89 4/8	17 2/8	17 5/8	6 7/8	6 7/8	3	2 7/8	9 4/8	5	5 6/8	Richard Steinmetz	Richard Steinmetz	Humboldt Co., NV	1977	46
89 4/8	17 7/8	17 5/8	7	7	3 2/8	3	10 4/8	3 2/8	6 3/8	Charles A. Grimmett	Charles A. Grimmett	Uintah Co., UT	1988	46
89 4/8	17 3/8	17 3/8	6 5/8	6 5/8	3 5/8	3 6/8	11 3/8	4 1/8	5 4/8	Brady J. Smith	Brady J. Smith	Catron Co., NM	1996	46
89 4/8	17 1/8	17 1/8	7	7	2 7/8	2 7/8	14 4/8	11 2/8	5 2/8	Brian B. Bingham	Brian B. Bingham	Yavapai Co., AZ	1999	46
89 2/8	17 7/8	17 7/8	7	7	3	3	10	6 2/8	6	Raymond R. Mong	Raymond R. Mong	Catron Co., NM	1999	54
89 2/8	18	18	7	7	2 7/8	3	9 1/8	3 4/8	5 2/8	Doug Millar	L.M. Edwards	Unknown	PR 1950	54
89 2/8	18 6/8	18 4/8	7 5/8	7 5/8	2 6/8	2 6/8	11 1/8	3 6/8	5 2/8	NM Dept. of Game & Fish	Jerry Saint	Grant Co., NM	1975	54
89 2/8	17 1/8	17 1/8	7	7	3 1/8	3 1/8	7 5/8	1 5/8	6	Gerald Scott	Gerald Scott	Moffat Co., CO	1982	54
89 2/8	17 2/8	17 2/8	6 6/8	6 7/8	3	2 7/8	12 4/8	4 4/8	6	Rene J. Dube, Jr.	Rene J. Dube, Jr.	Cochise Co., AZ	1985	54
89 2/8	16 3/8	16 3/8	6 7/8	6 6/8	3	3	9 6/8	6 6/8	5 7/8	Jack E. Beal	Jack E. Beal	Hudspeth Co., TX	1987	54
89 2/8	17 4/8	17 4/8	7 1/8	7	2 7/8	2 7/8	12 5/8	8 6/8	7 1/8	Jaime L. Fuentes	Jaime L. Fuentes	Washoe Co., NV	1990	54
89 2/8	15 4/8	15 4/8	7	7 5/8	2 4/8	2 4/8	10	4 4/8	8	Marjorie A. Puryear	Marjorie A. Puryear	Washoe Co., NV	1990	54
89 2/8	17 2/8	17 2/8	6 2/8	7 4/8	2 6/8	2 6/8	11 7/8	4 7/8	6 2/8	Michael R. Memmer	Michael R. Memmer	Mora Co., NM	1991	54
89 2/8	17 4/8	17 4/8	6 6/8	6 6/8	2 5/8	2 7/8	8 1/8	2 4/8	6 6/8	Harold P. Wales	Harold P. Wales	Lincoln Co., WY	1991	54
89 2/8	16 4/8	16 4/8	6 5/8	6 5/8	2 5/8	2 5/8	11 4/8	6 5/8	5 7/8	Glen E. Stinson	Glen E. Stinson	Moffat Co., CO	1997	54
89 2/8	18 4/8	18 4/8	6 7/8	6 7/8	3	3	15 3/8	12 1/8	5 3/8	Linda J. McBride	Linda J. McBride	Hudspeth Co., TX	2000	54
89 2/8	16 7/8	16 7/8	6 6/8	6 6/8	2 7/8	2 5/8	12	5 6/8	6 4/8	Robert E. Petersen	Robert E. Petersen	Coconino Co., AZ	2000	54
89	16 3/8	16 1/8	7 1/8	7 1/8	3 2/8	3	11 5/8	6 7/8	6	Harlan L. Legried	Harlan L. Legried	Johnson Co., WY	2003	67
89	17	17	7 4/8	7 4/8	3 1/8	3	11	5 2/8	6 5/8	Picked Up	George W. Conant	Lassen Co., CA	1985	67
89	18	18	7	7	3	3	11 2/8	8	7 1/8	Willis E. Haines	Willis E. Haines	Sweetwater Co., WY	1985	67
89	18 1/8	18 1/8	6 2/8	6 6/8	2 6/8	2 5/8	10 2/8	3 5/8	6	Arthur E. Long	Picked Up	Lincoln Co., NM	1985	67
89	16 2/8	16 2/8	6 4/8	6 7/8	3 1/8	3 1/8	10 2/8	4 5/8	6 4/8	Charles A. Grimmett	Charles A. Grimmett	Catron Co., NM	1989	67
89	16 3/8	16 3/8	6 6/8	7 5/8	2 4/8	2 4/8	10	5	6 2/8	Douglas G. DeVivo	Douglas G. DeVivo	Sweetwater Co., WY	1993	67
89	17 4/8	18 1/8	7 5/8	6 3/8	2 5/8	2 4/8	10 4/8	4 1/8	5 2/8	Wallace P. Riddell	Wallace P. Riddell	Hudspeth Co., TX	1996	67
89	16 4/8	16 4/8	7	7 3/8	3 1/8	3 2/8	11 3/8	7 3/8	7 3/8	David Meyer	David Meyer	Socorro Co., NM	2001	67
89	16 3/8	16 3/8	6 6/8	7 2/8	2 7/8	2 7/8	8 7/8	4 4/8	6 1/8	Patrick G. Nicholls	Patrick G. Nicholls	Washoe Co., NV	2002	67
88 6/8	18 1/8	18 1/8	6 2/8	6 5/8	2 5/8	2 5/8	10 5/8	5 4/8	6 3/8	Chris R. Winkel	Chris R. Winkel	Humboldt Co., NV	2002	76
88 6/8	16	16	7 2/8	6 5/8	2 6/8	3	11 7/8	10 1/8	6 2/8	J. Lyn Perry	J. Lyn Perry	Socorro Co., NM	1976	76
88 6/8	17 4/8	17 4/8	6 5/8	7 4/8	2 4/8	2 4/8	15 4/8	11 5/8	6 7/8	Bruce L. Zeller	Bruce L. Zeller	Washoe Co., NV	1986	76
88 6/8	18	18 4/8	7 4/8	6 3/8	2 6/8	2 6/8	8 4/8	4 7/8	5 5/8	William W. Diekmann	William W. Diekmann	White Pine Co., NV	1987	76
88 6/8	16 4/8	16 5/8	6 3/8	6 2/8	2 5/8	3	12	12	4 6/8	John W. Houchins	John W. Houchins	Brewster Co., TX	1988	76
88 6/8	18 4/8	16 3/8	7 6/8	6 3/8	2 5/8	2 5/8	15 6/8	12 7/8	5 7/8	Gerald Roland Gold	Gerald Roland Gold	Catron Co., NM	1990	76
88 6/8	16 5/8	18 1/8	6 3/8	7 3/8	3 1/8	3 1/8	13 6/8	12 2/8	5 7/8	Grant L. Perry	Grant L. Perry	Socorro Co., NM	1991	76
88 6/8	16 3/8	18	7 2/8	7 1/8	3 1/8	2 3/8	15 3/8	11 2/8	6	Kerry E. Kilgore	Kerry E. Kilgore	Washoe Co., NV	1992	76
88 6/8	18	18 4/8	7 1/8	6 2/8	3 1/8	3 1/8	18 2/8	15 6/8	5 4/8	Jerry P. Carver	Jerry P. Carver	Yavapai Co., AZ	1993	76
88 6/8	17 4/8	17 4/8	6 2/8	6 6/8	2 7/8	2 7/8	16	12 4/8	5 1/8	John D. Fetcho	John D. Fetcho	Mora Co., NM	1994	76
88 6/8	16 2/8	16 2/8	6 6/8	7 3/8	3	3	11 2/8	6 7/8	6 2/8	Werner Estes	Werner Estes	Humboldt Co., NV	1994	76
88 6/8	17 2/8	17 2/8	6 7/8	6 5/8	3 4/8	3 4/8	17 1/8	14 3/8	5 6/8	John C. Henkel	John C. Henkel	Colfax Co., NM	1995	76

PRONGHORN

Antilocapra americana americana and related subspecies

Score	Length of Horn R	L	Circumference of Base R	L	Circumference at Third Quarter R	L	Inside Spread	Tip to Tip Spread	Length of Prong R	L	Locality	Hunter	Owner	Date Killed	Rank
88 6/8	15 1/8	15	7 4/8	7 3/8	3 1/8	3 2/8	9	5 7/8	7 2/8	7 2/8	Washoe Co., NV	Todd B. Jaksick	Todd B. Jaksick	1996	76
88 6/8	16 1/8	15 5/8	7 4/8	7 1/8	3 4/8	3 3/8	12	7 7/8	6 3/8	6 6/8	Yavapai Co., AZ	Jerry Van Cleve	Jerry L. Van Cleve	1998	76
88 4/8	16 6/8	17 1/8	7	7	2 5/8	2 6/8	10	5 4/8	5 7/8	6 2/8	Fremont Co., WY	Terry N. TenBoer	Terry N. TenBoer	1974	89
88 4/8	17 7/8	17 6/8	7	7	3	3	15 6/8	11 6/8	5	5 1/8	Humboldt Co., NV	Clifford J. Heaverne	Clifford J. Heaverne	1983	89
88 4/8	19 2/8	18 6/8	6 5/8	6 5/8	2 6/8	2 6/8	13 4/8	10 4/8	5 4/8	5 3/8	Coconino Co., AZ	Harold R. Edgemon	Harold R. Edgemon	1984	89
88 4/8	18	17 5/8	6 4/8	6 4/8	2 6/8	2 5/8	13 2/8	8	6 4/8	6 7/8	Coconino Co., AZ	Randall W. Smith	Randall W. Smith	1985	89
88 4/8	16 5/8	16 2/8	7	6 7/8	3 4/8	3 7/8	8	2 1/8	5 6/8	5 7/8	Catron Co., NM	Douglas W. Kasey	Douglas W. Kasey	1987	89
88 4/8	17 7/8	17 7/8	6 6/8	6 6/8	2 7/8	3	13 7/8	5 7/8	5 5/8	5 6/8	Yavapai Co., AZ	Arthur C. Savoini	Arthur C. Savoini	1988	89
88 4/8	18 1/8	18 2/8	7	7 1/8	3 2/8	3	10	5 7/8	5 4/8	5 3/8	Coconino Co., AZ	Arthur R. Dubs	Arthur R. Dubs	1990	89
88 4/8	18 1/8	18	6 6/8	6 6/8	3 2/8	3 1/8	11 4/8	6 1/8	5 4/8	5 3/8	Cochise Co., AZ	Tom R. Braun	Tom R. Braun	1991	89
88 4/8	16 3/8	16 3/8	6 6/8	6 4/8	3 4/8	3 4/8	10 4/8	6 6/8	6 3/8	6 2/8	Catron Co., NM	R. Steve Bass	R. Steve Bass	1997	89
88 4/8	15 7/8	16 4/8	6 6/8	6 6/8	3 2/8	3 2/8	10 1/8	5 3/8	6 2/8	6 2/8	Coconino Co., AZ	Sam S. Jaksick, Jr.	Sam S. Jaksick, Jr.	1997	89
88 4/8	16 7/8	16 4/8	7 5/8	7 4/8	2 7/8	3 2/8	12 3/8	8 5/8	5 5/8	5 2/8	Mora Co., NM	Thomas J. Shaw	Thomas J. Shaw	1999	89
88 4/8	15 3/8	15 4/8	7 3/8	7 3/8	3	3	10	6 1/8	7	6 6/8	Carbon Co., WY	Shawn M. Hullinger	Shawn M. Hullinger	2000	89
88 4/8	16 2/8	16 3/8	7	6 7/8	2 7/8	2 7/8	9 1/8	8 1/8	5 5/8	5 6/8	Manyberries, AB	Fred J. Streleoff	Fred J. Streleoff	2003	89
88 2/8	17 2/8	17 2/8	7	7	2 6/8	2 6/8	17 3/8	14	5 5/8	5 6/8	Carter Co., MT	Carl T. Clapp	Carl T. Clapp	1955	102
88 2/8	18 2/8	18 2/8	6 6/8	6 6/8	3 1/8	3 1/8	11 4/8	8 4/8	5	5 3/8	Navajo Co., AZ	John M. Griffith, Jr.	John M. Griffith, Jr.	1983	102
88 2/8	17 4/8	16 5/8	6 6/8	6 5/8	3	2 6/8	20 5/8	20	7 2/8	6 4/8	Sweetwater Co., WY	Annette D. Lynch	Annette D. Lynch	1983	102
88 2/8	16 7/8	16 7/8	7	7	2 7/8	2 7/8	10 6/8	5 5/8	5 3/8	5 7/8	Yavapai Co., AZ	Larry D. Saylor	Larry D. Saylor	1984	102
88 2/8	18	17 5/8	6 3/8	6 7/8	3	2 5/8	13 4/8	10 6/8	6 5/8	6 4/8	Apache Co., AZ	Bob Howard	D.J. Hollinger & B. Howard	1987	102
88 2/8	18 2/8	18 1/8	6 7/8	7	3	2 7/8	16 4/8	12 4/8	5 3/8	5 6/8	Carbon Co., UT	James M. Machac	James M. Machac	1989	102
88 2/8	17 6/8	18 1/8	6 7/8	6 7/8	3	3	11 3/8	6 4/8	5 4/8	5 2/8	Mohave Co., AZ	Peter E. Mangelsdorf	Peter E. Mangelsdorf	1989	102
88 2/8	17 2/8	15 7/8	7 2/8	7 2/8	2 6/8	2 5/8	13 7/8	11 5/8	7 4/8	7	Goshen Co., WY	William P. Price	William P. Price	1991	102
88 2/8	17 2/8	17 4/8	7	7	2 4/8	2 4/8	13 1/8	10 5/8	6 7/8	7	Natrona Co., WY	John J. Heidel	John J. Heidel	1992	102
88 2/8	15 7/8	15 7/8	7	7	3 2/8	3 2/8	10 5/8	7 7/8	6 4/8	6 5/8	Washoe Co., NV	Todd B. Jaksick	Todd B. Jaksick	1997	102
88 2/8	18	18 2/8	6 3/8	6 2/8	3	3	6 4/8	3 4/8	6 6/8	5 7/8	Yavapai Co., AZ	John Mullins	John Mullins	1997	102
88 2/8	18 6/8	18 1/8	6 2/8	6 2/8	3 2/8	2 7/8	8 2/8	2	6 5/8	6	Socorro Co., NM	Burgh K. Johnson	Burgh K. Johnson	1998	102
88 2/8	17 1/8	17 1/8	7 1/8	6 6/8	2 7/8	2 7/8	13 5/8	13	6 4/8	6 4/8	Pershing Co., NV	Bryan L. Foote	Bryan L. Foote	2001	102
88 2/8	17 1/8	16 7/8	6 5/8	6 5/8	3	3	9 6/8	3 6/8	6	6	Lincoln Co., NM	John Timmons	John Timmons	2003	102
88	17 3/8	17	7 4/8	7 6/8	2 5/8	2 5/8	12 7/8	7 5/8	6	6	Sweet Grass Co., MT	William S. Amos	William S. Amos	1971	116
88	16 6/8	17 1/8	7	7	2 7/8	2 7/8	9 4/8	5 1/8	5 5/8	5 6/8	Coconino Co., AZ	Richard J. Hallock	Richard J. Hallock	1973	116
88	17 1/8	16 1/8	7 4/8	6 5/8	3	2 6/8	8 7/8	6 6/8	7 4/8	7 3/8	Hudspeth Co., TX	Gibson D. Lewis	Gibson D. Lewis	1986	116
88	17 1/8	17 4/8	7 1/8	7 1/8	2 6/8	2 6/8	14 1/8	9	5 7/8	6 1/8	Chaves Co., NM	Grant L. Perry	Grant L. Perry	1988	116
88	16 1/8	16 1/8	7	7	2 7/8	3	13	9 4/8	6 1/8	6	Uinta Co., WY	John V. Lockard	John V. Lockard	1990	116
88	16 7/8	16 7/8	6 6/8	6 6/8	2 7/8	2 7/8	11 3/8	8	6	6 2/8	Natrona Co., WY	F. Miles Hartung	F. Miles Hartung	1992	116
88	16 6/8	16 7/8	6 5/8	6 3/8	3 1/8	3 1/8	11 6/8	8 7/8	6 2/8	6 3/8	Apache Co., AZ	Richard L. Hazelwood	Richard L. Hazelwood	1992	116
88	18 6/8	18 1/8	6 5/8	6 5/8	2 6/8	2 6/8	9	3 1/8	5 5/8	6 3/8	Lincoln Co., NM	Vincent C. Gunn	Vincent C. Gunn	1994	116
88	16	16 2/8	7 2/8	7 3/8	2 6/8	2 6/8	10 7/8	6 1/8	6 2/8	6	Cassia Co., ID	Douglas G. Freestone, Sr.	Douglas G. Freestone, Sr.	1998	116

Score	Length of Horn R	Length of Horn L	Circ. of Base R	Circ. of Base L	Circ. 3rd Quarter R	Circ. 3rd Quarter L	Length of Prong R	Length of Prong L	Inside Spread	Tip to Tip Spread	Owner	Hunter	Locality	Date Killed	Rank
88	15 3/8	15 1/8	6 6/8	6 6/8	3 4/8	3 4/8	6 6/8	6 6/8	8 2/8	5 4/8	Burgh K. Johnson	Burgh K. Johnson	Emery Co., UT	1998	116
88	16 3/8	16 4/8	7	7	2 7/8	3	7	7 2/8	8 7/8	4 1/8	Mark G. Mahaney	Mark G. Mahaney	Yavapai Co., AZ	1998	116
88	16 2/8	16 2/8	7	7	2 5/8	2 6/8	7	7	10 1/8	6 7/8	Sherrie A. Rickman	Sherrie A. Rickman	Harney Co., OR	1998	116
88	16 4/8	17 2/8	7	7	2 7/8	2 7/8	7 3/8	7 3/8	14	12 7/8	Bill Drake	Bill Drake	Coconino Co., AZ	2001	116
88	16 2/8	16 2/8	6 5/8	6 5/8	2 6/8	2 6/8	6 5/8	7	12 3/8	8 2/8	Patrick J. Gilligan	Patrick J. Gilligan	Catron Co., NM	2002	116
87 6/8	17	17	7 4/8	7 4/8	2 6/8	3 1/8	7 4/8	6 3/8	15 2/8	12 1/8	William I. Crump	William I. Crump	Fremont Co., WY	1963	130
87 6/8	15	15 2/8	7 2/8	7 2/8	3 1/8	2 7/8	7 2/8	7 2/8	10 4/8	6 3/8	Frank Schuele	Frank Schuele	Fremont Co., WY	1975	130
87 6/8	17 2/8	16 6/8	6 6/8	6 6/8	2 7/8	2 6/8	6 6/8	6 6/8	14 4/8	9 5/8	Thomas R. Roberts	Thomas R. Roberts	Coconino Co., AZ	1986	130
87 6/8	15 3/8	15 3/8	7	7	2 7/8	3 1/8	7	7 1/8	13 6/8	11 2/8	Karey H. Stebner	Karey H. Stebner	Fremont Co., WY	1991	130
87 6/8	16	15	7 1/8	7 1/8	3 1/8	3 4/8	7 1/8	7 1/8	11 5/8	9 2/8	Paul A. Stewart	Paul A. Stewart	Socorro Co., NM	1993	130
87 6/8	15	15 3/8	7	7	3 5/8	2 7/8	7	7	13 2/8	10 3/8	Len H. Guldman	Len H. Guldman	Socorro Co., NM	1996	130
87 6/8	16 2/8	16 2/8	7 1/8	7 1/8	2 7/8	3 2/8	7 1/8	7	12 6/8	9 3/8	Robert R. Munro	Robert R. Munro	Natrona Co., WY	1998	130
87 6/8	16 6/8	16 5/8	7	7	3 3/8	3 3/8	7	7 1/8	10 7/8	6 1/8	Burgh K. Johnson	Burgh K. Johnson	Emery Co., UT	1999	130
87 6/8	16 5/8	16 2/8	6 6/8	6 6/8	3	3	6 6/8	6 6/8	10	5 1/8	Joseph R. Ellington	Joseph R. Ellington	Pershing Co., NV	2000	130
87 6/8	14 3/8	14 7/8	6 3/8	6 3/8	3	2 6/8	6 3/8	6 3/8	9 6/8	6 2/8	Jason L. Ridgeway	Jason L. Ridgeway	Sweetwater Co., WY	2000	130
87 4/8	18 1/8	18 1/8	7	7	2 6/8	3 4/8	7	7	12 2/8	6 3/8	A.J. Renkema	A.J. Renkema	Gillette, WY	2002	141
87 4/8	17 3/8	17 2/8	6 3/8	6 3/8	3 4/8	2 6/8	6 3/8	6 3/8	11 5/8	12	Stanley Scott	Stanley Scott	Modoc Co., CA	1961	141
87 4/8	17 4/8	16 3/8	7 2/8	7 2/8	2 6/8	3 7/8	7 2/8	7	11 2/8	2 4/8	Lynn M. Greene	Lynn M. Greene	Modoc Co., CA	1971	141
87 4/8	16	16 1/8	6 6/8	6 6/8	3 7/8	2 6/8	6 6/8	6 6/8	9 4/8	4 1/8	Ron L. Reasor	Ron L. Reasor	Socorro Co., NM	1979	141
87 4/8	16 2/8	16 7/8	7 2/8	7 2/8	2 7/8	2 7/8	7 2/8	7 2/8	8 3/8	7 2/8	Enoch D. Brandenburg	Enoch D. Brandenburg	Mora Co., NM	1987	141
87 4/8	16 3/8	16 2/8	7	7	3	3	7	6 6/8	11 7/8	2 7/8	Anthony J. Garrett	Anthony J. Garrett	Socorro Co., NM	1987	141
87 4/8	16 7/8	17	7 6/8	7 6/8	3	3	7 6/8	7 1/8	11 6/8	3 3/8	Kevin B. Oliver	Kevin B. Oliver	Colfax Co., NM	1993	141
87 4/8	17	16 3/8	6 5/8	6 5/8	3 4/8	3 4/8	6 5/8	6 5/8	8 2/8	13 3/8	Clay T. Robertson	Clay T. Robertson	Coconino Co., AZ	1994	141
87 4/8	16	16 5/8	6 6/8	6 6/8	2 4/8	2 4/8	6 6/8	6 6/8	8 6/8	4 4/8	Ken D. Langford	Ken D. Langford	Moffat Co., CO	1995	141
87 4/8	16 3/8	15 7/8	6 4/8	6 4/8	3 5/8	3 5/8	6 4/8	6 4/8	15 5/8	6 1/8	Preston J. Essex	Preston J. Essex	Socorro Co., NM	1997	141
87 4/8	16 5/8	16 1/8	7	7	2 7/8	2 7/8	7	7	9 7/8	8 5/8	Lesa A. Hall	Lesa A. Hall	Eureka Co., NV	1997	141
87 4/8	17	17	7 2/8	7 2/8	3 3/8	3 3/8	7 2/8	7 2/8	9 1/8	3	Nick Owen	Nick Owen	Socorro Co., NM	1997	141
87 2/8	17 2/8	17 2/8	6 6/8	6 6/8	2 7/8	2 7/8	6 6/8	6 6/8	9	11 4/8	Stephen C. LeBlanc	Stephen C. LeBlanc	Harney Co., OR	1998	155
87 2/8	16 7/8	16 7/8	7	7	2 7/8	2 7/8	7	7	12 7/8	11	Walt L. Kight	Walt L. Kight	Sage Creek, AB	1999	155
87 2/8	15 4/8	15 4/8	6 6/8	6 6/8	2 7/8	2 7/8	6 6/8	6 6/8	8	4 2/8	Drew Ramsay	Drew Ramsay	Lake Co., OR	2001	155
87 2/8	16 4/8	16 7/8	7 2/8	7 2/8	2 4/8	2 4/8	7 2/8	7 1/8	13 3/8	10 4/8	Ronald E. Hills	Ronald E. Hills	Fremont Co., WY	1966	155
87 2/8	16 3/8	15 4/8	7	7	2 5/8	2 5/8	7	7 2/8	13 5/8	9	Scott A. Trabing	Scott A. Trabing	Sweetwater Co., WY	1973	155
87 2/8	17 5/8	16 4/8	6 7/8	6 7/8	2 5/8	2 5/8	6 7/8	6 6/8	10 7/8	10 2/8	Jay R. Anderson	Jay R. Anderson	Niobrara Co., WY	1975	155
87 2/8	16 2/8	16 2/8	7 4/8	7 4/8	2 7/8	2 7/8	7 4/8	7 4/8	12 2/8	10	Steve Young	Steve Young	Carbon Co., WY	1975	155
87 2/8	17	17	7	7	2 7/8	2 7/8	7	7	12 1/8	8 2/8	Stephen M. Cameron	Stephen M. Cameron	Chaves Co., NM	1976	155
87 2/8	16 1/8	15 6/8	6 4/8	6 4/8	4 1/8	4 1/8	6 4/8	6 4/8	14 2/8	5 1/8	Lee Miller	Lee Miller	Humboldt Co., NV	1976	155
87 2/8	16 5/8	17 4/8	6 6/8	6 6/8	2 7/8	2 7/8	6 6/8	6 4/8	13 6/8	8	Charles A. Grimmett	Charles A. Grimmett	Washoe Co., NV	1988	155
87 2/8	16 5/8	16 6/8	6 7/8	6 7/8	2 7/8	2 7/8	6 7/8	6 7/8	11 7/8	10 2/8	Jared R. Nuffer	Jared R. Nuffer	Humboldt Co., NV	1988	155
87 2/8	19 1/8	18 3/8	7 1/8	7 1/8	2 6/8	2 6/8	7 1/8	7	10 2/8	15 6/8	Pierre M. Leautier	Pierre M. Leautier	Harney Co., OR	1989	155
87 2/8	16 4/8	17	7 2/8	7 2/8	3 1/8	3 1/8	7 2/8	7 2/8	15 6/8	12 4/8	Roy Holdridge	Roy Holdridge	Catron Co., NM	1991	155
87 2/8	18 1/8	17 6/8	7	7	2 7/8	2 7/8	7	7 4/8	14 4/8	8 7/8	Calvin H. Rabb, Jr.	Calvin H. Rabb, Jr.	Colfax Co., NM	1991	155
87 2/8	17 6/8	16 5/8	6 4/8	6 4/8	2 6/8	2 6/8	6 4/8	6 4/8	10 5/8	6 5/8	Ervin G. Rothfuss II	Ervin G. Rothfuss II	Yavapai Co., AZ	1991	155
87 2/8	16 7/8	17 2/8	7 1/8	7 1/8	2 3/8	2 3/8	7 1/8	7	9 4/8	5 6/8	Stephen C. LeBlanc	Stephen C. LeBlanc	Mora Co., NM	1992	155
87 2/8	17	17	6 7/8	6 7/8	2 7/8	2 7/8	6 7/8	6 4/8	14 7/8	11 1/8	James M. Machac	James M. Machac	Humboldt Co., NV	1992	155
87 2/8	15 6/8	16 5/8	7 2/8	7 2/8	2 6/8	2 6/8	7 2/8	6 7/8	12	6 4/8	Gary D. Bader	Gary D. Bader	Humboldt Co., NV	1994	155
87 2/8	17 4/8	17	6 5/8	6 5/8	3	3	6 5/8	7 2/8	10 4/8	3 6/8	Jay T. Gunter	Jay T. Gunter	Washoe Co., NV	1994	155
87 2/8	17 6/8	18 3/8	6 7/8	6 7/8	2 6/8	2 6/8	6 7/8	6 5/8	12 2/8	10 4/8	Brian F. Dolan	Brian F. Dolan	Yavapai Co., AZ	1996	155
87 2/8	16 5/8	17	7 1/8	7 1/8	2 6/8	2 6/8	7 1/8	6 7/8	12 2/8	8 7/8	Lester P. Everetts	Lester P. Everetts	Hudspeth Co., TX	1998	155

Antilocapra americana and related subspecies

Score	Length of Horn R	L	Circumference of Base R	L	Circumference at Third Quarter R	L	Inside Spread	Tip to Tip Spread	Length of Prong R	L	Locality	Hunter	Owner	Date Killed	Rank
87 2/8	16 2/8	17	7 1/8	7 1/8	2 7/8	3 1/8	15 6/8	14 2/8	5 7/8	5 6/8	Grant Co., NM	Bill Johnston	Bill Johnston	1998	155
87 2/8	15 2/8	15 3/8	6 7/8	6 7/8	3 4/8	3 5/8	12 5/8	11 2/8	6	6	Yavapai Co., AZ	David E. Evanow	David E. Evanow	1999	155
87 2/8	16 4/8	16 4/8	7	7	3	3	13 4/8	9 2/8	6 1/8	6	Socorro Co., NM	Kirk E. Winward	Kirk E. Winward	1999	155
87 2/8	18 5/8	16 4/8	7 4/8	7 4/8	3 1/8	2 4/8	13 7/8	8 5/8	5 3/8	6	Grant Co., NM	Edwin C. Broun III	Edwin C. Broun III	2000	155
87 2/8	16 7/8	16 7/8	6 5/8	6 5/8	3 1/8	3	11 1/8	4 4/8	5 5/8	5 6/8	Fremont Co., WY	Ben L. Wilkes	Ben L. Wilkes	2002	155
87 2/8	15 6/8	17 2/8	7 1/8	7 2/8	3	3 1/8	11 6/8	8 6/8	5 7/8	7 1/8	Navajo Co., AZ	Shatarra DeSpain	Shatarra DeSpain	2003	155
87	16 2/8	15 6/8	7 3/8	7 4/8	2 7/8	2 3/8	16	12 2/8	6 3/8	7	Hudspeth Co., TX	E.R. Rinehart	E.R. Rinehart	1959	179
87	17 6/8	17 4/8	6 3/8	6 3/8	3 1/8	3 1/8	15 4/8	10 4/8	5 2/8	5 3/8	Magdalena, NM	Picked Up	John L. Stein	1970	179
87	16 2/8	16 1/8	6 3/8	6 3/8	2 7/8	2 7/8	10 6/8	4 7/8	6 4/8	6 5/8	Washoe Co., NV	William E. Walker	William E. Walker	1976	179
87	15 7/8	15 7/8	7 1/8	7	2 4/8	2 4/8	10 5/8	5	6 1/8	6 5/8	Sweetwater Co., WY	Dell J. Barnes	Dell J. Barnes	1976	179
87	17 2/8	17 6/8	6 4/8	6 5/8	2 7/8	2 5/8	10 7/8	6 4/8	6 2/8	5 7/8	Lake Co., OR	JoAnn Hathaway	JoAnn Hathaway	1983	179
87	16 3/8	16 4/8	6 6/8	6 4/8	2 6/8	2 6/8	11 4/8	7 4/8	7 2/8	6 5/8	Sweetwater Co., WY	William S. Salisbury	William S. Salisbury	1984	179
87	15 6/8	16	6 4/8	6 4/8	3 2/8	3 2/8	11 5/8	5 6/8	6 1/8	6 2/8	Cochise Co., AZ	David J. Braun	David J. Braun	1984	179
87	17	17	6 6/8	6 6/8	2 7/8	2 5/8	10 4/8	8 2/8	6 1/8	6 6/8	Millard Co., UT	Duane Stanworth	Duane Stanworth	1987	179
87	16 2/8	16 6/8	6 6/8	6 7/8	2 4/8	2 4/8	12 3/8	6 7/8	6	6 4/8	Catron Co., NM	Laurie D. Scott	Laurie D. Scott	1988	179
87	15 1/8	16 2/8	7 4/8	7 4/8	2 7/8	3	18 2/8	17 1/8	5 4/8	5 4/8	Ochiltree Co., TX	Wayne Blue	Wayne Blue	1989	179
87	16 4/8	17 4/8	6 7/8	6 6/8	3	3	10 5/8	5 7/8	6 3/8	6 2/8	Yavapai Co., AZ	Robbie A. Jochim	Robbie A. Jochim	1990	179
87	16 5/8	16 6/8	6 7/8	6 5/8	3	3 1/8	9 1/8	2 6/8	5 2/8	5 3/8	Chouteau Co., MT	Darrell J. Woodahl	Darrell J. Woodahl	1991	179
87	16 2/8	15 4/8	6 6/8	6 6/8	2 6/8	2 5/8	9 6/8	5 2/8	8	7 4/8	Rosebud Co., MT	Shane A. Siewert	Shane A. Siewert	1991	179
87	16 3/8	16 3/8	8 1/8	8	2 5/8	2 4/8	11 5/8	11	6	6 4/8	Lincoln Co., WY	Jim S. Vilos	Jim S. Vilos	1994	179
87	16 1/8	16 2/8	7	7	3 3/8	3 4/8	9 5/8	7 3/8	6 1/8	5 6/8	Coconino Co., AZ	John P. Grimmett	John P. Grimmett	1995	179
87	16 1/8	16 1/8	7 2/8	7 1/8	3 2/8	3 2/8	13	8 3/8	5 7/8	6 1/8	Yavapai Co., AZ	Sam S. Jaksick, Jr.	Sam S. Jaksick, Jr.	1995	179
87	16 6/8	16 5/8	6 3/8	6 4/8	3 1/8	3 1/8	12 4/8	7 5/8	6	5 5/8	Yavapai Co., AZ	Garnet L. Kingsland	Garnet L. Kingsland	1996	179
87	16	16	6 6/8	6 6/8	3	3 2/8	13 6/8	13 5/8	6 4/8	6	Yavapai Co., AZ	Heidi A. Gunnell	Jeff K. Gunnell	1997	179
87	17 4/8	17 5/8	6 6/8	6 7/8	2 3/8	2 4/8	10 4/8	5 2/8	6	6 4/8	Washoe Co., NV	Donald R. Hilts	Donald R. Hilts	1997	179
87	16 6/8	16 2/8	6 5/8	6 4/8	2 6/8	3 2/8	9	5	5 6/8	5 5/8	Socorro Co., NM	Mark D. Nuessle	Mark D. Nuessle	1998	179
87	18 1/8	18 4/8	6 4/8	6 4/8	3 2/8	2 5/8	14 5/8	8 6/8	5 3/8	5 4/8	Harney Co., OR	Scott J. Bernards	Scott J. Bernards	1998	179
87	16 6/8	16 6/8	7 3/8	7 3/8	3	2 7/8	9 6/8	4 6/8	5 4/8	5 7/8	Carbon Co., WY	Larry S. Hicks	Larry S. Hicks	1999	179
87	16 4/8	16 1/8	7	7	3 2/8	2 7/8	9 3/8	4 5/8	7	7	Duchesne Co., UT	Joseph Machac	Joseph Machac	2001	179
87	18 3/8	17 3/8	6 7/8	6 7/8	2 5/8	2 6/8	10 5/8	5 1/8	5 3/8	5 5/8	Gilliam Co., OR	Jeff C. Wilkins	Jeff C. Wilkins	2002	179
86 6/8	16 6/8	17	6 7/8	6 7/8	2 5/8	2 6/8	15 3/8	9 6/8	6 6/8	6 6/8	South Dakota	Unknown	Dan E. McBride	PR 1940	203
86 6/8	18 7/8	18 6/8	6 7/8	6 3/8	2 4/8	2 4/8	12 4/8	7 1/8	4 6/8	5	Anderson Mesa, AZ	Gene Tolle	Gene Tolle	1941	203
86 6/8	17 4/8	17 3/8	6 3/8	6 4/8	2 7/8	2 6/8	15 5/8	13 4/8	7 4/8	6	Rock Springs, WY	Stanley Sinclair	Stanley Sinclair	1952	203
86 6/8	16 4/8	16 5/8	6 4/8	7 2/8	2 6/8	2 4/8	9 7/8	6 5/8	6 2/8	6 1/8	Rawlins Co., WY	C.M. Chandler	C.M. Chandler	1953	203
86 6/8	16 2/8	17	6 6/8	7	2 4/8	2 6/8	8 1/8	3 4/8	6 5/8	6 1/8	Jefferson Co., ID	Dale Nealis	Dale Nealis	1961	203
86 6/8	17 4/8	17 5/8	6 3/8	6 3/8	2 6/8	2 6/8	9 6/8	6 1/8	5 5/8	5 2/8	Yavapai Co., AZ	Louis R. Dees	Louis R. Dees	1963	203
86 6/8	16 3/8	16 3/8	7	7	3	2 7/8	11 6/8	9 4/8	5 5/8	6 1/8	Carbon Co., WY	Chuck Sanger	Chuck Sanger	1968	203
86 6/8	16 5/8	16 5/8	7	7	2 6/8	2 6/8	8 4/8	2 5/8	6 4/8	7	Fremont Co., WY	Richard A. Fruchey	Richard A. Fruchey	1973	203

Score	Length of Horn R	Length of Horn L	Circ. of Base R	Circ. of Base L	Circ. Third Qtr.	D-6	D-7	Prong R	Prong L	Locality	Hunter	Owner	Date	Rank
86 6/8	15 3/8	15 6/8	6 2/8	6 3/8	2 6/8	9 3/8	6	7 6/8	8 2/8	Sublette Co., WY	Mrs. Arvid J. Siegel	Mrs. Arvid J. Siegel	1974	203
86 6/8	17 3/8	17 1/8	6 6/8	7	2 6/8	10 2/8	6 5/8	5 4/8	5 2/8	Coconino Co., AZ	Ralph C. Stayner	Ralph C. Stayner	1980	203
86 6/8	17	17 1/8	6 7/8	7	3 1/8	14	9 1/8	5 5/8	5 2/8	Humboldt Co., NV	Rebecca J. Hall	Rebecca J. Hall	1981	203
86 6/8	18 3/8	18 1/8	6 5/8	6 5/8	3	8 7/8	5 6/8	4 6/8	5 3/8	Sublette Co., WY	Glenn A. Eiden	Glenn A. Eiden	1983	203
86 6/8	15 5/8	15 6/8	7 3/8	7 3/8	2 6/8	11 2/8	10 5/8	6 5/8	7	1983	Lloyd D. Kindsfater	Lloyd D. Kindsfater	1983	203
86 6/8	17 1/8	17 1/8	7	7	2 6/8	12 4/8	11 2/8	5 1/8	5 1/8	Catron Co., NM	John H. Bevel	John H. Bevel	1986	203
86 6/8	15 5/8	15 5/8	7 6/8	7 6/8	2 7/8	11	7 6/8	6 2/8	6 1/8	Carbon Co., WY	Troy T. Hall	Troy T. Hall	1987	203
86 6/8	16 7/8	16 7/8	6 6/8	6 6/8	3 1/8	8 5/8	5	5 5/8	5 5/8	Hudspeth Co., TX	Peter L. Bright	Peter L. Bright	1988	203
86 6/8	14 2/8	14 6/8	7 5/8	7 5/8	3 2/8	6	4 3/8	6 1/8	6 2/8	Perkins Co., SD	Scott R. Dell	Scott R. Dell	1990	203
86 6/8	17	17 3/8	7	7 1/8	3 3/8	11 3/8	2 2/8	6	5 7/8	Coconino Co., AZ	Ben E. Stayner	Ben E. Stayner	1991	203
86 6/8	16 6/8	16 3/8	6 7/8	7	2 7/8	13 3/8	11 1/8	6 5/8	6 1/8	Fremont Co., WY	Glen H. Taylor	Glen H. Taylor	1991	203
86 6/8	17 3/8	16 6/8	7 1/8	6 7/8	2 5/8	8 4/8	4 2/8	6 6/8	6	Coconino Co., AZ	Norman E. Gammons	Norman E. Gammons	1992	203
86 6/8	16 6/8	16 4/8	7 5/8	7 5/8	2 7/8	11	7 2/8	6	6 4/8	Bent Co., CO	Rodney D. Glaser	Rodney D. Glaser	1992	203
86 6/8	16 6/8	16 6/8	6 4/8	6 4/8	2 4/8	7 7/8	4 4/8	6 2/8	6 1/8	Blaine Co., ID	Johnny Unser	Johnny Unser	1992	203
86 6/8	17 2/8	17	7	7	2 5/8	12 4/8	9 4/8	6 2/8	5 2/8	Coconino Co., AZ	Harry L. Hussey	Harry L. Hussey	1993	203
86 6/8	16	16	7 1/8	7	2 6/8	12	8 1/8	6	6	Carbon Co., WY	James M. Machac	James M. Machac	1993	203
86 6/8	16	16 1/8	7 1/8	7 1/8	3	13 5/8	10 1/8	6 5/8	6 5/8	Coconino Co., AZ	Gary L. White	Gary L. White	1993	203
86 6/8	17 3/8	16 6/8	7 1/8	7 1/8	2 7/8	18 4/8	18 2/8	5 7/8	5 1/8	Jackson Co., CO	George V. Escobedo	George V. Escobedo	1994	203
86 6/8	17	17	7	7 2/8	2 7/8	10 6/8	7 6/8	5 4/8	5 5/8	Yavapai Co., AZ	Scott E. Raubach	Scott E. Raubach	1995	203
86 6/8	15 4/8	15 4/8	7 2/8	7 3/8	3	9 6/8	9 6/8	6 1/8	6 4/8	Yavapai Co., AZ	James M. Machac	James M. Machac	1998	203
86 6/8	17 2/8	17 2/8	7 3/8	7 3/8	3	10 3/8	10 6/8	5 6/8	6 1/8	Grand Co., UT	Kenneth F. Cook	Kenneth F. Cook	1999	203
86 6/8	17 2/8	16 2/8	6 4/8	6 2/8	3 1/8	8 7/8	3 4/8	7	2	Washoe Co., NV	Chris H. Darnell	Chris H. Darnell	1999	203
86 6/8	16 2/8	16 4/8	6 6/8	6 6/8	2 6/8	8 5/8	4 7/8	6 5/8	4 7/8	Washoe Co., NV	Don E. Perrien	Don E. Perrien	2000	203
86 6/8	19 1/8	16	6 6/8	6 6/8	2 5/8	6 2/8	3 2/8	6 4/8	3 2/8	Luna Co., NM	L. Victor Clark	L. Victor Clark	2000	203
86 6/8	16	16 7/8	6 4/8	6 4/8	2 4/8	14 7/8	10 4/8	4 7/8	4 3/8	Washoe Co., NV	William H. Moyer	William H. Moyer	2000	203
86 6/8	15 1/8	15	7	7	3 1/8	9 4/8	4 4/8	6	6	Washoe Co., NV	Jennifer M. Piccinini	Jennifer M. Piccinini	2000	203
86 4/8	16 4/8	16 4/8	6 6/8	6 6/8	2 7/8	12	12	5 7/8	5 3/8	Carbon Co., WY	Dale B. Jones	Dale B. Jones	2002	203
86 4/8	16 7/8	16 7/8	6 5/8	6 5/8	2 6/8	10 6/8	10 2/8	6 2/8	6 4/8	Carbon Co., WY	Gary A. Spina	Gary A. Spina	2002	203
86 4/8	15 7/8	15 7/8	6 4/8	6 4/8	2 7/8	10 5/8	10 7/8	6 3/8	5 4/8	Moffat Co., CO	Joseph R. Maynard	Joseph R. Maynard	1972	239
86 4/8	18	17	6 4/8	6 4/8	3	10 4/8	10 5/8	6 7/8	7	Lake Co., OR	James W. Greer	James W. Greer	1976	239
86 4/8	17	16 7/8	7 4/8	7 4/8	2 6/8	10 4/8	5 2/8	5 3/8	5 4/8	Navajo Co., AZ	John D. Higginbotham	John D. Higginbotham	1979	239
86 4/8	17 2/8	17 4/8	7 2/8	7 2/8	2 6/8	11	6 4/8	6	6	Sweetwater Co., WY	Rex A. Behrends	Rex A. Behrends	1980	239
86 4/8	15 7/8	15 7/8	6 6/8	6 6/8	2 5/8	9	6 7/8	6 7/8	5 6/8	Sweetwater Co., WY	Richard E. Hueckstaedt	Richard E. Hueckstaedt	1982	239
86 4/8	16 6/8	16 6/8	7 2/8	7 2/8	2 6/8	9 1/8	6 6/8	6 1/8	5 3/8	Catron Co., NM	Bruce D. Gallio	Bruce D. Gallio	1983	239
86 4/8	16 1/8	16 4/8	6 6/8	7	2 5/8	12 6/8	7 5/8	5 4/8	5 5/8	Fremont Co., WY	H. James Tonkin, Jr.	H. James Tonkin, Jr.	1987	239
86 4/8	16	16	6 7/8	7	2 4/8	11 2/8	5 7/8	5 3/8	5 3/8	Hay Lake, SK	Gerald G. Korell	Gerald G. Korell	1989	239
86 4/8	16 7/8	16 7/8	6 4/8	6 4/8	3 1/8	8 7/8	6 1/8	6 5/8	6 1/8	Billings Co., ND	Gerald W. Bien	Gerald W. Bien	1990	239
86 4/8	16 6/8	16 5/8	6 7/8	6 6/8	3 1/8	9	5 7/8	5 5/8	5 6/8	Coconino Co., AZ	Greg A. Ganje	Greg A. Ganje	1990	239
86 4/8	17 3/8	17 5/8	6 4/8	6 5/8	3 2/8	15	14	5 7/8	5 7/8	Coconino Co., AZ	Arthur R. Dubs	Arthur R. Dubs	1991	239
86 4/8	17 5/8	17 4/8	6 4/8	6 4/8	2 3/8	14 6/8	13	6 5/8	7	Malheur Co., OR	Nicholas J. Vidan	Nicholas J. Vidan	1991	239
86 4/8	17 4/8	16 6/8	6 6/8	6 6/8	2 6/8	10 7/8	4 2/8	5 4/8	6 1/8	Harney Co., OR	Sam L. Wilkins, Jr.	Sam L. Wilkins, Jr.	1991	239
86 4/8	16 6/8	16 6/8	6 7/8	6 7/8	2 5/8	14	9 5/8	6 1/8	5 3/8	Coconino Co., AZ	Sam S. Jaksick, Jr.	Sam S. Jaksick, Jr.	1992	239
86 4/8	15 6/8	15 6/8	7 2/8	7 2/8	2 7/8	9 5/8	5 3/8	6 1/8	6 1/8	Uinta Co., WY	Randy L. Mair	Randy L. Mair	1992	239
86 4/8	15 6/8	15 6/8	6 4/8	6 4/8	3 1/8	5 3/8	7 6/8	6 2/8	6 1/8	Rosebud Co., MT	Dennis J. Giese	Dennis J. Giese	1995	239
86 4/8	16 2/8	16 2/8	6 7/8	6 7/8	3 2/8	10 3/8	3 6/8	5 6/8	5 4/8	Las Animas Co., CO	Nicholas R. Russo	Nicholas R. Russo	1996	239
86 4/8	18 2/8	18 2/8	6 1/8	6 7/8	2 5/8	9 3/8	7 7/8	5 6/8	5 2/8	Catron Co., NM	Robert J. Seeds	Robert J. Seeds	1996	239
86 4/8	18 1/8	18 1/8	6 1/8	6 1/8	2 7/8	7 7/8	12 6/8	5 3/8	5 2/8	Catron Co., NM	David M. Asal	David M. Asal	1997	239
86 4/8	16 2/8	16 2/8	6 3/8	6 3/8	3	11	8 1/8	6 2/8	6	Elko Co., NV	Travis Branzell	Travis Branzell	1997	239

Antilocapra americana americana and related subspecies

Score	Length of Horn R	L	Circumference of Base R	L	Circumference at Third Quarter R	L	Inside Spread	Tip to Tip Spread	Length of Prong R	L	Locality	Hunter	Owner	Date Killed	Rank
86 4/8	16 2/8	16 4/8	7	6 7/8	2 7/8	2 7/8	12 2/8	8 4/8	6 4/8	6 2/8	Coconino Co., AZ	Jim Yarbrough	Jim L. Yarbrough	1998	239
86 4/8	16 5/8	16 4/8	6 6/8	6 7/8	3 2/8	3	14	7 4/8	5 4/8	6 2/8	Coconino Co., AZ	Rosemary B. Hume	Rosemary B. Hume	1999	239
86 4/8	16 6/8	16 3/8	6 7/8	6 7/8	3	2 7/8	12	9 4/8	5 5/8	5 6/8	Sierra Co., NM	Jimmy J. Liautaud	Jimmy J. Liautaud	1999	239
86 4/8	17 2/8	17 2/8	7	6 7/8	2 5/8	2 5/8	18 5/8	16 7/8	6 1/8	6	Judith Basin Co., MT	Michael D. Hannula	Michael D. Hannula	2001	239
86 4/8	14 5/8	14 2/8	7	7	3 3/8	3 1/8	12 2/8	9 2/8	5 2/8	5 2/8	Fremont Co., WY	Bill Chapman	Bill Chapman	2003	239
86 4/8	16	15 7/8	7 1/8	7 1/8	2 7/8	2 6/8	11 3/8	8	5 5/8	6 4/8	Humboldt Co., NV	James M. Hill	James M. Hill	2003	239
86 4/8	16 3/8	16 4/8	7 1/8	7	2 4/8	2 5/8	14 1/8	9 7/8	6	6 1/8	Carbon Co., WY	Garland E. Sawyers	Garland E. Sawyers	2003	239
86 2/8	16 7/8	16 6/8	6 7/8	6 5/8	3 1/8	3	13 5/8	10	5 4/8	5 7/8	Brooks, AB	S. Prescott Fay	Boston Mus. of Science	1913	266
86 2/8	16 6/8	16 2/8	6 4/8	6 3/8	3	3	11 4/8	10	7	6 1/8	Manville, WY	J.J. Hartnett	Roy Vail	1952	266
86 2/8	15 6/8	16 4/8	6 3/8	6 2/8	2 6/8	2 4/8	11	5 7/8	8 4/8	6 5/8	Otero Co., NM	Robert B. West	Dorothy West	1957	266
86 2/8	16	15 6/8	7 1/8	7 2/8	2 3/8	2 3/8	9 7/8	5 4/8	6 5/8	5 4/8	Coconino Co., AZ	Eugene Anderson	Eugene Anderson	1961	266
86 2/8	16 7/8	16 6/8	6 6/8	6 6/8	3	2 7/8	11 7/8	4 7/8	5 4/8	5	Du Gas, AZ	Rex Earl	Rex Earl	1962	266
86 2/8	15	15 2/8	7 6/8	7 6/8	2 7/8	2 7/8	9	5 6/8	6	5 6/8	Casper, WY	William W. Brummet	William W. Brummet	1963	266
86 2/8	17 6/8	17 6/8	6 3/8	6 3/8	2 7/8	3	10 6/8	7 4/8	5 3/8	5 3/8	Coconino Co., AZ	Jon H. Bryan	Jon H. Bryan	1970	266
86 2/8	16 1/8	16 1/8	6 5/8	6 6/8	2 6/8	2 6/8	12 1/8	7 2/8	6 5/8	6 4/8	Carbon Co., WY	Mike Davich	Mike Davich	1974	266
86 2/8	17 7/8	17 6/8	6 4/8	6 4/8	3 2/8	3 1/8	14 2/8	9 1/8	4 5/8	4 4/8	Ft. Apache Res., AZ	Jack Pierce	Jack Pierce	1974	266
86 2/8	16 6/8	16 6/8	6 4/8	7	2 7/8	2 6/8	12 3/8	9 4/8	6	6	Big Horn Co., WY	Robert N. Temme	Robert N. Temme	1974	266
86 2/8	17 2/8	17 2/8	7	7	2 6/8	2 5/8	12 6/8	10 7/8	5 6/8	5 7/8	Carbon Co., WY	Harold J. Rollison	Harold J. Rollison	1975	266
86 2/8	16 5/8	16 5/8	7 7/8	7	2 5/8	2 6/8	14 3/8	9 6/8	5	5 1/8	Fremont Co., WY	Douglas B. Stromberg	Douglas B. Stromberg	1976	266
86 2/8	17 3/8	17 3/8	6 7/8	7	2 6/8	2 4/8	13 7/8	13 7/8	5	5	Carbon Co., WY	James Poydack	James Poydack	1977	266
86 2/8	17 1/8	17 1/8	7 5/8	6 6/8	2 4/8	2 5/8	7 5/8	5	6 1/8	6 3/8	Sweetwater Co., WY	J. Robert Tigner	J. Robert Tigner	1980	266
86 2/8	16 5/8	16 5/8	7 5/8	7 2/8	2 7/8	2 7/8	14 3/8	8 1/8	5 2/8	5 1/8	El Paso Co., CO	Maurice Cutting	Maurice Cutting	1981	266
86 2/8	17	17	6 6/8	6 6/8	3 6/8	4	9 6/8	8 6/8	5	4 6/8	Hartley Co., TX	Ernie Davis	Ernie Davis	1983	266
86 2/8	15 2/8	15 2/8	6 4/8	6 4/8	2 6/8	2 6/8	11 4/8	7 3/8	5 2/8	5 3/8	Washoe Co., NV	Daniel E. Warren	Daniel E. Warren	1983	266
86 2/8	17 4/8	17 1/8	6 4/8	6 4/8	3 1/8	3 1/8	10 3/8	5 5/8	5 5/8	5 5/8	Colfax Co., NM	William E. Pipes III	William E. Pipes III	1985	266
86 2/8	16 3/8	16 3/8	6 7/8	6 6/8	3	3	17	5 3/8	6 2/8	6 1/8	Yavapai Co., AZ	Vincent J. Conti	Vincent J. Conti	1986	266
86 2/8	15 1/8	15 1/8	7 6/8	7 4/8	2 5/8	2 5/8	10 6/8	10 1/8	7	6 6/8	Sweetwater Co., WY	Kurt A. Mari	Kurt A. Mari	1988	266
86 2/8	17 6/8	17 5/8	6 5/8	6 4/8	2 7/8	2 7/8	15 6/8	13 4/8	4 7/8	5	Coconino Co., AZ	Scott J. Reger	Scott J. Reger	1988	266
86 2/8	15 4/8	15 3/8	7 1/8	7 1/8	2 4/8	2 4/8	12 1/8	10	7 1/8	6 6/8	Sweetwater Co., WY	Brian T. Gabbitas	Brian T. Gabbitas	1990	266
86 2/8	16 4/8	16 4/8	7 3/8	7 4/8	2 5/8	2 5/8	9 2/8	4	6 2/8	5 3/8	Sweetwater Co., WY	Daniel Daugherty	Daniel Daugherty	1991	266
86 2/8	16 3/8	16 3/8	7 3/8	7 4/8	2 7/8	2 7/8	9 2/8	2 6/8	6 1/8	6 2/8	Sweetwater Co., WY	Geraldine Hazzard	Geraldine Hazzard	1991	266
86 2/8	18	17 4/8	6 5/8	6 4/8	3	3	9 3/8	7	3 4/8	3 6/8	Mora Co., NM	Hub R. Grounds	Hub R. Grounds	1992	266
86 2/8	17 1/8	17 2/8	7 1/8	7 2/8	2 6/8	2 6/8	11 4/8	6 3/8	5 5/8	5 1/8	Mora Co., NM	Len H. Guldman	Len H. Guldman	1993	266
86 2/8	16 7/8	16 7/8	7 1/8	7	2 6/8	3 2/8	11	4 6/8	5	4 6/8	Colfax Co., NM	James D. Knight	James D. Knight	1994	266
86 2/8	16 2/8	17 2/8	7 2/8	7	2 7/8	2 7/8	9 1/8	4 4/8	4 6/8	5 5/8	Pershing Co., NV	Matthew K. Morris	Matthew K. Morris	1994	266
86 2/8	15 2/8	15	7 1/8	7 1/8	3 3/8	3 3/8	11	8 1/8	5 5/8	5 4/8	Humboldt Co., NV	David C. Rahn	David C. Rahn	1994	266
86 3/8	17 1/8	17	6 5/8	6 4/8	3	3	14 3/8	11	5 4/8	5 3/8	Coconino Co., AZ	Gregg L. Warne	Gregg L. Warne	1995	266
86 3/8	17 4/8	17 2/8	5 7/8	5 7/8	3 2/8	3	10 2/8	7 1/8	5 3/8	5	Yavapai Co., AZ	James E. Stark	James E. Stark	1996	266

Score	Length R	Length L	Circ. Base R	Circ. Base L	Circ. 3rd Qtr	Prong R	Prong L	Spread 1	Spread 2	Locality	Hunter	Owner	Date	Rank
86 2/8	15 5/8	16 2/8	6 6/8	6 6/8	6 6/8	4 4/8	4 3/8	9 6/8	9 6/8	Coconino Co., AZ	Jeffery A. Alt	Jeffery A. Alt	1997	266
86 2/8	15 6/8	15 6/8	6 7/8	6 7/8	6 6/8	3 1/8	3 2/8	10 1/8	4 6/8	Emery Co., UT	Len H. Guldman	Len H. Guldman	1997	266
86 2/8	17 2/8	16 7/8	6 7/8	6 7/8	6 7/8	2 6/8	2 6/8	8 7/8	3 2/8	Malheur Co., OR	Terry M. Dittrich	Terry M. Dittrich	1998	266
86 2/8	15 7/8	16	7 1/8	7 2/8	7 1/8	2 4/8	2 3/8	11 5/8	8 4/8	Sweetwater Co., WY	Tyler A. Jack	Tyler A. Jack	1998	266
86 2/8	16	15 7/8	6 7/8	6 7/8	7	3	3 2/8	10	6 2/8	Moffat Co., CO	Len H. Guldman	Len H. Guldman	2001	266
86 2/8	14 2/8	14 1/8	7 6/8	7 6/8	7 2/8	3 4/8	3 2/8	10 1/8	5 4/8	Sweetwater Co., WY	Jon W. Parker	Jon W. Parker	2003	266
86	15 4/8	15 1/8	7	7	6 7/8	3 4/8	3	6 6/8	4 2/8	Medicine Bow, WY	Jack R. Campbell	Jack R. Campbell	1959	303
86	17 3/8	18	6 6/8	7	6 7/8	2 3/8	2 5/8	12 6/8	8	Coconino Co., AZ	Richard R. Barney	Richard R. Barney	1969	303
86	16 2/8	16 3/8	7 3/8	7 1/8	7	2 5/8	2 3/8	9 7/8	6 3/8	Carter Co., MT	Jamie Byrne	Jamie Byrne	1972	303
86	15	15	7 2/8	7 1/8	7	3 2/8	3 3/8	13 6/8	4 4/8	Fremont Co., WY	Robert Hall	Robert Hall	1973	303
86	17 1/8	16 4/8	6 7/8	6 5/8	7 1/8	2 7/8	3	11 6/8	6 6/8	Yavapai Co., AZ	Ruth McCasland	Ruth McCasland	1975	303
86	16 4/8	16 4/8	6 5/8	6 6/8	7	2 7/8	2 7/8	7 6/8	6 7/8	Valley Co., MT	Ernie Freebury	Ernie Freebury	1981	303
86	17 3/8	17 3/8	7 1/8	7 1/8	7	2 4/8	3 1/8	11 3/8	5 6/8	Sweetwater Co., WY	F.A. Oliver	F.A. Oliver	1981	303
86	16 1/8	16	7 1/8	7 1/8	7	2 3/8	2 7/8	14 3/8	6 4/8	Natrona Co., WY	David M. Crum	David M. Crum	1983	303
86	16	16 5/8	6 5/8	6 5/8	7	3	2 4/8	10 1/8	5 6/8	McCone Co., MT	Danny L. Curtiss	Danny L. Curtiss	1983	303
86	16 5/8	16 6/8	6 7/8	6 6/8	6 7/8	2 4/8	2 4/8	9 4/8	5 7/8	Wibaux Co., MT	Raymond G. Marciniak	Raymond G. Marciniak	1984	303
86	16 4/8	16 4/8	6 6/8	6 6/8	6 7/8	2 6/8	2 5/8	10 4/8	6 7/8	Apache Co., AZ	Charles R. Sprung	Charles R. Sprung	1984	303
86	16 3/8	16 4/8	7 4/8	7 4/8	7 1/8	4 3/8	4 1/8	9 2/8	6	Lake Co., OR	Frank R. Biggs	Frank R. Biggs	1985	303
86	14 2/8	14 5/8	7 5/8	7 5/8	7 1/8	2 6/8	2 6/8	6 6/8	3 5/8	De Baca, NM	Bennie F. Hromadka	Bennie F. Hromadka	1985	303
86	17	17 1/8	6 2/8	6 3/8	6 7/8	2 3/8	2 4/8	10 2/8	7	Coconino Co., AZ	John S. Harrison	John S. Harrison	1986	303
86	15 2/8	15	7 4/8	7 3/8	7 1/8	2 6/8	2 7/8	0	6 2/8	Sierra Co., NM	Vicki L. Leonard	Vicki L. Leonard	1987	303
86	16 2/8	16 2/8	6 7/8	7	7 1/8	2 6/8	2 5/8	12 6/8	6 3/8	Lassen Co., CA	David A. Tye	David A. Tye	1987	303
86	16	15 6/8	6 6/8	6 6/8	6 7/8	2	2 6/8	11 7/8	6 7/8	Rosebud Co., MT	William E. Butler	William E. Butler	1989	303
86	14 6/8	14 2/8	8 1/8	8 1/8	6 6/8	3	3 1/8	13 4/8	6 2/8	Apache Co., AZ	Jennifer C. Flaherty	Jennifer C. Flaherty	1990	303
86	15 5/8	15 4/8	6 5/8	6 5/8	8 1/8	3 3/8	3 1/8	12	5 2/8	Catron Co., NM	NM Dept. of Game & Fish	Picked Up	1990	303
86	16 1/8	16	7	7	6 5/8	3 1/8	3 1/8	11	5 4/8	Natrona Co., WY	Bruce L. Bummer	Bruce L. Bummer	1991	303
86	15 5/8	15 5/8	6 7/8	6 7/8	7 1/8	2 5/8	2 7/8	11 4/8	6 2/8	Sweetwater Co., WY	Jason K. Faigl	Jason K. Faigl	1991	303
86	16 6/8	16 7/8	6 7/8	6 7/8	6 7/8	2 7/8	2 6/8	10 2/8	6 1/8	Catron Co., NM	Armando J. Garcia	Armando J. Garcia	1991	303
86	17 1/8	16 5/8	6 5/8	6 5/8	6 5/8	2 6/8	2 6/8	11 2/8	6 4/8	Garfield Co., UT	Lynn M. Greene	Lynn M. Greene	1991	303
86	17	16 4/8	6 5/8	6 5/8	6 5/8	2 6/8	2 6/8	10 6/8	6 6/8	Sweetwater Co., WY	William H. Miller, Jr.	William H. Miller, Jr.	1991	303
86	16 2/8	16 4/8	7	7	6 4/8	2 7/8	2 5/8	8 7/8	6 4/8	Socorro Co., NM	Joseph C. Sawyers	Joseph C. Sawyers	1992	303
86	17 2/8	18	6 4/8	6 3/8	6 3/8	2 7/8	2 7/8	9 5/8	5 4/8	Carter Co., MT	Keith L. Folk	Keith L. Folk	1994	303
86	15 6/8	15 6/8	6 3/8	6 5/8	6 4/8	2 7/8	2 7/8	14 4/8	5 5/8	Coconino Co., AZ	Walter E. George	Walter E. George	1994	303
86	17 2/8	16 1/8	6 5/8	6 5/8	6 7/8	3 1/8	3 1/8	13 1/8	5 4/8	Coconino Co., AZ	Sam S. Jaksick, Jr.	Sam S. Jaksick, Jr.	1995	303
86	16	16	7 1/8	7 1/8	7 1/8	3	3	10 6/8	6	Colfax Co., NM	Robert D. Jones	Robert D. Jones	1995	303
86	16 2/8	16 3/8	6 7/8	6 7/8	7 2/8	3 2/8	3 2/8	11 2/8	4 6/8	Gunnison Co., CO	James R. Dawson	James R. Dawson	1996	303
86	15	15	7 4/8	7 4/8	7	3 1/8	2 7/8	8 6/8	6 2/8	Washoe Co., NV	Len H. Guldman	Len H. Guldman	1995	303
86	17 3/8	17 2/8	6 7/8	6 7/8	7 2/8	2 7/8	2 7/8	7 5/8	5 5/8	Converse Co., WY	Charles J. White	Charles J. White	1996	303
86	15 5/8	15 4/8	6 5/8	6 5/8	6 6/8	3 4/8	3 5/8	9 4/8	6 2/8	Hudspeth Co., TX	Len H. Guldman	Len H. Guldman	1997	303
86	14 1/8	14 1/8	6 7/8	6 7/8	7	2 7/8	2 6/8	9 1/8	6 6/8	Cibola Co., NM	Bobby L. Beeman	Bobby L. Beeman	1997	303
86	15 4/8	15 6/8	6 3/8	6 3/8	6 6/8	2 6/8	2 5/8	16 3/8	4 7/8	Carbon Co., WY	J. Mike Clegg	J. Mike Clegg	2002	303
86	15 6/8	15 6/8	6 7/8	6 7/8	6 7/8	2 5/8	2 5/8	9 5/8	4 5/8	Mineral Co., NV	Roger L. Fawcett	Roger L. Fawcett	2002	303
85 6/8	18 2/8	17 7/8	6 4/8	6 3/8	6 3/8	3 5/8	3 5/8	12 1/8	4 6/8	Fergus Co., MT	H.H. Applegate	H.H. Applegate	1951	339
85 6/8	17 2/8	16 4/8	6 7/8	6 7/8	7	3 1/8	3 1/8	13 6/8	6	Carbon Co., WY	B.L. Holman	B.L. Holman	1953	339
85 6/8	16 5/8	17 5/8	6 4/8	6 4/8	7	2 6/8	2 6/8	7 7/8	5 6/8	Chugwater, WY	Louis C. Morrison	Louis C. Morrison	1955	339
85 6/8	18	15 4/8	6 4/8	6 4/8	7	3 4/8	3 4/8	12 5/8	5 3/8	Chihuahua, MX	Juan A. Saenz	Juan A. Saenz	1955	339
85 6/8	15 1/8	15	7 1/8	7 4/8	7 4/8	3 1/8	3 1/8	6	2 2/8	Sioux Co., NE	Gerald R. Larson	Gerald R. Larson	1962	339
85 6/8	16 2/8	16 1/8	6 5/8	6 5/8	6 1/8	2 6/8	2	12 5/8	9 6/8	Brooks, AB	Oliver Ost	Oliver Ost	1964	339

PRONGHORN

Antilocapra americana americana and related subspecies

	Length of Horn		Circumference of Base		Circumference at Third Quarter		Inside Spread	Tip to Tip Spread	Length of Prong					
Score	R	L	R	L	R	L			R	L	Locality	Hunter	Owner	Date Killed	Rank
85 6/8	18 4/8	18 1/8	6	6 1/8	2 4/8	2 6/8	6 5/8	0	6 1/8	6	Socorro Co., NM	V.F. Tannich	V.F. Tannich	1965	339
85 6/8	16	15 5/8	7	6 5/8	2 7/8	3	10 6/8	6 1/8	6 3/8	6 1/8	Boise City, OK	R.L. Williams	R.L. Williams	1966	339
85 6/8	16 4/8	16 5/8	6 6/8	6 5/8	3	3	9 1/8	5 1/8	6 1/8	6	Beaverhead Co., MT	Vern Hensley	Vern Hensley	1968	339
85 6/8	15 2/8	15 2/8	7 2/8	7 2/8	2 7/8	3	13 4/8	10 6/8	7	6 7/8	Rock Springs, WY	C.J. McElroy	C.J. McElroy	1969	339
85 6/8	15 7/8	16 3/8	6 2/8	6 2/8	3	3	10	9	4 4/8	4 4/8	Sweetwater Co., WY	E. Tom Thorne	E. Tom Thorne	1969	339
85 6/8	16 5/8	16 5/8	6 2/8	6 3/8	3	3	9 7/8	5 6/8	5 2/8	5 3/8	Sweetwater Co., WY	Roger A. Perkins	Roger A. Perkins	1971	339
85 6/8	16	16	6 5/8	6 5/8	2 5/8	3	13 1/8	8	6 2/8	6 2/8	Humboldt Co., NV	Thomas R. Pitts	Thomas R. Pitts	1973	339
85 6/8	16 4/8	16 5/8	6 4/8	6 5/8	2 5/8	2 5/8	9 6/8	4 4/8	6 4/8	6 4/8	Yavapai Co., AZ	Randy Modisett	Randy Modisett	1974	339
85 6/8	18 3/8	18 2/8	6 4/8	6 4/8	2 6/8	2 6/8	7 7/8	4 7/8	5 2/8	4 3/8	Carbon Co., WY	Robert F. Johnston	Robert F. Johnston	1977	339
85 6/8	16 1/8	16	7	7 1/8	2 5/8	2 6/8	11 2/8	8 7/8	6 2/8	6 1/8	Natrona Co., WY	Terrie L. Morrison	Terrie L. Morrison	1980	339
85 6/8	15 4/8	15 4/8	7 3/8	7 4/8	2 6/8	2 6/8	7 4/8	3	5 5/8	5 6/8	Carbon Co., WY	James M. Jagusch	James M. Jagusch	1981	339
85 6/8	15 7/8	16	6 7/8	6 7/8	2 7/8	2 7/8	9 4/8	4 3/8	5 4/8	5 5/8	Sweetwater Co., WY	Mark E. Nedrow	Mark E. Nedrow	1981	339
85 6/8	15 7/8	16 1/8	7 4/8	7 4/8	3	2 6/8	12 6/8	9 3/8	6 2/8	6 2/8	Navajo Co., AZ	C. Boyd Austin	C. Boyd Austin	1987	339
85 6/8	16	16 2/8	6 4/8	6 4/8	2 4/8	2 4/8	9	3	6 7/8	6 7/8	Sweetwater Co., WY	Steven J. Vanlerberghe	Steven J. Vanlerberghe	1988	339
85 6/8	15 7/8	15 7/8	7 6/8	7 6/8	2 6/8	2 6/8	8 6/8	2 3/8	5 5/8	6	Sweetwater Co., WY	Duane M. Smith	Duane M. Smith	1989	339
85 6/8	16 6/8	16 6/8	6 5/8	6 5/8	2 7/8	3	10 6/8	9 4/8	6	6	Carbon Co., WY	Herman A. Hatfield	Herman A. Hatfield	1990	339
85 6/8	17	16 7/8	7	7	2 5/8	2 5/8	11	4 7/8	5 6/8	5 4/8	Mora Co., NM	Michael J. Loomis	Michael J. Loomis	1990	339
85 6/8	16 3/8	16 5/8	6 2/8	6 2/8	2 5/8	2 5/8	8	1 7/8	6 5/8	6 6/8	Emery Co., UT	Jerry L. Oveson	Jerry L. Oveson	1991	339
85 6/8	15 4/8	15 4/8	7 2/8	7 2/8	2 6/8	2 6/8	8 3/8	3	6 4/8	6 2/8	Sweetwater Co., WY	Robert C. Sexton	Robert C. Sexton	1992	339
85 6/8	18 1/8	18	6 3/8	6 3/8	2 5/8	2 6/8	17 1/8	13	6 1/8	5 7/8	Coconino Co., AZ	Gene Coon	Gene Coon	1993	339
85 6/8	17 1/8	17 1/8	6 5/8	6 5/8	2 7/8	2 6/8	11 6/8	6 6/8	5 4/8	5 3/8	Mora Co., NM	Edward C. Joseph	Edward C. Joseph	1994	339
85 6/8	16 3/8	16 5/8	6 6/8	6 4/8	2 6/8	2 6/8	12 6/8	8 1/8	6 1/8	6	Yavapai Co., AZ	James W.P. Roe	James W.P. Roe	1994	339
85 6/8	15 4/8	15 4/8	7	7	2 7/8	3 1/8	11 1/8	7 3/8	5 6/8	5 4/8	Colfax Co., NM	Robert D. Jones	Robert D. Jones	1995	339
85 6/8	16 2/8	15 4/8	6 6/8	6 6/8	3 4/8	3 6/8	13 2/8	12 4/8	5 5/8	5 4/8	Coconino Co., AZ	Kevin E. Rector	Kevin E. Rector	1996	339
85 6/8	16 4/8	16 2/8	7 2/8	7 1/8	2 4/8	2 3/8	13 4/8	10 5/8	6 4/8	6 4/8	Malheur Co., OR	Klaus D. Pagel	Klaus D. Pagel	1998	339
85 6/8	15 7/8	16 7/8	6 6/8	6 6/8	3 1/8	3	11 2/8	10 1/8	6 1/8	6 4/8	Yoakum Co., TX	William S. Pickett III	William S. Pickett III	1999	339
85 6/8	15 4/8	15 3/8	7 7/8	7 6/8	3	3	10 6/8	8 3/8	5	5 3/8	Carbon Co., WY	Robert E. Bergquist	Robert E. Bergquist	2000	339
85 6/8	16 7/8	16 5/8	6 6/8	6 7/8	3	2 5/8	13	9 1/8	6 4/8	6 6/8	Goshen Co., WY	Billy G. Lee	Billy G. Lee	2000	339
85 6/8	15 3/8	15 7/8	6 6/8	6 6/8	2 5/8	2 5/8	8 7/8	5 6/8	7	7	Natrona Co., WY	Alex R. Bilek	Alex R. Bilek	2001	339
85 4/8	16 6/8	16 6/8	7 5/8	7 4/8	2 2/8	2 3/8	11 6/8	8 4/8	7 3/8	6 5/8	Rawlins Co., WY	Paul C. Himelright	Paul C. Himelright	1960	374
85 4/8	17 2/8	16 5/8	6 1/8	6 2/8	2 5/8	2 6/8	10 7/8	6 2/8	6 2/8	6 2/8	Campbell Co., WY	Eugene D. Springen	Brenda Clouser	1962	374
85 4/8	15 4/8	15 3/8	7 2/8	7 2/8	2 7/8	2 7/8	7 6/8	4 1/8	6 3/8	6 2/8	Saratoga Co., WY	Carlyn J. Ourada	Carlyn J. Ourada	1969	374
85 4/8	16	16 6/8	6 7/8	7 2/8	3	3	11 1/8	10 2/8	6 4/8	6 2/8	Rosebud Co., MT	Calvin F. Mayes	Calvin F. Mayes	1973	374
85 4/8	16 6/8	16 6/8	7 4/8	7 2/8	2 5/8	2 5/8	10 2/8	2 2/8	6 2/8	5 5/8	Washoe Co., NV	Mario E. Gildone	Mario E. Gildone	1977	374
85 4/8	17 2/8	17 1/8	6 4/8	6 3/8	2 5/8	2 5/8	15 1/8	11 1/8	6 1/8	6	Washoe Co., NV	Maryanne Robinson	M. & M. Robinson	1981	374
85 4/8	16	16	7	6 7/8	2 5/8	2 6/8	7 3/8	3 3/8	6 5/8	6 4/8	Sweetwater Co., WY	Lee Frudden	Lee Frudden	1982	374
85 4/8	17 2/8	17 3/8	6 6/8	6 3/8	2 7/8	2 7/8	11 4/8	9 4/8	6 7/8	6 2/8	Mora Co., NM	Roger B. Heemeier	Roger B. Heemeier	1982	374
85 4/8	16 4/8	17 1/8	7	6 7/8	2 6/8	3	13	9 3/8	5 7/8	5 5/8	Fremont Co., WY	Jerry A. Martin	Jerry A. Martin	1982	374

Score	Length of Horn R	L	Circ. of Base R	L	Circ. Third Quarter R	L	Inside Spread	Tip to Tip	Length of Prong R	L	Locality	Hunter	Owner	Date	Rank
85 4/8	15 5/8	15 6/8	6 7/8	6 7/8	2 5/8	2 5/8	8 4/8	2 3/8	6 3/8	6 3/8	Fremont Co., WY	Roger E. Udovich	Roger E. Udovich	1982	374
85 4/8	17 7/8	17 3/8	6 3/8	6 1/8	2 7/8	2 7/8	9 1/8	4 2/8	6 1/8	5 7/8	Lemhi Co., ID	Michael E. Wolf	Michael E. Wolf	1982	374
85 4/8	17	16 6/8	6 7/8	6 7/8	2 7/8	2 7/8	9 3/8	6	6 7/8	5 7/8	Sweetwater Co., WY	E. Jay Dawson	E. Jay Dawson	1983	374
85 4/8	16 1/8	15 7/8	7	7 1/8	2 4/8	2 4/8	10 4/8	5 6/8	7 1/8	7	Sioux Co., NE	John W. Hlavacek	John W. Hlavacek	1983	374
85 4/8	18 1/8	18 4/8	6 4/8	6 4/8	2 5/8	2 4/8	17 4/8	13 5/8	6 4/8	6 4/8	Apache Co., AZ	Don L. Corley	Don L. Corley	1985	374
85 4/8	17 6/8	17 3/8	7	7	2 4/8	2 4/8	14 1/8	12 2/8	7	7	Lake Co., OR	Edna J. Kettenburg	Edna J. Kettenburg	1985	374
85 4/8	16 5/8	16 5/8	6 7/8	6 7/8	2 6/8	2 6/8	9 3/8	4 1/8	6 7/8	6 7/8	Yavapai Co., AZ	Steven C. Dunn	Steven C. Dunn	1987	374
85 4/8	17 2/8	17 2/8	6 6/8	6 6/8	2 7/8	2 7/8	17 2/8	13 4/8	6 6/8	6 6/8	Washoe Co., NV	Peter K. Beers	Peter K. Beers	1988	374
85 4/8	16 5/8	16 5/8	6 6/8	6 6/8	2 5/8	2 6/8	15 1/8	11 1/8	6 6/8	6 6/8	Butte Co., ID	S. Eric Krasa	Picked Up	1988	374
85 4/8	16 6/8	16 4/8	6 6/8	6 7/8	3	3	9 2/8	5 1/8	6 7/8	6 7/8	Millard Co., UT	David J. Carter	David J. Carter	1989	374
85 4/8	16 5/8	16 6/8	6 6/8	6 7/8	2 6/8	3	7	1 1/8	6 7/8	5 5/8	Rosebud Co., MT	John A. Hill	John A. Hill	1989	374
85 4/8	16 4/8	16 4/8	6 4/8	6 5/8	3	3	11 2/8	5	6 5/8	6 6/8	Coconino Co., AZ	Lester E. Bradley	Lester E. Bradley	1990	374
85 4/8	16	16 2/8	7 1/8	7	3	3	12 5/8	8 3/8	7	7 1/8	Harney Co., OR	Van G. Decker	Van G. Decker	1990	374
85 4/8	16 5/8	16	6 4/8	6 4/8	2 7/8	2 7/8	12 6/8	7 7/8	6 4/8	6 4/8	Coconino Co., AZ	Don W. Drew	Don R. Drew	1990	374
85 4/8	16	16	6 6/8	6 6/8	3 1/8	3 3/8	8 4/8	3 7/8	6 6/8	6 6/8	Lassen Co., CA	Jeff R. Rogers	Jeff R. Rogers	1990	374
85 4/8	16 7/8	16 7/8	7	7	2 6/8	2 6/8	12 5/8	8 5/8	7	7	Washoe Co., NV	Gregg A. Menter	Gregg A. Menter	1991	374
85 4/8	15 7/8	15 5/8	6 4/8	6 4/8	2 6/8	2 6/8	9 7/8	5 6/8	6 4/8	6 4/8	Torrance Co., NM	James D. Moreland	James D. Moreland	1991	374
85 4/8	17 4/8	17 2/8	6	6	2 4/8	2 5/8	11 4/8	8	6	6 4/8	De Baca, NM	Samuel S. Pattillo	Samuel S. Pattillo	1991	374
85 4/8	15 6/8	15 6/8	6 7/8	7	3	3	12 3/8	10 2/8	6 7/8	6 6/8	Catron Co., NM	Tanya M. Horwath	Tanya M. Horwath	1992	374
85 4/8	15 5/8	15 5/8	6 6/8	6 5/8	2 6/8	2 6/8	12 4/8	9 1/8	6 6/8	6 5/8	Nye Co., NV	E. William Almberg	E. William Almberg	1993	374
85 4/8	17	16 6/8	6 7/8	6 7/8	2 5/8	2 5/8	8 4/8	8 2/8	6 7/8	6 7/8	Campbell Co., WY	Ronald R. Mobley	Ronald R. Mobley	1993	374
85 4/8	16 4/8	16 4/8	6 3/8	6 3/8	2 7/8	3	13 3/8	4 4/8	6 3/8	6 3/8	Coconino Co., AZ	Edward Boutonnet	Edward Boutonnet	1994	374
85 4/8	16 5/8	16 6/8	6 4/8	6 4/8	3 3/8	2 7/8	7 6/8	7 6/8	6 4/8	6 4/8	Catron Co., NM	Thomas J. Chavez	Thomas J. Chavez	1995	374
85 4/8	16 3/8	16 3/8	6 1/8	6 2/8	3	2 7/8	13 4/8	13 4/8	6 1/8	6 1/8	Cibola Co., NM	David M. Asal	David M. Asal	1996	374
85 4/8	18 1/8	18 1/8	6 2/8	6 2/8	2 7/8	2 5/8	3 5/8	3 5/8	6 2/8	6 2/8	Mohave Co., AZ	Ralph C. Stayner	Ralph C. Stayner	1996	374
85 4/8	17 4/8	17 6/8	6 4/8	6 4/8	3 2/8	3 2/8	5 2/8	5 2/8	6 4/8	6 4/8	Crook Co., OR	David T. Boyle	David T. Boyle	1997	374
85 4/8	16 1/8	16 2/8	6	6	3 1/8	3 1/8	9 6/8	14 1/8	6	6	Socorro Co., NM	Len H. Guldman	Len H. Guldman	1998	374
85 4/8	15 3/8	15 4/8	7 2/8	7 2/8	3	3	14 6/8	11	7 2/8	7 2/8	Colfax Co., NM	Robert D. Jones	Robert D. Jones	1998	374
85 4/8	17 2/8	17 2/8	6 6/8	6 6/8	3 2/8	3	13 3/8	13 7/8	6 5/8	6 6/8	Socorro Co., NM	Dale Hislop	Dale Hislop	1999	374
85 4/8	16 1/8	16 1/8	6 7/8	6 7/8	2 6/8	2 6/8	15	5 7/8	6 7/8	6 7/8	Lincoln Co., NM	Gary A. Lehnherr	Gary A. Lehnherr	1999	374
85 4/8	16 1/8	15 6/8	6 7/8	7	2 7/8	2 7/8	15 6/8	2 4/8	7 1/8	7 1/8	Carbon Co., WY	Lenard E. Brashier	Lenard E. Brashier	2000	374
85 4/8	17 2/8	17 1/8	7 2/8	7 1/8	3	3	11 4/8	4 5/8	6 6/8	6 6/8	Natrona Co., WY	Scotty J. Tuttle	Scotty J. Tuttle	2000	374
85 4/8	18	18	6 6/8	6 6/8	2 6/8	2 6/8	10 6/8	5 3/8	6 6/8	6 6/8	Colfax Co., NM	Donald E. Utecht	Donald E. Utecht	2000	374
85 4/8	18 1/8	18 1/8	6 5/8	6 5/8	2 4/8	2 4/8	15 7/8	5 6/8	6 5/8	6 5/8	Yavapai Co., AZ	David Meyer	David Meyer	2001	374
85 4/8	15 2/8	15 2/8	6 6/8	6 6/8	2 4/8	2 3/8	12 4/8	6	6 6/8	6 6/8	Duchesne Co., UT	John P. Grimmett	John P. Grimmett	2002	374
85 4/8	16 5/8	16 4/8	7 1/8	7	2 6/8	3	12 7/8	5 7/8	7 1/8	7 1/8	Colfax Co., NM	Ed Hengel, Jr.	Ed Hengel, Jr.	2002	374
85 2/8	16 3/8	16 3/8	7	7 1/8	3	3	12 4/8	5 1/8	7 2/8	7 2/8	Saratoga Co., WY	Russell C. Cutter	Russell C. Cutter	1957	419
85 2/8	17 4/8	17 6/8	7 1/8	7 1/8	2 8/8	2 6/8	8 6/8	5 4/8	7 1/8	7 1/8	Yavapai Co., AZ	Robert C. Bogart	Robert C. Bogart	1963	419
85 2/8	15 4/8	15 4/8	7 6/8	7 1/8	2 7/8	2 7/8	2	11 1/8	7 2/8	7 1/8	Lower Sweetwater, WY	John Kereszturi	John Kereszturi	1963	419
85 2/8	16 3/8	16 3/8	7 1/8	7	2 4/8	2 4/8	11 1/8	8	7 1/8	7 1/8	Maple Creek, SK	Glen A. Lewis	George Hooey	1964	419
85 2/8	17	17	6 5/8	6 3/8	2 7/8	2 7/8	8	8	6 4/8	6 3/8	Bow City, AB	Howard M. Stephens	Eric Wilson	1964	419
85 2/8	14 3/8	14 4/8	6 6/8	6 4/8	2 4/8	2 4/8	11 5/8	11 5/8	6 6/8	6 6/8	Sublette Co., WY	Mike Wilson	Mike Wilson	1966	419
85 2/8	16	15 5/8	6 3/8	6 3/8	2 6/8	2 6/8	7 4/8	7 4/8	6 3/8	6 3/8	Johnson Co., WY	Robert P. Murphy	Robert P. Murphy	1968	419
85 2/8	17 1/8	16 6/8	6 2/8	6 2/8	2 6/8	2 6/8	5 6/8	5 6/8	6 2/8	6 2/8	Sweetwater Co., WY	Mario Shassetz	Mario Shassetz	1968	419
85 2/8	14 4/8	14 4/8	7 6/8	7 2/8	2 6/8	2 6/8	9 7/8	9 7/8	7 6/8	7 2/8	S. Wamsutter, WY	William G. Hepworth	William G. Hepworth	1970	419
85 2/8	15 6/8	15 7/8	7 2/8	7 1/8	2 8/8	2 8/8	3 6/8	3 6/8	6 6/8	6 6/8	Carbon Co., WY	Daryl L. Frank	Daryl L. Frank	1973	419
85 2/8	15 6/8	15 6/8	6 6/8	6 6/8	2 5/8	2 6/8	8 2/8	8 2/8	6 6/8	6 6/8	Lincoln Co., WY	James R. Gunter	James R. Gunter	1976	419
85 2/8	17 5/8	17 4/8	7	7	2 7/8	2 7/8	6 1/8	6 1/8	7	7	Colfax Co., NM	Rick H. Jackson	Rick H. Jackson	1977	419

PRONGHORN

Antilocapra americana and related subspecies

Score	Length of Horn R	L	Circumference of Base R	L	Circumference at Third Quarter R	L	Inside Spread	Tip to Tip Spread	Length of Prong R	L	Locality	Hunter	Owner	Date Killed	Rank
85 2/8	16 4/8	16 3/8	7	7 1/8	3	3	8 5/8	4 3/8	5 6/8	5 2/8	Carbon Co., WY	Paul M. Ostrander	Paul M. Ostrander	1977	419
85 2/8	17 7/8	18 1/8	6 7/8	6 4/8	3	3 1/8	11 1/8	4 7/8	5	4 3/8	Colfax Co., NM	John D. Pearson	John D. Pearson	1977	419
85 2/8	15 2/8	15 1/8	7 5/8	7 3/8	2 5/8	2 4/8	10 6/8	6 3/8	4	4 1/8	Baker Co., OR	Robert Spears	Robert Spears	1977	419
85 2/8	14 4/8	14 4/8	5 7/8	5 7/8	2 7/8	2 7/8	9 7/8	6 7/8	6	5 7/8	Carbon Co., WY	Roland W. Anthony	Roland W. Anthony	1978	419
85 2/8	16 1/8	16 1/8	6 7/8	7	2 5/8	2 5/8	13 4/8	11 7/8	6 5/8	6 3/8	Lake Co., OR	James H. Hastings	James H. Hastings	1979	419
85 2/8	15 4/8	15 6/8	7 3/8	7 3/8	3 2/8	2 7/8	8	4 1/8	5 7/8	5 6/8	Baker Co., OR	Eldon L. Buckner	Eldon L. Buckner	1981	419
85 2/8	16	15 5/8	6 4/8	6 5/8	2 6/8	2 7/8	12	8 4/8	6	6 2/8	Fremont Co., WY	Richard A. Fruchey	Richard A. Fruchey	1981	419
85 2/8	17 4/8	17 3/8	6 1/8	6 1/8	2 6/8	2 6/8	9 3/8	6 5/8	5 4/8	5 7/8	Natrona Co., WY	Margery H.T. Torrey	Margery H.T. Torrey	1981	419
85 2/8	16 3/8	16 3/8	7	6 7/8	2 5/8	2 4/8	14 3/8	10 5/8	6 2/8	6 2/8	Carbon Co., WY	Patrick R. Adams	Patrick R. Adams	1982	419
85 2/8	16 7/8	16 7/8	6 6/8	6 7/8	3	3	11 6/8	6 5/8	5 1/8	5 3/8	Coconino Co., AZ	Philip S. Leiendecker	Philip S. Leiendecker	1982	419
85 2/8	16 1/8	16 1/8	7	6 7/8	2 7/8	2 5/8	10 5/8	7 1/8	5 5/8	6 1/8	Sweetwater Co., WY	L. Bill Miller	L. Bill Miller	1982	419
85 2/8	17 3/8	17 3/8	7 2/8	7	2 7/8	2 7/8	12	7 2/8	5 2/8	5 3/8	Rosebud Co., MT	Dale R. Brauer	Dale R. Brauer	1983	419
85 2/8	17	17 1/8	6 4/8	6 4/8	2 6/8	2 6/8	14 1/8	13 2/8	5 1/8	5 1/8	Colfax Co., NM	S.X. Callahan III	S.X. Callahan III	1983	419
85 2/8	17 1/8	17 2/8	6 4/8	6 4/8	2 4/8	2 4/8	7 1/8	2 4/8	6 6/8	6 2/8	Emery Co., UT	Marvin L. Thayn	Marvin L. Thayn	1986	419
85 2/8	16	18	6 6/8	6 6/8	2 7/8	2 7/8	13	9 2/8	5 7/8	6	Socorro Co., NM	L. Steve Waide	L. Steve Waide	1986	419
85 2/8	16 4/8	16 3/8	6 6/8	6 6/8	2 7/8	2 6/8	7 1/8	2 2/8	6 3/8	5 7/8	Navajo Co., AZ	Robert A. Dodson	Robert A. Dodson	1989	419
85 2/8	16 4/8	16 4/8	6 6/8	6 4/8	2 7/8	3	7 5/8	2 6/8	7	5 4/8	Natrona Co., WY	J. Brendan Bummer	J. Brendan Bummer	1990	419
85 2/8	15	14 7/8	7 1/8	7 1/8	3	2 7/8	10 3/8	7 3/8	6 3/8	5 7/8	McKenzie Co., ND	Michael A. Palmer	Michael A. Palmer	1990	419
85 2/8	17	16 7/8	6 5/8	6 3/8	2 7/8	2 7/8	12 3/8	7 4/8	5 4/8	6	Baker Co., OR	Gordon C. Van Patten	Gordon C. Van Patten	1990	419
85 2/8	16 5/8	17	7 1/8	7 2/8	2 3/8	2 3/8	12 6/8	10 7/8	5 4/8	6 2/8	Harney Co., OR	Sharon L. Ganos	Sharon L. Ganos	1992	419
85 2/8	15 7/8	15 6/8	7	6 6/8	2 7/8	2 7/8	11 1/8	7 1/8	5 7/8	5 6/8	Uinta Co., WY	Michael D. Wayman	Michael D. Wayman	1994	419
85 2/8	17	16 2/8	7 1/8	7	2 7/8	2 6/8	10 3/8	6 1/8	5 5/8	6 5/8	Coconino Co., AZ	Donald E. Wyckoff	Donald E. Wyckoff	1994	419
85 2/8	16 3/8	16 3/8	7	6 6/8	2 7/8	2 3/8	10 4/8	5 7/8	6 3/8	6 4/8	Carbon Co., WY	Michael S. Carrico	Michael S. Carrico	1996	419
85 2/8	16 4/8	16 2/8	6 7/8	7	3	3	6 4/8	0 4/8	5 3/8	5 2/8	Natrona Co., WY	Dwight O. Wicker	Dwight O. Wicker	1996	419
85 2/8	17 5/8	18	6 3/8	6 3/8	2 6/8	2 7/8	10 2/8	5 7/8	5 5/8	5 5/8	Socorro Co., NM	E. Lance Whary	E. Lance Whary	1998	419
85 2/8	17 1/8	17 6/8	6 6/8	6 5/8	2 5/8	2 6/8	10 2/8	4 5/8	5 3/8	5 6/8	Catron Co., NM	Joseph S. Brannen	Joseph S. Brannen	1999	419
85 2/8	16 2/8	16	7 6/8	7 6/8	3 1/8	3	12 1/8	10 3/8	5	4 7/8	Socorro Co., NM	Edward J. Bordovsky, Jr.	Edward J. Bordovsky, Jr.	2000	419
85 2/8	15 5/8	14 5/8	7 1/8	7 1/8	3 5/8	3 4/8	14 2/8	13	6	6 4/8	Harney Co., OR	Jeffrey H. Edwards	Jeffrey H. Edwards	2000	419
85 2/8	15 6/8	15 6/8	7	7 1/8	3 1/8	2 7/8	10 3/8	7 7/8	6 2/8	6 7/8	Harney Co., OR	Matthew J. Foster	Matthew J. Foster	2000	419
85 2/8	16 6/8	16 6/8	7 2/8	7 1/8	2 4/8	2 4/8	10 6/8	5 2/8	5	5 2/8	Harney Co., OR	Anthony J. Gardner	Anthony J. Gardner	2001	419
85 2/8	16 6/8	16 5/8	6 7/8	7 1/8	3	3 2/8	10	9 1/8	4 4/8	5 3/8	Hudspeth Co., TX	William G. Kyle	William G. Kyle	2002	419
85 2/8	16 5/8	15 4/8	6 7/8	6 3/8	3 4/8	3 4/8	11 1/8	10 3/8	5 6/8	5 6/8	Carbon Co., WY	Donald E. Perrien	Donald E. Perrien	2002	419
85 2/8	16 4/8	16 6/8	6 3/8	6 6/8	2 3/8	2 5/8	10	5 5/8	6 5/8	6 5/8	Carbon Co., WY	John V. Sjogren	John V. Sjogren	2002	419
85 2/8	17	17 1/8	6 2/8	6 2/8	2 4/8	2 5/8	11 1/8	5 2/8	6 4/8	6 7/8	Cypress Lake, SK	Bradley R. Jackle	Bradley R. Jackle	2003	419
85 2/8	17	16 6/8	6 5/8	6 5/8	3 2/8	3 2/8	15	10 3/8	4 6/8	5 3/8	Coconino Co., AZ	Levi M. Wilson	Levi M. Wilson	2003	419
85 2/8	15 4/8	15 2/8	7	6 7/8	2 6/8	2 6/8	10	8	6 2/8	6 3/8	Jackson Co., CO	Karl E. Wondrak	Karl E. Wondrak	2003	419
85	15 3/8	14 7/8	7 4/8	7 4/8	2 7/8	2 7/8	11 1/8	6 1/8	6	5 6/8	Douglas Co., WY	Floyd Bishop	Floyd Bishop	1937	467
85	16 4/8	16 4/8	6 5/8	6 5/8	2 6/8	2 6/8	13 2/8	9 6/8	6	5 3/8	Campbell Co., WY	O.P. Nicholson	Johnson Co. Museum	1937	467

Score	L.R	L.L	Circ. R	Circ. L	C3 R	C3 L	Spread	Tip-to-Tip	Prong R	Prong L	Locality	Hunter	Owner	Date	Rank
85	15 3/8	15 2/8	7 4/8	7 4/8	2 5/8	2 5/8	11	10 1/8	6 4/8	6	Henderson Co., NM	Ron Vance	Ron Vance	1943	467
85	17 5/8	17 4/8	5 5/8	5 5/8	2 5/8	2 5/8	9 7/8	7 2/8	6 2/8	6 2/8	Washoe Co., NV	Walter C. Bell	Walter C. Bell	1949	467
85	18	18 1/8	6 4/8	6 5/8	2 5/8	2 6/8	18 2/8	14 4/8	5 1/8	5 1/8	Plush, OR	Ernest E. Puddy	Ernest E. Puddy	1949	467
85	14 7/8	15 1/8	6 4/8	6 6/8	3	3 1/8	14 4/8	12 2/8	5 3/8	5 6/8	Brothers, OR	Orlo Flock	Orlo Flock	1955	467
85	15	15	6	6	3 1/8	3	14 1/8	10 7/8	5 7/8	5 6/8	Raleigh Co., ND	Archie Malm	Archie Malm	1958	467
85	15 5/8	15 6/8	6	6 2/8	3	3	9 6/8	8 1/8	6	6	Sage Creek Basin, WY	Robert A. Hill	Robert A. Hill	1959	467
85	19 3/8	18 6/8	6 2/8	6 6/8	2 4/8	3 2/8	14 1/8	8 5/8	4 5/8	3 6/8	Williams Co., AZ	Donovan E. Smith	Donovan E. Smith	1959	467
85	17 3/8	17 5/8	6 6/8	6 6/8	2 7/8	2 7/8	17 3/8	14 4/8	5 3/8	4 7/8	Forsyth Co., MT	John M. Broadwell	John M. Broadwell	1961	467
85	15 4/8	15 4/8	6 6/8	6 4/8	3 2/8	3 2/8	10	5 4/8	5	5 1/8	Brusett, MT	Unknown	Frank McKeever	PR 1962	467
85	16	15 7/8	7	7 1/8	2 5/8	2 5/8	8 6/8	4 6/8	5	4 6/8	Rawlins Co., WY	Clarence J. Becker	Clarence J. Becker	1965	467
85	16 1/8	15 6/8	6 7/8	8 1/8	2 7/8	2 7/8	10 4/8	7 4/8	5 6/8	5 7/8	Garfield Co., MT	W.A. Delaney	W.A. Delaney	1965	467
85	14 5/8	14 4/8	7 6/8	6 6/8	2 7/8	3	11 5/8	10 2/8	6 2/8	5 6/8	Saratoga Co., WY	Benny E. Bechtol	Benny E. Bechtol	1968	467
85	16 2/8	16 2/8	6 6/8	7 2/8	3	3	14 1/8	9 1/8	5 7/8	6	Rawlins Co., WY	H.H. Eighmy	H.H. Eighmy	1969	467
85	15 4/8	15 6/8	7 2/8	6 3/8	2 4/8	2 4/8	13 2/8	8 7/8	6 5/8	6 1/8	Uinta Co., WY	Joan Beachler	Joan Beachler	1974	467
85	16 3/8	16 1/8	6 3/8	6 2/8	3	3	9 2/8	3 5/8	5 5/8	5 5/8	Torrance Co., NM	Stephen A. Nisbet	Stephen A. Nisbet	1975	467
85	17 3/8	17 7/8	6 2/8	6 4/8	3 2/8	3 2/8	13 5/8	8 5/8	4 7/8	4 7/8	Yavapai Co., AZ	David M. Sanders	David M. Sanders	1976	467
85	18 2/8	18 5/8	6 4/8	6 6/8	2 6/8	2 6/8	13 4/8	9	5 3/8	5	Sierra Co., NM	Charles R. Bowen	Charles R. Bowen	1977	467
85	16 5/8	16 5/8	6 6/8	6 6/8	2 5/8	2 5/8	10 6/8	7 2/8	6	5 7/8	Lake Co., OR	Frank R. Biggs	Frank R. Biggs	1978	467
85	16 5/8	16 6/8	6 4/8	6 6/8	2 7/8	2 7/8	10 2/8	5 2/8	5 6/8	5 6/8	Lincoln Co., WY	Ross M. Wilde	Ross M. Wilde	1980	467
85	16 2/8	16	6 6/8	6 7/8	2 5/8	2 5/8	12 7/8	9 4/8	6 1/8	6 1/8	Carbon Co., WY	Kelly W. Hepworth	Kelly W. Hepworth	1982	467
85	16	16 6/8	6 3/8	6 3/8	2 7/8	2 7/8	10 2/8	3 5/8	5 5/8	5 5/8	Hudspeth Co., TX	Vernon Dodd	Vernon Dodd	1984	467
85	16 6/8	17 2/8	6 2/8	6 2/8	2 5/8	2 5/8	11 7/8	8 4/8	5 5/8	5 5/8	Millard Co., UT	Scott C. Rowley	Scott C. Rowley	1984	467
85	17	16	6 6/8	6 4/8	2 7/8	2 6/8	13 1/8	8 2/8	6 3/8	6 3/8	Garfield Co., MT	Jeff M. Busse	Jeff M. Busse	1988	467
85	16 1/8	16 1/8	6	6	2 6/8	2 6/8	11	8 3/8	5 6/8	5	Hudspeth Co., TX	Ronnie L. Hinze	Ronnie L. Hinze	1988	467
85	17 4/8	16 7/8	6 6/8	6 6/8	3	3	11 4/8	8 3/8	5	5	Rosebud Co., MT	Daniel D. Ova	Daniel D. Ova	1988	467
85	16 6/8	16 7/8	6 6/8	6 6/8	2 6/8	2 6/8	9 4/8	4 3/8	6 6/8	6 6/8	Sweetwater Co., WY	Ronald L. Barber	Ronald L. Barber	1989	467
85	15 5/8	15 3/8	6 3/8	6 3/8	2 7/8	2 7/8	10 7/8	3 1/8	5 3/8	5 2/8	Coconino Co., AZ	John L. Neely	John L. Neely	1989	467
85	17 5/8	18 1/8	7 2/8	7	2 4/8	2 5/8	7 3/8	4 5/8	6 4/8	6 3/8	Sweetwater Co., WY	Mary A. Barbour	Mary A. Barbour	1990	467
85	15 7/8	15 1/8	7 3/8	7 2/8	2 5/8	2 5/8	15 2/8	10 6/8	5 3/8	5 4/8	De Baca, NM	Ernie Davis	Ernie Davis	1991	467
85	15 1/8	15 1/8	7	7	3 3/8	3 4/8	12	9 7/8	5	5	Socorro Co., NM	Jess T. Jones	Jess T. Jones	1992	467
85	16 2/8	16 1/8	6 2/8	6 1/8	3	3	13	10 5/8	6 1/8	5 7/8	Dallam Co., TX	Charles R. Senter	Charles R. Senter	1992	467
85	16 6/8	17 6/8	6 5/8	6 5/8	2 6/8	2 6/8	12 3/8	8 2/8	5 4/8	5 3/8	Yavapai Co., AZ	Craig R. Johnson	Craig R. Johnson	1993	467
85	15 5/8	15 7/8	6 7/8	6 7/8	2 7/8	2 7/8	16	13 4/8	6	5 6/8	Coconino Co., AZ	Ruth L. Tasa	Ruth L. Tasa	1994	467
85	15 7/8	16 3/8	6 4/8	6 4/8	3 1/8	3	12 1/8	6 5/8	6 4/8	6 4/8	Yavapai Co., AZ	Rebecca R. Thomas	Rebecca R. Thomas	1994	467
85	15 1/8	15 3/8	7 2/8	6 2/8	2 6/8	2 6/8	10	5 6/8	6 2/8	5 7/8	Carbon Co., WY	Theodore Heimburger	Theodore Heimburger	1995	467
85	15 5/8	15 6/8	6 6/8	6 5/8	3 2/8	3 2/8	10 2/8	5 7/8	6	5 7/8	Hudspeth Co., TX	Len H. Guldman	Len H. Guldman	1997	467
85	16 1/8	16 1/8	7 1/8	7 1/8	3	3	13	11 1/8	5 7/8	6	Natrona Co., WY	Mark B. Steffen	Mark B. Steffen	1997	467
85	16 7/8	16 7/8	7	6 6/8	2 7/8	2 7/8	9 5/8	4 5/8	4 6/8	4 6/8	Carbon Co., WY	Tracey L. Arthur	Tracey L. Arthur	1999	467
85	16 5/8	16 4/8	6 6/8	6 5/8	2 7/8	2 7/8	9	5 1/8	5 6/8	5 6/8	Catron Co., NM	Mike J. Pilliken	Mike J. Pilliken	1999	467
85	16 1/8	16	6 5/8	6 3/8	2 4/8	2 4/8	14 6/8	10 6/8	5 1/8	5 1/8	Campbell Co., WY	Randall Russell	Randall Russell	1999	467
85	16 6/8	16 6/8	6 3/8	6 1/8	2 7/8	2 5/8	13	7 5/8	4 6/8	4 6/8	Socorro Co., NM	J. Bert Vargas	J. Bert Vargas	1999	467
85	16 6/8	16 6/8	6 5/8	6 5/8	2 5/8	2 5/8	4 2/8	3 3/8	6	6	Nye Co., NV	Jared R. Pekuri	Jared R. Pekuri	2000	467
85	16 1/8	16 3/8	7 1/8	7	2 7/8	2 7/8	3 3/8	10 4/8	5 7/8	5 7/8	Coconino Co., AZ	Robert E. Petersen	Robert E. Petersen	2000	467
85	16 3/8	16 3/8	6 6/8	6 5/8	3	3	13 1/8	13 1/8	5 6/8	5 6/8	Carbon Co., WY	Kenneth S. Sutter	Kenneth S. Sutter	2000	467
85	16	15 7/8	7	6 7/8	3	3	5 5/8	8 6/8	5 5/8	5 6/8	Baker Co., OR	Russell H. Elms	Russell H. Elms	2001	467
85	16	16 2/8	6 7/8	6 7/8	2 7/8	2 5/8	2 6/8	6 3/8	6 4/8	6 6/8	Emery Co., UT	Len H. Guldman	Len H. Guldman	2001	467
85	15	14 4/8	7 3/8	7 4/8	3	3 1/8	13 7/8	12	6	6	Carbon Co., WY	Larry S. Hicks	Larry S. Hicks	2001	467
85	17 2/8	16 4/8	6 7/8	6 7/8	2 3/8	2 2/8	9 2/8	2 5/8	6	6 1/8	Washoe Co., NV	Kawika Fisher	Kawika Fisher	2002	467

PRONGHORN

Antilocapra americana americana and related subspecies

Score	Length of Horn R	L	Circumference of Base R	L	Circumference at Third Quarter R	L	Inside Spread	Tip to Tip Spread	Length of Prong R	L	Locality	Hunter	Owner	Date Killed	Rank
85	16	15 6/8	6 6/8	6 6/8	2 5/8	2 5/8	10 6/8	4 6/8	5 2/8	5 4/8	Washoe Co., NV	Jelindo A. Tiberti II	Jelindo A. Tiberti II	2003	467
84 6/8	16 5/8	16 6/8	6 7/8	6 6/8	2 5/8	2 6/8	14 6/8	11 2/8	6 7/8	5 5/8	Anderson Mesa, AZ	Elgin T. Gates	Elgin T. Gates	1955	518
84 6/8	17 1/8	16 7/8	6 1/8	6 3/8	2 6/8	3	12 2/8	10 5/8	6 2/8	6 7/8	Slate Creek, WY	Jim Calkins	Jim Calkins	1956	518
84 6/8	16 4/8	16 4/8	6 5/8	6 5/8	2 4/8	2 4/8	8 3/8	3 4/8	6 1/8	5 5/8	Laramie Co., WY	Roger D. Ramsay	Roger D. Ramsay	1958	518
84 6/8	16 4/8	16 4/8	6 1/8	6	2 7/8	2 7/8	11 3/8	7 4/8	4 5/8	4 7/8	Laramie Peak, WY	Elmer Rupert	Elmer Rupert	1961	518
84 6/8	16	16 3/8	7 1/8	7 1/8	3	3	12 1/8	6 6/8	5	4 6/8	Alliance, NE	Joseph Nelson	Joseph Nelson	1962	518
84 6/8	17 3/8	16 7/8	7 1/8	7 1/8	2 7/8	2 7/8	14 6/8	12 4/8	5 4/8	4 4/8	Fremont Co., WY	Dick Cone	Dick Cone	1963	518
84 6/8	16 3/8	16 4/8	6 5/8	6 6/8	3	3	11 1/8	7	5	5	Sinclair, WY	John Kastner	John Kastner	1963	518
84 6/8	15 4/8	15 4/8	6 4/8	6 6/8	3 6/8	3 5/8	7 4/8	1 7/8	5 4/8	5 5/8	Harney Co., OR	D.R. Knoll	D.R. Knoll	1963	518
84 6/8	17	17 4/8	6 7/8	6 6/8	2 4/8	2 5/8	14 6/8	11 1/8	6 1/8	5 3/8	Jenner, AB	J.E. Edwards	J.E. Edwards	1964	518
84 6/8	16 5/8	16 5/8	6 7/8	7	2 7/8	2 7/8	12	11	5 2/8	4 7/8	Johnson Co., WY	John G. Carroll	John G. Carroll	1965	518
84 6/8	15 7/8	15 7/8	6 2/8	6 2/8	2 5/8	2 5/8	10 6/8	6 2/8	7	7	Rock Springs, WY	W. Daniel English	W. Daniel English	1966	518
84 6/8	17	16 6/8	6 5/8	6 5/8	2 4/8	2 4/8	17	16	5 3/8	5 1/8	Custer Co., ID	Claus Karlson	Claus Karlson	1966	518
84 6/8	16	16	6 6/8	6 4/8	2 6/8	2 6/8	11 2/8	5 4/8	6 4/8	6 4/8	Casper, WY	John E. Mohritz	John E. Mohritz	1966	518
84 6/8	16 2/8	16 3/8	6	6 1/8	2 4/8	2 3/8	8 5/8	3 5/8	7	6 7/8	Navajo Co., AZ	George M. Owen	George M. Owen	1966	518
84 6/8	15 5/8	15 7/8	7 1/8	7 6/8	2 5/8	2 7/8	10 2/8	5 7/8	5 6/8	5 5/8	Poison Spider Creek, WY	Robert F. Ziker	Robert F. Ziker	1969	518
84 6/8	16 5/8	17	6 2/8	6 2/8	2 3/8	2 3/8	10 4/8	5 1/8	6 5/8	6 5/8	Modoc Co., CA	Leland C. Lehman	Leland C. Lehman	1969	518
84 6/8	19 7/8	19 4/8	6 1/8	5 7/8	2 5/8	2 5/8	18	13 6/8	5 2/8	4 5/8	Boquillas Ranch, AZ	Bob Dixon	Bob Dixon	1970	518
84 6/8	15 7/8	15 6/8	6 5/8	6 5/8	3 6/8	3 5/8	13 5/8	8 6/8	5 4/8	5 2/8	Ft. Apache Res., AZ	Donald Smith	Donald Smith	1972	518
84 6/8	16 3/8	16 3/8	7	7 1/8	2 6/8	2 5/8	11	5 1/8	5 6/8	5 7/8	Moffat Co., CO	James C. MacLachlan	James C. MacLachlan	1975	518
84 6/8	15 6/8	15 5/8	7 1/8	7 1/8	2 6/8	2 7/8	10 2/8	7 1/8	6 3/8	5 7/8	Garden Co., NE	Richard Mosley	Richard Mosley	1978	518
84 6/8	16 6/8	16 5/8	6 1/8	6 1/8	2 5/8	2 6/8	9 7/8	5	6 3/8	6 1/8	Modoc Co., CA	Earnest Anacleto	Earnest Anacleto	1980	518
84 6/8	16 4/8	16 4/8	6 2/8	6 2/8	3	3	13 6/8	11 4/8	4 4/8	4 4/8	Lincoln Co., NM	Pat McCarty	Pat McCarty	1980	518
84 6/8	17 1/8	17 4/8	6 2/8	6 4/8	2 6/8	2 6/8	10	5	5 1/8	5 2/8	Washoe Co., NV	Lloyd B. Miller	Lloyd B. Miller	1980	518
84 6/8	15 4/8	15 6/8	6 3/8	6 3/8	2 7/8	2 6/8	8 5/8	3 2/8	6 5/8	6 4/8	Natrona Co., WY	W. Bruce Mouw	W. Bruce Mouw	1980	518
84 6/8	16 2/8	16 3/8	6 4/8	6 3/8	2 5/8	2 6/8	11 1/8	8 3/8	6 5/8	6 2/8	Baker Co., OR	Martin Vavra	Martin Vavra	1980	518
84 6/8	14 1/8	14 1/8	7 3/8	7 3/8	3 3/8	3 3/8	9 2/8	7 4/8	5	5 1/8	Fremont Co., WY	James E. Egger	James E. Egger	1981	518
84 6/8	16 7/8	16 3/8	6 5/8	6 5/8	2 2/8	2 3/8	11 4/8	8 4/8	7 1/8	6 7/8	Carbon Co., WY	Robb D. Hitchcock	Robb D. Hitchcock	1981	518
84 6/8	15 4/8	15 4/8	7 3/8	7 2/8	2 4/8	2 4/8	11 5/8	7 6/8	6 5/8	6 5/8	Sweetwater Co., WY	David L. Thompson	David L. Thompson	1982	518
84 6/8	17	16 5/8	6 5/8	6 5/8	2 6/8	2 7/8	8	1 5/8	6	5 4/8	Lemhi Co., ID	Sherl L. Chapman	Sherl L. Chapman	1983	518
84 6/8	16 3/8	16 3/8	6 4/8	6 4/8	3	3	9 3/8	4 2/8	5 2/8	5 3/8	Carbon Co., WY	Paul Herring	Paul Herring	1983	518
84 6/8	16 7/8	17 2/8	6 5/8	6 5/8	3 2/8	3 2/8	16 5/8	11 1/8	7 1/8	5	Hudspeth Co., TX	Ernie Davis	Ernie Davis	1986	518
84 6/8	16	16 1/8	6 6/8	6 6/8	3 1/8	3 1/8	8 6/8	6	4 7/8	5	Hudspeth Co., TX	Charles D. Tuttle	Charles D. Tuttle	1986	518
84 6/8	15 4/8	16 2/8	7 2/8	7 1/8	2 4/8	2 6/8	11 7/8	7 7/8	5 6/8	6 3/8	Mora Co., NM	William P. Boone	William P. Boone	1987	518
84 6/8	16 1/8	16	6 5/8	6 5/8	2 7/8	2 7/8	8 5/8	2 2/8	5 6/8	5 5/8	Catron Co., NM	John P. Grimmett	John P. Grimmett	1989	518
84 6/8	16 3/8	16 1/8	6 3/8	6 2/8	3	3 1/8	13 2/8	11 2/8	6 7/8	6 7/8	Sweetwater Co., WY	Melvin E. Killman	Melvin E. Killman	1989	518
84 6/8	16 4/8	16 5/8	6 4/8	6 4/8	2 5/8	2 5/8	11 1/8	6 3/8	6 3/8	7 1/8	Lassen Co., CA	Gary Caraccioli	Gary Caraccioli	1990	518
84 6/8	15 6/8	16	6 7/8	6 7/8	2 5/8	2 5/8	7 6/8	3 7/8	6 6/8	6 5/8	Natrona Co., WY	Warren N. Pearce	Warren N. Pearce	1990	518

Score											Locality	Owner	Hunter	Date	Rank
84 6/8	17	17 1/8	6 5/8	6 4/8	3	2 7/8	11 1/8	15 2/8	2 7/8	4 7/8	Otero Co., NM	William W. Shipton III	William W. Shipton III	1990	518
84 6/8	15 7/8	15 4/8	7	7 2/8	2 7/8	2 7/8	6 4/8	9 3/8	2 7/8	5 3/8	Hutchinson Co., TX	Rex A. Umbarger	Rex A. Umbarger	1990	518
84 6/8	15 2/8	15 3/8	7 3/8	7 4/8	2 5/8	2 6/8	9 6/8	11 3/8	2 5/8	5 7/8	Carbon Co., WY	Myron J. Wakkuri	Myron J. Wakkuri	1990	518
84 6/8	16 4/8	16 3/8	6 5/8	6 4/8	3	3	3 6/8	8 4/8	2 4/8	6 5/8	Cochise Co., AZ	David J. Braun	David J. Braun	1991	518
84 6/8	17 1/8	17 1/8	6 4/8	6 4/8	2 6/8	2 6/8	8 2/8	12 4/8	2 6/8	5 6/8	Coconino Co., AZ	Jerrell F. Coburn	Jerrell F. Coburn	1991	518
84 6/8	16 5/8	16 6/8	6 4/8	6 4/8	2 5/8	2 5/8	6 7/8	12 4/8	2 6/8	6 2/8	Socorro Co., NM	Charles A. Grimmett	Charles A. Grimmett	1991	518
84 6/8	16 3/8	16 3/8	6 4/8	6 4/8	2 4/8	2 4/8	7 2/8	7 2/8	2 5/8	4 6/8	Fremont Co., WY	Karen L. Jenson	Karen L. Jenson	1991	518
84 6/8	15 5/8	15 6/8	7	7	3 1/8	3 1/8	8 2/8	12	3 1/8	5 3/8		Brian T. King	Brian T. King	1991	518
84 6/8	14 6/8	14 6/8	7 1/8	7 1/8	2 6/8	2 7/8	11 7/8	14 5/8	2 7/8	5 2/8	Converse Co., WY	Michael R. Land	Michael R. Land	1991	518
84 6/8	16 1/8	16 1/8	7 1/8	7	3	3	7 4/8	11 1/8	3 1/8	5 6/8	Mora Co., NM	Linda J. McBride	Linda J. McBride	1991	518
84 6/8	16 2/8	16 2/8	6 6/8	6 5/8	2 3/8	2 4/8	5 2/8	10 2/8	2 3/8	5 6/8	Lake Co., OR	Patrick R. McConnell	Patrick R. McConnell	1991	518
84 6/8	17 4/8	17 5/8	6 5/8	6 5/8	2 4/8	2 4/8	11 6/8	10 2/8	2 5/8	6 5/8	Mora Co., NM	Robert Model	Robert Model	1991	518
84 6/8	17	17	6 7/8	7 1/8	3	3	11 6/8	11 4/8	2 5/8	4 6/8	Lincoln Co., NM	Jay B. Robert	Jay B. Robert	1991	518
84 6/8	16 3/8	16 2/8	6 5/8	6 2/8	2 4/8	2 4/8	11 4/8	15 2/8	2 4/8	5 4/8	Mora Co., NM	Donald W. Martin	Donald W. Martin	1992	518
84 6/8	16 2/8	16 1/8	7 2/8	7 2/8	3	2 7/8	3 1/8	9 3/8	2 7/8	6	Carter Co., MT	Daniel Goodman	Daniel Goodman	1993	518
84 6/8	15 3/8	15 3/8	7	7	2 4/8	2 4/8	11 4/8	14 6/8	2 4/8	5 4/8	Petroleum Co., MT	Daniel S. Wentz	Daniel S. Wentz	1993	518
84 6/8	15 2/8	15 2/8	6 7/8	7	3 1/8	3 1/8	4 7/8	10 6/8	3 2/8	5 5/8	Natrona Co., WY	Brian J. Bummer	Brian J. Bummer	1994	518
84 6/8	15 2/8	16 1/8	7	7	2 4/8	2 6/8	12	13 7/8	3 1/8	6	Mora Co., NM	Walter O. Ford, Jr.	Walter O. Ford, Jr.	1994	518
84 6/8	16 4/8	16 1/8	6 3/8	6 6/8	2 4/8	3	2	8 1/8	2 6/8	7	Emery Co., UT	Tomme L. Gold	Tomme L. Gold	1995	518
84 6/8	16 5/8	16 5/8	6 3/8	6 2/8	3	3	2	7 6/8	2 5/8	6	Mora Co., NM	Ilynn Guldman	Ilynn Guldman	1995	518
84 6/8	16 7/8	16 7/8	6 6/8	6 6/8	3	3	5 5/8	10 7/8	2 7/8	5 5/8	Rosebud Co., MT	John W. Lane	John W. Lane	1995	518
84 6/8	16	16	6 3/8	6 5/8	3 1/8	3	6 4/8	10 4/8	3 1/8	6 2/8	Socorro Co., NM	Kevin A. Teston	Kevin A. Teston	1996	518
84 6/8	16	16	8	8	2 6/8	2 7/8	9	13 3/8	3	5 4/8	Colfax Co., NM	Robert D. Jones	Robert D. Jones	1997	518
84 6/8	17	16 3/8	7 5/8	7 2/8	2 6/8	2 7/8	4 3/8	9 6/8	3	4 2/8	Navajo Co., AZ	Ronald D. Major	Ronald D. Major	1997	518
84 6/8	17 5/8	17 5/8	6 5/8	6 5/8	3 1/8	3	4 7/8	10 3/8	2 7/8	5 3/8	Yellowstone Co., MT	Michael E. Schieno	Michael E. Schieno	1997	518
84 6/8	17 7/8	17 6/8	6	6	3	3	5 3/8	11 1/8	3 4/8	5 5/8	Catron Co., NM	Frank P. DeYoung	Frank P. DeYoung	1998	518
84 6/8	16	16	6 3/8	6 2/8	3 3/8	2 7/8	8 2/8	11	2 3/8	5 4/8	Apache Co., AZ	Denise S. Rhodes	Denise S. Rhodes	1998	518
84 6/8	16 2/8	16 2/8	6 2/8	6 3/8	2 2/8	2 3/8	8 2/8	12 4/8	2 2/8	4 6/8	Elko Co., NV	David G. Paullin	David G. Paullin	2000	518
84 6/8	17	17	5 7/8	5 7/8	3	3 1/8	9	11 4/8	3 1/8	4 3/8	Mora Co., NM	Mark W. Streissguth	Mark W. Streissguth	2000	518
84 6/8	16 4/8	16 3/8	7	7 1/8	2 6/8	2 7/8	6 3/8	10 4/8	2 7/8	5 4/8	Harney Co., OR	Landon S. Blakeley	Landon S. Blakeley	2001	518
84 6/8	15 7/8	15 6/8	6 5/8	6 5/8	2 7/8	2 6/8	8 7/8	11 7/8	3 1/8	5 4/8	Colorado	Picked Up	Jim C. Femrite	PR 2001	518
84 6/8	15 5/8	15 7/8	5 5/8	5 5/8	2 6/8	2 7/8	5 6/8	9 6/8	2 6/8	6	Mohave Co., AZ	Lance M. Gatlin	Lance M. Gatlin	2001	518
84 6/8	15 7/8	14 7/8	6 1/8	6 1/8	3 1/8	3 1/8	9 7/8	12 3/8	2 6/8	6 1/8	Washakie Co., WY	Steve E. Johns	Steve E. Johns	2001	518
84 6/8	15	15	7 5/8	7 5/8	3	3	9 6/8	10 3/8	2 6/8	6 1/8	Socorro Co., NM	Mark I. Walker	Mark I. Walker	2002	518
84 6/8	15	15	7	7	2 7/8	2 7/8	7	10 5/8	2 4/8	6 1/8	Sheridan Co., NE	Gilbert T. Adams III	Gilbert T. Adams III	2002	518
84 6/8	16 6/8	16 5/8	6 5/8	6 5/8	3	3	2 2/8	5 5/8	2 6/8	5 5/8	Socorro Co., NM	Tim L. Bernard	Tim L. Bernard	2002	518
84 6/8	16 6/8	16 6/8	6 4/8	6 4/8	3 2/8	3 2/8	4 4/8	10 3/8	2 4/8	5 4/8	Sweetwater Co., WY	Roy G. Gamblin	Roy G. Gamblin	2003	518
84 6/8	16 4/8	16 4/8	6 2/8	6 1/8	3 3/8	3 3/8	9 7/8	11 3/8	2 4/8	5 1/8	Lincoln Co., WY	Angie D. Hall	Angie D. Hall	2003	518
84 6/8	15 5/8	15 5/8	7 1/8	7	2 5/8	2 5/8	8 6/8	12 2/8	2 5/8	6 3/8	Carbon Co., WY	Brad D. Lewis	Brad D. Lewis	2003	518
84 4/8	16 3/8	16 3/8	7 1/8	7 1/8	2 5/8	2 5/8	6	9 6/8	2 5/8	5 3/8	Chihuahua, MX	A.A. Carrey	A.A. Carrey	1944	594
84 4/8	16 4/8	16 2/8	6 2/8	6 2/8	2 5/8	2 6/8	9 2/8	12 7/8	2 6/8	7 5/8	North Dakota	Julio Estrada	Julio Estrada	1945	594
84 4/8	15 7/8	15 7/8	7 4/8	7 4/8	2 6/8	2 6/8	10 6/8	10 6/8	2 7/8	6 3/8	Fremont Co., WY	Dale Linderman	Dale Linderman	PR 1952	594
84 4/8	16	16	5 5/8	5 5/8	2 7/8	2 7/8	13 7/8	14 4/8	2 7/8	5	Tripp Co., SD	Ernest R. Novotny	Ernest R. Novotny	1954	594
84 4/8	16 6/8	16 5/8	6 1/8	6 1/8	2 6/8	2 6/8	4 2/8	10 3/8	2 6/8	6 3/8	Rawlins Co., WY	Roy Hazuka	Roy Hazuka	1962	594
84 4/8	15 6/8	15 7/8	7 5/8	7 5/8	2 4/8	2 4/8	10 3/8	14 2/8	2 4/8	5 6/8	Carbon Co., WY	Eloise Kees	Eloise Kees	1963	594
84 4/8	15 6/8	16 1/8	7 1/8	7 1/8	2 4/8	2 5/8	3 2/8	8 3/8	2 5/8	6 6/8	Seligman, AZ	Thomas McCulloch	Thomas McCulloch	1964	594
84 4/8	18	18 4/8	7	7	3	3	8 4/8	13	3	3 4/8	Seligman, AZ	Garth A. Brown	Garth A. Brown	1966	594
84 4/8	14 7/8	14 6/8	7 4/8	7 4/8	2 6/8	2 6/8	5 7/8	9 1/8	2 6/8	6 2/8	Baggs, WY	Tom Elberson	Tom Elberson		594

PRONGHORN

Antilocapra americana and related subspecies

Score	Length of Horn R	L	Circumference of Base R	L	Circumference at Third Quarter R	L	Inside Spread	Tip to Tip Spread	Length of Prong R	L	Hunter	Owner	Locality	Date Killed	Rank
84 4/8	17	17 1/8	6 4/8	6 5/8	2 4/8	2 4/8	11 1/8	5 1/8	5 6/8	5 6/8	Harvey B. Bartley	Harvey B. Bartley	Sweetwater Co., WY	1970	594
84 4/8	16 2/8	16 2/8	6	6	2 3/8	2 3/8	13	8	7 1/8	7	William G. Mackey	William G. Mackey	Carbon Co., WY	1972	594
84 4/8	14 5/8	14 7/8	6 7/8	7 1/8	2 6/8	2 4/8	12 6/8	8 6/8	6 1/8	6 5/8	Gene Cormie	Gene Cormie	Lake Co., OR	1973	594
84 4/8	16	16	6 4/8	6 5/8	2 4/8	2 4/8	12 3/8	7 3/8	6 6/8	6 6/8	George Kirkman	George Kirkman	Lincoln Co., WY	1973	594
84 4/8	16 3/8	16 4/8	7 2/8	7 1/8	2 3/8	2 4/8	13 3/8	7 7/8	5 6/8	5 6/8	Frances M. Hansell	Frances M. Hansell	Washoe Co., NV	1974	594
84 4/8	17	16 5/8	7 2/8	7 2/8	2 2/8	2 6/8	9 6/8	7 4/8	6	6 1/8	John H. Johnson	John H. Johnson	Fields, OR	1974	594
84 4/8	15	15 3/8	7 5/8	7 2/8	2 6/8	2 6/8	6 5/8	4 6/8	6 6/8	5 6/8	Stephen C. LeBlanc	Stephen C. LeBlanc	Carbon Co., WY	1976	594
84 4/8	15 6/8	16	7 4/8	7 4/8	3 1/8	3	10 4/8	6 6/8	5 1/8	5 3/8	John C. Sjogren	John C. Sjogren	Carbon Co., WY	1976	594
84 4/8	17 1/8	16 6/8	6 2/8	6 3/8	2 3/8	3	15 6/8	13 7/8	6 3/8	6 7/8	J. Bob Johnson	J. Bob Johnson	Modoc Co., CA	1978	594
84 4/8	16 3/8	16 3/8	7	6 7/8	3	3	14 6/8	12 5/8	6	5 4/8	Frankie Miller	Frankie Miller	Sweetwater Co., WY	1979	594
84 4/8	17 7/8	17 6/8	7 5/8	7 4/8	2 3/8	2 3/8	13 6/8	8 1/8	5 1/8	4 6/8	Rodger D. Bates	Rodger D. Bates	Lake Co., OR	1980	594
84 4/8	17 2/8	17	6 5/8	6 5/8	2 7/8	3	8 3/8	4 1/8	5 5/8	6	Lee Frudden	Lee Frudden	Sweetwater Co., WY	1981	594
84 4/8	16 1/8	16 4/8	6 6/8	6 5/8	3	2 6/8	15	12 2/8	5 5/8	5 5/8	Jack A. Berger	Jack A. Berger	Carbon Co., WY	1982	594
84 4/8	15	15	6 4/8	6 5/8	2 6/8	2 5/8	9 6/8	7 3/8	7	6 6/8	William J. Stokes	William J. Stokes	Carbon Co., WY	1982	594
84 4/8	15 4/8	15 2/8	7 4/8	7 4/8	3	3	13 6/8	10	5 6/8	5 5/8	Michael P. Hauffe	Michael P. Hauffe	Fremont Co., WY	1983	594
84 4/8	17 5/8	17 3/8	6 2/8	6 3/8	2 5/8	2 5/8	7 5/8	4 6/8	5 7/8	6	John E. Jerome, Jr.	John E. Jerome, Jr.	Yavapai Co., AZ	1983	594
84 4/8	16 6/8	16 7/8	7 3/8	7 2/8	2 5/8	2 5/8	14 4/8	8 6/8	4 5/8	4 5/8	William R. Suranyi	William R. Suranyi	Fremont Co., WY	1983	594
84 4/8	16 4/8	16 2/8	6 3/8	6	2 4/8	2 4/8	9	5 1/8	7 1/8	7	Donald W. Hellhake	Donald W. Hellhake	Phillips Co., MT	1984	594
84 4/8	16	16 2/8	7 2/8	7 4/8	2 4/8	2 5/8	8 4/8	4 4/8	5 5/8	5 5/8	Joe L. Ficken	Joe L. Ficken	Natrona Co., WY	1985	594
84 4/8	17	17 1/8	7	6 7/8	2 5/8	2 3/8	15	11	5 5/8	5 2/8	Rick Ward	Rick Ward	Deschutes Co., OR	1985	594
84 4/8	17 3/8	17 3/8	6 1/8	6 2/8	2 5/8	2 4/8	7 5/8	1 7/8	5 7/8	5 7/8	Bruce Gordon	Bruce Gordon	Emery Co., UT	1986	594
84 4/8	16 4/8	16 5/8	6 7/8	6 7/8	2 6/8	2 7/8	8 3/8	4	5 1/8	5 7/8	Michael D. McKell	Michael D. McKell	Sweetwater Co., WY	1986	594
84 4/8	16 1/8	16 5/8	7	7	2 6/8	2 6/8	7 3/8	2 5/8	4 6/8	5 1/8	Duane R. Pisk	Duane R. Pisk	Prairie Co., MT	1988	594
84 4/8	17 1/8	17 1/8	7	7	2 7/8	2 7/8	11 6/8	8 2/8	4 7/8	4 7/8	Tracy A. Tripp	Tracy A. Tripp	Washoe Co., NV	1989	594
84 4/8	14 7/8	15 1/8	7 3/8	7 2/8	3	3	8 6/8	4 6/8	5 6/8	5 6/8	Lyle D. Fruchey	Lyle D. Fruchey	Fremont Co., WY	1990	594
84 4/8	17 1/8	15 7/8	6 1/8	6 2/8	2 4/8	2 4/8	12 2/8	6 4/8	6 3/8	6 2/8	Shawn R. Hall	Shawn R. Hall	Humboldt Co., NV	1990	594
84 4/8	16 1/8	15 7/8	7	7	3	2 6/8	11 7/8	10 4/8	5 2/8	5 2/8	Cameron C. Owen	Cameron C. Owen	Cutbank Creek, AB	1990	594
84 4/8	14 2/8	14 1/8	6 7/8	6 7/8	3 7/8	3 7/8	8 6/8	4 4/8	6	6 1/8	Corey Urban	Corey Urban	Logan Co., KS	1990	594
84 4/8	16 3/8	16 5/8	6 4/8	6 2/8	2 5/8	2 6/8	13 4/8	9 7/8	6 4/8	6 2/8	Kenneth L. Ebbens	Kenneth L. Ebbens	Mora Co., NM	1991	594
84 4/8	16 7/8	17	6 3/8	6 2/8	2 6/8	2 7/8	12 2/8	6 4/8	6 2/8	5 7/8	Larry R. Price	Larry R. Price	Hudspeth Co., TX	1991	594
84 4/8	16 6/8	16 6/8	6 6/8	6 6/8	2 7/8	2 7/8	15	11 6/8	5	5 2/8	Walter R. Schreiner, Jr.	Walter R. Schreiner, Jr.	Union Co., NM	1991	594
84 4/8	16	15 6/8	7 2/8	7	3 2/8	3	13 7/8	14	4 5/8	4 7/8	Barry N. Strang	Barry N. Strang	Natrona Co., WY	1991	594
84 4/8	16 6/8	16 4/8	7 1/8	7	2 5/8	2 5/8	8 7/8	2 5/8	6	5 2/8	Clint N. Gibson	Clint N. Gibson	Sweetwater Co., WY	1992	594
84 4/8	15 6/8	15 5/8	6 7/8	6 6/8	2 4/8	2 4/8	10 3/8	9	6 4/8	6 5/8	Kirby C. Hornbeck	Kirby C. Hornbeck	Carbon Co., WY	1992	594
84 4/8	17 2/8	17 3/8	7	6 7/8	2 6/8	2 6/8	10	4 7/8	5 7/8	5 4/8	James P. Knudson	James P. Knudson	Carbon Co., WY	1992	594
84 4/8	16 5/8	16 7/8	7 1/8	7 1/8	2 4/8	2 4/8	10 7/8	6 1/8	4 5/8	4 4/8	Jeff A. Schweighart	Jeff A. Schweighart	Fremont Co., WY	1992	594
84 4/8	15 6/8	16	7 1/8	7 1/8	2 6/8	2 6/8	7 4/8	4	5 6/8	6 2/8	Stuart W. Shepherd	Stuart W. Shepherd	Fremont Co., WY	1992	594
84 4/8	15 7/8	15 6/8	6 3/8	6 3/8	2 7/8	2 6/8	12	6 6/8	6 2/8	6 2/8	David W. Ogilvie, Jr.	David W. Ogilvie, Jr.	Socorro Co., NM	1993	594

Score	Length of Horn R	Length of Horn L	Circ. of Base R	Circ. of Base L	Circ. at Third Quarter R	Circ. at Third Quarter L	Length of Prong R	Length of Prong L	Inside Spread	Tip to Tip Spread	Locality	Hunter	Owner	Date Killed	Rank
84 4/8	14 4/8	14 3/8	7 2/8	7 2/8	3	2 7/8	6 4/8	6 2/8	10 2/8	7 3/8	Humboldt Co., NV	Rebecca L. Webley	Rebecca L. Webley	1993	594
84 4/8	15 3/8	15 2/8	7	6 6/8	3	3	5 7/8	5 7/8	10 6/8	7 2/8	Humboldt Co., NV	Eric D. Olson	Eric D. Olson	1994	594
84 4/8	17 5/8	17 5/8	7	7	3	3	4 5/8	4 7/8	13 5/8	9 2/8	Yavapai Co., AZ	Ross F. Adams	Ross F. Adams	1995	594
84 4/8	17	17	6 5/8	6 3/8	2 6/8	2 4/8	5 7/8	5 7/8	15	12 2/8	Mora Co., NM	Dennis J. Sites	Dennis J. Sites	1996	594
84 4/8	16 6/8	16 6/8	6 3/8	6 4/8	3	3 1/8	5 7/8	5 4/8	9 5/8	3 6/8	Socorro Co., NM	Reuben R. Tipton III	Reuben R. Tipton III	1996	594
84 4/8	16 2/8	16 2/8	6 4/8	6 2/8	2 6/8	2 6/8	6	6	11 6/8	7 5/8	Moffat Co., CO	Patrick G. Diesing	Patrick G. Diesing	1997	594
84 4/8	16 2/8	16 7/8	6 3/8	6 3/8	2 6/8	2 6/8	5 4/8	5 4/8	10 4/8	6 1/8	Socorro Co., NM	Don W. Fullen	Don W. Fullen	1997	594
84 4/8	16 6/8	16 2/8	6	6	2 6/8	2 6/8	5 7/8	5 7/8	9 6/8	6 7/8	Catron Co., NM	D. Craig Heiner	D. Craig Heiner	1998	594
84 4/8	18 6/8	18 3/8	7 2/8	7 1/8	3	3	5 6/8	5 6/8	12 6/8	6 4/8	Catron Co., NM	R. Douglas Isbell	R. Douglas Isbell	1998	594
84 4/8	16 1/8	15 7/8	7 1/8	7 2/8	3	3	5 4/8	5 4/8	9	4 6/8	Colfax Co., NM	Michael B. Murphy	Michael B. Murphy	1999	594
84 4/8	15 3/8	15 2/8	6 5/8	7 1/8	2 6/8	2 6/8	5 7/8	4 6/8	13 2/8	11 3/8	Fremont Co., WY	Greg E. Fuechsel	Greg E. Fuechsel	2000	594
84 4/8	16 7/8	16 6/8	6	6 5/8	2 5/8	2 5/8	6 6/8	5 7/8	7 7/8	2 3/8	Lewis & Clark Co., MT	John T. Mandell	John T. Mandell	2000	594
84 4/8	16 4/8	15 2/8	6 7/8	5 7/8	3 3/8	3 5/8	6 6/8	6	10 1/8	7 6/8	Socorro Co., NM	Michael L. Braegelmann	Michael L. Braegelmann	2002	594
84 4/8	15	15	6	6	3 3/8	3 3/8	6 2/8	6 1/8	5 5/8	2 4/8	Emery Co., UT	Len H. Guldman	Len H. Guldman	2002	594
84 4/8	16 2/8	16 2/8	6 7/8	6 7/8	2 4/8	2 4/8	6 4/8	6 4/8	12 5/8	6 7/8	Consul, SK	Greg D. Illerbrun	Greg D. Illerbrun	2002	594
84 4/8	16 5/8	16 3/8	7	7	2 7/8	2 5/8	5 5/8	5 5/8	9 6/8	4 4/8	Brooks, AB	Shaun E. Steidel	Shaun E. Steidel	2002	594
84 4/8	16 2/8	16 2/8	6 2/8	6 2/8	2 6/8	2 6/8	6 5/8	6 6/8	9 1/8	3 7/8	Lincoln Co., NM	Charles W. Wolcott	Charles W. Wolcott	2002	594
84 4/8	17 3/8	17 3/8	6 5/8	6 5/8	2 6/8	2 6/8	5 3/8	5 1/8	16 3/8	9 6/8	Colfax Co., NM	Robert D. Jones	Robert D. Jones	2003	594
84 4/8	16 6/8	16 6/8	6 3/8	6 3/8	3	2 7/8	5 2/8	5 2/8	9	5 5/8	Apache Co., AZ	Mel L. Risch	Mel L. Risch	2003	594
84 2/8	16 6/8	16 4/8	6 6/8	6 6/8	2 6/8	2 6/8	5 4/8	5 2/8	10 2/8	5 7/8	Sweetwater River, WY	Kermit Platt	Kermit Platt	1952	660
84 2/8	15	15	6 3/8	6 3/8	3 2/8	3 1/8	4 3/8	4 4/8	11 4/8	11	Pumpkin Buttes, WY	John B. Miller	John B. Miller	1957	660
84 2/8	16 4/8	15	6 7/8	6 4/8	3 2/8	2 5/8	4 6/8	4 4/8	10 2/8	6 1/8	Sage Creek Basin, WY	Aydeen Auld	Aydeen Auld	1959	660
84 2/8	16 6/8	16 6/8	7	7	2 3/8	2 6/8	6	6	7 5/8	1 7/8	Natrona Co., WY	William A. Fisher	William A. Fisher	1960	660
84 2/8	16	16	6 7/8	6 7/8	2 5/8	2 3/8	6 2/8	6	11 5/8	7 6/8	Uinta Co., WY	Ross Lukenbill	Ross Lukenbill	1965	660
84 2/8	15 7/8	16 1/8	7	7	2 5/8	2 6/8	6 1/8	6 1/8	10 2/8	5 1/8	Rawlins Co., WY	Armin O. Baltensweiler	Armin O. Baltensweiler	1966	660
84 2/8	16 1/8	16 1/8	7 3/8	7 1/8	2 6/8	2 6/8	5 6/8	5 5/8	12 3/8	8 6/8	Fremont Co., WY	Edward S. Friend	Edward S. Friend	1967	660
84 2/8	14 7/8	14 7/8	6 5/8	6 5/8	3	3	6 6/8	6 1/8	7 2/8	7 1/8	Big Piney, WY	Lawrence M. Kick	Lawrence M. Kick	1967	660
84 2/8	17 7/8	17 7/8	6 1/8	6 1/8	2 7/8	3	4 6/8	4 5/8	12 1/8	7 6/8	Ft. Apache Res., AZ	Frank E. White	Frank E. White	1967	660
84 2/8	15	15	7 6/8	7 6/8	2 4/8	2 7/8	8	8	13 4/8	11 7/8	Fremont Co., WY	Lee Arce	Lee Arce	1968	660
84 2/8	17 4/8	17 4/8	7 2/8	7 2/8	2 4/8	2 4/8	4 1/8	6	8 4/8	5 4/8	Humboldt Co., NV	Gerald A. Lent	Gerald A. Lent	1970	660
84 2/8	15 2/8	15 2/8	6	6	2 5/8	2 6/8	4 7/8	4 7/8	11 6/8	8 2/8	Natrona Co., WY	Donald F. Mahnke	Donald F. Mahnke	1971	660
84 2/8	16 4/8	16 4/8	7	7	2 6/8	2 5/8	5 2/8	5 2/8	15 1/8	11 3/8	Albany Co., WY	George Panagos, Jr.	George Panagos, Jr.	1972	660
84 2/8	16 6/8	16 3/8	6 4/8	6 4/8	2 6/8	2 6/8	5 4/8	5 3/8	8 4/8	3 7/8	Apache Co., AZ	Alaine D. Neal	Alaine D. Neal	1973	660
84 2/8	17 1/8	17 3/8	7 3/8	7 3/8	3	3	5 3/8	7	14 2/8	13	Abbott, NM	George H. Ray III	George H. Ray III	1974	660
84 2/8	16 4/8	16 4/8	7 1/8	7	2 5/8	2 7/8	4 6/8	6 7/8	9	1 1/8	Meade Co., SD	John Hostetter	John Hostetter	1975	660
84 2/8	16	16	7 4/8	7	2 7/8	2 7/8	5 6/8	6	16	11 4/8	Carbon Co., WY	William O. Queen	William O. Queen	1975	660
84 2/8	15 5/8	15 5/8	6 7/8	6 7/8	2 4/8	3	4 5/8	4 5/8	9 7/8	7	Sweetwater Co., WY	Bill Jordan	Bill Jordan	1976	660
84 2/8	15 4/8	15 2/8	7 3/8	7 3/8	2 5/8	2 4/8	4 3/8	4 3/8	11 2/8	8 1/8	Humboldt Co., NV	Kenneth Mellin	Kenneth Mellin	1976	660
84 2/8	15 5/8	15 3/8	7 1/8	6 4/8	2 6/8	2 6/8	5 6/8	5 6/8	13	12 1/8	Carbon Co., WY	David Perondi	David Perondi	1976	660
84 2/8	15 2/8	16 3/8	6 3/8	7 3/8	3	3	6 1/8	6 1/8	8 2/8	5 1/8	Modoc Co., CA	Glenn F. Galbraith	Glenn F. Galbraith	1977	660
84 2/8	15 3/8	16 2/8	7 2/8	7	2 4/8	2 4/8	5 7/8	5 7/8	14 2/8	13	Fremont Co., WY	Jess T. Jones	Unknown	PR 1978	660
84 2/8	17 3/8	17 3/8	7 1/8	7	2 7/8	2 7/8	4 5/8	4 6/8	9	1 1/8	Humboldt Co., NV	William D. Baldwin	William D. Baldwin	1980	660
84 2/8	17	17	6 7/8	7 2/8	2 4/8	2 7/8	6 2/8	6 6/8	12 3/8	8	Sweetwater Co., WY	James R. Puryear	James R. Puryear	1980	660
84 2/8	16 1/8	16 1/8	6 6/8	6 4/8	2 4/8	2 4/8	6 6/8	6 6/8	6 4/8	8 1/8	Humboldt Co., NV	Richard D. Ullery	Richard D. Ullery	1980	660
84 2/8	15 5/8	15 5/8	7	6 7/8	2 4/8	2 4/8	5 7/8	6	13 4/8	2	Carbon Co., WY	John V. Wilgus	John V. Wilgus	1980	660
84 2/8	17 2/8	17 4/8	6 6/8	7 2/8	2 7/8	2 7/8	6 2/8	5 4/8	10 2/8	13 4/8	Modoc Co., CA	Larry A. Owens, Sr.	Larry A. Owens, Sr.	1981	660
84 2/8	16 4/8	17 2/8	6 2/8	6 2/8	3 1/8	3	6 3/8	6 2/8	14 6/8	10 4/8	Powder River Co., MT	Sam C. Borla	Sam C. Borla	1982	660
84 2/8	16 2/8	16 4/8	6	6 2/8	2 6/8	2 6/8	6 2/8	6	13 7/8	10 3/8	Malheur Co., OR	Matt J. Brundridge	Matt J. Brundridge	1982	660

PRONGHORN

Antilocapra americana americana and related subspecies

Score	Length of Horn R	L	Circumference of Base R	L	Circumference at Third Quarter R	L	Inside Spread	Tip to Tip Spread	Length of Prong R	L	Locality	Hunter	Owner	Date Killed	Rank
84 2/8	17	16 6/8	6 4/8	6 3/8	2 5/8	2 4/8	12 2/8	8 4/8	6	6 1/8	Coconino Co., AZ	Michael A. Cromer	Michael A. Cromer	1982	660
84 2/8	16	15 6/8	6 6/8	6 6/8	2 4/8	2 4/8	10	5 2/8	5 5/8	6	Carbon Co., WY	Ernest L. Tollini	Ernest L. Tollini	1982	660
84 2/8	15 5/8	15 5/8	6 7/8	6 5/8	2 5/8	2 4/8	9 3/8	4 5/8	6 1/8	5 5/8	Carbon Co., WY	J. Mike Clegg	J. Mike Clegg	1983	660
84 2/8	16 5/8	16 4/8	7 4/8	7 4/8	3	3	9 2/8	5 1/8	5 1/8	4 6/8	Natrona Co., WY	Allen J. Hogan	Allen J. Hogan	1983	660
84 2/8	17 2/8	17 3/8	6 4/8	6 6/8	2 4/8	2 5/8	8 5/8	2 2/8	5 6/8	5 4/8	Washoe Co., NV	Judy Taylor	Judy Taylor	1983	660
84 2/8	16 6/8	16 7/8	6 2/8	6 2/8	2 7/8	3	9 1/8	6 6/8	5 3/8	5 2/8	Coconino Co., AZ	William R. Vaughn	William R. Vaughn	1983	660
84 2/8	16	16 2/8	6 5/8	6 5/8	3	3	13 2/8	11	5 6/8	5 5/8	Fremont Co., WY	John A. Monje	John A. Monje	1985	660
84 2/8	15	15	6 7/8	7 3/8	2 5/8	2 5/8	12 5/8	10 2/8	6 2/8	6	White Pine Co., NV	Paul E. Podborny	Paul E. Podborny	1985	660
84 2/8	16	16 2/8	7 4/8	7	2 5/8	2 5/8	13 2/8	12	4 6/8	4 2/8	Washoe Co., NV	Eugene E. Belli	Eugene E. Belli	1986	660
84 2/8	16	16 2/8	6 7/8	6 7/8	2 3/8	2 5/8	12	7 2/8	6 2/8	6 4/8	Yellowstone Co., MT	Jim B. Cherpeski	Jim B. Cherpeski	1986	660
84 2/8	14 5/8	14 2/8	6 7/8	6 2/8	2 6/8	2 6/8	7 2/8	6 7/8	6 4/8	6 4/8	Carter Co., MT	Robert Cunningham	Robert Cunningham	1986	660
84 2/8	16 4/8	18 2/8	6 2/8	6 2/8	2 6/8	2 6/8	11 1/8	6 5/8	6 1/8	5 2/8	Coconino Co., AZ	Kevin B. Call	Kevin B. Call	1987	660
84 2/8	15 2/8	15 1/8	6 1/8	6	2 7/8	2 7/8	11 3/8	7 2/8	5 5/8	6 1/8	Baker Co., OR	Paul W. Schon	Paul W. Schon	1987	660
84 2/8	17	16 7/8	6 2/8	6 1/8	2 7/8	2 7/8	13 1/8	7 7/8	6 1/8	6	Hudspeth Co., TX	Sam H. Gann IV	Sam H. Gann IV	1988	660
84 2/8	16	16	6 6/8	6 5/8	2 3/8	2 3/8	10	4	7	7	Yavapai Co., AZ	Brian Murray	Brian Murray	1988	660
84 2/8	16 1/8	16 3/8	6 2/8	6 2/8	2 4/8	2 4/8	16 5/8	13	6	7	Hudspeth Co., TX	W. Wayne Spahn	W. Wayne Spahn	1988	660
84 2/8	15 7/8	15 7/8	6 7/8	6 7/8	2 7/8	2 7/8	9 2/8	4 6/8	6 5/8	7 1/8	Weld Co., CO	M. Wayne Hoeben	M. Wayne Hoeben	1989	660
84 2/8	15 7/8	15 1/8	7 1/8	7 1/8	2 5/8	2 5/8	10 1/8	6 3/8	6 2/8	6 2/8	Fremont Co., WY	Boyd E. Sharp, Jr.	Boyd E. Sharp, Jr.	1989	660
84 2/8	16 4/8	16 2/8	6 5/8	6 5/8	2 5/8	2 5/8	11 6/8	7 3/8	5 4/8	6 2/8	Mora Co., NM	Scott Steinkruger	Scott Steinkruger	1989	660
84 2/8	15 3/8	15 5/8	7 3/8	7 3/8	2 5/8	2 5/8	9 3/8	5 1/8	5 5/8	5 5/8	Washakie Co., WY	Douglas D. Stinnette	Douglas D. Stinnette	1989	660
84 2/8	17 1/8	17 1/8	7 1/8	7 1/8	2 5/8	2 5/8	12	7 7/8	6 7/8	6 2/8	San Miguel Co., NM	Larry R. Griffin	Larry R. Griffin	1990	660
84 2/8	15 6/8	15 6/8	7 2/8	7 2/8	2 4/8	2 4/8	9 6/8	5	6	5 7/8	Carbon Co., MT	Patrick I. Kalloch	Patrick I. Kalloch	1990	660
84 2/8	16 7/8	16 6/8	6 5/8	6 5/8	2 6/8	2 5/8	8 5/8	1 3/8	5 6/8	6	Harney Co., OR	Douglas J. Modey	Douglas J. Modey	1990	660
84 2/8	15 7/8	15 7/8	6 3/8	6 3/8	2 4/8	2 6/8	9 3/8	8 4/8	6 2/8	6 3/8	Sweetwater Co., WY	Kurt D. Olson	Kurt D. Olson	1990	660
84 2/8	15 2/8	15	7	7	2 6/8	2 4/8	11 1/8	8	6 4/8	7 1/8	Carbon Co., WY	Robert G. Wimpenny	Robert G. Wimpenny	1990	660
84 2/8	15 6/8	16	7	7	2 7/8	2 6/8	7 2/8	2 2/8	6 3/8	6 1/8	Jackson Co., CO	Jerrald L. Copple	Jerrald L. Copple	1991	660
84 2/8	17 2/8	15 5/8	7 5/8	7 5/8	2 3/8	2 3/8	12 6/8	12 6/8	5	5 5/8	Fremont Co., WY	Carl A. Engler	Carl A. Engler	1991	660
84 2/8	15 5/8	15 4/8	6 4/8	6 5/8	2 6/8	2 6/8	12 4/8	8 2/8	5	5	Quay Co., NM	Marvin S. Keating	Marvin S. Keating	1991	660
84 2/8	17 3/8	17 3/8	6 7/8	6 6/8	2 6/8	2 6/8	9 1/8	4 1/8	6 4/8	5 6/8	Box Elder Co., UT	O. Brent Maw	O. Brent Maw	1991	660
84 2/8	16 4/8	16 4/8	6 6/8	6 6/8	2 6/8	2 6/8	11 7/8	6 6/8	5 3/8	5 7/8	Mora Co., NM	Ralph C. Stayner	Ralph C. Stayner	1991	660
84 2/8	16	16 1/8	6 6/8	6 5/8	2 5/8	2 5/8	9 6/8	6 2/8	6 2/8	6	Carbon Co., WY	Lynn Woodard	Lynn Woodard	1991	660
84 2/8	13 7/8	13 7/8	7 1/8	7 1/8	2 7/8	2 7/8	9 1/8	3 1/8	5 6/8	5 6/8	Harney Co., OR	Timothy A. Barnhart	Timothy A. Barnhart	1992	660
84 2/8	15 4/8	15 4/8	7 1/8	7 2/8	2 4/8	2 4/8	12 2/8	10 1/8	7 3/8	7 3/8	Lassen Co., CA	Delbert W. Case	Delbert W. Case	1992	660
84 2/8	15 3/8	15 3/8	6 6/8	6 6/8	2 6/8	2 6/8	9 6/8	5 3/8	6 1/8	6 1/8	Dewey Co., SD	Bernard P. Fuhrmann	Bernard P. Fuhrmann	1993	660
84 2/8	16 4/8	16 3/8	6 6/8	6 4/8	3	3	8 2/8	4 1/8	5 1/8	5 1/8	Carbon Co., WY	Steven G. Sparks	Steven G. Sparks	1993	660
84 2/8	17 4/8	17 3/8	5 7/8	5 6/8	2 4/8	2 4/8	8 3/8	2	6	6	Hartley Co., TX	Ernie Davis	Ernie Davis	1994	660
84 2/8	17 1/8	17 1/8	6 3/8	6 3/8	2 5/8	2 5/8	10 4/8	4 4/8	5 3/8	5 5/8	Humboldt Co., NV	Gary J. Farotte	Gary J. Farotte	1994	660
84 2/8	17	17	6 2/8	6 2/8	2 4/8	2 4/8	9 3/8	3 2/8	6 6/8	6 4/8	Modoc Co., CA	Don E. Perrien	Don E. Perrien	1994	660

Score	L. Horn R	L. Horn L	Circ. Base R	Circ. Base L	Circ. 3rd Qtr R	Circ. 3rd Qtr L	L. Prong R	L. Prong L	Inside Spread	Tip to Tip	Locality	By whom killed	Owner	Date	Rank
84 2/8	17 5/8	17 5/8	7	7	2 2/8	2 5/8	5 2/8	2 5/8	9 1/8	2 2/8	Washoe Co., NV	Glen R. Barthold	Glen R. Barthold	1995	660
84 2/8	15 2/8	15 3/8	7 5/8	7 4/8	2 3/8	2 4/8	5 6/8	9 5/8	11 6/8	2 4/8	Sweetwater Co., WY	Jared Mason	Jared Mason	1995	660
84 2/8	13 6/8	13 6/8	8	7 2/8	2 6/8	2 7/8	5 6/8	13 4/8	14 7/8	2 7/8	Sweetwater Co., WY	Timothy M. Storey	Timothy M. Storey	1995	660
84 2/8	16	16 1/8	7 2/8	7	2 5/8	2 5/8	5 6/8	3 2/8	9 3/8	2 5/8	Natrona Co., WY	Ben P. Carlson	Ben P. Carlson	1996	660
84 2/8	15 4/8	15 4/8	7	6 2/8	2 5/8	2 5/8	6 3/8	3 4/8	7 3/8	2 5/8	Fremont Co., WY	Sandi K. Fruchey	Sandi K. Fruchey	1996	660
84 2/8	16 5/8	16 4/8	6 2/8	6 2/8	3 1/8	3 2/8	6 1/8	4 7/8	8 5/8	3 1/8	Yavapai Co., AZ	Caleb Miller	Caleb Miller	1996	660
84 2/8	16	16	6 1/8	6 3/8	3	3	6 5/8	6	10 1/8	3	Yavapai Co., AZ	Vernon S. Stenseng	Vernon S. Stenseng	1997	660
84 2/8	15 6/8	15 5/8	6 3/8	6 4/8	3 3/8	3	4 7/8	7 7/8	12 3/8	3 3/8	Colfax Co., NM	Lydia Dick	Lydia Dick	1997	660
84 2/8	16	16 4/8	6 4/8	6 7/8	2 4/8	2 4/8	7 2/8	10 7/8	13 1/8	2 4/8	Sublette Co., WY	John L. Hutchins	John L. Hutchins	1997	660
84 2/8	16 1/8	15 7/8	6 7/8	6 6/8	2 5/8	2 6/8	5 6/8	4 7/8	10 3/8	2 5/8	Baca Co., CO	William R. Kincade	William R. Kincade	1997	660
84 2/8	15 7/8	16	7 1/8	7 2/8	2 7/8	2 7/8	5 2/8	8 3/8	12 3/8	2 7/8	Socorro Co., NM	Stephen C. LeBlanc	Stephen C. LeBlanc	1997	660
84 2/8	16	15 6/8	6 7/8	6 6/8	3	3	5 7/8	1 3/8	6 4/8	3	Yavapai Co., AZ	Steven L. Long	Steven L. Long	1997	660
84 2/8	16 1/8	16 1/8	6 6/8	6 7/8	3 4/8	3 4/8	6 1/8	6 1/8	8 3/8	3 4/8	Yavapai Co., AZ	David W. Miller, Jr.	David W. Miller, Jr.	1998	660
84 2/8	15 3/8	15 5/8	7 1/8	7 1/8	2 5/8	2 5/8	6 5/8	5 6/8	8 1/8	2 5/8	Moffat Co., CO	Kenneth M. Appelgren	Kenneth M. Appelgren	1998	660
84 2/8	16 1/8	16	6 6/8	6 6/8	2 5/8	2 5/8	6 6/8	3	8 7/8	2 5/8	Harney Co., OR	Marvin K. Champ	Marvin K. Champ	1999	660
84 2/8	16 2/8	16 3/8	6 2/8	6 2/8	2 7/8	2 6/8	6 7/8	4 2/8	10 3/8	2 7/8	Hudspeth Co., TX	Michael Cottrell	Michael Cottrell	1999	660
84 2/8	16 5/8	16 5/8	6 6/8	6 6/8	2 6/8	2 4/8	6 3/8	5 1/8	10 2/8	2 6/8	Lassen Co., CA	Donald F. Housen	Donald F. Housen	1999	660
84 2/8	17	17	6 2/8	6 2/8	2 4/8	2 4/8	6 1/8	5 2/8	10 3/8	2 4/8	Catron Co., NM	Richard Jaramillo	Richard Jaramillo	1999	660
84 2/8	16 4/8	16 4/8	6 4/8	6 4/8	2 6/8	2 5/8	5 7/8	7	7 4/8	2 6/8	Moffat Co., CO	Doug Palmer	Doug Palmer	1999	660
84 2/8	16 2/8	16 3/8	6 4/8	6 1/8	2 5/8	2 5/8	6 4/8	10 3/8	13 7/8	2 5/8	Carbon Co., WY	Don E. Perrien	Don E. Perrien	1999	660
84 2/8	15 6/8	16	5 6/8	5 6/8	3 3/8	3 3/8	6 1/8	7 5/8	11 6/8	3 3/8	Sweetwater Co., WY	Joseph L. Koback	Joseph L. Koback	2000	660
84 2/8	16 3/8	16 1/8	6 6/8	6 4/8	3 1/8	3 1/8	6	21	21	3 1/8	Colfax Co., NM	William N. Utecht	William N. Utecht	2000	660
84 2/8	16 2/8	16 1/8	6 3/8	6 4/8	2 6/8	2 5/8	10 2/8	5 6/8	12 5/8	2 6/8	Carbon Co., WY	Kip T. Williams	Kip T. Williams	2001	660
84 2/8	16 2/8	16 3/8	7 1/8	7 3/8	2 6/8	2 6/8	9 6/8	9 6/8	12 6/8	2 6/8	Carbon Co., WY	Kim Cooper	Kim Cooper	2002	660
84 2/8	14 4/8	16 1/8	6 7/8	6 7/8	3	3 1/8	5 5/8	9 1/8	9 1/8	3	Lincoln Co., NM	Lee Frudden	Lee Frudden	2003	660
84 2/8	16 4/8	14 6/8	6 2/8	7 2/8	3 6/8	2 5/8	6 2/8	9 1/8	9 1/8	2 5/8	Logan Co., CO	Richard L. Smith	Richard L. Smith	2003	660
84 2/8	16 2/8	16 4/8	6 1/8	6 2/8	3	3	7	11 4/8	11 4/8	3	Custer Co., CO	Picked Up	Kevin Travnicek	2003	660
84	15 6/8	16	7 2/8	7 2/8	3 7/8	3 7/8	10 6/8	14 1/8	14 1/8	3 7/8	Lost Cabin, WY	Jack Henery	Jack Henery	1955	754
84	17 1/8	17 1/8	6 4/8	6 4/8	2 6/8	3 7/8	11 1/8	14 2/8	14 2/8	2 6/8	Meadowdale, WY	Mrs. Lodisa Pipher	Mrs. Lodisa Pipher	1956	754
84	17 2/8	16 5/8	6	6 2/8	2 7/8	5	5 2/8	10 6/8	14 2/8	2 7/8	Yavapai Co., AZ	Walter Tibbs	Walter Tibbs	1959	754
84	16 4/8	16 1/8	6 4/8	6 4/8	3 1/8	6	5 6/8	11 2/8	10 6/8	3 1/8	Campbell Co., WY	Fred J. Brogle	Fred J. Brogle	1960	754
84	15 6/8	14 2/8	7 5/8	7 3/8	3 1/8	13 6/8	6 4/8	14 4/8	14 4/8	3 1/8	Pinedale, WY	Edward Sturla	Edward Sturla	1960	754
84	16 3/8	16	6 6/8	6 6/8	2 4/8	9	5 7/8	11 4/8	11 4/8	2 4/8	Sage Creek, WY	Pat Swarts	Pat Swarts	1960	754
84	16 2/8	16 4/8	7	7 1/8	2 5/8	8 2/8	5 2/8	12 1/8	12 1/8	2 5/8	Coconino Co., AZ	Ross F. Adams	Don R. Adams	1961	754
84	17 1/8	17 4/8	6 4/8	6 3/8	3	12 5/8	6	13 4/8	13 4/8	3	Carbon Co., WY	Mrs. T.H. Green	Mrs. T.H. Green	1964	754
84	16 5/8	16 2/8	6 3/8	6 3/8	3	6	5 1/8	8 6/8	11 2/8	3	Fremont Co., WY	Robert E. Novotny	Robert E. Novotny	1964	754
84	16 1/8	16 1/8	6 5/8	6 5/8	2 5/8	5 2/8	6 1/8	8 6/8	8 6/8	2 5/8	Rawlins Co., WY	John M. Sell	John M. Sell	1964	754
84	17 2/8	16	7 1/8	7 1/8	2 5/8	6 7/8	4 7/8	12 2/8	12 2/8	2 5/8	Milk River, AB	George Vandervalk	George Vandervalk	1966	754
84	16 5/8	17	6 4/8	6 4/8	3	3	4 7/8	8	8	3	Washington Co., CO	Christian Heyden	Christian Heyden	1967	754
84	16 3/8	16 4/8	6 7/8	6 7/8	2 4/8	12 2/8	5 2/8	14 7/8	14 7/8	2 4/8	Leola, SD	Leonard Lahr	Leonard Lahr	1967	754
84	15 5/8	15 4/8	6 7/8	6 7/8	2 5/8	8 7/8	6 4/8	11 6/8	11 6/8	2 5/8	Chouteau Co., MT	W.E. Cherry	W.E. Cherry	1968	754
84	15 4/8	15 4/8	6 5/8	6 6/8	2 7/8	9	6 4/8	14 2/8	14 2/8	2 7/8	Washoe Co., NV	Robert L. Mallory	Robert L. Mallory	1969	754
84	14 4/8	14 4/8	6 6/8	7	2 7/8	11 5/8	6 2/8	11 5/8	11 5/8	2 7/8	Red Desert, WY	Fred Morgan	Fred Morgan	1969	754
84	16 6/8	16 1/8	6 7/8	6 7/8	2 6/8	3 5/8	4 6/8	7 3/8	7 3/8	2 6/8	Carbon Co., WY	Russ Allen	Russ Allen	1970	754
84	16 5/8	16 3/8	6 7/8	6 7/8	2 4/8	2 3/8	6 1/8	8 6/8	8 6/8	2 4/8	Humboldt Co., NV	Gary D. Bader	Gary D. Bader	1970	754
84	15	14 1/8	7	7	2 5/8	11 4/8	6	14 1/8	14 1/8	2 5/8	Albany Co., WY	Andy Pfaff	Andy Pfaff	1972	754
84	18 6/8	18 2/8	6 4/8	6	2 4/8	15 7/8	4 5/8	17 6/8	17 6/8	2 4/8	Sublette Co., WY	Dick Reilly	Dick Reilly	1974	754
84	17 2/8	16 6/8	7	7	2 4/8	9 7/8	5 3/8	13 1/8	13 1/8	2 4/8	Mora Co., NM	William E. Pipes III	William E. Pipes III	1977	754

PRONGHORN

Antilocapra americana americana and related subspecies

Score	Length of Horn R	Length of Horn L	Circumference of Base R	Circumference of Base L	Circumference at Third Quarter R	Circumference at Third Quarter L	Inside Spread	Tip to Tip Spread	Length of Prong R	Length of Prong L	Locality	Hunter	Owner	Date Killed	Rank
84	16 3/8	16 3/8	6 6/8	6 6/8	2 5/8	2 5/8	11 6/8	8 3/8	5 4/8	5 5/8	Presidio Co., TX	W. Wayne Roye	W. Wayne Roye	1977	754
84	15 1/8	14 7/8	6 4/8	6 5/8	3 3/8	3 1/8	11 1/8	9 6/8	6 6/8	5 7/8	Sioux Co., NE	Harvey Y. Suetsugu	Harvey Y. Suetsugu	1977	754
84	16 7/8	16 7/8	6 5/8	6 5/8	3	2 6/8	10 6/8	4 7/8	5 4/8	5 2/8	Coconino Co., AZ	Robert F. Veazey	Robert F. Veazey	1979	754
84	14 7/8	14 5/8	7 6/8	7 3/8	3	3	11 1/8	10	6 3/8	6	Natrona Co., WY	Bill E. Boatman	Bill E. Boatman	1980	754
84	17 6/8	17 4/8	6 2/8	6 1/8	2 5/8	2 5/8	6	5 3/8	6	5 3/8	Washoe Co., NV	Jamie L. Kent	Jamie L. Kent	1980	754
84	17 5/8	17 5/8	6 1/8	6 2/8	2 7/8	2 7/8	13 6/8	8 2/8	5	4 7/8	Yavapai Co., AZ	James O. Pierce	James O. Pierce	1980	754
84	16 1/8	16 4/8	6 7/8	6 6/8	2 5/8	2 7/8	11 2/8	5 7/8	6 4/8	5 6/8	Fremont Co., WY	Joel E. Hensley	Joel E. Hensley	1981	754
84	16	15 6/8	6 3/8	6 3/8	2 4/8	2 3/8	14 2/8	12 6/8	5	4 6/8	Blaine Co., ID	Charles R. Hisaw	Charles R. Hisaw	1981	754
84	15 2/8	15 7/8	7 2/8	7 1/8	2 4/8	2 5/8	15 3/8	13 6/8	6 2/8	6 2/8	Fremont Co., WY	Victor M. McCullough	Victor M. McCullough	1981	754
84	16	16 3/8	7	7	2 7/8	2 5/8	12 6/8	9 1/8	6 2/8	6 3/8	Carbon Co., WY	Dudley R. Elmgren	Dudley R. Elmgren	1982	754
84	16 7/8	16 3/8	6 6/8	6 6/8	2 5/8	2 5/8	10 4/8	6 4/8	5 2/8	5 4/8	Sweetwater Co., WY	Richard H. Maddock	Richard H. Maddock	1982	754
84	15 5/8	15 5/8	6 6/8	6 4/8	3 4/8	3 1/8	15 1/8	11 2/8	5 1/8	5 2/8	Coconino Co., AZ	Fred J. Nobbe, Jr.	Fred J. Nobbe, Jr.	1982	754
84	16 7/8	16 4/8	6 6/8	6 6/8	2 4/8	2 5/8	10 6/8	6	6 1/8	6	Sweetwater Co., WY	Lorio Verzasconi	Lorio Verzasconi	1982	754
84	16 2/8	16 2/8	6 4/8	6 4/8	3	3 2/8	12	9 5/8	5 3/8	5 1/8	Mora Co., NM	Roger B. Coit	Roger B. Coit	1983	754
84	16 4/8	16 4/8	6 3/8	6 3/8	2 6/8	2 6/8	11 6/8	7 4/8	5 6/8	5 7/8	Sweetwater Co., WY	Dennis W. Gallegos	Dennis W. Gallegos	1983	754
84	14 6/8	14 5/8	7 2/8	7 2/8	3	3	11 1/8	7 5/8	6 1/8	5 5/8	Sheridan Co., NE	Wayne M. Kelly	Wayne M. Kelly	1983	754
84	17 2/8	17 2/8	6 5/8	6 4/8	2 7/8	2 7/8	9 3/8	5 4/8	4 5/8	5 7/8	Bennett Co., SD	Paul R. Nelson	Paul R. Nelson	1983	754
84	16 7/8	16 6/8	6 5/8	6 5/8	2 4/8	2 3/8	10 4/8	6 4/8	6 3/8	6 3/8	Natrona Co., WY	Dale A. Ableidinger	Dale A. Ableidinger	1984	754
84	16	16	6 4/8	6 5/8	2 7/8	2 7/8	10	7 6/8	5 7/8	6 1/8	Washoe Co., NV	Bert F. Carder	Bert F. Carder	1984	754
84	17 4/8	17 2/8	6 7/8	6 7/8	3	2 6/8	18	14	4 5/8	4 5/8	Colfax Co., NM	David S. Dickenson	David S. Dickenson	1984	754
84	17 4/8	16 2/8	6 7/8	6 7/8	3 1/8	3	10 3/8	4 6/8	5 7/8	5 2/8	Yavapai Co., AZ	Frederick T. Lau	Frederick T. Lau	1985	754
84	16 4/8	16 1/8	6 7/8	6 6/8	2 5/8	2 7/8	9 7/8	5 7/8	5 6/8	5 5/8	Dawson Co., MT	Jeff S. Trangmoe	Jeff S. Trangmoe	1985	754
84	16 3/8	16 1/8	6 7/8	6 6/8	2 4/8	3	11	5 4/8	6	6	Lassen Co., CA	Al J. Accurso, Jr.	Al J. Accurso, Jr.	1986	754
84	15 2/8	15 3/8	6 2/8	6 3/8	2 5/8	2 4/8	12 3/8	8	7 1/8	7 2/8	Campbell Co., WY	Unknown	J. Michael Conoyer	PR 1986	754
84	16 4/8	16 2/8	7 2/8	7 2/8	2 6/8	2 4/8	10	6 3/8	5 7/8	5 3/8	Lake Co., OR	Del J. DeSart	Del J. DeSart	1986	754
84	16 7/8	17 2/8	6 6/8	6 6/8	2 4/8	2 4/8	12 6/8	7 3/8	5 4/8	5 2/8	Sierra Co., NM	Mike W. Leonard	Mike W. Leonard	1987	754
84	16 2/8	16 7/8	6 6/8	6 5/8	2 6/8	3 1/8	14 7/8	16 6/8	5 5/8	6 1/8	Yavapai Co., AZ	James K. McCasland	James K. McCasland	1987	754
84	15 6/8	15 6/8	6 2/8	6 2/8	2 7/8	3	12 3/8	11 1/8	5 7/8	5 6/8	Harney Co., OR	James E. Baley	James E. Baley	1988	754
84	17	16 7/8	6 6/8	6 6/8	2 4/8	2 4/8	11 7/8	8 6/8	5 7/8	5 7/8	Custer Co., MT	Don A. Bruendl	Don A. Bruendl	1988	754
84	14 2/8	14 5/8	7 1/8	7	3 1/8	3 2/8	11 1/8	7 3/8	5 4/8	5 3/8	Colfax Co., NM	Ruel Holt	Ruel Holt	1988	754
84	17 5/8	17	6 3/8	6 3/8	2 3/8	2 5/8	18 5/8	14 3/8	5 5/8	5 6/8	Hudspeth Co., TX	Gibson D. Lewis	Gibson D. Lewis	1988	754
84	16 3/8	16 3/8	6 6/8	6 5/8	2 7/8	2 7/8	11 3/8	8	5 3/8	5 3/8	Elko Co., NV	Raylene L. Naveran	Raylene L. Naveran	1989	754
84	15 7/8	15 7/8	6 6/8	6 5/8	2 6/8	2 6/8	11 3/8	6 1/8	5 6/8	5 5/8	Navajo Co., AZ	Alan K. Nulliner	Alan K. Nulliner	1989	754
84	17 2/8	16 6/8	6 6/8	6 6/8	2 4/8	2 4/8	14 6/8	8 5/8	5	4 6/8	Washoe Co., NV	Roger D. Puccinelli	Roger D. Puccinelli	1989	754
84	17	15 6/8	7	6 7/8	2 3/8	2 4/8	13 1/8	10 2/8	7 4/8	7	Lassen Co., CA	Larry R. Brower	Larry R. Brower	1990	754
84	16 2/8	16 2/8	6 5/8	6 5/8	2 5/8	2 5/8	9 7/8	6 2/8	5 5/8	5 3/8	Sweetwater Co., WY	Robert E. Bergquist	Robert E. Bergquist	1991	754
84	16 2/8	16 2/8	6 4/8	6 3/8	3	2 6/8	10 6/8	7 2/8	5 2/8	5 5/8	Coconino Co., AZ	William B. Bullock	William B. Bullock	1991	754
84	15 5/8	15 4/8	6 4/8	6 6/8	3 1/8	3 2/8	8 4/8	7 1/8	5 3/8	5 3/8	Mora Co., NM	Charles F. Marsh	Charles F. Marsh	1991	754

Score	Length of Horn	Circ. of Base R	Circ. of Base L	Circ. 3rd Qtr. R	Circ. 3rd Qtr. L	Length of Prong	Tip to Tip Spread	Name	By Whom Taken	Locality	Date	Rank
84	17 2/8	6 4/8	6 6/8	2 2/8	2 2/8	2 3/8	7	Andrew M. Specht	Andrew M. Specht	Humboldt Co., NV	1991	754
84	17	6 4/8	6 4/8	2 7/8	2 6/8	3 7/8	9 1/8	Charlinda Webster	Charlinda Webster	Apache Co., AZ	1991	754
84	15	7 2/8	7 2/8	3	2 7/8	5 2/8	10 4/8	John J. Weust	John J. Weust	Fremont Co., WY	1991	754
84	16 2/8	6 6/8	6 5/8	3 1/8	3	6 4/8	10 2/8	Joseph J. Bongiovi, Jr.	Joseph J. Bongiovi, Jr.	Mora Co., NM	1992	754
84	16 7/8	7 1/8	7	2 4/8	2 4/8	5	10	Mark A. Doner	Mark A. Doner	Harney Co., OR	1992	754
84	16 7/8	6 4/8	6 4/8	3	2 6/8	6 6/8	12 5/8	Mel L. Helm	Mel L. Helm	Mora Co., NM	1992	754
84	16 3/8	6 4/8	6 6/8	2 7/8	2 6/8	8 7/8	8 7/8	Timothy H. Humes	Timothy H. Humes	Washoe Co., NV	1993	754
84	15 6/8	6 2/8	6 6/8	2 6/8	2 7/8	4 4/8	14 5/8	Paul F. Musser	Paul F. Musser	Coconino Co., AZ	1993	754
84	16 6/8	7 6/8	8 2/8	2 7/8	2 6/8	14 4/8	16 4/8	Royce S. Schaeffer	Royce S. Schaeffer	Sioux Co., NE	1993	754
84	15 1/8	7 2/8	7 2/8	2 5/8	3 1/8	16 4/8	9 4/8	Barry A. Weaver	Barry A. Weaver	Jackson Co., CO	1993	754
84	16 3/8	6 6/8	6 5/8	2 6/8	2 6/8	3 6/8	9 4/8	Orlando J. Suris	Orlando J. Suris	Mora Co., NM	1995	754
84	17 1/8	7 1/8	7	3 2/8	3 3/8	9 4/8	5 5/8	Ken E. Ashley	Ken E. Ashley	Grand Co., UT	1996	754
84	15 5/8	6 7/8	6 6/8	3 4/8	2 5/8	8 1/8	10 4/8	Doug C. Brooks	Doug C. Brooks	Otero Co., NM	1996	754
84	15 3/8	6 5/8	6 6/8	2 7/8	2 5/8	0 4/8	13 6/8	Robert O. Crow	Robert O. Crow	Hudspeth Co., TX	1997	754
84	17 5/8	6 7/8	6 7/8	2 5/8	2 5/8	5 3/8	11 6/8	Craig L. Kling	Craig L. Kling	Sweetwater Co., WY	1997	754
84	16	6 6/8	6 2/8	2 7/8	2 7/8	10 5/8	9 3/8	Clyde E. Mandeville	Clyde E. Mandeville	Modoc Co., CA	1997	754
84	16 4/8	6 2/8	6 4/8	3	2 3/8	5 7/8	15 4/8	Trey Hickman	Trey Hickman	Modoc Co., CA	1998	754
84	15 6/8	6 4/8	6 2/8	2 3/8	3 1/8	4 1/8	12 1/8	Todd B. Jaksick	Todd B. Jaksick	Washoe Co., NV	1998	754
84	16 2/8	6 4/8	6 4/8	3 1/8	3 2/8	11 6/8	10	Jack W. Peters	Jack W. Peters	Elko Co., NV	1998	754
84	15 3/8	6 5/8	6 6/8	2 4/8	2 3/8	8 4/8	10	Scott J. Richins	Scott J. Richins	Washakie Co., WY	1998	754
84	16 4/8	6 2/8	6 3/8	2 7/8	2 5/8	7 2/8	14 3/8	Thomas R. Devereaux	Thomas R. Devereaux	Yavapai Co., AZ	1999	754
84	15 5/8	6 6/8	6 4/8	3 1/8	3 1/8	8	11 1/8	Jerry D. Johnson	Jerry D. Johnson	Sweetwater Co., WY	1999	754
84	15 7/8	6 4/8	5 4/8	3	3	11 4/8	7 1/8	Dennis J. Sites	Dennis J. Sites	Mora Co., NM	1999	754
84	17 1/8	6 6/8	6 2/8	2 7/8	2 5/8	5	10 1/8	Todd A. Wood	Todd A. Wood	Rosebud Co., MT	1999	754
84	17	6 5/8	6 4/8	2 4/8	2 4/8	6 1/8	11 2/8	Bob Nicholas	Bob Nicholas	Lincoln Co., NM	2000	754
84	16 1/8	6 2/8	6 6/8	2 3/8	2 3/8	1 2/8	13 2/8	Scott D. Isaak	Scott D. Isaak	Harney Co., OR	2001	754
84	15	6 6/8	6 3/8	3 2/8	3 2/8	3 6/8	10 1/8	Kevin A. Teston	Kevin A. Teston	Yavapai Co., AZ	2001	754
84	15 2/8	6 4/8	6 4/8	3 3/8	3 1/8	5 7/8	9	Brian J. Fagg	Brian J. Fagg	Eureka Co., NV	2002	754
84	16 3/8	6 6/8	6 6/8	2 6/8	3	8 6/8	7 1/8	Craig R. Pierce	Craig R. Pierce	Natrona Co., WY	2003	754
83 6/8	16 4/8	6 6/8	6 6/8	2 6/8	2 6/8	6 6/8	12 4/8	Marvin Redburn	Marvin Redburn	Coconino Co., AZ	1950	842
83 6/8	17	6 4/8	6 4/8	3	2 5/8	4 2/8	13	John T. Yarrington	John T. Yarrington	Sheridan Co., WY	1951	842
83 6/8	16	7 1/8	6 6/8	3 3/8	3 2/8	1	12 7/8	Bob Herbison	Bob Herbison	Saratoga Co., WY	1955	842
83 6/8	16 3/8	6 6/8	6 7/8	3	3	9 4/8	12 6/8	Max Durfee	Max Durfee	Chino Valley, AZ	1960	842
83 6/8	16 4/8	7	7 1/8	2 7/8	2 7/8	11	10 2/8	Bernie Wanhanen	Bernie Wanhanen	Plainview, SD	1960	842
83 6/8	16 1/8	6 6/8	6	2 6/8	2 5/8	8 6/8	10 4/8	Robert F. Ziker	Robert F. Ziker	Poison Spider, WY	1960	842
83 6/8	15 4/8	6	6 6/8	2 5/8	2 7/8	8 3/8	15 6/8	C.J. Adair	C.J. Adair	Yavapai Co., AZ	1961	842
83 6/8	16 7/8	6 4/8	6 3/8	2 7/8	2 5/8	6 3/8	10 6/8	Dave Blair	Dave Blair	Williams Co., AZ	1961	842
83 6/8	16 6/8	6 3/8	7	3	3 1/8	10 6/8	10 7/8	Jim Perry	Jim Perry	Hudspeth Co., TX	1963	842
83 6/8	17 5/8	7 2/8	7 2/8	3	3	6 7/8	8 6/8	Donald G. Gebers	Donald G. Gebers	Alcova, WY	1964	842
83 6/8	15 7/8	7	6 6/8	2 5/8	2 5/8	10 7/8	8 3/8	Basil C. Bradbury	Basil C. Bradbury	Hudspeth Co., TX	1966	842
83 6/8	15 6/8	6 5/8	6 2/8	2 6/8	2 6/8	5 6/8	10 3/8	Dale E. Beattie	Dale E. Beattie	Meridian, OR	1967	842
83 6/8	18 4/8	6 2/8	6 3/8	2 6/8	2 6/8	6 1/8	11 7/8	Ron Vandiver	Ron Vandiver	Motley Co., TX	1967	842
83 6/8	16 6/8	6 3/8	6 5/8	2 6/8	2 6/8	6 7/8	7 7/8	George M. Lewis	George M. Lewis	Black Tank, AZ	1968	842
83 6/8	15	6 5/8	6 3/8	3	3	8 3/8	10	R.L. Brown, Jr.	R.L. Brown, Jr.	Sweetwater Co., WY	1970	842
83 6/8	15 6/8	7 2/8	7	3	2 5/8	5 6/8	13 4/8	Dennis E. Carter	Dennis E. Carter	Lake Co., OR	1972	842
83 6/8	15 1/8	7	7 2/8	2 5/8	2 5/8	4 1/8	9 3/8	Betty J. Oliver	Betty J. Oliver	Sweetwater Co., WY	1974	842
83 6/8	14 4/8	6 5/8	6 5/8	2 7/8	2 6/8	11 2/8	14 2/8	Leslie Banford	Leslie Banford	Divide, SK	1975	842
83 6/8	16 2/8	6 4/8	6 4/8	2 2/8	2 1/8	7 4/8	10 6/8	Don F. Holt	D.F. & T. Holt	Park Co., WY	1975	842

PRONGHORN

Antilocapra americana and related subspecies

Score	Length of Horn R	L	Circumference of Base R	L	Circumference at Third Quarter R	L	Inside Spread	Tip to Tip Spread	Length of Prong R	L	Locality	Hunter	Owner	Date Killed	Rank
83 6/8	15 4/8	16	7 1/8	7 1/8	2 6/8	2 6/8	11 4/8	7	5 5/8	5 4/8	Sweetwater Co., WY	Dennis D. Seipp	Dennis D. Seipp	1975	842
83 6/8	16 6/8	16 6/8	6 4/8	6 1/8	2 6/8	2 6/8	7 1/8	2	6 4/8	6 4/8	Modoc Co., CA	William B. Steig	William B. Steig	1977	842
83 6/8	16 6/8	17 4/8	6 4/8	6 3/8	2 5/8	2 6/8	11 6/8	7 7/8	6 3/8	6 1/8	Wamsutter, WY	James A. White	James A. White	1980	842
83 6/8	15 4/8	14 7/8	7 5/8	7 4/8	2 7/8	2 6/8	9 2/8	6	5 5/8	5 4/8	Carbon Co., WY	Jack F. Schakel	Jack F. Schakel	1981	842
83 6/8	16 1/8	16 4/8	6 7/8	6 4/8	2 4/8	2 4/8	9 1/8	5 6/8	6 1/8	6 3/8	Humboldt Co., NV	Harold J. Ward	Harold J. Ward	1981	842
83 6/8	14 7/8	15 2/8	6 2/8	6 3/8	2 6/8	3	6 5/8	3 1/8	5	4 5/8	Washoe Co., NV	Robert A. Colon	Robert A. Colon	1982	842
83 6/8	16 3/8	16 7/8	6 2/8	6 1/8	2 6/8	2 6/8	8 5/8	2	6	6 5/8	Lincoln Co., NM	James R. Doverspike	James R. Doverspike	1982	842
83 6/8	15	15 1/8	6 7/8	6 6/8	2 6/8	2 7/8	10 2/8	6 6/8	6 6/8	6 2/8	Big Horn Co., MT	Michael Ferri	Michael Ferri	1982	842
83 6/8	17 2/8	16 3/8	6 6/8	6 6/8	2 5/8	2 3/8	7 1/8	2 5/8	6 4/8	6 1/8	Natrona Co., WY	Ronald K. Morrison	Ronald K. Morrison	1982	842
83 6/8	15 7/8	15 7/8	6 6/8	6 6/8	2 3/8	2 3/8	12 5/8	11	6 5/8	6 4/8	Sweetwater Co., WY	Robert Gilbert	Robert Gilbert	1983	842
83 6/8	16 2/8	16 5/8	7	6 6/8	2 5/8	2 5/8	12 6/8	8 4/8	5 6/8	5 5/8	Carbon Co., WY	Douglas L. Hancock	Douglas L. Hancock	1983	842
83 6/8	15 6/8	15 7/8	6 2/8	6 2/8	2 5/8	2 7/8	11	7 6/8	6	6 1/8	Jackson Co., CO	Cylestine A. Manguso	Cylestine A. Manguso	1983	842
83 6/8	16	16	7 4/8	7 5/8	2 3/8	2 4/8	15 5/8	11 6/8	5 6/8	6 3/8	Lake Co., OR	Barbara J. Smallwood	Barbara J. Smallwood	1983	842
83 6/8	16 1/8	16 1/8	6 4/8	6 3/8	2 6/8	2 6/8	12 7/8	9 6/8	6 2/8	6	Millard Co., UT	Arthur L. Biggs	Arthur L. Biggs	1984	842
83 6/8	15 6/8	16 1/8	6 6/8	6 5/8	3	2 5/8	12	7 2/8	5 2/8	5 1/8	Colfax Co., NM	Mitchell S. Bastian	Mitchell S. Bastian	1985	842
83 6/8	16 7/8	17	6 3/8	6 4/8	3	3	10 6/8	5 6/8	5	5 1/8	Catron Co., NM	Stephen C. LeBlanc	Stephen C. LeBlanc	1985	842
83 6/8	16 1/8	15 7/8	6 5/8	6 4/8	2 5/8	2 4/8	15 2/8	5 6/8	6 3/8	6	Colfax Co., NM	Charles A. Grimmett	Charles A. Grimmett	1986	842
83 6/8	15 4/8	15 4/8	7 3/8	7 4/8	2 4/8	2 2/8	13 1/8	9 6/8	6 2/8	5 6/8	Colfax Co., NM	LeGrand C. Kirby III	LeGrand C. Kirby III	1986	842
83 6/8	16 6/8	16 5/8	6 4/8	6 4/8	2 6/8	2 6/8	13 3/8	10	5 4/8	5 2/8	De Baca, NM	Ben L. Mueller	Ben L. Mueller	1986	842
83 6/8	14 7/8	15	6 5/8	6 5/8	2 6/8	2 7/8	9 4/8	7 7/8	6 2/8	6 6/8	Fremont Co., WY	Carl N. Anderson	Carl N. Anderson	1987	842
83 6/8	14 3/8	14 3/8	7 5/8	7 5/8	2 7/8	2 6/8	7	3 3/8	5 7/8	5 7/8	Carbon Co., WY	Thomas D. Widiker	Thomas D. Widiker	1987	842
83 6/8	15 7/8	15 7/8	6 4/8	6 3/8	3 1/8	3	9 6/8	3 5/8	5 7/8	6	Hudspeth Co., TX	A. Alan Griffin	A. Alan Griffin	1988	842
83 6/8	16 3/8	16 3/8	6 4/8	6 4/8	2 4/8	2 4/8	9 1/8	4 3/8	5 6/8	6 4/8	Harney Co., OR	Lyle W. Crawford	Lyle W. Crawford	1990	842
83 6/8	16 2/8	16 3/8	7	7 1/8	2 5/8	2 6/8	10 2/8	5 3/8	5 3/8	5 4/8	Harney Co., OR	John S. Hansen	John S. Hansen	1990	842
83 6/8	17	17 2/8	6 6/8	6 6/8	3 1/8	3	16	11 4/8	4 5/8	4 1/8	Washoe Co., NV	P.D. Kiser	P.D. Kiser	1990	842
83 6/8	15 4/8	15 2/8	7 2/8	6 6/8	2 3/8	2 3/8	13 4/8	10	5 5/8	5 6/8	Yavapai Co., AZ	Michael J. Rusing	Michael J. Rusing	1990	842
83 6/8	15 1/8	15	6 5/8	6 5/8	2 5/8	2 5/8	6	1 5/8	6 5/8	6 4/8	Fremont Co., WY	Stuart W. Shepherd	Stuart W. Shepherd	1990	842
83 6/8	16 4/8	16 6/8	6 5/8	6 5/8	2 4/8	2 4/8	9 6/8	6	5 6/8	5 7/8	Carbon Co., WY	Rod F. Waeckerlin	Rod F. Waeckerlin	1990	842
83 6/8	15 7/8	16	6 3/8	6 1/8	2 6/8	2 6/8	11 4/8	6 7/8	5 6/8	6 2/8	Yavapai Co., AZ	Roland J. Chooljian	Roland J. Chooljian	1991	842
83 6/8	17 1/8	17 3/8	6	6 1/8	3 2/8	2 7/8	9 5/8	4 3/8	5 2/8	5 4/8	Socorro Co., NM	William W. Klein	William W. Klein	1991	842
83 6/8	16 7/8	16 7/8	6 4/8	6 4/8	2 7/8	3	11 7/8	7	5 2/8	5	Humboldt Co., NV	Sam Lair	Sam Lair	1991	842
83 6/8	16 4/8	16 6/8	6 3/8	6 3/8	3	3	13 6/8	10	5	5 1/8	Mora Co., NM	Brody J. Bonnett	Brody J. Bonnett	1992	842
83 6/8	15 2/8	15 2/8	6 5/8	6 5/8	3 1/8	3	9	5 4/8	6	6 5/8	Rosebud Co., MT	William E. Butler	William E. Butler	1992	842
83 6/8	16 1/8	16 1/8	6 4/8	6 4/8	3 1/8	3	13 5/8	13 6/8	5 4/8	5 6/8	Yavapai Co., AZ	Jerry T. Harper	Jerry T. Harper	1992	842
83 6/8	15 6/8	15 5/8	6 7/8	6 6/8	2 4/8	2 4/8	10 4/8	5 7/8	6 2/8	6 2/8	Lake Co., OR	Brian R. Hayes	Brian R. Hayes	1992	842
83 6/8	16 6/8	16 5/8	6 6/8	6 6/8	2 6/8	2 6/8	9 5/8	4 1/8	5	4 7/8	Carbon Co., WY	John T. Johnson	John T. Johnson	1992	842
83 6/8	16 6/8	16 7/8	6 1/8	6 1/8	2 5/8	2 5/8	10 6/8	6	5 6/8	5 5/8	Mora Co., NM	Edward C. Joseph	Edward C. Joseph	1992	842
83 6/8	17	17	6 4/8	6 3/8	2 7/8	2 6/8	10 3/8	5 3/8	5 4/8	5 4/8	Campbell Co., WY	Loy D. Peters	Loy D. Peters	1992	842

Score	Length R	Length L	Circ. Base R	Circ. Base L	D3	D4	Prong/Spread	Prong/Spread	D7	D8	D9	Locality	Hunter	Owner	Date	Rank
83 6/8	16 3/8	16 3/8	6 6/8	6 6/8	2 4/8	6 6/8	14	10 7/8	2 4/8	5 7/8	5 6/8	Hot Springs Co., WY	Robert J. Ruiz	Robert J. Ruiz	1992	842
83 6/8	16 2/8	16 4/8	7	7	2 4/8	7	9 4/8	3 3/8	2 4/8	6 2/8	6 3/8	Sublette Co., WY	Delores Ball	Delores Ball	1993	842
83 6/8	15 4/8	15 4/8	6 6/8	6 6/8	2 7/8	6 6/8	14 2/8	11 4/8	2 7/8	6 1/8	6 2/8	Mora Co., NM	Richard E. Joseph	Richard E. Joseph	1993	842
83 6/8	16 4/8	16 4/8	6	6	2 6/8	6	10 1/8	6 4/8	2 6/8	6 7/8	6 4/8	Malheur Co., OR	Kenneth L. Barstad	Kenneth L. Barstad	1994	842
83 6/8	15 5/8	15 5/8	8	8	3 2/8	8	10 6/8	8 1/8	3 2/8	4 7/8	4 2/8	Jackson Co., CO	Stephen H. Porter	Stephen H. Porter	1994	842
83 6/8	16 5/8	16 5/8	7 3/8	7 3/8	2 3/8	7 3/8	14 4/8	10 4/8	2 3/8	5	4 4/8	Socorro Co., NM	John W. Bishop	John W. Bishop	1995	842
83 6/8	16 4/8	16 4/8	6 6/8	6 6/8	2 5/8	6 5/8	10 3/8	4 3/8	2 5/8	6 3/8	6 3/8	Natrona Co., NM	Miles B. Bundy	Miles B. Bundy	1996	842
83 6/8	17	17	6 7/8	6 7/8	2 4/8	6 7/8	11 3/8	4 3/8	2 4/8	6	6	Rosebud Co., MT	Douglas B. Colombik	Douglas B. Colombik	1996	842
83 6/8	16 7/8	16 6/8	6 3/8	6 3/8	3	6 3/8	11 5/8	7 7/8	3	5 7/8	5 4/8	Hudspeth Co., TX	James N. Gallagher, Jr.	James N. Gallagher, Jr.	1996	842
83 6/8	16 1/8	16 1/8	6 7/8	6 7/8	3 1/8	6 7/8	11 7/8	11 7/8	3 1/8	5 1/8	5 2/8	Socorro Co., NM	Ilynn Guldman	Ilynn Guldman	1996	842
83 6/8	16	16	7	7	2 4/8	7	13 6/8	7 1/8	2 4/8	5 5/8	5 3/8	Fremont Co., WY	Roger L. McCosker	Roger L. McCosker	1997	842
83 6/8	16 5/8	16 5/8	6 5/8	6 5/8	2 7/8	6 5/8	11 3/8	3 3/8	2 4/8	5 6/8	5 4/8	Lincoln Co., NM	G. Todd Ralstin	G. Todd Ralstin	1997	842
83 6/8	16 3/8	16 2/8	6 6/8	6 6/8	2 7/8	6 6/8	6 7/8	1 4/8	2 7/8	5 4/8	5 3/8	Humboldt Co., NV	Terry D. Scott	Terry D. Scott	1997	842
83 6/8	16 5/8	16 5/8	7	7	2 6/8	7	8	3	2 7/8	6	5 7/8	Sioux Co., NE	Moses Martinez	Moses Martinez	1998	842
83 6/8	15 4/8	15 7/8	5 7/8	5 7/8	2 5/8	5 7/8	18 4/8	15 5/8	2 6/8	5 3/8	5 4/8	Washakie Co., WY	Kevin P. Salzman	Kevin P. Salzman	1999	842
83 6/8	15 5/8	15 4/8	7 4/8	7 4/8	3 1/8	7 4/8	10 1/8	6 1/8	3 1/8	5 4/8	5 4/8	Carbon Co., WY	Larry S. Hicks	Larry S. Hicks	2000	842
83 6/8	16 6/8	16 6/8	7	7	2 7/8	7	10 7/8	6 1/8	3	6	6	Socorro Co., NM	Ken A. Kuhn	Ken A. Kuhn	2000	842
83 6/8	15 6/8	15 6/8	6 6/8	6 6/8	2 6/8	6 6/8	10	10	2 7/8	5 7/8	5 7/8	Hudspeth Co., TX	Brandon D. McBride	Brandon D. McBride	2000	842
83 6/8	16 1/8	16 1/8	6 4/8	6 4/8	3 1/8	6 4/8	3 4/8	4 3/8	3 1/8	6	5 7/8	Socorro Co., NM	Steve K. Scharf	Steve K. Scharf	2000	842
83 6/8	17 5/8	17 6/8	6 3/8	6 5/8	2 7/8	6 3/8	5 2/8	3 4/8	2 7/8	6 4/8	6	Catron Co., NM	R. Steve Bass	R. Steve Bass	2001	842
83 6/8	17 1/8	17 3/8	6 4/8	6 4/8	2 5/8	6 4/8	9 2/8	5 2/8	2 5/8	6 1/8	5 7/8	Catron Co., NM	Seth R. Edgar	Seth R. Edgar	2001	842
83 6/8	15 6/8	15 6/8	7	7	2 4/8	7	12 1/8	10 1/8	2 4/8	5 2/8	5 6/8	Socorro Co., NM	Todd A. Romsa	Todd A. Romsa	2001	842
83 6/8	18 7/8	18 6/8	6 6/8	6 6/8	2 5/8	6 6/8	10 4/8	8 3/8	2 5/8	6 3/8	5	Grant Co., NM	H. Hudson DeCray	H. Hudson DeCray	2002	842
83 6/8	17	17	6 2/8	6 2/8	2 4/8	6 2/8	16 2/8	14	2 4/8	5 4/8	4 7/8	Humboldt Co., NV	Victor Marcuerquiaga	Victor Marcuerquiaga	2002	842
83 6/8	15 5/8	15 2/8	6 4/8	6 4/8	2 5/8	6 4/8	9 6/8	11 2/8	2 5/8	5 2/8	5 2/8	Washakie Co., WY	Ronald D. Nelson	Ronald D. Nelson	2002	842
83 6/8	15 6/8	15 6/8	7	7	3 2/8	7	13	5 2/8	2 7/8	5 6/8	5 7/8	Coconino Co., AZ	Mark D. Roggenbuck	Mark D. Roggenbuck	2002	842
83 6/8	16 2/8	16 2/8	6 6/8	6 6/8	2 4/8	6 6/8	5 2/8	9 5/8	2 4/8	6	6	Uintah Co., UT	Timothy K. Krause	Timothy K. Krause	2003	842
83 4/8	17	17	6 4/8	6 6/8	2 7/8	6 4/8	14 1/8	11	2 6/8	6 4/8	6 1/8	Farson, WY	Geo. E. MacGillivray	Geo. E. MacGillivray	1951	926
83 4/8	16 7/8	16 6/8	6 3/8	6 6/8	3 2/8	6 4/8	10 4/8	6 7/8	2 5/8	5 2/8	5 2/8	Miles City, MT	J. Louis Mann	J. Louis Mann	1954	926
83 4/8	18 1/8	18 1/8	6 6/8	6 6/8	3 5/8	6 6/8	16	14 2/8	2 5/8	4 6/8	4 6/8	Arizona	William N. Henry	O. Patton	1956	926
83 4/8	14	14 4/8	7	7	2 5/8	7	10 2/8	5 7/8	2 4/8	5 7/8	6 2/8	Navajo Co., AZ	Mrs. Don Lambert	Mrs. Don Lambert	1961	926
83 4/8	15 6/8	15 6/8	6 4/8	6 4/8	2 5/8	6 4/8	12 5/8	10 1/8	2 4/8	5 1/8	6 2/8	Watford City, ND	Dean Etl	Dean Etl	1964	926
83 4/8	16	16	6 7/8	6 7/8	2 5/8	6 7/8	11 3/8	6 3/8	3 4/8	6 3/8	4 6/8	Shoshoni, WY	Collins F. Kellogg	Collins F. Kellogg	1965	926
83 4/8	15 6/8	15 6/8	7 1/8	7 1/8	2 6/8	7 1/8	10 5/8	5 7/8	3 1/8	5 7/8	6 6/8	Boone Co., CO	Mahlon T. White	Mahlon T. White	1966	926
83 4/8	15 5/8	15 5/8	6 4/8	6 4/8	2 7/8	6 4/8	9 6/8	6 7/8	2 4/8	6 7/8	5 3/8	Wamsutter, WY	Kenneth L. Swanson	Kenneth L. Swanson	1967	926
83 4/8	16 1/8	16 2/8	7 1/8	7	2 6/8	7 1/8	11 1/8	7 1/8	2 4/8	7 1/8	5 4/8	Craig Co., CO	Albert Johnson	Albert Johnson	1969	926
83 4/8	16 2/8	16 2/8	7 1/8	7 1/8	2 4/8	7 1/8	15 4/8	12 2/8	2 5/8	7 1/8	5 7/8	Red Desert, WY	David W. Knowles	David W. Knowles	1970	926
83 4/8	17	17	6 6/8	6 6/8	2 7/8	6 6/8	12	10 1/8	2 5/8	6 6/8	5 1/8	Carbon Co., WY	Billy C. Randall	Billy C. Randall	1970	926
83 4/8	17 1/8	17	6 6/8	6 6/8	2 5/8	6 6/8	15 5/8	10 6/8	2 6/8	6 6/8	5	Hoback Rim, WY	F. Larry Storey	F. Larry Storey	1973	926
83 4/8	17	15 3/8	6 5/8	6 6/8	2 7/8	7	6 2/8	1 3/8	2 7/8	6 5/8	4 5/8	Coconino Co., AZ	Cheryl Alderman	Cheryl Alderman	1974	926
83 4/8	15 3/8	15 3/8	7 2/8	7 2/8	2 4/8	7	8 1/8	2 2/8	2 4/8	2 2/8	5 1/8	Fremont Co., WY	James G. Allard	James G. Allard	1974	926
83 4/8	17 2/8	17 2/8	6 2/8	6 2/8	2 5/8	6 2/8	14 6/8	9 5/8	2 5/8	5 5/8	4 6/8	Coconino Co., AZ	Thomas A. Dunlap	Thomas A. Dunlap	1974	926
83 4/8	16	16	7 4/8	7 4/8	2 7/8	7 4/8	9	3 2/8	2 7/8	5 3/8	5 3/8	Fremont Co., WY	Ruth Muller	Ruth Muller	1974	926
83 4/8	17 3/8	17 3/8	6 4/8	6 3/8	2 5/8	6 4/8	9 5/8	9 5/8	2 6/8	5	5 1/8	Fremont Co., WY	Robert B. Cragoe, Sr.	Robert B. Cragoe, Sr.	1975	926
83 4/8	17	17	6 3/8	6 6/8	2 7/8	6 3/8	10 6/8	6 6/8	2 7/8	6 6/8	6 3/8	De Baca, NM	Glenn C. Conner	Glenn C. Conner	1977	926
83 4/8	16 3/8	16 2/8	6 3/8	6 3/8	2 5/8	6 3/8	9 4/8	3 6/8	2 5/8	5 1/8	4 3/8	Harney Co., OR	Craig Foster	Craig Foster	1977	926
83 4/8	16 4/8	16 4/8	6 5/8	6 6/8	2 5/8	6 5/8	10 4/8	5 3/8	2 5/8	5 2/8	4 7/8	Box Butte Co., NE	Derald E. Morgan	Derald E. Morgan	1977	926
83 4/8	15 3/8	15 3/8	6 3/8	6 1/8	3	6 3/8	10 3/8	6 1/8	3	6 1/8	6	Washoe Co., NV	James R. Cobb	James R. Cobb	1978	926

PRONGHORN

Antilocapra americana and related subspecies

Score	Length of Horn R	L	Circumference of Base R	L	Circumference at Third Quarter R	L	Inside Spread	Tip to Tip Spread	Length of Prong R	L	Locality	Hunter	Owner	Date Killed	Rank
83 4/8	15 2/8	16 1/8	6 6/8	6 5/8	2 5/8	2 6/8	10 2/8	6	6 2/8	6 3/8	Uinta Co., WY	Velma B. O'Neil	Velma B. O'Neil	1978	926
83 4/8	16 6/8	16 7/8	6 6/8	6 5/8	2 5/8	2 5/8	8 6/8	2 4/8	5 5/8	5 5/8	Sweetwater Co., WY	Otis T. Page	Otis T. Page	1978	926
83 4/8	14 6/8	14 7/8	6 3/8	6 3/8	2 3/8	2 2/8	9	3 5/8	7 3/8	7 4/8	Lake Co., OR	Thomas A. Jones	Thomas A. Jones	1980	926
83 4/8	15 4/8	15 5/8	6 6/8	6 7/8	3 1/8	3 1/8	13	10 1/8	5 1/8	5 3/8	Rosebud Co., MT	James D. Cameron	James D. Cameron	1981	926
83 4/8	16 6/8	16 6/8	6 4/8	6 4/8	2 4/8	2 5/8	11 4/8	5 6/8	5 4/8	5 4/8	Custer Co., ID	Wayne L. Coleman	Wayne L. Coleman	1981	926
83 4/8	16 7/8	17	6 6/8	6 5/8	2 7/8	2 6/8	10 3/8	4 6/8	5	5 1/8	Harding Co., SD	John R. Simpson	John R. Simpson	1981	926
83 4/8	17 5/8	17 3/8	6 1/8	6 1/8	2 4/8	2 3/8	6 7/8	0	6 3/8	5 7/8	Natrona Co., WY	Gerald J. Ahles	Gerald J. Ahles	1982	926
83 4/8	17 4/8	17	6 5/8	7 4/8	2 6/8	2 5/8	9 4/8	4 6/8	5	5 2/8	Colfax Co., NM	James H. Hoffman	James H. Hoffman	1982	926
83 4/8	16 4/8	16 6/8	6 4/8	6 3/8	2 3/8	2 3/8	10 1/8	2 7/8	6 4/8	6 2/8	Prairie Co., MT	Vern Lindquist	Vern Lindquist	1982	926
83 4/8	14 1/8	14 2/8	6 5/8	6 5/8	3 2/8	3 2/8	8 5/8	4	6 3/8	6 2/8	Jackson Co., CO	Cynthia L. Welle	Cynthia L. Welle	1982	926
83 4/8	18	18	7	7	3 7/8	3 2/8	9 3/8	6 2/8	4 6/8	3 1/8	Carbon Co., WY	Ronald K. Pettit	Ronald K. Pettit	1983	926
83 4/8	17 3/8	17 4/8	6 4/8	6 4/8	3 2/8	3	13 3/8	11 2/8	4 4/8	4 4/8	Coconino Co., AZ	Duane D. Backhaus	Duane D. Backhaus	1984	926
83 4/8	16 7/8	17	6 4/8	6 4/8	2 5/8	2 5/8	14 1/8	10 2/8	5 4/8	5 5/8	Lake Co., OR	Donald R. Davidson	Donald R. Davidson	1984	926
83 4/8	16 7/8	16 3/8	6 4/8	6 4/8	2 7/8	2 7/8	13 2/8	8 5/8	5 4/8	5 1/8	Yavapai Co., AZ	Glenn E. Leslie, Jr.	Glenn E. Leslie, Jr.	1984	926
83 4/8	17 5/8	17	6	6	2 6/8	2 7/8	10 7/8	8	5 3/8	5	Coconino Co., AZ	Arthur A. Smith	Arthur A. Smith	1984	926
83 4/8	16 4/8	16 5/8	6 1/8	6	3 2/8	3 2/8	12 4/8	9 1/8	5 2/8	5 2/8	Mora Co., NM	Brent Arrant	Brent Arrant	1986	926
83 4/8	17 3/8	17 4/8	6 3/8	6 3/8	2 7/8	2 7/8	8 4/8	1 6/8	4 6/8	4 6/8	Foremost, AB	Brian J. Gathercole	Brian J. Gathercole	1988	926
83 4/8	16 3/8	16 2/8	6 1/8	6 1/8	2 6/8	2 6/8	16 1/8	13 7/8	6	6	Wildhorse, AB	Ralph L. Cervo	Ralph L. Cervo	1989	926
83 4/8	16 5/8	16 5/8	6 4/8	6 5/8	2 6/8	2 6/8	9	3 6/8	5 1/8	5 3/8	Colfax Co., NM	David M. Lackie	David M. Lackie	1989	926
83 4/8	15 3/8	15 5/8	7	6 6/8	2 3/8	2 4/8	11 6/8	7 2/8	6	6 3/8	Sweetwater Co., WY	Charles R. Monroe	Charles R. Monroe	1989	926
83 4/8	17 2/8	17 2/8	6 2/8	6 2/8	2 6/8	2 6/8	10	4 3/8	6	5 2/8	Maple Creek, SK	Lynn P. Needham	Lynn P. Needham	1989	926
83 4/8	15 7/8	15 6/8	6 3/8	6 3/8	2 5/8	2 5/8	10 2/8	6 4/8	7	6 3/8	Carbon Co., UT	John R. Stevens	John R. Stevens	1989	926
83 4/8	15 5/8	16	6 5/8	6 4/8	2 6/8	2 6/8	15 5/8	12 4/8	5 7/8	5 2/8	Colfax Co., NM	Louie Alcon	Louie Alcon	1990	926
83 4/8	15 2/8	15 4/8	6 7/8	6 7/8	2 7/8	2 7/8	10 7/8	7 7/8	6 2/8	6 2/8	Sublette Co., WY	Heath Harrower	Heath Harrower	1990	926
83 4/8	15 6/8	15 5/8	6 6/8	6 7/8	2 4/8	2 4/8	15 5/8	12 4/8	6 3/8	6 3/8	Socorro Co., NM	Michael T. Miller	Michael T. Miller	1990	926
83 4/8	15 6/8	15 6/8	7	7	2 7/8	2 7/8	8 5/8	3 2/8	5 5/8	5 5/8	Moffat Co., CO	Brad A. Winder	Brad A. Winder	1990	926
83 4/8	16 7/8	16 7/8	5 4/8	5 5/8	2 6/8	2 5/8	9 3/8	4 5/8	6 2/8	6 4/8	Custer Co., ID	Michael J. Felton	Michael J. Felton	1991	926
83 4/8	16 1/8	15 6/8	6	6 1/8	3	2 6/8	10 2/8	5 1/8	4 7/8	5 2/8	Butte Co., ID	Sandie L. Goodson	Sandie L. Goodson	1991	926
83 4/8	16 4/8	16 6/8	6 2/8	6 1/8	2 4/8	2 4/8	8 7/8	3 2/8	6	6	Hudspeth Co., TX	Carl H. Green	Carl H. Green	1991	926
83 4/8	16 3/8	16 4/8	6 5/8	6 5/8	2 4/8	2 4/8	9 7/8	4 5/8	6 1/8	6 1/8	Moffat Co., CO	Rodney R. Hall, Jr.	Rodney R. Hall, Jr.	1991	926
83 4/8	18 3/8	18	5 7/8	6	2 4/8	2 4/8	10 3/8	8 4/8	6	5 6/8	Hudspeth Co., TX	Eduardo Padilla	Eduardo Padilla	1991	926
83 4/8	16 4/8	16 4/8	6 4/8	6 4/8	2 5/8	2 6/8	11 7/8	6 5/8	5 5/8	5 4/8	Elko Co., NV	Eugene E. Schain	Eugene E. Schain	1991	926
83 4/8	17 3/8	17 2/8	6 5/8	6 4/8	2 5/8	2 3/8	10	5	5 4/8	5 4/8	Humboldt Co., NV	William J. Swartz, Jr.	William J. Swartz, Jr.	1991	926
83 4/8	17 2/8	17 3/8	6	6	2 4/8	2 4/8	8 6/8	3 3/8	5 3/8	5 2/8	Socorro Co., NM	Randy W. Tonkin	Randy W. Tonkin	1991	926
83 4/8	15 7/8	16	6 6/8	7	3	3	14 7/8	11 5/8	6	5 2/8	Mora Co., NM	Jeffrey D. Warren	Jeffrey D. Warren	1991	926
83 4/8	17 3/8	16 7/8	6 3/8	6 3/8	2 3/8	2 2/8	8	4 7/8	6 3/8	6 4/8	Washoe Co., NV	Robert J. Cornelius	Robert J. Cornelius	1992	926
83 4/8	14 5/8	14 7/8	7 2/8	7 2/8	2 7/8	3	6 3/8	2 3/8	5 4/8	5 4/8	Carter Co., MT	Angelo J. Feroleto	Angelo J. Feroleto	1992	926
83 4/8	16 6/8	16 1/8	6 3/8	6 2/8	3	3	9 6/8	6	6 3/8	5 4/8	Hudspeth Co., TX	Ray O. Herzog	Ray O. Herzog	1992	926

Score	L. Horn R	L. Horn L	Circ. Base R	Circ. Base L	Circ. 3rd Qtr R	Circ. 3rd Qtr L	Inside Spread	Prong R	Prong L	Locality	Hunter	Owner	Date	Rank
83 4/8	17 5/8	17 5/8	6 3/8	6 3/8	2 5/8	2 6/8	12	6 7/8	5	Otero Co., NM	Harold W. Lisby	Harold W. Lisby	1992	926
83 4/8	14 3/8	14 4/8	7 4/8	7 1/8	2 5/8	2 5/8	13 4/8	12 1/8	6 2/8	Natrona Co., WY	Jerry A. Stoll	Jerry A. Stoll	1992	926
83 4/8	15 2/8	15 2/8	6 7/8	6 7/8	3 5/8	3 6/8	10 4/8	9 5/8	5	Weld Co., CO	Delmar C. Brewer	Delmar C. Brewer	1993	926
83 4/8	14 5/8	15	7	7	2 5/8	2 6/8	9 4/8	7	6 2/8	Sweetwater Co., WY	Keith A. Dana	Keith A. Dana	1994	926
83 4/8	15 7/8	16 2/8	6 5/8	6 5/8	3 1/8	2 6/8	8 3/8	1 6/8	5	Yavapai Co., AZ	Michael K. Giboney	Michael K. Giboney	1994	926
83 4/8	15 6/8	16	6 2/8	6 2/8	2 2/8	2 3/8	17	15	6 1/8	Washoe Co., NV	Thomas V. Guio	Thomas V. Guio	1994	926
83 4/8	15 6/8	16	5 7/8	6	3	3	10 1/8	5 3/8	6 1/8	Colfax Co., NM	Mark B. Henkel	Mark B. Henkel	1994	926
83 4/8	16 2/8	17 1/8	7	7 1/8	2 4/8	2 5/8	11 5/8	7 6/8	6 3/8	Lassen Co., CA	Jason W. Langslet	Jason W. Langslet	1995	926
83 4/8	17 1/8	16 6/8	6 6/8	6 6/8	2 6/8	2 5/8	15 7/8	11 4/8	5 3/8	Uintah Co., UT	Ben Dattage	Alan L. Dattage	1995	926
83 4/8	16 3/8	16 1/8	6 3/8	6 3/8	2 5/8	2 6/8	17 1/8	14 1/8	5 6/8	Washakie Co., WY	Chad D. Heiser	Chad D. Heiser	1995	926
83 4/8	17 1/8	16 4/8	6 4/8	6 4/8	2 3/8	2 3/8	7 6/8	3 2/8	5 4/8	Malheur Co., OR	Tom D. Johansen	Holly Johansen	1996	926
83 4/8	16 4/8	16 3/8	6 3/8	7	3	3	16 3/8	14 6/8	4 6/8	Navajo Co., AZ	Christopher H. Sipe	Christopher H. Sipe	1997	926
83 4/8	17 2/8	16 4/8	6 3/8	6 4/8	2 4/8	2 5/8	11 5/8	5 1/8	5 3/8	Socorro Co., NM	Holley W. Lacey	Holley W. Lacey	1997	926
83 4/8	16	16	6 4/8	6 3/8	2 7/8	2 5/8	11 4/8	7 2/8	5 3/8	Hudspeth Co., TX	Harold W. Hahn	Harold W. Hahn	1997	926
83 4/8	18 2/8	18 2/8	5 7/8	6	2 6/8	3	10 1/8	3 2/8	4 3/8	Hudspeth Co., TX	Thomas C. Merritt	Thomas C. Merritt	1998	926
83 4/8	15 5/8	15 5/8	6 6/8	6 6/8	2 6/8	2 7/8	9 1/8	3 6/8	6	Chaves Co., NM	Ben H. Ralston	Ben H. Ralston	1998	926
83 4/8	16 7/8	15 5/8	5 7/8	5 7/8	2 4/8	2 4/8	12 6/8	6 4/8	5 6/8	Catron Co., NM	Bill Bray	Bill Bray	1999	926
83 4/8	14 4/8	14 2/8	6 3/8	6 5/8	3 2/8	3	9 6/8	7	4 5/8	Grand Co., UT	Gordon W. Nelson	Gordon W. Nelson	1999	926
83 4/8	15 6/8	15 6/8	7	7	2 5/8	2 5/8	11 2/8	7 5/8	5 2/8	Navajo Co., UT	Thad R. Tucci	Thad R. Tucci	2000	926
83 4/8	16 1/8	16 1/8	7	7	3	2 5/8	9 1/8	3 5/8	5 3/8	Lincoln Co., NM	Bob Nicholas	Bob Nicholas	2000	926
83 4/8	16 4/8	16 3/8	6 3/8	6 3/8	2 4/8	2 6/8	8 5/8	5 2/8	6 3/8	Carbon Co., WY	Rita K. Pettit	Rita K. Pettit	2000	926
83 4/8	14 6/8	14 6/8	6 7/8	7	2 6/8	2 6/8	14 3/8	12 1/8	6 2/8	Fremont Co., WY	Patrick D. Austin	Patrick D. Austin	2000	926
83 4/8	16 1/8	16	6 6/8	6 7/8	3 1/8	2 6/8	13	9 5/8	4 7/8	Carbon Co., WY	Dale Hislop	Dale Hislop	2000	926
83 4/8	15 3/8	15 1/8	7 2/8	7 2/8	2 6/8	2 6/8	13 3/8	11 5/8	5 4/8	Moffat Co., CO	Bernard F. Kochevar, Jr.	Bernard F. Kochevar, Jr.	2001	926
83 4/8	15 5/8	15 3/8	6 5/8	6 5/8	2 7/8	2 6/8	13 2/8	11 7/8	4 1/8	Garfield Co., MT	Daniel J. Roberts	Daniel J. Roberts	2001	926
83 4/8	15 4/8	15 5/8	7 1/8	7 3/8	3	3	11 4/8	8 5/8	5 1/8	Mora Co., NM	Pate Stewart	Pate Stewart	2001	926
83 4/8	16	15 6/8	6 3/8	6 3/8	3 1/8	3	13 7/8	11 5/8	5 3/8	Coconino Co., AZ	Kyle L. Wells	Kyle L. Wells	2002	926
83 4/8	15 3/8	15 3/8	7	7	2 4/8	2 6/8	14 3/8	12 3/8	6	Lincoln Co., WY	LaDee N. Allred	LaDee N. Allred	2002	926
83 4/8	15 5/8	15 5/8	6 7/8	6 7/8	2 7/8	2 7/8	7 4/8	5 2/8	5 7/8	Jackson Co., CO	Robert B. Firth, Jr.	Robert B. Firth, Jr.	2003	926
83 4/8	15	14 7/8	7	7 4/8	6 1/8	2 6/8	11	6 1/8	6	Harney Co., OR	Randy Hopp	Randy Hopp	2003	926
83 4/8	15	14 4/8	7	6 7/8	6 7/8	3 4/8	10 6/8	8 7/8	6	Socorro Co., OR	John C. Perkins	John C. Perkins	2003	926
83 4/8	15	15 1/8	7	7	2 6/8	2 6/8	7 2/8	5 3/8	5 7/8	Sweetwater Co., WY	Aaron R. Carlson	Aaron R. Carlson	2003	926
83 2/8	14 7/8	15	6 2/8	6 2/8	3 6/8	3 1/8	9 2/8	3 6/8	5 6/8	Hudspeth Co., TX	James N. Gallagher, Jr.	James N. Gallagher, Jr.	2003	1021
83 2/8	15 3/8	15 3/8	7	7	2 6/8	2 6/8	10 7/8	7 2/8	5 5/8	Uintah Co., UT	J. Todd Hogan	J. Todd Hogan	1951	1021
83 2/8	15 6/8	16	6 7/8	7	2 6/8	2 5/8	15 1/8	11 6/8	4 7/8	Eureka Co., NV	Robert Loveridge	Robert Loveridge	1953	1021
83 2/8	16	16 2/8	6 6/8	6 2/8	3	2 7/8	14 5/8	10 2/8	5 4/8	Coconino Co., AZ	Jeffrey L. May	Jeffrey L. May	1955	1021
83 2/8	16 6/8	17 1/8	6 1/8	7	2 4/8	2 5/8	16 5/8	15 3/8	6	Arminto, WY	Edward H. Bohlin	Edward H. Bohlin	1958	1021
83 2/8	16 1/8	16	6 7/8	6 7/8	2 5/8	2 6/8	12 3/8	10 4/8	4 7/8	Newcastle, WY	Rupert Chisholm	Rupert Chisholm	1961	1021
83 2/8	15 3/8	14 7/8	8 2/8	8 2/8	2 1/8	2 4/8	8 5/8	6 3/8	6 7/8	Campbell Co., WY	Phillip M. Hodge	Phillip M. Hodge	1962	1021
83 2/8	15 5/8	16 1/8	6 3/8	6 3/8	2 5/8	2 3/8	9 5/8	6 4/8	6 5/8	Atlantic City, WY	James S. Kleinhammer	James S. Kleinhammer	1962	1021
83 2/8	15 5/8	15 5/8	6 2/8	6 2/8	2 4/8	2 4/8	5	6 6/8	7 1/8	Jeffrey City, WY	Harry G.M. Jopson	Harry G.M. Jopson	1969	1021
83 2/8	16 3/8	16 3/8	6 5/8	6 5/8	2 7/8	2 7/8	9 6/8	8 1/8	5	Kaycee, WY	R.B. Nienhaus	R.B. Nienhaus	1970	1021
83 2/8	14 7/8	14 7/8	6 2/8	6 2/8	2 5/8	2 5/8	6	6	4 5/8	Fergus Co., MT	Steven G. Ard	Steven G. Ard	1972	1021
83 2/8	16 3/8	16 4/8	6 4/8	6 4/8	2 4/8	3	4 3/8	4 6/8	6	Ferris Mt., WY	Ron Vance	Ron Vance	1972	1021
83 2/8	16 7/8	16 7/8	6 1/8	6 1/8	2 5/8	2 5/8	7 6/8	9 3/8	5 4/8	Capitan, NM	Lee H. Ingalls	Lee H. Ingalls		1021
83 2/8	15 2/8	17	7	7	2 2/8	2 2/8	11 2/8	11 2/8	5	Sweetwater Co., WY	Allen Tanner	Allen Tanner		1021
83 2/8	16 7/8	16 4/8	6 4/8	7 1/8	2 7/8	2 7/8	12 4/8	12 4/8	5 2/8	Coconino Co., AZ	Vernon E. North	Vernon E. North		1021
83 2/8	15 2/8	16 4/8	6 4/8	6 4/8	2 6/8	2 6/8	12	7 4/8	6 4/8	Coconino Co., AZ	Vernon E. North	Vernon E. North	1972	1021
83 2/8	17 1/8	17 1/8	6 5/8	6 6/8	2 4/8	2 3/8	8	2 4/8	5	Washoe Co., NV	David Pohl	David Pohl	1972	1021

PRONGHORN

Antilocapra americana americana and related subspecies

Score	Length of Horn R	L	Circumference of Base R	L	Circumference at Third Quarter R	L	Inside Spread	Tip to Tip Spread	Length of Prong R	L	Locality	Hunter	Owner	Date Killed	Rank
83 2/8	17	17	6 2/8	6 3/8	2 5/8	2 5/8	13 1/8	9 2/8	5 3/8	5 3/8	Culberson Co., TX	James L. Smith	James L. Smith	1972	1021
83 2/8	17 2/8	17 7/8	6 7/8	6 2/8	2 4/8	2 5/8	9 4/8	6 2/8	5	5 4/8	Coconino Co., AZ	Russell Fischer	Russell Fischer	1973	1021
83 2/8	16	16 2/8	6 1/8	6 2/8	2 4/8	2 6/8	11	8 4/8	7 1/8	7 2/8	Carbon Co., WY	Raymond Freitas	Raymond Freitas	1973	1021
83 2/8	16	15 6/8	6 1/8	6 1/8	3	3	8 3/8	5 5/8	5 2/8	5 2/8	Park Co., WY	Dwight Brunsvold	Dwight Brunsvold	1974	1021
83 2/8	16 4/8	16 2/8	6	6 1/8	2 7/8	2 6/8	10 6/8	4 1/8	6 3/8	6 5/8	Rolling Hills, AB	Dennis A. Andrews	Dennis A. Andrews	1975	1021
83 2/8	17 5/8	17 4/8	6 2/8	6 3/8	3 2/8	3 1/8	12 6/8	6 3/8	4 1/8	4 4/8	Yavapai Co., AZ	J. Mike Foley	J. Mike Foley	1975	1021
83 2/8	14 5/8	14 5/8	6 5/8	6 6/8	2 6/8	2 6/8	12 4/8	10	7 2/8	7 6/8	Carter Co., MT	Joseph Henderson	Joseph Henderson	1975	1021
83 2/8	16 3/8	17	6 7/8	7	2 4/8	2 5/8	15 4/8	12 6/8	6 5/8	5 1/8	Yavapai Co., AZ	Ralph Koepke	Ralph Koepke	1975	1021
83 2/8	17	17	6 2/8	6 2/8	2 6/8	2 5/8	15	11 3/8	5 2/8	5 4/8	Coconino Co., AZ	Edmond C. Morton	Edmond C. Morton	1975	1021
83 2/8	14 5/8	14 5/8	7	6 6/8	3 2/8	3 2/8	9 5/8	7 7/8	5 1/8	5 1/8	Jackson Co., CO	James R. Mosman	James R. Mosman	1975	1021
83 2/8	16	16	7	6 7/8	2 5/8	2 5/8	11 6/8	7 5/8	5 5/8	6	Harding Co., SD	Kathleen Prestjohn	Kathleen Prestjohn	1975	1021
83 2/8	15 6/8	15 2/8	6 1/8	6 1/8	2 5/8	2 6/8	11	4 1/8	7 2/8	7 5/8	Medicine Hat, AB	Roger H. Stone	Roger H. Stone	1975	1021
83 2/8	15 6/8	15 6/8	6 4/8	6 4/8	2 7/8	2 7/8	9	2 6/8	5 2/8	5	Cochise Co., AZ	Keith L. Miller	Keith L. Miller	1976	1021
83 2/8	14 6/8	14 6/8	7 1/8	7 1/8	3	3 2/8	13	10 6/8	4 2/8	5 1/8	Goshen Co., WY	William E. Patterson	William E. Patterson	1976	1021
83 2/8	15 2/8	15 2/8	7 1/8	6 6/8	2 7/8	2 7/8	14	10 5/8	6 1/8	6 1/8	Natrona Co., WY	Dean L. Johnson	Dean L. Johnson	1977	1021
83 2/8	15 6/8	16	6 5/8	6 6/8	2 4/8	2 5/8	9 6/8	4 4/8	6 3/8	6	Sweet Grass Co., MT	Dennis E. Moos	Dennis E. Moos	1977	1021
83 2/8	16 1/8	16 1/8	7 2/8	6 7/8	2 6/8	2 6/8	10 7/8	4 6/8	4 6/8	4	Humboldt Co., NV	Charles H.L. McLaughlin	Charles H.L. McLaughlin	1979	1021
83 2/8	17 5/8	17 7/8	6 5/8	6 4/8	2 6/8	2 5/8	15	9 1/8	4 2/8	4 7/8	Socorro Co., NM	Robert E. Stopper	Robert E. Stopper	1979	1021
83 2/8	17 1/8	17 2/8	6 2/8	6 2/8	2 6/8	2 5/8	16 1/8	13	4 6/8	4 7/8	Roosevelt Co., NM	Danny L. Tivis	Danny L. Tivis	1979	1021
83 2/8	16 2/8	16 2/8	6 6/8	6 6/8	2 6/8	2 5/8	8 5/8	5 2/8	5 2/8	5 2/8	Musselshell Co., MT	Caroll M. Lumpkin, Jr.	Caroll M. Lumpkin, Jr.	1980	1021
83 2/8	16 3/8	16 2/8	6 4/8	6 4/8	3	2 5/8	12 1/8	7 2/8	6	6 1/8	Beaverhead Co., MT	Scott Withers	Scott Withers	1980	1021
83 2/8	16	16	7	7	2 7/8	3	10 1/8	5 5/8	5	6 2/8	Natrona Co., WY	Bill E. Boatman	Bill E. Boatman	1981	1021
83 2/8	17 2/8	16 4/8	6 4/8	6 4/8	3 1/8	2 4/8	7 2/8	2 2/8	5 3/8	6	Fremont Co., WY	Benjamin T. Tonn	Benjamin T. Tonn	1981	1021
83 2/8	15 1/8	15 2/8	6 7/8	6 6/8	2 6/8	2 6/8	9 5/8	6 7/8	6	5 7/8	Natrona Co., WY	Andy Van Patten	Andy Van Patten	1981	1021
83 2/8	16 3/8	16 6/8	7 5/8	7 4/8	2 4/8	2 5/8	12 2/8	7 3/8	5 2/8	5 3/8	Harney Co., OR	Gary L. Wilfert	Gary L. Wilfert	1981	1021
83 2/8	17 4/8	17 3/8	6 2/8	6 2/8	3	2 7/8	8	2 4/8	5 1/8	4 6/8	Campbell Co., WY	Dwayne A. Anderson	Dwayne A. Anderson	1982	1021
83 2/8	16 3/8	16 1/8	6 4/8	6 4/8	3 2/8	3 2/8	8 7/8	3 5/8	4 6/8	4 7/8	Brewster Co., TX	Richard T. Delgado	Richard T. Delgado	1982	1021
83 2/8	16 4/8	16 5/8	6 2/8	6	3 2/8	3 3/8	11 5/8	8 1/8	4 7/8	4 7/8	Coconino Co., AZ	Gilbert S. Garside	Gilbert S. Garside	1982	1021
83 2/8	15 2/8	15 2/8	7 4/8	7 4/8	3 1/8	3 1/8	12	11 2/8	4 5/8	5 3/8	Natrona Co., WY	Gary A. Campbell	Gary A. Campbell	1983	1021
83 2/8	16 2/8	16 5/8	6	6	2 6/8	2 7/8	9 1/8	3 5/8	7	6 5/8	Carter Co., MT	Martin Crane	Martin Crane	1983	1021
83 2/8	16 1/8	16 3/8	6 6/8	6 5/8	3	3 1/8	14 3/8	10 1/8	5	5 2/8	Mora Co., NM	James E. Davenport, Jr.	James E. Davenport, Jr.	1983	1021
83 2/8	14 6/8	14 6/8	7 3/8	7 3/8	2 6/8	2 6/8	13 5/8	11 1/8	5 2/8	5 4/8	Lake Co., OR	Clyde L. Dehlinger	Clyde L. Dehlinger	1983	1021
83 2/8	16 4/8	16 2/8	6 6/8	6 6/8	2 2/8	2 2/8	8 6/8	3 4/8	6 6/8	6 2/8	Uinta Co., WY	Earl H. Heninger	Earl H. Heninger	1983	1021
83 2/8	16 6/8	17	6 4/8	6 4/8	2 6/8	2 6/8	9 5/8	3 7/8	5 2/8	5 3/8	Sweetwater Co., WY	Donald W. Kramer	Donald W. Kramer	1983	1021
83 2/8	15 2/8	15 7/8	6 6/8	6 7/8	2 4/8	2 6/8	11 6/8	6 5/8	5 5/8	5 5/8	Lake Co., OR	Richard L. Smith	Richard L. Smith	1983	1021
83 2/8	17 3/8	17 4/8	7	7	2 6/8	2 6/8	12 3/8	7	5 1/8	3 6/8	Apache Co., AZ	Robert A. Stacy	Robert A. Stacy	1983	1021
83 2/8	17 1/8	17 3/8	6 2/8	6 3/8	3	3 1/8	12 4/8	6 6/8	4 5/8	4 6/8	Coconino Co., AZ	Delroy Western	Delroy Western	1983	1021
83 2/8	16 2/8	15	6 6/8	6 4/8	3 3/8	3 1/8	11 4/8	7 3/8	6 1/8	6	Cochise Co., AZ	Jim Tomlin	B&C National Collection	1984	1021

Score	Length of Horn	Circ. Base R	Circ. Base L	Circ. 3rd Qtr R	Circ. 3rd Qtr L	Inside Spread	Tip to Tip Spread	Length of Prong	Locality	Hunter	Owner	Date Killed	Rank
83 2/8	15 6/8	6 2/8	6 2/8	3 2/8	3 3/8	8 5/8	4 5/8	4 7/8	Coconino Co., AZ	Matthew Dominy	Matthew Dominy	1984	1021
83 2/8	17	6 6/8	6 6/8	2 6/8	2 6/8	9 7/8	5	4 7/8	Colfax Co., NM	Stephen C. LeBlanc	Stephen C. LeBlanc	1984	1021
83 2/8	16	6 1/8	6 1/8	3 1/8	3 1/8	14	9 5/8	4 3/8	Lincoln Co., NV	Linda P. Allen	Linda P. Allen	1985	1021
83 2/8	15 3/8	7 1/8	7	3 1/8	3 2/8	15 3/8	4 4/8	4 6/8	Thomas Co., KS	Charles M. Barnett	Charles M. Barnett	1985	1021
83 2/8	18	7	6 4/8	3	2 7/8	10 2/8	4 2/8	6	Cochise Co., AZ	Neil G. Sutherland II	Neil G. Sutherland II	1986	1021
83 2/8	16 5/8	6 3/8	6 4/8	2 7/8	3	9 3/8	4 7/8	4 7/8	Sweetwater Co., WY	Rob M. Knight	Rob M. Knight	1987	1021
83 2/8	17 1/8	6 3/8	6 3/8	3 1/8	2 6/8	10 1/8	5 6/8	5 2/8	Coconino Co., AZ	H. Keith Neitch	H. Keith Neitch	1988	1021
83 2/8	17 2/8	6 2/8	6 2/8	2 6/8	2 4/8	9 6/8	5 6/8	5 5/8	Mora Co., NM	Patrick F. Taylor	Patrick F. Taylor	1988	1021
83 2/8	16 7/8	6	6	2 4/8	2 4/8	13 6/8	4 1/8	3 6/8	Hartley Co., TX	Ernie Davis	Ernie Davis	1989	1021
83 2/8	16	6 2/8	6 2/8	3 1/8	3	11 2/8	5 1/8	5 3/8	Socorro Co., NM	Arthur R. Dubs	Arthur R. Dubs	1989	1021
83 2/8	16	7	7	3	2 7/8	9	5 5/8	5 5/8	Rosebud Co., MT	Anthony J. Emmerich	Anthony J. Emmerich	1989	1021
83 2/8	17 1/8	7 1/8	7	2 7/8	3 3/8	8 4/8	6 1/8	6 2/8	Sweet Grass Co., MT	Daniel Phariss	Daniel Phariss	1989	1021
83 2/8	15 6/8	6 2/8	6 3/8	2 4/8	2 4/8	15 2/8	6	6	Navajo Co., AZ	Ray V. Pogue	Ray V. Pogue	1989	1021
83 2/8	16 3/8	6 2/8	6 1/8	3 1/8	2 7/8	16 5/8	6 3/8	6 2/8	Rosebud Co., MT	Gary M. Van Dyke	Gary M. Van Dyke	1990	1021
83 2/8	15 1/8	6 7/8	6 3/8	2 4/8	2 7/8	10 3/8	7	6	Natrona Co., WY	Dean Albanis	Dean Albanis	1990	1021
83 2/8	14 2/8	6 6/8	6 6/8	2 7/8	2 6/8	6 7/8	1 4/8	4 6/8	Modoc Co., CA	David T. Eveland	David T. Eveland	1990	1021
83 2/8	16 2/8	6 4/8	6 6/8	2 6/8	2 7/8	10 5/8	5 5/8	7	Washoe Co., NV	Steve F. Holmes	Steve F. Holmes	1990	1021
83 2/8	14 5/8	7	6 4/8	2 5/8	2 5/8	9 4/8	4	5 1/8	Uinta Co., WY	John W. McGehee	John W. McGehee	1990	1021
83 2/8	16	7	7	3 4/8	3 2/8	11 4/8	10 5/8	5	Carter Co., MT	Donald W. Mindemann, Jr.	Donald W. Mindemann, Jr.	1990	1021
83 2/8	16 1/8	6 6/8	6 7/8	2 7/8	3	10	6 7/8	4 7/8	Carbon Co., WY	Thomas W. Popham	Thomas W. Popham	1990	1021
83 2/8	16 1/8	7 1/8	7	2 6/8	2 5/8	13 1/8	9 7/8	5 6/8	Natrona Co., WY	Robert B. Poskie	Robert B. Poskie	1990	1021
83 2/8	16 1/8	6 5/8	6 5/8	2 7/8	2 4/8	9 6/8	6 5/8	5 2/8	Carbon Co., WY	Robert H. Ruegge	Robert H. Ruegge	1990	1021
83 2/8	17 1/8	6 6/8	6 6/8	2 7/8	2 5/8	13 2/8	9 5/8	5 7/8	Custer Co., MT	Eric S. Doeden	Eric S. Doeden	1991	1021
83 2/8	15 1/8	6 6/8	6 6/8	3	2 4/8	12 3/8	7 2/8	6 1/8	Albany Co., WY	Shawn E. Dovey	Shawn E. Dovey	1991	1021
83 2/8	17	7	7	2 2/8	2 3/8	10 7/8	10 6/8	6 4/8	Fremont Co., WY	John M. Dunsworth	John M. Dunsworth	1991	1021
83 2/8	16 7/8	6 6/8	6 6/8	2 6/8	2 5/8	11 6/8	6 3/8	5 2/8	Harney Co., OR	Patricia A. Kaiser	Patricia A. Kaiser	1991	1021
83 2/8	16 6/8	6 6/8	7	2 5/8	2 4/8	14 1/8	10 3/8	5 6/8	Colfax Co., NM	Robert J. Seeds	Robert J. Seeds	1991	1021
83 2/8	15 7/8	6 2/8	6 3/8	2 4/8	2 4/8	11 4/8	6 4/8	5 6/8	Mineral Co., NV	Victor Trujillo	Victor Trujillo	1991	1021
83 2/8	15 5/8	6 2/8	6 2/8	2 5/8	3 2/8	9 6/8	6 6/8	6 4/8	Lassen Co., CA	Timothy L. Hartin	Timothy L. Hartin	1992	1021
83 2/8	15 2/8	6 3/8	6 3/8	2 3/8	2 4/8	12 1/8	5 5/8	5 5/8	Natrona Co., WY	Sharnell I. Kamish	Sharnell I. Kamish	1992	1021
83 2/8	17 1/8	7	7	2 4/8	2 4/8	10 2/8	5 2/8	4 5/8	Carbon Co., WY	Kelly L. Sandry	Kelly L. Sandry	1992	1021
83 2/8	17 7/8	6 6/8	6	2 4/8	2 4/8	8 4/8	4 3/8	4 5/8	Apache Co., AZ	R. Steve Bass	R. Steve Bass	1993	1021
83 2/8	14 3/8	6 6/8	6 6/8	2 6/8	2 6/8	11 7/8	6 2/8	6 7/8	Coconino Co., AZ	Benjamin Piper	Benjamin Piper	1993	1021
83 2/8	16 3/8	6 2/8	6 1/8	3 1/8	2 4/8	14 7/8	6 7/8	6 7/8	Apache Co., AZ	Susanne W. Queenan	Susanne W. Queenan	1993	1021
83 2/8	14 2/8	6 4/8	6 4/8	3 6/8	3 6/8	11 5/8	9 7/8	5	Mora Co., NM	Robert J. Seeds	Robert J. Seeds	1993	1021
83 2/8	17	6 6/8	6 6/8	2 4/8	2 4/8	7 6/8	3 6/8	6 2/8	Sage Creek, AB	Leslie C. Wall	Leslie C. Wall	1993	1021
83 2/8	17 6/8	6 7/8	6 7/8	2 5/8	2 5/8	11 5/8	6 5/8	5 5/8	Coconino Co., AZ	Fred F. Brown	Fred F. Brown	1994	1021
83 2/8	15 5/8	6 7/8	6 1/8	2 5/8	2 5/8	12 4/8	9 4/8	5 7/8	Box Elder Co., UT	Larry D. Elliott	Larry D. Elliott	1994	1021
83 2/8	18 1/8	6 6/8	6 7/8	2 5/8	2 5/8	13 6/8	11 3/8	5 7/8	Apache Co., AZ	John W. Whitcombe	John W. Whitcombe	1994	1021
83 2/8	17 4/8	6	6	2 7/8	2 7/8	7 3/8	1 1/8	5 2/8	Colfax Co., NM	Herbert W. Eplee	Herbert W. Eplee	1995	1021
83 2/8	16 7/8	5 6/8	5 6/8	2 4/8	2 4/8	10 2/8	5 1/8	6 1/8	Catron Co., NM	Robert M. Kahute	Robert M. Kahute	1995	1021
83 2/8	16 1/8	6 4/8	6 4/8	2 4/8	2 3/8	14 4/8	10 5/8	6 6/8	Lea Co., NM	W. Don Byers	W. Don Byers	1996	1021
83 2/8	16 6/8	6 3/8	6 3/8	2 7/8	2 5/8	8 2/8	3 4/8	5 6/8	Catron Co., NM	Stephen K. May	Stephen K. May	1996	1021
83 2/8	15 5/8	6 2/8	6 2/8	2 5/8	2 7/8	12 5/8	4 7/8	5 5/8	Albany Co., WY	Felix A. Nieves	Felix A. Nieves	1996	1021
83 2/8	16 4/8	6 7/8	6 7/8	2 7/8	2 6/8	8 2/8	4	5 2/8	Navajo Co., AZ	David W. Pearson	David W. Pearson	1996	1021
83 2/8	16	6 6/8	6 6/8	2 6/8	3	8 6/8	4	5 6/8	Emery Co., UT	Kirk D. Taylor	Kirk D. Taylor	1996	1021
83 2/8	15 7/8	7 1/8	7 1/8	2 5/8	2 7/8	8 4/8	4 1/8	4 6/8	Natrona Co., WY	Gerald M. Schroder	Gerald M. Schroder	1997	1021
83 2/8	18 7/8	6 2/8	6 2/8	2 5/8	2 6/8	11	7	5 2/8	Washoe Co., NV	Terry D. Scott	Terry D. Scott	1998	1021

PRONGHORN

Antilocapra americana americana and related subspecies

Score	Length of Horn R	L	Circumference of Base R	L	Circumference at Third Quarter R	L	Inside Spread	Tip to Tip Spread	Length of Prong R	L	Locality	Hunter	Owner	Date Killed	Rank
83 2/8	15 1/8	15 3/8	7 3/8	7 2/8	2 5/8	3 3/8	13 6/8	13 2/8	5 2/8	5	Jackson Co., CO	Stanley W. Bouse	Stanley W. Bouse	1999	1021
83 2/8	15 3/8	15 4/8	6 3/8	6 2/8	3	2 7/8	11 6/8	8 5/8	6 6/8	6 2/8	Washoe Co., NV	John E. Christensen	John E. Christensen	1999	1021
83 2/8	16 3/8	16 5/8	7	7	2 6/8	2 6/8	8 4/8	5 4/8	6	5 7/8	Albany Co., WY	Gail D. Fibranz	Gail D. Fibranz	1999	1021
83 2/8	15 2/8	14 7/8	7 1/8	6 1/8	2 5/8	2 6/8	10 2/8	6 5/8	6	5 7/8	Carbon Co., WY	Tad W. Marshall	Tad W. Marshall	1999	1021
83 2/8	17	17	6 2/8	6 1/8	2 6/8	3	10 4/8	4 7/8	4 6/8	4 6/8	Mora Co., NM	Daniel K. Sites	Daniel K. Sites	1999	1021
83 2/8	15 6/8	15 5/8	6 6/8	6 6/8	2 7/8	3	13 3/8	14	5 4/8	5 4/8	Socorro Co., NM	Wade A. Boggs	Wade A. Boggs	2000	1021
83 2/8	15 1/8	16 1/8	7 4/8	7 2/8	2 7/8	3	10	4 2/8	5 4/8	6	Socorro Co., NM	Bonnie Cross	Bonnie Cross	2000	1021
83 2/8	16 6/8	16 6/8	6 5/8	6 2/8	2 7/8	2 7/8	8 3/8	2 2/8	5 5/8	5 3/8	Hudspeth Co., TX	Keith R. Eason	Keith R. Eason	2000	1021
83 2/8	16 3/8	17 3/8	6 4/8	6 4/8	2 6/8	2 7/8	7 6/8	3 4/8	4 4/8	4 4/8	Hudspeth Co., TX	Steve Whiteaker	Steve Whiteaker	2000	1021
83 2/8	15 7/8	15 5/8	7 1/8	6 7/8	2 4/8	2 4/8	9 4/8	3 2/8	6 3/8	6	Natrona Co., WY	Justin A. Fernandez	Justin A. Fernandez	2001	1021
83 2/8	15 6/8	15 5/8	7 4/8	7 4/8	2 6/8	2 4/8	12 1/8	8	4 6/8	4 6/8	Colfax Co., NM	Robert D. Jones	Robert D. Jones	2001	1021
83 2/8	16 3/8	16 3/8	6 7/8	6 5/8	2 5/8	2 5/8	12	7 6/8	6 2/8	5 6/8	Coconino Co., AZ	Charles H. Lewis	Charles H. Lewis	2001	1021
83 2/8	17 6/8	18 1/8	5 4/8	5 7/8	2 5/8	2 6/8	12 5/8	7 5/8	6	6 3/8	Red Deer River, AB	Ron Peshke	Ron Peshke	2001	1021
83 2/8	15 1/8	15	7 3/8	7 3/8	2 5/8	2 6/8	8 4/8	3 2/8	4 4/8	4 4/8	Carbon Co., WY	Charles P. Ruzicska	Charles P. Ruzicska	2001	1021
83 2/8	16 6/8	15	6 7/8	6 6/8	2 5/8	2 3/8	11 6/8	7 2/8	5 5/8	5 4/8	Harney Co., OR	Kenneth J. Zander, Jr.	Kenneth J. Zander, Jr.	2001	1021
83 2/8	16 7/8	16 1/8	5 7/8	6	2 3/8	2 4/8	11 6/8	7 1/8	6 2/8	6 6/8	Mineral Co., NV	George C. Mathias, Jr.	George C. Mathias, Jr.	2002	1021
83 2/8	15 4/8	15 5/8	6 1/8	6	3 4/8	3 4/8	10 1/8	7	5 4/8	6	Socorro Co., NM	Thomas J. Murphy	Thomas J. Murphy	2002	1021
83 2/8	15 4/8	15 6/8	6 4/8	6 4/8	2 6/8	2 6/8	9 4/8	3 4/8	5 5/8	5 3/8	Yavapai Co., AZ	John E. Pappas	John E. Pappas	2002	1021
83 2/8	15 6/8	15 7/8	6 4/8	6 4/8	2 3/8	2 5/8	12 2/8	8	6 3/8	6 3/8	Rosebud Co., MT	Todd D. Friez	Todd D. Friez	2003	1021
83 2/8	16 3/8	16 4/8	6 4/8	6 2/8	2 4/8	2 4/8	12 1/8	8	5 3/8	5 3/8	Albany Co., WY	Steven R. Maynard	Steven R. Maynard	2003	1021
83 2/8	17	17	6 2/8	6 2/8	2 6/8	2 5/8	12 5/8	8 1/8	5 7/8	5 4/8	Lincoln Co., NM	Bob Nicholas	Bob Nicholas	2003	1021
83	16 2/8	16 5/8	6 4/8	6 3/8	3 6/8	3	16 2/8	16 4/8	4 1/8	5 1/8	Shirley Basin, WY	Duncan G. Weibel	Duncan G. Weibel	1946	1140
83	15 7/8	15 4/8	7 1/8	7	2 5/8	3	9 1/8	3 1/8	5 5/8	5 4/8	Rawlins Co., WY	Richard Eisner	Richard Eisner	1951	1140
83	15 2/8	15 3/8	6 4/8	6 2/8	3 4/8	3 2/8	11 5/8	7 2/8	5 4/8	5	Hartley Co., TX	William G. Kendrick	William G. Kendrick	1953	1140
83	15 2/8	14 7/8	6 5/8	6 4/8	3	3 1/8	12 2/8	9 1/8	6	5 5/8	Heber, AZ	Grady L. Beard	Grady L. Beard	1954	1140
83	14 4/8	15 2/8	7 6/8	7 2/8	2 2/8	2 4/8	10 4/8	8 7/8	6 2/8	6 4/8	Casper, WY	Tom R. Frye	Tom R. Frye	1954	1140
83	15 2/8	15 1/8	6 5/8	6 4/8	2 5/8	2 5/8	14 6/8	13 4/8	6 5/8	6 2/8	Saratoga Co., WY	Dave Erickson	Dave Erickson	1957	1140
83	16 4/8	16 1/8	6 7/8	6 4/8	3	2 6/8	13 7/8	11 4/8	5 2/8	5 2/8	Rawlins Co., WY	Melvin Birks	Melvin Birks	1960	1140
83	16	16 1/8	6 4/8	6 4/8	2 7/8	2 7/8	11	5 1/8	5 7/8	5 7/8	Lame Deer, MT	G.E. Badgley	G.E. Badgley	1961	1140
83	16 3/8	16 7/8	6 2/8	6 2/8	2 3/8	2 3/8	11	5 7/8	5 6/8	6 1/8	Lake Co., OR	Kenneth Smith	Kenneth Smith	1962	1140
83	15 4/8	15 2/8	7 1/8	7 2/8	2 6/8	3	13 4/8	9 3/8	5 3/8	6 1/8	Plevna, MT	Joseph P. Burger	Joseph P. Burger	1963	1140
83	16 6/8	17 1/8	6 5/8	6 5/8	3	3	14 4/8	13 7/8	5 4/8	4 3/8	Thatcher, CO	M.A. May	M.A. May	1965	1140
83	16 2/8	16 2/8	6 7/8	6 7/8	2 5/8	2 5/8	8 7/8	3 7/8	5 5/8	5 5/8	Boyero, CO	Henry H. Zietz	Henry H. Zietz	1965	1140
83	18 2/8	18 2/8	6 3/8	6 2/8	2 5/8	2 5/8	12 5/8	8 3/8	4 4/8	4 2/8	Navajo Co., AZ	Joseph R. Rencher	Joseph R. Rencher	1970	1140
83	16 3/8	16 2/8	6 6/8	7	3 1/8	3	11	8 5/8	4 6/8	4 4/8	Wamsutter, WY	Marlene Simons	Marlene Simons	1970	1140
83	16 1/8	16 2/8	6 4/8	6 2/8	2 5/8	2 4/8	8 7/8	8	6 4/8	6 5/8	Moffat Co., CO	Michael Coleman	Michael Coleman	1971	1140
83	16	16	6 6/8	6 6/8	2 6/8	2 6/8	13 6/8	10 4/8	5	5	Springer, NM	Ronald E. McKinney	Ronald E. McKinney	1973	1140
83	16	15 5/8	7	7	2 5/8	2 4/8	9	4 2/8	5 7/8	6	Fremont Co., WY	Robert Cragoe, Jr.	Robert Cragoe, Jr.	1974	1140

Score												Locality	Hunter	Owner	Date	Rank
83	16 2/8	16 3/8	6 4/8	6 3/8	6 3/8	3	3	10 2/8	4 1/8	5 6/8	4 6/8	Colfax Co., NM	Jim Hoots	Jim Hoots	1975	1140
83	16 5/8	17	6 3/8	6 3/8	6 3/8	2 5/8	2 5/8	11	6 4/8	5 7/8	6	Yavapai Co., AZ	Artie L. Thrower	Artie L. Thrower	1975	1140
83	17	16 6/8	6 1/8	6 1/8	6 1/8	3	2 7/8	15	9 6/8	4 6/8	5 2/8	Wagon Mound, NM	Dale R. Leonard	Cabela's, Inc.	1976	1140
83	16 2/8	16 2/8	6 3/8	6 2/8	6 2/8	3 3/8	3 2/8	13 5/8	12 5/8	5 2/8	5 2/8	Valley Co., MT	Timothy R. Logan	Timothy R. Logan	1976	1140
83	16 1/8	16 1/8	6 6/8	6 5/8	6 5/8	2 5/8	2 5/8	11 6/8	10 7/8	5 7/8	5 4/8	Harding Co., NM	Stephen C. LeBlanc	Stephen C. LeBlanc	1977	1140
83	16 4/8	16 4/8	6 2/8	6 2/8	6 2/8	2 2/8	2 3/8	11 2/8	7 1/8	6 4/8	6 3/8	Lake Co., OR	Francis G. Dalrymple	Francis G. Dalrymple	1978	1140
83	16	16 1/8	6 4/8	6 4/8	6 4/8	2 6/8	2 5/8	9 5/8	4 2/8	6 1/8	6 4/8	Sweetwater Co., WY	Douglas Grantham	Douglas Grantham	1978	1140
83	16 1/8	16 2/8	7	7 1/8	7 1/8	2 6/8	2 4/8	9 5/8	5	6 1/8	6 2/8	Sublette Co., WY	Kenneth D. Knight	Kenneth D. Knight	1978	1140
83	16 2/8	17 1/8	6 2/8	6 2/8	6 2/8	2 6/8	2 6/8	8 3/8	2 2/8	5 3/8	6 2/8	Sublette Co., WY	Thomas A. Scott	Thomas A. Scott	1978	1140
83	17 1/8	16 1/8	6 4/8	6 4/8	6 4/8	2 6/8	2 7/8	15	14 2/8	5 2/8	5 3/8	Washington Co., CO	Gina R. Cass	Gina R. Cass	1979	1140
83	16 1/8	16	7 5/8	7 5/8	7 5/8	3	2 3/8	14 5/8	10 5/8	5 3/8	5 4/8	Sweetwater Co., WY	Glen W. Coates	Glen W. Coates	1979	1140
83	16 2/8	16 3/8	6 3/8	6 4/8	6 4/8	2 5/8	2 6/8	11 1/8	7 5/8	5 1/8	5 3/8	Custer Co., SD	Edward J. Schauer	Edward J. Schauer	1979	1140
83	16 3/8	16 3/8	5 5/8	5 5/8	5 5/8	2 6/8	2 6/8	8 1/8	1 2/8	4	5 1/8	Hudspeth Co., TX	Ernie Davis	Ernie Davis	1980	1140
83	15 7/8	16	6 4/8	6 4/8	6 4/8	3 1/8	3 2/8	10 1/8	8 5/8	5 7/8	4 2/8	Lake Co., OR	Jerry J. Peacore	Jerry J. Peacore	1980	1140
83	15 6/8	15 5/8	7 3/8	7 3/8	7 3/8	2 4/8	2 6/8	8 1/8	1 7/8	5 6/8	5 7/8	Campbell Co., WY	Keith Penner	Keith Penner	1982	1140
83	15 4/8	15 4/8	6 3/8	6 3/8	6 3/8	3 1/8	3 1/8	7 7/8	4 7/8	5 2/8	5 4/8	Meade Co., SD	Richard S. Alford	Richard S. Alford	1982	1140
83	16 4/8	16 5/8	6 4/8	6 2/8	6 2/8	2 4/8	2 4/8	11 1/8	5 6/8	6 2/8	6 6/8	Washoe Co., NV	Randy A. Cammack	Randy A. Cammack	1982	1140
83	15 7/8	15 7/8	6 7/8	7	7	2 5/8	2 5/8	8 6/8	6 1/8	5 2/8	5 4/8	Albany Co., WY	Richard J. Depaoli	Richard J. Depaoli	1982	1140
83	15 6/8	15 6/8	6 6/8	7	7	2 6/8	2 6/8	9	4 4/8	5 5/8	5 3/8	Humboldt Co., NV	Mark T. Gleason	Mark T. Gleason	1983	1140
83	15 4/8	15 6/8	6 6/8	7	7	2 5/8	2 5/8	10 6/8	4 6/8	5 6/8	5 4/8	Colfax Co., NM	Thomas S. Kelley	Thomas S. Kelley	1983	1140
83	15 7/8	15 7/8	7 2/8	7 1/8	7 1/8	2 6/8	2 6/8	13 6/8	9 3/8	5 6/8	5 4/8	Carbon Co., NM	John W. Ladd	John W. Ladd	1983	1140
83	16	15 7/8	7 1/8	7	7	2 5/8	2 4/8	10 1/8	8 4/8	5 2/8	5 4/8	Box Butte Co., NE	Frederick L. Proffitt II	Frederick L. Proffitt II	1984	1140
83	15 3/8	15 5/8	7	7	7	2 4/8	3	9	7	5 6/8	5 6/8	Jackson Co., CO	Lynda G. Sydow	Lynda G. Sydow	1985	1140
83	12 6/8	13	7	6	6	2 6/8	3 5/8	9 6/8	9 3/8	5 4/8	5 7/8	Fremont Co., WY	Charles J. Cesar	Charles J. Cesar	1985	1140
83	15 6/8	15 1/8	6 6/8	7	7	2 5/8	3	11 7/8	7 7/8	5 6/8	5 6/8	Sweetwater Co., WY	Thomas A. Dremel	Thomas A. Dremel	1985	1140
83	15 5/8	15 5/8	7 1/8	7 1/8	7 1/8	2 6/8	2 7/8	6 6/8	1 2/8	5 4/8	5 6/8	Humboldt Co., NV	Clifford Rockhold	Clifford Rockhold	1986	1140
83	16 5/8	17 1/8	7 1/8	7 1/8	7 1/8	3	2 6/8	15 6/8	13 6/8	4 5/8	4 5/8	Modoc Co., CA	Lenda Z. Azcarate	Lenda Z. Azcarate	1986	1140
83	16 5/8	16 6/8	6 4/8	6 2/8	6 2/8	3	3	11 7/8	7 7/8	5 2/8	5	Manyberries, AB	Richard Bishop	Richard Bishop	1986	1140
83	15 2/8	15 3/8	6 6/8	7	7	2 7/8	2 5/8	13 3/8	10 1/8	5 7/8	5 6/8	Baker Co., OR	Rae E. Cervo	Rae E. Cervo	1986	1140
83	15 5/8	16	7 1/8	7 2/8	7 2/8	2 5/8	2 4/8	13 4/8	10 7/8	4 7/8	5	Natrona Co., WY	Richard R. Mason	Richard R. Mason	1986	1140
83	15 4/8	15 7/8	7 1/8	6 6/8	6 6/8	2 6/8	2 6/8	11 7/8	9 4/8	5 7/8	5 6/8	Catron Co., NM	Gerald Utrup	Gerald Utrup	1987	1140
83	17 2/8	17 5/8	6	6	6	2 4/8	2 4/8	12 6/8	9	5 7/8	5 7/8	Emery Co., UT	Dan L. Harper	Dan L. Harper	1987	1140
83	16 4/8	16 6/8	6 6/8	7	7	2 6/8	2 6/8	10 1/8	6	6 1/8	5 6/8	Albany Co., WY	Dennis G. McElvain	Dennis G. McElvain	1987	1140
83	15 7/8	15 6/8	7	7	7	2 6/8	2 4/8	8 5/8	4 2/8	5 2/8	5 2/8	Washoe Co., NV	Robert J. Miller	Robert J. Miller	1987	1140
83	15 1/8	15	7 1/8	7 1/8	7 1/8	2 5/8	2 6/8	9 3/8	7	5 6/8	5 4/8	Graham Co., AZ	Christopher T. Rores	Christopher T. Rores	1987	1140
83	17 1/8	17	6 4/8	6 4/8	6 4/8	3 2/8	3 2/8	12 1/8	8 6/8	3 7/8	4 4/8	Moffat Co., CO	Marvin R. Selke	Marvin R. Selke	1987	1140
83	17 2/8	16 2/8	6 6/8	6 6/8	6 6/8	2 5/8	2 5/8	11 3/8	9 6/8	5 2/8	5 7/8	Washoe Co., NV	Marvin L. Shepard	Marvin L. Shepard	1987	1140
83	15 4/8	15 2/8	6 4/8	6 2/8	6 2/8	2 5/8	3 1/8	8	3	5 5/8	5	Coconino Co., AZ	Edward J. Smith	Edward J. Smith	1987	1140
83	17	17 4/8	6 2/8	6	6	2 7/8	2 7/8	15 3/8	12 2/8	5 6/8	5 5/8	Sierra Co., NM	Billie F. Bechtel	Billie F. Bechtel	1988	1140
83	17 4/8	17 4/8	6 1/8	6	6	3	3	14 4/8	10	5	4	Washakie Co., WY	Steven A. Berry	Steven A. Berry	1988	1140
83	16 4/8	16 2/8	6 4/8	6 4/8	6 4/8	3 1/8	3 2/8	16 2/8	16 4/8	4 3/8	4 5/8	Fremont Co., WY	Gordon E. Deromedi	Gordon E. Deromedi	1988	1140
83	16	16	6 4/8	6 4/8	6 4/8	2 6/8	2 6/8	14 6/8	11	5 4/8	5 4/8	Jackson Co., CO	Douglas R. Dow	Douglas R. Dow	1988	1140
83	15 6/8	15 6/8	6 6/8	6 7/8	6 7/8	2 3/8	2 6/8	5 4/8	8 4/8	5 6/8	5 2/8	Carbon Co., WY	Douglas A. Weimer	Douglas A. Weimer	1988	1140
83	16 5/8	16	6 3/8	7	7	2 1/8	2 3/8	13 1/8	9 7/8	6 2/8	6 3/8	Sheridan Co., WY	Gary Duggins	Gary Duggins	1989	1140
83	16 5/8	16 3/8	6 5/8	6 3/8	6 3/8	3 5/8	3 1/8	16 2/8	13 7/8	4 7/8	4 5/8	Moffat Co., CO	Tom W. Housh	Tom W. Housh	1989	1140
83	16 4/8	16 4/8	6 5/8	6 4/8	6 4/8	2 5/8	2 5/8	15 7/8	15 3/8	5 4/8	5 2/8	Carbon Co., WY	Mike Wallers	Mike Wallers	1989	1140
83	15 7/8	15 7/8	7 1/8	7 1/8	7 1/8	2 4/8	2 5/8	11 1/8	7 6/8	6	5 7/8	Carbon Co., WY	Robert G. Wimpenny	Robert G. Wimpenny	1989	1140
83	17 1/8	17	6 4/8	6 3/8	6 3/8	2 6/8	2 7/8	13 1/8	8 5/8	5 1/8	4 6/8	Socorro Co., NM	David A. Berry	David A. Berry	1990	1140

Score	Length of Horn R	L	Circumference of Base R	L	Circumference at Third Quarter R	L	Inside Spread	Tip to Tip Spread	Length of Prong R	L	Locality	Hunter	Owner	Date Killed	Rank
83	15 4/8	15 2/8	6 4/8	6 4/8	2 4/8	2 4/8	9 4/8	6	6 7/8	6 4/8	Fremont Co., WY	Tom Covert	Tom Covert	1990	1140
83	16 1/8	15 6/8	7 2/8	7 2/8	3	3 1/8	11 2/8	7	4 3/8	5 2/8	Perkins Co., SD	Dick D. Knock	Dick D. Knock	1990	1140
83	17 4/8	17 4/8	6 3/8	6 1/8	2 6/8	3 1/8	9 3/8	8 1/8	5 3/8	4 6/8	Greenlee Co., AZ	Paul E. Palmer	Paul E. Palmer	1990	1140
83	15 4/8	15 6/8	7	7	2 5/8	2 4/8	9 2/8	6 1/8	5	5 6/8	Mora Co., NM	Gerald W. Pullin	Gerald W. Pullin	1990	1140
83	16 1/8	15 6/8	6 2/8	6 1/8	2 6/8	2 4/8	10 1/8	4	5 7/8	5 6/8	Lincoln Co., NM	Robert M. Rogulic	Robert M. Rogulic	1990	1140
83	16 2/8	16 2/8	6 7/8	6 7/8	3	2 6/8	8 1/8	6	4 5/8	4 4/8	Coconino Co., AZ	Michael L. Allen	Michael L. Allen	1991	1140
83	16 5/8	16 5/8	6 2/8	6 3/8	2 5/8	2 5/8	16 3/8	12 4/8	5 2/8	5 4/8	Otero Co., NM	Steven A. Baldock	Steven A. Baldock	1991	1140
83	14	14 5/8	7	7	2 4/8	2 3/8	10 4/8	7 7/8	6 6/8	6 6/8	Lincoln Co., NM	Johnny Bliznak	Johnny Bliznak	1991	1140
83	16	16	7 3/8	7 3/8	2 3/8	2 5/8	9 3/8	3 4/8	5 7/8	6	Sweetwater Co., WY	Arnold DeCastro	Arnold DeCastro	1991	1140
83	16 3/8	16 2/8	6 4/8	6 4/8	2 5/8	2 5/8	10	5 5/8	5 6/8	5 3/8	Carbon Co., WY	Roger M. Green	Roger M. Green	1991	1140
83	16 2/8	16 4/8	6 6/8	6 5/8	2 6/8	2 7/8	10 7/8	7 3/8	5 3/8	4 7/8	Uinta Co., WY	Florence Kitchel	Florence Kitchel	1991	1140
83	17 2/8	17 1/8	6 1/8	6 2/8	3 1/8	3 1/8	15 2/8	6 2/8	4 4/8	4 4/8	Hudspeth Co., TX	Larry P. Panebaker	Larry P. Panebaker	1991	1140
83	17 4/8	17 2/8	6 4/8	6 6/8	2 6/8	3	12	7 6/8	5	4 7/8	Coconino Co., AZ	Gene Sewell	Gene Sewell	1991	1140
83	17	17 2/8	6 7/8	6 5/8	2 6/8	2 5/8	10 3/8	5 2/8	4 6/8	5 4/8	Carbon Co., WY	Gerald A. Steele	Gerald A. Steele	1991	1140
83	16 1/8	16	6 3/8	6 3/8	2 6/8	2 5/8	12 6/8	9	4 2/8	4 7/8	Lake Co., OR	Wil L. Wilson	Wil L. Wilson	1991	1140
83	15 1/8	15 3/8	7 1/8	7	2 6/8	2 5/8	14	13 4/8	5 5/8	5 3/8	Washoe Co., NV	Joseph A. Burkhamer	Joseph A. Burkhamer	1992	1140
83	16 1/8	15 7/8	7	7 1/8	2 3/8	2 3/8	12	4 2/8	5 6/8	6 4/8	Fremont Co., WY	Milo D. Smith	Marcia Darrow	1992	1140
83	15 6/8	16	6 6/8	6 7/8	2 4/8	2 7/8	10 2/8	6 4/8	5 5/8	5 6/8	Carbon Co., WY	Mark D. Gaines	Mark D. Gaines	1992	1140
83	15 5/8	15 3/8	6 2/8	6 3/8	2 6/8	2 5/8	10 2/8	5 3/8	6 1/8	5 7/8	Juab Co., UT	Alan L. Pfiefer	Alan L. Pfiefer	1992	1140
83	15 3/8	15 2/8	7	7	2 7/8	2 7/8	8	5 4/8	5 7/8	4 7/8	Kimball Co., NE	Mayda M. Zimmerman	Mayda M. Zimmerman	1992	1140
83	16 6/8	16 6/8	6	6	3 1/8	3 1/8	13 5/8	10 6/8	5 2/8	5 2/8	Milk River, AB	Lyle G. Andersen	Lyle G. Andersen	1993	1140
83	16 5/8	16 5/8	6 1/8	6	2 6/8	2 5/8	9 5/8	5 6/8	5 5/8	5 4/8	Colfax Co., NM	W. Douglas Appling	W. Douglas Appling	1993	1140
83	16	16	6 6/8	6 6/8	2 7/8	2 6/8	8 7/8	7 2/8	5 1/8	5	Las Animas Co., CO	Mike R. Caldarella	Mike R. Caldarella	1993	1140
83	15 7/8	15 5/8	6 4/8	6 3/8	2 7/8	2 7/8	10 6/8	6 2/8	5 4/8	5 2/8	Colfax Co., NM	Robert D. Jones	Robert D. Jones	1993	1140
83	16 3/8	17	7 5/8	7 5/8	2 5/8	2 6/8	7 4/8	1 6/8	5 1/8	4 4/8	Weld Co., CO	Gregory A. Peters	Gregory A. Peters	1993	1140
83	15 6/8	15 6/8	6 3/8	6 2/8	2 7/8	2 7/8	9 7/8	5	5 3/8	5 4/8	Mora Co., NM	William J. Smith	William J. Smith	1993	1140
83	15 7/8	16 2/8	7	7	2 5/8	2 5/8	6 3/8	2 4/8	5 3/8	5 3/8	Carbon Co., WY	John L. Anderson	John L. Anderson	1994	1140
83	15 6/8	16	6 1/8	6 1/8	2 6/8	2 7/8	8 1/8	3 3/8	6 6/8	6 6/8	Chouteau Co., MT	Brad Burney	Brad Burney	1994	1140
83	15 7/8	16	6 7/8	6 7/8	3	2 7/8	10 7/8	7 4/8	5 3/8	5 1/8	Humboldt Co., NV	Harvey J. Estes	Harvey J. Estes	1994	1140
83	15 6/8	16	7 1/8	7	2 4/8	2 4/8	12 5/8	9 7/8	5 7/8	5 3/8	Mora Co., NM	Ralph L. Galyan	Ralph L. Galyan	1994	1140
83	16	16	7 2/8	7 1/8	2 6/8	2 6/8	13 4/8	8 6/8	5 2/8	5 6/8	Mora Co., NM	Len H. Guldman	Len H. Guldman	1994	1140
83	15 2/8	14 6/8	7 2/8	7 2/8	2 5/8	2 3/8	8 1/8	5 5/8	6 5/8	6 2/8	Sweetwater Co., WY	William M. Henry III	William M. Henry III	1994	1140
83	16 6/8	16 6/8	6 6/8	6 4/8	2 5/8	2 5/8	12 6/8	9 2/8	6 5/8	5 6/8	Fremont Co., WY	James W. Gibson	James W. Gibson	1995	1140
83	16 4/8	16 5/8	6 1/8	6 2/8	2 7/8	3	9 1/8	4 5/8	5 2/8	5 7/8	Carbon Co., WY	Jeffery K. Harrow	Jeffery K. Harrow	1995	1140
83	15 2/8	15 1/8	7 3/8	7 3/8	2 6/8	2 6/8	11 2/8	10 2/8	5 3/8	5 2/8	Sweetwater Co., WY	David P. Nicholson	David P. Nicholson	1995	1140
83	16 7/8	17 2/8	6 1/8	6 1/8	2 4/8	2 6/8	9 4/8	7	5 2/8	5 3/8	Custer Co., ID	Stanley T. Riddle	Stanley T. Riddle	1995	1140
83	15 2/8	15 6/8	6 7/8	6 7/8	2 5/8	2 5/8	9 1/8	5	5 6/8	5 7/8	Carbon Co., WY	Todd D. Pope	Todd D. Pope	1996	1140
83	15 4/8	15 6/8	6 6/8	7 1/8	2 5/8	3	13 6/8	11 1/8	5 5/8	6	Socorro Co., NM	Len H. Guldman	Len H. Guldman	1997	1140

Score	Length R	Length L	Circ. Base R	Circ. Base L	Circ. 3rd Qtr R	Circ. 3rd Qtr L	Inside Spread	Tip to Tip	Prong R	Prong L	Locality	Hunter	Owner	Date Killed	Rank
83	15 4/8	15 1/8	6 7/8	6 6/8	2 5/8	2 3/8	9 6/8	7 3/8	6 7/8	6 5/8	Carbon Co., WY	John P. Hornbeck	John P. Hornbeck	1997	1140
83	16 3/8	16 1/8	6 7/8	6 6/8	2 5/8	2 4/8	7 4/8	1 4/8	5 1/8	4 7/8	Washoe Co., NV	Carolyn L. Bertoldi	Carolyn L. Bertoldi	1998	1140
83	16	15 7/8	7 1/8	7 2/8	2 5/8	2 4/8	11 1/8	8 7/8	5 3/8	5 3/8	Carbon Co., WY	Chuck Jaure	Chuck Jaure	1998	1140
83	16 5/8	16 3/8	6 4/8	6 4/8	2 6/8	2 6/8	11 2/8	8 1/8	4 7/8	5	Carbon Co., WY	Don E. Perrien	Don E. Perrien	1998	1140
83	16	15 4/8	6 6/8	6 6/8	2 6/8	2 6/8	8	5 3/8	5 7/8	5 7/8	Cascade Co., MT	Henry G. Sivumaki	Henry G. Sivumaki	1999	1140
83	17 2/8	17 3/8	6 3/8	6 3/8	2 7/8	2 6/8	11 2/8	7 1/8	5	4 4/8	Yavapai Co., AZ	Steven A. Bond	Steven A. Bond	1999	1140
83	16 1/8	16	7 1/8	6 7/8	3 1/8	3 1/8	11	6 5/8	6 1/8	5 2/8	Socorro Co., NM	Michael T. Don	Michael T. Don	1999	1140
83	16 5/8	16 3/8	7 1/8	7	2 4/8	2 4/8	12 2/8	6 3/8	6	5 3/8	Harney Co., OR	Ronald C. Garner	Ronald C. Garner	1999	1140
83	16 1/8	15 6/8	6 5/8	6 5/8	2 6/8	2 6/8	11 2/8	7 3/8	6 1/8	5 4/8	Sweetwater Co., WY	Calvin E. Snyder	Calvin E. Snyder	1999	1140
83	14 7/8	15	6 6/8	6 5/8	3	3	9 5/8	2 5/8	6 1/8	6 3/8	Socorro Co., NM	R. Steve Bass	R. Steve Bass	2000	1140
83	15 7/8	17	6 6/8	7 1/8	2 6/8	2 6/8	6 6/8	6 4/8	6 2/8	6	Sweetwater Co., WY	Vic R. Dana	Vic R. Dana	2000	1140
83	17	17	7 1/8	6 6/8	2 5/8	2 5/8	6 6/8	4 2/8	4 3/8	4 5/8	Union Co., NM	Brad DeSaye	Brad DeSaye	2000	1140
83	16 4/8	16 5/8	6 5/8	6 5/8	2 7/8	2 7/8	8 7/8	3 7/8	5	5	Humboldt Co., NV	David A. Hargrove	David A. Hargrove	2000	1140
83	17 1/8	16 7/8	6 5/8	6 4/8	2 6/8	2 6/8	9	9 5/8	5 4/8	4 6/8	Rich Co., UT	Charles A. Lantry	Charles A. Lantry	2000	1140
83	16 4/8	16 5/8	6 5/8	6 5/8	2 6/8	2 6/8	13 5/8	8 2/8	5 3/8	5 1/8	Socorro Co., NM	Michaux Nash, Jr.	Michaux Nash, Jr.	2000	1140
83	15	15 2/8	7 3/8	7 3/8	3	3	11 3/8	5 2/8	4 5/8	4 5/8	Carbon Co., WY	Dorin D. Blodgett	Dorin D. Blodgett	2001	1140
83	15 6/8	15 7/8	6 4/8	6 4/8	2 5/8	2 5/8	9 2/8	5 4/8	6 3/8	6 2/8	Humboldt Co., NV	Jevon W. Ziegler	Jevon W. Ziegler	2001	1140
83	15 7/8	15 4/8	6 1/8	6 3/8	2 4/8	2 4/8	10 6/8	5 6/8	7 2/8	7	Hudspeth Co., TX	Ernie Davis	Ernie Davis	2002	1140
83	15 4/8	15 7/8	6 6/8	6 6/8	2 6/8	2 6/8	11 4/8	5 2/8	6 3/8	7 2/8	Coconino Co., AZ	Ken Goodman	Ken Goodman	2002	1140
83	15 7/8	16 4/8	6 6/8	6 6/8	2 6/8	2 6/8	10 5/8	7 3/8	6 3/8	6 3/8	Harney Co., OR	Mark W. Scott	Mark W. Scott	2002	1140
83	16 2/8	16 3/8	6 2/8	6 3/8	3	3	13	7 7/8	5 6/8	6	Emery Co., UT	Susan Tuttle	Susan Tuttle	2002	1140
83	16 1/8	16 1/8	6 3/8	6 6/8	2 5/8	2 5/8	11 3/8	5 6/8	5 7/8	5 1/8	Carbon Co., WY	William L. Larson	William L. Larson	2003	1140
82 6/8	14 6/8	14 7/8	6 6/8	6 4/8	2 7/8	2 5/8	12 1/8	14 2/8	6 3/8	5 6/8	Natrona Co., WY	G.S. Peterson	Unknown	1948	1265
82 6/8	17 2/8	17	7	7	2 5/8	2 5/8	16 3/8	11 5/8	5 6/8	5 1/8	Navajo Co., AZ	Joe D. Sutton	Joe D. Sutton	1951	1265
82 6/8	15 4/8	15 5/8	5 5/8	5 7/8	2 4/8	2 4/8	12 1/8	14	5	5	Angora, NE	NE Game & Parks Comm.	Harold C. Rusk	1954	1265
82 6/8	16	16 2/8	6 2/8	6 4/8	3 3/8	3 2/8	14 3/8	11	6	5 1/8	Prairie Co., MT	Gordon Spears	Gordon Spears	1954	1265
82 6/8	16 6/8	17	6 4/8	6 4/8	3 2/8	2 6/8	14 2/8	9 1/8	5 4/8	6	Jelm Mt., WY	Guy Murdock	Guy Murdock	1955	1265
82 6/8	15 4/8	15 4/8	6 7/8	6 7/8	2 6/8	2 4/8	11 7/8	3 5/8	6 3/8	5	Glad Valley, SD	D.M. Davis	D.M. Davis	1958	1265
82 6/8	15 2/8	15 2/8	7 2/8	7	2 6/8	2 6/8	10 4/8	9 4/8	6 5/8	5	Butte Co., SD	P.T. Theodore	P.T. Theodore	1958	1265
82 6/8	17 3/8	17 4/8	6	6 4/8	3	3	13 3/8	8 3/8	6 5/8	5 6/8	Yavapai Co., AZ	Vaughan Rock	Vaughan Rock	1959	1265
82 6/8	17 6/8	17 6/8	6 4/8	6 4/8	2 7/8	3 1/8	8 3/8	8 3/8	4 7/8	5 2/8	Gillette, WY	R.R. Kirchner	R.R. Kirchner	1961	1265
82 6/8	14 6/8	14 7/8	7	6 7/8	2 7/8	2 4/8	8 3/8	5 3/8	4	5 7/8	Sweetwater Co., WY	A.L. Bruner	A.L. Bruner	1962	1265
82 6/8	15 6/8	15 6/8	6 7/8	6 7/8	2 6/8	2 7/8	11	5 7/8	6 1/8	6 3/8	Lake Co., OR	Kenneth Smith	Kenneth Smith	1963	1265
82 6/8	16 6/8	16 4/8	6 2/8	6 2/8	2 6/8	2 2/8	11 3/8	8 1/8	6 1/8	6 2/8	Natrona Co., WY	William S. Martin	William S. Martin	1964	1265
82 6/8	15 4/8	15 3/8	6 7/8	6 7/8	2 4/8	2 2/8	15 3/8	11 7/8	5 3/8	5 4/8	Sweetwater Co., WY	James C. Klum	James C. Klum	1965	1265
82 6/8	15 2/8	15 2/8	7 2/8	7	2 6/8	2 3/8	14 2/8	9 1/8	4 6/8	4 6/8	Ft. Apache Res., AZ	Robert L. Martin	Robert L. Martin	1965	1265
82 6/8	17 3/8	14 1/8	6	6	2 6/8	2 7/8	12 5/8	10 4/8	5	4 2/8	Alcova, WY	New Park Hotel	J. & V. Johnson	1965	1265
82 6/8	15 6/8	15 6/8	6 6/8	6 5/8	2 6/8	2 5/8	8 6/8	10 2/8	6 2/8	5 6/8	Converse Co., WY	Paul W. Tomlin	Paul W. Tomlin	1965	1265
82 6/8	17 3/8	17 3/8	6 6/8	6 5/8	3	2 7/8	14 6/8	1 6/8	5 6/8	5 6/8	Mora Co., NM	R.L. Wakefield	R.L. Wakefield	1965	1265
82 6/8	17 2/8	15 2/8	6 5/8	6 5/8	3	2 5/8	8 6/8	8 6/8	5 4/8	4 4/8	Round Mt., AZ	Dennis L. Fife	Dennis L. Fife	1967	1265
82 6/8	15 1/8	15 4/8	7	6 7/8	2 6/8	2 6/8	10 5/8	8 1/8	6 1/8	6 1/8	Rocky Ford, CO	Henry A. Helmke	Henry A. Helmke	1967	1265
82 6/8	15 2/8	15 4/8	6 4/8	6 4/8	2 6/8	2 6/8	10 5/8	8 1/8	6 1/8	6 1/8	Fremont Co., WY	Terry N. TenBoer	Terry N. TenBoer	1967	1265
82 6/8	16 3/8	16	6 7/8	6 7/8	2 4/8	2 4/8	10	4 7/8	5 5/8	5 5/8	Farson, WY	Ronald O. West	Ronald O. West	1969	1265
82 6/8	16	15 7/8	6 6/8	6 5/8	3 1/8	3	10 2/8	5 1/8	5 4/8	5 4/8	Uinta Co., WY	Barry Hyken	Barry Hyken	1969	1265
82 6/8	15 3/8	15 3/8	6 6/8	6 7/8	2 5/8	2 4/8	8 6/8	5 2/8	6 3/8	6 3/8	Carbon Co., WY	John M. Sell	John M. Sell	1970	1265
82 6/8	14 4/8	14	7 5/8	7 5/8	2 5/8	2 4/8	9	7 6/8	5 6/8	5 4/8	Sweetwater Co., WY	Keith F. Dunbar	Keith F. Dunbar	1970	1265
82 6/8	15 3/8	15 3/8	6 6/8	6 6/8	3 1/8	3 1/8	8 5/8	5 1/8	6 1/8	6	Custer Co., MT	George E. Sanquist	George E. Sanquist	1970	1265
82 6/8	16 5/8	16 5/8	6 3/8	6 3/8	2 3/8	2 3/8	15 4/8	13 2/8	5 1/8	5 1/8	Socorro Co., NM	Lawrence D. Vigil	Lawrence D. Vigil	1970	1265

PRONGHORN

Antilocapra americana americana and related subspecies

Score	Length of Horn R	L	Circumference of Base R	L	Circumference at Third Quarter R	L	Inside Spread	Tip to Tip Spread	Length of Prong R	L	Locality	Hunter	Owner	Date Killed	Rank
82 6/8	16 3/8	16 3/8	6 3/8	6 3/8	2 5/8	2 5/8	8 4/8	2 7/8	6 2/8	5 5/8	Natrona Co., WY	Kenneth Niedan	Kenneth Niedan	1971	1265
82 6/8	16 1/8	15 5/8	6 2/8	6 4/8	2 5/8	2 7/8	10 7/8	8 4/8	6 6/8	6 7/8	Medicine Bow, WY	Raymond Freitas	Raymond Freitas	1973	1265
82 6/8	15 4/8	15 4/8	6 3/8	6 1/8	3 5/8	2 7/8	9 2/8	4 6/8	5	4 5/8	Carbon Co., WY	Roger D. George	Roger D. George	1975	1265
82 6/8	16 3/8	16	6 2/8	6 2/8	2 7/8	3 2/8	13	7 4/8	6	5 2/8	Modoc Co., CA	Dennis McClelland	Dennis McClelland	1977	1265
82 6/8	16 6/8	17 2/8	6 6/8	6 6/8	2 3/8	2	10 5/8	6	5 1/8	5 2/8	Catron Co., NM	David Chavez	David Chavez	1978	1265
82 6/8	15 5/8	16 3/8	6 3/8	6 3/8	2 5/8	2 6/8	10 6/8	5 6/8	6 4/8	6 5/8	Weld Co., CO	Chester N. Erwin	Ronald G. Erwin	1978	1265
82 6/8	14 5/8	14 5/8	6 6/8	6 6/8	2 1/8	2 2/8	11 2/8	7 5/8	7 2/8	7 2/8	Grant Co., OR	A. Paul Malstrom	A. Paul Malstrom	1978	1265
82 6/8	15 6/8	15 7/8	6 4/8	6 5/8	2 7/8	2 7/8	8	5 3/8	5 5/8	5 6/8	Hudspeth Co., TX	L.A. Grelling	L.A. Grelling	1980	1265
82 6/8	15 6/8	15 3/8	6 5/8	6 5/8	2 6/8	2 6/8	10 5/8	8 2/8	6 5/8	6 1/8	Carbon Co., WY	Robert J. Smith	Robert J. Smith	1980	1265
82 6/8	16 1/8	16 1/8	7 4/8	7 3/8	2 4/8	2 6/8	8 7/8	2 1/8	5 2/8	5 2/8	Natrona Co., WY	Bill E. Boatman	Bill E. Boatman	1982	1265
82 6/8	15	15	7 2/8	6 7/8	2 5/8	2 5/8	10	6	5 3/8	5 5/8	Carbon Co., WY	Dailen R. Jones	Dailen R. Jones	1982	1265
82 6/8	15 3/8	15 4/8	6 6/8	6 6/8	2 6/8	2 6/8	12	9	5 6/8	6 1/8	Carter Co., MT	Lloyd R. Norvell	Lloyd R. Norvell	1982	1265
82 6/8	15 5/8	16	6 5/8	6 4/8	2 6/8	2 5/8	9 2/8	6 3/8	6 3/8	5 6/8	Natrona Co., WY	Eugene Turner, Jr.	Eugene Turner, Jr.	1982	1265
82 6/8	16 7/8	16 6/8	6 2/8	6 2/8	2 6/8	2 6/8	11 3/8	8 3/8	4 7/8	5	Mora Co., NM	Donald R. Warren	Donald R. Warren	1982	1265
82 6/8	14 6/8	15	7 5/8	7 2/8	2 6/8	2 6/8	14 6/8	12 3/8	6 3/8	5 6/8	Carbon Co., WY	Kenneth E. Grail	Kenneth E. Grail	1983	1265
82 6/8	17 1/8	17 4/8	6 6/8	6 5/8	2 2/8	2 3/8	11 1/8	4 5/8	5 2/8	5 3/8	Washoe Co., NV	Michael J. Lange	Michael J. Lange	1983	1265
82 6/8	15 6/8	15 5/8	6 3/8	6 2/8	2 4/8	2 4/8	15 7/8	13	6 3/8	6 2/8	Yavapai Co., AZ	Joseph C. Cancilliere	Joseph C. Cancilliere	1984	1265
82 6/8	16 3/8	16 4/8	6	6	2 5/8	2 6/8	13 7/8	10 1/8	5 2/8	5 2/8	Yellowstone Co., MT	Robert M. Labert	Robert M. Labert	1984	1265
82 6/8	16 3/8	16 2/8	6 2/8	6 2/8	2 4/8	2 4/8	8 4/8	2 5/8	6 4/8	6 2/8	Sweetwater Co., WY	Craig B. Argyle	Craig B. Argyle	1985	1265
82 6/8	17 3/8	17	6	6	2 6/8	2 5/8	9 5/8	5 1/8	5 4/8	5 3/8	Custer Co., ID	William P. Benscoter	William P. Benscoter	1985	1265
82 6/8	15 7/8	15 5/8	7 3/8	7 2/8	2 4/8	2 3/8	14 5/8	10 6/8	6 2/8	6	Natrona Co., WY	Michael L. Brownell	Michael L. Brownell	1985	1265
82 6/8	15 4/8	15 3/8	6 6/8	6 5/8	2 4/8	2 4/8	10 5/8	4 3/8	6 4/8	7 1/8	Yavapai Co., AZ	Roy T. Hume	Roy T. Hume	1985	1265
82 6/8	16 2/8	16 4/8	6 5/8	6 3/8	2 6/8	2 6/8	12 4/8	9 3/8	6 1/8	5 6/8	Larimer Co., CO	James D. Brink	James D. Brink	1986	1265
82 6/8	17	17 1/8	6 3/8	6 3/8	2 5/8	2 5/8	10	4 4/8	5 6/8	5 2/8	Lake Co., OR	Steve W. Thompson	Steve W. Thompson	1986	1265
82 6/8	16 6/8	16 7/8	7	7	2 5/8	2 5/8	13 3/8	8 4/8	5 3/8	5 5/8	Lake Co., OR	Wayne W. Wingert	Wayne W. Wingert	1986	1265
82 6/8	15 3/8	15 3/8	7	7	3 1/8	2 5/8	8 5/8	3 2/8	5 7/8	6 1/8	Natrona Co., WY	Tom Covert	Tom Covert	1987	1265
82 6/8	15 5/8	15 6/8	6 2/8	6 2/8	3 1/8	2 4/8	15 3/8	11 7/8	6 1/8	5 7/8	Lemhi Co., ID	Richard W. Feagan	Richard W. Feagan	1988	1265
82 6/8	17	16 6/8	6 6/8	6 4/8	2 5/8	2 4/8	9 3/8	2	5 6/8	5 5/8	Washoe Co., NV	David Messmann	David Messmann	1988	1265
82 6/8	16 1/8	15 4/8	6 2/8	6 2/8	2 5/8	2 4/8	12 4/8	8 2/8	6 2/8	6 6/8	Sweetwater Co., WY	Roy D. Sessions	Roy D. Sessions	1988	1265
82 6/8	16 2/8	16	6 4/8	6 3/8	2 5/8	2 4/8	10 7/8	8 1/8	6	6 2/8	Malheur Co., OR	Terrence L. Vaughan	Terrence L. Vaughan	1988	1265
82 6/8	15 4/8	15 5/8	7 2/8	7 1/8	2 4/8	2 4/8	12 1/8	7 2/8	6 3/8	5 7/8	Humboldt Co., NV	Darren K. Bader	Darren K. Bader	1989	1265
82 6/8	17 3/8	17 5/8	6 3/8	6 3/8	2 6/8	2 5/8	12 4/8	9 7/8	4 7/8	4 6/8	Humboldt Co., NV	Christopher C. Hornbarger	Christopher C. Hornbarger	1989	1265
82 6/8	16	15 4/8	6 7/8	6 6/8	3	3	8 6/8	4 1/8	5 7/8	5 7/8	Campbell Co., WY	Richard H. Stasiak	Richard H. Stasiak	1989	1265
82 6/8	17 4/8	17 6/8	6 3/8	6 3/8	2 4/8	2 4/8	11	5 5/8	6	4 7/8	Fremont Co., WY	Ronald E. Cebuhar	Ronald E. Cebuhar	1990	1265
82 6/8	16 2/8	16 3/8	6 3/8	6 3/8	2 6/8	2 6/8	12 1/8	8 7/8	6 1/8	6 1/8	Catron Co., NM	H. James Tonkin, Jr.	H. James Tonkin, Jr.	1990	1265
82 6/8	16 2/8	16 2/8	7	6 7/8	2 4/8	2 6/8	13 3/8	9 6/8	5 7/8	5	Harney Co., OR	Garry L. Whitmore	Garry L. Whitmore	1990	1265
82 6/8	16 3/8	16 2/8	6 1/8	6 2/8	3	3	8	1 6/8	5 2/8	5 7/8	Cypress Lake, SK	Jack Clary	Jack Clary	1991	1265

Score													Owner	Hunter	Locality	Date	Rank
82 6/8	17 6/8	18	6	6	2 3/8	2 5/8	13	8 6/8	5	5 1/8	6	6	Louise G. Davis	Louise G. Davis	Hudspeth Co., TX	1991	1265
82 6/8	15 4/8	15 1/8	6 7/8	6 7/8	2 5/8	2 5/8	9 1/8	4 6/8	5 6/8	5 6/8	6 6/8	6 5/8	Rebecca J. Miller	Rebecca J. Miller	Carbon Co., WY	1991	1265
82 6/8	15 6/8	15 6/8	6 5/8	6 6/8	2 5/8	2 5/8	12 5/8	9 3/8	5 7/8	6 2/8	6 1/8	6 6/8	Timothy L. Schuckman	Timothy L. Schuckman	Sweetwater Co., WY	1991	1265
82 6/8	16 4/8	16 3/8	6 1/8	6 1/8	2 2/8	2 2/8	9 4/8	7 3/8	6 2/8	6 2/8	6 6/8	6 1/8	Gilbert T. Adams	Gilbert T. Adams	Mora Co., NM	1992	1265
82 6/8	16 4/8	16 3/8	7	7	2 3/8	2 2/8	13 2/8	10 1/8	6 4/8	6 4/8	7	7	Robby Aston	Robby Aston	Rich Co., UT	1992	1265
82 6/8	16	15 7/8	6 4/8	6 4/8	2 3/8	2 5/8	10 5/8	7 6/8	7	6 4/8	6 4/8	6 4/8	Mary L. Crabtree	Mary L. Crabtree	Modoc Co., CA	1992	1265
82 6/8	16 6/8	16 6/8	6 5/8	6 5/8	2 3/8	2 3/8	14 1/8	10 6/8	5 6/8	5 6/8	6 5/8	6 6/8	Kevin D. Fabig	Kevin D. Fabig	Modoc Co., CA	1992	1265
82 6/8	15	15	6 6/8	7	2 5/8	2 6/8	9 5/8	5 3/8	6 2/8	6 2/8	7	7	William S. Franzen	William S. Franzen	Natrona Co., WY	1992	1265
82 6/8	15 2/8	16	7 3/8	7 4/8	2 5/8	2 4/8	8 7/8	5 4/8	6	6	7 3/8	7 4/8	Lyle D. Fruchey	Lyle D. Fruchey	Fremont Co., WY	1992	1265
82 6/8	16 2/8	16 1/8	6 6/8	6 6/8	2 5/8	2 5/8	13 5/8	8 4/8	5 7/8	5 8/8	6 6/8	6 6/8	Edward A. Greaves	Edward A. Greaves	Goshen Co., WY	1992	1265
82 6/8	15 7/8	16	7 3/8	7 5/8	2 5/8	2 6/8	9 7/8	4 2/8	5 1/8	5 1/8	7 5/8	7	Joe Ingrao	Joe Ingrao	Sweetwater Co., WY	1992	1265
82 6/8	15 6/8	16	6 7/8	7	3	3	14	13 2/8	4 6/8	4 6/8	6 6/8	6 6/8	Brian T. King	Brian T. King	Sweetwater Co., WY	1992	1265
82 6/8	16 2/8	16 1/8	6 5/8	6 4/8	2 6/8	2 7/8	9	4 1/8	5 5/8	5 5/8	6 4/8	6 5/8	David B. Nielsen	David B. Nielsen	Juab Co., UT	1992	1265
82 6/8	16 1/8	15 5/8	6 1/8	6 2/8	2 6/8	2 7/8	7 1/8	0 5/8	6 6/8	6 6/8	6	6	Michael R. Tiffany	Michael R. Tiffany	Lincoln Co., NM	1992	1265
82 6/8	16	16 2/8	6 4/8	6 4/8	2 6/8	2 7/8	10 2/8	5 2/8	5 3/8	5 3/8	6 5/8	6 4/8	Darryl D. Bartos	Darryl D. Bartos	Milk River, AB	1993	1265
82 6/8	17 7/8	17 6/8	6 5/8	6 6/8	2 4/8	2 4/8	15 2/8	10 7/8	5 1/8	5 1/8	6 5/8	6 7/8	Ernie Davis	Ernie Davis	Mora Co., NM	1993	1265
82 6/8	15 5/8	15 4/8	6 7/8	6 6/8	2 5/8	2 5/8	11 5/8	8	5 7/8	6 2/8	7	6 7/8	Tim A. Erich	Tim A. Erich	Sweetwater Co., WY	1993	1265
82 6/8	16 4/8	16 4/8	7 2/8	7	2 4/8	2 4/8	10 7/8	5 4/8	4 7/8	4 7/8	7 4/8	7	Linda J. McBride	Linda J. McBride	Mora Co., NM	1993	1265
82 6/8	15 2/8	15 4/8	7 4/8	7 4/8	2 6/8	2 6/8	11 5/8	5 4/8	5 3/8	5 3/8	7 4/8	7 4/8	Lawrence L. Searles	Lawrence L. Searles	Carbon Co., WY	1993	1265
82 6/8	16	16 2/8	6 7/8	6 7/8	2 5/8	2 4/8	13 5/8	12 7/8	5 2/8	5 2/8	6 6/8	6 4/8	Linda J. McBride	Linda J. McBride	Hudspeth Co., TX	1994	1265
82 6/8	16 2/8	14 4/8	6 1/8	6	2 7/8	2 7/8	10 2/8	6	5	5	6 1/8	6 3/8	Hammond R. Collins	Hammond R. Collins	Rio Grande Co., CO	1995	1265
82 6/8	14 3/8	17 2/8	6 2/8	6 3/8	2 4/8	2 5/8	9 6/8	7 2/8	5 2/8	5 2/8	6 1/8	6 2/8	Alan Hamberlin	Alan Hamberlin	Navajo Co., NV	1995	1265
82 6/8	17 3/8	17	6 1/8	7	2 4/8	2 4/8	15 5/8	11 7/8	5	5	6 3/8	6 1/8	John M. Porter	John M. Porter	Washoe Co., NV	1995	1265
82 6/8	17 4/8	15 7/8	6 1/8	6 1/8	2 5/8	2 6/8	8 7/8	6 5/8	5 4/8	5 4/8	6 3/8	6 2/8	Noel J. Poux	Noel J. Poux	Navajo Co., AZ	1996	1265
82 6/8	16 5/8	16 4/8	6 2/8	6 6/8	2 7/8	2 8/8	11 1/8	4 6/8	5 1/8	5 1/8	6 5/8	6 6/8	Richard Tripp	Richard Tripp	Washoe Co., NV	1996	1265
82 6/8	17 4/8	17	6 6/8	7	3 4/8	3	11	8	4 4/8	4 4/8	6 5/8	7	T. Bottari & B. Anderson	Picked Up	Elko Co., NV	1997	1265
82 6/8	15 5/8	16 1/8	6 2/8	6 2/8	2 5/8	2 6/8	8 5/8	6 7/8	4 2/8	4 2/8	6 6/8	6 7/8	Paul S. Keltner	Paul S. Keltner	Yavapai Co., AZ	1997	1265
82 6/8	16 1/8	16	6 3/8	6 4/8	2 6/8	2 6/8	10 3/8	6 5/8	5 2/8	5 2/8	6 4/8	6 4/8	Paul I. Fritzinger	Paul I. Fritzinger	Yavapai Co., AZ	1998	1265
82 6/8	16	17 1/8	7	7	3 3/8	3	8 3/8	4 4/8	5 2/8	5 2/8	6 7/8	6 7/8	David R. Harrow	David R. Harrow	Socorro Co., NM	1998	1265
82 6/8	17 1/8	17	6 4/8	7	2 5/8	2 7/8	11 6/8	6 6/8	4 4/8	4 4/8	6 4/8	6 6/8	Edward C. Joseph	Edward Joseph	Lincoln Co., NM	1998	1265
82 6/8	17	15 7/8	6 4/8	6 1/8	3	3	15 1/8	11 7/8	4 6/8	5 1/8	6 1/8	6 3/8	Zeev Nederman	Zeev Nederman	Grant Co., NM	1998	1265
82 6/8	15 7/8	16 4/8	6 1/8	6 1/8	2 7/8	3	15 1/8	7	5 1/8	5	7 1/8	7	Christopher D. Rarig	Christopher D. Rarig	Custer Co., MT	1998	1265
82 6/8	16 4/8	16 3/8	6 3/8	6 2/8	2 7/8	2 5/8	12 1/8	7	5	5	7 1/8	7	Clifford I. Bergman	Clifford I. Bergman	Socorro Co., NM	1999	1265
82 6/8	15 6/8	16	6 6/8	6 6/8	2 7/8	2 7/8	9 5/8	4 3/8	5 7/8	5 7/8	7	7	Larry Gross	Larry Gross	Uintah Co., UT	1999	1265
82 6/8	15 3/8	17	6 6/8	6 3/8	2 5/8	2 4/8	7 4/8	1 2/8	4 7/8	4 7/8	6 5/8	7	Rodney Olson	Rodney Olson	Brown Co., NE	1999	1265
82 6/8	15 7/8	16 1/8	6 7/8	6 4/8	2 5/8	2 5/8	10 2/8	6 7/8	5 5/8	5 5/8	6 6/8	6 6/8	Bonnie M. Powell	Bonnie M. Powell	Carbon Co., UT	1999	1265
82 6/8	15	15 7/8	6 4/8	7	2 6/8	2 6/8	11 2/8	5 6/8	5 1/8	5 1/8	6 7/8	6 7/8	Kevin E. Robison	Kevin E. Robison	Humboldt Co., NV	2000	1265
82 6/8	15 4/8	15 4/8	6 2/8	7	2 7/8	2 7/8	8 4/8	5 4/8	6	6	6 2/8	6 2/8	Bonnie B. Schaefer	Bonnie B. Schaefer	Mora Co., NM	2000	1265
82 6/8	16 3/8	16 1/8	6 3/8	6 4/8	2 7/8	2 7/8	11	2 2/8	5 5/8	5 3/8	6 3/8	6 3/8	Joshua M. Panger	Joshua M. Panger	Quay Co., NM	2001	1265
82 6/8	16	16 1/8	6 2/8	6 1/8	2 6/8	2 6/8	8 2/8	2 2/8	5 5/8	5 5/8	6 1/8	6 2/8	Ken Wilkinson	Ken Wilkinson	Fremont Co., WY	2001	1265
82 6/8	16 6/8	16 4/8	6 3/8	6 4/8	2 7/8	2 6/8	10 4/8	6 2/8	5 7/8	5 5/8	6 2/8	6 3/8	Mike B. Holt	Mike B. Holt	Eureka Co., NV	2002	1265
82 6/8	15 4/8	16 4/8	6 3/8	6 6/8	2 7/8	2 7/8	9 1/8	7 2/8	4 6/8	4 6/8	7 2/8	7	William P. Stuver	William P. Stuver	Powder River Co., MT	2002	1265
82 6/8	15 5/8	15 5/8	6 6/8	6 6/8	2 5/8	2 5/8	12 4/8	9 5/8	6 2/8	6 2/8	6 4/8	6 6/8	Isaac W. Wilson	Isaac W. Wilson	Coconino Co., AZ	2003	1265
82 4/8	14 6/8	14 3/8	7	7	3 4/8	3 3/8	8	4 4/8	5	5	6	7	Foster's Bighorn Rest.	Bill Foster	California	1930	1371
82 4/8	16 4/8	16 4/8	6 5/8	6 1/8	2 6/8	2 6/8	9 3/8	4 4/8	5 3/8	5 3/8	6 5/8	6 4/8	Helen R. Peterson	Helen R. Peterson	Saratoga Co., WY	1945	1371
82 4/8	16 1/8	15 7/8	6 2/8	6 2/8	2 7/8	2 7/8	10 4/8	6 5/8	6 1/8	6 1/8	6 2/8	6 1/8	William E. Randall	William E. Randall	Park Co., MT	1947	1371
82 4/8	16 1/8	16 6/8	6 6/8	6 6/8	2 3/8	2 4/8	11 2/8	5 6/8	5 3/8	5 4/8	6 6/8	6 8/8	Charles J. Boyd	Charles J. Boyd	Catron Co., NM	1952	1371
82 4/8	14 2/8	14 2/8	7 6/8	7 6/8	2 5/8	2 5/8	12 3/8	11 2/8	6	6	7 6/8	7 6/8	Donald Anderson	Donald Anderson	Ferris Mt., WY	1959	1371

PRONGHORN

Antilocapra americana americana and related subspecies

Score	Length of Horn R	L	Circumference of Base R	L	Circumference at Third Quarter R	L	Inside Spread	Tip to Tip Spread	Length of Prong R	L	Locality	Hunter	Owner	Date Killed	Rank
82 4/8	16 7/8	16 6/8	6 1/8	6 1/8	2 7/8	2 6/8	10	6 7/8	5 4/8	5 4/8	Seligman, AZ	Cleo E. Wallace	Cleo E. Wallace	1959	1371
82 4/8	16 1/8	15 7/8	6 5/8	6 6/8	3	3	11 1/8	8	5 3/8	5 3/8	Campbell Co., WY	Fred J. Brogle	Fred J. Brogle	1960	1371
82 4/8	16 2/8	16	6 6/8	6 6/8	2 3/8	2 4/8	10 7/8	7 4/8	4 7/8	5 1/8	Shirley Basin, WY	Walter B. Hester	Walter B. Hester	1960	1371
82 4/8	16 4/8	16 4/8	6 5/8	6 4/8	3	2 6/8	13 1/8	8 7/8	3 5/8	3 5/8	Poison Spider, WY	Clarence Meddock	Clarence Meddock	1961	1371
82 4/8	16 4/8	16 7/8	6 1/8	6	2 2/8	2 4/8	14 2/8	10	5 3/8	5 6/8	Green Mt., WY	Forrest H. Burnett	Forrest H. Burnett	1962	1371
82 4/8	16	16 1/8	6 6/8	6 6/8	2 4/8	2 4/8	16 5/8	14 2/8	5 6/8	5 6/8	Shirley Basin, WY	G.C. Cunningham	G.C. Cunningham	1962	1371
82 4/8	17	17	6 2/8	6 2/8	2 4/8	2 6/8	10 4/8	6 3/8	5 4/8	5	Springerville, AZ	Malcolm Silvia	Malcolm Silvia	1962	1371
82 4/8	15 2/8	16 3/8	6 7/8	6 7/8	2 4/8	2 5/8	11 1/8	7 2/8	6 1/8	5 7/8	Medicine Hat, AB	Nick Mandryk	Nick Mandryk	1963	1371
82 4/8	16 3/8	16 6/8	7 5/8	7 5/8	2 5/8	2 7/8	10 2/8	4 1/8	4 6/8	5	Park Co., CO	Mrs. Cotton Gordon	Mrs. Cotton Gordon	1964	1371
82 4/8	16 6/8	16 6/8	6 2/8	6 2/8	2 6/8	2 7/8	10 5/8	7 3/8	5 4/8	5 4/8	Seligman, AZ	Glenn Olson	Glenn Olson	1965	1371
82 4/8	16 6/8	16	6 1/8	6 2/8	2 4/8	2 4/8	16 1/8	11 4/8	5	5 7/8	Ingomar, MT	L.P. Treaster	L.P. Treaster	1965	1371
82 4/8	15 5/8	16	6 4/8	6 5/8	2 6/8	3	9	4 3/8	5 3/8	5	Natrona Co., WY	Charles P. Weber	Charles P. Weber	1965	1371
82 4/8	15 6/8	15 7/8	6 7/8	7 1/8	2 6/8	2 5/8	11	7 1/8	5 5/8	6	Laramie Co., WY	Noel Weidner	Noel Weidner	1966	1371
82 4/8	15 1/8	16	6 5/8	6 3/8	3	3	6 3/8	4 5/8	6 1/8	6 4/8	Butte Co., ND	E.J. Weigel	E.J. Weigel	1966	1371
82 4/8	16 1/8	16 5/8	7 1/8	6 7/8	2 4/8	2 5/8	9 7/8	5 7/8	5 3/8	5 4/8	Hartley Co., TX	Marvin Willis	Marvin Willis	1968	1371
82 4/8	15 5/8	15 5/8	6 5/8	6 6/8	2 5/8	2 4/8	14	10 7/8	5 3/8	5 4/8	Washoe Co., NV	James R. Stoner, Jr.	James R. Stoner, Jr.	1969	1371
82 4/8	16 1/8	16 1/8	6 5/8	6 6/8	2 4/8	2 4/8	12 1/8	6 3/8	5 6/8	5 6/8	Lake Co., OR	Charles R. Waite	Charles R. Waite	1969	1371
82 4/8	15 6/8	15 3/8	6 6/8	6 5/8	2 6/8	2 4/8	8 7/8	6 4/8	5 4/8	5 4/8	Humboldt Co., NV	Robert C. Lawson	Robert C. Lawson	1970	1371
82 4/8	15 1/8	15 3/8	6 6/8	6 7/8	3	3 1/8	8 5/8	4	3 6/8	3 6/8	Brewster Co., TX	Joseph W. Burkett III	Joseph W. Burkett III	1971	1371
82 4/8	16 1/8	16	6 5/8	6 5/8	2 7/8	2 7/8	9 7/8	6 3/8	5 2/8	5 6/8	Platte Co., WY	Dwight E. Farr	William R. Brewer	1972	1371
82 4/8	16 1/8	17 1/8	6 5/8	6 4/8	2 7/8	2 7/8	10 2/8	5	5 2/8	4 6/8	Coconino Co., AZ	Robert J. Hallock	Robert J. Hallock	1973	1371
82 4/8	14 5/8	16 5/8	6 2/8	6	2 5/8	2 4/8	11 7/8	10 6/8	5 5/8	5 5/8	Converse Co., WY	J.A. Merrill, Jr. & C. Davis	J.A. Merrill, Jr.	1973	1371
82 4/8	14 3/8	14 3/8	7	6 7/8	3	3 1/8	9 5/8	5 5/8	5 5/8	5 4/8	Rosebud Co., MT	Norman G. Kern	Norman G. Kern	1974	1371
82 4/8	14 4/8	14 6/8	7 1/8	7	3	3 1/8	11	9 3/8	6	5 6/8	Cimarron Co., NM	Ronald E. McKinney	Ronald E. McKinney	1974	1371
82 4/8	16	16 3/8	6 3/8	6 2/8	2 4/8	2 4/8	11 1/8	6 6/8	5 6/8	5 7/8	Custer Co., MT	Harry Zirwas	Harry Zirwas	1974	1371
82 4/8	16 7/8	17	6 2/8	6 1/8	2 6/8	2 7/8	10 2/8	6 1/8	5 2/8	5 5/8	Slope Co., ND	Marlin J. Kapp	Marlin J. Kapp	1975	1371
82 4/8	17 2/8	17	6 2/8	6 2/8	2 5/8	2 5/8	11 6/8	7 6/8	5 3/8	5	Coconino Co., AZ	David S. Hibbert	David S. Hibbert	1976	1371
82 4/8	15 3/8	15 3/8	6 4/8	6 3/8	2 5/8	2 4/8	13 5/8	10 4/8	6 3/8	7	Lassen Co., CA	Brad L. Ayotte	Brad L. Ayotte	1977	1371
82 4/8	15	15	6 4/8	6 4/8	2 6/8	2 6/8	9 4/8	4	6 4/8	6 4/8	Sublette Co., WY	Larry W. Cross	Larry W. Cross	1977	1371
82 4/8	14 7/8	14 7/8	7	7	3	2 7/8	11 7/8	8 7/8	5 2/8	5 4/8	Richland Co., MT	Lloyd Holland	Lloyd Holland	1977	1371
82 4/8	16 3/8	16 4/8	6 6/8	6 6/8	2 5/8	2 5/8	11 1/8	5 4/8	5 6/8	5 4/8	Fremont Co., WY	Wayne D. Kleinman	Wayne D. Kleinman	1977	1371
82 4/8	16	15 5/8	6 4/8	6 6/8	2 2/8	2 5/8	14 1/8	5 4/8	5 7/8	5 4/8	Washakie Co., WY	Greg Warner	Greg Warner	1977	1371
82 4/8	16	16 1/8	6 6/8	6 6/8	2 5/8	2 2/8	14 3/8	8 1/8	5 7/8	5 1/8	Carter Co., MT	James A. White	James A. White	1977	1371
82 4/8	15 4/8	15 2/8	6 6/8	6 5/8	2 5/8	2 4/8	12 2/8	7 1/8	5 5/8	5	Modoc Co., CA	Mark Hansen	Mark Hansen	1978	1371
82 4/8	16 5/8	16 3/8	6 4/8	6 3/8	2 7/8	2 6/8	9 1/8	5 3/8	5 2/8	5 1/8	Sweetwater Co., WY	Fred B. Keyes	Fred B. Keyes	1978	1371
82 4/8	14 6/8	14 7/8	6 6/8	6 5/8	2 7/8	2 7/8	13 7/8	11 7/8	6 4/8	6 4/8	Carbon Co., WY	Michael Boender	Michael Boender	1979	1371
82 4/8	15 4/8	15 5/8	6 4/8	6 6/8	2 5/8	2 5/8	9 4/8	4 5/8	5 3/8	5 3/8	Millard Co., UT	William R. Houston	William R. Houston	1979	1371
82 4/8	16 2/8	16 3/8	7	6 7/8	2 3/8	2 4/8	8 1/8	6 2/8	5 5/8	5 3/8	Siskiyou Co., CA	Rodney F. Royer	Rodney F. Royer	1979	1371

Score	Locality	Hunter	Owner	Date Killed	Rank
82⁴/₈	Hudspeth Co., TX	Ray A. Acker, Sr.	Ray A. Acker, Sr.	1980	1371
82⁴/₈	Carbon Co., WY	Barry L. Alger	Barry L. Alger	1980	1371
82⁴/₈	White Pine Co., NV	Tom I. Papagna, Jr.	Tom I. Papagna, Jr.	1980	1371
82⁴/₈	Socorro Co., NM	Clyde C. Brumley	Clyde C. Brumley	1981	1371
82⁴/₈	Campbell Co., WY	Larry L. Helgerson	Larry L. Helgerson	1981	1371
82⁴/₈	Moffat Co., CO	Charles W. Klaassens	Charles W. Klaassens	1981	1371
82⁴/₈	Sweetwater Co., WY	Donald R. Williamson	Donald R. Williamson	1981	1371
82⁴/₈	Natrona Co., WY	Edgar M. Artecona	Edgar M. Artecona	1982	1371
82⁴/₈	Carbon Co., WY	John T. Butters	John T. Butters	1982	1371
82⁴/₈	Union Co., NM	John W. Saunders	John W. Saunders	1982	1371
82⁴/₈	Washoe Co., NV	Vernon E. Benney	Vernon E. Benney	1983	1371
82⁴/₈	Natrona Co., WY	Bill E. Boatman	Bill E. Boatman	1983	1371
82⁴/₈	Carbon Co., WY	Merlyn J. Kiel	Merlyn J. Kiel	1983	1371
82⁴/₈	Sweetwater Co., WY	Richard E. Knox, Jr.	Richard E. Knox, Jr.	1983	1371
82⁴/₈	Navajo Co., AZ	Perry H. Finger	Perry H. Finger	1984	1371
82⁴/₈	Humboldt Co., NV	Frank K. Azcarate, Jr.	Frank K. Azcarate, Jr.	1985	1371
82⁴/₈	Sweetwater Co., WY	W.A. Chambers	W.A. Chambers	1985	1371
82⁴/₈	Rosebud Co., MT	Robert B. DeLattre	Robert B. DeLattre	1985	1371
82⁴/₈	Hudspeth Co., TX	Ernest M. Elbert, Jr.	Ernest M. Elbert, Jr.	1985	1371
82⁴/₈	Lassen Co., CA	Bob Freed	Bob Freed	1985	1371
82⁴/₈	Saguache Co., CO	Michael J. Atwood, Sr.	Michael J. Atwood, Sr.	1986	1371
82⁴/₈	Chouteau Co., MT	Jack Willson	Jack Willson	1986	1371
82⁴/₈	Campbell Co., WY	Robert J. Anderson	Robert J. Anderson	1987	1371
82⁴/₈	Colfax Co., NM	John A. Jones	John A. Jones	1987	1371
82⁴/₈	Sweetwater Co., WY	Eric M. Berg	Eric M. Berg	1988	1371
82⁴/₈	Humboldt Co., NV	Michael K. McBeath	Michael K. McBeath	1988	1371
82⁴/₈	Custer Co., ID	Ronald E. Pruyn	Ronald E. Pruyn	1988	1371
82⁴/₈	Yavapai Co., AZ	Chris Skoczylas	Chris Skoczylas	1988	1371
82⁴/₈	Yellowstone Co., MT	Jon J. Wilson	Jon J. Wilson	1988	1371
82⁴/₈	Fremont Co., WY	Ben L. Adamson	Ben L. Adamson	1989	1371
82⁴/₈	Box Elder Co., UT	Curtis K. Blasingame	Curtis K. Blasingame	1989	1371
82⁴/₈	Hudspeth Co., TX	Peter L. Bright	Peter L. Bright	1989	1371
82⁴/₈	Graham Co., AZ	Daniel C. Hicks	Daniel C. Hicks	1989	1371
82⁴/₈	Colfax Co., NM	Roy G. Jones	Roy G. Jones	1989	1371
82⁴/₈	Fremont Co., WY	James M. Machac	James M. Machac	1989	1371
82⁴/₈	Carbon Co., WY	Lance E. Novak	Lance E. Novak	1989	1371
82⁴/₈	Jackson Co., CO	Loren D. Reid	Loren D. Reid	1989	1371
82⁴/₈	Humboldt Co., NV	Richard Vanderkous	Richard Vanderkous	1989	1371
82⁴/₈	Converse Co., WY	Larry E. Zumbrum	Larry E. Zumbrum	1989	1371
82⁴/₈	Natrona Co., WY	Robert W. Genner	Robert W. Genner	1990	1371
82⁴/₈	McKenzie Co., ND	Nathan S. Gilbertson	Nathan S. Gilbertson	1990	1371
82⁴/₈	San Juan Co., UT	Wayne A. Hines	Wayne A. Hines	1990	1371
82⁴/₈	Converse Co., WY	Farrell M. McQuiddy	Farrell M. McQuiddy	1990	1371
82⁴/₈	Fremont Co., WY	James J. Person	James J. Person	1990	1371
82⁴/₈	Mora Co., NM	Gilbert T. Adams	Gilbert T. Adams	1991	1371
82⁴/₈	Judith Basin Co., MT	Sarah M. Brown	Sarah M. Brown	1991	1371
82⁴/₈	Box Elder Co., UT	Roudy Christensen	Roudy Christensen	1991	1371
82⁴/₈	Hot Springs Co., WY	Brett W. Jones	Brett W. Jones	1991	1371

PRONGHORN

Antilocapra americana americana and related subspecies

Score	Length of Horn R	L	Circumference of Base R	L	Circumference at Third Quarter R	L	Inside Spread	Tip to Tip Spread	Length of Prong R	L	Locality	Hunter	Owner	Date Killed	Rank
82 4/8	15 5/8	16	7	6 7/8	2 2/8	2 5/8	15 4/8	15 2/8	6 2/8	6 3/8	Sweetwater Co., WY	Robert S. Lund	Robert S. Lund	1991	1371
82 4/8	17 2/8	17 6/8	6 1/8	6	2 3/8	2 4/8	10 1/8	4 7/8	6 2/8	5 6/8	Mora Co., NM	Dan E. McBride	Dan E. McBride	1991	1371
82 4/8	16	15 7/8	6 3/8	6 4/8	2 5/8	2 5/8	6 3/8	0 3/8	5 5/8	5 5/8	Cascade Co., MT	John P. Michalies	John P. Michalies	1991	1371
82 4/8	15 5/8	15 5/8	7	7 2/8	2 3/8	2 4/8	9 4/8	4 5/8	5 7/8	6	Uinta Co., WY	Velma B. O'Neil	Velma B. O'Neil	1991	1371
82 4/8	15 4/8	15 5/8	6 5/8	6 5/8	2 7/8	2 7/8	8 2/8	3 7/8	6 1/8	6 4/8	Moffat Co., CO	S. Wayne Olson	S. Wayne Olson	1991	1371
82 4/8	17	16 6/8	6 3/8	6 3/8	2 4/8	2 3/8	9	2 6/8	5 2/8	5 1/8	Mora Co., NM	Kenneth G. Planet	Kenneth G. Planet	1991	1371
82 4/8	15 4/8	15 6/8	7 1/8	7	2 5/8	2 5/8	12 2/8	8 4/8	6 3/8	5 5/8	Sweetwater Co., WY	Justin C. Shadrick	Justin C. Shadrick	1991	1371
82 4/8	15 6/8	15 4/8	6 6/8	6 7/8	2 5/8	2 4/8	8 6/8	2 6/8	5 4/8	5 4/8	Treasure Co., MT	David W. Shannon	David W. Shannon	1991	1371
82 4/8	16 2/8	16 3/8	6 5/8	6 6/8	2 5/8	2 7/8	9 7/8	5	4 5/8	4 7/8	Washoe Co., NV	Dean C. Tischler	Dean C. Tischler	1991	1371
82 4/8	17	15 5/8	6 7/8	6 7/8	2 7/8	2 6/8	11 2/8	9 7/8	5 1/8	5	Natrona Co., WY	Hubert C. Wightman	Hubert C. Wightman	1991	1371
82 4/8	16 4/8	16 7/8	6 2/8	6 2/8	2 6/8	2 5/8	10	8 6/8	5 5/8	5 1/8	Harney Co., OR	Terry L. Greene	Terry L. Greene	1992	1371
82 4/8	15 7/8	15 7/8	6 5/8	6 4/8	2 6/8	2 5/8	8 5/8	3 5/8	6 1/8	6	Milk River, AB	Carey Karl	Carey Karl	1992	1371
82 4/8	15 5/8	15 5/8	6 3/8	6 6/8	2 3/8	2 4/8	13 4/8	9 7/8	7	7	Jefferson Co., MT	Tom R. Osborne	Tom R. Osborne	1992	1371
82 4/8	16 4/8	16 1/8	6 2/8	6 2/8	2 6/8	2 5/8	10 7/8	5 5/8	5 6/8	5 4/8	Colfax Co., NM	Robert J. Seeds	Robert J. Seeds	1992	1371
82 4/8	15 4/8	15 4/8	6 1/8	6	2 3/8	2 3/8	7 2/8	4 1/8	6 3/8	6 3/8	Carbon Co., WY	David Shadrick	David Shadrick	1992	1371
82 4/8	15 5/8	16 2/8	6 6/8	6 4/8	2 7/8	3	9 3/8	7 6/8	6	5 4/8	Washoe Co., NV	Sydney M. Smith	Sydney M. Smith	1992	1371
82 4/8	16	16	6 3/8	6 2/8	2 4/8	2 5/8	6 5/8	1 6/8	6	6	Moffat Co., CO	Brad A. Winder	Brad A. Winder	1992	1371
82 4/8	14 6/8	14 4/8	7 1/8	7 2/8	3 2/8	3	11 7/8	10 3/8	5 6/8	5 6/8	Park Co., WY	Dan Barngrover	Dan Barngrover	1993	1371
82 4/8	16 5/8	16 5/8	6 5/8	6 4/8	2 7/8	2 6/8	9	4	5 1/8	5 2/8	Fergus Co., MT	Scott D. Boelman	Scott D. Boelman	1993	1371
82 4/8	16 5/8	16 6/8	6 6/8	6 7/8	2 6/8	2 6/8	8 7/8	7 6/8	5	4 6/8	Hudspeth Co., TX	Bruce Kettler	Bruce Kettler	1993	1371
82 4/8	14 2/8	14 1/8	7	6 7/8	2 5/8	2 5/8	10 1/8	7 6/8	6 2/8	6	Elko Co., NV	Paul M. Adams	Paul M. Adams	1994	1371
82 4/8	15 6/8	15 5/8	6 4/8	6 4/8	2 7/8	2 7/8	10 2/8	6 5/8	5 4/8	5 7/8	Mora Co., NM	Luke C. Kellogg	Luke C. Kellogg	1994	1371
82 4/8	16 1/8	16 1/8	6 3/8	6 1/8	3 1/8	3	8 1/8	2 6/8	5 3/8	5 3/8	Moffat Co., CO	Brad A. Winder	Brad A. Winder	1994	1371
82 4/8	16 4/8	16 4/8	6 4/8	6 1/8	3	3	13 2/8	8 4/8	4 5/8	4 4/8	Deaf Smith Co., TX	Russell W. Casteel	Russell W. Casteel	1995	1371
82 4/8	15 7/8	16 1/8	7 1/8	7 1/8	2 4/8	2 4/8	8 5/8	4	5 4/8	5 4/8	Mora Co., NM	Len H. Guldman	Len H. Guldman	1995	1371
82 4/8	16 7/8	15 4/8	6 4/8	6 3/8	3	3	11 2/8	8 3/8	6	6	Socorro Co., NM	Jess T. Jones	Jess T. Jones	1995	1371
82 4/8	15 4/8	16 6/8	6 6/8	6 7/8	2 7/8	2 6/8	8 4/8	5 5/8	5 5/8	6 2/8	Niobrara Co., WY	William F. King	William F. King	1995	1371
82 4/8	16 6/8	16 6/8	6 4/8	6 4/8	2 7/8	2 7/8	12 2/8	8 7/8	5	5 4/8	Liberty Co., MT	Stuart Stone	Stuart Stone	1995	1371
82 4/8	17 2/8	17 2/8	6 4/8	6 1/8	2 5/8	2 4/8	11 6/8	6 2/8	5 4/8	5 6/8	Coconino Co., AZ	Thomas Bowman	Thomas Bowman	1996	1371
82 4/8	15 6/8	15 5/8	6 5/8	6 5/8	2 4/8	2 3/8	9 6/8	7 2/8	5 6/8	6	Carbon Co., WY	Kristopher P. Cobbley	Kristopher P. Cobbley	1996	1371
82 4/8	17 4/8	17 1/8	6 1/8	6 2/8	2 4/8	2 3/8	12 1/8	7 1/8	5 4/8	5 2/8	Hudspeth Co., TX	Gerald P. McBride	Gerald P. McBride	1996	1371
82 4/8	16 7/8	16 6/8	6 6/8	6	2 7/8	2 7/8	8 7/8	6 3/8	5 3/8	5 5/8	Navajo Co., AZ	Herman C. Meyer	Herman C. Meyer	1996	1371
82 4/8	16	16	6 6/8	6 6/8	2 7/8	2 7/8	12 1/8	9	5 6/8	5 1/8	Socorro Co., NM	Gerald L. Warnock	Gerald L. Warnock	1996	1371
82 4/8	18	17 7/8	5 6/8	5 7/8	2 5/8	2 5/8	8 6/8	5 1/8	4 6/8	4 5/8	Albany Co., WY	Brian N. Beisher	Brian N. Beisher	1997	1371
82 4/8	16 1/8	16	6 5/8	6 4/8	2 6/8	2 6/8	9 4/8	4 1/8	5 4/8	5 1/8	Mora Co., NM	Dennis J. Sites	Dennis J. Sites	1997	1371
82 4/8	16 1/8	16 2/8	7	6 5/8	2 6/8	2 3/8	10 3/8	5 4/8	6 3/8	5 5/8	Carbon Co., WY	John Strand	John Strand	1997	1371
82 4/8	14 7/8	14 7/8	6 4/8	6 4/8	2 6/8	2 6/8	10 3/8	7 3/8	5	5	Colfax Co., NM	Kevin W. Underwood	Kevin W. Underwood	1997	1371
82 4/8	17 1/8	17	6 3/8	6 2/8	2 7/8	2 6/8	8 4/8	1 7/8	6 2/8	5 4/8	Hot Springs Co., WY	Arthur W. Andersen	Arthur W. Andersen	1998	1371

Score	L. Horn R	L. Horn L	Circ. Base R	Circ. Base L	Circ. 3rd Qtr R	Circ. 3rd Qtr L	Tip to Tip	Inside Spr.	Prong R	Prong L	Prong L2	Locality	Hunter	Owner	Date	Rank
82 4/8	15 5/8	15 2/8	7 3/8	7 2/8	2 5/8	2 4/8	9 7/8	2 4/8	5 2/8	5 3/8	5 5/8	Washington Co., CO	Timothy A. Baker	Timothy A. Baker	1998	1371
82 4/8	15 4/8	15 4/8	6 6/8	6 7/8	2 5/8	2 6/8	8	2 5/8	3 4/8	6 2/8	6 2/8	Sweetwater Co., WY	Gilbert K. Davies	Gilbert K. Davies	1998	1371
82 4/8	14 7/8	14 6/8	6 7/8	6 7/8	2 6/8	2 6/8	7 2/8	2 6/8	3 2/8	5	5 5/8	Campbell Co., WY	Richard F. LaCrone	Richard F. LaCrone	1998	1371
82 4/8	16	16 2/8	6 4/8	6 2/8	2 7/8	2 7/8	13 2/8	3 1/8	3 1/8	5 5/8	5 4/8	Socorro Co., NM	Whitney Moore	Whitney M. Moore	1998	1371
82 4/8	14 5/8	14 7/8	6 3/8	6 7/8	3 5/8	3	9	3 5/8	3	3 1/8	4 7/8	Coconino Co., AZ	Thomas J. Pawlacyk	Thomas J. Pawlacyk	1998	1371
82 4/8	16 3/8	16 1/8	6 7/8	6 7/8	2 6/8	2 5/8	12 2/8	2 6/8	3	4 5/8	4 5/8	Fremont Co., WY	Wade Sikkink	Wade A. Sikkink	1998	1371
82 4/8	17	17 1/8	6 2/8	6 3/8	2 5/8	2 5/8	15 6/8	2 5/8	2 5/8	4 5/8	5 7/8	Coconino Co., AZ	Jeffrey Stone	Jeffrey R. Stone	1998	1371
82 4/8	16 2/8	16 5/8	6 7/8	7	2 6/8	2 4/8	10 5/8	2 6/8	2 4/8	5 3/8	5 7/8	Sweetwater Co., WY	Bradley A. Thoren	Bradley A. Thoren	1998	1371
82 4/8	15 4/8	15 1/8	7	7	2 6/8	2 6/8	7 6/8	2 6/8	2 4/8	7	5 2/8	Weld Co., CO	Bob Chapman	Bob Chapman	1999	1371
82 4/8	15	15	7 4/8	7 3/8	2 7/8	2 5/8	11 2/8	2 5/8	2 4/8	5 6/8	6 3/8	Musselshell Co., MT	Matt M. Marvel	Matt M. Marvel	1999	1371
82 4/8	15 6/8	15 6/8	6 3/8	6 6/8	2 7/8	2 7/8	14 3/8	2 7/8	2 7/8	9 2/8	5 1/8	Grant Co., NM	Zeev Nederman	Zeev Nederman	1999	1371
82 4/8	14 6/8	14 4/8	6 4/8	6 4/8	3 1/8	3	14 6/8	3 1/8	3	10 5/8	4 6/8	Harney Co., OR	Michael D. Tyrholm	Michael D. Tyrholm	1999	1371
82 4/8	16 3/8	16 3/8	6 3/8	6 6/8	2 4/8	3	15	2 4/8	3	13	5 4/8	Washakie Co., WY	Turner R. Allen	Turner R. Allen	1999	1371
82 4/8	17	16 4/8	6 4/8	6 3/8	2 6/8	2 4/8	10 6/8	2 4/8	2 4/8	10 6/8	5	Navajo Co., AZ	Byron L. Eiler	Byron L. Eiler	2000	1371
82 4/8	16	16 1/8	6 3/8	6 4/8	2 6/8	2 6/8	10 6/8	2 6/8	2 6/8	9 2/8	4 7/8	Harney Co., OR	Travis E. Ingram	Travis E. Ingram	2000	1371
82 4/8	16 3/8	16 5/8	6 7/8	6 7/8	2 6/8	2 5/8	11 5/8	2 5/8	2 5/8	8 6/8	5 5/8	Socorro Co., NM	J. Fred Ketcham	J. Fred Ketcham	2000	1371
82 4/8	17	17	6 7/8	6 7/8	2 5/8	2 5/8	7 7/8	2 5/8	2 5/8	1 2/8	5 1/8	Catron Co., NM	Scott M. Kohrs	Scott M. Kohrs	2000	1371
82 4/8	16 3/8	17	6 4/8	6 4/8	3	3	11 4/8	3	3	7 7/8	4 4/8	Humboldt Co., NV	M. Todd McLean	M. Todd McLean	2000	1371
82 4/8	16 6/8	16 3/8	6 2/8	6 2/8	2 3/8	2 3/8	11 3/8	2 3/8	2 3/8	6 7/8	6 1/8	Carbon Co., WY	James E. Schmid	James E. Schmid	2000	1371
82 4/8	15	15	6 6/8	6 6/8	2 5/8	2 6/8	9 6/8	2 6/8	2 6/8	7 4/8	6	Fremont Co., WY	Picked Up	William J. Waller, Jr.	2000	1371
82 4/8	15 6/8	15 6/8	6 6/8	6 5/8	3 4/8	2 5/8	11 1/8	3 4/8	2 5/8	7 5/8	6 1/8	Luna Co., NM	Hanspeter Giger	Hanspeter Giger	2001	1371
82 4/8	15 7/8	15 7/8	6 6/8	6 6/8	2 4/8	2 4/8	14 1/8	2 4/8	3 4/8	12 4/8	5 2/8	Humboldt Co., NV	John H. Parker	John H. Parker	2001	1371
82 4/8	14 4/8	14 5/8	6 6/8	6 6/8	2 5/8	2 5/8	8	2 5/8	2 4/8	1 3/8	5 3/8	Sweetwater Co., WY	Paul H. Comino	Paul H. Comino	2002	1371
82 4/8	15 7/8	15 7/8	6 4/8	6 4/8	2 5/8	2 5/8	9	2 5/8	2 5/8	5 1/8	5 6/8	Colfax Co., NM	Robert D. Jones	Robert D. Jones	2002	1371
82 4/8	15 3/8	15 2/8	6 7/8	6 7/8	3	3	16 3/8	3	3	12 3/8	4 5/8	Owyhee Co., ID	Donald E. Perrien	Donald E. Perrien	2002	1371
82 4/8	15 7/8	15 5/8	6 4/8	6 4/8	3 3/8	3 3/8	9 4/8	3 3/8	3 2/8	6 5/8	5	Otero Co., NM	George C. Billings	George C. Billings	2003	1371
82 4/8	15 2/8	15 7/8	6 3/8	6 2/8	2 6/8	2 6/8	14 2/8	2 6/8	2 6/8	5 5/8	5 4/8	Powder River Co., MT	Floyd Michell	Floyd Michell	2003	1371
82 4/8	15 7/8	16 4/8	6 1/8	6 1/8	2 7/8	2 7/8	13 2/8	2 7/8	2 7/8	7 1/8	5 2/8	Natrona Co., WY	Cory L. Wolff	Cory L. Wolff	2003	1371
82 2/8	16 4/8	17	6 4/8	6 2/8	2 6/8	2 6/8	11 4/8	3	7	7 1/8	5 3/8	Chaves Co., NM	Harvey Pirtle	Glenn Marshall	1939	1528
82 2/8	17	14 6/8	6 5/8	6 3/8	3 5/8	2 4/8	14 5/8	2 4/8	2 4/8	12 6/8	6 3/8	Henderson Co., NM	Ron Vance	Ron Vance	1947	1528
82 2/8	14 5/8	16 7/8	6	6 2/8	2 4/8	2 4/8	8 2/8	2 4/8	2 6/8	6 2/8	5 5/8	Split Rock, WY	Herb Klein	Dallas Mus. of Natl. Hist.	1952	1528
82 2/8	16 7/8	14 4/8	7 1/8	6 5/8	2 7/8	2 7/8	15 7/8	3 1/8	6 4/8	7 2/8	5 7/8	Anderson Mesa, AZ	Roy Stevens	Roy Stevens	1953	1528
82 2/8	16 6/8	16 5/8	6 6/8	6 3/8	2 6/8	2 4/8	14 1/8	2 4/8	2 6/8	10	4 4/8	Weld Co., CO	Roy Stevens	Howard E. Bates	1955	1528
82 2/8	17 4/8	17 3/8	6 2/8	6 3/8	2 7/8	2 5/8	11 3/8	2 5/8	2 4/8	5 5/8	5 4/8	Rawlins Co., WY	James Gertson, Jr.	Thomas B. McNeill	1955	1528
82 2/8	16	16 4/8	6 2/8	6 4/8	2 6/8	2 4/8	8 6/8	2 6/8	2 4/8	5 5/8	6 3/8	Saratoga Co., WY	Thomas B. McNeill	Thomas B. McNeill	1955	1528
82 2/8	15 4/8	15	6 6/8	6 5/8	2 4/8	2 4/8	8 6/8	3 1/8	4 4/8	4 4/8	5	Hettinger Co., ND	J.E. Prothroe	J.E. Prothroe	1955	1528
82 2/8	16 5/8	16 6/8	6 4/8	6 3/8	3	3	10 5/8	3	3	4 5/8	4 4/8	Sage Creek, WY	Art Score	Art Score	1957	1528
82 2/8	15 2/8	15 7/8	7 1/8	7	2 7/8	2 4/8	13 2/8	2 7/8	6	8 6/8	6 1/8	Williams Co., AZ	Glenn P. Anderson	Glenn P. Anderson	1959	1528
82 2/8	16 7/8	16 4/8	6 1/8	6 4/8	2 4/8	2 4/8	13 2/8	2 4/8	5 5/8	10 3/8	5 5/8	Anderson Mesa, AZ	Fred Udine	Fred Udine	1959	1528
82 2/8	16 2/8	16 2/8	6 4/8	6 5/8	2 6/8	2 4/8	13	2 7/8	5 1/8	6 7/8	5 1/8	Park Co., WY	Bill Gray	Bill Gray	1960	1528
82 2/8	16 2/8	16 2/8	6 5/8	6 5/8	2 4/8	2 4/8	6 4/8	2 4/8	4 4/8	4 4/8	5 5/8	Sierra Blanca, TX	Don A. Johnson	Don A. Johnson	1960	1528
82 2/8	16 7/8	16 2/8	6 6/8	6 6/8	2 7/8	2 7/8	13 2/8	2 7/8	4 6/8	13 2/8	4 6/8	Arpan, SD	Charles Nichols	Charles Nichols	1960	1528
82 2/8	16 5/8	16 1/8	6	6	2 5/8	2 5/8	11 1/8	2 5/8	5	11 1/8	5 4/8	Crook Co., SD	Dell Shanks	Dell Shanks	1960	1528
82 2/8	16 1/8	16 2/8	6 3/8	6	2 4/8	2 4/8	10 2/8	2 4/8	6	5	6 6/8	Crook Co., WY	John P. Wood	John P. Wood	1960	1528
82 2/8	16 6/8	16	6 6/8	6	2 4/8	2 4/8	14	3 1/8	6	12 6/8	5	Shirley Basin, WY	T.C. Gonya	T.C. Gonya	1961	1528
82 2/8	17 2/8	16 2/8	6 2/8	6	2 4/8	2 7/8	7 2/8	2 4/8	6 2/8	7 1/8	6 3/8	New Mexico	Joan V. Gordon	Joan V. Gordon	1961	1528
82 2/8	16 2/8	16 2/8	6 3/8	6 4/8	2 7/8	3	11 2/8	2 7/8	5 2/8	11 2/8	5 5/8	Poison Spider, WY	Unknown	Robert F. Ziker	1961	1528
82 2/8	15 4/8	15 4/8	6 6/8	6 5/8	2 3/8	2 4/8	10 1/8	2 3/8	5 6/8	10 1/8	6	Lewis & Clark Co., MT	Leo M. Bergthold	Leo M. Bergthold	1963	1528
82 2/8	15 7/8	15 6/8	7 1/8	7 1/8	2 6/8	2 7/8	11 4/8	2 6/8	5 2/8	6 4/8	5 3/8	Casper, WY	Frank Gardner	Frank Gardner	1963	1528

759

PRONGHORN

Antilocapra americana americana and related subspecies

Score	Length of Horn R	L	Circumference of Base R	L	Circumference at Third Quarter R	L	Inside Spread	Tip to Tip Spread	Length of Prong R	L	Locality	Hunter	Owner	Date Killed	Rank
82 2/8	15 6/8	16	6 4/8	6 4/8	2 5/8	2 6/8	13 1/8	9	6 3/8	5 7/8	Lavina, MT	W.J. Morrelle	W.J. Morrelle	1963	1528
82 2/8	15 7/8	16	7	7	2 6/8	3	11 7/8	7 6/8	5 2/8	5 1/8	Hanna, AB	Rita Shumka	C.W. Edwards	1964	1528
82 2/8	16 2/8	16 1/8	6 6/8	6 6/8	2 6/8	2 6/8	12	9 4/8	5	5	Laramie Co., WY	Susan W. Tupper	Susan W. Tupper	1964	1528
82 2/8	16 3/8	16 2/8	6 2/8	6 2/8	2 6/8	2 6/8	13 2/8	9 1/8	5 4/8	5 2/8	Knappen, AB	Ken Bosch	Ken Bosch	1965	1528
82 2/8	16 4/8	16 2/8	6 3/8	6 4/8	2 6/8	2 6/8	10 2/8	4 1/8	5 3/8	5 2/8	Foremost, AB	Les Gordon	Les Gordon	1966	1528
82 2/8	16 6/8	16 3/8	6 5/8	6 4/8	2 5/8	2 5/8	11	11 4/8	5	5	Bowen, ND	Lee Atkinson	Sioux Sporting Goods	1966	1528
82 2/8	16 6/8	16 3/8	6 4/8	6 5/8	2 4/8	2 4/8	9 1/8	5 6/8	6 2/8	6 2/8	Weld Co., CO	Mrs. Paul Goodwin	Mrs. Paul Goodwin	1967	1528
82 2/8	14 7/8	15	6 6/8	6 4/8	2 4/8	2 4/8	9 6/8	4 5/8	6	6 1/8	Powderville, MT	Morrel W. Ivie	Morrel W. Ivie	1969	1528
82 2/8	15 7/8	15 7/8	6 6/8	6 6/8	2 5/8	2 5/8	11 2/8	7 3/8	6 4/8	6 6/8	Vivian, SD	Larry K. Lantz	Larry K. Lantz	1969	1528
82 2/8	15	15 4/8	6 7/8	6 6/8	2 6/8	2 6/8	10 3/8	8 1/8	5 3/8	6 2/8	Natrona Co., WY	R.O. Marshall, Jr.	R.O. Marshall, Jr.	1970	1528
82 2/8	16 4/8	16 3/8	6 5/8	6 7/8	1 5/8	1 5/8	7 1/8	3 1/8	4 7/8	4 7/8	Wild Horse, AB	Adam Schmick	Adam Schmick	1970	1528
82 2/8	17 3/8	17 2/8	6 7/8	6 7/8	2 6/8	2 6/8	10 7/8	4 4/8	5 5/8	5 7/8	Fergus Co., MT	Carl Aus	Carl Aus	1971	1528
82 2/8	15 6/8	15 7/8	6 6/8	6 6/8	2 6/8	2 6/8	13	8 3/8	5 4/8	5 5/8	Coconino Co., AZ	William L. Butler	William L. Butler	1973	1528
82 2/8	16 5/8	15 5/8	6 4/8	6 5/8	2 4/8	2 6/8	9 6/8	5 7/8	5 5/8	5 5/8	Treasure Co., MT	Joseph A. Balmelli	Joseph A. Balmelli	1974	1528
82 2/8	15 5/8	15 5/8	6 4/8	6 4/8	2 7/8	2 7/8	9 6/8	9 4/8	5 2/8	5 2/8	Fremont Co., WY	Collins F. Kellogg	Collins F. Kellogg	1974	1528
82 2/8	15	15 2/8	6	6	2 4/8	2 4/8	10 2/8	3 3/8	5 6/8	5 2/8	Gillette, WY	Gary Simonson	Gary Simonson	1975	1528
82 2/8	15 3/8	15 2/8	6 3/8	6 3/8	2 7/8	2 7/8	7 7/8	5 7/8	5 6/8	5 7/8	Duchesne Co., UT	David L. Peterson	David L. Peterson	1976	1528
82 2/8	15 3/8	15 2/8	7 1/8	7 2/8	2 6/8	2 6/8	8 7/8	9 6/8	6 1/8	6 2/8	Harney Co., OR	Dean Dunson	Dean Dunson	1977	1528
82 2/8	15 3/8	15 3/8	6 6/8	6 6/8	2 5/8	2 5/8	13 2/8	10	6 3/8	6 3/8	Morgan Co., CO	Kenneth L. Kelly	Kenneth L. Kelly	1977	1528
82 2/8	16	15 6/8	6 1/8	6 1/8	3	3	13 2/8	9	6	5 4/8	Lassen Co., CA	Del S. Oliver	Del S. Oliver	1978	1528
82 2/8	16 6/8	16 2/8	6 3/8	6 4/8	2 4/8	2 4/8	12 4/8	11	6 4/8	7	Otero Co., NM	Heber Simmons, Jr.	Heber Simmons, Jr.	1978	1528
82 2/8	16 2/8	16 2/8	6 5/8	6 5/8	2 4/8	2 4/8	15	8	6 1/8	6 1/8	Apache Co., AZ	Richard L. Simmons, Sr.	Richard L. Simmons, Sr.	1978	1528
82 2/8	15 3/8	15 2/8	6 7/8	6 7/8	2 4/8	2 3/8	12 2/8	14 5/8	5 6/8	5 6/8	Carbon Co., WY	Jerry G. Hagen	Jerry G. Hagen	1980	1528
82 2/8	15 1/8	15 5/8	6 6/8	6 6/8	2 5/8	2 5/8	15 5/8	7	6 4/8	5 7/8	Lake Co., OR	Richard R. Delfs	Richard R. Delfs	1981	1528
82 2/8	15 7/8	15	6 6/8	6 6/8	2 6/8	2 6/8	9 5/8	14 1/8	6 2/8	5 3/8	Natrona Co., WY	Wade Dumont	Wade Dumont	1981	1528
82 2/8	15 3/8	15	7 2/8	7 1/8	2 5/8	2 5/8	16 1/8	11 7/8	6 2/8	6 2/8	Niobrara Co., WY	W.L. McMillan	W.L. McMillan	1981	1528
82 2/8	17 3/8	17 4/8	6 2/8	6 3/8	2 4/8	2 3/8	14 5/8	4 3/8	5 3/8	5 4/8	Butte Co., ID	Jon L. Wadkins	Jon L. Wadkins	1981	1528
82 2/8	15 4/8	15 4/8	6 5/8	6 5/8	2 4/8	2 4/8	10 2/8	5 6/8	5 5/8	5 6/8	Brewster Co., TX	McLean Bowman	McLean Bowman	1982	1528
82 2/8	16 7/8	16	6 1/8	6	2 7/8	2 7/8	11 1/8	0 6/8	5 1/8	5 1/8	Sweetwater Co., WY	Len H. Guldman	Len H. Guldman	1982	1528
82 2/8	17	17	6	6	2 5/8	2 5/8	9 2/8	6 2/8	5 4/8	6	Sweetwater Co., WY	Gregg R. Landrum	Gregg R. Landrum	1982	1528
82 2/8	14 5/8	14 7/8	6 5/8	6 5/8	2 4/8	2 4/8	9 5/8	8 6/8	6 5/8	6 2/8	Washoe Co., NV	Thomas O. Malone	Thomas O. Malone	1982	1528
82 2/8	16 6/8	16 4/8	6 5/8	6 5/8	2 4/8	2 6/8	11 5/8	11	4 7/8	4 7/8	Fremont Co., WY	Michael C. Meeker	Michael C. Meeker	1982	1528
82 2/8	16 2/8	16 2/8	6 4/8	6 4/8	2 4/8	2 4/8	13 7/8	5 6/8	4 7/8	4 7/8	Valley Co., MT	David D. Rittenhouse	David D. Rittenhouse	1982	1528
82 2/8	15 6/8	15 6/8	6 5/8	6 5/8	2 5/8	2 5/8	14 1/8	13 6/8	5 6/8	5 6/8	Carbon Co., WY	Larry J. Thoney	Larry J. Thoney	1982	1528
82 2/8	16 4/8	16 4/8	6 3/8	6 3/8	2 4/8	2 4/8	13 1/8	9 2/8	5 5/8	5 6/8	Fremont Co., WY	Richard L. Bostrom	Richard L. Bostrom	1983	1528
82 2/8	16 2/8	16 2/8	6 4/8	6 4/8	2 7/8	2 7/8	9 5/8	3 5/8	5 4/8	5 4/8	Garfield Co., MT	William E. Butler	William E. Butler	1983	1528
82 2/8	16	16	6 1/8	6 1/8	2 7/8	2 6/8	10 2/8	6	6	6	Navajo Co., AZ	Collins L. Cochran	Collins L. Cochran	1983	1528
82 2/8	15 7/8	15 6/8	6 6/8	6 5/8	2 6/8	2 6/8	10 3/8	10	5 4/8	5 4/8	Washakie Co., WY	Carol Greet	Carol Greet	1983	1528

Score	Length of Horn R	Length of Horn L	Circ. Third Quarter R	Circ. Third Quarter L	Circ. of Base R	Circ. of Base L	Inside Spread	Tip to Tip Spread	Length of Prong R	Length of Prong L	Locality	Hunter	Owner	Date Killed	Rank
82 2/8	16 3/8	16 5/8	2 5/8	2 4/8	6 2/8	6 2/8	13 3/8	8 3/8	5 6/8	5 6/8	Fremont Co., WY	Evelyn A. Maxon	Evelyn A. Maxon	1983	1528
82 2/8	14	14 3/8	2 4/8	2 4/8	7 7/8	7 6/8	10 4/8	8 4/8	6 2/8	6 2/8	Sweetwater Co., WY	Peter B. Shaw	Peter B. Shaw	1983	1528
82 2/8	16 2/8	16 2/8	2 7/8	2 7/8	6 4/8	6 6/8	15	11	5 1/8	5	Navajo Co., AZ	Unknown	A.T. Boultinghouse	1983	1528
82 2/8	16 3/8	15 7/8	2 3/8	2 4/8	6 3/8	6 3/8	10 5/8	6 3/8	6 1/8	5 7/8	Butte Co., ID	Chris Tiller	Chris Tiller	1983	1528
82 2/8	18 2/8	18 7/8	2 5/8	2 2/8	6 2/8	6 3/8	9 5/8	5 5/8	5 2/8	5 2/8	Humboldt Co., NV	David E. Boyles, Sr.	David E. Boyles, Sr.	1984	1528
82 2/8	15 7/8	15 6/8	2 5/8	2 7/8	6 1/8	6 1/8	12 6/8	8 7/8	6 3/8	6 3/8	Hartley Co., TX	Ernie Davis	Ernie Davis	1984	1528
82 2/8	15 4/8	15 4/8	3	2 5/8	6 4/8	6 4/8	10	4 7/8	6	6	Fremont Co., WY	Charles D. Day	Charles D. Day	1984	1528
82 2/8	16	16 7/8	2 6/8	2 5/8	6	6	13 4/8	12	6 4/8	6 4/8	Sweetwater Co., WY	William Holland	Carl Holland	1984	1528
82 2/8	17 3/8	15 6/8	2 2/8	2 4/8	6 3/8	6 2/8	11 7/8	9 4/8	6 2/8	5 5/8	Siskiyou Co., CA	Laird E. Marshall	Laird E. Marshall	1984	1528
82 2/8	16	15	2 6/8	2 5/8	7 1/8	6 3/8	12 1/8	8 6/8	6 2/8	6 2/8	Natrona Co., WY	Michael D. Samuelson	Michael D. Samuelson	1984	1528
82 2/8	15 2/8	15 5/8	3	3	6 4/8	6 5/8	9 4/8	5	5 2/8	5 2/8	Humboldt Co., NV	Andrew S. Burnett	Andrew S. Burnett	1986	1528
82 2/8	15 2/8	15	2 7/8	2 7/8	7 4/8	7 3/8	11 1/8	7 6/8	7 1/8	5 4/8	Fergus Co., MT	Patricia M. Dreeszen	Patricia M. Dreeszen	1986	1528
82 2/8	17	17 2/8	3	3 2/8	6 2/8	6 2/8	10 2/8	3 4/8	6 2/8	4 4/8	Natrona Co., WY	Steven N. Levin	Steven N. Levin	1986	1528
82 2/8	14 1/8	14 5/8	3 1/8	2 5/8	7 5/8	7 3/8	8 6/8	14 2/8	7 3/8	6 1/8	Torrance Co., NM	Michael F. Killoy	Michael F. Killoy	1987	1528
82 2/8	16 5/8	16 4/8	3 2/8	2 5/8	6	6	15 6/8	6 7/8	6	6	Converse Co., WY	Barbara Moore	Barbara Moore	1987	1528
82 2/8	15 6/8	15 6/8	2 6/8	2 6/8	6 3/8	6 1/8	11	4 6/8	6 1/8	5 5/8	Catron Co., NM	Harry J. Turiello	Harry J. Turiello	1987	1528
82 2/8	14 6/8	14 7/8	2 7/8	2 7/8	7 1/8	7 1/8	10 3/8	5 3/8	5 6/8	6 1/8	Mohave Co., AZ	Ronald D. Wood	Ronald D. Wood	1987	1528
82 2/8	16	16 6/8	2 6/8	2 6/8	6	6	8 1/8	13 4/8	6 2/8	5 6/8	Rosebud Co., MT	Cory Nissen	Cory Nissen	1988	1528
82 2/8	16 2/8	15 7/8	2 7/8	2 5/8	6 5/8	6 5/8	14 1/8	2 6/8	6 1/8	6 1/8	Navajo Co., AZ	Brian Reece	Brian Reece	1988	1528
82 2/8	16 2/8	16 6/8	2 5/8	2 5/8	6	6 4/8	7 7/8	3 4/8	6 3/8	6 3/8	Carbon Co., WY	Robert Depellegrini	Robert Depellegrini	1989	1528
82 2/8	16 1/8	16 1/8	2 5/8	2 5/8	6 4/8	6 6/8	9 5/8	5 5/8	6 4/8	6 4/8	Fremont Co., WY	John A. Monje	John A. Monje	1989	1528
82 2/8	17	17	2 5/8	2 4/8	6 2/8	6	12 1/8	12 1/8	6 2/8	6 2/8	Natrona Co., WY	Valentine Novicki II	Valentine Novicki II	1989	1528
82 2/8	16 4/8	16 7/8	2 4/8	3 1/8	6 1/8	6 2/8	16 3/8	6 1/8	5 6/8	5	Middle Creek Res., AB	Donald P. Penner	Donald P. Penner	1989	1528
82 2/8	16	15 5/8	3 1/8	2 6/8	6 2/8	6 2/8	10 4/8	10 1/8	6 3/8	6 1/8	Catron Co., NM	Todd Garrison	Todd Garrison	1990	1528
82 2/8	14 4/8	14 4/8	2 6/8	3	6 5/8	6 4/8	14 2/8	6 6/8	5 3/8	5 2/8	Washoe Co., NV	Robert E. Hill	Robert E. Hill	1990	1528
82 2/8	15 5/8	15 6/8	3	2 6/8	6 5/8	6 6/8	10 5/8	7 6/8	5 2/8	5 4/8	Colfax Co., NM	Virgil A. Lair	Virgil A. Lair	1990	1528
82 2/8	16 2/8	16 5/8	2 5/8	2 6/8	6 4/8	6 6/8	10 3/8	7 1/8	5 4/8	4 6/8	Mora Co., NM	Allen E. Thomas	Allen E. Thomas	1990	1528
82 2/8	18 7/8	19 4/8	3 1/8	2 6/8	6 5/8	5 6/8	9 3/8	15 4/8	4 6/8	4 5/8	Weston Co., WY	Scott H. Eia	Scott H. Eia	1991	1528
82 2/8	15 6/8	15 5/8	2 3/8	3	5 6/8	7	17 7/8	7 7/8	5 4/8	6 2/8	Modoc Co., CA	Rod Eisenbeis	Rod Eisenbeis	1991	1528
82 2/8	15 1/8	15 1/8	2 4/8	2 7/8	7	7 1/8	9 7/8	8 2/8	5 3/8	5 1/8	Natrona Co., WY	Brian G. Elliott	Brian G. Elliott	1991	1528
82 2/8	17 2/8	16 7/8	2 7/8	2 5/8	6 4/8	6 3/8	10 6/8	5	6 2/8	6 1/8	Coconino Co., AZ	Dale H. Haggard	Dale H. Haggard	1991	1528
82 2/8	14 5/8	14 5/8	2 7/8	2 5/8	7 1/8	7	11 1/8	6 7/8	5 1/8	6 1/8	Sierra Co., NM	Gerald S. Janos	Gerald S. Janos	1991	1528
82 2/8	17	16 7/8	2 5/8	2 4/8	6 2/8	6 4/8	10 3/8	3 4/8	6 1/8	6 7/8	Dewey Co., SD	Roger T. Ralph	Roger T. Ralph	1991	1528
82 2/8	16 6/8	16 5/8	2 4/8	2 5/8	6 2/8	6 1/8	9	7	6 1/8	6 1/8	Slope Co., ND	Alan Ruhlman	Alan Ruhlman	1991	1528
82 2/8	15	15	2 6/8	2 5/8	6 7/8	7 2/8	11	5 2/8	5 2/8	5	Butte Co., SD	Marty Beard	Marty Beard	1992	1528
82 2/8	16 5/8	16 6/8	2 5/8	2 6/8	6 5/8	6 3/8	10	8 2/8	5 5/8	5 5/8	Catron Co., NM	Bernerd E. Emery	Bernerd E. Emery	1992	1528
82 2/8	16 2/8	16 3/8	3 3/8	3	6 7/8	7	8 2/8	2 7/8	4 6/8	4 6/8	Sweetwater Co., WY	Sam S. Jaksick, Jr.	Sam S. Jaksick, Jr.	1992	1528
82 2/8	17 1/8	17	2 4/8	2 4/8	5 7/8	6	17 3/8	14 4/8	5	4 7/8	Colfax Co., NM	Dan E. McBride	Dan E. McBride	1992	1528
82 2/8	15 3/8	15 3/8	2 4/8	2 6/8	7 2/8	7 1/8	10 4/8	5 7/8	6	5 6/8	Quay Co., NM	Cooper Moore	Cooper Moore	1992	1528
82 2/8	16 1/8	16 1/8	2 6/8	2 6/8	6 3/8	6 2/8	9 1/8	4 5/8	5 6/8	5 2/8	Natrona Co., WY	Lonnie L. Ritchey	Lonnie L. Ritchey	1992	1528
82 2/8	17 5/8	17 2/8	2 6/8	2 5/8	6 3/8	6 3/8	11 7/8	11 7/8	5 2/8	5 3/8	Mora Co., NM	Charles K. Williams	Charles K. Williams	1992	1528
82 2/8	16 4/8	16 5/8	2 6/8	2 5/8	6	6	7 7/8	7 7/8	5 3/8	5 4/8	Big Horn Co., MT	Anses Joseph, Jr.	Anses Joseph, Jr.	1993	1528
82 2/8	16 3/8	16 3/8	2 5/8	2 5/8	5 7/8	5 7/8	9	9	5 4/8	6	Coconino Co., AZ	Valley C. Sian	Valley C. Sian	1993	1528
82 2/8	16 6/8	15 5/8	2 3/8	2 3/8	5 6/8	5 6/8	10 2/8	4 3/8	6 2/8	6 6/8	Socorro Co., NM	Charles M. Wiedmaier	Charles M. Wiedmaier	1993	1528
82 2/8	15 5/8	15 5/8	3 1/8	3	6 2/8	6 3/8	11 5/8	8 5/8	6 7/8	6 6/8	Catron Co., NM	Mark A. Cadwallader	Mark A. Cadwallader	1994	1528
82 2/8	15 7/8	15 7/8	3	3	6 3/8	6 7/8	10 5/8	5 3/8	5	5	Sweetwater Co., WY	David Fulson	David Fulson	1994	1528
82 2/8	16	16	2 7/8	2 7/8	6 7/8	6 7/8	9	5 2/8	5	5 2/8	Carbon Co., WY	Casey Hunter	Casey Hunter	1994	1528
82 2/8	16	16	3 4/8	2 6/8	7	7	9 4/8	5 7/8	4 5/8	4 5/8	Carbon Co., WY	Richard D. Lumpkins	Richard D. Lumpkins	1994	1528

PRONGHORN

Antilocapra americana and related subspecies

Score	Length of Horn R	L	Circumference of Base R	L	Circumference at Third Quarter R	L	Inside Spread	Tip to Tip Spread	Length of Prong R	L	Locality	Hunter	Owner	Date Killed	Rank
82 2/8	14 6/8	14 5/8	6 5/8	6 4/8	3 1/8	3 2/8	8	4 3/8	5 3/8	5 3/8	Washoe Co., NV	Mark A. Mannens	Mark A. Mannens	1994	1528
82 2/8	16	16 2/8	6 1/8	6 1/8	3	3	9 4/8	5 2/8	5 3/8	5 4/8	Yavapai Co., AZ	Jason L. Sims	Jason L. Sims	1994	1528
82 2/8	16 1/8	16 1/8	7 1/8	7 1/8	3 1/8	3 1/8	12 5/8	8	4 7/8	4 6/8	Mora Co., NM	Edward C. Joseph	Edward C. Joseph	1995	1528
82 2/8	17 2/8	17	6 4/8	6 4/8	1 7/8	1 7/8	16 4/8	15 6/8	5	4 4/8	Socorro Co., NM	David L. Swenson	David L. Swenson	1995	1528
82 2/8	16 1/8	16	6 4/8	6 4/8	2 3/8	2 3/8	11 6/8	7	6 4/8	6 6/8	Washoe Co., NV	Kent Burroughs	Kent Burroughs	1996	1528
82 2/8	15 5/8	15 5/8	6 6/8	6 7/8	2 6/8	2 6/8	12 1/8	7	5 5/8	5 4/8	Colfax Co., NM	Robert D. Jones	Robert D. Jones	1996	1528
82 2/8	16 5/8	16 6/8	6 4/8	6 4/8	2 6/8	3 1/8	8 7/8	2 6/8	5 1/8	4 7/8	Hudspeth Co., TX	Dan E. McBride	Dan E. McBride	1996	1528
82 2/8	16 5/8	16 5/8	6 3/8	6 2/8	3 2/8	3 2/8	10 6/8	7 4/8	4 6/8	4 4/8	Socorro Co., NM	William S. Pickett III	William S. Pickett III	1996	1528
82 2/8	16 4/8	16 5/8	6 6/8	6 6/8	2 4/8	2 4/8	8 4/8	2	5 6/8	6 2/8	Pershing Co., NV	Randy C. Rasley	Randy C. Rasley	1996	1528
82 2/8	17	17	6 6/8	6 6/8	2 7/8	2 7/8	9 3/8	5 6/8	5 4/8	5 4/8	Colfax Co., NM	Bill K. Ritchey	Bill K. Ritchey	1996	1528
82 2/8	15 2/8	14 5/8	7 2/8	7 2/8	2 4/8	2 3/8	8 6/8	7 2/8	5 3/8	5 3/8	Converse Co., WY	David Tinson	David Tinson	1996	1528
82 2/8	16 2/8	16	6 5/8	6 5/8	2 4/8	2 3/8	9 3/8	4 4/8	5 3/8	5 4/8	Mora Co., NM	Howard M. Barnett	Howard M. Barnett	1997	1528
82 2/8	16	16 1/8	6 2/8	6 2/8	3	2 4/8	10 4/8	7 1/8	6 4/8	6 5/8	Beaverhead Co., MT	Kenneth A. Bujok	Kenneth A. Bujok	1997	1528
82 2/8	15 4/8	15 1/8	6 5/8	6 5/8	3	3	18 5/8	17	5 6/8	5 6/8	Arapahoe Co., CO	Joseph P. Emily	Joseph P. Emily	1998	1528
82 2/8	16 4/8	16 4/8	5 6/8	5 6/8	2 7/8	2 6/8	9 1/8	4 1/8	5 5/8	5 6/8	Socorro Co., NM	Peeler Lacey	Peeler G. Lacey	1998	1528
82 2/8	16 4/8	16 4/8	6 4/8	6 3/8	2 6/8	2 3/8	8 6/8	4 2/8	6 3/8	6 4/8	Emery Co., UT	Rick M. Rasmussen	Rick M. Rasmussen	1998	1528
82 2/8	15	14 4/8	6 4/8	6	2 5/8	2 6/8	13 5/8	9 1/8	5 7/8	5 3/8	Coconino Co., AZ	James Shaff	James R. Shaff	1998	1528
82 2/8	16 3/8	16 3/8	6 1/8	6	2 5/8	2 5/8	10	4 3/8	4 3/8	4 3/8	Mora Co., NM	Justin Stewart	Justin Stewart	1998	1528
82 2/8	16 3/8	16 2/8	7	7 2/8	2 6/8	2 6/8	9 2/8	4 5/8	5 7/8	5 7/8	Taos Co., NM	William R. Balsi, Jr.	William R. Balsi, Jr.	1999	1528
82 2/8	16 2/8	16 2/8	6 4/8	6 4/8	2 4/8	2 4/8	12 2/8	8 5/8	4 6/8	5	Carbon Co., WY	Jeffrey J. Bode	Jeffrey J. Bode	1999	1528
82 2/8	15 6/8	15 5/8	7 3/8	7 2/8	2 4/8	2 4/8	12 2/8	9 7/8	5 2/8	5	Socorro Co., NM	Mark T. Donovan	Mark T. Donovan	1999	1528
82 2/8	14 7/8	14 5/8	6 4/8	6 4/8	3 3/8	3 3/8	13 1/8	10 2/8	6	5 3/8	Natrona Co., WY	Garrett Henry	Garrett Henry	1999	1528
82 2/8	16	15 6/8	6 7/8	7	2 4/8	2 4/8	13	10	5 4/8	4 5/8	Carbon Co., WY	Michael D. Hirsch	Michael D. Hirsch	1999	1528
82 2/8	16 6/8	16 4/8	7	7 2/8	2 6/8	2 6/8	10	7 2/8	5	5	Uinta Co., WY	Dolores M. Larson	Dolores M. Larson	1999	1528
82 2/8	15 2/8	14 7/8	7 5/8	7 5/8	2 6/8	3	8 7/8	3 5/8	5 3/8	5 4/8	Fremont Co., WY	Michael D. Schauer	Michael D. Schauer	1999	1528
82 2/8	15 5/8	15 3/8	6 3/8	6 3/8	2 4/8	2 4/8	12 4/8	9 1/8	5 7/8	5 5/8	Washakie Co., WY	Carol A. Schuette	Carol A. Schuette	1999	1528
82 2/8	15 2/8	15 1/8	6 5/8	6 5/8	3 1/8	3 1/8	10	7 1/8	6 1/8	5 4/8	Socorro Co., NM	Ernie Davis	Ernie Davis	2000	1528
82 2/8	17 1/8	16	6 3/8	6 4/8	2 4/8	2 4/8	9 2/8	4 5/8	6 5/8	5 5/8	Modoc Co., CA	Ronald V. Giese	Ronald V. Giese	2000	1528
82 2/8	15 2/8	15 6/8	6 4/8	6 7/8	2 5/8	2 4/8	13 6/8	10	6 5/8	5 5/8	S. Saskatchewan River, AB	John D. Gordon	John D. Gordon	2000	1528
82 2/8	15 3/8	15 3/8	6 2/8	6 2/8	2 6/8	2 6/8	8 3/8	3 3/8	5 7/8	5 7/8	Rosebud Co., MT	Eugene F. Himmel	Eugene F. Himmel	2000	1528
82 2/8	15 2/8	15 4/8	6 7/8	7	2 7/8	2 7/8	12	7 2/8	5 4/8	5 3/8	Cibola Co., NM	Russell E. Livingston II	Russell E. Livingston II	2000	1528
82 2/8	16 4/8	16 4/8	5 5/8	6	2 6/8	3	14 2/8	12 4/8	6 1/8	6 1/8	Coconino Co., AZ	Keith Martin	Keith Martin	2000	1528
82 2/8	15 3/8	15 2/8	6 6/8	6 6/8	2 5/8	2 6/8	14 7/8	12 3/8	5 7/8	4 5/8	Hudspeth Co., TX	Timothy L. Orton	Timothy L. Orton	2001	1528
82 2/8	16 2/8	15 7/8	7 2/8	7 2/8	2 5/8	2 3/8	12 2/8	10	5 5/8	5 6/8	Sweetwater Co., WY	Kevin Burns	Kevin Burns	2001	1528
82 2/8	14 7/8	14 5/8	7 2/8	7 1/8	2 5/8	2 6/8	11 3/8	8 2/8	5 7/8	6 1/8	Campbell Co., WY	Derek E. Emter	Orin Edwards	2001	1528
82 2/8	16	16	7	7	2 4/8	2 4/8	9 7/8	7	6	6 1/8	Fremont Co., WY	Jeffery K. Harrow	Jeffery K. Harrow	2001	1528
82 2/8	15 7/8	15 1/8	6 4/8	6 4/8	2 5/8	2 2/8	9	4 2/8	6 6/8	6 6/8	Albany Co., WY	Janan B. Jones	Janan B. Jones	2001	1528

Score	Locality	By Whom Killed	Owner	Date Killed	Rank
82 2/8	Union Co., OR	David J. Barlet	David J. Barlet	2002	1528
82 2/8	Hudspeth Co., TX	Gerald P. McBride	Gerald P. McBride	2002	1528
82 2/8	Santa Fe Co., NM	Johnny L. Montoya	Johnny L. Montoya	2002	1528
82 2/8	Wibaux Co., MT	Gary A. Nunberg	Gary A. Nunberg	2002	1528
82 2/8	Taos Co., NM	Donald E. Perrien	Donald E. Perrien	2002	1528
82 2/8	Laramie Co., WY	Blake C. Prather	Blake C. Prather	2002	1528
82 2/8	Coconino Co., AZ	Robert M. Young	Robert M. Young	2002	1528
82 2/8	Golden Valley Co., ND	Sean M. Finneman	Sean M. Finneman	2003	1528
82 2/8	Carbon Co., WY	Larry S. Hicks	Larry S. Hicks	2003	1528
82 2/8	Socorro Co., NM	Timothy K. Krause	Timothy K. Krause	2003	1528
82 2/8	Yavapai Co., AZ	Rick J. Levine	Rick J. Levine	2003	1528
82 2/8	Humboldt Co., NV	Valerie J. Moser	Valerie J. Moser	2003	1528
82	Pahsimeroi Valley, ID	Elmer Keith	Elmer Keith	1936	1683
82	Catron Co., NM	Floyd Todd	Floyd Todd	1947	1683
82	Mormon Lake, AZ	Bob Householder	Bob Householder	1949	1683
82	Shirley Basin, WY	Earl Fisher	Earl Fisher	1951	1683
82	Williams Co., AZ	Paul D. Hosman	Paul D. Hosman	1951	1683
82	Anderson Mesa, AZ	Mrs. C.C. Cooper	Mrs. C.C. Cooper	1953	1683
82	Santa Rosa Co., NM	Frank C. Hibben	Frank C. Hibben	1955	1683
82	Bow Island, AB	R.F. Dunmire	R.F. Dunmire	1957	1683
82	Limon, CO	Walt Paulk	Walt Paulk	1958	1683
82	Sage Creek, WY	Mrs. Ramon Somavia	Mrs. Ramon Somavia	1960	1683
82	Encampment, WY	G.A. Surface	G.A. Surface	1960	1683
82	Natrona Co., WY	Fred Deiss	Fred Deiss	1961	1683
82	Shirley Basin, WY	Norman Miller	Norman Miller	1961	1683
82	Shirley Basin, WY	Henry Macagni	Henry Macagni	1962	1683
82	Hartley Co., TX	Walter O. Ford, Jr.	Walter O. Ford, Jr.	1964	1683
82	Arco, ID	Ernest L. Ellis, Jr.	Ernest L. Ellis, Jr.	1965	1683
82	McKinley Co., NM	W.R. Phillips	W.R. Phillips	1965	1683
82	Navajo Co., AZ	John Welch III	John Welch III	1965	1683
82	Eston, SK	Dennis Crowe	Dennis Crowe	1966	1683
82	Lake Co., OR	Eldon Hayes	Eldon Hayes	1966	1683
82	Garfield Co., MT	Dean V. Ashton	Dean V. Ashton	1968	1683
82	Carbon Co., WY	C.W. Hermanson	C.W. Hermanson	1968	1683
82	Farson, WY	Larry N. Garner	Larry N. Garner	1969	1683
82	Albany Co., WY	Edwin J. Keppner	Edwin J. Keppner	1969	1683
82	Wamsutter, WY	Frank Simons	Frank Simons	1969	1683
82	Carbon Co., WY	Martin J. Stuart	Martin J. Stuart	1969	1683
82	Washoe Co., NV	Oliver V. Iveson	Josh Iveson	1970	1683
82	Brewster Co., TX	Joseph W. Burkett III	Joseph W. Burkett III	1972	1683
82	Sweet Rock, WY	Alphonse Cuomo, Jr.	Alphonse Cuomo, Jr.	1973	1683
82	Sublette Co., WY	Gary D. Jorgensen	Gary D. Jorgensen	1973	1683
82	Coconino Co., AZ	Jerry R. Killman	Jerry R. Killman	1973	1683
82	Garfield Co., MT	Don E. Traughber	Don E. Traughber	1973	1683
82	Wolf Point, MT	Raymond A. Gould	Raymond A. Gould	1974	1683
82	Carbon Co., WY	Reg. R. Smith	Reg. R. Smith	1974	1683
82	Campbell Co., WY	Gilbert Steinen, Jr.	Gilbert Steinen, Jr.	1975	1683
82	Lake Co., OR	Calvin M. Auvil	Calvin M. Auvil	1976	1683

PRONGHORN

Antilocapra americana and related subspecies

Score	Length of Horn R	L	Circumference of Base R	L	Circumference at Third Quarter R	L	Inside Spread	Tip to Tip Spread	Length of Prong R	L	Locality	Hunter	Owner	Date Killed	Rank
82	14 1/8	13 6/8	7	6 6/8	3	3	11 4/8	9 6/8	4 4/8	4 4/8	Sweetwater Co., WY	Starla L. Cairns	Starla L. Cairns	1976	1683
82	15 2/8	15 3/8	6 6/8	6 4/8	3 2/8	3 2/8	9	2 7/8	5 6/8	5 6/8	Wallace Co., KS	Curtis R. Penner	Curtis R. Penner	1976	1683
82	16 4/8	16 4/8	6 6/8	6 6/8	2 3/8	2 2/8	11 4/8	8 2/8	5 4/8	5 4/8	Fremont Co., WY	Daniel R. Hahn	Daniel R. Hahn	1977	1683
82	15 6/8	15 6/8	7	6 7/8	2 4/8	2 3/8	10	7 3/8	6 1/8	5 7/8	Carbon Co., WY	William E. Pipes III	William E. Pipes III	1977	1683
82	15	15	7 3/8	7 1/8	2 5/8	2 5/8	12 4/8	10 3/8	5 6/8	5	Carbon Co., WY	Peck Rollison	Peck Rollison	1977	1683
82	16	16	6	6	3	3 2/8	9	6 2/8	5 4/8	5 4/8	Hartley Co., TX	John A. Wright	John A. Wright	1978	1683
82	17 7/8	17 6/8	5 5/8	5 4/8	2 4/8	2 2/8	12 7/8	6 7/8	5 4/8	5 3/8	Otero Co., NM	Robert E. Anton	Robert E. Anton	1978	1683
82	16 4/8	16 3/8	7 5/8	7	2 5/8	2 7/8	12 6/8	10 3/8	5 4/8	5	Fremont Co., WY	John J. Eichhorn	John J. Eichhorn	1978	1683
82	16 4/8	16 4/8	6 2/8	6 2/8	2 6/8	2 5/8	8 7/8	4	5 1/8	5 2/8	Hudspeth Co., TX	Luther V. Oliver	Luther V. Oliver	1978	1683
82	17 1/8	17 4/8	6 4/8	6 4/8	3 1/8	3 1/8	0	0	4 2/8	4 4/8	Culberson Co., TX	Charles Seidensticker	Charles Seidensticker	1978	1683
82	14 5/8	15 1/8	6 7/8	6 7/8	2 4/8	2 4/8	10 7/8	6 7/8	6 3/8	5 1/8	Sweetwater Co., WY	Dan B. Artery	Dan B. Artery	1979	1683
82	17	17	6 4/8	6 3/8	2 5/8	2 4/8	8 6/8	6 4/8	4 6/8	5 5/8	Brewster Co., TX	Peggy F. Brady	Peggy F. Brady	1979	1683
82	16 1/8	16 1/8	6 5/8	6 4/8	2 6/8	2 6/8	12 6/8	7 3/8	5 5/8	5 5/8	Lassen Co., CA	Robert D. Luna, Jr.	Robert D. Luna, Jr.	1979	1683
82	16 1/8	16	7	6 7/8	2 5/8	2 5/8	9	2 1/8	5 2/8	4 6/8	Fremont Co., WY	Steven E. Clingman	Steven E. Clingman	1980	1683
82	16 6/8	16 5/8	6 3/8	6 2/8	2 2/8	2 2/8	15	11 5/8	5 5/8	5 2/8	Natrona Co., WY	Theresa Fulfaro	Theresa Fulfaro	1980	1683
82	16 3/8	16 2/8	6 3/8	6 4/8	2 5/8	2 5/8	9 6/8	3 5/8	5 5/8	5 5/8	Coconino Co., AZ	Fred W. Fernow, Jr.	Fred W. Fernow, Jr.	1981	1683
82	16 1/8	16	6 1/8	6 1/8	2 2/8	2 2/8	14	10 1/8	6 4/8	6 4/8	Washoe Co., NV	Jerry L. Nelms	Jerry L. Nelms	1981	1683
82	17	17	6 2/8	6 1/8	2 4/8	2 4/8	6 6/8	1 6/8	5 5/8	5 4/8	Lincoln Co., WY	Tom Crank	Tom Crank	1982	1683
82	15 6/8	15 6/8	7	7	2 6/8	2 6/8	8 4/8	2 6/8	5 2/8	5 2/8	Crook Co., WY	Jay D. Hacklin	Jay D. Hacklin	1982	1683
82	15 5/8	15 3/8	6 2/8	6 6/8	2 6/8	2 5/8	10 4/8	6 3/8	6 2/8	6 4/8	Fremont Co., WY	Thomas O. Martens	Thomas O. Martens	1982	1683
82	16 2/8	16 1/8	6 1/8	6 6/8	2 5/8	2 5/8	12	8 3/8	5 2/8	5 1/8	Natrona Co., WY	Joseph P. Prinzi	Joseph P. Prinzi	1982	1683
82	15 2/8	15 2/8	6 5/8	6 4/8	3	3 1/8	10	6 4/8	5 2/8	5 4/8	Carbon Co., WY	Eric J. Swanson	Eric J. Swanson	1982	1683
82	14 1/8	14	7 2/8	7 1/8	2 5/8	2 5/8	10 6/8	7 5/8	6 2/8	6 1/8	Sweetwater Co., WY	Brett A. Ward	Brett A. Ward	1982	1683
82	15	14 5/8	7	7 1/8	2 6/8	2 6/8	12	10 6/8	5 5/8	5 5/8	Carbon Co., WY	Albert Gregg	Albert Gregg	1983	1683
82	16 2/8	15 6/8	6 5/8	6 5/8	2 4/8	2 4/8	7 2/8	1	5 7/8	5 7/8	Washoe Co., NV	Jack D. Bothwell	Jack D. Bothwell	1984	1683
82	16 5/8	16 3/8	6 1/8	6 4/8	2 3/8	2 4/8	14 1/8	10 1/8	5 6/8	5 6/8	Quay Co., NM	Donald E. Fritz	Donald E. Fritz	1984	1683
82	16	15 7/8	6 2/8	6 3/8	2 7/8	2 6/8	9 6/8	5	5	5 3/8	Coconino Co., AZ	Charles L. Holland	Charles L. Holland	1984	1683
82	15 5/8	16 1/8	6 7/8	6 6/8	2 5/8	2 5/8	8 4/8	5	5 6/8	5 6/8	Carbon Co., WY	James A. Rademacher	James A. Rademacher	1986	1683
82	16 4/8	17	6 3/8	6 4/8	2 5/8	2 5/8	10 2/8	7 4/8	5 3/8	5	Johnson Co., WY	Thomas F. Williams	Thomas F. Williams	1986	1683
82	15 5/8	15 7/8	6 6/8	6 6/8	2 6/8	2 6/8	8 4/8	3 4/8	5 5/8	5 5/8	Catron Co., NM	John P. Grimmett	John P. Grimmett	1987	1683
82	16 1/8	16	6 6/8	6 5/8	2 4/8	2 4/8	11 6/8	7 5/8	6	5 3/8	Apache Co., AZ	Leonard J. Imperial	Leonard J. Imperial	1987	1683
82	17 4/8	18	6 6/8	5 6/8	2 7/8	2 7/8	18	16 2/8	4 6/8	4 5/8	Graham Co., AZ	James P. Kniffin	James P. Kniffin	1987	1683
82	15 4/8	15 4/8	6 6/8	6 6/8	2 6/8	2 6/8	8 4/8	5 7/8	5 6/8	4 6/8	Alberta	Peter M. Parkyn	Peter M. Parkyn	1987	1683
82	16 4/8	16 2/8	6 4/8	6 4/8	2 4/8	2 4/8	7 5/8	5 7/8	5 7/8	5 7/8	Sweetwater Co., WY	Jeffrey A. Schalow	Jeffrey A. Schalow	1988	1683
82	15 3/8	15 3/8	6 6/8	6 2/8	2 2/8	2 2/8	7 2/8	3 4/8	6 2/8	6 2/8	Elko Co., NV	Roger L. Curry	Roger L. Curry	1988	1683
82	15 7/8	15 7/8	6 3/8	6 3/8	3	3	14 4/8	11	5 3/8	5 4/8	Billings Co., ND	Curtis D. Decker	Curtis D. Decker	1988	1683
82	17 1/8	16 6/8	6 4/8	6 3/8	2 3/8	2 3/8	11 5/8	6 5/8	5 5/8	5 4/8	Fremont Co., WY	Timothy A. Kiefer	Timothy A. Kiefer	1988	1683
82	16	15 3/8	6 4/8	6 4/8	2 6/8	2 6/8	11	8 1/8	4 6/8	4 6/8	Harding Co., NM	Andrew J. Ortega	Andrew J. Ortega	1988	1683

Score	Length of Horn R	Length of Horn L	Circ. of Base R	Circ. of Base L	Circ. 3/4 R	Circ. 3/4 L	Length of Prong	Inside Spread	Tip to Tip Spread	Locality	Hunter	Owner	Date	Rank
82	14 2/8	14 3/8	7 2/8	7 2/8	2 5/8	2 6/8	5 7/8	9 3/8	5 4/8	Carbon Co., WY	Donald L. Soderberg	Donald L. Soderberg	1988	1683
82	14 3/8	14 3/8	7 2/8	7 2/8	2 3/8	2 3/8	6 3/8	11 5/8	10 2/8	Carbon Co., WY	Becky Strand	Becky Strand	1988	1683
82	16 7/8	17	6 3/8	6 4/8	2 5/8	2 6/8	4 6/8	11 2/8	6	Mora Co., NM	Horace P. Wood	Horace P. Wood	1988	1683
82	14 4/8	14 3/8	7 6/8	7 6/8	2 5/8	2 6/8	5 5/8	10 6/8	8 6/8	Sweetwater Co., WY	Mark E. Gillespie	Mark E. Gillespie	1989	1683
82	15 4/8	15 6/8	6	6	2 5/8	2 7/8	6	10 2/8	4 1/8	Mohave Co., AZ	Jeff K. Gunnell	Jeff K. Gunnell	1989	1683
82	17 4/8	17	6 1/8	6 4/8	2 2/8	2 2/8	5 6/8	12 6/8	8 5/8	Guadalupe Co., NM	Kenneth J. Morga	Kenneth J. Morga	1989	1683
82	16 2/8	16 2/8	6 4/8	6 4/8	2 4/8	2 3/8	6 3/8	9 5/8	5 4/8	Washoe Co., NV	James E. Puryear	James E. Puryear	1989	1683
82	16 2/8	16 2/8	6 1/8	6 4/8	2 3/8	2 7/8	6 1/8	8 6/8	5 5/8	Lincoln Co., NV	Michael H. Romney	Michael H. Romney	1989	1683
82	15 5/8	15 5/8	6 3/8	6 4/8	2 7/8	2 7/8	5 6/8	8 2/8	5	Natrona Co., WY	Victor Colonna	Victor Colonna	1990	1683
82	15 3/8	15 2/8	6 4/8	7	2 6/8	2 4/8	5 6/8	8 4/8	4	Albany Co., WY	Phil Darnell	Phil Darnell	1990	1683
82	15	15 1/8	7	7 1/8	2 3/8	3	6 5/8	8 6/8	4	Carbon Co., WY	Allen A. Ehrke	Allen A. Ehrke	1990	1683
82	16 6/8	16 2/8	6 7/8	7	3	2 6/8	6 6/8	9 6/8	3	Moffat Co., CO	Len H. Guldman	Len H. Guldman	1990	1683
82	16 2/8	16	6 3/8	6 4/8	2 6/8	2 4/8	5	10 3/8	5 5/8	Washakie Co., WY	Jake Hanson	Jake Hanson	1990	1683
82	15 7/8	15 7/8	6 2/8	6 2/8	2 5/8	2 3/8	6 1/8	8 2/8	4 6/8	Mora Co., NM	Todd S. Hyden	Todd S. Hyden	1990	1683
82	17 4/8	17 3/8	6 6/8	6 6/8	2 3/8	2 7/8	4 7/8	9 2/8	2 7/8	Washoe Co., NV	Paul J. Jesch	Paul J. Jesch	1990	1683
82	17	17	6 6/8	6 1/8	3	3	3 5/8	16 3/8	3	Lincoln Co., NM	Steve A. Marasovich, Jr.	Steve A. Marasovich, Jr.	1990	1683
82	16 5/8	16 7/8	6 1/8	6 4/8	2 4/8	2 4/8	5 2/8	8 7/8	12 3/8	Slope Co., ND	Todd M. Quinn	Todd M. Quinn	1990	1683
82	17 6/8	17 4/8	6 3/8	6 4/8	2 4/8	2 5/8	6 1/8	10 4/8	4 4/8	Hudspeth Co., TX	E. Scott Smith	E. Scott Smith	1990	1683
82	16	16	6 3/8	6 4/8	2 4/8	2 4/8	7 1/8	12	8 7/8	Albany Co., WY	James T. Sprinkle	James T. Sprinkle	1990	1683
82	15 3/8	15 4/8	6 5/8	6 5/8	3	2 4/8	6 5/8	11 4/8	8 1/8	Lassen Co., CA	Tommy B. Esperance	Tommy B. Esperance	1991	1683
82	15 7/8	15 3/8	7 1/8	7	2 4/8	3	6 4/8	9 7/8	8 7/8	Mora Co., NM	Raymond R. Gonzales	Charlie Hooser	1991	1683
82	15 4/8	15	6 4/8	6 4/8	2 5/8	2 5/8	7 2/8	10 6/8	7 2/8	Washoe Co., NV	James D. Jones	James D. Jones	1991	1683
82	16 3/8	16 4/8	7 2/8	6 6/8	2 7/8	2 7/8	6 5/8	9 7/8	5 3/8	Lassen Co., CA	Joseph D. Nolan	Joseph D. Nolan	1991	1683
82	16 1/8	16 2/8	6 2/8	6 6/8	2 5/8	2 7/8	6 1/8	9 5/8	7 3/8	Converse Co., WY	Rick P. Sakovitz	Rick P. Sakovitz	1991	1683
82	13 4/8	13 2/8	7 1/8	6 4/8	2 7/8	2 6/8	7 1/8	11 7/8	3 7/8	Frenchman River, SK	Larry Schmidt	Larry Schmidt	1991	1683
82	16 4/8	16 7/8	6 5/8	6 5/8	3	3	6 5/8	7	10 6/8	Carbon Co., WY	Andrew W. Serres	Andrew W. Serres	1991	1683
82	16 2/8	16 3/8	6 5/8	6 4/8	2 4/8	2 4/8	6 3/8	6 3/8	2 3/8	Cochise Co., AZ	Brad Wedding	Brad Wedding	1992	1683
82	16 2/8	16 2/8	6 4/8	6 6/8	2 5/8	3	5 1/8	13 3/8	0 1/8	Washoe Co., NV	Richard T. Adams	Richard T. Adams	1992	1683
82	15 1/8	15 7/8	6	6	3	3	5	8 3/8	8 6/8	Catron Co., NM	Spence Dupree	Spence Dupree	1992	1683
82	16 1/8	16	6 4/8	6 4/8	2 5/8	2 5/8	6 2/8	10 7/8	8 6/8	Carbon Co., WY	Jeffrey L. Engel	Jeffrey L. Engel	1992	1683
82	16 3/8	16 3/8	6 3/8	6 3/8	2 7/8	2 7/8	5 4/8	13 6/8	6 6/8	Sweetwater Co., WY	Dennis L. Haan	Dennis L. Haan	1992	1683
82	16 1/8	16 1/8	6 6/8	6 6/8	2 3/8	2 1/8	5 5/8	10 1/8	4 4/8	Rosebud Co., MT	Denver W. Holt	Denver W. Holt	1992	1683
82	15	15	6 4/8	6 4/8	2 5/8	2 5/8	6	13 6/8	10 2/8	Colfax Co., NM	Kyle G. Hyden	Kyle G. Hyden	1992	1683
82	16 3/8	16 3/8	6 6/8	7 1/8	2 6/8	2 6/8	4 7/8	10	7 6/8	Garfield Co., MT	Kip K. Karges	Kip K. Karges	1992	1683
82	16 2/8	16 1/8	6 4/8	6 5/8	2 5/8	2 6/8	6 1/8	7	2 5/8	Mora Co., NM	Luke C. Kellogg	Luke C. Kellogg	1992	1683
82	17 1/8	16 5/8	5 6/8	5 6/8	2 7/8	2 6/8	5 5/8	10 7/8	5 4/8	Catron Co., NM	Donald K. Lash	Donald K. Lash	1992	1683
82	16 1/8	16	6 6/8	6 6/8	2 1/8	2 2/8	4 6/8	13 6/8	11 4/8	Washoe Co., NV	Andy H. Riddell	Andy H. Riddell	1992	1683
82	16 1/8	16 1/8	6 4/8	6 4/8	3	3	4 6/8	9 2/8	3	Colfax Co., NM	Maurice R. Strawn	Maurice R. Strawn	1992	1683
82	16 5/8	16 5/8	6 7/8	6 7/8	2 5/8	2 5/8	5 2/8	12	7 4/8	Colfax Co., NM	James D. Verbrugge	James D. Verbrugge	1992	1683
82	15 5/8	15 4/8	6 2/8	6 2/8	2 6/8	2 6/8	5 3/8	7 6/8	4	Lincoln Co., NM	Earl K. Wahl, Jr.	Earl K. Wahl, Jr.	1993	1683
82	16 7/8	16	7	7	2 7/8	3 1/8	5	10 3/8	6 4/8	Rich Co., UT	William B. Bullen	William B. Bullen	1993	1683
82	15 4/8	15 3/8	6 4/8	6 4/8	3 1/8	2 3/8	6 4/8	11 1/8	6 3/8	Coconino Co., AZ	John P. Grimmett	John P. Grimmett	1993	1683
82	14 6/8	14 6/8	6 2/8	6 2/8	2 3/8	3 7/8	4 2/8	13 5/8	9	Milk River, AB	Lance Hartley	Lance Hartley	1993	1683
82	16 2/8	15 4/8	6 3/8	6 3/8	3	3	5 7/8	6 3/8	1 3/8	Apache Co., AZ	Shane D. Koury	Shane D. Koury	1993	1683
82	17	17	6	6	2 6/8	2 5/8	6 3/8	11 1/8	6 3/8	Slope Co., ND	Sherry L. Niesar	Sherry L. Niesar	1993	1683
82	15 7/8	15 5/8	6 2/8	6 3/8	2 5/8	2 5/8	5 6/8	15 6/8	14	Colfax Co., NM	David R. Raemisch	David R. Raemisch	1993	1683
82	17 1/8	17 1/8	6 2/8	6 2/8	3 1/8	3	4 1/8	9 7/8	4 3/8	Lincoln Co., NM	Nicholas A. Baldock	Nicholas A. Baldock	1994	1683
82								13	7 7/8	Harney Co., OR	Errol W. Claire	Errol W. Claire	1994	1683

Score	Length of Horn R	L	Circumference of Base R	L	Circumference at Third Quarter R	L	Inside Spread	Tip to Tip Spread	Length of Prong R	L	Locality	Hunter	Owner	Date Killed	Rank
82	17 4/8	17 3/8	6	6 1/8	2 4/8	2 6/8	15 2/8	9 2/8	5	5 1/8	Navajo Co., AZ	Earl A. Petznick, Jr.	Earl A. Petznick, Jr.	1994	1683
82	15 4/8	15 4/8	7	7	2 6/8	2 6/8	9 5/8	4 6/8	5 7/8	5 2/8	Colfax Co., NM	R. Terrell McCombs	R. Terrell McCombs	1995	1683
82	15	15 4/8	6 6/8	6 6/8	2 5/8	2 7/8	11 4/8	8 4/8	5 2/8	5 2/8	Banner Co., NE	Timothy H. Ruzicka	Timothy H. Ruzicka	1995	1683
82	17 6/8	17 4/8	6 6/8	6 4/8	2 4/8	2 4/8	11 7/8	6 5/8	4 3/8	5	Humboldt Co., NV	Joseph D. Anelli	Joseph D. Anelli	1996	1683
82	16 2/8	16 2/8	6 4/8	6 2/8	2 5/8	2 5/8	11	5 5/8	5 1/8	5 3/8	Catron Co., NM	Mark J. Etcheberry	Mark J. Etcheberry	1996	1683
82	16 4/8	16 2/8	6 6/8	6 6/8	2 4/8	2 3/8	8 7/8	4 4/8	5 4/8	6	Washoe Co., NV	Robert A. Johnson	Robert A. Johnson	1996	1683
82	15 3/8	15 2/8	7 1/8	7 1/8	2 4/8	2 4/8	13 2/8	9 1/8	5 4/8	5 3/8	Rosebud Co., MT	Gary L. Reed	Gary L. Reed	1996	1683
82	15 4/8	15 6/8	6 2/8	6 3/8	3	3	8 2/8	4	5 4/8	5 2/8	Malheur Co., OR	Ursula E. Sporrer-Cain	Ursula E. Sporrer-Cain	1996	1683
82	16 3/8	15 4/8	6 6/8	6 6/8	2 4/8	2 4/8	9 5/8	4 2/8	6 5/8	6	Humboldt Co., NV	Donald D. Van Dyken	Donald D. Van Dyken	1996	1683
82	16 4/8	16 4/8	6 2/8	6 2/8	2 4/8	2 4/8	9 6/8	2 5/8	6 2/8	6 3/8	Lincoln Co., NM	Russell J. Jackson	Russell J. Jackson	1997	1683
82	16 4/8	16 3/8	6 3/8	6 3/8	3	3	10 2/8	9	5 4/8	5 2/8	Mora Co., NM	Robert I. Kelly	Robert I. Kelly	1997	1683
82	15 1/8	15 1/8	6 6/8	6 7/8	3 1/8	2 5/8	9 6/8	5 6/8	5	5	Logan Co., CO	Andrew R. Paxton	Andrew R. Paxton	1997	1683
82	16 2/8	16 2/8	6 1/8	6 4/8	2 5/8	2 6/8	8	2 4/8	6 2/8	5 7/8	Platte Co., WY	Rick L. Wiley	Rick L. Wiley	1998	1683
82	16	16	7 1/8	7 1/8	2 4/8	2 5/8	12 2/8	9 1/8	5	4 7/8	Carbon Co., CA	Jon D. Crowley	Jon D. Crowley	1998	1683
82	15 7/8	15 7/8	6 5/8	6 5/8	2 5/8	2 5/8	10 4/8	5 2/8	5 6/8	5 3/8	Carbon Co., WY	Jerry L. Hamel, Jr.	Jerry L. Hamel, Jr.	1998	1683
82	16 2/8	15 7/8	6 7/8	6 7/8	3 1/8	2 7/8	15	11 6/8	5 3/8	5	Socorro Co., NM	William R. Hemphill	William R. Hemphill	1998	1683
82	16 3/8	16 3/8	6 6/8	6 5/8	2 5/8	2 5/8	9 5/8	5 1/8	5 2/8	5	Socorro Co., NM	Alan W. Krause	Alan W. Krause	1998	1683
82	15 5/8	15 1/8	6 4/8	6 4/8	2 2/8	2 2/8	8 2/8	5 5/8	6 4/8	6 4/8	Harney Co., OR	Dale R. Thornton	Dale R. Thornton	1998	1683
82	16 5/8	16 2/8	6 4/8	6 4/8	2 7/8	2 6/8	13	8	5 2/8	5 2/8	Yavapai Co., AZ	Larry Adkins	Larry Adkins	1999	1683
82	15 4/8	15 4/8	6 3/8	6 2/8	3 3/8	3 3/8	9 3/8	5 3/8	5	5	Yavapai Co., AZ	Lisa K. Beeman	Lisa K. Beeman	1999	1683
82	15 5/8	16	6 5/8	6 3/8	2 6/8	2 6/8	12 1/8	8 6/8	5 1/8	5 6/8	Lomond, AB	Eric W. Dirks	Eric W. Dirks	1999	1683
82	15 2/8	15 4/8	7 4/8	7 4/8	2 5/8	2 6/8	11 5/8	8 3/8	4 7/8	4 6/8	Cassia Co., ID	David R. Harrow	David R. Harrow	1999	1683
82	16 2/8	16	6 4/8	6 4/8	2 7/8	3	7 3/8	2	5 6/8	5 5/8	Converse Co., WY	James E. Herren	James E. Herren	1999	1683
82	16 3/8	16 6/8	6 3/8	6 3/8	2 6/8	3	11	6 1/8	5 4/8	5 1/8	Harney Co., OR	Earl E. Kessler	Earl E. Kessler	1999	1683
82	17 4/8	17 5/8	6 1/8	6 1/8	3	3 3/8	11 4/8	7 6/8	3 7/8	4 5/8	Hudspeth Co., TX	Timothy L. Orton	Timothy L. Orton	1999	1683
82	14	13 2/8	6 7/8	6 7/8	3	3 3/8	10	8 6/8	6 2/8	6 1/8	Washoe Co., NV	Harry B. Swanson	Harry B. Swanson	1999	1683
82	16 3/8	16 3/8	6 2/8	6 2/8	2 5/8	2 5/8	10 1/8	5 6/8	5 4/8	5 6/8	Moffat Co., CO	George F. Bailey	George F. Bailey	2000	1683
82	14 7/8	15	7	7	3	3	12 3/8	8 6/8	5	5 3/8	Rio Grande Co., CO	Andrew L. Farish	Andrew L. Farish	2000	1683
82	15 4/8	15 5/8	6 4/8	6 4/8	2 4/8	2 4/8	13	8 5/8	6	6	Liberty Co., MT	Joel H. Fenger	Joel H. Fenger	2000	1683
82	16	15 6/8	6 4/8	6 4/8	3	3	12	8 2/8	5 5/8	5 3/8	Washoe Co., NV	Warren T. Goodale	Warren T. Goodale	2000	1683
82	16 6/8	16 5/8	6 4/8	6 5/8	2 6/8	2 6/8	12 2/8	8 4/8	5 2/8	5	Washoe Co., NV	Anthony V. Guillen, Jr.	Anthony V. Guillen, Jr.	2000	1683
82	15 3/8	15 1/8	7 2/8	7 1/8	3 2/8	3	11	7 7/8	4 2/8	4 7/8	Box Elder Co., UT	David R. Harrow	David R. Harrow	2000	1683
82	17 3/8	17 3/8	6 1/8	6 3/8	2 6/8	2 4/8	9 3/8	5	5 1/8	5 1/8	Tide Lake, AB	Dale W. Heinz	Dale W. Heinz	2000	1683
82	15 5/8	16 1/8	6 3/8	6 3/8	3 2/8	3 2/8	9 4/8	6 3/8	6 1/8	5 5/8	Hartley Co., TX	John K. Mikeman	John K. Mikeman	2000	1683
82	16 1/8	16 1/8	6 6/8	6 5/8	2 5/8	2 5/8	8 2/8	2 4/8	5 4/8	5 1/8	Platte Co., WY	Michael Perkowski	Michael Perkowski	2000	1683
82	15 4/8	15 4/8	6 2/8	6 2/8	2 7/8	2 7/8	12 5/8	8 2/8	6	5 4/8	Washoe Co., NV	Thomas W. Caron	Thomas W. Caron	2001	1683
82	15 2/8	15 2/8	6 3/8	6 3/8	3	2 7/8	8	7 4/8	5 6/8	5 6/8	Albany Co., WY	Curt Apel	Curt Apel	2002	1683
82	15 3/8	15 4/8	6 6/8	6 5/8	2 6/8	2 7/8	15 4/8	12 4/8	5 2/8	5 1/8	Larimer Co., CO	Paul W. Hansen	Paul W. Hansen	2002	1683

Score											Hunter	Location		
82	15 4/8	15 1/8	7	6 7/8	2 5/8	2 3/8	12 2/8	9 3/8	6 1/8	5 4/8	John L. O'Brien	Fremont Co., WY	2002	1683
82	14 6/8	14 5/8	6 6/8	6 6/8	2 6/8	2 7/8	10 3/8	6 7/8	6 1/8	6 2/8	Lew W. Raderschadt	Washakie Co., WY	2002	1683
82	15	16 1/8	7	7	2 6/8	2 6/8	13	9 4/8	5 4/8	5 4/8	Tom L. Swartz	Natrona Co., WY	2002	1683
82	14 6/8	14 6/8	6 2/8	6 1/8	2 5/8	3 3/8	11 4/8	7 4/8	5 7/8	5 6/8	Brent V. Trumbo	Socorro Co., NM	2002	1683
82	16 1/8	15 5/8	6 4/8	6 2/8	2 5/8	3 2/8	11	6	6 1/8	5 4/8	Robert J. Smalley	Lincoln Co., NM	2003	1683
82	15 3/8	15 3/8	6 4/8	6 4/8	2 5/8	2 4/8	9 5/8	6 4/8	5 7/8	5 6/8	Scott R. Strand	Carbon Co., WY	2003	1683
82	15 6/8	15 5/8	6 2/8	6 4/8	3	3 3/8	10 2/8	10 2/8	5 1/8	5	Robert B. Williams	Socorro Co., NM	2003	1683
92 6/8*	16 5/8	16 5/8	7 6/8	7 5/8	3 2/8	3 2/8	9 1/8	5 5/8	7 2/8	6 7/8	R. Steve Bass	Socorro Co., NM	1999	
91 2/8*	17 7/8	17 5/8	6 6/8	6 7/8	3 3/8	3 3/8	8 3/8	4 3/8	6	5 7/8	R. Steve Bass	Socorro Co., NM	1998	
90 6/8*	17 4/8	17 3/8	7 1/8	7	4 3/8	3 7/8	10 2/8	6 6/8	5 1/8	4 6/8	Kirk E. Winward	Catron Co., NM	2003	

* Final score is subject to revision by additional verifying measurements.

CATEGORY
PRONGHORN

SCORE
90-4/8

HUNTER
DALE HISLOP (BELOW)

LOCATION
LINCOLN COUNTY, NEW MEXICO

DATE OF KILL
SEPTEMBER 2003

CATEGORY
PRONGHORN

SCORE
90-2/8

HUNTER
LANNY S. ROMINGER (ABOVE)

LOCATION
GRAND COUNTY, NEW MEXICO

DATE OF KILL
OCTOBER 2002

CATEGORY
PRONGHORN

SCORE
89-2/8

HUNTER
LINDA J. MCBRIDE

LOCATION
HUDSPETH COUNTY,
TEXAS

DATE OF KILL
OCTOBER 2000

CATEGORY
PRONGHORN

SCORE
84-6/8

HUNTER
MARK W. STREISSGUTH

LOCATION
MORA COUNTY,
NEW MEXICO

DATE OF KILL
AUGUST 2000

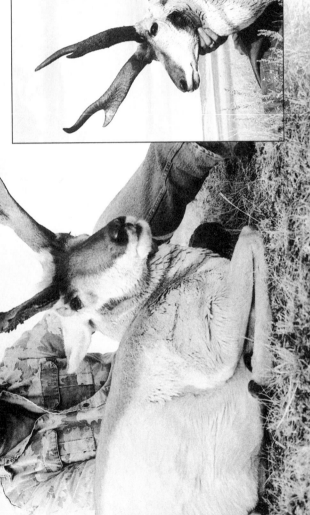

CATEGORY
PRONGHORN

SCORE
82-2/8

HUNTER
JOHN D. GORDON

LOCATION
SOUTH SASKATCHEWAN RIVER,
ALBERTA

DATE OF KILL
OCTOBER 2000

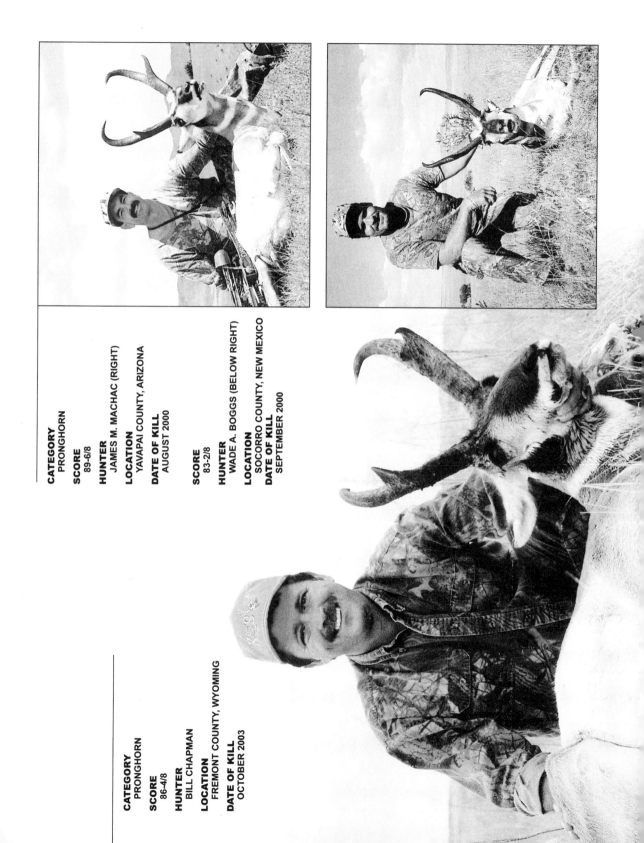

CATEGORY
PRONGHORN

SCORE
89-6/8

HUNTER
JAMES M. MACHAC (RIGHT)

LOCATION
YAVAPAI COUNTY, ARIZONA

DATE OF KILL
AUGUST 2000

SCORE
83-2/8

HUNTER
WADE A. BOGGS (BELOW RIGHT)

LOCATION
SOCORRO COUNTY, NEW MEXICO

DATE OF KILL
SEPTEMBER 2000

CATEGORY
PRONGHORN

SCORE
86-4/8

HUNTER
BILL CHAPMAN

LOCATION
FREMONT COUNTY, WYOMING

DATE OF KILL
OCTOBER 2003

CATEGORY
PRONGHORN

SCORE
84-6/8

HUNTER
LANDON S. BLAKELEY
(RIGHT)

LOCATION
NATRONA COUNTY,
WYOMING

DATE OF KILL
OCTOBER 2001

CATEGORY
PRONGHORN

SCORE
83-4/8

HUNTER
J. TODD HOGAN

LOCATION
UINTA COUNTY, UTAH

DATE OF KILL
SEPTEMBER 2003

CATEGORY
PRONGHORN

SCORE
82-6/8

HUNTER
DAVID R. HARROW

LOCATION
SOCORRO COUNTY, NEW MEXICO

DATE OF KILL
SEPTEMBER 1998

CATEGORY
PRONGHORN

SCORE
92-6/8*

HUNTER
R. STEVE BASS

LOCATION
SOCORRO COUNTY, NEW MEXICO

DATE OF KILL
AUGUST 1999

CATEGORY
PRONGHORN

SCORE
83-6/8

HUNTER
H. HUDSON DECRAY (LEFT)

LOCATION
GRANT COUNTY, NEW MEXICO

DATE OF KILL
OCTOBER 2002

SCORE
87-6/8

HUNTER
A.J. RENKEMA (BELOW LEFT)

LOCATION
COCONINO COUNTY, ARIZONA

DATE OF KILL
SEPTEMBER 2002

BISON
WORLD'S RECORD

TROPHY INFO

RANK
World's Record

SCORE
136 4/8

LOCATION
Yellowstone
National Park

HUNTER
Sam T. Woodring

OWNER
Fishing Bridge
Museum

DATE KILLED
1925

For years, tourists visiting Yellowstone National Park have been awed by a bison skull that hangs in the Chief Ranger's office in Mammoth Hot Springs. This replica is based off the original skull that is currently stored in the Albright Visitor Center. Shot by Chief Ranger Sam Woodring in 1926, "Old Tex" was not taken for sport but in the course of reducing the Yellowstone Park herd in order to balance it with the land's grazing capacity.

The record was almost toppled by a very outstanding trophy shot by Samuel Israel in Northwest Territories in 1961, with a score of 136-2/8. Though the Canadian subspecies of the wood bison is considered to have a larger head than the plains bison, its horns are not necessarily as large as Woodring's long-standing record of 136-4/8. The dense cushioning of matted hair between their wide, black crescent horns, said to be thick enough to stop a bullet, is used as a sort of shock absorber when colliding with a competitor during the rut. It is an awesome sight, but at times devastating as a horn can deliver a mortal wound.

Bison are capable of galloping up to 32 miles per hour and have been known to charge and injure careless tourists that have approached too closely. However, this supreme power along with an immense appearance is really their only means of defense. Consequently, the plains bison became an easy target for market shooters who greatly contributed to their ruthless butchering in the late nineteenth century. This act was a tragic blow to the Plains Indians who were dependent on these animals for meat, clothes, shelter, fuel and as the basis of their culture. By the turn of the 20th century fewer than a thousand bison were in existence. Luckily, there was a call to rescue their plight by organizations and individuals such as Theodore Roosevelt, founder of the Boone and Crockett Club, and William T. Hornaday, an early Club member and founder of the Bison Society and the National Bison Range in western Montana. ∎

Records of
North American
Big Game

BOONE AND CROCKETT CLUB®

OFFICIAL SCORING SYSTEM FOR NORTH AMERICAN BIG GAME TROPHIES

BISON

250 Station Drive
Missoula, MT 59801
(406) 542-1888

MINIMUM SCORES
AWARDS ALL-TIME
115   115

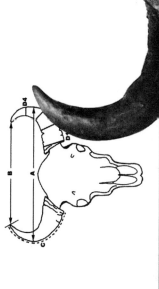

BISON
WORLD'S RECORD SCORE CHART

BOUNDARY FOR BISON

Bison are eligible from states and provinces that recognize them as wild and free-ranging and which require a hunting license and/or big-game tag for hunting them.

SEE OTHER SIDE FOR INSTRUCTIONS	COLUMN 1	Right Horn		
A. Greatest Spread	35 3/8			
B. Tip to Tip Spread	27			
C. Length of Horn		21 2/8	23 2/8	
D-1. Circumference of Base		16	15	1
D-2. Circumference at First Quarter		13 4/8	13	4/8
D-3. Circumference at Second Quarter		11 4/8	11	4/8
D-4. Circumference at Third Quarter		8 2/8	8	2/8
TOTALS		70 4/8	70 2/8	4 2/8

ADD	Column 1	70 4/8
	Column 2	70 2/8
	Subtotal	140 6/8
SUBTRACT	Column 3	4 2/8
	FINAL SCORE	**136 4/8**

Exact Locality Where Killed: Yellowstone National Park, WY

Date Killed: 1925   Hunter: Sam T. Woodring

Owner: Yellowstone National Park   Telephone #:

Owner's Address:

Guide's Name and Address:

Remarks: (Mention Any Abnormalities or Unique Qualities:)

I, __Grancel Fitz__ , certify that I have measured this trophy on __09/24/1951__
   PRINT NAME   MM/DD/YYYY

at __Yellowstone National Park__ _____ __WY__
  STREET ADDRESS   CITY   STATE/PROVINCE

and that these measurements and data are, to the best of my knowledge and belief, made in accordance with the instructions given.

Witness: _____   Signature: __Grancel Fitz__   I.D. Number _____
                              B&C OFFICIAL MEASURER

TOP 10 BISON

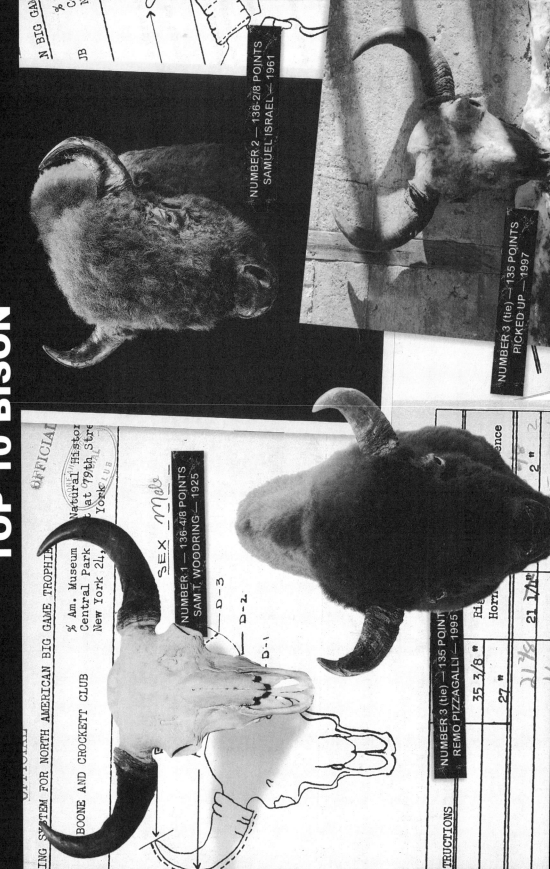

NUMBER 2 — 136-2/8 POINTS
SAMUEL ISRAEL — 1961

NUMBER 3 (tie) — 135 POINTS
PICKED-UP — 1997

NUMBER 1 — 136-4/8 POINTS
SAM T. WOODRING — 1925

NUMBER 3 (tie) — 135 POINT
REMO PIZZAGALLI — 1995

NUMBER 5 — 134-2/8 POINTS
PICKED UP — 1977

NUMBER 9 (tie) — 131-6/8 POINTS
DUANE R. RICHARDSON — 2002

The following top 10 bison do not have photographs available

NUMBER 6 — 133-4/8 POINTS
MIKE DEMPSEY — 1935

NUMBER 7 (tie) — 132-2/8 POINTS
JAMES H. LOCKHART — Prior to 1939

NUMBER 9 (tie) — 131-6/8 POINTS
PICKED UP — 1945

NUMBER 7 (tie) — 132-2/8 POINTS
KEN COOPER — 1961

775

BISON

Bison bison bison and Bison bison athabascae

MINIMUM SCORE 115

Score	Length of Horn R	L	Circumference of Base R	L	Circumference at Third Quarter R	L	Greatest Spread	Tip to Tip Spread	Locality	Hunter	Owner	Date Killed	Rank
136 4/8	21 2/8	23 2/8	16	15	8 2/8	8	35 3/8	27	Yellowstone Natl. Park, WY	Sam T. Woodring	Yellowstone Natl. Park	1925	1
136 2/8	19	18 6/8	18 4/8	18 4/8	6 5/8	6 7/8	30 1/8	22 3/8	Northwest Territories	Samuel Israel	Samuel Israel	1961	2
135	18 2/8	18	16	15 4/8	8 6/8	8 7/8	32 2/8	28 4/8	Custer Co., SD	Remo Pizzagalli	Remo Pizzagalli	1995	3
135	23	24 4/8	14 4/8	14 1/8	6	7	31 3/8	20	Park Co., MT	Picked Up	Glenn M. Smith	1997	3
134 2/8	21 2/8	20 6/8	14 4/8	14 7/8	8 6/8	7 6/8	33 7/8	26 2/8	Park Co., WY	Picked Up	H.A. Moore	1977	5
133 4/8	19 2/8	18 6/8	17	17	7	7	29 2/8	21 2/8	Great Slave Lake, AB	Mike Dempsey	Natl. Mus. of Canada	1935	6
132 2/8	21 2/8	22 2/8	16 4/8	16 7/8	6	7 5/8	35 4/8	26 6/8	Unknown	James H. Lockhart	Carnegie Museum	PR 1939	7
132 2/8	21 2/8	21 7/8	14 1/8	14 1/8	6 6/8	6 5/8	32 6/8	24 3/8	Sweet Grass, AB	Ken Cooper	Univ. of Sask.	1961	7
131 6/8	20 5/8	20 6/8	15	15	7	7	30	20 7/8	Hell Roaring Creek, MT	Picked Up	Philip L. Wright Zool. Mus.	1945	9
131 6/8	21 5/8	21 4/8	16	15 1/8	5 4/8	5 4/8	30	19 5/8	Coconino Co., AZ	Duane R. Richardson	Duane R. Richardson	2002	9
130 6/8	24 2/8	23 5/8	14 3/8	14 1/8	6 6/8	6	34 1/8	20 1/8	Falaise Lake, NT	Rene Picard	Rene Picard	1992	11
129	21 1/8	20 2/8	14 1/8	14 4/8	7 5/8	7 5/8	29 4/8	18 6/8	Big Horn Mts., WY	Picked Up	George S. Burnap, Jr.	1953	12
129	18 6/8	18 3/8	15 7/8	15 7/8	7 1/8	7 3/8	29 4/8	23 2/8	Custer Co., SD	Collins F. Kellogg, Sr.	Collins F. Kellogg, Sr.	2000	12
128 6/8	19 1/8	18 7/8	17 1/8	16 7/8	6 4/8	6 4/8	33 2/8	25	Northwest Territories	Bert Klineburger	Bert Klineburger	1960	14
128 6/8	19 5/8	20	15 2/8	15 4/8	6 3/8	6 4/8	35 1/8	33 6/8	Custer Co., SD	Rick E. Matzick	Rick E. Matzick	1996	14
128 6/8	19	19	14 7/8	15	7 4/8	7 5/8	29 4/8	21 4/8	Garfield Co., UT	Steven R. Farr	Steven R. Farr	2000	14
128 4/8	18 4/8	18 5/8	14 6/8	14 6/8	8 2/8	8 4/8	28 1/8	20 4/8	Yellowstone Natl. Park, WY	Unknown	U.S. Natl. Museum	1913	17
128 4/8	18 7/8	18 6/8	15 1/8	14 7/8	7 6/8	7 4/8	31	23 5/8	Custer Co., SD	Stephanie Altimus	Wildlife Mus. of the West	1989	17
128 2/8	23	23	14 5/8	14 5/8	4 4/8	4 4/8	33 4/8	24 3/8	Sikanni Chief River, BC	George E. Salazar	George E. Salazar	2001	19
128 2/8	20 6/8	20 6/8	15 3/8	15 3/8	5 7/8	6	33 6/8	29 6/8	Custer Co., SD	William D. Gentner	William D. Gentner	2002	19
128	21 5/8	20 4/8	14 5/8	14 6/8	6 6/8	5 7/8	23 7/8	27	Custer Co., SD	Larry L. Altimus	Larry L. Altimus	1990	21
128	19 2/8	19 6/8	16 2/8	16 2/8	5 6/8	6	31 1/8	26	Cub Mt., YT	Richard Ward	Richard Ward	2001	21
127 6/8	19 2/8	20 1/8	15 6/8	15 3/8	5 5/8	6	31 2/8	22 2/8	Northwest Territories	Leslie Bowling	Leslie Bowling	1961	23
127 6/8	19 5/8	19 6/8	15 5/8	15 3/8	6 3/8	6 4/8	32 2/8	25 3/8	Northwest Territories	Wilbur Hilgar	Wilbur Hilgar	1961	23
127	21 7/8	22 3/8	13 2/8	13 6/8	6 6/8	7 7/8	29	18 4/8	Canada	Unknown	Raymond Brown	1899	25
127	18 7/8	19	15 4/8	15 6/8	6 7/8	7 1/8	26 3/8	23 5/8	Custer Co., SD	Henry E. McLemore	Henry E. McLemore	1980	25
127	19 6/8	19 5/8	14 4/8	14 5/8	8 6/8	8 6/8	30 6/8	25 4/8	Coconino Co., AZ	William G. Cummard II	William G. Cummard II	1997	25
126 6/8	19 6/8	19 6/8	15 2/8	15 1/8	7 2/8	7 3/8	27 6/8	18 2/8	Gillette, WY	D.C. Basolo, Jr.	D.C. Basolo, Jr.	1963	28
126 6/8	20 7/8	21 1/8	14 2/8	14 4/8	6 2/8	6 2/8	30 3/8	19 6/8	Garfield Co., UT	Holland D. Butler	Holland D. Butler	1990	28
126 6/8	19 7/8	20 1/8	14	14	7	7	31 7/8	26 6/8	Custer Co., SD	Thomas P. Powers	Thomas P. Powers	2002	28
126 4/8	18 7/8	18 7/8	15	14 6/8	6 5/8	6 2/8	29	22	Park Co., MT	Picked Up	M.J. Young	1990	31
126 2/8	17 4/8	18 3/8	15 6/8	15 6/8	7 2/8	7	30 4/8	24 3/8	Yellowstone River, MT	Picked Up	Edward J. Melby	1935	32
126 2/8	18 3/8	18 1/8	16 2/8	16	6 2/8	6 4/8	29 6/8	21 7/8	Fort Smith, NT	V.N. Holderman	V.N. Holderman	1961	32
126 2/8	20 1/8	20 5/8	15 6/8	15 4/8	5 7/8	5 4/8	32 2/8	23 6/8	Custer Co., SD	Norman F. Taylor	Norman F. Taylor	1994	32
126	20 2/8	20 3/8	15	15 4/8	5 7/8	5 4/8	27 2/8	13 2/8	Slave River, NT	Edward A. Feser	Edward A. Feser	1975	35
126	18 1/8	21	15 2/8	15 2/8	6 4/8	7 2/8	31 7/8	24 6/8	Wrangell Mts., AK	Walter H. Hammer	Walter H. Hammer	1977	35
126	18 2/8	19 1/8	15 6/8	15 4/8	6 5/8	5 6/8	32 1/8	29 1/8	Custer Co., SD	Brian K. Yeoman	Brian K. Yeoman	1994	35
125 6/8	19 4/8	19 4/8	15	15	6	6 2/8	30 2/8	24	Yellowstone Natl. Park, WY	Lee L. Coleman	Jackson Hole Museum	1958	38

Score								Locality	Hunter	Owner	Date Killed	Rank
125 6/8	17 7/8	17 2/8	14	14	8	26 7/8	21 6/8	Park Co., WY	Unknown	James Patterson	PR 1970	38
125 6/8	20	19 2/8	15	15 3/8	6 2/8	31 2/8	24 6/8	Custer Co., SD	Edward Orestad	Edward Orestad	1991	38
125 6/8	20 4/8	20 1/8	14 6/8	14 5/8	6 3/8	30 4/8	21 2/8	Custer Co., SD	Robert B. Williams	Robert B. Williams	1999	38
125 4/8	19 5/8	19 6/8	14 7/8	14 6/8	5 7/8	31 5/8	25	Custer Co., SD	C. Brent Morgan	C. Brent Morgan	1986	42
125 2/8	20	19 7/8	14 3/8	13 4/8	7 1/8	28 4/8	19 5/8	Montana	Unknown	O.P. Chisholm	PR 1891	43
125 2/8	19	18 6/8	14 2/8	14 1/8	8	31 6/8	26 2/8	Park Co., MT	Richard Olson	Richard Olson	1989	43
125 2/8	18 4/8	18 4/8	14 7/8	14 3/8	8 2/8	3? 2/8	29 1/8	Custer Co., SD	Robert J. Fair	Robert J. Fair	1992	43
125 2/8	17 7/8	17	15 1/8	14 7/8	8 2/8	2? 2/8	24 4/8	Custer Co., SD	Romaine L. Marshall	Romaine L. Marshall	1993	43
125 2/8	19 5/8	19 5/8	15 2/8	15 2/8	5 7/8	2? 6/8	21 6/8	Custer Co., SD	Adam Ziolkowski	Adam Ziolkowski	2001	43
125	19 7/8	19 7/8	14 4/8	14 4/8	6	2?	20 3/8	Manitoba	Unknown	James Fredrick	1928	48
125	18 7/8	18 7/8	15	14 5/8	6 2/8	2? 3/8	18 5/8	Fort Smith, NT	Leonard J. Ostrom	Leonard J. Ostrom	1959	48
125	18 4/8	18 4/8	15 7/8	15 3/8	6	2? 1/8	18 4/8	Halfway River, BC	Mary-Anne Faiers	Mary-Anne Faiers	1996	48
124 6/8	20 2/8	20 3/8	15 1/8	15 1/8	6 1/8	3? 1/8	21 7/8	Wyoming	Lord Rendlesham	B&C National Collection	1892	51
124 6/8	18 2/8	18 2/8	14 3/8	14 3/8	8 1/8	3? 7/8	25 6/8	Custer Co., SD	Picked Up	Dick Rossum	1991	51
124 6/8	18	19 2/8	15	15	6 2/8	31	26	Custer Co., SD	Donald A. Peterson	Donald A. Peterson	1998	51
124 4/8	18 1/8	18 1/8	14 7/8	13 3/8	7 3/8	29 6/8	24 2/8	Teton Co., WY	Heidi Anderson	Heidi Anderson	1999	51
124 4/8	20 1/8	20 2/8	14 2/8	14 2/8	6 4/8	33 6/8	28 4/8	Custer Co., SD	William J. Smith	William J. Smith	2000	51
124 4/8	20 4/8	20 4/8	14 7/8	15 1/8	6 1/8	31 6/8	24	Copper River, AK	Earl E. Knutson	Earl E. Knutson	1965	56
124 4/8	19 4/8	20	15 1/8	15 1/8	5 5/8	29 3/8	20 4/8	Delta Junction, AK	Mike Stagno	Mike Stagno	1975	56
124 2/8	19 6/8	19 6/8	15	14 6/8	6 2/8	30	23 3/8	Delta Junction, AK	Ted J. Forsi, Jr.	Ted J. Forsi, Jr.	1992	56
124 2/8	18 5/8	18	15	14 7/8	7	31 1/8	27 2/8	Custer Co., SD	Anthony J. Visentin	Anthony J. Visentin	1994	56
124 2/8	17 6/8	17 5/8	16 3/8	16 2/8	6 2/8	32 4/8	28 4/8	Fort Smith, NT	Margaret Buckner	Margaret Buckner	1960	60
124 2/8	17 6/8	17 2/8	14 6/8	14 6/8	7 4/8	31 3/8	27 3/8	Custer Co., SD	Stuart Godin	Stuart Godin	1975	60
124 2/8	19 1/8	19 2/8	15 6/8	15 6/8	5 6/8	31	25 2/8	Chitina River, AK	Robert E. Day	Robert E. Day	1976	60
124 2/8	19	19 4/8	14 4/8	14 4/8	6 6/8	30 6/8	24 4/8	Custer Co., SD	Robert D. Taylor	Robert D. Taylor	1986	60
124 2/8	18 3/8	18 3/8	15 4/8	15 4/8	7 2/8	29 4/8	23 7/8	Delta Junction, AK	Gary D. Wolfe	Gary D. Wolfe	1990	60
124 2/8	18 1/8	18 1/8	15 6/8	15 6/8	6 4/8	28 1/8	22 2/8	Teton Co., WY	Terry Mathes	Terry Mathes	1998	60
124	18 4/8	18	15 2/8	15 2/8	6 7/8	30 6/8	25	Custer Co., SD	Richard C. Sturm	Richard C. Sturm	1999	60
124	21 2/8	20 3/8	14	14	6 7/8	29 7/8	20 4/8	Jardine, MT	Unknown	Kerry J. Constan	1962	67
124	16 6/8	16 3/8	13 3/8	13 4/8	5 7/8	25 5/8	18 6/8	Slave River, NT	Rudolf Sand	Rudolf Sand	1972	67
124	19 4/8	19 2/8	15 4/8	14 2/8	7 7/8	30 6/8	22 4/8	Hook Lake, NT	Manfred Kurtz	Manfred Kurtz	1973	67
124	18 6/8	18 4/8	14	14	6 4/8	33 2/8	27 6/8	Coconino Co., AZ	Philip A. Sturgill	Philip A. Sturgill	1984	67
124	19 2/8	18 3/8	14 5/8	14 5/8	6 1/8	33	28	Custer Co., SD	William H. Smith	William H. Smith	1991	67
124	20 4/8	19	14 3/8	14 3/8	5 4/8	33 1/8	26 4/8	Custer Co., SD	Jack S. Snider	Jack S. Snider	1993	67
124	20 6/8	20 6/8	13 6/8	13 6/8	7	31 4/8	23	Custer Co., SD	George Tulowetzke	George Tulowetzke	1997	67
123 6/8	20 2/8	20 2/8	16	16	5 1/8	31	20 7/8	Northwest Territories	J.S. Sanders	J.S. Sanders	1961	74
123 6/8	17 4/8	17 4/8	15	15	7 2/8	25	15 2/8	Gillette, WY	D.C. Basolo, Jr.	D.C. Basolo, Jr.	1963	74
123 6/8	19	17 6/8	16 1/8	16	5 6/8	29	22 3/8	Calais Lake, NT	Warren D. St. Germaine	Warren D. St. Germaine	1988	74
123 6/8	19	19	14 1/8	14 1/8	7 1/8	26 6/8	16 3/8	Garfield Co., UT	Gregory N. Brian	Gregory N. Brian	2002	74
123 4/8	19 6/8	19 5/8	14 2/8	14 4/8	6 3/8	28 6/8	21 4/8	Yellowstone Natl. Park, WY	Harry Trishman	James B. Minter	1924	78
123 4/8	18	18	15 6/8	15 6/8	5 7/8	29 4/8	21 5/8	Yellowstone Natl. Park, WY	Picked Up	C. Watters & D. Moore	1956	78
123 4/8	20	20 7/8	15 1/8	15 1/8	5 2/8	32 5/8	22 5/8	Delta Junction, AK	Donald A. Prescott	Donald A. Prescott	1963	78
123 2/8	20 2/8	20 2/8	15 5/8	15 4/8	7	29 2/8	19	Gillette, WY	H.I.H. Prince Abdorreza Pahlavi	H.I.H. Prince Abdorreza Pahlavi	1967	78
123 2/8	18 6/8	19 2/8	14 6/8	15	7 3/8	26	21 4/8	Fort Smith, NT	Earl H. Harris	Earl H. Harris	1969	78
123 2/8	19 4/8	19 1/8	15 5/8	15 4/8	5 3/8	31	25 4/8	Custer Co., SD	Jack L. Blachly	Jack L. Blachly	1997	78
123 2/8	18 4/8	18 4/8	14 7/8	15 5/8	4 4/8	32 1/8	26 4/8	Custer Co., SD	Lonnie R. Henriksen	Lonnie R. Henriksen	2001	78
123 2/8	17 5/8	18	16 2/8	15 4/8	6	29 1/8	22 1/8	Custer Co., SD	Tim P. Matzinger	Tim P. Matzinger	1983	85

BISON

Bison bison bison and Bison bison athabascae

Score	Length of Horn R	L	Circumference of Base R	L	Circumference at Third Quarter R	L	Greatest Spread	Tip to Tip Spread	Locality	Hunter	Owner	Date Killed	Rank
123 2/8	18 3/8	18 1/8	13 6/8	14 2/8	7 6/8	7 5/8	28	22 1/8	Garfield Co., UT	Carl R. Albrecht	Carl R. Albrecht	1986	85
123 2/8	19	18 5/8	15 2/8	14 7/8	6 1/8	5 7/8	32	26 4/8	Chitina River, AK	Gerald H. Phillips	Gerald H. Phillips	1987	85
123	16 4/8	17	14 5/8	14 6/8	8	7	27 6/8	24	Custer Co., SD	Jerry Ippolito	Jerry Ippolito	1990	88
122 6/8	20 3/8	19 3/8	15 2/8	15 2/8	5 4/8	5 3/8	31 4/8	24 7/8	Big Delta, AK	Unknown	Chuck Sutter	1950	89
122 6/8	18 3/8	18 3/8	14 5/8	14 3/8	6 5/8	7 1/8	29 4/8	21 6/8	Park Co., MT	Picked Up	James J. Darr	1991	89
122 4/8	20 4/8	20 4/8	14 4/8	14 4/8	5	5	26 4/8	16 5/8	Garfield Co., UT	Greg Harper	Greg Harper	1978	91
122 4/8	18 4/8	18 5/8	14 6/8	14 2/8	6 6/8	6	25	23 7/8	Custer Co., SD	Donald F. Senter	Donald F. Senter	1989	91
122 4/8	19 1/8	19 1/8	14	14	5 7/8	5 6/8	27 2/8	19 6/8	Garfield Co., UT	Shawn M. Ward	Shawn M. Ward	1991	91
122 4/8	19 6/8	19 2/8	14 3/8	14 3/8	6 3/8	6	33 2/8	29 4/8	Custer Co., UT	Robert D. Jones	Robert D. Jones	1995	91
122 2/8	20 5/8	20 4/8	13 7/8	13 4/8	6 4/8	6 4/8	32 7/8	26 2/8	Absarokee Wilder., MT	H.E. Lillis	H.E. Lillis	1953	95
122 2/8	18 4/8	18	14 2/8	14 1/8	7 2/8	7 3/8	29 6/8	23 2/8	Fort Greely, AK	Picked Up	McClaren Johnson, Jr.	PR 1961	95
122 2/8	19 2/8	19 3/8	15	15 1/8	6 2/8	9 3/8	28 4/8	19 1/8	Northwest Territories	A. Sanford	A. Sanford	1961	95
122 2/8	18 2/8	18 3/8	14 4/8	14 5/8	7 4/8	7 4/8	28 6/8	20 3/8	Gillette, WY	Tom R. Bowles	Tom R. Bowles	1963	95
122 2/8	18 1/8	20 1/8	15 4/8	15 5/8	5 6/8	6 1/8	31 5/8	27 5/8	Lawrence Co., SD	Kenneth H. Jones	Kenneth H. Jones	1986	95
122 2/8	18 7/8	19	15	15	6 4/8	5 4/8	29 1/8	22	Custer Co., SD	Kent Deligans	Kent Deligans	2001	95
122	18 5/8	18 3/8	16 1/8	16	5 2/8	5	29 1/8	22 6/8	Hook Lake, NT	Picked Up	Robert C. Jones	1974	101
122	19 3/8	19 6/8	15 1/8	15 4/8	5 3/8	5 3/8	29 4/8	21 3/8	Goodpastor River, AK	Charles W. Jackson	Charles W. Jackson	1989	101
122	19 1/8	19 4/8	15 2/8	15 6/8	5 2/8	5 3/8	30 4/8	25 3/8	Gerstle River, AK	Richard Voss	Richard Voss	1990	101
122	17 4/8	18 3/8	14 7/8	14 6/8	7	7 5/8	31 1/8	26 2/8	Custer Co., SD	Kent Deligans	Kent Deligans	1999	101
122	19	19	15 4/8	15 6/8	5 6/8	6 2/8	31 4/8	24 5/8	Custer Co., SD	Charles A. LeKites	Charles A. LeKites	2001	101
121 6/8	19 4/8	20 3/8	14 6/8	14 4/8	5 5/8	5 7/8	29 3/8	21 3/8	Wayne Co., UT	Ardell K. Woolsey	Ardell K. Woolsey	1974	106
121 6/8	18 2/8	18 2/8	14 3/8	14 3/8	7	7 2/8	23 7/8	23 7/8	Custer Co., SD	Jon R. Stephens	Jon R. Stephens	1982	106
121 6/8	18 6/8	18 6/8	13 4/8	13 2/8	7 4/8	7 3/8	32 4/8	30 3/8	Custer Co., SD	Thomas H. Coe	Thomas H. Coe	1991	106
121 6/8	19 5/8	18 5/8	14 6/8	14 7/8	5 7/8	5 7/8	31 2/8	24 2/8	Custer Co., MT	Horace Smith, Jr.	Horace Smith, Jr.	1999	106
121 4/8	21 1/8	22 1/8	13 5/8	14	5 3/8	5 3/8	29 7/8	18 7/8	Custer Co., MT	Picked Up	Martin Sorensen, Jr.	1962	110
121 4/8	19 2/8	18 3/8	15 3/8	14 5/8	6 2/8	6 7/8	31 4/8	26 4/8	Custer Co., SD	Glen Taylor	Glen Taylor	1993	110
121 4/8	14 4/8	14 4/8	18 2/8	17 6/8	5 7/8	6	30 3/8	25 4/8	Custer Co., SD	Gary W. Derrick	Gary W. Derrick	2001	110
121 2/8	16	14 1/8	16	16 3/8	8 2/8	8	29 4/8	25 6/8	Ogalala Sioux G. R., SD	Robert B. Peregrine	Robert B. Peregrine	1972	113
121 2/8	18	18 6/8	14	14 3/8	6 3/8	7	28 3/8	17 2/8	Fort Smith, NT	W.C. Whitt	W.C. Whitt	1972	113
121 2/8	18 1/8	18 4/8	15	15 1/8	5 5/8	6	28 4/8	21 4/8	Custer Co., SD	Robert L. Trupe	Robert L. Trupe	1979	113
121 2/8	16 7/8	17 2/8	13 5/8	13 4/8	7 4/8	7 4/8	30 4/8	25 3/8	Custer Co., SD	Bradley D. Hanson	Bradley D. Hanson	1988	113
121 2/8	20 1/8	20 4/8	14	14 2/8	4 6/8	5 1/8	29	21 6/8	Garfield Co., UT	Travis S. Myers	Travis S. Myers	1995	113
121	16 7/8	18 3/8	14 3/8	14 2/8	7 1/8	7 1/8	29 2/8	21 5/8	Slave River, NT	Franz M. Wilhelmsen	Franz M. Wilhelmsen	1959	118
121	20 4/8	18 3/8	14 4/8	14 4/8	6 4/8	6 4/8	28 5/8	20	Shoshone Natl. For., WY	Picked Up	G.A. Cadwalader	PR 1965	118
121	17 4/8	18 2/8	14 4/8	15 2/8	6 6/8	7 1/8	28	21 7/8	Coconino Co., AZ	Larry R. French	Larry R. French	1965	118
121	18 2/8	18	14 4/8	14 1/8	6 6/8	6 7/8	27 6/8	19 6/8	Big Horn Co., MT	Picked Up	Larry Edgar	1972	118
121	19 2/8	18 3/8	14 5/8	14 3/8	5 7/8	5 4/8	30 2/8	24 6/8	Custer Co., SD	Dave Ramey	Dave Ramey	1978	118
121	17 7/8	17 4/8	15 2/8	15 1/8	7 5/8	6 1/8	25 5/8	19 5/8	Custer Co., SD	Wilson W. Crook III	Wilson W. Crook III	1982	118

Score	Length of Horn R	Length of Horn L	Circumference of Base R	Circumference of Base L	Greatest Spread	Circ. at Third Quarter R	Circ. at Third Quarter L	Tip to Tip Spread	Locality	Hunter	Owner	Date	Rank
121	17 5/8	17 2/8	14 4/8	15 1/8	29 6/8	7 2/8	7	23 3/8	Park Co, MT	Dale K. Jackson	Dale K. Jackson	1986	118
121	17 4/8	17 4/8	14 4/8	14 2/8	29 2/8	6 5/8	7	22 4/8	Custer Co, SD	James J. Ceccolini	James J. Ceccolini	1992	118
121	15 7/8	16 4/8	14 7/8	15	28	7 5/8	7 6/8	22 2/8	Custer Co, SD	Jerry Landa	Jerry Landa	1993	118
120 6/8	17	17 4/8	15 3/8	15 2/8	31 2/8	5 3/8	5 6/8	29 6/8	Delta Junction, AK	George R. Horner	George R. Horner	1950	127
120 6/8	18 2/8	18 2/8	15 3/8	15 3/8	26 6/8	5 3/8	5 3/8	24 7/8	Hook Lake, NT	George W. Parker	George W. Parker	1961	127
120 6/8	17 7/8	17 5/8	15 6/8	15 7/8	26	5 3/8	5 2/8	25 6/8	Afton, WY	Bernard Domries	Bernard Domries	1968	127
120 6/8	17	16 6/8	14 4/8	14 4/8	26 1/8	5	7	24 1/8	Custer Co, SD	Louis Vaughn	Louis Vaughn	1968	127
120 6/8	16 6/8	20 7/8	15 2/8	15 1/8	31 3/8	5 1/8	5 1/8	24	Gillette, WY	C.J. McElroy	C.J. McElroy	1970	127
120 6/8	20 7/8	16 5/8	16 1/8	13 7/8	26 2/8	7 4/8	7 4/8	24 1/8	Park Co, WY	Picked Up	James Patterson	PR 1970	127
120 6/8	16 5/8	18	15 4/8	15 1/8	26 1/8	7 6/8	7 4/8	24	Coconino Co, AZ	Greg V. Parker	Greg V. Parker	1975	127
120 6/8	17 4/8	18 3/8	15 6/8	15 3/8	26 1/8	6 2/8	6 2/8	24	Custer Co, SD	Lucky Simpson	Lucky Simpson	1985	127
120 6/8	18	14 4/8	14 3/8	14 2/8	28 1/8	5 3/8	5 1/8	26 4/8	Custer Co, SD	Douglas M. Dreeszen	Douglas M. Dreeszen	1988	127
120 6/8	18 3/8	16 6/8	14 6/8	14 6/8	28	8 2/8	6 6/8	25	Park Co, MT	Matthew P. Wheeler	Matthew P. Wheeler	1989	127
120 6/8	15 1/8	18 7/8	14 6/8	14 5/8	27	6 3/8	6 4/8	24 7/8	Custer Co, SD	William D. Bradley	William D. Bradley	1996	127
120 6/8	16 6/8	19 4/8	14 5/8	14 3/8	31 6/8	5 7/8	6 2/8	21	Pink Mt., BC	Chester L. Greene	Chester L. Greene	1996	127
120 4/8	18 7/8	20 6/8	14 3/8	14 4/8	29 7/8	6 3/8	6 3/8	17 3/8	Northwest Territories	Charles H. Stoll	Charles H. Stoll	1961	139
120 4/8	19 4/8	17	14 2/8	14	29 2/8	5 2/8	5 1/8	23 2/8	Custer Co, SD	Philip L. Nare	Philip L. Nare	1974	139
120 4/8	20 6/8	17 2/8	14 5/8	14 5/8	28 7/8	7 1/8	7 4/8	26 3/8	Custer Co, SD	Dale L. Martin	Dale L. Martin	1983	139
120 4/8	17 1/8	17 3/8	15	14 6/8	30 4/8	7 3/8	6 6/8	24 4/8	Custer Co, SD	Morgan D. Silvers	Morgan D. Silvers	2002	139
120 2/8	17 5/8	17 2/8	14 4/8	14 1/8	30 4/8	6 7/8	6 1/8	21 1/8	Slave River, NT	Unknown	Mrs. Malcom McKenzie	1960	143
120 2/8	19 7/8	20	15 2/8	15 1/8	27 7/8	6 6/8	6 1/8	27 1/8	Delta Junction, AK	James M. Hill	James M. Hill	1978	143
120 2/8	18 2/8	17 4/8	14 3/8	14 3/8	31 3/8	5	5 1/8	27 6/8	Custer Co, SD	Richard A. Bonander	Richard A. Bonander	1996	143
120 2/8	16 3/8	17 1/8	13 2/8	13 4/8	31 5/8	6 4/8	7	26 6/8	Teton Co, WY	Herbert C. Hazen	Herbert C. Hazen	2000	143
120 2/8	17 5/8	17 5/8	14 1/8	14 4/8	32 4/8	8	7 7/8	24 5/8	Teton Co, WY	Jim P. Collins, Jr.	Jim P. Collins, Jr.	2001	143
120 2/8	18 3/8	18 2/8	13 7/8	14 4/8	31 6/8	6	5 4/8	18 1/8	Custer Co, SD	Gary E. Janssen	Gary E. Janssen	2002	143
120	21	20 2/8	14	13 7/8	29 7/8	6 7/8	6 4/8	18 1/8	Lamar River, WY	Frank Oberhansley	Natl. Park Service	1939	149
120	15 1/8	17	14 2/8	15 7/8	28 7/8	4 5/8	4 5/8	24 4/8	Big Delta, AK	Unknown	Robert C. Reeve	1950	149
120	18 1/8	20 2/8	14 1/8	14 7/8	28 1/8	7 1/8	7 1/8	23	Big Delta, AK	Thomas B. Hite	Thomas B. Hite	1983	149
120	18 4/8	19 3/8	14 5/8	14 1/8	29 5/8	5 1/8	4 5/8	27 6/8	Park Co, MT	Luke G. Eighorn	Luke G. Eighorn	1986	149
120	19 5/8	19 4/8	14 6/8	14 5/8	31 2/8	5 3/8	5	22 3/8	Wayne Co, UT	Bryant S. Furness	Bryant S. Furness	1986	149
120	18 2/8	19 4/8	14 1/8	14 2/8	28 4/8	5	5	27 7/8	Custer Co, SD	Donald G. Allen	Donald G. Allen	1994	149
120	16 2/8	16 6/8	15	15	31 5/8	5 6/8	5 6/8	28	Custer Co, SD	Robert D. Jones	Robert D. Jones	1997	149
120	16 7/8	16 2/8	13 7/8	14	30 6/8	7	7 2/8	20 4/8	Custer Co, SD	Gregory S. Oliver	Gregory S. Oliver	1998	149
120	17 1/8	18 2/8	15	14 7/8	26 7/8	7 4/8	7 1/8	24 4/8	Teton Co, WY	Brandon Egbert	Brandon Egbert	2001	149
120	19 3/8	18 6/8	15	14 1/8	30	6 7/8	6	18 4/8	Garfield Co, UT	David Dastrup	David Dastrup	2002	149
119 6/8	17 5/8	17 1/8	14 1/8	14 4/8	27 4/8	5	5 1/8	16	Northwest Territories	Patrick Britell	Patrick Britell	1961	159
119 6/8	19 6/8	19 2/8	14 4/8	14 5/8	25 7/8	6 4/8	6 4/8	23 1/8	Big Delta, AK	Ann Denardo	Ann Denardo	1961	159
119 6/8	18 1/8	18 5/8	14 7/8	14 7/8	30 6/8	5	5	20 3/8	Northwest Territories	Pitt Sanders	Pitt Sanders	1961	159
119 6/8	17 5/8	20	15 1/8	14 6/8	28 4/8	6 2/8	6 2/8	21 3/8	Fort Smith, NT	Sheldon H. Weinstein	Sheldon H. Weinstein	1975	159
119 6/8	18 4/8	17 4/8	15 2/8	15 2/8	28 6/8	5 3/8	5 3/8	30 4/8	Custer Co, SD	Charles E. Ferguson	Charles E. Ferguson	1985	159
119 6/8	20 2/8	19 2/8	14 6/8	14 6/8	23 1/8	6 1/8	6 2/8	25	Custer Co, SD	Bruce W. Anderson	Bruce W. Anderson	1998	159
119 4/8	18	18 6/8	13 7/8	13 7/8	32 2/8	6 7/8	6 2/8	26 7/8	Northwest Territories	Picked Up	Tupper A. Blake	PR 1940	165
119 4/8	19	18	14 2/8	14 2/8	30	6	6	32	Gillette, WY	Glenn Ellingson	Glenn Ellingson	1961	165
119 4/8	17	17 4/8	15 6/8	15 4/8	29	5 6/8	5 6/8	29	Gillette, WY	Walt Paulk	Walt Paulk	1962	165
119 4/8	19 2/8	17 4/8	13 4/8	15 4/8	25 5/8	6 6/8	6 6/8	15 4/8	Yellowstone Natl. Park, WY	Picked Up	James A. Ford	1970	165
119 4/8	18	17 3/8	16 1/8	13 2/8	30 3/8	5 4/8	5 5/8	24 5/8	Coconino Co, AZ	Dorothy B. Gilliam	Dorothy B. Gilliam	1980	165
119 4/8	17 7/8	17 7/8	14 2/8	15 6/8	30 4/8	6 2/8	6 5/8	24 4/8	Custer Co, SD	Paul L.C. Snider	Paul L.C. Snider	1992	165
119 4/8	18	18 1/8	13 5/8	14 3/8	29 7/8	6 1/8	6	24 3/8	Custer Co, SD	Robert M. Anderson	Robert M. Anderson	1998	165

BISON

Bison bison bison and Bison bison athabascae

Score	Length of Horn R	L	Circumference of Base R	L	Circumference at Third Quarter R	L	Greatest Spread	Tip to Tip Spread	Locality	Hunter	Owner	Date Killed	Rank
119 4/8	19 1/8	19 1/8	13 6/8	13 6/8	6	5 7/8	27 5/8	19 3/8	Garfield Co., UT	Darin D. Kerr	Darin D. Kerr	2000	165
119 4/8	18 6/8	18 6/8	14 3/8	14	6 5/8	7 5/8	31	24 4/8	Custer Co., SD	Charles F. Harris	Charles F. Harris	2001	165
119 2/8	18 1/8	18 5/8	15 5/8	15 1/8	6 2/8	5 4/8	27 5/8	18 1/8	Ravalli Co., MT	Unknown	Harold G. Arnold	1975	174
119 2/8	19 6/8	19 3/8	14 4/8	14 4/8	5	5 1/8	26 6/8	15 4/8	San Juan Co., UT	Janice N. Wahlstrom	Janice N. Wahlstrom	1979	174
119 2/8	16 7/8	17 4/8	14 5/8	14 6/8	6 2/8	6 2/8	29 5/8	24 4/8	Custer Co., SD	Merlynn K. Jones	Merlynn K. Jones	1986	174
119 2/8	18 6/8	19	14 6/8	14 2/8	6 4/8	6 5/8	28 7/8	21 3/8	Custer Co., SD	John L. Van Horn	John L. Van Horn	1986	174
119 2/8	17 4/8	17 2/8	14	14 4/8	6 4/8	7	28 3/8	21 5/8	Coconino Co., AZ	James R. Brown	James R. Brown	1988	174
119 2/8	19	17 7/8	15 1/8	15	5 7/8	5 5/8	31 7/8	27 6/8	Park Co., MT	Michael D. Cadwell	Michael D. Cadwell	1988	174
119 2/8	19 2/8	19 2/8	13 5/8	13 4/8	5 5/8	5 5/8	30	21 6/8	Black Rapids Glacier, AK	Picked Up	Ashley L. Thompson	1991	174
119 2/8	18 1/8	19 7/8	14 3/8	13 3/8	5 4/8	6 5/8	28 2/8	20 2/8	Custer Co., SD	Robert G. Kinna	Robert G. Kinna	2000	174
119	17 6/8	17 4/8	13 6/8	13 5/8	6 2/8	6 7/8	25 4/8	16 4/8	Fort Smith, NT	John H. Epp	John H. Epp	1960	182
119	18 6/8	18 6/8	15 1/8	15 2/8	4 7/8	5	25 4/8	18	Hook Lake, NT	John G. Zelenka	John G. Zelenka	1971	182
119	16 7/8	16 7/8	14 5/8	14 6/8	6 5/8	6 4/8	27 2/8	18 7/8	Coconino Co., AZ	Melvin C. Kincaid	Melvin C. Kincaid	1983	182
119	20 7/8	21 4/8	13 6/8	13 2/8	4 7/8	5 2/8	30 7/8	24 4/8	Pink Mt., BC	Wendy E. Olson	Wendy E. Olson	1998	182
119	18 4/8	18 6/8	13 7/8	14 1/8	6	6	30 3/8	24 1/8	Teton Co., WY	Kathryn H. Rommel	Kathryn H. Rommel	2000	182
119	18 5/8	18 1/8	13 5/8	13 4/8	6 2/8	6 6/8	28 2/8	18 2/8	Teton Co., WY	Slaton J. Reynoldson	Slaton J. Reynoldson	2002	182
118 6/8	18	18 1/8	14 1/8	14	7 1/8	7 1/8	28 7/8	19 1/8	Northwest Territories	Herb Klein	Dallas Mus. of Natl. Hist.	1960	188
118 6/8	17 2/8	16 6/8	15 3/8	15 2/8	6	5 6/8	29	22 4/8	Fort Smith, NT	W.J. Nixon	W.J. Nixon	1960	188
118 6/8	15 4/8	17 1/8	15 6/8	15 6/8	6 2/8	5 7/8	27 3/8	20 6/8	Fort Smith, NT	D.N. Rowe	D.N. Rowe	1960	188
118 6/8	19 1/8	18	14 7/8	15 1/8	5 3/8	4 7/8	28 7/8	22 6/8	Fort Smith, NT	Charles Sides	Charles Sides	1960	188
118 6/8	16 2/8	16 5/8	14 2/8	14 6/8	7	7 5/8	29 7/8	26 3/8	Big Delta, AK	Richard P. Platz	Richard P. Platz	1961	188
118 6/8	15 3/8	14	15 4/8	15 4/8	7 1/8	7 6/8	28 2/8	25	Big Horn Co., MT	Basil C. Bradbury	Basil C. Bradbury	1968	188
118 6/8	19 6/8	19 6/8	15 2/8	15 3/8	4 6/8	4 6/8	31 1/8	23 6/8	Lake Co., MT	Jack A. Shane, Sr.	Jack A. Shane, Sr.	1968	188
118 6/8	17 6/8	15 6/8	16 4/8	16 4/8	6 3/8	6 2/8	31 1/8	26	Hook Lake, NT	G.A. Treschow	G.A. Treschow	1972	188
118 6/8	20 1/8	20 2/8	14 2/8	14 1/8	5	5	29	23 1/8	Garfield Co., UT	David G. Hansen	David G. Hansen	1975	188
118 6/8	17 7/8	17 5/8	15 6/8	16	5 4/8	5 5/8	30 4/8	24 7/8	Custer Co., SD	Joel J. Torgerson	Joel J. Torgerson	1981	188
118 6/8	17 7/8	17 7/8	13 2/8	13 4/8	7	7 1/8	29 1/8	22 3/8	Copper River, AK	G. Michael Miller	G. Michael Miller	1988	188
118 6/8	18 7/8	18	14	14 3/8	5 6/8	6 6/8	33 5/8	29	Custer Co., SD	William J. Ahern	William J. Ahern	1992	188
118 6/8	17 3/8	18 3/8	14 5/8	14 5/8	5 4/8	6 5/8	31	25 5/8	Custer Co., SD	Robert B. Williams	Robert B. Williams	1995	188
118 4/8	18 1/8	18 1/8	14 4/8	14 4/8	5 7/8	6	28 4/8	23 6/8	Copper River, AK	Jim Harrower	Jim Harrower	1964	201
118 4/8	20 1/8	20 3/8	14 7/8	15 2/8	4 5/8	4 5/8	28 4/8	21 3/8	Pine Ridge Indian Res., SD	Mary L. Pipp	Mary L. Pipp	1972	201
118 4/8	20	19 4/8	14 5/8	14 3/8	5 1/8	4 6/8	27 5/8	20 2/8	Garfield Co., UT	Robert B. Williams	Robert B. Williams	1986	201
118 4/8	20 2/8	20 2/8	14 2/8	14 3/8	4 6/8	5	26 6/8	14 4/8	Davis Co., UT	Ronald J. Dallin	Ronald J. Dallin	1987	201
118 4/8	17 5/8	19 1/8	13 7/8	13 6/8	6 6/8	6 6/8	32	27	Custer Co., SD	Patrick C. Allen	Patrick C. Allen	1992	201
118 4/8	17 7/8	18 1/8	13 6/8	14 2/8	6 4/8	6 5/8	30 6/8	24 4/8	Custer Co., SD	Max G. Bauer, Jr.	Max G. Bauer, Jr.	2001	201
118 2/8	19 4/8	18 7/8	14 7/8	15 4/8	4 6/8	5 3/8	31	28	Wyoming	Sidney Snow	Snow Museum	PR 1900	207
118 2/8	18 6/8	19 4/8	14 2/8	14 1/8	5 3/8	5 5/8	28 2/8	22 4/8	Pierre, SD	Earl Mumaw	Earl Mumaw	1962	207
118 2/8	19 1/8	19 6/8	14 2/8	14 4/8	5 2/8	5 4/8	29	18 4/8	Coconino Co., AZ	Fred Shook	Fred Shook	1967	207

Score	Length of Horn R	Length of Horn L	Circ. of Base R	Circ. of Base L	Circ. Third Quarter R	Circ. Third Quarter L	Greatest Spread	Tip to Tip Spread	Locality	Hunter	Owner	Date Killed	Rank
118 2/8	18 1/8	18 7/8	15	15 1/8	5 6/8	5 4/8	30 5/8	23 5/8	Teton Co., WY	Steven C. Kobold	Steven C. Kobold	1990	207
118 2/8	17 7/8	16 5/8	15 5/8	15 2/8	5 4/8	5 6/8	29 4/8	25	Custer Co., SD	Robert M. McCarten	Robert M. McCarten	1993	207
118 2/8	14 6/8	15	14 1/8	14 3/8	8 6/8	8 7/8	28 1/8	22 3/8	Custer Co., SD	Robert D. Jones	Robert D. Jones	1995	207
118	17 4/8	18 6/8	15 4/8	15	6 2/8	6 2/8	29 4/8	21	Yellowstone Natl. Park, WY	Unknown	Alfred C. Berol	1927	213
118	17 2/8	17 3/8	14 2/8	13 7/8	6 2/8	6 7/8	30	26 2/8	Crow Indian Res., MT	Pete Laird	Curt Laird	1956	213
118	16	16	16	16	7	7	27 6/8	20 2/8	Gillette, WY	D.C. Basolo, Jr.	D.C. Basolo, Jr.	1962	213
118	17 4/8	16 7/8	14 1/8	14 1/8	5 7/8	5 7/8	25 5/8	19	Garfield Co., UT	John Goldenstein	John Goldenstein	1962	213
118	18 4/8	19 4/8	15 1/8	15 1/8	5 1/8	5 4/8	31 7/8	25 5/8	Custer Co., SD	Harry T. Scharfenberg	Harry T. Scharfenberg	1984	213
118	18 7/8	18 1/8	14	14 2/8	4 7/8	5	29 3/8	25 1/8	Garfield Co., UT	Sharon G. Polley	Sharon G. Polley	1994	213
118	18 4/8	18 1/8	14 3/8	14 3/8	5 7/8	5 4/8	30	24 6/8	Coconino Co., AZ	Chuck Adams	Chuck Adams	2000	213
117 6/8	18 2/8	17 6/8	14 1/8	14 3/8	6 2/8	5 5/8	30 6/8	25 6/8	Farewell, AK	Thomas R. Keele	Thomas R. Keele	1975	220
117 6/8	17 5/8	17 4/8	13 5/8	14 2/8	5 5/8	5 6/8	26	20 4/8	Garfield Co., UT	Sheldon D. Worthen	Sheldon D. Worthen	1977	220
117 6/8	17 4/8	16 4/8	14 5/8	14 5/8	6	6	27 4/8	23	Park Co., MT	Thomas D. Roe	Thomas D. Roe	1988	220
117 4/8	16 3/8	18 6/8	15 6/8	15 4/8	6 6/8	6	29	23	Custer Co., SD	Thomas J. Radoumis	Thomas J. Radoumis	1973	223
117 4/8	19	18 6/8	14 2/8	14 4/8	5 1/8	5 2/8	26 7/8	19 1/8	Delta Junction, AK	Kenneth L. Carlson	Kenneth L. Carlson	2001	223
117 4/8	18 6/8	17 3/8	14 3/8	14 3/8	5 2/8	5 3/8	27 6/8	20	Coconino Co., AZ	Chuck Adams	Chuck Adams	2002	223
117 2/8	17 6/8	18 7/8	14 2/8	14 2/8	6 3/8	6 5/8	30	25	Garfield Co., UT	Don Genessy	Don Genessy	1960	226
117 2/8	18 7/8	17 7/8	14 6/8	14 4/8	4 5/8	4 7/8	27	16	Gillette, WY	D.C. Basolo, Jr.	D.C. Basolo, Jr.	1963	226
117 2/8	19	18 6/8	14 2/8	14 1/8	5	5	31	27	Campbell Co., WY	Leroy Van Buggenum	Leroy Van Buggenum	1968	226
117 2/8	17 7/8	16 3/8	14 1/8	14 6/8	5 6/8	5 6/8	28 5/8	24 4/8	Park Co., MT	Donald E. Franklin	Donald E. Franklin	1986	226
117 2/8	19 1/8	18	14 6/8	15	5	4 7/8	27 5/8	18 4/8	Wayne Co., UT	Tony K. Cross	Tony K. Cross	1987	226
117 2/8	16 6/8	17 5/8	14 2/8	14 6/8	6 1/8	5 4/8	27 3/8	23 1/8	Garfield Co., UT	L. Scot Jenkins	L. Scot Jenkins	1987	226
117 2/8	17 5/8	17	14 6/8	14 6/8	5 6/8	5 6/8	29 1/8	23 4/8	Custer Co., SD	Louis J. Peterson	Louis J. Peterson	1998	226
117 2/8	17	16 5/8	14 7/8	14 4/8	5 7/8	6 3/8	28	22 4/8	Davis Co., UT	Jacob B. Mecham	Jacob B. Mecham	2000	226
117	18 2/8	18	14 1/8	14 4/8	5 4/8	5 4/8	30 6/8	25	Fort Smith, NT	Fred Burke	Fred Burke	1960	234
117	17 4/8	17 6/8	15 1/8	14 1/8	5	5	28 4/8	22 7/8	Gillette, WY	D.C. Basolo, Jr.	D.C. Basolo, Jr.	1963	234
117	18 4/8	18 5/8	15	15 1/8	5 4/8	4 6/8	29 5/8	26	Dadina River, AK	Joe Van Conia	Joe Van Conia	1965	234
117	19	19 3/8	14 6/8	14 6/8	4 6/8	4 6/8	29 6/8	29 6/8	Delta Junction, AK	William T. Warren	William T. Warren	1978	234
117	19 6/8	20 2/8	14 6/8	14 5/8	4 4/8	4 4/8	30 4/8	24 3/8	Donnelly Dome, AK	Debra S. Darland	Debra S. Darland	1981	234
117	17 7/8	19 7/8	14 2/8	14 2/8	6 1/8	6 6/8	29	23 7/8	Delta Junction, AK	Elizabeth B. McConkey	Elizabeth B. McConkey	1981	234
117	19 5/8	18 4/8	14	14 2/8	5	5	29 4/8	26 4/8	Farewell, AK	Kevin G. Meyer	Kevin G. Meyer	1982	234
117	19	19 3/8	13 6/8	14	6	6	28 4/8	19 6/8	Custer Co., SD	William E. Butler	William E. Butler	1986	234
117	19 3/8	18 6/8	14 3/8	14 2/8	4 6/8	4 6/8	27 3/8	21	Delta Junction, AK	Rodney D. Bradford	Rodney D. Bradford	1994	234
117	18 1/8	18	13 7/8	13 5/8	6 3/8	7 1/8	31 2/8	25 1/8	Custer Co., SD	Richard H. Manly	Richard H. Manly	1998	234
117	18 5/8	15 6/8	13 5/8	13 4/8	6 5/8	6 5/8	30 3/8	23 5/8	Custer Co., SD	Duncan B. Gilchrist	Duncan B. Gilchrist	1999	234
116 6/8	16 2/8	15 7/8	14 7/8	14 7/8	6 5/8	6 3/8	38 1/8	32 7/8	Raymond Ranch, AZ	Unknown	Jack Brooks	1954	245
116 6/8	16 3/8	19 4/8	13 6/8	14 3/8	7	7 6/8	28	28	Custer Co., SD	Merle G. Smith	Merle G. Smith	1974	245
116 6/8	19 4/8	18 5/8	14 3/8	14 2/8	4 4/8	4 5/8	29 5/8	24 6/8	Coconino Co., AZ	Stanley W. Gaines	Stanley W. Gaines	1977	245
116 6/8	19 1/8	17 7/8	14 1/8	14 1/8	5	5	30 5/8	25	Post River, AK	Elizabeth A. Bassney	Elizabeth A. Bassney	1990	245
116 6/8	17 5/8	18	13 2/8	13 2/8	6 2/8	6	29 4/8	20 5/8	Garfield Co., UT	Chris S. Eggli	Chris S. Eggli	1990	245
116 6/8	17 6/8	20 5/8	14	13 4/8	5 4/8	5 2/8	27	20 4/8	Delta Junction, AK	Wallace J. Niles	Wallace J. Niles	1998	245
116 6/8	17 5/8	16 3/8	13 7/8	14	5	5 2/8	27 7/8	20 3/8	Sekulmun Lake, YT	Terry L. Fretz	Terry L. Fretz	2000	245
116 4/8	21	18 1/8	12 2/8	13 1/8	5 2/8	5 5/8	29 7/8	17 5/8	Donnelly Dome, AK	F. Glaser & R. Tremblay	Univ. of Alaska	1954	252
116 4/8	16 7/8	16 3/8	14 6/8	14 6/8	5 5/8	7	28	22	Gillette, WY	D.C. Basolo, Jr.	D.C. Basolo, Jr.	1963	252
116 4/8	17 6/8	17 6/8	13 6/8	13 2/8	5 7/8	5 5/8	29 6/8	25	Park Co., MT	Picked Up	Glenn M. Smith	1990	252
116 4/8	18 4/8	18 1/8	14	13 6/8	5 6/8	6 3/8	27 7/8	19 3/8	Pink Mt., BC	Jerry E. Mason	Jerry E. Mason	1992	252
116 4/8	17 2/8	17 3/8	13 4/8	13 4/8	6 6/8	6 6/8	30 1/8	25 3/8	Custer Co., SD	Ken G. Wilson	Ken G. Wilson	1998	252
116 2/8	18	18 2/8	15	14 5/8	4 7/8	4 7/8	30 1/8	26 6/8	Alberta	Casper Whitney	B&C National Collection	1907	257

BISON

Bison bison bison and Bison bison athabascae

Score	Length of Horn R	Length of Horn L	Circumference of Base R	Circumference of Base L	Circumference at Third Quarter R	Circumference at Third Quarter L	Greatest Spread	Tip to Tip Spread	Locality	Hunter	Owner	Date Killed	Rank
116 2/8	20 3/8	20 5/8	13 4/8	14 1/8	4 5/8	4 6/8	30 3/8	23 4/8	Osage Co., OK	H.A. Yocum	H.A. Yocum	1943	257
116 2/8	17 1/8	17 3/8	17	16 6/8	4 7/8	5	25 6/8	18 1/8	Slave River, NT	Jim Wellman	Jim Wellman	1960	257
116 2/8	18 4/8	20	14 2/8	14 3/8	5	5 2/8	23 2/8	23 2/8	Delta Junction, AK	Alma Eades	Alma Eades	1963	257
116 2/8	17 4/8	17 3/8	14 4/8	14 4/8	5 3/8	6 4/8	33	28 5/8	Hook Lake, NT	Jerry Bick	Jerry Bick	1970	257
116 2/8	16 5/8	16 4/8	14 4/8	14 3/8	6 2/8	6 2/8	25 3/8	17	Hook Lake, NT	Jens K. Touborg	Jens K. Touborg	1972	257
116 2/8	19 6/8	18	14 4/8	14 3/8	5 2/8	4 4/8	28 7/8	20 2/8	Custer Co., SD	James B. Wade	James B. Wade	1976	257
116 2/8	19 4/8	19 3/8	13 6/8	13 4/8	5 1/8	4 7/8	27 3/8	18 5/8	Garfield Co., UT	Jed D. Topham	Jed D. Topham	1989	257
116 2/8	18 2/8	19 4/8	13	13 2/8	6 4/8	6	29 4/8	20 4/8	Custer Co., SD	Gene C. Lasch	Gene C. Lasch	1995	257
116 2/8	17 4/8	17 5/8	13 4/8	14 1/8	6 7/8	6 1/8	30 3/8	24 2/8	Custer Co., SD	Mark J. Long	Mark J. Long	1998	257
116 2/8	16 4/8	16 4/8	14 2/8	14 1/8	5 7/8	6 6/8	27 3/8	23 5/8	Garfield Co., UT	Jelindo A. Tiberti II	Jelindo A. Tiberti II	2002	257
116	15	15 4/8	14 7/8	15 5/8	6 5/8	6 4/8	27 4/8	22 6/8	Gillette, WY	D.C. Basolo, Jr.	D.C. Basolo, Jr.	1962	268
116	17 2/8	18	14 7/8	15 4/8	5 6/8	5 6/8	30 4/8	24 6/8	Copper River, AK	Tony Oney	Tony Oney	1964	268
116	17 5/8	18 1/8	14 6/8	14 6/8	5 4/8	5 3/8	30 1/8	23 7/8	Coconino Co., AZ	John Renkema, Jr.	John Renkema, Jr.	1977	268
116	19 2/8	19 2/8	14 3/8	14 2/8	5 1/8	4 6/8	27 1/8	19 1/8	Garfield Co., UT	Gary B. Brosig	Gary B. Brosig	1995	268
116	20	19 3/8	13	12 5/8	5 5/8	5 4/8	27	19 1/8	Halfway River, BC	Picked Up	Gus Heather	PR 1998	268
115 6/8	18 5/8	18 2/8	14	14	5 4/8	6	33	25	Big Delta, AK	Barbara A. Nagengast	Barbara A. Nagengast	1963	273
115 6/8	15 3/8	17	14 6/8	14 5/8	6 4/8	6	25 5/8	21	Park Co., MT	Hilary J. Benbenek	Hilary J. Benbenek	1989	273
115 6/8	16 7/8	16 6/8	13 4/8	13 6/8	7 7/8	7 2/8	31 2/8	25	Custer Co., SD	C.J. Fuller	C.J. Fuller	1991	273
115 6/8	22 5/8	20 5/8	14 3/8	14	4 3/8	3 7/8	31	23 6/8	Nickolai Village, AK	Picked Up	Robert D. Jones	1994	273
115 6/8	17	17 2/8	14 1/8	14 2/8	5 5/8	5 4/8	26 4/8	21 1/8	Garfield Co., UT	Leo W. Mack, Jr.	Leo W. Mack, Jr.	1997	273
115 6/8	19 4/8	20 2/8	14	13 6/8	5	5 1/8	28 4/8	15	Sikanni Chief River, BC	Brian Nelson	Brian Nelson	1997	273
115 6/8	18 1/8	17 6/8	13 1/8	13 7/8	7 1/8	6 3/8	30	24 7/8	Custer Co., SD	James R. Weatherly	James R. Weatherly	1998	273
115 4/8	17 4/8	18	14 3/8	14 6/8	4 7/8	5 1/8	28 3/8	20 4/8	Sanders Co., MT	Glenn W. Slade, Jr.	Glenn W. Slade, Jr.	1961	280
115 4/8	19 4/8	19 7/8	14	14	4 6/8	5 1/8	27 1/8	15 4/8	Delta Junction, AK	W.S. Jarusiewicz	W.S. Jarusiewicz	1963	280
115 4/8	19 1/8	19	13 7/8	13 7/8	5	5	29 6/8	22 6/8	Hook Lake, NT	Robert C. Jones	Robert C. Jones	1974	280
115 4/8	19 4/8	20	13 4/8	13 2/8	5	5 2/8	29 3/8	24 1/8	Chitina River, AK	Ronald A. Sturgeon	Ronald A. Sturgeon	1979	280
115 4/8	17 7/8	17 4/8	13 4/8	14 1/8	5 6/8	5 7/8	32 1/8	25 7/8	Garfield Co., UT	Roger Stewart	Roger Stewart	1984	280
115 4/8	19 6/8	19 4/8	13 4/8	13 3/8	5	5 1/8	29 4/8	20	Gerstle River, AK	Robert F. Wiese	Robert F. Wiese	1987	280
115 4/8	19 1/8	20 2/8	13 7/8	13 7/8	4 7/8	5 3/8	27 4/8	24	Gerstle River, AK	Frank H. Talerico	Frank H. Talerico	1990	280
115 4/8	16	16 4/8	15 3/8	15 3/8	5	5 2/8	28 5/8	24	Garfield Co., UT	Kirk S. Jessop	Kirk S. Jessop	1992	280
115 4/8	18 2/8	18 6/8	14 2/8	14 2/8	5	5 4/8	31	22 4/8	Delta Junction, AK	Barbara G. Rekowski	Barbara G. Rekowski	1992	280
115 4/8	19 4/8	19 5/8	14	13 7/8	5	5 1/8	30 5/8	24 4/8	Pink Mt., BC	Jim Popil	Jim Popil	1996	280
115 4/8	18 1/8	18 6/8	13 4/8	13 2/8	5 6/8	5 7/8	27 6/8	20 3/8	Park Co., MT	Picked Up	Glenn M. Smith	1998	280
115 4/8	17 5/8	18 4/8	13	13 2/8	6	5 7/8	27 3/8	21 2/8	Garfield Co., UT	Norman L. Reese	Norman L. Reese	1999	280
115 4/8	19	18 4/8	13 6/8	13 5/8	5	4 6/8	28 2/8	23 2/8	Garfield Co., UT	Thomas M. Sorensen	Thomas M. Sorensen	2001	280
115 2/8	16 2/8	17 2/8	13 6/8	13 5/8	6 7/8	7 2/8	28 6/8	21	Black Hills, SD	Unknown	John H. Brandt	1969	293
115 2/8	18 2/8	19 1/8	14 7/8	15 2/8	4 3/8	5 6/8	28 4/8	24 1/8	Custer Co., SD	James P. Moon, Jr.	James P. Moon, Jr.	1983	293
115 2/8	17	17 4/8	13 7/8	14	5 4/8	5 4/8	28 4/8	24 1/8	Garfield Co., UT	Marsha Nickle	Marsha Nickle	1986	293

Score									Location	Owner	Date	Rank
115 2/8	19 7/8	19 5/8	13 6/8	13 4/8	5	4 7/8	27 4/8	19 6/8	Garfield Co., UT	Rodney J. Davis	1997	293
115 2/8	18 6/8	18 6/8	13 4/8	14 2/8	6 1/8	6 1/8	29	22	Kenney Lake, AK	Gloria M. Lannen	1999	293
115 2/8	16 3/8	17 1/8	13 4/8	13 7/8	6 4/8	6 6/8	28 7/8	23 7/8	Teton Co., WY	Barry Remington	2000	293
115 2/8	15 4/8	15 4/8	15 6/8	15 7/8	6	5 2/8	26 -/8	21 1/8	Davis Co., UT	Douglas S. Christensen	2002	293
115	19 2/8	18 3/8	14	13 6/8	5 3/8	4 7/8	28 7/8	18 1/8	Fort Smith, NT	Jules R. Ashlock	1973	300
115	16 6/8	16 6/8	15	15	5 4/8	6 2/8	29 7/8	27 6/8	Custer Co., SD	Rodger E. Warwick	1982	300
115	18 1/8	18 6/8	14	14 2/8	5 6/8	5 3/8	30 7/8	25 6/8	Custer Co., SD	August Benz, Jr.	1983	300
115	18 2/8	17 4/8	14	14	5 1/8	5	26	18	Garfield Co., UT	LaMar K. Cox	1985	300
115	18 2/8	19 2/8	14 4/8	12 4/8	7 2/8	6	30	23 2/8	Custer Co., SD	Picked Up	1987	300
115	17 3/8	18 5/8	13 4/8	13 4/8	5	5 6/8	27 7/8	18 6/8	Davis Co., UT	Willie T. Southern	1990	300
115	17	17	13 1/8	13 2/8	7 2/8	7 3/8	26 6/8	26 1/8	Park Co., MT	Picked Up	1992	300
115	17 6/8	17 6/8	13 2/8	13 5/8	5 2/8	5	27 6/8	24 4/8	Garfield Co., UT	Joanne L. Flesch	1993	300
115	16 4/8	17 4/8	13 5/8	13 4/8	6 2/8	6 6/8	28	26 3/8	Davis Co., UT	Michael D. Vincent	1998	300
115	18	18 2/8	13 2/8	13 2/8	5 7/8	6 1/8	30 6/8	26 6/8	Halfway River, BC	Rudell B. Willey	1999	300
132 *	21 3/8	21 2/8	15 1/8	15 1/8	7	6 7/8	32 4/8	21 3/8	Copper River, AK	Brenda K. Bergen	2002	
122 7/8*	20 6/8	19 7/8	15 3/8	14 2/8	6 2/8	6 6/8	28	15 7/8	Pink Mt., BC	Timothy L. Hastings	1997	
120 7/8*	19 7/8	19 7/8	13 4/8	13 4/8	6 4/8	7	30 4/8	21 7/8	Halfway River, BC	Norman L. Teng	1996	

* Final score is subject to revision by additional verifying measurements.

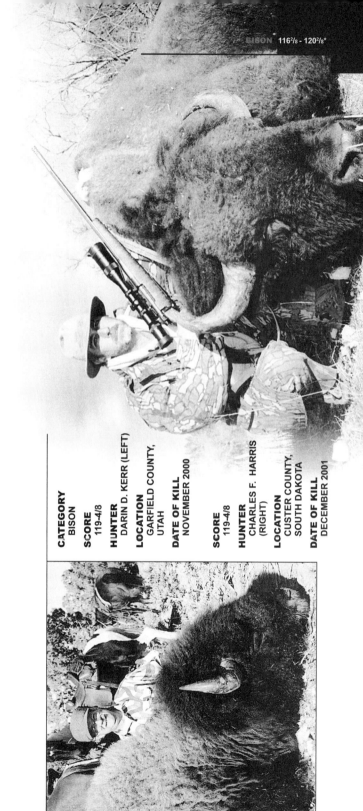

CATEGORY
BISON

SCORE
119-4/8

HUNTER
DARIN D. KERR (LEFT)

LOCATION
GARFIELD COUNTY, UTAH

DATE OF KILL
NOVEMBER 2000

SCORE
119-4/8

HUNTER
CHARLES F. HARRIS (RIGHT)

LOCATION
CUSTER COUNTY, SOUTH DAKOTA

DATE OF KILL
DECEMBER 2001

CATEGORY
BISON

SCORE
122-2/8

HUNTER
KENT DELIGANS

LOCATION
CUSTER COUNTY,
SOUTH DAKOTA

DATE OF KILL
DECEMBER 2001

CATEGORY
BISON

SCORE
126-6/8

HUNTER
THOMAS P. POWERS

LOCATION
CUSTER COUNTY,
SOUTH DAKOTA

DATE OF KILL
DECEMBER 2002

CATEGORY
BISON

SCORE
115-6/8

HUNTER
LEO W. MACK, JR.

LOCATION
GARFIELD COUNTY, UTAH

DATE OF KILL
SEPTEMBER 1997

B&C HISTORY

HENRY FAIRFIELD OSBORN
1857-1935

By Leonard H. Wurman

Twenty years after it was founded in 1869, the American Museum of Natural History in New York was poorly run and in debt. The museum's board, realizing that dinosaurs attracted visitors, recruited Osborn, then America's pre-eminent vertebrate paleontologist, to head the paleontology section. Osborn's administrative and fundraising skills were immediately appreciated and in 1901 he was appointed to the museum's board of directors. Seven years later, he became its president, a position he held for 25 years. It was under his leadership that the museum sponsored explorations to all corners of the globe. Osborn himself coined the name Tyrannosaurus Rex. A strong conservationist, Osborn assisted in writing the legislation that resulted in the Migratory Bird Treaty Act of 1918. ■

ROCKY MOUNTAIN GOAT
NEW WORLD'S RECORD (TIE)

After 50 years standing alone atop the record books, E.C Haase's majestic Rocky Mountain goat (*Oreamnos americanus*) now shares the World's Record title. Amazingly, Haase's goat taken in 1949, as well as Gernot Wober's goat taken in 1999, share not only a title, but also a history. Both hunters were awarded the prestigious Sagamore Hill Award, the Boone and Crockett Club's highest honor. As lofty as Gernot Wober's place in history is, he was lucky to even be on the hunt.

Lawrence Michalchuk's wife opted out of their planned mountain goat hunt, so with less than 24 hours notice, longtime friend Gernot played the fill-in role. He drove nearly 500 miles to join Lawrence in Bella Coola, British Columbia. The next morning, still weary from the long drive, Gernot and Lawrence climbed up the soggy Bella Coola Valley. They gained nearly 5,000 feet of elevation before making camp and spending the few remaining hours of daylight glassing for goats. For Gernot, it was a long day.

The first day was relatively uneventful, with the exception of a few unsuccessful stalks. Things picked up the second day however, as the men hiked North along the ridge. As they glassed a secluded valley, Lawrence noticed a billy standing in thick brush approximately 50 feet above the base of a distant cliff. As he looked through the spotting scope, Lawrence said, "The bases of those horns are the biggest I've ever seen. Too bad we can't get to him from here." They watched the big goat for a while and then headed back toward camp. At the time, neither man realized they had spotted a potential World's Record.

For the next two days, they stalked numerous animals, coming up short on several attempts. At night, as they cooked their meager meals, all they could talk about was the large goat they had seen and the problems of accessing the area he was in. They discussed moving camp closer to the goat but knew they couldn't climb down the cliffs at the headwall. They hatched a plan. The men hiked off the ridge the next morning to re-stock their supplies, get a hot shower, and attempt to take the big goat from the bottom.

On their ascent the following day, they thrashed up a nasty alder and devil's club hillside to get to the new valley. By noon, they were across from where they'd last seen the huge goat. At first they didn't see any activity, but soon Lawrence whispered, "He's there."

Lawrence carried his bow and Gernot a .270 with the understanding that Lawrence would get the first try at the billy, and if unsuccessful, Gernot would take him with the rifle. With Lawrence in the lead, they arrived at the base of the cliff where the goat hid, only to find he'd moved. As Lawrence climbed higher and circled around, Gernot waited. Suddenly, Lawrence gestured wildly toward some thick brush. Gernot could make out the outline of the huge billy.

After about 25 minutes of Lawrence trying without luck to get into bow range, Gernot heard him yell in desperation, "Just shoot him!" Before the echo faded into the valley, Gernot Wober had shot a goat that equaled the largest ever taken, at 56-6/8 points. ∎

ROCKY MOUNTAIN GOAT
WORLD'S RECORD SCORE CHART

Records of
North American
Big Game

250 Station Drive
Missoula, MT 59801
(406) 542-1888

BOONE AND CROCKETT CLUB®
OFFICIAL SCORING SYSTEM FOR NORTH AMERICAN BIG GAME TROPHIES

ROCKY MOUNTAIN GOAT

MINIMUM SCORES

AWARDS	47
ALL-TIME	50

SEE OTHER SIDE FOR INSTRUCTIONS		COLUMN 1	COLUMN 2	COLUMN 3
		Right Horn	Left Horn	Difference
A. Greatest Spread	8 7/8			
B. Tip to Tip Spread	8 2/8			
C. Length of Horn		11 7/8	10 6/8	1 1/8
D-1. Circumference of Base		6 4/8	6 4/8	—
D-2. Circumference at First Quarter		5 2/8	5 2/8	—
D-3. Circumference at Second Quarter		3 6/8	3 6/8	—
D-4. Circumference at Third Quarter		2 1/8	2 1/8	—
	TOTALS	29 4/8	28 3/8	1 1/8

ADD	Column 1	29 4/8	
	Column 2	28 3/8	
	Subtotal	57 7/8	
SUBTRACT Column 3		1 1/8	
FINAL SCORE		**56 6/8**	

Exact Locality Where Killed: Bella Coola, British Columbia

Date Killed: September 1999 Hunter: G. Wober & L. Mich

Owner: Gernot Wober Telephone #:

Owner's Address:

Guide's Name and Address:

Remarks: (Mention Any Abnormalities or Unique Qualities)

I, Ronald L. Scherer , certify that I have measured this trophy on
PRINT NAME

at Bass Pro Shops Springfield, MO
STREET ADDRESS CITY

and that these measurements and data are, to the best of my knowledge and belief, made in accordance with the instruct

Witness: Albert C. England Signature: B&C OFFICIAL MEASURER I.D. Number

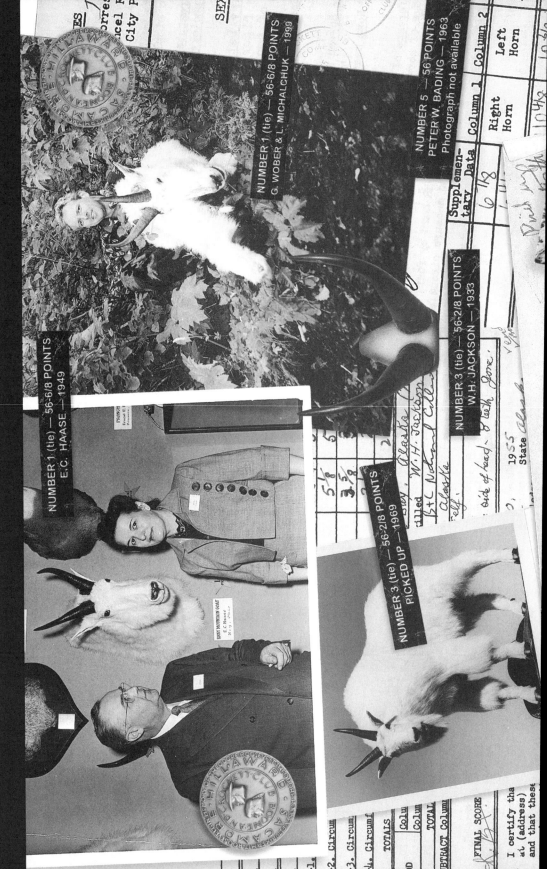

NUMBER 1 (tie) — 56-6/8 POINTS
G. WOBER & L. MICHALCHUK — 1999

NUMBER 5 — 56 POINTS
PETER W. BADING — 1963
Photograph not available

NUMBER 3 (tie) — 56-2/8 POINTS
W.H. JACKSON — 1933

NUMBER 1 (tie) — 56-6/8 POINTS
E.C. HAASE — 1949

NUMBER 3 (tie) — 56-2/8 POINTS
PICKED UP — 1969

Records of North A...
% Co...

RECORDS OF NORTH AMERICAN... CROCKETT CLUB

...TAIN GOAT

NUMBER 7 — 55-2/8 POINTS
PATRICK P. MOLESKI — 1994

NUMBER 8 (tie) — 55 POINTS
JAMES WILSON — 1969

NUMBER 6 — 55-6/8 POINTS
PICKED UP — 1970

NUMBER 8 (tie) — 55 POINTS
DAVID K. MUELLER — 1997

NUMBER 8 (tie) — 55 POINTS
ELMER W. COPSTEAD — 1939

1965

Column 1   Left
Right

...irst Quarter
... Quarter

BOONE & CROCKETT... N.A.B.G. COMPET. TI... 1973

RECOR...
BI...
Goat M...

ROCKY MOUNTAIN GOAT — 1st Prize
Score—55

Length—(R) 11-7/8 (L) 11-7/8
Basal Circumference—(R) 11-7/8
Locality—Cleveland Pe...
Hunter—Fl...

MINIMUM SCORE 50

ROCKY MOUNTAIN GOAT

Oreamnos americanus americanus and related subspecies

Score	Length of Horn R	L	Circumference of Base R	L	Circumference at Third Quarter R	L	Greatest Spread	Tip to Tip Spread	Locality	Hunter	Owner	Date Killed	Rank
56 6/8	12	12	6 4/8	6 4/8	2	2	9 2/8	9	Babine Mts., BC	E.C. Haase	B&C National Collection	1949	1
56 6/8	11 7/8	10 6/8	6 4/8	6 4/8	2 1/8	2 1/8	8 7/8	8 2/8	Bella Coola, BC	G. Wober & L. Michalchuk	Gernot Wober	1999	1
56 2/8	11 5/8	11 5/8	5 5/8	5 5/8	2 1/8	2	7 2/8	6 4/8	Helm Bay, AK	W.H. Jackson	B&C National Collection	1933	3
56 2/8	11 3/8	11 3/8	6 3/8	6 4/8	2 1/8	2	8 6/8	8 3/8	Hedley, BC	Picked Up	Robert Kitto	1969	3
56	10 4/8	10 6/8	6 1/8	6	2 5/8	2 6/8	6 7/8	6 4/8	Kenai Pen., AK	Peter W. Bading	Peter W. Bading	1963	5
55 6/8	10 5/8	10 4/8	6 1/8	6 1/8	2 2/8	2 2/8	7 6/8	6 3/8	Blunt Mt., BC	Picked Up	Jack Adams	1970	6
55 2/8	10 6/8	11	6 2/8	6 3/8	2	2 1/8	7 6/8	7 2/8	Oliver Creek, BC	Patrick P. Moleski	Patrick P. Moleski	1994	7
55	11 7/8	11 7/8	5 4/8	5 3/8	2	2	8 3/8	6 4/8	Cleveland Pen., AK	Elmer W. Copstead	Jonas Bros. of Seattle	1939	8
55	12 1/8	12 1/8	5 2/8	5 1/8	2 2/8	2	7 7/8	5 6/8	Alex. Archipelago, AK	James Wilson	James Wilson	1969	8
55	11 4/8	11 2/8	6 2/8	6 2/8	2	2	7	5 5/8	Cleveland Pen., AK	David K. Mueller	David K. Mueller	1997	8
54 6/8	10 5/8	11 3/8	6 2/8	6 2/8	2	1 7/8	8 3/8	7 5/8	Coquihalla Mts., BC	Fred D. Fouty	Fred D. Fouty	1959	11
54 6/8	10 7/8	11 2/8	6	6	2 3/8	2 3/8	7 5/8	6 5/8	Telkwa Range, BC	Mrs. V. Goudie	Mrs. V. Goudie	1964	11
54 6/8	11 3/8	11 3/8	5 6/8	5 5/8	2	2	7 6/8	5 5/8	Reflection Lake, AK	Lue Wilson, Jr.	Lue Wilson, Jr.	1979	11
54 6/8	11 3/8	11 2/8	5 7/8	6	2	2	8 1/8	7 7/8	Chupaka Mts., BC	Dennis F. Gaines	Dennis F. Gaines	1991	11
54 6/8	11 3/8	11 2/8	6 2/8	6 1/8	1 7/8	2	7 6/8	6 3/8	Bowser Lake, BC	Perley E. Holmes	Perley E. Holmes	1993	11
54 6/8	11 4/8	11 4/8	5 6/8	5 6/8	2	2	6 1/8	6 1/8	Vixen Inlet, AK	Ross M. Groben	Ross M. Groben	2001	11
54 2/8	11	11	6 3/8	6 3/8	1 7/8	1 7/8	10 1/8	10	Fairmont Range, BC	Ira McLemore	Ira McLemore	1947	17
54 2/8	11 2/8	11 4/8	6	5 7/8	1 7/8	1 7/8	10	9 3/8	Hastings Arm, BC	Rupert Maier	Rupert Maier	1963	17
54 2/8	10 3/8	10 4/8	6	5 7/8	2 2/8	2 2/8	8 2/8	7 4/8	Cassiar Mts., BC	Richard J. Wristen	Richard J. Wristen	1978	17
54 2/8	11	10 6/8	6 2/8	6 2/8	2	2	9 6/8	9 4/8	Cassiar Mts., BC	Raymond M. Stenger	Raymond M. Stenger	1979	17
54 2/8	10 5/8	10 5/8	6 2/8	6 2/8	2 1/8	2	7 5/8	6 7/8	Mt. Meehaus, BC	Denis J. Chagnon	Denis J. Chagnon	1989	17
54 2/8	11 6/8	12	5 4/8	5 4/8	1 7/8	2	7 2/8	5 2/8	Yes Bay, AK	Wally L. Grover	Wally L. Grover	1991	17
54	11 2/8	11 1/8	6 2/8	6 2/8	2	2	9 2/8	9 2/8	Bow Summit, AB	Native American	N.K. Luxton	1907	23
54	11	11	6 1/8	6 1/8	2	2	8 1/8	8 1/8	Terminus Mt., BC	Herb Klein	Dallas Mus. of Natl. Hist.	1965	23
54	10 7/8	10 6/8	6	6 1/8	2 1/8	2 1/8	9 1/8	8 5/8	Sicintine Range, BC	Thomas R. VanEvery	Thomas R. VanEvery	1994	23
54	12 3/8	11 7/8	6	6	1 6/8	1 6/8	9 2/8	7 6/8	Flathead Co., MT	Jason D. Beatty	Jason D. Beatty	1998	23
54	10 3/8	10 2/8	6 1/8	6	2 1/8	2 1/8	7 6/8	7	Stikine River, BC	Shawn K. MacFarlane	Shawn K. MacFarlane	2003	23
53 6/8	11 1/8	11 2/8	5 7/8	5 7/8	2	1 7/8	9 4/8	8 4/8	Telegraph Creek, BC	Vernon D.E. Smith	Vernon D.E. Smith	1954	28
53 6/8	10 7/8	10 7/8	6	6	1 7/8	1 7/8	7 6/8	6 6/8	Tumeka Lake, BC	Robert H. Edwards	Robert H. Edwards	1972	28
53 6/8	10 3/8	10 3/8	5 7/8	6	2 1/8	2 1/8	7 7/8	7 5/8	Elko Co., NV	Robert D. Kennedy	Robert D. Kennedy	1978	28
53 6/8	10 6/8	10 6/8	6	6	2	2	8 6/8	8	Sheslay River, BC	Dan Stobbe	Dan Stobbe	1987	28
53 6/8	10 6/8	10 6/8	6 1/8	6 2/8	2 1/8	2 1/8	8 3/8	8 2/8	Telegraph Creek, BC	Steven M. Gross	Steven M. Gross	1991	28
53 6/8	10 2/8	10 2/8	5 7/8	5 7/8	2	2	7 4/8	7 3/8	Del Creek, BC	Dora L. Hetzel	Dora L. Hetzel	2003	28
53 4/8	11 4/8	11 4/8	6	6 1/8	2 1/8	2	7 4/8	6 7/8	Stikine River, BC	John Creyke	John Creyke	1926	34
53 4/8	10 6/8	11	6	6	1 7/8	1 7/8	9 2/8	8 7/8	Coldstream Creek, BC	R.J. Pop	Herb Klein	1952	34
53 4/8	11 4/8	11	5 6/8	5 7/8	1 7/8	1 7/8	8 1/8	7 4/8	Kitimat, BC	Fred Hahn	Fred Hahn	1966	34
53 4/8	10 7/8	9 5/8	6 5/8	6 6/8	2	2 3/8	7	6	Bella Coola, BC	Darryl Hodson	Darryl Hodson	1966	34

Score	Length of Horn R	Length of Horn L	Circ. of Base R	Circ. of Base L	Circ. 3rd Quarter R	Circ. 3rd Quarter L	Greatest Spread	Tip to Tip Spread	Locality	Hunter	Owner	Date Killed	Rank
53 4/8	11 4/8	11 3/8	5 5/8	5 5/8	2	2	9 2/8	8 7/8	Cassiar Mts., BC	William Rohlfs	William Rohlfs	1971	34
53 4/8	10 6/8	10 3/8	6 2/8	6 2/8	2	2	7	5 2/8	Mt. Horetzky, BC	Jackie O. Arnold	Jackie O. Arnold	1980	34
53 4/8	10 4/8	10 6/8	6 1/8	6 2/8	2	2	8 5/8	8 1/8	Beggerlay Creek, BC	Joe Hamelink	Joe Hamelink	1986	34
53 4/8	10 5/8	10 5/8	6 1/8	6	2	2	6 4/8	8 6/8	Sheslay River, BC	Gregory A. Hurst	Gregory A. Hurst	1996	34
53 4/8	10 4/8	10 6/8	6	6	2	2	7 4/8	7 1/8	Elko Co., NV	R. Dean Conley	R. Dean Conley	2002	34
53 2/8	11 1/8	11	6 6/8	5 6/8	2	2	6 7/8	7 7/8	Cassiar Mts., BC	W. Reuen Fisher	W. Reuen Fisher	1945	43
53 2/8	10 6/8	11 1/8	5 7/8	6 6/8	2	2	7 7/8	5 6/8	Ketchikan, AK	Charles E. Slajer	Charles E. Slajer	1966	43
53 2/8	10 7/8	11	5 7/8	6 3/8	1 6/8	1 7/8	7	7 2/8	Mt. Findlay, BC	Glenn Welsh	Glenn Welsh	1971	43
53 2/8	11 2/8	11 5/8	6 3/8	5 4/8	2	2 1/8	7 6/8	6 1/8	Halfmoon Lake, AK	Robert A. Hewitt	Robert A. Hewitt	1980	43
53 2/8	10 3/8	10 3/8	5 4/8	5 7/8	2	2 1/8	6 2/8	7 2/8	Skeena River, BC	Robin B. Freeman	Robin B. Freeman	1985	43
53 2/8	10 4/8	10 4/8	5 7/8	5 7/8	2	2	5 1/8	5 1/8	Cleveland Pen., AK	Robert M. Ortiz	Robert M. Ortiz	2001	43
53	10	10 1/8	5 7/8	5 7/8	2	2	6 2/8	6 2/8	Skagway, AK	Charles R. Heath	Charles R. Heath	1965	49
53	10 7/8	10 7/8	5 7/8	5 7/8	2	2	7 4/8	7 4/8	Skeena-Copper Rivers, BC	John A. Paetkau	John W. Kroeker	1967	49
53	11	11	6	6	2	2	8 7/8	8 7/8	James Creek, BC	Manfred Beier	Manfred Beier	1968	49
53	10	10 6/8	5 4/8	5 4/8	2	2	4 7/8	4 7/8	Cassiar Mts., BC	Jack Thorndike	Jack Thorndike	1970	49
53	11 2/8	10 7/8	6 2/8	6 1/8	2	2	8 2/8	8 1/8	Aaron Mt., AK	John Sturgeon	John Sturgeon	1973	49
53	10 4/8	10 7/8	6	6	1 7/8	2	10 1/8	9 3/8	Homer, AK	Robert W. Hertz, Jr.	Robert W. Hertz, Jr.	1974	49
53	10 7/8	10 7/8	5 7/8	5 4/8	2	2	9 6/8	9 3/8	Sheslay Mt., BC	Wallace E. Sills	Wallace E. Sills	1985	49
53	11	11 1/8	5 4/8	5 6/8	2	1 7/8	8 6/8	8 5/8	Tagish Lake, BC	Larry W. White	Larry W. White	1987	49
53	11 2/8	11 1/8	6	6	1 7/8	2	8 1/8	7 5/8	Toms Creek, BC	Tommy B. Lee, Jr.	Tommy B. Lee, Jr.	1988	49
53	11	10 6/8	6	6	2	1 7/8	7 1/8	6 2/8	Morice River, BC	Elizabeth D. Saunders	Rob Saunders	1989	49
53	10 7/8	11	6	6	1 7/8	2	8	7 4/8	Skeena River, BC	Russil Tanner	Russil Tanner	1990	49
53	11	10 5/8	6	6	2	1 7/8	8 6/8	8 3/8	Nahlin River, BC	James T. Kruger	James T. Kruger	1992	49
53	10 5/8	10 5/8	6	6	2	2	7 2/8	6 7/8	Tahltan River, BC	Terry Schulist	Terry Schulist	1997	49
53	10 5/8	10 4/8	5 6/8	5 6/8	2	2	8 3/8	7 6/8	Shoemaker Creek, BC	Klauss Wolff	Klauss Wolff	2002	49
53	11	10 5/8	5 6/8	5 6/8	2	2	7 6/8	7 3/8	Skeena River, BC	Randy Kucharyshen	Randy Kucharyshen	2003	49
52 6/8	11 4/8	11 4/8	5 6/8	5 5/8	1 7/8	2	7 3/8	8 2/8	Idaho Co., ID	A.C. Gilbert	Farrell M. Trenary	1933	64
52 6/8	11	11	5 5/8	5 5/8	2 1/8	1 7/8	8 2/8	7 4/8	Kootenay, BC	Jules V. Lane	Jules V. Lane	1935	64
52 6/8	11 4/8	11 4/8	5 7/8	5 6/8	1 6/8	2 1/8	7 4/8	5 6/8	Whatcom Co., WA	Arie Vanderhoek, Jr.	Arie Vanderhoek, Jr.	1966	64
52 6/8	10 1/8	10 1/8	5 1/8	5 7/8	2 3/8	2	5 6/8	8 1/8	Cold Fish Lake, BC	Stanley W. Glasscock	Stanley W. Glasscock	1967	64
52 6/8	10 2/8	10 2/8	5 7/8	5 7/8	2 1/8	2	8 1/8	5 5/8	Ashnola Valley, BC	Brian Chipperfield	Brian Chipperfield	1968	64
52 6/8	11 1/8	11 3/8	5 6/8	5 6/8	2	2	6 3/8	7	Vernon, BC	Robert B. Procter	Robert B. Procter	1968	64
52 6/8	10 3/8	10 4/8	6	6	2	2	7 5/8	7 4/8	Terrace, BC	R.P. Kolterman	R.P. Kolterman	1971	64
52 6/8	10 4/8	10 2/8	6	6	1 7/8	1 7/8	8 2/8	6	Cassiar Mts., BC	H. Scott Whyel	H. Scott Whyel	1981	64
52 6/8	10 5/8	11 3/8	5 7/8	5 7/8	2	2 1/8	7 6/8	6 4/8	Foch Lake, BC	Albert S. Griffin, Jr.	Albert S. Griffin, Jr.	1985	64
52 6/8	10 4/8	10 1/8	5 6/8	5 6/8	1 7/8	2 1/8	7 3/8	8 2/8	Reflection Lake, AK	Timothy F. McGinn	Timothy F. McGinn	1985	64
52 6/8	11 3/8	10 6/8	5 6/8	5 7/8	2	2	8 2/8	7 5/8	Park Co., CO	Lyle K. Willmarth	Lyle K. Willmarth	1988	64
52 6/8	10 5/8	11	5 7/8	5 7/8	1 7/8	1 7/8	7 6/8	8 2/8	Inklin River, BC	Anthony C. Ruggeri	Anthony C. Ruggeri	1993	64
52 4/8	10 4/8	10 1/8	5 4/8	5 4/8	2	2	7 1/8	7 3/8	Skeena River, BC	Michael Moleski	Michael Moleski	1996	64
52 4/8	10 4/8	10 4/8	5 7/8	5 7/8	1 7/8	1 7/8	8 2/8	7 2/8	Okanogan Co., WA	Richard Shatto	Richard Shatto	1962	64
52 4/8	11 1/8	11	6	6	2	2	7 3/8	6	Whatcom Co., WA	John W. Bullene	John W. Bullene	1965	64
52 4/8	10 1/8	10 6/8	5 7/8	6	1 6/8	1 6/8	7 4/8	6 6/8	Colt Lake, BC	George P. Jackson, Jr.	George P. Jackson, Jr.	1965	64
52 4/8	10 6/8	10 7/8	6	6	2	2	7 4/8	9 1/8	Terminus Mt., BC	Herb Klein	Dallas Mus. of Natl. Hist.	1965	64
52 4/8	10	10 2/8	5 5/8	5 7/8	2	2	10	7 6/8	Sheep Creek, WA	R.C. Dukart	R.C. Dukart	1967	77
52 4/8	10 7/8	10 6/8	5 7/8	6	2 1/8	2	7 7/8	7 7/8	Cassiar, BC	Otto Machek	Otto Machek	1968	77
52 4/8	10 1/8	10 2/8	6	5 7/8	2 1/8	2 1/8	8 7/8	7 3/8	Spectrum Range, BC	Kelly Good	Kelly Good	1973	77
52 4/8	10 2/8	10 2/8	5 7/8	6	2 1/8	2 1/8	8 7/8	8 7/8	Rock Island Lake, BC	Joe E. Coleman	Joe E. Coleman	1976	77
52 4/8	10	10	5 7/8	5 6/8	2 1/8	2 1/8	8 7/8	7 5/8	Skeena Mts., BC	Hardy Murr	Hardy Murr	1977	77

ROCKY MOUNTAIN GOAT
Oreamnos americanus americanus and related subspecies

Score	Length of Horn R	Length of Horn L	Circumference of Base R	Circumference of Base L	Circumference at Third Quarter R	Circumference at Third Quarter L	Greatest Spread	Tip to Tip Spread	Locality	Hunter	Owner	Date Killed	Rank
52 4/8	9 6/8	9 7/8	6	5 7/8	2 1/8	2	8 1/8	7 5/8	Taku River, BC	Fritz Stork	Fritz Stork	1985	77
52 4/8	10 6/8	10 7/8	5 3/8	5 5/8	2	2 1/8	7 3/8	6 6/8	Granite Basin Lake, AK	Scott D. Hansen	Scott D. Hansen	1988	77
52 4/8	11	11 3/8	6	6	1 6/8	1 7/8	10 1/8	10	Sicintine Lake, BC	Albert C. Nassan	Albert C. Nassan	1992	77
52 4/8	10 1/8	10 1/8	6	6	1 7/8	2	7 2/8	7 1/8	Keremeos, BC	Jerrell Coburn	Jerrell Coburn	1994	77
52 4/8	10 5/8	10 1/8	6	6	1 7/8	1 7/8	6 7/8	6 5/8	Kittitas Co., WA	James L. Hawk, Jr.	James L. Hawk, Jr.	1998	77
52 4/8	10 5/8	10 6/8	5 6/8	5 6/8	2	2	6 2/8	5 4/8	Cleveland Pen., AK	Robert M. Ortiz	Robert M. Ortiz	2001	77
52 4/8	10 5/8	10 6/8	5 7/8	5 7/8	1 7/8	1 7/8	7 6/8	7 2/8	Tahltan Highland, BC	Peter A. Walker	Peter A. Walker	2001	77
52 4/8	10 5/8	10 4/8	5 4/8	5 5/8	2	2	6 6/8	5 5/8	Boca De Quadra, AK	Jason C. Wrinkle	Jason C. Wrinkle	2001	77
52 4/8	11	11 1/8	6	6	1 7/8	2	8 3/8	5 5/8	Swan Lake, BC	A.C. Gilbert	The Old State House, CT	1938	77
52 2/8	10 3/8	10 3/8	6	6	2	2	7 1/8	6	Cassiar, BC	Frank H. Schramm	Frank H. Schramm	1947	94
52 2/8	10 1/8	10 1/8	5 6/8	5 6/8	2	2	7 3/8	6 6/8	Hastings Arm, BC	Ernest Dietschi	Ernest Dietschi	1963	94
52 2/8	10 4/8	10 2/8	5 7/8	5 7/8	2	2	8 2/8	7 6/8	Copper River, AK	Fritz Maier	Fritz Maier	1964	94
52 2/8	10 3/8	10 3/8	5 7/8	5 7/8	1 7/8	1 7/8	6 5/8	5 3/8	Bella Bella, BC	William B. Chivers	William B. Chivers	1965	94
52 2/8	10 7/8	10 7/8	5 2/8	5 3/8	1 7/8	1 7/8	8	7 5/8	Boca De Quadra, AK	Dan Hook	Dan Hook	1968	94
52 2/8	10 7/8	10 7/8	5 4/8	5 4/8	2	1 7/8	7 6/8	7 1/8	Boca De Quadra, AK	Doug Vann	Doug Vann	1968	94
52 2/8	11	11	5 6/8	5 3/8	2	2	8 5/8	8	Whatcom Co., WA	Al Hershey	Al Hershey	1969	94
52 2/8	10 6/8	10 6/8	5 7/8	5 7/8	2	2	8 2/8	7 7/8	Seward, AK	Donald R. Platt, Sr.	Donald R. Platt, Sr.	1969	94
52 2/8	10 5/8	10 5/8	6		1 6/8		9 3/8	8 3/8	Cassiar Mts., BC	Peter Fenchak	Peter Fenchak	1970	94
52 2/8	11	11 1/8	6	6	1 6/8	1 7/8	6 7/8	5 2/8	Mt. Cronin, BC	Vinko Strgar	Vinko Strgar	1972	94
52 2/8	10 6/8	10 4/8	6 1/8	6 1/8	1 7/8	1 7/8	8 2/8	7 6/8	Chelan Co., WA	John W. Lane	John W. Lane	1973	94
52 2/8	10 6/8	10 5/8	6	6	1 7/8	1 7/8	9 4/8	8 6/8	Cold Fish Lake, BC	Larry Bonetti	Larry Bonetti	1975	94
52 2/8	10	10	5 7/8	5 4/8	1 5/8	1 6/8	8 4/8	8 3/8	Kutcho Creek, BC	J.C. Page	J.C. Page	1975	94
52 2/8	10 1/8	10 2/8	5 4/8	5 6/8	2	2	6 7/8	6 4/8	Chelan Co., WA	Thomas A. Lovas	Thomas A. Lovas	1976	94
52 2/8	10 1/8	10 4/8	5 6/8	6 1/8	1 6/8	1 7/8	7	6 2/8	Chelan Co., WA	Nat C. Steele	Nat C. Steele	1980	94
52 2/8	10 2/8	10 2/8	5 6/8	5 6/8	2	2	7 3/8	7	Lewis & Clark Co., MT	Charles N. Johns	Charles N. Johns	1981	94
52 2/8	10 4/8	10 4/8	6 2/8	6 1/8	2	2	7 5/8	7 1/8	Sheslay River, BC	Frank L. Stukel	Frank L. Stukel	1984	94
52 2/8	10 2/8	10	5 6/8	5 5/8	1 7/8	1 7/8	6 7/8	6	Mt. Meehaus, BC	George A. Angello, Jr.	George A. Angello, Jr.	1988	94
52 2/8	11 1/8	11 1/8	5 5/8	5 4/8	1 7/8	1 7/8	9 5/8	9 3/8	Little Oliver Creek, BC	James K. Hansen	James K. Hansen	1988	94
52 2/8	11	10 5/8	5 4/8	5 4/8	2	2	10	9 7/8	Sheslay River, BC	Stephan A. Parks	Stephan A. Parks	1988	94
52 2/8	10 5/8	10 6/8	5 6/8	5 6/8	2	2	7 5/8	7 1/8	Bradfield Canal, AK	C. Wayne Treadway	C. Wayne Treadway	1988	94
52 2/8	10 6/8	10 2/8	5 7/8	5 7/8	2 1/8	2 1/8	6 7/8	6 2/8	Cassiar Mts., BC	Debbie S. Sanowski	Debbie S. Sanowski	1989	94
52 2/8	10 2/8	10 2/8	5 4/8	5 4/8	1 7/8	1 7/8	7 7/8	6 6/8	Lynn Canal, AK	Charles F. Roy	Charles F. Roy	1990	94
52 2/8	10 2/8	10 3/8	5 7/8	6 1/8	1 7/8	1 6/8	7 7/8	5 7/8	Fife Creek, BC	George M. Klein	George M. Klein	1991	94
52 2/8	10 4/8	10 4/8	5 4/8	5 7/8	1 7/8	1 7/8	6 4/8	6 2/8	Elko Co., NV	Daniel E. Warren	Daniel E. Warren	1994	94
52 2/8	10 1/8	10 2/8	6	6	2	2	7 1/8	6 3/8	Seton Lake, BC	Jerry M. Smith	Jerry M. Smith	1995	94
52 2/8	10 2/8	10 2/8	5 6/8	5 6/8	1 7/8	1 7/8	8 2/8	7 4/8	Resurrection Bay, AK	James L. Kedrowski	James L. Kedrowski	1997	94
52 2/8	10 7/8	10 6/8	5 6/8	5 6/8	1 7/8	1 7/8	9 6/8	8 7/8	Telegraph Creek, BC	Paul L.C. Snider	Paul L.C. Snider	1998	94
52 2/8	10 2/8	10 4/8	5 7/8	6 1/8	2	1 7/8	8 7/8	8 4/8	Sheslay River, BC	R. Terrell McCombs	R. Terrell McCombs	2002	94

Score	Length of Horn R	L	Circumference of Base R	L	Circ. Third Quarter R	L	Greatest Spread	Tip to Tip	Locality	Hunter	Owner	Date Killed	Rank
52 2/8	9 4/8	9 4/8	6 2/8	6 2/8	2	2	8 1/8	7 6/8	Piute Co., UT	Cloys D. Seegmiller	Cloys D. Seegmiller	2002	94
52 2/8	9 6/8	9 4/8	6 4/8	6 4/8	1 6/8	1 7/8	6 4/8	5 5/8	Adams Co., ID	Rusty P. Kirtley	Rusty P. Kirtley	2003	94
52 2/8	9 7/8	9 7/8	5 7/8	5 7/8	2	2	8 6/8	8 3/8	Morice Lake, BC	Rebecca M. Werner	Rebecca M. Werner	2003	94
52	11 2/8	10 7/8	5 4/8	5 4/8	1 6/8	1 6/8	8 3/8	7 7/8	Idaho Co., ID	Jeff R. Seagle	Joseph A. Seagle	1927	127
52	10 1/8	10 4/8	6 1/8	6 1/8	2	2	8 6/8	8 4/8	Cassiar, BC	Walter R. Peterson	Walter R. Peterson	1937	127
52	10 4/8	10	5 6/8	5 6/8	2	2	9	9	Tweedsmuir Park, BC	Chester G. Moore	Chester G. Moore	1946	127
52	10 3/8	10 3/8	5 4/8	5 4/8	2 1/8	2 1/8	6 7/8	4 5/8	Jumbo Mt., WA	Clyde Lewis	Clyde Lewis	1948	127
52	10 7/8	11	5 5/8	5 5/8	1 7/8	1 7/8	7 4/8	6 7/8	Watson Peak, AK	Harold M. Wright	Harold M. Wright	1957	127
52	10 6/8	10 3/8	5 4/8	5 4/8	2	2	6 7/8	6 2/8	Idaho Co., ID	Charlie T. Knox	Charlie T. Knox	1959	127
52	10 2/8	10 3/8	5 6/8	5 6/8	2	2	7 6/8	7 5/8	Mission Ridge, BC	Barry Naimark	Barry Naimark	1960	127
52	10 4/8	11	6	6	2 1/8	2 1/8	8 7/8	8 2/8	Bulkley Ranges, BC	Ingvar Wickstrom	Ingvar Wickstrom	1960	127
52	10 1/8	10 2/8	5 7/8	5 7/8	1 7/8	1 7/8	7 2/8	6 1/8	Kootenay River, BC	Howard Paish	Howard Paish	1961	127
52	10 3/8	10 2/8	5 7/8	5 7/8	2 1/8	2 1/8	7 3/8	7 1/8	Coquihalla, BC	Fred D. Fouty	Fred D. Fouty	1962	127
52	10	10	6	6	2	2	7	7	Sundial Lake, AK	Arnold W. Johnson	Arnold W. Johnson	1962	127
52	11 4/8	11 3/8	5 3/8	5 3/8	2	2	9 1/8	4 5/8	Boca De Quadra, AK	James Todahl	James Todahl	1963	127
52	10 1/8	10 2/8	5 7/8	5 7/8	2	2	7 2/8	7 6/8	Skeena River, BC	R.H. Simonds	R.H. Simonds	1965	127
52	10 5/8	10 6/8	6	6	1 7/8	1 7/8	6 1/8	6	Kitsumgallum Lake, BC	Manfred Beier	Manfred Beier	1965	127
52	9 7/8	9 7/8	5 5/8	5 5/8	1 7/8	1 7/8	7 3/8	5 4/8	Hart Mt., BC	Donna Loewenstein	Donna Loewenstein	1966	127
52	10 1/8	10 2/8	6 1/8	6 1/8	2 1/8	2 1/8	6 3/8	6 1/8	Southgate River, BC	R.T. Ostby	R.T. Ostby	1967	127
52	10 7/8	10 2/8	5 4/8	5 4/8	2	2	6 1/8	5 4/8	Okanogan Co., WA	E.W. Butler	E.W. Butler	1968	127
52	9 6/8	10 2/8	5 4/8	5 4/8	1 7/8	1 7/8	9 6/8	9 2/8	Auke Bay, AK	Kenneth L. Klawunder	Kenneth L. Klawunder	1970	127
52	10 1/8	9 6/8	5 6/8	5 6/8	2	2	7 5/8	7	Skagit Co., WA	John C. Casebeer	John C. Casebeer	1971	127
52	11	10 3/8	6	6	2	2	6 3/8	6 3/8	Chelan Co., WA	Robert A. Beckton	Robert A. Beckton	1971	127
52	10 1/8	9 5/8	5 7/8	5 7/8	2 2/8	2 2/8	8 5/8	5 7/8	Camp Island Lake, BC	C.N. Hoffman	C.N. Hoffman	1974	127
52	10 2/8	11	5 7/8	5 7/8	2 2/8	2 2/8	5 7/8	5 7/8	Skeena Mts., BC	William F. Jury	William F. Jury	1971	127
52	10 7/8	10 1/8	6 1/8	6 1/8	1 6/8	1 6/8	8 4/8	7 7/8	Kispiox Range, BC	John W. Allen	John W. Allen	1971	127
52	9 7/8	10 6/8	6	6	2 1/8	2 1/8	6 3/8	6 3/8	Elko Co., NV	Les Boni	Les Boni	1974	127
52	10 1/8	10 1/8	6	6	2 1/8	2 1/8	5 3/8	5 3/8	Whatcom Co., WA	George W. Bowen	George W. Bowen	1978	127
52	10 1/8	10 6/8	6 2/8	6 2/8	1 6/8	1 6/8	5 7/8	5 7/8	Chilkat River, AK	Terry L. Friske	Terry L. Friske	1980	127
52	10 2/8	12 1/8	5 3/8	5 3/8	1 7/8	1 7/8	8 1/8	5 7/8	Horn Cliffs, AK	Jack W. McKernan	Jack W. McKernan	1981	127
52	10 5/8	10 2/8	5 6/8	5 6/8	1 7/8	1 7/8	8 1/8	4 7/8	Burnie Lake, BC	Paul R. Levan	Paul R. Levan	1983	127
52	10 6/8	10 3/8	5 7/8	5 7/8	2	2	7 4/8	6 7/8	Old Tom Creek, BC	Dusty R. Cooper	Dusty R. Cooper	1986	127
52	9 7/8	9 4/8	6	6	1 7/8	1 7/8	6 3/8	5 2/8	Telegraph Creek, BC	Britt W. Wilson	Britt W. Wilson	1986	127
52	10	10 1/8	5 6/8	5 6/8	2 2/8	2 2/8	5 2/8	7	Yes Bay, AK	Roddy Shelton	Roddy Shelton	1987	127
52	10 2/8	10 6/8	5 5/8	5 5/8	2 1/8	2 1/8	7	7	Shemes River, BC	Russil Tanner	Russil Tanner	1990	127
52	10 1/8	10	5 4/8	5 4/8	2	2	8	6 4/8	Whatcom Co., WA	Gary W. Cunningham	Gary W. Cunningham	1991	127
52	10 3/8	10 3/8	5 7/8	5 7/8	1 7/8	1 7/8	7 1/8	6 3/8	Kumealon Inlet, BC	Steven D. Einarson	Steven D. Einarson	1998	127
52	10 1/8	10 1/8	5 5/8	5 5/8	1 7/8	1 7/8	8 1/8	8 1/8	Atlin Lake, BC	Frank J. Provencal	Frank J. Provencal	2002	127
52	10 3/8	10 3/8	5 7/8	5 7/8	2	2	8 4/8	7 5/8	Atlin Lake, BC	Frank W. Provencal	Frank W. Provencal	2002	127
52	10 6/8	10	6	6	1 7/8	1 7/8	6 5/8	5	Beaver Co., UT	Patrick J. Gilligan	Patrick J. Gilligan	2003	127
51 6/8	10 3/8	10 3/8	5 6/8	5 6/8	2	2	8 6/8	8 3/8	Telegraph Creek, BC	John S. McCormick, Jr.	John S. McCormick, Jr.	1936	164
51 6/8	10 6/8	10 6/8	5 4/8	5 4/8	1 7/8	1 7/8	7 5/8	7 4/8	Mile 402, AK	E.J. Blumenshine	E.J. Blumenshine	1948	164
51 6/8	10 3/8	10 2/8	6 1/8	6 1/8	1 7/8	1 7/8	6 3/8	6 2/8	Lake Co., MT	Glenn Conklin	Glenn Conklin	1958	164
51 6/8	10 4/8	10 4/8	5 6/8	5 6/8	1 6/8	1 6/8	8 4/8	8 2/8	Wolf Creek, MT	Jim B. Beard	Jim B. Beard	1963	164
51 6/8	11 2/8	11	5 6/8	5 6/8	1 6/8	1 6/8	7 4/8	6 7/8	Flathead Co., MT	John J. Allmaras	John J. Allmaras	1965	164
51 6/8	10 2/8	10	5 7/8	5 7/8	1 7/8	1 6/8	9 3/8	7	Telegraph Creek, BC	John Caputo, Sr.	John Caputo, Sr.	1965	164
51 6/8	10	10 4/8	5 7/8	5 7/8	1 7/8	1 7/8	9 1/8	7 1/8	Atlin, BC	W.H. Slikker	W.H. Slikker	1965	164
51 6/8	10 4/8	10 1/8	5 6/8	5 6/8	2	2	7 1/8	7 1/8	Kildala River, BC	Lorne Hallman	Lorne Hallman	1966	164

ROCKY MOUNTAIN GOAT

Oreamnos americanus americanus and related subspecies

Score	Length of Horn R	L	Circumference of Base R	L	Circumference at Third Quarter R	L	Greatest Spread	Tip to Tip Spread	Locality	Hunter	Owner	Date Killed	Rank
51 6/8	11 5/8	12	5 1/8	5 1/8	1 6/8	1 6/8	13	13	Cassiar Mts., BC	Bruce N. Spencer	Bruce N. Spencer	1966	164
51 6/8	10 4/8	10 3/8	5 6/8	5 6/8	1 7/8	1 7/8	7 4/8	5 7/8	Copper-Skeena Rivers, BC	Henry Dyck	Henry Dyck	1967	164
51 6/8	10 1/8	10	5 7/8	5 7/8	2	2	6 6/8	5 7/8	Ecstall River, BC	W.A. Kristmanson	W.A. Kristmanson	1967	164
51 6/8	10 5/8	10 7/8	5 5/8	5 6/8	2	2	6 2/8	5 1/8	The Pinnacles Mt., BC	Michael Bigford	Michael Bigford	1968	164
51 6/8	10 5/8	10 2/8	5 7/8	5 6/8	1 7/8	1 7/8	8 4/8	5 1/8	Wrangell Mts., AK	Basil C. Bradbury	Basil C. Bradbury	1968	164
51 6/8	10 1/8	10 3/8	5 6/8	5 6/8	1 6/8	1 6/8	7	6 2/8	Turnagain River, BC	John R. Braun	John R. Braun	1968	164
51 6/8	10 2/8	11 3/8	5 6/8	5 6/8	1 5/8	1 5/8	10	9 7/8	Clearwater Creek, BC	Stephen W. Cook	Stephen W. Cook	1968	164
51 6/8	11 2/8	11 3/8	5 4/8	5 6/8	1 7/8	1 7/8	7 7/8	7 5/8	Skeena-Exstew Rivers, BC	Frans Fait	Frans Fait	1968	164
51 6/8	10 5/8	10 4/8	5 4/8	6 1/8	1 6/8	1 7/8	9 2/8	8 7/8	Hobo Creek, BC	Roy K. Pysher	Roy K. Pysher	1969	164
51 6/8	10 3/8	10 4/8	6	6 1/8	2	2	7 6/8	7 1/8	Burns Lake, BC	Ellis D. Skidmore	Ellis D. Skidmore	1969	164
51 6/8	10 3/8	10 2/8	5 6/8	5 5/8	1 7/8	2	6 3/8	5	Tongass Natl. For., AK	Roderick Martin	Roderick Martin	1970	164
51 6/8	10 6/8	10 7/8	5 5/8	5 5/8	2	1 7/8	6 6/8	5 1/8	Bradfield River, AK	James M. Remza	James M. Remza	1970	164
51 6/8	10	10	5 6/8	5 7/8	1 7/8	2	7 2/8	6 3/8	Cleveland Pen., AK	H.D. Costello	H.D. Costello	1973	164
51 6/8	10 7/8	10 6/8	6	6	1 7/8	2	6	5 2/8	Snohomish Co., WA	Des F. Hinds	Des F. Hinds	1974	164
51 6/8	10 5/8	10 6/8	5 4/8	5 4/8	2	1 7/8	6	4 5/8	Mt. Allard, BC	David Brousseau	David Brousseau	1975	164
51 6/8	10 2/8	10 3/8	6	6	1 7/8	1 7/8	7 3/8	7	Ketchikan, AK	Donald K. Oldenburg	Donald K. Oldenburg	1977	164
51 6/8	11	10 6/8	6	5 6/8	2	1 7/8	8 6/8	7 6/8	Zymoetz River, BC	William E. Bond	William E. Bond	1978	164
51 6/8	10 5/8	10 3/8	5 4/8	5 6/8	2	2	6 6/8	5 4/8	Mt. Carthew, BC	Harry McCowan	Harry McCowan	1980	164
51 6/8	10 3/8	10 4/8	5 5/8	5 6/8	1 6/8	2	6 5/8	5 4/8	Kaza Lake, BC	J.C. Priebe & W.A. Bolles	J.C. Priebe & W.A. Bolles	1980	164
51 6/8	10 3/8	10 3/8	5 3/8	5 7/8	2	2	7 7/8	7 2/8	Behm Canal, AK	Michael L. Ward	Michael L. Ward	1980	164
51 6/8	10 2/8	10 1/8	5 6/8	5 4/8	2 1/8	2 2/8	6 4/8	5 5/8	Snohomish Co., WA	Michael J. Simon	John M. Mitchell	1981	164
51 6/8	9 7/8	10 5/8	5 4/8	5 5/8	2 1/8	2 1/8	6 5/8	6	Tyee Lake, AK	Daniel G. Bowden	Daniel G. Bowden	1982	164
51 6/8	10 2/8	10 2/8	5 5/8	5 3/8	2	2 1/8	7 1/8	6	Leduc Lake, AK	Steve Lepschat	Steve Lepschat	1982	164
51 6/8	10 6/8	10 5/8	5 6/8	5 5/8	2 1/8	2	6 3/8	5 1/8	Lake Rowena, AK	George T. Law	George T. Law	1983	164
51 6/8	10 6/8	10 4/8	6	5 5/8	2	2	6	4 4/8	Cleveland Pen., AK	Michael L. Ward	Michael L. Ward	1983	164
51 6/8	9 6/8	9 6/8	5 5/8	6	2	2	7 7/8	7 4/8	Bonneville Co., ID	K. Rands Wiley	K. Rands Wiley	1984	164
51 6/8	10 1/8	10 3/8	6	5 5/8	1 5/8	1 5/8	7 1/8	6 1/8	Snohomish Co., WA	Edward M. Beitner	Edward M. Beitner	1985	164
51 6/8	10 5/8	10 4/8	5 7/8	6 1/8	1 7/8	1 7/8	6 5/8	5 6/8	Whatcom Co., WA	Desmond J. Iverson	Desmond J. Iverson	1986	164
51 6/8	10 3/8	10 5/8	5 6/8	5 7/8	1 7/8	1 7/8	7 3/8	7 1/8	Spatsizi Plateau, BC	Gary R. Schneider	Gary R. Schneider	1987	164
51 6/8	10 3/8	10 2/8	5 4/8	6	1 7/8	2	8	6 6/8	McGavin Creek, BC	Charles H. Menzer	Charles H. Menzer	1987	164
51 6/8	10 2/8	10 4/8	5 4/8	5 6/8	2	2	7	6 3/8	Chita Creek, BC	Anthony D. Tindall	Anthony D. Tindall	1989	164
51 6/8	10 1/8	10 1/8	6	5 4/8	2	2	6 6/8	6 2/8	Snohomish Co., WA	Terry L. Wagner	Terry L. Wagner	1990	164
51 6/8	10	9 6/8	6	5 5/8	2	1 7/8	7 2/8	6 3/8	Gallatin Co., MT	Todd E. Barry	Todd E. Barry	1994	164
51 6/8	11	10 7/8	6	5 5/8	2 1/8	2 1/8	6 7/8	6 2/8	Lillooet, BC	Greg C. Bond	Greg C. Bond	1997	164
51 6/8	9 6/8	9 5/8	5 5/8	6	1 7/8	1 7/8	8	7 5/8	Chouteau Co., MT	Rhonda H. Tylinski	Rhonda H. Tylinski	1997	164
51 6/8	10 3/8	10 3/8	5 5/8	6	2	2	8 1/8	7 5/8	Kiniskan Lake, BC	Caroline R. Larsen	Caroline R. Larsen	1999	164
51 6/8	10	9 7/8	6 1/8	6 1/8	2 1/8	2	6 4/8	5 6/8	Skeena River, BC	James F. Sullivan	James F. Sullivan	1999	164
51 6/8	10 3/8	10 3/8	5 7/8	5 7/8	2	2	7 3/8	6 2/8	Little Tahltan River, BC	Leon E. Procknow	Leon E. Procknow	2000	164

Score	Length of Horn R	Length of Horn L	Circ. of Base R	Circ. of Base L	Owner	Hunter	Locality	Date	Rank
51 6/8	10 2/8	10 1/8	6	6	Troy Christensen	Troy Christensen	Beaver Co., UT	2001	164
51 6/8	10 7/8	10 7/8	5 5/8	5 5/8	Doug H. Cundy	Doug H. Cundy	Flint Creek, BC	2001	164
51 6/8	9 6/8	10 1/8	6	6	John C. Marsh	John C. Marsh	Telegraph Creek, BC	2001	164
51 6/8	9 6/8	10	6	6	Eric Torgerson	Eric Torgerson	Pine Tree Lake, BC	2001	164
51 4/8	10	10 3/8	6	5 7/8	Mark D. Larson	Mark D. Larson	Kittitas Co., WA	2002	164
51 4/8	11	11 2/8	5 6/8	5 6/8	Dallas Mus. of Natl. Hist.	Herb Klein	Kootenay, BC	1946	215
51 4/8	11 3/8	11 5/8	5 4/8	5 4/8	Walter Ozorowski	Lee G. Smith	Ella Lake, BC	1950	215
51 4/8	10 2/8	10 1/8	5 6/8	5 6/8	George W. Hooker	George W. Hooker	Cold Fish Lake, BC	1956	215
51 4/8	10	10	5 6/8	5 6/8	G.F. Juhl	G.F. Juhl	Jarvis Lake, BC	1960	215
51 4/8	10	10	5 7/8	5 7/8	Adolf Doerre	Adolf Doerre	Cassiar, BC	1961	215
51 4/8	10 4/8	10 3/8	5 6/8	5 6/8	Dan M. Edwards, Jr.	Dan M. Edwards, Jr.	Cold Fish Lake, BC	1961	215
51 4/8	10 3/8	10 3/8	5 6/8	5 6/8	Allen E. Linn	Allen E. Linn	Cleveland Pen., AK	1961	215
51 4/8	10 2/8	10 2/8	5 5/8	5 5/8	Charles E. Simmons	Charles E. Simmons	Boca De Quadra, AK	1961	215
51 4/8	10 5/8	10 7/8	5 6/8	5 6/8	Alan Olson	Alan Olson	Kenai Pen., AK	1962	215
51 4/8	9 5/8	9 5/8	5 6/8	5 6/8	Donald A. Turcke	Donald A. Turcke	Chugach Mts., AK	1964	215
51 4/8	10 6/8	10 7/8	5 4/8	5 4/8	W.C. Dabney, Jr.	W.C. Dabney, Jr.	Kechika Range, BC	1965	215
51 4/8	11 1/8	11 1/8	5 4/8	5 3/8	Arthur N. Wilson, Jr.	Arthur N. Wilson, Jr.	Boca De Quadra, AK	1965	215
51 4/8	10 1/8	9 7/8	5 3/8	5 7/8	Russell A. Fischer	Russell A. Fischer	Sheep Creek, AB	1967	215
51 4/8	10 1/8	10 2/8	6 1/8	6 1/8	S. Lantenhammer	S. Lantenhammer	Coast Range, BC	1967	215
51 4/8	10 6/8	10 5/8	6	6	Richard H. Leedy	Richard H. Leedy	Clearwater Creek, BC	1967	215
51 4/8	9 5/8	9 6/8	5 7/8	5 7/8	William E. Goosman	William E. Goosman	Toad River, BC	1970	215
51 4/8	10 3/8	10 3/8	5 6/8	5 6/8	Ted A. Dedmon	Ted A. Dedmon	Bowen Lake, AK	1971	215
51 4/8	10 2/8	10 2/8	5 7/8	5 7/8	George A. Shaw	George A. Shaw	Terrace, BC	1972	215
51 4/8	10 1/8	10 2/8	5 4/8	5 4/8	Virgil N. Carpenter	Virgil N. Carpenter	Chelan Co., WA	1973	215
51 4/8	11	11	5 6/8	5 7/8	Kevin Downey	Kevin Downey	Ketchikan, AK	1973	215
51 4/8	10 2/8	10 2/8	5 7/8	5 6/8	Donald E. Fossen	Donald E. Fossen	Stikine River, AK	1973	215
51 4/8	10 4/8	10 4/8	5 4/8	5 7/8	L.A. Candelaria	L.A. Candelaria	Stikine Range, BC	1974	215
51 4/8	9 4/8	10 3/8	5 6/8	5 6/8	A. Coe Frankhauser	A. Coe Frankhauser	Mt. Edziza, BC	1974	215
51 4/8	10 2/8	10 1/8	5 7/8	5 7/8	Charles H. Duke, Jr.	Charles H. Duke, Jr.	Pine Lake, BC	1975	215
51 4/8	11 5/8	11 2/8	5 7/8	5 6/8	Gordon Hannas	Gordon Hannas	Bulkley Ranges, BC	1976	215
51 4/8	10 4/8	10 4/8	5 6/8	5 6/8	John Reinhart	John Reinhart	Castle Creek, BC	1976	215
51 4/8	9 7/8	9 7/8	5 4/8	5 4/8	Ron Eller	Ron Eller	Kodiak Island, AK	1978	215
51 4/8	9 7/8	9 7/8	5 7/8	5 7/8	Casey G. Terry	Casey G. Terry	Telegraph Creek, BC	1979	215
51 4/8	10 4/8	10 4/8	6 1/8	6 1/8	Steven D. Skipper	Steven D. Skipper	Big Wideen River, BC	1980	215
51 4/8	10 1/8	10 2/8	5 6/8	5 7/8	James Fredrick	Unknown	Montana	PR 1981	215
51 4/8	10 3/8	10 1/8	5 6/8	5 6/8	Kurt W. Kuehl	Kurt W. Kuehl	Halfmoon Lake, AK	1982	215
51 4/8	10 1/8	10 7/8	5 4/8	5 4/8	Larry W. Lander	Larry W. Lander	Chouteau Co., MT	1983	215
51 4/8	10 7/8	10 4/8	5 4/8	5 4/8	JoAnn F. Flemming	JoAnn F. Flemming	Little Oliver Creek, BC	1985	215
51 4/8	10 4/8	10 1/8	5 7/8	5 7/8	Theadore H. Kiser	Theadore H. Kiser	Snohomish Co., WA	1985	215
51 4/8	10 3/8	10 3/8	5 7/8	5 7/8	Jack D. Yadon	Jack D. Yadon	Gallatin Co., MT	1986	215
51 4/8	11 1/8	11	5 6/8	5 6/8	Bernard Sippin	Bernard Sippin	Taku River, BC	1987	215
51 4/8	10	10	5 4/8	5 4/8	John P. Katrichak	John P. Katrichak	Maiyuk Creek, BC	1988	215
51 4/8	10	10 6/8	5 7/8	5 7/8	Wayne H. Kingsley	Wayne H. Kingsley	Tahltan River, BC	1988	215
51 4/8	11	10	5 6/8	5 6/8	Scott McDonald	Scott McDonald	Nass River, BC	1988	215
51 4/8	9 5/8	9 5/8	6	6	Daniel E. Gorecki	Daniel E. Gorecki	Sheslay River, BC	1989	215
51 4/8	10 1/8	10 1/8	6	6	Paul H. Ross	Paul H. Ross	Bradley Lake, AK	1989	215
51 4/8	9 7/8	10	6	6	Shawn M. Probst	Shawn M. Probst	Beaverhead Co., MT	1990	215
51 4/8	10 2/8	10 3/8	5 5/8	5 5/8	Rodney G. Chinn	Rodney G. Chinn	Little Oliver Creek, BC	1993	215

ROCKY MOUNTAIN GOAT

Oreamnos americanus americanus and related subspecies

Score	Length of Horn R	L	Circumference of Base R	L	Circumference at Third Quarter R	L	Greatest Spread	Tip to Tip Spread	Locality	Hunter	Owner	Date Killed	Rank
51 4/8	9 7/8	9 7/8	5 7/8	5 7/8	1 7/8	1 7/8	7	6 4/8	Salt Lake Co., UT	Joyce A. Christensen	Joyce A. Christensen	1993	215
51 4/8	10 2/8	10 2/8	5 7/8	5 6/8	2	2	8 2/8	7 2/8	Nanika Lake, BC	Reg Meisner	Reg Meisner	1995	215
51 4/8	10 3/8	10 4/8	5 7/8	6	1 6/8	1 7/8	8 5/8	8 2/8	Knik River, AK	Richard J. Jacob	Richard J. Jacob	1997	215
51 4/8	10 1/8	10	5 6/8	5 7/8	2	2	7 1/8	7 1/8	Scoop Lake, BC	Robert McCarter	Robert McCarter	1997	215
51 4/8	10 2/8	10 3/8	5 7/8	5 7/8	1 7/8	1 7/8	6 3/8	5 1/8	Gilltoyees Creek, BC	Gerald Volz	Gerald Volz	1997	215
51 4/8	10	10 2/8	5 7/8	5 7/8	2	2	7 7/8	7 3/8	Sinawa Eddy Mt., BC	Jeffrey A. Sackett	Jeffrey A. Sackett	2002	215
51 2/8	10 7/8	10 7/8	5 6/8	6	1 6/8	1 6/8	8 1/8	7 7/8	Kootenay, BC	Teddy MacLachlan	W.K. Porter	1925	264
51 2/8	10 2/8	10 4/8	6 1/8	6 1/8	1 6/8	1 6/8	7 7/8	7 5/8	Hard Scrabble Pass, AB	Justus von Lengerke	Justus von Lengerke	1937	264
51 2/8	10 1/8	10 1/8	5 4/8	5 4/8	2	2	8 1/8	8 1/8	Katalla, AK	John Goeres	John Goeres	1943	264
51 2/8	10	10	6 1/8	6 1/8	2	2	6 6/8	6	Mt. Robson, BC	E.T. Reilly	E.T. Reilly	1948	264
51 2/8	10 6/8	10 6/8	5 6/8	5 6/8	1 6/8	1 5/8	8 7/8	8 5/8	Cassiar, BC	Elmer E. Rasmuson	Elmer E. Rasmuson	1952	264
51 2/8	10 4/8	10 6/8	5 5/8	5 6/8	1 7/8	1 6/8	7 2/8	6 7/8	Bulkley Ranges, BC	Mrs. Billie Gardiner	Mrs. Billie Gardiner	1959	264
51 2/8	10	10 4/8	6	6	2 1/8	1 7/8	7 7/8	7 5/8	Kechika Range, BC	Paul A. Bagalio	Paul A. Bagalio	1965	264
51 2/8	9 6/8	9 6/8	5 7/8	5 7/8	2	2	7 5/8	7	Gataga River, BC	Robert C. McAtee	Robert C. McAtee	1965	264
51 2/8	9 3/8	9 2/8	6 1/8	6 1/8	2 2/8	2 1/8	7 7/8	7 5/8	Anchorage, AK	Wade Charles	Wade Charles	1966	264
51 2/8	10 3/8	10 3/8	5 6/8	5 5/8	2 1/8	2	8 4/8	7 5/8	Atlin, BC	Nolan Martins	Nolan Martins	1967	264
51 2/8	9 6/8	10	5 6/8	5 6/8	2	2	7 4/8	6 7/8	Atlin Lake, BC	Walter O. Johnston	Walter O. Johnston	1968	264
51 2/8	10 3/8	10 3/8	5 6/8	5 7/8	1 7/8	1 7/8	7 4/8	6 6/8	Vetter Peak, BC	Tracy Skead	Tracy Skead	1969	264
51 2/8	10 1/8	10 1/8	5 6/8	5 6/8	2	2	6 4/8	5 6/8	Kechika Range, BC	W.A. McKay	W.A. McKay	1970	264
51 2/8	10 1/8	10 4/8	5 3/8	5 2/8	2 1/8	2 2/8	8 2/8	7 6/8	Wrangell Mts., AK	John E. Meyers	John E. Meyers	1971	264
51 2/8	10 5/8	10 7/8	5 6/8	5 6/8	1 7/8	1 7/8	8 4/8	8 2/8	Skeena Mts., BC	Michael A. Wright	Michael A. Wright	1972	264
51 2/8	10 3/8	10 3/8	5 6/8	5 5/8	1 7/8	1 7/8	7 3/8	6 3/8	Tsetia Creek, BC	Douglas V. Turner	Douglas V. Turner	1973	264
51 2/8	10 4/8	10 2/8	6	5 7/8	2	2	6 4/8	5 3/8	Pend Oreille Co., WA	William R. Stevens	William R. Stevens	1975	264
51 2/8	10 2/8	10	5 7/8	5 7/8	2	2	7 2/8	6 3/8	Morice Lake, BC	G. Fitchett & L. Austin	George Fitchett	1978	264
51 2/8	10 5/8	10 6/8	5 4/8	5 4/8	1 7/8	1 7/8	10 4/8	10 3/8	Marker Lake, YT	James K. Montgomery	James K. Montgomery	1978	264
51 2/8	10 4/8	10 3/8	5 5/8	5 5/8	1 7/8	1 7/8	7 2/8	6 4/8	Idaho Co., ID	Lorraine Ravary	Lorraine Ravary	1978	264
51 2/8	10 5/8	10 6/8	5 4/8	5 3/8	2	2	8 3/8	7 7/8	Kittitas Co., WA	Michael W. Duby	Michael W. Duby	1980	264
51 2/8	10 6/8	10 6/8	5 6/8	5 5/8	1 6/8	1 6/8	7 3/8	6 5/8	Chilkat Mt., AK	Terry L. Friske	Terry L. Friske	1980	264
51 2/8	10 6/8	10 7/8	6 1/8	6 1/8	1 6/8	1 6/8	8 2/8	7 5/8	Swan Lake, BC	John Dobish	John Dobish	1981	264
51 2/8	9 6/8	10 2/8	5 5/8	5 5/8	2	2	7	8 1/8	Duti Lake, BC	T.J. Tucker	T.J. Tucker	1981	264
51 2/8	10	10 2/8	5 5/8	5 5/8	2 1/8	2 1/8	5 7/8	5	Tyee Lake, AK	David L. Bowden	David L. Bowden	1982	264
51 2/8	10 1/8	10 1/8	5 5/8	5 6/8	1 7/8	1 7/8	6 6/8	6 2/8	Okanogan Co., WA	Richard D. Grant	Richard D. Grant	1982	264
51 2/8	10 5/8	10 5/8	6	5 7/8	1 7/8	1 7/8	7 4/8	6 7/8	Kaustua Creek, BC	Duane Pankratz	Duane Pankratz	1982	264
51 2/8	10 4/8	10	5 5/8	5 7/8	1 7/8	1 7/8	8 3/8	7 6/8	Glennallen, AK	Kirk Z. Smith	Kirk Z. Smith	1982	264
51 2/8	10 6/8	10 3/8	5 4/8	5 4/8	2 1/8	2	8 4/8	8 2/8	Nass River, BC	Larry Zilinski	Larry Zilinski	1982	264
51 2/8	9 1/8	9 1/8	5 5/8	5 5/8	2 4/8	2 4/8	7 4/8	6 6/8	Taku River, BC	Charles W. Schmidt	Charles W. Schmidt	1985	264
51 2/8	10 1/8	9 1/8	5 6/8	5 6/8	1 7/8	1 7/8	6 7/8	6 6/8	Crown Mt., AK	Robert L. Hales	Robert L. Hales	1986	264
51 2/8	10 2/8	10 1/8	5 6/8	5 4/8	2	2	7	6 2/8	Mt. Guanton, BC	Charles R. McKinley	Charles R. McKinley	1986	264
51 2/8	9 7/8	9 7/8	5 4/8	5 6/8	2	2	6 2/8	5 3/8	Snehumption Creek, BC	Raymond C. Croissant	Raymond C. Croissant	1989	264

Score								Locality	Owner	By whom taken	Date	Rank
51 2/8	10 6/8	5 5/8	5 6/8	1 7/8	1 7/8	7 2/8	6 2/8	Cassiar Mts, BC	Robert A. Lenzini	Robert A. Lenzini	1991	264
51 2/8	10 6/8	5 6/8	5 5/8	1 7/8	1 7/8	3	7 2/8	Taku River, BC	John H. Garnett, Sr.	John H. Garnett, Sr.	1992	264
51 2/8	10 2/8	6	6	1 6/8	1 6/8	3 1/8	7 2/8	Moose Creek, AK	Michael R. Morava	Michael R. Morava	1993	264
51 2/8	10 6/8	5 5/8	5 7/8	1 7/8	1 7/8	7 7/8	6 4/8	Hugh Creek, BC	Gerhard Volz	Gerhard Volz	1993	264
51 2/8	11	5 7/8	5 6/8	2	2	3 1/8	6 2/8	Washout Creek, BC	Brian L. Davis	Brian L. Davis	1994	264
51 2/8	9 5/8	5 6/8	6 1/8	1 7/8	1 6/8	5 5/8	7 2/8	Bond Sound, BC	Richard R. Ford	Richard R. Ford	1994	264
51 2/8	9 7/8	6 1/8	5 4/8	1 7/8	1 7/8	7 5/8	7 4/8	Nahlin Mt., BC	Daniel W. Brockman	Daniel W. Brockman	1995	264
51 2/8	10 4/8	5 4/8	5 5/8	1 7/8	1 7/8	7 5/8	8 4/8	Sand Lake, BC	William J. Kuehn	William J. Kuehn	1999	264
51 2/8	10 7/8	5 5/8	6	1 7/8	1 7/8	3 6/8	6 2/8	Inklin River, BC	John A. Morrison	John A. Morrison	1999	264
51 2/8	10 1/8	6	5 4/8	1 7/8	1 7/8	6 6/8	5 7/8	Baker Co., OR	Kenneth R. Mellow	Kenneth R. Mellow	2000	264
51 2/8	9 3/8	6	6	2	2	6 4/8	8	Okanogan Co., WA	Carey D. Mott	Carey D. Mott	2000	264
51 2/8	10 6/8	5 4/8	5 7/8	2	2	3 1/8	7 7/8	Bob Quinn Lake, BC	Larry G. Snyder	Larry G. Snyder	2000	264
51	9 6/8	5 7/8	5 7/8	2 1/8	2 2/8	3 2/8	6 1/8	Morice Lake, BC	Warren Bodeker	Warren Bodeker	1958	309
51	9 6/8	5 6/8	5 7/8	2 1/8	2 1/8	6 6/8	4 4/8	Resurrection Bay, AK	Peter W. Bading	Peter W. Bading	1961	309
51	9 4/8	5 6/8	5 5/8	1 6/8	1 7/8	6 6/8	6 4/8	Terrace, BC	Gerald Prosser	Gerald Prosser	1962	309
51	11	5 7/8	5 4/8	2	2	7 2/8	6 1/8	Smithers, BC	John Strban	John Strban	1962	309
51	10 2/8	5 5/8	5 2/8	1 6/8	1 7/8	7 5/8	6 6/8	Butte Inlet, BC	Reuben C. Carlson	Reuben C. Carlson	1963	309
51	10 7/8	5 2/8	5 3/8	2	1 6/8	7 1/8	7	Kootenay Range, BC	Norbert M. Welch	Norbert M. Welch	1963	309
51	10	5 3/8	5	1 7/8	1 7/8	7 6/8	7 3/8	Dease Lake, BC	W.M. Rudd	W.M. Rudd	1964	309
51	10 2/8	5 6/8	5 5/8	1 6/8	1 7/8	7 4/8	6 2/8	Telegraph Creek, BC	John Caputo, Jr.	John Caputo, Jr.	1965	309
51	10 3/8	5 4/8	5 7/8	1 7/8	1 6/8	7 2/8	5 5/8	Flathead Co., MT	Johnny Powell	Johnny Powell	1965	309
51	10 6/8	5 6/8	6	2	1 7/8	7 1/8	7 7/8	Alaska Panhandle, AK	Donald W. Moody	Donald W. Moody	1966	309
51	10 2/8	6	5 7/8	1 7/8	1 7/8	8 3/8	6 6/8	Okanagan, BC	Earl Dawson	Earl Dawson	1967	309
51	10 1/8	5 7/8	5 5/8	2	2	7 3/8	7 2/8	Tete Jaune, BC	George Hanschen	George Hanschen	1967	309
51	9 6/8	5 5/8	5 5/8	1 7/8	1 7/8	7 2/8	7 3/8	Hart Mt., BC	Marvin F. Lawrence	Marvin F. Lawrence	1967	309
51	10 2/8	5 5/8	5 6/8	2	1 7/8	8	9	Telegraph Creek, BC	George McCullough	George McCullough	1967	309
51	10 6/8	5 7/8	5 5/8	2	1 7/8	9 2/8	5 5/8	Terrace, BC	Gary Townsend	Gary Townsend	1967	309
51	10 4/8	5 6/8	5 7/8	1 6/8	1 6/8	7 3/8	7 6/8	Nuka Bay, AK	Curt Henning	Curt Henning	1968	309
51	9 4/8	5 7/8	5 2/8	1 7/8	1 7/8	5 6/8	6	McBride, BC	Ervin Voelk	Ervin Voelk	1968	309
51	10 5/8	5 5/8	5 7/8	2 1/8	2	8 3/8	5 7/8	Lillooet, BC	Helmut Krieger	Helmut Krieger	1969	309
51	10	5 6/8	5 2/8	2	2	6 6/8	7 5/8	Yakutat, AK	Robert Sinko	Robert Sinko	1971	309
51	10 2/8	5 2/8	5 7/8	2	2	6 6/8	0	Snohomish Co., WA	David T. Lewis	David T. Lewis	1972	309
51	10 3/8	5 7/8	6	1 7/8	1 7/8	8	5 7/8	Findlay Creek, BC	Sharon Robey	Sharon Robey	1978	309
51	10 6/8	6	5 6/8	1 6/8	1 6/8	7 2/8	6 6/8	Ravalli Co., MT	John K. Frederikson	John K. Frederikson	1979	309
51	10 4/8	5 6/8	5 7/8	1 7/8	1 7/8	7 3/8	4 6/8	Tahtsa Lake, BC	Vernon J. Boose	Vernon J. Boose	1981	309
51	10 5/8	5 6/8	5 4/8	1 7/8	1 7/8	6 4/8	5 6/8	Snohomish Co., WA	John W. Lane	John W. Lane	1982	309
51	9 7/8	5 7/8	5 3/8	1 7/8	1 7/8	6 4/8	6 7/8	Granite Basin, AK	Gerry D. Downey	Gerry D. Downey	1983	309
51	10 7/8	5 4/8	5 6/8	1 7/8	1 7/8	7 3/8	7 2/8	Gallatin Co., MT	Ronald K. Lewis	Ronald K. Lewis	1984	309
51	10 4/8	5 6/8	5 6/8	1 7/8	1 7/8	5 6/8	8 2/8	Sheslay River, BC	Steven M. Sullivan	Steven M. Sullivan	1985	309
51	8 6/8	6	6	2 3/8	2 2/8	8 3/8	6 4/8	Salt Lake Co., UT	Andrea L. Shaffer	Andrea L. Shaffer	1987	309
51	10 4/8	5 5/8	5 6/8	1 6/8	1 6/8	7	7 1/8	Skilak Glacier, AK	Mark A. Gaede	Mark A. Gaede	1988	309
51	10 3/8	6	5 6/8	2	2	7	5 5/8	Clear Creek Co., CO	Janice L. Hemingson	Janice L. Hemingson	1988	309
51	10 1/8	5 4/8	5 4/8	1 7/8	1 7/8	6 2/8	5	Serrated Peak, BC	Philip E. Blacher, Jr.	Philip E. Blacher, Jr.	1989	309
51	10 4/8	5 5/8	5 6/8	2	2	6 1/8	6 3/8	Cleveland Pen., AK	Lynn K. Herbert	Lynn K. Herbert	1989	309
51	10 2/8	5 6/8	5 8/8	2	2	6 4/8	6 7/8	Wrangell, AK	Kerry Kammer	Kerry Kammer	1992	309
51	9 3/8	6 2/8	6 2/8	1 7/8	1 7/8	6 4/8	—	Yakima Co., WA	Stephanie L. Peyser	Stephanie L. Peyser	1992	309
51	10 2/8	6 1/8	6	1 6/8	1 6/8	7	—	Nanika Lake, BC	Gary Eby	Gary Eby	1993	309
51	10 2/8	5 5/8	5 5/8	2	2	7 1/8	—	Similkameen River, BC	Charles H. Veasey	Charles H. Veasey	1993	309

ROCKY MOUNTAIN GOAT

Oreamnos americanus americanus and related subspecies

Score	Length of Horn R	L	Circumference of Base R	L	Circumference at Third Quarter R	L	Greatest Spread	Tip to Tip Spread	Locality	Hunter	Owner	Date Killed	Rank
51	9 6/8	9 6/8	5 7/8	5 7/8	2	2	6 6/8	6 2/8	Morice Lake, BC	Keith Thompson	Keith Thompson	1994	309
51	10 3/8	10 2/8	5 6/8	5 6/8	1 6/8	1 6/8	6 4/8	5 3/8	Granite Creek, BC	Erich Unterberger	Erich Unterberger	1996	309
51	9 5/8	9 7/8	5 7/8	5 7/8	2	1 7/8	6 4/8	5 1/8	Tatla Lake, BC	James A. Kelley	James A. Kelley	1998	309
51	10 5/8	10 4/8	5 4/8	5 4/8	1 6/8	1 7/8	6 2/8	4 5/8	Cleveland Pen., AK	David K. Mueller	David K. Mueller	1998	309
51	10 3/8	10 4/8	5 7/8	5 7/8	1 5/8	1 6/8	7 6/8	7 3/8	Sweet Grass Co., MT	Brad Zundel	Brad Zundel	1998	309
51	10 3/8	10 2/8	5 2/8	5 3/8	1 7/8	2 1/8	7	6 2/8	Taku River, BC	Clifford D. Graham	Clifford D. Graham	1999	309
51	11 1/8	11 4/8	5 6/8	5 7/8	1 6/8	1 6/8	6 4/8	4 6/8	Horn Cliffs, AK	C. Don Wall	C. Don Wall	2002	309
50 6/8	10 1/8	10 3/8	5 6/8	5 5/8	1 7/8	2	9	7 1/8	Cassiar, BC	William N. Beach	Shelburne Museum	1918	352
50 6/8	10 4/8	11 1/8	5 4/8	5 4/8	1 5/8	2	9	8 5/8	Cassiar, BC	Clement B. Newbold	Clement B. Newbold	1926	352
50 6/8	11	11 1/8	5 4/8	5 4/8	1 6/8	1 6/8	5 4/8	4 3/8	Flathead Co., MT	Picked Up	Charlie Shaw	1936	352
50 6/8	9 4/8	9 4/8	5 7/8	5 7/8	2 1/8	2 1/8	7 7/8	7 6/8	Similkameen, BC	Peter Braun	John D. Rempel	1939	352
50 6/8	10 2/8	10 2/8	5 5/8	5 6/8	1 7/8	1 7/8	6 7/8	6 7/8	Cordova, AK	Ralph E. Renner	Ralph E. Renner	1950	352
50 6/8	10 4/8	10 2/8	5 5/8	5 4/8	2	2	8 3/8	7 6/8	Cassiar, BC	Peter Schramm	Peter Schramm	1950	352
50 6/8	10 7/8	11 2/8	5 5/8	5 5/8	1 6/8	1 7/8	9 1/8	8	Telegraph Creek, BC	Wayne C. Eubank	Wayne C. Eubank	1953	352
50 6/8	9 5/8	10 1/8	5 6/8	5 7/8	1 7/8	2	9 4/8	7 2/8	Telegraph Creek, BC	A.J. Duany	A.J. Duany	1954	352
50 6/8	10 1/8	10 2/8	5 7/8	5 6/8	2 1/8	1 7/8	8	7 3/8	Knik River, AK	C.M. Van Meter	C.M. Van Meter	1956	352
50 6/8	9 6/8	10 1/8	5 6/8	5 6/8	2	2	7 1/8	5 7/8	Boca De Quadra Inlet, AK	Lyman Reynoldson	Lyman Reynoldson	1957	352
50 6/8	10 4/8	10 3/8	5 6/8	5 6/8	2	2	8 2/8	7 5/8	Kenai Pen., AK	Elgin T. Gates	Elgin T. Gates	1961	352
50 6/8	9 6/8	9 6/8	6	6	2	2	7 1/8	5 6/8	Maxan Lake, BC	K.J. Nysven	K.J. Nysven	1961	352
50 6/8	10 2/8	10	6	6	1 7/8	1 7/8	7 4/8	6 6/8	Cold Fish Lake, BC	Howard Boazman	Howard Boazman	1962	352
50 6/8	10 4/8	10 5/8	5 6/8	5 5/8	1 7/8	1 7/8	9 4/8	8 3/8	Gataga River, BC	Herb Klein	Dallas Mus. of Natl. Hist.	1963	352
50 6/8	9 6/8	9 6/8	5 7/8	6	1 6/8	2	6 1/8	5 5/8	Keremeos, BC	Bill Postill	Bill Postill	1963	352
50 6/8	10	9 4/8	6	6	2 1/8	2 1/8	9 2/8	8 6/8	Atlin, BC	G. Vernon Boggs	G. Vernon Boggs	1964	352
50 6/8	9 3/8	9 3/8	5 7/8	5 7/8	1 7/8	1 7/8	6 2/8	6	Kechika Range, BC	Basil C. Bradbury	Unknown	1965	352
50 6/8	10 3/8	10 3/8	5 3/8	5 2/8	2 1/8	2 1/8	8	7 5/8	Cold Fish Lake, BC	Armin O. Baltensweiler	Armin O. Baltensweiler	1965	352
50 6/8	10 1/8	10 1/8	5 6/8	5 6/8	1 7/8	1 7/8	7 7/8	7 4/8	Cassiar Mts., BC	Ernest Granum	Ernest Granum	1965	352
50 6/8	9 7/8	9 6/8	5 7/8	5 7/8	1 7/8	1 7/8	8 7/8	8 1/8	Klappan Range, BC	Larry P. Miller	Larry P. Miller	1965	352
50 6/8	9 2/8	9 5/8	6 1/8	6 1/8	1 7/8	2	6 7/8	6 3/8	Hedley, BC	Donald J. Robb	Donald J. Robb	1965	352
50 6/8	10 2/8	10 3/8	6 1/8	6	1 5/8	1 5/8	6	5 7/8	Mt. Antero, CO	Leroy C. Wood	Leroy C. Wood	1965	352
50 6/8	10 1/8	10 1/8	5 3/8	5 3/8	1 7/8	1 7/8	7 5/8	7 3/8	Ashnola River, BC	Robert C. Bateson	Robert C. Bateson	1966	352
50 6/8	10 5/8	10 5/8	5 5/8	5 5/8	1 7/8	1 7/8	6 6/8	5 6/8	Skeena River, BC	G. Best	G. Best	1966	352
50 6/8	9 7/8	9 6/8	5 6/8	5 7/8	2 1/8	2 1/8	8 3/8	8 2/8	Toad River, BC	Walt Paulk	Walt Paulk	1966	352
50 6/8	10 1/8	10 7/8	5 6/8	5 6/8	2	2	8 3/8	6 5/8	Horsethief Creek, BC	Bill Pitt	Bill Pitt	1966	352
50 6/8	10 2/8	10 4/8	5 7/8	5 7/8	1 7/8	1 7/8	6 6/8	5 7/8	Black Hills, SD	Lloyd Weaver	Lloyd Weaver	1967	352
50 6/8	9 7/8	9 7/8	5 7/8	5 7/8	2	2	7 7/8	7 1/8	Kenai Mts., AK	Stephen D. LaBelle	Stephen D. LaBelle	1971	352
50 6/8	9 6/8	9 4/8	5 5/8	5 6/8	2 2/8	2 2/8	7 3/8	7 1/8	Dease Lake, BC	John H. Epp	John H. Epp	1972	352
50 6/8	10 4/8	10 4/8	5 5/8	5 6/8	1 6/8	1 6/8	8 4/8	8 1/8	Chelan Co., WA	Raymond J. Hammer	Raymond J. Hammer	1973	352
50 6/8	10 1/8	9 7/8	5 5/8	5 7/8	2	2	8 5/8	8 3/8	Kechika River, BC	Dennis Laabs	Dennis Laabs	1973	352

Score									Locality	By whom killed	Owner	Date	Rank
50 6/8	10 1/8	10	5 7/8	5 7/8	1 7/8	1 7/8	7 2/8	7 7/8	Kenai Pen., AK	Jack E. Allen	Jack E. Allen	1974	352
50 6/8	10	8 7/8	6	6 1/8	2 1/8	2 1/8	6 5/8	7 2/8	Cassiar Mts., BC	Kenneth E. Bishop	Kenneth E. Bishop	1979	352
50 6/8	10 3/8	10 2/8	5 6/8	5 5/8	1 7/8	1 7/8	7 2/8	7 6/8	Johnston Lake, BC	Brian A. Halina	Brian A. Halina	1979	352
50 6/8	9 5/8	9 5/8	5 6/8	5 7/8	2	2	7 5/8	8	Klastline River, BC	Glenn E. Hisey	Glenn E. Hisey	1979	352
50 6/8	10 3/8	10 4/8	5 7/8	5 6/8	1 6/8	1 6/8	6 1/8	7 1/8	Dutch Creek, BC	Tom W. Housh	Tom W. Housh	1982	352
50 6/8	10 4/8	10	5 5/8	5 5/8	2	2	7	7 4/8	Stewart, BC	Harry J. McCowan	Harry J. McCowan	1983	352
50 6/8	10	10 3/8	5 7/8	5 7/8	1 7/8	1 7/8	7 2/8	7 5/8	Okanogan Co., WA	Jerrel R. Harmon	Jerrel R. Harmon	1984	352
50 6/8	10 3/8	11 7/8	5 5/8	5 5/8	1 6/8	1 6/8	9 5/8	9 5/8	Day Harbor, AK	Steen Henriksen	Steen Henriksen	1984	352
50 6/8	11 7/8	10 5/8	5 5/8	5 7/8	1 5/8	1 5/8	7	7 7/8	Beaverfoot Range, BC	Kelley Knight	Kelley Knight	1984	352
50 6/8	11	10	6	5 7/8	2	2	6 2/8	7 3/8	Little Oliver Creek, BC	David J. Flemming	David J. Flemming	1985	352
50 6/8	10	9 6/8	5 7/8	6	1 6/8	1 6/8	6 3/8	6 5/8	Okanogan Co., WA	Susan M. Fletcher	Susan M. Fletcher	1985	352
50 6/8	9 6/8	10 5/8	6	5 7/8	1 7/8	1 7/8	5 4/8	5 7/8	Salt Lake Co., UT	Picked Up	UT Div. of Wildl. Resc.	1985	352
50 6/8	10 5/8	10 1/8	5 7/8	6	1 7/8	1 7/8	6 5/8	6 7/8	Chelan Co., WA	David L. Metzler	David L. Metzler	1986	352
50 6/8	10 1/8	10 1/8	5 4/8	5 4/8	1 7/8	1 7/8	7 7/8	8 2/8	Okanogan Co., WA	Monica M. Knight	Monica M. Knight	1987	352
50 6/8	10 1/8	9 5/8	5 6/8	5 6/8	1 7/8	1 7/8	5 6/8	6 2/8	Williams Lake, BC	Norwood N. Kern	Norwood N. Kern	1988	352
50 6/8	9 5/8	9 7/8	5 6/8	5 6/8	1 7/8	1 7/8	6 2/8	6 6/8	Salt Lake Co., UT	Macie J. Manire	Macie J. Manire	1988	352
50 6/8	9 7/8	10 5/8	5 7/8	5 7/8	1 6/8	1 6/8	7 6/8	5 7/8	Belcourt Creek, BC	Cameron Todd	Cameron Todd	1988	352
50 6/8	10 5/8	10 2/8	5 6/8	5 6/8	1 6/8	1 6/8	6 1/8	7 2/8	Kootenay Mt., BC	Ted A. Trout	Ted A. Trout	1988	352
50 6/8	10 2/8	10 2/8	5 5/8	5 5/8	1 7/8	1 7/8	7 7/8	6 5/8	Chouteau Co., MT	Craig L. Nowak	Craig L. Nowak	1990	352
50 6/8	10 2/8	10	5 4/8	5 4/8	2	2	7 2/8	8 1/8	Chopaka Mts., BC	John D. Chalk III	John D. Chalk III	1991	352
50 6/8	10	10 2/8	5 7/8	5 7/8	1 7/8	1 7/8	5 2/8	5 3/8	Coldstream Creek, BC	Richard P. Price	Richard P. Price	1991	352
50 6/8	10 2/8	10 3/8	6	6	1 6/8	1 6/8	8 6/8	9	Atlin Lake, BC	John R. Busby	John R. Busby	1992	352
50 6/8	10 2/8	10 1/8	6	6	2	2	6	6	Lardeau River, BC	Rod Smaldon	Rod Smaldon	1993	352
50 6/8	11 2/8	12 4/8	5 5/8	4 6/8	2	2	7 1/8	8	Whatcom Co., WA	James C. Zevely	James C. Zevely	1993	352
50 6/8	10 1/8	10 5/8	6	5 4/8	1 7/8	1 7/8	5	7 6/8	Castle Creek, BC	Curtis Neudorf	Curtis Neudorf	1996	352
50 6/8	10 5/8	9 5/8	5 4/8	5 5/8	1 7/8	1 7/8	7 6/8	6 1/8	Cleveland Pen., AK	Stephen Elenberger	Stephen Elenberger	1997	352
50 6/8	9 5/8	10 2/8	6	6 1/8	1 7/8	1 7/8	6 7/8	8 1/8	Chugach Mts., AK	Bill Gregory	Bill Gregory	1997	352
50 6/8	10 2/8	10 1/8	6	6	1 6/8	1 6/8	6 7/8	7 2/8	Syncline Hills, AB	Gilbert W. Davis	Gilbert W. Davis	1998	352
50 6/8	10 1/8	10 3/8	6	5 5/8	1 7/8	1 7/8	5 6/8	6 6/8	Park Co., MT	Dustin J. Hartl	Dustin J. Hartl	2001	352
50 6/8	10 2/8	10 2/8	5 5/8	5 5/8	1 6/8	1 6/8	7 2/8	7 3/8	Beaver Co., UT	Patrick J. Gilligan	Patrick J. Gilligan	2002	352
50 6/8	10 3/8	11 1/8	5 5/8	5 4/8	1 7/8	1 7/8	6 4/8	7 1/8	Cub Lake, BC	Jeffrey A. Grant	Jeffrey A. Grant	2003	352
50 4/8	12 1/8	10 4/8	5 4/8	5 5/8	2	2	7	5	Cassiar, BC	A. Bryan Williams	Mrs. N.S. Gooch	PR 1916	414
50 4/8	10 2/8	10 1/8	5 5/8	5 3/8	1 7/8	1 7/8	7 2/8	7 4/8	Cassiar, BC	George E. Burghard	George E. Burghard	1925	414
50 4/8	10 1/8	9 7/8	5 2/8	5	2	2	7	7 2/8	Telegraph Creek, BC	John S. McCormick, Jr.	John S. McCormick, Jr.	1936	414
50 4/8	10 4/8	10 4/8	5	5 5/8	2	2	5	7	Brazeau River, AB	Walter B. McClurkan	Walter B. McClurkan	1942	414
50 4/8	11 1/8	10 1/8	5 5/8	5 4/8	1 7/8	1 6/8	6	7	Stikine River, AK	W.F. Littleton	W.F. Littleton	1953	414
50 4/8	10 4/8	10 5/8	5 4/8	5 6/8	2 1/8	2 1/8	7 1/8	7 1/8	Bull Co., MT	Albert Markstein	Albert Markstein	1954	414
50 4/8	10 1/8	9 7/8	5 6/8	5 6/8	1 6/8	1 6/8	8 2/8	8 2/8	Cold Fish Lake, BC	Joseph Smith	Joseph Smith	1955	414
50 4/8	10	10	5 6/8	5 4/8	1 7/8	1 7/8	6 5/8	6 5/8	Okanogan Mts., WA	Neil Castner	Neil Castner	1956	414
50 4/8	10 1/8	10 1/8	5 6/8	5 6/8	2	2	7 2/8	7 2/8	Cold Fish Lake, BC	Patrick Britell	Patrick Britell	1957	414
50 4/8	10 2/8	9 6/8	5 4/8	5 4/8	2	2	8 1/8	8 1/8	Bennett Lake, YT	H. Kennedy	H. Kennedy	1958	414
50 4/8	9 6/8	10 4/8	5 6/8	5 6/8	1 7/8	1 6/8	7 5/8	7 4/8	Chugach Mts., AK	Elmer A. Patson	Elmer A. Patson	1958	414
50 4/8	10 4/8	10 3/8	5 6/8	5 1/8	2	2	6 3/8	6 6/8	Cold Fish Lake, BC	L.A. Wunsch	L.A. Wunsch	1958	414
50 4/8	10 3/8	10 2/8	5 4/8	5 6/8	2	2	7 5/8	7 7/8	Okanogan Co., WA	Bob Hazelbrook	Bob Hazelbrook	1960	414
50 4/8	10 1/8	10 3/8	5 6/8	5 1/8	1 6/8	1 6/8	6 7/8	7	Smithers, BC	A.S. Langan	A.S. Langan	1960	414
50 4/8	10 2/8	10 1/8	5 1/8	5 1/8	2 1/8	2 1/8	5 1/8	7	Chilco Lake, BC	G. Best & R. Reed	C. Marc Miller	1960	414
50 4/8	10	10 2/8	5 6/8	5 6/8	1 7/8	1 7/8	6 7/8	8 1/8	Kenai Pen., AK	Gordon Best	Gordon Best	1962	414
50 4/8	10	10	5 4/8	5 4/8	2	2	7	7 5/8	Atlin Lake, BC	Wendell Bever	Wendell Bever	1962	414

ROCKY MOUNTAIN GOAT
Oreamnos americanus and related subspecies

Score	Length of Horn R	L	Circumference of Base R	L	Circumference at Third Quarter R	L	Greatest Spread	Tip to Tip Spread	Locality	Hunter	Owner	Date Killed	Rank
50 4/8	9 3/8	9 3/8	5 5/8	5 5/8	2 1/8	2 1/8	6 3/8	5 4/8	Mt. Stoyoma, BC	Frank S.T. Bradley	Frank S.T. Bradley	1962	414
50 4/8	10 1/8	9 7/8	5 6/8	5 6/8	1 7/8	2	7	6 2/8	White Sales Mt., BC	Robert McDonald	Robert McDonald	1962	414
50 4/8	9 7/8	10	5 7/8	5 7/8	1 7/8	2	7 2/8	7 2/8	Kechika Range, BC	G.W. Hawkins	G.W. Hawkins	1963	414
50 4/8	10 5/8	10 6/8	5 4/8	5 4/8	1 6/8	1 6/8	7 2/8	6 7/8	Cape Yakataga, AK	Lynn M. Castle	Lynn M. Castle	1964	414
50 4/8	10 3/8	10 4/8	5 5/8	5 5/8	1 7/8	1 7/8	7 6/8	6 6/8	Lake Kinniskan, BC	Michel Boel	Michel Boel	1965	414
50 4/8	10	10	5 7/8	5 7/8	1 6/8	1 5/8	7 1/8	5 4/8	Wrangell Mts., AK	Charles S. Moses	Charles S. Moses	1965	414
50 4/8	9 4/8	9 4/8	5 6/8	5 6/8	2 1/8	2 1/8	8	8	Smoky River, AB	Terry Thrift, Jr.	Terry Thrift, Jr.	1965	414
50 4/8	9 6/8	9 4/8	5 5/8	5 5/8	2	2	8 1/8	7 6/8	Atlin, BC	Raymond Bartram	Raymond Bartram	1966	414
50 4/8	10 1/8	10 2/8	5 4/8	5 6/8	2	1 7/8	7 3/8	6 2/8	McDonald Lake, BC	Henry P. Foradora	Henry P. Foradora	1966	414
50 4/8	9 6/8	9 7/8	5 5/8	5 6/8	2	2	8	7 5/8	Sloko Lake, BC	John Haefeli, Jr.	John Haefeli, Jr.	1966	414
50 4/8	10 2/8	10 3/8	5 4/8	5 4/8	1 7/8	1 7/8	6	5 1/8	Revelstoke, BC	Picked Up	George Lines	1966	414
50 4/8	10 4/8	10 3/8	5 5/8	5 5/8	1 7/8	1 6/8	7 3/8	7 7/8	Seward, AK	Frank W. Pinkerton	Frank W. Pinkerton	1966	414
50 4/8	10 5/8	10 3/8	5 4/8	5 3/8	1 7/8	1 7/8	7 3/8	5 4/8	Winstanley Lakes, AK	James R. Simms	James R. Simms	1966	414
50 4/8	10 5/8	10 5/8	5 3/8	5 3/8	1 6/8	1 6/8	7 2/8	6 3/8	Black Hills, SD	Robert M. Aalseth	Robert M. Aalseth	1967	414
50 4/8	10 1/8	10 1/8	5 6/8	5 6/8	1 7/8	1 7/8	9 2/8	9 2/8	Cassiar Mts., BC	Donovan N. Branch	Donovan N. Branch	1967	414
50 4/8	10 2/8	10 2/8	5 4/8	5 4/8	1 7/8	1 7/8	8 4/8	7 6/8	Goat Mt., BC	T.T. Stroup	T.T. Stroup	1968	414
50 4/8	10 2/8	10 2/8	5 7/8	6	2	1 7/8	6 5/8	5 4/8	Turnagain River, BC	Howard S. Duffield	Howard S. Duffield	1969	414
50 4/8	10 1/8	9 7/8	5 4/8	5 5/8	1 7/8	1 6/8	7 1/8	5 1/8	Stikine River, AK	Donald E. Fossen	Donald E. Fossen	1973	414
50 4/8	11	11	5 4/8	6	1 7/8	1 6/8	7 1/8	7 7/8	Lewis & Clark Co., MT	Robert F. Thelen	Donald C. Thelen	1974	414
50 4/8	10 3/8	10 4/8	5 6/8	6	1 6/8	1 6/8	7 7/8	7 5/8	Dease Lake, BC	James T. Knutson	James T. Knutson	1975	414
50 4/8	10	10 2/8	5 6/8	5 6/8	2	2	7 7/8	7 5/8	Pennington Co., SD	Floyd J. Campbell	Floyd J. Campbell	1978	414
50 4/8	10	10	5 7/8	5 7/8	1 7/8	1 7/8	7	6 6/8	Wrangell Mts., AK	Leonard O. Farlow	Leonard O. Farlow	1978	414
50 4/8	9 7/8	9 6/8	5 6/8	5 6/8	1 7/8	1 6/8	6 7/8	6 4/8	Bingay Creek, BC	Clayton P. Podrasky	Clayton P. Podrasky	1981	414
50 4/8	10 4/8	10 4/8	5 5/8	5 5/8	1 6/8	1 6/8	9 1/8	5 7/8	Stikine Canyon, BC	Reuben F. Gerecke	Reuben F. Gerecke	1982	414
50 4/8	10	9 7/8	5 6/8	5 6/8	2	2	7 7/8	9	Mt. Cummins, BC	Rod Aune	Rod Aune	1984	414
50 4/8	10 4/8	10 3/8	5 7/8	5 7/8	1 6/8	1 6/8	7 7/8	7 3/8	Icy Bay, AK	David W. Dillard	David W. Dillard	1985	414
50 4/8	10 6/8	10 6/8	5 3/8	5 3/8	1 7/8	1 7/8	8	7 5/8	Leduc Lake, AK	James M. Judd	James M. Judd	1985	414
50 4/8	10 7/8	10 7/8	5 3/8	5 3/8	1 5/8	1 5/8	7 4/8	6 4/8	Missoula Co., MT	Bill R. Tillerson	Bill R. Tillerson	1985	414
50 4/8	10 1/8	10 1/8	5 6/8	5 6/8	1 4/8	1 5/8	6 4/8	5 5/8	Madison Co., MT	Corey M. Halvorson	Corey M. Halvorson	1986	414
50 4/8	10	10 1/8	5 6/8	5 6/8	1 7/8	1 7/8	5 6/8	5	Beaver Lake, BC	Richard G. Henke	Richard G. Henke	1986	414
50 4/8	11	11	5 5/8	5 4/8	1 6/8	1 6/8	5 6/8	4 4/8	Lewis & Clark Co., MT	Don St. Clair	Don St. Clair	1986	414
50 4/8	9 7/8	10	5 6/8	5 6/8	1 6/8	1 6/8	6 2/8	5 5/8	Bonneville Co., ID	Bill D. Stoddard	Bill D. Stoddard	1986	414
50 4/8	10	10 1/8	5 5/8	5 5/8	1 7/8	1 7/8	6 7/8	6 7/8	Cassiar Mts., BC	Charles Reichenau	Charles Reichenau	1991	414
50 4/8	9 7/8	10 2/8	5 6/8	5 6/8	2 1/8	2 1/8	8 2/8	7 5/8	Jug Lake, BC	Larry W. Steeley	Larry W. Steeley	1991	414
50 4/8	10	10	5 5/8	5 5/8	1 7/8	1 7/8	7	6 1/8	Tahtsa Lake, BC	Melvin Bromels	Melvin Bromels	1992	414
50 4/8	10 4/8	10 3/8	5 4/8	5 4/8	2	2	8 1/8	8	Puget Bay, AK	Ross Darst	Ross Darst	1992	414
50 4/8	10 4/8	10 3/8	5 5/8	5 6/8	1 7/8	1 7/8	7 6/8	7 3/8	Palliser River, BC	Ernie F. Knight	Ernie F. Knight	1992	414
50 4/8	9 4/8	10	5 6/8	5 5/8	2 1/8	2	8 3/8	7 7/8	Eagle Nest Mt., BC	Paul Green	Paul Green	1993	414

Score	Length R	Length L	Circ. Base R	Circ. Base L	Circ. 3rd Q. R	Circ. 3rd Q. L	Greatest Spread	Tip to Tip	Owner	Hunter	Locality	Date Killed	Rank
50 4/8	10 1/8	10 1/8	5 5/8	5 4/8	2	2	7	6 2/8	Thomas R. LeMasters	Thomas R. LeMasters	Stikine River, AK	1994	414
50 4/8	10 2/8	10 2/8	5 6/8	5 6/8	1 6/8	1 7/8	6 3/8	5 7/8	Glenn P. Anderson	Glenn P. Anderson	Lewis & Clark Co., MT	1995	414
50 4/8	10 3/8	10 3/8	5 5/8	5 5/8	1 7/8	1 7/8	7 7/8	7 4/8	Mike Young	Mike Young	Tuktsayda Mt., BC	1995	414
50 4/8	10 1/8	10	6 1/8	6	1 7/8	1 7/8	8 6/8	7 6/8	Mark S. Calkins	Mark S. Calkins	Kakesta Mt., BC	1996	414
50 4/8	10 2/8	10 1/8	5 6/8	5 5/8	1 7/8	1 7/8	7 7/8	6 1/8	Emile Matte	Emile Matte	Telegraph Creek, BC	1996	414
50 4/8	10	10	5 5/8	5 5/8	1 7/8	1 7/8	7 7/8	7 7/8	Alvin Schmoyer	Alvin Schmoyer	Fox River, AK	1996	414
50 4/8	10 1/8	10 5/8	5 4/8	5 4/8	1 7/8	1 7/8	6 7/8	6 3/8	William J. Swartz, Jr.	William J. Swartz, Jr.	Gallatin Co., MT	1996	414
50 4/8	10 5/8	10 6/8	5 6/8	5 6/8	1 7/8	1 7/8	8	7	Ricardo L. Garza	Ricardo L. Garza	Inklin River, BC	1997	414
50 4/8	10 2/8	10 2/8	5 4/8	5 6/8	2	2	7 6/8	6 5/8	William B. Deuink	William B. Deuink	Sunset Creek, BC	1999	414
50 4/8	9 5/8	9 5/8	5 7/8	5 7/8	1 6/8	1 6/8	5 7/8	5 1/8	Davin J. Jaatteenmaki	Davin J. Jaatteenmaki	Quartz Creek, BC	1999	414
50 4/8	10	10	5 6/8	5 6/8	1 6/8	1 6/8	7 3/8	5 6/8	Carlo Kathriner	Carlo Kathriner	Brewer Creek, BC	1999	414
50 4/8	10 1/8	10 1/8	5 6/8	5 6/8	1 7/8	1 7/8	6 7/8	6 5/8	Norman A. Kingsland	Norman A. Kingsland	Judith Basin Co., MT	2000	414
50 4/8	9 7/8	10	5 5/8	5 5/8	2	2	7 7/8	7 6/8	Garry G. Mathews	Garry G. Mathews	Kittitas Co., WA	2001	414
50 4/8	10 2/8	10 1/8	5 7/8	5 7/8	1 7/8	1 7/8	7 4/8	7	L. Dale Gaugler	L. Dale Gaugler	Tom Creek, BC	2001	414
50 4/8	9 2/8	9 1/8	6	6	2 1/8	2	7 4/8	7 1/8	Karl-Heinz Seitzinger	Karl-Heinz Seitzinger	Coles Lake, BC	2001	414
50 4/8	10 6/8	9 4/8	5 6/8	5 6/8	2	2	6 5/8	5 5/8	Eugene L. Webb	Eugene L. Webb	Middle River, BC	2002	414
50 4/8	9 7/8	9 6/8	5 4/8	5 4/8	1 7/8	1 7/8	8 1/8	8 1/8	Tarek C. Wetzel	Tarek C. Wetzel	Revillagigedo Island, AK	2002	414
50 4/8	10 2/8	9 7/8	5 7/8	5 7/8	2	2	7 4/8	7 4/8	Frank F. Flynn	Frank F. Flynn	Spatsizi Plateau, BC	2002	414
50 4/8	9 6/8	9 5/8	5 4/8	5 7/8	2	2	7 2/8	6 7/8	Roy B. Hisler	Roy B. Hisler	Mt. Stinenia, AK	2002	414
50 4/8	10 1/8	10 1/8	5 4/8	5 4/8	1 7/8	1 7/8	8 2/8	7 6/8	Bryan C. Bailey	Bryan C. Bailey	Dease Lake, BC	2003	414
50 4/8	10 3/8	10 3/8	5 5/8	5 5/8	1 7/8	1 7/8	8 2/8	6 1/8	Kevin A. McLain	Kevin A. McLain	Okanogan Co., WA	2003	414
50 4/8	10 2/8	10 2/8	5 4/8	5 4/8	1 6/8	1 6/8	6 5/8	6 1/8	Blane E. Rogers	Blane E. Rogers	Swan Lake, BC	2003	414
50 4/8	10 4/8	10 4/8	5 6/8	5 6/8	1 6/8	1 6/8	8 5/8	6 7/8	A.C. Gilbert	A.C. Gilbert	Taseko Lakes, BC	1938	491
50 4/8	9 5/8	9 7/8	5 5/8	5 5/8	2	2	7 4/8	7 4/8	L.W. Howell	L.W. Howell	Cold Fish Lake, BC	1952	491
50 4/8	10	10	5 6/8	5 6/8	1 6/8	1 6/8	7	6 4/8	Univ. of BC	T.A. Walker	Blue Goat Mt., WA	1952	491
50 4/8	10	10	5 4/8	5 4/8	1 6/8	1 6/8	6 6/8	6 6/8	Charles F. Martinsen	Picked Up	Pentagon Mt., MT	1956	491
50 4/8	10 4/8	10 3/8	5 6/8	5 6/8	1 6/8	1 6/8	6 2/8	6	Guy Brash	Guy Brash	Unknown	1957	491
50 4/8	9 7/8	10	5 4/8	5 4/8	1 5/8	1 5/8	6	6	Buckhorn Mus. & Saloon, Ltd.	Unknown		PR 1957	491
50 2/8	10 4/8	10 3/8	5 4/8	5 4/8	1 6/8	1 6/8	7 2/8	7	John La Rocca	John La Rocca	Turnagain River, BC	1957	491
50 2/8	10	10 1/8	5 6/8	5 6/8	2	1 7/8	7 6/8	8	Victor E. Moss	Victor E. Moss	Okanogan Co., WA	1957	491
50 2/8	10 2/8	10 4/8	5 1/8	5 1/8	1 7/8	1 7/8	0	0	A.D. Stenger	Picked Up	Seward, AK	PR 1957	491
50 2/8	10 1/8	10 3/8	5 5/8	5 5/8	1 7/8	1 7/8	7 4/8	8	Nolan Rad	Nolan Rad	Shuswap Creek, BC	1958	491
50 2/8	10 2/8	10 2/8	5 5/8	5 5/8	1 6/8	1 6/8	6	6	Leslie B. Maxwell	Leslie B. Maxwell	Sheridan Glacier, AK	1959	491
50 2/8	9 4/8	9 1/8	5 6/8	5 6/8	2 1/8	2	7 2/8	6 3/8	William Stallone	William Stallone	Smithers, BC	1960	491
50 2/8	10 1/8	10 1/8	5 5/8	5 5/8	1 6/8	1 6/8	7 2/8	7	Billy Ross	Billy Ross	Ft. St. John, BC	1962	491
50 2/8	10 2/8	10 2/8	5 5/8	5 5/8	1 7/8	1 7/8	8 4/8	8 4/8	Robert C. Sutton	Robert C. Sutton	Sukunka River, BC	1962	491
50 2/8	10 5/8	9 5/8	6	6	1 6/8	1 6/8	7 3/8	7 4/8	James E. Kelley	James E. Kelley	Cassiar, BC	1963	491
50 2/8	11 2/8	10 6/8	5 5/8	5 5/8	1 6/8	1 6/8	8 4/8	7 7/8	Emile Gele	Emile Gele	Elk Valley, BC	1964	491
50 2/8	10 2/8	10 6/8	5 4/8	5 4/8	1 6/8	1 6/8	7 5/8	7 3/8	Pat Archibald	Pat Archibald	Koch Creek, BC	1965	491
50 2/8	10 2/8	10 1/8	5 6/8	5 6/8	1 7/8	1 7/8	6 4/8	7 5/8	Fred E. Harper	Fred E. Harper	Chehalis Lake, BC	1965	491
50 2/8	10 4/8	10 3/8	5 5/8	5 5/8	1 6/8	1 6/8	8	7 2/8	Mark J. Jakobson	Mark J. Jakobson	Ravalli Co., MT	1965	491
50 2/8	10 5/8	10 3/8	5 4/8	5 4/8	1 6/8	1 6/8	6 6/8	5 2/8	Laszlo Molnar	Laszlo Molnar	Invermere, BC	1965	491
50 2/8	10 7/8	11	5 3/8	5 3/8	1 7/8	1 7/8	8 4/8	8 1/8	Walter F. Ramage	Walter F. Ramage	Atlin, BC	1965	491
50 2/8	10 6/8	10 7/8	5 4/8	5 4/8	1 6/8	1 6/8	6 6/8	5 6/8	Jack E. Monet	Jack E. Monet	Skeena River, BC	1966	491
50 2/8	10	10	5 7/8	5 7/8	1 6/8	1 6/8	7 4/8	6 5/8	Ned Shiflett	Ned Shiflett	Chelan Co., WA	1966	491
50 2/8	10 2/8	10 3/8	5 6/8	5 6/8	1 5/8	1 4/8	6 3/8	5 1/8	A.W. Phillips	A.W. Phillips	Telkwa, BC	1967	491
50 2/8	9 4/8	9 4/8	5 6/8	5 6/8	2	2	7	7	John A. Mueller	John A. Mueller	Cassiar, BC	1968	491

Oreamnos americanus and related subspecies

Score	Length of Horn R	L	Circumference of Base R	L	Circumference at Third Quarter R	L	Greatest Spread	Tip to Tip Spread	Locality	Hunter	Owner	Date Killed	Rank
50 2/8	10 1/8	10 1/8	5 3/8	5 4/8	2	2	7 5/8	7 5/8	Lynn Canal, AK	Jacques M. Norvell, Sr.	Jacques M. Norvell, Sr.	1968	491
50 2/8	10	9 6/8	6	5 7/8	1 7/8	1 7/8	6 4/8	6	Lake Chelan, WA	Gary L. Aichlmayr	Gary L. Aichlmayr	1969	491
50 2/8	10 5/8	10 2/8	5 3/8	5 4/8	1 7/8	2	6 5/8	5	Ecstall River, BC	Thomas J. Perry	Thomas J. Perry	1970	491
50 2/8	9 7/8	9 5/8	5 5/8	5 5/8	2	2	6 7/8	6 2/8	Juneau, AK	Jerry Kressin	Jerry Kressin	1971	491
50 2/8	10 1/8	10 2/8	5 6/8	5 6/8	1 7/8	1 7/8	7 1/8	6 2/8	Tumeka Lake, BC	Dan M. Edwards, Jr.	Dan M. Edwards, Jr.	1972	491
50 2/8	10 1/8	10 1/8	5 3/8	5 4/8	1 7/8	1 7/8	7 7/8	7 5/8	Dease Lake, BC	Carl K. Beaudry	Carl K. Beaudry	1975	491
50 2/8	10 6/8	10 1/8	5 4/8	5 5/8	1 6/8	1 7/8	8 7/8	8 2/8	Stikine River, BC	R.H. Weaver	R.H. Weaver	1976	491
50 2/8	9 7/8	10 6/8	5 6/8	5 6/8	1 7/8	1 7/8	7 3/8	6 4/8	Cassiar Mts., BC	Ron R. Ragan	Ron R. Ragan	1978	491
50 2/8	9 7/8	9 7/8	5 7/8	5 7/8	2	2	7 5/8	7 5/8	Ice Mt., BC	J.S. Van Alsburg	J.S. Van Alsburg	1978	491
50 2/8	10 2/8	10 2/8	5 4/8	5 6/8	1 7/8	1 7/8	6 5/8	5 4/8	Eagle Lake, AK	Dale E. Gibbons	Dale E. Gibbons	1982	491
50 2/8	10 1/8	10	5 6/8	5 6/8	1 7/8	1 7/8	6 6/8	5 5/8	Pemberton, BC	Weldon Talbot	Weldon Talbot	1982	491
50 2/8	9 3/8	9 1/8	5 7/8	5 7/8	1 7/8	1 7/8	6 7/8	6 3/8	Okanogan Co., WA	Richard J. Wristen	Richard J. Wristen	1982	491
50 2/8	10 7/8	10 5/8	5 6/8	5 4/8	1 6/8	1 6/8	8	7 2/8	Skeena, BC	Clarence J. Fields	Clarence J. Fields	1983	491
50 2/8	10 3/8	10 3/8	5 5/8	5 5/8	1 6/8	1 6/8	7 6/8	7 4/8	Mt. Stockdale, BC	James C. King	James C. King	1983	491
50 2/8	10 1/8	10 1/8	5 5/8	5 4/8	2	2	8 1/8	7 3/8	Kildala River, BC	Philip Perrone	Philip Perrone	1983	491
50 2/8	10 3/8	10 2/8	5 6/8	5 4/8	1 6/8	1 6/8	7 4/8	6 7/8	Chouteau Co., MT	Robert E. Young	Robert E. Young	1983	491
50 2/8	10 5/8	10 5/8	5 4/8	5 6/8	1 6/8	1 7/8	6 7/8	6 3/8	Bleasdell Creek, BC	Daniel Fediuk	Daniel Fediuk	1984	491
50 2/8	9 4/8	9 5/8	5 6/8	5 6/8	2	2	7	6 5/8	Snohomish Co., WA	Wayne E. Ritter	Wayne E. Ritter	1985	491
50 2/8	9 7/8	9 5/8	5 6/8	5 6/8	1 7/8	1 7/8	7	6 4/8	Kudwat Creek, BC	William R. Orth	William R. Orth	1986	491
50 2/8	9 2/8	9 2/8	5 7/8	5 7/8	1 7/8	1 7/8	7 1/8	6 6/8	Sicintine Range, BC	Roger L. Pock	Roger L. Pock	1988	491
50 2/8	9 6/8	10	5 6/8	5 6/8	1 7/8	1 7/8	8 1/8	7 5/8	Kitimat, BC	Steven M. Cooper	Steven M. Cooper	1990	491
50 2/8	10 4/8	10 6/8	5 4/8	5 4/8	1 7/8	1 6/8	7 5/8	7 3/8	Kenai Pen., AK	David W. Doner	David W. Doner	1992	491
50 2/8	10 4/8	10 6/8	5 4/8	5 4/8	1 6/8	1 6/8	6 7/8	6 4/8	Whatcom Co., WA	Darrel Van Kekerix	Darrel Van Kekerix	1992	491
50 2/8	10 1/8	10 2/8	5 5/8	5 5/8	1 6/8	1 6/8	7 6/8	7	Bonneville Co., ID	Arnae R. Hillam	Arnae R. Hillam	1993	491
50 2/8	10 1/8	9 5/8	5 6/8	5 6/8	2	2	9 4/8	9	Gataga River, BC	Wilson S. Stout	Wilson S. Stout	1993	491
50 2/8	10 4/8	10 1/8	5 5/8	5 5/8	1 6/8	1 6/8	5 6/8	4 3/8	Niblack Hollow, AK	Stan Colton	Stan Colton	1994	491
50 2/8	10 7/8	10 2/8	5 5/8	5 5/8	1 7/8	1 7/8	8 5/8	8 2/8	Kluachon Lake, BC	Eugene E. Hafen	Eugene E. Hafen	1994	491
50 2/8	10 1/8	10 2/8	5 6/8	5 6/8	1 7/8	1 7/8	6 3/8	5 5/8	Hidden Basin, AK	Chester J. McConnell, Jr.	Chester J. McConnell, Jr.	1994	491
50 2/8	10	10 2/8	5 5/8	5 5/8	1 6/8	1 6/8	7 2/8	6 2/8	Flameau Creek, BC	Robert Reisert	Robert Reisert	1994	491
50 2/8	9 6/8	9 6/8	5 6/8	5 6/8	1 7/8	1 7/8	7 7/8	7 3/8	Meziadin Lake, BC	John A. Monk	John A. Monk	1995	491
50 2/8	10	10	5 5/8	5 6/8	2	2	7 6/8	7 1/8	Chukachida River, BC	Lynn C. Street	Lynn C. Street	1995	491
50 2/8	10 1/8	10 2/8	5 7/8	5 7/8	1 7/8	1 7/8	6 2/8	5 1/8	Goldstream River, BC	Jo-Anne Meissner	Jo-Anne Meissner	1996	491
50 2/8	10 2/8	10 2/8	5 5/8	5 6/8	1 6/8	1 7/8	8 2/8	8 2/8	Kenai Pen., AK	William G. Boyce	William G. Boyce	1997	491
50 2/8	9 7/8	10 1/8	5 6/8	5 6/8	1 7/8	1 7/8	7 1/8	6 5/8	Idaho Co., ID	Joseph M. Coelho III	Joseph M. Coelho III	1997	491
50 2/8	10 3/8	10 4/8	5 6/8	5 6/8	1 6/8	1 6/8	6 2/8	6	Park Co., CO	Heath A. Hibbard	Heath A. Hibbard	1998	491
50 2/8	10 1/8	10 1/8	5 5/8	5 5/8	1 7/8	1 7/8	6	4 4/8	Bella Coola River, BC	Douglas N. Langkow	Douglas N. Langkow	1998	491
50 2/8	9 7/8	10	5 5/8	5 6/8	1 7/8	1 7/8	7 2/8	6 2/8	Little Oliver Creek, BC	Richard C. Berreth	Richard C. Berreth	1999	491
50 2/8	9 4/8	9 4/8	5 5/8	5 5/8	1 7/8	1 7/8	6 6/8	6 2/8	Gold River, BC	Wade Derby	Wade Derby	1999	491

Score	Length R	Length L	Circ. Base R	Circ. Base L	Circ. 3rd Qtr R	Circ. 3rd Qtr L	Greatest Spread	Tip to Tip	Locality	By whom killed	Owner	Date Killed	Rank
50 2/8	10 4/8	10 4/8	5 4/8	5 4/8	1 6/8	1 6/8	6	5 2/8	Nakusp, BC	J. Henry Scown	J. Henry Scown	1999	491
50 2/8	9 5/8	9 4/8	5 6/8	5 6/8	2	2	6	5 2/8	Elko Co., NV	Rafael Betancourt, Jr.	Rafael Betancourt, Jr.	2000	491
50 2/8	10 5/8	10 4/8	5 5/8	5 5/8	1 6/8	1 6/8	7 7/8	6 3/8	Kechika River, BC	Stephen A. Nelson	Stephen A. Nelson	2001	491
50 2/8	10 7/8	11	5 4/8	5 4/8	1 5/8	1 5/8	8 5/8	8 1/8	Blue Lake, BC	Charles M. Bloom	Charles M. Bloom	2002	491
50	10 2/8	10 6/8	5 5/8	5 5/8	1 7/8	1 7/8	8 5/8	7	Klinaklini River, BC	Powhatan Robinson	Camp Fire Club of America	1916	558
50	10 1/8	10	5 7/8	5 7/8	1 6/8	1 6/8	7	6 4/8	Rudyerd Bay, AK	Joseph H. Keeney	Joseph H. Keeney	1946	558
50	10 1/8	10	5 4/8	5 4/8	2	2	4 5/8	5 5/8	British Columbia	John Oshea	Donnie J. Allen	1947	558
50	10 1/8	9 6/8	5 6/8	5 6/8	2	2	6 5/8	7 1/8	Cassiar Mts., BC	James King	James King	1947	558
50	10 1/8	10 1/8	5 4/8	5 4/8	1 7/8	1 7/8	7 1/8	7 6/8	Okanogan Co., WA	John Hutchinson	Ralph Hutchinson	1950	558
50	9 3/8	9 4/8	6	6	1 7/8	1 7/8	7 6/8	7 5/8	Kenai Pen., AK	Coke Elms	Coke Elms	1956	558
50	10 1/8	10	5 6/8	5 6/8	2 1/8	2 1/8	7 5/8	6 4/8	Prophet River, BC	Frank C. Hibben	Frank C. Hibben	1956	558
50	9 6/8	9 6/8	5 6/8	5 6/8	1 7/8	1 7/8	6	6 7/8	Keremeos Mt., BC	Robert Quaedvlieg	Robert Quaedvlieg	1956	558
50	10 4/8	10 2/8	5 4/8	5 4/8	1 7/8	1 7/8	7 5/8	5 5/8	Flathead River, MT	Gene Biddle	Gene Biddle	1957	558
50	10 7/8	10 6/8	5 6/8	5 6/8	2	2	6	5 6/8	Squaw Creek, ID	William A. Callaway	William H. Lockhart	1959	558
50	9 3/8	10	5 7/8	5 7/8	1 6/8	1 6/8	7 3/8	6 6/8	Cape Yakataga, AK	Edward I. Worst	Edward I. Worst	1960	558
50	9 6/8	9 6/8	5 7/8	5 7/8	1 7/8	1 7/8	7 5/8	5 6/8	K-Mountain, BC	Fred D. Fouty	Fred D. Fouty	1961	558
50	10	10	5 6/8	5 6/8	2 1/8	2 1/8	6 5/8	6 4/8	Bear Point, ID	Aaron U. Jones	Aaron U. Jones	1961	558
50	9 7/8	10 2/8	6	6	1 6/8	1 6/8	7	7 3/8	Girdwood, AK	Franklin Maus	Franklin Maus	1961	558
50	9 6/8	10 2/8	6	6	1 7/8	1 7/8	7	6	Grand Forks, BC	Norman Dawson, Jr.	Norman Dawson, Jr.	1962	558
50	9 3/8	10 2/8	5 6/8	5 6/8	1 7/8	1 7/8	6 6/8	6 6/8	Lake Chelan, WA	Ed Pariseu	Ed Pariseu	1962	558
50	9 6/8	9 4/8	5 4/8	5 6/8	2 2/8	2 2/8	6 7/8	6 6/8	Telegraph Creek, BC	Anthony Bechik	Anthony Bechik	1963	558
50	10 3/8	9 5/8	5 3/8	5 4/8	2	2	6 6/8	6 7/8	Lincoln Co., MT	James A. Gunn III	James A. Gunn III	1963	558
50	10 7/8	10 3/8	5 7/8	5 3/8	1 6/8	1 6/8	9 5/8	6 1/8	Gataga River, BC	Herb Klein	Dallas Mus. of Natl. Hist.	1963	558
50	9 6/8	10 7/8	5 4/8	5 7/8	1 7/8	1 7/8	7	8 2/8	Oroville, WA	G. Pickering	G. Pickering	1963	558
50	10 4/8	9 6/8	5 4/8	5 4/8	1 7/8	1 7/8	6 7/8	6 4/8	Spatsizi, BC	William L. Searle	William L. Searle	1963	558
50	10 7/8	10 2/8	5 7/8	5 4/8	2 1/8	2 1/8	7 5/8	7 5/8	Halfway River, BC	Victor Tullis	Victor Tullis	1964	558
50	9 6/8	9 5/8	5 5/8	5 7/8	1 7/8	1 7/8	6	5 1/8	Blue Sheep Lake, BC	O.A. McClintock	O.A. McClintock	1964	558
50	10 4/8	10 3/8	5 4/8	5 5/8	1 6/8	1 6/8	7 6/8	6 6/8	Smithers, BC	John Rienhart	John Rienhart	1964	558
50	9 7/8	10 7/8	5 4/8	5 4/8	1 5/8	1 5/8	7	6	Missoula Co., MT	Charles Barry	Charles Barry	1965	558
50	10 1/8	9 6/8	5 3/8	5 4/8	1 6/8	1 6/8	6 5/8	6 7/8	Keremeos, BC	Picked Up	Robert Kitto	1965	558
50	11 2/8	10 1/8	5 4/8	5 4/8	1 7/8	1 7/8	7 4/8	5 6/8	Hope, BC	Peter Konrad	Peter Konrad	1965	558
50	9 3/8	9 7/8	5 6/8	5 6/8	2 1/8	2 1/8	8 2/8	6 2/8	Heart Peaks, BC	Bob Loewenstein	Bob Loewenstein	1965	558
50	10 1/8	10 1/8	5 6/8	5 6/8	1 6/8	1 6/8	8 4/8	8	Chilkat Range, AK	Jacques M. Norvell	Jacques M. Norvell	1965	558
50	9 7/8	11 2/8	5	5	2	2	8 4/8	7 2/8	Morice River, BC	Dennis A. Sperling	Dennis A. Sperling	1966	558
50	9 6/8	9 3/8	5 7/8	5 7/8	1 6/8	1 6/8	8 3/8	7 6/8	Petersburg, AK	James Briggs	James Briggs	1966	558
50	10 3/8	10 1/8	5 6/8	5 6/8	1 7/8	1 7/8	6 3/8	5 2/8	Lake Chelan, WA	Don Francis	Don Francis	1966	558
50	9 7/8	9 7/8	5 7/8	5 7/8	1 7/8	1 7/8	6 4/8	8 3/8	Seward, AK	John Lee	John Lee	1966	558
50	10 2/8	9 6/8	5 4/8	5 4/8	1 7/8	1 7/8	7 5/8	5 6/8	Nass River, BC	Vernon Rydde	Vernon Rydde	1966	558
50	10	10 3/8	5 4/8	5 4/8	1 7/8	1 7/8	7 4/8	6 3/8	Tatla Lake, BC	Jack Close	Jack Close	1967	558
50	9 6/8	9 7/8	5 6/8	5 4/8	1 6/8	1 6/8	7 3/8	6 4/8	Kenai Pen., AK	A.P. Funk	A.P. Funk	1967	558
50	9 7/8	9 6/8	5 4/8	5 4/8	1 7/8	1 7/8	7 3/8	7 4/8	Nass River, BC	D.E. O'Shea	D.E. O'Shea	1967	558
50	10 2/8	10 2/8	5 4/8	5 4/8	1 6/8	1 6/8	8 6/8	7 3/8	Cassiar Mts., BC	Arthur M. Scully, Jr.	Arthur M. Scully, Jr.	1967	558
50	10	10	5 4/8	5 4/8	2	2	7 4/8	6 7/8	Cassiar Mts., BC	E. David Slye	E. David Slye	1968	558
50	9 6/8	9 6/8	5 5/8	5 5/8	1 7/8	1 7/8	7 4/8	8 6/8	Whittier, AK	Myron D. Cowell	Myron J. Eisele	1968	558
50	9 7/8	9 7/8	5 2/8	5 2/8	2	2	7 4/8	7 6/8	Hastings Arm, BC	Walter J. Eisele	Walter J. Eisele	1968	558
50	10 2/8	10 2/8	5 4/8	5 4/8	1 7/8	1 7/8	6	6 5/8	Chelan Co., WA	Carl Lewis	Carl Lewis	1968	558
50	10 2/8	10 2/8	5 4/8	5 4/8	1 6/8	1 6/8	7 1/8	4 6/8	Skagway, AK	Don Sather	Don Sather	1968	558
50	10 5/8	10 6/8	5 5/8	5 5/8	1 5/8	1 5/8	6 6/8	6 2/8	St. Mary River, BC	Frederick Brahniuk	Frederick Brahniuk	1969	558

ROCKY MOUNTAIN GOAT

Oreamnos americanus americanus and related subspecies

Score	Length of Horn R	L	Circumference of Base R	L	Circumference at Third Quarter R	L	Greatest Spread	Tip to Tip Spread	Locality	Hunter	Owner	Date Killed	Rank
50	9 7/8	9 7/8	5 6/8	5 7/8	1 6/8	1 7/8	5	4 3/8	Chelan Co., WA	John F. Hooper	William R. Hooper	1970	558
50	9 6/8	9 6/8	5 5/8	5 5/8	2	2	6 6/8	5 7/8	Lake Kitchener, BC	Aubrey W. Minshall	Aubrey W. Minshall	1971	558
50	10 2/8	10 3/8	5 2/8	5 3/8	2	2	8 6/8	8 6/8	Port Dick, AK	Neil Smith	Neil Smith	1972	558
50	9 6/8	9 6/8	5 5/8	5 5/8	1 7/8	1 7/8	6 5/8	6	Hendon River, BC	R.A. Wiseman	R.A. Wiseman	1973	558
50	10 3/8	10 3/8	5 6/8	5 6/8	1 7/8	1 7/8	8 3/8	8	Goodwin Lake, BC	Bill R. Moomey	Bill R. Moomey	1974	558
50	9 6/8	9 7/8	5 6/8	5 5/8	1 7/8	1 7/8	6 4/8	6	Rudyerd Bay, AK	Gerry D. Downey	Gerry D. Downey	1975	558
50	10 1/8	9 7/8	5 4/8	5 3/8	2	1 7/8	7 3/8	6 5/8	Gataga River, BC	Jerald T. Waite	Jerald T. Waite	1975	558
50	9 7/8	9 7/8	5 4/8	5 4/8	1 7/8	1 7/8	8 2/8	7 7/8	Cassiar Mts., BC	Gordon A. Read	Gordon A. Read	1976	558
50	10 2/8	10 5/8	5 5/8	5 5/8	1 7/8	1 7/8	7 5/8	7 5/8	Terrace, BC	Joe Zucchiatti	Joe Zucchiatti	1976	558
50	10 3/8	10 5/8	5 6/8	5 5/8	1 6/8	1 6/8	8 2/8	7 5/8	Cassiar Mts., BC	Murray B. Wilson	Murray B. Wilson	1977	558
50	10 2/8	10 1/8	5 3/8	5 2/8	1 7/8	1 7/8	8 2/8	7 4/8	Prince William Sound, AK	Ernest H. Youngs	Ernest H. Youngs	1978	558
50	10 1/8	10 2/8	5 5/8	5 6/8	1 6/8	1 7/8	7 4/8	6 6/8	Skeena Mts., BC	Dee J. Burnett	Dee J. Burnett	1982	558
50	10 3/8	10 2/8	5 5/8	5 5/8	1 7/8	2	8 2/8	7	Yeth Creek, BC	Michael Follett	Michael Follett	1983	558
50	9 2/8	9 2/8	5 2/8	5 2/8	1 7/8	1 7/8	7 4/8	7 1/8	Bonneville Co., ID	Charles E. Wood	Charles E. Wood	1983	558
50	10 1/8	10 1/8	5 4/8	5 5/8	1 7/8	1 7/8	7 4/8	8	Inklin River, BC	John Macaluso	John Macaluso	1984	558
50	9 7/8	10	5 6/8	5 7/8	1 6/8	1 6/8	7 1/8	7	Kodiak Island, AK	Terry R. Stockman	Terry R. Stockman	1986	558
50	9 5/8	9 7/8	5 7/8	5 7/8	1 7/8	1 7/8	6 7/8	6 1/8	Yohetta Creek, BC	Terry R. Wagner	Terry R. Wagner	1986	558
50	10 3/8	10 6/8	5 5/8	5 5/8	1 6/8	1 6/8	6 7/8	6 1/8	Lincoln Co., MT	Wayne Hill	Wayne Hill	1988	558
50	9 7/8	9 7/8	5 5/8	5 5/8	1 7/8	1 7/8	7 7/8	7 7/8	Nass River, BC	Murray McDonald	Murray McDonald	1988	558
50	10 2/8	10 5/8	5 5/8	5 6/8	2	2	8 1/8	7 4/8	Rapid River, BC	Michael D. Rowe	Michael D. Rowe	1988	558
50	10 2/8	10 5/8	5 2/8	5 2/8	1 6/8	1 7/8	6 3/8	5	Bradfield Canal, AK	James L. Beskin	James L. Beskin	1989	558
50	10 1/8	9 7/8	5 2/8	5 2/8	2	2	7 4/8	6 3/8	Snohomish Co., WA	Jeffrey J. Nelson	Jeffrey J. Nelson	1989	558
50	10 3/8	10 2/8	5 5/8	5 5/8	1 7/8	1 7/8	7 7/8	7 3/8	Palliser River, BC	Louis B. Wood, Jr.	Louis B. Wood, Jr.	1989	558
50	10 4/8	10 2/8	5 5/8	5 4/8	1 7/8	1 6/8	6 2/8	5 7/8	King Co., WA	Spencer C. Davis	Spencer C. Davis	1990	558
50	9 1/8	9 3/8	5 6/8	5 6/8	2	2	7 3/8	7 1/8	Thunder Mt., BC	Jimmy E. Dixon	Jimmy E. Dixon	1990	558
50	9 3/8	9 3/8	5 6/8	5 7/8	2	2	6 4/8	5 3/8	Checats Lake, AK	Mark W. Agnew	Mark W. Agnew	1992	558
50	10 2/8	10	5 7/8	5 7/8	1 7/8	1 6/8	7 1/8	6 5/8	Bradley Lake, AK	John L. Hendrix	John L. Hendrix	1992	558
50	9 6/8	9 6/8	5 6/8	5 6/8	1 6/8	1 6/8	7 3/8	7	Elko Co., NV	Tammy H. Bawcom	Tammy H. Bawcom	1993	558
50	10 1/8	10	5 6/8	5 6/8	1 6/8	1 6/8	7	6 3/8	Kodiak Island, AK	Michael K. Odin	Michael K. Odin	1993	558
50	9 6/8	9 6/8	5 4/8	5 4/8	1 6/8	1 6/8	6 7/8	6	Kenai Pen., AK	Les Rainey	Les Rainey	1993	558
50	9 4/8	10 2/8	5 6/8	5 6/8	1 7/8	1 7/8	7 1/8	6 2/8	Elk River, BC	Santo Rocca	Santo Rocca	1993	558
50	9 4/8	9 4/8	5 6/8	5 6/8	1 7/8	1 7/8	6 6/8	6 2/8	Utah Co., UT	Ned W. Walker	Ned W. Walker	1994	558
50	10 7/8	10 7/8	5 4/8	5 4/8	1 5/8	1 5/8	7 3/8	6 5/8	Brewer Creek, BC	Donald L. Butler	Donald L. Butler	1995	558
50	10	10	5 6/8	5 6/8	1 7/8	1 7/8	8	8	Dease Lake, BC	Beau Beck	Beau Beck	1996	558
50	10	9 5/8	5 5/8	5 5/8	2	2	7 6/8	7 1/8	Flint Creek, BC	Doug H. Cundy	Doug H. Cundy	1996	558
50	10 2/8	10 4/8	5 4/8	5 4/8	1 6/8	1 6/8	7 6/8	7 4/8	Clark Co., ID	Brian G. Edgerton	Brian G. Edgerton	1996	558
50	9 7/8	10 1/8	5 7/8	5 7/8	1 6/8	1 7/8	7 3/8	6 6/8	Lake Tatsamenie, BC	Philip W. Geisse	Philip W. Geisse	1996	558
50	9 7/8	9 6/8	5 7/8	5 7/8	1 7/8	1 6/8	6 3/8	5 2/8	Salt Lake Co., UT	Brad B. Kimball	Brad B. Kimball	1996	558

Score									Hunter	Location	Date	Rank
50	10 2/8	10 2/8	5 5/8	5 5/8	1 6/8	1 6/8	7	6 5/8	Eric J. Horst	Yakima Co, WA	1998	558
50	10 3/8	10 2/8	5 5/8	5 5/8	1 6/8	1 6/8	7 1/8	7 2/8	Carl R. Kyser	Sunset Creek, BC	1998	558
50	10 6/8	10 3/8	5 6/8	5 5/8	1 6/8	1 6/8	8 5/8	8 5/8	Daniel M. Mikutel	Tahltan River, BC	1998	558
50	9 7/8	9 6/8	5 7/8	5 6/8	1 6/8	1 6/8	5 4/8	7	John J. Provost	Utah Co, UT	1999	558
50	9 7/8	9 7/8	5 5/8	5 6/8	1 7/8	1 7/8	5 4/8	3 7/8	Troy N. Ginn	Williston Lake, BC	2000	558
50	10	9 6/8	6	6	1 6/8	2	5 7/8	7 6/8	David J. Hucke	Kaketsa Mt., BC	2000	558
50	9 5/8	9 5/8	5 6/8	5 6/8	1 7/8	1 7/8	5 6/8	4 7/8	Rick M. Santos	Cleveland Pen., AK	2000	558
50	9 6/8	9 6/8	5 5/8	5 5/8	1 7/8	1 7/8	6 6/8	6 2/8	William J. Smith	Stikine River, BC	2000	558
50	10 1/8	10 2/8	5 5/8	5 5/8	1 6/8	1 6/8	7 1/8	6 5/8	Mark A. Wayne	Deadwood River, BC	2000	558
50	10 7/8	10 3/8	5 5/8	5 5/8	1 6/8	1 6/8	7	6 1/8	Kirk E. Winward	Utah Co, UT	2001	558
50	10 7/8	11	5 4/8	5 3/8	1 5/8	1 6/8	6 4/8	6	Mark D. Etchart	Park Co, MT	2002	558
50	9 5/8	9 5/8	6	6	1 7/8	1 7/8	6 4/8	5 7/8	Mike G. Harrigan	Elko Co, NV	2002	558
50	10 2/8	10 2/8	5 5/8	5 5/8	1 6/8	1 6/8	8 5/8	8	Melvin S. Matthews	Portlock Glacier, AK	2002	558
54 *	11	11 1/8	6	6	1 7/8	1 7/8	8 2/8	8	John G. Jones	Big Olive Creek, BC	1997	
53 4/8*	10 5/8	10 6/8	6 2/8	6 2/8	1 6/8	1 6/8	6 7/8	5 7/8	Frank Boling	Lake Co, MT	1999	
52 6/8*	10 3/8	10 5/8	6	6	2	2	8 2/8	7 6/8	Rodney G. Chinn	Shames River, BC	1997	

* Final score is subject to revision by additional verifying measurements.

CATEGORY
ROCKY MOUNTAIN GOAT

SCORE
50

HUNTER
TROY N. GINN

LOCATION
WILLISTON LAKE,
BRITISH COLUMBIA

DATE OF KILL
SEPTEMBER 2000

CATEGORY
ROCKY MOUNTAIN GOAT

SCORE
50

HUNTER
RICK M. SANTOS

LOCATION
CLEVELAND PENINSULA,
ALASKA

DATE OF KILL
OCTOBER 2000

CATEGORY
ROCKY MOUNTAIN GOAT

SCORE
50-2/8

HUNTER
DOUGLAS N. LANGKOW

LOCATION
BELLA COOLA RIVER,
BRITISH COLUMBIA

DATE OF KILL
OCTOBER 1998

CATEGORY
ROCKY MOUNTAIN GOAT

SCORE
50

HUNTER
KIRK E. WINWARD (LEFT)

LOCATION
UTAH COUNTY, UTAH

DATE OF KILL
SEPTEMBER 2001

SCORE
51-2/8

HUNTER
JOHN A. MORRISON
(BOTTOM LEFT)

LOCATION
INKLIN RIVER,
BRITISH COLUMBIA

DATE OF KILL
SEPTEMBER 1999

CATEGORY
ROCKY MOUNTAIN GOAT

SCORE
52-4/8

HUNTER
JAMES L. HAWK, JR. (LEFT)

LOCATION
KITTITAS COUNTY,
WASHINGTON

DATE OF KILL
OCTOBER 1998

SCORE
53

HUNTER
KLAUSS WOLFF (BELOW)

LOCATION
SHOEMAKER CREEK,
BRITISH COLUMBIA

DATE OF KILL
NOVEMBER 2002

CATEGORY
ROCKY MOUNTAIN GOAT

SCORE
53-4/8*

HUNTER
FRANK BOLING (BELOW)

LOCATION
LAKE COUNTY, MONTANA

DATE OF KILL
NOVEMBER 1999

Musk ox (*Ovibos moschatus*) populations in the Northwest Territories have been doing very well over the last few decades, after having been virtually eliminated during the early part of the last century. They have rebounded in both numbers and distribution to the point where limited-entry trophy hunting is again possible. Craig Scott was absolutely delighted when he found out his name had been drawn for a permit.

Craig had no previous musk ox hunting experience. He'd never even seen one in the wild. To get more information, Craig visited Richard Popko, a biologist in the local Department of Resources, Wildlife & Economic Development (DRWED) office. Richard had many years of experience with musk ox that he gladly shared. Richard then showed Craig a large, framed picture of a massive bull musk ox that had been taken not far from Norman Wells. "This is what you want to look for," said Richard.

On March 22, 2002, Craig and friends Garth Hummelle and Mark Kelly, set out to hunt in a series of rocky hills near Kelly Lake, about 18 miles northwest of Norman Wells. These hills are covered in alpine tundra and surrounded by thick boreal forest. They are a favorite habitat for the musk ox throughout the year, but particularly in late winter when snow depths in other areas can make movement and feeding a little more difficult for the animals.

After walking about a mile and a half, the men spied four animals in the distance. They snuck around a series of plateaus until they were 150 yards away. As they glassed, Garth told Craig there was a really big one in the group.

After watching them for 20 minutes, Craig took careful aim and his first shot hit the big bull square in the chest. The bull took the shot, then turned and ran. Craig worked hard to catch up to the bull again and managed to finish off the animal...or so he thought. The valiant old bull managed to get back to its feet, turn, and chase Craig for 20 feet before falling for the last time not far from where Craig stood.

After letting the horns dry in his shed for almost three weeks, Craig again visited the DRWED office to shoot the breeze about his hunt. He was describing the size of his bull's horns when the biologist asked him to bring them in.

Biologist Alasdair Veitch unofficially scored the horns at 128-6/8 points, well above the standing record of 127 inches. While Alasdair reminded Craig that he was not a Boone and Crockett Club Official Measurer, Richard disappeared for a few minutes and returned with the framed print of the big bull he'd shown Craig earlier in the year. The shape of the horns and the distinctive scars and cracks showed that Craig had taken Richard's advice to heart — he'd shot the bull featured in the photograph!

After the requisite 60-day drying period was over, Craig took his musk ox horns to Warren St. Germaine — a Boone and Crockett Club Official Measurer. When it was over, Craig Scott's musk ox was scored higher than any other musk ox in history at 129 points. ∎

MUSK OX
WORLD'S RECORD SCORE CHART

Records of
North American
Big Game

250 Station Drive
Missoula, MT 59801
(406) 542-1888

BOONE AND CROCKETT CLUB®
OFFICIAL SCORING SYSTEM FOR NORTH AMERICAN BIG GAME TROPHIES

MUSK OX

MINIMUM SCORES
AWARDS	ALL-TIME
105	105

SEE OTHER SIDE FOR INSTRUCTIONS	COLUMN 1	COLUMN 2	COLUMN 3
	Right Horn	Left Horn	Difference
A. Greatest Spread	29 1/8		
B. Tip to Tip Spread	27 1/8		
C. Length of Horn	29 5/8	28 3/8	1 2/8
D-1. Width of Boss	11 0/8	11 0/8	—
D-2. Width at First Quarter	7 6/8	7 5/8	1/8
D-3. Circumference at Second Quarter	13 0/8	12 0/8	1 0/8
D-4. Circumference at Third Quarter	6 2/8	5 4/8	6/8
TOTALS	67 5/8	64 4/8	3 1/8

ADD	Column 1	67 5/8
	Column 2	64 4/8
	Subtotal	132 1/8
SUBTRACT	Column 3	3 1/8
	FINAL SCORE	129 0/8

Exact Locality Where Killed: **Norman Wells, Northwest Territories**

Date Killed: **March 2002**   Hunter: **Craig D. Scott**

Owner: **Craig D. Scott**   Telephone #:

Owner's Address:

Guide's Name and Address:

Remarks: (Mention Any Abnormalities or Unique Qualities)

I, **Albert C. England** , certify that I have measured this trophy on **04/30/2004**

PRINT NAME   MM/DD/YYYY

at **Cabela's** **Kansas City, Kansas**

STREET ADDRESS   CITY   STATE

and that these measurements and data are, to the best of my knowledge and belief, made in accordance with instructions given.

Witness: **Frederick J. King** Signature: **Albert C. England** B&C OFFICIAL MEASURER

COPYRIGHT © 2004 BY BOONE AND CROCKETT CLUB®

809

TOP 10 MUSK OX

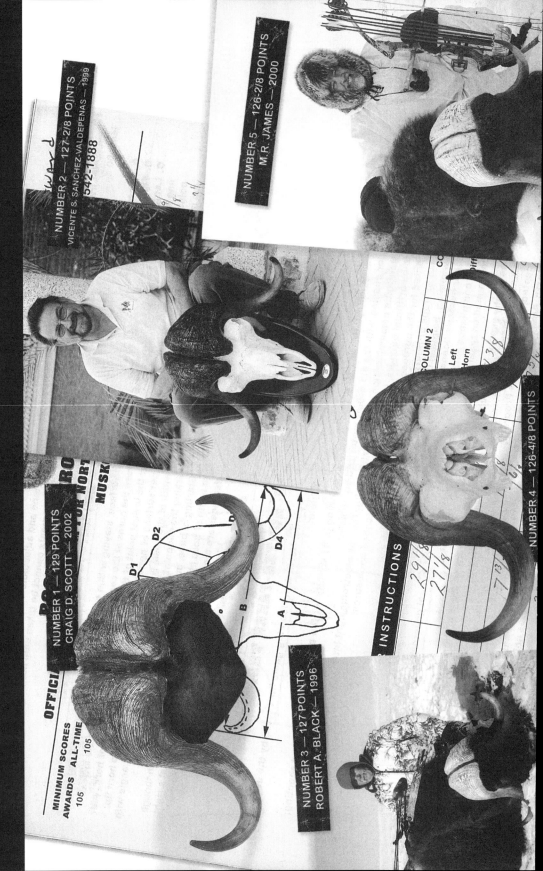

NUMBER 2 — 127-2/8 POINTS
VICENTE S. SANCHEZ-VALDEPENAS — 1999
542-1888

NUMBER 5 — 126-2/8 POINTS
M.R. JAMES — 2000

NUMBER 1 — 129 POINTS
CRAIG D. SCOTT — 2002

NUMBER 3 — 127 POINTS
ROBERT A. BLACK — 1996

NUMBER 4 — 126-4/8 POINTS

MINIMUM SCORES   ALL-TIME
AWARDS   105   105

NUMBER 6 — 126 POINTS
ERIC LLANES — 1997

250 Station Drive
Missoula, MT 59801
(406) 542-1888

... BIG GAME TROPHIES

NUMBER 9 — 125-2/8 POINTS
DONALD NICHOLSON — 1988

NUMBER 10 (tie) — 125 POINTS
WILLIAM L. COX — 1998

10 5/8

Hunter: CRAIG SCOTT

Telephone #:

...ress:

Abnor...

NUMBER 7 — 125-6/8 POINTS
WILLIAM J. SMITH — 2002

NUMBER 8 — 125-4/8 POINTS
STEVEN PERSSON — 1935

NUMBER 10 (tie) — 125 POINTS
ANTON GOSSEIN — 2001

KODAK 5062 PX

NUMBER 10 (tie) — 125 POINTS
STEPHEN A. KROFLICH — 1990

KODAK 5062 PX

KODAK 5062 PX

MUSK OX

Ovibos moschatus moschatus and certain related subspecies

MINIMUM SCORE 105

Score	Length of Horn R	L	Width of Boss R	L	Circumference at Third Quarter R	L	Greatest Spread	Tip to Tip Spread	Locality	Hunter	Owner	Date Killed	Rank
129	29 5/8	28 3/8	11	11	6 2/8	5 4/8	29 1/8	27 1/8	Norman Wells, NT	Craig D. Scott	Craig D. Scott	2002	1
127 2/8	29 2/8	29 7/8	10 6/8	11	6	5 6/8	29 6/8	28 6/8	Kugluktuk, NU	Vicente S. Sanchez-Valdepenas	Vicente S. Sanchez-Valdepenas	1999	2
127	29 7/8	29 6/8	10 1/8	10 1/8	6	5 4/8	30 4/8	29 5/8	Kugluktuk, NU	Robert A. Black	Robert A. Black	1996	3
126 4/8	30 6/8	30 7/8	10 3/8	10 5/8	5 7/8	5 4/8	29 7/8	28 6/8	Coppermine River, NU	Robert M. Ortiz	Robert M. Ortiz	2003	4
126 2/8	29 2/8	28 3/8	10 5/8	11	5 4/8	5 5/8	27 7/8	27 4/8	Kugaryuak River, NU	M.R. James	M.R. James	2000	5
126	30	29 1/8	10 1/8	10 2/8	6 2/8	6	29 7/8	29	Kugluktuk, NU	Eric Llanes	Eric Llanes	1997	6
125 6/8	29 7/8	29 3/8	10 3/8	10 5/8	6 1/8	6	28 7/8	27 3/8	Coppermine River, NU	William J. Smith	William J. Smith	2002	7
125 4/8	28 1/8	27 6/8	10 1/8	10 4/8	5 7/8	5 7/8	29	28 4/8	Perry River, NU	Steven Persson	Steven Persson	1995	8
125 2/8	27 2/8	27 1/8	10 5/8	10 2/8	6 5/8	6 4/8	30 4/8	30 1/8	Umingmaktok, NU	Donald Nicholson	Donald Nicholson	1988	9
125	30 2/8	31 6/8	10 4/8	10 1/8	5	6 3/8	31 4/8	30 5/8	Umingmaktok, NU	Stephen A. Kroflich	Stephen A. Kroflich	1990	10
125	28 4/8	28 7/8	11 1/8	11 3/8	5 6/8	5 7/8	29 1/8	27 4/8	Kugluktuk, NU	William L. Cox	William L. Cox	1998	10
125	28 3/8	28 7/8	10 6/8	11 2/8	6	6 4/8	30 5/8	30 5/8	Kugluktuk, NU	Anton Gossein	Anton Gossein	2001	10
124 6/8	30 1/8	29 6/8	9 2/8	9	6	5 7/8	31 4/8	31	Perry River, NU	Robert D. Jones	Robert D. Jones	1988	13
124 6/8	27 2/8	27 6/8	11 1/8	11	5 5/8	6 2/8	28 2/8	27 3/8	Tree River, NU	John V. Lattimore, Jr.	John V. Lattimore, Jr.	1995	13
124 6/8	27 2/8	28 1/8	12	12	5 6/8	6 3/8	28 3/8	27	Kugluktuk, NU	Thomas L. Straka	Thomas L. Straka	2003	13
124 4/8	30	29 7/8	10 2/8	10 7/8	6 2/8	6	29 4/8	29	Kugaryuak River, NU	Ronald G. McKnight	Ronald G. McKnight	2000	16
123 6/8	28 1/8	28 3/8	10 4/8	10 5/8	6 2/8	6 5/8	31 2/8	31	Northwest Territories	Unknown	Sam Pancotto	PR 1976	17
123 2/8	27	27 2/8	10 5/8	10 4/8	6 4/8	6 6/8	25 4/8	24	Norman Wells, NT	Darcy Hernblad	Darcy Hernblad	1999	18
123	29 1/8	28 7/8	10 2/8	10 3/8	6	5 4/8	28 2/8	27 6/8	Kent Pen., NU	Raymond L. Howell, Sr.	Raymond L. Howell, Sr.	2000	19
122 6/8	28 3/8	29 3/8	9 7/8	9 6/8	5 7/8	7 1/8	27 2/8	26 6/8	Kent Pen., NU	Jeffery L. Meyerl	Jeffery L. Meyerl	1993	20
122 4/8	27 6/8	27 6/8	10 7/8	11	6 6/8	5 5/8	30 2/8	29 4/8	Rendez-vous Lake, NT	William R. Powers	William R. Powers	1991	21
122 4/8	27 5/8	28 1/8	11 3/8	11 1/8	6 1/8	5 2/8	29 2/8	27 2/8	Asiak River, NU	Bruce T. Berger	Bruce T. Berger	1993	21
122 2/8	27 4/8	27 3/8	10 5/8	10 7/8	5 7/8	5 6/8	29 5/8	29 2/8	Kikerk Lake, NU	Bill Pastorek	Bill Pastorek	1996	21
122 2/8	29 2/8	27 7/8	11	11 7/8	6	5 4/8	29 2/8	28 3/8	Coppermine River, NU	Larry C. Fisher	Larry C. Fisher	1997	21
122 2/8	29	30 3/8	10 4/8	10 1/8	5 4/8	6 2/8	27	25 1/8	Kugluktuk, NU	R. Stephen Irwin	R. Stephen Irwin	1995	25
122	29	28 1/8	10	9 7/8	6 5/8	5 7/8	30 5/8	30 3/8	Perry River, NU	Picked Up	Robert J. Decker	1979	26
122	30 2/8	30 6/8	10 3/8	10 3/8	5 2/8	5 4/8	31 1/8	30 6/8	Kikerk Lake, NU	Bill McDowell	Bill McDowell	1994	26
121 6/8	28 2/8	29	9 7/8	9 7/8	5 6/8	6 2/8	32 4/8	32 2/8	Cambridge Bay, NU	Tom Gross	Tom Gross	1986	28
121 6/8	26 7/8	26 4/8	10 1/8	10 5/8	6 4/8	6 2/8	27	26 6/8	Cambridge Bay, NU	Michael J. Drewnowski	Michael J. Drewnowski	1997	28
121	28 2/8	29 6/8	9 7/8	9 7/8	5 5/8	6 4/8	31 4/8	31	Ellice River, NU	Picked Up	B&C National Collection	1983	30
121	29	27	10 5/8	10 6/8	6 4/8	5 5/8	28 5/8	28	Inulik Lake, NU	Richard N. Gubler	Richard N. Gubler	1994	30
120 6/8	28 6/8	30	11 3/8	11 1/8	4 7/8	5 3/8	25 7/8	22 4/8	Coppermine River, NU	Ralph E. Post	Ralph E. Post	1993	32
120 6/8	29 5/8	29	10	10	5 5/8	4 7/8	26 7/8	26 2/8	Paulatuk, NT	Derek A. Burdeny	Derek A. Burdeny	2000	32
120 6/8	29 2/8	29 2/8	10 1/8	10 2/8	5 6/8	5 6/8	29 6/8	26 2/8	Kugluktuk, NU	Kent Deligans	Kent Deligans	2003	32
120 4/8	28	28 4/8	10	9 6/8	6	6 1/8	27 4/8	26 4/8	Kugluktuk, NU	Robert W. Ehle	Robert W. Ehle	2000	35
120 2/8	27 6/8	28 7/8	10 1/8	10 3/8	5 7/8	6	28 6/8	26 7/8	Inulik Lake, NU	Mike Stockton	Mike Stockton	1994	36
120	28 5/8	28 3/8	10 1/8	10 6/8	5 4/8	5 2/8	28 4/8	27	Rendez-vous Lake, NT	Jim Moellman	Jim Moellman	1989	37

Score									Location	By	Owner	Date Killed	Rank
120	27 2/8	26 7/8	10 3/8	10 3/8	5 6/8	5 3/8	28 3/8	28	Kikerk Lake, NU	Charles A. LeKites	Charles A. LeKites	1999	37
119 6/8	29 4/8	29 2/8	10 2/8	10 2/8	5 2/8	5 1/8	27	24 1/8	Coppermine River, NU	Glenn M. Smith	Glenn M. Smith	1994	39
119 4/8	28 7/8	29 1/8	10	9 5/8	5 4/8	5 4/8	29 1/8	28 7/8	McNaughton River, NU	Picked Up	Robert D. Jones	1991	40
119 4/8	29 1/8	28 4/8	9 6/8	9 6/8	6 1/8	5 5/8	28 4/8	26 7/8	Back River, NU	Michael N. Van Handel	Michael N. Van Handel	1997	40
119 1/8	28 6/8	29	8 6/8	8 6/8	5 7/8	5 3/8	25 2/8	23 6/8	Cambridge Bay, NU	Collins F. Kellogg, Sr.	Collins F. Kellogg, Sr.	1998	40
119 1/8	28 3/8	27 4/8	10 2/8	10 2/8	5 7/8	5 3/8	29 5/8	27 5/8	Kugluktuk, NU	John Gehan	John Gehan	2000	40
119 1/8	28 5/8	28 1/8	11 1/8	11 1/8	5 7/8	5 2/8	29	27 4/8	Kugluktuk, NU	William A. Keebler	William A. Keebler	2001	40
119	28 4/8	29 3/8	10 5/8	10 5/8	5 2/8	5 2/8	29 1/8	26 7/8	Kugluktuk, NU	John Zimmerman	John Zimmerman	1998	45
119 2/8	29	29 3/8	10 1/8	9 7/8	5 3/8	5 7/8	32 4/8	29 1/8	Rendez-vous Lake, NT	Ray E. Dukes	Ray E. Dukes	1999	45
119 2/8	29 3/8	27 2/8	9 7/8	9 2/8	6 4/8	6 2/8	28 6/8	28 6/8	Ellice River, NU	Greg C. Bond	Greg C. Bond	1995	47
119	29 3/8	29	9 2/8	10 3/8	5 2/8	5 3/8	28 1/8	25 6/8	Paulatuk, NT	Mark S. Rau	Mark S. Rau	2003	47
119	27 5/8	28 2/8	10 3/8	10 4/8	5	5 2/8	29 3/8	28 3/8	Umingmaktok, NU	Doyle V. Toliver	Doyle V. Toliver	1989	49
118 6/8	29 4/8	28 5/8	10 4/8	10	5 7/8	5 2/8	28 5/8	27 1/8	Umingmaktok, NU	Lance K. Parks	Lance K. Parks	1993	49
118 3/8	28 3/8	28 1/8	10	10	5 4/8	5 1/8	29 4/8	26 5/8	Rendez-vous Lake, NT	John J. Grabenstein	John J. Grabenstein	1994	49
118 3/8	28 3/8	29 1/8	9 3/8	9 3/8	5 7/8	5 7/8	32	31 6/8	Perry Island, NU	Lawrence T. Epping	Lawrence T. Epping	1990	49
118 4/8	27 4/8	27 5/8	10 2/8	10 6/8	5 2/8	5 4/8	28 6/8	28 4/8	Coppermine River, NU	Glenn M. Smith	Glenn M. Smith	1998	52
118 4/8	28 4/8	28 7/8	9 5/8	9 5/8	5 2/8	5 6/8	29 6/8	28 5/8	Kugluktuk, NU	Frank S. Noska IV	Frank S. Noska IV	2003	52
118 4/8	27 2/8	27 2/8	10 4/8	10 6/8	5 1/8	5 4/8	26 7/8	24 6/8	Rendez-vous Lake, NT	Victor E. Moss	Victor E. Moss	1989	52
118 2/8	28 7/8	28 7/8	10 6/8	10 5/8	5 4/8	5 1/8	27 4/8	25 6/8	Kugluktuk, NU	Louis E. Dunyon	Louis E. Dunyon	1994	55
118 2/8	28 4/8	28 4/8	9 3/8	10 6/8	5 6/8	5 6/8	27 3/8	27 3/8	Rendez-vous Lake, NT	Roy L. Jacobs	Roy L. Jacobs	1996	55
118	27 5/8	27 7/8	10 4/8	9 3/8	5 4/8	5 1/8	30 2/8	29 2/8	Coppermine River, NU	Robert M. Anderson	Robert M. Anderson	2000	55
118	27 7/8	27 7/8	9	10 4/8	5 6/8	5 6/8	29 2/8	27 3/8	Victoria Island, NT	James D. Verbrugge	James D. Verbrugge	1996	57
117 6/8	28 3/8	28 3/8	11 2/8	9 4/8	4 6/8	5 3/8	27 3/8	26 3/8	Kugluktuk, NU	Sean J. Lancaster	Sean J. Lancaster	1999	57
117 4/8	28 2/8	28 2/8	9 4/8	9 2/8	5 4/8	5 6/8	27 6/8	29 4/8	Franklin Bay, NT	Bruce B. Faulkner	Bruce B. Faulkner	2000	59
117	29 5/8	25 7/8	9 3/8	10	5	5 2/8	30 3/8	28 6/8	Perry Island, NU	Robert D. Jones	Robert D. Jones	1989	60
117	26	26 3/8	10 1/8	10 4/8	6 2/8	6 5/8	28 5/8	28 5/8	Cambridge Bay, NU	Jay Archibald	Jay Archibald	1996	60
116 6/8	26 3/8	26 6/8	10 4/8	10 2/8	5 5/8	5 6/8	27 2/8	27 2/8	Ellice River, NU	George M. Dirgo	George M. Dirgo	1991	62
116 6/8	26 6/8	26	9 7/8	9 7/8	4 7/8	5 4/8	24 4/8	22 4/8	Rendez-vous Lake, NT	Picked Up	Hubert R. Kennedy	PR 1991	62
116 6/8	27 3/8	28 5/8	11	11	5 1/8	5 3/8	28 2/8	27 3/8	Kugluktuk, NU	Rob W. Shatzko	Rob W. Shatzko	1996	64
116 6/8	29 4/8	29 5/8	10 5/8	10 4/8	4 6/8	4 6/8	24 6/8	18 6/8	Horton River, NT	Marion H. Scott	Marion H. Scott	2003	64
116	29 7/8	29 7/8	10 4/8	10 4/8	6 1/8	4 4/8	26 4/8	24 2/8	Inulik Lake, NU	Russell G. Brice	Russell G. Brice	1994	64
115 6/8	27 3/8	28	9 5/8	9 5/8	5	5	24 7/8	24 1/8	Kugluktuk, NU	Michael Gajeske	Michael Gajeske	2001	64
115 6/8	28 3/8	28 5/8	10 1/8	10 1/8	5 7/8	5 5/8	27 1/8	26 6/8	Perry Island, NU	Delbert E. Rieckers	Delbert E. Rieckers	1988	64
115 6/8	28 3/8	28 3/8	9 6/8	9 6/8	4 3/8	5 1/8	28 5/8	26 3/8	Rendez-vous Lake, NT	Hubert R. Kennedy	Hubert R. Kennedy	1990	68
115 4/8	26 1/8	26 1/8	10 1/8	10 1/8	5 1/8	5 2/8	25 4/8	19	Paulatuk, NT	John F. Babler	John F. Babler	1999	69
115 4/8	29 5/8	29 5/8	9 6/8	9 6/8	4 6/8	4 4/8	26 1/8	24 3/8	Smoking Hills, NT	Jack A. Michaelson	Jack A. Michaelson	1999	70
115 4/8	28	28	8 7/8	8 7/8	5 4/8	5 4/8	26 1/8	25 1/8	Adelaide Pen., NU	Jack A. Wilkinson	Jack A. Wilkinson	1992	70
115 2/8	27 7/8	27 7/8	9 2/8	9 2/8	5 2/8	5 2/8	28 3/8	27 5/8	Umingmaktok, NU	Richard Persson	Richard Persson	1995	70
115	27	30	11 3/8	11 3/8	4	6	30 7/8	29 7/8	Kugluktuk, NU	James D. Verbrugge	James D. Verbrugge	1995	70
115	27 1/8	29 1/8	9 4/8	9 4/8	6	5 3/8	28 2/8	27 5/8	Buchan Hills, NU	Craig S. Mortz	Craig S. Mortz	2000	70
114 6/8	27 3/8	26 6/8	9 1/8	9 1/8	5 3/8	5 2/8	31 5/8	30 7/8	Perry Island, NU	Richard A. Jones	Richard A. Jones	1988	74
114 4/8	26	27 2/8	10 6/8	10 6/8	5 4/8	5 4/8	27	27	Ellesmere Island, NU	I.S. Wombath	Harvard Univ. Mus.	1900	74
114 4/8	27	26 4/8	9 5/8	9 5/8	6	5 4/8	26 4/8	26 4/8	Canoe Lake, NT	Ronald W. Wangerow	Ronald W. Wangerow	2000	74
114 1/8	25 4/8	25 7/8	9 2/8	9 2/8	5 2/8	5 4/8	28 3/8	27 7/8	Kent Pen., NU	Archie J. Nesbitt	Archie J. Nesbitt	1989	74
114 6/8	27 6/8	28 6/8	10 5/8	10 6/8	5	5 7/8	28 6/8	27 3/8	Horton River, NT	Kevin Crowe	Kevin Crowe	1999	74
114 4/8	23 2/8	26 4/8	10 6/8	10 5/8	6 6/8	5 7/8	24 6/8	24 4/8	Melbourne Island, NU	Brian Knusta	Brian Knusta	2002	78
114 4/8	28 1/8	27 7/8	9 3/8	9 3/8	5	4 7/8	25 5/8	22 4/8	Banks Island, NT	Don L. Corley	Don L. Corley	1985	79
114 1/8	26	26 1/8	9 6/8	9 6/8	5 4/8	5 2/8	25 2/8	22 5/8	Horton River, NT	Jerry K. Davis	Jerry K. Davis	1992	79

Ovibos moschatus moschatus and certain related subspecies

Score	Length of Horn R	L	Width of Boss R	L	Circumference at Third Quarter R	L	Greatest Spread	Tip to Tip Spread	Locality	Hunter	Owner	Date Killed	Rank
114 4/8	25 6/8	26 5/8	11	10 4/8	5 1/8	5 7/8	31 5/8	31 2/8	Melville Sound, NU	Robert D. Taylor	Robert D. Taylor	1996	84
114 2/8	29 6/8	29 4/8	9 5/8	9 7/8	5 2/8	5	26	25 5/8	Hudson Bay, NU	Monjo	Carnegie Museum	1910	87
114 2/8	27 6/8	25 5/8	9 7/8	10 2/8	6 2/8	5 2/8	26 6/8	26 1/8	Ellice River, NU	Gary Loghry	Gary Loghry	1990	87
114 2/8	26 6/8	27 4/8	10 4/8	10 2/8	5	5 6/8	26	24 6/8	Rendez-vous Lake, NT	James C. Johnson	James C. Johnson	1991	87
114	26	25 7/8	9 5/8	9 6/8	5 4/8	5 2/8	27 6/8	27	Rendez-vous Lake, NT	Richard E. Aniballi	Richard E. Aniballi	1992	90
114	25 5/8	25 6/8	10 7/8	10 6/8	5 2/8	4 7/8	26 6/8	25 6/8	Ellice River, NU	Leo C. Potter	Leo C. Potter	1999	90
113 6/8	27 5/8	28	9 1/8	9 6/8	5 1/8	4 7/8	26 4/8	24 6/8	Rendez-vous Lake, NT	Shawn Andres	Shawn Andres	1990	92
113 6/8	27 3/8	28 3/8	9 7/8	9 6/8	5 2/8	5	29 1/8	28	Kikerk Lake, NU	Ronald J. Pavlik	Ronald J. Pavlik	1994	92
113 6/8	27 1/8	26 2/8	10 2/8	10 1/8	5 5/8	5 2/8	29 4/8	28 5/8	Inulik Lake, NU	Heber Simmons, Jr.	Heber Simmons, Jr.	1998	92
113 4/8	29	28	8 7/8	9 3/8	5 5/8	5 1/8	28 6/8	28	Ellice River, NU	Steve Munier	Steve Munier	1988	95
113 4/8	28 2/8	27 2/8	9 5/8	9 3/8	5 7/8	5 1/8	28 1/8	27 4/8	Bathurst Inlet, NT	George R. Skaggs	George R. Skaggs	1988	95
113 4/8	27 1/8	27 2/8	9 7/8	9 6/8	5 2/8	5 4/8	28 6/8	27 2/8	Paulatuk, NT	Duane Fujiye	Duane Fujiye	1996	95
113 2/8	28	29	8 5/8	8 6/8	4 7/8	4 7/8	29 5/8	28 5/8	Barren Grounds, NT	Gift of H. Casmir de Rham	B&C National Collection	PR 1910	98
113 2/8	26 6/8	26 7/8	9 7/8	10 1/8	4 7/8	5 1/8	28	26 1/8	Swan Lake, NT	Basil C. Bradbury	Basil C. Bradbury	1982	98
113 2/8	26 6/8	28	9 4/8	9	5 2/8	5 1/8	23 6/8	22 4/8	Kuuk River, NT	Roger L. Gregg	Roger L. Gregg	1992	98
113 2/8	26 6/8	26 6/8	9 1/8	9 1/8	5	5 3/8	24 6/8	28 3/8	Rendez-vous Lake, NT	Dale A. Rivers	Dale A. Rivers	1992	98
113 2/8	27 4/8	28 2/8	10	10 1/8	4 5/8	5	28 7/8	28 3/8	Inulik Lake, NU	William H. Crawford	William H. Crawford	1994	98
113	27 6/8	27 1/8	9 4/8	9	5 4/8	5 6/8	30	29 6/8	Umingmaktok, NU	David B. Dentoni, Sr.	David B. Dentoni, Sr.	1990	103
113	27 2/8	27 5/8	10 1/8	10 4/8	5	5 1/8	27 1/8	25 2/8	Rendez-vous Lake, NT	Picked Up	Victor E. Moss	PR 1990	103
112 6/8	28 4/8	26 7/8	10 6/8	11 4/8	5 6/8	4 5/8	25 1/8	23 3/8	Paulatuk, NT	Picked Up	Roger A. Hansen	1988	105
112 6/8	25 7/8	27 3/8	10 7/8	11	4 2/8	5 5/8	30 2/8	30	Kugluktuk, NU	Al Houston	Al Houston	1995	105
112 6/8	26 2/8	26	9 3/8	9 6/8	5 4/8	5 1/8	28 6/8	28 1/8	Dease Strait, NU	Neil A. Briscoe, Jr.	Neil A. Briscoe, Jr.	1998	105
112 6/8	27 2/8	28 6/8	10 4/8	10 2/8	4 2/8	5 2/8	31	30	Coronation Gulf, NU	William E. Wilson	William E. Wilson	1999	105
112 6/8	27 4/8	26 4/8	9	8 7/8	6	5 2/8	27 1/8	25 6/8	Ellice River, NU	Paul W. Hansen	Paul W. Hansen	2001	105
112 6/8	28	27 4/8	8 5/8	8 4/8	5 3/8	5 4/8	27 6/8	27 4/8	Garfield Creek, AK	H. Appel & M.W. Smith	Howard Appel	2002	105
112 4/8	27 5/8	27 5/8	8 2/8	8 2/8	5	5	31 1/8	30 2/8	Thirty Mile Lake, NU	Joe Scotti	Neale Wortley	1983	111
112 4/8	31 2/8	30 4/8	9 2/8	9	5 2/8	4 2/8	27 7/8	25 5/8	Victoria Island, NT	Patrick H. Ackerman	Patrick H. Ackerman	1992	111
112 4/8	25 2/8	25 6/8	10 3/8	10	5 3/8	5 3/8	28 7/8	28 3/8	Rendez-vous Lake, NT	Victor E. Moss	Victor E. Moss	1992	111
112 4/8	25 7/8	26 3/8	9 2/8	9 4/8	5 4/8	5 4/8	26	25 1/8	Canoe Lake, NU	Randy Kaszeta	Randy Kaszeta	2000	111
112 2/8	27 7/8	27 3/8	9 1/8	9 1/8	4 7/8	4 6/8	27 4/8	24	Rendez-vous Lake, NT	Michael E. Kuglitsch	Michael E. Kuglitsch	1994	115
112 2/8	25 3/8	25 4/8	9 2/8	9 4/8	5 6/8	5 6/8	29	27	Melbourne Island, NU	Terry L. McVey	Terry L. McVey	1998	115
112	27 3/8	27 1/8	8 2/8	8 4/8	5 4/8	5 3/8	28 1/8	28	Nunivak Island, AK	Robert J. Condon	Robert J. Condon	2002	117
111 6/8	24 7/8	26 1/8	9	9 1/8	6 3/8	7 4/8	27 7/8	28 1/8	Perry River, NU	Robert H. Hanson	Robert H. Hanson	1987	118
111 6/8	25 4/8	26 3/8	9 5/8	9 3/8	5 4/8	5 7/8	29 1/8	29	Ellice River, NU	William G. Farley	William G. Farley	1990	118
111 6/8	26 4/8	26 3/8	9 2/8	9	5	4 7/8	27 7/8	27 4/8	Nunivak Island, AK	Danny Pankoski	Danny Pankoski	1991	118
111 4/8	27 4/8	26 2/8	9 4/8	9 7/8	5 6/8	4 5/8	26 5/8	24 6/8	Rendez-vous Lake, NT	Richard J. Larson	Richard J. Larson	1992	118
111 4/8	24 3/8	24 4/8	10 1/8	10 2/8	5 6/8	5 1/8	26 4/8	25 3/8	Prince of Wales Island, NU	Picked Up	J. William Kerr	1970	122
111 4/8	27 6/8	27	9 1/8	8 6/8	5 6/8	5 2/8	28 4/8	28	Nightmute, AK	Picked Up	B. & T. Jorgensen	1988	122

Score	Length R	Length L	Width of Boss R	Width of Boss L	Circ. R	Circ. L	Greatest Spread	Tip to Tip	Locality	Hunter	Owner	Date
111 4/8	27 7/8	27 4/8	9 3/8	9 5/8	5 2/8	5 1/8	23 6/8	22 5/8	Kaleet River, NU	Collins F. Kellogg, Sr.	Collins F. Kellogg, Sr.	1993
111 4/8	28	28 1/8	9 3/8	9 3/8	5	5 3/8	27 7/8	25 3/8	Kugluktuk, NU	George W. Windolph	George W. Windolph	2001
111 2/8	28 1/8	28 5/8	10 1/8	10 1/8	5 5/8	4 4/8	28 1/8	26 4/8	Perry River, NU	Douglas G. Williams	Douglas G. Williams	1987
111 2/8	26 6/8	26 6/8	8 6/8	8 4/8	6	5 7/8	26 7/8	25 6/8	Nunivak Island, AK	Willard G. Waite	Willard G. Waite	1989
111 2/8	27	27 1/8	8 3/8	8 1/8	5 4/8	5 5/8	27 7/8	27 5/8	Nunivak Island, AK	David L. Richards	David L. Richards	1990
111 2/8	26 2/8	26 6/8	9 5/8	10	5 1/8	5 1/8	23	21 1/8	Rendez-vous Lake, NT	Mark A. Adams	Mark A. Adams	1991
111 2/8	26 7/8	28 1/8	9 6/8	9	4 5/8	5 3/8	28 1/8	27 5/8	Kugluktuk, NU	Robert W. Kubick	Robert W. Kubick	1991
111 2/8	25 2/8	25 2/8	10	10	5 6/8	5 4/8	26 7/8	25 2/8	Kugluktuk, NU	Douglas G. Lynn	Douglas G. Lynn	1995
111 2/8	27 3/8	26 4/8	9 4/8	9 3/8	5 6/8	5	27 7/8	25 7/8	Rendez-vous Lake, NT	Jonathan M. Olson	Jonathan M. Olson	2000
111	27 4/8	26 6/8	9 7/8	9 3/8	4 6/8	5	26 7/8	24 5/8	Rendez-vous Lake, NT	Michael Andres	Michael Andres	1994
111	26 1/8	26 2/8	9 1/8	9	5 2/8	5 2/8	26	25	Paulatuk, NT	Dale L. Hedgpeth	Dale L. Hedgpeth	1994
110 6/8	27	27	9	8 2/8	5 6/8	5 5/8	26 4/8	26 1/8	McNaughton River, NU	Hugo K. Kilian	Hugo K. Kilian	1992
110 4/8	26 6/8	26 6/8	9 4/8	9 3/8	5 4/8	5 4/8	28 1/8	25 7/8	Holman, NT	Adam Ovilek	Roger Britton	1981
110 4/8	26 3/8	26 3/8	9 2/8	9	5	5 4/8	26 1/8	27 2/8	Thelon River, NT	Picked Up	H.P.L. Kiliaan	1982
110 4/8	25	25 1/8	10	10	5	5 4/8	28 2/8	21 5/8	Holman, NT	William M. Phillippe, Jr.	William M. Phillippe, Jr.	1982
110 4/8	26	26	9 6/8	9 6/8	4 5/8	5	25 5/8	27 4/8	Banks Island, NT	David V. Collis	David V. Collis	1985
110 4/8	27	27 2/8	8 4/8	8 4/8	5 3/8	5 4/8	28	27 6/8	Nelson Island, AK	William McNamara	William McNamara	1993
110 4/8	27 2/8	26 4/8	9 2/8	9 2/8	4 5/8	5 1/8	28	28	Rendez-vous Lake, NT	Joseph G. Zapotosky	Joseph G. Zapotosky	2000
110 2/8	26 4/8	25 2/8	8 6/8	8 6/8	5 3/8	5 3/8	28	26 5/8	Kougarok River, AK	Mark W. Smith	Mark W. Smith	2001
110	25 2/8	25 2/8	9 5/8	9 5/8	5	5	27	26 4/8	Delesse Lake, NT	Michael T. Warn	Michael T. Warn	1995
110	26 2/8	26 6/8	9 1/8	8 6/8	4 6/8	5 4/8	28	26 1/8	Banks Island, NT	William R. Ellis III	William R. Ellis III	1982
110	26 4/8	26 4/8	8 6/8	8 5/8	5 4/8	5 1/8	27	28 4/8	Sadlerochit River, AK	Ronald L. Deis	Ronald L. Deis	1985
110	26 6/8	25 2/8	9 7/8	9 6/8	5	5 7/8	28 7/8	27	Pelly Island, NT	Jurgen Blattgerste	Jurgen Blattgerste	1990
110	26 2/8	27 4/8	8 7/8	8 6/8	5 4/8	5	28 7/8	28 6/8	Nunivak Island, AK	Abed S. Radwan	Abed S. Radwan	2002
109 6/8	27 4/8	27 2/8	8 1/8	8 4/8	5 1/8	5 1/8	26 4/8	26 2/8	Nelson Island, AK	Brent R. Akers	Brent R. Akers	1986
109 6/8	27 2/8	27 2/8	10 1/8	9 7/8	5 3/8	5	26 4/8	26 4/8	Victoria Island, NT	Virgil R. Graber	Virgil R. Graber	1987
109 6/8	26 1/8	27 4/8	9	9	5 1/8	4 6/8	27 3/8	26 6/8	Nunivak Island, AK	Scott Hebertson	Scott Hebertson	1988
109 6/8	27 5/8	25 5/8	9 3/8	9 5/8	5	4 7/8	23 3/8	21 5/8	Victoria Island, NU	Richard E. Bennett	Richard E. Bennett	1991
109 6/8	25 4/8	26 2/8	8 5/8	8 6/8	5 2/8	5 4/8	27 1/8	23 4/8	Rendez-vous Lake, NT	F. Dee Rea	F. Dee Rea	1994
109 6/8	26 2/8	26 3/8	9 1/8	9 2/8	4 6/8	4 5/8	27 1/8	27 4/8	Victoria Island, NT	Harold B. Biggs	Harold B. Biggs	1996
109 6/8	27 3/8	26 3/8	9 4/8	9 4/8	5 4/8	5 7/8	27	27	Banks Island, NT	James M. Domokos	James M. Domokos	1981
109 6/8	26	26 5/8	9 7/8	9 1/8	5 1/8	5	28 1/8	25 1/8	Nunivak Island, AK	Carolyn K. Elledge	Carolyn K. Elledge	1983
109 4/8	26 4/8	26	10 1/8	9 7/8	5 3/8	5	27	27	Nelson Island, AK	Jeff C. Rogers	Jeff C. Rogers	1986
109 4/8	26 3/8	26 4/8	8	8 6/8	5 5/8	5 4/8	26 4/8	26 4/8	Canning River, AK	Gregory L. Venable	Gregory L. Venable	1990
109 2/8	26 5/8	26 5/8	9	9 2/8	5 4/8	5 7/8	28	25 4/8	Nunivak Island, AK	David R. Lautner	David R. Lautner	1991
109 2/8	25 3/8	26	9 6/8	9 7/8	5 2/8	5 1/8	29	26 6/8	Rendez-vous Lake, NT	Joe Novak	Joe Novak	2001
109	28 5/8	28 5/8	9 3/8	9 4/8	5 2/8	5 3/8	29 4/8	29 4/8	Nunivak Island, AK	Bill C. Hicks, Jr.	Bill C. Hicks, Jr.	2002
109	27	26 6/8	8 7/8	9 1/8	4 6/8	4 5/8	26 4/8	26 4/8	Parry Pen., NT	Douglas J. Dollhopf	Douglas J. Dollhopf	1983
109	26 6/8	26 6/8	9 7/8	9 7/8	5 4/8	4 2/8	25 5/8	25 4/8	Banks Island, NT	Audrey E. Crabtree	Audrey E. Crabtree	1985
109 2/8	28	26 6/8	9 7/8	9 7/8	5 2/8	5 1/8	30 3/8	30 3/8	Nunivak Island, AK	Wayne L. Evans	Wayne L. Evans	1999
109	26 4/8	26 6/8	8 4/8	8 3/8	5	5	27	27 7/8	Nunivak Island, AK	Ron D. King	Ron D. King	1986
109	26 4/8	27	9	8 7/8	5 2/8	5 4/8	27 1/8	26 5/8	Ellice River, NU	Gerald L. Warnock	Gerald L. Warnock	1988
109	27 3/8	26 3/8	8 2/8	8 2/8	5 2/8	4 5/8	26 3/8	25 6/8	Nunivak Island, AK	Butch Hautanen	Butch Hautanen	1989
109	26 3/8	24 3/8	9 2/8	9 2/8	5 4/8	5 7/8	28 1/8	28	Ellice River, NU	Thomas D. Suedmeier	Thomas D. Suedmeier	1989
109	26 5/8	26 5/8	8 1/8	8 2/8	5 4/8	5 7/8	24 7/8	24 7/8	Nunivak Island, AK	James A. Reid	James A. Reid	1991
109	27 7/8	30	9 1/8	9 1/8	4 2/8	4	23 3/8	23 3/8	Rendez-vous Lake, NT	George B. Hubbard, Jr.	George B. Hubbard, Jr.	1993
109	27	27	8 1/8	8 1/8	5 1/8	5 1/8	26 6/8	22 4/8	Rendez-vous Lake, NT	Jos Van Hage	Jos Van Hage	2000
108 6/8	25 1/8	25 1/8	10	10 1/8	5	5	28 6/8	27 3/8	Banks Island, NT	William M. Wheless III	William M. Wheless III	1980

MUSK OX

Ovibos moschatus moschatus and certain related subspecies

Score	Length of Horn R	L	Width of Boss R	L	Circumference at Third Quarter R	L	Greatest Spread	Tip to Tip Spread	Locality	Hunter	Owner	Date Killed	Rank
108 6/8	25 3/8	25 7/8	8 7/8	8 3/8	5 7/8	5 7/8	27 7/8	27 6/8	Nunivak Island, AK	James P. Moon, Jr.	James P. Moon, Jr.	1985	171
108 6/8	24 7/8	26 1/8	10 5/8	10 4/8	5	5 2/8	27	24 5/8	Sachs Harbour, NT	Charles D. Lein	Charles D. Lein	1986	171
108 6/8	26 6/8	26 1/8	8 1/8	8 1/8	5 3/8	5 2/8	26 6/8	26 4/8	Nunivak Island, AK	William C. Cloyd	William C. Cloyd	1991	171
108 6/8	27 2/8	27	7 6/8	7 7/8	5 6/8	5 1/8	26 6/8	26 4/8	Nunivak Island, AK	Joseph E. Hardy	Joseph E. Hardy	1991	171
108 6/8	26 7/8	28	9	8 6/8	4 1/8	5 1/8	26 3/8	26	Nunivak Island, AK	Loren B. Hollers	Loren B. Hollers	1991	171
108 6/8	25 7/8	25 6/8	8 7/8	8 7/8	5 1/8	5 1/8	28	27 2/8	Nunivak Island, AK	Travis D. House	Travis D. House	1994	171
108 6/8	26 4/8	27 7/8	9 6/8	9 4/8	4 5/8	4 7/8	25 4/8	22 2/8	Rendez-vous Lake, NT	Chilton E. Miles, Jr.	Chilton E. Miles, Jr.	1997	171
108 6/8	27	25 6/8	9 1/8	8 7/8	5 4/8	5 1/8	26 3/8	24 1/8	Rendez-vous Lake, NT	Joe Hocevar	Joe Hocevar	2003	171
108 4/8	25	23	9 1/8	9 4/8	6 6/8	6 7/8	25 3/8	23 1/8	Hornaday River, NT	Picked Up	Dan Murphy	PR 1976	180
108 4/8	27	26 3/8	9 2/8	9 4/8	4 6/8	4 6/8	25 5/8	23 6/8	Banks Island, NT	James W. Owens	James W. Owens	1981	180
108 4/8	25 4/8	26 3/8	9 7/8	10 2/8	4 4/8	5 6/8	27 6/8	26 6/8	Banks Island, NT	Herman A. Bennett	Herman A. Bennett	1982	180
108 4/8	27	26 7/8	8 3/8	8 4/8	5 1/8	5	27 1/8	26 3/8	Nunivak Island, AK	Jaci A. Crace	Jaci A. Crace	1986	180
108 4/8	26 5/8	26 6/8	8 2/8	8 2/8	4 7/8	5	24 5/8	24 2/8	Nunivak Island, AK	Lloyd E. Laborde	Lloyd E. Laborde	1986	180
108 4/8	27 7/8	27 4/8	7 7/8	8	5	5	28 5/8	28 3/8	Nunivak Island, AK	Jerry M. Wylie	Jerry M. Wylie	1989	180
108 4/8	26	26 1/8	9 6/8	10 4/8	4 7/8	5 4/8	28	26 6/8	Kikerk Lake, NU	Daryl W. Schreiner	Daryl W. Schreiner	1994	180
108 4/8	24 7/8	28	11 4/8	10 7/8	4 4/8	6 1/8	29 6/8	28 6/8	Kugluktuk, NU	Deborah K. DeBruyn	Deborah K. DeBruyn	1997	180
108 2/8	25 3/8	27	8 5/8	8 5/8	4 7/8	5 3/8	29	28 2/8	Ellice River, NU	Jerry E. Mason	Jerry E. Mason	1989	188
108 2/8	25 3/8	25 7/8	9 3/8	9 3/8	4 7/8	6	25 3/8	24 2/8	Lady Franklin Point, NU	Perry Harwell	Perry Harwell	1990	188
108 2/8	26 2/8	27	9	9	5	5 2/8	26 7/8	25 7/8	Gjoa Haven, NU	Chuck Adams	Chuck Adams	2002	188
108	24 5/8	25 6/8	9 6/8	10 1/8	4 6/8	4 7/8	26 6/8	24	Hudson Bay, NU	Native American	N.K. Luxton	PR 1890	191
108	24 6/8	25 2/8	9 4/8	9 5/8	5 2/8	5 4/8	26 5/8	26	Barren Grounds, NT	Gift of J.B. Marvin	Unknown	PR 1951	191
108	30 1/8	30 4/8	7 4/8	7 4/8	5 6/8	6 2/8	27	26 6/8	Nunivak Island, AK	Helga Schroeder	Helga Schroeder	1977	191
108	26 6/8	25 7/8	9 4/8	9 4/8	4 2/8	5 6/8	25 3/8	23 4/8	Cape Mendenhall, AK	Donald E. Franklin	Donald E. Franklin	1978	191
108	26 6/8	25 7/8	9 4/8	9 6/8	5 1/8	5	25 6/8	25 3/8	Paulatuk, NT	Don J. McVittie	Don J. McVittie	1983	191
108	26 7/8	25 3/8	9 4/8	9 1/8	5	4 5/8	28	26 2/8	Sachs Harbour, NT	John G. Munsinger	John G. Munsinger	1985	191
108	26 1/8	25 3/8	8 4/8	9 1/8	5	5 1/8	28 2/8	27 1/8	Perry River, NU	Robert D. Jones	Robert D. Jones	1988	191
108	27	25 6/8	8 4/8	8 4/8	5 1/8	5 1/8	26 7/8	26 3/8	Nunivak Island, AK	Terrance E. Burlew	Terrance E. Burlew	1990	191
108	25 2/8	24 1/8	8 7/8	8 7/8	6 1/8	4 7/8	28 5/8	28 2/8	Queen Maud Gulf, NU	Archie J. Nesbitt	Archie J. Nesbitt	1990	191
108	26 7/8	24 1/8	10 6/8	10 1/8	5 2/8	4 3/8	28 1/8	27 6/8	Victoria Island, NT	David L. Currier	David L. Currier	1993	191
108	26 7/8	27 4/8	9 2/8	9 2/8	4 3/8	4 5/8	23 7/8	21 1/8	Victoria Island, NT	George F. Dennis, Jr.	George F. Dennis, Jr.	1993	191
108	26 2/8	26 3/8	9 5/8	9 2/8	4 6/8	5 1/8	27 4/8	22 7/8	Rendez-vous Lake, NT	Thomas J. Merkley	Thomas J. Merkley	1993	191
108	24 7/8	26 1/8	9 4/8	9 1/8	5 3/8	5 4/8	24 7/8	23 6/8	Victoria Island, NT	Robert C. Balkman	Robert C. Balkman	1994	191
108	25 5/8	26 5/8	9 6/8	9 6/8	4 7/8	5	28 7/8	27 7/8	Brock River, NT	Craig W. Barnes	Craig W. Barnes	1994	191
108	26	26	9 2/8	9 3/8	5	5 2/8	25 3/8	25	Banks Island, NT	K-Tal G. Johnson	K-Tal G. Johnson	1997	191
107 6/8	25 6/8	25 1/8	9 3/8	9 5/8	5 5/8	5	25 5/8	24 6/8	Melville Island, NT	Picked Up	D.C. Thomas	1974	206
107 6/8	26 3/8	26 2/8	8 3/8	8 3/8	5	4 7/8	27 3/8	27 1/8	Nunivak Island, AK	John H. Taucher II	John H. Taucher II	1976	206
107 4/8	27 4/8	26 2/8	9 7/8	9 7/8	4 7/8	4 1/8	26 5/8	24 5/8	Victoria Island, NT	Picked Up	John Behrns	1982	206
107 6/8	26 7/8	26 2/8	9 6/8	9 7/8	4 7/8	5 1/8	26	24 7/8	Pellatt Lake, NT	Robert A. Skrzypek	Robert A. Skrzypek	1988	206

Score	Length of Horn R	Length of Horn L	Width of Boss R	Width of Boss L	Circumf. R	Circumf. L	Greatest Spread	Locality	Hunter	Owner	Date	Rank
107 6/8	25 2/8	25 5/8	9 5/8	9 4/8	5	5 4/8	23 7/8	Perry River, NU	Robert L. Killett	Robert L. Killett	1989	206
107 6/8	24 7/8	24 4/8	9 2/8	9 2/8	5 6/8	5 3/8	22 5/8	Banks Island, NT	John M. Schaffter	John M. Schaffter	1996	206
107 6/8	26 1/8	25 6/8	8 2/8	8 3/8	5 4/8	5 2/8	26 6/8	Ivishak River, AK	James L. Kedrowski	James L. Kedrowski	1999	206
107 4/8	26 5/8	27 7/8	8 2/8	8	5 3/8	5 4/8	25 2/8	Canada	George Vaux	Acad. Nat. Sci., Phil.	PR 1951	213
107 4/8	26 2/8	26 1/8	9 3/8	9 2/8	4 5/8	4 5/8	24	Victoria Island, NT	Craig T. Boddington	Craig T. Boddington	1981	213
107 4/8	25 3/8	25 6/8	9 2/8	9 4/8	5	5	25 7/8	Banks Island, NT	Jack Fiske	Jack Fiske	1981	213
107 4/8	25 2/8	26	8 4/8	8 4/8	5	4 6/8	27 2/8	Cape Mohican, AK	Tommy L. Ramsey	Tommy L. Ramsey	1990	213
107 4/8	25 5/8	26 6/8	9 3/8	9 4/8	4 4/8	4 6/8	28	Victoria Island, NT	Vernon J. Boose	Vernon J. Boose	1992	213
107 4/8	25	25 1/8	8 1/8	8 1/8	5 4/8	5 4/8	24 1/8	Nunivak Island, AK	Timothy A. Gleason	Timothy A. Gleason	1992	213
107 4/8	26 1/8	25 7/8	9 1/8	9 3/8	5 3/8	5 1/8	26 3/8	Contwoyto Lake, NU	John P. Burdette	John P. Burdette	1993	213
107 4/8	25 4/8	27 2/8	9 7/8	9 7/8	4 3/8	6	29 4/8	Kent Pen., NU	Raymond Venissat	Raymond Venissat	1993	213
107 4/8	26 2/8	25 5/8	8 4/8	8 3/8	5 4/8	5 1/8	29 2/8	Nunivak Island, AK	Merle R. Frank	Merle R. Frank	1997	213
107 2/8	26 2/8	24 7/8	8 3/8	8 6/8	5 1/8	5	27 1/8	Greenland	Bill Foster	Foster's Bighorn Rest.	PR 1945	222
107 2/8	26 3/8	26 6/8	9	9	5 6/8	5	29 4/8	Nunivak Island, AK	William A. Keller	William A. Keller	1977	222
107 2/8	26 2/8	27 3/8	8 7/8	8 1/8	5	4 6/8	27 6/8	Nunivak Island, AK	Normand Poulin	Normand Poulin	1977	222
107 2/8	26 3/8	26 2/8	8 1/8	8 1/8	5	5 4/8	28	Nunivak Island, AK	Jacob Metzger	Jacob Metzger	1978	222
107 2/8	25 2/8	26 3/8	8 4/8	8 4/8	5 2/8	5 4/8	27 6/8	Cambridge Bay, NU	Picked Up	Manfred Huellbusch	1979	222
107 2/8	26 4/8	25 2/8	9 1/8	9	5 2/8	5 4/8	24 4/8	Banks Island, NT	Karen K. Jacobsen	Karen K. Jacobsen	1987	222
107 2/8	26 2/8	26 4/8	9 1/8	9	4 5/8	4 5/8	27	Victoria Island, NT	Johnnie R. Walters	Johnnie R. Walters	1993	222
107 2/8	26 6/8	26 6/8	8 5/8	9 1/8	4 3/8	4 5/8	27 3/8	Rendez-vous Lake, NT	Terence L. Andres	Terence L. Andres	1994	222
107 2/8	25 6/8	27 1/8	9 6/8	9 7/8	4 5/8	4 5/8	26 6/8	Umingmaktok, NU	Dyrk T. Eddie	Dyrk T. Eddie	1998	222
107 2/8	26	27 3/8	8 2/8	8 5/8	4 6/8	4 7/8	27 4/8	Paulatuk, NT	Mitchel C. Arnold	Mitchel C. Arnold	1999	222
107 2/8	25 4/8	26 4/8	9 4/8	9 4/8	3 7/8	5 2/8	29 6/8	McDonald Lake, NT	W.G. Hawes	W.G. Hawes	2000	222
107	27 4/8	28 2/8	10 1/8	9 4/8	5 3/8	4 3/8	28 6/8	Kugluktuk, NU	George E. Mann	George E. Mann	2000	234
107	25	25	8 5/8	10 1/8	5	5	28	Nunivak Island, AK	Russell Reed	Russell Reed	1978	234
107	24 3/8	26 6/8	8 4/8	9	5 6/8	5 2/8	26 1/8	Delesse Lake, NT	Franco Mazzucchelli	Franco Mazzucchelli	1981	234
107	26 1/8	25	9	9 4/8	5 4/8	4 2/8	23 5/8	Holman, NT	I.D. Shapiro	I.D. Shapiro	1982	234
107	24 7/8	25 5/8	9 7/8	10 1/8	5 5/8	4 2/8	22 7/8	Rendez-vous Lake, NT	Jack W. Claypoole	Jack W. Claypoole	1993	234
107	26 1/8	25 7/8	9 3/8	9	4 7/8	5	24	Falaise Lake, NT	Robert D. Hansen	Robert D. Hansen	1994	234
107	27 2/8	24 6/8	7 7/8	8 5/8	4 5/8	4 6/8	25 4/8	Horton River, NT	Dwain Spray	Dwain Spray	1996	234
107	25 7/8	26 1/8	8 4/8	8 2/8	5 3/8	5 2/8	25 7/8	Nunivak Island, AK	David R. Lautner	David R. Lautner	1999	234
107	27 3/8	27 3/8	8 2/8	8 2/8	5	5 4/8	29 1/8	Granite Falls, NT	Pete Studwell	Pete Studwell	1999	234
107	28 1/8	28 1/8	8 3/8	8 6/8	5 3/8	5 4/8	26 4/8	Greenland	Unknown	Rudolf Sand	1930	234
106 6/8	25	25 5/8	8 2/8	8 5/8	5	5 3/8	25 5/8	Greenland	Alvin Pedersen	Zool. Mus., Copenhagen	1935	242
106 6/8	25 1/8	25 1/8	8 4/8	8 3/8	5	5	27 6/8	Nunivak Island, AK	Bert Klineburger	Bert Klineburger	1959	242
106 6/8	26 1/8	27 1/8	8 6/8	9 3/8	5 2/8	5	27 5/8	Nunivak Island, AK	Ethel D. Leedy	Ethel D. Leedy	1975	242
106 6/8	26 3/8	26 3/8	9 3/8	9 3/8	4 7/8	4 7/8	27	Sachs Harbour, NT	John R. Blanton	John R. Blanton	1984	242
106 6/8	26 2/8	26 3/8	8 1/8	7 7/8	5 1/8	5	26 1/8	Nunivak Island, AK	Jerald M. Finney	Jerald M. Finney	1987	242
106 6/8	25	25	8 3/8	8 2/8	5 6/8	5 4/8	27 6/8	Roberts Mt., AK	Jack D. Adams	Jack D. Adams	1993	242
106 6/8	27 3/8	27 3/8	9 5/8	9 5/8	4 2/8	4 7/8	27 3/8	Sachs Harbour, NT	James R. Gall	James R. Gall	1995	242
106 6/8	25 4/8	25 4/8	10	10	5 6/8	4 4/8	29	Umingmaktok, NU	David G. Miller	David G. Miller	1996	242
106 6/8	25 1/8	25 1/8	9 3/8	9 3/8	5 2/8	4 6/8	26 7/8	Holman, NT	David A. Justmann	David A. Justmann	1997	242
106 6/8	24	24 4/8	12 4/8	12 4/8	5 2/8	4 7/8	22 6/8	Cambridge Bay, NU	William Kneer	William F. Kneer	1999	242
106 6/8	25 6/8	25 2/8	8 4/8	8 4/8	4 6/8	5	27 5/8	Nunivak Island, AK	Bud Junger	Bud Junger	2000	242
106 4/8	25 7/8	26 1/8	8 4/8	8 1/8	5 1/8	4 7/8	28	Karon Lake, AK	R. Kim Francisco	R. Kim Francisco	1985	254
106 4/8	25 4/8	25 5/8	9 3/8	9 2/8	5	5	25 1/8	Banks Island, NT	Keith C. Halstead	Keith C. Halstead	1986	254
106 4/8	25 6/8	26 2/8	8 2/8	8 4/8	5 3/8	4 7/8	22 6/8	Nunivak Island, AK	Richard McIntyre	Richard McIntyre	1988	254
106 4/8	26 4/8	26 4/8	8	8 1/8	5 3/8	5	25 3/8	Sadlerochit River, AK	Donald L. Willis	Donald L. Willis	1990	254

Ovibos moschatus moschatus and certain related subspecies

Score	Length of Horn R	L	Width of Boss R	L	Circumference at Third Quarter R	L	Greatest Spread	Tip to Tip Spread	Locality	Hunter	Owner	Date Killed	Rank
106 4/8	25	25 2/8	8 5/8	8 3/8	5 3/8	5 3/8	27 6/8	27 4/8	Nunivak Island, AK	Paulette R. Knutson	Paulette R. Knutson	1992	254
106 4/8	26 5/8	28 1/8	9 5/8	9 5/8	4	5 2/8	25 1/8	24 3/8	Sachs Harbour, NT	James E. Kapuscinski	James E. Kapuscinski	1994	254
106 4/8	26 2/8	27 2/8	8 4/8	8 1/8	4 5/8	5 2/8	25 4/8	24 5/8	Kuparuk River, AK	David F. Neel	David F. Neel	1995	254
106 4/8	25 6/8	25 2/8	8 6/8	8 5/8	5 3/8	5 1/8	30 4/8	30 2/8	Nunivak Island, AK	Derek D. Nord	Derek D. Nord	2001	254
106 2/8	26	25 6/8	8 4/8	8 2/8	4 7/8	4 4/8	29 6/8	29 4/8	Nunivak Island, AK	L.G. Sullivan	L.G. Sullivan	1977	262
106 2/8	24 6/8	25 2/8	9	8 6/8	6	5 2/8	27	26 4/8	Nunivak Island, AK	Frank N. Rome	Frank N. Rome	1985	262
106 2/8	25 2/8	25 3/8	9 3/8	9 4/8	5 7/8	4 7/8	27 6/8	21 2/8	Victoria Island, NT	Lawrence T. Epping	Lawrence T. Epping	1986	262
106 2/8	26 4/8	25 7/8	7 6/8	8 1/8	4 7/8	5 3/8	27 6/8	26 7/8	Perry River, NU	Jack Downing	Jack Downing	1988	262
106 2/8	25 4/8	26 5/8	9 1/8	9	5	5 2/8	26 6/8	26 6/8	Nunivak Island, AK	Elwin J. Lawler	Elwin J. Lawler	1990	262
106 2/8	25 7/8	25 2/8	8 5/8	8 6/8	5 7/8	5 1/8	26 2/8	25 6/8	Canning River, AK	Carl L. Yowell	Carl L. Yowell	1990	262
106 2/8	25 2/8	25 6/8	8 7/8	9	4 7/8	5 4/8	25 5/8	24 4/8	Cambridge Bay, NU	Donald E. Twa	Donald E. Twa	1991	262
106 2/8	26 3/8	26 5/8	9 2/8	9 5/8	5 1/8	4 7/8	26 5/8	25 7/8	Ellice River, NU	David L. Gayer	David L. Gayer	2001	262
106	26 3/8	25 1/8	10 4/8	10 5/8	4 4/8	4 5/8	27	27	Nunivak Island, AK	Gail W. Holderman	Gail W. Holderman	1976	270
106	26 5/8	26 5/8	8 6/8	9	5 1/8	4 2/8	26 4/8	25 1/8	Banks Island, NT	Norman F. Taylor	Norman F. Taylor	1981	270
106	26 1/8	25 2/8	8	8 3/8	5 3/8	5	27 4/8	27 2/8	Canning River, AK	Darrel W. Sauder	Darrel W. Sauder	1983	270
106	25 1/8	25 2/8	8 6/8	8 6/8	5	4 6/8	26 6/8	26 4/8	Rendez-vous Lake, NT	Lanny L. Walker	Lanny L. Walker	1988	270
106	26 7/8	26 2/8	8 4/8	8 3/8	4 6/8	4 5/8	25 6/8	24 6/8	Cambridge Bay, NU	Collins F. Kellogg, Jr.	Collins F. Kellogg, Jr.	1998	270
106	26 1/8	25 4/8	10 1/8	10 1/8	4 7/8	4 4/8	28 3/8	27 5/8	Ellice River, NU	Gary A. Rose	Gary A. Rose	2000	270
106	25 6/8	27 2/8	9 4/8	9 6/8	4 4/8	5 2/8	27	24 6/8	Barren Grounds, NT	Unknown	Snow Museum	1890	276
105 6/8	25 2/8	25 1/8	8 5/8	8 7/8	5 5/8	5	25 2/8	24 4/8	Nunivak Island, AK	Lynn M. Castle	Lynn M. Castle	1977	276
105 6/8	25 6/8	25 2/8	8 4/8	8 4/8	4 6/8	4 6/8	27 2/8	26 4/8	Nunivak Island, AK	William K. Leech	William K. Leech	1977	276
105 6/8	26	25 2/8	9 2/8	9 1/8	4 5/8	4 5/8	25 7/8	23 6/8	Nunivak Island, AK	Gary E. Brown	Gary E. Brown	1978	276
105 6/8	25	24 7/8	9 4/8	9 6/8	4 6/8	4 6/8	27 5/8	25 6/8	Coronation Gulf, NU	Donald J. Craite	Donald J. Craite	1987	276
105 6/8	25 2/8	25 6/8	9	8 7/8	5 1/8	5 1/8	23 6/8	21 5/8	Sachs Harbour, NT	James A. Hale	James A. Hale	1987	276
105 6/8	26 2/8	26 6/8	7 7/8	7 7/8	5 2/8	5 2/8	29 5/8	29 2/8	Nunivak Island, AK	Henry M. Hills III	Henry M. Hills III	1987	276
105 6/8	25	26	9 7/8	9 5/8	4 3/8	5	27 1/8	26 5/8	Banks Island, NT	Bernard Sippin	Bernard Sippin	1988	276
105 6/8	25	28	9 3/8	9 5/8	4 2/8	4 1/8	26	25 4/8	Ellice River, NU	Christopher J. Harvey	Christopher J. Harvey	1992	276
105 6/8	26 5/8	26 5/8	9 4/8	9 5/8	4	4 1/8	23 6/8	22 7/8	Montresor River, NU	David J. DuFlo	David J. DuFlo	1993	276
105 6/8	25 5/8	26 3/8	8	8 1/8	5	5 6/8	27 5/8	27 3/8	Nunivak Island, AK	Gregory A. Stoick	Gregory A. Stoick	1993	276
105 6/8	25 5/8	25 5/8	8 5/8	8 4/8	4 6/8	5 1/8	26 1/8	23 5/8	Rendez-vous Lake, NT	Paul E. Hostetler	Paul E. Hostetler	1996	276
105 6/8	25 6/8	26	8 3/8	8 2/8	4 7/8	4 4/8	26 2/8	25	Rendez-vous Lake, NT	Jody C. Hostetler	Jody C. Hostetler	1996	276
105 6/8	24 3/8	26 2/8	10 1/8	9 7/8	4 6/8	5 5/8	26	24 1/8	Rendez-vous Lake, NT	David L. Hussey	David L. Hussey	1998	276
105 6/8	25 1/8	25 3/8	8 7/8	8 7/8	4 7/8	4 7/8	25 3/8	27 3/8	Nanwaksjiak Crater, AK	Robert R. Halpin	Robert R. Halpin	1999	276
105 6/8	24 3/8	25 4/8	8 6/8	8 5/8	5 3/8	5 3/8	26 3/8	24 2/8	Nunivak Island, AK	A. Timothy Toth	A. Timothy Toth	2000	276
105 6/8	26 7/8	25 3/8	9 4/8	9 4/8	5 1/8	4 2/8	24 2/8	18 5/8	Rendez-vous Lake, NT	Metod Novak	Metod Novak	2001	276
105 4/8	26	26 7/8	8 2/8	8 2/8	4 7/8	4 6/8	26 2/8	26 2/8	Nunivak Island, AK	Sam C. Arnett III	Sam C. Arnett III	1976	293
105 4/8	25 7/8	25 7/8	8 2/8	8 3/8	5	4 6/8	27	26 6/8	Nunivak Island, AK	Robert E. Speegle	Robert E. Speegle	1976	293
105 4/8	26	25 7/8	8 1/8	8 1/8	5 2/8	5	26 3/8	25 1/8	Nunivak Island, AK	Jean Louis L'Ecuyer	Jean Louis L'Ecuyer	1978	293

Score	Length of Horn		Width of Boss		Circumference		Greatest Spread	Tip to Tip Spread	Locality	Hunter	Owner	Date Killed	Rank
105 4/8	25 4/8	25 4/8	8 1/8	8 2/8	5 2/8	5 1/8	25 6/8	24 4/8	Nunivak Island, AK	Curtis S. Williams	Curtis S. Williams	1978	293
105 4/8	25 4/8	25 3/8	8 7/8	9 1/8	4 6/8	4 6/8	28	27	Nunivak Island, AK	Roland Stickney	Roland Stickney	1979	293
105 4/8	25 3/8	26 3/8	8 7/8	8 6/8	5 1/8	4 3/8	29 4/8	29	Nunivak Island, AK	Joseph A. Carr	Joseph A. Carr	1984	293
105 4/8	26 4/8	26 7/8	7 7/8	8	4 5/8	4 7/8	27 3/8	26 3/8	Nunivak Island, AK	John D. Frost	John D. Frost	1986	293
105 4/8	25 4/8	25 6/8	9 5/8	9 4/8	4 6/8	5 1/8	26 4/8	25 4/8	Sachs Harbour, NT	William H. Bynum	William H. Bynum	1989	293
105 4/8	26 4/8	27	8 6/8	8 2/8	4 5/8	4 5/8	24 3/8	23 2/8	Bluenose Lake, NU	George P. Mann	George P. Mann	1990	293
105 4/8	25 6/8	26 1/8	8 3/8	8 3/8	5 4/8	5 7/8	27 7/8	27 6/8	Nunivak Island, AK	Frederick D. Overly	Frederick D. Overly	1994	293
105 4/8	25 7/8	25 5/8	9 5/8	9 3/8	4 7/8	4 7/8	25 4/8	24 4/8	Banks Island, NT	Jerry Boettcher	Jerry Boettcher	1996	293
105 4/8	27 1/8	26 6/8	9	8 6/8	4 2/8	4 2/8	26 5/8	25 6/8	Banks Island, NT	Clyde M. Sasser	Clyde M. Sasser	1999	293
105 2/8	25 5/8	26	7 5/8	7 4/8	5 3/8	5 3/8	27 5/8	26 7/8	Nunivak Island, AK	G.A. Treschow	G.A. Treschow	1978	305
105 2/8	26 1/8	25 3/8	8 2/8	8 1/8	6	5 4/8	25 6/8	24	Nunivak Island, AK	F. Phillips Williamson	F. Phillips Williamson	1978	305
105 2/8	25 6/8	25 5/8	8 3/8	8 3/8	4 6/8	4 6/8	27 2/8	26 4/8	Nunivak Island, AK	David A. Schuller	David A. Schuller	1982	305
105 2/8	24 5/8	24 4/8	9 6/8	9 6/8	4 5/8	5	25 1/8	23 7/8	Richardson River, NU	Ronald L. Fuller	Ronald L. Fuller	1988	305
105 2/8	27	27	9 2/8	9 1/8	5 1/8	5 2/8	26 5/8	26	Gjoa Haven, NU	James J. McBride	James J. McBride	1991	305
105 2/8	26 3/8	25 4/8	8 6/8	8 6/8	4 4/8	4 7/8	27 7/8	27 7/8	Nunivak Island, AK	Michael L. Frost, Jr.	Michael L. Frost, Jr.	1993	305
105 2/8	24 7/8	24 2/8	8 3/8	9	5 2/8	5 4/8	25 6/8	24 6/8	Banks Island, NT	Thomas A. Shimak, Sr.	Thomas A. Shimak, Sr.	1993	305
105 2/8	25 5/8	25 7/8	8	9	4 7/8	4 7/8	27 3/8	27	Nelson Island, AK	Samuel H. Schurig	Samuel H. Schurig	1994	305
105 2/8	25 6/8	26 2/8	9 7/8	7 7/8	5 2/8	5 2/8	26 5/8	26 2/8	Gjoa Haven, NU	Ken G. Wilson	Ken G. Wilson	1998	305
105 2/8	26	27	9 5/8	9 5/8	3 7/8	5 2/8	29 7/8	29 5/8	Hudson Bay, NU	Dudley K. White	Dudley K. White	2003	305
105	26 5/8	25 3/8	7 6/8	7 7/8	5	4 7/8	24 4/8	23 4/8	Nunivak Island, AK	Native American	N.K. Luxton	1905	315
105	26	26	8 3/8	8 7/8	4 7/8	4 7/8	26 7/8	26 1/8	Nunivak Island, AK	Carlo Bonomi	Carlo Bonomi	1976	315
105	25 7/8	26 6/8	8 2/8	8 2/8	4 7/8	4 6/8	27 7/8	27	Bering Sea, AK	Dan H. Brainard	Dan H. Brainard	1977	315
105	26 2/8	25 4/8	8 7/8	9	4 6/8	4 5/8	27 5/8	26	Cambridge Bay, NU	Jack M. Holland, Jr.	Jack M. Holland, Jr.	1979	315
105	24 7/8	27 5/8	8 4/8	8 3/8	4 3/8	5 1/8	24 6/8	24	Cambridge Bay, NU	Picked Up	Manfred Huellbusch	1989	315
105	26 2/8	25 6/8	9 1/8	8 2/8	5 1/8	5 4/8	24 5/8	19	Nelson Island, AK	Norman L. Epley	Norman L. Epley	PR 1992	315
105	27 1/8	25 5/8	8 1/8	7 7/8	4 5/8	4 3/8	27 4/8	26	Banks Island, NT	Unknown	Thomas W. Oatis	1992	315
105	27 2/8	26 6/8	8 3/8	8 4/8	4 6/8	6	26 6/8	24 7/8	Victoria Island, NT	William O. West	William O. West	1995	315
105	25 7/8	26 7/8	9 4/8	9 4/8	4 1/8	4 7/8	27 1/8	25 6/8	Mekoryuk, AK	Robert B. Nancarrow	Robert B. Nancarrow	1996	315
105	23 5/8	25 1/8	9 2/8	9 2/8	4 7/8	4 5/8	28 1/8	27 5/8	Cape Mendenhall, AK	Kenneth L. Jenson	Kenneth L. Jenson	1998	315
105	25 6/8	26 2/8	8 4/8	8 2/8	4 5/8	5	28 6/8	28 4/8	Nunivak Island, AK	Steven J. Bries	Steven J. Bries	1998	315
105	26 4/8	26 1/8	8 3/8	8 3/8	4 5/8	4 5/8	27 3/8	27 3/8	Bekere Lake, NT	Todd D. Bergman	Todd D. Bergman	2002	315
105	27	27	8 2/8	8 2/8	4 5/8	4 5/8	26 2/8	26 2/8	Horton River, NT	David A. Garganta	David A. Garganta	2002	315
105	25 4/8	26 5/8	7 7/8	8 2/8	4 4/8	4 4/8	28	28	Baldy Mt., AK	Michael D. Moore	Michael D. Moore	2002	315
105	26 5/8	27	8	8 5/8	4 2/8	4 2/8	26 6/8	26 2/8	Umingmaktok, NU	Mary C. Scott	Mary C. Scott	2003	315
105	25 5/8	27 7/8	9 2/8	8 5/8	4 2/8	5 4/8	31	30 3/8	Kugluktuk, NU	Mark W. Smith	Mark W. Smith	2003	315
125 2/8*	28 7/8	29 6/8	11	10 7/8	6	6 2/8	29 2/8	27 2/8	Kugluktuk, NU	Kent L. Prouty	Kent L. Prouty	2000	
125 *	29 4/8	28 7/8	11 1/8	11 3/8	6 2/8	5 3/8	28 4/8	27 6/8	Kugluktuk, NU	James A. Cummings	James A. Cummings	2000	
122 4/8*	28 1/8	28 4/8	11	11 5/8	6 1/8	5 6/8			Kugluktuk, NU	Jack L. Blachly	Jack L. Blachly	1999	

* Final score is subject to revision by additional verifying measurements.

CATEGORY
MUSK OX

SCORE
125*

HUNTER
JAMES A. CUMMINGS

LOCATION
KUGLUKTUK, NUNAVUT

DATE OF KILL
APRIL 2000

SCORE
112-6/8

HUNTER
PAUL W. HANSEN
(BELOW RIGHT)

LOCATION
ELLICE RIVER, NUNAVUT

DATE OF KILL
AUGUST 2001

CATEGORY
MUSK OX

SCORE
124-6/8

HUNTER
THOMAS L. STRAKA

LOCATION
KUGLUKTUK, NUNAVUT

DATE OF KILL
MARCH 2003

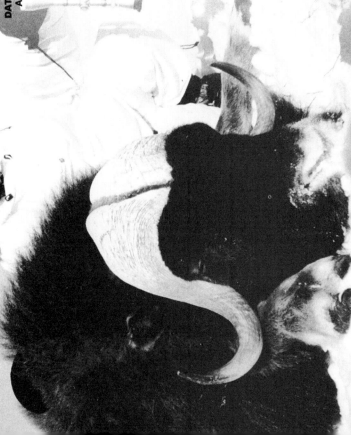

820

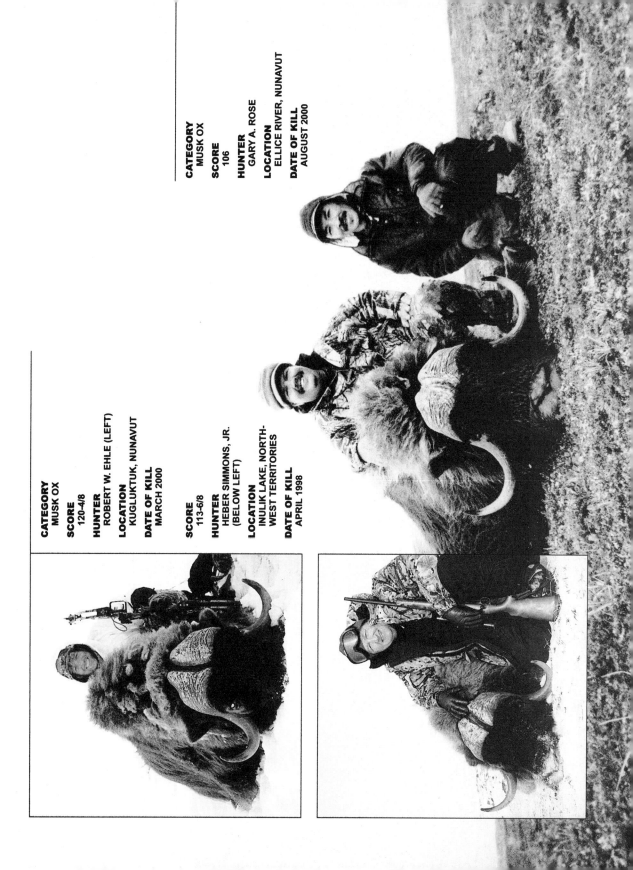

CATEGORY
MUSK OX

SCORE
106

HUNTER
GARY A. ROSE

LOCATION
ELLICE RIVER, NUNAVUT

DATE OF KILL
AUGUST 2000

CATEGORY
MUSK OX

SCORE
120-4/8

HUNTER
ROBERT W. EHLE (LEFT)

LOCATION
KUGLUKTUK, NUNAVUT

DATE OF KILL
MARCH 2000

SCORE
113-6/8

HUNTER
HEBER SIMMONS, JR.
(BELOW LEFT)

LOCATION
INULIK LAKE, NORTH-
WEST TERRITORIES

DATE OF KILL
APRIL 1998

BIGHORN SHEEP
NEW WORLD'S RECORD

It was late in the afternoon on November 28, 2000, on Luscar Mountain in Alberta's Rockies. The echoes of Guinn Crousen's .270 Weatherby Magnum had died away and the great ram was down. Many men would have run forward to see their prize up close. But, Crousen is both patient and practical. He'd waited more than a dozen years to finish his Grand Slam with a Rocky Mountain bighorn (*Ovis canadensis canadensis*)—not just any bighorn, but the right one. He'd tried to obtain this particular tag for four years, believing that Alberta offered the best opportunity for the kind of ram he wanted. With the right tag finally in hand, he'd tried for 15 days to get a shot at this particular ram.

Now it was getting dark and cold in the Alberta mountains. He was tired and his bad knees hurt. The ram could wait a little bit longer. So, while his hunting partners sprang forward, Crousen turned back to retrieve his pack and jacket, dropped during the final moments of the stalk.

A few minutes later, moving more slowly with adrenaline levels dropping, Crousen approached his ram. His hunting team—Randy Babala, Ron McKenzie, and Lyle Moberly—were sitting quietly, looking at the downed monarch. Crousen approached from the rear, seeing the full curl of the ram's horns. "My gosh, boys, he's big," he said.

Randy Babala looked up and spoke quietly in the silence of the moment. "Guinn, you may have a new World's Record." Guinn Crousen sat down and cried a little.

The story of Crousen's march into history began in 1985 when a friend convinced him to attend his first Foundation for North American Wild Sheep convention. From that day on, Crousen worked to fulfill the requirements of a Grand Slam. With three-fourths of his goal met, Crousen settled on trophy-rich western Alberta as his final destination.

After three days of hard hunting, Crousen glassed a very big ram, unique and recognizable because of his exceptional length. Although located just inside an area closed to hunting, they kept close tabs on him. On the fifth day they lost him, and didn't see him again for six long days. Eventually, they found the long-horned ram again, still in his sanctuary.

On the 15th day, a pack of coyotes dashed into the herd of sheep as they fed on the protected side of the line. Suddenly sheep were running everywhere. Babala said, "There's the ram, there's the boundary stake. He's out. Take him!" It was a going-away shot at just about 70 yards, and the ram that would become the new World's Record Rocky Mountain bighorn belonged to Guinn Crousen, his team, and all of us who care about such things.

The ram was officially scored on August 15, 2001, by a B&C Special Judges Panel at 208-3/8 points. It is the new World's Record bighorn by two eighths of an inch. Crousen and his team were absolutely correct when they recognized its incredible length. At 47-4/8 and 46-5/8 inches for the right and left, respectively, its horns are the second longest of any bighorn sheep in the All-time records book. ■

BIGHORN SHEEP
WORLD'S RECORD SCORE CHART

RANK
New World's Record

SCORE
208 3/8

LOCATION
Luscar Mt., AB

HUNTER
Guinn D. Crousen

OWNER
Guinn D. Crousen

DATE KILLED
2000

Records of
North American
Big Game

250 Station Drive
Missoula, MT 59801
(406) 542-1888

BOONE AND CROCKETT CLUB®
OFFICIAL SCORING SYSTEM FOR NORTH AMERICAN BIG GAME TROPHIES

SHEEP

MINIMUM SCORES

	AWARDS	ALL-TIME
bighorn	175	180
desert	165	168
Dall's	160	170
Stone's	165	170

KIND OF SHEEP (check one)
- ☒ bighorn
- ☐ desert
- ☐ Dall's
- ☐ Stone's

PLUG NUMBER
00AB382

Measure to a
Point in Line
With Horn T...

SEE OTHER SIDE FOR INSTRUCTIONS	COLUMN 1	COLUMN 2	3
	Right Horn	Left Horn	...nce
A. Greatest Spread (Is Often Tip to Tip Spread)	23 1/8		
B. Tip to Tip Spread	23 1/8		
C. Length of Horn	47 4/8	46 5/8	
D-1. Circumference of Base	15 7/8	15 7/8	—
D-2. Circumference at First Quarter	15 2/8	15 3/8	1/8
D-3. Circumference at Second Quarter	14 7/8	14 5/8	2/8
D-4. Circumference at Third Quarter	12 0/8	11 3/8	5/8
TOTALS	105 4/8	103 7/8	1 0/8

ADD	Column 1	105 4/8
	Column 2	103 7/8
	Subtotal	209 3/8
SUBTRACT	Column 3	1 0/8
FINAL SCORE		**208 3/8**

Exact Locality Where Killed: Luscar Mt., Alberta

Date Killed: November 2000   Hunter: Guinn D. Crousen

Owner: Guinn D. Crousen   Telephone #:

Owner's Address:

Guide's Name and Address:

Remarks: (Mention Any Abnormalities or Unique Qualities)

I, _____ Ken Witt _____ , certify that I have measured this trophy on _____ 01/28/2001 _____
PRINT NAME   MM/DD/YYYY

at _____ Dallas, Texas _____
STREET ADDRESS   CITY   STATE/PROVINCE

and that these measurements and data are, to the best of my knowledge and belief, made in accordance with the instructions given.

Witness: _____ Tommy Caruthers _____   Signature: _____   B&C OFFICIAL MEASURER   I.D. Number

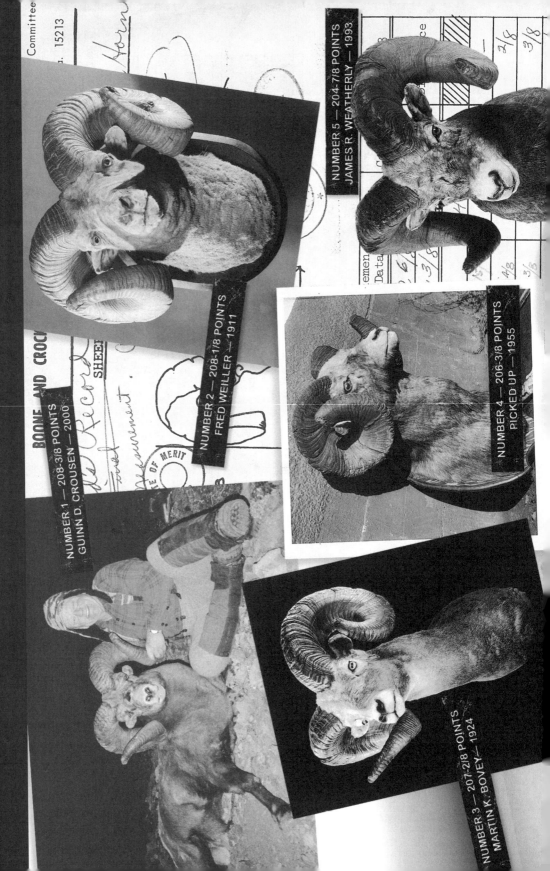

TOP 10 BIGHORN SHEEP

NUMBER 1 — 208-3/8 POINTS
GUINN D. CROUSEN — 2000

NUMBER 2 — 208-1/8 POINTS
FRED WEILLER — 1911

NUMBER 3 — 207-2/8 POINTS
MARTIN K. BOVEY — 1924

NUMBER 4 — 206-3/8 POINTS
PICKED UP — 1955

NUMBER 5 — 204-7/8 POINTS
JAMES R. WEATHERLY — 1993

OFFICI[...]

By whom killed
Clarence [...]

where killed

SYSTEM FOR NORTH AMERICAN BIG GAME TROPHIES
% Am. Museum of Natural History
Central Park West at 79th St
[...] New York

NE AND CROCKETT CLUB

NUMBER 7 — 203-5/8 POINTS
PICKED UP — 1992

| | Column 1 | Column 2 |
Supplemen- tary Data	Right Horn	Left Horn
	46 7/8	44 5/8
	15 5/8	15 2/8
23 2/8	15 1/8	15 [...]
23 2/8		

NUMBER 10 — 202-2/8 POINTS
TOM KERQUITS — 1918
Photograph not available

Tip Spread)

ONS

NUMBER 6 — 204 POINTS
JAMES SIMPSON — 1920

THE FAMOUS JAMES SIMPSON BIGHORN RAM
Now Number Two, in the Habitat Group in the
American Museum of Natural History, New York
SCORE 204

ph by Grancel Fits

KODAK 5062 P

17

NUMBER 9 — 202-3/8 POINTS
RICHARD B. WIANT — 1992

KODAK SOE

16

NUMBER 8 — 203-4/8 POINTS
KATHERINE A. PYRA — 1992

BIGHORN SHEEP

Ovis canadensis canadensis and certain related subspecies

MINIMUM SCORE 180

Score	Length of Horn R	L	Circumference of Base R	L	Circumference at Third Quarter R	L	Greatest Spread	Tip to Tip Spread	Locality	Hunter	Owner	Date Killed	Rank
208 3/8	47 4/8	46 5/8	15 7/8	15 7/8	12	11 3/8	23 1/8	23 1/8	Luscar Mt., AB	Guinn D. Crousen	Guinn D. Crousen	2000	1
208 1/8	44 7/8	45	16 5/8	16 5/8	11 2/8	11 7/8	22 6/8	19 3/8	Blind Canyon, AB	Fred Weiller	Clarence Baird	1911	2
207 2/8	45	45 2/8	15 6/8	16	11 6/8	11 7/8	23 1/8	19 3/8	Oyster Creek, AB	Martin K. Bovey	Aly M. Bruner	1924	3
206 3/8	44 4/8	44 3/8	15 7/8	15 7/8	12 1/8	12 1/8	21 4/8	21 4/8	Burnt Timber Creek, AB	Picked Up	Gordon L. Magnussen	1955	4
206 3/8	43 1/8	41 6/8	17 1/8	16 7/8	11 4/8	11 7/8	23 4/8	18 6/8	Granite Co., MT	James R. Weatherly	James R. Weatherly	1993	5
204 7/8	49 4/8	48 2/8	15 2/8	15 3/8	10 5/8	10 2/8	23 7/8	23 7/8	Sheep River, BC	James Simpson	Am. Mus. Nat. Hist.	1920	6
204	43 2/8	41 5/8	17 2/8	17 4/8	11 3/8	10 2/8	20 7/8	23 4/8	Beaverhead Co., MT	Picked Up Wildl., & Parks	MT Dept. of Fish,	1992	7
203 5/8	43 1/8	42 5/8	16 4/8	16 4/8	11 3/8	11 1/8	25 4/8	19 4/8	Sheep River, AB	Katherine A. Pyra	Katherine A. Pyra	1992	8
203 4/8	41	40 7/8	17 2/8	17 2/8	11	11	26 2/8	25 3/8	Granite Co., MT	Richard B. Wiant	D.J. Hollinger & B. Howard	1992	9
202 3/8	46 7/8	44 5/8	15 5/8	15 5/8	10 6/8	11	23 2/8	23 3/8	Panther River, AB	Tom Kerquits	Unknown	1918	10
202 2/8	45	44 7/8	15 6/8	15 6/8	11 6/8	11 5/8	24 6/8	24 1/8	Leyland Mt., AB	Guinn D. Crousen	Guinn D. Crousen	2001	11
202 1/8	46 5/8	45 1/8	15 2/8	15 3/8	10 4/8	10 4/8	22 6/8	22 5/8	Canmore, AB	Picked Up	AB Fish & Wildl. Div.	1987	12
202	43 2/8	42 4/8	16 3/8	16 3/8	10 7/8	10 7/8	22 3/8	17 6/8	Nikanassin Range, AB	Larry Strawson	Cabela's, Inc.	1997	13
201 2/8	44	43 7/8	15 5/8	15 5/8	11 3/8	11 4/8	25	25	Jasper, AB	Picked Up	A.H. Hilbert	1932	14
201 1/8	49 2/8	44 5/8	15 2/8	15 1/8	9 4/8	9 2/8	26 2/8	25 6/8	Cross River, BC	David L. Onerheim	David L. Onerheim	1987	14
201 1/8	43 6/8	43 3/8	16 5/8	16 7/8	9	9 2/8	22 5/8	20 3/8	Fernie, BC	H.J. Johnson	Royal Ontario Mus.	1902	16
200 7/8	45 7/8	49 2/8	15 2/8	15 2/8	9 1/8	9 1/8	28 5/8	28 5/8	Deer Lodge Co., MT	Lester A. Kish	Lester A. Kish	1990	16
200 7/8	44	44 7/8	17	16 7/8	8 6/8	9 6/8	26 1/8	25 7/8	Sanders Co., MT	Jack M. Greenwood	Jack M. Greenwood	2001	16
200 7/8	44	44 7/8	16 7/8	16 7/8	9 6/8	9 6/8	23 7/8	23 7/8	Blaine Co., MT	Eugene R. Knight	Eugene R. Knight	1991	19
200 2/8	42 4/8	43 6/8	15 1/8	15 2/8	11 6/8	10 7/8	23	23	Brazeau River, AB	Unknown	Norman Lougheed	1937	20
200 1/8	44 3/8	44	16 3/8	16 3/8	11 3/8	11 3/8	22 2/8	18 5/8	Alberta	Picked Up	Otis Chandler	1955	20
200 1/8	40 4/8	41 3/8	16 1/8	16 2/8	10 4/8	10 1/8	23 3/8	22 6/8	Granite Co., MT	Mavis M. Lorenz	Mavis M. Lorenz	1993	20
200 1/8	44	44 1/8	16 3/8	16 6/8	10 7/8	12	20 5/8	19 3/8	Jarvis Creek, AB	Picked Up	Robert E. Sonnenberg	2002	20
200 1/8	40 4/8	42 1/8	16 3/8	16 5/8	10 7/8	10 7/8	26 6/8	26 2/8	Fergus Co., MT	David J. Nygard	David J. Nygard	2003	25
200	44 3/8	41 6/8	16 3/8	15	11 2/8	9 4/8	22	19 6/8	Wind River Range, WY	Mr. Crawford	Duncan G. Weibel	1883	26
199 6/8	42 6/8	43 6/8	16 4/8	16 2/8	11 4/8	9 7/8	22 7/8	21 6/8	Granite Co., MT	Kevin E. Williams	Kevin E. Williams	1993	27
199 3/8	42 4/8	45 3/8	16	16	9 4/8	10	22 2/8	20 6/8	Sanders Co., MT	Michael D. Turner	Michael D. Turner	1992	27
199 2/8	42 6/8	42 4/8	17 3/8	17 2/8	9 2/8	9 4/8	25 5/8	25 2/8	Granite Co., MT	Marvin C. Skinner	Marvin C. Skinner	1995	28
199 1/8	43 5/8	42 4/8	16	16	10 1/8	10	22 2/8	22 2/8	Salmo, BC	Picked Up	Municipality of Trail, BC	1993	29
199	45	45 4/8	15 1/8	15	10 3/8	10 6/8	22 5/8	22 5/8	Spences Bridge, BC	Picked Up	Parliament Bldg., BC	1969	30
198 6/8	43 4/8	43 6/8	15 4/8	15 4/8	10 7/8	11 3/8	24 6/8	24 6/8	Alberta	Bill Foster	Foster's Bighorn Rest.	PR 1947	31
198 1/8	42 4/8	41 3/8	15 6/8	15 6/8	12	11 3/8	23 3/8	23 3/8	Saskatchewan Lake, AB	Herb Klein	Dallas Mus. of Natl. Hist.	1965	32
198	42 4/8	43 4/8	16 5/8	16 5/8	10	9 4/8	25	18 4/8	Wallowa Co., OR	Todd B. Jaksick	Todd B. Jaksick	1988	33
197 7/8	43 2/8	42 7/8	14 7/8	15	11 4/8	11 5/8	21 6/8	21 2/8	Wallowa Co., OR	Daniel R. Schwenk	OR Dept. of Fish & Wildl.	1986	34
197 7/8	42 5/8	42 6/8	16 4/8	16 4/8	9 4/8	9 5/8	23 4/8	23 1/8	Sanders Co., MT	Picked Up	Daniel R. Schwenk	1992	34
197 7/8	45 4/8	45	15 4/8	15 4/8	9 2/8	9 3/8	24 1/8	21 2/8	Nez Perce Co., ID	Picked Up	Bob Landrus	1996	34
197 7/8	41	39 7/8	16 4/8	16 5/8	10 6/8	11 5/8	22 2/8	15	Costilla Co., CO	West Ward	West Ward	1998	34

Score									Locality	Hunter	Owner	Date	Rank
197 6/8	44 6/8	42	16	16 1/8	10 2/8	9 6/8	23	23 7/8	Sanders Co., MT	Steven M. Inabnit	Steven M. Inabnit	1995	38
197 5/8	41 1/8	42 4/8	15 7/8	16 1/8	11 1/8	11	22 3/8	22 3/8	Deer Lodge Co., MT	Arthur R. Dubs	Arthur R. Dubs	1987	39
197 3/8	44 7/8	43 4/8	14 6/8	14 6/8	11 1/8	10 6/8	23 4/8	18 3/8	Alberta	Bill Foster	Foster's Bighorn Rest.	PR 1947	40
197 2/8	39 1/8	42 3/8	17	17	9 5/8	9 6/8	23 4/8	20	East Kootenay, BC	Picked Up	Victoria Fish & Game Assn.	PR 1930	41
197 1/8	44 3/8	45 4/8	15 7/8	15 5/8	8 5/8	9 4/8	28 7/8	28 7/8	Sanders Co., MT	Armand H. Johnson	Armand H. Johnson	1979	42
197 1/8	42	41 5/8	16 5/8	16 4/8	10 5/8	10 6/8	23 5/8	23 2/8	Granite Co., MT	Lee Hart	Lee Hart	1990	42
197 1/8	41 2/8	40 7/8	16 6/8	16 6/8	10 4/8	10 2/8	20 7/8	18 4/8	Granite Co., MT	Mary E. Schroeder	Mary E. Schroeder	1992	42
197 1/8	41 1/8	41 1/8	16 3/8	16 2/8	10 1/8	9 6/8	23 1/8	18 2/8	Costilla Co., CO	Renee Snider	Renee Snider	2000	42
196 7/8	43	40 4/8	17 4/8	17 3/8	10	9 7/8	23 2/8	18 1/8	Yarrow Creek, AB	George W. Biron	George W. Biron	1968	46
196 7/8	41 2/8	40 7/8	16 3/8	16 2/8	9 7/8	10 1/8	20 2/8	20	Granite Co., MT	Keith J. Koprivica	Keith J. Koprivica	1990	46
196 6/8	45 2/8	44 2/8	16 4/8	16 4/8	9 7/8	10 1/8	22 3/8	20	Badlands, ND	Howard Eaton	Richard K. Mellon	1880	48
196 6/8	41 5/8	41 3/8	16 1/8	16 1/8	9 3/8	8 7/8	23	19 4/8	Wardner, BC	Jim Buss	Jim Buss	1961	48
196 5/8	39 5/8	41 6/8	16 2/8	16	10 7/8	10 6/8	22 2/8	20	Brazeau River, AB	Donald S. Hopkins	Donald S. Hopkins	1924	50
196 5/8	45 2/8	44 3/8	16	16	11 4/8	10 5/8	21 2/8	19 1/8	Alberta	Bill Foster	Foster's Bighorn Rest.	1938	50
196 5/8	40 6/8	40 2/8	14 5/8	14 6/8	10 4/8	10 4/8	24 4/8	24 3/8	Sun River, MT	Don Anderson	Don Anderson	1961	50
196 4/8	40 4/8	45	15 4/8	15 4/8	12	12	24	19 2/8	Badlands Natl. Park, SD	Picked Up	SD Game, Fish, & Parks Dept.	1984	53
196 4/8	43 7/8	42 4/8	16	16	10 1/8	10 5/8	24 2/8	21 4/8	Silver Bow Co., MT	Verne O. Barnett	Verne O. Barnett	1991	53
196 4/8	42 4/8	42 4/8	16	16 1/8	11 5/8	11 4/8	22 7/8	22 7/8	Cadomin, AB	Rick Stelter	Rick Stelter	1996	53
196 2/8	44 6/8	43 6/8	16 2/8	16 2/8	10	9 5/8	21 5/8	16 5/8	Highwood, AB	Joseph F. Kubasek	Joseph F. Kubasek	1953	56
196 2/8	44 7/8	44 3/8	14 7/8	14 7/8	11	11 2/8	22 7/8	22 1/8	Sanders Co., MT	Earl V. Cole	Earl V. Cole	1993	56
196	45 3/8	44 3/8	15 5/8	15 7/8	10 3/8	9 1/8	16 5/8	16 5/8	Cadomin, AB	Al Leary	Al Leary	1962	58
196	45 4/8	44 3/8	15 5/8	15 6/8	7 7/8	9 2/8	16 6/8	15 6/8	Nez Perce Co., ID	Richard N. Aznaran	Richard N. Aznaran	1994	58
195 7/8	45	45	16 1/8	16	8 6/8	9 2/8	15 6/8	15 6/8	Montana	Unknown	Dole & Bailey, Inc.	1890	60
195 7/8	41	41 4/8	15 4/8	15 4/8	8 3/8	8 3/8	16 2/8	16 1/8	Lewis & Clark Co., MT	Steven J. King	Steven J. King	2001	60
195 6/8	41 5/8	40 2/8	16 2/8	16 3/8	10	10	27 1/8	26 4/8	Line Creek, BC	Danny Whiting	Danny Whiting	1994	62
195 5/8	40 2/8	43 6/8	16 5/8	16 3/8	11 3/8	10 4/8	23	22 7/8	Castle River, AB	R.E. Woodward	R.E. Woodward	1965	63
195 4/8	43	41	14 7/8	14 7/8	11 1/8	11	23	19 4/8	Bow River, AB	Native American	N.K. Luxton	1890	64
195 4/8	46 2/8	42	16 3/8	16 1/8	9	9	29 4/8	29 6/8	Deer Lodge Co., MT	Thomas J. Matosich	Thomas J. Matosich	1986	64
195 4/8	42	43 4/8	15 6/8	15 6/8	10 1/8	9	26	25 3/8	Fergus Co., MT	Patricia A. Slivka	Patricia A. Slivka	2001	64
195 3/8	42 3/8	42 4/8	15 7/8	15 7/8	10 1/8	10 1/8	22 7/8	20 7/8	West Sundre, AB	Jim Neeser	Jim Neeser	1961	67
195 3/8	44 5/8	43 4/8	15 4/8	15 4/8	10 4/8	9	24 7/8	23 2/8	Missoula Co., MT	Leonard G. Thompson	Leonard G. Thompson	1990	67
195 3/8	40 4/8	40 4/8	16 3/8	16 1/8	10 2/8	10 2/8	22 7/8	21 3/8	Granite Co., MT	Craig R. Johnson	Craig R. Johnson	1994	67
195 2/8	41 4/8	41 7/8	15 7/8	15 7/8	10 3/8	10 3/8	22 7/8	20 7/8	Taos Co., NM	Greg Koons	Greg Koons	2003	70
195	44 2/8	42 2/8	16 4/8	16 3/8	11	11	22 7/8	26 7/8	Sun River, MT	Gold White	B&C National Collection	1911	71
195	41 6/8	42 3/8	16 3/8	16 4/8	11 6/8	11 6/8	26 7/8	26 7/8	Huerfano Co., CO	Donald W. Snyder	Donald W. Snyder	2000	71
195	42 4/8	38 4/8	16 3/8	16 3/8	10 4/8	10 4/8	24 3/8	17	Taos Co., NM	Jennifer L. Chapel	Jennifer L. Chapel	2002	71
194 7/8	40 4/8	42 4/8	15 3/8	15 3/8	11 2/8	11 2/8	24 1/8	20 4/8	Ram River, AB	G.M. De Witt	G.M. De Witt	1944	74
194 7/8	42	41 6/8	16 2/8	16 2/8	10 3/8	10 3/8	23 1/8	19 6/8	Granite Co., MT	Rick L. Barkell	Rick L. Barkell	1992	74
194 6/8	40 4/8	41 3/8	15 1/8	15 3/8	10 7/8	10 5/8	23 1/8	22 4/8	Storm Mt., AB	Bryan M. Watts	Bryan M. Watts	1957	76
194 3/8	44 2/8	41 3/8	15 7/8	15 7/8	10 6/8	10 4/8	20 5/8	20	Sheep River, AB	Picked Up	Harry McElroy	1966	77
194 3/8	45 2/8	44	15 3/8	15 4/8	10 4/8	10 5/8	22 4/8	17 4/8	Beaverhead Co., MT	Glenn M. Smith	Glenn M. Smith	1992	77
194 2/8	42 7/8	43 1/8	14 7/8	15	10 3/8	9 7/8	22 4/8	20 6/8	Panther River, AB	Picked Up	N.K. Luxton	1930	79
194 2/8	41 4/8	43 2/8	15 7/8	15 6/8	10 2/8	9 7/8	21 4/8	21 4/8	Cadomin, AB	Al D. Kuffner	Al D. Kuffner	1994	79
194 2/8	42 2/8	40 5/8	15 6/8	15 6/8	9 6/8	10	20 7/8	18 7/8	Broadwater Co., MT	Bud Breining	Bud Breining	2003	79
194 1/8	44	42 6/8	16	16	10 1/8	10	24 3/8	18 1/8	Nez Perce Co., ID	George R. Harms	George R. Harms	1995	82
194	37 6/8	42 6/8	14 4/8	14 4/8	10 6/8	10 6/8	22 3/8	21 2/8	Alberta	Bill Foster	Foster's Bighorn Rest.	PR 1947	83
194	39 4/8	38 4/8	17	17 1/8	10 3/8	10 6/8	23 3/8	22 3/8	Fergus Co., MT	Donald R. Hecht	Donald R. Hecht	1998	83
193 6/8	39 4/8	42 4/8	16 2/8	16 2/8	9 4/8	9 4/8	22 1/8	16 7/8	Yarrow Creek, AB	F.H. Riggall	F.H. Riggall	1906	85

BIGHORN SHEEP

Ovis canadensis canadensis and certain related subspecies

Score	Length of Horn R	L	Circumference of Base R	L	Circumference at Third Quarter R	L	Greatest Spread	Tip to Tip Spread	Locality	Hunter	Owner	Date Killed	Rank
193 6/8	41	42	16	16	10 5/8	10 2/8	24	18 1/8	Cameron Pass, CO	F. Cotter	Herbert J. Havemann	1954	85
193 6/8	40 5/8	40 5/8	15 4/8	15 4/8	10 6/8	10 6/8	22 1/8	17 4/8	Tornado Pass, BC	John Stuber	John Stuber	1956	85
193 6/8	40 4/8	39 6/8	16 5/8	16 4/8	9 7/8	9 7/8	23 7/8	22 7/8	Granite Co., MT	Michael L. Girard	Michael L. Girard	1986	85
193 6/8	40 2/8	42	15 6/8	15 7/8	11 1/8	10 6/8	22 6/8	20 1/8	Granite Co., MT	Kenneth L. Getz	Kenneth L. Getz	1992	85
193 6/8	40 6/8	41 4/8	16 5/8	16 4/8	9 6/8	9 5/8	23 3/8	22 6/8	Granite Co., MT	Rex V. Blackwell	Rex V. Blackwell	1997	85
193 6/8	40 6/8	41 2/8	15 4/8	15 4/8	10 4/8	10 4/8	22 4/8	19 4/8	Sheep River, AB	Gary H. Cain	Gary H. Cain	1990	91
193 5/8	43 1/8	41 2/8	16 3/8	16 3/8	8 3/8	8 4/8	23	23	Lincoln Co., MT	Al Bratkovich	Al Bratkovich	1993	91
193 5/8	42 2/8	43 3/8	16 4/8	16 1/8	10 6/8	10	22 7/8	22 2/8	Granite Co., MT	Eric W. Burdette	Eric W. Burdette	2000	91
193 5/8	39 6/8	41 1/8	16 1/8	15 2/8	11 7/8	11 5/8	20 5/8	15 4/8	Wallowa Co., OR	Picked Up	OR Dept. of Fish & Wildlife	2002	91
193 5/8	40 2/8	39 5/8	15 2/8	16 3/8	10 6/8	10 7/8	26 7/8	23 2/8	Silver Bow Co., MT	Thomas R. Webster	Thomas R. Webster	1990	95
193 4/8	39	39 4/8	16 4/8	15 7/8	10 2/8	10	22 3/8	17 1/8	Coleman, AB	George Hagglund	George Hagglund	1952	96
193 3/8	42 1/8	40 4/8	15 5/8	16 4/8	10	10	22 4/8	19 1/8	Sanders Co., MT	Jerry Landa	Jerry Landa	1989	97
193 2/8	39 7/8	39 7/8	16 4/8	16	9	8 7/8	23 2/8	20	Luscar Mt., AB	Marion McLean	Marion McLean	1994	97
193 2/8	42 2/8	42 6/8	16	16	9 7/8	10 1/8	21 7/8	21 7/8	Spences Bridge, BC	M. Da Rosa	M. Da Rosa	1961	99
193 1/8	44 5/8	42 4/8	15 1/8	15 2/8	9 7/8	10 1/8	23 6/8	21 4/8	Missoula Co., MT	Bonnie A. Ford	Bonnie A. Ford	1982	99
193 1/8	41 7/8	43 4/8	15 1/8	15 5/8	9 7/8	9 7/8	19 7/8	15	Ewin Creek, BC	Gary N. Goode	Carl Iacona	1989	99
193 1/8	40 1/8	39 2/8	16 3/8	16 4/8	10 3/8	10 3/8	23 5/8	23	Fergus Co., MT	Joan L. Gallentine	Joan L. Gallentine	2002	99
193 1/8	38 6/8	41 1/8	16	16	10 2/8	10 4/8	22 1/8	22 1/8	Spences Bridge, BC	Norman Holland	Norman Holland	1971	103
193	43 1/8	43 5/8	14 6/8	14 4/8	10 1/8	9 7/8	22 1/8	21 7/8	Granite Co., MT	Phillip S. Benson	Phillip S. Benson	1992	103
193	39 2/8	41 2/8	16 3/8	16 2/8	9 6/8	9 7/8	23	21 3/8	Granite Co., MT	Raymond J. Dvorak	Raymond J. Dvorak	1989	105
192 7/8	40 6/8	41 3/8	16 2/8	16 2/8	10	9 5/8	21 3/8	21 3/8	Clearwater, AB	Edward L. Fuchs	Edward L. Fuchs	1943	106
192 6/8	44 6/8	43 2/8	14 2/8	14 2/8	10 7/8	11 1/8	22 1/8	22 1/8	Wallowa Co., OR	Bryan C. Bailey	Bryan C. Bailey	1998	106
192 6/8	38 4/8	42 4/8	16 7/8	17	9	9 2/8	24 4/8	24 4/8	Sun River, MT	Leyton Z. Yearout	Leyton Z. Yearout	1963	108
192 5/8	42 7/8	44 3/8	14 3/8	14 3/8	10 3/8	10 6/8	24	24	Clearwater River, AB	Unknown	James Allan	1977	108
192 5/8	39 5/8	41 4/8	15 6/8	15 4/8	11 4/8	11 4/8	21 2/8	17 4/8	Mt. Gregg, AB	Eric Satre	Eric Satre	1992	110
192 4/8	38 4/8	41 2/8	16 1/8	16 1/8	10 6/8	10 4/8	22	18 6/8	Granite Co., MT	James E. Ratcliffe	James E. Ratcliffe	1999	110
192 4/8	41 3/8	41 5/8	15 7/8	15 6/8	10 4/8	10	23	22 2/8	Alberta	Henry Graves, Jr.	Unknown	PR 1931	112
192 3/8	40 7/8	40 7/8	15 6/8	15 4/8	10 5/8	11 3/8	22 7/8	18 4/8	Granite Co., MT	Robert L. Sandman	Robert L. Sandman	1991	112
192 3/8	40 6/8	42 4/8	15 4/8	15 5/8	10 5/8	10 5/8	20 5/8	17 6/8	Teton Co., MT	Darwin T. Scott	Darwin T. Scott	1995	112
192 3/8	42 4/8	42 3/8	16 2/8	16 1/8	8 4/8	8 5/8	22 2/8	21 6/8	Sanders Co., MT	Richard W. Browne	Richard W. Browne	1968	115
192 2/8	45 2/8	43	16	16	8 6/8	8 3/8	21	21	Sanders Co., MT	Michael A. Jorgenson	Michael A. Jorgenson	1978	115
192 2/8	40 5/8	40 5/8	16 7/8	16 7/8	9 2/8	9 1/8	22	17 6/8	Granite Co., MT	John P. Steele	John P. Steele	1991	115
192 2/8	43 3/8	41 7/8	16 2/8	16 2/8	8 4/8	8 6/8	22 2/8	21 3/8	Sanders Co., MT	Charles M. LaRance	Dale Manning	1995	115
192 2/8	40 7/8	40 1/8	17 1/8	17 1/8	9 1/8	8 1/8	22	21 3/8	Nez Perce Co., ID	Paul Koslowski	Paul Koslowski	2001	115
192 2/8	40 2/8	42 4/8	16 6/8	16 5/8	8 6/8	8 6/8	20 6/8	18 1/8	Deer Lodge Co., MT	Mitchell A. Thorson	Mitchell A. Thorson	1987	120
192 1/8	42 7/8	42 4/8	16	16 2/8	9 1/8	8 6/8	22 4/8	19 1/8	Fergus Co., MT	John Benes	John Benes	1997	120
192 1/8	41	40 5/8	15 7/8	15 6/8	10 1/8	10 4/8	21 7/8	21 2/8	Fergus Co., MT	George R. Harms	George R. Harms	1998	120
192 1/8	36 6/8	37 5/8	16 2/8	16 2/8	12	11 5/8	26 4/8	24	Fergus Co., MT	George R. Harms	George R. Harms	1998	120
192 1/8	41 4/8	41 1/8	15 3/8	15 4/8	10 6/8	10 3/8	21 3/8	16 3/8	Luscar Mt., AB	William C. Cloyd	William C. Cloyd	2000	120

Score							Locality	By whom taken	Owner	Date	Rank
192	41 6/8	15 1/8	15	10 3/8	10	21 5/8 · 20 1/8	Narrow Creek, AB	Henry Mitchell	Henry Mitchell	1910	124
192	43 3/8	15 5/8	15 6/8	9 6/8	9	24 2/8 · 24 2/8	Wallowa Co., OR	H. James Tonkin, Jr.	H. James Tonkin, Jr.	1991	124
192	41 3/8	15 6/8	15 7/8	9 3/8	9 2/8	20 1/8 · 20 1/8	Granite Co., MT	Greg A. Stavish	Greg A. Stavish	1999	124
191 7/8	40 4/8	15	15	11 6/8	11 1/8	23 3/8 · 21 4/8	Lake Co., CO	Emory Whilton	Kern Co. CA Mus.	1901	127
191 7/8	44	15 3/8	15 3/8	8 7/8	9 6/8	24 4/8 · 22 2/8	Lake Co., MT	Picked Up	Philip L. Wright Zool. Mus.	1961	127
191 7/8	41 6/8	15 3/8	15 3/8	8 7/8	9 6/8	22 4/8 · 22	Alberta	Clarence Hardy	Russel Vanslett	PR 1961	127
191 7/8	41 3/8	16	16	10 1/8	10 1/8	24 · 24	Granite Co., MT	Steven L. Gingras	Steven L. Gingras	1984	127
191 7/8	41 3/8	15 7/8	15 7/8	9 5/8	8 6/8	24 3/8 · 21 7/8	Missoula Co., MT	Carl W. Schmidt	Carl W. Schmidt	1989	127
191 7/8	39 5/8	16	16	9 4/8	9 7/8	24 3/8 · 21 2/8	Granite Co., MT	Dale E. Garrison	Dale E. Garrison	1996	127
191 7/8	41 4/8	16 6/8	16	10 2/8	10 2/8	21 2/8 · 18 2/8	Sanders Co., MT	Michael L. Knaff	Michael L. Knaff	1996	127
191 6/8	40	16 6/8	16 5/8	8 4/8	8 3/8	21 4/8 · 20 6/8	Smoky River, AB	Picked Up	Carl M. Borgh	1944	134
191 6/8	41 7/8	15 5/8	15 5/8	10 3/8	9 7/8	23 3/8 · 22 6/8	Silver Bow Co., MT	James G. Dennehy	James G. Dennehy	1992	134
191 6/8	41 6/8	16 1/8	16	9	9 1/8	25 · 23 6/8	Missoula Co., MT	Shelley Goodman	Shelley Goodman	1993	134
191 6/8	43 4/8	16 2/8	16 3/8	8 5/8	8 4/8	24 5/8 · 20 4/8	Granite Co., MT	Blair G. McGavin	Blair G. McGavin	1995	134
191 6/8	40 4/8	14 6/8	14 6/8	9 2/8	9 4/8	23 2/8 · 20 4/8	Fergus Co., MT	Randy C. Orley	Randy C. Orley	2000	134
191 6/8	39 2/8	16 3/8	16 3/8	8 4/8	8 5/8	21 7/8 · 21 5/8	Pennington Co., SD	Scott E. Vander Meulen	Scott E. Vander Meulen	2000	134
191 5/8	40 2/8	16 3/8	16 3/8	9 7/8	9 5/8	23 4/8 · 16 1/8	Dinwoody Creek, WY	Oris Miller	Oris Miller	1954	140
191 4/8	42 3/8	14 6/8	14 6/8	10 1/8	10 2/8	22 1/8 · 15	Lincoln Co., MT	Picked Up	Ed Boyes	PR 1961	141
191 4/8	44 3/8	15 7/8	16	9 7/8	9 3/8	22 6/8 · 20 3/8	Wallowa Co., OR	Sam S. Jaksick, Jr.	Sam S. Jaksick, Jr.	1987	141
191 4/8	41 5/8	16	16	10 1/8	10 1/8	23 6/8 · 25 6/8	Missoula Co., MT	Roy R. Wickman	Roy R. Wickman	1994	141
191 4/8	40 7/8	15 5/8	16	10 4/8	10 4/8	26 · 17	Line Creek, BC	Stephen Babijowski	Stephen Babijowski	1996	141
191 3/8	40 7/8	15	15 4/8	10 5/8	10 4/8	20 5/8 · 20 7/8	Canada	Unknown	A.H. Hilbert	PR 1930	145
191 3/8	42 3/8	16 1/8	16 1/8	10 7/8	10 6/8	22 1/8 · 15 2/8	Natal, BC	John A. Morais	John A. Morais	1960	145
191 3/8	39 6/8	16 1/8	16 1/8	10 6/8	10 4/8	21 4/8 · 18 3/8	Cadomin, AB	Tony Oney	Tony Oney	1966	145
191 3/8	40	15 7/8	15 7/8	10 4/8	10 3/8	21 · 19	Sanders Co., MT	Robert A. Larsson	Robert A. Larsson	1994	145
191 2/8	41 5/8	15 3/8	15 3/8	10 5/8	10 5/8	22 · 20 5/8	Brazeau River, AB	Donald S. Hopkins	Donald S. Hopkins	1937	149
191 2/8	45 6/8	15 2/8	15 2/8	7 7/8	7 7/8	24 5/8 · 24 5/8	Grassmere, BC	Donald F. Letcher	Donald F. Letcher	1965	149
191 2/8	42	14 4/8	14 5/8	10 6/8	10 6/8	22 1/8 · 19 4/8	Leyland Mt., AB	Rick J. Tymchuk	Rick J. Tymchuk	1982	149
191 2/8	39 5/8	16 1/8	16 1/8	10 4/8	10 5/8	22 1/8 · 21 4/8	Sanders Co., MT	Charles V. Gordon	Charles V. Gordon	1993	149
191 2/8	39 6/8	15 6/8	15 6/8	9 7/8	9 7/8	23 · 23	Fording River, BC	Ryan D. Jones	Ryan D. Jones	1993	149
191 2/8	39 6/8	15 2/8	15 2/8	10	10	23 1/8 · 16 4/8	Huerfano Co., CO	Timothy K. Rushing	Timothy K. Rushing	1997	149
191 2/8	40 1/8	15 3/8	15 3/8	11	10 7/8	19 6/8 · 18 3/8	Cadomin, AB	Frank Nuspel	Frank Nuspel	1962	149
191 1/8	39 3/8	15 4/8	15 4/8	9 6/8	10	22 · 25 1/8	Castle River, AB	Picked Up	E.B. Cunningham	PR 1967	155
191 1/8	43 2/8	16	16	10 7/8	11 1/8	25 1/8 · 21 6/8	Wolverine Creek, AB	James R. Gaines	James R. Gaines	1990	155
191 1/8	44	15 7/8	15 7/8	8 2/8	8 1/8	21 6/8 · 18	Sheep River, AB	Harvey Pyra	Harvey Pyra	1991	155
191 1/8	40 4/8	15 3/8	15 4/8	9	9	22 5/8 · 22 5/8	Kvass Creek, AB	Joseph W. Dent	Joseph W. Dent	1962	155
191	40	16 5/8	16 5/8	9 1/8	11	24 · 21 1/8	Granite Co., MT	Harry W. Miller	Harry W. Miller	1985	159
191	39 4/8	16 1/8	16	9 6/8	9 6/8	21 1/8 · 22 2/8	Sanders Co., MT	Lenora L. Liberty	Lenora L. Liberty	1995	159
191	43 3/8	16	15 7/8	9 5/8	9 5/8	22 5/8 · 21 1/8	Cardinal River, AB	Eugene Kirk	Eugene Kirk	1997	159
191	39 6/8	15 7/8	16	9 4/8	9 6/8	23 4/8 · 22 5/8	Sanders Co., MT	Teresa L. Stoneman	Teresa L. Stoneman	1988	159
190 7/8	42 5/8	15 4/8	15 4/8	9 7/8	9 7/8	25 2/8 · 23 4/8	Lewis & Clark Co., MT	Rodney H. Eaton	Rodney H. Eaton	1992	163
190 7/8	39 1/8	16 5/8	16 5/8	9 3/8	9 3/8	23 4/8 · 25 7/8	Apache Co., AZ	Jeffery P. Augustine	Jeffery P. Augustine	1995	163
190 7/8	43	14 4/8	14 3/8	10 1/8	10 2/8	25 7/8 · 23 3/8	Park Co., MT	Craig Kamps	Craig Kamps	2003	163
190 6/8	42 4/8	14 7/8	15	9 1/8	9 1/8	23 3/8 · 22	Fernie, BC	J.J. Osman	J.J. Osman	1950	163
190 6/8	37 1/8	16 7/8	16 7/8	11	11 1/8	22 · 25 6/8	Elko, BC	Charles Weikert	Charles Weikert	1970	167
190 6/8	42 3/8	15 5/8	15 5/8	8 7/8	8 7/8	25 5/8 · 23 3/8	Missoula Co., MT	Arthur R. Dubs	Arthur R. Dubs	1986	167
190 6/8	40 6/8	15 7/8	15 7/8	9 7/8	10 3/8	23 · 24 7/8	Granite Co., MT	Scott A. Campbell	Scott A. Campbell	1990	167
190 6/8	41 1/8	15 7/8	15 7/8	9 2/8	9 4/8	24 7/8 · 22 2/8	Sanders Co., MT	H. Gene Warren	H. Gene Warren	1991	167

BIGHORN SHEEP

Ovis canadensis canadensis and certain related subspecies

Score	Length of Horn R	L	Circumference of Base R	L	Circumference at Third Quarter R	L	Greatest Spread	Tip to Tip Spread	Locality	Hunter	Owner	Date Killed	Rank
190 6/8	40 2/8	41 4/8	15 2/8	15 2/8	10	10 1/8	22	20 3/8	Gregg River, AB	Mike Wasylyshen	Mike Wasylyshen	1994	167
190 6/8	40 3/8	40 5/8	15 7/8	16	9 4/8	9 5/8	24	23 2/8	Sanders Co., MT	Timothy B. Johnston	Timothy B. Johnston	1995	167
190 6/8	43 4/8	40 2/8	16	16 2/8	9 3/8	8 2/8	24	23 7/8	Fergus Co., MT	David E. Buschena	David E. Buschena	1998	167
190 5/8	41 5/8	39 4/8	17	16 7/8	8 6/8	9	23 4/8	16 7/8	Brazeau River, AB	Julio Estrada	Julio Estrada	1936	175
190 5/8	43 5/8	43 2/8	15 6/8	15 5/8	8 6/8	8 4/8	24 5/8	24 5/8	Missoula Co., MT	John J. Ottman	John J. Ottman	1985	175
190 5/8	40 4/8	42 5/8	15 6/8	16 1/8	9 2/8	9 2/8	24 2/8	23 4/8	Missoula Co., MT	Chris L. Mostad	Chris L. Mostad	1986	175
190 5/8	40 2/8	40 1/8	16	16	9 4/8	9 4/8	25 2/8	19 2/8	Asotin Co., WA	Picked Up	WA Dept. of Fish & Wildl.	1995	175
190 5/8	38 6/8	39 5/8	15 6/8	16	10 5/8	10 4/8	23	20 5/8	Blaine Co., MT	Wilbur J. Helzer	Wilbur J. Helzer	1996	175
190 5/8	41 1/8	41 2/8	14 3/8	14 2/8	12	11 7/8	21	17	Taos Co., NM	Donald E. Wenner	Donald E. Wenner	1996	175
190 5/8	39 1/8	40 4/8	15 2/8	15 2/8	10 3/8	10	25	18 4/8	Missoula Co., MT	Picked Up	Lolo Natl. Forest	1998	175
190 5/8	42 6/8	41 1/8	16 1/8	16 1/8	8 7/8	8 4/8	23	22 6/8	Granite Co., MT	Mark A. Donovan	Mark A. Donovan	1999	175
190 5/8	41 2/8	41 5/8	15 6/8	15 5/8	9 5/8	10 1/8	21 4/8	20 5/8	Taos Co., NM	Rick C. Hooley	Rick C. Hooley	2002	175
190 4/8	42 2/8	40 6/8	16 1/8	16 1/8	9 6/8	8 7/8	24 3/8	24 3/8	Silver Bow Co., MT	James A. Barnett	James A. Barnett	1990	184
190 4/8	40 6/8	41 6/8	14 5/8	14 6/8	11 1/8	11 3/8	19 4/8	19	Berry's Creek, AB	Bernard A. Fiedeldey, Jr.	Bernard A. Fiedeldey, Jr.	1996	184
190 3/8	46 3/8	40	15 1/8	15 1/8	8 4/8	8 3/8	22 6/8	22 6/8	Highwood, AB	Nick Sekella	Nick Sekella	1953	186
190 3/8	39 2/8	39 1/8	16	16	10 4/8	10 3/8	21 7/8	21 7/8	Sun River, MT	F.P. Murray	F.P. Murray	1957	186
190 2/8	39 2/8	37 6/8	16 5/8	16 4/8	10 2/8	9 7/8	22 4/8	18 1/8	Sanders Co., MT	Duane Dauenhauer	Duane Dauenhauer	1992	188
190 2/8	39 2/8	44 6/8	14 7/8	14 5/8	9 4/8	9 2/8	23 3/8	22 5/8	Sanders Co., MT	Scott W. Johnson	Scott W. Johnson	1994	188
190 2/8	39 7/8	44 5/8	16 1/8	16 1/8	8 6/8	8 7/8	25 4/8	24 3/8	Sanders Co., MT	S. Douglas Shear	S. Douglas Shear	1999	188
190 1/8	41 6/8	40 3/8	15 7/8	15 7/8	9 2/8	9 2/8	23 4/8	21	Missoula Co., MT	Joseph C. Turner	Joseph C. Turner	1987	191
190 1/8	39 3/8	41	15 6/8	15 6/8	10	10	24	17 4/8	Nez Perce Co., ID	Gary E. Hansen	Gary E. Hansen	1996	191
190	40	39 6/8	15 4/8	15 4/8	10 5/8	10 5/8	22 1/8	14	Alberta	Native American	Acad. Nat. Sci., Phil.	1901	193
190	40 7/8	39 7/8	15 1/8	15 1/8	10 2/8	10 3/8	19 4/8	19 4/8	Brazeau River, AB	Donald S. Hopkins	Acad. Nat. Sci., Phil.	1927	193
190	40 5/8	40 1/8	16	16	10 5/8	10 5/8	22 6/8	22	Granite Co., MT	Rick L. Williams	Rick L. Williams	1991	193
190	41	40	14 6/8	14 6/8	11 2/8	11 5/8	24 3/8	20 4/8	Jackson Co., CO	Tracy C. Atkinson	Tracy C. Atkinson	1999	193
190	38 7/8	39 7/8	16 2/8	16 2/8	10 1/8	9 4/8	23 7/8	22 1/8	Granite Co., MT	Richard N. King	Richard N. King	2001	193
190	44 4/8	43 4/8	14	14 1/8	10 2/8	10 4/8	23 3/8	23 3/8	Lewis & Clark Co., MT	Robert L. Freeman	Robert L. Freeman	2002	193
189 7/8	40 4/8	39 1/8	16	16 2/8	9 7/8	10 3/8	21 5/8	21 5/8	Clearwater Forest, AB	George Bugbee	Sally Bugbee	1928	199
189 7/8	40 5/8	41 4/8	15 4/8	15 4/8	9	9 1/8	21 3/8	17 1/8	Ribbon Lake, AB	Ovar Uggen	Ovar Uggen	1957	199
189 6/8	41	40 4/8	15 1/8	15 1/8	9 5/8	9 5/8	23 4/8	20 1/8	Highwood Range, AB	Unknown	Earl Johnson	1928	201
189 6/8	40 6/8	40 6/8	16	16	9 1/8	9 1/8	21 6/8	14 1/8	Swan Lake, BC	Billy Stork	A.C. Gilbert	1936	201
189 6/8	42 7/8	43 1/8	15 6/8	15 5/8	8 2/8	8 3/8	23 6/8	23 3/8	Sanders Co., MT	Eric C. Hastings	Eric C. Hastings	1995	201
189 5/8	42 4/8	41 5/8	15 5/8	15 4/8	8 7/8	9	22	21 3/8	Valley Co., MT	Picked Up	Carl Iacona	PR 1918	204
189 5/8	38 6/8	40 1/8	16	15	9 4/8	9 3/8	23	20 2/8	Yarrow Creek, AB	Allan Foster	Allan Foster	1963	204
189 5/8	39 4/8	42 3/8	15 4/8	15 4/8	9 7/8	10 1/8	22 3/8	21 4/8	Deer Lodge Co., MT	Lawrence A. Jany	Lawrence A. Jany	1990	204
189 5/8	41 3/8	45 4/8	15 2/8	15 3/8	8 2/8	8 3/8	25 6/8	25 4/8	Fergus Co., MT	Edmund C. Bishop	Edmund C. Bishop	1999	204
189 4/8	41	40 4/8	14 5/8	14 5/8	11 4/8	11 2/8	23 3/8	21	Park Co., WY	Picked Up	Dale McWilliams	1975	208
189 4/8	41 2/8	39 2/8	15 7/8	15	9 7/8	9 6/8	19 6/8	19 3/8	Nikanassin Range, AB	Colleen Bodenchuk	Colleen Bodenchuk	1976	208

Score	Length R	Length L	Base R	Base L	Qtr R	Qtr L	Gr. Spread	Tip to Tip	Locality	Hunter	Owner	Date	Rank
189 4/8	43	43	14 2/8	14 2/8	10 2/8	10 2/8	21 6/8	21 6/8	Mora Co., NM	Matthew D. Liljenquist	Matthew D. Liljenquist	2003	208
189 3/8	40 3/8	41 2/8	14 4/8	14 4/8	11 4/8	11 3/8	13 6/8	17 2/8	Panther River, AB	Picked Up	George Browne	1928	211
189 3/8	43 7/8	43	14 2/8	14 4/8	9 4/8	10 1/8	22 3/8	22 3/8	Spences Bridge, BC	Bert Walkem	Bert Walkem	1964	211
189 3/8	40 7/8	40 4/8	16 4/8	16 4/8	8 5/8	8 4/8	23	19 1/8	Teton Co., MT	R.L. Kennedy	R.L. Kennedy	1983	211
189 3/8	40 1/8	41 4/8	16 6/8	16 6/8	8	8 5/8	23 2/8	21 6/8	Asotin Co., WA	Edwin L. Harris	Edwin L. Harris	1987	211
189 3/8	40 7/8	41	15 7/8	15 7/8	8 6/8	8 5/8	20 5/8	18 6/8	Sheep Creek, AB	Norman G. Miller	Norman G. Miller	2001	216
189 2/8	41	40 3/8	15 6/8	15 6/8	9 7/8	9 7/8	21	20 2/8	Canal Flat, BC	Robert Lemaster	Robert Lemaster	1962	216
189 2/8	40 7/8	40 5/8	16 6/8	16 6/8	8 2/8	8 1/8	23	25 6/8	Sanders Co., MT	Linda Phillips	Linda Phillips	1989	218
189 1/8	40 5/8	42	14 7/8	14 5/8	10 5/8	10 5/8	21 3/8	17 4/8	Alberta	Bill Foster	Foster's Bighorn Rest.	PR 1947	218
189 1/8	37 3/8	38	15 7/8	15 6/8	11 1/8	11	20 7/8	19	Sheep River, AB	Patrick J. Downey	Patrick J. Downey	1986	218
189 1/8	39 3/8	39 3/8	16 4/8	15 6/8	9 1/8	9	21 6/8	18	Lost Creek, BC	Les J. Husband	Les J. Husband	1992	221
189 1/8	39	40	16 4/8	16 4/8	9 4/8	9 4/8	19 5/8	17	Highwood Co., AB	Hanson Bearspaw	W.S. Armstrong	1917	221
189	41	41	15 4/8	15 4/8	9 4/8	9 5/8	21 6/8	20 5/8	Granite Co., MT	Mark M. Morgan	Mark M. Morgan	1991	221
189	40 1/8	41 5/8	15 3/8	15 3/8	9 5/8	9 5/8	20 5/8	17 2/8	Panther River, AB	Picked Up	D. James Turner	1994	221
189	40 4/8	37 4/8	15 7/8	15 7/8	10 3/8	10 3/8	22 4/8	24 3/8	Blaine Co., MT	Greg D. Beach	Greg D. Beach	1997	221
189	43 1/8	39 3/8	15 6/8	15 6/8	8 7/8	8 7/8	25	25	Fergus Co., MT	Mark B. Hathaway	Mark B. Hathaway	2003	221
189	40 2/8	40 2/8	15 3/8	15 4/8	10 3/8	10 3/8	25 1/8	18	Ram Creek, AB	William N. Beach	Shelburne Museum	1928	221
188 7/8	41	41	14 5/8	14 5/8	11 1/8	11	25 6/8	25 6/8	Bow Valley, AB	Picked Up	Joseph Kovach	PR 1952	226
188 7/8	43 1/8	41 1/8	15 1/8	15 1/8	9	9	24	17	Gannet Peak, WY	James Huffman	James Huffman	1962	226
188 7/8	44 5/8	40 4/8	15	15 1/8	8 7/8	8 7/8	24 4/8	23 6/8	Gallatin Range, MT	Alden B. Walrath	Alden B. Walrath	1965	226
188 7/8	39 6/8	38 7/8	14 7/8	15 7/8	10 6/8	10 6/8	22	22	Wallowa Co., OR	Nicholas J. Gianopoulos	Nicholas J. Gianopoulos	1986	226
188 7/8	39 4/8	39 2/8	15 7/8	15 2/8	8 4/8	8 4/8	26 6/8	26 4/8	Silver Bow Co., MT	Jerry J. Joseph	Cabela's, Inc.	1990	226
188 7/8	39 5/8	41	15	15 4/8	10 2/8	10 2/8	22 5/8	18 4/8	Whitehorse Creek, AB	Wally Nicklin	Wally Nicklin	1995	226
188 7/8	41	43 1/8	15 4/8	15 1/8	9 3/8	9 3/8	23 2/8	19 6/8	Ewin Creek, BC	Marshall J. Collins, Jr.	Marshall J. Collins, Jr.	2001	226
188 6/8	44 7/8	39 2/8	17 1/8	17 1/8	8 4/8	8 4/8	24 7/8	20 5/8	Highwood, AB	Steve Kubasek	Steve Kubasek	1953	234
188 6/8	39 5/8	41	15 1/8	15 1/8	10 7/8	11	20 4/8	16 4/8	Onion Lake, AB	Martin M. Reddy	Martin M. Reddy	1985	234
188 6/8	38 7/8	45 4/8	15 4/8	15 4/8	10 3/8	10 3/8	20	20 6/8	Deer Lodge Co., MT	Mike J. Bartoletti	Mike J. Bartoletti	1991	234
188 6/8	41	40	15	15	10 5/8	10 5/8	20	17 2/8	Line Creek, BC	Jim Musil	Jim Musil	1998	234
188 6/8	39 2/8	40	15	15 4/8	10	10	19 6/8	19 6/8	Alberta	Bill Foster	Foster's Bighorn Rest.	PR 1947	234
188 5/8	41	39 7/8	15 5/8	15 6/8	9 5/8	9 4/8	23 1/8	21 3/8	Sun River, MT	Bruce McCracken	Bruce McCracken	1955	238
188 5/8	45 4/8	38 7/8	15 6/8	15 3/8	10 1/8	10 6/8	20 4/8	19 2/8	Simpson River, BC	Patrick Deuling	Patrick Deuling	1985	238
188 5/8	41	40 5/8	15 3/8	15 2/8	10 2/8	10 3/8	20 3/8	18 2/8	Sanders Co., MT	Richard L. Grimes	Richard L. Grimes	1990	238
188 5/8	40 2/8	43 1/8	15 1/8	15 1/8	9 3/8	9 3/8	19 2/8	17 3/8	Burnt Timber Creek, AB	Robert P. Erickson	Robert P. Erickson	1993	238
188 5/8	38	39 2/8	15 4/8	15 2/8	10 5/8	10 4/8	20 4/8	19	Luscar Mt., AB	Dwayne W. Oneski	Dwayne W. Oneski	1997	238
188 4/8	40 4/8	41	14 6/8	14 6/8	9 1/8	9 1/8	27	27	Clearwater, AB	Unknown	Norman Lougheed	1936	244
188 4/8	37 4/8	40 4/8	16 2/8	15 7/8	8 6/8	8 5/8	22 1/8	19 4/8	Opal Range, AB	Robert Zebedee	Robert Zebedee	1977	244
188 4/8	42 5/8	39	15 7/8	15 7/8	9 5/8	9 5/8	24 4/8	22 4/8	Ravalli Co., MT	Sandy Rose	Cabela's, Inc.	1978	244
188 4/8	39 2/8	40 4/8	15 7/8	15 7/8	8 1/8	8 1/8	23 6/8	17 4/8	Blaine Co., MT	Lanny L. Walker	Lanny L. Walker	1991	244
188 4/8	40 6/8	42 5/8	16	16	10 6/8	10 6/8	23 2/8	22 6/8	Sanders Co., MT	Dean M. Vaughan	Dean M. Vaughan	1993	244
188 3/8	40 5/8	37 4/8	16	16	9	9	20 1/8	20	Blaine Co., MT	Brian W. Evans	Brian W. Evans	1997	250
188 3/8	42 1/8	40 6/8	16 1/8	16 1/8	9	9	25 7/8	21	White Swan Lake, BC	A.C. Gilbert	The Old State House, CT	1940	250
188 3/8	39 6/8	40 5/8	15 4/8	15 4/8	9 2/8	9 2/8	20 6/8	17 2/8	Surprise Lake, BC	Herb Klein	Dallas Mus. of Natl. Hist.	1950	250
188 3/8	39 3/8	38	16	16	9 7/8	9 7/8	21 6/8	20 6/8	Alberta	Arthur Smith	Arthur Smith	1959	250
188 3/8	40	39 1/8	15 6/8	15 6/8	10 4/8	10 4/8	21 6/8	15 4/8	Burnt Timber Creek, AB	Walter O. Ford, Jr.	Walter O. Ford, Jr.	1966	250
188 3/8	40 7/8	39 3/8	15 3/8	15 3/8	9 7/8	9 7/8	22 4/8	14	Gibraltar Mt., AB	Leslie Kish	Leslie Kish	1981	250
188 3/8	39 3/8	40	15 4/8	15 4/8	11	11	24	23 1/8	Deer Lodge Co., MT	Paul J. Druyvestein	Paul J. Druyvestein	1986	250
188 3/8	40 4/8	39 3/8	15 2/8	15 2/8	10 7/8	10 7/8	22 6/8	20 6/8	Granite Co., MT	Larry J. Antonich	Larry J. Antonich	1990	250
188 3/8	40	39 7/8	16	16	8 7/8	9	22 1/8	20 1/8	Sheep River, AB	Katherine A. Pyra	Katherine A. Pyra	1990	250

BIGHORN SHEEP

Ovis canadensis canadensis and certain related subspecies

Score	Length of Horn R	L	Circumference of Base R	L	Circumference at Third Quarter R	L	Greatest Spread	Tip to Tip Spread	Locality	Hunter	Owner	Date Killed	Rank
188 3/8	38 7/8	40 2/8	15 5/8	15 7/8	10 1/8	10 2/8	22 4/8	20 4/8	Granite Co., MT	Michael R. Priddy	Michael R. Priddy	2002	250
188 2/8	40	40 6/8	15 4/8	15 1/8	9 3/8	10 4/8	21 4/8	19	Sun River, MT	Bruce Neal	Bruce Neal	1912	259
188 2/8	45 4/8	44 2/8	13 6/8	13 6/8	9 4/8	9 7/8	23 4/8	22 7/8	Panther River, AB	Unknown	Harvey A. Trimble	1932	259
188 2/8	40 4/8	40 6/8	15 1/8	15	10	10 5/8	22 4/8	21 1/8	Sun River, MT	J.R. Pfeifer	J.R. Pfeifer	1958	259
188 2/8	38 5/8	37 7/8	15 6/8	15 6/8	10 7/8	10 4/8	21 2/8	15	Kananaskis, AB	Terry Webber	Terry Webber	1961	259
188 2/8	42 5/8	42 5/8	15 6/8	15 6/8	8 3/8	8 4/8	25 7/8	25 7/8	Spences Bridge, BC	Romeo Leduc	Romeo Leduc	1982	259
188 2/8	43	42	15 6/8	15 6/8	7 7/8	8 1/8	24 3/8	24 3/8	Deer Lodge Co., MT	Walter F. Smith	Walter F. Smith	1986	259
188 2/8	39 4/8	42	15 5/8	15 7/8	9 1/8	9 5/8	25 6/8	25 2/8	Beaverhead Co., MT	Corey J. Buhl	Corey J. Buhl	1992	259
188 2/8	40 6/8	40 4/8	17	17	8	8	25 4/8	25 3/8	Granite Co., MT	Donald O. Cure	Donald O. Cure	1994	259
188 2/8	38	39 4/8	15 7/8	14 7/8	10	10 1/8	21 3/8	19 4/8	Sanders Co., MT	Anders J. Brooker	Anders J. Brooker	1997	259
188 1/8	44 3/8	42 2/8	14 3/8	14 3/8	9 6/8	9 2/8	25 3/8	25 3/8	Lincoln Co., MT	Alfred E. Journey	Alfred E. Journey	1980	268
188 1/8	38 5/8	39 4/8	16 6/8	16 5/8	9	9 2/8	26 4/8	21	Sanders Co., MT	Patti L. Lewis	Patti L. Lewis	1984	268
188 1/8	40 1/8	40 4/8	15 1/8	15 2/8	10 1/8	10	23 4/8	23 4/8	Blaine Co., MT	Curtis L. Kostelecky	Curtis L. Kostelecky	1991	268
188 1/8	41 2/8	40 7/8	15 3/8	15 4/8	9 6/8	9 6/8	21 5/8	19 7/8	Cadomin, AB	Randy Hancock	Randy Hancock	1997	268
188	41 6/8	40 6/8	14 6/8	14 7/8	10	10 2/8	21 2/8	16 6/8	Kananaskis River, AB	C. Allenhof	C. Allenhof	1958	272
188	39 7/8	39 1/8	15 4/8	15 4/8	10 6/8	10 5/8	23 7/8	23 4/8	Kananaskis Summit, AB	Ted Howell	Ted Howell	1963	272
188	41 1/8	39 5/8	15	15 3/8	10 4/8	10 5/8	20 5/8	16 6/8	Cardinal River, AB	Lawrence N. Baraniuk	Lawrence N. Baraniuk	1986	272
188	39 2/8	41	16 2/8	16 2/8	9 1/8	8 4/8	22 2/8	16 4/8	Asotin Co., WA	Glen A. Landrus	Glen A. Landrus	1995	272
188	41 7/8	41 3/8	16	16 1/8	8 2/8	8 3/8	21 7/8	21 2/8	Leyland Mt., AB	Norman P. Harasym	Norman P. Harasym	1997	272
188	39 6/8	38 6/8	16 4/8	16 6/8	8 5/8	9 1/8	21 3/8	20 7/8	Granite Co., MT	Anna F. Anderson	Anna F. Anderson	2002	272
187 7/8	41 6/8	41 3/8	15 7/8	15 7/8	8 7/8	8 3/8	24 2/8	18	Sanders Co., MT	Richard L. Carlson	Richard L. Carlson	1994	278
187 7/8	41 6/8	40 1/8	15 5/8	15 4/8	9	9	22 6/8	19 1/8	Missoula Co., MT	Ronald C. Gibson	Ronald C. Gibson	1995	278
187 7/8	40 5/8	40	15 3/8	15 3/8	9 1/8	9 1/8	22 6/8	20	Little Elbow River, AB	David W. Sowers	David W. Sowers	1995	278
187 7/8	41 7/8	39 2/8	15 4/8	15 5/8	10 2/8	9 1/8	21 7/8	20	Granite Co., MT	Richard M. Mierva	Richard M. Mierva	1996	278
187 7/8	40 4/8	40 7/8	16 4/8	16 2/8	8 4/8	8 6/8	23 1/8	20	Missoula Co., MT	Richard P. Hughes	Richard P. Hughes	1998	278
187 6/8	43 4/8	44 2/8	14 2/8	14 7/8	8 4/8	8 2/8	24 2/8	24 2/8	Salmon River, ID	Picked Up	Dwight Smith	1951	283
187 6/8	42 1/8	42 3/8	14 5/8	15	9 2/8	9 2/8	21 4/8	21 4/8	Chase, BC	L. McNary & J. Langer	Lloyd McNary	1956	283
187 6/8	44	43 2/8	15 1/8	15 2/8	8 4/8	7 6/8	24 3/8	24 3/8	Ram River, AB	George W. Parker	George W. Parker	1961	283
187 6/8	39 3/8	38 7/8	14 5/8	15 2/8	11 3/8	11 3/8	22 3/8	15	Wildhay River, AB	Jim Papst	Jim Papst	1967	283
187 6/8	39 4/8	42	15 6/8	15 6/8	8 7/8	8 7/8	23 2/8	23 1/8	Deer Lodge Co., MT	William H. Shurte	William H. Shurte	1984	283
187 6/8	40 1/8	39 7/8	16	16	9 6/8	8 4/8	21	12	Ghost River, AB	Gerald Molnar	Gerald Molnar	1988	283
187 6/8	38	37	15 6/8	15 7/8	11	10 7/8	20 1/8	20 1/8	Fergus Co., MT	Gordon L. Lencioni	Gordon L. Lencioni	1995	283
187 5/8	39 3/8	40 4/8	15 2/8	15 2/8	9 6/8	9 6/8	21 2/8	21 2/8	Glacier Natl. Park, MT	Olmstead, Dow, & Hawley	MT Dept. of Fish, Wildl. & Parks	1956	290
187 5/8	40 5/8	43 6/8	14 4/8	14 4/8	10 3/8	10 2/8	22 1/8	22	Butcher Creek, AB	Vince Bruder	Vince Bruder	1958	290
187 5/8	42 4/8	39 5/8	16 1/8	16	8 7/8	8	26 1/8	25 4/8	Teton Co., WY	William R. Flagg	William R. Flagg	1967	290
187 5/8	45 7/8	42	14 7/8	14 4/8	8 6/8	8 7/8	23	22 2/8	Spences Bridge, BC	J. David Smith	J. David Smith	1969	290
187 5/8	39 6/8	39 7/8	15 6/8	15 2/8	9 3/8	9 3/8	22 6/8	20 5/8	El Paso Co., CO	Picked Up	Michael D. Swanson	1988	290

Score									Locality	Hunter	Owner	Date	Rank
187 5/8	40 5/8	38 4/8	16 5/8	16 7/8	8 2/8	8 3/8	24 7/8	21 1/8	Granite Co., MT	Polly A. Tate	Polly A. Tate	1997	290
187 4/8	39 5/8	43 1/8	15 5/8	15 4/8	9	8 4/8	26 4/8	19	Crystal Creek, WY	Picked Up	Melvin R. Fowlkes	1970	296
187 4/8	40 5/8	39 7/8	15 3/8	15 3/8	9 4/8	9 3/8	20 7/8	19 2/8	Ram Range, AB	John F. Snyder	John F. Snyder	1978	296
187 4/8	35	37 4/8	16 1/8	16 2/8	10 7/8	10 7/8	24 3/8	23 5/8	Deer Lodge Co., MT	Dorothy A. Pennington	Dorothy A. Pennington	1991	296
187 3/8	39 3/8	39 3/8	15 4/8	15 4/8	9 6/8	9 7/8	21 1/8	20	Sundre, AB	Stan Burrell	Stan Burrell	1953	299
187 3/8	40 4/8	40 3/8	16 2/8	16 1/8	8 3/8	8 4/8	22 7/8	22 7/8	Elbow River, AB	Sam R. Sloan	Sam R. Sloan	1962	299
187 3/8	42	41 7/8	15 3/8	15 4/8	8 4/8	8 4/8	21 4/8	21 6/8	Lytton, BC	R.G. Jones & P.B. Wilmot	R. George Jones	1973	299
187 3/8	41 4/8	40 7/8	15 7/8	16	8 3/8	8 4/8	22 7/8	21 6/8	Ravalli Co., MT	James A. Martin	James A. Martin	1997	299
187 2/8	40 3/8	43 1/8	14 7/8	15 1/8	9 1/8	9 3/8	22 3/8	19 7/8	McDonald Creek, AB	Ernest F. Greenwood	Ernest F. Greenwood	1965	303
187 2/8	38 4/8	39 4/8	15 6/8	15 1/8	10	10 3/8	22 5/8	17 3/8	Plateau Mt., AB	Randy Jackson	Randy Jackson	1984	303
187 2/8	41 1/8	38 3/8	17	17	7 7/8	7 7/8	24 5/8	20 1/8	Asotin Co., WA	Roger S. Brazier	Roger S. Brazier	1986	303
187 2/8	39 2/8	40 4/8	15 7/8	15 7/8	8 6/8	8 6/8	23 7/8	22 6/8	Thornton Creek, AB	Donald A. Chamberlain	Donald A. Chamberlain	1987	303
187 2/8	36 3/8	37 1/8	16 5/8	16 5/8	9 7/8	9 7/8	22 7/8	20	Granite Co., MT	John Gehan	John Gehan	1988	303
187 2/8	42 4/8	39 4/8	15 7/8	15 7/8	8 3/8	8 7/8	22 5/8	21 5/8	Granite Co., MT	Chuck Houtz	Chuck Houtz	1988	303
187 2/8	40 3/8	41 1/8	16	16 1/8	8 4/8	8 7/8	21 7/8	20 2/8	Beaverhead Co., MT	Charles R. Moe	Charles R. Moe	1994	303
187 1/8	38 5/8	37 5/8	16 3/8	16 1/8	9 4/8	9 6/8	20 1/8	18	Elk Valley, BC	Mike Podrasky	Mike Podrasky	1998	303
187 1/8	41 3/8	41 4/8	15 4/8	16 3/8	9 1/8	9 1/8	21	21	White Swan Lake, BC	Lucius A. Chase	Lucius A. Chase	1961	311
187 1/8	41 5/8	43 4/8	15	15 4/8	8 5/8	8 5/8	23 1/8	23	Fallen Timber Creek, AB	Picked Up	J.F. Blakemore	1968	311
187 1/8	41	38 5/8	15 6/8	15 7/8	9 3/8	9 3/8	22 6/8	15 2/8	Red Deer River, AB	Richard B. Smith	Richard B. Smith	1984	311
187 1/8	40 7/8	40 4/8	14 5/8	14 4/8	10 5/8	10 3/8	23 1/8	23 4/8	Deer Lodge Co., MT	David J. Etzwiler	David J. Etzwiler	1985	311
187 1/8	40	40 3/8	15 6/8	15 6/8	8 7/8	8 5/8	25	25	Deer Lodge Co., MT	Jeffrey A. Mikunda	Jeffrey A. Mikunda	1995	311
187 1/8	38 3/8	38	16 2/8	16 1/8	9 5/8	9 6/8	23 6/8	20 3/8	Huerfano Co., CO	Joshua S. Gunning	Joshua S. Gunning	1998	311
187	39	39 4/8	15	15	10 5/8	10 4/8	22 6/8	17 4/8	Wind River Mts., WY	Ralph E. Platt, Jr.	Ralph E. Platt, Jr.	1963	317
187	36 6/8	38	15 6/8	15 7/8	10 3/8	10 6/8	23 3/8	22 7/8	Colorado	Picked Up	E.H. Brown	PR 1964	317
187	37 7/8	38 1/8	16	16 1/8	10	10 2/8	17 6/8	22 5/8	Unknown	Unknown	Dale Selby	PR 1968	317
187	40 6/8	40 6/8	15 5/8	15 5/8	8 4/8	8 6/8	22 1/8	20 7/8	Sanders Co., MT	Bruce L. Hartford	Bruce L. Hartford	1978	317
187	37 4/8	38 4/8	16 3/8	16 5/8	9 4/8	9 7/8	25	22 4/8	Sanders Co., MT	Richard F. Lukes	Richard F. Lukes	1980	317
187	40 4/8	38 6/8	16	15 7/8	9 4/8	8 6/8	22 7/8	15	Elbow River, AB	Ralph L. Cervo	Ralph L. Cervo	1981	317
187	39 6/8	38	16 7/8	17	8 1/8	8 1/8	21 7/8	20	Highwood Range, AB	Sten B. Lundberg	Sten B. Lundberg	1984	317
187	40 6/8	40 4/8	16 4/8	16 4/8	7 6/8	8	21 6/8	21 6/8	Deer Lodge Co., MT	Wayne E. Bousfield	Wayne E. Bousfield	1985	317
187	41 3/8	41 3/8	15 6/8	16	8 2/8	8 2/8	24 4/8	24 4/8	Sanders Co., MT	Mark S. Eaton	Mark S. Eaton	1985	317
187	38 4/8	40	16	16	8 7/8	8 5/8	22 4/8	22	Granite Co., MT	Norman C. Dunkle	Norman C. Dunkle	1989	317
187	39	38 4/8	15 2/8	15 2/8	10 3/8	11	22 7/8	22 1/8	Sanders Co., MT	William V. Kuchera	William V. Kuchera	1990	317
187	40 4/8	39 4/8	15 5/8	15 5/8	10	9 6/8	20 7/8	17 4/8	Granite Co., MT	Pearl E. Foust	Cabela's, Inc.	1991	317
187	38 7/8	39 1/8	16 3/8	16 3/8	9 6/8	8 7/8	22 7/8	19 7/8	Granite Co., MT	Jim Zumbo	Jim Zumbo	1995	317
187	40 4/8	38 4/8	16 2/8	16 2/8	8 7/8	9 5/8	23 4/8	22 6/8	Sanders Co., MT	James E. Solecki	James E. Solecki	1997	317
187	38	36 4/8	15	14 7/8	10	8 7/8	23 5/8	23 5/8	Valley Co., ID	Steven M. Morgan	Steven M. Morgan	1999	317
187	40	40 2/8	16 2/8	16 4/8	9 7/8	10 3/8	25	19	Sanders Co., MT	Fred L. Cavill	Fred L. Cavill	2000	317
187	41 3/8	40 2/8	14 7/8	14 6/8	10	10 2/8	20 5/8	17 2/8	Granite Co., MT	Nathan L. Mattioli	Nathan L. Mattioli	2000	317
187	38 4/8	41 3/8	15 5/8	15 5/8	8 2/8	8 2/8	20 7/8	16 2/8	Grace Creek, BC	David A. Halko	David A. Halko	2002	317
187	40 2/8	40	15 6/8	15 2/8	10 4/8	10 5/8	22 1/8	18 6/8	Granite Co., MT	Raymond M. Hanke	Raymond M. Hanke	2002	317
186 7/8	34 3/8	38 4/8	15 6/8	15 6/8	10 5/8	10 5/8	22 3/8	18 6/8	Burnt Timber, AB	C.J. McElroy	C.J. McElroy	1965	336
186 7/8	40 1/8	38 4/8	16 1/8	16	9	9	24 3/8	19	Ghost River, AB	D. James Turner	D. James Turner	1990	336
186 7/8	40 1/8	39 4/8	15 1/8	15	10 2/8	10 2/8	22 1/8	21 4/8	Asotin Co., WA	Ron Willenborg	Ron Willenborg	1991	336
186 6/8	39 4/8	38 4/8	16 2/8	16 3/8	9 2/8	9 2/8	23 1/8	18 7/8	East Kootenay, BC	Jerry Mortimer	Jerry Mortimer	1959	339
186 6/8	39 1/8	39 7/8	15 1/8	15 2/8	10 4/8	10 2/8	22	17 4/8	Whitehorse Creek, AB	Philip H.R. Stepney	Prov. Mus. of Alberta	1978	339
186 6/8	41 7/8	42 7/8	15 7/8	15 7/8	7 4/8	7 3/8	22 3/8	21 6/8	Whitman Co., WA	Picked Up	Inland Empire Big Game Council	1983	339

Ovis canadensis and certain related subspecies

Score	Length of Horn R	L	Circumference of Base R	L	Circumference at Third Quarter R	L	Greatest Spread	Tip to Tip Spread	Locality	Hunter	Owner	Date Killed	Rank
186 6/8	38 6/8	38 2/8	16 3/8	16 3/8	8 7/8	8 7/8	23 3/8	18 5/8	Highwood River, AB	Ross Nikonchuk	Ross Nikonchuk	1984	339
186 6/8	41 2/8	40 2/8	15	15	9 6/8	9 6/8	22 5/8	18 7/8	Tornado Creek, BC	Clive J. Endicott	Clive J. Endicott	1988	339
186 6/8	39 1/8	37 5/8	15 2/8	15 3/8	11 1/8	10 5/8	22 3/8	20 4/8	Sanders Co., MT	Bill Mitchell	Bill Mitchell	1988	339
186 6/8	41 1/8	41 1/8	15 4/8	15 4/8	8 5/8	8 6/8	22 3/8	21 6/8	Granite Co., MT	Carol K. Chudy	Carol K. Chudy	1991	339
186 6/8	39 4/8	40	15 3/8	15 4/8	10 1/8	9 1/8	20 4/8	15	Sheep River, AB	Percy Pyra	Percy Pyra	1991	339
186 6/8	40 2/8	38 2/8	16 2/8	16 1/8	9	9 2/8	25 2/8	24 4/8	Granite Co., MT	Anthony D. Orizotti	Anthony D. Orizotti	1995	339
186 6/8	41	40 6/8	14 1/8	14 4/8	10 6/8	10 6/8	19 6/8	17 4/8	Whitehorse Creek, AB	Brian T. Panylyk	Brian T. Panylyk	1995	339
186 6/8	40 6/8	39 6/8	15 4/8	15 5/8	9	8 5/8	22	22	Missoula Co., MT	Dustyn W. Strachan	Dustyn W. Strachan	2001	339
186 6/8	39 3/8	38 5/8	16 6/8	16 6/8	8 2/8	8 2/8	22	21 6/8	Sanders Co., MT	Richard J. Briskin	Richard J. Briskin	2002	339
186 5/8	42 4/8	41 3/8	14 6/8	14 5/8	9 4/8	9 4/8	24 4/8	21 6/8	Panther River, AB	Picked Up	Belmore Browne	1936	351
186 5/8	42 1/8	42 1/8	15	15	8 3/8	8 2/8	25 6/8	25 6/8	Shell Rock, ID	Lea J. Bacos	Lea J. Bacos	1953	351
186 5/8	38 6/8	38 3/8	15 3/8	15 3/8	10 1/8	10	22	17 7/8	Blind Canyon, AB	Picked Up	AB Fish & Wildl. Div.	1983	351
186 5/8	41	40 7/8	16 1/8	16 1/8	8	8 6/8	23 6/8	23 6/8	Beaverhead Co., MT	Gary L. Peltomaa	Gary L. Peltomaa	1989	351
186 5/8	37 5/8	38 4/8	15 6/8	15 6/8	9 7/8	9 6/8	22 3/8	16 3/8	Sanders Co., MT	Robert G. Blenker	Robert G. Blenker	1991	351
186 5/8	37 5/8	38	17 2/8	17 3/8	8 5/8	8 2/8	25	25	Blaine Co., MT	Gary A. Morton	Gary A. Morton	1995	351
186 5/8	40	39 5/8	15 4/8	15 4/8	9 2/8	9 2/8	25 2/8	25 2/8	Missoula Co., MT	Paul Bjerke	Paul Bjerke	1996	351
186 5/8	40	38 7/8	16 6/8	17	8 2/8	8 4/8	22	17 4/8	Sanders Co., MT	Cathryn Powell	Cathryn Powell	1997	351
186 5/8	39 3/8	38 4/8	16 3/8	16 3/8	9	9 3/8	21 4/8	21 4/8	Sanders Co., MT	G. Michael Martin	G. Michael Martin	1998	351
186 5/8	38 6/8	39 1/8	15 7/8	15 7/8	9 3/8	9 2/8	22 5/8	19 5/8	Blaine Co., MT	Gerald A. Brown	Gerald A. Brown	2000	351
186 4/8	40 5/8	39 1/8	15 6/8	15 7/8	9 3/8	8 7/8	22 6/8	19	Fording River, BC	Martin C. Baher	Martin C. Baher	1942	361
186 4/8	38	38 4/8	17 3/8	17 3/8	8 1/8	8 4/8	20 2/8	17 2/8	Rocky Mt. House, AB	Robert B. Johnson	Robert B. Johnson	1960	361
186 4/8	40 1/8	39 7/8	16 3/8	16 2/8	8 6/8	8 4/8	21 7/8	20 4/8	Mt. Assiniboine, BC	Shirley A. Malberg	Shirley A. Malberg	1990	361
186 4/8	41	40 4/8	14 4/8	14 4/8	9 6/8	9 6/8	23 6/8	17 2/8	Sanders Co., MT	Picked Up	C.F. Dupuis & I. Dupuis	1995	361
186 3/8	41 7/8	40 4/8	14 1/8	14 1/8	10 4/8	10 4/8	20	18	Tyrrell Creek, AB	Picked Up	John H. Batten	1949	365
186 3/8	41	41 7/8	14 1/8	14	10 6/8	11 1/8	22 1/8	17 6/8	Ventre-Flat, WY	John Evasco	John Evasco	1953	365
186 3/8	38 1/8	36	16	16 1/8	10	10	22 4/8	18 2/8	Castle River, AB	Ed Burton	Ed Burton	1954	365
186 3/8	42	41 1/8	15 3/8	15 1/8	8 6/8	8 7/8	21 6/8	16 6/8	Fernie, BC	Thomas Krall	Thomas Krall	1963	365
186 3/8	42 3/8	40 1/8	15 1/8	15 1/8	8 2/8	8 7/8	20 1/8	20 1/8	Simpson River, BC	James A. Walls	James A. Walls	1981	365
186 3/8	43 4/8	40 5/8	14 1/8	14 1/8	10 2/8	9 7/8	23 3/8	23	Grant Co., NM	Clyde Reed	Clyde Reed	1992	365
186 3/8	39	40 1/8	14 6/8	14 6/8	10 6/8	10 6/8	23 5/8	19 4/8	Emery Co., UT	Stephen C. Walker	Stephen C. Walker	1992	365
186 3/8	38	38 3/8	15 1/8	15 3/8	10 2/8	10 3/8	22 4/8	14 4/8	Luscar Mt., AB	Max Howard	Max Howard	1998	365
186 3/8	39 5/8	39 4/8	15 5/8	15 5/8	9 4/8	9 2/8	21 7/8	18 4/8	Blaine Co., MT	Martin Lyders	Martin K. Lyders	1998	365
186 3/8	37 6/8	36 5/8	16 1/8	16 1/8	10 5/8	10 4/8	19 3/8	17 4/8	Missoula Co., MT	Dale Truett	Dale H. Truett	1998	365
186 2/8	41 7/8	42 1/8	14	14	9 7/8	9 7/8	22 4/8	21 4/8	Cadomin, AB	R.A. Craig	R.A. Craig	1936	375
186 2/8	42 3/8	41 3/8	14 5/8	14 6/8	9 4/8	9 4/8	24 2/8	20 6/8	Clearwater River, AB	Picked Up	John H. Batten	1954	375
186 2/8	40 3/8	40 1/8	15 1/8	15 3/8	9 5/8	9 7/8	21 4/8	19 5/8	Sheep Creek, AB	G.A. Reiche	G.A. Reiche	1960	375
186 2/8	37	38 4/8	15 7/8	15 7/8	9 4/8	10	20 1/8	17	Junction Mt., AB	Robert R. Willis	Robert R. Willis	1978	375
186 2/8	40	41 4/8	16	16	8 3/8	8	22 2/8	22 2/8	Rabbit Creek, BC	Lanny E. Kniert	Lanny E. Kniert	1982	375

Score	Length of Horn R	Length of Horn L	Circ. of Base R	Circ. of Base L	Circ. 3rd Qtr. R	Circ. 3rd Qtr. L	Greatest Spread	Tip to Tip	Locality	Owner	By Whom Killed	Date Killed	Rank
186 2/8	39 6/8	39 4/8	16 1/8	16 1/8	8 5/8	8 4/8	23 3/8	17 4/8	Little Elbow River, AB	John Liefso	John Liefso	1982	375
186 2/8	40	41	16 1/8	16 1/8	8 5/8	8 1/8	20 7/8	13	Riverside Mt., BC	Paul A. Templin	Paul A. Templin	1983	375
186 2/8	41 3/8	38 7/8	16 2/8	16 2/8	8 2/8	8 3/8	24 2/8	24	Deer Lodge Co., MT	Jennifer Jaap	Jennifer Jaap	1997	375
186 2/8	37	39	15 4/8	15 5/8	10 3/8	8 3/8	23 3/8	19	Granite Co., MT	Jeff J. Krier	Jeff J. Krier	2001	375
186 1/8	43 2/8	44 5/8	16 4/8	16 5/8	6 7/8	10 5/8	24 5/8	24 5/8	Yellowstone Park, MT	James K. Weatherford	William H. Dirrett	1913	384
186 1/8	39 4/8	38 3/8	15 2/8	15 3/8	10 4/8	6 7/8	22 3/8	15 6/8	Highwood, AB	Terry J. Webber	Terry J. Webber	1959	384
186 1/8	41 5/8	41 2/8	15 4/8	15 4/8	8 2/8	8 5/8	20 7/8	19 1/8	Sun River Canyon, MT	Glen Roberts	Glen Roberts	1961	384
186 1/8	39 5/8	38	15 6/8	15 3/8	8 3/8	8 2/8	22	17 4/8	Waterton Natl. Park, AB	Robert Thompson	Picked Up	PR 1966	384
186 1/8	40 2/8	38	15 5/8	16 1/8	9 6/8	10 2/8	20 4/8	20 4/8	Cougar Mt., AB	Alan E. Schroeder	Alan E. Schroeder	1989	384
186 1/8	41 4/8	36 7/8	16	16	9 1/8	9 2/8	22 1/8	18	Fergus Co., MT	Henry M. Kengerski	Henry M. Kengerski	1993	384
186 1/8	38 5/8	41 2/8	14 5/8	14 5/8	10 6/8	10 4/8	20 6/8	20 4/8	Fremont Co., WY	Ben L. Wilkes	Picked Up	1994	384
186 1/8	36 7/8	38 5/8	16 4/8	16 6/8	9 2/8	9 7/8	22	11 2/8	Emery Co., UT	Kenneth M. Labrum	Kenneth M. Labrum	2002	384
186	40 2/8	40 2/8	15 2/8	15	9 7/8	9 3/8	22	18 6/8	Sparwood, BC	H. Bruce Freeman	Unknown	PR 1910	392
186	40 4/8	39	16	16	8 4/8	8 7/8	19 5/8	19 5/8	Clearwater, AB	Herb Hamilton	Herb Hamilton	1964	392
186	39 4/8	39	14 6/8	14 6/8	10 6/8	10 6/8	21	21	Granite Co., MT	Dale W. Hoth	Dale W. Hoth	1981	392
186	36 5/8	40 1/8	17 4/8	17 4/8	8 3/8	7 7/8	24 4/8	24 4/8	Granite Co., MT	Thomas J. Kubichek	Thomas J. Kubichek	1987	392
186	40 6/8	40 2/8	15 4/8	15 4/8	9	9	22	20 4/8	Line Creek, BC	Sam W. Stephenson	Sam W. Stephenson	1991	392
186	39 4/8	37 4/8	16 2/8	16	9 4/8	9 2/8	21 1/8	21 1/8	Fergus Co., MT	Kenneth R. Brandt	Kenneth Brandt	1998	392
186	38 6/8	39 2/8	15 6/8	15 6/8	9 3/8	9 2/8	24 5/8	24	Pershing Co., NV	Sam S. Jaksick, Jr.	Sam S. Jaksick, Jr.	2001	392
185 7/8	40 3/8	40 4/8	15	15	9 5/8	9 6/8	21	17 3/8	Panther River, AB	J.F. Blakemore	J.F. Blakemore	1961	399
185 7/8	41 2/8	41 3/8	14 2/8	14 2/8	10 6/8	10 3/8	22 5/8	17 3/8	Mystery Lake, AB	Jim Baballa	Jim Baballa	1962	399
185 7/8	35	37 3/8	14 4/8	14 4/8	13	13	20 3/8	17 5/8	Ural, MT	Curtis Gatson	Curtis Gatson	1962	399
185 7/8	38 7/8	38 2/8	15 6/8	15 5/8	10	10	21 5/8	17 1/8	Burnt Timber Creek, AB	John T. Blackwell	John T. Blackwell	1967	399
185 7/8	40 3/8	41	15 6/8	15 6/8	8 5/8	8 4/8	21 5/8	21	Botanie Creek, BC	William J. Pincock	William J. Pincock	1988	399
185 7/8	40	40	14 6/8	14 7/8	10 1/8	9 5/8	21 1/8	17	Gregg River, AB	Thomas J. Pawlacyk	Thomas J. Pawlacyk	1997	399
185 7/8	37 7/8	43 4/8	16 1/8	16	8 3/8	8 3/8	26 4/8	26 4/8	Granite Co., MT	Dale A. Carpenter	Dale A. Carpenter	1999	399
185 7/8	39 7/8	36 4/8	16 1/8	16 1/8	9 4/8	9 7/8	23 6/8	21 2/8	Missoula Co., MT	Charles F. MacIntire	Charles F. MacIntire	2000	399
185 6/8	40 2/8	40 2/8	15	15	10 1/8	10 1/8	21	21	Ghost River, AB	William D. Cox	William D. Cox	1959	407
185 6/8	39 6/8	39 6/8	15 2/8	15 2/8	9 6/8	9 7/8	20 4/8	20	Granite Co., MT	James M. Milligan	James M. Milligan	1990	407
185 6/8	38 4/8	36 6/8	16	16	10 2/8	10 5/8	21	18 3/8	Granite Co., MT	Donald A. Dwyer	Donald A. Dwyer	1992	407
185 5/8	39 1/8	39 3/8	14 6/8	14 7/8	13	13	22 4/8	18	Black Diamond, AB	Gordon Lait	Picked Up	1962	410
185 5/8	40 5/8	40	15 2/8	15 2/8	9	8 7/8	23 4/8	23 4/8	Lemhi Co., ID	W.R. Franklin	W.R. Franklin	1963	410
185 5/8	40 6/8	39 3/8	15 6/8	15 5/8	8 2/8	8 3/8	24 3/8	18 4/8	Simpson River, BC	Thomas R. VanEvery	Thomas R. VanEvery	1995	410
185 5/8	39 2/8	39 2/8	15 3/8	15 3/8	9 4/8	9 4/8	21 5/8	21 4/8	Lewis & Clark Co., MT	Rick R. Rosekelly	Rick R. Rosekelly	1999	410
185 4/8	42 6/8	41	14	14	9 7/8	8 7/8	21 2/8	20	Wind River Mts., WY	Elgin T. Gates	Elgin T. Gates	1954	414
185 4/8	40	40	14 6/8	14 6/8	10	10	22 4/8	19 4/8	Saskatchewan River, AB	Dallas Mus. of Natl. Hist.	Herb Klein	1963	414
185 4/8	38 5/8	38 5/8	15 4/8	15	10	9 7/8	22	20 4/8	Highwood River, AB	M.R. Wagner	W. Erdman	1964	414
185 4/8	40 2/8	40 2/8	14 4/8	14 4/8	10 1/8	8 7/8	27 3/8	27 3/8	Canyon Creek, AB	Edith J. Nagy	Edith J. Nagy	1981	414
185 4/8	39 7/8	39 7/8	16 3/8	16 4/8	8 2/8	8 7/8	21 7/8	21 7/8	Granite Co., MT	Lawrence R. Simkins	Lawrence R. Simkins	1986	414
185 4/8	40 5/8	39 4/8	16 3/8	16 4/8	8 3/8	9 5/8	21	18 4/8	Deer Lodge Co., MT	Douglas C. Landers	Douglas C. Landers	1987	414
185 4/8	38 4/8	40 4/8	14 7/8	14 7/8	10 4/8	10 4/8	20 5/8	20 3/8	Barrier Mt., AB	Ronald K. Smith	Ronald K. Smith	1988	414
185 4/8	40 7/8	40 3/8	14 5/8	14 5/8	10 2/8	10 2/8	25	22 2/8	Lewis & Clark Co., MT	Darlene K. Kechely	Darlene K. Kechely	1992	414
185 4/8	41 1/8	39 3/8	15 7/8	15 6/8	8 3/8	8 3/8	23 1/8	17	Missoula Co., MT	Thomas J. Dux	Thomas J. Dux	1993	414
185 4/8	38 4/8	37 4/8	16	16	9 5/8	9 7/8	22 3/8	19	Blaine Co., MT	Eugene W. Bell	Eugene W. Bell	1995	414
185 4/8	42	39	15 1/8	15 1/8	8 6/8	8 6/8	23 1/8	22 2/8	Highwood Range, AB	James Collings	James Collings	1998	414
185 4/8	40 1/8	39 5/8	15 7/8	15 7/8	8 4/8	8 4/8	23 1/8	21 5/8	Blaine Co., MT	Joseph A. Blades	Joseph A. Blades	1999	414
185 3/8	39 6/8	39 6/8	16 3/8	16 3/8	8 1/8	8	16 3/8	13 4/8	Natal, BC	Myles Travis	H. Beard	1921	426
185 3/8	39 4/8	38 3/8	15 1/8	14 7/8	10 2/8	10 2/8	22	17 4/8	Lewis & Clark Co., MT	Richard Tyler	Richard Tyler	1954	426

BIGHORN SHEEP

Ovis canadensis canadensis and certain related subspecies

Score	Length of Horn R	Length of Horn L	Circumference of Base R	Circumference of Base L	Circumference at Third Quarter R	Circumference at Third Quarter L	Greatest Spread	Tip to Tip Spread	Locality	Hunter	Owner	Date Killed	Rank
185 3/8	39 5/8	39	16	16	9 6/8	9 1/8	21	20 5/8	Fremont Co., CO	Leonard L. Kiser	Leonard L. Kiser	1955	426
185 3/8	40 3/8	39 6/8	14 6/8	14 7/8	10 1/8	9 5/8	23 4/8	19 4/8	Lillooet, BC	Glen E. Park	Glen E. Park	1964	426
185 3/8	39 3/8	40 2/8	15 4/8	15 6/8	10 1/8	10 6/8	21 4/8	15 6/8	Banff, AB	Unknown	E. Kent. Univ.	PR 1974	426
185 3/8	38 1/8	40 6/8	15 7/8	15 7/8	9 4/8	9 3/8	22 6/8	17 6/8	Sanders Co., MT	Chad R. Jones	Chad R. Jones	1990	426
185 3/8	40 1/8	38 2/8	14 6/8	14 6/8	10 1/8	10 2/8	22 5/8	18 6/8	Grand Co., UT	Picked Up	Ute Indian Tribe	1990	426
185 3/8	36 7/8	38 2/8	17 2/8	17 2/8	8	8 2/8	22	16 4/8	Kananaskis, AB	Bruce Stewart	Bruce Stewart	1996	426
185 3/8	38 1/8	38 4/8	15 7/8	15 6/8	9 3/8	10 2/8	22 3/8	19 1/8	Granite Co., MT	John C. Lundt	John C. Lundt	1997	426
185 3/8	37 1/8	39 6/8	15 6/8	15 6/8	9	9 1/8	23	14 6/8	Rio Arriba Co., NM	Robert D. Mac Millan	Robert D. Mac Millan	1999	426
185 2/8	42 2/8	38	15 6/8	16	8 5/8	8 6/8	21	17 3/8	Unknown	Unknown	Art Esslinger	1930	436
185 2/8	38 1/8	37 1/8	16	15 3/8	10 4/8	9 7/8	20 1/8	20 1/8	Big Creek, ID	Edson Piers	Edson Piers	1962	436
185 2/8	40 6/8	41	15 3/8	15 3/8	8 7/8	8 6/8	23 2/8	20 1/8	Spences Bridge, BC	J.C. Atkinson	J.C. Atkinson	1965	436
185 2/8	38 1/8	37 5/8	16 5/8	16 5/8	9 1/8	8 5/8	22 4/8	21	Fremont Co., CO	Robert W. Wallace	Robert W. Wallace	1978	436
185 2/8	38 5/8	41 3/8	15 5/8	15	8 6/8	9 2/8	21 4/8	20 4/8	Teton Co., MT	Picked Up	Tim French	1980	436
185 2/8	39 2/8	38	15	15 2/8	11 3/8	10 3/8	22 7/8	17	Phillips Co., MT	Patrick R. Trujillo	Patrick R. Trujillo	1992	436
185 2/8	40 5/8	40 3/8	16	16	8 5/8	8 3/8	23 1/8	22 4/8	Missoula Co., MT	Mayline K. Robertson	Mayline K. Robertson	1996	436
185 2/8	39 6/8	39	15	15	9 6/8	9 6/8	23 5/8	18 4/8	Teton Co., MT	Doug Larson	Doug E. Larson	1998	436
185 1/8	41 3/8	40 6/8	14 5/8	14 4/8	9 3/8	9 3/8	22 7/8	19 2/8	Dubois Co., WY	B.N. Lively	B.N. Lively	1953	444
185 1/8	40 1/8	38 6/8	15 3/8	15 3/8	9 2/8	8 7/8	23	15 2/8	Tornado Mt., BC	Vincent Kehm	Vincent Kehm	1958	444
185 1/8	40 2/8	37 5/8	15 7/8	15 7/8	9 4/8	9	23 2/8	18 2/8	Big Horn River, AB	Chris Klineburger	Chris Klineburger	1962	444
185 1/8	40 5/8	37 6/8	16	16	8 3/8	8 7/8	21 7/8	18	Sheep River, AB	Garner D. Jacobs	Garner D. Jacobs	1989	444
185 1/8	38	38 5/8	16 4/8	16 2/8	8 5/8	9	25 1/8	22 4/8	Blaine Co., MT	Mark K. Weiser	Mark K. Weiser	1989	444
185 1/8	41	40 1/8	14 2/8	14 1/8	11	10 7/8	21	17 6/8	Lewis & Clark Co., MT	Eugene R. Lewis	Eugene R. Lewis	1990	444
185 1/8	36 2/8	37 7/8	16 4/8	16 4/8	9 2/8	10 5/8	24 6/8	18	Greenlee Co., AZ	Gary L. Asmus	Gary L. Asmus	1994	444
185 1/8	38	39 1/8	16 2/8	16 2/8	9	9	22 2/8	18 2/8	Sanders Co., MT	Marcus M. Nichols	Marcus M. Nichols	1994	444
185	40 1/8	39 5/8	16 2/8	16 2/8	8 4/8	8 2/8	22	19 4/8	Alberta	Gift of Lynford Biddle	Acad. Nat. Sci., Phil.	1901	452
185	40 1/8	39 1/8	14 7/8	14 7/8	10 4/8	10 4/8	23	17 6/8	Green River, WY	Floyd J. Stalnaker	Elsie Stalnaker	1913	452
185	38 6/8	41 2/8	15 1/8	15 2/8	9 2/8	9 4/8	18 4/8	17 7/8	Mitchell River, BC	Mr. & Mrs. N.A. Meckstroth	Mr. & Mrs. N.A. Meckstroth	1963	452
185	40 4/8	39 4/8	15 1/8	14 7/8	9 3/8	9	20 2/8	17 2/8	Cadomin, AB	Rita Oney	Rita Oney	1966	452
185	40	41	14 7/8	15	10	9	23 3/8	18 1/8	Sanders Co., MT	Patrick M. Woolard	Patrick M. Woolard	1992	452
185	41 2/8	38 2/8	15 6/8	15 5/8	8 6/8	8 6/8	22 3/8	21 1/8	Missoula Co., MT	William G. Crandall	William G. Crandall	1994	452
185	40 6/8	40 2/8	14 7/8	15	9 3/8	9 4/8	21 4/8	20 7/8	Granite Co., MT	Matt A. Noble	Matt A. Noble	2001	452
184 7/8	40 4/8	39 5/8	14 6/8	14 7/8	9 5/8	9 4/8	23 5/8	23 5/8	Westhorse Mts., ID	Cecil Dodge	Cecil Dodge	1953	459
184 7/8	37 6/8	37 7/8	15	15 3/8	10 4/8	10 2/8	22 3/8	20	Glenwood Springs, CO	Picked Up	Mark E. Cook	1960	459
184 7/8	37 6/8	37 3/8	15 7/8	16	10 1/8	9 7/8	22 6/8	21 2/8	Silver Bow Co., MT	Leslie D. Barnett	Leslie D. Barnett	1994	459
184 7/8	39 1/8	40 4/8	15 4/8	15 4/8	9	8 5/8	25 2/8	25 2/8	Harney Co., OR	Thomas P. Weil	Thomas P. Weil	1997	459
184 7/8	40	40 7/8	15 2/8	15	8 5/8	9	23 2/8	20 4/8	Cheviot Mt., AB	Leo D. Paquin	Leo D. Paquin	1999	459
184 6/8	38 7/8	39 1/8	15 1/8	15 4/8	10 4/8	10 2/8	21 3/8	21 3/8	Unknown	Unknown	George Ostashek	PR 1920	464

Score	Length of Horn R	Length of Horn L	Circ. of Base R	Circ. of Base L	Circ. 3rd Qtr R	Circ. 3rd Qtr L	Greatest Spread	Tip to Tip Spread	Locality	Hunter	Owner	Date	Rank
184 6/8	40 1/8	40 1/8	15 2/8	15 2/8	9 7/8	9 6/8	21 5/8	19 3/8	Brazeau River, AB	Grancel Fitz	Mrs. Grancel Fitz	1931	464
184 6/8	41 2/8	41 2/8	14 4/8	14 4/8	9 6/8	9 4/8	21	20 6/8	Castle Mt., MT	E.L. Anderson	E.L. Anderson	1954	464
184 6/8	40	40 4/8	14 2/8	14 2/8	10 2/8	10 5/8	23 7/8	21 6/8	Jackson Hole, WY	Johnny Kretschman	Johnny Kretschman	1962	464
184 6/8	39 4/8	39 2/8	16 3/8	16 1/8	7 6/8	8 1/8	21 1/8	17 3/8	Little Elbow River, AB	Alex Cornett	Alex Cornett	1976	464
184 6/8	37 7/8	37 3/8	15 4/8	15 4/8	10 1/8	10 2/8	19 7/8	18 4/8	Sanders Co., MT	William J. Alexander	William J. Alexander	1991	464
184 6/8	40 2/8	40 6/8	15 7/8	15 5/8	8 1/8	8 2/8	23 4/8	24 4/8	Sanders Co., MT	Klinton K. Curtis	Klinton K. Curtis	1994	464
184 6/8	37 6/8	40 4/8	15 5/8	15 4/8	8 4/8	8 5/8	20 2/8	20 4/8	Granite Co., MT	Bruce A. Hover	Bruce A. Hover	1995	464
184 6/8	39 1/8	37 5/8	16 5/8	16 5/8	6 7/8	6 6/8	22 4/8	19 7/8	Ravalli Co., MT	Bill A. Richichi	Bill A. Richichi	1996	464
184 6/8	41	41	16 6/8	16 6/8	8 3/8	8 3/8	26 6/8	21 1/8	Wallowa Co., OR	Mark D. Armstrong	Mark D. Armstrong	1997	464
184 6/8	40 2/8	40	15 3/8	15 4/8	9 4/8	9 4/8	22 3/8	26 2/8	Ravalli Co., MT	David G. Paullin	David G. Paullin	1999	464
184 6/8	38 5/8	37 4/8	15 6/8	15 3/8	9 6/8	9 6/8	20 2/8	20 7/8	Salmon River, ID	Ted Biladeau	Ted Biladeau	1939	464
184 5/8	39 2/8	39 2/8	14 7/8	14 7/8	9 7/8	9 7/8	22 1/8	17 6/8	Clearwater, AB	G.C. Matthews	G.C. Matthews	1942	475
184 5/8	41 1/8	42 3/8	14 2/8	14 1/8	10 6/8	10 4/8	22 1/8	20 2/8	Burnt Timber Creek, AB	Berry B. Brooks	Berry B. Brooks	1960	475
184 5/8	39 2/8	39 1/8	14 7/8	14 7/8	9 3/8	9 3/8	22 5/8	18 3/8	Rock Lake, AB	Bill Bodenchuk	Clifford Wolfe	1960	475
184 5/8	38 2/8	39 2/8	15 4/8	15 3/8	10	10	22	21 4/8	Ruby Lake, AB	Picked Up	Carl Iacona	1965	475
184 5/8	39	40 5/8	15	15	10	10	22	18 2/8	Luscar Creek, AB	Doug W. Whiteside	Doug W. Whiteside	1976	475
184 5/8	41 6/8	37 7/8	16	16 3/8	7 7/8	8 1/8	22 1/8	21 3/8	Asotin Co., WA	Thomas J. Pawlacyk	Thomas J. Pawlacyk	1994	475
184 5/8	38 6/8	38 6/8	16	16	8 7/8	8 6/8	26 2/8	25 2/8	Fergus Co., MT	Jason R. Cargill	Jason R. Cargill	1997	475
184 5/8	41 1/8	41 1/8	16	16	8 1/8	8 1/8	21	20 4/8	Missoula Co., MT	Lloyd D. Hanson	Lloyd D. Hanson	1999	475
184 5/8	41 1/8	41 1/8	14	13 6/8	9 4/8	9 4/8	22 2/8	19 2/8	Taos Co., NM	Perry D. Harper	Perry D. Harper	1999	475
184 5/8	39 2/8	39 2/8	16	16	8 1/8	8 4/8	22 3/8	17 4/8	Smoky River, AB	W.C. Barthman	W.C. Barthman	1946	475
184 4/8	39 5/8	39 5/8	15 1/8	15	10 1/8	10 1/8	21 5/8	17 7/8	Sun River, MT	Picked Up	W.H. Stecker	1948	485
184 4/8	38 7/8	38 5/8	16	16 1/8	10 1/8	10 1/8	22 4/8	18 5/8	Custer Co., ID	Stanley V. Potts	Stanley V. Potts	1981	485
184 4/8	36 7/8	36 7/8	16 1/8	16 2/8	8 4/8	8 5/8	24 6/8	23 7/8	Granite Co., MT	Kevin R. Bouley	Kevin R. Bouley	1988	485
184 4/8	39 3/8	39 1/8	15 7/8	15 7/8	8 5/8	8 3/8	21 2/8	18 1/8	Exshaw Creek, AB	Kenneth F. Bills	Kenneth F. Bills	1993	485
184 4/8	38 6/8	38 6/8	15 5/8	15 5/8	8 6/8	8 7/8	22 7/8	17 4/8	Kindersley Creek, BC	James C. Johnson	James C. Johnson	1993	485
184 4/8	40 6/8	40 4/8	15	15	9 5/8	9 6/8	19 6/8	19 6/8	Park Co., MT	Cliff Harden	Cliff Harden	1994	485
184 4/8	38 3/8	38 5/8	15 6/8	15 6/8	9 2/8	9 2/8	22	19 4/8	Ravalli Co., MT	Brenda M. Lewis	Brenda M. Lewis	1994	485
184 4/8	37 7/8	40 6/8	16 1/8	16 2/8	8 3/8	8 3/8	21 1/8	19 1/8	Nez Perce Co., ID	Robert P. Ellingson III	Robert P. Ellingson III	1999	485
184 4/8	40 7/8	38 5/8	15 7/8	15 7/8	8	7 3/8	23 3/8	23	Fergus Co., MT	Mathew W. Birdwell	Mathew W. Birdwell	2002	485
184 4/8	41 4/8	40 2/8	15 2/8	15 2/8	9	8 4/8	31	30 3/8	Phillips Co., MT	Colby L. Loudon	Colby L. Loudon	2002	485
184 4/8	36 4/8	38 2/8	15 2/8	15 2/8	11	10 2/8	21 6/8	13 7/8	Gunnison Co., CO	Billy Prior	Daniel C. Harrington	1915	485
184 3/8	37 4/8	39 6/8	14	14	11	10 2/8	22 1/8	17 6/8	Cadomin, AB	John H. Marcum	John H. Marcum	1969	496
184 3/8	37 3/8	41	14 1/8	14 1/8	9	8 7/8	22	21	Carbon Co., MT	Picked Up	Monte Berzel	1977	496
184 3/8	39 6/8	41 7/8	14 2/8	14 2/8	11 6/8	11	24 2/8	18 2/8	Burnt Timber Creek, AB	Terrance S. Marcum	Terrance S. Marcum	1988	496
184 3/8	41	42 4/8	15 4/8	15 4/8	10	10	18 6/8	18 6/8	Sanders Co., MT	Charles Hall	Charles Hall	1992	496
184 3/8	42 4/8	39 5/8	16 4/8	16 3/8	7 4/8	7 4/8	23 3/8	19	Hinton, AB	James S. Robinson	James S. Robinson	1994	496
184 3/8	39 5/8	41 6/8	15 7/8	15 4/8	8 4/8	8 5/8	23 4/8	16 2/8	Missoula Co., MT	James A. Schott	James A. Schott	1995	496
184 3/8	41 6/8	37 2/8	15 7/8	15 7/8	8 2/8	9 1/8	22 4/8	21 4/8	Baker Co., OR	Craig R. Droke	Craig R. Droke	2000	496
184 3/8	37 2/8	39 3/8	15 4/8	15 4/8	10 3/8	10 5/8	20 6/8	21 4/8	Granite Co., MT	John A. Slevin	John A. Slevin	2001	496
184 3/8	39 3/8	39 2/8	14 4/8	14 4/8	9 6/8	9 1/8	24	16	Clearwater River, AB	Alan J. Douglas	Alan J. Douglas	2002	496
184 3/8	39 2/8	37 6/8	14 6/8	14 6/8	10 4/8	10 7/8	20 1/8	18 4/8	Middle Mts., WY	William Underwood	William Underwood	1959	496
184 2/8	37 6/8	38 7/8	15 4/8	15	10 7/8	10 7/8	20 7/8	20 1/8	Drinnan Creek, AB	John H. Epstein	John H. Epstein	1963	506
184 2/8	38 7/8	41	15	15	8 5/8	9 2/8	21 7/8	17	Elk Valley, BC	Bernard A. Fiedeldey, Jr.	Bernard A. Fiedeldey, Jr.	1992	506
184 2/8	41	39 3/8	15 1/8	15	9 6/8	9 6/8	22 1/8	17 6/8	Granite Co., MT	Keith Bomstad	Keith Bomstad	1996	506
184 2/8	39 3/8	40 2/8	15 1/8	15 1/8	11 1/8	11 1/8	22 4/8	22	Mystery Lake, AB	David S. Stelter	David S. Stelter	1998	506
184 2/8	40 2/8	39 4/8	15 3/8	15 3/8	10	10	22 1/8	20 2/8	Granite Co., MT	Garry D. Seaman	Garry D. Seaman	2000	506
184 2/8	39 2/8	39 2/8	14 7/8	15 1/8	9 7/8	9 5/8	22 4/8	20 2/8	Condor Mt., AB	Keith C. Brown	Keith C. Brown	2001	506

Ovis canadensis and certain related subspecies

Score	Length of Horn R	L	Circumference of Base R	L	Circumference at Third Quarter R	L	Greatest Spread	Tip to Tip Spread	Locality	Hunter	Owner	Date Killed	Rank
184 2/8	38	43 2/8	15	15	9 6/8	9 3/8	26 2/8	26 1/8	Ravalli Co., MT	Thomas J. O'Neill	Thomas J. O'Neill	2001	506
184 1/8	40 2/8	38 1/8	15 2/8	15 3/8	9 6/8	8 6/8	23	22	Vaseux Lake, BC	Robert E. McDowell	Robert E. McDowell	1960	514
184 1/8	39 5/8	42	15 2/8	15 1/8	8 5/8	8 1/8	22 5/8	22 5/8	Alberta	Bob Wood	N. Am. Wildl. Mus.	1964	514
184 1/8	38 7/8	39	17	17	7 7/8	7 6/8	23 1/8	23 1/8	Castle River, AB	E.B. Cunningham	E.B. Cunningham	1965	514
184 1/8	39 7/8	39 4/8	15 4/8	15 4/8	9 1/8	9 3/8	24	21 7/8	Panther River, AB	Picked Up	Paul Ujfalusi	1966	514
184 1/8	39	38 1/8	16	15 7/8	9 5/8	9 5/8	25	23 5/8	Silver Bow Co., MT	John D. Truzzolino	John D. Truzzolino	1990	514
184 1/8	38 1/8	38 4/8	16 6/8	15 5/8	8 3/8	8 2/8	22 1/8	13 5/8	Fording River, BC	Cam McGregor	Cam McGregor	1995	514
184 1/8	38 6/8	38 3/8	15	15 1/8	9 7/8	9 7/8	21 3/8	16 1/8	Cadomin Creek, AB	David F. Thomson	David F. Thomson	1997	514
184 1/8	41	39 3/8	16 5/8	15 5/8	6 6/8	6 7/8	22	22	Lost Mt., BC	Paul R. D'Andrea	Paul R. D'Andrea	2000	514
184 1/8	39	39 3/8	14 6/8	15	10	9 7/8	24 6/8	24	Graham Co., AZ	James A. Jamison	James A. Jamison	2001	514
184	40 5/8	37 7/8	14 6/8	14 7/8	9 2/8	9 4/8	22 4/8	22 3/8	Valley Co., ID	Picked Up	LaVarr Jacklin	1949	523
184	41 1/8	41 1/8	14 2/8	14 1/8	10	10	20 5/8	19	Ghost River, AB	W.D. Norwood	W.D. Norwood	1955	523
184	39 1/8	39 1/8	14 7/8	14 7/8	10 1/8	10 3/8	21 6/8	21 6/8	Sun River, MT	Carl Mehmke	Carl Mehmke	1957	523
184	35	36 4/8	16 2/8	15 1/8	10 6/8	11	21	20	Cardston, AB	August Glander	August Glander	1969	523
184	37 5/8	39 5/8	16 4/8	15 3/8	8 2/8	8 7/8	25 5/8	20	Sanders Co., MT	Don Robinson	Cabela's, Inc.	1980	523
184	40 4/8	43 4/8	15	15	8 2/8	8 3/8	25 5/8	25 5/8	Deer Lodge Co., MT	David M. Bisch	Davis M. Bisch	1988	523
184	40	38 4/8	15 3/8	15 3/8	9	9	20 1/8	17	Unknown	Unknown	Paul L.C. Snider	PR 1989	523
184	39	40 2/8	14 4/8	14 4/8	10 2/8	10 4/8	22	19 7/8	Mineral Co., MT	Ronald A. Snyder	Ronald A. Snyder	1991	523
184	36 6/8	37 4/8	15 4/8	15 4/8	10 7/8	11	22 2/8	18 4/8	Sanders Co., MT	Robert Schultz	Robert Schultz	1994	523
184	39 4/8	32	16 2/8	16 4/8	9 5/8	9 4/8	25	22	Missoula Co., MT	Billy J. Olsen	Billy J. Olsen	1997	523
184	38 6/8	37 4/8	15 7/8	15 5/8	9 2/8	9 4/8	23 7/8	21	Blaine Co., MT	Jim M. Forman	Jim M. Forman	1999	523
184	38 6/8	37	15 4/8	15 4/8	9 3/8	9 4/8	25 4/8	18 3/8	Blaine Co., MT	George Willeford	George Willeford	2000	523
184	39 4/8	41 2/8	16 2/8	16 3/8	7 4/8	7 4/8	24 6/8	24 4/8	Sanders Co., MT	Gary N. Hill	Gary N. Hill	2001	523
184	38 3/8	38 3/8	15	14 7/8	10 6/8	10 6/8	21 2/8	14 3/8	Taos Co., NM	Dick A. Jacobs	Dick A. Jacobs	2001	523
183 7/8	41 1/8	40	14 4/8	14 4/8	9 6/8	9 4/8	23	20 5/8	Saskatchewan River, AB	Basil C. Bradbury	Basil C. Bradbury	1968	537
183 7/8	43 5/8	35 2/8	17	17	7 5/8	6 6/8	24 4/8	23	Beaverhead Co., MT	James C. Garrett	James C. Garrett	1983	537
183 7/8	41	41 1/8	15 1/8	15 1/8	8 4/8	8 2/8	24 3/8	24 3/8	Sanders Co., MT	Lyndell C. Stahn	Lyndell C. Stahn	1988	537
183 7/8	39 2/8	39 3/8	16	16	8 2/8	8 6/8	21 5/8	18 3/8	Garfield Co., WA	Klaus H. Meyn	Klaus H. Meyn	1990	537
183 7/8	39 1/8	39 2/8	15 6/8	15 5/8	8 7/8	8 4/8	23 7/8	21 6/8	Granite Co., MT	Gordon H. Brandenburger	Gordon H. Brandenburger	1992	537
183 7/8	38 1/8	39	16 4/8	16	8 4/8	9	20 5/8	20 2/8	Nez Perce Co., ID	Michael L. Lohman	Michael L. Lohman	1993	537
183 7/8	37 4/8	37 1/8	16 4/8	16	9	8 7/8	23 2/8	23	Beaverhead Co., MT	Arthur E. Nuthak	Arthur E. Nuthak	1993	537
183 7/8	38 3/8	39 6/8	16	16	8 5/8	9 5/8	23 6/8	16 2/8	Huerfano Co., CO	Mark D. Thomson	Mark D. Thomson	1997	537
183 7/8	37 6/8	38 7/8	15 4/8	15 4/8	10 4/8	9 6/8	20 6/8	20 2/8	Granite Co., MT	Bruce Stell	Bruce Stell	2002	537
183 6/8	37 2/8	37 2/8	15 5/8	15 5/8	9 5/8	9 6/8	20 4/8	17 4/8	Fernie, BC	Unknown	Fred Braatz	1930	546
183 6/8	38 4/8	41 4/8	14 4/8	15 4/8	9 1/8	8 3/8	25 2/8	25 2/8	Diorite Creek, BC	Leon Cloarec	F.P. Bills Family	1936	546
183 6/8	39 7/8	39 3/8	14 6/8	14 6/8	9 7/8	10	21 4/8	15 7/8	Natal, BC	Mrs. A.L. Musser	A.L. Musser	1947	546
183 6/8	40 1/8	39 5/8	14 4/8	14 4/8	10 2/8	10 2/8	19 5/8	18 1/8	Castle River, AB	George Hagglund	George Hagglund	1959	546
183 6/8	37 2/8	38	15 4/8	15 4/8	10	10	21 4/8	18 2/8	Highwood Range, AB	K. Fred Coleman	K. Fred Coleman	1977	546
183 6/8	37 6/8	36 4/8	16 5/8	16 5/8	9	9	23 4/8	23 4/8	Ravalli Co., MT	Sandra L. Gann	Les Towner	1985	546

Score	Length R	Length L	Circ. Base R	Circ. Base L	Circ. 3rd Qtr R	Circ. 3rd Qtr L	Greatest Spread	Tip to Tip	Locality	By Whom Killed	Owner	Date Killed	Rank
183 6/8	37 4/8	37 4/8	16	16	9 3/8	9 4/8	24	22 4/8	Silver Bow Co., MT	Emmett O. Riordan	Emmett O. Riordan	1986	546
183 6/8	38 4/8	39	15 6/8	15 6/8	8 7/8	8 6/8	23 2/8	14 4/8	Wallowa Co., OR	Tom R. Croswell	Tom R. Croswell	1992	546
183 6/8	36	36	16 2/8	16 2/8	9 5/8	10 1/8	21 7/8	15 3/8	Teton Co., MT	Greg D. Gilbert	Greg D. Gilbert	1992	546
183 6/8	37 1/8	36 1/8	17 2/8	17 2/8	8 1/8	8	21 4/8	21	Blaine Co., MT	John H. Miller	John H. Miller	1992	546
183 6/8	38 5/8	40 3/8	14 7/8	14 7/8	9 6/8	9 7/8	23 6/8	17 6/8	Granite Co., MT	Janice J. Kauffman	Janice J. Kauffman	1993	546
183 6/8	39	37 6/8	15 2/8	15 2/8	9 7/8	9 6/8	23 5/8	17 7/8	Lewis Co., ID	Earl G. Lunceford, Jr.	Earl G. Lunceford, Jr.	1993	546
183 6/8	38 3/8	40 7/8	16 7/8	16 7/8	7 5/8	7 2/8	22 3/8	20 4/8	Blaine Co., MT	Kathy M. Peterson	Kathy M. Peterson	1995	546
183 5/8	38 2/8	37 3/8	16 3/8	16 3/8	9 2/8	9 3/8	21 6/8	17 2/8	Mystery Lake, AB	Paul Inzanti	Paul Inzanti	1960	559
183 5/8	37 7/8	39 3/8	15 6/8	15 5/8	9 5/8	9 2/8	19 4/8	18 7/8	Marble Creek, ID	Joseph T. Pelton	Joseph T. Pelton	1961	559
183 5/8	39	39	15 3/8	15 3/8	10 1/8	10 1/8	22	16 1/8	Burnt Timber, AB	Jay H. Giese	Jay H. Giese	1966	559
183 5/8	37	37	16 1/8	16 1/8	9 6/8	9 5/8	24 7/8	24 7/8	Granite Co., MT	Sandy C. Antonich	Sandy C. Antonich	1982	559
183 5/8	36 7/8	36 7/8	15	15	9 1/8	9 2/8	22	21 2/8	Lemhi Co., ID	Ronald D. Carlson	Ronald D. Carlson	1989	559
183 5/8	39 4/8	41 5/8	16 5/8	15 4/8	8 4/8	8 5/8	21 6/8	21 2/8	Phillips Co., CO	Dee Strickler	Jack F. Strickler	1993	559
183 5/8	38 3/8	38 3/8	15 4/8	15 4/8	9	9	23 3/8	17 4/8	Pitkin Co., CO	D. Dean Spatz	D. Dean Spatz	1998	559
183 5/8	40	40	16	16 2/8	8 4/8	8 7/8	23 4/8	23	Granite Co., MT	Gary L. Zabel	Gary L. Zabel	1999	559
183 5/8	39 7/8	39 4/8	15 4/8	15 4/8	9	9 7/8	21 4/8	21 4/8	Fergus Co., MT	Marvin L. Dahl	Marvin L. Dahl	2000	559
183 4/8	38	39 3/8	15 6/8	15 6/8	10 4/8	10 4/8	22 3/8	18 2/8	Sweet Grass Co., MT	Basil C. Bradbury	Basil C. Bradbury	1965	568
183 4/8	33 4/8	39	14 7/8	16	9 7/8	9 4/8	21 2/8	21 1/8	Mystery Lake, AB	Armando Tomasso	Armando Tomasso	1967	568
183 4/8	42	36 6/8	15 6/8	15 4/8	9 5/8	9 5/8	20 4/8	20 4/8	C.M. Russell Game Range, MT	Mrs. Gordon Pagenkopf	Mrs. Gordon Pagenkopf	1970	568
183 4/8	38 2/8	39 2/8	16 2/8	16 1/8	8 6/8	8 1/8	18	13 7/8	Granite Co., MT	Karen Throckmorton	Karen Throckmorton	1987	568
183 4/8	39 1/8	37 5/8	16 4/8	16 6/8	8 1/8	7 1/8	22 6/8	14 2/8	Chauncey Creek, BC	Stewart Cockshutt	Stewart Cockshutt	1990	568
183 4/8	39 2/8	38 6/8	16 1/8	16 1/8	8	8 2/8	21 2/8	21 2/8	Galatea Creek, AB	Karlo Miklic	Karlo Miklic	1990	568
183 4/8	39	39 6/8	16	16	8	9 3/8	21 2/8	20 3/8	Lewis & Clark Co., MT	Lynn E. Valtinson	Lynn E. Valtinson	1991	568
183 4/8	39	38 4/8	15 6/8	15 6/8	9 2/8	9 2/8	22 7/8	19	Sanders Co., MT	Clinton R. Fitchett	Clinton R. Fitchett	1996	568
183 4/8	38 4/8	40	15 1/8	15 1/8	7 7/8	7 7/8	21 4/8	19 3/8	Granite Co., MT	Robert D. Mattie	Robert D. Mattie	1996	568
183 4/8	41	41 7/8	15 7/8	15 7/8	8 3/8	8 3/8	24 5/8	24 3/8	Fergus Co., MT	Jack R. Sater	Jack R. Sater	1997	568
183 4/8	42 3/8	38 3/8	15 4/8	15 7/8	9	9	22 7/8	19	Sanders Co., MT	Jeffrey M. Shouse	Jeffrey M. Shouse	1999	568
183 4/8	38 7/8	38 7/8	15 7/8	15 4/8	9 5/8	8 6/8	22 4/8	20	Elko Co., NV	S. Kim Elliott	S. Kim Elliott	2002	568
183 4/8	39 6/8	39 4/8	16	15 7/8	9 4/8	9 4/8	23 4/8	23 1/8	Lewis & Clark Co., MT	Jim R. Marques	Jim R. Marques	2003	568
183 3/8	38 6/8	36 6/8	15 6/8	16	8 3/8	8 3/8	24 1/8	23 5/8	Lewis & Clark Co., MT	John Coston	John Coston	1961	581
183 3/8	41	38 1/8	15 3/8	15 3/8	10 7/8	10 1/8	22	16 2/8	Clearwater River, AB	C.J. McElroy	C.J. McElroy	1969	581
183 3/8	37 3/8	38 7/8	16 4/8	16 4/8	8 2/8	7 7/8	21	15 6/8	Sanders Co., MT	John P. Dilley	John P. Dilley	1981	581
183 3/8	38 7/8	42 7/8	15 2/8	15 2/8	6 7/8	7 4/8	27 4/8	27 4/8	Sanders Co., MT	Edward W. Blackwood	Rocky Mt. Elk Foundation	1985	581
183 3/8	42 7/8	40 4/8	15 6/8	15 6/8	7 4/8	7 5/8	21 5/8	21 5/8	Sanders Co., MT	Ilse R. Knight	Ilse R. Knight	1986	581
183 3/8	40 4/8	38 3/8	16 4/8	16 4/8	7 7/8	8	20 5/8	18 4/8	Mt. Sparrowhawk, AB	Gregory Kondro	Gregory Kondro	1989	581
183 3/8	38 3/8	37 5/8	16 1/8	16 1/8	9 6/8	9 2/8	22 6/8	19 4/8	Silver Bow Co., MT	Travis T. Schluessler	Travis T. Schluessler	1990	581
183 3/8	37 5/8	39 3/8	15 5/8	15 5/8	9 2/8	9 5/8	21 7/8	21 2/8	Beaverhead Co., MT	Austin S. Rosenbaum	Austin S. Rosenbaum	1993	581
183 3/8	39 3/8	36 6/8	15 3/8	15 3/8	9 5/8	9 3/8	23	21 4/8	Granite Co., MT	Terry R. Screnar	Terry R. Screnar	1996	581
183 3/8	36 6/8	41 1/8	15 6/8	15 6/8	8 6/8	8 3/8	21 2/8	22 6/8	Lewis & Clark Co., MT	Scott A. Van Dyken	Scott A. Van Dyken	1997	581
183 3/8	41 1/8	40 7/8	16 2/8	16 2/8	7 5/8	7 5/8	23 4/8	22 1/8	Granite Co., MT	Nanette M. Cox	Nanette Cox	1998	581
183 3/8	40 7/8	40	15 5/8	15 4/8	8 6/8	8 6/8	22 3/8	23 4/8	Blaine Co., MT	Richard Bardwell	Richard Bardwell	2000	581
183 3/8	40	39 5/8	15	15	8 4/8	10	23 4/8	18 1/8	Granite Co., MT	Leanna E. Olson	Leanna E. Olson	2000	581
183 3/8	39 5/8	39 5/8	15 3/8	15 3/8	10	8 5/8	18 6/8	17 6/8	Missoula Co., MT	Rich Lamb	Rich Lamb	2002	581
183 2/8	39 5/8	39 4/8	14 3/8	14 2/8	11 5/8	11 1/8	20	19 6/8	Snake-Indian River, AB	O. Fowler & J. Brewster	Fred Brewster	1919	595
183 2/8	39 4/8	38	15 7/8	15 7/8	9 7/8	9 4/8	19 6/8	23 2/8	Smoky River, AB	Frank C. Hibben	Frank C. Hibben	1957	595
183 2/8	38	38 4/8	14 7/8	14 6/8	9 6/8	9 7/8	23 2/8	18 2/8	Sun River, MT	Earl Hofland	Earl Hofland	1957	595
183 2/8	39 6/8	40 4/8	15 1/8	14 6/8	9	9	23 1/8	23 1/8	Clearwater River, AB	Joseph C. Sellitti	Joseph C. Sellitti	1981	595

BIGHORN SHEEP

Ovis canadensis and certain related subspecies

Score	Length of Horn R	Length of Horn L	Circumference of Base R	Circumference of Base L	Circumference at Third Quarter R	Circumference at Third Quarter L	Greatest Spread	Tip to Tip Spread	Locality	Hunter	Owner	Date Killed	Rank
183 2/8	38 4/8	40 2/8	15 6/8	15 6/8	8	8 4/8	22 3/8	18 4/8	Granite Co., MT	John L. Wozniak	John L. Wozniak	1984	595
183 2/8	41	42 6/8	15 2/8	15 2/8	7 4/8	7 7/8	23 7/8	23 7/8	Deer Lodge Co., MT	Phillip DeMers	Phillip DeMers	1985	595
183 2/8	38 2/8	38 6/8	15 6/8	16	8 5/8	8 6/8	20 5/8	20 5/8	Bow River, AB	Guy R. Woods	Guy R. Woods	1985	595
183 2/8	41 1/8	40 2/8	16 2/8	16 2/8	7 3/8	7 6/8	22 2/8	21 1/8	Sanders Co., MT	Alma E. Arnold	Alma E. Arnold	1986	595
183 2/8	40 2/8	40 2/8	15 7/8	15 4/8	8 1/8	8 1/8	23 6/8	23 3/8	Sanders Co., MT	Thorne R. Johnson	Thorne R. Johnson	1987	595
183 2/8	39 5/8	36 3/8	16 2/8	16 3/8	8 7/8	8 5/8	28 2/8	28 2/8	Granite Co., MT	Scott R. Rossow	Scott R. Rossow	1988	595
183 2/8	39 4/8	39 6/8	15 3/8	15 4/8	8 6/8	9 1/8	20 2/8	18 2/8	Simpson River, BC	Robert T. White	Robert T. White	1988	595
183 2/8	39	39	15 2/8	15 2/8	9 3/8	9 4/8	21 4/8	18 6/8	Prospect Creek, AB	Bruce E. Williams	Bruce E. Williams	1989	595
183 2/8	37 5/8	37 1/8	16 1/8	16 1/8	9 1/8	9 2/8	20 4/8	17 7/8	Grizzly Creek, AB	William J. Herchuk	William J. Herchuk	1993	595
183 2/8	41 6/8	40 4/8	14 6/8	14 5/8	9 3/8	9 2/8	26	26	Park Co., WY	T.K. Atkinson	T.K. Atkinson	1994	595
183 2/8	41	39 4/8	15 1/8	15 1/8	8 6/8	8 2/8	24 6/8	24	Silver Bow Co., MT	Jeffrey T. Fisher	Jeffrey T. Fisher	1994	595
183 2/8	37 7/8	36 7/8	15 1/8	15 2/8	10 2/8	10 2/8	21 6/8	20 1/8	Deer Lodge Co., MT	Dan J. Burns	Dan J. Burns	2001	595
183 1/8	40	37 1/8	16	16	9	8 6/8	22 4/8	20	Unknown	Unknown	Jonas Bros. of Seattle	PR 1939	611
183 1/8	34 7/8	36	16 2/8	16 2/8	9 7/8	10 1/8	24 5/8	20	S. Platte Canyon, CO	Harold C. Eastwood	Harold C. Eastwood	1957	611
183 1/8	38 4/8	38 5/8	15 5/8	15 5/8	9	9 1/8	22 2/8	16 7/8	Kootenay River, BC	W. Vernon Walsh	W. Vernon Walsh	1962	611
183 1/8	36 7/8	37 2/8	15 3/8	15 3/8	10 3/8	10	22	18 4/8	Fraser River, BC	Karl P. Willms	Karl P. Willms	1977	611
183 1/8	36 3/8	36 1/8	16 1/8	16 2/8	9 5/8	9 4/8	21 1/8	16 3/8	Mt. Sparrowhawk, AB	Randy Ward	Randy Ward	1984	611
183 1/8	36 1/8	40 2/8	16	16	8 7/8	9	20 3/8	20 2/8	Deer Lodge Co., MT	Jeffrey R. Shellenberg	Jeffrey R. Shellenberg	1990	611
183 1/8	39 6/8	39 5/8	15 4/8	15 4/8	9	8 5/8	22 7/8	20 4/8	Granite Co., MT	Stephen E. Brown	Stephen E. Brown	1993	611
183 1/8	41 1/8	39 6/8	14 6/8	14 5/8	9 5/8	9 4/8	22	18 4/8	Sanders Co., MT	Robert A. Parker	Robert A. Parker	1993	611
183 1/8	39 3/8	39 4/8	15 4/8	15 4/8	8 6/8	8 4/8	21 2/8	18 2/8	Wallowa Co., OR	Kenneth W. Kirsch	Kenneth W. Kirsch	1994	611
183 1/8	38 1/8	39	13 2/8	13 2/8	8	8 4/8	22	21 7/8	Sanders Co., MT	Diana L. Ross	Diana L. Ross	1994	611
183 1/8	38 4/8	39 3/8	15 4/8	15 5/8	8 6/8	9 1/8	23 2/8	17 5/8	Taos Co., NM	Clinton L. Kuchan	Clinton L. Kuchan	2000	611
183 1/8	39 6/8	39 7/8	14 1/8	14 1/8	10 2/8	10 5/8	22 4/8	17 6/8	Taos Co., NM	James G. Petersen	James G. Petersen	2002	611
183	39 4/8	38	16 2/8	16 2/8	8 2/8	8 4/8	21 4/8	17 6/8	Teton Basin, WY	William A. Baillie-Grohman	John H. Batten	1876	623
183	37 5/8	39 1/8	15 5/8	15 5/8	10 3/8	10 5/8	19 4/8	15 6/8	Clearwater River, AB	John H. Batten	John H. Batten	1931	623
183	39 2/8	40	15 4/8	15 4/8	8 3/8	8 5/8	21 5/8	21 5/8	Cadomin, AB	Otis Chandler	Otis Chandler	1969	623
183	38	38 6/8	15 1/8	15 1/8	9	9 2/8	21 1/8	21 1/8	Solomon Creek, AB	Picked Up	William Gosney	1977	623
183	40 5/8	40 7/8	13 7/8	14 1/8	10 5/8	10 4/8	20 2/8	19 4/8	Ram River, AB	Robert G. Morgan	Robert G. Morgan	1980	623
183	38	38 4/8	15 5/8	15 5/8	9 2/8	9 2/8	20 6/8	15 6/8	Galatea Mt., AB	Mario G. Giustini	Mario G. Giustini	1996	623
183	37 2/8	37 2/8	14 5/8	14 4/8	11 2/8	11 4/8	24	22 7/8	Timber Creek, AB	Picked Up	John E. Cassidy	1997	623
183	39	39 4/8	15 7/8	16	8 2/8	8 2/8	22 2/8	21 2/8	Granite Co., MT	Joseph M. Walsh	Joseph M. Walsh	1998	623
183	40 5/8	38 7/8	15 1/8	15 1/8	9 3/8	9 4/8	22 4/8	21 5/8	Granite Co., MT	Carole J. Beebe	Carole J. Beebe	1999	623
182 7/8	40 5/8	38 6/8	15 1/8	15 1/8	9 4/8	9 4/8	22	17 4/8	Alberta	G.L. Gibbons	G.L. Gibbons	1963	632
182 7/8	37 6/8	38 5/8	16 4/8	16 6/8	8 1/8	7 6/8	22 1/8	17	Line Creek, BC	Kevin J. Galla	Kevin J. Galla	1989	632
182 7/8	39	37 5/8	14 7/8	15	9 7/8	10 6/8	21	19	Harlequin Creek, AB	Bob Wasylyshen	Bob Wasylyshen	1997	632
182 6/8	37 5/8	37 5/8	15 2/8	15 2/8	9 7/8	10	23 7/8	20 4/8	Lake Louise, AB	Picked Up	Howard Bronsdon	1952	635
182 6/8	39 6/8	38	14 3/8	14 4/8	10 2/8	10	22 4/8	18	Salmon River, ID	Picked Up	Wayne Demaray	1963	635

Score									Locality	Owner	Hunter	Date	Rank
182 6/8	38 4/8	37 4/8	15	14 6/8	15	10 5/8	10 3/8	21 7/8	15 5/8	Burnt Timber, AB	Mrs. W.E. Anderson	Mrs. W.E. Anderson	1964	635
182 6/8	39 2/8	39	15	15	15	9 7/8	9 4/8	22	18 6/8	Wildhay River, AB	Jim Papst	Jim Papst	1968	635
182 6/8	40 4/8	40 4/8	14 6/8	14 6/8	14 5/8	9	9 1/8	22 6/8	22 6/8	Lower Salmon River, ID	Glenn H. Schubert	Deloras A. Schubert	1970	635
182 6/8	40 6/8	39 2/8	16 1/8	16 1/8	16	7 7/8	7 7/8	22 6/8	19 6/8	Sanders Co., MT	Terrence Pond	Terrence Pond	1978	635
182 6/8	42	40 4/8	16	16	16	7	7 1/8	25 7/8	25 3/8	Deer Lodge Co., MT	Kirk G. Stovall	Kirk G. Stovall	1990	635
182 6/8	40 1/8	40 3/8	15 2/8	15 2/8	15 2/8	9	8 4/8	23	23	Ravalli Co., MT	Robert S. Wood	Robert S. Wood	1993	635
182 6/8	42 1/8	40 5/8	15	15	15	9 1/8	9 1/8	22	22	Blaine Co., MT	Mike Crites	Mike Crites	1996	635
182 6/8	42	40	14 7/8	14 7/8	14 7/8	8 1/8	8 2/8	22	21 2/8	Missoula Co., MT	Shawn M. Conrad	Shawn M. Conrad	1997	635
182 6/8	39 4/8	36 4/8	15 5/8	15 5/8	15 5/8	8 7/8	9	24 4/8	23 1/8	Redcap Mt., AB	Glenn Funfer	Glenn Funfer	1997	635
182 6/8	38 2/8	39	15	15 1/8	15 1/8	9 6/8	9 2/8	22	18 3/8	Teton Co., MT	Audie Anderson	Audie Anderson	2000	635
182 6/8	37 5/8	36 3/8	15 2/8	15 2/8	15 2/8	10 1/8	10 1/8	20 7/8	20 7/8	Chelan Co., WA	Kenneth R. Harris	Kenneth R. Harris	2002	635
182 5/8	44 1/8	42 4/8	14	13 7/8	13 7/8	8 4/8	8 4/8	23 1/8	23 1/8	Alberta	John D. Hazen	Unknown	1918	648
182 5/8	37 7/8	38 6/8	16 6/8	16 6/8	16 6/8	7 3/8	7 3/8	19 4/8	16	Brazeau Forest, AB	H.A. Yocum	H.A. Yocum	1941	648
182 5/8	40 3/8	39 4/8	15 2/8	15	15	8 6/8	8 4/8	22 7/8	13 4/8	Bull River, BC	Ralph W. Stearns	Ralph W. Stearns	1950	648
182 5/8	42 1/8	40 4/8	15 2/8	15	15	7 5/8	7 3/8	20 2/8	20	Sun River, MT	Martin Alzheimer	Martin Alzheimer	1955	648
182 5/8	39 1/8	36 4/8	15 4/8	15 5/8	15 5/8	9 4/8	9 4/8	21 4/8	20 6/8	Narraway River, AB	John C. Seidensticker	John C. Seidensticker	1959	648
182 5/8	38 1/8	38 4/8	14 7/8	15	15	10 2/8	10 2/8	21 2/8	15 6/8	Storm Mt., AB	W. Glaser	W. Glaser	1961	648
182 5/8	38 4/8	37 3/8	16	16	16	8 7/8	8 7/8	19 2/8	13 1/8	Junction Creek, AB	Robert F. Brooks	Robert F. Brooks	1978	648
182 5/8	38	38 7/8	14 7/8	14 7/8	14 7/8	9 2/8	9 6/8	21 2/8	20 7/8	Missoula Co., AB	Brad A. Sweeney	Brad A. Sweeney	1996	648
182 5/8	38 3/8	37 4/8	16 2/8	15 7/8	15 7/8	9 6/8	9 1/8	20 7/8	18 6/8	Lewis & Clark Co., MT	Gary M. Zadick	Gary M. Zadick	1996	648
182 5/8	38 5/8	39	15 1/8	15 1/8	15 1/8	9 2/8	9 2/8	20 2/8	15	Rocky Mt. House, AB	Chris Blower	Chris Blower	1997	648
182 5/8	34 7/8	37 2/8	16 2/8	16 2/8	16 2/8	9 6/8	10 2/8	20 3/8	15 6/8	Galatea Creek, AB	Leo Ouellette	Leo Ouellette	1998	648
182 5/8	37 6/8	37 3/8	16 1/8	16	16	9	9	20 5/8	14 5/8	Granite Co., MT	Gerald L. Fischer	Gerald L. Fischer	2000	648
182 5/8	39 7/8	38 4/8	14 4/8	14 4/8	14 4/8	10	10 1/8	2—	20 5/8	Mora Co., NM	Robert G. Ringer	Robert G. Ringer	2000	648
182 4/8	35 4/8	35 2/8	16 4/8	16 4/8	16 4/8	10	9 4/8	24	22 5/8	Waterton, CO	William D. Jenkins	William D. Jenkins	1956	661
182 4/8	37	35	15 3/8	15 4/8	15 4/8	11 2/8	10 4/8	23	21	Wind River, WY	Hubert Weibel	Hubert Weibel	1956	661
182 4/8	36 7/8	37 7/8	16 3/8	16 1/8	16 1/8	8 5/8	8 7/8	23 5/8	17 6/8	S. Castle River, AB	Leon Atwood	Leon Atwood	1962	661
182 4/8	38 4/8	39 2/8	15 5/8	15 5/8	15 5/8	8 4/8	8 2/8	22 1/8	19 1/8	Kananaskis Summit, AB	Ted Howell	Ted Howell	1964	661
182 4/8	38 3/8	37 5/8	14 6/8	14 6/8	14 6/8	10 6/8	10 5/8	22 1/8	18 2/8	Turtle Creek, WY	Russell C. Cutter	Russell C. Cutter	1968	661
182 4/8	41 1/8	40 5/8	15	15	15	8 1/8	8 2/8	22	18 4/8	Edgewater, BC	William N. Ward	William N. Ward	1969	661
182 4/8	40 2/8	40	15 3/8	15 3/8	15 3/8	8 2/8	8 1/8	23 1/8	20	Spences Bridge, BC	Don Ticehurst	Don Ticehurst	1973	661
182 4/8	38 4/8	41 2/8	15 4/8	15 4/8	15 4/8	9	9	22 5/8	17 2/8	Mary Ann Creek, BC	Jack Bridgewater	Jack Bridgewater	1981	661
182 4/8	38 6/8	35 6/8	15 3/8	15 3/8	15 3/8	10 1/8	10 1/8	23 2/8	23 2/8	Wallowa Co., OR	Randy Craddock	Randy Craddock	1981	661
182 4/8	35 7/8	36 3/8	16 2/8	16 2/8	16 2/8	9 7/8	9 7/8	22 4/8	19	Blind Canyon, AB	Alan W. Foster	Alan W. Foster	1981	661
182 4/8	39 3/8	39 3/8	15 5/8	15 5/8	15 5/8	8 4/8	8 4/8	2— 5/8	19	Sanders Co., MT	Thorne R. Johnson	Thorne R. Johnson	1989	661
182 4/8	37 2/8	39 2/8	15 2/8	15 2/8	15 2/8	9 1/8	9 3/8	23 4/8	23 4/8	Blaine Co., MT	Daniel D. Doran	Daniel D. Doran	1997	661
182 4/8	39	41 2/8	14 7/8	14 7/8	14 7/8	8 7/8	9 3/8	23 5/8	15 5/8	Gregg River, AB	William Cloyd	William C. Cloyd	1998	661
182 4/8	39 7/8	40 1/8	14 6/8	14 5/8	14 5/8	9 3/8	9 2/8	21 4/8	21 4/8	Teton Co., MT	Josh B. Johns	Josh B. Johns	1998	661
182 4/8	41	44 2/8	15 1/8	15 1/8	15 1/8	7 4/8	7 6/8	24 3/8	23 4/8	Sanders Co., MT	Colin E. White	Colin E. White	2001	661
182 3/8	38 7/8	38 2/8	15 3/8	15 4/8	15 4/8	9 1/8	9 5/8	20	18 1/8	Montana	Unknown	Joseph P. Scurti	PR 1949	676
182 3/8	38 3/8	37 4/8	14 6/8	14 5/8	14 5/8	10 2/8	10 4/8	22	16 2/8	Banff, AB	Gift of Madison Grant to NCHH	Unknown	PR 1951	676
182 3/8	37 2/8	37 3/8	15 2/8	15 3/8	15 3/8	10 4/8	10 4/8	2— 7/8	17	Teton River, MT	Geoffrey A. Morrison	Geoffrey A. Morrison	1969	676
182 3/8	38 6/8	37 1/8	16	16	16	8 3/8	8 7/8	23 7/8	18 6/8	West Sulphur River, AB	Robert Highberg	Robert Highberg	1980	676
182 3/8	38 7/8	39 2/8	15 6/8	15 6/8	15 6/8	9 4/8	8 7/8	20 6/8	20 1/8	Pigeon Mt., AB	Len H. Guldman	Len H. Guldman	1990	676
182 2/8	40 3/8	40 1/8	14 5/8	14 5/8	14 5/8	9 7/8	9 6/8	23 4/8	21	Shoshone N. Fork, WY	Herb Klein	Dallas Mus. of Natl. Hist.	1934	681
182 2/8	40 7/8	40 1/8	15	15	15	8 7/8	8 6/8	23 4/8	20 4/8	Dubois Co., WY	George Pate	Larry Pate	1960	681
182 2/8	39 5/8	39 7/8	15 2/8	15	15	9 1/8	9 4/8	2— 4/8	17 4/8	Ram River, AB	Louise McConnell	Louise McConnell	1961	681

BIGHORN SHEEP

Ovis canadensis canadensis and certain related subspecies

Score	Length of Horn R	L	Circumference of Base R	L	Circumference at Third Quarter R	L	Greatest Spread	Tip to Tip Spread	Locality	Hunter	Owner	Date Killed	Rank
182 2/8	36	36 6/8	15 4/8	15 4/8	10	10	21 3/8	16	Sulphur River, AB	Unknown	Roy Everest	1963	681
182 2/8	40 1/8	39 7/8	15	14 5/8	9 4/8	10 2/8	21 2/8	21 2/8	Wildhay River, AB	James H. Duke, Jr.	James H. Duke, Jr.	1967	681
182 2/8	36 4/8	35 6/8	16 1/8	16 2/8	9 1/8	9 1/8	23 3/8	18 7/8	Rocky Creek, AB	Randy A. Desabrais	Randy A. Desabrais	1982	681
182 2/8	37 5/8	39 1/8	14 5/8	14 7/8	10 1/8	10 1/8	22 5/8	21 3/8	Park Co., MT	Rodney W. Cole	Rodney W. Cole	1985	681
182 2/8	39 3/8	39 1/8	15 7/8	16 1/8	8	7 7/8	23 1/8	23 5/8	Beaverhead Co., MT	Raymond L. Cote	Raymond L. Cote	1989	681
182 2/8	38 5/8	38 7/8	15 1/8	15 1/8	9 3/8	9 6/8	19 7/8	19 1/8	Silver Bow Co., MT	John T. LaPierre	John T. LaPierre	1990	681
182 2/8	39	40 2/8	14 4/8	14 7/8	9 1/8	9 1/8	22 2/8	22 2/8	Lewis & Clark Co., MT	Ben E. Arps	Ben E. Arps	1996	681
182 2/8	40	40 6/8	15 7/8	15 7/8	7	7 3/8	20 4/8	20 4/8	Elbow River, AB	Glen R. Pickering	Glen R. Pickering	1998	681
182 2/8	39	37 2/8	16	16	8 4/8	8 6/8	20 4/8	20 2/8	Missoula Co., MT	John B. Smith	John B. Smith	2002	681
182 2/8	37 5/8	39 1/8	15 3/8	15 3/8	9 2/8	8 7/8	23 3/8	23	Ravalli Co., MT	Virginia G. Karstetter	Virginia G. Karstetter	2003	681
182 1/8	41 5/8	39	12 7/8	13 1/8	11 6/8	11 5/8	22 6/8	22 6/8	Salmon River, ID	Picked Up	Anson Eddy	PR 1959	694
182 1/8	35 4/8	39 3/8	15 2/8	15 2/8	11 2/8	9 2/8	24 6/8	24 6/8	Lemhi Co., ID	Leonard C. Miller, Sr.	Leonard C. Miller, Sr.	1963	694
182 1/8	38 3/8	37 4/8	15 2/8	15 1/8	9 4/8	9 4/8	22 1/8	17 3/8	Panther River, AB	W.H. Slikker	W.H. Slikker	1966	694
182 1/8	37 7/8	37 4/8	16	16 2/8	8 5/8	8 5/8	20 1/8	18 2/8	Crowsnest Lake, AB	John Truant	John Truant	1970	694
182 1/8	39	39 3/8	16 1/8	16 1/8	7 6/8	7 6/8	22 4/8	22 4/8	Silver Bow Co., MT	Eric L. Jacobson	Eric L. Jacobson	1990	694
182 1/8	37 7/8	44	15 3/8	15	7 6/8	8 2/8	23 5/8	22 6/8	Ravalli Co., MT	Bret A. Sourbrine	Bret A. Sourbrine	1994	694
182 1/8	39 2/8	38 3/8	14 6/8	14 6/8	9 7/8	9 7/8	22 2/8	21 7/8	Granite Co., MT	Roy H. Rogers	Roy H. Rogers	1995	694
182	40	41	14 5/8	14 7/8	8 5/8	8 7/8	24	24	Salmon River, ID	Picked Up	Elmer Keith	1957	701
182	41	37 6/8	15	14 7/8	9 2/8	9 1/8	21 5/8	17 4/8	Canal Flat, BC	Allen Cudworth	Allen Cudworth	1958	701
182	37 5/8	36 7/8	15 6/8	15 7/8	9 7/8	10	21	16 4/8	Pincher Creek, AB	Delton Smith	Delton Smith	1958	701
182	39 1/8	41 7/8	14 4/8	14 3/8	8 3/8	7 6/8	23 5/8	23 3/8	Lewis & Clark Co., MT	Allan L. Davies	Allan L. Davies	1981	701
182	38 6/8	38 4/8	14 4/8	14 3/8	10 3/8	10 4/8	19	17 4/8	Mt. Kidd, AB	Picked Up	Dirk Kieft	1982	701
182	37 4/8	39 2/8	15 3/8	15 3/8	8 6/8	8 7/8	20 3/8	17 1/8	Mt. Kidd, AB	Dwayne W. Oneski	Dwayne W. Oneski	1982	701
182	39 7/8	40 1/8	15 2/8	15 4/8	8	8 1/8	20 4/8	20 4/8	Murray Creek, BC	Nancy J. Koopman	Nancy J. Koopman	1986	701
182	40 7/8	39 5/8	16 2/8	16 3/8	7 1/8	7 3/8	22 5/8	22 2/8	Wallowa Co., OR	Dale R. Dotson	Dale R. Dotson	1988	701
182	39 4/8	39 6/8	15	15 1/8	8 7/8	9 4/8	20 1/8	19 1/8	Sanders Co., MT	Kevin K. Harris	Kevin K. Harris	1988	701
182	37	38 6/8	15 3/8	15 1/8	10 4/8	9 6/8	22 1/8	20 2/8	Deer Lodge Co., MT	George A. Kovacich	George A. Kovacich	1988	701
182	37 5/8	37 5/8	16 2/8	16 2/8	8 2/8	8 2/8	22 4/8	18 4/8	Wigwam River, BC	Grant W. Markoski	Grant W. Markoski	1990	701
182	39 4/8	38 6/8	15	15	8 7/8	9	24	24	Saguache Co., CO	Ralph G. Hejny	Ralph G. Hejny	1992	701
182	38 3/8	38 1/8	15 2/8	15 2/8	9 5/8	9 4/8	21 1/8	17 2/8	Missoula Co., MT	Jeff S. Putnam	Jeff S. Putnam	1993	701
182	39 6/8	39 6/8	16 2/8	16 2/8	8 1/8	8 1/8	22 4/8	20 3/8	Mineral Co., MT	Billy D. Queen	Billy D. Queen	1994	701
182	37 4/8	38	14 4/8	14 7/8	10 6/8	10 5/8	25 6/8	20 7/8	Las Animas Co., CO	Picked Up	U.S. Army	1994	701
182	40	40 4/8	15 6/8	15 6/8	8 1/8	8 1/8	22 6/8	22 6/8	Missoula Co., MT	Kenneth B. Henegar	Kenneth B. Henegar	1996	701
182	39 6/8	41 2/8	14 4/8	14 4/8	9 6/8	9 6/8	22 6/8	21 2/8	Catron Co., NM	D. Scott Annala	D. Scott Annala	1997	701
182	36 1/8	37 1/8	15 4/8	15 4/8	10 6/8	10	20 1/8	14 2/8	Elk River, BC	Harry E. Seratt	Harry E. Seratt	1997	701
182	39 1/8	40 1/8	15 7/8	15 6/8	7 6/8	7 6/8	23 4/8	23 4/8	Sanders Co., MT	Bernard Robinson	Bernard L. Robinson	1998	701
182	37 3/8	38 3/8	15 3/8	15 3/8	9 2/8	8 6/8	21 4/8	18 5/8	Elk River, BC	W. Joe Putz	W. Joe Putz	2001	701
182	40	40 6/8	15	15	7 7/8	8 1/8	22 4/8	22 1/8	Mt. Allen, AB	Dale A. Fournier	Dale A. Fournier	2003	701

Score									Location	Hunter	Owner	Date	Rank
181 7/8	39 2/8	39 1/8	14 3/8	14 2/8	10 5/8	10 1/8	20 7/8	20 4/8	Coal Branch, AB	John Caputo, Sr.	John Caputo, Sr.	1962	722
181 7/8	36 5/8	36 2/8	16 5/8	16 4/8	8 4/8	8	20 7/8	20	Elko, BC	Percy McGregor	Percy McGregor	1974	722
181 7/8	38 3/8	39	15 2/8	15 1/8	9 4/8	9 4/8	21 1/8	19	Hinton, AB	Darla J. Smith	Ben Morris	1980	722
181 7/8	39 5/8	40 6/8	15 1/8	14 7/8	8 6/8	8 4/8	21 1/8	21 1/8	Sundre, AB	Dennis G. Overguard	Dennis G. Overguard	1980	722
181 7/8	39 1/8	38 4/8	15 1/8	15 1/8	9 1/8	9	20	19	Kakwa River, AB	Donald C. Fobert	Donald C. Fobert	1983	722
181 7/8	38	38 7/8	15 7/8	15 5/8	8 6/8	8 3/8	23 2/8	22 7/8	Cataract Creek, AB	Michael J. Hogan	Michael J. Hogan	1984	722
181 7/8	38 5/8	39 4/8	15 3/8	15 3/8	8 4/8	9	22	20 2/8	Teton Co., MT	Deborah Conway	Deborah Conway	1991	722
181 7/8	38 6/8	38 2/8	16	16	8 5/8	8 4/8	23 2/8	21 7/8	Granite Co., MT	Don Syvrud	Don Syvrud	1991	722
181 7/8	35 5/8	36 1/8	15	15	12	12	21 7/8	16 4/8	Taos Co., NM	Reuben R. Tipton III	Reuben R. Tipton III	1994	722
181 7/8	43 4/8	43	14 7/8	14 6/8	6 1/8	5 6/8	22 4/8	17 1/8	Missoula Co., MT	Warren W. Dennis	Warren W. Dennis	1997	722
181 7/8	37 4/8	37 3/8	16 1/8	16	8 6/8	8 6/8	12 6/8	12 6/8	Pennington Co., SD	Tad B. Jacobs	Tad B. Jacobs	2001	722
181 6/8	37	37 2/8	15 4/8	15 4/8	9 5/8	9 5/8	13	14 4/8	Ghost River, AB	L.C. Nowlin	L.C. Nowlin	PR 1940	733
181 6/8	38 1/8	38 5/8	15	15 2/8	10	10	20 6/8	16 1/8	Prospect Creek, AB	Wayne Tarnasky	Wayne Tarnasky	1983	733
181 6/8	36 4/8	36 4/8	17	15 1/8	9 6/8	8 4/8	23 4/8	20 6/8	Gunnison Co., CO	Paula D. Darner	Paula D. Darner	1986	733
181 6/8	40 5/8	39 5/8	15 2/8	15 2/8	8 4/8	8 4/8	25	24 4/8	Teton Co., WY	Richard L. Grabowski	Richard L. Grabowski	1989	733
181 6/8	38 3/8	39 7/8	14 7/8	14 7/8	8	9 1/8	22 2/8	22 2/8	Blaine Co., MT	Betty L. Ramsey	Betty L. Ramsey	1989	733
181 6/8	39 3/8	37 3/8	15	14 7/8	8 4/8	9 4/8	23 1/8	20	Graham Co., AZ	Terrance S. Marcum	Terrance S. Marcum	1995	733
181 6/8	36 4/8	38 2/8	15 7/8	15 5/8	9 3/8	8 7/8	23 1/8	22 2/8	Blaine Co., MT	Dennis M. McCleary	Dennis M. McCleary	1997	733
181 6/8	38 1/8	37 3/8	16	16	9	9	22	19 4/8	Granite Co., MT	Guy D. Buyan	Guy D. Buyan	1999	733
181 6/8	40	37	15 6/8	15 6/8	8 5/8	8 5/8	22	21	Missoula Co., MT	James A. Hoiland	James A. Hoiland	1999	733
181 5/8	38	37 6/8	16 1/8	16 2/8	8 1/8	8 1/8	21 1/8	19 2/8	Baker Co., OR	Steven W. Brooks	Steven W. Brooks	2001	733
181 5/8	42	40 1/8	15 2/8	15 1/8	7 6/8	7 6/8	20 2/8	20 2/8	Ghost River, AB	Jack S. Parker	Jack S. Parker	1954	743
181 5/8	39 1/8	37	15 6/8	15 6/8	9 3/8	9 4/8	21 2/8	21 2/8	Custer Co., MT	Picked Up	Picked Up	1959	743
181 5/8	36 7/8	39 2/8	15 4/8	15 4/8	8 7/8	9	23 4/8	23 4/8	Elbow River, AB	Ernest F. Dill	Ernest F. Dill	1961	743
181 5/8	39 6/8	40 1/8	15 3/8	15 3/8	7 6/8	8 4/8	22 7/8	22 7/8	Sun River, MT	Walter L. Bodie	Walter L. Bodie	1965	743
181 5/8	41 5/8	37 6/8	14 2/8	14 4/8	10 2/8	10	20 4/8	20 4/8	Burnt Timber Creek, AB	George H. Glass	George H. Glass	1967	743
181 5/8	39 3/8	39 3/8	14 4/8	14 6/8	9 6/8	9 2/8	23 5/8	23 5/8	Park Co., WY	Keith Frick	Keith Frick	1972	743
181 5/8	39 3/8	37	16 4/8	16 3/8	7 5/8	7 3/8	20	20	Fisher Range, AB	Reginald Zebedee	Reginald Zebedee	1982	743
181 5/8	38 1/8	34 4/8	16 2/8	16 2/8	9 2/8	9 4/8	23	23	Pigeon Mt., AB	Paul S. Inzanti	Paul S. Inzanti	1984	743
181 5/8	39 6/8	39 5/8	15 4/8	15 4/8	8 1/8	8 1/8	21 4/8	21 4/8	Goat Range, AB	Christian D. Pagenkopf	Christian D. Pagenkopf	1984	743
181 5/8	39	38 1/8	15 3/8	15 2/8	9 7/8	9 7/8	20	20 6/8	Lemhi Co., ID	David Freel	David Freel	1986	743
181 5/8	37 7/8	39	16	16	8 3/8	8 3/8	13 4/8	19 5/8	Kootenay River, BC	Arthur V. Parsons	Arthur V. Parsons	1986	743
181 5/8	35 6/8	36 2/8	16	15 7/8	10 4/8	9 5/8	22 5/8	22 5/8	Lewis & Clark Co., MT	Pamela J. Bennett	Pamela J. Bennett	1989	743
181 5/8	39 1/8	35 1/8	15 4/8	15 4/8	8 7/8	8 4/8	20 1/8	20 1/8	Teton Co., MT	Neil L. Hamm	Neil L. Hamm	1990	743
181 5/8	39	38 2/8	15 2/8	15 2/8	9 3/8	9	24 4/8	23 4/8	Deer Lodge Co., MT	Roy A. Wiant	David P. Moore	1990	743
181 5/8	37 4/8	39 1/8	14 6/8	14 6/8	10 4/8	10 4/8	21 7/8	14 3/8	Sanders Co., MT	Peter J. Bachmeier	Peter J. Bachmeier	1995	743
181 5/8	37 1/8	36 7/8	16 1/8	16 1/8	8 3/8	8 3/8	23 3/8	21 7/8	Blaine Co., MT	Clifford Wilber	Clifford Wilber	1999	743
181 4/8	40	37 6/8	15 2/8	15 2/8	8 2/8	8 2/8	22	22 1/8	Sulphur River, AB	John E. Hammett	John E. Hammett	1938	759
181 4/8	38 6/8	40 5/8	14 4/8	14 4/8	8 4/8	8 5/8	22 2/8	22 2/8	Castle River, AB	Cliff Johnson	Cliff Johnson	1957	759
181 4/8	36	41 2/8	15 1/8	14 4/8	11 1/8	11 1/8	23	21	Dubois Co., WY	Jack Adams	Jack Adams	1959	759
181 4/8	38 5/8	36	15 3/8	15 1/8	9	8 6/8	23 1/8	19 6/8	Cadomin, AB	John Caputo, Sr.	John Caputo, Sr.	1961	759
181 4/8	43	43 4/8	16	16	6 2/8	6 7/8	29 4/8	29 4/8	Gallatin Co., MT	Richard D. Gilman	Richard D. Gilman	1967	759
181 4/8	41 3/8	39 7/8	15 2/8	15 2/8	7 7/8	7 7/8	22 5/8	22 5/8	Lewis & Clark Co., MT	William L. Wesland	Picked Up	1973	759
181 4/8	39 7/8	37 6/8	15 1/8	15 1/8	9 1/8	8	18 6/8	18 6/8	Spray Lake, AB	George R. Willows	George R. Willows	1974	759
181 4/8	39	41 2/8	16 1/8	16	6 6/8	6 5/8	21 4/8	21 4/8	Deer Lodge Co., MT	Gerald P. Wendt	Gerald P. Wendt	1978	759
181 4/8	37	39	16 2/8	16 3/8	8 3/8	8 4/8	24 3/8	24 3/8	Lewis & Clark Co., MT	Donel G. Hayes	Donel G. Hayes	1980	759
181 4/8	38 3/8	41 3/8	16 2/8	16 3/8	6 7/8	6 7/8	24	24	Granite Co., MT	Michael B. Murphy	Michael B. Murphy	1987	759
181 4/8	38 6/8	36 4/8	16 5/8	16 5/8	7 3/8	7 5/8	19 4/8	11 7/8	Mt. Evans-Thomas, AB	William E. MacDougall	William E. MacDougall	1988	759

BIGHORN SHEEP

Ovis canadensis and certain related subspecies

Score	Length of Horn R	L	Circumference of Base R	L	Circumference at Third Quarter R	L	Greatest Spread	Tip to Tip Spread	Locality	Hunter	Owner	Date Killed	Rank
181 4/8	35 7/8	36 7/8	16 3/8	16 3/8	8 5/8	9 2/8	22 3/8	21	Granite Co., MT	Bronwyn B. Price	Bronwyn B. Price	1989	759
181 4/8	38 3/8	31 1/8	17	17	9	9	23 5/8	19 3/8	Greenlee Co., AZ	Timothy R. Lacy, Sr.	Timothy R. Lacy, Sr.	1991	759
181 4/8	38 3/8	38 7/8	15 5/8	15 6/8	7 7/8	8 2/8	21 4/8	13 6/8	Burnt Timber Creek, AB	Lambert VanDongen	Lambert VanDongen	1991	759
181 4/8	40 4/8	40 7/8	15 2/8	15 2/8	8 2/8	8 2/8	22 1/8	21 5/8	Sanders Co., MT	Thomas L. Judge	Thomas L. Judge	1992	759
181 4/8	38 1/8	38 5/8	16 2/8	16 4/8	8 1/8	8 1/8	20 4/8	18 4/8	Granite Co., MT	Jacob A. Streitz	Jacob A. Streitz	1992	759
181 4/8	36 3/8	35 7/8	15 1/8	15 1/8	10 7/8	10 6/8	22 5/8	18	Saguache Co., CO	Darrel L. Moberly	Darrel L. Moberly	1994	759
181 4/8	40 1/8	39 5/8	15 6/8	15 6/8	7 6/8	7 4/8	21 3/8	17 6/8	Wildhorse Creek, BC	Dan VanZanten	Dan VanZanten	1994	759
181 4/8	39	39	15 6/8	15 6/8	8 2/8	8 5/8	20 6/8	19 6/8	Kootenay River, BC	Gerry Favreau	Gerry Favreau	1998	759
181 4/8	37 6/8	37 6/8	16 2/8	16 1/8	8 4/8	8 4/8	20	20	Granite Co., MT	Michael D. Swanson	Michael D. Swanson	1999	759
181 4/8	39 2/8	37 4/8	15 4/8	15 4/8	9 3/8	8 5/8	23 7/8	19 7/8	Blaine Co., MT	Doug D. Stout	Doug D. Stout	2002	759
181 4/8	39 4/8	37	15	15	10 2/8	10	21	16 6/8	Fremont Co., CO	J. Chad Carter	J. Chad Carter	2003	759
181 3/8	39 3/8	39 6/8	15 1/8	14 6/8	9 4/8	9 1/8	25	21	Clearwater River, AB	Phil Temple	Phil Temple	1951	781
181 3/8	38 2/8	39 3/8	15 1/8	15 2/8	9 2/8	9 4/8	20 4/8	14 4/8	Big Horn Creek, AB	Earl Foss	Earl Foss	1960	781
181 3/8	37 2/8	36 7/8	17	17	8	8 1/8	20 4/8	15 4/8	Park Co., CO	Richard L. Rudeen	Richard L. Rudeen	1963	781
181 3/8	37 7/8	37 7/8	14 7/8	14 7/8	9 3/8	9 3/8	20 4/8	19 6/8	Clearwater River, AB	Joseph T. Pelton	Joseph T. Pelton	1966	781
181 3/8	38 3/8	38 4/8	15	15	9 5/8	9 5/8	21 4/8	15	Beartooth Plateau, MT	Olav E. Nelson	Olav E. Nelson	1970	781
181 3/8	39	39 5/8	15 4/8	15 5/8	8 3/8	8 2/8	22 3/8	19 4/8	Lincoln Co., MT	Lowell Olin	Lowell Olin	1977	781
181 3/8	38 4/8	39 5/8	14 6/8	14 7/8	9 3/8	9	20 6/8	20 3/8	Lake Co., MT	Picked Up	J. Michael Conoyer	1978	781
181 3/8	37 5/8	37 4/8	15	15	10 5/8	10 5/8	19	15 3/8	Cardinal River, AB	Randy Babala	Randy Babala	1980	781
181 3/8	39 1/8	38 3/8	15 6/8	15 5/8	8 1/8	7 7/8	21 2/8	20 5/8	Granite Co., MT	David D. Rittenhouse	David D. Rittenhouse	1980	781
181 3/8	38 3/8	38 3/8	15 6/8	15 6/8	8 2/8	8 5/8	21 2/8	20 5/8	Lewis & Clark Co., MT	Elmer T. Crawford	Elmer T. Crawford	1986	781
181 3/8	38 5/8	40 2/8	14 5/8	14 7/8	9 2/8	9 1/8	22 6/8	22 1/8	Wallowa Co., OR	Michael L. Taylor	Michael L. Taylor	1987	781
181 3/8	37 7/8	39 2/8	15	15	9 7/8	9 5/8	20 2/8	16 4/8	Fairholme Range, AB	Eldon Hoff	Eldon Hoff	1989	781
181 3/8	39 3/8	39	15	15	10 2/8	9 6/8	23 3/8	21 4/8	Grant Co., NM	Dan Pocapalia	Dan Pocapalia	1990	781
181 3/8	40 3/8	38 6/8	16	15 6/8	7 6/8	7 7/8	23 2/8	18 5/8	Teton Co., MT	Chad J. Bouma	Chad J. Bouma	1997	781
181 3/8	36 7/8	39 2/8	16 2/8	16 1/8	8 4/8	8 4/8	23 5/8	23 5/8	Deer Lodge Co., MT	Kenneth B. Fitte	Kenneth B. Fitte	1997	781
181 3/8	38 1/8	38 6/8	14 6/8	14 6/8	9 1/8	9 5/8	23 2/8	11 3/8	Hinsdale Co., CO	Mary J. Johnson	Mary J. Johnson	2000	781
181 3/8	38 7/8	37	15	15	9 5/8	10 3/8	18 6/8	17 7/8	Granite Co., MT	Randall L. Kanter	Randall L. Kanter	2001	781
181 2/8	42	41 4/8	14	14	8 5/8	8 2/8	24 6/8	24 6/8	Teton Basin, WY	Michael Huppuch	Philip Schlegel	1901	798
181 2/8	41 1/8	40 5/8	14	13 7/8	10 1/8	9 5/8	21 2/8	19 6/8	Highwood River, AB	Ralph Rink	George Beach	1946	798
181 2/8	40 3/8	40 7/8	15 4/8	15 4/8	7 2/8	7 5/8	22 4/8	22 4/8	McBride, BC	Alfred Saulnier	Alfred Saulnier	1966	798
181 2/8	39 2/8	40 2/8	14 1/8	14 1/8	10	10 2/8	20 5/8	16 4/8	Timber Creek, AB	Jason G. Hindes	Jason G. Hindes	1985	798
181 2/8	40 3/8	40 3/8	14 3/8	14 3/8	8 7/8	9	23 7/8	23 7/8	Lewis & Clark Co., MT	Brandon C. Johns	Brandon C. Johns	1987	798
181 2/8	41 3/8	39 5/8	15 4/8	15 3/8	7 5/8	7 6/8	21	21	Granite Co., MT	Tom J. Lewis	Tom J. Lewis	1989	798
181 2/8	38 3/8	38 5/8	16 4/8	16 1/8	7 4/8	8	19 5/8	17 6/8	Calgary, AB	Max Howard	Max Howard	1990	798
181 2/8	37 1/8	37 3/8	15 4/8	15 5/8	9 4/8	9 5/8	20 7/8	20 4/8	Fergus Co., MT	Leda R. McReynolds	Leda R. McReynolds	1991	798
181 2/8	40	40 6/8	15 1/8	15	7 6/8	7 6/8	21 4/8	21	Ghost River, AB	Mike Michalezki	Mike Michalezki	1991	798
181 2/8	38 4/8	38 4/8	15 4/8	15 4/8	8 6/8	8 5/8	19 5/8	19 5/8	Whiteswan Lake, BC	Larry Tooze	Larry Tooze	1995	798

Score	Horn R	Horn L	Base R	Base L	3rd Qtr R	3rd Qtr L	Gr. Spread	Tip to Tip	Locality	Owner	Hunter	Date	Rank
181 2/8	38 2/8	37 6/8	15 4/8	15 4/8	9	9 3/8	21 3/8	19 6/8	Teton Co., MT	Joseph R. Balazs	Joseph R. Balazs	1996	798
181 2/8	36	36 4/8	15 4/8	15 3/8	9 5/8	10	21 6/8	16 2/8	Gregg River, AB	Mike Michalezki	Mike Michalezki	1997	798
181 1/8	38 2/8	38 5/8	14	14 2/8	11	10 3/8	20 2/8	15 1/8	Cooke City, MT	Larry L. Altimus	Larry L. Altimus	1969	810
181 1/8	38 7/8	35	15 5/8	15 5/8	9 1/8	9	20 4/8	15	Spray Lakes Reservoir, AB	G. Robert Willows	G. Robert Willows	1977	810
181 1/8	38 2/8	40 3/8	15	15 2/8	8 5/8	8 3/8	21	17 3/8	Scalp Creek, AB	James Mills	James Mills	1984	810
181 1/8	39 4/8	39 3/8	14 5/8	14 4/8	9 5/8	9 4/8	22 5/8	22 5/8	Deer Lodge Co., MT	Thomas R. Puccinelli	Thomas R. Puccinelli	1984	810
181 1/8	39	38 5/8	15 4/8	15 3/8	8 5/8	8 3/8	20 6/8	17 4/8	Mt. Inflexible, AB	Carl Gallant	Carl Gallant	1987	810
181 1/8	39 3/8	39 2/8	16 4/8	16 3/8	7 4/8	7 7/8	22	21	Sanders Co., MT	David O. Conrad	David O. Conrad	1993	810
181 1/8	40 4/8	38 3/8	16 1/8	16 1/8	7 5/8	7 5/8	20 4/8	20 3/8	Sanders Co., MT	Darren J. Page	Darren J. Page	1995	810
181 1/8	35 3/8	41 2/8	15 7/8	16	8 6/8	8	22 6/8	22	Granite Co., MT	Shannon V. Taylor	Shannon V. Taylor	2003	810
181	40 5/8	45 7/8	14 1/8	13 7/8	7 7/8	7 5/8	23 1/8	26 1/8	Kootenay, BC	A.E. Matthew	A.E. Matthew	1950	818
181	39 2/8	39 4/8	14 7/8	14 7/8	8 3/8	8 6/8	23 5/8	17 6/8	Lincoln Co., MT	Hal Kanzler	Hal Kanzler	1960	818
181	39 2/8	39 2/8	15 2/8	15 2/8	8 6/8	8 6/8	21	17	Brule, AB	Peter Lazio	Picked Up	1963	818
181	37 6/8	37	15 5/8	15 5/8	9	9	23	15	Mystery Lake, AB	Peter Lazio	Peter Lazio	1967	818
181	38 7/8	37 5/8	14 3/8	14 2/8	11 1/8	11	19 1/8	19 1/8	Simpson Creek, BC	Walt Failor	Walt Failor	1968	818
181	37 5/8	39 1/8	14 4/8	14 4/8	9 5/8	9 3/8	21 3/8	18 3/8	Cadomin, AB	Carl Iacona	Picked Up	1968	818
181	39 1/8	41 1/8	15	15	7 7/8	8 1/8	22 4/8	24 7/8	Kindersley Creek, BC	Karl Dorr	Karl Dorr	1989	818
181	41 1/8	43	16 6/8	16 6/8	5 7/8	6 4/8	25	25	Granite Co., MT	Misty D. Fischer	Misty D. Fischer	1995	818
181	38	40 6/8	15 4/8	15 1/8	8 2/8	8 1/8	20 5/8	20 2/8	Missoula Co., MT	Daniel M. Rockwood	Daniel M. Rockwood	1995	818
181	38 2/8	38 6/8	15 1/8	15 1/8	9 2/8	9 5/8	21 3/8	19 4/8	Cadomin, AB	Steven A. Bowick	Steven A. Bowick	1999	818
180 7/8	37 4/8	38	15 2/8	15 2/8	10 1/8	10 3/8	19 6/8	19 6/8	Granite Co., MT	Robert W. Ehle	Robert W. Ehle	1999	829
180 7/8	36 6/8	38 3/8	14	14	9 4/8	9 4/8	22 6/8	22 3/8	Park Co., WY	Jay Thomas	Picked Up	1979	829
180 7/8	39 2/8	39 2/8	14 6/8	14 6/8	9 3/8	9 3/8	25 5/8	22 4/8	Clearwater River, AB	Kevin Peters	Kevin Peters	1989	829
180 7/8	39 2/8	38 1/8	15 3/8	15 3/8	7 7/8	7 7/8	19 4/8	13 4/8	Sanders Co., MT	Raymond J. Smith	Raymond J. Smith	1990	829
180 7/8	37 4/8	37 4/8	15	16	9 1/8	9 2/8	24 4/8	16 4/8	Line Creek, BC	Kevin J. Galla	Kevin J. Galla	1991	829
180 7/8	41	41	14 6/8	15 2/8	8 4/8	7 7/8	23	24 4/8	Deer Lodge Co., MT	Jack D. Shanstrom	Jack D. Shanstrom	1991	829
180 6/8	39 6/8	39 5/8	15 2/8	15 3/8	7 7/8	8 1/8	20 6/8	23	Washout Creek, AB	Joseph P. Ambrose	Joseph P. Ambrose	1998	836
180 6/8	39 7/8	39 7/8	15	14 7/8	10	10 2/8	22 7/8	20 6/8	Grant Co., NM	Naim S. Bashir	Naim S. Bashir	2002	836
180 6/8	38 2/8	38 2/8	15 7/8	16 2/8	8 7/8	8 4/8	22 5/8	22 7/8	Seebe, AB	Ted Trueblood	Ted Trueblood	1956	836
180 6/8	37	37	15 2/8	15 3/8	7 6/8	7 6/8	22 5/8	22 5/8	Bull River, BC	Walter J. Ruehle	Walter J. Ruehle	PR 1963	836
180 6/8	35	34 2/8	16 2/8	16 2/8	8	8	21	15	Texas Creek, CO	Jack D. Putnam	Picked Up	1964	836
180 6/8	37 4/8	37 4/8	15 1/8	15 2/8	8 5/8	8 3/8	21 3/8	15 3/8	Flat Creek, AB	G.I. Franklin	G.I. Franklin	1964	836
180 6/8	37 5/8	38 3/8	16	16 2/8	10 6/8	10 6/8	21	16 4/8	Panther Creek, AB	C.D. Sharp	C.D. Sharp	1966	836
180 6/8	37 2/8	36 4/8	16	15 1/8	8 6/8	8 4/8	22 7/8	21	Junction Creek, AB	Spencer T. Nichols	Spencer T. Nichols	1981	836
180 6/8	39 6/8	39 4/8	15 1/8	15	9 7/8	9 7/8	21 4/8	16	Mineral Co., MT	Roberta A. Hartford	Roberta A. Hartford	1982	836
180 6/8	37 6/8	37 6/8	15 7/8	15 7/8	8 7/8	9 2/8	24 4/8	19 1/8	Park Co., WY	Dwight Lyman	Dwight Lyman	1982	836
180 6/8	37 1/8	37 1/8	16 2/8	16 2/8	8 4/8	8 7/8	21 1/8	17 5/8	Forbidden Creek, AB	Dennis H. Russell	Dennis H. Russell	1984	836
180 6/8	38 7/8	38 7/8	16 2/8	16 2/8	10 1/8	10	21 6/8	21	Sanders Co., MT	Bob L. Jacks	Bob L. Jacks	1990	836
180 6/8	36 2/8	39	15 3/8	15 3/8	8 7/8	8 7/8	21 4/8	18 7/8	Ewin Pass, BC	Sam W. Stephenson	Sam W. Stephenson	1992	836
180 6/8	38 6/8	38 6/8	15 1/8	15 1/8	7 6/8	7 6/8	22 4/8	19 4/8	Columbia Co., WA	Karie K. Kominski	Karie K. Kominski	1994	836
180 6/8	38	38	15 3/8	15 1/8	8	8	21	21	Sanders Co., MT	MT Dept. of Fish, Wildl., & Parks	Picked Up	1998	836
180 6/8	39	39	15 3/8	15 3/8	8 2/8	8 2/8	18 4/8	18	Mt. Solomon, AB	Dennis Tucker	Dennis Tucker	1998	836
180 6/8	38 1/8	38 5/8	14 7/8	14 7/8	9 4/8	9 4/8	23 4/8	23 1/8	Ravalli Co., MT	Richard J. Hayden	Carl Hayden	2001	836
180 6/8	37 3/8	37 3/8	15 3/8	15 2/8	10	10	23	23	Gilliam Co., OR	Jerry R. Tyrrell	Jerry R. Tyrrell	2001	836
180 5/8	39 4/8	39 4/8	13 6/8	13 6/8	11	11	22	22	Wind River Mts., WY	Alfred Hume	Alfred Hume	1960	852
180 5/8	38 1/8	38 2/8	14 6/8	14 6/8	10	10	21 1/8	21 1/8	Sun River, MT	Robert W. Boucher	Robert W. Boucher	1966	852
180 5/8	38	39 3/8	14 3/8	14 3/8	10 3/8	9 6/8	19 4/8	19 4/8	Salmon River, ID	Emerson Hall	Emerson Hall	1968	852

BIGHORN SHEEP

Ovis canadensis canadensis and certain related subspecies

Score	Length of Horn R	L	Circumference of Base R	L	Circumference at Third Quarter R	L	Greatest Spread	Tip to Tip Spread	Locality	Hunter	Owner	Date Killed	Rank
180 5/8	37 1/8	35	15 4/8	15 5/8	9 4/8	9 4/8	22 4/8	15 4/8	Waterton Lake, BC	Victor T. Zarnock, Jr.	Victor T. Zarnock, Jr.	1972	852
180 5/8	40 5/8	39 4/8	15 3/8	15 4/8	8 1/8	7 6/8	20	18 6/8	Lewis & Clark Co., MT	William J. McRae	William J. McRae	1980	852
180 5/8	37 3/8	36	15 3/8	15 3/8	9 5/8	9 6/8	22 1/8	16 2/8	Ghost River, AB	Robert W. Hodge	Robert W. Hodge	1985	852
180 5/8	41 4/8	41 7/8	14 7/8	14 7/8	7 5/8	7 6/8	27 2/8	27 1/8	Sanders Co., MT	Raymond J. Baenen	Raymond J. Baenen	1986	852
180 5/8	38 7/8	40 2/8	14 4/8	14 4/8	9 5/8	10	21 6/8	21	Lemhi Co., ID	Eugene L. Chesler	Eugene L. Chesler	1990	852
180 5/8	39 4/8	38 7/8	15 5/8	15 3/8	8 2/8	8 1/8	21 2/8	19 6/8	Blaine Co., MT	Mark D. Farnam	Mark D. Farnam	1990	852
180 5/8	38 3/8	36 2/8	16	16	8 3/8	8 2/8	22 3/8	16 4/8	Chouteau Co., MT	Edward J. Lehman	Edward J. Lehman	1994	852
180 4/8	39	41 1/8	14 5/8	16	8	8 2/8	22 5/8	22	Smoky River, AB	H.P. Brandenburg	H.P. Brandenburg	1924	862
180 4/8	40 2/8	38 2/8	15 5/8	15 4/8	8 3/8	8	21 2/8	17	White Swan Lake, BC	John Barton	John Barton	1936	862
180 4/8	35 6/8	38 2/8	15 2/8	15	10 7/8	9 3/8	22	20	Lake Louise, AB	Unknown	Martin Bonack	PR 1951	862
180 4/8	38	39	14 2/8	14 2/8	10 6/8	10 6/8	22 3/8	18 2/8	Coal Branch, AB	R.G.F. Brown	R.G.F. Brown	1962	862
180 4/8	38	38 4/8	15	15	8 7/8	9	19 7/8	18 6/8	Moosehorn Lake, AB	Maynard Mathews	Maynard Mathews	1964	862
180 4/8	41	39	14	14	10 1/8	9 6/8	21 4/8	18 3/8	Simpson River, BC	Picked Up	Sharon Buck	1967	862
180 4/8	38 6/8	39 2/8	13 6/8	13 6/8	10 3/8	10 5/8	20 6/8	20 6/8	Park Co., WY	Picked Up	Sam L. Beasom	1974	862
180 4/8	34 7/8	35 5/8	15 4/8	15 4/8	10 1/8	10 2/8	21 2/8	13 1/8	Thistle Creek, AB	Paul H. Chance	Paul H. Chance	1975	862
180 4/8	40 1/8	40 1/8	15 4/8	14 5/8	7 6/8	7 5/8	22 6/8	20 2/8	Luscar Mt., AB	Jerry L. Christian	Jerry L. Christian	1979	862
180 4/8	40 6/8	38 2/8	14 5/8	14 5/8	9 2/8	9 3/8	23 2/8	22 6/8	Deer Lodge Co., MT	Jan J. Henry	Jan J. Henry	1983	862
180 4/8	39 1/8	37 5/8	14 6/8	14 7/8	9 4/8	9	25 2/8	24 6/8	Sanders Co., MT	Terry F. Brown	Terry F. Brown	1991	862
180 4/8	39 4/8	39 2/8	14	14	10	10 2/8	20	17 2/8	Skeleton Creek, AB	James W. Campbell	James W. Campbell	1991	862
180 4/8	40 2/8	40	14 3/8	14 4/8	8 4/8	8 4/8	23 1/8	23	Granite Creek, MT	Maxallen D. Jackson	Maxallen D. Jackson	1993	862
180 4/8	34 6/8	37 6/8	15 5/8	15 4/8	9 7/8	10 1/8	21 2/8	19	Elko Co., NV	Picked Up	Cabela's, Inc.	1994	862
180 4/8	36 2/8	35 6/8	15 7/8	16	10 1/8	9 6/8	21 7/8	18 4/8	Costilla Co., CO	Picked Up	Shawn Espinosa	1996	862
180 4/8	34 4/8	36 6/8	16	16	10 1/8	10 1/8	22 4/8	16	Columbia Co., WA	John M. Gebbia	John M. Gebbia	1999	862
180 4/8	38	38	15 6/8	15 6/8	8 4/8	8 3/8	23 3/8	19 1/8	Lewis & Clark Co., MT	Graham G. Weiss	Graham G. Weiss	1999	862
180 4/8	38 7/8	38 5/8	15 6/8	15 6/8	7 6/8	8 1/8	18 4/8	18 1/8	Elko Co., NV	Bruce E. Keaster	Bruce E. Keaster	2000	862
180 4/8	35 4/8	37 4/8	15 7/8	16	9 6/8	9 1/8	26 5/8	25 4/8	Lewis & Clark Co., MT	Michael J. Nannini	Michael J. Nannini	2002	862
180 3/8	38 6/8	40 1/8	15 1/8	15 1/8	8 6/8	9 3/8	20 1/8	19	Bow Lake, AB	Robert D. Layton	Robert D. Layton	1942	881
180 3/8	39 6/8	39 7/8	16 2/8	16	8 6/8	7 1/8	22 1/8	22 1/8	Sulphur River, AB	W.D. Parker	W.D. Parker	1955	881
180 3/8	41	36 7/8	15 4/8	15 5/8	8 1/8	8 1/8	19 7/8	19 7/8	Ghost River, AB	Art Brewster	Art Brewster	1960	881
180 3/8	37 5/8	38 6/8	14 6/8	14 4/8	9 4/8	10 1/8	22 6/8	19	Sheep Creek, WY	Picked Up	Loren L. Lutz	1962	881
180 3/8	36 1/8	37 2/8	15 4/8	15 2/8	9 6/8	10	22	19 4/8	Jakey's Fork, WY	Eugene Schilling	Eugene Schilling	1962	881
180 3/8	38 1/8	39 4/8	15	14 7/8	9 4/8	9	21 4/8	17	Ghost River, AB	J.E. Edwards	J.E. Edwards	1964	881
180 3/8	39 5/8	39 4/8	14 6/8	15	8 7/8	9	23 2/8	23 2/8	Wallowa Co., OR	Kirk W. Jones	Kirk W. Jones	1979	881
180 3/8	40 7/8	40 2/8	14 4/8	14 6/8	8 5/8	8 3/8	22 7/8	22 7/8	Lemhi Co., ID	Picked Up	R. Munn & F. Porter	1982	881
180 3/8	35 5/8	38 2/8	16 3/8	16 4/8	8 2/8	8 3/8	24 4/8	21 5/8	Silver Bow Co., MT	Robert C. Carlson	Robert C. Carlson	1983	881
180 3/8	37	37 7/8	15 1/8	15 2/8	9 5/8	9 5/8	23	19	Park Co., WY	Robert G. Curtis	Robert G. Curtis	1984	881
180 3/8	39 4/8	39 1/8	15 3/8	15 3/8	8 5/8	8 1/8	22 5/8	19 6/8	Mineral Co., MT	J. Ray Lake	J. Ray Lake	1984	881
180 3/8	37 5/8	41 4/8	15 2/8	15 3/8	7 7/8	8 3/8	23 4/8	23 4/8	Silver Bow Co., MT	Scott A. Shuey	Scott A. Shuey	1985	881

Score	Length of Horn R	Length of Horn L	Circ. Base R	Circ. Base L	Circ. 3rd Qtr R	Circ. 3rd Qtr L	Greatest Spread	Tip to Tip	Locality	Hunter	Owner	Date	Rank
180 3/8	37 1/8	38	15 5/8	15 5/8	8 6/8	9	21	19	Sanders Co., MT	Calvin L. Pomrenke	Calvin L. Pomrenke	1986	881
180 3/8	38	38 1/8	15 5/8	15 5/8	9 3/8	8 3/8	19 3/8	19 3/8	Ravalli Co., MT	Terry Frey	Terry Frey	1988	881
180 3/8	35 1/8	37 2/8	15 4/8	15 5/8	9 7/8	9 4/8	24	15 6/8	Greenlee Co., AZ	James A. Gerrettie II	James A. Gerrettie II	1988	881
180 3/8	40 4/8	40 3/8	15	14 6/8	8	8 1/8	25 6/8	25 6/8	Chouteau Co., MT	Scott D. Rubin	Scott D. Rubin	1989	881
180 3/8	38 4/8	38 5/8	15 3/8	15 1/8	8 7/8	8 7/8	23 1/8	22 4/8	Deer Lodge Co., MT	Max W. Leishman	Max W. Leishman	1990	881
180 3/8	41 6/8	32 5/8	16 4/8	16 4/8	7 3/8	9 1/8	25	22 4/8	Beaverhead Co., MT	James M. Linscott	James M. Linscott	1990	881
180 3/8	38 3/8	37 4/8	15 6/8	15 2/8	8 3/8	8 6/8	22 1/8	15 4/8	Sheep Creek, AB	Barry Gramlich	Barry Gramlich	1992	881
180 3/8	37 6/8	36 5/8	15 2/8	15 2/8	10	10	19 5/8	17 6/8	Mora Co., NM	Ronald D. Rod	Ronald D. Rod	1992	881
180 3/8	40 4/8	38 3/8	16 1/8	15 5/8	8 3/8	7 6/8	23 1/8	21 2/8	Asotin Co., WA	Brian J. Greenhaw	Brian J. Greenhaw	1993	881
180 3/8	41 5/8	36	16	16	7 6/8	9	23 4/8	23 4/8	Greenlee Co., AZ	Hoover L. Lee	Hoover L. Lee	1993	881
180 3/8	36 6/8	36 1/8	16 2/8	16 2/8	9	9 2/8	22 4/8	22 4/8	Nez Perce Co., ID	Don R. Scoles	Don R. Scoles	1994	881
180 3/8	38 7/8	39 4/8	14 7/8	14 6/8	8 5/8	8 6/8	26 4/8	26 4/8	Fergus Co., MT	Dan T. Brelsford	Dan T. Brelsford	1995	881
180 3/8	37 5/8	38 4/8	16 3/8	16 3/8	7 5/8	7 5/8	23 7/8	23 7/8	Sanders Co., MT	Daniel C. Wahle	Daniel C. Wahle	1995	881
180 3/8	38 5/8	38 2/8	15 4/8	15 4/8	8 4/8	8 5/8	23 2/8	23 2/8	Sanders Co., MT	Sara C. Reeder	Sara C. Reeder	1998	881
180 3/8	39 5/8	39 6/8	15 7/8	15 7/8	7 2/8	7 3/8	22 1/8	22 2/8	Fergus Co., MT	William R. Gibson, Jr.	William R. Gibson, Jr.	1999	881
180 3/8	38 7/8	38 7/8	14 6/8	14 6/8	9 2/8	9 2/8	19 6/8	22 7/8	Fremont Co., WY	John F. Babler	John F. Babler	2000	881
180 3/8	34 3/8	34 4/8	16	16	10 1/8	10 3/8	14 6/8	19 5/8	Mount Kidd, AB	Jay J. Fuller	Jay J. Fuller	2000	881
180 3/8	35 6/8	36 5/8	15 6/8	15 5/8	10 2/8	10 2/8	18	21 2/8	Costilla Co., CO	David D. Dillon	David D. Dillon	2001	881
180 2/8	38	39 2/8	16	16	10 4/8	10 2/8	14	21	British Columbia	James T. Wilson	Kevin D. O'Connell	1928	911
180 2/8	36 4/8	38 6/8	14 4/8	14 4/8	9	9	20 4/8	20 4/8	Cecelia Lake, BC	Dan Auld	Pat Auld Appersen	1950	911
180 2/8	39 3/8	38 1/8	15	15	10	10 6/8	20 3/8	20 7/8	Salmon River, ID	Ralph Puckett	Ralph Puckett	1958	911
180 2/8	38 6/8	37 2/8	14 1/8	14 6/8	9 6/8	10 3/8	15	21 1/8	Burnt Timber Creek, AB	Ruth Mahoney	Ruth Mahoney	1963	911
180 2/8	39 5/8	39 5/8	14 6/8	15 3/8	7 6/8	7 7/8	19 1/8	21 1/8	Invermere, BC	Lyle O. Fett	Lyle O. Fett	1982	911
180 2/8	37 6/8	37 6/8	15 4/8	15	9 5/8	10 1/8	12 7/8	20 1/8	Ewin Creek, BC	Bob Hildebrandt	Bob Hildebrandt	1988	911
180 2/8	38 2/8	38 2/8	15 3/8	15 2/8	8 6/8	9 1/8	16 3/8	19 5/8	Cross River, BC	Daryl G. Stech	Daryl G. Stech	1988	911
180 2/8	39 1/8	39 1/8	14 4/8	14 5/8	9 1/8	9 1/8	20 2/8	22	Lincoln Co., MT	Bradley G. Osler	Bradley G. Osler	1989	911
180 2/8	35 3/8	35 7/8	15 6/8	15 5/8	9 7/8	10	14 2/8	21 1/8	Warden Rock, AB	Brian N. Holthe	Brian N. Holthe	1990	911
180 2/8	39 4/8	39 4/8	15 1/8	15 3/8	8	7 7/8	18 5/8	19	Rocky Creek, AB	Donald R. Smith	Donald R. Smith	1991	911
180 2/8	39	39 2/8	15	15	8 2/8	8 3/8	25 4/8	25 4/8	Lemhi Co., ID	Picked Up	Thomas C. Pike	1993	911
180 2/8	36 5/8	36 3/8	15 4/8	15 4/8	8 2/8	8 2/8	26 2/8	26 2/8	Missoula Co., MT	Joel D. Cusker	Joel D. Cusker	1994	911
180 2/8	40 5/8	36 3/8	16 3/8	15 5/8	8 2/8	7 1/8	18 1/8	21 5/8	Kootenay River, BC	Gerry Favreau	Gerry Favreau	1994	911
180 2/8	41	40 4/8	14 7/8	14 3/8	7 1/8	7 2/8	22 2/8	22 2/8	Blaine Co., MT	Roxana L. Laeupple	Roxana L. Laeupple	1997	911
180 2/8	37 7/8	39 7/8	15 5/8	14 7/8	7 7/8	7 6/8	19	23	Mt. Cornwall, AB	Fred Thomson	Fred Thomson	1997	911
180 2/8	36 4/8	36	16 1/8	15 5/8	8	8	22 4/8	21	Greenlee Co., AZ	Daniel J. Tout	Daniel J. Tout	1997	911
180 2/8	39	39	16	16	8 6/8	9 1/8	23 6/8	23 6/8	Sanders Co., MT	Jon W. Cole	Jon W. Cole	2000	911
180 2/8	38 3/8	35 4/8	16 2/8	16 2/8	7 5/8	7 6/8	22 2/8	22 2/8	Taos Co., NM	George J. Elledge, Sr.	George J. Elledge, Sr.	2000	911
180 2/8	35 4/8	37 7/8	15 3/8	15 5/8	9 4/8	9 2/8	21 2/8	21 6/8	Granite Co., MT	Joseph F. Maloney	Joseph F. Maloney	2000	911
180 2/8	37 7/8	38 2/8	16 2/8	16 2/8	7 2/8	7 5/8	21 6/8	21 6/8	Condor Peak, AB	Flint J. Simpson	Flint J. Simpson	2001	911
180 2/8	39 4/8	36 4/8	14 6/8	14 6/8	9 4/8	9 4/8	26 1/8	26 1/8	Gunnison Co., CO	Oliver R. Biggers	Oliver R. Biggers	2001	911
180 2/8	36 4/8	37 6/8	16 4/8	16 4/8	7 6/8	7 6/8	22	22	Fremont Co., CO	Lonnie Lasha	Lonnie Lasha	2001	911
180 2/8	37 6/8	38 6/8	14 5/8	14 3/8	9 2/8	9 5/8	21 1/8	21 1/8	Gila Co., AZ	George F. Dennis, Jr.	George F. Dennis, Jr.	2002	911
180 1/8	38 4/8	38 6/8	14 5/8	14 5/8	10 3/8	10 2/8	18 4/8	21 1/8	Blaine Co., MT	Roy L. Thompson	Roy L. Thompson	2003	911
180 1/8	40	40	15 6/8	15 1/8	7 4/8	10 7/8	18 4/8	17 4/8	Sugarloaf Mt., CO	Picked Up	Henry H. Zietz	1947	935
180 1/8	36 4/8	34 5/8	15 1/8	15 4/8	9 1/8	9 1/8	22 1/8	22 1/8	Green River, WY	John N. Leonard	John N. Leonard	1953	935
180 1/8	36 5/8	37 2/8	15 3/8	15 4/8	9 1/8	8 5/8	23 3/8	20 5/8	Sun River, MT	Dennis Reichelt	Dennis Reichelt	1958	935
180 1/8	36 1/8	40 6/8	15 2/8	15 4/8	8 3/8	8 5/8	18	20 4/8	Salmon River, ID	C.A. Schwope	C.A. Schwope	1959	935
180 1/8	39 5/8	40 3/8	15	14 7/8	8 5/8	9 4/8	23	22 7/8	Kootenay Mts., BC	Picked Up	Gary E. Brown	1963	935
180 1/8	37 2/8	34 5/8	15 3/8	15 4/8	9 4/8	9 6/8	22 1/8	16 5/8	Gannet Peak, WY	Wilbur Rickett	Wilbur Rickett	1964	935

BIGHORN SHEEP

Ovis canadensis canadensis and certain related subspecies

Score	Length of Horn R	L	Circumference of Base R	L	Circumference at Third Quarter R	L	Greatest Spread	Tip to Tip Spread	Locality	Hunter	Owner	Date Killed	Rank
180 1/8	37 3/8	37 6/8	14 4/8	14 6/8	10	10	22 4/8	19 1/8	Ghost River, AB	Lloyd E. Zeman	Jenifer D. Schmidt	1968	935
180 1/8	36 4/8	34 3/8	15 6/8	15 7/8	9 7/8	9 5/8	22 5/8	18 2/8	Castle River, AB	Don W. Caldwell	Don W. Caldwell	1969	935
180 1/8	37 6/8	38 1/8	15 7/8	15 7/8	8 1/8	8	18 6/8	18 6/8	Nye Co., MT	Ira H. Kent	Ira H. Kent	1974	935
180 1/8	37 5/8	37 4/8	16 4/8	16 4/8	8 1/8	8	20	20	Sanders Co., MT	Gene N. Meyer	Gene N. Meyer	1976	935
180 1/8	41 3/8	41 4/8	15	15	7	7 2/8	28 6/8	28 6/8	Deer Lodge Co., MT	Arden Holden	Arden Holden	1979	935
180 1/8	37 4/8	35 3/8	15 4/8	15 5/8	9 7/8	9 7/8	19 4/8	16	Coral Creek, AB	Leonard W. King	Leonard W. King	1983	935
180 1/8	37 6/8	37 7/8	16	16	7 7/8	8	21 4/8	14 6/8	Cougar Mt., AB	Norman Howg	Norman Howg	1984	935
180 1/8	38 5/8	42 6/8	15 7/8	15 7/8	6 3/8	6 3/8	24 3/8	24 3/8	Granite Co., MT	Leonard W. Bowen	Leonard W. Bowen	1985	935
180 1/8	38	37 1/8	16 4/8	16 4/8	7 5/8	7 5/8	19 3/8	19 3/8	Sanders Co., MT	Bruce P. Allen	Bruce P. Allen	1986	935
180 1/8	39 4/8	38 5/8	15 4/8	15	8 5/8	8 2/8	23 1/8	20 7/8	Custer Co., ID	Leland S. Speakes, Jr.	Leland S. Speakes, Jr.	1987	935
180 1/8	36 2/8	38 1/8	15 4/8	15 4/8	9 5/8	9 6/8	19 2/8	17 4/8	Granite Co., MT	Scott M. Willumsen	Scott M. Willumsen	1989	935
180 1/8	40	39 5/8	14 1/8	14 2/8	9 3/8	9 1/8	22 6/8	22 4/8	Lemhi Co., ID	JoAnn Basso	JoAnn Basso	1990	935
180 1/8	37 4/8	37 3/8	15 2/8	15 2/8	9 2/8	9	22 7/8	18 2/8	Clear Creek Co., CO	Charles W. Hanawalt	Charles W. Hanawalt	1990	935
180 1/8	37 2/8	35 3/8	16	16 1/8	8 4/8	8 4/8	21	19 3/8	Drinnan Mt., AB	Everitt N. Davis	Everitt N. Davis	1992	935
180 1/8	39 1/8	34 4/8	16 1/8	16 2/8	8	9 5/8	25 1/8	22 2/8	Greenlee Co., AZ	Mark E. McCullough	Mark E. McCullough	1994	935
180 1/8	37 2/8	37 1/8	16 1/8	16 1/8	8 3/8	8 5/8	23 2/8	23 1/8	Granite Co., MT	Dan Beck	Dan Beck	1995	935
180 1/8	37 7/8	38	15	15	9 3/8	9 1/8	22 1/8	18 3/8	Mineral Co., MT	Michael P. Hogan	Michael P. Hogan	1999	935
180 1/8	38 2/8	38 5/8	14 7/8	14 7/8	8 7/8	9 3/8	21 4/8	21 4/8	Lewis & Clark Co., MT	Brian L. Martinez	Brian L. Martinez	1999	935
180 1/8	39 7/8	38 6/8	14 2/8	14 1/8	10 1/8	10 1/8	23 2/8	17 6/8	Greenlee Co., AZ	Robert J. Stokes	Robert J. Stokes	2001	935
180 1/8	38 7/8	39	14 1/8	14 2/8	11	11 1/8	21	14 2/8	Taos Co., NM	Branko Terkovich	Branko Terkovich	2001	935
180 1/8	38 5/8	40 6/8	14 6/8	14 5/8	8 1/8	8 1/8	26 3/8	25 4/8	Ravalli Co., MT	E. Earl Willard	E. Earl Willard	2001	935
180 1/8	36 5/8	36	15 7/8	15 6/8	9 3/8	9 2/8	21 7/8	20 2/8	Broadwater Co., MT	Gerry R. Jones	Gerry R. Jones	2002	935
180 1/8	40 6/8	39 1/8	14 3/8	14 2/8	9 1/8	9	23 1/8	23 1/8	Lewis & Clark Co., MT	Anthony P. Swartz	Anthony P. Swartz	2002	935
180	37 1/8	38 7/8	15	15	9 4/8	10	22	18 2/8	Seebe, AB	Anson Brooks	Anson Brooks	1956	964
180	39 1/8	37 1/8	15	15 2/8	9 4/8	9 6/8	21	19 4/8	Forbidden Creek, AB	James Haugland	James Haugland	1958	964
180	38 1/8	38 3/8	15 2/8	15 2/8	9	9	21 5/8	18 2/8	Kootenay, BC	Walter L. Bjorkman	Walter L. Bjorkman	1963	964
180	37 6/8	37 2/8	14 4/8	14 4/8	10 4/8	10 4/8	22 3/8	22 3/8	Panther Creek, AB	Walter R. Schubert	Walter R. Schubert	1966	964
180	38 5/8	41 1/8	14 5/8	14 5/8	8 3/8	8 4/8	24	23 4/8	Lewis & Clark Co., MT	James G. Braddee, Jr.	James G. Braddee, Jr.	1978	964
180	39 6/8	39 2/8	15 3/8	15 3/8	8	8	22 4/8	20 6/8	Wallowa Co., OR	F. Carter Kerns	F. Carter Kerns	1978	964
180	38 5/8	37 3/8	15 4/8	15 4/8	9	8 4/8	20 4/8	16 3/8	Whitehorse Creek, AB	Philip H. R. Stepney	Prov. Mus. of Alberta	1978	964
180	40 2/8	37 2/8	15 3/8	15 3/8	8 2/8	8 7/8	22 6/8	22 6/8	Granite Co., MT	Jerry E. Gallagher	Jerry E. Gallagher	1980	964
180	40 2/8	40 1/8	14 5/8	14 5/8	8 4/8	8 4/8	25	25	Wallowa Co., OR	Jerome V. Epping	Jerome V. Epping	1984	964
180	39 7/8	40 2/8	15 5/8	15 5/8	7 4/8	7 5/8	22 2/8	22 2/8	Granite Co., MT	James A. Crepeau	James A. Crepeau	1986	964
180	37 1/8	39 5/8	15 6/8	15 6/8	7 7/8	8 1/8	21 6/8	21 6/8	Beaverhead Co., MT	Kory McGavin	Kory McGavin	1988	964
180	38 2/8	40	14 4/8	14 6/8	9 2/8	9 1/8	21 2/8	20 6/8	Lewis & Clark Co., MT	Brian J. Boehm	Brian J. Boehm	1989	964
180	38 1/8	37 5/8	15 3/8	15 2/8	9 1/8	9	23 1/8	22 4/8	Deer Lodge Co., MT	Michael P. Lorello	Michael P. Lorello	1990	964
180	37 4/8	37	15 3/8	15 5/8	9 2/8	9 1/8	21	17 4/8	Granite Co., MT	Thomas I. Jenni	Thomas I. Jenni	1991	964
180	40 5/8	40 1/8	14 4/8	14 4/8	8 4/8	8 6/8	20 7/8	19 5/8	Lemhi Co., ID	A. Oscar Carlson	A. Oscar Carlson	1993	964

Score									Location	Hunter	Owner	Date Killed	Rank
180	38 5/8	40 1/8	14 6/8	14 7/8	8 2/8	8 5/8	22 3/8	17 2/8	Fortress Mt., AB	Mike Michalezki	Mike Michalezki	1993	964
180	37 1/8	36 1/8	15 3/8	15 3/8	9 7/8	9 3/8	21 6/8	16 2/8	Mist Creek, AB	Morgan J. Williams	Morgan J. Williams	1995	964
180	37 1/8	37 3/8	15 5/8	15 5/8	9 3/8	8 7/8	21 6/8	20 5/8	Sanders Co., MT	Gino R. Fasano	Gino R. Fasano	1996	964
180	40	37 4/8	14 6/8	15 1/8	9 3/8	9	20 7/8	18 6/8	Granite Co., MT	William J. Leehan	William J. Leehan	1996	964
180	42	41 2/8	15	15	7 3/8	7 3/8	21 7/8	21 3/8	Sanders Co., MT	Jeff A. Hockaday	Jeff A. Hockaday	2000	964
180	40 5/8	38 3/8	16 2/8	16 2/8	6 6/8	6 6/8	23 3/8	23 1/8	Ravalli Co., MT	Vicki Stiller	Vicki Stiller	2002	964
204 4/8*	42 4/8	42 4/8	16 4/8	16 5/8	12 1/8	12	23 1/8	21 2/8	Cardinal River, AB	Picked Up	AB Govt. Natl. Resc. Ser.	1998	
202 *	41 6/8	41 4/8	16 4/8	16 4/8	11 1/8	10 6/8	23 6/8	17	Pennington Co., SD	Picked Up	SD Game, Fish, & Parks Dept.	PR 1997	
200 6/8*	40 7/8	40 7/8	16 6/8	17 1/8	11 3/8	11 3/8	25 3/8	20 7/8	Whitehorse Creek, AB	Todd K. Kirk	Todd K. Kirk	1998	
199 5/8*	42 6/8	43 1/8	16 2/8	16	10 3/8	10 6/8	22 5/8	22 4/8	Mystery Lake, AB	Ross D. Stelter	Ross D. Stelter	1998	
197 4/8*	41 4/8	41 2/8	15 7/8	15 7/8	11	11 4/8	25	20 5/8	Drinnan Creek, AB	Dean B. Erickson	Dean B. Erickson	2002	

CATEGORY
BIGHORN SHEEP

SCORE
195

HUNTER
JENNIFER L. CHAPEL (LEFT)

LOCATION
TAOS COUNTY, NEW MEXICO

DATE OF KILL
SEPTEMBER 2002

SCORE
180-1/8

HUNTER
BRANKO TERKOVICH (RIGHT)

LOCATION
TAOS COUNTY, NEW MEXICO

DATE OF KILL
SEPTEMBER 2001

CATEGORY
BIGHORN SHEEP

SCORE
187-1/8

HUNTER
JOSHUA S. GUNNING

LOCATION
HUERFANO COUNTY,
COLORADO

DATE OF KILL
SEPTEMBER 1998

CATEGORY
BIGHORN SHEEP

SCORE
183

HUNTER
CAROLE J. BEEBE

LOCATION
GRANITE COUNTY,
MONTANA

DATE OF KILL
OCTOBER 1999

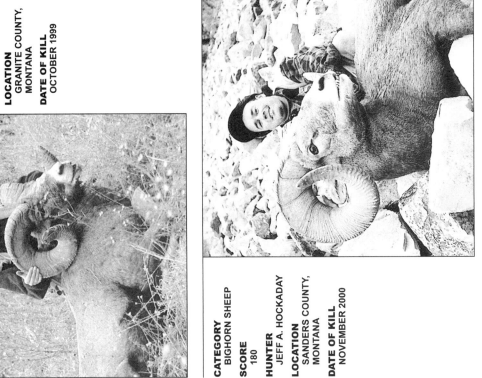

CATEGORY
BIGHORN SHEEP

SCORE
180

HUNTER
JEFF A. HOCKADAY

LOCATION
SANDERS COUNTY,
MONTANA

DATE OF KILL
NOVEMBER 2000

CATEGORY
BIGHORN SHEEP

SCORE
180-2/8

HUNTER
GEORGE F. DENNIS, JR.

LOCATION
GILA COUNTY, ARIZONA

DATE OF KILL
OCTOBER 2002

CATEGORY
BIGHORN SHEEP

SCORE
193-1/8

HUNTER
JOAN L. GALLENTINE

LOCATION
FERGUS COUNTY,
MONTANA

DATE OF KILL
SEPTEMBER 2002

CATEGORY
BIGHORN SHEEP

SCORE
184-6/8

HUNTER
DAVID G. PAULLIN

LOCATION
RAVALLI COUNTY,
MONTANA

DATE OF KILL
NOVEMBER 1999

CATEGORY
BIGHORN SHEEP

SCORE
182-4/8

HUNTER
JOSH B. JOHNS (LEFT)

LOCATION
TETON COUNTY, MONTANA

DATE OF KILL
NOVEMBER 1998

SCORE
192-1/8

HUNTER
JOHN BENES (RIGHT)

LOCATION
FERGUS COUNTY, MONTANA

DATE OF KILL
NOVEMBER 1997

CATEGORY
BIGHORN SHEEP

SCORE
182-5/8

HUNTER
GERALD L. FISCHER

LOCATION
GRANITE COUNTY,
MONTANA

DATE OF KILL
OCTOBER 2000

CHARLES SHELDON
1867-1928

By Leonard H. Wurman

Blessed with uncommonly good judgment, a predilection for hard work, and an engaging personality, Sheldon retired in his mid-30s and devoted the rest of his life to hunting and conservation. He spent years studying and was the first to accurately describe the characteristics separating the Dall's, Fannin, and Stone's sheep. After wintering in the Mourt McKinley area, Sheldon devoted the next ten years until he succeeded in getting legislation passed to create Denali National Park. President Wilson gave Sheldon the pen he used to sign the act. When the Tennessee and North Carolina governors recommended low altitude, cut-over lands for inclusion in a park, the Secretary of the Interior asked Sheldon to intervene. It was Sheldon who recommended the present borders for the Great Smokey Mountains National Park. The Boone and Crockett Club remembered this ardent conservationist by establishing the Charles Sheldon National Wildlife Refuge in northwest Nevada. ■

DESERT SHEEP
WORLD'S RECORD

Carl M. Scrivens of Jackson, Wyoming, has taken impressive desert sheep (*Ovis canadensis nelsoni*) in the past, but this accomplished hunter has not yet shot a ram that had topped the extraordinary trophy he found in 1941.

In a 1992 article for *Wild Sheep*, Scrivens gave an account of his discovery that occurred during a hunting trip on the Baja Peninsula of Mexico, and his subsequent determination to obtain the trophy.

"We finally arrived at our destination, a remote rancho on the southern end of the Sierra San Pedro Martir. While the vaqueros were rounding up the mules, we took a stroll around the rancho. We looked inside an old dilapidated wagon, and there was a skull and horns of a desert ram. What a head it was!!! My brothers and family were fairly knowledgeable about the size of desert rams, but this beat anything we had ever seen — and I was determined to have it before we left."

Scrivens added that he wished he had more background on the actual circumstances of the hunt for this ram.

"The history of the taking of this head is meager. According to the vaqueros at the rancho, the ram had been killed the previous year by a Native American meat hunter, who left the head lying. A vaquero brought the head to the rancho.

"When I acquired the head there was still a scrap of hide adhered to the skull, and it was black. Frequently rams with black, or nearly black pelts are found in that area. We hunted this same area at later times and took other rams, but none as large as the one I bartered for."

Scrivens' find was measured by Samuel Webb of the Boone and Crockett Club in 1946 and scored at 205-1/8 points. This magnificent ram was still the World's Record in 1992 when it was bequeathed to the Arizona Desert Bighorn Sheep Society, of which Scrivens has been a lifelong member. After locating a suitable cape for the ram from the Arizona Department of Fish and Game, the restored mount was hung in the Boone and Crockett Club's National Collection of Heads and Horns at the Buffalo Bill Historical Center in Cody, Wyoming, on June 27, 1992. ∎

DESERT SHEEP
WORLD'S RECORD SCORE CHART

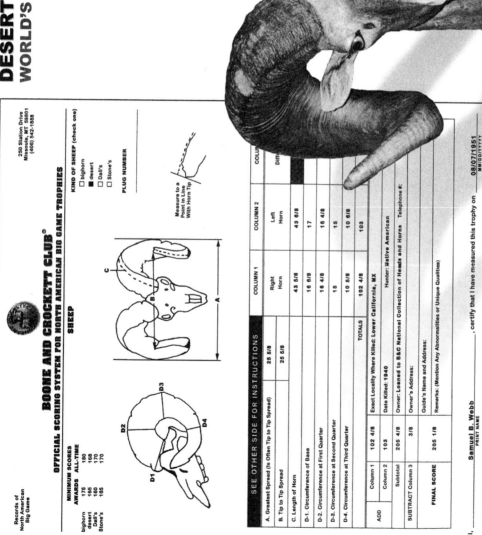

Records of
North American
Big Game

250 Station Drive
Missoula, MT 59801
(406) 542-1888

BOONE AND CROCKETT CLUB®

OFFICIAL SCORING SYSTEM FOR NORTH AMERICAN BIG GAME TROPHIES

SHEEP

MINIMUM SCORES

	AWARDS	ALL-TIME
bighorn	175	180
desert	165	168
Dall's	160	170
Stone's	165	170

KIND OF SHEEP (check one)
- ☐ bighorn
- ■ desert
- ☐ Dall's
- ☐ Stone's

PLUG NUMBER

Measure to a
Point in Line
With Horn Tip

SEE OTHER SIDE FOR INSTRUCTIONS		COLUMN 1	COLUMN 2	COLUMN
		Right Horn	Left Horn	Diff
A. Greatest Spread (Is Often Tip to Tip Spread)	25 5/8			
B. Tip to Tip Spread	25 5/8			
C. Length of Horn		43 5/8	43 6/8	
D-1. Circumference of Base		16 6/8	17	
D-2. Circumference at First Quarter		16 4/8	16 4/8	
D-3. Circumference at Second Quarter		15	15	
D-4. Circumference at Third Quarter		10 5/8	10 6/8	
TOTALS		102 4/8	103	

ADD	Column 1	102 4/8	Exact Locality Where Killed: **Lower California, MX**
	Column 2	103	Date Killed: **1940** Hunter: **Native American**
	Subtotal	205 4/8	Owner: **Loaned to B&C National Collection of Heads and Horns** Telephone #:
SUBTRACT	Column 3	3/8	Owner's Address:
			Guide's Name and Address:
FINAL SCORE		**205 1/8**	Remarks: (Mention Any Abnormalities or Unique Qualities)

I, **Samuel B. Webb** , certify that I have measured this trophy on **08/07/1951**
PRINT NAME MM/DD/YYYY

at **11600 South Denver Ave,** **Los Angeles** **CA**
STREET ADDRESS CITY STATE/PROVINCE

and that these measurements and data are, to the best of my knowledge and belief, made in accordance with the instructions given.

Witness: **Carl M. Scrivens** Signature: **Samuel B. Webb** I.D. Number
B&C OFFICIAL MEASURER

COPYRIGHT © 1999 BY BOONE AND CROCKETT CLUB®

855

TOP 10 DESERT SHEEP

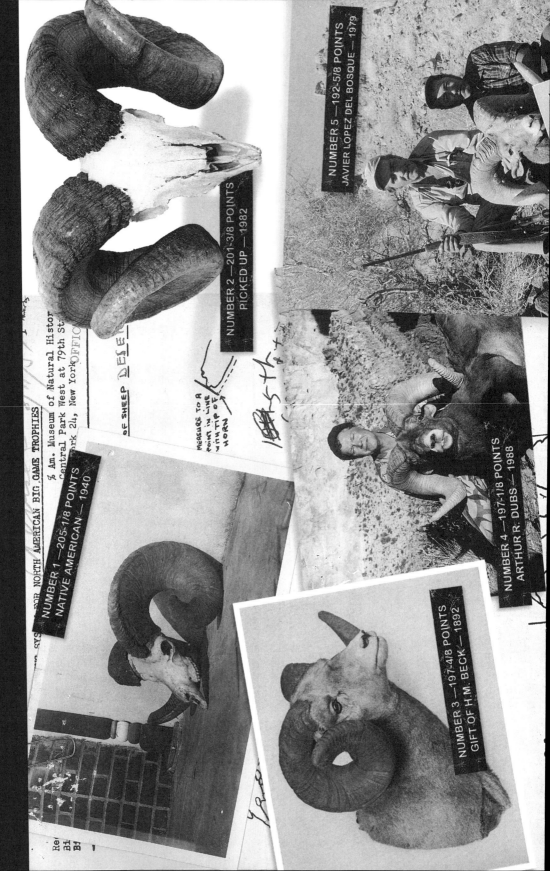

NUMBER 2 — 201-3/8 POINTS
PICKED UP — 1982

NUMBER 5 — 192-5/8 POINTS
JAVIER LÓPEZ DEL BOSQUE — 1979

NUMBER 4 — 197-1/8 POINTS
ARTHUR R. DUBS — 1988

NUMBER 1 — 205-1/8 POINTS
NATIVE AMERICAN — 1940

NUMBER 3 — 197-4/8 POINTS
GIFT OF H.M. BECK — 1892

856

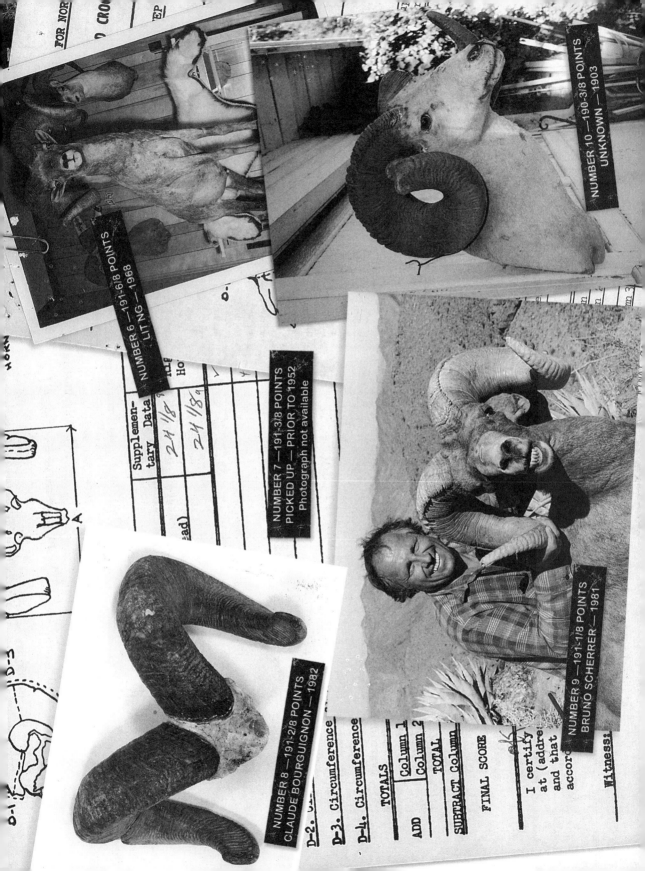

NUMBER 10 — 190-3/8 POINTS
UNKNOWN — 1903

NUMBER 6 — 191-6/8 POINTS
LIT NG — 1968

NUMBER 7 — 191-3/8 POINTS
PICKED UP — PRIOR TO 1952
Photograph not available

NUMBER 9 — 191-1/8 POINTS
BRUNO SCHERRER — 1981

NUMBER 8 — 191-2/8 POINTS
CLAUDE BOURGUIGNON — 1982

Supplementary Data

24 1/8

24 1/8

D-2.

D-3. Circumference

D-4. Circumference

TOTALS | Column 1

ADD | Column 2

TOTAL

SUBTRACT Column

FINAL SCORE

I certify
at (addre
and that
accord

Witness:

DESERT SHEEP

MINIMUM SCORE 168

Ovis canadensis nelsoni and certain related subspecies

Score	Length of Horn R	L	Circumference of Base R	L	Circumference at Third Quarter R	L	Greatest Spread	Tip to Tip Spread	Locality	Hunter	Owner	Date Killed	Rank
205 1/8	43 5/8	43 6/8	16 6/8	17	10 5/8	10 6/8	25 5/8	25 5/8	Lower Calif, MX	Native American	Loaned to B&C Natl. Coll.	1940	1
201 3/8	45 5/8	46 2/8	15 5/8	15 5/8	11 2/8	11 5/8	20 4/8	20	Pima Co., AZ	Picked Up	Greg Koons	1982	2
197 4/8	44	43 4/8	15 7/8	15 7/8	10 5/8	10	23 7/8	23 7/8	Lower Calif, MX	Gift of H.M. Beck	Acad. Nat. Sci., Phil.	1892	3
197 1/8	42 3/8	41 6/8	16 1/8	16 1/8	10 5/8	11	26	26	Graham Co., AZ	Arthur R. Dubs	Arthur R. Dubs	1988	4
192 5/8	41 6/8	42 3/8	15	15 1/8	10 6/8	10 4/8	25 4/8	25	Baja Calif, MX	Javier Lopez del Bosque	Javier Lopez del Bosque	1979	5
191 6/8	42	43 4/8	15 4/8	15 3/8	9 6/8	9 6/8	23 4/8	23 4/8	Baja Calif, MX	Lit Ng	Lit Ng	1968	6
191 3/8	40	41 3/8	16 5/8	16 5/8	9 1/8	9 5/8	24 1/8	24 1/8	Mexico	Picked Up	Snow Museum	PR 1952	7
191 2/8	38 4/8	40 4/8	16 2/8	16 2/8	10 3/8	10 7/8	21 6/8	17 2/8	Baja Calif, MX	Claude Bourguignon	Claude Bourguignon	1982	8
191 1/8	39 3/8	39 2/8	16 3/8	16 4/8	10	10	19 3/8	19 2/8	Baja Calif, MX	Bruno Scherrer	Bruno Scherrer	1981	9
190 3/8	41	43 7/8	15 3/8	15 5/8	9 1/8	9 1/8	23 7/8	23 7/8	Arizona	Unknown	Bruce R. Kemp, Sr.	1903	10
189 3/8	39 5/8	39 4/8	16 6/8	16 7/8	10 3/8	11	21 3/8	21 3/8	Lower Calif, MX	M.B. Silva	M.B. Silva	1939	11
189	41	40 2/8	16 6/8	16 7/8	8 7/8	8 7/8	23 2/8	23 2/8	Gila Co., AZ	Sam S. Jaksick, Jr.	Sam S. Jaksick, Jr.	1988	12
188 4/8	40 2/8	40 2/8	15 4/8	15 6/8	10 2/8	10 1/8	21 5/8	19	Grant Co., NM	Picked Up	NM Dept. of Game & Fish	1992	13
188 4/8	41 2/8	38 4/8	15 7/8	16	9 4/8	10	21 2/8	16 4/8	Grant Co., NM	Picked Up	NM Dept. of Game & Fish	2000	13
188 2/8	43	43	14 4/8	14 5/8	9 5/8	9 4/8	27 3/8	27 3/8	Baja Calif, MX	A. Cal Rossi, Jr.	A. Cal Rossi, Jr.	1974	15
188 2/8	38 2/8	37 4/8	16 3/8	16 2/8	10 3/8	10 6/8	24 3/8	21 5/8	Maricopa Co., AZ	Jerry Fletcher	Jerry Fletcher	1993	15
187 7/8	39 6/8	39 5/8	15 6/8	15 7/8	9 4/8	9 4/8	21 4/8	16 6/8	Pima Co., AZ	Carl A. Mattias, Sr.	Carl A. Mattias, Sr.	1982	17
187 5/8	42	40	15 2/8	15 2/8	10 1/8	10 1/8	23 5/8	23 5/8	Baja Calif, MX	Ed Stedman, Jr.	Ed Stedman, Jr.	1976	18
187 5/8	38 4/8	40 5/8	16 2/8	16 2/8	9	9 4/8	21 4/8	20 6/8	Baja Calif, MX	Romulo Sanchez Mireles	Romulo Sanchez Mireles	1969	19
187 3/8	39 2/8	39 7/8	15 1/8	15 2/8	10 2/8	10 5/8	21	21	Sonora, MX	Herb Klein	Dallas Mus. of Natl. Hist.	1952	20
187 3/8	39 1/8	39 2/8	16	16	10 2/8	10 3/8	17 6/8	17 6/8	Sonora, MX	Oscar J. Brooks	Oscar J. Brooks	1955	20
187 1/8	39 3/8	39 3/8	15 4/8	15 4/8	9 3/8	9 5/8	24 3/8	22	Yuma Co., AZ	Rick Wood	Rick Wood	1996	22
187	39 1/8	39 3/8	16	16	9 6/8	9 6/8	24 5/8	24 5/8	Lower Calif, MX	Unknown	Snow Museum	PR 1952	23
187	40 4/8	40 2/8	15 4/8	15 6/8	9 6/8	10	26	26	Kofa Mts., AZ	Louis R. Dees	Louis R. Dees	1965	23
187	41 4/8	42 4/8	14 7/8	14 7/8	11 3/8	11 3/8	28	28	California	Picked Up	CA Dept. of Fish & Game	PR 1970	23
186 5/8	38 3/8	38 4/8	15 7/8	15 7/8	9 3/8	9 4/8	22	20 1/8	Sonora, MX	F.B. Heider	O.M. Corbett	1927	26
186 3/8	41 1/8	39	16	16	9 3/8	9 1/8	24	22 3/8	Gila Co., AZ	Steven E. Wright	Steven E. Wright	1990	27
186 2/8	40 5/8	38 3/8	16	16	9	9	21 1/8	20 7/8	Maricopa Co., AZ	Ralph Grossman	Ralph Grossman	1961	28
186 2/8	40 6/8	40 2/8	14 6/8	14 7/8	10	10	23	20 2/8	Baja Calif, MX	Robert P. Miller	Robert P. Miller	1981	28
186	37	36	15 7/8	16	11 7/8	11 7/8	21 4/8	19	Arizona	Unknown	J. Michael Conoyer	1960	30
186	38 3/8	38 4/8	15 4/8	15 5/8	10 6/8	10 6/8	22 3/8	19 5/8	Yuma Co., AZ	Gerry W. Nikolaus	Gerry W. Nikolaus	1979	30
185 5/8	39 5/8	40	16	16	10 2/8	9 2/8	22 3/8	19 7/8	Baja Calif, MX	Graciano Guichard	Graciano Guichard	1970	32
185 3/8	38 3/8	39 4/8	16 1/8	16 1/8	8 7/8	9	23 2/8	19 6/8	Baja Calif, MX	Robert L. Williamson	Robert L. Williamson	1987	32
185 3/8	39 7/8	38 7/8	15 5/8	15 6/8	9	9 3/8	19 4/8	16 3/8	Baja Calif, MX	Wilmer C. Hansen	Wilmer C. Hansen	1972	34
185 2/8	39 2/8	39 2/8	15 3/8	15 4/8	10 4/8	9 7/8	25 2/8	20 2/8	Baja Calif, MX	Albert Pellizzari	Albert Pellizzari	1978	34
185 2/8	41	40 2/8	15 7/8	15 7/8	8 2/8	9	21 1/8	20 3/8	Graham Co., AZ	John W. Harris	John W. Harris	1982	34
185	39 4/8	39 2/8	15 7/8	15 7/8	8 7/8	9	20 3/8	18 6/8	San Borjas Mts., MX	Alice J. Landreth	Alice J. Landreth	1969	37

Score	Length R	Length L	Base Circ. R	Base Circ. L	Third Qtr. R	Third Qtr. L	Greatest Spread	Tip to Tip	Locality	Hunter	Owner	Date Killed	Rank
185	38 6/8	37 2/8	16 4/8	16 4/8	9	8 7/8	24 5/8	21	Baja Calif., MX	Miguel Zaldavar De Valasco	Miguel Zaldavar De Valasco	1979	37
184 6/8	42	40 6/8	14 6/8	15	9 4/8	9 2/8	29 4/8	29 4/8	Kofa Mts., AZ	W.A. Rudd	W.A. Rudd	1965	39
184 6/8	39 4/8	38 4/8	16 2/8	16 3/8	8 5/8	8 7/8	22 5/8	21 1/8	Baja Calif., MX	Burton L. Smith, Sr.	Burton L. Smith, Sr.	1973	39
184 6/8	42 6/8	41	15	15 1/8	8 4/8	8 3/8	27 1/8	26 6/8	Nye Co., NV	Alfred L. Raiche, Sr.	Alfred L. Raiche, Sr.	1988	39
184 5/8	40 1/8	37 4/8	15 1/8	15 1/8	10	10 3/8	22 4/8	21 2/8	Baja Calif., MX	Steven L. Rose	Steven L. Rose	1967	42
184 4/8	38 6/8	39	15 5/8	15 5/8	9 2/8	9 4/8	20 6/8	21	Baja Calif., MX	H. Clayton Poole	H. Clayton Poole	1966	43
184 4/8	43 1/8	45 3/8	13 7/8	13 7/8	8 6/8	8 6/8	26 4/8	26 4/8	Santa Teresa Mts., AZ	Picked Up	AZ Game & Fish Dept.	1967	43
184 4/8	40 4/8	40	15 2/8	15 2/8	9 2/8	9	22	22	Baja Calif., MX	Clint Heiber	Clint Heiber	1978	43
184 2/8	40 4/8	37 2/8	15 4/8	15 4/8	9 2/8	9 2/8	22 1/8	22	Pinal Co., AZ	Everett A. Hodge	Everett A. Hodge	1988	46
184 1/8	38 5/8	40	15 2/8	15 2/8	9 2/8	9 4/8	22	20 1/8	Papago Indian Res., AZ	Ralph J. Murrietta	Ollie O. Barney, Jr.	1965	47
184	40 1/8	38 7/8	14 6/8	14 6/8	10 1/8	9 4/8	25 6/8	25 4/8	Santa Rosa Mts., CA	Picked Up	Fred L. Jones	1955	48
184	41 6/8	40 4/8	15 4/8	15 4/8	8 3/8	8 7/8	25 6/8	25 6/8	Baja Calif., MX	Thomas J. Brimhall	Thomas J. Brimhall	1981	48
183 7/8	39 3/8	38 4/8	16	16	9 5/8	9 3/8	23 5/8	23 5/8	Gonzaga, MX	Glenn P. Napierskie	Glenn P. Napierskie	1970	50
183 3/8	40	40 3/8	13 7/8	14	10 4/8	9 6/8	24 7/8	24 1/8	Pinkley, AZ	Picked Up	Organ Pipe Cactus Natl. Mon.	1957	51
183 2/8	39 4/8	41 6/8	15 2/8	15 2/8	9	9	25 3/8	25 3/8	Lower Calif., MX	George H. Gould	George H. Gould	1894	52
183 2/8	39 7/8	39 1/8	15 2/8	15 3/8	9 7/8	9 6/8	23	23	Clark Co., NV	Gerald A. Lent	Gerald A. Lent	1976	52
183 2/8	37	37	14 7/8	14 7/8	10 7/8	11 1/8	14 3/8	14 2/8	Pima Co., NV	LeRoy Van Buggenum	LeRoy Van Buggenum	1987	52
183 2/8	40 5/8	41 5/8	15 2/8	15 2/8	8 3/8	8 6/8	27 2/8	27 2/8	Clark Co., NV	Alan G. Means	Alan G. Means	1988	52
182 6/8	39 2/8	37 5/8	14 6/8	14 6/8	11	10 7/8	22	22	Colorado River, AZ	Picked Up	John E. Luster	1956	56
182 6/8	41 6/8	38 6/8	15 4/8	15 4/8	8 2/8	8 4/8	23 4/8	23 4/8	Baja Calif., MX	Rita Oney	Rita Oney	1976	56
182 5/8	36	35 5/8	16 3/8	16 4/8	9 4/8	9 6/8	22 2/8	19 5/8	Pima Co., AZ	Charles W. Fisher	Charles W. Fisher	1972	58
182 5/8	39	39 1/8	15 5/8	15 5/8	8 6/8	9 2/8	22 6/8	22 6/8	Baja Calif., MX	Duane H. Loomis	Duane H. Loomis	1972	58
182 4/8	39 7/8	39 3/8	14 5/8	14 6/8	9 6/8	9 7/8	21 1/8	21 1/8	Lower Calif., MX	C.G. Clare	C.G. Clare	1958	60
182 4/8	37	37 4/8	14 7/8	14 7/8	10	10 2/8	22 3/8	22 3/8	Riverside Co., CA	Picked Up	Orson Morgan	1963	60
182 3/8	38 5/8	37 6/8	14 6/8	14 6/8	10 5/8	10 1/8	22 1/8	22 1/8	Lower Calif., MX	Elgin T. Gates	Elgin T. Gates	1940	62
182 3/8	39 3/8	40	14 7/8	15	9 5/8	9 5/8	22	22	Baja Calif., MX	Robert Zachrich	Robert Zachrich	1978	62
182 2/8	39 5/8	39 5/8	15 3/8	15 3/8	9	7 3/8	22 3/8	22 3/8	Graham Co., AZ	Beverly M. Nuessle	Beverly M. Nuessle	1986	64
182 2/8	40 7/8	39 6/8	15 4/8	15 2/8	8 4/8	9 4/8	22 2/8	22 2/8	Graham Co., AZ	James W. Ferguson	James W. Ferguson	1984	65
182 1/8	37 7/8	37	14 7/8	14 7/8	10 2/8	10 1/8	23 6/8	23 6/8	Baja Calif., MX	Jesus H. Garza-Villarreal	Jesus H. Garza-Villarreal	1984	65
182	38	36 6/8	15 6/8	15 6/8	9 2/8	9 2/8	22 1/8	22	Baja Calif., MX	John M. Griffith, Jr.	John M. Griffith, Jr.	1974	67
181 6/8	42 2/8	40	14 3/8	14 3/8	8 5/8	9	24	24	Sonora, MX	George W. Parker	George W. Parker	1939	68
181 5/8	39 2/8	41 3/8	15 2/8	15 2/8	8 7/8	8 7/8	24 1/8	24 1/8	Sheep Mt. Range, NV	David Ingram	David Ingram	1962	69
181 5/8	36 2/8	36 3/8	16 1/8	16 1/8	10 3/8	10 3/8	22	20 1/8	Baja Calif., MX	Elvin Hawkins	Elvin Hawkins	1978	69
181 4/8	39	38 4/8	16 2/8	16 2/8	9 4/8	9 5/8	21 5/8	19 2/8	Graham Co., AZ	Mark A. Clark	Mark A. Clark	1995	71
181 4/8	38 2/8	39 2/8	15 1/8	15 1/8	9 1/8	9	21 6/8	16	Hidalgo Co., NM	Thomas J. Pawlacyk	Thomas J. Pawlacyk	1995	71
181 2/8	37	37	15	15	10 6/8	10 3/8	21 7/8	21 1/8	Sonora, MX	Ira C. Green	Ira C. Green	1939	73
180 7/8	40	38 1/8	15 4/8	15 4/8	9 1/8	8 7/8	22 5/8	22 5/8	Baja Calif., MX	George H. Landreth	George H. Landreth	1969	74
180 7/8	37 7/8	34 4/8	15 6/8	15 6/8	9 6/8	9 6/8	20 6/8	20 6/8	Baja Calif., MX	Jack Atcheson, Jr.	Jack Atcheson, Jr.	1978	74
180 6/8	38	38 1/8	15 2/8	15 2/8	9 4/8	9 3/8	22 6/8	16 3/8	Yuma Co., AZ	Michael J. Pace	Michael J. Pace	1991	74
180 6/8	38 6/8	39	14 7/8	14 7/8	10 2/8	10 2/8	26	26	Mohave Co., AZ	Larry F. Snead	Larry F. Snead	1993	77
180 5/8	37 7/8	40	15	15	9 2/8	9 2/8	28 7/8	21 5/8	Brewster Co., TX	Picked Up	TX Parks & Wildlife	2002	78
180 4/8	35 7/8	37 3/8	16 1/8	16 1/8	9	8 6/8	19 1/8	18 4/8	Dragon Teeth Mt., AZ	Raymond White	Raymond White	1966	79
180 4/8	36 7/8	37 5/8	16 2/8	16 2/8	9 4/8	9 5/8	21 5/8	17 3/8	Yuma Co., AZ	Weldon A. Rogers	Weldon A. Rogers	1990	79
180 3/8	38 1/8	40 2/8	15 1/8	15 1/8	9	9 1/8	20 3/8	20 3/8	Baja Calif., MX	Arthur R. Dubs	Arthur R. Dubs	1966	81
180 3/8	39 2/8	39 5/8	14 5/8	14 5/8	9 3/8	9 6/8	22 4/8	22 4/8	Yuma Co., AZ	Fritz A. Nachant	Fritz A. Nachant	1970	81
180 3/8	38	37 5/8	15	14 7/8	10 2/8	9 4/8	21 7/8	17	Baja Calif., MX	James K. McCasland	James K. McCasland	1978	81
180 3/8	37 2/8	38 5/8	15 1/8	15 2/8	9 4/8	9 3/8	21 6/8	19 1/8	Baja Calif., MX	Emory C. Thompson	Emory C. Thompson	1985	81

DESERT SHEEP

Ovis canadensis nelsoni and certain related subspecies

Score	Length of Horn R	L	Circumference of Base R	L	Circumference at Third Quarter R	L	Greatest Spread	Tip to Tip Spread	Locality	Hunter	Owner	Date Killed	Rank
180 2/8	36 2/8	36 4/8	15 5/8	15 4/8	9 7/8	10 1/8	22 4/8	21 1/8	Baja Calif., MX	Hector A. Parada	Hector A. Parada	1988	85
180 2/8	41 2/8	39 6/8	14 4/8	14 4/8	8 7/8	9 7/8	22 6/8	22 2/8	Baja Calif., MX	Bernard Sippin	Bernard Sippin	1988	85
180 2/8	38 6/8	37 6/8	14 4/8	14 5/8	10 2/8	10	21 5/8	17 1/8	La Paz Co., AZ	Bruce Liddy	Bruce Liddy	1992	85
180 1/8	37 4/8	39 1/8	14 3/8	14 2/8	9 3/8	9 6/8	22 5/8	22 2/8	Tank Mts., AZ	Picked Up	Calvin C. Wallerich	1960	88
180 1/8	36 5/8	35 4/8	16 5/8	16 5/8	9 1/8	8 5/8	22 4/8	21 5/8	Pima Co., AZ	Robert A. Christy	Robert A. Christy	1986	88
180 1/8	38 1/8	38 2/8	15 1/8	15 4/8	9	8 7/8	26 7/8	26 5/8	Mohave Co., AZ	Gary D. Barcom	Gary D. Barcom	1996	88
180	36 1/8	38 1/8	15 6/8	15 6/8	9 4/8	10 1/8	21 3/8	17 3/8	Pima Co., AZ	Clifford W. Saylor	Clifford W. Saylor	1976	91
180	38 2/8	38 6/8	15 2/8	15 2/8	9	9 2/8	22	20 6/8	Clark Co., NV	John V. Zenz	John V. Zenz	1980	91
179 7/8	38 7/8	36 4/8	15 3/8	15 4/8	10 2/8	9 4/8	25 4/8	23 5/8	Clark Co., NV	Sal Quilici	NV State Museum	1978	93
179 7/8	37 5/8	37 2/8	15 4/8	15 2/8	8 7/8	9 2/8	19 5/8	17 5/8	Baja Calif., MX	George W. Vogt	George W. Vogt	1978	93
179 7/8	37 6/8	37 5/8	16	16 1/8	8 4/8	9	24 3/8	24 3/8	Baja Calif., MX	Paul E. Robey	Paul E. Robey	1979	93
179 6/8	39 1/8	37	16	16	7 5/8	7 4/8	24	24	Baja Calif., MX	Don L. Corley	Don L. Corley	1978	96
179 5/8	36 7/8	37	16 5/8	16 1/8	8 2/8	8 4/8	21 2/8	19 4/8	Pima Co., AZ	Brian F. Dolan	Brian F. Dolan	1995	97
179 4/8	38 1/8	37 3/8	15 3/8	15 4/8	9 4/8	9 7/8	21	19 6/8	Baja Calif., MX	Mrs. Carroll Pistell	Mrs. Carroll Pistell	1969	98
179 4/8	38 1/8	37 7/8	15 5/8	15 6/8	8 7/8	8 5/8	26 6/8	26 6/8	Baja Calif., MX	Ronald J. Wade	Ronald J. Wade	1987	98
179 3/8	37 1/8	37 2/8	15 6/8	15 6/8	9 2/8	9 7/8	21 3/8	16 1/8	Hidalgo Co., NM	James A. Schneider	MaHUNT	2001	100
179 3/8	36 5/8	35 7/8	16 2/8	16 2/8	9 1/8	9 1/8	20 5/8	19 3/8	Baja Calif., MX	Jim Buss	Jim Buss	1966	101
179 2/8	38 2/8	37	15 2/8	15 2/8	9 6/8	9 4/8	21 2/8	21 3/8	Baja Calif., MX	Francisco Salido	Francisco Salido	1968	101
179 2/8	36 7/8	36 7/8	14 7/8	14 7/8	9 7/8	9 6/8	20 4/8	20 4/8	Clark Co., NV	Andy S. Burnett	Andy S. Burnett	1979	101
179 2/8	38 3/8	40 1/8	15 1/8	15 2/8	9 3/8	9 3/8	23 4/8	23	Clark Co., NV	Tammy H. Bawcom	Tammy H. Bawcom	1988	101
179 2/8	38	35 2/8	15 2/8	15 2/8	9 4/8	9 4/8	28 6/8	27 5/8	Nye Co., NV	Picked Up	John V. Zenz II	1994	101
179 2/8	38 2/8	37 7/8	14 1/8	14 4/8	11 2/8	10 6/8	23 7/8	18 3/8	Cochise Co., AZ	Steven E. Krook	Steven E. Krook	1996	101
179 1/8	36 1/8	38 2/8	15 4/8	15 4/8	8 4/8	8 6/8	21 4/8	18 4/8	Baja Calif., MX	W.J. Boynton, Jr.	W.J. Boynton, Jr.	1974	107
179 1/8	39 5/8	40	14 4/8	14 4/8	9	9	25 1/8	24 5/8	Clark Co., NV	Gary D. Selmi	Gary D. Selmi	1989	107
179	37 3/8	36 1/8	16 2/8	16 1/8	8 5/8	8 6/8	19 4/8	18 7/8	Baja Calif., MX	Graciano G. Michel	Graciano G. Michel	1970	109
178 7/8	39 1/8	36	16 2/8	16 2/8	8	7 5/8	20 5/8	20	Hidalgo Co., NM	L.P. McKinney	Frank McKinney	1921	110
178 7/8	36 7/8	37	15 3/8	15 4/8	9 7/8	10 1/8	23	22 6/8	Sauceda Mts., AZ	Picked Up	Edward Hunt	1962	110
178 7/8	35 2/8	36 3/8	15 2/8	15 2/8	9 7/8	10 2/8	29 5/8	29 5/8	Mohave Co., AZ	Earle H. Smith	Earle H. Smith	1981	110
178 7/8	39 6/8	39 5/8	14 6/8	14 7/8	9 7/8	9	28 1/8	27	Mohave Co., AZ	Ronald A. Norman	Ronald A. Norman	1994	110
178 6/8	39 6/8	39 4/8	14 3/8	14 4/8	9 1/8	9	27	27	Colorado River, NV	E.A. Goldman	U.S. Natl. Museum	1913	114
178 6/8	37 2/8	37	14 6/8	14 6/8	10 2/8	10 2/8	22 3/8	18 5/8	Sonora, MX	Oscar J. Brooks	Oscar J. Brooks	1950	114
178 6/8	37 2/8	36 6/8	15 7/8	15 7/8	8 4/8	8 3/8	21 4/8	21 4/8	Baja Calif., MX	Hobson L. Sanderson, Jr.	Hobson L. Sanderson, Jr.	1981	114
178 6/8	35 6/8	36 2/8	15 7/8	16	8 6/8	9 2/8	25 2/8	22 6/8	Sonora, MX	George R. Harms	George R. Harms	2000	114
178 6/8	36 2/8	38 2/8	15 7/8	15 7/8	8 5/8	9	22 1/8	21 3/8	Mohave Co., AZ	Ernie Bombardieri	Ernie Bombardieri	2002	114
178 5/8	35 2/8	36 5/8	15 5/8	15 5/8	9 5/8	9 2/8	23 4/8	22	Lincoln Co., NV	William A. Bertelson	William A. Bertelson	1984	119
178 5/8	37 7/8	37 2/8	15 3/8	15 3/8	8 7/8	8 7/8	21 2/8	20 2/8	La Paz Co., AZ	Wayne B. Smith	Wayne B. Smith	1993	119
178 4/8	38 3/8	35 3/8	15 5/8	15 5/8	9 1/8	9 5/8	22 3/8	20	Pima Co., AZ	Ken Broyles	Ken Broyles	1971	121
178 4/8	36 4/8	36 2/8	15 6/8	15 6/8	9	9 2/8	20 4/8	19 2/8	Baja Calif., MX	Henry Culp	Henry Culp	1978	121

Score	Length of Horn	Circ. of Base	Circ. of Base	Circ. 3rd Qtr	Circ. 3rd Qtr	Greatest Spread	Tip to Tip	Locality	By Whom Killed	Owner	Date	Rank
178 4/8	40 4/8	14 1/8	13 7/8	9 6/8	10	25 7/8	25 7/8	Clark Co., NV	Stephen E. Aiazzi	Stephen E. Aiazzi	1985	121
178 4/8	38	14	13 7/8	10 4/8	10 4/8	22 5/8	21 5/8	Coconino Co., AZ	Picked Up	Carl Iacona	1996	121
178 2/8	38 6/8	14 2/8	14 2/8	10 1/8	10 4/8	23 5/8	22 4/8	Clark Co., NV	Kenneth A. Brunk	Kenneth A. Brunk	1989	125
178 1/8	34	15	14 6/8	9 5/8	10 2/8	19 7/8	18	Maricopa Co., AZ	Michael Holt	Michael Holt	1970	126
178 1/8	39 4/8	14 5/8	14 4/8	9 6/8	9 5/8	25 4/8	25 1/8	Lincoln Co., NV	David R. Montrose	David R. Montrose	1993	126
178 1/8	36 2/8	15 2/8	15 2/8	9 1/8	9 5/8	18 1/8	18 1/8	Sonora, MX	Dennis H. Dunn	Dennis H. Dunn	1997	126
178	38 3/8	15	15	9 3/8	9 6/8	21 4/8	19 4/8	Sonora, MX	Basil C. Bradbury	Basil C. Bradbury	1969	129
178	36	16	16	8 6/8	9	22	22	Baja Calif, MX	Aaron Saenz, Jr.	Aaron Saenz, Jr.	1969	129
178	35 4/8	16	16	8 2/8	8 2/8	24	24	Baja Calif, MX	James G. Lagiss	James G. Lagiss	1980	129
177 7/8	39 7/8	15 1/8	15 3/8	8 3/8	8	26 5/8	26 5/8	San Borjas Mts., MX	Jerald T. Waite	Jerald T. Waite	1972	132
177 7/8	38 1/8	15	15 1/8	9 2/8	9 2/8	20 5/8	20 5/8	Baja Calif, MX	Richard C. Hansen	Richard C. Hansen	1973	132
177 7/8	37	14 7/8	15	9 5/8	9 5/8	21	21	Mohave Co., AZ	William C. Duffy, Jr.	William C. Duffy, Jr.	1981	132
177 7/8	36	15 4/8	14 7/8	9 3/8	9 3/8	22 7/8	22 7/8	Yuma Co., AZ	J. Dorsey Smith	J. Dorsey Smith	1983	132
177 7/8	36 5/8	16 2/8	15 6/8	8 3/8	8 4/8	24	24	Graham Co., AZ	William N. Willis	William N. Willis	1989	132
177 4/8	34 2/8	16 2/8	15 1/8	9 1/8	9 4/8	23 1/8	23 1/8	Tiburon Island, MX	Donald W. Snyder	Donald W. Snyder	2001	138
177 4/8	37 1/8	15 5/8	14 4/8	9 4/8	8 3/8	27 6/8	27 6/8	Lower Calif, MX	Earl A. Garrettson	William Foster	1912	138
177 4/8	38	14 4/8	14 6/8	9 4/8	9 3/8	24	24	Baja Calif, MX	Herb Klein	Dallas Mus. of Natl. Hist.	1966	138
177 3/8	38	14 5/8	15 1/8	9 4/8	9 5/8	18 7/8	18 7/8	Baja Calif, MX	Joe Osterbauer	Joe Osterbauer	1978	142
177 3/8	36 7/8	14 7/8	14 2/8	9 5/8	10 4/8	20 3/8	20 3/8	Pima Co., AZ	Mark D. Morris	Mark D. Morris	1990	142
177 3/8	35 7/8	14 7/8	14 5/8	9 6/8	9 5/8	21	21	Lower Calif, MX	F. Stephens	U.S. Natl. Museum	1902	142
177 3/8	35 5/8	14 3/8	14 3/8	8 7/8	9 6/8	22 6/8	22 6/8	Yuma Co., AZ	George I. Parker	George I. Parker	1968	142
177 2/8	38 4/8	15 4/8	15 4/8	8	8 7/8	21 7/8	21 7/8	Baja Calif, MX	Arthur W. Carlsberg	Arthur W. Carlsberg	1970	147
177 2/8	36 6/8	16	16 2/8	10 4/8	8	16	16	Baja Calif, MX	Don McBride	Don McBride	1980	147
177 2/8	37 3/8	15 1/8	15 3/8	8 7/8	8 4/8	28 5/8	28 5/8	Clark Co., NV	Ralph W. McClintock	Ralph W. McClintock	1980	147
177 2/8	37	15 2/8	15 3/8	9	9	20 2/8	20 2/8	San Borjas Mts., MX	Robert M. Bransford	Robert M. Bransford	1966	147
177 2/8	34 6/8	15 3/8	15 2/8	9 3/8	9 1/8	20 6/8	20 6/8	Yuma Co., AZ	Lloyd E. Zeman	Jenifer D. Schmidt	1970	147
177 1/8	39 2/8	15 2/8	15 2/8	9 3/8	9 3/8	21 7/8	21 7/8	Yuma Co., AZ	Robert Fritzinger	Robert Fritzinger	1976	153
177 1/8	37 1/8	15 1/8	15 4/8	9 1/8	9 3/8	21 7/8	21 7/8	Sonora, MX	Julian W. Chancellor	Julian W. Chancellor	1992	153
177 1/8	37	15 4/8	15 5/8	8 6/8	10	19	19	Yuma Co., AZ	Anthony J. Conte	Anthony J. Conte	1999	153
177	36 4/8	15 3/8	15 3/8	9 3/8	10 1/8	22 2/8	22 2/8	La Paz Co., AZ	Bruce D. Kroeger	Bruce D. Kroeger	2002	156
177	38 2/8	14 5/8	14 5/8	8 6/8	8 6/8	21 4/8	21 4/8	Pima Co., AZ	Michael A. Jensen	Michael A. Jensen	1978	156
177	36 4/8	15 1/8	15 6/8	8 6/8	8 7/8	22 5/8	22 5/8	Baja Calif, MX	G. Dale Monson	G. Dale Monson	1982	156
177	37 6/8	15 2/8	15 2/8	8 1/8	8 2/8	18 1/8	18 1/8	Yuma Co., AZ	Michael A. Longoria	Michael A. Longoria	1994	156
176 7/8	37 6/8	15 2/8	15 4/8	8 3/8	9 2/8	18	18	Baja Calif, MX	Alain Ferraris	Alain Ferraris	1966	160
176 6/8	36 4/8	14 6/8	14 6/8	9 2/8	9 2/8	21 3/8	21 3/8	Sonora Desert, MX	Herb Klein	Dallas Mus. of Natl. Hist.	1969	161
176 6/8	36 4/8	15	15 6/8	9 1/8	9 1/8	18 6/8	18 6/8	Baja Calif, MX	Roy A. Woodward	Roy A. Woodward	1969	161
176 6/8	38	14 2/8	14 2/8	9 2/8	9 2/8	22 7/8	22 7/8	Clark Co., NV	Scott J. Weyrick	Scott J. Weyrick	1996	161
176 6/8	37 4/8	14 6/8	14 6/8	9 1/8	8 7/8	20 2/8	20 2/8	Mexico	Bill Foster	Foster's Bighorn Rest.	PR 1967	161
176 6/8	38 1/8	14 1/8	13 6/8	8 7/8	10 7/8	23 3/8	23 3/8	Kofa Range, AZ	Picked Up	D.B. Sanford	1957	161
176 5/8	38	15 5/8	15 5/8	8 4/8	10 5/8	21 6/8	21 6/8	Santa Rosa Mts., CA	Picked Up	John C. Belcher	PR 1958	166
176 5/8	36 3/8	14 6/8	15	8 6/8	8 2/8	22 1/8	22 1/8	Pinal Co., AZ	Travis Holder	Travis Holder	1984	166
176 5/8	37 4/8	15	14 6/8	9 1/8	9	21 1/8	21 1/8	Clark Co., NV	Douglas E. Wendt	Douglas E. Wendt	1989	166
176 5/8	37	15	15	8 4/8	8 7/8	20	20	Yuma Co., AZ	Steven E. Hopkins	Steven E. Hopkins	1998	166
176 5/8	35 6/8	15 6/8	15 6/8	9 1/8	8 4/8	22 3/8	22 3/8	Baja Calif, MX	Fernando Garcia	Fernando Garcia	1968	166
176 5/8	39	14 4/8	14 4/8	9 1/8	8 6/8	28 3/8	28 3/8	Clark Co., NV	Allan R. Sundell	Kent A. Sundell	1979	166
176 5/8	35 4/8	15 6/8	15 6/8	9 6/8	9 1/8	14 5/8	14 5/8	Baja Calif, MX	Douglas J. Dollhopf	Douglas J. Dollhopf	1983	166
176 5/8	39 7/8	14 1/8	14 1/8	8 6/8	9 4/8	21	21	Cochise Co., AZ	William R. Whitworth	William R. Whitworth	1995	166
176 5/8	36 6/8	15	15 4/8	9 5/8	9 6/8	21 6/8	21 6/8	Pima Co., AZ	Benjamin J. Hooper	Benjamin J. Hooper	1996	166

DESERT SHEEP

Ovis canadensis nelsoni and certain related subspecies

Score	Length of Horn R	L	Circumference of Base R	L	Circumference at Third Quarter R	L	Greatest Spread	Tip to Tip Spread	Locality	Hunter	Owner	Date Killed	Rank
176 4/8	38 6/8	37 2/8	15 2/8	15 1/8	8 3/8	8 4/8	23 2/8	23 2/8	Lower Calif., MX	E.W. Funcke	U.S. Natl. Museum	1905	171
176 4/8	38	38 2/8	13 6/8	14	10 1/8	9 7/8	21 6/8	21 6/8	Baja Calif., MX	Picked Up	Leland Brand	1973	171
176 4/8	36 7/8	38 3/8	16	16	7 7/8	7 7/8	20 6/8	18 4/8	Pinal Co., AZ	Robbie A. Brown	Robert L. Brown	1985	171
176 4/8	35 2/8	36 2/8	15 1/8	15	9 6/8	10 2/8	21 2/8	19 2/8	Yuma Co., AZ	Gail C. Ferguson	Gail C. Ferguson	1988	171
176 3/8	34 5/8	34 6/8	16 4/8	16 5/8	8 5/8	9	19 7/8	18 1/8	Baja Calif., MX	William L. Baker, Jr.	William L. Baker, Jr.	1974	175
176 3/8	35 2/8	37 1/8	15 3/8	16	9	9 2/8	21 1/8	15 6/8	Baja Calif., MX	Joe E. Coleman	Joe E. Coleman	1976	175
176 3/8	37 5/8	36	15 3/8	15 2/8	8 2/8	8 5/8	29 1/8	29 1/8	Baja Calif., MX	C.J. McElroy	C.J. McElroy	1978	175
176 3/8	36 5/8	36 6/8	15 7/8	15 7/8	8 4/8	8 4/8	19 7/8	14 7/8	Baja Calif., MX	Richard Wehling	Richard Wehling	1978	175
176 2/8	35 6/8	36 6/8	14 3/8	14 3/8	9 6/8	10	23 1/8	22 4/8	Clark Co., NV	F. Lorin Ronnow	F. Lorin Ronnow	1957	179
176 2/8	35 6/8	37 5/8	15	15 3/8	8 4/8	8 4/8	21 5/8	21 5/8	Yuma Co., AZ	Vicki L. Clark	Vicki L. Clark	1980	179
176 2/8	38 2/8	36	15 3/8	15 3/8	8 4/8	8 4/8	21 6/8	19 4/8	Clark Co., NV	Christine J. Burrows	Christine J. Burrows	1981	179
176 2/8	38 6/8	37 4/8	14 4/8	14 4/8	8 7/8	9	21	21	Pinal Co., AZ	D. Mark Exline	D. Mark Exline	1982	179
176 2/8	34	37	15 2/8	15 2/8	9 1/8	9 5/8	23	21 2/8	Clark Co., NV	Jack Oberly	Jack Oberly	1983	179
176 1/8	37 2/8	36 5/8	15	15 1/8	9 2/8	9 2/8	25 3/8	25 3/8	Baja Calif., MX	N.J. Segal, Jr.	N.J. Segal, Jr.	1972	184
176 1/8	36 5/8	36 4/8	14 6/8	14 6/8	9 3/8	9 4/8	21 6/8	20	Pinal Co., AZ	Warren A. Adams	Warren A. Adams	1985	184
176 1/8	37 7/8	38 2/8	15 1/8	15 4/8	8 3/8	8	21 5/8	21 1/8	Clark Co., NV	Timothy L. Iveson	Timothy L. Iveson	1985	184
176 1/8	34 7/8	37	15 6/8	16	8 4/8	8 4/8	22 4/8	22 4/8	Pima Co., AZ	Donald P. Petersen	Donald P. Petersen	1988	184
176 1/8	38 2/8	38 3/8	14 5/8	14 6/8	8 4/8	8 6/8	21 3/8	20 7/8	Culberson Co., TX	Daniel F. Boone	Daniel F. Boone	1997	184
176	38 3/8	39 7/8	15 1/8	15 1/8	7 4/8	8 1/8	22 1/8	20 5/8	Sonora, MX	Fritz Katz	Fritz Katz	1941	189
176	37 2/8	38 2/8	14 4/8	15	9	9 4/8	25	25	Black Mts., AZ	Picked Up	R.A. Wagner	1954	189
176	37 4/8	34 2/8	15 4/8	15 4/8	9 2/8	9 2/8	21 4/8	18 4/8	Kofa Mts., AZ	Robin Underdown	Robin Underdown	1966	189
176	34 6/8	34 4/8	17 1/8	17 1/8	8 3/8	8 3/8	19 6/8	17	Sonora, MX	Ollie O. Barney, Jr.	Ollie O. Barney, Jr.	1968	189
176	36	36	15 4/8	15 4/8	9	9 1/8	18 2/8	18 2/8	Baja Calif., MX	Paul S. Inzanti	Paul S. Inzanti	1982	189
176	36 2/8	35 6/8	14 6/8	14 6/8	10 2/8	10	19 1/8	16 4/8	Baja Calif., MX	Pedro S. Montano	Pedro S. Montano	1986	189
175 7/8	35 7/8	35 4/8	15	15	9 7/8	9 3/8	22 4/8	22	Yuma Co., AZ	J. Don McGaffee	J. Don McGaffee	1978	195
175 7/8	39 5/8	38 6/8	14	14	8 6/8	9 2/8	22 5/8	22 5/8	Yuma Co., AZ	Fred W. Jerome	Fred W. Jerome	1979	195
175 7/8	36 7/8	37	15 2/8	15 1/8	9 4/8	9 6/8	22 4/8	19	Pinal Co., AZ	Tracy L. Contreras	Tracy L. Contreras	1980	195
175 6/8	35 5/8	36 1/8	14 1/8	14	10 4/8	10 4/8	21 2/8	17 5/8	San Diego Co., CA	Picked Up	Anza-Borrego Desert State Park	1951	198
175 6/8	35 3/8	35 3/8	16 1/8	16 3/8	8 5/8	8 3/8	18 6/8	18 6/8	Baja Calif., MX	Jack Leeds	Jack Leeds	1976	198
175 6/8	36 6/8	36 4/8	14 3/8	14 3/8	9 6/8	9 6/8	21	21	Lincoln Co., NV	Denny L. Frook	Denny L. Frook	1977	198
175 6/8	33 3/8	35 5/8	16	16	9 4/8	9 1/8	22	20 6/8	Pima Co., AZ	Robert F. Lebo	Robert F. Lebo	1977	198
175 6/8	35 2/8	35 2/8	16	16	8 7/8	9 1/8	20	17 4/8	Baja Calif., MX	William C. Cloyd	William C. Cloyd	1984	198
175 6/8	34 5/8	35 1/8	15 5/8	15 6/8	9	9 3/8	22 4/8	18 4/8	Yuma Co., AZ	Robert A. Brannan	Robert A. Brannan	1994	198
175 6/8	37 1/8	37 7/8	15 4/8	15 2/8	8 7/8	8 6/8	25 3/8	24 7/8	Clark Co., NV	David L. Mode	David L. Mode	1994	198
175 6/8	37 4/8	39	15 3/8	15 3/8	8 6/8	8 6/8	21	21	Maricopa Co., AZ	Mark A. Thorsrud	Mark A. Thorsrud	2001	198
175 4/8	36	36 4/8	15 4/8	15 4/8	8 4/8	8 4/8	20 6/8	19 3/8	Yuma Co., AZ	Picked Up	Tom D. Moore	1956	206
175 4/8	37 2/8	36	15	15	9 4/8	10	21 4/8	21 4/8	Maricopa Co., AZ	Picked Up	Robert B. Thompson	1963	206

Score	Length R	Length L	Circ. Base R	Circ. Base L	Circ. Third R	Circ. Third L	Greatest Spread	Tip to Tip	Location	Hunter	Owner	Date Killed	Rank
175 4/8	37 3/8	36 5/8	14 4/8	14 6/8	9 3/8	9 4/8	21 6/8	19	Baja Calif., MX	Tony Oney	Tony Oney	1968	206
175 4/8	36 4/8	37 4/8	14 7/8	14 7/8	8 7/8	9 7/8	22 3/8	21 6/8	Plomosa Mts., AZ	J. James Froelich	J. James Froelich	1969	206
175 4/8	36 3/8	36 1/8	14 3/8	14 2/8	10 1/8	10 1/8	21 6/8	18 4/8	Yuma Co., AZ	Anton E. Rimsza	Anton E. Rimsza	1982	206
175 4/8	37 2/8	36 6/8	15 4/8	15	8 5/8	8 6/8	20 7/8	17 5/8	Pima Co., AZ	David R. Howell	David R. Howell	1991	206
175 3/8	37	37 3/8	14 5/8	14 5/8	8 6/8	9 2/8	21 2/8	21 2/8	Lincoln Co., NV	Robert Fagan	Robert Fagan	1968	212
175 3/8	35 6/8	35 3/8	15 4/8	15 3/8	9 2/8	9 4/8	21 6/8	18 4/8	Plomosa Mts., AZ	M.S. Mac Collum	M.S. Mac Collum	1968	212
175 3/8	38 2/8	38 3/8	14 5/8	14 5/8	8 5/8	8 5/8	22	19 4/8	Yuma Co., AZ	Patrick E. Hurley	Patrick E. Hurley	1981	212
175 3/8	37 5/8	39 4/8	14	13 7/8	9 4/8	9 2/8	19 1/8	17 7/8	Baja Calif., MX	Isidro Lopez del Bosque	Isidro Lopez del Bosque	1984	212
175 2/8	37 4/8	37 4/8	14 3/8	14 2/8	9 1/8	9 1/8	21 5/8	21 3/8	Baja Calif., MX	Keith C. Brown	Keith C. Brown	1966	216
175 2/8	37 4/8	37 3/8	14 2/8	15 2/8	9 2/8	9 2/8	17 4/8	17 1/8	Yuma Co., AZ	Ted Phoenix	Ted Phoenix	1995	216
175 2/8	36 2/8	36 4/8	15 2/8	15 6/8	8 4/8	7 7/8	23 4/8	21 2/8	Riverside Co., CA	David E. Combs	David E. Combs	1996	216
175 1/8	36 1/8	36 1/8	15 1/8	15 2/8	8 5/8	8 4/8	19 3/8	19 3/8	Mexico	Bill Foster	Foster's Bighorn Rest.	1950	219
175 1/8	36 5/8	36 5/8	14 7/8	15 1/8	8 7/8	9 4/8	19 4/8	17 4/8	Sonora, MX	Unknown	Paul W. Hughes	1952	219
175 1/8	37 2/8	37 3/8	14 2/8	14 2/8	8 5/8	9 2/8	20 1/8	20 1/8	Lamb Springs, NV	D.B. Walkington	D.B. Walkington	1965	219
175 1/8	37 1/8	38 3/8	14 6/8	14 6/8	9 2/8	9 5/8	25 7/8	25 7/8	Clark Co., NV	Wayne C. Matley	Wayne C. Matley	1966	219
175 1/8	37 1/8	37	13 7/8	13 7/8	9 3/8	8 6/8	22 6/8	20 5/8	Riverside Co., CA	Picked Up	George F. Stewart, Jr.	PR 1967	219
175 1/8	36 6/8	40	15 2/8	13 7/8	8 6/8	8 7/8	31 1/8	18 6/8	Baja Calif., MX	C.J. Wimer	C.J. Wimer	1977	219
175 1/8	36 4/8	35 5/8	15 2/8	15 2/8	8 4/8	8 4/8	23 1/8	23 1/8	Clark Co., NV	Lenda Z. Azcarate	Lenda Z. Azcarate	1979	219
175 1/8	36 2/8	36 1/8	15	15 1/8	9 5/8	9	23 7/8	23 7/8	Clark Co., NV	Lloyd G. Bare	Lloyd G. Bare	1980	219
175 1/8	34 4/8	36 5/8	15	15	9 6/8	10	23 2/8	22	Clark Co., NV	William J. Conner	William J. Conner	1989	219
175 1/8	34 2/8	34 7/8	15 2/8	15 2/8	10 1/8	10 5/8	21 6/8	20	San Bernardino Co., CA	Arthur D. Bailey	Arthur D. Bailey	1993	219
175	35	36	15	15	9 2/8	10	22 4/8	22 4/8	Sonora, MX	Juan A. Saenz, Jr.	Juan A. Saenz, Jr.	1969	229
175	37 4/8	33 6/8	15 5/8	15 3/8	8 4/8	8 4/8	20 4/8	18 4/8	Yuma Co., AZ	Harry B. Cook	Harry B. Cook	1982	229
175	37 4/8	37 4/8	15	15	9 6/8	9 2/8	26 6/8	26 6/8	Clark Co., NV	Timothy P. Ryan	Timothy P. Ryan	1983	229
175	35 6/8	35 6/8	14 6/8	14 6/8	9 5/8	9 5/8	20 6/8	20 2/8	Baja Calif., MX	Craig Leerberg	Craig Leerberg	1990	229
175	35 6/8	36 4/8	14 6/8	15	9	9	23 2/8	23 2/8	Maricopa Co., AZ	Matthew D. Liljenquist	Matthew D. Liljenquist	2002	229
174 7/8	37	36 2/8	15	15	8 6/8	9 3/8	20 3/8	19 6/8	Pima Co., AZ	Picked Up	Robert J. Kirkpatrick	PR 1968	234
174 7/8	37 1/8	35 1/8	13 5/8	13 5/8	9 4/8	9 3/8	23 3/8	21	Arizona	Picked Up	Nathan Frisby	1974	234
174 7/8	35 1/8	38 4/8	15 7/8	15 7/8	8 7/8	8 7/8	23 5/8	23 1/8	Clark Co., NV	Herman H. Storey, Jr.	Herman H. Storey, Jr.	1980	234
174 7/8	35 7/8	35	15 6/8	15 2/8	8 5/8	8 4/8	19 6/8	19 6/8	Clark Co., NV	Cleldon E. Nelson	Cleldon E. Nelson	1987	234
174 7/8	41 4/8	41 1/8	13 5/8	14 2/8	8	8 1/8	29	29	Clark Co., NV	Michael J. Ellena	Michael J. Ellena	1993	234
174 7/8	34 5/8	35 4/8	14 6/8	13 6/8	9 7/8	9 3/8	21 5/8	19	Hidalgo Co., NM	James L. Daubendiek	James L. Daubendiek	2002	234
174 6/8	39	38 4/8	15	14 6/8	8 6/8	9 5/8	22 1/8	22 1/8	Barstow, CA	Picked Up	Thomas Hodges	1941	240
174 6/8	33 6/8	34 6/8	15	15	7 5/8	7 7/8	25 4/8	25 4/8	Clark Co., NV	Ron W. Biggs	Ron W. Biggs	1980	240
174 6/8	37 4/8	35 4/8	15 6/8	15 2/8	9 1/8	8 7/8	21 4/8	17	Pima Co., AZ	Collins L. Cochran	Collins L. Cochran	1992	240
174 5/8	36 3/8	34 6/8	15 4/8	15 4/8	9 2/8	9	24	23	Brewster Co., TX	William W. Britain	William W. Britain	1997	244
174 5/8	34 7/8	37 5/8	14 6/8	15 7/8	9 3/8	9 5/8	18 7/8	16 4/8	Baja Calif., MX	Stanley S. Gray	Stanley S. Gray	1972	244
174 5/8	36 4/8	36	14 4/8	14 6/8	9 4/8	8	25 1/8	25 1/8	Clark Co., NV	Roseanne K. Wilkinson	Roseanne K. Wilkinson	1980	244
174 4/8	36 4/8	36 6/8	14	14 2/8	7 6/8	7 6/8	19 4/8	19 4/8	Maricopa Co., AZ	Picked Up	Robert B. Thompson	1963	246
174 4/8	37	37 4/8	15 1/8	15 7/8	8 3/8	8 3/8	20 6/8	20 6/8	Baja Calif., MX	Jack Walters	Jack Walters	1966	246
174 4/8	37 2/8	37 6/8	14 2/8	14 2/8	7 5/8	7 7/8	26 2/8	25 7/8	Clark Co., NV	Stanley R. Galvin, Jr.	Stanley R. Galvin, Jr.	1983	246
174 4/8	36 6/8	34 7/8	15 2/8	15 5/8	9 1/8	9 1/8	21 4/8	18 5/8	Clark Co., NV	Larry G. Marshall	Larry G. Marshall	1983	246
174 4/8	33 7/8	38 4/8	15	15	9 6/8	9 5/8	21	13 2/8	Hidalgo Co., NM	Glen A. Landrus	Glen A. Landrus	2002	246
174 3/8	38 1/8	36	14 4/8	14 4/8	8	7 7/8	24 4/8	23 5/8	Clark Co., NV	Kathy E. Seaberg	K.E. & G. Seaberg	1981	251
174 2/8	37	38 2/8	15 7/8	15 7/8	10 1/8	10 1/8	20 4/8	18 3/8	Baja Calif., MX	Basil C. Bradbury	Basil C. Bradbury	1968	252
174 2/8	37	36	14	14 1/8	10 1/8	10	20 7/8	21 7/8	Las Vegas, NV	Thomas R. McElhenney	Thomas R. McElhenney	1969	252
174 2/8	35 3/8	35 6/8	14 7/8	14 7/8	9 7/8	9 7/8	25 5/8	25 5/8	Mohave Co., AZ	Susan C. Nelson	Susan C. Nelson	1979	252
174 2/8	34 4/8	35 6/8	15 3/8	15 2/8	9	9 7/8	26	26	Lincoln Co., NV	Larry M. Evans	Larry M. Evans	1982	252

Ovis canadensis nelsoni and certain related subspecies

Score	Length of Horn R	L	Circumference of Base R	L	Circumference at Third Quarter R	L	Greatest Spread	Tip to Tip Spread	Locality	Hunter	Owner	Date Killed	Rank
174 2/8	35 6/8	40 4/8	14 4/8	14 5/8	8 1/8	8 3/8	30 3/8	30 1/8	Mohave Co., AZ	Howard Grounds	Howard Grounds	1984	252
174 2/8	34 2/8	33 3/8	15 4/8	15 5/8	9 4/8	9 3/8	24 4/8	21 6/8	Maricopa Co., AZ	Debi L. Adair	Debi L. Adair	1987	252
174 2/8	34 6/8	35 4/8	15 1/8	15 1/8	9 7/8	9 7/8	23 6/8	23 6/8	Washington Co., UT	Margaret Barnett	Margaret Barnett	2001	252
174 1/8	38 1/8	37 4/8	14 2/8	14 3/8	9	8 6/8	22 2/8	21 6/8	Baja Calif., MX	Scott Jankowski	Scott Jankowski	2001	259
174	40	38 4/8	15 2/8	15 4/8	7 4/8	7 6/8	25 2/8	25 2/8	Lower Calif., MX	E.W. Funcke	Harvard Univ. Mus.	1911	260
174	36 4/8	37 4/8	15 4/8	15 3/8	9	8	21 5/8	21	Yuma Co., MX	Wynn Robestal	U.S. Fish & Wild. Serv.	1913	260
174	37 2/8	36 2/8	14 4/8	14 4/8	9 2/8	9	19 4/8	18	Sonora, MX	Frank C. Hibben	Frank C. Hibben	1940	260
174	36 6/8	37 4/8	13 4/8	13 5/8	10	10	24 4/8	24 4/8	McCullough Mts., NV	Picked Up	William H. Pogue	PR 1958	260
174	31 6/8	34 4/8	15 6/8	15 6/8	9 5/8	9 5/8	22	20	Pima Co., AZ	George Martin	George Martin	1978	260
174	36 3/8	35 1/8	15 2/8	15 1/8	9 1/8	8 6/8	23	23	Baja Calif., MX	James W. Owens	James W. Owens	1983	260
174	37 2/8	38 2/8	14 3/8	14 2/8	8 7/8	8 7/8	22	17 5/8	Clark Co., NV	H. James Tonkin, Jr.	H. James Tonkin, Jr.	1990	260
174	35 5/8	35 5/8	14 3/8	14 3/8	10 1/8	10 1/8	22 1/8	18	La Paz Co., AZ	Craig R. Johnson	Craig R. Johnson	1993	260
174	35 6/8	37 2/8	15 2/8	15 2/8	8 3/8	8 1/8	23 5/8	23 2/8	Sonora, MX	Donald W. Jacklin	Donald W. Jacklin	2000	260
174	36	36	14 1/8	14 1/8	10 4/8	9 7/8	24 6/8	23	Hudspeth Co., TX	Robert H. Torstenson	Double H Ranch	2001	260
173 7/8	37 2/8	37 1/8	14 3/8	14 5/8	8 4/8	8 7/8	24 5/8	24 5/8	Kofa Mts., AZ	William L. Snider	William L. Snider	1965	270
173 7/8	36 5/8	37	13 1/8	13 4/8	10 3/8	10 4/8	22 2/8	19 3/8	Anza-Borrego Desert, CA	Picked Up	Anza-Borrego Desert State Park	1971	270
173 7/8	34 6/8	34 7/8	15 6/8	15 6/8	9 1/8	9 1/8	22 5/8	22 2/8	Baja Calif., MX	Erwin Dykstra	Erwin Dykstra	1978	270
173 7/8	37	37 5/8	15	14 6/8	8 6/8	9 3/8	21 4/8	20 4/8	Yuma Co., AZ	John C. Marsalla	John C. Marsalla	1982	270
173 7/8	35 5/8	35 6/8	15 3/8	15 2/8	9 2/8	9 3/8	18 3/8	17 5/8	Sonora, MX	A. Oscar Carlson	A. Oscar Carlson	1996	270
173 7/8	36 4/8	35 3/8	15 3/8	15 1/8	9 2/8	9	22 1/8	21 1/8	Clark Co., NV	Bob Wells	Bob Wells	2002	270
173 6/8	34 6/8	34 4/8	14 2/8	14 4/8	9 6/8	10 2/8	22 4/8	21 6/8	Yuma Co., AZ	Picked Up	Bob Housholder	1953	276
173 6/8	35 7/8	36 1/8	16 2/8	16 2/8	8 4/8	8	20 5/8	20 5/8	Baja Calif., MX	Fritz A. Nachant	Fritz A. Nachant	1969	276
173 6/8	36 2/8	35 6/8	15 7/8	15 6/8	7 7/8	7 5/8	22 4/8	23	Mohave Co., AZ	Steve Clonts	Steve Clonts	1991	276
173 6/8	35 3/8	35 7/8	15 4/8	15 4/8	8 5/8	8 6/8	20 5/8	17 5/8	Sonora, MX	Ronald F. Mobley	Ronald F. Mobley	1998	276
173 5/8	37	37 1/8	15 1/8	15 3/8	8 4/8	8 6/8	20 7/8	20 4/8	Baja Calif., MX	James H. Duke, Jr.	James H. Duke, Jr.	1969	280
173 5/8	35 4/8	34 5/8	15 1/8	15 1/8	9	8 7/8	22 2/8	22 2/8	Baja Calif., MX	John H. Batten	John H. Batten	1975	280
173 5/8	37 1/8	36 6/8	15 2/8	15	8 6/8	8 6/8	23 4/8	23 4/8	Clark Co., NV	Buddy H. Fujii	Buddy H. Fujii	1980	280
173 5/8	36 6/8	34 5/8	15 2/8	15 5/8	9 3/8	8 7/8	24 4/8	19 7/8	Yuma Co., AZ	David C. Root	David C. Root	1983	280
173 5/8	37 1/8	34 2/8	15	15	9	9	19 2/8	15 1/8	Sonora, MX	Douglas G. Williams	Douglas G. Williams	1983	280
173 5/8	37 3/8	36 2/8	14 4/8	14 4/8	8 3/8	8 3/8	22	21 3/8	Baja Calif., MX	Patrick C. Allen	Patrick C. Allen	1987	280
173 5/8	37 5/8	36 6/8	14 6/8	14 5/8	8 2/8	8 3/8	21 6/8	20	Clark Co., NV	Dale O. Milliren	Dale O. Milliren	1987	280
173 5/8	35 4/8	36 3/8	15 6/8	15 4/8	8 2/8	8 7/8	21	20 4/8	Baja Calif., MX	John P. Reilly	John P. Reilly	1989	280
173 5/8	36 3/8	35 4/8	15	14 7/8	8 7/8	8 5/8	19 5/8	18 6/8	Baja Calif., MX	Stephen B. Clark	Stephen B. Clark	1999	280
173 4/8	35 6/8	36 6/8	15 6/8	15 6/8	8 1/8	8	21 3/8	21 3/8	Muleje Baja, MX	Victor M. Ruiza	Victor M. Ruiza	1966	289
173 4/8	35	33 4/8	16	16	8 4/8	8 2/8	23 1/8	23 1/8	Clark Co., NV	Ira H. Kent	Ira H. Kent	1978	289
173 4/8	34 6/8	33 6/8	16 2/8	16 2/8	8 2/8	9	19 7/8	15	Sonora, MX	Walter Snoke	Walter Snoke	1978	289
173 4/8	34	33 4/8	15 4/8	15 4/8	9 4/8	9 4/8	25 7/8	25 4/8	Mohave Co., AZ	Gordon M. Osborn	Gordon M. Osborn	1989	289
173 4/8	33 7/8	35 7/8	14 4/8	14 3/8	10	10 5/8	20 5/8	17 7/8	San Bernardino Co., CA	Jerry K. Chandler	Jerry K. Chandler	1993	289

Score	Length R	Length L	Circ. Base R	Circ. Base L	Circ. 3rd Qtr R	Circ. 3rd Qtr L	Greatest Spread	Tip to Tip	Locality	By whom killed	Owner	Date	Rank
173 4/8	33 5/8	33 7/8	16 2/8	16 3/8	8 7/8	9	20 3/8	20	Sonora, MX	Robert E. Manger	Robert E. Manger	1993	289
173 4/8	34 4/8	34 2/8	15 6/8	15 6/8	8 6/8	8 7/8	24 1/8	24 1/8	Nye Co., NV	Seth Puryear	Seth Puryear	1995	289
173 3/8	36 6/8	36 1/8	14 5/8	14 5/8	8 6/8	8 5/8	21 1/8	17 7/8	Baja Calif., MX	M. Alessio Robles	M. Alessio Robles	1956	296
173 3/8	36 2/8	36 3/8	15 5/8	15 5/8	8 1/8	8 2/8	21 3/8	20 3/8	Sonora, MX	Gaston Cano	Gaston Cano	1968	296
173 3/8	36 6/8	37 3/8	14 6/8	14 7/8	8 1/8	8 4/8	22 3/8	22	Baja Calif., MX	Roy A. Schultz	Roy A. Schultz	1971	296
173 3/8	37	37 7/8	15 1/8	15	8 4/8	8 6/8	22	22	Baja Calif., MX	Dale R. Leonard	Dale R. Leonard	1972	296
173 3/8	40 5/8	38	13 7/8	14 6/8	8 2/8	8 1/8	21 3/8		Baja Calif., MX	Tim C. Boyd	Tim C. Boyd	1981	296
173 3/8	36	36 3/8	15 3/8	15 3/8	8 2/8	8 3/8	23 4/8	19 1/8	Mohave Co., AZ	Donald E. Franklin	Donald E. Franklin	1982	296
173 3/8	36 4/8	35 1/8	14 6/8	14 7/8	8 7/8	9	25 3/8	22 5/8	Maricopa Co., AZ	James D. Thorne	James D. Thorne	1989	303
173 3/8	34 7/8	35 3/8	15 4/8	15 4/8	8 6/8	8 5/8	25 3/8	25 3/8	Little Horn Mts., AZ	Joseph J. Sobotka	Joseph J. Sobotka	1969	303
173 2/8	36 3/8	36 1/8	15 2/8	15 2/8	8 2/8	8 2/8	21 1/8	19 6/8	Baja Calif., MX	Ernest Righetti	Ernest Righetti	1974	303
173 2/8	35 2/8	35 2/8	15 4/8	15 3/8	8 6/8	8 6/8	26 1/8	21 5/8	Baja Calif., MX	Marion H. Scott	Marion H. Scott	1978	303
173 2/8	35 4/8	35 6/8	15 1/8	15 1/8	8 6/8	9 1/8	23 4/8	25 4/8	Lincoln Co., NV	Ken G. Gerg	Ken G. Gerg	1990	303
173 2/8	36 4/8	35 4/8	15 5/8	15 5/8	8 5/8	9 2/8	21	20 6/8	Pima Co., AZ	Ben H. Mattausch	Ben H. Mattausch	1994	303
173 1/8	37 1/8	35 2/8	14 1/8	14 1/8	9 4/8	9	25 4/8	21	Little Horn Mts., AZ	Picked Up	Duane J. Hall	1960	308
173 1/8	37 5/8	37 3/8	14 6/8	14 5/8	9	11	24 4/8	25 4/8	Lincoln Co., NV	Picked Up	Billy D. Stoddard	1965	308
173 1/8	32 6/8	32 6/8	13 6/8	13 6/8	11	11 6/8	21 3/8	23	Tulelake, CA	Picked Up	Natl. Park Service	1968	308
173 1/8	37 4/8	30 7/8	14	14 1/8	7 7/8	9 7/8	27 5/8	18	Sonora Desert, MX	Picked Up	Herb Klein	1969	308
173 1/8	37 1/8	40 1/8	14 3/8	14 4/8	9 1/8	8 3/8	24	27 5/8	Clark Co., NV	Chris Hurtado	Chris Hurtado	1975	308
173 1/8	36 5/8	37 1/8	14 7/8	14 7/8	9 5/8	9 5/8	20 3/8	24	Lincoln Co., NV	Michael D. Rowe	Michael D. Rowe	1988	308
173 1/8	35 6/8	36 5/8	14 5/8	14 5/8	8 7/8	8 7/8	22	16 4/8	Yuma Co., AZ	Robert S. Holyoak	Robert S. Holyoak	1994	308
173 1/8	36 1/8	36 4/8	16 1/8	16	9 3/8	9 6/8	21 1/8	16 1/8	Hidalgo Co., NM	James A. Schneider	MaHUNT	2000	308
173	35 2/8	36 5/8	14 6/8	14 7/8	9	8 4/8	24 4/8	16 4/8	Yuma Co., AZ	Heath Lewis	Heath Lewis	2002	317
173	36	36	15	15	8 2/8	9 1/8	19 1/8	21 4/8	Lower Calif., MX	Henry H. Blagden	Henry H. Blagden	1914	317
173	38	38 3/8	14 6/8	14 6/8	8 4/8	8 4/8	21 6/8	19 1/8	Sheep Mt. Range, NV	Gilbert A. Helsel	Gilbert A. Helsel	1960	317
173	36 1/8	35 2/8	14 3/8	14 3/8	9 4/8	9 1/8	20 7/8	16 6/8	Aguila Mts., AZ	Picked Up	C.G. Clare	1961	317
173	36	36	15 1/8	15 1/8	8 7/8	9	20	20 1/8	Baja Calif., MX	James H. Russell	James H. Russell	1970	317
173	35 6/8	35 6/8	13 6/8	13 7/8	10 3/8	10 5/8	24	17 5/8	Maricopa Co., AZ	Stephen K. Weisser	Stephen K. Weisser	1973	317
173	37 1/8	37 1/8	15	15	8 3/8	8 3/8	20 4/8	24	Baja Calif., MX	Charles Oyer	Charles Oyer	1975	317
173	39	35	15 5/8	15 5/8	8 6/8	8 2/8	20 2/8	17 2/8	Baja Calif., MX	P. Franklin Bays, Jr.	P. Franklin Bays, Jr.	1976	317
173	34 4/8	35 3/8	16	16 1/8	8 1/8	8 1/8	21 3/8	19 4/8	Maricopa Co., AZ	Tom W. Housh	Tom W. Housh	1988	317
172 7/8	35 1/8	35 6/8	14 7/8	14 6/8	9 4/8	9 4/8	21 4/8	21 2/8	Cochise Co., AZ	Jim L. Boyer	Jim L. Boyer	1993	327
172 7/8	35 4/8	35 2/8	15 3/8	15 4/8	9 3/8	8 6/8	20 5/8	20 4/8	Baja Calif., MX	Jon A. Ancell	Jon A. Ancell	1997	327
172 7/8	34	34 1/8	15 2/8	15	9 7/8	9 3/8	22 1/8	19 4/8	Gila Co., AZ	Mahlon T. White	Mahlon T. White	1969	327
172 7/8	34 6/8	34 6/8	15	14 4/8	10	9 7/8	22	18 2/8	Clark Co., NV	Picked Up	Michael T. Miller	1990	327
172 6/8	35 6/8	35 1/8	14 4/8	14 2/8	8 7/8	9 4/8	19 2/8	19 6/8	Baja Calif., MX	William R. Slattery	William R. Slattery	1992	331
172 6/8	35 3/8	35 2/8	15 5/8	15 3/8	9	8 1/8	23 7/8	19 2/8	Baja Calif., MX	James G. Petersen	James G. Petersen	2000	331
172 6/8	37 1/8	38 5/8	13 5/8	13 4/8	8 7/8	9	21 2/8	23 7/8	Baja Calif., MX	Otis Chandler	Otis Chandler	1966	331
172 6/8	37 2/8	35 4/8	15 7/8	15 5/8	8 7/8	8 4/8	20 3/8	21 2/8	Yuma Co., AZ	Graciano Guichard	Graciano Guichard	1969	331
172 6/8	36 3/8	36 3/8	14 3/8	14 3/8	8 4/8	8 5/8	19 1/8	19	Yuma Co., AZ	Norman F. Mathews	Norman F. Mathews	1977	331
172 6/8	36	36 5/8	15 5/8	15 3/8	8 5/8	8 2/8	19 6/8	18 3/8	Pima Co., AZ	Paul H. Harrison	Paul H. Harrison	1981	331
172 6/8	36 5/8	36 5/8	14	13 7/8	10 1/8	9 2/8	24 5/8	19 6/8	Yuma Co., AZ	Larry J. Landes	Larry J. Landes	1981	331
172 5/8	41 4/8	37 2/8	14 2/8	14 3/8	9 4/8	9 4/8	22	24 3/8	Gila Co., AZ	Bryon Wiley	Bryon Wiley	1986	338
172 5/8	36 4/8	35	15 2/8	15 3/8	8 7/8	8 4/8	20 6/8	19 1/8	Gila Co., AZ	Richard P. Carlsberg	Richard P. Carlsberg	1989	338
172 5/8	34 1/8	36 4/8	15 3/8	15 2/8	8 1/8	9 2/8	19 6/8	18 2/8	Sonora, MX	Lloyd O. Barrow	Lloyd O. Barrow	1969	338
172 5/8	35 7/8	35 2/8	14 4/8	14 4/8	9 6/8	10	21 3/8	19 6/8	Baja Calif., MX	G. David Edwards	G. David Edwards	1973	338
172 5/8	37 3/8	37 3/8	15 5/8	15 4/8	8	8	19 2/8	21 3/8	Baja Calif., MX	Daniel Smith	Daniel Smith	1975	338
172 5/8	32 3/8	35 4/8	15 2/8	15 2/8	8 3/8	9	19 2/8	18 6/8	Clark Co., NV	Charles W. Knittle	Charles W. Knittle	1976	338

DESERT SHEEP

Ovis canadensis nelsoni and certain related subspecies

Score	Length of Horn R	L	Circumference of Base R	L	Circumference at Third Quarter R	L	Greatest Spread	Tip to Tip Spread	Locality	Hunter	Owner	Date Killed	Rank
172 5/8	40 3/8	38 6/8	13 3/8	12 6/8	8 6/8	8 2/8	26 5/8	26 5/8	White Mts., CA	Picked Up	Danny Lowe	1978	338
172 5/8	37 4/8	36 5/8	14 2/8	14 3/8	8 5/8	8 5/8	20	17	Sonora, MX	C. Alan Still	C. Alan Still	2000	338
172 4/8	36 2/8	34 6/8	15 3/8	15 5/8	8 3/8	8 2/8	22 1/8	19 6/8	Yuma Co., AZ	Margaret Wood	Margaret Wood	1958	344
172 4/8	36	34 4/8	15	15	8 4/8	8 4/8	23	23	Yuma Co., AZ	Picked Up	Donald Ogan	1964	344
172 4/8	40	36	14 4/8	14 5/8	8	7 6/8	25	25	Clark Co., NV	Scott D. Oxborrow	Scott D. Oxborrow	1983	344
172 4/8	33 4/8	33 4/8	15 1/8	15 3/8	9 3/8	9 2/8	21 4/8	21	Baja Calif, MX	Hector A. Parada	Hector A. Parada	1985	344
172 4/8	37 2/8	35 2/8	15 4/8	15 4/8	8	8	25 5/8	23	Yuma Co., AZ	William J. Paul	William J. Paul	1987	344
172 4/8	36 4/8	37 6/8	14 4/8	14 1/8	8 6/8	9 3/8	29 5/8	28 4/8	Mohave Co., AZ	Densel M. Strang	Densel M. Strang	1989	344
172 4/8	35 6/8	35 4/8	14 7/8	14 7/8	9 6/8	9 5/8	20 3/8	17 6/8	Lincoln Co., NV	Craig S. Boyack	Craig S. Boyack	1990	344
172 4/8	36 2/8	36 2/8	14 3/8	14 3/8	8 7/8	9	23 6/8	21 2/8	Coconino Co., AZ	Frank J. Tucek	Frank J. Tucek	1993	344
172 3/8	34 6/8	32 5/8	15	15 1/8	9 6/8	9 2/8	21 5/8	21 1/8	Sauceda Mts., AZ	Wayne Grippin	Wayne Grippin	1962	352
172 3/8	35 1/8	34 6/8	15 2/8	15 1/8	9	9	23 1/8	23 1/8	Clark Co., NV	Ronald L. Giovanetti	Ronald L. Giovanetti	1980	352
172 3/8	36 3/8	35 2/8	14 5/8	14 3/8	9 4/8	9 4/8	20 1/8	19 1/8	Baja Calif, MX	H. Varley Grantham	H. Varley Grantham	1980	352
172 3/8	35 3/8	36	14 7/8	14 7/8	8 4/8	9 5/8	21 2/8	21 2/8	Clark Co., NV	John F. Lohse	John F. Lohse	1982	352
172 3/8	33 5/8	34	16 1/8	16 1/8	8 6/8	9	20 2/8	16 2/8	Pima Co., AZ	Loren G. Pederson, Jr.	Loren G. Pederson, Jr.	1985	352
172 3/8	41	41 3/8	13 3/8	13 4/8	8	8 3/8	28 2/8	28	Nye Co., NV	James G. Pedersen	James G. Pedersen	2000	352
172 2/8	38	37 4/8	15	15 4/8	7 3/8	7 4/8	27 1/8	27 1/8	Baja Calif, MX	W.E. Humphrey	WA State Museum	1909	358
172 2/8	35 2/8	35 2/8	15 6/8	15 4/8	9	8 6/8	19 1/8	16 6/8	Baja Calif, MX	Armando de la Parra	Armando de la Parra	1966	358
172 2/8	36 5/8	35 3/8	15 1/8	15 1/8	8 5/8	8 4/8	20 2/8	20 2/8	Baja Calif, MX	Herb Klein	Dallas Mus. of Natl. Hist.	1966	358
172 2/8	35	35 6/8	15 3/8	15 3/8	8 6/8	8 6/8	22 6/8	18 5/8	Clark Co., NV	Ralph A. Shoberg	Ralph A. Shoberg	1986	358
172 2/8	37 3/8	37 1/8	14 2/8	14 4/8	8 5/8	8 4/8	22 2/8	22 2/8	Clark Co., NV	Verner J. Fisher, Jr.	Verner J. Fisher, Jr.	1988	358
172 2/8	35 3/8	34 3/8	15 3/8	15 1/8	9	8 7/8	22 2/8	22 2/8	Baja Calif, MX	R. Fred Fortier	R. Fred Fortier	1989	358
172 2/8	36 4/8	36 4/8	14	13 7/8	10	10 1/8	21 1/8	19 6/8	Clark Co., NV	Nicholas J. Coussoulis	Nicholas J. Coussoulis	1990	358
172 2/8	34 3/8	34 7/8	15 4/8	15 4/8	9 5/8	8 4/8	20 3/8	18 1/8	La Paz Co., AZ	John H. Gannaway	John H. Gannaway	1997	358
172 2/8	36	36	15 2/8	15 2/8	8 4/8	8 7/8	20 6/8	20 6/8	Pima Co., AZ	Wallace Duncan	Wallace H. Duncan	1998	358
172 2/8	36	36 4/8	14 3/8	14 5/8	9	8 6/8	22 7/8	22 4/8	Yuma Co., AZ	Dyanne L. Edwards	Dyanne L. Edwards	2000	358
172 2/8	36 4/8	35 6/8	15	15	8 5/8	8 5/8	23 6/8	23 6/8	San Bernardino Co., CA	Oliver R. Biggers	Oliver R. Biggers	2002	358
172 1/8	36	35 7/8	15 2/8	15 2/8	8 4/8	8 4/8	23	14	Kofa Range, AZ	Picked Up	AZ Game & Fish Dept.	1953	369
172 1/8	35 3/8	36 6/8	14 5/8	14 3/8	9 3/8	9 2/8	22 6/8	21 4/8	Clark Co., NV	Robert F. Sievert	Robert F. Sievert	1985	369
172 1/8	35 5/8	35 6/8	14 7/8	15	9 2/8	8 6/8	20 7/8	20 4/8	Baja Calif, MX	Greg A. Strait	Greg A. Strait	1989	369
172 1/8	36 3/8	35 6/8	15 4/8	15 4/8	7 7/8	8	19	17 7/8	Sonora, MX	Kevin S. Small	Kevin S. Small	2002	369
172	33	36	15	15 4/8	9	8 4/8	30 2/8	30 2/8	Tulelake, CA	Picked Up	Natl. Park Service	1963	373
172	34 6/8	35	16 4/8	16 1/8	8 7/8	8 7/8	20 6/8	20 6/8	Baja Calif, MX	Robert O. Cromwell	Robert O. Cromwell	1974	373
172	34 5/8	34 5/8	14 2/8	14 3/8	8 3/8	8 5/8	21 3/8	20 3/8	Baja Calif, MX	Bill Silveira	Bill Silveira	1974	373
172	36 4/8	36	14 6/8	14 3/8	9 3/8	9 2/8	22 4/8	22 4/8	Clark Co., NV	Mike W. Steele	Mike W. Steele	1986	373
172	34	36 4/8	14 6/8	14 4/8	9 4/8	9 3/8	23 3/8	22 5/8	Clark Co., NV	Jerry J. Long	Jerry J. Long	1987	373
172	36 7/8	37 3/8	15 1/8	14 7/8	8 5/8	8 6/8	25 7/8	25 7/8	Clark Co., NV	Dan Pocapalia	Dan Pocapalia	1988	373
172	35	35	15 4/8	15 3/8	8 2/8	8 2/8	24 6/8	22 1/8	Lincoln Co., NV	Gary R. Quarisa	Gary R. Quarisa	1993	373

Score									Locality	Hunter	Owner	Date Killed	Rank
171 7/8	33 1/8	32 6/8	16 1/8	15 7/8	8 6/8	8 6/8	19 7/8	17 7/8	Baja Calif, MX	Joan Leeds	Joan Leeds	1976	380
171 7/8	33 7/8	35 4/8	15 2/8	15 4/8	9 7/8	9 7/8	22 1/8	21 4/8	Baja Calif, MX	Don L. Corley	Don L. Corley	1978	380
171 7/8	35 3/8	36 2/8	15	15	9	9 1/8	20 2/8	18 2/8	Graham Co., AZ	Rodger J. Stolp	Rodger J. Stolp	1985	380
171 7/8	34 7/8	33 2/8	15 6/8	15 4/8	8 7/8	9 4/8	2_ 5/8	18 4/8	La Paz Co., AZ	Robert M.H. Gray	Robert M.H. Gray	1987	380
171 7/8	36 6/8	36 3/8	14	14 3/8	9 2/8	9 3/8	22 7/8	21 5/8	Clark Co., NV	John R. Chase	John R. Chase	1990	380
171 7/8	36 4/8	35 3/8	15 1/8	15 2/8	8 1/8	8 2/8	2_ 5/8	21 5/8	Yuma Co., AZ	John F. Heskett	John F. Heskett	1990	380
171 6/8	37 2/8	36 4/8	14	13 4/8	9 5/8	9 4/8	20 1/8	20 1/8	Kofa Range, AZ	Harvey Davison	Harvey Davison	1953	386
171 6/8	36	36	15 6/8	15 6/8	7 6/8	8 3/8	2_	18 2/8	Baja Calif, MX	Earl H. Harris	Earl H. Harris	1968	386
171 6/8	35 6/8	35 2/8	14	14	10	10 1/8	23	20 7/8	Lincoln Co., NV	William A. Molini	William A. Molini	1977	386
171 6/8	35 6/8	34 4/8	15	15	9 4/8	9 5/8	22	22	San Bernardino Co., CA	Lee R. Anderson, Jr.	Lee R. Anderson, Jr.	1997	386
171 6/8	37 1/8	37	14 4/8	14 4/8	8 2/8	8 4/8	24 6/8	24 6/8	Maricopa Co., AZ	Roxane R. Kelso	Roxane R. Kelso	2001	386
171 5/8	38 6/8	38 1/8	15 4/8	15 4/8	7	7	23	23	Sonora, MX	Julio Estrada	Julio Estrada	1931	391
171 5/8	33 3/8	35	15 5/8	15 4/8	8 6/8	8 7/8	20	18 4/8	Sonora, MX	Dan L. Quen	Dan L. Quen	1968	391
171 5/8	35 3/8	35 4/8	15 2/8	15 4/8	8 7/8	8 7/8	21 4/8	20	Baja Calif, MX	Roberto M. del Campo	Roberto M. del Campo	1969	391
171 5/8	35 6/8	35 3/8	14 7/8	15	9 1/8	8 7/8	19 3/8	19 3/8	Baja Calif, MX	C.J. McElroy	C.J. McElroy	1969	391
171 5/8	36 4/8	36 3/8	14 3/8	14 5/8	8 7/8	8 5/8	21 4/8	21 4/8	Sonora, MX	Robert C. Jones	Robert C. Jones	1970	391
171 5/8	34 3/8	32 2/8	15 3/8	15 4/8	9 3/8	9 6/8	21 7/8	20 4/8	Clark Co., NV	Edward M. Evans	Edward M. Evans	1977	391
171 5/8	35 4/8	35 4/8	14 5/8	14 6/8	9 3/8	9	20 5/8	20 5/8	Clark Co., NV	George Hueftle	George Hueftle	1977	391
171 5/8	34 6/8	34 7/8	14 7/8	15	9	8 4/8	23 3/8	18	Yuma Co., AZ	Miles R. Brown	Miles R. Brown	1989	391
171 5/8	33 2/8	33 3/8	15 1/8	15 2/8	9 6/8	10 2/8	23 6/8	22	Lincoln Co., NV	James D. Buonamici	James D. Buonamici	1989	391
171 5/8	36 7/8	34 2/8	16 2/8	15 2/8	7 6/8	7 5/8	20 5/8	19 7/8	Baja Calif, MX	Marshall J. Collins, Jr.	Marshall J. Collins, Jr.	1994	391
171 4/8	35 1/8	34 7/8	14	14	10 2/8	10	19 4/8	19 4/8	Bullion Mts., CA	Fred L. Jones	Picked Up	1950	401
171 4/8	37 4/8	37 6/8	13 6/8	13 6/8	8 3/8	8 3/8	23	22 6/8	Clark Co., NV	Jerry P. Devin	Jerry P. Devin	1976	401
171 4/8	33 6/8	35	15 1/8	15 1/8	8 6/8	9 2/8	21 4/8	20 2/8	Maricopa Co., AZ	Clarence House	Unknown	PR 1979	401
171 4/8	35	35	14 4/8	14 1/8	10	10	21 4/8	20 4/8	San Bernardino Co., CA	Leon A. Pimentel	Leon A. Pimentel	1989	401
171 4/8	36 5/8	35 7/8	14 1/8	14 1/8	8 7/8	8 7/8	22 6/8	20 4/8	Gila Co., AZ	Earl R. LaForge	Earl R. LaForge	1991	401
171 4/8	35 1/8	34 3/8	14 6/8	14 6/8	10 2/8	10 2/8	23	19 4/8	Clark Co., NV	L. Alan Forman	L. Alan Forman	2001	401
171 3/8	36 7/8	36 4/8	14 3/8	14 3/8	8 5/8	8 4/8	22 2/8	22 2/8	Anvil Mt., AZ	George F. Stewart, Jr.	George F. Stewart, Jr.	1961	407
171 3/8	34 2/8	34 3/8	15 5/8	15 6/8	8 2/8	8 5/8	19 7/8	16 1/8	Crater Mts., AZ	Raymond I. Skipper, Jr.	Raymond I. Skipper, Jr.	1971	407
171 3/8	38 1/8	37	14 1/8	14 2/8	9 3/8	9 2/8	24	23 5/8	Clark Co., NV	Daniel T. Magee	Daniel T. Magee	1980	407
171 3/8	37 6/8	35	14 1/8	14 1/8	9 2/8	9	25	25	Lincoln Co., NV	Roy F. Lerg	Roy D. Lerg	1984	407
171 3/8	35 3/8	35 2/8	13 7/8	13 7/8	9 1/8	9 5/8	24 2/8	23 5/8	Mohave Co., AZ	Picked Up	Dan Priest	1985	407
171 3/8	37 6/8	37	14 6/8	14 6/8	8	8 5/8	25 1/8	24	Lincoln Co., NV	Steven C. Hall	Steven C. Hall	1987	407
171 3/8	35 5/8	37	16 4/8	16 5/8	7 2/8	7 2/8	19 5/8	19 4/8	Baja Calif, MX	Milton Schultz, Jr.	Milton Schultz, Jr.	1995	407
171 3/8	35 5/8	34 4/8	15 3/8	15 5/8	8 5/8	9 1/8	23 6/8	23 6/8	Clark Co., NV	Mitch Buzzetti	Mitch Buzzetti	2001	407
171 3/8	36 5/8	36 6/8	15 1/8	15 5/8	8 1/8	9	13	16 5/8	Pima Co., AZ	Frank E. Zuern, Jr.	Frank E. Zuern, Jr.	2001	407
171 2/8	35 2/8	35 2/8	14 2/8	14 4/8	8 6/8	8 2/8	21 2/8	18 3/8	Growler Mts., AZ	David E. Brown	David E. Brown	1967	416
171 2/8	35 1/8	36 7/8	14 4/8	14 4/8	8 5/8	8 6/8	2_ 2/8	20 2/8	Clark Co., NV	Bill R. Balsi, Jr.	Bill R. Balsi, Jr.	1979	416
171 2/8	34 4/8	35	15 4/8	15 4/8	8 4/8	8 4/8	24	24	Baja Calif, MX	David L. Harshbarger	David L. Harshbarger	1983	416
171 2/8	38 2/8	38	14 3/8	14 6/8	9 4/8	9 3/8	21 6/8	21 4/8	Yuma Co., AZ	Loren W. Hogan	Loren W. Hogan	1984	416
171 2/8	35 6/8	35 4/8	14 7/8	14 7/8	9 1/8	9 3/8	21	17 3/8	Baja Calif, MX	L. Irvin Barnhart	L. Irvin Barnhart	1992	416
171 2/8	34 6/8	34 4/8	15	15 4/8	8 1/8	8 3/8	21 1/8	20 4/8	Coconino Co., AZ	Merlynn K. Jones	Merlynn K. Jones	1994	416
171 2/8	36 6/8	35 4/8	14 6/8	14 7/8	9	8 2/8	23 6/8	29 6/8	Mohave Co., AZ	Jayson K. Hatfield	Jayson K. Hatfield	1997	416
171 1/8	35 4/8	35 1/8	16 4/8	16 4/8	7 2/8	7 6/8	13 1/8	19 1/8	Yuma Co., AZ	Elizabeth Barganski	Elizabeth Barganski	1959	423
171 1/8	36 4/8	36 7/8	14 3/8	14 4/8	8 3/8	8 2/8	22 2/8	19 7/8	Palomas Mts., AZ	James F. Pierce	James F. Pierce	1967	423
171 1/8	37 3/8	35 2/8	14 2/8	14 4/8	9 1/8	9 4/8	21 1/8	21	Clark Co., NV	James Gay, Sr.	James B. Sisco III	1974	423
171 1/8	35 3/8	35 5/8	14 7/8	14 7/8	8 6/8	8 6/8	25 2/8	25 2/8	Baja Calif, MX	Ray W. Diehl	Ray W. Diehl	1979	423
171 1/8	35 5/8	36 6/8	14 6/8	14 7/8	8 3/8	8 2/8	22	21 1/8	Yuma Co., AZ	Robert J. Cordes III	Robert J. Cordes III	1988	423

Ovis canadensis nelsoni and certain related subspecies

Score	Length of Horn R	L	Circumference of Base R	L	Circumference at Third Quarter R	L	Greatest Spread	Tip to Tip Spread	Locality	Hunter	Owner	Date Killed	Rank
171 1/8	37 4/8	33 3/8	15	14 6/8	8 1/8	8 1/8	23 1/8	22 6/8	Mohave Co., AZ	Gary C. Bateman	Gary C. Bateman	1991	423
171 1/8	36 2/8	35 1/8	14 5/8	14 6/8	8 7/8	8 6/8	21	18	Yuma Co., AZ	Robert J. Zent	Robert J. Zent	1991	423
171 1/8	36 1/8	35 6/8	15	15	8 1/8	8 1/8	23 4/8	23 2/8	Churchill Co., NV	Vincent L. Euse	Vincent L. Euse	1993	423
171 1/8	37 5/8	37 4/8	13 7/8	13 6/8	8 5/8	8 3/8	25	24 4/8	Mohave Co., AZ	Donald G. McMurry	Donald G. McMurry	1993	423
171 1/8	34 6/8	34 5/8	15	15 1/8	8 6/8	8 4/8	24	24	Mohave Co., AZ	William H. Smith	William H. Smith	1995	423
171 1/8	36 7/8	37	14 6/8	14 7/8	8	8 1/8	24 3/8	24	Clark Co., NV	Joel McMillin	Joel A. McMillin	1998	423
171 1/8	36 1/8	35 6/8	15 6/8	15 2/8	8 4/8	8 2/8	20 4/8	20 2/8	Baja Calif, MX	Thomas P. Wittmann	Thomas P. Wittmann	2000	423
171	36	36 2/8	14 3/8	14 4/8	8 4/8	8 7/8	20 3/8	19 4/8	Sauceda Mts., AZ	Kelly S. Neal, Jr.	Kelly S. Neal, Jr.	1969	435
171	36 4/8	35 4/8	14 4/8	14 4/8	8 7/8	8 6/8	22 1/8	22 1/8	Baja Calif, MX	George S. Gayle III	George S. Gayle III	1975	435
171	36 4/8	35 2/8	14 5/8	14 6/8	9 7/8	9 3/8	23 1/8	21 4/8	Clark Co., NV	Richard A. Bell	Richard A. Bell	1986	435
171	35 5/8	36 1/8	14 7/8	14 7/8	8 5/8	8 5/8	18 3/8	17	Pima Co., AZ	Don J. Parks, Jr.	Don J. Parks, Jr.	1986	435
171	37 5/8	37 1/8	14 5/8	14 2/8	7 7/8	8 1/8	24 4/8	24 4/8	Clark Co., NV	Toni M. Venturacci	Toni M. Venturacci	1986	435
171	36 1/8	35 5/8	14 7/8	14 7/8	8 2/8	8 2/8	26 5/8	26	Mohave Co., AZ	Michael A. Gwaltney	Michael A. Gwaltney	1990	435
171	35 4/8	35 4/8	15 3/8	15 4/8	8 5/8	8 6/8	27 2/8	27 2/8	Mohave Co., AZ	Tanner D. Henry	Tanner D. Henry	1994	435
170 7/8	35 5/8	35 4/8	16	16	8	8 1/8	22 5/8	22 5/8	Sonora Desert, MX	Herb Klein	Dallas Mus. of Natl. Hist.	1962	442
170 7/8	38 1/8	37 4/8	14	14 2/8	9 3/8	8 2/8	21 5/8	21 5/8	Baja Calif, MX	Michaux Nash, Jr.	Michaux Nash, Jr.	1964	442
170 7/8	32 7/8	36 4/8	14 4/8	14 4/8	9 7/8	9 5/8	19 2/8	17 6/8	Baja Calif, MX	John T. Blackwell	John T. Blackwell	1966	442
170 7/8	36 5/8	37	15	15	8 2/8	8 2/8	21 4/8	21	Baja Calif, MX	Daniel B. Moore	Daniel B. Moore	1979	442
170 7/8	33	35 7/8	15 3/8	15 3/8	8	8 7/8	21 4/8	18 7/8	Pima Co., AZ	Barbara J. Ridgeway	Barbara J. Ridgeway	1984	442
170 7/8	37	36 1/8	15 2/8	14 6/8	8 1/8	8 7/8	24 1/8	23 1/8	Mohave Co., AZ	Dale A. Kelling	Dale A. Kelling	1987	442
170 7/8	34 1/8	35 4/8	14 4/8	15 4/8	8 4/8	8 7/8	22 6/8	19 3/8	Yuma Co., AZ	Gary L. Major	Gary L. Major	1989	442
170 7/8	34 5/8	36 2/8	14 4/8	14 2/8	9 4/8	9 5/8	24 2/8	24 2/8	Clark Co., NV	John V. Zenz	John V. Zenz	1991	442
170 7/8	34 7/8	36	14	13 7/8	9 5/8	10 1/8	24 3/8	23 7/8	Clark Co., NV	Richard D. Kendall	Richard D. Kendall	1995	442
170 7/8	36	35 5/8	15 4/8	15 3/8	8	8	21 2/8	20 4/8	Mohave Co., AZ	Jeffrey J. Anderson	Jeffrey J. Anderson	2000	442
170 6/8	33 3/8	35 1/8	14	14	9 5/8	10 2/8	23 1/8	23 1/8	San Bernardino Co., CA	Picked Up	John M. Parrish	1960	452
170 6/8	36 7/8	36 3/8	15 6/8	15 3/8	7 6/8	7 5/8	21 6/8	20 7/8	Little Horn Mts., AZ	Dale Wagner	Dale Wagner	1963	452
170 6/8	35 2/8	34 6/8	15 6/8	15 6/8	7 7/8	7 7/8	20 5/8	20 5/8	Baja Calif, MX	Enrique C. Cicero	Enrique C. Cicero	1968	452
170 6/8	36 7/8	36 7/8	16 3/8	16 3/8	7 2/8	7 3/8	21 4/8	21 4/8	Baja Calif, MX	Gino Perfetto	Gino Perfetto	1968	452
170 6/8	39 4/8	37 4/8	13 1/8	13 7/8	9 4/8	8 4/8	22 6/8	22 6/8	Clark Co., NV	Roy Gamblin	Roy G. Gamblin	1977	452
170 6/8	36 4/8	35 4/8	14 2/8	14 2/8	9 2/8	9 4/8	24 4/8	24	Nye Co., NV	Donald A. Leveille	Donald A. Leveille	1986	452
170 6/8	34 1/8	36 7/8	15	15 1/8	8 1/8	8 2/8	19 4/8	17 4/8	Yuma Co., AZ	Bryan L. Rogers	Bryan L. Rogers	1986	452
170 6/8	36 3/8	37 7/8	13 6/8	14	8 4/8	8 6/8	24	24	Clark Co., NV	Picked Up	Lacel Bland	1991	452
170 6/8	35 6/8	35 6/8	15 1/8	15 1/8	8	8 4/8	22	20 4/8	Pima Co., AZ	Andrew D. Langmade	Andrew D. Langmade	1991	452
170 6/8	36 3/8	36 3/8	14 4/8	14 4/8	8 2/8	8 1/8	21 4/8	20 3/8	Graham Co., AZ	William A. Keebler	William A. Keebler	1993	452
170 6/8	34 4/8	37 4/8	14 7/8	14 7/8	8 4/8	8 2/8	22 4/8	21 2/8	Clark Co., NV	Timothy H. Humes	Timothy H. Humes	1999	452
170 6/8	34	38 5/8	13 6/8	13 5/8	9 2/8	9 1/8	24 4/8	24 4/8	Death Valley, CA	Picked Up	Fred L. Jones	1955	463
170 5/8	34 2/8	35 3/8	15	15 2/8	8 4/8	8 2/8	19 3/8	17 6/8	Baja Calif, MX	Bill Lewis	Bill Lewis	1969	463
170 5/8	32 6/8	35 7/8	16 1/8	16 1/8	8 6/8	8 6/8	23 1/8	23 1/8	Pima Co., AZ	David Chavez	David Chavez	1972	463

Score									Locality	By	Owner	Date	Rank
170 5/8	34 7/8	32 2/8	15	14 7/8	22 6/8	22 6/8	9 4/8	9 5/8	Clark Co., NV	George W. Wilkinson, Jr.	George W. Wilkinson, Jr.	1976	463
170 5/8	35 2/8	35 5/8	14 4/8	14 4/8	21 2/8	21 2/8	9	8 7/8	Yuma Co., AZ	James R. Ammons	James R. Ammons	1995	463
170 4/8	34 7/8	34 7/8	15 2/8	15 1/8	19 3/8	19 3/8	9	9	Mohave Co., AZ	John H. Houzenga, Jr.	John H. Houzenga, Jr.	1961	468
170 4/8	36	35	14 1/8	14 3/8	20 2/8	20 2/8	10 1/8	9 1/8	Clark Co., NV	Robert E. Coons	Robert E. Coons	1971	468
170 4/8	34 6/8	34 6/8	15 7/8	16	18 7/8	13 7/8	7 5/8	7 6/8	Baja Calif., MX	Don Turner	Don Turner	1980	468
170 4/8	32 6/8	34 2/8	16 2/8	16 2/8	24	24	8	8 3/8	Baja Calif., MX	Stephen P. Connell	Stephen P. Connell	1986	468
170 4/8	34 7/8	35 7/8	15 1/8	15	18 7/8	19 4/8	8 7/8	8 3/8	Baja Calif., MX	Edward J. Huxen	Edward J. Huxen	1988	468
170 4/8	34 5/8	32 1/8	15 2/8	15 3/8	23	23 6/8	8 6/8	8 5/8	Lincoln Co., NV	Robert Del Porto	Robert Del Porto	1989	468
170 4/8	33 4/8	35	14 6/8	14 6/8	17 4/8	19 4/8	9 2/8	10	La Paz Co., AZ	Oscar B. Oland	Oscar B. Oland	1992	468
170 4/8	38 5/8	38 5/8	13 7/8	14	22 6/8	22 6/8	7 6/8	7 6/8	Clark Co., NV	Gregory K. Goodin	Gregory K. Goodin	1997	468
170 3/8	32	34 3/8	16 2/8	16 2/8	19 2/8	19 2/8	8 7/8	8 7/8	Sonora, MX	Frank C. Hibben	Frank C. Hibben	1935	476
170 3/8	35 3/8	36 2/8	15	15	19 7/8	19 7/8	7 7/8	7 7/8	Chemehuevi Mts., AZ	James B. Lingo	James B. Lingo	1970	476
170 3/8	32 5/8	32 4/8	16	16	20 2/8	20 2/8	9 1/8	9 3/8	Hermosillo, MX	Michael Follett	Michael Follett	1979	476
170 3/8	35 5/8	35 6/8	14 1/8	14 4/8	23 6/8	23 6/8	8 4/8	9	Yuma Co., AZ	Gary V. Harmon	Gary V. Harmon	1979	476
170 3/8	35	35 7/8	14 2/8	14 2/8	23 3/8	23 3/8	9 6/8	9 6/8	Lincoln Co., NV	Robert S. Mastronardi	Robert S. Mastronardi	1982	476
170 3/8	35 1/8	35 6/8	14 4/8	14 4/8	23 4/8	23 4/8	9 5/8	9 5/8	Clark Co., NV	Tracy L. Wilkinson	Tracy L. Wilkinson	1982	476
170 3/8	36 1/8	36 1/8	14	14	20 6/8	20 6/8	9 2/8	9 2/8	La Paz Co., AZ	Rick P. Palmer	Rick P. Palmer	1989	476
170 3/8	34 3/8	38 4/8	14	14 1/8	29	29	9 2/8	9 2/8	Mohave Co., AZ	Picked Up	Carl Iacona	PR 1996	476
170 2/8	35 2/8	36 4/8	15	15 2/8	20 1/8	20 1/8	8	8 4/8	Baja Calif., MX	Richard Buffington	Richard Buffington	1966	484
170 2/8	37 7/8	34 7/8	14 7/8	14 4/8	24 1/8	24 1/8	8 2/8	8 4/8	Clark Co., NV	Landon D. Mack	Landon D. Mack	1977	484
170 2/8	37 2/8	35	14 4/8	15 4/8	21 3/8	21 3/8	8	7 5/8	Baja Calif., MX	James W. Owens	James W. Owens	1978	484
170 2/8	37 2/8	34 2/8	15	15	18 1/8	18 1/8	9 5/8	9 4/8	Baja Calif., MX	A. Verne Crowell	A. Verne Crowell	1979	484
170 2/8	34 5/8	33 7/8	14 6/8	14 6/8	21 2/8	21 2/8	9 2/8	9 1/8	Sonora, MX	Leonard E. Brewster	Leonard E. Brewster	1982	484
170 2/8	36	35 2/8	15 1/8	15 1/8	21 7/8	21 7/8	8 1/8	8 2/8	Baja Calif., MX	David C. Southard, Jr.	David C. Southard, Jr.	1987	484
170 2/8	37 6/8	37 2/8	15 2/8	15 3/8	24 7/8	24 7/8	7	7 4/8	Clark Co., NV	Raymond B. Graber II	Raymond B. Graber II	1987	484
170 2/8	34 2/8	35	14 4/8	14 5/8	19 5/8	21 6/8	9 4/8	10	Yuma Co., AZ	Lance K. Parks	Lance K. Parks	1987	484
170 2/8	33	33	14 7/8	14 7/8	21 6/8	21	10 1/8	10 1/8	Yuma Co., AZ	Valentino J. Pugnea	Valentino J. Pugnea	1992	484
170 2/8	34 1/8	34 5/8	14 5/8	14 5/8	24	24	9 2/8	9 5/8	Mohave Co., AZ	Wily S. Addis	Wily S. Addis	1996	484
170 2/8	36 3/8	36 1/8	15 6/8	15 6/8	24 5/8	24	7 3/8	7	Maricopa Co., AZ	Gregory C. Hintze	Gregory C. Hintze	2000	484
170 2/8	36 6/8	33 6/8	15	15	25	24 4/8	8 4/8	8 5/8	La Paz Co., AZ	Michael J. Bertoldi	Michael J. Bertoldi	2000	484
170 2/8	34	34	14 6/8	14 6/8	20 4/8	16 4/8	9	9	Yuma Co., AZ	James S. Lee	James S. Lee	2000	484
170 2/8	35 2/8	36 6/8	14 7/8	14 7/8	21 6/8	18	9 1/8	8 7/8	Clark Co., NV	Paul J. Harris	Paul J. Harris	2001	484
170 1/8	36	35 6/8	14 3/8	14 5/8	23 4/8	19	8 7/8	9	Clark Co., NV	William H. Taylor	William H. Taylor	2001	499
170 1/8	34 6/8	34 7/8	14 6/8	15	19 1/8	18 2/8	9	9	Baja Calif., MX	Fred T. LaBean	Fred T. LaBean	2001	499
170 1/8	34 2/8	34 2/8	13 6/8	13 6/8	25 4/8	25 4/8	8 3/8	8 3/8	Mineral Co., NV	Picked Up	NV Dept. of Wildl.	1969	499
170 1/8	37	40 3/8	15 5/8	15 5/8	22 4/8	22 4/8	7 1/8	7 1/8	Baja Calif., MX	Arthur E. Davis	Arthur E. Davis	1969	499
170 1/8	36 3/8	37 1/8	15 3/8	15 3/8	19 2/8	19 2/8	7 7/8	7 7/8	Baja Calif., MX	Edward V. Wilson	Edward V. Wilson	1972	499
170 1/8	34 4/8	36	15 3/8	15 3/8	20 4/8	20 4/8	8 4/8	8 4/8	Clark Co., NV	William F. Zenz, Jr.	William F. Zenz, Jr.	1974	499
170 1/8	35 5/8	34 4/8	14 2/8	14 2/8	20 1/8	20 1/8	8 7/8	9 1/8	Baja Calif., MX	Alfred Barone	Alfred Barone	1980	499
170 1/8	35 4/8	35 3/8	14 3/8	14 3/8	19 5/8	19 5/8	8 5/8	8 5/8	Mineral Co., NV	Jeff Lund	Jeff Lund	1994	499
170	36 1/8	35 2/8	15 5/8	15 3/8	21 4/8	21 4/8	9 1/8	9 1/8	Little Horn Mts., AZ	Ivan L. Shiflet	Ivan L. Shiflet	1966	506
170	33	33	15 2/8	15 1/8	22 2/8	22 7/8	7 6/8	7 6/8	Baja Calif., MX	Warren K. Parker	Warren K. Parker	1970	506
170	37 4/8	34 6/8	15 1/8	14 2/8	20 7/8	20 7/8	10 2/8	10 2/8	Clark Co., NV	Lee R. Williamson	Lee R. Williamson	1972	506
170	33	35 2/8	14 2/8	14 6/8	18 5/8	19 5/8	8 6/8	8 6/8	Baja Calif., MX	Rudolf Sand	Rudolf Sand	1973	506
170	35 2/8	34 1/8	14 6/8	14 4/8	19 5/8	19 5/8	8 5/8	9 5/8	Clark Co., NV	Jim Lathrop, Jr.	Jim Lathrop, Jr.	1976	506
170	35 6/8	35 2/8	14 4/8	14 4/8	21 2/8	20 1/8	10 1/8	9	Clark Co., NV	Roy A. Walker	Roy A. Walker	1985	506
170	36	36	15	14 7/8	19 4/8	22 3/8	9 2/8	9 6/8	Yuma Co., AZ	Cheryl Machac	Cheryl Machac	1988	506
170	33 4/8	36	15	14 5/8	23 4/8	24 7/8	9 1/8	9 2/8	Mohave Co., AZ	Ross F. Adams	Ross F. Adams	1993	506

DESERT SHEEP

Ovis canadensis nelsoni and certain related subspecies

Score	Length of Horn R	L	Circumference of Base R	L	Circumference at Third Quarter R	L	Greatest Spread	Tip to Tip Spread	Locality	Hunter	Owner	Date Killed	Rank
170	33 4/8	33 6/8	15 2/8	15 6/8	8 4/8	8 5/8	18	18	Baja Calif, MX	Dennis Campbell	Dennis C. Campbell	1995	506
169 7/8	35 3/8	35 2/8	14 6/8	14 6/8	8 3/8	8 4/8	20 4/8	19 5/8	Baja Calif, MX	Harold Hallick	Harold Hallick	1971	515
169 7/8	35 5/8	34 6/8	15 2/8	15 2/8	8	7 6/8	26 1/8	26	Nye Co, NV	William R. Rohel	William R. Rohel	1993	515
169 7/8	35 3/8	35 4/8	14 2/8	14 2/8	8 5/8	8 7/8	25 2/8	25 2/8	Mohave Co, AZ	Rita E. Steele	Rita E. Steele	1996	515
169 7/8	34 5/8	35 4/8	15 2/8	15	8 2/8	7 7/8	22 3/8	22	La Paz Co, AZ	Wilson W. Allen, Jr.	Wilson W. Allen, Jr.	1999	515
169 6/8	35 2/8	35 6/8	14 1/8	14	9 3/8	9 5/8	21 2/8	21 2/8	Baja Calif, MX	William M. Wheless III	William M. Wheless III	1974	519
169 6/8	36 4/8	36 6/8	15 3/8	15	7 4/8	7 3/8	21	20 1/8	Baja Calif, MX	Richard L. Larson	Richard L. Larson	1985	519
169 6/8	33 5/8	34 1/8	14	14 2/8	10	10 2/8	22	20 5/8	Yuma Co, AZ	Gary S. Sitton	Gary S. Sitton	1986	519
169 6/8	37 2/8	37	13 6/8	14	9 1/8	9	20 7/8	18 4/8	San Bernardino Co, CA	Charles E. Cook	Charles E. Cook	1989	519
169 6/8	38 2/8	36	13 3/8	13 5/8	9 3/8	9 3/8	23	21 7/8	Clark Co, NV	Harold D. Humes	Harold D. Humes	1990	519
169 6/8	33 4/8	36	15 3/8	15 2/8	7 7/8	8 1/8	25 4/8	25 4/8	Nye Co, NV	Kevin B. Oliver	Kevin B. Oliver	1994	519
169 6/8	35	35	14 6/8	14 6/8	8 3/8	8 5/8	19	16 4/8	Sonora, MX	William R. Pritchard	William R. Pritchard	1999	519
169 6/8	36 4/8	35 2/8	14 2/8	14 1/8	9	9	19 4/8	15 3/8	Yuma Co, AZ	Joseph M. Del Re	Joseph M. Del Re	2001	519
169 6/8	34 5/8	32	14 6/8	14 7/8	10	9 1/8	23 3/8	22 2/8	Nye Co, NV	Mark R. Forsmark	Mark R. Forsmark	2002	519
169 5/8	35 1/8	36 2/8	14 3/8	14 4/8	9 1/8	9 1/8	23	19	Muddy Mts., NV	Peter Dietrick	Peter Dietrick	1962	528
169 5/8	35 3/8	34	15	15	8	8 1/8	20	18 7/8	Baja Calif, MX	Leonard W. Gilman	Leonard W. Gilman	1969	528
169 5/8	35 5/8	34	15 4/8	15 4/8	8 2/8	8 2/8	20 4/8	20 4/8	San Borjas Mts., MX	John T. Blackwell	John T. Blackwell	1970	528
169 5/8	33 6/8	34 5/8	15 7/8	15	9	8 7/8	18 2/8	16 3/8	Baja Calif, MX	Gunter M. Paefgen	Gunter M. Paefgen	1975	528
169 5/8	34	33 7/8	15 1/8	15 1/8	7 6/8	8 3/8	21 6/8	21 6/8	Baja Calif, MX	Emerson Hall	Emerson Hall	1978	528
169 5/8	33	34	15 2/8	15 1/8	8 7/8	8 6/8	20 7/8	18 4/8	Yuma Co, AZ	Brad J. Ullery	Brad J. Ullery	1981	528
169 5/8	34 5/8	34 5/8	15 2/8	15 2/8	8 4/8	8 5/8	18 6/8	18 4/8	Coconino Co, AZ	Terrance S. Marcum	Terrance S. Marcum	1990	528
169 5/8	31 3/8	33	15 2/8	15 2/8	9 6/8	9 5/8	19 6/8	19 6/8	Mesa Co, CO	Steven K. Allen	Steven K. Allen	1996	528
169 5/8	36 6/8	37 7/8	14	14 1/8	8 3/8	8 6/8	22 4/8	22 1/8	Clark Co, NV	Gwendolyn C. Jaksick-Dixon	Gwendolyn C. Jaksick-Dixon	1996	528
169 5/8	34 3/8	34 3/8	14 6/8	14 5/8	9 1/8	8 7/8	22 3/8	21 6/8	Mohave Co, AZ	James Hicks	James E. Hicks	1998	528
169 5/8	35 5/8	35 2/8	14 5/8	14 5/8	8 4/8	8 4/8	23 1/8	22 3/8	Clark Co, NV	Jelindo A. Tiberti II	Jelindo A. Tiberti II	1999	528
169 4/8	33	36	15 4/8	15 4/8	8 6/8	8 4/8	25 4/8	25 4/8	Lower Calif, MX	Henry H. Blagden	Henry H. Blagden	1914	539
169 4/8	34 4/8	34 6/8	14 1/8	14 3/8	9 6/8	10 5/8	21	18 5/8	Hart Tank, AZ	Picked Up	Greg Diley	PR 1970	539
169 4/8	35 6/8	35 6/8	14 5/8	14 4/8	8 4/8	8 5/8	18	18	Baja Calif, MX	Lowell C. Hansen II	Lowell C. Hansen II	1974	539
169 4/8	33 6/8	36	14 6/8	14 7/8	9 2/8	8 5/8	22 7/8	22 5/8	Quartzite, AZ	Maurice D. Mathews	Maurice D. Mathews	1975	539
169 4/8	39	37 2/8	15 2/8	15	6 6/8	6 7/8	19 4/8	19 4/8	Baja Calif, MX	James A. Bush, Jr.	James A. Bush, Jr.	1981	539
169 4/8	34 4/8	34 2/8	14 6/8	14 6/8	9 4/8	9 1/8	23 3/8	20 4/8	San Bernardino Co, CA	Jefre R. Bugni	Jefre R. Bugni	1989	539
169 4/8	34 4/8	35 2/8	15 1/8	15 1/8	8 1/8	8 5/8	22 5/8	21 5/8	Baja Calif, MX	Steven D. Bacon	Steven D. Bacon	1990	539
169 4/8	32 2/8	34 4/8	15 3/8	15 4/8	9 2/8	10	21 2/8	20	Coconino Co, AZ	Warren K. Winkler	Warren K. Winkler	1990	539
169 4/8	36 6/8	33 6/8	14 3/8	14 3/8	8 4/8	8 4/8	21 3/8	18 4/8	Maricopa Co, AZ	David T. Demaree	David T. Demaree	1993	539
169 4/8	35	35 2/8	14 6/8	14 7/8	8 7/8	8 7/8	20 6/8	20 4/8	Maricopa Co, AZ	Jay Senkerik	Jay Senkerik	2000	539
169 4/8	35 4/8	36 2/8	14 2/8	14 2/8	8 6/8	8 6/8	20 4/8	18 7/8	Sonora, MX	Normand Berube	Normand Berube	2001	539
169 3/8	35 3/8	35	15 7/8	16	7 2/8	7 2/8	20 4/8	20 4/8	Sonora, MX	Unknown	Unknown	PR 1939	550

Score	Length of Horn R	Length of Horn L	Circ. of Base R	Circ. of Base L	Circ. 3rd Qtr R	Circ. 3rd Qtr L	Greatest Spread	Tip to Tip	Locality	By Whom Taken	Owner	Date	Rank
169 3/8	38 2/8	33 3/8	15	15	8	8	23	22	Pima Co, AZ	Don L. Mattausch	Don L. Mattausch	1979	550
169 2/8	34 7/8	34 5/8	13 7/8	14	9 6/8	9 7/8	21 2/8	21 2/8	White Mts, CA	Picked Up	Fred L. Jones	1951	552
169 2/8	34 7/8	33 7/8	15 2/8	15 2/8	8 4/8	9 1/8	18 4/8	18 3/8	Baja Calif, MX	Joe Osterbauer	Joe Osterbauer	1977	552
169 2/8	36 1/8	35 3/8	15 4/8	15 5/8	7 5/8	7 5/8	20 4/8	20 4/8	Baja Calif, MX	Steve F. Reiter	Steve F. Reiter	1984	552
169 2/8	34 6/8	34 4/8	14 6/8	14 6/8	8 1/8	8 1/8	23 4/8	23 4/8	Clark Co, NV	Richard M. McDrew	Richard M. McDrew	1986	552
169 2/8	34 4/8	33 3/8	15 1/8	15 1/8	8 7/8	8 6/8	21 3/8	21 3/8	La Paz Co, AZ	James F. Phelps	James F. Phelps	1988	552
169 2/8	34 3/8	35 3/8	14 2/8	14 2/8	10	9 1/8	23 4/8	23 7/8	Mohave Co, AZ	William A. Doty	William A. Doty	1991	552
169 2/8	34 5/8	35 5/8	15 2/8	15 3/8	8 2/8	8 2/8	20 2/8	20 2/8	Sonora, MX	Timothy K. Krause	Timothy K. Krause	1998	552
169 2/8	33 4/8	33 2/8	14 6/8	14 4/8	10 1/8	10 1/8	20 1/8	20 1/8	Yuma Co, AZ	W. Jason Sherwood	W. Jason Sherwood	2001	552
169 2/8	35 7/8	35 7/8	14 6/8	14 6/8	9 4/8	8 4/8	18 2/8	17	Sonora, MX	Stephen A. Nelson	Stephen A. Nelson	2002	552
169 2/8	33 4/8	33 4/8	14 4/8	14 2/8	10	10	20 6/8	20 6/8	Lower Calif, MX	Picked Up	William W. Renfrew	1953	552
169 1/8	34 1/8	35	14 2/8	14 2/8	9	10	25 4/8	22 4/8	Chocolate Mts., AZ	Dan Oliver	Dan Oliver	1966	561
169 1/8	38 7/8	35 6/8	15	15	7 3/8	7 1/8	25 4/8	22 4/8	Baja Calif, MX	James W. Owens	James W. Owens	1977	561
169 1/8	35 5/8	34 4/8	14	14	10 1/8	10	21 6/8	21 6/8	Clark Co, NV	Lee M. Smith, Jr.	Lee M. Smith, Jr.	1979	561
169 1/8	36 7/8	36	15	14 7/8	7 1/8	7	23 5/8	22	Clark Co, NV	Vernon C. Tays	Vernon C. Tays	1987	561
169	36 3/8	36 1/8	15 4/8	15 6/8	6 5/8	6 4/8	22 2/8	22 3/8	Baja Calif, MX	W.E. Humphrey	WA State Museum	1909	566
169	36	37	13 4/8	14	8 4/8	8	27	27	Yuma Co, AZ	Picked Up	Dean Bowdoin	1964	566
169	34 3/8	34 3/8	15 1/8	15 1/8	7 7/8	8	21	21	Baja Calif, MX	Gordon L. Schuster	Gordon L. Schuster	1980	566
169	34 1/8	34 1/8	13 6/8	13 6/8	10	10	20 5/8	20 5/8	Baja Calif, MX	Arthur L. Wehner	Arthur L. Wehner	1980	566
169	35	35	15 2/8	15 2/8	7 6/8	7 6/8	25 6/8	25 6/8	Clark Co, NV	Charles E. Sibley	Charles E. Sibley	1986	566
169	33 7/8	33 7/8	15	15	8 2/8	8 2/8	22 1/8	22 1/8	Maricopa Co., AZ	C. Ames Thompson	C. Ames Thompson	1988	566
168 7/8	34 1/8	34 1/8	15 5/8	15 5/8	8 6/8	8 6/8	16 1/8	20 1/8	Sonora, MX	Marshall J. Collins, Jr.	Marshall J. Collins, Jr.	1999	574
168 7/8	34 7/8	35	15 1/8	15 1/8	8 4/8	8 6/8	22 6/8	23 3/8	Mohave Co., AZ	George F. Dennis, Jr.	George F. Dennis, Jr.	1999	574
168 7/8	33 7/8	34 1/8	16	16	8 1/8	7 7/8	21 4/8	20 1/8	Aquila Mts., AZ	John Carr	John Carr	1969	574
168 7/8	35	35	14 7/8	14 6/8	7 5/8	7 6/8	18 4/8	20 1/8	Baja Calif, MX	Larry R. Price	Larry R. Price	1973	574
168 7/8	36 2/8	36 5/8	13 3/8	13 5/8	8 2/8	8 2/8	22	22	Baja Calif, MX	Gary Davis	Gary Davis	1975	574
168 7/8	33 2/8	33 4/8	15 2/8	15 2/8	9 2/8	9 2/8	20 6/8	20 5/8	Clark Co, NV	Robert Darakjy	Robert Darakjy	1978	574
168 7/8	37 4/8	36 2/8	13	13	8 7/8	8	20 5/8	20 5/8	Lincoln Co, NV	Melvin J. Lowe	Melvin J. Lowe	1981	574
168 7/8	36 1/8	36	14 3/8	14 4/8	8 5/8	8 5/8	17 5/8	20 6/8	Tiburon Island, MX	Kevin A. Dettler	Kevin A. Dettler	1997	574
168 7/8	35 1/8	36 6/8	14 4/8	14 4/8	8 2/8	8 6/8	17 2/8	20 5/8	Sonora, MX	Donald W. Snyder	Donald W. Snyder	1999	574
168 6/8	35 2/8	35 2/8	14	14	10 1/8	9 6/8	16 4/8	19 7/8	Little Horn Mts., AZ	Jack O'Connor	Univ. of ID	1946	581
168 6/8	36 2/8	36 4/8	14 3/8	14 2/8	7 7/8	7 7/8	21 7/8	22 5/8	Lincoln Co, NV	Dean Bowdoin	Dean Bowdoin	1966	581
168 6/8	36 6/8	35 2/8	13 3/8	13 5/8	9 2/8	9 2/8	22 4/8	22 4/8	Sierra De Jaraguay, MX	Von A. Mitton	Von A. Mitton	1966	581
168 6/8	35 2/8	34 6/8	15 2/8	15 2/8	8 2/8	8 2/8	19	19	Yuma Co, AZ	Jack A. Shane, Sr.	Jack A. Shane, Sr.	1972	581
168 6/8	34 6/8	34 4/8	15 2/8	15 2/8	8 6/8	8 6/8	21 2/8	22 2/8	Clark Co, NV	Frances B. Boggess	Frances B. Boggess	1980	581
168 6/8	36 4/8	36 3/8	13	13	7 7/8	8	22 2/8	23 2/8	Mohave Co., AZ	Martha F. Dudley	Martha F. Dudley	1998	581
168 6/8	32 2/8	32 3/8	15 2/8	15 2/8	9 3/8	9 5/8	22 2/8	22 2/8	Mohave Co., AZ	Cerene Paul	Cerene J. Paul	1998	581
168 6/8	33	33	14 4/8	14 4/8	9	9	23 4/8	23 6/8	Arizona	Lawrence R. Lundin	Lawrence R. Lundin	2000	581
168 5/8	33 6/8	36	13 7/8	13 7/8	9 4/8	9 4/8	20 7/8	23 6/8	Castle Dome Peak, AZ	Picked Up	Don McBride	PR 1961	589
168 5/8	36 1/8	36 4/8	14 4/8	14 5/8	8 7/8	8 7/8	17 3/8	17 3/8	Aquila Mts., AZ	Tommy G. Moore	Tommy G. Moore	1966	589
168 5/8	34 4/8	34 4/8	14 5/8	14 3/8	8 7/8	9	18 2/8	18 3/8	Sonora, MX	David C. Thornburg	David C. Thornburg	1969	589
168 5/8	34 6/8	34 3/8	14 3/8	14 3/8	9	8 7/8	22 1/8	24 1/8	Clark Co, NV	Lionel Heinrich	Lionel Heinrich	1982	589
168 5/8	35 5/8	35 5/8	15	15	8	8 2/8	19 1/8	19 1/8	Sonora, MX	Joseph Machac	Joseph Machac	1989	589
168 4/8	34 5/8	34 6/8	16	16	8 7/8	8 7/8	18 5/8	18 5/8	Clark Co, NV	John M. Gebbia	John M. Gebbia	1998	595
168 4/8	33 6/8	33 6/8	15	15 4/8	9 1/8	8 4/8	17 4/8	18 5/8	Sonora, MX	Russell C. Cutter	Russell C. Cutter	1964	595
168 4/8	32 3/8	35 3/8	15	15	8 4/8	8 4/8	25 4/8	25 4/8	Baja Calif, MX	Judy Franks	Judy Franks	1965	595
168 4/8	35	35	16 3/8	16 3/8	7	7 2/8	20 3/8	21 2/8	Kofa Game Range, AZ	Jerald S. Wagner	Jerald S. Wagner	1977	595
168 4/8	35 5/8	36 3/8	13 5/8	13 6/8	9 4/8	9	18 5/8	18 5/8	Baja Calif, MX	W.T. Yoshimoto	W.T. Yoshimoto	1978	595

DESERT SHEEP

Ovis canadensis nelsoni and certain related subspecies

Score	Length of Horn R	L	Circumference of Base R	L	Circumference at Third Quarter R	L	Greatest Spread	Tip to Tip Spread	Locality	Hunter	Owner	Date Killed	Rank
168 4/8	37 2/8	37	15 2/8	15 1/8	7 2/8	7 1/8	23 4/8	23 4/8	Baja Calif, MX	Dan L. Duncan	Dan L. Duncan	1979	595
168 4/8	36	35 4/8	14 2/8	14 5/8	8 2/8	7 7/8	18 7/8	18 7/8	Baja Calif, MX	John W. Whitcombe	John W. Whitcombe	1983	595
168 4/8	34 7/8	35 5/8	14 6/8	14 7/8	8 3/8	8 5/8	25 5/8	24 4/8	Mohave Co., AZ	Louise B. Ellison	Louise B. Ellison	1984	595
168 4/8	35 5/8	35 5/8	15 3/8	15 3/8	7 3/8	7 5/8	23 5/8	23 5/8	Clark Co., NV	James M. Machac	James M. Machac	1987	595
168 4/8	33 6/8	35	14 6/8	14 5/8	9	8 7/8	22 6/8	22 6/8	Nye Co., NV	David E. Underwood	David E. Underwood	1992	595
168 4/8	35 4/8	36 4/8	16	15 7/8	6 6/8	6 6/8	20 6/8	20 6/8	Pima Co., AZ	Carl L. Plasterer	Carl L. Plasterer	1995	595
168 4/8	34 2/8	33 4/8	13 6/8	14	10 2/8	10 4/8	23 1/8	19 5/8	Yuma Co., AZ	Dan L. Mattausch	Dan L. Mattausch	1996	595
168 3/8	34 5/8	34 2/8	15 5/8	15 5/8	8	7 6/8	17 6/8	17 4/8	Sand Tank Mts., AZ	Homer Coppinger	Homer Coppinger	1960	606
168 3/8	35	34 3/8	14	14 5/8	9 6/8	9 2/8	19 1/8	17 6/8	Yuma Co., AZ	Leanna G. Mendenhall	Leanna G. Mendenhall	1975	606
168 3/8	34 6/8	34 3/8	15 1/8	15	9	8 4/8	21 6/8	20 1/8	Maricopa Co., AZ	Peter C. Knagge	Peter C. Knagge	1985	606
168 3/8	35 4/8	37 1/8	13 6/8	13 4/8	9 3/8	9 4/8	24 2/8	24	Clark Co., NV	Leonard L. Lerg	Leonard L. Lerg	1985	606
168 3/8	34	32 3/8	14 3/8	14 4/8	10 1/8	9 3/8	23	20 2/8	Garfield Co., UT	Douglas L. Marx	Douglas L. Marx	1996	606
168 2/8	34 4/8	35 2/8	14 7/8	14 6/8	8	8 4/8	21 6/8	21 6/8	Baja Calif, MX	George H. Glass	George H. Glass	1964	611
168 2/8	34 7/8	34 1/8	15 5/8	15 6/8	7 4/8	7 5/8	20 7/8	14	Sonora, MX	Sergio Rios Aguilera	Sergio Rios Aguilera	1968	611
168 2/8	34 1/8	34 7/8	14 4/8	14 4/8	9	8 5/8	21 4/8	19 7/8	Clark Co., NV	Marie F. Reuter	Marie F. Reuter	1969	611
168 2/8	33 6/8	33 6/8	15 3/8	15 3/8	8 1/8	8 5/8	22 2/8	19 3/8	Clark Co., NV	Charles J. Lindberg	Charles J. Lindberg	1971	611
168 2/8	34 1/8	35 5/8	14 7/8	15 1/8	8 3/8	8 1/8	22	22	Yuma Co., AZ	Ervin Black	Ervin Black	1972	611
168 2/8	33 5/8	34 5/8	14	13 6/8	9 2/8	9 5/8	23 3/8	23 3/8	Lincoln Co., NV	Dale Deming	Dale Deming	1977	611
168 2/8	37	36	13 6/8	13 6/8	10 2/8	9 3/8	20	19 4/8	Lincoln Co., NV	Lee A. Raine	Lee A. Raine	1982	611
168 2/8	35 7/8	37 1/8	14 3/8	14 4/8	7 7/8	8 2/8	25 3/8	25 3/8	Clark Co., NV	Ronald E. Brown	Ronald E. Brown	1983	611
168 2/8	35 1/8	33 1/8	15 1/8	15 1/8	8 4/8	8 3/8	19 6/8	19	Baja Calif, MX	Roger R. Card	Roger R. Card	1985	611
168 2/8	34 6/8	36	13 5/8	14	8 7/8	9 1/8	24	23	Yuma Co., AZ	Ralph C. Stayner	Ralph C. Stayner	1985	611
168 2/8	34 4/8	35 4/8	14 3/8	14 3/8	8 4/8	8 4/8	20 7/8	19 1/8	Culberson Co., TX	Ben Hollingsworth, Jr.	Ben Hollingsworth, Jr.	1993	611
168 2/8	34 7/8	34 7/8	15 1/8	15 3/8	8	8	30 4/8	30 1/8	Mohave Co., AZ	Stephen A. Miller	Stephen A. Miller	1997	611
168 2/8	35	34 4/8	14 3/8	14 5/8	8 4/8	8 3/8	23 3/8	23 1/8	Mineral Co., NV	Brenda K. Stinson	Brenda K. Stinson	1997	611
168 2/8	36 4/8	36	14 5/8	14 6/8	7 3/8	7 3/8	24 4/8	24 4/8	Lincoln Co., NV	Todd G. DeLong	Todd G. DeLong	2001	611
168 2/8	33 4/8	35 2/8	14 5/8	14 6/8	9 3/8	9 3/8	23 3/8	22 2/8	Brewster Co., TX	Doyle R. Powers	Doyle R. Powers	2002	611
168 1/8	34 3/8	37 6/8	14	15	8	7 7/8	24 4/8	24 4/8	Lower Calif., MX	G.L. Harrison	Acad. Nat. Sci., Phil.	1903	626
168 1/8	34 4/8	34 5/8	14 1/8	14	8 6/8	9 2/8	20 7/8	18 3/8	Baja Calif, MX	James C. Nystrom	James C. Nystrom	1969	626
168 1/8	32 3/8	31 6/8	16 1/8	16 1/8	8 6/8	8 4/8	19 4/8	18 5/8	Pima Co., AZ	Jeff R. Snodgrass	Jeff R. Snodgrass	1970	626
168 1/8	34 6/8	35 3/8	14 6/8	14 4/8	8 5/8	8 7/8	22 2/8	22 2/8	Baja Calif, MX	C. Robert Palmer	C. Robert Palmer	1979	626
168 1/8	32 2/8	34 3/8	15 2/8	15 2/8	8 5/8	8 5/8	20	15 4/8	Sonora, MX	David V. Collis	David V. Collis	1985	626
168 1/8	35 6/8	36 5/8	14 6/8	14 6/8	7 1/8	7 3/8	23	21 1/8	Clark Co., NV	Richard L. Deane	Richard L. Deane	1988	626
168 1/8	31 4/8	31 1/8	15 2/8	15 2/8	9 6/8	9 5/8	21 2/8	20 4/8	Yuma Co., AZ	Charles H. Criss	Charles H. Criss	1996	626
168	35	35	14	14	10	10	25	25	Lamb Springs, NV	Leslie H. Farr	Leslie H. Farr	1966	633
168	34 4/8	34 4/8	14 6/8	14 6/8	8 3/8	8 6/8	21 4/8	21	Clark Co., NV	Edward Friel	Edward Friel	1969	633
168	34 4/8	35 6/8	15 1/8	15 1/8	8	8 3/8	21 1/8	21 1/8	Baja Calif, MX	Lee Frudden	Lee Frudden	1972	633
168	35	35 4/8	14 2/8	14 3/8	9 1/8	9	23	23	Clark Co., NV	Leonard M. Faike	Leonard M. Faike	1973	633

Score									Location	Hunter	Owner	Date	Rank
168	33 1/8	34 3/8	14 6/8	14 6/8	8 4/8	9 3/8	18 4/8	17 4/8	Mohave Co., AZ	Robert L. Fletcher	Robert L. Fletcher	1974	633
168	37 2/8	35 2/8	14 6/8	14 6/8	6 6/8	6 5/8	26 3/8	26 3/8	Mohave Co., AZ	Tom H. Martin	Tom H. Martin	1980	633
168	36 4/8	35 6/8	14 2/8	14 4/8	8 4/8	8 1/8	23 5/8	22 2/8	Clark Co., NV	Dennis K. Evans	Dennis K. Evans	1981	633
168	35 1/8	35 3/8	14 6/8	14 6/8	8 3/8	8 2/8	25	24 2/8	Mohave Co., AZ	Picked Up	Dean Priest	1984	633
168	34	35	14 3/8	14 3/8	9 2/8	8 7/8	21	20	Mohave Co., AZ	Perry H. Finger	Perry H. Finger	1985	633
168	35 4/8	35	15 4/8	14 3/8	7 7/8	7 7/8	20	19 4/8	Baja Calif, MX	Carl E. Jacobson	Carl E. Jacobson	1985	633
168	34	34 2/8	15 5/8	15 4/8	8 1/8	8 2/8	21 6/8	18 2/8	Pinal Co., AZ	Peter A. Inorio	Peter A. Inorio	1986	633
168	33 4/8	32 4/8	14 7/8	14 6/8	9 2/8	9 1/8	25 3/8	24 5/8	Mohave Co., AZ	Joseph D. Lynch	Joseph D. Lynch	1987	633
168	36 7/8	36 3/8	14 2/8	14 1/8	8 1/8	8 1/8	20 5/8	20 1/8	Yuma Co., AZ	Alan D. Maynard	Alan D. Maynard	1987	633
168	35 2/8	35 2/8	14 1/8	14 2/8	8 7/8	8 7/8	19 6/8	17 3/8	Baja Calif, MX	Mclean Bowman	Mclean Bowman	1989	633
168	34 3/8	35 1/8	14 6/8	14 6/8	9	9	20 5/8	19	Yuma Co., AZ	Richard M. Cordova	Richard M. Cordova	1991	633
168	34 3/8	34 1/8	14 3/8	14 4/8	9 2/8	9 1/8	22	20 6/8	San Bernardino Co., CA	Charles L. Rensing	Charles L. Rensing	1992	633
168	35 6/8	37 2/8	13	13 3/8	9 5/8	9 5/8	22 1/8	17 3/8	San Bernardino Co., CA	Ron Smith	Ron Smith	1992	633
168	32 6/8	32 6/8	14 5/8	14 3/8	9 6/8	9 4/8	19 5/8	16 5/8	Yuma Co., AZ	Kennmth L. Blank	Kenneth L. Blank	1993	633
168	33 6/8	36 2/8	13 5/8	13 5/8	9 4/8	9 6/8	21	20 2/8	Clark Co., NV	Gino Aramini	Gino J. Aramini	1998	633
168	36	34 6/8	13 5/8	13 5/8	8 7/8	9 3/8	21 4/8	20 2/8	Garfield Co., UT	Lee Howard	Lee Howard	2001	633
184 7/8*	38	38 5/8	17 2/8	17 1/8	8 3/8	8 4/8	20 2/8	15 5/8	Sonora, MX	Mirrel R. Kephart, Jr.	Mirrel R. Kephart, Jr.	2001	633
184 4/8*	36 6/8	38	15 5/8	16	10 6/8	10 6/8	24	24	Clark Co., NV	Henry J. Moreda	Henry J. Moreda	2002	633
182 6/8*	37 3/8	36 1/8	16 1/8	16	10 1/8	9 3/8	24 2/8	24 2/8	Tiburon Island, MX	Dick A. Jacobs	Dick A. Jacobs	2000	633
182 2/8*	37 7/8	37 1/8	16	16	9 1/8	9 2/8	24 1/8	23 5/8	San Bernardino Co., CA	John D. Bauder	John D. Bauder	1999	633
181 5/8*	36 3/8	36 4/8	15 7/8	16	9 6/8	9 6/8	22 1/8	21 5/8	Pima Co., AZ	Marshall G. Varner, Sr.	Marshall G. Varner, Sr.	1993	633
181 *	39 6/8	37 4/8	15 2/8	15 1/8	8 6/8	8 7/8	23 4/8	23 4/8	Churchill Co., NV	Dennis J. Sites	Dennis J. Sites	1999	633
179 *	38 2/8	39 6/8	14 6/8	14 6/8	8 7/8	9	22 6/8	22 6/8	Gila Co., AZ	Donald W. Snyder	Donald W. Snyder	2002	633
178 2/8*	41	39 4/8	15 1/8	15 4/8	7 6/8	8 2/8	21 6/8	21 3/8	Graham Co., AZ	Jason J. Gisi	Jason J. Gisi	1998	633

* Final score is subject to revision by additional verifying measurements.

CATEGORY
DESERT SHEEP

SCORE
181-4/8

HUNTER
THOMAS J. PAWLACYK

LOCATION
HIDALGO COUNTY, NEW MEXICO

DATE OF KILL
1995

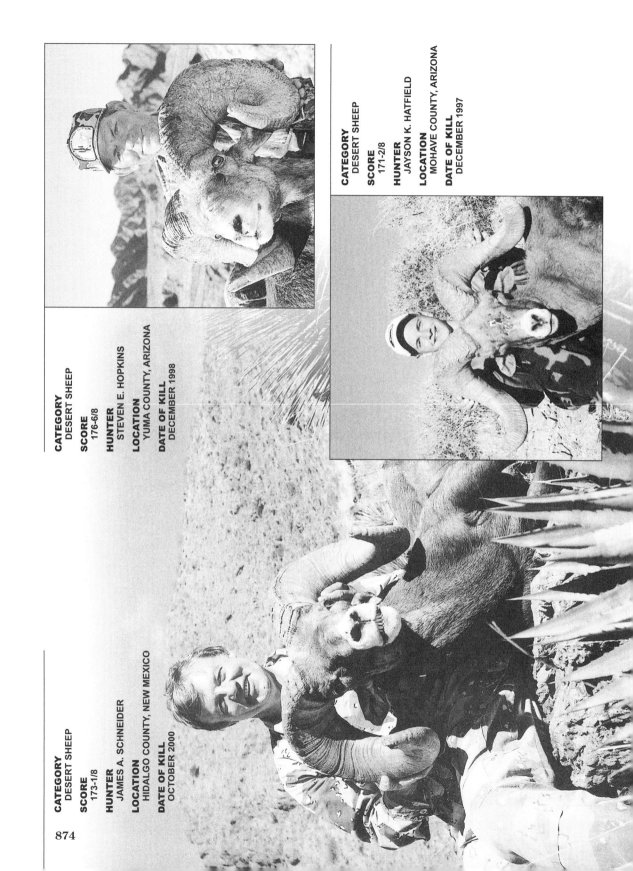

CATEGORY
DESERT SHEEP

SCORE
176-6/8

HUNTER
STEVEN E. HOPKINS

LOCATION
YUMA COUNTY, ARIZONA

DATE OF KILL
DECEMBER 1998

CATEGORY
DESERT SHEEP

SCORE
171-2/8

HUNTER
JAYSON K. HATFIELD

LOCATION
MOHAVE COUNTY, ARIZONA

DATE OF KILL
DECEMBER 1997

CATEGORY
DESERT SHEEP

SCORE
173-1/8

HUNTER
JAMES A. SCHNEIDER

LOCATION
HIDALGO COUNTY, NEW MEXICO

DATE OF KILL
OCTOBER 2000

874

CATEGORY
DESERT SHEEP

SCORE
177-7/8

HUNTER
DONALD W. SNYDER

LOCATION
TIBURON ISLAND, MEXICO

DATE OF KILL
DECEMBER 2001

CATEGORY
DESERT SHEEP

SCORE
174

HUNTER
ROBERT H. TORSTENSON (LEFT)

LOCATION
HUDSPETH COUNTY, TEXAS

DATE OF KILL
MAY 2001

SCORE
173-6/8

HUNTER
RONALD F. MOBLEY
(BOTTOM LEFT)

LOCATION
SONORA, MEXICO

DATE OF KILL
MARCH 1998

Having gained the experience he needed on some earlier hunts for Dall's sheep (*Ovis dalli dalli*) in Alaska, Harry Swank, Jr., a resident of Anchorage, decided to try for a really outstanding ram in the Wrangell Mountains. He knew there were some wonderful heads to be found there, even though the World's Record up to that time had come from the Chugach Mountains. Swank's story occurred in September 1961, and it offers another good example of trophy hunting at its very best.

"A man must want a trophy pretty badly to put in all that time, and that man was me. So last season I went into the wild Wrangell Mountains of Alaska with my hunting partner, Perley Jones, and guide, Jack Wilson. From Jack's base camp at Gulkana we made a number of reconnaissance flights deep into the mountains and finally, picked an area that was so shockingly rough and remote that it is seldom, if ever, visited by hunters. Then in September, I was put down on a big, tilted glacier — an operation that called for infinite skill. The country was as hostile as any a man is likely to meet; forbidding glaciers bounded by treacherous crevasses; cliffs whose sheer faces seemed insurmountable, and the weather was miserable.

"After a good night's sleep, Perley and I made a blood-curdling descent down the side of the main glacier into the valley of a lesser one. Moving slowly up the canyon we carefully glassed the surrounding ridges. There were sheep, but nothing that looked like a World's Record. By now it was well into the afternoon, but I decided to have a look at what lay beyond the next hill. The hill proved to be farther away than I'd estimated and the sun was getting dangerously low when I finally glassed the valley beyond it. Seeing nothing, I was about to return to camp when two rams suddenly appeared on a ridge a quarter mile away. One was only a youngster but the other was huge — bigger than any sheep I'd ever seen.

"Caught out in the open, there was nothing I could do but try to get closer to the ram, and, strangely enough, I managed to get within a few hundred yards of it before the young sheep noticed me and started to act nervous. Groaning inwardly, I dropped to the ground and brought my .264 against my shoulder. The great white sheep moved closer to the edge of the ridge and peered down curiously. Instantly I brought the crosshairs to bear, but as my finger tightened on the trigger, doubts began to assail me. Should I shoot or wait? I was not sure he was of World's Record stature, and if I shot him my hunt would be over for the year. Maybe-Wham! The rifle went off, almost by itself, before I'd made up my mind. The big ram leaped convulsively, then slumped to the ground. By now it was almost dark. Not until the next morning did I know my seven-year quest was over. Carefully I measured the curl. The head was a new World's Record! Later on, the Boone and Crockett Club officially scored it at 189-6/8 points."

This trophy won the coveted Sagamore Hill Award in the 1961 Competition, signifying both trophy excellence and a hunt exhibiting the finest standards of Fair Chase. ∎

DALL'S SHEEP
WORLD'S RECORD SCORE CHART

Records of
North American
Big Game

250 Station Drive
Missoula, MT 59801
(406) 542-1888

BOONE AND CROCKETT CLUB®
OFFICIAL SCORING SYSTEM FOR NORTH AMERICAN BIG GAME TROPHIES

SHEEP

MINIMUM SCORES

	AWARDS	ALL-TIME
bighorn	175	180
desert	165	168
Dall's	160	170
Stone's	165	170

KIND OF SHEEP (check one)
- ☐ bighorn
- ☐ desert
- ■ Dall's
- ☐ Stone's

PLUG NUMBER ____

Measure to a
Point in Line
With Horn Tip

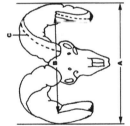

SEE OTHER SIDE FOR INSTRUCTIONS	COLUMN 1	COLUMN 2	COLUMN 3
	Right Horn	Left Horn	Difference
A. Greatest Spread (Is Often Tip to Tip Spread)	34 3/8		
B. Tip to Tip Spread	34 3/8		
C. Length of Horn	48 5/8	47 7/8	1/8
D-1. Circumference of Base	14 5/8	14 6/8	1/8
D-2. Circumference at First Quarter	13 5/8	13 6/8	1/8
D-3. Circumference at Second Quarter	11 6/8	11 7/8	1/8
D-4. Circumference at Third Quarter	6 5/8	6 7/8	2/8
TOTALS	95 2/8	95 1/8	5/8

ADD	Column 1	95 2/8	Exact Locality Where Killed: Wrangell Mts., AK
	Column 2	95 1/8	Date Killed: 1961 Hunter: Harry L. Swank, Jr.
	Subtotal	190 3/8	Owner: Mrs. Harry L. Swank, Jr. Telephone #:
SUBTRACT Column 3		5/8	Owner's Address:
FINAL SCORE		189 6/8	Guide's Name and Address:

Remarks: (Mention Any Abnormalities or Unique Qualities)

I, __Grancel Fitz__, certify that I have measured this trophy on __12/08/1961__
PRINT NAME   MM/DD/YYYY

at __5 Tudor City Place__ __New York__ __NY__
STREET ADDRESS   CITY   STATE/PROVINCE

and that these measurements and data are, to the best of my knowledge and belief, made in accordance with the instructions given.

Witness: __Elmer Rusten__ Signature: __Grancel Fitz__ I.D. Number ____
B&C OFFICIAL MEASURER

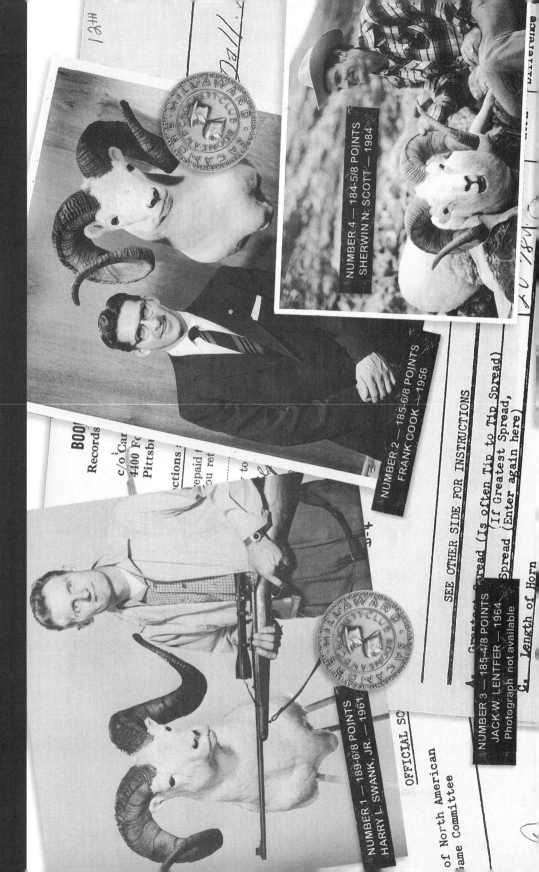

TOP 10 DALL'S SHEEP

NUMBER 4 — 184-5/8 POINTS
SHERWIN N. SCOTT — 1984

NUMBER 2 — 185-6/8 POINTS
FRANK COOK — 1956

NUMBER 1 — 189-6/8 POINTS
HARRY L. SWANK, JR. — 1961

NUMBER 3 — 185-4/8 POINTS
JACK W. LENTFER — 1964
Photograph not available

SEE OTHER SIDE FOR INSTRUCTIONS

Greatest Spread (Is often Tip to Tip Spread)
(If Greatest Spread,
Spread (Enter again here)

G. Length of Horn

OFFICIAL SC

of North American
Game Committee

BONUS PHOTO
NUMBER 11 — 182-2/8 POINTS
EARL J. THEE — 1948

NUMBER 7 — 183-7/8 POINTS
TONEY ONEY — 1963

NUMBER 6 — 184 POINTS
THOMAS C. SHEETS — 1962
Photograph not available

NUMBER 10 — 183 POINTS
GENE M. EFFLER — 1959
Photograph not available

NUMBER 5 — 184-4/8 POINTS
B.L. BURKHOLDER — 1958

NUMBER 8 — 183-6/8 POINTS
JONATHAN T. SUMMAR. JR. — 1965

NUMBER 9 — 183-4/8 POINTS
W. NEWHALL — 1924
Photograph not available

DALL'S SHEEP
Ovis dalli dalli and Ovis dalli kenaiensis

MINIMUM SCORE 170

Score	Length of Horn R	L	Circumference of Base R	L	Circumference at Third Quarter R	L	Greatest Spread	Tip to Tip Spread	Locality	Hunter	Owner	Date Killed	Rank
189 6/8	48 5/8	47 7/8	14 5/8	14 6/8	6 5/8	6 7/8	34 3/8	34 3/8	Wrangell Mts., AK	Harry L. Swank, Jr.	Mrs. Harry L. Swank, Jr.	1961	1
185 6/8	49 4/8	44 2/8	14	13 7/8	6 6/8	7 3/8	24 3/8	24 3/8	Chugach Mts., AK	Frank Cook	Frank Cook	1956	2
185 4/8	43 6/8	40 4/8	14 7/8	14 7/8	9 4/8	9 3/8	20 7/8	20 7/8	Chugach Mts., AK	Jack W. Lentfer	Jack W. Lentfer	1964	3
184 5/8	44 7/8	47	14 1/8	14	7 1/8	7 2/8	26 6/8	26 6/8	Jacksina Creek, AK	Sherwin N. Scott	Foundation for N. American Wild Sheep	1984	4
184 4/8	43 6/8	46	14 1/8	14 3/8	9	7 6/8	21 6/8	21 6/8	Wrangell Mts., AK	B.L. Burkholder	B.L. Burkholder	1958	5
184	44 6/8	44 4/8	14 2/8	14 2/8	7 1/8	7 2/8	24 5/8	24 5/8	Chugach Mts., AK	Thomas C. Sheets	Thomas C. Sheets	1962	6
183 7/8	46 5/8	47 4/8	13 6/8	13 6/8	6 4/8	6 4/8	31	31	Chugach Mts., AK	Tony Oney	Tony Oney	1963	7
183 6/8	48	47 4/8	14	14	6 2/8	6 5/8	33 4/8	33 4/8	Alaska Range, AK	Jonathan T. Summar, Jr.	Jonathan T. Summar, Jr.	1965	8
183 4/8	45 7/8	45 1/8	13 7/8	14	7 1/8	7 6/8	27 7/8	27 7/8	Whitehorse, YT	W. Newhall	Robert E. Barnes	1924	9
183	42 3/8	39 3/8	14 6/8	14 6/8	9 5/8	9 5/8	22 5/8	19 4/8	Wrangell Mts., AK	Gene M. Effler	Gene M. Effler	1959	10
182 2/8	44 4/8	43 6/8	14 1/8	14 5/8	7 2/8	7 1/8	23 4/8	23 4/8	Champagne, YT	Earl J. Thee	Earl J. Thee	1948	11
182	38 6/8	39	15 2/8	15 1/8	10 1/8	10 1/8			Kenai Pen., AK	Picked Up	C.E. Lyons	PR 1969	12
181 6/8	44 4/8	44 4/8	14 5/8	14 5/8	6 4/8	6 6/8	27 2/8	27 2/8	Knik River, AK	Matthew Lahti	Unknown	1930	13
181 5/8	46 2/8	46 5/8	14	14 1/8	6	6 2/8	32 6/8	32 6/8	McCarthy, AK	Bud Nelson	Bud Nelson	1953	14
181 3/8	42 6/8	42 5/8	15 2/8	15 1/8	7 4/8	7 6/8	24 2/8	24 2/8	Wrangell Mts., AK	James K. Harrower	James K. Harrower	1961	15
181 3/8	46 6/8	46 5/8	13	13	6 5/8	6 5/8	28 3/8	28 3/8	Hartman River, AK	Carl E. Jacobson	Carl E. Jacobson	1989	15
181	46 3/8	46 7/8	13 4/8	13 6/8	6 2/8	6 2/8	28 7/8	28 7/8	Mt. Selous, YT	George C. Morris, Sr.	George C. Morris, Sr.	1962	17
180 7/8	44 2/8	44 1/8	14 7/8	14 5/8	6 4/8	6 4/8	30 1/8	30 1/8	Wrangell Mts., AK	Robert W. Engstrom	Robert W. Engstrom	1973	18
180 6/8	43 1/8	43 7/8	14 1/8	14 1/8	7 2/8	7 2/8	27	25 3/8	Kluane Lake, YT	Moose Johnson	Ollie Wirth	1953	19
180 6/8	42 4/8	44 2/8	15	15	6 2/8	7	26 5/8	26 5/8	Yukon Territory	Billy Jack	Yukon Territory Govt.	1966	19
180 3/8	45 7/8	46 2/8	13 4/8	13 5/8	6	6 5/8	29 1/8	29 1/8	Johnson River, AK	P.A. Johnson & J.N. Brennan	P.A. Johnson & J.N. Brennan	1950	21
180 1/8	39 2/8	46 1/8	14 6/8	15 2/8	7 2/8	7	27	27	Wrangell Mts., AK	Harry H. Wilson	Harry H. Wilson	1961	22
180	39 2/8	40 6/8	14 6/8	14 4/8	8 2/8	8 1/8	23	21	Grand View, AK	Nellie Neal	Nellie Neal	1917	23
179 7/8	45 6/8	45 5/8	13	13	6 4/8	7 4/8	27 2/8	27 2/8	Kenai Pen., AK	A.B. Learned	A.B. Learned	1936	24
179 6/8	41 5/8	41 1/8	14 6/8	14 6/8	7	7	28 3/8	28 3/8	Chugach Mts., AK	J.H. Esslinger	J.H. Esslinger	1959	25
179 5/8	40 7/8	41 4/8	14 5/8	14 4/8	8	8	26 2/8	26 2/8	Kluane Lake, YT	George E. Thompson	George E. Thompson	1956	26
179 1/8	44 5/8	44 2/8	14 2/8	14 2/8	6 5/8	6 4/8	27	27	Chugach Mts., AK	Boyd Howard	Boyd Howard	1957	27
178 7/8	40 7/8	40 4/8	14 6/8	14 7/8	7 5/8	7 3/8	24	23 7/8	Chugach Mts., AK	Daniel A. Story	Daniel A. Story	1954	28
178 6/8	42 4/8	42 2/8	13 6/8	13 2/8	8 5/8	8 2/8	25 5/8	25 5/8	Knik River, AK	V.A. Morgan	V.A. Morgan	1899	29
178 6/8	40 2/8	40 4/8	15 5/8	15 6/8	7	7	30 2/8	30 2/8	Champagne, YT	V.B. Seigel	V.B. Seigel	1964	29
178 3/8	45 3/8	43 6/8	13 5/8	13 4/8	7	6 4/8	23 6/8	23 6/8	Alaska Hwy., YT	William H. Miller	William H. Miller	1947	31
178 3/8	43 2/8	42 5/8	13 7/8	14	6 7/8	6 6/8	27 1/8	27 1/8	Chugach Mts., AK	Sam S. Jaksick, Jr.	Sam S. Jaksick, Jr.	1966	31
178 2/8	45 6/8	46 4/8	13	13	6 5/8	6 3/8	26 3/8	26 3/8	Pelly Mts., YT	Eric W. French	Eric W. French	1958	33
178 2/8	45 4/8	42 2/8	14 6/8	14 6/8	6 3/8	6	31 5/8	31 5/8	Wrangell Mts., AK	Wilbur Ternyik	Wilbur Ternyik	1958	33
178 1/8	45 7/8	43 6/8	14 4/8	13 5/8	7 1/8	6 2/8	23 6/8	23 6/8	Wrangell Mts., AK	Unknown	Jeff Sievers	PR 1950	35
178 1/8	45 7/8	44	14	13 7/8	7 4/8	7 3/8	28	28	Chugach Mts., AK	Joseph S. Lichtenfels	Joseph S. Lichtenfels	1956	35
178	43 4/8	43	15	15	6 4/8	6 4/8	30 2/8	30 2/8	Chitina River, AK	Frank C. Hibben	Frank C. Hibben	1963	37

Score	Length of Horn R	Length of Horn L	Circumf. of Base R	Circumf. of Base L	Circumf. 3rd Qtr. R	Circumf. 3rd Qtr. L	Greatest Spread	Tip to Tip Spread	Locality	Hunter	Owner	Date Killed	Rank
177 7/8	44 5/8	45	14 3/8	14	6 3/8	6 2/8	28 3/8	28 3/8	Chugach Mts., AK	William R. Champlain	William R. Champlain	1965	38
177 6/8	43 3/8	44 3/8	14 4/8	14 2/8	6 2/8	6 1/8	27 4/8	27 4/8	Chugach Mts., AK	Chris Klineburger	Chris Klineburger	1957	39
177 5/8	41 7/8	43 2/8	13 4/8	13 2/8	9 1/8	8 7/8	22	22	Rainy Pass, AK	F. Edmond Blanc	F. Edmond Blanc	1937	40
177 5/8	44	43 5/8	14 4/8	14 4/8	6	6	27 6/8	27 6/8	Kenai Pen., AK	John T. Swiss	John T. Swiss	1959	40
177 5/8	43 2/8	44 4/8	14 1/8	14 1/8	6 6/8	6 4/8	26 5/8	26 5/8	Wrangell Mts., AK	Elgin T. Gates	Elgin T. Gates	1961	43
177 4/8	44	44	14	14	6 4/8	6 3/8	25 6/8	25 6/8	Aishihik Lake, YT	Eleanor O'Connor	Univ. of ID	1963	43
177 4/8	45 4/8	44 4/8	14 2/8	14 2/8	6 4/8	6 2/8	28 7/8	28 7/8	Wrangell Mts., AK	Rita Oney	Rita Oney	1963	43
177 4/8	44 4/8	44	14 3/8	14 3/8	6 2/8	6 2/8	28 5/8	28 5/8	Chugach Mts., AK	Robert Kraai	Robert Kraai	1977	46
177 2/8	43 4/8	43 4/8	13 6/8	13 6/8	6	6	23 6/8	23 6/8	Kenai Pen., AK	Luke Elwell	Luke Elwell	1936	46
177 1/8	38	40 6/8	15 2/8	15 2/8	7	7	20 1/8	20 1/8	Chugach Mts., AK	Harry H. Wilson	Harry H. Wilson	1960	46
177 1/8	43 4/8	43 4/8	14	14	7 2/8	7 3/8	27 2/8	27 2/8	Kenai Pen., AK	C.R. Cross, Jr.	Harvard Club of Boston	1907	48
177 1/8	43 7/8	43 3/8	13 6/8	13 6/8	6 6/8	6 6/8	22 1/8	22 1/8	Ship Creek, AK	Oliver Towsen	Oliver Towsen	1940	48
177 1/8	45 3/8	44	13 1/8	13	7 1/8	7	22 1/8	22 1/8	Chugach Mts., AK	James Milito	James Milito	1971	48
177	44 6/8	44 6/8	14	14	5 7/8	6	30 7/8	30 7/8	Mackenzie River, NT	Joseph Scott	Joseph Scott	1973	48
177	40 1/8	45 4/8	13 5/8	13 5/8	6 1/8	6	25 3/8	25 3/8	Chugach Mts., AK	Paul E. Huling	Paul E. Huling	1959	52
176 7/8	43 5/8	44 6/8	13 7/8	13 7/8	6	6	27 1/8	27 1/8	Chugach Mts., AK	William J. Dunbar	William J. Dunbar	1994	52
176 6/8	41 3/8	39 7/8	15	15 1/8	7 1/8	7 1/8	21 4/8	21 4/8	Sifton Range, YT	Jack O'Connor	Univ. of ID	1950	54
176 6/8	43	42 2/8	14 7/8	14 6/8	6 3/8	6 1/8	23 1/8	23 1/8	Wrangell Mts., AK	Vic S. Sears	Vic S. Sears	1960	54
176 6/8	43 1/8	42	14 7/8	14 7/8	6 4/8	6 6/8	23 4/8	23 4/8	Wrangell Mts., AK	Ed Bilderback	Ed Bilderback	1959	56
176 4/8	44 7/8	43	15	15	6 2/8	5 7/8	28	28	Chugach Mts., AK	Charles H. Rohrer	Charles H. Rohrer	1982	56
176 4/8	45	43 1/8	14 3/8	14 6/8	6 4/8	6 4/8	23 3/8	23 3/8	Chugach Mts., AK	C.L. Bestoule	C.L. Bestoule	1960	58
176 4/8	46 2/8	44 7/8	13 1/8	13 1/8	6 6/8	6 4/8	27	27	Mayo, YT	Olof Erickson	Mrs. Jacquot	1933	59
176 3/8	43 5/8	45 6/8	13 3/8	13	7 2/8	7	26 1/8	26 1/8	Donjek, YT	Philip English	Philip English	1954	59
176 2/8	41 7/8	40 6/8	13 7/8	13 7/8	6 4/8	7	32	32	Knik River, AK	Daniel E. Yaeger	Daniel E. Yaeger	1973	59
176 2/8	40 4/8	43 5/8	14	14	6 6/8	6 7/8	22 7/8	22 7/8	Mt. River, NT	Lloyd Ronning	Lloyd Ronning	1953	62
176 2/8	42 2/8	41 7/8	14	14	7 6/8	8	25 6/8	25 6/8	Chugach Mts., AK	H.W. Meisch	H.W. Meisch	1957	63
176	40 7/8	42 2/8	14 4/8	14 4/8	7	6 4/8	24 2/8	24 2/8	Champagne, YT	J. Martin Benchoff	J. Martin Benchoff	1963	63
176	41 6/8	41 3/8	13 5/8	13 4/8	8 2/8	8 4/8	24	24	Ruby Range, NT	Donald P. Chase	Donald P. Chase	1978	63
176	42	42	14 4/8	14 4/8	7 1/8	7	21 2/8	21 2/8	Chugach Mts., AK	John S. Lahti	John S. Lahti	1930	66
176	42	42	14 3/8	14	7	7	27 5/8	27 5/8	Knik River, AK	William D. Backman, Jr.	William D. Backman, Jr.	1960	66
176	39	40 3/8	14 2/8	14 2/8	6 4/8	6 5/8	23	23	Chugach Mts., AK	Horace E. Groff	Horace E. Groff	1960	66
176	46	46 6/8	14 7/8	15	7 6/8	9 6/8	28 7/8	28 7/8	Tonsina Lake, AK	Picked Up	T.H. Rowe	PR 1960	66
175 6/8	41 2/8	42	15	15	6 4/8	6 4/8	26	26	Alaska	Harold Meeker	Harold Meeker	1965	66
175 6/8	40 4/8	43 3/8	14 3/8	13 3/8	6 4/8	6	31 4/8	31 4/8	Wrangell Mts., AK	Paul D. Weingart	Paul D. Weingart	1974	66
175 6/8	42 3/8	41 4/8	14 2/8	13 2/8	6	6	25	25	Wrangell Mts., AK	John K. Hansen	John K. Hansen	1960	72
175 5/8	43 7/8	46 6/8	15	13 4/8	6 7/8	6	23 4/8	23 4/8	Ruby Range, YT	William E. Portman	William E. Portman	1966	72
175 4/8	41 4/8	42 7/8	14 7/8	14 7/8	6 2/8	6 2/8	22 7/8	22 7/8	Yukon Territory	Ben C. Boynton	Ben C. Boynton	1971	72
175 3/8	42	43 7/8	13 5/8	13 5/8	6 4/8	6 4/8	30 3/8	30 3/8	Wrangell Mts., AK	Harry Anderson	Harry Anderson	1955	75
175 2/8	37 6/8	42 3/8	13 4/8	14	7 5/8	7 4/8	24	24	Chugach Mts., AK	Swen Honkola	Swen Honkola	1958	76
175 2/8	40 4/8	42	14	14	6 7/8	7	24	24	Wrangell Mts., AK	Burt Ahlstrom	Burt Ahlstrom	1959	77
175 2/8	41 4/8	40 3/8	14 4/8	14 4/8	8 3/8	8 2/8	23 5/8	23 5/8	Chitina River, AK	Henry Boyden	Am. Mus. Nat. Hist.	1936	78
175 2/8	41 7/8	46 6/8	14 6/8	14 6/8	6 3/8	6 2/8	26 4/8	26 4/8	Wrangell Mts., AK	Grant Smith	Grant Smith	1963	78
175 1/8	39	42	14 3/8	14 5/8	6 6/8	6 4/8	26 2/8	26 2/8	Chugach Mts., AK	Miles Hajny	Miles Hajny	1969	78
175 1/8	43 3/8	43 3/8	14 2/8	14 4/8	6 6/8	6 7/8	30 3/8	30 3/8	Wrangell Mts., AK	Russell A. Reed	Russell A. Reed	1983	78
175 1/8	42 3/8	39 4/8	15	15	7 3/8	7 3/8	26 3/8	26 3/8	Talkeetna Mts., AK	Dale Caldwell	Dale Caldwell	1957	82
175 1/8	42 1/8	44 2/8	14 2/8	14 2/8	6 4/8	6 4/8	29	29	Wrangell Mts., AK	Herman F. Wyman	Herman F. Wyman	1964	82
175 1/8	41	37	14 3/8	14 3/8	8 2/8	8	20 2/8	20 2/8	Chugach Mts., AK	Edward A. Champlain	Edward A. Champlain	1965	82
175 1/8	41 3/8	40 7/8	14 3/8	15	6 7/8	6 7/8	23	23	Wrangell Mts., AK	John M. Griffith, Jr.	John M. Griffith, Jr.	1976	82

DALL'S SHEEP

Ovis dalli dalli and Ovis dalli kenaiensis

Score	Length of Horn R	L	Circumference of Base R	L	Circumference at Third Quarter R	L	Greatest Spread	Tip to Tip Spread	Locality	Hunter	Owner	Date Killed	Rank
175	42 4/8	42 2/8	14 2/8	14 2/8	6 4/8	6 3/8	23 2/8	23 2/8	Kenai Pen., AK	Russel Gainer	Russel Gainer	1959	86
175	42 7/8	42 7/8	13 7/8	14	6 6/8	6 4/8	23 4/8	23 4/8	Chugach Mts., AK	Arthur R. Dubs	Arthur R. Dubs	1961	86
174 7/8	44 5/8	44	13 3/8	13 3/8	6 6/8	6 5/8	26 5/8	26 5/8	Lake Arkell, YT	J.J. Elliott	J.J. Elliott	1924	88
174 7/8	41 3/8	40 4/8	13 7/8	13 7/8	8 2/8	8	19 7/8	19 7/8	Chugach Mts., AK	Leroy Holen	Leroy Holen	1957	88
174 7/8	42 2/8	40 3/8	13 7/8	14	7 4/8	7 7/8	28 2/8	28 2/8	Aishihik Lake, YT	Abe Goldberg	Abe Goldberg	1962	88
174 7/8	43 1/8	43	13 5/8	13 7/8	6 6/8	6 6/8	29	29	Wrangell Mts., AK	R.W. Ulman	R.W. Ulman	1962	88
174 7/8	44 6/8	42 1/8	13 6/8	13 4/8	7	6 5/8	29	29	Chitina River, AK	Ray B. Nienhaus	Ray B. Nienhaus	1966	88
174 6/8	47 4/8	47	13	12 6/8	5 6/8	5 6/8	26	26	Carcross, YT	Billy Smith	Acad. Nat. Sci., Phil.	1927	93
174 6/8	46 6/8	43	13	13	7 1/8	6 1/8	25 4/8	25 4/8	Sifton Range, YT	Herb Klein	Dallas Mus. of Natl. Hist.	1950	93
174 6/8	45 2/8	45	13 1/8	13	9 4/8	6 2/8	28 5/8	28 5/8	Wrangell Mts., AK	Warren W. Wilbur	Warren W. Wilbur	1952	93
174 6/8	40 5/8	40 3/8	14 4/8	14 3/8	6 6/8	6 7/8	26 3/8	26 3/8	Wrangell Mts., AK	Peter W. Bading	Peter W. Bading	1963	93
174 6/8	41 3/8	43 5/8	14 4/8	14 5/8	6 4/8	6 1/8	28 2/8	28 2/8	Wheaton, YT	Herbert Carlson	Herbert Carlson	1963	93
174 6/8	42	42 4/8	14	13 6/8	6 7/8	7	24 1/8	24 1/8	Chugach Mts., AK	Bill Silveira	Bill Silveira	1969	93
174 6/8	40 1/8	40 7/8	15 3/8	15 4/8	6 4/8	6 4/8	20 4/8	20 4/8	Wrangell Mts., AK	Tod Reichert	Tod Reichert	1976	93
174 6/8	41 2/8	41 2/8	14	14	6 7/8	7 3/8	27 3/8	27 3/8	Wrangell Mts., AK	Don L. Corley	Don L. Corley	1978	93
174 5/8	40 4/8	43 5/8	14 2/8	14 3/8	6 4/8	6 4/8	22 3/8	22 3/8	Kenai Mts., AK	Charles A. Brauch	Charles A. Brauch	1959	101
174 5/8	40 5/8	42 2/8	14 5/8	14 5/8	7 2/8	6 4/8	27 1/8	27 1/8	Raft Creek, YT	Marvin Wood	Marvin Wood	1961	101
174 5/8	43 4/8	42 3/8	13 7/8	14 1/8	6 5/8	6 6/8	26 1/8	26 1/8	Kusawa Lake, YT	Lawrence J. Kolar	Lawrence J. Kolar	1973	101
174 5/8	43	42 3/8	14 2/8	14 2/8	6 1/8	6	26 4/8	26 4/8	Barnard Glacier, AK	Rodney Lane	Rodney Lane	1995	101
174 5/8	42 2/8	40 7/8	14 1/8	14 1/8	6 2/8	6 1/8	22	22	Chugach Mts., AK	Carl W. Schmidt	Carl W. Schmidt	1996	101
174 4/8	41	41 4/8	13 5/8	13 6/8	8 2/8	8 5/8	21 3/8	21 3/8	Wrangell Mts., AK	Lloyd B. Walker	Lloyd B. Walker	1959	106
174 4/8	42 2/8	41 6/8	13 7/8	13 7/8	8	7 4/8	20 1/8	20 1/8	Wrangell Mts., AK	Robert L. Jenkins	Robert L. Jenkins	1963	106
174 4/8	40 3/8	40 5/8	15 1/8	14 7/8	6 4/8	6 7/8	23 7/8	23 5/8	Chugach Mts., AK	Lawrence T. Keenan	Lawrence T. Keenan	1976	106
174 4/8	42 1/8	41 3/8	15 1/8	15	6 3/8	6 4/8	27 5/8	27 3/8	Snowcap Mt., AK	Brenton J. Whaley	Brenton J. Whaley	1992	106
174 3/8	43 2/8	43 1/8	14 3/8	14 3/8	6 2/8	6 2/8	24	24	Wrangell Mts., AK	John J. Liska	John J. Liska	1963	110
174 3/8	42 1/8	42 4/8	14 1/8	14 2/8	6 4/8	6 5/8	25 6/8	25 6/8	Nahanni Range, NT	Nick Trenke	Nick Trenke	1979	110
174 2/8	41 5/8	41 5/8	14 4/8	14 2/8	6 4/8	6 3/8	26 4/8	26 4/8	Talkeetna Mts., AK	William J. Konesky	William J. Konesky	1958	112
174 2/8	40 7/8	41 5/8	14 4/8	14 4/8	7 4/8	7	22	22	Wrangell Mts., AK	Jerry L. Beason	Jerry L. Beason	1961	112
174 2/8	41 4/8	43 4/8	13 7/8	14	6 3/8	6 3/8	31 1/8	31 1/8	Coast Mts., YT	Clarence Hinkle	Clarence Hinkle	1963	112
174 1/8	40	42 7/8	14 5/8	14 4/8	6 4/8	6 4/8	25	25	Ruby Range, YT	Lawrence S. Kellogg	T.A. Alujevic	1958	115
174 1/8	43 6/8	43 3/8	14 1/8	14 1/8	5 7/8	6	30 7/8	30 7/8	Wrangell Mts., AK	Sven Johanson	Sven Johanson	1960	115
174	40 7/8	42 3/8	13 5/8	13 7/8	7 4/8	7 6/8	21 7/8	21 7/8	Kenai Pen., AK	Basil C. Bradbury	James B. Sisco III	1960	117
174	42 4/8	45	14	14	6 1/8	6 1/8	27	27	Wrangell Mts., AK	Howard Gilmore, Jr.	Howard Gilmore, Jr.	1969	117
174	43 3/8	44 7/8	14	14	5 5/8	5 7/8	32 1/8	31 6/8	Wrangell Mts., AK	Dan Parker	Dan Parker	1972	117
174	43 5/8	42 1/8	14 3/8	14 4/8	5 7/8	5 4/8	29	29 2/8	Alaska Range, AK	Harry R. Hannon	Harry R. Hannon	1976	117
174	42 6/8	41 2/8	14 2/8	14 3/8	6 1/8	6 1/8	23 4/8	23 4/8	Keele River, NT	Kelly R. Elmer	Kelly R. Elmer	1997	117
173 7/8	44 1/8	42 4/8	14 2/8	13 7/8	6 2/8	6 5/8	26	26	Twitya River, NT	Lewis W. Lindemer	Lewis W. Lindemer	1970	122
173 6/8	42 6/8	43 2/8	14 2/8	14 5/8	6 1/8	6 4/8	29 3/8	29 3/8	Talkeetna Mts., AK	Frank Cook	Frank Cook	1961	123
173 6/8	36 2/8	41 6/8	15 1/8	15	7 2/8	7 2/8	24 6/8	24 6/8	Wrangell Mts., AK	Gene Effler	Gene Effler	1964	123

Score	Length of Horn R	Length of Horn L	Circ. of Base R	Circ. of Base L	Circ. 3rd Qtr R	Circ. 3rd Qtr L	Greatest Spread	Tip to Tip	Locality	Hunter	Owner	Date Killed	Rank
173 6/8	40 2/8	40 2/8	14 7/8	14 6/8	5 4/8	5 4/8	30 4/8	30 4/8	Keele River, NT	John M. Azevedo	John M. Azevedo	1975	123
173 6/8	43 6/8	43 6/8	13 7/8	13 7/8	5 6/8	5 6/8	28 1/8	28 1/8	Robertson River, AK	Thomas A. Berg	Thomas A. Berg	1992	123
173 6/8	45 1/8	42 6/8	13 1/8	13 2/8	6 4/8	6 5/8	26	26	Brooks Range, AK	Chris E. Kneeland	Chris E. Kneeland	2003	123
173 5/8	41 6/8	45 3/8	12 7/8	13	6 7/8	7	24 6/8	24 6/8	Ruby Range, YT	John E. Hammett, Jr.	John E. Hammett, Jr.	1949	128
173 5/8	45 2/8	45 1/8	13 2/8	13 2/8	5 6/8	5 7/8	30 7/8	30 6/8	Chitina, AK	Dene Leonard, Jr.	Dene Leonard, Jr.	1959	128
173 5/8	38 5/8	38 2/8	13 7/8	13 7/8	9 3/8	9 3/8	21 1/8	19 6/8	Wrangell Mts., AK	B.L. Burkholder	B.L. Burkholder	1960	128
173 5/8	42 1/8	42 6/8	14 6/8	14 3/8	5 4/8	5 4/8	28	28	Chugach Mts., AK	Richard T. Kopsack	Richard T. Kopsack	1961	128
173 5/8	43 4/8	41 3/8	13 4/8	13 2/8	7 2/8	7 2/8	23 3/8	22 2/8	Champagne, YT	Edmund D. Patterson, Jr.	Edmund D. Patterson, Jr.	1963	128
173 5/8	41 4/8	41 7/8	14 2/8	14 2/8	6 7/8	6 7/8	24 2/8	24 2/8	Lake Clark, AK	Melvin C. Paxton	Melvin C. Paxton	1968	128
173 5/8	40 2/8	40 2/8	14 5/8	14 5/8	6 5/8	6 5/8	25 6/8	25 6/8	Chugach Mts., AK	Keith A. Douglas	Keith A. Douglas	1993	128
173 4/8	43 5/8	43 5/8	14	13 6/8	5 7/8	5 7/8	29 7/8	29 7/8	Primrose River, YT	W.R. Collier	W.R. Collier	1962	135
173 4/8	42	44 4/8	13 7/8	13 7/8	6 3/8	6 4/8	29 7/8	29 7/8	Wrangell Mts., AK	James K. Harrower	James K. Harrower	1963	135
173 4/8	41 1/8	41 1/8	14 7/8	14 6/8	6 4/8	6 4/8	31 1/8	30 6/8	Chitina Glacier, AK	Robert W. Kubick	Robert W. Kubick	1967	135
173 4/8	41 7/8	41 5/8	13 6/8	13 6/8	6 6/8	6 6/8	26 4/8	26 4/8	Troublesome Creek, AK	David G. Urban	David G. Urban	1991	135
173 3/8	43 5/8	43	13 5/8	13 5/8	6 5/8	6 6/8	28 4/8	28 4/8	Tonsina Lake, AK	James St. Amour	James St. Amour	1957	139
173 3/8	40 1/8	40 1/8	15	15	6 1/8	6 2/8	27 5/8	27 5/8	Whitehorse, YT	Francis X. Bouchard	Francis X. Bouchard	1961	139
173 3/8	44 6/8	44 7/8	13 3/8	13 3/8	5 6/8	5 6/8	28 6/8	28 6/8	Chugach Mts., AK	Howard Haney	Howard Haney	1961	139
173 3/8	42 2/8	43 3/8	13 1/8	13 2/8	6 2/8	6 2/8	19 4/8	19 4/8	Kenai Pen., AK	Spud Dillon	Spud Dillon	1966	139
173 3/8	39 7/8	44 4/8	13 7/8	13 5/8	6 2/8	6 4/8	25 3/8	24 4/8	Wrangell Mts., AK	Basil C. Bradbury	Basil C. Bradbury	1968	139
173 3/8	42	42 7/8	13 3/8	13 4/8	7	7	22 3/8	22 3/8	Alaska Range, AK	Arthur L. Spicer	Arthur L. Spicer	1970	139
173 3/8	44	43	14 4/8	14 7/8	5 3/8	5 3/8	30 2/8	30 2/8	Cache Lake, NT	Lester Behrns	Lester Behrns	1980	139
173 2/8	35 2/8	45	14 3/8	13 5/8	6 2/8	6 2/8	25 2/8	23 3/8	Wrangell Mts., AK	J.H. Shelton	J.H. Shelton	1958	146
173 1/8	46 4/8	41 5/8	13 3/8	13 3/8	6	6	26 7/8	26 7/8	Kenai Pen., AK	W.R. Shellhorn	D. Shellhorn	1936	147
173 1/8	41 2/8	39 7/8	14 3/8	14 3/8	7 4/8	7 3/8	21 7/8	21 7/8	Dawson Range, YT	William E. Goosman	William E. Goosman	1972	147
173	40 3/8	40 3/8	15	15	6 3/8	6 4/8	28 6/8	28 6/8	Whitehorse, YT	Earl DuBois	Earl DuBois	1961	149
173	42	42 4/8	13 4/8	13 4/8	6 4/8	6 4/8	28 1/8	28 1/8	Wrangell Mts., AK	Kenneth Knudson	Kenneth Knudson	1961	149
173	45 6/8	45 2/8	13 3/8	13 3/8	5 4/8	5 4/8	33	33	Wrangell Mts., AK	Bob Merz	Bob Merz	1966	149
173	40 5/8	41 5/8	13 5/8	13 5/8	7 2/8	7 2/8	20 5/8	20 5/8	Chugach Mts., AK	J.C. Hemming	J.C. Hemming	1970	149
173	40 6/8	43	14 7/8	14 7/8	5 7/8	5 7/8	28 3/8	27 7/8	Wrangell Mts., AK	Charles A. Pohland	Charles A. Pohland	1971	149
173	43 6/8	44	13 5/8	13 5/8	6	6	28	28	Chugach Mts., AK	Thomas Clark	Thomas Clark	1975	149
173	40 4/8	40 6/8	13 7/8	14	6 7/8	6 7/8	24 3/8	24 1/8	Chugach Mts., AK	Daniel G. Montgomery	Daniel G. Montgomery	1991	149
173	41 6/8	41 6/8	14 1/8	14 2/8	6 4/8	6 4/8	28	28	Mackenzie Mts., NT	F. Michael Parkowski	F. Michael Parkowski	1991	149
172 7/8	40 1/8	40 4/8	14 2/8	14 2/8	6 3/8	6 2/8	25 1/8	25 1/8	Chugach Mts., AK	Peter W. Bading	Peter W. Bading	1961	157
172 7/8	39 1/8	39	14 2/8	14 2/8	7 7/8	7 7/8	25 1/8	25 1/8	Alaska Range, AK	Ralph Cox	Ralph Cox	1971	157
172 7/8	43 7/8	42 6/8	13 4/8	13 5/8	6 1/8	6 1/8	24 2/8	24	Kusawa Lake, YT	George Faerber	George Faerber	1976	157
172 6/8	40 3/8	40 3/8	14 2/8	14 1/8	7 6/8	7 7/8	22	20 6/8	Nabesna River, AK	John I. Moore	Buckhorn Mus. & Saloon, Ltd.	1955	160
172 6/8	38 7/8	39	14 1/8	14 2/8	8	8	27 7/8	27 7/8	Chugach Mts., AK	Jack C. Phillips	Jack C. Phillips	1956	160
172 6/8	41 2/8	42 6/8	13 5/8	13 5/8	6 6/8	6 6/8	25 6/8	25 6/8	Chugach Mts., AK	Ruby Wyatt	Ruby Wyatt	1960	160
172 6/8	43 5/8	40 3/8	13 4/8	13 5/8	6 4/8	6 4/8	33	33	Wrangell Mts., AK	Richard T. Kopsack	Richard T. Kopsack	1963	160
172 6/8	41 2/8	43 5/8	14 2/8	14 1/8	6 3/8	6 4/8	28 5/8	28 5/8	Wrangell Mts., AK	Alvin W. Huba, Jr.	Alvin W. Huba, Jr.	1968	160
172 6/8	40	41 2/8	14 4/8	14 4/8	7	7	30 3/8	30 3/8	Gerstle River, AK	John A. Shilling	John A. Shilling	1968	160
172 6/8	41 7/8	40 4/8	14 1/8	14 1/8	6 3/8	6 5/8	29	29	Radelet Creek, BC	Norman W. Dougan	Norman W. Dougan	1972	160
172 6/8	43 2/8	41 7/8	13 6/8	13 5/8	6 1/8	5 7/8	28 5/8	28 5/8	Chandalar River, AK	Robert M. Welch	Robert M. Welch	1974	160
172 6/8	43 1/8	43	14	14	5 6/8	5 6/8	30 3/8	30 1/8	Wrangell Mts., AK	Robert J. Wykel	Robert J. Wykel	1976	160
172 6/8	40 2/8	43 7/8	15	15	5 7/8	5 7/8	29	28 5/8	Mountain River, NT	Edmond D. Henley	Edmond D. Henley	1983	160
172 6/8	41	41 2/8	14 1/8	14 1/8	7 2/8	7 2/8	27	27	White Mts., AK	John P. Bast	John P. Bast	1995	160
172 5/8	43 4/8	42 3/8	12 7/8	13 2/8	7	7	29 4/8	29 4/8	Knik Glacier, AK	Picked Up	Howard G. Romig	1932	171
172 5/8	42 4/8	42 4/8	13 4/8	13 6/8	6 6/8	6 6/8	26 3/8	26 3/8	Mt. Arkell, YT	Stuart Hall	Stuart Hall	1957	171

DALL'S SHEEP

Ovis dalli dalli and Ovis dalli kenaiensis

Score	Length of Horn R	L	Circumference of Base R	L	Circumference at Third Quarter R	L	Greatest Spread	Tip to Tip Spread	Locality	Hunter	Owner	Date Killed	Rank
172 5/8	42	41 3/8	14 5/8	14 6/8	5 7/8	5 6/8	32	32	Wrangell Mts., AK	William T. Ellis	William T. Ellis	1960	171
172 5/8	38 7/8	39 2/8	14 7/8	15 3/8	6 5/8	6 7/8	33 7/8	33 1/8	Caribou Creek, YT	Harold J. Lund	Harold J. Lund	1963	171
172 5/8	41 5/8	42	14 4/8	14 2/8	8 6/8	6 2/8	27 1/8	27 1/8	Yukon Territory	S.P. Viezner	S.P. Viezner	1964	171
172 5/8	41 1/8	41 6/8	14 1/8	14 1/8	6 3/8	6 3/8	29 7/8	29 7/8	Knik River, AK	Miles G. France	Miles G. France	1969	171
172 5/8	42	41 3/8	13	13	7 6/8	7 3/8	21 6/8	21 6/8	Talbot Creek, YT	Lloyd E. Zeman	Jenifer D. Schmidt	1969	171
172 4/8	42 4/8	41 4/8	14 2/8	14 2/8	6 6/8	6 6/8	26 1/8	26 1/8	Wrangell Mts., AK	W.A. Bailey, Jr.	W.A. Bailey, Jr.	1959	178
172 4/8	43 4/8	42 6/8	13 1/8	13 1/8	7 2/8	6 7/8	24 3/8	24 3/8	Wrangell Mts., AK	H.E. Eldred	H.E. Eldred	1960	178
172 4/8	39 5/8	45 1/8	14 1/8	14	5 6/8	5 6/8	27 5/8	27 5/8	Chugach Mts., AK	Raymond Capossela	Raymond Capossela	1963	178
172 4/8	41 1/8	42 1/8	14 2/8	14 2/8	6 1/8	6	31 3/8	31 3/8	Primrose Lake, YT	Walter Sutton	Walter Sutton	1968	178
172 4/8	40 6/8	42	14 6/8	15	6 4/8	6 3/8	26 6/8	26 6/8	Mackenzie Mts., NT	Leslie C. Finger	Leslie C. Finger	1985	178
172 3/8	41 5/8	41 2/8	13 6/8	13 6/8	6 6/8	6 6/8	25 1/8	25	Chugach Mts., AK	Chuck Moe	Chuck Moe	1979	183
172 3/8	42 7/8	41 6/8	14 2/8	14 2/8	6 5/8	6 1/8	21 1/8	21 1/8	Granite Lake, YT	William E. Medley II	William E. Medley II	1980	183
172 3/8	41 4/8	41 7/8	14 1/8	14 1/8	6 4/8	6 6/8	23	22 7/8	Mackenzie Mts., NT	Dan L. Johnerson	Dan L. Johnerson	1989	183
172 3/8	45	41 3/8	14	13 7/8	5 5/8	5 6/8	27 2/8	27 2/8	Alaska Range, AK	Joseph C. LoMonaco	Joseph C. LoMonaco	1992	183
172 2/8	45 7/8	44 7/8	13 2/8	13 2/8	5 5/8	6	32	32	Copper River, AK	C.J. McElroy	C.J. McElroy	1977	187
172 2/8	43 1/8	43 3/8	13 5/8	13 4/8	6 2/8	6 3/8	26 6/8	26 4/8	Chugach Mts., AK	Michael L. Kasterin	Michael L. Kasterin	1986	187
172 2/8	42 3/8	41 3/8	13 4/8	13 5/8	6 5/8	6 5/8	23	22 7/8	Chugach Mts., AK	Ethan Williams	Ethan Williams	1988	187
172 2/8	40 6/8	43	14 3/8	14 3/8	6 1/8	6 6/8	25 2/8	23 6/8	Chugach Mts., AK	William J. Dunbar	William J. Dunbar	1991	187
172 2/8	41 1/8	42 5/8	13 2/8	13 2/8	7 3/8	7	23 6/8	23 6/8	McCarthy, AK	Picked Up	John W. Adams	1996	187
172 1/8	40	39 7/8	14 2/8	14 2/8	6 4/8	6 6/8	24 3/8	24 3/8	Wrangell Mts., AK	Kirk Gay	Kirk Gay	1958	192
172 1/8	39 7/8	39	15 4/8	15 3/8	7	6 5/8	26	26	Wrangell Mts., AK	Horace Groff	Horace Groff	1961	192
172 1/8	38 5/8	42	14 1/8	14 1/8	7	7	21 7/8	21 3/8	Chugach Mts., AK	E.F. Craig	E.F. Craig	1963	192
172 1/8	42	41 7/8	14 5/8	14 6/8	6	6 2/8	25 6/8	25 6/8	Wrangell Mts., AK	Walter E. Cox	Walter E. Cox	1966	192
172 1/8	43	38 7/8	14 4/8	14 4/8	5 7/8	5 7/8	29 2/8	29 2/8	Kuskokwim River, AK	Ken M. Wilson	Ken M. Wilson	1973	192
172	41 3/8	41 7/8	14 5/8	14 6/8	6 2/8	5 7/8	26 2/8	26 2/8	Wrangell Mts., AK	Carroll W. Gibbs	Carroll W. Gibbs	1957	197
172	43 6/8	44 6/8	13 6/8	13 6/8	5 6/8	6	26 1/8	26 1/8	Chugach Mts., AK	M.L. Magnusson	M.L. Magnusson	1957	197
172	41 6/8	42	13 5/8	13 6/8	6 4/8	7	25 3/8	25 3/8	Sheep Mt., YT	Ray Hoffman III	Ray Hoffman III	1961	197
172	36	39	15	15 1/8	8	8	22 6/8	20	Chugach Mts., AK	Ward Gay, Jr.	Ward Gay, Jr.	1962	197
172	41 4/8	41 4/8	14 4/8	14 2/8	6 2/8	6 2/8	22 3/8	22 3/8	Sekwi Mt., NT	J.D. Martin, Jr.	J.D. Martin, Jr.	1978	197
171 7/8	45 2/8	42 7/8	13 1/8	13 1/8	6	6 7/8	27 6/8	27 6/8	McCarthy, AK	Eugene E. Saxton	Eugene E. Saxton	1953	202
171 7/8	43 2/8	41 3/8	13 5/8	13 4/8	6 2/8	6 1/8	25 4/8	25 4/8	Talkeetna Mts., AK	Paul S. Lawrence	Paul S. Lawrence	1960	202
171 7/8	39 5/8	38	15 6/8	15 7/8	6	6 2/8	25 6/8	25 6/8	Wrangell Mts., AK	Kenneth Knudson	Kenneth Knudson	1963	202
171 7/8	41 4/8	40 1/8	13 3/8	13 3/8	7 6/8	7 3/8	24 4/8	24 4/8	Chugach Mts., AK	Herb Klein	Dallas Mus. of Natl. Hist.	1964	202
171 7/8	41 5/8	40 2/8	14 6/8	14 6/8	6 1/8	6 3/8	22 6/8	22 2/8	Chugach Mts., AK	Frank Cook	Frank Cook	1965	202
171 7/8	40 4/8	40 5/8	14 1/8	14 2/8	6 3/8	6 3/8	28 2/8	28 2/8	Wrangell Mts., AK	Brent R. Hanks	Brent R. Hanks	1983	202
171 7/8	42 7/8	43	13 1/8	13 1/8	6 7/8	6 6/8	25 1/8	25 1/8	Robertson River, AK	David C. Sharp	David C. Sharp	1987	202
171 6/8	38 7/8	42 5/8	14	13 7/8	6 4/8	6 4/8	28 4/8	28 4/8	Wrangell Mts., AK	Charles C. Parsons	Charles C. Parsons	1955	209
171 6/8	42 7/8	42 3/8	13 7/8	14	6 3/8	6 2/8	30 7/8	30 7/8	Wrangell Mts., AK	Ross Jardine	Ross Jardine	1960	209

Score	Length of Horn R	L	Circumference of Base R	L	Circumference at Third Quarter R	L	Greatest Spread	Tip to Tip Spread	Locality	Hunter	Owner	Date	Rank
171 6/8	35 4/8	42	14 7/8	14 7/8	6 5/8	6 7/8	24 3/8	24 3/8	Chugach Mts, AK	C.J. McElroy	C.J. McElroy	1969	209
171 6/8	44 2/8	40 2/8	13 7/8	13 7/8	6 3/8	6 2/8	30 3/8	30 3/8	Ivishak River, AK	Charles W. Troutman	Charles W. Troutman	1987	209
171 6/8	41 5/8	42 1/8	14 7/8	14 6/8	5 6/8	5 5/8	23 5/8	23 5/8	Chugach Mts, AK	Mark D. Truax	Mark D. Truax	1992	209
171 6/8	42	41	14 5/8	14 5/8	5 4/8	5 5/8	24 2/8	24 3/8	Canyon Creek, YT	George F. Dennis, Jr.	George F. Dennis, Jr.	1993	209
171 6/8	43 3/8	44 1/8	13 4/8	13 2/8	6 4/8	6	25 6/8	25 6/8	Chandalar River, AK	Reed J. Morisky	Reed J. Morisky	1999	209
171 6/8	41 6/8	43 2/8	14 1/8	14 1/8	6 1/8	6 2/8	24 5/8	24 6/8	Talkeetna Mts, AK	Andrew G. Kelso	Andrew G. Kelso	2003	217
171 5/8	41 7/8	41 6/8	14 3/8	14 1/8	6 1/8	5 7/8	26 5/8	26 5/8	Chugach Mts, AK	Justin L. Smith	Justin L. Smith	1963	217
171 5/8	40 3/8	41	14 4/8	14 4/8	6 7/8	6 7/8	22 1/8	22 1/8	Nabesna Glacier, AK	John F. Saltz	John F. Saltz	1983	219
171 4/8	40 5/8	40 5/8	13 6/8	13 6/8	6 7/8	6 7/8	23 4/8	23 4/8	Kenai Pen., AK	C.R. Wright	C.R. Wright	1936	219
171 4/8	40 6/8	39 4/8	14 6/8	14 6/8	6 2/8	6 3/8	28	28	Whitehorse, YT	Howard Creason	Howard Creason	1969	219
171 4/8	41 5/8	42 5/8	13 5/8	13 5/8	6 3/8	6 3/8	26	26	Wrangell Mts, AK	Robert V. Walker	Robert V. Walker	1971	222
171 3/8	44 3/8	45 2/8	13	12 7/8	6 7/8	6 6/8	34 2/8	34 2/8	Wood River, AK	R.R.M. Carpenter	Acad. Nat. Sci., Phil.	1940	222
171 3/8	39 4/8	40 1/8	13 6/8	13 5/8	7 5/8	7 7/8	27 2/8	27 2/8	Coal Creek, AK	W.W. Fultz	W.W. Fultz	1955	222
171 3/8	41 1/8	41 2/8	14	14	6 3/8	6 2/8	30 3/8	30 3/8	Chugach Mts, AK	Perley Colbeth	Perley Colbeth	1958	222
171 3/8	42	42 3/8	13 3/8	13 3/8	7 3/8	7 2/8	29 2/8	29 2/8	Wrangell Mts, AK	Arthur R. Dubs	Arthur R. Dubs	1962	222
171 3/8	36 3/8	44	14 6/8	14 5/8	6 3/8	6 7/8	25 6/8	26 4/8	Wrangell Mts, AK	Doug McRae, Sr.	Doug McRae, Sr.	1972	222
171 3/8	41 1/8	42 2/8	14	14	6	6 7/8	26 6/8	26 6/8	Chugach Mts, AK	Michael J. Ebner	Michael J. Ebner	1977	222
171 3/8	42 2/8	42 3/8	14	14	5 6/8	5 7/8	32 2/8	32 2/8	Caracjou River, NT	Colin J. Kure	Colin J. Kure	1980	222
171 3/8	42 1/8	42 4/8	14	13 6/8	5 4/8	5 6/8	22 2/8	22 2/8	Chugach Mts, AK	Anthony R. Russ	Anthony R. Russ	1988	222
171 3/8	41	40 7/8	13 6/8	13 5/8	6 5/8	6 5/8	22 7/8	22 7/8	Chugach Mts, AK	Michael J. Pace	Michael J. Pace	2003	222
171 2/8	36 3/8	38 1/8	14 7/8	14 7/8	7 6/8	7 6/8	24 3/8	24 3/8	Wrangell Mts, AK	Gordon Madole	Gordon Madole	1956	231
171 2/8	39 4/8	40	12 4/8	12 3/8	9 4/8	9 3/8	21 6/8	21 6/8	Ruby Range, YT	William J. Joslin	William J. Joslin	1960	231
171 2/8	39	39 6/8	14 3/8	14 3/8	7	7 1/8	19 6/8	19 6/8	Kluane River, YT	Phil Temple	Phil Temple	1972	231
171 2/8	39 6/8	41 2/8	14 7/8	14 6/8	6 5/8	6 5/8	23 7/8	24 1/8	Wrangell Mts, AK	Rudolpho Valladolid	Rudolpho Valladolid	1974	231
171 2/8	40 7/8	41 5/8	13 7/8	13 6/8	6 2/8	6 2/8	24	24 3/8	Chugach Mts, AK	Donald W. Snyder	Donald W. Snyder	2000	231
171 2/8	41 2/8	41 2/8	14 4/8	14 4/8	5 5/8	5 6/8	28	28 1/8	Mackenzie Mts, NT	Dan H. Whitelock	Dan H. Whitelock	2002	237
171 1/8	45	44 1/8	12 1/8	12 1/8	6 2/8	6 2/8	26 4/8	26 4/8	Wrangell Mts, AK	Picked Up	Dick Gunlogson	1968	237
171 1/8	42	42 5/8	13 7/8	13 7/8	6	6 1/8	24	24	Kusawa Lake, YT	Picked Up	Maurice G. Katz	1970	237
171 1/8	40 7/8	40 6/8	13 6/8	13 6/8	6 4/8	6 5/8	22 2/8	22 2/8	Robertson River, AK	Maurice G. Katz	Beuron A. McKenzie	1971	237
171 1/8	39 7/8	39 4/8	14 6/8	14 6/8	6 5/8	6	25	25	Godlin Lakes, NT	Paul Tadlock	Paul Tadlock	1980	237
171 1/8	43 2/8	42 7/8	13 2/8	13 2/8	6	6	26 4/8	26 4/8	Chugach Mts, AK	Emil V. Nelson	Emil V. Nelson	1988	237
171 1/8	38 4/8	40 1/8	14	14	7 6/8	7 5/8	21	20 1/8	Blackstone River, YT	Randy Pittman	Randy Pittman	1998	237
171	42 7/8	43 1/8	13 5/8	13 5/8	5 7/8	5 6/8	30 4/8	30 4/8	Carcross, YT	Henry Brockhouse	Henry Brockhouse	1955	243
171	36 7/8	39 3/8	14	14	8 3/8	8	20 6/8	19 3/8	Chugach Mts, AK	Raymond Capossela	Raymond Capossela	1961	243
171	42 1/8	41 1/8	13 7/8	14	6 2/8	6 1/8	26 7/8	26 7/8	Alligator Lake, YT	D. Graham	D. Graham	1968	243
171	40 6/8	41 2/8	14	14	6 3/8	6 4/8	26 3/8	26 3/8	Ruby Range, YT	Harry T. Scharfenberg	Harry T. Scharfenberg	1977	243
171	40 6/8	40 6/8	14 2/8	14 2/8	6 1/8	6 1/8	29	29	Greyling Creek, AK	Michael M. Stitzel	Michael M. Stitzel	1986	243
171	43	42 6/8	13 3/8	13 3/8	6 6/8	6 6/8	28 6/8	28 6/8	Little Tok River, AK	Kenneth L. House	Kenneth L. House	1992	243
171	39	39	14 3/8	14 3/8	6 7/8	6 7/8	22 7/8	22 7/8	Chugach Mts, AK	James P. Driskell	James P. Driskell	1998	243
170 7/8	41 5/8	41 4/8	14 6/8	14 6/8	5 4/8	5 3/8	26 3/8	26 3/8	Kenai Pen., AK	David Jones	David Jones	1963	250
170 7/8	35 3/8	39 6/8	15 2/8	15 2/8	7 2/8	7 1/8	25 7/8	25 7/8	Wrangell Mts, AK	Richard Stingley	Richard Stingley	1965	250
170 7/8	42	41 5/8	14 1/8	14 4/8	6 3/8	6 5/8	29 5/8	29 5/8	Wrangell Mts, AK	Thomas Sperstad	Thomas Sperstad	1969	250
170 7/8	36	36 5/8	14	14 2/8	9 1/8	9 1/8	24 5/8	25 4/8	Chugach Mts, AK	Gerald L. Warnock	Gerald L. Warnock	1970	250
170 7/8	40 6/8	40 6/8	14 2/8	14 2/8	6	6	25 7/8	25 7/8	Trench Lake, NT	Wayne G. Myers	Wayne G. Myers	1974	250
170 7/8	41 6/8	41 5/8	14 1/8	14 1/8	6 1/8	6 1/8	29	29	Wrangell Mts, AK	Unknown	J. Michael Conoyer	1980	250
170 7/8	41 1/8	41 1/8	13 5/8	13 4/8	6 4/8	6 4/8	24 6/8	25 3/8	Chugach Mts, AK	Kenneth P. Meinzer	Kenneth P. Meinzer	1992	250
170 6/8	41 5/8	41 7/8	14 1/8	14 1/8	5 6/8	5 6/8	26 4/8	26 4/8	Wrangell Mts, AK	Joseph A. Tedesco	Joseph A. Tedesco	1959	257
170 6/8	39 2/8	39 2/8	14 7/8	14 6/8	6 6/8	6 6/8	28 2/8	28 2/8	Wrangell Mts, AK	George Stelious	George Stelious	1962	257

DALL'S SHEEP

Ovis dalli dalli and Ovis dalli kenaiensis

Score	Length of Horn R	L	Circumference of Base R	L	Circumference at Third Quarter R	L	Greatest Spread	Tip to Tip Spread	Locality	Hunter	Owner	Date Killed	Rank
170 6/8	42 2/8	42 4/8	13 6/8	13 6/8	6	6 1/8	26 4/8	26 4/8	Wrangell Mts., AK	Robert V. Broadbent	Robert V. Broadbent	1965	257
170 6/8	44	44	13 4/8	13 3/8	5 7/8	5 5/8	30 6/8	30 6/8	Teepee Mt., BC	Steve Snider	Jon K. Mahoney	1983	257
170 5/8	41 4/8	41 7/8	14	14	6 2/8	6 2/8	30 1/8	30 1/8	Nabesna River, AK	J.S. Rutherford	J.S. Rutherford	1956	261
170 5/8	42 1/8	40 6/8	12 7/8	12 7/8	7 4/8	7 6/8	21 3/8	21 3/8	Wrangell Mts., AK	W.A. Fisher	W.A. Fisher	1959	261
170 5/8	41 3/8	42 2/8	13 7/8	13 7/8	6 3/8	6 4/8	25 1/8	25 1/8	Wrangell Mts., AK	Gene Sperstad	Gene Sperstad	1961	261
170 5/8	43 2/8	40 7/8	14 1/8	14 1/8	5 5/8	5 6/8	25 6/8	25 6/8	Nutzotin Mts., AK	Dorothy Andersen	Larry Folger	1965	261
170 5/8	41 2/8	42 1/8	15	14 6/8	5 2/8	5 3/8	28	28	Chugach Mts., AK	Harry C. Heckendorn	Harry C. Heckendorn	1972	261
170 5/8	39 4/8	41 1/8	14	14	7	6 4/8	19 2/8	18 6/8	S. Nahanni River, NT	Lionel G. Heinrich	Lionel G. Heinrich	1987	261
170 5/8	41 4/8	41 1/8	14 4/8	14 4/8	6 2/8	6	25 3/8	25 1/8	Hawkins Glacier, AK	Terrance S. Marcum	Terrance S. Marcum	1997	261
170 5/8	43 6/8	44 1/8	13 2/8	13	6	5 7/8	27 7/8	27 6/8	Mt. Hesperus, AK	Scott T. Doxey	Scott T. Doxey	2000	261
170 5/8	41	41 5/8	14	14	5 7/8	5 7/8	27 5/8	27 3/8	Chugach Mts., AK	Glen A. Landrus	Glen A. Landrus	2001	261
170 4/8	44 2/8	38	13 5/8	13 6/8	6 4/8	6 4/8	29 3/8	29 3/8	Wrangell Mts., AK	Harry L. Swank, Jr.	Mrs. Harry L. Swank, Jr.	1962	270
170 4/8	40 2/8	40 6/8	14 4/8	14 4/8	6 2/8	6 4/8	21 3/8	21 3/8	Ruby Range, YT	Harold C. Casey	Harold C. Casey	1964	270
170 4/8	41 2/8	41 3/8	14 2/8	14 2/8	6 3/8	6 4/8	23 6/8	23 6/8	Brooks Range, AK	Donald E. Harrell	Donald E. Harrell	1979	270
170 4/8	41 3/8	41 3/8	13 5/8	13 5/8	6 7/8	6 7/8	26 3/8	26 3/8	Ogilvie River, YT	Charles L. Baldridge	Charles L. Baldridge	1987	270
170 4/8	43 1/8	43 7/8	13 2/8	13 2/8	6	6 3/8	25 7/8	25 6/8	Eklutna River, AK	Robert L. Lynch	Robert L. Lynch	1994	270
170 4/8	42 1/8	42 1/8	14	14	6	6 1/8	25 6/8	25 6/8	Talkeetna Mts., AK	William C. Cloyd	William C. Cloyd	1995	270
170 3/8	40	40 3/8	14 2/8	14 2/8	6 2/8	6 2/8	22	22	Kenai Pen., AK	Vance Corrigan	Vance Corrigan	1957	276
170 3/8	39 7/8	43	14 2/8	14 2/8	6 2/8	6 2/8	28	28	Wrangell Mts., AK	J.A. Tadesco	J.A. Tadesco	1960	276
170 3/8	41 5/8	42 4/8	14 2/8	14 2/8	5 6/8	5 7/8	27 7/8	27 7/8	Wrangell Mts., AK	Willie Bogner, Sr.	Willie Bogner, Sr.	1961	276
170 3/8	42 4/8	43 5/8	13 2/8	13 2/8	5 7/8	6 4/8	31 2/8	31 2/8	Chugach Mts., AK	William H. Smith	William H. Smith	1961	276
170 3/8	40 6/8	40 3/8	13 7/8	13 7/8	6 7/8	6 6/8	23 7/8	23 7/8	Alaska Range, AK	James W. Thompson	James W. Thompson	1986	276
170 3/8	42	38 7/8	14 4/8	14 2/8	6 1/8	6 2/8	25 4/8	25 4/8	Chugach Mts., AK	Gene N. Meyer	Gene N. Meyer	1996	276
170 3/8	46	42 1/8	13 1/8	12 7/8	6	5 3/8	28 7/8	28 5/8	Wrangell Mts., AK	James H. Duke, Jr.	James H. Duke, Jr.	1999	276
170 2/8	40 5/8	41 3/8	14 1/8	14 1/8	5 6/8	6 1/8	22 2/8	22 2/8	Kenai Pen., AK	C.R. Wright	C.R. Wright	1935	283
170 2/8	39 7/8	39 7/8	14 5/8	14 5/8	6 2/8	6 4/8	25 3/8	25 3/8	Champagne, YT	Walter W. Butcher	Walter W. Butcher	1956	283
170 2/8	39 5/8	41 7/8	15 3/8	15 3/8	5 6/8	5 6/8	23 3/8	23 3/8	Tonsina Creek, AK	Russell J. Uhl	Cabela's, Inc.	1959	283
170 2/8	38 7/8	39 7/8	13 6/8	13 6/8	7 6/8	7 6/8	19 6/8	19 6/8	Chugach Mts., AK	Donald Stroble	Donald Stroble	1961	283
170 2/8	37 2/8	38	14 7/8	14 7/8	7	6 7/8	20 6/8	19 4/8	Kenai Pen., AK	Lee Miller	Lee Miller	1963	283
170 2/8	40 3/8	40	14 6/8	14 7/8	6 2/8	6 2/8	27 2/8	27 2/8	Wrangell Mts., AK	C. Driskell	C. Driskell	1965	283
170 2/8	41	40	14 6/8	14 5/8	6 5/8	5 7/8	28 3/8	28 3/8	Wrangell Mts., AK	Jim Baballa	Jim Baballa	1967	283
170 2/8	38 2/8	37 6/8	13 6/8	13 7/8	8 2/8	9 2/8	21	20 5/8	Robertson River, AK	John W. Redmond	John W. Redmond	1970	283
170 2/8	41 2/8	41 4/8	13 6/8	13 7/8	6 4/8	6 4/8	25 7/8	25 7/8	Talkeetna Mts., AK	H. Albertas Hall	H. Albertas Hall	1971	283
170 2/8	40	40	14 4/8	14 4/8	6 4/8	7	26 6/8	23 6/8	Wrangell Mts., AK	Bernard J. Meinerz	Bernard J. Meinerz	1972	283
170 2/8	42 7/8	42 7/8	13 4/8	13 4/8	5 7/8	6	29 2/8	29 2/8	Snake River, YT	Norman M. Thachuk	Norman M. Thachuk	1982	283
170 2/8	39 4/8	40	15	15	6 2/8	6 2/8	26	26	Alaska Range, AK	Jon A. Shiesl	Jon A. Shiesl	1988	283
170 2/8	41 1/8	41 1/8	14	13 7/8	6 5/8	6 6/8	21 4/8	21 2/8	Mackenzie Mts., NT	Alan Means	Alan Means	1991	283
170 2/8	39 6/8	39	14 3/8	14 2/8	6 4/8	6 2/8	29 2/8	29	Hunter Creek, AK	James C. Becker	James C. Becker	1993	283

Score	Length R	Length L	Base Circ. R	Base Circ. L	Third Qtr. R	Third Qtr. L	Greatest Spread	Tip to Tip	Locality	Hunter	Owner	Date Killed	Rank
170 2/8	41	41	13 6/8	13 5/8	6 4/8	6 4/8	27	27	Talkeetna Mts., AK	Robert L. Hodson	Robert L. Hodson	1995	283
170 1/8	42	42 7/8	13 5/8	13 5/8	6 5/8	6 7/8	28	28	Donjek, YT	Unknown	Acad. Nat. Sci., Phil.	1921	298
170 1/8	40 1/8	41	14 5/8	14 5/8	6 3/8	6 2/8	25 4/8	25 4/8	Mt. Arkell, YT	Ed Steiner	Ed Steiner	1955	298
170 1/8	40 2/8	40 3/8	13 2/8	13 4/8	7 6/8	7 5/8	22	22	Wrangell Mts., AK	Chester Beer	Chester Beer	1959	298
170 1/8	41 4/8	41 1/8	14	14	5 5/8	5 5/8	24 5/8	24 5/8	Chugach Mts., AK	James A. Kirsch	James A. Kirsch	1961	298
170 1/8	38	37 3/8	14 2/8	14	8 3/8	8 2/8	20 3/8	20 3/8	Wrangell Mts., AK	W.T. Yoshimoto	W.T. Yoshimoto	1967	298
170	42	42 2/8	13 1/8	13 1/8	6 1/8	6 2/8	30 1/8	30 1/8	Wrangell Mts., AK	Ralph Morava, Jr.	Ralph Morava, Jr.	1954	303
170	40 6/8	42 2/8	14 3/8	14 1/8	6 1/8	6 1/8	27 3/8	27 3/8	Nabesna River, AK	Raymond A. Talbott	Raymond A. Talbott	1958	303
170	40 2/8	39 4/8	13 4/8	13 1/8	7 5/8	8 2/8	23 3/8	23 3/8	Kluane Lake, YT	Herb Graham	Herb Graham	1959	303
170	41 5/8	42 5/8	13 5/8	13 6/8	6 1/8	6 1/8	23 4/8	23 4/8	Wrangell Mts., AK	Mrs. Melvin Soder	Mrs. Melvin Soder	1961	303
170	42	39	13 7/8	14 2/8	6 6/8	6	21	21	Mackenzie Mts., NT	William C. Mills	William C. Mills	1979	303
170	41 6/8	42	13 3/8	13 3/8	6 4/8	6 5/8	23 5/8	23 5/8	Farewell Lake, AK	Frank G. Merz	Frank G. Merz	1983	303
170	41 7/8	42 7/8	13 7/8	14	5 7/8	5 6/8	24 4/8	24 4/8	Haley Creek, AK	Larry C. Munn	Larry C. Munn	1985	303
170	38 7/8	40 7/8	14	14 1/8	6 6/8	6 5/8	24	24	Snake River, YT	Clark D. Johnson	Clark D. Johnson	1988	303
170	40 5/8	37 7/8	13 6/8	13 7/8	7 2/8	7 2/8	22 1/8	22 1/8	Chugach Mts., AK	Russell Scribner	Russell Scribner	1988	303
170	41 1/8	40 1/8	13 7/8	13 7/8	6 7/8	6 6/8	28 2/8	28 2/8	Arctic Red River, NT	Philipp Heuchert	Philipp Heuchert	1991	303
170	39 5/8	37 1/8	14	14	7 4/8	7 4/8	19 2/8	21 6/8	Ptarmigan Creek, AK	Mark W. Bills	Mark W. Bills	1993	303
170	42 4/8	42	13 2/8	13 2/8	6 3/8	6	26	26	Chugach Mts., AK	Picked Up	John Greenwood	1996	303
170	42 7/8	42 1/8	13 4/8	13 5/8	5 5/8	5 5/8	28	28	Alaska Range, AK	John F. Murray	John F. Murray	2000	303
177 *	41 6/8	41 4/8	15	15	6 7/8	7	23 6/8	23 3/8	Chugach Mts., AK	Richard Ballow	R. & C. Ballow	1997	
176 *	46	44 4/8	14 4/8	14 5/8	5 3/8	5 3/8	31 4/8	31 4/8	Tok, AK	Roscoe D. Uscola	Roscoe D. Uscola	1995	
174 4/8*	40 4/8*	43 2/8	14 2/8	14 2/8	6 2/8	6 3/8	23 5/8	23 7/8	Chugach Mts., AK	Curt D. Menard	Curt D. Menard	1998	
174 1/8*	41 5/8	42	13 6/8	13 6/8	6 6/8	6 6/8	23	23	Ship Creek, AK	Dick A. Jacobs	Dick A. Jacobs	1999	
173 7/8*	43 4/8	42 7/8	13 4/8	13 4/8	6 4/8	6 5/8	30	30	Sheenjek River, AK	Jerry D. Lees	Jerry D. Lees	2002	
173 *	42 6/8	40	15	14 7/8	5 6/8	5 6/8	22 3/8	24 3/8	Aishihik Lake, YT	Fred K. Koken	Fred K. Koken	1998	
171 3/8*	41 3/8	41 6/8	14 3/8	14 4/8	6	5 7/8	26 1/8	26 4/8	Takhini River, BC	Abe J.N. Dougan	Abe J.N. Dougan	1999	

* Final score is subject to revision by additional verifying measurements.

CATEGORY
DALL'S SHEEP

SCORE
171-3/8*

HUNTER
ABE J.N. DOUGAN

LOCATION
TAKHINI RIVER, BRITISH COLUMBIA

DATE OF KILL
AUGUST 1999

CATEGORY
DALL'S SHEEP

SCORE
171

HUNTER
JAMES P. DRISKELL (RIGHT)

LOCATION
CHUGACH MOUNTAINS, ALASKA

DATE OF KILL
DECEMBER 1998

SCORE
170-4/8

HUNTER
WILLIAM C. CLOYD (BELOW RIGHT)

LOCATION
TALKEETNA MOUNTAINS, ALASKA

DATE OF KILL
SEPTEMBER 1995

CATEGORY
DALL'S SHEEP

SCORE
171-2/8

HUNTER
DONALD W. SNYDER

LOCATION
CHUGACH MOUNTAINS, ALASKA

DATE OF KILL
AUGUST 2000

B&C HISTORY

JOHN F. LACEY
1841-1913

By Leonard H. Wurman

Major John Lacey served with distinction during the Civil War. From 1889 until 1907, as a United States Congressman from Iowa, Lacey proved to be an ardent conservationist. When Yellowstone Park was established in 1872, there were no rules defining what a national park should be. The Yellowstone Park Protection Act (the Lacey Act of 1894) not only established such laws, but also became the benchmark model for laws and policies when the National Park Service was established in 1916. But it was the Lacey Act of 1900, otherwise known as the Game and Wild Bird Disposition Act, which became the cornerstone of all federal and state fish and game laws. Prohibiting the interstate shipment of illegally taken game, the Lacey Act put an end to market hunting and led the way for the recovery of wild game in North America. ∎

STONE'S SHEEP
WORLD'S RECORD

L.S. Chadwick was enterprising enough to hunt Stone's sheep (*Ovis dalli stonei*) in the upper Muskwa River country of British Columbia in 1936, long before the Alcan Highway made a formerly virgin game range more accessible. He was accompanied by Roy Hargreaves, with whom he had hunted several times in that region, as well as local guides Walter (Curly) Cochrane and Frank Golata.

On the evening the campsite was reached, Hargreaves looked the country over with a 20x spotting scope and saw a few sheep on a distant mountain. The next morning, the whole party rode in that direction. In the early afternoon, they saw three rams on the skyline of a ridge, about a mile and a half away. The horses were left with the guides, while Chadwick started off with Hargreaves for the final approach.

"We went up pretty fast for a man close to 62 years of age, but when my hatband, which was tight, banked up a large pool of perspiration, I would remove the hat and scoop off several handfuls of water, take a short rest, then plod on toward the top, with dry mouth and my shoes slowly filling with perspiration.

"When we arrived at the top, the sheep were gone, as was to be expected, but we sighted them down in the Muskwa Valley, two thousand feet or more below. Then down over the rock slide, with sore feet and trembling knees, we went, until we got to within about 200 yards of them. We stopped and took movies of the three, and I undertook to shoot the big one.

"My first shot was low, through his brisket. I used the scope for the first time. He started off at a terrible speed, and I started to pour lead into him. I shot four times, one of these hitting him lightly in the hip. Roy followed him on the run and, when he started up the mountain, he could not keep up with the other rams and this gave Roy a chance to get in the finishing shot.

"He fell down a sharp ravine into a little brook. I was about all in and, of course, could not keep up with Roy. It was a very bad place to get to, but we both got down to the sheep without a fall, and when we got to him, we saw that he was well worth the hard work.

"He had the most magnificent head I had ever seen, but not an overly large body. He had two almost perfect horns. The right horn was slightly broken on the end and only measured 50-4/8 inches. The left horn was pointed clear to the end and measured 52-1/8 inches. They were both a little over 15-3/8 inches at the base and the spread was 31-2/8 inches. All told, he was the finest head I had ever seen. If he is not a record head, he is close to it."

While Chadwick's field measurements were unofficial, his hunch was absolutely correct. Scored at a World's Record 196-6/8 points, this is the only recorded ram ever taken in North America with horns over 50 inches long, and it is widely regarded as the best big game trophy this continent has produced. ∎

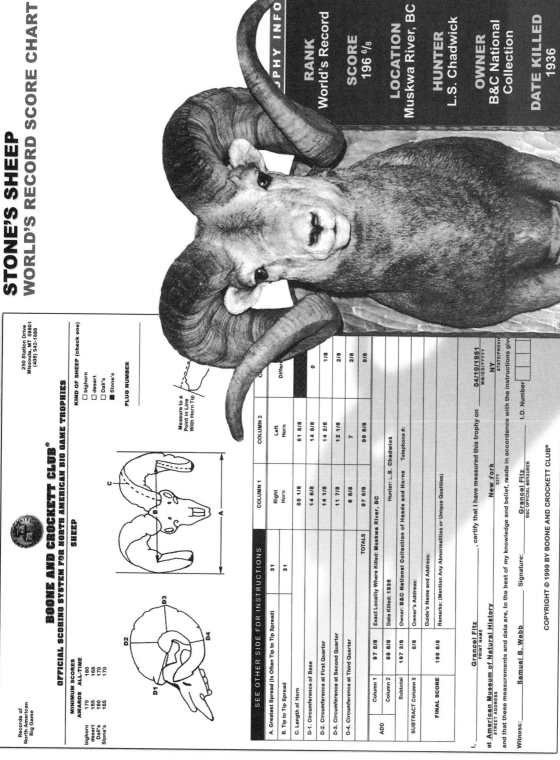

STONE'S SHEEP
WORLD'S RECORD SCORE CHART

Records of North American Big Game

250 Station Drive
Missoula, MT 59801
(406) 542-1888

BOONE AND CROCKETT CLUB®
OFFICIAL SCORING SYSTEM FOR NORTH AMERICAN BIG GAME TROPHIES

SHEEP

MINIMUM SCORES	AWARDS	ALL-TIME
bighorn	175	180
desert	165	168
Dall's	160	170
Stone's	165	170

KIND OF SHEEP (check one)
- ☐ bighorn
- ☐ desert
- ☐ Dall's
- ■ Stone's

PLUG NUMBER _____

Measure to a
Point in Line
With Horn Tip

SEE OTHER SIDE FOR INSTRUCTIONS

	COLUMN 1 Right Horn	COLUMN 2 Left Horn	Difference
A. Greatest Spread (Is Often Tip to Tip Spread)	31		
B. Tip to Tip Spread	31		
C. Length of Horn	50 1/8	51 5/8	
D-1. Circumference of Base	14 6/8	14 6/8	0
D-2. Circumference at First Quarter	14 1/8	14 2/8	1/8
D-3. Circumference at Second Quarter	11 7/8	12 1/8	2/8
D-4. Circumference at Third Quarter	6 6/8	7	2/8
TOTALS	97 5/8	99 6/8	5/8

ADD	Column 1	97 5/8	Exact Locality Where Killed: Muskwa River, BC
	Column 2	99 6/8	Date Killed: 1936 Hunter: L.S. Chadwick
	Subtotal	197 3/8	Owner: B&C National Collection of Heads and Horns Telephone #:
SUBTRACT Column 3		5/8	Owner's Address:
FINAL SCORE		196 6/8	Guide's Name and Address:

Remarks: (Mention Any Abnormalities or Unique Qualities)

I, **Grancel Fitz** (PRINT NAME), certify that I have measured this trophy on **04/10/1951** (MM/DD/YYYY)
at **American Museum of Natural History** (STREET ADDRESS) **New York** (CITY) **NY** (STATE/PROVINCE)
and that these measurements and data are, to the best of my knowledge and belief, made in accordance with the instructions given.

Witness: **Samuel B. Webb**   Signature: **Grancel Fitz**   I.D. Number _____
B&C OFFICIAL MEASURER

COPYRIGHT © 1999 BY BOONE AND CROCKETT CLUB®

TROPHY INFO

RANK
World's Record

SCORE
196 6/8

LOCATION
Muskwa River, BC

HUNTER
L.S. Chadwick

OWNER
B&C National Collection

DATE KILLED
1936

891

TOP 10 STONE'S SHEEP

NUMBER 3 — 189-6/8 POINTS
G.C.F. DALZIEL — 1965

NUMBER 2 — 190 POINTS
NORMAN BLANK — 1962

STONE SHEEP

Hunter—Herman F. W
Guide—James F. Wood

NUMBER 1 — 196-6/8 POINTS
L.S. CHADWICK — 1936

KIND OF SHEEP STONE

MEASURE TO A
POINT IN LINE
WITH TIP OF
HORN

5th Compe

Locality—Mts. east of Blue Sheep Lake, B. C. — 1965.
Hunter—George C. F. Dalziel

NUMBER 4 — 187-4/8 POINTS
PAUL D. WEINGART — 1970

NUMBER 9 — 184-2/8 POINTS
ARTHUR R. DUBS — 1966

...three view... show the astonishing... positions to show the author in his hunting clothes in the top view is the author in his hunting clothes.

The following top 10 Stone's sheep do not have photographs available

NUMBER 5 — 185-3/8 POINTS
FELIPE PALAU — 1970

NUMBER 7 — 184-4/8 POINTS
JOHN W. PITNEY — 1936

NUMBER 8 — 184-3/8 POINTS
LLOYD E. HALL — 1963

NUMBER 9 — 184-2/8 POINTS
G.C.F. DALZIEL — 1964

NUMBER 6 — 184-6/8 POINTS
JOSEPH H. SHIRK — 1948

...base ...
...o dep...
...owin...
...r e...
...the ...
...to ...
...whic...
...gh...

...e whether the trophy has any characteristics ...the normal for this species.

NUMBER 9 — 184-2/8 POINTS
HERB KLEIN — 1965

All mea...

A Length ...
tip. C...
f...

C

STONE'S SHEEP
Ovis dalli stonei

MINIMUM SCORE 170

Score	Length of Horn R	L	Circumference of Base R	L	Circumference at Third Quarter R	L	Greatest Spread	Tip to Tip Spread	Locality	Hunter	Owner	Date Killed	Rank
196 6/8	50 1/8	51 5/8	14 6/8	14 6/8	6 6/8	7	31	31	Muskwa River, BC	L.S. Chadwick	B&C National Collection	1936	1
190	46 6/8	46 6/8	15 2/8	15 1/8	6 5/8	6 6/8	30 6/8	30 6/8	Sikanni Chief River, BC	Norman Blank	Norman Blank	1962	2
189 4/8	48 2/8	46 2/8	14 7/8	14 7/8	7 2/8	7 4/8	28	28	Blue Sheep Lake, BC	G.C.F. Dalziel	G.C.F. Dalziel	1965	3
187 4/8	43	44	14 6/8	14 6/8	8 4/8	8 4/8	22	22	Ospika River, BC	Paul D. Weingart	Paul D. Weingart	1970	4
185 6/8	45 6/8	44 3/8	15 7/8	15 6/8	6 1/8	5 7/8	29 3/8	29 3/8	Prophet River, BC	Felipe Palau	Felipe Palau	1970	5
185 3/8	43	43 4/8	15 6/8	15 6/8	7	7 1/8	28 4/8	28 4/8	Prophet River, BC	Joseph H. Shirk	Mrs. C. Barnaby	1948	6
184 6/8	44 4/8	45	15 4/8	15 3/8	6 3/8	6 4/8	26 3/8	26 3/8	Hudson Hope, BC	John W. Pitney	Am. Mus. Nat. Hist.	1936	7
184 4/8	44 3/8	46	14 1/8	14 2/8	7	7	28 6/8	28 6/8	Colt Lake, BC	Lloyd E. Hall	Lloyd E. Hall	1963	8
184 2/8	42 1/8	42 3/8	16 2/8	16 2/8	7 1/8	7 1/8	24 4/8	24 4/8	Blue Sheep Lake, BC	G.C.F. Dalziel	G.C.F. Dalziel	1964	9
184 2/8	47 5/8	45 3/8	14 2/8	14 2/8	6 6/8	6 3/8	31 3/8	31 3/8	Colt Lake, BC	Herb Klein	Dallas Mus. of Natl. Hist.	1965	9
184 2/8	45 7/8	42 7/8	14 7/8	15	7 3/8	7 3/8	22 5/8	22 3/8	Kechika Range, BC	Arthur R. Dubs	Arthur R. Dubs	1966	9
183 7/8	44 4/8	45 5/8	13 7/8	13 7/8	7 5/8	7 5/8	23 7/8	23 7/8	Hudson Hope, BC	Picked Up	Bill Beattie	1961	12
183 6/8	44 3/8	44 5/8	14 6/8	14 6/8	7	6 7/8	20 5/8	19	Dease Lake, BC	Otis Chandler	Otis Chandler	1966	13
183 5/8	43 3/8	43 2/8	14 7/8	14 7/8	7 1/8	7	25 7/8	25 7/8	Sikanni Chief River, BC	Picked Up	B. & D. Beattie	1962	14
183 5/8	43 3/8	44	14 4/8	14 4/8	8 1/8	8	22 6/8	22 6/8	Muncho Lake, BC	Jeff Browne	Jeff Browne	1990	14
183 3/8	44 6/8	44 1/8	15	15	6 6/8	6 4/8	26 3/8	26 1/8	Kechika Range, BC	John Caputo, Jr.	John Caputo, Jr.	1961	16
183 3/8	49 2/8	44 7/8	13 4/8	13 4/8	6 6/8	6 5/8	25	25	Terminus Mt., BC	Picked Up	Herb Klein	1969	16
183 2/8	44 1/8	43 5/8	15 6/8	15 6/8	5 7/8	5 7/8	27	27	Buckinghorse River, BC	Keith C. Brown	Keith C. Brown	1971	18
183 1/8	44 7/8	46 4/8	14 1/8	14 1/8	6 7/8	7	29 6/8	29 5/8	Cassiar Mts., BC	Robert S. Jackson	Robert S. Jackson	1968	19
183	45 4/8	44 4/8	14	14	7 6/8	7 6/8	25 3/8	25 3/8	Muskwa River, BC	T.E. Shillingburg	T.E. Shillingburg	1937	20
183	44	44 4/8	14 5/8	14 5/8	7	7	25 7/8	25 7/8	Kechika Range, BC	John Caputo, Sr.	John Caputo, Sr.	1966	20
183	45 6/8	44 6/8	14 6/8	14 6/8	6 5/8	6 4/8	27 6/8	27 6/8	Cassiar Mts., BC	Gordon Studer	Gordon Studer	1967	20
182 6/8	46 1/8	45 7/8	14 4/8	14 4/8	6 6/8	6 5/8	26 3/8	26 2/8	Cassiar Mts., BC	Alex Cox	Alex Cox	1959	23
182 6/8	43	42 2/8	14 2/8	14 2/8	6 6/8	6 6/8	24 7/8	24 7/8	Cassiar Mts., BC	James P. Winters	James P. Winters	1970	23
182 4/8	42 5/8	41 7/8	15 1/8	15 1/8	7 1/8	7 1/8	24	24	Redfern Lake, BC	Gary F. Bogner	Gary F. Bogner	1987	25
182 3/8	45 1/8	45 6/8	14 6/8	14 6/8	7 7/8	7 7/8	31 4/8	31 2/8	Chlotapecta Creek, BC	Mrs. John Crowe	Mrs. John Crowe	1967	26
182 3/8	43	44 7/8	14 5/8	14 4/8	6 4/8	6 4/8	26 6/8	26 6/8	Telegraph Creek, BC	Hallett Ward, Jr.	Hallett Ward, Jr.	1967	26
182	41	42	15 4/8	15 4/8	8	8	27	27	Kechika Range, BC	John E. Hammett, Jr.	John E. Hammett, Jr.	1944	28
182	45 6/8	45 4/8	14 2/8	14 2/8	6 7/8	7 1/8	26 4/8	26 4/8	Prophet River, BC	Al Robbins	Al Robbins	1963	28
182	45 1/8	44 5/8	14 3/8	14 3/8	6 5/8	6 5/8	26	26	Sand Pile Lake, BC	G.F. Moore	G.F. Moore	1965	28
181 7/8	43 3/8	43 4/8	15 1/8	15	6 5/8	6 5/8	26 5/8	26 5/8	Gataga River, BC	Norman Lougheed	Norman Lougheed	1965	31
181 6/8	47 3/8	47 5/8	14 4/8	14 3/8	6 2/8	6 2/8	28 7/8	28 7/8	Cassiar Mts., BC	Robert Landis	Robert Landis	1969	32
181 4/8	39	45 2/8	14 3/8	14 4/8	7 6/8	7 6/8	23 6/8	23 6/8	Atlin, BC	Lloyd E. Zeman	Jenifer D. Schmidt	1970	33
181 3/8	44 3/8	44 6/8	15	14 7/8	6 4/8	6 4/8	27 2/8	27 2/8	Toad River, BC	Jerry E. Dahl	Jerry E. Dahl	1971	34
181	44 3/8	44 7/8	14 3/8	14 3/8	6 2/8	6 3/8	30 5/8	30 5/8	Watson Lake, BC	C.W. Houle	C.W. Houle	1967	35
180 7/8	41 4/8	42 3/8	15	14 7/8	7 2/8	7 3/8	26 6/8	26 6/8	Hudson Hope, BC	Don Beattie	Don Beattie	1945	36
180 7/8	44	43 1/8	14 7/8	14 6/8	6 7/8	6 7/8	26 2/8	26 2/8	Sand Pile Lake, BC	David S. Loos	David S. Loos	1967	36
180 5/8	40 5/8	43	14 1/8	14 2/8	7 7/8	8	22 4/8	22 2/8	Hudson Hope, BC	David Slutker	David Slutker	1966	38

Score	L.R	L.L	Base R	Base L	3rd Qtr R	3rd Qtr L	Gr. Spread	Tip to Tip	Locality	Hunter	Owner	Date Killed	Rank
180 5/8	38 5/8	38 6/8	15 1/8	15 2/8	9 2/8	9 1/8	19	23 2/8	Prophet River, BC	Joseph Madonia	Joseph Madonia	1970	38
180 4/8	44 4/8	44 4/8	14 2/8	14 3/8	6 6/8	6 6/8	23 6/8	23 6/8	Kechika Range, BC	Tucker Davis	Tucker Davis	1965	40
180 3/8	45 6/8	44 5/8	14 3/8	14 2/8	6 3/8	6	29	29	Telegraph Creek, BC	John B. Winsor	John B. Winsor	1966	41
180 2/8	44 4/8	44	14 2/8	14 2/8	6 5/8	7	26 3/8	26 3/8	Burnt Rose Lake, BC	E.L. Cook	E.L. Cook	1970	42
179 7/8	42 7/8	42 2/8	14 4/8	14 5/8	7 7/8	8	24 7/8	24 7/8	Prophet River, BC	Bill Thomas	Bill Thomas	1963	43
179 7/8	42 1/8	43 3/8	14 2/8	14 1/8	7 5/8	7 1/8	28	28	Ice Mt., BC	Jerry E. Mason	Jerry E. Mason	1966	43
179 5/8	39 4/8	44 5/8	13 7/8	13 6/8	8 6/8	9	21 3/8	21 3/8	Cassiar Mts., BC	Ralph W. Hull	Ralph W. Hull	1963	45
179 3/8	43 2/8	39 3/8	14 5/8	14 6/8	7 5/8	7 3/8	21 3/8	21 3/8	Pink Mt., BC	Gerald E. Howe	Gerald E. Howe	1970	46
179 3/8	45 4/8	44 7/8	14 3/8	14 2/8	6 3/8	6 5/8	24	24	Gathto Creek, BC	Gary J. Powell	Gary J. Powell	1970	46
179 2/8	43 3/8	44 5/8	13 7/8	13 6/8	6 6/8	7 2/8	26 3/8	26 3/8	Toad River, BC	Dennis Callison	Dennis Callison	1957	48
179 1/8	40 2/8	40 5/8	14 6/8	14 5/8	8 4/8	8 2/8	19 2/8	22 6/8	Eydee Creek, BC	Jack McNeill	Jack McNeill	1967	49
178 7/8	41 7/8	42 2/8	14 6/8	15	6 5/8	7	26	26 6/8	Muskwa River, BC	Cliff C. Cory	Cliff C. Cory	1987	49
178 7/8	39 3/8	45 5/8	13 6/8	13 6/8	7 3/8	6 7/8	28 3/8	28 3/8	Muskwa River, BC	W.C. Waldron	W.C. Waldron	1967	51
178 3/8	43 4/8	48	14 4/8	14 4/8	6 4/8	7	26	26	Moody Lake, BC	J. Martin Benchoff	J. Martin Benchoff	1966	52
178 3/8	43 6/8	42 4/8	14 2/8	14 2/8	6 5/8	6 4/8	27 6/8	27 6/8	Muskwa River, BC	Don S. Hopkins	Don S. Hopkins	1948	53
178 2/8	40 7/8	44 2/8	14 7/8	14 7/8	7 4/8	7 4/8	24 2/8	24 2/8	Tuchodi Lakes, BC	Ross Peck	Ross Peck	1963	53
178 2/8	43 3/8	41 1/8	14	14	7 4/8	7	24	24	Moody Lake, BC	Raymond G. Speer	Raymond G. Speer	1966	53
178 1/8	44 2/8	43 3/8	13 7/8	13 7/8	6 6/8	6 7/8	26 4/8	26 4/8	Gataga Mts., BC	Dan Auld	Pat Auld Appersen	1960	56
178 1/8	44 3/8	43 7/8	14 4/8	14 4/8	6 3/8	7 1/8	27 4/8	27 4/8	Watson Lake, BC	James C. Maly	James C. Maly	1963	56
177 7/8	42 1/8	43 2/8	13 4/8	13 5/8	8 1/8	8	31	31	Skookum Mt., YT	Ira H. Kent	Ira H. Kent	1968	58
177 7/8	42 2/8	42	13 7/8	13 7/8	7 5/8	7 2/8	24 3/8	24 3/8	Frog River, BC	Don Palmer	Don Palmer	1968	58
177 6/8	41 5/8	42	13 6/8	13 6/8	6 2/8	6 4/8	27 3/8	27 5/8	Kechika Range, BC	John Caputo, Sr.	John Caputo, Sr.	1961	60
177 6/8	43 1/8	44 7/8	15 1/8	15 1/8	6 6/8	6 5/8	28 2/8	26 4/8	Sikanni Chief River, BC	Steven L. Rose	Steven L. Rose	1961	60
177 3/8	44	44	14 6/8	14 5/8	6 3/8	9	22 2/8	22 2/8	Telegraph Creek, BC	Byron Dalziel	Byron Dalziel	1970	60
177 2/8	39 1/8	39 1/8	14 2/8	14 2/8	6 7/8	6 2/8	26 2/8	26 2/8	Toad River, BC	Paul O'Hollaren	Paul O'Hollaren	1967	63
177 1/8	45 2/8	44	13	13	6 6/8	7	27 6/8	27 6/8	Watson Lake, YT	Dewey Rawlings	Dewey Rawlings	1969	63
177 1/8	44 2/8	44 3/8	14 5/8	14 4/8	6 3/8	6 5/8	24 2/8	24 2/8	Toad River, BC	Edgar A. Robertson	Edgar A. Robertson	1968	65
177	40 7/8	42 2/8	14 2/8	13 4/8	8 1/8	8	23 4/8	23 4/8	Racing River, BC	John Huml	John Huml	1969	66
177	42 1/8	42 1/8	13 5/8	13 5/8	7 5/8	7 2/8	22 4/8	22 4/8	Atlin, BC	Robert H. Kunzli	Robert H. Kunzli	1959	67
177	42 1/8	42	13 7/8	13 7/8	6 2/8	6 4/8	24 6/8	24 6/8	Ft. St. John, BC	Delmar Aldrich	Delmar Aldrich	1964	67
176 7/8	36	44 3/8	13 6/8	13 6/8	6 6/8	6 2/8	20 7/8	20 2/8	Watson Lake, YT	Ted T. Dabrowski	Ted T. Dabrowski	1967	67
176 7/8	44 5/8	44 5/8	15 1/8	15	6 3/8	6 5/8	29 4/8	29 4/8	Cassiar Mts., BC	Keith Thompson	Keith Thompson	1969	67
176 6/8	41 6/8	41 6/8	14 5/8	14 5/8	8 7/8	9	27 7/8	27 7/8	Redfern Lake, BC	H.H. Kissinger	H.H. Kissinger	1970	67
176 4/8	44 2/8	40 3/8	14 6/8	14 6/8	6 1/8	6 1/8	23 5/8	23 5/8	Mt. Lady Laurier, BC	W.H. Kirk	Unknown	1923	72
176 4/8	40	40 6/8	15	15	6	6	27	27 2/8	Muskwa River, BC	Chet Gifford	Chet Gifford	1963	72
176 4/8	43 7/8	40 7/8	14 2/8	14 3/8	7 2/8	7 1/8	25 6/8	25 6/8	Prophet River, BC	Gerald A. Paille	Gerald A. Paille	1986	72
176 4/8	42 7/8	42 1/8	15 3/8	15 4/8	6 4/8	6 4/8	21 6/8	21 6/8	Sikanni Chief River, BC	Wade Martin	Wade Martin	1960	75
176 3/8	45 3/8	40 3/8	14 4/8	14 5/8	6 6/8	6 6/8	29	29	Dease Lake, BC	Don R. Hughes	Don R. Hughes	1988	75
176 3/8	41 2/8	41 6/8	13 1/8	13 1/8	6 7/8	6 8/8	25 3/8	25 3/8	Rabbit River, BC	Thomas M. Dye	Thomas M. Dye	1966	77
176 3/8	45	44	15 2/8	15 2/8	7 4/8	7 1/8	24 3/8	24 3/8	Cassiar Mts., BC	George H. Rhoads	George H. Rhoads	1971	77
176 3/8	40 7/8	41 6/8	14	14	6	6	23	23	Muskwa River, BC	Donald J. Robb	Donald J. Robb	1969	79
176 3/8	44	42 7/8	14 4/8	13 6/8	7	8 3/8	21 5/8	21 5/8	Prophet River, BC	T.E. Shillingburg	T.E. Shillingburg	1947	80
176 3/8	44 5/8	45 3/8	14 3/8	14 3/8	5 5/8	5 4/8	28 1/8	28 1/8	Gataga River, BC	Jim Caves	Jim Caves	1959	81
176 3/8	41	44 3/8	14 6/8	14 6/8	7	7	24	24	Tuchodi River, BC	David C. Coleman	David C. Coleman	1980	81
176 3/8	43	45	14 3/8	14 3/8	6 6/8	6 3/8	31	31	Burnt Rose Lake, BC	James M. Peek	James M. Peek	1993	81
176 3/8	40 2/8	41	15 4/8	14 3/8	6 4/8	6 2/8	23 6/8	23 6/8	Prophet River, BC	Michael G. Adams	Michael G. Adams	1994	81
176 3/8	44 7/8	40 7/8	15 4/8	15 4/8	6 7/8	6 7/8	23 6/8	23 6/8	Prophet River, BC	O.B. Kahn	O.B. Kahn	1965	85
176 3/8	44	44 7/8	14 2/8	14 2/8	6 3/8	6 3/8	28 3/8	28 3/8	Cassiar Mts., BC	Eugene D. Klineburger	Eugene D. Klineburger	1965	85

Score	Length of Horn R	L	Circumference of Base R	L	Circumference at Third Quarter R	L	Greatest Spread	Tip to Tip Spread	Locality	Hunter	Owner	Date Killed	Rank
176 3/8	42 7/8	43 4/8	15	15	5 6/8	5 5/8	29 4/8	29 2/8	Nabesche River, BC	Kenneth W. Kleiman	Kenneth W. Kleiman	1973	85
176 3/8	45	38 7/8	14 4/8	14 4/8	7 2/8	6 5/8	23	23	Wokkpash Creek, BC	Hub R. Grounds	Hub R. Grounds	1987	85
176 2/8	41 6/8	44	14 4/8	14 4/8	6 1/8	6 1/8	26 7/8	26 7/8	Prophet River, BC	W.A. Newmiller	W.A. Newmiller	1958	89
176 1/8	36 3/8	39 2/8	15	15	8 7/8	7 7/8	22 6/8	18 6/8	Richard Creek, BC	James Milito	James Milito	1967	90
176 1/8	40 7/8	36	15	15	7 4/8	7 6/8	21 7/8	19 7/8	Pink Mt., BC	Roland Schroeder	Roland Schroeder	1968	90
176 1/8	43 3/8	43 2/8	14 1/8	14 1/8	6 5/8	6 5/8	25 4/8	25 4/8	Watson Lake, BC	Elgin T. Gates	Elgin T. Gates	1969	93
176	45 7/8	41 1/8	13 7/8	13 6/8	6 6/8	7	25 4/8	25 4/8	Cassiar Mts., BC	Walter O. Ford, Jr.	Walter O. Ford, Jr.	1967	93
176	39	41 2/8	15 2/8	15 2/8	6 5/8	6 4/8	23 6/8	23 6/8	Tetsa River, BC	Ron Sedor	Ron Sedor	1988	93
176	41 2/8	40 2/8	14 2/8	14 4/8	8 1/8	8 1/8	21 6/8	21 6/8	Tuchodi Lakes, BC	Terry Filas	Terry Filas	1989	93
176	42	40	15 2/8	15 2/8	6 4/8	6 5/8	25 1/8	25 1/8	Gathto Creek, BC	Dyrk T. Eddie	Dyrk T. Eddie	1997	97
175 6/8	41 4/8	39 6/8	14 7/8	14 7/8	7 2/8	7 2/8	22 4/8	22 4/8	Prophet River, BC	Jack O'Connor	Univ. of ID	1946	97
175 6/8	41 4/8	40 4/8	13 3/8	13 3/8	8 7/8	9	23 1/8	23 1/8	Terminus Mt., BC	Irvin Hart	Irvin Hart	1964	97
175 6/8	42 1/8	37 1/8	15 5/8	15 5/8	7	7 1/8	21 1/8	20 7/8	Turnagain River, BC	Lester C. Brewick	Lester C. Brewick	1967	97
175 6/8	43 2/8	43 4/8	14 1/8	13 7/8	6 6/8	6 7/8	29 2/8	29 2/8	Blue Sheep Lake, BC	John M. Griffith, Jr.	John M. Griffith, Jr.	1971	97
175 6/8	39 2/8	39 2/8	14 1/8	14 1/8	8 4/8	8 4/8	20 4/8	20	Tuchodi River, BC	Roy D. Brown	Roy D. Brown	1992	102
175 5/8	42 5/8	42 6/8	14 4/8	14 2/8	6 2/8	6 3/8	22	22	Pelly Mts., YT	John Caputo, Sr.	John Caputo, Sr.	1953	102
175 5/8	42 4/8	41 5/8	14	14	6 6/8	6 7/8	21 6/8	21 6/8	Top Lake, BC	Richard Buffington	Richard Buffington	1964	102
175 5/8	46 3/8	43 4/8	13 5/8	13 5/8	5 5/8	5 4/8	28	27 7/8	Hudson Hope, BC	Jim Papst	Jim Papst	1966	102
175 4/8	46 6/8	48	12 6/8	12 6/8	5 5/8	5 5/8	30 6/8	30 6/8	Lake Kinniskan, BC	Richard Stough	Richard Stough	1961	105
175 4/8	41 2/8	41 2/8	14	14 2/8	7 3/8	7 5/8	23 6/8	23 6/8	Frog River, BC	Robert McMurray	Robert McMurray	1968	105
175 4/8	42 2/8	42	14 7/8	14 6/8	6 3/8	6 2/8	28 1/8	28 1/8	Colt Lake, BC	Marsh Dear	Marsh Dear	1970	105
175 4/8	40 1/8	36 3/8	14 4/8	14 4/8	8	7 7/8	22 2/8	19 4/8	Prophet River, BC	Sam C. Arnett III	Sam C. Arnett III	1972	105
175 4/8	38 2/8	38	15	15	8	8	23 7/8	21 1/8	Muskwa River, BC	Robert M. Case	Robert M. Case	1980	105
175 3/8	43	42 5/8	14 2/8	14 4/8	6 4/8	6 4/8	26	26	Pelly Mts., YT	Pat S. McInturff	Pat S. McInturff	1962	110
175 2/8	41 3/8	42 3/8	12 7/8	12 7/8	8 7/8	9 2/8	22	21 6/8	Tetsa River, BC	Stanley Walchuk, Jr.	Stanley Walchuk, Jr.	1992	111
175	42 2/8	41 6/8	14 2/8	14 2/8	6 5/8	6 5/8	26 5/8	26 5/8	Hudson Hope, BC	Harry M. Haywood	Harry M. Haywood	1949	112
175	40 5/8	41 3/8	14 1/8	14 2/8	7	7 1/8	22	21 5/8	Cassiar, BC	John Sochor	John Sochor	1962	112
175	42 6/8	42 6/8	13 7/8	13 7/8	6 5/8	6 5/8	28 5/8	28 5/8	Cold Fish Lake, BC	Chris Reynolds	Chris Reynolds	1963	112
175	42 4/8	43 2/8	14 2/8	14 2/8	6 1/8	6 2/8	24	24	Colt Lake, BC	Warren Page	Warren Page	1965	112
175	40 4/8	42	14	14 1/8	8 2/8	7 6/8	22 5/8	20 1/8	Toad River, BC	William E. Butler	William E. Butler	1975	112
174 7/8	41 6/8	42 3/8	14 6/8	14 5/8	6 7/8	6 4/8	21 7/8	21 7/8	Cassiar, BC	John W. Hull	John W. Hull	1962	117
174 7/8	38 2/8	38 3/8	13 7/8	14	9 3/8	9 1/8	19 6/8	17	Summit Lake, BC	John D. Chalk III	John D. Chalk III	1989	117
174 7/8	44 7/8	46	14	14	5 5/8	5 5/8	26 2/8	26 2/8	Johiah Lake, BC	Robert Joseph	Robert Joseph	1997	117
174 6/8	38 6/8	38 2/8	14 5/8	14 5/8	7 7/8	8	21 4/8	19 7/8	Watson Lake, BC	Philip English	Philip English	1965	120
174 6/8	39 3/8	42 3/8	14 4/8	14 3/8	6 6/8	6 6/8	24 6/8	24 6/8	Muncho Lake, BC	Donald L. Mann	Donald L. Mann	2000	120
174 5/8	42 1/8	41 1/8	14 6/8	14 6/8	6 1/8	6	30 2/8	30 2/8	Stikine River, BC	Hugh J. O'Dower	Hugh J. O'Dower	1952	122
174 5/8	41 4/8	41 5/8	14 1/8	14 1/8	7 3/8	7 3/8	24 7/8	24 7/8	Sikanni Chief River, BC	Joseph W. Quarto	Joseph W. Quarto	1965	122
174 5/8	36 7/8	39	14 6/8	14 6/8	8 3/8	8 4/8	20 7/8	20 2/8	Prophet River, BC	Craig R. Johnson	Craig R. Johnson	1989	122

Score	Length R	Length L	Circ. Base R	Circ. Base L	Circ. 3rd Qtr R	Circ. 3rd Qtr L	Greatest Spread	Tip to Tip	Locality	Hunter	Owner	Date	Rank
174 4/8	40 6/8	41 2/8	15	14 6/8	8	8 2/8	27 4/8	27 4/8	Dease Lake, BC	Alice J. Landreth	Alice J. Landreth	1964	125
174 4/8	42 6/8	42	14 5/8	14 6/8	5 6/8	6	24 6/8	24 6/8	Ram Lake, BC	Walter Smetaniuk	Walter Smetaniuk	1966	125
174 4/8	40	40 2/8	15	15	6 7/8	6 7/8	21	22 6/8	Dall Lake, BC	Darrell Orth	Darrell Orth	1990	125
174 4/8	42 3/8	41 1/8	14 3/8	14 3/8	6 3/8	6 2/8	22 5/8	22 6/8	Drury Lake, YT	Samuel E. Sanders	Samuel E. Sanders	1997	125
174 3/8	41 2/8	40 1/8	13 5/8	13 4/8	7 5/8	8	20 5/8	20 5/8	Racing River, BC	Lash Callison	Lash Callison	1959	129
174 3/8	39 4/8	41 5/8	14 6/8	14 6/8	7 3/8	8 4/8	21 6/8	21 6/8	Top Lake, BC	W.E. Fisher	W.E. Fisher	1964	129
174 3/8	37	38 5/8	14 4/8	14 4/8	8 7/8	8 6/8	21	21 6/8	Cassiar Mts., BC	Gordon Studer	Gordon Studer	1966	129
174 3/8	40 3/8	40 6/8	15 1/8	15	6 1/8	6 4/8	24	24	Tuchodi Lakes, BC	Lydell Johnson	Lydell Johnson	1993	129
174 2/8	46 4/8	46 2/8	13 3/8	13 3/8	5 4/8	5 3/8	33	33	Watson Lake, BC	G.C.F. Dalziel	G.C.F. Dalziel	1962	133
174 2/8	42 2/8	46 2/8	12 4/8	12 5/8	6 5/8	6 5/8	26 3/8	26 3/8	W. Toad River, BC	N.B. Sorenson	Unknown	PR 1969	133
174 2/8	39 7/8	39 1/8	15 1/8	15 1/8	6 6/8	6 6/8	22 5/8	22 5/8	Toad River, BC	Bill Hicks, Jr.	Bill Hicks, Jr.	1990	133
174 2/8	38 2/8	39 2/8	15 4/8	15 4/8	6 7/8	7	26 4/8	26 6/8	Redfern Lake, BC	Wilf Klingsat	Wilf Klingsat	1990	133
174 1/8	42 2/8	40 7/8	14	14	7 6/8	5 2/8	23	23	Cold Fish Lake, BC	Roberto De La Garza	Roberto De La Garza	1961	137
174 1/8	39 2/8	41 3/8	15 2/8	15 1/8	5 2/8	6 2/8	25 3/8	25 3/8	Gold Bar, BC	Henry O. Carlson	Henry O. Carlson	1962	137
174 1/8	41 1/8	43 3/8	14 4/8	14 4/8	6 4/8	6 7/8	23 5/8	23 5/8	Mt. Winston, BC	Norman A. Hill	Norman A. Hill	1967	137
174 1/8	43 7/8	41 4/8	14 2/8	14 1/8	6 5/8	6 5/8	23 6/8	23 6/8	Muskwa River, BC	Gary J. Powell	Gary J. Powell	1974	137
174 1/8	41	41	14	13 7/8	6 3/8	6 3/8	23 6/8	23 6/8	Marker Lake, YT	Ronald G. Selby	Ronald G. Selby	2001	137
174	41	40	13 6/8	14	6 4/8	6 7/8	22 7/8	22 7/8	Muskwa River, BC	Wade Martin	Wade Martin	1961	142
174	44 6/8	38 4/8	14 1/8	14 1/8	6 6/8	6 4/8	27	27	Cassiar Mts., BC	Russell Castner	Russell Castner	1966	142
174	41 6/8	41	14 1/8	14 1/8	6 7/8	6 7/8	26 3/8	26 3/8	Cassiar Mts., BC	George H. Glass	George H. Glass	1966	142
174	40	41	14 6/8	14 5/8	6 6/8	6 6/8	19 4/8	20 3/8	Muskwa Area, BC	W.R. Collie	W.R. Collie	1972	142
174	40 1/8	40 1/8	15 3/8	15 2/8	6 4/8	6 4/8	24 7/8	25 1/8	Muskwa River, BC	R.L. Gearhart	R.L. Gearhart	1983	142
173 7/8	44 2/8	43 5/8	13 4/8	13 4/8	6 2/8	6 2/8	27 2/8	27 2/8	Stikine River, BC	Vernon D.E. Smith	Vernon D.E. Smith	1960	147
173 7/8	44 3/8	44 2/8	13 2/8	13 2/8	7	7	29 7/8	25 7/8	Cassiar, BC	Fred F. Wells	Fred F. Wells	1961	147
173 7/8	39 6/8	38 4/8	14 4/8	14 4/8	8 3/8	9	25	25	Gataga River, BC	H.L. Hale	H.L. Hale	1968	147
173 6/8	40 1/8	38 1/8	13 6/8	13 4/8	8 3/8	8 3/8	16	20 2/8	Tetsa River, BC	Eugene P. LaSota	Eugene P. LaSota	1973	147
173 6/8	41 5/8	41 5/8	14 5/8	15	6 6/8	6 6/8	21 5/8	21 5/8	Rabbit River, BC	Terry J. Ridley	Terry J. Ridley	1994	147
173 6/8	47 3/8	43 1/8	13 4/8	13 4/8	5 3/8	5 3/8	25 2/8	25 2/8	Halfway River, BC	R. Lynn Ross	R. Lynn Ross	1957	152
173 6/8	43 4/8	43 4/8	13 6/8	13 5/8	6 2/8	6 2/8	28 2/8	28 2/8	Terminus Mt., BC	Chester A. Crago	Chester A. Crago	1962	152
173 6/8	41 4/8	43	14	14	6 3/8	6 4/8	30 4/8	30 4/8	Kechika Range, BC	Russell C. Cutter	Russell C. Cutter	1965	152
173 6/8	41 5/8	40 7/8	14 4/8	14 4/8	7 2/8	7 2/8	25 6/8	25 6/8	Muskwa River, BC	W. Michalsky	W. Michalsky	1965	152
173 6/8	41 4/8	40 6/8	14 1/8	14 1/8	6 5/8	6 5/8	22 6/8	22 6/8	Toad River, BC	Peter C. Swenson	Peter C. Swenson	1993	152
173 5/8	45 4/8	40 1/8	13 4/8	13 4/8	6 5/8	6 5/8	26 2/8	26 2/8	Peace River, BC	Unknown	Melvin Shearer	1933	157
173 5/8	42 5/8	42	14 3/8	14 3/8	5 7/8	5 7/8	23 2/8	23 2/8	Hudson Hope, BC	G.F. Moore	G.F. Moore	1963	157
173 5/8	42 3/8	42	14 3/8	14 3/8	6 2/8	6 2/8	22 4/8	22 4/8	Rose Mt., YT	Karl Fritzsche	Karl Fritzsche	1972	157
173 5/8	40	41 5/8	15 2/8	15 4/8	6	6	22 3/8	22 5/8	Muskwa River, BC	Valerie Carter-Green	Valerie Carter-Green	1994	157
173 4/8	40 2/8	41 2/8	13 4/8	13 4/8	8 1/8	7 7/8	20 4/8	20 4/8	Cassiar, BC	Charles F. Haas	Charles F. Haas	1960	161
173 4/8	41 6/8	41 6/8	14 1/8	14 1/8	6 2/8	6 2/8	28 5/8	28 5/8	Telegraph Creek, BC	L. Iverson	L. Iverson	1961	161
173 4/8	39	42	15	15	7 4/8	6 4/8	22 4/8	22 4/8	Dease Lake, BC	George I. Parker	George I. Parker	1963	161
173 4/8	41	41	14	14	9 4/8	9	27	27	Dease Lake, BC	John T. Blackwell	John T. Blackwell	1964	161
173 4/8	39 4/8	39 4/8	14 2/8	14	8 1/8	8	23	23	Watson Lake, YT	Harry S. Rinker	Harry S. Rinker	1964	161
173 4/8	41 3/8	41 5/8	14 4/8	14 4/8	6 2/8	6 2/8	26 4/8	26 4/8	Cold Fish Lake, BC	Roger M. Britton	Roger M. Britton	1986	161
173 4/8	39 6/8	40 2/8	15 3/8	15 4/8	6 1/8	6 2/8	24 7/8	24 7/8	Schooler Creek, BC	Wade Nielsen	Wade Nielsen	1992	161
173 4/8	41 2/8	41	14 2/8	14 2/8	7	7	22 4/8	22 4/8	Muncho Lake, BC	Harold L. Brander	Harold L. Brander	1996	161
173 4/8	42 4/8	43	14 7/8	14 7/8	5 5/8	5 5/8	26 4/8	26 4/8	Through Creek, BC	Peter W. Spear	Peter W. Spear	1997	161
173 3/8	43 3/8	44	13 4/8	13 4/8	6 6/8	6 6/8	28	28	Toad River, BC	H.L. Vidricksen	H.L. Vidricksen	1960	170
173 3/8	38 3/8	38 4/8	14 6/8	14 4/8	8 3/8	8	19 3/8	20 6/8	Tuchodi Lakes, BC	George S. Gayle III	George S. Gayle III	1972	170
173 3/8	41 5/8	42 6/8	14 3/8	14 3/8	5 5/8	5 5/8	26 4/8	26 4/8	Delano Creek, BC	Richard W. Sullivan	Richard W. Sullivan	1982	170

STONE'S SHEEP
Ovis dalli stonei

Score	Length of Horn R	L	Circumference of Base R	L	Circumference at Third Quarter R	L	Greatest Spread	Tip to Tip Spread	Locality	Hunter	Owner	Date Killed	Rank
173 3/8	39 3/8	38 6/8	15 3/8	15 4/8	6 3/8	6 6/8	21 6/8	20 6/8	Sikanni Chief River, BC	Ray M. Fabri	Ray M. Fabri	1992	170
173 2/8	41 6/8	41 2/8	14 4/8	14 3/8	6 4/8	6 2/8	24 6/8	24 6/8	Cassiar Mts., BC	John Caputo, Sr.	John Caputo, Sr.	1962	174
173 2/8	44 4/8	45	13 2/8	13 2/8	5 7/8	5 5/8	26 6/8	26 5/8	Cassiar Mts., BC	William H. Warrick	William H. Warrick	1963	174
173 1/8	40 1/8	41 2/8	14	14	7	6 7/8	24 5/8	24 5/8	Halfway River, BC	Frank H. Rogers	Frank H. Rogers	1962	176
173 1/8	40 4/8	41 3/8	14 7/8	14 7/8	6	6 3/8	27 4/8	27 4/8	Cassiar Mts., BC	Charles F. Nadler	Charles F. Nadler	1967	176
173 1/8	41 3/8	40	14 1/8	14 2/8	7 2/8	7 2/8	21 6/8	21 6/8	Summit Lake, BC	Henry L. Baddley	Henry L. Baddley	1979	176
173	39 4/8	38	14 4/8	14 4/8	8	8	26	26	Muskwa River, BC	Elmer Keith	Elmer Keith	1937	179
173	34	45	15	15	7 1/8	7 1/8	24 2/8	24 2/8	Gataga River, BC	Wilson Southwell	Wilson Southwell	1958	179
173	40 3/8	41 3/8	13 6/8	13 7/8	7 2/8	7 5/8	23 4/8	21 4/8	Prophet River, BC	Merrimen M. Watkins	Merrimen M. Watkins	1965	179
173	42	42 2/8	14 2/8	14 3/8	5 6/8	5 6/8	22 5/8	22 5/8	Watson Lake, YT	E.P. Gray	E.P. Gray	1968	179
173	42	42 2/8	13 6/8	14	6 6/8	6 5/8	23 2/8	23 2/8	Prophet River, BC	Robert E. Hammond	Robert E. Hammond	1969	179
173	42 5/8	42 3/8	14	14	5 6/8	5 7/8	27 1/8	27 1/8	Cold Fish Lake, BC	A.H. Clise	A.H. Clise	1970	179
173	41 5/8	42 5/8	14 1/8	13 7/8	5 5/8	5 7/8	24 3/8	24 3/8	Alaska Hwy., Mile 422, BC	Garland N. Teich	Garland N. Teich	1971	179
173	41 4/8	42 4/8	13 6/8	13 5/8	6 6/8	7	24	23 5/8	Rapid River, BC	Bill Silveira	Bill Silveira	1983	179
173	41 7/8	42 7/8	13 3/8	13 3/8	6 4/8	6 2/8	25 5/8	25 5/8	Racing River, BC	Len J. Smith	Len J. Smith	1995	179
173	41 7/8	41 7/8	14 2/8	14 2/8	6 2/8	6 2/8	27 6/8	27 6/8	Cassiar Mts., BC	Michael J. Borel	Michael J. Borel	1997	179
172 7/8	40 4/8	39 5/8	14 3/8	14 4/8	6 6/8	6 6/8	24 1/8	24 1/8	Prophet River, BC	Harry M. Haywood	Harry M. Haywood	1956	189
172 7/8	40 7/8	42 4/8	14 7/8	14 7/8	5 4/8	6	25 3/8	25 3/8	Summit Lake, BC	A. Tony Mathisen	Bill Malast	1958	189
172 7/8	42 7/8	42 2/8	13 7/8	13 7/8	6 3/8	6 4/8	25 1/8	25 1/8	Cassiar Mts., BC	Wayne C. Eubank	Wayne C. Eubank	1963	189
172 7/8	46 3/8	35	14	14	6 4/8	6 4/8	21 2/8	21 2/8	Cassiar Mts., BC	Orval H. Ause	Orval H. Ause	1968	189
172 7/8	37 7/8	37	15	14 6/8	7 5/8	7 7/8	23	20	Cassiar Mts., BC	Greg Williams	Greg Williams	1976	189
172 7/8	42 7/8	42 4/8	13 7/8	13 7/8	6 4/8	6 4/8	27 1/8	27 1/8	Coal Creek, YT	Dennis C. Campbell	Dennis C. Campbell	1998	189
172 6/8	36 4/8	37	14 6/8	15	8 3/8	8 4/8	19 1/8	19 1/8	Sikanni Chief River, BC	Mrs. Maitland Armstrong	Mrs. Maitland Armstrong	1962	195
172 6/8	40 2/8	41 6/8	14 2/8	14 3/8	6 5/8	7	22	22	Gataga River, BC	Basil C. Bradbury	Basil C. Bradbury	1968	195
172 6/8	36 4/8	36 2/8	14 6/8	15	8 6/8	8 4/8	21 3/8	15 3/8	Muskwa River, BC	Andrew A. Samuels, Jr.	Andrew A. Samuels, Jr.	1969	195
172 6/8	42	41 6/8	14 5/8	14 4/8	6 2/8	6 1/8	27 5/8	27 5/8	Dall Lake, BC	Robert J. Rood	Robert J. Rood	1971	195
172 6/8	41 2/8	41	14 5/8	14 5/8	6 6/8	6 3/8	22 7/8	22 5/8	Toad River, BC	Robert E. Zaiglin	Robert E. Zaiglin	1995	195
172 5/8	40 3/8	40 4/8	14 2/8	14 2/8	7 2/8	7 1/8	24 5/8	24 5/8	Liard River, BC	Jack N. Allen	Jack N. Allen	1959	200
172 5/8	38 7/8	40	14 7/8	14 7/8	6 6/8	6 6/8	24 6/8	23	Blue Sheep Lake, BC	John Deromedi	John Deromedi	1989	200
172 5/8	43 2/8	42 5/8	14 1/8	14 1/8	5 7/8	5 4/8	26 1/8	26 1/8	Kechika River, BC	William B. McClelland	William B. McClelland	1991	200
172 4/8	42 2/8	42	13 7/8	13 5/8	6 1/8	5 7/8	29 4/8	29 4/8	Halfway River, BC	Cecil V. Mumbert	Cecil V. Mumbert	1958	203
172 4/8	40 4/8	41 6/8	14 4/8	14 2/8	6 4/8	6 2/8	25	25	Dease Lake, BC	John T. Blackwell	John T. Blackwell	1963	203
172 4/8	37 2/8	38	15 2/8	15 5/8	6 6/8	6	27 5/8	27 5/8	Prophet River, BC	William A. Miller	William A. Miller	1969	203
172 4/8	39 6/8	42	14 4/8	14 3/8	6 6/8	7	25 3/8	25 3/8	Watson Lake, BC	Julian Gutierrez	Julian Gutierrez	1970	203
172 4/8	37 3/8	41 7/8	14 4/8	14 3/8	6 4/8	7	23 3/8	23 1/8	Muskwa River, BC	L.A. Denson	L.A. Denson	1971	203
172 4/8	41 1/8	41 1/8	15 1/8	15 1/8	6	6 1/8	28 2/8	28 2/8	Mile Creek, BC	H.D. Miller	H.D. Miller	1980	203
172 4/8	40 5/8	40 5/8	14 4/8	14 4/8	5 7/8	5 7/8	24 2/8	24	Sikanni Chief River, BC	Ben F. Carter III	Ben F. Carter III	1997	203
172 3/8	37 1/8	38 4/8	14 2/8	14 2/8	8 3/8	8 4/8	23 1/8	17 2/8	Sandbar Creek, BC	John La Rocca	Cabela's, Inc.	1957	210

Score	Length of Horn R	Length of Horn L	Circ. of Base R	Circ. of Base L	Circ. 3rd Qtr R	Circ. 3rd Qtr L	Greatest Spread	Tip to Tip	Locality	Hunter	Owner	Date Killed	Rank
172 3/8	41 6/8	42 3/8	14 3/8	14 4/8	5 7/8	5 7/8	27 6/8	27 6/8	Pelly Mts., YT	Walter R. Michael	Walter R. Michael	1960	210
172 3/8	45 1/8	45 2/8	13	13	5 7/8	5 5/8	28	28	Cold Fish Lake, BC	Juan Brittingham	Juan Brittingham	1961	210
172 3/8	39 3/8	39 6/8	15 5/8	15 5/8	6	6 6/8	20 2/8	20 2/8	Ospika Drainage, BC	Mark Swenson	Mark Swenson	1964	210
172 3/8	41 5/8	41 4/8	14 5/8	14 5/8	6 1/8	6 2/8	23 4/8	23 4/8	Dall Lake, BC	Paul M. Rothermel, Jr.	Paul M. Rothermel, Jr.	1965	210
172 3/8	38 6/8	38 7/8	15 2/8	15 1/8	6 5/8	6 5/8	25 1/8	25 1/8	Muskwa River, BC	Kenneth W. Scheer	Kenneth W. Scheer	1985	210
172 2/8	40 1/8	41 1/8	14 1/8	14 2/8	6	6 5/8	21 4/8	21 4/8	Prophet River, BC	George F. Crain	George F. Crain	1961	216
172 2/8	42 4/8	38 2/8	14 3/8	14 4/8	7	6 7/8	20	20	Muskwa River, BC	Arvid F. Benson	Arvid F. Benson	1963	216
172 2/8	41 6/8	36 6/8	14 4/8	14 4/8	5 4/8	5 6/8	29	29	Prophet River, BC	S.E. Burrell	S.E. Burrell	1967	216
172 2/8	39 6/8	42 2/8	14 4/8	14 2/8	8	7 4/8	23 1/8	23 1/8	Sikanni Chief River, BC	John B. Collier IV	John B. Collier IV	1967	216
172 2/8	41 6/8	41 2/8	14 2/8	14 2/8	6 6/8	7 7/8	26 4/8	26 4/8	Cassiar Mts., BC	Michaux Nash, Jr.	Michaux Nash, Jr.	1967	216
172 2/8	39	38 4/8	14	14	6 1/8	6	28 4/8	28 4/8	Akie River, BC	O.J. Baggenstoss	O.J. Baggenstoss	1968	216
172 2/8	41 5/8	41	14 5/8	14 4/8	7 3/8	7 4/8	20 2/8	20 2/8	Prophet River, BC	Larry Ciejka	Larry Ciejka	1977	216
172 1/8	37 6/8	40	14 4/8	14 4/8	6 3/8	6 2/8	22 1/8	22 1/8	Chlotapecta Creek, BC	Merle Freyborg	Merle Freyborg	1992	224
172 1/8	34 5/8	40 5/8	13	13	9 2/8	9 2/8	30	30	Dease Lake, BC	W.M. Rudd	W.M. Rudd	1964	224
172 1/8	39	38 1/8	14 2/8	14	9 1/8	9 1/8	19	19	Cassiar Mts., BC	Keith M. Kissinger	Keith M. Kissinger	1968	224
172 1/8	40 2/8	41	14 2/8	14 4/8	6 7/8	7 1/8	23 3/8	23 2/8	Alaska Hwy., BC	Robert Murdock	Robert Murdock	1968	224
172	40 3/8	40 2/8	14 2/8	14 2/8	7 2/8	7 3/8	23 2/8	23 2/8	Burnt Rose Lake, BC	John K. De Broux	John K. De Broux	1970	229
172	41	43 3/8	14 3/8	14 3/8	6 4/8	6 3/8	23 2/8	23 2/8	Muskwa River, BC	Greg L. Stires	Greg L. Stires	1984	229
172	39 2/8	41 6/8	15	15	6 5/8	6 5/8	20 5/8	20 3/8	Hudson Hope, BC	Don Stewart	Don Stewart	1961	229
172	45 5/8	40	12 7/8	13	6 2/8	6 2/8	23 2/8	23 2/8	Atlin, BC	Thomas E. Francis	Thomas E. Francis	1964	229
172	40 2/8	41 4/8	14 2/8	14 4/8	6	6 1/8	25 7/8	25 7/8	Pelly Creek, BC	Robert A. Lubeck	Robert A. Lubeck	1968	229
172	40 2/8	42 1/8	14 5/8	14 5/8	6 1/8	6 2/8	25 2/8	25 2/8	Prairie River, BC	C.J. McElroy	C.J. McElroy	1969	229
172	41 2/8	40 6/8	14	14	6 2/8	6 2/8	29	29	Denetiah Lake, BC	Michael G. Meeker	Michael G. Meeker	1969	229
171 7/8	42 1/8	38 1/8	13 4/8	13 4/8	6 5/8	6 7/8	26 6/8	26 6/8	Toad River, BC	David G. Kidder	David G. Kidder	1975	236
171 7/8	41 2/8	43	14 2/8	14 2/8	7 5/8	7 3/8	25 1/8	25 1/8	Toad River, BC	Steve Best	Steve Best	1988	236
171 7/8	38 6/8	41 3/8	13 7/8	13 7/8	8 7/8	8 5/8	23	23	Akie River, BC	Henry K. Leworthy	Henry K. Leworthy	1966	236
171 7/8	38 3/8	39 6/8	14 1/8	14 1/8	5 6/8	5 6/8	20 2/8	20 2/8	Island Lake, BC	Martin F. Wood	Martin F. Wood	1970	236
171 6/8	43 2/8	41	14 1/8	14 1/8	6 3/8	6 2/8	20 4/8	20 4/8	Cache Creek, BC	Kenneth A. Jeronimus	Kenneth A. Jeronimus	1974	240
171 6/8	42 3/8	42 6/8	14 2/8	14 2/8	5 4/8	5 4/8	30 2/8	30 2/8	Toad River, BC	Larry Jenkins	Larry Jenkins	1988	240
171 6/8	39 2/8	37	13 4/8	13 4/8	8	8	23 5/8	23 5/8	Gataga River, BC	Pat Auld Appersen	Dan Auld	1958	240
171 6/8	40 4/8	41 2/8	14 1/8	14 1/8	5 4/8	5 4/8	27 4/8	27 4/8	Cassiar Mts., BC	John Caputo, Sr.	John Caputo, Sr.	1960	240
171 6/8	36 2/8	39 2/8	14 5/8	14 5/8	7 2/8	6 4/8	27 1/8	27 1/8	Trimble Lake, BC	Roy E. Stare	Roy E. Stare	1962	240
171 6/8	39 2/8	37 6/8	14 7/8	14 7/8	8 3/8	8 3/8	24 6/8	24 6/8	Muskwa River, BC	William I. Spencer	William I. Spencer	1963	240
171 6/8	37 6/8	38 4/8	16	16	6 4/8	6 4/8	21 6/8	21 6/8	Dease Lake, BC	Michaux Nash, Jr.	Michaux Nash, Jr.	1965	240
171 5/8	38 4/8	42 6/8	15 5/8	15 5/8	6 3/8	6 3/8	21 3/8	21 3/8	Gataga River, BC	D.R. Seabaugh	D.R. Seabaugh	1971	248
171 5/8	40 4/8	37 1/8	14 2/8	14	6 7/8	6 7/8	24 2/8	24 2/8	Prophet River, BC	Don Haemmerlein	Don Haemmerlein	1977	248
171 5/8	37 2/8	42 3/8	14	14	6	6	24 7/8	24 7/8	Rock Island Lakes, BC	William K. Mortlock	William K. Mortlock	1988	248
171 5/8	42 4/8	40	14 6/8	14 6/8	8 6/8	8 6/8	20 3/8	20 3/8	Tuchodi Lakes, BC	Win Condict	Win Condict	1951	248
171 4/8	44 1/8	36 3/8	13 4/8	13 4/8	6 2/8	6 1/8	26	26	Dease Lake, BC	C.E. Krieger	C.E. Krieger	1962	253
171 4/8	38 6/8	45 3/8	13 5/8	13 4/8	6 2/8	6 3/8	25 6/8	25 6/8	Muncho Lake, BC	H.W. Julien	John W. Julien	1966	253
171 4/8	37 2/8	40 4/8	14 2/8	14 2/8	8 5/8	8 5/8	20 1/8	20 1/8	Toad River, BC	H.W. Julien	John W. Julien	1969	253
171 4/8	37	38 4/8	14 1/8	14 1/8	6 1/8	6	24	24	Prophet River, BC	John W. Whitcombe	John W. Whitcombe	1981	253
171 4/8	37	38 4/8	14 2/8	14 2/8	6 2/8	6 2/8	23 3/8	23 3/8	Prophet River, BC	L.A. Denson	L.A. Denson	1963	253
171 4/8	39	43 5/8	14 4/8	14 4/8	7 6/8	7 4/8	17	17	Trutch, BC	Charles F. Waterman	Charles F. Waterman	1964	253
171 4/8	45 4/8	45	13 6/8	13 6/8	7	7	23	23	Cassiar Mts., BC	Robert R. Bridges	Robert R. Bridges	1966	253
171 4/8	42 5/8	43 5/8	13 5/8	13 5/8	5 4/8	5 6/8	29 7/8	29 7/8	Turnagain River, BC	George H. Landreth	George H. Landreth	1966	253
171 4/8	45	43 6/8	13 1/8	13 1/8	6 1/8	5 7/8	29 7/8	29 7/8	Turnagain River, BC	Lewis M. Mull	Lewis M. Mull	1966	253
171 4/8	45	43 6/8	13 2/8	13 1/8	5 4/8	5 4/8	28 4/8	28 4/8	Cassiar Mts., BC	William A. Kelly	William A. Kelly	1969	253

STONE'S SHEEP
Ovis dalli stonei

Score	Length of Horn R	L	Circumference of Base R	L	Circumference at Third Quarter R	L	Greatest Spread	Tip to Tip Spread	Locality	Hunter	Owner	Date Killed	Rank
171 4/8	39	34 4/8	15 6/8	15 5/8	7	7 2/8	25 6/8	23	Lower Besa River, BC	Peter Hochleitner	Peter Hochleitner	1977	253
171 4/8	39 7/8	40 3/8	14 4/8	14 4/8	5 7/8	6 1/8	27 3/8	27 3/8	Gundahoo River, BC	A.J. Goertz	John McCall	2001	253
171 3/8	43	42 7/8	13 6/8	14	6	6	30 4/8	30 4/8	Kechika Range, BC	H.I.H. Prince Abdorreza Pahlavi	H.I.H. Prince Abdorreza Pahlavi	1960	261
171 3/8	37 7/8	37	14	14 -/8	8 4/8	8 7/8	21 7/8	18 3/8	Horseshoe Lake, YT	Jack G. Giannola	Jack G. Giannola	1973	261
171 3/8	39 2/8	38 5/8	14 1/8	14	7 4/8	7 3/8	22 4/8	22 4/8	Besa River, BC	Dale Webber	Dale Webber	1984	264
171 2/8	42 5/8	42 5/8	13 5/8	13 6/8	6 4/8	6 6/8	24 3/8	24 3/8	Muskwa River, BC	Bernard J. Brown	Bernard J. Brown	1953	264
171 2/8	41	41	13 7/8	13 7/8	6 3/8	6	26 2/8	26 2/8	Pelly Mts., YT	Jack Tillotson	Jack Tillotson	1955	264
171 2/8	41 6/8	43	13 6/8	13 6/8	5 7/8	6 2/8	27 2/8	27 2/8	Cold Fish Lake, BC	Robert Brittingham	Robert Brittingham	1961	264
171 2/8	44 1/8	43 1/8	12 7/8	12 7/8	5 7/8	5 6/8	27 3/8	27 3/8	Pelly Lake, BC	Robert M. Mallett	Robert M. Mallett	1966	264
171 2/8	41	39 6/8	14 3/8	14 4/8	6 7/8	6 6/8	21 6/8	20 6/8	Cassiar Mts., BC	G.A. Treschow	G.A. Treschow	1966	264
171 2/8	38	45 4/8	13	13 3/8	6 2/8	7 2/8	20 4/8	20 4/8	Telegraph Creek, BC	Picked Up	John Crowe	PR 1967	264
171 2/8	39 1/8	40 3/8	15 2/8	15 3/8	5 7/8	6	25 1/8	25 1/8	Colt Lake, BC	Roscoe Hurd	Roscoe Hurd	1969	264
171 2/8	42	42 2/8	13 5/8	13 5/8	6 3/8	6	26 3/8	26 3/8	Cassiar, BC	Herb Parsons	Herb Parsons	1969	264
171	41	42	14	14 3/8	6	6	30	30	Cassiar, BC	Wilson Potter	Harvard Univ. Mus.	1906	272
171	40 3/8	39 7/8	15	15	5 5/8	5 5/8	28 7/8	28 7/8	Sandbar Creek, BC	John La Rocca	Cabela's, Inc.	1958	272
171	40	40	14 2/8	14 2/8	6 4/8	6 4/8	25 5/8	25 5/8	Halfway River, BC	S.J. Seidensticker	S.J. Seidensticker	1962	272
171	41 7/8	41 3/8	14	14 2/8	5 7/8	5 7/8	24 7/8	24 7/8	Cassiar Mts., BC	Sam S. Jaksick, Jr.	Sam S. Jaksick, Jr.	1967	272
171	35 6/8	40 6/8	14 4/8	14 1/8	6 7/8	6 1/8	22 3/8	22 3/8	Wrede Creek, BC	Jack Feightner	Jack Feightner	1972	272
171	38 5/8	38 7/8	14 7/8	15	6 1/8	6 1/8	24 5/8	24 5/8	Ice Mt., BC	David P. Jacobson	David P. Jacobson	1974	272
171	41	44 4/8	13 4/8	13 5/8	5 7/8	6	27 1/8	27 1/8	Cassiar Mts., BC	Ed Stedman, Jr.	Ed Stedman, Jr.	1974	272
171	39 5/8	40 1/8	14 7/8	14 7/8	6 2/8	6 4/8	21 3/8	18 6/8	Burnt Rose Lake, BC	John Drift	John Drift	1977	272
171	40 2/8	39 6/8	14 6/8	14 5/8	6	5 7/8	20 6/8	20 5/8	Ice Lakes, YT	Terrance S. Marcum	Terrance S. Marcum	1992	272
170 7/8	41 7/8	41 5/8	13 3/8	13 3/8	7	7 1/8	26 5/8	26 5/8	Watson Lake, BC	Ed Ball	Ed Ball	1960	281
170 7/8	44 5/8	41 4/8	13 2/8	13 3/8	6 1/8	6 1/8	28	28	Watson Lake, YT	Richard G. Peters	Richard G. Peters	1962	281
170 7/8	39 6/8	39 5/8	14 4/8	15	6 3/8	6 3/8	19 6/8	19 6/8	Prophet River, BC	John J. LoMonaco	John J. LoMonaco	1963	281
170 7/8	38	38 1/8	14 2/8	14	7 7/8	8	19 7/8	19	Prophet River, BC	Ted Howell	Ted Howell	1964	281
170 7/8	37 5/8	38 4/8	14 5/8	14 5/8	7 3/8	7 4/8	24 6/8	18 1/8	Tuchodi Lakes, BC	Robert C. Ries	Robert C. Ries	1965	281
170 7/8	39 2/8	41 1/8	14 4/8	14 4/8	6 3/8	6 2/8	28 1/8	28 1/8	Telegraph Creek, BC	R.B. England	R.B. England	1966	281
170 7/8	37 3/8	38 6/8	14 6/8	14 6/8	7 2/8	7 2/8	23	22 3/8	Cassiar Mts., BC	W.G. Rathmann	W.G. Rathmann	1971	281
170 7/8	39 7/8	41	14	13 7/8	6 6/8	6 7/8	19 6/8	19 6/8	Toad River, BC	Rick G. Ferrara	Rick G. Ferrara	1998	281
170 6/8	42 2/8	42 4/8	13 7/8	13 7/8	6 4/8	6 2/8	32	32	Pink Mt., BC	Unknown	J. Michael Conoyer	1960	289
170 6/8	42	41	14	14	6 5/8	6 3/8	24 4/8	24 4/8	Peace River, BC	C.A. Freese	C.A. Freese	1960	289
170 6/8	41	41	14	14	6	6	27 4/8	27 4/8	Gataga River, BC	Herb Klein	Dallas Mus. of Natl. Hist.	1963	289
170 6/8	43	42 2/8	13 4/8	13 5/8	5 6/8	5 7/8	22 2/8	22 2/8	Pelly Creek, BC	Jon A. Jourdonnais	Jon A. Jourdonnais	1968	289
170 6/8	40 6/8	41	14 1/8	14 4/8	6 3/8	6 3/8	25 3/8	25 3/8	Kechika Range, BC	Ferdinand Stemann	Ferdinand Stemann	1970	289
170 6/8	41 6/8	37 6/8	14	14 1/8	6 6/8	7	25 5/8	25 5/8	Tuchodi Lakes, BC	Larry Tooze	Larry Tooze	1986	289
170 6/8	43 5/8	45 1/8	12 6/8	12 6/8	6 3/8	6 2/8	26 3/8	26 3/8	Anvil Range, YT	John A. Capdeville	John A. Capdeville	1991	289

Score									Location	Hunter	Owner	Year	Rank
170 6/8	40 2/8	40 4/8	14 2/8	14 2/8	6 5/8	6 4/8	22 5/8	22 6/8	Anvil Range, YT	Alan A. Terril	Alan A. Terril	1997	289
170 5/8	43 2/8	43 3/8	13 4/8	13 5/8	5 5/8	6 1/8	29 6/8	29 6/8	Cassiar, BC	John W. Beban	John W. Beban	1956	297
170 5/8	40 4/8	40 1/8	14 4/8	14 4/8	6	6	29 5/8	29 5/8	Prophet River, BC	E.R. Wells	E.R. Wells	1967	297
170 5/8	41 3/8	39	14 2/8	14 2/8	6 4/8	6 7/8	21 1/8	21 2/8	Toad River, BC	Jay Stewart	Jay Stewart	1969	297
170 5/8	40 7/8	40 6/8	14	14	6 2/8	6 4/8	24 2/8	24 3/8	Prophet River, BC	Robert E. Speegle	Robert E. Speegle	1983	297
170 5/8	41 1/8	42 2/8	14	14 1/8	6 1/8	6 4/8	25 1/8	25 4/8	Prophet River, BC	Steven J. DeRicco	Steven J. DeRicco	1990	297
170 5/8	41 7/8	41 4/8	14	14	6	6 3/8	25 1/8	24 7/8	Sharktooth Mt., BC	Mark R. Redman	Mark R. Redman	1990	297
170 5/8	42 4/8	42 1/8	14 6/8	14 6/8	5 3/8	5 3/8	25 7/8	25 7/8	Fox Mt., YT	George L. Wilson	George L. Wilson	1995	297
170 5/8	40 4/8	40 4/8	13 4/8	13 4/8	7 2/8	7	23 1/8	23 1/8	Turnagain River, BC	Chuck Pridgeon	Chuck Pridgeon	1996	297
170 5/8	40 6/8	40 6/8	14 2/8	14 2/8	7	7	20 5/8	20 5/8	Williston Lake, BC	Kenneth R. Hamer	Kenneth R. Hamer	1997	297
170 5/8	39	39	15 5/8	15 3/8	5 1/8	5 6/8	27 5/8	27 4/8	Muskwa River, BC	Don W. Hansen	Don W. Hansen	1997	297
170 5/8	40	41 1/8	14 6/8	14 6/8	5 5/8	6 1/8	25 4/8	25 4/8	Prophet River, BC	Steven J. LaFleur	Steven J. LaFleur	1999	297
170 5/8	39 3/8	40 2/8	14	14 1/8	7 5/8	8	23 2/8	22 2/8	Gathto Creek, BC	Joel D. Bedgood	Joel D. Bedgood	2000	297
170 4/8	42 7/8	42 5/8	13 4/8	13 4/8	6	5 7/8	33 4/8	33 1/8	McDonald Creek, BC	William A. Fisher	William A. Fisher	1957	309
170 4/8	42	42	13 4/8	13 4/8	6 1/8	6 1/8	26 4/8	26 4/8	Pelly Mts, YT	Joseph T. Pelton	Joseph T. Pelton	1963	309
170 4/8	40	40	14	14	7	6 4/8	22	20 4/8	Telegraph Creek, BC	Fred Sothmann	Fred Sothmann	1963	309
170 4/8	40 7/8	39 3/8	14 2/8	14 2/8	6 7/8	6 3/8	21 6/8	21 6/8	Toad River, BC	Melvin A. Hetland	Melvin A. Hetland	1965	309
170 4/8	40	40 4/8	14 3/8	14 4/8	6 7/8	6 4/8	22 4/8	22 4/8	Dease Lake, BC	W. Brandon Macomber	W. Brandon Macomber	1966	309
170 4/8	41 2/8	40	14 4/8	14 4/8	6 2/8	6 2/8	26 1/8	26 1/8	Watson Lake, BC	Rita Oney	Rita Oney	1966	309
170 4/8	32	41 4/8	14 6/8	14 6/8	8	8 4/8	24	24	Pink Mt., BC	E.C. Eickhoff	Donald P. Eickhoff	1968	309
170 4/8	42 2/8	40 2/8	13 5/8	13 4/8	6 4/8	6 4/8	25 4/8	25 4/8	Muskwa River, BC	William J. Pollard	William J. Pollard	1974	309
170 4/8	38 5/8	40 5/8	14 1/8	14 2/8	5 7/8	6 4/8	19 7/8	18 2/8	Mt. Edziza, BC	James G. Petersen	James G. Petersen	1997	309
170 4/8	42 3/8	42 3/8	14 2/8	13 7/8	5 7/8	5 5/8	22 6/8	21 3/8	Muncho Lake, BC	Steven C. Rudd	Steven C. Rudd	1999	309
170 3/8	41 3/8	40 2/8	13 7/8	14	6 2/8	6 2/8	22 3/8	22 3/8	Ice Lake, YT	W.A.K. Seale	W.A.K. Seale	1961	319
170 3/8	39 6/8	40 7/8	14	14 6/8	6 1/8	6 3/8	28	28	Sikanni, BC	Basil C. Bradbury	Basil C. Bradbury	1965	319
170 3/8	37 5/8	38 2/8	14 6/8	14	6 5/8	6 5/8	22 4/8	22 4/8	Kechika Range, BC	Ray E. Bigler	Ray E. Bigler	1972	319
170 3/8	41	41 1/8	14	14	6 3/8	6 1/8	25 7/8	25 7/8	Ospika Area, BC	Michael H. Baldwin	Michael H. Baldwin	1997	319
170 2/8	40	43 2/8	13 4/8	13 4/8	6 4/8	5 5/8	25 4/8	25 6/8	Muncho Lake, BC	John Forester	John Forester	1963	323
170 2/8	35	35 2/8	14 6/8	14 6/8	8	8 2/8	21 6/8	19 2/8	Beale Lake, BC	Herbert A. Leupold	Herbert A. Leupold	1965	323
170 2/8	38 4/8	39	14 7/8	15	6 7/8	6 5/8	22 6/8	22 6/8	Richards Creek, BC	Steven L. Rose	Steven L. Rose	1967	323
170 2/8	41	41	14 2/8	14 2/8	6 1/8	6 1/8	26	26	Halfway River, BC	Fritz A. Nachant	Fritz A. Nachant	1970	323
170 2/8	39 4/8	39 6/8	14 6/8	14 6/8	6 3/8	6 3/8	21 7/8	21 2/8	Keohka River, BC	James S. Griffin	James S. Griffin	1972	323
170 2/8	38 4/8	43 2/8	14 1/8	14 1/8	6 2/8	6 2/8	23 6/8	23 6/8	Muskwa River, BC	Jerald T. Waite	Jerald T. Waite	1976	323
170 2/8	36 2/8	37	13 3/8	14 7/8	6 1/8	6	20 7/8	19 4/8	Turnagain River, BC	Robert L. Williamson	Robert L. Williamson	1981	323
170 2/8	41	39 2/8	14 7/8	14 5/8	6 1/8	6 1/8	24 2/8	24 2/8	Townsley Creek, BC	Bill Stevenson	Bill Stevenson	1983	323
170 2/8	39 2/8	39 2/8	13 4/8	13 4/8	6 4/8	6 6/8	25 3/8	25 3/8	Racing Creek, BC	Steve J. Polich	Steve J. Polich	1984	323
170 2/8	40 4/8	40 7/8	14 5/8	14 2/8	6 1/8	5 6/8	27 1/8	27 1/8	Prophet River, BC	Brett M. Moore	Brett M. Moore	1987	323
170 2/8	39 5/8	39 5/8	14 2/8	14 1/8	6 6/8	5 6/8	27 2/8	27 2/8	Cutbank Creek, BC	Ralph L. Albright	Ralph L. Albright	1995	323
170 2/8	41 6/8	42	14 1/8	14 1/8	5 6/8	6 2/8	32 2/8	32 2/8	Blue Lake, BC	Dennis L. Merrey	Dennis L. Merrey	1999	323
170 1/8	41	42 4/8	14 1/8	14 1/8	6 2/8	6 4/8	30 7/8	30 7/8	Pelly Mts, YT	George W. Young	George W. Young	1965	335
170 1/8	42 4/8	41	13 3/8	13 7/8	5 5/8	5 7/8	24 6/8	24 6/8	Rabbit River, BC	Kim Cox	Kim Cox	1966	335
170 1/8	42 6/8	43 1/8	14 6/8	14 6/8	6 2/8	6 2/8	21 5/8	21 5/8	Ram Creek, BC	Roy Fukunaga	Roy Fukunaga	1974	335
170 1/8	38 1/8	38 1/8	13 4/8	13 4/8	6 4/8	5 7/8	27 5/8	27 5/8	Needham Creek, BC	James H. Duke, Jr.	James H. Duke, Jr.	1976	335
170 1/8	39 2/8	39 5/8	12 5/8	12 5/8	6 4/8	6 2/8	24 7/8	24 7/8	Cassiar Mts., BC	Frank F. Azcarate	Frank F. Azcarate	1985	335
170 1/8	43 2/8	42 3/8	14 1/8	14 1/8	6 4/8	6 2/8	23	23	Rabbit River, BC	Kenneth Baker, Jr.	Kenneth Baker, Jr.	1995	335
170 1/8	40	40 1/8	14 6/8	14 6/8	5 7/8	5 7/8	23	22 6/8	Prophet River, BC	Lawrence W. Dossman	Lawrence W. Dossman	1995	335
170 1/8	39 7/8	39	15 4/8	15 1/8	6 2/8	5 5/8	26 4/8	23 1/8	The Pillar, BC	Dwight Clower	Dwight Clower	1997	335
170 1/8	40 2/8	40 1/8	14	14	6	6 1/8	23 5/8	23 5/8	Toad River, BC	Timothy K. Krause	Timothy K. Krause	1997	335

STONE'S SHEEP
Ovis dalli stonei

Score	Length of Horn R	L	Circumference of Base R	L	Circumference at Third Quarter R	L	Greatest Spread	Tip to Tip Spread	Locality	Hunter	Owner	Date Killed	Rank
170	42 4/8	38 6/8	14 1/8	14 2/8	6	6	24 3/8	24 3/8	Prophet River, BC	Walter B. McClurkan	Walter B. McClurkan	1945	344
170	39 2/8	43 4/8	13 7/8	13 5/8	6 3/8	6	25	25	Cold Fish Lake, BC	Howard Boazman	Howard Boazman	1962	344
170	42	37	14 1/8	14 1/8	6 4/8	6 5/8	22 4/8	22 4/8	Alaska Hwy., BC	Arthur Gordon	Arthur Gordon	1965	344
170	39 4/8	39 2/8	14 5/8	14 6/8	6 4/8	6 3/8	27 3/8	27 3/8	Cassiar Mts., BC	Neil Castner	Neil Castner	1966	344
170	39 5/8	40 1/8	14 2/8	14 4/8	6 4/8	6 4/8	21 5/8	16 5/8	Cassiar Mts., BC	Glen E. Park	Glen E. Park	1967	344
170	38 4/8	39 4/8	13 6/8	13 7/8	7 2/8	7 3/8	21	17 5/8	Tetsa River, BC	Owen R. Walker	Owen R. Walker	1967	344
170	41	41	14	14	6 2/8	6 4/8	20 6/8	20 6/8	Prophet River, BC	James C. Nystrom	James C. Nystrom	1968	344
170	40	39 2/8	15 4/8	15 1/8	5 2/8	5 2/8	22 6/8	22 6/8	Muskwa River, BC	W.J. Boynton III	W.J. Boynton III	1970	344
170	42 3/8	43 7/8	13 2/8	13 2/8	6	6 1/8	29 2/8	29 2/8	Gataga River, BC	Paul L.C. Snider	Paul L.C. Snider	1970	344
170	37	37 6/8	14 6/8	14 5/8	7 2/8	7 4/8	22 2/8	18 1/8	Prophet River, BC	Doug Heinrich	Doug Heinrich	1992	344
170	35 4/8	37	14 1/8	14 1/8	8 4/8	8 5/8	19 6/8	17 1/8	Toad River, BC	Rick Davis	Rick Davis	1993	344
170	42 2/8	42	13 4/8	13 6/8	6 1/8	6 1/8	23 3/8	23 1/8	Toad River, BC	Robert M. Hall	Robert M. Hall	1995	344
170	41 3/8	39 1/8	14 2/8	14 2/8	5 7/8	5 7/8	23 2/8	23	Muncho Lake, BC	Ken Jagersma	Ken Jagersma	1996	344
182 6/8*	43 5/8	43 7/8	15 1/8	15 2/8	6 3/8	6 4/8	24 6/8	24 6/8	Tuchodi Lakes, BC	Aldo Guglielmini	Aldo Guglielmini	1998	344
178 2/8*	43	42 4/8	14 6/8	14 6/8	7	6 7/8	25 2/8	25 1/8	Ram Creek, BC	Roger M. Britton	Roger M. Britton	1993	
177 4/8*	41 5/8	42 1/8	14 4/8	14 3/8	7 2/8	7 3/8	25	24 6/8	Racing River, BC	Floyd W. Ternier	F.W. & C. Ternier	1994	
177 1/8*	44 7/8	45 2/8	14	14	5 6/8	6	31	31	Muskwa River, BC	Kevin H. Olmstead	Kevin H. Olmstead	1993	
172 7/8*	42 3/8	39 6/8	13 7/8	14	6 3/8	6 3/8	22 5/8	22 5/8	McDonald Creek, BC	Rod Parkin	Rod Parkin	1997	
171 6/8*	40 5/8	42 7/8	14 5/8	14 5/8	5 5/8	5 5/8	23 2/8	23	Scoop Lake, BC	Craig A. Miller	Craig A. Miller	1998	
171 6/8*	45	38	14 3/8	14 4/8	6 4/8	6 3/8	25 3/8	25 3/8	Laurier Creek, YT	Shayne D. Parker	Shayne D. Parker	2000	
171 2/8*	39 3/8	40 5/8	14 4/8	14 4/8	7 5/8	6 6/8	26 2/8	25 7/8	Quash Creek, BC	Dick A. Jacobs	Dick A. Jacobs	2001	

* Final score is subject to revision by additional verifying measurements.

CATEGORY
STONE'S SHEEP

SCORE
171-6/8*

HUNTER
SHAYNE D. PARKER

LOCATION
LAURIER CREEK,
YUKON TERRITORY

DATE OF KILL
AUGUST 2000

CATEGORY
STONE'S SHEEP

SCORE
172-7/8

HUNTER
DENNIS C. CAMPBELL (RIGHT)

LOCATION
COAL CREEK, YUKON TERRITORY

DATE OF KILL
SEPTEMBER 1998

SCORE
182-6/8*

HUNTER
ALDO GUGLIELMINI
(BELOW RIGHT)

LOCATION
TUCHODI LAKES,
BRITISH COLUMBIA

DATE OF KILL
AUGUST 1998

CATEGORY
STONE'S SHEEP

SCORE
171-4/8

HUNTER
A.J. GOERTZ

LOCATION
GUNDAHOO RIVER, BRITISH COLUMBIA

DATE OF KILL
AUGUST 2001

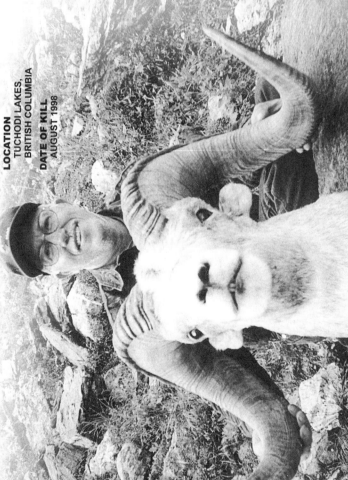

ACKNOWLEDGEMENTS
RECORDS OF NORTH AMERICAN BIG GAME

DATA COMPILED WITH THE ABLE ASSISTANCE OF:

Eldon L. "Buck" Buckner - Chair, Records of North American Big Game Committee

Jack Reneau - Director of Big Game Records

Ryan Hatfield - Assistant Director of Big Game Records

Sandy Poston - Office Manager and Data Guru

Amy Hutchison - Customer Service

Wendy Nickelson - Customer Service

WORLD'S RECORD ACCOUNTS GATHERED AND EDITED BY:

Jeffrey Buchanan Miller - Jackson, Wyoming

NEW WORLD'S RECORD ACCOUNTS EDITED BY:

A.E. Walsh - Powhatan, Virginia

BOOK LAYOUT, DUST JACKET, AND COVER DESIGNED BY:

Julie T. Houk - Director of Publications

WHITETAIL DEER PAINTING BY:

Ken Carlson - Kerrville, Texas

COPY EDITING BY:

Eldon L. "Buck" Buckner - Chair, Records of North American Big Game Committee

Jack Reneau - Director of Big Game Records

Ryan Hatfield - Assistant Director of Big Game Records

PRINTED AND BOUND HARDCOVER TRADE EDITIONS BY:

R.R. Donnelley & Sons Company

Crawfordsville, Indiana

phy on **Dec 15** City **JOHNSTOWN** 19 5...
...ts and data are, to the best of my knowledge and be... State

New Foundland 1951

I certify
at (addre
and that
accordan

Witnes

All
Off
Ple

Su
c

EW

CARIBOU

AND